Essentials of
Abnormal Psychology

EIGHTH EDITION

gawrav/E+/Getty Images

V. Mark Durand
University of South Florida-St. Petersburg

David H. Barlow
Boston University

Stefan G. Hofmann
Boston University

 CENGAGE

Australia • Brazil • Mexico • Singapore • United Kingdom • United States

Essentials of Abnormal Psychology, **Eighth Edition**
V. Mark Durand, David H. Barlow,
Stefan G. Hofmann

Product Director: Marta Lee-Perriard

Product Team Manager: Star Burruto

Product Manager: Erin Schnair

Content Developer: Tangelique Williams-Grayer

Product Assistant: Leah Jenson

Marketing Manager: Heather Thompson

Content Project Manager: Ruth Sakata Corley

Production and Composition Service: Lumina
Datamatics

Photo Researcher: Ragav Seshadri, Lumina Datamatics

Text Researcher: Ramesh Muthuramalingam, Lumina
Datamatics

Art Director: Vernon Boes

Text and Cover Designer: Cheryl Carrington

Cover Image(s): gawrav/E+/Getty Images

For product information and technology assistance, contact us at
Cengage Learning Customer & Sales Support, 1-800-354-9706.

For permission to use material from this text or product, submit all
requests online at **www.cengage.com/permissions**.
Further permissions questions can be e-mailed to
permissionrequest@cengage.com.

Library of Congress Control Number: 2017943789

Student Edition:
ISBN: 978-1-337-61937-0

Loose-leaf Edition:
ISBN: 978-1-337-61939-4

Cengage Learning
20 Channel Center Street
Boston, MA 02210
USA

Cengage Learning is a leading provider of customized learning solutions
with employees residing in nearly 40 different countries and sales in more
than 125 countries around the world. Find your local representative at:
www.cengage.com.

Cengage Learning products are represented in Canada by
Nelson Education, Ltd.

To learn more about Cengage Learning Solutions,
visit **www.cengage.com.**

Purchase any of our products at your local college store or at our preferred
online store **www.cengagebrain.com.**

Printed in the United States of America
Print Number: 01   Print Year: 2017

About the Authors

V. Mark Durand

V. Mark Durand is known worldwide as an authority in the area of autism spectrum disorder. He is a professor of psychology at the University of South Florida–St. Petersburg, where he was the founding Dean of Arts & Sciences and Vice Chancellor for Academic Affairs. Dr. Durand is a fellow of the American Psychological Association. He has received more than $4 million in federal funding since the beginning of his career to study the nature, assessment, and treatment of behavior problems in children with disabilities. Before moving to Florida, he served in a variety of leadership positions at the University at Albany, including associate director for clinical training for the doctoral psychology program from 1987 to 1990, chair of the psychology department from 1995 to 1998, and interim dean of Arts and Sciences from 2001 to 2002. There he established the Center for Autism and Related Disabilities at the University at Albany–SUNY. He received his B.A., M.A., and Ph.D.—all in psychology—at the State University of New York–Stony Brook.

Dr. Durand was awarded the University Award for Excellence in Teaching at SUNY–Albany in 1991 and was given the Chancellor's Award for Excellence in Research and Creative Scholarship at the University of South Florida–St. Petersburg in 2007. He was named a 2014 Princeton Lecture Series Fellow and received the 2015 Jacobson Award for Critical Thinking from the American Psychological Association for his body of work in the field of autism spectrum disorder. Dr. Durand was elected to serve as President of the American Psychological Association's Division 33 (Intellectual and Developmental Disabilities/Autism Spectrum Disorders) for 2019. Dr. Durand is currently a member of the Professional Advisory Board for the Autism Society of America and was on the board of directors of the International Association of Positive Behavioral Support. He was co-editor of the *Journal of Positive Behavior Interventions,* serves on a number of editorial boards, and has more than 125 publications on functional communication, educational programming, and behavior therapy. His books include *Severe Behavior Problems: A Functional Communication Training Approach; Sleep Better! A Guide to Improving Sleep for Children with Special Needs; Helping Parents with Challenging Children: Positive Family Intervention;* the multiple national award-winning *Optimistic Parenting: Hope and Help for You and Your Challenging Child;* and most recently *Autism Spectrum Disorder: A Clinical Guide for General Practitioners.*

Dr. Durand developed a unique treatment for severe behavior problems that is currently mandated by states across the country and is used worldwide. He also developed an assessment tool that is used internationally and has been translated into more than 15 languages. Most recently he developed an innovative approach to help families work with their challenging child (Optimistic Parenting), which was validated in a five-year clinical trial. He has been consulted by the departments of education in numerous states and by the U.S. Departments of Justice and Education. His current research program includes the study of prevention models and treatments for such serious problems as self-injurious behavior.

In his leisure time, he enjoys long-distance running and has completed three marathons.

To Wendy and Jonathan, whose patience,

understanding, and love provided me

the opportunity to complete such

an ambitious project.

—V. M. D.

To my mother, Doris Elinor Barlow-Lanigan,

for her multidimensional influence

across my life span.

—D. H. B.

To Benjamin and Lukas for helping me

integrate the many dimensions of life.

—S. G. H.

David H. Barlow

David H. Barlow is an internationally recognized pioneer and leader in clinical psychology. Currently Professor Emeritus of Psychology and Psychiatry at Boston University, Dr. Barlow is Founder and Director Emeritus of the Center for Anxiety and Related Disorders, one of the largest research clinics of its kind in the world. From 1996 to 2004, he directed the clinical psychology programs at Boston University. From 1979 to 1996, he was distinguished professor at the University at Albany–State University of New York. From 1975 to 1979, he was professor of psychiatry and psychology at Brown University, where he also founded the clinical psychology internship program. From 1969 to 1975, he was professor of psychiatry at the University of Mississippi Medical Center, where he founded the psychology residency program. Dr. Barlow received his B.A. from the University of Notre Dame, his M.A. from Boston College, and his Ph.D. from the University of Vermont.

A fellow of every major psychological association, Dr. Barlow has received many awards in honor of his excellence in scholarship, including the National Institute of Mental Health Merit Award for his long-term contributions to the clinical research effort; the Distinguished Scientist Award for applications of psychology from the American Psychological Association; and the James McKeen Cattell Fellow Award from the Association for Psychological Science honoring individuals for their lifetime of significant intellectual achievements in applied psychological research. Other awards include the Distinguished Scientist Award from the Society of Clinical Psychology of the American Psychological Association and a certificate of appreciation from the APA section on the clinical psychology of women for "outstanding commitment to the advancement of women in psychology." He was awarded an Honorary Doctorate of Science from the University of Vermont, an Honorary Doctorate of Humane Letters from William James College, as well as the C. Charles Burlingame Award from the Institute of Living in Hartford Connecticut

"for his outstanding leadership in research, education, and clinical care." In 2014 he was awarded a Presidential Citation from the American Psychological Association "for his lifelong dedication and passion for advancing psychology through science, education, training, and practice."

He also has received career/lifetime contribution awards from the Massachusetts, Connecticut, and California Psychological Associations, as well as the University of Mississippi Medical Center and the Association for Behavioral and Cognitive Therapies. In 2000, he was named Honorary Visiting Professor at the Chinese People's Liberation Army General Hospital and Postgraduate Medical School in Beijing, China, and in 2015 was named Honorary President of the Canadian Psychological Association. In addition, the annual Grand Rounds in Clinical Psychology at Brown University was named in his honor. During the 1997–1998 academic year, he was Fritz Redlich Fellow at the Center for Advanced Study in the Behavioral Sciences in Palo Alto, California. His research has been continually funded by the National Institute of Mental Health for over 40 years.

Dr. Barlow has edited several journals including *Clinical Psychology: Science and Practice* and *Behavior Therapy*, has served on the editorial boards of more than 20 different journals, and is currently Editor in Chief of the "Treatments that Work" series for Oxford University Press. He has published more than 600 scholarly articles and written or edited more than 80 books and clinical manuals, including *Anxiety and Its Disorders*, 2nd edition, Guilford Press; *Clinical Handbook of Psychological Disorders: A Step-by-Step Treatment Manual*, 5th edition, Guilford Press; *Single-Case Experimental Designs: Strategies for Studying Behavior Change*, 3rd edition, Allyn & Bacon (with Matthew Nock and Michael Hersen); *The Scientist–Practitioner: Research and Accountability in the Age of Managed Care*, 2nd edition, Allyn & Bacon (with Steve Hayes and Rosemary Nelson-Gray); *Mastery of Your Anxiety and Panic*, Oxford University Press (with Michelle Craske); and, more recently, *The Unified Protocol for Transdiagnostic Treatment of Emotional Disorders with the Unified Team* at Boston University. The books and manuals have been translated into more than 20 languages, including Arabic, Chinese, and Russian.

Dr. Barlow was one of three psychologists on the task force that was responsible for reviewing the work of more than 1,000 mental health professionals who participated in the creation of *DSM-IV,* and he continued on as an Advisor to the *DSM-5* task force. He also chaired the APA task force on Psychological Intervention Guidelines, which created a template for the creation of clinical practice guidelines. His current research program focuses on the nature and treatment of anxiety and related emotional disorders.

At leisure he plays golf, skis, and retreats to his home on Nantucket Island, where he loves to write, walk on the beach, and visit with his island friends.

Stefan G. Hofmann

Stefan G. Hofmann is an international expert on psychotherapy for emotional disorders. He is a professor of psychology at Boston University, where he directs the Psychotherapy and Emotion Research Laboratory. He was born in a little town near Stuttgart in Germany, which may explain his thick German accent. He studied psychology at the University of Marburg, Germany, where he received his B.A., M.S., and Ph.D. A brief dissertation fellowship to spend some time at Stanford University turned into a longer research career in the United States. He eventually moved to the United States in 1994 to join Dr. Barlow's team at the University at Albany–State University of New York, and has been living in Boston since 1996.

Dr. Hofmann has an actively funded research program studying various aspects of emotional disorders with a particular emphasis on anxiety disorders, cognitive behavioral therapy, and neuroscience. More recently, he has been interested in mindfulness approaches, such as yoga and meditation practices, as treatment strategies of emotional disorders. Furthermore, he has been one of the leaders in translational research methods to enhance the efficacy of psychotherapy and to predict treatment outcome using neuroscience methods.

He has won many prestigious professional awards, including the Aaron T. Beck Award for Significant and Enduring Contributions to the Field of Cognitive Therapy by the Academy of Cognitive Therapy. He is a fellow of the American Psychological Association and the Association for Psychological Science and was president of various national and international professional societies, including the Association for Behavioral and Cognitive Therapies and the International Association for Cognitive Psychotherapy. He was an advisor to the *DSM-5* Development Process and a member of the *DSM-5* Anxiety Disorder Sub-Work Group. As part of this, he participated in the discussions about the revisions of the *DSM-5* criteria for various anxiety disorders, especially social anxiety disorder, panic disorder, and agoraphobia. Dr. Hofmann is a Thomson Reuters' Highly Cited Researcher.

Dr. Hofmann has been the editor in chief of *Cognitive Therapy and Research* and is also the Associate Editor of *Clinical Psychological Science*. He has published more than 300 peer-reviewed journal articles and 15 books, including *An Introduction of Modern CBT* (Wiley-Blackwell) and *Emotion in Therapy* (Guilford Press).

At leisure, he enjoys playing with his sons. He likes traveling to immerse himself into new cultures, make new friends, and reconnect with old ones. When time permits, he occasionally gets out his flute.

Brief Contents

1   Abnormal Behavior in Historical Context   **2**

2   An Integrative Approach to Psychopathology   **32**

3   Clinical Assessment, Diagnosis, and Research in Psychopathology   **69**

4   Anxiety Disorders   **117**

5   Somatoform and Dissociative Disorders   **172**

6   Mood Disorders and Suicide   **200**

7   Physical Disorders and Health Psychology   **248**

8   Eating and Sleep Disorders   **282**

9   Sexual and Gender Identity Disorders   **326**

10   Substance-Related and Impulse-Control Disorders   **366**

11   Personality Disorders   **408**

12   Schizophrenia and Other Psychotic Disorders   **444**

13   Developmental and Cognitive Disorders   **480**

14   Mental Health Services: Legal and Ethical Issues   **528**

Contents

Preface   **xix**

1 Abnormal Behavior in Historical Context   2

Understanding Psychopathology   3
■ *Judy: The Girl Who Fainted at the Sight of Blood*   3
What Is a Psychological Disorder?   4
The Science of Psychopathology   6
Historical Conceptions of Abnormal Behavior   8

The Supernatural Tradition   9
Demons and Witches   9
Stress and Melancholy   9
■ *Charles VI: The Mad King*   10
Treatments for Possession   10
Mass Hysteria   10
Modern Mass Hysteria   10
The Moon and the Stars   11
Comments   11

The Biological Tradition   11
Hippocrates and Galen   11

The 19th Century   12
■ *Discussing Diversity: Biological Explanations for Psychopathology in Women: A Brief History of Hysteria*   13
The Development of Biological Treatments   14
Consequences of the Biological Tradition   14

The Psychological Tradition   15
Moral Therapy   15
Asylum Reform and the Decline of Moral Therapy   16
Psychoanalytic Theory   16
Humanistic Theory   22
The Behavioral Model   22

An Integrative Approach   25

Summary   26

Key Terms   27

Answers to Concept Checks   28

Chapter Quiz   28

2 An Integrative Approach to Psychopathology   32

One-Dimensional versus Multidimensional Models   34
What Caused Judy's Phobia?   34
Outcome and Comments   35

Genetic Contributions to Psychopathology   36
The Nature of Genes   36
New Developments in the Study of Genes and Behavior   37
The Interaction of Genes and the Environment   38
Epigenetics and the Nongenomic "Inheritance" of Behavior   40

Neuroscience and Its Contributions to Psychopathology   41
The Central Nervous System   41
The Structure of the Brain   44

The Peripheral Nervous System   45
Neurotransmitters   47
Implications for Psychopathology   51
Psychosocial Influences on Brain Structure and Function   52
Interactions of Psychosocial Factors and Neurotransmitter Systems   53
Psychosocial Effects on the Development of Brain Structure and Function   54

Behavioral and Cognitive Science   55
Conditioning and Cognitive Processes   55
Learned Helplessness   55
Social Learning   56
Prepared Learning   57
Cognitive Science and the Unconscious   57

Emotions 58
  The Physiology and Purpose of Fear 58
  Emotional Phenomena 59
  The Components of Emotion 59
  Anger and Your Heart 60
  Emotions and Psychopathology 61

Cultural, Social, and Interpersonal Factors 61
  Voodoo and the Evil Eye 61
  Gender 62
  Social Effects on Health and Behavior 62

  ■ *Discussing Diversity: Fear: Evolutionary and Social Influences* 63
  Global Incidence of Psychological Disorders 64

Life-Span Development 64

Conclusions 65

Summary 66

Key Terms 67

Answers to Concept Checks 68

Chapter Quiz 68

3 Clinical Assessment, Diagnosis, and Research in Psychopathology 69

Assessing Psychological Disorders 70
  ■ *Frank: Young, Serious, and Anxious* 70
  Key Concepts in Assessment 71
  The Clinical Interview 72
  Physical Examination 74
  Behavioral Assessment 75
  Psychological Testing 76
  Neuropsychological Testing 81
  Neuroimaging: Pictures of the Brain 81
  Psychophysiological Assessment 82

Diagnosing Psychological Disorders 84
  Classification Issues 85
  Diagnosis before 1980 87
  DSM-III and *DSM-III-R* 87
  DSM-IV and *DSM-IV-TR* 88
  DSM-5 88
  Beyond *DSM-5:* Dimensions and Spectra 90

Conducting Research in Psychopathology 92
  Basic Components of a Research Study 92
  Statistical versus Clinical Significance 94
  The "Average" Client 95

Types of Research Methods 95
  Studying Individual Cases 95
  Research by Correlation 96
  Research by Experiment 98
  Single-Case Experimental Designs 100

Genetics and Behavior across Time and Cultures 104
  Studying Genetics 104
  Studying Behavior over Time 106
  Studying Behavior across Cultures 108
  The Power of a Program of Research 109
  Replication 110
  ■ *Discussing Diversity: Do Psychological Disorders Look the Same across Countries?* 111

Research Ethics 111

Summary 113

Key Terms 114

Answers to Concept Checks 115

Chapter Quiz 115

4 Anxiety, Trauma- and Stressor-Related, and Obsessive-Compulsive and Related Disorders 117

The Complexity of Anxiety Disorders 118
  Anxiety, Fear, and Panic: Some Definitions 118
  ■ *Gretchen: Attacked by Panic* 119
  Causes of Anxiety and Related Disorders 120
  ■ *Discussing Diversity: Cultural Influences on Anxiety* 121
  Comorbidity of Anxiety and Related Disorders 123

Anxiety Disorders 124

Generalized Anxiety Disorder 124
  ■ *Irene: Ruled by Worry* 124
  Clinical Description 125
  Statistics 125
  Causes 126
  Treatment 127

Panic Disorder and Agoraphobia 128
  ■ *Mrs. M: Self-Imprisoned* 129

Clinical Description **129**
Statistics **130**
Nocturnal Panic **131**
Causes **132**
Treatment **132**

Specific Phobia 135
Clinical Description **135**
Statistics **137**
Causes **138**
Treatment **140**

Social Anxiety Disorder (Social Phobia) 141
■ *Billy: Too Shy* **141**
Clinical Description **141**
■ *Chuck Knoblauch: Star Players?* **141**
Statistics **142**
Causes **142**
Treatment **144**
Selective Mutism **145**

Trauma and Stressor-Related Disorders 146

Posttraumatic Stress Disorder (PTSD) 146
Clinical Description **146**
■ *The Joneses: One Victim, Many Traumas* **147**
Statistics **148**
Causes **149**
Treatment **151**

Other Trauma- and Stressor-Related Disorders 152

Obsessive-Compulsive and Related Disorders 153

Obsessive-Compulsive Disorder 153
Clinical Description **154**
■ *Richard: Enslaved by Ritual* **154**
Statistics **155**
Causes **156**
Treatment **157**

Body Dysmorphic Disorder 158
■ *Jim: Ashamed to Be Seen* **158**
Clinical Description **159**
Statistics **159**
Causes and Treatment **160**

Other Obsessive-Compulsive and Related Disorders 161
Hoarding Disorder **161**
Trichotillomania (Hair Pulling Disorder) and Excoriation (Skin Picking Disorder) **164**

Summary 164

Key Terms 167

Answers to Concept Checks 168

Chapter Quiz 168

5 Somatic Symptom and Related Disorders and Dissociative Disorders 172

Somatic Symptom and Related Disorders 174
Somatic Symptom Disorder **174**
■ *Linda: Full-Time Patient* **174**
■ *The Medical Student: Temporary Pain* **175**
Illness Anxiety Disorder **175**
■ *Gail: Invisibly Ill* **175**
■ *Discussing Diversity: Somatic Symptoms around the World* **179**
Psychological Factors Affecting Medical Conditions **179**
Conversion Disorder (Functional Neurological Symptom Disorder) **180**
■ *Eloise: Unlearning Walking* **180**
■ *Celia: Seeing Through Blindness* **182**

Dissociative Disorders 184
Depersonalization-Derealization Disorder **185**
■ *Bonnie: Dancing Away from Herself* **185**
Dissociative Amnesia **185**
■ *The Woman Who Lost Her Memory* **186**
■ *Jeffrey: A Troubled Trip* **186**
Dissociative Identity Disorder **188**
■ *Jonah: Bewildering Blackouts* **188**
■ *Kenneth: The Hillside Strangler* **189**

Summary 196

Key Terms 196

Answers to Concept Checks 196

Chapter Quiz 197

6 Mood Disorders and Suicide 200

Understanding and Defining Mood Disorders 201
- ■ *Katie: Weathering Depression* 201
- An Overview of Depression and Mania 202
- The Structure of Mood Disorders 203
- Depressive Disorders 204
- ■ *Jack: A Life Kept Down* 205
- From Grief to Depression 206
- Other Depressive Disorders 207
- Disruptive Mood Dysregulation Disorder 208
- Bipolar Disorders 209
- ■ *Jane: Funny, Smart, and Desperate* 209
- ■ *Billy: The World's Best at Everything* 210

Prevalence of Mood Disorders 212
- Prevalence in Children, Adolescents, and Older Adults 212
- Life Span Developmental Influences on Mood Disorders 213
- Across Cultures 215

Causes of Mood Disorders 215
- Biological Dimensions 216
- Psychological Dimensions 219
- ■ *Katie: No Easy Transitions* 221
- Social and Cultural Dimensions 223
- An Integrative Theory 225

Treatment of Mood Disorders 227
- Medications 227
- Electroconvulsive Therapy and Transcranial Magnetic Stimulation 230
- Psychological Treatments for Depression 230
- ■ *Beck and Irene: A Dialogue* 231
- Combined Treatments for Depression 233
- Preventing Relapse of Depression 233
- Psychological Treatments for Bipolar Disorder 234
- ■ *Katie: The Triumph of the Self* 235

Suicide 236
- Statistics 236
- Causes 237
- ■ *Discussing Diversity: Suicide Behaviors around the World* 238
- Risk Factors 238
- Is Suicide Contagious? 240
- Treatment 240

Summary 243

Key Terms 244

Answers to Concept Checks 244

Chapter Quiz 244

7 Physical Disorders and Health Psychology 248

Psychological and Social Factors that Influence Health 249
- Health and Health-Related Behavior 250
- The Nature of Stress 251
- The Physiology of Stress 251
- Contributions to the Stress Response 252
- Stress, Anxiety, Depression, and Excitement 253
- Stress and the Immune Response 254
- How the Immune System Works 255

Psychosocial Effects on Physical Disorders 257
- AIDS 257
- Cancer 258
- Cardiovascular Problems 260
- ■ *John: The Human Volcano* 260
- Chronic Pain 264

- ■ *Discussing Diversity: The Influence of Culture on Individual Health and Development: Female Reproduction around the World* 267

Psychosocial Treatment of Physical Disorders 270
- Biofeedback 271
- Relaxation and Meditation 272
- A Comprehensive Stress- and Pain-Reduction Program 272
- ■ *Sally: Improving Her Perception* 272
- Drugs and Stress-Reduction Programs 273
- Denial as a Means of Coping 274
- Modifying Behaviors to Promote Health 274

Summary 277

Key Terms 278

Answers to Concept Checks 278

Chapter Quiz 278

8 Eating and Sleep–Wake Disorders 282

Major Types of Eating Disorders 283
Bulimia Nervosa 284
■ *Phoebe: Apparently Perfect* 284
Anorexia Nervosa 286
■ *Julie: The Thinner, the Better* 286
Binge-Eating Disorder 288
Statistics 289
■ *Discussing Diversity: Cultural Influences on Eating Disorders* 291

Causes of Eating Disorders 292
Social Dimensions 292
■ *Phoebe: Dancing to Destruction* 295
Biological Dimensions 295
Psychological Dimensions 296
An Integrative Model 297

Treatment of Eating Disorders 298
Drug Treatments 298
Psychological Treatments 298
■ *Phoebe: Taking Control* 299
Preventing Eating Disorders 301

Obesity 302
Statistics 302
Disordered Eating Patterns in Cases of Obesity 303

Causes 304
Treatment 304

Sleep–Wake Disorders: The Major Dyssomnias 306
An Overview of Sleep–Wake Disorders 306
Insomnia Disorder 308
■ *Sonja: School on Her Mind* 308
Hypersomnolence Disorders 311
■ *Ann: Sleeping in Public* 311
Narcolepsy 312
Breathing-Related Sleep Disorders 312
Circadian Rhythm Sleep Disorder 313

Treatment of Sleep Disorders 315
Medical Treatments 315
Environmental Treatments 315
Psychological Treatments 316
Preventing Sleep Disorders 317
Parasomnias and Their Treatment 317

Summary 320
Key Terms 321
Answers to Concept Checks 322
Chapter Quiz 322

9 Sexual Dysfunctions, Paraphilic Disorders, and Gender Dysphoria 326

What Is Normal Sexuality? 327
Gender Differences 329
Cultural Differences 330
The Development of Sexual Orientation 330

An Overview of Sexual Dysfunctions 332
Sexual Desire Disorders 333
■ *Mr. and Mrs. C: Getting Started* 334
Sexual Arousal Disorders 334
■ *Bill: Long Marriage, New Problem* 334
Orgasm Disorders 335
■ *Greta and Will: Loving Disunion* 336
■ *Gary: Running Scared* 336
Sexual Pain Disorder 337
■ *Jill: Sex and Spasms* 337
Assessing Sexual Behavior 338

Causes and Treatment of Sexual Dysfunction 339
Causes of Sexual Dysfunction 339
Treatment of Sexual Dysfunction 342
■ *Carl: Never Too Late* 342

Paraphilic Disorders: Clinical Descriptions 345
Fetishistic Disorder 346
Voyeuristic and Exhibitionistic Disorders 346
■ *Robert: Outside the Curtains* 346
Transvestic Disorder 346
■ *Mr. M: Strong Man in a Dress* 346
Sexual Sadism and Sexual Masochism Disorders 347
Pedophilic Disorder and Incest 348
■ *Tony: More and Less a Father* 349
Causes of Paraphilic Disorders 349
■ *Robert: Revenge on Repression* 350
■ *Tony: Trained Too Young* 350

Assessing and Treating Paraphilic Disorders 351
Psychological Treatment 351
■ *Tony: Imagining the Worst* 352
Drug Treatments 353
Summary 353

Gender Dysphoria 354
■ *Joe: Trapped in the Wrong Body* 354
Defining Gender Dysphoria 355
■ *Discussing Diversity: Alternative or Mixed Gender Identity* 356
Causes 356
■ *Bruce/Brenda: Gender and Biology* 356

Treatment 358
Summary 360
Key Terms 362
Answers to Concept Checks 362
Chapter Quiz 363

10 Substance-Related, Addictive, and Impulse-Control Disorders 366

Perspectives on Substance-Related and Addictive Disorders 367
■ *Danny: Comorbid Substance Use Disorders* 368
Levels of Involvement 368
Diagnostic Issues 370

Depressants 371
Alcohol-Related Disorders 371
Sedative-, Hypnotic-, or Anxiolytic-Related Disorders 375

Stimulants 377
Stimulant-Related Disorders 377
Tobacco-Related Disorders 380
Caffeine-Related Disorders 381

Opioid-Related Disorders 382

Cannabis-Related Disorders 383

Hallucinogen-Related Disorders 385

Other Drugs of Abuse 386

Causes of Substance-Related Disorders 387
Biological Dimensions 387
Psychological Dimensions 389

Cognitive Dimensions 390
Social Dimensions 390
Cultural Dimensions 391
An Integrative Model 391
■ *Discussing Diversity: Alcohol, Drugs, and Sex* 392

Treatment of Substance-Related Disorders 393
Biological Treatments 394
Psychosocial Treatments 395
Prevention 397

Gambling Disorder 398

Impulse-Control Disorders 399
Intermittent Explosive Disorder 400
Kleptomania 400
Pyromania 400

Summary 402
Key Terms 403
Answers to Concept Checks 404
Chapter Quiz 404

11 Personality Disorders 408

An Overview of Personality Disorders 409
Aspects of Personality Disorders 409
Categorical and Dimensional Models 409
Personality Disorder Clusters 410
Statistics and Development 410
Gender Differences 412
Comorbidity 413
Personality Disorders under Study 414

Cluster A Personality Disorders 415
Paranoid Personality Disorder 415
■ *Jake: Research Victim* 415
Schizoid Personality Disorder 416

■ *Mr. Z: All on His Own* 416
Schizotypal Personality Disorder 418
■ *Mr. S: All on His Own* 418

Cluster B Personality Disorders 420
Antisocial Personality Disorder 420
■ *Ryan: The Thrill Seeker* 420
Borderline Personality Disorder 426
■ *Claire: A Stranger Among Us* 426
■ *Discussing Diversity: Gender and Personality Disorder* 430
Histrionic Personality Disorder 430
■ *Pat: Always Onstage* 430
Narcissistic Personality Disorder 432

■ *Willie: It's All About Me* **432**

Cluster C Personality Disorders **434**

Avoidant Personality Disorder **434**

■ *Jane: Not Worth Noticing* **434**

Dependent Personality Disorder **435**

■ *Karen: Whatever You Say* **435**

Obsessive-Compulsive Personality Disorder **436**

■ *Daniel: Getting It Exactly Right* **436**

Summary **438**

Key Terms **439**

Answers to Concept Checks **439**

Chapter Quiz **440**

12 Schizophrenia Spectrum and Other Psychotic Disorders **444**

Perspectives on Schizophrenia **445**

Early Figures in Diagnosing Schizophrenia **445**

Identifying Symptoms **446**

■ *Arthur: Saving the Children* **446**

Clinical Description, Symptoms, and Subtypes **447**

Positive Symptoms **448**

■ *David: Missing Uncle Bill* **449**

Negative Symptoms **450**

Disorganized Symptoms **451**

Historic Schizophrenia Subtypes **452**

Other Psychotic Disorders **453**

Prevalence and Causes of Schizophrenia **456**

Statistics **456**

Development **457**

Cultural Factors **457**

Genetic Influences **458**

Neurobiological Influences **461**

Psychological and Social Influences **464**

Treatment of Schizophrenia **467**

Biological Interventions **467**

Psychosocial Interventions **469**

Treatment across Cultures **471**

Prevention **472**

■ *Discussing Diversity: Treatment and Understanding of Psychosis across Cultures* **472**

Summary **473**

Key Terms **475**

Answers to Concept Checks **475**

Chapter Quiz **476**

13 Neurodevelopmental and Neurocognitive Disorders **480**

Overview of Neurodevelopmental Disorders **481**

Attention-Deficit/Hyperactivity Disorder **483**

■ *Danny: The Boy Who Couldn't Sit Still* **483**

Clinical Description **484**

■ *Discussing Diversity: ADHD across Age and Gender* **484**

Statistics **485**

Causes **486**

Treatment of ADHD **487**

Specific Learning Disorder **488**

■ *Alice: Taking a Learning Disorder to College* **488**

Clinical Description **489**

Statistics **489**

Causes **490**

Treatment of Learning Disorders **491**

Autism Spectrum Disorder **492**

Clinical Description **492**

■ *Amy: In Her Own World* **492**

Statistics **494**

Causes: Psychological and Social Dimensions **495**

Causes: Biological Dimensions **495**

Treatment of Autism Spectrum Disorder **496**

Psychosocial Treatments **496**

Intellectual Disability (Intellectual Developmental Disorder) **498**

■ *James: Up to the Challenge* **498**

Clinical Description **499**

Statistics **500**

Causes **500**

Treatment of Intellectual Disability **503**

Prevention of Neurodevelopmental Disorders **504**

Overview of Neurocognitive Disorders **505**

Delirium **505**

■ *Mr. J: Sudden Distress* **505**

Clinical Description and Statistics **506**

Causes **506**

Treatment **507**

Prevention **507**

Major and Mild Neurocognitive Disorders **508**

■ *Pat Summitt: Grit and Determination* **509**
Clinical Description and Statistics **509**
Neurocognitive Disorder Due to Alzheimer's Disease **511**
Vascular Neurocognitive Disorder **512**
Other Medical Conditions That Cause Neurocognitive
  Disorder **512**
Substance/Medication-Induced Neurocognitive
  Disorder **515**

Causes of Neurocognitive Disorder **515**
Treatment **517**
Prevention **520**

Summary **521**

Key Terms **522**

Answers to Concept Checks **523**

Chapter Quiz **523**

14 Mental Health Services: Legal and Ethical Issues 528

■ *Arthur: A Family's Dilemma* **529**
Civil Commitment **529**
  Criteria for Civil Commitment **530**
Procedural Changes Affecting Civil Commitment **532**
■ *Joyce Brown: Homeless but Not Helpless* **533**
■ *Discussing Diversity: Mental Illness, Homelessness,
  and Culture* **534**
An Overview of Civil Commitment **535**

Criminal Commitment **535**
  The Insanity Defense **535**
  Reactions to the Insanity Defense **537**
  Therapeutic Jurisprudence **539**
  Competence to Stand Trial **539**
  Duty to Warn **539**
  Mental Health Professionals as Expert Witnesses **540**

**Patients' Rights and Clinical Practice
Guidelines** **541**
  The Right to Treatment **541**
  The Right to Refuse Treatment **541**
  The Rights of Research Participants **542**
  ■ *Greg Aller: Concerned About Rights* **542**
  Evidence-Based Practice and Clinical Practice
    Guidelines **543**

Summary **545**

Key Terms **546**

Answers to Concept Checks **546**

Chapter Quiz **546**

Appendix A Answers to Chapter Quizzes **A-1**

Glossary **G-1**

References **R-1**

Name Index **I-1**

Subject Index **I-22**

Preface

Science is a constantly evolving field, but every now and then something groundbreaking occurs that alters our way of thinking. For example, evolutionary biologists, who long assumed that the process of evolution was gradual, suddenly had to adjust to evidence that says evolution happens in fits and starts in response to such cataclysmic environmental events as meteor impacts. Similarly, geology has been revolutionized by the discovery of plate tectonics.

Until recently, the science of psychopathology had been compartmentalized, with psychopathologists examining the separate effects of psychological, biological, and social influences. This approach is still reflected in popular media accounts that describe, for example, a newly discovered gene, a biological dysfunction (chemical imbalance), or early childhood experiences as a "cause" of a psychological disorder. This way of thinking still dominates discussions of causality and treatment in some psychology textbooks: "The psychoanalytic views of this disorder are . . . ," "the biological views are . . . ," and, often in a separate chapter, "psychoanalytic treatment approaches for this disorder are . . . ," "cognitive behavioral treatment approaches are . . . ," or "biological treatment approaches are . . ."

In the first edition of this text, we tried to do something very different. We thought the field had advanced to the point that it was ready for an integrative approach in which the intricate interactions of biological, psychological, and social factors are explicated in as clear and convincing a manner as possible. Recent explosive advances in knowledge confirm this approach as the only viable way of understanding psychopathology. To take just two examples, Chapter 2 contains a description of a study demonstrating that stressful life events can lead to depression but that not everyone shows this response. Rather, stress is more likely to cause depression in individuals who already carry a particular gene that influences serotonin at the brain synapses. Similarly, Chapter 7 describes how the pain of social rejection activates the same neural mechanisms in the brain as physical pain. In addition, the entire section on genetics has been rewritten to highlight the new emphasis on gene–environment interaction, along with recent thinking from leading behavioral geneticists that the goal of basing the classification of psychological disorders on the firm foundation of genetics is fundamentally flawed. Descriptions of the emerging field of epigenetics, or the influence of the environment on gene expression, is also woven into the chapter, along with new studies on the seeming ability of extreme environments to largely override the effects of genetic contributions. Studies elucidating the mechanisms of epigenetics or specifically how environmental events influence gene expression are described.

These results confirm the integrative approach in this book: Psychological disorders cannot be explained by genetic or environmental factors alone but rather arise from their interaction. We now understand that psychological and social factors directly affect neurotransmitter function and even genetic expression. Similarly, we cannot study behavioral, cognitive, or emotional processes without appreciating the contribution of biological and social factors to psychological and psychopathological expression. Instead of compartmentalizing psychopathology, we use a more accessible approach that accurately reflects the current state of our clinical science.

As colleagues, you are aware that we understand some disorders better than others. But we hope you will share our excitement in conveying to students both what we currently know about the causes and treatments of psychopathology and how far we have yet to go in understanding these complex interactions.

Integrative Approach

As noted earlier, the first edition of *Essentials of Abnormal Psychology* pioneered a new generation of abnormal psychology textbooks, which offer an integrative and multidimensional perspective. (We acknowledge such one-dimensional approaches as biological, psychosocial, and supernatural as historic perspectives on our field.) We include substantial current evidence of the reciprocal influences of biology and behavior and of psychological and social influences on biology. Our examples hold students' attention; for example, we discuss genetic contributions to divorce, the effects of early social and behavioral experience on later brain function and structure, new information on the relation of social networks to the common cold, and new data on psychosocial treatments for cancer. We note that in the phenomenon of implicit memory and blind sight, which may have parallels in dissociative experiences, psychological science verifies the existence of the unconscious (although it does not much resemble the seething caldron of conflicts envisioned by Freud). We present new evidence confirming the effects of psychological treatments on neurotransmitter flow and brain function. We acknowledge the often-neglected area of emotion theory for its rich contributions to psychopathology (e.g., the effects of anger on cardiovascular disease). We weave scientific findings from the study of emotions together with behavioral, biological, cognitive, and social discoveries to create an integrated tapestry of psychopathology.

Life-Span Developmental Influences

No modern view of abnormal psychology can ignore the importance of life-span developmental factors in the manifestation and treatment of psychopathology. Studies highlighting developmental windows for the influence of the environment on gene expression are explained. Accordingly, although we include a chapter describing Neurodevelopmental Disorders (Chapter 13), we consider the importance of development throughout the text; we discuss childhood and geriatric anxiety, for example, in the context of the Anxiety, Trauma- and Stressor-Related, and Obsessive-Compulsive and Related Disorders (Chapter 4). This system of organization, which is for the most part consistent with *DSM-5*, helps students appreciate the need to study each disorder from childhood through adulthood and old age. We note findings on developmental considerations in separate sections of each disorder chapter and, as appropriate, discuss how specific developmental factors affect causation and treatment.

Scientist–Practitioner Approach

We go to some lengths to explain why the scientist–practitioner approach to psychopathology is both practical and ideal. Like most of our colleagues, we view this as something more than simple awareness of how scientific findings apply to psychopathology. We show how every clinician contributes to general scientific knowledge through astute and systematic clinical observations, functional analyses of individual case studies, and systematic observations of series of cases in clinical settings. For example, we explain how information on dissociative phenomena provided by early psychoanalytic theorists remains relevant today. We also describe the formal methods used by scientist–practitioners, showing how abstract research designs are actually implemented in research programs.

Clinical Cases of Real People

We have enriched the book with authentic clinical histories to illustrate scientific findings on the causes and treatment of psychopathology. We have run active clinics for years, so 95% of the cases are from our own files, and they provide a fascinating frame of reference for the findings we describe. The beginnings of most chapters include a case description, and most of the discussion of the latest theory and research is related to these very human cases.

Disorders in Detail

We cover the major psychological disorders in 10 chapters, focusing on three broad categories: clinical description, causal factors, and treatment and outcomes. We pay considerable attention to case studies and *DSM-5* criteria, and we include statistical data, such as prevalence and incidence rates, sex ratio, age of onset, and the general course or pattern for the disorder as a whole. Since several of us were appointed Advisors to the *DSM-5* task force, we are able to include the reasons for changes as well as the changes themselves. Throughout, we explore how biological, psychological, and social dimensions may interact to cause a particular disorder. Finally, by covering treatment and outcomes within the context of specific disorders, we provide a realistic sense of clinical practice.

Treatment

One of the best-received innovations in the first seven editions was our strategy of discussing treatments in the same chapter as the disorders themselves instead of in a separate chapter, an approach that is supported by the development of specific psychosocial and pharmacological treatment procedures for specific disorders. We have retained this integrative format and have improved upon it, and we include treatment procedures in the key terms and glossary.

Legal and Ethical Issues

In our closing chapter, we integrate many of the approaches and themes that have been discussed throughout the text. We include case studies of people who have been involved directly with many legal and ethical issues and with the delivery of mental health services. We also provide a historical context for current perspectives so students will understand the effects of social and cultural influences on legal and ethical issues.

Diversity

Issues of culture and gender are integral to the study of psychopathology. Throughout the text, we describe current thinking about which aspects of the disorders are culturally specific and which are universal, and about the strong and sometimes puzzling effects of gender roles. This is accomplished both in the narrative and in "Discussing Diversity" boxes throughout the disorders chapters. For instance, we discuss the current information on such topics as the gender imbalance in depression, how panic disorders are expressed differently in various Asian cultures, the ethnic differences in eating disorders, treatment of schizophrenia across cultures, and the diagnostic differences of attention deficit/hyperactivity disorder (ADHD) in boys and girls. Clearly, our field will grow in depth and detail as these subjects and others become standard research topics. For example, why do some disorders overwhelmingly affect females and others appear predominantly in males? And why does this apportionment sometimes change from one culture to another? In answering questions like these, we adhere closely to science, emphasizing that gender and culture are each one dimension among several that constitute psychopathology.

New to This Edition

A Thorough Update

This exciting field moves at a rapid pace, and we take particular pride in how our book reflects the most recent developments. Therefore, once again, every chapter has been carefully revised to reflect the latest research studies on psychological disorders. Hundreds of new references from 2015 to 2017 (and some still "in press") appear for the first time in this edition, and some of the information they contain stuns the imagination. Non-essential material has been eliminated, some new headings have been added, and *DSM-5* criteria are included in their entirety as tables in the appropriate disorder chapters.

Anxiety, Trauma- and Stressor-Related, and Obsessive-Compulsive and Related Disorders (Chapter 4), Mood Disorders and Suicide (Chapter 6), Physical Disorders and Health Psychology (Chapter 7), Eating and Sleep–Wake Disorders (Chapter 8), Substance-Related, Addictive, and Impulse-Control Disorders (Chapter 10), Schizophrenia Spectrum and Other Psychotic Disorders (Chapter 12), and Neurodevelopmental Neurocognitive Disorders (Chapter 13) have been the most heavily revised to reflect new research, but all chapters have been significantly updated and freshened.

Chapter 1, Abnormal Behavior in Historical Context, features updated nomenclature to reflect new titles in *DSM-5*, updated descriptions of research on defense mechanisms, and fuller and deeper descriptions of the historical development of psychodynamic and psychoanalytic approaches.

Chapter 2, An Integrative Approach to Psychopathology, includes an updated discussion of developments in the study of genes and behavior with a focus on gene–environment interaction; new data illustrating the gene–environment correlation model; new studies illustrating the psychosocial influence on the development of brain structure and function in general and on neurotransmitter systems specifically; updated, revised, and refreshed sections on behavioral and cognitive science including new studies illustrating the influence of positive psychology on physical health and longevity; new studies supporting the strong influence of emotions, specifically anger, on cardiovascular health; new studies illustrating the influence of gender on the presentation and treatment of psychopathology; a variety of powerful new studies confirming strong social effects on health and behavior; and new studies confirming the puzzling "drift" phenomenon resulting in a higher prevalence of schizophrenia among individuals living in urban areas.

Chapter 3, Clinical Assessment, Diagnosis, and Research in Psychopathology now presents references to "intellectual disability" instead of "mental retardation" to be consistent with *DSM-5* and changes within the field; (a new discussion about how information from the MMPI-2—although informative—does not necessarily change how clients are treated and may not improve their outcomes;) a description of the organization and structure of *DSM-5* along with major changes from *DSM-IV*; a description of methods to coordinate the development of *DSM-5* with the forthcoming ICD 11; and a description of likely directions of research as we begin to head toward *DSM-6*. In addition, a new example of how behavioral scientists develop research hypotheses is presented and a new example of longitudinal designs which look at how the use of spanking predicts later behavior problems in children (Gershoff, Lansford, Sexton, Davis-Kean, & Sameroff, 2012).

Chapter 4, entitled Anxiety, Trauma- and Stressor-Related, and Obsessive-Compulsive and Related Disorders, is organized according to the three major groups of disorders: anxiety disorders, trauma- and stressor-related disorders, and obsessive-compulsive and related disorders. Two disorders new to *DSM-5* (separation anxiety disorder and selective mutism) are presented, and the Trauma- and Stressor-Related Disorders section includes not only post-traumatic stress disorder and acute stress disorder but also adjustment disorder and attachment disorders. The final new grouping, Obsessive-Compulsive and Related Disorders, includes not only obsessive-compulsive disorder but also body dysmorphic disorder, hoarding disorder, and finally trichotillomania (hair pulling disorder) and excoriation (skin picking disorder). Some of the revisions to Chapter 4 include the following:

- Updated information about the neuroscience and genetics of fear and anxiety;
- Updated information on the relationship of anxiety and related disorders to suicide;
- Updated information on the influence of personality and culture on the expression of anxiety;
- Updated generalized anxiety disorder discussion, especially about newer treatment approaches;
- Updated information on description, etiology, and treatment for specific phobia, social anxiety disorder, and posttraumatic stress disorder.

The grouping of disorders in Chapter 5, titled Somatic Symptom and Related Disorders and Dissociative Disorders, reflects a major overarching change, specifically for somatic symptom disorder, illness anxiety disorder (formerly known as hypochondriasis), and psychological factors affecting medical conditions. The chapter discusses the differences between these overlapping disorders and provides a summary of the causes and treatment approaches of these problems. In addition, Chapter 5 now has an updated discussion on the false memory debate related to trauma in individuals with dissociative identity disorder.

Chapter 6, Mood Disorders and Suicide, provides an updated discussion on the psychopathology and treatment of the *DSM-5* Mood Disorders, including persistent depressive disorder, seasonal affective disorder, disruptive mood dysregulation disorder, bipolar disorder, and suicide. The chapter discusses new data on the genetic and environmental risk factors and protective factors, such as optimism. Also included is an update on the pharmacological and psychological treatments.

Chapter 7, Physical Disorders and Health Psychology, includes updated data on the leading causes of death in the United States; a review of the increasing depth of knowledge on the influence of psychological social factors on brain structures and function; new data supporting the efficacy of stress management on cardiovascular disease; an updated review of developments into causes and treatment of chronic pain; updated information eliminating certain viruses (XMRV and pMLV) as possible causes of chronic fatigue syndrome; and updated review of psychological and behavioral procedures for preventing injuries.

Thoroughly rewritten and updated, Chapter 8, Eating and Sleep–Wake Disorders, contains new information on mortality and suicide rates in anorexia nervosa; new epidemiological information on the prevalence of eating disorders in adolescents; new information on the increasing globalization of eating disorders and obesity; updated information on typical patterns of comorbidity accompanying eating disorders; and new and updated research on changes in the incidence of eating disorders among males, racial and ethnic differences on the thin-ideal body image associated with eating disorders, the substantial contribution of emotion dysregulation to etiology and maintenance of anorexia, the role of friendship cliques in the etiology of eating disorders, mothers with eating disorders who also restrict food intake by their children, the contribution of parents and family factors in the etiology of eating disorders, biological and genetic contributions to causes of eating disorders including the role of ovarian hormones, transdiagnostic treatment applicable to all eating disorders, results from a large multinational trial comparing CBT to psychoanalysis in the treatment of bulimia, the effects of combining Prozac with CBT in the treatment of eating disorders, racial and ethnic differences in people with binge eating disorder seeking treatment, the phenomenon of night eating syndrome and its role in the development of obesity, and new public health policy developments directed at the obesity epidemic.

Realigned coverage of Sleep–Wake Disorders, also in Chapter 8, with new information on sleep in women is now reported—including risk and protective factors, an updated section on narcolepsy to describe new research on the causes of this disorder, and new research on the nature and treatment of nightmares are now included.

In Chapter 9, Sexual Dysfunctions, Paraphilic Disorders, and Gender Dysphoria, a revised organization of sexual dysfunctions, paraphilic disorders, and gender dysphoria to reflect the fact that both paraphilic disorders and gender dysphoria are separate chapters in *DSM-5*, and gender dysphoria disorder, is, of course, not a sexual disorder but a disorder reflecting incongruence between natal sex and expressed gender, in addition to other major revisions—new data on developmental changes in sexual behavior from age of first intercourse to prevalence and frequency of sexual behavior in old age; new reports contrasting differing attitudes and engagement in sexual activity across cultures even within North America; updated information on the development of sexual orientation; and a thoroughly updated description of gender dysphoria with an emphasis on emerging conceptualizations of gender expression that are on a continuum.

Chapter 9 also includes updated information on contributing factors to gender dysphoria as well as the latest recommendations on treatment options, recommended treatment options (or the decision not to treat) for gender non-conformity in children, a full description of disorders of sex development (formerly called intersexuality), and a thoroughly revamped description of paraphilic disorders to reflect the updated system of classification with a discussion of the controversial change in the name of these disorders from paraphilia to paraphilic disorders.

A thoroughly revised Chapter 10, Substance-Related, Addictive, and Impulse-Control Disorders, features new discussion of how the trend to mix caffeinated energy drinks with alcohol may increase the likelihood of later abuse of alcohol; new research on chronic use of MDMA ("Ecstasy") leading to lasting memory problems (Wagner, Becker, Koester, Gouzoulis-Mayfrank, & Daumann, 2013); and new research on several factors predicting early alcohol use, including when best friends have started drinking, whether family members are at high risk for alcohol dependence, and the presence of behavior problems in these children (Kuperman *et al.*, 2013).

Chapter 11, Personality Disorders, now features a completely new section on gender differences to reflect newer, more sophisticated analyses of prevalence data, and a new section on criminality and antisocial personality disorder is now revised to better reflect changes in *DSM-5*.

Chapter 12, Schizophrenia Spectrum and Other Psychotic Disorders, presents a new discussion of schizophrenia spectrum disorder and the dropping of subtypes of schizophrenia from *DSM-5;* new research on deficits in emotional prosody comprehension and its role in auditory hallucinations (Alba-Ferrara, Fernyhough, Weis, Mitchell, & Hausmann, 2012); a discussion of a new proposed psychotic disorder suggested in *DSM-5* for further study—Attenuated Psychosis Syndrome; and a new discussion of the use of transcranial magnetic stimulation.

In Chapter 13 (Neurodevelopmental and Neurocognitive Disorders), the neurodevelopmental disorders are presented, instead of Pervasive Developmental Disorders, to be consistent with the major changes in *DSM-5*. In addition, Chapter 13 now describes new research to show that gene–environment interaction can lead to later behavior problems in children with ADHD (Thapar, Cooper, Jefferies, & Stergiakouli, 2012; Thapar *et al.*, 2005); new research on ADHD (and on other disorders) that is finding that in many cases mutations occur that either create extra copies of a gene on one chromosome or result in the deletion of genes (called copy number variants—CNVs) (Elia *et al.*, 2009; Lesch *et al.*, 2010); and new research findings that show a variety of genetic mutations, including de novo disorders (genetic mutations occurring in the sperm or egg or after fertilization), are present in those children with intellectual disability (ID) of previously unknown origin (Rauch *et al.*, 2012). Chapter 13 also features descriptions of research assessing brain activity (fMRI) in individuals during active episodes of delirium as well as after these episodes; data from the Einstein Aging Study concerning the prevalence of a disorder new in *DSM-5*, mild neurocognitive disorder (Katz *et al.*, 2012); and a discussion of new neurocognitive disorders (e.g., neurocognitive disorder due to Lewy bodies or prion disease).

And Chapter 14, Mental Health Services: Legal and Ethical Issues, presents a brief, but new, discussion of the recent trend to provide individuals needing emergency treatment with court-ordered assisted outpatient treatment (AOT) to avoid commitment in a mental health facility (Nunley, Nunley, Cutleh, Dentingeh, & McFahland, 2013); a new discussion of a major meta-analysis showing that current risk assessment tools are best at identifying persons at low risk of being violent but only marginally successful at accurately detecting who will be violent at a later point (Fazel, Singh, Doll, & Grann, 2012); and an updated section on legal rulings on involuntary medication.

Additional Features

In addition to the changes highlighted earlier, *Essentials of Abnormal Psychology* features other distinct features:

- *Student Learning Outcomes* at the start of each chapter assist instructors in accurately assessing and mapping questions throughout the chapter. The outcomes are mapped to core American Psychological Association goals and are integrated throughout the instructor resources and testing program.
- In each disorder chapter a feature called *DSM Controversies,* which discusses some of the contentious and thorny decisions made in the process of creating *DSM-5.* Examples include the creation of new and sometimes controversial disorders appearing for the first time in *DSM-5*, such as premenstrual dysphoric disorder, binge eating disorder, and disruptive mood dysregulation disorder. Another example is removing the "grief" exclusion criteria for diagnosing major depressive disorder so that someone can be diagnosed with major depression even if the trigger was the death of a loved one. Finally, changing the title of the "paraphilia" chapter to "paraphilic disorders" implies that paraphilic sexual arousal patterns such as pedophilia are not disorders in themselves, but only become disorders if they cause impairment or harm to others.

DSM-IV, DSM-IV-TR, and DSM-5

Much has been said about the mix of political and scientific considerations that resulted in *DSM-5*, and naturally there are controversial views on this. Psychologists and psychiatrists are often concerned about their own specific areas of interest in what has become—for better or worse—the nosological standard in our field, and with good reason: in previous *DSM* editions, scientific findings sometimes gave way to personal opinions. For *DSM-IV* and *DSM-5*, however, most professional biases were left at the door while the task force almost endlessly debated the data. This process produced enough new information to fill every psychopathology journal for a year with integrative reviews, reanalysis of existing databases, and new data from field trials. From a scholarly point of view, the process was both stimulating and exhausting. This book contains highlights of various debates that created the nomenclature, as well as recent updates. For example, in addition to the controversies described above, we summarize and update the data and discussion of premenstrual dysphoric disorder, which was designated a new disorder in *DSM-5*, and mixed anxiety depression, a disorder that did not make it into the final criteria. Students can thus see the process of making diagnoses, as well as the combination of data and inferences that are part of it.

We also discuss the intense continuing debate on categorical and dimensional approaches to classification. We describe some of the compromises the task force made to accommodate data, such as why dimensional approaches to personality disorders did not make it into *DSM-5*, and why the proposal to do so was rejected at the last minute and included in Section III under "Conditions for Further Study" even though almost everyone agrees that these disorders should not be categorical but rather dimensional.

Prevention

Looking into the future of abnormal psychology as a field, it seems our ability to prevent psychological disorders may help the most. Although this has long been a goal of many, we now appear to be at the cusp of a new age in prevention research. Scientists from all over the globe are developing the methodologies and techniques that may at long last provide us with the means to interrupt the debilitating toll of emotional distress caused by the disorders chronicled in this book. We therefore highlight these cutting-edge prevention efforts—such as preventing eating disorders, suicide, and health problems, including HIV and injuries—in appropriate chapters as a means to celebrate these important advancements, as well as to spur on the field to continue this important work.

Retained Features

Visual Summaries

At the end of each disorder chapter is a colorful, two-page visual overview that succinctly summarizes the causes, development, symptoms, and treatment of each disorder covered in the chapter. Our integrative approach is instantly evident in these diagrams, which show the interaction of biological, psychological, and social factors in the etiology and treatment of disorders. The visual summaries will help instructors wrap up discussions, and students will appreciate them as study aids.

Pedagogy

Each chapter contains several Concept Checks, which let students verify their comprehension at regular intervals. Answers are listed at the end of each chapter along with a more detailed Summary; the Key Terms are listed in the order they appear in the text and thus form a sort of outline that students can study.

MindTap for Durand, Barlow, and Hofmann's *Essentials of Abnormal Psychology*

MindTap is a personalized teaching experience with relevant assignments that guide students to analyze, apply, and improve thinking, allowing you to measure skills and outcomes with ease.

- Guide Students: A unique learning path of relevant readings, media, and activities that moves students up the learning taxonomy from basic knowledge and comprehension to analysis and application.
- Personalized Teaching: Becomes yours with a Learning Path that is built with key student objectives. Control what students see and when they see it. Use it as-is or match to your syllabus exactly—hide, rearrange, add, and create your own content.
- Promote Better Outcomes: Empower instructors and motivate students with analytics and reports that provide a snapshot of class progress, time in course, engagement, and completion rates.
- In addition to the benefits of the platform, MindTap for Durand, Barlow, and Hofmann's *Essentials of Abnormal Psychology* includes:
  - Profiles in Psychopathology, an exciting new product that guides users through the symptoms, causes, and treatments of individuals who live with mental disorders.
  - Videos, assessment, and activities from the *Continuum Video Project.*
  - *Concept Clip Videos* that visually elaborate on specific disorders and psychopathology in a vibrant, engaging manner.
  - Case studies to help students humanize psychological disorders and connect content to the real world.

- Section quizzes aid student understanding.
- Master Training, powered by Cerego, for student personalized learning plans to help them understand and retain key topics and discussions.

Teaching and Learning Aids

Instructor Resource Center

Everything you need for your course in one place! This collection of book-specific lecture and class tools is available online via www.cengage.com/login. Access and download videos, PowerPoint presentations, images, instructor's manual, and more.

Cognero

Cengage Learning Testing Powered by Cognero is a flexible, online system that allows you to author, edit, and manage test bank content from multiple Cengage Learning solutions, create multiple test versions in an instant, and deliver tests from your LMS, your classroom, or wherever you want.

Instructor's Manual

The Online Instructor's Manual contains chapter overviews, learning objectives, lecture outlines with discussion points, key terms, classroom activities, demonstrations, and lecture topics, suggested supplemental reading material, handouts, video resources, and internet resources.

Profiles in Psychopathology

In Profiles of Psychopathology, students explore the lives of individuals with mental disorders to better understand the etiology, symptoms, and treatment. Each of the ten modules focuses on one type of disorder. Students learn about six individuals—historical and popular culture figures—and then match the individual to the disorder that best explains their symptoms and causes. The experiences of a real-life person from the population-at-large is also featured, with video footage of that individual discussing their experience with psychopathology.

Continuum Video Project

The Continuum Video Project provides holistic, three-dimensional portraits of individuals dealing with psychopathologies. Videos show clients living their daily lives, interacting with family and friends, and displaying—rather than just describing—their symptoms. Before each video segment, students are asked to make observations about the individual's symptoms, emotions, and behaviors, and then rate them on the spectrum from normal to severe. The Continuum Video Project allows students to "see" the disorder and the person, humanly; the videos also illuminate student understanding that abnormal behavior can be viewed along a continuum.

PowerPoint

The Online PowerPoints feature lecture outlines and important images from the text.

Titles of Interest

- *DSM-5 Supplement* by Boettcher, Wu, Barlow, and Durand is a thorough comparison of the changes made in *DSM-5* with the previous criteria and language in *DSM-IV-TR*. Also includes discussion of major controversies resulting from the proposed and realized modifications to the latest diagnostic manual. ISBN: 9781285848181
- *Looking into Abnormal Psychology: Contemporary Readings* by Scott O. Lilienfeld is a fascinating 234-page reader consisting of 40 articles from popular magazines and journals. Each article explores ongoing controversies regarding mental illness and its treatment. ISBN: 0534354165
- *Casebook in Abnormal Psychology*, 5th edition, by Timothy A. Brown and David H. Barlow, is a comprehensive casebook fully updated to be consistent with *DSM-5* that reflects the integrative approach, which considers the multiple influences of genetic, biological, familial, and environmental factors into a unified model of causality as well as maintenance and treatment of the disorder. The casebook discusses treatment methods that are the most effective interventions developed for a particular disorder. It also presents three undiagnosed cases in order to give students an appreciation for the complexity of disorders. The cases are strictly teaching/learning exercises, similar to what many instructors use on their examinations. ISBN: 9781305971714.

Acknowledgments

Finally, this book in all of its editions would not have begun and certainly would not have been finished without the inspiration and coordination of our senior editors at Cengage, Erin Schnair and Carly McJunkin, who always keep their eyes on the ball. A special note of thanks to senior content developer Tangelique Williams-Grayer and her eye for detail and organization. And we are incredibly grateful for Shannon LeMay-Finn whose work on this edition made it as smooth a process as we could have imagined. The book is much better for your efforts. We hope to work with you on many subsequent editions. We appreciate the expertise of marketing coordinator, Quynton Johnson. Leah Jenson, product assistant, was hardworking, enthusiastic, and organized from beginning to end.

In the production process, many individuals worked as hard as we did to complete this project. In Boston, Hannah Boettcher, Clair Cassiello-Robbins, Amantia Ametaj and Olenka S. Olesnycky assisted enormously in integrating a vast amount of new information into each chapter. Their ability to find missing references and track down information was remarkable, and Hannah and Jade Wu also took the lead in putting together a remarkably useful supplement detailing all of the changes in diagnostic criteria from *DSM-IV* to *DSM-5* in an easy-to-read, side-by-side format. It is an understatement to say we couldn't have done it without you. In St. Petersburg, Ashley Smith's professionalism and attention to detail helped smooth this process immensely. At Cengage, Vernon Boes guided the design down to the last detail. Cengage Content Production Manager Ruth Sakata-Corley and Lumina Datamatics Project Manager Suganya Radjaradjane coordinated all production details with grace under pressure. We thank Ragav Seshadri with Lumina Datamatics for his commitment to licensing the best photos possible

Numerous colleagues and students provided superb feedback on the previous editions, and to them we express our deepest gratitude. Although not all comments were favorable, all were important. Readers who take the time to communicate their thoughts offer the greatest reward to writers and scholars.

Finally, you share with us the task of communicating knowledge and discoveries in the exciting field of psychopathology, a challenge that none of us takes lightly. In the spirit of collegiality, we would greatly appreciate your comments on the content and style of this book and recommendations for improving it further.

Reviewers

Creating this book has been both stimulating and exhausting, and we could not have done it without the valuable assistance of colleagues who read one or more chapters and provided extraordinarily perceptive critical comments, corrected errors, pointed to relevant information, and, on occasion, offered new insights that helped us achieve a successful, integrative model of each disorder.

We thank the following expert reviewers and survey participants:

Kanika Bell, *Clark Atlanta University*
Jamie S Bodenlos, *Hobart and William Smith Colleges*
Lawrence Burns, *Grand Valley State University*
Don Evans, *Simpson College*
Susan Frankel, *Lamar Community College*
Tammy Hanna, *Albertus Magnus College*
Sarah Heavin, *University of Puget Sound*
Stephen T. Higgins, *University of Vermont*
Fiyyaz Karim, *University of Minnesota*
Maureen C. Kenny, *Florida International University*
Lissa Lim, *California State University–San Marcos*
Barbara S. McCrady, *University of New Mexico*
Winfried Rief, *University of Marburg–Germany*
Robert Rotunda, *University of West Florida*
Kyle Stephenson, *Willamette University*
Lynda Szymanski, *St. Catherine University*
Amanda Sesko, *University of Alaska–Southeast*
Dale Alden, *Lipscomb University*
Kerm Almos, *Capital University*
Frank Andrasik, *University of Memphis*
Robin Apple, *Stanford University Medical Center*
Barbara Beaver, *University of Wisconsin*
James Becker, *University of Pittsburgh*
Evelyn Behar, *University of Illinois–Chicago*
Dorothy Bianco, *Rhode Island College*
Sarah Bisconer, *College of William & Mary*
Susan Blumenson, *City University of New York, John Jay College of Criminal Justice*
Robert Bornstein, *Adelphi University*
James Calhoun, *University of Georgia*
Montie Campbell, *Oklahoma Baptist University*
Robin Campbell, *Brevard Community College*
Shelley Carson, *Harvard University*
Richard Cavasina, *California University of Pennsylvania*
Antonio Cepeda-Benito, *Texas A&M University*
Kristin Christodulu, *State University of New York–Albany*
Bryan Cochran, *University of Montana*
Julie Cohen, *University of Arizona*

Dean Cruess, *University of Connecticut*
Sarah D'Elia, *George Mason University*
Robert Doan, *University of Central Oklahoma*
Juris Draguns, *Pennsylvania State University*
Melanie Duckworth, *University of Nevada–Reno*
Mitchell Earleywine, *State University of New York–Albany*
Chris Eckhardt, *Purdue University*
Elizabeth Epstein, *Rutgers University*
Donald Evans, *University of Otago*
Ronald G. Evans, *Washburn University*
Janice Farley, *Brooklyn College, CUNY*
Anthony Fazio, *University of Wisconsin–Milwaukee*
Diane Finley, *Prince George's Community College*
Allen Frances, *Duke University*
Louis Franzini, *San Diego State University*
Maximillian Fuhrmann, *California State University–Northridge*
Aubyn Fulton, *Pacific Union College*
Noni Gaylord-Harden, *Loyola University–Chicago*
Trevor Gilbert, *Athabasca University*
David Gleaves, *University of Canterbury*
Frank Goodkin, *Castleton State College*
Irving Gottesman, *University of Minnesota*
Laurence Grimm, *University of Illinois–Chicago*
Mark Grudberg, *Purdue University*
Marjorie Hardy, *Eckerd College*
Keith Harris, *Canyon College*
Christian Hart, *Texas Women's University*
William Hathaway, *Regent University*
Brian Hayden, *Brown University*
Stephen Hinshaw, *University of California, Berkeley*
Alexandra Hye-Young Park, *Humboldt State University*
William Iacono, *University of Minnesota*
Heidi Inderbitzen-Nolan, *University of Nebraska–Lincoln*
Thomas Jackson, *University of Arkansas*
Kristine Jacquin, *Mississippi State University*
James Jordan, *Lorain County Community College*
Boaz Kahana, *Cleveland State University*
Arthur Kaye, *Virginia Commonwealth University*
Christopher Kearney, *University of Nevada–Las Vegas*
Ernest Keen, *Bucknell University*
Elizabeth Klonoff, *San Diego State University*
Ann Kring, *University of California–Berkeley*
Marvin Kumler, *Bowling Green State University*
Thomas Kwapil, *University of North Carolina–Greensboro*
George Ladd, *Rhode Island College*
Michael Lambert, *Brigham Young University*
Travis Langley, *Henderson State University*
Christine Larson, *University of Wisconsin–Milwaukee*

Elizabeth Lavertu, *Burlington County College*
Cynthia Ann Lease, *VA Medical Center, Salem, VA*
Richard Leavy, *Ohio Wesleyan University*
Karen Ledbetter, *Portland State University*
Scott Lilienfeld, *Emory University*
Kristi Lockhart, *Yale University*
Michael Lyons, *Boston University*
Jerald Marshall, *Valencia Community College*
Janet Matthews, *Loyola University–New Orleans*
Dean McKay, *Fordham University*
Mary McNaughton-Cassill, *University of Texas at San Antonio*
Suzanne Meeks, *University of Louisville*
Michelle Merwin, *University of Tennessee–Martin*
Thomas Miller, *Murray State University*
Scott Monroe, *University of Notre Dame*
Greg Neimeyer, *University of Florida*
Sumie Okazaki, *New York University*
John Otey, *South Arkansas University*
Christopher Patrick, *University of Minnesota*
P. B. Poorman, *University of Wisconsin–Whitewater*
Katherine Presnell, *Southern Methodist University*
Lynn Rehm, *University of Houston*
Kim Renk, *University of Central Florida*
Alan Roberts, *Indiana University–Bloomington*
Melanie Rodriguez, *Utah State University*
Carol Rothman, *City University of New York, Herbert H. Lehman College*
Steve Schuetz, *University of Central Oklahoma*
Stefan Schulenberg, *University of Mississippi*

Paula K. Shear, *University of Cincinnati*
Steve Saiz, *State University of New York–Plattsburgh*
Jerome Small, *Youngstown State University*
Ari Solomon, *Williams College*
Michael Southam-Gerow, *Virginia Commonwealth University*
John Spores, *Purdue University–North Central*
Brian Stagner, *Texas A&M University*
Irene Staik, *University of Montevallo*
Rebecca Stanard, *State University of West Georgia*
Chris Tate, *Middle Tennessee State University*
Lisa Terre, *University of Missouri–Kansas City*
Gerald Tolchin, *Southern Connecticut State University*
Michael Vasey, *Ohio State University*
Larry Ventis, *College of William & Mary*
Richard Viken, *Indiana University*
Lisa Vogelsang, *University of Minnesota–Duluth*
Philip Watkins, *Eastern Washington University*
Kim Weikel, *Shippensburg University of Pennsylvania*
Amy Wenzel, *University of Pennsylvania*
W. Beryl West, *Middle Tennessee State University*
Michael Wierzbicki, *Marquette University*
Richard Williams, *State University of New York–College at Potsdam*
John Wincze, *Brown University*
Bradley Woldt, *South Dakota State University*
Nancy Worsham, *Gonzaga University*
Ellen Zaleski, *Fordham University*
Raymond Zurawski, *St. Norbert College*

1

Abnormal Behavior in Historical Context

CHAPTER OUTLINE

Understanding
Psychopathology

   What Is a Psychological Disorder?
   The Science of Psychopathology
   Historical Conceptions of Abnormal
     Behavior

The Supernatural Tradition

   Demons and Witches
   Stress and Melancholy
   Treatments for Possession
   Mass Hysteria
   Modern Mass Hysteria
   The Moon and the Stars
   Comments

The Biological Tradition

   Hippocrates and Galen
   The 19th Century
   The Development of Biological
     Treatments
   Consequences of the Biological
     Tradition

The Psychological Tradition

   Moral Therapy
   Asylum Reform and the Decline of
     Moral Therapy
   Psychoanalytic Theory
   Humanistic Theory
   The Behavioral Model

An Integrative Approach

PhotoAlto/Alamy Stock Photo

Describe key concepts, principles, and overarching themes in psychology	▶ Explain why psychology is a science with the primary objectives of describing, understanding, predicting, and controlling behavior and mental processes (APA SLO 1.1b) (see textbook pages 3–6, 22–25) ▶ Use basic psychological terminology, concepts, and theories in psychology to explain behavior and mental processes (APA SLO 1.1a) (see textbook pages 3–5, 7–13, 16–20, 22–26)
Develop a working knowledge of the content domains of psychology	▶ Summarize important aspects of history of psychology, including key figures, central concerns, methods used, and theoretical conflicts (APA SLO 1.2c) (see textbook pages 8–27, 30–31) ▶ Identify key characteristics of major content domains in psychology (e.g., cognition and learning, developmental, biological, and sociocultural) (APA SLO 1.2a) (see textbook pages 3–5, 11–25)
Use scientific reasoning to interpret behavior	▶ See APA SLO 1.1b listed above ▶ Incorporate several appropriate levels of complexity (e.g., cellular, individual, group/ system, society/cultural) to explain behavior (APA SLO 2.1c) (see textbook pages 8–9, 11–16, 18–26)

* Portions of this chapter cover learning outcomes suggested by the American Psychological Association (2013) in their guidelines for the under-graduate psychology major. Chapter coverage of these outcomes is identified above by APA Goal and APA Suggested Learning Outcome (SLO).

Understanding Psychopathology

▶ How do psychologists define a psychological disorder?

▶ What is a scientist–practitioner?

Today you may have gotten out of bed, had breakfast, gone to class, studied, and, at the end of the day, enjoyed the company of your friends before dropping off to sleep. It probably did not occur to you that many physically healthy people are not able to do some or any of these things. What they have in common is a **psychological disorder**, a psychological dysfunction within an individual associated with distress or impairment in functioning and a response that is not typical or culturally expected. Before examining exactly what this means, let's look at one individual's situation.

Judy... • The Girl Who Fainted at the Sight of Blood

Judy, a 16-year-old, was referred to our anxiety disorders clinic after increasing episodes of fainting. About 2 years earlier, in Judy's first biology class, the teacher had shown a movie of a frog dissection.

This was a graphic film, with vivid images of blood, tissue, and muscle. About halfway through, Judy felt lightheaded and left the room. But the images did not leave her. She continued to be bothered by them and occasionally felt queasy. She began to avoid situations in which she might see blood or injury. She found it difficult to look at raw meat, or even Band-Aids, because

they brought the feared images to mind. Eventually, anything anyone said that evoked an image of blood or injury caused Judy to feel lightheaded. It got so bad that if one of her friends exclaimed, "Cut it out!" she felt faint.

Beginning about 6 months before her visit to the clinic, Judy fainted when she unavoidably encountered something bloody. Physicians could find nothing wrong with her. By the time she was referred to our clinic, she was fainting 5 to 10 times a week, often in class. Clearly, this was problematic and disruptive; each time Judy fainted, the other students flocked around her, trying to help, and class was interrupted. The principal finally concluded that she was being manipulative and suspended her from school, even though she was an honor student.

Judy was suffering from what we now call *blood–injection–injury phobia*. Her reaction was severe, thereby meeting the criteria for **phobia**, a psychological disorder characterized by marked and persistent fear of an object

---

psychological disorder Psychological dysfunction associated with distress or impairment in functioning that is not a typical or culturally expected response.

phobia A psychological disorder characterized by marked and persistent fear of an object or situation.

or situation. But many people have similar reactions that are not as severe when they receive an injection or see someone who is injured. For people who react as severely as Judy, this phobia can be disabling. They may avoid certain careers, such as medicine or nursing, and, if they are so afraid of needles and injections that they avoid them even when they need them, they put their health at risk.

What Is a Psychological Disorder?

A psychological disorder, or problematic **abnormal behavior**, is a psychological dysfunction that is associated with distress or impairment in functioning and a response that is not typical or culturally expected (see ● Figure 1.1). These three criteria may seem obvious, but they were not easily arrived at and it is worth a moment to explore what they mean.

Psychological Dysfunction

Psychological dysfunction refers to a breakdown in cognitive, emotional, or behavioral functioning. For example, if you are out on a date, it should be fun. But if you experience severe fear all evening, even though there is nothing to be afraid of, and the fear happens on every date, your emotions are not functioning properly. However, if your friends agree that the person who asked you out is unpredictable and dangerous in some way, it would not be dysfunctional to be fearful.

A dysfunction was clearly present for Judy. But many people experience a mild version of this reaction (feeling queasy at the sight of blood) without meeting the criteria for the disorder. Drawing the line between normal and abnormal dysfunction is often difficult. For this reason, these problems are often considered to be on a continuum rather than either present or absent (McNally, 2011; Widiger & Crego, 2013). This, too, is a reason why just having a dysfunction is not enough to meet the criteria for a psychological disorder.

● **Figure 1.1** The criteria defining a psychological disorder.

Distress or Impairment

That the behavior must be associated with distress to be classified as a disorder seems clear: The criterion is satisfied if the individual is extremely upset. We can certainly say that Judy was distressed. But remember, by itself this criterion does not define problematic **abnormal behavior**. It is often normal to be distressed—for example, if someone close to you dies. Suffering and distress are part of life. Furthermore, for some disorders, by definition, suffering and distress are absent. Consider the person who feels elated and acts impulsively as part of a manic episode. As you will see in Chapter 6, one of the major difficulties with this problem is that some people enjoy the manic state so much they are reluctant to receive treatment for it. Thus, defining psychological disorder by distress alone doesn't work.

The concept of *impairment* is useful, although not entirely satisfactory. For example, many people consider themselves shy or lazy. This doesn't mean they're abnormal. But if you are so shy that you find it impossible to interact with people even though you would like to have friends, your social functioning is impaired.

Judy was clearly impaired by her phobia, but many people with less severe reactions are not impaired. This difference again illustrates the important point that most psychological disorders are extreme expressions of otherwise normal emotions, behaviors, and cognitive processes.

Atypical or Not Culturally Expected

The criterion that the response be *atypical* or *not culturally expected* is also insufficient to determine if a disorder is present by itself. At times, something is considered abnormal because it deviates from the average. The greater the deviation, the more abnormal it is. You might say that someone is abnormally short or abnormally tall, but this obviously isn't a definition of disorder. Many people's behavior is far from average, but we call them *talented or eccentric*, not disordered. For example, it's not normal to wear a dress made out of meat, but when Lady Gaga wore this to an awards show, it only enhanced her celebrity. In most cases, the more productive you are in the eyes of society, the more eccentricities society will tolerate. Therefore, "deviating from the average" doesn't work well as a definition for problematic abnormal behavior.

Another view is that your behavior is disordered if you are violating social norms. This definition is useful in considering cultural differences in psychological disorders. For example, to enter a trance state and believe you are possessed reflects a psychological disorder in most Western cultures but not in many other societies, where the behavior is accepted and expected (see Chapter 5). An example is provided by Robert Sapolsky (2002), a neuroscientist who worked closely with the Masai tribe in East Africa. One day, Sapolsky's Masai friend Rhoda asked him to bring his jeep to the village where a woman had been acting aggressively and hearing voices. The woman had killed a goat with her own hands. Sapolsky and several Masai were able to subdue her and transport her to a health center. Realizing this was an opportunity to learn more of the Masai's view of psychological disorders, Sapolsky had the following discussion:

"So, Rhoda," I began laconically, "what do you suppose was wrong with that woman?"

She looked at me as if I was mad.

"She is crazy."

"But how can you tell?"

"She's crazy. Can't you just see from how she acts?"

"But how do you decide that she is crazy? What did she do?"

"She killed that goat."

"Oh," I said with anthropological detachment, "but Masai kill goats all the time."

She looked at me as if I were an idiot. "Only the men kill goats," she said.

"Well, how else do you know that she is crazy?"

"She hears voices."

Again, I made a pain of myself. "Oh, but the Masai hear voices sometimes." (At ceremonies before long cattle drives, the Masai trance-dance and claim to hear voices.) And in one sentence, Rhoda summed up half of what anyone needs to know about cross-cultural psychiatry.

"But she hears voices at the wrong time." (p. 138)

A social standard of *normal* can be misused, however. Consider the practice of committing political dissidents to mental institutions because they protest the policies of their government, which was common in Iraq before the fall of Saddam Hussein. Although such behavior clearly violates social norms, it should not alone be cause for commitment.

Jerome Wakefield (1999, 2009) uses the shorthand definition of *harmful dysfunction*. A related concept is to determine whether the behavior is out of the individual's control (something the person doesn't want to do) (Widiger & Crego, 2013; Widiger & Sankis, 2000). Variants of these approaches are most often used in current diagnostic practice, as outlined in the fifth edition of the Diagnostic and Statistical Manual (American Psychiatric Association, 2013), which contains the current listing of criteria for psychological disorders (Stein *et al.*, 2010).

An Accepted Definition

In conclusion, it is difficult to define what constitutes a psychological disorder (Lilienfeld & Marino, 1999)—and the debate continues (Blashfield, Keeley, Flanagan, & Miles, 2014; McNally, 2011; Zachar & Kendler, 2014). The most widely accepted definition used in the *Diagnostic and Statistical Manual of Mental Disorders* (5th ed.; American Psychiatric Association, 2013) describes behavioral, psychological, or biological dysfunctions that are unexpected in their cultural context and associated with present distress and impairment in functioning, or increased risk of suffering, death, pain, or impairment. This definition can

Steve Granitz/Wireimage/Getty Images

▲ We accept extreme behaviors by entertainers, such as Lady Gaga, that would not be tolerated in other members of our society.

be useful across cultures if we pay attention to what is dysfunctional (or out of control) in a given society. But it is never easy to decide what represents dysfunction, and some scholars have argued that we can never satisfactorily define *disease* or *disorder* (see, for example, Lilienfeld & Marino, 1995, 1999; Zachar & Kendler, 2014). The best we may be able to do is to consider how the apparent disease or disorder matches a "typical" profile of a disorder—for example, major depression or schizophrenia—when most or all symptoms that experts would agree are part of the disorder are present. We call this typical profile a *prototype*, and, as described in Chapter 3, the diagnostic criteria from *DSM-5* found throughout this book are all prototypes. This means that the patient may have only some features or symptoms of the disorder and still meet criteria for the disorder because those symptoms are close to the prototype. But one of the differences between *DSM-5* and its predecessor, *DSM-IV*, is the addition of dimensional estimates of the severity of specific disorders in *DSM-5* (American Psychiatric Association, 2013; Regier , Narrow, Kuhl, & Kupfer, 2009). Thus, for the anxiety disorders, for example, the intensity and frequency of anxiety within a given disorder is

abnormal behavior Actions that are unexpected and often evaluated negatively because they differ from typical or usual behavior.

rated on a 0 to 4 scale, where a rating of 1 indicates mild or occasional symptoms and a rating of 4 indicates continual and severe symptoms (Beesdo-Baum *et al.*, 2012; LeBeau, Bogels, Moller, & Craske, 2015).

The Science of Psychopathology

Psychopathology is the scientific study of psychological disorders. Within this field are clinical and counseling psychologists, psychiatrists, psychiatric social workers, and psychiatric nurses, as well as marriage and family therapists and mental health counselors. *Clinical psychologists* and *counseling psychologists* receive the Ph.D., doctor of philosophy, degree (or sometimes an Ed.D., doctor of education, or Psy.D., doctor of psychology) and follow a course of graduate-level study lasting approximately 5 years, which prepares them to conduct research into the causes and treatment of psychological disorders and to diagnose, assess, and treat these disorders. Counseling psychologists tend to study and treat adjustment and vocational issues encountered by relatively healthy individuals, and clinical psychologists usually concentrate on more severe psychological disorders. Psychologists with other specialty training, such as experimental and social psychologists, investigate the basic determinants of behavior but do not assess or treat psychological disorders.

Psychiatrists first earn an M.D. degree in medical school and then specialize in psychiatry during residency training that lasts 3 to 4 years. Psychiatrists also investigate the nature and causes of psychological disorders, make diagnoses, and offer treatments. Many psychiatrists emphasize drugs or other biological treatments, although most use psychosocial treatments as well.

Psychiatric social workers typically earn a master's degree in social work as they develop expertise in collecting information relevant to the social and family situation of the individual with a psychological disorder. Social workers also treat disorders, often concentrating on family problems associated with them. *Psychiatric nurses* have advanced degrees and specialize in the care and treatment of patients with psychological disorders, usually in hospitals as part of a team.

Finally, *marriage and family therapists* and *mental health counselors* typically spend 1 to 2 years earning a master's degree and are employed to provide clinical services by hospitals or clinics.

The Scientist-Practitioner

The most important recent development in psychopathology is the adoption of scientific methods to learn more about psychological disorders, their causes, and treatment. Many mental health professionals take a scientific approach to their clinical work and therefore are called **scientist-practitioners** (Barlow, Hayes, & Nelson, 1984; Hayes, Barlow, & Nelson-Gray, 1999). Mental health

Mental health professional

Consumer of science
• Enhancing the practice

Evaluator of science
• Determining the effectiveness of the practice

Creator of science
• Conducting research that leads to new procedures useful in practice

Kevin Peterson/Photodisc/Getty Images

● **Figure 1.2** Functioning as a scientist-practitioner.

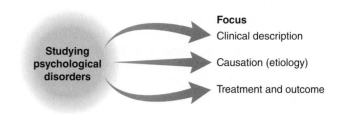

Studying psychological disorders

Focus
Clinical description

Causation (etiology)

Treatment and outcome

● **Figure 1.3** Three major categories make up the study and discussion of psychological disorders.

practitioners function as scientist-practitioners in three ways (see ● Figure 1.2). First, they keep up with the latest developments in their field and use the most current diagnostic and treatment procedures. In this sense, they are consumers of the science of psychopathology. Second, they evaluate their own assessments or treatment procedures to see whether they work. They are accountable not only to their patients but also to government agencies and insurance companies that pay for the treatments, so they must demonstrate whether their treatments are effective. Third, scientist-practitioners conduct research that produces new information about disorders or their treatment. Such research attempts three basic things: to describe psychological disorders, to determine their causes, and to treat them (see ●Figure 1.3). These three categories compose an organizational structure that recurs throughout this book. A general overview of them will give you a clearer perspective on our efforts to understand abnormality.

Clinical Description

In hospitals and clinics, we often say that a patient "presents" with a specific problem or we discuss the **presenting problem**. Describing Judy's presenting problem is the first step in determining her **clinical description**, the unique combination of behaviors, thoughts, and feelings that make up a specific disorder. The word *clinical* refers both to the types of disorders you would find in a clinic or hospital and to the activities connected with assessment and treatment.

An important function of the clinical description is to specify what makes the disorder different from normal behavior or from other disorders. Statistical data may also be relevant. For example, how many people in the population as a whole have the disorder? This figure is called the **prevalence** of the disorder. Statistics on how many new cases occur during a given period, such as a year, represent the **incidence** of the disorder. Other statistics include the *sex ratio*—what percentage of males and females has the disorder—and the typical age of onset.

In addition, most disorders follow a particular pattern, or **course**. For example, some disorders, such as schizophrenia (see Chapter 12), follow a *chronic course*, meaning they tend to last a long time. Other disorders, like mood disorders (see Chapter 6), follow an *episodic course,* in that the individual is likely to recover within a few months only to suffer a recurrence of the disorder. Still other disorders may have a *time-limited course,* meaning they will improve without treatment in a relatively short period with little or no risk of recurrence.

Closely related to differences in course of disorders are differences in onset. Some disorders have an *acute onset,* meaning they begin suddenly; others develop gradually over an extended period, which is sometimes called an *insidious onset.* It is important to know the typical course of a disorder so we can know what to expect and how best to deal with the problem. For example, if someone is suffering from a mild disorder with acute onset that we know is time limited, we might advise the individual not to bother with expensive treatment. If the disorder is likely to last a long time (become chronic) however, the individual might want to seek treatment. The anticipated course of a disorder is called the **prognosis**.

The patient's age may be an important part of the clinical description. A psychological disorder occurring in childhood may present differently from the same disorder in adulthood or old age. For example, children experiencing severe anxiety often assume they are physically ill. Because their thoughts and feelings are different from those experienced by adults with anxiety, children are often misdiagnosed and treated for a medical disorder.

We call the study of changes in behavior over time *developmental psychology* and we refer to the study of changes in abnormal behavior as *developmental psychopathology.* Because we change throughout our lives, researchers study development in children, adolescents, and adults. Study of abnormal behavior across the entire age span is referred to as *life-span developmental psychopathology.*

Causation, Treatment, and Etiology Outcomes

Etiology, or the study of origins, has to do with why a disorder begins and includes biological, psychological, and

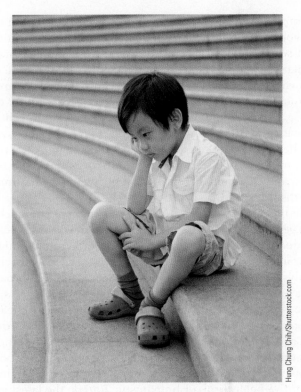

▲ Children experience anxiety differently from adults, so their reactions may be mistaken for symptoms of physical illness.

social dimensions. Chapter 2 is devoted to this key aspect of abnormal psychology.

Treatment is also important to the study of psychological disorders. If a new drug or psychosocial treatment is successful in treating a disorder, it may give us some hints about the nature of the disorder and its causes. For

psychopathology Scientific study of **psychological disorders**.

scientist-practitioners Mental health professional expected to apply scientific methods to his or her work. A scientist–practitioner must know the latest research on **diagnosis** and treatment, must evaluate his or her methods for effectiveness, and may generate research to discover information about disorders and their treatment.

presenting problem Original complaint reported by the client to the therapist. The actual treated problem may be a modification derived from the presenting problem.

clinical description Details of the combination of behaviors, thoughts, and feelings of an individual that make up a particular disorder.

prevalence Number of people displaying a disorder in the total population at any given time (compare with **incidence**).

incidence Number of new cases of a disorder appearing during a specific period (compare with **prevalence**).

course Pattern of development and change of a disorder over time.

prognosis Predicted development of a disorder over time.

course Pattern of development and change of a disorder over time.

etiology Cause or source of a disorder.

example, if a drug with a specific known effect within the nervous system alleviates a specific disorder, we know that something in that part of the nervous system might either be causing the disorder or helping maintain it. As you will see in the next chapter, psychopathology is rarely simple because the *effect* does not necessarily imply the *cause*. For example, you might take an aspirin to relieve a headache. If you then feel better, that does not mean the headache was caused by a lack of aspirin. Nevertheless, many people seek treatment for psychological disorders, and treatment can provide hints about the nature of the disorder.

In the past, textbooks emphasized treatment approaches in a general sense, with little attention to the disorder being treated. For example, a mental health professional might be trained in a single theoretical approach, such as psychoanalysis or behavior therapy, and then use that approach on every disorder. More recently, we have developed specific effective treatments that do not always adhere neatly to one theoretical approach or another but that have grown out of a deeper understanding of the disorder in question. For this reason, there are no separate chapters in this book on such types of treatment approaches as psychodynamic, cognitive behavioral, or humanistic. Rather, the latest and most effective treatments are described in the context of specific disorders in keeping with our integrative multidimensional perspective.

We now survey many early attempts to describe and treat abnormal behavior and to comprehend its causes. In Chapter 2, we examine contemporary views of causation and treatment. In Chapter 3, we discuss efforts to describe, or classify, abnormal behavior. In Chapter 4, we review research methods—our systematic efforts to discover the truths underlying description, cause, and treatment that allow us to function as scientist-practitioners. In Chapters 4 through 13, we examine specific disorders. Finally, in Chapter 14 we examine legal, professional, and ethical issues relevant to psychological disorders and their treatment. With that overview in mind, let us turn to the past.

Historical Conceptions of Abnormal Behavior

For thousands of years, humans have tried to explain and control problematic behavior. But our efforts always derive from the theories or models of behavior popular at the time. Three major models that have guided us date back to the beginnings of civilization.

Humans have always supposed that agents outside our bodies and environment influence our behavior, thinking, and emotions. These agents—which might be divinities, demons, spirits, or other phenomena such as magnetic fields or the moon or the stars—are the driving forces behind the *supernatural model*. In addition, the mind has

---

1.1 Concept CHECK

Part A

Write the letter for any or all of the following definitions of abnormality in the blanks: (a) societal norm violation, (b) impairment in functioning, (c) dysfunction, and (d) distress.

1. Miguel recently began feeling sad and lonely. Although still able to function, he finds himself feeling down much of the time and worries about what is happening to him. Which of the definitions of abnormality apply to Miguel's situation?
   _____

2. Three weeks ago, Jane, a 35-year-old business executive, stopped showering, refused to leave her apartment, and started watching television talk shows. Threats of being fired have failed to bring Jane back to reality. Which of the definitions seems to describe Jane's behavior? _____

Part B

Match the following words that are used in clinical descriptions with their corresponding examples: (a) presenting problem, (b) prevalence, (c) incidence, (d) prognosis, (e) course, and (f) etiology.

3. Maria should recover quickly with no intervention. Without treatment, John will deteriorate rapidly.
   _____

4. Three new cases of bulimia have been reported in this county during the past month and only one in the next county. _____

5. Elizabeth visited the campus mental health center because of her increasing feelings of guilt and anxiety _____

6. Biological, psychological, and social influences all contribute to a variety of disorders. _____

7. The pattern a disorder follows can be chronic, time-limited, or episodic. _____

8. How many people in the population as a whole suffer from obsessive-compulsive disorder?
   _____

---

often been called the *soul* or the *psyche* and considered separate from the body. Although many have thought that the mind can influence the body and, in turn, the body can influence the mind, most philosophers looked for causes of abnormal behavior in one or the other. This split gave rise to two traditions of thought about abnormal behavior, the *biological model* and the *psychobiological model*.

▶ What supernatural influences were formerly believed to explain abnormal behavior?

For much of our recorded history, deviant behavior has been considered a reflection of the battle between good and evil. When confronted with unexplainable, irrational behavior and by suffering and upheaval, people have perceived evil.

Demons and Witches

One current of opinion put the causes and treatment of psychological disorders in the realm of the supernatural. During the late 14th century, religious and lay authorities supported these popular superstitions, and society as a whole increasingly turned to magic and sorcery to solve their problems. During these times, the bizarre behavior of

▲ During the Middle Ages, individuals with psychological disorders were sometimes thought to be possessed by evil spirits and exorcisms were attempted through rituals.

people afflicted with psychological disorders was seen as the work of the devil and witches. It followed that individuals "possessed" by evil spirits were probably responsible for any misfortune experienced by people in the community, which inspired action against the possessed. Treatments included **exorcism**, in which religious rituals were performed to rid the victim of evil spirits. Other approaches included shaving the pattern of a cross in the hair of the victim's head and securing sufferers to a wall near the front of a church so that they might benefit from hearing Mass.

The conviction that sorcery and witches are causes of madness and other evils continued into the 15th century, and evil continued to be blamed for unexplainable behavior, even after the founding of the United States, as evidenced by the Salem, Massachusetts witch trials in the late 17th century, which resulted in the hanging deaths of 20 women.

Stress and Melancholy

An equally strong opinion reflected the view that insanity was a natural phenomenon, caused by mental or emotional stress, and was curable (Alexander & Selesnick, 1966; Maher & Maher, 1985a). Mental depression and anxiety were recognized as illnesses (Kemp, 1990; Schoeneman, 1977), although symptoms such as despair and lethargy were often identified by the church with the sin of *acadia* or sloth (Tuchman, 1978). Common treatments were rest, sleep, and a healthy environment. Other treatments included baths, ointments, and potions. Indeed, during the 14th and 15th centuries, people with insanity, along with those with physical deformities or disabilities, were often moved from house to house in medieval villages as neighbors took turns caring for them. We now know that this medieval practice of keeping people with psychological disturbances in their own community is beneficial (see Chapter 13).

In the 14th century, one of the chief advisers to the king of France, Nicholas Oresme, suggested that melancholy (depression) was the source of some bizarre behavior, rather than demons. Oresme pointed out that much of the evidence for the existence of sorcery and witchcraft, particularly among those considered insane, was obtained from people who were tortured and who, quite understandably, confessed to anything.

These conflicting natural and supernatural explanations for mental disorders are represented more or less strongly in historical works, depending on the sources consulted by

exorcism Religious ritual that attributes disordered behavior to possession by demons and seeks to treat the individual by driving the demons from the body.

historians. Some assumed that demonic influences were the predominant explanations of abnormal behavior during the Middle Ages (for example, Zilboorg & Henry, 1941); others believed that the supernatural had little or no influence. As we see in the handling of the severe psychological disorder experienced by late-14th-century King Charles VI of France, both influences were strong, sometimes alternating in the treatment of the same case.

Charles VI... • *The Mad King*

In the summer of 1392, King Charles VI of France was under a great deal of stress. As he rode with his army to Brittany, an aide dropped his lance with a loud clatter and the King, thinking he was under attack, turned on his own army, killing several knights before being subdued. The King's lieutenants and advisers concluded he was mad.

During the following years, at his worst the King hid in a corner of his castle believing he was made of glass or roamed the corridors howling like a wolf. At other times, he couldn't remember who or what he was. He became fearful and enraged whenever he saw his own royal coat of arms and would try to destroy it if it was brought near him.

The people of Paris were devastated by their leader's apparent madness. Some thought it reflected God's anger; others thought it was divine punishment for heavy taxes. But most thought the King's madness was caused by sorcery, a belief strengthened by a drought that caused cattle to die of thirst. Merchants claimed their worst losses in 20 years.

Naturally, the King was given the best care available at the time. The most famous healer in the land was a 92-year-old physician whose treatment included moving the King to the country where the air was thought to be the cleanest. The physician prescribed rest, relaxation, and recreation. After some time, the King seemed to recover. Unfortunately, the physician died and the insanity of the King returned. This time, however, he came under the influence of the conflicting crosscurrent of supernatural causation. "An unkempt evil-eyed charlatan and pseudo-mystic named Arnaut Guilhem was allowed to treat Charles on his claim of possessing a book given by God to Adam by means of which man could overcome all affliction resulting from original sin" (Tuchman, 1978, p. 514). Guilhem insisted that the King's malady was caused by sorcery, but his treatments failed to bring about a cure.

A variety of remedies and rituals were tried, but none worked. High-ranking officials and doctors called for the "sorcerers" to be discovered and punished. "On one occasion, two Augustinian friars, after getting no results from magic incantations and a liquid made from powdered pearls, proposed to cut incisions in the King's head. When this was not allowed by the King's council, the friars accused those who opposed their recommendation of sorcery" (Tuchman, 1978, p. 514). Even the King himself, during his lucid moments, came to believe that the source of madness was evil and sorcery.

Treatments for Possession

Early treatments for possession included exorcisms, which at least have the virtue of being relatively painless. Interestingly, they sometimes work, as do other forms of faith healing, for reasons we explore in subsequent chapters. But what if they did not? In the Middle Ages, if exorcism failed, some authorities thought that steps were necessary to make the body uninhabitable by evil spirits, and many people were subjected to confinement, beatings, and other forms of torture (Kemp, 1990).

Somewhere along the way, a creative "therapist" decided that hanging people over a pit full of poisonous snakes might scare the evil spirits right out of their bodies. Strangely, this approach sometimes worked; the most disturbed individuals would suddenly come to their senses and experience relief from their symptoms, if only temporarily. Many other treatments based on the hypothesized therapeutic element of shock were developed, including dunkings in ice-cold water.

Mass Hysteria

Another fascinating phenomenon is characterized by large-scale outbreaks of bizarre behavior. During the Middle Ages, they lent support to the notion of possession by the devil. In Europe, whole groups of people were simultaneously compelled to run out in the streets, dance, shout, rave, and jump around in patterns as if they were at a particularly wild party (still called a *rave* today, but with music). This behavior was known by several names, including Saint Vitus's Dance and tarantism. Several reasons were offered in addition to possession. One reasonable guess was reaction to insect bites. Another possibility was what we now call *mass hysteria* (Veith, 1965). Consider the following example.

Modern Mass Hysteria

One Friday afternoon, an alarm sounded over the public address system of a hospital, calling all physicians to the emergency room. Arriving from a local school in ambulances were 17 students and 4 teachers who reported dizziness, headache, nausea, and stomach pains. Some were vomiting; most were hyperventilating.

All the students and teachers had been in four classrooms, two on each side of the hallway. The incident began when a 14-year-old girl reported a funny smell coming from

▲ In hydrotherapy, patients were shocked back to their senses by applications of ice-cold water.

a vent. She fell to the floor, crying and complaining that her stomach hurt and her eyes stung. Soon, many of the students and teachers in the four adjoining classrooms, who could see and hear what was happening, experienced similar symptoms. Of 86 susceptible people (82 students and four teachers in the four classrooms), 21 patients (17 students and four teachers) experienced symptoms severe enough to be evaluated at the hospital. Inspection of the school building by public health authorities revealed no apparent cause for the reactions, and physical examinations revealed no abnormalities. All the patients were sent home and quickly recovered (Rockney & Lemke, 1992).

Mass hysteria may simply demonstrate the phenomenon of *emotion contagion,* in which the experience of an emotion spreads to those around us (Hatfield, Cacioppo, & Rapson, 1994; Ntika, Sakellariou, Kefalas, & Stamatpoulou, 2014; Wang, 2006). If someone nearby becomes frightened, chances are that, for the moment, you also will feel fear. When this experience escalates into full-blown panic, whole communities are affected (Barlow, 2002). People are also suggestible when they are in states of high emotion.

Therefore, if one person identifies a "cause" of the problem, others may assume their own reactions have the same source. In popular language, this response is referred to as *mob psychology.* Until recently, it was assumed that victims had to be in contact with each other for the contagion to occur, but there have been recent documented cases of emotion contagion occurring across social networks as well (Bartholomew, Wessely, & Rubin, 2012; Dimon, 2013).

The Moon and the Stars

Paracelsus, a Swiss physician who lived from 1493 to 1541, rejected notions of possession by the devil, suggesting instead that the movements of the moon and stars had effects on people's psychological functioning. This influential theory inspired the word *lunatic,* which is derived from the Latin word meaning "moon." You might hear some of your friends explain something crazy they did one night by saying, "It must have been the full moon." The belief that heavenly bodies affect human behavior is most noticeable today in followers of astrology, who hold that their behavior and the major events in their lives can be predicted by their relationship to the position of the planets. No serious evidence has ever confirmed such a connection, however.

Comments

The supernatural tradition in psychopathology is alive and well, although it is relegated, for the most part, to small religious sects and primitive cultures. Members of organized religions look to psychology and medical science for help with psychological disorders; in fact, the Roman Catholic Church requires that all health-care resources be exhausted before spiritual solutions such as exorcism can be considered. Nonetheless, miraculous cures are sometimes achieved by exorcism, rituals, and other methods that seem to have little connection with modern science. But such cases are relatively rare, and almost no one would advocate supernatural treatment for severe psychological disorders except, perhaps, as a last resort.

The Biological Tradition

▶ What are the underlying assumptions of the biological approach to understanding abnormal behavior?

Physical causes of mental disorders have been sought since antiquity. Important to the biological tradition are a man, Hippocrates; a disease, syphilis; and the early consequences of believing that psychological disorders are biologically caused.

Hippocrates and Galen

The Greek physician Hippocrates (460–377 B.C.) is considered to be the father of modern Western medicine. In a body of work called the *Hippocratic Corpus* written between

450 and 350 B.C. (Maher & Maher, 1985a), he and others suggested that psychological disorders could be treated like any other disease. They did not limit their search for the causes of psychopathology to the general area of "disease"; they believed that psychological disorders might also be caused by brain pathology or head trauma and could be influenced by heredity (genetics). Hippocrates considered the brain to be the seat of wisdom, consciousness, intelligence, and emotion. Therefore, disorders involving these functions would logically be located in the brain. Hippocrates also recognized the importance of psychological and interpersonal contributions to psychopathology, such as the sometimes-negative effects of family stress.

The Roman physician Galen (approximately A.D. 129–198) adopted these ideas and developed them further, creating an influential school of thought that extended well into the 19th century. One of the more influential legacies of the Hippocratic-Galenic approach is the *humoral theory* of disorders. Hippocrates assumed that normal brain functioning was related to four bodily fluids or *humors:* blood, black bile, yellow bile, and phlegm. Blood came from the heart, black bile from the spleen, phlegm from the brain, and choler or yellow bile from the liver. Physicians believed that disease resulted from too much or too little of one of the humors; for example, too much black bile was thought to cause melancholia (depression). In fact, the term *melancholy,* which means "black bile," is still used to refer to aspects of depression. The humoral theory was, perhaps, the first example of associating psychological disorders with a "chemical imbalance," an approach that is widespread today.

The four humors were related to the Greeks' conception of the four basic qualities: heat, dryness, moisture, and cold. Terms derived from the four humors are still sometimes applied to personality traits. For example, *sanguine* (literal meaning "red, like blood") describes someone who is ruddy in complexion, presumably from copious blood flowing through the body, and cheerful and optimistic, although insomnia and delirium were thought to be caused by excessive blood in the brain. *Melancholic* means depressive (depression was thought to be caused by black bile flooding the brain). A *phlegmatic* personality (from the humor phlegm) indicates apathy and sluggishness but can also mean being calm under stress. A *choleric* person (from yellow bile or choler) is hot tempered (Maher & Maher, 1985a).

Excess humors were treated by regulating the environment to increase or decrease heat, dryness, moisture, or cold, depending on which humor was out of balance. One reason King Charles VI's physician moved him to the countryside was to restore the balance in his humors (Kemp, 1990). In addition to rest, good nutrition, and exercise, two treatments were developed. In one, *bleeding* or *bloodletting,* a carefully measured amount of blood was removed from the body, often with leeches. The other was to induce vomiting. If Judy (the student afraid of blood who we discussed at the beginning of the chapter) had lived 300 years ago, she might have been diagnosed with an illness, a brain disorder, or some other physical problem, perhaps related to excessive humors, and been given the proper medical treatments of the day: bed rest, a healthful diet, and exercise.

In ancient China and throughout Asia, a similar idea existed. But rather than "humors," the Chinese focused on the movement of air or "wind" throughout the body. Unexplained mental disorders were caused by blockages of wind or the presence of cold, dark wind (yin) as opposed to warm, life-sustaining wind (yang). Treatment involved restoring proper flow of wind through various methods, including acupuncture.

▲ Bloodletting, the extraction of blood from patients, was intended to restore the balance of humors in the body.

Hippocrates also coined the word *hysteria* to describe a concept he learned about from the Egyptians, who had identified what we now call the *somatic symptom disorders.* In these disorders, symptoms, such as paralysis and some kinds of blindness, appear to be the result of a problem for which no physical cause can be found. Because these disorders occurred primarily in women, the Egyptians (and Hippocrates) mistakenly assumed that they were restricted to women. They also presumed a cause: The empty uterus wandered to parts of the body in search of conception (the Greek word for "uterus" is *hysteron*). Numerous symptoms reflected the location of the wandering uterus. The prescribed cure might be marriage or, occasionally, fumigation of the vagina to lure the uterus back to its natural location (Alexander & Selesnick, 1966). Knowledge of physiology eventually disproved the wandering uterus theory; however, the tendency to stigmatize dramatic women as hysterical continued into the 1970s. As you will learn in Chapter 5, somatic symptom disorders are not limited to one sex or the other.

The 19th Century

The biological tradition waxed and waned during the centuries after Hippocrates and Galen but was reinvigorated in the 19th century because of two factors: the discovery of the nature and cause of syphilis and strong support from the well-respected American psychiatrist John P. Grey.

Syphilis

Behavioral and cognitive symptoms of what we now know as *advanced syphilis,* a sexually transmitted disease caused by a bacterial microorganism entering the brain, include believing that everyone is plotting against you (delusion of persecution) or that you are God (delusion of grandeur).

Adriana is an 18-year-old who is concerned about her excessive nervousness, irritability, loss of appetite, and insomnia. According to the biological tradition of abnormal behavior, what is the best explanation for Adriana's experiences? How should they be treated?

As the understanding of human biology has changed over time, so too have the biological models that guide the conceptualization and treatment of psychopathology. Unfortunately, some approaches to understanding and treating psychopathology have been unfavorable for women. One example is the diagnosis of hysteria to describe general psychological complaints among women. In ancient times, the Greek physician Hippocrates would have attributed Adriana's symptoms to a biological condition known as "wandering womb," or the movement of Adriana's uterus around her body because of a lack of sexual intercourse. Hippocrates often prescribed marriage as a treatment for hysteria. Although this may seem absurd in retrospect, hysteria was a diagnosis for a range of psychological complaints expressed by women. As recently as the late 19th century, Adriana's complaints would have been attributed to hysteria, although by that time the idea of a wandering womb had been replaced with the belief that hysteria was caused by sexual dissatisfaction. As a result, the prescribed treatment often was vaginal massage to enhance sexual satisfaction.

In the early 20th century, Sigmund Freud (1856–1939) proposed that hysteria actually worked in the opposite direction and suggested that many physical complaints reported by women in the 1900s were the result of the "conversion" of unacceptable sexual fantasies into more acceptable outlets. This was an influential theory and one that ultimately led to the inclusion of a diagnosis of conversion hysteria in the DSM.

More recent scientific advances have abandoned the concept of hysteria, which has been replaced with more objective, specific, and gender-neutral diagnoses such as anxiety disorders, depressive disorders, and somatoform disorders. As a result of research on genetics and neuroscience, simple biological explanations such as the wandering womb theory also have been replaced with more sophisticated models of biological influences on psychopathology. Despite these advances, history suggests that our current approaches to conceptualizing and treating psychopathology will someday be looked on as primitive. In the meantime, psychologists continue to use currently available science as a guide to explaining and treating psychopathology. ∎

Although these symptoms are similar to those of *psychosis*—psychological disorders characterized in part by beliefs that are not based in reality (delusions), perceptions that are not based in reality (hallucinations), or both—researchers recognized that a subgroup of apparently psychotic patients deteriorated steadily, becoming paralyzed and dying within 5 years of onset. This course of events contrasted with that of most psychotic patients, who remained fairly stable. In 1825, the condition was designated a disease, *general paresis,* because it had consistent symptoms (presentation) and a consistent course that resulted in death. The relationship between general paresis and syphilis was only gradually established. Louis Pasteur's germ theory of disease, developed in about 1870, facilitated the identification of the microorganism that caused syphilis.

Of equal importance was the discovery of a cure for general paresis. Physicians observed a surprising recovery in patients with general paresis who had contracted malaria, so they injected other patients with blood from a soldier who was ill with malaria. Many recovered because the high fever "burned out" the syphilis bacteria. Obviously, this type of experiment would not be ethically possible today. Ultimately, investigators discovered that penicillin cures syphilis, but with the malaria cure, "madness" and associated symptoms for the first time were traced directly to a curable infection. Many mental health professionals assumed that comparable causes and cures might be discovered for all psychological disorders.

John P. Grey

The champion of the biological tradition in the United States was the most influential American psychiatrist of the time, John P. Grey (Bockoven, 1963). In 1854, Grey was appointed superintendent of the Utica State Hospital in New York and became editor of the *American Journal of Insanity,* the precursor of the *American Journal of Psychiatry*. Grey held that the causes of insanity were physical. Therefore, mentally ill patients should be treated as physically ill, with treatment including rest, diet, and proper room temperature and ventilation. Grey even invented the rotary fan to ventilate his hospital.

Under Grey's leadership, conditions in hospitals improved and they became more humane institutions. But in subsequent years they also became so large that individual attention was not possible. In fact, leaders in psychiatry became alarmed at the increasing size and impersonality of mental hospitals and recommended that they be downsized. It was almost 100 years before the community mental health movement was successful in reducing the population of mental hospitals with the controversial policy of deinstitutionalization, in which patients were released into their communities. Unfortunately, this practice has as many negative consequences as positive ones, including a large increase in the number of chronically disabled patients homeless on city streets.

In the 19th century, psychological disorders were attributed to mental or emotional stress, so patients were often treated sympathetically in a restful and hygienic environment.

The Development of Biological Treatments

Renewed interest in the biological origin of psychological disorders led to greatly increased understanding of biological contributions to psychopathology and to the development of new treatments. In the 1930s, electric shock and brain surgery were often used. Their effects, and the effects of new drugs, were discovered by accident. For example, insulin was occasionally given to stimulate appetite in psychotic patients who were not eating, but it also seemed to calm them down. In 1927, a Viennese physician, Manfred Sakel, began using increasingly higher dosages until, finally, patients convulsed and became temporarily comatose (Sakel, 1958). Some actually recovered their mental health, much to the surprise of everybody, and their recovery was attributed to the convulsions. The procedure became known as *insulin shock therapy*, but it was abandoned because it was too dangerous, often resulting in prolonged coma or death. Other methods of producing convulsions had to be found.

In the 1920s, Hungarian psychiatrist Joseph von Meduna observed that schizophrenia was rarely found in individuals with epilepsy (which ultimately did not prove to be true). Some of his followers concluded that induced brain seizures might cure schizophrenia. Following suggestions on the possible benefits of applying electric shock directly to the brain, a surgeon in London treated a depressed patient by sending six small shocks directly through his brain, producing convulsions (Hunt, 1980). The patient recovered. Although greatly modified, shock treatment is still used. The controversial modern uses of *electroconvulsive therapy* are described in Chapter 6.

During the 1950s, the first effective drugs for severe psychotic disorders were developed in a systematic way. Before that time, a number of medicinal substances, including

opium, had been used as sedatives, along with herbs and folk remedies (Alexander & Selesnick, 1966). With the discovery of *Rauwolfia serpentine* (later renamed *reserpine*) and another class of drugs called *neuroleptics* (major tranquilizers), for the first time hallucinatory and delusional thought processes could be diminished in some patients; these drugs also controlled agitation and aggressiveness. Other discoveries included *benzodiazepines* (minor tranquilizers), which seemed to reduce anxiety. By the 1970s, the benzodiazepines (such as Valium and Librium) were among the most widely prescribed drugs in the world. As drawbacks of tranquilizers became apparent, prescriptions decreased somewhat (we discuss the benzodiazepines in more detail in Chapters 4 and 10).

Throughout the centuries, as Alexander and Selesnick point out, "[t]he general pattern of drug therapy for mental illness has been one of initial enthusiasm followed by disappointment" (1966, p. 287). For example, bromides, a class of sedating drugs, were used at the end of the 19th century and beginning of the 20th century to treat anxiety and other psychological disorders. By the 1920s, they were reported as being effective for many serious psychological and emotional symptoms. When their side effects became widely known and experience began to show that their effectiveness was modest, bromides largely disappeared.

Neuroleptics have also been used less as attention has focused on their side effects, such as tremors and shaking. However, the positive effects of these drugs on some patients' psychotic symptoms revitalized the search both for biological contributions to psychological disorders and for new and more powerful drugs.

Consequences of the Biological Tradition

In the late 19th century, Grey and his colleagues ironically reduced or eliminated interest in treating mental patients, because they thought mental disorders were the result of some as-yet-undiscovered brain pathology and were therefore incurable. The only available course of action was to hospitalize these patients. Around the turn of the century, some nurses documented success in treating mental patients but were prevented from treating others for fear of raising hopes of a cure among family members. In place of treatment, interest centered on diagnosis and the study of brain pathology itself.

Emil Kraepelin (1856–1926) was the dominant figure during this period. He was influential in advocating the major ideas of the biological tradition, but he was little involved in treatment. His lasting contribution was in the area of diagnosis and classification. Kraepelin (1913) was one of the first to distinguish among various psychological disorders, seeing that each may have a different age of onset and time course, different symptoms, and probably a different cause.

By the end of the 1800s, a scientific approach to psychological disorders and their classification had begun with the search for biological causes. Furthermore, treatment was based on humane principles. There were many drawbacks however, the most unfortunate being that treatment was all but eliminated in some settings, despite the availability of some effective approaches. It is to these that we now turn.

The Psychological Tradition

▶ How do the psychological approaches of psychoanalysis, humanism, and behaviorism explain abnormal behavior?

It is a long leap from evil spirits to brain pathology as the cause of psychological disorders. In the intervening centuries, how did psychological development come to be viewed in an interpersonal and social context? In fact, this approach has a long tradition. Plato, for example, thought that the two causes of maladaptive behavior were the social and cultural influences in one's life and the learning that took place in that environment. If something was wrong in the environment, such as abusive parents, one's impulses and emotions would overcome reason. The best treatment was to re-educate the individual through rational discussion so that the power of reason would predominate (Maher & Maher, 1985a). This was a precursor to modern **psychosocial treatment** approaches to the causation of psychopathology, which focus not only on psychological factors but also on social and cultural ones. Other early philosophers, including Aristotle, also emphasized the influence of social environment and early learning on psychopathology. These philosophers wrote about the importance of fantasies, dreams, and cognitions and thus anticipated later developments in psychoanalytic thought and cognitive science. They also advocated humane care for individuals with psychological disturbances.

Moral Therapy

During the first half of the 19th century, a psychosocial approach to mental disorders called **moral therapy** became influential. The term *moral* actually referred more to emotional or psychological factors rather than to a code of conduct. Its tenets included treating institutionalized patients as normally as possible in a setting that encouraged normal social interaction (Bockoven, 1963). Relationships were carefully nurtured. Individual attention emphasized positive consequences for appropriate interactions and behavior, and restraint and seclusion were eliminated.

As with the biological tradition, the principles of moral therapy date back to Plato and beyond. For example, the Greek Asclepiad Temples of the 6th century B.C. housed the chronically ill, including those with psychological disorders. Here, patients were well cared for, massaged, and provided with soothing music. Similar practices were evident in Muslim countries in the Middle East (Millon, 2004). But moral therapy as a system originated with French psychiatrist Philippe Pinel (1745–1826) and his associate Jean-Baptiste Pussin (1746–1811), the superintendent of the Parisian hospital La Bicêtre (Gerard, 1997; Zilboorg & Henry, 1941).

When Pinel arrived in 1791, Pussin had already instituted reforms by removing all chains used to restrain patients and instituting humane psychological interventions. Pussin persuaded Pinel to go along with the changes. Much to Pinel's credit, he did, first at La Bicêtre and then at the women's hospital Salpétrière (Gerard, 1997; Maher & Maher, 1985b).

After William Tuke (1732–1822) followed Pinel's lead in England, Benjamin Rush (1745–1813), often considered the founder of U.S. psychiatry, introduced moral therapy at Pennsylvania Hospital. *Asylums* had appeared in the

....

psychosocial treatment Treatment practices that focuses on social and cultural factors (such as family experience), as well as psychological influences. These approaches include cognitive, behavioral, and interpersonal methods.

moral therapy Psychosocial approach in the 19th century that involved treating patients as normally as possible in normal environments.

16th century, but they were more like prisons than hospitals. It was the rise of moral therapy in Europe and the United States that made asylums habitable and even therapeutic.

In 1833, Horace Mann, chairman of the board of trustees of the Worcester State Hospital, reported on 32 patients who had been given up as incurable. These patients were treated with moral therapy, cured, and released to their families. Of 100 patients who were viciously assaultive before treatment, only 12 continued to be violent a year after beginning treatment. Before treatment, 40 patients had routinely torn off clothes provided by attendants; only 8 continued this behavior after a period of treatment. These statistics would be remarkable even today (Bockoven, 1963).

Asylum Reform and the Decline of Moral Therapy

Unfortunately, after the mid-19th century, humane treatment declined. It was widely recognized that moral therapy worked best when the number of patients in an institution was 200 or fewer, allowing for a great deal of individual attention. But after the Civil War, enormous waves of immigrants arrived in the United States, and patient loads in hospitals increased to 1,000 or 2,000, and even more. Because immigrants were thought not to deserve the same privileges as "native" Americans (whose ancestors had immigrated perhaps only 50 or 100 years earlier!), they were not given moral treatments even when there were sufficient hospital personnel.

A second reason for the decline of moral therapy has an unlikely source. The great crusader Dorothea Dix (1802–1887) campaigned for reform in the treatment of insanity. Having worked in various institutions, she had firsthand knowledge of the deplorable conditions imposed on patients with insanity, and she made it her life's work to inform the American public and their leaders of these abuses. Her work became known as the **mental hygiene movement**.

In addition to improving the standards of care, Dix worked to make sure everyone who needed care received it. Through her efforts, humane treatment became more widely available in U.S. institutions. Unfortunately, an unforeseen consequence of Dix's efforts was a substantial increase in the number of mental patients. This influx led to a transition from moral therapy to custodial care because hospitals were inadequately staffed. Dix reformed our asylums and inspired the construction of new institutions here and abroad. But even her tireless efforts and advocacy could not ensure sufficient staffing to allow the individual attention necessary to moral therapy. A final blow to the practice of moral therapy was the decision, in the middle of the 19th century, that mental illness was caused by brain pathology and, therefore, was incurable.

The psychological tradition lay dormant for a time, only to re-emerge in several schools of thought in the 20th century. The first major approach was **psychoanalysis**, based on Sigmund Freud's (1856–1939) theory of the structure of the mind and the role of unconscious processes in behavior. The second was **behaviorism**, associated with John B. Watson, Ivan Pavlov, and B. F. Skinner, which focuses on how learning and adaptation affect the development of psychopathology.

Psychoanalytic Theory

Have you ever felt as if someone cast a spell on you? Have you ever been mesmerized by a look across the classroom from a beautiful man or woman? If so, you have something in common with the patients of Franz Anton Mesmer (1734–1815) and with millions of people who have been hypnotized. Mesmer suggested to his patients that their problem was caused by an undetectable fluid found in all living organisms called "animal magnetism," which could become blocked.

Mesmer had his patients sit in a dark room around a vat of chemicals with rods extending from it and touching them. Dressed in flowing robes, he might then identify and tap various areas of their bodies where their "animal magnetism" was blocked while suggesting that they were

▲ Dorothea Dix (1802–1887) began the mental hygiene movement and spent much of her life campaigning for reform in the treatment of the mentally ill.

▲ Franz Anton Mesmer (1734–1815) and other early therapists often used hypnosis and/or strong suggestions to cure their patients.

being cured. Because of his unusual techniques, Mesmer was considered an oddity and was opposed by the medical establishment (Winter, 1998). However, many scientists and physicians were interested in Mesmer's methods of suggestion. One of the best known, Jean-Martin Charcot (1825–1893), was head of the Salpêtrière Hospital in Paris, where Philippe Pinel had introduced psychological treatments several generations earlier. A distinguished neurologist, Charcot demonstrated that some techniques of mesmerism were effective with a number of psychological disorders, and he did much to legitimize the practice of hypnosis. In 1885 a young man named Sigmund Freud came from Vienna to study with Charcot.

After returning from France, Freud teamed up with Josef Breuer (1842–1925), who had experimented with a somewhat different hypnotic procedure. While his patients were in the highly suggestible state of hypnosis, Breuer asked them to describe their problems, conflicts, and fears. Breuer observed two important phenomena during this process. First, patients often became emotional as they talked and felt relieved and improved after emerging from the hypnotic state. Second, seldom would they have gained an understanding of the relationship between their emotional problems and their psychological disorder. In fact, it was difficult or impossible for them to recall some details they had described under hypnosis. In other words, the material seemed to be beyond the awareness of the patient. With this observation, Breuer and Freud had "discovered" the **unconscious** mind and its apparent influence on the production of psychological disorders.

They also discovered that it is therapeutic to recall and relive emotional trauma that has been made unconscious and to release the accompanying tension. This release of emotional material became known as **catharsis**. A fuller understanding of the relationship between current emotions and earlier events is referred to as *insight*. As you shall see throughout this book, the existence of "unconscious" memories and feelings and the importance of processing emotion-filled information have been verified.

Freud and Breuer's theories were based on case observations. An example is Breuer's description of his treatment of "hysterical" symptoms in Anna O. in 1895 (Breuer & Freud, 1895/1957). Anna O. was a bright, attractive young woman who was healthy until she reached 21 years of age. Shortly before her problems began, her father developed a chronic illness that led to his death. Throughout his illness, Anna O. had cared for him, spending endless hours at his bedside. Five months after her father became ill, Anna noticed that during the day her vision blurred and that from time to time she had difficulty moving her right arm and both legs. Soon, she began to experience difficulty speaking, and her behavior became unpredictable. Shortly thereafter, she consulted Breuer.

In a series of treatment sessions, Breuer dealt with one symptom at a time through hypnosis and subsequent "talking through," tracing each symptom to its hypothetical

causation in circumstances surrounding the death of Anna's father. One at a time, her "hysterical" ailments disappeared, but only after treatment was administered for each behavior. This process of treating one behavior at a time fulfills a basic requirement for drawing scientific conclusions about the effects of treatment in an individual case study. Freud expanded these basic observations into the **psychoanalytic model**, the most comprehensive theory yet constructed on the development and structure of our personalities. He also speculated on where this development could go wrong and produce psychological disorders. Although many of Freud's views changed over time, the basic principles of mental functioning that he originally proposed remained constant through his writings and are still applied by psychoanalysts today.

▲ Bertha Pappenheim (1859–1936), famous as Anna O., was described as "hysterical" by Breuer.

Although most of it remains unproven, psychoanalytic theory has had a strong influence, and it is important to be familiar with its basic ideas; what follows is a brief outline of the theory. We focus on its three major facets: (1) the structure of the mind and the functions of personality that sometimes clash with one another; (2) the defense mechanisms with which the mind defends itself from these conflicts; and (3) the stages of psychosexual development that contribute to our inner conflicts.

· ·

mental hygiene movement Mid-19th-century effort to improve care of the mentally disordered by informing the public of their mistreatment.

psychoanalysis Assessment and therapy pioneered by Sigmund Freud that emphasizes exploration of, and insight into, unconscious processes and conflicts.

behaviorism Explanation of human behavior, including dysfunction, based on principles of learning and adaptation derived from experimental psychology.

unconscious Part of the psychic makeup that is outside the awareness of the person.

catharsis Rapid or sudden release of emotional tension thought to be an important factor in psychoanalytic therapy.

psychoanalytic model Complex and comprehensive theory originally advanced by Sigmund Freud that seeks to account for the development and structure of personality, as well as the origin of **abnormal behavior**, based primarily on inferred inner entities and forces.

The Structure of the Mind

The mind, according to Freud, has three major parts or functions: the id, the ego, and the superego (see ● Figure 1.4). Although you may have heard these terms, you may not be aware of their meaning. The **id** is the source of our strong sexual and aggressive feelings or energies. It is, basically, the animal within us; if totally unchecked, it would make us all rapists or killers. The energy or drive within the id is the *libido*. Even today, some people explain low sex drive as an absence of libido. A less important source of energy is the death instinct, or *thanatos*. These two basic drives, toward life and fulfillment on the one hand and death and destruction on the other, are continually in opposition.

The id operates according to the *pleasure principle*, with a goal of maximizing pleasure and eliminating associated tension or conflicts. The goal of pleasure, which is particularly prominent in childhood, often conflicts with social rules. The id has its own characteristic way of processing information; referred to as the *primary process*, this type of thinking is emotional, irrational, illogical, filled with fantasies, and preoccupied with sex, aggression, selfishness, and envy.

Fortunately for all of us, in Freud's view, the id's selfish and sometimes dangerous drives do not go unchecked. In fact, only a few months into life, we know we must find ways to meet our basic needs without offending everyone around us. Put yet another way, we must act realistically. The part of our mind that ensures that we act realistically is called the **ego**, and it operates according to the *reality principle* instead of the pleasure principle. The cognitive operations or thinking styles of the ego are characterized by logic and reason and are referred to as the *secondary process,* as opposed to the illogical and irrational primary process of the id.

The third important structure within the mind, the **superego**, or what we might call *conscience*, represents the *moral principles* instilled in us by our parents and culture. It is the voice within us that nags at us when we know we're doing something wrong. Because the purpose of the superego is to counteract the potentially dangerous aggressive and sexual drives of the id, the basis for conflict is apparent.

AP Images

▲ Sigmund Freud (1856–1939) is considered the founder of psychoanalysis.

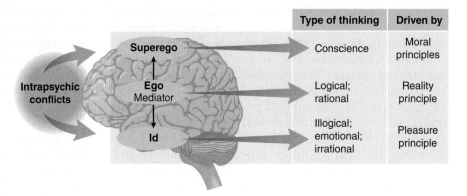

	Type of thinking	Driven by
Superego	Conscience	Moral principles
Ego Mediator	Logical; rational	Reality principle
Id	Illogical; emotional; irrational	Pleasure principle

Intrapsychic conflicts

● **Figure 1.4** Freud's structure of the mind.

The role of the ego is to mediate conflict between the id and the superego. The ego is often referred to as the executive or manager of our minds. If it mediates successfully, we can go on to higher intellectual and creative pursuits. If it is unsuccessful and the id or superego becomes too strong, conflict will overtake us and psychological disorders will develop. Because these conflicts are all within the mind, they are referred to as **intrapsychic conflicts**. Freud believed that the id and the superego are almost entirely unconscious. We are fully aware only of the secondary processes of the ego, which is a relatively small part of the mind.

Defense Mechanisms

The ego fights a continual battle to stay on top of the warring id and superego. Occasionally, their conflicts produce anxiety. The anxiety alerts the ego to marshal **defense mechanisms**, unconscious protective processes that keep emotions associated with conflicts in check so that the ego can continue to function. Although Freud first conceptualized defense mechanisms, it was his daughter, Anna Freud, who developed the ideas more fully.

Defense mechanisms may be adaptive or maladaptive. For example, have you ever done poorly on a test because the grading was unfair? And then when you got home you yelled at your younger brother or your dog? This is an example of the defense mechanism of *displacement*. The ego adaptively decides that expressing anger at your professor might not be in your best interest. Because your brother and your dog don't have the authority to affect you in an adverse way, your anger is displaced to one of them. Some people may redirect energy from conflict or underlying anxiety into a more constructive outlet such as work. This process is called *sublimation*.

More severe internal conflicts that produce a lot of anxiety or other emotions can trigger self-defeating defensive processes or symptoms. Phobic and obsessive symptoms are especially common self-defeating defensive reactions that, according to Freud, reflect an inadequate attempt to deal with such conflict. Phobic symptoms typically incorporate elements of the conflict. For example, a dog phobia may be connected to an infantile fear of castration; that is, a man's internal conflict involves a fear of being attacked and castrated, a fear that is consciously expressed as a fear of being attacked and bitten by a dog, even if he knows the dog is harmless.

Examples of defense mechanisms are listed below (APA, 2000a):

Denial: Refuses to acknowledge some aspect of objective reality or subjective experience that is apparent to others

Displacement: Transfers a feeling about, or a response to, an object that causes discomfort onto another, usually less-threatening, object or person

Projection: Falsely attributes own unacceptable feelings, impulses, or thoughts to another individual or object

Rationalization: Conceals the true motivations for actions, thoughts, or feelings through elaborate reassuring or self-serving but incorrect explanations

Reaction formation: Substitutes behavior, thoughts, or feelings that are the direct opposite of unacceptable ones

Repression: Blocks disturbing wishes, thoughts, or experiences from conscious awareness

Sublimation: Directs potentially maladaptive feelings or impulses into socially acceptable behavior

Psychosexual Stages of Development

Freud also theorized that during infancy and early childhood we pass through a number of **psychosexual stages of development**. The stages—oral, anal, phallic, latency, and genital—represent distinctive patterns of gratifying our basic needs and satisfying our drive for physical pleasure. For example, the oral stage (birth to about age 2) is characterized by a focus on the need for food. In the act of sucking, necessary for feeding, the lips, tongue, and mouth become the focus of libidinal drives and, therefore, the principal source of pleasure. Freud hypothesized that if we did not receive gratification during a stage or if a stage left a particularly strong impression (which he termed *fixation*), an individual's personality would reflect the stage throughout adult life. For example, fixation at the oral stage might result in excessive thumb sucking and emphasis on oral stimulation through eating, chewing pencils, or biting fingernails. Adult personality characteristics theoretically associated with oral fixation include dependency and passivity or, in reaction to these tendencies, rebelliousness and cynicism.

One of the more controversial psychosexual conflicts occurs during the phallic stage (from age 3 to age 5 or 6), which is characterized by early genital self-stimulation. This conflict is the subject of the Greek tragedy *Oedipus Rex*, in which Oedipus is fated to kill his father and, unknowingly, to marry his mother. Freud asserted that all young boys relive this fantasy when genital self-stimulation is accompanied by images of sexual interactions with their mothers. These fantasies, in turn, are accompanied by strong feelings of envy and perhaps anger toward their fathers, with whom they identify but whose place they wish to take. Furthermore,

strong fears develop that the father may punish that lust by removing the son's penis—thus, the phenomenon of **castration anxiety**. This fear helps the boy keep his lustful impulses toward his mother in check. The battle of the lustful impulses on the one hand and castration anxiety on the other creates a conflict that is internal, or intrapsychic, called the *Oedipus complex*. The phallic stage passes uneventfully only if several things happen. First, the child must resolve his ambivalent relationship with his parents. If this happens, he may channel his libidinal impulses into heterosexual relationships while retaining harmless affection for his mother.

The counterpart conflict in girls, called the *Electra complex*, is even more controversial. Freud viewed the young girl as wanting to replace her mother and possess her father. Central to this possession is the girl's desire for a penis—hence the term *penis envy*. According to Freud, the conflict is resolved when females develop healthy heterosexual relationships and look forward to having a baby, which he viewed as a healthy substitute for having a penis. Needless to say, this theory has provoked marked consternation over the years as being sexist and demeaning. It is important to remember that it is theory, not fact; no systematic research exists to support it.

In Freud's view, all nonpsychotic psychological disorders resulted from unconscious conflicts, the anxiety that resulted from those conflicts, and the implementation of defense mechanisms. Freud called such disorders **neuroses**, or *neurotic disorders*.

Later Developments in Psychoanalytic Thought

Freud's original psychoanalytic theories have been modified and developed in different directions. Some theorists

id In **psychoanalysis**, the **unconscious** psychic entity present at birth representing basic drives.

ego In **psychoanalysis**, the psychic entity responsible for finding realistic and practical ways to satisfy **id** drives.

superego In **psychoanalysis**, the psychic entity representing the internalized moral standards of parents and society.

intrapsychic conflicts In psychoanalytic theory, a struggle among the **id**, **ego**, and **superego**.

defense mechanisms Common pattern of behavior, often an adaptive coping style when it occurs in moderation, observed in response to a particular situation. Psychoanalytic theory suggests that defense mechanisms are **unconscious** processes originating in the **ego**.

psychosexual stages of development Psychoanalytic concept of the sequence of phases a person passes through during development. Each stage is named for the location on the body where **id** gratification is maximal at that time.

castration anxiety In **psychoanalysis**, the fear in young boys that they will be mutilated genitally because of their lust for their mothers.

neurosis (*plural* neuroses) Obsolete psychodynamic term for a **psychological disorder** thought to result from an **unconscious** conflict and the **anxiety** it causes. Plural is *neuroses*.

▲ Anna Freud (1895–1982), here with her father, contributed the concept of defense mechanisms to the field of psychoanalysis.

simply took one component of psychoanalytic theory and developed it more fully. Others broke with Freud and went in new directions.

Anna Freud (1895–1982), Freud's daughter, concentrated on how defensive mechanisms determine our behavior. In so doing, she was the first proponent of the modern field of **ego psychology**. According to Anna Freud, the individual slowly accumulates adaptational capacities, skill in reality testing, and defenses. Abnormal behavior develops when the ego is deficient in regulating such functions as controlling impulses or in marshaling appropriate defenses to internal conflicts. In another modification of Freud's theories, Heinz Kohut (1913–1981) focused on the formation of self-concept and the attributes of the self that allow an individual to progress toward health, or conversely, to develop **neurosis**. This psychoanalytic approach became known as **self-psychology** (Kohut, 1977).

A related area is **object relations**—the study of how children incorporate the images, the memories, and sometimes the values of a person to whom they were (or are) emotionally attached. *Object* in this sense refers to these important people, and the process of incorporation is called *introjection*. Introjected objects can become an integrated part of the ego or may assume conflicting roles in determining the identity, or self. For example, your parents may have conflicting views on relationships or careers, which, in turn, may differ from your own. To the extent that these varying positions have been incorporated, the potential for conflict

arises. One day you may feel one way about your career direction, and the next day you may feel differently. According to object relations theory, you tend to see the world through the eyes of the person incorporated into yourself. Object relations theorists focus on how these disparate images come together to make up a person's identity.

Carl Jung (1875–1961) and Alfred Adler (1870–1937) were students of Freud who formed their own schools of thought. Jung, rejecting many of the sexual aspects of Freud's theory, introduced the concept of the **collective unconscious**, a wisdom stored deep in individual memories and passed down from generation to generation. Jung also suggested that spiritual and religious drives are as much a part of human nature as are sexual drives; this emphasis and the idea of the collective unconscious continue to draw the attention of mystics.

Adler focused on feelings of inferiority and the striving for superiority; he created the term *inferiority complex*. Unlike Freud, both Jung and Adler believed that the basic quality of human nature is positive and that there is a strong drive toward self-actualization (realizing one's full potential). Jung and Adler believed that by removing barriers to both internal and external growth, the individual would flourish.

Others emphasized development over the life span and the influence of culture and society on personality. Karen Horney (1885–1952) and Erich Fromm (1900–1980) are associated with these ideas, but the best-known theorist is Erik Erikson (1902–1994). Erikson's greatest contribution was his theory of development across the life span, in which he described the crises and conflicts that accompany eight specific stages. For example, in the *mature stage*, beginning about age 65, individuals review their lives, experiencing both satisfaction at having completed goals, and despair at having failed at others. Scientific developments have borne out the wisdom of considering psychopathology from a developmental point of view.

Psychoanalytic Psychotherapy

Many techniques of psychoanalytic psychotherapy, or psychoanalysis, are designed to reveal the nature of unconscious mental processes through catharsis and insight. Freud developed techniques of **free association**, in which patients are instructed to say whatever comes to mind. Free association is intended to reveal emotionally charged material that may be repressed because it is too painful or threatening to bring into consciousness. Freud's patients lay on a couch, and he sat behind them so that they would not be distracted. Other techniques include **dream analysis** (still quite popular today), in which the therapist interprets the content of dreams, supposedly reflecting the primary-process thinking of the id, and relates the dreams to symbolic aspects of unconscious conflicts. This procedure is often difficult because the patient may resist the efforts of the therapist to uncover repressed conflicts and may deny the interpretations. The goal of this stage of therapy is to help the patient gain insight into the nature of the conflicts.

The relationship between the therapist, called the **psychoanalyst**, and the patient is important. In the context of this relationship, the therapist may discover the nature of the patient's intrapsychic conflict. This is because, in a phenomenon called **transference**, patients come to relate to the therapist much as they did to important figures in their childhood, particularly their parents. Patients who resent the therapist but can verbalize no good reason for it may be re-enacting childhood resentment toward a parent. More often, the patient will fall in love with the therapist, which reflects positive feelings that existed earlier for a parent. In the phenomenon of *countertransference*, therapists project their own issues and feelings, usually positive, onto the patient. Therapists are trained to deal with their own feelings as well as those of their patients, whatever the mode of therapy, and relationships outside therapy are forbidden.

Classical psychoanalysis requires therapy four to five times a week for 2 to 5 years to analyze unconscious conflicts, resolve them, and restructure the personality to put the ego back in charge. Reduction of symptoms (psychological disorders) is relatively inconsequential because they are only expressions of underlying intrapsychic conflicts that arise from psychosexual developmental stages. Thus, eliminating a phobia or depressive episode would be of little use unless the underlying conflict was dealt with adequately, because another set of symptoms would almost certainly emerge *(symptom substitution)*. Because of the extraordinary expense of classical psychoanalysis, and the lack of evidence that it is effective, this approach is seldom used today.

Psychoanalysis is still practiced, but many psychotherapists employ a loosely related set of approaches referred to as **psychodynamic psychotherapy**. Although conflicts and unconscious processes are still emphasized, and efforts are made to identify trauma and defense mechanisms, therapists use a mixture of tactics, including (1) a focus on affect and the expression of patients' emotions; (2) an exploration of patients' attempts to avoid topics or hinder the progress of therapy; (3) the identification of patterns in patients' actions, thoughts, feelings, experiences, and relationships; (4) an emphasis on past experiences; (5) a focus on interpersonal experiences; (6) an emphasis on the therapeutic relationship; and (7) an exploration of patients' wishes, dreams, or fantasies (Blagys & Hilsenroth, 2000). Two additional features characterize psychodynamic psychotherapy. First, it is significantly briefer than classical psychoanalysis. Second, psychodynamic therapists de-emphasize the goal of personality reconstruction, focusing instead on relieving the suffering associated with psychological disorders.

Comments

Pure psychoanalysis as a treatment has been diminishing in popularity for years. A criticism of psychoanalysis is that it is unscientific, relying on reports by the patient of events that happened years ago. These events have been filtered through the experience of the observer and then interpreted by the psychoanalyst in ways that could be questioned and might differ from one analyst to the next. Finally, there has been no careful measurement of any of these phenomena and no obvious way to prove or disprove the hypotheses of psychoanalysis. This is important because measurement and the ability to prove or disprove a theory are the foundations of the scientific approach.

Nevertheless, psychoanalytic concepts and observations have been valuable. Scientific studies of psychopathology have supported the observation of unconscious mental processes, the notion that emotional responses are often triggered by hidden or symbolic cues, and the understanding that memories can be repressed and avoided in a variety of ways. The relationship of the therapist and the patient, called the *therapeutic alliance*, is an important area of study. These concepts, along with the importance of coping styles or defense mechanisms, will appear throughout this book.

Many of these psychodynamic ideas had been in development for more than a century, culminating in Freud's influential writings (e.g., Lehrer, 1995), and they stood in stark contrast to witch trials and ideas of incurable brain pathology. In early years, the source of good and evil and of urges and prohibitions was conceived as external and spiritual, usually in the guise of demons confronting the forces of good. From the psychoanalytic point of view, we

. . . .

ego psychology Psychoanalytic theory that emphasizes the role of the ego in development and attributes psychological disorders to failure of the ego to manage impulses and internal conflicts. Also known as self-psychology.

neurosis (*plural* neuroses) Obsolete psychodynamic term for a **psychological disorder** thought to result from an **unconscious** conflict and the **anxiety** it causes. Plural is *neuroses*.

self-psychology See **ego psychology**.

object relations Modern development in psychodynamic theory involving the study of how children incorporate the memories and values of people who are close and important to them.

collective unconscious Accumulated wisdom of a culture collected and remembered across generations, a psychodynamic concept introduced by Carl Jung.

free association Psychoanalytic therapy technique intended to explore threatening material repressed into the **unconscious**. The patient is instructed to say whatever comes to mind without censoring.

dream analysis Psychoanalytic therapy method in which dream content is examined as symbolic of **id** impulses and **intrapsychic conflicts**.

psychoanalyst Therapist who practices **psychoanalysis** after earning either an M.D. or a Ph.D. degree and receiving additional specialized postdoctoral training.

transference Psychoanalytic concept suggesting that clients may seek to relate to the therapist as they do to important authority figures, particularly their parents.

psychodynamic psychotherapy Contemporary version of **psychoanalysis** that still emphasizes **unconscious** processes and conflicts but is briefer and more focused on specific problems.

ourselves became the battleground for these forces, and we are inexorably caught up in the battle, sometimes for better and sometimes for worse.

Humanistic Theory

We have seen that Jung and Adler broke sharply with Freud. Their fundamental disagreement concerned the very nature of humanity. Freud portrayed life as a battleground where we are continually in danger of being overwhelmed by our darkest forces. Jung and Adler emphasized the positive, optimistic side of human nature. Jung talked about setting goals, looking toward the future, and realizing one's potential. Adler believed that human nature reaches its potential when we contribute to the welfare of others. He believed that we all strive to reach superior levels of intellectual and moral development. Nevertheless, both Jung and Adler retained many principles of psychodynamic thought. Their general philosophies were adopted in the middle of the century by personality theorists and became known as *humanistic psychology.*

Self-actualizing was the watchword for this movement. The underlying assumption is that all of us could reach our highest potential if we had the freedom to grow. Inevitably, a variety of conditions may block our actualization, usually originating outside the individual. Difficult living conditions or stressful experiences may move you away from your true self.

Abraham Maslow (1908–1970) was most systematic in describing the structure of personality. He postulated a *hierarchy of needs,* beginning with our most basic needs for food and sex and ranging up to our needs for self-actualization, love, and self-esteem. Social needs such as friendship fall somewhere between. Maslow hypothesized that we cannot progress up the hierarchy until we have satisfied the needs at lower levels.

Carl Rogers (1902–1987) is the most influential humanist. Rogers (1961) originated client-centered therapy, later known as **person-centered therapy**. In this approach, the therapist takes a passive role, making as few interpretations as possible. The point is to give the individual a chance to develop unfettered by threats to the self. **Unconditional positive regard**, the complete acceptance of most of the client's feelings and actions, is critical to the humanistic approach. *Empathy* is the sympathetic understanding of the individual's view of the world. The hoped-for result of person-centered therapy is that clients will be more straightforward and honest with themselves and will access their innate tendencies toward growth.

Like psychoanalysis, the humanistic approach has had a substantial effect on theories of interpersonal relationships. For example, the human potential movements popular in the 1960s and 1970s were a result of humanistic theorizing. This approach also emphasized the importance of the therapeutic relationship in a way quite different from Freud's approach. Rather than seeing the relationship as a means to an end (transference), humanistic therapists believed that relationships, including the therapeutic relationship, were the single most positive influence in facilitating human growth. Nevertheless, the humanistic model contributed relatively little new information to the field of psychopathology. One reason for this is that its proponents stressed the unique, nonquantifiable experiences of the individual, emphasizing that people are more different than alike. As Maslow noted, the humanistic model found its greatest application among individuals without psychological disorders. The application of person-centered therapy to more severe psychological disorders has decreased substantially over the decades.

The Behavioral Model

The **behavioral model**, also known as the *cognitive-behavioral model* or *social learning model*, brought a more scientific approach to psychological aspects of psychopathology.

Pavlov and Classical Conditioning

In his classic study examining why dogs salivate before the presentation of food, Russian physiologist Ivan Petrovich Pavlov (1849–1936) initiated the study of **classical conditioning**, a type of learning in which a neutral stimulus is paired with a response until it elicits that response. Conditioning is one way in which we acquire new information. This process is not as simple as it first seems, and we continue to uncover many more facts about its complexity (Lissek *et al.*, 2014; Prenoveau, Craske, Liao, & Ornitz, 2013; Rescorla, 1988). But it can be quite automatic. Let's look at a powerful contemporary example.

Chemotherapy, a common treatment for some forms of cancer, has side effects including severe nausea and vomiting. But patients often experience these effects when they merely see the personnel who administered the chemotherapy or any equipment associated with the treatment (Morrow & Dobkin, 1988; Kamen *et al.*, 2014). For some patients, this reaction becomes associated with stimuli that evoke people or things present during chemotherapy—anybody in a nurse's uniform or even the sight of the hospital. This phenomenon is called *stimulus generalization* because the response generalizes

▲ Ivan Pavlov (1849–1936) identified the process of classical conditioning, which is important to many emotional disorders.

to similar stimuli. Psychologists have had to develop specific treatments to overcome this response (Mustian *et al.*, 2011).

Whether the stimulus is food, as in Pavlov's laboratory, or chemotherapy, the classical conditioning process begins with a stimulus that would elicit a response in almost anyone and requires no learning; no conditions must be present for the response to occur. For these reasons, the food or chemotherapy is called the *unconditioned stimulus (UCS)*. The natural or unlearned response to this stimulus—in these cases, salivation or nausea—is called the *unconditioned response (UCR)*. Now the learning comes in. As we have seen, any person or object associated with the UCS (food or chemotherapy) acquires the power to elicit the same response, but now the response, because it was elicited by the conditional or *conditioned stimulus (CS)*, is termed a *conditioned response (CR)*. Thus, the nurse associated with the chemotherapy becomes a CS. The nauseous sensation (upon seeing the nurse), which is almost the same as that experienced during chemotherapy, becomes the CR.

With unconditioned stimuli as powerful as chemotherapy, a CR can be learned in one trial. Most learning of this type, however, requires repeated pairing of the UCS (for example, chemotherapy) and the CS (for instance, nurses' uniforms or hospital equipment). When Pavlov began to investigate this phenomenon, he substituted a metronome for the footsteps of his assistants so that he could quantify the stimulus more accurately. He found that presentation of the CS (for example, the metronome) *without* the food for a long enough period would eventually eliminate the CR to the food. In other words, the dog learned that the metronome no longer meant that a meal might be on the way. This process was called **extinction**.

Because Pavlov was a physiologist, it was natural for him to study these processes in a laboratory and to be scientific about it. This required precision in measuring and observing relationships and in ruling out alternative explanations. Although this scientific approach is common in biology, it was uncommon in psychology at that time. For example, it was impossible for psychoanalysts to measure unconscious conflicts precisely, or even observe them. Even early experimental psychologists such as Edward Titchener (1867–1927) emphasized the study of **introspection**. Subjects reported on their thoughts and feelings after experiencing certain stimuli, but the results of this "armchair" psychology were inconsistent.

Watson and the Rise of Behaviorism

American psychologist John B. Watson (1878–1958) is considered the founder of behaviorism. Watson decided that to base psychology on introspection was to head in the wrong direction; that psychology could be made as scientific as physiology (Watson, 1913). Most of Watson's time was spent developing behavioral psychology as an empirical science, but he did dabble briefly in the study of psychopathology. In 1920, he and a student, Rosalie Rayner, presented an 11-month-old boy named Albert with a harmless fluffy white rat to play with. Albert was not afraid of the animal and enjoyed playing with it. Every time Albert reached for the rat, however, the experimenters made a loud noise behind him. After only five trials, Albert showed signs of fear if the white rat came near. The experimenters then determined that Albert displayed mild fear of any white furry object, even a Santa Claus beard. You may not think this is surprising, but this was one of the first examples ever recorded in a laboratory of producing fear of an object not previously feared. Of course, this experiment would be considered unethical today, and it turns out Albert may have also had some neurological impairment that could have contributed to developing fear (Fridlund, Beck, Goldie, & Irons, 2012), but the study remains a classic one.

Another student of Watson's, Mary Cover Jones (1896–1987), thought that if fear could be conditioned, perhaps it could also be unlearned or extinguished. She worked

▲ Mary Cover Jones (1896–1987) was one of the first psychologists to use behavioral techniques to free a patient from phobia.

self-actualizing Process emphasized in humanistic psychology in which people strive to achieve their highest potential against difficult life experiences.

person-centered therapy Therapy method in which the client, rather than the counselor, primarily directs the course of discussion, seeking self-discovery and self-responsibility.

unconditional positive regard Acceptance by the counselor of the client's feelings and actions without judgment or condemnation.

behavioral model Explanation of human behavior, including dysfunction, based on principles of learning and adaptation derived from experimental psychology.

classical conditioning Fundamental learning process first described by Ivan Pavlov. An event that automatically elicits a response is paired with another stimulus event that does not (a neutral stimulus). After repeated pairings, the neutral stimulus becomes a **conditioned stimulus** that by itself can elicit the desired response.

extinction Learning process in which a response maintained by **reinforcement** in **operant conditioning** or pairing in **classical conditioning** decreases when that reinforcement or pairing is removed; also the procedure of removing that reinforcement or pairing.

introspection Early, nonscientific approach to the study of psychology involving systematic attempts to report thoughts and feelings that specific stimuli evoked.

with a 2-year-old boy named Peter, who was already afraid of furry objects. Jones decided to bring a white rabbit into the room where Peter was playing for a short time each day. She also arranged for other children, who did not fear rabbits, to be in the same room. Peter's fear gradually diminished. Jones brought the rabbit closer. Eventually Peter was touching and playing with the rabbit (Jones, 1924a, 1924b), and years later the fear had not returned.

The Beginnings of Behavior Therapy

The implications of Jones's research were largely ignored for two decades, but in the late 1940s and early 1950s, South African psychiatrist Joseph Wolpe (1915–1997) became dissatisfied with prevailing psychoanalytic interpretations of psychopathology. He turned to the field of behavioral psychology and developed behavioral procedures for treating his patients, many of whom suffered from phobias. His best-known technique was termed **systematic desensitization**. It was similar to the treatment of little Peter: Individuals were gradually introduced to the objects or situations they feared so their fear could extinguish; that is, they could test reality and see that nothing bad happened in the presence of the phobic object or scene. Wolpe also had his patients do something that was incompatible with fear while they were in the presence of the dreaded object or situation. Because he could not always reproduce the phobic object in his office, Wolpe had his patients systematically *imagine* the phobic scene while relaxing. For example, Wolpe treated a man with a phobia of dogs by training him to relax and then imagine he was looking at a dog across the park. Gradually, he could imagine the dog across the park and remain relaxed. Wolpe then had him imagine he was closer to the dog. Eventually, the man imagined he was touching the dog while maintaining a relaxed, almost trancelike state.

Wolpe reported success with systematic desensitization, one of the first wide-scale applications of the science of behaviorism to psychopathology. Wolpe, working with fellow pioneers Hans Eysenck and Stanley Rachman in London, called this approach **behavior therapy**. Although Wolpe's procedures are seldom used today, they paved the way for modern-day procedures in which severe phobias can be eliminated in as little as 1 day (see Chapter 4).

B. F. Skinner and Operant Conditioning

Freud's influence extended far beyond psychopathology into many aspects of our cultural and intellectual history. Only one other behavioral scientist has made a similar impact: Burrhus Frederic (B. F.) Skinner (1904–1990). In 1938 he published *The Behavior of Organisms*, in which he laid out the principles of *operant conditioning*, a type of learning in which behavior changes as a function of what follows the behavior.

Skinner was strongly influenced by Watson's conviction that a science of human behavior must be based on observable events and relationships among those events; he was also influenced by the work of Edward L. Thorndike (1874–1949). Thorndike is best known for the *law of effect*, which states that behavior is either strengthened (likely to be repeated more frequently) or weakened (likely to occur less frequently) depending on the consequences of that behavior. Skinner took the notions that Thorndike had tested in the animal laboratories, using food as a reinforcer, and developed them in complex ways to apply to much of our behavior. For example, if a 5-year-old boy starts shouting at the top of his lungs in a restaurant, it is unlikely his behavior was automatically elicited by a UCS. Also, he will be less likely to do it in the future if his parents scold him, take him out to the car, or consistently reinforce more appropriate behavior. Then again, if the parents think his behavior is cute and laugh, chances are he will do it again.

Skinner coined the term *operant conditioning* because behavior operates on the environment and changes it in some way. For example, the boy's behavior affects his parents' behavior and probably the behavior of other customers. Most things that we do socially provide the context for other people to respond to us in one way or another, thereby providing consequences for our behavior. The same is true of our physical environment, although the consequences may be long term (polluting the air eventually will poison us). Skinner preferred the term **reinforcement** to "reward" because it connotes the effect on the behavior. He pointed out that all our behavior is governed to some degree by reinforcement, which can be arranged in a variety of schedules of reinforcement (Ferster & Skinner, 1957). He also believed that using punishment is relatively ineffective in the long run and that the primary way to develop new behavior is to positively reinforce desired behavior. Skinner did not deny the influence of biology or the existence of subjective states of emotion or cognition; he simply

▲ B. F. Skinner (1904–1990) studied operant conditioning, a form of learning that is central to psychopathology.

explained these phenomena as relatively inconsequential side effects of a particular history of reinforcement.

The subjects of Skinner's research were usually pigeons and rats. Skinner taught the animals a variety of tricks, including dancing, playing Ping-Pong, and playing a toy piano. To do this he used **shaping**, a process of reinforcing successive approximations to a final behavior or set of behaviors. For example, if you want a pigeon to play Ping-Pong, first you provide it with a pellet of food every time it moves its head slightly toward a Ping-Pong ball tossed in its direction. Gradually you require the pigeon to move its head ever closer to the Ping-Pong ball until it touches it. Finally, receiving the food pellet is contingent on the pigeon hitting the ball back with its head.

Comments

The behavioral model has contributed greatly to the understanding and treatment of psychopathology. Nevertheless, it is incomplete and inadequate to account for what we now know about psychopathology. In the past, there was little or no room for biology in behaviorism, because disorders were considered, for the most part, environmentally determined reactions. The model also fails to account for development of psychopathology across the life span. Advances in our knowledge of how information is processed have added a layer of complexity. Integrating all these dimensions requires a new model of psychopathology.

An Integrative Approach

▶ Why is the scientific method so important in studying abnormal behavior?

We have just reviewed three traditions or ways of thinking about causes of psychopathology: the supernatural, the biological, and the psychological (further subdivided into two major historical components: psychoanalytic and behavioral).

Supernatural explanations of psychopathology are still with us. This tradition has little influence on scientists and other professionals, however. Biological, psychoanalytic, and behavioral models, by contrast, continue to further our knowledge of psychopathology.

Each tradition has failed in important ways. First, scientific methods were not often applied to the theories and treatments within a tradition, mostly because methods that would have produced the evidence necessary to confirm or disprove the theories and treatments had not been developed. Lacking such evidence, many people accepted fads and superstitions that proved to be untrue or useless. New fads often superseded useful theories and treatment procedures. King Charles VI was subjected to a variety of procedures, some of which have since been proved useful and others that were fads or even harmful. How we use scientific methods to confirm or disconfirm findings in psychopathology is described in Chapter 3.

Second, health professionals tend to look at psychological disorders from their own point of view alone. Grey assumed that psychological disorders were the result of brain disease and that other factors had no influence. Watson assumed that all behaviors, including disordered behavior, were the result of psychological and social influences and that the contribution of biological factors was inconsequential.

In the 1990s, two developments came together to shed light on the nature of psychopathology: (1) the increasing sophistication of scientific tools and methodology, and (2) the realization that no one influence—biological, behavioral, cognitive, emotional, or social—occurs in isolation. Every time we think, feel, or do something, the brain and the rest of the body are hard at work. Perhaps not as obvious, however, is that our thoughts, feelings, and actions influence the function and even the structure of the brain. In other words, our behavior is the product of a continual interaction of psychological, biological, and social influences.

By 2000, the young fields of cognitive science and neuroscience were growing rapidly as we learned more about

- -

systematic desensitization Behavioral therapy technique to diminish excessive fears, involving gradual exposure to the feared stimulus paired with a positive coping experience, usually relaxation.

behavior therapy Array of therapeutic methods based on the principles of behavioral and **cognitive science**, as well as principles of learning as applied to clinical problems. It considers specific behaviors rather than inferred conflicts as legitimate targets for change.

reinforcement In **operant conditioning**, consequences for behavior that strengthen it or increase its frequency. Positive reinforcement involves the contingent delivery of a desired consequence. Negative reinforcement is the contingent escape from an aversive consequence. Unwanted behaviors may result from reinforcement of those behaviors or the failure to reinforce desired behaviors.

shaping In **operant conditioning**, the development of a new response by reinforcing successively more similar versions of that response. Both desirable and undesirable behaviors may be learned in this manner.

the brain and about how we process, remember, and use information. At the same time, new findings from behavioral science revealed the importance of early experience in determining later development. It was clear that a new model was needed that would consider biological, psychological, and social influences on behavior. This approach to psychopathology would combine findings from all areas with our rapidly growing understanding of how we experience life during different developmental periods. In 2010, the National Institute of Mental Health (NIMH) instituted a plan to support research and development on the interrelationship of these factors with the aim of translating research findings to treatment settings (Cuthbert, 2014; Insel, 2009). In the remainder of this book, we explore the reciprocal influences among neuroscience, cognitive science, behavior science, and developmental science and demonstrate that the only currently valid model of psychopathology is multidimensional and integrative.

1.3 Concept CHECK

Match the treatment with the corresponding theory of behavior: (a) behavioral model, (b) moral therapy, (c) psychoanalytic theory, and (d) humanistic theory.

1. Treating institutionalized patients as normally as possible and encouraging social interaction and relationship development. _____

2. Hypnosis, psychoanalysis-like free association and dream analysis, and balance of the id, ego, and superego. _____

3. Person-centered therapy with unconditional positive regard. _____

4. Classical conditioning, systematic desensitization, and operant conditioning. _____

SUMMARY

Understanding Psychopathology

How do psychologists define a psychological disorder?

▶ A psychological disorder is (1) a psychological dysfunction that is (2) associated with distress or impairment in functioning and (3) a response that is not typical or culturally expected. All three basic criteria must be met; no one criterion alone has yet been identified that defines the essence of abnormality.

▶ Psychopathology is concerned with the scientific study of psychological disorders. Mental health professionals range from clinical and counseling psychologists to psychiatrists and psychiatric social workers and nurses. Each profession requires a specific type of training.

What is a scientist–practitioner?

▶ Mental health professionals can function as scientist-practitioners. They not only keep up with the latest findings but also use scientific data to evaluate their own work, and they often conduct research within their clinics or hospitals.

▶ Research about psychological disorders falls into three categories: description, causation, and treatment and outcomes.

The Supernatural, Biological, and Psychological Traditions

What supernatural influences were formerly believed to explain abnormal behavior?

What are the underlying assumptions of the biological approach to understanding abnormal behavior?

How do the psychological approaches of psychoanalysis, humanism, and behaviorism explain abnormal behavior?

▶ Historically, there have been three approaches to abnormal behavior. In the supernatural tradition, abnormal behavior is attributed to outside agents, such as demons or spirits. In the biological tradition, disorders are attributed to disease or biochemical imbalances; in the psychological tradition, abnormal behavior is attributed to faulty psychological development and to social context.

▶ Each tradition has its own ways of treating individuals. Supernatural treatments include exorcism to rid the body of the supernatural spirits. Biological treatments emphasize physical care and medical cures, especially drugs. Psychological approaches use psychosocial treatments, beginning with moral therapy and including modern psychotherapy.

▶ Sigmund Freud, the founder of psychoanalytic therapy, offered an elaborate conception of the unconscious mind. In therapy, Freud focused on tapping into the unconscious through such techniques as catharsis, free association, and dream analysis. Although Freud's followers veered from his path in many ways, Freud's influence can still be felt today.

▶ One outgrowth of Freudian therapy is humanistic psychology, which focuses on human potential and self-actualizing. Therapy that has evolved from this approach is known as person-centered therapy; the therapist shows almost unconditional positive regard for the client's feelings and thoughts.

▶ The behavioral model moved psychology into the realm of science. Both research and therapy focus on things that are measurable, including such techniques as systematic desensitization, reinforcement, and shaping.

An Integrative Approach

Why is the scientific method so important in studying abnormal behavior?

▶ With the increasing sophistication of our scientific tools, and new knowledge from cognitive science, behavioral science, and neuroscience, we now realize that no contribution to psychological disorders occurs in isolation. Our behavior, both normal and abnormal, is a product of a continual interaction of psychological, biological, and social influences.

▆ Key Terms

psychological disorder, 3
phobia, 3
abnormal behavior, 4
psychopathology, 6
scientist-practitioner, 6
presenting problem, 6
clinical description, 6
prevalence, 7
incidence, 7
course, 7
prognosis, 7
etiology, 7
exorcism, 9
psychosocial treatment, 15
moral therapy, 15
mental hygiene movement, 16
psychoanalysis, 16

behaviorism, 16
unconscious, 17
catharsis, 17
psychoanalytic model, 17
id, 18
ego, 18
superego, 18
intrapsychic conflicts, 18
defense mechanisms, 18
psychosexual stages of
    development, 19
castration anxiety, 19
neurosis (*plural* neuroses), 19, 20
ego psychology, 20
self-psychology, 20
object relations, 20
collective unconscious, 20

free association, 20
dream analysis, 20
psychoanalyst, 21
transference, 21
psychodynamic psychotherapy, 21
self-actualizing, 22
person-centered therapy, 22
unconditional positive regard, 22
behavioral model, 22
classical conditioning, 22
extinction, 23
introspection, 23
systematic desensitization, 24
behavior therapy, 24
reinforcement, 24
shaping, 25

Answers to Concept Checks

1.1

Part A

1. d; 2. b, c

Part B

3. d; 4. c; 5. a; 6. f; 7. e; 8. b

1.2

1. c; 2. a; 3. b

1.3

1. b; 2. c; 3. d; 4. a

Chapter Quiz

1. Dr. Roberts, a psychiatrist, often prescribes medication to his patients for their psychological problems. Dr.Roberts has what type of degree?

   a. PhD

   b. MD

   c. PsyD

   d. EdD

2. All of the following are part of a clinical description EXCEPT?:

   a. thoughts

   b. feelings

   c. causes

   d. behaviors

3. The _____ describes the number of people in a population who have a disorder, whereas the _____ describes how many new cases of a disorder occur within a given period?

   a. ratio; prevalence

   b. incidence; ratio

   c. incidence; prevalence

   d. prevalence; incidence

4. Which of the following is NOT a historical model of abnormal behavior?

   a. the psyche model

   b. the supernatural model

   c. the biological model

   d. the psychological model

5. During the 19th century, the biological tradition of psychological disorders was supported by the discovery that a bacterial microorganism, _____, could result in psychotic symptoms and bizarre behaviors in advanced stages.

   a. malaria

   b. yellow fever

   c. dengue

   d. syphilis

6. Which of the following describes the order in which biological treatments for mental disorders were introduced?

   a. neuroleptic drug therapy, insulin therapy, electroconvulsive therapy

   b. insulin therapy, electroconvulsive therapy, neuroleptic drug therapy

   c. electroconvulsive therapy, neuroleptic drug therapy, insulin therapy

   d. electroconvulsive therapy, insulin therapy, neuroleptic drug therapy

7. _____ is the release of tension following the disclosure of emotional trauma, whereas _____ is the increased understanding of current feelings and past events.

   a. Insight; catharsis

   b. Catharsis; insight

   c. Catharsis; mediation

   d. Mediation; catharsis

8. Which of the following is an example of the Freudian defense mechanism known as displacement?

   a. Terry despises the fact that his brother is a star athlete. Instead of letting his brother know how he feels, Terry cheers him on at every game.

   b. Erika is attracted to her friend's husband and flirts with him. When her friend confronts her, Erika disagrees and refuses to believe what her friend is saying.

   c. Adam is criticized by his teacher in front of other students. When he goes home, his dog runs to him, and Adam kicks the dog.

   d. Judith feels uncomfortable around people with ethnic backgrounds different from her own. During a group discussion at work, she tells a coworker that his ideas are racist.

9. Before feeding her dog, Anna always gets his food out of the pantry. When she opens the pantry door, her dog begins to salivate. The dog's salivation is a(n):

   a. unconditioned stimulus

   b. unconditioned response

   c. conditioned stimulus

   d. conditioned response

10. B. F. Skinner is known for introducing the concept of _____, the belief that behavior can influence and change the environment.

   a. classical conditioning

   b. systematic desensitization

   c. operant conditioning

   d. extinction

(See Appendix A for answers.)

Timeline of Significant Events

400 B.C.–1875

400 B.C.: Hippocrates suggests that psychological disorders have both biological and psychological causes.

1300s: Superstition runs rampant and mental disorders are blamed on demons and witches; exorcisms are performed to rid victims of evil spirits.

DEA PICTURE LIBRARY/ De Agostini/Getty Images

Source: National Library of Medicine

1400–1800: Bloodletting and leeches are used to rid the body of unhealthy fluids and restore balance.

1793: Philippe Pinel introduces moral therapy and makes French mental institutions more humane.

400 B.C.	1300s	1500s	1825–1875

200 B.C.: Galen suggests that normal and abnormal behavior are related to four bodily fluids, or humors.

1400s: Enlightened view that insanity is caused by mental or emotional stress gains momentum, and depression and anxiety are again regarded by some as disorders.

1500s: Paracelsus suggests that the moon and the stars, not possession by the devil, affect people's psychological functioning.

1825–1875: Syphilis is differentiated from other types of psychosis in that it is caused by a specific bacterium; ultimately, penicillin is found to cure syphilis.

1930–1968

1930: Insulin shock therapy, electric shock treatments, and brain surgery begin to be used to treat psychopathology.

1943: The Minnesota Multiphasic Personality Inventory is published.

1950: The first effective drugs for severe psychotic disorders are developed. Humanistic psychology (based on ideas of Carl Jung, Alfred Adler, and Carl Rogers) gains some acceptance.

1958: Joseph Wolpe effectively treats patients with phobias using systematic desensitization based on principles of behavioral science.

1930	1943	1950	1968

1938: B. F. Skinner publishes *The Behavior of Organisms*, which describes the principles of operant conditioning.

1946: Anna Freud publishes *Ego and the Mechanisms of Defense.*

1952: The first edition of the *Diagnostic and Statistical Manual (DSM-I)* is published.

1968: *DSM-II* is published.

Bettmann/Getty Images

Imagno/Hulton Archive/Getty Images

1848–1920

1848: Dorothea Dix successfully campaigns for more humane treatment in U.S. mental institutions.

1870: Louis Pasteur develops his germ theory of disease, which helps identify the bacterium that causes syphilis.

1900: Sigmund Freud publishes *The Interpretation of Dreams*.

1913: Emil Kraepelin classifies various psychological disorders from a biological point of view and publishes work on diagnosis.

1848	1870	1900	1920

1854: John P. Grey, head of New York's Utica Hospital, believes that insanity is the result of physical causes, thus de-emphasizing psychological treatments.

1895: Josef Breuer treats the "hysterical" Anna O., leading to Freud's development of psychoanalytic theory.

1904: Ivan Pavlov receives the Nobel Prize for his work on the physiology of digestion, which leads him to identify conditioned reflexes in dogs.

1920: John B. Watson experiments with conditioned fear in Little Albert, using a white rat.

1980–Present

1990s: Increasingly sophisticated research methods are developed; no one influence—biological or environmental—is found to cause psychological disorders in isolation from the other.

1980: *DSM-III* is published.

2000: *DSM-IV-TR* is published.

1980	1990s	2000	2010

1987: *DSM-III-R* is published.

1994: *DSM-IV* is published.

2013: *DSM-5* is published.

2

An Integrative Approach to Psychopathology

CHAPTER OUTLINE

One-Dimensional versus Multidimensional Models

What Caused Judy's Phobia?
Outcome and Comments

Genetic Contributions to Psychopathology

The Nature of Genes
New Developments in the Study of Genes and Behavior
The Interaction of Genes and the Environment
Epigenetics and the Nongenomic "Inheritance" of Behavior

Neuroscience and Its Contributions to Psychopathology

The Central Nervous System
The Structure of the Brain
The Peripheral Nervous System
Neurotransmitters
Implications for Psychopathology
Psychosocial Influences on Brain Structure and Function
Interactions of Psychosocial Factors and Neurotransmitter Systems
Psychosocial Effects on the Development of Brain Structure and Function

Behavioral and Cognitive Science

Conditioning and Cognitive Processes
Learned Helplessness
Social Learning
Prepared Learning
Cognitive Science and the Unconscious

Emotions

The Physiology and Purpose of Fear
Emotional Phenomena
The Components of Emotion
Anger and Your Heart
Emotions and Psychopathology

Cultural, Social, and Interpersonal Factors

Voodoo and the Evil Eye
Gender
Social Effects on Health and Behavior
Global Incidence of Psychological Disorders

Life-Span Development

Conclusions

iStock.com/Wavebreak

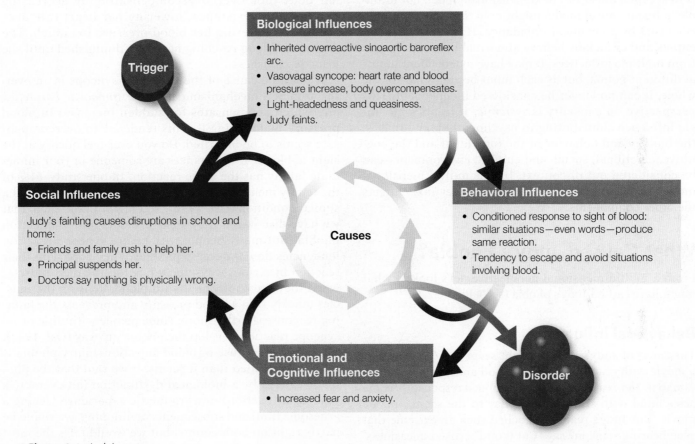

● **Figure 2.1** Judy's case.

Remember Judy from Chapter 1? We knew she suffered from blood–injection–injury phobia but we did not know why. Here, we address the issue of causation. This chapter examines the specific components of a **multidimensional integrative approach** to psychopathology (see ● Figure 2.1). Biological dimensions include causal factors from the fields of genetics and neuroscience. Psychological dimensions include causal factors from behavioral and cognitive processes, including learned helplessness, social learning, prepared learning, and even unconscious processes. Emotional influences contribute in a variety of ways to psychopathology, as do social and interpersonal influences. Finally, developmental influences figure in any discussion of causes of psychological disorders. But remember that no influence operates in isolation. Each dimension is influenced by the others and by development, and they weave together in intricate ways to create a psychological disorder.

....

multidimensional integrative approach Approach to the study of **psychopathology** that holds **psychological disorders** are always the products of multiple interacting causal factors.

Here, we explain briefly why we have adopted a multi-dimensional integrative model of psychopathology. Then we preview causal influences and interactions, using Judy's case as background. After that, we look more deeply at specific causal influences in psychopathology.

One-Dimensional versus Multidimensional Models

▶ How does a multidimensional model of causality differ from a unidimensional model?

▶ What are the key influences comprising the multidimensional model of abnormal behavior?

To say that psychopathology is caused by a single cause is to accept a linear or one-dimensional model. For example, a linear causal model might hold that schizophrenia is caused by a chemical imbalance. However, most scientists and clinicians believe abnormal behavior results from multiple influences. It may have independent inputs at different points, but as each input becomes part of the whole, it can no longer be considered independent. This perspective on causality is *systemic;* it implies no single influence contributing to psychopathology—that is, the biology and behavior of the individual and the cognitive, emotional, social, and cultural environment—can be considered out of context. In this multidimensional model, each component of the system inevitably affects the other components.

What Caused Judy's Phobia?

From a multidimensional perspective, let's look at what might have caused Judy's phobia (see ● Figure 2.1).

Behavioral Influences

The cause of Judy's phobia might seem obvious. She saw a movie with graphic scenes of blood and had a bad reaction to it. Her reaction, an unconditioned response, became associated with situations similar to the scenes in the movie. But Judy's reaction reached such an extreme that even hearing someone say "Cut it out!" evoked queasiness. Is Judy's phobia a straightforward case of classical conditioning? It might seem so, but why didn't the other kids in Judy's class develop the same phobia?

Biological Influences

We now know that more is involved in blood–injection–injury phobia than a simple conditioning experience (Antony & Barlow, 2002; Ritz, Meuret, & Ayala, 2010). Physiologically, Judy experienced a *vasovagal syncope,* a common cause of fainting. *Syncope* means "sinking feeling" or "swoon" caused by low blood pressure in the head. When she saw the film, she became mildly distressed, and her heart rate and blood pressure increased. Then her body took over, overcompensating by decreasing her vascular resistance, lowering her heart rate and, eventually, lowering her blood pressure too much. The amount of blood reaching her brain diminished until she lost consciousness.

A possible cause of the vasovagal syncope is an overreaction of a mechanism called the *sinoaortic baroreflex arc,* which compensates for sudden increases in blood pressure by lowering it. This tendency to overcompensate seems to be inherited. Do you ever feel queasy at the sight of blood? If so, chances are someone in your immediate family has the same reaction. In one study, 61% of the family members of individuals with this phobia had a similar condition (Öst, 1992). You might think, then, that we have discovered the cause of blood–injury–injection phobia. But many people with severe syncope reaction tendencies do *not* develop phobias. They cope with their reaction in various ways, including tensing their muscles when they are confronted with blood. Tensing the muscles quickly raises blood pressure and prevents the fainting response. Furthermore, some people with little or no syncope reaction develop the phobia anyway (Öst, 1992). Therefore, the cause of blood–injection–injury phobia is more complicated than it seems. If we said that the phobia is caused by a biological dysfunction (an overactive vasovagal reaction) or a traumatic experience (seeing a gruesome film) and subsequent conditioning, we would be partly right on both counts, but we would miss the most important point: To cause blood–injection–injury phobia, a complex *interaction* must occur between emotional, cognitive, social, biological, and behavioral factors. Inheriting a strong syncope reaction definitely puts a person at risk for developing this phobia, but other influences are at work as well.

Emotional Influences

Judy's case is a good example of biology influencing behavior. But behavior can also influence biology. What role did Judy's fear play in the development of her phobia? Emotions can affect physiological responses such as

▲ People who experience the same traumatic event will have different long-term reactions.

blood pressure, heart rate, and respiration, particularly if we know there is nothing to fear, as Judy did. In her case, rapid increases in heart rate caused by her emotions may have triggered a stronger and more intense baroreflex. Emotions also changed the way she thought about situations involving blood and injury and motivated her to avoid all situations connected with blood, even if it was important not to avoid them. As we see throughout this book, emotions play a substantial role in the development of many disorders.

Social Influences

Social and cultural factors contribute to biology and behavior. Judy's friends and family rushed to her aid when she fainted. Did their support help or hurt? Her principal dismissed her problem. What effect did this behavior have on her phobia? Rejection, particularly by authority figures, can make psychological disorders worse. Then again, being supportive only when somebody is experiencing symptoms is not always helpful because the attention may actually increase the frequency and intensity of the reaction.

Developmental Influences

As time passes, many things about ourselves and our environments change, causing us to react differently at different ages. Thus, at certain times we may enter a *developmental critical period* when we are more or less reactive to a given situation or influence than at other times. To go back to Judy, it is possible she was previously exposed to other situations involving blood. Why did this problem develop when she was 16 and not before? Is it possible that her susceptibility to having a vasovagal reaction was highest in her teenage years? It may be that the timing of her physiological reaction, along with viewing the disturbing film, provided just the right combination to initiate her severe phobic response.

Outcome and Comments

Fortunately for Judy, she responded well to brief but intensive treatment at one of our clinics, and she was back in school within seven days. Judy was gradually exposed to words, images, and situations describing or depicting blood and injury, while a sudden drop in blood pressure was prevented. We began with something mild, such as the phrase "Cut it out!" By the end of the week Judy was witnessing surgical procedures at the local hospital.

As you can see, finding the causes of abnormal behavior is a complex process. Focusing on biological or behavioral factors would not have given us a full picture of the causes of Judy's disorder; we had to consider a variety of influences and how they might interact. We now examine the research underlying the biological, psychological, and social influences that must be considered as causes of any psychological disorder.

2.1 Concept CHECK

Match each of the following scenarios to its most likely influence or influences: (a) behavioral, (b) biological, (c) emotional, (d) social, and (e) developmental.

1. The fact that some phobias are more common than others (such as fear of heights and snakes) and may have contributed to the survival of the species in the past suggests that phobias may be genetically prewired. This is evidence for which influence?

   _____

2. Jan's husband, Jinx, was an unemployed jerk who spent his life chasing women other than his wife. Jan, happily divorced for years, cannot understand why the smell of Jinx's brand of aftershave causes her to become nauseated. Which influence best explains her response? _____

3. Nathan, age 16, finds it more difficult than his seven-year-old sister to adjust to his parents' recent separation. This may be explained by what influences?

   _____

4. A traumatic ride on a Ferris wheel at a young age was most likely to have been the initial cause of Juanita's fear of heights. Her strong emotional reaction to heights is likely to maintain or even increase her fear. The initial development of the phobia is likely a result of _____ influences; however, _____ influences are likely perpetuating the phobia.

Genetic Contributions to Psychopathology

▶ How do genes interact with environmental factors to affect behavior?

▶ What kinds of models have been proposed to describe this interaction?

What causes you to look like one or both of your parents or, perhaps, your grandparents? Obviously, the genes you inherit are from your parents and from your ancestors before them. **Genes** are long molecules of deoxyribonucleic acid (DNA) at various locations on chromosomes within the cell nucleus. Physical characteristics are determined—or at least strongly influenced—by our genetic endowment. Other factors in the environment influence our physical appearance, however. To some extent, our weight and even our height are affected by nutritional, social, and cultural factors. Consequently, our genes seldom determine our physical development in any absolute way. They do provide some boundaries to our development. Exactly where we go within these boundaries depends on environmental influences.

Although this is true for most of our characteristics, it is not true for all of them. Some of our characteristics are strongly determined by genes, including hair and eye color. A few rare disorders are determined in the same way, including Huntington's disease, a degenerative brain disease that appears in early to middle age. Except for identical twins, every person has a unique set of genes unlike those of anyone else in the world. Because there is room for the environment to influence our development within the constraints set by our genes, there are many reasons for the development of individual differences.

What about our behavior and traits, our likes and dislikes? Do genes influence personality and abnormal behavior? This question of nature (genes) versus nurture (upbringing and other environmental influences) is age-old in psychology, and the answers beginning to emerge are fascinating. Before discussing them, let's review what we know about genes and environmental factors.

The Nature of Genes

We have known for a long time that each normal human cell has 46 chromosomes arranged in 23 pairs. One chromosome in each pair comes from the father and one from the mother. The first 22 pairs of chromosomes provide programs or directions for the development of the body and brain, and the last pair, the *sex chromosomes*, determines an individual's sex. In females, both chromosomes in the 23rd pair are called *X chromosomes*. In males, the mother contributes an X chromosome but the father contributes a *Y chromosome*. Abnormalities in the sex chromosomal pair can cause ambiguous sexual characteristics.

The DNA molecules that contain genes have a certain structure, a double helix. The shape of a helix is like a spiral staircase. A double helix is two spirals intertwined, turning in opposite directions. Located on this double spiral are pairs of molecules bound together and arranged in different orders. The ordering of these base pairs influences how the body develops and works.

A *dominant gene* is one of a pair of genes that strongly influences a particular trait, and we need only one of them to determine, for example, our eye or hair color. A *recessive gene*, by contrast, must be paired with another (recessive) gene to determine a trait. Gene dominance occurs when one member of a gene pair is consistently expressed over the other (for example, a brown-eyed gene is dominant over a blue-eyed gene). When we have a dominant gene, we can predict fairly accurately how many offspring will develop a certain trait, characteristic, or disorder, depending on whether one or both parents carry that dominant gene.

Most of the time, predictions are not so simple. Much of our development and most of our behavior, our personality, and even our intelligence are probably *polygenic*—that is, influenced by many genes, each contributing only a tiny effect, all of which may be influenced by the environment. The same is true for psychiatric disorders (Geschwind & Flint, 2015). And because the human *genome*—an individual's complete set of genes—consists of more than 20,000 genes (U.S. Department of Energy Office of Science, 2009), polygenic interactions can be complex. For this reason, most genetic scientists use sophisticated procedures such as quantitative genetics and molecular genetics that allow them to look for patterns of influence across many genes (Kendler, 2011, 2013; Rutter, Moffitt, & Caspi, 2006). *Quantitative genetics* basically sums up all the tiny effects across many genes without necessarily telling us which genes are responsible for which effects. *Molecular genetics* focuses on examining the actual structure of genes with technologies such as *DNA microarrays;* these technologies allow scientists to analyze thousands of genes at once and identify broad networks of genes that may be contributing to a particular trait (Kendler, 2011; Plomin & Davis, 2009). Such studies have indicated that hundreds of genes can contribute to the heritability of a single trait (Hariri *et al.*, 2002; Rutter *et al.*, 2006).

Genes exert influences on our bodies and behavior through a series of steps that produce proteins. Although all cells contain our entire genetic structure, only a small proportion of the genes in any one cell are "turned on" or expressed. In this way, cells become specialized, with some influencing liver function and others affecting personality. Environmental factors, in the form of social and

NORMAL FEMALE

▲ A normal female has 23 pairs of chromosomes.

▲ A DNA molecule, which contains genes, resembles a double spiral, or helix.

cultural influences, can determine whether genes are "turned on" (Cole, 2011). For example, in studies with rat pups, researchers have found that the absence of normal maternal behavior of "licking and grooming" prevents the genetic expression of a glucocorticoid receptor that modulates stress hormones. This means rats with inadequate maternal care have greater sensitivity to stress (Meaney & Szyf, 2005). There is evidence that a similar model may be relevant in humans (Dickens, Turkheimer, & Beam, 2011; Hyman, 2009).

New Developments in the Study of Genes and Behavior

Scientists have now identified, in a preliminary way, the genetic contribution to psychological disorders and related behavioral patterns. The best estimates attribute about half of our enduring personality traits and cognitive abilities to

genetic influence (Rutter, 2006). For example, McClearn and colleagues (1997) compared 110 Swedish identical twin pairs, at least 80-years-old, with 130 same-sex fraternal twin pairs of a similar age and found heritability estimates for specific cognitive abilities, such as memory, ranged from 32% to 62%. This work built on earlier twin studies, with different age groups showing similar results (for example, Bouchard, Lykken, McGue, Segal, & Tellegen, 1990). Furthermore, a study of more than 1,200 twins spanning 35 years confirmed that during adulthood, genetic factors determined stability in cognitive abilities, whereas environmental factors were responsible for any changes (Lyons *et al.*, 2009).

It has also become clear that adverse life events such as a "chaotic" childhood can overwhelm the influence of genes (Turkheimer, Haley, Waldron, D'Onofrio, & Gottesman, 2003). For example, one member of a set of twins in the Lyons and colleagues (2009) study showed marked change in cognitive abilities if his or her environment changed dramatically from the other twin's because of some stressful event such as death of a loved one.

For psychological disorders, evidence indicates that genetic factors make some contribution to all disorders but account for less than half of the explanation. This means that if one of a pair of identical twins has schizophrenia, there is a less-than-50% likelihood that the other twin will also have schizophrenia (Gottesman, 1991). Similar or lower rates exist for other psychological disorders (Kendler & Prescott, 2006; Rutter, 2006).

Behavioral geneticists have concluded that specific genes or small groups of genes may ultimately be found to be associated with certain psychological disorders. But much of the evidence suggests that contributions to psychological disorders come from many genes, each having a relatively small effect (Flint, 2009; Rutter, 2006). Advances in gene mapping, molecular genetics, and linkage studies help us track the genes implicated in various disorders (for example, Gershon Kelsoe, Kendler, & Watson, 2001; Hettema, Prescott, Myers, Neale, & Kendler, 2005). In linkage studies, scientists study individuals who have the same disorder, such as bipolar disorder, and also share other features, such as eye color; because the location of the gene for eye color is known, this allows scientists to attempt to "link" known gene locations with the possible location of a gene contributing to the disorder (Flint, 2009).

It has become increasingly clear that genetic contributions cannot be studied in the absence of interactions with events in the environment that trigger genetic vulnerability or "turn on" specific genes (Kendler *et al.*, 2011; Rutter, 2010). It is to this fascinating topic that we now turn.

genes Long deoxyribonucleic acid (DNA) molecule, the basic physical unit of heredity that appears as a location on a chromosome.

The Interaction of Genes and the Environment

In 1983, neuroscientist Eric Kandel speculated that the process of learning affects more than behavior. He suggested that the very genetic structure of cells may change as a result of learning if genes that were inactive interact with the environment in such a way that they become active. In other words, the environment may occasionally turn on certain genes. This type of mechanism may lead to changes in the number of receptors at the end of a neuron, which would affect biochemical functioning in the brain.

Most of us assume that the brain, like other parts of the body, may be influenced by environmental changes during development. But we also assume that once maturity is reached, the structure and function of our internal organs and most of our physiology are set or, in the case of the brain, hard-wired. The competing idea is that the brain and its functions are plastic, subject to continual change in response to the environment, even at the level of genetic structure. Now there is additional strong evidence supporting that view (Dick, 2011; Kendler *et al.*, 2011).

With these new findings in mind, we can now explore gene–environment interactions as they relate to psychopathology. Two models have received the most attention: the diathesis–stress model and reciprocal gene–environment model (or gene–environment correlations).

The Diathesis–Stress Model

For years, scientists have assumed a specific method of interaction between genes and environment. According to this **diathesis–stress model**, individuals inherit tendencies to express certain traits or behaviors, which may then be activated under conditions of stress (see ● Figure 2.2). Each inherited tendency is a *diathesis*, a condition that makes someone susceptible to developing a disorder. When the right kind of life event, such as a certain type of stressor, comes along, the disorder develops. For example, according to the diathesis–stress model, Judy inherited a *tendency* to faint at the sight of blood. This tendency is the diathesis,

or **vulnerability**. It would not become prominent until certain environmental events occurred. For Judy, this event was the sight of an animal being dissected when she was in a situation in which escape was not acceptable. The stress of seeing the dissection under these conditions activated her genetic tendency to faint. Together, these factors led to her developing a disorder. If she had not taken biology, she might have gone through life without ever knowing she had this tendency, at least to such an extreme, although she might have felt queasy about minor cuts. You can see that the diathesis is genetically based and the stress is environmental but that they must interact to produce a disorder.

We might also take the case of someone who inherits a vulnerability to alcoholism. During college, both this person and a friend who lacks the tendency engage in extended drinking bouts, but only the individual with the so-called addictive genes begins the downward spiral into alcoholism. Having a particular vulnerability doesn't mean you will necessarily develop the associated disorder. The smaller the vulnerability, the greater the life stress required to produce the disorder; conversely, with greater vulnerability, less life stress is required.

This relationship was demonstrated in a landmark study by Caspi and colleagues (2003), who have been studying a group of 847 individuals in New Zealand for more than two decades, starting at the age of three. They noted whether the participants, at age 26, had been depressed during the past year. Overall, 17% of the study participants reported that they had experienced a major depressive episode, and 3% felt suicidal. The investigators also identified the genetic makeup of the individuals and, in particular, a gene that produces a substance called a *chemical transporter* that affects the transmission of serotonin in the brain, called the *5-HTT gene*. Serotonin, a neurotransmitter, is implicated in depression and related disorders. But the gene that Caspi and colleagues were studying comes in two common versions, or *alleles:* one long and one short. There was reason to believe, from prior work with animals, that individuals with at least two copies of the long allele (LL) were able to cope better with stress than individuals with two copies of the short allele (SS).

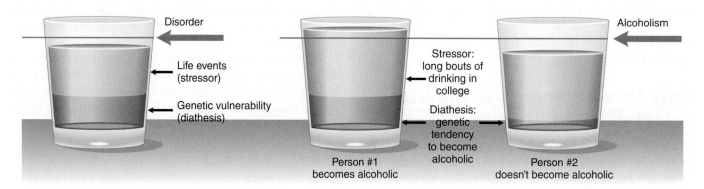

● **Figure 2.2** In the diathesis–stress model, the greater the underlying vulnerability, the less stress is needed to trigger a disorder.

Because the investigators have been recording stressful life events in these individuals most of their lives, they were able to test this relationship. In people with two S alleles, the risk for having a major depressive episode doubled if they had at least four stressful life events, compared with participants experiencing four stressful events who had two L alleles. Moreover, in people with the SS alleles, severe maltreatment during childhood more than doubled their risks of depression in adulthood compared with those individuals carrying the SS alleles who were not maltreated (63% versus 30%). For individuals carrying the LL alleles, stressful childhood experiences did not affect the incidence of depression in adulthood; 30% of this group became depressed whether they had experienced stressful childhoods or not. (This relationship is shown in ● Figure 2.3.) Therefore, unlike this SS group, depression in the LL allele group seems related to stress in their recent past rather than childhood experiences. This study was important in demonstrating that neither genes nor life experiences (environmental events) can solely explain the onset of a disorder such as depression. It takes a complex interaction of the two factors. Other studies have replicated or supported these findings (Binder, 2008; Karg, Burmeister, Shedden, & Sen, 2011; Kilpatrick *et al.*, 2007).

The Gene–Environment Correlation Model

With additional study, psychologists have found the web of interrelationships between genes and environment to be even more complex. Some evidence now indicates that genetic endowment may *increase the probability* that an

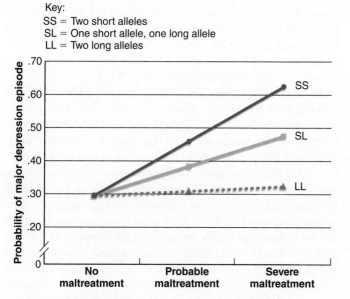

Key:
SS = Two short alleles
SL = One short allele, one long allele
LL = Two long alleles

● **Figure 2.3** Interaction of genes and early environment in producing adult major depression. (Reprinted, with permission, from Caspi, A., Sugden, K., Moffitt, T. E., Taylor, A., Craig, I. W., Harrington, H., *et al.* [2003]. Influence of life stress on depression: Moderation by a polymorphism in the 5-HTT gene. *Science, 301,* 386–389, © 2003 AAAS.)

individual will experience stressful life events (see Kendler, 2006; Rutter, 2006). For example, people with a genetic vulnerability to develop a certain disorder, such as blood–injury–injection phobia, may also have a personality trait—say impulsiveness—that makes them more likely to be involved in minor accidents that would result in their seeing blood. In other words, they may be accident prone because they are continually rushing to complete things or to get to places without regard for their physical safety. These people, then, might have a genetically determined tendency to create the very environmental risk factors that trigger a genetic vulnerability to blood–injury–injection phobia.

This is the **gene–environment correlation model** or reciprocal gene–environment model (Jaffee, 2011; Kendler, 2011) (see ● Figure 2.4). Some evidence indicates that it applies to the development of depression, because some people tend to seek out difficult relationships or other circumstances that lead to depression (Eley, 2011). McGue and Lykken (1992) have even applied the gene–environment correlation model to some fascinating data on the influence of genes on the divorce rate. For example, if you and your spouse each have an identical twin, and both identical twins have been divorced, the chance that you will divorce increases greatly. Furthermore, if your identical twin and your parents and your spouse's parents have been divorced, the chance that you will divorce is 77.5%. Conversely, if none of your family members has been divorced, the probability that you will divorce is only 5.3%.

This is an extreme example, but McGue and Lykken (1992) demonstrated that the probability of your divorcing doubles over the probability in the population at large if your fraternal twin is also divorced and increases sixfold if your identical twin is divorced. Why would this happen? To the extent that it is genetically determined, the tendency to divorce is almost certainly related to various inherited traits, such as being highly-strung, impulsive, or short-tempered, that make someone hard to *get al*ong with (Jockin, McGue, & Lykken, 1996). Another possibility is that an inherited trait makes it more likely you will choose an incompatible spouse. For example, if you are unassertive, you may choose a dominant mate who turns out to be difficult to live with. You get divorced but then find yourself attracted to another individual with the same traits. Some people would attribute this pattern to poor judgment. Nevertheless, social, interpersonal, psychological, and environmental factors play major roles in whether we stay married, and it's possible our genes contribute to how we create our own environment.

. . . .

diathesis–stress model Hypothesis that both an inherited tendency (a **vulnerability**) and specific stressful conditions are required to produce a disorder.

vulnerability Susceptibility or tendency to develop a disorder.

gene–environment correlation model Hypothesis that people with a genetic predisposition for a disorder may also have a genetic tendency to create environmental risk factors that promote the disorder.

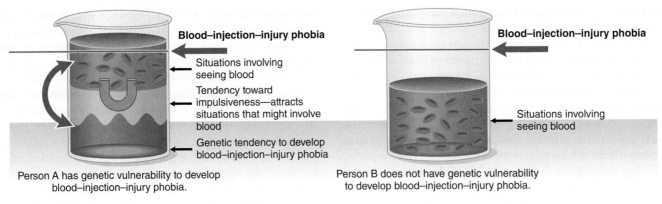

● **Figure 2.4** Gene–Environment Correlation Model.

Epigenetics and the Nongenomic "Inheritance" of Behavior

Reports suggest that studies to date have overemphasized the extent of genetic influence on our personalities, our temperaments, and their contribution to psychological disorders (Mill, 2011). This overemphasis may be partly the result of the manner in which these studies have been conducted (Moore, 2001; Turkheimer & Waldron, 2000). Several lines of evidence have come together in recent years to buttress this conclusion.

For example, Crabbe, Wahlsten, and Dudek (1999) conducted an experiment in which three types of mice with different genetic makeups were raised in virtually identical environments at three sites. Each mouse of a given type was genetically indistinguishable from all other mice of that type at each site. The experimenters made sure the environments were the same at each site. If genes determine the behavior of the mice, mice with virtually identical genetic makeup (type A) should have performed the same at all three sites on tests, as should have type B and type C mice. But the results showed that this did not happen. Although a certain type of mouse might perform similarly on a specific test across all three sites, on other tests that type of mouse performed differently. Robert Sapolsky, a prominent neuroscientist, concluded, "genetic influences are often a lot less powerful than is commonly believed. The environment, even working subtly, can still mould and hold its own in the biological interactions that shape who we are" (Sapolsky, 2000, p. 15).

In research with rodents (Francis, Diorio, Liu, & Meaney, 1999; Weaver *et al.*, 2004), investigators studied stress reactivity and how it is passed through generations, using a procedure called *cross-fostering*, in which a rat pup born to one mother is assigned to another mother for rearing. They first demonstrated that maternal behavior affected how the young rats tolerated stress. If the mothers were calm and supportive, their rat pups were less fearful and better able to tolerate stress. But we don't know if this effect results from genetic influences or from being raised by calm mothers.

This is where cross-fostering comes in. Francis *et al.* (1999) took some newly born rat pups of easily stressed mothers and placed them for rearing with calm mothers. Other young rats remained with their easily stressed mothers. They found that calm and supportive behavior by the mothers could be passed down through generations of rats *independent of genetic influences,* because rats born to easily stressed mothers but reared by calm mothers grew up more calm and supportive.

Strong effects of the environment have also been observed in humans. For example, Tienari *et al.* (1994) found that children whose parents had schizophrenia and who were adopted away as babies demonstrated a tendency to develop psychiatric disorders (including schizophrenia) themselves only if they were adopted into dysfunctional families. Those children adopted into functional families with high-quality parenting did not develop the disorders. Thus, it is probably too simplistic to say the genetic contribution to a personality trait or to a psychological disorder is approximately 50%. We can talk of a heritable (genetic) contribution only in the context of the individual's past and present environment (Dickens *et al.*, 2011).

In support of this conclusion, Suomi (2000) demonstrated that for young monkeys with a specific genetic pattern associated with a highly reactive temperament (emotional or susceptible to the effects of stress), early maternal deprivation (disruptions in mothering) have a powerful effect on their neuroendocrine functioning and their later behavioral and emotional reactions. For animals not carrying this genetic characteristic, however, maternal deprivation will have little effect, just as was found in the New Zealand study in humans by Caspi *et al.* (2003), and it is likely this effect will be carried down through the generations. But chaotic early environments can override genetic factors and alter neuroendocrine function to increase the likelihood of later behavioral and emotional disorders (Dickens *et al.*, 2011; Ouellet-Morin *et al.*, 2008).

How does this work? Although the environment cannot change our DNA, it can change the gene expression. It seems that genes are turned on or off by cellular material that is located just outside of the genome ("epi," as in the word **epigenetics**, means on or around) and that stress, nutrition, or other factors can affect this epigenome, which is passed down to the next generation and maybe for several generations (Arai, Li, Hartley, & Feig, 2009; Mill, 2011). The genome itself isn't changed, so if the stressful environment disappears, eventually the epigenome will fade. That is, it seems that environmental manipulations, particularly early in life, may do much to override the genetically influenced tendency to develop undesirable behavioral and emotional reactions (Mill, 2011; Ouellet-Morin et al., 2008).

Nowhere is the complexity of the interaction of genetic and environmental influences more apparent than in the famous cases of Chang and Eng, identical twins born in 1810 in Thailand (known as Siam at the time) who were joined at the chest. These individuals, who were successful entertainers, were the source of the name "Siamese twins." They obviously shared identical genes, as well as nearly identical environments throughout their lives. Thus, we would expect them to behave in similar ways when it comes to personality features, temperaments, and psychological disorders. But the twins had distinct personalities. Chang was prone to moodiness and depression and started drinking heavily. Eng, on the other hand, was more cheerful, quiet, and thoughtful (Moore, 2001).

In summary, a complex interaction between genes and the environment plays an important role in every psychological disorder (Kendler et al., 2011; Rutter, 2010). Our genes do contribute to our behavior, emotions, and cognitive processes and constrain the influence of environmental factors, such as upbringing, on our later behavior

(Caspi et al., 2003). Environmental events, in turn, seem to affect our genetic structure by determining whether certain genes are activated (Kendler, 2011; Landis & Insel, 2008). Furthermore, strong environmental influences alone may be sufficient to override genetic diatheses. Thus, neither nature (genes) nor nurture (environmental events) alone, but rather a complex interaction of the two, influences the development of our behavior and personalities.

2.2 Concept CHECK

Determine whether these statements are true (T) or false (F).

1. _____ The first 20 pairs of chromosomes program the development of the body and brain.

2. _____ No individual genes have been identified that cause psychological disorders.

3. _____ According to the diathesis–stress model, people inherit a vulnerability to express certain traits that may be activated under certain stress conditions.

4. _____ The idea that individual genes may increase the probability that they will experience stressful life events and therefore trigger a vulnerability is in accordance with the diathesis–stress model.

5. _____ Environmental events alone influence the development of our behavior and personalities.

Neuroscience and Its Contributions to Psychopathology

▶ What are neurotransmitters, and how are they involved in abnormal behavior?

▶ What are the functions of different brain regions, and what are their roles in psychopathology?

Knowing how the nervous system and brain work is central to any understanding of our behavior, emotions, and cognitive processes. This is the focus of **neuroscience**. To comprehend research in this field, we first need an overview of how the brain and the nervous system function. The human nervous system includes the *central nervous system*, consisting of the brain and the spinal cord, and the *peripheral nervous system*, consisting of the somatic nervous system and the autonomic nervous system (see ● Figure 2.5).

The Central Nervous System

The central nervous system processes all information received from our sense organs and reacts as necessary. It sorts out what is relevant, such as a certain taste or a new

sound, from what isn't, such as a familiar view or ticking clock; checks the memory banks to determine why the information is relevant; and implements the right reaction, whether it is to answer a simple question or to play a Mozart sonata. This is a lot of exceedingly complex work. The spinal cord is part of the central nervous system, but its primary function is to facilitate the sending of messages to and from the brain, which is the other major component of the central nervous system (CNS). The brain uses

....

epigenetics The study of factors other than inherited DNA sequence, such as new learning or stress, that alter the phenotypic expression of **genes**.

neuroscience Study of the nervous system and its role in behavior, thoughts, and **emotions**.

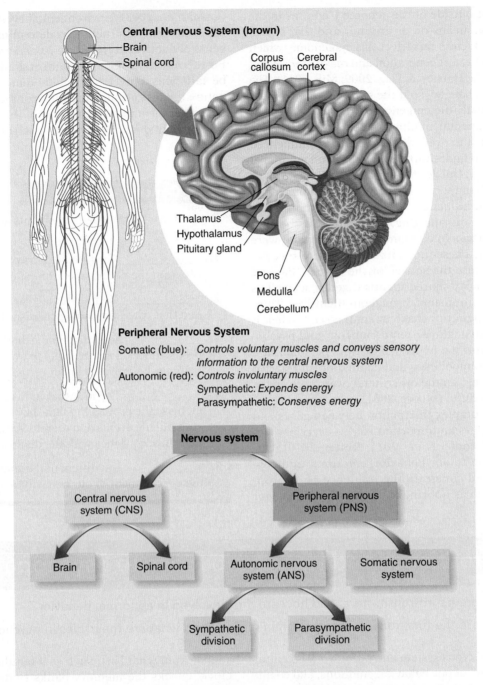

● **Figure 2.5** Divisions of the nervous system. (Reprinted from Kalat, J. W. [2009]. *Biological Psychology*, 10th edition, © 2009 Wadsworth.)

an average of 140 billion nerve cells, called **neurons**, to control our thoughts and action. Neurons transmit information throughout the nervous system.

The typical neuron contains a central cell body with two kinds of branches. One kind of branch is called a *dendrite*. Dendrites have numerous *receptors* that receive messages in the form of chemical impulses from other nerve cells, which are converted into electrical impulses. The other kind of branch, called an *axon*, transmits these impulses to other neurons. Any one nerve cell may have multiple connections to other neurons. These connections are called *synapses*. The brain has billions of nerve cells, more than 100 billion by some estimates, and trillions of synapses, so you can see how complicated the system becomes.

The smallest building blocks of the brain are the neurons that form a highly complex network of information flow. Within each neuron, information is transmitted through electrical impulses, called **action potentials**, traveling along the axon of a neuron. The end of an axon is called a **terminal button**. Neurons are not actually connected directly to each other. There is a small space through which the impulse must pass to get to the next neuron. The space between the terminal button of one neuron and the dendrite of another is called the **synaptic cleft**. The biochemicals that are released from the axon of one neuron and transmit the impulse to the dendrite receptors of another neuron are called **neurotransmitters** (see ● Figure 2.6). Using increasingly sensitive equipment and techniques, scientists have identified many types of neurotransmitters.

In addition to neurons, another type of cell comprises the nervous system—*glia* (or glial) cells. Even though these cells outnumber neurons by a ratio of about ten to one, for many years scientists believed they were passive cells that merely served to connect and insulate neurons (Koob, 2009). More recently, scientists have discovered that glia play active roles in neural activity (Eroglu & Barres, 2010). It is now known that there are different types of glia cells with several specific functions, some of which serve to modulate neurotransmitter activity (Allen & Barres, 2009; Perea & Araque, 2007). Better understanding of the role of glia cells in neurotransmitter processes is an important new area of research. To date, however, most neuroscience research in psychopathology has focused on neurons.

Major neurotransmitters relevant to psychopathology include *norepinephrine* (also known as noradrenaline), *serotonin, dopamine, gamma-aminobutyric acid (GABA)*, and *glutamate*. Some neurotransmitters are **excitatory** because they increase the likelihood that the connecting neuron will fire, whereas other neurotransmitters are **inhibitory** because they decrease the likelihood that the connecting neuron will fire. Some neurons can receive input from both excitatory and inhibitory neurotransmitters. Excesses or insufficiencies in some neurotransmitters are associated with different psychological disorders.

. . . .

neuron Individual nerve cell responsible for transmitting information.

action potentials Short periods of electrical activity at the membrane of a neuron, responsible for the transmission of signals within the neuron.

terminal button The end of an axon (of a neuron) where neurotransmitters are stored before release.

synaptic cleft Space between nerve cells where chemical transmitters act to move impulses from one **neuron** to the next.

neurotransmitters Chemical that crosses the **synaptic cleft** between nerve cells to transmit impulses from one **neuron** to the next. Relative excess or deficiency of neurotransmitters is involved in several **psychological disorders**.

excitatory Causing excitation. Activating.

inhibitory Causing inhibition. Suppressing.

Cell body

1 Synthesis of neurotransmitter and formation of vesicles

2 Transport of neurotransmitter down axon

3 Release of neurotransmitter

4 Interaction of neuro-transmitter with receptor, exciting or inhibiting post-synaptic neuron

5 Separation of neurotransmitter molecules from receptors

6 Reuptake of neuro-transmitter to be recycled

7 Vesicles without neurotransmitter transported back to cell body

Postsynaptic neuron

● **Figure 2.6** The transmission of information from one neuron to another. (Adapted from Goldstein, B. [1994]. *Psychology*, © 1994 Brooks/Cole Publishing Company.)

The Structure of the Brain

The brain (see • Figure 2.7) includes the *brain stem* and the *forebrain*. The brain stem is the lower and more ancient part of the brain. Found in most animals, this structure handles most of the essential automatic functions, such as breathing, sleeping, and moving around in a coordinated way. The forebrain is more advanced and evolved more recently.

The lowest part of the brain stem, the *hindbrain*, contains the *medulla*, the *pons*, and the *cerebellum*. The hindbrain regulates many automatic activities, such as breathing, the

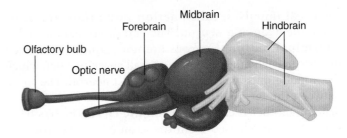

• **Figure 2.7a** Three divisions of the brain. (Reprinted, with permission, from Kalat, J. W. [2009]. *Biological Psychology,* 10th edition, © 2009 Wadsworth.)

• **Figure 2.7b** Major structures of the brain. (Reprinted, with permission, from Kalat, J. W. [2009]. *Biological Psychology,* 10th edition, © 2009 Wadsworth.)

• **Figure 2.7c** The limbic system. (Reprinted, with permission, from Kalat, J. W. [2009]. *Biological Psychology,* 10th edition, © 2009 Wadsworth.)

Thalamus

Globus
pallidus
(medial)

Caudate
nucleus

Putamen
(lateral)

Amygdala

● **Figure 2.7d** The basal ganglia. (Reprinted, with permission, from Kalat, J. W. [2009]. *Biological Psychology*, 10th edition, © 2009 Wadsworth.)

pumping action of the heart (heartbeat), and digestion. The cerebellum controls motor coordination.

Also located in the brain stem is the *midbrain*, which coordinates movement with sensory input and contains parts of the *reticular activating system*, which contributes to processes of arousal and tension, such as whether we are awake or asleep.

At the top of the brain stem are the *thalamus* and *hypothalamus*, which are involved broadly with regulating behavior and emotion. These structures function primarily as a relay between the forebrain and the remaining lower areas of the brain stem. Some anatomists consider the thalamus and hypothalamus to be parts of the forebrain.

At the base of the forebrain, just above the thalamus and hypothalamus, is the *limbic system*. *Limbic* means border, so named because it is located around the edge of the center of the brain. The limbic system, which figures prominently in much of psychopathology, includes such structures as the *hippocampus* (sea horse), *cingulate gyrus* (girdle), *septum* (partition), and *amygdala* (almond), all of which are named for their approximate shapes. This system helps regulate our emotional experiences and expressions and, to some extent, our ability to learn and to control our impulses. It is also involved with the basic drives of sex, aggression, hunger, and thirst.

The *basal ganglia*, also at the base of the forebrain, include the *caudate* (tailed) *nucleus*. Because damage to these structures is involved in changing our posture or twitching or shaking, they are believed to control motor activity.

The largest part of the forebrain is the *cerebral cortex*, which contains more than 80% of all neurons in the central nervous system. This part of the brain provides us with our distinctly human qualities, allowing us to plan, reason, and create. The cerebral cortex is divided into two hemispheres.

Although the hemispheres look alike structurally and operate relatively independently (both are capable of perceiving, thinking, and remembering), each has different specialties. The left hemisphere seems to be chiefly responsible for verbal and other cognitive processes. The right hemisphere seems to be better at perceiving the world around us and creating images. The hemispheres may play differential roles in specific psychological disorders.

Each hemisphere consists of four separate areas, or *lobes*: temporal, parietal, occipital, and frontal (see ● Figure 2.8). Each is associated with different processes: The *temporal lobe* is associated with recognizing sights and sounds and with long-term memory storage, the *parietal* lobe is associated with recognizing sensations of touch and monitoring body positioning, and the *occipital lobe* is associated with integrating and making sense of visual inputs. These three lobes, located toward the back (posterior) of the brain, process sight, touch, hearing, and other signals from our senses.

The *frontal lobe* is the most interesting from the point of view of psychopathology. The front (or anterior) of the frontal lobe is called the *prefrontal cortex* and is responsible for higher cognitive functions such as thinking and reasoning, planning for the future, and long-term memory. This area of the brain synthesizes all information received from other parts of the brain and decides how to respond. When studying areas of the brain for clues to psychopathology, most researchers focus on the frontal lobe of the cerebral cortex, as well as on the limbic system and the basal ganglia.

The Peripheral Nervous System

The peripheral nervous system coordinates with the brain stem to make sure the body is working properly. Its two major components are the *somatic nervous system* and the

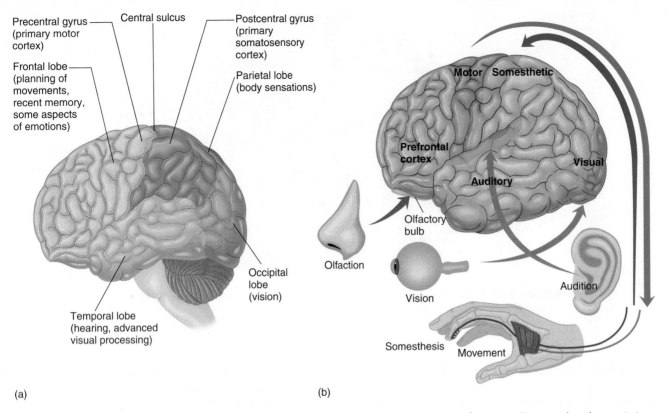

(a)

(b)

● **Figure 2.8** Some major subdivisions of the human cerebral cortex and a few of their primary functions. (Reprinted, with permission, from Kalat, J. W. [2009]. *Biological Psychology,* 10th edition, © 2009 Wadsworth.)

autonomic nervous system. The somatic nervous system controls the muscles. The autonomic nervous system includes the *sympathetic nervous system* and *parasympathetic nervous system.* The autonomic nervous system regulates the cardiovascular and endocrine systems and performs other functions, including aiding digestion and regulating body temperature (see ● Figure 2.9).

The *endocrine system* includes a number of glands, each of which produces its own chemical messenger, called a **hormone**, and releases it directly into the bloodstream. The adrenal glands produce *epinephrine* (also called *adrenaline*) in response to stress, as well as salt-regulating hormones; the thyroid gland produces *thyroxine,* which facilitates energy metabolism and growth; the pituitary is a master gland that produces a variety of regulatory hormones; and the gonadal glands produce sex hormones such as estrogen and testosterone. The endocrine system is closely related to the immune system; it is also implicated in a variety of disorders. In addition to contributing to stress-related physical disorders, endocrine regulation may play a role in depression, anxiety, schizophrenia, and other disorders (McEwen, 2013). Some studies have found, for example, that depressed patients may respond better to an antidepressant medication if it is administered in combination with a thyroid hormone (Nierenberg *et al.,* 2006), This interdisciplinary area of research is termed *psychoneuroendocrinology* and is a growing subfield.

Sympathetic and parasympathetic divisions of the autonomic nervous system operate in a complementary fashion. The sympathetic nervous system is primarily responsible for mobilizing the body during times of stress or danger by rapidly activating the organs and glands under its control. When the sympathetic division goes on alert, the heart beats faster, thereby increasing the flow of blood to the muscles; respiration increases, allowing more oxygen to get into the blood and brain; and the adrenal glands are stimulated. All three changes help mobilize us for action. When you read in the newspaper that a woman lifted a heavy object to free a trapped child, you can be sure her sympathetic nervous system was working overtime. This system mediates a substantial part of our "emergency" or "alarm" reaction, discussed later in this chapter and in Chapter 4.

One of the functions of the parasympathetic system is to balance the sympathetic system. In other words, because we could not operate in a state of hyperarousal and preparedness forever, the parasympathetic nervous system takes over after the sympathetic nervous system has been active for a while, normalizing our arousal and facilitating the storage of energy by helping the digestive process.

One brain connection implicated in some psychological disorders involves the hypothalamus and the endocrine system. The hypothalamus connects to the adjacent

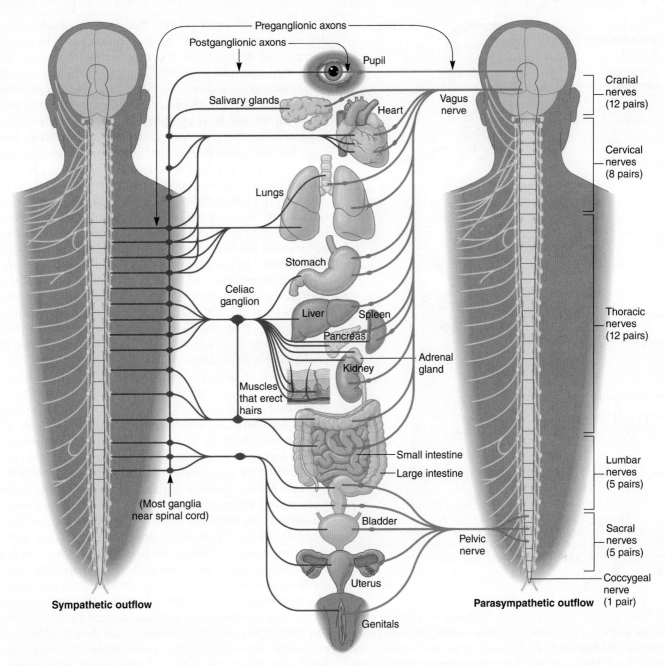

Preganglionic axons
Postganglionic axons
Pupil
Salivary glands
Heart
Vagus nerve
Lungs
Stomach
Celiac ganglion
Liver
Spleen
Pancreas
Kidney
Adrenal gland
Muscles that erect hairs
Small intestine
Large intestine
(Most ganglia near spinal cord)
Bladder
Pelvic nerve
Uterus
Genitals

Cranial nerves (12 pairs)
Cervical nerves (8 pairs)
Thoracic nerves (12 pairs)
Lumbar nerves (5 pairs)
Sacral nerves (5 pairs)
Coccygeal nerve (1 pair)

Sympathetic outflow

Parasympathetic outflow

● **Figure 2.9** The sympathetic nervous system (red lines) and parasympathetic nervous system (blue lines). (Reprinted, with permission, from Kalat, J. W. [2009]. *Biological Psychology*, 10th edition, © 2009 Wadsworth.)

pituitary gland, which is the master or coordinator of the endocrine system. The pituitary gland, in turn, may stimulate the cortical part of the adrenal glands on top of the kidneys. As we noted previously, surges of epinephrine tend to energize us, arouse us, and get our bodies ready for threat or challenge. The cortical part of the adrenal glands also produces the stress hormone cortisol. This system is called the *hypothalamic–pituitary–adrenocortical axis*, or *HPA axis* (see ● Figure 2.10); it has been implicated in several psychological disorders, including depression (Burke, Davis, Otte, & Mohr, 2005).

Neurotransmitters

The biochemical neurotransmitters in the brain and nervous system that carry messages from one neuron to another continue to receive attention from psychopathologists (Iverson, 2006; Nestler, Hyman, & Malenka, 2008). One example is the role of the neurotransmitter serotonin in some studies of gene–environment interactions described earlier

hormone Chemical messenger produced by the endocrine glands.

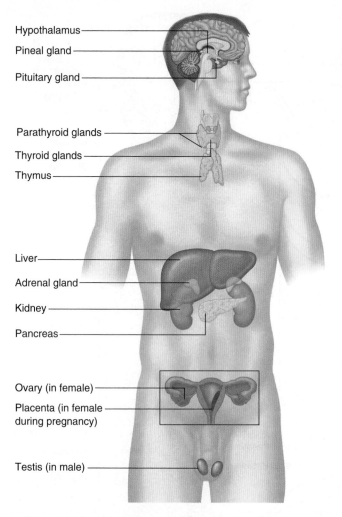

Hypothalamus
Pineal gland
Pituitary gland

Parathyroid glands
Thyroid glands
Thymus

Liver
Adrenal gland
Kidney
Pancreas

Ovary (in female)
Placenta (in female during pregnancy)

Testis (in male)

● **Figure 2.10** Location of some major endocrine glands. (Reprinted, with permission, from Kalat, J. W. [2009]. *Biological Psychology*, 10th edition, © 2009 Wadsworth.)

(e.g., Karg *et al.*, 2011). This biochemical was discovered in the past several decades, and only in the past few years have we developed the sophisticated procedures necessary to study them. One way to think of neurotransmitters is as narrow currents flowing through the ocean of the brain. Sometimes they run parallel with other currents, only to separate again. Often they seem to meander aimlessly, looping back on themselves before moving on. Neurons that are sensitive to one type of neurotransmitter cluster together and form paths from one part of the brain to the other.

These paths may overlap with the paths of other neurotransmitters, but, as often as not, they end up going their separate ways (Bloom, Nelson, & Lazerson, 2001; Dean, Kelsey, Heller, & Ciaranello, 1993). There are thousands, perhaps tens of thousands, of these **brain circuits**, and we are just beginning to discover and map them (Arenkiel & Ehlers, 2009). Neuroscientists have identified several neural pathways that seem to play roles in various psychological disorders (Fineberg *et al.*, 2010; Tau & Peterson, 2010).

You may still read reports that certain psychological disorders are "caused" by biochemical imbalances, excesses, or deficiencies in certain neurotransmitter systems. For example, abnormal activity of the neurotransmitter serotonin is often described as causing depression, and abnormalities in the neurotransmitter dopamine have been implicated in schizophrenia. Increasing evidence indicates that this is an enormous oversimplification, however. We are now learning that the effects of neurotransmitter activity are less specific. They often seem to be related to the way we process information (Harmer *et al.*, 2009; Sullivan & LeDoux, 2004). Changes in neurotransmitter activity may make people more or less likely to exhibit certain kinds of behavior in certain situations without causing the behavior directly. In addition, broad-based disturbances in our functioning are almost always associated with interactions of the neurotransmitters rather than with alterations in the activity of any one system (Fineberg *et al.*, 2010; Stahl, 2008). In other words, the currents intersect so often that changes in one neurotransmitter result in changes in the other, often in a way scientists have not yet been able to predict.

Research on neurotransmitter function focuses primarily on what happens when activity levels change. We can study this in several ways. We can introduce substances called **agonists** that effectively *increase* the activity of a neurotransmitter by mimicking its effects; substances called **antagonists** that *decrease*, or block, a neurotransmitter; or substances called **inverse agonists** that produce effects *opposite* to those produced by the neurotransmitter. By manipulating the production of a neurotransmitter in different parts of the brain, we can learn more about its effects. Most drugs could be classified as either agonistic or antagonistic—that is, they work by either increasing or decreasing the flow of specific neurotransmitters. Some drugs inhibit, or block, the production of a neurotransmitter. Others increase the production of competing biochemical substances that may deactivate the neurotransmitter. Yet other drugs do not affect neurotransmitters directly but prevent the chemical from reaching the next neuron by closing down, or occupying, the receptors in that neuron. After a neurotransmitter is released, it is quickly broken down and brought back from the synaptic cleft into the same neuron that released it. This process is called **reuptake**. Some drugs work by blocking the reuptake process, thereby causing continued stimulation along the brain circuit; other drugs work by stimulating or blocking the release of a neurotransmitter into the synaptic gap or by blocking the receptor of a neurotransmitter.

Two types of neurotransmitters, *monoamines* and *amino acids*, have been most studied in regard to psychopathology. Neurotransmitters in the monoamine class include norepinephrine (also known as *noradrenaline*), serotonin, and dopamine. Amino-acid neurotransmitters include gamma-aminobutyric acid (GABA) and glutamate.

Glutamate and GABA

Two major neurotransmitters affect much of what we do. The first, **glutamate**, is an excitatory transmitter that "turns on" many different neurons, leading to action. A second, **gamma-aminobutyric acid (GABA)** is an inhibitory neurotransmitter. Its job is to inhibit (or regulate) the transmission of information and action potentials. Glutamate and GABA operate relatively independently at a molecular level, but the relative balance of each in a cell will determine whether the neuron is activated (fires) or not. Another characteristic of these "chemical brothers" (LeDoux, 2002) is that they are fast acting, as they would have to be for the brain to keep up with the many influences from the environment that require action or restraint.

As noted earlier, GABA reduces postsynaptic activity, which, in turn, inhibits a variety of behaviors and emotions. Its best-known effect is to reduce anxiety (Griebel & Holmes, 2013). A particular class of drugs, the *benzodiazepines,* or minor tranquilizers, makes it easier for GABA molecules to attach themselves to the receptors of specialized neurons. Thus, the higher the level of benzodiazepine, the more GABA becomes attached to neuron receptors and the calmer we become (to a point). Because benzodiazepines have certain addictive properties, scientists are working to identify other substances that may also modulate levels of GABA; these include certain natural steroids in the brain (Eser, Schule, Baghai, Romeo, & Rupprecht, 2006; Rupprecht *et al.*, 2009).

As with other neurotransmitter systems, we now know that GABA's effect is not specific to anxiety but has a broader influence. GABA seems to reduce overall arousal somewhat and to temper our emotional responses. For example, in addition to reducing anxiety, minor tranquilizers have an anticonvulsant effect, relaxing muscle groups that may be subject to spasms. Drug compounds that increase GABA are also under evaluation as treatments for insomnia (Sullivan, 2012; Sullivan & Guilleminault, 2009). Furthermore, the GABA system seems to reduce levels of anger, hostility, aggression, and perhaps even positive emotional states such as eager anticipation and pleasure, making GABA a generalized inhibiting neurotransmitter, much as glutamate has a generalized excitatory function (Bond & Lader, 1979; Sharp, 2009).

Serotonin

The technical name for **serotonin** is 5-hydroxytryptamine (5HT). It is in the monoamine category of neurotransmitters, along with norepinephrine and dopamine, discussed next. Approximately six major circuits of serotonin spread from the midbrain, looping around its various parts (Azmitia, 1978) (see ● Figure 2.11). Serotonin is believed to influence a great deal of our behavior, particularly the way we process information (Harmer, 2008; Merens, Willem Van der Does, & Spinhoven, 2007). It was genetically influenced dysregulation in this system that contributed to depression in the New Zealand study described earlier (Caspi *et al.*, 2003).

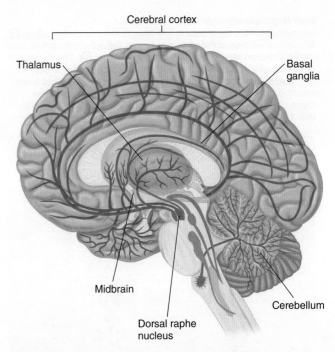

● **Figure 2.11** Major serotonin pathways in the brain.

The serotonin system regulates our behavior, moods, and thought processes. Extremely low activity levels of serotonin are associated with less inhibition and with instability, impulsivity, and the tendency to overreact to situations. Low serotonin activity has been associated with aggression, suicide, impulsive overeating, and excessive sexual behavior (Berman, McCloskey, Fanning, Schumacher, & Coccaro, 2009). These behaviors do not *necessarily* happen if serotonin activity is low, however. Other currents in the brain, or other psychological or social influences, may compensate for low serotonin activity. Therefore, low serotonin

brain circuits **Neurotransmitter** current or neural pathway in the brain.

agonist In **neuroscience**, a chemical substance that effectively increases the activity of a **neurotransmitter** by imitating its effects.

antagonist In **neuroscience**, a chemical substance that decreases or blocks the effects of a **neurotransmitter**.

inverse agonist In **neuroscience**, a chemical substance that produces effects opposite those of a particular **neurotransmitter**.

reuptake Action by which a **neurotransmitter** is quickly drawn back into the discharging **neuron** after being released into a **synaptic cleft**.

glutamate Amino acid **neurotransmitter** that excites many different **neurons**, leading to action.

gamma-aminobutyric acid (GABA) Neurotransmitter that reduces activity across the **synaptic cleft** and thus inhibits a range of behaviors and **emotions**, especially generalized **anxiety**.

serotonin Neurotransmitter involved in processing of information and coordination of movement, as well as inhibition and restraint. It also assists in the regulation of eating, sexual, and aggressive behaviors, all of which may be involved in different **psychological disorders**. Its interaction with **dopamine** is implicated in **schizophrenia**.

How Neurotransmitters Work

Neurotransmitters are stored in tiny sacs at the end of the neuron **A**. An electric jolt makes the sacs merge with the outer membrane, and the neurotransmitter is released into the synapse **B**. The molecules diffuse across the gap and bind receptors, specialized proteins, on the adjacent neuron **C**. When sufficient neurotransmitter has been absorbed, the receptors release the molecules, which are then broken down or reabsorbed by the first neuron and stored for later use **D**.

How Serotonin Drugs Work

Prozac enhances serotonin's effects by preventing it from being absorbed **E**. Redux and fenfluramine (antiobesity drugs) cause the release of extra serotonin into the synapse **F**. These drugs have been recalled by the FDA for dangerous cardiovascular side effects (see Chapter 8).

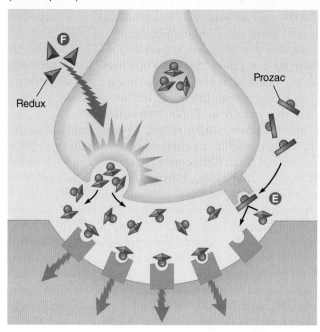

Receptor Variation

There are at least 15 different serotonin receptors, each associated with a different function.

● **Figure 2.12** Manipulating serotonin in the brain.

activity may make us more vulnerable to certain behavior without directly causing it. On the other end, high levels of serotonin may interact with GABA to counteract glutamate.

Several classes of drugs primarily affect the serotonin system. However, the class of drugs called *selective-serotonin reuptake inhibitors (SSRIs),* including fluoxetine (Prozac) (see ● Figure 2.12), affects serotonin more directly than other drugs, including the tricyclic antidepressants. SSRIs are used to treat a number of psychological disorders, particularly anxiety, mood, and eating disorders. The herbal medication St. John's wort, available in many drugstores, also affects serotonin levels.

Norepinephrine

A third neurotransmitter system in the monoamine class important to psychopathology is **norepinephrine** (also known as **noradrenaline**) (see ● Figure 2.13).

Norepinephrine seems to stimulate at least two groups (and probably more) of receptors called *alpha-adrenergic* and *beta-adrenergic receptors.* A widely-used class of drugs called *beta-blocker are used to treat* hypertension or difficulties with

regulating heart rate. These drugs block the beta-receptors so that their response to a surge of norepinephrine is reduced, which keeps blood pressure and heart rate down. In the central nervous system, a number of norepinephrine circuits have been identified. One major circuit begins in the hindbrain, an area that controls basic bodily functions such as respiration. Another circuit appears to influence the emergency reactions or alarm responses (Charney & Drevets, 2002; Sullivan & LeDoux, 2004) that occur when we find ourselves in a dangerous situation, suggesting that norepinephrine may bear some relationship to states of panic (Charney *et al.*, 1990; Gray & McNaughton, 1996). More likely, however, is that this system acts in a more general way to regulate certain behavioral tendencies and is not directly involved in specific patterns of behavior or in psychological disorders.

Dopamine

Dopamine is a major neurotransmitter in the monoamine class. Dopamine has been implicated in the pathophysiology of schizophrenia (see ● Figure 2.14) and disorders of addiction (Le Foll, Gallo, Le Strat, Lu, & Gorwood, 2009).

Figure 2.13 Major norepinephrine pathways in the human brain. (Adapted from Kalat, J. W. [2009]. *Biological Psychology*, 10th edition, © 2009 Wadsworth.)

Figure 2.14 Two major dopamine pathways. The mesolimbic system is apparently implicated in schizophrenia; the path to the basal ganglia contributes to problems in the locomotor system, such as tardive dyskinesia, which sometimes results from use of neuroleptic drugs. (Adapted from Kalat, J. W. [2009]. *Biological Psychology*, 10th edition, © 2009 Wadsworth.)

Some research also indicates it may play a significant role in depression (Dunlop & Nemeroff, 2007) and attention-deficit hyperactivity disorder (Volkow *et al.*, 2009). Remember the wonder drug reserpine mentioned in Chapter 1 that reduced

psychotic behaviors associated with schizophrenia? This drug and more modern antipsychotic treatments affect a number of neurotransmitter systems, but their greatest impact may be that they block specific dopamine receptors, thus lowering dopamine activity (see, for example, Snyder, Burt, & Creese, 1976).

In its various circuits throughout specific regions of the brain, dopamine also seems to have a more general effect, best described as a switch that turns on brain circuits possibly associated with certain types of behavior. Once the switch is turned on, other neurotransmitters may then inhibit or facilitate emotions or behavior (Armbruster *et al.*, 2009; Stahl, 2008). Dopamine circuits merge and cross with serotonin circuits at many points and therefore influence many of the same behaviors. For example, dopamine activity is associated with exploratory, outgoing, pleasure-seeking behaviors (Elovainio, Kivimaki, Viikari, Ekelund, & Keltikangas-Jarvinen, 2005), and serotonin is associated with inhibition and constraint; thus, in a sense they balance each other (Depue, Luciana, Arbisi, Collins, & Leon, 1994).

Researchers have discovered at least five different receptor sites that are selectively sensitive to dopamine (Beaulieu & Gainetdinov, 2011). One of a class of drugs that affects the dopamine circuits specifically is L-dopa, a dopamine agonist (increases levels of dopamine). One of the systems that dopamine switches on is the locomotor system, which regulates the ability to move in a coordinated way and, once turned on, is influenced by serotonin activity. Because of these connections, deficiencies in dopamine have been associated with disorders such as Parkinson's disease, in which a deterioration in motor behavior includes tremors, rigidity of muscles, and difficulty with judgment. L-dopa has been successful in reducing some of these motor disabilities.

Implications for Psychopathology

Psychological disorders typically mix emotional, behavioral, and cognitive symptoms, so identifiable lesions (or damage) localized in specific structures of the brain do not, for the most part, cause the disorders. Even widespread damage most often results in motor or sensory deficits, which are usually the province of the medical specialty of

norepinephrine (also noradrenaline) Neurotransmitter active in the **central** and **peripheral nervous systems**, controlling heart rate, blood pressure, and respiration, among other functions. Because of its role in the body's alarm reaction, it may also contribute generally and indirectly to **panic attacks** and other disorders. Also known as *noradrenaline*.

dopamine Neurotransmitter whose generalized function is to activate other neurotransmitters and to aid in exploratory and pleasure-seeking behaviors (thus balancing **serotonin**). A relative excess of dopamine is implicated in **schizophrenia** (although contradictory evidence suggests the connection is not simple), and its deficit is involved in **Parkinson's disease**.

neurology; neurologists often work with neuropsychologists to identify specific lesions. But psychopathologists have been focusing lately on the more general role of brain function in the development of personality, with the goal of considering how different types of biologically driven personalities might be more vulnerable to developing certain types of psychological disorders. For example, genetic contributions might lead to patterns of neurotransmitter activity that influence personality. Thus, some impulsive risk takers may have low serotonergic activity and high dopaminergic activity.

Remember that one of the roles of serotonin seems to be to moderate our reactions. Eating behavior, sexual behavior, and aggression are under better control with adequate levels of serotonin. Research, mostly on animals, demonstrates that lesions (damage) that interrupt serotonin circuits seem to impair the ability to ignore irrelevant external cues, making the organism overactive. Thus, if we were to experience damage or interruption in this brain circuit, we might find ourselves acting on every thought or impulse that enters our heads.

Thomas Insel (1992) described a case originally reported by Eslinger and Damasio (1985) of a man who had been successful as an accountant, husband, and father of two before undergoing surgery for a brain tumor. He made a good recovery from surgery, but in the following year his business failed and he separated from his family. Although his scores on IQ tests were as high as ever and his mental functions were intact, he was unable to keep a job or even be on time for an appointment. What was causing all these problems? He was engaging in lengthy and uncontrollable compulsive rituals. Most of his days were consumed with washing, dressing, and rearranging things in the single room where he lived. In other words, he had classic obsessive-compulsive symptoms. The area of his brain damaged by removal of the tumor was a small area of his orbital frontal cortex.

This information seems to support a biological cause for OCD. You might think there is no need to consider social or psychological influences here. But Insel and other neuroscientists interpret these findings cautiously. First, this case involves only one individual. Other individuals with the *same* lesion might react differently. Also, brain-imaging studies are often inconsistent with one another. Sometimes pinpointing the increased or decreased activity is difficult because brains differ in their structure. Also, the orbital frontal cortex is implicated in other anxiety disorders and maybe other emotional disorders (Gansler *et al.*, 2009; Goodwin, 2009), so the damage in this area of the brain may just increase negative affect more generally rather than OCD specifically. Therefore, more work has to be done, and perhaps technology has to improve further, before we can be confident about the relation of the orbital frontal cortex to OCD. It is also important to note that today, neuroscientists focus more on the connectivity between certain brain areas (the brain circuitry) than the activity of any particular brain region that might be associated with a specific mental disorder (e.g., Whitfield-Gabrieli *et al.*, 2016).

Psychosocial Influences on Brain Structure and Function

Sometimes the effects of treatment tell us about the nature of psychopathology. For example, if a clinician thinks OCD is caused by brain dysfunction or by learned anxiety, this view would determine choice of treatment. Directing a treatment at one or the other of these theoretical causes and then observing whether the patient gets better will prove or disprove the theory. This strategy has one weakness. Successfully treating a patient's toothache with aspirin does not mean the toothache was caused by an aspirin deficiency, because an effect does not imply a cause. So the reasons why a problem develops (*the initiating factors*) are not necessarily the same as the reasons why the problem persists (*the maintaining factors*). In order to treat the problem, it is typically more important to know and target the maintaining factors than the initiating factors. Nevertheless, this line of evidence gives us hints about causes of psychopathology, particularly when it is combined with other experimental evidence.

If you knew that someone with OCD might have a somewhat faulty brain circuit, what treatment would you choose? Maybe you would recommend brain surgery, or neurosurgery. Neurosurgery to correct severe psychopathology (sometimes called "psychosurgery") is an option still chosen today, particularly in the case of OCD when the suffering is severe and other treatments have failed (Bear, Fitzgerald, Rosenfeld, & Bittar, 2010; Denys *et al.*, 2010). For the man described previously, the removal of his brain tumor seems to have eliminated an inhibitory part of the brain circuit implicated in OCD. Precise surgical lesions might dampen the runaway activity that seems to occur in or near this area of the brain. This result would probably be welcome if all other treatments have failed, although psychosurgery is used seldom and has not been studied systematically.

Nobody wants to do surgery if less intrusive treatments are available. We now have drugs that do seem to be beneficial in treating OCD. As you might suspect, most of them act by increasing serotonin activity in one way or another. But is it possible to get at this brain circuit without either surgery or drugs? Could psychological treatment be powerful enough to affect the circuit directly? The answer seems to be yes. Lewis R. Baxter and his colleagues used brain imaging on patients who had not been treated and then treated the patients with a cognitive-behavioral therapy known to be effective in OCD called *exposure and response prevention* (Baxter *et al.*, 1992). They discovered that the brain circuit had been changed (normalized) by a psychological intervention. They replicated the experiment with a different group of patients and found the same changes in brain function (Schwartz, Stoessel, Baxter, Martin, & Phelps, 1996). In other examples, investigating teams noted changes in brain function after successful psychological treatment for depression, PTSD, obsessive-compulsive disorder, panic disorder, social anxiety disorder, specific phobias, and schizophrenia (Barsaglini, Sartori, Benetti,

Pettersson-Yeo, & Mechelli, 2014). A review of the evidence suggests that, depending on the disorder, psychotherapy results in either a normalization of abnormal patterns of activity, the recruitment of additional areas, which did not show altered activation prior to treatment, or both.

The study of placebo effects offers another window on psychological factors directly affecting brain function. It is common for inactive placebo medications, which are sugar pills, or other "sham" (inactive) treatments to result in behavioral and emotional changes in patients, presumably as a result of psychological factors such as increasing hope and expectations or conditioning effects (Brody & Miller, 2011). Several studies have examined the conditions under which placebos are active. For example, one study administered medications for pain or anxiety after surgery by means of an infusion pump that was either in plain view of the patients or was hidden behind a screen (Colloca, Lopiano, Lanotte, & Benedetti, 2004). Even though the same dosage of medicine was administered, the effect was consistently greater when patients knew they were receiving the drug because they could see the pump working. No placebos were actually given in this study, but the difference in effects between knowing and not knowing whether the drug was given was considered a good estimate of the placebo effect.

Another area of research is exploring the specific ways in which drug or active psychological treatments work in terms of changes in brain function. Are the changes in brain function similar or different as a function of drug or psychological treatment? Kennedy *et al.* (2007) treated individuals with major depressive disorder with either a psychological treatment, cognitive-behavioral therapy (CBT), or the antidepressant drug venlafaxine. Although some brain changes were similar among the three treatment groups, complex differences were also noted, primarily in the way in which CBT facilitated changes in thinking patterns in the cortex that, in turn, affected the emotional brain. Sometimes this is called a "top down" change because it originates in the cortex and works its way down into the lower brain. Drugs, on the other hand, often seem to work more in a "bottom up" manner, reaching higher areas of the cortex (where thinking occurs) last. Because we know that some people respond better to psychological treatments, and others respond better to drugs, this research provides hope that we will one day be able to choose the best treatments or better combine treatments based on an analysis of the individual's brain function.

Our team has been able to use brain imaging as a tool to predict psychotherapy response (Doehrmann *et al.*, 2013; Whitfield-Gabrieli, 2016) in certain individuals. This is an example for *precision medicine* (i.e., tailoring the treatment to the individual patient in order to optimize therapy outcome).

Interactions of Psychosocial Factors and Neurotransmitter Systems

Several experiments illustrate the interaction of psychosocial factors and brain function on neurotransmitter activity. Some even indicate that psychosocial factors directly affect levels of neurotransmitters. In one experiment, Insel, Scanlan, Champoux, and Suomi (1988) raised two groups of rhesus monkeys identically except for their ability to control things in their cages. One group had free access to toys and food treats, but the second group got these toys and treats only when the first group did. In other words, members of the second group had the same number of toys and treats but could not choose when they got them. The monkeys in the first group grew up with a sense of control over things in their lives and those in the second group didn't.

Later in their lives, all these monkeys were administered a benzodiazepine inverse agonist, a neurochemical that has the *opposite* effect of the neurotransmitter GABA; the effect is an extreme burst of anxiety. The monkeys that had been raised with little control over their environment ran to a corner of their cage and displayed signs of severe anxiety and panic. But the monkeys that had a sense of control did not seem anxious. Rather, they seemed angry and aggressive, even attacking other monkeys. Thus, the same level of a neurochemical substance, acting as a neurotransmitter, had different effects, depending on the psychological and environmental histories of the monkeys. Other experiments suggest that psychosocial influences directly affect the functioning and perhaps even the structure of the central nervous system. Scientists have observed that psychosocial factors routinely change the activity levels of many of our neurotransmitter systems (Marinelli & McCutcheon, 2014; Sandi & Haller, 2015).

In another example of the interaction among psychosocial factors, brain structure, and brain function as reflected in neurotransmitter activity, Yeh, Fricke, and Edwards (1996) studied two male crayfish battling to establish

▲ Rhesus monkeys injected with a specific neurotransmitter react with anger or fear, depending on their early psychological experiences.

dominance in their social group. When one of the crayfish won the battle and established dominance, serotonin made a specific set of neurons more likely to fire. In the animal that lost the battle, serotonin made the same neurons less likely to fire. Thus, Yeh and colleagues (1996) discovered that naturally occurring neurotransmitters have different effects depending on the previous psychosocial experience of the organism. Furthermore, this experience affects the structure of neurons at the synapse by altering the sensitivity of serotonin receptors. The researchers also discovered that the effects of serotonin are reversible if the losers again become dominant.

In another example, Berton and colleagues (2006) discovered that putting into a cage big mice that then proceeded to "bully" a smaller mouse produced changes in the mesolimbic dopamine system of the smaller mouse. These changes were associated with the smaller mouse wanting no part of other mice under any circumstances. The mesolimbic system is ordinarily associated with reward and even addiction. But in this case, certain chemicals that produce new learning and other changes in other parts of the brain, specifically brain development neurotrophic factor (BDNF; a protein involved in learning by stimulating growth of new neurons), were turned on in the mesolimbic dopamine system by a psychological experience—bullying—such that the mesolimbic dopamine system had different effects on the mouse than it usually does. That is, the "bullying" experience produced BDNF, which changed the usual functioning of the mesolimbic dopamine system from facilitating reinforcement to facilitating avoidance. More recent research implicates glucocorticoid receptors located on dopaminergic neurons specifically in facilitating and maintaining this social aversion (Barik et al., 2013).

Psychosocial Effects on the Development of Brain Structure and Function

It also seems that the structure of neurons themselves, including the number of receptors on a cell, can be changed by learning and experience during development (Clemenson, Deng, & Gage, 2015; Kandel, Dudai, & Mayford, 2014) and that these effects on the central nervous system continue throughout our lives (Spinelli et al., 2009; Suárez et al., 2009). For example, William Greenough and his associates (Greenough, Withers, & Wallace, 1990) discovered that the nervous systems of rats raised in a rich environment requiring a lot of learning and motor behavior develop differently from the nervous systems in rats that were couch potatoes. The active rats had more connections between nerve cells in the cerebellum and grew more dendrites. Similarly, stress during early development can lead to substantial changes in the functioning of the HPA axis that make primates more or less susceptible to stress later in life (Barlow, 2002;

Spinelli et al., 2009). More recent experiments with monkeys indicate that housing monkeys in larger groups increases the amount of grey matter in parts of the brain involved in social cognition. This is important because social cognition, including such skills as being able to interpret facial expressions and gestures, makes one more successful socially and, in monkeys, increases one's social ranking (Sallet et al., 2011).

So, we can conclude that early psychological experience affects the development of the nervous system and thus determines vulnerability to psychological disorders later in life. It seems that the very structure of the nervous system is constantly changing as a result of learning and experience, even into old age, and that some of these changes become permanent (Barlow, Ellard, Sauer Zavala, Bullis, & Carl, 2014). This plasticity of the central nervous system helps us adapt more readily to our environment. These findings will be important when we discuss the causes of anxiety disorders and mood disorders in Chapters 4 and 6.

2.3 Concept CHECK

Match each of the following with its description below: (a) frontal lobe, (b) brain stem, (c) GABA, (d) midbrain, (e) serotonin, (f) dopamine, (g) norepinephrine, and (h) cerebral cortex.

1. Movement, breathing, and sleeping depend on the ancient part of the brain, which is present in most animals. _____

2. Which neurotransmitter binds to neuron receptor sites, inhibiting postsynaptic activity and reducing overall arousal? _____

3. Which neurotransmitter is a switch that turns on various brain circuits? _____

4. Which neurotransmitter seems to be involved in our emergency reactions or alarm responses? _____

5. This area contains part of the reticular activating system and coordinates movement with sensory output. _____

6. Which neurotransmitter is believed to influence the way we process information, as well as to moderate or inhibit our behavior? _____

7. More than 80% of the neurons in the human central nervous system are contained in this part of the brain, which gives us distinct qualities. _____

8. This area is responsible for most of our memory, thinking, and reasoning capabilities and makes us social animals. _____

▶ What are the key differences between behavioral and cognitive explanations of the origins of mental illness?

Enormous progress has been made in understanding behavioral and cognitive influences in psychopathology. Some new information has come from the field of **cognitive science**, which is concerned with how we acquire and process information and how we store and retrieve it. Scientists have also discovered that we are not necessarily aware of a great deal of what goes on inside our heads. Because, technically, these cognitive processes are unconscious, some findings recall the unconscious mental processes that are so much a part of Sigmund Freud's theory of psychoanalysis (although they do not look much like the ones he envisioned). A brief account of current thinking on what is happening during the process of classical conditioning will start us on our way.

Conditioning and Cognitive Processes

During the 1960s and 1970s, behavioral scientists in animal laboratories began to uncover the complexity of the basic processes of classical conditioning (Bouton, Mineka, & Barlow, 2001; Eelen & Vervliet, 2006). Robert Rescorla (1988) concluded that simply pairing two events closely in time (such as the meat powder and the metronome in Ivan Pavlov's laboratories) is not what's important in this type of learning. Rather, a variety of judgments and cognitive processes combine to determine the final outcome of this learning, even in lower animals such as rats.

To take one simple example, Pavlov would have predicted that if the meat powder and the metronome were paired, say, 50 times, then a certain amount of learning would take place. But Rescorla and others discovered that if one animal never saw the meat powder except for the 50 trials following the metronome sound, whereas the meat powder was brought to a second animal many times *between* the 50 times it was paired with the metronome, the two animals would learn different things; that is, even though the metronome and the meat powder were paired 50 times for each animal, the metronome was less meaningful to the second animal (see ● Figure 2.15). Put another way, the first animal learned that the sound of the metronome meant meat powder came next; the second animal learned that the meat sometimes came after the sound and sometimes without the sound. That two different conditions produce two different learning outcomes is a commonsense notion, but it demonstrates, along with many far more complex scientific findings, that basic classical (and operant) conditioning paradigms facilitate the learning of the relationship among events in the environment.

This type of learning enables us to develop working ideas about the world that allow us to make appropriate judgments. We can then respond in a way that will benefit, or at least not hurt, us. In other words, complex cognitive processing of information, as well as emotional processing, is involved when conditioning occurs, even in animals.

Learned Helplessness

Along similar lines, Martin Seligman and his colleague Steven Maier, also working with animals, described the phenomenon of **learned helplessness**, which occurs when animals encounter conditions over which they have no control (Maier & Seligman, 1976). If rats are confronted with a situation in which they receive occasional foot shocks, they can function well if they learn they can cope with these shocks by doing something to avoid them (say, pressing a lever). But if the animals learn their behavior has no effect on their environment—sometimes they get shocked and sometimes they don't, no matter what they do—they become "helpless"; in other words, they give up attempting to cope and seem to develop the animal equivalent of depression.

Seligman theorized that the same phenomenon may happen with people who are faced with uncontrollable stress. Subsequent work revealed this to be true under one important condition: People become depressed if they "decide" or "think" they can do little about the stress in their lives, even if it seems to others that there is something they could do. People make an *attribution* that they have no control, and they become depressed (Abramson, Seligman, & Teasdale, 1978; Miller & Norman, 1979). This finding illustrates, again, the necessity of recognizing that different people process information about events in the environment in different ways. These cognitive differences are an important component of psychopathology.

Lately, Seligman has turned his attention to a different set of attributions, which he terms *learned optimism* (Seligman, 1998, 2002). In other words, if people faced with considerable stress and difficulty in their lives nevertheless display an optimistic, upbeat attitude, they are

....

cognitive science Field of study that examines how humans and other animals acquire, process, store, and retrieve information.

learned helplessness Martin Seligman's theory that people become anxious and depressed when they make an attribution that they have no control over the **stress** in their lives (whether or not they do in reality).

Contiguity only

Neutral stimulus

Unconditioned stimulus

♪ = 🥩

Meat always comes with sound.

Contiguity and random

Neutral stimulus

Unconditioned stimulus

♪ = 🥩 ?

Meat comes with and without sound.

● **Figure 2.15** Robert Rescorla's experiment that showed contiguity—pairing a neutral stimulus and an unconditioned stimulus— does not result in the same kind of conditioning. The dog in the contiguity-only group (top panel) experiences the usual conditioning procedure: Pairing a tone and meat causes the tone to take on properties of the meat. For the dog in the contiguity-and-random group, the meat appeared away from the tones, as well as with it, making the tone less meaningful.

likely to function better psychologically and physically. In a classic study by Levy, Slade, Kunkel, and Kasl (2002), individuals between ages 50 and 94 who had positive views about themselves and positive attitudes toward aging lived 7.5 years longer than those without such positive attitudes. This connection was still true after the investigators controlled for age, sex, income, loneliness, and physical capability to engage in household and social activities. This effect exceeds the one to four years of added life associated with other factors, such as low blood pressure, low cholesterol levels, and no history of obesity or cigarette smoking. These results have been strongly supported in more recent studies (Steptoe & Wardle, 2012). Studies such as this have created interest in a new field of study called *positive psychology,* in which investigators explore factors that account for positive attitudes and happiness (Diener, 2000; Lyubomirsky, 2001).

Social Learning

Another influential psychologist, Albert Bandura (1973, 1986), observed that organisms do not have to experience certain events in their environment to learn effectively.

Rather, they can learn just as much by observing what happens to someone else in a given situation, a process termed **modeling** or **observational learning**. Even in animals, this type of learning requires integration of the experiences of others with judgments of what might happen to oneself; in other words, even an animal such as a monkey must make a decision about the conditions under which its own experiences would be similar to those of the animal it is observing. Bandura concluded that behavior, cognitive factors, and environmental influences converge to produce the complexity of behavior that confronts us. He also specified the importance of the social context of our learning; that is, much of what we learn depends on our interactions with other people around us. These ideas have been integrated with new findings on the genetic and biological bases of social behavior in a new field of study called social neuroscience (Cacioppo *et al.,* 2007).

The basic idea in all Bandura's work is that a careful analysis of cognitive processes may produce the most accurate scientific predictions of behavior. Concepts of probability learning, information processing, and attention have become increasingly important in psychopathology (Barlow, 2002; Yiend, 2010).

Prepared Learning

It is clear that biology and, probably, our genetic endowment influence what we learn. This conclusion is based on our learning to fear some objects more easily than others. In other words, we learn fears and phobias selectively (Morris, Öhman, & Dolan, 1998; Öhman & Mineka, 2001). Why might this be? According to the concept of **prepared learning**, we have become highly prepared for learning about certain types of objects or situations over the course of evolution because this knowledge contributes to the survival of the species (Mineka, 1985; Seligman, 1971). Even without any contact, we are more likely to learn to fear snakes or spiders than rocks or flowers, even if we know rationally that the snake or spider is harmless (for example, Fredrikson, Annas, & Wik, 1997; Pury & Mineka, 1997). In the absence of experience, however, we are less likely to fear guns, cars, or electrical outlets, even though they are potentially deadlier.

Why do we so readily learn to fear snakes or spiders? One possibility is that our ancestors who avoided snakes and spiders eluded deadly varieties and therefore survived in greater numbers to pass down their genes to us, thus contributing to the survival of the species. In fact, recent research has found that a sex difference may exist for this type of learning: Females are particularly sensitive to this learning and, unlike males, demonstrate it as early as 11 months of age (Rakison, 2009). Thus, "prepared learning" may account for the greater incidence of snake and spider phobias in adult women (see Chapter 4). According to the theory it would have been more important for women, in their roles as gatherers, to develop a tendency to avoid snakes and spiders than males, in their roles as risk-taking hunters (Rakison, 2009).

In any case, something within us recognizes the connection between a signal and a threatening event. If you've ever gotten sick on an exotic alcoholic drink, chances are you won't make the same mistake again. This quick, or "one-trial," learning also occurs in animals that eat something that tastes bad, causes nausea, or may contain poison. It is easy to see that survival is associated with quickly learning to avoid poisonous food. If animals are shocked instead of poisoned when eating certain foods, however, they do not learn this association as quickly, probably because in nature shock is not a consequence of eating, whereas food is more closely associated with getting poisoned. Perhaps these selective associations are also facilitated by our genes and depend on the context and nature of the associated stimuli (Barlow, 2002; Mallan, Lipp, & Cochrane, 2013).

Cognitive Science and the Unconscious

Advances in cognitive science have revolutionized our conceptions of the unconscious. We are not aware of much of what goes on inside our heads, but our unconscious is not necessarily the cauldron of primitive emotional conflicts envisioned by Freud. Rather, we simply seem able to process and store information, and act on it, without having awareness of what the information is or why we are acting on it (Bargh & Chartrand, 1999; Uleman, Saribay, & Gonzalez, 2008). Is this surprising? Consider briefly two examples.

Lawrence Weiskrantz in a classic study (1992) describes a phenomenon called *blind sight* or *unconscious vision*. He relates the case of a young man who, for medical reasons, had a small section of his visual cortex (the center for the control of vision in the brain) surgically removed. Although the operation was considered a success, the man became blind in both eyes. Later, during tests, a physician raised his hand to the left of the patient who, much to the shock of his doctors, reached out and touched it. Subsequently, scientists determined that he could not only reach accurately for objects but could also distinguish among objects and perform most of the functions usually associated with sight. Yet, when asked about his abilities, he would say, "I couldn't see anything, not a darn thing," and that all he was doing was guessing.

The phenomenon in this case is associated with brain damage. More interesting, from the point of view of psychopathology, is that the same thing seems to occur in healthy individuals who have been hypnotized (Hilgard, 1992; Kihlstrom, 1992); that is, normal individuals, provided with hypnotic suggestions that they are blind, are able to function visually but have no awareness or memory of their visual abilities. This condition, which illustrates a process of *dissociation* between behavior and consciousness, is the basis of the dissociative disorders discussed in Chapter 5.

A second example, more relevant to psychopathology, is called **implicit memory** (Kandel *et al.*, 2014; Schacter, Chiu, & Ochsner, 1993). Implicit memory is apparent when someone acts on the basis of things that have happened in the past but can't remember the events. (A conscious memory for events is called *explicit memory*.) But implicit memory can be selective for only certain events or circumstances. An example of implicit memory at work is the story of Anna O., the case described by Breuer and Freud (1895/1957) to demonstrate the existence of the unconscious. It was only after therapy that Anna O. remembered events surrounding her father's death and the connection of these events to her paralysis. Thus, Anna O.'s behavior (occasional paralysis) was evidently connected to implicit memories of her father's death. Many scientists have concluded that Freud's

modeling (also observational learning) Learning through observation and imitation of the behavior of other individuals and consequences of that behavior.

prepared learning Ability adaptive for evolution, allowing certain associations to be learned more readily than others.

implicit memory Condition of memory in which a person cannot recall past events despite acting in response to them.

1. RED	6. GREEN	11. BLUE
2. PURPLE	7. PURPLE	12. PURPLE
3. GREEN	8. BROWN	13. BROWN
4. BLUE	9. BLUE	14. RED
5. BROWN	10. RED	15. GREEN

▲ The Stroop paradigm. Have someone keep time as you name the colors of the words but not the words themselves and again while you read the words aloud.

speculations on the nature and structure of the unconscious went beyond the evidence, but the existence of unconscious processes has since been demonstrated, and we must take them into account as we study psychopathology.

Several methods for studying the unobservable unconscious have been made possible by advances in technology. One of them is the Stroop color-naming paradigm, in which participants are shown a variety of words, each printed in a different color, and are asked to name the colors in which the words are printed while ignoring their meaning (e.g., the person is asked to say "blue" if she sees the word

red printed in a blue color). Color naming is delayed when the meaning of the word attracts the participant's attention, despite efforts to concentrate on the color; that is, the meaning of the word interferes with the participant's ability to process color information. For example, experimenters have determined that people with certain disorders, like Judy, are much slower at naming the colors of words associated with their problem (for example, *blood*) than the colors of words that have no relation to the disorder. Thus, psychologists can uncover patterns of emotional significance, even if the participant cannot verbalize them or is not aware of them.

Recently, cognitive neuroscientists using brain imaging methods (functional magnetic resonance imaging [fMRI]) have noticed differences in the processing of neural activity in the brain depending on whether the person is aware of the information or not (Uehara *et al.*, 2013). Generally, the greater the duration, intensity, and coherence of the neural representation of a piece of information in the brain, the more likely that the person will be conscious of the information (e.g., Kandel *et al.*, 2014). So far, this work has been carried out only in experiments with normal individuals. It remains to be seen if the unconscious experience of people with psychological disorders will look similar during brain imaging.

Emotions

▶ What role do emotions play in psychopathology?

Emotions can contribute in major ways to the development of psychopathology (Barrett, 2012; Gross, 2015). Consider fear. For example, have you ever been swimming in the ocean and realized you were caught in a current? If so, you would have felt an incredible surge of arousal. As Charles Darwin (1872) pointed out more than 100 years ago, this kind of reaction seems to be programmed in all animals, including humans, which suggests that it serves a useful evolutionary function. The alarm reaction that activates during potentially life-threatening emergencies is called the **flight or fight response**. If you are caught in ocean currents, your almost instinctive tendency is to struggle toward shore. You might realize rationally that you're best off just floating until the current runs its course and then, more calmly, swimming in later. Yet somewhere, deep within, ancient instincts for survival won't let you relax, even though struggling against the ocean will wear you out and increase your chance of drowning. Still, this kind of reaction might momentarily give you the strength to lift a car off your trapped brother or fight off an attacker. The whole purpose of the physical rush of adrenaline that we feel in extreme danger is to mobilize us to escape the danger (flight) or to fend it off (fight).

The Physiology and Purpose of Fear

How do physical reactions prepare us to respond this way? According to physiologist Walter Cannon (1929), fear activates your cardiovascular system. Your blood vessels constrict, raising arterial pressure and decreasing the blood flow to your extremities. Excess blood is redirected to the skeletal muscles, where it is available to the vital organs that may be needed in an emergency. Breathing becomes faster and, usually, deeper to provide oxygen to rapidly circulating blood. Increased blood circulation carries oxygen to the brain, stimulating cognitive processes and sensory functions, which make you more alert and able to think more quickly. An increased amount of glucose (sugar) is released from the liver into the bloodstream, energizing various muscles and organs, including the brain. Pupils dilate, presumably to allow a better view of the situation. Hearing becomes more acute, and digestive activity is suspended, resulting in a reduced flow of saliva (the "dry mouth" of fear). In the short term, voiding the body of all waste material and eliminating digestive processes further prepare the

▲ Charles Darwin (1809–1882) drew this cat frightened by a dog to show the flight or fight reaction.

organism for concentrated action and activity, so there is often pressure to urinate and defecate and, occasionally, to vomit.

It is easy to see why the flight or fight reaction is important. Millennia ago, when our ancestors lived in unstable circumstances, those with strong emergency reactions were more likely to live through attacks and other dangers than those with weak emergency responses, and the survivors passed their genes down to us.

Emotional Phenomena

The **emotion** of fear is a subjective feeling of terror, a strong motivation for behavior (escaping or fighting), and a complex physiological or arousal response. To define "emotion" is difficult, but most theorists agree that it is linked to an *action tendency* (Barlow *et al.*, 2014; Barlow, 2002); that is, a tendency to behave in a certain way (for example, escape), elicited by an external event (a threat) and a feeling state (terror) and accompanied by a (possibly) characteristic physiological response (Fairholme, Boisseau, Ellard, Ehrenreich, & Barlow, 2010; Gross, 2015). One purpose of a feeling state is to motivate us to carry out a behavior: If we escape, our terror will be decreased, so decreasing unpleasant feelings motivates us to escape (Campbell-Sills, Ellard, & Barlow, 2015; Hofmann, 2016). As Öhman (1996; Öhman, Flykt, & Lundquist, 2000) points out, the principal function of emotions can be understood as a means to get us to do what we have to do to pass on our genes successfully. How do you think this works with anger or with love? What is the feeling state? What is the behavior?

Emotions are usually short-lived, temporary states lasting from several minutes to several hours, occurring in response to an external event. **Mood** is a more persistent period of affect or emotionality. Thus, in Chapter 6 we describe enduring or recurring states of depression or excitement (mania) as *mood disorders*. But *anxiety disorders*, described in Chapter 4, are characterized by enduring or chronic anxiety and, therefore, could also be called *mood disorders*. Alternatively, both anxiety disorders and mood disorders could be called *emotional disorders*, a term not formally used in psychopathology. This is only one example of the occasional inconsistencies in the terminology of abnormal psychology. A related term is **affect**, which often refers to the valence dimension (i.e., pleasant or positive vs. unpleasant or negative) of an emotion. For example, positive affect is experienced during joy, whereas negative affect is experienced during anger and fear. Together with arousal dimension (i.e., activated or high arousal vs deactivated or low arousal), any emotional experience can be assigned as a point on this two-dimensional system. This two dimensional system is known as the **circumplex model** of emotions (e.g., Colibazzi *et al.*, 2010). A third dimension (time) could be added to specify whether the emotional experience is short or long-lasting (e.g., surprise vs joy).

The Components of Emotion

Emotion is composed of three related components—*behavior*, *physiology*, and *cognition*—but most emotion scientists tend to concentrate on one component or another (see ● Figure 2.16). Emotion scientists who concentrate on behavior think that basic patterns of emotion differ from one another in fundamental ways; for example, anger may differ from sadness not only in how it feels but also behaviorally and physiologically. These scientists also emphasize that emotion is a way of communicating between one member of the species and another. One function of fear is to motivate immediate and decisive action, such as running away. But if you look scared, your facial expression will quickly communicate the possibility of danger to your friends, who may not have been aware that a threat is imminent. Your facial communication increases their chance for survival because they can now respond more quickly to the threat when it occurs. This may be one reason emotions are contagious (Hatfield, Cacioppo, & Rapson, 1994; Wang, 2006).

Other scientists have concentrated on the physiology of emotions. Cannon (1929) viewed emotion as primarily a brain function. Research in this tradition suggests that areas of the brain associated with emotional expression are generally more ancient and primitive than areas associated with higher cognitive processes, such as reasoning. Other research demonstrates direct neurobiological connections between emotional centers of the brain and parts of the eye (the retina) or the ear that allow emotional activation without the influence of higher cognitive processes (LeDoux, 2002; Zajonc, 1984). In other words, you may experience various emotions quickly and directly without necessarily thinking about them or being aware of why you feel the way you do.

flight or fight response Biological reaction to alarming stressors that musters the body's resources (for example, blood flow and respiration) to resist or flee a threat.

emotion Pattern of action elicited by an external event and a feeling state, accompanied by a characteristic physiological response.

mood Enduring period of emotionality.

affect Conscious, subjective aspect of an **emotion** that accompanies an action at a given time.

circumplex model A model describing different emotions as points in a 2-dimensional space of valence and arousal.

Emotion and Behavior
• Basic patterns of emotional behavior (freeze, escape, approach, attack) that differ in fundamental ways.
• Emotional behavior is a means of communication.

Cognitive Aspects of Emotion
• Appraisals, attributions, and other ways of processing the world around you that are fundamental to emotional experience.

Physiology of Emotion
• Emotion is a brain function involving (generally) the more primitive brain areas.
• Direct connection between these areas and the eyes may allow emotional processing to bypass the influence of higher cognitive processes.

● **Figure 2.16** Emotion has three important and overlapping components: behavior, cognition, and physiology.

Finally, a number of prominent emotion scientists concentrate on studying the cognitive aspects of emotion. Notable among these theorists was the late Richard S. Lazarus (for example, 1968, 1991, 1995), who proposed that changes in a person's environment are appraised in terms of their potential impact on that person. The type of appraisal you make determines the emotion you experience. For example, if you see somebody holding a gun in a dark alley, you will probably appraise the situation as dangerous and experience fear. You would make a different appraisal if you saw a tour guide displaying an antique gun in a museum. Lazarus would suggest that thinking and feeling cannot be separated, but other scientists are concluding otherwise by suggesting that, although cognitive and emotional systems interact and overlap, they are fundamentally separate (Teasdale, 1993). All components of emotion—behavior, physiology, and cognition—are important, and theorists are adopting more integrative approaches by studying their interaction (Gross, 2015; Hofmann, 2016).

Anger and Your Heart

When we discussed Judy's blood phobia, we observed that behavior and emotion may strongly influence biology. We have known for years that negatively valenced emotions such as hostility and anger increase a person's risk of developing heart disease (Chesney, 1986; MacDougall, Dembroski, Dimsdale, & Hackett, 1985). Sustained hostility with angry outbursts and repeatedly and continually suppressing anger contributes more strongly to death from heart disease than other risk factors, including smoking, high blood pressure, and high cholesterol levels (Harburg, Kaciroti, Gleiberman, Julius, & Schork, 2008; Williams, Haney, Lee, Kong, & Blumenthal, 1980).

Why is this? Ironson and colleagues (1992) asked people with heart disease to recall something that made them angry. They then compared the experience of anger with stressful events that increased heart rate but were not associated with anger. For example, some participants imagined making a speech to defend themselves against a charge of shoplifting. Heart rates during these angry and stressful situations were then compared with heart rates that increased as a result of exercise. Investigators found that the ability of the heart to pump blood efficiently through the body dropped significantly during anger but not during stress or exercise. In fact, remembering being angry was sufficient to cause the anger effect. If participants were really angry, their heart-pumping efficiency dropped more, putting them at risk for dangerous disturbances in heart rhythm.

This study was the first to prove that anger affects the heart through decreased pumping efficiency, at least in people who have heart disease. This was confirmed in a large study examining 13,171 participants (Kucharska-Newton *et al.*, 2014). The incidence of heart failure was greater among those with high trait anger as compared to those with low or moderate trait anger, and men had a higher risk for heart failure than women. Suarez and colleagues (2002) demonstrated how inflammation produced by an overactive immune system in particularly hostile individuals may contribute to clogged arteries (and decreased heart-pumping efficiency).

Interestingly, it seems that adopting a forgiving attitude can neutralize the effects of anger on cardiovascular activity. Larsen *et al.* (2012) had participants think about a previous offense from either an angry or a forgiving perspective or while they were distracted by focusing on a neutral topic. All of them were then distracted by focusing on the neutral topic for five minutes, after which they could ruminate on the offense. As expected, thinking about the offense from an angry perspective had negative effects on cardiovascular measures (increased blood pressure and heart rate, etc.) compared with the distraction condition, but taking a forgiving attitude not only reduced this cardiovascular reactivity to a level present in the distraction condition, but these effects were still present during the follow-up free rumination period, even compared to the distraction condition as that group began ruminating on the offense causing increases in their reactivity.

Taken together, these results provide support for the effects of anger on the heart, but shall we conclude that too much anger causes heart attacks? This would be another example of one-dimensional causal modeling. Increasing evidence, including the studies just mentioned, suggests that anger and hostility contribute to heart disease, but so do many other factors, including a genetically determined biological vulnerability. We discuss cardiovascular disease in Chapter 7.

Emotions and Psychopathology

We now know that suppressing almost any kind of emotional response, such as anger or fear, increases sympathetic nervous system activity, which may contribute to psychopathology (Barlow, Sauer-Zavala, Carl, Bullis, & Ellard, 2014, Campbell-Sills et al., 2015; Fairholme, Boisseau, Ellard, Ehrenreich, & Barlow, 2010). Other emotions seem to have a more direct effect. In Chapter 4, we study the phenomenon of *panic* and its relationship to anxiety disorders. One possibility is that a panic attack is the normal emotion of fear occurring at the wrong time, when there is nothing to fear (Barlow, 2002). Some patients with mood disorders become overly excited and joyful. Every little event is the most wonderful and exciting experience they have ever had. These individuals are suffering from *mania*, which is part of the mood disorder called *bipolar disorder*. People who suffer from mania usually alternate periods of excitement with periods of extreme sadness and distress, when they are unable to experience pleasure in life and may find it difficult to get out of bed and move around. If hopelessness becomes acute, they are at risk for suicide. This emotional state is *depression*, a defining feature of many mood disorders.

Thus, basic emotions of fear, anger, sadness or distress, and excitement may contribute to many psychological disorders and may even define them. Emotions and mood also affect our cognitive processes: If your mood is positive, then your associations, interpretations, and impressions also tend to be positive (Diener, Oishi, & Lucas, 2003). Your impression of people you first meet and even your memories of past events are colored to a great extent by your current mood. If you are consistently negative or depressed, then your memories of past events are likely to be unpleasant. The pessimist or depressed person sees the bottle as half empty, whereas the cheerful optimist sees the bottle as half full. This is a rich area of investigation for cognitive and emotion scientists (Rottenberg & Johnson, 2007; Teasdale, 1993), particularly those interested in the interconnection of cognitive and emotional processes. Leading psychopathologists are beginning to outline the nature of emotion disruption (or dysregulation) and to understand how these disruptions interfere with thinking and behavior in various psychological disorders (Barlow, Allen, & Choate, 2004; Campbell-Sills et al., 2015; Hofmann, Sawyer, Fang, & Asnaani, 2012).

2.4 Concept CHECK

Identify the following descriptions as either (a) learned helplessness, (b) modeling, (c) prepared learning, or (d) implicit memory.

1. Karen noticed that every time Tyrone behaved well at lunch, the teacher praised him. Karen decided to behave better to receive praise herself. _____

2. Josh stopped trying to please his father because he never knows whether his father will be proud or outraged. _____

3. Greg fell into a lake as a baby and almost drowned. Even though Greg has no recollection of the event, he hates to be around large bodies of water. _____

4. Juanita was scared to death of the tarantula, even though she knew it wasn't likely to hurt her. _____

Cultural, Social, and Interpersonal Factors

▶ How do cultural, social, and interpersonal factors influence abnormal behavior?

Given the neurobiological and psychological variables impinging on our lives, is there room for the influence of social, interpersonal, and cultural factors? Studies are beginning to demonstrate the substantial power and depth of such influences. Consider the following example.

Voodoo and the Evil Eye

In many cultures, individuals may suffer from *fright disorders*, which are characterized by exaggerated startle responses, and other observable fear and anxiety reactions. One example is the Latin American *susto*, which describes various anxiety-based symptoms, including insomnia, irritability, phobias, and the marked somatic symptoms of sweating and increased heart rate (tachycardia). But *susto* has only one cause: The individual believes that he or she has become the object of black magic, or witchcraft. In some cultures, the sinister influence is called the *evil eye* (Good & Kleinman, 1985; Tan, 1980), and the resulting fright disorder can be fatal. Cannon (1942), examining the Haitian phenomenon of voodoo death, suggested that the sentence of death by a medicine man may create an intolerable autonomic arousal in the participant, who has little ability to cope because there is no social support.

▲ A "possessed" person receives treatment in a voodoo ritual.

That is, friends and family ignore the individual after a brief period of grieving because they assume death has already occurred. Ultimately, the condition leads to damage to internal organs and death. Thus, from all accounts, an individual who is from a physical and psychological point of view functioning in a perfectly healthy and adaptive way suddenly dies because of marked changes in the social environment.

Gender

Gender roles have a strong and sometimes puzzling effect on psychopathology (Kistner, 2009; Maeng & Milad, 2015). The likelihood of your having a particular phobia is powerfully influenced by your gender. For example, someone who complains of an insect or small-animal phobia severe enough to prohibit field trips or visits to friends in the country is almost certain to be female, as are 90% of the people with this phobia (possible reasons for this were mentioned on pp. 62 and 63). But a social phobia strong enough to keep someone from attending parties or meetings affects men and women more or less equally but perhaps for different reasons.

We think these substantial differences have to do with, at least in part, cultural expectations of men and women, or our *gender roles*. For example, an equal number of men and women may have an experience that could lead to an insect or small-animal phobia, such as being bitten by one, but in our society it isn't always acceptable for a man to show or even admit fear. So a man is more likely to hide or endure the fear until he gets over it. It is more acceptable for women to acknowledge fearfulness, so a phobia develops.

It is also more acceptable for a man to be shy than to show fear, so he is more likely to admit social discomfort.

It even seems that men and women may respond differently to the same standardized psychological treatment (Felmingham & Bryant, 2012). After exposure therapy for post-traumatic stress disorder, both groups benefited, but women maintained their gains significantly better during a follow-up period. The authors suggest that the well-established ability of women to recall emotional memories somewhat better than men may facilitate emotional processing and long term treatment gains.

Bulimia nervosa, the severe eating disorder, occurs almost entirely in young females. Why? As you will see in Chapter 8, a cultural emphasis on female thinness plagues our society and, increasingly, societies around the world. The pressures for males to be thin are less apparent, and of the few males who develop bulimia, a substantial percentage are gay; for these individuals, cultural imperatives to be thin are present in many specific instances (Rothblum, 2002).

Finally, Taylor (2002, 2006; Taylor *et al.*, 2000) described a unique way in which females in many species respond to stress in their lives. This unique response to stress is called "tend and befriend" and refers to protecting themselves and their young through nurturing behavior (tend) and forming alliances with larger social groups, particularly other females (befriend). Taylor *et al.* (2000) supposed that this response fits better with the way females respond to stress because it builds on the brain's attachment–caregiving system and leads to nurturing and affiliative behavior. Furthermore, the response is characterized by identifiable neurobiological processes in the brain that are gender specific.

Our gender doesn't cause psychopathology. But because gender role is a social and cultural factor that influences the form and content of a disorder, we attend closely to it in the chapters that follow.

Social Effects on Health and Behavior

Many studies have demonstrated that the greater the number and frequency of social relationships and contacts, the longer you are likely to live (Miller, 2011). Conversely, the lower you score on a social index that measures the richness of your social life, the shorter your life expectancy. Studies documenting this finding have been reported in the United States (Berkman & Syme, 1979; House, Robbins, & Metzner, 1982), as well as in Sweden and Finland. They take into account existing physical health and other risk factors for dying young, such as high blood pressure, high cholesterol levels, and smoking habits, and they still produce the same result. Studies also show that social relationships seem to protect individuals against many physical and psychological disorders, such as high blood pressure, depression, alcoholism, arthritis, the progression to AIDS, and

Some fears are evolutionarily ingrained and found in people from all different cultures. However, other fears are learned and are present only within specific cultures.

Perhaps the most salient example of evolutionarily ingrained fear that people from all cultures experience is that related to physical illness from food and subsequent fear or repulsion of similar food in the future. The strong aversion to foods that make us ill was first written about by Garcia, Ervin, and Koelling (1966) and is referred to as *conditioned taste aversion*. These researchers found that unlike other negative stimuli (e.g., electric shock), this type of aversion is learned from a single pairing of food with illness. Once you have become physically ill, your brain says, "I am not taking a chance on that food again."

Whereas this is an evolutionarily ingrained fear that affects all people, there also are fears that are uniquely influenced by culture/social learning. An interesting example of a socially learned fear is that of "Koro" seen in parts of Asia. Koro refers to a fear that the penis will shrink or retract into one's abdomen, with some people even fearing that this will result in death (Garlipp, 2006). Although the perceived cause of Koro has changed over time, it has long been attributed to social influences such as witchcraft. Moreover, reports of mass episodes of Koro suggest that beliefs about the possibility of one's genitals shrinking or retracting into the body are spread through social means (such as word-of-mouth). Treatment often includes providing education about the impossibility of spontaneous genital retraction, as well as treatment for the anxiety associated with this condition.

Cases of Koro are rare in the United States, where episodes of sudden and intense anxiety generally are not accompanied by concerns about genital retraction (American Psychiatric Association, 2000). Instead, anxiety in Americans often occurs along with concerns about more widely accepted medical concerns, including that the person is having a heart attack or "going crazy." What seems to be an unbelievable fear in one culture can appear reasonable to people in other cultures. ∎

---

bearing low birth weight babies (Cobb, 1976; House, Landis, & Umberson, 1988). Conversely, the risk of depression for people who live alone is approximately 80% higher than for people who live with others, based on a count of new prescriptions for anti-depressant medication (Pulkki-Raback *et al.*, 2012). Even whether or not we come down with a cold is strongly influenced by the quality and extent of our social network (Cohen, Doyle, Skoner, Rabin, & Gwaltney, 1997).

How do social relationships have such a profound impact on our physical and psychological characteristics? We don't know for sure, but there are some intriguing hints (Cacioppo & William, 2008; Cacioppo *et al.*, 2007). Some people think interpersonal relationships give meaning to life and that people who have something to live for can overcome physical deficiencies and even delay death. You may have known an elderly person who far outlived his or her expected time to witness a significant family event, such as a grandchild's graduation from college. Once the event has passed, the person dies. Another common observation is that if one spouse in a long-standing marital relationship dies, particularly an elderly wife, the other often dies soon after, regardless of health status. It is also possible that social relationships facilitate health-promoting behaviors, such as restraint in the use of alcohol and drugs, getting proper sleep, and seeking appropriate health-care (House, Landis, & Umberson, 1988; Leserman *et al.*, 2000).

Sometimes social upheaval is an opportunity for studying the impact of social networks on individual functioning. For example, whether you live in a city or the country may be associated with your chances of developing schizophrenia, a severe disorder. Lewis, David, Andreasson, and Allsbeck (1992) found that the incidence of schizophrenia was 38% greater in men who had been raised in cities than in those raised in rural areas. We have known for a long time that more schizophrenia exists in the city than in the country, but researchers thought people with schizophrenia who drifted to cities *after* developing schizophrenia or other endemic urban factors, such as drug use or unstable family relationships, might account for the disparity. But Lewis and associates carefully controlled for such factors, and it now seems something about cities beyond those influences may contribute to the development of schizophrenia (Boydell & Allardyce, 2011; Vassos, Pederson, Murray, Collier, & Lewis, 2012). We do not yet know what it is. This finding, if it is replicated and shown to be true, may be important in view of the mass migration of individuals to overcrowded urban areas, particularly in less developed countries.

The effect of social and interpersonal factors on the expression of physical and psychological disorders also may differ with age (Charles & Carstensen, 2010; Holland & Gallagher-Thompson, 2011). Grant, Patterson, and Yager (1988) studied 118 men and women 65 years or older who lived independently. Those with fewer meaningful contacts and less social support from relatives had consistently higher levels of depression and more reports of unsatisfactory quality of life. If these individuals became physically ill, however, they had more substantial support from their families than those who were not physically ill. This finding raises the unfortunate possibility that it may be advantageous for elderly people to become physically ill, because illness allows them to re-establish the social support that makes life worth living. If further research confirms this

▲ In developing countries, personal upheaval because of political strife affects mental health.

Global Incidence of Psychological Disorders

Surveys from the World Health Organization (WHO) reveal that mental disorders account for 13% of the global burden of disease (WHO, 2015). Behavioral and mental health problems in developing countries are exacerbated by political strife, technological change, and massive movements from rural to urban areas. 10% to 20% of all primary medical services in poor countries are sought by patients with psychological disorders (WHO, 2015). Treatments for disorders such as depression and addictive behaviors that are successful in the United States can't be administered in countries where mental health-care is limited. In Cambodia, during and after the bloody reign of the Khmer Rouge, all mental health professionals either died or disappeared. As of 2006, only 26 psychiatrists were available to see 12 million people. In sub-Saharan Africa it's even worse, with only one psychiatrist per 2 million people (WHO, 2011). And despite the efforts of the Bill and Melinda Gates Foundation, there is no mention of mental health among the goals of the foundation's "Grand Challenges in Global Health" initiative. Mental disorders—especially the most common ones, such as anxiety disorders and depression—not only impose great suffering on the affected individuals, they also lead to high economic costs to society by being undertreated (Laird & Clark, 2014). In addition to their role in causation, social and cultural factors substantially maintain disorders because most societies have not yet developed the social context for alleviating and ultimately preventing them. Changing societal attitudes is just one of the challenges facing us as the century unfolds.

finding, we will know for fact what seems to make intuitive sense: involvement with their families before they become ill might help elderly people maintain their physical health (and significantly reduce health-care costs).

Finally, psychological disorders continue to carry a substantial stigma in our society (Hinshaw & Stier, 2008). To be anxious or depressed is to be weak and cowardly. To be schizophrenic is to be unpredictable and crazy. For physical injuries in times of war, we award medals. For psychological injuries, the unfortunate soldiers earn scorn and derision. Often a patient with psychological disorders does not seek health insurance reimbursement for fear a co-worker might learn about the problem. With far less social support than for physical illness, there is less chance of full recovery. We discuss some consequences of social attitudes toward psychological disorders in Chapters 3 and 14.

Life-Span Development

▶ Why should psychological disorders be considered from a life-span developmental perspective?

To understand psychopathology, we must appreciate how experiences during different periods of development may influence our vulnerability to other types of stress or to differing psychological disorders (Charles & Carstensen, 2010; Rutter, 2002).

Important developmental changes occur at all points in life. For example, adulthood, far from being a relatively stable period, is highly dynamic, with important changes occurring into old age. Erik Erikson (1982) suggested that

we go through eight major crises during our lives, each determined by our biological maturation and the social demands made at particular times. Although aspects of Erikson's theory of psychosocial development have been criticized as being too vague and not supported by research (Shaffer, 1993), it illustrates the comprehensive approach to human development advocated by life-span developmentalists. Research is beginning to confirm the importance of this approach. In one experiment, Kolb, Gibb, and

Gorny (2003) placed animals in complex environments as juveniles, as adults, or in old age when cognitive abilities were beginning to decline (senescence). They found that the environment had different effects on the brains of these animals depending on their developmental stage. Basically, the complex and challenging environments increased the size and complexity of neurons in the motor and sensory cortical regions in the adult and aged animals; however, unlike the older groups, in young animals the complex and challenging environments decreased the size and complexity of neurons in the spine. Nevertheless, this decrease was associated with enhanced motor and cognitive skills when the animals became adults, indicating that stimulating environments can affect brain function in a positive way at any age. Even prenatal experience seems to affect brain structure, because the offspring of an animal housed in a rich and complex environment during the term of her pregnancy have the advantage of more complex cortical brain circuits after birth (Kolb, Gibb, & Robinson, 2003).

Thus, we can infer that the influence of developmental stage and prior experience has an impact on the development and presentation of psychological disorders, an inference that is receiving confirmation from life-span developmental psychologists such as Laura Carstensen (Charles & Carstensen, 2010; Isaacowitz, Smith, & Carstensen, 2003). For example, in depressive (mood) disorders, children and adolescents do not receive the same benefit from antidepressant drugs as do adults (Hazell, O'Connell, Heathcote, Robertson, & Henry, 1995; Santosh, 2009), and for many of them these drugs pose risks that are not present in adults (Santosh, 2009). Also, the gender distribution in depression is approximately equal until puberty, when it becomes more common in girls (Compas *et al.*, 1997; Hankin, Wetter, & Cheely, 2007).

Like a fever, a particular behavior or disorder may have a number of causes. The principle of **equifinality** is used in developmental psychopathology to indicate that we must consider a number of paths to a given outcome (Cicchetti, 1991). There are many examples of this principle. A delusional syndrome may be an aspect of schizophrenia, but it can also arise from amphetamine abuse. Delirium, which involves difficulty focusing attention, often occurs in older adults after surgery, but it can also result from thiamine deficiency or renal (kidney) disease.

Different paths can also result from the interaction of psychological and biological factors during various stages of development. How someone copes with impairment resulting from physical causes may have a profound effect on that person's overall functioning. For example, people with documented brain damage of approximately equal severity may have different levels of disorder. Those with healthy systems of social support, consisting of family and friends, as well as highly adaptive personality characteristics, such as confidence in their abilities to overcome challenges, may experience only mild behavioral and cognitive disturbance despite physical (organic) pathology. Those without comparable support and personality may be incapacitated. Even the content of delusions and hallucinations that may accompany a disorder, and the degree to which they are difficult to cope with, is partly determined by psychological and social factors.

Researchers are exploring not only what makes people experience particular disorders but what protects others from having the same difficulties. If you were interested in why someone would be depressed, for example, you would look at people who display depression. But you could also study people in similar situations and from similar backgrounds who are not depressed. An example of this approach is research on "resilient" children, which suggests that social factors may protect some children from being hurt by stressful experiences, such as one or both parents suffering a psychiatric disturbance (Becvar, 2013; Goldstein, & Brooks, 2013). The presence of a caring adult friend or relative can offset the negative stresses of this environment, as can the child's own ability to understand and cope with unpleasant situations. More recently, scientists are discovering strong biological differences in responsiveness to trauma and stress as a result of protective factors such as social support or having a strong purpose or meaning of life (Charney, 2004; Ozbay *et al.*, 2007). Perhaps if we better understand why some people do not encounter the same problems as others in similar circumstances, we can better understand particular disorders, assist those who suffer from them, and even prevent some cases from occurring.

Conclusions

In this overview of modern approaches to psychopathology, we have seen that contributions from (1) psychoanalytic theory, (2) behavioral and cognitive science, (3) emotional influences, (4) social and cultural influences, (5) genetics, (6) neuroscience, and (7) life-span developmental factors must be considered when we think about psychopathology. Even though our knowledge is incomplete, you can see why we could never resume the one-dimensional thinking typical of the various historical traditions described in Chapter 1.

equifinality Developmental psychopathology principle that a behavior or disorder may have several causes.

And yet, books about psychological disorders and news reports in the popular press often describe the causes of disorders in one-dimensional terms without considering other influences. For example, how many times have you heard that a psychological disorder such as depression is caused by a "chemical imbalance" without considering other possible causes? When you read that a disorder is *caused* by a chemical imbalance, it sounds like all you have to do is correct the imbalance in neurotransmitter activity to "cure" the problem.

There is no question that psychological disorders are associated with altered neurotransmitter activity and other aspects of brain function (a chemical imbalance). But you have learned in this chapter that a chemical imbalance could, in turn, be caused by psychological or social factors such as stress, strong emotional reactions, difficult family interactions, changes caused by aging, or, most likely, some interaction of these factors. Therefore, it is inaccurate and misleading to say that a psychological disorder is "caused" by a chemical imbalance, even though chemical imbalances almost certainly exist.

If you learn one thing from this book, it should be that psychological disorders do not have just one cause. They have many causes—these causes all interact with one another—and we must understand this interaction to appreciate the origins of psychological disorders. To do this requires a multidimensional integrative approach. In chapters covering specific psychological disorders, we return to

cases like Judy's and consider them from this multidimensional integrative perspective. But first we must explore the processes of assessment and diagnosis used to measure and classify psychopathology.

2.5 Concept CHECK

Fill in the blanks to complete these statements relating to the cultural, social, and developmental factors influencing psychopathology.

1. What we _____ is strongly influenced by our social environments.

2. The likelihood of your having a particular phobia is powerfully influenced by your _____.

3. A large number of studies have demonstrated that the greater the number and frequency of _____ relationships and _____, the longer you are likely to live.

4. The effect of social and interpersonal factors on the expression of physical and psychological disorders may differ with _____.

5. The principle of _____ is used in developmental psychopathology to indicate that we must consider a number of paths to a given outcome.

SUMMARY

One-Dimensional versus Multidimensional Models

How does a multidimensional model of causality differ from a unidimensional model?

▸ The causes of abnormal behavior are complex and fascinating. Psychological disorders are caused by a complex interplay of nature (biology) and nurture (psychosocial factors).

What are the key influences comprising the multidimensional model of abnormal behavior?

▸ To identify the causes of a psychological disorder in a given person we must consider the interaction of all relevant dimensions: genetic contributions, the role of the nervous system, behavioral and cognitive processes, emotional influences, social and interpersonal influences, and developmental factors. Thus, we have arrived at a multidimensional integrative approach to the causes of psychological disorders.

Genetic Contributions to Psychopathology

How do genes interact with environmental factors to affect behavior?

▸ The genetic influence on much of our development and most of our behavior, personality, and even IQ score is polygenic—that is, influenced by many genes. This is assumed to be the case in abnormal behavior as well, although research is beginning to identify specific small groups of genes that relate to some major psychological disorders.

What kinds of models have been proposed to describe this interaction?

▸ In studying causal relationships in psychopathology, researchers look at the interactions of genetic and environmental effects. In the diathesis–stress model, individuals are assumed to inherit certain vulnerabilities that make them susceptible to a disorder when the right kind of stressor comes along. In the gene–environment correlation or reciprocal gene–environment model, the individual's genetic vulnerability toward a certain disorder may make it more likely that the person will experience the stressor that, in turn, triggers the genetic vulnerability and thus the disorder. In epigenetics, the immediate effects of the environment (such as early stressful experiences) influence cells that turn certain genes on or off. This effect may be passed down through several generations.

Neuroscience and Its Contributions to Psychopathology

What are neurotransmitters, and how are they involved in abnormal behavior?

▶ Within the nervous system, levels of neurotransmitter and neuroendocrine activity interact to modulate and regulate emotions and behavior and contribute to psychological disorders. Of the neurotransmitters that may play a key role, we investigated five: serotonin, gamma-aminobutyric acid (GABA), glutamate, norepinephrine, and dopamine.

What are the functions of different brain regions, and what are their roles in psychopathology?

▶ The brain includes the *brain stem*, which handles most essential automatic functions, and the *forebrain*. The *hindbrain* contains the *medulla*, *pons*, and *cerebellum; it* regulates many automatic activities, such as breathing. The *midbrain* coordinates movement. At the top of the brain stem are the *thalamus* and *hypothalamus*, which regulate behavior and emotion. The *limbic system* includes the *hippocampus, cingulate gyrus, septum,* and *amygdala*, which help regulate our emotions and are involved with the basic drives of sex, aggression, hunger, and thirst. The *cerebral cortex* allows us to plan, reason, and create.

Behavioral and Cognitive Science

What are the key differences between behavioral and cognitive explanations of the origins of mental illness?

▶ The field of cognitive science provides a valuable perspective on how behavioral and cognitive influences affect learning and adaptation. Clearly, such influences not only contribute to psychological disorders but also may modify brain functioning, brain structure, and even genetic expression. We examined some research in this field by looking at learned helplessness, modeling, prepared learning, and implicit memory.

Emotions

What role do emotions play in psychopathology?

▶ Emotions have a direct and dramatic impact on our functioning and play a central role in many mental disorders. Mood, a persistent period of emotionality, is often evident in psychological disorders.

Cultural, Social, and Interpersonal Factors

How do cultural, social, and interpersonal factors influence abnormal behavior?

▶ Social and interpersonal influences affect both psychological disorders and biology.

Life-Span Development

Why should psychological disorders be considered from a life-span developmental perspective?

▶ In considering a multidimensional integrative approach to psychopathology, it is important to remember the principle of equifinality, which reminds us that we must consider the various paths to a particular outcome, not just the result.

▰ Key Terms

multidimensional integrative approach, 33
genes, 36
diathesis–stress model, 38
vulnerability, 38
gene–environment correlation model, 39
epigenetics, 41
neuroscience, 41
neuron, 42
action potentials, 43
terminal button, 43
synaptic cleft, 43
neurotransmitters, 43

excitatory, 43
inhibitory, 43
hormone, 46
brain circuits, 48
agonist, 48
antagonist, 48
inverse agonist, 48
reuptake, 48
glutamate, 49
gamma-aminobutyric acid (GABA), 49
serotonin, 49
norepinephrine (also known as noradrenaline), 50

dopamine, 50
cognitive science, 55
learned helplessness, 55
modeling (or observational learning), 56
prepared learning, 57
implicit memory, 57
flight or fight response, 58
emotion, 59
mood, 59
affect, 59
circumplex model, 59
equifinality, 65

Answers to Concept Checks

2.1

1. b; 2. a (best answer) or c; 3. e;
4. a (initial), c (maintenance)

2.2

1. F (first 22 pairs); 2. T; 3. T; 4. F
(reciprocal gene–environment model);
5. F (complex interaction of both
nature and nurture)

2.3

1. b; 2. c; 3. f; 4. g; 5. d; 6. e; 7. h; 8. a

2.4

1. b; 2. a; 3. d; 4. c

2.5

1. fear; 2. gender; 3. social, contacts;
4. age; 5. Equifinality

Chapter Quiz

1. Which approach to psychopathology considers biological, social, behavioral, emotional, cognitive, and developmental influences?
   a. genetic
   b. multidimensional
   c. interpersonal
   d. psychodynamic

2. Much of our development and most of our behavior, personality, and IQ are influenced by many genes, each contributing only a portion of the overall effect. This type of influence is known as:
   a. reciprocal
   b. polygenic
   c. integrative
   d. recessive

3. Behavioral genetics research has concluded that:
   a. genetic factors do not contribute to most psychological disorders
   b. genetic factors that contribute to psychological disorders account for most of the explanation
   c. for any one psychological disorder there is probably one gene that explains most of its development
   d. genetic factors that contribute to psychological disorders account for less than half of the explanation

4. Which portion of the brain is responsible for complex cognitive activities such as reasoning, planning, and creating?
   a. limbic system
   b. basal ganglia
   c. hindbrain
   d. cerebral cortex

5. John is startled by a loud crash in his apartment. His heart immediately starts beating rapidly and the pace of his breathing increases. What part of the nervous system is responsible for this physiological response?
   a. central nervous system
   b. sympathetic nervous system
   c. limbic system
   d. parasympathetic nervous system

6. Which neurotransmitter appears to reduce overall arousal and dampen emotional responses?
   a. serotonin
   b. gamma-aminobutyric acid
   c. norepinephrine
   d. dopamine

7. Martin Seligman noted that when rats or other animals encounter conditions over which they have no control, they give up attempting to cope and seem to develop the animal equivalent of depression. This is referred to as:
   a. learned depression
   b. learned fear
   c. learned helplessness
   d. learned defenselessness

8. Which concept explains why fears of snakes and heights are more common (or more easily learned) than fears of cats and flowers?
   a. equifinality
   b. vulnerability
   c. prepared learning
   d. observational learning

9. Recent research on implicit memory suggests that:
   a. people can recall colors more quickly than words
   b. memories can change based on the implicit structures of the brain
   c. implicit memory is more relevant to psychopathology than explicit memory
   d. memories outside our awareness may influence psychopathology, just as Freud speculated

10. Emotion comprises all of the following components EXCEPT:
    a. behavior
    b. cognition
    c. genetics
    d. physiology
    (See Appendix A for answers.)

Clinical Assessment, Diagnosis, and Research in Psychopathology

3

CHAPTER OUTLINE

Assessing Psychological Disorders

Key Concepts in Assessment
The Clinical Interview
Physical Examination
Behavioral Assessment
Psychological Testing
Neuropsychological Testing
Neuroimaging: Pictures
 of the Brain
Psychophysiological Assessment

Diagnosing Psychological Disorders

Classification Issues
Diagnosis before 1980
DSM-III and *DSM-III-R*
DSM-IV and *DSM-IV-TR*
DSM-5
Beyond *DSM-5:* Dimensions
 and Spectra

Conducting Research in Psychopathology

Basic Components of a
 Research Study
Statistical versus Clinical
 Significance
The "Average" Client

Types of Research Methods

Studying Individual Cases
Research by Correlation
Research by Experiment
Single-Case Experimental Designs

Genetics and Behavior across Time and Cultures

Studying Genetics
Studying Behavior over Time
Studying Behavior across Cultures
The Power of a Program of Research
Replication
Research Ethics

iStock.com/izusek

Use scientific reasoning to interpret behavior:	▶ Identify basic biological, psychological, and social components of behavioral explanations (e.g., inferences, observations, operational definitions and interpretations) (APA SLO 2.1a) *(see textbook pages 81–82, 104–106)*
Describe applications that employ discipline-based problem solving:	▶ Describe examples of relevant and practical applications of psychological principles to everyday life (APA SLO 4.1, 4.4) *(see textbook pages 71–84)*
Interpret, design, and conduct basic psychological research:	▶ Describe research methods used by psychologists including their respective advantages and disadvantages [APA SLO 2.4a] *(see textbook pages 95–110)* ▶ Define and explain the purpose of key research concepts that characterize psychological research (e.g., hypothesis, operational definition) [APA SLO 2.4c] *(see textbook pages 92–95)*
Incorporate sociocultural factors in scientific inquiry:	▶ Recognize the systematic influences of sociocultural, theoretical, and personal biases on the research enterprise and evaluate the effectiveness with which researchers address those influences in psychological research [APA SLO 2.5a] *(see textbook pages 85–91)*
Apply ethical standards to psychological science and practice:	▶ Discuss relevant ethical issues that reflect principles in the APA Code of Ethics [APA SLO 3.1c] *(see textbook page 111)*

* Portions of this chapter cover learning outcomes suggested by the American Psychological Association (2013) in their guidelines for the undergraduate psychology major. Chapter coverage of these outcomes is identified above by APA Goal and APA Suggested Learning Outcome (SLO).

Assessing Psychological Disorders

▶ What are clinical assessment and diagnosis?

▶ What are the main methods used in clinical assessment?

The processes of clinical assessment and diagnosis are central to the study of psychopathology and, ultimately, to the treatment of psychological disorders. **Clinical assessment** is the systematic evaluation and measurement of psychological, biological, and social factors in an individual presenting with a possible psychological disorder. **Diagnosis** is the process of determining whether the particular problem afflicting the individual meets all criteria for a psychological disorder, as set forth in the fifth edition of the *Diagnostic and Statistical Manual of Mental Disorders,* or *DSM-5* (American Psychiatric Association, 2013). In this chapter, we examine the development of the *DSM* into a widely used classification system for abnormal behavior. Then we review the many assessment techniques available to the clinician as well as diagnostic issues and the related challenges of classification. But first, let's consider the case of Frank.

Frank... • *Young, Serious, and Anxious*

Frank was referred to one of our clinics for evaluation and possible treatment of severe distress and anxiety centering on his marriage. He reported that he was 24-years-old and that this was the first time he had ever seen a mental health professional. He wasn't sure that he needed (or wanted) to be there, but he felt he was beginning to "come apart" because of his marital difficulties. He figured that it wouldn't hurt to come once to see whether we could help. What follows is a transcript of parts of this first interview.

Therapist: What sorts of problems have been troubling you during the past month?

Frank: I'm beginning to have a lot of marital problems. I was married about 9 months ago, but I've been really tense around the house and we've been having a lot of arguments.

Therapist: Is this something recent?

Frank: Well, it wasn't too bad at first, but it's been worse lately. I've also been really uptight in my job, and I haven't been getting my work done.

Note that we always begin by asking the patient to describe the difficulties that brought him or her to the office. When dealing with adults, or children old enough (or verbal enough) to tell us their story, this strategy tends to break the ice. After Frank described this major problem in some detail, we asked him about his marriage, his job, and other current life circumstances.

Frank reported that he had worked in an auto body repair shop for the past 4 years and that, 9 months previously, he had married a 17-year-old woman. After getting a better picture of his current situation, we returned to his feelings of distress and anxiety.

Therapist: When you feel uptight at work, is it the same kind of feeling you have at home?

Frank: Pretty much; I just can't seem to concentrate, and lots of times I lose track of what my wife's saying to me, which makes her mad and then we'll have a big fight.

Therapist: Are you thinking about something when you lose your concentration, such as your work, or maybe other things?

Frank: Oh, I don't know; I guess I just worry a lot.

Therapist: What do you find yourself worrying about most of the time?

Frank: Well, I worry about getting fired and then not being able to support my family. A lot of the time I feel like I'm going to catch something—you know, get sick and not be able to work. Basically I guess I'm afraid of getting sick and then failing at my job and in my marriage, and having my parents and her parents both telling me what an ass I was for getting married in the first place.

During the first 10 minutes or so of the interview, Frank seemed to be quite tense and anxious and would often look down at the floor while he talked, glancing up only occasionally to make eye contact. Sometimes his right leg would twitch a bit. Although it was not easy to see at first because he was looking down, Frank was also closing his eyes tightly for a period of 2 to 3 seconds. It was during these periods when his eyes were closed that his right leg would twitch.

The interview proceeded for the next half hour, exploring marital and job issues. It became increasingly clear that Frank was feeling inadequate and anxious about handling situations in his life. By this time, he was talking freely and looking up a little more at the therapist, but he was continuing to close his eyes and twitch his right leg slightly.

Therapist: Are you aware that once in a while you're closing your eyes while you're telling me this?

Frank: I'm not aware all the time, but I know I do it.

Therapist: Do you know how long you've been doing that?

Frank: Oh, I don't know, maybe a year or two.

Therapist: Are you thinking about anything when you close your eyes?

Frank: Well, actually I'm trying not to think about something.

Therapist: What do you mean?

Frank: Well, I have these really frightening and stupid thoughts, and it's hard to even talk about it.

Therapist: The thoughts are frightening?

Frank: Yes, I keep thinking I'm going to take a fit, and I'm just trying to get that out of my mind.

Therapist: Could you tell me more about this fit?

Frank: Well, you know, it's those terrible things where people fall down and they froth at the mouth, and their tongues come out, and they shake all over. You know, seizures. I think they call it epilepsy.

Therapist: And you're trying to get these thoughts out of your mind?

Frank: Oh, I do everything possible to get those thoughts out of my mind as quickly as I can.

Therapist: I've noticed you moving your leg when you close your eyes. Is that part of it?

Frank: Yes, I've noticed if I really jerk my leg and pray real hard for a little while the thought will go away.

(Excerpt from Nelson, R. O., & Barlow, D. H., 1981. Behavioral assessment: Basic strategies and initial procedures. In D. H. Barlow, Ed., *Behavioral assessment of adult disorders*. New York: Guilford Press.)

What's wrong with Frank? The first interview reveals an insecure young man experiencing substantial stress as he questions whether he is capable of handling marriage and a job. He reports that he loves his wife and wants the marriage to work and is attempting to be conscientious in his job, from which he derives a lot of satisfaction. Also, for some reason, he is having troubling thoughts about seizures. How do we determine whether Frank has a psychological disorder or is simply suffering the normal stresses of a new marriage and could benefit from marital counseling? The purpose of this chapter is to illustrate how mental health clinicians address these types of questions to make diagnoses and plan treatment.

Key Concepts in Assessment

The process of clinical assessment in psychopathology has been likened to a funnel (Antony & Barlow, 2010; Urbina, 2014). The clinician begins by collecting information across a broad range of the individual's functioning to determine

....

clinical assessment Systematic evaluation and measurement of psychological, biological, and social factors in a person presenting with a possible **psychological disorder**.

diagnosis Process of determining whether a **presenting problem** meets the established criteria for a specific **psychological disorder**.

where the source of the problem may lie. The clinician then narrows the focus by ruling out problems in some areas and concentrating on areas that seem most relevant.

Three basic concepts help determine the value of clinicians' assessments: reliability, validity, and standardization (Ayearst & Bagby, 2010) (see ● Figure 3.1). One of the more important requirements of these assessments is that they be reliable. **Reliability** is the degree to which a measurement is consistent. One way psychologists improve their reliability is by carefully designing their assessment devices and then conducting research on them to ensure that two or more raters will get the same answers (called *interrater reliability*). They also determine whether these assessment techniques are stable across time. In other words, if you go to a clinician on Tuesday and are told you have an IQ of 110, you should expect a similar result if you take the same test again on Thursday. This is known as *test–retest reliability*.

Validity is whether something measures what it is designed to measure. Comparing the results of an assessment measure under consideration with the results of others that are better known helps determine the validity of the first measure. This comparison is called *concurrent* or *descriptive validity*. For example, if the results from a standard, but long, IQ test were essentially the same as the results from a new, brief version, you could conclude that the brief version had concurrent validity. *Predictive validity* is how well your assessment tells you what will happen in the future. For example, does it predict who will succeed in school (which is one of the goals of an IQ test)?

Standardization is the process by which a certain set of standards or norms is determined for a technique to make its use consistent across different measurements.

The standards might apply to the procedures of testing, scoring, and evaluating data. For example, the assessment might be given to large numbers of people who differ on important factors such as age, race, gender, socioeconomic status, and diagnosis; their scores would be pooled with other individuals like them and then be used as a standard, or norm, for comparison purposes. For example, if you are an African American male, 19-years-old, and from a middle-class background, your score on a psychological test should be compared with the scores of others like you and not to the scores of different people, such as a group of women of Asian descent in their 60s from working-class backgrounds. Reliability, validity, and standardization are important to all forms of psychological assessment.

Clinical assessment consists of a number of strategies and procedures that help clinicians acquire the information they need to understand their patients and assist them. These procedures include a clinical interview and mental status exam; often a physical examination; a behavioral observation and assessment; and psychological tests (if needed).

The Clinical Interview

The clinical interview gathers information on current and past behavior, attitudes, and emotions, as well as a detailed history of the individual's life in general and of the presenting problem. Clinicians determine when the problem started and identify other events (for example, trauma or physical illness) that might have occurred about the same time. In addition, most clinicians gather information on the patient's interpersonal and social history, including family makeup, and on the individual's upbringing. Information on sexual development, religious attitudes, cultural concerns (such as stress induced by discrimination), and educational history are also collected.

The Mental Status Exam

To organize information obtained during an interview, many clinicians use a **mental status exam**. A mental status exam involves the systematic observation of an individual's behavior. We all perform mental status exams whenever we interact with others, but clinicians must organize their observations in a way that gives them sufficient information to determine whether a psychological disorder might be present (Nelson & Barlow, 1981). Mental status exams can be structured and detailed (Cooper, Sartorius, & Wing, 1974; Mooney & Wiger, 2015), but mostly they are performed in the course of interviewing or observing a patient. The exam covers five categories:

1. *Appearance and behavior.* The clinician notes any overt physical behaviors, such as Frank's leg twitch, as well as the individual's dress, general appearance, posture, and facial expression. For example, slow and effortful motor behavior, sometimes referred to as *psychomotor retardation,* may indicate severe depression.

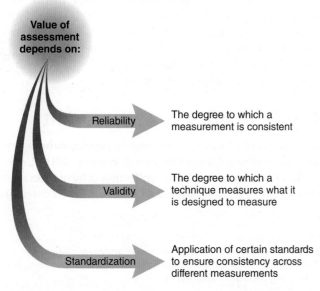

● **Figure 3.1** Concepts that determine the value of clinical assessments.

Value of assessment depends on:

Reliability → The degree to which a measurement is consistent

Validity → The degree to which a technique measures what it is designed to measure

Standardization → Application of certain standards to ensure consistency across different measurements

2. *Thought processes.* When clinicians listen to a patient talk, they're getting a good idea of that person's thought processes. What is the rate or flow of speech? Does the person talk quickly or slowly? What about continuity of speech? Does the patient make sense when talking, or are ideas presented with no apparent connection? In some patients with schizophrenia, a disorganized speech pattern, referred to as *loose association* or *derailment,* is quite noticeable. Clinicians sometimes ask specific questions. If the patient shows difficulty with continuity or rate of speech, a clinician might ask, "Can you think clearly, or do your thoughts tend to be mixed up or come slowly?" In addition to rate or flow and continuity of speech, what about the content? Is there any evidence of *delusions* (distorted views of reality)? The individual might also have *ideas of reference,* in which everything everyone else does somehow relates back to the individual. The most common example would be thinking that a conversation between two strangers on the other side of the room must be about you. *Hallucinations* are things a person sees or hears when those things really aren't there.

3. *Mood and affect.* Determining mood and affect is an important part of the mental status exam. *Mood* is the predominant feeling state of the individual. Does the person appear to be down in the dumps or continually elated? Does the individual talk in a depressed or hopeless fashion? How pervasive is this mood? *Affect,* by contrast, refers to the feeling state that accompanies what we say at a given point. Usually our affect is "appropriate"; that is, we laugh when we say something funny or look sad when we talk about something sad. If a friend just told you his mother died and is laughing about it, you would think it strange, to say the least. A mental health clinician would note that your friend's affect is "inappropriate." Then again, you might observe your friend talking about a range of happy and sad things with no affect whatsoever. In this case, a mental health clinician would say the affect is "blunted" or "flat."

4. *Intellectual functioning.* Clinicians make a rough estimate of others' intellectual functioning just by talking to them. Do they seem to have a reasonable vocabulary? Can they talk in abstractions and metaphors? How is the person's memory? Clinicians usually make a rough estimate of intelligence that is noticeable only if it deviates from normal.

5. *Sensorium.* The term *sensorium* refers to our general awareness of our surroundings. Does an individual know what the date is, what time it is, who or where he or she is, and who you are? People with brain damage or dysfunction may not know the answer to these questions. If the patient knows who he is and who the clinician is and has a good idea of the time and place, the clinician would say that the patient's sensorium is "clear" and is "oriented times three" (to person, place, and time).

These observations allow the clinician to make a preliminary determination of which areas of the patient's behavior and condition should be assessed in more detail. If psychological disorders remain a possibility, the clinician may begin to hypothesize which disorders might be present.

Returning to our case, what have we learned from this mental status exam (see ● Figure 3.2)? Observing Frank's persistent motor behavior in the form of a twitch led to the discovery of a connection (functional relationship) with his thoughts regarding seizures. Beyond this, his appearance was appropriate, and the flow and content of his speech was reasonable; his intelligence was within normal limits, and he was oriented. He did display an anxious mood; however, his affect was appropriate to what he was saying. These observations suggested that we attempt to identify the possible existence of a disorder characterized by intrusive, unwanted thoughts and the attempt to resist them—in other words, *obsessive-compulsive disorder (OCD).* Later we describe some specific assessment strategies that we would use with Frank.

Patients usually have a good idea of their major concerns in a general sense ("I'm depressed" or "I'm phobic"); occasionally, the problem reported by the patient may not be the major issue in the eyes of the clinician. The case of Frank illustrates this point well: He complained of distress relating to marital problems, but the clinician decided that the principal difficulties lay elsewhere. Frank wasn't attempting to hide anything from the clinician. Frank just didn't think his intrusive thoughts were the major problem; in addition, talking about them was difficult for him because they were frightening.

This example illustrates the importance of conducting the clinical interview in a way that elicits the patient's trust. Mental health professionals are trained in methods that put patients at ease and facilitate communication, including non-threatening ways of seeking information and appropriate listening skills. Information provided by patients to clinicians is protected by laws of "privileged communication" or confidentiality in most states; that is, even if authorities want the information the therapist has received from the patient, they cannot have access to it without the expressed consent of the patient. The only

reliability Degree to which a measurement is consistent—for example, over time or among different raters.

validity Degree to which a technique measures what it purports to measure.

standardization Process of establishing specific norms and requirements for a measurement technique to ensure it is used consistently across measurement occasions. This includes instructions for administering the measure, evaluating its findings, and comparing these to data for large numbers of people.

mental status exam Relatively coarse preliminary test of a client's judgment, orientation to time and place, and emotional and mental state; typically conducted during an initial interview.

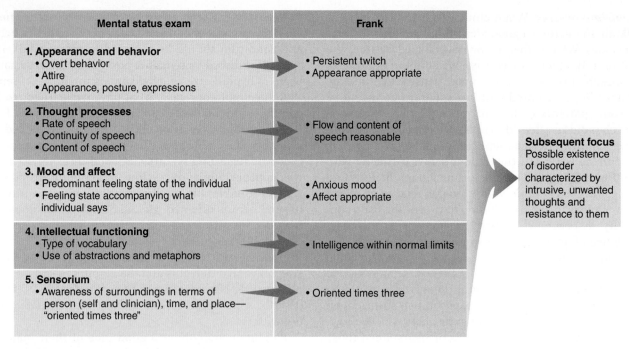

Mental status exam	Frank
1. Appearance and behavior • Overt behavior • Attire • Appearance, posture, expressions	• Persistent twitch • Appearance appropriate
2. Thought processes • Rate of speech • Continuity of speech • Content of speech	• Flow and content of speech reasonable
3. Mood and affect • Predominant feeling state of the individual • Feeling state accompanying what individual says	• Anxious mood • Affect appropriate
4. Intellectual functioning • Type of vocabulary • Use of abstractions and metaphors	• Intelligence within normal limits

5. Sensorium
• Awareness of surroundings in terms of
   person (self and clinician), time, and place—
   "oriented times three"
	• Oriented times three

Subsequent focus
Possible existence of disorder characterized by intrusive, unwanted thoughts and resistance to them

● **Figure 3.2** Components of the mental status exam.

exception to this rule occurs when the clinician judges that some harm or danger to either the patient or someone else is imminent. At the outset of the initial interview, the therapist should inform the patient of the confidential nature of their conversation and the conditions under which that confidence would not hold.

Semistructured Clinical Interviews

Unstructured interviews follow no systematic format. *Semistructured interviews* are made up of questions that have been carefully phrased and tested to elicit useful information in a consistent manner so that clinicians can be sure they have inquired about the most important aspects of particular disorders (Galletta, 2013; Summerfeldt, Kloosterman, & Antony, 2010). Clinicians may also depart from set questions to follow up on specific issues—thus the label "semistructured." Because the wording and sequencing of questions has been carefully worked out over a number of years, the clinician can feel confident that a semistructured interview will accomplish its purpose. The disadvantage is that it robs the interview of some of the spontaneous quality of two people talking about a problem. Also, if applied too rigidly, a semistructured interview may inhibit the patient from volunteering useful information that is not directly relevant to the questions being asked. Because of these few drawbacks associated with semistructured interviews, fully structured interviews administered wholly by a computer have not caught on, although they are used in some settings.

An increasing number of mental health professionals, however, do routinely use semistructured interviews. Some

are quite specialized. For example, Frank's clinician, in probing further into a possible obsessive-compulsive disorder, might use the *Anxiety and Related Disorders Interview Schedule for DSM-5* (*ADIS-5*; Brown & Barlow, 2014). According to this interview schedule the clinician first asks if the patient is bothered by thoughts, images, or impulses (obsessions) or feels driven to experience some behavior or thought repeatedly (compulsions). Based on a 9-point rating scale that ranges from "never" to "constantly," the clinician then asks the patient to rate each obsession on two measures: persistence–distress (how often it occurs and how much distress it causes) and resistance (types of attempts the patient makes to get rid of the obsession). For compulsions, the patient provides a rating of their frequency.

Physical Examination

Many patients with problems first go to a family physician and are given a physical. If the patient presenting with psychological problems has not had a physical exam in the past year, a clinician might recommend one. Many problems presenting as disorders of behavior, cognition, or mood may have a relationship to a temporary toxic state caused by bad food, the wrong amount or type of medicine, or onset of a medical condition. For example, thyroid difficulties may produce symptoms that mimic certain anxiety disorders. Withdrawal from cocaine often produces panic attacks, but many patients presenting with panic attacks are reluctant to volunteer information about their addiction, which may lead to an inappropriate diagnosis and improper treatment.

If a current medical condition or substance abuse situation exists, the clinician must ascertain whether it is merely co-existing or is causal, usually by looking at the onset of the problem. If a patient has suffered from severe bouts of depression for the past five years but within the past year has also developed hypothyroid problems or begun taking a sedative drug, the clinician would not conclude the depression was caused by the medical or drug condition. On the other hand, if the depression developed simultaneously with the initiation of sedative drugs and diminished considerably when the drugs were discontinued, the clinician would be likely to conclude the depression was part of a substance-induced mood disorder.

Behavioral Assessment

The mental status exam is one way to begin to sample how people think, feel, and behave and how these actions might contribute to or explain their problems. **Behavioral assessment** takes this process one step further by using direct observation to formally assess an individual's thoughts, feelings, and behavior in specific contexts. Behavioral assessment may be more appropriate than an interview in terms of assessing individuals who are not old enough or skilled enough to report their problems and experiences.

In behavioral assessment, target behaviors are identified and observed with the goal of determining the factors that seem to influence them. It may seem easy to identify what is bothering a particular person (i.e., the target behavior), but even this aspect of assessment can be challenging. For example, when the mother of a 7-year-old child with a severe conduct disorder came to one of our clinics for assistance, she told the clinician, after much prodding, that her son "didn't listen to her" and he sometimes had an "attitude." The boy's schoolteacher, however, painted a different picture. She spoke candidly of his verbal violence—of his threats toward other children and to herself. To get a clearer picture of the situation at home, the clinician visited one afternoon. Approximately 15 minutes after the visit began, the boy got up from the kitchen table without removing the drinking glass he was using. When his mother meekly asked him to put the glass in the sink, he picked it up and threw it across the room, sending broken glass throughout the kitchen. He giggled and went into his room to watch television. "See," she said. "He doesn't listen to me!"

Obviously, this mother's description of her son's behavior at home didn't portray what he was really like. It also didn't accurately describe her response to his violent outbursts. Clearly this was more than simple disobedience. We developed strategies to teach the mother how to make requests of her son and how to follow up if he was violent.

Most clinicians assume that a complete picture of a person's problems requires direct observation in naturalistic environments. But going into a person's home, workplace, or school isn't always possible or practical, so clinicians sometimes arrange *analogue*, or similar, settings (Haynes, Yoshioka, Kloezeman, & Bello, 2009). For example, one of us studies children with autism spectrum disorder (a disorder characterized by social withdrawal and communication problems). The reasons for self-hitting (called *self-injurious*) behavior in this disorder are discovered by placing the children in simulated situations, such as sitting alone at home, playing with a sibling, or being asked to complete a difficult task (Durand, Hieneman, Clarke, Wang, & Rinaldi, 2013). Observing how the children behave in these different situations helps determine why they hit themselves so that we can design a successful treatment to eliminate the behavior.

The ABCs of Observation

Observational assessment is usually focused on the here and now. Therefore, the clinician's attention is usually directed to the immediate behavior, its antecedents (what happened just before the behavior), and its consequences (what happened afterward) (Haynes, O'Brien, & Kaholokula, 2011). To use the example of the violent boy, an observer would note that the sequence of events was (1) his mother asking him to put his glass in the sink (antecedent), (2) the boy throwing the glass (behavior), and (3) his mother's lack of response (consequence). This antecedent–behavior–consequence sequence (the ABCs) might suggest that the boy was being reinforced for his violent outburst by not having to clean up his mess. And because there was no negative consequence for his behavior (his mother didn't scold or reprimand him), he will probably act violently the next time he doesn't want to do something (see ● Figure 3.3).

This is an example of a relatively *informal observation*. A problem with this type of observation is that it relies on the observer's recollection, as well as interpretation, of the events. *Formal observation* involves identifying specific

● **Figure 3.3** The ABCs of observation.

behavioral assessment Measuring, observing, and systematically evaluating (rather than inferring) the client's thoughts, feelings, and behavior in the actual problem situation or context.

behaviors that are observable and measurable (called an *operational definition*). For example, it would be difficult for two people to agree on what "having an attitude" looks like. An operational definition, however, clarifies this behavior by specifying that this is "any time the boy does not comply with his mother's reasonable requests." Once the target behavior is selected and defined, an observer writes down each time it occurs, along with what happened just before (antecedent) and just after (consequence). The goal of collecting this information is to see whether there are any obvious patterns of behavior and then to design a treatment based on these patterns.

Self-Monitoring

People can also observe their own behavior to find patterns, a technique known as **self-monitoring** or self-observation (Haynes *et al.*, 2011). People trying to quit smoking may write down the number of cigarettes they smoke and the times when and places where they smoke. This observation can tell them exactly how big their problem is (for example, they smoke two packs a day) and what situations lead them to smoke more (for example, talking on the phone). The use of smartphones is becoming common in these types of assessments (e.g., Faurholt-Jepsen *et al.*, 2015; Swenderman *et al.*, 2015).

A more formal and structured way to observe behavior is through checklists and *behavior rating scales*, which are used as assessment tools before treatment and then periodically during treatment to assess changes in the person's behavior (Maust *et al.*, 2012). Of the many such instruments for assessing a variety of behaviors, the *Brief Psychiatric Rating Scale* (Clarkin, Howieson, & McClough, 2008), assesses 18 general areas of concern. Each symptom is rated on a 7-point scale from 0 (not present) to 6 (extremely severe). The rating scale screens for moderate to severe psychotic disorders and includes items such as somatic concern (preoccupation with physical health, fear of physical illness), guilt feelings (shame, remorse for past behavior), and grandiosity (exaggerated self-opinion, conviction of unusual power or abilities) (American Psychiatric Association, 2006).

A phenomenon known as *reactivity* can distort any observational data. Any time you observe how people behave, the mere fact of your presence may cause them to change their behavior (Haynes *et al.*, 2011). To test reactivity, you can tell a friend you are going to record every time she says the word *like*. Just before you reveal your intent, however, count the times your friend uses this word in a 5-minute period. You will probably find that your friend uses the word less often when you are recording it. The same phenomenon occurs if you observe your own behavior, or self-monitor. Behaviors people want to increase, such as talking more in class, tend to increase, and behaviors people want to decrease, such as smoking, tend to decrease when they are self-monitored (Cohen, Edmunds, Brodman, Benjamin, & Kendall, 2012).

Psychological Testing

We are confronted with so-called psychological tests in the popular press almost every week: "12 Questions to Test Your Relationship," "Are You a Type 'Z' Personality?" Many such tests are no more than entertainment. They are typically made up for the purposes of the article and include questions that, on the surface, seem to make sense. In reality, they tell us little. In contrast, the tests used to assess psychological disorders must meet the strict standards we have noted. They must be reliable so that two or more people administering the same test to the same person will come to the same conclusion about the problem, and they must be valid so that they measure what they say they are measuring (Barker, Pistrang, & Elliot, 2016).

Psychological tests include specific tools to determine cognitive, emotional, or behavioral responses that might be associated with a specific disorder and more general tools that assess long-standing personality features, such as a tendency to be suspicious. For example, intelligence testing is designed to determine the structure and patterns of cognition. Neuropsychological testing determines the possible contribution of brain damage or cognitive dysfunction to the patient's condition. Neuroimaging uses sophisticated technology to assess brain structure and function.

Projective Testing

To assess unconscious processes in psychological disorders, psychoanalysts have developed several assessment measures known as **projective tests**. They include a variety of methods in which ambiguous stimuli, such as pictures of people or things, are presented to people who are asked to describe what they see. The theory is that people project their own personality and unconscious fears onto other people and things—in this case, the ambiguous stimuli—and, without realizing it, reveal their unconscious thoughts to the therapist.

Because these tests are based in psychoanalytic theory, they are controversial. Even so, the use of projective tests is quite common, with a majority of clinicians administering them at least occasionally (Butcher, 2009). Two of the more widely used are the Rorschach inkblot test and the Thematic Apperception Test. The *Rorschach inkblot test* is one of the early projective tests. In its current form, the test includes 10 inkblot pictures that serve as the ambiguous stimuli (see ● Figure 3.4). The examiner presents the inkblots one by one to the person being assessed, who responds by telling what he sees. Unfortunately, much of the early use of the Rorschach is extremely controversial because of the lack of data on reliability or validity, among other things. Until relatively recently, therapists administered the test in any way they saw fit, although one of the most important tenets of assessment is that the same test be given in the same way each time—that is, according to standardized procedures. If you encourage someone to give more detailed

● **Figure 3.4** This inkblot resembles the ambiguous figures presented in the Rorschach test.

like the Rorschach, the TAT is based on the notion that people will reveal their unconscious mental processes in their stories about the pictures (McGrath & Carroll, 2012).

Several variations of the TAT have been developed for different groups, including a Children's Apperception Test (CAT) and a Senior Apperception Test (SAT). In addition, modifications of the test have evolved for use with a variety of racial and ethnic groups (Aronow, Weiss, & Reznikoff, 2013). These modifications have included changes not only in the appearance of people in the pictures but also in the situations depicted. Like the Comprehensive System used with the Rorschach, researchers have developed formal scoring systems for TAT stories, including the Social Cognition and Object Relations Scale (Stein, Hilsenroth, Slavin-Mulford, & Pinkser, 2011; Westen, 1991).

Unfortunately, the TAT and its variants continue to be used inconsistently. How the stories people tell about these pictures are interpreted depends on the examiner's frame of reference, as well as what the patient may say. It is not surprising, therefore, that questions remain about its use in psychopathology (Hunsley & Mash, 2011).

Most clinicians who use projective tests have their own methods of administration and interpretation. When used to get people to open up and talk about how they feel, the ambiguous stimuli in these tests can be valuable tools. Their relative lack of reliability and validity, however, makes them less useful as diagnostic tests.

Personality Inventories

The questions in psychological tests published in mainstream magazines typically make sense when you read them. This is called having *face validity:* The wording of the questions seems to fit the type of information desired. But is this necessary? Paul Meehl presented his position on this issue more than 60 years ago and subsequently influenced a whole field of study on **personality inventories** (self-report questionnaires that assess personal traits) (Meehl, 1945). Meehl pointed out that what is necessary from these types of tests is not whether the questions necessarily make sense on the surface but, rather, what the answers to these questions predict. If we find that people who have schizophrenia tend to respond "true" to "I have never been in love with

answers during one testing session but not during a second session, for example, you may get different responses as the result of your administering the test differently on the two occasions—not because of problems with the test or administration by another person (interrater reliability).

To respond to the concerns about reliability and validity, John Exner developed a standardized version of the Rorschach inkblot test, called the *Comprehensive System* (Exner, 2003). Exner's system of administering and scoring the Rorschach specifies how the cards should be presented, what the examiner should say, and how responses should be recorded (Mihura, Meyer, Dumitrascu, & Bombel, 2012). Still, critics of the Rorschach question whether research on the Comprehensive System supports its use as a valid assessment technique for people with psychological disorders (Mihura *et al.*, 2012; Wood, Garb, Nezworski, Lillienfeld, & Duke, 2015).

The *Thematic Apperception Test (TAT)* is perhaps the best-known projective test after the Rorschach (Clarkin *et al.*, 2008). It consists of a series of 31 cards—30 with pictures on them and one blank card—although only 20 cards are typically used during each administration. The instructions ask the person to tell a dramatic story about the picture. The tester presents the pictures and tells the patient, "This is a test of imagination, one form of intelligence". The person being assessed can "let your imagination have its way, as in a myth, fairy story, or allegory" (Stein, 1978, p. 186). Again,

self-monitoring Action by which clients observe and record their own behaviors as either an assessment of a problem and its change or a treatment procedure that makes them more aware of their responses. Also known as *self-observation*.

projective tests Psychoanalytically based measure that presents ambiguous stimuli to clients on the assumption that their responses can reveal their **unconscious** conflicts. Such tests are inferential and lack high **reliability** and **validity**.

personality inventories Self-report questionnaire that assesses personal traits by asking respondents to identify descriptions that apply to themselves.

anyone," then it doesn't matter whether we have a theory of love and schizophrenia. What matters is if people with certain disorders tend, as a group, to answer certain questions in a certain way, this pattern may predict who else has this disorder. The content of the questions becomes irrelevant; again, the importance lies in what the answers predict.

Although many personality inventories are available, we look at the most widely used personality inventory in the United States, the *Minnesota Multiphasic Personality Inventory (MMPI)*. The MMPI was developed in the late 1930s and early 1940s and first published in 1943 (Hathaway & McKinley, 1943). In stark contrast to projective tests, which rely heavily on theory for an interpretation, the MMPI and similar inventories are based on an *empirical* approach, that is, the collection and evaluation of data. The administration of the MMPI is straightforward. The individual being assessed reads statements and answers either "true" or "false." Following are some statements from the MMPI:

▶ Cry readily
▶ Often happy for no reason
▶ Am being followed
▶ Fearful of things or people that can't hurt me

There is little room for interpretation of MMPI responses. A problem with administering the MMPI, however, is the time and tedium of responding to the 550 items on the original version and now the 567 items on the MMPI-2 (published in 1989). A version of the MMPI that is appropriate for adolescents is also available—MMPI-A (published in 1992)—and other versions are being adapted for people in different cultures (Okazaki, Okazaki, & Sue, 2009). Individual responses on the MMPI are not examined; instead, the pattern of responses is reviewed to see whether it resembles patterns from groups of people who have specific disorders. Each group is represented on separate standard scales (Nichols, 2011) (see Table 3.1).

TABLE 3.1 | Scales of the MMPI-2

Validity Scales	Characteristics of High Scorers
Cannot Say (reported as a raw score) — (?CNS)	Reading difficulties, guardedness, confusion and distractibility, depression, rebellion, or obsessiveness
Variable Response Inconsistency (VRIN)	Responding to questions in a manner inconsistent with psychological disorder
True Response Inconsistency (TRIN)	Answering questions all true or all false
Infrequency (F)	Exhibit randomness of responses or psychotic psychopathology
Back F (F_b)	Changing the way the questions are answered at the end of the test
Infrequency — Psychopathology (F_r)	Claiming more psychiatric symptoms than expected
Symptom Validity (FBS)	Trying to appear to have more disabilities but not psychotic
Lie (L)	Dishonest, deceptive, and/or defended
Correction (K)	Person is very guarded and defensive
Superlative Self-Presentation (S)	Believes in human goodness and denies personal flaws
Clinical Scales	**Characteristics of High Scorers**
Hypochondriasis	Somatizers, possible medical problems
Depression	Dysphoric, possibly suicidal
Hysteria	Highly reactive to stress, anxious, and sad at times
Psychopathic deviate	Antisocial, dishonest, possible drug abusers
Masculinity–femininity	Exhibit lack of stereotypical masculine interests, aesthetic and artistic
Paranoia	Exhibit disturbed thinking, ideas of persecution, possibly psychotic
Psychasthenia	Exhibit psychological turmoil and discomfort, extreme anxiety
Schizophrenia	Confused, disorganized, possible hallucinations
Mania	Manic, emotionally labile, unrealistic self-appraisal
Social introversion	Very insecure and uncomfortable in social situations, timid

SOURCE: Excerpted from the MMPI®-2 (Minnesota Multiphasic Personality Inventory®-2) Manual for Administration, Scoring, and Interpretation, revised edition. Copyright © 2001 by the Regents of the University of Minnesota. Used by permission of the University of Minnesota Press. All rights reserved. "MMPI-2" and "Minnesota Multiphasic Personality Inventory-2" are trademarks owned by the Regents of the University of Minnesota.

Fortunately, clinicians can have these responses scored by computer; the program also includes an interpretation of the results, thereby reducing problems of reliability. One concern that arose early in the development of the MMPI was the potential of some people to answer in ways that would downplay their problems; skilled individuals would ascertain the intent of statements such as "Worry about saying things that hurt people's feelings," and fake the answers. To assess this possibility, the MMPI includes additional scales that determine the validity of each administration. For example, on the Lie scale, a statement such as "Have hurt someone when angry," when answered "false" might be an indication that the person may be falsifying answers to look good. The other scales are the Infrequency scale, which measures false claims about psychological problems or determines whether the person is answering randomly, and the Subtle Defensiveness scale, which assesses whether the person sees herself in unrealistically positive ways (Nichols, 2011).

● Figure 3.5 is an MMPI *profile* or summary of scores from an individual being clinically assessed. Before we tell you why this 27-year-old man (we'll call him James S.) was being evaluated, let's see what his MMPI profile tells us about him (note that these scores were obtained on the original version of the MMPI). The first three data points represent scores on the validity scales; the high scores on these scales were interpreted to mean that James S. made a naive attempt to look good for the evaluator and may have

● **Figure 3.5** Minnesota Multiphasic Personality Inventory Profile Form. (Copyright © 1942, 1943, 1948, 1970, 1948, 1976, 1982 by the Regents of the University of Minnesota. Used by permission of the University of Minnesota Press. All rights reserved. "MMPI" and "Minnesota Multiphasic Personality Inventory" are trademarks owned by the Regents of the University of Minnesota.)

been trying to fake an appearance of having no problems. Another important part of his profile is the very high score on the psychopathic deviation scale, which measures the tendency to behave in antisocial ways. The interpretation of this score from the assessing clinician is that James S. is "aggressive, unreliable, irresponsible; unable to learn from experience; may initially make a good impression but then psychopathic features will surface in longer interactions or under stress."

Why was James S. being evaluated? He was a young man with a criminal record that began in his childhood. He was evaluated as part of his trial for kidnapping, raping, and murdering a middle-aged woman. Throughout his trial, he made up a number of contradictory stories to make himself look innocent (remember his high scores on the validity scales), including blaming his brother. There was overwhelming evidence of his guilt, however, and he was sentenced to life in prison. His answers on the MMPI resembled those of others who act in violent and antisocial ways.

The MMPI is one of the most extensively researched assessment instruments in psychology (Cox, Weed, & Butcher, 2009; Friedman, Bonlinskey, Levak, & Nichols, 2014). The original standardization sample—the people who first responded to the statements and set the standard for answers—included people from Minnesota who had no psychological disorders and several groups of people who had particular disorders. The more recent versions of this test, including the MMPI-2-Revised Form (Ben-Porath & Tellegen, 2008), eliminate problems with the original version, problems partly resulting from the original selective sample of people and partly resulting from the wording of questions (Ranson, Nichols, Rouse, & Harrington, 2009). For example, some questions were sexist. One item on the original version asks the respondent to say whether she has ever been sorry she is a girl (Worell & Remer, 1992). Other items were criticized as insensitive to cultural diversity. Items dealing with religion, for example, referred almost exclusively to Christianity (Butcher, Graham, Williams, & Ben-Porath, 1990). The MMPI-2 has also been standardized with a sample that reflects the 1980 U.S. Census figures, including African Americans and Native Americans for the first time. In addition, new items have been added that deal with contemporary issues such as type A personality, low self-esteem, and family problems.

Intelligence Testing

In 1904, a French psychologist, Alfred Binet, and his colleague, Théodore Simon, were commissioned by the French government to develop a test that would identify "slow learners" who would benefit from remedial help. The psychologists identified tasks that presumably measured the skills children need to succeed in school, including tasks of attention, perception, memory, reasoning, and verbal comprehension. Binet and Simon gave their series of tasks to a large number of children; they then eliminated tasks that did not separate the slow learners from the children who did well in school. After several revisions and administrations, they had a test that was easy to administer and did what it was designed to do—predict academic success. In 1916, Lewis Terman of Stanford University translated a revised version of this test for use in the United States; it became known as the *Stanford-Binet test*.

The test provided a score known as an **intelligence quotient**, or **IQ**. Initially, IQ scores were calculated by using the child's *mental age*. For example, a child who passed all questions on the 7-year-old level and none on the 8-year-old level received a mental age of 7. This mental age was then divided by the child's *chronological age* and multiplied by 100 to get the IQ score. There were problems, however, with using this formula for calculating an IQ score. For example, a 4-year-old needed to score only 1 year above his or her chronological age to be given an IQ score of 125, although an 8-year-old had to score 2 years above his or her chronological age to be given the same score. Current tests use what is called a *deviation IQ*. A person's score is compared only with scores of others of the same age. The IQ score, then, is an estimate of how much a child's performance in school will deviate from the average performance of others of the same age (Fletcher & Hattie, 2011).

In addition to the revised version of the Stanford-Binet (*Stanford-Binet 5;* Roid, 2003), there is another widely used set of intelligence tests, developed by psychologist David Wechsler. The Wechsler tests include versions for adults (*Wechsler Adult Intelligence Scale*, fourth edition, or *WAIS-IV*), children (*Wechsler Intelligence Scale for Children*, fifth edition, or *WISC-V*), and young children (*Wechsler Preschool and Primary Scale of Intelligence*, fourth edition, or *WPPSI-IV*). All these tests contain *verbal scales* (which measure vocabulary, knowledge of facts, short-term memory, and verbal reasoning skills) and *performance scales* (which assess psychomotor abilities, non-verbal reasoning, and ability to learn new relationships) (Weiss *et al.*, 2015).

One of the biggest mistakes non-psychologists (and a distressing number of psychologists) make is to confuse IQ with intelligence. An IQ score significantly higher than average means the person has a significantly greater than average chance of doing well in our educational system. By contrast, a score significantly lower than average suggests the person will probably not do well in school. Does a lower-than-average IQ score mean a person is not intelligent? Not necessarily. First, there are numerous reasons for a low score. For example, if the IQ test is administered in English and that is not the person's native language, the results will be affected.

Perhaps more important, however, is the continued development of models that answer the question "What constitutes intelligence?" Remember that the IQ tests measure abilities such as attention, perception, memory, reasoning, and verbal comprehension. But do these skills represent the totality of what we consider intelligence?

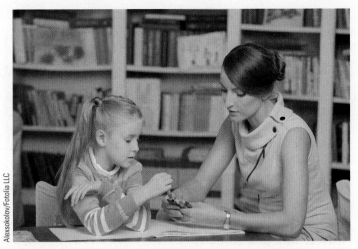

▲ This child is concentrating on a standard psychological assessment test.

Some recent theorists believe that what we think of as intelligence involves more, including the ability to adapt to the environment, the ability to generate new ideas, and the ability to process information efficiently (Gottfredson & Saklofske, 2009). In general, however, IQ tests tend to be reliable, and to the extent that they predict academic success, they are valid assessment tools.

Neuropsychological Testing

Sophisticated tests now exist that can pinpoint the location of brain dysfunction. Fortunately, these techniques are generally available and relatively inexpensive, and technological advances in interactive teleconferencing have led to efforts to conduct such assessments for people in remote areas (Lezak, Howieson, Bigler, & Tranel, 2012). **Neuropsychological tests** measure abilities in areas such as receptive and expressive language, attention and concentration, memory, motor skills, perceptual abilities, and learning and abstraction.

A fairly simple neuropsychological test often used with children is the *Bender Visual–Motor Gestalt Test* (Brannigan & Decker, 2006). A child is given a series of cards on which are drawn various lines and shapes. The task is for the child to copy what is drawn on the card. The errors on the test are compared with test results of other children of the same age; if the number of errors exceeds a certain figure, then brain dysfunction is suspected. Two advanced tests of organic (brain) damage that allow more precise determinations of the location of the problem are the *Luria-Nebraska Neuropsychological Battery* (Golden, Hammeke, & Purisch, 1980) and the *Halstead-Reitan Neuropsychological Battery* (Reitan & Davison, 1974).

Research on the validity of neuropsychological tests suggests they may be useful for detecting organic damage. One study found that the Halstead-Reitan and the Luria-Nebraska test batteries were equivalent in their abilities to detect damage and were about 80% correct (Goldstein & Shelly, 1984). These types of studies, however, raise the issue of **false positives** and **false negatives**. For any assessment strategy, there will be times when the test shows a problem when none exists (false positive) and times when no problem is found even though some difficulty is present (false negative). Neuropsychological tests are therefore used primarily as screening devices and are routinely paired with other assessments to improve the likelihood that real problems will be found.

Neuroimaging: Pictures of the Brain

In recent years we have developed the ability to take increasingly accurate pictures of the structure and function of the brain, using a technique called **neuroimaging** (Filippi, 2015). Neuroimaging can be divided into two categories: (1) procedures that examine the structure of the brain, such as the size of various parts and whether there is any damage, and (2) procedures that examine the actual functioning of the brain by mapping blood flow and other metabolic activity.

Images of Brain Structure

The first neuroimaging technique, developed in the early 1970s, uses multiple X-ray exposures of the brain from different angles. As with any X-ray, these are partially blocked or attenuated more by bone and less by brain tissue. The degree of blockage is picked up by detectors in the opposite side of the head. A computer then reconstructs pictures of various slices of the brain. This procedure, which takes about 15 minutes, is called a *computerized axial tomography (CAT) scan* or *CT scan*. CT scans are particularly useful in locating brain tumors, injuries, and other structural and anatomical abnormalities. One difficulty, however, is that these scans, like all X-rays, involve repeated x-radiation, which poses some risk of cell damage (Filippi, 2015).

Several more recently developed procedures give greater resolution (specificity and accuracy) than a CT scan without the risks of X-ray tests. In nuclear *magnetic resonance imaging (MRI)*, the patient's head is placed in a high-strength magnetic field through which radio

intelligence quotient (IQ) Score on an intelligence test estimating a person's deviation from average test performance.

neuropsychological test Assessment of brain and nervous system functioning by testing an individual's performance on behavioral tasks.

false positive Assessment error in which pathology is reported (i.e., test results are positive) when none is actually present.

false negative Assessment error in which no pathology is noted (i.e., test results are negative) when one is actually present.

neuroimaging Sophisticated computer-aided procedure that allows nonintrusive examination of nervous system structure and function.

iStock.com/JohnnyGreig

▲ The patient is being positioned for an MRI scan.

have been reported for obsessive-compulsive disorder and bipolar disorder. Because PET scanning is expensive, these facilities are available only in large medical centers.

A second procedure used to assess brain functioning is called *single photon emission computed tomography (SPECT)*. It works much like PET, although a different tracer substance is used; this procedure is somewhat less accurate. It is also less expensive, however, and requires far less sophisticated equipment to pick up the signals. Therefore, SPECT is used more often than PET scans.

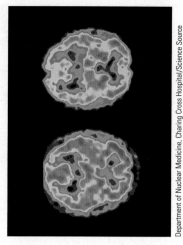

Department of Nuclear Medicine, Charing Cross Hospital/Science Source

▲ PET scans display areas of high and low neurological activity, as in these scans of a brain affected by HIV.

frequency signals are transmitted. These signals "excite" the brain tissue, altering the protons in the hydrogen atoms. The alteration is measured, along with the time it takes the protons to "relax" or return to normal. Where there are lesions or damage, the signal is lighter or darker (Filippi, 2015). Technology now exists that allows the computer to view the brain in layers, which enables precise examination of the structure. Although an MRI is more expensive than a CT scan and originally took as long as 45 minutes, this is changing as technology improves. Another disadvantage of MRI at present is that someone undergoing the procedure is totally enclosed inside a narrow tube with a magnetic coil surrounding the head. People who are somewhat claustrophobic often cannot tolerate an MRI.

Images of Brain Functioning

Several widely used procedures are capable of measuring the actual functioning of the brain, as opposed to its structure. The first is called *positron emission tomography (PET) scan*. Subjects undergoing a PET scan are injected with a tracer substance attached to radioactive isotopes, or groups of atoms that react distinctively. This substance interacts with blood, oxygen, or glucose. When parts of the brain become active, blood, oxygen, or glucose rushes to these areas of the brain, creating "hot spots" picked up by detectors that identify the location of the isotopes. Thus, we can learn what parts of the brain are working and what parts are not. These images can be superimposed on MRI images to show the precise location of the active areas. PET scans are used increasingly to look at varying patterns of metabolism that might be associated with different disorders. Recent PET scans have demonstrated that many patients with early Alzheimer's-type dementia show reduced glucose metabolism in the parietal lobes. Other intriguing findings

The most exciting advances involve MRI procedures that have been developed to work more quickly than the regular MRI (Filippi, 2015). These procedures take only milliseconds and, therefore, can actually take pictures of the brain at work, recording its changes from one second to the next. Because these procedures measure the functioning of the brain, they are called *functional MRI*, or *fMRI*. fMRI procedures have largely replaced PET scans in the leading brain-imaging centers because they allow researchers to see the immediate response of the brain to a brief event, such as seeing a new face. BOLD-fMRI (Blood-Oxygen-Level-Dependent fMRI) is currently the most common fMRI technique used to study psychological disorders (Filippi, 2015).

Psychophysiological Assessment

Yet another method for assessing brain structure and function specifically and nervous system activity generally is called **psychophysiological assessment**. As the term implies, *psychophysiology* refers to measurable changes in the nervous system that reflect emotional or psychological events. The measurements may be taken either directly from the brain or peripherally from other parts of the body.

Frank feared that he might have seizures. If we had any reason to suspect he might have periods of memory loss or exhibit bizarre, trance-like behavior, if only for a short period, it would be important for him to have an **electroencephalogram (EEG)**. Measuring electrical activity in the head related to the firing of a specific group of neurons reveals brain wave activity; brain waves come from the low-voltage electrical current that runs through the neurons. In an EEG, electrodes are placed directly

Carl Friston of Stichman Medical Equipment, Medford, MA

(a) (b) (c)

▲ A horizontal brain section (a) in a SPECT image clearly reveals parietal lobe damage in a person with schizophrenia. Images (b) and (c) are MRI photographs. SPECT images show metabolic activity and thus indicate the relationship between the person's brain and the person's behavior. The higher-resolution MRI images show tissue variations.

on various places on the scalp to record the different low-voltage currents.

We have learned much about EEG patterns in the past decades (Kim, Schulz, Wilde, & Yudofsky, 2008). Usually we measure ongoing electrical activity in the brain. When brief periods of EEG patterns are recorded in response to specific events, such as hearing a psychologically meaningful stimulus, the response is called an *event-related potential (ERP)* or *evoked potential*. We have learned that EEG patterns are often affected by psychological or emotional factors and can be an index of these reactions, or a psychophysiological measure. In a normal, healthy, relaxed adult, waking activities are characterized by a regular pattern of changes in voltage termed *alpha waves*.

Many types of stress-reduction treatments attempt to *increase* the frequency of the alpha waves, often by relaxing the patients in some way. The alpha wave pattern is associated with relaxation and calmness. During sleep, we pass through several stages of brain activity, at least partially identified by EEG patterns. During the deepest, most relaxed stage, typically occurring 1 to 2 hours after a person falls asleep, EEG recordings show a pattern of *delta waves*. These brain waves are slower and more irregular than the alpha waves, which is normal for this stage of sleep. If frequent delta wave activity occurred during the waking state, it might indicate dysfunction of localized areas of the brain.

Psychophysiological assessment of other bodily responses may also play a role in assessment. These responses include heart rate, respiration, and *electrodermal responding*, formerly referred to as *galvanic skin response (GSR)*, which is a measure of sweat gland activity controlled by the peripheral nervous system. Assessing psychophysiological response to emotional stimuli is important in many disorders, one being post-traumatic

stress disorder. Stimuli such as sights and sounds associated with the trauma evoke strong psychophysiological responses, even if the patient is not fully aware that this is happening.

Physiological measures are also important in the assessment and treatment of conditions such as headaches and hypertension (Hazlett-Stevens & Bernstein, 2012); they form the basis for the treatment we call *biofeedback*. In biofeedback, levels of physiological responding, such as blood pressure readings, are fed back to the patient (provided on a continuous basis) by meters or gauges so that the patient can try to regulate these responses.

Physiological assessment requires a great deal of skill and some technical expertise. Even when administered properly, the measures sometimes produce inconsistent results because of procedural or technical difficulties or the nature of the response itself. Therefore, only clinicians specializing in certain disorders in which these measures are particularly important are likely to make extensive use of psychophysiological recording equipment, although more straightforward applications, such as monitoring heart rate during relaxation exercises, are more common. More sophisticated psychophysiological assessment is most often used in theoretical investigations of the nature of certain psychological disorders, particularly emotional disorders (Barlow, 2002; Ovsiew, 2005).

· ·

psychophysiological assessment Measurement of changes in the nervous system reflecting psychological or emotional events such as **anxiety**, **stress**, and sexual arousal.

electroencephalogram (EEG) Measure of electrical activity patterns in the brain, taken through electrodes placed on the scalp.

Part A

The mental status exam includes five categories: (a) appearance and behavior, (b) thought processes, (c) mood and affect, (d) intellectual functioning, and (e) sensorium. Identify which part of the mental status exam is being performed in the following situations.

1. Dr Swan listened carefully to Joyce's speech pattern, noting its speed, content, and continuity. He noticed no loose association but did hear indications of delusional thoughts and visual hallucinations. _____

2. Andrew arrived at the clinic accompanied by police, who had found him dressed only in shorts although the temperature was 23°F. He was reported to the police by someone who saw him walking slowly down the street, making strange faces, and talking to himself. _____

3. When Lisa was brought to Dr Miller's office, he asked if she knew the date and time, her identity, and where she was. _____

4. Dr Jones viewed as inappropriate Tim's laughter after discussing his near-fatal incident and noted that Tim appeared to be elated. _____

5. Holly's vocabulary and memory seemed adequate, leading Dr Adams to estimate that she was of average intelligence. _____

Part B

Check your understanding of reliability and validity by marking each test R (reliable) or NR (not reliable) and V (valid) or NV (not valid).

6. ___, ___ EEG to show electrical activity in the brain of someone who has seizures

7. ___, ___ Rorschach inkblots

8. ___, ___ Structured interviews with definite answers

Diagnosing Psychological Disorders

▶ How is psychiatric diagnosis carried out?

Thus far, we have looked at Frank's functioning on an individual basis; that is, we have closely observed his behavior, cognitive processes, and mood, and we have conducted *semistructured interviewing*, **behavioral assessment**, and psychological tests. These operations tell us what is unique about Frank, and what he may have in common with other individuals.

Learning how Frank may resemble other people in terms of the problems he presents is important for several reasons. If in the past people came in with similar problems or psychological profiles, we can go back and find a lot of information from their cases that might be applicable to Frank's case. We can see how the problems began for those other individuals, what factors seemed influential, and how long the problem or disorder lasted. Did the problem in the other cases just go away on its own? If not, what kept it going? Did it need treatment? Most important, what treatments seemed to relieve the problem for those other individuals? These general questions are useful because they evoke a wealth of clinical and research information that enables the investigator to make certain inferences about what will happen next and what treatments may work. In other words, the clinician can form general conclusions and establish a *prognosis*, a term we discussed in Chapter 1 that refers to the likely future course of a disorder under certain conditions.

Both strategies are essential in the study and treatment of psychopathology. If we want to determine what is unique about an individual's personality, cultural background, or circumstances, we use what is known as an **idiographic strategy** (Barlow & Nock, 2009). This information lets us tailor our treatment to the person. But to take advantage of the information already accumulated on a particular problem or disorder, we must be able to determine a general class of problems to which the presenting problem belongs. This is known as a **nomothetic strategy**. When we identify a specific psychological disorder, we are making a diagnosis. We can also identify a general class or grouping of problems by determining a particular personality profile on a psychological test such as the MMPI. Before proceeding, let's define some additional terms more precisely.

The term **classification** itself is broad, referring simply to any effort to construct groups or categories and to assign objects or people to these categories on the basis of their shared attributes or relations—a nomothetic strategy. If the classification is in a scientific context, it is most often called **taxonomy**, which is the classification of entities for scientific purposes, such as insects, rocks, or—if the subject is psychology—behaviors. If you apply a taxonomic system to psychological or medical phenomena or other clinical areas, you use the word **nosology**. All diagnostic systems used in health-care settings, such as those for infectious diseases, are nosological systems. The term **nomenclature** describes the names or labels of the disorders that make up the nosology (for example, anxiety or mood disorders). Most mental health professionals in North America use the classification system contained in the *DSM-5* (American Psychiatric Association, 2013).

Classification Issues

Classification is at the heart of any science, and much of what we have said about it is common sense. When we are dealing with human behavior, however, the subject of classification becomes controversial. Some people have questioned whether it is proper or ethical to classify human behavior. Even among those who recognize the necessity of classification, major controversies have arisen in several areas. Within psychopathology, for example, definitions of "normal" and "abnormal" are questioned, as is the assumption that a behavior or cognition is part of one disorder and not another. Some would prefer to talk about behavior and feelings on a continuum from happy to sad or fearful to non-fearful rather than to create such categories as mania, depression, and phobia. For better or worse, classifying behavior and people is something we all do. Few of us talk about our own emotions or those of our friends by using a number on a scale (where 0 is totally unhappy and 100 is totally happy), although this approach might be more accurate. ("How do you feel about that?" "About 65.") Rather, we talk about being happy, sad, angry, depressed, fearful, and so on.

Categorical and Dimensional Approaches

How can we classify human behavior? We have already alluded to two possibilities. We can have distinct categories of disorders that have little or nothing in common with one another; for example, you either hear voices talking to you from the refrigerator (auditory hallucination) and have other symptoms of schizophrenia, or you don't. Alternatively, we can quantify the various attributes of a psychological disorder along several dimensions, coming up with a composite score. An MMPI profile is a good example; another is "dimensionalizing" a disorder—for example, depression, on a continuum of severity from feeling mildly depressed in the morning (something most of us experience once in a while) to feeling so deeply depressed and hopeless that suicide seems the only solution. Each system has its strengths and its faults (Blashfield *et al.*, 2014; LeBeau, Bogels, Moller, & Craske, 2015). Let's look at both.

The **classical (or pure) categorical approach** to classification assumes that every diagnosis has a clear underlying pathophysiological cause, such as a bacterial infection or a malfunctioning endocrine system, and that each disorder is unique. When diagnoses are thought of in this way, the causes could be psychological or cultural instead of pathophysiological, but there is still only one set of causative

factors per disorder, which does not overlap with those of other disorders. Because each disorder is fundamentally different from every other, we need only one set of defining criteria, which everybody in the category has to meet. If the criteria for a major depressive episode are (1) the presence of depressed mood, (2) significant weight loss or gain when not dieting, (3) diminished ability to think or concentrate, and seven additional specific symptoms, then, to be diagnosed with depression, an individual would have to meet all of the criteria. In that case, according to the classical categorical approach, the clinician would know the cause of the disorder.

Classical categorical approaches are quite useful in medicine. It is extremely important for a physician to make accurate diagnoses. If a patient has a fever accompanied by stomach pain, the doctor must determine quickly whether the cause is stomach flu or an infected appendix. To understand the cause of symptoms (infected appendix) is to know what treatment will be effective (surgery). But if someone is depressed or anxious, is there a similar type of underlying cause? Probably not. Most psychopathologists believe psychological and social factors interact with biological factors to produce a disorder. Therefore, the mental health field has not adopted a classical categorical model of psychopathology. The classical categorical approach is clearly inappropriate to the complexity of psychological disorders (Lillienfeld, 2014; Widiger & Edmundson, 2011).

A second strategy is a **dimensional approach**, in which we note the variety of cognitions, moods, and behaviors with which the patient presents and quantify them on a scale. For example, on a scale of 1 to 10, a patient might be rated as severely anxious (10), moderately depressed (5), and mildly manic (2) to create a profile of emotional functioning (10, 5, 2). Although dimensional approaches have

....

idiographic strategy A close and detailed investigation of an individual emphasizing what makes that person unique. (Compare with **nomothetic strategy**.)

nomothetic strategy Identification and examination of large groups of people with the same disorder to note similarities and develop general laws.

classification Assignment of objects or people to categories on the basis of shared characteristics.

taxonomy System of naming and **classification** (for example, of specimens) in science.

nosology **Classification** and naming system for medical and psychological phenomena.

nomenclature In a naming system or **nosology**, the actual labels or names that are applied. In **psychopathology**, these include **mood disorders** and eating disorders.

classical categorical approach **Classification** method founded on the assumption of clear-cut differences among disorders, each with a different known cause. Also known as *pure categorical approach*.

dimensional approach Method of categorizing characteristics on a continuum rather than on a binary, either-or, or all-or-none basis.

▲ Despite their wide physical variation, all dogs belong to the same class of animals.

DSM
5

DISORDER CRITERIA SUMMARY
Major Depressive Episode

Five (or more) of the following symptoms have been present during the same two-week period and represent a change from previous functioning; at least one of the symptoms is either (a) depressed mood or (b) loss of interest or pleasure.

Note: Do not include symptoms that are clearly attributable to another medical condition.

1. Depressed mood most of the day, nearly every day.
2. Markedly diminished interest or pleasure in all, or almost all, activities most of the day, nearly every day.
3. Significant weight loss when not dieting or weight gain.
4. Insomnia or hypersomnia nearly every day.
5. Psychomotor agitation or retardation nearly every day.
6. Fatigue or loss of energy nearly every day.
7. Feelings of worthlessness or excessive or inappropriate guilt nearly every day.
8. Diminished ability to think or concentrate or indecisiveness nearly every day.
9. Recurrent thoughts of death (not just fear of dying), recurrent suicidal ideation without a specific plan, or a suicide attempt or a specific plan for committing suicide.

From American Psychiatric Association. (2013). *Diagnostic and statistical manual of mental disorders* (5th ed.). Washington, DC.

been applied to psychopathology in the past—particularly to personality disorders (Blashfield *et al.*, 2014; Krueger, Hopwood, Wright, & Markon, 2014)—they have been relatively unsatisfactory (Brown & Barlow, 2009; Widiger & Edmundson, 2011). Most theorists have not been able to agree on how many dimensions are required: Some say one dimension is enough; others have identified as many as 33 (Millon, 1991, 2004).

Prototypical Approach

A third strategy for organizing and classifying behavioral disorders has found increasing support in recent years. Called a **prototypical approach**, this alternative identifies certain essential characteristics of a disorder, but it also allows certain non-essential features that do not affect the classification. For example, if someone were to ask you to describe a dog, you could easily give a general description, but you might not exactly describe a specific dog. Dogs come in different colors, sizes, and even breeds (the non-essential, dimensional features), but they all share certain characteristics that allow you to classify them separately from cats. Thus, requiring a certain number of prototypical criteria and only some of an additional number of criteria is adequate. This system is not perfect because there is a greater blurring at the boundaries of categories, and some symptoms apply to more than one disorder. For this reason, these categories are often called "fuzzy." It has the advantage, however, of fitting better with the current state of our knowledge of psychopathology than a categorical approach, and it is relatively user-friendly.

When a prototypical approach is used in classifying a psychological disorder, many possible features or properties of the disorder are listed, and any candidate must meet enough of them to fall into that category. Consider the *DSM-5* criteria defining a major depressive episode. As you can see, the criteria include many non-essential symptoms, but if you have either depressed mood or marked loss of interest or pleasure in most activities and at least four of the remaining eight symptoms, you come close enough to the prototype to meet the criteria for a major depressive

episode. One person might have depressed mood, significant weight loss, insomnia, psychomotor agitation, and loss of energy, whereas another person who also meets the criteria for major depressive episode might have markedly diminished interest or pleasure in activities, fatigue, feelings of worthlessness, difficulty thinking or concentrating, and ideas of committing suicide. Although both have the requisite five symptoms that bring them close to the prototype, they look different because they share only one symptom. This is a good example of a prototypical category. The *DSM-5* is based on this approach.

Reliability

Any system of classification should describe specific subgroups of symptoms that are clearly evident and can be readily identified by experienced clinicians. If two clinicians interview the patient at separate times on the same day (and assuming the patient's condition does not change during the day), the two clinicians should see, and perhaps measure, the same set of behaviors and emotions. The psychological disorder can thus be identified reliably (Chmielewski, Clark, Bagby, & Watson, 2015; Kraemer, 2014). If the disorder is not readily apparent to both clinicians, the resulting diagnoses might represent bias.

As we noted before, unreliable classification systems are subject to bias by clinicians making diagnoses. One of the most unreliable categories in current classification is the area of personality disorders—chronic, trait-like sets of inappropriate behaviors and emotional reactions that characterize a person's way of interacting with the world. Although great progress has been made, particularly with certain personality disorders, determining the presence or absence of this type of disorder during one interview is still difficult (Krueger *et al.*, 2014). The lack of agreement among clinicians when diagnosing personality disorders indicates that more reliable criteria are needed and may be on the way for future revisions described below (Krueger *et al.*, 2014).

Validity

In addition to being reliable, a system of nosology must be valid. Earlier we described *validity* as whether something measures what it is designed to measure. There are several types of diagnostic validity. For one, the system should have *construct validity*. This means the signs and symptoms chosen as criteria for the diagnostic category are consistently associated or "go together" and what they identify differs from other categories. Someone meeting the criteria for depression should be discriminable from someone meeting the criteria for social phobia. This discriminability might be evident not only in presenting symptoms but also in the course of the disorder and possibly in the choice of treatment. It may also predict **familial aggregation**, the extent to which the disorder would be found among the patient's relatives (Kupfer, First, & Regier, 2002; Lillienfeld, 2014).

In addition, a valid diagnosis tells the clinician what is likely to happen with the prototypical patient; it may predict the course of the disorder and the likely effect of one treatment or another. This type of validity is referred to often as *predictive validity* and sometimes as *criterion validity*, when the outcome is the criterion by which we judge the usefulness of the diagnostic category (e.g., Klaus *et al.*, 2015). Finally, there is *content validity*, which simply means that if you create criteria for a diagnosis of, say, social phobia, it should reflect the way most experts in the field think of social phobia, as opposed to, say, depression. In other words, you need to get the label right.

Diagnosis before 1980

Early efforts to classify psychopathology arose out of the biological tradition, particularly the work of Emil Kraepelin. Kraepelin first identified what we now know as the disorder of schizophrenia. His term for the disorder at the time was *dementia praecox* (Kraepelin, 1919). Dementia praecox refers to deterioration of the brain that sometimes occurs with advancing age (dementia) and develops earlier than it is supposed to, or "prematurely" (praecox). This label (later changed to *schizophrenia*) reflected Kraepelin's belief that brain pathology is the cause of this particular disorder. Kraepelin's landmark 1913 book (*Psychiatry: A Textbook for Students and Physicians*) described not only dementia

praecox but also bipolar disorder, then called *manic depressive psychosis*. Kraepelin also described a variety of organic brain syndromes. Other well-known figures in their time, such as French psychiatrist Philippe Pinel, characterized psychological disorders, including depression (melancholia), as separate entities, but Kraepelin's theorizing that psychological disorders are basically biological disturbances had the greatest impact on the development of our nosology and led to an early emphasis on classical categorical strategies.

It was not until 1948 that the World Health Organization (WHO) added a section classifying mental disorders to the sixth edition of the *International Classification of Diseases and Related Health Problems (ICD)*. This early system did not have much influence, however. Nor did the first *Diagnostic and Statistical Manual (DSM-I)*, published in 1952 by the American Psychiatric Association. Only in the late 1960s did systems of nosology begin to have some real influence on mental health professionals. In 1968, the American Psychiatric Association published a second edition of its *Diagnostic and Statistical Manual (DSM-II)*, and in 1969, WHO published the eighth edition of the *ICD*, which was all but identical to *DSM-II*, since leaders in mental health began to realize the importance of at least trying to develop a uniform system of classification. Nevertheless, these systems lacked precision, often relying heavily on unproven theories of etiology not widely accepted by all mental health professionals. To make matters worse, the systems had little reliability. Even as late as the 1970s, many countries, such as France and Russia, had their own systems of nosology. In these countries, the same disorders would be labeled and interpreted differently.

DSM-III and *DSM-III-R*

The year 1980 brought a landmark in the history of nosology: the third edition of the *Diagnostic and Statistical Manual (DSM-III)* (American Psychiatric Association, 1980). Under the leadership of Robert Spitzer, *DSM-III* departed radically from its predecessors. Two changes stood out. First, *DSM-III* attempted to take an atheoretical approach to diagnosis, relying on precise descriptions of the disorders as they presented to clinicians rather than on psychoanalytic or biological theories of etiology. With this focus, *DSM-III* became a tool for clinicians with a variety of points of view. For example, rather than classifying phobia under the broad category "neurosis," defined by intrapsychic conflicts and defense mechanisms, it was assigned its own category within a new broader group, "anxiety disorders."

The second major change in *DSM-III* was that the specificity and detail with which the criteria for identifying a disorder were listed made it possible to study their reliability

....

prototypical approach System for categorizing disorders using both essential, defining characteristics and a range of variation on other characteristics.

familial aggregation Extent to which a disorder would be found among a patient's relatives.

and validity. Although not all categories in *DSM-III* (and its 1987 revision, *DSM-III-R*) achieved perfect or even good reliability and validity, this system was a vast improvement over what was available before.

Despite numerous shortcomings, such as low reliability in identifying some disorders and arbitrary decisions on criteria for many disorders, *DSM-III* and *DSM-III-R* had a substantial impact. Maser, Kaelber, and Weise (1991) surveyed the international usage of various diagnostic systems at that time and found that *DSM-III* had become popular for a number of reasons. Primary among them were its precise descriptive format and its neutrality with regard to presuming a cause for diagnosis. The multiaxial format, which emphasizes a broad consideration of the whole individual rather than a narrow focus on the disorder alone, was also thought to be useful. Therefore, more clinicians around the world used *DSM-III-R* at the beginning of the 1990s than the *ICD* system designed to be applicable internationally (Maser *et al.*, 1991).

DSM-IV and *DSM-IV-TR*

By the late 1980s, clinicians and researchers realized once again the importance of a consistent, worldwide system of nosology. The 10th edition of the *International Classification of Diseases (ICD-10;* World Health Organization, 1992) would be published in 1992, and the United States is required by treaty obligations to use the *ICD-10* codes in all matters related to health. To make the *ICD-10* and *DSM* as compatible as possible, work proceeded more or less simultaneously on both the *ICD-10* and the fourth edition of the *DSM (DSM-IV)*, published in 1994. The *DSM-IV* task force attempted to review the voluminous literature in all areas pertaining to the diagnostic system (Widiger *et al.*, 1996; Widiger *et al.*, 1998) and to identify large sets of data that might have been collected for other reasons but that, with reanalysis, would be useful to *DSM-IV*. Finally, 12 independent studies or field trials examined the reliability and validity of alternative sets of definitions or criteria and, in some cases, the possibility of creating a new diagnosis. (See Widiger *et al.*, 1998; Zinbarg *et al.*, 1994, 1998, for examples.)

Perhaps the most substantial change in *DSM-IV* was that the distinction between organically based disorders and psychologically based disorders that was present in previous editions was eliminated. We now know that even disorders associated with known brain pathology are substantially affected by psychological and social influences. Similarly, disorders previously described as psychological in origin certainly have biological components and, most likely, identifiable brain circuits.

In 2000, a committee updated the text that describes the research literature accompanying the *DSM-IV* diagnostic category and made minor changes to some of the criteria themselves to improve consistency (American Psychiatric Association, 2000a; First & Pincus, 2002). This text revision *(DSM-IV-TR)* helped clarify many issues related to the diagnosis of psychological disorders.

DSM-5

In the almost 20 years since the publication of *DSM-IV*, our knowledge has advanced considerably and, after over 10 years of effort, *DSM-5* was published in 2013. This massive undertaking was also carried out in collaboration with international leaders working simultaneously on *ICD-11* (due to be published in 2018) such that each "workgroup" responsible for a set of disorders had an international expert involved in the work of the committee. The general consensus is that *DSM-5* is largely unchanged from *DSM-IV* although some new disorders are introduced and other disorders have been reclassified. Also, there have been some organizational and structural changes in the manual itself. For example, the manual is divided into three main sections. The first section introduces the manual and describes how best to use it. The second section presents the disorders, and the third section includes descriptions of disorders or conditions that need further research before they can qualify as official diagnoses.

The use of dimensional axes for rating severity, intensity, frequency, or duration of specific disorders in a relatively uniform manner across all disorders is also a feature of *DSM-5* (LeBeau *et al.*, 2015). In addition to dimensional assessments of severity or intensity for individual disorders, the *DSM-5* introduces cross-cutting dimensional symptom measures. These assessments are not specific to any particular disorder but rather evaluate in a global sense important symptoms that are often present across disorders in almost all patients. Examples include anxiety, depression, and problems with sleep (Narrow *et al.*, 2013). The idea would be to monitor the symptoms, if present, across the course of treatment for the presenting disorder. Thus, one might diagnose bipolar disorder and provide a dimensional rating of the degree of anxiety also present because a greater degree of anxiety seems to predict a poorer response to treatment and thus may require additional treatment (Deckersbach *et al.*, 2014; Howland *et al.*, 2009).

Notice that this does not represent a change to the categories of disorders themselves; rather, these dimensions are added on to the categorical diagnoses in order to provide clinicians with additional information for assessment, treatment planning, and treatment monitoring. Specific changes to diagnostic categories as well as new diagnoses will be described in subsequent chapters.

DSM-5 and Frank

In Frank's case, initial observations indicated an obsessive-compulsive disorder diagnosis. He might also, however, have long-standing personality traits that lead him systematically to avoid social contact. If so, there might also be a diagnosis of schizoid personality disorder. Job and marital difficulties might be indicated where clinicians note psychosocial or environmental problems that are not part of the disorder but might make it worse or affect treatment planning. Similarly, overall severity and impairment would be rated in a dimensional fashion periodically, as described above for PTSD, to monitor response to treatment using a *DSM-5* scale devised for that purpose (LeBeau *et al.*, 2013).

It is important to emphasize that impairment is a crucial determination in making any diagnosis. For example, if someone, such as Frank, has all of the symptoms of obsessive-compulsive disorder but finds them only mildly annoying because the intrusive thoughts are not severe and don't occur that often, that person would not meet criteria for a psychological disorder. It is essential that the various behaviors and cognitions comprising the diagnosis interfere with functioning in some substantial manner. Thus, the criteria for disorders include the provision that the disorder must cause clinically significant distress or impairment in social, occupational, or other important areas of functioning. Individuals who have all the symptoms as noted earlier but do not cross this "threshold" of impairment could not be diagnosed with a disorder. As noted above, one change in *DSM-5* is to make this judgment of severity and impairment more systematic by using a dimensional scale. In one of our own clinics, we have been doing something similar to this for many years (Brown & Barlow, 2014). That is, in addition to rating overall impairment, impairment specifically associated with the disorder (if present) is also rated. We have used a scale of 0 to 8, where 0 is no impairment and 8 is severely disturbing or disabling (usually housebound and barely functional). The disorder must be rated at least a 4 in severity (definitely disturbing or disabling) to meet criteria for a psychological disorder. Many times, disorders such as obsessive-compulsive disorder would be rated a 2 or 3, meaning that all of the symptoms are there but in too mild a form to impair functioning; in this case, the disorder would be termed *subthreshold*. Using Frank as an example again, the severity of his obsessive-compulsive disorder would be rated 5.

Social and Cultural Considerations in *DSM-5*

By emphasizing levels of stress in the environment, *DSM-III* and *DSM-IV* facilitated a more complete picture of the individual. Furthermore, *DSM-IV* corrected a previous omission by including a plan for integrating important social and cultural influences on diagnosis, a feature that remains in *DSM-5*. "Culture" refers to the values, knowledge, and practices that individuals derive from membership in different ethnic groups, religious groups, or other social groups, as well as how membership in these groups may affect the individual's perspective on their experience with psychological disorders (American Psychiatric Association, 2013). The plan, referred to as "cultural formulation," allows the disorder to be described from the perspective of the patient's personal experience and in terms of his or her primary social and cultural group, such as Hispanic or Chinese. Answering suggested culture-related questions from the *DSM-5 Cultural Formulation Interview* (American Psychiatric Association, 2013) will help accomplish these goals:

1. What is the primary cultural reference group of the patient? For recent immigrants to the country, as well as other ethnic minorities, how involved are they with their "new" culture versus their old culture? Have they mastered the language of their new country, or is language a continuing problem?
2. Does the patient use terms and descriptions from his or her "old" country to describe the disorder? For example, *ataques de nervios* in the Hispanic subculture is a type of anxiety disorder close to panic disorder. Does the patient accept Western models of disease or disorder for which treatment is available in health-care systems, or does the patient also have an alternative health-care system in another culture (for example, traditional herbal doctors in Chinese subcultures)?
3. What does it mean to be "disabled?" Which kinds of "disabilities" are acceptable in a given culture and which are not? For example, is it acceptable to be physically ill but not to be anxious or depressed? What are the typical family, social, and religious supports in the culture? Are they available to the patient? Does the clinician understand the first language of the patient, as well as the cultural significance of the disorder?

These cultural considerations must not be overlooked in making diagnoses and planning treatment, and they are assumed throughout this book. But, as yet, there is no research supporting the use of these cultural formulation guidelines (Aggarwal, Nicasio, DeSilva, Boiler, & Lewis-Fernandez, 2013). The consensus is that we have a lot more work to do in this area to make our nosology truly culturally sensitive.

Criticisms of *DSM-5*

Because the collaboration among groups creating the *ICD-11* and *DSM-5* was largely successful, it is clear that *DSM-5* (and the closely related *ICD-11* mental disorder section) are the most advanced, scientifically based systems of nosology ever developed. Nevertheless, any nosological system should be considered a work in progress (Frances & Widiger, 2012; Regier *et al.*, 2009), and *DSM-5* has attempted to put operations in place allowing for interim revisions to categories as new information becomes available (American Psychiatric Association, 2013).

For the time being, we still have "fuzzy" categories that blur at the edges, making diagnostic decisions difficult at times. As a consequence, individuals are often diagnosed with more than one psychological disorder at the same time, which is called **comorbidity**. How can we conclude anything definite about the course of a disorder, the response to treatment, or the likelihood of associated problems if we are dealing with combinations of disorders (Brown & Barlow,

....

comorbidity Presence of two or more disorders in an individual at the same time.

2009; Krueger *et al.*, 2014)? Is there a way to identify essential features of comorbid disorders and, perhaps, rate them dimensionally (Brown & Barlow, 2009; Rosellini, Boettcher, Brown, & Barlow, 2015)? Resolution of these tough problems simply awaits the long, slow process of science.

Criticisms center on two other aspects of *DSM-5* and the forthcoming *ICD-11*. First, the systems strongly emphasize reliability, sometimes at the expense of validity. This is understandable, because reliability is so difficult to achieve unless you are willing to sacrifice validity. If the sole criterion for establishing depression were to hear the patient say at some point during an interview, "I feel depressed," the clinician could theoretically achieve perfect reliability. But this achievement would be at the expense of validity because many people with differing psychological disorders, or none, occasionally say they are depressed. Thus, clinicians could agree that the statement occurred, but it would be of little use (Meehl, 1989). Second, methods of constructing a nosology of mental disorders have a way of perpetuating definitions handed down to us from past decades, even if they might be fundamentally flawed (Lilienfield, 2014). Some (e.g., Markon, 2013) think that it might be better to start fresh once in a while and create a new system of disorders, or several new systems, based on emerging scientific knowledge and see which one turns out to be best rather than to simply fine-tune old definitions, but this is unlikely to happen because of the enormous effort and expense involved, and the necessity of discarding the accumulated wisdom of previous versions.

A Caution about Labeling and Stigma

A related problem that occurs any time we categorize people is **labeling**. You may remember Kermit the Frog from *Sesame Street* sharing with us that "It's not easy being green." Something in human nature causes us to use a label, even one as superficial as skin color, to characterize the totality of an individual ("He's green . . . he's different from me"). We see the same phenomenon among psychological disorders ("He's a schizo"). Furthermore, if the disorder is associated with an impairment in cognitive or behavioral functioning, the label itself has negative connotations and contributes to stigma, which is a combination of stereotypical negative beliefs, prejudices, and attitudes resulting in reduced life opportunities for the devalued group in question, such as individuals with mental disorders (Martinez, Piff, Mendoza-Denton, & Hinshaw, 2011; Parcesepe & Cabassa, 2013).

Once labeled, individuals with a disorder may identify with the negative connotations associated with the label (Hinshaw & Stier, 2008). This affects their self-esteem. We have to remember that terms in psychopathology do not describe people but identify patterns of behavior that may or may not occur in certain circumstances. Thus, whether the disorder is medical or psychological, we must resist the temptation to identify the person with the disorder:

Tristan Fewings/Getty Images Entertainment/Getty Images

▲ Would we label this man? Stephen Hawking, one of the world's leading physicists, is severely disabled by amyotrophic lateral sclerosis, a rare progressive degenerative disease of the spinal cord. Because he cannot activate his voice box or move his lips, Hawking types his words into an electronic voice synthesizer that "speaks" for him. He uses his thumbprint to autograph his books. "I have been lucky," he says. "I don't have anything to be angry about."

Note the different implications of "John is a diabetic" and "John is a person who has diabetes."

Beyond *DSM-5:* Dimensions and Spectra

The process of changing the criteria for existing diagnoses and creating new ones will continue as our science advances. New findings on brain circuits, cognitive processes, and cultural factors that affect our behavior could date diagnostic criteria relatively quickly.

As mentioned above, although some new disorders have been added, and others relocated from one section to another, overall the *DSM-5* has not changed substantially from *DSM-IV*. Nevertheless, it has been clear to most professionals involved in this process that an exclusive reliance on discrete diagnostic categories has not achieved its objective in achieving a satisfactory system of nosology (Blashfield *et al.*, 2014; Krueger, Watson, & Barlow, 2005). In addition to problems noted earlier with comorbidity and the fuzzy boundary between diagnostic categories, little evidence has emerged validating these categories, such as discovering specific underlying causes associated with each category (Regier *et al.*, 2009). In fact, not one biological marker, such as a laboratory test, that would clearly distinguish one disorder from another has been discovered (Frances, 2009; Widiger & Crego, 2013). It is also clear that the current categories lack treatment specificity. That is, certain treatments such as cognitive behavioral therapies or specific antidepressant drugs are effective for a large number of diagnostic categories that are not supposed to be all that similar (Kennedy & Barlow, 2018). Therefore, although some progress has been made, many are beginning to assume that the limitations of the current diagnostic system are substantial enough that continued research on these diagnostic categories may never be successful in uncovering their underlying causes or helping us develop new treatments.

It may be time for a new approach, a suggestion strongly supported by the last two directors of the National Institute of Mental Health (Hyman, 2010; Insel *et al.*, 2010; Insel, 2014). Most people agree that this approach will incorporate a dimensional strategy to a much greater extent than in *DSM-5* (Krueger & Markon, 2014; Widiger & Crego, 2013). The term "spectrum" is another way to describe groups of disorders that share certain basic biological or psychological qualities or dimensions. For example, in Chapter 13 you will read about one of the notable advances in *DSM-5* where the term "Asperger's syndrome" (a mild form of autism) was integrated with autistic disorder into a new category of "autism spectrum disorder." But it is also clear at this point that research is not sufficiently advanced to attempt a wholesale switch to a dimensional or spectrum approach, so the categories in *DSM-5* for the most part look very much like the categories in *DSM-IV* with some updated language and increased precision and clarity. But, sparked by research and conceptual advances during the process of creating *DSM-5*, more conceptually substantial and consistent dimensional approaches are in development, and may be ready for the sixth edition of the *DSM* in 10 to 20 years.

For example, in the area of personality disorders, most investigators in this area, in studying both clinical samples of patients with personality disorders and community samples, have concluded that personality disorders are not qualitatively distinct from the personalities of normal-functioning individuals in community samples (Krueger *et al.*, 2014; Trull, Carpenter, & Widiger, 2013). Instead, personality disorders simply represent maladaptive, and perhaps extreme, variants of common personality traits (Widiger & Edmundson, 2011; Widiger, Livesley, & Clark, 2009). For the anxiety and mood disorders, Brown and Barlow (2009) have proposed a new dimensional system of

classification based on previous research (Brown, Chorpita, & Barlow, 1998) demonstrating that anxiety and depression have more in common than previously thought and may best be represented as points on a continuum of negative affect or a spectrum of emotional disorders (see Brown & Barlow, 2009; Rosellini *et al.*, 2015). Even for severe disorders with seemingly stronger genetic influences, such as schizophrenia, it appears that dimensional classification strategies or spectrum approaches might prove superior (Ahmed *et al.*, 2013; Harvey & Bowie, 2013).

At the same time, exciting new developments from the area of neuroscience relating to brain structure and function will provide enormously important information on the nature of psychological disorders. This information could then be integrated with more psychological, social, and cultural information into a diagnostic system. But even neuroscientists are abandoning the notion that groups of genes or brain circuits will be found that are specifically associated with *DSM-5* diagnostic categories. Rather, it is now assumed that neurobiological processes will be discovered that are associated with specific cognitive, emotional, and behavioral patterns or traits (for example, behavioral inhibition) that do not necessarily correspond closely with current diagnostic categories.

3.2 Concept CHECK

Identify each of the following statements related to diagnosing psychological disorders as either true (T) or false (F).

1. _____ The classical categorical approach to classification assumes there is only one set of causative factors per disorder with no overlap between disorders, and the prototypical approach uses essential, defining features, as well as a range of other characteristics.

2. _____ As in earlier versions, *DSM-5* retains a distinction between organically and psychologically based disorders.

3. _____ The *DSM-5* eradicated the problem of comorbidity, the identification of two or more disorders in an individual at one time, which was previously caused by imprecise categories.

4. _____ If two or more clinicians agree on a patient's classification, the assessments are said to be valid.

5. _____ A danger in psychological classification is that a diagnostic label might be used to characterize personally the total individual.

labeling Applying a name to a phenomenon or a pattern of behavior. The label may acquire negative connotations or be applied erroneously to the person rather than that person's behaviors.

Conducting Research in Psychopathology

▶ **What are the basic components of research in psychopathology?**

As you've already seen, abnormal behavior is a challenging subject because of the interaction of biological and psychological dimensions. In addition to the obvious complexity of human nature, another factor that makes an objective study of abnormal behavior difficult is the inaccessibility of many important aspects of this phenomenon. We can't get inside the minds of people except indirectly. Fortunately, some creative individuals have accepted this challenge and developed many methods of studying scientifically what behaviors constitute problems, why people suffer from behavioral disorders, and how to treat these problems. Many critical questions regarding abnormal behavior have yet to be answered, and we hope that some of you will be inspired to take them on. Understanding research methods is extremely important for everyone, however. You or someone close to you may need the services of a psychologist, psychiatrist, or other mental health provider. You may have questions such as these:

▶ Should childhood aggression be cause for concern, or is it just a phase my child will grow out of?

▶ A TV news program just reported that increased exposure to sunlight alleviates depression. Instead of seeing a therapist, should I buy a ticket to Hawaii?

▶ My brother has been in therapy for 3 years but doesn't seem to be any better. Should I tell him to look elsewhere for help?

▶ My mother is still in her 50s but seems to be forgetting things. Friends tell me this is natural as you grow older. Should I be concerned?

To answer such questions, you need to be a good consumer of research. When you understand the correct ways of obtaining information—that is, research methodology—you will know when you are dealing with fact and not fiction.

Basic Components of a Research Study

The basic research process is simple. You start with an educated guess, called a **hypothesis**, about what you expect to find. When you decide how you want to test this hypothesis, you formulate a **research design** that includes the aspects you want to measure in the people you are studying (the **dependent variable**) and the influences on these characteristics or behaviors (the **independent variable**). Finally, two forms of validity are specific to research studies: internal validity and external validity. **Internal validity** is the extent to which you can be confident that the independent variable is causing the dependent variable to change. **External validity** refers to how well the results relate to things

TABLE 3.2 | The Basic Components of a Research Study

Component	Description
Hypothesis	An educated guess or statement to be supported by data.
Research design	The plan for testing the hypothesis. Affected by the question addressed, by the hypothesis, and by practical considerations.
Dependent variable	Some aspect of the phenomenon that is measured and is expected to be changed or influenced by the independent variable.
Independent variable	The aspect manipulated or thought to influence the change in the dependent variable.
Internal validity	The extent to which the results of the study can be attributed to the independent variable.
External validity	The extent to which the results of the study can be generalized or applied outside the immediate study.

outside your study—in other words, how well your findings describe similar individuals who were not among the study participants. Although we discuss a variety of research strategies, they all have these basic elements. Table 3.2 shows the essential components of a research study.

Hypothesis

Human beings look for order and purpose. We want to know why the world works as it does, and why people behave the way they do. Robert Kegan describes us as "meaning-making" organisms, constantly striving to make sense of what is going on around us (Lefrancois, 1990). In an attempt to make sense of these phenomena, behavioral scientists construct hypotheses and then test them. Hypotheses are nothing more than educated guesses about the world (ideally informed by reviewing previous research on the subject of interest). You may believe that watching violent television programs will cause children to be more aggressive. You may think that bulimia is influenced by media depictions of supposedly ideal female body types. You may suspect that someone abused as a child is likely to abuse his or her significant other or child. These concerns are all testable hypotheses.

Once a scientist decides what to study, the next step is to put it in words that are unambiguous and in a form that is testable. Consider a study of how the use of the drug MDMA (also known as "ecstasy") affects long-term memory (Wagner, Becker, Koester, Gouzoulis-Mayfrank, & Daumann, 2012). Researchers from the University of Cologne in Germany followed 109 young adults over the course of a year to see if those who used MDMA performed as well on tests of memory as those who did not use the drug. In their study, these researchers posed the following research question: "Does the use of MDMA over a period of one year lead to a decrease in cognitive performance?" They didn't know what they would find until the study was completed, but phrasing the hypothesis in this way made it testable. If, for example, people with a history of MDMA use performed as well on cognitive tasks as those who do not use the drug, then other effects (e.g., psychological changes such as depression or anxiety with continued chronic use) would be studied. This concept of **testability** (the ability to support the hypothesis) is important for science because it allows us to say that in this case, either (1) regular MDMA use impairs learning and memory in users, or (2) there is no relationship between MDMA use and cognitive performance. The researchers did find a strong relationship between MDMA use and poor performance on certain visually oriented learning tasks, which may prove useful for understanding the nature of the drug as well as instructive for potential users (Wagner *et al.*, 2012).

When they develop an experimental hypothesis, researchers also specify dependent and independent variables. A **dependent variable** is what is measured, and it may be influenced directly by the study. Psychologists studying abnormal behavior typically measure an aspect of the disorder in question, such as overt behaviors, self-reported thoughts and feelings, or biological symptoms. In the study by Wagner and colleagues, the main dependent variable (cognitive performance) was measured using several different types of measures of learning and memory (e.g., digit span test, Stroop test, Trail-making test). **Independent variables** are those factors thought to affect the dependent variables and may be directly manipulated by the researchers. The independent variable in the study was measured by reports of MDMA use—with users defined as ingesting at least 10 MDMA pills over the previous year. In other words, changes in MDMA use over the year were thought to influence later cognitive abilities.

Internal and External Validity

The researchers in the study of MDMA on cognitive performance used responses on a neuropsychological test battery. Suppose they found that those who used MDMA happened to have lower IQ scores than those who did not use MDMA.

▲ Studying people as part of a group sometimes masks individual differences.

In other words, there was a systematic difference (i.e., IQ scores) in the whole group who used MDMA. This would have affected the data in a way that would limit what they could conclude about MDMA and cognitive ability and would change the meaning of their results. This situation, which relates to internal validity, is called a **confound** (or **confounding variable**), defined as any factor occurring in a study that makes the results uninterpretable because a variable (in this instance, the type of population being studied) other than the independent variable (MDMA use) may also affect the dependent variable (scores on cognitive abilities). Of course, you may point out that many different things can affect a dependent variable like cognitive ability, and you would be right. In the example given here,

hypothesis Educated guess or statement to be tested by research.

research design Plan of experimentation used to test a **hypothesis**.

dependent variable In an experimental study, the phenomenon that is measured and expected to be influenced (compare with **independent variable**).

independent variable Phenomenon manipulated by the experimenter in a study and expected to influence the **dependent variable**.

internal validity Extent to which the results of a study can be attributed to the **independent variable** after confounding alternative explanations have been ruled out.

external validity Extent to which research findings generalize, or apply, to people and settings not involved in the study.

testability Ability of a **hypothesis**, for example, to be subjected to scientific scrutiny and to be accepted or rejected, a necessary condition for the hypothesis to be useful.

confound Any factor occurring in a study that makes the results uninterpretable because its effects cannot be separated from those of the variables being studied.

confounding variable Variable in a research study that was not part of the intended design and that may contribute to changes in the **dependent variable**.

however, the confounding variable is problematic because it differs systematically between the two groups being compared (MDMA users and non-users).

Scientists use many strategies to ensure internal validity in their studies, three of which we discuss here: control groups, randomization, and analogue models. In a **control group**, people are similar to the experimental group in every way except that members of the experimental group are exposed to the independent variable and those in the control group are not. Because researchers can't prevent people from being exposed to many things around them that could affect the outcomes of the study, they try to compare people who receive the treatment with people who go through similar experiences except for the treatment (control group). For example, scientists studying whether a new type of therapy reduces anxiety might compare people who receive the therapy against people who are similar but who do not receive the therapy. Control groups help rule out alternative explanations for results (e.g., anxiety reducing simply due to the passage of time), thereby strengthening internal validity.

Randomization is the process of assigning people to different research groups in such a way that each person has an equal chance of being placed in any group. Researchers can, for example, randomly place people in groups in the hope that there will be approximately equal numbers of certain people (for example, people with more severe depression) in all groups. Placing people in groups by flipping a coin or using a random number table helps improve internal validity by eliminating any systematic bias in assignment. If random assignment is not used, people sometimes "put themselves in groups," and this self-selection can affect study results.

Analogue models recreate and study a real-world phenomenon in the controlled conditions of the laboratory. For example, bulimia researchers could ask volunteers to binge eat in the laboratory, questioning them before they ate, while they were eating, and after they finished, to learn whether eating in this way made them feel more or less anxious, guilty, and so on. If they used volunteers of any age, gender, race, or background, the researchers could rule out influences on the participants' attitudes about eating that they might not be able to dismiss if the group contained only people with bulimia. In this way, such "artificial" studies help improve internal validity.

In a research study, internal and external validity often seem to be in opposition. On the one hand, we want to be able to control as many things as possible to conclude that the independent variable (the aspect of the study we manipulated) was responsible for the changes in the dependent variables (the aspects of the study we expected to change). On the other hand, we want the results to apply to people other than the participants of the study and in other settings; this is **generalizability**, the extent to which results apply to everyone in a certain population (e.g., people with a particular disorder). If we control all aspects of a study so that only the independent variable changes, the result is

not relevant to the real world. For example, if you reduce the influence of gender issues by studying only males, and if you reduce age variables by selecting only people from 25 to 30 years of age, and finally, if you limit your study to those with college degrees so that education level isn't an issue—then what you study (in this case, 25- to 30-year-old male college graduates) may not be relevant to many other populations. Internal and external validity are in this way often inversely related. Researchers constantly try to balance these two concerns and, as you will see later in this chapter, the best solution for achieving both internal and external validity may be to conduct several related studies.

Statistical versus Clinical Significance

In psychological research, statistical significance typically means that the probability of obtaining the observed effect by chance is small. As an example, consider a study evaluating whether watching a video designed to promote a positive mood affects the amount of food eaten by subjects with eating disorders (Cardi, Esposito, Clarke, Schifano, & Treasure, 2015). The study found that participants with anorexia nervosa consumed 75 milliliters of a fruit smoothie after watching the positive video clip, compared to 38 milliliters consumed on average by subjects with anorexia nervosa after watching a neutral video clip. This difference was statistically significant. But is it an important difference? The difficulty is in the distinction between **statistical significance** (a mathematical calculation about the difference between groups) and **clinical significance** (whether or not the difference was meaningful for those affected) (Thirthalli & Rajkumar, 2009).

Closer examination of the results leads to concern about the size of the effect. Despite this difference in consumption between the positive-mood and neutral-mood groups, overall these subjects with anorexia nervosa ate less of the smoothie than a group of subjects without eating disorders (who consumed approximately 199 milliliters of the smoothie on average). Therefore, the difference may not be clinically significant because it did not elevate consumption to "non-disordered" levels.

Fortunately, concern for the clinical significance of results has led researchers to develop statistical methods that address not just that groups are different but also how large these differences are, or **effect size**. Calculating the actual statistical measures involves fairly sophisticated procedures that take into account how much each treated and untreated person in a research study improves or worsens (Durand & Wang, 2011; Fritz, Morris, & Richler, 2012). In other words, instead of just looking at the results of the group as a whole, individual differences are considered as well. Some researchers have used more subjective ways of determining whether truly important change has resulted from treatment. The late behavioral scientist Montrose Wolf (1978) advocated the assessment of what he called *social validity*. This technique involves obtaining input from the person being treated, as well as from significant others, about the importance of the changes that have occurred. In the example here, we might ask the participants and family members if they thought the positive video clip led to lasting changes in eating behavior (e.g., eating more over the week following the study). If the effect of the treatment is large enough to impress those who are directly involved, the treatment effect is clinically significant.

The "Average" Client

Too often we look at results from studies and make generalizations about the group, ignoring individual differences. Kiesler (1966) labeled the tendency to see all participants as one homogeneous group, the **patient uniformity myth**. This myth leads researchers to make inaccurate generalizations about disorders and their treatments. To continue with our previous example, what if the researchers studying the treatment of eating disorders concluded watching positive video clips was a good approach? And suppose we found that, although some participants improved with treatment, others worsened. Such differences would be averaged out in the analysis of the group as a whole, but for the person who continued to suffer from eating disorder symptoms, it would make little difference that "on the average" people improved.

Because people differ in such ways as age, cognitive abilities, gender, and history of treatment, a simple group comparison may be misleading.

3.3 Concept CHECK

Fill in the blanks with one of the following: hypothesis, dependent variable, independent variable, internal validity, external validity, or confound.

1. In a treatment study, the introduction of the treatment to the participants is referred to as the _____.

2. After the treatment study has been completed, you find that many people in the control group received treatment outside of the study. This is called a _____.

3. A researcher's guess about what a study might find is labeled the _____.

4. Scores on a depression scale improved for a treatment group after therapy. The change in these scores would be referred to as a change in the _____.

5. A relative lack of confounds in a study would indicate good _____, whereas good generalizability of the results would be called good _____.

Types of Research Methods

▶ What methods are used to conduct research on the causes of behavior?

Researchers who study human behavior use several forms of research when studying the causes of behavior. We now examine individual case studies, correlational research, experimental research, and single-case experimental studies.

Studying Individual Cases

Consider the following scenario: A psychologist thinks she has discovered a new disorder. She has observed several men who seem to have similar characteristics. All complain of a specific sleep disorder: falling asleep at work. Each man has obvious cognitive impairments that were evident during the initial interviews, and all are similar physically, each with significant hair loss and a pear-shaped physique. Finally, their personality styles are extremely egocentric, or self-centered. On the basis of these preliminary observations, the psychologist has come up with a tentative name, the Homer Simpson disorder, and she has decided to investigate this condition and possible treatments. But what is

control group Group of individuals in a study who are similar to the experimental subjects in every way but are not exposed to the treatment received by the experimental group. Their presence allows for a comparison of the differential effects of the treatment.

randomization Method for placing individuals into research groups that assures each an equal chance of being assigned to any group, thus eliminating any systematic differences across groups.

analogue models Approach to research that employs subjects who are similar to clinical clients, allowing replication of a clinical problem under controlled conditions.

generalizability Extent to which research results apply to a range of individuals not included in the study.

statistical significance Small probability of obtaining the observed research findings by chance.

clinical significance Degree to which research findings have useful and meaningful applications to real problems.

effect size A statistical process that eliminates how large a change in measure occurred. Often used before and after a clinical treatment to determine its relative success.

patient uniformity myth Tendency to consider all members of a category as more similar than they are, ignoring their individual differences.

the best way to begin exploring a relatively unknown disorder? One method is to use the **case study method**, investigating intensively one or more individuals who display the behavioral and physical patterns (Yin, 2012).

One way to describe the case study method is by noting what it is not. It does not use the scientific method. Few efforts are made to ensure internal validity and, typically, many confounding variables are present that can interfere with conclusions. Instead, the case study method relies on a clinician's observations of differences among one person or one group with a disorder, people with other disorders, and people with no psychological disorders. The clinician usually collects as much information as possible to obtain a detailed description of the person. Historically, interviewing the person under study yields a great deal of information on personal and family background, education, health, and work history, as well as the person's opinions about the nature and causes of the problems being studied.

Case studies are important in the history of psychology. Sigmund Freud developed psychoanalytic theory and the methods of psychoanalysis on the basis of his observations of dozens of cases. Freud and Josef Breuer's description of Anna O. (see Chapter 1) led to development of the clinical technique known as free association. Sexuality researchers Virginia Johnson and William Masters based their work on many case studies and helped shed light on numerous myths regarding sexual behavior (Masters & Johnson, 1966). Joseph Wolpe, author of the landmark book *Psychotherapy by Reciprocal Inhibition* (1958), based his work with systematic desensitization on more than 200 cases. As our knowledge of psychological disorders has grown, psychological researchers' reliance on the case study method has gradually decreased.

Research by Correlation

One of the fundamental questions posed by scientists is whether two variables relate to each other. A statistical relationship between two variables is called a **correlation**. For example, is schizophrenia related to the size of ventricles (spaces) in the brain? Are people with depression more likely to have negative attributions (negative explanations for their own and others' behavior)? Is the frequency of hallucinations higher among older people? The answers depend on determining how one variable (for example, number of hallucinations) is related to another (for example, age). Unlike experimental designs, which involve manipulating or changing conditions, correlational designs are used to study phenomena just as they occur. The result of a correlational study—whether variables occur together—is important to the ongoing search for knowledge about abnormal behavior.

One of the clichés of science is that correlation does not imply causation. In other words, if two things occur together, this does not necessarily mean that one caused the other. For example, the occurrence of marital problems

in families is correlated with behavior problems in children (e.g., Yoo & Huang, 2012). If you conduct a correlational study in this area, you will find that in families with marital problems, you tend to see children with behavior problems; in families with fewer marital problems, you are likely to find children with fewer behavior problems. The most obvious conclusion is that having marital problems will cause children to misbehave. If only it were as simple as that! The nature of the relationship between marital discord and childhood behavior problems can be explained in a number of ways. It may be that problems in a marriage cause disruptive behavior in the children. Some evidence suggests, however, the opposite may be true as well: The disruptive behavior of children may cause marital problems (Rutter & Giller, 1984). In addition, evidence suggests genetic influences may play a role in conduct disorders and in marital discord (D'Onofrio *et al.*, 2006; Lynch *et al.*, 2006). So parents who are genetically more inclined to argue pass on those genes to children, who then have an increased tendency to misbehave.

This example points out the problems in interpreting the results of a correlational study. We know that variable A (marital problems) is correlated with variable B (child behavior problems). We do not know from these studies whether A causes B (marital problems cause child problems), whether B causes A (child problems cause marital problems), or whether some third variable, C, causes both (genes influence both marital problems and child problems).

The association between marital discord and child problems represents a **positive correlation**. This means that great strength or quantity in one variable (a great deal of marital distress) is associated with great strength or quantity in the other variable (more child disruptive behavior). At the same time, lower strength or quantity in one variable (marital distress) is associated with lower strength or quantity in the other (disruptive behavior). If you have trouble conceptualizing statistical concepts, you can think about this mathematical relationship in the same way you would a social relationship. Two people who are getting along well tend to go places together: "Where I go, you will go!" The correlation (or **correlation coefficient**) is represented as +1.00. The plus sign means there is a positive relationship, and the 1.00 means that it is a "perfect" relationship, in which the people are inseparable. Obviously, two people who like each other do not go everywhere together. The strength of their relationship ranges between 0.00 and +1.00 (0.00 means no relationship exists). The higher the number, the stronger the relationship, whether the number is positive or negative (for example, a correlation of +0.80 is "stronger" than a correlation of +0.75). You would expect two strangers, for example, to have a relationship of 0.00, because their behavior is not related; they sometimes end up in the same place together, but this occurs rarely and randomly. Two people who know each other but do not like each other would be represented by a negative sign,

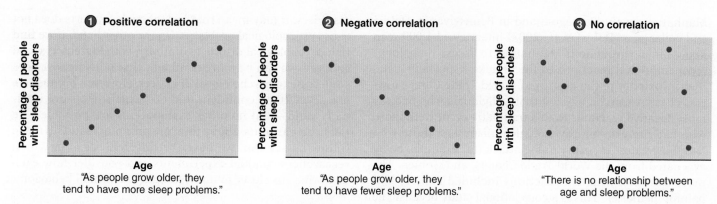

① Positive correlation

Percentage of people with sleep disorders

Age

"As people grow older, they
tend to have more sleep problems."

② Negative correlation

Percentage of people with sleep disorders

Age

"As people grow older, they
tend to have fewer sleep problems."

③ No correlation

Percentage of people with sleep disorders

Age

"There is no relationship between
age and sleep problems."

● **Figure 3.6** These three graphs represent hypothetical correlations between age and sleep problems.

with the strongest negative relationship being –1.00, which means "Anywhere you go, I won't be there!"

Using this analogy, marital problems in families and behavior problems in children have a relatively strong positive correlation represented by a number around +0.50. They tend to go together. On the other hand, other variables are strangers to each other. Schizophrenia and height are not related, so they don't go together and probably would be represented by a number close to 0.00. If A and B have no correlation, their correlation coefficient would approximate 0.00. Other factors have negative relationships: As one increases, the other decreases. (See ● Figure 3.6 for an illustration of positive and negative correlations.) We used an example of **negative correlation** in Chapter 2, when we discussed social supports and illness. The more social supports that are present, the less likely it is that a person will become ill. The negative relationship between social supports and illness could be represented by a number such as –0.40.

A correlation allows us to see whether a relationship exists between two variables but not to draw conclusions about whether either variable causes the effects. This is a problem of **directionality**. In this case, it means that we do not know whether A causes B, B causes A, or a third variable, C, causes A and B. Therefore, even an extremely strong relationship between two variables (+0.90) shows nothing about the direction of causality.

Epidemiological Research

Scientists often think of themselves as detectives, searching for the truth by studying clues. One type of correlational research that is much like the efforts of detectives is called **epidemiology**, the study of the incidence, distribution, and consequences of a problem or set of problems in one or more populations. Epidemiologists expect that by tracking a disorder among people they will find clues as to why the disorder exists. One strategy involves determining *prevalence*, the number of people with a disorder at any one time. For example, the prevalence of binge drinking (having

five or more drinks in a row) among U.S. college students is about 40% (Substance Abuse and Mental Health Services Administration, 2014). A related strategy is to determine the *incidence* of a disorder, the estimated number of new cases during a specific period. For example, incidence of binge drinking among college students has lowered only slightly from 1980 until the present (Substance Abuse and Mental Health Services Administration, 2014), suggesting that despite efforts to reduce such heavy drinking, it continues to be a problem. Epidemiologists study the incidence and prevalence of disorders among different groups of people. For instance, data from epidemiological research indicate that the prevalence of alcohol abuse among African Americans is lower than that among whites (Substance Abuse and Mental Health Services Administration, 2012).

Researchers have used epidemiological techniques to study the effects of stress on psychological disorders. On the morning of September 11, 2001, approximately 3,000 people died from three separate terrorist attacks in lower

case study method Research procedure in which a single person or small group is studied in detail. The method does not allow conclusions about cause-and-effect relationships, and findings can be generalized only with great caution (contrast with **single-case experimental design**).

correlation Degree to which two variables are associated. In a **positive correlation**, the two variables increase or decrease together. In a **negative correlation**, one variable decreases as the other increases.

positive correlation Association between two variables in which one increases as the other increases.

correlation coefficient Computed statistic reflecting the strength and direction of any association between two variables. It can range from 21.00 through 0.00 (indicating no association) to 11.00, with the absolute value indicating the strength and the sign reflecting the direction.

negative correlation Association between two variables in which one increases as the other decreases.

directionality Possibility that when two variables, A and B, are correlated variable A causes variable B or variable B causes variable A.

epidemiology Psychopathology research method examining the prevalence, distribution, and consequences of disorders in populations.

Manhattan, at the Pentagon, and in Pennsylvania. DeLisi and colleagues (DeLisi *et al.*, 2003) interviewed 1,009 men and women throughout Manhattan to assess their long-term emotional reactions to the attacks, especially given their proximity to the destroyed World Trade Center towers. These researchers found that individuals who had the most negative reactions to this traumatic event were those who had pre-existing psychological disorders, those who had the greatest exposure to the attack (for example, being evacuated from the World Trade Center), and women. The most common negative reactions included anxiety and painful memories. This is a correlational study because the investigators did not manipulate the independent variable. (The attack was not part of an experiment.)

Like other types of correlational research, epidemiological research can't tell us conclusively what causes a particular phenomenon. Knowledge about the prevalence and course of psychological disorders is extremely valuable to our understanding, however, because it points researchers in the right direction.

Research by Experiment

An **experiment** involves the manipulation of an independent variable and the observation of its effects. We manipulate the independent variable to answer the question of causality. For example, if we observe a correlation between social supports and psychological disorders, we can't conclude which of these factors influenced the other. We can, however, change the extent of social supports and see whether there is an accompanying change in the prevalence of psychological disorders—in other words, do an experiment.

What will this experiment tell us about the relationship between these two variables? If we increase social supports and find no change in the frequency of psychological

▲ The more social supports people have, the less likely it is that they will become ill.

disorders, it may mean that lack of such supports does not cause psychological problems. On the other hand, if we find that psychological disorders diminish with increased social support, we can be more confident that non-support does contribute to psychological disorders. However, because we are never 100% confident that our experiments are internally valid—that no other explanations are possible—we must be cautious about interpreting our results. In the following section, we describe different ways in which researchers conduct experiments and consider how each one brings us closer to understanding abnormal behavior.

Group Experimental Designs

With correlational designs, researchers observe groups to see how different variables are associated. In group experimental designs, researchers are more active. They actually change an independent variable to see how the behavior of the people in the group is affected. Suppose researchers design an intervention to help reduce insomnia in older adults, who are particularly affected by the condition (Karlin, Trockel, Spira, Taylor, & Manber, 2015). They treat a number of individuals and follow them for 10 years to learn whether their sleep patterns improve. The treatment is the independent variable; that is, it would not have occurred naturally. They then assess the treated group to learn whether their behavior changed as a function of what the researchers did. Introducing or withdrawing a variable in a way that would not have occurred naturally is called *manipulating a variable.*

Unfortunately, a decade later the researchers find that the older adults treated for sleep problems still, as a group, sleep less than 8 hours per night. Is the treatment a failure? Maybe not. The question that can't be answered in this study is what would have happened to group members if they hadn't been treated. Perhaps their sleep patterns would have been worse. Fortunately, researchers have devised ingenious methods to help sort out these complicated questions.

A special type of group experimental design is used more and more frequently in the treatment of psychological disorders and is referred to as a *clinical trial* (Durand & Wang, 2011; Pocock, 2013). A clinical trial is an experiment used to determine the effectiveness and safety of a treatment or treatments. The term *clinical trial* implies a level of formality with regard to how it is conducted. As a result, a clinical trial is not a design by itself but rather a method of evaluation that follows a number of generally accepted rules. For example, these rules cover how you should select the research participants, how many individuals should be included in the study, how they should be assigned to groups, and how the data should be analyzed—and this represents only a partial list. Also, treatments are usually applied using formal protocols to ensure that everyone is treated the same.

Control Groups

One answer to the what-if dilemma is to use a control group—people who are similar to the experimental group in every way except they are not exposed to the independent variable. In the study looking at sleep in older adults, suppose another group who didn't receive treatment was selected. Further, suppose that the researchers also follow this group of people, assess them 10 years later, and look at their sleep patterns over this period of time. They probably observe that, without intervention, people tend to sleep fewer hours as they age (Cho *et al.*, 2008). Members of the control group, then, might sleep significantly less than people in the treated group, who might themselves sleep somewhat less than they did 10 years earlier. Using a control group allows the researchers to see that their treatment did help the treated participants keep their sleep time from decreasing further.

Ideally, a control group is nearly identical to the treatment group in such factors as age, gender, socioeconomic backgrounds, and the problems they are reporting. Furthermore, a researcher would do the same assessments before and after the independent variable manipulation (for example, a treatment) to people in both groups. Any later differences between the groups after the change would, therefore, be attributable only to what was changed.

People in a treatment group often expect to get better. When behavior changes as a result of a person's expectation of change rather than as a result of any manipulation by an experimenter, the phenomenon is known as a **placebo effect**. Conversely, people in the control group may be disappointed that they are not receiving treatment. Depending on the type of disorder they experience (for example, depression), disappointment may make them worse. This phenomenon would also make the treatment group look better by comparison.

One way that researchers address the expectation concern is through **placebo control groups**. The word *placebo* typically refers to inactive medications such as sugar pills. The placebo is given to members of the control group to make them believe they are getting treatment (Kendall & Comer, 2014). A placebo control in a medication study can be carried out with relative ease because people in the untreated group receive something that looks like the medication administered to the treatment group. In psychological treatments, however, it is not always easy to devise something that people believe may help them but does not include the component the researcher believes is effective. Clients in these types of control groups are often given part of the actual therapy—for example, the same homework as the treated group—but not the portions the researchers believe are responsible for improvements.

Note that you can look at the placebo effect as one portion of any treatment (Kendall & Comer, 2014). If someone you provide with a treatment improves, you would have to attribute the improvement to a combination of your treatment and the client's expectation of improving (placebo

effect). Therapists want their clients to expect improvement; this helps strengthen the treatment. When researchers conduct an experiment to determine what portion of a particular treatment is responsible for the observed changes, however, the placebo effect is a confound that can dilute the validity of the research. Thus, researchers use a placebo control group to help distinguish the results of positive expectations from the results of actual treatment.

The **double-blind control** is a variant of the placebo control group procedure. As the name suggests, not only are the participants in the study "blind," or unaware of what group they are in or what treatment they are given (single blind), but so are the researchers or therapists providing treatment (double blind). This type of control eliminates the possibility that an investigator might bias the outcome. For example, a researcher comparing two treatments who expected one to be more effective than the other might "try harder" if the "preferred" treatment wasn't working as well as expected. On the other hand, if the treatment that wasn't expected to work seemed to be failing, the researcher might not push as hard to see it succeed. This reaction might not be deliberate, but it does happen. This phenomenon is referred to as an *allegiance effect* (Dragioti, Dimoliatis, Fountoulakis, & Evangelou, 2015). If, however, both the participants and the researchers or therapists are "blind" there is less chance that bias will affect the results.

Comparative Treatment Research

As an alternative to using no-treatment control groups to help evaluate results, some researchers compare different treatments. In this design, the researcher gives different treatments to two or more comparable groups of people with a particular disorder and can then assess how or whether each treatment helped the people who received it. This is called **comparative treatment research**. In the sleep study we discussed, two groups of older adults could be selected, with one group given medication for insomnia, the other given a cognitive-behavioral intervention, and the results compared.

The process and outcome of treatment are two important issues to be considered when different approaches

. . . .

experiment Research method that can establish causation by manipulating the variables in question and controlling for alternative explanations of any observed effects.

placebo effect Behavior change resulting from the person's expectation of change rather than from the experimental manipulation itself.

placebo control group In **outcome research**, a **control group** that does not receive the experimental manipulation but is given a similar procedure with an identical expectation of change, allowing the researcher to assess any **placebo effect**.

double-blind control Procedure in **outcome research** that prevents bias by ensuring that neither the subjects nor the providers of the experimental treatment know who is receiving treatment and who is receiving a **placebo**.

comparative treatment research Outcome research that contrasts two or more treatment methods to determine which is most effective.

are studied. *Process research* focuses on the mechanisms responsible for behavior change, or "why does it work?" In an old joke, someone goes to a physician for a new miracle cold cure. The physician prescribes the new drug and tells the patient the cold will be gone in 7 to 10 days. As most of us know, colds typically improve in 7 to 10 days without so-called miracle drugs. The new drug probably does nothing to further the improvement of the patient's cold. The process aspect of testing medical interventions involves evaluating biological mechanisms responsible for change. Does the medication cause lower serotonin levels, for example, and does this account for the changes we observe? Similarly, in looking at psychological interventions, we determine what is "causing" the observed changes. This is important for several reasons. First, if we understand what the "active ingredients" of our treatment are, we can often eliminate aspects that are not important, thereby saving clients' time and money. For an example, one study of treatments for anxiety in youth found that the introduction of relaxation training did not speed up an individual's progress in treatment, whereas the introduction of treatment elements that focused on thoughts or behaviors did. These results allow clinicians to focus their treatment on only those aspects most likely to improve anxiety (for example, cognitive restructuring and exposures; Peris *et al.*, 2015). In addition, knowing what is important about our interventions can help us create more powerful, newer versions that may be more effective.

Outcome research focuses on the positive, negative, or both results of the treatment. In other words, does it work? Remember, *treatment process* involves finding out why or how your treatment works. In contrast, *treatment outcome* involves finding out what changes occur after treatment.

Single-Case Experimental Designs

B. F. Skinner's innovations in scientific methodology were among his most important contributions to psychopathology. Skinner formalized the concept of **single-case experimental designs**. This method involves the systematic study of individuals under a variety of experimental conditions. Skinner thought it was much better to know a lot about the behavior of one individual than to make only a few observations of a large group for the sake of presenting the "average" response. Psychopathology is concerned with the suffering of specific people, and this methodology has greatly helped us understand the factors involved in individual psychopathology (Barlow, Nock, & Hersen, 2009; Kazdin, 2011). Many applications throughout this book reflect Skinnerian methods.

Single-case experimental designs differ from case studies in their use of various strategies to improve internal validity, thereby reducing the number of confounding variables. As you will see, these strategies have strengths and weaknesses in comparison with traditional group designs.

Although we use examples from treatment research to illustrate the single-case experimental designs, they, like other research strategies, can help explain why people engage in abnormal behavior, as well as how to treat them.

Repeated Measurements

One of the more important strategies used in single-case experimental design is **repeated measurement**, in which a behavior is measured several times instead of only once before you change the independent variable and once afterward. The researcher takes the same measurements repeatedly to learn how variable the behavior is (how much does it change from day to day?) and whether it shows any obvious trends (is it getting better or worse?). Suppose a young woman, Wendy, comes into the office complaining about feelings of anxiety. When asked to rate the level of her anxiety, she gives it a 9 (10 is the worst). After several weeks of treatment, Wendy rates her anxiety at 6. Can we say that the treatment reduced her anxiety? Not necessarily.

Suppose we had measured Wendy's anxiety each day during the weeks before her visit to the office (repeated measurement) and observed that it differed greatly. On particularly good days, she rated her anxiety from 5 to 7. On bad days, it was between 8 and 10. Suppose further that, even after treatment, her daily ratings continued to range from 5 to 10. The rating of 9 before treatment and 6 after treatment may only have been part of the daily variations she experienced normally. Wendy could just as easily have had a good day and reported a 6 before treatment and then had a bad day and reported a 9 after treatment, which would imply that the treatment made her worse!

Repeated measurement is part of each single-subject experimental design. It helps identify how a person is doing before and after intervention and whether the treatment accounted for any changes. ● Figure 3.7 summarizes Wendy's anxiety and the added information obtained by repeated measurements. The top graph shows Wendy's original before-and-after ratings of her anxiety. The middle graph shows that with daily ratings her reports are variable and that just by chance the previous measurement was probably misleading. She had good and bad days both before and after treatment and doesn't seem to have changed much.

The bottom graph shows a different possibility: Wendy's anxiety was on its way down before the treatment, which would also have been obscured with just before-and-after measurements. Maybe she was getting better on her own and the treatment didn't have much effect. Although the middle graph shows how the **variability** from day to day could be important in an interpretation of the effect of treatment, the bottom graph shows how the **trend** itself can also be important in determining the cause of any change. The three graphs illustrate important parts of

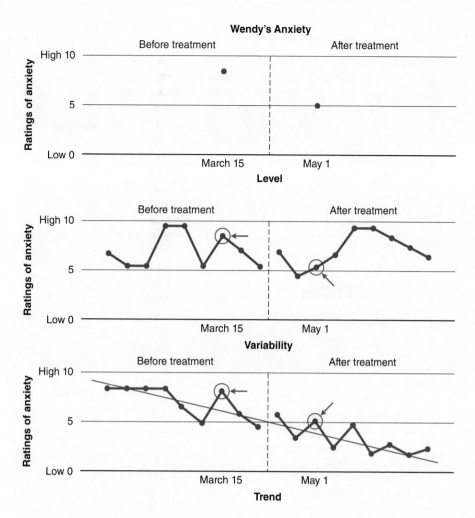

Figure 3.7 The top graph seems to show Wendy's anxiety dropping significantly after treatment (measuring level). When you look at repeated measures before and after treatment, however, the middle graph reveals little change because her anxiety fluctuated a great deal (measuring variability). A different scenario is illustrated in the bottom graph (measuring trend), where her anxiety also varied. In general, there was a downward movement (improved anxiety) even before treatment, suggesting that she might have improved without help. Examining variability and trend can provide more information about the true nature of the change.

repeated measurements: (1) the **level** or degree of behavior change with different interventions (top), (2) the variability or degree of change over time (middle), and (3) the trend or direction of change (bottom). Again, before-and-after scores alone do not necessarily show what is responsible for behavioral changes.

Withdrawal Designs

One of the more common strategies used in single-subject research is a **withdrawal design**, in which a researcher tries to determine whether the independent variable is responsible for changes in behavior. The effect of Wendy's treatment could be tested by stopping it for some time to see whether her anxiety increased. A simple withdrawal design has three parts. First, a person's condition is evaluated before treatment, to establish a **baseline**. Then comes the change in the independent variable—in Wendy's case, the beginning of treatment. Last, treatment is withdrawn ("return to baseline") and the researcher assesses whether Wendy's anxiety level changes again as a function of this last step. If with the treatment her anxiety lessens in comparison to baseline and then worsens after treatment is

withdrawn, the researcher can conclude the treatment has reduced Wendy's anxiety.

....

single-case experimental design Research tactic in which an **independent variable** is manipulated for a single individual, allowing cause-and-effect conclusions but with limited **generalizability** (contrast with **case study method**).

repeated measurement When responses are measured on more than two occasions (not just before and after intervention) to assess **trends**.

variability Degree of change in a phenomenon over time.

trend Direction of change of a behavior or behaviors (for example, increasing or decreasing).

level Degree of behavior change with different interventions (for example, high or low).

withdrawal design Removing a treatment to note whether it has been effective. In **single-case experimental designs**, a behavior is measured (**baseline**), an **independent variable** is introduced (intervention), and then the intervention is withdrawn. Because the behavior continues to be measured throughout (**repeated measurement**), any effects of the intervention can be noted.

baseline Measured rate of a behavior before introduction of an intervention that allows comparison and assessment of the effects of the intervention.

How is this design different from a case study? An important difference is that the change in treatment is designed specifically to show whether treatment caused the changes in behavior. Although case studies often involve treatment, they don't include any effort to learn whether the person would have improved without the treatment. A withdrawal design gives researchers a better sense of whether or not the treatment itself caused behavior change.

Despite their advantages, withdrawal designs are not always appropriate. The researcher is required to remove what might be an effective treatment, a decision that is sometimes difficult to justify for ethical reasons. In Wendy's case, a researcher would have to decide there was a sufficient reason to risk making her anxious again. A withdrawal design is also unsuitable when the treatment can't be removed. Suppose Wendy's treatment involved visualizing herself on a beach on a tropical island. It would be difficult—if not impossible—to stop her from imagining something. Similarly, some treatments involve teaching people skills, which might be impossible to unlearn. If Wendy learned how to be less anxious in social situations, how could she revert to being socially apprehensive?

Several counterarguments support the use of withdrawal designs (Barlow *et al.*, 2009). Treatment is routinely withdrawn when medications are involved. *Drug holidays* are periods when the medication is withdrawn so that clinicians can determine whether it is responsible for the treatment effects. Any medication can have negative side effects, and unnecessary medication should be avoided. Sometimes treatment withdrawal happens naturally. Withdrawal does not have to be prolonged; a brief withdrawal may still clarify the role of the treatment.

Multiple Baseline

Another single-case experimental design strategy used often that doesn't have some of the drawbacks of a withdrawal design is the **multiple baseline**. Rather

● **Figure 3.8** This figure shows how a multiple baseline design was used to illustrate that the treatment—functional communication training—was responsible for improvements in the children's behaviors. The circles represent how often each child exhibited behavior problems (called challenging behavior), and the blue-shaded areas show how often they communicated without help from the teacher (referred to as unprompted communication). (From Durand, V. M. (1999). Functional communication training using assistive devices: recruiting natural communities of reinforcement, Journal of Applied Behavior Analysis, 32(3), 247–267. Reprinted by permission of the Society for the Experimental Analysis of Human Behavior.)

than stopping the intervention to see whether it is effective, the researcher starts treatment at different times across settings (home versus school), behaviors (yelling at spouse/partner or boss), or people. As an example of treatment across settings, suppose that after waiting for a while and taking repeated measures of Wendy's anxiety both at home and at her office (the baseline), the clinician treats her first at home. When the treatment begins to be effective, intervention could begin at work. If she improves only at home after beginning treatment but improves at work after treatment is used there also, we could conclude the treatment was effective. This is an example of using a multiple baseline across settings.

Suppose a researcher wanted to assess the effectiveness of a treatment for a child's problem behaviors. Treatment could focus first on the child's crying then on a second problem, such as fighting with siblings. If the treatment was first effective only in reducing crying, and effective for reducing fighting only after the second intervention, the researcher could conclude that the treatment, not something else, accounted for the improvements. This is a multiple baseline conducted across behaviors.

Single-case experimental designs are sometimes criticized because they tend to involve only a small number of cases, leaving their external validity in doubt. In other words, we can't say the results we saw with a few people would be the same for everyone. However, although they are called *single-case* designs, researchers can and often do use them with several people at once, in part to address the issue of external validity. One of us studied the effectiveness of a treatment for the severe behavior problems of children with autism spectrum disorder (Durand, 1999) (see ● Figure 3.8). We taught the children to communicate instead of misbehave, using a procedure known as *functional communication training* (we discuss this in more detail in Chapter 14). Using a multiple baseline, we introduced this treatment to a group of five children. Our dependent variables were the incidence of the children's behavior problems and their newly acquired communication skills. As ● Figure 3.8 shows, only when we began treatment did each child's behavior problems improve and communication begin. This multiple baseline design let us rule out coincidence or some other change in the children's lives as explanations for the improvements.

Among the advantages of the multiple baseline design in evaluating treatments is that it does not require withdrawal of treatment and, as you've seen, withdrawing treatment is sometimes difficult or impossible. Furthermore, the multiple baseline typically resembles the way treatment would naturally be implemented. A clinician can't help a client with numerous problems simultaneously but can take repeated measures of the relevant behaviors and observe when they change. A clinician who sees predictable and orderly changes related to where and when the treatment is used can conclude the treatment is causing the change.

3.4 Concept CHECK

Indicate which research method would be most appropriate in each of the following situations. Choose from (a) case study, (b) correlation, (c) randomized clinical trials, (d) epidemiology, (e) experiment, and (f) single-case experimental design.

1. A researcher changes the level of noise several times to see how it affects concentration in a group of people. _____

2. A group of researchers uses chance assignment to include participants in one of two treatment groups and uses published protocols to make sure treatment is applied uniformly. _____

3. A researcher wants to investigate the hypothesis that as children go through adolescence they listen to louder music. _____

4. A researcher is interested in studying a woman who had no contact with civilization and created her own language. _____

5. A researcher wants to know how different kinds of music will affect a 5-year-old who has never spoken. _____

- -

multiple baseline **Single-case experimental design** in which measures are taken on two or more behaviors or on a single behavior in two or more situations. A particular intervention is introduced for each at different times. If behavior change is coincident with each introduction, this is strong evidence the intervention caused the change.

Genetics and Behavior across Time and Cultures

▶ How do researchers study the interaction between environment and genetics?

▶ Why do researchers study behavior over time and across cultures?

Examining the origin and strategies for treating an individual's behavior problem or disorder requires several factors to be considered so that multiple possible influences are taken into account. The factors include determining any inherited influences, how behavior will change or remain the same over time, and the effects of culture.

Studying Genetics

We tend to think of genetics in terms of what we inherit from our parents: "He's got his mother's eyes." "She's thin, just like her dad." "She's stubborn, like her mother." This simplistic view of how we become individuals suggests that how we look, think, feel, and behave is predetermined. Yet we now know that the interaction between our genetic makeup and our experiences is what determines how we will develop. The goal of behavioral geneticists (people who study the genetics of behavior) is to tease out the role of genetics in these interactions.

Genetic researchers examine **phenotypes**, the observable characteristics or behavior of the individual, and **genotypes**, the unique genetic makeup of individual people. For example, a person with Down syndrome typically has some level of intellectual disability and a variety of other physical characteristics, such as slanted eyes and a thick tongue. These characteristics are the phenotype. The genotype is the extra 21st chromosome that causes Down syndrome.

Our knowledge of the phenotypes of different psychological disorders exceeds our knowledge of the genotypes, but that may soon change. Beginning in 1990, scientists around the world, in a coordinated effort, began the **human genome project** (*genome* means "all the genes of an organism"). Using the latest advances in molecular biology, scientists working on this project completed a rough draft of the mapping of the approximately 25,000 human genes. This work identified hundreds of genes that contribute to inherited diseases. These exciting findings represent truly astounding progress in deciphering the nature of genetic endowment and its role in psychological disorders.

With the rapid advance of science, a third concept is now the focus of intense study—**endophenotypes**. Endophenotypes are the genetic mechanisms that ultimately contribute to the underlying problems causing the symptoms and difficulties experienced by people with psychological disorders (Greenwood *et al.*, 2016). In the case of schizophrenia, for example, researchers are not looking for a "schizophrenia gene" (genotype); instead, they are searching for the gene or genes responsible for the working memory problems characteristic of people with this disorder (endophenotype), as well as the genes responsible for other problems experienced by people with this disorder.

What follows is a brief review of the research strategies that scientists use as they study the interaction between environment and genetics in psychological disorders: family studies, adoption studies, twin studies, genetic linkage analysis, and association studies.

Family Studies

In **family studies**, scientists simply examine a behavioral pattern or emotional trait in the context of the family. The family member with the trait singled out for study is called the **proband**. If there is a genetic influence, presumably the trait should occur more often in first-degree relatives (parents, siblings, or offspring) than in second-degree or more distant relatives. The presence of the trait in distant relatives, in turn, should be somewhat greater than in the population as a whole. In Chapter 1 you met Judy, the adolescent with blood–injury–injection phobia who fainted at the sight of blood. The tendency of a trait to run in families, or familial aggregation, is as high as 60% for this disorder; that is, 60% of the first-degree relatives of someone with blood–injury–injection phobia have the same reaction to at least some degree.

The problem with family studies is that family members tend to live together and there might be something in their shared environment that causes the high familial aggregation. For example, Mom might have developed a bad reaction to blood as a young girl after witnessing a serious accident. Every time she sees blood she has a strong emotional response. Because emotions are contagious, the young children watching Mom probably react similarly. In adulthood, they pass it on, in turn, to their own children.

Adoption Studies

How do we separate environmental from genetic influences in families? One way is through **adoption studies**. Scientists identify adoptees that have a particular behavioral pattern or psychological disorder and attempt to locate first-degree relatives who were raised in different family settings. Suppose a young man has a disorder and scientists discover his brother was adopted as a baby and brought up in a different home. The researchers would then examine the brother to see whether he also displays signs of the disorder. If they can identify enough sibling pairs (and they usually do after a lot of hard work), they can assess whether siblings brought up in different families display the disorder to the same extent as the original participant. If the siblings raised with different families have the disorder more often than would be expected by chance, the researchers can infer that genetic endowment is a contributor.

Twin Studies

Nature presents an elegant experiment that gives behavioral geneticists their closest possible look at the role of genes in development: identical (monozygotic) twins (Jansen, Mous, White, Posthuma, & Polderman, 2015). These twins not only look a lot alike but also have identical genes. Some changes do occur in chemical markers (called epigenetic markers) in the womb, which explains the subtle differences even in identical twins (van Dongen *et al.*, 2014). Fraternal (dizygotic) twins, on the other hand, come from different eggs and have only about 50% of their genes in common, as do all first-degree relatives. In **twin studies**, the obvious scientific question is whether identical twins share the same trait—say, fainting at the sight of blood—more often than fraternal twins. Determining whether a trait is shared is easy with some physical traits, such as height. As Plomin (1990) points out, correlations in height are 0.45 for both first-degree relatives and fraternal twins and 0.90 for identical twins. These findings show that heritability of height is about 90%, so approximately 10% of the variance is the result of environmental factors. But the case of conjoined identical twins with different personalities reminds us that the 90% estimate is the *average* contribution. An identical twin who was severely physically abused or selectively deprived of proper foods might be substantially different in height from the other twin.

Michael Lyons and his colleagues (1995) conducted a study of antisocial behavior among members of the Vietnam Era Twin Registry. The individuals in the study were about 8,000 twin men who served in the military from 1965 to 1975. The investigators found that among identical twins there was a greater degree of resemblance for antisocial traits than among fraternal twins. The difference was greater for adult antisocial behavior—that is, identical twins' behavior was more similar than fraternal twins' behavior in adulthood—than for juvenile antisocial behavior (meaning that non-adult identical and fraternal twin pairs were more similar in childhood than in adulthood). The researchers concluded that the family environment is a stronger influence than genetic factors on juvenile antisocial traits and that antisocial behavior in adulthood is more strongly influenced by genetic factors. In other words, after the individual grew up and left the family of origin, early environmental influences mattered less and less.

This way of studying genetics isn't perfect. You can assume identical twins have the same genetic makeup and fraternal twins do not. A complicating concern, however, is whether identical twins have the same experiences or environment as fraternal twins. Some identical twins are dressed alike and are even given similar names. Yet the twins themselves influence each other's behavior, and in some cases, identical twins may affect each other more than fraternal twins (Johnson, Turkheimer, Gottesman, & Bouchard, 2009). One way to address this problem is by combining the adoption study and twin study methods. If you can find identical twins, one or both of whom were adopted as an infant, you can estimate the relative roles of genes and the environment (nature versus nurture) in the development of behavioral patterns.

Genetic Linkage Analysis and Association Studies

The results of a series of family, twin, and adoption studies may suggest that a particular disorder has a genetic component, but they can't provide the location of the implicated gene or genes. To locate a defective gene, there are two general strategies: genetic linkage analysis and association studies (Flanagan, 2015).

The basic principle of **genetic linkage analysis** is simple. When a family disorder is studied, other inherited characteristics are assessed at the same time. These

. . . .

phenotypes Observable characteristics or behaviors of an individual.

genotypes Specific genetic makeup of an individual.

human genome project Ongoing scientific attempt to develop a comprehensive map of all human **genes**.

endophenotypes Genetic mechanism that contributes to the underlying problems causing the symptoms and difficulties experienced by people with **psychological disorders**.

family studies Genetic study that examines patterns of traits and behaviors among relatives.

proband In genetics research, the individual displaying the trait or characteristic being studied.

adoption studies In genetics research, the study of first-degree relatives reared in different families and environments. If they share common characteristics, such as a disorder, this finding suggests that those characteristics have a genetic component.

twin studies In genetics research, the comparison of twins with unrelated or less closely related individuals. If twins, particularly monozygotic twins who share identical **genotypes**, share common characteristics such as a disorder, even if they were reared in different environments, then strong evidence of genetic involvement in those characteristics exists.

genetic linkage analysis Study that seeks to match the inheritance pattern of a disorder to that of a **genetic marker**. This helps researchers establish the location of the **gene** responsible for the disorder.

▲ Family members often resemble each other in physical appearance but their shared genetics can influence many other aspects of their lives.

other characteristics—called **genetic markers**—are selected because we know their exact location. If a match or link is discovered between the inheritance of the disorder and the inheritance of a genetic marker, the genes for the disorder and the genetic marker are probably close together on the same chromosome. For example, bipolar disorder (manic depression) was studied in a large Amish family (Egeland *et al.*, 1987). Researchers found that two markers on chromosome 11—genes for insulin and a known cancer gene—were linked to the presence of mood disorder in this family, suggesting that a gene for bipolar disorder might be on chromosome 11. Unfortunately, although this is a genetic linkage study, it also illustrates the danger of drawing premature conclusions from research. This linkage study and a second study that purported to find a linkage between bipolar disorder and the X chromosome (Baron *et al.*, 1987) have yet to be replicated; that is, different researchers have not been able to show similar linkages in other families (Merikangas & Risch, 2014).

The second strategy for locating specific genes, **association studies**, also uses genetic markers. Whereas linkage studies compare markers in a large group of people with a particular disorder, association studies compare such people to people without the disorder. If certain markers occur significantly more often in the people with the disorder, it is assumed the markers are close to the genes involved with the disorder. This type of comparison makes association studies better able to identify genes that may only be weakly associated with a disorder. Both strategies for locating specific genes shed new light on the origins of specific disorders and may inspire new approaches to treatment (Flanagan, 2015).

Studying Behavior over Time

Sometimes we want to ask, "How will a disorder or behavior pattern change (or remain the same) over time?" This question is important for several reasons. First, the answer helps us decide whether to treat a particular person. For example, should we begin an expensive and time-consuming program for a young adult who is depressed over the loss of a grandparent? You might not if you knew that with normal social supports the depression is likely to diminish over the next few months without treatment. On the other hand, if you have reason to believe a problem isn't likely to go away on its own, you might decide to begin treatment. For example, aggression among young children does not usually go away naturally and should be dealt with as early as possible.

It is also important to understand the developmental changes in abnormal behavior because sometimes these can provide insight into how problems are created and how they become more serious. For example, you will see that some researchers identify newborns that are at risk for autism spectrum disorder (ASD) because they are siblings of a child with ASD and then follow them through infancy until some develop the disorder themselves. This type of study is showing us that the pattern of the onset of this disorder is actually much different than parents report after the fact (they tend to remember drastic changes in the child's behavior when, in fact, the changes occur gradually) (Zwaigenbaum, Bryson, & Garon, 2013).

Prevention Research

An additional reason for studying clinical problems over time is that we may be able to design interventions and services to prevent these problems. Clearly, preventing mental health difficulties would save countless families significant emotional distress, and the financial savings could be substantial. Prevention research has expanded over the years to include a broad range of approaches. These different methods can be viewed in four broad categories: positive development strategies (health promotion), universal prevention strategies, selective prevention strategies, and indicated prevention strategies (Kalra *et al.*, 2012).

Health promotion or *positive development strategies* involve efforts to blanket entire populations of people—even those who may not be at risk—to prevent later problems and promote protective behaviors. The intervention is not designed to fix existing problems but, instead, focuses on skill building to keep problems from developing. For example, the Seattle Social Development Program targets young children in public elementary schools in the Seattle school system that are in high-crime areas, providing intervention with teachers and parents to engage the children in learning and positive behaviors. Although this approach does not target one particular problem (for example, drug use), long-term follow-up of these children suggests multiple positive effects in achievement, reductions in delinquency, and lower odds of contracting a sexually transmitted illness by age 30 (Bailey, 2009; Hill, et al., 2014; Lonczak, Abbott, Hawkins, Kosterman, & Catalano, 2002). *Universal prevention strategies* focus on entire populations and target certain specific risk factors (for example, behavior problems in inner-city classrooms) without focusing on specific individuals. The third approach to prevention intervention—*selective prevention*—specifically targets whole groups at risk (for example, children who have parents who have died) and designs specific interventions aimed at helping them avoid future problems. Finally, *indicated prevention* is a strategy for those individuals who are beginning to show signs of problems (for example, depressive symptoms) but do not yet have a psychological disorder.

To evaluate the effectiveness of each of these approaches, the research strategies used in prevention research for examining psychopathology across time combine individual and group research methods, including both correlational and experimental designs. We look next at two of the most often used: cross-sectional and longitudinal designs.

Cross-Sectional Designs A variation of correlation research is to compare different people at different ages. For a **cross-sectional design**, researchers take a cross section of a population across the different age groups and compare them on some characteristic. For example, if they were trying to understand the development of alcohol abuse and dependence, they could take groups of adolescents at 12, 15, and 17 years of age and assess their beliefs about alcohol use. In an early comparison, Brown and Finn (1982) made some interesting discoveries. They found that 36% of the 12-year-olds thought the primary purpose of drinking was to get drunk. This percentage increased to 64% with 15-year-olds, but dropped again to 42% for the 17-year-old students. The researchers also found that 28% of the 12-year-olds reported drinking with their friends at least sometimes, a rate that increased to 80% for the 15-year-olds and to 88% for the 17-year-olds. Brown and Finn used this information to develop the hypothesis that the reason for excessive drinking among teens is a deliberate attempt to get drunk rather than a mistake in judgment once they are under the influence of alcohol.

In cross-sectional designs, the participants in each age group are called **cohorts**; Brown and Finn studied three cohorts: 12-year-olds, 15-year-olds, and 17-year-olds. The members of each cohort are the same age at the same time and thus have all been exposed to similar experiences. Members of one cohort differ from members of other cohorts in age and in their exposure to cultural and historical experiences. You would expect a group of

12-year-olds in the 1980s to have received a great deal of education about drug and alcohol use (such as the "Just Say No" program), whereas the 17-year-olds may not have. Differences among cohorts in their opinions about alcohol use may be related to their respective cognitive and emotional development at these different ages and to their dissimilar experiences. This **cohort effect**, the confounding of age and experience, is a limitation of the cross-sectional design.

Researchers prefer cross-sectional designs to study changes over time partly because they are easier to use than longitudinal designs (discussed next). In addition, some phenomena are less likely to be influenced by different cultural and historical experiences and therefore less susceptible to cohort effects. For example, the prevalence of Alzheimer's disease among people at ages 60 and 70—assumed to be strongly influenced by biology—is not likely to be greatly affected by different experiences among the study participants.

One question not answered by cross-sectional designs is how problems develop in individuals. For example, do children who refuse to go to school grow up to have anxiety disorders? Researchers cannot answer this question simply by comparing adults with anxiety problems and children who refuse to go to school. They could ask the adults whether they were anxious about school when they were children, but this **retrospective information** (looking back) is usually less than accurate. To get a better picture of how individuals develop over the years, researchers use longitudinal designs.

Longitudinal Designs Rather than looking at different groups of people of differing ages, researchers may follow one group over time and assess change in its members directly. The advantages of **longitudinal designs** are that they do not suffer from cohort effect problems and they allow the researchers to assess individual change.

genetic marker Inherited characteristic for which the chromosomal location of the responsible **gene** is known.

association studies Research strategy for comparing **genetic markers** in groups of people with and without a particular disorder.

cross-sectional design Methodology to examine a characteristic by comparing individuals of different ages (contrast with **longitudinal design**).

cohort Participants in each age group of a study with a **cross-sectional design**.

cohort effect Observation that people of different age groups differ in their values and experiences.

retrospective information Literally "the view back;" data collected by examining records or recollections of the past. It is limited by the accuracy, **validity**, and thoroughness of the sources.

longitudinal design Systematic study of changes in the same individual or group examined over time (contrast with **cross-sectional design**).

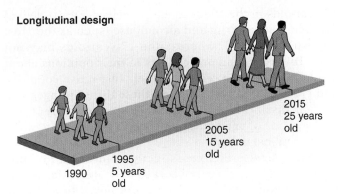

Longitudinal design

2015
25 years
old

2005
15 years
old

1995
5 years
old

1990

Same people followed across time

Cross-sectional design

5 yrs.

15 yrs

25 yrs.

People of different ages viewed at the same time

● **Figure 3.9** Two types of research designs: longitudinal and cross-sectional.

(● Figure 3.9 illustrates both longitudinal and cross-sectional designs.) In one such study, researchers followed a large number of patients (3,440) over 17 years to assess how consuming dairy products was associated with changes in their weight. Every three years, participants completed a physical exam and filled out a food frequency assessment to determine how much dairy they had consumed in the past year. The results of this study suggested that participants who had consumed three or more servings of dairy per day gained less weight over the year than those who had not (Wang, *et al.*, 2014). This study lends support to advocates of healthy dairy consumption and shows the value of longitudinal designs when assessing health outcomes over time.

Imagine conducting a major longitudinal study. Not only must the researcher persevere over months and years, but so must the people who participate in the study. They must remain willing to continue in the project, and the researcher must hope they will not move away or, worse, die. Longitudinal research is costly and time consuming; it is also possible that the research question will have become irrelevant by the time the study is complete.

Finally, longitudinal designs can suffer from a phenomenon similar to the cohort effect on cross-sectional designs. The **cross-generational effect** involves trying to generalize the findings to groups whose experiences are different from those of the study participants. For example, the drug-use histories of people who were young adults in the 1960s and early 1970s are vastly different from those of people born in the 1990s.

Sometimes psychopathologists combine longitudinal and cross-sectional designs in a strategy called **sequential design**, which involves repeated study of different cohorts over time. As an example, we will look at work by Laurie Chassin and her colleagues, who study children's beliefs about cigarette smoking (Chassin, Presson, Rose, & Sherman, 2001). These researchers have followed 10 cohorts of middle- and high-school-age children (cross-sectional design) since the early 1980s (longitudinal design). Through questionnaires, they have tracked how these children (and later, adults) viewed the health risks associated with smoking from their youth into their mid-30s. The results suggest that as middle schoolers (ages 11–14) the children viewed smoking as less risky to them personally and believed that there were positive psychological benefits (for example, making them appear more mature). These beliefs changed as the children went into high school and entered adulthood, but they point to the importance of targeting smoking prevention programs during the middle-school period (Macy, Chassin, & Presson, 2012).

Studying Behavior across Cultures

Just as we can become narrowly focused when we study people only at a certain age, we can also miss important aspects by studying people from only one culture. Studying the differences in behavior of people from different cultures can tell us a great deal about the origins and possible treatments of abnormal behaviors. Unfortunately, most research literature originates in Western cultures, producing an ethnocentric view of psychopathology that can limit our understanding of disorders in general and can restrict the way we approach treatment (Christopher, Wendt, Marecek, & Goodman, 2014). Increasing awareness of the limited cultural scope of our research is creating a corresponding increase in cross-cultural research on psychopathology.

The designs we have described are adapted for studying abnormal behavior across cultures. Some researchers view the effects of different cultures as though they were different treatments (López & Guarnaccia, 2012). In other words, the independent variable is the effect of different cultures on behavior, rather than, say, the effect of cognitive therapy versus simple exposure for the treatment of fears. The difference between looking at culture as a "treatment" and our typical design, however, is important. In cross-cultural research, we can't randomly assign infants to different cultures and observe how they develop. People from varying cultures can differ in any number of important ways—their genetic backgrounds, for one—that could explain variations in their behavior for reasons other than culture.

The characteristics of different cultures can also complicate research efforts. Symptoms, or descriptions of symptoms, can be dissimilar in different societies (Paniagua & Yamada, 2013). Nigerians who are depressed complain of heaviness or heat in the head, crawling sensations in the head or legs, burning sensations in the body, and a feeling that the belly is bloated with water (Ebigno, 1982; James, Jenkins, & Lawani, 2012). In contrast, people in the United States report feeling worthless, being unable to start or finish anything, losing interest in usual activities, and thinking of suicide. Natives of China, on the other hand, are less likely to report feeling depressed or losing interest in favorite things but may have thoughts of suicide or worthlessness (Yu, Tam, Wong, Lam, & Stewart, 2012). These few examples illustrate that applying a standard definition of depression across different cultures will result in vastly different outcomes (Corrigan, Druss, & Perlick, 2014).

An additional complicating factor is varying tolerances, or thresholds, for abnormal behavior. If people in different cultures see the same behaviors differently, researchers will have trouble comparing incidence and prevalence rates. For example, traditional Chinese customs include talking to deceased relatives and local deities—behaviors, which might be characteristic of schizophrenia in other cultures (Fuji, Tsushima, Murakami-Brundage, & Kamath, 2014). Understanding cultural attitudes and customs is essential to such research (Paniagua & Yamada, 2013).

Finally, treatment research is also complicated by cross-cultural differences. Cultures develop treatment models that reflect their own values. In Japan, psychiatric hospitalization is organized in terms of a family model, with caregivers assuming parental roles. A family model was common in psychiatric institutions in 19th-century North America until it was replaced with the medical model common today (Colp, 2009). In Saudi Arabia, women are veiled when outside the home, which prevents them from uncovering their faces in the presence of therapists; custom thus complicates efforts to establish a trusting and intimate therapeutic client–therapist relationship and may also

▲ The same behavior—in this case a woman baring her legs and having her head uncovered in public—would be acceptable in some cultures but not in others.

prevent the therapist from gathering information about a patient's affective state from her facial expression (Ali, Liu, & Humedian, 2004; Dubovsky, 1983; Mistry, Bhugra, Chaleby, Khan, & Sauer, 2009). Because in the Islamic perspective medicine and religion are inseparable, medical and religious treatments are combined (Tober & Budiani, 2014). As you can see, something as basic as comparing treatment outcomes is highly complex in a cross-cultural context.

The Power of a Program of Research

When we examine different research strategies independently, as we have done here, we often have the impression that some approaches are better than others. It is important to understand that this is not true. Depending on the type of question you are asking and the practical limitations inherent in the inquiry, any of the research techniques would be appropriate. Significant issues often are resolved not by one perfectly designed study but rather by a series of studies that examine different aspects of the problem—in a program of research. The research of one of

cross-generational effect Limit on the **generalizability** of longitudinal research because the group under study may differ from others in culture and experience.

sequential design Combination of **cross-sectional** and **longitudinal designs** involving repeated study of different **cohorts** over time.

this book's authors will be used to illustrate how complex research questions are answered with a variety of different research designs.

One of us (Durand) studies why children with autism spectrum disorder display seemingly irrational behaviors such as self-injury (hitting or biting oneself) or aggression. The expectation is that the more we understand why these behaviors occur, the better the chances of designing an effective treatment. In an early study we used a single-subject design (withdrawal design) to test the influence of adult attention and escaping from unpleasant educational tasks on these problem behaviors (Carr & Durand, 1985). We found that some children hit themselves more when people ignore them, and others will hit themselves to get out of school assignments that are too difficult, showing that these disturbing behaviors can be understood by looking at them as primitive forms of communication (for example, "Please come here" or "This is too hard"). This led us to consider what would happen if we taught these children to communicate with us more appropriately (Durand, 1990). The next series of studies again used single-subject designs and demonstrated that teaching more acceptable ways of getting attention or help from others did significantly reduce these challenging behaviors (e.g., Durand & Carr, 1992). Several decades of research on this treatment (called functional communication training) demonstrates its value in significantly improving the lives of people with these once severe behavior problems by reducing the severity of the misbehavior through improving communication skills (Durand, 2012).

One of the questions that faces researchers in this area is why some children develop more severe forms of these behavior problems, while others do not. To begin to answer this question, we conducted a three-year prospective longitudinal study on more than 100 children with autism spectrum disorder to see what factors might cause more problems (Durand, 2001). We studied the children at age three and later at age six to determine what about the child or the family led to more severe problems. We found the following two factors to be the most important indicators of severe behavior problems in the children: (1) the parents were pessimistic about their ability to help their child or (2) the parents were doubtful about their child's ability to change. These parents would "give up" and allow their child to dictate many of the routines around the house (for example, eating dinner in the living room, or not going out to the movies because it would cause tantrums) (Durand, 2001).

This important finding then led to the next question: Could we make pessimistic parents more optimistic, and would this help prevent their children from developing more severe behavior problems? To answer this question we next relied on a randomized clinical trial to see if adding a cognitive behavior intervention (described in more detail in the later chapters on the individual disorders) would help make pessimistic parents more optimistic. We wanted to teach these parents to examine their own pessimistic thoughts ("I have no control of my child." "My child won't improve because of his/her disorder.") and replace them with more hopeful views of their world ("I can help my child" or "My child can improve his/her behavior"). We hypothesized that this cognitive intervention would help them carry out the parenting strategies we offer them (including functional communication training) and in turn improve the outcomes of our behavioral interventions. We randomly assigned groups of pessimistic parents who also had a child with very severe behavior problems to either a group that taught them how to work with their child or a group that used the same techniques but also helped them explore their pessimistic thinking and helped them view themselves and their child in a better light. The treatments were applied very formally, using written protocols to make sure that each group received the treatment as designed (Durand & Hieneman, 2008). What we found was that addition of the cognitive behavioral intervention had the expected effect—improving optimism and also improving child outcomes (Durand, Hieneman, Clarke, Wang, & Rinaldi, 2013).

As this example indicates, research is conducted in stages, and a complete picture of any disorder and its treatment can be seen only after looking at it from many perspectives. An integrated program of research can help researchers explore various aspects of abnormal behavior.

Replication

Scientists in general, and behavioral scientists in particular, are never really convinced something is "true." Replicating findings is what makes researchers confident that what they are observing isn't a coincidence. The strength of a research program is in its ability to replicate findings in different ways to build confidence in the results. If you look back at the research strategies we have described, you will find that replication is one of the most important aspects of each. The more times researchers repeat a process (and the behavior they are studying changes as expected), the surer they are about what caused the changes.

Since the end of World War II, researchers have been conducting national surveys to determine what percentages of people in the population have different psychological disorders. In such surveys, researchers typically conduct household, face-to-face diagnostic interviews with a large (approximately 5,000), randomly selected group of people within a given country and use the information to make inferences about what percentage of people in that country have each psychological disorder. Surveys like these are how we know what percentage of the population has the disorders discussed in this book. Most of these surveys are done only within individual countries and so have not been able to address whether psychological disorders occur at the same rate or look the same across different countries.

To address such questions, in the late 1990s, researchers from 28 countries began a series of coordinated and rigorously implemented population surveys to estimate the prevalence of psychological disorders around the world and to identify risk, protective factors, and treatments used for each disorder. This project, called the World Health Organization (WHO) World Mental Health Survey Initiative, has yielded some noteworthy findings. Of note, the rates of each psychological disorder vary significantly across the 28 countries; however, when they occur, disorders look similar across the countries. For instance, when disorders are present, their age of onset is remarkably consistent cross-nationally, and approximately half of all disorders begin before adulthood in each country. The results of this study suggest that despite differences in rates and in the manifestation of different disorders, many characteristics of psychological disorders look the same around the world. To learn more about this study and its findings, go to www.hcp.med.harvard.edu/wmh. ∎

Research Ethics

▶ Why are ethical principles so important in the research process?

An important final issue involves the ethics of doing research in abnormal psychology. For example, the appropriateness of a clinician's delaying treatment to people who need it, just to satisfy the requirements of an experimental design, is often questioned. One single-case experimental design, the withdrawal design, can involve removing treatment for some time. Treatment is also withheld when placebo control groups are used in group experimental designs. Researchers continue to discuss and caution others about just when it is appropriate to use placebo-controlled trials (Boot, Simons, Stohart, & Stutts, 2013). The fundamental question is this: When does a scientist's interest in preserving the internal validity of a study outweigh a client's right to treatment?

One answer to this question involves **informed consent**—a research participant's formal agreement to cooperate in a study following full disclosure of the nature of the research and the participant's role in it (Boot *et al.*, 2013). In studies using some form of treatment delay or withdrawal, the participant is told why it will occur and the risks and benefits, and permission to proceed is then obtained. In placebo control studies, participants are told they may not receive an active treatment (all participants are blind to or unaware of which group they are placed in), but they are usually given the option of receiving treatment after the study ends.

True informed consent is at times elusive. The basic components are competence, voluntarism, full information, and comprehension on the part of the participant (Snyder, 2012). In other words, research participants must be capable of consenting to participation in the research, they must volunteer or not be coerced into participating, they must have all the information they need to make the decision, and they must understand what their participation will involve. In some circumstances, all these conditions are difficult to attain. Children, for example, often do not fully appreciate what will occur during research. Similarly, individuals with cognitive impairments such as intellectual disability or schizophrenia may not understand their role or their rights as participants. In institutional settings, participants should not feel coerced into taking part in research. And individuals from different cultures can have different perspectives about what is important in informed consent (Lakes *et al.*, 2012).

Certain general protections help ensure that these concerns are properly addressed. First, research in university and medical settings must be approved by an institutional

....

informed consent Ethical requirement whereby research subjects agree to participate in a study only after they receive full disclosure about the nature of the study and their own role in it.

review board (IRB; Fisher & Vacanti-Shova, 2012). These are committees made up of university faculty and non-academic people from the community, and their purpose is to see that the rights of research participants are protected. The committee structure allows people other than the researcher to look at the research procedures to determine whether sufficient care is being taken to protect the welfare and dignity of the participants.

To safeguard those who participate in psychological research and to clarify the responsibilities of researchers, the American Psychological Association has published *Ethical Principles of Psychologists and Code of Conduct*, which includes general guidelines for conducting research (Knapp, Gottlieb, Handelsman, & Vande-Creek, 2012a, 2012b). People in research experiments must be protected from both physical and psychological harm. In addition to the issue of informed consent, these principles stress the investigators' responsibility for the research participants' welfare, because the researcher must ensure that the welfare of the research participants is given priority over any other consideration, including experimental design.

Psychological harm is difficult to define, but its definition remains the responsibility of the investigators. Researchers must hold in confidence all information obtained from participants, who have the right to concealment of their identity on all data, either written or informal. Whenever deception is considered essential to research, the investigator must satisfy a committee of peers that this judgment is correct. If deception or concealment is used, participants must be debriefed—that is, told in language they can understand the true purpose of the study and why it was necessary to deceive them.

A final and important development in the field that will help to "keep the face" on psychological disorders is the involvement of consumers in important aspects of this research—referred to as participatory action research (Chevalier & Buckles, 2013). The concern over not only how people are treated in research studies but also how the information is interpreted and used has resulted in many government agencies providing guidance on how the people who are the targets of the research (for example, those with schizophrenia, depression, or anxiety disorders) should be involved in the process. The hope is that if people who experience these disorders are partners in designing, running, and interpreting this research, the relevance of the research, as well as the treatment of the participants in these studies, will be markedly improved.

3.5 Concept CHECK

Part A

The following are some advantages and limitations of methods used in research across time. Sort them out by marking *CS* for cross-sectional designs and L for longitudinal designs.

Benefits:

1. _____ Shows individual development

2. _____ Easier

3. _____ No cohort effects

Limitations:

4. _____ Cohort effects

5. _____ Cross-generational effect

6. _____ No individual development data

Part B

Indicate whether the following statements are true (T) or false (F).

7. _____ After participants are told the nature of the experiment and their role in it, they must be allowed to refuse or agree to sign an informed consent form.

8. _____ If the participant is in the control group or taking a placebo, informed consent is not needed.

9. _____ Research in universities or medical settings must be approved by the institution's review board regarding whether or not the participants lack the cognitive skills to protect themselves from harm.

10. _____ Participants have a right to concealment of their identity on all data collected and reported.

11. _____ When deception is essential to the research, participants do not have to be debriefed regarding the true pose of the study.

SUMMARY

Assessing Psychological Disorders

What are clinical assessment and diagnosis?

▶ Clinical assessment is the systematic evaluation and measurement of psychological, biological, and social factors in an individual with a possible psychological disorder; diagnosis is the process of determining that those factors meet all criteria for a specific psychological disorder.

▶ Reliability, validity, and standardization are important components in determining the value of a psychological assessment.

What are the main methods used in clinical assessment?

▶ To assess various aspects of psychological disorders, clinicians may first interview and take an informal mental status exam of the patient. More systematic observations of behavior are called behavioral assessment.

▶ A variety of psychological tests can be used during assessment, including projective tests, in which the patient responds to ambiguous stimuli by projecting unconscious thoughts; personality inventories, in which the patient takes a self-report questionnaire designed to assess personal traits; and intelligence testing, which provides a score known as an intelligence quotient (IQ).

▶ Biological aspects of psychological disorders may be assessed through neuropsychological testing designed to identify possible areas of brain dysfunction. Neuroimaging can be used more directly to identify brain structure and function. Finally, psychophysiological assessment refers to measurable changes in the nervous system, reflecting emotional or psychological events that might be relevant to a psychological disorder.

Diagnosing Psychological Disorders

How is psychiatric diagnosis carried out?

▶ The term *classification* refers to any effort to construct groups or categories and to assign objects or people to the categories on the basis of their shared attributes or relations. Methods of classification include classical categorical, dimensional, and prototypical approaches. Our current system of classification, the *Diagnostic and Statistical Manual*, fifth edition (*DSM-5*), is based on a prototypical approach in which certain essential characteristics are identified but certain "non-essential" variations do not necessarily change the classification.

The *DSM-5* categories are based on empirical findings to identify the criteria for each diagnosis. Although this system is the best to date in terms of scientific underpinnings, it is far from perfect, and research continues on the most useful way to classify psychological disorders.

Conducting Research in Psychopathology

What are the basic components of research in psychopathology?

▶ Research involves establishing a hypothesis that is then tested. In abnormal psychology, research focuses on hypotheses meant to explain the nature, the causes, or the treatment of a disorder.

Types of Research Methods

What methods are used to conduct research on the causes of behavior?

▶ The individual case study is used to study one or more individuals in depth. Although case studies have an important role in the theoretical development of psychology, they are not subject to experimental control and must necessarily be suspect in terms of both internal and external validity.

▶ Research by correlation can tell us whether a relationship exists between two variables, but it does not tell us if that relationship is a causal one. Epidemiological research is a type of correlational research that reveals the incidence, distribution, and consequences of a particular problem in one or more populations.

▶ Research by experiment can follow one of two designs: group or single case. In both designs, a variable (or variables) is manipulated and the effects are observed to determine the nature of a causal relationship.

Genetics and Behavior across Time and Cultures

How do researchers study the interaction between environment and genetics?

▶ Genetic research focuses on the role of genetics in behavior. These research strategies include family studies, adoption studies, twin studies, genetic linkage analyses, and association studies.

Why do researchers study behavior over time and across cultures?

▶ Research strategies that examine psychopathology across time include cross-sectional and longitudinal designs. Both focus on differences in behavior or attitudes at different ages, but the former does so by looking at different individuals at different ages and the latter looks at the same individuals at different ages.

▶ Prevention research can be viewed in four broad categories: health promotion or positive development strategies, universal prevention strategies, selective prevention strategies, and indicated prevention strategies.

▶ The clinical picture, causal factors, and treatment process and outcome can all be influenced by cultural factors.

▶ The more the findings of a research program are replicated, the more they gain in credibility.

Research Ethics

Why are ethical principles so important in the research process?

▶ Ethics are important to the research process, and ethical guidelines are spelled out by many professional organizations in an effort to ensure the well-being of research participants.

▶ Ethical concerns are being addressed through informed consent and through the inclusion of consumers in research design, implementation, and interpretation.

Key Terms

clinical assessment, 70
diagnosis, 70
reliability, 72
validity, 72
standardization, 72
mental status exam, 72
behavioral assessment, 75, 84
self-monitoring, 76
projective tests, 76
personality inventories, 77
intelligence quotient (IQ), 80
neuropsychological test, 81
false positive, 81
false negative, 81
neuroimaging, 81
psychophysiological assessment, 82
electroencephalogram (EEG), 82
idiographic strategy, 84
nomothetic strategy, 84
classification, 84
taxonomy, 84
nosology, 84
nomenclature, 85
classical (or pure)
    categorical approach, 85
dimensional approach, 85
prototypical approach, 86
familial aggregation, 87
comorbidity, 89
labeling, 90

hypothesis, 92
research design, 92
dependent variable, 92, 93
independent variable, 92, 93
internal validity, 92
external validity, 92
testability, 93
confound, 93
confounding variable, 93
control group, 94
randomization, 94
analogue models, 94
generalizability, 94
statistical significance, 94
clinical significance, 94
effect size, 94
patient uniformity myth, 95
case study method, 96
correlation, 96
positive correlation, 96
correlation coefficient, 96
negative correlation, 97
directionality, 97
epidemiology, 97
experiment, 98
placebo effect, 99
placebo control groups, 99
double-blind control, 99
comparative treatment
    research, 99

single-case experimental
    designs, 100
repeated measurement, 100
variability, 100
trend, 100
level, 101
withdrawal design, 101
baseline, 101
multiple baseline, 102
phenotypes, 104
genotypes, 104
human genome project, 104
endophenotypes, 104
family studies, 104
proband, 104
adoption studies, 104
twin studies, 105
genetic linkage analysis, 105
genetic markers, 106
association studies, 106
cross-sectional design, 107
cohorts, 107
cohort effect, 107
retrospective
    information, 107
longitudinal designs, 107
cross-generational effect, 108
sequential design, 108
informed consent, 111

Answers to Concept Checks

3.1

Part A

1. b; 2. a; 3. e; 4. c; 5. d

Part B

6. R, V; 7. NR, NV; 8. R, V

3.2

1. T; 2. F; 3. F (still a problem);
4. F (reliable); 5. T

3.3

1. independent variable; 2. confound;
3. hypothesis; 4. dependent variable;
5. internal validity, external validity

3.4

1. e; 2. c; 3. b; 4. a; 5. f

3.5

Part A

1. L; 2. CS; 3. L; 4. CS; 5. L; 6. CS

Part B

7. T; 8. F; 9. T; 10. T; 11. F

Chapter Quiz

1. During a clinical interview a psychologist notes that a client is not aware of what the date is or even where she is. The psychologist has gained information about what aspect of the client's mental status?
   a. reliability
   b. affect
   c. sensorium
   d. intellectual functioning

2. One criticism of the Rorschach inkblot test and other projective assessment techniques is that different therapists administer and interpret them in different ways. Because of that variability, the tests lack what key attribute?
   a. random sampling
   b. standardization
   c. validity
   d. testability

3. What type of test would you use to explore whether an individual might have some sort of brain damage or injury?
   a. neuropsychological test
   b. projective test
   c. electrodermal test
   d. personality test

4. Measuring electrical activity in the brain with an electroencephalogram (EEG) would be most appropriate to answer which of the following questions?
   a. Will this client perform at the same level with his peers in school?
   b. Does this client have excessive fears and worries?

   c. Is this client well suited to pursue a career in the creative arts?
   d. Is this client benefiting from relaxation training?

5. Which approach to diagnostic classification identifies both essential characteristics of a disorder that everyone with the disorder shares and non-essential characteristics that might vary from person to person?
   a. prototypical
   b. standardized
   c. dimensional
   d. categorical

6. Despite improvements in *DSM-IV, DSM-IV-TR*, and *DSM-5* which of the following criticisms can still be leveled at that classification system?
   a. It provides no opportunity to describe biological or social factors that might influence psychological health.
   b. It relies on a purely dimensional approach, and the number of relevant dimensions on which to describe clients is infinite.
   c. The system emphasizes validity at the expense of reliability.
   d. It categorizes and labels people, which can be pejorative or even self-fulfilling.

7. In most experiments, researchers explore the expected influence of the _____ on the _____.
   a. incidence; prevalence
   b. independent variable; dependent variable
   c. external validity; internal validity
   d. testability; generalizability

8. When behavior change occurs because of a person's expectation of change rather than (or in addition to) the result of any manipulation by the experimenter, it is known as the?:

a. clinical significance

b. cohort effect

c. placebo effect

d. prevalence

9. What type of research design is used if an experiment examines life satisfaction in different groups of 20-, 40-, and 60-year-olds to draw conclusions about age differences?

a. cross-sectional

b. longitudinal

c. multiple baseline

d. case study

10. One way that participants in research projects are protected from harm is by making sure they are not coerced into participating and that they have full knowledge of what their participation will involve. What is that ethical protection called?

a. internal validity

b. positive correlation

c. informed consent

d. clinical significance

(See Appendix A for answers.)

Anxiety, Trauma- and Stressor-Related, and Obsessive-Compulsive and Related Disorders

4

CHAPTER OUTLINE

The Complexity of Anxiety Disorders
    Anxiety, Fear, and Panic: Some
        Definitions
    Causes of Anxiety and Related Disorders
    Comorbidity of Anxiety and Related
        Disorders
ANXIETY DISORDERS
Generalized Anxiety Disorder
    Clinical Description
    Statistics
    Causes
    Treatment
Panic Disorder and Agoraphobia
    Clinical Description
    Statistics
    Causes
    Treatment
Specific Phobia
    Clinical Description
    Statistics
    Causes
    Treatment
    Separation Anxiety Disorder
Social Anxiety Disorder (Social
Phobia)
    Clinical Description
    Statistics
    Causes
    Treatment
TRAUMA- AND STRESSOR-
RELATED DISORDERS
Posttraumatic Stress Disorder
    Clinical Description
    Statistics
    Causes
    Treatment
Other Trauma- and Stressor-
Related Disorders
OBSESSIVE-COMPULSIVE AND
RELATED DISORDERS
Obsessive-Compulsive Disorder
    Clinical Description
    Statistics
    Causes
    Treatment
Body Dysmorphic Disorder
    Clinical Description
    Statistics
    Causes and Treatment
Other Obsessive-Compulsive
and Related Disorders
    Hoarding Disorder
    Trichotillomania (Hair Pulling
        Disorder) and Excoriation (Skin
        Picking Disorder)

Blend Images/Shutterstock.com

Use scientific reasoning to interpret behavior:	▶ Identify basic biological, psychological, and social components of behavioral explanations (e.g., inferences, observations, operational definitions and interpretations) [APA SLO 2.1a] *(see textbook pages 120–122, 127, 133, 139, 143, 151, 156, 164)*
Engage in innovative and integrative thinking and problem solving:	▶ Describe problems operationally to study them empirically [APA SLO 2.3A, 2.4b] *(see textbook pages 119, 125, 130–131, 136, 142, 148, 154, 159)*
Describe applications of psychology:	▶ Correctly identify antecedents and consequences of behavior and mental processes [APA SLO 1.3b] *(see textbook pages 120, 127, 133, 139, 144–143).* ▶ Describe examples of relevant and practical applications of psychological principles to everyday life [APA SLO 1.3a] *(see textbook pages 118–119, 129, 135–139, 141, 147, 158–159)*

* Portions of this chapter cover learning outcomes suggested by the American Psychological Association (2012) in their guidelines for the under-graduate psychology major. Chapter coverage of these outcomes is identified above by APA Goal and APA Suggested Learning Outcome (SLO).

The Complexity of Anxiety Disorders

▶ What are the similarities and differences among anxiety, fear, and panic attacks?

Anxiety is complex and mysterious, as Sigmund Freud realized many years ago. In some ways, the more we learn about it, the more baffling it seems. "Anxiety" is a specific type of disorder, but it is more than that. It is an emotion implicated so heavily across the full range of psychopathology that our discussion explores its general nature, both biological and psychological. Next, we consider fear, a somewhat different but clearly related emotion. Related to fear is a panic attack, which we propose is fear that occurs when there is nothing to be afraid of and, therefore, at an inappropriate time. With these important ideas clearly in mind, we focus on specific anxiety and related disorders.

Anxiety, Fear, and Panic: Some Definitions

Anxiety is a common and normal experience. It is a neg-ative mood state characterized by bodily symptoms of physical tension and by apprehension about the future (American Psychiatric Association, 2013; Barlow, 2002). In humans, it can be a subjective sense of unease, a set of behaviors (looking worried and anxious or fidget-ing), or a physiological response originating in the brain and reflected in elevated heart rate and muscle tension. Because anxiety is difficult to study in humans, much of the research has been done with animals such as rats. But is a rat's experience of anxiety the same as that of a human? It seems to be similar, but we don't know for sure. It could even be argued that any emotional experience in

humans, including fear and anxiety, involves conscious-ness. This would obviously limit what we can say about human emotions when studying animals (LeDoux, 2015). Thus, anxiety remains a mystery, and we are only begin-ning our journey of discovery. Anxiety is also closely related to depression (Brown & Barlow, 2009; Kessler, Petukhova, Sampson Zaslavsky, & Wittchen, 2012), so much of what we say here is relevant to Chapter 6.

Surprisingly, anxiety is good for us, at least in moderate amounts. Psychologists have known for over a century that we perform better when we are a little anxious (Yerkes & Dodson, 1908). In fact, Howard Liddell (1949) called anx-iety the "shadow of intelligence." He thought the human ability to plan in some detail for the future was connected to that gnawing feeling that things could go wrong and we had better be prepared for them. This is why anxiety is a future-oriented mood state.

But what happens when you have too much anxi-ety? You might actually fail an exam you are anxious for because you can't concentrate on the questions. All you can think about when you're too anxious is how terri-ble it will be if you fail. Too much of a good thing can be harmful, and few sensations are more harmful than severe anxiety that is out of control. What makes the situation worse is that severe anxiety usually doesn't go away—that is, even if we "know" there is nothing to be afraid of, we remain anxious.

All the disorders discussed in this chapter are charac-terized by excessive anxiety, which takes many forms. In Chapter 2 you saw that **fear** is an immediate alarm reaction to danger. Like anxiety, fear can be good for us. It protects us by activating a massive response from the autonomic nervous system (increased heart rate and blood pressure, for example), which, along with our subjective sense of terror, motivates us to escape (flee) or, possibly, to attack (fight). As such, this emergency reaction is often called the flight or fight response.

There is much evidence that fear and anxiety reactions differ psychologically and physiologically (Barlow, 2002; Tovote, Fadok, & Lüthi, 2015). As noted earlier, anxiety is a future-oriented mood state, characterized by apprehension because we cannot predict or control upcoming events. Fear, on the other hand, is an immediate emotional reaction to current danger characterized by strong escapist action tendencies and, often, a surge in the sympathetic branch of the autonomic nervous system (Barlow, Brown, & Craske, 1994; Craske *et al.*, 2010).

What happens if you experience the alarm response of fear when there is nothing to be afraid of—that is, if you have a false alarm? Consider the case of Gretchen, who appeared at one of our clinics.

Gretchen... • *Attacked by Panic*

I was 25 when I had my first attack. It was a few weeks after I'd come home from the hospital. I had had my appendix out. The surgery had gone well, and I wasn't in any danger, which is why I don't understand what happened. But one night I went to sleep and I woke up a few hours later—I'm not sure how long—but I woke up with this vague feeling of apprehension. Mostly I remember how my heart started pounding. And my chest hurt; it felt like I was dying—that I was having a heart attack. And I felt kind of queer, as if I were detached from the experience. It seemed like my bedroom was covered with a haze. I ran to my sister's room, but I felt like I was a puppet or a robot who was under the control of somebody else while I was running. I think I scared her almost as much as I was frightened myself. She called an ambulance (Barlow, 2002).

This sudden overwhelming reaction came to be known as **panic**, after the Greek god Pan who terrified travelers with bloodcurdling screams. In psychopathology, a **panic attack** is defined as an abrupt experience of intense fear or acute discomfort, accompanied by physical symptoms that usually include heart palpitations, chest pain, shortness of breath, and, possibly, dizziness.

Two basic types of panic attacks are described in *DSM-5*: expected and unexpected. If you know you are afraid of high places or of driving over long bridges, you might have a panic attack in these situations but not anywhere else; this is an *expected (cued) panic attack*. By contrast, you might experience *unexpected (uncued) panic attacks* if you don't have a clue when or where the next attack will occur. We mention these types of attacks because they play a role in several anxiety disorders. Unexpected attacks are important in panic disorder. Expected attacks are more common in specific phobias or social anxiety disorder (see ● Figure 4.1).

Remember that fear is an intense emotional alarm accompanied by a surge of energy in the autonomic nervous system that motivates us to flee from danger. Does Gretchen's panic attack sound as if it could be the emotion of fear? A variety of evidence suggests it is (Craske & Barlow, 2014; Bouton, 2005), including similarities in reports of the experience of fear and panic, similar behavioral tendencies to escape, and similar underlying neurobiological processes.

DSM 5 | DISORDER CRITERIA SUMMARY
Panic Attack

An abrupt surge of intense fear or intense discomfort that reaches a peak within minutes, and during which time four (or more) of the following symptoms occur:

1. Palpitations, pounding heart, or accelerated heart rate
2. Sweating
3. Trembling or shaking
4. Sensations of shortness of breath or smothering
5. Feeling of choking
6. Chest pain or discomfort
7. Nausea or abdominal distress
8. Feeling dizzy, unsteady, lightheaded, or faint
9. Chills or heat sensations
10. Paresthesias (numbness or tingling sensations)
11. Derealization (feelings of unreality) or depersonalization (being detached from oneself)
12. Fear of losing control or going crazy
13. Fear of dying

From American Psychiatric Association. (2013). *Diagnostic and statistical manual of mental disorders* (5th ed.). Washington, DC.

- -

anxiety **Mood** state characterized by marked **negative affect** and bodily symptoms of tension in which a person apprehensively anticipates future danger or misfortune. Anxiety may involve feelings, behaviors, and physiological responses.

fear **Emotion** of an immediate alarm reaction to present danger or life-threatening emergencies.

panic Sudden, overwhelming fright or terror.

panic attack Abrupt experience of intense **fear** or discomfort accompanied by several physical symptoms, such as dizziness or heart palpitations.

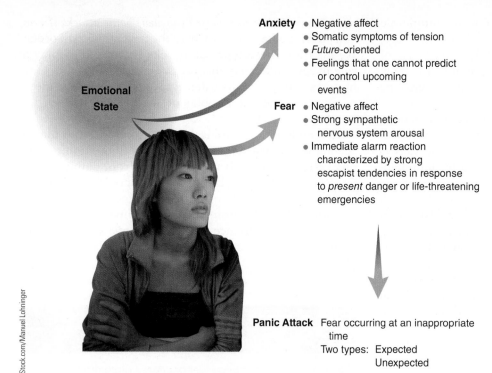

Animage labels:

Emotional
State

Anxiety
- Negative affect
- Somatic symptoms of tension
- *Future*-oriented
- Feelings that one cannot predict or control upcoming events

Fear
- Negative affect
- Strong sympathetic nervous system arousal
- Immediate alarm reaction characterized by strong escapist tendencies in response to *present* danger or life-threatening emergencies

Panic Attack   Fear occurring at an inappropriate time
Two types: Expected
            Unexpected

Figure 4.1 The relationships among anxiety, fear, and panic attack.

iStock.com/Manuel Lohninger

Causes of Anxiety and Related Disorders

You learned in Chapters 1 and 2 that excessive emotional reactions have no simple one-dimensional cause but come from multiple sources. Next, we explore the biological, psychological, and social contributors and how they interact to produce anxiety and related disorders.

Biological Contributions

Increasing evidence shows that we inherit a tendency to be tense, uptight, and anxious (Barlow *et al.*, 2014; Clark, 2005; Gray & McNaughton, 2003). The tendency to panic also seems to run in families and probably has a genetic component that differs somewhat from genetic contributions to anxiety (Craske & Barlow, 2014; Ollendick & Muris, 2015). As with almost all emotional traits and psychological disorders, no single gene seems to cause anxiety or panic or any other psychiatric disorder (Gratten, Wray, Keller, & Visscher, 2014). Instead, contributions from collections of genes in several areas on chromosomes make us vulnerable when the right psychological and social factors are in place. Furthermore, a genetic vulnerability does not cause anxiety and/or panic directly. That is, stress or other factors in the environment can "turn on" these genes, as we reviewed in Chapter 2 (Owens *et al.*, 2012; Smoller, 2013).

Anxiety is also associated with specific brain circuits (Hermans, Henckens, Joels, & Fernandez, 2014; Tovote

et al., 2015) and neurotransmitter systems (Durant, Christmas, & Nutt, 2010). For example, depleted levels of gamma-aminobutyric acid (GABA), part of the GABA–benzodiazepine system, are associated with increased anxiety, although the relationship is not quite so direct. The noradrenergic system has also been implicated in anxiety (Hermans *et al.*, 2011), and evidence from basic animal studies, as well as studies of normal anxiety in humans, suggests the serotonergic neurotransmitter system is also involved (Canli & Lesch, 2007). But increasing attention in the past several years has focused on the role of the corticotropin-releasing factor (CRF) system as central to the expression of anxiety (and depression) and the groups of genes that increase the likelihood that this system will be turned on (Essex, Klein, Slattery, Goldsmith, & Kalin, 2010; Durant *et al.*, 2010). This is because CRF activates the hypothalamic–pituitary–adrenocortical (HPA) axis, described in Chapter 2, which is part of the CRF system, and this CRF system has wide-ranging effects on areas of the brain implicated in anxiety, including the emotional brain (the limbic system), particularly the hippocampus and the amygdala; the locus coeruleus in the brain stem; the prefrontal cortex; and the dopaminergic neurotransmitter system. The CRF system is also directly related to the GABA–benzodiazepine system and the serotonergic and noradrenergic neurotransmitter systems.

The area of the brain most often associated with anxiety is the limbic system (Hermans *et al.*, 2011; LeDoux, 2002, 2015), which acts as a mediator between the brain stem and the cortex. The more primitive brain stem monitors

Anxiety is experienced by people all over the world. However, significant differences are found in the reported rates of anxiety disorders and how people experience them across different countries. A recent study analyzed previous epidemiological research encompassing nearly half a million individuals from 44 countries. While fewer than 1% of individuals in China reported a current anxiety disorder, a full 28% did so in Afghanistan. Just 2.4% of Italians had suffered from anxiety disorders in the past year, while almost 30% of Mexicans had (in Baxter, Scott, Vos, & Whiteford, 2013). This could reflect a true difference in the rate of anxiety across these countries but may largely result from how anxiety is experienced and reported.

For instance, the criteria used to assess the presence of anxiety disorders around the world typically are based on the Western conceptualization of each disorder. In the case of panic disorder, this includes the experience of extreme physiological distress (such as heart racing and sweating), which is usually accompanied by fears that one is going crazy or losing control, as well as persistent worry about future attacks. The physiological symptoms associated with panic appear to be universal and are reported in virtually all countries. However, the psychological manifestations of panic differ across countries, and this may lead to lower numbers of people in other countries meeting diagnostic criteria for panic disorder as defined by Western standards. In many Third World countries, for example, anxiety and mood disorders are experienced as bodily sensations but symptoms like fear and dread are not reported (Hinton, Chhean, Fama, Pollack, & McNally, 2007).

In addition to differences in the experience of anxiety, some people may be more willing to report anxiety than others. This appears to be the explanation behind the large sex differences in the prevalence of anxiety disorders in the United States—that is, women consistently report higher rates of fears and phobias, whereas men are less inclined to admit to such disorders (Kessler, Petukhova, Sampson, Zaslavsky, & Wittchen, 2012). So what happens to men with severe anxiety that goes unnoticed and untreated? A large portion of them seem to cope with their anxiety by drinking alcohol, often leading to the development of an alcohol use disorder (DeMartini & Carey, 2011).

Although more is known about sex differences in rates of anxiety disorders, researchers are just beginning to learn how cultural factors can influence the experience and reporting of anxiety disorders. It will be important for future work to continue to enhance our ability to understand and treat anxiety disorders around the world.

and senses changes in bodily functions and relays these potential danger signals to higher cortical processes through the limbic system. The late Jeffrey Gray, a prominent British neuropsychologist, identified a brain circuit in the limbic system of animals that seems heavily involved in anxiety (Gray & McNaughton, 2003) and may be relevant to humans. This circuit leads from the septal and hippocampal area in the limbic system to the frontal cortex. The system that Gray calls the **behavioral inhibition system (BIS)** is activated by signals from the brain stem of unexpected events, such as major changes in body functioning that might signal danger. Danger signals in response to something we see that might be threatening descend from the cortex to the septal–hippocampal system. The BIS also receives a big boost from the amygdala (LeDoux, 1996, 2002, 2015). When the BIS is activated by signals that arise from the brain stem or descend from the cortex, our tendency is to freeze, experience anxiety, and apprehensively evaluate the situation to confirm that danger is present.

The BIS circuit is distinct from the circuit involved in panic. Gray and McNaughton (2003) and Graeff (2004) identified what Gray and others call the **fight/flight system (FFS)**. This circuit originates in the brain stem and travels through several midbrain structures, including the amygdala, the ventromedial nucleus of the hypothalamus, and the central gray matter. When stimulated in animals, this circuit produces an immediate alarm-and-escape response that looks very much like panic in humans (Gray & McNaughton, 2003). The FFS is activated partly by deficiencies in serotonin, suggest Gray and McNaughton (2003) and Graeff (2004). As is true for other anxiety disorders (such as social anxiety disorder, which we will discuss later), activation of a network that involves the prefrontal cortex and the amygdala while performing certain tasks, can predict response to cognitive behavioral therapy.

It is likely that factors in your environment can change the sensitivity of these brain circuits, making you more or less susceptible to developing anxiety and its disorders, a finding that has been demonstrated in several laboratories (Francis, Diorio, Plotsky, & Meaney, 2002; Stein, Schork, & Gelernter, 2007). For example, one study suggested that cigarette smoking as a teenager is associated with greatly increased risk for developing anxiety disorders as an adult, particularly panic disorder and generalized anxiety disorder (Johnson *et al.*, 2000). The complex interaction between smoking and anxiety disorders has been confirmed in more recent research (Leventhal & Zvolensky, 2015). The current thinking about the link between smoking and anxiety is that

. . . .

behavioral inhibition system (BIS) Brain circuit in the **limbic system** that responds to threat signals by inhibiting activity and causing **anxiety**.

fight/flight system (FFS) Brain circuit in animals that when stimulated causes an immediate alarm-and-escape response resembling human **panic**.

anxiety sensitivity (the tendency to fear bodily sensations), distress tolerance (how much distress a person can tolerate), and anhedonia (the inability to feel pleasure) all contribute to smoking, which could be one reason why so many people with anxiety find it very difficult to quit smoking.

Brain-imaging procedures are yielding more information about the neurobiology of anxiety and panic (Britton *et al*, 2013; Shin & Liberzon, 2010). For example, there is now general agreement that in people with anxiety disorders, the limbic system, including the amygdala, is overly responsive to stimulation or new information (abnormal bottom-up processing); at the same time, controlling functions of the cortex that would down-regulate the hyperexcitable amygdala are deficient (abnormal top-down processing), consistent with Gray's BIS model (Ellard, 2013; Ochsner *et al.*, 2009). Despite these biological abnormalities, psychological treatments, and in particular cognitive-behavioral treatment (CBT), can effectively treat these disorders (Kendall & Peterman, 2015; Hofmann, Asnaani, Vonk, Sawyer, & Fang, 2012).

Psychological Contributions

New and accumulating evidence supports an integrated model of anxiety involving a variety of psychological factors (see, for example, Barlow, 2002; Barlow, Ellard *et al*, 2014). In childhood, we may acquire an awareness that events are not always in our control (Chorpita & Barlow, 1998; Gallagher, Bentley, & Barlow, 2014). The continuum of this perception may range from total confidence in our control of all aspects of our lives to deep uncertainty about ourselves and our ability to deal with upcoming events. If you are anxious about schoolwork, for example, you may worry you will do poorly in the next exam, even though all your grades have been As and Bs. A general "sense of uncontrollability" may develop early as a function of upbringing and other disruptive or traumatic environmental factors.

Interestingly, the actions of parents in early childhood seem to do a lot to foster this sense of control or uncontrollability (Barlow, Ellard *et al.*, 2014; Gunnar, Hostinar, Sanches, Tottenam, & Sullivan, 2015). Generally, it seems that parents who interact in a positive and predictable way with their children by responding to their needs, particularly when the child communicates needs for attention, food, relief from pain, and so on, perform an important function. These parents teach their children that they have control over their environment and their responses have an effect on their parents and their environment. In addition, parents who provide a "secure home base" but allow their children to explore their world and develop the necessary skills to cope with unexpected occurrences enable their children to develop a healthy sense of control (Chorpita & Barlow, 1998). In contrast, parents who are overprotective and overintrusive and who "clear the way" for their children, never letting them experience any adversity, create a situation in which children never learn how to cope with adversity when it comes along. Therefore, these children don't learn that they can control their environment. A variety of evidence has accumulated supporting these ideas (Fulton, Kiel, Tull, & Gratz, 2014; Gallagher *et al.* 2014). A sense of control (or lack of it) that develops from these early experiences is the psychological factor that makes us more or less vulnerable to anxiety in later life.

Another feature among patients with panic is the tendency to respond fearfully to anxiety symptoms. This is known as *anxiety sensitivity*, which appears to be an important personality trait that determines who will and will not experience problems with anxiety under certain stressful conditions (Reiss, 1991).

Most psychological accounts of panic (as opposed to anxiety) invoke conditioning and cognitive explanations that are difficult to separate (Bouton, Mineka, & Barlow, 2001). Thus, a strong fear response initially occurs during extreme stress or perhaps as a result of a dangerous situation in the environment (a true alarm). This emotional response then becomes associated with a variety of external and internal cues. In other words, these cues, or conditioned stimuli, provoke the fear response and an assumption of danger, even if the danger is not actually present (Bouton *et al.*, 2001; Razran, 1961), so it is really a learned or false alarm. This is the conditioning process described in Chapter 2. External cues are places or situations similar to the one where the initial panic attack occurred. Internal cues are increases in heart rate or respiration that were associated with the initial panic attack, even if they are now the result of normal circumstances, such as exercise. Thus, when your heart is beating fast, you are more likely to think of and, perhaps, experience a panic attack than when it is beating normally. Furthermore, you may not be aware of the cues or triggers of severe fear; that is, they are unconscious as recently demonstrated in patients with panic disorder (Meuret *et al.*, 2011).

Social Contributions

Stressful life events trigger our biological and psychological vulnerabilities to anxiety. Most are social and interpersonal in nature—marriage, divorce, difficulties at work, death of a loved one, pressures to excel in school, and so on. Some might be physical, such as an injury or illness.

The same stressors can trigger physical reactions, such as headaches or hypertension, and emotional reactions, such as panic attacks (Barlow, 2002). The particular way we react to stress seems to run in families. If you get headaches when under stress, chances are other people in your family also get headaches. If you have panic attacks, other members of your family probably do also. This finding suggests a possible genetic contribution, at least to initial panic attacks.

An Integrated Model

Putting the factors together in an integrated way, we have described a theory of the development of anxiety called

● **Figure 4.2** The three vulnerabilities that contribute to the development of anxiety disorders. If individuals possess all three, the odds are greatly increased that they will develop an anxiety disorder after experiencing a stressful situation. (From Barlow, D. H. (2002). Anxiety and its disorders: The nature and treatment of anxiety and panic (2nd ed.). New York: Guilford Press.)

the *triple vulnerability theory* (Barlow, 2000, 2002; Barlow, Ellard *et al.*, 2014). The first vulnerability (or diathesis) is a *generalized biological vulnerability.* We can see that a tendency to be uptight or highly-strung might be inherited. But a generalized biological vulnerability to develop anxiety is not sufficient to produce anxiety itself. The second vulnerability is a *generalized psychological vulnerability.* That is, you might also grow up believing the world is dangerous and out of control and you might not be able to cope when things go wrong, based on your early experiences. If this perception is strong, you have a generalized psychological vulnerability to anxiety. The third vulnerability is a *specific psychological vulnerability* in which you learn from early experience, such as being taught by your parents, that some situations or objects are fraught with danger (even if they really aren't). For example, if one of your parents is afraid of dogs, or expresses anxiety about being evaluated negatively by others, you may well develop a fear of dogs or of social evaluation. These triple vulnerabilities are presented in ● Figure 4.2. If you are under a lot of pressure, particularly from interpersonal stressors, a given stressor could activate your biological tendencies to be anxious and your psychological tendencies to feel you might not be able to deal with the situation and control the stress. Once this cycle starts, it tends to feed on itself, so it might not stop even when the particular life stressor has long since passed. Anxiety can be general, evoked by many aspects of your life. But it is usually focused on one area, such as social evaluations or grades (Barlow, 2002).

Comorbidity of Anxiety and Related Disorders

Before describing the specific disorders, it is important to note that the disorders often co-occur. As we described in Chapter 3, the co-occurrence of two or more disorders in a single individual is referred to as *comorbidity*. The high rates of comorbidity among anxiety and related disorders (and

depression) emphasize how all of these disorders share the common features of anxiety and panic described here. They also share the same vulnerabilities—biological and psychological—to develop anxiety and panic. The various disorders differ only in what triggers the anxiety and, perhaps, the patterning of panic attacks. Of course, if each patient with an anxiety or related disorder also had every other anxiety disorder, there would be little sense in distinguishing among the specific disorders. But this is not the case, and, although rates of comorbidity are high, they vary somewhat from disorder to disorder (Allen *et al.*, 2010; Bruce *et al.*, 2005). A large-scale study completed at one of our centers examined the comorbidity of *Diagnostic and Statistical Manual of Mental Disorders*, fourth edition (*DSM-IV-TR*) anxiety and mood disorders (Brown & Barlow, 2005; Brown, Campbell, Lehman, Grisham, & Mancill, 2001). Data were collected from 1,127 patients carefully diagnosed using a semistructured interview in our center. If we examine just rates of comorbidity at the time of assessment, the results indicate that 55% of the patients who received a principal diagnosis of an anxiety or depressive disorder had at least one additional anxiety or depressive disorder at the time of the assessment. If we consider whether the patient met criteria for an additional diagnosis at any time in his or her life, rather than just at the time of the assessment, the rate increases to 76%.

By far the most common additional diagnosis for all anxiety disorders was major depression, which occurred in 50% of the cases over the course of the patient's life, probably due to the shared vulnerabilities between depression and anxiety disorders in addition to the disorder-specific vulnerability. This becomes important when we discuss the relationship of anxiety and depression later in this chapter. Also important is the finding that additional diagnoses of depression or alcohol or drug abuse makes it less likely that you will recover from an anxiety disorder and more likely that you will relapse if you do recover (Bruce *et al.*, 2005; Ciraulo *et al.*, 2013 Huppert, 2009).

Complete the following statements about anxiety and its causes with the following terms: (a) comorbidity, (b) panic attack, (c) expected, (d) neurotransmitter, (e) brain circuits, and (f) stressful.

1. A(n) _____ is an abrupt experience of intense fear or acute discomfort accompanied by physical symptoms, such as chest pain and shortness of breath.

2. A(n) _____ panic attack often occurs in certain situations but not anywhere else.

3. Anxiety is associated with specific _____ (for example, behavioral inhibition system or fight/flight system) and _____ systems (for example, noradrenergic).

4. The rates of _____ among anxiety and related disorders are high because they share the common features of anxiety and panic.

5. _____ life events can trigger biological and psychological vulnerabilities to anxiety.

ANXIETY DISORDERS

Disorders traditionally grouped together as anxiety disorders include generalized anxiety disorder, panic disorder and agoraphobia, specific phobia, and social anxiety disorder, as well as two new disorders, separation anxiety disorder and selective mutism. These specific anxiety disorders are complicated by panic attacks or other features that are the focus of the anxiety. But in generalized anxiety disorder, the focus is generalized to the events of everyday life. Therefore, we consider generalized anxiety disorder first.

Generalized Anxiety Disorder

▶ What are the essential features, possible causes, and available treatment approaches for generalized anxiety disorder?

Most of us worry to some extent. As we have said, worry can be useful. It helps us plan for the future, make sure that we're prepared for that test, or double-check that we've thought of everything before we head home for the holidays. But what if you worry indiscriminately about everything? Furthermore, what if worrying is unproductive? What if no matter how much you worry, you can't seem to decide what to do about an upcoming problem or situation? And what if you can't stop worrying, even if you know it is doing you no good and probably making everyone else around you miserable? These features characterize **generalized anxiety disorder (GAD)**. Consider the case of Irene.

Irene... • *Ruled by Worry*

Irene, a 20-year-old college student, came to the clinic complaining of excessive anxiety and general difficulties in controlling her life. Everything was a catastrophe for Irene. Although she carried a 3.7 grade point average, she was convinced she would flunk every test she took.

Irene worried until she dropped out of the first college she attended after one month. She felt depressed for a while and then decided to take a couple of courses at a local junior college, believing she could handle the work there better. After achieving straight As at the junior college for two years, she enrolled once again in a four-year college as a junior. After a short time, she began calling the clinic in a state of extreme agitation, saying she had to drop this or that course because she couldn't handle it. With great difficulty, her therapist and parents persuaded her to stay in the courses and to seek further help. In any course Irene completed, her grade was between an A and a B-minus, but she still worried about every test and every paper.

Irene was also concerned about relationships with her friends. Whenever she was with her new boyfriend, she feared making a fool of herself and losing his interest. She reported that each date went extremely well, but she knew the next one would probably be a disaster.

Irene was also concerned about her health. She had minor hypertension, probably because she was somewhat overweight. She was also very worried about eating the wrong types or amounts of food. She became reluctant to have her blood pressure checked for fear it would be high or to weigh herself for fear she was not losing weight. She severely restricted her eating and as a result had an occasional episode of binge eating.

Although Irene had an occasional panic attack, this was not a major issue to her. As soon as the panic subsided, she focused on the next possible catastrophe. In addition to high blood pressure, Irene had tension headaches and a "nervous stomach," with a lot of gas, occasional diarrhea, and some abdominal pain. Irene's life was a series of impending catastrophes. Her mother reported that she dreaded a phone call from Irene, let alone a visit, because she knew she would have to see her daughter through a crisis. For the same reason, Irene had few friends.

Clinical Description

Irene suffered from GAD. The *DSM-5* criteria specify that at least six months of excessive anxiety and worry (apprehensive expectation) must be ongoing more days than not. Furthermore, it must be difficult to turn off or control the worry process. Most of us worry for a time but can set the problem aside and go on to another task. Even if the upcoming challenge is a big one, as soon as it is over, the worrying stops. For Irene, it never stopped. She turned to the next crisis as soon as the current one was over.

The physical symptoms associated with generalized anxiety and GAD differ somewhat from those associated with panic attacks and panic disorder (covered next). Whereas panic is associated with autonomic arousal, presumably as a result of a sympathetic nervous system surge (for instance, increased heart rate, palpitations, perspiration, and trembling), GAD is characterized by muscle tension, mental agitation (Brown, Marten, & Barlow, 1995), susceptibility to fatigue (probably the result of chronic excessive muscle tension), some irritability, and difficulty sleeping (Campbell-Sills & Brown, 2010). Focusing one's attention is difficult, as the mind quickly switches from crisis to crisis. People with GAD mostly worry about minor, everyday life events, a characteristic that distinguishes GAD from other anxiety disorders. When asked, "Do you worry excessively about minor things?" 100% of individuals with GAD respond "yes," compared with approximately 50% of individuals whose anxiety disorder falls within other categories (Barlow, 2002). Major events quickly become the focus of anxiety and worry, too. Adults typically focus on possible misfortune to their children, family health, job responsibilities, and more minor things such as household chores or being on time for appointments. Children with GAD most

often worry about competence in academic, athletic, or social performance, as well as family issues (Furr, Tiwari, Suveg, & Kendall, 2009; Weems, Silverman, & La Greca, 2000). Older adults tend to focus, understandably, on health (Wetherell *et al.*, 2010; Beck & Averill, 2004; they also have difficulty sleeping, which seems to make the anxiety worse (Beck & Stanley, 1997; Brenes, Miller, Stanley, Williamson, Knudson, & McCall, 2009).

Statistics

Although worry and physical tension are common, the severe generalized anxiety experienced by Irene is quite rare. Approximately 3.1% of the population meets criteria for GAD during a given one-year period (Kessler, Chiu, Demler, & Walters, 2005) and 5.7% at some point during their lifetime (Kessler, Berglund, Demler, Jin, & Walters, 2005), making GAD one of the most common anxiety disorders. Similar rates are reported from around the world, for example, from rural South Africa (Bhagwanjee, Parekh, Paruk, Petersen, & Subedar, 1998). Relatively few people with GAD come for treatment, however, compared with

generalized anxiety disorder (GAD) Anxiety disorder characterized by intense, uncontrollable, unfocused, chronic, and continuous worry that is distressing and unproductive, accompanied by physical symptoms of tenseness, irritability, and restlessness.

patients with panic disorder. Anxiety clinics like ours report that only approximately 10% of their patients meet criteria for GAD compared with 30% to 50% for panic disorder. This may be because most patients with GAD seek help from their primary care doctors, where they are found in large numbers (Roy-Byrne & Katon, 2000; Wittchen, 2002).

About twice as many individuals with GAD are female than male in epidemiological studies (where individuals with GAD are identified from population surveys), which include people who do not necessarily seek treatment (Grant et al., 2005). But this sex ratio may be specific to developed countries. In the South African study mentioned here, GAD was more common in males. In the United States, the prevalence of the disorder is significantly lower among Asian, Hispanic, and Black adults compared to Whites (Grant et al., 2005).

Some people with GAD report onset in early adulthood, usually in response to a life stressor. Nevertheless, most studies find that GAD is associated with an earlier and more gradual onset than most other anxiety disorders (Barlow, 2002; Beesdo, Pine, Lieb, & Wittchen, 2010). The median age of onset based on interviews is 31 (Kessler, Berglund, Demler, Jin, & Walters, 2005), but like Irene, many people have felt anxious and tense all their lives. Once it develops, GAD follows a chronic course, characterized by waxing and waning of symptoms.

GAD is prevalent among older adults. In the large national comorbidity study and its replication, GAD was found to be most common in the group over 45 years-of-age and least common in the youngest group, ages 15 to 24 (Wittchen, Zhao, Kessler, & Eaton, 1994; Byers, Yaffe, Covinsky, Friedman, & Bruce, 2010); reported prevalence rates of GAD in older adults were as high as 10%. We also know that the use of minor tranquilizers in the elderly is high. For example, in 2008, 5.2% of U.S. adults used benzodiazepines, and the percentage increased with age (Olfson, King, & Schoenbaum, 2015). The study showed that only 2.6% of the 18- to 35- year-olds but 8.7% of the 65- to 80-year-olds filled at least one prescription of benzodiazepines during the year. It is not clear why drugs are prescribed with such frequency for the elderly. One possibility is that the drugs may not be entirely intended for anxiety but rather for sleeping problems or other effects of medical illnesses. In any case, benzodiazepines interfere with cognitive function and put the elderly at greater risk for falling and breaking bones (Barlow, 2002). Difficulties that hamper the investigation of anxiety in the elderly include the lack of good assessment instruments and treatment studies, largely because of insufficient research interest (Ayers, Thorp, & Wetherell, 2009; Campbell-Sills & Brown, 2010).

In a classic study, Rodin and Langer (1977) demonstrated that older adults may be particularly susceptible to anxiety about failing health or other life situations that begin to diminish whatever control they retain over events in their lives. This increasing lack of control, failing health, and gradual loss of meaningful functions may be a particularly unfortunate by-product of the way the elderly are treated in Western culture. The result is substantial impairment in quality of life in older adults with GAD (Wetherell et al., 2004). If it were possible to change our attitudes and behavior, we might well reduce the frequency of anxiety, depression, and early death among elderly people.

Causes

What causes GAD? As with most anxiety disorders, there seems to be a generalized biological vulnerability. This is reflected in studies examining a genetic contribution to GAD, although Kendler and colleagues (1995; Hettema, Neale, & Kendler, 2001; Hettema, Prescott, Myers, Neale, & Kendler, 2005) confirmed that what seems to be inherited is the tendency to become anxious rather than GAD itself. Heritability has been found for the trait of anxiety sensitivity, the tendency to become distressed in response to arousal-related sensations arising from beliefs that these sensations have harmful consequences (Davies et al., 2015).

For years, clinicians thought that people who were generally anxious had simply not focused their anxiety on anything specific. Thus, such anxiety was described as "free floating." But now scientists have looked more closely and have discovered some interesting distinctions from other anxiety disorders.

The first hints of difference were found in the physiological responsivity of individuals with GAD. It is interesting that individuals with GAD do not respond as strongly to stressors as individuals with anxiety disorders in which panic is more prominent. Several studies have found that individuals with GAD show *less responsiveness* on most physiological measures, such as heart rate, blood pressure, skin conductance, and respiration rate (Borkovec & Hu, 1990; Roemer & Orsillo, 2013), than do individuals with other anxiety disorders. Moreover, GAD patients often show a comparatively low *cardiac vagal tone* (the vagus nerve is the largest parasympathetic nerve innervating the heart and decreasing its activity), leading to *autonomic inflexibility*, because the heart is less responsive to certain tasks (Hofmann, Moscovitch, Litz, Kim, Davis, & Pizzagalli, 2005). Therefore, people with GAD have been called *autonomic restrictors* (Barlow, Chorpita, & Turovsky, 1996; Thayer, Friedman, & Borkovec, 1996).

When individuals with GAD are compared with nonanxious "normal" participants, the one physiological measure that consistently distinguishes the anxious group is muscle tension—people with GAD are chronically tense (Andrews et al., 2010; Marten, Brown, Borkovec, Shear, & Lydiard, 1993). To understand this phenomenon of chronic muscle tension, we may have to know what's going on in the minds of people with GAD. The evidence indicates that individuals with GAD are highly sensitive to threat in general, particularly to a threat that has personal relevance. That is, they allocate their attention more readily to sources of threat than do people who are not anxious (Roemer & Orsillo, 2013; Bradley, Mogg, White, Groom, & de Bono, 1999). This high sensitivity may have arisen in early stressful experiences where they learned that the world is dangerous and out of control, and they might not be able to cope (generalized psychological vulnerability). Furthermore, this acute awareness of potential threat, particularly if it is personal, seems to be entirely automatic or unconscious.

How do mental processes link up with the tendency of individuals with GAD to be autonomic restrictors? Tom Borkovec and his colleagues noticed that although the peripheral autonomic arousal of individuals with GAD is restricted, they showed intense cognitive processing in the frontal lobes as indicated by EEG activity, particularly in the left hemisphere. This finding would suggest frantic, intense thought processes or worry without accompanying images (which would be reflected by activity in the right hemisphere of the brain rather than the left) (Borkovec, Alcaine, & Behar, 2004). Borkovec suggests that this kind of worry may be what causes these individuals to be autonomic restrictors (Borkovec, Shadick, & Hopkins, 1991; Roemer & Orsillo, 2013). That is, they are thinking so hard about upcoming problems that they don't have the attentional capacity left for the all-important process of creating images of the potential threat, images that would elicit more substantial negative affect and autonomic activity. In other words, they *avoid* images associated with the threat (Borkovec *et al.*, 2004; Fisher & Wells, 2009). But from the point of view of therapy, it is important to "process" the images and negative affect associated with anxiety (Craske & Barlow, 2006; Zinbarg, Craske, & Barlow, 2006). Because people with GAD do not seem to engage in this process, they may avoid much of the unpleasantness and pain associated with the negative affect and imagery, but they are never able to work through their problems and arrive at solutions. Therefore, they become chronic worriers, with accompanying autonomic inflexibility and quite severe muscle tension.

In summary, some people inherit a tendency to be tense (generalized biological vulnerability), and they develop a sense early on that important events in their lives may be uncontrollable and potentially dangerous (generalized psychological vulnerability). Significant stress makes them apprehensive and vigilant. This sets off intense worry with resulting physiological changes, leading to GAD (Roemer, Orsillo, & Barlow, 2002; Turovsky & Barlow, 1996). Time will tell if the current model is correct, although there is much supporting data (Borkovec, Alcaine, & Behar, 2004; Mineka & Zinbarg, 2006). In any case, it is consistent with our view of anxiety as a future-oriented mood state focused on potential danger or threat, as opposed to an emergency or alarm reaction to actual present danger. A model of the development of GAD is presented in ● Figure 4.3.

Treatment

GAD is quite common, and available treatments, both drug and psychological, are reasonably effective. Benzodiazepines are most often prescribed for generalized anxiety, and

● **Figure 4.3** An integrative model of GAD.

the evidence indicates that they give some relief, at least in the short term. Few studies have looked at the effects of these drugs for a period longer than eight weeks (Mathew & Hoffman, 2009). But the therapeutic effect is relatively modest. Furthermore, benzodiazepines carry some risks. First, they seem to impair both cognitive and motor functioning (see, for example, Hindmarch, 1990; van Laar, Volkerts, & Verbaten, 2001). The drugs may impair driving, and in older adults they seem to be associated with falls (Ray, Gurwitz, Decker, & Kennedy, 1992; Wang, Bohn, Glynn, Mogun, & Avorn, 2001). More important, benzodiazepines seem to produce both psychological and physical dependence, making it difficult for people to stop taking them (Noyes, Garvey, Cook, & Suelzer, 1991; Rickels, Schweizer, Case, & Greenblatt, 1990). There is reasonably wide agreement that the optimal use of benzodiazepines is for the short-term relief of anxiety associated with a temporary crisis or stressful event, such as a family problem (Craske & Barlow, 2006). Under these circumstances, a physician may prescribe a benzodiazepine until the crisis is resolved but for no more than a week or two. There is stronger evidence for the usefulness of antidepressants in the treatment of GAD, such as paroxetine (also called Paxil) (Rickels, Rynn, Ivengar, & Duff, 2006) and venlafaxine (also called Effexor) (Schatzberg, 2000). These drugs may prove to be a better choice (Brawman-Mintzer, 2001; Mathew & Hoffman, 2009).

In the short term, psychological treatments seem to confer about the same benefit as drugs in the treatment of GAD, but psychological treatments are more effective in the long term (Barlow, Allen, & Basden, 2007; Roemer & Orsillo, 2013). Recent reports of innovations in brief psychological treatments are encouraging. Because we now know that individuals with GAD seem to avoid "feelings" of anxiety and the negative affect associated with threatening images, clinicians have designed treatments to help patients with GAD process the threatening information on an emotional level, using images, so that they will experience (rather than avoid feeling) the emotion associated with the images. In the early 1990s, we developed a cognitive-behavioral treatment (CBT) for GAD in which patients evoke the worry process during therapy sessions and confront threatening images and thoughts head-on. The patient learns to use cognitive therapy and other coping techniques to counteract and control the worry process (Craske & Barlow, 2006; Wetherell, Gatz, & Craske, 2003). In a major study, a brief adaptation of this treatment was also used successfully to decrease anxiety and improve quality of life in a primary care office (family doctors and nurses) where GAD is a frequent complaint (Rollman et al., 2005).

Despite this success, it is clear we need more powerful treatments for GAD. Recently, a psychological treatment has been developed that incorporates procedures focusing on acceptance rather than avoidance of distressing thoughts and feelings in addition to cognitive therapy. Meditational- and mindfulness-based approaches help teach the patient to be more tolerant of these feelings (Hofmann, Sawyer, Witt, & Oh, 2010; Khoury et al., 2013). Results from a clinical trial reported some of the highest success rates yet to appear in the literature (Hayes-Skelton, Roemer, & Orsillo, 2013).

There is particularly encouraging evidence that psychological treatments are effective with children who suffer from generalized anxiety (Albano & Hack, 2004; Furr et al., 2009). Also, mindfulness-based therapies for GAD are being adapted and tested with youth with some indications of success (Semple & Burke, 2012). Similarly, progress is being made in adapting psychological treatments for older adults (Beck & Stanley, 1997; Stanley et al., 2003; Wetherell, Lenze, & Stanley, 2005). One large clinical trial demonstrated the efficiency of this treatment for adults over 60 compared to the usual care they received (Stanley et al., 2009). Other promising new strategies are to train patients in increasing their tolerance to uncertainty about the future (Dugas, Schwartz, & Francis, 2012) and changing their beliefs about worrying (Wells, Welford, King, Papageorgiou, Wisely, & Mendel, 2010), because often patients hold maladaptive beliefs about worrying, referred to as *meta-cognitions*.

After trying a number of different drugs, Irene was treated with the CBT approach developed at our clinic. She completed college and graduate school, married, and is successful in her career as a counselor in a nursing home. But even now, Irene continues to experience mild to moderate anxiety, particularly when under stress; she occasionally takes minor tranquilizers to support her psychological coping skills.

4.2 Concept CHECK

True (T) or false (F)?

1. _____ GAD is characterized by muscle tension, mental agitation, irritability, sleeping difficulties, and susceptibility to fatigue.

2. _____ Most studies show that in the majority of cases of GAD, onset is early in adulthood as an immediate response to a life stressor.

3. _____ GAD is prevalent in the elderly and in females in our society.

4. _____ GAD has no genetic basis.

5. _____ Cognitive-behavioral treatment and other psychological treatments for GAD are probably better than drug therapies in the long run.

Panic Disorder and Agoraphobia

▶ What are the essential features of panic disorder and agoraphobia?

Have you had a relative—an eccentric great-aunt, for example—who never seemed to leave her house? Perhaps you attributed her behavior to her being a little odd or not fond of travel. But your aunt may not have been just odd or eccentric. She may have suffered from **panic disorder (PD)**, an anxiety disorder in which individuals experience severe, unexpected panic attacks; they may think they're dying or otherwise losing control. In many cases,

PD is accompanied by a closely related disorder called **agoraphobia**, which is fear and avoidance of situations in which a person feels unsafe or unable to escape to get home or to a hospital in the event of a developing panic, panic-like symptoms, or other physical symptoms, such as loss of bladder control. In severe cases, people with agoraphobia are unable to leave the house, sometimes for years on end, as in the example of Mrs. M.

Mrs. M... • *Self-Imprisoned*

Mrs. M. was 67-years-old and lived in a second-floor walk-up apartment in a lower-middle-class section of the city. Her adult daughter, one of her few remaining contacts with the world, had requested an evaluation with Mrs. M.'s consent. I rang the bell and entered a narrow hallway; Mrs. M. was nowhere in sight. Knowing that she lived on the second floor, I walked up the stairs and knocked on the door at the top. When I heard Mrs. M. ask me to come in, I opened the door. She was sitting in her living room, and I could quickly see the layout of the rest of the apartment. The living room was in the front; the kitchen was in the back, adjoining a porch. To the right of the stairs was the one bedroom, with a bathroom opening from it.

Mrs. M. was glad to see me and seemed very friendly, offering me coffee and homemade cookies. I was the first person she had seen in three weeks. Mrs. M. had not left that apartment in 20 years, and she had suffered from panic disorder and agoraphobia for more than 30 years.

As she told her story, Mrs. M. conveyed vivid images of a wasted life. And yet she continued to struggle in the face of adversity and to make the best she could of her limited existence. Even areas in her apartment signaled the potential for terrifying panic attacks. She had not answered the door herself for the past 15 years because she was afraid to look into the hallway. She could enter her kitchen and go into the areas containing the stove and refrigerator, but for the past 10 years she had not been to the part of the room that overlooked the backyard or out onto the back porch. Thus, her life for the past decade had been confined to her bedroom, her living room, and the front half of her kitchen. She relied on her adult daughter to bring groceries and visit once a week. Her only other visitor was the parish priest, who came to deliver communion every two to three weeks when he could. Her only other contact with the outside world was through the television and the radio. Her husband, who had abused both alcohol and Mrs. M., had died 10 years earlier of alcohol-related causes. Early in her stressful marriage, she had her first terrifying panic attack and had gradually withdrawn from the world. As long as she stayed in her apartment, she was relatively free of panic. Therefore, and because in her mind there were few reasons left near the end of her life to venture out, she declined treatment.

Clinical Description

In *DSM-IV*, panic disorder and agoraphobia were integrated into one disorder called panic disorder with agoraphobia, but investigators discovered that many people experienced panic disorder without developing agoraphobia and some

people develop agoraphobia in the absence of panic disorder (Wittchen, Gloster, Beesdo-Baum, Fava, & Craske, 2010). Often, however, they go together, so we discuss both disorders in this section.

At the beginning of the chapter, we talked about the related phenomena of anxiety and panic. In PD, anxiety and panic are combined in an intricate relationship that can become as devastating as it was for Mrs. M. Many people who have panic attacks do not necessarily develop panic disorder. To meet criteria for panic disorder, a person must experience an unexpected panic attack *and* develop substantial anxiety over the possibility of having another attack or about the implications of the attack or its consequences. In other words, the person must think that each attack is a sign of impending death or incapacitation. A few individuals do not report concern about another attack but still change their behavior in a way that indicates the distress the attacks cause them. They may avoid going to certain places or neglect their duties around the house for fear an attack might occur if they are too active.

Most agoraphobic avoidance behavior is simply a complication of severe, unexpected panic attacks (Barlow, 2002; Craske & Barlow, 2014). Simply put, if you have had unexpected panic attacks and are afraid you may have another one, you want to be in a safe place or at least with a safe person who knows what you are experiencing if another attack occurs so that you can quickly get to a hospital or at least go into your bedroom and lie down (the home is usually a safe place). We know that anxiety is diminished for individuals with agoraphobia if they think a location or person is "safe," even if there is nothing effective the person could do if something bad did happen to the patient. For these reasons, when they do venture outside their homes, people with agoraphobia always plan for rapid escape (for example, by sitting near the door). A list of typical situations commonly avoided by someone with agoraphobia is found in Table 4.1.

Even if agoraphobic behavior is closely tied to the occasions of panic initially, it can become relatively independent of panic attacks (Craske & Barlow, 1988; White & Barlow, 2002). In other words, an individual who has not had a panic attack for years may still have strong agoraphobic avoidance, like Mrs. M. Agoraphobic avoidance seems to be determined for the most part by the extent to which you think or expect you might have another attack rather than by how many attacks you actually have or how severe they are. Thus, agoraphobic avoidance is simply one way of coping with unexpected panic attacks.

Other methods of coping with panic attacks include using (and sometimes abusing) drugs and/or alcohol. Some individuals do not avoid agoraphobic situations but

panic disorder (PD) Recurrent unexpected panic attacks accompanied by concern about future attacks and/or a lifestyle change to avoid future attacks.

agoraphobia Anxiety about being in places or situations from which escape might be difficult.

TABLE 4.1 | Typical Situations Avoided by People with Agoraphobia

Shopping malls	Being far from home
Cars (as driver or passenger)	Staying at home alone
Buses	Waiting in line
Trains	Supermarkets
Subways	Stores
Wide streets	Crowds
Tunnels	Planes
Restaurants	Elevators
Theaters	Escalators

SOURCE: Adapted, with permission, from Barlow, D. H., & Craske, M. G. (2007). *Mastery of your anxiety and panic* (4th ed., p. 5). New York: Oxford University Press.

endure them with "intense dread." For example, people who must go to work each day or, perhaps, travel as part of the job will suffer untold agonies of anxiety and panic simply to achieve their goals. Thus, *DSM-5* notes that agoraphobia may be characterized either by avoiding the situations or by enduring them with intense fear and anxiety.

Most patients with panic disorder and agoraphobic avoidance also display another cluster of avoidant behaviors that we call *interoceptive avoidance*, or avoidance of internal physical sensations (Craske & Barlow, 2014; Shear *et al.*, 1997). These behaviors involve removing oneself from situations or activities that might produce the physiological arousal that somehow resembles the beginnings of a panic attack. Some patients might avoid exercise because it produces increased cardiovascular activity or faster respiration, which reminds them of panic attacks and makes them think one might be beginning. Other patients might avoid sauna baths or any rooms in which they might perspire. Psychopathologists are beginning to recognize that this cluster of avoidance behaviors is every bit as important as more classical agoraphobic avoidance.

Statistics

PD is fairly common. Approximately 2.7% of the population meet criteria for PD during a given one-year period (Kessler, Chiu, *et al.*, 2005; Kessler, Chiu, Jin, *et al.*, 2006) and 4.7% met them at some point during their lives, two-thirds of them women (Eaton, Kessler, Wittchen, & Magee, 1994; Kessler, Berglund, Demler, Jin, Merikangas, & Walters, 2005). Another smaller group (1.4% at some point during their lives) develops agoraphobia without ever having a full-blown panic attack.

Onset of panic disorder usually occurs in early adult life—from mid-teens through about 40 years-of-age.

The median age of onset is between 20 and 24 (Kessler, Berglund, Demler, Jin, & Walters, 2005). Most initial unexpected panic attacks begin at or after puberty. Furthermore, many prepubertal children who are seen by general medical practitioners have symptoms of hyperventilation that may well be panic attacks. These children do not report fear of dying or losing control, however, perhaps because they are not at a stage of their cognitive development where they can make these attributions (Nelles & Barlow, 1988).

Important work on anxiety in the elderly suggests that health and vitality are the primary focus of anxiety in the elderly population (Mohlman *et al.*, 2012; Wolitzky-Taylor, Castriotta, Lenze, Stanley, & Craske, 2010). In general, the prevalence of PD or comorbid panic disorder and agoraphobia decreases among the elderly, from 5.7% at ages 30–44 to 2.0% or less after age 60 (Kessler, Berglund, Demler, Jin, Merikangas, & Walters, 2005).

As we have said, most (75% or more) of those who suffer from agoraphobia are women (Barlow, 2002; Myers *et al.*, 1984; Thorpe & Burns, 1983). For a long time, we didn't know why, but now it seems the most logical explanation is cultural (Arrindell *et al.*, 2003a; Wolitzky-Taylor *et al.*, 2010). It is more accepted for women to report fear and to avoid numerous situations. Men, however, are expected to be stronger and braver, to "tough it out." The higher the severity of agoraphobic avoidance, the greater the proportion of women. For example, in our clinic, out of a group of patients suffering from panic disorder with mild agoraphobia, 72% were women. If the agoraphobia was moderate, however, the percentage was 81%. Similarly, if agoraphobia was severe, the percentage was 89%.

What happens to men who have severe unexpected panic attacks? Is cultural disapproval of fear in men so strong that most of them simply endure panic? The answer seems to be "no." A large proportion of males with unexpected panic attacks cope in a culturally acceptable way: They consume large amounts of alcohol. The problem is

---

DSM 5 | **DSM DISORDER CRITERIA SUMMARY**
Panic Disorder

Features of panic disorder include the following:

A. Recurrent unexpected panic attacks are present.

B. At least one of the attacks has been followed by one month or more of one or both of the following: (a) persistent concern or worry about additional panic attacks or their consequences or (b) a significant maladaptive change in behavior related to the attacks.

C. The disturbance is not attributable to the physiological effects of a substance (e.g., a drug of abuse, a medication) or another medical condition and is not better explained by another mental disorder.

From American Psychiatric Association. (2013). *Diagnostic and statistical manual of mental disorders* (5th ed.). Washington, DC.

that people then become dependent on alcohol, and many begin the long downward spiral into serious addiction. Thus, males may end up with an even more severe problem. Because these men are so impaired by alcohol abuse, clinicians may not realize they also have panic disorder and agoraphobia. Furthermore, even if they are successfully treated for their addiction, the anxiety disorder will require treatment (McHugh, 2015).

Cultural Influences

Panic disorder exists worldwide, although its expression may vary from place to place. Prevalence rates for panic disorder show some degree of cross-cultural variability, with Asian and African countries usually showing the lowest rates. These findings mirror cross-ethnic comparisons within the United States, with Asian Americans showing the lowest, and White Americans showing the highest prevalence rates (Lewis-Fernandez *et al.*, 2010; Hofmann & Hinton, 2014). Furthermore, rates of recovery from panic disorder is lower among African Americans as compared to non-Latino White individuals (Sibrava *et al.*, 2013).

In addition to differences in prevalence rates and chronicity, cross-cultural studies have also identified interesting differences in the expression of the anxiety. An anxiety-related, culturally defined syndrome prominent among Hispanic Americans, particularly those from the Caribbean, is called *ataques de nervios* (Hinton, Chong, Pollack, Barlow, & McNally, 2008; Hinton, Lewis-Fernández, & Pollack, 2009). The symptoms of an *ataque* seem quite similar to those of a panic attack, although such manifestations as shouting uncontrollably or bursting into tears may be associated more often with *ataque* than with panic.

Nocturnal Panic

Think back to the case of Gretchen, whose panic attack was described earlier. She was sound asleep when it happened. Approximately 60% of the people with panic disorder have experienced such nocturnal attacks (Craske & Rowe, 1997; Uhde, 1994). In fact, panic attacks occur more often between 1:30 A.M. and 3:30 A.M. than any other time. In some cases, people are afraid to go to sleep at night. What's happening to them? Are they having nightmares? Research indicates they are not. Nocturnal attacks are studied in a sleep laboratory. Patients spend a few nights sleeping while attached to an electroencephalograph machine that monitors their brain waves. Nocturnal panic attacks occur during delta wave or slow wave sleep, which typically occurs several hours after we fall asleep and is the deepest stage of sleep. People with panic disorder often begin to panic when they start sinking into delta sleep, and then they awaken amid an attack. Because there is no obvious reason for them to be anxious or panicky when they are sound asleep,

most of these individuals think they are dying (Craske & Barlow, 1988; Craske & Barlow, 2014).

What causes nocturnal panic? Currently, our best information is that the change in stages of sleep to slow wave sleep produces physical sensations of "letting go" that are frightening to an individual with panic disorder (Craske, Lang, Mystkowski, Zucker, & Bystritsky, 2002). Several other events also occur during sleep that resemble nocturnal panic and are mistakenly thought by some to be the cause of nocturnal panic. Initially, these events were thought to be nightmares, but nightmares and other dreamlike activity occur only during a stage of sleep characterized by rapid eye movement (REM) sleep, which typically occurs much later in the sleep cycle. Therefore, people are not dreaming when they have nocturnal panics, a conclusion consistent with patient reports.

A related phenomenon occurring in children is called *sleep terrors* (Durand, 2006). Often children scream and get out of bed as if something were after them. However, they do not wake up and have no memory of the event in the morning. In contrast, individuals experiencing nocturnal panic attacks do wake up and later remember the event clearly. Sleep terrors also tend to occur at a later stage of sleep (stage 4 sleep), a stage associated with sleepwalking.

Finally, there is a fascinating condition called *isolated sleep paralysis* that seems culturally determined. Isolated sleep paralysis occurs during the transitional state between sleep and waking, when a person is either falling asleep or waking up, but mostly when waking up. During this period, the individual is unable to move and experiences a surge of terror that resembles a panic attack; occasionally, there are also vivid hallucinations. One possible explanation is that REM sleep is spilling over into the waking cycle. This seems likely because one feature of REM sleep is lack of bodily movement. Another is vivid dreams, which could account for the experience of hallucination. Interestingly, rates of sleep paralysis vary by ethnic groups and samples. Sharpless and Barber (2011) showed that rates of sleep paralysis are highest among African American samples in the general population (40.2%) and psychiatric samples (44.3%), and also among Asian American student samples (39.9%). In contrast, the rate in the general population across all groups is 7.6%. Also interesting is that the disorder does not seem to occur in Nigerian blacks. The prevalence in Nigerian blacks is about the same as it is in American whites. The reasons for this distribution are not clear, although all factors point to a cultural explanation.

Causes

It is not possible to understand panic disorder without referring to the triad of contributing factors mentioned throughout this book: biological, psychological, and social. Strong evidence indicates that agoraphobia often develops after a person has unexpected panic attacks (or panic-like sensations), but whether agoraphobia develops and how severe it becomes seem to be socially and culturally determined, as we noted earlier. Panic attacks and panic disorder, however, seem to be related most strongly to biological and psychological factors and their interaction.

According to the triple vulnerability model (Bouton *et al.*, 2001; White & Barlow, 2002) (see ● Figure 4.2), we all inherit—some more than others—a vulnerability to stress, which is a tendency to be generally neurobiologically overreactive to the events of daily life (generalized biological vulnerability). But some people are also more likely than others to have an emergency alarm reaction (unexpected panic attack) when confronted with stress-producing events. Particular situations quickly become associated in an individual's mind with external and internal cues that were present during the panic attack (Bouton *et al.*, 2001). The next time the person's heart rate increases during exercise, she might assume she is having a panic attack (conditioning). Being in a movie theater when panic first occurred would be an external cue that might become a conditioned stimulus for future panics. Because these cues become associated with a number of different internal and external stimuli through a learning process, we call them *learned alarms*.

But none of this would make much difference without the next step. Why would some people think something terrible is going to happen when they have an attack but others wouldn't? In an important study, young women at risk for developing anxiety disorders were followed prospectively for several years. Those women who had a history of various physical disorders and were anxious about their health tended to develop panic disorder rather than another anxiety disorder such as social anxiety disorder (Rudaz, Craske, Becker, Ledermann, & Margraf, 2010). Thus, these women may have learned in childhood that unexpected bodily sensations may be dangerous—whereas other people experiencing panic attacks do not. This tendency to believe that unexpected bodily sensations are dangerous reflects a specific psychological vulnerability to develop panic and related disorders. The causal sequence for the development of panic disorder is depicted in ● Figure 4.4.

Approximately 8% to 12% of the population has an occasional unexpected panic attack, often during a period of intense stress over the previous year (Kessler, Chiu *et al.*, 2006; Mattis & Ollendick, 2002). Most of these people do not develop anxiety (Telch *et al.*, 1989). They seem to attribute the attack to events of the moment, such as an argument with a friend, something they ate, or a bad day, and go on with their lives.

The influential cognitive theories of David Clark (1986, 1996) explicate in more detail some cognitive processes that may be ongoing in panic disorder. Clark emphasizes the specific psychological vulnerability of people with this disorder to interpret normal physical sensations in a catastrophic way. In other words, although we all typically experience rapid heartbeat after exercise, if you have a psychological or cognitive vulnerability, you might interpret the response as dangerous and feel a surge of anxiety. This anxiety, in turn, produces more physical sensations because of the action of the sympathetic nervous system; you perceive these additional sensations as even more dangerous, and a vicious cycle begins that results in a panic attack. Thus, Clark emphasizes the cognitive process as most important in panic disorder.

Treatment

As we noted in Chapter 1, research on the effectiveness of new treatments is important to psychopathology. Responses to certain specific treatments, whether drug or psychological, may indicate the causes of the disorder. We now discuss the benefits and some drawbacks of medication, psychological interventions, and a combination of these two treatments.

Medication

A large number of drugs affecting the noradrenergic, serotonergic, or GABA–benzodiazepine neurotransmitter systems, or some combination, seem effective in treating

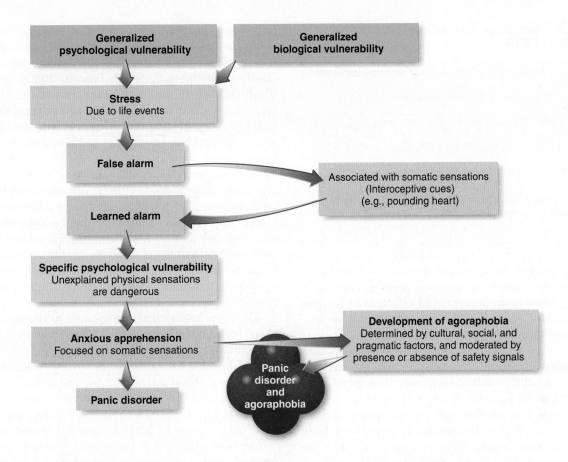

● **Figure 4.4** A model of the causes of panic disorder with or without agoraphobia. (Reprinted, with permission, from White, K. S., & Barlow, D. H. (2002). Panic disorder and agoraphobia. In D. H. Barlow, Anxiety and its disorders: The nature and treatment of anxiety and panic, 2nd ed. New York: Guilford Press, © 2002 by Guilford Press.)

panic disorder, including high-potency benzodiazepines, the newer selective-serotonin re-uptake inhibitors (SSRIs) such as Prozac and Paxil, and the closely related serotonin-norepinephrine re-uptake inhibitors (SNRIs), such as venlafaxine (Barlow & Craske, 2013; Pollack & Simon, 2009).

There are advantages and disadvantages to each class of drugs. SSRIs are currently the indicated drug for panic disorder based on all available evidence, although sexual dysfunction seems to occur in 75% or more of people taking these medications (Lecrubier, Bakker *et al.*, 1997; Lecrubier, Judge *et al.*, 1997). On the other hand, high-potency benzodiazepines such as alprazolam (Xanax), commonly used for panic disorder, work quickly but are hard to stop taking because of psychological and physical dependence and addiction. Therefore, they are not recommended as strongly as the SSRIs. Nevertheless, benzodiazepines remain the most widely used class of drugs in practice (Blanco *et al.*, 2004) and their use continues to increase (Comer, Mojtabai, & Olfson, 2011).

Approximately 60% of patients with panic disorder are free of panic as long as they stay on an effective drug (Lecrubier, Bakker *et al.*, 1997; Pollack & Simon, 2009),

but 20% or more stop taking the drug before treatment is done (Otto, Behar, Smits, & Hofmann, 2009), and relapse rates are high (approximately 50%) once the medication is stopped (Hollon *et al.*, 2005). The relapse rate is closer to 90% for those who stop taking benzodiazepines (see, for example, Fyer *et al.*, 1987).

Psychological Intervention

Psychological treatments have proved quite effective for panic disorder. Originally, such treatments concentrated on reducing agoraphobic avoidance, using strategies based on exposure to feared situations. The strategy of exposure-based treatments is to arrange conditions in which the patient can gradually face the feared situations and learn there is nothing to fear. Sometimes the therapist accompanies the patients on their exposure exercises. At other times, the therapist simply helps patients structure their own exercises and provides them with a variety of psychological coping mechanisms to help them complete the exercises, which are typically arranged from least to most difficult. A sample of these is listed in Table 4.2.

TABLE 4.2 | Situation-Exposure Tasks (From Least to Most Difficult)

Shopping in a crowded supermarket for 30 minutes alone
Walking five blocks away from home alone
Driving on a busy highway for 5 miles with spouse and alone
Eating in a restaurant, seated in the middle
Watching a movie while seated in the middle of the row

SOURCE: Adapted, with permission, from Barlow, D. H., & Craske, M. G. (2007). Mastery of your anxiety and panic (4th ed., p. 133). New York: Oxford University Press.

Gradual exposure exercises, sometimes combined with anxiety-reducing coping mechanisms such as relaxation or breathing retraining, have proved effective in helping patients overcome agoraphobic behavior whether associated with panic disorder or not (Craske & Barlow, 2014). As many as 70% of patients undergoing these treatments substantially improve as their anxiety and panic are reduced and their agoraphobic avoidance is greatly diminished. Few, however, are cured, because many still experience some anxiety and panic attacks, although at a less severe level.

Effective psychological treatments have recently been developed that treat panic disorder directly even in the absence of agoraphobia (Barlow & Craske, 2007; Craske & Barlow, 2014). **Panic control treatment (PCT)** developed at one of our clinics concentrates on exposing patients with panic disorder to the cluster of interoceptive (physical) sensations that remind them of their panic attacks. The therapist attempts to create "mini" panic attacks in the office by having the patients exercise to elevate their heart rates or perhaps by spinning them in a chair to make them dizzy. A variety of exercises have been developed for this purpose. Patients also receive cognitive therapy. Basic attitudes and perceptions concerning the dangerousness of the feared but objectively harmless situations are identified and modified. As discussed earlier, many of these attitudes and perceptions are beyond the patient's awareness. Uncovering these unconscious cognitive processes requires a great deal of therapeutic skill. Sometimes, in addition to exposure to interoceptive sensations and cognitive therapy, patients are taught relaxation or breathing retraining to help them reduce anxiety and excess arousal, but we are using these strategies less often because we find they are not necessary.

Combined Psychological and Drug Treatments

How do psychological and drug treatments compare with each other? And do they work together? One major study sponsored by the National Institute of Mental Health looked at the separate and combined effects of psychological and drug treatments (Barlow, Gorman, Shear, & Woods, 2000). In this double-blind study, patients were randomized into five treatment conditions: psychological treatment alone (CBT); drug treatment alone (imipramine—IMI—a tricyclic antidepressant, was used because this study was begun before the SSRIs were available); a combined treatment condition (IMI + CBT); and two "control" conditions, one using placebo alone (PBO), and one using PBO + CBT (to determine the extent to which any advantage for combined treatment was caused by placebo contribution). The data indicate that all treatment groups responded significantly better than the placebo group, but approximately the same number of patients responded to both drug and psychological treatments. Combined treatment was no better than individual treatments.

After six additional months of maintenance treatment (nine months after treatment was initiated), during which patients were seen once per month, the results looked much as they did after initial treatment, except there was a slight advantage for combined treatment at this point and the number of people responding to placebo had diminished. ● Figure 4.5 shows the last set of results, six months after treatment was discontinued (15 months after it was initiated). At this point, patients on medication, whether combined with CBT or not, had deteriorated somewhat, and those receiving CBT without the drug had retained most of their gains. For example, 14 of 29 patients (48% of those who began the six-month follow-up phase) who were taking the drug combined with CBT (IMI + CBT) relapsed, with those who dropped

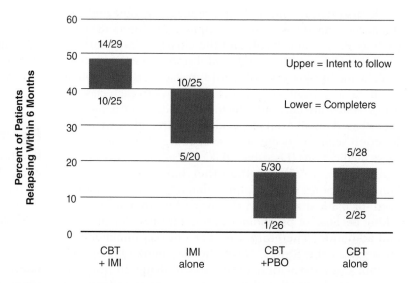

● **Figure 4.5** Posttreatment relapse rates in patients with panic disorder. (Adapted from Barlow, D. H., Gorman, J. M., Shear, K. M., & Woods, S. W. (2000). Cognitive-behavioral therapy, imipramine, or their combination for panic disorder: A randomized controlled trial. Journal of the American Medical Association, 283(19), 2529–2536.)

out during this period counted as failures (intent to follow). Forty percent, or 10 of 25, of those patients who completed the follow-up phase relapsed. Notice the much lower relapse figure for the conditions containing CBT. Thus, treatments containing CBT without the drug tended to be superior at this point, because they had more enduring effects.

Most studies show that drugs, particularly benzodiazepines, may interfere with the effects of psychological treatments (Craske & Barlow, 2014). Furthermore, benzodiazepines taken over a long period are associated with cognitive impairment (Deckersbach, Moshier, Tuschen-Caffier, & Otto, 2011). Because of this, our multisite collaborative team asked whether a sequential strategy in which one treatment was delayed until later and only given to those patients who didn't do as well as hoped would work better than giving both treatments at the same time. This study, which was the second part of our long-term strategies research described above (Payne et al., 2016), examined 58 of the original 256 patients treated with CBT who did not respond adequately to the initial treatment and randomized these patients to a study where they either received continued CBT or the SSRI drug paroxetine. Paroxetine was administered for up to 12 months, whereas the CBT was delivered for three months. At the end of the three-month period, patients receiving paroxetine responded better than those receiving continued CBT, but these differences had disappeared by the one-year follow-up. So clinicians must judge if the more rapid response among some patients is worth trying drug treatment given that subsequent improvement will be about the same at a later date.

What about those patients already taking drugs? In the primary care setting, adding CBT to the treatment of patients already on medications resulted in significant further improvement compared with those patients on medication who did not have CBT added (Craske et al., 2005).

General conclusions from these studies suggest no advantage to combining drugs and CBT initially for panic disorder and agoraphobia. Furthermore, the psychological treatments seemed to perform better in the long run (six months after treatment had stopped). This suggests that psychological treatment should be offered initially, followed by drug treatment for those patients who do not respond adequately or for whom psychological treatment is not available.

4.3 Concept CHECK

True (T) or false (F)?

1. _____ Panic disorder is a disorder in which an individual experiences anxiety and panic triggered by being in an "unsafe" situation.

2. _____ About 40% of the population meets the criteria for panic disorder at some point in life.

3. _____ Some individuals with panic disorder are suicidal, have nocturnal panic, and/or are agoraphobic.

4. _____ Psychological treatments like PCT or CBT are highly effective for treating panic disorder.

Specific Phobia

▶ What are the principal causes of specific phobia?

▶ What strategies are typically used to treat specific phobia?

Remember Judy in Chapter 1? When she saw a film of the frog being dissected, Judy began feeling queasy. Eventually she reached the point of fainting if someone simply said, "Cut it out." Judy has what we call a *specific phobia*.

Clinical Description

A **specific phobia** is an irrational fear of a specific object or situation that markedly interferes with an individual's ability to function. Many of you might be afraid of something that is not dangerous, such as going to the dentist, or have a greatly exaggerated fear of something that is only slightly dangerous, such as driving a car. Surveys indicate that specific fears of a variety of objects or situations occur in a majority of the population (Myers et al., 1984). But the very commonness of fears, even severe fears, often causes people to trivialize the more serious psychological disorder known as a specific phobia. These phobias can be extremely disabling, as we saw with Judy.

For many people, phobias are a nuisance—sometimes an extremely inconvenient nuisance—but people can adapt to life with a phobia by simply working around it somehow. In upstate New York and New England, some people are afraid

....

panic control treatment (PCT) Cognitive–behavioral treatment for panic attacks, involving gradual exposure to feared somatic sensations and modification of perceptions and attitudes about them.

specific phobia Unreasonable **fear** of a specific object or situation that markedly interferes with daily life functioning.

TABLE 4.3 | Phobias Beginning with "A"

Term	Fear of:
Acarophobia	Insects, mites
Achluophobia	Darkness, night
Acousticophobia	Sounds
Acrophobia	Heights
Aerophobia	Air currents, drafts, wind
Agoraphobia	Open spaces
Agyiophobia	Crossing the street
Aichmophobia	Sharp, pointed objects; knives; being touched by a finger
Ailurophobia	Cats
Algophobia	Pain
Amathophobia	Dust
Amychophobia	Laceration; being clawed, scratched
Androphobia	Men (and sex with men)
Anemophobia	Air currents, wind, drafts
Anginophobia	Angina pectoris (brief attacks of chest pain)
Anthropophobia	Human society
Antlophobia	Floods
Apeirophobia	Infinity
Aphephobia	Physical contact, being touched
Apiphobia	Bees, bee stings
Astraphobia	Thunderstorms, lightning
Ataxiophobia	Disorder
Atephobia	Ruin
Auroraphobia	Northern lights
Autophobia	Being alone, solitude, oneself, being egotistical

SOURCE: Reprinted, with permission, from Maser, J. D. (1985). List of phobias. In A. H. Tuma & J. D. Maser (Eds.), *Anxiety and the anxiety disorders* (p. 805). Mahwah, NJ: Erlbaum, © 1985 Lawrence Erlbaum Associates.

to drive in the snow. We have had people come to our clinics who have been so severely phobic that during the winter they were ready to uproot, change their jobs and their lives, and move south. That is one way of dealing with a phobia. We discuss some other ways at the end of this chapter.

Judy's phobia meets the *DSM-5* criterion of marked fear and anxiety about a specific object or situation. She recognized that her fear and anxiety were out of proportion to any actual danger and went to considerable lengths to avoid situations in which her phobic response might occur.

There are as many phobias as there are objects and situations. The variety of Greek and Latin names contrived to describe phobias stuns the imagination. Table 4.3 gives only the phobias beginning with the letter "a" from a long list compiled by Jack D. Maser from medical dictionaries and other diverse sources (Maser, 1985). This sort of list has little or no value for people studying psychopathology, but it does show the extent of the named phobias.

Before the publication of *DSM-IV* in 1994, no meaningful classification of specific phobias existed. We have now learned, however, that distinct types of specific phobia differ in major ways. Four major subtypes of specific phobia have been identified: blood–injection–injury type, situational type (such as planes, elevators, or enclosed places), natural environment type (for example, heights, storms, and water), and animal type. A fifth category, "other," includes phobias that do not fit any of the four major subtypes (for example, situations that may lead to choking, vomiting, or contracting an illness or, in children, avoidance of loud sounds or costumed characters). Although this subtyping strategy is useful, we also know that most people who suffer from phobia tend to have multiple phobias of several types (LeBeau *et al.*, 2010; Hofmann, Lehman, & Barlow, 1997).

Blood–Injection–Injury Phobia

How do phobia subtypes differ from each other? We have already seen one major difference in the case of Judy. Rather than the usual surge of activity in the sympathetic nervous system and increased heart rate and blood pressure, Judy experienced a marked drop in heart rate and blood pressure and fainted as a consequence. Many people who suffer from phobias and experience panic attacks in their feared situations report that they feel like they are going to faint, but they never do because their heart rate and blood pressure are actually increasing. Therefore, those with **blood–injection–injury phobias** almost always differ in their physiological reaction from people with other types of phobia (Barlow & Liebowitz, 1995; Hofmann, Alpers, & Pauli, 2009). We also noted in Chapter 2 that blood–injection–injury phobia runs in families more strongly than any phobic disorder we know. This is probably because people with this phobia inherit a strong vasovagal response to blood, injury, or the possibility of an injection, all of which cause a drop in blood pressure and a tendency to faint. The phobia develops over the possibility of having this response. The average age of onset for this phobia is approximately nine years (LeBeau *et al.*, 2010).

Situational Phobia

Phobias characterized by fear of public transportation or enclosed places are called **situational phobias**. Claustrophobia, a fear of small enclosed places, is situational, as is a phobia of flying. Psychopathologists first thought that situational phobia was similar to panic disorder and agoraphobia. Situational phobia, as well as panic disorder and agoraphobia, tends to emerge from mid-teens to mid-20s (Craske *et al.*, 2006; LeBeau *et al.*, 2010). The extent to which PD, agoraphobia, and situational phobias run in families is also similar (Curtis, Hill, & Lewis, 1990; Fyer *et al.*, 1990), with approximately 30% of first-degree relations having the same or a similar phobia. But some analyses do not support the similarity as anything more than superficial (Antony, Brown, & Barlow, 1997a, 1997b). The main difference between situational phobia and panic disorder is that people with situational phobia never experience panic attacks outside the context of their phobic object or situation. Therefore, they can relax when they don't have to confront their phobic situation. People with panic disorder, in contrast, might experience unexpected, uncued panic attacks at any time.

Natural Environment Phobia

Sometimes very young people develop fears of situations or events occurring in nature. These fears are called **natural environment phobias**. The major examples are heights, storms, and water. These fears also seem to cluster together (Antony & Barlow, 2002; Hofmann *et al.*, 1997): If you fear one situation or event, such as deep water, you are likely to fear another, such as storms. Many of these situations have some danger associated with them and, therefore, mild to moderate fear can be adaptive. For example, we should be careful in a high place or in deep water. It is entirely possible that we are somewhat prepared to be afraid of these situations; as we discussed in Chapter 2, something in our genes makes us sensitive to these situations if any sign of danger is present. In any case, these phobias have a peak age of onset of about seven years. They are not phobias if they are only passing fears. They have to be persistent (lasting at least six months) and to interfere substantially with the person's functioning, leading to avoidance of boat trips or summer vacations in the mountains where there might be a storm.

Animal Phobia

Fears of animals and insects are called **animal phobias**. Again, these fears are common but become phobic only if severe interference with functioning occurs. For example, we have seen cases in our clinic in which people with snake or mice phobias are unable to read magazines for fear of unexpectedly coming across a picture of one of these animals. There are many places that these people are unable to go, even if they want to very much, such as to the country to visit someone. The fear experienced by people with animal phobias is different from an ordinary mild revulsion. The age of onset for these phobias, like that of natural environment phobias, peaks at around seven years (Antony *et al.*, 1997a; LeBeau *et al.*, 2010).

Statistics

Specific fears occur in a majority of people. The ones most commonly found in the population at large, categorized by Agras, Sylvester, and Oliveau (1969), are presented in Table 4.4. Not surprisingly, fears of snakes and heights rank near the top. Few people who report specific fears qualify as having a phobia. During a given one-year period the prevalence is 8.7% overall (Kessler, Berglund, Demler *et al.*, 2005), but 15.8% in adolescents (Kessler, Petukhova *et al.*, 2012). This is a high percentage, making specific phobia one of the most common psychological disorders in the United States and around the world (Arrindell *et al.*, 2003b). As with common fears, the sex ratio for specific phobias is, at 4:1, overwhelmingly female; this is also consistent around the world (Craske *et al.*, 2006; LeBeau *et al.*, 2010).

Even though phobias may interfere with an individual's functioning, only the most severe cases come for treatment, because more mildly affected people tend to work around their phobias. For example, someone with a fear of heights

blood–injection–injury phobia Unreasonable **fear** and avoidance of exposure to blood, injury, or the possibility of an injection. Victims experience fainting and a drop in blood pressure.

situational phobia Anxiety involving enclosed places (for example, claustrophobia) or public transportation (for example, **fear** of flying).

natural environment phobia Fear of situations or events in nature, especially heights, **storms, and water.**

animal phobia Unreasonable, enduring **fear** of animals or insects that usually develops early in life.

TABLE 4.4 | Prevalence of Intense Fears and Phobias

Intense Fear	Prevalence per 1,000 Population	Sex Distribution	SE by Sex
Snakes	253	M: 118 F: 376	M: 34 F: 48
Heights	120	M: 109 F: 128	M: 33 F: 36
Flying	109	M: 70 F: 144	M: 26 F: 38
Enclosures	50	M: 32 F: 63	M: 18 F: 25
Illness	33	M: 31 F: 35	M: 18 F: 19
Death	33	M: 46 F: 21	M: 21 F: 15
Injury	23	M: 24 F: 22	M: 15 F: 15
Storms	31	M: 9 F: 48	M: 9 F: 22
Dentists	24	M: 22 F: 26	M: 15 F: 16
Journeys alone	16	M: 0 F: 31	M: 0 F: 18
Being alone	10	M: 5 F: 13	M: 7 F: 11

SOURCE: Adapted, with permission, from Agras, W. S., Sylvester, D., & Oliveau, D. (1969). The epidemiology of common fears and phobias. *Comprehensive Psychiatry*, 10, 151–156, © 1969 Elsevier.

arranges her life so she never has to be in a tall building or other high place. People with situational phobias of such things as driving, flying, or small enclosed places most often come for treatment.

Once a phobia develops, it tends to last a lifetime (run a chronic course) (see, for example, Barlow, 2002; Kessler, Berglund, Demler *et al.*, 2005); thus, the issue of treatment, described shortly, becomes important.

Although most anxiety disorders look much the same in adults and in children, clinicians must be aware of the types of normal fears and anxieties experienced throughout childhood so that they can distinguish them from specific phobias (Albano *et al.*, 1996; Silverman & Rabian, 1993). Infants, for example, show marked fear of loud noises and strangers. At one to two years of age, children quite normally are anxious about separating from parents, and fears of animals and the dark also develop and may persist into

the fourth or fifth year of life. Fear of various monsters and other imaginary creatures may begin about age three and last for several years. At age 10, children may fear evaluation by others and feel anxiety over their physical appearance. Generally, reports of fear decline with age, although performance-related fears of such activities as taking a test or talking in front of a large group may increase with age. Specific phobias seem to decline with old age (Ayers *et al.*, 2009; Blazer, George, & Hughes, 1991; Sheikh, 1992).

The prevalence of specific phobias varies from one culture to another (Hinton & Good, 2009). Hispanics are two times more likely to report specific phobias than white non-Hispanic Americans (Magee, Eaton, Wittchen, McGonagle, & Kessler, 1996), for reasons not entirely clear. A variant of phobia in Chinese cultures is called *Pa-leng*, sometimes *frigo phobia* or "fear of the cold." *Pa-leng* can be understood only in the context of traditional ideas—in this case, the Chinese concepts of *yin* and *yang* (Tan, 1980). Chinese medicine holds that there must be a balance of yin and yang forces in the body for health to be maintained. Yin represents the cold, dark, windy, energy-sapping aspects of life; yang refers to the warm, bright, energy-producing aspects of life. Individuals with *Pa-leng* have a morbid fear of the cold. They ruminate over loss of body heat and may wear several layers of clothing even on a hot day. As discussed earlier, these ideas also play a role in phobia and anxiety disorders in other Asian cultures (Hinton, Park, Hsia, Hofmann, & Pollack, 2009; Hinton, Pich, Chhean, Pollack, & Barlow, 2004).

Causes

For a long time, we thought that most specific phobias began with an unusual traumatic event. For example, if you were bitten by a dog, you would develop a phobia of dogs. We now know this is not necessarily the case (Barlow, 2002; Craske *et al.*, 2006). This is not to say that traumatic conditioning experiences do not result in subsequent phobic behavior. Almost every person with a choking phobia has had some kind of a choking experience. An individual with claustrophobia who recently came to our clinic reported being trapped in an elevator for an extraordinarily long period. These are examples of phobias acquired by *direct experience*, where real danger or pain results in an alarm response (a true alarm). This is one way of developing a phobia, and there are at least three others: *experiencing* a false alarm (panic attack) in a specific situation, *observing* someone else experiencing severe fear (vicarious experience), or, under the right conditions, *being told* about danger.

Studies show that many people with specific phobias do not necessarily experience a true alarm resulting from real danger at the onset of their phobia. Many initially have an unexpected panic attack in a specific situation, perhaps related to current life stress. A specific phobia of that situation may then develop. This was evident in a study with driving phobia (Ehlers, Hofmann, Herda, & Roth, 1994).

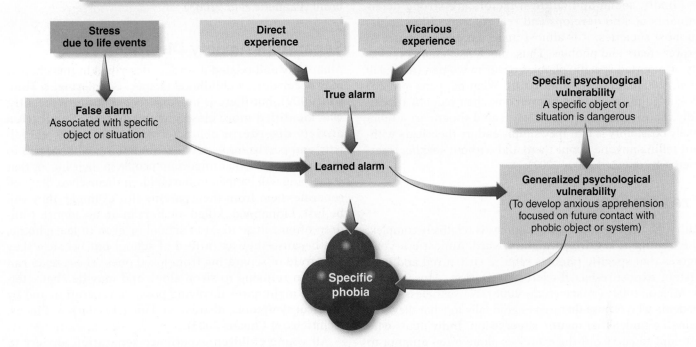

Generalized biological vulnerability
Includes heritable tendency to be "prepared" to associate fear with objects or situations that have been dangerous to the human species (e.g., heights, snakes, spiders), and low threshold for specific defensive reactions (e.g., alarms—tendency to faint at sight of blood) (vasovagal response)

Stress due to life events

Direct experience

Vicarious experience

True alarm

False alarm
Associated with specific object or situation

Specific psychological vulnerability
A specific object or situation is dangerous

Learned alarm

Generalized psychological vulnerability
(To develop anxious apprehension focused on future contact with phobic object or system)

Specific phobia

● **Figure 4.6** A model of the various ways a specific phobia may develop. (From Barlow, D. H. (2002). Anxiety and its disorders: The nature and treatment of anxiety and panic (2nd ed.). New York: Guilford Press.)

Although only a minority (14%) met criteria for panic disorder, the majority (81%) of people with excessive fear of driving an automobile reported having had panic attacks. When asked about the primary reason for their phobia, only 15% attributed it to an accident, whereas 53% attributed it to the possibility of having panic attacks. These people were also more concerned about anxiety symptoms while driving than those who gave other, non-accident-related reasons for their driving phobia.

We also learn fears vicariously. Seeing someone else have a traumatic experience or endure intense fear may be enough to instill a phobia in the watcher. Sometimes just being warned repeatedly about a potential danger is sufficient for someone to develop a phobia (Muris & Field, 2010). We call this mode of developing a phobia *information transmission*.

Terrifying experiences alone do not create phobias. As we have said, a true phobia also requires anxiety over the possibility of another extremely traumatic event or false alarm, and we are likely to avoid situations in which that terrible thing might occur. If we don't develop anxiety, our reaction would presumably be in the category of normal fears experienced by more than half the population. Normal fear can cause mild distress, but it is usually ignored and forgotten. This point is best illustrated by Peter DiNardo and his colleagues (1988), who studied a group of dog phobics, as well as a matched group who

did not have the phobia. Only about 50% of the dog phobics had had a frightening encounter with a dog, usually involving a bite. In the other group of individuals who did not have dog phobia, however, about 50% had also had a frightening encounter with a dog. Why hadn't they become phobics as well? They had not developed anxiety about another encounter with a dog, unlike the people who did become phobic (reflecting a generalized psychological vulnerability). A diagram of the etiology of specific phobia is presented in ● Figure 4.6.

In summary, several things have to occur for a person to develop a phobia. First, a traumatic conditioning experience often plays a role (even hearing about a frightening event is sufficient for some individuals). Second, fear is more likely to develop if we are "prepared"; that is, we seem to carry an inherited tendency to fear situations that have always been dangerous to the human race, such as being threatened by wild animals or trapped in small places (see Chapter 2).

Third, we also have to be susceptible to developing anxiety about the possibility that the event will happen again. We have discussed the biological and psychological reasons for anxiety and have seen that at least one phobia, blood–injection–injury phobia, is highly heritable (Öst, 1989; Ayala, Meuret, & Ritz, 2009; Page & Martin, 1998). Patients with blood phobia probably also inherit a strong vasovagal response that makes them susceptible to fainting. This alone would not be sufficient to ensure their becoming phobic, but it combines with anxiety to produce strong vulnerability.

Finally, social and cultural factors are strong determinants of who develops and reports a specific phobia. In most societies, it is almost unacceptable for males to express fears and phobias. Thus, the overwhelming majority of reported specific phobias occur in women (Arrindell et al., 2003b; LeBeau et al., 2010). What happens to men? Possibly they work hard to overcome their fears by repeatedly exposing themselves to their feared situations. A more likely possibility is that they simply endure their fears without telling anyone about them and without seeking treatment (Antony & Barlow, 2002).

Treatment

Although the development of phobias is relatively complex, the treatment is fairly straightforward. Almost everyone agrees that specific phobias require structured and consistent exposure-based exercises (Barlow, Moscovitch, & Micco, 2004; Craske et al., 2006). Nevertheless, most patients who expose themselves gradually to what they fear must be under therapeutic supervision. Individuals who attempt to carry out the exercises alone often attempt to do too much too soon and end up escaping the situation, which may strengthen the phobia. In addition, if they fear having another unexpected panic attack in this situation, it is helpful to direct therapy at panic attacks in the manner described for panic disorder (Antony, Craske, & Barlow, 2006; Craske et al., 2006).

In cases of blood–injection–injury phobia, where fainting is a real possibility, graduated exposure-based exercises must be done in specific ways. Individuals must tense various muscle groups during exposure exercises to keep their blood pressure sufficiently high to complete the practice (Ayala, Meuret, & Ritz, 2009; Öst & Sterner, 1987). New developments make it possible to treat many specific phobias, including blood phobia, in a single, session taking anywhere from approximately two to six hours (see, for example, Hauner, Mineka, Voss, & Paller, 2012; Oar, Farrell, Waters, Conlon, & Ollendick, 2015). Basically, the therapist spends most of the session with the individual, working through exposure exercises with the phobia object or situation. The patient then practices approaching the phobic situation at home, checking in occasionally with the therapist. It is interesting that in these cases, not only does the phobia disappear, but in blood phobia the tendency to experience the vasovagal response at the sight of blood also lessens considerably. It is also now clear, based on brain-imaging work, that these treatments change brain functioning in an enduring way by modifying neural circuitry in such areas as the amygdala, insula, and cingulate cortex (Hauner et al., 2012). After treatment, responsiveness is diminished in this fear-sensitive network but increased in prefrontal cortical areas, suggesting that more rational appraisals were inhibiting emotional appraisals of danger. Thus, these treatments "rewire" the brain (Paquette et al., 2003).

Separation Anxiety Disorder

All anxiety and related disorders described in this chapter may occur during childhood (Rapee, Schniering, & Hudson, 2009), but there is one disorder that, until recently, was identified more closely with children. **Separation anxiety disorder** is characterized by children's unrealistic and persistent worry that something will happen to their parents or other important people in their life, or that something will happen to the children themselves that will separate them from their parents (for example, they will be lost, kidnapped, killed, or hurt in an accident). Children often refuse to go to school or even to leave home, not because they are afraid of school but because they are afraid of separating from loved ones. These fears can result in refusing to sleep alone and may be characterized by nightmares involving possible separation and by physical symptoms, distress, and anxiety (Barlow, Pincus, Heinrichs, & Choate, 2003).

All young children experience separation anxiety to some extent; this fear usually decreases as they grow older. Therefore, a clinician must judge whether the separation anxiety is greater than would be expected at that particular age (Allen, Lavallee, Herren, Ruhe, & Schneider, 2010; Barlow et al., 2003). It is also important to differentiate separation anxiety from school phobia. In school phobia, the fear is clearly focused on something specific to the school situation; the child can leave the parents or other attachment figures to go somewhere other than school. In separation anxiety, the act of separating from the parent or attachment figure provokes anxiety and fear; 4.1% of children have separation anxiety at a severe enough level to meet criteria for a disorder (Shear, Jin, Ruscio, Walters, & Kessler, 2006).

Several years ago it was discovered that separation anxiety, if untreated, can extend into adulthood in approximately 35% of cases (Shear et al., 2006). Furthermore, evidence suggests that it occurs in approximately 6.6% of the adult population over the course of a lifetime (Shear et al., 2006). In some cases, the onset is in adulthood rather than carrying over from childhood. The focus of anxiety in adults is the same: that harm may befall loved ones during separation (Manicavasagar et al., 2010; Silove, Marnane, Wagner, Manicavasagar, & Rees, 2010). With the recognition that separation anxiety disorder occurs across the life span and is characterized by a unique presentation, a decision was made to elevate this disorder to a full status as a diagnostic category in DSM-5. As with any new disorder, the expectation is that this problem will receive greater attention from a research point of view and that individuals in all age ranges suffering from this problem will find it easier to get the help they need.

In treating separation anxiety in children, parents are often included to help structure the exercises and also to address parental reaction to childhood anxiety (Choate, Pincus, Eyberg, & Barlow, 2005; Pincus, Santucci, Ehrenreich, & Eyberg, 2008). More recently, researchers have explored the use of real-time coaching of parents using a small microphone in parents' ears to allow therapists to actively instruct parents in how to best respond when their child resists separation (Sacks, Comer, Pincus, Comacho, & Hunter, 2013; Puliafico, Comer, & Pincus, 2012). Innovative formats for treatment have also proven highly successful, including, as noted above, an intensive one-week program for girls with separation anxiety disorder aged 8 to 11 in which the girls end up having a sleepover at the clinic on the final day of treatment (Santucci *et al.*, 2009).

Social Anxiety Disorder (Social Phobia)

▶ What are the principal causes of social anxiety disorder (social phobia)?

▶ What strategies are used to treat social anxiety disorder (social phobia)?

Are you shy? If so, you have something in common with 20% to 50% of college students, depending on which survey you read. A much smaller number of people, who suffer severely around others, have **social anxiety disorder (SAD)**, also called **social phobia**. Consider the case of Billy, a 13-year-old boy.

Clinical Description

SAD is more than exaggerated shyness (Hofmann, Alpers, & Pauli, 2009; Morrison, & Heimberg, 2013). The cases described here are typical of many that appear occasionally in the press over the years.

Billy... • *Too Shy*

Billy was the model boy at home. He did his homework, stayed out of trouble, obeyed his parents, and was generally so quiet and reserved he didn't attract much attention. When he got to junior high school, however, something his parents had noticed earlier became painfully evident. Billy had no friends. He was unwilling to attend social or sporting activities connected with school, even though most of the other kids in his class went to these events. When his parents decided to check with the guidance counselor, they found that she had been about to call them. She reported that Billy did not socialize or speak up in class and was sick to his stomach all day if he knew he was going to be called on. His teachers had difficulty getting anything more than a yes or no answer from him. More troublesome was that he had been found hiding in a stall in the boy's restroom during lunch, which he said he had been doing for several months instead of eating. After Billy was referred to our clinic, we diagnosed a severe case of social anxiety disorder, an irrational and extreme fear of social situations. Billy's phobia took the form of extreme shyness. He was afraid of being embarrassed or humiliated in the presence of almost everyone except his parents.

Chuck Knoblauch... • *Star Players?*

Chuck Knoblauch won a Golden Glove Award at second base in 1997 but led the league in errors in 1999 with 26, most of them throwing errors. Announcers and reporters observed that his throws would be hard and on target to first base if he made a difficult play and had to quickly turn and throw the ball "without thinking about it." But if he fielded a routine ground ball and had time to think about the accuracy of his throw, he would throw awkwardly and slowly—and often off target. The announcers and reporters concluded that, because his arm seemed fine on the difficult plays, his problem must be "mental." For the 2001 season, he was moved to left field to avoid having to make that throw, and by 2003 was out of baseball.

....

separation anxiety disorder Excessive, enduring **fear** in some children that harm will come to them or their parents while they are apart.

social anxiety disorder (SAD) Extreme, enduring, irrational **fear** and avoidance of social or performance situations.

social phobia Extreme, enduring, irrational **fear** and avoidance of social or performance situations.

NFL player Ricky Williams also interrupted his career partly because of severe social anxiety. Whereas Knoblauch continued to struggle, Williams overcame his problems. Many other athletes are not so fortunate. This problem is not limited to athletes. Actress Scarlett Johansson avoided doing Broadway for many years due to intolerable performance anxiety, in this case called "stage fright." The inability of a skilled athlete to throw a baseball to first base or a seasoned performer to appear on stage certainly does not match the concept of "shyness" with which we are all familiar. What holds these seemingly different conditions together within the category of social anxiety disorder? Billy, Knoblauch, and Johansson all experienced marked fear or anxiety focused on one or more social or performance situations. In Billy's case, these situations were any in which he might have to interact with people. For Knoblauch and Johansson, they were specific to performing some special behavior in public. Individuals with just performance anxiety, which is a subtype of SAD, usually have no difficulty with social interaction, but when they must do something specific in front of people, anxiety takes over and they focus on the possibility that they will embarrass themselves.

The most common type of performance anxiety, to which most people can relate, is public speaking. Other situations that commonly provoke performance anxiety are eating in a restaurant or signing a paper or check in front of a person or people who are watching. Anxiety-provoking physical reactions include blushing, sweating, trembling, or, for males, urinating in a public restroom ("bashful bladder" or paruresis). Males with this problem must wait until a stall is available, a difficult task at times. What these examples have in common is that the individual is very anxious only while others are present and maybe watching and, to some extent, evaluating their behavior. This is truly social anxiety disorder because the people have no difficulty eating, writing, or urinating in private. Only when others are watching does the behavior deteriorate.

Statistics

As many as 12.1% of the general population suffer from SAD at some point in their lives (Kessler, Berglund, Demler *et al.*, 2005). In a given one-year period, the prevalence is 6.8% (Kessler, Chiu *et al.*, 2005), and 8.2% in adolescents (Kessler *et al.*, 2012). This makes SAD second only to specific phobia as the most prevalent anxiety disorder, afflicting more than 35 million people in the United States alone. Unlike other anxiety disorders for which females predominate (Hofmann, Alpers, & Pauli, 2009; Magee *et al.*, 1996), the sex ratio for SAD is nearly 50:50 (Hofmann & Barlow, 2002; Marks, 1985). Overall, 45.6% of people suffering from SAD sought professional help in a recent 12-month period (Wang *et al.*, 2005). SAD usually begins during adolescence, with a peak age of onset around 13 years (Kessler, Berglund, Demler *et al.*, 2005). SAD also tends to be more prevalent in people who are young (18–29 years), undereducated, single, and

of low socioeconomic class. It is less than half as prevalent among individuals over 60 (6.6%) as it is among individuals 18 to 29 (13.6%) (Kessler, Berglund, Demler *et al.*, 2005).

Considering their difficulty meeting people, it is not surprising that a greater percentage of individuals with SAD are single than in the population at large. In the United States, white Americans are typically more likely to be diagnosed with social anxiety disorder (as well as GAD and PD) than African Americans, Hispanic Americans, and Asian Americans (Asnaani, Richey, Dimaite, Hinton, & Hofmann, 2010). Cross-national data suggest that Asian cultures show the lowest rates of SAD, whereas Russian and U.S. samples show the highest rates (Hofmann, Asnaani, & Hinton, 2010). In Japan, the clinical presentation of anxiety disorders is best summarized under the label *shinkeishitsu*. One of the most common subcategories is referred to as *taijin kyofusho*, which resembles SAD in some of its forms (Hofmann, Asnaani, & Hinton, 2010; Kleinknecht, Dinnel, Kleinknecht, Hiruma, & Harada, 1997). Japanese people with this form of SAD strongly fear that some aspect of their personal presentation (blushing, stuttering, body odor, and so on) will appear reprehensible, causing other people to feel embarrassed. Thus, the focus of anxiety in this disorder is on offending or embarrassing others rather than embarrassing oneself, as in SAD, although these two disorders overlap considerably (Dinnel, Kleinknecht, & Tanaka-Matsumi, 2002).

Causes

We have noted that we seem to be prepared by evolution to fear certain wild animals and dangerous situations in the natural environment. Similarly, it seems we are also prepared to fear angry, critical, or rejecting people (Blair *et al.*, 2008; Mineka & Zinbarg, 2006). In a series of studies, Öhman and colleagues (see, for example, Dimberg & Öhman, 1983; Öhman & Dimberg, 1978) noted that we learn more quickly to fear angry expressions than other facial expressions, and this fear diminishes more slowly than other types of learning. Lundh and Öst (1996) demonstrated that people with SAD who saw a number of pictures of faces were likely to remember critical expressions; Mogg and colleagues (2004) showed that socially anxious individuals more quickly recognized angry faces than "normals," whereas "normals" remembered the accepting expressions (Navarrete *et al.*, 2009).

Why should we inherit a tendency to fear angry faces? Our ancestors probably avoided hostile, angry, domineering people who might attack or kill them. In all species, dominant, aggressive individuals, high in the social hierarchy, tend to be avoided. Possibly, individuals who avoided people with angry faces were more likely to survive and pass their genes down to us. Of course, this is just a theory.

Jerome Kagan (see, for example, Kagan, 2014a,b) has demonstrated that some infants are born with a temperamental profile or trait of inhibition or shyness that is evident

as early as four months of age. Four-month-old infants with this trait become more agitated and cry more frequently when presented with toys or other age-appropriate stimuli than infants without the trait. There is now evidence that individuals with excessive behavioral inhibition are at increased risk for developing phobic behavior (Essex *et al.*, 2010; Hirschfeld *et al.*, 1992).

A model of the etiology of SAD would look somewhat like models of PD and specific phobia. Three pathways to SAD are possible, as depicted in ● Figure 4.7. First, someone could inherit a generalized biological vulnerability to develop anxiety, a biological tendency to be socially inhibited, or both. The existence of a generalized psychological vulnerability—such as the belief that events, particularly stressful events, are potentially uncontrollable—would increase an individual's vulnerability. When under stress, a person could have anxiety and self-focused attention increase to the point of disrupting performance, even in the absence of a false alarm (panic attack). Second, when under stress, someone might have an unexpected panic attack in a social situation that would become associated (conditioned) to social cues. The individual would then

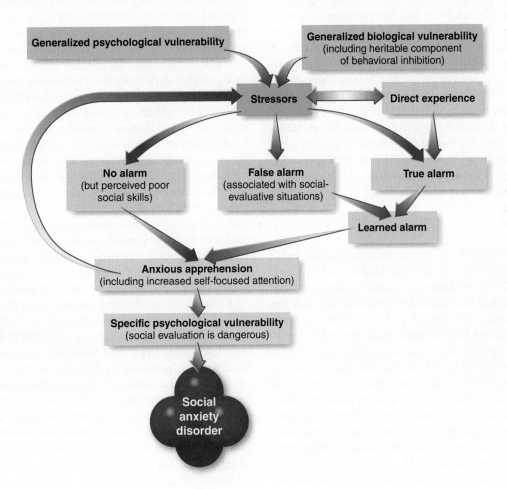

● **Figure 4.7** A model of the various ways a social anxiety disorder may develop. (From Barlow, D. H. (2002). Anxiety and its disorders: The nature and treatment of anxiety and panic. (2nd ed.). New York: Guilford Press.)

become anxious about having additional panic attacks in the same or similar social situations. Third, someone might experience a real social trauma resulting in a true alarm. Anxiety would then develop (be conditioned) in the same or similar social situations. Traumatic social experiences may also extend back to difficult periods in childhood. Early adolescence—usually ages 12 through 15—is when children may be brutally taunted by peers who are attempting to assert their own dominance. This experience may produce anxiety and panic that are reproduced in future social situations. For example, McCabe, Anthony, Summerfeldt, Liss, and Swinson (2003) noted that 92% of adults with social anxiety disorder in their sample experienced severe teasing and bullying in childhood, compared with only 35% to 50% among people with other anxiety disorders.

But one more factor must fall into place to make it SAD. The individual with the vulnerabilities and experiences just described must also have learned growing up that social evaluation in particular can be dangerous, creating a specific psychological vulnerability to develop social anxiety. Evidence indicates that some people with SAD are predisposed to focus their anxiety on events involving social evaluation. Some investigators (Bruch & Heimberg, 1994; Rapee & Melville, 1997) suggest that the parents of patients with SAD are significantly more socially fearful and concerned with the opinions of others than are the parents of patients with panic disorder and that they pass this concern on to their children (Lieb et al., 2000). Fyer, Mannuzza, Chapman, Liebowitz, and Klein (1993) reported that the relatives of people with SAD had a significantly greater risk of developing it than the relatives of individuals without SAD (16% versus 5%)—thus, the specific psychological vulnerability depicted in ● Figure 4.7. As you can see, a combination of biological and psychological events seems to lead to the development of SAD.

Treatment

Effective treatments have been developed for SAD (Hofmann & Otto, 2008; Heimberg & Magee, 2014). Clark and colleagues (2006) evaluated a cognitive therapy program that emphasized real-life experiences during therapy to disprove automatic perceptions of danger. This program substantially benefited 84% of individuals receiving treatment, and these results were maintained at a one-year follow-up. This outcome is the best yet for this condition and significantly better than previous approaches to which it has been compared. Subsequent studies indicated that this treatment was superior to a second credible treatment, interpersonal psychotherapy (IPT), both immediately after treatment and at a one-year follow-up (Stangier, Schramm, Heidenreich, Berger, & Clark, 2011).

A similar approach was developed at our center (Hofmann, 2007b; Hofmann & Otto, 2008). This treatment targets the factors maintaining the disorder. One reason why SAD is maintained in the presence of repeated exposure to social cues is because individuals with SAD engage in avoidance behaviors to reduce the risk of rejection and, more generally, prevent patients from evaluating their catastrophic beliefs about how foolish they will look if they interact with somebody. Social mishap exposures target the patients' beliefs by confronting them with the actual consequences of such mishaps, such as what would happen if you spilled something on yourself while talking to somebody for the first time (Hofmann & Otto, 2008). As a group intervention, this treatment was associated with an 82% completion rate and a 73% response rate, which was maintained at six-month follow-up (Hofmann et al., 2013). Brain imaging studies showed that brain measures before treatment can strongly predict the extent to which CBT reduces symptoms in patients with SAD (Doehrmann et al., 2013; Whitfield-Gabrieli et al., 2016 and that CBT leads to changes in brain activity associated with emotional processing (Klumpp, Fitzgerald, & Phan, 2013; Månsson et al., 2013).

We have adapted these protocols for adolescents, involving parents in the treatment process. Studies suggest that severely socially anxious adolescents can attain relatively normal functioning after receiving CBT (Albano & Barlow, 1996; Garcia-Lopez et al., 2006). Clinical trials have compared individual and family-based treatment approaches for youth with social anxiety; while both treatments appear to be equally efficacious (Barmish & Kendall 2005), family-based treatment outperforms individual treatment when the child's parents also have an anxiety disorder (Kendall, Hudson, Gosch, Flannery-Schroeder, & Suveg, 2008). A long-term follow-up study indicates that youths who receive a parent component as part of treatment are more likely to be diagnosis-free three years following treatment (Cobham, Dadds, Spence & McDermott, 2010), and a family-based intervention can prevent the onset of anxiety disorders in the children of anxious parents (Ginsburg, Drake, Tein, Teetsel, & Riddle, 2015). Once the child develops an anxiety disorder, early treatment with CBT can treat the symptoms or prevent future problems with anxiety (Benjamin, Harrison, Settipani, Brodman, & Kendall, 2013; Ginsburg et al., 2014), with a slight advantage of family-based CBT over child-based CBT (Schneider et al., 2013).

Effective drug treatments have been discovered as well (Van Ameringen, Mancini, Patterson, & Simpson, 2009). For a time, clinicians assumed that beta-blockers (drugs that lower heart rate and blood pressure, such as Inderal) would work, particularly for performance anxiety, but the evidence did not seem to support that contention (Liebowitz et al., 1992; Turner, Beidel, & Jacob, 1994). Since 1999, the SSRIs Paxil, Zoloft, and Effexor have received approval from the Food and Drug Administration for treatment of SAD based on studies showing effectiveness compared with placebo (see, for example, Stein et al., 1998).

Several major studies have compared psychological and drug treatments. One impressive study compared Clark's cognitive therapy described earlier with the SSRI drug Prozac, along with instructions to the patients with SAD to attempt to engage in more social situations (self-exposure). A third group received placebos plus instructions to attempt to engage in more social activities. Assessments were conducted before the 16-week treatment, at the midpoint of treatment, post-treatment, and then after three months of booster sessions. Finally, researchers followed up with patients in the two treatment groups 12 months later (Clark *et al.*, 2003). Results show that both treatments did well, but the psychological treatment was substantially better at all times, with most patients cured or nearly cured with few remaining symptoms. Also, gains made during CT were maintained when assessed after five years (Mörtberg, Clark, & Bejerot, 2011).

The evidence is mixed on the usefulness of combining SSRIs or related drugs with psychological treatments. Davidson, Foa, and Huppert (2004) found that a cognitive-behavioral treatment and an SSRI were comparable in efficacy but that the combination was no better than the two individual treatments. Several exciting studies suggest that adding the drug D-cycloserine (DCS) to cognitive-behavioral treatments can enhance exposure therapy (Chasson *et al.*, 2010; Wilhelm *et al.*, 2008). Neuroscientists working with rats in the laboratory, such as Michael Davis at Emory University, learned that DCS made extinction work faster and last longer (Walker, Ressler, Lu, & Davis, 2002). Further research indicated that this drug works in the amygdala, a structure in the brain involved in the learning and unlearning of fear and anxiety. Unlike SSRIs, this drug is known to facilitate extinction of anxiety by modifying neurotransmitter flow in the glutamate system as described in Chapter 2 (Hofmann, 2007a). SSRIs and other antidepressants might even interact with DCS to block its facilitating effect on exposure therapy (Andersson *et al.*, 2015).

Selective Mutism

Now grouped with the anxiety disorders in *DSM-5*, **selective mutism (SM)** is a rare childhood disorder characterized by a lack of speech in one or more settings in which speaking is socially expected. As such, it seems clearly driven by social anxiety, since the failure to speak is not because of a lack of knowledge of speech or any physical difficulties, nor is it due to another disorder in which speaking is rare or can be impaired such as autism spectrum disorder. In fact, speech in selective mutism commonly occurs in some settings, such as home, but not others, such as school, hence the term "selective." In order to meet diagnostic criteria for SM, the lack of speech must occur for more than one month and cannot be limited to the first month of school. Further evidence that this disorder is strongly related to social anxiety is found in the high rates of comorbidity of SM and anxiety disorders, particularly SAD (Bögels *et al.* 2010). In fact, in one study, nearly 100% of a series of 50 children with selective mutism also met criteria for SAD (Dummit *et al.*, 1997). Another recent study found substantially more social anxiety in children with SM than a matched control group without SM (Buzzella, Ehrenreich-May, & Pincus, 2011). Estimates of the prevalence of SM average about 0.5% of children with girls more affected than boys (Kumpulainen, 2002; Viana, Beidal, & Rabian, 2009).

Why does lack of speech in certain situations emerge as the specific symptom in selective mutism instead of other socially anxious behaviors? It is not entirely clear yet, but there is some evidence that well-meaning parents enable this behavior by being more readily able to intervene and "do their talking for them" (Buzzella *et al.*, 2011).

Treatment employs many of the same cognitive behavioral principles used successfully to treat social anxiety in children but with a greater emphasis on speech (Carpenter, Puliafico, Kurtz, Pincus, & Comer, 2014). For example, in one of our clinics, we run a specialized program called "The Boston University Brave Buddies Camp." This is a week-long intensive group treatment program for children ages four to eight who have been diagnosed with selective mutism or have difficulty speaking in social or school situations with familiar and/or unfamiliar peers and adults. The BU Brave Buddies

4.4 Concept CHECK

Identify the following phobias: (a) blood–injection–injury, (b) acrophobia, (c) animal, (d) social, (e) natural environment, and (f) other. The same phobia may apply to more than one statement.

1. Mark had no friends at school and hid in the boys' bathroom during both lunch and recess. _____

2. Dennis fears and strenuously avoids storms. Not surprisingly, on his first ocean-going cruise, he found that deep water terrified him, too. _____

3. Rita was comfortable at the zoo until the old terror gripped her at the insect display. _____

4. Armando would love to eat fish with his fishing buddies, but he experiences an inordinate fear of choking on a bone. _____

5. John had to give up his dream of becoming a surgeon because he faints at the sight of blood. _____

6. Rachel turned down several lucrative job offers that involved public speaking and took a low-paying desk job instead. _____

7. Farrah can't visit her rural friends because of her fear of snakes. _____

selective mutism (SM) A rare childhood disorder characterized by a lack of speech in one or more settings in which speaking is socially expected.

Camp provides guided opportunities for children to interact with a number of new children and adults, participate in classroom-like activities, engage in field trips, and play socializing games that promote verbal participation ("brave talking") and spontaneous speaking. This approach utilizes behavioral interventions such as modeling, stimulus fading, and shaping that allow for gradual exposure to the speaking situation; these techniques are combined with a behavioral reward system for participation in treatment (Sacks, Comer, Furr, Pincus, & Kurtz, 2011; Furr *et al.*, 2012). Results from this program have been very encouraging: 80 percent of 15 children who participated in this camp successfully initiating speech and maintaining speech productivity at a two-year follow-up. Unfortunately, these highly specialized programs are not readily available at the present time.

Trauma and Stressor-Related Disorders

DSM-5 consolidates a group of formerly disparate disorders that all develop after a relatively stressful life event, often an extremely stressful or traumatic life event. This set of disorders—**trauma and stressor-related disorders**—include attachment disorders in childhood following inadequate or abusive child-rearing practices, adjustment disorders characterized by persistent anxiety and depression following a stressful life event, and reactions to trauma such as posttraumatic stress disorder and acute stress disorder. Investigators working in this area concluded that these disorders did not fit as neatly with other classes of disorders, such as the anxiety disorders as previously assumed. This is because trauma and stressor-related disorders all share a proximal instigating stressful event followed by intense emotional responses. Also, a wider range of emotions—such as rage, horror, guilt, and shame, in addition to fear and anxiety—may be implicated in the onset, particularly for posttraumatic stress disorder (Friedman *et al.*, 2011; Keane, Marx, Sloan, & DePrince, 2011; Miller, Wolf, & Keane, 2014). We begin with a description of posttraumatic stress disorder.

Posttraumatic Stress Disorder (PTSD)

▶ What are the essential features and possible causes of posttraumatic stress disorder?

▶ What treatment approaches are available for posttraumatic stress disorder?

In recent years, we have heard a great deal about the severe and long-lasting emotional disorders that can occur after a variety of traumatic events. For Americans, perhaps the most notorious traumatic events of this century have been the wars in Iraq and Afghanistan, the terrorist attacks on September 11, 2001, or hurricanes (such as Hurricane Sandy in 2012). Still, emotional disorders also occur after physical assault (particularly rape), car accidents, natural catastrophes, or the sudden death of a loved one. **Posttraumatic stress disorder (PTSD)** is the best known of these disorders.

Clinical Description

DSM-5 describes the setting event for PTSD as exposure to a traumatic event during which an individual experiences or witnesses death or threatened death, actual or threatened serious injury, or actual or threatened sexual violation. Learning that the traumatic event occurred to a close family member or friend or enduring repeated exposure to details of a traumatic event (as in first responders to a terrorist attack dealing with human remains) are also setting events. Afterward, victims re-experience the event through memories and nightmares. When memories occur suddenly, accompanied by strong emotion, and the victims find themselves reliving the event, they are having a *flashback*. Victims most often avoid anything that reminds them of the trauma. They often display a characteristic restriction or numbing of emotional responsiveness, which may be disruptive to interpersonal relationships. They are sometimes unable to remember certain aspects of the event. It is possible that victims unconsciously attempt to avoid the experience of emotion itself, like people with panic disorder, because intense emotions could bring back memories of the trauma. Finally, victims typically are chronically over-aroused, easily startled, and quick to anger.

New to *DSM-5* is the addition of "reckless or self-destructive behavior" under the PTSD E criteria as one sign of increased arousal and reactivity. Also new to *DSM-5* is the addition of a "dissociative" subtype describing victims who do not necessarily react with the re-experiencing or hyperarousal, characteristic of PTSD. Rather, individuals with PTSD who experience dissociation have less arousal than normal along with (dissociative) feelings of unreality (Wolf, Lunney *et al.*, 2012; Wolf, Miller *et al.*, 2012). Victims with PTSD seem to respond somewhat differently to treatment if they meet criteria for a dissociative subtype (Lanius, Brand, Vermetten, Frewen, & Spiegel, 2012).

Consider the case of the Joneses from one of our clinics.

The Joneses... • *One Victim, Many Traumas*

Mrs. Betty Jones and her four children arrived at a farm to visit a friend. (Mr. Jones was at work.) Jeff, the oldest child, was eight-years-old. Marcie, Cathy, and Susan were six, four, and two years-of- age. Mrs. Jones parked the car in the driveway, and they all started across the yard to the front door. Suddenly Jeff heard growling somewhere near the house. Before he could warn the others, a large German Shepherd charged and leapt at Marcie, the six-year-old, knocking her to the ground and tearing viciously at her face. The family, too stunned to move, watched the attack helplessly. After what seemed like an eternity, Jeff lunged at the dog and it moved away. The owner of the dog, in a state of panic, ran to a nearby house to get help. Mrs. Jones immediately put pressure on Marcie's facial wounds in an attempt to stop the bleeding. The owner had neglected to retrieve the dog, and it stood a short distance away, growling and barking at the frightened family. Eventually, the dog was restrained and Marcie was rushed to the hospital. Marcie, who was hysterical, had to be restrained on a padded board so that emergency room physicians could stitch her wounds.

This case is unusual because not only did Marcie develop PTSD, but so did her eight-year-old brother. In addition, Cathy, four, and Susan, two, although quite young, showed symptoms of the disorder, as did their mother (see Table 5.7) (Albano, Miller, Zarate, Côté, & Barlow, 1997). Jeff evidenced classic survivor guilt symptoms, reporting that he should have saved Marcie or at least put himself between Marcie and the dog. Both Jeff and Marcie regressed developmentally, wetting the bed (nocturnal enuresis) and experiencing nightmares and separation fears. In addition, Marcie, having been strapped down and given a local anesthetic and stitches, became frightened of any medical procedures and even of such routine daily events as having her nails trimmed or taking a bath. Furthermore, she refused to be tucked into bed, something she had enjoyed all her life, probably because it reminded her of the hospital board. Jeff started sucking his fingers, which he had not done for years. These behaviors, along with intense separation anxiety, are common, particularly in younger children (Eth, 1990; Silverman & La Greca,

2002). Cathy, the four-year-old, evidenced considerable fear and avoidance when tested but denied having any problem when she was interviewed by a child psychologist. Susan, the two-year-old, also had some symptoms, as shown in Table 4.5, but was too young to talk about them. For several months following the trauma, however, she repeatedly said, without provocation, "Doggy bit sister."

Since many individuals experience strong reactions to stressful events that typically disappear within a month, the diagnosis of PTSD cannot be made until at least one

TABLE 4.5 | Symptoms of Posttraumatic Stress Disorder (PTSD) Evidenced by Marcie and her Siblings

Symptoms	Jeff	Marcie	Cathy	Susan
Repetitive play—trauma themes		×	×	×
Nightmares	×	×	×	×
Re-experiencing	×			
Distress at exposure to similar stimuli	×	×	×	×
Avoidance of talk of trauma	×	×		
Avoidance of trauma recollections	×			
Regressive behavior	×	×		
Detachment	×	×		
Restricted affect	×	×		
Sleep disturbance	×	×	×	×
Anger outbursts	×	×		
Hypervigilance	×	×		
Startle response	×	×		
DSM-III-R PTSD diagnosis met	×	×		

SOURCE: From Albano, A. M., Miller, P. P., Zarate, R., Côté, G., & Barlow, D. H. (1997). Behavioral assessment and treatment of PTSD in prepubertal children: Attention to developmental factors and innovative strategies in the case study of a family. *Cognitive and Behavioral Practice, 4,* 245–262.

trauma and stressor-related disorders A group of mental disorders distinguished by their origin in stressful events (e.g., traumatic experience, major life stressor, childhood neglect)

posttraumatic stress disorder (PTSD) Enduring, distressing emotional disorder that follows exposure to a severe helplessness-or fear-inducing threat. The victim reexperiences the trauma, avoids stimuli associated with it, and develops a numbing of responsiveness and an increased vigilance and arousal.

month after the occurrence of the traumatic event. In *PTSD with delayed onset*, individuals show few or no symptoms immediately or for months after a trauma, but at least six months later, and perhaps years afterward, develop full-blown PTSD (O'Donnell *et al.*, 2013). Why onset is delayed in some individuals is not yet clear.

As we noted, PTSD cannot be diagnosed until a month after the trauma. In *DSM-IV* a disorder called **acute stress disorder** was introduced. This is similar to PTSD, occurring within the first month after the trauma, but the different name emphasizes the severe reaction that some people have immediately (Cardeña & Carlson, 2011). According to a recent survey, approximately 50% of individuals with acute stress disorder went on to develop PTSD (Bryant, 2010; Bryant, Friedman, Spiegel, Ursano, & Strain, 2011). But these surveys also indicated that as many as 52% of a sample of trauma survivors who went on to develop PTSD did not meet criteria for acute stress disorder in the month following the trauma (Bryant *et al.*, 2011). Acute stress disorder was included in *DSM-IV* because many people with severe early reactions to trauma could not otherwise be diagnosed and, therefore, could not receive insurance coverage for immediate treatment. The surveys described above confirm that people with early severe reactions to traumatic stress are severely impacted and can benefit from treatment. But these early reactions are not particularly good predictors of who will go on to develop PTSD.

Statistics

A number of studies have demonstrated the remarkably low prevalence of PTSD in populations of trauma victims. Rachman, in a classic study, reported on the British citizenry who endured numerous life-threatening air raids during World War II. He concluded that "a great majority of people endured the air raids extraordinarily well, contrary to the universal expectation of mass panic. Exposure to repeated bombings did not produce a significant increase in psychiatric disorders. Although short-lived fear reactions were common, surprisingly few persistent phobic reactions emerged" (Rachman, 1991, p. 162). Similar results have been observed from classic studies following disastrous fires, earthquakes, and floods (e.g., Green, Grace, Lindy, Titchener, & Lindy, 1983).

Large studies are also available on the prevalence of PTSD in veterans of the wars in Iraq and Afghanistan. Based on experiences during the Vietnam War, military mental health officials were very concerned that rates of PTSD might be as high as 30% or more (McNally, 2012b). A recent survey of women who were active-duty military personnel during the Vietnam War suggested that the lifetime prevalence rate of PTSD among the 4,219 women who responded to the survey was 20.1% (Magruder *et al.*, 2015). In contrast, the results of other investigations are less dire than expected. Based on a study of more than 47,000 members of the armed forces, "only" 4.3% of personnel developed PTSD. For those

experiencing combat, exposure rates increased to 7.6% versus 1.4% among those not experiencing combat (Smith *et al.*, 2008). Of course, given the large number of personnel deployed over the past decade, this still amounts to an enormous number of soldiers suffering from PTSD.

In the population as a whole, surveys indicate that 6.8% have experienced PTSD at some point in their life (Kessler, Berglund, Demler *et al.*, 2005) and 3.5% during the past year (Kessler, Chiu *et al.*, 2005). For adolescents, the corresponding figure is 3.9% (Kessler *et al.*, 2012). Breslau (2012) reports, based on large population surveys, the highest rates of PTSD are associated with experiences of rape; being held captive, tortured, or kidnapped; or being badly assaulted. Compared with those for non-victims, the rates of PTSD are 2.4 to 3.5 times higher for women experiencing a single sexual assault or rape and 4.3 to 8.2 times higher for those who have been re-victimized (Walsh *et al.*, 2012).

What accounts for the discrepancies between the low rate of PTSD in citizens who endured bombing and shelling in London and the relatively high rate in victims of assaultive violence? Investigators have now concluded that during air raids, many people may not have directly experienced the horrors of dying, death, and direct attack. Close exposure to the trauma seems to be necessary to developing this disorder (Friedman, M. J., 2009; Keane & Barlow, 2002). But this is also evident among Vietnam veterans, among whom 18.7% developed PTSD, with prevalence rates directly related to amount of combat exposure (Dohrenwend, Turner, & Turse, 2006). Surveys of 76 victims of Hurricane Katrina in 2005 also report a doubling of severe mental illness based on extent of direct exposure to danger (Kessler, Galea, Jones, & Parker, 2006). The connection between proximity to the traumatic event and the development of PTSD was starkly evident following the tragedy of 9/11. Galea and colleagues (2002) contacted a representative sample of adults living south of 110th Street in Manhattan and found that 7.5% reported symptoms consistent with a diagnosis of acute stress disorder or PTSD. But among respondents who lived close to the World Trade Center (south of Canal Street), the prevalence of the disorder was 20%. Again, those who experienced

the disaster most personally and directly seemed to be the ones most affected.

But is this the whole story? It seems not. Some people experience the most horrifying traumas imaginable and emerge psychologically healthy. For others, even relatively mild stressful events are sufficient to produce a full-blown disorder. To better understand why trauma influences some people more than others, we must consider the etiology of PTSD.

Causes

PTSD is the one disorder for which we know the cause at least in terms of the precipitating event: Someone experiences a trauma and develops a disorder. Whether or not a person develops PTSD, however, is a complex issue involving biological, psychological, and social factors. We know that intensity of exposure to assaultive violence contributes to the etiology of PTSD (Dohrenwend, Yager, Wall, & Adams, 2012; Friedman, 2009) but does not account for all of it. For example, approximately 67% of prisoners of war in Vietnam developed PTSD (Foy, Resnick, Sipprelle, & Carroll, 1987). This means that 33% of the prisoners who endured long-term deprivation and torture *did not* develop the disorder. Similarly, children experiencing severe burns are likely to develop PTSD in proportion to the severity and pain of the burns (Saxe *et al.*, 2005). At lower levels of trauma, some people develop PTSD, but most do not. What accounts for these differences?

As with other disorders, we bring our own generalized biological and psychological vulnerabilities with us. The greater the vulnerability, the more likely we are to develop PTSD. If certain characteristics run in your family, you have a much greater chance of developing the disorder. A family history of anxiety suggests a generalized biological vulnerability for PTSD. True and colleagues (1993) reported that, given the same amount of combat exposure and one twin with PTSD, a monozygotic (identical) twin was more likely to develop PTSD than a dizygotic (fraternal) twin, which suggests some genetic influence in the development of PTSD. Nevertheless, as with other disorders, there is little or no evidence that genes directly cause PTSD (Norrholm & Ressler, 2009). Rather, the stress–diathesis model described in Chapter 2 comes into play again since genetic factors predispose individuals to be easily stressed and anxious, which then may make it more likely that a traumatic experience will result in PTSD (Uddin, Amstadter, Nugent, & Koenen, 2012).

Breslau, Davis, and Andreski (1995; Breslau, 2012) demonstrated among a random sample of 1,200 individuals that characteristics such as a tendency to be anxious,

Andy Nelson/The Christian Science Monitor/Getty Images

▲ Exposure to a traumatic event may create profound fear and helplessness. People who suffer from PTSD may re-experience such feelings in flashbacks, involuntarily reliving the horrifying event.

acute stress disorder Severe reaction immediately following a terrifying event, often including amnesia about the event, emotional numbing, and **derealization**. Many victims later develop **posttraumatic stress** disorder.

as well as factors such as minimal education, predict exposure to traumatic events in the first place and therefore an increased risk for PTSD. Breslau, Lucia, and Alvarado (2006) elaborated on this finding by showing that six-year-old children with externalizing (acting out) problems were more likely to encounter trauma (such as assaults), probably because of their acting out, and later develop PTSD. Higher intelligence predicted decreased exposure to these types of traumatic events. That is, personality and other characteristics, some of them at least partially heritable, may predispose people to the experience of trauma by making it likely that they will be in (risky) situations where trauma is likely to occur (Norrholm & Ressler, 2009).

Also, there seems to be a generalized psychological vulnerability described in the context of other disorders based on early experiences with unpredictable or uncontrollable events. Family instability is one factor that may instill a sense that the world is an uncontrollable, potentially dangerous place (Chorpita & Barlow, 1998; Suárez et al., 2009), so it is not surprising that individuals from unstable families are at increased risk for developing PTSD if they experience trauma. Family instability was found to be a pre-war risk factor for the development of PTSD in a study of more than 1,600 male and female Vietnam veterans (King et al., 1996, 2012).

In addition, certain biological individual characteristics (biomarkers) appear to increase the likelihood for developing PTSD. In one study, Telch and colleagues (Telch, Rosenfield, Lee, & Pai, 2012) asked 158 soldiers before their deployment to Iraq to inhale air that was enriched with 35% carbon dioxide. Inhaling such gas mixture typically leads to strong physiological symptoms (shortness of breath, tingling, sweating, etc.) and anxiety in some people. Telch and colleagues found that those who reported more emotional reactivity to the gas mixture were at greater risk for developing PTSD symptoms and other anxiety and stress symptoms later. This example illustrates how certain vulnerabilities can lead to a disorder when the person is exposed to stressors.

Finally, social factors play a major role in the development of PTSD (Ruzek, 2012; King et al., 2012). A number of studies have shown that it is much less likely you will develop PTSD after a trauma if you have a supportive group of people around you (Friedman, 2009). In one study, Vernberg, La Greca, Silverman, and Prinstein (1996) studied 568 elementary school children three months after Hurricane Andrew hit the coast of south Florida. More than 55% of these children reported moderate to severe levels of PTSD symptoms, a typical result for this type of disaster (La Greca & Prinstein, 2002). When the authors examined factors contributing to who developed PTSD symptoms and who didn't, social support from parents, friends, classmates, and teachers was an important protective factor. Similarly, positive coping strategies involving active problem solving seemed to be protective, whereas becoming angry and placing blame on others were associated with higher levels of PTSD. The broader and deeper the network of social support, the less the chance of developing PTSD. Longer-term follow-up of children at nine and 21 months after hurricane Charley hit Florida in 2004 confirmed that strong social support systems reduced the persistence of posttraumatic stress symptoms over time (La Greca, Silverman, Lai, & Jaccard, 2010).

Why is this? As you saw in Chapter 2, we are all social animals, and something about having a loving, caring group of people around us directly affects our biological and psychological responses to stress. A number of studies show that support from loved ones reduces cortisol secretion and hypothalamic–pituitary–adrenocortical (HPA) axis activity in children during stress (see, for example, Tarullo & Gunnar, 2006). It is likely that one reason for the high prevalence of PTSD in Vietnam veterans compared with veterans from Iraq and Afghanistan was the tragic absence of social support when those veterans returned from Vietnam.

It seems clear that PTSD involves a number of neurobiological systems, particularly elevated or restricted corticotropin-releasing factor (CRF), which indicates heightened activity in the HPA axis, as described earlier in this chapter and in Chapter 2 (Amat et al., 2005; Yehuda, Pratchett, & Pelcovitz, 2012). Chronic arousal associated with HPA axis and some other symptoms of PTSD may be related to changes in brain function and structure (Bremner, 1999; McEwen & Magarinos, 2004) that influence treatment response (Rauch et al., 2014). For example, evidence of damage to the hippocampus has appeared in groups of patients with war-related PTSD (Gurvits et al., 1996; Wang et al., 2010), adult survivors of childhood sexual abuse (Bremner et al., 1995), and firefighters exposed to extreme trauma (Shin et al., 2004). The hippocampus is a part of the brain that plays an important role in regulating the HPA axis and in learning and memory. Thus, if there is damage to the hippocampus, we might expect persistent and chronic arousal as well as some disruptions in learning and memory. These memory deficits are evident in veterans of the Gulf War (Vasterling, Brailey, Constans, & Sotker, 1998) and Holocaust survivors with PTSD, as compared with Holocaust survivors without PTSD or healthy Jewish adults (Golier et al., 2002).

Earlier we described a panic attack as an adaptive fear response occurring at an inappropriate time. We have speculated that the "alarm reaction" that is a panic attack is similar in both panic disorder and PTSD but that in panic disorder the alarm is false. In PTSD, the initial alarm is true in that real danger is present (Jones & Barlow, 1990; Keane & Barlow, 2002). If the alarm is severe enough, we may develop a conditioned or learned alarm reaction to stimuli that remind us of the trauma (for example, being tucked into bed may have reminded Marcie of the emergency room board) (Lissek & Grillon, 2012). We may also develop anxiety about the possibility of additional uncontrollable emotional experiences (such as flashbacks, which

Figure 4.8 A model of the causes of PTSD. (Reprinted, with permission, from Barlow, D. H. (2002). Anxiety and its disorders: The nature and treatment of anxiety and panic (2nd ed.). New York: Guilford Press, © 2002 Guilford Press.)

are common in PTSD). Whether or not we develop anxiety partly depends on our vulnerabilities. This model of the etiology of PTSD is presented in ● Figure 4.8.

Treatment

Most clinicians agree that victims of PTSD should face the original trauma, process the intense emotions, and develop coping procedures to overcome the debilitating effects of the disorder (Beck & Sloan, 2012; Monson, Resick, & Rizvi, 2014). In psychoanalytic therapy, reliving emotional trauma to relieve emotional suffering is called *catharsis*. The trick is in arranging the re-exposure so that it will be therapeutic rather than traumatic. Unlike the object of a specific phobia, a traumatic event is difficult to recreate, and few therapists want to try. Therefore, *imaginal exposure*, in which the content of the trauma and the emotions associated with it are worked through systematically, has been used for decades under a variety of names. At present, the most common strategy to achieve this purpose with adolescents or adults is to work with the victim to develop a narrative

of the traumatic experience and to expose the patients for an extended period of time to the image (*prolonged exposure therapy*) that is then reviewed extensively in treatment (Eftekhari *et al.*, 2013; Foa, McLean, Capaldi, & Rosenfield, 2013). Recent research suggests the effects of the exposure practices may be strengthened by strategically timing the exposure treatment with sleep. Patients in the study were asked to take a nap soon after an exposure, because extinction learning appears to take place during slow wave sleep and also because sleep quality reduces anxiety (Pace-Schott, Germain, & Milad, 2015). Cognitive therapy to correct negative assumptions about the trauma—such as blaming oneself in some way, feeling guilty, or both—is another part of treatment (Ehlers *et al.*, 2014; Monson *et al.*, 2014).

Another complication is that trauma victims often repress the emotional side of their memories of the event and sometimes, it seems, the memory itself. This happens automatically and unconsciously. Occasionally, with treatment, the memories flood back and the patient dramatically relives the episode. Although this may be frightening to both patient and therapist, it can be therapeutic if handled appropriately. Evidence is now accumulating that early, structured interventions delivered as soon after the trauma as possible to those who require help are useful in preventing the development of PTSD (Ehlers *et al.*, 2003; Kearns, Ressler, Zatzick, & Rothbaum, 2012), and these preventive psychological approaches seem more effective than medications (Shalev *et al.*, 2012). For example, in the study by Ehlers and colleagues (2003) of patients who had experienced a scary car accident and were clearly at risk for developing PTSD, only 11% developed PTSD after 12 sessions of cognitive therapy, compared with 61% of those receiving a detailed self-help booklet or 55% of those who were just assessed repeatedly over time but had no intervention. All patients who needed it were then treated with cognitive therapy. On the other hand, there is evidence that subjecting trauma victims to a single debriefing session, in which they are forced to express their feelings as to whether they are distressed or not, can be harmful (Ehlers & Clark, 2003).

Both Marcie, the young girl bitten by the dog, and her brother were treated at our clinic. The primary difficulty was Marcie's reluctance to be seen by a doctor or to undergo any physical examinations, so a series of experiences was arranged from least to most intense (see Table 4.6). Mildly anxiety-provoking procedures for Marcie included having her pulse taken and lying on an examination table. The most intense challenge was being strapped on a restraining board. First Marcie watched her brother go through these exercises. He was not afraid of these particular procedures, although he was anxious about being strapped to a board because of Marcie's terror at the thought. After she watched her brother experience these situations with little or no fear, Marcie tried each one in turn. The therapist took photos of her that she kept after completing the procedures. Marcie was also asked to draw pictures of the situations.

TABLE 4.6 | Fear and Avoidance Hierarchy for Marcie

	Pretreatment Fear Rating	Posttreatment Fear Rating
Being strapped on a board	4	0
Having an electrocardiogram	4	0
Having a chest X-ray	4	0
Having doctor listen to heart with stethoscope	3	0
Lying on examination table	3	0
Taking a bath after sustaining an accidentally inflicted cut	3	0
Allowing therapist to put Band-Aid on a cut	2	0
Letting therapist listen to heart with stethoscope	1	0
Having pulse taken	1	0
Allowing therapist to examine throat with tongue depressor	1	0

SOURCE: From Albano, A. M., Miller, P. P., Zarate, R., Côté, G., & Barlow, D. H. (1997). Behavioral assessment and treatment of PTSD in prepubertal children: Attention to developmental factors and innovative strategies in the case study of a family. *Cognitive and Behavioral Practice*, 4, 254, © 1997 Association for Advancement of Behavior Therapy.

The therapist and her family congratulated her as she completed each exercise. Because of Marcie's age, she was not adept at imaginatively recreating memories of the traumatic medical procedures. Therefore, her treatment offered experiences designed to alter her current perceptions of the situations. Marcie's PTSD was successfully treated, and her brother's guilt was greatly reduced as a function of helping in her treatment.

We now have evidence that the strategies described above produce lasting changes. 144 female rape survivors who were treated with evidence-based psychological treatments were reassessed five to ten years after treatment. The substantial decreases in symptoms originally observed were maintained with very little change over this period of time (Resick, Williams, Suvak, Monson, & Gradus, 2012). Another important study evaluated treatment for 40 heterosexual and same-sex couples, in which one partner met criteria for PTSD. However, in this study the partner was directly included in treatment in order to address the severe disruptions in intimate relationships that often accompany PTSD and may lead to relapse (Monson *et al.*, 2012). The outcome was significant improvement in PTSD symptoms, but also in relationship satisfaction that might contribute substantially to long-term adjustment. Drugs can also be effective for symptoms of PTSD (Dent & Bremner, 2009; Schneier *et al.*, 2012). Some of the drugs, such as SSRIs (e.g., Prozac and Paxil), that are effective for anxiety disorders in general have been shown to be helpful for PTSD, perhaps because they relieve the severe anxiety and panic attacks so prominent in this disorder. Promising, but mixed, results have been reported for the use of d-cycloserine (DCS) as an augmentation strategy of CBT for PTSD (de Kleine, Hendriks, Kusters, Broekman, & van Minnen, 2012; Rothbaum *et al.*, 2014).

Other Trauma- and Stressor-Related Disorders

▶ What are the originals of other trauma- and stress-related disorders?

Several other disorders in addition to PTSD are included in this general category. **Adjustment disorders** describe anxious or depressive reactions to life stress that are milder than one would see in acute stress disorder or PTSD but are nevertheless impairing in terms of interfering with work or school performance, interpersonal relationships, or other areas of living (Friedman *et al.*, 2011; Strain & Friedman, 2011). Sometimes, particularly in adolescence, the life stress may provoke conduct problems. The stressful events themselves would not be considered traumatic, but it is clear that the individual is unable to cope with the demands of the situation and some intervention is typically required.

If the symptoms persist for more than six months after the removal of the stress or its consequences, the adjustment disorder would be considered "chronic."

Attachment disorders refers to disturbed and developmentally inappropriate behaviors in children, emerging before five years of age, in which the child is unable or unwilling to form normal attachment relationships with caregiving adults. These seriously maladaptive patterns are due to inadequate or abusive child-rearing practices. In many cases, these inadequate child-rearing practices might be caused by frequent changes in the primary caregiver because of multiple foster care placements, or possibly just neglect in the home. In either case, the result is a failure to meet the child's basic emotional needs for affection, comfort, or even providing for the basic necessities of daily living. As such, these disorders are considered to be pathological reactions to early extreme stress (Kay & Green, 2013).

In **reactive attachment disorder**, the child will seldom seek out a caregiver for protection, support, and nurturance and will seldom respond to offers from caregivers to provide this kind of care. Generally they would evidence lack of responsiveness, limited positive effect, and additional heightened emotionality, such as fearfulness and intense sadness. In **disinhibited social engagement disorder**, a similar set of child-rearing circumstances—perhaps including early persistent harsh punishment—would result in a pattern of behavior in which the child shows no inhibitions whatsoever to approaching adults. Such a child might engage in inappropriately intimate behavior by showing a willingness to immediately accompany an unfamiliar adult figure somewhere without first checking back with a caregiver.

4.5 Concept CHECK

Match the correct preliminary diagnosis with the cases below: (a) posttraumatic stress disorder, (b) acute stress disorder, and (c) delayed onset posttraumatic stress disorder:

1. Judy witnessed a horrific tornado leveling her farm three weeks ago. Since then, she's had many flashbacks of the incident, trouble sleeping, and a fear of going outside in storms. _____

2. Jack was involved in a car accident six weeks ago in which the driver of the other car was killed. Since then, Jack has been unable to get into a car because it brings back the horrible scene he witnessed. Nightmares of the incident haunt him and interfere with his sleep. He is irritable and has lost interest in his work and hobbies. _____

3. Patricia was raped 30 years ago at the age of 17. Just recently, she has been having flashbacks of the event, difficulty sleeping, and fear of sexual contact with her husband. _____

Obsessive-Compulsive and Related Disorders

Another new class of disorders in *DSM-5* brings together several disorders that share a number of characteristics, such as driven repetitive behaviors and some other symptoms, and a similar course and treatment response (Abramowitz & Jacoby, 2015). Previously these disorders had been scattered in other areas of *DSM-IV*. In addition to obsessive-compulsive disorder, which has been classified as an anxiety disorder until *DSM-5*, this grouping now includes a separate diagnostic category for hoarding disorder, body dysmorphic disorder (previously located with the somatoform disorders), and trichotillomania (previously grouped with the impulse control disorders). Also, another new disorder in this group is excoriation (skin picking) disorder. We begin with the most prominent disorder in this group, obsessive-compulsive disorder.

Obsessive-Compulsive Disorder

▶ What are the symptoms of obsessive-compulsive disorder?

▶ How is obsessive-compulsive disorder treated?

Among the persons suffering from anxiety and related disorders, a client who needs hospitalization is likely to have **obsessive-compulsive disorder (OCD)**. A client referred for psychosurgery (neurosurgery for a psychological disorder) because every psychological and pharmacological treatment has failed, and the suffering is unbearable, probably has OCD. OCD is the devastating culmination of the anxiety disorders. It is not uncommon for someone with OCD to experience severe generalized anxiety, recurrent panic attacks, debilitating avoidance, and major depression, all occurring simultaneously with obsessive-compulsive

adjustment disorders Clinically significant emotional and behavioral symptoms in response to one or more specific stressors.

attachment disorders Developmentally inappropriate behaviors in which a child is unable or unwilling to form normal attachment relationships with caregiving adults.

reactive attachment disorder Attachment disorder in which a child with disturbed behaviour neither seeks out a caregiver nor responds to offers of help from one; fearfulness and sadness are often evident.

disinhibited social engagement disorder Condition in which a child shows no inhibitions whatsoever in approaching adults.

symptoms. With OCD, establishing even a foothold of control and predictability over the dangerous events in life seems so utterly hopeless that victims resort to magic and rituals.

Clinical Description

In other anxiety disorders, the danger is usually in an external object or situation, or at least in the memory of one. In OCD, the dangerous event is a thought, image, or impulse that the client attempts to avoid as completely as someone with a snake phobia avoids snakes (Clark & O'Connor, 2005). For example, has anyone ever told you not to think of pink elephants? If you really concentrate on not thinking of pink elephants, using every mental means possible, you will realize how difficult it is to suppress a suggested thought or image. Individuals with OCD fight this battle all day, every day, sometimes for most of their lives, and they usually fail miserably. In Chapter 3, we discussed the case of Frank, who experienced involuntary thoughts of epilepsy or seizures and prayed or shook his leg to try to distract himself. **Obsessions** are intrusive and mostly nonsensical thoughts, images, or urges that the individual tries to resist or eliminate. **Compulsions** are the thoughts or actions used to suppress the obsessions and provide relief. Frank had both obsessions and compulsions, but his disorder was mild compared with the case of Richard.

Richard... • *Enslaved by Ritual*

Richard, a 19-year-old college freshman majoring in philosophy, withdrew from school because of incapacitating ritualistic behavior. He abandoned personal hygiene because the compulsive rituals that he had to carry out during washing or cleaning were so time consuming that he could do nothing else. Almost continual showering gave way to no showering. He stopped cutting and washing his hair and beard, brushing his teeth, and changing his clothes. He left his room infrequently and, to avoid rituals associated with the toilet, defecated on paper towels, urinated in paper cups, and stored the waste in the closet. He ate only late at night when his family was asleep. To be able to eat, he had to exhale completely, making a lot of hissing noises, coughs, and hacks, and then fill his mouth with as much food as he could while no air was in his lungs. He would eat only a mixture of peanut butter, sugar, cocoa, milk, and mayonnaise. All other foods he considered contaminants. When he walked, he took small steps on his toes while continually looking back, checking and rechecking. Occasionally, he ran quickly in place. He withdrew his left arm completely from his shirt sleeve as if he were crippled and his shirt was a sling.

Like everyone with OCD, Richard experienced intrusive and persistent thoughts and impulses; in his case, they were about sex, aggression, and religion. His various behaviors were efforts to suppress sexual and aggressive thoughts or to ward off the disastrous consequences he thought would ensue if he did not perform his rituals. Richard performed most of the repetitive behaviors and mental acts mentioned in the *DSM-5* criteria. Compulsions can be either behavioral (hand-washing or checking) or mental (thinking about certain words in a specific order, counting, praying, and so on) (Purdon, 2009; Steketee & Barlow, 2002). The important thing is that they are believed to reduce stress or prevent a dreaded event. Compulsions are often "magical" in that they may bear no logical relation to the obsession.

DSM 5 DISORDER CRITERIA SUMMARY
Obsessive-Compulsive Disorder

Features of OCD include the following:

A. Presence of obsessions, compulsions or both:

- Obsessions: Recurrent and persistent thoughts, urges, or images that are experienced, at some time during the disturbance, as intrusive and inappropriate and that in most individuals cause marked anxiety or distress; the individual attempts to ignore or suppress such thoughts, impulses, or images, or to neutralize them with some other thought or action.

- Compulsions: Repetitive behaviors (e.g., handwashing, checking) or mental acts (e.g., counting, repeating words silently) that the individual feels driven to perform in response to an obsession, or according to rules that must be applied rigidly; the behaviors or mental acts are aimed at preventing or reducing distress or preventing some dreaded event or situation; however, these behaviors or mental acts either are not connected in a realistic way with what they are designed to neutralize or prevent, or are clearly excessive.

B. The obsessions or compulsions are time-consuming (e.g., take more than one hour per day), or cause clinically significant distress or impairment in important areas of functioning.

C. The disturbance is not due to the direct physiological effects of a substance or another medical condition and is not better explained by the symptoms of another mental disorder.

From American Psychiatric Association. (2013). *Diagnostic and statistical manual of mental disorders* (5th ed.). Washington, DC.

Types of Obsessions and Compulsions

Based on statistically associated groupings, there are four major types of obsessions (Bloch, Landeros-Weisenberger, Rosario, Pittenger, & Leckman, 2008; Mathews, 2009) and each is associated with a pattern of compulsive behavior (see Table 4.7). Symmetry obsessions account for most

TABLE 4.7 | Types of Obsessions and Associated Compulsions

Symptom Subtype	Obsession	Compulsion
Symmetry/ exactness/ "just right"	Needing things to be symmetrical/ aligned just so Urges to do things over and over until they feel "just right"	Putting things in a certain order Repeating rituals
Forbidden thoughts or actions (aggressive/ sexual/religious)	Fears, urges to harm self or others Fears of offending God	Checking Avoidance Repeated requests for reassurance
Cleaning/contamination	Germs Fears of germs or contaminants	Repetitive or excessive washing Using gloves, masks to do daily tasks
Hoarding	Fears of throwing anything away	Collecting/saving objects with little or no actual or sentimental value such as food wrappings

SOURCE: Adapted from Mathews (2009) and Bloch *et al*. (2008).

obsessions (26.7%), followed by "forbidden thoughts or actions" (21%), cleaning and contamination (15.9%), and hoarding (15.4%) (Bloch *et al*., 2008). Symmetry refers to keeping things in perfect order or doing something in a specific way. As a child, were you careful not to step on cracks in the sidewalk? You and your friends might have kept this up for a few minutes before tiring of it. But what if you had to spend your whole life avoiding cracks, on foot or in a car, to prevent something bad from happening? You wouldn't have much fun. People with aggressive (forbidden) obsessive impulses may feel they are about to yell out a swear word in church. One patient of ours, a young and moral woman, was afraid to ride the bus for fear that if a man sat down beside her she would grab his crotch! In reality, this would be the last thing she would do, but the aggressive urge was so horrifying that she made every attempt possible to suppress it and to avoid riding the bus or similar situations where the impulse might occur.

Certain kinds of obsessions are strongly associated with certain kinds of rituals (Bloch *et al*., 2008; Calamari *et al*., 2004; Leckman *et al*., 1997). For example, forbidden thoughts or actions, as indicated in Table 4.7, seem to lead to checking rituals. Checking rituals serve to prevent an imagined disaster or catastrophe. Many are logical, such as repeatedly checking the stove to see whether you turned it off, but severe cases can be illogical. For example, Richard thought that if he did not eat in a certain way he might become possessed. If he didn't take small steps and look back, some disaster might happen to his family. A mental act, such as counting, can also be a compulsion. Obsessions with symmetry lead to ordering and arranging or repeating rituals; obsessions with contamination lead to washing rituals that may restore a sense of safety and control (Rachman, 2006). Like Richard, many patients have several kinds of obsessions and compulsions.

Tic Disorder and OCD

It is also common for tic disorder, characterized by involuntary movement (sudden jerking of limbs, for example), to co-occur in patients with OCD (particularly children) or in their families (Browne *et al*., 2015; Mataix-Cols *et al*., 2013). More complex tics with involuntary vocalizations are referred to as Tourette's disorder (Leckman *et al*., 2010; see Chapter 13). In some cases, these movements are not tics but may be compulsions. Approximately 10% to 40% of children and adolescents with OCD also have had tic disorder at some point (Leckman *et al*., 2010). The obsessions in tic-related OCD are almost always related to symmetry. CBT has been found to be quite effective for treating tic disorders (McGuire *et al*., 2015).

Statistics

Estimates of the lifetime prevalence of OCD range from 1.6% to 2.3% (Calamari, Chik, Pontarelli, & DeJong, 2012; Kessler, Berglund, Demler *et al*., 2005), and in a given one-year period the prevalence is 1% (Calamari *et al*., 2012; Kessler, Chiu *et al*., 2005). Not all cases meeting criteria for OCD are as severe as Richard's. Obsessions and compulsions can be arranged along a continuum, like most clinical features of anxiety disorders. Intrusive and distressing thoughts are common in non-clinical ("normal") individuals (Boyer & Liénard, 2008; Fullana *et al*., 2009). Spinella (2005) found that 13% of a "normal" community

obsessions Recurrent intrusive thought or impulse the client seeks to suppress or neutralize while recognizing it is not imposed by outside forces.

compulsions Repetitive, ritualistic, time-consuming behavior or mental act a person feels driven to perform.

sample of people had moderate levels of obsessions or compulsions that were not severe enough to meet diagnostic criteria for OCD.

It would also be unusual *not* to have an occasional intrusive or strange thought. Many people have bizarre, sexual, or aggressive thoughts, particularly if they are bored—for example, when sitting in class. Steketee and Barlow (2002) collected examples of thoughts from ordinary people who do not have OCD. Some of these thoughts are listed in Table 4.8.

Have you had any of these thoughts? Most people do, but they are passing worries. Certain individuals, however, are horrified by such thoughts, considering them signs of an alien, intrusive, evil force. Unlike other anxiety and related disorders, OCD has a ratio of female to male that is nearly 1:1. Although there is some evidence in children that there are more males than females (Hanna, 1995), this seems to be because boys tend to develop OCD earlier. By mid-adolescence, the sex ratio is approximately equal (Albano et al., 1996). Age of onset ranges from childhood through the 30s, with a median age of onset of 19 (Kessler, Berglund, Demler et al., 2005). The age of onset peaks earlier in males (13 to 15) than in females (20 to 24) (Rasmussen & Eisen, 1990). Once OCD develops, it tends to become chronic (Calamari et al., 2012; Steketee & Barlow, 2002).

OCD looks remarkably similar across cultures. Studies from England, Hong Kong, India, Egypt, Japan, and Norway found essentially similar types and proportions of obsessions and compulsions, as did studies from Canada, Finland, Taiwan, Africa, Puerto Rico, Korea, and New Zealand (Horwath & Weissman, 2000; Weissman et al., 1994).

Causes

Many of us sometimes have intrusive, even horrific, thoughts and occasionally engage in ritualistic behavior, especially when we are under stress (Parkinson & Rachman, 1981a, 1981b). But few of us develop OCD. Again, as with panic disorder and PTSD, someone must develop anxiety focused on the possibility of having additional intrusive thoughts.

The repetitive, intrusive, unacceptable thoughts of OCD may well be regulated by the hypothetical brain circuits described in Chapter 2. The tendency to develop anxiety over having additional compulsive thoughts, however, may have the same generalized biological and psychological precursors as anxiety in general (Barlow et al., 2014; Suárez et al., 2009).

Why would people with OCD focus their anxiety on the occasional intrusive thought rather than on the possibility of a panic attack or some other external situation? One hypothesis is that early experiences taught them that some thoughts are dangerous and

TABLE 4.8 | Obsessions and Intrusive Thoughts Reported by Nonclinical Samples*

Harming

Impulse to jump out of a high window

Idea of jumping in front of a car

Impulse to push someone in front of a train

Wishing a person would die

While holding a baby, having a sudden urge to kick it

Thoughts of dropping a baby

The thought that if I forget to say goodbye to someone, they might die

Thought that thinking about horrible things happening to a child will cause it

Contamination or Disease

Thought of catching a disease from public pools or other public places

Thoughts I may have caught a disease from touching toilet seat

Idea that dirt is always on my hand

Inappropriate or Unacceptable Behavior

Idea of swearing or yelling at my boss

Thought of doing something embarrassing in public, like forgetting to wear a top

Hoping someone doesn't succeed

Thought of blurting out something in church

Thought of "unnatural" sexual acts

Doubts about Safety, Memory, and So On

Thought that I haven't locked the house up properly

Idea of leaving my curling iron on the carpet and forgetting to pull out the plug

Thought that I've left the heater and stove on

Idea that I've left the car unlocked when I know I've locked it

Idea that objects are not arranged perfectly

* Examples were obtained from Rachman and de Silva (1978) and from unpublished research by Dana Thordarson, Ph.D., and Michael Kyrios, Ph.D. (personal communications, 2000). Source: Reprinted, with permission, from Steketee, G., & Barlow, D. H. (2002). Obsessive-compulsive disorder. In D. H. Barlow, *Anxiety and its disorders: The nature and treatment of anxiety and panic* (2nd ed., p. 529), © 2002 Guilford Press.

unacceptable because the terrible things they are thinking might happen and they would be responsible. These early experiences would result in a specific psychological vulnerability to develop OCD. When clients with OCD equate thoughts with the specific actions or activity represented by the thoughts, this is called *thought–action fusion.* Thought–action fusion may, in turn, be caused by attitudes of excessive responsibility and resulting guilt developed during childhood, when even a bad thought is associated with evil intent (Steketee & Barlow, 2002; Taylor, Abramowitz, McKay, & Cuttler, 2012). They may learn this through the same process of misinformation that convinced the person with snake phobia that snakes were dangerous and could be everywhere. One patient believed thinking about abortion was the moral equivalent of having an abortion. Richard finally admitted to having strong homosexual impulses that were unacceptable to him and to his minister father, and he believed the impulses were as sinful as actual acts. Many people with OCD who believe in the tenets of fundamental religions, whether Christian, Jewish, or Islamic, present with similar attitudes of inflated responsibility and thought–action fusion. Several studies showed that the strength of religious belief, but not the type of belief, was associated with thought–action fusion and severity of OCD (Rassin & Koster, 2003; Steketee, Quay, & White, 1991). Of course, most people with fundamental religious beliefs do not develop OCD. But what if the most frightening thing in your life was not a snake or speaking in public, but a terrible thought that happened to pop into your head? You can't avoid it as you would a snake, so you resist this thought by attempting to suppress it or "neutralize" it using mental or behavioral strategies, such as distraction, praying, or checking. These strategies become compulsions, but they are doomed to fail in the long term, because these strategies backfire and actually in-crease the frequency of the thought (Franklin & Foa, 2014; Wegner, 1989).

Again, generalized biological and psychological vulnerabilities must be present for this disorder to develop. Believing some thoughts are unacceptable and therefore must be suppressed (a specific psychological vulnerability) may put people at greater risk of OCD (Parkinson & Rachman, 1981b; Salkovskis & Campbell, 1994). A model of the etiology of OCD that is somewhat similar to other models of anxiety disorders is presented in ● Figure 4.9.

Treatment

The effects of drugs on OCD have been evaluated extensively (Dougherty, Rauch, & Jenike, 2012; Stewart, Jenike, & Jenike, 2009). The most effective seem to be those that inhibit the re-uptake of serotonin, such as clomipramine or the SSRIs, which benefit up to 60% of patients with OCD, with no particular advantage to one drug over another. Relapse often occurs when the drug is

● **Figure 4.9** A model of the causes of obsessive-compulsive disorder. (Reprinted, with permission, from Steketee, G., & Barlow, D. H. (2002). Obsessive-Compulsive Disorder. In Anxiety and its Disorders: The Nature and Treatment of Anxiety and Panic (2nd ed., p. 536). New York: Guilford Press, © 2002 Guilford Press.)

discontinued, however (Dougherty *et al.*, 2012; Lydiard, Brawman-Mintzer, & Ballenger, 1996).

Highly structured psychological treatments work somewhat better than drugs, but they are not readily available. The most effective approach is called *exposure and ritual prevention (ERP)*, a process whereby the rituals are prevented and the patient is systematically exposed to the feared thoughts or situations (Abramowitz, Taylor, & McKay, 2012; Franklin & Foa, 2014). These procedures seem to facilitate "reality testing," because clients soon learn, at an emotional level, that no harm will result whether they carry out the rituals or not. More recent innovations to evidence-based psychological treatments for OCD have examined the efficacy of cognitive treatments with a focus on the overestimation of threat, the importance and control of intrusive thoughts, the sense of inflated responsibility present in patients with OCD who think they alone may be responsible for preventing a catastrophe, and the need for perfectionism and certainty in these patients (Whittal & Robichaud, 2012). Initial results indicate that these strategies are perhaps as effective as ERP.

Studies have evaluated the combined effects of medication and psychological treatments (Romanelli, Wu, Gamba, Mojtabai, & Segal, 2014; Simpson *et al.*, 2013). In one study (Foa *et al.*, 2005), ERP was compared with clomipramine, as well as with a combined condition. ERP, with or without the drug, produced superior results to the drug alone, with 86% responding to ERP alone versus 48% to the drug alone. Combining the treatments did not produce any additional advantage. Also, relapse rates were high from the medication-only group when the drug was withdrawn. Furthermore, medication such as SSRIs appear to be only effective in a subgroup of patients, possibly because these drugs primarily dampen the symptoms but do not correct the dysregulated neural circuits (Ressler & Rothbaum, 2013). Therefore, adding ERP to people who continue to have OCD symptoms after starting an SSRI

can be more beneficial than adding another medication (Simpson *et al.*, 2013).

Psychosurgery is one of the more radical treatments for OCD. "Psychosurgery" is a misnomer that refers to neurosurgery for a psychological disorder. Jenike and colleagues (1991) reviewed the records of 33 patients with OCD, most of them extremely severe cases who had failed to respond to either drug or psychological treatment. After a surgical procedure to lesion the cingulate bundle (cingulotomy), approximately 30% benefited substantially. Similarly, Rück *et al.* (2008) performed a related surgery (capsulotomy) on 25 patients who had not responded to five years of previous treatment; 35% (nine patients) benefited substantially, but six of those nine patients suffered from serious adverse side effects of the surgery. These results seem typical (Greenberg, Rauch, & Haber, 2010) and are similar to results from a procedure called deep brain stimulation in which electrodes are placed through small holes drilled in the skull and are connected to a pacemaker-like device in the brain. The advantage of deep brain stimulation over more traditional surgery is that it is reversible (McLaughlin & Greenberg, 2012). Considering that these patients seemed to have no hope from other treatments, surgery deserves consideration as a last resort.

Body Dysmorphic Disorder

▶ What are the features of body dysmorphic disorder and how is it treated?

Did you ever wish you could change part of your appearance? Maybe the size of your nose or the way your ears stick out? Most people fantasize about improving something, but some relatively normal-looking people think they are so ugly they refuse to interact with others or otherwise function normally for fear that people will laugh at their ugliness. This curious affliction is called **body dysmorphic disorder (BDD)**, and at its center is a preoccupation with some imagined defect in appearance by someone who actually looks reasonably normal (Fang & Wilhelm, 2015). The disorder has been referred to as "imagined ugliness" (Phillips, 1991). Consider the case of Jim.

Jim... • *Ashamed to Be Seen*

In his mid-20s, Jim was diagnosed with suspected social anxiety disorder. He had just finished rabbinical school and had been offered a position at a synagogue in a nearby city. He found himself unable to accept, however, because of marked social difficulties. Lately he had given up leaving his small apartment for fear of

running into people he knew and being forced to stop and interact with them.

Jim was a good-looking young man of about average height, with dark hair and eyes. Although he was somewhat depressed, a mental status exam and a brief interview focusing on current functioning and past history did not reveal any remarkable problems. There was no sign of a psychotic process (he was not out of touch with reality). We then focused on Jim's social difficulties. We expected the usual kinds of anxiety about interacting with people or "doing something" (performing) in front of them. But this was not Jim's concern. Rather, he was convinced that everyone, even his good friends, was staring at a part of his body that he found grotesque. He reported that strangers would never mention his deformity and his friends felt too sorry for him to mention it. Jim thought his head was square! To hide his condition, Jim wore floppy hats and was most comfortable in winter, when he could cover his head with a stocking cap. To us, Jim looked normal.

Clinical Description

For many years, BDD was considered a somatoform disorder because its central feature is a psychological preoccupation with somatic (physical) issues. But increasing evidence indicated it was more closely related to OCD, accounting for its relocation to the obsessive-compulsive and related disorders section in *DSM-5*. For example, OCD often co-occurs with BDD and is found among family members of BDD patients (Chosak *et al.*, 2008; Gustad & Phillips, 2003; Phillips *et al.*, 2010; Phillips & Stout, 2006; Tynes, White, & Steketee, 1990; Zimmerman & Mattia, 1998). There are other similarities. People with BDD complain of persistent, intrusive, and horrible thoughts about their appearance, and they engage in such compulsive behaviors as repeatedly looking in mirrors to check their physical features. BDD and OCD also have approximately the same age of onset and run the same course. One brain-imaging study demonstrated similar abnormal brain functioning between patients with BDD and patients with OCD (Rauch *et al.*, 2003).

To give you a better idea of the types of concerns people with BDD present to health professionals, the locations of imagined defects in 200 patients are shown in Table 4.9. The average number of body areas of concern to these individuals was five to seven (Phillips, Menard, Fay, & Weisberg, 2005). In another group of 23 adolescents with BDD, 61% focused on their skin and 55% on their hair (Albertini & Phillips, 1999). A variety of checking or compensating rituals are common in people with BDD in attempts to alleviate their concerns. For example, excessive tanning is common, with 25% of one group of 200 patients tanning themselves in an attempt to hide skin defects (Phillips, Menard, Fay, & Weisberg, 2005). Excessive grooming and skin picking are also common. Many people with this disorder become fixated on mirrors (Veale & Riley, 2001). They often check their presumed ugly feature to see whether any change has taken

TABLE 4.9 | Location of Imagined Defects in 200 Patients with Body Dysmorphic Disorder*

Location	%	Location	%
Skin	80	Overall appearance of face	19
Hair	58	Small body build	18
Nose	39	Legs	18
Stomach	32	Face size or shape	16
Teeth	30	Chin	15
Weight	29	Lips	14.5
Breasts	26	Arms or wrists	14
Buttocks	22	Hips	13
Eyes	22	Cheeks	11
Thighs	20	Ears	11
Eyebrows	20		

Adapted from Phillips, K. A., Menard, B. A., Fay, C., & Weisberg, R. (2005). Demographic characteristics, phenomenology, comorbidity, and family history in 200 individuals with body dysmorphic disorder. *Psychosomatics*, 46(4), 317–325. © 2005 The Academy of Psychosomatic Medicine.

place. Others avoid mirrors to an almost phobic extent. Quite understandably, suicidal ideation, suicide attempts, and suicide itself are typical consequences of this disorder (Phillips, Menard, Fay, & Weisberg, 2005; Zimmerman & Mattia, 1998). People with BDD also have "ideas of reference," which means they think everything that goes on in their world somehow is related to them—in this case, to their imagined defect. This disorder can cause considerable disruption in the patient's life. Many patients with severe cases become housebound for fear of showing themselves to other people.

Statistics

The prevalence of BDD is hard to estimate because by its very nature it tends to be kept secret. The best estimates, however, are that it is far more common than we had previously thought. Without some sort of treatment, it tends to run a lifelong course (Phillips, 1991; Veale, Boocock *et al.*, 1996). One of the patients with BDD reported by Phillips and colleagues (1993) had suffered from her condition for 71 years, since the age of nine. Studies suggest that as many as 70% of college students report at least some dissatisfaction with their bodies, with 4% to 28% of these appearing to meet all the criteria for the disorder (Fitts, Gibson, Redding, & Deiter, 1989; Phillips, 2005). This study was done by questionnaire, however, and may have reflected the large percentage of students who are concerned simply with weight.

DSM 5 | DISORDER CRITERIA SUMMARY
Body Dysmorphic Disorder

Features of BDD include the following:

A. Preoccupation with one or more imagined defects or flaws in physical appearance.

B. Repetitive behaviors (e.g., mirror checking) or mental acts (e.g., comparing his or her appearance with that of others) in response to the appearance concerns.

C. The preoccupation causes clinically significant distress or impairment in important areas of functioning.

D. The appearance preoccupation is not better explained by concerns with body fat or weight in an individual whose symptoms meet diagnostic criteria for an eating disorder.

From American Psychiatric Association. (2013). *Diagnostic and statistical manual of mental disorders* (5th ed.). Washington, DC.

Another study investigated the prevalence of BDD, specifically in an ethnically diverse sample of 566 adolescents between the ages of 14 and 19. The overall prevalence of BDD in this group was 2.2%, with adolescent girls more dissatisfied with their bodies than boys and African Americans of both genders more satisfied with their bodies than Caucasians, Asians, and Hispanics (Mayville, Katz, Gipson, & Cabral, 1999; Roberts, Cash, Feingold, & Johnson, 2006). Overall, about 1% to 2% of individuals in community samples and from 2% to 13% of student samples meet criteria for BDD (Koran, Abujaoude, Large, & Serpe, 2008; Woolfolk & Allen, 2011). A somewhat higher proportion of individuals with BDD are interested in art or design compared with individuals without BDD, reflecting, perhaps, a strong interest in aesthetics or appearance (Veale, Ennis, & Lambrou, 2002).

In mental health clinics, the disorder is also uncommon because most people with BDD seek other types of health professionals, such as plastic surgeons and dermatologists. BDD is seen equally in men and women. In the larger series of 200 individuals reported by Phillips, Menard, Fay, and Weisberg (2005), 68.5% were female, but 62% of a large number of individuals with BDD in Japan were males. Generally, there are more similarities than differences between men and women with BDD, but some differences have been noted (Phillips, Menard, & Fay, 2006). Men tend to focus on body build, genitals, and thinning hair and tend to have more severe BDD. A focus on muscle defects and body building is nearly unique to men with the disorder (Pope *et al.*, 2005). Women focus on more varied body areas and are more likely to also have an eating disorder.

Age of onset ranges from early adolescence through the 20s, peaking at the age of 16–17 (Phillips, Menard, Fay, & Weisberg, 2005; Zimmerman & Mattia, 1998). Individuals are somewhat reluctant to seek treatment. In many cases, a relative will force the issue, demanding the individual get help; this insistence may reflect the disruptiveness of the disorder for family members. Severity is also reflected in the high percentage (24%) of past suicide attempts among the 50 cases described by Veale, Boocock, and colleagues (1996); 27.5% of the 200 cases described by Phillips, Menard, Fay, and Weisberg (2005); and 21% of a group of 33 adolescents (Albertini & Phillips, 1999).

One study of 62 consecutive outpatients with BDD found that the degree of psychological stress, quality of life, and impairment were generally worse than comparable indices in patients with depression, diabetes, or a recent myocardial infarction (heart attack) on several questionnaire measures (Phillips, Dufresne, Wilkel, & Vittorio, 2000). Similar results were reported on a larger sample of 176 patients (Phillips, Menard, Fay, & Pagano, 2005). Thus, BDD is among the more serious of psychological disorders,

and depression and substance abuse are common consequences of BDD (Gustad & Phillips, 2003; Phillips *et al.*, 2010). As you might suspect, few people with this disorder get married. Further reflecting the intense suffering that accompanies this disorder, Veale (2000) collected information on 25 patients with BDD who had sought cosmetic surgery in the past. Of these, nine patients who could not afford surgery, or were turned down for other reasons, had attempted by their own hand to alter their appearance dramatically, often with tragic results. One example was a man preoccupied by his skin, who believed it was too "loose." He used a staple gun on both sides of his face to try to keep his skin taut. The staples fell out after 10 minutes and he narrowly missed damaging his facial nerve. In a second example, a woman was preoccupied by her skin and the shape of her face. She filed down her teeth to alter the appearance of her jawline. Yet another woman who was preoccupied by what she perceived as the ugliness of multiple areas of her body and desired liposuction, but could not afford it, used a knife to cut her thighs and attempted to squeeze out the fat. BDD is also stubbornly chronic. In a prospective study of 183 patients, only 21% were somewhat improved over the course of a year, and 15% of that group relapsed during that year (Phillips, Pagano, Menard, & Stout, 2006).

Causes and Treatment

We know little about the etiology of BDD specifically. What little evidence we do have on etiology comes from the pattern of comorbidity of BDD with OCD described earlier. The marked similarities to OCD suggest, perhaps, somewhat similar patterns of etiology. Interestingly, approximately 15% of a series of 100 patients with eating disorders suffered from comorbid BDD, with their body dysmorphic concerns unrelated to weight and shape (Kollei, Schieber, de Zwaan, Svitak, & Martin, 2013).

Perhaps more significantly, there are two, and only two, treatments for BDD with any evidence of effectiveness, and these treatments are the same found effective in OCD. First, drugs that block the re-uptake of serotonin, such as clomipramine (Anafranil) and fluvoxamine (Luvox), provide relief to at least some people (Hadley, Kim, Priday, & Hollander, 2006). Second, exposure and response prevention, the type of cognitive-behavioral therapy effective with OCD, has also been successful with BDD (McKay *et al.*, 1997; Rosen, Reiter, & Orosan, 1995; Veale, Gournay *et al.*, 1996; Wilhelm, Otto, Lohr, & Deckersbach, 1999). Furthermore, patients with BDD and OCD have similar rates of response to these treatments (Saxena *et al.*, 2001; Williams *et al.*, 2006). As with OCD, cognitive-behavioral therapy tends to produce better and longer lasting outcomes compared to medication alone (Buhlmann, Reese,

Renaud, & Wilhelm, 2008). But CBT is not as readily available as drugs.

Another interesting lead on causes of BDD comes from cross-cultural explorations of similar disorders. You may remember the Japanese variant of social anxiety disorder, *taijin kyofusho* (see page 151). But people with *taijin kyofusho* also have all the other characteristics of social anxiety disorder. Some patients diagnosed with BDD in our culture might simply be considered to have severe social anxiety in Japan and Korea. Possibly, then, social anxiety is fundamentally related to BDD, a connection that would give us further hints on the nature of the disorder. Indeed, a study of BDD in Western countries indicates that concerns relating to perceived negative evaluation of their appearance by others are every bit as important as self-evaluation of the imagined defects in appearance (Anson, Veale, & de Silva, 2012). Studies of comorbidity indicate that social anxiety disorder, along with OCD, is also commonly found in people with BDD (Fang & Hofmann, 2010; Phillips & Stout, 2006).

Plastic Surgery and Other Medical Treatments

Patients with BDD believe they are physically deformed in some way and go to medical doctors to attempt to correct their deficits (Woolfolk & Allen, 2011). Phillips, Grant, Siniscalchi, and Albertini (2001) studied the treatments sought by 289 patients with BDD, including 39 children or adolescents, and found that fully 76.4% had sought this type of treatment and 66% were receiving it. Dermatology (skin) treatment was the most often received (45.2%), followed by plastic surgery (23.2%). Looking at it another way, in one study of 268 patients seeking care from a dermatologist, 11.9% met criteria for BDD (Phillips *et al.*, 2000).

Because the concerns of people with BDD involve mostly the face or head, it is not surprising that the disorder is big business for the plastic surgery profession. Investigators estimate that as many as 8% to 25% of all patients who request plastic surgery may have BDD (Barnard, 2000; Crerand

▲ Michael Jackson as a child and as an adult. Many people alter their features through surgery. However, people with body dysmorphic disorder are seldom satisfied with the results.

et al., 2004). The most common procedures are rhinoplasties (nose jobs), facelifts, eyebrow elevations, liposuction, breast augmentation, and surgery to alter the jawline. Between 2000 and 2012, according to the American Society of Plastic Surgeons (2012), the total number of cosmetic procedures increased 98%. The problem is that surgery on the proportion of these people with BDD seldom produces the desired results. These individuals return for additional surgery on the same defect or concentrate on some new defect. Phillips, Menard, Fay, and Pagano (2005) report that 81% of 50 individuals seeking surgery or similar medical consults were dissatisfied with the result. In 88% of a large group of people with BDD seeking medical rather than psychological treatment, the severity of the disorder and accompanying distress either did not change or *increased* after surgery. Similar discouraging or negative results are evident from other forms of medical treatment, such as skin treatments (Phillips *et al.*, 2001). It is important that plastic surgeons screen out these patients; many do so by collaborating with medically trained psychologists (Pruzinsky, 1988).

Other Obsessive-Compulsive and Related Disorders

▶ What are the other obsessive-compulsive and related disorders and how are they treated?

Hoarding Disorder

Several years ago, a group of patients came to the attention of specialty clinics because they compulsively hoard things, fearing that if they throw something away, even a 10-year-old newspaper, they then might urgently need it.

At first, the specialty clinics assumed that this was just a strange variant of OCD, but it soon became apparent that it was a major problem unto itself, as is obvious to anyone who has seen the recent spate of television programs showing individuals with this disorder in their almost unlivable homes. Estimates of prevalence range between

2% and 5% of the population, which is twice as high as the prevalence of OCD, with nearly equal numbers of men and women, and is found worldwide (Frost, Steketee, & Tolin, 2012). The three major characteristics of this problem are excessive acquisition of things, difficulty discarding anything, and living with excessive clutter under conditions best characterized as gross disorganization (Frost & Rasmussen, 2012; Grisham & Barlow, 2005). It is not uncommon for some patients' houses and yards to come to the attention of public health authorities (Tolin, 2011). One patient's house and yard was condemned, because junk was piled so high it was both unsightly and a fire hazard. Among her hoard was a 20-year collection of used sanitary napkins! Although only a tiny percentage of fires in residences occur in the homes of individuals who hoard, these fires account for 24% of all fire-related fatalities (Frost *et al.*, 2012).

Basically, these individuals usually begin acquiring things during their teenage years and often experience great pleasure, even euphoria, from shopping or otherwise collecting various items. Shopping or collecting things may be a response to feeling down or depressed and is sometimes

DSM 5 CONTROVERSY Classifying Anxiety and Related Disorders

The anxiety disorders as classified in *DSM-5* are now divided into three separate groupings or classes of disorders, and 10 disorders have been added to these groupings either by splitting existing disorders, relocating disorders from other diagnostic sections such as the somatoform disorders, or introducing new disorders appearing for the first time in the DSM. In Chapter 3, we introduced the idea that emerging conceptions of psychopathology move us away from an emphasis on categorical (individual) diagnoses to a consideration of larger dimensions, or spectra, in which similar and related diagnoses might be grouped. One such spectrum consists of what some call emotional disorders, including anxiety and depression (Leyfer & Brown, 2011). But how would this dimensional approach to psychopathology change the way we make diagnoses? Recently, we speculated on how a future diagnostic system using dimensional approaches for emotional disorders might work (Brown & Barlow, 2009), and emerging theoretical development and empirical evidence should be more satisfactory than having to consider a very large number of individual categorical diagnoses as represented in this chapter as well as chapters 6 and 7 (Barlow, Sauer-Zavala, Carl, Bullis, & Ellard, 2014). To illustrate this approach, let's first consider a case from our clinic.

Mr. S. was a high school teacher in his mid-50s who had been in a very serious car accident several months before coming in and was suffering from symptoms related to that accident.

These included intrusive memories of the crash, "flashbacks" of the accident itself that were very intense emotionally, and images of the cuts and bruises on his wife's face. He also had a very strong startle reaction to any cues that reminded him of the accident and avoided driving in certain locations that were somewhat similar to where he had his accident. These symptoms intermingled with a similar set of symptoms emerging from a series of traumatic experiences that had occurred during his service in the Vietnam War. In addition to these trauma symptoms, he also spent a lot of his day worrying about various life events, including his own health and that of his family. He also worried about his performance at work and whether he would be evaluated poorly by other staff members, despite his having received consistently high evaluations for his teaching.

After considering everything he said and evaluating him clinically, therapists found that he clearly met criteria for PTSD. He also met criteria for GAD given his substantial worry that was occurring every day about life events unrelated to the trauma. In addition, he had some mild depression, perhaps due in part to all of the anxiety he was experiencing. In summary, the patient could be diagnosed with PTSD although he had substantial features of GAD as well as depression. But what would it look like if we attempted to describe his symptoms on a series of dimensions rather than on whether they meet criteria for one category or another? • Figure 4.10 displays a simplified version of one

possible dimensional system (Brown & Barlow, 2009). In this dimensional scheme, "anxiety" (AN) is represented on the left because all individuals with anxiety or depressive disorders have some level of anxiety. Many individuals, but not all, are also depressed (DEP) (as was Mr. S.). Mr. S. would score fairly high on anxiety and somewhat lower on depression. Looking to the far right of the figure, Mr. S. displayed a lot of behavioral avoidance as well as avoidance of physical sensations (interoceptive avoidance) (AV-BI). Mostly he was having difficulty driving and also would avoid cues connected with his earlier trauma by refusing if at all possible to engage in activities or conversations associated with the war. Another related type of avoidance is when you avoid experiencing intense emotions or thoughts about emotional experiences. We call this cognitive and emotional avoidance (AV-CE) and Mr. S. also scored relatively high on this aspect of avoidance.

But what was the focus of Mr. S.'s anxiety? Here we look at five characteristics that currently categorize anxiety and related disorder diagnoses. Looking first at trauma (TRM) focus, obviously, this earned the highest score on Mr. S.'s profile. He also was suffering from frequent flashbacks to his traumatic experiences, which as you may remember, are very similar to panic attacks and consist of strong autonomic surges, such as rapidly increasing heart rate. Thus, he scored high on panic and related autonomic surges (PAS). Other kinds of intrusive obsessive thoughts were not present, and he scored low on this dimension (IC). His worry about his health and the health of his family caused him to score moderately high on somatic anxiety (SOM), but social anxiety (SOC) was not particularly high.

As you can see, this dimensional profile provides a more complete picture of Mr. S.'s clinical presentation than simply noting that he met criteria for PTSD. This is because the profile captures the relative severity of a number of key features of anxiety and mood disorders that are often present together in patients who might meet criteria for only a single diagnosis in the current categorical system. This profile also captures the fact that Mr. S. had some depression that was below the severity threshold to meet criteria for mood disorder. Knowing all of this by glancing at Mr. S.'s profile in ● Figure 4.10 should help clinicians match therapy more closely to his presenting problems.

This is just one possible example, but it does provide some idea of what a diagnostic system might look like in the future. Although this system was not ready for *DSM-5* because much more research is needed on how best to make it work, a system like this might be ready for *DSM-6*. ●

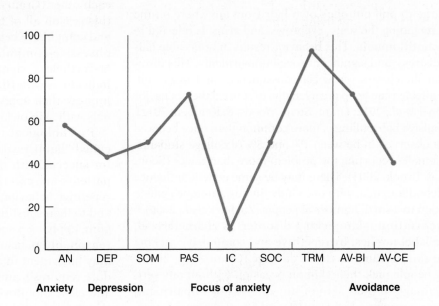

● **Figure 4.10** Proposed DSM-6 Dimensional Diagnosis of a Patient with PTSD. AN, anxiety; DEP, unipolar depression; SOM, somatic anxiety; PAS, panic and related autonomic surges; IC, intrusive cognitions; SOC, social evaluation; TRM, past trauma; AV-BI, behavioral and interoceptive avoidance; AV-CE, cognitive and emotional avoidance. Higher scores on the y-axis (0–100) indicate higher levels of the x-axis dimension, but otherwise the y-axis metric is arbitrary and is used for illustrative purposes. (Adapted from Brown, T. A., & Barlow, D. H. (2009). A proposal for a dimensional classification system based on the shared features of the DSM-IV anxiety and mood disorders: Implications for assessment and treatment. Psychological Assessment, 21(3), 267. © 2009 by American Psychological Association. Reprinted with permission.)

called, facetiously, "retail therapy." But unlike most people who like to shop or collect, these individuals then experience strong anxiety and distress about throwing anything away, because everything has either some potential use or sentimental value in their minds, or simply becomes an extension of their own identity. Most of these individuals don't consider that they have a problem until family members or authorities insist that they seek help.

Careful analysis of what we know about hoarding suggests it has similarities and differences with both OCD and impulse control disorders. Therefore, it is best considered a separate disorder and now appears as such in the *DSM-5*. For example, OCD tends to wax and wane, whereas hoarding behavior can begin early in life and get worse with each passing decade (Ayers, Saxena, Golshan, & Wetherell, 2010). One study examined the neural mechanisms of decision-making

about whether to keep or discard possessions among individuals with hoarding disorder compared with individuals with OCD without hoarding. The study found specific differences in areas of the brain related to problems identifying the emotional significance of an object and generating the appropriate emotional response (Tolin *et al.*, 2012).

CBT is a promising treatment for hoarding disorder (Tolin, Frost, Steketee, & Muroff, 2015). These treatments developed at our clinic teach people to assign different values to objects and to reduce anxiety about throwing away items that are somewhat less valued (Grisham *et al.*, 2012; Steketee & Frost, 2007a). Preliminary results are promising, but results are more modest than those achieved with OCD. Also, more information on long-term effects of these treatments is needed. Little or nothing is known about effective interventions for individuals who hoard animals.

Trichotillomania (Hair Pulling Disorder) and Excoriation (Skin Picking Disorder)

The urge to pull out one's own hair from anywhere on the body, including the scalp, eyebrows, and arms, is referred to as **trichotillomania**. This behavior results in noticeable hair loss, distress, and significant social impairments. This disorder can often have severe social consequences, and, as a result, those affected can go to great lengths to conceal their behavior (Lochner *et al.*, 2012; Grant, Stein, Woods, & Keuthen, 2012). Compulsive hair pulling is more common than once believed and is observed in between 1% and 5% of college students, with females reporting the problem more than males (Scott, Hilty, & Brook, 2003). There may be some genetic influence on trichotillomania, with one study finding a unique genetic mutation in a small number of people (Zuchner *et al.*, 2006).

Excoriation (skin picking disorder) is characterized, as the label implies, by repetitive and compulsive picking of the skin, leading to tissue damage (Grant *et al.*, 2012). Many people pick their skin on occasion without any serious damage to their skin or any distress or impairment, but for somewhere between 1% and 5% of the population, noticeable damage to skin occurs, sometimes requiring medical attention. There can be significant embarrassment, distress, and impairment in terms of social and work functioning. Excoriation is largely a female disorder.

Prior to *DSM-5*, both disorders were classified under impulse control disorders, but it has been established that these disorders often co-occur with obsessive-compulsive disorder and body dysmorphic disorder, as well as with each other (Grant *et al.*, 2012; Odlaug & Grant, 2012). For this reason all of these disorders, which share repetitive and compulsive behaviors, are now grouped together under obsessive-compulsive and related disorders in *DSM-5*. Nevertheless, significant differences exist. For example, individuals with BDD may pick at their skin occasionally to improve their appearance, which is not the case for individuals with skin picking disorder.

Psychological treatments, particularly an approach called "habit reversal training," have the most evidence for success with these two disorders. In this treatment, patients are carefully taught to be more aware of their repetitive behavior, particularly as it is just about to begin, and to then substitute a different behavior, such as chewing gum, applying a soothing lotion to the skin, or some other reasonably pleasurable but harmless behavior. Results may be evident in as little as four sessions, but the procedure requires teamwork between the patient and therapist and close monitoring of the behavior throughout the day (Nock *et al.*, 2011). Drug treatments, mostly serotonin-specific re-uptake inhibitors, hold some promise, particularly for trichotillomania (Chamberlain, Menzies, Sahakian, & Fineberg, 2007), but the results have been mixed with excoriation (Grant *et al.*, 2012).

4.6 Concept CHECK

Fill in the blanks to form facts about OCD:

1. _____ are intrusive and nonsensical thoughts, images, or urges an individual tries to eliminate or suppress.

2. The practices of washing, counting, and checking to suppress obsessions and provide relief are called _____.

3. The lifetime prevalence of OCD is approximately _____, or even lower.

4. _____ is a radical treatment for OCD involving a surgical lesion to the cingulate bundle.

---

trichotillomania People's urge to pull out their own hair from anywhere on the body, including the scalp, eyebrows, and arm.

excoriation Recurrent, difficult-to-control picking of one's skin leading to significant impairment or distress.

SUMMARY

The Complexity of Anxiety Disorders

What are the similarities and differences among anxiety, fear, and panic attacks?

▶ Anxiety is a future-oriented state characterized by negative affect in which a person focuses on the possibility of uncontrollable danger or misfortune; in contrast, fear is a present-oriented state characterized by strong escapist tendencies and a surge in the sympathetic branch of the autonomic nervous system in response to current danger.

▶ A panic attack represents the alarm response of real fear, but there is no actual danger.

▶ Panic attacks may be (1) unexpected (without warning), or (2) expected (always occurring in a specific situation).

ANXIETY DISORDERS

Generalized Anxiety Disorder

What are the essential features, possible causes, and available treatment approaches for generalized anxiety disorder?

▶ In generalized anxiety disorder (GAD), anxiety focuses on minor, everyday events and not on one major worry or concern.

▶ Both genetic and psychological vulnerabilities seem to contribute to the development of GAD.

▶ Although drug and psychological treatments may be effective in the short term, drug treatments are no more effective in the long term than placebo treatments. Successful treatment may help individuals with GAD focus on what is really threatening to them in their lives.

Panic Disorder and Agoraphobia

What are the essential features of panic disorder and agoraphobia?

▶ In panic disorder, which may or may not be accompanied by agoraphobia (a fear and avoidance of situations considered to be "unsafe"), anxiety is focused on the next panic attack. For some people, agoraphobia develops in the absence of panic attacks or panic-like symptoms.

▶ We all have some genetic vulnerability to stress, and many of us have had a neurobiological overreaction to some stressful event—that is, a panic attack. Individuals who develop panic disorder and then develop anxiety over the possibility of having another panic attack.

▶ Both drug and psychological treatments have proved successful in the treatment of panic disorder. One psychological method, panic control treatment, concentrates on exposing patients to clusters of sensations that remind them of their panic attacks. For agoraphobia, therapeutically-supervised exposure to feared situations is most effective.

Specific Phobia

What are the principal causes of specific phobia?

▶ In phobic disorders, the individual avoids situations that produce severe anxiety, panic, or both. In specific phobia, the fear is focused on a particular object or situation.

▶ Phobias can be acquired by experiencing some traumatic event; they can also be learned vicariously or even be taught.

What strategies are typically used to treat specific phobia?

▶ Treatment of phobias is rather straightforward, with a focus on structured and consistent exposure-based exercises.

Social Anxiety Disorder (Social Phobia)

What are the principal causes of social anxiety disorder (social phobia)?

▶ Social anxiety disorder is a fear of being around others, particularly in situations that call for some kind of "performance" in front of other people.

What strategies are used to treat social anxiety disorder (social phobia)?

▶ Although the causes of social anxiety disorder are similar to those of specific phobias, treatment has a different focus that includes rehearsing or role-playing socially phobic situations. In addition, drug treatments have been effective.

TRAUMA- AND STRESSOR-RELATED DISORDERS

Posttraumatic Stress Disorder

What are the essential features and possible causes of posttraumatic stress disorder?

▶ Posttraumatic stress disorder (PTSD) focuses on avoiding thoughts or images of past traumatic experiences.

▶ The precipitating cause of PTSD is obvious—a traumatic experience. But mere exposure to trauma is not enough. The intensity of the experience seems to be a factor in whether an individual develops PTSD; biological vulnerabilities, as well as social and cultural factors, appear to play a role as well.

What treatment approaches are available for posttraumatic stress disorder?

▶ Treatment involves re-exposing the victim to the trauma and re-establishing a sense of safety to overcome the debilitating effects of PTSD.

Other Trauma- and Stressor-Related Disorders

What are the origins of other trauma- and stress-related disorders?

▸ Adjustment disorder is the development of anxiety or depression in response to stressful, but not traumatic, life events. Individuals prone to anxiety or depression generally may experience increases during stressful life events.

▸ Children experiencing inadequate, abusive, or absent caregiving in early childhood fail to develop normal attachment relationships with caregivers, resulting in two different disorders.

▸ Reactive attachment disorder describes children who are inhibited and emotionally withdrawn and unable to form attachment with caregivers.

▸ Disinhibited social engagement disorder describes children who inappropriately approach all strangers, behaving as if they had always had strong loving relationships with them.

◼ OBSESSIVE-COMPULSIVE AND RELATED DISORDERS

Obsessive-Compulsive Disorder

What are the symptoms of obsessive-compulsive disorder?

▸ Obsessive-compulsive disorder (OCD) focuses on avoiding frightening or repulsive intrusive thoughts (obsessions) or neutralizing these thoughts through the use of ritualistic behavior (compulsions).

▸ As with all anxiety disorders, biological and psychological vulnerabilities seem to be involved in the development of OCD.

How is obsessive-compulsive disorder treated?

▸ Drug treatment seems to be only modestly successful in treating OCD. The most effective treatment approach is a psychological treatment called exposure and ritual prevention (ERP).

Body Dysmorphic Disorder

What are the features of body dysmorphic disorder and how is it treated?

▸ In body dysmorphic disorder (BDD), a person who looks normal is obsessively preoccupied with some imagined defect in appearance (imagined ugliness). These patients typically have more insight into their problem and may seek out plastic surgery as a remedy. Psychological treatment approaches are also similar to those for OCD and are approximately equally successful.

Other Obsessive-Compulsive and Related Disorders

What are the other obsessive-compulsive and related disorders and how are they treated?

▶ Hoarding disorder is characterized by excessive acquisition of things, difficulty discarding anything, and living with excessive clutter under conditions best characterized as gross disorganization.

▶ Treatment approaches are similar to those for OCD but are less successful.

▶ Repetitive and compulsive hair pulling, resulting in significant noticeable loss of hair or repetitive and compulsive picking of the skin, leading to tissue damage, characterize trichotillomania and excoriation disorders respectively.

■ Key Terms

anxiety, 118
fear, 118
panic, 119
panic attack, 119
behavioral inhibition
    system (BIS), 121
fight/flight system (FFS), 121
generalized anxiety
    disorder (GAD), 124
panic disorder (PD), 128
agoraphobia, 128
panic control treatment (PCT), 134

specific phobia, 135
blood–injection–injury phobia, 137
situational phobia, 137
natural environment phobia, 137
animal phobia, 137
separation anxiety disorder, 140
social anxiety disorder (SAD), 141
social phobia, 141
posttraumatic stress
    disorder (PTSD), 146
acute stress disorder, 148
adjustment disorders, 152

attachment disorders, 152
reactive attachment disorder, 153
disinhibited social engagement
    disorder, 153
obsessive-compulsive
    disorder (OCD), 153
obsessions, 154
compulsions, 154
body dysmorphic disorder
    (BDD), 158
trichotillomania, 164
excoriation, 164

Answers to Concept Checks

4.1

1. b; 2. c; 3. e, d; 4. a; 5. f

4.2

1. T; 2. F (more gradual); 3. T; 4. F; 5. T

4.3

1. F (panic attacks occur unexpectedly in panic disorder, even in "safe" situations); 2. F (3.5%); 3. T; 4. T

4.4

1. d; 2. e; 3. c; 4. f; 5. a; 6. d; 7. c

4.5

1. b; 2. a; 3. c

4.6

1. obsessions; 2. compulsions; 3. 1.6%; 4. Psychosurgery

Chapter Quiz

1. _____ is a psychological experience characterized by concern about future events, and _____ is characterized by concern about current circumstances.
   a. Panic; anxiety
   b. Fear; anxiety
   c. Anxiety; fear
   d. Depression; anxiety

2. In an integrated model of anxiety, which childhood experience appears to make an individual more vulnerable to anxiety in adulthood?
   a. negative and inconsistent attention from parents
   b. exposure to situations that reinforce a rigid sense of personal control
   c. interactions with peers that are violent
   d. academic failures in pre-school

3. Which of the following is true about generalized anxiety disorder?
   a. It is most common in individuals aged 15–24 years.
   b. Its course tends to be chronic.
   c. It is the least common of the anxiety disorders.
   d. It is more common in men.

4. Why are the majority of people who suffer from agoraphobia women?
   a. Chromosomal features related to sensitivity of the hypothalamus–pituitary axis are more common in women.
   b. Women are more likely to use cognitive distortions in which they appraise events as threatening.
   c. The hormonal system in women sensitizes the female nervous system to stress.
   d. Cultural factors make it more acceptable for women to avoid situations and to report their fears.

5. Marty has a fear of dogs. Which of the following suggests that his fear qualifies as a specific phobia rather than just an everyday fear?

a. Marty's fear of dogs comes and goes following an episodic pattern.

b. Marty owns a cat but no dog.

c. Marty believes that his fear of dogs is reasonable and appropriate.

d. Marty will only work night shifts, a time when he thinks all dogs will be safely inside.

6. Which technique appears to be the most effective treatment for phobias?

a. exposure to the feared stimulus under therapeutic supervision.

b. rapid and repeated exposure to the feared stimulus followed by immediate escape.

c. hypnosis during which fear-related conflicts are banished from the unconscious.

d. challenging the client to see that the fears are irrational, unrealistic, and excessive.

7. Which of the following is the most essential characteristic of social anxiety disorder (social phobia)?

a. fear of being in public places.

b. fear of being left alone.

c. fear of evaluation by other people.

d. fear of having a panic attack.

8. Which feature differentiates posttraumatic stress disorder from acute stress disorder?

a. the time since the traumatic event occurred.

b. the severity of the symptoms.

c. the nature of the symptoms.

d. the presence of emotional numbing.

9. Every morning when he leaves for work Anthony has recurring doubts about whether he locked his front door. He continues thinking about this throughout the day, to the distraction of his work. Anthony is experiencing:

a. obsession

b. derealization

c. panic

d. compulsion

10. When a person believes that thinking about hurting someone is just as bad as actually hurting someone, that person is experiencing:

a. obsession

b. a false alarm

c. a panic attack

d. thought-action fusion

(See Appendix A for answers.)

People with anxiety disorders:

▶ Feel overwhelming tension, apprehension, or fear when there is no actual danger

▶ May take extreme action to avoid the source of their anxiety

Trigger

Biological Influences

■ Inherited vulnerability to experience anxiety and/or panic attacks

■ Activation of specific brain circuits, neurotransmitters, and neurohormonal systems

Causes

Social Influences

■ Social support reduces intensity of physical and emotional reactions to triggers or stress

■ Lack of social support intensifies symptoms

Behavioral Influences

■ Marked avoidance of situations and/or people associated with fear, anxiety, or panic attacks

Disorder

Emotional and Cognitive Influences

■ Heightened sensitivity to situations or people perceived as threats

■ Unconscious feeling that physical symptoms of panic are catastrophic (intensifies physical reaction)

TREATMENT FOR ANXIETY DISORDERS

Cognitive–Behavioral Therapy

■ Systematic exposure to anxiety-provoking situations or thoughts
■ Learning to substitute positive behaviors and thoughts for negative ones
■ Learning new coping skills: relaxation exercises, controlled breathing, etc.

Drug Treatment

■ Reduces the symptoms of anxiety disorders by influencing brain chemistry
—antidepressants (Tofranil, Paxil, Effexor)
—benzodiazepines (Xanax, Klonopin)

Other Treatments

■ Managing stress through a healthy lifestyle: rest, exercise, nutrition, social support, and moderate alcohol or other drug intake

Obsessive-Compulsive and Related Disorders

TYPES OF DISORDERS

Panic

People with panic disorders have had one or more panic attacks and are anxious and fearful about having future attacks.

Photodisc/Getty Images

What is a panic attack?
A person having a panic attack feels:
- Apprehension leading to intense fear
- Sensation of "going crazy" or of losing control
- Physical signs of distress: racing heartbeat, rapid breathing, dizziness, nausea, or sensation of heart attack or imminent death

When/why do panic attacks occur?
Panic attacks can be:
- Expected: Always occurring in a specific situation
- Unexpected: Occurring without warning

Phobias

People with phobias avoid situations that produce severe anxiety and/or panic. There are three main types:

Eyewire/Getty Images

Agoraphobia
- Fear and avoidance of situations, people, or places where it would be unsafe to have a panic attack: malls, grocery stores, buses, planes, tunnels, etc.
- In the extreme, inability to leave the house or even a specific room
- Begins after a panic attack but can continue for years even if no other attacks occur

Specific Phobia
- Fear of specific object or situation that triggers attack: heights, closed spaces, insects, snakes, or flying
- Develops from personal or vicarious experience of traumatic event with the triggering object or situation or from misinformation

Social Anxiety Disorder (social phobia)
- Fear of being called for some kind of "performance" that may be judged: speaking in public, using a public restroom (for males), or generally interacting with people

Other Types

Eyewire/Getty Images

Generalized Anxiety
- Uncontrollable unproductive worrying about everyday events
- Feeling impending catastrophe even after successes
- Inability to stop the worry–anxiety cycle: e.g., Irene's fear of failure about school relationships and health even though everything seemed fine
- Physical symptoms of muscle tension

Posttraumatic Stress
- Fear of reexperiencing a traumatic event: rape, war, life-threatening situation, etc.
- Nightmares or flashbacks (of the traumatic event)
- Avoidance of the intense feelings of the event through emotional numbing

Obsessive-Compulsive
- Fear of unwanted and intrusive thoughts (obsessions)
- Repeated ritualistic actions or thoughts (compulsions) designed to neutralize the unwanted thoughts: e.g., Richard's attempts to suppress "dangerous" thoughts about sex, aggression, and religion with compulsive washing and cleaning rituals

5

Somatic Symptom and Related Disorders and Dissociative Disorders

CHAPTER OUTLINE

Somatic Symptom
and Related Disorders

Somatic Symptom Disorder
Illness Anxiety Disorder
Psychological Factors Affecting
    Medical Condition
Conversion Disorder (Functional
    Neurological Symptom Disorder)

Dissociative Disorders

Depersonalization-Derealization
    Disorder
Dissociative Amnesia
Dissociative Identity Disorder

Tinxi/Shutterstock.com

STUDENT LEARNING OUTCOMES*

Engage in innovative and integrative thinking and problem solving:	▶ Describe problems operationally to study them empirically [APA SLO 2.3a] *(see textbook pages 176–178, 175, 182–185, 186–189, 191–192)*
Describe applications that employ discipline-based problem solving:	▶ Correctly identify antecedents and consequences of behavior and mental processes [APA SLO 1.3b] *(see textbook pages 179–180, 185–186)* Describe examples of relevant and practical applications of psychological principles to everyday life [APA SLO 1.3a] *(see textbook pages 176, 179–181)*

* Portions of this chapter cover learning outcomes suggested by the American Psychological Association (2013) in their guidelines for the undergraduate psychology major. Chapter coverage of these outcomes is identified above by APA Goal and APA Suggested Learning Outcome (SLO).

Do you know somebody who's a hypochondriac? Most of us do. Maybe it's you! The popular image of this condition, now called "illness anxiety disorder" in the fifth edition of the *Diagnostic and Statistical Manual of Mental Disorders (DSM-5)* (American Psychiatric Association, 2013) is of someone who exaggerates the slightest physical symptom. Many people continually run to the doctor even though there is nothing really wrong with them. This is usually a harmless tendency, but for a few individuals, the preoccupation with their health or appearance becomes so great that it dominates their lives. Their problems fall under the heading of **somatic symptom disorders**. *Soma* means body, and the problems preoccupying these people seem, initially, to be physical disorders. What the somatic symptom disorders have in common is that there is an excessive or maladaptive response to physical symptoms or to associated health concerns. These disorders are sometimes grouped under the label of "medically unexplained physical symptoms" (Dimsdale *et al.*, 2013; Woolfolk & Allen, 2011), but in some cases the medical cause of the presenting physical symptoms is known but the emotional distress or level of impairment in response to this symptom is clearly excessive and may even make the condition worse.

Have you ever felt "detached" from yourself or your surroundings? ("This isn't really me" or "There's something unreal about this place.") During these experiences, some people feel as if they are dreaming. These sensations that most people experience occasionally are slight alterations, or detachments, in consciousness or identity called *dissociation* or *dissociative experiences*, but they are normal. For a few people, these experiences are so intense and extreme that they lose their identity entirely and assume a new one, or they lose their memory or sense of reality and are unable to function. We discuss several types of **dissociative disorders** in the second half of this chapter.

Somatic symptom and dissociative disorders used to be categorized under one general heading, "hysterical neurosis." The term *hysteria* suggests that the cause of these disorders, which were thought to occur primarily in women, can be traced to a "wandering uterus." But the term *hysterical* came to refer more generally to physical symptoms without known organic cause or to dramatic or "histrionic" behavior thought to be characteristic of women. Sigmund Freud (1894–1962) suggested that in a condition called *conversion hysteria*, unexplained physical symptoms indicated the conversion of unconscious emotional conflicts into a more acceptable form. The historical term *conversion* remains with us (without the theoretical implications); however, the prejudicial and stigmatizing term *hysterical* is no longer used.

Somatic symptom disorders and dissociative disorders have intrigued psychopathologists and the public for centuries. A fuller understanding provides a rich perspective on the extent to which normal, everyday traits found in all of us can evolve into distorted, strange, and incapacitating disorders.

....

somatic symptom disorders Disorder involving extreme and long-lasting focus on multiple physical symptoms for which no medical cause is evident.

dissociative disorder Disorder in which individuals feel detached from themselves or their surroundings and feel reality, experience, and identity may disintegrate.

▶ What are the defining features of somatic symptom and related disorders?

▶ What treatments have been developed for somatic symptom and related disorders?

DSM-5 lists five basic somatic symptom and related disorders: *somatic symptom disorder, illness anxiety disorder, psychological factors affecting medical condition, conversion disorder*, and *factitious disorder*. In each, individuals are pathologically concerned with the functioning of their bodies. The first three disorders covered in this section—somatic symptom disorder, illness anxiety disorder, and psychological factors affecting medical condition—overlap considerably since each focuses on a specific somatic symptom, or set of symptoms, about which the patient is so excessively anxious or distressed that it interferes with his or her functioning, or the anxiety or distress is focused on just the possibility of developing an illness as in illness anxiety disorder.

Somatic Symptom Disorder

In 1859, Pierre Briquet, a French physician, described patients who came to see him with seemingly endless lists of somatic complaints for which he could find no medical basis (American Psychiatric Association, 1980). Despite his negative findings, patients returned shortly with either the same complaints or new lists containing slight variations. For many years, this disorder was called *Briquet's syndrome,* but now would be considered **somatic symptom disorder**. Consider the case of Linda.

Linda... • *Full-Time Patient*

Linda, an intelligent woman in her 30s, came to our clinic looking distressed and pained. As she sat down, she noted that coming into the office was difficult for her because she had trouble breathing and considerable swelling in the joints of her legs and arms. She was also in pain from chronic urinary tract infections and might have to leave at any moment to go to the restroom, but she was happy she had kept the appointment. She said she knew we would have to go through a detailed initial interview, but she had something that might save time. At this point, she pulled out several sheets of paper and handed them over. One section, some five pages long, described her contacts with the health-care system for *major difficulties only*. Times, dates, potential diagnoses, and days hospitalized were noted. The second section, one-and-a-half single-spaced pages, consisted of a list of all medications she had taken for various complaints.

Linda felt she had any one of a number of chronic infections that nobody could properly diagnose. Drawn to hospitals and medical clinics, she had entered nursing school after high school. During hospital training, however, she noticed her physical condition deteriorating: She seemed to pick up the diseases she was learning about. A series of stressful emotional events resulted in her leaving nursing school.

After developing unexplained paralysis in her legs, Linda was admitted to a psychiatric hospital, and after a year she regained her ability to walk. On discharge she obtained disability status, which freed her from having to work full time. She was currently seeing a family practitioner and six specialists, who monitored various aspects of her physical condition.

Linda met all *DSM-5* diagnostic criteria for somatic symptom disorder. She was severely impaired and had suffered in the past from symptoms of paralysis (which we refer to as a conversion symptom; see page 180). People with somatic symptom disorder do not always feel the urgency to take action but continually feel weak and ill, and they avoid exercising, thinking it will make them worse (Rief, Hiller, & Margraf, 1998). Linda's entire life revolved around her symptoms. She once told her therapist that her symptoms were her identity: Without them, she would not know who she was. By this she meant that she would not know how to relate to people except in the context of discussing her symptoms much as other people might talk about their day at the office or their kids' accomplishments at school. Her few friends who were not health-care professionals had the patience to relate to her sympathetically, through the veil of her symptoms, and she thought of them as friends because they "understood" her suffering.

Another common example of a somatic symptom disorder would be the experience of severe pain in which psychological factors play a major role in maintaining or exacerbating the pain whether there is a clear physical reason for the pain or not. Consider the case of the medical student.

The Medical Student... • *Temporary Pain*

During her first clinical rotation, a 25-year-old third-year medical student in excellent health was seen at her student health service for intermittent abdominal pain of several weeks' duration. The student claimed no past history of similar pain. Physical examination revealed no physical problems, but she told the physician that she had recently separated from her husband. The student was referred to the health service psychiatrist. No other psychiatric problems were found. She was taught relaxation techniques and given supportive therapy to help her cope with her current stressful situation. The student's pain subsequently disappeared, and she successfully completed medical school.

Once again, the important factor in this condition is not whether the physical symptom, in this case pain, has a clear medical cause or not, but rather that psychological or behavioral factors, particularly anxiety and distress, are compounding the severity and impairment associated with the physical symptoms. The new emphasis in *DSM-5* on the psychological symptoms in these disorders is useful to clinicians since it highlights the psychological experiences of anxiety and distress focused on the somatic symptoms as the most important target for treatment (Tomenson *et al.*, 2012; Voigt *et al.*, 2012). But an important feature of these physical symptoms, such as pain, is that it is real and it hurts, whether there are clear physical reasons for pain or not (Asmundson & Carleton, 2009; Dersh, Polatin, & Gatchel, 2002).

DSM 5 DISORDER CRITERIA SUMMARY
Somatic Symptom Disorder

Features of somatic symptom disorder include the following:

- One or more somatic symptoms that are distressing and/or result in significant disruption of daily life

- Excessive thoughts, feelings, and behaviors related to the somatic symptoms or associated health concerns as manifested by at least one of the following: (1) disproportionate and persistent thoughts about the seriousness of one's symptoms; (2) high level of health-related anxiety; (3) excessive time and energy devoted to these symptoms or health concerns

- Although any one symptom may not be continuously present, the state of being symptomatic is persistent (typically more than six months)

From American Psychiatric Association. (2013). *Diagnostic and statistical manual of mental disorders* (5th ed.). Washington, DC.

Illness Anxiety Disorder

Illness anxiety disorder was formerly known as "hypochondriasis," which is still the term widely used among the public. In illness anxiety disorder, physical symptoms are either not experienced at the present time or are very mild, but severe anxiety is focused on the possibility of having or developing a serious disease. (Note that if one or more physical symptoms are relatively severe and are associated with anxiety and distress, the diagnosis would be somatic symptom disorder.) In illness anxiety disorder the concern is primarily with the idea of being sick instead of the physical symptom itself. And the threat seems so real that reassurance from physicians does not seem to help. Consider the case of Gail.

Gail... • *Invisibly Ill*

Gail was married at 21 and looked forward to a new life. As one of many children in a lower-middle-class household, she felt weak and somewhat neglected and suffered from low self-esteem. But she believed that marriage would solve everything; she was finally someone special. Unfortunately, it didn't work out that way. She soon discovered her husband was continuing an affair with an old girlfriend.

Three years after her wedding, Gail came to our clinic. Although she complained initially of anxiety and stress, it soon became clear that her major concerns were about her health. Any time she experienced minor physical symptoms such as breathlessness or a headache, she was afraid she had a serious illness. A headache indicated a brain tumor. Breathlessness was an impending heart attack. Other sensations were quickly elaborated into the possibility of AIDS or cancer. Gail was afraid to go to sleep at night for fear that she would stop breathing. She avoided exercise, drinking, and even laughing because the resulting sensations upset her.

The major trigger of uncontrollable anxiety and fear was the news. Each time an article appeared on the "disease of the month," Gail found herself irresistibly drawn into it, intently noting symptoms that were part of the disease. For days afterward she was vigilant, looking for the symptoms in herself and others. Only with great effort could she dismiss these thoughts. Real illness in a friend or relative would incapacitate her for days.

somatic symptom disorders Disorder involving extreme and long-lasting focus on multiple physical symptoms for which no medical cause is evident.

illness anxiety disorder Somatic symptom disorder (previously known as *somatoform disorder*) involving severe **anxiety** over belief in having a disease process without any evident physical cause.

Gail's fears developed during the first year of her marriage, around the time she learned of her husband's affair. Over the years, she heard the same thing during each doctor's visit: "There's nothing wrong with you; you're perfectly healthy." Finally, she stopped going, as she became convinced her concerns were excessive, but her fears did not go away and she was chronically miserable.

Clinical Description

Do you notice any differences between Linda, who presented with somatic symptom disorder, and Gail, who presented with illness anxiety disorder? Gail was somewhat less concerned with any specific physical symptom and more worried about the idea that she was either ill or developing an illness. Gail's problems are fairly typical of illness anxiety disorder.

Research indicates that illness anxiety disorder and somatic symptom disorder share many features with the anxiety and mood disorders, particularly panic disorder (Craske et al., 1996; Creed & Barsky, 2004), including similar age of onset, personality characteristics, and patterns of familial aggregation (running in families). Indeed, anxiety and mood disorders are often comorbid with somatic symptom disorders; that is, if individuals with somatic symptom disorders have additional diagnoses, these most likely are anxiety or mood disorders (Wollburg, Voigt, Braukhaus, Herzog, & Lowe, 2013).

In illness anxiety disorder, the individual is preoccupied with bodily symptoms, misinterpreting them as indicative of illness or disease. Another important feature of this

disorder is that reassurances from numerous doctors that all is well and the individual is healthy have, at best, only a short-term effect. It isn't long before patients like Gail or Linda are back in the office of another doctor on the assumption that the previous doctors have missed something. This is because many of these individuals mistakenly believe they have a disease, a difficult-to-shake belief sometimes referred to as "disease conviction" (Haenen, de Jong, Schmidt, Stevens, & Visser, 2000). Therefore, along with anxiety focused on the possibility of disease or illness, disease conviction is a core feature of the disorder (Fergus & Valentiner, 2010; Woolfolk & Allen, 2011).

Statistics

We can only estimate prevalence of somatic symptom disorders in the general population, mostly from studies of similar *DSM-IV* disorders that were defined a bit differently than the current *DSM-5* disorders. For example, the prevalence of *DSM-IV* hypochondriasis, which would encompass illness anxiety disorder and part of somatic symptom disorder, has been estimated to be from 1% to 5% (American Psychiatric Association, 2000). In primary care settings, the median prevalence rate for hypochondriasis is 6.7% but as high as 16.6% for distressing somatic symptoms, which should closely approximate the prevalence of somatic symptom disorder and illness anxiety disorder combined in these settings (Creed & Barsky, 2004). Severe illness anxiety has a late age of onset, possibly because more physical health problems occur with aging (El-Gabalawy, Mackenzie, Thibodeau, Asmundson, & Sareen, 2013).

Linda's disorder developed during adolescence. A number of studies have demonstrated that individuals with what would now be somatic symptom disorder tend to be women, unmarried, and from lower socioeconomic groups (see, for example, Creed & Barsky, 2004; Lieb et al., 2002). In addition to a variety of somatic complaints, individuals may have psychological complaints, usually anxiety or mood disorders (Rief et al., 1998; Simms, Prisciandaro, Krueger, & Goldberg, 2012). Obviously, individuals with somatic symptom disorders overuse and misuse the healthcare system, with medical bills as much as nine times more than the average patient (Barsky, Orav, & Bates, 2005; Woolfolk & Allen, 2011). In one study, 19% of people with this disorder were on disability (Allen, Woolfolk, Escobar, Gara, & Hamer, 2006). Although symptoms may come and go, somatic symptom disorders and the accompanying sick role behavior are chronic, often continuing into old age.

Causes

Almost everyone agrees that these disorders are basically disorders of cognition or perception with strong emotional contributions (Hartman et al., 2009; Witthöft & Hiller, 2010).

Individuals with somatic symptom disorders experience physical sensations common to all of us, but they quickly focus their attention on these sensations. Remember that

---

DSM 5
DISORDER CRITERIA SUMMARY
Illness Anxiety Disorder

Features of illness anxiety disorder include the following:

- Preoccupation with fears of having or acquiring a serious illness.

- Somatic symptoms are not present or, if present, are only mild in intensity; if another medical condition is present or there is a high risk for developing one, the preoccupation is clearly excessive or disproportionate.

- A high level of anxiety about health.

- The individual performs excessive health-related behaviors (e.g., repeatedly checks his or her body for signs of illness) or exhibits maladaptive avoidance (e.g., avoids doctors' appointments).

- Illness preoccupation has been present for at least six months, but the specific illness that is feared may change.

From American Psychiatric Association. (2013). *Diagnostic and statistical manual of mental disorders* (5th ed.). Washington, DC.

▲ In illness anxiety disorder, normal experiences and sensations are often transformed into life-threatening illnesses.

enhanced perceptual sensitivity to illness cues. They also tend to interpret ambiguous stimuli as threatening (Haenen *et al.*, 2000). Thus, they quickly become aware (and frightened) of any sign of possible illness or disease. A minor headache, for example, might be interpreted as a sure sign of a brain tumor. More fundamentally, they have a restrictive concept of health as being symptom-free (Rief *et al.*, 1998).

What causes individuals to develop this pattern of somatic sensitivity and distorted beliefs? Although it is not certain, the cause is unlikely to be found in isolated biological or psychological factors. For some patients, the fundamental causes of these disorders are similar to those implicated in the anxiety disorders (Barlow, 2002; Barlow *et al.*, 2014). For example, evidence shows that somatic symptom disorders run in families (Guze, Cloninger, Martin, & Clayton, 1986; Katon, 1993), and that there is a modest genetic contribution (Taylor, Thordarson, Jang, & Asmundson, 2006). But this contribution may be non-specific, such as a tendency to overrespond to stress, and thus may be indistinguishable from the non-specific genetic contribution to anxiety disorders. Hyperresponsivity might combine with a tendency to view negative life events as unpredictable and uncontrollable and, therefore, to be guarded against at all times (Barlow *et al.*, 2014; Noyes *et al.*, 2004). As we noted in Chapter 4, these factors would constitute biological and psychological vulnerabilities to anxiety.

Why does this anxiety focus on physical sensations and illness? We know that children with these concerns often report the same kinds of symptoms that other family members may have reported at one time (Kirmayer, Looper, & Taillefer, 2003). It is therefore quite possible, as in panic disorder, that some individuals who develop somatic

the very act of focusing on yourself increases arousal and makes the physical sensations seem more intense than they are (see Chapter 4). If you also tend to misinterpret these as symptoms of illness, your anxiety will increase further. Increased anxiety produces additional physical symptoms, which creates a vicious cycle (see ● Figure 5.1, which was developed to apply to *DSM-IV* hypochondriasis, but in fact applies to *DSM-5* somatic symptom disorder and illness anxiety disorder) (Warwick & Salkovskis, 1990; Witthöft & Hiller, 2010).

Using procedures from cognitive science such as the Stroop test (see Chapter 2), a number of investigators (Hitchcock & Mathews, 1992; Pauli & Alpers, 2002) have confirmed that participants with these disorders show

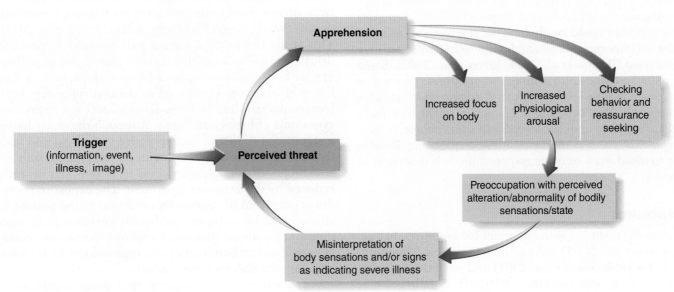

● **Figure 5.1** Integrative model of causes of hypochondriasis. (Based on Warwick, H. M., & Salkovskis, P. M. [1990]. Hypochondriasis. *Behaviour Research Therapy, 28,* 105–117.)

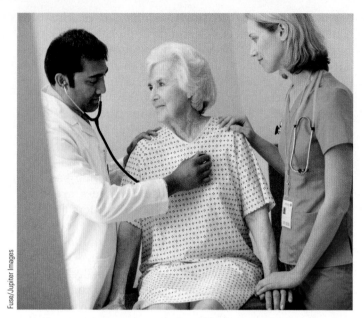
▲ In somatic symptom disorder, primary relationships are often with medical caregivers; one's symptoms are one's identity.

symptom disorder or illness anxiety disorder have *learned* from family members to focus their anxiety on specific physical conditions and illness.

Three other factors may contribute to this etiological process. First, these disorders seem to develop in the context of a stressful life event, as do many disorders, including anxiety disorders. Such events often involve death or illness (Noyes *et al.*, 2004; Sandin, Chorot, Santed, & Valiente, 2004). (Gail's traumatic first year of marriage seemed to coincide with the beginning of her disorder.) Second, people who develop these disorders tend to have had a disproportionate incidence of disease in their family when they were children. Thus, even if they did not develop somatic symptom disorders until adulthood, they carry strong memories of illness that could easily become the focus of anxiety. Third, an important social and interpersonal influence may be involved (Barlow *et al.*, 2014; Noyes *et al.*, 2003). Some people who come from families where illness is a major issue seem to have learned that an ill person often gets a lot of attention. The "benefits" of being sick might contribute to the development of the disorder in some people. A "sick person" who receives increased attention for being ill and is able to avoid work or other responsibilities is described as adopting a "sick role."

Treatment

Studies have shown some support for cognitive behavioral treatment (CBT) for health anxiety (e.g., Bouman, 2014; Taylor & Asmundon, 2009) and somatic symptom disorder (e.g., Kleinstäuber, Witthöft, & Hiller, 2011; Sharma & Manjula, 2013). Surprisingly, clinical reports indicate that reassurance and education can be effective

in some cases with health anxiety (Haenen *et al.*, 2000; Kellner, 1992)—"surprisingly" because, by definition, patients with these disorders are not supposed to benefit from reassurance about their health. Reassurance is usually given only briefly, however, by family doctors who have little time to provide the ongoing support and reassurance that might be necessary. Mental health professionals may be able to offer reassurance in a more effective manner, devote sufficient time to concerns the patient may have, and attend to the "meaning" of the symptoms (for example, their relation to the patient's life stress). "Explanatory therapy" in which the clinician goes over the source and origins of the patient's symptoms in some detail shows some promise (Fava, Grandi, Rafanelli, Fabbri, & Cazzaro, 2000), but the benefits might be limited to those with more mild forms of the disorders (Taylor, Asmundson, & Coons, 2005).

Evaluations of more robust treatments are now available (for a review, see Bouman, 2014). For example, in one study, Barsky and Ahern (2005) randomized 187 patients with *DSM-IV* hypochondriasis to receive either six sessions of CBT from trained therapists or treatment as usual from primary care physicians. CBT focused on identifying and challenging illness-related misinterpretations of physical sensations and on showing patients how to create "symptoms" by focusing attention on certain body areas. Bringing on their own symptoms persuaded many patients that such events were under their control. Patients were also coached to seek less reassurance regarding their concerns. CBT was more effective after treatment and at each follow-up point for both symptoms of hypochondriasis and overall changes in functioning and quality of life. But results were still "modest," and many eligible patients refused to enter treatment because they were convinced their problems were medical rather than psychological.

Interestingly, one trial suggests that cognitive interventions do not seem to be necessary for treating hypochondriasis (Weck, Neng, Richtberg, Jakob, & Stangier, 2015). This study randomly assigned patients with hypochondriasis to receive cognitive therapy alone, exposure therapy without explicit cognitive interventions, or to a wait list control group. Compared to the control group, both treatments resulted in large-sized effects for improving symptoms of hypochondriasis. Although the study found a significant reduction in depressive symptoms and bodily complaints for both treatments in comparison with the control group, anxiety symptoms were only significantly reduced by the exposure treatment. The exposure procedures consisted of repeatedly confronting the patient to stimuli that are relevant for health anxieties (e.g., documentaries about diseases) without using any avoidance and safety behaviors (e.g., reassurance by doctors, checking the abdomen for cancer).

A few other reports suggest that drugs (antidepressants) may help some with somatic symptom disorders (Fallon *et al.*, 2003; Kroenke, 2007). In one study, CBT and

Some bodily concerns are unique to certain cultures, highlighting the importance of the cultural context in evaluating somatic symptom disorders. Among these is the disorder of *koro*, in which there is the belief, accompanied by severe anxiety, that the genitals are retracting into the abdomen. Most victims of this disorder are Chinese males. Why does *koro* occur in Chinese cultures? Rubin (1982) points to the central importance of sexual functioning among Chinese males. He notes that typical sufferers are guilty about excessive masturbation, unsatisfactory intercourse, or promiscuity. These kinds of events may predispose men to focus their attention on their sexual organs, which could exacerbate anxiety and emotional arousal.

Another culture-specific somatic disorder, prevalent in India, is a concern about losing semen. The disorder, called *dhat*, is associated with a vague mix of physical symptoms, including dizziness, weakness, and fatigue. These low-grade depressive or anxious symptoms are thought by some Indians, particularly those living in rural areas, to be due to a physical factor, semen loss (Ranjith & Mohan, 2004).

Kyol goeu, or "wind overload," is another example of a culture-bound somatic concern. Found in the Khmer people of Cambodia, this is a fear that the vessels thought to allow for circulation of blood and "wind" through the body may become blocked, leading to possible death. The Khmer interpret certain somatic complaints as indicative of this blockage, including sore neck, dizziness, weakness, fatigue, or shaking. Because these sensations cause severe anxiety (as they would to anyone who thought they were dying), *kyol goeu* closely resembles panic disorder (see Chapter 4).

In Japan, physical symptoms play a major role in a disorder called *shinkeishitsu*, which resembles Western anxiety disorders (Reynolds, 1976). Individuals may become intensely preoccupied by somatic complaints like headaches, constipation, and blushing, or they may worry that these symptoms will offend others (e.g., body odor). Other specific culture-bound somatic symptoms associated with emotional factors include hot sensations in the head or a sensation of something crawling in the head, specific to African patients (Ebigno, 1986), and a sensation of burning in the hands and feet in Pakistani or Indian patients (Kirmayer & Weiss, 1993). For a long time, researchers thought that expressing psychological distress as somatic complaints was particularly common in non-Western or developing countries. But on closer inspection, this does not seem to be the case. The rates are relatively uniform around the world, as is the sex ratio (Gureje, Simon, Ustun, & Goldberg, 1997). When the problem is severe enough to meet criteria for disorder, the sex ratio is approximately 2:1 female to male. ∎

the drug paroxetine (Paxil), a selective-serotonin re-uptake inhibitor (SSRI), were both moderately effective, but only CBT was significantly different from a placebo condition (Greeven *et al.*, 2007).

In our clinic, we concentrate on initially providing reassurance, reducing stress, and, in particular, reducing the frequency of help-seeking behaviors. One of the most common problems is the person's tendency to visit numerous medical specialists, causing an extraordinary cost to the health-care system (Barsky *et al.*, 2005; Witthöft & Hiller, 2010). In treatment, to limit these visits, a gatekeeper physician is often assigned to each patient to screen all physical complaints. Subsequent visits to specialists must be specifically authorized by this gatekeeper. In the context of a positive therapeutic relationship, most patients are amenable to this arrangement.

Additional therapeutic attention is directed at reducing the supportive consequences of relating to significant others on the basis of physical symptoms alone. More appropriate methods of interacting with others are encouraged, along with additional procedures to promote healthy social and personal adjustment without relying on being "sick." In this context, CBT may then be the most helpful (Allen *et al.*, 2006; Woolfolk & Allen, 2011).

Psychological Factors Affecting Medical Conditions

A related somatic symptom disorder is called **psychological factors affecting medical condition**. The essential feature of this disorder is the presence of a diagnosed medical condition—such as asthma, diabetes, or severe pain clearly caused by a known medical condition such as cancer—that is adversely affected (increased in frequency or severity) by one or more psychological or behavioral factors. These behavioral or psychological factors would have a direct influence on the course or perhaps the treatment of the medical condition. One example would be anxiety severe enough to clearly worsen an asthmatic condition. Another example would be a patient with diabetes who is in denial about the need to regularly check blood sugar levels and intervene when necessary. In this case, the pattern would have to be consistent in the neglect of appropriate monitoring and intervention, but the neglect is clearly a behavioral or psychological factor that is adversely affecting the medical condition. This diagnosis would need to be

....

psychological factors affecting medical conditions Psychological factors that seem to influence the course of medical disorders.

distinguished from the development of stress or anxiety in response to having a severe medical condition that would more appropriately be diagnosed as an adjustment disorder (see Chapter 4). In Chapter 7, we discuss health psychology and the contribution of psychological factors to physical disorders including cardiovascular disease, cancer, AIDS, and chronic pain.

Conversion Disorder (Functional Neurological Symptom Disorder)

The term *conversion* has been used off and on since the Middle Ages (Mace, 1992) but was popularized by Freud, who believed the anxiety resulting from unconscious conflicts somehow was "converted" into physical symptoms to find expression. In *DSM-5*, "functional neurological symptom disorder" is a subtitle to conversion disorder because the term is more often used by neurologists who see the majority of patients receiving a conversion disorder diagnosis, and because the term is more acceptable to patients. "Functional" refers to a symptom without an organic cause (Stone, LaFrance, Levenson, & Sharpe, 2010).

Clinical Description

Conversion disorders generally have to do with physical malfunctioning, such as paralysis, blindness, or difficulty speaking (aphonia), without any physical or organic pathology to account for the malfunction. Most conversion symptoms suggest that some kind of neurological disease is affecting sensory–motor systems, although conversion symptoms can mimic the full range of physical malfunctioning.

Conversion disorders provide some of the most intriguing, sometimes astounding, examples of psychopathology. What could possibly account for somebody going blind when all visual processes are normal or experiencing paralysis of the arms or legs when there is no neurological damage? Consider the case of Eloise.

Examinations revealed no physical problems. Eloise presented with a classic case of conversion disorder. Although she was not paralyzed, her symptoms included weakness in her legs and difficulty keeping balance. This particular type of conversion symptom is called *astasia-abasia*. Eloise lived with her mother, who ran a gift shop in the front of her house in a small rural town. Eloise had been schooled through special education programs until she was about 15; after this, no programs were available. When Eloise began staying home, her walking began to deteriorate.

In addition to blindness, paralysis, and aphonia, conversion symptoms may include total mutism and the loss of the sense of touch. Some people have seizures, which may be psychological in origin, because no significant electroencephalogram (EEG) changes can be documented. These "seizures" are usually called psychogenic non-epileptic seizures. Another relatively common symptom is *globus hystericus*, the sensation of a lump in the throat that makes it difficult to swallow, eat, or sometimes talk (Finkenbine & Miele, 2004).

Closely Related Disorders

Distinguishing among conversion reactions, medically explained symptoms, and outright **malingering** (faking) is sometimes difficult. Several factors can help. Conversion symptoms often seem to be precipitated by marked stress. Often this stress takes the form of a physical injury. In one large survey, 324 out of 869 patients (37%) reported prior physical injury (Stone, Carson, Aditya et al., 2009). But the occurrence of some identifiable stressor has not been a reliable sign of conversion disorder, since many other disorders are associated with stressful events and stressful events often occur in the lives of people without any disorders. For this reason, the diagnostic criterion that

Eloise... • *Unlearning Walking*

Eloise sat on a chair with her legs under her, refusing to put her feet on the floor. Her mother sat close by, ready to assist her if she needed to get up. Her mother had made the appointment and, with the help of a friend, had all but carried Eloise into the office. Eloise was a 20-year-old of borderline intelligence who was friendly during the initial interview.

Eloise's difficulty walking developed over five years. Her right leg had given way and she began falling. Gradually, the condition worsened to the point that six months before her admission to the hospital Eloise could move around only by crawling.

DSM 5 **DISORDER CRITERIA SUMMARY**
Conversion Disorder (Functional Neurological Symptom Disorder)

Features of conversion disorder (functional neurological symptom disorder) include the following:

- One or more symptoms of altered voluntary motor or sensory function
- Evidence of incompatibility between the symptom and recognized neurological or medical conditions
- The symptom or deficit causes clinically significant distress or impairment in social, occupational, or other important areas of functioning or warrants medical evaluation

From American Psychiatric Association. (2013). *Diagnostic and statistical manual of mental disorders* (5th ed.). Washington, DC.

TABLE 5.1 | Child Abuse Associated with Munchausen Syndrome by Proxy versus Typical Child Abuse

	Typical Child Abuse	Atypical Child Abuse (Munchausen Syndrome by Proxy)
Physical presentation of the child	Results from direct physical contact with the child; signs often detected on physical examination	Misrepresentation of an acute or accidental medical or surgical illness not usually obvious on physical examination
Obtaining the diagnosis	The perpetrator does not invite the discovery of the manifestation of the abuse	The perpetrator usually presents the manifestations of the abuse to the health-care system
Victims	Children are either the objects of frustration and anger or are receiving undue or inappropriate punishment	Children serve as the vector in gaining the attention the mother desires; anger is not the primary causal factor
Awareness of abuse	Usually present	Not usually present

SOURCE: Reprinted, with permission, from Check, J. R. (1998). Munchausen syndrome by proxy: An atypical form of child abuse. *Journal of Practical Psychiatry and Behavioral Health*, 4(6), p. 341, Table 6.2. © 1998 Lippincott, Williams & Wilkins.

conversion disorder is associated with preceding stress does not appear in *DSM-5*. Although people with conversion symptoms can usually function normally, they seem truly unaware either of this ability or of sensory input. For example, individuals with the conversion symptom of blindness can usually avoid objects in their visual field, but they will tell you they can't see the objects. Similarly, individuals with conversion symptoms of paralysis of the legs might suddenly get up and run in an emergency and then be astounded they were able to do this. (It is possible that at least some people who experience miraculous cures during religious ceremonies may have been suffering from conversion reactions.) These factors may help in distinguishing between conversion and organically based physical disorders, but clinicians sometimes make mistakes, although it is not common with modern diagnostic techniques. In any case, ruling out medical causes for the symptoms is crucial to making a diagnosis of conversion and, given advances in medical screening procedures, this is the principal diagnostic criterion in *DSM-5* (APA, 2013; Stone *et al.*, 2010).

It can also be difficult to distinguish between individuals who are truly experiencing conversion symptoms in a seemingly involuntary way and malingerers who are good at faking symptoms. Once malingerers are exposed, their motivation is clear: They are either trying to get out of something, such as work or legal difficulties, or they are attempting to gain something, such as a financial settlement. Malingerers are fully aware of what they are doing and are clearly attempting to manipulate others to gain a desired end.

More puzzling is a set of conditions called **factitious disorders**, which fall somewhere between malingering and conversion disorders. The symptoms are under voluntary control, as with malingering, but there is *no obvious reason* for voluntarily producing the symptoms except, possibly, to assume the sick role and receive increased attention.

Tragically, this disorder may extend to other members of the family. An adult, almost always a mother, may purposely make her child sick, evidently for the attention and pity given to her as the mother of a sick child. When an individual deliberately makes someone else sick, the condition is called *factitious disorder imposed on another*. It was also known previously as *Munchausen syndrome by proxy*. In any case, it is really an atypical form of child abuse (Check, 1998). Table 5.1 presents differences between typical child abuse and factitious disorder imposed on another (Munchausen syndrome by proxy).

The offending parent may resort to extreme tactics to create the appearance of illness in the child. For example, one mother stirred her child's urine specimen with a vaginal tampon obtained during menstruation. Another mother mixed feces into her child's vomit (Check, 1998). Because the mother typically establishes a positive relationship with a medical staff, the true nature of the illness is most often unsuspected and the staff members perceive the parent as remarkably caring, cooperative, and involved in providing for her child's well-being. Therefore, the mother is often successful at eluding suspicion.

Helpful procedures to assess the possibility of factitious disorder imposed on another include a trial separation of the mother and the child or video surveillance of the child while in the hospital.

. . . .

conversion disorder Physical malfunctioning, such as blindness or paralysis, suggesting neurological impairment but with no organic pathology to account for it.

malingering Deliberate faking of a physical or **psychological disorder** motivated by gain.

factitious disorder Non-existent physical or **psychological disorder** deliberately faked for no apparent gain except, possibly, sympathy and attention.

Unconscious Mental Processes

Unconscious cognitive processes seem to play a role in much of psychopathology (although not necessarily as Freud envisioned it), but nowhere is this phenomenon more readily and dramatically apparent than when we attempt to distinguish between conversion disorders and related conditions. Information (reviewed in Chapter 2) on unconscious cognitive processes becomes important in this context. We are all capable of receiving and processing information in a number of sensory channels (such as vision and hearing) without being aware of it. Remember the phenomenon of blind sight or unconscious vision? Weiskrantz (1980) and others discovered that people with small, localized damage to certain parts of their brains could identify objects in their field of vision but that they had no awareness whatsoever that they could see. Could this happen to people without brain damage? Consider the case of Celia.

Celia... • *Seeing Through Blindness*

A 15-year-old girl named Celia suddenly was unable to see. Shortly thereafter, she regained some of her sight, but her vision was so severely blurred that she could not read. When she was brought to a clinic for testing, psychologists arranged a series of sophisticated vision tests that did not require her to report when she could or could not see. One of the tasks required her to examine three triangles displayed on three separate screens and to press a button under the screen containing an upright triangle. Celia performed perfectly on this test without being aware that she could see anything (Grosz & Zimmerman, 1970). Was Celia faking? Evidently not, or she would have purposely made a mistake.

Someone who is truly blind would perform at a chance level on visual discrimination tasks. People with conversion symptoms, on the other hand, can see objects in their visual field and therefore would perform well on these tasks, but this experience is dissociated from their awareness of sight.

Statistics

We have already seen that conversion disorder may occur with other disorders, particularly somatic symptom disorder, as in the case of Linda. Linda's paralysis passed after several months and did not return, although on occasion she would report "feeling as if" it were returning. Comorbid anxiety and mood disorders are also common (Rowe, 2010; Stone, Carson, Duncan *et al.*, 2009). Conversion disorders are relatively rare in mental health settings, but remember that people who seek help for this condition are more likely to consult neurologists or other specialists. The prevalence estimate in neurological settings is high, averaging about 30% (Rowe, 2010; Stone, Carson, Duncan *et al.*, 2009).

Like severe somatic symptom disorder, conversion disorders are found primarily in women (Brown & Lewis-Fernandez, 2011; Deveci *et al.*, 2007) and typically develop during adolescence or slightly thereafter. Conversion reactions have also been reported in soldiers exposed to severe combat, mainly during World War I and II (Mucha & Reinhardt, 1970; Perez-Sales, 1990). The conversion symptoms often disappear after a time, only to return later in the same or similar form when a new stressor occurs. In other cultures, some conversion symptoms are common aspects of religious or healing rituals. Seizures, paralysis, and trances are common in some rural fundamentalist religious groups in the United States (Griffith, English, & Mayfield, 1980), and they are often seen as evidence of contact with God. Individuals who exhibit such symptoms are thus held in high esteem by their peers. These symptoms do not meet criteria for a "disorder" unless they persist and interfere with an individual's functioning.

Causes

Freud described four basic processes in the development of conversion disorder. First, the individual experiences a traumatic event—in Freud's view, an unacceptable, unconscious conflict. Second, because the conflict and the resulting anxiety are unacceptable, the person represses the conflict, making it unconscious. Third, the anxiety continues to increase and threatens to emerge into consciousness, and the person "converts" it into physical symptoms, thereby relieving the pressure of having to deal directly with the conflict. This reduction of anxiety is considered to be the *primary gain* or reinforcing event that maintains the conversion symptom. Fourth, the individual receives greatly increased attention and sympathy from loved ones and may also be allowed to avoid a difficult situation or task. Freud considered such attention or avoidance to be the *secondary gain*, the secondarily reinforcing set of events.

We believe Freud was basically correct on at least three counts but probably not on the fourth, although firm evidence supporting any of these ideas is sparse and Freud's views were far more complex than represented here. Most often, individuals with conversion disorder have experienced a traumatic event that must be escaped at all costs (Brown &

Lewis-Fernandez, 2011; Stone, Carson, Aditya *et al.*, 2009). This might be combat, where death is imminent, or an impossible interpersonal situation. Because simply running away is unacceptable in most cases, the socially acceptable alternative of getting sick is substituted; but getting sick on purpose is also unacceptable, so this motivation is detached from the person's consciousness. Finally, because the escape behavior (the conversion symptoms) is successful to an extent in obliterating the traumatic situation, the behavior continues until the underlying problem is resolved.

One study confirms these hypotheses, at least partially (Wyllie, Glazer, Benbadis, Kotagal, & Wolgamuth, 1999). In this study, child and adolescent patients were evaluated after receiving a diagnosis of psychologically based pseudo-seizures (psychogenic non-epileptic seizures). Many of these patients presented with additional psychological disorders, including mood and anxiety disorders. When the extent of psychological stress in the lives of these children was examined, it was found that most of the patients had substantial stress, including a history of sexual abuse, recent parental divorce or death of a close family member, and physical abuse. This suggests that major mood disorders and severe traumatic stress, especially sexual abuse, are common among children and adolescents with the conversion disorder of pseudo-seizures, as other studies have similarly indicated (Roelofs *et al.*, 2002).

The one step in Freud's progression of events about which some questions remain is the issue of primary gain. The notion of primary gain accounts for the feature of *la belle indifférence*, where individuals seem not the least bit distressed about their symptoms. In other words, Freud thought that because symptoms reflected an unconscious attempt to resolve a conflict, the patient would not be upset by them. But formal tests of this feature provide little support for Freud's claim. For example, Stone and colleagues (2006) in the study described earlier on "indifference" to conversion symptoms found no difference in distress over

symptoms among patients with conversion disorder compared with patients with organic disease.

Social and cultural influences also contribute to conversion disorder, which, like somatic symptom disorder, tends to occur in less educated, lower socioeconomic groups where knowledge about disease and medical illness is not well developed (Brown & Lewis-Fernandez, 2011; Woolfolk & Allen, 2011). For example, Binzer and colleagues (Binzer, Andersen, & Kullgren, 1997) noted that 13% of 30 adult patients with motor disabilities resulting from conversion disorder had attended high school, compared with 67% in a control group of patients with motor symptoms because of a physical cause. Prior experience with real physical problems, usually among other family members, tends to influence the later choice of specific conversion symptoms; that is, patients tend to adopt symptoms with which they are familiar (see, for example, Brady & Lind, 1961). Furthermore, the incidence of these disorders has decreased over the decades (Kirmayer *et al.*, 2003). The most likely explanation is that increased knowledge of the real causes of physical problems by both patients and loved ones eliminates much of the possibility of secondary gain so important in these disorders.

Finally, many conversion symptoms seem to be part of a larger constellation of psychopathology. Linda had broad-ranging somatic symptom disorder, as well as the severe conversion symptoms, that resulted in her hospitalization. In similar cases, individuals may have a marked biological vulnerability to develop conversion disorder when under stress, with biological processes like those discussed in the context of somatic symptom disorder. Neuroscientists are increasingly finding a strong connectivity between the conversion symptom and parts of the brain regulating emotion, such as the amygdala, using brain-imaging procedures (Bryant & Das, 2012; Rowe, 2010).

For countless other cases, however, biological contributory factors seem to be less important than the overriding influence of interpersonal factors (the actions of Eloise's mother, for example), as we will discuss in the next section.

▲ The seizures and trances that may be symptomatic of conversion disorder are also common in some rural fundamentalist religious groups in the United States.

Treatment

Because conversion disorder has much in common with somatic symptom disorder, many of the treatment principles are similar. A principal strategy in treating conversion disorder is to identify and attend to the traumatic or stressful life event, if it is still present (either in real life or in memory). The therapist must also work hard to reduce any reinforcing or supportive consequences of the conversion symptoms (secondary gain). For example, it was quite clear that Eloise's mother found it convenient if Eloise stayed in one place most of the day while her mother attended to the store in the front of the house. Eloise's immobility was thus strongly reinforced by motherly attention and concern. Any unnecessary mobility was punished. The therapist must collaborate with both the patient and the family to eliminate such self-defeating behaviors.

Diagnose the somatic symptom and related disorders described here by choosing one of the following: (a) illness anxiety disorder, (b) somatic symptom disorder, (c) conversion disorder:

1. Emily constantly worries about her health. She has been to numerous doctors for her concerns about cancer and other serious diseases—even though she doesn't report current notable physical symptoms—only to be reassured of her well-being. Emily's anxiety is exacerbated by each small ailment (for example, mild headaches or stomach pains) that she considers to be indications of a major illness. _____

2. D. J. arrived at Dr. Blake's office with a folder crammed full of medical records, symptom documentation, and lists of prescribed treatments and drugs. Several doctors are monitoring him for his complaints, ranging from marked chest pain to difficulty swallowing. D. J. recently lost his job for using too many sick days. _____

3. Sixteen-year-old Chad suddenly lost the use of his arms with no medical cause. The complete paralysis slowly improved to the point that he could slightly raise them. However, Chad cannot drive, pick up objects, or perform most tasks necessary for day-to-day life. _____

Dissociative Disorders

▶ What are the defining features and different types of dissociative disorders?

▶ What factors influence the etiology and treatment of dissociative disorders?

At the beginning of the chapter, we said that when individuals feel detached from themselves or their surroundings, almost as if they are dreaming or living in slow motion, they are having dissociative experiences. It might be likely to happen after an extremely stressful event, such as an accident (Spiegel, 2010). It also is more likely to happen when you're tired or sleep deprived from staying up all night cramming for an exam (Giesbrecht, Smeets, Leppink, Jelicic, & Merckelbach, 2007). If you have had an experience of dissociation, it may not have bothered you much, perhaps because you knew the cause (Barlow, 2002). On the other hand, it may have been extremely frightening. Transient experiences of dissociation will occur in about half of the general population at some point in their lives, and studies suggest that if a person experiences a traumatic event, between 31% and 66% will have this feeling at that time (Hunter, Sierra, & David, 2004; Keane, Marx, Sloan, & DePrince, 2011). Because it's hard to measure dissociation, the connection between trauma and dissociation is controversial (Giesbrecht, Lynn, Lilienfeld, & Merckelbach, 2008).

These kinds of experiences can be divided into two types. During an episode of *depersonalization,* your perception alters so that you temporarily lose the sense of your own reality, as if you were in a dream and you were watching yourself. During an episode of **derealization**, your sense of the reality of the external world is lost. Things may seem to change shape or size; people may seem dead or mechanical. These sensations of unreality are characteristic of the dissociative disorders because, in a sense, they are a psychological mechanism whereby one "dissociates" from reality. Depersonalization is often part of a serious set of conditions in which reality, experience, and even identity seem to disintegrate. As we go about our day-to-day lives, we ordinarily have an excellent sense of who we are and a general knowledge of the identity of other people. We are also aware of events around us, of where we are, and of why we are there. Finally, except for occasional small lapses, our memories remain intact so that events leading up to the current moment are clear in our minds.

But what happens if we can't remember why we are in a certain place or even who we are? What happens if we lose our sense that our surroundings are real? Finally, what happens if we not only forget who we are but also begin thinking we are somebody else—somebody who has a different personality, different memories, and even different physical reactions, such as allergies we never had? These are examples of disintegrated experience (Dell & O'Neil, 2009; Spiegel *et al.*, 2013). In each case, there are alterations in our relationship to the self, to the world, or to memory processes.

Although we have much to learn about these disorders, we briefly describe two of them—depersonalization-derealization disorder, and dissociative amnesia—before examining the fascinating condition of dissociative identity disorder. As you will see, the influence of social and cultural factors is strong in dissociative disorders. Even in severe cases, the expression of the pathology does not stray far from socially and culturally sanctioned forms (Giesbrecht *et al.*, 2008; Kihlstrom, 2005a).

Depersonalization-Derealization Disorder

When feelings of unreality are so severe and frightening that they dominate an individual's life and prevent normal functioning, clinicians may diagnose the rare **depersonalization-derealization disorder**. Consider the case of Bonnie.

Bonnie... • *Dancing Away from Herself*

Bonnie, a dance teacher in her late 20s, was accompanied by her husband when she first visited the clinic and complained of "flipping out." When asked what she meant, she said, "It's the most scary thing in the world. It often happens when I'm teaching my modern dance class. As I'm demonstrating the steps, I just feel like it's not really me and that I don't really have control of my legs. Sometimes I feel like I'm standing in back of myself just watching. Also I get tunnel vision. It seems like I can only see in a narrow space right in front of me and I just get totally separated from what's going on around me. Then I begin to panic and perspire and shake." It turns out that Bonnie's problems began after she smoked marijuana for the first time about 10 years before. She had the same feeling then and found it scary, but with the help of friends she got through it. Lately the feeling recurred more often and more severely, particularly when she was teaching dance class.

You may remember from Chapter 4 that during an intense panic attack, many people (approximately 50%) experience feelings of unreality. People undergoing intense stress or experiencing a traumatic event may also experience these symptoms, which characterize the newly defined *acute stress disorder*. Feelings of depersonalization and derealization are part of several disorders (Spiegel *et al.*, 2011; Spiegel *et al.*, 2013). But when severe depersonalization and derealization are the primary problem, the individual meets criteria for depersonalization-derealization disorder (APA, 2013). Surveys suggest that this disorder exists in approximately 0.8% to 2.8% of the population (Johnson, Cohen, Kasen, & Brook, 2006; Spiegel *et al.*, 2011). Simeon, Knutelska, Nelson, and Guralnik (2003) described 117 cases approximately equally split between men and women. Mean age of onset was 16 years, and the course tended to be chronic. All patients were substantially impaired. Anxiety, mood, and personality disorders were also commonly found in these individuals. Among the 117 patients described, 73% suffered from additional mood disorders and 64% from anxiety disorders at some point in their lives.

Two studies (Guralnik, Giesbrecht, Knutelska, Sirroff, & Simeon, 2007; Guralnik, Schmeidler, & Simeon, 2000) compared patients who had what we now call depersonalization-derealization disorder with matched

normal-comparison participants on a comprehensive neuropsychological test battery that assessed cognitive function. Although both groups were of equal intelligence, the participants with depersonalization disorder showed a distinct cognitive profile, reflecting some specific cognitive deficits on measures of attention, processing of information, short-term memory, and spatial reasoning. Basically, these patients were easily distracted and were slow to perceive and process new information. It is not clear how these cognitive and perceptual deficits develop, but they seem to correspond with reports of "tunnel vision" (perceptual distortions) and "mind emptiness" (difficulty absorbing new information) that characterize these patients.

Specific aspects of brain functioning are also associated with depersonalization (see, for example, Sierra & Berrios, 1998; Simeon *et al.*, 2000). Brain-imaging studies confirm deficits in perception (Simeon, 2009; Simeon *et al.*, 2000) and emotion regulation (Phillips *et al.*, 2001). Other studies note dysregulation in the hypothalamic–pituitary–adrenocortical (HPA) axis among these patients, compared with normal controls (Simeon, Guralnik, Knutelska, Hollander, & Schmeidler, 2001; Spiegel *et al.*, 2013), suggesting, again, deficits in emotional responding. Prozac did not show any treatment effect compared with placebo (Simeon, Guralnik, Schneider, & Knutelska, 2004).

Dissociative Amnesia

Perhaps the easiest to understand of the severe dissociative disorders is one called **dissociative amnesia**, which includes several patterns. People who are unable to

. . . .

derealization Situation in which the individual loses a sense of the reality of the external world.

depersonalization-derealization disorder Dissociative disorder in which feelings of depersonalization are so severe they dominate the client's life and prevent normal functioning.

dissociative amnesia Dissociative disorder featuring the inability to recall personal information; usually of a stressful or traumatic nature.

remember anything, including who they are, are said to suffer from **generalized amnesia**. Generalized amnesia may be lifelong or may extend from a period in the more recent past, such as six months or a year previously. Consider the case study described here.

The Woman Who Lost Her Memory

Several years ago, a woman in her early 50s brought her daughter to one of our clinics because of the girl's refusal to attend school and other severely disruptive behavior. The father, who refused to come to the session, was quarrelsome, a heavy drinker, and, on occasion, abusive. The girl's brother, now in his mid-20s, lived at home and was a burden on the family. Several times a week a major battle erupted, complete with shouting, pushing, and shoving, as each member of the family blamed the others for all their problems. The mother, a strong woman, was clearly the peacemaker responsible for holding the family together. Approximately every six months, usually after a family battle, the mother lost her memory and the family had her admitted to the hospital. After a few days away from the turmoil, the mother regained her memory and went home, only to repeat the cycle in the coming months. Although we did not treat this family (they lived too far away), the situation resolved itself when the children moved away and the stress decreased.

Far more common than general amnesia is **localized or selective amnesia**, a failure to recall specific events, usually traumatic, that occur during a specific period. Dissociative amnesia is common during war (Cardeña & Gleaves, 2003; Spiegel *et al.*, 2013). An interesting case of a woman whose father deserted her when she was young and who then was forced to have an abortion at the age of 14 is described by Sackeim and Devanand (1991). Years later, she came for treatment for frequent headaches. In therapy she reported early events (for example, the abortion) rather matter-of-factly, but under hypnosis she would relive, with intense emotion, the early abortion and remember that subsequently she was raped by the abortionist. She also had images of her father attending a funeral for her aunt, one of the few times she ever saw him. Upon awakening from the hypnotic state, she had no memory of emotionally re-experiencing these events, and she wondered why she had been crying. In this case, the woman did not have amnesia for the *events themselves* but rather for her intense *emotional reactions to the events*. Absence of the subjective experience of emotion that is often present in depersonalization-derealization disorder and confirmed by brain-imaging studies (Phillips *et al.*, 2001) becomes prominent here. In most cases of dissociative amnesia, the forgetting is selective for traumatic events or memories rather than generalized.

DSM 5 DISORDER CRITERIA SUMMARY
Dissociative Amnesia

Features of dissociative amnesia include the following:

- An inability to recall important autobiographical information, usually of a traumatic or stressful nature, that is inconsistent with ordinary forgetting.

- The symptoms cause clinically significant distress or impairment in social, occupational, or other important areas of functioning.

- The disturbance is not attributable to the physiological effects of a substance (e.g., alcohol or other drug of abuse), a neurological or other medical condition, or a different psychological disorder.

From American Psychiatric Association. (2013). *Diagnostic and statistical manual of mental disorders* (5th ed.). Washington, DC.

A subtype of dissociative amnesia is referred to as **dissociative fugue** (Ross, 2009) with *fugue* literally meaning "flight" (*fugitive* is from the same root). In these curious cases, memory loss revolves around a specific incident—an unexpected trip (or trips). Mostly, individuals just take off and later find themselves in a new place, unable to remember why or how they got there. Usually they have left behind an intolerable situation. During these trips, a person sometimes assumes a new identity or at least becomes confused about the old identity. Consider the case of Jeffrey Ingram, a 40-year-old male from Washington state, who found himself unexpectedly in Denver.

Jeffrey... • *A Troubled Trip*

An amnesia sufferer who had been searching for his identity for more than a month was back in Washington state with his fiancée on Tuesday, but he still doesn't remember his past life or what happened, his mother said.

Jeffrey Alan Ingram, 40, was diagnosed in Denver with dissociative fugue, a type of amnesia.

He has had similar bouts of amnesia in the past, likely triggered by stress, once disappearing for nine months. When he went missing this time, on September 6, he had been on his way to Canada to visit a friend who was dying of cancer, said his fiancée, Penny Hansen.

"I think that the stress, the sadness, the grief of facing a best friend dying was enough, and leaving me was enough to send him into an amnesia state," Hansen told KCNC-TV.

When Ingram found himself in Denver on September 10, he didn't know who he was. He said he walked around for about six hours asking people for help, then ended up at a hospital, where police spokeswoman

Virginia Quinones said Ingram was diagnosed with a type of amnesia known as dissociative fugue.

Searched for his identity. Ingram's identity came to light last weekend after he appeared on several news shows asking the public for help: "If anybody recognizes me, knows who I am, please let somebody know."

"Penny's brother called her right away and told her 'Did you watch this newscast?' and 'I think that's Jeff that they're showing on television,'" said Marilyn Meehan, a spokeswoman for Hansen.

Hansen had filed a missing person report after Ingram failed to show up at her mother's home in Bellingham, Washington, on his way to Canada, but officials searching for him had turned up nothing.

On Monday night, two Denver police detectives accompanied Ingram on a flight to Seattle, where he was reunited with his fiancée.

His mother, Doreen Tompkins of Slave Lake, Alberta, was in tears as she talked about the struggle her son and the family still face.

"It's going to be very difficult again, but you know what, I can do it," she told CTV news of Edmonton, Alberta. "I did it before, I can do it again. I'll do it as many times as I have to just so I can have my son."

Memory never fully regained. Ingram had experienced an episode of amnesia in 1995 when he disappeared during a trip to a grocery store. Nine months later, he was found in a Seattle hospital, according to Thurston County, Washington, officials. His mother said he never fully regained his memory.

Meehan, who works with Hansen at the state Utilities and Transportation Commission, said the couple would not give interviews because they want to concentrate on Ingram's effort to regain his memory.

"They're taking it one step at a time," Meehan said.

"He said that while her face wasn't familiar to him, her heart was familiar to him," she said. "He can't remember his home, but he said their home felt like home to him."

Dissociative amnesia seldom appears before adolescence and usually occurs in adulthood. It is rare for dissociative amnesia to appear for the first time after an individual reaches the age of 50 (Sackeim & Devanand, 1991). Once dissociative disorders do appear, however, they may continue well into old age. Estimates of prevalence range anywhere from 1.8% to 7.3%, suggesting that dissociative amnesia is the most prevalent of all the dissociative disorders (Spiegel *et al.*, 2011).

Fugue states usually end rather abruptly, and the individual returns home, recalling most, if not all, of what happened. In this disorder, the disintegrated experience is

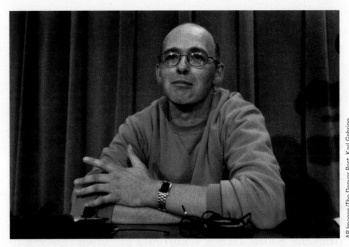

▲ Jeffrey Alan Ingram found himself in Denver not knowing who he was or why he was there after having gone missing a month earlier from Washington state.

AP Images/The Denver Post, Karl Gehring

more than memory loss, involving at least some disintegration of identity, if not the complete adoption of a new one.

An apparently distinct dissociative state not found in Western cultures is called *amok* (as in "running amok"). Most people with this disorder are males. Amok has attracted attention because individuals in this trance-like state often brutally assault and sometimes kill people or animals. If the person is not killed himself, he probably will not remember the episode. Running amok is only one of a number of "running" syndromes in which an individual enters a trance-like state and suddenly, imbued with a mysterious source of energy, runs or flees for a long time. Except for amok, the prevalence of running disorders is somewhat greater in women, as with most dissociative disorders. Among native peoples of the Arctic, running disorder is termed *pivloktoq*. Among the Navajo tribe, it is called *frenzy witchcraft*. Despite their different culturally determined expression, running disorders seem to resemble dissociative fugue, with the possible exception of amok.

Dissociative disorders differ in important ways across cultures. In many areas of the world, dissociative phenomena may occur as a trance or possession. The usual sorts of dissociative symptoms, such as sudden changes in personality, are attributed to possession by a spirit important in the particular culture. Often this spirit demands and receives gifts or favors from the family and friends of the victim. Like other dissociative states, trance or possession seems to be most common in women and is often

....

generalized amnesia Loss of memory of all personal information, including identity.

localized or selective amnesia Memory loss limited to specific times and events, particularly traumatic events.

dissociative fugue Dissociative disorder featuring sudden, unexpected travel away from home, along with an inability to recall the past, sometimes with assumption of a new identity.

associated with stress or trauma, which, as in dissociative amnesia and fugue states, is current rather than in the past.

Trance and possession are a common part of some traditional religious and cultural practices and are not considered abnormal in that context. Dissociative trances commonly occur in India, Nigeria (where they are called *vinvusa*), Thailand *(phii pob)*, and other Asian and African countries (Mezzich *et al.*, 1992; van Duijil, Cardeña, & de Jong, 2005). In the United States, culturally accepted dissociation commonly occurs during African American prayer meetings (Griffith *et al.*, 1980), Native American rituals (Jilek, 1982), and Puerto Rican spiritist sessions (Comas-Diaz, 1981). Among Bahamians and African Americans from the South, trance syndromes are often referred to colloquially as "falling out." The personality profiles of 58 cases of dissociative trance disorder in Singapore, derived from objective testing, revealed that these individuals tended to be nervous, excitable, and emotionally unstable relative to "normals" in Singapore (Ng, Yap, Su, Lim, & Ong, 2002). Although trance and possession are almost never seen in Western cultures, they are among the most common forms of dissociative states elsewhere. When the state is *undesirable* and considered pathological by members of the culture, particularly if the trance involves a perception of being possessed by an evil spirit or another person (described next), the individual would be diagnosed with an "other specified dissociative disorder (**dissociative trance**)" (APA, 2013).

Dissociative Identity Disorder

People with **dissociative identity disorder (DID)** may adopt as many as 100 new identities, all simultaneously co-existing, although the average number is closer to 15. In some cases, the identities are complete, each with its own behavior, tone of voice, and physical gestures. But in many cases, only a few characteristics are distinct, because the identities are only partially independent, so it is not true that there are "multiple" complete personalities. Therefore, the name of the disorder was changed in the previous edition of the *DSM, DSM-IV,* from multiple personality disorder to DID. Consider the case of Jonah, originally reported by Ludwig, Brandsma, Wilbur, Bendfeldt, and Jameson (1972).

Jonah... • *Bewildering Blackouts*

Jonah, 27-years-old and black, suffered from severe headaches that were unbearably painful and lasted for increasingly longer periods. Furthermore, he couldn't remember things that happened while he had a headache, except that sometimes a great deal of time passed. Finally, after a particularly bad night, when he could stand it no longer, he arranged for admission to the local hospital. What prompted Jonah to come to the hospital, however, was that other people told him what he did during his severe headaches. For example, he was told that the night before he had a violent fight with another man and attempted to stab him. He fled the scene and was shot at during a high-speed chase by the police. His wife told him that during a previous headache he chased her and his three-year-old daughter out of the house, threatening them with a butcher's knife. During his headaches, and while he was violent, he called himself "Usoffa Abdulla, son of Omega." Once he attempted to drown a man in a river. The man survived, and Jonah escaped by swimming a quarter of a mile upstream. He woke up the next morning in his own bed, soaking wet, with no memory of the incident.

Clinical Description

During Jonah's hospitalization, the staff were able to observe his behavior directly, both when he had headaches and during other periods that he did not remember. He claimed other names at these times, acted differently, and generally seemed to be another person entirely. The staff distinguished three separate identities, or **alters**, in addition to Jonah. (*Alters* is the shorthand term for the different identities or personalities in DID.) The first alter was named Sammy. Sammy seemed rational, calm, and in control. The second alter, King Young, seemed to be in charge of all sexual activity and was particularly interested in having as many heterosexual interactions as possible. The third alter was the violent and dangerous Usoffa Abdulla. Characteristically, Jonah knew nothing of the three alters. Sammy was most aware of the other personalities. King Young and Usoffa Abdulla knew a little bit about the others but only indirectly.

In the hospital, psychologists determined that Sammy first appeared when Jonah was about six, immediately after Jonah saw his mother stab his father. Jonah's mother sometimes dressed him as a girl in private. On one of these occasions, shortly after Sammy emerged, King Young appeared. When Jonah was nine or ten, he was brutally attacked by a group of white youths. At this point, Usoffa Abdulla emerged, announcing that his sole reason for existence was to protect Jonah.

DSM-5 criteria for DID include amnesia, as in dissociative amnesia. In DID, however, identity has also fragmented. How many personalities live inside one body is relatively unimportant, whether there are three, four, or even 100 of them. Again, the defining feature of this disorder is that certain aspects of the person's identity are dissociated (Spiegel *et al.*, 2013).

Characteristics

The person who becomes the patient and asks for treatment is usually a "host" identity. Host personalities usually attempt to hold various fragments of identity together but end up being overwhelmed. The first personality to seek treatment is seldom the original personality of the person. Usually, the host personality develops later (Putnam, 1992). Many patients have at least one impulsive alter who handles sexuality and generates income, sometimes by acting as a prostitute. In other cases, all alters may abstain from sex. Cross-gendered alters are not uncommon. For example, a small agile woman might have a strong powerful male alter who serves as a protector.

The transition from one personality to another is called a *switch*. Usually, the switch is instantaneous (although in movies and on television it is often drawn out for dramatic effect). Physical transformations may occur during switches. Posture, facial expressions, patterns of facial wrinkling, and even physical disabilities may emerge. In one study, changes in handedness occurred in 37% of the cases (Putnam, Guroff, Silberman, Barban, & Post, 1986).

Can DID Be Faked?

Are the fragmented identities "real," or is the person faking them to avoid responsibility or stress? As with conversion disorders, it is difficult to answer this question, for several reasons (Kluft, 1999). First, evidence indicates that individuals with DID are suggestible (Giesbrecht *et al.*, 2008; Kihlstrom, 2005a). It is possible that alters are created in response to leading questions from therapists, either during psychotherapy or while the person is in a hypnotic state. In other cases, multiple identities may be simulated purposefully for individual gain. Consider the case of Kenneth.

Kenneth... • *The Hillside Strangler*

During the late 1970s, Kenneth Bianchi brutally raped and murdered 10 women in the Los Angeles area and left their bodies naked and in full view on hills. Despite overwhelming evidence that Bianchi was the "Hillside Strangler," he continued to assert his innocence, prompting some professionals to think he might have DID. His lawyer brought in a clinical psychologist, who hypnotized him and asked whether there were another part of Ken with whom he could speak. Guess what? Somebody called "Steve" answered and said he had done all the killing. Steve also said that Ken knew nothing about the murders. With this evidence, the lawyer entered a plea of not guilty by reason of insanity.

The prosecution called on Martin Orne, a distinguished clinical psychologist and psychiatrist who was one of the world's leading experts on hypnosis and dissociative disorders (Orne, Dinges, & Orne, 1984). Orne suggested during an in-depth interview with Bianchi that a true multiple personality disorder included at least three personalities. Bianchi soon produced a third personality. By interviewing Bianchi's friends and relatives, Orne established that there was no independent corroboration of different personalities before Bianchi's arrest. Psychological tests also failed to show significant differences among the personalities. Orne concluded that Bianchi responded like someone simulating hypnosis, not someone deeply hypnotized. On the basis of Orne's testimony, Bianchi was found guilty and sentenced to life in prison.

Some investigators have studied the ability of individuals to fake dissociative experiences. Spanos, Weeks, and Bertrand (1985) demonstrated in an experiment that a college student could simulate an alter if it was suggested that faking was plausible, as in the interview with Bianchi. All the students in the group were told to play the role of an accused murderer claiming his innocence. The participants received exactly the same interview as Orne administered to Bianchi, word for word. More than 80% simulated an alternate personality to avoid conviction. Groups given vaguer instructions, and no direct suggestion an alternate personality might exist, were much less likely to use one in their defense.

....

dissociative trance Altered state of consciousness in which people firmly believe they are possessed by spirits; considered a disorder only where there is distress and dysfunction.

dissociative identity disorder (DID) Disorder in which as many as 100 personalities or fragments of personalities coexist within one body and mind. Formerly known as *multiple personality disorder*.

alters Shorthand term for *alter ego*, one of the different personalities or identities in **dissociative identity disorder**.

Objective assessment of memory, particularly implicit (unconscious) memory, reveals that the memory processes in patients with DID do not differ from "normals" when the methodologies of cognitive science are used (Huntjens *et al.*, 2002; Huntjens, Postma, Peters, Woertman, & van der Hart, 2003). Huntjens and colleagues (2006) showed that patients with DID acted more like simulators concerning other identities, about which they profess no memory (interidentity amnesia), suggesting the possibility of faking. This is in contrast to reports from interviews with patients with DID that suggest that memories are different from one alter to the next. Furthermore, Kong, Allen, and Glisky (2008) found that, much as with normal participants, patients with DID who memorized words as one identity, could remember the words just as well after switching to another identity, contrary to their self-report of interidentity amnesia.

These findings on faking and the effect of hypnosis led Spanos (1996) to suggest that the symptoms of DID could mostly be accounted for by therapists who inadvertently suggested the existence of alters to suggestible individuals, a model known as the "sociocognitive model" because the possibility of identity fragments and early trauma is socially reinforced by a therapist (Kihlstrom, 2005a; Lilienfeld *et al.*, 1999). A survey of American psychiatrists showed little consensus on the scientific validity of DID, with only one-third in the sample believing that the diagnosis should have been included without reservation in the *DSM* (Pope, Oliva, Hudson, Bodkin, & Gruber, 1999). (We return to this point of view when we discuss false memories.)

The diagnosis captured the fascination of the public after popular books, movies, and TV series appeared on the topic. Chris Costner Sizemore was the real-life subject of a popular book and movie *The Three Faces of Eve*. Ms. Sizemore, who used the pseudonym Evelyn Lancaster in her book, was played by Joanne Woodward, who later also played the psychiatrist who treated another patient with DID in the 1976 TV mini-series, *Sybil*. Although these cases of DID became very popular, critics soon questioned the patients' reports and accuracy of the diagnosis. On the other hand, in the case of Ms. Sizemore, some objective tests suggest that many people with fragmented identities are not consciously and voluntarily simulating (Kluft, 1991, 1999). Condon, Ogston, and Pacoe (1969) examined Ms. Sizemore and determined that one of the personalities (Eve Black) showed a transient microstrabismus (difference in joined lateral eye movements) that was not observed in the other personalities. These optical differences have been confirmed by S. D. Miller (1989), who demonstrated that DID patients had 4.5 times the average number of changes in optical functioning in their alter identities than control patients who simulated alter personalities. Miller concludes that such optical changes would be difficult to fake. Ludwig

▲ The 1957 film *The Three Faces of Eve* dramatized the case of Chris Sizemore, whose experiences with dissociative identity disorder drew this controversial diagnosis into the public eye.

and colleagues (1972) found that Jonah's various identities had different physiological responses to emotionally laden words, including electrodermal activity, a measure of otherwise imperceptible sweat gland activity, and EEG brain waves.

Using functional magnetic resonance imaging (fMRI) procedures, changes in brain function were observed in one patient while switching from one personality to another. Specifically, this patient showed changes in hippocampal and medial temporal activity after the switch (Tsai, Condie, Wu, & Chang, 1999). A number of subsequent studies confirm that various alters have unique psychophysiological profiles (Cardeña & Gleaves, 2003; Putnam, 1997). Kluft (1999) suggests a number of additional clinical strategies to distinguish malingerers from patients with DID, including the observations that malingerers are usually eager to demonstrate their symptoms and do so in a fluid fashion. Patients with DID, on the other hand, are more likely to attempt to hide symptoms.

Statistics

Jonah had four identities, but the average number of alter personalities is reported by clinicians as closer to 15 (Ross, 1997; Sackeim & Devanand, 1991). Of people with DID, the ratio of females to males is as high as 9:1, although these data are based on accumulated case studies rather than survey research (Maldonado, Butler, & Spiegel, 1998). The onset is almost always in childhood, often as young as four years of age, although it is usually approximately seven years after the appearance of symptoms before the disorder is identified (Maldonado *et al.*, 1998; Putnam *et al.*, 1986). Once established, the disorder tends to last a lifetime in the absence of treatment. The form DID takes does not seem to vary substantially over the person's lifespan, although some evidence indicates the frequency of switching decreases with age (Sackeim & Devanand, 1991). Different personalities may emerge in response to new life situations, as was the case with Jonah.

There are no good epidemiological studies on the prevalence of the disorder in the population at large, although investigators now think it is more common than previously estimated (Kluft, 1991; Ross, 1997). For example, semistructured interviews of large numbers of severely disturbed inpatients found prevalence rates of DID of between 3% and 6% in North America (Ross, 1997; Saxe *et al.*, 1993) and approximately 2% in Holland (Friedl & Draijer, 2000). In the best survey to date in a non-clinical (community) setting, a prevalence of 1.5% was found during the previous year (Johnson *et al.*, 2006). A large percentage of DID patients have simultaneous psychological disorders that may include anxiety, substance abuse, depression, and personality disorders (Giesbrecht *et al.*, 2008; Johnson *et al.*, 2006; Kluft, 1999).

Causes

Life circumstances that encourage the development of DID seem quite clear in at least one respect. Almost every patient presenting with this disorder reports to their mental health professional being horribly, often unspeakably, abused as a child.

Imagine you are a child in a situation like this. What can you do? You're too young to run away or to call the authorities. Although the pain may be unbearable, you have no way of knowing it is unusual or wrong. But you can do one thing. You can escape into a fantasy world; you can be somebody else. If the escape blunts the physical and emotional pain just for a minute or makes the next hour bearable, chances are you'll escape again. Your mind learns there is no limit to the identities that can be created as needed. You do whatever it takes to get through life. Most surveys report a high rate of childhood trauma in cases of DID (Gleaves, 1996; Ross, 1997). Putnam and colleagues (1986) examined 100 cases and found that 97% of the patients had experienced significant trauma, usually sexual or physical abuse. Sixty-eight percent reported incest. Not all the trauma is caused by abuse. Putnam (1992) describes a young girl in a war zone who saw both her parents blown to bits in a minefield. In a heart-wrenching response, she tried to piece the bodies back together, bit by bit.

Such observations have led to wide-ranging agreement that DID is rooted in a natural tendency to escape or "dissociate" from the unremitting negative affect associated with severe abuse (Kluft, 1984, 1991). A lack of social support during or after the abuse also seems implicated. A study of 428 adolescent twins demonstrated that a surprisingly major portion of the cause of dissociative experience could be attributed to a chaotic, non-supportive family environment. Individual experience and personality factors also contributed to dissociative experiences (Waller & Ross, 1997).

The behavior and emotions that make up dissociative disorders seem related to otherwise normal tendencies present in all of us to some extent. It is quite common for otherwise normal individuals to escape in some way from emotional or physical pain (Butler, Duran, Jasiukaitis, Koopman, & Spiegel, 1996; Spiegel *et al.*, 2013). Dissociative amnesia and fugue states are clearly reactions to severe life stress. But the life stress or trauma is in the present rather than the past, as in the case of the overwrought mother who suffered from dissociative amnesia. Many patients are escaping from legal difficulties or severe stress at home or on the job (Sackeim & Devanand, 1991). But sophisticated statistical analyses indicate that "normal" dissociative reactions differ substantially from the pathological experiences we've described (Waller, Putnam, & Carlson, 1996; Waller & Ross, 1997) and that at least some people do not develop severe pathological dissociative experiences, no matter how extreme the stress. These findings are consistent with our diathesis–stress model in that only with the appropriate vulnerabilities (the diathesis) will someone react to stress with pathological dissociation.

You may have noticed that DID seems similar in its etiology to posttraumatic stress disorder (PTSD). One perspective suggests that DID is an extreme subtype of PTSD, with a much greater emphasis on the process of dissociation than on symptoms of anxiety, although both are present in each disorder (Butler *et al.*, 1996). Some evidence also shows that the "developmental window" of vulnerability to the abuse that leads to DID closes at approximately nine years of age (Putnam, 1997). After that, DID is unlikely to develop, although severe PTSD might. If true, this is a particularly good example of the role of development in the etiology of psychopathology.

We also must remember that we know relatively little about DID. Our conclusions are based on retrospective case studies or correlations rather than on the prospective examination of people who may have undergone the severe trauma that seems to lead to DID (Kihlstrom, 2005a; Kihlstrom, Glisky, & Anguilo, 1994). Therefore, it is hard to say what psychological or biological factors might contribute, but there are hints concerning individual differences that might play a role.

Suggestibility

Suggestibility is a personality trait distributed normally across the population, much like weight and height. Some people are more suggestible than others; some are relatively immune to suggestibility; and the majority fall in the mid-range.

Did you ever have an imaginary childhood playmate? Many people did, and it is one sign of the ability to lead a rich fantasy life, which can be helpful and adaptive. But it also seems to correlate with being suggestible or easily hypnotized (some people equate the terms *suggestibility* and *hypnotizability*). A hypnotic trance is also similar to dissociation (Butler *et al.*, 1996; Spiegel *et al.*, 2013). People in a trance tend to be focused on one aspect of their world, and they become vulnerable to suggestions by the hypnotist. There is also the phenomenon of self-hypnosis, in which individuals can dissociate from most of the world around them and "suggest" to themselves that, for example, they won't feel pain in one of their hands.

According to the *autohypnotic model,* people who are suggestible may be able to use dissociation as a defense against extreme trauma (Putnam, 1991). As many as 50% of DID patients clearly remember imaginary playmates in childhood (Ross *et al.*, 1990); whether they were created before or after the trauma is not entirely clear. According to this view, when the trauma becomes unbearable, the person's very identity splits into multiple dissociated identities. Children's ability to distinguish clearly between reality and fantasy as they grow older may be what closes the developmental window for developing DID at approximately age nine. People who are less suggestible may develop a severe posttraumatic stress reaction but not a dissociative reaction.

Biological Contributions

As in PTSD, where the evidence is more solid, there is almost certainly a biological vulnerability to DID, but it is difficult to pinpoint. For example, in a large twin study (Waller & Ross, 1997), none of the variance or identifiable causal factors was attributable to heredity: All of it was environmental. As with anxiety disorders, more basic heritable traits, such as tension and responsiveness to stress, may increase vulnerability. On the other hand, much as in PTSD, there is some evidence of smaller hippocampal and amygdala volume in patients with DID compared with "normals" (Vermetten, Schmahl, Lindner, Loewenstein, & Bremner, 2006).

Head injury and resulting brain damage may induce amnesia or other types of dissociative experience. But these conditions are usually easily diagnosed because they are generalized and irreversible and are associated with an identifiable head trauma (Butler *et al.*, 1996). Finally, strong evidence exists that sleep deprivation produces dissociative symptoms such as hallucinations (Giesbrecht *et al.*, 2007; van der Kloet, Giesbrecht, Lynn, Merckelbach, & de Zutter, 2012).

Real Memories and False

One of the most controversial issues in the field of abnormal psychology today concerns the extent to which memories of early trauma, particularly sexual abuse, are accurate or not. This issue is not specific to any one particular mental disorder. Rather, whenever clinical decisions are based on a person's memory, it is important to consider the fact that memories are not always very accurate or even

▲ A person in a hypnotic trance is suggestible and may become absorbed in a particular experience.

true, even if they *feel* true. Sometimes, we can't remember important things that did happen and other times, we seem to remember things that actually never happened. But this controversy often arises in the context of studying traumatic memories, particularly as identified in DID. The stakes in this controversy are enormous, with considerable opportunity for harm to innocent people on each side of the controversy.

On the one hand, if early sexual abuse did occur but is not remembered because of dissociative amnesia, it is crucially important to re-experience aspects of the trauma under the direction of a skilled therapist to relieve current suffering. Without therapy, the patient is likely to suffer from PTSD or a dissociative disorder indefinitely. It is also important that perpetrators are held accountable for their actions because abuse of this type is a crime and prevention is an important goal.

On the other hand, if memories of early trauma are inadvertently created in response to suggestions by a careless therapist but seem real to the patient, false accusations against loved ones could lead to irreversible family breakup and, perhaps, unjust prison sentences for those falsely accused as perpetrators. In recent years, allegedly inaccurate accusations based on false memories have led to substantial lawsuits against therapists, resulting in awards of millions of dollars in damages. There is irrefutable evidence that false memories *can* be created by reasonably well-understood psychological processes (Loftus & Davis, 2006; McNally, 2003, 2012a; Wilson, Mickes, Stolarz-Fantino, Evrard, & Fantino, 2015). Some authors contend that early traumatic experiences can cause selective dissociative amnesia, with substantial implications for psychological functioning (Dahlenberg *et al.*, 2012; Spiegel *et al.*, 2013). In contrast, others question the assumption that people can encode traumatic experiences without being able to recall them (e.g., Lynn *et al.*, 2014).

Evidence supporting the existence of distorted or illusory memories comes from experiments like one by the distinguished cognitive psychologist Elizabeth Loftus and her colleagues (Loftus, 2003; Loftus & Davis, 2006). Loftus, Coan, and Pickrell (1996) successfully convinced a number of individuals that they had been lost for an extended period when they were approximately five-years-old, which was not true. A trusted companion was recruited to "plant" the memory. In one case, a 14-year-old boy was told by his older brother that he had been lost in a nearby shopping mall when he was five years old, rescued by an older man, and reunited with his mother and brother. Several days after receiving this suggestion, the boy reported remembering the event and even that he felt frightened when he was lost. As time went by, the boy remembered more and more details of the event, beyond those described in the "plant," including an exact description of the older man. When he was finally told the incident never happened, the boy was surprised, and he continued to describe details of the event as if they were true. More recently, Bernstein and Loftus (2009) reviewed a series of experiments demonstrating that, for example, creating a false memory of becoming ill after eating egg salad led to eating less egg salad and reporting a distaste for egg salad up to four months later during a test in which the participants didn't know they were being tested for food preferences.

Young children are quite unreliable in reporting accurate details of events (Bruck, Ceci, Francouer, & Renick, 1995), particularly emotional events (Howe, 2007; Toth et al., 2011). In one study (Bruck et al., 1995), 35 three-year-old girls were given a genital exam as part of their routine medical checkup; another 35 girls were not (the control group). Shortly after the exam, with her mother present, each girl was asked to describe where the doctor had touched her. She was then presented with an anatomically correct doll and asked again to point out where the doctor had touched her. The findings indicated that the children were inaccurate in reporting what happened. Approximately 60% of those who were touched in the genital region refused to indicate this, whether the dolls were used or not. On the other hand approximately 60% of the control group indicated genital insertions or other intrusive acts by the doctor, even though nothing of the sort had occurred.

In another set of studies (Ceci, 2003), pre-school children were asked to think about actual events that they had experienced, such as an accident, and about fictitious events, such as having to go to the hospital to get their fingers removed from a mousetrap. Each week for 10 consecutive weeks, an interviewer asked each child to choose one of the scenes and to "think very hard and tell me if this ever happened to you." The child thus experienced thinking hard and visualizing both real and fictitious scenes over an extended period. After 10 weeks, the children were examined by a new interviewer who had not participated in the experiment.

Clancy and colleagues, in a fascinating experiment, studied the process of false memory creation in a group who reported having recovered memories of traumatic events unlikely to have occurred: abduction by space aliens. Among three groups—those reporting recovered memories of alien abduction, those who believe they were abducted but have no memories of it (repressed memories), and people who have no such beliefs or memories—some interesting differences emerged (Clancy, McNally, Schacter, Lenzenweger, & Pitman, 2002; McNally 2012). Those reporting recovered and repressed memories of abduction also evidenced more false recall and recognition on some cognitive tasks in the laboratory and scored higher on measures of suggestibility and depression than control participants. These studies collectively indicate that memories are malleable and easily distorted, particularly in some individuals with certain personality traits and characteristics such as vivid imaginal capabilities (absorption), and an openness to unusual ideas (McNally, 2012a).

But there is also plenty of evidence that therapists need to be sensitive to signs of trauma that may not be fully remembered in patients presenting with symptoms of dissociative disorder or PTSD. Even if patients are unable to report or remember early trauma, it can sometimes be confirmed through corroborating evidence (Coons, 1994). In one study, Williams (1994) interviewed 129 women with documented histories, such as hospital records, of having been sexually abused as children. Thirty-eight percent did not recall the incidents that had been reported to authorities at least 17 years earlier, even with extensive probing of their abuse histories. This lack of recall was more extensive if the victim had been young and knew the abuser. But Goodman and colleagues (2003) interviewed 175 individuals with documented child sexual abuse histories and found that most participants (81%) remembered and reported the abuse. Older age when the abuse ended and emotional support following initial disclosure of the abuses were associated with higher rates of disclosures. McNally and Geraerts (2009) also present evidence suggesting that some people, after many years, simply forget these early experiences and recall them after encountering some reminders outside of therapy. In this group, then, it's not necessary to invoke the concepts of repression, trauma, or false memory. It is simple forgetting. In summary, among those individuals reporting memories of sexual abuse, some may have experienced it and remembered it all along, some people may have false memories, some may have recovered memories in therapy of "repressed" sexual abuse, and some may have simply forgotten the incident, but remember later.

How will this controversy be resolved? Because false memories can be created through strong repeated suggestions by an authority figure, therapists must be fully aware of the conditions under which this is likely to occur, particularly when dealing with young children. This requires extensive knowledge of the workings of memory and other aspects of psychological functioning, and illustrates, again, the dangers of dealing with inexperienced or inadequately trained psychotherapists. Elaborate tales of satanic abuse of children under the care of elderly women in day care centers are most likely cases of memories implanted by aggressive and careless therapists or law enforcement officials (Loftus & Davis, 2006; McNally, 2003). In some cases, elderly caregivers have been sentenced to life in prison.

On the other hand, many people with dissociative disorder and PTSD have suffered documented extreme abuse and trauma, which could then become dissociated from awareness. It may be that future research will find that the severity of dissociative amnesia is directly related to the severity of the trauma in vulnerable individuals with certain specific coping styles (Toth *et al.*, 2011), and this type of severe dissociative reaction is also likely to be proved as qualitatively different from "normal" dissociative experiences we all have occasionally, such as feeling unreal or not here for a moment or two (see, for example, Kluft, 1999; Waller *et al.*, 1996). Advocates on both sides of this issue

agree that clinical science must proceed as quickly as possible to specify the processes under which the implantation of false memories is likely and to define the presenting features that indicate a real but dissociated traumatic experience (Frenda *et al.*, 2011; Goodman, Quas, & Ogle, 2010; Kihlstrom, 2005a; Lilienfeld *et al.*, 1999; Pope, 1997). Until then, mental health professionals must be extremely careful not to prolong unnecessary suffering among both victims of actual abuse and victims falsely accused as abusers (e.g., Lynn *et al.*, 2014).

Treatment

Individuals who experience dissociative amnesia or a fugue state usually get better on their own and remember what they have forgotten. The episodes are so clearly related to current life stress that prevention of future episodes usually involves therapeutic resolution of the distressing situations and increasing the strength of personal coping mechanisms. When necessary, therapy focuses on recalling what happened during the amnesic or fugue states, often with the help of friends or family who know what happened, so

---

DSM 5 CONTROVERSY   Radical Changes in Classification

Somatic symptom and related disorders and dissociative disorders are among the oldest recognized mental disorders. And yet, evidence indicates that we have much to learn about the nature of these disorders and that neither grouping of disorders may comprise a uniform category that reflects shared characteristics for purposes of classification (Mayou *et al.*, 2005). For example, the grouping of somatic symptom disorders was based until recently on the assumption that "somatization" is a common process in which a mental disorder manifests itself in the form of physical symptoms. The specific disorders, then, simply reflect the ways in which symptoms can be expressed physically. But major questions arose concerning the classification of these disorders (Noyes, Stuart, & Watson, 2008; Voigt *et al.*, 2010).

Specifically, the somatic symptom disorders all share presentations of somatic symptoms accompanied by cognitive distortions in the form of misattributions of, or excessive preoccupation with, symptoms. These cognitive distortions may include

excessive anxiety about health or physical symptoms, a tendency to "catastrophize" about these symptoms, and strong beliefs that physical symptoms might be more serious than health-care professionals have recognized. Also, people presenting with these disorders often make health concerns a central part of their lives. For this reason, *DSM-5* has changed substantially the definitions of these disorders to focus on two major factors: the severity and number of physical symptoms, as well as the severity of anxiety focused on the symptoms and the degree of behavior change as a consequence of the symptoms. In illness anxiety disorder, physical symptoms need not be present beyond mild complaints, and the focus is solely on severe anxiety over the prospect that one is ill or will become ill. Preliminary explorations of the validity and utility of this strategy indicate that this new dimensional approach, reflecting both physical and psychological symptom severity, may be helpful to clinicians in predicting the course of the disorder as well as

selecting treatments (Voigt *et al.*, 2010; Voigt *et al.*, 2012; Wollburg *et al.*, 2013).

Another advantage of this approach is that there is less burden on physicians to make tricky determinations on whether the symptoms have physical causes as was the case in *DSM-IV*. Rather, the combination of chronic physical symptoms accompanied by the psychological factors of misattributing the meaning of the symptoms and excessive concern is sufficient to make the diagnosis. This new category also includes psychological factors affecting medical condition and the factitious disorders because all involve the presentation of physical symptoms and/or concern about medical illness. Needless to say, the very radical nature of change in this major category of disorders is proving to be very controversial, primarily because so little data exist on the validity of these new categories or even the reliability with which they can be diagnosed. But they appear to be an improvement, and clinical investigators are already busy attempting to confirm or disconfirm the utility of this new approach. •

---

that patients can confront the information and integrate it into their conscious experience.

For DID, however, the process is not so easy. With the person's very identity shattered into many elements, reintegrating the personality might seem hopeless. Fortunately, this is not always the case. Although no controlled research has been reported on the effects of treatment, there are some documented successes of attempts to reintegrate identities through long-term psychotherapy (Brand *et al.*, 2009; Kluft, 2009). Nevertheless, the prognosis for most people remains guarded. Coons (1986) found that only five of 20 patients achieved a full integration of their identities. Ellason and Ross (1997) reported that 12 of 54 (22.2%) patients had achieved integration two years after presenting for treatment, which in most cases had been continuous. These results could be attributed to other factors than therapy because no experimental comparison was present (Powell & Howell, 1998).

The strategies that therapists use today in treating DID are based on accumulated clinical wisdom, as well as on procedures that have been successful with PTSD (Gold & Seibel, 2009; Keane *et al.*, 2011; see Chapter 4). The fundamental goal is to identify cues or triggers that provoke memories of trauma, dissociation, or both, and to neutralize them. More important, the patient must confront and relive the early trauma and gain control over the horrible events, at least as they recur in the patient's mind (Kluft, 2009; Ross, 1997). To instill this sense of control, the therapist must skillfully, and slowly, help the patient visualize and relive aspects of the trauma until it is simply a terrible memory instead of a current event. Because the memory is unconscious, aspects of the experience are often not known to either the patient or the therapist until they emerge during treatment. Hypnosis is often used to access unconscious memories and bring various alters into awareness. Because the process of dissociation may be similar to the process of hypnosis, the latter may be a particularly efficient way to access traumatic memories (Maldonado *et al.*, 1998). (There is as yet no evidence that hypnosis is a *necessary* part of treatment.) DID seems to run a chronic course and seldom improves spontaneously, which confirms that current treatments, primitive as they are, have some effectiveness.

It is possible that re-emerging memories of trauma may trigger further dissociation. The therapist must be on guard against this happening. Trust is important to any therapeutic relationship, but it is essential in the treatment of DID. Occasionally, medication is combined with therapy, but there is little indication that it helps much. What little clinical evidence there is indicates that antidepressant drugs might be appropriate in some cases (Kluft, 1996; Putnam & Loewenstein, 1993).

5.2 Concept CHECK

Diagnose the dissociative disorders described here by choosing one of the following: (a) dissociative fugue, (b) depersonalization-derealization disorder, (c) generalized amnesia, (d) dissociative identity disorder, and (e) localized amnesia.

1. Ann was found wandering the streets, unable to recall any important personal information. After searching her purse and finding an address, doctors were able to contact her mother. They learned that Ann had just been in a terrible accident and was the only survivor. Ann could not remember her mother or any details of the accident. She was distressed. _____

2. Karl was brought to a clinic by his mother. She was concerned because at times his behavior was strange. His speech and his way of relating to people and situations would change dramatically, almost as if he were a different person. What bothered her and Karl most was that he could not recall anything he did during these periods. _____

3. Terry complained about feeling out of control. She said she felt sometimes as if she were floating under the ceiling and just watching things happen to her. She also experienced tunnel vision and felt uninvolved in the things that went on in the room around her. This always caused her to panic and perspire.

_____

4. Henry is 64 and recently arrived in town. He does not know where he is from or how he got here. His driver's license proves his name, but he is unconvinced it is his. He is in good health and not taking any medication. _____

5. Rosita cannot remember what happened last weekend. On Monday she was admitted to a hospital, suffering from cuts, bruises, and contusions. It also appeared that she had been sexually assaulted.

_____

SUMMARY

Somatic Symptom and Related Disorders

What are the defining features of somatic symptom and related disorders?

▶ Individuals with somatic symptom and related disorders are pathologically concerned with the functioning of their bodies and bring these concerns to the attention of health professionals, who usually find no identifiable medical basis for the physical complaints.

▶ There are several types of somatic symptom disorders. Somatic symptom disorder is characterized by a focus on one or more physical symptoms accompanied by marked distress focused on the symptom that is disproportionate to the nature or severity of the physical symptoms. Illness anxiety disorder is a condition in which individuals believe they are seriously ill and become anxious over this possibility, even though they are not experiencing any notable physical symptoms at the time. In conversion disorder, there is physical malfunctioning, such as paralysis, without any apparent physical problems.

▶ The causes of somatic symptom disorder are not well understood. In the case of illness anxiety disorder, the person experiences significant anxiety about having or developing a serious medical disease. The latter diagnosis is similar to an anxiety disorder.

What treatments have been developed for somatic symptom and related disorders?

▶ Treatment of somatic symptom disorders ranges from basic techniques of reassurance and social support to interventions meant to reduce stress and remove any secondary gain for the behavior. Recently, specifically tailored cognitive-behavioral therapy has proved successful with these conditions.

Dissociative Disorders

What are the defining features and different types of dissociative disorders?

▶ Dissociative disorders are characterized by alterations in perceptions: a sense of detachment from one's own self, from the world, or from memories.

▶ Dissociative disorders include depersonalization-derealization disorder, in which the individual's sense of personal reality is temporarily lost (depersonalization), as is the reality of the external world (derealization). In dissociative amnesia, the individual may be unable to remember important personal information. In generalized amnesia, the individual is unable to remember anything; more commonly, the individual is unable to recall specific events that occur during a specific period (localized or selective amnesia). In dissociative fugue, a subtype of dissociative amnesia, memory loss is combined with an unexpected trip (or trips). In the extreme, new identities, or alters, may be formed, as in dissociative identity disorder (DID).

What factors influence the etiology and treatment of dissociative disorders?

▶ The causes of dissociative disorders are not well understood but often seem related to the tendency to escape psychologically from stress or memories of traumatic events.

▶ Treatment of dissociative disorders involves helping the patient re-experience the traumatic events in a controlled therapeutic manner to develop better coping skills. In the case of DID, therapy is often long term. Particularly essential with this disorder is a sense of trust between therapist and patient.

▬▬ Key Terms

somatic symptom disorder, 173, 174
dissociative disorder, 173
illness anxiety disorder, 175
psychological factors affecting
   medical condition, 179
conversion disorder, 180
malingering, 180

factitious disorder, 181
derealization, 184
depersonalization-derealization
   disorder, 185
dissociative amnesia, 185
generalized amnesia, 186
localized or selective amnesia, 186

dissociative fugue, 186
dissociative trance, 188
dissociative identity
   disorder (DID), 188
alters, 188

▬▬ Answers to Concept Checks

5.1

1. a; 2. b; 3. c

5.2

1. c; 2. d; 3. b; 4. a; 5. e

Chapter Quiz

1. The primary symptom of illness anxiety disorder is:
   a. fear of developing a disease
   b. fear of spreading a disease
   c. fear of contact with diseased individuals
   d. fear of currently having a disease

2. Someone who presents with the following symptoms might have illness anxiety disorder:
   a. interpreting momentary flutters in the stomach as a sign of illness
   b. reluctance to visit the doctor for fear of having a panic attack
   c. enjoyment of the immediate attention received when visiting a doctor
   d. realization that the presence of an illness could qualify the individual for full-time disability benefits

3. Choose the scenario that best demonstrates somatic symptom disorder:
   a. Lisa reports that she has continuous nausea and is unable to work, but a medical exam finds no sign of illness. Lisa claims she only feels better when her husband stays home to nurse her.
   b. Eddie frequently has episodes in which he feels like his body is not his own.
   c. Sherry has physical complaints that have lasted at least 10 years. Her symptoms include pain in her feet, hands, and neck; alternating diarrhea and constipation; and difficulty walking. Sherry's physician cannot find any illness to account for these complaints.
   d. Pedro stops working because he thinks that his ears are twice the size they should be and that he looks like a freak. His therapist observes, however, that Pedro's ears are a normal size.

4. In factitious disorder:
   a. the individual is faking symptoms for personal gain
   b. the individual is voluntarily producing the symptoms without any obvious financial or other external incentives
   c. the individual is not in control of the symptoms but there is no physical explanation
   d. the symptoms are caused by a yet-to-be-identified virus

5. Jorge, a 19-year-old male, was hospitalized after his legs collapsed under him while walking to class. He could not regain his stance and has been unable to walk since, although he desperately wants to walk again. A neurological exam revealed no medical problem. Jorge's behavior is consistent with:
   a. somatic symptom disorder
   b. conversion disorder
   c. malingering
   d. illness anxiety disorder

7. Mrs. Thompson brought her four-year-old daughter, Carmen, to the emergency room, stating that the child had been vomiting non-stop throughout the morning. Carmen's condition improved over the course of several days. On the day of her discharge from the hospital, a nurse walked in as Mrs. Thompson was giving Carmen a drink of floor cleaner. Mrs. Thompson's behavior is consistent with:
   a. parental illness anxiety disorder
   b. Factitious disorder imposed on another
   c. conversion syndrome by proxy
   d. parental somatic symptom disorder

8. _____ describes the experience of losing a sense of your own reality, whereas _____ describes losing your sense of reality of the external world:
   a. Depersonalization; derealization
   b. Derealization; somatization
   c. Derealization; depersonalization
   d. Somatization; derealization

9. Michael's wife, Jennifer, reported him missing to the police in 1998. Two years later she saw Michael in an airport. He lived two states away from Jennifer, was married to another woman, and had two children with her. Michael told Jennifer that his name was Danny, not Michael, and that he had never met her before. Michael's presentation is consistent with:
   a. depersonalization–derealization disorder
   b. dissociative trance disorder
   c. dissociative identity disorder
   d. dissociative fugue

10. The different identities or personalities in dissociative identity disorder are called _____, whereas the change from one personality to another is called a _____:
    a. masks; transition
    b. faces; switch
    c. façades; transition
    d. alters; switch

(See Appendix A for answers.)

Exploring Somatic Symptom and Dissociative Disorders

These two sets of disorders share some common features and are strongly linked historically as "hysterical neuroses." Both are relatively rare and not yet well understood.

SOMATIC SYMPTOM AND RELATED DISORDERS
Characterized by a pathological concern with physical functioning or appearance

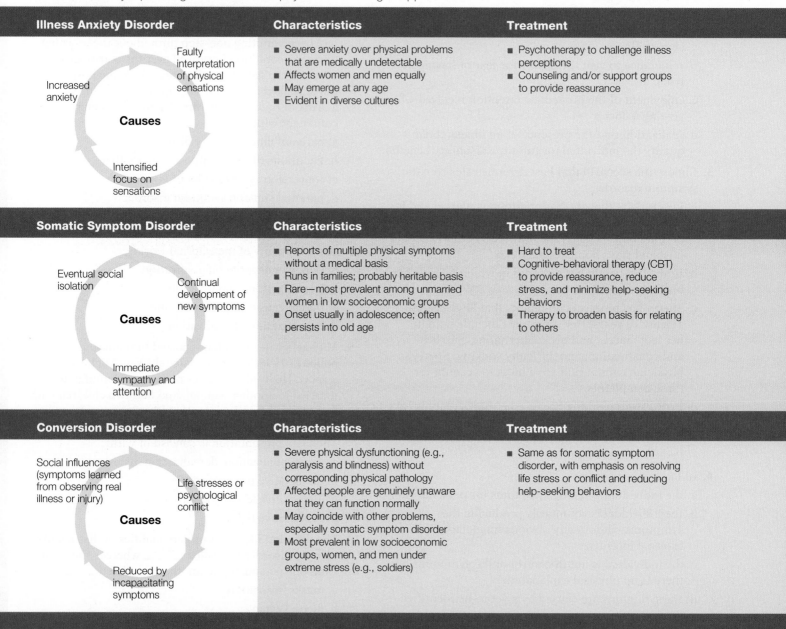

Illness Anxiety Disorder

Causes cycle: Increased anxiety → Faulty interpretation of physical sensations → Intensified focus on sensations → (Causes)

Characteristics

- Severe anxiety over physical problems that are medically undetectable
- Affects women and men equally
- May emerge at any age
- Evident in diverse cultures

Treatment

- Psychotherapy to challenge illness perceptions
- Counseling and/or support groups to provide reassurance

Somatic Symptom Disorder

Causes cycle: Eventual social isolation → Continual development of new symptoms → Immediate sympathy and attention → (Causes)

Characteristics

- Reports of multiple physical symptoms without a medical basis
- Runs in families; probably heritable basis
- Rare—most prevalent among unmarried women in low socioeconomic groups
- Onset usually in adolescence; often persists into old age

Treatment

- Hard to treat
- Cognitive-behavioral therapy (CBT) to provide reassurance, reduce stress, and minimize help-seeking behaviors
- Therapy to broaden basis for relating to others

Conversion Disorder

Causes cycle: Social influences (symptoms learned from observing real illness or injury) → Life stresses or psychological conflict → Reduced by incapacitating symptoms → (Causes)

Characteristics

- Severe physical dysfunctioning (e.g., paralysis and blindness) without corresponding physical pathology
- Affected people are genuinely unaware that they can function normally
- May coincide with other problems, especially somatic symptom disorder
- Most prevalent in low socioeconomic groups, women, and men under extreme stress (e.g., soldiers)

Treatment

- Same as for somatic symptom disorder, with emphasis on resolving life stress or conflict and reducing help-seeking behaviors

DISSOCIATIVE DISORDERS

Characterized by detachment from the self (depersonalization) and objective reality (derealization)

Similar etiology to posttraumatic stress disorder

Causes

Severe abuse during childhood
- Fantasy life is the only "escape"
- Process becomes automatic and then involuntary

High suggestibility a possible trait

Interacts with biological vulnerability

istock.com/track5

Controversy

The scientific community is divided over the question of whether multiple identities are a genuine experience or faked. Studies have shown that "false memories" can be created ("implanted") by therapists. Other tests confirm that various alters are physiologically distinct.

Disorder	Characteristics	Treatment
Dissociative Identity Disorder (DID)	■ Affected person adopts new identities, or alters, that coexist simultaneously; the alters may be complete and distinct personalities or only partly independent ■ Average number of alters is 15 ■ Childhood onset; affects more women than men ■ Patients often suffer from other psychological disorders simultaneously ■ Rare outside of Western cultures	■ Long-term psychotherapy may reintegrate separate personalities in 25% of patients ■ Treatment of associated trauma similar to posttraumatic stress disorder; lifelong condition without treatment
Depersonalization-Derealization Disorder	■ Severe and frightening feelings of detachment dominate the person's life ■ Affected person feels like an outside observer of his or her own mental or body processes ■ Causes significant distress or impairment in functioning, especially emotional expression and deficits in perception ■ Some symptoms are similar to those of panic disorder ■ Rare; onset usually in adolescence	■ Psychological treatments similar to those for panic disorder may be helpful ■ Stresses associated with onset of disorder should be addressed ■ Tends to be lifelong
Dissociative Amnesia	■ Generalized: Inability to remember anything, including identity; comparatively rare ■ Localized: Inability to remember specific events (usually traumatic); frequently occurs in war ■ More common than general amnesia ■ Usually adult onset for both types ■ Dissociative Fugue Subtype: Memory loss is accompanied by purposeful travel or bewildered wandering	■ Usually self-correcting when current life stress is resolved ■ If needed, therapy focuses on retrieving lost information
Dissociative Trance	■ Sudden changes in personality accompany a trance or "possession" ■ Causes significant distress and/or impairment in functioning ■ Often associated with stress or trauma ■ Prevalent worldwide, usually in a religious context; rarely seen in Western cultures ■ More common in women than in men	■ Little is known

Photodisc/Getty Images

6

Mood Disorders and Suicide

CHAPTER OUTLINE

Understanding and Defining Mood Disorders

An Overview of Depression and Mania
The Structure of Mood Disorders
Depressive Disorders
Other Depressive Disorders
Bipolar Disorders

Prevalence of Mood Disorders

Prevalence in Children, Adolescents, and Older Adults
Life Span Developmental Influences on Mood Disorders
Across Cultures
Among Creative Individuals

Causes of Mood Disorders

Biological Dimensions
Psychological Dimensions
Social and Cultural Dimensions
An Integrative Theory

Treatment of Mood Disorders

Medications
Electroconvulsive Therapy and Transcranial Magnetic Stimulation
Psychological Treatments for Depression
Combined Treatments for Depression
Preventing Relapse of Depression
Psychological Treatments for Bipolar Disorder

Suicide

Statistics
Causes
Risk Factors
Is Suicide Contagious?

Treatment

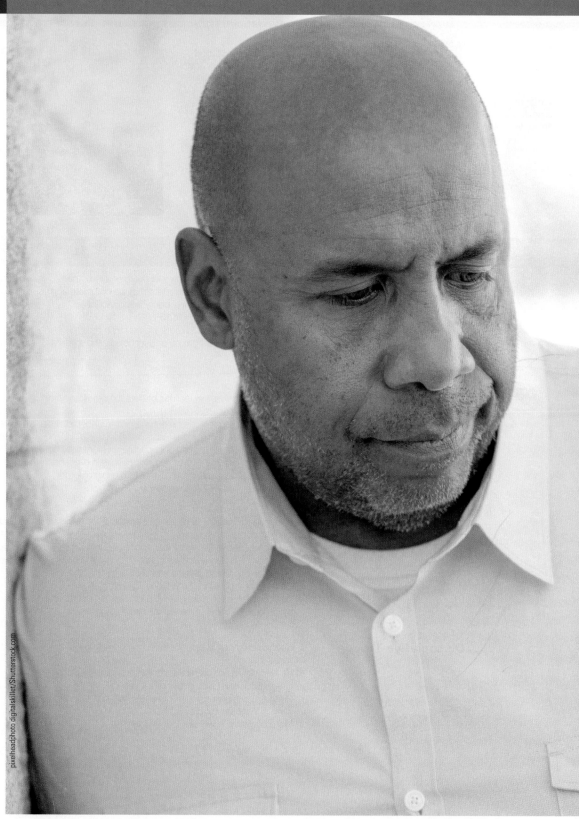

pixelheadphoto digitalskillet/Shutterstock.com

Use scientific reasoning to interpret behavior:	▶ Identify basic biological, psychological, and social components of behavioral explanations (e.g., inferences, observations, operational definitions and interpretations) (APA SLO 2.1a) *(see textbook pages 201–202, 219–226, 227–230)*
Describe key concepts, principles, and overarching themes in psychology:	▶ Analyze the variability and continuity of behavior and mental processes within and across animal species (APA SLO 1.2d2) *(see textbook pages 218, 221, 225–226)*
Engage in innovative and integrative thinking and problem solving:	▶ Describe problems operationally to study them empirically (APA SLO 2.3a) *(see textbook pages 204–205, 206–208, 209–211, 213–214)*
Develop a working knowledge of the content domains of psychology:	▶ Recognize major historical events, theoretical perspectives, and figures in psychology and their link to trends in contemporary research (APA SLO 1.2c) *(see textbook pages 225–226, 234–235)*
Describe applications that employ discipline-based problem solving:	▶ Correctly identify antecedents and consequences of behavior and mental processes (APA SLO 1.3c) *(see textbook pages 218–230)* ▶ Describe examples of relevant and practical applications of psychological principles to everyday life (APA SLO 1.3a) *(see textbook pages 205–206, 212, 242)*

* Portions of this chapter cover learning outcomes suggested by the American Psychological Association (2013) in its guidelines for the undergraduate psychology major. Chapter coverage of these outcomes is identified above by APA Goal and APA Suggested Learning Outcome (SLO).

Understanding and Defining Mood Disorders

▶ What is the difference between a depressive episode and a manic or hypomanic episode?

▶ What are the clinical symptoms of major depressive disorder, persistent depressive disorder, and bipolar disorder?

Think back over the last month of your life. It may seem normal in most respects; you studied during the week, socialized on the weekend, and thought about the future once in a while. Perhaps you were anticipating with some pleasure the next school break or seeing an old friend. But maybe sometime during the past month you also felt kind of down, because you got a lower mark than you expected on a test or broke up with your boyfriend or girlfriend. Think about your feelings during this period. Were you sad? Maybe you couldn't seem to get up the energy to study or go out with your friends. It may be that you feel this way once in a while for no good reason and your friends think you're moody.

If you are like most people, you know that such a mood will pass. You will be back to your old self in a few days or a week. If you never felt down and always saw only what was good in a situation, it would be more unusual than if you were depressed once in a while. Feelings of depression (and joy) are universal, which makes it all the more difficult to understand disorders of mood, disorders that can be so incapacitating that violent suicide may seem by far a better option than living. Consider the case of Katie.

Katie... • *Weathering Depression*

Katie was an attractive but shy 16-year-old who came to our clinic with her parents. For several years, Katie had seldom interacted with anybody outside her family because of her considerable social anxiety. Going to school was difficult, and as her social contacts decreased, her days became empty and dull. By the time she was 16, a deep, all-encompassing depression blocked the sun from her life. Here is how she described it later:

The experience of depression is like falling into a deep, dark hole that you cannot climb out of. You scream as you fall, but it seems like no one hears you. Some days you float upward without even trying; on other days, you wish that you would hit bottom so that you would never fall again. Depression affects the way you interpret events. It influences the way you see yourself and the way you see other people. I remember looking in the mirror and thinking that I was the ugliest creature in the world.

Later in life, when some of these ideas would come back, I learned to remind myself that I did not have those thoughts yesterday and chances were that I would not have them tomorrow or the next day. It is a little like waiting for a change in the weather.

But at 16, in the depths of her despair, Katie had no such perspective. She often cried for hours at the end of the day. She had begun drinking alcohol the year before, with the blessing of her parents, strangely enough, because the pills prescribed by her family doctor did no good. A glass of wine at dinner had a temporary soothing effect on Katie, and both she and her parents, in their desperation, were willing to try anything that might make her a more functional person. But one glass was not enough. She drank increasingly more often. She began drinking herself to sleep. It was a means of escaping what she felt: "I had very little hope of positive change. I do not think that anyone close to me was hopeful, either. I was angry, cynical, and in a great deal of emotional pain."

For several years, Katie had thought about suicide as a solution to her unhappiness. At 13, in the presence of her parents, she reported these thoughts to a psychologist. Her parents wept, and the sight of their tears deeply affected Katie. From that point on, she never expressed her suicidal thoughts again, but they remained with her. By the time she was 16, her preoccupation with her own death had increased.

I think this was just exhaustion. I was tired of dealing with the anxiety and depression, day in and day out. Soon I found myself trying to sever the few interpersonal connections that I did have, with my closest friends, with my mother, and my oldest brother. I was almost impossible to talk to. I was angry and frustrated all the time. One day I went over the edge. My mother and I had a disagreement about some unimportant little thing. I went to my bedroom where I kept a bottle of whiskey or vodka or whatever I was drinking at the time. I drank as much as I could until I could pinch myself as hard as I could and feel nothing. Then I got out a very sharp knife that I had been saving and slashed my wrist deeply. I did not feel anything but the warmth of the blood running from my wrist.

The blood poured out onto the floor next to the bed that I was lying on. The sudden thought hit me that I had failed, that this was not enough to cause my death. I got up from the bed and began to laugh. I tried to stop the bleeding with some tissues. I stayed calm and frighteningly pleasant. I walked to the kitchen and called my mother. I cannot imagine how she felt when she saw my shirt and pants covered in blood. She was amazingly calm. She asked to see the cut and said that it was not going to stop bleeding on its own and that I needed to go to the doctor immediately. I remember as the doctor shot novocaine into the cut he remarked that I must have used an anesthetic before cutting myself. I never felt the shot or the stitches.

After that, thoughts of suicide became more frequent and more real. My father asked me to promise that I would never do it again, and I said I would not, but that promise meant nothing to me. I knew it was to ease his pains and fears and not mine, and my preoccupation with death continued.

Clearly, Katie's depression was outside the boundaries of normal experience because of its intensity and duration. In addition, her severe or "clinical" depression interfered substantially with her ability to function. Finally, a number of associated psychological and physical symptoms accompany clinical depression.

Sometimes, **mood disorders** lead to tragic consequences. So developing a full understanding of them is key. In the following sections, we describe how various emotional experiences and symptoms interrelate to produce specific mood disorders. We offer detailed descriptions of different mood disorders and examine the many criteria that define them. We discuss the relationship of anxiety and depression and the causes and treatment of mood disorders. We conclude with a discussion of suicide.

An Overview of Depression and Mania

The fundamental experiences of *depression* and *mania* contribute, either singly or together, to all the mood disorders. The most commonly diagnosed and most severe depression is called a **major depressive episode**. The *DSM-5* criteria describes it as an extremely depressed mood state that lasts at least two weeks and includes cognitive symptoms (such as feelings of worthlessness and indecisiveness) and disturbed physical functions (such as altered sleeping patterns, significant changes in appetite and weight, or a notable loss of energy) to the point that even the slightest activity or movement requires an overwhelming effort. The episode is typically accompanied by a general loss of interest in things and an inability to experience any pleasure from life, including interactions with family or friends or accomplishments at work or at school. Although all symptoms are important, evidence suggests that the most central indicators of a full major depressive episode are the physical changes (sometimes called *somatic* or *vegetative* symptoms) (Bech, 2009; Kessler & Wang, 2009), along with the behavioral and emotional "shutdown," as reflected by low behavioral activation (Dimidjian, Barrera, Martell, Muñoz, & Lewinsohn, 2011). *Anhedonia* (loss of energy and inability to engage in pleasurable activities or have any "fun") is more characteristic of these severe episodes of depression than are, for example, reports of sadness or distress (Pizzagalli, 2014). Nor does the tendency to cry, which occurs equally in depressed and non-depressed individuals (mostly women in both cases) reflect severity—or even the presence of a depressive episode (Vingerhoets, Rottenberg, Cevaal, & Nelson, 2007). This anhedonia reflects that these episodes represent a state of low positive affect and not just high negative affect (Brown & Barlow, 2009). The duration of a major depressive episode, if untreated, is approximately four to nine months (Hasin, Goodwin, Stinson, & Grant, 2005; Kessler & Wang, 2009).

The second fundamental state in mood disorders is abnormally exaggerated elation, joy, or euphoria. In **mania**, individuals find extreme pleasure in every activity; some patients compare their daily experience of mania with a continuous sexual orgasm. They become extraordinarily active (hyperactive), require little sleep, and may develop grandiose plans, believing they can accomplish anything they desire. *DSM-5* highlights this feature by adding "persistently increased goal-directed activity or energy" to the criteria (American Psychiatric Association, 2013). Speech

is typically rapid and may become incoherent, because the individual is attempting to express so many exciting ideas at once; this feature is typically referred to as *flight of ideas*.

DSM-5 also defines a **hypomanic episode**, a less severe version of a manic episode that does not cause marked impairment in social or occupational functioning and need last only four days rather than a full week. (*Hypo* means "below"; thus the episode is below the level of a manic episode.) A hypomanic episode is not in itself necessarily problematic, but its presence does contribute to the definition of several mood disorders.

The Structure of Mood Disorders

Individuals who experience either depression or mania are said to suffer from a *unipolar mood disorder*, because their mood remains at one "pole" of the usual depression–mania continuum. Mania by itself (unipolar mania) probably does occur (Angst & Grobler, 2015; Baek, Eisner, & Nierenberg, 2014 but seems to be rare, because most people with a unipolar mood disorder eventually develop depression. On the

. . . .

mood disorders One of a group of disorders involving severe and enduring disturbances in emotionality ranging from elation to severe depression.

major depressive episode Most common and severe experience of depression, including feelings of worthlessness, disturbances in bodily activities such as sleep, loss of interest, and inability to experience pleasure, persisting at least 2 weeks.

mania Period of abnormally excessive elation or euphoria associated with some **mood disorders**.

hypomanic episode Less severe and less disruptive version of a **manic episode** that is one of the criteria for several **mood disorders**.

other hand, manic episodes alone may be somewhat more frequent in adolescents (Merikangas *et al.*, 2012). Someone who alternates between depression and mania is said to have a *bipolar mood disorder* traveling from one "pole" of the depression–elation continuum to the other and back again. This label is somewhat misleading, however, because depression and elation may not be at exactly opposite ends of the same mood state; although related, they are often relatively independent. An individual can experience manic symptoms but feel somewhat depressed or anxious at the same time, or be depressed with a few symptoms of mania. This episode is characterized as having "**mixed features**" (Angst, 2009; Angst *et al.*, 2011; Swann *et al.*, 2013). In *DSM-5,* the term "mixed features" requires specifying whether a predominantly manic or predominantly depressive episode is present and then noting if enough symptoms of the opposite polarity are present to meet the mixed features criteria.

Depressive Disorders

DSM-5 describes several types of depressive disorders. These disorders differ from one another in the frequency and severity with which depressive symptoms occur and the course of the symptoms (chronic—meaning almost continuous—or non-chronic). In fact, a strong body of evidence indicates that the two factors that most importantly describe mood disorders are severity and chronicity (Klein, 2010, and see below).

Clinical Descriptions

The most easily recognized mood disorder is **major depressive disorder**, defined by the presence of depression and the absence of manic, or hypomanic episodes, before or during the disorder. An occurrence of just one isolated depressive episode in a lifetime is now known to be relatively rare (Eaton *et al.*, 2008; Kessler & Wang, 2009).

If two or more major depressive episodes occurred and were separated by at least two months during which the individual was not depressed, the major depressive disorder is noted as being **recurrent**. Recurrence is important in predicting the future course of the disorder, as well as in choosing appropriate treatments. From 35% to 85% of people with single-episode occurrences of major depressive disorder later experience a second episode (Angst, 2009; Souery *et al.*, 2012), based on follow-ups as long as 23 years (Eaton *et al.*, 2008). In the first year following an episode, the risk of recurrence is 20%, but it rises as high as 40% in the second year (Boland & Keller, 2009). Because of this finding and others reviewed later, clinical scientists have recently concluded that unipolar depression is often a chronic condition that waxes and wanes over time but seldom disappears (Judd, 2012). The median lifetime number

of major depressive episodes is four to seven; in one large sample, 25% experienced six or more episodes (Angst, 2009; Kessler & Wang, 2009). The median duration of recurrent major depressive episodes is four to five months (Boland & Keller, 2009; Kessler *et al.*, 2003), somewhat shorter than the average length of the first episode.

On the basis of these criteria, how would you diagnose Katie? Katie suffered from a severely depressed mood, feelings of worthlessness, difficulty concentrating, recurrent thoughts of death, sleep difficulties, and loss of energy. She clearly met the criteria for major depressive disorder, recurrent. Katie's depressive episodes were quite severe when they occurred, but she tended to cycle in and out of them.

Persistent depressive disorder (dysthymia) shares many of the symptoms of major depressive disorder but differs in its course. There may be fewer symptoms, but depression remains relatively unchanged over long periods, sometimes 20 or 30 years or more (Cristancho, Kocsis, & Thase, 2012; Murphy & Byrne, 2012).

Persistent depressive disorder is defined as depressed mood that continues at least two years, during which the patient cannot be symptom free for more than two months at a time even though they may not experience all of the symptoms of a major depressive episode. It identifies patients who were formerly diagnosed with dysthymic disorder and other depressive disorders (Rhebergen & Graham, 2014). Persistent depressive disorder differs from a major depressive disorder in the number of symptoms required, but mostly it is in the chronicity. It is considered more severe, since patients with persistent depression present with higher rates of comorbidity with other mental disorders, are less responsive to treatment, and show a slower rate of improvement over time. About 20% of patients with a major depressive episode report chronicity of this episode for at least two years, thereby meeting criteria for persistent depressive disorder (Klein, 2010).

Also, 22% of people suffering from persistent depression with fewer symptoms (specified as "with pure dysthymic syndrome," see below) eventually experienced a major depressive episode (Klein *et al.*, 2006). These individuals who suffer from both major depressive episodes and persistent depression with fewer symptoms are said to have **double depression**. Typically, a few depressive symptoms develop first, perhaps at an early age, and then one or more major depressive episodes occur later only to revert to the underlying pattern of depression once the major depressive episode has run its course (Boland & Keller, 2009; Klein *et al.*, 2006). Identifying this pattern is important because it is associated with more severe psychopathology and a problematic future course (Boland & Keller, 2009; Rubio, Markowitz, Alegria, Perez-Fuentes, Liu, Lin, & Blanco, 2011). For example, Klein *et al.* (2006) found that the relapse rate of depression among people meeting criteria for *DSM-IV* dysthymia was 71.4%. Consider the case of Jack.

Jack... • *A Life Kept Down*

Jack was a 49-year-old divorced white man who lived at his mother's home with his 10-year-old son. He complained of chronic depression, saying he finally realized he needed help. Jack reported that he had been a pessimist and a worrier for much of his adult life. He consistently felt kind of down and depressed and did not have much fun. He had difficulty making decisions, was generally pessimistic about the future, and thought little of himself. During the past 20 years, the longest period he could remember in which his mood was "normal" or less depressed lasted only four or five days.

About five years before coming to the clinic, Jack had experienced a bout of depression worse than anything he had previously known. His self-esteem went from low to non-existent. From indecisiveness, he became unable to decide anything. He was exhausted all the time and felt as if lead had filled his arms and legs, making it difficult even to move. He became unable to complete projects or to meet deadlines. Seeing no hope, he began to consider suicide. After tolerating a listless performance for years from someone they had expected to rise through the ranks, Jack's employers finally fired him.

After about six months, the major depressive episode resolved and Jack returned to his chronic but milder state of depression. He could get out of bed and accomplish some things, although he still doubted his own abilities. He was unable to obtain another job, however. After several years of waiting for something to turn up, he realized he was unable to solve his own problems and that without help his depression would continue. After a thorough assessment, we determined that Jack suffered from a classic case of double depression.

Onset and Duration

Generally the risk for developing major depression is fairly low until the early teens, when it begins to rise in a steady (linear) fashion (Rohde, Lewinsohn, Klein, Seeley, & Gau, 2013). A longitudinal study with 2,320 individuals from the Baltimore Longitudinal Study of Aging spanning from age 19 to 95 showed that symptoms of depression followed a U-shaped pattern, such that symptoms of depression were highest in young adults, decreased across middle adulthood, and then increased again in older age, with older people also experiencing an increase in distress associated with these symptoms (Sutin *et al.*,

2013). Another alarming finding is that the incidence of depression and consequent suicide seem to be steadily increasing. Kessler and colleagues (2003) compared four age groups and found that fully 25% of people 18 to 29 years had already experienced major depression, a rate far higher than the rate for older groups when they were that age.

As we noted previously, the length of depressive episodes is variable, with some lasting as little as two weeks; in more severe cases, an episode might last for several years, with the typical duration of the first episode being two to nine months if untreated (Boland & Keller, 2009; Rohde *et al.*, 2013). Although nine months is a long time to suffer with a severe depressive episode, evidence indicates that, even in the most severe cases, the probability of remission of the episode within one year approaches 90% (Kessler & Wang, 2009). In those severe cases in which the episode lasts five years or longer, 38% can be expected to eventually recover (Mueller *et al.*, 1996). Occasionally, however, episodes may not entirely clear up, leaving some residual symptoms. In this case, the likelihood of a subsequent episode with another incomplete recovery is much higher (Boland & Keller, 2009; Judd, 2012). Awareness of this increased likelihood is important to treatment planning, because treatment should be continued much longer in these cases.

Investigators have found a lower (0.07%) prevalence of persistent mild depressive symptoms in children compared with adults (3% to 6%) (Klein, Schwartz, Rose, & Leader, 2000), but symptoms tend to be stable throughout childhood (Garber, Gallerani, & Frankel, 2009). Kovacs, Akiskal, Gatsonis, and Parrone (1994) found that 76% of a sample of children with persistent mild depressive symptoms later developed major depressive disorder.

Persistent depressive disorder may last 20 to 30 years or more, although studies have reported a median duration of approximately five years in adults (Klein *et al.*, 2006) and four years in children (Kovacs *et al.*, 1994). Klein and colleagues (2006), in the study mentioned earlier, conducted a 10-year follow-up of 97 adults with

mixed features Condition in which the individual experiences both elation and depression or **anxiety** at the same time. Also known as *dysphoric manic episode or mixed manic episode.*

major depressive disorder **Mood disorder** involving one (*single episode*) or more (separated by at least 2 months without depression, *recurrent*)

recurrent Repeatedly occurring.

persistent depressive disorder (dysthymia) **Mood disorder** involving persistently depressed **mood**, with low self-esteem, **withdrawal**, pessimism, or despair, present for at least 2 years, with no absence of symptoms for more than 2 months.

double depression Severe **mood disorder** typified by **major depressive episodes** superimposed over a background of **dysthymic disorder**.

DSM-IV dysthymia (now known as persistent depressive disorder, which is characterized by fewer or more mild symptoms of depression) and found that 74% had recovered at some point but 71% of those had relapsed. The whole sample of 97 patients spent approximately 60% of the 10-year follow-up period meeting full criteria for a mood disorder. This compares with 21% of a group of patients with major depressive disorder also followed for 10 years. Even worse, patients with persistent depressive disorder with less severe depressive symptoms (dysthymia) were more likely to attempt suicide than a comparison group with (non-persistent) episodes of major depressive disorder during a five-year period. As noted above, it is relatively common for major depressive episodes and dysthymia (now persistent depressive disorder) to co-occur (double depression) (Boland & Keller, 2009; McCullough *et al.*, 2000).

From Grief to Depression

If someone you love has died, you may have experienced a number of depressive symptoms as well as anxiety, emotional numbness, and denial (Shear, 2012; Simon, 2012). Usually the natural grieving process has peaked within the first six months, although some people grieve for a year or longer (Currier, Neimeyer, & Berman, 2008; Maciejewski *et al.*, 2007). The acute grief most of us would feel eventually evolves into what is called **integrated grief**, in which the finality of death and its consequences are acknowledged and the individual adjusts to the loss. New, bittersweet, but mostly positive memories of the deceased person that are no longer dominating or interfering with functioning are then incorporated into memory (Shear *et al.*, 2011).

Integrated grief often recurs at significant anniversaries, such as the birthday of the loved one, holidays, and other meaningful occasions, including the anniversary of the death. This is all a very normal and positive reaction. In fact, mental health professionals are concerned when someone does not grieve after a death, because grieving is our natural way of confronting and handling loss. When grief lasts beyond the typical time, mental health professionals again become concerned (Neimeyer & Currier, 2009). After six months to a year or so, the chance of recovering from severe grief without treatment is considerably reduced, and for approximately 7% of bereaved individuals, a normal process becomes a disorder (Kersting, Brahler, Glaesmer, & Wagner, 2011; Shear *et al.*, 2011). At this stage, suicidal thoughts increase substantially and focus mostly on joining the beloved deceased (Stroebe, Stroebe, & Abakoumkin, 2005). The ability to imagine events in the future is generally impaired, since it is difficult to think of a future without the deceased (MacCallum & Bryant, 2011; Robinaugh, & McNally, 2013). Individuals also have difficulty regulating their own emotions, which tend to become rigid and

▲ Queen Victoria remained in such deep mourning for her husband, Prince Albert, that she was unable to perform as monarch for several years after his death.

Bob Thomas/Popperfoto/Getty Images

inflexible (Gupta & Bonanno, 2011). Many of the psychological and social factors related to mood disorders in general, including a history of past depressive episodes, also predict the development of what is called the syndrome of **complicated grief**, although this reaction can develop without a preexisting depressed state (Bonanno, Wortman, & Nesse, 2004).

Features of normal grief, integrated grief, and complicated grief are listed in Table 6.1 (Shear *et al.*, 2011). Indeed, some have proposed that this unique cluster of symptoms, combined with other differences, should be sufficient to make complicated grief a separate diagnostic category distinct from depression (Bonanno, 2006; Shear *et al.*, 2011). For example, the very strong yearning in complicated grief seems to be associated with the activation of the dopamine neurotransmitter system; this is in contrast to major depressive disorder, in which activation is reduced in this system (O'Connor *et al.*, 2008). Also, brain-imaging

TABLE 6.1 | Normal and Complicated Grief

Common symptoms of acute grief that are within normal limits within the first 6–12 months after:

- Recurrent, strong feelings of yearning, wanting very much to be reunited with the person who died; possibly even a wish to die in order to be with deceased loved one
- Pangs of deep sadness or remorse, episodes of crying or sobbing, typically interspersed with periods of respite and even positive emotions
- Steady stream of thoughts or images of deceased, may be vivid or even entail hallucinatory experiences of seeing or hearing deceased person
- Struggle to accept the reality of the death, wishing to protest against it; there may be some feelings of bitterness or anger about the death
- Somatic distress, e.g., uncontrollable sighing, digestive symptoms, loss of appetite, dry mouth, feelings of hollowness, sleep disturbance, fatigue, exhaustion or weakness, restlessness, aimless activity, difficulty initiating or maintaining organized activities, and altered sensorium
- Feeling disconnected from the world or other people, indifferent, not interested, or irritable with others

Symptoms of integrated grief that are within normal limits:

- Sense of having adjusted to the loss
- Interest and sense of purpose, ability to function, and capacity for joy and satisfaction are restored
- Feelings of emotional loneliness may persist
- Thoughts and memories of the deceased person accessible and bittersweet but no longer dominate the mind
- Occasional hallucinatory experiences of the deceased may occur
- Surges of grief in response to calendar days or other periodic reminders of the loss may occur

Complicated grief:

- Persistent intense symptoms of acute grief
- The presence of thoughts, feelings, or behaviors reflecting excessive or distracting concerns about the circumstances or consequences of the death

SOURCE: Shear, M. K., Simon, N., Wall, M., Zisook, S., Neimeyer, R., Duan, N., & Keshaviah, A. (2011). Complicated grief and related bereavement issues for *DSM-5*. *Depression and Anxiety, 28*, 103–117.

studies indicate that areas of the brain associated with close relationships and attachment are active in grieving people, in addition to areas of the brain associated with more general emotional responding (Gündel, O'Connor, Littrell, Fort, & Lane, 2003). *Persistent Complex Bereavement Disorder* is now included as a diagnosis requiring further study in section III of *DSM-5*.

Other Depressive Disorders

Premenstrual dysphoric disorder (PMDD) and **disruptive mood dysregulation disorder**, both depressive disorders, were added to *DSM-5*.

Premenstrual Dysphoric Disorder (PMDD)

The history of the development of PMDD over the past several decades as a diagnosis was described in some detail in Chapter 3. Basically clinicians identified a small group of women, from 2% to 5%, who suffered from severe and sometimes incapacitating emotional reactions during the premenstrual period (Epperson *et al.*, 2012). But strong objections to making this condition an official diagnosis

were based on concerns that women who were experiencing a very normal monthly physiological cycle, as part of being female, would now be classified as having a disorder, which would be very stigmatizing. It has now been clearly established that this small group of women differs in a number of ways from the 20% to 40% of women who experience uncomfortable premenstrual symptoms (PMS) that, nevertheless, are not associated with impairment of functioning. Criteria defining PMDD are presented in the nearby DSM Disorder Criteria Summary. A combination

integrated grief Grief that evolves from acute grief into a condition in which the individual accepts the finality of a death and adjusts to the loss.

complicated grief Grief characterized by debilitating feelings of loss and emotions so painful that a person has trouble resuming a normal life; designated for further study as a disorder by *DSM-5*.

premenstrual dysphoric disorder Clinically significant emotional problems that can occur during the premenstrual phase of the reproductive cycle of a woman.

disruptive mood dysregulation disorder Condition in which a child has chronic negative moods such as anger and irritability without any accompanying mania.

Features of premenstrual dysphoric disorder include the following:

- In the majority of menstrual cycles, at least five symptoms must be present in the final week before the onset of menses, start to improve within a few days after the onset of menses, and become minimal or absent in the week post-menses.

- One (or more) of the following symptoms must be present: (1) marked affective lability (e.g., mood swings) (2) marked irritability or anger (3) marked depressed mood (4) marked anxiety and tension.

- One (or more) of the following symptoms must additionally be present, to reach a total of five symptoms when combined with symptoms above: (1) decreased interest in usual activities (2) difficulty in concentration (3) lethargy, fatigability, lack of energy (4) marked change in appetite; overeating; or specific food cravings (5) hypersomnia or insomnia (5) a sense of being overwhelmed or out of control (7) physical symptoms such as breast tenderness or swelling.

- Clinically significant distress or interference with work, school, usual social activities, or relationships.

- Symptoms are not attributable to the effects of a substance (e.g., drug abuse) or another medical condition.

From American Psychiatric Association. (2013). *Diagnostic and statistical manual of mental disorders* (5th ed.). Washington, DC.

of physical symptoms, severe mood swings, and anxiety are associated with incapacitation during this period of time (Hartlage, Freels, Gotman, & Yonkers, 2012). All of the evidence indicates that PMDD is best considered a disorder of mood as opposed to a physical disorder (such as an endocrine disorder), and, as pointed out in Chapter 3, the creation of this diagnostic category should greatly assist the thousands of women suffering from this disorder to receive the treatment they need to relieve their suffering and improve their functioning.

Disruptive Mood Dysregulation Disorder

Children and adolescents are being diagnosed with bipolar disorder (which we discuss next) at greatly increasing rates over the past several years. In fact, from 1995 to 2005, the diagnosis of bipolar disorder in children increased 40-fold overall and has quadrupled in U.S. community hospitals (up to 40%) (Leibenluft & Rich, 2008; Moreno *et al.*, 2007). Why the increase? Many clinicians are now using much broader diagnostic criteria that would not correspond to current definitions of bipolar I or bipolar II disorder, but rather fall under the relatively vague category of bipolar

disorder not otherwise specified (NOS) and include children with chronic irritability, anger, aggression, hyperarousal, and frequent temper tantrums that are not limited to an occasional episode.

But the most important observation is that these children show no evidence of periods of elevated mood (mania), which has been a requirement for a diagnosis of bipolar disorder (Liebenluft, 2011). Additional research demonstrated that these children with chronic and severe irritability and difficulty regulating their emotions resulting in frequent temper tantrums are at increased risk for additional depressive and anxiety disorders rather than manic episodes and that there is no evidence of excessive rates of bipolar disorder in their families, which one would expect if this condition were truly bipolar disorder. It was also recognized that this severe irritability is more common than bipolar disorder but has not been well studied (Brotman *et al.*, 2006). This irritability is associated with substantial suffering in the children themselves, reflecting as it does chronically high rates of negative affect and marked disruption of family life. Though these broader definitions of symptoms do display some similarities with more classic bipolar disorder symptoms (Biederman *et al.*, 2005; Biederman *et al.*, 2000), the danger is that these children are being misdiagnosed when they might better meet criteria for more classic diagnostic categories, such as attention-deficit/hyperactivity disorder (ADHD) or conduct disorder (see Chapter 13). In that case, the very potent drug treatments for bipolar disorder with substantial side effects would pose more risks for these children than they would benefits. But these cases also differ from more typical conduct or ADHD conditions as well, since it is the intense negative affect that seems to be driving the irritability and marked inability to regulate mood.

In view of the distinctive features of this condition, it seemed important to better describe these children up to 18 years of age as suffering from a diagnosis termed **disruptive mood dysregulation disorder** rather than have them continue to be mistakenly diagnosed with bipolar disorder or perhaps conduct disorder (Roy, Lopes, & Klein, 2014). Criteria for this new disorder are presented in the DSM Disorder Criteria Summary below. In one case seen at our clinic, a nine-year-old girl we will call Betsy was brought in by her father for evaluation for severe anxiety. The father described a situation in which Betsy, although a very bright child who had done well in school, was continually irritable and increasingly unable to get along at home, engaging in intense arguments at the slightest provocation. Her mood would then deteriorate into a full-blown aggressive temper tantrum and she would run to her room and on occasion begin throwing things. She began refusing to eat meals with the family, since bitter arguments would often arise and it just became easier to allow her to eat in her

Features of disruptive mood dysregulation disorder include the following:

- Severe recurrent (three or more times per week present for 12 or more months) temper outburst manifested verbally and/or behaviorally that are grossly out of proportion in intensity or duration to the situation or provocation and are inconsistent with developmental level.

- The mood between temper outbursts is persistently irritable or angry most of the day, nearly every day, and is observable by others in at least two of three settings (i.e., at home, at school) and is severe in at least one of these.

- The diagnosis should not be made for the first time before age six years or after age 18 years.

- There has never been a distinct period lasting more than one day during which the full symptom criteria, except duration, for a manic or hypomanic episode have been met.

- The symptoms are not attributable to the physiological effects of a substance or to another medical or neurological condition.

From American Psychiatric Association. (2013). *Diagnostic and statistical manual of mental disorders* (5th ed.). Washington, DC.

room. Since nothing else seemed to work to calm her down, her father resorted to something he used to do when she was a baby: take her for a long ride in the family car. After a while, Betsy would begin to relax but during one long ride turned to her father and said, "Daddy, please help me feel better, because if I keep feeling like this I just want to die."

Adults with a history of disruptive mood dysregulation disorder are at increased risk for developing mood and anxiety disorders as well as many other adverse health outcomes (Copeland, Shanahan, Egger, Angold, & Costello, 2014). Therefore, a very important objective for the immediate future will be developing and evaluating treatments for this difficult condition, both psychological and drug. For example, it is very possible that new psychological treatments under development for severe emotional dysregulation in children may be useful with this condition (Ehrenreich, Goldstein, Wright, & Barlow, 2009).

Bipolar Disorders

The key identifying feature of bipolar disorders is the tendency of manic episodes to alternate with major depressive episodes in an unending roller-coaster ride from the peaks of elation to the depths of despair. Beyond that, bipolar disorders are parallel in many ways to depressive disorders. For example, a manic episode might occur only once or repeatedly. Consider the case of Jane.

Jane... • *Funny, Smart, and Desperate*

Jane was the wife of a well-known surgeon and the loving mother of three children. She was nearly 50; her older children had moved out; her youngest son, 16-year-old Mike, was having academic difficulties in school and seemed anxious. Jane brought Mike to the clinic to find out why he was having problems.

As they entered the office, I observed that Jane was well dressed, vivacious, and personable; she had a bounce to her step. She began talking about her successful family before she and Mike even reached their seats. Mike, by contrast, was quiet and reserved. He seemed resigned and perhaps relieved that he would have to say little during the session. By the time Jane sat down, she had mentioned the personal virtues and material achievement of her husband, and the brilliance and beauty of one of her older children, and she was proceeding to describe the second child. But before she finished, she noticed a book on anxiety disorders and, having read voraciously on the subject, began a litany of various anxiety-related problems that might be troubling Mike.

In the meantime, Mike sat in the corner with a small smile on his lips that seemed to be masking considerable distress and uncertainty over what his mother might do next. It became clear as the interview progressed that Mike suffered from obsessive-compulsive disorder, which disturbed his concentration both in and out of school. He was failing all his courses.

It also became clear that Jane herself was in the midst of a hypomanic episode, evident in her unbridled enthusiasm, grandiose perceptions, "uninterruptable" speech, and report that she needed little sleep these days. She was also easily distracted, as when she quickly switched from describing her children to the book on the table. When asked about her own psychological state, Jane readily admitted that she was a "manic depressive" (the old name for bipolar disorder) and that she alternated rather rapidly between feeling on top of the world and feeling depressed; she was taking

disruptive mood dysregulation disorder Condition in which a child has chronic negative moods such as anger and irritability without any accompanying mania.

bipolar II disorder Alternation of **major depressive episodes** with **hypomanic episodes** (not full **manic episodes**).

bipolar I disorder Alternation of **major depressive episodes** with full **manic episodes**.

medication for her condition. I immediately wondered if Mike's obsessions had anything to do with his mother's condition.

Mike was treated intensively for his obsessions and compulsions but made little progress. He said that life at home was difficult when his mother was depressed. She sometimes went to bed and stayed there for three weeks. During this time, she seemed to be in a depressive stupor, essentially unable to move for days. It was up to the children to care for themselves and their mother, whom they fed by hand. Because the older children had now left home, much of the burden had fallen on Mike. Jane's profound depressive episodes would remit after about three weeks, and she would immediately enter a hypomanic episode that might last several months or more. During hypomania, Jane was mostly funny, entertaining, and a delight to be with—if you could get a word in edgewise. Consultation with her therapist, an expert in the area, revealed that he had prescribed a number of medications but was so far unable to bring her mood swings under control.

DSM 5 DISORDER CRITERIA SUMMARY
Bipolar II Disorder

Features of bipolar II disorder include the following:

- Presence (or history) of one or more major depressive episodes
- Presence (or history) of at least one hypomanic episode
- No history of a full manic episode
- Mood symptoms are not better accounted for by another disorder
- Clinically significant distress or impairment of functioning

From American Psychiatric Association. (2013). *Diagnostic and statistical manual of mental disorders* (5th ed.). Washington, DC.

Jane suffered from **bipolar II disorder**, in which major depressive episodes alternate with hypomanic episodes rather than full manic episodes. As we noted earlier, hypomanic episodes are less severe. Although she was noticeably "up," Jane functioned pretty well while in this mood state. The criteria for **bipolar I disorder** are the same, except the individual experiences a full manic episode. As in the criteria set for major depressive disorder, for the manic episodes to be considered separate, there must be a symptom-free period of at least two months between them. Otherwise, one episode is seen as a continuation of the last.

The case of Billy illustrates a full manic episode. This individual was first encountered when he was admitted to a hospital.

Billy... • *The World's Best at Everything*

Before Billy reached the ward, you could hear him laughing and carrying on in a deep voice; it sounded as if he was having a wonderful time. As the nurse brought Billy down the hall to introduce him to the staff, he spied the Ping-Pong table. Loudly, he exclaimed, "Ping-Pong! I love Ping-Pong! I have only played twice, but that is what I am going to do while I am here; I am going to become the world's greatest Ping-Pong player! And that table is gorgeous! I am going to start work on that table immediately and make it the finest Ping-Pong table in the world. I am going to sand it down, take it apart, and rebuild it until it gleams and every angle is perfect!" Billy soon went on to something else that absorbed his attention.

The previous week, Billy had emptied his bank account, taken his credit cards and those of his elderly parents with whom he was living, and bought every piece of fancy stereo equipment he could find. He thought that he would set up the best sound studio in the city and make millions of dollars by renting it to people who would come from far and wide. This episode had precipitated his admission to the hospital.

During manic or hypomanic phases, patients often deny they have a problem, which was characteristic of Billy. Even after spending inordinate amounts of money or making foolish business decisions, these individuals, particularly if they are in the midst of a full manic episode, are so wrapped up in their enthusiasm and expansiveness that their behavior seems reasonable to them. The high during a manic state is so pleasurable that people may stop taking their medication during periods of distress or discouragement in an attempt to bring on a manic state again; this is a serious challenge to professionals.

Returning to the case of Jane, we continued to treat Jane's son Mike for several months. We made little progress before the school year ended. Because Mike was doing so poorly, the school administrators informed his parents that he would not be accepted back the next year. Mike and his parents wisely decided it might be a good idea if he got away from the house and did something different for a while, and he began working and living at a ski and tennis resort. Several months later, his father called to tell us that Mike's obsessions and compulsions had completely lifted since he'd been away from home. The father thought Mike should continue living at the resort, where he had entered school and was doing better academically. He now agreed with our previous assessment that Mike's condition might be related to his relationship with his mother. Several years later, we heard that Jane, in a depressive stupor, had killed herself, an all-too-tragic outcome in bipolar disorder.

DISORDER CRITERIA SUMMARY
Cyclothymic Disorder

Features of cyclothymic disorder include the following:

- For at least two years, numerous periods with hypomanic symptoms and numerous periods with depressive symptoms that do not meet the criteria for a major depressive episode.

- Since onset, the person has not been without the symptoms for more than two months at a time.

- No major depressive episode, manic episode, or hypomanic episode has been present during the first two years of the disturbance.

- Mood symptoms are not better accounted for by another disorder, the physiological effects of a substance, or a general medical condition.

- Clinically significant distress or impairment of functioning.

From American Psychiatric Association. (2013). *Diagnostic and statistical manual of mental disorders* (5th ed.). Washington, DC.

A milder but more chronic version of bipolar disorder is called **cyclothymic disorder** (Akiskal, 2009; Parker, McCraw, & Fletcher, 2012). Cyclothymic disorder is a chronic alternation of mood elevation and depression that does not reach the severity of manic or major depressive episodes. Individuals with cyclothymic disorder tend to be in one mood state or the other for years with relatively few periods of neutral (or euthymic) mood. This pattern must last for at least two years (one year for children and adolescents) to meet criteria for the disorder. Individuals with cyclothymic disorder alternate between the kinds of mild depressive symptoms Jack experienced during his dysthymic states and the sorts of hypomanic episodes Jane experienced. In neither case was the behavior severe enough to require hospitalization or immediate intervention. Much of the time, such individuals are just considered moody. However, the chronically fluctuating mood states are, by definition, substantial enough to interfere with functioning. Furthermore, people with cyclothymia should be treated because of their increased risk to develop the more severe bipolar I or bipolar II disorder (Goodwin & Jamison, 2007; Otto & Applebaum, 2011).

Onset and Duration

The average age of onset for bipolar I disorder is from 15 to 18 and for bipolar II disorder from 19 to 22, although cases of both can begin in childhood (Judd *et al.*, 2003; Merikangas & Pato, 2009). This is somewhat younger than the average age of onset for major depressive disorder, and bipolar disorders begin more acutely; that is, they develop more suddenly (Angst & Sellaro, 2000; Johnson *et al.*, 2009). About one-third of the cases of bipolar disorder begin in adolescence, and the onset is often preceded by minor oscillations in mood or mild cyclothymic mood swings (Goodwin & Jamison, 2007; Merikangas *et al.*, 2007). Between

10% and 25% of people with bipolar II disorder will progress to full bipolar I disorder (Birmaher *et al.*, 2009; Coryell *et al.*, 1995).

Though unipolar and bipolar disorder have been thought distinct disorders some studies suggest they may be on a continuum (called a "spectrum" in psychopathology) (Johnson *et al.*, 2009; Merikangas *et al.*, 2011).

It is relatively rare for someone to develop bipolar disorder after the age of 40. Once it does appear, the course is chronic; that is, mania and depression alternate indefinitely. Therapy usually involves managing the disorder with ongoing drug regimens that prevent recurrence of episodes. Suicide is an all-too-common consequence of bipolar disorder, almost always occurring during depressive episodes, as it did in the case of Jane (Angst, 2009; Valtonen *et al.*, 2007). A large Swedish study showed that, on average, people with bipolar disorder died eight to nine years earlier of various medical diseases and suicide compared to the general population (Crump, Sundquist, Winkleby, & Sundquist, 2013). However, when patients receive treatment early, the mortality rate was comparable to that of the general population. Bipolar disorder is associated with a high risk of suicide attempts and suicide death, the latter being associated with the male sex and having a first-degree relative who committed suicide (Schaffer *et al.*, 2015). The risk of suicide is not limited to Western countries but occurs in countries around the world (Merikangas *et al.*, 2011).

In typical cases, cyclothymia is chronic and lifelong. In about one-third to one-half of patients, cyclothymic mood swings develop into full-blown bipolar disorder (Kochman *et al.*, 2005; Parker *et al.*, 2012). In one sample of cyclothymic patients, 60% were female, and the age of onset was often during the teenage years or before, with some data suggesting the most common age of onset to be 12 to 14 years (Goodwin & Jamison, 2007). The disorder is often not recognized, and sufferers are thought to be highlystrung, explosive, moody, or hyperactive (Akiskal, 2009; Goodwin & Jamison, 2007). One subtype of cyclothymia is based on the predominance of mild depressive symptoms, one on the predominance of hypomanic symptoms, and another on an equal distribution of both.

▲ In April 2013, Catherine Zeta-Jones again sought help for bipolar II disorder, a condition for which she has received years of treatment.

s_bukley/Shutterstock.com

cyclothymic disorder Chronic (at least 2 years) **mood disorder** characterized by alternating **mood** elevation and depression levels that are not as severe as **manic** or **major depressive episodes**.

Match each description or case by choosing its corresponding disorder: (a) mania, (b) double depression, (c) persistent depressive disorder, (d) major depressive episode, and (e) bipolar I disorder:

1. Last week, as he does about every three months, Ryan went out with his friends, buying rounds of drinks, socializing until early morning, and feeling on top of the world. Today Ryan will not even get out of bed to go to work, see his friends, or even turn on the lights. _____

2. Feeling certain he would win the lottery, Charles went on an all-night shopping spree, maxing out all his credit cards without a worry. We know he's done this several times, feeling abnormally extreme elation, joy, and euphoria. _____

3. Ayana has had some mood disorder problems in the past, although some days she's better than others. Many days it seems like she has fallen into a rut. Although she manages to get by, she has trouble making decisions because she doesn't trust herself. _____

4. For the past few weeks, Jennifer has been sleeping a lot. She feels worthless, can't get up the energy to leave the house, and has lost a lot of weight. Her problem is the most common and extreme mood disorder. _____

5. Eusebio is always down and a bit blue, but occasionally he becomes so depressed that nothing pleases him. _____

Prevalence of Mood Disorders

▶ How does the prevalence of mood disorders vary across a life span?

Several large epidemiological studies estimating the prevalence of mood disorders have been carried out in recent years (Kessler & Bromet, 2013; Merikangas & Pato, 2009). The best estimates of the worldwide prevalence of mood disorders suggest that approximately 16% of the population experience major depressive disorder over a lifetime and approximately 6% have experienced a major depressive disorder in the last year (Hasin et al., 2005; Kessler, Chiu, Demler, & Walters, 2005). The prevalence rates for the combination of persistent depressive disorder and chronic major depression are approximately 3.5%, both for lifetime and in the past year (Kessler & Wang, 2009). And for bipolar disorder, the estimates are 1% lifetime prevalence and 0.8% during the past year (Merikangas & Pato, 2009; Merikangas et al., 2011). The similarity of the lifetime and past-year rates for persistent depressive disorder (dysthymia) and bipolar disorders reflects the fact that these disorders are chronic conditions that last much of one's life.

Studies indicate that women are twice as likely to have mood disorders as men (Kessler, 2006; Kessler & Wang, 2009), but the imbalance in prevalence between males and females is accounted for solely by major depressive disorder and persistent depressive disorder (dysthymia), because bipolar disorders are distributed approximately equally across gender (Merikangas & Pato, 2009). Although equally prevalent, there are some sex-based differences in bipolar disorder. As noted above, women are more likely than men to experience rapid cycling, but also to be anxious, and to be in a depressive phase rather than a manic phase (Altshuler et al., 2010).

It is interesting that the prevalence of major depressive disorder and persistent depressive disorder (dysthymia) is significantly lower among blacks than among whites (Hasin et al., 2005), although, again, no differences appear in bipolar disorders. One study of major depressive disorder in a community sample of African Americans found a prevalence of 3.1% during the previous year (Brown, Ahmed, Gary, & Milburn, 1995), and another found a prevalence of 4.52% during the previous year (Hasin et al., 2005), compared with 5.53% among whites. Fair or poor health status was the major predictor of depression in African Americans. Few of these individuals received appropriate treatment, with only 11% coming in contact with a mental health professional (Brown et al., 1995). Native Americans, on the other hand, present with a significantly higher prevalence of depression (Hasin et al., 2005), although difficulties in translating the concept of depression to Native American cultures suggest this finding needs more study (Beals et al., 2005; Kaufmann et al., 2013).

Prevalence in Children, Adolescents, and Older Adults

Estimates on the prevalence of mood disorders in children and adolescents vary widely, although more sophisticated studies are beginning to appear. The general conclusion is that depressive disorders occur less often in prepubertal children than in adults but rise dramatically in adolescence (Kessler *et al.*, 2012; Rohde *et al.*, 2013). Among children ages two to five, rates of major depression are about 1.5% and a bit lower later in childhood (Garber *et al.*, 2009), but as many as 20% to 50% of children experience some depressive symptoms that are not frequent or severe enough to meet diagnostic criteria, though are nevertheless impairing (Kessler, Avenevoli, Ries, & Merikangas, 2001; Rudolph, 2009). Adolescents experience major depressive disorder about as often as adults (Kessler *et al.*, 2012; Rohde *et al.*, 2013). In children, the sex ratio for depressive disorders is approximately 50:50, but this changes dramatically in adolescence. Major depressive disorder in adolescents is largely a female disorder, as it is in adults, with puberty and greater interpersonal stress in adolescent girls than boys seemingly triggering this sex imbalance (Garber, Clarke *et al.*, 2009; Hamilton, Stange, Abramson, & Alloy, 2015). Interestingly, this sex imbalance is not evident for more mild depression.

The overall prevalence of major depressive disorder for individuals over 65 is about half that of the general population (Byers, Yaffe, Covinsky, Friedman, & Bruce, 2010; Fiske, Wetherell, & Gatz, 2009), perhaps because stressful life events that trigger major depressive episodes decrease with age. But milder symptoms that do not meet criteria for major depressive disorder seem to be more common among the elderly (Beekman *et al.*, 2002; Gotlib & Nolan, 2001), and may be associated with illness and infirmity (Alexopoulos, 2005; Delano-Wood & Abeles, 2005).

Bipolar disorder seems to occur at about the same rate (1%) in childhood and adolescence as in adults (Kessler *et al.*, 2012; Merikangas & Pato, 2009). The rates of diagnosis of bipolar disorder in clinics has increased substantially, however, due to greater interest and a controversial tendency described above to broaden the diagnostic criteria in children to include what will now be subsumed under disruptive mood dysregulation disorder. Considering the chronicity and seriousness of mood disorders (Gotlib & Hammen, 2009), the prevalence in all age groups is high indeed, demonstrating a substantial impact not only on the affected individuals and their families but also on society.

Life Span Developmental Influences on Mood Disorders

You might assume that depression requires some experience with life, that an accumulation of negative events or disappointments might create pessimism, which then leads to depression. Like many reasonable assumptions in psychopathology, this one is not uniformly correct. There is some evidence that three-month-old babies can become depressed! Infants of depressed mothers display marked depressive behaviors (sad faces, slow movement, lack of responsiveness) even when interacting

with a non-depressed adult (Garber *et al.*, 2009; Guedeney, 2007). Whether this behavior or temperament is caused by a genetic tendency inherited from the mother, the result of early interaction patterns with a depressed mother or primary caregiver, or a combination is not yet clear.

Most investigators agree that mood disorders are fundamentally similar in children and in adults (Brent & Birmaher, 2009; Garber *et al.*, 2009). Therefore, no "childhood" mood disorders in *DSM-5* are specific to a developmental stage, with the exception of disruptive mood dysregulation disorder, which can be diagnosed only up to 18 years of age. This is unlike the anxiety disorders, in which a number of conditions occur only early in development. It seems clear, however, that the "look" of depression changes with age. For example, children under three years of age might manifest depression by sad facial expressions, irritability, fatigue, fussiness, and tantrums, as well as by problems with eating and sleeping. In the extreme, this could develop into disruptive mood dysregulation disorder. In children between the ages of nine and 12, many of these features would not occur. Also, for pre-school children (six years old and under), Luby and colleagues (2003) report the necessity of setting aside the strict two-week duration requirement for major depression, because it is normal for mood to fluctuate at this young age. However, once depression develops, it cannot be expected that children simply "grow out of it" (Luby, 2012). For example, a recent study by Luby and colleagues (2014) found that preschool depression was a significant and robust predictor for later depression at the ages of six to 13. Preschool depression was also a risk factor for other problems, such as anxiety disorders and ADHD at school age.

As far as mania is concerned, children under the age of nine seem to present with more irritability and emotional swings as compared with classic manic states, particularly irritability (Fields & Fristad, 2009; Leibenluft & Rich, 2008), but it is also important to recognize that irritability alone is insufficient to diagnose mania, because it is associated with many different types of problems in childhood (it is non-specific to mania). "Emotional swing," or oscillating manic states that are less distinct than in adults, may also be characteristic of children, as are brief or rapid-cycling manic episodes lasting only part of a day (Youngstrom, 2009).

▲ Children of depressed mothers may show depressive behavior at less than a year old.

One developmental difference between children and adolescents compared with adults concerns patterns of comorbidity. For example, childhood depression (and mania) is often associated with and sometimes misdiagnosed as ADHD or, more often, conduct disorder in which aggression and even destructive behavior are common (Fields & Fristad, 2009; Garber et al., 2009). Conduct disorder and depression often co-occur in bipolar disorder. But, once again, many of these children might now meet criteria for disruptive mood dysregulation disorder, which would better account for this comorbidity. In any case, successful treatment of the underlying depression (or spontaneous recovery) may resolve the associated ADHD or conduct disorder in these patients.

Whatever the presentation, mood disorders in children and adolescents are serious because of their likely consequences (Garber et al., 2009). Fergusson and Woodward (2002), in a large prospective study, identified 13% of a group of 1,265 adolescents who developed major depressive disorder between 14 and 16 years of age. Later, between ages 16 and 21, this group was significantly at risk for occurrence of major depression, anxiety disorders, nicotine dependence, suicide attempts, and drug and alcohol abuse, as well as educational underachievement and early parenting, compared with adolescents who were not depressed. Fergusson, Horwood, Ridder, and Beautrais (2005) found that extent and severity of depressive symptoms as an adolescent predicted extent of depression and suicidal behaviors as an adult. Clearly, becoming depressed as a child or adolescent is a dangerous, threatening event to be treated immediately or prevented if possible. Fortunately, cognitive behavioral therapy (CBT) can effectively prevent the onset of depressive episodes in at-risk youth (Beardslee et al., 2013).

Age-Based Influences on Older Adults

The problem of depression in the elderly has only been considered fairly recently (Wang & Blazer, 2015; Wittchen, 2012). Some studies estimate that 14% to 42% of nursing home residents may experience major depressive episodes (Djernes, 2006; Fiske et al., 2009). In one large study, depressed patients between 56 and 85 years of age were followed for six years; approximately 80% did not remit but continued to be depressed (or cycled in and out of depression) even if their depressive symptoms were not severe enough to meet diagnostic criteria for a disorder (Beekman et al., 2002). Late-onset depressions are associated with sleep difficulties, illness anxiety disorder (anxiety focused on possibly being sick or injured in some way), and agitation (Baldwin, 2009). It can be difficult to diagnose depression in older adults because elderly people who become physically ill or begin to show signs of dementia might become depressed about it, but the signs of depression or mood disorder would be attributed to the illness or dementia and thus missed (see, for example, Blazer & Hybels, 2009; Delano-Wood & Abeles, 2005). As many as 50% of patients with Alzheimer's disease suffer from comorbid depression, which makes life more difficult for their families (Lyketsos & Olin, 2002; Modrego, 2010).

Anxiety disorders accompany depression in one-third to one-half of elderly patients, particularly generalized anxiety disorder and panic disorder (Fiske et al., 2009; Lenze et al., 2000), and when they do, patients are more severely depressed. One-third will also suffer from comorbid alcohol abuse (Devanand, 2002). Several studies have shown that entering menopause also increases rates of depression among women who have never previously been depressed (Cohen, Soares, Vitonis, Otto, & Harlow, 2006; Freeman, Sammel, Lin, & Nelson, 2006).

Depression can also contribute to physical disease and death in the elderly (Blazer & Hybels, 2009). Being depressed doubles the risk of death in elderly patients who have suffered a heart attack or stroke (Schulz, Drayer, & Rollman, 2002; Whooley & Wong, 2013). Wallace and O'Hara (1992), in a longitudinal study, found that elderly citizens became increasingly depressed over a three-year period. They suggest that this trend is related to increasing illness and reduced social support (Wittchen, 2012). Bruce (2002) confirmed that death of a spouse, caregiving burden for an ill spouse, and loss of independence because of medical illness are among the strongest risk factors for depression in this age group. This vicious cycle is deadly, because suicide rates are higher in older adults than in any other age group (Conwell, Duberstein, & Caine, 2002), although rates have been decreasing lately (Blazer & Hybels, 2009). In contrast, optimism prevents depression after medical illnesses and promotes longevity. For example, Galatzer-Levy and Bonanno (2014) studied more than 2,000 older adults from six years prior to their first heart attack to four years after their first heart attack. People were more likely to die if they became depressed after their first heart attack, as compared with people who did not become depressed. However, optimism measured before the heart attack distinguished all people who became depressed from those who did not become depressed after the first heart attack, suggesting that optimism prospectively predicted depression and thereby also mortality following the first heart attack. Approximately half of the sample in this study was male, and the results were similar in both sexes.

The earlier gender imbalance in depression lessens considerably after the age of 65. In early childhood, boys are more likely to be depressed than girls, but an overwhelming surge of depression in adolescent girls produces an imbalance in the sex ratio that is maintained until old age, when just as many women are depressed but increasing numbers of men are also affected (Fiske et al., 2009). From the perspective of the life span, this is the first time since early childhood that the sex ratio for depression is more closely balanced.

Across Cultures

We noted the strong tendency of anxiety to take somatic (physical) forms in some cultures; instead of talking about fear, panic, or general anxiety, many people describe stomachaches, chest pains or heart distress, and headaches. Much the same tendency exists across cultures for mood disorders (Kim & Lopez, 2014), which is not surprising given the close relationship of anxiety and depression (Kessler & Bromet, 2013). Feelings of weakness or tiredness particularly characterize depression that is accompanied by mental or physical slowing or retardation (Kleinman, 2004; Ryder *et al.*, 2008). Some cultures have their own idioms for depression; for instance, the Hopi, a Native American tribe, say they are "heartbroken" (Manson & Good, 1993), whereas aboriginal men in central Australia who are clearly depressed attribute it to weakness or injury of the spirit (Brown, Scales *et al.*, 2012).

Although somatic symptoms that characterize mood disorders seem roughly equivalent across cultures, it is difficult to compare subjective feelings. The way people think of depression may be influenced by the cultural view of the individual and the role of the individual in society (Kleinman, 2004; Ryder *et al.*, 2008). For example, in societies that focus on the *individual* instead of the *group*, it is common to hear statements such as, "I feel blue" or "I am depressed." In cultures where the individual is tightly integrated into the larger group, however, someone might say, "Our life has lost its meaning," referring to the group in which the individual resides (Manson & Good, 1993).

In specific locations, prevalence of depression can differ dramatically. A structured interview was used by Kinzie, Leung, Boehnlein, and Matsunaga (1992) to determine the percentage of adult members of a Native American village who met criteria for mood disorders. The lifetime prevalence for any mood disorder was 19.4% in men, 36.7% in women, and 28% overall, approximately four times higher than in the general population. Examined by disorder, almost all the increase is accounted for by greatly elevated rates of major depression. Findings in the same village for substance abuse are similar to the results for major depressive disorder (see Chapter 10). Hasin and colleagues (2005) found a somewhat lower overall percentage of 19.17% in a different village, which was still 1.5 times higher than the percentage found in Caucasians, a significant difference. Beals and colleagues (2005), on the other hand, reported a considerably lower prevalence in two tribes they studied, perhaps because of differences in interviewing methods or because conditions and culture can differ greatly from tribe to tribe. Still, appalling social and economic conditions on many reservations fulfill all requirements for chronic major life stress, which is so strongly related to the onset of mood disorders, particularly major depressive disorder.

6.2 Concept CHECK

Identify the following statements as true (T) or false (F):

1. _____ Women are approximately twice as likely as men to be diagnosed with a mood disorder.

2. _____ Depression requires some life experience, indicating that babies and young children cannot experience the disorder.

3. _____ It's often difficult to diagnose depression in the elderly because its symptoms are similar to those of medical ailments or dementia.

4. _____ Somatic symptoms characterizing mood disorders are nearly equivalent across cultures.

Causes of Mood Disorders

▶ What biological, psychological, and sociocultural factors contribute to the development of mood disorders?

Psychopathologists are identifying biological, psychological, and social factors that seem strongly implicated in the etiology of mood disorders, whatever the precipitating factor. An integrative theory of the etiology of mood disorders considers the interaction of biological, psychological, and social dimensions and notes the strong relationship of anxiety and depression. Before describing these interactions, we review evidence pertaining to each contributing factor.

Biological Dimensions

Conducting research to determine the genetic contribution to a particular disorder or class of disorders is complex and difficult to do. But several traditional strategies—such as family studies and twin studies—can help us estimate this contribution.

Familial and Genetic Influences

In *family studies,* we look at the prevalence of a given disorder in the first-degree relatives of an individual known to have the disorder (the *proband*). We have found that, despite wide variability, the rate in relatives of probands with mood disorders is consistently about two to three times greater than in relatives of controls who don't have mood disorders (Lau & Eley, 2010; Levinson, 2009). Increasing severity, recurrence of major depression, and earlier age of onset in the proband is associated with the highest rates of depression in relatives (Kendler, Gatz, Gardner, & Pedersen, 2007; Weissman *et al.*, 2005).

The best evidence that genes have something to do with mood disorders comes from *twin studies,* in which we examine the frequency with which identical twins (with identical genes) have the disorder, compared with fraternal twins, who share only 50% of their genes (as do all first-degree relatives). If a genetic contribution exists, the disorder should be present in identical twins to a much greater extent than in fraternal twins. A number of twin studies suggest that mood disorders are heritable (see, for example, Hodgson & McGuffin, 2013; Kendler, Neale, Kessler, Heath, & Eaves, 1993; McGuffin *et al.*, 2003). One of the strongest studies demonstrates that an identical twin is two to three times more likely to present with a mood disorder than a fraternal twin if the first twin has a mood disorder (66.7% of identical twins compared with 18.9% of fraternal twins if the first twin has bipolar disorder; 45.6% versus 20.2% if the first twin has unipolar disorder). However, if one identical twin has unipolar disorder, the chances of a co-twin having bipolar disorder are slim to none. In a large meta-analysis of twin studies, Sullivan *et al.* (2000) estimated the heritability of depression to be 37%. Shared environmental factors have little influence, whereas 63% of the variance in depression can be attributed to non-shared environmental factors.

Two reports have appeared suggesting sex differences in genetic vulnerability to depression. Bierut and colleagues (1999) studied 2,662 twin pairs in the Australian twin registry and found the characteristically higher rate of depressive disorders in women. Estimates of heritability in women ranged from 36% to 44%, consistent with other studies. But estimates for men were lower and ranged from 18% to 24%. These results mostly agree with an important study of men in the United States by Lyons and colleagues (1998). The authors conclude that environmental events play a larger role in causing depression in men than in women.

Note from the studies just described that bipolar disorder confers an increased risk of developing some mood disorder in close relatives, but not necessarily bipolar disorder. This conclusion supports an assumption noted previously that bipolar disorder may simply be a more severe variant of mood disorders rather than a fundamentally different disorder. Then again, of identical twins both having (concordant for) a mood disorder, 80% are also concordant for polarity. In other words, if one identical twin is unipolar, there is an 80% chance the other twin is unipolar as opposed to bipolar. This finding suggests these disorders may be inherited separately and therefore be separate disorders after all (Nurnberger, 2012; Nurnberger & Gershon, 1992).

McGuffin and colleagues (2003) conclude that both points are partially correct. Basically, they found that the genetic contributions to depression in both disorders are the same or similar but that the genetics of mania are distinct from depression. Thus, individuals with bipolar disorder are genetically susceptible to depression and independently genetically susceptible to mania. This hypothesis still requires further confirmation.

Although these findings do raise continuing questions about the relative contributions of psychosocial and genetic factors to mood disorders, overwhelming evidence suggests that such disorders are familial and almost certainly reflect an underlying genetic vulnerability, particularly for women. As described in some detail in Chapter 2 (see pp. 36–41), studies are now beginning to identify different patterns of genes that may confer this vulnerability, at least for some types of depression (Kendler, Aggen, & Neale, 2013; Nurnberger, 2012). In this complex field, it is likely that many additional patterns of gene combinations will be found to contribute to varieties of depression.

In conclusion, the best estimates of genetic contributions to depression fall in the range of approximately 40% for women but seem to be significantly less for men (around 20%). Genetic contributions to bipolar disorder seem to be somewhat higher. This means that from 60% to 80% of the causes of depression can be attributed to environmental factors. Also, recent findings underscore the enormous heterogeneity of genetic associations with any mental disorder. So these percentages (40% for women, 20% for men) may not reflect any one pattern of genetic contribution associated with specific groups of genes but perhaps many different patterns from different groups of genes (Kendler, Jaffee, & Roemer, 2011; McClellan & King, 2010). For example, one of our most distinguished behavioral geneticists, Ken Kendler, has recently reported, along with his colleagues, that three separate genetic factors underlie the syndrome of major depression with one factor associated with cognitive and psychomotor symptoms, a second factor associated with mood, and a third factor with neurovegetative (melancholic) symptoms (Kendler *et al.*, 2013). As we noted in Chapter 3, behavioral geneticists break down environmental factors into events shared by twins (experiencing the same upbringing in the same house and, perhaps, experiencing the same stressful events) and events not shared. What part of our experience causes depression? There is wide agreement that it is the unique, non-shared events rather than the shared ones that interact with biological vulnerability to cause depression (Lau & Eley, 2010; Plomin, DeFries, McClearn, & Rutter, 1997).

Depression and Anxiety: Same Genes?

Although most studies have looked at specific disorders in isolation, a growing trend is to examine the heritability of related groups of disorders. Evidence supports the assumption of a close relationship among depression, anxiety, and panic (as well as other emotional disorders). For example, data from family studies indicate that the more signs and symptoms of anxiety and depression there are in a given patient, the greater the rate of anxiety, depression, or both in first-degree relatives and children (Hudson *et al.*, 2003; Leyfer & Brown, 2011). In several important reports from a major set of data on more than 2,000 female twins, Kendler and his colleagues (Kendler, Neale, Kessler, Heath, & Eaves, 1992b; Kendler *et al.*, 1995) found that the same genetic factors contribute to both anxiety and depression. Social and psychological explanations seemed to account for the factors that differentiate anxiety from depression rather than genes. These findings again suggest that, with the possible exception of mania, the biological vulnerability for mood disorders may not be specific to that disorder but may reflect a more general predisposition to anxiety or mood disorders, or, more likely to a basic temperament underlying all emotional disorders, such as neuroticism (Barlow *et al.*, 2013). The specific form of the disorder would be determined by unique psychological, social, or additional biological factors (Rutter, 2010; Slavich & Irwin, 2014).

Neurotransmitter Systems

In Chapter 2, we observed that we now know that neurotransmitter systems have many subtypes and interact in many complex ways with one another and with neuromodulators (products of the endocrine system). Research implicates low levels of serotonin in the causes of mood disorders, but only in relation to other neurotransmitters, including norepinephrine and dopamine (see, for example, Thase, 2005, 2009). Remember that the apparent primary function of serotonin is to regulate our emotional reactions. For example, we are more impulsive, and our moods swing more widely, when our levels of serotonin are low. This may be because one of the functions of serotonin is to regulate systems involving norepinephrine and dopamine. According to the "permissive" hypothesis, when serotonin levels are low, other neurotransmitters are "permitted" to range more widely, become dysregulated, and contribute to mood irregularities, including depression. Current thinking is that the balance of the various neurotransmitters

and their interaction with systems of self-regulation are more important than the absolute level of any one neurotransmitter (Whisman, Johnson, & Smolen, 2011; Yatham *et al.*, 2012).

In the context of this delicate balance, there is continued interest in the role of dopamine, particularly in relationship to manic episodes, atypical depression, or depression with psychotic features (Dunlop & Nemeroff, 2007; Thase, 2009). For example, the dopamine agonist L-dopa seems to produce hypomania in bipolar patients (see, for instance, Van Praag & Korf, 1975), along with other dopamine agonists (Silverstone, 1985). Chronic stress also reduces dopamine levels and produces depressive-like behavior (Thase, 2009). But, as with other research in this area, it is quite difficult to pin down any relationships with certainty.

The Endocrine System

During the past several years, most attention has shifted away from a focus on neurotransmitters to the endocrine system and the "stress hypothesis" of the etiology of depression (Nemeroff, 2004). This hypothesis focuses on overactivity in the hypothalamic–pituitary–adrenocortical (HPA) axis (discussed later), which produces stress hormones. Again, notice the similarity with the description of the neurobiology of anxiety in Chapter 4 (see, for example, Barlow *et al.*, 2014; Britton & Rauch, 2009). Investigators became interested in the endocrine system when they noticed that patients with diseases affecting this system sometimes became depressed. For example, hypothyroidism, or Cushing's disease, which affects the adrenal cortex, leads to excessive secretion of cortisol and often to depression (and anxiety).

In Chapter 2, and again in Chapter 4, we discussed the brain circuit called the HPA axis, beginning in the hypothalamus and running through the pituitary gland, which coordinates the endocrine system (see Figure 2.10, p. 48). Investigators have also discovered that neurotransmitter activity in the hypothalamus regulates the release of hormones that affect the HPA axis. These **neurohormones** are an increasingly important focus of study in psychopathology (see, for example, Hammen & Keenan-Miller, 2013; Thase, 2009). There are thousands of neurohormones. Sorting out their relationship to antecedent neurotransmitter systems (as well as determining their independent effects on the central nervous system) is likely to be a complex task indeed. One of the glands influenced by the pituitary is the cortical section of the adrenal gland, which produces the stress hormone cortisol that completes the HPA axis. Cortisol is called a *stress hormone* because it is elevated during stressful life events. (We discuss this system in more detail in Chapter 7.) For now, it is enough to

....

neurohormones **Hormone** that affects the brain and is increasingly the focus of study in **psychopathology**.

know that cortisol levels are elevated in depressed patients, a finding that makes sense considering the relationship between depression and severe life stress (Barlow *et al.*, 2014; Thase, 2009).

Recognizing that stress hormones are elevated in patients with depression (and anxiety), researchers have begun to focus on the consequences of these elevations. Preliminary findings indicate that these hormones can be harmful to neurons in that they decrease a key ingredient that keeps neurons healthy and growing. You saw in Chapter 4 on anxiety disorders that individuals experiencing heightened levels of stress hormones over a long period undergo some shrinkage of a brain structure called the *hippocampus*. The hippocampus, among other things, is responsible for keeping stress hormones in check and serves important functions in facilitating cognitive processes such as short-term memory. But the new finding, at least in animals, is that long-term overproduction of stress hormones makes the organism unable to develop new neurons (neurogenesis). Thus, some theorists suspect that the connection between high stress hormones and depression is the suppression of neurogenesis in the hippocampus (Glasper, Schoenfeld, & Gould, 2012; Snyder, Soumier, Brewer, Pickel, & Cameron, 2011). Evidence reveals that healthy girls at risk for developing depression because their mothers suffer from recurrent depression have reduced hippocampal volume compared with girls with non-depressed mothers (Chen, Hamilton, & Gotlib, 2010). This finding suggests that low hippocampal volume may precede and perhaps contribute to the onset of depression. Scientists have already observed that successful treatments for depression, including electroconvulsive therapy, seem to produce neurogenesis in the hippocampus, thereby reversing this process (Duman, 2004; Santarelli *et al.*, 2003). More recently it has been demonstrated in animal laboratories that exercise increases neurogenesis, which could possibly be one mechanism of action in successful psychological treatments utilizing exercise, such as behavioral activation described below (Speisman, Kumar, Rani, Foster, & Ormerod, 2013). Despite strong preliminary evidence, this is just a theory that must now undergo the slow process of scientific confirmation.

Sleep and Circadian Rhythms

We have known for several years that sleep disturbances are a hallmark of most mood disorders. Most important, in people who are depressed, there is a significantly shorter period after falling asleep before *rapid eye movement (REM) sleep* begins. As you may remember from your introductory psychology or biology course, there are two major stages of sleep: REM sleep and non-REM sleep. When we first fall asleep, we go through several substages of progressively deeper sleep during which we achieve most of our rest. After about 90 minutes, we begin to experience REM sleep, when the brain arouses, and we begin to dream. Our eyes move rapidly back and forth under our eyelids—hence

the name *rapid eye movement* sleep. As the night goes on, we have increasing amounts of REM sleep. In addition to entering REM sleep more quickly, depressed patients experience REM activity that is more intense, and the stages of deepest sleep, called *slow wave sleep*, don't occur until later, if at all (Jindal *et al.*, 2002; Thase, 2009). It seems that some sleep characteristics occur only while we are depressed and not at other times (Riemann, Berger, & Voderholzer, 2001; Rush *et al.*, 1986). But other evidence suggests that, at least in more severe cases with recurrent depression, disturbances in sleep continuity, as well as reduction of deep sleep, may be present even when the individual is not depressed (Kupfer, 1995; Thase, 2009). In addition, unusually short and long sleep durations were associated with an increased risk for depression in adults (Zhai, Zhang, & Zhang, 2015).

Sleep pattern disturbances in depressed children are less pronounced than in adults, perhaps because children are very deep sleepers, illustrating once again the importance of developmental stage to psychopathology (Brent & Birmaher, 2009; Garber *et al.*, 2009). But sleep disturbances are even more severe among depressed older adults. In fact, insomnia, frequently experienced by older adults, is a risk factor for both the onset and persistence of depression (Fiske *et al.*, 2009; Talbot *et al.*, 2012). Talbot and colleagues (2012) studied the relationship between sleep and mood in patients with bipolar disorder who were not currently in a depressed or manic state (inter-episode), compared with a group of patients suffering from insomnia. Both the bipolar and insomnia patients had greater sleep disturbance compared with a healthy control group. But the investigators discovered that the relationship between sleep and mood was bidirectional in both groups. That is, negative mood predicted sleep disruptions and sleep disruptions subsequently resulted in negative mood. Treating the insomnia of bipolar I patients between episodes with CBT has been shown to reduce the risk of relapse and improve sleep, mood, and functioning (Harvey *et al.*, 2015). Thus, it seems that the relationship between sleep and mood may cut across different diagnoses and that treating sleep disruptions directly might positively affect mood not only in insomnia but also in mood disorders.

Another interesting finding is that depriving depressed patients of sleep, particularly during the second half of the night, causes temporary improvement in their condition (Giedke & Schwarzler, 2002; Thase, 2009), particularly for patients with bipolar disorder in a depressive state (Harvey, 2008; Johnson *et al.*, 2009), although the depression returns when the patients start sleeping normally again. In any case, because sleep patterns reflect a biological rhythm, there may be a relationship among seasonal affective disorder (SAD), sleep disturbances in depressed patients, and a more general disturbance in biological rhythms (Soreca, Frank, & Kupfer, 2009). This would not be surprising if it were true, because most mammals are exquisitely sensitive to day length at the latitudes at which they live, and this "biological clock" controls eating, sleeping, and weight changes. Thus, substantial disruption in circadian rhythm might be particularly problematic for some vulnerable individuals (Moore, 1999; Sohn & Lam, 2005; Soreca *et al.*, 2009).

Psychological Dimensions

Thus far we have reviewed genetic and biological factors, including findings from studies of neurotransmitters, the endocrine system, sleep and circadian rhythms, and relative activity in certain areas of the brain associated with depression. But these factors are all inextricably linked to psychological and social dimensions where scientists are also discovering strong associations with depression. We now review some of these findings.

Stressful Life Events

Stress and trauma are among the most striking unique contributions to the etiology of all psychological disorders. This is reflected throughout psychopathology and is evident in the wide adoption of the diathesis–stress model of psychopathology presented in Chapter 2 (and referred to throughout this book), which describes possible genetic and psychological vulnerabilities. But in seeking what activates this vulnerability (diathesis), we usually look for a stressful or traumatic life event.

Stress and Depression You would think it would be sufficient to ask people whether anything major had happened in their lives before they developed depression or some other psychological disorder. Most people who develop depression report losing a job, getting divorced, having a child, or graduating from school and starting a career. But, as with most issues in the study of psychopathology, the significance of a major event is not easily discovered (Carter & Garber, 2011; Hammen & Keenan-Miller, 2013), so most investigators have stopped simply asking patients whether something bad (or good) happened and have begun to look at the context of the event, as well as the meaning it has for the individual.

For example, losing a job is stressful for most people, but it is far more difficult for some than others. A few people might even see it as a blessing. If you were laid off as a manager in a large corporation because of a restructuring but your wife is the president of another corporation and makes more than enough money to support the family, it might not be so bad. Furthermore, if you are an aspiring writer or artist who has not had time to pursue your art, becoming jobless might be the opportunity you have been waiting for, particularly if your wife has been telling you for years to devote yourself to your creative pursuits.

Now consider losing your job if you are a single mother of two young children living from paycheck to paycheck and, on account of a recent doctor's bill, you have to choose

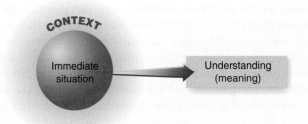

● **Figure 6.1** Context and meaning in life stress situations. (Reprinted, with permission, from Brown, G. W. [1989b]. Life events and measurement. In G. W. Brown & T. O. Harris, Eds., *Life events and illness.* New York, NY: Guilford Press, © 1989 New York, NY: Guilford Press.)

between paying the electric bill or buying enough food. The stressful life event is the same, but the context is different and transforms the significance of the event substantially. To complicate the scenario further, think for a minute about how various women in this situation might react to losing their job. One woman might well decide she is a total failure and thus become unable to carry on and provide for her children. Another woman might realize the job loss was not her fault and take advantage of a job training program while scraping by somehow. Thus, both the context of the life event and its meaning are important. This approach to studying life events, developed by George W. Brown (1989b) and associates in England, is represented in ● Figure 6.1.

Brown's study of life events is difficult to carry out, and the methodology is still evolving. Psychologists such as Scott Monroe and Constance Hammen (Hammen, 2005; Monroe *et al.*, 2009; Monroe, Rohde, Seeley, & Lewinsohn, 1999) have developed new methods. One crucial issue is the bias inherent in remembering events. If you ask people who are currently depressed what happened when they first became depressed more than five years ago, you will probably get answers different from those that they would give if they were not currently depressed. Because current moods distort memories, many investigators have concluded that the only useful way to study stressful life events is to follow people *prospectively* to determine more accurately the precise nature of events and their relation to subsequent psychopathology.

In any case, in summarizing a large amount of research, it is clear that stressful life events are strongly related to the onset of mood disorders (Grant, Kendler, & Gardner, 2010; Monroe & Reid, 2009). Measuring the context of events and their impact in a random sample of the population, a number of studies have found a marked relationship between severe and, in some cases, traumatic life events and the onset of depression (Brown, Harris, & Hepworth, 1994; Kendler *et al.*, 1999b). Severe events precede all types of depression except, perhaps, for a small group of patients with melancholic or psychotic features who are experiencing subsequent episodes where depression emerges in the absence of life events (Brown *et al.*, 1994). For example, childhood sexual abuse (in addition to a family history of depression and anxiety disorders) is a significant predictor of a first onset of depression in young adults (Klein *et al.*, 2013). In addition, for people with recurrent depression, the clear occurrence of a severe life stress before or early in the latest episode predicts a poorer response to treatment and a longer time before remission (Monroe *et al.*, 2009; Monroe, Kupfer, & Frank, 1992), as well as a greater likelihood of recurrence (Monroe *et al.*, 2009; Monroe, Roberts, Kupfer, & Frank, 1996).

Although the context and meaning are often more important than the exact nature of the event itself, there are some events that are particularly likely to lead to depression. One of them is the breakup of a relationship, which is difficult for both adolescents (Carter & Garber, 2011; Monroe, Rohde, Seeley, & Lewinsohn, 1999) and adults (Kendler, Hettema, Butera, Gardner, & Prescott, 2003). Kendler and colleagues (2003) demonstrated in an elegant twin study that if one twin experienced a loss, such as the death of a loved one, that twin was 10 times more likely to become depressed than the twin who didn't experience the loss. But if one twin is also humiliated by the loss, as when, for example, a boyfriend or husband leaves the twin for a best friend and the twin still sees them all the time, then that twin would be 20 times more likely to get depressed than a twin with the same genes who didn't experience the event. Scientists have confirmed that humiliation, loss, and social rejection are the most potent stressful life events likely to lead to depression (Monroe *et al.*, 2009).

Clearly there is a strong relationship between stress and depression, and scientists are discovering that the cause-and-effect connection between the two might go both ways. Remember in Chapter 2 where we noted that our genetic endowment might increase the probability that we will experience stressful life events? We referred to this as the *gene–environment correlation model* (Kendler, 2011; Kendler, Jaffee, & Roemer, 2011). One example would be people who tend to seek difficult relationships because of genetically based personality characteristics that then lead to depression. Kendler and colleagues (1999a) report that about one third of the association between stressful life events and depression is not the usual arrangement where stress triggers depression but rather individuals vulnerable to depression who are placing themselves in high-risk stressful environments, such as difficult relationships or other risky situations where bad outcomes are common. What is important about the reciprocal model is that it can happen both ways in the same individual; stress triggers depression, and depressed individuals create or seek stressful events. Interestingly, if you ask mothers, they tend to say their depressed adolescents created the problem, but adolescents blame the stressful event itself (Carter, Garber,

Cielsa, & Cole, 2006; Eley, 2011). According to the reciprocal model, the truth lies somewhere between these two views. Moreover, the relative importance of the contribution of genetic factors versus environmental effects seems to differ depending on age: Whereas heritability depression (and anxiety) symptoms is high during childhood, the importance of environmental effects increases with age (Nivard *et al.*, 2015).

Stress and Bipolar Disorder The relationship of stressful events to the onset of episodes in bipolar disorder is also strong (Johnson, Gruber, & Eisner, 2007; Johnson *et al.*, 2008). Several issues may be particularly relevant to the causes of bipolar disorders, however (Goodwin & Ghaemi, 1998). First, typically negative stressful life events trigger depression, but a somewhat different, more positive, set of stressful life events seems to trigger mania (Alloy *et al.*, 2012; Johnson *et al.*, 2008). Specifically, experience associated with striving to achieve important goals, such as getting accepted into graduate school, obtaining a new job or promotion, getting married, or any goal striving activity for popularity or financial success trigger mania in vulnerable individuals (Alloy *et al.*, 2012). Second, stress seems to initially trigger mania and depression, but as the disorder progresses, these episodes seem to develop a life of their own. In other words, once the cycle begins, a psychological or pathophysiological process takes over and ensures the disorder will continue (see, for example, Post, 1992; Post *et al.*, 1989). Third, some precipitants of manic episodes seem related to loss of sleep, as in the postpartum period (Harvey, 2008; Soreca *et al.*, 2009) or as a result of jet lag—that is, disturbed circadian rhythms (Alloy, Nusslock, & Boland, 2015). In most cases of bipolar disorder, nevertheless, stressful life events are substantially indicated not only in provoking relapse but also in preventing recovery (Alloy, Abramson, Urosevic, Bender, & Wagner, 2009; Johnson & Miller, 1997).

Finally, although almost everyone who develops a mood disorder has experienced a significant stressful event, most people who experience such events do not develop mood disorders. Although the data are not yet as precise as we would like, somewhere between 20% and 50% of individuals who experience severe events develop mood disorders. Thus, between 50% and 80% of individuals do *not* develop mood disorders or, presumably, any other psychological disorder. Again, data strongly support the interaction of stressful life events with some kind of vulnerability: genetic, psychological, or, more likely, a combination of the two influences (Barlow, 2002; Haeffel & Hames, 2014).

Given a genetic vulnerability (diathesis) and a severe life event (stress), what happens then? Research has isolated a number of psychological and biological processes. To illustrate one, let's return to Katie. Her stressful life event was attending a new school. Katie's feeling of loss of control leads to another important psychological factor in depression: learned helplessness.

I was a serious and sensitive 11-year-old at the edge of puberty and at the edge of an adventure that many teens and pre-teens embark on—the transition from elementary to junior high school. A new school, new people, new responsibilities, new pressures. Academically, I was a good student up to this point, but I didn't feel good about myself and generally lacked self-confidence.

Katie began to experience severe anxiety reactions. Then she became quite ill with the flu. After recovering and attempting to return to school, Katie discovered that her anxieties were worse than ever. More important, she began to feel she was losing control.

As I look back, I can identify events that precipitated my anxieties and fears, but then everything seemed to happen suddenly and without cause. I was reacting emotionally and physically in a way that I didn't understand. I felt out of control of my emotions and body. Day after day I wished, as a child does, that whatever was happening to me would magically end. I wished that I would awake one day to find that I was the person I was several months before.

Learned Helplessness

As discussed in Chapter 2, Martin Seligman discovered that dogs and rats have an interesting emotional reaction to events over which they have no control. If rats receive occasional shocks, they can function reasonably well as long as they can cope with the shocks by doing something to avoid them, such as pressing a lever. But if they learn that nothing they do helps them avoid the shocks, they eventually become helpless, give up, and manifest an animal equivalent of depression (Seligman, 1975).

Do humans react the same way? Seligman suggests we seem to, but only under one important condition: People become anxious and depressed when they decide that they have no control over the stress in their lives (Abramson, Seligman, & Teasdale, 1978; Miller & Norman, 1979). These findings evolved into an important model called the **learned helplessness theory of depression**. Often overlooked is Seligman's point that anxiety is the first response to a stressful situation. Depression may follow marked hopelessness about coping with the difficult life events (Barlow, 1988, 2002). The depressive attributional style is (1) *internal*, in that the individual attributes negative events to personal failings ("it is all my fault"); (2) *stable*, in that, even after a particular negative event passes, the attribution that "additional bad things will always be my fault" remains; and (3) *global*, in that the attributions extend across a variety of issues. Research continues on this

interesting concept, but you can see how it applies to Katie. Early in her difficulties with attending school, she began to believe events were out of her control and that she was unable even to begin to cope. More important, in her eyes the bad situation was all her fault: "I blamed myself for my lack of control." A downward spiral into a major depressive episode followed.

But a major question remains: Is learned helplessness a cause of depression or a correlated side effect of becoming depressed? If it were a cause, learned helplessness would have to exist *before* the depressive episode. Results from a classic five-year longitudinal study of children shed some light on this issue. Nolen-Hoeksema, Girgus, and Seligman (1992) reported that negative attributional style did not predict later symptoms of depression in young children; rather, stressful life events seemed to be the major precipitant of symptoms. As children under stress grew older, however, they tended to develop more negative cognitive styles, which did tend to predict symptoms of depression in reaction to additional negative events. Nolen-Hoeksema and colleagues speculate that meaningful negative events early in childhood may lead to negative attributional styles, making these children more vulnerable to future depressive episodes when stressful events occur. Indeed, most studies support the finding that negative cognitive styles precede and are a risk factor for depression (Garber & Carter, 2006; Garber *et al.*, 2009).

This thinking recalls the types of psychological vulnerabilities theorized to contribute to the development of anxiety disorders (Barlow, 1988, 2002; Barlow *et al.*, 2013). That is, in a person who has a non-specific genetic vulnerability to either anxiety or depression, stressful life events activate a psychological sense that life events are uncontrollable (Barlow, 2002; Chorpita & Barlow, 1998). Evidence suggests that negative attributional styles are not specific to depression but also characterize people with anxiety (Barlow, 2002; Barlow *et al.*, 2013). This may indicate that a psychological (cognitive) vulnerability is no more specific for mood disorders than a genetic vulnerability. Both types of vulnerabilities may underlie numerous disorders.

Abramson, Metalsky, and Alloy (1989) revised the learned helplessness theory to de-emphasize the influence of negative attributions and highlight the development of a sense of hopelessness as a crucial cause of many forms of depression. Attributions are important only to the extent that they contribute to a sense of hopelessness. This fits well with recent thinking on crucial differences between anxiety and depression. Both anxious and depressed individuals feel helpless and believe they lack control, but only in depression do they give up and become hopeless about ever regaining control (Barlow, 1991, 2002; Chorpita & Barlow, 1998).

....

learned helplessness theory of depression Martin Seligman's theory that people become anxious and depressed when they make an attribution that they have no control over the **stress** in their lives (whether or not they actually have control).

According to the learned helplessness theory of depression, people become depressed when they believe they have no control over the stress in their lives.

Negative Cognitive Styles

In 1967, Aaron T. Beck (1967, 1976) suggested that depression may result from a tendency to interpret everyday events in a negative way. According to Beck, people with depression make the worst of everything; for them, the smallest setbacks are major catastrophes. In his extensive clinical work, Beck observed that all of his depressed patients thought this way, and he began classifying the types of "cognitive errors" that characterized this style. From the long list he compiled, two representative examples are *arbitrary inference* and *overgeneralization*. Arbitrary inference is evident when a depressed individual emphasizes the negative rather than the positive aspects of a situation. A high school teacher may assume he is a terrible instructor because two students in his class fell asleep. He fails to consider other reasons they might be sleeping (up all night partying, perhaps) and "infers" that his teaching style is at fault. As an example of overgeneralization, when your professor makes one critical remark on your paper, you then assume you will fail the class despite a long string of positive comments and good grades on other papers. You are overgeneralizing from one small remark. According to Beck, people who are depressed think like this all the time. They make cognitive errors in thinking negatively about themselves, their immediate world, and their future, three areas that together are called the **depressive cognitive triad** (see ● Figure 6.2).

In addition, Beck theorized, after a series of negative events in childhood, individuals may develop a deep-seated *negative schema*, an enduring negative cognitive belief system about some aspect of life (Alloy et al., 2012; Young, Rygh, Weinberger, & Beck, 2014). In a self-blame schema, individuals feel personally responsible for every bad thing that happens. With a negative self-evaluation schema, they believe they can never do anything correctly. In Beck's view, these cognitive errors and schemas are automatic, that is, not necessarily conscious. Indeed, an individual might not even be aware of thinking negatively and illogically. Thus, minor negative events can lead to a major depressive episode.

A variety of evidence supports a cognitive theory of emotional disorders in general and depression in particular (Gotlib, Joormann, & Foland-Ross, 2014; Hammen & Keenan-Miller, 2013). The thinking of depressed individuals is consistently more negative than that of nondepressed individuals (Gotlib & Abramson, 1999; Gotlib *et al.*, 2014) in each dimension of the cognitive triad—the self, the world, and the future (see, for example, Garber & Carter, 2006). Depressive cognitions seem to emerge from distorted and probably automatic methods of processing information. People prone to depression are more likely to recall negative events when they are depressed than when they are not depressed or than are nondepressed individuals (Gotlib *et al.*, 2014).

The implications of this theory are important. By recognizing cognitive errors and the underlying schemas, we can correct them and alleviate depression and related emotional disorders. In developing ways to do this, Beck became the father of cognitive therapy, one of the most important developments in psychotherapy in the past 50 years. Individuals with bipolar disorder also exhibit negative cognitive styles, but with a twist. Cognitive styles in

Self · About · World · About · Future · Negative cognitions

● **Figure 6.2** Beck's cognitive triad for depression.

these individuals are characterized by ambitious striving for goals, perfectionism, and self-criticism in addition to the more usual depressive cognitive styles (Alloy & Abramson, 2010; Johnson *et al.*, 2008).

Cognitive Vulnerability for Depression: An Integration

Seligman and Beck developed their theories independently, and good evidence indicates their models are independent in that some people may have a negative outlook (dysfunctional attitudes), whereas others may explain things negatively (hopeless attributes) (Joiner & Rudd, 1996; Spangler, Simons, Monroe, & Thase, 1997). Nevertheless, the basic premises overlap a great deal and considerable evidence suggests depression is always associated with pessimistic explanatory style and negative cognitions. Evidence also exists that cognitive vulnerabilities predispose some people to view events in a negative way, putting them at risk for depression (see, for example, Abela *et al.*, 2011; Alloy *et al.*, 2012).

Good evidence supporting this conclusion comes from the Temple-Wisconsin study of cognitive vulnerability to depression conducted by Lauren Alloy and Lyn Abramson (Alloy & Abramson, 2006; Alloy, Abramson, Safford, & Gibb, 2006). University freshmen who were not depressed at the time of the initial assessment were assessed every several months for up to five years to determine whether they experienced any stressful life events or diagnosable episodes of depression or other psychopathology. At the first assessment, the investigators determined whether the students were cognitively vulnerable to developing depression or not on the basis of their scores on questionnaires that measure dysfunctional attitudes and hopelessness attributions. Results indicated students at high risk because of dysfunctional attitudes reported higher rates of depression in the past compared with the low-risk group. But the really important results come from the prospective portion of the study. Negative cognitive styles do indicate a vulnerability to later depression. Even if participants had never suffered from depression before in their lives, high-risk participants (who scored high on the measures of cognitive vulnerability) were six to 12 times more likely than low-risk participants to experience a major depressive episode. In addition, 16% of the high-risk participants versus only 2.7% of the low-risk participants experienced major depressive episodes, and 46% versus 14% experienced minor depressive symptoms (Alloy & Abramson, 2006).

Social and Cultural Dimensions

A number of social and cultural factors contribute to the onset or maintenance of depression. Among these, marital relationships, gender, and social support are most prominent.

Marital Relations

Depression and bipolar disorder are strongly influenced by interpersonal stress (Sheets & Craighead, 2014; Vrshek-Schallhorn *et al.*, 2015), and especially marital dissatisfaction, as suggested earlier when it was noted that disruptions in relationships often lead to depression (Davila, Stroud, & Starr, 2009). Bruce and Kim (1992) collected data on 695 women and 530 men and then re-interviewed them up to one year later. During this period, a number of participants separated from or divorced their spouses, although the majority reported stable marriages. Approximately 21% of the women who reported a marital split during the study experienced severe depression, a rate three times higher than that for women who remained married. Nearly 17% of the men who reported a marital split developed severe depression, a rate *nine times* higher than that for men who remained married. When the researchers considered only those participants with no history of severe depression, however, 14% of the men who separated or divorced during the period experienced severe depression, as did approximately 5% of the women. In other words, *only the men* faced a heightened risk of developing a mood disorder for the first time immediately following a marital split.

Another finding with considerable support is that depression including bipolar disorder, particularly if it continues, may lead to substantial deterioration in marital relationships (Beach, Jones, & Franklin, 2009; Davila *et al.*, 2009). It is not hard to figure out why. Being around someone who is continually negative, ill tempered, and pessimistic becomes tiring after a while. Because emotions are contagious, the spouse probably begins to feel bad also. These kinds of interactions precipitate arguments or, worse, make the non-depressed spouse want to leave (Joiner & Timmons, 2009; Whisman, Weinstock, & Tolejko, 2006).

But conflict within a marriage seems to have different effects on men and women. Depression seems to cause men to withdraw or otherwise disrupt the relationship. For women, on the other hand, problems in the relationship most often cause depression. Thus, for both men and women, depression and problems in marital relations are associated, but the causal direction is different (Fincham, Beach, Harold, & Osborne, 1997), a result also found by Spangler, Simons, Monroe, and Thase (1996). Given these factors, Beach, Jones, and Franklin (2009) suggest that therapists treat disturbed marital relationships at the same time as the mood disorder to ensure the highest level of success for the patient and the best chance of preventing future relapses.

Mood Disorders in Women

Data on the prevalence of mood disorders indicate dramatic gender imbalances. Although bipolar disorder is

....

depressive cognitive triad Thinking errors by depressed people negatively focused in three areas: themselves, their immediate world, and their future.

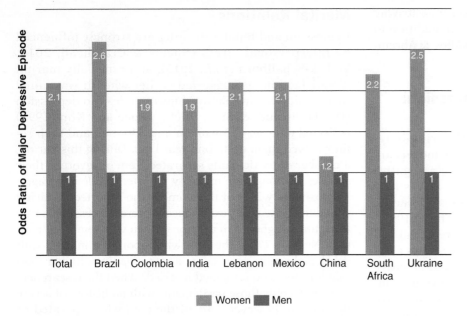

Women ■ Men

● **Figure 6.3** The gender disparity in depression diagnoses worldwide, expressed as odds ratios. These odds ratios express the comparative likelihood of women experiencing a major depressive episode in the past year, relative to men. In Brazil, for example, women are 2.6 times more likely than men to report having had a major depressive episode in the last year. (Adapted from Bromet et al. [2011], p. 11 of 16.)

evenly divided between men and women, almost 70% of the individuals with major depressive disorder and persistent depressive disorder (dysthymia) are women (Kessler, 2006; Kessler & Bromet, 2013). What is particularly striking is that this gender imbalance is constant around the world, even though overall rates of disorder may vary from country to country (Kessler & Bromet, 2013; Seedat *et al.*, 2009; see ● Figure 6.3). Often overlooked is the similar ratio for most anxiety disorders, particularly panic disorder and generalized anxiety disorder. Women represent an even greater proportion of specific phobias, as we noted in Chapter 2. What could account for this?

It may be that gender differences in the development of emotional disorders are strongly influenced by perceptions of uncontrollability (Barlow, 1988; Barlow *et al.*, 2014). If you feel a sense of mastery over your life and the difficult events we all encounter, you might experience occasional stress, but you will not feel the helplessness central to anxiety and mood disorders. The source of these differences is cultural, in the sex roles assigned to men and women in our society. Males are strongly encouraged to be independent, masterful, and assertive; females, by contrast, are expected to be more passive, sensitive to other people, and, perhaps, to rely on others more than males do (needs for affiliation) (Cyranowski, Frank, Young, & Shear, 2000; Hankin & Abramson, 2001). Although these stereotypes are slowly changing, they still describe current sex roles to a large extent. But this culturally induced dependence and passivity may well put women at heightened risk for emotional disorders by increasing their feelings of uncontrollability and helplessness.

Evidence has accumulated that parenting styles encouraging stereotypic gender roles are implicated in the development of early psychological vulnerability to later depression or anxiety (Barlow *et al.*, 2013; Chorpita & Barlow, 1998), specifically, a smothering, overprotective style that prevents the child from developing initiative. Also interesting is the "sudden surge" in depression among girls mentioned earlier that occurs during puberty. Many thought this might be biologically-based. Kessler (2006) notes, however, that low self-esteem emerges quickly in girls in seventh grade if the school system has a seventh- through ninth-grade middle school, but low self-esteem among girls does not emerge until ninth grade when the school has a kindergarten through eighth-grade primary school and a four-year high school (Simmons & Blyth, 1987). These results suggest that the younger girls just entering a new school, whether it is seventh, ninth, or some other grade, find it stressful. Also, girls who mature early physically have more distress and depression than girls who don't (Ge, Conger, & Elder, 1996).

Women tend to place greater value on intimate relationships than men, which can be protective if social networks are strong, but it may also put them at risk. Disruptions in such relationships, combined with an inability to cope with the disruptions, seem to be far more damaging to women than to men (Kendler & Gardner, 2014; Nolen-Hoeksema & Hilt, 2009). Cyranowski and associates (2000) note that the tendency for adolescent girls to express aggression by rejecting other girls, combined with a greater sensitivity to rejection, may precipitate more depressive episodes in these adolescent girls compared with boys. Kendler, Myers, and Prescott (2005) also observed that women tend to have larger and more intimate social networks than men and that emotionally supportive groups of friends protect against depression. However, data from Bruce and Kim (1992), reviewed earlier, suggest that if the disruption in a marital relationship reaches the stage of divorce, men who had previously been functioning well are at greater risk for depression.

Another potentially important gender difference has been suggested by Susan Nolen-Hoeksema (1990, 2000; Nolen-Hoeksema, Wisco, & Lyubomirsky, 2008). Women tend to ruminate more than men about their situation and blame themselves for being depressed. This response style predicted the later development of depression when under stress (Abela & Hankin, 2011). Men tend to ignore their feelings, perhaps engaging in activity to take their minds off them (Addis, 2008). This male behavior may be therapeutic because "activating" people (getting them busy doing something) is a common element of successful therapy for depression (Dimidjian, Martell, Herman-Dunn, & Hubley, 2014; Jacobson, Martell, & Dimidjian, 2001).

Women are at a disadvantage in our society: They experience more discrimination, poverty, sexual harassment, and abuse than do men. They also earn less respect and accumulate less power. Three quarters of the people living in poverty in the United States are women and children. Women, particularly single mothers, have a difficult time entering the workplace. Interestingly, married women employed full time outside the home report levels of depression no greater than those of employed married men. Single, divorced, and widowed women experience significantly more depression than men in the same categories (Davila *et al.*, 2009). This does not necessarily mean that anyone should get a job to avoid becoming depressed. Indeed, for a man or woman, feeling mastery, control, and value in a strongly socially supported role of homemaker and parent should be associated with low rates of depression.

Finally, other disorders may reflect gender role stereotypes but in the opposite direction. Disorders associated with aggressiveness, overactivity, and substance abuse occur far more often in men than in women (Barlow, 1988, 2002). Identifying the reasons for gender imbalances across the full range of psychopathological disorders may prove important in discovering causes of disorders.

Social Support

In Chapter 2, we examined the powerful effect of social influences on our psychological and biological functioning. It is not surprising, then, that social factors influence whether we become depressed (Beach *et al.*, 2009). To take one example, the risk of depression for people who live alone is almost 80% higher than for people who live with others (Pulkki-Råback *et al.*, 2012) In an early landmark study, Brown and Harris (1978) first suggested the important role of social support in the onset of depression. In a study of a large number of women who had experienced a serious life stress, they discovered that only 10% of the women who had a friend in whom they could confide became depressed, compared with 37% of the women who did not have a close supportive relationship. Later prospective studies have also confirmed the importance of social support (or lack of it) in predicting the onset of depressive symptoms at a later time (see, for instance, Kendler, Kuhn *et al.*, 2005; Monroe *et al.*, 2009). The importance of social support in preventing depression holds true in China (Wang, Wang, & Shen, 2006) and every other country in which it has been studied. Other studies have established the importance of social support in speeding recovery from depressive episodes (Keitner *et al.*, 1995; Sherbourne, Hays, & Wells, 1995). These and related findings on the importance of social support have led to an exciting new psychological therapeutic approach for emotional disorders called interpersonal psychotherapy, which we discuss later in this chapter.

An Integrative Theory

How do we put all this together? Basically, depression and anxiety may often share a common, genetically determined biological vulnerability (Barlow, 2002) that can be described as an overactive neurobiological response to stressful life events. Again, this vulnerability is simply a general tendency to develop depression (or anxiety) rather than a specific vulnerability for depression or anxiety itself. To understand the causes of depression, we must look at psychological vulnerabilities as well as life experiences that interact with genetic vulnerabilities.

People who develop mood disorders also possess a psychological vulnerability experienced as feelings of inadequacy for coping with the difficulties confronting them as well as depressive cognitive styles. As with anxiety, we may develop this sense of control in childhood (Barlow, 2002; Chorpita & Barlow, 1998). It may range on a continuum from total confidence to a complete inability to cope. When vulnerabilities are triggered, the pessimistic "giving up" process seems crucial to the development of depression (Alloy *et al.*, 2000; Alloy & Abramson, 2006).

These psychological processes of inadequate coping and depressive cognitive style in combination with certain genetic patterns comprise the temperament of neuroticism or negative affect (Barlow *et al.*, 2014). You will remember from Chapter 4 that neuroticism is associated with biochemical markers of stress and depression (see, for example, Nemeroff, 2004; Thase, 2009), as well as differential levels of arousal in different hemispheres in the brain (hemispheric lateral asymmetry and activation of specific brain circuits (Barlow *et al.*, 2013; Davidson *et al.*, 2009). Recent research illustrates the strong associations between the genetic and generalized psychological vulnerabilities (e.g., Whisman, Johnson, & Smolen, 2011). There is also good evidence that stressful life events trigger the onset of depression in most cases in these vulnerable individuals, particularly initial episodes (Jenness, Hankin, Abela, Young, & Smollen, 2011). How do these factors interact? Current thinking is that stressful life events in vulnerable individuals activate stress hormones, which, in turn, have wide-ranging effects on neurotransmitter systems, particularly those involving serotonin, norepinephrine, and the corticotropin-releasing factor system.

What we have so far is a possible mechanism for the diathesis–stress model. Finally, it seems clear that factors such as interpersonal relationships (Tsai, Lucas, & Kawachi, 2015) or cognitive style (Gotlib *et al.*, 2014) may protect us from the effects of stress and therefore from developing mood disorders. Alternatively, these factors may at least determine whether we quickly recover from these disorders or not. But remember that bipolar disorder, and particularly activation of manic episodes, seems to have a somewhat different genetic basis, as well as a different response to social support. Scientists are beginning to theorize that individuals with bipolar disorder, in addition to factors outlined so far, are also highly sensitive to the experience of life events connected with striving to reach important goals, perhaps because of an overactive brain circuit called the behavioral approach system (BAS) (Alloy & Abramson, 2010; Gruber, Johnson, Oveis, & Keltner, 2008). In these cases, stressful life events that are more positive but still stressful, such as starting a new job, or pulling all-nighters to finish an important term paper, might precipitate a manic episode in vulnerable individuals instead of a depressive episode. Individuals with bipolar disorder are also highly sensitive to disruptions in circadian rhythm. So individuals with bipolar disorder might possess brain circuits that predispose them to both depression and mania. Research of this hypothesis is just commencing.

In summary, biological, psychological, and social factors all influence the development of mood disorders, as depicted in ● Figure 6.4. This model does not fully account for the varied presentation of mood disorders—seasonal, bipolar, and so on—although mania in bipolar disorder seems to be associated with unique genetic contributions and is triggered by relatively unique life events as noted above. But why would someone with an underlying genetic vulnerability who experiences a stressful life event develop a mood disorder rather than an anxiety or somatic symptom disorder? As with the anxiety disorders and other stress disorders, specific psychosocial circumstances, such as early learning experiences, may interact with specific genetic vulnerabilities and personality characteristics to produce the rich variety of emotional disorders.

● **Figure 6.4** An integrative model of mood disorders.

Answer these questions about the various causes of mood disorders:

1. List five biological sources that can contribute to mood disorders. _____ _____ _____ _____ _____

2. What psychological factors can have an impact on mood disorders? _____ _____ _____ _____

3. Name several social and cultural dimensions that contribute to mood disorders. _____ _____ _____

Treatment of Mood Disorders

▶ What medical and psychological treatments have been successful in treating mood disorders?

Researchers have learned a great deal about the neurobiology of mood disorders during the past several years. Findings on the complex interplay of neurochemicals are beginning to shed light on the nature of mood disorders. As we have noted, the principal effect of medications is to alter levels of these neurotransmitters and other related neurochemicals. Other biological treatments, such as electroconvulsive therapy, dramatically affect brain chemistry. A more interesting development, however, alluded to throughout this book, is that powerful psychological treatments also alter brain chemistry. Despite these advances, most cases of depression go untreated because neither health-care professionals nor patients recognize and correctly identify or diagnose depression. Similarly, many professionals and patients are unaware of the existence of effective and successful treatments (Delano-Wood & Abeles, 2005; Hirschfeld *et al.*, 1997).

Medications

A number of medications are effective treatments for depression. New information often becomes available on new medications or the latest estimates of effectiveness of older medications.

Antidepressants

Four basic types of antidepressant medications are used to treat depressive disorders: selective-serotonin reuptake inhibitors (SSRIs), mixed reuptake inhibitors, tricyclic antidepressants, and monoamine oxidase (MAO) inhibitors. It is important to note at the outset that there are few, if any, differences in effectiveness among the different antidepressants; approximately 50% of patients receive some benefit, with about half of the 50% coming very close to normal functioning (remission). If dropouts are excluded and only those who complete treatment are counted, the percentage of patients receiving at least some benefit increases to between 60% and 70% (American Psychiatric Association, 2010), but

one thoroughgoing meta-analysis indicated that antidepressants were relatively ineffective for mild to moderate depression compared with placebo. Only in severely depressed patients is there a clear advantage for taking an antidepressant compared with placebo (Fournier *et al.*, 2010).

The class of drugs currently considered the first choice in drug treatment for depression seems to have a specific effect on the serotonin neurotransmitter system (although such drugs affect other systems to some extent). These *selective*-serotonin reuptake inhibitors (SSRIs) specifically block the presynaptic reuptake of serotonin. This temporarily increases levels of serotonin at the receptor site, but again the precise long-term mechanism of action is unknown, although levels of serotonin are eventually increased (Gitlin, 2009; Thase & Denko, 2008). Perhaps the best-known drug in this class is *fluoxetine* (Prozac). Like many other medications, Prozac was initially hailed as a breakthrough drug; it even made the cover of *Newsweek* (Cowley & Springen, 1990). Then reports began to appear that it might lead to suicidal preoccupation, paranoid reactions, and, occasionally, violence (see, for example, Mandalos & Szarek, 1990; Teicher, Glod, & Cole, 1990). Prozac went from being a wonder drug in the eyes of the press to a potential menace to modern society. Neither conclusion was true. Findings indicated that the risks of suicide with this drug for the general population were no greater than with any other antidepressant (Fava & Rosenbaum, 1991), and the effectiveness is about the same as that of other antidepressants.

Several years ago, concerns about suicidal risks (increased thoughts, and so on) surfaced again, particularly among adolescents, and this time it looks like the concerns are justified, at least for adolescents (Berman, 2009; Olfson, Marcus, & Schaffer, 2006). These findings have led to warnings from the Food and Drug Administration (FDA) and other regulatory agencies around the world about these drugs. On the other hand, Gibbons, Hur, Bhaumik, and Mann (2006) found that actual suicide rates were lower in sections of the United States where prescriptions for SSRIs

▲ Of the synthetic drugs for depression, fluoxetine (Prozac) is the most widely used.

were higher. In addition, the SSRIs were also associated with a small but statistically significant *decrease* in actual suicides among adolescents compared with depressed adolescents not taking these drugs, based on a large community survey (Olfson, Shaffer, Marcus, & Greenberg, 2003). These findings are *correlational*, meaning we can't conclude that increased prescriptions for SSRIs caused lower suicide rates. Research will continue on this important question. One possible conclusion is that SSRIs cause increased thoughts about suicide in the first few weeks in some adolescents but, once they start working after a month or more, may prevent the depression from leading to suicide (Berman, 2009; Simon, 2006).

Prozac and other SSRIs have their own set of side effects, the most prominent of which are physical agitation, sexual dysfunction, low sexual desire (which is prevalent, occurring in 50% to 75% of cases), insomnia, and gastrointestinal upset. But these side effects, on the whole, seem to bother most patients less than the side effects associated with tricyclic antidepressants, with the possible exception of the sexual dysfunction. Another class of antidepressants (sometimes termed *mixed reuptake inhibitors*) seem to have somewhat different mechanisms of neurobiological action. The best known, venlafaxine (Effexor) is related to tricyclic antidepressants, but acts in a slightly different manner, blocking reuptake of norepinephrine as well as serotonin. Some side effects associated with the SSRIs are reduced with venlafaxine, as is the risk of damage to the cardiovascular system. Other typical side effects remain, including nausea and sexual dysfunction.

MAO inhibitors work differently. As their name suggests, they block the enzyme MAO that breaks down such neurotransmitters as norepinephrine and serotonin. The result is roughly equivalent to the effect of the tricyclics. Because they are not broken down, the neurotransmitters pool in the synapse, leading to a down-regulation. The MAO inhibitors seem to be as effective as the tricyclics (American Psychiatric Association, 2010), with somewhat fewer side effects. Some evidence suggests they are relatively more

effective for depression with atypical features (American Psychiatric Association, 2010; Thase & Kupfer, 1996). But MAO inhibitors are used far less often because of two potentially serious consequences: Eating and drinking foods and beverages containing tyramine, such as cheese, red wine, or beer, can lead to severe hypertensive episodes and, occasionally, death. In addition, many other drugs that people take daily, such as cold medications, are dangerous and even fatal in interaction with a MAO inhibitor. Therefore, MAO inhibitors are usually prescribed only when other antidepressants are not effective.

Tricyclic antidepressants were the most widely used treatments for depression before the introduction of SSRIs, but are now used less commonly (Gitlin, 2009; Thase & Denko, 2008). The best-known variants are probably imipramine (Tofranil) and amitriptyline (Elavil). It is not yet clear how these drugs work, but initially, at least, they block the reuptake of certain neurotransmitters, allowing them to pool in the synapse and, as the theory goes, desensitize or down-regulate the transmission of that particular neurotransmitter (so less of the neurochemical is transmitted). Tricyclic antidepressants seem to have their greatest effect by down-regulating norepinephrine, although other neurotransmitter systems, particularly serotonin, are also affected. This process then has a complex effect on both presynaptic and postsynaptic regulation of neurotransmitter activity, eventually restoring appropriate balance. Side effects include blurred vision, dry mouth, constipation, difficulty urinating, drowsiness, weight gain (at least 13 pounds on average), and, sometimes, sexual dysfunction. Therefore, as many as 40% of these patients may stop taking the drug, thinking the cure is worse than the disease. Nevertheless, with careful management, many side effects disappear over time. Another issue clinicians must consider is that tricyclics are *lethal* if taken in excessive doses; therefore, they must be prescribed with great caution to patients with suicidal tendencies.

Because the SSRIs and other drugs relieve symptoms of depression to some extent in about 50% of all patients treated but eliminate depression or come close to it in only 25% to 30% of all patients treated (termed *remission*) (Trivedi *et al.*, 2006), the question remains: What do clinicians do when depression does not respond adequately to drug treatment, often called treatment-resistant depression? A large study called the Sequenced Treatment Alternatives to Relieve Depression (STAR*D) examined whether offering those individuals who did not achieve remission the alternatives of either adding a second drug or switching to a second drug is useful. Among those who were willing, approximately 20% (for switching) to approximately 30% (for adding a second drug) achieved remission. When repeating this with a third drug among those who had failed to achieve remission with the first two drugs, the results weren't as good (between 10% and 20% achieved remission) (Insel, 2006; Rush, 2007), and very few clinicians would go to a third drug in the same class after failing on the first two (Gitlin, 2009). The conclusion is that it's worth being persistent, as long as individuals with depression are still willing to try a second drug, because some people who don't improve with the first drug could improve with a different drug. Later, we report on combining psychological treatments with drugs. In summary, all antidepressant medications work about the same in large clinical trials, but sometimes a patient will not do well on one drug but respond better to another.

Current studies indicate that drug treatments effective with adults are not necessarily effective with children (American Psychiatric Association, 2010; Kaslow, Davis, & Smith, 2009). Sudden deaths of children under 14 who were taking tricyclic antidepressants have been reported, particularly during exercise, as in routine school athletic competition (Tingelstad, 1991). Cardiac side effects have been implicated in these deaths. But evidence indicates that, unlike tricyclic antidepressants, at least one of the SSRIs, fluoxetine (Prozac), is safe and has some evidence for efficacy with adolescents both initially (Kaslow et al., 2009; Treatment for Adolescents with Depression Study [TADS] Team, 2004) and at follow-up (TADS Team, 2009), particularly if combined with CBT (March & Vitiello, 2009). Traditional antidepressant drug treatments are usually effective with the elderly, but administering them takes considerable skill because older people may suffer from a variety of side effects not experienced by younger adults, including memory impairment and physical agitation (Blazer & Hybels, 2009; Fiske et al., 2009). Use of a depression care manager to deliver care to depressed elderly patients right in the office of their primary medical care doctor including encouraging compliance with drug taking, monitoring side effects unique to older adults, and delivering a bit of psychotherapy was more effective than usual care (Alexopoulos et al., 2005; Unutzer et al., 2002).

Clinicians and researchers have concluded that recovery from depression, although important, may not be the most important therapeutic outcome (Frank et al., 1990; Thase, 2009). Most people eventually recover from a major depressive episode, some rather quickly. A more important goal is often to delay the next depressive episode or even prevent it entirely (National Institute of Mental Health, 2003; Thase, 2009). This is particularly important for patients who retain some symptoms of depression or have a past history of chronic depression or multiple depressive episodes (Forand & DeRubeis, 2013; Hammen & Keenan-Miller, 2013). Because all these factors put people at risk for relapse, it is recommended that drug treatment go well beyond the termination of a depressive episode, continuing perhaps six to 12 months after the episode is over, or even longer (American Psychiatric Association, 2010; Insel, 2006). The drug is then gradually withdrawn over weeks or months. (We return later to strategies for maintaining therapeutic benefits.) Long-term administration of antidepressants has not been studied extensively, and there is even some evidence that long-term treatment lasting several years may worsen the course of depression (Fava, 2003).

Antidepressant medications have relieved severe depression and undoubtedly prevented suicide in tens of thousands of patients around the world, particularly in cases of more severe depression. Although these medications are readily available, many people refuse or are not eligible to take them. Some are wary of long-term side effects. Women of childbearing age must protect themselves against the possibility of conceiving while taking antidepressants, because of possible damage to the fetus. In one recent study of all births over a 10-year period in the country of Denmark, infants of mothers who were taking SSRIs during pregnancy, but not other antidepressants, had an almost two-fold increased risk of having a low Apgar score (a measure of infant health immediately after birth that predicts IQ scores, performance in school, as well as neurological disability including cerebral palsy, epilepsy, and cognitive impairment lasting for many years after birth) (Jensen et al., 2013). On the other hand, a large population-based prospective study in the US showed that depressed mothers who were taking SSRIs during pregnancy had a *lower* risk for birth complications (e.g., preterm birth, caesarean delivery) than those who did not take SSRIs, suggesting that SSRIs may also have a protective effect on the process of giving birth (Malm et al., 2015). The current recommendation is to individualize clinical decision making.

Lithium

Another type of antidepressant drug, *lithium carbonate*, is a common salt widely available in the natural environment (Alda, 2015). It is found in our drinking water in amounts too small to have any effect. The side effects of therapeutic doses of lithium are potentially more serious, however, than the side effects of other antidepressants. Dosage has to be carefully regulated to prevent toxicity (poisoning) and lowered thyroid functioning, which might intensify the lack of energy associated with depression. Substantial weight gain is also common. Lithium, however, has one major advantage that distinguishes it from other antidepressants: It is also often effective in preventing and treating manic episodes. Therefore, it is most often referred to as a **mood-stabilizing drug**. Antidepressants can induce manic episodes, even in individuals without pre-existing bipolar disorder (Goodwin & Ghaemi, 1998; Goodwin & Jamison, 2007), and lithium remains the gold standard for treatment of bipolar disorder, although the mechanism of action remains only partially understood (Alda, 2015; Nivoli, Murru, & Vieta, 2010). Other pharmacological treatments for acute bipolar depression include antidepressants, anticonvulsants, and antipsychotics (Vazques, Holtzman, Tondo, & Baldessarini, 2015).

Results indicate that 50% of bipolar patients respond well to lithium initially, meaning at least a 50% reduction in manic symptoms (Goodwin & Jamison, 2007). Thus, although

mood-stabilizing drug A medication used in the treatment of **mood disorders**, particularly bipolar disorder, that is effective in preventing and treating pathological shifts in mood.

effective, lithium provides many people with inadequate therapeutic benefit. Patients who don't respond to lithium can take other drugs with antimanic properties, including anticonvulsants such as carbamazepine and valproate (Divalproex), as well as calcium channel blockers such as verapamil (Sachs & Rush, 2003; Thase & Denko, 2008). Valproate has recently overtaken lithium as the most commonly prescribed mood stabilizer for bipolar disorder (Thase & Denko, 2008) and is equally effective, even for patients with rapid-cycling symptoms (Calabrese et al., 2005). But newer studies show that these drugs have one distinct disadvantage: They are less effective than lithium in preventing suicide (Thase & Denko, 2008; Tondo, Jamison, & Baldessarini, 1997).

For those patients who do respond to lithium, studies following patients for up to five years report that approximately 70% relapse, even if they continue to take the lithium (Frank et al., 1999; Hammen & Keenan-Miller, 2013). Nevertheless, for almost anyone with recurrent manic episodes, maintenance on lithium or a related drug is recommended to prevent relapse (Yatham et al., 2006). Another problem with drug treatment of bipolar disorder is that people usually like the euphoric or high feeling that mania produces and they often stop taking lithium to maintain or regain the state; that is, they do not comply with the medication regimen. Because the evidence now clearly indicates that individuals who stop their medication are at considerable risk for relapse, other treatment methods, usually psychological in nature, are used to increase compliance.

Electroconvulsive Therapy and Transcranial Magnetic Stimulation

When someone does not respond to medication (or in an extremely severe case), clinicians may consider a more dramatic treatment, **electroconvulsive therapy (ECT)**, the most controversial treatment for psychological disorders after psychosurgery. In Chapter 1, we described how ECT was used in the early 20th century. Despite many unfortunate abuses along the way, ECT is considerably changed today. It is now a safe and reasonably effective treatment for those cases of severe depression that do not improve with other treatments (American Psychiatric Association, 2010; Kellner et al., 2012).

In current administrations, patients are anesthetized to reduce discomfort and given muscle-relaxing drugs to prevent bone breakage from convulsions during seizures. Electric shock is administered directly through the brain for less than a second, producing a seizure and a series of brief convulsions that usually lasts for several minutes. In current practice, treatments are administered once every other day for a total of six to 10 treatments (fewer if the patient's mood returns to normal). Side effects are generally limited to short-term memory loss and confusion that disappear after a week or two, although some patients may have long-term memory problems. For severely depressed inpatients with psychotic features, controlled studies indicate that approximately 50% of those *not responding* to medication will benefit. Continued treatment with medication or psychotherapy is then necessary because the relapse rate approaches 60% or higher (American Psychiatric Association, 2010a; Gitlin, 2009).

We do not really know why ECT works. Repeated seizures induce massive functional and perhaps structural changes in the brain, which seems to be therapeutic. There is some evidence that ECT increases levels of serotonin, blocks stress hormones, and promotes neurogenesis in the hippocampus.

Recently, another method for altering electrical activity in the brain by setting up a strong magnetic field has been introduced. This procedure is called *transcranial magnetic stimulation (TMS)*, and it works by placing a magnetic coil over the individual's head to generate a precisely localized electromagnetic pulse. Anesthesia is not required, and side effects are usually limited to headaches. Initial reports, as with most new procedures, showed promise in treating depression (George, Taylor, & Short, 2013), and recent observations and reviews have confirmed that TMS can be effective (De Raedt et al., 2015; Mantovani et al., 2012; Schutter, 2009). But results from several important clinical trials with severe or treatment-resistant psychotic depression reported ECT to be clearly more effective than TMS (Eranti et al., 2007). It may be that TMS is more comparable to antidepressant medication than to ECT, and one study reported a slight advantage for combining TMS and medication compared to using either treatment alone (Brunoni et al., 2013; Gitlin, 2009).

Several other non-drug approaches for treatment-resistant depression are in development. Vagus nerve stimulation involves implanting a pacemaker-like device that generates pulses to the vagus nerve in the neck, which, in turn, is thought to influence neurotransmitter production in the brain stem and limbic system (Gitlin, 2009; Marangell et al., 2002). Sufficient evidence has accumulated so that the FDA has approved this procedure, but results are generally weak and it has been little-used. Deep brain stimulation has been used with a few severely depressed patients. In this procedure, electrodes are surgically implanted in the limbic system (the emotional brain). These electrodes are also connected to a pacemaker-like device (Mayberg et al., 2005). Initial results show some promise in treatment-resistant patients, but time will tell if this is a useful treatment (Kennedy et al., 2011; Lozano et al., 2012).

Psychological Treatments for Depression

Of the effective psychological treatments now available for depressive disorders, two major approaches have the most evidence supporting their efficacy. The first is a cognitive-behavioral approach; Aaron T. Beck, the founder of cognitive therapy, is most closely associated with this approach. The second approach, interpersonal psychotherapy, was developed by Myrna Weissman and Gerald Klerman.

Cognitive-Behavioral Therapy

Beck's **cognitive therapy** grew directly out of his observations of the role of deep-seated negative thinking in generating depression (Beck, 1967, 1976; Young *et al.*, 2014). Clients are taught to examine carefully their thought processes while they are depressed and to recognize "depressive" errors in thinking. This task is not always easy, because many thoughts are automatic and beyond clients' awareness. Clients are taught that errors in thinking can directly cause depression. Treatment involves correcting cognitive errors and substituting less depressing and (perhaps) more realistic thoughts and appraisals. Later in therapy, underlying negative cognitive schemas (characteristic ways of viewing the world) that trigger specific cognitive errors are targeted, not only in the clinic but also as part of the client's day-to-day life. The therapist purposefully takes a Socratic approach (teaching by asking questions—see the dialogue below), making it clear that therapist and client are working as a team to uncover faulty thinking patterns and the underlying schemas from which they are generated. Therapists must be skillful and highly trained. Following is an example of an actual interaction between Beck and a depressed client named Irene.

Beck and Irene... • *A Dialogue*

Because an intake interview had already been completed by another therapist, Beck did not spend time reviewing Irene's symptoms in detail or taking a history. Irene began by describing her "sad states." Beck almost immediately started to elicit her automatic thoughts during these periods.

Therapist: What kind of thoughts go through your mind when you've had these sad feelings this past week?

Patient: Well . . . I guess I'm thinking what's the point of all this. My life is over. It's just not the same. . . . I have thoughts like, "What am I going to do? . . . Sometimes I feel mad at him, you know my husband. How could he leave me? Isn't that terrible of me? What's wrong with me? How can I be mad at him? He didn't want to die a horrible death. . . . I should have done more. I should have made him go to the doctor when he first started getting headaches. . . . Oh, what's the use. . . ."

T: It sounds like you are feeling quite bad right now. Is that right?

P: Yes.

T: Keep telling me what's going through your mind right now.

P: I can't change anything. . . . It's over. . . . I don't know. . . . It all seems so bleak and hopeless. . . . What do I have to look forward to . . . sickness and then death. . . .

T: So one of the thoughts is that you can't change things and that it's not going to get any better?

P: Yes.

T: And sometimes you believe that completely?

P: Yeah, I believe it, sometimes.

T: Right now do you believe it?

P: I believe it—yes.

T: Right now you believe that you can't change things and it's not going to get better?

P: Well, there is a glimmer of hope but it's mostly. . . .

T: Is there anything in your life that you kind of look forward to in terms of your own life from here on?

P: Well, what I look forward to—I enjoy seeing my kids, but they are so busy right now. My son is a lawyer and my daughter is in medical school. . . . So, they are very busy. . . . They don't have time to spend with me.

Related cognitive-behavioral approaches to depression include the Cognitive-Behavioral Analysis System of Psychotherapy (CBASP) (McCullough, 2000, 2014), which integrates cognitive, behavioral, and interpersonal strategies and focuses on problem-solving skills, particularly in the context of important relationships. This treatment was designed for individuals with persistent (chronic) depression and has been tested in a large clinical trial (see below). Finally, mindfulness-based therapy has been found to be effective for treating depression (Hofmann, Sawyer, Witt, & Oh, 2010; Khoury *et al.*, 2013) and preventing future depressive relapse and recurrence (Kuyken *et al.*, 2015). These techniques have also been combined with cognitive therapy in mindfulness-based cognitive therapy (MBCT) (Barnhofer *et al.*, 2015; Michalak, Schultze, Heidenreich, & Schramm, 2015; Segal, Williams, & Teasdale, 2002; Williams, Teasdale, Segal, & Kabat-Zinn, 2007). MBCT has been evaluated and found effective for the most part in the context of preventing relapse or recurrence in patients who are in remission from their depressive episode. This approach seems particularly effective for individuals with more severe disorders, as indicated by a history of three or more prior depressive episodes (Segal *et al.*, 2002; Segal *et al.*, 2010).

The late Neil Jacobson and colleagues have shown that increased activities alone can improve self-concept and lift

electroconvulsive therapy (ECT) Biological treatment for severe, chronic depression involving the application of electrical impulses through the brain to produce seizures. The reasons for its effectiveness are unknown.

cognitive therapy Treatment approach that involves identifying and altering negative thinking styles related to **psychological disorders** such as depression and **anxiety** and replacing them with more positive beliefs and attitudes—and, ultimately, more adaptive behavior and coping styles.

depression (Dimidjian *et al.*, 2014; Jacobson *et al.*, 1996). This more behavioral treatment has been reformulated because initial evaluation suggests it is as effective as, or more effective than, cognitive approaches (Hollon, 2011; Jacobson, Martell, & Dimidjian, 2001). The new focus of this approach is on preventing avoidance of social and environmental cues that produce negative affect or depression and result in avoidance and inactivity. Rather, the individual is helped to face the cues or triggers and work through them and the depression they produce, with the therapist, by developing better coping skills. Similarly, programmed exercise over the course of weeks or months is surprisingly effective in treating depression (Mead *et al.*, 2009; Stathopoulou, Powers, Berry, Smits, & Otto, 2006). Babyak and colleagues (2000) demonstrated that programmed aerobic exercise three times a week was as effective as treatment with antidepressive medication (Zoloft) or the combination of exercise and Zoloft after four months. More important, exercise was *better* at preventing relapse in the six months following treatment compared with the drug or combination treatment, particularly if the patients continued exercising. It was noted above that there is some new evidence that exercise increases neurogenesis in the hippocampus, which is known to be associated with resilience to depression. This general approach of focusing on fitness activities is also consistent with findings about the most powerful methods to change dysregulated emotions (Barlow, Allen, & Choate, 2004; Campbell-Sills, Ellard, & Barlow, 2015), and we are likely to see more research on this approach in the near future.

Interpersonal Psychotherapy

Interpersonal psychotherapy (IPT) (Bleiberg & Markowitz, 2014; Weissman, 1995) focuses on resolving problems in existing relationships and learning to form important new interpersonal relationships. Like cognitive-behavioral approaches, IPT is highly structured and seldom takes longer than 15 to 20 sessions, usually scheduled once a week (Cuijpers *et al.*, 2011). After identifying life stressors that seem to precipitate the depression, the therapist and patient work collaboratively on the patient's current interpersonal problems. Typically, these include one or more of four interpersonal issues: *dealing with interpersonal role disputes*, such as marital conflict; *adjusting to the loss of a relationship*, such as grief over the death of a loved one; *acquiring new relationships*, such as getting married or establishing professional relationships; and *identifying and correcting deficits in social skills* that prevent the person from initiating or maintaining important relationships.

To take a common example, the therapist's first job is to identify and define an interpersonal dispute (Bleiberg & Markowitz, 2014; Weissman, 1995), perhaps with a wife who expects her spouse to support her but has had to take an outside job to help pay bills. The husband might expect the wife to share equally in generating income. If this dispute seems to be associated with the onset of depressive symptoms and

to result in a continuing series of arguments and disagreements without resolution, it would become the focus for IPT.

After helping identify the dispute, the next step is to bring it to a resolution. First, the therapist helps the patient determine the stage of the dispute.

1. *Negotiation stage.* Both partners are aware it is a dispute, and they are trying to renegotiate it.
2. *Impasse stage.* The dispute smolders beneath the surface and results in low-level resentment, but no attempts are made to resolve it.
3. *Resolution stage.* The partners are taking some action, such as divorce, separation, or recommitting to the marriage.

The therapist works with the patient to define the dispute clearly for both parties and develop specific strategies for resolving it. Studies comparing the results of cognitive therapy and IPT with those of antidepressant drugs and other control conditions have found that psychological approaches and medication are equally effective immediately following treatment, and all treatments are more effective than placebo conditions, brief psychodynamic treatments, or other appropriate control conditions for both major depressive disorder and persistent depressive disorder (Hollon, 2011; Paykel & Scott, 2009). Depending on how "success" is defined, approximately 50% or more of people benefit from treatment to a significant extent, compared with approximately 30% in placebo or control conditions (Hollon, 2011; Hollon & Dimidjian, 2009).

Similar results have been reported in depressed children and adolescents (Kaslow *et al.*, 2009). In one notable clinical trial, Brent and colleagues (2008) demonstrated that, in more than 300 severely depressed adolescents who had failed to respond to an SSRI antidepressant, CBT was significantly more effective than switching to another antidepressant. Kennard and colleagues (2009) showed that this was particularly true if the adolescents received at least nine sessions of the CBT. Furthermore, studies have not found differences in treatment effectiveness based on severity of depression (Fournier *et al.*, 2010; Hollon, Stewart, & Strunk, 2006).

Prevention

In view of the seriousness of mood disorders in children and adolescents, work has begun on preventing these disorders in these age groups (Horowitz & Garber, 2006; Muñoz, Beardslee, & Leykin, 2012). The Institute of Medicine (IOM) delineated three types of programs: *universal* programs, which are applied to everyone; *selected* interventions, which target individuals at risk for depression because of factors such as divorce, family alcoholism, and so on; and *indicated* interventions, in which the individual is already showing mild symptoms of depression (Muñoz *et al.*, 2009). As an example of selected interventions, Gillham and colleagues (2012) taught cognitive and social problem-solving techniques to more than 400 middle school children ages 10 to 15 who were at risk for depression because of negative thinking styles. Compared with children in a matched no-treatment control group, the prevention group reported fewer depressive symptoms during follow up. Seligman, Schulman, DeRubeis, and Hollon (1999) conducted a similar course for university students who were also at risk for depression based on a pessimistic cognitive style. After three years, students taking the eight-session program experienced less anxiety and depression than a control group receiving the assessments only. This suggests that it might be possible to "psychologically immunize" at-risk children and adolescents against depression by teaching appropriate cognitive and social skills before they enter puberty.

Results from a major clinical trial that combined "selected" and "indicated" approaches have been reported targeting adolescents at risk for depression (Garber *et al.*, 2009). Three hundred sixteen adolescent offspring of parents with current or prior depressive disorders were entered into the trial and randomized to a CBT prevention program or to usual care. To be included, adolescents had to have either a past history of depression, or current depressive symptoms that would not be severe enough to meet criteria for a disorder, or both. The adolescents in the CBT prevention group received eight weekly group sessions as well as six monthly continuation sessions. The usual care group included a fairly active use of mental health or other health-care services that, however, did not include any of the procedures used in the CBT group. The results indicate that the CBT prevention program was significantly more effective than usual care in preventing future episodes of depression, but only for those adolescents whose parents were not currently in a depressive episode themselves. If the parents were in a depressive episode while the adolescents were receiving care, the adolescents became somewhat less depressed based on their own report but did not have significantly fewer depressive episodes during the follow-up period. These results are very important because they show not only that preventive programs are potentially powerful but also that living with a depressed parent lessens the power of preventive programs to some degree (Hammen, 2009). The results also suggest that to prevent future depressive episodes, it is necessary to treat depression in the whole family in a coordinated manner.

In view of the enormous burden depression places on society, a consensus has developed that preventing depression is a global priority in public health (Cuijpers, Beekman, & Reynolds, 2012).

Combined Treatments for Depression

One important question is whether combining psychosocial treatments with medication is more effective than either treatment alone in treating depression or preventing relapse. In a large study reported by Keller and colleagues (2000) on the treatment of persistent (chronic) major

depression, 681 patients at 12 clinics around the country were assigned to receive antidepressant medication (nefazodone), a CBT constructed specifically for chronically depressed patients (CBASP, discussed earlier) (McCullough, 2014), or the combination of two treatments. Researchers found that 48% of patients receiving each of the individual treatments went into remission or responded in a clinically satisfactory way, compared with 73% of the patients receiving combined treatment. Because this study was conducted with only a subset of depressed patients, those with persistent depression, the findings would need to be replicated before researchers could say combined treatment was useful for depression in general. In addition, because the study did not include a fifth condition in which the CBT was combined with placebo, we cannot rule out that the enhanced effectiveness of the combined treatment was the result of placebo factors. Nevertheless, the consensus is that combined treatment does provide some advantage.

Preventing Relapse of Depression

Given the high rate of recurrence in depression, one important question has to do with **maintenance treatment** to prevent relapse or recurrence over the long term. In a number of studies, cognitive therapy reduced rates of subsequent relapse in depressed patients by more than 50% over groups treated with antidepressant medication (see, for example, Hollon *et al.*, 2005, 2006; Teasdale *et al.*, 2000). A study by Jarrett and colleagues (Jarrett, Minhajuddin, Gershenfeld, Friedman, & Thase, 2013) compared CBT, an SSRI (fluoxetine) and a pill placebo as a relapse prevention strategy for people with recurrent major depressive disorder. The study showed that, overall, both CBT and the SSRI prevented relapse equally well and more so than the placebo. Interestingly, relapse rates after having received CBT and fluoxetine did not differ.

In another study, patients were treated with either antidepressant medication or cognitive therapy compared with placebo (see DeRubeis *et al.*, 2005), and then the study began (Hollon *et al.*, 2005; Hollon, Stewart, & Strunk, 2006). All patients who had responded well to treatment were followed for two years. During the first year, one group of patients who were originally treated with antidepressant medication continued on the medication but then stopped for the second year. Also included in this figure is

··

interpersonal psychotherapy (IPT) Brief treatment approach that emphasizes resolution of interpersonal problems and stressors, such as role disputes in marital conflict, forming relationships in marriage, or a new job. It has demonstrated effectiveness for such problems as depression.

maintenance treatment Combination of continued **psychosocial treatment**, medication, or both designed to prevent **relapse** following therapy.

a subgroup of patients from the antidepressant medication group who took their medication exactly as prescribed and, therefore, should have received maximum benefit from the drugs (perfect adherence). A second group of patients originally receiving cognitive therapy were given up to three additional (booster) sessions during that first year but none after that. A third group was also originally treated with antidepressant medication but then switched to placebo.

During the first year, patients who were withdrawn from medication and placed onto pill placebo were considerably more likely to relapse over the ensuing 12-month interval than were patients continued on medication (23.8% did not relapse on placebo versus 52.8% on medication). In comparison, 69.2% of patients with a history of cognitive therapy did not relapse. At this point, there was no statistically significant difference in relapse rates among patients who had received cognitive therapy versus those who continued on antidepressant medication. This suggests that prior cognitive therapy has an enduring effect that is at least as large in magnitude as keeping the patients on medications. In the second year, when all treatments had stopped, patients who had received medications were more likely to experience a recurrence than patients who had originally received cognitive therapy. Thus, the adjusted recurrence rates were 17.5% for prior cognitive therapy versus 56.3% for prior continuation of antidepressant medication. Stangier and colleagues (2013) compared the effects of CBT with psychoeducation (a control condition) as a maintenance intervention for recurrent depression and found that CBT was only more effective than the control treatment in patients with five or more previous depressive episodes. These studies would seem to confirm that psychological treatments for depression are most notable for their enduring ability to prevent relapse or recurrence, especially for the more chronic or severe cases.

Early intervention of high-risk children and adolescents is an important area of future research. A recent trial compared CBT with usual care for preventing depression in high-risk adolescents (Beardslee *et al.*, 2013; Brent *et al.*, 2015). Subjects received eight weekly sessions followed by six monthly continuation sessions. The results showed that CBT was more effective than usual care (consisting of family-initiated mental health treatment) at preventing the onset of depression within three years (Beardslee *et al.*, 2013) and six years (Brent *et al.*, 2015) following the treatment.

Psychological Treatments for Bipolar Disorder

Although medication, particularly lithium, seems a necessary treatment for bipolar disorder, most clinicians emphasize the need for psychological interventions to manage interpersonal and practical problems (for example, marital and job difficulties that result from the disorder) (Otto & Applebaum, 2011). Until recently, the principal objective of psychological intervention was to increase compliance with medication regimens such as lithium. We noted before that the "pleasures" of a manic state make refusal to take lithium a major therapeutic obstacle. Giving up drugs between episodes or skipping dosages during an episode significantly undermines treatment. Therefore, increasing compliance with drug treatments is important (Goodwin & Jamison, 2007). For example, Clarkin, Carpenter, Hull, Wilner, and Glick (1998) evaluated the advantages of adding a psychological treatment to medication in inpatients and found it improved adherence to medication for all patients and resulted in better overall outcomes for the most severe patients compared with medication alone.

More recently, psychological treatments have also been directed at psychosocial aspects of bipolar disorder. Ellen Frank and her colleagues developed a psychological treatment that regulates circadian rhythms by helping patients regulate their eating and sleep cycles and other daily schedules as well as cope more effectively with stressful life events, particularly interpersonal issues (Frank *et al.*, 2005; Frank *et al.*, 1997). In an evaluation of this approach, called *interpersonal and social rhythm therapy* (IPSRT), patients receiving IPSRT survived longer without a new manic or depressive episode compared with patients undergoing standard, intensive clinical management. Initial results with adolescents are also promising (Hlastala, Kotler, McClellan, & McCauley, 2010).

David Miklowitz and his colleagues found that family tension is associated with relapse in bipolar disorder. Preliminary studies indicate that treatments directed at helping families understand symptoms and develop new coping skills and communication styles do change communication styles (Simoneau, Miklowitz, Richards, Saleem, & George, 1999) and prevent relapse (Miklowitz, 2014). Miklowitz, George, Richards, Simoneau, and Suddath (2003) demonstrated that their family-focused treatment combined with medication results in significantly less relapse one year following initiation of treatment than occurs in patients receiving crisis management and medication over the same period. Specifically, only 35% of patients receiving family therapy plus medication relapsed, versus 54% in the comparison group. Similarly, family therapy patients averaged over a year and a half (73.5 weeks) before relapsing, significantly longer than the comparison group.

Rea, Tompson, and Miklowitz (2003) compared this approach to an individualized psychotherapy in which patients received the same number of sessions over the same period and continued to find an advantage for the family therapy after two years. Reilly-Harrington and colleagues (2007) found some evidence that CBT is effective for bipolar patients with the rapid-cycling feature. In view of the relative ineffectiveness of antidepressant medication for the depressive stage of bipolar disorder reviewed above, Miklowitz and colleagues (2007) reported an important study showing that up to 30 sessions of an intensive psychological treatment was significantly more effective than usual and customary best treatment in promoting recovery from bipolar depression and remaining well. A more recent trial compared the effects of a four-month family-focused therapy and an educational control condition on preventing on the one-year course of mood symptoms in youths who are at high risk for developing bipolar disorder based on their family history and environment (Miklowitz *et al.*, 2013). The study showed that participants who received the family-focused therapy had a more rapid recovery from their initial mood symptoms and were more often in remission over the one year following treatment than those in the education control condition.

Let us now return to Katie, who, you will remember, had made a serious suicide attempt amid a major depressive episode.

Katie... • *The Triumph of the Self*

Like the overwhelming majority of people with serious psychological disorders, Katie had never received an adequate course of treatment, although she was evaluated occasionally by various mental health professionals. She lived in a rural area where competent professional help was not readily available. Her life ebbed and flowed with her struggle to subdue anxiety and depression. When she could manage her emotions sufficiently, she took an occasional course in the high school independent study program. Katie discovered that she was fascinated by learning. She enrolled in a local community college at the age of 19 and did extremely well, even though she had not progressed beyond her freshman year in high school. At the college, she earned a high school equivalency degree. She went to work in a local factory. But she continued to drink heavily and to take Valium; occasionally, anxiety and depression would return and disrupt her life.

Finally, Katie left home, attended college full time, and fell in love. But the romance was one-sided, and she was rejected.

One night after a phone conversation with him, I nearly drank myself to death. I lived in a single room alone in the dorm. I drank as much vodka as quickly as I could. I fell asleep. When I awoke, I was covered in vomit and couldn't recall falling asleep or being sick. I was drunk for much of the next day. When I awoke the following morning, I realized I could have killed myself by choking on my own vomit. More importantly, I wasn't sure if I fully wanted to die. That was the last of my drinking.

Katie decided to make some changes. Taking advantage of what she had learned in the little treatment she had received, she began looking at life and herself differently. Instead of dwelling on how inadequate and evil she was, she began to pay attention to her strengths. "But I now realized that I needed to accept myself as is,

and work with any stumbling blocks that I faced. I needed to get myself through the world as happily and as comfortably as I could. I had a right to that." Other lessons learned in treatment now became valuable, and Katie became more aware of her mood swings:

I learned to objectify periods of depression as [simply] periods of "feeling." They are a part of who I am, but not the whole. I recognize when I feel that way, and I check my perceptions with someone that I trust when I feel uncertain of them. I try to hold on to the belief that these periods are only temporary.

Katie developed other strategies for coping successfully with life:

I try to stay focused on my goals and what is important to me. I have learned that if one strategy to achieve some goal doesn't work, there are other strategies that probably will. My endurance is one of my blessings. Patience, dedication, and discipline are also important. None of the changes that I have been through occurred instantly or automatically. Most of what I have achieved has required time, effort, and persistence.

Katie dreamed that if she worked hard enough she could help other people who had problems similar to her own. Katie pursued that dream and earned her Ph.D. in psychology.

6.4 Concept CHECK

Indicate which type of treatment for mood disorders is being described in each statement:

1. The controversial but somewhat successful treatment involving the production of seizures through electrical current to the brain. _____

2. This teaches clients to carefully examine their thought process and recognize "depressive" styles in thinking. _____

3. These come in three main types (tricyclics, MAO inhibitors, and SSRIs) and are often prescribed but have numerous side effects. _____

4. This antidepressant must be carefully regulated to avoid illness but has the advantage of affecting manic episodes. _____

5. This therapy focuses on resolving problems in existing relationships and learning to form new interpersonal relationships. _____

6. This is an effort to prevent relapse or recurrence over the long run. _____

Suicide

▶ What is the relationship between suicide and mood disorders?

Most days we are confronted with news about the war on cancer or the frantic race to find a cure for AIDS. We also hear never-ending admonitions to improve our diet and to exercise more to prevent heart disease. But another cause of death ranks right up there with the most frightening and dangerous medical conditions. This is the seemingly inexplicable decision to kill themselves made by approximately 40,000 people a year in the United States alone.

Statistics

Suicide is officially the 11th leading cause of death in the United States (Nock, Borges, Bromet, Cha *et al.*, 2008), and most epidemiologists agree that the actual number of suicides may be two to three times higher than what is reported. Many of these unreported suicides occur when people deliberately drive into a bridge or off a cliff (Blumenthal, 1990), and in the past, it was not uncommon to attribute deaths by suicide to medical causes out of respect to the deceased (Marcus, 2010). Around the world, suicide causes more deaths per year than homicide or HIV/AIDS (Nock, Borges, Bromet, Cha *et al.*, 2008).

Suicide is overwhelmingly a white phenomenon. Most minority groups, including African Americans and Hispanics, seldom resort to this desperate alternative. As you might expect from the incidence of depression in Native Americans, however, their suicide rate is extremely high, far outstripping the rates in other ethnic groups (Centers for Disease Control and Prevention [CDC], 2015); although there is great variability across tribes—among the Apache, the rates are nearly four times the national average (Mullany *et al.*, 2009). Even more alarming is the dramatic increase in death by suicide beginning in adolescence. In 2012 in the United States, the number of deaths by suicide per 100,000 people rose from 1.73 in the 10 to 14 age group to 14.26 in the 20 to 24 age group (CDC, 2015). Firearms account for almost half of all suicides in this age group (CDC, 2015). Sadly, adolescents who are at risk for suicide have just as easy access to firearms (one in three adolescents live in a home with a firearm) as those who are not at risk (Simonetti *et al.*, 2015). Prevalence rates for suicide in adolescents differ greatly depending on ethnic group. This fact underscores the importance of attending to cultural considerations in the prevention and treatment of adolescent suicide (Goldston *et al.*, 2008).

There is also a dramatic increase in suicide rates among the elderly compared with rates for younger age groups. This rise has been connected to the growing incidence of medical illness in our oldest citizens and to their increasing loss of social support (Conwell, Duberstein, & Caine, 2002) and resulting depression (Boen, Dalgard, & Bjertness, 2012; Fiske *et al.*, 2009). As we have noted, a strong relationship exists between illness or infirmity and hopelessness or depression.

Suicide is not attempted only by adolescents and adults. Several reports exist of children two to five years of age who had attempted suicide at least once, many injuring themselves severely (Rosenthal & Rosenthal, 1984; Tishler, Reiss, & Rhodes, 2007), and suicide is the fifth leading cause of death from ages five to 14 (Minino *et al.*, 2002).

Regardless of age, in every country around the world except China, males are four times more likely to *commit* suicide than females (Nock *et al.*, 2011; World Health Organization, 2010). This startling fact seems to be related partly to gender differences in the types of suicide *attempts*. Males generally choose far more violent methods, such as guns and hanging; females tend to rely on less violent options, such as drug overdose (Callanan & Davis, 2012; Nock *et al.*, 2011). More men commit suicide during old age and more women during middle age, partly because most attempts by older women are unsuccessful (Berman, 2009; Kuo, Gallo, & Tien, 2001).

Uniquely in China, more women commit suicide than men, particularly in rural settings (Sun, 2011; Wu, 2009). What accounts for this culturally determined reversal? Chinese scientists agree that China's suicide rates, probably the highest in the world, are the result of an absence of stigma. Suicide, particularly among women, is often portrayed in classical Chinese literature as a reasonable solution to problems. A rural Chinese woman's family is her entire world, and suicide is an honorable solution if the family collapses. Furthermore, highly toxic farm pesticides are readily available, and it is possible that many women who did not necessarily intend to kill themselves die after accidentally swallowing poison.

In addition to completed suicides, three other important indices of suicidal behavior are **suicidal ideation** (thinking seriously about suicide), **suicidal plans** (the formulation of a specific method for killing oneself), and **suicidal attempts** (the person survives) (Kessler *et al.*, 2005; Nock *et al.*, 2011). Also, Nock and Kessler (2006) distinguish "attempters" (self-injurers with the intent to die) from "gesturers" (self-injurers who intend not to die but to influence or manipulate somebody or communicate a cry for help). In a carefully done cross-national study using consistent definitions, the prevalence of suicide ideation has been estimated at 9.2%; 3.1% reported a suicide plan, and 2.7% attempted suicide during their lifetime (Nock, Borges, Bromet, Alonso *et al.*, 2008).

Although males *commit* suicide more often than females in most of the world, females *attempt* suicide at least three times as often (Berman & Jobes, 1991; Kuo *et al.*, 2001). And the overall rate of non-lethal suicidal thoughts, plans, and (unsuccessful) attempts is 40% to 60% higher in women than in men (Nock *et al.*, 2011). This high incidence may reflect that more women than men are depressed and that depression is strongly related to suicide attempts (Berman, 2009). It is also interesting that despite the much higher rate of completed suicides among whites, there are no significant ethnic or racial differences in rates of suicide ideation, plans, or attempts (Kessler *et al.*, 2005). Among adolescents, the ratio of *thoughts* about suicide to *attempts* is also between 3:1 and 6:1. In other words, between 16% and 30% of adolescents who think about killing themselves actually attempt it (Kovacs, Goldston, & Gatsonis, 1993; Nock, Borges, Bromet, Cha *et al.*, 2008). "Thoughts" in this context does not refer to a fleeting philosophical type of consideration but rather to a serious contemplation of the act. The first step down the dangerous road to suicide is thinking about it.

▲ Men often choose violent methods of committing suicide. Actor Robin Williams, shown here, hanged himself. Singer Kurt Cobain shot himself.

In a study of college students (among whom suicide is the second leading cause of death), approximately 12% had serious thoughts about suicide during the past 12 months (Wilcox *et al.*, 2010). Only a minority of these college students with thoughts of suicide (perhaps around 10%) attempt to kill themselves, and only a few succeed (Schwartz, 2011). Nevertheless, given the enormity of the problem, suicidal thoughts are taken seriously by mental health professionals.

Causes

The great sociologist Emile Durkheim (1951) defined a number of suicide types, based on the social or cultural conditions in which they occurred. One type is "formalized" suicides that were approved of, such as the ancient custom of *hara-kiri* in Japan, in which an individual who brought dishonor to himself or his family was expected to impale himself on a sword. Durkheim referred to this as *altruistic suicide*. Durkheim also recognized the loss of social supports as an important provocation for suicide; he called this *egoistic suicide*. (Older adults who kill themselves after losing touch with their friends or family fit into this category.) Magne-Ingvar, Ojehagen, and Traskman-Bendz (1992) found that only 13% of 75 individuals who had seriously attempted suicide had an adequate social network of friends and relationships. Similarly, a recent study found that suicide attempters perceived themselves to have lower social support than did non-attempters (Riihimaki, Vuorilehto, Melartin, Haukka, & Isometsa, 2013). *Anomic suicides* are the result of marked disruptions, such as the sudden loss of a high-prestige job. (*Anomie* is feeling lost and confused.) Finally, *fatalistic suicides* result from a loss of control over one's own destiny. The mass suicide of 39 Heaven's Gate cult members in 1997 is an example of this type because the lives of those people were largely in the hands of Marshall Applewhite, a supreme and charismatic leader. Durkheim's work was important in alerting us to the social contribution to suicide. Sigmund Freud (1917/1957) believed that suicide (and depression, to some extent) indicated unconscious hostility directed inward to the self rather than outward to the person or situation causing the anger. Indeed, suicide victims often seem to be psychologically "punishing" others who may have rejected them or caused some other personal hurt. Current thinking considers social and psychological factors but also highlights the potential importance of biological contributions.

suicidal ideation Serious thoughts about committing suicide.

suicidal plans The formulation of a specific method of killing oneself.

suicidal attempts Effort made to kill oneself.

Consider a group of 1000 people, randomly selected from the world's population. Each year, four of these people will commit suicide, seven will make plans to kill themselves, and twenty will seriously consider suicide (Borges et al., 2010). Although suicide is a leading cause of death, it is difficult to predict and prevent, partly because many people who die by suicide leave behind few clues about the factors that influenced their decision to end their life. In an effort to better understand and predict suicide, researchers now often study people who have experienced suicidal thoughts and have made non-lethal suicide attempts. The results of such studies have provided interesting information about suicidal behaviors around the world.

Data from a recent survey of people in 17 countries indicate that approximately 9% of all adults report that they have seriously considered suicide at some point in their life, 3% have made an actual suicide plan, and just under 3% have made a suicide attempt (Nock, Borges, Bromet, Alonso et al., 2008). However, the rate of suicidal thoughts and attempts varies significantly across countries. For instance, only 3% of people in Italy have had suicidal thoughts, compared to 16% of people in New Zealand. Although the greatest absolute number of suicides occurs in populous countries like China and India, in recent years the highest suicide rates have been found in Japan, Hungary, Lithuania, and South Korea (Värnik, 2012).

Researchers are still trying to understand why these rates are so dissimilar across countries. Of note, once people report that they have had suicidal thoughts or made a suicide attempt, the characteristics look quite similar across countries. For instance, in every country examined, the rate of suicidal thoughts sharply increases during adolescence, approximately one-third of those with suicidal thoughts go on to make a suicide attempt, and more than 60% of those who do attempt suicide do so within the first year after they initially had suicidal thoughts. In addition, risk factors for suicidal thoughts and attempts are quite consistent cross-nationally and include being female, younger, less educated, and unmarried and having a mental disorder (Nock, Borges, Bromet, Alonso et al., 2008). Unfortunately, although an increasing number of risk factors for suicidal behaviors have been identified, to date no theories of suicide have been able to tie them together into a clear model that allows us to accurately predict who is most at risk and how to prevent them from engaging in suicidal behavior. ■

Risk Factors

Edward Shneidman pioneered the study of risk factors for suicide (Shneidman, 1989; Shneidman, Farberow, & Litman, 1970). Among the methods he and others have used to study those conditions and events that make a person vulnerable is **psychological autopsy**. The psychological profile of the person who committed suicide is reconstructed through extensive interviews with friends and family members who are likely to know what the individual was thinking and doing in the period before death. This and other methods have allowed researchers to identify a number of risk factors for suicide.

Family History

If a family member committed suicide, there is an increased risk that someone else in the family will also (Brent et al., 2015; Nock et al., 2011). In fact, among depressed patients, the strongest predictor of suicidal behavior was having a family history of suicide (Hantouche et al., 2010). Brent and colleagues (2002) noted that offspring of family members who had attempted suicide had six times the risk of suicide attempts compared with offspring of non-attempters. If a sibling was also a suicide attempter, the risk increased even more (Brent et al., 2003). This may not be surprising, because so many people who kill themselves are depressed or have some related mental disorder, and these disorders run in families (Nock et al., 2011). Nevertheless, the question remains: Are people who kill themselves simply adopting a familiar solution that they've witnessed in family members, or does an inherited trait, such as impulsivity, account for increased suicidal behavior in families? It seems both factors may contribute. If individuals have an early onset of their mood disorder, as well as aggressive or impulsive traits, then their families are at a greater risk for suicidal behavior (Mann et al., 2005). The possibility that something is inherited is also supported by several adoption studies. One found an increased rate of suicide in the biological relatives of adopted individuals who had committed suicide compared with a control group of adoptees who had not committed suicide (Nock et al., 2011). Also, reviewing studies of adopted children and their biological and adopted families, Brent and Mann (2005) found that adopted individuals' suicidal behavior was predicted only by suicidal behavior in their biological relatives. This suggests some biological (genetic) contribution to suicide, even if it is relatively small, although it may not be independent of genetic contribution to depression or associated disorders.

Neurobiology

A variety of evidence suggests that low levels of serotonin may be associated with suicide and with violent suicide attempts (Cremniter et al., 1999; Pompili et al., 2010).

As we have noted, extremely low levels of serotonin are associated with impulsivity, instability, and the tendency to overreact to situations. It is possible then that low levels of serotonin may contribute to creating a vulnerability to act impulsively. This may include killing oneself, which is sometimes an impulsive act. The studies by Brent and colleagues (2002) and Mann and colleagues (2005) suggest that transmission of vulnerabilities for a mood disorder, including the trait of impulsivity, may mediate family transmission of suicide attempts.

Existing Psychological Disorders and Other Psychological Risk Factors

More than 80% of people who kill themselves suffer from a psychological disorder, usually mood, substance use, or impulse control disorders (Berman, 2009; Nock, Hwang, Sampson, & Kessler, 2009). Suicide is often associated with mood disorders, and for good reason. As many as 60% of suicides (75% of adolescent suicides) are associated with an existing mood disorder (Berman, 2009; Oquendo et al., 2004). But many people with mood disorders do not attempt suicide, and, conversely, many people who attempt suicide do not have mood disorders. Therefore, depression and suicide, although strongly related, are still independent. Looking more closely at the relationship of mood disorder and suicide, some investigators have isolated hopelessness, a specific component of depression, as strongly predicting suicide (Beck, 1986; Goldston, Reboussin, & Daniel, 2006). But hopelessness also predicts suicide among individuals whose primary mental health problem is not depression (David Klonsky et al., 2012; Simpson, Tate, Whiting, & Cotter, 2011), a finding that also holds true in China (Cheung, Law, Chan, Liu, & Yip, 2006). A recent important theoretical account of suicide termed the "interpersonal theory of suicide" cites a perception of oneself as a burden on others and a diminished sense of belonging as powerful predictors of hopelessness and subsequently suicide (van Orden et al., 2010).

Alcohol use and abuse are associated with approximately 25% to 50% of suicides and are particularly evident in suicide among college students (Lamis, Malone, Langhinrichsen-Rohling, & Ellis, 2010) and adolescents (Berman, 2009; Pompili et al., 2012). In fact, Brent and colleagues (1988) found that about one-third of adolescents who commit suicide were intoxicated when they died and that many more might have been under the influence of drugs. Combinations of disorders, such as substance abuse and mood disorders in adults or mood disorders and conduct disorder in children and adolescents, seem to create a stronger vulnerability than any one disorder alone (Nock, Hwang et al., 2010; Woods et al., 1997). For example, Nock, Hwang, and colleagues (2010) noticed that depression alone did not predict suicidal ideation or attempts, but depression combined with impulse control problems and anxiety/agitation did. Woods and colleagues (1997) also found that

substance abuse with other risk-taking behaviors—such as getting into fights, carrying a gun, or smoking—were predictive of teenage suicide, possibly reflecting impulsivity in these troubled adolescents. A closely related trait termed *sensation-seeking* predicts teenage suicidal behavior as well, above and beyond its relationship with depression and substance use (Ortin, Lake, Kleinman, & Gould, 2012). Past suicide attempts are another strong risk factor and must be taken seriously (Berman, 2009). Cooper and colleagues (2005) followed almost 8,000 individuals who were treated in the emergency room for deliberate self-harm for up to four years. Sixty of these people later killed themselves, which equates to 30 times the rate for the general population.

A disorder characterized more by impulsivity than depression is borderline personality disorder (see Chapter 11). Individuals with this disorder, known for making manipulative and impulsive suicidal gestures without necessarily wanting to destroy themselves, sometimes kill themselves by mistake in as many as 10% of the cases. The combination of borderline personality disorder and depression is particularly deadly (Perugi et al., 2013; Soloff, Lynch, Kelly, Malone, & Mann, 2000).

The association of suicide with severe psychological disorders, especially depression, belies the myth that it is a response to disappointment in people who are otherwise healthy.

Stressful Life Events

Perhaps the most important risk factor for suicide is a severe, stressful event experienced as shameful or humiliating, such as a failure (real or imagined) in school or at work, an unexpected arrest, or rejection by a loved one (Conwell et al., 2002; Joiner & Rudd, 2000). Physical and sexual abuse are also important sources of stress (Wagner, 1997). Evidence confirms that the stress and disruption of natural disasters increase the likelihood of suicide (Krug et al., 1998; Stratta et al., 2012), particularly in the case of extreme catastrophes like massive earthquakes (Matsubayashi, Sawada, & Ueda, 2012). Based on data from 337 countries experiencing natural disasters in the 1980s, Krug and colleagues (1998) concluded that the rates of suicide increased 13.8% in the four years after severe floods, 31% in the two years after hurricanes, and 62.9% in the first year after an earthquake. Given pre-existing vulnerabilities—including psychological disorders, traits of impulsiveness, and lack of social support—a stressful event can often put a person over the edge. An integrated model of the causes of suicidal behavior is presented in ● Figure 6.5.

....

psychological autopsy Postmortem psychological profile of a suicide victim constructed from interviews with people who knew the person before death.

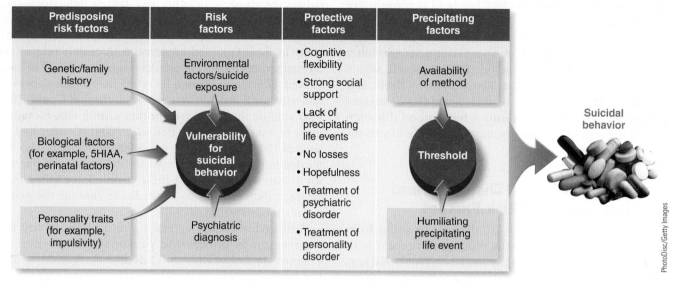

● **Figure 6.5** Threshold model for suicidal behavior. 5-hydroxy-indole acetic acid (5HIAA). (Based on Blumenthal, S. J., & Kupfer, D. J. (1988). Clinical assessment and treatment of youth suicide. *Journal of Youth and Adolescence, 17,* 1–24.)

Is Suicide Contagious?

Most people react to hearing the news of a suicide with sadness and curiosity. Some people react by attempting suicide themselves, often by the same method they have just heard about. Gould (1990) reported an increase in suicides during a nine-day period after widespread publicity about a suicide, and a recent review found a positive relationship between suicidal behavior and exposure to media coverage related to suicide (Sisask & Varnik, 2012). Clusters of suicides (several people copying one person) seem to predominate among teenagers, with as many as 5% of all teenage suicides reflecting an imitation (Gould, 1990; Gould, Greenberg, Velting, & Shaffer, 2003).

Why would anyone want to copy a suicide? First, suicides are often romanticized in the media: An attractive young person under unbearable pressure commits suicide and becomes a martyr to friends and peers by getting even with the (adult) world for creating such a difficult situation. Also, media accounts often describe in detail the methods used in the suicide, thereby providing a guide to potential victims. Little is reported about the paralysis, brain damage, and other tragic consequences of the incomplete or failed suicide or about how suicide is almost always associated with a severe psychological disorder. More important, even less is said about the futility of this method of solving problems (Gould, 1990, 2001; O'Carroll, 1990). To prevent these tragedies, mental health professionals must intervene immediately in schools and other locations with people who might be depressed or otherwise vulnerable to the contagion of suicide (Boyce, 2011). But it isn't clear that suicide is "contagious" in the infectious disease sense. Rather, the stress of a friend's suicide or some other major stress may affect several individuals who are vulnerable because of existing psychological disorders (Blasco-Fontecilla, 2012; Joiner, 1999).

Treatment

Despite the identification of important risk factors, predicting suicide is still an uncertain art. Individuals with few precipitating factors unexpectedly kill themselves, and many who live with seemingly insurmountable stress and illness and have little social support or guidance somehow survive and overcome their difficulties.

Mental health professionals are thoroughly trained in assessing for possible suicidal ideation (Fowler, 2012; Joiner *et al.*, 2007). Others might be reluctant to ask leading questions for fear of putting the idea in someone's head. We know, however, it is far more important to check for these "secrets" than to do nothing, because the risk of inspiring suicidal thoughts is small to non-existent and the risk of leaving them undiscovered is enormous (Berman, 2009). Gould and colleagues (2005) found that more than 1,000 high school students who were asked about suicidal thoughts or behaviors during a screening program showed no risk of increased suicidal thoughts compared with a second group of 1,000 students who had the screening program without the questions about suicide. Therefore, if there is any indication that someone is suicidal, the mental health professional will inquire, "Has there been any time recently when you've thought that life wasn't worth living or had some thoughts about hurting yourself or possibly killing yourself?"

One difficulty with this approach is that sometimes these thoughts are implicit or out of awareness. Now Cha, Najmi, Park, Finn, and Nock (2010) have developed measures of implicit (unconscious) cognition, adapted from the labs of cognitive psychology, to assess implicit suicidal ideation. In this assessment using the Stroop test described in Chapter 2, people who demonstrated an implicit association between the words *death/suicide* and *self*, even if they weren't aware of it, were six times more likely to make a suicide attempt in the next six months than those without this specific association; thus, this assessment is a better predictor of suicide attempts than both patients' own predictions and clinicians' predictions (Nock, Park *et al.*, 2010).

The mental health professional will also check for possible recent humiliations and determine whether any of the factors are present that might indicate a high probability of suicide. For example, does a person who is thinking of suicide have a detailed plan or just a vague fantasy? If a plan is discovered that includes a specific time, place, and method, the risk is high. Does the detailed plan include putting all personal affairs in order, giving away possessions, and other final acts? If so, the risk is higher still. What specific method is the person considering? Generally, the more lethal and violent the method (guns, hanging, poison, and so on), the greater the risk it will be used. Does the person understand what might actually happen? Many people do not understand the effects of the pills on which they might overdose. Finally, has the person taken any precautions against being discovered? If so, the risk is extreme (American Psychiatric Association, 2003).

If a risk is present, clinicians attempt to get the individual to agree to or perhaps even sign a "no-suicide" contract. Usually this includes a promise not to do anything remotely connected with suicide without contacting the mental health professional first. Although signing

---

DSM 5 CONTROVERSY — When Should Normal Grief be Considered Major Depressive Disorder?

Prior to *DSM-5*, if you met criteria for a major depressive episode in the two months following the loss, you would not receive a diagnosis of major depressive disorder, even if you otherwise met criteria for it (unless you had very severe symptoms such as strong suicidal ideation or psychotic features). This was called the "bereavement exclusion." This exclusion was dropped in *DSM-5* for several reasons (Zisook et al., 2012). For example, it was noted that major depressive episodes often are triggered by stressful events other than loss of a loved one in vulnerable individuals and, if all of the criteria are otherwise met for a major depressive episode, there seemed no reason to exclude people simply because the precipitating event was the death of a loved one. Furthermore, data from a number of sources suggested no differences between depressive episodes triggered by loss or not triggered by loss, and that the biological, psychological, and social factors that make one vulnerable to developing major depression are the same whether the trigger is loss of a loved one or not (Shear et al., 2011; Zisook et al., 2012). Finally, the data indicated that eliminating the two months bereavement exclusion would not greatly increase the numbers of people requiring treatment for major depression (Gilman et al., 2012; Zisook et al., 2012).

Nevertheless, this change was controversial, since some concluded that *DSM-5* would be making the natural grieving process a disorder resulting in, among other things, frequent prescriptions of antidepressant medication to those who might be undergoing a normal process of grieving (Fox & Jones, 2013; Maj, 2008)! This is one part of the larger criticism levied at *DSM-5* that the major purpose of *DSM* is to increase business for mental health professionals and make sure that large drug companies remain profitable. Advocates for dropping the bereavement exclusion point out that the diagnosis of major depressive disorder or posttraumatic stress disorder in response to other major life stressors is not controversial, nor should the development of major depressive disorder in some people in response to the loss of a loved one. Furthermore, the advocates continue, there are differences between a major depressive episode and grief. Individuals undergoing grief experience feelings of emptiness and loss, and these feelings come in waves sometimes referred to as the "pangs of grief," always triggered by thoughts of the loss of the loved one. Furthermore, grieving individuals are most usually able to experience some positive emotions, and even humor and self-esteem is generally intact. In a major depressive episode, feelings of depression are persistent and seldom accompanied by any positive emotions. Thought processes are typically very generally pessimistic and self-critical accompanied by very low self-esteem and a sense of worthlessness (APA, 2013).

In response, some mental health professionals propose that all intense sadness or stress—or even depression that is proportionate to the loss, the trauma, or the stress—should not be considered a disorder, since it is a natural experience of being human (Wakefield, Schmitz, First, & Horwitz, 2007). Time will tell if removing the bereavement exclusion from the diagnosis of major depressive disorder is a positive or negative development. •

a contract will not prevent a suicide attempt in someone who is determined, if the person at risk refuses a contract (or the clinician has serious doubts about the patient's sincerity) and the suicidal risk is judged to be high, immediate hospitalization is indicated, even against the will of the patient. Whether the person is hospitalized or not, treatment aimed at resolving underlying life stressors and treating existing psychological disorders should be initiated immediately.

In view of the public health consequences of suicide, a number of programs have been implemented to reduce the rates of suicide. Most research indicates that such curriculum-based programs targeting the general population (universal programs) in schools or organizations on how to handle life stress or increase social support are not effective (Berman, 2009; Garfield & Zigler, 1993). More helpful are programs targeted to at-risk individuals, including adolescents in schools where a student has committed suicide. The Institute of Medicine (2002) recommends making services available immediately to friends and relatives of victims. An important step is limiting access to lethal weapons for anyone at risk for suicide. A recent analysis suggests that this may be the most powerful part of a suicide prevention program (Mann and colleagues, 2005). Telephone hotlines and other crisis intervention services also seem to be useful. Nevertheless, as Garfield and Zigler (1993) point out, hotline volunteers must be backed up by competent mental health professionals who can identify potentially serious risks. One large health maintenance organization carefully screened all of its approximately 200,000 members who came in for services for suicide risk and then intervened if any risk was noted. Suicides were greatly reduced in this very promising program (Hampton, 2010).

Specific treatments for people at risk have also been developed. Suicide prevention programs for the elderly, for example, tend to focus on decreasing risk factors (e.g., treating depression) rather than shoring up protective factors like familial support, and could be improved by greater involvement of individuals' social networks (Lapierre et al., 2011). Other interventions target specific mental health problems associated with suicide. For instance, Marsha Linehan and colleagues developed a noteworthy treatment for borderline personality disorder that addresses impulsive suicidal behavior associated with this condition (see Chapter 11).

Empirical research indicates that cognitive-behavioral interventions can be efficacious in decreasing suicide risk. For example, David Rudd and colleagues developed a brief psychological treatment targeting young adults who were at risk for suicide because of the presence of suicidal ideation accompanied by previous suicidal attempts, mood or substance use disorders, or both (Rudd et al., 1996). Patients were assessed up to two years following treatment, and results indicated reductions in suicidal ideation and behavior, as well as marked improvement in problem-solving ability. This program was expanded into a psychological treatment for suicidal behavior with empirical support for its efficacy (Rudd, Joiner, & Rajab, 2001). One of the more important studies to date has demonstrated that 10 sessions of cognitive therapy for recent suicide attempters cuts the risk of additional attempts by 50% over the next 18 months (Brown et al., 2005). Specifically, 24% of those in the cognitive therapy group made a repeat attempt compared with 42% in the care-as-usual group. Because cognitive therapy is relatively widely available, this is an important development in suicide prevention (Joiner, 2014).

With the increased rate of suicide, particularly in adolescents, the tragic and paradoxical act is receiving increased scrutiny from public health authorities. The quest will go on to determine more effective and efficient ways of preventing one of the most serious consequences of any psychological disorder, the taking of one's own life.

6.5 Concept CHECK

Match each of the following summaries with the correct suicide type, choosing from (a) altruistic, (b) egoistic, (c) anomic, and (d) fatalistic:

1. Ralph's wife left him and took the children. He is a well-known television personality, but, because of a conflict with the new station owners, he was recently fired. If Ralph kills himself, his suicide would be considered _____.

2. Sam killed himself while a prisoner of war in Vietnam. _____

3. Sheiba lives in a remote village in Africa. She was recently caught in an adulterous affair with a man in a nearby village. Her husband wants to kill her but won't have to because of a tribal custom that requires her to kill herself. She leaps from the nearby "sinful woman's cliff." _____

4. Mabel lived in a nursing home for many years. At first, her family and friends visited her often; now they come only at Christmas. Her two closest friends in the nursing home died recently. She has no hobbies or other interests. Mabel's suicide would be identified as what type? _____

SUMMARY

Understanding and Defining Mood Disorders

What is the difference between a depressive episode and a manic or hypermanic episode?

▶ Mood disorders are among the most common psychological disorders, and the risk of developing them is increasing worldwide, particularly in younger people.

▶ Two fundamental experiences can contribute either singly or in combination to all specific mood disorders: a major depressive episode and mania. A less severe episode of mania that does not cause impairment in social or occupational functioning is known as a hypomanic episode. An episode of mania coupled with anxiety or depression is known as a mixed episode or mixed state.

▶ An individual who suffers from episodes of depression only is said to have a unipolar disorder. An individual who alternates between depression and mania has a bipolar disorder.

What are the clinical symptoms of major depressive disorder, persistent depressive disorder, and bipolar disorder?

▶ Major depressive disorder may be a single episode or recurrent, but it is always time-limited; in another form of depression, persistent depressive disorder (dysthymia), the symptoms are often somewhat milder but remain relatively unchanged over long periods. In some cases, fewer symptoms are observed than in a major depressive episode, but they persist for at least two years (persistent depressive disorder) (dysthymia); in other cases, a major depressive episode will last at least two years (chronic major depressive episode). In cases of double depression, a form of persistent depressive disorder, an individual experiences both major depressive episodes and persistent depressive disorder (dysthymia).

▶ Approximately 20% of bereaved individuals may experience a complicated grief reaction in which the normal grief response develops into a full-blown mood disorder.

▶ The key identifying feature of bipolar disorders is an alternation of manic episodes and major depressive episodes. Cyclothymic disorder is a milder but more chronic version of bipolar disorder.

▶ Patterns of additional features that sometimes accompany mood disorders, called *specifiers,* may predict the course or patient response to treatment, as does the temporal patterning or course of mood disorders. One pattern, seasonal affective disorder, most often occurs in winter.

Prevalence of Mood Disorders

How does the prevalence of mood disorders vary across a life span?

▶ Mood disorders in children are fundamentally similar to mood disorders in adults.

▶ Symptoms of depression are increasing dramatically in our elderly population.

▶ The experience of anxiety across cultures varies, and it can be difficult to make comparisons—especially, for example, when we attempt to compare subjective feelings of depression.

Causes of Mood Disorders

What biological, psychological, and sociocultural factors contribute to the development of mood disorders?

▶ The causes of mood disorders lie in a complex interaction of biological, psychological, and social factors. From a biological perspective, researchers are particularly interested in the stress hypothesis and the role of neurohormones. Psychological theories of depression focus on learned helplessness and the depressive cognitive schemas, as well as interpersonal disruptions.

Treatment of Mood Disorders

What medical and psychological treatments have been successful in treating mood disorders?

▶ A variety of treatments, both biological and psychological, have proved effective for the mood disorders, at least in the short term. For those individuals who do not respond to antidepressant drugs or psychosocial treatments, a more dramatic physical treatment, electroconvulsive therapy, is sometimes used. Two psychological treatments—cognitive therapy and interpersonal psychotherapy—seem effective in treating depressive disorders.

▶ Relapse and recurrence of mood disorders are common in the long term, and treatment efforts must focus on maintenance treatment, that is, on preventing relapse or recurrence.

Suicide

What is the relationship between suicide and mood disorders?

▶ Suicide is often associated with mood disorders but can occur in their absence or in the presence of other disorders. It is the 10th leading cause of death among all people in the United States, but among adolescents, it is the 3rd leading cause of death.

▶ In understanding suicidal behavior, three indices are important: suicidal ideation (serious thoughts about committing suicide), suicidal plans (a detailed method for killing oneself), and suicidal attempts (that are not successful). Important, too, in learning about risk factors for suicides is the psychological autopsy, in which the psychological profile of an individual who has committed suicide is reconstructed and examined for clues.

Key Terms

mood disorders, 202
major depressive episode, 202
mania, 203
hypomanic episode, 203
mixed features, 204
major depressive disorder, 204
recurrent, 204
persistent depressive disorder
    (dysthymia), 204
double depression, 204
integrated grief, 206

complicated grief, 206
premenstrual dysphoric disorder, 207
disruptive mood dysregulation
    disorder, 207, 208
bipolar II disorder, 210
bipolar I disorder, 210
cyclothymic disorder, 211
neurohormones, 217
learned helplessness theory
    of depression, 221
depressive cognitive triad, 222

mood-stabilizing drug, 229
electroconvulsive therapy (ECT), 230
cognitive therapy, 231
interpersonal psychotherapy
    (IPT), 232
maintenance treatment, 233
suicidal ideation, 236
suicidal plans, 236
suicidal attempts, 236
psychological autopsy, 238

Answers to Concept Checks

6.1

1. e; 2. a; 3. c; 4. d; 5. b

6.2

1. T; 2. F (it does not require life experience); 3. T; 4. T

6.3

1. Genetics, neurotransmitter system abnormalities, endocrine system, circadian or sleep rhythms, neurohormones; 2. Stressful life events, learned helplessness, depressive cognitive triad, a sense of uncontrollability; 3. Marital dissatisfaction, gender, few social supports

6.4

1. Electroconvulsive therapy; 2. Cognitive therapy; 3. Antidepressants; 4. Lithium; 5. Interpersonal psychotherapy; 6. Maintenance treatment

6.5

1. c; 2. d; 3. a; 4. b

Chapter Quiz

1. An individual who is experiencing an elevated mood, a decreased need for sleep, and distractibility is most likely experiencing:
   a. panic disorder
   b. mania
   c. depersonalization
   d. hallucinations.

2. What is the general agreement among mental health professionals about the relationship between bereavement and depression?
   a. Bereavement is less severe than depression in all cases.
   b. Depression can lead to bereavement in many cases.
   c. Bereavement can lead to depression in many cases.
   d. Symptoms of bereavement and depression rarely overlap.

3. Bipolar I disorder is characterized by _____, whereas bipolar II is characterized by _____.
   a. full manic episodes; hypomanic episodes
   b. hypomanic episodes; full manic episodes
   c. both depressive and manic episodes; full manic episodes
   d. full manic episodes; both depressive and manic episodes.

4 Treatment for bereavement often includes:
   a. finding meaning in the loss
   b. replacing the lost person with someone else
   c. finding humor in the tragedy
   d. replacing sad thoughts about the lost person with more happy thoughts.

5. Which statement best characterizes the relationship between anxiety and depression?
   a. Anxiety usually precedes the development of depression.
   b. Depression usually precedes the development of anxiety.
   c. Almost all depressed patients are anxious, but not all anxious patients are depressed.
   d. Almost all anxious patients are depressed, but not all depressed patients are anxious.

6. Which theory suggests that depression occurs when individuals believe that they have no control over the circumstances in their lives?
   a. attribution theory
   b. learned helplessness
   c. social learning theory
   d. theory of equifinality.

7. In treating depressed clients, a psychologist helps them think more positively about themselves, about their place in the world, and about the prospects for the future. This psychologist is basing her techniques on whose model of depression?

a. Sigmund Freud

b. Carl Rogers

c. Rollo May

d. Aaron Beck

8. Maintenance treatment for depression can be important because it can prevent:

a. transmission

b. bereavement

c. incidence

d. relapse

9. Which of the following explains why some people refuse to take medications to treat their depression or take those medications and then stop?

a. The medications are in short supply and are unavailable.

b. The medications don't work for most people.

c. For some people the medications cause serious side effects.

d. The medications work in the short term but not the long term.

10. Which of the following is a risk factor for suicide?

a. having a relative who committed suicide

b. playing aggressive, full-contact sports

c. a history of multiple marriages

d. an abstract, philosophical cognitive

(See Appendix A for answers.)

Exploring Mood Disorders

People with mood disorders experience one or both of the following:

▶ **Mania:** A frantic "high" with extreme overconfidence and energy, often leading to reckless behavior
▶ **Depression:** A devastating "low" with extreme lack of energy, interest, confidence, and enjoyment of life

- Negative or positive life changes (death of a loved one, promotion, etc.)
- Physical illness

Trigger

Brand X Pictures/Getty Images

Biological Influences

- Inherited vulnerability
- Altered neurotransmitters and neurohormonal systems
- Sleep deprivation
- Circadian rhythm disturbances

Social Influences

- Women and minorities—social inequality and oppression and a diminished sense of control
- Social support can reduce symptoms
- Lack of social support can aggravate symptoms

Causes

Disorder

Behavioral Influences

Depression
- General slowing down
- Neglect of responsibilities and appearance
- Irritability; complaints about matters that used to be taken in stride

Mania
- Hyperactivity
- Reckless or otherwise unusual behavior

SW Productions/Stockbyte/Getty Images

Emotional and Cognitive Influences

Depression
- Emotional flatness or emptiness
- Inability to feel pleasure
- Poor memory
- Inability to concentrate
- Hopelessness and/or learned helplessness
- Loss of sexual desire
- Loss of warm feelings for family and friends
- Exaggerated self-blame or guilt
- Overgeneralization
- Loss of self-esteem
- Suicidal thoughts or actions

Mania
- Exaggerated feelings of euphoria and excitement

PhotoDisc/Getty Images

TYPES OF MOOD DISORDERS

Depressive

Major Depressive Disorder
Symptoms of major depressive disorder:
- begin suddenly, often triggered by a crisis, change, or loss
- are extremely severe, interfering with normal functioning
- can be long term, lasting months or years if untreated

Some people have only one episode, but the pattern usually involves repeated episodes or lasting symptoms.

Persistent Depressive Disorder (Dysthymia)
Long-term unchanging symptoms of mild depression, sometimes lasting 20 to 30 years if untreated. Daily functioning not as severely affected, but over time impairment is cumulative.

Double Depression
Alternating periods of major depression and dysthymia

PhotoDisc/Getty Images

Bipolar

People who have a bipolar disorder live on an unending emotional roller coaster.

Types of Bipolar Disorders
- **Bipolar I:** major depression and full mania
- **Bipolar II:** major depression and mild mania
- **Cyclothymia:** mild depression with mild mania, chronic and long term

During the **Depressive Phase**, the person may:
- lose all interest in pleasurable activities and friends
- feel worthless, helpless, and hopeless
- have trouble concentrating
- lose or gain weight without trying
- have trouble sleeping or sleep more than usual
- feel tired all the time
- feel physical aches and pains that have no medical cause
- think about death or attempt suicide

During the **Manic Phase**, the person may:
- feel extreme pleasure and joy from every activity
- be extraordinarily active, planning excessive daily activities
- sleep little without getting tired
- develop grandiose plans leading to reckless behavior: unrestrained buying sprees, sexual indiscretions, foolish business investments, etc.
- have "racing thoughts" and talk on and on
- be easily irritated and distracted

TREATMENT OF MOOD DISORDERS
Treatment for mood disorders is most effective and easiest when it's started early. Most people are treated with a combination of these methods.

Treatment

Medication
Antidepressants can help to control symptoms and restore neurotransmitter functioning.
Common types of antidepressants:

- Tricyclics (Tofranil, Elavil)
- Monamine oxidase inhibitors (MAO inhibitors): (Nardil, Parnate); MAO inhibitors can have severe side effects, especially when combined with certain foods or over-the-counter medications
- Selective-serotonin reuptake inhibitors or SSRIs (Prozac, Zoloft) are newer and cause fewer side effects than tricyclics or MAO inhibitors
- Lithium is the preferred drug for bipolar disorder; side effects can be serious; and dosage must be carefully regulated

PhotoDisc/Getty Images

Cognitive-Behavioral Therapy
Helps depressed people:

- learn to replace negative depressive thoughts and attributions with more positive ones
- develop more effective coping behaviors and skills

Interpersonal Psychotherapy
Helps depressed people:

- focus on the social and interpersonal triggers for their depression (such as the loss of a loved one)
- develop skills to resolve interpersonal conflicts and build new relationships

Electroconvulsive Therapy (ECT)

- For severe depression, ECT is used when other treatments have been ineffective. It usually has temporary side effects, such as memory loss and lethargy. In some patients, certain intellectual and/or memory functions may be permanently lost.

David Buffington/Photodisc/Jupiter Images

Light Therapy

- For seasonal affective disorder

7 Physical Disorders and Health Psychology

CHAPTER OUTLINE

Psychological and Social Factors That Influence Health

Health and Health-Related Behavior
The Nature of Stress
The Physiology of Stress
Contributions to the Stress Response
Stress, Anxiety, Depression, and Excitement
Stress and the Immune Response

Psychosocial Effects on Physical Disorders

AIDS
Cancer
Cardiovascular Problems
Chronic Pain
Chronic Fatigue Syndrome

Psychosocial Treatment of Physical Disorders

Biofeedback
Relaxation and Meditation
A Comprehensive Stress- and Pain-Reduction Program
Drugs and Stress-Reduction Programs
Denial as a Means of Coping
Modifying Behaviors to Promote Health

Use scientific reasoning to interpret behavior:	▶ Identify basic biological, psychological, and social components of behavioral explanations (e.g., inferences, observations, operational definitions and interpretations) (APA SLO 2.1a) *(see textbook pages 255–258, 272)* ▶ Evaluate how the mind and body interact to influence psychological and physical health (APA SLO 1.3b) *(see textbook pages 258–276)*
Engage in innovative and integrative thinking and problem solving:	▶ Describe problems operationally to study them empirically (APA SLO 2.3a) *(see textbook pages 341–348)* ▶ Correctly identify antecedents and consequences of behavior and mental processes (APA SLO 1.3c) *(see textbook pages 257–258, 272, 275)*
Describe applications that employ discipline-based problem solving:	▶ Summarize psychological factors that can influence the pursuit of a healthy lifestyle (APA SLO 1.3b) *(see textbook pages 269, 276–278)*

* Portions of this chapter cover learning outcomes suggested by the American Psychological Association (2013) in their guidelines for the undergraduate psychology major. Chapter coverage of these outcomes is identified above by APA Goal and APA Suggested Learning Outcome (SLO).

Psychological and Social Factors that Influence Health

▶ What is the difference between behavioral medicine and health psychology?

▶ How are immune system function, stress, and physical disorders related?

At the beginning of the 20th century, the leading causes of death were infectious diseases such as influenza, pneumonia, diphtheria, tuberculosis, typhoid fever, measles, and gastrointestinal infections. Since then, the percentage of yearly total deaths from these diseases has been reduced greatly, from 38.9% to 4% (see Table 7.1). This reduction represents the first revolution in public health that eliminated many infectious diseases and controlled many more. But the success of our health-care system in reducing mortality from disease has revealed a more complex and challenging problem: At present, some major contributing factors to illness and death in this country are *psychological* and *behavioral* (Ezzati & Riboli, 2012; Marteau, Hollands, & Fletcher, 2012).

In Chapter 2, we described the effects of psychological and social factors on brain structure and function. These factors seem to influence neurotransmitter activity, the secretion of neurohormones, and, at a more fundamental level, gene expression. We have looked at the interplay of biological, psychological, and social factors in the production and maintenance of psychological disorders. But psychological and social factors are important to a number of additional disorders, including endocrinological disorders such as type 2 diabetes, cardiovascular disorders, and disorders of the immune system such as acquired immune deficiency syndrome (AIDS). These and the other disorders discussed in this chapter are *physical disorders*. They have known (or strongly inferred) physical causes and mostly observable physical pathology (for example, genital herpes, damaged heart muscle, malignant tumors, or measurable

hypertension). Contrast this with the somatic symptom disorders discussed in Chapter 5—in conversion disorders, for example, clients complain of physical damage or disease but show no physical pathology.

The study of how psychological and social factors affect physical disorders used to be distinct and somewhat separate from the remainder of psychopathology. Early on, the field was called *psychosomatic medicine* (Alexander, 1950), which meant that *psychological* factors affected *somatic* (physical) function. The label *psychophysiological disorders* was used to communicate a similar idea. Such terms are less often used today because they are misleading. Describing as psychosomatic a disorder with an obvious physical component gave the impression that psychological (mental) disorders of mood and anxiety did not have a strong biological component. As we now know, this assumption is not viable. Biological, psychological, and social factors are implicated in the cause and maintenance of virtually every disorder, both mental and physical.

The contribution of psychosocial factors to the etiology and treatment of physical disorders is widely studied. Some of the discoveries are among the more exciting findings in all of psychology and biology. For example, we described briefly in Chapter 2 that lowering stress levels and having a rich social network are associated with better health, living longer, and less cognitive decline as one ages (Cohen & Janicki-Deverts, 2009). Remember, too, the tragic physical and mental deterioration among elderly people who are removed from social networks of family and friends (Hawkley & Cacioppo, 2007).

TABLE 7.1 | The 10 Leading Causes of Death in the United States in 1900 and in 2010 (Percentage of Total Deaths)

1900	Percentage	2010	Percentage
Pneumonia and Influenza	11.8	Heart disease	24.2
Tuberculosis	11.3	Cancer	23.3
Diarrhea, enteritis, and ulceration of the intestines	8.3	Chronic lower respiratory disease	5.6
Diseases of the heart	8.0	Stroke (cerebrovascular diseases)	5.2
Intracranial lesions of vascular origin	6.2	Accidents (unintentional injury)	4.9
Nephritis (Kidney Disease)	5.2	Alzheimer's disease	3.4
Accidents (Unintentional Injury)	4.2	Diabetes	2.8
Cancer and other malignant tumors	3.7	Nephritis, nephritic syndrome, and nephrosis	2.0
Senility	2.9	Influenza and pneumonia	2.0
Diphtheria	2.3	Intentional self-harm (suicide)	1.6
Other	36.1	Other	25.0

SOURCE: Figures for 1900 from Historical Tables: Center for Disease Control, National Vital Statistics System. Leading Causes of Death, 1900–1998. Figures for 2010 from Murphy, S. L., Xu, J., & Kochanek, K. D. (2013). *Deaths: Final data for 2010.* National Vital Statistics Reports, 61(4). Retrieved from http://www.cdc.gov/nchs/data/nvsr/nvsr61/nvsr61_04.pdf.

Health and Health-Related Behavior

The shift in focus from infectious disease to psychological factors has been called the second revolution in public health. Two closely related new fields of study have developed. In the first, **behavioral medicine** (Feldman & Christensen, 2014), knowledge derived from behavioral science is applied to the prevention, diagnosis, and treatment of medical problems. This is an interdisciplinary field in which psychologists, physicians, and other health professionals work together to develop treatments and preventive strategies. A second field, **health psychology**, is not interdisciplinary, and is usually considered a subfield of behavioral medicine. Practitioners study psychological factors that are important to the promotion and maintenance of health; they also analyze and recommend improvements in health-care systems and health-policy formation within the discipline of psychology (Nicassio, Greenberg, & Motivala, 2010; Taylor, 2009).

Psychological and social factors influence health and physical problems in *two* ways (see ● Figure 7.1). First, they can affect the basic biological processes that lead to illness and disease. Second, long-standing behavior patterns may put people at risk to develop certain physical disorders. Sometimes both these avenues contribute to the etiology or maintenance of disease (Ezzati & Riboli, 2012; Miller & Blackwell, 2006). Consider the example of *genital herpes*, an incurable sexually transmitted infection. Estimates indicate that more than 15.5% of

1 Psychosocial factors (such as negative emotions and stress) disrupt basic biological processes, which may lead to physical disorders and disease.

Stress   Lack of control

2 "Risky" behaviors cause or contribute to a variety of physical disorders and disease.

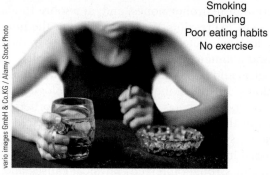

Smoking
Drinking
Poor eating habits
No exercise

●**Figure 7.1** Psychosocial factors directly affect physical health in two ways.

Americans aged 14 to 49 years are infected by the herpes simplex virus affecting either oral or genital areas (Center of Disease Control, 2015). Because the disease is concentrated in young adults, the percentage in that group is much higher. The virus remains dormant until it is reactivated periodically. When it recurs in the genital region, infected individuals usually experience any of a number of symptoms, including pain, itching, vaginal or urethral discharge, and, most commonly, ulcerative lesions (open sores) in the genital area. Lesions recur approximately four times each year but can appear more often. Cases of genital herpes have increased dramatically over the years, for reasons that are as much psychological and behavioral as biological. Although genital herpes is a biological disease, it spreads rapidly because people choose not to reduce their risk by changing their behavior, such as by simply using a condom.

Stress also plays a role in triggering herpes recurrences (Chida & Mao, 2009; Coe 2010). Stress-control procedures, particularly stress management, seem to decrease recurrences of genital herpes, as well as the duration of each episode, most likely through the positive effects of such practices on the immune system (Goldmeier, Garvey, & Barton, 2008; Pereira, Antoni, Danielson, Simon, Efantis-Potter, Carver et al., 2003).

Consider also the tragic example of AIDS. AIDS is a disease of the immune system that is directly affected by stress (Kennedy, 2000), so stress may promote the deadly progression of AIDS. This is an example of how psychological factors may influence biological processes. We also know that a variety of things we may choose to do put us at risk for AIDS—for example, having unprotected sex or sharing contaminated needles. Because there is no medical cure for AIDS yet, our best weapon is large-scale behavior modification to *prevent acquisition* of the disease (Fauci & Folkers, 2012; Mermin & Fenton, 2012).

Other behavioral patterns contribute to disease. The roots of many of the leading causes of death, such as heart disease, cancer, and type 2 diabetes, can be traced to lifestyle factors, principally smoking, diet, and physical activity (Ford et al., 2013). Smoking is the leading preventable cause of death in the United States and has been estimated to cause nearly half a million of premature deaths every year in the nation and reduces life expectancy by more than a decade (U.S. Department of Health and Human Services, 2014). Other unhealthy behaviors include poor eating habits, lack of exercise, and insufficient injury control (not wearing seat belts, for example). These behaviors are grouped under the label *lifestyle* because they are mostly enduring habits that are an integral part of a person's daily living pattern (Lewis, Statt, & Marcus, 2011; Oldenburg, de Courten, & Frean, 2010). Available evidence suggests that the same kinds of causal factors active in psychological disorders—social, psychological, and biological—play a role in some physical disorders (Mostofsky & Barlow, 2000; Uchino, 2009). But the factor attracting the most attention is *stress*, particularly the neurobiological components of the stress response.

The Nature of Stress

In 1936, a young scientist in Montreal, Canada, named Hans Selye noticed that one group of rats he injected with a certain chemical extract developed ulcers and other physiological problems, including atrophy of immune system tissues. But a control group of rats that received a daily saline (salty water) injection that should not have had any effect developed the *same* physical problems. Selye pursued this unexpected finding and discovered that the daily injections themselves seemed to be the culprit rather than the injected substance. Furthermore, many types of environmental changes produced the same results. Borrowing a term from engineering, he decided the cause of this non-specific reaction was *stress*. As so often happens in science, an accidental or serendipitous observation led to a new area of study, in this case, *stress physiology* (Selye, 1936).

Selye theorized that the body goes through several stages in response to *sustained stress*. The first phase is a type of *alarm* response to immediate danger or threat. With continuing stress, we seem to pass into a stage of *resistance*, in which we mobilize various coping mechanisms to respond to the stress. Finally, if the stress is too intense or lasts too long, we may enter a stage of *exhaustion*, in which our bodies suffer permanent damage or death (Selye, 1936, 1950). Selye called this sequence the **general adaptation syndrome (GAS)**.

The word *stress* means many things in modern life. In engineering, stress is the strain on a bridge when a heavy truck drives across it; stress is the *response* of the bridge to the truck's weight. But stress is also a *stimulus*. The truck is a "stressor" for the bridge, just as being fired from a job or facing a difficult final exam is a stimulus or stressor for a person. These varied meanings can create some confusion, but we concentrate on **stress** as the physiological response of the individual to a stressor.

The Physiology of Stress

In Chapter 2, we described the physiological effects of the early stages of stress, noting its activating effect on the sympathetic nervous system, which mobilizes our

....

behavioral medicine Interdisciplinary approach applying behavioral science to the prevention, diagnosis, and treatment of medical problems. Also known as *psychosomatic medicine*.

stress Physiological response of the individual to a stressor.

health psychology Subfield of behavioural medicine that studies psychological factors important in health promotion and maintenance.

general adaptation syndrome (GAS) Sequence of reactions to sustained stress described by Hans Selye. These stages are alarm, resistance, and exhaustion, which may lead to death.

resources during times of threat or danger by activating internal organs to prepare the body for immediate action, either fight or flight. These changes increase our strength and mental activity. We also noted that the activity of the endocrine system increases when we are stressed, primarily through activation of the hypothalamic–pituitary–adrenocortical (HPA) axis. Although a variety of neurotransmitters begin flowing in the nervous system, much attention has focused on the endocrine system's neuromodulators or neuropeptides, hormones affecting the nervous system that are secreted by the glands directly into the bloodstream (Chaouloff & Groc, 2010; Owens, Mulchahey, Taylor, Maloney, Dearborn, & Weiss, 2009). These neuromodulating hormones act much like neurotransmitters in carrying the brain's messages to parts of the body. One of the neurohormones, *corticotropin-releasing factor (CRF)*, is secreted by the hypothalamus and stimulates the pituitary gland. Farther down the chain of the HPA axis, the pituitary gland (along with the autonomic nervous system) activates the adrenal gland, which secretes, among other things, the hormone *cortisol*. Because of their close relationship to the stress response, cortisol and other related hormones are known as the *stress hormones*. Remember that the HPA axis is closely related to the limbic system. The hypothalamus, at the top of the brain stem, is right next to the limbic system, which contains the hippocampus and seems to control our emotional memories. The hippocampus is responsive to cortisol. When stimulated by this hormone during HPA axis activity, the hippocampus helps to *turn off* the stress response, completing a feedback loop between the limbic system and the various parts of the HPA axis.

This loop may be important for a number of reasons. Working with primates, Robert Sapolsky and his colleagues (see, for example, Sapolsky & Meaney, 1986; Sapolsky, 2000b, 2007) showed that increased levels of cortisol in response to chronic stress may kill nerve cells in the hippocampus. If hippocampal activity is thus compromised, excessive cortisol is secreted and, over time, the ability to turn off the stress response decreases, which leads to further aging of the hippocampus. These findings indicate that chronic stress leading to chronic secretion of cortisol may have long-lasting effects on physical function, including brain damage. Cell death may, in turn, lead to deficient problem-solving abilities among the aged and, ultimately, dementia. This physiological process may also affect susceptibility to infectious disease and recovery from it in other pathophysiological systems. Sapolsky's work is important because we now know that hippocampal cell death associated with chronic stress and anxiety occurs in humans with, for example, posttraumatic stress disorder (see Chapter 4) and depression (see Chapter 6). The long-term effects of this cell death are not yet known.

▲ Baboons at the top of the social hierarchy have a sense of predictability and control that allows them to cope with problems and maintain physical health; baboons at the bottom of the hierarchy suffer the symptoms of stress because they have little control over access to food, resting places, and mates.

Contributions to the Stress Response

Stress physiology is profoundly influenced by psychological and social factors (Adler, 2013; Lovallo, 2010). This link has been demonstrated by Sapolsky and others (Gesquiere *et al.*, 2011; Sapolsky, 2007). Sapolsky studied baboons living freely in a national reserve in Kenya because their primary sources of stress, like those of humans, are psychological rather than physical. As with many species, baboons arrange themselves in a social hierarchy with dominant members at the top and submissive members at the bottom. The lives of subordinate animals are made difficult (Sapolsky calls it "stressful") by continual bullying from the dominant animals, and they have less access to food, preferred resting places, and sexual partners. Particularly interesting are Sapolsky's findings on levels of cortisol in the baboons as a function of their social rank in a dominance hierarchy.

Remember from our description of the HPA axis that the secretion of cortisol from the adrenal glands is the final step in a cascade of hormone secretion that originates in the limbic system in the brain during periods of stress. The secretion of cortisol contributes to our arousal and mobilization in the short run but, if produced chronically, it can damage the hippocampus. In addition, muscles atrophy, fertility is affected by declining testosterone, hypertension develops in the cardiovascular system, and the immune response is impaired. Sapolsky discovered that dominant males in the baboon hierarchy ordinarily had *lower* resting levels of cortisol than subordinate males. When an emergency occurred, however, cortisol levels rose more quickly in the dominant males than in the subordinate males.

Sapolsky and his colleagues sought the causes of these differences by working backward up the HPA axis. They found an excess secretion of CRF by the hypothalamus in subordinate animals, combined with a diminished sensitivity of the pituitary gland (which is stimulated by CRF). Therefore, subordinate animals, unlike dominant animals, continually secrete cortisol, probably because their lives are so stressful. In addition, their HPA system is less sensitive to the effects of cortisol and therefore less efficient in turning off the stress response.

Sapolsky also discovered that subordinate males have fewer circulating lymphocytes (white blood cells) than dominant males, a sign of immune system suppression. In addition, subordinate males evidence less circulating high-density lipoprotein cholesterol, which puts them at higher risk for atherosclerosis and coronary heart disease.

What is it about being on top that produces positive effects? Sapolsky concluded that it is primarily the psychological benefits of having *predictability* and *controllability* concerning events in one's life. Parts of his data were gathered during years in which a number of male baboons were at the top of the hierarchy, with no clear "winner." Although these males dominated the rest of the animals in the group, they constantly attacked one another. Under these conditions, they displayed hormonal profiles more like those of subordinate males. Thus, dominance combined with stability produced optimal stress hormone profiles. But the most important factor in regulating stress physiology seems to be a sense of control (Sapolsky & Ray, 1989), a finding confirmed in subsequent research (Kemeny, 2003; Sapolsky, 2007). Control of social situations and the ability to cope with tension that arises go a long way toward blunting the long-term effects of stress.

Stress, Anxiety, Depression, and Excitement

Is there any relationship between psychological and physical disorders? There seems to be a strong one. In a classic study, George Vaillant (1979) studied more than 200 Harvard University sophomore men between 1942 and 1944 who were mentally and physically healthy. He followed these men closely for more than 30 years. Those who developed psychological disorders or who were highly stressed became chronically ill or died at a significantly higher rate than men who remained well adjusted and free from psychological disorders, a finding that has been repeatedly confirmed (see, for example, Robles *et al.*, 2005; Scott *et al.*, 2016). The study by Scott and colleagues (2016) surveyed more than 47,000 individuals across 17 countries to examine the temporal relationship between 16 different mental disorders (e.g., mood and anxiety disorders, substance use disorders, etc.) and 10 chronic physical conditions (such as arthritis, cancer, chronic pain, heart disease, etc.). The results showed that mental disorders of all kinds were associated with an increased risk for developing chronic physical conditions. This suggests that the same types of stress-related psychological factors that contribute to psychological disorders may contribute to the later development of physical disorders and that stress, anxiety, and depression are closely related. Can you tell the difference among feelings of stress, anxiety, depression, and excitement? You might say, "No problem," but these four states have a lot in common. Which one you experience may depend on your *sense of control* at the moment or how well you think you can cope with the threat or challenge you are facing (Barlow, 2002; Barlow, Sauer-Zavala, Carl, Bullis, & Ellard, 2014). This continuum of feelings from excitement to stress to anxiety to depression is shown in ● Figure 7.2.

Consider how you feel when you are excited. You might experience a rapid heartbeat, a sudden burst of energy, or a jumpy stomach. But if you're prepared for the challenge—for example, if you're an athlete, up for the game and confident in your abilities—these feelings of *excitement* can be pleasurable and might even enhance your performance.

Sometimes when you face a challenging task, you feel you could handle it if you only had the time or help you need, but because you don't have these resources, you feel pressured. In response, you may work harder to do better, even though you think you will be all right in the end. If you are under too much pressure, you may become tense and irritable or develop a headache or an upset stomach. This is what *stress* feels like. If something really is threatening and you believe there is little you can do about it, you may feel *anxiety*. The threatening situation could be anything from a physical attack to making a fool of yourself in front of someone. As your body prepares for the challenge, you worry about it incessantly. In some cases, we are anxious for no reason except that we feel certain aspects of our lives are out of control. Finally, individuals who always perceive life as threatening may lose hope about ever having control and slip into a state of *depression*, no longer trying to cope.

To sum up, the underlying physiology of these emotional states seems similar in basic ways. This is why we refer to a similar pattern of sympathetic arousal and activation of specific neurotransmitters and hormones in discussing anxiety, depression, and stress-related physical disorders. On the other hand, there seem to be some differences. Blood pressure may increase when the challenges seem to overwhelm coping resources, resulting in a low sense of control (anxiety, depression), but blood pressure will be unchanged during excitement or marked stress (Blascovich & Tomaka, 1996). Nevertheless, it is psychological factors—specifically a sense of control and confidence that we can cope with stress or challenges,

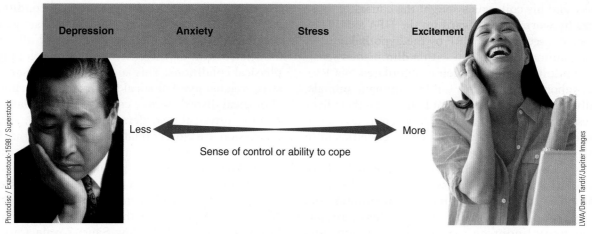

Depression   Anxiety   Stress   Excitement

Less ← → More

Sense of control or ability to cope

● **Figure 7.2** Responses to threats and challenges. Our feelings range along a continuum from depression to anxiety to stress to excitement, depending partly on our sense of control and ability to cope. (Adapted, with permission, from Barlow, D. H., Rapee, R. M., & Reisner, L. C. [2001]. *Mastering stress 2001: A lifestyle approach.* Dallas, TX: American Health, ©2001 American Health Publishing.)

called **self-efficacy** by Bandura (1986)—that differ most markedly among these emotions, leading to different feelings (Taylor *et al.*, 1997).

Stress and the Immune Response

Have you had a cold recently? How did you pick it up? Did you spend the day with someone else who had a cold? Exposure to cold viruses is a necessary factor in developing a cold, but, as mentioned in Chapter 2, your level of stress seems to play a major role in whether the exposure results in a cold. Sheldon Cohen and his associates (Cohen, 1996; Cohen, Doyle, & Skoner, 1999) exposed volunteer participants to a dosage of a cold virus and found that the chance a participant would get sick was related to how much stress the person had experienced during the past year. Cohen and colleagues (1995) also linked the intensity of stress and negative affect at the time of exposure to the later *severity* of the cold, as measured by mucus production. In an interesting twist, Cohen, Doyle, Turner, Alper, and Skoner (2003) have demonstrated that the quantity and quality of your social relationships affects whether you come down with a cold when exposed to the virus, perhaps because socializing relieves stress (Cohen & Janicki-Devarts, 2009). Finally, an optimistic cognitive style protects against developing a cold (Cohen & Pressman, 2006).

Almost certainly, the effect of stress on susceptibility to infections is mediated through the **immune system**, which protects the body from foreign materials that may enter it. Humans under stress show increased rates of infectious diseases, including colds, herpes, and mononucleosis (Coe 2010; Taylor, 2009). Direct evidence links a number of stressful situations to lowered immune system functioning,

including marital discord or relationship difficulties (Kiecolt-Glaser & Newton, 2001; Uchino, 2009), job loss, and the death of a loved one (Hawkley & Cacioppo, 2007).

We have noted that psychological disorders seem to make us more susceptible to developing physical disorders (Robles *et al.*, 2005; Scott *et al.*, 2016). In fact, evidence indicates that depression lowers immune system functioning (Herbert & Cohen, 1993; Miller & Blackwell, 2006), particularly in older adults (Herbert & Cohen, 1993), whereas optimism and positive affect is associated with a stronger immune system (Segerstrom & Sephton, 2010). It may be that the level of depression—and, more importantly, the underlying sense of uncontrollability—is the crucial mechanism in lowering immune system functioning, a mechanism present during most negative stressful life events (Miller & Blackwell, 2006; Robles *et al.*, 2005). Depression can also lead to poor self-care and a tendency to engage in riskier behaviors. For humans, like Sapolsky's baboons, the ability to retain a sense of control over events in our lives may be one of the most important psychological contributions to good health.

Most studies concerning stress and the immune system have examined a sudden or acute stressor. But *chronic stress* may be more problematic because the effects last longer (Schneiderman, 2004). For example, lowered immune system functioning has been reported for people who care for chronically ill family members, such as Alzheimer's disease patients (Holland & Gallagher-Thompson, 2011; Mills *et al.*, 2004).

To understand how the immune system protects us, we must first understand how it works. We take a brief tour of the immune system next, using ● Figure 7.3 as a visual guide, and then we examine psychological contributions to the biology of two diseases strongly related to immune system functioning: AIDS and cancer.

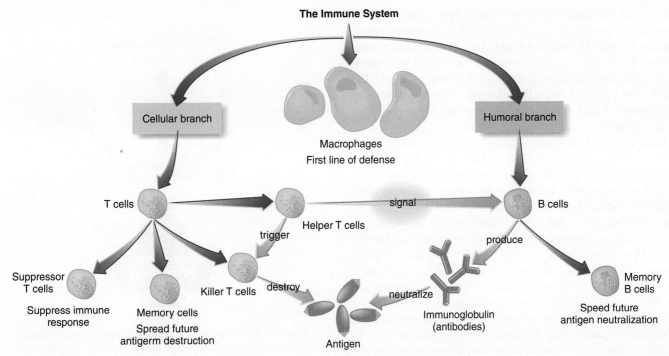

The Immune System

Cellular branch

Macrophages
First line of defense

Humoral branch

T cells

signal

B cells

Helper T cells

trigger

produce

Suppressor
T cells

Killer T cells

destroy

neutralize

Memory
B cells

Suppress immune
response

Memory cells

Spread future
antigerm destruction

Immunoglobulin
(antibodies)

Speed future
antigen neutralization

Antigen

• **Figure 7.3** An overview of the immune system.

How the Immune System Works

The immune system identifies and eliminates foreign materials, called **antigens**, in the body. Antigens can be any of a number of substances, usually bacteria, viruses, or parasites. But the immune system also targets the body's own cells that have become aberrant or damaged, perhaps as part of a malignant tumor. Donated organs are foreign, so the immune system attacks them after surgical transplant; consequently, it is necessary to suppress the immune system temporarily after transplant surgery.

The immune system has two main parts: the humoral and the cellular. Specific types of cells function as agents of both. White blood cells, called *leukocytes,* do most of the work. There are several types of leukocytes. *Macrophages* might be considered one of the body's first lines of defense: They surround identifiable antigens and destroy them. They also signal *lymphocytes,* which consist of two groups, B cells and T cells.

The *B cells* operate within the humoral part of the immune system, releasing molecules that seek antigens in blood and other bodily fluids with the purpose of neutralizing them. The B cells produce highly specific molecules called *immunoglobulins* that act as *antibodies,* which combine with the antigens to neutralize them. After the antigens are neutralized, a subgroup called *memory B cells* are created so that the next time that antigen is encountered, the immune system response will be faster. This action accounts for the success of inoculations, or vaccinations,

you may have received as a child. An inoculation contains small amounts of the targeted organism but not enough to make you sick. Your immune system then "remembers" this antigen and prevents you from coming down with the full disease when you are exposed to it.

Members of the second group of lymphocytes, called *T cells,* operate in the cellular branch of the immune system. These cells don't produce antibodies. Instead, one subgroup, *killer T cells,* directly destroys viruses and cancer cells (Dustin & Long, 2010; Wan, 2010). When the process is complete, *memory T cells* are created to speed future responses to the same antigen. Other subgroups of T cells help regulate the immune system. For example, *T4 cells* are called *helper T cells* because they enhance the immune system response by signaling B cells to produce antibodies and telling other T cells to destroy the antigen. *Suppressor T cells* suppress the production of antibodies by B cells when they are no longer needed.

We should have twice as many T4 (helper) cells as suppressor T cells. With too many T4 cells, the immune system

self-efficacy Perception of having the ability to cope with stress or challenges.

immune system Body's means of identifying and eliminating any foreign materials (for example, bacteria, parasites, and even transplanted organs) that enter.

antigens Foreign material that enters the body, including bacteria and parasites.

may attack the body's normal cells rather than antigens. When this happens, we have what is called an **autoimmune disease**, such as **rheumatoid arthritis**. With too many suppressor T cells, the body is subject to invasion by a number of antigens. The human immunodeficiency virus (HIV) attacks the helper T cells, lymphocytes that are crucial to both humoral and cellular immunity, thereby weakening the immune system and causing AIDS.

Aside from autoimmune disease and AIDS, the immune system has become a central focus for other fields in medicine as well. In fact, some of the most promising new treatments for cancer involve the immune system. This approach builds on clinical observations during the course of more than a century. Physicians in the 1800s noted that occasionally their cancer patients unexpectedly went into remission after a viral infection. In the 1950s and 1960s, these reports inspired doctors to inject cancer patients with a menagerie of viruses. Sometimes, the therapy destroyed the tumor, but often it also killed the person (Ledford, 2015). Today, anticancer viruses are genetically engineered to enter the cancer cells, stimulating the patient's own immune system to destroy the cancer throughout the patient's body. In the field of cancer research, *immunotherapy* is one of the most promising new developments.

Until the mid-1970s, most scientists believed the brain and the immune system operated independently of each other. However, in 1974, Robert Ader and his colleagues (see, for example, Ader & Cohen, 1975, 1993) made a discovery. Working with a classical conditioning paradigm, they gave sugar-flavored water to rats, together with a drug that suppresses the immune system. Ader and Cohen then demonstrated that giving the same rats only the sweet-tasting water produced similar changes in the immune system. In other words, the rats had "learned" (through classical conditioning) to respond to the water by suppressing their immune systems. We now know there are many connections between the nervous system and the immune system. These findings have generated a field of study known as **psychoneuroimmunology**, or **PNI** (Ader & Cohen, 1993; Coe, 2010), which simply means the object of study is *psycho*logical influences on the *neuro*logical responding implicated in our *immune* response.

Researchers have learned a great deal about pathways through which psychological and social factors may influence immune system functioning. Direct connections among the brain (central nervous system), the HPA axis (hormonal), and the immune system have already been described. Behavioral changes in response to stressful events, such as increased smoking or poor eating habits, may also suppress the immune system (Cohen & Herbert, 1996) (see • Figure 7.4). Now scientists have uncovered a chain of molecules that connects stress to the onset of disease by turning on certain genes (Cole *et al.*, 2010). Basically, stress seems to activate certain molecules in cells that activate genes (called a transcription factor), in this case the GABA-1 transcription factor that activates the interleukin-6

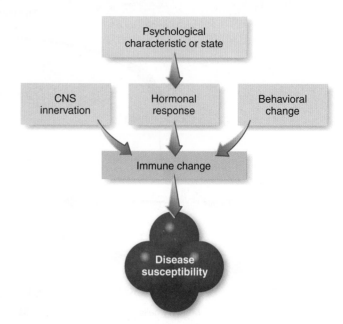

• **Figure 7.4** Pathways through which psychological factors might influence onset and progression of immune system–mediated disease. For simplicity, arrows are drawn in only one direction, from psychological characteristics to disease. No lack of alternative paths is implied. CNS = central nervous system. (From Cohen, S., & Herbert, T. B. [1996]. Health psychology: Psychological factors and physical disease from the perspective of human psychoneuroimmunology. *Annual Review of Psychology, 47,* 113–142.)

gene. This gene makes a protein that turns on the inflammatory response, which brings infection-fighting cells of the immune system to the area. This is great if you've cut yourself, but very damaging if it occurs over a long period of time. It is this chronic inflammatory response that exacerbates cancer, heart disease, and diabetes, and shortens life. Of course other genes, such as the serotonin transporter gene mentioned in Chapter 2, are also implicated in making one vulnerable to certain types of stressors (Way & Taylor, 2010). Undoubtedly many more groups of genes and integrative psychobiological paths implicated in the effects of the stress response will be discovered (Segerstrom & Sephton, 2010).

7.1 Concept CHECK

Match components of the immune system with their function in the body: (a) macrophages, (b) B cells, (c) immunoglobulins, (d) killer T cells, (e) suppressor T cells, and (f) memory B cells:

1. This subgroup targets viral infections within the cells by directly destroying the anti gens. _____

2. A type of leukocyte that surrounds identifiable antigens and destroys them. _____

3. Highly specific molecules that act as antibodies. They combine with antigens to neutralize them. _____

4. Lymphocytes that operate within the humoral part of the system and circulate in the blood and bodily fluids. _____

5. These are created so that when a specific antigen is encountered in the future, the immune response will be faster. _____

6. These T cells stop the production of antibodies by B cells when they are no longer needed. _____

Psychosocial Effects on Physical Disorders

▶ How is stress related to AIDS, cancer, and cardiovascular disease?
▶ What are the potential causes of acute and chronic pain, and how do the types of pain differ?

With an enhanced understanding of the effects of emotional and behavioral factors on the immune system, we can now examine how these factors influence specific physical disorders.

AIDS

The ravages of the AIDS epidemic have made this disease the highest priority of public health systems around the world. The number of people worldwide living with HIV continues to grow, reaching an estimated 34.2 million in 2011, which is 22% higher than in 2000 (Kaiser Family Foundation, Kates, Carbaugh, Rousseau, & Jankiewicz, 2012). Only in 2004 did adult and child deaths begin to level off with aggressive treatment and prevention efforts in some parts of the world (Bongaarts & Over, 2010; Fauci & Folkers, 2012). Despite this modest success, 1.8 million people died of AIDS in 2010 alone (Fauci & Folkers, 2012). In the hardest hit regions in southern Africa, between 15% and 28% of the adult population are believed to be HIV positive, comprising two-thirds of cases worldwide, with approximately 18 million children orphaned by the disease (Kates et al., 2012; Klimas, Koneru, & Fletcher, 2008). AIDS is also spreading rapidly to the densely populated regions of India and China (Normile, 2009), and in Latin America, rates are projected to rise from two million in 2006 to 3.5 million by 2015 (Cohen, 2006). About a decade after the HIV/AIDS pandemic swept through central Africa, Europe, the Caribbean, and North America, it began to expand rapidly in southern Africa, making it now the highest priority region for HIV prevention and care (Vermund, Sheldon, & Sidat, 2015). With the exception of Asians, minority groups are disproportionately affected by this deadly disease. In fact, the epidemic is clearly concentrated in the United States in disenfranchised sexual minorities and communities of color, with effective treatment alternatives few and far between (Pellowski, Kalichman, Matthews, & Adler,

2013). And yet, the perceived urgency of this problem in the United States and around the world has decreased considerably over the past decade.

Once a person is infected with HIV, the course of the disease is variable. After several months to years with no symptoms, patients may develop minor health problems such as weight loss, fever, and night sweats—symptoms that make up the condition known as **AIDS-related complex (ARC)**. A diagnosis of AIDS itself is not made until one of several serious diseases appears, such as pneumocystis pneumonia, cancer, dementia, or a wasting syndrome in which the body literally withers away. The median time from initial infection to the development of full-blown AIDS has been estimated to range from 7.3 to 10 years or more (Pantaleo, Graziosi, & Fauci, 1993). Clinical scientists have developed powerful combinations of drugs referred to as highly active antiretroviral therapy (HAART) that suppress the virus in those infected with HIV, even in advanced cases (Hammer et al., 2006; Thompson et al., 2010). This has been a positive development that has slowed disease progression and decreased mortality. For example, most people with AIDS die within one year of diagnosis without treatment, as is the case in many developing countries (Zwahlen & Egger, 2006). But the proportion of people who receive treatment

autoimmune disease Condition in which the body's immune system attacks healthy tissue rather than antigens.

rheumatoid arthritis Painful, degenerative disease in which the immune system essentially attacks itself, resulting in stiffness, swelling, and even destruction of the joints. Cognitive–behavioral treatments can help relieve pain and stiffness.

psychoneuroimmunology (PNI) Study of psychological influences on the neurological responding involved in the body's immune response.

AIDS-related complex (ARC) Group of minor health problems such as weight loss, fever, and night sweats that appears after HIV infection but before development of full-blown AIDS.

surviving with AIDS for two years or longer increased to 85% by 2005, and the death rates from AIDS from 2002 to 2010 declined by at least 50% in the United States, where the drugs are most available (Fauci & Folkers, 2012).

Nevertheless, HAART does not seem to be a cure, because the evidence suggests the virus is not eliminated but rather lies dormant in reduced numbers; thus, infected patients face a lifetime of taking multiple medications (Buscher & Giordano, 2010; Thompson et al., 2012). Also, the percentage who drop out of HAART because of severe side effects, such as nausea and diarrhea, is high—61% in one study (O'Brien, Clark, Besch, Myers, & Kissinger, 2003; Thompson et al., 2012). For this reason, earlier recommendations were to postpone treatment until those infected are in imminent danger of developing symptomatic disease (Cohen, 2002; Hammer et al., 2006), but in view of the success of this treatment regimen with cases of newly acquired HIV, current recommendations are to start as early as possible after detecting infection and to work with patients to increase adherence to the schedule for the medication (Mermin & Fenton, 2012; Thompson et al., 2012). Some studies have even shown that this treatment regimen can prevent acquisition of the virus in high-risk populations (Cohen, 2011; Mermin & Fenton, 2012). Unfortunately, drug-resistant strains of HIV are now being transmitted.

Because AIDS is a relatively new disease, we are still learning about the factors that extend survival (Klimas et al., 2008; Taylor, 2009). Investigators identified a group of people who have been exposed repeatedly to the AIDS virus but have not contracted the disease. A major distinction of these people is that their immune systems, particularly the cellular branch, are robust and strong (Ezzel, 1993), partly due to genetic factors (Kaiser, 2006), but psychological factors also seem to play a role. For example, one study demonstrated that people with the virus who have not progressed to AIDS were characterized by particularly strong confidence in their clinical providers and strong social support, factors that have been linked to stronger immune system functioning (Ruffin, Ironson, Fletcher, Balbin, & Schneiderman, 2012). Therefore, efforts to boost the immune system may contribute to the prevention of AIDS.

Because psychological factors impact immune system functioning, investigators have begun to examine whether these psychological factors influence the progression of HIV. For example, high levels of stress and depression and low levels of social support have been associated with a faster progression to disease (Leserman, 2008; Leserman et al., 2000). One reason for this faster progression is that depression is strongly associated with decreased adherence to the drug regimen (Gonzalez, Batchelder, Psaros, & Safren, 2011). But an even more intriguing question is whether psychological interventions can slow the progression of the disease, even among those who are symptomatic

(Cole, 2008; Gore-Felton & Koopman, 2008). In fact, several important studies suggest that cognitive-behavioral stress-management (CBSM) programs may have positive effects on the immune systems of individuals who are already symptomatic (Carrico & Antoni, 2008; Lerner, Kibler, & Zeichner, 2013). Specifically, Lutgendorf and colleagues (1997) used an intervention program that significantly decreased depression and anxiety compared with a control group that did not receive the treatment. More important, there was a significant reduction in antibodies to the herpes simplex virus II in the treatment group compared with the control group, which reflects the greater ability of the cellular component of the immune system to control the virus.

If stress and related variables *are* clinically significant to immune response, functioning, and disease progression in HIV-infected patients, as suggested by a number of studies (Cole, 2008; Leserman, 2008), then psychosocial interventions to bolster the immune system might increase survival rates and, in the most optimistic scenario, prevent the deterioration of the immune system (Carrico & Antoni, 2008; Kennedy, 2000). Of course, the most effective interventions focus on changing behavior to prevent acquiring HIV in the first place, such as reducing risky behavior and promoting safe sexual practices (Mermin & Fenton, 2012; Temoshok, Wald, Synowski, & Garzino-Demo, 2008).

Cancer

Among the more mind-boggling developments in the study of illness and disease is the discovery that the development and course of different varieties of **cancer** are subject to psychosocial influences (Fagundes et al., 2012; Giese-Davis et al., 2011). This has resulted in a field of study called **psychoncology** (Antoni & Lutgendorf, 2007; Lutgendorf, Costanzo, & Siegel, 2007). *Oncology* means the study of cancer. David Spiegel and his colleagues (Spiegel, Bloom, Kramer, & Gotheil, 1989; Spiegel, 2013) studied 86 women with advanced breast cancer that had metastasized to other areas of their bodies and was expected to kill them within two years. Although Spiegel and his colleagues had little hope of affecting the disease itself, they thought that by treating these people in group psychotherapy at least they could relieve some of their anxiety, depression, and pain.

All patients had routine medical care for their cancer. In addition, 50 patients (of the 86) met with their therapist for psychotherapy once a week in small groups. Much to everyone's surprise, including Spiegel's, the therapy group's survival time was significantly longer than that of the control group who did not receive psychotherapy but otherwise benefited from the best care available. The group receiving therapy lived twice as long on average (approximately three years) as the controls (approximately 18 months). Four years after the study began, one-third of the therapy patients were still alive, and all the patients receiving the best medical care available *without* therapy had died. Subsequently, a careful reanalysis of medical treatment received by each group revealed no differences that could account for the effects of psychological treatment (Kogon, Biswas, Pearl, Carlson, & Spiegel, 1997). These findings do not mean that psychological interventions cured advanced cancer. At 10 years, only three patients in the therapy group still survived.

In another study, Andersen and colleagues (2008) randomized 227 patients who had been surgically treated for breast cancer to a psychological intervention plus assessment or to an assessment-only condition. The intervention included strategies to reduce stress, improve mood, alter important health behaviors (increasing exercise, etc.), and maintain adherence to cancer treatment and care. The treatment was successful in reducing stress and increasing positive mood and healthy behavior (Andersen *et al.*, 2007). More important, after a median of 11 years follow up, patients receiving the psychological intervention reduced their risk of dying by breast cancer by 56% and their risk of breast cancer recurrence by 45%. Similarly, the positive effects of reducing depressive symptoms on survival in patients with metastatic breast cancer have been demonstrated (Giese-Davis *et al.*, 2011).

As a result of these studies, psychosocial treatment for various cancers to reduce stress, improve quality of life, and even to increase survival and reduce recurrence are now more available (Jacobsen & Andrykowski, 2015; McDonald, O'Connell, & Suls, 2015). The initial success of these treatments on length of survival in at least some studies generated a great deal of interest in how they might work (Emery *et al.*, 2011; Nemeroff, 2013). Possibilities include better health habits, closer adherence to medical treatment, and improved endocrine functioning and response to stress, all of which may improve immune function (Emery *et al.*, 2011; Foley, Baillie, Huxter, Price, & Sinclair, 2011). For example, the experience of a severely stressful life event in the past year, particularly in individuals with troubled early parent–child relationships, predicted decreased immune system reactivity to a basal cell carcinoma tumor (skin cancer) (Fagundes *et al.*, 2012).

In addition, anything that promotes more supportive relationships in cancer patients is important, because it buffers stress (Hostinar, Sullivan, & Gunnar, 2013) and slows disease progression (Antoni *et al.*, 2006; Foley, Baillie, Huxter, Price, & Sinclair, 2010). There is even preliminary evidence that psychological factors may contribute not only to the *course* but also to the *development* of cancer and other diseases (Antoni & Lutgendorf, 2007; Lutgendorf *et al.*, 2007). Perceived lack of control, inadequate coping responses, overwhelmingly stressful life events, or the use of inappropriate coping responses (such as denial) may contribute to the development of cancer, probably through changes in immune function but also through regulating the activity of cancer-causing viruses, deoxyribonucleic acid (DNA) repair processes, and the expression of genes that control the growth of tumors (Antoni & Lutgendorf, 2007; Nemeroff, 2013).

These studies have also led to a renewed emphasis on an overlooked result of cancer: Some people discover some positive consequences. For example, many patients with breast cancer experience an enhanced sense of purpose, deepening spirituality, closer ties to others, and changes in life priorities (Park, Edmondson, Fenster, & Blank, 2008; Yanez *et al.*, 2009). These experiences have been called "benefit finding" and may reflect the types of traits, such as coping skills, a sense of control, and optimism, that underlie resiliency and reduce the harmful effect of stress (Bower, Moskowitz, & Epel, 2009).

Psychological factors are also prominent in treatment and recovery from cancer in children (Kazak & Noll, 2015). Many types of cancer require invasive and painful medical procedures. Children usually struggle and cry, so to complete many of the procedures, they must be physically restrained. Not only does their behavior interfere with successful completion, but also the stress and anxiety associated with repeated painful procedures may have their own detrimental effect on the disease process. Psychological procedures designed to reduce pain and stress in these children include breathing exercises, watching films of exactly what happens to take the uncertainty out of the procedure, and rehearsal of the procedure with dolls, all of which make the interventions more tolerable and therefore more successful for young patients (Brewer, Gleditsch, Syblik, Tietjens, & Vacik, 2006; Hubert, Jay, Saltoun, & Hayes, 1988). Much of this work is based on the pioneering efforts of Barbara Melamed and her colleagues, who demonstrated the importance of incorporating psychological procedures into children's medical care, particularly children about to undergo surgery (see, for example, Melamed & Siegel, 1975).

David H. Wells/Corbis Documentary/Getty Images

▲ Psychological preparation reduces suffering and facilitates recovery in children who undergo surgery.

cancer Category of often-fatal medical conditions involving abnormal cell growth and malignancy.

psychoncology Study of psychological factors involved in the course and treatment of cancer.

Reducing stress in parents who could then provide more supportive care is important because almost all parents develop posttraumatic stress symptoms after hearing that their children have cancer (Kazak, Boeving, Alderfer, Hwang, & Reilly, 2005). Sahler and colleagues (2005) treated mothers of children with newly diagnosed cancer with a cognitive-behavioral problem-solving intervention and compared the results to the usual care available to these mothers. Mothers in the problem-solving group became less negative, less stressed, and better problem solvers, certainly a positive outcome in parents who have to deal with cancer in their children.

Cardiovascular Problems

The *cardiovascular system* consists of the heart, blood vessels, and complex control mechanisms for regulating their function. Many things can go wrong with this system and lead to **cardiovascular disease**. For example, many individuals, particularly older individuals, suffer **strokes**, also called **cerebral vascular accidents (CVAs)**. Strokes are temporary blockages of blood vessels leading to the brain or a rupture of blood vessels in the brain that result in temporary or permanent brain damage and loss of functioning. The cardiovascular problems receiving the most attention these days are hypertension and coronary heart disease. Let's consider the case of John.

John... • *The Human Volcano*

John is a 55-year-old business executive, married, with two teenage children. For most of his adult life, John has smoked a pack of cigarettes a day. Although he maintains a busy schedule, John is mildly obese. He has been taking several medications for high blood pressure since age 42. John's doctor has warned him to cut down on his smoking and to exercise more, especially because John's father died of a heart attack. Although John has episodes of chest pain, he continues his busy and stressful lifestyle. It is difficult for John to slow down, as his business has been doing extremely well during the past 10 years.

Moreover, John believes that life is too short, that there is no time to slow down. He sees relatively little of his family and works late most evenings. Even when he's at home, John works into the night. It is difficult for him to relax; he feels a constant urgency to get as many things done as possible, and prefers to work on several tasks simultaneously. He attributes much of the success of his business to his working style. Despite his success, his co-workers often find him to be overbearing, easily frustrated, and even hostile. His subordinates in particular claim he is overly impatient and critical of their performance.

Most people would recognize that John's behaviors and attitudes make his life unpleasant and possibly lethal. Some of these behaviors and attitudes appear to operate on the cardiovascular system and may result in hypertension and coronary heart disease. John's personality could be described as a *type A personality*. We will come back to this further when we discuss coronary heart disease.

Hypertension

Hypertension (high blood pressure) is a major risk factor not only for stroke and heart disease but also for kidney disease. This makes hypertension an extremely serious medical condition. Blood pressure increases when the blood vessels leading to organs and peripheral areas constrict (become narrower), forcing increasing amounts of blood to muscles in central parts of the body. Because so many blood vessels have constricted, the heart muscles must work harder to force the blood to all parts of the body, which causes increased pressure. These factors produce wear and tear on the ever-shrinking blood vessels and lead to cardiovascular disease. A small percentage of cases of hypertension can be traced to specific physical abnormalities, such as kidney disease or tumors on the adrenal glands (Chobanian *et al.*, 2003; Papillo & Shapiro, 1990), but the majority, (close to 90%), have no specific verifiable physical cause and are considered **essential hypertension**. Blood pressure is defined as high by the World Health Organization if it exceeds 160 over 95 (Papillo & Shapiro, 1990), although measures of 140/90 or higher are cause for concern and more usually used to define hypertension (James *et al.*, 2013; Taylor, 2009). The first value is called the *systolic blood pressure*, the pressure when the heart is pumping blood. The second value is the *diastolic blood pressure*, the pressure between beats when the heart is at rest. Elevations in systolic pressure seem to be more worrisome in terms of risk of disease.

According to a comprehensive survey, 27.6% of individuals between the ages of 35 and 64 suffer from hypertension in North America, with a corresponding and shocking figure of 44.2% in six European countries (Wolf-Maier *et al.*, 2003). One survey examined hypertension rates by county in the United States, and found a staggering median prevalence of 38% for men and 40% for women (Olives, Myerson, Mokdad, Murray, & Lim, 2013). These are extraordinary numbers when you consider that hypertension, contributing to as many fatal diseases as it does, has been called the "silent killer" because there are few—if any—symptoms and most people don't know they have it. These numbers are much higher than for any single psychological disorder. Even more striking is that African Americans, both men and women, are between 1.5 and two times as likely to develop hypertension as whites (CDC, 2011; Egan *et al.*, 2010; Lewis *et al.*, 2006). Furthermore, among people with hypertension and other cardiovascular concerns, minority groups have poorer management of these conditions compared with white Americans (McWilliams, Meara, Zaslavsky, & Ayanian, 2009). More important, African Americans have hypertensive vascular diseases at a rate five to 10 times greater than whites. Saab and colleagues (1992) demonstrated in a classic study that during laboratory stress tests, African Americans without high blood pressure show greater vascular responsiveness, including heightened blood pressure. Thus, African Americans in general may be at greater risk to develop hypertension. You will not be surprised to learn there are biological, psychological, and social contributions to the development of this potentially deadly condition. It has long been clear that hypertension runs in families and likely is subject to marked genetic influences (e.g., Padmanabhan, Caufrield, & Dominiczak, 2015). When stressed in the laboratory, even individuals with *normal* blood pressure show greater reactivity in their blood pressure if their parents have high blood pressure than do individuals with normal blood pressure whose parents also had normal blood pressure (Clark, 2003; Fredrikson & Matthews, 1990). In other words, it doesn't take much to activate an inherited vulnerability to hypertension. The offspring of parents with hypertension are at twice the risk of developing hypertension as children of parents with normal blood pressure (Taylor, 2009). Nevertheless, others have pointed out that genetics (as opposed to other related factors, such as upbringing) may not be the whole story; specific gene variations account for only a small percentage of hypertension risk (Kurtz, 2010).

Studies examining neurobiological causes of hypertension have centered on two factors central to the regulation of blood pressure: autonomic nervous system activity and mechanisms regulating sodium in the kidneys. When the sympathetic branch of the autonomic nervous system becomes active, one consequence is the constriction of blood vessels, which produces greater resistance against circulation; that is, blood pressure is elevated (Chida & Steptoe, 2010; Joyner, Charkoudian, & Wallin, 2010). Because the sympathetic nervous system is responsive to stress, many investigators have long assumed that stress is a major contributor to essential hypertension. Sodium and water regulation, one of the functions of the kidneys, is also important in regulating blood pressure. Retaining too much salt increases blood volume and heightens blood pressure. This is one reason that people with hypertension are often told to restrict their intake of salt.

Psychological factors, such as personality, coping style, and level of stress, have been used to explain individual differences in blood pressure (Lehman, Taylor, Kiefe, & Seeman, 2009; Winters & Schneiderman, 2000). In addition, social support is an important contributor to cardiovascular health (Cuffee *et al.*, 2014; Hawkley, Thisted, Masi, & Cacioppo, 2010). Similarly, loneliness, depression, and feelings of uncontrollability contribute to cardiovascular problems (Wooley & Wong, 2013), whereas happiness and optimism are associated with cardiovascular health (Boehm & Kubzansky, 2012).

A long-term study identified two psychological factors, each of which almost doubles the risk of hypertension: hostility, particularly in interpersonal relations, and a sense of time urgency or impatience. To reach this conclusion, more than 5,000 adults (including both blacks and whites) were followed for 15 years in the Coronary Artery Risk Development in Young Adults (CARDIA) study (Yan *et al.*, 2003). It is likely that the combination of these factors creates an even more powerful risk. Also, both anger and hostility have been associated with increases in blood pressure in laboratory and applied settings (Mezick *et al.*, 2010; Miller, Smith, Turner, Guijarro, & Hallet, 1996).

The notion that hostility or repressed hostility predicts hypertension (and other cardiovascular problems) can be traced back to Alexander (1939), who suggested that an inability to express anger could result in hypertension and other cardiovascular problems. What may be more important is not whether anger is suppressed but rather how often anger and hostility are experienced during stressful situations and expressed to others (Brondolo *et al.*, 2009; Winters & Schneiderman, 2000). Let's return to the case of John, who clearly suffered from hypertension. John's hypertension may well be related to his stressful lifestyle, frustration levels, and hostility. The ability to control anger by expressing these feelings constructively is associated with markedly lower blood pressure in the general population (Haukkala, Konttinen, Laatikainen, Kawachi, & Utela, 2010; Taylor, 2009), suggesting it might help patients with hypertension, too. So the causes of hypertension seem to

Creatas/Superstock

▲ African Americans suffer from hypertension in disproportionately high numbers.

....

cardiovascular disease Afflictions in the mechanisms, including the heart, blood vessels, and their controllers, responsible for transporting blood to the body's tissues and organs. Psychological factors may play important roles in such diseases and their treatments.

stroke/cerebral vascular accident (CVA) Temporary blockage of blood vessels supplying the brain, or a rupture of vessels in the brain, resulting in temporary or permanent loss of brain functioning.

hypertension Major risk factor for stroke and heart and kidney disease that is intimately related to psychological factors. Also known as *high blood pressure*.

essential hypertension High blood pressure with no verifiable physical cause, which makes up the overwhelming majority of high blood pressure cases.

include the interaction of high stress reactivity (possibly genetically-based), high exposure to stress, and inappropriate coping skills and reactions, often involving hostility and anger (Brondolo *et al.*, 2009; Taylor, 2009).

Coronary Heart Disease

Coronary heart disease (CHD) is a blockage of the arteries supplying blood to the heart muscle (the *myocardium*). Chest pain resulting from partial obstruction of the arteries is called *angina pectoris* or just *angina*. *Atherosclerosis* occurs when a fatty substance or plaque builds up inside the arteries and causes an obstruction. *Ischemia* is the name for deficiency of blood to a body part caused by the narrowing of the arteries by too much plaque. And *myocardial infarction,* or *heart attack,* is the death of heart tissue when a specific artery becomes clogged with plaque. Arteries can constrict or become blocked for a variety of reasons other than plaque. For example, a blood clot might lodge in the artery.

It seems clear that we inherit a vulnerability to CHD (and to many other physical disorders), and other factors such as diet, exercise, and culture contribute to our cardiovascular status (Allender, Peto, Scarborough, Boxer, & Rayner, 2007; Cuffee *et al.*, 2014). But what sort of psychological factors contribute to CHD?

A variety of studies suggest that stress, anxiety, and anger, combined with poor coping skills and low social support, are implicated in CHD (Jiang *et al.*, 2013; Taylor, 2009). Severe stress, as in learning that a family member suddenly died, can lead on rare occasions to a condition called *myocardial stunning,* which is basically heart failure (Wittstein *et al.*, 2005). Some evidence suggests that heart attacks in response to emotional triggers, though rare, are found with disproportionate frequency among individuals high in negative affectivity and social inhibition to begin with (Compare *et al.*, 2013).

There is a great deal of evidence on the value of stress-reduction procedures in preventing future heart attacks and prolonging life (Emery *et al.*, 2011; Orth-Gomer *et al.*, 2009). In one report summarizing results from 37 studies, the effects of stress-reduction programs on CHD were apparent. Specifically, as a group, these studies yielded a 34% reduction in death from heart attacks; a 29% reduction in the recurrence of heart attacks; and a positive effect on blood pressure, cholesterol levels, body weight, and other risk factors for CHD (Dusseldorp, van Elderen, Maes, Meulman, & Kraaij, 1999). Clinical studies confirmed the benefits of CBT focusing on stress reduction and exercise in reducing emotional distress and improving heart function and risk for future attacks in a group of individuals with established heart disease (Blumenthal *et al.*, 2005; Gulliksson *et al.*, 2011). For example, the study by Gulliksson and colleagues (2011) showed that a CBT program focusing on stress management can prevent recurrent

heart problems in patients who experienced their first cardiovascular events.

This brings us to an important question: Can we identify, before an attack, people who are under a great deal of stress that might make them susceptible to a first heart attack? The answer seems to be yes, but the answer is more complex than we first thought.

Clinical investigators reported several decades ago that certain groups of people engage in a cluster of behaviors in stressful situations that seem to put them at considerable risk for CHD. These behaviors include excessive competitive drive, a sense of being pressured for time, impatience, incredible amounts of energy that may show up in accelerated speech and motor activity, and angry outbursts. This set of behaviors, which came to be called the **type A behavior pattern**, was first identified by two cardiologists, Meyer Friedman and Ray Rosenman (1959, 1974). The **type B behavior pattern**, also described by these clinicians, applies to people who basically do not have type A attributes. In other words, the type B individual is more relaxed, less concerned about deadlines, and seldom feels the pressure or, perhaps, the excitement of challenges or overriding ambition.

The concept of the type A personality or behavior pattern is widely accepted in our hard-driving, goal-oriented culture. Indeed, some early studies supported the concept of type A behavior as putting people at risk for CHD (Friedman & Rosenman, 1974; Matthews, 2013), and individual elements of the type A personality, such as anger, continue to emerge as presenting increased cardiovascular risk (Chida & Steptoe, 2009). But the most convincing evidence came from two large prospective studies that followed thousands of patients over a long period to determine the relationship of their behavior to heart disease. The first study was the Western Collaborative Group Study (WCGS). In this project, 3,154 healthy men, aged 39 to 59, were interviewed at the beginning of the study to determine their typical behavioral patterns. They were then followed for eight years. The basic finding was that the men who displayed a type A behavior pattern at the beginning of the study were at least twice as likely to develop CHD as the men with a type B behavior pattern. When the investigators analyzed the data for the younger men in the study (aged 39 to 49), the results were even more striking, with CHD developing approximately six times more often in the type A group than in the type B group (Rosenman *et al.*, 1975).

A second major study is the Framingham Heart Study (Haynes, Feinleib, & Kannel, 1980). In this study, 1,674 healthy men and women were categorized by a type A or type B behavior pattern and followed for eight years. Again, both men and women with a type A pattern were more than twice as likely to develop CHD as their type B counterparts (in men, the risk was nearly three times as great). For women with type A behavior pattern, the likelihood of developing CHD was highest for those with a low level of education (Eaker, Pinsky, & Castelli, 1992).

Population-based studies in Europe essentially replicated these results (De Backer, Kittel, Kornitzer, & Dramaix, 1983; French-Belgian Collaborative Group, 1982). It is interesting that a large study of Japanese men conducted in Hawaii did *not* replicate these findings (Cohen & Reed, 1985). The prevalence of type A behavior among Japanese men is much lower than among men in the United States (18.7% versus approximately 50%). Similarly, the prevalence of CHD is equally low in Japanese men (4%, compared with 13% in U.S. men in the Framingham study) (Haynes & Matthews, 1988). In a study that illustrates the effects of culture more dramatically, 3,809 Japanese Americans were classified into groups according to how "traditionally Japanese" they were (in other words, they spoke Japanese at home, retained traditional Japanese values and behaviors, and so on). Japanese Americans who were the "most Japanese" had the lowest incidence of CHD, not significantly different from Japanese men in Japan. In contrast, the group that was the "least Japanese" had a three to five times greater incidence of CHD levels (Marmot & Syme, 1976; Matsumoto, 1996). Clearly, sociocultural differences are important.

Yet the type A concept has proved more complex and elusive than scientists had hoped. First, it is difficult to determine whether someone is type A from structured interviews, questionnaires, or other measures of this construct, because the measures often do not agree with one another. Many people have *some* characteristics of type A but not all of them, and others present with a mixture of types A and B. As a result, subsequent studies did not necessarily support the relationship of type A behavior to CHD (Dembroski & Costa, 1987; Hollis, Connett, Stevens, & Greenlick, 1990).

The Role of Chronic Negative Emotions

At this point, investigators decided that something might be wrong with the type A construct itself (Matthews, 1988; Rodin & Salovey, 1989). A consensus developed that some behaviors and emotions representative of the type A personality might be important in the development of CHD, but not all of them. One factor that seems to be responsible for much of the type A–CHD relationship is anger (Chida & Steptoe, 2009; Miller *et al.*, 1996). Ironson and colleagues (1992) compared increased heart rate when they instructed individuals with heart disease to imagine situations or events in their own lives that made them angry with heart rates when they imagined other situations, such as exercise. They found that anger impaired the pumping efficiency of the heart, putting these individuals at risk for dangerous disturbances in heart rhythm (arrhythmias). This study confirms earlier findings relating the frequent experience of anger to later CHD (Houston, Chesney, Black, Cates, & Hecker, 1992; Smith, 1992).

Is type A irrelevant to the development of heart disease? Most investigators conclude that some components of the type A construct are important determinants of CHD, particularly a chronically high level of negative affect (such as anger) and the time urgency or impatience factor (Matthews, 2005; Williams, Barefoot, & Schneiderman, 2003). But what about people who experience closely related varieties of negative affect on a chronic basis? Look back to Figure 7.2 and notice the close relationship between stress, anxiety, and depression. Some evidence indicates that the physiological components of these emotions and their effects on the cardiovascular system may be identical, or at least similar (Suls & Bunde, 2005). We also know that the emotion of anger, commonly associated with stress, is closely related to fear, as evidenced in flight or fight response. Fight is the typical behavioral action tendency associated with anger, and flight or escape is associated with fear. But our bodily alarm response, activated by an immediate danger or threat, is associated with both emotions.

Some investigators, after reviewing the literature, have concluded that anxiety and depression are as important as anger in the development of CHD (Barlow, 1988; Strike & Steptoe, 2005), even anxious and depressive features noticeable at an early age (Grossardt, Bower, Geda, Colligan, & Rocca, 2009). In a study of 1,017 patients with CHD, Whooley and colleagues (2008) found a 31% higher rate of cardiovascular events such as heart attacks or arrhythmias in patients with depressive symptoms compared with those without depressive symptoms. Severe depression, as in major depressive episodes, is particularly implicated in cardiovascular damage (Agatisa *et al.*, 2005; Emery *et al.*, 2011). Also in a study of 80,000 women aged 54 to 79, those women with a history of depression had a 29% greater risk of having a stroke than women who were not depressed (Pan *et al.*, 2011). Thus, it may be that the chronic experience of the negative emotions of stress (anger), anxiety (fear), and depression (ongoing) and the neurobiological activation that accompanies these emotions provide the most important psychosocial contributions to CHD, and perhaps to other physical disorders. Indeed, studies have confirmed that not only depression but also anxiety predicts future cardiovascular events in people with CHD (Martens *et al.*, 2010; Shen *et al.*, 2008). A large study

. . . .

coronary heart disease (CHD) Blockage of the arteries supplying blood to the heart muscle; a major cause of death in Western culture, with social and psychological factors involved.

type A behavior pattern Cluster of behaviors including excessive competitiveness, time-pressured impatience, accelerated speech, and anger, originally thought to promote high risk for heart disease.

type B behavior pattern Cluster of behaviors including a relaxed attitude, indifference to time pressure, and less forceful ambition; originally thought to promote low risk for heart disease.

following nearly 50,000 Swedish men over four decades found that early onset anxiety was predictive of later CHD (Janszky, Ahnve, Lundberg, & Hemmingsson, 2010).

Partly because of these findings, some investigators are proposing another personality type, type D, which is characterized by social inhibition and heightened negative emotions. Type D personality has been implicated in CHD in some research (Compare *et al.*, 2013), although not all studies have found an association between D-type behavior and cardiovascular risk (Larson, Barger, & Sydeman, 2013), highlighting a need for further research (Hausteiner, Klupsch, Emeny, Baumert, & Ladwig, 2010).

Investigators are also learning more about the process through which negative emotions contribute to CHD. Once again, the inflammatory processes associated with the stress response (and with all negative emotions) play a major role, because inflammation directly contributes to atherosclerosis and heart failure (Matthews *et al.*, 2007; Taylor, 2009). Matthews and colleagues (Gallo & Matthews, 2003; Matthews, 2005, 2013) provide a model of the contribution of psychosocial factors to CHD (see ● Figure 7.5). Lower socioeconomic status and relatively few resources or low prestige is in the first box. Stressful life events are in the second. Coping skills and social support contribute to a reserve capacity that may buffer the effects of stress, as represented in the third box. Both negative emotions and negative cognitive styles then constitute a major risk

factor. Positive emotions and an optimistic style, on the other hand, reduce the risk of CHD (Davidson, Mostofsky, & Whang, 2010; Giltay, Geleijnse, Zitman, Hoekstra, & Schouten, 2004) and may turn out to be just as important as negative emotions in their effects on CHD. Both negative and positive emotions are in the fourth box. This model summarizes what we know about the influence of psychosocial factors on CHD.

Chronic Pain

The National Institutes of Health have identified chronic pain as the costliest medical problem in the United States, affecting at least 100 million individuals and costing the nation 560 to 635 billion dollars each year in medical treatment and lost productivity (Institute of Medicine, 2014). This report, which reflects data from 2008, shows that 2.1 million people every year visit the ER for acute headache alone, and the majority (62%) of nursing home residents suffer from pain, with arthritis being the most common painful condition. Clearly, pain is a common, undertreated, and costly problem.

There are two kinds of clinical pain: acute and chronic. **Acute pain** typically follows an injury and disappears once the injury heals or is effectively treated, often within a month. **Chronic pain**, by contrast, may begin with an acute episode but *does not decrease* over time, even when

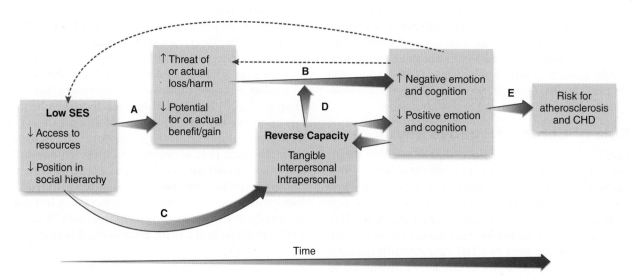

● **Figure 7.5** The reserve capacity model for associations among environments of low socioeconomic status (SES), stressful experiences, psychosocial resources, and emotions and cognitions, which represent pathways to increased risk for CHD. *Note:* Arrow A depicts the direct influence of SES on exposure to stressful experiences. Arrow B indicates the direct impact of stress experiences on emotion and cognition. Arrow C shows that SES conditions and shapes the bank of resources (that is, the reserve capacity) available to manage stress. Arrow D shows that reserve capacity represents a potential moderator of the association between stress and emotional-cognitive factors. Arrow E indicates the direct effects of emotional-cognitive factors on intermediate pathways and risk for atherosclerosis and CHD. The dashed lines note the possible reverse influences. (Adapted from Gallo, L. C., & Matthews, K. A. [2003]. Understanding the association between socioeconomic status and physical health: Do negative emotions play a role?" *Psychological Bulletin, 129*, 34 (Figure 1), ©2003 American Psychological Association. Reprinted, with permission, from Matthews, K. A. [2005]. Psychological perspectives on the development of coronary heart disease. *American Psychologist, 60* (8), 791 (Figure 2), ©2005 American Psychological Association.)

the injury has healed or effective treatments have been administered. Typically, chronic pain is in the muscles, joints, or tendons, particularly in the lower back. Vascular pain because of enlarged blood vessels may be chronic, as may headaches; pain caused by the slow degeneration of tissue, as in some terminal diseases; and pain caused by the growth of cancerous tumors that impinge on pain receptors (Otis & Pincus, 2008; Taylor, 2009).

To better understand the experience of pain, clinicians and researchers generally make a clear distinction between the subjective experience termed *pain,* reported by the patient, and the overt manifestations of this experience, termed *pain behaviors.* Pain behaviors include changing the way one sits or walks, continually complaining about pain to others, grimacing, and, most important, avoiding various activities, particularly those involving work or leisure. Finally, an emotional component of pain called *suffering* sometimes accompanies pain (Fordyce, 1988; Liebeskind, 1991). We first review psychological and social contributions to pain, because they are so important.

Psychological and Social Aspects of Pain

In mild forms, chronic pain can be an annoyance that eventually wears you down and takes the pleasure out of your life. Severe chronic pain may cause you to lose your job, withdraw from your family, give up the fun in your life, and focus your entire awareness on seeking relief. What is interesting for our purposes is that the *severity* of the pain does not seem to predict the *reaction* to it. Some individuals experience intense pain frequently yet continue to work productively, rarely seek medical services, and lead reasonably normal lives; others become invalids. These differences appear to be primarily the result of psychological factors (Dersh *et al.,* 2002; Flor & Turk, 2011). It will come as no surprise that these factors are the same as those implicated in the stress response and other negative emotional states, such as anxiety and depression (Ohayon & Schatzberg, 2003; Otis, Pincus, and Murawski, 2011). The determining factor seems to be the individual's general sense of control over the situation: whether he or she can deal with the pain and its consequences in an effective way. When a positive sense of control is combined with an optimistic outlook about the future, there is substantially less distress and disability (Keefe & France, 1999; Otis & Pincus, 2008). Positive psychological factors are also associated with active attempts to cope, such as exercise and other regimens, as opposed to suffering passively (Otis *et al.,* 2011; Zautra *et al.,* 2005), and successfully treating depression diminishes the experience of chronic pain (Teh, Zaslavsky, Reynolds, & Cleary, 2009).

In one classic example, Philips and Grant (1991) studied 117 patients who suffered from back and neck pain after an injury. Almost all were expected to recover quickly, but 40% of them still reported substantial pain at six months, thereby qualifying for "chronic pain" status. Of the 60%

who reported no pain at the six-month point, most had been pain-free since approximately one month after the accident. Furthermore, Philips and Grant reported that the relationship between the experience of pain and the subsequent disability was not as strongly related to the intensity of the pain as other factors, such as personality and socioeconomic differences and whether the person planned to initiate a lawsuit concerning the injury. Pre-existing anxiety and personality problems predict who will suffer chronic pain (Flor & Turk, 2011; Taylor, 2009). Generally, a profile of negative emotion such as anxiety and depression, poor coping skills, low social support, and the possibility of being compensated for pain through disability claims predict most types of chronic pain (Dersh *et al.,* 2002; Gatchel *et al.,* 2007). Conversely, developing a greater sense of control and less anxiety focused on the pain results in less severe pain and less impairment (Burns, Glenn, Bruehl, Harden, & Lofland, 2003; Edwards *et al.,* 2009).

That the experience of pain can be largely disconnected from disease or injury is perhaps best exemplified by *phantom limb pain.* In this condition, people who have lost an arm or leg feel pain in the limb that is no longer there. Furthermore, they can describe in detail the location of the pain and its type, such as a dull ache or a sharp pain. They are aware the limb is amputated, but this does nothing to relieve the pain. Victims of the Boston Marathon bombing in April 2013 have reported this experience and have benefited from sharing their feelings among themselves and ways they have discovered to cope with it. These coping methods include looking in a full-length mirror for several minutes each morning so that the brain can register that the limb is no longer there. Evidence suggests that changes in the sensory cortex of the brain may contribute to this phenomenon (Flor *et al.,* 1995; Katz & Gagliese, 1999; Ramachandran, 1993).

Social factors also influence how we experience pain (Koban & Wager, 2015). For example, family members who were formerly critical and demanding may become caring and sympathetic (Kerns, Rosenberg, & Otis, 2002; Otis & Pincus, 2008). This phenomenon is referred to as *operant control* of pain behavior because the behavior clearly seems under the control of social consequences (Flor & Turk, 2011). But these consequences have an uncertain relation to the amount of pain being experienced.

By contrast, a strong network of social support may reduce pain. Jamison and Virts (1990) studied 521 chronic pain patients (with back, abdominal, and chest conditions) and discovered that those who lacked social

. . . .

acute pain Pain that typically follows an injury and disappears once the injury heals or is effectively treated.

chronic pain Enduring pain that does not decrease over time; may occur in muscles, joints, and the lower back; and may be caused by enlarged blood vessels or degenerating or cancerous tissue. Other significant factors are social and psychological.

▲ It is not uncommon for people to feel specific pain in limbs that are no longer part of them.

support from their families reported more pain sites and showed more pain behavior, such as staying in bed. These patients also exhibited more emotional distress *without* rating their pain as any more intense than participants with strong socially supportive families. The participants with strong support returned to work earlier, showed less reliance on medications, and increased their activity levels more quickly than the others. Even having just a photo of a loved one to look at reduces the experience of pain (Master *et al.*, 2009).

Although these results may seem to contradict studies on the operant control of pain, different mechanisms may be at work (Burns *et al.*, 2014). General social support may reduce the stress associated with pain and injury and promote more adaptive coping procedures and control. Specifically reinforcing pain behaviors, however, particularly in the absence of social supports, may powerfully increase such behavior.

Biological Aspects of Pain

No one thinks pain is entirely psychological, just as no one thinks it is entirely physical. As with other disorders, we must consider how psychological and physical factors interact.

Mechanisms of Pain Experience and Pain Control The *gate control theory of pain* (Melzack & Wall, 1965, 1982) accommodates both psychological and physical factors. According to this theory, nerve impulses from painful

stimuli make their way to the spinal column and from there to the brain. An area called the *dorsal horns of the spinal column* acts as a "gate" and may open and transmit sensations of pain if the stimulation is sufficiently intense. Specific nerve fibers referred to as *small fibers* (A-delta and C fibers) and *large fibers* (A-beta fibers) determine the pattern, as well as the intensity, of the stimulation. Small fibers tend to open the gate, thereby increasing the transmission of painful stimuli, whereas large fibers tend to close the gate.

Most important for our purpose is that the brain sends signals back down the spinal cord that may affect the gating mechanism. For example, a person with strong negative emotions such as fear or anxiety may experience pain more intensely because the basic message from the brain is to be vigilant against possible danger or threat. Then again, in a person whose emotions are more positive or who is absorbed in an engaging activity (such as a runner intent on finishing a long race), the brain sends down an inhibitory signal that closes the gate, thus reducing their experience of pain. Although many think that the gate control theory is overly simplistic (and it has been updated periodically; see Melzack, 1999, 2005), research findings continue to support its basic elements, particularly as it describes the complex interaction of psychological and biological factors in the experience of pain (Edwards *et al.*, 2009; Gatchel et al., 2007).

Endogenous Opioids The neurochemical means by which the brain inhibits pain is an important discovery (Taylor, 2009). Drugs such as heroin and morphine are manufactured from opioid substances. It now turns out that **endogenous (natural) opioids** exist within the body. Called *endorphins* or *enkephalins*, they act much like neurotransmitters. Because endogenous opioids are distributed widely throughout the body, they may be implicated in a variety of psychopathological symptoms and conditions, including tolerance and dependence, eating disorders, and stress reactions (Bodnar, 2012). They are commonly associated with the "runner's high" that occurs after intense (and sometimes painful) physical activity. The brain uses endorphins to shut down pain, even in the presence of marked tissue damage or injury. Bandura and colleagues (1987) found that people with a greater sense of self-efficacy and control had a higher tolerance for pain than individuals with low self-efficacy and that they increased their production of endogenous opioids when they were confronted with a painful stimulus. Edwards and colleagues (2009) have articulated the neurobiological processes underlying the effectiveness of psychological coping procedures that successfully alter the experience of pain. Certain procedures, such as reappraising the significance of the pain instead of catastrophizing or thinking the worst about it, activate a variety of brain circuits that modulate or diminish pain experience and allow for more normal functioning.

The study of psychology and the mental states and disorders experienced by individuals requires a high degree of sensitivity to the fact that people are inexorably intertwined with the cultural values and experiences in which they are raised. A fascinating example of varying cultural influences, and the psychological and physical effects of such experiences, can be seen through an examination of female reproduction around the world. It turns out that even this most basic aspect of human biology is heavily influenced by cultural, environmental, and psychological components.

Women's ability to reproduce begins during a process called menarche, which refers to a girl's first menstrual bleeding. Women generally are able to reproduce until they reach menopause, which refers to the cessation of the menstrual cycle.

Although all women experience the events of menarche and menopause, the experience and timing can be different depending on the cultural, environmental, and psychological context in which these processes occur. For instance, differences in nutrition may help explain differences in the age of onset of menarche seen in different parts of the world (Euling et al., 2008). In addition, girls in more stressful home environments and in father-absent homes experience menarche earlier, perhaps because from an evolutionary perspective these events signal the need to leave the home and start one's own family (Weisfeld & Woodward, 2004).

There also are significant cross-cultural differences in the psychological and social experience of menopause. For instance, in some cultures the loss of the ability to reproduce may be associated with diminished health or social standing (such as in Italy), whereas in other cultures (such as in China and India) menopause confers a more prestigious place in society (Fu, Anderson & Courtney, 2003; Gifford, 1994). Interestingly, these different perceptions of menopause not only influence how cultures react to menopausal women but also can affect the occurrence of menopausal symptoms, with those for whom menopause is seen as a positive life transition experiencing fewer or no negative symptoms (Fu et al., 2003). These findings point out how sensitive clinicians must be to the cultural differences clients bring with them to therapy and how culture might influence how clients experience and describe their problems (e.g., Ryder et al., 2008). ∎

Gender Differences in Pain

Men and women seem to experience different types of pain. In addition to menstrual cramps and labor pains, women suffer more often than men from migraine headaches, arthritis, carpal tunnel syndrome, and temporomandibular joint (TMJ) pain in the jaw (Lipchik, Holroyd, & Nash, 2002; Smitherman, Burch, Sheikh, & Loder, 2013). Men have more cardiac pain and backache. Both males and females have endogenous opioid systems, although in males it may be more powerful. But women seem to have additional pain-regulating mechanisms that may be different. The female neurochemistry may be based on an estrogen-dependent neuronal system that may have evolved to cope with the pain associated with reproductive activity (Mogil, Sternberg, Kest, Marek, & Liebeskind, 1993). It is an "extra" pain-regulating pathway in females that, if taken away by removing hormones, has no implications for the remaining pathways, which continue to work. One implication of this finding is that males and females may benefit from different kinds of drugs, different kinds of psychological interventions, or unique combinations of these treatments to best manage and control pain.

The Inseparability of Psychological and Physical Experience of Pain In this chapter and earlier chapters, we have described the influence of psychological factors on brain function and structure, showing how, for example, psychological interventions may affect physical illnesses such as CHD and AIDS. The study of the placebo response adds another layer to the discussion. To take one example, do "phony" placebo pills really decrease pain, or is it just that individuals think or report that they are feeling less pain? This is one of the controversies in the study of placebo responses, not only for pain but also for other mental health conditions, such as depression.

With the help of brain-imaging technology, several experiments have demonstrated that when pain is induced in some volunteers (for example, by injecting salt water in their jaws) after they are given a placebo, their brains operate in such a way that they actually feel less pain as opposed to simply thinking they feel less pain or reporting that they feel less pain (Wager, 2005; Zubieta et al., 2005). Broad areas of the brain are affected, but the most important system activated may be the endogenous opioid system (or endorphins), which, among other functions, suppresses pain. Increased endorphin activity across broad areas of the brain was associated with lower ratings of pain intensity, as well as reductions in the sensations of pain and emotional reactions to it.

endogenous (natural) opioids Substance occurring naturally throughout the body that functions like a neurotransmitter to shut down pain sensation even in the presence of marked tissue damage. These opioids may contribute to psychological problems such as eating disorders. Also known as an *endorphin* or *enkephalin*.

One study examined whether distraction operates through the same brain circuits as the placebo response (Buhle, Stevens, Friedman, & Wager, 2012). Participants were subjected to thermal pain on their arms while they were either absorbed in a distracting task, received a placebo (a cream that was applied to the participants' skin that, they were told, would reduce pain), or assigned to a control condition in which they were told that a different cream would have no pain reducing effects. Both the placebo and the distraction task separately reduced the experience of pain, but when they were combined, there was an additive effect in that pain was reduced substantially more than it was with either condition alone. This suggests that these procedures operate through somewhat different brain circuits. Thus, the studies show that the placebo effect is certainly not "all in your head." "Phony" pills or other placebo substances really do spur chemical changes in the brain that reduce pain, even if the pill only contains sugar.

But does it also work the other way? Do medical treatments, such as drugs, affect what are clearly psychological processes, and if they do, are drugs affecting different regions in the brain compared with purely psychological interventions to achieve the same end? For example, we know that drugs can relieve anxiety and depression, but the presumption is that these medications are having their effects in different areas of the brain compared with psychological treatments. Several studies have demonstrated that physical pain (such as that caused by physical injury) and social pain (such as hurt feelings caused by social rejection) may rely on some of the same behavioral and neural mechanisms (DeWall et al., 2010; Eisenberger, 2012). In one experiment, participants took a drug commonly used for physical pain, acetaminophen (Tylenol), while another group took a placebo. They then recorded on a form their hurt feelings every day for three weeks. Subjects taking the acetaminophen reported substantially fewer hurt feelings than the placebo group. In a second experiment, the investigators found that the acetaminophen reduced neural responses to social rejection in brain regions known to be associated with both social pain as well as physical pain (the dorsal anterior cingulate cortex and the anterior insula). These findings indicate substantial overlap between social and physical pain (Eisenberger, 2012; Wager, 2005). All of these findings illustrate again the theme of this book: You cannot easily separate brain function induced biochemically from brain function induced by psychological factors, including expectancies and appraisals. The body and the mind are inseparable, and only a multidimensional integrative approach focusing on the full spectrum of responding will produce a complete understanding of behavior, either normal or pathological.

Chronic Fatigue Syndrome

Chronic fatigue syndrome (CFS) is prevalent throughout the Western world (Brown, Bell, Jason, Christos, & Brown, 2012; Prins, van der Meer, & Bleijenberg, 2006).

The symptoms of CFS, listed in Table 7.2, were initially attributed to XMRV (xenotropic murine leukemia virus-related virus), a retrovirus with some similarities to HIV and the so-called polytropic murine leukemia virus (pMLV) (Lombardi et al., 2009; Lo et al., 2010). However, after unusually heated scientific debates, which even resulted in the imprisonment of a senior scientist who manipulated the data (Dr. Judy Mikovits) and a retraction of original studies (one published in the prestigious journal *Science*), the evidence now clearly shows that XMRV and pMLV are not related to CFS (Alter et al., 2012).

Jason and colleagues (1999) conducted a sophisticated study of the prevalence of CFS in the community and reported that 0.4% of their sample was determined to have CFS, with higher rates in Latino and African American respondents compared with whites. CFS occurs in up to 3% of patients in a primary care clinic, predominantly in women, and usually begins in early adulthood (Afari & Buchwald, 2003), but it can occur in children as young as seven years (Sankey, Hill, Brown, Quinn, & Fletcher, 2006). A study of 4,591 twins yielded a 2.7% prevalence rate (Furberg et al., 2005), and a prospective study of a larger birth cohort revealed that by age 53, 1.1% reported

TABLE 7.2 | Definition of Chronic Fatigue Syndrome

Inclusion Criteria
Clinically evaluated, medically unexplained fatigue of at least six months duration that is:
of new onset (not lifelong)
not resulting from ongoing exertion
not substantially alleviated by rest
a substantial reduction in previous level of activities
The occurrence of four or more of the following symptoms:
Subjective memory impairment
Sore throat
Tender lymph nodes
Muscle pain
Joint pain
Headache
Unrefreshing sleep
Post-exertional malaise lasting more than 24 hours

SOURCE: Adapted from Fukuda, K., Straus, S. E., Hickie, I., Sharpe, M. B., Dobbins, J. G., & Komaroff, A. L. (1994). Chronic fatigue syndrome: A comprehensive approach to its diagnosis and management. *Annals of Internal Medicine, 121,* 953–959.

a diagnosis of CFS (Harvey, Wadsworth, Wessely, & Hotopf, 2008). To get a better idea of prevalence, psychologists will need to do large-scale population studies.

People with CFS suffer considerably and often must give up their careers, because the disorder runs a chronic course (Clayton, 2015; Taylor *et al.*, 2003). In a group of 100 patients followed for 18 months, chronic fatigue symptoms did not decrease significantly in 79% of cases. Better mental health to begin with—as well as less use of sedating medications and a more "psychological" as opposed to medical attribution for causes—led to better outcomes (Schmaling, Fiedelak, Katon, Bader, & Buchwald, 2003). Results from longer-term follow-ups are more encouraging. Of 25 patients diagnosed with CFS 25 years ago, only five self-reported that they maintained a diagnosis of CFS, while 20 reported no longer having a diagnosis. But even those 20 patients were significantly more impaired than a control group that had never had the diagnosis (Brown *et al.*, 2012). Of course this was a small study so results must be interpreted cautiously. Fortunately, CFS patients do not seem to be at risk for increased mortality (death) through disease or suicide compared with the general population (Smith, Noonan, & Buchwald, 2006).

It is possible that a virus or a specific immune system dysfunction will someday be found to account for CFS, although, as noted above, the search has been disappointing so far. Another possibility suggested by Abbey and Garfinkel (1991) is that the condition represents a rather non-specific response to stress, and Heim and colleagues (2006) found a higher level of adverse early stressful events in people with CFS compared with non-fatigued controls, reminiscent of Sapolsky's monkeys (discussed earlier in the chapter). Furthermore, a large study looking at personality factors that may contribute to CFS found pre-existing stress and emotional instability to be important factors (Kato, Sullivan, Evengard, & Pederson, 2006). But it is not clear why certain individuals respond to stress with chronic fatigue instead of some other psychological or physical disorder.

Michael Sharpe (1997) has developed one of the first models of the causes of CFS that accounts for all of its features (see ● Figure 7.6). Sharpe theorizes that individuals with particularly achievement-oriented lifestyles (driven, perhaps, by a basic sense of inadequacy) undergo a period of extreme stress or acute illness. They misinterpret the lingering symptoms of fatigue, pain, and inability to function at their usual high levels as a continuing disease that is worsened by activity and improved by rest. This results in behavioral avoidance, helplessness, depression, and frustration. They think they should be able to conquer the problem and cope with its symptoms. Chronic inactivity leads to lack of stamina, weakness, and increased feelings of depression and helplessness that in turn result in episodic bursts of long activity followed by further fatigue. Genetic factors probably influence the impact of stress and

● **Figure 7.6** A complex-specific model of CFS. (Adapted, with permission, from Sharpe, M. [1997]. Chronic fatigue syndrome. In D. M. Clark & C. G. Fairburn, Eds., *Science and Practice of Cognitive Behavior Therapy*. Oxford, UK: Oxford University Press, pp. 381–414, ©1997 Oxford University Press.)

chronic fatigue syndrome (CFS) Incapacitating exhaustion following only minimal exertion, accompanied by fever, headaches, muscle and joint pain, depression, and anxiety.

psychological variables in causing CFS, as is the case with all disorders (Kaiser, 2006).

Harvey and colleagues (2008) studied 34 individuals with CFS and found very high levels of exercise prior to the development of CFS and increased long bursts of exercise even after the onset of CFS, perhaps as an attempt to compensate for feelings of fatigue. On the other hand, physical activity that is too vigorous can perpetuate CFS symptoms (Nijs, Paul, & Wallman, 2008). As a result, some patients restrict their physical activity, which can also perpetuate fatigue. A meta-analytic review suggests that a behavioral intervention that encourages patients to slowly increase and maintain their physical activities (such as aerobic exercise and housework) without leading to exertion has sustained benefits on CFS symptoms (Marques, De Gucht, Gouveia, Leal, & Maes, 2015).

Pharmacological treatment has not proved effective for CFS (Afari & Buchwald, 2003; Chalder *et al.*, 2000), but Sharpe has developed a cognitive-behavioral program that includes procedures to increase activity, regulate periods of rest, and direct cognitive therapy at the cognitions specified in ● Figure 7.6. This treatment also includes relaxation, breathing exercises, and general stress-reduction procedures (Sharpe, 1992, 1993, 1997). Seventy-four percent of individuals who completed cognitive-behavioral therapy achieved substantial improvement in physical functioning at a six-month follow up, compared with only 19% of those in the relaxation-only group. A five-year follow-up indicates the gains were largely maintained (Deale, Husain, Chalder, & Wessely, 2001). Increasing emphasis is now placed on preventing bursts of over-exercise (e.g., Harvey & Wessely, 2009; Jason *et al.*, 2010). There is some evidence that moderate and graded as opposed to intense exercise can be useful in treatment, but CBT seems clearly indicated when patients have comorbid anxiety and depression (Castell, Kazantzis, & Moss-Morris, 2011; White *et al.*, 2011), since cognitive reappraisal of the meaning of fatigue in one's life and increased self-efficacy seem important (Friedberg & Sohl, 2009).

7.2 Concept CHECK

Answer the following questions about the psychosocial effects on physical disorders.

1. Which of the following is not considered part of the experience of pain?

   a. The subjective impression of pain as reported by the patient

   b. Pain behaviors or overt manifestations of pain

   c. Cuts, bruises, and other injuries

   d. An emotional component called suffering

2. Some evidence shows that psychological factors may contribute to both the course and the _____ of cancer, AIDS, and other diseases, as well as treatment and recovery.

3. Psychosocial and biological factors contribute to the development of _____, a potentially deadly condition of high blood pressure, and to the development of _____, the blockage of arteries supplying blood to the heart muscle.

4. Psychologists have found that behavior pattern "types" impact physical health. _____ is associated with the development of illness to a greater extent than is _____

5. No confirmed evidence exists to show that there is a physical cause for the disease of _____ that often causes individuals to give up their careers and suffer considerably.

Psychosocial Treatment of Physical Disorders

▶ What procedures and strategies are used in stress management and in prevention and intervention programs?

Certain experiments suggest that pain not only is bad for you but also may kill you. Several years ago, John Liebeskind and his colleagues (Page, Ben-Eliyahu, Yirmiya, & Liebeskind, 1993) demonstrated that postsurgical pain in rats doubles the rate at which a certain cancer metastasizes (spreads) to the lungs. Rats undergoing abdominal surgery *without* morphine developed twice the number of lung metastases as rats who were given morphine for the same surgery. The rats undergoing surgery with the pain-killing drug had even lower rates of metastases than rats that did not have surgery.

This effect may result from the interaction of pain with the immune system. Pain may reduce the number of natural killer cells in the immune system, perhaps because of the general stress reaction to the pain. Thus, if a rat is in *extreme* pain, the associated stress may further enhance the pain, completing a vicious circle. Because this finding also seems to apply to humans (Flor & Turk, 2011; Taylor, 2009), it is important, because the consensus is that we are reluctant to use pain-killing medication in chronic diseases such as cancer. Some estimates suggest that fewer than half of all cancer patients in the United States receive sufficient pain relief. Direct evidence is available on the benefits of early pain relief in patients undergoing surgery (Coderre, Katz, Vaccarino, & Melzack, 1993; Keefe & France, 1999). Patients receiving pain medication before surgery reported less pain after surgery and requested less pain medication. Adequate pain-management procedures, either medical or psychological, are an essential part of the management of chronic disease.

A variety of psychological treatments have been developed for physical disorders and pain, including biofeedback, relaxation procedures, and hypnosis (Kerns, Sellinger, & Goodin, 2011; Otis & Pincus, 2008; Otis *et al.*, 2011). But because of the overriding role of stress in the cause and maintenance of many physical disorders, comprehensive stress-management programs are increasingly incorporated into medical centers where such disorders are treated.

Biofeedback

Biofeedback is a process of making patients aware of physiological functions that, ordinarily, they would not notice consciously, such as heart rate, blood pressure, muscle tension in specific areas of the body, electroencephalogram rhythms (brain waves), and patterns of blood flow (Kerns *et al.*, 2011; Schwartz & Andrasik, 2003). Clinicians use physiological monitoring equipment to make the response, such as heart rate, visible or audible to the patient. The patient then works with the therapist to learn to control the response. A successful response produces some type of signal. For example, if the patient is successful in lowering their blood pressure by a certain amount, the pressure reading will be visible on a gauge and a tone will sound. It wasn't long before researchers discovered that humans could discriminate changes in autonomic nervous system activity with a high degree of accuracy (Blanchard & Epstein, 1977).

One goal of biofeedback has been to reduce tension in the muscles of the head and scalp, thereby relieving headaches. Pioneers such as Ed Blanchard, Ken Holroyd, and

▲ In biofeedback, the patient learns to control physiological responses that are visible on a screen.

Frank Andrasik found that biofeedback was successful in this area (Holroyd, Andrasik, & Noble, 1980), although no more successful than deep muscle relaxation procedures (Andrasik, 2000; Holroyd & Penzien, 1986). Because of these results, some have thought that biofeedback might achieve its effects with tension headaches by simply teaching people to relax. However, Holroyd and colleagues (1984) concluded instead that the success of biofeedback, at least for headaches, may depend not on the reduction of tension but on the extent to which the procedures instill a sense of *control* over the pain. (How do you think this relates to the study of stress in baboons described in the beginning of the chapter?)

Whatever the mechanism, biofeedback and relaxation are more effective treatments than, for example, placebo medication interventions, and the results of these two treatments are not altogether interchangeable, in that some people benefit more from biofeedback and others benefit from relaxation procedures. Therefore, applying one treatment or the other is a safe strategy (Andrasik, 2000; Kerns *et al.*, 2011). Several reviews have found that 38% to 63% of patients undergoing relaxation or biofeedback achieve significant reductions in headaches compared with approximately 35% who receive placebo medication (Blanchard, 1992; Holroyd & Penzien, 1986). Furthermore, the effects of biofeedback and relaxation seem to be long lasting (Andrasik, 2000; Kerns *et al.*, 2011).

....

biofeedback Use of physiological monitoring equipment to make individuals aware of their own bodily functions, such as blood pressure or brain waves, that they cannot normally access, with the purpose of controlling these functions.

Relaxation and Meditation

Various types of relaxation and meditation procedures have also been used, either alone or with other procedures, to treat physical disorder and pain patients (Kerns et al., 2011). In *progressive muscle relaxation*, devised by Edmund Jacobson in 1938, people tense different muscle groups in a sequential fashion (lower arm, upper arm, etc.) followed by relaxing each specific muscle group. In this way they learn to recognize tension in different muscle groups and how to reduce it. A number of meditation-based procedures focus attention either on a specific part of the body or on a single thought or image. This attentional focus is often accompanied by regular, slowed breathing.

Herbert Benson developed a brief procedure he calls the **relaxation response**, in which a person silently repeats a mantra (focusing attention solely on a repeated syllable) to minimize distraction by closing the mind to intruding thoughts. Individuals who meditate for 10 or 20 minutes a day report feeling calmer or more relaxed throughout the day. These brief, simple procedures can be powerful in reducing the flow of certain neurotransmitters and stress hormones, an effect that may be mediated by an increased sense of control and mastery (Benson, 1975, 1984). Relaxation has generally positive effects on headaches, hypertension, and acute and chronic pain, although the results are sometimes modest (Taylor, 2009). In addition, mindfulness meditation appears to be effective for a range of problems, including stress, anxiety, and depression (Goyal et al., 2014; Hofmann et al., 2010; Khoury et al., 2013; Kuyken et al., 2015). Therefore, relaxation and meditation are almost always part of a comprehensive pain-management program.

A Comprehensive Stress- and Pain-Reduction Program

In our own stress-management program (Barlow, Rapee, & Parini, 2014), individuals practice a variety of stress-management procedures. First, they learn to monitor their stress closely and to identify the stressful events in their daily lives. (A sample of a daily stress record is in • Figure 7.7.) Note that clients are taught to be specific about recording the times they experience stress, the intensity of the stress, and what seems to trigger the stress. They also note the somatic symptoms and thoughts that occur when they are stressed.

After learning to monitor stress, clients are taught deep muscle relaxation, which first involves tensing various muscles to identify the location of different muscle groups. Clients are then taught to relax the muscle groups beyond the point of inactivity—that is, to actively let go of the muscle so that no tension remains in it. Appraisals and attitudes are an important part of stress, and clients learn how they

exaggerate the negative impact of events in their lives. In the program, therapist and client use cognitive therapy to develop more realistic appraisals and attitudes, as exemplified in the case of Sally.

Sally... • *Improving Her Perception*

(Sally is a 45-year-old real estate agent.)

Patient: My mother is always calling just when I'm in the middle of doing something important and it makes me so angry, I find that I get short with her.

Therapist: Let's try and look at what you just said in another way. When you say that she *always* phones in the middle of something, it implies 100% of the time. Is that true? How likely is it really that she will call when you are doing something important?

P: Well, I suppose that when I think back over the last 10 times she's called, most of the times I was just watching TV or reading. There was once when I was making dinner and it burned because she interrupted me. Another time, I was busy with some work I had brought home from the office, and she called. I guess that makes it 20% of the time.

T: OK, great; now let's go a bit further. So what if she calls at an inconvenient time?

P: Well, I know that one of my first thoughts is that she doesn't think anything I do is important. But before you say anything, I know that is a major overestimation since she obviously doesn't know what I'm doing when she calls. However, I suppose I also think that it's a major interruption and inconvenience to have to stop at that point.

T: Go on. What is the chance that it is a major inconvenience?

P: When I was doing my work, I forgot what I was up to and it took me 10 minutes to work it out again. I guess that's not so bad; it's only 10 minutes. And when the dinner burned, it was really not too bad, just a little burned. Part of that was my fault anyway, because I could have turned the stove down before I went to the phone.

T: So, it sounds like quite a small chance that it would be a major inconvenience, even if your mother does interrupt you.

P: True. And I know what you are going to say next. Even if it is a major inconvenience, it's not the end of the world. I have handled plenty of bigger problems than this at work.

In this program, individuals work to identify unrealistic negative thoughts and to develop new appraisals and attitudes almost instantaneously when negative

Daily Stress Record
(sample)

Week of _____

	(1) Starting time	(2) Ending time	(3) Highest stress (0–8)	(4) Triggers	(5) Symptoms	(6) Thoughts
Date						
1-5	10:00am	11:00am	7	Sales meeting	Sweating, headache	My figures are bad
1-7	5:15pm	5:35pm	6	Traffic jam	Tension, impatience	I'll never get home
1-8	12:30pm	12:32pm	3	Lost keys	Tension	I can't find my keys
1-9	3:30pm	4:30pm	4	Waiting for guests	Sweating, nausea	Are they lost ?

Stress scale: 8 Extreme stress / 7 / 6 Much stress / 5 / 4 Moderate stress / 3 / 2 Mild stress / 1 / 0 No stress

● **Figure 7.7** Methods for monitoring stress. (Adapted, with permission, from Barlow, D. H., Rapee, R. M., & Reisner, L. C. [2001]. *Mastering stress 2001: A lifestyle approach* [p. 28]. Dallas, TX: American Health, © 2001 American Health Publishing.)

thoughts occur. After the session just related, Sally began using what she had learned in cognitive therapy to reappraise stressful situations. Finally, clients in stress-reduction programs develop new coping strategies, such as time management and assertiveness training. During *time-management training*, patients are taught to prioritize their activities and pay less attention to non-essential demands. During *assertiveness training*, they learn to stand up for themselves in an appropriate way. Clients also learn other procedures for managing every-day problems.

A number of studies have evaluated some version of this comprehensive program. The results suggest that it is generally more effective than individual components alone, such as relaxation or biofeedback, for chronic pain (Otis & Pincus, 2008; Turk & Monarch, 2002), CFS (Deale *et al.*, 1997), tension headaches (Lipchik *et al.*, 2002), hypertension (Ward, Swan, & Chesney, 1987), temporomandibular joint (jaw) pain (Turner, Mancl, & Aaron, 2006), and cancer pain (Andersen *et al.*, 2007; Crichton & Morey, 2003). A summary "meta-analysis" of 22 studies of treatments for chronic lower back pain also found comprehensive psychological treatments effective (Hoffman, Papas, Chatkoff, & Kerns, 2007).

Drugs and Stress-Reduction Programs

Some evidence suggests that chronic reliance on over-the-counter analgesic (pain reliever) medications lessens the efficacy of comprehensive programs in the treatment of headache and may make headaches worse because patients experience *increased* headache pain every time the medication wears off or is stopped (rebound headaches) (Capobianco, Swanson, & Dodick, 2001).

Traditional medical advice for people suffering from headache is to avoid the triggers leading to headache. However, it is possible that avoiding triggers is not as effective as learning how to cope with the triggers (Martin & MacLeod, 2009; Martin *et al.*, 2014), which includes general stress-reduction techniques and "planned exposures" to achieve desensitization and to examine whether an alleged trigger does, in fact, precipitate headaches.

. . . .

relaxation response Active components of meditation methods, including repetitive thoughts of a sound to reduce distracting thoughts and closing the mind to other intruding thoughts, that decrease the flow of stress hormones and neurotransmitters and cause a feeling of calm.

Pain medication is an obvious and commonly practiced strategy to avoid pain. Despite its frequent use, it is not overly effective and can lead to overuse and even dependency. Grazzi and colleagues (2002) treated 61 patients with migraine headaches and analgesic overuse by withdrawing the patients from analgesics and then starting them on a more comprehensive but non-addictive medication regimen, either with biofeedback and relaxation or without these (drugs only). After three years, significantly more individuals in the medication-only condition had relapsed by resuming analgesic use and were experiencing more headache pain. It is important that psychological treatment also seems to reduce drug consumption fairly consistently as it did in the study by Grazzi and colleagues (2002), not only for headaches but also for severe hypertension.

Denial as a Means of Coping

Mental health professionals have long recognized the importance of reliving or processing intense emotional experiences to put them behind us and to develop better coping responses. For example, individuals undergoing coronary artery bypass surgery who were optimistic recovered more quickly, returned to normal activities more rapidly, and reported a stronger quality of life six months after surgery than those who were not optimistic (Scheier et al., 1989). Scheier and colleagues also discovered that optimistic people are less likely to use denial as a means of coping with a severe stressor such as surgery. Most mental health professionals work to eliminate denial because it has many negative effects. For example, people who deny the severe pain connected with disease may not notice meaningful variations in their symptoms, and they typically avoid treatment regimens or rehabilitation programs.

But is denial always harmful? The well-known health psychologist Shelley Taylor (2009) points out that most individuals who are functioning well deny the implications of a potentially serious condition, at least initially. A common reaction is to assume that what they have is not serious or will go away quickly. Most people with serious diseases react this way, including those with cancer and CHD. Several groups of investigators (see, for example, Hackett & Cassem, 1973; Meyerowitz, 1983) have found that during that extremely stressful period when a person is first diagnosed, denial may help patients endure the shock. They are then better able to develop coping responses later. The value of denial as a coping mechanism may depend more on timing than on anything else. In the long run, however, all evidence indicates that at some point we must face the situation, process our emotions, and come to terms with what is happening (Compas et al., 2006).

Modifying Behaviors to Promote Health

As early as 1991, the director of the National Institutes of Health said, "Our research is teaching us that many common diseases can be prevented and others can be postponed or controlled simply by making possible lifestyle changes" (U.S. Department of Health and Human Services, 1991). Unhealthy eating habits, lack of exercise, and smoking are three of the most common behaviors that put us at risk in the long term for a number of physical disorders (Lewis et al., 2011). Other high-risk behaviors and conditions include unprotected sex, failure to take precautions to avoid injuries, excessive use of alcohol, and excessive exposure to the sun, just to name a few. Many of these behaviors contribute to diseases and physical disorders that are among the leading causes of death, including not only CHD and cancer but also accidents of various kinds (related to consumption of alcohol and the non-use of safety restraints), cirrhosis of the liver (related to excessive consumption of alcohol), and a variety of respiratory diseases, including influenza and pneumonia (related to smoking and stress) (Lewis et al., 2011).

Considerable work is ongoing to develop effective behavior modification procedures that improve diet, increase adherence to drug and medical treatment programs, and develop optimal exercise programs. Here we review briefly four areas of interest: injury prevention, AIDS prevention, efforts to reduce smoking in China, and a community intervention known as the Stanford Three Community Study.

Injury Prevention

Accidents are the leading cause of death for people age one to 45 and the fifth leading cause of death among all causes in the United States (see Table 7.1). Furthermore, the loss of productivity to the individual and society, as well as years of life lost from injuries, is far greater than from the other four leading causes of death: heart disease, cancer, stroke, and respiratory disease (Institute of Medicine, 1999; National Safety Council, 2013). Therefore, the U.S. government has become interested in methods for reducing injury (CDC, 2010; Scheidt, Overpeck, Trifiletti, & Cheng, 2000). Spielberger and Frank (1992) pointed out that psychological variables are crucial in leading to virtually all factors that lead to injury. A good example is the work of the late Lizette Peterson and her colleagues (see, for example, Damashek, Williams, Sher, & Peterson, 2009; Peterson & Roberts, 1992). Peterson was particularly interested in preventing accidents in children. Injuries kill more children than the next six causes of childhood death combined (Scheidt et al., 1995; Taylor, 2009), and nearly half of all cases of poisoning each year occur in children under six (CDC, 2006).

A variety of programs focusing on behavior change have proved effective for preventing injuries in children. For example, children have been systematically and successfully taught to prevent burns, escape fires, and prevent other serious injuries (Gielen, McDonald, & Shields, 2015; Kendrick *et al.*, 2012). In many of these programs, the participating children maintained the safety skills they had learned for months after the intervention—as long as assessments were continued, in most cases. Because little evidence indicates that repeated warnings are effective in preventing injuries, programmatic efforts to change behavior are important. Such programs, however, are non-existent in most communities. Fortunately, parental responses to childhood injury can be improved through cognitive behavioral interventions, leading to more informed care for recovering children (Marsac, Kassam-Adams, Hildenbrand, Kohser, & Winston, 2011).

AIDS Prevention

Earlier we documented the horrifying spread of AIDS, particularly in developing countries. Table 7.3 illustrates modes of transmission of AIDS in the United States and the world as they existed through 2008 and 2009. In developing countries, such as in Africa, for instance, AIDS is almost exclusively linked to heterosexual intercourse with an infected partner. There is no vaccine for the disease. *Changing high-risk behavior is the most effective prevention strategy* (Grossman, Purcell, Rotheram-Borus, & Veniegas, 2013; Mermin & Fenton, 2012).

TABLE 7.3 | AIDS Cases by Mode of Transmission (World, 2009; U.S., 2008) Percentage Estimates of Total Cases

Transmission Category	World	United States*
Male-to-male sexual contact	5–10%	50%
Injection drug use	10%	17%
Male-to-male sexual contact and injection drug use		5%
Heterosexual contact	59–69%	32%
Other**	16–21%	1%

* Because totals were calculated independently from the subpopulations, the percentages may not sum exactly to 100%.
** Includes hemophilia, blood transfusion, perinatal exposure, transmission within health-care settings, and risk not reported or identified.

SOURCE: Figures for the world adapted from UNAIDS (2009, November), *AIDS epidemic update*. Figures for the U.S. adapted from Centers for Disease Control and Prevention (2010), *Diagnosis of HIV infection and AIDS in the U.S. and dependent areas, 2008* (HIV Surveillance Report, Volume 20).

Comprehensive programs are particularly important because testing alone to learn whether one is HIV positive or HIV negative does little to change behavior (see, for example, Grossman *et al.*, 2013). Even educating at-risk individuals is generally ineffective in changing high-risk behavior. One of the most successful behavior-change programs was carried out in San Francisco relatively early in the development of the AIDS epidemic. In this program, specific behaviors were targeted and certain methods were used to achieve behavior change in various groups. Before this program was introduced, frequent unprotected sex was reported by 37.4% of one sample of gay men and 33.9% of another sample (Stall, McKusick, Wiley, Coates, & Ostrow, 1986). At a follow-up point in 1988, the incidence had dropped to 1.7% and 4.2%, respectively, in the same two samples (Ekstrand & Coates, 1990). These changes did not occur in comparable groups where a program of this type had not been instituted.

It is crucial that these programs be extended to minorities and women, who often do not consider themselves at risk, probably because most media coverage in the United States has primarily focused on gay white males. In 2003, women accounted for 50% of new AIDS cases (World Health Organization, 2003). Furthermore, the age of highest risk for women is between 15 and 25 years; the peak risk for men is during their late 20s and early 30s. In view of the different circumstances in which women put themselves at risk for HIV infection—for example, prostitution in response to economic deprivation—effective behavior-change programs for them must be different from those developed for men (World Health Organization, 2000).

In Africa, where the primary mode of transmission of HIV is heterosexual, a greater focus on the interpersonal and social system of the individual at risk has also begun. One important new initiative is to focus prevention techniques on couples rather than individuals (Grabbe & Bunnell, 2010). This is important, because studies demonstrate that only 22% of adults aged 15 to 49 years know their HIV status in Africa, and condom use within regular partnerships is very low because the assumption is that their partner is "safe" and they are at low risk. Because 55% to 93% of new HIV infections occur within cohabiting relationships, this means that most transmissions occur within couples who are unaware of their HIV status. The successful initiation of couples counseling and testing has occurred in Rwanda, Uganda, and Kenya. Couples counseling for HIV prevention also provides opportunities for delivering and providing more comprehensive maternal and child health services.

Smoking in China

Despite efforts by the government to reduce smoking among its citizens, China has one of the most tobacco-addicted populations in the world. Approximately 320 million people in China are habitual smokers, a number that is greater than the entire population of the United States. About 90 % of China's smokers are male. China consumes 33% of all cigarettes in the world, and smoking is projected to kill 100 million Chinese people in the next 50 years (Gu *et al.*, 2009; Lam, Ho, Hedley, Mak, & Peto, 2001).

Unger and colleagues (2001) reported that 47% of Chinese boys in the seventh through ninth grades—but only 16% of girls—had already smoked cigarettes. In one early attempt to reach these individuals, health professionals took advantage of the strong family ties in China and decided to persuade the *children* of smokers to intervene with their fathers. In so doing, they conducted the largest study yet reported of attempted behavior modification to promote health. In 1989, they developed an antismoking campaign in 23 primary schools in Hangzhou, capital of Zhejiang province. Children took home antismoking literature and questionnaires to almost 10,000 fathers. They then wrote letters to their fathers asking them to quit smoking, and they submitted monthly reports on their fathers' smoking habits. Approximately nine months later, the results were assessed. Almost 12% of the fathers in the intervention group had quit smoking for at least six months. By contrast, in a control group of another 10,000 males, the quit rate was only 0.2%.

Since then, the Chinese government has become more involved in smoking prevention efforts. For example, Ma and colleagues (2008) identified several myths that characterize Chinese smokers. These include (1) the identification of smoking as a symbol of personal freedom, (2) a perception that tobacco is important in social and cultural interactions, (3) the perception that the health effects of smoking can be controlled through reasonable and measured use, and (4) the importance of tobacco to the economy. At present, the Chinese government is considering ways to counter these prevailing misconceptions as a prelude to developing more effective preventative programs.

The Stanford Three Community Study

One of the best-known and most successful efforts to reduce risk factors for disease in the community is the Stanford Three Community Study (Meyer, Nash, McAlister, Maccoby, & Farquhar, 1980). Although it was conducted several decades ago, it remains a model program. Rather than assemble three groups of people, these investigators studied three entire communities in central California that were reasonably alike in size and type of residents between 1972 and 1975. The target was reduction of risk factors for CHD. The positive behaviors that

were introduced focused on smoking, high blood pressure, diet, and weight reduction. In Tracy, the first community, no interventions were conducted, but detailed information was collected from a random sample of adults to assess any increases in their knowledge of risk factors, as well as any changes in risk factors over time. In addition, participants in Tracy received a medical assessment of their cardiovascular factors. The residents of Gilroy and part of Watsonville were subjected to a media blitz on the dangers of behavioral risk factors for CHD, the importance of reducing these factors, and helpful hints for doing so. Most residents of Watsonville, the third community, also had a face-to-face intervention in which behavioral counselors worked with the townspeople judged to be at particularly high risk for CHD. Participants in all three communities were surveyed once a year for a three-year period following the intervention. Results indicate that the interventions were markedly successful at reducing risk factors for CHD in these communities (see ● Figure 7.8). Furthermore, for the residents of Watsonville who also received individual counseling, risk factors were substantially lower than for people in Tracy or even for those in Gilroy and people in the part of Watsonville that received only the media blitz, and their knowledge of risk factors was substantially higher.

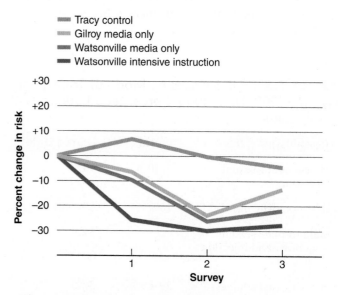

● **Figure 7.8** Results of the Stanford Three Community Study. (Reprinted, with permission, from Meyer, A. J., Nash, J. D., McAlister, A. L., Maccoby, N., & Farquhar, J. W. [1980]. Skills training in a cardiovascular health education campaign. *Journal of Consulting and Clinical Psychology, 48,* 129–142, © 1980 American Psychological Association.)

Match the treatments to the correct scenarios or statements: (a) biofeedback, (b) meditation and relaxation, (c) cognitive coping procedures, (d) denial, (e) modify behaviors to promote health, and (f) Stanford Three Community Study:

1. Mary is often upset by stupid things other people are always doing. Her doctor wants her to realize her exaggeration of these events and suggests _____.

2. Tyrone can't seem to focus on anything at work. He feels too stressed. He needs _____, a way of minimizing intruding thoughts, that he can do at work in a short amount of time.

3. Harry's blood pressure soars when he feels stressed. His doctor showed him how to become aware of his body process to control them better by using _____.

4. At a world conference, leaders met to discuss how to reduce the risk of childhood injuries, AIDS risks, and the number of smoking-related diseases. Professionals suggested programs involving teaching individuals how to _____.

5. Initially, strong _____ can help a patient endure the shock of bad news; however, later it can inhibit or prevent the healing process.

6. The _____ is one of the best-known efforts to reduce community disease risk factors.

SUMMARY

Psychological and Social Factors That Influence Health

What is the difference between behavioral medicine and health psychology?

▶ Psychological and social factors play a major role in developing and maintaining a number of physical disorders.

▶ Two fields of study have emerged as a result of a growing interest in psychological factors contributing to illness. Behavioral medicine involves the application of behavioral science techniques to prevent, diagnose, and treat medical problems. Health psychology is a subfield that focuses on psychological factors involved in the promotion of health and well-being.

How are immune system function, stress, and physical disorders related?

▶ Psychological and social factors may contribute directly to illness and disease through the psychological effects of stress on the immune system and other physical functioning.

▶ If the immune system is compromised, it may no longer be able to attack and eliminate antigens from the body effectively, or it may even begin to attack the body's normal tissue instead, a process known as autoimmune disease.

▶ Growing awareness of the many connections between the nervous system and the immune system has resulted in a field of study called *psychoneuroimmunology*.

▶ Diseases that may be partly related to the effects of stress on the immune system include AIDS, cardiovascular disease, and cancer.

Psychosocial Effects on Physical Disorders

How is stress related to AIDS, cancer, and cardiovascular disease?

▶ Long-standing patterns of behavior or lifestyle may put people at risk for developing certain physical disorders. For example, unhealthy sexual practices can lead to AIDS and other sexually transmitted diseases, and unhealthy behavioral patterns, such as poor eating habits, lack of exercise, or type A behavior pattern, may contribute to cardiovascular diseases such as stroke, hypertension, and coronary heart disease.

▶ Of the 10 leading causes of death in the United States, fully 50% of deaths can be traced to lifestyle behaviors.

What are the potential causes of acute and chronic pain, and how do the types of pain differ?

▶ Psychological and social factors also contribute to chronic pain. The brain inhibits pain through naturally occurring endogenous opioids, which may also be implicated in a variety of psychological disorders.

- Chronic fatigue syndrome is a disorder that is attributed at least partly to stress but may also have an as yet undiscovered viral or immune system dysfunction component.

Psychosocial Treatment of Physical Disorders

What procedures and strategies are used in stress management and in prevention and intervention programs?

- A variety of psychosocial treatments have been developed with the goal of either treating or preventing physical disorders. Among these are biofeedback and the relaxation response.

- Comprehensive stress- and pain-reduction programs include not only relaxation and related techniques but also new methods to encourage effective coping, including stress management, realistic appraisals, and improved attitudes through cognitive therapy.
- Comprehensive programs are generally more effective than individual components delivered singly.
- Other interventions aim to modify such behaviors as unsafe sexual practices, smoking, and unhealthy dietary habits. Such efforts have been made in a variety of areas, including injury control, AIDS prevention, smoking cessation campaigns, and programs to reduce risk factors for diseases such as CHD.

Key Terms

behavioral medicine, 250
health psychology, 250
general adaptation syndrome (GAS), 251
self-efficacy 254
immune system 254
antigens 255
rheumatoid arthritis 256
psychoneuroimmunology (PNI) 256

AIDS-related complex (ARC) 257
cancer 258
psychoncology 258
cardiovascular disease 260
stroke/cerebral vascular accident (CVA) 260
hypertension 260
essential hypertension 260
coronary heart disease (CHD) 262

type A behavior pattern 262
type B behavior pattern 262
acute pain 264
chronic pain 264
endogenous (natural) opioids 266
chronic fatigue syndrome (CFS) 268
biofeedback 271
relaxation response 272

Answers to Concept Checks

7.1

1. d; 2. a; 3. c; 4. b; 5. f; 6. e

7.2

1. c; 2. development; 3. hypertension, coronary heart disease; 4. type A (hard-driving, impatient), type B (relaxed, less concerned); 5. chronic fatigue syndrome

7.3

1. c; 2. b; 3. a; 4. e; 5. d; 6. f

Chapter Quiz

1. Which of the following is an interdisciplinary field that applies knowledge about human thoughts, emotions, and activities to prevent, diagnose, and treat medical problems?

   a. behavioral medicine

   b. endogenous medicine

   c. health psychology

   d. medical psychology

2. The general adaptation syndrome describes several stages people experience in response to sustained stress. These stages occur in which order?

   a. alarm, resistance, exhaustion

   b. resistance, alarm, exhaustion

   c. resistance, exhaustion, alarm

   d. exhaustion, alarm, resistance

3. Cortisol is:
   a. a neurotransmitter that reduces anxiety
   b. a neurohormone whose chronic secretion enhances hippocampal and immune functioning
   c. a portion of the brain that stimulates the HPA axis in response to stress
   d. a hormone that stimulates the hippocampus to turn off the stress response

4. Next month Shanti has to take an important college entrance exam. Which factor is most likely to influence whether her response to the exam is positive or negative?
   a. the genetic vulnerability to stress that Shanti has inherited from her parents
   b. whether Shanti will be taking the exam in a room by herself or with other students
   c. Shanti's beliefs about how much control she has over the situation
   d. how much time Shanti has to study before the exam

5. Joan has been living with HIV for three years and has just started participating in a stress-management support group. Based on previous research, what might Joan expect from her participation?
   a. an increase in the activity of T helper and natural killer cells
   b. an increase in the amount of antigens in her system
   c. an increase in depression as she discusses her illness
   d. an increase in immune functioning, but only for the first few weeks of the group

6. The study of how psychosocial factors influence cancer is known as:
   a. psychopathology
   b. psychopharmacology
   c. psychoncology
   d. oncosociology

7. Which of the following is a risk factor for coronary heart disease?
   a. anger that is part of the type A behavior pattern
   b. belligerence that is part of the type B behavior pattern
   c. competitive drive that is part of the type B behavior pattern
   d. carefree disregard for deadlines that is part of the type A behavior pattern

8. Biofeedback can be used to teach people how to:
   a. reduce their competitive drive and sense of urgency
   b. consciously control physiological functions that are outside awareness
   c. develop more supportive social support networks
   d. control their facial expressions to control their mood

9. Which of the following accurately characterizes the effects of denial as a coping strategy?
   a. Individuals who undergo coronary artery bypass surgery return to normal activities more rapidly if they deny their pain.
   b. Denial may have damaging short-term consequences in terms of the stress response, but it seems to be helpful to rehabilitation in the long term.
   c. People who deny their disease may not notice meaningful variations in their symptoms.
   d. Denial appears to have exclusively negative consequences on health and adaptation.

10. Which three behaviors, all of which can be modified, put people at the most risk for physical problems?
    a. unhealthy diet, lack of exercise, smoking
    b. pollution, unhealthy diet, lack of exercise
    c. lack of exercise, smoking, reckless driving
    d. smoking, alcohol use, "road rage"
    (See Appendix A for answers.)

Exploring Physical Disorders and Health Psychology

Psychological and behavioral factors are major contributors to illness and death.

▶ Behavioral medicine applies behavioral science to medical problems.

▶ Health psychology focuses on psychological influences on health and improving health care.

PSYCHOLOGICAL AND SOCIAL FACTORS INFLUENCE BIOLOGY

Stress

Anxiety

Causes

Depression

Weakened immune system/ compromised nervous system

Responses to threats and challenges may predict the effect of stress on the immune system.

Depression Anxiety Stress Excitement

Sense of control or ability to cope

Less control

More control

PhotoDisc/Getty Images

PhotoDisc/Getty Images

ILLNESS

PhotoDisc/Getty Images

AIDS (Acquired Immune Deficiency Syndrome)

- The human immunodeficiency virus (HIV) attacks the immune system and opportunistic infections develop uncontrollably.
- Psychological treatments focus on strengthening the immune system and gaining a sense of control.
- Although drug therapy may control the virus, there is so far no biological means of prevention and the disease is still always fatal.

Cardiovascular Problems

- The heart and blood vessels can be damaged by
  - *Stroke:* Blockage or rupture of blood vessels in the brain
  - *Hypertension:* Constriction of blood vessels at organs and extremities puts extra pressure on the heart, which eventually weakens
  - *Coronary heart disease:* Blockage of arteries supplying blood to the heart
- Biological, psychological, and social factors contribute to all these conditions and are addressed in treatment.

Chronic Pain

- May begin with an acute episode but does not diminish when injury heals.
- Typically involves joints, muscles, and tendons; may result from enlarged blood vessels, tissue degeneration, or cancerous tumors.
- Psychological and social influences may cause and maintain chronic pain to a significant degree.

Cancer

- Abnormal cell growth produces malignant tumors.
- Psychosocial treatments may prolong life, alleviate symptoms, and reduce depression and pain.
- Different cancers have different rates of recovery and mortality.
- Psychoncology is the study of psychosocial factors involved in the course and treatment of cancer.

PSYCHOSOCIAL TREATMENTS FOR PHYSICAL DISORDERS

The stress reaction associated with pain may reduce the number of natural killer cells in the immune system:

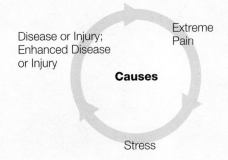

Disease or Injury;
Enhanced Disease
or Injury

Extreme
Pain

Causes

Stress

Biofeedback

- Electronic monitors make physiological responses such as heartbeat visible on a computer screen.
- Patient learns to increase or decrease the response, thereby improving functioning (decreasing tension).
  - Developing a sense of control may be therapeutic.

PhotoDisc/Getty Images

Relaxation and Meditation

- ***Progressive muscle relaxation:*** Person learns to locate physical tension and to counteract it by relaxing a specific muscle group.
- ***Meditation:*** Focusing attention on a specific body part or process or on an affirming thought or image; in some forms, focusing on a single silently repeated syllable (mantra) "empties" the mind. Meditation is accompanied by slow, regular breathing.
  - Meditating daily for at least 10 to 20 minutes imparts calm and relaxation by reducing certain neurotransmitters and stress hormones and increasing a sense of control.

PhotoDisc/Getty Images

BEHAVIOR MODIFICATION TO PROMOTE HEALTH

Many injuries and diseases can be prevented or controlled through lifestyle changes involving diet, substance use, exercise, and safety precautions.

Injury Control

- Injuries are the leading cause of death for people age 1 to 45, especially children.
- Most people consider injuries to be out of their control and therefore do not change high-risk behaviors.
- In children, prevention focuses on
  - escaping fires
  - crossing streets
  - using car seats, seat belts, and bicycle helmets
  - first aid

PhotoDisc/Getty Images

AIDS Prevention

- Changing high-risk behavior through individual and community education is the only effective strategy.
  - Eliminate unsafe sexual practices through cognitive-behavioral self-management training and social support networks.
  - Show drug abusers how to clean needles and make safe injections.
- Target minorities and women, groups that do not perceive themselves to be at risk.
  - Media coverage focuses on gay white males.
  - More women are infected through heterosexual interactions than through intravenous drug use.

PhotoDisc/Getty Images

8

Eating and Sleep–Wake Disorders

CHAPTER OUTLINE

Major Types of Eating Disorders

Bulimia Nervosa
Anorexia Nervosa
Binge-Eating Disorder
Statistics

Causes of Eating Disorders

Social Dimensions
Biological Dimensions
Psychological Dimensions
An Integrative Model

Treatment of Eating Disorders

Drug Treatments
Psychological Treatments
Preventing Eating Disorders

Obesity

Statistics
Disordered Eating Patterns in
    Cases of Obesity
Causes
Treatment

Sleep–Wake Disorders: The Major Dyssomnias

An Overview of Sleep–Wake
    Disorders
Insomnia Disorder
Hypersomnolence Disorders
Narcolepsy
Breathing-Related Sleep Disorders
Circadian Rhythm Sleep Disorder

Treatment of Sleep Disorders

Medical Treatments
Environmental Treatments
Psychological Treatments
Preventing Sleep Disorders
Parasomnias and Their Treatment

PeopleImages/E+/Getty Images

Use scientific reasoning to interpret behavior:	▶ Identify basic biological, psychological, and social components of behavioral explanations (e.g., inferences, observations, operational definitions and interpretations) [APA SLO 2.1a] *(see textbook pages 292–298, 304, 309–311)*
Engage in innovative and integrative thinking and problem solving:	▶ Describe problems operationally to study them empirically [APA SLO 2.3a] *(see textbook pages 285–289, 302–303, 308, 311–314)*
Describe applications that employ discipline-based problem solving:	▶ Correctly identify antecedents and consequences of behavior and mental processes [APA SLO 1.3b]. Describe examples of relevant and practical applications of psychological principles to everyday life [APA SLO 1.3a] *(see textbook pages 298–301, 304–305, 315–319)*

* Portions of this chapter cover learning outcomes suggested by the American Psychological Association (2013) in its guidelines for the undergraduate psychology major. Chapter coverage of these outcomes is identified above by APA Goal and APA Suggested Learning Outcome (SLO).

Most of us take our bodies for granted. We wake up in the morning assuming we will be alert enough to handle our required daily activities; we eat; we may engage in some exercise and, on some days, in sexual activity. We don't focus on our functioning to a great degree unless it is disrupted by illness or disease. Yet psychological and social factors can significantly disrupt these "activities of survival."

In this chapter, we talk about psychological disruptions of two of our relatively automatic behaviors, eating and sleeping, which substantially affect the rest of our behavior.

Major Types of Eating Disorders

▶ What are the defining features of bulimia nervosa and anorexia nervosa?

▶ How does binge-eating disorder differ from bulimia?

Although some disorders we discuss in this chapter can be deadly, many of us are not aware how widespread they are among us. Eating disorders began to increase during the 1950s or early 1960s and have spread insidiously over the ensuing decades. In **bulimia nervosa**, out-of-control eating episodes, or **binges**, are followed by self-induced vomiting, excessive use of laxatives, or other attempts to purge (get rid of) the food. In **anorexia nervosa**, the person eats only minimal amounts of food or exercises vigorously to offset food intake so body weight sometimes drops dangerously. In **binge-eating disorder**, individuals may binge repeatedly and find it distressing, but they do not attempt to purge the food. The chief characteristic of these related disorders is an overwhelming, all-encompassing drive to be thin. Of the people with anorexia nervosa who are followed over a sufficient period, up to 20% die as a result of their disorder, with slightly more than 5% dying within 10 years (see, for example, Franko *et al.*, 2013; Millar *et al.*, 2005; Papadopoulos, Ekbom, Brandt, & Ekselius, 2009). Around 20% to 30% of anorexia-related deaths are suicides, which is 50 times higher than the risk of death from suicide in the general population (Arcelus, Mitchell, Wales, & Nielsen, 2011; Chavez & Insel, 2007).

A growing number of studies in different countries indicate that eating disorders are widespread and increased dramatically in Western countries from about 1960 to 1995, before seeming to level off somewhat (Russell, 2009; Steiger, Bruce, & Israel, 2013). Most dramatic are the data for bulimia nervosa (Russell, 2009). Garner and Fairburn (1988) reviewed rates of referral to a major eating disorder center in Canada. Between 1975 and 1986, the referral rates for anorexia rose slowly, but the rates for bulimia rose dramatically—from virtually none to more

. . . .

bulimia nervosa Eating disorder involving recurrent episodes of uncontrolled excessive (**binge**) eating followed by compensatory actions to remove the food (e.g., deliberate vomiting, laxative abuse, and excessive exercise).

binge Relatively brief episode of uncontrolled, excessive consumption, usually of food or **alcohol**.

anorexia nervosa Eating disorder characterized by recurrent food refusal, leading to dangerously low body weight.

binge-eating disorder (BED) Pattern of eating involving distress-inducing **binges** not followed by purging behaviors; being considered as a new *DSM* diagnostic category.

than 140 per year. Similar findings have been reported from other parts of the world (Hay & Hall, 1991; Lacey, 1992), although more recent surveys suggest that rates for bulimia may be leveling off or even beginning to drop from highs reached in the 1990s (Keel, Heatherton, Dorer, Joiner, & Zalta, 2006).

The figures on mortality mentioned above represent six times the increase in death rates from eating disorders compared with death rates in the normal population (Arcelus et al., 2011; Franko et al., 2013; Papadopoulos et al., 2009). Eating disorders were included for the first time as a separate group of disorders in the fourth edition of the *Diagnostic and Statistical Manual (DSM-IV)*, published by the American Psychiatric Association in 2000.

The increases in eating disorders during the second half of the 20th century would be puzzling enough if they occurred across the population. What makes them even more intriguing is that they tend to be culturally specific. Until recently, eating disorders, particularly bulimia, were not found in developing countries, where access to sufficient food is so often a daily struggle; only in the West, where food was generally plentiful, have they been rampant. Now this has changed; evidence suggests that eating disorders are going global. For example, recent studies show estimates of prevalence in China and Japan are approaching those in the United States and other Western countries (Chisuwa & O'Dea, 2010; Steiger et al., 2013). Not everyone in the world is at risk. Eating disorders tend to occur in a relatively small segment of the population. More than 90% of the severe cases are young females who live in a socially competitive environment. Increasingly, this group of girls and young women with eating disorders seek one another out on the internet through "pro-ana" (anorexia), "pro-mia" (bulimia), and "thinspiration" websites and social networks, where they find support and, in some cases, inspiration (e.g., my-pro-ana, 2013; Peng, 2008), much to the detriment of their health.

The very specificity of these disorders in terms of sex and age is unparalleled and makes the search for causes all the more interesting. In these disorders, unlike most others, the strongest contributions to etiology seem to be sociocultural rather than psychological or biological factors.

Obesity is not considered an official disorder in the *DSM*, but we consider it here because it is thought to be one of the most dangerous epidemics confronting public health authorities around the world today. The latest surveys indicate that close to 70% of adults in the United States are overweight, more than 35% meet criteria for obesity (Flegal, Carroll, Kit, & Ogden, 2012) and over 100 million people in the United States alone are dieting at any one time (Mann, Tomiyama, & Ward, 2015). These rates have been increasing for decades, although they may now be leveling off, at least in North America (Flegal et al., 2012; Ogden et al., 2006). Definitions of underweight, overweight, and

obesity will be discussed further later, but they are based in part on body mass index (BMI), which is highly correlated with body fat. The more overweight someone is at a given height, the greater the risks to health (Convit, 2012). These risks are widespread and involve greatly increased prevalence of cardiovascular disease, type 2 diabetes, hypertension, stroke, gallbladder disease, respiratory disease, muscular skeletal problems, and hormone-related cancers (Convit, 2012; Flegal, Graubard, Williamson, & Gail, 2005). And, more recent evidence indicates that these risks may be even greater than previously thought (Stokes & Preston, 2015). Obesity is produced by the consumption of a greater number of calories than are expended in energy. The behavior that produces this distorted energy equation contradicts a common assumption—namely, that people with obesity do not necessarily eat more or exercise less than their lean counterparts. They do. Although the tendency to overeat and exercise too little unquestionably has a genetic component, as described later, the excessive eating at the core of the problem is the reason that obesity could be considered a disorder of eating.

Bulimia Nervosa

You are probably familiar with bulimia nervosa from your own experience or a friend's. It is one of the most common psychological disorders on college campuses. Consider the case of Phoebe.

Phoebe... • *Apparently Perfect*

Phoebe was a classic all-American girl: popular, attractive, intelligent, and talented. By the time she was a senior in high school, she had accomplished a great deal. She was a class officer throughout high school, homecoming princess her sophomore year, and junior prom queen. She played on school athletic teams, maintained an A-minus average, and was headed for a top-ranked university.

But Phoebe had a secret: She was haunted by her belief that she was fat and ugly. Every bite of food that she put in her mouth was, in her mind, a step down the inexorable path that led to the end of her success and popularity. Phoebe had been concerned about her weight since she was 11. Ever the perfectionist, she began regulating her eating in junior high. She would skip breakfast (over the protestations of her mother), eat a small bowl of pretzels at noon, and allow herself one half of whatever she was served for dinner.

This behavior continued into high school, but as Phoebe struggled to restrict her eating, occasionally she would binge on junk food. Sometimes she stuck her fingers down her throat after a binge, but this tactic was unsuccessful. By the time she was a senior, Phoebe was obsessed with what she would eat and when. She used every bit of her willpower to restrict her eating, but occasionally she failed. One day during her senior year, she came home after school and ate two big boxes of candy. Depressed, guilty, and desperate, she went to the bathroom and stuck her fingers farther down her throat than she had before dared. She vomited. And she kept vomiting. Although physically exhausted, Phoebe had never felt such an overwhelming sense of relief from the anxiety, guilt, and tension that accompanied her binges. She realized that she had gotten to eat all that candy and now her stomach was empty. It was the perfect solution to her problems.

Phoebe learned quickly what foods she could easily vomit. And she always drank lots of water. She began to restrict her eating even more and her bingeing increased. This routine went on for about six months, until April of her senior year in high school. By this time, Phoebe had lost much of her energy, and her schoolwork was deteriorating. She was continually tired, her skin was broken out, and her face puffed up. Her teachers and mother suspected she might have an eating problem. When they confronted her, she was relieved her problem was out in the open and stopped binging for a while, but afraid of gaining weight and losing her popularity, Phoebe resumed her pattern, but she was now better at hiding it. For six months, Phoebe binged and purged approximately 15 times a week.

When Phoebe went away to college, things became more difficult. Now she had a roommate, and she was more determined than ever to keep her problem a secret. Although the student health service offered workshops on eating disorders, Phoebe knew that she could not break her cycle without the risk of gaining weight. To avoid the communal bathroom, she went to a deserted place behind a nearby building to vomit.

She kept her secret until the beginning of her sophomore year. One night, after drinking beer and eating fried chicken at a party, she attempted to cope with her guilt anxiety and tension in the usual manner, but when she tried to vomit, her gag reflex seemed to be gone. Breaking into hysterics, she called her boyfriend and told him she was ready to kill herself. Her loud sobbing and crying attracted the attention of her friends, and she confessed her problem to them. She also called her parents. At this point, Phoebe realized that her life was out of control and that she needed professional help.

Clinical Description

The hallmark of bulimia nervosa is eating a larger amount of food—typically, more junk food than fruits and vegetables—than most people would eat under similar circumstances (Fairburn & Cooper, 1993, 2014). Patients with bulimia readily identify with this description, even though the actual caloric intake for binges varies significantly from person to person (Franko, Wonderlich, Little, & Herzog, 2004). Just as important as the *amount* of food eaten is that the eating is experienced as *out of control* (Fairburn & Cooper, 2014; Sysko & Wilson, 2011), a criterion that is an integral part of the definition of binge-eating.

Another important criterion is that the individual attempts to *compensate* for the binge eating and potential weight gain, almost always by **purging techniques**. Techniques include self-induced vomiting immediately after eating, as in the case of Phoebe, and using laxatives (drugs that relieve constipation) and diuretics (drugs that result in loss of fluids through greatly increased frequency of urination). Some people use both methods; others attempt to compensate in other ways. Some exercise excessively (although rigorous exercising is more usually a characteristic of anorexia nervosa). Others fast for long periods between binges. Bulimia nervosa was subtyped in *DSM-IV-TR* into *purging type* (e.g., vomiting, laxatives, or diuretics) or *non-purging type* (e.g., exercise and/or fasting). But the non-purging type has turned out to be quite rare, accounting for only 6% to 8% of patients with bulimia (Hay &

obesity Excess of body fat resulting in a body mass index (BMI, a ratio of weight to height) of 30 or more.

purging techniques In the eating disorder **bulimia nervosa**, the self-induced vomiting or laxative abuse used to compensate for excessive food ingestion.

Fairburn, 1998; Striegel-Moore *et al.*, 2001). Furthermore, these studies found little evidence of any differences between purging and non-purging types of bulimia, nor were any differences evident in severity of psychopathology, frequency of binge episodes, or prevalence of major depression and panic disorder (van Hoeken, Veling, Sinke, Mitchell, & Hoek, 2009). As a result, this distinction was dropped in *DSM-5*.

Purging is not a particularly efficient method of reducing caloric intake (Fairburn, 2013). Vomiting reduces approximately 50% of the calories just consumed—less if it is delayed at all (Kaye, Weltzin, Hsu, McConaha, & Bolton, 1993); laxatives and related procedures have little effect, acting, as they do, so long after the binge (Fairburn, 2013).

One of the more important additions to the *DSM-IV* criteria in 1994 was the specification of a psychological characteristic clearly present in Phoebe. Despite her accomplishments and success, she felt her continuing popularity and self-esteem would largely be determined by the weight and shape of her body. Garfinkel (1992) noted that of 107 women seeking treatment for bulimia nervosa, only 3% did not share this attitude. Recent investigations confirm that the major features of the disorder (bingeing, purging, over-concern with body shape, and so on) "cluster together" in someone with this problem, which strongly supports the validity of the diagnostic category (Fairburn, & Cooper, 2014; Fairburn, Stice *et al.*, 2003).

Medical Consequences

Chronic bulimia with purging has a number of medical consequences (Mehler, Birmingham, Crow, & Jahraus, 2010; Russell, 2009). One is salivary gland enlargement caused by repeated vomiting, which gives the face a chubby appearance. This was noticeable with Phoebe. Repeated vomiting also may erode the dental enamel on the inner surface of the front teeth as well as tear the esophagus. More important, continued vomiting may upset the chemical balance of bodily fluids, including sodium and potassium levels. This condition, called an *electrolyte imbalance,* can result in serious medical complications if unattended, including cardiac arrhythmia (disrupted heartbeat), seizures, and kidney failure, all of which can be fatal. Surprisingly, young women with bulimia also develop more body fat than age- and weight-matched healthy controls (Ludescher *et al.*, 2009), the very effect they are trying to avoid! Normalization of eating habits will quickly reverse the imbalance. Intestinal problems resulting from laxative abuse are also potentially serious; they can include severe constipation or permanent colon damage.

Associated Psychological Disorders

An individual with bulimia usually presents with additional psychological disorders, particularly anxiety and mood disorders (Steiger *et al.*, 2013; Sysko & Wilson, 2011). Results from a definitive national survey on the prevalence of eating disorders and associated psychological disorders found that 80.6% of individuals with bulimia had an anxiety disorder at some point during their lives (Hudson *et al.*, 2007), and 66% of adolescents with bulimia presented with a co-occurring anxiety disorder when interviewed (Swanson *et al.*, 2011). Mood disorders, particularly depression, also commonly co-occur with bulimia, with about 20% of bulimic patients meeting criteria for a mood disorder when interviewed, and between 50% and 70% meeting criteria at some point during the course of their disorder (Hudson *et al.*, 2007; Swanson *et al.*, 2011).

For a number of years, one prominent theory suggested that eating disorders are simply a way of expressing depression. But most evidence indicates that depression *follows* bulimia and may be a reaction to it (Brownell & Fairburn, 1995; Steiger *et al.*, 2013). Finally, substance abuse commonly accompanies bulimia nervosa. For example, Hudson and colleagues (2007) reported that 36.8% of individuals with bulimia and 27% of individuals with anorexia were also current substance abusers, with even higher lifetime rates of substance abuse. In summary, bulimia seems strongly related to anxiety disorders and somewhat less so to mood and substance use disorders. Underlying traits of emotional instability and novelty seeking in these individuals may account for these patterns of comorbidity.

Anorexia Nervosa

Like Phoebe, the overwhelming majority of individuals with bulimia are within 10% of their normal weight (Fairburn & Cooper, 2014; Hsu, 1990). In contrast, individuals with anorexia nervosa differ in one important way from individuals with bulimia. They are so successful at losing weight that they put their lives in danger. Both anorexia and bulimia are characterized by a morbid fear of gaining weight and losing control over eating. The major difference seems to be whether the individual is successful at losing weight. People with anorexia are proud of both their diets and their extraordinary control. People with bulimia are ashamed of both their eating issues and their lack of control (Brownell & Fairburn, 1995). Consider the case of Julie.

Julie... • *The Thinner, the Better*

Julie was 17-years-old when she first came for help. She looked emaciated and unwell. Eighteen months earlier she had been overweight, weighing 140 pounds at five feet one inch. Her mother, a well-meaning but overbearing woman, nagged Julie about her appearance. Her friends were kinder but no less relentless. Julie, who had never had a date, was told by a friend she was cute and would have no trouble getting dates if she lost some weight. So she did! After many previous unsuccessful attempts, she was determined to succeed this time.

After several weeks on a strict diet, Julie noticed she was losing weight. She felt a control and mastery that she had never known before. It wasn't long before she received positive comments, not only from her friends but also from her mother. Julie began to feel good about herself. The difficulty was that she was losing weight too fast. She stopped menstruating. But now nothing could stop her from dieting. By the time she reached our clinic, she weighed 75 pounds but she thought she could stand to lose a bit more weight. Still, Julie did not initially seek treatment for her eating behavior. Rather, she had developed a numbness in her left lower leg and a left foot drop—an inability to lift up the front part of the foot—that a neurologist determined was caused by peritoneal nerve paralysis believed to be related to inadequate nutrition. The neurologist referred her to our clinic.

Like most people with anorexia, Julie said she probably should put on a little weight, but she didn't mean it. She thought she looked fine, but she had "lost all taste for food," a report that may not have been true because most people with anorexia crave food at least some of the time but control their cravings. Nevertheless, she was participating in most of her usual activities and continued to do well in school and in her extracurricular pursuits. Her parents were happy to buy her most of the workout tapes available, and she began doing one every day, and then two. When her parents suggested she was exercising enough, perhaps too much, she worked out when no one was around. After every meal, she exercised until, in her mind, she burned up all the calories she had just taken in.

▲ These women are at different stages of anorexia.

The tragic consequences of anorexia among young celebrities and within the modeling world have been well publicized in the media. In November 2010, 28-year-old French model and actress Isabelle Caro died, weighing 93 pounds. At five feet five inches, she had a BMI of 15.47 (16 is considered starvation). Around 2006, first Spain, then Italy, Brazil, and India, instituted bans on models with BMIs less than 18 from their top fashion shows (30% of models in Spain were turned away). In 2015, France instituted a similar ban. It is not clear yet whether the bans have impacted popular perception of ideal body size in these countries.

Clinical Description

Anorexia nervosa is less common than bulimia, but there is a great deal of overlap. For example, many individuals with bulimia have a history of anorexia; that is, they once used fasting to reduce their body weight below desirable levels (Fairburn & Cooper, 2014; Fairburn, Welch et al., 1997).

Although decreased body weight is the most notable feature of anorexia nervosa, it is not the core of the disorder.

Many people lose weight because of a medical condition, but people with anorexia have an intense fear of obesity and relentlessly pursue thinness (Fairburn & Cooper, 2014; Hsu, 1990; Russell, 2009). As with Julie, the disorder most commonly begins in an adolescent who is overweight or who perceives herself to be. She then starts a diet that escalates into an obsessive preoccupation with being thin. As we noted, severe, almost punishing exercise is common (Davis et al., 1997; Russell, 2009), as with Julie. Dramatic weight loss is achieved through severe caloric restriction or by combining caloric restriction and purging.

DSM-5 specifies two subtypes of anorexia nervosa. In the restricting type, individuals diet to limit calorie intake; in the binge-eating–purging type, they rely on purging. Unlike individuals with bulimia, binge-eating–purging anorexics binge on relatively small amounts of food and purge more consistently, in some cases each time they eat. Approximately half the individuals who meet criteria for anorexia engage in binge-eating and purging (Fairburn & Cooper, 2014). However, few differences exist between these two subtypes on severity of symptoms or personality based on prospective data collected over eight years on 136 individuals with anorexia (Eddy et al., 2002). After eight years, fully 62% of the restricting subtype had begun bingeing or purging. Another study showed few differences between these subtypes on comorbidity with anxiety disorders (Kaye et al., 2014). Thus, subtyping may not be useful in predicting the future course of the disorder but rather may reflect a certain phase or stage of anorexia, a finding confirmed in a more recent study (Eddy et al., 2008). For this reason, DSM-5 criteria specify that subtyping refer only to the past three months (Peat, Mitchell, Hoek, & Wonderlich, 2009).

Individuals with anorexia are never satisfied with their weight loss. Staying the same weight from one day to the next or gaining any weight is likely to cause intense panic, anxiety, and depression. Only continued weight loss every day for weeks on end is satisfactory. Although *DSM-5* criteria specify only "significantly low" body weight 15% below that expected, one study suggests that BMI averages are close to 15.8 by the time treatment is sought (Berner, Shaw, Witt, & Lowe, 2013). Another key criterion of anorexia is a marked disturbance in body image. When Julie looked at herself in the mirror, she saw something different from what others saw. They saw an emaciated, sickly, frail girl in the throes of semistarvation. Julie saw a girl who still needed to lose at least a few pounds from some parts of her body.

After seeing numerous doctors, people like Julie become good at mouthing what others expect to hear. They may agree they are underweight and need to gain a few pounds—but they do not really believe it. Question further and they will tell you the girl in the mirror is fat. Therefore, individuals with anorexia seldom seek treatment on their own. Usually pressure from somebody in the family leads to the initial visit (Agras, 1987; Fairburn & Cooper, 2014), as in Julie's case. Perhaps as a demonstration of absolute control over their eating, some individuals with anorexia show increased interest in cooking and food. Some have become expert chefs, preparing all the food for the family. Others hoard food in their rooms, looking at it occasionally.

Medical Consequences

One common medical complication of anorexia nervosa is cessation of menstruation (amenorrhea), which also occurs relatively often in bulimia (Crow, Thuras, Keel, & Mitchell, 2002). This feature can be an objective physical index of the degree of food restriction but is inconsistent because it does not occur in all cases (Franko *et al.*, 2004). Because of this inconsistency, amenorrhea was dropped as a diagnostic criterion in *DSM-5* (Attia & Roberto, 2009; Fairburn & Cooper, 2014). Other medical signs and symptoms of anorexia include dry skin, brittle hair or nails, and sensitivity to or intolerance of cold temperatures. Also, it is relatively

common to see *lanugo*, downy hair on the limbs and cheeks. Cardiovascular problems, such as chronically low blood pressure and heart rate, can also result. If vomiting is part of the anorexia, electrolyte imbalance and resulting cardiac and kidney problems can result (Mehler *et al.*, 2010).

Associated Psychological Disorders

As with bulimia nervosa, anxiety disorders and mood disorders are often present in individuals with anorexia (Russell, 2009; Sysko & Wilson, 2011), with rates of depression occurring at some point during their lives in as many as 71% of cases (Godart *et al.*, 2007). Interestingly, one anxiety disorder that seems to co-occur often with anorexia is obsessive-compulsive disorder (OCD) (see Chapter 4; Cederlöf *et al.*, 2015; Kaye *et al.*, 2014; Keel *et al.*, 2004). In anorexia, unpleasant thoughts are focused on gaining weight, and individuals engage in a variety of behaviors, some of them ritualistic, to rid themselves of such thoughts. Substance abuse is also common in individuals with anorexia nervosa (Root *et al.*, 2010; Swanson *et al.*, 2011), and, in conjunction with anorexia, is a strong predictor of mortality, particularly by suicide.

Binge-Eating Disorder

Beginning in the 1990s, research focused on a group of individuals who experience marked distress because of binge-eating but do *not* engage in extreme compensatory behaviors and therefore cannot be diagnosed with bulimia (Castonguay, Eldredge, & Agras, 1995; Fairburn *et al.*, 1998). These individuals have binge-eating disorder (BED). After classification in *DSM-IV* as a disorder needing further study, BED is now included as a fully fledged disorder in *DSM-5* (Wonderlich, Gordon, Mitchell, Crosby, & Engel, 2009). Evidence that supports its elevation to disorder status includes somewhat different patterns of heritability compared with other eating disorders (Bulik *et al.*, 2000), as well as a greater likelihood of occurring in males and a later age of onset. There is also a greater likelihood of remission and a better response to treatment in BED compared with other eating disorders (Striegel-Moore & Franko, 2008; Wonderlich *et al.*, 2009).

Individuals who meet preliminary criteria for BED are often found in weight-control programs. The general consensus is that about 20% of obese individuals in weight-loss programs engage in binge-eating, with the number rising to approximately 50% among candidates for bariatric surgery (surgery to correct severe or morbid obesity).

About half of individuals with BED try dieting before bingeing, and half start with bingeing and then attempt to diet (Abbott *et al.*, 1998); those who begin bingeing first become more severely affected by BED and are more likely to have additional disorders (Brewerton, Rance, Dansky, O'Neil, & Kilpatrick, 2014; Spurrell, Wilfley, Tanofsky, &

DIAGNOSTIC CRITERIA SUMMARY
Binge-Eating Disorder

Features of binge-eating disorder include the following:

- Recurrent episodes of binge-eating

- The binge-eating episodes are associated with three (or more) of the following: (1) eating much more rapidly than normal, (2) eating until feeling uncomfortably full, (3) eating large amounts of food when not feeling physically hungry, (4) eating alone because of feeling embarrassed by how much one is eating, and (5) feeling disgusted with oneself, depressed, or very guilty afterward

- Marked distress regarding binge-eating is present

- The binge-eating occurs, on average, at least once a week for three months

- The binge-eating is not associated with the recurrent use of inappropriate compensatory behavior

From American Psychiatric Association. (2013). *Diagnostic and statistical manual of mental disorders* (5th ed.). Washington, DC.

Brownell, 1997). Individuals with BED have some of the same concerns about shape and weight as people with anorexia and bulimia, which distinguishes them from individuals who are obese without BED (Fairburn & Cooper, 2014; Grilo, Masheb, & White, 2010). Approximately 33% of those with BED binge to alleviate "bad moods" or negative affect (see, for example, Grilo, Masheb, & Wilson, 2001; Steiger *et al.*, 2013). These individuals are more severe, both in their weight/shape concerns and levels of depression, than the 67% who do not use bingeing to regulate mood (Grilo *et al.*, 2001).

Statistics

Clear cases of bulimia have been described for thousands of years (Parry-Jones & Parry-Jones, 2002), but bulimia nervosa was recognized as a distinct psychological disorder only in the 1970s (Boskind-Lodahl, 1976; Russell, 1979). Therefore, information on prevalence has been acquired relatively recently.

Among those who present for treatment, the overwhelming majority (90% to 95%) of individuals with bulimia are women. Males with bulimia have a slightly later age of onset, and a large minority are gay males or bisexual (Matthews-Ewald, 2014; Rothblum, 2002). For example, Carlat, Camargo, and Herzog (1997) accumulated information on 135 male patients with eating disorders who were seen over 13 years and found that 42% were either gay males or bisexual (Feldman & Meyer, 2007). Male athletes in sports that require weight regulation, such as wrestling, are another large group of males with eating disorders (Ricciardelli & McCabe, 2004). Studies suggest the incidence among males is increasing (Dominé, Berchtold, Akré, Michaud, &

Suris, 2009) with one study showing 0.8% of a large group of males having at least some of the symptoms of bulimia with another 2.9% having at least some of the symptoms of BED (Field *et al.*, 2014).

Among women, adolescent girls are most at risk. A prospective eight-year survey of 496 adolescent girls reported that more than 13% experienced some form of eating disorder by the time they were 20 (Stice, Marti, Shaw, & Jaconis, 2009; Stice *et al.*, 2013). In another study, eating-related problems of 1,498 freshmen women at a large university were studied over the four-year college experience. Only 28% to 34% had no eating-related concerns. But 29% to 34% consistently attempted to limit their food intake because of weight/shape concerns; 14% to 18% engaged in overeating and binge-eating; another 14% to 17% combined attempts to limit intake with binge-eating; and 6% to 7% had pervasive bulimic-like concerns. And these tendencies were stable for the most part throughout their four years of college (Cain, Epler, Steinley, & Sher, 2010).

A somewhat different view of the prevalence of bulimia comes from studies of the population rather than of specific groups of adolescents, with the most definitive study appearing in 2007 (Hudson *et al.*, 2007). These results from the National Comorbidity Survey reflect lifetime and 12-month prevalence, not only for the three major eating disorders described here but also for "subthreshold" BED, where binge-eating occurred at a high-enough frequency but some additional criteria, such as "marked distress" regarding the binge-eating, were not met. Therefore, the disorder did not meet the diagnostic "threshold" for BED. Although the study was conducted prior to the publication of *DSM-5*, the three-month duration required for BED (or subthreshold BED), found in *DSM-5*, rather than the six months required in *DSM-IV-TR*, was used. Finally, if binge-eating occurred at least twice a week for three months—even if it was just a symptom of the four other disorders in Table 8.1 rather than a separate condition—the case was listed under "Any binge-eating." This latter category provides an overall picture of the prevalence of binge-eating. As you can see in Table 8.1, lifetime prevalence was consistently two to three times greater for females, with the exception of subthreshold BED. This sex ratio reflects a somewhat higher proportion of males than found in other samples, but it agrees with data from the Field and colleagues (2014) study showing that some binge-eating symptoms are relatively common in males. In the adolescent supplement to the National Comorbidity Survey that reports results just for adolescents from ages 13 to 18, lifetime prevalence rates were 0.3% for anorexia (compared with 0.6% for the full age range in Table 8.1), 0.9% for bulimia (compared with 1.0% in Table 8.1), and 1.6% for BED (compared with 2.8% in Table 8.1) (Swanson *et al.*, 2011). This suggests that many cases of anorexia and BED, but not bulimia, begin after age 18.

TABLE 8.1 | Lifetime and 12-Month Prevalence Estimates of *DSM-IV-TR* Eating Disorders and Related Problems

	Male	Female	Total
	%	%	%
I. Lifetime prevalence			
Anorexia nervosa	0.3	0.9	0.6
Bulimia nervosa	0.5	1.5	1.0
Binge-eating disorder	2.0	3.5	2.8
Subthreshold binge-eating disorder	1.9	0.6	1.2
Any binge-eating	4.0	4.9	4.5
II. 12-month prevalence*			
Bulimia nervosa	0.1	0.5	0.3
Binge-eating disorder	0.8	1.6	1.2
Subthreshold binge-eating disorder	0.8	0.4	0.6
Any binge-eating	1.7	2.5	2.1
(n) Number of participants	(1,220)	(1,760)	(2,980)

* None of the respondents met criteria for 12-month anorexia nervosa.

SOURCE: From Hudson *et al.* (2007). The prevalence and correlates of eating disorders in the national comorbidity survey replication. *Biological Psychiatry, 61*, 348–358. © Society for Biological Psychiatry.

The median age of onset for all eating-related disorders occurred in a narrow range of 18 to 21 years (Hudson *et al.*, 2007), which is consistent with more recent findings (Stice *et al.*, 2013). For anorexia, this age of onset was fairly consistent, with younger cases tending to begin at age 15, but it was more common for cases of bulimia to begin as early as age 10.

Once bulimia develops, it tends to be chronic if untreated (Fairburn, Stice *et al.*, 2003; Hudson *et al.*, 2007). Fairburn and colleagues (2000) identified a group of 102 females with bulimia nervosa and followed 92 of them prospectively for five years. About a third improved to the point where they no longer met diagnostic criteria each year, but another third who had improved previously relapsed. Between 50% and 67% exhibited serious eating disorder symptoms at the end of each year of the five-year study, indicating this disorder has a relatively poor prognosis. In a follow-up study, Fairburn, Stice, and colleagues (2003) reported that the strongest predictors of persistent bulimia were a history of childhood obesity and a continuing overemphasis on the importance of being thin.

Similarly, once anorexia develops, its course seems chronic—although not so chronic as bulimia, based on data from Hudson and colleagues (2007), particularly if it is caught early and treated. But individuals with anorexia tend to maintain a low BMI over a long period, along with distorted perceptions of shape and weight, indicating that even if they no longer meet criteria for anorexia they continue to restrict their eating (Fairburn & Cooper, 2014). Perhaps for this reason, anorexia is thought to be more resistant to treatment than bulimia, based on clinical studies (Vitiello & Lederhendler, 2000). In one seven-year study following individuals who had received treatment, 33% of those with anorexia versus 66% of those with bulimia reached full remission at some point during the follow-up (Eddy *et al.*, 2008).

Cross-Cultural Considerations

We have already discussed the highly culturally specific nature of anorexia and bulimia. A particularly striking finding is that these disorders develop in immigrants who have recently moved to Western countries (Anderson-Fye, 2009). One of the more interesting classic studies is Nasser's survey of 50 Egyptian women in London universities and 60 Egyptian women in Cairo universities (Nasser, 1988). There were no instances of eating disorders in Cairo, but 12% of the Egyptian women in England had developed eating disorders. Mumford, Whitehouse, and Platts (1991) found comparable results with Asian women living in the United States.

The prevalence of eating disorders varies somewhat among most North American minority populations, including African Americans, Hispanics, Native Americans, and Asians. Earlier surveys revealed that African-American adolescent girls have less body dissatisfaction, fewer weight concerns, a more positive self-image, and perceive themselves to be thinner than they are, compared with the attitudes of Caucasian adolescent girls (Celio, Zabinski, & Wilfley, 2002). Greenberg and LaPorte (1996) observed in an experiment that young white males preferred somewhat thinner figures in women than African-American males, which may contribute to the somewhat lower incidence of eating disorders in African-American women. But a more recent survey suggests some of these ethnic differences may be changing. Marques and colleagues (2011) found that the prevalence of eating disorders is now more similar among non-Hispanic whites, African American, Asian American, and Hispanic females. Eating disorders are generally more common among Native Americans than other ethnic groups (Crago, Shisslak, & Estes, 1997).

In conclusion, anorexia and bulimia are relatively homogeneous, and both—particularly bulimia—were overwhelmingly associated with Western cultures until

Olesia Bilkei/Shutterstock.com

▲ Anorexia seldom occurs among North American black women.

recently. In addition, the frequency and pattern of occurrence among minority Western cultures differed somewhat in the past, but those differences seem to be diminishing (Marques *et al.*, 2011; Pike, Hoek, & Dunne, 2014).

Developmental Considerations

Because the overwhelming majority of cases begin in adolescence, it is clear that anorexia and bulimia are strongly related to development (Smith, Simmons, Flory,

Annus, & Hill, 2007; Steiger *et al.*, 2013). As pointed out in classic studies by Striegel-Moore, Silberstein, and Rodin (1986) and Attie and Brooks-Gunn (1995), differential patterns of physical development in girls and boys interact with cultural influences to create eating disorders. After puberty, girls gain weight primarily in fat tissue, whereas boys develop muscle and lean tissue. As the ideal look in Western countries is tall and muscular for men and thin and prepubertal for women, physical development brings boys closer to the ideal and takes girls further away.

Eating disorders, particularly anorexia nervosa, occasionally occur in children under the age of 11 (Walsh, 2010). Negative attitude toward being overweight emerges as early as three years of age, and more than half of girls age six to eight would like to be thinner (Striegel-Moore & Franko, 2002). By nine years of age, 20% of girls reported trying to lose weight, and by 14, 40% were trying to lose weight (Field *et al.*, 1999).

Both bulimia and anorexia can occur in later years, particularly after the age of 55. Hsu and Zimmer (1988) reported that most of these individuals had had an eating disorder for decades with little change in their behavior. In a few cases, however, onset did not occur until later years, and it is not yet clear what factors were involved. Generally, concerns about body image decrease with age (Peat, Peyeri, & Muehlenkamp, 2008; Tiggemann & Lynch, 2001; Whitbourne & Skultety, 2002).

Discussing Diversity Cultural Influences on Eating Disorders

We all eat. However, what and how much we eat is strongly influenced by the culture in which we live. As mentioned earlier, cultural influences contribute to differences in the rates of eating disorders, such as anorexia nervosa and bulimia nervosa, across sexes, ethnicities, and geographic regions. Eating disorders are much more prevalent among women than men and occur significantly more often among European American women than African-American women (Striegel-Moore et al., 2003).

How is it that culture influences eating in ways that makes eating disorders more prevalent among these groups? A leading possibility is the beliefs held in different cultures about the ideal body shape. The more a culture values thinness, the greater the

desire of people within that culture to attain a lower weight. Studies have shown that as the ideal body shape for women has become thinner, the rates of eating disorders among young girls in Western cultures have increased (Keel & Klump, 2003).

Evidence of the influence of cultural factors—and not some genetic or other biological factor operating within Western cultures—comes from studies that have shown that women from Eastern and Middle Eastern cultures who attend Western universities have higher rates of eating disorders while in the Western culture compared with women in their home country (Mumford, Whitehouse, & Platts, 1991; Nasser, 1988).

Further evidence of the influence of Western culture comes from a study on

the development of eating problems among girls on the island of Fiji after the introduction of television on Fiji in 1995. Within one month of seeing television for the first time, 7.9% of Fijian girls reported binge-eating, and the rate of self-induced vomiting increased from 0% to 11% over the next three years (Becker, Burwell, Gilman, Herzog, & Hamburg, 2002). Interviews with Fijian girls revealed that they had begun to model themselves after the girls observed on television, providing evidence for the influence of Western culture on their eating behavior. Overall, although there appears to be a genetic basis for eating disorders, these studies highlight the strong influence that culture can have on a person's self-image, eating habits, and likelihood of developing an eating disorder. ■

Check your understanding by identifying the proper disorder in the following scenarios: (a) bulimia nervosa, (b) anorexia nervosa, and (c) binge-eating disorder:

1. Manny has been having episodes lately when he eats prodigious amounts of food. He's been putting on a lot of weight because of it. _____

2. I noticed Elena eating a whole pie, a cake, and two bags of potato chips the other day when she didn't know I was there. She ran to the bathroom when she was finished and it sounded like she was vomiting. This disorder can lead to an electrolyte imbalance, resulting in serious medical problems. _____

3. Joo-Yeon eats large quantities of food in a short time. She then takes laxatives and exercises for long periods to prevent weight gain. She has been doing this almost daily for several months and feels she will become worthless and ugly if she gains even an ounce. _____

4. Kirsten has lost several pounds and now weighs less than 90 pounds. She eats only a small portion of the food her mother serves her and fears that intake above her current 500 calories daily will make her fat. Since losing the weight, Kirsten has stopped having periods. She sees a fat person in the mirror. _____

Causes of Eating Disorders

▶ What social, psychological, and neurobiological factors might cause eating disorders?

As with all disorders discussed in this book, biological, psychological, and social factors contribute to the development of these serious eating disorders. The evidence is increasingly clear, however, that the most dramatic factors are social and cultural.

Social Dimensions

Remember that anorexia and particularly bulimia are the most culturally specific psychological disorders yet identified. What drives so many young people into a punishing and life-threatening routine of semistarvation or purging? For many young women, looking good is more important than being healthy. For young females in competitive environments, self-worth, happiness, and success are largely determined by body measurements and percentage of body fat, factors that have little or no correlation with personal happiness and success in the long run. The cultural imperative for thinness directly results in dieting, the first dangerous step down the slippery slope to anorexia and bulimia.

Levine and Smolak referred over 20 years ago (1996) to "the glorification of slenderness" in magazines and on television, where most females are thinner than the average American woman. Because overweight men are two to five times more common as television characters than overweight women, the message from the media to be thin is clearly aimed at women, and the message got through loud and clear and is still getting through. Grabe, Ward, and Hyde (2008), reviewing 77 studies, demonstrated a strong relationship between exposure to media images depicting the thin-ideal body and body image concerns in women. Interestingly, a recent analysis of images of women in *Ebony* magazine,

which has wide African-American readership, generally does not show this thin-ideal body image, seemingly reflecting the somewhat lower prevalence of body image disturbances in African-American women (Thompson-Brenner, Boisseau, & St. Paul, 2011). Finally, Thompson and Stice (2001) found that risk for developing eating disorders was directly related to the extent to which women internalize or "buy in" to media messages and images glorifying thinness, a finding also confirmed by Cafri, Yamamiya, Brannick, and Thompson (2005) as well as Keel and Forney (2013).

The problem with today's standards is that they are increasingly difficult to achieve, because the size and weight of the average woman has increased over the years with improved nutrition; there is also a general increase in size throughout history (Brownell, 1991; Brownell & Rodin, 1994). Whatever the cause, the collision between our culture and our physiology (Brownell, 1991; Fairburn & Brownell, 2002) has had some negative effects, one of which is that women became dissatisfied with their bodies.

In a classic case study, Fallon and Rozin (1985), enlisting male and female undergraduates, found that men rated their current size, their ideal size, and the size they figured would be most attractive to the opposite sex as approximately equal; indeed, they rated their ideal body weight as *heavier* than the weight females thought most attractive in men (see ● Figure 8.1). Women, however, rated their current figures as much heavier than what they judged the most attractive, which in turn, was rated as heavier than what they thought was ideal. This conflict between reality and fashion seems most closely related to the current epidemic of eating disorders.

Other researchers have presented data that support Fallon and Rozin's findings that men have different body

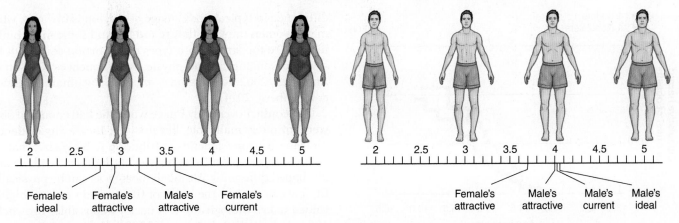

● **Figure 8.1** Male and female ratings of body size. (Based on Fallon & Rozin [1985].)

image perceptions than women. Several studies confirmed that men generally desire to be heavier and more muscular than they are (Field *et al.*, 2014; Neumark-Sztainer & Eisenberg, 2014). Pope and colleagues (2000) measured the height, weight, and body fat of college-age men in three countries—Austria, France, and the United States. They asked the men to choose the body image that they felt represented (1) their own body, (2) the body they ideally would like to have, (3) the body of an average man of their age, and (4) the male body they believed was preferred by women. In all three countries, men chose an ideal body weight that was approximately 28 pounds more muscular than their current one. They also estimated that women would prefer a male body about 30 pounds more muscular than their current one. In contradiction to this impression in men, Pope and colleagues (2000) demonstrated, in a pilot study, that most women preferred an ordinary male body without the added muscle. Men who abuse anabolic–androgenic steroids to increase muscle mass and "bulk up" possess these distorted attitudes toward muscles, weight, and the "ideal man" to a greater degree than men who don't use steroids (Kanayama, Barry, & Pope, 2006), and utilizing these unhealthy substances can lead to other serious problems such as binge-drinking or other drug addictions (Field *et al.*, 2014; Neumark-Sztainer & Eisenberg, 2014).

We have some specific information on how these attitudes are socially transmitted in adolescent girls. In an early study, Paxton, Schutz, Wertheim, and Muir (1999) explored the influence of close friendship groups on attitudes concerning body image, dietary restraint, and extreme weight-loss behaviors. In a clever experiment, the authors identified 79 different friendship cliques in a group of 523 adolescent girls. They found that these friendship cliques tended to share the same attitudes toward body image, dietary restraint, and the importance of attempts to lose weight. They assumed from the study that these friendship cliques are significantly associated with individual body image concerns and eating behaviors. In other words, if your friends tend to use extreme dieting or other weight-loss techniques, there is a greater chance that you

will, too (Hutchinson & Rapee, 2007). A recent, more definitive study concludes that while young girls do tend to share body image concerns, these friendship cliques do not necessarily cause these attitudes or the disordered eating that follows. Rather, adolescent girls simply tend to choose friends who already share these attitudes (Rayner, Schniering, Rapee, Taylor, & Hutchinson, 2012). Nevertheless, any attempts to treat eating disorders must take into account the influence of the social network in maintaining these attitudes.

The abhorrence of fat can have tragic consequences. In one early study, toddlers with affluent parents appeared at hospitals with "failure to thrive" syndrome, in which growth and development are severely retarded because of inadequate nutrition. In each case, the parents had put their young, healthy, but somewhat chubby toddlers on diets in the hope of preventing obesity at a later date (Pugliese, Weyman-Daun, Moses, & Lifshitz, 1987). Mothers who have anorexia restrict food intake in not only themselves but also their children, sometimes to the detriment of their children's health (Russell, 2009).

Most people who diet don't develop eating disorders, but Patton, Johnson-Sabine, Wood, Mann, and Wakeling (1990) determined in a prospective study that adolescent girls who dieted were eight times more likely to develop an eating disorder one year later than those who weren't dieting. And Telch and Agras (1993) noted marked increases in bingeing during and after rigorous dieting in 201 obese women. Stice and colleagues (1999) demonstrated that one of the reasons attempts to lose weight may lead to eating disorders is that weight-reduction efforts in adolescent girls are more likely to result in weight *gain* than weight loss! To establish this finding, 692 girls, initially the same weight, were followed for four years. Girls who attempted dieting faced more than 300% greater risk of obesity than those who did not diet. Results are presented in ● Figure 8.2.

Why does dieting cause weight gain? Cottone and colleagues (2009) began feeding rats junk food, which the rats came to love, instead of a boring diet of pellets. They then withdrew the junk food but not the pellets. Based on

● **Figure 8.2** The onset of obesity over four years for self-labeled dieters versus self-labeled non-dieters. (From Stice, E., Cameron, R. P., Killen, J. D., Hayward, C., & Taylor, C. B. [1999]. Naturalistic weight-reduction efforts prospectively predict growth in relative weight and onset of obesity among female adolescents. *Journal of Consulting and Clinical Psychology, 67*, 967–974.)

observations of brain function compared with rats that never had junk food, it was clear that these rats became extremely stressed and anxious. Furthermore, the "junk food" rats began eating more of the pellets than the control group; which then seemed to relieve the stress. Thus, repeated cycles of "dieting" seems to produce stress-related withdrawal symptoms in the brain, much like other addictive substances, resulting in more eating than would have occurred without dieting.

Fairburn, Cooper, Doll, and Davies (2005) examined a group of 2,992 young women who were dieting and identified 104 who developed an eating disorder over the next two years. Among all of these dieters, several risk factors were identified. Those most at risk for developing an eating disorder were already binge-eating and purging, were eating in secret, expressed a desire to have an empty stomach, were preoccupied with food, and were afraid of losing control over eating.

Distortions of body image in some males can also have tragic consequences. Olivardia, Pope, and Hudson (2000) have described a syndrome in men, particularly male weight lifters, that they initially termed "reverse anorexia nervosa." Men with this syndrome reported they were extremely concerned about looking small, even though they were muscular. These men were prone to using anabolic–androgenic steroids to bulk up, risking both the medical and psychological consequences of taking steroids. Thus, although a marked gender

difference in typical body image distortion is obvious, with many women thinking they're too big and some men thinking they're too small, both types of distortion can result in severe psychological and physical consequences (Corson & Andersen, 2002; Kanayama *et al.*, 2006; Neumark-Sztainer & Eisenberg, 2014).

The conflict over body image would be bad enough if size were infinitely malleable, but it is not. Increasing evidence indicates a strong genetic contribution to body size; that is, some of us are born to be heavier than others, and we are all shaped differently. Although most of us can be physically fit, few can achieve the levels of fitness and shape so highly valued today. Biologically, it is nearly impossible (Brownell, 1991; Brownell & Fairburn, 2002). Nevertheless, many young people in our society fight biology to the point of starvation. In adolescence, cultural standards are often experienced as peer pressure and are more influential than reason and fact. The high number of males who are homosexual among the relatively small numbers of males with eating disorders has also been attributed to pressures among gay men to be physically trim (Carlat *et al.*, 1997; Feldman & Meyer, 2007; Hadland, Austin, Goodenow, & Calzo, 2014). Conversely, pressure to appear more fit and muscular is also apparent for a substantial proportion of men (Neumark-Sztainer & Eisenberg, 2014; Pope *et al.*, 2000).

Dietary Restraint

If cultural pressures to be thin are as important as they seem to be in triggering eating disorders, then such disorders would be expected to occur where these pressures are particularly severe, which is just what happens to ballet dancers, who are under extraordinary pressures to be thin. Garner, Garfinkel, Rockert, and Olmsted (1987) followed a group of 11- to 14-year-old female students in ballet school. The conservative estimate was that at least 25% of these girls developed eating disorders during the two years of the study. Similar results are apparent among athletes, particularly females, such as gymnasts. What goes on in ballet classes that has such a devastating effect on girls?

▲ Changing concepts of ideal weight are evident in a 17th-century painting by Peter Paul Rubens and in a photograph of a current fashion model.

Consider the case of Phoebe again.

Phoebe... • *Dancing to Destruction*

Phoebe remembered clearly that during her early years in ballet the older girls talked incessantly about their weight. The ballet mistress seemed to comment more on weight than on dance technique, often remarking, "You'd dance better if you lost weight." If one little girl lost a few pounds through heroic dieting, the instructor always pointed it out: "You've done well working on your weight; the rest of you had better follow this example." One day, without warning, the instructor said to Phoebe, "You need to lose five pounds before the next class." At that time, Phoebe was five feet two inches and weighed 98 pounds. The next class was in two days. After one of these admonitions and several days of restrictive eating, Phoebe experienced her first uncontrollable binge.

Early in high school, Phoebe gave up the rigors of ballet to pursue a variety of other interests. But in college, as she stuck her head in the toilet bowl, vomiting her guts out for perhaps the third time that day, she realized there was one lesson she had learned in ballet class more thoroughly than any other—the life-or-death importance of being thin at all costs.

Thus, dieting is one factor that can contribute to eating disorders (Polivy & Herman, 2002), and, along with dissatisfaction with one's body, is a primary risk factor for later eating disorders (Stice, Ng, & Shaw, 2010).

Family Influences

In the past, much has been made of the possible significance of family interaction patterns in cases of eating disorders. A number of clinicians and investigators (see, for example, Attie & Brooks-Gunn, 1995; Bruch, 1985) observed that the "typical" family of someone with anorexia is successful, hard-driving, concerned about external appearances, and eager to maintain harmony. To accomplish these goals, family members often deny or ignore conflicts or negative feelings and tend to attribute their problems to other people at the expense of frank communication among themselves (Fairburn, Shafran, & Cooper, 1999; Hsu, 1990). Pike and Rodin (1991) confirmed some differences in interactions within the families of girls with disordered eating in comparison with control families. But more recent evidence downplays the contribution of parents or family factors in causing eating disorders specifically (Russell, 2009; Steiger *et al.*, 2013). Reflecting this development, the Academy for Eating Disorders (le Grange, Lock, Loeb, & Nicholls, 2010) concluded:

"It is the position of the Academy for Eating Disorders (AED) that whereas family factors can play a role in the genesis and maintenance of eating disorders, current knowledge refutes the idea that they are either the exclusive or even the primary mechanisms that underlie risk." (p. 1)

Whatever the pre-existing relationships, after the onset of an eating disorder, particularly anorexia, family relationships can deteriorate quickly. Educated and knowledgeable parents, including psychologists and psychiatrists with full understanding of the disorder, have reported resorting to physical violence (e.g., hitting or slapping) in moments of extreme frustration, in a vain attempt to get their daughters to put some food, however little, in their mouths. The parents' guilt and anguish was considerable, and this kind of behavior is associated with poorer outcomes of the eating disorder (Ducios, Vibert, Mattar, & Godart, 2012).

Biological Dimensions

Eating disorders run in families and seem to have a genetic component (Trace, Baker, Penas-Lledo, & Bulik, 2013). Studies suggest that relatives of patients with eating disorders are four to five times more likely than the general population to develop eating disorders, with the risks for female relatives of patients with anorexia higher (see, for example, Strober, Freeman, Lampert, Diamond, & Kaye, 2000). In twin studies of bulimia by Kendler and colleagues (1991) and of anorexia by Walters and Kendler (1995), researchers ascertained the prevalence of the disorders among 2,163 female twins. In 23% of identical twin pairs, both twins had bulimia, as compared with 9% of fraternal twins. Because no adoption studies have been reported, strong sociocultural influences cannot be ruled out, and other studies have produced inconsistent results (Fairburn, Cowen, & Harrison, 1999). For anorexia, numbers were too small for precise estimates, but the disorder in one twin did seem to confer a significant risk for both anorexia and bulimia in the co-twin. The consensus is that genetic makeup is about half the equation among causes of anorexia and bulimia (Trace *et al.*, 2013).

Again, there is no clear agreement on *what* is inherited (Steiger *et al.*, 2013; Trace *et al.*, 2013). Hsu (1990) and Steiger and colleagues (2013) speculate that personality traits such as emotional instability and poor impulse control might be inherited. In other words, a person might inherit a tendency to be emotionally responsive to stress and might eat impulsively to relieve stress (Kaye, 2008; Pearson, Wonderlich, & Smith, 2015; Strober, 2002). Klump and colleagues (2001) mention perfectionist traits, along with negative affect. Wade and colleagues (2008) found support for this idea in a study of 1,002 same-sex twins in which anorexia was associated with, and maybe a reflection of, a trait of perfectionism and a need for order that runs in families.

Biological processes are active in the regulation of eating and thus of eating disorders, and investigators have studied the hypothalamus and the major neurotransmitter systems—including norepinephrine, dopamine, and serotonin—that pass through it to determine whether something is malfunctioning when eating disorders occur (Kaye, 2008; Vitiello & Lederhendler, 2000). Low levels of serotonergic activity, the system most often associated with eating disorders (Russell, 2009; Steiger, Bruce, & Groleau, 2011), are associated with impulsivity and binge-eating. Thus, most drugs under study as treatments for eating disorders target the serotonin system (see, for example, Grilo, Crosby, Wilson, & Masheb, 2012; Kaye, 2008).

Investigators are also interested in the influence of hormones on eating behavior, particularly binge-eating. Kelly Klump and colleagues found strong associations between ovarian hormones and dysregulated or impulsive eating in women prone to binge-eating episodes (Klump *et al.*, 2014). Furthermore, emotional eating behavior (eating to relieve stress or anxiety) and binge-eating peaked in the post-ovulatory phases of the menstrual cycle for all women whether they binged or not during other phases of their cycle. High levels of hormones at least partially accounted for these peaks. Klump and her colleagues, noting the association between the onset of bulimia and puberty, speculate that the onset of puberty and hormonal changes may "turn on" certain hormone-responsive risk genes in women prone to binge-eating. If true, this would be an example of the gene–environment interactions discussed in Chapter 2.

If investigators do find a strong association between neurobiological functions and eating disorders, the question of cause or effect remains. At present, the consensus is that some neurobiological abnormalities do exist in people with eating disorders (e.g., Mainz, Schulte-Rüther, Fink, Herpertz-Dahlmann, & Konrad, 2012; Marsh *et al.*, 2011) but that they may be a *result* of semistarvation or a binge–purge cycle rather than a cause, although they may well contribute to the *maintenance* of the disorder once it is established.

Psychological Dimensions

Clinical observations have indicated that many young women with eating disorders have a diminished sense of personal control and confidence in their own abilities and talents (Striegel-Moore, Silberstein, & Rodin, 1993; Walters & Kendler, 1995). This may manifest as strikingly low self-esteem (Fairburn, Cooper, & Shafran, 2003). They also display more perfectionistic attitudes, which may reflect attempts to exert control over their lives (Boone, Soenens, Vansteenkiste, & Braet, 2012; Bulik *et al.*, 2014; Fairburn, Halmi *et al.*, 2012; Joiner *et al.*, 1997; Martinez & Craighead, 2015; Welch *et al.*, 1997). Shafran, Lee, Payne, and Fairburn (2006) artificially raised perfectionistic standards in otherwise normal women by instructing them to

pursue the highest possible standards in everything they did for the next 24 hours. These instructions caused them to eat fewer high-calorie foods, to restrict their eating, and to have more regret after eating than women told to just do the minimum for 24 hours. This occurred even though eating was not specifically mentioned as part of pursuing the "highest standards." Perfectionism alone, however, is only weakly associated with the development of an eating disorder, because individuals must consider themselves overweight and manifest low self-esteem before the trait of perfectionism makes a contribution (Vohs, Bardone, Joiner, Abramson, & Heatherton, 1999). But when perfectionism is directed to distorted perception of body image, a powerful engine to drive eating disorder behavior is in place (Lilenfeld, Wonderlich, Riso, Crosby, & Mitchell, 2006; Shafran, Cooper, & Fairburn, 2002).

Women with eating disorders are intensely preoccupied with how they appear to others (Fairburn, Stice *et al.*, 2003; Smith *et al.*, 2007). They also perceive themselves as frauds, considering false any impressions they make of being adequate, self-sufficient, or worthwhile. In this sense, they feel like impostors in their social groups and experience heightened levels of social anxiety (Bardone-Cone *et al.*, 2010; Clance & Imes, 1978; Smolak & Levine, 1996), which may explain why they choose social groups with similar attitudes toward eating and body shape (Rayner *et al.*, 2012). Striegel-Moore and colleagues (1993) suggest these social self-deficits are likely to increase as a consequence of the eating disorder, further isolating the woman from the larger social world.

Specific distortions in perception of body shape change often, depending on day-to-day experience. McKenzie, Williamson, and Cubic (1993) found that women with bulimia judged that their bodies were larger after they ate a candy bar and soft drink, whereas the judgments of women in control groups were unaffected by snacks. Thus, rather minor events related to eating may activate fear of gaining weight, further distortions in body image, and corrective schemes such as purging.

Another important observation is that at least a subgroup of these patients has difficulty tolerating any negative emotion and may binge or engage in other behaviors, such as self-induced vomiting or intense exercise, in an attempt to reduce their anxiety or distress (Haynos & Fruzzetti, 2011; Paul, Schroeter, Dahme, & Nutzinger, 2002). For example, Mauler, Hamm, Weike, and Tuschen-Caffier (2006) discovered that women with bulimia evidenced more intense negative affect after overeating, which could lead to extreme food restriction or intense exercise. Fairburn and Cooper (2014) noted the importance in treatment of countering the tendency to overly restrict food intake and the associated negative attitudes about body image that lead to bingeing and purging. What these studies suggest is that the common factors driving eating disorders include the experience of intense emotions triggered by food cues and fear of becoming fat as well as faulty attempts to regulate these emotions.

An Integrative Model

In putting together what we know about eating disorders, it is important to remember, again, that no one factor seems sufficient to cause them (see ● Figure 8.3). Individuals with eating disorders may have some of the same biological vulnerabilities (such as being highly responsive to stressful life events) as individuals with anxiety disorders (Kendler *et al.*, 1995; Klump *et al.*, 2014; Rojo, Conesa, Bermudez, & Livianos, 2006). Anxiety and mood disorders are also common in the families of individuals with eating disorders (Steiger *et al.*, 2013), and negative emotions, along with "mood intolerance," seem to trigger binge-eating in many patients. In addition, as you will see, drug and psychological treatments with proven effectiveness for anxiety disorders are also the treatments of choice for eating disorders. Indeed, we could conceptualize eating disorders as anxiety disorders focused exclusively on a fear of becoming overweight.

In any case, it is clear that social and cultural pressures to be thin motivate significant restriction of eating, usually through severe dieting. Remember, however, that many people, including adolescent females, go on strict diets, but only a small minority develops eating disorders, so dieting alone does not account for the disorders. It is also important to note that the social interactions in high-achieving families play at least some role. An

● **Figure 8.3** An integrative causal model of eating disorders.

emphasis in these families on looks and achievement, and perfectionistic tendencies, may help establish strong attitudes about the overriding importance of physical appearance to popularity and success, attitudes reinforced in peer groups. These attitudes result in an exaggerated focus on body shape and weight.

Finally, there is the question of why a small minority of individuals with eating disorders can control their intake through dietary restraint, resulting in alarming weight loss (anorexia), whereas the majority are unsuccessful at losing weight and compensate in a cycle of bingeing and purging (bulimia) (Eddy *et al.*, 2002, 2008). These differences, at least initially, may be determined by biology or physiology, such as a genetically determined disposition to be somewhat thinner initially. Then again, perhaps preexisting personality characteristics, such as a tendency to be overcontrolling, are important determinants of which disorder an individual develops. In any case, most individuals with anorexia do go on to bingeing and purging at some point.

Treatment of Eating Disorders

▶ How does the use of medications compare with psychological therapies for the treatment of eating disorders?

Only since the 1980s have there been treatments for bulimia; treatments for anorexia have been around much longer but were not initially well-developed. Rapidly accumulating evidence indicates that at least one, and possibly two, psychological treatments are effective, particularly for bulimia nervosa. Certain drugs may also help, although the evidence is not so strong.

Drug Treatments

At present, drug treatments have not been found to be effective in the treatment of anorexia (see, for example, Crow, Mitchell, Roerig, & Steffen, 2009; Wilson & Fairburn, 2007). For example, one definitive study reported that fluoxetine (Prozac) had no benefit in preventing relapse in patients with anorexia after weight has been restored (Walsh *et al.*, 2006).

On the other hand, there is some evidence that drugs may be useful for some people with bulimia, particularly during the bingeing and purging cycle. The drugs generally considered the most effective for bulimia are the same antidepressant medications proven effective for mood disorders and anxiety disorders (Broft, Berner, & Walsh, 2010; Wilson & Fairburn, 2007). The Food and Drug Administration (FDA) in 1996 approved Prozac as effective for eating disorders. Effectiveness is usually measured by reductions in the frequency of binge eating, as well as by the percentage of patients who stop binge eating and purging altogether, at least for a while. However, although antidepressants are more effective than placebo in the short term, and they may enhance the effects of psychological treatment somewhat (Whittal, Agras, & Gould, 1999; Wilson *et al.*, 1999), the evidence suggests that antidepressants alone do not have substantial long-lasting effects on bulimia nervosa, and current expert opinions suggest that medications are likely most useful in conjunction with psychological treatments (Reas & Grilo, 2014; Walsh, 1995; Wilson & Fairburn, 2007).

Psychological Treatments

Until the 1980s, psychological treatments for people with eating disorders were directed at the patient's low self-esteem as well as disordered patterns of family interaction and communication. These treatments alone, however, did not have the effectiveness that clinicians hoped they might (see, for example, Minuchin *et al.*, 1978; Russell, Szmukler, Dare, & Eisler, 1987). Instead, short-term cognitive-behavioral treatments that target problem eating behavior and attitudes about body weight and shape became the treatment of choice for bulimia (Fairburn & Cooper, 2014; Sysko & Wilson, 2011).

More recently, this approach has been updated to target all eating disorders (i.e., has become "transdiagnostic"). A variety of new procedures intended to improve outcomes have been added. For example, individuals with anorexia and a very low weight—BMI of 17.5 or less—who would need inpatient treatment would be excluded until their weight was restored to an adequate level when they could then benefit from the program. In addition, factors common to all eating disorders are targeted in an integrated way with essential components of cognitive-behavioral therapy (CBT). Thus, the principal focus of this protocol is on the distorted evaluation of body shape and weight, and maladaptive attempts to control weight in the form of strict dieting, possibly accompanied by binge-eating, and methods to compensate for overeating such as purging. Fairburn refers to this treatment as cognitive-behavioral therapy-enhanced (CBT-E) (Fairburn & Cooper, 2014). Nevertheless, since there are some differences in outcomes across the eating disorders, we will review treatment of each separately.

Bulimia Nervosa

In the CBT-E pioneered by Fairburn (2008), the first stage is teaching the patient the physical consequences of binge-eating and purging, as well as the ineffectiveness of vomiting and laxative abuse for weight control. The adverse effects of dieting are also described, and patients are scheduled to eat small amounts of food five or six times per day with no more than a three-hour interval between any planned meals and snacks, which eliminates the alternating periods of overeating and dietary restriction that are hallmarks of bulimia. In later stages of treatment, CBT-E focuses on altering dysfunctional thoughts and attitudes about body shape, weight, and eating. Coping strategies for resisting the impulse to binge and/or purge are also developed, including arranging activities so that the individual will not spend time alone after eating during the early stages of treatment (Fairburn & Cooper, 2014). Evaluations of the earlier versions of short-term (approximately three months) cognitive-behavioral treatments for bulimia have been good, showing superior efficacy to credible alternative psychological treatments not only for bingeing and purging but also for distorted attitudes and accompanying depression. Furthermore, these results seem to last (Pike, Walsh, Vitousek, Wilson, & Bauer, 2003; Thompson-Brenner, Glass, & Westen, 2003), although a number of patients improved only modestly or did not benefit.

In a widely noted study using the earlier version of treatment, Agras, Walsh, Fairburn, Wilson, and Kraemer (2000) randomly assigned 220 patients meeting diagnostic criteria for bulimia to 19 sessions of either CBT or interpersonal psychotherapy (IPT) focused on improving interpersonal functioning. The investigators found that, for those who completed treatment, CBT was superior to IPT at the end of treatment. The percentage who remitted (no longer met diagnostic criteria for an eating disorder but still had some problems) was 67% in the CBT group versus 40% in the IPT group. After one year, however, these differences were no longer significant, as patients in the IPT group tended to "catch up" to patients in the CBT group.

More recent evaluations of CBT-E are very promising (e.g., Fairburn *et al.*, 2009). Results from a clinical trial comparing 20 weeks of CBT-E with two years of weekly psychoanalytic psychotherapy (PPT) in 70 patients with bulimia revealed that at five months (when the CBT-E treatment concluded), 42% of CBT-E patients were recovered compared to 6% of PPT patients. After two years (when the PPT treatment concluded), the comparable figures were 44% and 15% (Poulsen *et al.*, 2014). Recently, results have been reported from a major clinical trial similar to the Agras and colleagues (2000) study described above, but comparing the transdiagnostic version of CBT (CBT-E) to IPT in 130 patients with any form of eating disorder (Fairburn *et al.*, 2015). Just after treatment, 65.5% of the CBT-E participants met criteria for remission compared to 33.3% of the IPT participants. One year later, the figures were 69.4% for CBT-E compared to 49% for IPT. Therefore, at the present time, CBT-E would seem to be the treatment of choice for adults based on these studies.

There is also evidence that family therapy directed at the painful conflicts present in families with an adolescent who has an eating disorder can be helpful (le Grange, Crosby, Rathouz, & Leventhal, 2007). Integrating family and interpersonal strategies into CBT is a promising new direction (Sysko & Wilson, 2011). Clearly, we need to understand more about how to improve such treatments to deal more successfully with the growing number of patients with eating disorders.

Phoebe... • *Taking Control*

During her sophomore year in college, Phoebe entered a short-term CBT program similar to the program discussed here. She made good progress during the first several months and worked to eat regularly and gain control over her eating. She also made sure that she was with somebody during her high-risk times and planned alternative activities that would reduce her temptation to purge if she felt she had eaten too much at a restaurant or drunk too much beer at a party. During the first two months, Phoebe had three slips, and she and her therapist discussed what led to her temporary relapse. Much to Phoebe's surprise, she did not gain weight on this program, even though she did not have time to increase her exercise. Nevertheless, she still was preoccupied with food, was concerned about her weight and appearance, and had strong urges to vomit if she thought she had overeaten the slightest amount.

During the nine months following treatment, Phoebe reported that her urges seemed to decrease somewhat, although she had one major slip after eating a big pizza and drinking a lot of beer. She reported that she was thoroughly disgusted with herself for purging and was quite careful to return to her program after this episode. Two years after finishing treatment, Phoebe reported that her urges to vomit had disappeared, a report confirmed by her parents.

Binge-Eating Disorder

Early studies adapting CBT for bulimia to obese binge eaters were quite successful (Smith, Marcus, & Kaye, 1992). To take one example, Agras, Telch, Arnow, Eldredge, and Marnell (1997) followed 93 obese individuals with BED for one year and found that immediately after treatment with CBT, 41% of the participants abstained from bingeing and 72% binged less frequently. After one year, binge-eating was reduced by

64%, and 33% of the group refrained from bingeing altogether. Importantly, those who had stopped binge-eating during CBT maintained a weight loss of approximately nine pounds over this one-year follow-up period; those who continued to binge gained approximately eight pounds. Thus, stopping binge-eating is critical to sustaining weight loss in obese patients, a finding consistent with other studies of weight-loss procedures (Marcus et al., 1990).

In contrast to results with bulimia, it appears that IPT is as effective as CBT for binge-eating. Wilfley and colleagues (2002) treated 162 overweight or obese men and women with BED with either CBT or IPT and found comparable results from each treatment. Fully 60% refrained from bingeing at a one-year follow-up. But, in a study examining the effectiveness of the antidepressant Prozac compared with CBT for BED, Prozac was ineffective (compared with placebo) and did not add anything to CBT when the two treatments were combined (Grilo, Masheb, & Wilson, 2005). The positive results from CBT were reasonably durable at follow up one year later (Grilo et al., 2012). If individuals began to respond rapidly to CBT treatment (by the fourth week), the response was particularly good, both short term and long term (Grilo, Masheb, & Wilson, 2006).

Widely available behavioral weight loss programs for obese patients with BED, such as Weight Watchers, have some positive effect on binging, but not so much as CBT (Grilo, Masheb, Wilson, Gueorguieva, & White, 2011). Some racial and ethnic differences are apparent in people with BED seeking treatment (Franko et al., 2012). African-American participants tend to have higher BMI, and Hispanic participants have greater concerns with shape and weight than Caucasian participants. Thus, it would seem that tailoring treatment to these ethnic groups would be useful. Also, males may respond differently than females to treatment. One recent study demonstrated that men with lower shape/weight concerns responded well to brief treatments, whereas females with shape/weight concerns at any level of severity, and men at more severe levels, all required longer treatment (Shingleton, Thompson, Pratt, & Franko, 2015).

It appears that self-help procedures may be useful in the treatment of BED (Carter & Fairburn, 1998; Wilson & Zandberg, 2012). For example, CBT delivered as guided self-help was demonstrated to be more effective than a standard behavioral weight-loss program for BED both after treatment and at a two-year follow-up (Wilson, Wilfley, Agras, & Bryson, 2010), and this same program is effective when delivered out of a doctor's office in a primary care setting (Striegel-Moore et al., 2010). In view of these results, it would seem a self-help approach should probably be the first treatment offered for BED before engaging in more expensive and time-consuming therapist-led treatments. Much as with bulimia, however, more severe cases may need the more intensive treatment delivered by a therapist, particularly cases with multiple (comorbid) disorders in addition to BED, as well as low self-esteem (Wilson et al., 2010). Matching treatment to individuals on the basis of their personal characteristics or patterns of responding (personalized medicine) is regarded by many as the next important step for improving success rates of treatments.

Anorexia Nervosa

In anorexia, the most important initial goal is to restore the patient's weight to a point that is at least within the low–normal range (American Psychiatric Association, 2010b). If body weight is below approximately 75% of average healthy body weight, or if weight has been lost rapidly and the individual continues to refuse food, inpatient treatment is recommended (Schwartz, Mansbach, Marion, Katzman & Forman, 2008; Russell, 2009) because severe medical complications, particularly acute cardiac failure, could occur if weight is not restored immediately. If the weight loss has been more gradual and seems to have stabilized, weight restoration can be accomplished on an outpatient basis. Clinicians who treat patients in different settings, as reported in a variety of studies, find that at least 85% will be able to gain weight. The gain is often as much as a half-pound to a pound a day until weight is within normal range. Weight gain is important, since starvation induces loss of gray matter and hormonal dysregulation in the brain (Mainz et al., 2012), changes that are reversible when weight is restored.

However, as Hsu (1988) and others have demonstrated, initial weight gain is a poor predictor of long-term outcome in anorexia. Without attention to the patient's dysfunctional attitudes about body shape, as well as interpersonal disruptions in her life, she will almost always relapse. For restricting anorexics, the focus of treatment must shift to their anxiety over becoming obese and losing control of eating, as well as to their emphasis on thinness as a determinant of self-worth. In this regard, treatments for restricting anorexics are similar to those for patients with bulimia, particularly in the CBT-E approach (Fairburn & Cooper, 2014). Recent results from 99 adults with anorexia treated with CBT-E suggest the efficiency of this treatment (only "suggest" because there was no control or comparison group). In the 64% who completed treatment after 40 sessions, weight increased substantially and eating disorder features improved; this improvement was stable at a 60-week follow-up (Fairburn et al., 2013). One recent study underscored the importance of reducing anxiety concerning shape/weight in the treatment of anorexia. Racine and Wildes (2015) followed 191 patients who had received inpatient or day hospital treatment who had recovered sufficiently to be discharged and demonstrated that the presence of continued emotion dysregulation at discharge predicted an increase in anorexia over the following year, whereas low emotion dysregulation predicted a decrease in anorexic symptoms.

In addition, every effort is made to include the family. First, the dysfunctional communication in the family regarding eating must be eliminated and meals must be made more structured and reinforcing. Second, attitudes toward body shape and image are discussed in family sessions. Family therapy directed at these goals seems effective, particularly with young girls (less than 19 years of age) with a short history of the disorder (Eisler *et al.*, 2000; Lock, le Grange, Agras, & Dare, 2001). In a recent clinical trial, 121 adolescents with anorexia received 24 sessions of either family-based treatment (FBT) in which the parents became involved in the treatment, or individual psychotherapy. At treatment conclusion, 42% met criteria for remission in the FBT condition and 49% at a one-year follow-up, compared with 23% at both points in time in the individual psychotherapy condition (Lock *et al.*, 2010). A subsequent study demonstrated that FBT was at least as effective as, and less costly than other forms of family therapy addressing general family processes (Agras *et al.*, 2014). As in some studies of bulimia, a positive early response (gaining at least five pounds in the first four weeks) predicts a better outcome (Lock *et al.*, 2015). At present, FBT has the most support from clinical trials for treating adolescents with anorexia (Lock *et al.*, 2015), but there is some support for its efficacy in treating bulimia (Le Grange, Lock, Agras, Bryson, & Jo, 2015). Also, promising results have been reported with CBT-E for adolescents with anorexia (Dalle Grave, Calugi, Doll, & Fairburn, 2013).

Preventing Eating Disorders

Attempts are being made to prevent the development of eating disorders (Field *et al.*, 2012; Stice, Rohde, Shaw, & Marti, 2012). If successful methods are confirmed, they will be important, because many cases of eating disorders are resistant to treatment, and most individuals who do not receive treatment suffer for years, in some cases all of their lives (Eddy *et al.*, 2008). The development of eating disorders during adolescence is a risk factor for a variety of problems and disorders during adulthood, including cardiovascular symptoms, chronic fatigue and infectious diseases, binge-drinking and drug use, and anxiety and mood disorders (Field *et al.*, 2012; Johnson, Cohen, Kasen, & Brook, 2002).

Before implementing a prevention program, however, it is necessary to target specific behaviors to change. Stice, Shaw, and Marti (2007) concluded after a review of prevention programs that selecting girls age 15 or over and focusing on eliminating an exaggerated focus on body shape or weight and encouraging acceptance of one's body stood the best chance of success in preventing eating disorders. A program developed by Stice and colleagues (2012) called

"Healthy Weight" was compared with just handing out educational material in 398 college women at risk for developing eating disorders because of weight and shape concerns. During four weekly hour-long group sessions with 6,210 participants, the women were educated about food and eating habits (and motivated to alter these habits using motivational enhancement procedures). Eating disorder risk factors and symptoms were substantially reduced in the "Healthy Weight" group compared with the comparison group, particularly for the most severely at risk women, and the effect was durable at a six-month follow-up.

Could these preventive programs be delivered over the internet? It seems they can! Winzelberg and colleagues (2000) studied a group of university women who did not have eating disorders at the time of the study but were concerned about their body image and the possibility of being overweight. The investigators developed the "Student Bodies" program (Winzelberg *et al.*, 1998), a structured, interactive health education program designed to improve body image satisfaction and delivered through the internet. Program participants, compared to controls, reported a significant improvement in body image and a decrease in drive for thinness. Recently, developers have added an online-guided discussion group to accompany the program with initial results indicating more substantially reduced weight/shape concerns in students at risk for eating disorders (Kass *et al.*, 2014).

A briefer and more efficient program termed "The Body Project" has now been adapted as a standalone intervention delivered over the internet (eBody Project; Stice, Rohde, Durant, & Shaw, 2012), with no clinician required. Initial results indicate that this program is just as good as the program delivered in groups by a clinician, and it avoids problems with relying on institutions (in this case universities) to sustain these programs after the initial trial (Rohde, Shaw, Butryn, & Stice, 2015).

8.2 Concept CHECK

Mark the following statements about the causes and treatment of eating disorders as either true (T) or false (F):

1. _____ Many young women with eating disorders have a diminished sense of personal control and confidence in their own abilities, are perfectionists, and/or are preoccupied with how they appear.

2. _____ Biological limitations, as well as the societal pressure to use diet and exercise to achieve nearly impossible weight goals, contribute to the number of people with anorexia and bulimia.

(Continued next page)

3. _____ One study showed that males consider a smaller female body to be more attractive than women do.

4. _____ Antidepressants help individuals overcome anorexia but have no effect on bulimia.

5. _____ Cognitive-behavioral treatment (CBT) and interpersonal psychotherapy (IPT) are both successful treatments for bulimia nervosa, although CBT is the preferred method.

6. _____ Attention must be focused on dysfunctional attitudes about body shape in anorexia, or relapse will most likely occur.

Obesity

▶ What are some possible causes of obesity?

▶ What treatments are available?

As noted at the beginning of the chapter, obesity is not formally considered an eating disorder in the *DSM*. But in the year 2000, the number of adults with excess weight worldwide surpassed the number of those who were underweight (Caballero, 2007). Indeed, the prevalence of obesity is so high that one might consider it statistically "normal" if it weren't for the serious implications for health, as well as for social and psychological functioning.

Statistics

The prevalence of obesity (BMI 30 or greater) among adults in the United States in 2000 was fully 30.5% of the population, increasing to 37.7% in 2013–2014 with no difference in prevalence between men and women (Flegal *et al.*, 2010, 2012; Flegal, Kruszon-Moran, Carroll, Fryar, & Ogden, 2016; Ogden *et al.*, 2006). This prevalence of obesity represents close to a tripling from 12% of adults in 1991. Medical costs for obesity and overweight are estimated at $147 billion, or 9.1% of U.S. health-care expenditures (Brownell *et al.*, 2009). The direct relationship between obesity and mortality (dying prematurely) is shown in ● Figure 8.4. At a BMI of 30, risk of mortality increases by 30%, and at a BMI of 40 or more, risk of mortality is 100% or more (Manson *et al.*, 1995; Wadden, Brownell, & Foster, 2002). Because 6.3% of the U.S. adult population has a BMI over 40 (Flegal *et al.*, 2012), a substantial number of people, perhaps 10 million or more, are in serious danger, and recent evidence indicates that this may be an underestimate (Stokes & Preston, 2015).

In the past decade, the obesity rates for children ages 2 to 19 (defined as above the 95th percentile for sex-specific BMI for that age) have increased from 13.9% in 2000 to 17.1% in 2004 (Ogden *et al.*, 2006), but they now may be leveling off with a 16.9% rate in 2008, 2010, and 2011 (Ogden, Carroll, Curtin, Lamb, & Flegal, 2010; Ogden, Carroll, Kit, & Flegal, 2012, 2014; Ogden *et al.*, 2016). Rates may be even dropping a bit in pre-schoolers (Ogden *et al.*,

2016; Pan, Blanck, Sherry, Dalenius, & Grummer-Strawn, 2012), indicating, perhaps, that public education campaigns are beginning to have an effect. If one looks at children and adolescents either overweight (above the 85th percentile in BMI) or obese, the rate is 30.4%.

The stigma of obesity has a major impact on quality of life (Gearhardt *et al.*, 2012; Neumark-Sztainer & Haines,

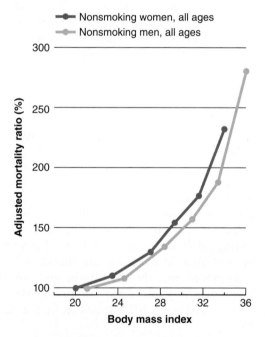

● **Figure 8.4** Mortality rates in relation to the BMI of non-smoking men and women (of all ages) who participated in the American Cancer Society study. (Reprinted, with permission, from Vanitallie, T. B., & Lew, E. A. [1992]. Assessment of morbidity and mortality risk in the overweight patient. In T. A. Wadden and T. B. Vanitallie, Eds., *Treatment of the seriously obese patient* [p. 28]. New York: Guilford Press, © 1992 Guilford Press.)

2004). For example, most overweight individuals are subjected to prejudice and discrimination in college, at work, and in housing (Gearhardt *et al.*, 2012). Further, the experience of weight discrimination is associated with increased mortality risk (Sutin, Stephan, & Terracciano, 2015). Ridicule and teasing in children may increase obesity through depression and binge-eating (Schwartz & Brownell, 2007).

Ethnicity also is a factor in rates of obesity. In the United States, 47.8% of African American women and 42% of Hispanic American women are obese, compared with 33.4% of Caucasian women (Ogden *et al.*, 2014). Rates among minority adolescents are even more concerning, with considerably higher rates of obesity and being overweight among black and Hispanic adolescents compared with white adolescents.

Obesity is not limited to North America. Rates of obesity in eastern and southern European nations are as high as 50% (Berghöfer *et al.*, 2008; Bjorntorp, 1997; Ng *et al.*, 2014), and the rate is increasing in developing nations. In Japan, although still comparatively low, obesity rates in men have doubled since 1992 and have nearly doubled in young women (Organization for Economic Co-operation and Development, 2012). Although less extreme, increases in obesity are also occurring in China (Henderson & Brownell, 2004), where the proportion of Chinese who are overweight increased from 6% to 8% in a seven-year period (Holden, 2005). Obesity is also the main driver of type 2 diabetes, which has reached epidemic status (Yach, Stuckler, & Brownell, 2006).

Disordered Eating Patterns in Cases of Obesity

There are two forms of maladaptive eating patterns in people who are obese. The first is binge-eating, and the second is **night eating syndrome** (Lundgren, Allison, & Stunkard,

2012; Vander Wal, 2012). We discussed BED earlier in the chapter, but it is important to note that only 7% and 19% of patients with obesity present with patterns of binge-eating. When they do, treatment for binge-eating reviewed earlier should be integrated into weight-loss programs.

More interesting is the pattern of night eating syndrome that occurs in between 6% and 16% of obese individuals seeking weight-loss treatment but in as many as 55% of those with extreme obesity seeking bariatric surgery (discussed later; Colles & Dixon, 2012; Stunkard, Allison, & Lundgren, 2008). Individuals with night eating syndrome consume a third or more of their daily intake after their evening meal and get out of bed at least once during the night to have a high-calorie snack. In the morning, however, they are not hungry and do not usually eat breakfast. These individuals do not binge during their night eating and seldom purge. Occasionally, non-obese individuals will engage in night eating, but the behavior is overwhelmingly associated with being overweight or obese (Gallant, Lundgren, & Drapeau, 2012; Lundgren *et al.*, 2012; Striegel-Moore *et al.*, 2010).

Notice the relationship of night eating syndrome with increasing levels of obesity in ● Figure 8.5 (Colles, Dixon, & O'Brien, 2007). This condition is not the same as the nocturnal eating syndrome described later in the chapter. In that condition, individuals get up during the night and raid the refrigerator but never wake up. On the contrary, in night eating syndrome, the individuals are awake as they go

night eating syndrome Consuming a third or more of daily food intake after the evening meal and getting out of bed at least once during the night to have a high-calorie snack. In the morning, however, individuals with night eating syndrome are not hungry and do not usually eat breakfast. These individuals do not **binge** during their night eating and seldom purge.

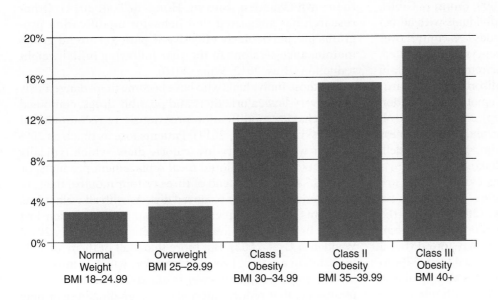

● **Figure 8.5** Prevalence of night eating syndrome by level of obesity. (Colles, S.L., Dixon, J. B., & O'Brien, P.E. [2007]. Night eating syndrome and nocturnal snacking: Association with obesity, binge-eating, and psychological distress. *International Journal of Obesity, 31,* 1722–1730.)

about their nightly eating patterns. Night eating syndrome is an important target for treatment in any obesity program to re-regulate patterns of eating so that individuals eat more during the day, when their energy expenditure is highest.

Causes

Henderson and Brownell (2004) make a point that the obesity epidemic is clearly related to the spread of modernization. That is, the promotion of an inactive, sedentary lifestyle and the consumption of a high-fat, energy-dense diet is the largest single contributor to the obesity epidemic (Caballero, 2007; Levine *et al.*, 2005). Kelly Brownell (2003; Brownell *et al.*, 2010) notes that in our modern society, individuals are continually exposed to heavily advertised, inexpensive fatty foods that have low nutritional value. When consumption of these is combined with an increasingly inactive lifestyle, it is not surprising that the prevalence of obesity is increasing (Esparza-Romero *et al.*, 2015; Gearhardt *et al.*, 2012). Brownell has referred to this as the "toxic environment" (Schwartz & Brownell, 2007).

However, not everyone exposed to the modernized environment becomes obese, and this is where genetics, physiology, and personality come in. On average, genetic contributions may constitute a smaller portion of the cause of obesity than cultural factors, but it helps explain why some people become obese and some don't when exposed to the same environment. For example, genes influence the number of fat cells an individual has, the likelihood of fat storage, satiety, and, most likely, activity levels (Cope, Fernandez, & Allison, 2004; Hetherington & Cecil, 2010; Llewellyn, Trzaskowski, Jaarsveid, & Plomin, 2014). Generally, genes are thought to account for about 30% of the equation in causation of obesity (Bouchard, 2002), but this is misleading because it takes a "toxic" environment to turn on these genes. Physiological processes, particularly hormonal regulation of appetite, play a large role in the initiation and maintenance of eating and vary considerably from individual to individual (Friedman, 2009; Smith & Gibbs, 2002; Yeo & Heisler, 2012). Indeed, individuals with addictive obese eating behavior, which includes less control over eating and feelings of withdrawal if access to food is limited, show similar patterns of reward neurocircuitry in the brain as do individuals with substance use disorders (Gearhardt *et al.*, 2011). Psychological processes of emotional regulation (e.g., eating to try to cheer yourself up), impulse control, attitudes and motivation toward eating, and responsiveness to the consequences of eating are also important (Blundell, 2002; Stice, Presnell, Shaw, & Rohde, 2005).

Many of these attitudes as well as eating habits are strongly influenced by family and close friends. In an important study, Christakis and Fowler (2007) studied the social networks (close friends and neighbors) of more than 12,000 people for more than 30 years. They found that a person's chance of becoming obese increased from 37% to 57% if a spouse, sibling, or even a close friend was obese, but it did not if a neighbor or co-worker with whom the person did not socialize was obese. Thus, it seems that obesity spreads through social networks. Although the etiology of obesity is extraordinarily complex, as with most disorders, an interaction of biological and psychological factors with a notably strong environmental and cultural contribution provides the most complete account.

Treatment

The treatment of obesity is only moderately successful at the individual level (Bray, 2012; Ludwig, 2012), with somewhat greater long-term evidence for effectiveness in children compared to adults (Sarwer *et al.*, 2004; Waters *et al.*, 2011). The first step is usually a self-directed weight-loss program. The most common result is that some individuals may lose some weight in the short term but almost always regain that weight (Mann, Tomiyama, & Ward, 2015). Similarly, there is little evidence that physician counseling results in any changes (Wing, 2010). Nevertheless, physicians can play an important role by providing specific treatment recommendations, including referral to professionals (Sarwer *et al.*, 2004).

The next step is commercial self-help programs such as Weight Watchers and Jenny Craig. These programs stand a better chance of achieving some success, at least compared with self-directed programs (Jakicic *et al.*, 2012; Johnston, Rost, Miller-Kovach, Moreno, & Foreyt, 2013; Wing, 2010). In an earlier study (Heshka *et al.*, 2003) among members who successfully lost weight initially and kept their weight off for at least six weeks after completing the program, between 19% and 37% weighed within five pounds of their goal weight at least five years after treatment (Lowe, Miller-Kovach, Frie, & Phelan, 1999; Sarwer *et al.*, 2004). But this means that up to 80% of individuals are not successful in the long run.

The most successful programs are professionally directed behavior modification programs. A recent study suggested that the combination of restricted calorie intake, increased physical activity, and behavior therapy tends to lead to more weight loss than any of these components on their own (Wadden, Butryn, Hong, & Tsai, 2014). Other research has suggested that behavior modification programs are particularly effective if patients attend group maintenance sessions in the year following initial weight reduction (Bray, 2012; Wing, 2010).

For those individuals who have become more dangerously obese, very-low-calorie diets and possibly drugs, combined with behavior modification programs, are recommended (Yanovski & Yanovski, 2014). Patients lose as much as 20% of their weight on very-low-calorie diets, which typically consist of four to six liquid meal replacement products, or "shakes," a day. At the end of three or four months, they are placed on a low-calorie balanced diet. As with all weight-loss programs, patients typically regain up to 50% of their lost weight in the year following treatment (Ames *et al.*, 2014; Wadden & Osei, 2002). But more than half of them are able to maintain a weight loss of at least 5%, which is important in very obese people (Sarwer *et al.*, 2004). Similarly, drug treatments that reduce internal cues signaling hunger may have some effect, particularly if combined with a behavioral approach targeting lifestyle change, but concerns about cardiovascular side effects have plagued these medications (Morrato & Allison, 2012, Yanovski & Yanovski, 2014).

Finally, the surgical approach to extreme obesity—**bariatric surgery**—is an increasingly popular approach for individuals with a BMI of at least 40 (Adams *et al.*, 2012; Courcoulas, 2012; Livingston, 2012; Arteburn & Fisher, 2014). Such surgery is usually more successful than diets, with patients losing approximately 20% to 30% of their body weight post-operatively and maintaining these results over a number of years (Adams *et al.*, 2012; Buchwald *et al.*, 2004; Courcoulas *et al.*, 2013). Bariatric surgery is also associated with lower mortality in obese individuals up to 14 years after the procedure (Arteburn *et al.*, 2015). This surgery is reserved only for the most severely obese individuals for whom the obesity is an imminent health risk. Surgeons typically require patients to exhaust all other treatment options and to undergo a thorough psychological assessment to ascertain whether they can adapt to the radically changed eating patterns required postsurgery (Kral, 2002; Livingston, 2010; Sarwer *et al.*, 2004).

Approximately 15% of patients who have bariatric surgery fail to lose significant weight, or they regain lost weight after surgery (Latfi, Kellum, DeMaria, & Sugarman, 2002; Livhits *et al.*, 2012). A small percentage of individuals, from 0.1% to 0.5%, do not survive the operation, and an additional 15% to 20% experience severe complications requiring rehospitalization and additional surgery within the first year after surgery and in each of the next two years after that (Birkmeyer *et al.*, 2013; O'Brien *et al.*, 2010; Zingmond, McGory, & Ko, 2005).

Turning to public health policy approaches, many states are removing soft drink machines and other unhealthy foods from public schools. Nine states have requested permission from the federal government to eliminate the option of buying sugar-sweetened beverages with food stamps, a proposal supported by the American Medical Association (Brownell & Ludwig, 2011). Food taxes have also been discussed as a way to raise revenue that could be used to promote education and policy changes on food consumption. Could the government make it more attractive to eat healthy foods and less attractive to eat unhealthy foods by making the former less expensive and the latter more expensive? The Rudd Center for Food Policy and Obesity at Yale is studying the issue. By 2009, 40 states had put into place some taxes on snack foods or soft drinks (Brownell & Frieden, 2009). The thinking is that taxes would have to be increased considerably to provide a substantial disincentive. Of course, any substantial tax, with its implications of government control of our behavior, would be controversial and criticized by many. But counterarguments point out the obligation of the government to create policy that supports the efforts of all people to be healthy (Brownell *et al.*, 2010).

Another public health approach is choice architecture—that is, designing different ways in which choices can be presented to consumers. One line of research has explored the effects of labeling foods with traffic light colors (i.e., red, yellow, or green) based on their nutritional value. In two studies (Thorndike, Sonnenberg, Riis, Barraclough, & Levy, 2012; Thorndike, Riis, Sonnenberg, & Levy, 2014) researchers found that labeling food in this manner led to decreases in purchases of red (i.e., unhealthy) foods and increases in purchases of green (i.e., healthy) foods. While promising, more research is needed in this area.

In contrast to adults, the treatment of obesity in children and adolescents has achieved somewhat better outcomes (Cooperberg & Faith, 2004; Oude Luttikhuis *et al.*, 2011), particularly for children. A number of studies report that behavior modification programs, especially those that include parents, may produce a 20% reduction in overweight children or adolescents, a change maintained for at least several years. These behavior modification programs include a number of strategies to change dietary habits, particularly decreasing high-calorie, high-fat snacks, and also targeting reduction of sedentary habits in children and adolescents, such as playing video games. Parents are typically fully engaged in the program in a constructive way and provide constant support (Altman & Wilfey, 2015; Ludwig, 2012). This is important because many parents who are not part of a structured program have a tendency to pressure their overweight children not to eat, which has the opposite effect of causing them to eat more (Agras *et al.*, 2012). Also, dietary habits in children are less engrained than in adults. For the most severely obese adolescents with a BMI greater than 35, a less intrusive and safer bariatric surgical procedure than the one typically done on adults is now being evaluated, and initial results suggest short-term reduction in weight, but the long-term effects remain to be seen (Black, White, Viner, & Simmons, 2013; O'Brien *et al.*, 2010).

8.3 Concept CHECK

Mark the following statements about obesity as either true (T) or false (F):

1. _____ Obesity is the single most expensive health problem in the United States, surpassing both smoking and alcohol abuse.

2. _____ Individuals with night eating syndrome consume at least half their daily intake after their evening meal.

3. _____ Fatty foods and technology are not to blame for the obesity epidemic in the United States.

4. _____ Professionally directed behavior modification programs represent the most successful treatment for obesity.

bariatric surgery Surgical approach to extreme **obesity**, usually accomplished by stapling the stomach to create a small stomach pouch or bypassing the stomach through gastric bypass surgery.

Sleep–Wake Disorders: The Major Dyssomnias

▶ What are the critical diagnostic features of the major sleep–wake disorders?

▶ What medical and psychological treatments are used for the treatment of sleep_____ disorders?

▶ How are rapid eye movement and nonrapid eye movement sleep related to the parasomnias?

We spend about one-third of our lives asleep. That means most of us sleep nearly 3,000 hours per *year*. For many of us, sleep is energizing, both mentally and physically. Unfortunately, most people do not get enough sleep, and 28% of people in the United States report feeling excessively sleepy during the day (Ohayon, Dauvilliers, & Reynolds, 2012). Research tells us that even minor sleep deprivation over only 24 hours impedes our ability to think clearly (Joo, Yoon, Koo, Kim, & Hong, 2012). People who do not get enough sleep are also more susceptible to illnesses such as the common cold, perhaps because immune system functioning is reduced with the loss of even a few hours of sleep (Ruiz et al., 2012).

Here you might ask yourself how sleep–wake disorders fit into a textbook on abnormal psychology. Different variations of disturbed sleep clearly have physiological bases and therefore could be considered purely medical concerns. Like other physical disorders, however, sleep problems interact in important ways with psychological factors.

An Overview of Sleep–Wake Disorders

The study of sleep has long influenced concepts of abnormal psychology. Moral treatment, used in the 19th century for people with severe mental illness, included encouraging patients to get adequate amounts of sleep (Charland, 2008). Researchers who prevented people from sleeping for prolonged periods found that chronic sleep deprivation often had profound effects. A number of the disorders covered in this book are often associated with sleep complaints, including autism spectrum disorder, schizophrenia, major depression, bipolar disorder, and anxiety-related disorders. Sleep problems may also cause the difficulties people experience in everyday life (e.g., Kreutzmann, Havekes, Abel, & Meerlo, 2015; Almklov, Drummond, Orff, & Alhassoon, 2015), or they may result from some disturbance common to a psychological disorder.

In Chapter 4, we explained how a brain circuit in the limbic system may be involved with anxiety. We know that this region of the brain is also involved with our dream sleep, which is called **rapid eye movement (REM) sleep** (Steiger, 2008). This mutual neurobiological connection suggests that anxiety and sleep may be interrelated, although the nature of the relationship is unknown. Insufficient sleep, for example, can stimulate overeating (Hanlon & Knutson, 2014). Similarly, REM sleep seems related to depression (Wiebe, Cassoff, & Gruber, 2012). Furthermore, sleep

deprivation has temporary antidepressant effects on some people, although in people who are not already depressed, sleep deprivation may bring on a depressed mood (Voderhozer et al., 2014). We do not fully understand how psychological disorders are related to sleep, yet research points to the importance of understanding sleep if we are to complete the broader picture of abnormal behavior.

Sleep–wake disorders are divided into two major categories: **dyssomnias** and **parasomnias** (see Table 8.2). Dyssomnias involve difficulties in getting enough sleep, problems with sleeping when you want to, and complaints about the quality of sleep. Parasomnias are characterized by abnormal behavioral or physiological events that occur during sleep, such as nightmares and sleepwalking.

The clearest and most comprehensive picture of a person's sleep habits can be determined by a **polysomnographic (PSG) evaluation** (Mindell & Owens, 2015). The

▲ This participant is undergoing a polysomnograph, an overnight electronic evaluation of sleep patterns.

TABLE 8.2 | Summary of *DSM-5* Sleep–Wake Disorders

Sleep Disorder	Description
DYSSOMNIAS	(Problems in the amount, timing, or quality of sleep)
Insomnia Disorder	Difficulty falling asleep at bedtime, problems staying asleep throughout the night, or sleep that does not result in the person feeling rested even after normal amounts of sleep.
Hypersomnolence Disorders	Excessive sleepiness that is displayed as either sleeping longer than is typical or frequent falling asleep during the day.
Narcolepsy	Episodes of irresistible attacks of refreshing sleep occurring daily, accompanied by episodes of brief loss of muscle tone (cataplexy).
Breathing-Related Sleep Disorders (Obstructive Sleep Apnea Hypopnea Syndrome, Central Sleep Apnea and Sleep-Related Hypoventilation)	A variety of breathing disorders that occur during sleep and that lead to excessive sleepiness or insomnia.
Circadian Rhythm Sleep–Wake Disorder	A discrepancy between the sleep–wake schedule required by a person to be rested and the requirements of the person's environment (e.g., work schedules) that leads to excessive sleepiness or insomnia.
PARASOMNIAS	
Disorder of Arousal	Motor movements and behaviors that occur during NREM sleep including incomplete awakening (confusional arousals), sleep walking, or sleep terrors (abrupt awakening from sleep that begins with a panicky scream).
Nightmare Disorder	Frequently being awakened by extended and extremely frightening dreams that cause significant distress and impaired functioning.
Rapid Eye Movement Sleep Behavior Disorder	Episodes of arousal during REM sleep that result in behaviors that can cause harm to the individual or others.
Restless Legs Syndrome	Irresistible urges to move the legs as a result of unpleasant sensations (sometimes labeled "creeping," "tugging," or "pulling" in the limbs) (otherwise referred to as Willis-Ekbom disease).
Substance-Induced Sleep Disorder	Severe sleep disturbance that is the result of substance intoxication or withdrawal.

SOURCE: Adapted from American Psychiatric Association. (2013). *Diagnostic and statistical manual of mental disorders* (5th ed.). Washington, DC.: American Psychiatric Association.

patient spends one or more nights sleeping in a laboratory and being monitored on a number of measures, including respiration and oxygen desaturation (a measure of airflow); leg movements; brain wave activity, measured by an *electroencephalogram;* eye movements, measured by an *electrooculogram;* muscle movements, measured by an *electromyogram;* and heart activity, measured by an *electrocardiogram.* Daytime behavior and typical sleep patterns are also noted—for example, whether the person uses drugs or alcohol, is anxious about work, takes afternoon naps, or has a psychological disorder. Collecting all these data can be both time consuming and costly, but it is important to ensure an accurate diagnosis and treatment plan.

One alternative to the comprehensive assessment of sleep is to use a wristwatch-size device called an **actigraph**. This instrument records the number of arm movements, and the data can be downloaded into a computer to determine the length and quality of sleep. Several studies have tested the usefulness of this device in measuring the sleep of astronauts during space travel, and they find it can

rapid eye movement (REM) sleep Periodic intervals of sleep during which the eyes move rapidly from side to side, and dreams occur, but the body is inactive.

dyssomnias Problems in getting to sleep or in obtaining sufficient quality sleep.

parasomnias Abnormal behaviors such as **nightmares** or **sleepwalking** that occur during sleep.

polysomnographic (PSG) evaluation Assessment of sleep disorders in which a client sleeping in the lab is monitored for heart, muscle, respiration, brain wave, and other functions.

actigraph Small electronic device that is worn on the wrist like a watch and records body movements. This device can be used to record sleep–wake cycles.

reliably detect when they fall asleep, when they wake up, and how restful their in-space sleep is (e.g., Barger *et al.*, 2014). Smartphone apps and wristband devices can also provide some of this information (de Zambotti, Claudatos, Inkelis, Colrain, & Baker, 2015).

In addition, clinicians find it helpful to know the average number of hours the individual sleeps each day, taking into account **sleep efficiency (SE)**, the percentage of time actually spent asleep, not just lying in bed trying to sleep. SE is calculated by dividing the amount of time sleeping by the amount of time in bed. An SE of 100% would mean you fall asleep as soon as your head hits the pillow and do not wake up during the night. In contrast, an SE of 50% would mean half your time in bed is spent trying to fall asleep.

One way to determine whether a person has a problem with sleep is to observe his or her behavior while awake. For example, if it takes you 90 minutes to fall asleep, but this doesn't bother you and you feel rested, you do not have a problem. A friend who also takes 90 minutes to fall asleep but finds this delay anxiety provoking and is fatigued the next day might be considered to have a sleep problem. It is, to some degree, a subjective decision, partly depending on how the person perceives the situation and reacts to it.

Insomnia Disorder

Insomnia is one of the most common sleep–wake disorders. You may picture someone with insomnia as being awake all the time. It isn't possible to go completely without sleep, however. For example, after being awake for one or two nights, a person begins having **microsleeps** that last several seconds or longer (Morin *et al.*, 2012). Despite the common use of the term *insomnia* to mean "not sleeping," it actually applies to a number of complaints. People are considered to have insomnia if they have trouble falling asleep at night, if they wake up frequently or too early and can't go back to sleep, or even if they sleep a reasonable number of hours but are still not rested the next day (non-restorative sleep). Consider the case of Sonja.

Clinical Description

Sonja's symptoms meet the *DSM-5* criteria for **insomnia disorder** (also referred to as **primary insomnia**) because her sleep problems were not related to other medical or psychiatric problems. Looking at sleep–wake disorders as primary recalls the overlap of sleep problems with psychological disorders such as anxiety and depression. Because not sleeping makes you anxious and anxiety further interrupts your sleep—which makes you more anxious, and so on—it is uncommon to find a person with a simple sleep–wake disorder and no related problems.

Sonja... • *School on Her Mind*

Sonja was a 23-year-old law student with a history of sleep problems. She reported that she never slept well, having trouble falling asleep and awakening again in the early morning. Since she started law school last year, her sleep problems had grown worse. She would lie in bed awake until the early morning hours thinking about school, getting only three to four hours of sleep on a typical night. In the morning, she had difficulty getting out of bed and was frequently late for her early morning class.

Sonja's sleep problems and their interference with her schoolwork were causing her to experience increasingly severe depression. In addition, she recently reported having a severe anxiety attack that woke her in the middle of the night. All of these difficulties caused her to be increasingly isolated from family and friends, who finally convinced her to seek help.

We return to Sonja later in this chapter.

Sonja's is a typical case of insomnia disorder. She had trouble both initiating and maintaining sleep. Other people sleep all night but still feel as if they've been awake for hours. Although most people can carry out day-to-day activities, their inability to concentrate can have serious consequences, such as debilitating accidents when they attempt to drive long distances (like bus drivers) or handle dangerous material (like electricians). Students with insomnia like Sonja's may do poorly in school because of difficulty concentrating.

Statistics

Approximately one-third of the population reports some symptoms of insomnia during any given year (Chung *et al.*, 2015). For many of these individuals, sleep difficulties are a lifetime affliction (Lind, Aggen, Kirkpatrick, Kendler, & Amstadter, 2015). Approximately 15% of older adults report excessive daytime sleepiness, with older black men reporting the most problems, and this contributes to increased risk for falling (Green, Ndao-Brumblay, & Hart-Johnson, 2009; Hayley *et al.*, 2015).

A number of psychological disorders are associated with insomnia. Total sleep time often decreases with depression, substance use disorders, anxiety disorders, and neurocognitive disorder due to Alzheimer's disease. The interrelationship between alcohol use and sleep disorders can be particularly troubling. Alcohol is often used to initiate sleep (Morin *et al.*, 2012). In small amounts, it helps make people drowsy, but it also interrupts ongoing sleep. Interrupted

DISORDER CRITERIA SUMMARY
Insomnia Disorder

Features of insomnia disorder include the following:

- A predominant complaint of dissatisfaction with sleep quantity or quality associated with one or more of the following: (1) difficulty initiating sleep, (2) difficulty maintaining sleep, (3) early morning awakening with inability to return to sleep.

- The sleep disturbance causes significant distress in social, occupational, educational, academic, behavioral, or other important areas of functioning.

- The sleep difficulty occurs at least three nights per week and is present for at least three months.

- The sleep difficulty occurs despite adequate opportunity for sleep.

- The insomnia is not better explained by and does not occur exclusively during the course of another sleep–wake disorder and is not attributable to the effects of a substance (e.g., a drug abuse) or a co-existing mental disorders or medical conditions.

From American Psychiatric Association. (2013). *Diagnostic and statistical manual of mental disorders* (5th ed.). Washington, DC.

sleep causes anxiety, which often leads to repeated alcohol use and an obviously vicious cycle.

Women report insomnia twice as often as men. Women more often report problems initiating sleep, which may be related to hormonal differences or to differential reporting of sleep problems, with women generally more negatively affected by poor sleep than men (Jaussent *et al.*, 2011). Interestingly, there may be some protective factors that can improve sleep in women, including moderate alcohol and caffeine use and following a Mediterranean diet (e.g., high intake of vegetables, legumes, fruits, and unsaturated fatty acids mostly in the form of olive oil) (Jaussent *et al.*, 2011).

Just as people's needs concerning normal sleep change over time, complaints of insomnia differ in frequency among people of different ages. Approximately one in five young children experiences insomnia (Calhoun, Fernandez-Mendoza, Vgontzas, Liao, & Bixler, 2014). Growing evidence points to both biological and cultural explanations for poor sleep among adolescents. As children move into adolescence, their biologically determined sleep schedules shift toward a later bedtime (Skeldon, Dirks, & Dijk, 2015). At least in the United States, however, children are still expected to rise early for school, causing chronic sleep deprivation. The percentage of individuals who complain of sleep problems increases as they become older adults. This higher rate in reports of sleeping problems among older people makes sense when you remember that the number of hours we sleep decreases as we age. It is not uncommon for someone over 65 to sleep fewer than six hours and wake up several times each night.

Causes

Insomnia accompanies many medical and psychological disorders, including pain and physical discomfort, physical inactivity during the day, and respiratory problems. Sometimes insomnia is related to problems with the biological clock and its control of temperature. Some people who can't fall asleep at night may have a delayed temperature rhythm: Their body temperature doesn't drop, and they don't become drowsy until later at night. As a group, people with insomnia seem to have higher body temperatures than good sleepers, and their body temperatures seem to vary less; this lack of fluctuation may interfere with sleep (Taylor, Gehrman, Dautovich, Lichstein, & McCrae, 2014).

Among the other factors that can interfere with sleeping are drug use and a variety of environmental influences such as changes in light, noise, or temperature. People admitted to hospitals often have difficulty sleeping, because the noises and routines differ from those at home. Other sleep disorders, such as *sleep apnea* (a disorder that involves obstructed nighttime breathing) or *periodic limb movement disorder* (excessive jerky leg movements), can cause interrupted sleep and may seem similar to insomnia. Finally, various psychological stresses can also disrupt sleep.

People with insomnia may have unrealistic expectations about how much sleep they need ("I need a full eight hours") and about how disruptive disturbed sleep will be ("I won't be able to think or do my job if I sleep for only five hours") (Hiller, Johnston, Dohnt, Lovato, & Gradisar, 2015). The actual amount of sleep each person needs varies and is assessed by how it affects you during the day. It is important to recognize the role of cognition in insomnia; our thoughts alone may disrupt our sleep.

Is poor sleeping a learned behavior? It is generally accepted that people suffering from sleep problems associate the bedroom and bed with the frustration and anxiety that go with insomnia. Eventually, the arrival of bedtime itself may cause anxiety (Morin & Benca, 2012). Interactions associated with sleep may contribute to children's sleep problems. For example, one study found that a parent's depression and negative thoughts about child sleep negatively influenced infant night waking (Teti & Crosby, 2012). Researchers think that some children learn to fall asleep only with a parent present; if they wake up at night, they are frightened at finding themselves alone, and their sleep is disrupted.

sleep efficiency (SE) Percentage of time actually spent sleeping of the total time spent in bed.

microsleeps Short, seconds-long periods of sleep that occur in people who have been deprived of sleep.

insomnia disorder Condition in which insufficient sleep interferes with normal functioning.

primary insomnia Difficulty in initiating, maintaining, or gaining from sleep; not related to other medical or psychological problems.

▲ In the United States, children usually sleep alone (left). In many cultures, all family members share the same bed (right).

Cross-cultural sleep research has focused primarily on children. In the predominant culture in the United States, infants are expected to sleep on their own, in a separate bed, and, if possible, in a separate room. In other cultures as diverse as rural Guatemala and Korea and urban Japan, however, the child spends the first few years of life in the same room and sometimes the same bed as the mother (Burnham & Gaylor, 2011). In many cultures, mothers report that they do not ignore the cries of their children (Giannotti & Cortesi, 2009), in stark contrast to the United States, where many pediatricians recommend that parents ignore the cries of their infants over a certain age at night (Moore, 2012). One conclusion from this research is that sleep can be affected by cultural norms. Unmet demands can result in stress that negatively affects the ultimate sleep outcome for children (Durand, 2008, 2014).

An Integrative Model

An integrative view of sleep disorders includes several assumptions. The first is that, at some level, both biological and psychological factors are present in most cases. A second assumption is that these multiple factors are reciprocally related. This can be seen in the study we noted earlier, where a parent's depression and negative thoughts about child sleep negatively influenced infant night waking (Teti & Crosby, 2012). In other words, personality characteristics, sleep difficulties, and parental reaction interact in a reciprocal manner to produce and maintain sleep problems.

People may be biologically vulnerable to disturbed sleep. This vulnerability differs from person to person and can range from mild to more severe disturbances. For example, a person may be a light sleeper (easily aroused at night) or have a family history of insomnia, narcolepsy, or obstructed breathing. All these factors can lead to eventual sleeping problems. Such influences have been referred to as *predisposing conditions* (Spielman & Glovinsky, 1991); they may not, by themselves, always cause problems, but they may

combine with other factors to interfere with sleep (see ● Figure 8.6).

Biological vulnerability may, in turn, interact with *sleep stress* (Durand, 2008), which includes a number of events that can negatively affect sleep. For example, poor bedtime habits (such as having too much alcohol or caffeine) can interfere with falling asleep (Morin *et al.*, 2012). Note that biological vulnerability and sleep stress influence each other (as shown in ●Figure 8.6). Although we may intuitively assume that biological factors come first, extrinsic influences such as poor sleep hygiene (the daily activities that affect how we sleep) can affect the physiological activity of sleep. One of the most striking examples of this phenomenon is jet lag, in which people's sleep patterns are disrupted when they fly across time zones. Whether disturbances continue or become more severe may depend on how they are managed. For example, many people react to disrupted sleep by taking over-the-counter sleeping pills. Unfortunately, most people are not aware that **rebound insomnia**—where sleep problems reappear, sometimes worse—may occur when the medication is withdrawn. This rebound leads people to think they still have a sleep problem, re-administer the medicine, and go through the cycle repeatedly. In other words, taking sleep aids can perpetuate sleep problems.

Other ways of reacting to poor sleep can also prolong problems. It seems reasonable that a person who hasn't had enough sleep can make up for this loss by napping during the day. Unfortunately, naps that alleviate fatigue during the day can also disrupt sleep that night. Anxiety can also extend the problem. Lying in bed worrying about school, family problems, or even about not being able to sleep will interfere with sleep (O'Kearney & Pech, 2014). The behavior of parents can also help maintain these problems in children. Children who receive a great deal of positive attention at night when they wake up may wake up during the night more often (Durand, 2014). Such maladaptive reactions, when combined with a biological predisposition to sleep problems and sleep stress, may account for continuing problems.

● **Figure 8.6** An integrative, multidimensional model of sleep disturbance.

Hypersomnolence Disorders

Insomnia disorder involves not getting enough sleep (the prefix *in* means "lacking" or "without"), and **hypersomnolence disorders** involve sleeping too much (*hyper* means "in great amount" or "abnormal excess"). Many people who sleep all night find themselves falling asleep several times the next day. Consider the case of Ann.

Ann... • *Sleeping in Public*

Ann, a college student, came to my office to discuss her progress in class. We talked about several questions that she got wrong on the last exam, and as she was about to leave she said that she never fell asleep during my class. This seemed like faint praise, but I thanked her for the feedback. "No," she said, "you don't understand. I usually fall asleep in *all* of my classes, but not in yours." Again, I didn't quite understand what she was trying to tell me and joked that she must pick her professors more carefully. She laughed. "That's probably true. But I also have this problem with sleeping too much."

As we talked more seriously, Ann told me that excessive sleeping had been a problem since her teenage years. In situations that were monotonous or boring, or when she couldn't be active, she fell asleep. This could happen several times a day, depending on what she was doing. Recently, large lecture classes had become a problem unless the lecturer was particularly interesting

or animated. Watching television and driving long distances were also problematic.

Ann reported that her father had a similar problem. He had recently been diagnosed with narcolepsy (which we discuss next) and was now getting help at a clinic. Both she and her brother had been diagnosed with hypersomnolence disorder. Ann had been prescribed Ritalin (a stimulant medication) about four years ago and said that it was only somewhat effective in keeping her awake during the day. She said the drug helped reduce the sleep attacks but did not eliminate them altogether.

The *DSM-5* diagnostic criteria for hypersomnolence include not only the excessive sleepiness that Ann described but also the subjective impression of this problem (American Psychiatric Association, 2013). Remember that whether insomnia disorder is a problem depends on how it affects each person. Ann found her disorder disruptive because it interfered with driving and paying attention in class. Hypersomnolence caused her to be less successful academically and upset her personally, both of which are defining features of this disorder. She slept approximately eight hours each night, so her daytime sleepiness couldn't be attributed to insufficient sleep.

Several factors that can cause excessive sleepiness would not be considered hypersomnolence. For example, people with insomnia disorder (who get inadequate amounts of sleep) often report being tired during the day. In contrast, people with hypersomnolence sleep through the night and appear rested upon awakening but still complain of being excessively tired throughout the day. Another sleep problem that can cause a similar excessive sleepiness is a breathing-related sleep disorder called **sleep apnea**. People with this problem have difficulty breathing at night. They often snore loudly, pause between breaths, and wake in the morning with a dry mouth and headache. In identifying hypersomnolence, the clinician needs to rule out insomnia, sleep apnea, or other reasons for sleepiness during the day (American Psychiatric Association, 2013).

We are just beginning to understand the nature of hypersomnolence, so relatively little research has been done on its causes. Genetic influences seem to be involved in a portion of cases (Buysse *et al.*, 2008). A significant subgroup of people diagnosed with hypersomnolence disorder previously were exposed to a viral infection such as mononucleosis, hepatitis, and viral pneumonia, which suggests there may be more than one cause (Hirshkowitz, Seplowitz, & Sharafkhaneh, 2009).

rebound insomnia In a person with insomnia, the worsened sleep problems that can occur when medications are used to treat insomnia and then withdrawn.

hypersomnolence disorders Sleep dysfunction involving an excessive amount of sleep that disrupts normal routines.

sleep apnea Disorder involving brief periods when breathing ceases during sleep.

Narcolepsy

Ann described her father as having **narcolepsy**, a different form of the sleeping problem she and her brother shared (Goodrick, 2014). In addition to daytime sleepiness, some people with narcolepsy experience *cataplexy*, a sudden loss of muscle tone. Cataplexy occurs while the person is awake and can range from slight weakness in the facial muscles to complete physical collapse. Cataplexy lasts from several seconds to several minutes; it is usually preceded by strong emotion such as anger or happiness. Cataplexy appears to result from a sudden onset of REM sleep. Instead of falling asleep normally and going through the four nonrapid eye movement (NREM) stages that typically precede REM sleep, people with narcolepsy periodically progress right to this dream-sleep stage almost directly from the state of being awake. One outcome of REM sleep is the inhibition of input to the muscles, and this seems to be the process that leads to cataplexy.

Two other characteristics distinguish people who have narcolepsy (Ahmed & Thorpy, 2012). They commonly report *sleep paralysis*, a brief period after awakening when they can't move or speak that is often frightening to those who go through it. The last characteristic of narcolepsy is *hypnagogic hallucinations*, vivid and often terrifying experiences that begin at the start of sleep and are said to be unbelievably realistic because they include not only visual aspects but also touch, hearing, and even the sensation of body movement. Narcolepsy is relatively rare, occurring in 0.03% to 0.16% of the population, with the numbers approximately equal among males and females. Although some cases have been reported in young children, the problems associated with narcolepsy usually are first seen during the teenage years. Excessive sleepiness usually occurs first, with cataplexy appearing either at the same time or with a delay of up to 30 years. Fortunately, the cataplexy, hypnagogic hallucinations, and sleep paralysis often decrease in frequency over time, although sleepiness during the day does not seem to diminish with age.

Specific genetic models of narcolepsy are now being developed (Peall & Robertson, 2014). Previous research with Doberman pinschers and Labrador retrievers, which also inherit this disorder, suggests that narcolepsy is associated with a cluster of genes on chromosome 6, and it may be an autosomal recessive trait. It appears that there is a significant loss of a certain type of nerve cell (hypocretin neurons) in those with narcolepsy.

Breathing-Related Sleep Disorders

For some people, sleepiness during the day or disrupted sleep at night has a physical origin—namely, problems with breathing while asleep. In *DSM-5*, these problems are diagnosed as **breathing-related sleep disorders**. People whose breathing is interrupted during their sleep often experience numerous brief arousals throughout the night and do not feel rested even after eight or nine hours asleep (Mindell & Owens, 2015). For all of us, the muscles in the upper airway relax during sleep, constricting the passageway somewhat and making breathing a little more difficult. For some, unfortunately, breathing is constricted a great deal and may be labored (*hypoventilation*) or, in the extreme, there may be short periods (10 to 30 seconds) when they stop breathing altogether, called *sleep apnea*. Often the affected person is only minimally aware of breathing difficulties and doesn't attribute the sleep problems to the breathing. A bed partner usually notices loud snoring (which is one sign of this problem), however, or will have noticed frightening episodes of interrupted breathing. Other signs that a person has breathing difficulties are heavy sweating during the night, morning headaches, and episodes of falling asleep during the day *(sleep attacks)* with no resulting feeling of being rested (Overeem & Reading, 2010).

There are three types of apnea, each with different causes, daytime complaints, and treatment: obstructive, central, and mixed sleep apnea. *Obstructive sleep apnea hypopnea syndrome* occurs when airflow stops despite continued activity by the respiratory system (Mbata & Chukwuka, 2012). In some people, the airway is too narrow; in others, some abnormality or damage interferes with the ongoing effort to breathe. Everyone in a group of people with obstructive sleep apnea hypopnea syndrome reported snoring at night (Goel, Talwar, & Jain, 2015). Obesity is sometimes associated with this problem, as is increasing age. Obstructive sleep apnea is most common in males and is thought to occur in approximately 20% of the population (Franklin & Lindberg, 2015).

The second type of apnea, *central sleep apnea*, involves the complete cessation of respiratory activity for brief periods and is often associated with certain central nervous system disorders, such as cerebral vascular disease, head trauma, and degenerative disorders (Badr, 2012). Unlike people with obstructive sleep apnea hypopnea syndrome, those with central sleep apnea wake up frequently during the night but they tend not to report excessive daytime sleepiness and often are not aware of having a serious breathing problem. Because of the lack of daytime symptoms, people tend not to seek treatment, so we know relatively little about this disorder's prevalence or course. The third breathing disorder, *sleep-related hypoventilation*, is a

DSM 5 DISORDER CRITERIA SUMMARY
Obstructive Sleep Apnea Hypopnea

Features of obstructive sleep apnea hypopnea include the following:

- Either (1) evidence by polysomnography of at least five obstructive apneas or hypopneas per hour of sleep and either (a) nocturnal breathing disturbances (snoring, snorting/gasping, or breathing pauses or (b) daytime sleepiness, fatigue, or unrefreshing sleep despite sufficient opportunities to sleep that is not better explained by another mental disorder or medical condition
- Evidence by polysomnography of 15 or more obstructive apneas and/or hypopneas per hour of sleep regardless of accompanying symptoms.

From American Psychiatric Association. (2013). *Diagnostic and statistical manual of mental disorders* (5th ed.). Washington, DC .

DSM 5 DISORDER CRITERIA SUMMARY
Central Sleep Apnea

Features of central sleep apnea include the following:

- Evidence by polysomnography of five or more central apneas per hour of sleep.
- The disorder is not better explained by another current sleep disorder.

From American Psychiatric Association. (2013). *Diagnostic and statistical manual of mental disorders* (5th ed.). Washington, DC.

DSM 5 DISORDER CRITERIA SUMMARY
Sleep-Related Hypoventilation

Features of sleep-related hypoventilation include the following:

- Polysomnography demonstrates episodes of decreased respiration associated with elevated CO_2 levels.
- The disorder is not better explained by another current sleep disorder.

From American Psychiatric Association. (2013). *Diagnostic and statistical manual of mental disorders* (5th ed.). Washington, DC.

decrease in airflow without a complete pause in breathing. This tends to cause an increase in carbon dioxide (CO_2) levels, because insufficient air is exchanged with the environment. All these breathing difficulties interrupt sleep and result in symptoms similar to those of insomnia.

Circadian Rhythm Sleep Disorder

In the 1960s, German and French scientists identified several bodily rhythms that seem to persist without cues from the environment, rhythms that are self-regulated (Aschoff & Wever, 1962; Siffre, 1964). Because these rhythms don't exactly match our 24-hour day, they are called circadian (from *circa* meaning "about" and *dian* meaning "day"). If our circadian rhythms don't match the 24-hour day, why isn't our sleep completely disrupted over time?

Fortunately, our brains have a mechanism that keeps us in sync with the outside world. Our biological clock is in the *suprachiasmatic nucleus* in the hypothalamus. Connected to the suprachiasmatic nucleus is a pathway that comes from our eyes. The light we see in the morning and the decreasing light at night signal the brain to reset the biological clock each day. Unfortunately, some people have trouble sleeping when they want to because of problems

narcolepsy Sleep disorder involving sudden and irresistible sleep attacks.

breathing-related sleep disorders Sleep disruption leading to excessive sleepiness or insomnia, caused by a breathing problem such as interrupted (**sleep apnea**) or labored (hypoventilation) breathing.

with their circadian rhythms. The causes may be outside the person (e.g., crossing several time zones in a short amount of time) or internal. A **circadian rhythm sleep disorder** is characterized by disturbed sleep (either insomnia or excessive sleepiness during the day) brought on by the brain's inability to synchronize its sleep patterns with the current patterns of day and night.

There are several types of circadian rhythm sleep disorders. *Jet lag type* is, as its name implies, caused by rapidly crossing multiple time zones (Abbott, Soca, & Zee, 2014). People with jet lag usually report difficulty going to sleep at the proper time and feeling fatigued during the day. Traveling more than two time zones westward usually affects people the most. Traveling eastward and/or less than three time zones are usually tolerated better (Kolla, Auger, & Morgenthaler, 2012). Research with mice suggests that the effects of jet lag can be quite serious—at least among older adults. When older mice were exposed to repeated artificial jet lag, a significant number of them lived shorter lives (Davidson *et al.*, 2006), and artificial jet lag has also been shown to increase cancer risk in mice (van Dycke *et al.*, 2015). *Shift work type* sleep problems are associated with work schedules (Abbott *et al.*, 2012). Many people, such as hospital employees, police, or emergency personnel, work at night or must work irregular hours; as a result, they may have problems sleeping or experience excessive sleepiness during waking hours. Unfortunately, the problems of working (and thus staying awake) at unusual times can go beyond sleep and may contribute to cardiovascular disease, ulcers, and breast cancer in women (Truong *et al.*, 2014). Working rotating shifts is consistently predictive of poor sleep (Linton *et al.*, 2015).

In contrast with jet lag and shift work sleep-related problems, which have external causes, several circadian rhythm sleep disorders seem to arise from within the person experiencing the problems. Extreme night owls, people who stay up late and sleep late, may have a problem known as *delayed sleep phase type*, where sleep is delayed or there is a later than normal bedtime. At the other extreme, people with an *advanced sleep phase type* of circadian rhythm disorder are "early to bed and early to rise." Here, sleep is advanced or earlier than normal bedtime. Finally, two other types, *irregular sleep–wake type* (people who experience highly varied sleep cycles) and *non-24-hour sleep–wake type* (e.g., sleeping on a 25- or 26-hour cycle with later and later bedtimes ultimately going throughout the day), illustrate the diversity of circadian rhythm sleep–wake problems.

Research on why our sleep rhythms are disrupted is advancing at a great pace, and we are beginning to understand the circadian rhythm process. Scientists believe the hormone *melatonin* contributes to the setting of our biological clocks that tell us when to sleep. This hormone is produced by the pineal gland in the center of the brain. When our eyes see that it is nighttime, this information is passed on to the pineal gland, which, in turn, begins producing melatonin. Researchers believe that both light and melatonin help set the biological clock (Stevens & Zhu, 2015).

8.4 Concept CHECK

Match the following descriptions of sleeping problems with the correct term: (a) cataplexy, (b) hypersomnolence disorder, (c) insomnia disorder, (d) sleep apnea, (e) sleep paralysis, (f) narcolepsy, (g) circadian rhythm sleep disorder, and (h) breathing-related sleep disorder:

1. Timothy wakes up frequently every night because he feels he is about to hyperventilate. He can't seem to get enough air, and many times his wife will wake him to tell him to quit snoring. He is suffering from a(n) _____.

2. Sonia has problems staying awake throughout the day. Even while talking on the phone or riding the bus, she unexpectedly loses muscle tone and falls asleep. This is due to _____.

3. Jaime sometimes awakens and cannot move or speak. This is a frightening experience known as _____.

4. Brett has started a new job that requires him to change shifts monthly. He sometimes has day shifts and at other times has night shifts. Since then he has had considerable trouble sleeping. _____

5. Rama is extremely overweight. His wife suspects he may be suffering from _____ because he snores every night and often wakes up exhausted.

6. Melinda sleeps all night and still finds herself falling asleep throughout the next day. This happens even when she goes to bed early and gets up as late as possible. _____

DSM 5 DISORDER CRITERIA SUMMARY
Circadian Rhythm Sleep–Wake Disorders

Features of circadian rhythm sleep–wake disorders include the following:

- A persistent or recurrent pattern of sleep disruption that is primarily due to an alteration of the circadian system or to a misalignment between the endogenous circadian rhythm and the sleep–wake schedule required by an individual's physical environment or social or professional schedule.

- The sleep disruption leads to excessive sleepiness or insomnia, or both.

- The sleep disturbance causes clinically significant distress or impairment in social, occupational, and other important areas of functioning.

From American Psychiatric Association. (2013). *Diagnostic and statistical manual of mental disorders* (5th ed.). Washington, DC.

When we can't fall asleep or when we awaken frequently or when sleep does not restore our energy and vitality, we need help. A number of biological and psychological interventions have been designed and evaluated to help people regain the benefits of normal sleep.

Medical Treatments

People who complain of insomnia to a medical professional are likely prescribed one of several benzodiazepine or related medications. Short-acting drugs (those that cause only brief drowsiness) are preferred because long-acting drugs sometimes do not stop working by morning and people report more daytime sleepiness. The long-acting medications are sometimes preferred when negative effects such as daytime anxiety are observed in people taking the short-acting drugs (Neubauer, 2009). Newer medications, such as those that work directly with the melatonin system (e.g., ramelteon [Rozerem]), are also being developed to help people fall and stay asleep. People over the age of 65 are most likely to use medication to help them sleep, although people of all ages, including young children (Durand, 2008), have been prescribed medications for insomnia.

There are several drawbacks to medical treatments for insomnia. First, benzodiazepine medications can cause excessive sleepiness. Second, people can easily become dependent on them and misuse them, deliberately or not. Third, these medications are meant for short-term treatment no longer than four weeks. Longer use can cause dependence and rebound insomnia. A newer concern for some medications (e.g., Ambien) is that they may increase the likelihood of sleepwalking-related problems, such as sleep-related eating disorder (Nzwalo, Ferreira, Peralta, & Bentes, 2013). Therefore, although medications may be helpful for sleep problems that will correct themselves in a short period (e.g., insomnia because of anxiety related to hospitalization), they are not intended for long-term chronic problems.

To help people with hypersomnolence or narcolepsy, physicians usually prescribe a stimulant such as methylphenidate (Ritalin) or modafinil (Nevsimalova, 2009). Cataplexy, or loss of muscle tone, can be treated with antidepressants, not because people with narcolepsy are depressed but because antidepressants suppress REM (or dream) sleep. Also, sodium oxybate is recommended to treat cataplexy (Bogan, Roth, Schwartz, & Miloslavsky, 2014).

Treatment of breathing-related sleep disorders focuses on helping the person breathe better during sleep. For some, this means recommending weight loss. In some people who are obese, the neck's soft tissue compresses the airways. Unfortunately, voluntary weight loss is rarely successful in the long term; as a result, it is not an adequate standalone treatment for breathing-related sleep disorders (Anandam, Akinnusi, Kufel, Porhomayon, & El-Solh, 2013).

The gold standard for the treatment of obstructive sleep apnea involves a mechanical device—called the continuous positive air pressure (CPAP) machine—that improves breathing (Patel, White, Malhotra, Stanchina, & Ayas, 2003). Patients wear a mask that provides slightly pressurized air during sleep and it helps them breathe more normally throughout the night. Unfortunately, many people have difficulty using the device because of issues of comfort, and some even experience a form of claustrophobia. Severe breathing problems may require surgery to help remove blockages in airways.

An interesting treatment for people with mild apnea was developed by researchers in collaboration with a Swiss didgeridoo instructor. A didgeridoo is a long instrument constructed from tree limbs hollowed out by termites. The instructor observed that people who practiced this instrument had less daytime sleepiness. Evidence points to the effectiveness of several months of daily practice using this instrument in improving the sleep of people with interrupted breathing (Puhan *et al.*, 2006; Sutherland & Cistulli, 2015).

Environmental Treatments

Because medication as a primary treatment isn't usually recommended, other ways of getting people back in step with their sleep rhythms are usually tried. One general principle for treating circadian rhythm disorders is that *phase delays* (moving bedtime later) are easier than *phase advances* (moving bedtime earlier). In other words, it is easier to stay up several hours later than usual than to force yourself to go to sleep several hours earlier. Scheduling shift changes in a clockwise direction (going from day to evening schedule) seems to help workers adjust better. People can best readjust their sleep patterns by going to bed several hours later each night until bedtime is at the desired hour (Sack *et al.*, 2007). A drawback of this approach is that it requires the person to sleep during the day for several days, which is difficult for people with regularly scheduled responsibilities.

Another strategy to help people with sleep problems involves using bright light to trick the brain into readjusting the biological clock. Research indicates that bright light (also referred to as *phototherapy*) may help people with circadian rhythm problems readjust their sleep patterns (Burkhalter *et al.*, 2015).

....

circadian rhythm sleep disorder Sleep disturbances resulting in sleepiness or insomnia, caused by the body's inability to synchronize its sleep patterns with the current pattern of day and night.

Psychological Treatments

Limitations of using medication to help people sleep better have led to the development of psychological treatments. Table 8.3 describes some psychological approaches to insomnia.

Research shows that some psychological treatments for insomnia may be more effective than others. For adult sleep problems, stimulus control may be recommended. People are instructed to use the bedroom only for sleeping and for sex and *not* for work or other anxiety-provoking activities (e.g., watching the news on television). Progressive relaxation or sleep hygiene (changing daily habits that may interfere with sleep) alone may not be as effective as stimulus control alone for some people (Means & Edinger, 2006). Because sleep problems are so widespread, there is a growing interest in developing internet-based treatments to determine if certain sufferers can help themselves with appropriate guidance. One study, for example, randomly assigned adults to a control group or an internet-based education group (Ritterband *et al.*, 2009). The internet group received online instruction on the proper use of several of the psychological treatments (e.g., sleep restriction, stimulus control, sleep hygiene, cognitive restructuring, and relapse prevention). The findings were striking, suggesting that not only could the treatment be delivered over the internet but also that sleep improved in this group even six months later. Under certain circumstances people are able to use *evidence-based instruction* (education on the use of a treatment that has empirical support) to improve a variety of psychological problems.

Often, psychological treatment of insomnia takes the form of a "package" of different skills known as cognitive-behavioral therapy for insomnia (CBT-i; Trauer, Qian, Doyle, Rajaratnam, & Cunnington, 2015). Such

was the case for Sonja, the student we profiled in the beginning of this section, who was helped with her sleep problems using several techniques. She was instructed to limit her time in bed to about four hours of sleep time (sleep restriction), about the amount of time she slept each night. The period was lengthened when she began to sleep through the night. Sonja was also asked not to do any schoolwork while in bed and to get out of bed if she couldn't fall asleep within 15 minutes (stimulus control). Finally, therapy involved confronting her unrealistic expectations about how much sleep was enough for a person of her age (cognitive therapy). Within about three weeks of treatment, Sonja was sleeping longer (six to seven hours per night as opposed to four to five hours previously) and had fewer interruptions in her sleep. Also, she felt more refreshed in the morning and had more energy during the day. Sonja's results mirror those of studies that find combined treatments to be effective in older adults with insomnia (Savard, Savard, & Morin, 2011). One study found that CBT may be more successful treating sleep disorders in older adults than a medical (drug) intervention (Siddiqui & D'Ambrosio, 2012). In contrast, a recent review of insomnia treatments found almost no differences in the effectiveness of drug interventions compared to CBT interventions, except that behavioral interventions more effectively reduced sleep latency (the time it takes to fall asleep) (Smith *et al.*, 2014).

For young children, some cognitive treatments may not be possible. Instead, treatment often includes setting up bedtime routines such as a bath, followed by a parent reading a story, to help children go to sleep at night. Graduated extinction (described in Table 8.3) has been used with some success for bedtime problems, as well as for waking up at night (Durand, 2014; Hill, 2011).

TABLE 8.3 | Psychological Treatments for Insomnia

Sleep Treatment	Description
Cognitive	This approach focuses on changing the sleepers' unrealistic expectations and beliefs about sleep ("If I get less than eight hours of sleep, it will make me ill"). The therapist attempts to alter beliefs and attitudes about sleeping by providing information on topics such as normal amounts of sleep and a person's ability to compensate for lost sleep.
Guided Imagery Relaxation	This approach uses meditation or imagery to help with relaxation at bedtime or after a night waking.
Graduated Extinction	Used for children who have tantrums at bedtime or wake up crying at night, this treatment instructs the parent to check on the child after progressively longer periods until the child falls asleep on his or her own.
Paradoxical Intention	This technique involves instructing individuals in the opposite behavior from the desired outcome. Telling poor sleepers to lie in bed and try to stay awake as long as they can is used to try to relieve the performance anxiety surrounding efforts to try to fall asleep.
Progressive Relaxation	This technique involves relaxing the muscles of the body in an effort to introduce drowsiness.

Preventing Sleep Disorders

Sleep professionals generally agree that a significant portion of the sleep problems people experience daily can be prevented by following a few steps during the day. Referred to as *sleep hygiene*, these changes in lifestyle can be relatively simple to follow and can help avoid problems such as insomnia for some people (Goodman & Scott, 2012). Some sleep hygiene recommendations rely on allowing the brain's normal drive for sleep to take over, replacing the restrictions we place on our activities that interfere with sleep. For example, setting a regular time to go to sleep and awaken each day can help make falling asleep at night easier. Avoiding the use of caffeine and nicotine—which are both stimulants—can also help prevent problems such as nighttime awakening. Table 8.4 illustrates a number of the sleep hygiene steps recommended for preventing sleep problems. Although there is little controlled prospective research on preventing sleep disorders, practicing good sleep hygiene appears to be among the most promising techniques available.

Parasomnias and Their Treatment

Parasomnias are not problems with sleep itself but abnormal events that occur either during sleep or during that twilight time between sleeping and waking. Some events

TABLE 8.4 | Good Sleep Habits

Establish a set bedtime routine.
Develop a regular bedtime and a regular time to awaken.
Eliminate all foods and drinks that contain caffeine six hours before bedtime.
Limit any use of alcohol or tobacco.
Try drinking milk before bedtime.
Eat a balanced diet, limiting fat.
Go to bed only when sleepy and get out of bed if you are unable to fall asleep or back to sleep after 15 minutes.
Do not exercise or participate in vigorous activities in the hours before bedtime.
Do include a weekly program of exercise during the day.
Restrict activities in bed to those that help induce sleep.
Reduce noise and light in the bedroom.
Increase exposure to natural and bright light during the day.
Avoid extreme temperature changes in the bedroom (that is, too hot or too cold).

SOURCE: Adapted, with permission, from Durand, V. M. (2014). Good sleep habits. In V. M. Durand (Ed.), *Sleep better: A guide to improving sleep for children with special needs* (p. 60). Baltimore: Paul H. Brookes.

associated with parasomnia are not unusual if they happen while you are awake (e.g., walking to the kitchen to look into the refrigerator) but can be distressing if they take place while you are sleeping.

DSM-5 identifies a number of different parasomnias (American Psychiatric Association, 2013). As you might have guessed, **nightmares** (or nightmare disorder) occur during REM or dream sleep (Augedal, Hansen, Kronhaug, Harvey, & Pallesen, 2013). About 10% to 50% of children and about 9% to 30% of adults experience them regularly (Schredl, 2010). To qualify as a nightmare disorder, according to *DSM-5* criteria, these experiences must be so distressful that they impair a person's ability to carry on normal activities (such as making a person too anxious to try to sleep at night). Some researchers distinguish nightmares from bad dreams by whether or not you wake up as a result. Nightmares are defined as disturbing dreams that awaken the sleeper; bad dreams are those that do not awaken the person experiencing them. Based on this definition, college students report an average of 30 bad dreams and 10 nightmares per year (Zadra & Donderi, 2000).

Nightmares are thought to be influenced by genetics (Barclay & Gregory, 2013), trauma, medication use, and are associated with some psychological disorders (e.g., substance abuse, anxiety, borderline personality disorder, and schizophrenia spectrum disorders) (Augedal *et al.*, 2013). Research on the treatment of nightmares suggests that both psychological intervention (e.g., cognitive-behavioral therapy) and pharmacological treatment (i.e., prazosin) can help reduce these unpleasant sleep events (Augedal *et al.*, 2013; Aurora *et al.*, 2010).

Disorder of arousal includes a number of motor movements and behaviors during NREM sleep such as sleepwalking, sleep terrors, and incomplete awakening. **Sleep terrors**, which most commonly afflict children, usually begin with a piercing scream. The child is extremely upset, often sweating, and frequently has a rapid heartbeat. On the surface, sleep terrors appear to resemble nightmares—the child cries and appears frightened—but they occur during NREM sleep and therefore are not caused by frightening dreams. During sleep terrors, children cannot be easily awakened and comforted, as they can during a nightmare. Children do not remember sleep terrors, despite their often dramatic effect on the observer (Durand, 2008). As many as one-third of 18-month-old children may experience sleep terrors, but this number drops to 13% by age five and just 5% by age

nightmares Frightening and anxiety-provoking dreams occurring during **rapid eye movement sleep**. The individual recalls the bad dreams and recovers alertness and orientation quickly.

disorder of arousal Category of sleep disorder during NREM sleep that includes **sleepwalking** and **sleep terrors**.

sleep terrors Episodes of apparent awakening from sleep, accompanied by signs of **panic**, followed by disorientation and amnesia for the incident. These occur during **nonrapid eye movement sleep** and so do not involve frightening dreams.

13 (Petit *et al.*, 2015). We know relatively little about sleep terrors, although several theories have been proposed—including the possibility of a genetic component, because the disorder tends to occur in families (Durand, 2008). Treatment for sleep terrors usually begins with a recommendation to wait and see if they disappear on their own.

One approach to reducing chronic sleep terrors is the use of *scheduled awakenings*. In the first controlled study of its kind, Durand and Mindell (1999) instructed parents of children who were experiencing almost nightly sleep terrors to awaken their child briefly approximately 30 minutes before a typical episode (these usually occur around the same time each evening). This simple technique, which was faded out over several weeks, was successful in almost eliminating these disturbing events.

It might surprise you to learn that **sleepwalking** (also called **somnambulism**) occurs during NREM sleep (Perrault, Carrier, Desautels, Montplaisir, & Zadra, 2014). This means that when people walk in their sleep, they are probably not acting out a dream. This parasomnia typically occurs during the first few hours while a person is in the deep stages of sleep. The *DSM-5* criteria for sleepwalking require that the person leave the bed, although less active episodes can involve small motor behaviors, such as sitting up in bed and picking at the blanket or gesturing. Because sleepwalking occurs during the deepest stages of sleep, waking someone during an episode is difficult; if the person is wakened, she typically will not remember what has happened. It is not true, however, that waking a sleepwalker is somehow dangerous. Sleepwalking is primarily a problem during childhood, affecting more than 10% of school-aged children (Petit *et al.*, 2015), but a small proportion of adults are affected. Mostly, the course of sleepwalking is short, and few people over the age of 15 continue to exhibit this parasomnia.

We do not yet clearly understand why some people sleepwalk, although factors such as extreme fatigue, previous sleep deprivation, the use of sedative or hypnotic drugs, and stress have been implicated (Shatkin & Ivanenko, 2009). On occasion, sleepwalking episodes have been associated with violent behavior, including homicide and suicide (Cartwright, 2006). In one case, a man drove to his in-laws' house, succeeded in killing his mother-in-law, and attempted to kill his father-in-law. He was acquitted of the charges of murder, using sleepwalking as his legal defense (Broughton, Billings, & Cartwright, 1994). These cases are still controversial, although there is evidence for the legitimacy of some violent behavior coinciding with sleepwalking episodes. There also seems to be a genetic component to sleepwalking, with a higher incidence observed and within families (Petit *et al.*, 2015).

A related disorder, *nocturnal eating syndrome,* is when individuals rise from their beds and eat while they are still asleep (Yamada, 2015). This problem, which is different from the *night eating syndrome* discussed earlier in the chapter in the eating disorders section, may be more frequent than previously thought; it was found in almost 6% of individuals in one study who were referred because of insomnia complaints (Manni, Ratti, & Tartara, 1997; Winkelman, 2006). Another uncommon parasomnia is *sexsomnia*; acting out sexual behaviors such as masturbation and sexual intercourse with no memory of the event (Béjot *et al.*, 2010). This rare problem can cause relationship problems and, in extreme cases, legal problems when cases occur without consent or with minors (Howell, 2012; Schenck, Arnulf, & Mahowald, 2007).

There is an increasing awareness that sleep is important for both our mental and our physical well-being. Sleep problems are also comorbid with many other disorders and therefore can compound the difficulties of people with significant psychological difficulties. Researchers are coming

8.5 Concept CHECK

Diagnose the sleep problems of these cases using one of the following: (a) nocturnal eating syndrome, (b) sleep terrors, and (c) nightmares:

1. Jaclyn's dad is sometimes awakened by his daughter's screams. He runs to Jaclyn's room to comfort her and is eventually able to calm her down. Jaclyn usually explains that she was being chased by a big, one-eyed, purple monster. The events typically happen after watching scary movies with friends. _____

2. Sho-jen's parents hear her piercing screams on many nights and rush to comfort her, but she does not respond. During these episodes, her heart rate is elevated, and her pajamas are soaked in sweat. When she gets up the next day, she has no memory of the experience. _____

3. Jack has made a serious commitment to his diet for more than a month but continues to gain weight. He has no memory of eating but noticed that food is always missing from the refrigerator. _____

DSM 5 CONTROVERSY Binge Eating Disorder

Binge-eating disorder is a new diagnosis in *DSM-5*, but as with most new disorders, some controversy has surrounded its inclusion. Alan J. Frances, the psychiatrist who chaired the task force that created *DSM-IV*, has criticized binge-eating disorder as he has many of the new disorders introduced into *DSM-5*. He notes that the history of our system of nosology in mental health has been littered with fad diagnoses that in retrospect have done more harm than good (Frances, 2012). And, in his view, binge-eating disorder may be one of those fads. He notes that eating excessively at least 12 times over a period of three months (part of the criteria for binge-eating disorder on page 000) could really be considered just a manifestation of modern-day gluttony caused by the easy availability

of great-tasting food (Frances, 2012). How many of us have "overeaten" approximately once a week over the past month? If you continued that for three months, you might be eligible for this diagnosis.

But look again at the description of binge-eating disorder. Notice that only a small minority of individuals who are obese and have joined commercial weight control programs to deal with their problem also evidence binge-eating. Notice also that the percentage of obese individuals who binge rises considerably in groups who are so severely obese that they would be candidates for bariatric surgery. Also note that these individuals, but not those who are obese without bingeing, share the same concerns about shape and weight as people with anorexia

and bulimia, and their binging is often driven by attempts to alleviate bad moods. This, along with other factors such as the tendency of binge-eating to run in families and have a heritable component and its responsiveness to the same types of treatments effective for other eating disorders (something that is not the case for individuals who are obese without bingeing), was sufficient to convince the eating disorders workgroup and the *DSM-5* task force that this condition should be a diagnosis. With this designation, this condition will now achieve greater recognition and its treatment can be reimbursed by health insurance, thereby increasing the likelihood that individuals suffering from this disorder will receive appropriate care. •

closer to understanding the basic nature of sleep and its disorders, and we anticipate significant treatment advances in the years to come.

sleepwalking (somnambulism) Parasomnia that involves leaving the bed during **nonrapid eye movement sleep**. See also **somnambulism**.

Bulimia Nervosa, Binge-Eating Disorder, and Anorexia Nervosa

▶ The prevalence of eating disorders has increased rapidly over the past half century. As a result, they were included for the first time as a separate group of disorders in *DSM-IV*.

What are the defining features of bulimia nervosa, binge-eating disorder, and anorexia nervosa?

▶ There are three prevalent eating disorders. In bulimia nervosa, dieting results in out-of-control binge-eating episodes that are often followed by purging the food through vomiting or other means. In binge-eating disorder, a pattern of binge-eating is not followed by purging. Anorexia nervosa, in which food intake is cut dramatically, results in substantial weight loss and sometimes dangerously low body weight.

▶ Bulimia nervosa and anorexia nervosa are largely confined to young women in developed countries who are pursuing a thin body shape that is culturally mandated and biologically inappropriate, making it extremely difficult to achieve.

▶ Without treatment, eating disorders become chronic and can, on occasion, result in death.

Causes of Eating Disorders

What social, psychological, and neurobiological factors might cause eating disorders?

▶ In addition to sociocultural pressures, causal factors include possible biological and genetic vulnerabilities (the disorders tend to run in families), psychological factors (low self-esteem), social anxiety (fears of rejection), and distorted body image (relatively normal-weight individuals view themselves as fat and ugly).

Treatment of Eating Disorders

How does the use of medications compare with psychological therapies for the treatment of eating disorders?

▶ Several psychosocial treatments are effective, including cognitive-behavioral approaches combined with family therapy and interpersonal psychotherapy. Drug treatments are less effective at the current time.

Obesity

What are some possible causes of obesity?
What treatments are available?

▶ Obesity is not a disorder in *DSM* but is one of the more dangerous epidemics confronting the world today. Cultural norms that encourage eating high-fat foods combine with genetic and other factors to cause obesity, which is difficult to treat.

▶ Professionally directed behavior modification programs emphasizing diet and exercise are moderately successful, but prevention effort in the form of changes in government policy on nutrition seem the most promising.

Sleep–Wake Disorders

What are the critical diagnostic features of the major sleep–wake disorders?

▶ Sleep–wake disorders are highly prevalent in the general population and are of two types: dyssomnias (disturbances of sleep) and parasomnias (abnormal events such as nightmares and sleepwalking that occur during sleep).

▶ Of the dyssomnias, the most common disorder, insomnia disorder, involves the inability to initiate sleep, problems maintaining sleep, or failure to feel refreshed after a full night's sleep. Other dyssomnias include hypersomnolence (excessive sleep), narcolepsy (sudden and irresistible sleep attacks), circadian rhythm sleep disorders (sleepiness or insomnia caused by the body's inability to synchronize its sleep patterns with day and night), and breathing-related sleep disorders (disruptions that have a physical origin, such as sleep apnea, that leads to excessive sleepiness or insomnia).

▶ The formal assessment of sleep disorders, a polysomnographic evaluation, is typically done by monitoring the heart, muscles, respiration, brain waves, and other functions of a sleeping client in the lab. In addition to such monitoring, it is helpful to determine the individual's sleep efficiency, a percentage based on the time the individual actually sleeps as opposed to time spent in bed trying to sleep.

What medical and psychological treatments are used for the treatment of sleep disorders?

▶ Benzodiazepine medications have been helpful for short-term treatment of many of the dyssomnias, but they must be used carefully or they might cause rebound insomnia, a withdrawal experience that can cause worse sleep problems after the medication is stopped. Any long-term treatment of sleep problems should include psychological interventions such as stimulus control and sleep hygiene.

How are rapid eye movement and nonrapid eye movement sleep related to the parasomnias?

▶ Parasomnias such as nightmares occur during rapid eye movement (or dream) sleep, and sleep terrors and sleepwalking occur during nonrapid eye movement sleep.

■ Key Terms

bulimia nervosa, 283
binge, 283
anorexia nervosa, 283
binge-eating disorder (BED), 283
obesity, 284
purging techniques, 285
night eating syndrome, 303
bariatric surgery, 305
rapid eye movement (REM) sleep, 306
dyssomnias, 306

parasomnias, 306
polysomnographic (PSG) evaluation, 306
actigraph, 307
sleep efficiency (SE), 308
microsleeps, 308
insomnia disorder, 308
primary insomnia, 308
rebound insomnia, 310
hypersomnolence disorders, 311

sleep apnea, 311
narcolepsy, 312
breathing-related sleep disorders, 312
circadian rhythm sleep disorders, 314
nightmares, 317
disorder of arousal, 317
sleep terrors, 317
sleepwalking (somnambulism), 318

Answers to Concept Checks

8.1

1. c; 2. a; 3. a; 4. b

8.2

1. T; 2. T; 3. F (females find a smaller size more attractive than do men);

4. F (they help with bulimia nervosa, not anorexia); 5. T; 6. T

8.3

1. T; 2. F (it's at least one third or more); 3. F; 4. T

8.4

1. h; 2. f; 3. e; 4. g; 5. d; 6. b

8.5

1. c; 2. b; 3. a

Chapter Quiz

1. It is estimated that _____ of individuals with eating disorders die as a result of the disorder, with as many as 50% of those deaths coming from _____.
   a. 20%; homicide
   b. 20%; suicide
   c. 50%; homicide
   d. 50%; suicide

2. Dr. Thompson sees a patient with a chubby face, calluses on her fingers, and small scars on the back of her hand. Tests indicate that the patient weighs slightly more than her expected weight and that she has an electrolyte imbalance. The patient reports that she is having persistent constipation and that she feels as if her heart has been skipping beats. These symptoms are consistent with:
   a. depression
   b. anxiety
   c. anorexia nervosa
   d. bulimia nervosa

3. Research on bulimia nervosa suggests that it most often co-occurs with:
   a. anxiety disorders
   b. mood disorders

   c. psychotic disorders
   d. substance use disorders

4. The typical age of onset for anorexia nervosa and bulimia nervosa is _____, with younger cases of anorexia tending to begin at _____ and younger cases of bulimia tending to begin at _____.
   a. 30; 25; 20
   b. 20; 15; 10
   c. 15; 10; 5
   d. 15; 13; 12

5. In a study by Fallon and Rozin, female undergraduates:
   a. rated their current body size the same as the ideal body size
   b. rated the ideal body size smaller than the attractive body size
   c. rated the ideal body size heavier than the attractive body size
   d. rated their current body size smaller than the ideal body size

6. Which of the following statements is true of cognitive–behavioral therapy (CBT) and interpersonal therapy (IPT) in the treatment of bulimia?

a. CBT appears to work faster than IPT, but they both seem to have the same positive effect at a one-year follow-up.

b. CBT and IPT appear to have the same impact in both the short term and the long term.

c. IPT appears to work faster than CBT, but they both seem to have the same positive effect at a one-year follow-up.

d. Neither CBT nor IPT appears to be effective in the treatment of bulimia.

7. Which of the following is used to measure arm movements as an indicator of sleep activity and sleep quality?

a. electrocardiogram

b. electromyograph

c. electroencephalograph

d. actigraph

8. While sleeping, Michael, a 55-year-old overweight male, experiences a cessation in his breathing for short periods. Michael's wife reports that he snores continuously and never feels rested. Michael's symptoms are consistent with:

a. narcolepsy

b. sleep apnea

c. sleep–wake schedule disorder

d. cataplexy

9. Mr. Dunn has been experiencing insomnia for several weeks. His doctor recommends that he only lie in bed for three hours, the amount of time that he actually sleeps each night. The amount of time Mr. Dunn lies in bed is then increased as he begins to sleep more. This treatment is known as:

a. sleep hygiene

b. sleep restriction

c. phase delay

d. progressive relaxation

10. The primary difference between sleep terrors and nightmares is:

a. sleep terrors usually begin with a scream

b. children do not remember nightmares

c. sleep terrors occur during NREM sleep

d. sleep terrors are more prevalent in the population

(See Appendix A for answers.)

Exploring Eating Disorders

Individuals with eating disorders:

◗ Feel a relentless, all-encompassing drive to be thin

◗ Are overwhelmingly young females from middle- to upper-class families, who live in socially competitive environments

◗ Lived only in Western countries until recently

Psychological—Diminished sense of personal control and self-confidence, causing low self-esteem. Distorted body image.

Social—Cultural and social emphasis on slender ideal, leading to body dissatisfaction and pre-occupation with food and eating.

Causes

Biological—Possible genetic tendency to poor impulse control, emotional instability, and perfectionistic traits

EATING DISORDERS

Disorder	Characteristics	Treatment
Bulimia Nervosa	■ Out-of-control consumption of excessive amounts of mostly non-nutritious food within a short time ■ Elimination of food through self-induced vomiting and/or abuse of laxatives or diuretics ■ To compensate for binges, some bulimics exercise excessively or fast between binges ■ Vomiting may enlarge salivary glands (causing a chubby face), erode dental enamel, and cause electrolyte imbalance resulting in cardiac failure or kidney problems ■ Weight usually within 10% of normal ■ Age of onset is typically 18 to 21 years of age, although it can be as early as 10	■ Drug treatment, such as antidepressants ■ Short-term cognitive-behavioral therapy (CBT) to address behavior and attitudes on eating and body shape ■ Interpersonal psychotherapy (IPT) to improve interpersonal functioning ■ Tends to be chronic if left untreated
Anorexia Nervosa	■ Intense fear of obesity and persistent pursuit of thinness; perpetual dissatisfaction with weight loss ■ Severe caloric restriction, often with excessive exercise and sometimes with purging, to the point of semistarvation ■ Severely limiting caloric intake may cause cessation of menstruation, downy hair on limbs and cheeks, dry skin, brittle hair or nails, sensitivity to cold, and danger of acute cardiac or kidney failure ■ Weight at least 15% below normal ■ Average age of onset is between 18 and 21 years of age, with younger cases tending to begin at 15	■ Hospitalization (at 70% below normal weight) ■ Outpatient treatment to restore weight and correct dysfunctional attitudes on eating and body shape ■ Family therapy ■ Tends to be chronic if left untreated; more resistant to treatment than bulimia
Binge-Eating	■ Similar to bulimia with out-of-control food binges, but no attempt to purge the food (vomiting, laxatives, diuretics) or compensate for excessive intake ■ Marked physical and emotional stress; some sufferers binge to alleviate bad moods ■ Binge eaters share some concerns about weight and body shape as individuals with anorexia and bulimia ■ Tends to affect more older people than either bulimia or anorexia	■ Short-term CBT to address behavior and attitudes on eating and body shape ■ IPT to improve interpersonal functioning ■ Drug treatments that reduce feelings of hunger ■ Self-help approaches

Photodisc/Getty Images

Disorder	Characteristics	Treatment
Obesity	■ Up to 70% of U.S. adults are over-weight, and over 35% are obese ■ Worldwide problem; increased risk in urban rather than rural settings ■ Two forms of maladaptive eating patterns associated with obesity—binge eating and night eating syndrome ■ Increases risk of cardiovascular disease, diabetes, hypertension, stroke, and other physical problems.	■ Self-directed weight loss programs ■ Commercial self-help programs, such as Weight Watchers ■ Professionally directed behavior modification programs, which are the most effective treatment ■ Surgery, as a last resort

Stockbyte/Getty Images

Psychological—Affects impulse control, attitudes, and motivation towards eating, and responsive-ness to the consequenc-es of eating.

Social—Advancing technology promotes sedentary lifestyle and consumption of high fat foods.

Causes

Biological—Genes influence an individual's number of fat cells, tendency toward fat storage, and activity levels.

Exploring Sleep–Wake Disorders

Characterized by extreme disruption in the everyday lives of affected individuals, and are an important factor in many psychological disorders.

SLEEP–WAKE DISORDERS

Diagnosing Sleep–Wake Disorders

A polysomnographic (PSG) evaluation assesses an individual's sleep habits with various electronic tests to measure airflow, brain activity, eye movements, muscle movements, and heart activity. Results are weighed with a measure of sleep efficiency (SE), the percentage of time spent asleep.

Burger/Phanie/Science Source

Dyssomnias
Disturbances in the timing, amount, or quality of sleep

Disorder	Characteristics	Causes	Treatment
Insomnia Disorder	■ Characteristics include difficulty initiating sleep, difficulty maintaining sleep, or nonrestorative sleep.	■ Causes include pain, insufficient exercise, drug use, environmental influences, anxiety, respiratory problems, and biological vulnerability.	■ Treatment may be medical (benzodiazepines) or psychological (anxiety reduction, improved sleep hygiene); combined approach is usually most effective.
Narcolepsy	■ Characteristics include sudden daytime onset of REM sleep combined with cataplexy, a rapid loss of muscle tone that can be quite mild or result in complete collapse. Often accompanied by sleep paralysis and/or hypnagogic hallucinations.	■ Causes are likely to be genetic.	■ Treatment is medical (stimulant drugs).
Hypersomnolence Disorder	■ Characteristics include abnormally excessive sleep and sleepiness, and involuntary daytime sleeping. Classified as a disorder only when it's subjectively perceived as disruptive.	■ Causes may involve genetic link and/or excess serotonin.	■ Treatment is usually medical (stimulant drugs).
Breathing-Related Sleep Disorders	■ Characteristics include disturbed sleep and daytime fatigue resulting from hypoventilation (labored breathing) or sleep apnea (suspended breathing).	■ Causes may include narrow or obstructed airway, obesity, and increasing age.	■ Treatment using continuous positive air pressure (CPAP) machines is the gold standard; weight loss is also often prescribed.
Circadian Rhythm Sleep–Wake Disorders	■ Characteristics include sleepiness or insomnia.	■ Caused by inability to synchronize sleep patterns with current pattern of day and night due to jet lag, shift work, delayed sleep, or advanced sleep (going to bed earlier than normal bedtime).	■ Treatment includes phase delays to adjust bedtime and bright light to readjust biological clock.

Parasomnias
Abnormal behaviors that occur during sleep.

Nightmares

Frightening REM dreams that awaken the sleeper. Nightmares qualify as nightmare disorder when they are stressful enough to impair normal functioning. Causes are unknown, but they tend to decrease with age.

Royalty-Free/Corbis

Sleep Terrors

Occur during non-REM (nondreaming) sleep and most commonly afflict children. Sleeping child screams, cries, sweats, sometimes walks, has rapid heartbeat, and cannot easily be awakened or comforted. More common in boys than girls, and possible genetic link since they tend to run in families. May subside with time.

Sleepwalking

Occurs at least once during non-REM sleep in 15% to 30% of children under age 15. Causes may include extreme fatigue, sleep deprivation, sedative or hypnotic drugs, and stress. Adult sleepwalking is usually associated with other psychological disorders. May have a genetic link.

9 Sexual Dysfunctions, Paraphilic Disorders, and Gender Dysphoria

CHAPTER OUTLINE

What Is Normal Sexuality?

Gender Differences
Cultural Differences
The Development of Sexual
    Orientation

**An Overview of Sexual
Dysfunctions**

Sexual Desire Disorders
Sexual Arousal Disorders
Orgasm Disorders
Sexual Pain Disorder
Assessing Sexual Behavior

**Causes and Treatment
of Sexual Dysfunction**

Causes of Sexual Dysfunction
Treatment of Sexual Dysfunction

**Paraphilic Disorders: Clinical
Descriptions**

Fetishistic Disorder
Voyeuristic and Exhibitionistic
    Disorders
Transvestic Disorder
Sexual Sadism and Sexual Masochism
    Disorders
Pedophilic Disorder and Incest
Paraphilic Disorders in Women
Causes of Paraphilic Disorders

**Assessing and Treating
Paraphilic Disorders**

Psychological Treatment
Drug Treatments
Summary

Gender Dysphoria

Defining Gender Dysphoria
Causes
Treatment

iStock.com/hayunne

Use scientific reasoning to interpret behavior:	▶ Identify basic biological, psychological, and social components of behavioral explanations (e.g., inferences, observations, operational definitions, and interpretations) [APA SLO 2.1a] *(see textbook pages 330–331, 339–342, 349–351, 356–357, 360–361)*
Engage in innovative and integrative thinking and problem solving:	▶ Describe problems operationally to study them empirically. [APA SLO 2.3a] *(see textbook pages 333–339, 346–350; 354–356)*
Describe applications that employ discipline-based problem solving:	▶ Correctly identify antecedents and consequences of behavior and mental processes [APA SLO 1.3c] *(see textbook pages 339–342; 350–351; 356–357)* ▶ Describe examples of relevant and practical applications of psychological principles to everyday life [APA SLO 1.3a]*(see textbook pages 334–338; 342; 346–347;349–350; 352; 354; 356–357)*

* Portions of this chapter cover learning outcomes suggested by the American Psychological Association (2013) in their guidelines for the undergraduate psychology major. Chapter coverage of these outcomes is identified above by APA Goal and APA Suggested Learning Outcome (SLO).

What Is Normal Sexuality?

▶ **How do sociocultural factors influence what are considered "normal" sexual behaviors?**

What is normal sexual behavior? As you will see, it depends. More to the point, when is sexual behavior that is somewhat different from the norm a disorder? Again, it depends. Current views tend to be quite tolerant of a variety of sexual expressions, even if they are unusual, unless the behavior is associated with a substantial impairment in functioning or involves non-consenting individuals such as children. Two kinds of sexual behavior meet this definition. Individuals with *sexual dysfunction* find it difficult to function adequately while having sex; for example, they may not become aroused or achieve orgasm. In *paraphilic disorders*, the relatively new term for sexual deviation, sexual arousal occurs primarily in the context of inappropriate objects or individuals. *Philia* refers to a strong attraction or liking, and *para* indicates the attraction is abnormal. In actuality, paraphilic disorders have little to do with sexual dysfunctions except for the fact that they both involve sexual behavior. For this reason, paraphilic disorders now comprise a separate category of disorders in *DSM-5*. Another condition that has been separated from sexual disorders is *gender dysphoria*. In gender dysphoria there is incongruence and psychological distress and dissatisfaction with the gender one has been assigned at birth (boy or girl). The disorder is not sexual but rather a disturbance in the person's sense of being a male or a female.

Accurately determining the prevalence of sexual practices requires careful surveys that randomly sample the population. In a scientifically sound survey, Mosher, Chandra, and Jones (2005) reported data from 12,571 men and women in the United States ages 15 to 44, as part of the National Survey of Family Growth by the Centers for Disease Control and Prevention (CDC). These data are presented in ● Figure 9.1. The most recent survey from the National Survey of Family Growth sponsored by the CDC was reported in 2011 (Chandra, Mosher, & Copen, 2011). More than 13,000 men and women participated in this study, which provides some updated data, although the areas of sexual behavior sampled were more limited.

Virtually all men and women studied by Mosher and colleagues and Chandra and colleagues were sexually experienced, with vaginal intercourse a nearly universal experience, even for those who had never been married. By age 15, over a quarter of males and females have engaged in vaginal intercourse, and the prevalence rate increases with the age of individuals. In the overall sample, 81.3% of men and 80.1% of women in the study by Chandra and colleagues (2011) also engaged in oral sex, but only 35.8 and 30.7 %, respectively, had engaged in anal sex, a particularly high-risk behavior for AIDS transmission. Slightly more troublesome is an earlier finding by Billy and colleagues (1993) that 23.3% of men had had sex with 20 or more partners, which is another high-risk behavior. Then again, more than 70% had had only one sexual partner during the previous year, and fewer than 10% had had four or more partners during the same period. The Chandra and colleagues study (2011) reports similar figures, with 21.4% of men having sex with 15 or more partners during their lifetime (compared with 8.3% of women). Also, only 6.0% of men and 2.9% of women reported four or more partners during the past year.

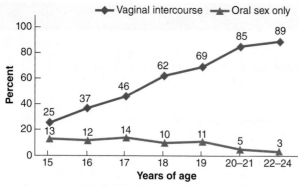

Percentage of males 15–24 years of age who have had vaginal intercourse, and percent who have had oral sex with a female but not vaginal intercourse, by age: United States, 2002

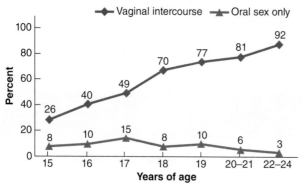

Percentage of females 15–24 years of age who have had vaginal intercourse, and percentage who have had oral sex with a male but not vaginal intercourse, by age: United States, 2002

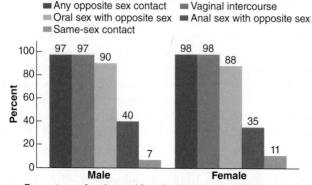

Percentage of males and females 25–44 years of age who have had each type of sexual contact: United States, 2002

● **Figure 9.1** Results of a survey of male and female sexual experiences: United States, 2006–2008. (Chandra, A., Mosher, W. D., & Copen, C. [2011]. *Sexual behavior, sexual attraction, and sexual identity in the United States: data from the 2006-2008 National Survey of Family Growth*. Atlanta, GA: US Department of Health and Human Services, Centers for Disease Control and Prevention, National Center for Health Statistics.)

The overwhelming majority of the men in the Mosher and colleagues study (2005) had engaged exclusively in **heterosexual behavior** (sex with the opposite sex), with only 6.5% of adult men having ever engaged in any

homosexual behavior (sex with the same sex). In this sample, 92% of men reported being attracted only to females, 3.9% mostly to females, 1.0% to both males and females, and 2.2% were attracted only to males, with similar numbers reported by women. Similarly, another survey found that nearly 9% of women and 10% of men reported some homosexual attractions or behavior. For adolescents, 5% of male teenagers and 11% of female teenagers report some homosexual behavior, albeit mostly in addition to heterosexual behavior, and most of these teenagers identify as heterosexual (Diamond, Butterworth, & Savin-Williams, 2011; Mosher, Chandra, & Jones, 2005).

One study from Britain (Johnson, Wadsworth, Wellings, Bradshaw, & Field, 1992) and one from France (Spira *et al.*, 1992) surveyed sexual behavior and practices among more than 20,000 men and women in each country. The results were similar to those reported for U.S. men. More than 70% of the respondents from all age groups in the British and French studies reported no more than one sexual partner during the past year. Women were somewhat more likely than men to have had fewer than two partners. Only 4.1% of French men and 3.6% of British men reported ever having had a male sexual partner, and this figure drops to 1.5% for British men if we consider only the past five years. Almost certainly, the percentage of males engaging exclusively in homosexual behavior would be considerably lower. The consistency of these

▲ Sexual behavior often continues well into old age.

data across three countries suggests strongly that the results represent something close to the norm, at least for Western countries. Also interesting is that sexual practices and the determinants of sexual satisfaction are now remarkably similar around the world, as demonstrated in a large survey of Chinese urban adults (Garcia, Kincannon, Poston, & Walther, 2014).

Sexual behavior can continue well into old age, even past 80 for some people. Notably, 38.5% of men and 16.7% of women aged 75 to 85 were sexually active. Reasons for the discrepancy between men and women are not clear, although given the earlier mortality of men, many older women lack a suitable partner; it is also possible that some women are married to men in an older age bracket. Many older women also indicated that sex was "not at all important" and generally reported less interest in sex than their male counterparts. Decreases in sexual activity are mostly correlated with decreases in general mobility and various disease processes and consequent medication, which may reduce arousal. Furthermore, the speed and intensity of various vasocongestive responses decrease with age.

Gender Differences

Although both men and women tend toward a monogamous (one partner) pattern of sexual relationships, gender differences in sexual behavior exist. One common finding among sexual surveys is a much higher percentage of men than women report that they masturbate (self-stimulate to orgasm) (Oliver & Hyde, 1993; Petersen & Hyde, 2010). When Richters and colleagues (2014) surveyed Australian adults, they also found this discrepancy (72% of men versus only 42% of women reported masturbating in the past year).

Why women masturbate less frequently than men puzzles sex researchers (Clement, 1990; Petersen & Hyde, 2010). One traditional view accounting for differences in masturbatory behavior is that women have been taught to associate sex with emotional intimacy, whereas men are more interested in physical gratification. But the discrepancy continues despite decreases in gender-specific attitudes toward sexuality. A more likely reason is anatomical. Because of the nature of the erectile response in men and their relative ease in providing sufficient stimulation to reach orgasm, masturbation may simply be more convenient for men. This may explain why gender differences in masturbation are also evident in primates and other animals (Ford & Beach, 1951).

Another continuing gender difference is reflected in the incidence of casual sex, attitudes toward casual premarital sex, and pornography use, with men expressing more permissive attitudes and behaviors than women (e.g., England & Bearak, 2014). One current term for

casual sex, particularly among college students, is "hooking up," which refers to a range of physically intimate behaviors outside of a committed relationship (Owen, Rhoades, Stanley, & Fincham, 2010). Studies of "hooking up" demonstrate similar findings to older studies of casual sex, in that it is often precipitated by alcohol, and women are less likely to consider it a positive experience than men (Olmstead, Pasley, & Fincham, 2013; Strokoff, Owen, Fincham, 2014). For example, Owen & Fincham (2011) found that greater alcohol use leads to greater engagement in "friends with benefits" relationships (a type of "hooking up" that involves an ongoing non-romantic relationship), and this was especially true for women. Even when women deliberately engage in casual sex, having a greater number of partners is associated with greater worry and vulnerability on the part of the woman, while the opposite was true for men (Furman & Collibee, 2014; Townsend & Wasserman, 2011). Despite the high prevalence of hooking up, with 40% of female students engaging in it during their first year at college in one study, sex within a romantic relationship was twice as common as "hook-up" sex for young women (Fielder, Carey, & Carey, 2013). However, longitudinal studies show no association between the number of sex partners and later anxiety or depression, although there is an association with increased risk for substance abuse (Ramrakha et al., 2013).

By contrast, studies suggest that *no* gender differences are apparent in attitudes about homosexuality (generally acceptable), the experience of sexual satisfaction (important for both), or attitudes toward masturbation (generally accepting). Small-to-moderate gender differences were evident in attitudes toward premarital intercourse when the couple was engaged or in a committed relationship (with men more approving than women) and in attitudes toward extramarital sex (sex outside of the marital relationship, which men also approved of more than women). As in the British and French studies, the number of sexual partners and the frequency of intercourse were slightly greater for men, and men were slightly younger at age of first sexual intercourse. Examining trends from 1943 to 1999, we find that almost all existing gender differences became smaller over time, especially in regard to attitudes toward premarital sex. Specifically, only 12% of young women approved of premarital sex in 1943, compared with 73% in 1999. The figures for men were 40% in 1943 and 79% in 1999 (Wells & Twenge, 2005). More recently, in the late 1990s and after 2000, investigators

heterosexual behavior Sexual activity with members of the opposite gender.

homosexual behavior Sexual activity with members of the same gender.

have noted a *decrease* in number of sexual partners and a tendency to delay sexual intercourse among adolescent boys, perhaps due to a fear of AIDS. Few changes over this time period were noted for adolescent girls (Petersen & Hyde, 2010).

Although they are decreasing, differences still exist between men and women in sexual behavior and attitudes toward sexuality (Peplau, 2003; Petersen & Hyde, 2010). For example, differences seem to exist in patterns of sexual arousal (Chivers, Rieger, Latty, & Bailey, 2004; Samson & Janssen, 2014). Men are more specific and narrow in their patterns of arousal. That is, heterosexual men are aroused by female sexual stimuli but not male sexual stimuli. For gay men, it's the opposite. Men with gender dysphoria (discussed later) who had surgery to become female retained this specificity (attracted to males but not females). Females, on the other hand, whether heterosexual or lesbian, experience arousal to both male and female sexual stimuli, demonstrating a broader, more general pattern of arousal.

Barbara Andersen and her colleagues have assessed gender differences in basic or core beliefs about sexual aspects of one's self (or "sexual self-schemas"). Specifically, in a series of studies (Andersen & Cyranowski, 1994; Andersen, Cyranowski, & Espindle, 1999), Andersen and colleagues demonstrated that women tend to report the experience of romantic feelings as an integral part of their sexuality, as well as an openness to sexual experience. A substantial number of women, however, also hold an embarrassed, conservative, or self-conscious schema that sometimes conflicts with more positive aspects of their sexual attitudes. Men, on the other hand, evidence a strong component of feeling powerful, independent, and aggressive as part of their sexuality, in addition to being passionate, loving, and open to experience. Also, men do not generally possess negative core beliefs reflecting self-consciousness, embarrassment, or feeling behaviorally inhibited.

Peplau (2003) summarizes research on gender differences in human sexuality as highlighting four themes: (1) men show more sexual desire and arousal than women; (2) women emphasize committed relationships as a context for sex more than men; (3) men's sexual self-concept, unlike women's, is characterized partly by power, independence, and aggression; and (4) women's sexual beliefs are more "plastic" in that they are more easily shaped by cultural, social, and situational factors. For example, women are more likely to change sexual orientation over time (Diamond, 2007; Diamond *et al.*, 2011; Mock & Eibach, 2012) or may be more variable in frequency of sex.

It also seems there are differences in sexual behavior based on sexual orientation. For example, in one study using U.S. college students (Oswalt & Wyatt, 2013), researchers found that men who identified "unsure" had more partners than those who identified as gay, bisexual, or heterosexual and that heterosexual men had fewer partners than gay, bisexual, and "unsure" men. On the other hand, women who identified as bisexual had more partners than women who identified with other orientations.

Cultural Differences

What is normal in some countries may not be normal in others (McGoldrick, Loonan, & Wohlsifer, 2007). For example, the Sambia in Papua New Guinea believe semen is an essential substance for growth and development in young boys of the tribe. They also believe semen is *not* produced naturally; that is, the body is incapable of producing it spontaneously. Therefore, all young boys in the tribe, beginning at approximately age seven, become semen recipients by engaging in homosexual oral sex with teenage boys. Only oral sexual practices are permitted; masturbation is forbidden and absent. Early in adolescence, the boys switch roles and become semen providers to younger boys. Heterosexual relations and even contact with the opposite sex are prohibited until the boys become teenagers. Late in adolescence, the boys are expected to marry and begin exclusive heterosexual activity. And they do, with no exceptions (Herdt, 1987; Herdt & Stoller, 1989). By contrast, the Munda of north-east India require adolescents and children to live together. But in this group, both male and female children live in the same setting, and the sexual activity, consisting mostly of petting and mutual masturbation, is all heterosexual (Bancroft, 1989).

In about half of more than 100 societies surveyed worldwide, premarital sexual behavior is culturally accepted and encouraged; in the remaining half, premarital sex is unacceptable and discouraged (Bancroft, 1989; Broude & Greene, 1980). Thus, what is normal sexual behavior in one culture is not necessarily normal in another, even among cultures in the same country, and the range of sexual expression must be considered in diagnosing the presence of a disorder.

The Development of Sexual Orientation

In studying the development of sexual orientation, the recent emphasis is on the breadth and variety of sexual arousal patterns within otherwise normal and adaptive sexual expression. This was not always the case. Until the 1970s, many forms of sexual expression, including homosexuality, were considered pathological. After homosexuality was eliminated as a diagnosis, many societies began to re-evaluate the nature and origins of consensual sexual behavior in adults, but because of the "taboos" on sexual research by government granting agencies and other funding sources, this inquiry is in its infancy. Most research to date has occurred in the context of the development of homosexual arousal patterns.

Some reports suggest that there may be a genetic component to sexual orientation because homosexuality runs in families (Bailey & Benishay, 1993) and concordance for homosexuality is more common among identical twins than among fraternal twins or natural siblings (Jannini, Burri, Jern, & Novelli, 2015). In two twin studies, homosexual orientation was shared in approximately 50% of identical twins compared with 16% to 22% of fraternal twins. Approximately the same or a slightly lower percentage of non-twin brothers or sisters were homosexual (Bailey & Pillard, 1991; Bailey, Pillard, Neale, & Agyei, 1993). Other studies reveal that in men, genes account for 34% to 39% of the cause, and in women, 18% to 19%, with the remainder accounted for by environmental influences (Långström, Rahman, Carlström, & Lichtenstein, 2010), including unique biological experiences, such as differential hormone exposure in utero. Other reports indicate that homosexuality and also gender atypical behavior during childhood is associated with differential exposure to hormones, particularly atypical androgen levels in utero (Auyeng et al., 2009; Gladue, Green, & Hellman, 1984) and that the actual structure of the brain might be different in individuals with homosexual arousal patterns as compared with those with heterosexual arousal patterns (Allen & Gorski, 1992; LeVay, 1991).

The principal conclusion drawn in the media over the years is that sexual orientation has a biological cause. Some gay rights activists were initially pleased with the biological interpretation, because people could no longer assume that gays had made a "morally depraved" choice of supposedly "deviant" arousal patterns. Others, however, noted how quickly some members of the public pounced on the implication that something was biologically wrong with individuals with homosexual arousal patterns, assuming that someday the abnormality would be detected in the fetus and prevented, perhaps through genetic engineering.

Do such arguments over biological causes sound familiar? Think back to studies described in Chapter 2 that attempted to link complex behavior to particular genes. In almost every case, these studies could not be replicated, and investigators fell back on a model in which genetic contributions to behavioral traits and psychological disorders come from many genes, each making a small contribution to a *vulnerability*. This generalized biological vulnerability interacts in a complex way with environmental conditions, personality traits, and other contributors to determine behavioral patterns. We also discussed reciprocal gene–environment interactions in which learning experiences and environmental events may affect brain structure and function and genetic expression.

The same thing is now happening with sexual orientation. Most theoretical models outlining these complex interactions for sexual orientation imply that there may be many pathways to the development of heterosexuality or homosexuality and that no one factor—biological or psychological—can predict the outcome (Bancroft, 1994; Brakefield et al., 2014). One of the more intriguing findings from the twin studies of Bailey and his colleagues is that approximately 50% of the identical twins with exactly the same genetic structure, as well as the same environment, *did not* have the same sexual orientation (Bailey & Pillard, 1991). Also intriguing is the finding in a study of 302 gay males that those growing up with older brothers are more likely to be gay, whereas having older sisters or younger brothers or sisters is not correlated with sexual orientation. This study found that each additional older brother increased the odds of being gay by one third. This finding, which has been replicated several times and is referred to as the "fraternal birth order hypothesis," may suggest the importance of environmental influences (Blanchard, 2008; Cantor, Blanchard, Paterson, & Bogaert, 2002). Research has implicated the importance of the mother's immunological response to Y-linked proteins (a substance important in male fetal development) as a potential explanation for this finding (Bogaert & Skorska, 2011). Finally, recent research has found that epigenetic effects (chemical modifications of the genome without changing the actual DNA sequence) may influence sexual orientation (Balter, 2015).

It is likely, too, that different types of homosexuality (and, perhaps, heterosexuality), with different patterns of cause, may be discovered (Diamond et al., 2011; Savin-Williams, 2006). It may even be that sexual orientation is changeable over time, at least for some people (Mock & Eibach, 2012). Lisa Diamond has discovered that interpersonal and situational factors exert a substantial influence on women's patterns of sexual behavior and sexual identities, a finding much less true for men (Diamond, 2007; Diamond et al., 2011). Among women who initially identified themselves as heterosexual, lesbian, bisexual, or "unlabeled," after 10 years more than two-thirds of women had changed their identity label a few times. When women changed their sexual identities, they typically broadened rather than narrowed their potential range of attractions and relationships.

In any case, almost certainly, biology sets certain limits within which social and psychological factors affect development. Scientists will ultimately pin down biological contributions to the formation of sexual orientation, and the environment and experience will be found to influence how these patterns of potential sexual arousal develop (Diamond et al., 2011; Långström et al., 2010).

An Overview of Sexual Dysfunctions

▶ How do psychologists define sexual dysfunction?

▶ How is sexual dysfunction related to the sexual response cycle?

Before we describe **sexual dysfunction**, it's important to note that the problems that arise in the context of sexual interactions may occur in both heterosexual and homosexual relationships. Inability to become aroused or reach orgasm seems to be as common in homosexual as in heterosexual relationships, but we discuss them in the context of heterosexual relationships, which are the majority of cases we see in our clinic. Of the different stages in the sexual response cycle, three of them—desire, arousal, and orgasm (see ● Figure 9.2)—are each associated with specific sexual dysfunctions. In addition, pain can become associated with sexual functioning in women, which leads to an additional dysfunction.

An overview of the *DSM-5* categories of the sexual dysfunctions we examine is in Table 9.1. As you can see, both males and females can experience parallel versions of most disorders, which take on specific forms determined by anatomy and other gender-specific characteristics. However,

two disorders are sex specific: Premature (early) ejaculation occurs only in males, and genito-pelvic pain/penetration disorder—which includes difficulties with penetration during intercourse due in many cases to painful contractions or spasms of the vagina—appears only in females. Sexual dysfunctions can be either lifelong or acquired. *Lifelong* refers to a chronic condition that is present during a person's entire sexual life; *acquired* refers to a disorder that begins after sexual activity has been relatively normal. In addition, disorders can either be *generalized*, occurring every time the individual attempts sex, or they can be *situational*, occurring with some partners or at certain times but not with other partners or at other times.

Before we describe the prevalence of specific sexual dysfunctions, we need to note a classic study by Ellen Frank and her colleagues (1978), who carefully interviewed 100 well-educated, happily married couples who were not

Desire phase
Sexual urges occur in response to sexual cues or fantasies.

Arousal stage
A subjective sense of sexual pleasure and physiological signs of sexual arousal: in males, penile tumescence (increased flow of blood into the penis); in females, vasocongestion (blood pools in the pelvic area) leading to vaginal lubrication and breast tumescence (erect nipples).

Resolution phase
Decrease in arousal occurs after orgasm (particularly in men).

Orgasm phase
In males, feelings of the inevitability of ejaculation, followed by ejaculation; in females, contractions of the walls of the lower third of the vagina.

Plateau phase
Brief period occurs before orgasm.

T.T./DigitalVision/Getty Images

● **Figure 9.2** The human sexual response cycle. (Based on Kaplan, H. S. [1979]. *Disorders of sexual desire*. New York, NY: Brunner/Mazel and Masters, W. H., & Johnson, V. E. [1966]. *Human sexual response*. Boston, MA: Little, Brown.)

TABLE 9.1 | Categories of Sexual Dysfunction among Men and Women

	Sexual Dysfunction	
Type of Disorder	**Men**	**Women**
Desire	Male hypoactive sexual desire disorder (little or no desire to have sex)	Female sexual interest/arousal disorder (little or no desire to have sex)
Arousal	Erectile disorder (difficulty attaining or maintaining erections)	Female sexual interest/arousal disorder (little or no desire to have sex)
Orgasm	Delayed ejaculation; premature (early) ejaculation	Female orgasmic disorder
Pain		Genito-pelvic pain/penetration disorder (pain, anxiety, and tension associated with sexual activity; vaginismus, i.e., muscle spasms in the vagina that interfere with penetration)

SOURCE: American Psychiatric Association. (2013). *Diagnostic and statistical manual of mental disorders* (5th ed.). Washington, DC: Author.

seeking treatment. More than 80% of these couples reported that their marital and sexual relations were happy and satisfying. Surprisingly, 40% of the men reported occasional erectile and ejaculatory difficulties, and 63% of the women reported occasional dysfunctions of arousal or orgasm. But the crucial finding was that these dysfunctions did not detract from the respondents' overall sexual satisfaction. In another study, only 45% of women experiencing difficulties with orgasm reported the issue as problematic (Fugl-Meyer & Sjogren Fugl-Meyer, 1999). Bancroft, Loftus, and Long (2003) extended this analysis in a survey of close to 1,000 U.S. women involved in a heterosexual relationship for at least six months. The results indicate that, although 44.3% met criteria for one of the disorders in Table 9.1, only 24.4% of these individuals were distressed about it. Indeed, the best predictors of sexual distress among these women were deficits in general emotional well-being or emotional relationships with the partner during sexual relations, not lack of lubrication or orgasm. These studies indicate that sexual satisfaction and occasional sexual dysfunction are not mutually exclusive categories (Bradford & Meston, 2011; Graham, 2010). But this does raise problems for diagnosing sexual dysfunctions. Should a sexual problem be identified as a diagnosis when dysfunction is present but the person is not distressed (Balon, Segraves, & Clayton, 2007; Zucker, 2010)? In *DSM-5*, the symptoms must clearly cause clinically significant distress in the individual or in the couple.

Sexual Desire Disorders

Three disorders reflect problems with the desire or arousal phase of the sexual response cycle. Two of these disorders are characterized by little or no interest in sex that is causing significant distress in the individual or couple. The two disorders differ somewhat for females and males, however. In females, low sexual interest is almost always

accompanied by a diminished ability to become excited or aroused by erotic cues or sexual activity. Thus, deficits in interest and/or the ability to become aroused is combined in women in a disorder called **female sexual interest/arousal disorder** (Brotto, 2010a; Brotto & Luria, 2014). For males, disorders of interest and arousal are separate. There is a specific disorder of arousal—erectile dysfunction. The disorder referring to lack of interest is called **male hypoactive sexual desire disorder**.

Male Hypoactive Sexual Desire Disorder and Female Sexual Interest/Arousal Disorder

Males with **hypoactive sexual desire disorder** and females with sexual interest/arousal disorder have little or no interest in any type of sexual activity. It is difficult to assess low sexual desire, and a great deal of clinical judgment is required (Leiblum, 2010; Wincze, Bach, & Barlow, 2008; Wincze & Weisberg, 2015). You might gauge it by frequency of sexual activity, or you might determine whether someone ever thinks about sex or has sexual fantasies. Then, there is the person who has sex twice a week but really doesn't want to and thinks about it only because his wife is on his case to live up to his end of the marriage. This individual might have no desire, despite having frequent sex. Consider the case of Mr. and Mrs. C.

....

sexual dysfunction Sexual disorder in which the client finds it difficult to function adequately while having sex.

female sexual interest/arousal disorder Recurrent inability in some women to attain or maintain adequate lubrication and sexual excitement swelling responses until completion of sexual activity.

male hypoactive sexual desire disorder Dysfunction in which a man feels distress from having little or no sexual interest.

Mr. and Mrs. C... • *Getting Started*

Mrs. C., a 31-year-old successful businesswoman, was married to a 32-year-old lawyer. They had two children, ages two and five, and had been married eight years when they entered therapy. The presenting problem was Mrs. C.'s lack of sexual desire. Mr. and Mrs. C. were interviewed separately during the initial assessment, and both professed attraction to and love for their partner. Mrs. C. reported that she could enjoy sex once she got involved and almost always was orgasmic. The problem was her lack of desire to get involved. She avoided her husband's sexual advances and looked on his affection and romanticism with skepticism and, usually, anger and tears. Mrs. C. was raised in an upper-middle-class family that was supportive and loving. From age 6 to age 12, however, she had been repeatedly pressured into sexual activity by a male cousin who was five years her senior. She did not tell her parents because she felt guilty, as the boy did not use physical force to make her comply. It appeared that romantic advances by Mr. C. triggered memories of abuse by her cousin.

Best estimates suggest that more than 50% of patients who come to sexuality clinics for help complain of low sexual desire or interest (Leiblum 2010; Pridal & LoPiccolo, 2000). In many clinics, it is the most common presenting complaint of women; men present more often with erectile dysfunction (Hawton, 1995). The U.S. survey confirmed that 22% of women and 5% of men suffer from low sexual interest. But in a larger international survey, as many as 43% of women reported this problem (Laumann *et al.*, 2005).

DSM 5 DISORDER CRITERIA SUMMARY
Male Hypoactive Sexual Desire Disorder

A. Persistently or recurrently deficient (or absent) sexual/erotic thoughts or fantasies and desire for sexual activity. The judgment of deficiency is made by the clinician, taking into account factors that affect sexual functioning, such as age and the context of the person's life.

B. The symptoms have persisted for a minimum of approximately six months and cause clinically significant distress in the individual.

C. The sexual dysfunction is not better explained by a non-sexual mental disorder or as a consequence of severe relationship distress or other significant stressors and is not attributable to the effects of a substance/medication or another medical condition.

From American Psychiatric Association. (2013). *Diagnostic and statistical manual of mental disorders* (5th ed.). Washington, DC.

For men, the prevalence increases with age; for women, it decreases with age (Fileborn *et al.*, 2015; Laumann, Paik, & Rosen, 1999). Schreiner-Engel and Schiavi (1986) noted that patients with this disorder rarely have sexual fantasies, seldom masturbate (35% of the women and 52% of the men never masturbated, and the remaining majority masturbated no more than once a month), and attempt intercourse once a month or less.

Sexual Arousal Disorders

Erectile disorder is a specific disorder of arousal. The problem here is not desire. Many males with erectile dysfunction have frequent sexual urges and fantasies and a strong desire to have sex. Their problem is in becoming physically aroused. Consider the case of Bill below.

Bill... • *Long Marriage, New Problem*

Bill, a 58-year-old white man who had been married for 29 years to his 57-year-old wife, was referred to our clinic by his urologist. For the past several years, Bill had had difficulty obtaining and maintaining an erection. He reported a rather rigid routine he and his wife had developed to deal with the problem. They scheduled sex for Sunday mornings. Bill had to do a number of chores first, however, including letting the dog out, washing the dishes, and shaving. The couple's current behavior consisted of mutual hand stimulation. Bill was "not allowed" to attempt insertion until after his wife had climaxed. Bill's wife was adamant that she was not going to change her sexual behavior. This included refusing to try a lubricant appropriate to her postmenopausal decrease in lubrication.

Bill and his wife agreed that they had always maintained a good sexual relationship until the onset of the current problem. Useful information was obtained in separate interviews. Bill masturbated on Saturday night in an attempt to control his erection the following morning; his wife was unaware of this. In addition, he quickly and easily achieved a full erection when viewing erotica in the privacy of the sexuality clinic laboratory (surprising the assessor). Bill's wife privately acknowledged being angry at her husband for an affair that he had had 20 years earlier.

At the final session, three specific recommendations were made: for Bill to cease masturbating the evening before sex, for the couple to use a lubricant, and for them to delay the morning routine until after they had had sexual relations. The couple called back one month later to report that their sexual activity was much improved.

For females with sexual arousal difficulties, who are also likely to have low interest, deficits are reflected in an inability to achieve or maintain adequate lubrication (Wincze *et al.*, 2008; Wincze & Weisberg, 2015).

The old and somewhat derogatory terms for male erectile disorder and female interest and arousal difficulties are *impotence* and *frigidity*, but these are imprecise labels that do not identify the specific phase of the sexual response in which the problems are localized. A man typically feels more impaired by his problem than a woman does by hers. Inability to achieve and maintain an erection makes intercourse difficult or impossible. Women who are unable to achieve vaginal lubrication, however, may be able to compensate by using a commercial lubricant (Leiblum 2010; Wincze, 2009). In women, arousal and lubrication may decrease at any time but, as in men, such problems tend to accompany aging (Basson, 2007; Shamloul & Ghanem, 2013). It is unusual for a man to be completely unable to achieve an erection. More typical is a situation like Bill's, where full erections are possible during masturbation and partial erections occur during attempted intercourse, but with insufficient rigidity to allow penetration.

The prevalence of erectile dysfunction is startlingly high and increases with age. Although data from the U.S. survey indicate that 5% of men between 18 and 59 fully meet a stringent set of criteria for erectile dysfunction (Laumann *et al.*, 1999), this figure certainly underestimates the prevalence because erectile dysfunction increases rapidly in men after age 60. Rosen, Wing, Schneider, and Gendrano (2005) reviewed evidence from around the world and found that 60% of men 60 and over suffered from erectile dysfunction. Data from another study (shown in ● Figure 9.3) suggest that at least some impairment is present in approximately

40% of men in their 40s and 70% of men in their 70s (Feldman, Goldstein, Hatzichristou, Krane, & McKunlay, 1994; Rosen, 2007). Erectile disorder is the most common problem for which men seek help, accounting for 50% or more of the men referred to specialists for sexual problems (Hawton, 1995).

The prevalence of female interest and arousal disorders is somewhat more difficult to estimate because many women do not consider absence of arousal to be a problem, let alone a disorder. The U.S. survey reports a prevalence of 14% of females experiencing an arousal disorder (Laumann *et al.*, 1999). A more recent study (Rosen *et al.*, 2014) reported a prevalence of 7.4%. Because disorders of desire, arousal, and orgasm often overlap, it is difficult to estimate how many women with specific interest and arousal disorders present to sex clinics (Basson, 2007; Wincze & Weisberg, 2015).

Orgasm Disorders

The orgasm phase of the sexual response cycle can also become disrupted in one of several ways. As a result, either the orgasm occurs at an inappropriate time or it does not occur.

An inability to achieve orgasm despite adequate sexual desire and arousal is commonly seen in women and less commonly seen in men. Males who achieve orgasm only with great difficulty or not at all meet criteria for a

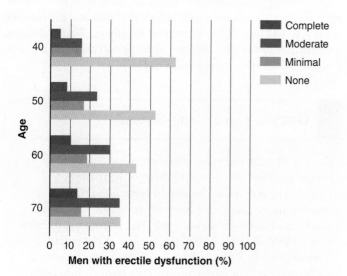

● **Figure 9.3** Estimated prevalence and severity of erectile dysfunction in a sample of 1,290 men between 40 and 70 years of age. Adapted from Feldman *et al.* (1994). Impotence and its medical and psychosocial correlates: Results of the Massachusetts male aging study. *Journal of Urology*, 51, 54–61.

erectile disorder Recurring inability in some men to attain or maintain adequate penile erection until completion of sexual activity.

condition called **delayed ejaculation**. In women the condition is referred to as **female orgasmic disorder** (Kleinplatz *et al.*, 2013; Wincze & Weisberg, 2015). Consider the case of Greta and Will.

Greta and Will... • *Loving Disunion*

Greta and Will were an attractive couple who came to the first interview and entered the office clearly showing affection for each other. They had been married for five years and were in their late 20s. When asked about the problems that had brought them to the office, Greta quickly reported that she didn't think she had ever had an orgasm—"didn't think" because she wasn't really sure what an orgasm was.

Will certainly didn't think Greta was reaching orgasm. In any case, he reported, they were clearly going in "different directions" sexually, in that Greta's interest was decreasing. She had progressed from initiating sex occasionally early in their marriage to almost never doing so, except for an occasional spurt every six months or so. But Greta noted that it was the physical closeness she wanted most during these times rather than sexual pleasure. Further inquiry revealed that she did become sexually aroused occasionally but had never reached orgasm, even during several attempts at masturbation mostly before her marriage.

Greta had been brought up in a strict but loving and supportive Catholic family that more or less ignored sexuality. The parents were always careful not to display their affection in front of Greta, and when her mother caught Greta touching her genital area, she was cautioned rather severely to avoid that kind of activity.

An inability to reach orgasm is the most common complaint among women who seek therapy for sexual problems. Although the U.S. survey did not estimate the prevalence of **female orgasmic disorder** specifically, approximately 25% of women report significant difficulty reaching orgasm (Heiman, 2000; Laumann *et al.*, 1999), although estimates vary widely (Graham, 2010). The problem is equally present in different age groups, and unmarried women were 1.5 times more likely than married women to experience orgasm disorder. In diagnosing this problem, it is necessary to determine that the women "never or almost never" reach orgasm (Wincze & Weisberg, 2015). This distinction is important because only approximately 20% of all women reliably experience regular orgasms during sexual intercourse (Graham, 2010; Lloyd, 2005). Therefore, approximately 80% do not achieve orgasm with every sexual encounter, unlike most men, who tend to experience orgasm more consistently. Thus, the "never or almost never"

DSM 5 DISORDER CRITERIA SUMMARY
Female Orgasmic Disorder

A. Presence of either of the following symptoms and experienced on almost all or all occasions of sexual activity: (1) marked delay in, marked infrequency of, or absence of orgasm; (2) markedly reduced intensity of orgasmic sensations.

B. The symptoms have persisted for approximately six months and cause clinically significant distress in the individual.

C. The sexual dysfunction is not better explained by a non-sexual mental disorder or as a consequence of severe relationship distress or other significant stressors and is not attributable to the effects of a substance/medication or another medical condition.

From American Psychiatric Association. (2013). *Diagnostic and statistical manual of mental disorders* (5th ed.). Washington, DC.

inquiry is important, along with establishing the extent of the woman's distress, in diagnosing orgasmic dysfunction.

In the U.S. survey, approximately 8% of men report having delayed ejaculation or none during sexual interactions (Laumann *et al.*, 1999). Men seldom seek treatment for this condition. It is quite possible that in many cases some men reach climax through alternative forms of stimulation and that this condition is accommodated by the couple (Apfelbaum, 2000). Some men who are unable to ejaculate with their partners can obtain an erection and ejaculate during masturbation. Occasionally men suffer from *retrograde ejaculation,* in which ejaculatory fluids travel backward into the bladder rather than forward. This is almost always caused by certain drugs or a co-existing medical condition and should not be confused with delayed ejaculation.

A far more common male orgasmic disorder is **premature ejaculation**, that occurs well before the man and his partner wish it to (Althof, 2006; Wincze & Weisberg, 2015), defined as approximately one minute after penetration in *DSM-5*. Consider the rather typical case of Gary.

Gary... • *Running Scared*

Gary, a 31-year-old sales representative, engaged in sexual activity with his wife three or four times a month. He noted that he would have liked to have had sex more often, but his busy schedule kept him working about 80 hours a week. His primary difficulty was an inability to control the timing of his ejaculation. Approximately 70% to 80% of the time, he ejaculated within seconds of penetration. This pattern had been constant since he met his wife approximately 13 years earlier. Previous experience with other women, although limited, was not characterized by premature ejaculation. In an attempt to delay his ejaculation, Gary distracted himself by thinking of non-sexual things and sometimes attempted sex soon after a previous attempt because he seemed not to climax as quickly under these circumstances. Gary reported masturbating three or four times a year at most. When he did masturbate, he usually attempted to reach orgasm quickly, a habit he acquired during his teens to avoid being caught by a family member.

One of his greatest concerns was that he was not pleasing his wife, and under no circumstances did he want her told that he was seeking treatment. Further inquiry revealed that he made many extravagant purchases at his wife's request, even though it strained their finances, because he wished to please her. He felt that if they had met recently, his wife probably would not even accept a date with him because he had lost much of his hair and she had lost weight and was more attractive than she used to be.

In the U.S. survey, 21% of all men met criteria for premature ejaculation, making it the most common male sexual dysfunction (Laumann *et al.*, 1999; Serefoglu & Saitz, 2012). Although *DSM-5* specifies a duration of less than approximately one minute, it is difficult to define "premature." An adequate length of time before ejaculation varies from individual to individual. Patrick and colleagues (2005) found that men who complain of premature ejaculation ejaculated 1.8 minutes after penetration, compared with 7.3 minutes in individuals without this complaint. A perceived lack of control over orgasm, however, may be the more important psychological determinant of premature ejaculation (Wincze *et al.*, 2008). Although occasional early ejaculation is normal, consistent premature ejaculation appears to occur primarily in inexperienced men with less education about sex (Laumann *et al.*, 1999).

DSM 5 DISORDER CRITERIA SUMMARY
Premature Ejaculation

A. A persistent or recurrent pattern of ejaculation occurring during partnered sexual activity within approximately one minute following vaginal penetration and before the person wishes it.

B. The symptom has been present for at least six months, must be experienced on almost all or all occasions of sexual activity, and causes clinically significant distress in the individual.

C. The sexual dysfunction is not better explained by a non-sexual mental disorder or as a consequence of severe relationship distress or other significant stressors and is not attributable to the effects of a substance/medication or another medical condition.

From American Psychiatric Association. (2013). *Diagnostic and statistical manual of mental disorders* (5th ed.). Washington, DC.

Sexual Pain Disorder

A sexual dysfunction specific to women refers to difficulties with penetration during attempted intercourse or significant pain during intercourse. This disorder is called **genito-pelvic pain/penetration disorder**. For some women, sexual desire is present, and arousal and orgasm are easily attained, but the pain during attempted intercourse is so severe that sexual behavior is disrupted. In other cases, severe anxiety or even panic attacks may occur in anticipation of possible pain during intercourse.

But the most usual presentation of this disorder is **vaginismus**, in which the pelvic muscles in the outer third of the vagina undergo involuntary spasms when intercourse is attempted (Binik *et al.*, 2007; Kleinplatz *et al.*, 2013). The spasm reaction of vaginismus may occur during any attempted penetration, including a gynecological exam or insertion of a tampon (Beck, 1993; Bradford & Meston, 2011). Women report sensations of "ripping, burning, or tearing during attempted intercourse" (Beck, 1993, p. 384). Consider the case of Jill.

Jill... • *Sex and Spasms*

Jill was referred to our clinic by another therapist because she had not consummated her marriage of one year. At 23 years of age, she was an attractive and loving wife who managed a motel while her husband worked as an accountant. Despite numerous attempts in a variety of positions to engage in intercourse, Jill's severe vaginal spasms prevented penetration of any kind. Jill was also unable to use tampons. With great reluctance, she submitted to gynecological exams at infrequent intervals. Jill, an anxious young woman, came from a family in which sexual matters were seldom discussed and sexual contact between the parents had ceased some years before. Although she enjoyed petting, Jill's

delayed ejaculation Disorder in which a man achieves orgasm only with great difficulty.

female orgasmic disorder Recurring delay or absence of orgasm in some women following a normal sexual excitement phase, relative to their prior experience and current stimulation. Also known as inhibited orgasm (female).

premature ejaculation Recurring ejaculation before the person wishes it, with minimal sexual stimulation.

genito-pelvic pain/penetration disorder Sexual dysfunction in which a woman experiences pain or difficulty with penetration during intercourse; may include **vaginismus**.

vaginismus Recurring involuntary muscle spasms in the outer third of the vagina that interfere with sexual intercourse.

general attitude was that intercourse was disgusting. Furthermore, she expressed fears of becoming pregnant despite taking adequate contraceptive measures. She also thought that she would perform poorly when she did engage in intercourse, therefore embarrassing herself with her new husband.

DSM 5 DISORDER CRITERIA SUMMARY
Genito-Pelvic Pain/Penetration Disorder

A. Persistent or recurrent difficulties with one (or more) of the following: (1) vaginal penetration during intercourse, (2) marked vulvovaginal or pelvic pain during vaginal intercourse or penetration attempts, (3) marked fear or anxiety about vulvovaginal or pelvic pain in anticipation of, during, or as a result of vaginal penetration, (4) marked tensing or tightening of the pelvic floor muscles during attempted vaginal penetration.

B. The symptoms have persisted for approximately six months and cause clinically significant distress in the individual.

C. The sexual dysfunction is not better explained by a non-sexual mental disorder or as a consequence of severe relationship distress or other significant stressors and is not attributable to the effects of a substance/medication or another medical condition.

From American Psychiatric Association. (2013). *Diagnostic and statistical manual of mental disorders* (5th ed.). Washington, DC.

Although there are no data on the prevalence of vaginismus, best estimates are that it affects 6% of women (Bradford & Meston, 2011). Twenty-five percent of women who report suffering from some sexual dysfunction experience vaginismus (Crowley, Richardson, & Goldmeir, 2006). Because vaginismus and the experience of pain during intercourse overlap quite a bit, these conditions have been combined in *DSM-5* into genito-pelvic pain/penetration disorder (Binik, 2010; Bradford & Meston, 2011). Results from the U.S. survey indicate that approximately 7% of women suffer from one or the other type of sexual pain disorder, with higher proportions of younger and less educated women reporting this problem (Laumann *et al.*, 1999). Somewhat higher estimates of 15% of women in North America endorsing recurring pain during intercourse have been reported in *DSM-5* (APA, 2013).

Assessing Sexual Behavior

There are three major aspects to the assessment of sexual behavior (Wiegel, Wincze, & Barlow, 2002):

1. *Interviews*, usually supported by questionnaires because patients may provide more information on paper than in a verbal interview

2. A *thorough medical evaluation*, to rule out medical conditions that can contribute to sexual problems
3. A *psychophysiological assessment*, to measure the physiological aspects of sexual arousal.

Clinicians who conduct interviews for sexual problems must be aware of several useful assumptions (Wiegel *et al.*, 2002; Wincze, 2009). For example, they must demonstrate to the patient that they are comfortable talking about sexual issues. Because many patients do not know the clinical terms professionals use to describe aspects of sexual behavior, clinicians must also be prepared to use the language familiar to the patient. In addition, clinicians must be careful to ask questions in a manner that puts patients at ease.

During a medical evaluation, clinicians inquire about medical conditions that affect sexual functioning. A variety of drugs, including some prescribed for hypertension, anxiety, and depression, often disrupt sexual arousal and functioning. Recent surgery or concurrent medical conditions must be evaluated for their impact on sexual functioning. Specialists may check levels of sexual hormones necessary for adequate sexual functioning and, in the case of males, evaluate vascular functioning necessary for an erectile response.

Clinicians also may take psychophysiological measurements to assess the ability of individuals to become sexually aroused under a variety of conditions. In men, penile erection is measured directly, using, for example, a *penile strain gauge* developed in our clinic (Barlow, Becker, Leitenberg, & Agras, 1970). As the penis expands, the strain gauge picks up the changes and records them on a polygraph, indicating levels of sexual arousal. The comparable device for women is a *vaginal photoplethysmograph*, developed by James Geer and his associates (Geer, Morokoff, & Greenwood, 1974; Prause & Janssen, 2006). This device, which is inserted by the woman into her vagina, measures the amount of light reflected back from the vaginal walls. Because blood flows to the vaginal walls during arousal, the amount of light passing through them decreases with increasing arousal.

Typically in our clinic, individuals undergoing physiological assessment view an erotic video or listen to an erotic audiotape (see, for example, Bach, Brown, & Barlow, 1999; Weisburg, Brown, Wincze, & Barlow, 2001). The patient's sexual responsivity during this time is assessed using the strain gauge or photoplethysmograph just described. Patients also report subjectively on the sexual arousal they experience. This assessment allows clinicians to observe the conditions under which arousal is possible for the patient. For example, many individuals with psychologically-based sexual dysfunctions may achieve strong arousal in a laboratory but be unable to become aroused with a partner (Bradford & Meston, 2011; Sakheim, Barlow, Abrahamson, & Beck, 1987).

Diagnose the following sexual dysfunctions:

1. After Bob's football team won the championship, his interest in sexual activity diminished. All his thoughts and fantasies centered on football and winning again next season, and his wife was threatening to leave him. Bob is probably displaying (a) male hypoactive sexual desire disorder, (b) vaginismus, (c) penile strain gauge, or (d) male orgasmic disorder.

2. Kelly has no desire for sex. She has sex only because she feels that otherwise her husband may leave her. Kelly suffers from (a) sexual insecurities, (b) hypoactive sexual desire disorder, (c) boredom, or (d) female sexual interest/arousal disorder.

3. Aadarsh lacks the ability to control ejaculation. The majority of the time he ejaculates within seconds of penetration. He suffers from (a) erectile disorder, (b) stress, (c) premature ejaculation, or (d) both a and b.

4. Samantha came into the office because she is unable to reach orgasm. She loves her husband but stopped initiating sex. She is most likely suffering from (a) female orgasmic disorder, (b) female sexual interest/arousal arousal disorder, (c) vaginismus, or (d) dislike for her husband.

Causes and Treatment of Sexual Dysfunction

▶ What are the defining features and known causes of sexual dysfunction?

▶ What psychosocial and medical treatments are available, and are they effective?

As with most disorders, biological, psychological, and social factors contribute to the development of sexual dysfunction. And these problems can be treated either psychologically or medically.

Causes of Sexual Dysfunction

Individual sexual dysfunctions seldom occur in isolation. Usually, a patient referred to a sexuality clinic complains of a wide assortment of sexual problems, although one may be of most concern (Rosen, 2007; Wincze, 2009). Because of the frequency of such combinations, we discuss the causes of various sexual dysfunctions together, reviewing briefly the biological, psychological, and social contributions and specifying causal factors thought to be associated exclusively and specifically with one or another dysfunction.

Biological Contributions

A number of physical and medical conditions contribute to sexual dysfunction (Bradford & Meston, 2011; Wincze & Weisburg, 2015). For example, neurological diseases and other conditions that affect the nervous system, such as diabetes and kidney disease, may interfere with sexual functioning by reducing sensitivity in the genital area, and they are a common cause of erectile dysfunction (Rosen, 2007; Wincze & Weisburg, 2015). Vascular disease is a major cause of sexual dysfunction, because erections in men and vaginal engorgement in women depend on adequate blood flow. The two relevant vascular problems in men are arterial insufficiency (constricted arteries), which makes it difficult for blood to reach the penis, and venous leakage (blood flows out too quickly for an erection to be maintained) (Wincze & Weisburg, 2015).

Chronic illness can also indirectly affect sexual functioning. For example, it is not uncommon for individuals who have had heart attacks to be wary of the physical exertion involved in sexual activity and become unable to achieve arousal despite being assured by physicians that sexual activity is safe (Cooper, 1988). Also, coronary artery disease and sexual dysfunction commonly co-exist, and it is now recommended that men presenting with erectile dysfunction be screened for cardiovascular disease (Gandaglia et al., 2014; Jackson, Rosen, Kloner, & Kostis, 2006).

A major physical cause of sexual dysfunction is prescription medication. Drug treatments for high blood pressure, for example, may contribute to sexual dysfunction. Antidepressant medications and antianxiety drugs may also interfere with sexual desire and arousal (Balon, 2006; Kleinplatz et al., 2013). A number of these drugs, particularly the psychoactive drugs, may dampen sexual desire and arousal by altering levels of certain subtypes of serotonin in the brain.

Some people are aware that alcohol suppresses sexual arousal, but they may not know that most other drugs of abuse, such as cocaine and heroin, also produce sexual dysfunction in frequent users and abusers (Cocores, Miller, Pottash, & Gold, 1988; Macdonald, Waldorf, Reinarman, & Murphy, 1988). There is also the misconception that alcohol facilitates sexual arousal and behavior. What actually happens is that alcohol at low and moderate levels reduces social inhibitions so that people feel more like having sex (and perhaps are more willing to request it) (Wiegel, Scepkowski, & Barlow, 2006). Physically, alcohol is a central nervous system suppressant, and for men to achieve erection and women to achieve lubrication is more difficult when the central nervous system is suppressed (Schiavi, 1990). Chronic alcohol abuse may cause permanent neurological damage and may virtually eliminate the sexual response cycle. Such abuse may lead to liver and testicular damage, resulting in decreased testosterone levels and related decreases in sexual desire and arousal.

Many people report that cocaine or marijuana enhances sexual pleasure. Although little is known about the effects of marijuana, it is unlikely that chemical effects increase pleasure. Rather, in those individuals who report enhancement of sexual pleasure, the effect may be psychological in that their attention is focused more completely on sensory stimulation (Buffum, 1982), a factor important to sexual functioning. If so, imagery and attentional focus can be enhanced with non-drug procedures such as meditation.

Nicotine is similarly associated with impaired sexual performance. One report from Mannino, Klevens, and Flanders (1994), studying more than 4,000 male army veterans, found that cigarette smoking alone was associated with increased erectile dysfunction. A more recent study found that nicotine used before viewing an erotic film was associated with reduced erectile response (Harte & Meston, 2008a). A parallel study found decreased arousal in women who used nicotine before viewing the film (Harte & Meston, 2008b).

Psychological Contributions

How do we account for sexual dysfunction from a psychological perspective? Basically, we have to break the concept of performance anxiety into several components. One component is arousal, another is cognitive processes, and the third is negative affect (Wiegel *et al.*, 2006; Wincze & Weisburg, 2015).

When confronted with the possibility of having sexual relations, individuals with dysfunctions tend to expect the worst and find the situation to be relatively negative (Weisburg *et al.*, 2001; Wincze & Weisburg, 2015). As far as possible, they avoid becoming aware of sexual cues (and therefore are not aware of how aroused they are physically, thus underreporting their arousal). They also may distract themselves with negative thoughts, such as, "I'll never be able to get aroused; she [or he] will think I'm stupid." We know that as arousal increases, a person's attention focuses more intently and consistently, but the person who is focusing on negative thoughts will find it impossible to become sexually aroused.

People with normal sexual functioning react to a sexual situation positively. They focus their attention on the erotic cues and do not become distracted. When they become aroused, they focus even more strongly on the sexual and erotic cues, allowing themselves to become increasingly sexually aroused. The model presented in ● Figure 9.4 illustrates both functional and dysfunctional sexual arousal (Barlow, 1986, 2002). These experiments demonstrate that sexual arousal is strongly determined by psychological factors, particularly cognitive and emotional factors, that are powerful enough to determine whether blood flows to the appropriate areas of the body, such as the genitals, confirming again the strong interaction of psychological and biological factors in most of our functioning.

Though little is known about the psychological (or biological) factors associated with premature ejaculation (Bradford & Meston, 2011; Malavige & Jayawickrema, 2015), the condition is most prevalent in young men and excessive physiological arousal in the sympathetic nervous system may lead to rapid ejaculation. These observations suggest some men may require less stimulation and arousal to ejaculate. Unfortunately, the psychological factor of anxiety also increases sympathetic arousal. Thus, when a man becomes anxiously aroused about ejaculating too quickly, his concern only makes the problem worse. We return to the role of anxiety in sexual dysfunctions later.

Social and Cultural Contributions

The model of sexual dysfunction displayed in Figure 9.4 helps explain why some individuals may experience dysfunction *at the present time* but it does not explain how they *became* that way. Although it is not known for sure why some people develop problems, many people learn early that sexuality can be negative and threatening, and the responses they develop reflect this belief. Donn Byrne and his colleagues call this negative cognitive set *erotophobia*. They have demonstrated that erotophobia, presumably learned in childhood from families, religious authorities, or others, seems to predict sexual difficulties later in life (Byrne & Schulte, 1990). In other cases, men and women may experience negative or traumatic events after a period of relatively well-adjusted sexuality. These negative events might include sudden failure to become aroused or actual sexual trauma such as rape.

Laumann and colleagues (1999), in the U.S. sex survey, found a substantial impact of early traumatic sexual events on later sexual functioning, particularly in women. For example, if women were sexually victimized by an adult before puberty or were forced to have sexual contact of some kind, they were approximately twice as likely to have orgasmic dysfunction as women who had not been touched before puberty or forced to have sex at any time.

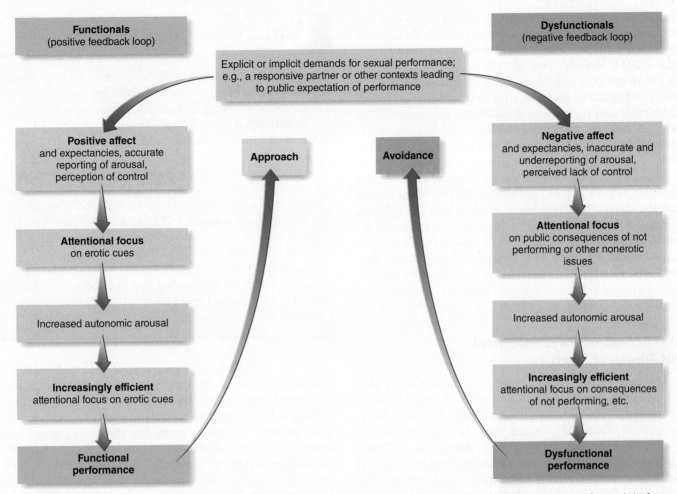

Functionals
(positive feedback loop)

Dysfunctionals
(negative feedback loop)

Explicit or implicit demands for sexual performance; e.g., a responsive partner or other contexts leading to public expectation of performance

Positive affect
and expectancies, accurate reporting of arousal, perception of control

Approach

Avoidance

Negative affect
and expectancies, inaccurate and underreporting of arousal, perceived lack of control

Attentional focus
on erotic cues

Attentional focus
on public consequences of not performing or other nonerotic issues

Increased autonomic arousal

Increased autonomic arousal

Increasingly efficient
attentional focus on erotic cues

Increasingly efficient
attentional focus on consequences of not performing, etc.

Functional performance

Dysfunctional performance

● **Figure 9.4** A model of functional and dysfunctional sexual arousal. (Adapted from Barlow, D. H. [1986]. Causes of sexual dysfunction: The role of anxiety and cognitive interference. *Journal of Consulting and Clinical Psychology, 54*, 140–148.)

For male victims of adult–child contact, the probability of experiencing erectile dysfunction is more than three times greater than if they had not had the contact. Interestingly, men who admitted sexually assaulting women are 3.5 times as likely to report erectile dysfunction as those who did not. Thus, traumatic sexual acts of all kinds have effects on subsequent sexual functioning, in both men and women, sometimes lasting decades beyond the occurrence of the original event (Hall, 2007; Meston & Lorenz, 2013). Such stressful events may initiate negative affect, in which individuals experience a loss of control over their sexual response cycle, throwing them into the kind of dysfunctional pattern depicted in Figure 9.4. It is common for people who experience erectile failure during a stressful time to continue sexual dysfunction long after the stressful situation has ended.

In addition to generally negative attitudes or experiences associated with sexual interactions, a number of other factors may contribute to sexual dysfunction. The most common is a marked deterioration in close interpersonal relationships (Burri, Spector, & Rahman, 2013; Wincze, Bach, & Barlow, 2008). It is difficult to have a satisfactory sexual relationship in the context of growing dislike for a partner. Occasionally, the partner may no longer seem physically attractive. Finally, it is also important to feel attractive yourself. Koch, Mansfield, Thurau, and Carey (2005) found that women who perceived themselves as less attractive than before, increased their likelihood of sexual problems. Poor sexual skills might also lead to sexual failure and, ultimately, lack of desire. For example, men with erectile dysfunction report a greatly restricted range of sexual behaviors compared with men without these problems (Wincze *et al.*, 2008; Wincze & Weisberg, 2015).

Thus, social and cultural factors seem to affect later sexual functioning. John Gagnon has studied this phenomenon and constructed an important concept called *script theory* of sexual functioning, according to which we all operate by following "scripts" that reflect social and cultural expectations and guide our behavior (Gagnon, 1990; Laumann, Gagnon, Michael, & Michaels, 1994). For example, a person who learns that sexuality is potentially dangerous, dirty, or forbidden is more vulnerable to developing sexual dysfunction. This pattern is most evident in cultures with restrictive attitudes toward sex (McGoldrick *et al.*, 2007).

For example, vaginismus is relatively rare in North America but is considerably more prevalent in Ireland, Turkey, and Iran (Doğan, 2009; Farnam, Janghorbani, Merghati-Khoei, & Raisi, 2014; McGoldrick et al., 2007).

Even in our own culture, socially communicated expectations and attitudes may stay with us despite our relatively enlightened and permissive attitude toward sex. Barbara Andersen and her colleagues (see, for example, Cyranowski et al., 1999) have demonstrated that being self-conscious about sex (having a negative sexual self-schema) may lead to sexual difficulties under stressful situations. Bernie Zilbergeld (1999), one of the foremost authorities on male sexuality, described a number of myths about sex believed by many men, and Baker and DeSilva (1988) converted a version of Zilbergeld's male myths into a questionnaire and presented it to groups of sexually functional and dysfunctional men. They found that men with dysfunctions showed greater belief in the myths than did men who were sexually functional.

Interaction of Psychological and Physical Factors

Having reviewed the various causes, we must now say that seldom is any sexual dysfunction associated exclusively with either psychological or physical factors (Rosen, 2007; Wiegel et al., 2006). More often, there is a combination of factors. For example, a young man, vulnerable to developing anxiety and holding to a certain number of sexual myths (the social contribution), may experience erectile failure after using alcohol, as many men do (the biological contribution). He will anticipate the next sexual encounter with anxiety, wondering if the failure might happen again. This combination of experience and apprehension activates the psychological sequence depicted in Figure 9.4, regardless of whether he's had a few drinks.

In summary, socially transmitted negative attitudes about sex may interact with a person's relationship difficulties and predispositions to develop performance anxiety and, ultimately, lead to sexual dysfunction. From a psychological point of view, it is not clear why some individuals develop one dysfunction and not another, although it is common for several dysfunctions to occur in the same patient. Possibly, an individual's specific biological predispositions interact with psychological factors to produce a specific sexual dysfunction.

Treatment of Sexual Dysfunction

Unlike most other disorders discussed in this book, one surprisingly simple treatment is effective for a large number of individuals who experience sexual dysfunction: education. Ignorance of the most basic aspects of the sexual response cycle and intercourse often leads to dysfunctions (Bach, Wincze, & Barlow, 2001; Wincze et al., 2008). Consider the case of Carl.

Carl... • *Never Too Late*

Carl, a 55-year-old white man, was referred to our clinic by his urologist because he had difficulty maintaining an erection. Although he had never been married, he was involved in a relationship with a 50-year-old woman. An interview revealed that Carl engaged in sex twice a week, but requests by the clinician for a step-by-step description of his sexual activities revealed an unusual pattern: Carl skipped foreplay and immediately proceeded to intercourse. Unfortunately, because his partner was not aroused and lubricated, he was unable to penetrate her. His efforts sometimes resulted in painful abrasions for both of them. Two sessions of sex education, including step-by-step instructions for foreplay, provided Carl with a new outlook on sex. For the first time, he had successful, satisfying intercourse, much to his and his partner's delight.

In the case of hypoactive sexual desire disorder, a marked difference within a couple often leads to one partner being labeled as having low desire. For example, if one partner is happy with sexual relations once a week but the other partner desires sex every day, the latter partner may accuse the former of having low desire and, unfortunately, the former partner might agree. Facilitating better conditions often resolves these misunderstandings. Fortunately, for people with this and more complex sexual dysfunctions, treatments are available, both psychosocial and medical.

Psychosocial Treatments

Among the many advances in our knowledge of sexual behavior, none was more dramatic than the publication in 1970 by William Masters and Virginia Johnson of *Human Sexual Inadequacy*. The procedures outlined in this book revolutionized sex therapy by providing a brief, direct, and reasonably successful therapeutic program for sexual dysfunctions. Underscoring again the common basis of most sexual dysfunctions, a similar approach to therapy is taken with all patients, male and female, with slight variations depending on the sexual problem (e.g., premature ejaculation or orgasmic disorder). This intensive program involves a male and a female therapist to facilitate communication between the dysfunctional partners. (Masters and Johnson were the original male and female therapists.) Therapy is conducted daily over a two-week period.

The actual program is straightforward. In addition to providing basic education about sexual functioning, altering deep-seated myths, and increasing communication, the clinicians' primary goal is to eliminate psychologically-based performance anxiety (refer back to Figure 9.4). To accomplish this, Masters and Johnson introduced *sensate focus* and *non-demand pleasuring*. In this exercise, couples are instructed to refrain from intercourse or genital caressing and simply to explore and enjoy each other's body through touching, kissing, hugging, massaging, or similar kinds of behavior. In the first phase, non-genital pleasuring, breasts and genitals are excluded from the exercises. After successfully accomplishing this phase, the couple moves to genital pleasuring but with a ban on orgasm and intercourse and clear instructions to the man that achieving an erection is not the goal.

At this point, arousal should be re-established and the couple should be ready to attempt intercourse. So as not to proceed too quickly, this stage is also broken down into parts. For example, a couple might be instructed to attempt the beginnings of penetration; that is, the depth of penetration and the time it lasts are only gradually built up, and both genital and non-genital pleasuring continue. Eventually, full intercourse and thrusting are accomplished. After this two-week intensive program, recovery was reported by Masters and Johnson for the vast majority of more than 790 sexually dysfunctional patients, with some differences in the rate of recovery depending on the disorder. Close to 100% of individuals with premature ejaculation recovered, whereas the rate for more difficult cases of lifelong generalized erectile dysfunction was closer to 60%.

Sex therapists have expanded on and modified these procedures over the years to take advantage of recent advances in knowledge (see, for example, Bradford & Meston, 2011; Weiner & Avery-Clark, 2014). Results with sex therapy for erectile dysfunction indicate that as many as 60% to 70% of the cases show a positive treatment outcome for at least several years, although results are mixed and there may be some slipping after that (Frühauf, Gerger, Schmidt, Munder, & Barth, 2013; Rosen, 2007; Segraves & Althof, 1998). For better treatment of specific sexual dysfunctions, sex therapists integrate specific procedures into the context of general sex therapy. For example, to treat premature ejaculation, most sex therapists use a procedure developed by Semans (1956), sometimes called the *squeeze* technique, in which the penis is stimulated, usually by the partner, to nearly full erection. At this point, the partner firmly squeezes the penis near the top where the head of the penis joins the shaft, which quickly reduces arousal. These steps are repeated until (for heterosexual partners) eventually the penis is briefly inserted in the vagina without thrusting. If arousal occurs too quickly, the penis is withdrawn and the squeeze technique is employed again. In this way, the man develops a sense of control over arousal and ejaculation. Reports of success with this approach over the past 20 years suggest that 60% to 90% of men benefit, but the success rates drop to about 25% after three years or more of follow up (Althof, 2007; Malavige & Jayawickrema, 2015). Gary, the 31-year-old sales representative, was treated with this method, and his wife was cooperative during the procedures. Brief marital therapy also persuaded Gary that his insecurity over his perception that his wife no longer found him attractive was unfounded. After treatment, he reduced his work hours somewhat, and the couple's marital and sexual relations improved.

Lifelong female orgasmic disorder may be treated with explicit training in masturbatory procedures (Bradford & Meston, 2011). For example, Greta was still unable to achieve orgasm with manual stimulation by her husband, even after proceeding through the basic steps of sex therapy. At this point, following certain standardized treatment programs for this problem (see, for example, Heiman, 2000; Heiman & LoPiccolo, 1988), Greta and Will purchased a vibrator and Greta was taught to let go of her inhibitions by talking out loud about how she felt during sexual arousal, even shouting or screaming if she wanted. In the context of appropriate genital pleasuring and disinhibition exercises, the vibrator brought on Greta's first orgasm. With practice and good communication, the couple eventually learned how to bring on Greta's orgasm without the vibrator. Summaries of results from a number of studies suggest 70% to 90% of women benefit from treatment, and these gains are stable and even improve further over time (Fruhauf *et al.*, 2013; Heiman, 2007).

To treat vaginismus and pain related to penetration in genito-pelvic pain/penetration disorder, the woman and, eventually, the partner gradually insert increasingly larger dilators at the woman's pace. After the woman (and then the partner) can insert the largest dilator, in a heterosexual couple, the woman gradually inserts the man's penis. These exercises are carried out in the context of genital and non-genital pleasuring so as to retain arousal. Close attention must be accorded to any increased fear and anxiety that may be associated with the process, which may trigger memories of early sexual abuse that may have contributed to the onset of the condition. These procedures are highly successful, with 80% to 100% of women overcoming vaginismus in a relatively short period (Binik *et al.*, 2007; ter Kuile, Melles, de Groot, Tuijnman-Raasveld, & van Lankveld, 2013).

Treatment procedures have also been developed for low sexual desire (see, for example, Wincze, 2009; Wincze

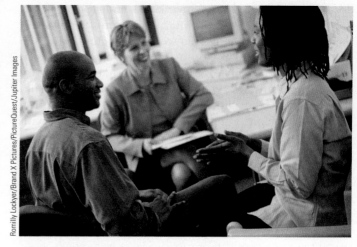

▲ A therapist usually treats a dysfunction in one partner by seeing the couple together.

& Weisberg, 2015). At the heart of these treatments are the standard re-education and communication phases of traditional sex therapy with, possibly, the addition of masturbatory training and exposure to erotic material. Each case may require individual strategies. Remember Mrs. C., who was sexually abused by her cousin? Therapy involved helping the couple understand the impact of the repeated, unwanted sexual experiences in Mrs. C.'s past and to approach sex so that Mrs. C. was more comfortable with foreplay. She gradually lost the idea that once sex was started she had no control. She and her husband worked on starting and stopping sexual encounters. Cognitive restructuring was used to help Mrs. C. interpret her husband's amorousness in a positive rather than a skeptical light. In general, 50% to 70% of individuals with low sexual desire benefit from sex therapy, at least initially (Basson, 2007; Brotto, 2006).

Medical Treatments

Pharmacological and surgical techniques have been developed in recent years to treat sexual dysfunction, almost all focusing on male erectile disorder. We look at the four most popular procedures: oral medication (such as Viagra), injection of vasoactive substances into the penis, surgery, and vacuum device therapy. Note that it is important to combine any medical treatment with a comprehensive educational and sex therapy program to ensure maximum benefit.

In 1998, the drug sildenafil (trade name Viagra) was introduced for erectile dysfunction. Approval from the Food and Drug Administration occurred early in 1998, and results from several clinical trials suggested that between 50% and 80% of a large number of men benefit from this treatment (Conti, Pepine, & Sweeney, 1999; Goldstein *et al.*, 1998) in that erections become sufficient for intercourse, compared with approximately 30% who benefit from placebo. Results are similar with Cialis and Levitra (Carrier *et al.*, 2005). As many as 30% of men may suffer severe headaches as a side effect, however, particularly at higher doses (Rosen, 2000, 2007; Virag, 1999), and reports of sexual satisfaction are not optimal. For example, only 32% men reported that the results were satisfactory. Also, the large majority of men stop using the drug after several months or a year, also indicating less than satisfactory long-term results (Rosen, 2007). To address this issue, Bach, Barlow, and Wincze (2004) evaluated the addition of cognitive-behavioral treatment (CBT) to treatment with Viagra. Couples reported greater satisfaction and increased sexual activity after combined drug therapy and CBT, compared with a period when only the drug was used.

There was also hope that Viagra would be useful for dysfunction in postmenopausal women, but results were disappointing (Bradford & Meston, 2011; Kaplan *et al.*, 1999). Interest is now centered on a new drug, flibanserin, as a possible treatment for hypoactive sexual desire in women. There is preliminary evidence for increases in sexual desire and reduced distress associated with hypoactive sexual desire in women who take this drug (DeRogatis *et al.*, 2012; Katz *et al.*, 2013). However, the effects of what has been called "pink Viagra" are relatively unnoticeable for many women, leading some to question whether pharmaceutical companies may be misleading the public in order to cash in on a sexual enhancement drug for women (Laan & Tiefer, 2014; Levine, 2015). This research is still in its infancy.

Some urologists teach male patients to inject vasodilating drugs such as *papaverine* or *prostaglandin* directly into the penis when they want to have sexual intercourse. These drugs dilate the blood vessels, allowing blood to flow to the penis and thereby producing an erection within 15 minutes that can last from one to four hours (Rosen, 2007; Segraves & Althof, 1998). Because this procedure is a bit painful (although not as much as one might think), usually 50% to 60% of men stop using it after a short time (Lakin, Montague, Vanderbrug Medendorp, Tesar, & Schover, 1990; Segraves & Althof, 1998).

Insertion of *penile prostheses* or implants has been a surgical option for almost 100 years; only recently have they become good enough to approximate normal sexual functioning. One procedure involves implanting a semi-rigid silicone rod that can be bent by the male into correct position for intercourse and maneuvered out of the way at other times. In a more popular procedure, the male squeezes a small pump that is surgically implanted into the scrotum, forcing fluid into an inflatable cylinder and thus producing an erection. A newer penile prosthetic device is an inflatable rod that contains the pumping device, which is more convenient than having the pump outside the rod. However, surgical implants fall short of restoring pre-surgical sexual functioning or assuring satisfaction in most patients (Gregoire, 1992; Kim & Lipshultz, 1997); they are now generally used only if other approaches don't work.

Another approach is *vacuum device therapy*, which works by creating a vacuum in a cylinder placed over the penis. The vacuum draws blood into the penis, which is then trapped by a ring placed around the base of the penis. Between 70% and 100% of users report satisfactory erections, particularly if psychological sex therapy is ineffective (Segraves & Althof, 1998; Witherington, 1988). The procedure is less intrusive than surgery or injections, but it remains awkward and artificial (Delizonna *et al.*, 2001). However, in recent years, this therapy has gained traction as a first-line therapy for men who have been treated for prostate cancer (Pahlajani, Raina, Jones, & Zippe, 2012).

▲ An inflatable penile implant may be used for men with inadequate sexual functioning.

Larry Mulvehill/The Image Works

Summary

Treatment programs offer hope to most people who suffer from sexual dysfunctions. Unfortunately, such programs are not available in many locations because few health and mental health professionals are trained to apply them. Further, government agencies have been slow to fund research dedicated to understanding sexual dysfunctions and their treatments. Psychological treatment of sexual arousal disorders requires further improvement, and treatments for low sexual desire are largely untested. Most treatments are still intrusive and clumsy, although drugs such as Viagra and Levitra exhibit some success for erectile dysfunction. New medical developments, including medications, topical creams, and gene therapy, are under investigation as potential treatments, but research on these interventions is just beginning.

Unfortunately, most health professionals ignore the issue of sexuality in older adults. Along with the usual emphasis on communication, education, and sensate focus, appropriate lubricants for women and a discussion of methods to maximize erectile response in men should be a part of any sexual counseling for older couples. More important, continued sexual relations, not necessarily including intercourse, should be an enjoyable and important part of an aging couple's relationship.

9.2 Concept CHECK

Determine whether the following statements are true (T) or false (F):

1. _____ Many physical and medical conditions and their treatments (e.g., prescription medications) contribute to sexual dysfunction; however, many doctors are unaware of the connection.

2. _____ Anxiety always decreases or even eradicates sexual arousal.

3. _____ Sexual dysfunctions can result from a growing dislike for a partner, traumatic sexual events, or childhood lessons about the negative consequences of sexual behavior.

4. _____ A simple, effective treatment for many disorders is education.

5. _____ All sexual dysfunctions are treated with the same psychosocial technique.

6. _____ Most surgical and pharmacological treatments of recent years have focused on erectile disorder.

Paraphilic Disorders: Clinical Descriptions

▶ What are the clinical features of the major paraphilias?

▶ What is known about the causes of paraphilias?

If you are like most people, your sexual interest is directed to other physically mature adults (or late adolescents), all of whom are capable of freely offering or withholding their consent. But what if you are sexually attracted to something or somebody other than another adult, such as animals (particularly horses and dogs) (Williams & Weinberg, 2003) or a vacuum cleaner? (Yes, it does happen!) Or what if your only means of obtaining sexual satisfaction was to commit a brutal murder? Such patterns of sexual arousal and countless others exist in a large number of individuals, causing untold human suffering both for them and, if their behavior involves other people, for their victims. As noted in the beginning of the chapter, these disorders of sexual arousal, if they cause distress or impairment to the individual or cause personal harm or the risk of harm to others, are called **paraphilic disorders**. It is important to note that *DSM-5* does not consider a paraphilia a disorder unless it is associated with distress and impairment or harm or the threat of harm to others. Thus, unusual patterns of sexual attraction are not considered to be sufficient to meet criteria for a disorder. This is a controversial change in *DSM-5*.

Over the years, we have assessed and treated a large number of individuals with paraphilias and paraphilic disorders, ranging from the slightly eccentric to dangerous killer-rapists. Many of our patients present with two, three, or more patterns, although one is usually dominant (American Psychiatric Association, 2013; Brownell, Hayes, & Barlow, 1977). Furthermore, it is not uncommon for individuals with paraphilic disorders to suffer from comorbid mood, anxiety, and substance abuse disorders (Kafka & Hennen, 2003; Krueger & Kaplan, 2015; Raymond, Coleman, Ohlerking, Christenson, & Miner, 1999). Although paraphilic disorders are not widely prevalent and estimates of their frequency are hard to come by, some disorders, such as transvestic disorder (cross-dressing, discussed later), seem relatively common (Bancroft, 1989; Mason, 1997).

....

paraphilic disorders Sexual disorders and deviations in which sexual arousal occurs almost exclusively in the context of inappropriate objects or individuals.

You may have been the victim of **frotteuristic disorder** in a large city, typically on an extremely crowded subway or bus. In this situation, women have been known to experience more than the usual jostling and pushing from behind. What they discover, much to their horror, is a male with a frotteuristic arousal pattern rubbing against them until he is stimulated to the point of ejaculation. Because the victims cannot escape easily, the frotteuristic act is usually successful (Lussier & Piché, 2008).

Fetishistic Disorder

In **fetishistic disorder**, a person is sexually attracted to non-living objects. There are almost as many types of fetishes as there are objects, although women's undergarments and shoes are popular (Darcangelo, 2008; Kafka, 2010). Fetishistic arousal is associated with two classes of objects or activities: (1) an inanimate object or (2) a source of specific tactile stimulation, such as rubber, particularly clothing made out of rubber. Shiny black plastic is also used (Bancroft, 1989; Junginger, 1997). Most of the person's sexual fantasies, urges, and desires focus on this object. A third source of attraction (sometimes called *partialism*) is a part of the body, such as the foot, buttocks, or hair.

Voyeuristic and Exhibitionistic Disorders

Voyeuristic disorder is the practice of observing an unsuspecting individual undressing or naked to become aroused. **Exhibitionistic disorder**, by contrast, is achieving sexual arousal and gratification by exposing genitals to unsuspecting strangers (Långström, 2010). Consider the case of Robert.

Robert... • *Outside the Curtains*

Robert, a 31-year-old, married, blue-collar worker, reported that he first started "peeping" into windows when he was 14. He rode around the neighborhood on his bike at night, and when he spotted a female through a window, he stopped and stared. During one of these episodes, he felt the first pangs of sexual arousal. Eventually he began masturbating while watching, thereby exposing his genitals, although out of sight. When he was older, he drove around until he spotted some prepubescent girls. He parked his car near them, unzipped his fly, called them over, and attempted to carry on a non-sexual conversation. Later he was sometimes able to talk a girl into mutual masturbation and *fellatio*, or oral stimulation of the penis. Although he was arrested several times, paradoxically, the threat of arrest increased his arousal (Barlow & Wincze, 1980).

Although prevalence is unknown (Murphy & Page, 2008), in a random sample of 2,450 adults in Sweden, 31% reported at least one incident of being sexually aroused by exposing their genitals to a stranger, and 7.7% reported at least one incident of being sexually aroused by spying on others having sex (Långström & Seto, 2006). To meet diagnosis for exhibitionistic disorder, the behavior must occur repeatedly and be compulsive or out of control.

Transvestic Disorder

In **transvestic disorder**, sexual arousal is strongly associated with the act of (or fantasies of) dressing in clothes of the opposite sex, or cross-dressing (Blanchard, 2010; Wheeler, Newring, & Draper, 2008). Consider the case of Mr. M.

Mr. M... • *Strong Man in a Dress*

Mr. M., a 31-year-old married police officer, came to our clinic seeking treatment for uncontrollable urges to dress in women's clothing and appear in public. He had been doing this for 16 years and had been discharged from the Marine Corps for cross-dressing. Since then, he had risked public disclosure on several occasions. Mr. M.'s wife had threatened to divorce him because of the cross-dressing, yet she often purchased women's clothing for him and was "compassionate" while he wore them.

Note that Mr. M. was in the Marine Corps before he joined the police force. It is not unusual for males who are strongly inclined to dress in female clothes to compensate by associating with so-called macho organizations. Nevertheless, most individuals with this disorder do not seem to display any compensatory behaviors. The same survey in Sweden mentioned earlier found 2.8% of men and 0.4% of women reported at least one episode of transvestic disorder (Långström & Zucker, 2005). The 3% prevalence rate in males, while a rough estimate, is generally accepted (APA, 2013).

Interestingly, the wives of many men who cross-dress have accepted their husbands' behavior and can be quite supportive if it is a private matter between them. Docter and Prince (1997) reported that 60% of more than 1,000 men with transvestic disorder were married at the time of the survey. Some people, both married and single, join cross-dressing clubs or subscribe to newsletters devoted to the topic. If sexual arousal is primarily focused on the clothing itself, the diagnostic criteria require a specification

"with fetishism." Another specifier for transvestic disorder describes a pattern of sexual arousal associated not with clothing itself but rather with thoughts or images of oneself as a female. This specifier is called "autogynephilia." This specifier is controversial because the "sexual confusion" experienced by those who experience autogynephilia overlaps to some degree with gender dysphoria (described below), and some think this confusion is better captured by the concept of gender dysphoria. Indeed, there is a somewhat greater risk that individuals with this paraphilic disorder will develop gender dysphoria and request transition through sex reassignment surgery (Blanchard, 2010; Lawrence, 2013).

Sexual Sadism and Sexual Masochism Disorders

Sexual sadism and **sexual masochism** are associated with either inflicting pain or humiliation (sadism) or suffering pain or humiliation (masochism) (Hucker, 2008; Krueger,

frotteuristic disorder Paraphilic disorder in which the person gains sexual gratification by rubbing against unwilling victims in crowds from which they cannot escape.

fetishistic disorder Long-term, recurring, intense sexually arousing urges, fantasies, or behavior that involve the use of nonliving, unusual objects and that cause distress or impairment in life functioning.

voyeuristic disorder Paraphilic disorder in which sexual arousal is derived from observing unsuspecting individuals undressing or naked.

exhibitionistic disorder Sexual gratification attained by exposing genitals to unsuspecting strangers.

transvestic disorder Paraphilia in which individuals, usually males, are sexually aroused or receive gratification by wearing clothing of the opposite sex.

sexual sadism Paraphilia in which sexual arousal is associated with inflicting pain or humiliation.

sexual masochism Paraphilia in which sexual arousal is associated with experiencing pain or humiliation.

2010a, 2010b), and becoming sexually aroused is specifically associated with violence and injury in these conditions (Seto, Lalumiere, Harris, & Chivers, 2012). Although Mr. M. was extremely concerned about his cross-dressing, he was also disturbed by another problem: To maximize his sexual pleasure during intercourse, he had his wife wear a collar and leash, tied her to the bed, and handcuffed her. He sometimes tied himself with ropes, chains, handcuffs, and wires, all while he was cross-dressed. Mr. M. was concerned he might injure himself seriously. As a member of the police force, he had heard of cases in which an individual was found dead, tightly and completely bound in harnesses, handcuffs, and ropes. In many such cases, the individual accidentally hangs himself, an event that should be distinguished from the closely related condition called *hypoxiphilia*, which involves self-strangulation to reduce the flow of oxygen to the brain and enhance the sensation of orgasm.

It may seem paradoxical that someone has to either inflict or receive pain to become sexually aroused, but these types of cases are not uncommon. On many occasions, the behaviors themselves are quite mild and harmless (Krueger, 2010a, 2010b), but they can become dangerous and costly.

Sadistic Rape

After murder, rape is the most devastating assault one person can make on another. It is not classified as a paraphilic disorder because most instances of rape are better characterized as an assault by a male (or, quite rarely, a female) whose patterns of sexual arousal are not paraphilic. Instead, many rapists meet criteria for antisocial personality disorder (see Chapter 11) and may engage in a variety of antisocial and aggressive acts (Davison & Janca, 2012; Quinsey, 2010). Many rapes can be described as opportunistic, in that an aggressive or antisocial individual with a marked lack of empathy and disregard for inflicting pain on others (Bernat, Calhoun, & Adams, 1999) spontaneously takes advantage of a vulnerable and unsuspecting woman. These unplanned assaults often occur during robberies or other criminal events. Rapes can also be motivated by anger and vindictiveness against specific women and may have been planned in advance (Rebocho & Silva, 2014; Quinsey, 2010).

A number of years ago, we determined in our sexuality clinic that certain rapists do closely fit definitions of paraphilic disorder and could probably better be described as sadists, a finding that has since been confirmed (Quinsey, 2010; Seto *et al.*, 2012). We constructed two audiotapes on which were described (1) mutually enjoyable sexual intercourse and (2) sexual intercourse involving force on the part of the male (rape). Each tape was played twice for selected listeners. The non-rapists became sexually aroused to descriptions of mutually consenting intercourse but not

to those involving force. Rapists, however, became aroused by both types of descriptions (Abel, Barlow, Blanchard, & Guild, 1977).

Pedophilic Disorder and Incest

Perhaps the most tragic sexual deviance is sexual attraction to children (or young adolescents generally aged 13 years or younger) called **pedophilia** (Blanchard, 2010; Seto, 2012). People have become more aware of this problem following the well-publicized scandal in the Catholic Church, where priests, many of whom undoubtedly met criteria for pedophilic disorder, abused children repeatedly, only to be transferred to another church and repeat these offences. Individuals with this pattern of arousal may be attracted to male children, female children, or both. In one survey, as many as 12% of men and 17% of women reported being touched inappropriately by adults when they were children (Fagan, Wise, Schmidt, & Berlin, 2002). A more recent study estimated the prevalence of sexual abuse before age 18 to be 10.14% (Pérez-Fuentes *et al.*, 2013). Approximately 90% of abusers are male, and 10% are female (Fagan *et al.*, 2002; Seto, 2009). Much as with adult rape, as many as 40% to 50% of sexual offenders do not have pedophilic arousal patterns and do not meet criteria for pedophilic disorder. Rather, their offenses are associated with brutal antisocial and aggressive opportunistic acts (Blanchard, 2010; Seto, 2009). Child pornography investigations have made much news lately, and individuals convicted of downloading child pornography often defend themselves by pointing out that they were "just looking" and are not pedophiles. But an important study indicates that being charged with a child pornography offense is one of the best diagnostic indications of pedophilic disorder (Seto, Cantor, & Blanchard, 2006).

If the children are the person's relatives, the pedophilia takes the form of **incest**. Although pedophilia and incest have much in common, victims of pedophilic disorder tend to be young children, and victims of incest tend to be girls beginning to mature physically (Rice & Harris, 2002). By using penile strain gauge measures, Marshall, Barbaree, and Christophe (1986) and Marshall (1997) demonstrated that incestuous males are, in general, more aroused by adult women than are males with pedophilic disorder, who tend to focus exclusively on children. Thus, incestuous relations may have more to do with availability and interpersonal issues ongoing in the family than pedophilia, as in the case of Tony.

Tony... • *More and Less a Father*

Tony, a 52-year-old married television repairman, came in depressed. About 10 years earlier, he had begun sexual activity with his 12-year-old daughter. Light kissing and some fondling gradually escalated to heavy petting and, finally, mutual masturbation. When his daughter was 16-years-old, his wife discovered the ongoing incestuous relationship. She separated from her husband and eventually divorced him, taking her daughter with her. Soon, Tony remarried. Just before his initial visit to our clinic, Tony visited his daughter, then 22-years-old, who was living alone in a different city. They had not seen each other for five years. A second visit, shortly after the first, led to a recurrence of the incestuous behavior. At this point, Tony became extremely depressed and told his new wife the whole story. She contacted our clinic with his full cooperation while his daughter sought treatment in her own city.

We return to the case of Tony later, but several features are worth noting. First, Tony loved his daughter and was bitterly disappointed and depressed over his behavior. Occasionally, a child molester is abusive and aggressive, sometimes killing the victims; in these cases, the disorder is often both sexual sadism and pedophilia. But most child molesters are *not* physically abusive. Rarely is a child physically forced or injured. From the molester's perspective, no harm is done because there is no physical force or threats. Child molesters often rationalize their behavior as "loving" the child or teaching the child

useful lessons about sexuality. The child molester almost never considers the psychological damage the victim suffers, yet these interactions often destroy the child's trust and ability to share intimacy. Child molesters rarely gauge their power over the children, who may participate in the molestation without protest yet be frightened and unwilling. Often children feel responsible for the abuse because no outward force or threat was used by the adult, and only after the abused children grow up are they able to understand they were powerless to protect themselves and not responsible for what was done to them.

Causes of Paraphilic Disorders

Although no substitute for scientific inquiry, case histories often provide hypotheses that can then be tested by controlled scientific observations. Let's return to the cases of Robert and Tony to see if their histories contain any clues.

These cases remind us that deviant patterns of sexual arousal often occur in the context of other sexual and social problems. Undesired kinds of arousal may be associated with deficiencies in levels of "desired" arousal with consensual adults; this was certainly true for both Tony and Robert, whose sexual relationships with adults were incomplete. In many cases, an inability to develop

....

pedophilia Paraphilia involving strong sexual attraction toward children.

incest Deviant sexual attraction (**pedophilia**) directed toward a family member; often the attraction of a father toward a daughter who is maturing physically.

Robert... • *Revenge on Repression*

Robert (who sought help for exhibitionism) was raised by a stern authoritarian father and a passive mother in a small Texas town. His father, who was a firm believer in old-time religion, often preached the evils of sexual intercourse to his family. Robert learned little about sex from his father except that it was bad, so he suppressed any emerging heterosexual urges and fantasies and as an adolescent felt uneasy around girls his own age. By accident, he discovered a private source of sexual gratification: staring at attractive and unsuspecting females through the window. This led to his first masturbatory experience.

Robert reported in retrospect that being arrested was not so bad because it disgraced his father, which was his only way of getting back at him. The courts treated him lightly (which is not unusual), and his father was publicly humiliated, forcing the family to move from their small Texas town (Barlow & Wincze, 1980).

Tony... • *Trained Too Young*

Tony, who sought help because of an incestuous relationship with his daughter, reported an early sexual history that contained a number of interesting events. Although he was brought up in a reasonably loving and outwardly normal Catholic family, he had an uncle who did not fit the family pattern. When he was 9 or 10, Tony was encouraged by his uncle to observe a game of strip poker that the uncle was playing with a neighbor's wife. During this period, he also observed his uncle fondling a waitress at a drive-in restaurant and shortly thereafter was instructed by his uncle to fondle his young female cousin. Thus, he had an early model for mutual fondling and masturbation and obtained some pleasure from interacting in this way with young girls. Although the uncle never touched Tony, his behavior was clearly abusive. When Tony was about 13, he engaged in mutual manipulation with a sister and her girlfriend, which he remembers as pleasurable. Later, when Tony was 18, a brother-in-law took him to a prostitute, and he first experienced sexual intercourse. He remembered this visit as unsatisfactory because, on that and subsequent visits to prostitutes, he ejaculated prematurely—a sharp contrast to his early experience with young girls. Other experiences with adult women were also unsatisfactory. When he joined the service and was sent overseas, he sought out prostitutes who were often as young as 12.

adequate social relations with the appropriate people for sexual relationships seems to be associated with developing of inappropriate sexual outlets (Marshall, 1997). Indeed, integrated theories of the causes of paraphilic disorders all note the presence of disordered relationships during childhood and adolescence with resulting deficits in healthy sexual development (Marshall & Barbaree, 1990; Ward & Beech, 2008). Many people with deficient sexual and social skills do not develop deviant patterns of arousal, however.

Early experience seems to have an effect that may be quite accidental. Tony's early sexual experiences just happened to be of the type he later found sexually arousing. Many individuals with pedophilic disorder also report being abused themselves as children, which turns out to be a strong predictor of later sexual abuse by the victim (Fagan *et al.*, 2002; Nunes, Hermann, Malcom, & Lavoie, 2013). Robert's first erotic experience occurred while he was "peeping." But, many of us do not find our early experiences reflected in our sexual patterns.

Another factor may be the nature of the person's early sexual fantasies. For example, Rachman and Hodgson (1968; see also Bancroft, 1989) demonstrated that sexual arousal could become associated with a neutral object—a boot, for example—if the boot was repeatedly presented while the individual was sexually aroused. One of the most powerful engines for developing unwanted arousal may be early sexual fantasies that are repeatedly reinforced through the strong sexual pleasure associated with masturbation (Bradford & Meston, 2011). Before an individual with a pedophilic or sadism disorder ever acts on his behavior, he may fantasize about it thousands of times while masturbating. Expressed as a clinical or operant-conditioning paradigm, this is another example of a learning process in which a behavior (sexual arousal to a specific object or activity) is repeatedly reinforced through association with a pleasurable consequence (orgasm). This mechanism may explain why paraphilic disorders are almost exclusively male disorders. The basic differences in frequency of masturbation between men and women that exist across cultures may contribute to the differential development of paraphilic disorders. However, if early experiences contribute strongly to later sexual arousal patterns, then what about the Sambia males who practice exclusive homosexual behavior during childhood and early adolescence and yet are exclusively heterosexual as adults? In such cohesive societies, the social demands or "scripts" for sexual interactions are stronger and more rigid than in our culture and thus may override the effects of early experiences (Baldwin & Baldwin, 1989).

In addition, therapists and sex researchers who work with individuals with paraphilic disorders have observed what seems to be an incredibly strong sex drive. It is not uncommon for some individuals to masturbate three or four times a day. In one case seen in our clinic, a sadistic rapist masturbated approximately every half hour all day long, just as often as it was physiologically possible. We have speculated elsewhere that activity this consuming may be related to the obsessional processes of obsessive-compulsive disorder (Barlow, 2002). In both instances, the very act of trying to suppress unwanted, emotionally charged thoughts and fantasies seems to have the paradoxical effect of *increasing* their frequency and intensity (see Chapter 4).

Psychopathologists are also becoming interested in the phenomenon of weak inhibitory control across these paraphilic disorders, which may indicate a weak biologically-based behavioral inhibition system (BIS) in the brain (Ward & Beech, 2008) that might repress serotonergic functioning. (You may remember from Chapter 4 that the BIS is a brain circuit associated with anxiety and inhibition.) The model shown in ● Figure 9.5 incorporates the factors thought to contribute to the development of paraphilic disorders. Nevertheless, all speculations, including the hypotheses we have described, have little scientific support at this time. For example, this model does not include the biological dimension. Excess arousal in paraphilic disorders could be biologically-based. Before we can make any steadfast conclusions, more research is needed.

● **Figure 9.5** A model of the development of paraphilia.

Assessing and Treating Paraphilic Disorders

▶ What psychosocial and drug treatments are available for paraphilias, and how effective are they?

In recent years, researchers have developed sophisticated methods for assessing specific patterns of sexual arousal (Ponseti *et al.*, 2012; Wincze, 2009; Wincze & Weisberg, 2015). This development is important in studying paraphilic disorder because sometimes even the individual presenting with the problem is not fully aware of what caused arousal. Using the model of paraphilic disorders described previously, we assess each patient not only for the presence of paraphilic arousal but also for levels of desired arousal to adults, for social skills, and for the ability to form relationships. Tony had no problems with social skills: He was 52-years-old and generally compatible with his second wife. His major difficulty was his continuing strong, incestuous attraction to his daughter. Nevertheless, he loved his daughter and wished strongly to interact in a normal fatherly way with her.

Psychological Treatment

A number of treatment procedures are available for decreasing unwanted arousal. Most are behavior therapy procedures directed at changing the associations and context from arousing and pleasurable to neutral. One procedure, carried out entirely in the imagination of the patient, called **covert sensitization**, was first described by Joseph Cautela (1967; see also Barlow, 2004). In this treatment, patients associate sexually arousing images in their imagination

....

covert sensitization Cognitive-behavioral intervention to reduce unwanted behaviors by having clients imagine the extremely aversive consequences of the behaviors and establish negative rather than positive associations with them.

with some reasons why the behavior is harmful or dangerous. Before treatment, the patient knows about these reasons, but the immediate pleasure and strong reinforcement the sexual activity provides is enough to overcome any thoughts of possible harm or danger that might arise in the future. In imagination, harmful or dangerous consequences can be associated quite directly with the unwanted behavior and arousal in a powerful and emotionally meaningful way. One of the most powerful negative aspects of Tony's behavior was his embarrassment over the thought of being discovered by his current wife, other family members, or, most important, the family priest. Therefore, he was guided through the fantasy described here.

During six or eight sessions, the therapist narrates such scenes dramatically, and the patient is then instructed to imagine them daily until all arousal disappears. Tony's incestuous arousal was largely eliminated after three to four weeks. These results were confirmed by psychophysiological measurement of his arousal response. A return of some arousal at a three-month follow up prompted us to ask Tony if anything unusual was happening in his life.

Tony... • *Imagining the Worst*

You are alone with your daughter in your trailer. You realize that you want to caress her breasts. So you put your arm around her, slip your hand inside her blouse, and begin to caress her breasts. Unexpectedly the door to the trailer opens and in walks your wife with Father X (the family priest). Your daughter immediately jumps up and runs out the door. Your wife follows her. You are left alone with Father X. He is looking at you as if waiting for an explanation of what he has just seen. Seconds pass, but they seem like hours. You know what Father X must be thinking as he stands there staring at you. You are embarrassed and want to say something, but you can't seem to find the right words. You realize that Father X can no longer respect you as he once did. Father X finally says, "I don't understand this; this is not like you." You both begin to cry. You realize that you may have lost the love and respect of both Father X and your wife, who are important to you. Father X asks, "Do you realize what this has done to your daughter?" You think about this and you hear your daughter crying; she is hysterical. You want to run, but you can't. You are miserable and disgusted with yourself. You don't know if you will ever regain the love and respect of your wife and Father X.

(Reproduced, with permission of the authors and publisher, from Harbert, T. L., Barlow, D. H., Hersen, M., & Austin, J. B. [1974]. Measurement and modification of incestuous behavior: A case study. *Psychological Reports, 34*, 79–86, © 1974 Psychological Reports.)

He confessed that his marriage had taken a turn for the worse, and sexual relations with his wife had all but ceased. A period of marital therapy restored the therapeutic gains. Several years later, after his daughter's therapist decided she was ready, she and Tony resumed a non-sexual relationship, which they both wanted.

Most individuals with paraphilic arousal patterns need a great deal of attention to family functioning or other interpersonal systems (Fagan *et al.*, 2002; Rice & Harris, 2002). In addition, many require intervention to help strengthen appropriate desired patterns of arousal. In **orgasmic reconditioning**, patients are instructed to masturbate to their usual fantasies but to substitute more desirable ones just before ejaculation. With repeated practice, patients should be able to begin the desired fantasy earlier in the masturbatory process and retain their arousal. This technique, first described by Gerald Davison (1968), has been used with some success in a variety of settings (Brownell *et al.*, 1977; Maletzky, 2002). Finally, as with most strongly pleasurable but undesirable behaviors (including addiction), care must be taken to provide the patient with coping skills to prevent slips or relapses. *Relapse prevention* treatment created for addictions (Laws & O'Donohue, 1997) does just that. Patients are taught to recognize the early signs of temptation and to institute a variety of self-control procedures before their urges become too strong.

Evidence on the effects of psychological treatments for sexual offenders is mixed. For sexual offenders who have come into contact with the legal system, including those who are incarcerated, the results are modest at best in terms of preventing later occurrences of offending (termed recidivism). Reviews of large numbers of studies with these populations are hampered because of the different methods and procedures in accessing recidivism rates. But several large surveys following up sexual offenders for a period of four to five years indicate reductions in sexual recidivism among patients who received psychological treatments of up to 11% to 20% over what would be expected with the customary treatment, with cognitive-behavioral programs the most effective (Hanson *et al.*, 2002; Lösel & Schmucker, 2005). On the other hand, a large study from California with participants who were incarcerated for their sexual offense showed little effect of any intervention in rates of sexual or violent offending over an eight-year follow-up period after these individuals were released (Marques, Wiederanders, Day, Nelson, & van Ommeren, 2005). Recently, new techniques have been incorporated into psychological treatments for sex offenders, including techniques to enhance motivation (motivational interviewing), and a focus on the patient's strengths, with the hope that these techniques will increase the efficacy of treatment; however, more research is needed (Marshall & Marshall, 2014).

For outpatients, on the other hand, there is at least some evidence for success when treatment is carried out by an experienced professional. For example, Barry Maletzky and his staff reported on the treatment of more than 8,000 sexual offenders over 20 years (Maletzky, 2002). A variety of procedures were used in a program of three to four months in a clinic devoted exclusively to this type of treatment. What makes the report notable is that Maletzky collected objective physiological outcome measures using the penile strain gauge described earlier with almost every participant in the program, in addition to patients' reports of progress. In many cases, he also obtained corroborating information from families and legal authorities.

In his follow up of these patients, Maletzky (2002) defined a treatment as successful when someone had (1) completed all treatment sessions, (2) demonstrated no deviant sexual arousal on objective physiological testing at any annual follow-up testing session, (3) reported no deviant arousal or behavior at any time since treatment ended, and (4) had no legal record of any charges of deviant sexual activity, even if unsubstantiated. He defined as a treatment failure anyone who was not a success. Any offender who did not complete treatment for any reason was counted as a failure, even though some may well have benefited from the partial treatment and gone on to recover. Using these criteria, from 75% to 95% of individuals, depending on the type of sexual offense, had a successful outcome. Maletzky's results were not derived from a scientifically-controlled clinical trial, however.

Men who rape had the lowest success rate among all offenders with a single diagnosis (75%), and individuals with multiple paraphilic disorders had the lowest success rate of any group. Maletzky (2002) also examined factors associated with failure. Among the strongest predictors were a history of unstable social relationships, an unstable employment history, strong denial the problem exists, a history of multiple victims, and a situation in which the offender continues to live with a victim (as might be typical in cases of incest).

Other groups using similar treatment procedures have achieved comparable success rates (Abel, 1989; Becker, 1990; Fagan *et al.*, 2002). Therapist knowledge and expertise seem to be important in successfully carrying out these treatments.

Drug Treatments

The most popular drug used to treat individuals with paraphilic disorders is an antiandrogen called *cyproterone acetate* (Assumpção, Garcia, Garcia, Bradford, & Thibaut, 2014; Bradford, 1997; Seto, 2009). This "chemical castration" drug eliminates sexual desire and fantasy by reducing testosterone levels, but fantasies and arousal return as soon as the drug is removed. A second drug is *medroxyprogesterone* (Depo-Provera is the injectable form), a hormonal agent that reduces testosterone (Assumpção *et al.*, 2014; Fagan *et al.*, 2002). These drugs may be useful for dangerous sexual offenders who do not respond to alternative treatments or to temporarily suppress sexual arousal in patients who require it, but they are not always successful.

Summary

Evidence for the psychosocial treatment of paraphilic disorders is mixed, with more success reported in outpatient settings with presumably less severe, more stable patients. But most results are uncontrolled observations from a small number of clinical research centers, and results may not be as good in other clinics and offices. In any case, as with treatment for sexual dysfunctions, psychosocial approaches to paraphilic disorders are not readily available outside of specialized treatment centers. In the meantime, the outlook for most individuals with these disorders is bleak because paraphilic disorders run a chronic course and recurrence is common.

9.3 Concept CHECK

Check your understanding of sexual paraphilic disorders by matching the scenarios with the correct label: (a) exhibitionistic disorder, (b) voyeuristic disorder, (c) fetishistic disorder, or (d) sexual masochism disorder:

1. Mae enjoys being slapped with leather whips during foreplay. Without such stimulation, she is unable to achieve orgasm during sex. _____

2. Kai has a collection of women's panties that arouse him. He loves to look at, collect, and wear them. _____

3. Sam finds arousal in walking up to strangers in the park and showing them his genitals. _____

4. Peeping Tom loves to look through Susie's bedroom window and watch her undress. He gets extremely excited as she disrobes. He is practicing _____.

5. What Peeping Tom does not realize is that Susie knows that he is watching. She is aroused by slowly undressing while others are watching, and she fantasizes about what they are thinking. Susie's behavior is called _____.

6. What Peeping Tom will be shocked to find out is that "Susie" is actually Scott, a man who can become aroused only if he wears feminine clothing. Scott's behavior is _____.

orgasmic reconditioning Learning procedure to help clients strengthen appropriate patterns of sexual arousal by pairing appropriate stimuli with the pleasurable sensations of masturbation.

Gender Dysphoria

▶ What are the defining clinical features, causes, and treatments of gender dysphoria?

What is it that makes you think you are a man or a woman? Clearly, it's more than your sexual arousal patterns or your anatomy. It's also more than the reactions and experiences of your family and society. The essence of your masculinity or femininity is a deep-seated personal sense called gender identity or the gender you actually experience. **Gender dysphoria** is present if a person's physical sex (male or female anatomy, also called "natal" sex) is not consistent with the person's sense of who he or she really is or with his or her experienced gender. While gender dysphoria can occur on a continuum (American Psychological Association [APA] Task Force of Gender Identity and Gender Variance, 2008; Cohen-Kettenis & Pfäfflin, 2010), at the extreme end of the continuum are individuals who reject their natal sex altogether and wish to change it. People with this disorder often feel trapped in a body of the wrong sex. Consider the case of Joe.

Joe... • *Trapped in the Wrong Body*

Joe was a 17-year-old male and the last of five children. Although his mother had wanted a girl, he became her favorite child. His father worked long hours and had little contact with the boy. For as long as Joe could remember, he had thought of himself as a girl. He began dressing in girls' clothes of his own accord before he was five-years-old and continued cross-dressing into junior high school. He developed interests in cooking, knitting, crocheting, and embroidering, skills he acquired by reading an encyclopedia.

Joe associated mostly with girls during this period, although he remembered being strongly attached to a boy in the first grade. In his sexual fantasies, which developed around 12 years of age, he pictured himself as a female having intercourse with a male. His extremely effeminate behavior made him the object of scorn and ridicule when he entered high school at age 15. Usually passive and unassertive, he ran away from home and attempted suicide. Unable to continue in high school, he attended secretarial school, where he was the only boy in his class. During his first interview with a therapist, he reported, "I am a woman trapped in a man's body, and I would like to have surgery to become a woman."

If the natal sex is female but the experienced gender (gender identity) is strongly male, the individual is typically referred to as a transsexual man or "transman,"

and a natal male would be a transwoman. If the individual has made the transition to full-time living in their experienced gender (by interacting with people in their daily lives in a consistent manner in their desired gender) and they are preparing for or have undergone sex reassignment surgery, then they are referred to as "posttransition," and this is specified in the diagnostic criteria for gender dysphoria.

DSM 5 DISORDER CRITERIA SUMMARY
Gender Dysphoria

In Children:

A. A marked incongruence between one's experienced/expressed gender and assigned gender, of at least six months' duration, as manifested by at least six of the following (one of which must be Criterion 1): (1) a strong desire to be of the other gender or an insistence that one is the other gender, (2) in boys, a strong preference for cross-dressing or simulating female attire; or in girls, a strong preference for wearing only typical masculine clothing and a strong resistance to the wearing of typical feminine clothing, (3) a strong preference for cross-gender roles in make-believe play or fantasy play, (4) a strong preference for the toys, games, or activities stereotypically used or engaged in by the other gender, (5) a strong preference for playmates of the other gender, (6) in boys, a strong rejection of typically masculine toys, games, and activities and a strong avoidance of rough-and-tumble play or in girls, a strong rejection of typically feminine toys, games, and activities, (7) a strong dislike of one's sexual anatomy, (8) a strong desire for the primary and/or secondary sex characteristics that match one's experienced gender.

B. The condition is associated with clinically significant distress or impairment in social, school, or other important areas of functioning.

In Adolescents and Adults:

A. A marked incongruence between one's experienced/expressed gender and assigned gender, of at least six months' duration, as manifested by at least two of the following: (1) a marked incongruence between one's experienced/expressed gender and primary and/or secondary sex characteristics (or in young adolescents, the anticipated secondary sex characteristics), (2) a strong desire to be rid of one's primary and/or secondary sex characteristics because of a marked incongruence with one's experienced/expressed gender (or in young adolescents, a desire to prevent the development of the anticipated secondary sex characteristics), (3) a strong desire for the primary and/or secondary sex characteristics of the other gender, (4) a strong desire to be of the other

Defining Gender Dysphoria

Gender dysphoria must be distinguished from transvestic fetishism, a paraphilic disorder (discussed earlier) in which individuals, usually males, are sexually aroused by wearing articles of clothing associated with the opposite sex. There is an occasional preference on the part of the male with transvestite patterns of sexual arousal for the female role, but the primary purpose of cross-dressing is sexual gratification. In the case of gender dysphoria, the primary goal is not sexual gratification but rather the desire to live life openly in a manner consistent with that of the other gender.

Gender dysphoria can also occur among individuals with disorders of sex development (DSD), formerly known as *intersexuality or hermaphroditism* who are born with ambiguous genitalia associated with documented hormonal or other physical abnormalities. Depending on their particular mix of characteristics, individuals with DSDs are usually "assigned" to a specific sex at birth, sometimes undergoing surgery as well as hormonal treatments to alter their sexual anatomy. If gender dysphoria occurs in the context of a DSD, this should be specified when making a diagnosis. But most individuals with gender dysphoria have no demonstrated physical abnormalities.

Finally, gender dysphoria must be distinguished from the same-sex arousal patterns of a male who sometimes behaves effeminately, or a woman with same-sex arousal patterns and masculine mannerisms. Such an individual does not feel like a woman trapped in a man's body or have any desire to be a woman, or vice versa. Note also, as the *DSM-5* criteria do, that gender identity is independent of sexual arousal patterns (APA, 2013; Savin-Williams, 2006). For example, a transwoman (a biological [natal] male with a strongly experienced feminine gender identity) may be sexually attracted to females. Similarly, Eli Coleman and his associates (Coleman, Bockting, & Gooren, 1993) reported on nine transmen in which the individuals were sexually attracted to men. Thus, heterosexual women before surgery were gay men after surgery. Chivers and Bailey (2000) compared a group of transmen who were attracted to men (a rare occurrence) with a group of transmen who were attracted to women (the usual pattern) both before and after surgery. They found the groups did not differ in the strength of their gender identity (as males), although the latter group was more sexually assertive and,

understandably, more interested in surgery to create an artificial penis.

Gender dysphoria resulting in a rejection of natal sex is relatively rare. The estimated prevalence in natal males is between 5 and 14 per 1,000 and for natal females between two and three per 1,000 (American Psychiatric Association, 2013; American Psychological Association, 2008). Many countries require a series of legal steps to change gender. In Germany, between 2.1 and 2.4 per 100,000 in the population took at least the first legal step of changing their first names in the 1990s; in that country, the male:female ratio of people with gender dysphoria is 2.3:1 (Weitze & Osburg, 1996). Since 2006 in New York City, people may choose to alter the natal sex listed on their birth certificates following surgery.

In some cultures, individuals with a different gender experience are often accorded the status of "shaman" or "seer" and treated as wisdom figures. A shaman is almost always a male adopting a female role (see, for example, Coleman, Colgan, & Gooren, 1992). Stoller (1976) reported on two contemporary feminized Native American men who were not only accepted but also esteemed by their tribes for their expertise in healing rituals. Contrary to the respect accorded these individuals in some cultures, social tolerance for them remains relatively low in Western cultures, although that is changing particularly as individuals such as Caitlyn Jenner openly discuss gender dysphoria. In recent years, books such as "Becoming Nicole" and movies such as *The Danish Girl* have also begun to raise awareness about gender dysphoria.

▲ Born identical twin boys in 1998, one of the twins realized early on that she didn't feel like a boy and at age 17 came out as transgender followed by gender confirmation surgery.

gender dysphoria Psychological dissatisfaction with biological gender, a disturbance in the sense of identity as a male or female. The primary goal is not sexual arousal but rather to live the life of the opposite gender.

Discussing Diversity   Alternative or Mixed Gender Identity

Transgender is an umbrella term for someone with unconventional gender expression (i.e., not identifying with their physical sex at birth). Such individuals are recognized differently across cultures.

In Western culture, it is usually believed that people are firmly male or female. Therefore, transgendered individuals are most often considered to have gender dysphoria and are required to fully assert their identity with their non-birth gender before being approved for sex reassignment surgery. Interestingly, in many cultures around the world, gender is not fixed as only male or female, but a mix or alternative gender expression is accepted. Take for instance "hijras" in India or "kathoey" or "ladyboys" in Thailand. In both of these groups, the biological male dresses

in women's clothing and identifies with femininity; such individuals are accepted by their society as a third gender. For instance, the hijras, who are considered "neither man, nor woman" (Nanda, 1999), may have actually had castration surgery, receive religious and cultural legitimacy through Hindu mythology (e.g., tranvestism existed before the conception of mankind), and are believed by some to have divine power (Bakshi, 2004). In fact, hijras serve a special function within their culture, performing at weddings and birth rituals, and their behavior is considered to be natural. Similarly kathoey, biological males with what the Thai refer to as a *female heart*, are recognized as a third gender. In some places, these individuals even have been given their own restroom with a

symbol on the door of a human divided in half with a blue side wearing pants and a red side dressed in a skirt (Beech, 2008). Whereas those within Western cultures believe that people are fully male or female and places such as India and Thailand accept hijras and kathoeys as a third sex, other cultures completely fail to accept transgendered individuals. For example, in Iran being transsexual can result in death, as was the case with a 24-year-old transsexual woman (born a male and underwent sex reassignment surgery) who was found strangled to death by her own brothers, a form of murder, known as an *honor killing*. Although the understanding and treatment of transgendered individuals vary across cultures, increased knowledge will ultimately reduce stigma and prejudice. ■

Causes

Research has yet to uncover any specific biological contributions to gender dysphoria or alternative gender experience for that matter, although it seems likely that a biological predisposition will be discovered. Coolidge, Thede, and Young (2002) estimated that genetics contributed about 62% to creating a vulnerability to experience gender dysphoria in their twin sample. Thirty-eight percent of the vulnerability came from non-shared (unique) environmental events. A study from the Netherlands twin registry suggested that 70% of the vulnerability for cross-gender behavior (behaving in a manner consistent with the opposite natal sex) was genetic as opposed to environmental, but this behavior is not the same as gender identity, which was not measured (as explained later) (van Beijsterveldt, Hudziak, & Boomsma, 2006). Gomez-Gil and colleagues (2010) found a somewhat higher prevalence of gender dysphoria than would be expected by chance in non-twin siblings of a larger group (995) of individuals with gender dysphoria. Segal (2006), on the other hand, found two monozygotic (identical) female twin pairs in which one twin had gender dysphoria and the other did not; no unusual medical or life history factors were identified to account for this difference. Nevertheless, genetic contributions are clearly part of the picture (Heylens *et al.*, 2012).

Early research suggested that, as with sexual orientation, slightly higher levels of testosterone or estrogen at certain critical periods of development might masculinize a female fetus or feminize a male fetus (see, for example, Keefe, 2002). Variations in hormonal levels could occur naturally or because of medication that a pregnant mother

is taking. However, scientists have yet to establish a link between pre-natal hormonal influence and later gender identity, although it is still possible that one exists.

At least some evidence suggests that gender identity firms up between 18 months and three years of age (Ehrhardt & Meyer-Bahlburg, 1981; Money & Ehrhardt, 1972) and is relatively fixed after that. But newer studies suggest that possible pre-existing biological factors have already had their impact. One interesting case illustrating this phenomenon was originally reported by Green and Money (1969), who described the sequence of events that occurred in the case of Bruce/Brenda.

Bruce/Brenda... • *Gender and Biology*

A set of male identical twins was born into a well-adjusted family. Several months later, an unfortunate accident occurred. Although circumcision went routinely for one of the boys, the physician's hand slipped so that the electric current in the device burned off the penis of the second baby. After working through their hostility toward the physician, the parents consulted specialists in children with intersexual problems and were faced with a choice. The specialists pointed out that the easiest solution would be to reassign their son Bruce as a girl, and the parents agreed. At the age of several months, Bruce became "Brenda." The parents purchased a new wardrobe and treated the child in every way possible as a girl.

These twins were followed through childhood and, upon reaching puberty, the young girl was given hormonal replacement therapy. After six years, the doctors lost track of the case but assumed the child had adjusted well.

However, Brenda endured almost intolerable inner turmoil. We know this because two clinical scientists found this individual and reported a long-term follow up (Diamond & Sigmundson, 1997). Brenda never adjusted to her assigned gender. As a child, she preferred rough-and-tumble play and resisted wearing girls' clothes. In public bathrooms, she often insisted on urinating while standing up, which usually made a mess. By early adolescence, Brenda was pretty sure she was a boy, but her doctors pressed her to act more feminine. When she was 14, she confronted her parents, telling them she was so miserable she was considering suicide. At that point, they told her the true story, and the muddy waters of her mind began to clear. Shortly thereafter, Brenda had additional surgery changing her back to Bruce, who married and became the father of three adopted children. But the turmoil of his early life never fully resolved. Perhaps because of this, perhaps because his twin brother had recently died and he had lost his job and was divorcing, or perhaps because of a combination of these factors, David Reimer (his real name) committed suicide at age 38 in 2004.

Str Old/Reuters

▲ After gender reassignment as a baby and subsequently being raised as a girl, David Reimer reclaimed his male gender identity in his teens and lived his life as a man. He spoke out against infant gender reassignment until his death in 2004.

Richard Green, a pioneering researcher in this area, has studied boys who behave in feminine ways and girls who behave in masculine ways, investigating what makes them that way and following what happens to them (Green, 1987). This set of behaviors and attitudes is referred to as **gender nonconformity** (see, for example, Skidmore, Linsenmeier, & Bailey, 2006). Green discovered that when most young boys spontaneously display "feminine"

interests and behaviors, they are typically discouraged by most families, and these behaviors usually cease. Boys who consistently display these behaviors are not discouraged, however, and are sometimes encouraged.

Other factors, such as excessive attention and physical contact on the part of the mother, may also play some role, as may a lack of male playmates during the early years of socialization. These are just some factors identified by Green as characteristic of gender-nonconforming boys. Remember that as-yet-undiscovered biological factors may also contribute to the spontaneous display of cross-gender behaviors and interests. For example, one recent study found that exposure to higher levels of fetal testosterone was associated with more masculine play behavior in both boys and girls during childhood (Auyeng *et al.*, 2009). In following up with these boys, however, Green discovered that few seem to develop the gender incongruence. The most likely outcome is the development of homosexual preferences, but even this particular sexual arousal pattern seems to occur exclusively in only approximately 40% of the gender-nonconforming boys. Another 32% show some degree of *bisexuality*, sexual attraction to both their own and the opposite sex. Looking at it from the other side, 60% were functioning heterosexually. These results were replicated in subsequent prospective studies of boys (Zucker, 2005).

Girls with gender-nonconforming behavior are seldom studied because their behavior attracts much less attention in Western societies. But one recent study followed 25 girls prospectively, beginning at approximately nine years of age, whose behavior was extreme enough that they were referred to a gender identity clinic. Most of these girls met criteria for childhood gender dysphoria disorder or came very close to it. At a follow up, when these girls (now women) averaged 25 years of age, only three met criteria for gender dysphoria. Another six reported bisexual/homosexual behavior; eight more would have homosexual fantasies but not behavior. The remaining eight women were heterosexual (Drummond, Bradley, Peterson-Badali, & Zucker, 2008).

This finding of only a very loose relationship between gender-nonconforming behavior and later sexual development is not unique to American culture. For example, similar relationships between early gender-nonconforming behavior and later development exist among the Fa'afafine, a group of males with homosexual orientation in the Pacific Islands country of Samoa (Bartlett & Vasey, 2006). And even in strict Muslim societies where any hint of gender-nonconforming behavior is severely discouraged, gender-nonconforming behavior, gender dysphoria, or both may develop (Doğan & Doğan, 2006). We can safely say that the causes of the development of incongruent experienced gender is still something of a mystery.

gender nonconformity A phenomenon in which pre-pubescent children do not identify with their biological sex, but instead identify strongly with the gender of the opposite sex and display varying degrees of behavior more characteristic of the opposite sex.

Treatment

Treatment is available for gender dysphoria in specialty clinics around the world, although much controversy surrounds treatment (Carroll, 2007; Meyer-Bahlburg, 2010). For adults requesting full sex transition treatment, guidelines from both the American Psychiatric Association and the American Psychological Association have now been published (American Psychological Association, 2015; Byne *et al.*, 2012). Recommendations from the American Psychiatric Association begin with the least intrusive step of full psychological evaluation and education before proceeding to partially reversible steps such as administration of gonadal hormones to bring about desired secondary sex characteristics. The final non-reversible step is to alter anatomy physically to be consistent with gender identity through **sex reassignment surgery**.

Sex Reassignment Surgery

To qualify for surgery at a reputable clinic, individuals must live in the desired gender for one to two years so that they can be sure they want to change sex. They also must be stable psychologically, financially, and socially. In transwomen, hormones are administered to promote *gynecomastia* (the growth of breasts) and the development of other secondary sex characteristics. Facial hair is typically removed through electrolysis. If the individual is satisfied with the events of the trial period, the genitals are removed and a vagina is constructed.

For transmen, an artificial penis is typically constructed through plastic surgery, using sections of skin and muscle from elsewhere in the body, such as the thigh. Breasts are surgically removed. Genital surgery is more difficult and complex in natal females. Estimates of satisfaction with surgery indicate predominantly successful adjustment (between 75% and 100% generally satisfied) among those who could be reached for follow-ups, with transmen generally adjusting better than transwomen (Byne *et al.*, 2012; Costantino *et al.*, 2013). Approximately 1% to 7% of individuals who have sex reassignment surgery and were reached for follow-up later regret having the surgery to some extent (Byne *et al.*, 2012; Dhejne, Öberg, Aryer, & Landén, 2014). This is unfortunate, because the surgery is irreversible. Also, as many as 2% attempt suicide after surgery, a rate much higher than the rate for the general population. Nevertheless, surgery has made life worth living for many people who suffered the effects of existing in what they felt to be the wrong body with rates of satisfaction in recent years averaging about 90% (Johansson *et al.*, 2010).

Treatment of Gender Nonconformity in Children

More controversial is the treatment of gender-nonconforming children. On the one hand, some segments of society are becoming open to gender variations in both children

▲ Laverne Cox and Caitlin Jenner are both male-to-female transgender (transwomen) who are strong and effective advocates for the transgender community. Laverne Cox has an identical twin brother who identifies as male, and gay.

and adults. Indeed, one study suggests that gender non-conforming children who present themselves according to their gender identity exhibit cognitions more consistent with their expressed gender than their natal sex (Olson, Key, & Eaton, 2015). On the other hand, research has found that gender nonconformity is associated with lower levels of psychological well-being (Rieger & Savin-Williams, 2012).

Treatment guidelines developed by the American Psychiatric Association and the American Psychological Association for gender nonconformity in youth simply outline the options available (American Psychological Association, 2015; Byne *et al.*, 2012). One option is to work with the child and caregivers to lessen gender dysphoria and decrease cross-gender behaviors and identification on the assumption that these behaviors are unlikely to persist and the negative consequences of social rejection could be avoided. A second approach is letting expressed gender unfold naturally. This goal requires strong support from caregivers and the community because of the social and interpersonal risks. A third approach advocates affirming and encouraging cross-gender identification, but critics point out that gender nonconformity usually does not persist and that taking this course increases the likelihood of persistence.

More recently, new treatment approaches have been developed for children who clearly identify as transsexual. Given the irreversible nature of many treatments for gender dysphoria, treatment for these children must be administered with caution. One specialty clinic for these children at Children's Hospital in Boston has attracted attention. In pre-pubescent children, treatments include psychoeducation and therapy to help clarify gender identity and navigate the social issues associated with cross-gender identification. In individuals closer to puberty, psychotherapy is also recommended. However, a medical intervention that blocks puberty is also available. This medication allows the adolescents time to explore gender identity issues without the stress of beginning puberty in a gender inconsistent with their identify (Tishelman *et al.*, 2014). Although this treatment has received some positive press, it still remains controversial in many parts of the United States.

Treatment of Disorders of Sex Development (Intersexuality)

As we noted, surgery and hormonal replacement therapy has been standard treatment for many individuals with DSDs who may be born with physical characteristics of both sexes in order to make their sexual anatomy match as closely to their assigned gender as possible. These procedures usually take place soon after birth. But in later years, gender dysphoria may also develop in these individuals, and, if it does, a similar sequence of treatment steps beginning with the least intrusive would be initiated as described above (Byne *et al.*, 2012). Of course, treatment for gender dysphoria in any form has always been controversial and particularly so when a DSD is present. For example, one alternative approach has been proposed by Anne Fausto-Sterling, who suggests that there are actually five sexes: males; females; "herms," who are named after true hermaphrodites, or people born with both testes and ovaries; "merms," who are anatomically more male than female but possess some aspect of female genitalia; and "ferms," who have ovaries but possess some aspect of male genitalia (Fausto-Sterling, 2000a, 2000b, 2015). She estimates, based on the best evidence available, that for every 1,000 children born, 17, or 1.7%, may be present with a DSD in some form. What Fausto-Sterling (2000b) and others have noted is that individuals in this group are often dissatisfied with surgery.

Fausto-Sterling suggests that an increasing number of pediatric endocrinologists, urologists, and psychologists are examining the wisdom of early genital surgery that results in an irreversible gender assignment. Instead, health professionals may want to examine the precise nature of the DSD and consider surgery only as a last resort, and only when they are quite sure the particular condition will lead to a specific psychological gender identity. Otherwise, psychological treatments to help individuals adapt to their particular sexual anatomy, or their emerging gender experience, might be more appropriate.

9.4 Concept CHECK

Answer the following questions about normal sexuality and gender dysphoria:

1. Name some gender differences that exist in sexual attitudes and sexual behavior. _____

2. Which sexual preference or preferences are normal, and how are they developed? _____

3. Charlie always felt out of place with the boys. At a young age, he preferred to play with girls and insisted that his parents call him "Charlene." He later claimed that he felt like a woman trapped in a man's body. What disorder could Charlie have? _____

4. What could be the cause(s) of Charlie's disorder? _____

5. What treatments could be given to Charlie? _____

sex reassignment surgery Surgical procedures to alter a person's physical anatomy to conform to that person's psychological gender identity.

DSM 5 CONTROVERSY Paraphilia or Paraphilic Disorder?

In *DSM-IV*, a paraphilia was diagnosed based on the presence of intense and persistent sexual interest as determined by the presence of strong sexual fantasies, sexual urges, or behaviors generally involving non-human objects, the suffering or humiliation of oneself or one's partner, or children or other non-consenting persons. It was also noted that these fantasies, urges, or behaviors cause clinically significant distress or impairment. In *DSM-5*, an explicit distinction is made between paraphilia, which denotes any intense and persistent sexual interest other than sexual interest and behaviors with phenotypically normal, physically mature, consenting human partners, and paraphilic disorder.

A paraphilic disorder is a paraphilia which either causes distress or impairment to the individual or personal harm or risk of harm to others. This change was made to accommodate the high prevalence of "paraphilic" type fantasies that might occasionally occur among people without mental disorders (Ahlers et al., 2011). An example would be a harmless fetish for an article of clothing that is incorporated into sexual activity with a willing partner. Here, the individual would have a paraphilia but not a paraphilic disorder. But what if the paraphilia focused on sex with small children or inflicting grievous harm on other individuals? Advocates of the change would point out that if these fantasies are not acted upon in any way, no harm is done and it is not a disorder, and that it does more harm to pathologize this very private behavior than to call it a mental disorder. Critics would point out that it is highly unlikely that anyone with such a strong and persistent pattern of sexual arousal would not at least watch an occasional video on the internet if it were readily available, and in so doing, harm would occur. This example is yet another point of contention in the fundamental question of what defines a mental disorder, discussed in Chapter 1. •

What Is Normal Sexuality?

How do sociocultural factors influence what are considered "normal" sexual behaviors?

▶ Patterns of sexual behavior, both heterosexual and homosexual, vary around the world in terms of both behavior and risks. Approximately 20% of individuals who have been surveyed engage in sex with numerous partners, which puts them at risk for sexually transmitted diseases such as AIDS.

▶ Two types of disorders are associated with sexual functioning—sexual dysfunctions and paraphilic disorders. Gender dysphoria is not specifically a sexual disorder, but rather a marked incongruence between one's natal (biological) sex and the gender one experiences or identifies with.

An Overview of Sexual Dysfunctions

How do psychologists define sexual dysfunction?
How is sexual dysfunction related to the sexual response cycle?

▶ Sexual dysfunction includes a variety of disorders in which people find it difficult to function adequately during sexual relations.

▶ Specific sexual dysfunctions include disorders of sexual desire (hypoactive sexual desire disorder in males and female sexual interest/arousal disorder) in which interest in sexual relations is extremely low or non-existent, disorders of sexual arousal (erectile disorder and female sexual interest/arousal disorder) in which achieving or maintaining adequate penile erection or sexual excitement and vaginal lubrication is problematic; and orgasmic disorders (female orgasmic disorder

and delayed or premature ejaculation in males) in which orgasm occurs too quickly or not at all. The most common disorder in this category is premature ejaculation, which occurs in males; inhibited orgasm is commonly seen in females.

▶ Sexual pain disorder, specifically genito-pelvic pain/penetration disorder in women, refers to unbearable pain associated with sexual relations, including vaginismus, in which the pelvic muscles in the outer third of the vagina undergo involuntary spasms when intercourse is attempted .

▶ The three components involved in assessing sexual behavior include interviews, a complete medical evaluation, and a psychophysiological assessment.

Causes and Treatment of Sexual Dysfunction

What are the defining features and known causes of sexual dysfunction?
What psychosocial and medical treatments are available, and are they effective?

▶ Sexual dysfunction is associated with socially transmitted negative attitudes about sex, current relationship difficulties, and anxiety focused on sexual activity as well as occasional medical issues.

▶ In recent years, various medical approaches have become available, including the drug Viagra and similar drugs. These treatments focus mostly on erectile dysfunction and are effective for about one-third of patients who try them. Some preliminary evidence exists on a new drug, flibanserin, as a possible treatment for hypoactive sexual desire in women, but more research is needed.

Paraphilic Disorders: Clinical Descriptions

What are the clinical features of the major paraphilias? What is known about the causes of paraphilias?

▶ Paraphilia is sexual attraction to inappropriate people, such as children, or to inappropriate objects, such as articles of clothing. Paraphilia becomes a paraphilic disorder when the sexual attraction causes significant distress or impairment to the individual or causes harm or the risk of harm to others.

▶ The paraphilic disorders include fetishistic disorder, in which sexual arousal occurs almost exclusively in the context of inappropriate objects or individuals; exhibitionistic disorder, in which sexual gratification is attained by exposing one's genitals to unsuspecting strangers; voyeuristic disorder, in which sexual arousal is derived from observing unsuspecting individuals undressing or naked; transvestic disorder, in which individuals are sexually aroused by wearing clothing of the opposite sex; sexual sadism disorder, in which sexual arousal is associated with inflicting pain or humiliation; sexual masochism disorder, in which sexual arousal is associated with experiencing pain or humiliation; and pedophilic disorder, in which there is a strong sexual attraction toward children. Incest is a type of pedophilia in which the victim is related, often a son or daughter.

▶ The development of paraphilic disorders is associated with deficiencies in consensual adult sexual arousal, deficiencies in consensual adult social skills, deviant sexual fantasies that may develop before or during puberty, and attempts by the individual to suppress thoughts associated with these arousal patterns.

Assessing and Treating Paraphilic Disorders

What psychosocial and drug treatments are available for paraphilias, and how effective are they?

▶ Psychosocial treatments of these disorders are only modestly effective at best among individuals who are incarcerated, but somewhat more successful in less severe outpatients.

Gender Dysphoria

What are the defining clinical features, causes, and treatments of gender dysphoria?

▶ Gender dysphoria is a dissatisfaction with one's natal (biological) sex and the sense that one is really the opposite gender (e.g., a woman trapped in a man's body). A person develops a sense of gender or gender identity between 18 months and three years of age, and it seems that both congruent gender identity and incongruent gender identity have biological roots influenced by learning.

▶ Treatment for adults with marked gender incongruence (transsexualism) may include sex reassignment surgery integrated with psychological approaches.

Key Terms

heterosexual behavior, 329
homosexual behavior, 328
sexual dysfunction, 333
male hypoactive sexual desire
   disorder, 333
female sexual interest/arousal
   disorder, 333
erectile disorder, 335
delayed ejaculation, 337
female orgasmic disorder, 337

premature ejaculation, 337
genito-pelvic pain/penetration
   disorder, 337
vaginismus, 337
paraphilic disorders, 345
frotteuristic disorder, 347
fetishistic disorder, 347
voyeuristic disorder, 347
exhibitionistic disorder, 347
transvestic disorder, 347

sexual sadism, 347
sexual masochism, 347
pedophilia, 349
incest, 349
covert sensitization, 351
orgasmic reconditioning, 353
gender dysphoria, 355
gender nonconformity, 357
sex reassignment surgery, 359

Answers to Concept Checks

9.1

1. a; 2. d; 3. c; 4. a

9.2

1. T; 2. F (sometimes increases arousal); 3. T; 4. T; 5. F (non-demand pleasuring, squeeze technique, and so on); 6. T

9.3

1. d; 2. c; 3. a; 4. b; 5. a; 6. c

9.4

1. More men masturbate and do it more often; men are more permissive about casual sex; women want more intimacy from sex, and so on.
2. Both heterosexuality and homosexuality are normal; genetics appear to play some role in the development of sexual preference.
3. Gender dysphoria
4. Abnormal hormone levels during development; social or parental influences
5. Sex reassignment surgery; psychosocial treatment to adjust to expressed or desired gender.

Chapter Quiz

1. Statistics about sexual activity have suggested that:
   a. more people engage in oral intercourse than vaginal intercourse
   b. the majority of people engage in heterosexual, vaginal intercourse in the context of a relationship with one partner
   c. 10% to 15% of the population has exclusively homosexual sex
   d. in the 1990s, people were more likely to be having sex with multiple partners than they were to be in a monogamous sexual relationship

2. Research evidence on the origins of homosexuality has suggested a possible role for all of the following EXCEPT:
   a. genetic or chromosomal influences
   b. emotionally distant fathers
   c. size or function of brain structures
   d. exposure to hormones

3. The most common form of treatment for gender dysphoria is:
   a. exposure therapy
   b. antidepressant medication
   c. cognitive–behavioral therapy
   d. sexual reassignment surgery

4. In which phase of the sexual response cycle can men experience difficulty attaining or maintaining erections?
   a. resolution
   b. orgasm
   c. arousal
   d. plateau

5. Simone and her partner have sexual intercourse about once a month. Simone says she wants to have sex but can't seem to achieve adequate lubrication to make sex enjoyable. Simone's symptoms are most consistent with:
   a. impotence
   b. sexual aversion disorder
   c. sexual arousal disorder
   d. vaginismus

6. Which component is essential to the diagnosis of female orgasmic disorder?
   a. orgasms occur less frequently than desired
   b. a 20% to 30% reduction in the frequency of orgasms in the past six months
   c. a 70% to 80% reduction in the frequency of orgasms in the past year
   d. orgasm never or almost never occurs

7. The overarching goal of Masters and Johnson's psychosocial treatment for sexual dysfunction was:
   a. reducing or eliminating psychologically-based performance anxiety
   b. helping couples to increase the frequency of their sexual encounters to normalize sexual experiences
   c. encouraging couples to be more willing to try medical treatments, despite their potential side effects
   d. helping both individuals in a couple to understand past parental influences on contemporary sexual relations within the couple

8. A disorder in which an inappropriate, inanimate object is the source of sexual arousal is known as a:
   a. parapathology
   b. paranormality
   c. paraphilia
   d. paraphasia

9. Which of the following statements is an accurate characterization of pedophilia?
   a. It involves an attraction to male children more often than female children.
   b. It is most commonly directed at girls who are beginning to mature physically.
   c. It is often rationalized by the perpetrator as an acceptable way to teach children about sexuality.
   d. It involves the use of physical force to get a child to perform sexual acts.

10. Shane is being treated for a paraphilia by imagining harmful consequences occurring in response to his unwanted behavior and arousal. Shane is receiving what kind of treatment?
    a. covert sensitization
    b. marital therapy
    c. relapse prevention
    d. orgasmic reconditioning
    (See Appendix A for answers.)

Exploring Sexual Disorders and Gender Dysphoria

▶ Sexual behavior is considered normal in our culture unless it is associated with one of three kinds of impaired functioning—gender dysphoria, sexual dysfunction, or paraphilic disorders.

▶ Sexual orientation probably has a strong biological basis that is influenced by environmental and social factors.

GENDER DYSPHORIA

Present when a person feels trapped in a body that is the "wrong" sex, that does not match his or her innate sense of personal identity. (Gender identity is independent of sexual arousal patterns.) Relatively rare.

Thinkstock/Getty Images

Causes

Biological Influences

- Not yet confirmed, although likely to involve prenatal exposure to hormones
  - Hormonal variations may be natural or result from medication

Psychological Influences

- Gender identity develops between 1½ and 3 years of age
  - "Masculine" behaviors in girls and "feminine" behaviors in boys evoke different responses in different families

Treatment

- Sex reassignment surgery: removal of breasts or penis; genital reconstruction
  - Requires rigorous psychological preparation and financial and social stability
- Psychosocial intervention to change gender identity
  - Usually unsuccessful except as temporary relief until surgery

PARAPHILIC DISORDERS

Sexual arousal occurs almost exclusively in the context of inappropriate objects or individuals.

Types

- **Fetishistic disorder:** Sexual attraction to nonliving objects
- **Voyeuristic disorder:** Sexual arousal achieved by viewing unsuspecting person undressing or naked
- **Exhibitionistic disorder:** Sexual gratification from exposing one's genitals to unsuspecting strangers
- **Transvestic disorder:** Sexual arousal from wearing opposite-sex clothing (cross-dressing)
- **Sexual sadism disorder:** Sexual arousal associated with inflicting pain or humiliation
- **Sexual masochism disorder:** Sexual arousal associated with experiencing pain or humiliation
- **Pedophilic disorder:** Strong sexual attraction to children
- **Incest:** Sexual attraction to family member

Causes

- Preexisting deficiencies
  - In levels of arousal with consensual adults
  - In consensual adult social skills
- Treatment received from adults during childhood
- Early sexual fantasies reinforced by masturbation
- Extremely strong sex drive combined with uncontrollable thought processes

Treatment

- *Covert sensitization:* Repeated mental reviewing of aversive consequences to establish negative associations with behavior
- *Relapse prevention:* Therapeutic preparation for coping with future situations
- *Orgasmic reconditioning:* Pairing appropriate stimuli with masturbation to create positive arousal patterns
- *Medical:* Drugs that reduce testosterone to suppress sexual desire; fantasies and arousal return when drugs are stopped

PhotoDisc/Getty Images

Thinkstock/Getty Images

PhotoDisc/Getty Images

SEXUAL DYSFUNCTIONS

Sexual dysfunctions can be
- *Lifelong:* Present during entire sexual history
- *Acquired:* Interrupts normal sexual pattern
- *Generalized:* Present in every encounter
- *Situational:* Present only with certain partners or at certain times

The Human Sexual Response Cycle
A dysfunction is an impairment in one of the sexual response stages.

Desire
Resolution
Causes
Arousal
Orgasm
Plateau

Types of Sexual Dysfunctions

Sexual Desire Disorders
- *Male hypoactive sexual desire disorder:* Apparent lack of interest in sexual activity or fantasy

Sexual Arousal Disorders
- *Erectile disorder:* Recurring inability to achieve or maintain adequate erection
- *Female sexual interest/arousal disorder:* Recurring inability to achieve or maintain adequate lubrication

Orgasm Disorders
- *Female orgasmic disorder:* Inability to achieve orgasm despite adequate desire and arousal
- *Premature ejaculation:* Ejaculation before it is desired, with minimal stimulation

Sexual Pain Disorders
- *Genito-pelvic pain/penetration disorder:* Marked pain, anxiety, and tension associated with intercourse for which there is no medical cause; vaginismus (i.e., involuntary muscle spasms in the front of the vagina that prevent or interfere with intercourse); occurs in females

Psychological Contributions
- Distraction
- Underestimates of arousal
- Negative thought processes

Psychological and Physical Interactions
- A combination of influences is almost always present
  - Specific biological predisposition *and* psychological factors may produce a particular disorder

Causes

Sociocultural Contributions
- Erotophobia, caused by formative experiences of sexual cues as alarming
- Negative experiences, such as rape
- Deterioration of relationship

Biological Contributions
- Neurological or other nervous system problems
- Vascular disease
- Chronic illness
- Prescription medication
- Drugs of abuse, including alcohol

Treatment

- *Psychosocial:* Therapeutic program to facilitate communication, improve sexual education, and eliminate anxiety. Both partners participate fully.
- *Medical:* Almost all interventions focus on male erectile disorder, including drugs, prostheses, and surgery. Medical treatment is combined with sexual education and therapy to achieve maximum benefit.

Romilly Lockyer/Brand X Pictures/PictureQuest/Jupiter Images

10 Substance-Related, Addictive, and Impulse-Control Disorders

CHAPTER OUTLINE

Perspectives on Substance-Related and Addictive Disorders
Levels of Involvement
Diagnostic Issues

Depressants
Alcohol-Related Disorders
Sedative-, Hypnotic-, or Anxiolytic-Related Disorders

Stimulants
Stimulant-Related Disorders
Tobacco-Related Disorders
Caffeine-Related Disorders

Opioid-Related Disorders

Cannabis-Related Disorders

Hallucinogen-Related Disorders

Other Drugs of Abuse

Causes of Substance-Related Disorders
Biological Dimensions
Psychological Dimensions
Cognitive Dimensions
Social Dimensions
Cultural Dimensions
An Integrative Model

Treatment of Substance-Related Disorders
Biological Treatments
Psychosocial Treatments
Prevention

Gambling Disorder

Impulse-Control Disorders
Intermittent Explosive Disorder
Kleptomania
Pyromania

iStock.com/coldsnowstorm

Use scientific reasoning to interpret behavior:	▶ Identify basic biological, psychological, and social components of behavioral explanations (e.g., inferences, observations, operational definitions and interpretations) [APA SLO 2.1a] (*see textbook pages 370–374, 387–391*)
Engage in innovative and integrative thinking and problem solving:	▶ Describe problems operationally to study them empirically. [APA SLO 2.3a] (*see textbook pages 391–393*)
Describe applications that employ discipline-based problem solving:	▶ Correctly identify antecedents and consequences of behavior and mental processes [APA SLO 5.3c] Describe examples of relevant and practical applications of psychological principles to everyday life [APA SLO 1.3c] (*see textbook pages 387–391*)

* Portions of this chapter cover learning outcomes suggested by the American Psychological Association (2013) in its guidelines for the undergraduate psychology major. Chapter coverage of these outcomes is identified above by APA Goal and APA Suggested Learning Outcome (SLO).

In this chapter, we explore **substance-related and addictive disorders**, which are associated with the abuse of drugs and other substances people take to alter the way they think, feel, and behave. In addition, the newly added disorder to this category in *DSM-5*—gambling disorder—will be discussed.

Equally disruptive to the people affected, **impulse-control disorders** represent a number of related problems that involve the inability to resist acting on a drive or temptation. Included in this group are those who cannot resist aggressive impulses or the impulse to steal, for example,

or to set fires. Controversy surrounds substance-related, addictive, and impulse-control disorders because our society sometimes believes that these problems result simply from a lack of "will." If you wanted to stop drinking, using cocaine, or gambling, well, you would just stop. We first examine those individuals who are being harmed by their use of a variety of chemical substances (substance-related disorders) or their addictive behaviors (gambling disorder) and then turn our attention to the puzzling array of disorders that are under the heading of impulse-control disorders.

Perspectives on Substance-Related and Addictive Disorders

▶ What are substance-related and addictive disorders?

The cost in lives, money, and emotional turmoil has made the issue of drug abuse a major concern worldwide. Currently, around 9.7% of the general population (12 years or older) are believed to use illegal drugs (Substance Abuse and Mental Health Services Administration [SAMHSA], 2013). Many U.S. presidential administrations have declared various "wars on drugs," but the problem remains. The Roman Catholic Church issued a universal catechism in 1992 that officially declared drug abuse and drunk driving to be sins (Riding, 1992). Yet from the drug-related deaths of rock stars Jimi Hendrix and Janis Joplin in 1970 to contemporary celebrities such as Amy Winehouse and Prince, drug use continues to negatively impact the lives of

many. Consider the case of Danny, who has the disturbing but common habit of **alcohol use disorder**, and several substance use disorders.

substance-related and addictive disorders Range of problems associated with the use and abuse of drugs such as **alcohol, cocaine**, heroin, and other substances people use to alter the way they think, feel, and behave. These are extremely costly in human and financial terms.

impulse-control disorders A disorder in which a person acts on an irresistible, but potentially harmful, impulse.

alcohol use disorder A cognitive, biological, behavioral, and social problem associated with **alcohol** use and abuse.

At the age of 43, Danny was in jail, awaiting trial on vehicular manslaughter charges stemming from a DUI accident that left one woman dead. Danny grew up in the suburbs in the United States, the youngest of three children. He was well liked in school and an average student. Like many of his friends, he smoked cigarettes in his early teens and drank beer with his friends at night behind his high school. Unlike most of his friends, however, Danny almost always drank until he was obviously drunk; he also experimented with other drugs, including cocaine, heroin, "speed" (amphetamines), and "downers" (barbiturates).

After high school, Danny attended a community college for one semester, but he dropped out after failing most of his courses. His performance in school seemed to be related to his missing most classes rather than to an inability to learn. He had difficulty getting up for classes after partying most of the night, which he did frequently. Danny's family knew he occasionally drank too much, but they didn't know (or didn't want to know) about his other drug use. He had for years forbidden anyone to go into his room after his mother found packets of white powder (probably cocaine) in his sock drawer. He said he was keeping them for a friend and was furious that his family might suspect him of using drugs. Money was sometimes missing from the house, and once some stereo equipment "disappeared," but if his family members suspected Danny they never admitted it.

Danny held a series of low-paying jobs, and when he was working his family reassured themselves that he was back on track. Unfortunately, he rarely held a job for more than a few months. Because he continued to live at home, Danny could survive despite frequent periods of unemployment. When he was in his late 20s, Danny seemed to have a revelation. He announced that he needed help and planned to check into an alcohol rehabilitation center. His family's joy and relief were overwhelming, and no one questioned his request for several thousand dollars to pay for the program. Danny disappeared for several weeks, presumably because he was in the rehab program. However, a call from the police put an end to this fantasy: Danny had been found high, living in an abandoned building. Danny's deceptiveness and financial irresponsibility strained his relationship with his family. He was allowed to live at home, but his family excluded him from their emotional lives. Following this, Danny seemed to straighten out, and he held a job at a gas station for almost two years. He became friendly with the station owner and his son, but without any obvious warning, Danny resumed drinking and using drugs and was arrested for robbing the very place that had kept him employed for many months.

Although he received probation for that offense upon promising to attend drug treatment, his pattern continued. Years later while driving under the influence of multiple substances, he hit another car and killed the 28-year-old driver.

Why did Danny's drug use become problematic when many of his friends' and siblings' use did not? What ultimately became of him? We return to Danny's story later when we look at the causes and treatment of substance-related disorders.

Levels of Involvement

Although each drug described in this chapter has unique effects, there are similarities in the ways they are used and how people who abuse them are treated. First, we present some concepts that apply to substance-related disorders in general, noting important terminology and addressing several diagnostic issues.

Can you use drugs without meeting criteria for a disorder? Can you use drugs and not become addicted to them? To answer these important questions, we first need to outline what we mean by *substance use, substance intoxication, substance use disorder, and substance dependence/addiction.* The term *substance* refers to chemical compounds that are ingested to alter mood or behavior. **Psychoactive substances** alter mood, behavior, or both. Although you might first think of drugs such as cocaine and heroin, this definition also includes more commonplace legal drugs such as alcohol, the nicotine found in tobacco, and the caffeine in coffee, soft drinks, and chocolate. As you will see, these so-called safe drugs also affect mood and behavior, they can be addictive, and they account for more health problems and a greater mortality rate than all illegal drugs combined.

Substance Use

Substance use is the ingestion of psychoactive substances in moderate amounts that does not significantly interfere with social, educational, or occupational functioning. Drinking a cup of coffee in the morning to wake up or smoking a cigarette and having a drink with a friend to relax are examples of substance use, as is the occasional ingestion of illegal drugs such as cannabis, cocaine, amphetamines, or barbiturates.

Intoxication

Our physiological reaction to ingested substances—drunkenness or getting high—is **substance intoxication**.

▲ Substance use.

For a person to become intoxicated, many variables interact, including the type of drug taken, the amount ingested, and the person's individual biological reaction. For many of the substances we discuss here, intoxication is experienced as impaired judgment, mood changes, and lowered motor ability (for example, problems walking or talking).

Substance Use Disorders

Defining **substance use disorders** by how much of a substance is ingested is problematic. For example, is drinking two glasses of wine in an hour abuse? Three glasses? Six? Is taking one injection of heroin considered abuse? The fifth edition of the *Diagnostic and Statistical Manual (DSM-5)* (American Psychiatric Association, 2013) defines substance use disorders in terms of how significantly the use interferes with the user's life. If substances disrupt your education, job, or relationships with others, and put you in physically dangerous situations (for example, while driving) you would be considered to have a disorder. Some evidence suggests that drug use can predict later job outcomes. In one study, researchers controlled for factors such as educational interests and other problem behavior, and still found that repeated hard drug use (using one or more of the following: amphetamines, barbiturates, crack, cocaine, PCP, LSD, other psychedelics, crystal meth, inhalants, heroin, or other narcotics) predicted poor job outcomes after college (Arria *et al.*, 2013).

Danny seems to fit this definition of a disorder. His inability to complete a semester of community college was a direct result of drug use. Danny often drove while drunk or under the influence of other drugs, and he had been arrested twice. Danny's use of multiple substances was so relentless and pervasive that he would probably be diagnosed with severe forms of the disorders.

Substance use disorder is usually described as addiction. Although we use the term *addiction* routinely when we describe people who seem to be under the control of drugs, there is some disagreement about how to define addiction (Edwards, 2012; Rehm *et al.*, 2013). In order to meet criteria for a disorder, a person must meet criteria for at least two symptoms in the past year that interfered with his/her life or bothered him/her a great deal. When a person has four or five symptoms, he or she is considered to fall in the moderate range. A severe substance use disorder would be someone like Danny who has six or more symptoms.

Symptoms for substance use disorders can include a **physiological dependence** on the drug or drugs, meaning the use of increasingly greater amounts of the drug to experience the same effect (**tolerance**) and a negative physical response when the substance is no longer ingested (**withdrawal**) (Higgins, Sigmon, & Heil, 2014). Tolerance and withdrawal are physiological reactions to the chemicals being ingested. Have you ever experienced a headache when you didn't get your morning coffee? You were probably going through caffeine withdrawal. In a more extreme example, withdrawal from alcohol can cause alcohol withdrawal delirium, in which a person can experience frightening hallucinations and body tremors. Withdrawal from many substances can bring on chills, fever, diarrhea, nausea and vomiting, and aches and pains. Not all substances are physiologically addicting, however. For example, you do not go through severe physical withdrawal when you stop taking LSD. Cocaine withdrawal has a pattern that includes anxiety, sleep changes, lack of motivation, and boredom (*DSM-5*; American Psychiatric Association, 2013), and withdrawal from cannabis includes such symptoms as irritability, nervousness, appetite change, and sleep disturbance (*DSM-5*).

psychoactive substances Substances, such as a drug, that alter **mood** or behavior.

substance use The ingestion of psychoactive substances in moderate amounts that does not significantly interfere with social, educational, or occupational functioning.

substance intoxication A physiological reaction, such as impaired judgment and motor ability, as well as **mood** change, resulting from the ingestion of a **psychoactive substance**.

substance use disorders When the recurrent use of alcohol and/or drugs causes clinically and functionally significant impairment, such as health problems, disability, and failure to meet major responsibilities at work, school, or home.

physiological dependence The use of increasingly greater amounts of the drug to experience the same effect (**tolerance**) and a negative physical response when the substance is no longer ingested.

tolerance The need for increased amounts of a substance to achieve the desired effect, and a diminished effect with continued use of the same amount.

withdrawal A severely negative physiological reaction to removal of a **psychoactive substance**, which can be alleviated by the same or a similar substance.

Other symptoms that make up a substance use disorder include "drug-seeking behaviors." The repeated use of a drug, a desperate need to ingest more of the substance (stealing money to buy drugs, standing outside in the cold to smoke), and the likelihood that use will resume after a period of abstinence are behaviors that define the extent of substance use disorders. Such behavioral reactions are different from the physiological responses to drugs we described before and are sometimes referred to in terms of psychological dependence. The previous version of the *DSM* considered substance abuse and **substance dependence** as separate diagnoses. The *DSM-5* combines the two into the general definition of substance-related disorders based on research that suggests the two co-occur (American Psychiatric Association, 2013; Dawson, Goldstein, & Grant, 2012; O'Brien, 2011).

Let's go back to the questions we started with: "Can you use drugs and not abuse them?" and "Can you abuse drugs and not become addicted to them?" The answer to the first question is yes. Some people drink wine or beer regularly without drinking to excess. And contrary to popular belief, some people use drugs such as heroin, cocaine, or crack (a form of cocaine) occasionally (for instance, several times

a year) without abusing them (Ray, 2012). What is disturbing is that we do not know ahead of time who might be likely to lose control and abuse these drugs and who is likely to become dependent with even a passing use of a substance.

It may seem counterintuitive, but dependence can be present without abuse. For example, cancer patients who take morphine for pain may become dependent on the drug—build up a tolerance and go through withdrawal if it is stopped—without abusing it (Flemming, 2010; Portenoy & Mathur, 2009). Later in this chapter, we discuss biological and psychosocial theories of the causes of substance-related disorders and why we have individualized reactions to these substances.

Diagnostic Issues

In early editions of the *DSM*, alcoholism and drug abuse weren't treated as separate disorders. Instead, they were categorized as "sociopathic personality disturbances"—a forerunner of the current *antisocial personality disorder* we discuss in Chapter 11, because substance use was seen as a symptom of other problems. It was considered a sign of moral weakness, and the influence of genetics and biology was hardly acknowledged. A separate category was created for **substance abuse** disorders in *DSM-III*, in 1980, and since then we have acknowledged the complex biological and psychological nature of the problem.

The *DSM-5* term *substance-related disorders* include 11 symptoms that range from relatively mild (e.g., substance use results in a failure to fulfill major role obligations) to more severe (e.g., occupational or recreational activities are given up or reduced because of substance use). *DSM-5* removed the previous symptom that related to substance-related legal problems and added a symptom that indicates the presence of craving or a strong desire to use the substance (Dawson *et al.*, 2012). These distinctions help clarify the problem and focus treatment on the appropriate aspect of the disorder.

Symptoms of other disorders can complicate the substance use disorder picture significantly. For example, do some people take drugs to excess because they are depressed, or does drug use and its consequences (for example, loss of friends, job) create depression? Researchers estimate that almost three-quarters of the people in addiction treatment centers have an additional psychiatric disorder, with mood disorders (such as major depression) observed in more than 40% and anxiety disorders and posttraumatic stress disorder seen in more than 25% of the cases (Dawson *et al.*, 2012; Lieb, 2015).

Substance use might occur concurrently with other disorders for several reasons. Substance-related disorders and anxiety and mood disorders are highly prevalent in our society and may occur together so often just by chance. Drug intoxication and withdrawal can cause symptoms of anxiety, depression, and psychosis. Disorders such as schizophrenia and antisocial personality disorder are highly likely to include a secondary problem of substance use.

ACE STOCK LIMITED/Alamy Stock Photo

▲ Intoxication.

Because substance-related disorders can be so complicated, *DSM-5* tries to define when a symptom is a result of substance use and when it is not. Basically, if symptoms seen in schizophrenia or in extreme states of anxiety appear during intoxication or within six weeks after withdrawal from drugs, they are not considered signs of a separate psychiatric disorder. So, for example, individuals who show signs of severe depression just after they have stopped taking heavy doses of stimulants would not be diagnosed with a major mood disorder. However, individuals who were severely depressed before they used stimulants and those whose symptoms persist more than six weeks after they stop might have a separate disorder (Sheperis, Lionetti, & Snook, 2015).

We now turn to the individual substances themselves, their effects on our brains and bodies, and how they are used in our society. We have grouped the substances into six general categories.

- **Depressants**: These substances result in behavioral sedation and can induce relaxation. They include alcohol (ethyl alcohol) and the sedative and hypnotic drugs in the families of barbiturates (for example, Seconal) and benzodiazepines (for example, Valium, Xanax).
- **Stimulants**: These substances cause us to be more active and alert and can elevate mood. Included in this group are amphetamines, cocaine, nicotine, and caffeine.
- **Opiates**: The major effect of these substances is to produce analgesia temporarily (reduce pain) and euphoria. Heroin, opium, codeine, and morphine are included in this group.
- **Hallucinogens**: These substances alter sensory perception and can produce delusions, paranoia, and hallucinations. Cannabis and LSD are included in this category.
- **Other drugs of abuse**: Other substances that are abused but do not fit neatly into one of the categories here include inhalants (for example, airplane glue), anabolic steroids, and other over-the-counter and prescription medications (for example, nitrous oxide). These substances produce a variety of psychoactive effects that are characteristic of the substances described in the previous categories.
- **Gambling disorder:** As with the ingestion of the substances just described, individuals who display gambling disorder are unable to resist the urge to gamble which, in turn, results in negative personal consequences (e.g., divorce, loss of employment).

Depressants

▶ What are the physiological and psychological effects of depressants?

Depressants primarily *decrease* central nervous system activity. Their principal effect is to reduce our levels of physiological arousal and help us relax. Included in this group are alcohol and the sedative, hypnotic, and anxiolytic drugs, such as those prescribed for insomnia (see Chapter 8). These substances are among those most likely to produce symptoms of physical dependence, tolerance, and withdrawal. We first look at the most commonly used of these substances—**alcohol**—and the **alcohol-related disorders** that can result.

Alcohol-Related Disorders

Clinical Description

Apparent stimulation is the initial effect of alcohol, although it is a depressant. We generally experience a feeling of well-being, our inhibitions are reduced, and we become more outgoing. This is because the inhibitory centers in the brain are initially depressed—or slowed. With continued drinking, however, alcohol depresses more areas of the brain, which impedes the ability to function properly. Motor coordination is impaired (staggering, slurred

speech), reaction time is slowed, we become confused, our ability to make judgments is reduced, and even vision and hearing can be negatively affected, all of which help explain why driving while intoxicated is clearly dangerous.

Effects

Alcohol affects many parts of the body (see ● Figure 10.1). After it is ingested, it passes through the esophagus (1 in Figure 10.1) and into the stomach (2), where small amounts are absorbed . From there, most of it travels to

· ·

substance dependence A maladaptive pattern of substance use characterized by the need for increased amounts to achieve the desired effect, negative physical effects when the substance is withdrawn, unsuccessful efforts to control its use, and substantial effort expended to seek it or recover from its effects. Also known as *addiction*.

substance abuse A pattern of **psychoactive substance** use leading to significant distress or impairment in social and occupational roles and in hazardous situations.

alcohol By-product of the fermentation of yeasts, sugar, and water; the most commonly used and abused **depressant** substance.

alcohol-related disorders Cognitive, biological, behavioral, and social problems associated with **alcohol** use and abuse.

1. Ingestion
2. Stomach
3. Small intestine
4. Heart
5. Liver

● **Figure 10.1** The path traveled by alcohol throughout the body (see text for complete description).

the small intestine (3), where it is easily absorbed into the bloodstream. The circulatory system distributes the alcohol throughout the body, where it contacts every major organ, including the heart (4). Some of the alcohol goes to the lungs, where it vaporizes and is exhaled, a phenomenon that is the basis for the *breathalyzer test* that measures levels of intoxication. As alcohol passes through the liver (5), it is broken down or metabolized into carbon dioxide and water by enzymes (Maher, 1997).

Most substances we describe in this chapter, including cannabis, opiates, and tranquilizers, interact with specific receptors in the brain cells. The effects of alcohol, however, are more complex. Alcohol influences a number of neuroreceptor systems, which makes it difficult to study (Ray, 2012). For example, the *gamma-aminobutyric acid (GABA)* system, which we discussed in Chapters 2 and 4, seems to be particularly sensitive to alcohol. GABA, as you will recall, is an inhibitory neurotransmitter. Its major role is to interfere with the firing of the neuron it attaches to. Because the GABA system seems to effect the emotion of anxiety, alcohol's antianxiety properties may result from its interaction with the GABA system. Also, when GABA attaches to its receptor, chloride ions enter the cell and make it less sensitive to the effects of other neurotransmitters. Alcohol seems to reinforce the movement of these chloride ions; as a result, the neurons have difficulty firing. In other words, although alcohol seems to loosen our tongues and makes us more sociable, it makes it difficult for neurons to communicate with one another (Joslyn, Ravindranathan, Brush, Schuckit, & White, 2010).

The *glutamate system* is under study for its role in the effects of alcohol. In contrast to the GABA system, the glutamate system is excitatory, helping neurons fire. It is suspected to involve learning and memory, and it may be the avenue through which alcohol affects our cognitive abilities. Blackouts, the loss of memory for what happens during intoxication, may result from the interaction of alcohol with the glutamate system. The serotonin system also appears to be sensitive to alcohol. This neurotransmitter system affects mood, sleep, and eating behavior and is thought to be responsible for alcohol cravings (Sari, Johnson, & Weedman, 2011; Strain, 2009). Because alcohol affects so many neurotransmitter systems, we should not be surprised that it has such widespread and complex effects.

The long-term effects of heavy drinking are often severe. Withdrawal from chronic alcohol use typically includes hand tremors and, within several hours, nausea or vomiting, anxiety, transient hallucinations, agitation,

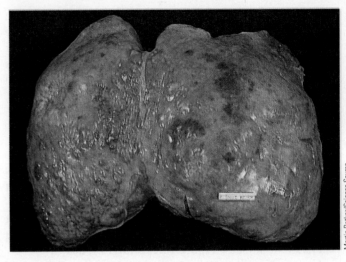

▲ A healthy liver (left), and a cirrhotic liver scarred by years of alcohol abuse (right).

insomnia, and, at its most extreme, **withdrawal delirium** (or **delirium tremens**—the **DTs**), a condition that can produce frightening hallucinations and body tremors. The devastating experience of delirium tremens can be reduced with adequate medical treatment (Schuckit, 2014b).

Whether alcohol will cause organic damage depends on genetic vulnerability, the frequency of use, the length of drinking binges, the blood alcohol levels attained during the drinking periods, and whether the body is given time to recover between binges. Consequences of long-term excessive drinking include liver disease, pancreatitis, cardiovascular disorders, and brain damage.

Part of the folklore concerning alcohol is that it permanently kills brain cells (neurons). As you will see later, this may not be true. Some evidence for brain damage comes from the experiences of people who are alcohol dependent and experience blackouts, seizures, and hallucinations. Memory and the ability to perform certain tasks may also be impaired. More seriously, two types of organic brain syndromes may result from long-term heavy alcohol use: dementia and **Wernicke-Korsakoff syndrome**. *Dementia (or neurocognitive disorder)*, which we discuss in Chapter 13, involves the general loss of intellectual abilities and can be a result of neurotoxicity or "poisoning of the brain" by excessive amounts of alcohol (Ridley, Draper, & Withall, 2013). *Wernicke-Korsakoff syndrome* results in confusion, loss of muscle coordination, and unintelligible speech (Isenberg-Grzeda, Kutner, & Nicolson, 2012); it is believed to be caused by a deficiency of thiamine, a vitamin metabolized

poorly by heavy drinkers. The dementia caused by this disease does not go away once the brain is damaged. It is important to note that mild to moderate intake of alcohol (especially wine) may actually serve a protective role in cognitive decline as we age (Panza *et al.*, 2012).

withdrawal delirium (delirium tremens/DTs) The frightening hallucinations and body tremors that result when a heavy drinker withdraws from **alcohol**. Also known as *delirium tremens (DT)*.

wernicke-korsakoff syndrome Organic brain syndrome resulting from prolonged heavy **alcohol** use, involving confusion, unintelligible speech, and loss of motor coordination. It may be caused by a deficiency of thiamine, a vitamin metabolized poorly by heavy drinkers.

46 yr old alcoholic man
lifetime alcohol consumption=1516 kg

45 yr old healthy community male volunteer
lifetime alcohol consumption=28 kg

▲ The dark areas in the top brain images show the extensive loss of brain tissue caused by heavy alcohol use.

The effects of alcohol abuse extend beyond the health and well-being of the drinker. **Fetal alcohol syndrome (FAS)** is now generally recognized as a combination of problems that can occur in a child whose mother drank while she was pregnant. These problems include fetal growth retardation, cognitive deficits, behavior problems, and learning difficulties (Douzgou *et al.*, 2012).

Statistics on Use and Abuse

Most adults in the United States characterize themselves as light drinkers or abstainers. On the other hand, about half of all Americans over the age of 12 report being current drinkers of alcohol. Caucasians report the highest frequency of drinking (56.8%); drinking is lowest among Asians (40.0%) (see ● Figure 10.2; SAMHSA, 2012).

About 63 million Americans (24.6%) over the age of 18 report binge-drinking (typically four or more drinks for women and five or more drinks for men over the span of two hours) in the past month (SAMHSA, 2013). Asians report the lowest level of binge-drinking (12.4%) and Caucasians (24.0%) and Hispanics or Latinos (24.1%) report the highest. Peak lifetime alcohol use happens around the late teens to early adolescence. In surveys across 100 four-year universities and colleges, about 36% of respondents said they had gone on a binge of heavy drinking once in the preceding two weeks (Johnston, O'Malley, Bachman, & Schulenberg, 2012). Unfortunately, this binge-drinking

trend seems to have increased in college students along with drunk driving and alcohol-related deaths (Whiteside, Bittinger, Kilmer, Lostutter, & Larimer, 2015). Men were more likely to report several binges in the two-week period (White & Hingson, 2014; Presley & Meilman, 1992). The same survey found that students with a grade point average of A had no more than three drinks per week, whereas D and F students averaged 11 drinks per week (Presley & Meilman, 1992).

We know that not everyone who drinks develops an alcohol use disorder. Researchers estimate, however, that more than 16.6 million adults ages 18 and older meet criteria for an alcohol use disorder and the same is true of 697,000 adolescents ages 12 to 17 (SAMHSA, 2013). Lifetime prevalence rates for alcohol use disorders, meaning a person met criteria for an alcohol use disorder at some point in his or her life, are more than 29% (Grant *et al.*, 2015).

Outside the United States, rates of alcohol use problems and dependence vary widely. The prevalence of alcohol use disorders in 2004 as measured by the World Health Organization was highest in eastern European countries (in Russia it was close to 19%), followed by Colombia at 13%, South Korea at 13.5%, and Thailand at 11%. The prevalence for alcohol use disorders in 2004 was lowest in Northern Africa (e.g., in Libya at 0.05%) and the Middle East (e.g., in Afghanistan at 0.2%) (World Health Organization, 2004). Such cultural differences can be accounted for by different attitudes toward drinking, the availability of alcohol, physiological reactions, and family norms and patterns.

Progression

Many people with an alcohol use disorder fluctuate between drinking heavily, drinking "socially" without negative effects, and being abstinent (not drinking) (McCrady, 2014). About 20% of people with severe alcohol dependence have a spontaneous remission (they are able to stop drinking on their own) and do not re-experience problems with drinking.

It used to be thought that once problems arose with drinking they would become steadily worse (Sobell & Sobell, 1993). In other words, like a disease that isn't treated properly, alcoholism will get progressively worse if left unchecked. First championed by Jellinek more than 50 years ago, this view continues to influence the way people view and treat the disorder (Jellinek, 1946, 1952, 1960). Unfortunately, Jellinek based his model of the progression of alcohol use on a now famous but faulty study (Jellinek, 1946).

It appears that the course of a severe alcohol use disorder may indeed be progressive for most people. However, this progressive pattern is not inevitable for everyone who abuses alcohol, although we do not as yet understand what distinguishes those who are and those who

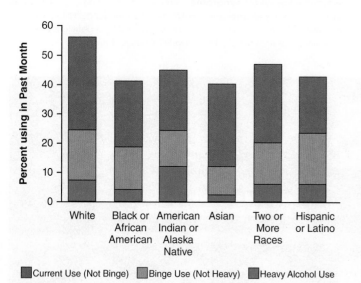

● **Figure 10.2** Alcohol use across racial groups. Binge-drinking is defined as drinking five or more drinks on one occasion at least once per month, and heavy alcohol use is defined as binge-drinking for five or more days in a month. (From Substance Abuse and Mental Health Services Administration, Office of Applied Studies. [2012]. *Results from the 2011 National Survey on Drug Use and Health: National Findings*, NSDUH Series H-44, DHHS Publication No. (SMA) 12-4713. Rockville, MD: Author.)

are not susceptible (Krenek & Maisto, 2013). A study of almost 6,000 lifetime drinkers found that drinking at an early age—from ages 11 to 14—was predictive of later alcohol-related disorders (DeWitt, Adlaf, Offord, & Ogborne, 2000). Another study followed 636 male inpatients in an alcohol rehabilitation center (Schuckit *et al.*, 1993). Among these chronically alcohol-dependent men, a general progression of alcohol-related life problems did emerge, although not in the specific pattern proposed by Jellinek. Three-quarters of the men reported moderate consequences of their drinking, such as demotions at work, in their 20s. During their 30s, the men had more serious problems, such as regular blackouts. By their late 30s and early 40s, these men demonstrated long-term serious consequences of their drinking, including hallucinations, withdrawal convulsions, and hepatitis or pancreatitis.

Research on the mechanism responsible for the differences in early alcohol use suggests that those individuals who tend not to develop the slurred speech, staggering, and other sedative effects of alcohol use are more likely to abuse it in the future (Chung & Martin, 2009; Schuckit, 2014a). This is of particular concern given the trend to mix caffeinated energy drinks with alcohol (McKetin, Coen, & Kaye, 2015). This combination of drinks can reduce the sedative effect of alcohol, which may increase the likelihood of later abuse.

Finally, statistics often link alcohol with violent behavior (Boden, Fergusson, & Horwood, 2012; Bye, 2007). Numerous studies have found that many people who commit violent acts such as murder, rape, and assault are intoxicated at the time of the crime (Rossow & Bye, 2012). We hope you are skeptical of this type of correlation. Just because drunkenness and violence overlap does not mean that alcohol will necessarily make you violent. Laboratory studies show that alcohol may increase participants' aggression (Bushman, 1993). Whether a person behaves aggressively outside the laboratory, however, probably involves a number of factors, such as the quantity and timing of alcohol consumed, the person's history of violence, expectations about drinking, and what happens to the individual while intoxicated. Alcohol does not *cause* aggression, but it may increase a person's likelihood of engaging in impulsive acts and it may impair the ability to consider the consequences of acting impulsively (Bye, 2007). Given the right circumstances, such impaired thinking may increase a person's risk of behaving aggressively.

▲ Intoxication is often involved in cases of domestic violence.

Sedative-, Hypnotic-, or Anxiolytic-Related Disorders

The general group of depressants also includes sedative (calming), hypnotic (sleep-inducing), and anxiolytic (anxiety-reducing) drugs (Bond & Lader, 2012). These drugs include barbiturates and benzodiazepines. **Barbiturates** (which include Amytal, Seconal, and Nembutal) are a family of sedative drugs prescribed to help people sleep. Barbiturates were widely prescribed by physicians during the 1930s and 1940s, before their addictive properties were fully understood. By the 1950s, they were among the drugs most abused by adults in the United States (Franklin & Frances, 1999).

Benzodiazepines (which today include Valium, Xanax, and Ativan) have been used since the 1960s, primarily to reduce anxiety. These drugs were originally touted as a miracle cure for the anxieties of living in our highly pressured technological society. Although in 1980 the U.S. Food and Drug Administration ruled that they are not appropriate for reducing the tension and anxiety resulting from everyday stresses and strains, an estimated 85 million prescriptions are written for benzodiazepines in the United States each year (Olfson, King, & Schoenbaum, 2015). In general, benzodiazepines are considered much safer than barbiturates, with less risk of abuse and dependence. Reports on the misuse of Rohypnol, however, show how dangerous some benzodiazepines can be. Rohypnol (otherwise known as "forget-me-pill," "roofenol," "roofies," "ruffies") has the same effect as alcohol without the telltale odor. There have been numerous incidents of men giving the drug to women without their knowledge, making it easier for them to engage in date rape (Albright, Stevens, & Beussman, 2012).

Clinical Description

At low doses, barbiturates relax the muscles and can produce a mild feeling of well-being. Larger doses can produce slurred speech and problems walking, concentrating, and working. At extremely high doses, the diaphragm muscles can relax so much that they cause death by suffocation. Overdosing on barbiturates is a common means of suicide.

....

barbiturates A sedative (and addictive) drug such as Amytal, Seconal, or Nembutal that is used as a sleep aid.

benzodiazepines An antianxiety drug such as Valium, Xanax, Dalmane, or Halcion also used to treat insomnia. Effective against **anxiety** (and, at high potency, **panic disorder**), benzodiazepines show some side effects, such as some cognitive and motor impairment, and may result in **substance dependence**. **Relapse** rates are extremely high when such a drug is discontinued.

Like the barbiturates, benzodiazepines are used to calm an individual and induce sleep. In addition, drugs in this class are prescribed as muscle relaxants and anticonvulsants (antiseizure medications) (Bond & Lader, 2012). People who use them for non-medical reasons report first feeling a pleasant high and a reduction of inhibition, similar to the effects of drinking alcohol. With continued use, however, tolerance and dependence can develop. Users who try to stop taking the drug experience symptoms like those of alcohol withdrawal (anxiety, insomnia, tremors, and delirium).

The *DSM-5* criteria for **sedative-, hypnotic-, and anxiolytic-related disorders** do not differ substantially from those for alcohol disorders. Both include maladaptive behavioral changes such as inappropriate sexual or aggressive behavior, variable moods, impaired judgment, impaired social or occupational functioning, slurred speech, motor coordination problems, and unsteady gait.

Sedative, hypnotic, and anxiolytic drugs affect the brain by influencing the GABA neurotransmitter system (Bond & Lader, 2012), although by mechanisms slightly different from those involving alcohol. As a result, when people use alcohol with any of these drugs or combine multiple types there can be synergistic effects. In other words, if you drink alcohol after taking a benzodiazepine or barbiturate or combine these drugs, the total effects can reach dangerous levels.

Statistics

Barbiturate use has declined and benzodiazepine use has increased since 1960 (SAMHSA, 2012). Of those seeking treatment for substance-related problems, less than 1% present problems with benzodiazepines compared with other drugs of abuse. Those who do seek help with abuse of these drugs tend to be female, Caucasian, and over the age of 35.

DSM 5

DISORDER CRITERIA SUMMARY

Sedative-, Hypnotic-, or Anxiolytic-Related Disorders

A. A problematic pattern of sedative, hypnotic, or anxiolytic use leading to clinically significant impairment or distress, as manifested by at least two of the following, occurring within a 12-month period: (1) Sedatives, hypnotics, or anxiolytics are often taken in larger amounts or over a longer period than was intended. (2) There is a persistent desire or unsuccessful efforts to cut down or control sedative, hypnotic, or anxiolytic use. (3) A great deal of time is spent in activities necessary to obtain the sedative, hypnotic, or anxiolytic; use the sedative, hypnotic, or anxiolytic; or recover from its effects. (4) Craving, or a strong desire to use the sedative, hypnotic, or anxiolytic. (5) Recurrent sedative, hypnotic, or anxiolytic use resulting in a failure to fulfill major role obligations at work, school, or home. (6) Continued sedative, hypnotic or anxiolytic use despite having persistent or recurrent social or interpersonal problems caused or exacerbated by the effects of sedatives, hypnotics or anxiolytics. (7) Important social, occupational, or recreational activities are given up or reduced because of sedative, hypnotic or anxiolytic use. (8) Recurrent sedative, hypnotic or anxiolytic use in situations in which it is physically hazardous. (9) Sedative, hypnotic, or anxiolytic use is continued despite knowledge of having a persistent or recurrent physical or psychological problem that is likely to have been caused or exacerbated by the sedative, hypnotic, or anxiolytic. (10) Tolerance, as defined by either (a) a need for markedly increased amounts of sedative, hypnotic, or anxiolytic to achieve intoxication or desired effect or (b) a markedly diminished effect with continued use of the same amount of sedative, hypnotic or anxiolytic. (11) Withdrawal, as manifested by either (a) the characteristic withdrawal syndrome for sedatives, hypnotics, or anxiolytics or (b) sedatives, hypnotics, or anxiolytics (or closely related substance, such as alcohol) are taken to relieve or avoid withdrawal symptoms.

Specify current severity:
Mild: Presence of two to three symptoms
Moderate: Presence of four to five symptoms
Severe: Presence of six or more symptoms

From American Psychiatric Association. (2013). *Diagnostic and statistical manual of mental disorders* (5th ed.). Washington, DC.

10.1 Concept CHECK

Part A

Check your understanding of substance use definitions by stating whether the following case summaries describe (a) use, (b) intoxication, or (c) use disorder:

1. Giya started a new job five weeks ago and is about to be fired. This is her third job this year. She has been absent from work at least once a week for the past five weeks. She was reprimanded in the past after being seen at a local pub in a drunken state during regular office hours although she called in sick. At her previous job, she was fired after she came to work unable to conduct herself appropriately and with alcohol on her breath. When confronted about her problems, Giya went to the nearest bar and drank some more to try to forget about the situation.

2. Brennan scored the winning goal for his high school soccer team and his friends take him out to celebrate. He doesn't smoke, but he doesn't mind drinking alcohol occasionally. Because Brennan had such a good game, he decides to have a few drinks. Despite his great performance in the game, he is easily irritated, laughing one minute and yelling

---

the next. The more Brennan rambles on about his game-winning goal, the more difficult it is to understand him. _____

3. Marti is a 24-year-old college student who started drinking heavily when he was 15. Marti drinks a moderate amount every night. In high school, he would become drunk after about four beers; now his tolerance has more than doubled. Marti claims alcohol relieves the pressures of college life. He once attempted to quit drinking, but he had chills, fever, diarrhea, nausea and vomiting, and body aches and pains. _____

4. Over the past year Henry picked up a habit of having a cigarette every day after lunch. Instead of sitting in the lounge with his friends he goes to his favorite spot in the courtyard and has his cigarette. If for some reason he is unable to have his cigarette after lunch, he is not dependent on it and can still function normally.

_____

Part B

Match the following disorders with their corresponding effects: (a) substance-related and addictive disorder, (b) dementia, (c) impulse-control disorder, (d) alcohol use disorder, and (e) Wernicke-Korsakoff syndrome:

5. Disorder that deprives a person of the ability to resist acting on a drive or temptation. _____

6. Disorder in which the effects of the drug impede the ability to function properly by affecting vision, motor control, reaction time, memory, and hearing.

_____

7. The decline of intellectual abilities through, for example, excess consumption of alcohol.

_____

8. A class of disorders that effects the way people think, feel, and behave. _____

Stimulants

▶ **What are the physiological and psychological effects of stimulants?**

Of all the **psychoactive** drugs used in the United States, the most commonly consumed are stimulants. Included in this group are caffeine (in coffee, chocolate, and many soft drinks), nicotine (in tobacco products such as cigarettes), amphetamines, and cocaine. In contrast to the depressant drugs, stimulants make you more alert and energetic. We describe several stimulants and their effects on behavior, mood, and cognition.

Stimulant-Related Disorders

Amphetamines

At low doses, **amphetamines** can induce feelings of elation and vigor and can reduce fatigue. You feel "up." After a period of elevation, however, you come back down and "crash," feeling depressed or tired. Amphetamines are manufactured in laboratories; they were first synthesized in 1887 and later used as a treatment for asthma and as a nasal decongestant (Carvalho *et al.*, 2012). Because amphetamines also reduce appetite, some people take them to lose weight. Long-haul truck drivers, pilots, and some college students trying to "pull all-nighters" use amphetamines to get an extra energy "boost" and stay awake. Some of these drugs (Ritalin, Adderall) are even given to children with attention-deficit/hyperactivity

disorder (ADHD) (discussed in Chapter 13). Amphetamines are often misused for their psychostimulant effects. One large study found that almost two-thirds of college students in their fourth year had been offered illegal prescription stimulants and 31% used them—usually to improve studying (Garnier-Dykstra, Caldeira, Vincent, O'Grady, & Arria, 2012).

DSM-5 diagnostic criteria for intoxication in **amphetamine use disorders** include significant behavioral symptoms, such as euphoria or affective blunting (a lack of emotional expression), changes in sociability, interpersonal sensitivity, anxiety, tension, anger, stereotyped behaviors, impaired judgment, and impaired social or occupational functioning. In addition, physiological symptoms occur during or shortly after amphetamine or related substances are ingested and can include heart rate or blood pressure changes, perspiration or chills, nausea or vomiting, weight loss, muscular weakness, respiratory

. . . .

amphetamines Stimulant medication used to treat hypersomnia by keeping the person awake during the day, and to treat **narcolepsy**, including sudden onset episodes, by suppressing **rapid eye movement sleep**.

amphetamine use disorders Psychological, biological, behavioral, and social problems associated with **amphetamine** use and abuse.

depression, chest pain, seizures, or coma. Severe intoxication or overdose can cause hallucinations, panic, agitation, and paranoid delusions (Carvalho *et al.*, 2012). Amphetamine tolerance builds quickly, making it doubly dangerous. Withdrawal often results in apathy, prolonged periods of sleep, irritability, and depression.

Periodically, certain "designer drugs" appear in local mini-epidemics. An amphetamine called methylenedioxymethamphetamine (MDMA) was used as an appetite suppressant (McCann & Ricaurte, 2009). Recreational use of this drug, now commonly called Ecstasy, rose sharply in the late 1980s. After cocaine and methamphetamine, MDMA is the club drug most often bringing people to emergency rooms, and it has surpassed LSD in frequency of use (SAMHSA, 2011). Its effects are described by users in a variety of ways: Ecstasy makes you "feel happy" and "love everyone and everything"; "music feels better" and "it's more fun to dance" (Levy, O'Grady, Wish, & Arria, 2005, p. 1431). Recent years have seen a rise in a variation of MDMA called "Molly" that is a purified powder in capsules instead of the pressed pills of Ecstasy (National Institute of Drug Abuse, 2013).

A purified, crystallized form of amphetamine, called methamphetamine (commonly referred to as "crystal meth" or "ice"), is ingested through smoking. This drug causes marked aggressive tendencies and stays in the system longer than cocaine, making it particularly dangerous. This drug gained and dropped in popularity since it was invented in the 1930s, although its use has now spread wider than before (Maxwell & Brecht, 2011). However enjoyable these various amphetamines may be in the short term, the potential for users to become dependent on them is extremely high, with great risk for long-term difficulties. Some research also shows that repeated use of MDMA can cause lasting memory problems (Wagner, Becker, Koester, Gouzoulis-Mayfrank, & Daumann, 2013).

Amphetamines stimulate the central nervous system by enhancing the activity of norepinephrine and dopamine. Specifically, amphetamines help the release of these neurotransmitters and block their reuptake, thereby making more of them available throughout the system (Carvalho *et al.*, 2012). Too much amphetamine—and therefore too much dopamine and norepinephrine—can lead to hallucinations and delusions. As we see in Chapter 12, this effect has stimulated theories on the causes of schizophrenia, which can also include hallucinations and delusions.

Cocaine

Cocaine is derived from the leaves of the coca plant, a flowering bush indigenous to South America. In small amounts cocaine increases alertness, produces euphoria, increases blood pressure and pulse, and causes insomnia and loss of appetite. Remember that Danny occasionally snorted (inhaled) cocaine. He later said the drug made him feel

DSM 5 DIAGNOSTIC CRITERIA SUMMARY
Stimulant Use Disorder

A. A pattern of amphetamine-type substance, cocaine, or other stimulant use leading to clinically significant impairment or distress, as manifested by at least two of the following, occurring within a 12-month period: (1) The stimulant is often taken in larger amounts or over a longer period than was intended. (2) There is a persistent desire or unsuccessful efforts to cut down or control stimulant use. (3) A great deal of time is spent in activities necessary to obtain the stimulant, use the stimulant, or recover from its effects. (4) Craving, or a strong desire or urge to use the stimulant. (5) Recurrent stimulant use resulting in a failure to fulfill major role obligations at work, school, or home. (6) Continued stimulant use despite having persistent or recurrent social or interpersonal problems caused or exacerbated by the effects of the stimulant. (7) Important social, occupational, or recreational activities are given up or reduced because of stimulant use. (8) Recurrent stimulant use in situations in which it is physically hazardous. (9) Stimulant use is continued despite knowledge of having a persistent or recurrent physical or psychological problem that is likely to have been caused or exacerbated by the stimulant. (10) Tolerance, as defined by either (a) a need for markedly increased amounts of the stimulant to achieve intoxication or desired effect or (b) a markedly diminished effect with continued use of the same amount of the stimulant. (11) Withdrawal, as manifested by either (a) the characteristic withdrawal syndrome for the stimulant or (b) the stimulant (or a closely related substance) is taken to relieve or avoid withdrawal symptoms.

Specify current severity:
Mild: Presence of two to three symptoms
Moderate: Presence of four to five symptoms
Severe: Presence of six or more symptoms

From American Psychiatric Association. (2013). *Diagnostic and statistical manual of mental disorders* (5th ed.). Washington, DC.

invincible. The effects of cocaine are short lived; for Danny they lasted less than an hour, and he had to snort repeatedly to keep himself up. During these binges, he often became paranoid, experiencing exaggerated fears that he would be caught or that someone would steal his cocaine. Such paranoia—referred to as *cocaine-induced paranoia*—is common among persons with **cocaine use disorders**, occurring in two-thirds or more (Daamen *et al.*, 2012). Cocaine also makes the heart beat more rapidly and irregularly, and it can have fatal consequences, depending on a person's physical condition and the amount of the drug ingested. It has also been suspected that the use of cocaine (especially crack) by pregnant women may adversely affect their babies.

Worldwide, almost 5% of adults report using cocaine at some point in their lives, and in the United States, more than 1.5 million people (0.6% of U.S. population) report using cocaine, including crack-cocaine, each year. Those

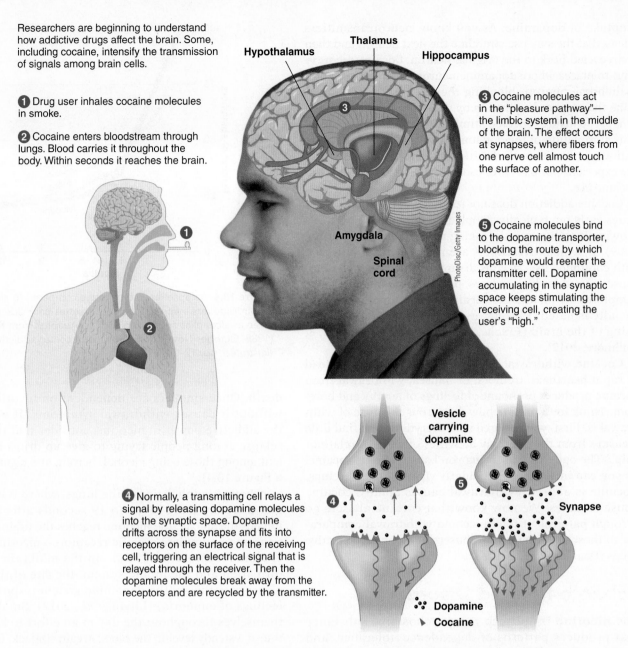

Researchers are beginning to understand how addictive drugs affect the brain. Some, including cocaine, intensify the transmission of signals among brain cells.

1 Drug user inhales cocaine molecules in smoke.

2 Cocaine enters bloodstream through lungs. Blood carries it throughout the body. Within seconds it reaches the brain.

Hypothalamus

Thalamus

Hippocampus

3 Cocaine molecules act in the "pleasure pathway"— the limbic system in the middle of the brain. The effect occurs at synapses, where fibers from one nerve cell almost touch the surface of another.

Amygdala

Spinal cord

PhotoDisc/Getty Images

5 Cocaine molecules bind to the dopamine transporter, blocking the route by which dopamine would reenter the transmitter cell. Dopamine accumulating in the synaptic space keeps stimulating the receiving cell, creating the user's "high."

Vesicle carrying dopamine

4 Normally, a transmitting cell relays a signal by releasing dopamine molecules into the synaptic space. Dopamine drifts across the synapse and fits into receptors on the surface of the receiving cell, triggering an electrical signal that is relayed through the receiver. Then the dopamine molecules break away from the receptors and are recycled by the transmitter.

Synapse

•° **Dopamine**

▶ **Cocaine**

● **Figure 10.3** Anatomy of a high. (Reprinted, with permission, from Booth, W. [1990]. The anatomy of a high. *Washington Post National Weekly Edition*, March 26–April 1, p. 38, © 1990 The Washington Post.)

aged 18 to 25 are about twice as likely to use cocaine compared with other age groups. Also, men are twice as likely to use cocaine as women (SAMHSA, 2014). Black individuals account for close to half of admissions to emergency rooms for cocaine-related problems (47%), followed by Caucasian individuals (37%) and Hispanic individuals (10%). Also, men were twice as likely as women to be in the emergency room (SAMHSA, 2011). Approximately 17% of cocaine users have also used crack cocaine (a crystallized form of cocaine that is smoked) (Closser, 1992). One estimate is that about 0.1% of people in the United States have tried crack and that an increasing proportion of the

abusers seeking treatment are young, unemployed adults living in urban areas (SAMHSA, 2014).

Cocaine is in the same group of stimulants as amphetamines because it has similar effects on the brain. The "up" seems to come primarily from the effect of cocaine on the dopamine system. Look at ● Figure 10.3 to see how this action occurs. Cocaine enters the bloodstream and is carried to the brain. There the cocaine molecules block the

cocaine use disorders Cognitive, biological, behavioral, and social problems associated with the use and abuse of **cocaine**.

reuptake of dopamine. As you know, neurotransmitters released at the synapse stimulate the next neuron and then are recycled back to the original neuron. Cocaine seems to bind to places where dopamine neurotransmitters re-enter their home neuron, blocking their reuptake. The dopamine that cannot be taken in by the neuron remains in the synapse, causing repeated stimulation of the next neuron. This stimulation of the dopamine neurons in the "pleasure pathway" (the site in the brain that seems to be involved in the experience of pleasure) causes the high associated with cocaine use.

Cocaine addiction does not resemble that of many other drugs early on; typically, people find only that they have a growing inability to resist taking more (Weiss & Iannucci, 2009). Few negative effects are noted at first; however, with continued use, sleep is disrupted, increased tolerance causes a need for higher doses, paranoia and other negative symptoms set in, and the cocaine user gradually becomes socially isolated. Chronic use may result in premature aging of the brain (Ersche, Jones, Williams, Robbins, & Bullmore, 2012).

Cocaine withdrawal isn't like that of alcohol. Instead of rapid heartbeat, tremors, or nausea, withdrawal from cocaine produces pronounced feelings of apathy and boredom. Think for a minute how dangerous this type of withdrawal is. First, you're bored with everything and find little pleasure from the everyday activities of work or relationships. The one that can "bring you back to life" is cocaine. As you can imagine, a particularly vicious cycle develops: Cocaine is abused, withdrawal causes apathy, cocaine abuse resumes. We now know that cocaine abusers go through patterns of tolerance and withdrawal comparable to those experienced by abusers of other psychoactive drugs (Daamen *et al.*, 2012).

Tobacco-Related Disorders

The **nicotine** in tobacco is a psychoactive substance that produces patterns of dependence, tolerance, and withdrawal—**tobacco-related disorders**—comparable to those of the other drugs we have discussed so far (Litvin, Ditre, Heckman, & Brandon, 2012). Today, about 20% of all people in the United States smoke, which is down from the 42.4% who were smokers in 1965 (Litvin *et al.*, 2012).

DSM-5 does not describe an intoxication pattern for tobacco-related disorders. Rather, it lists withdrawal symptoms, which include depressed mood, insomnia, irritability, anxiety, difficulty concentrating, restlessness, and increased appetite and weight gain. Nicotine in small doses stimulates the central nervous system; it can relieve stress and improve mood. But it can also cause high blood pressure and increase the risk of heart disease and cancer (Litvin *et al.*, 2012). High doses can blur your vision, cause confusion, lead to convulsions, and sometimes even cause

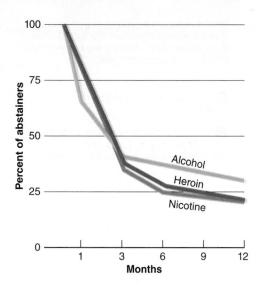

● **Figure 10.4** Relapse rates for nicotine compared to alcohol and heroin. Smokers trying to give up cigarettes backslide about as often as alcoholics and heroin addicts. Adapted from Kanigel, R. (1988, October/November). Nicotine becomes addictive. *Science Illustrated*, pp. 12–14, 19–21.

death. Once smokers are dependent on nicotine, going without it causes withdrawal symptoms. If you doubt the addictive power of nicotine, consider that the rate of relapse among people trying to give up drugs is equivalent among those using alcohol, heroin, and cigarettes (see ● Figure 10.4).

Nicotine is inhaled into the lungs, where it enters the bloodstream. Only seven to 19 seconds after a person inhales the smoke, the nicotine reaches the brain. Nicotine appears to stimulate specific receptors—nicotinic acetylcholine receptors (nAChRs)—in the midbrain reticular formation and the limbic system, the site of the brain's pleasure pathway (the dopamine system responsible for feelings of euphoria) (Litvin *et al.*, 2012). Smokers dose themselves throughout the day in an effort to keep nicotine at a steady level in the bloodstream (Dalack, Glassman, & Covey, 1993). Some evidence also points to how maternal smoking can predict later substance-related disorders in their children, but this appears to be an environmental (e.g., home environment) rather than biological influence (D'Onofrio *et al.*, 2012).

Smoking has been linked with signs of negative affect, such as depression, anxiety, and anger (Rasmusson, Anderson, Krishnan-Sarin, Wu, & Paliwal, 2006). For example, many people who quit smoking but later resume report that feelings of depression or anxiety were responsible for the relapse (Kahler, Litvin Bloom, Leventhal, & Brown, 2015). Due to this association between smoking and symptoms of depression and anxiety, relapse may be especially higher for women as compared to men, because women more than men tend to have these symptoms (Nakajima & al'Absi, 2012).

A. A problematic pattern of tobacco use leading to clinically significant impairment or distress, as manifested by at least two of the following, occurring within a 12-month period: (1)Tobacco is often taken in larger amounts or over a longer period than was intended. (2)There is a persistent desire or unsuccessful efforts to cut down or control tobacco use. (3)A great deal of time is spent in activities necessary to obtain or use tobacco. (4) Craving, or a strong desire or urge to use tobacco. (5) Recurrent tobacco use resulting in a failure to fulfill major role obligations at work, school, or home. (6) Continued tobacco use despite having persistent or recurrent social or interpersonal problems caused or exacerbated by the effects of tobacco. (7) Important social, occupational, or recreational activities are given up or reduced because of tobacco use. (8) Recurrent tobacco use in situations in which it is physically hazardous (e.g., smoking in bed). (9) Tobacco use is continued despite knowledge of having a persistent or recurrent physical or psychological problem that is likely to have been caused or exacerbated by tobacco. (10) Tolerance, as defined by either (a) a need for markedly increased amounts of tobacco to achieve the desired effect or (b) a markedly diminished effect with continued use of the same amount of tobacco. (11) Withdrawal, as manifested by either (a) the characteristic withdrawal syndrome for tobacco or (b) tobacco (or a closely related substance such as nicotine) is taken to relieve or avoid withdrawal symptoms.

Specify current severity:
Mild: Presence of two to three symptoms
Moderate: Presence of four to five symptoms
Severe: Presence of six or more symptoms

From American Psychiatric Association. (2013). *Diagnostic and statistical manual of mental disorders* (5th ed.). Washington, DC.

Caffeine-Related Disorders

Caffeine is the most common of the psychoactive substances; upwards of 85% of the U.S. population has at least one caffeinated beverage per day (Mitchell, Knight, Hockenberry, Teplansky, & Hartman, 2014). Called the "gentle stimulant" because it is thought to be the least harmful of all addictive drugs, caffeine can still lead to problems similar to that of other drugs (e.g., interfering with social and work obligations; Meredith, Juliano, Hughes & Griffiths, 2013). This drug is found in tea, coffee, many soda drinks, and cocoa products. High levels of caffeine are added to the "energy drinks" that are widely consumed in the United States today but are banned in some European countries (including France, Denmark, and Norway) due to health concerns (Price, Hilchey, Darredeau, Fulton, & Barrett, 2010; Thorlton, Colby, & Devine, 2014).

Caffeine in small doses can elevate your mood and decrease fatigue. In larger doses, it can make you feel jittery and cause insomnia. Because caffeine takes a relatively long time to leave our bodies (about six hours), sleep can be disturbed if the caffeine is ingested in the hours close to bedtime. This effect is especially pronounced among those already suffering from insomnia (Byrne *et al.*, 2012). As with the other psychoactive drugs, people react variously to caffeine; some are sensitive to it, and others can consume relatively large amounts with little effect. Research suggests that moderate use of caffeine (a cup of coffee per day) by pregnant women does not harm the developing fetus (Loomans *et al.*, 2012).

DSM-5 includes caffeine use disorder—defined problematic caffeine use that causes significant impairment and distress—as a condition for further study (American Psychiatric Association, 2013). As with other stimulants, regular caffeine use can result in tolerance and dependence on the drug. Those of you who have experienced headaches, drowsiness, and a generally unpleasant mood when denied your morning coffee have had the withdrawal symptoms characteristic of this drug (Meredith *et al.*, 2013). Caffeine's effect on the brain seems to involve the neuromodulator *adenosine* and, to a lesser extent, the neurotransmitter *dopamine* (Juliano, Ferré, & Griffiths, 2015). Caffeine seems to block adenosine reuptake. Adenosine plays an important role on the release of dopamine and glutamate in the striatum, which may explain the elation and increased energy that come with caffeine use (Juliano *et al.*, 2015).

A. Recent consumption of caffeine (typically a high dose well in excess of 250 mg).

B. Five (or more) of the following signs or symptoms developing during, or shortly after, caffeine use: (1) Restlessness. (2) Nervousness. (3) Excitement. (4) Insomnia. (5) Flushed face. (6) Diuresis. (7) Gastrointestinal disturbance. (8) Muscle twitching. (9) Rambling flow of thought and speech. (10) Tachycardia or cardiac arrhythmia. (11) Periods of inexhaustibility. (12) Psychomotor agitation.

C. The signs or symptoms in Criterion B cause clinically significant distress or impairment in social, occupational, or other important areas of functioning.

D. The signs or symptoms are not attributable to another medical condition and are not better explained by another mental disorder, including intoxication with another substance.

From American Psychiatric Association. (2013). *Diagnostic and statistical manual of mental disorders* (5th ed.). Washington, DC.

nicotine Toxic and addictive substance found in tobacco leaves.

tobacco-related disorders Cognitive, biological, behavioral, and social problems associated with the use and abuse of **nicotine**.

Determine whether the following statements about stimulants are true (T) or false (F):

1. _____ Use of crack cocaine by a pregnant woman always adversely affects the developing fetus.

2. _____ Regular use of stimulants can result in tolerance and dependence on the drugs.

3. _____ Amphetamines have been used as appetite suppressants.

4. _____ Compared with all other drugs, caffeine can produce the most variable reactions in people.

5. _____ Amphetamines are naturally occurring drugs that induce feelings of elation and vigor and can reduce fatigue.

6. _____ An ingredient of the beverage Coca-Cola in the 1800s was cocaine.

7. _____ Stimulants are produced only in a laboratory.

Opioid-Related Disorders

▶ What are the physiological and psychological effects of opiates?

The word *opiate* refers to the natural chemicals in the opium poppy that have a narcotic effect (they relieve pain and induce sleep). In some circumstances, they can cause **opioid-related disorders**. The broader term *opioids* refers to the family of substances that includes natural opiates, synthetic variations (heroin, methadone, hydrocodone, oxycodone), and the comparable substances that occur naturally in the brain (enkephalins, beta-endorphins, and dynorphins) (Borg *et al.*, 2015). Opiates induce euphoria, drowsiness, and slowed breathing. High doses can lead to death if respiration is completely depressed. Opiates are also analgesics, substances that help relieve pain. People are sometimes given morphine before and after surgery to calm them and help block pain.

Withdrawal from opioids can be so unpleasant that people may continue to use these drugs despite a sincere desire to stop. People who cease or reduce their opioid intake begin to experience symptoms within six to 12 hours; these include excessive yawning, nausea and vomiting, chills, muscle aches, diarrhea, and insomnia—temporarily disrupting work, school, and social relationships. The symptoms can persist for one to three days, and the withdrawal process is completed in about a week.

Addiction to heroin is reported in almost a half million people in the United States, double the number estimated between 2002 and 2013. Illicit use of opioid-containing prescription medicines—the most commonly abused opiate class—has also risen in recent years with 4.13 million people over the age of 12 reporting nonmedical use (SAMHSA, 2014). Illicit use of opioid-containing prescription was the second most common type of illicit drug use in 2014 after marijuana. This rise in opioid use has been deemed an epidemic and public health crisis in the United States; in fact, 1.9 million people met criteria for opioid use disorder in 2013 (SAMHSA, 2014). Additionally, illicit opioid use was the leading cause of death for drug users in 2013, a 360% increase from 1999 (Centers for Disease Control, National Center for Health Statistics, 2014). Research also suggests that individuals who first became addicted to prescription pain medication transitioned to using heroin (Muhuri, Gfroerer, & Davies, 2013). People who use opiates face risks beyond addiction and the threat of overdose. Because these drugs are usually injected intravenously, users are at increased risk for life-threatening illness such as Hepatitis C and HIV infection and therefore AIDS (Compton, Boyle, & Wargo, 2015).

▲ The pop icon Prince died in 2016 at the age of 57 from an accidental overdose of the prescribed opioid, fentanyl.

Kevin Mazur/ WireImage/ Getty Images

Research suggests that mortality rates for opiate addicts are 6 to 20 times higher than the general population. Those addicts who do live face hardship recovering from addiction, with stable abstinence rates as low as 30%, and with most individuals undergoing relapses. Even those who discontinue opioids often use alcohol and other drugs in their place (Hser, Evans, Grella, Ling, & Anglin, 2015). Results from a 33-year follow-up study of more than 80 opioid users in an English town highlight this pessimistic view (Rathod, Addenbrooke, & Rosenbach, 2005). At the follow up, 22% of opioid users had died—about twice the rate of about 12% for the general population. More than half the deaths were the result of drug overdose, and several took their own lives. The good news from this study was that of those who survived, 80% were no longer using opioids, and the remaining 20% were being treated with methadone. Long-term recovery has been shown to be associated with family and social support, employment, and opioid abstinence of at least five years (Hser *et al.*, 2015).

The high or "rush" experienced by users comes from activation of the body's natural opioid system. In other words, the brain already has its own opioids—called enkephalins and endorphins—that provide narcotic effects (Ballantyne, 2012). Heroin, opium, morphine, and other opiates activate this system. The discovery of the natural opioid system was a major breakthrough in the field of psychopharmacology: Not only does it allow us to study the effects of addictive drugs on the brain, but it also has led to important discoveries that may help us treat people dependent on these drugs.

DSM 5 — DISORDER CRITERIA SUMMARY
Opioid Use Disorder

A. A problematic pattern of opioid use leading to clinically significant impairment or distress, as manifested by at least two of the following, occurring within a 12-month period: (1) Opioids are often taken in larger amounts or over a longer period than was intended. (2) There is a persistent desire or unsuccessful efforts to cut down or control opioid use. (3) A great deal of time is spent in activities necessary to obtain the opioid, use the opioid, or recover from its effects. (4) Craving, or a strong desire or urge to use opioids. (5) Recurrent opioid use resulting in a failure to fulfill major role obligations at work, school, or home. (6) Continued opioid use despite having persistent or recurrent social or interpersonal problems caused or exacerbated by the effects of opioids. (7) Important social, occupational, or recreational activities are given up or reduced because of opioid use. (8) Recurrent opioid use in situations in which it is physically hazardous. (9) Continued opioid use despite knowledge of having a persistent or recurrent physical or psychological problem that is likely to have been caused or exacerbated by the substance. (10) Tolerance, as defined by either (a) a need for markedly increased amounts of opioids to achieve intoxication or desired effect or (b) a markedly diminished effect with continued use of the same amount of an opioid. (11) Withdrawal, as manifested by either (a) the characteristic opioid withdrawal syndrome or (b) opioids (or a closely related substance) are taken to relieve or avoid withdrawal symptoms.

Specify current severity:
Mild: Presence of two to three symptoms
Moderate: Presence of four to five symptoms
Severe: Presence of six or more symptoms

From American Psychiatric Association. (2013). *Diagnostic and statistical manual of mental disorders* (5th ed.). Washington, DC.

Cannabis-Related Disorders

▶ What are the physiological and psychological effects of cannabis?

Cannabis (marijuana) is the most routinely used illegal substance, with 22.2 million individuals in the United States aged 12 or older reporting they have used marijuana in the past 30 days (SAMHSA, 2014). Marijuana is the name given to the dried parts of the cannabis or hemp plant. Cannabis grows wild throughout the tropical and temperate regions of the world, which accounts for one of its nicknames, "weed."

Reactions to cannabis usually include mood swings. Otherwise-normal experiences seem extremely funny, or the person might enter a dreamlike state in which time seems to stand still. Users often report heightened sensory experiences, seeing vivid colors, or appreciating the subtleties of music. Perhaps more than any other drug, however, cannabis can produce different reactions in people. It is not uncommon for someone to report having no reaction to the first use of the drug; it also appears that people can "turn off" the high if they are sufficiently motivated (Jager, 2012). The feelings of well-being produced by small doses can change to paranoia, hallucinations, and dizziness when larger doses are taken. High school–age marijuana smokers get lower grades and are less likely to graduate, although

opioid-related disorders Cognitive, biological, behavioral, and social problems associated with the use and abuse of **opiates** and their synthetic variants.

cannabis (*cannabis* sativa) (marijuana) See **marijuana**.

▲ Marijuana

it is not clear if this is the direct result of cannabis use or concurrent other drug use (Jager, 2012). Research on frequent cannabis users suggests that impairments of memory, concentration, relationships with others, and employment may be negative outcomes of long-term use (possibly leading to **cannabis use disorders**), although some researchers suggest that some psychological problems precede usage—increasing the likelihood that someone will use cannabis (Heron *et al.*, 2013; Macleod *et al.*, 2004). The introduction of synthetic marijuana (referred to with names such as "fake weed," "K2" or "Spice" and marketed as "herbal incense") has caused alarm because in many places it can be purchased legally and the reaction to its use can be extremely harmful (e.g., hallucinations, seizures, heart rhythm problems, etc.) (Palamar & Barratt, 2016; Wells & Ott, 2011).

The evidence for cannabis tolerance is contradictory. Chronic and heavy users report tolerance, especially to the euphoric high (Mennes, Ben Abdallah, & Cottler, 2009); they are unable to reach the levels of pleasure they experienced earlier. However, evidence also indicates "reverse tolerance," when regular users experience more pleasure from the drug after repeated use. Major signs of withdrawal do not usually occur with cannabis. Chronic users who stop taking the drug report a period of irritability, restlessness, appetite loss, nausea, and difficulty sleeping (Jager, 2012).

Controversy surrounds the use of cannabis for medicinal purposes. However, there appears to be an increasing database documenting the successful use of cannabis and its by-products for the symptoms of certain diseases. In Canada and 24 states including Washington, D.C., cannabis products are available for medical use, including a herbal cannabis extract (Sativex—delivered in a nasal spray), dronabinol (Marinol), nabilone (Cesamet), and the herbal form of cannabis that is typically smoked (Borgelt, Franson, Nussbaum, & Wang, 2013; Wang, Collet, Shapiro, & Ware, 2008). These cannabis-derived products are prescribed for chemotherapy-induced nausea and vomiting, HIV-associated anorexia, neuropathic pain in multiple sclerosis, and cancer pain. Unfortunately, marijuana smoke may contain as many carcinogens as tobacco smoke, although one study that followed more than 5,000 men and women over 20 years suggested that occasional use does not appear to have a negative effect on lung functioning (Pletcher *et al.*, 2012).

Most cannabis users inhale the drug by smoking the dried leaves in marijuana cigarettes; others use preparations such as hashish, which is the dried form of the resin in the leaves of the female plant. Marijuana contains more than 80 varieties of the chemicals called *cannabinoids,* which are believed to alter mood and behavior. The most common of these chemicals includes the *tetrahydrocannabinols,* otherwise known as *THC.* An exciting finding in the area of cannabis research was that the brain makes its own version of THC, a neurochemical called *anandamide* (Sedlak & Kaplin, 2009; Volkow, Baler, Compton, & Weiss, 2014). Subsequent research points to several other naturally occurring brain chemicals including 2-AG (2-arachidonylglcerol), noladin ether, virodhamine, and N-arachidonoyldopamine (Mechoulam & Parker, 2013; Piomelli, 2003). Scientists continue to explore how this neurochemical affects the brain and behavior (Piomelli, 2014).

DSM 5 DISORDER CRITERIA SUMMARY
Cannabis Use Disorder

A. A problematic pattern of cannabis use leading to clinically significant impairment or distress, as manifested by at least two of the following, occurring within a 12-month period: (1) Cannabis is often taken in larger amounts or over a longer period than was intended. (2) There is a persistent desire or unsuccessful efforts to cut down or control cannabis use. (3) A great deal of time is spent in activities necessary to obtain cannabis, use cannabis, or recover from its effects. (4) Craving, or a strong desire or urge to use cannabis. (5) Recurrent cannabis use resulting in a failure to fulfill major role obligations at work, school, or home. (6) Continued cannabis use despite having persistent or recurrent social or interpersonal problems caused or exacerbated by the effects of cannabis. (7) Important social, occupational, or recreational activities are given up or reduced because of cannabis use. (8) Recurrent cannabis use in situations in which it is physically hazardous. (9) Cannabis use is continued despite knowledge of having a persistent or recurrent physical or psychological problem that is likely to have been caused or exacerbated by cannabis. (10) Tolerance, as defined by either (a) a need for markedly increased amounts of cannabis to achieve intoxication or desired effect or (b) a markedly diminished effect with continued use of the same amount of cannabis. (11) Withdrawal, as manifested by either (a) the characteristic withdrawal syndrome for cannabis or (b) cannabis (or a closely related substance) is taken to relieve or avoid withdrawal symptoms.

Specify current severity:
Mild: Presence of two to three symptoms
Moderate: Presence of four to five symptoms
Severe: Presence of six or more symptoms

From American Psychiatric Association. (2013). *Diagnostic and statistical manual of mental disorders* (5th ed.). Washington, DC.

Hallucinogen-Related Disorders

▶ What are the physiological and psychological effects of hallucinogenics?

LSD (*d*-lysergic acid diethylamide), sometimes referred to as "acid," is the most common hallucinogenic drug. It is produced synthetically in laboratories, although naturally occurring derivatives of this grain fungus (ergot) have been found historically. LSD largely remained in the laboratory until the 1960s, when it was first produced illegally for recreational use. There are a number of other hallucinogens, some occurring naturally in a variety of plants: *psilocybin* (found in certain species of mushrooms), *lysergic acid amide* (found in the seeds of the morning glory plant), *dimethyltryptamine (DMT)* (found in the bark of the Virola tree, which grows in South and Central America); and *mescaline* (found in the peyote cactus plant). Phencyclidine (or PCP) is snorted, smoked, or injected intravenously, and it causes impulsivity and aggressiveness.

The *DSM-5* diagnostic criteria for hallucinogen intoxication are similar to those for cannabis: perceptual changes such as the subjective intensification of perceptions, depersonalization, and hallucinations. Physical symptoms include pupillary dilation, rapid heartbeat, sweating, and blurred vision (American Psychiatric Association, 2013). Many users have written about hallucinogens, and they describe a variety of experiences. In one well-designed placebo-controlled study of hallucinogens, researchers at Johns Hopkins School of Medicine gave volunteers either the hallucinogen psilocybin or a control drug (the ADHD medication Ritalin) and assessed their reactions (Griffiths, Richards, McCann, & Jesse, 2006). Psilocybin ingestion resulted in individualized reactions including perceptual changes (for example, mild visual hallucinations) and mood changes (for example, joy or happiness, anxiety, or fearfulness). Interestingly, the drug increased reports of mystical experiences (for example, deeply felt positive mood), and even 14 months later many rated the experience as having a spiritual significance (Griffiths, Richards, Johnson, McCann, & Jesse, 2008). Some research is showing that psilocybin may be helpful for anxiety and depression among those receiving cancer care (Nutt, 2016). More research is needed to explore how these types of drugs work with increased specificity, and this research may also tell us how our brains process experiences such as personal meaning and spirituality (TylŠ, Páleníček, & Horáček, 2014).

Tolerance develops quickly to a number of hallucinogens, including LSD, psilocybin, and mescaline (**hallucinogen use disorders**) (Passie & Halpern, 2015). If taken repeatedly over a period of days, these drugs lose their effectiveness. Sensitivity returns after about a week of abstinence, however. For most hallucinogens, no withdrawal symptoms are reported. Even so, a number of concerns have been expressed about their use. One is the possibility of psychotic reactions. Stories in the press about people who jumped out of windows because they believed they could fly have provided for sensational reading, but little evidence suggests that using hallucinogens produces a greater risk than being drunk or under the influence of any other drug. People do report having "bad trips"; these are the sort of frightening episodes in which clouds turn into monsters or feelings of paranoia take over. Usually someone on a bad trip can be "talked down" by people who provide reassurance that the experience is just a temporary effect of the drug (Parrott, 2012).

DSM 5 DISORDER CRITERIA SUMMARY
Other Hallucinogen Use Disorder

A. A problematic pattern of hallucinogen (other than phencyclidine) use leading to clinically significant impairment or distress, as manifested by at least two of the following, occurring within a 12-month period: (1) The hallucinogen is often taken in larger amounts or over a longer period than was intended. (2) There is a persistent desire or unsuccessful efforts to cut down or control hallucinogen use. (3) A great deal of time is spent in activities necessary to obtain the hallucinogen, use the hallucinogen, or recover from its effects. (4) Craving, or a strong desire or urge to use the hallucinogen. (5) Recurrent hallucinogen use resulting in a failure to fulfill major role obligations at work, school, or home. (6) Continued hallucinogen use despite having persistent or recurrent social or interpersonal problems caused or exacerbated by the effects of the hallucinogen. (7) Important social, occupational, or recreational activities are given up or reduced because of hallucinogen use. (8) Recurrent hallucinogen use in situations in which it is physically hazardous. (9) Hallucinogen use is continued despite knowledge of having a persistent or recurrent physical or psychological problem that is likely to have been caused or exacerbated by the hallucinogen. (10) Tolerance, as defined by either (a) a need for markedly increased amounts of the hallucinogen to achieve intoxication or desired effect or (b) a markedly diminished effect with continued use of the same amount of the hallucinogen.

Specify current severity:
Mild: Presence of two to three symptoms
Moderate: Presence of four to five symptoms
Severe: Presence of 6 or more symptoms

From American Psychiatric Association. (2013). *Diagnostic and statistical manual of mental disorders* (5th ed.). Washington, DC.

· ·

hallucinogen use disorders Cognitive, biological, behavioral, and social problems associated with the use and abuse of hallucinogenic substances.

hallucinogenic substances Any psychoactive substance, such as LSD, that can produce delusions, hallucinations, paranoia, and altered sensory perception.

Hallucinogens seem to affect the brain in diverse and non-specific ways. It is thought that this broad impact on brain receptors may lead to the consciousness expanding experienced by some (Passie & Halpern, 2015). Most of these drugs bear some resemblance to neurotransmitters; LSD, psilocybin, lysergic acid amide, and DMT are chemically similar to serotonin; mescaline resembles norepinephrine; and a number of other hallucinogens we have not discussed are similar to acetylcholine. Research in human and animal laboratory studies shows no short-term or long-toxicity with regards to hallucinogens, meaning one's body processes the substances without incurring any harm to organs including the brain. This may be in part why some researchers are exploring psilocybin as a substance with possible therapeutic potential (TylŠ et al., 2014).

Other Drugs of Abuse

▶ What are the physiological and psychological effects of other drugs, including inhalants, steroids, and designer drugs?

A number of other substances are used by individuals to alter sensory experiences. These drugs do not fit neatly into the classes of substances just described but are of concern because they can be physically damaging to those who ingest them. We describe inhalants, steroids, and a group of drugs referred to as designer drugs.

Inhalants include substances found in volatile solvents—making them available to breathe into the lungs directly. Common inhalants used abusively include spray paint, hair spray, paint thinner, gasoline, amyl nitrate, nitrous oxide ("laughing gas"), nail polish remover, felt-tipped markers, airplane glue, contact cement, dry-cleaning fluid, and spot remover (Ridenour & Howard, 2012). Inhalant use is highest during early adolescence, especially in those in correctional or psychiatric institutions. Higher rates of use are also found among Native Americans and Caucasians, as well as those who live in rural or small towns, come from disadvantaged backgrounds, have higher levels of anxiety and depression, and show more impulsive and fearless temperaments (Garland, Howard, Vaughn, & Perron, 2011; Halliburton & Bray, 2016). Inhalants are rapidly absorbed into the bloodstream through the lungs when inhaled from containers or on a cloth held up to the mouth and nose. The high associated with inhalants resembles that of alcohol intoxication and usually includes dizziness, slurred speech, lack of coordination, euphoria, and lethargy (American Psychiatric Association, 2013). Users build up a tolerance to the drugs, and withdrawal—which involves sleep disturbance, tremors, irritability, and nausea—can last from two to five days. Use can also increase aggressive and antisocial behavior, and long-term use can damage bone marrow, the kidneys, liver, lungs, the nervous system, and the brain (Ford, Sutter, Owen, & Albertson, 2014). If users are startled, this can cause a cardiac event that can lead to death (called "sudden sniffing death") (Ridenour & Howard, 2012).

DSM 5 — DISORDER CRITERIA SUMMARY
Inhalant Use Disorder

A. A problematic pattern of use of a hydrocarbon-based inhalant substance leading to clinically significant impairment or distress, as manifested by at least two of the following, occurring within a 12-month period: (1) The inhalant substance is often taken in larger amounts or over a longer period than was intended. (2) There is a persistent desire or unsuccessful efforts to cut down or control use of the inhalant substance. (3) A great deal of time is spent in activities necessary to obtain the inhalant, use it, or recover from its effects. (4) Craving, a strong desire or urge to use the inhalant substance. (5) Recurrent use of the inhalant substance resulting in a failure to fulfill major role obligations at work, school, or home. (6) Continued use of the inhalant substance despite having persistent or recurrent social or interpersonal problems caused or exacerbated by the effects of its use. (7) Important social, occupational, or recreational activities are given up or reduced because of use of the inhalant substance. (8) Recurrent use of the inhalant substance in situations in which it is physically hazardous. (9) Use of the inhalant substance is continued despite knowledge of having a persistent or recurrent physical or psychological problem that is likely to have been caused or exacerbated by the substance. (10) Tolerance, as defined by either (a) a need for markedly increased amounts of inhalant substance to achieve intoxication or desired effect or (b) a markedly diminished effect with continued use of the same amount of the inhalant substance.

Specify current severity:
Mild: Presence of two to three symptoms
Moderate: Presence of four to five symptoms
Severe: Presence of six or more symptoms

From American Psychiatric Association. (2013). *Diagnostic and statistical manual of mental disorders* (5th ed.). Washington, DC.

Anabolic–androgenic steroids (more commonly referred to as steroids or "roids" or "juice") are derived from or are a synthesized form of the hormone testosterone (Pope & Kanayama, 2012). The legitimate medical uses of these drugs focus on people with asthma, anemia, breast cancer, and males with inadequate sexual development. However, the anabolic action of these drugs (that can produce increased body mass) has resulted in their illicit use by those wishing to try to improve their physical abilities by increasing muscle bulk. Steroids can be taken orally or through injection, and some estimates suggest that approximately 2% to 6% of males will use the drug illegally at some point in their lives (Pope & Kanayama, 2012). Users sometimes administer the drug on a schedule of several weeks or months followed by a break from its use—called "cycling"—or combine several types of steroids—called "stacking." Steroid use differs from other drug use because the substance does not produce a desirable high but instead is used to enhance performance and body size. Dependence on the substance therefore seems to involve the desire to maintain the performance gains obtained rather than a need to re-experience an altered emotional or physical state. Research on the long-term effects of steroid use seems to suggest that mood disturbances are common (for example, depression, anxiety, and panic attacks) (Pope & Kanayama, 2012), and there is a concern that more serious physical consequences may result from regular use.

Another class of drugs—dissociative anesthetics—causes drowsiness, pain relief, and the feeling of being out of one's body (Domino & Miller, 2015; Javitt & Zukin, 2009). Sometimes referred to as designer drugs, this growing group of drugs was originally developed by pharmaceutical companies to target specific diseases and disorders. It was only a matter of time before some began using the technology to design "recreational drugs." We have already described one common illicit designer drug—MDMA (street names include Ecstasy or Molly). These drugs are able to heighten a person's auditory and visual perception, as well as the senses of taste and touch. A drug associated with the "drug club" scene is ketamine (street names include K, Special K, and Cat Valium), a dissociative anesthetic that produces a sense of detachment and a reduced awareness of pain (Wolff, 2012). Gamma-hydroxybutyrate (GHB, or liquid Ecstasy) is a depressant that at low doses can produce a state of relaxation and increased tendency to verbalize, but at higher doses or with alcohol or other drugs can result in seizures, severe respiratory depression, and coma. These drugs taken at high doses may be especially dangerous for the developing teenage brain due to their high toxicity, which may cause irreversible memory loss and other cognitive problems (Domino & Miller, 2015).

Since 2010 there has been a rise in the use of synthetic stimulants (called "bath salts") including *3,4-methylenedioxypyrovalerone (MDPV)*, a synthetic form of a stimulant found in the khat plant (Baumann, 2014). The effects of these synthetic drugs are much stronger and, though similar to stimulants, they have an excitatory or agitating effect that can include paranoia, delirium, hallucinations, and panic attacks (Baumann *et al.*, 2013). Use of these drugs can result in tolerance and dependence, and their increasing popularity among adolescents and young adults raises significant public health concerns.

Causes of Substance-Related Disorders

We saw that despite his clear potential as an individual, Danny continued to use drugs to his detriment. Various factors help explain why people like Danny persist in using drugs. Drug abuse and dependence, once thought to be the result of moral weakness, are now understood to be influenced by a combination of biological and psychosocial factors.

Why do some people use psychoactive drugs without abusing or becoming dependent on them? Why do some people stop using these drugs or use them in moderate amounts after being dependent on them and others continue a lifelong pattern of dependence despite their efforts to stop? These questions continue to occupy the time and attention of numerous researchers throughout the world.

Biological Dimensions

Familial and Genetic Influences

As you already have seen throughout this book, many psychological disorders are influenced in important ways by genetics. Mounting evidence indicates that drug abuse follows this pattern. Researchers conducting twin, family, and adoption and other genetic studies have found that certain people are genetically vulnerable to drug abuse (Strain, 2009; Volkow & Warren, 2015). Twin studies of smoking, for example, indicate a moderate genetic influence (e.g., Hardie, Moss, & Lynch, 2006; Seglem, Waaktaar, Ask, & Torgersen, 2015). Most genetic data on substance abuse come from research on alcoholism, which is widely studied because alcohol use is legal and many people are dependent on it. Research in general suggests that genetic risk factors cut across all mood-altering drugs (Kendler *et al.*, 2012).

In a major twin study, the role of the environment, as well as the role of genetics, was examined in substance use problems. Researchers studied more than 1,000 pairs of male twins and questioned them about their use of cannabis, cocaine, hallucinogens, sedatives, stimulants, and opiates (Kendler, Jacobson, Prescott, & Neale, 2003). The findings suggest that there are common genetic influences on the use of all of these drugs. Although it is clear that genetics plays an important role in substance-related disorders, specific genes and their influence on these disorders are still being explored (Ray, 2012; Volkow & Warren, 2015). As the search for the genes influencing substance use disorders continues, the next obvious question is how these genes function when it comes to addiction—a field of research called *functional genomics* (Demers, Bogdan, & Agrawal, 2014; Khokhar, Ferguson, Zhu, & Tyndale, 2010).

Genetic factors may affect how people experience and metabolize certain drugs, which in turn may partly determine who will or will not become regular users (Volkow & Warren, 2015). Just to illustrate how complex these relationships can be, research has found that certain genes are associated with a greater likelihood of heroin addiction in Hispanic and African American populations (Nielsen *et al.*, 2008). Other research points out that a pharmacological treatment for alcohol use disorder—naltrexone (an opioid antagonist)—may be most effective with individuals who have a particular genetic variant in their opioid receptors (the OPRM1 gene) (Ray, 2012). In other words, your genetics may not only influence whether you develop a substance-related disorder but also help predict which treatments may be effective in reducing these problems.

Neurobiological Influences

In general, the pleasurable experiences reported by people who use psychoactive substances partly explain why people continue to use them. In behavioral terms, people are positively reinforced for using drugs. But what mechanism is responsible for such experiences? Studies indicate the brain appears to have a natural "pleasure pathway" that mediates our experience of reward. All abused substances seem to affect this internal reward center in the same way as you experience pleasure from certain foods or from sex (Ray, 2012). In other words, what psychoactive drugs may have in common is their ability to activate this reward center and provide the user with a pleasurable experience, at least for a time.

The pleasure center was discovered more than 50 years ago by James Olds, who studied the effects of electrical stimulation on rat brains (Olds, 1956; Olds & Milner, 1954).

If certain areas were stimulated with small amounts of electricity, the rats behaved as if they had received something pleasant, such as food. The exact location of the area in the human brain is still subject to debate. It is believed that the *dopaminergic system* and its *opioid-releasing neurons* are involved.

How do different drugs that affect different neurotransmitter systems all converge to activate the pleasure pathway, which is primarily made up of dopamine-sensitive neurons? Researchers are only beginning to sort out the answers to this question, but some surprising findings have emerged in recent years. For example, we know that amphetamines and cocaine act directly on the dopamine system. Other drugs, however, appear to increase the availability of dopamine in more roundabout and intricate ways. For example, the neurons in the brain's ventral tegmental area are kept from continuous firing by GABA neurons. One thing that keeps us from being on an unending high is the presence of these GABA neurons, which act as the "brain police," or superegos of the reward neurotransmitter system. Opiates (opium, morphine, heroin) inhibit GABA, which in turn stops the GABA neurons from inhibiting dopamine, which makes more dopamine available in the brain's pleasure pathway. Drugs that stimulate the reward center directly or indirectly include not only amphetamine, cocaine, and opiates but also nicotine and alcohol (Strain, 2009; Volkow & Warren, 2015).

This complicated picture is far from complete. We now understand that other neurotransmitters in addition to dopamine—including serotonin and norepinephrine—are involved in the brain's reward system (Khokhar *et al.*, 2010; Volkow & Warren, 2015). The coming years should yield interesting insights into the interaction of drugs and the brain. One aspect that awaits explanation is how drugs not only provide pleasurable experiences (positive reinforcement) but also help remove unpleasant experiences such as pain, feelings of illness, or anxiety (negative reinforcement). Aspirin is a negative reinforcer: We take it not because it makes us feel good but because it stops us from feeling bad. In much the same way, one property of the psychoactive drugs is that they stop people from feeling bad, an effect as powerful as making them feel good.

With several drugs, negative reinforcement is related to the anxiolytic effect, the ability to reduce anxiety. Alcohol has an anxiolytic effect. The neurobiology of how these drugs reduce anxiety seems to involve the septal–hippocampal system (Ray, 2012), which includes a large number of GABA-sensitive neurons. Certain drugs may reduce anxiety by enhancing the activity of GABA in this region, thereby inhibiting the brain's normal reaction (anxiety or fear) to anxiety-producing situations.

Researchers have identified individual differences in the way people respond to alcohol. Understanding these response differences is important because they may help explain why some people continue to use drugs until they acquire a dependence on them, whereas others stop before this happens. A number of studies compare individuals with and without a family history of alcoholism (Gordis, 2000). They concluded that, compared with the sons of non-alcoholics, the sons of alcoholics may be more sensitive to alcohol when it is first ingested and then become less sensitive to its effects as the hours pass after drinking. This finding is significant because the euphoric effects of alcohol occur just after drinking but the experience after several hours is often sadness and depression. People who are at risk for developing alcoholism (in this case, the sons of alcoholics) may be better able to appreciate the initial highs of drinking and be less sensitive to the lows that come later, making them ideal candidates for continued drinking. In support of this observation, follow-up research over a 10-year period found that those men who tended to be less sensitive to alcohol also tended to drink more heavily and more often (Schuckit, 1994, 1998).

Psychological Dimensions

We have shown that the substances people use to alter mood and behavior have unique effects. The high from heroin differs substantially from the experience of smoking a cigarette, which in turn differs from the effects of amphetamines or LSD. Nevertheless, it is important to point out the similarities in the way people mentally react to most of these substances.

Positive Reinforcement

The feelings that result from using psychoactive substances are pleasurable in some way, and people will continue to take the drugs to recapture the pleasure. Research shows that many drugs used and abused by humans also seem to be pleasurable to animals (Young & Herling, 1986). Laboratory animals will work to have their bodies injected with drugs such as cocaine, amphetamines, opiates, sedatives, and alcohol, which demonstrates that even without social and cultural influences these drugs are pleasurable. Human research also indicates that to some extent all psychoactive drugs provide a pleasurable experience (Ray, 2012). In addition, the social contexts for drug taking may encourage its use, even when the use alone is not the desired outcome. One study found that among volunteers who preferred not to take Valium, pairing money with pill taking caused participants to switch from a placebo to Valium (Alessi, Roll, Reilly, & Johanson, 2002). Positive reinforcement in the use and the situations surrounding the use of drugs contributes to whether or not people decide to try to continue using drugs.

Negative Reinforcement

Most researchers have looked at how drugs help reduce unpleasant feelings through negative reinforcement. In addition to the initial euphoria, many drugs provide escape from physical pain (opiates), from stress (alcohol), or from panic and anxiety (benzodiazepines). This phenomenon has been explored under a number of different names, including *tension reduction*, *negative affect*, and *self-medication*, each of which has a somewhat different focus (Ray, 2012).

One premise is that substance use becomes a way for users to cope with the unpleasant feelings. For example, one study of 1,252 U.S. Army soldiers returning home from Operation Iraqi Freedom found that those exposed to violent combat, human trauma, and having direct responsibility for taking the life of another person were at increased risk for risk-taking and for more frequent and greater alcohol use (Killgore *et al.*, 2008; Stappenbeck, Hellmuth, Simpson, & Jakupcak, 2014). People who experience other types of trauma such as sexual abuse are also more likely to abuse alcohol (Breckenridge, Salter, & Shaw, 2012). These observations emphasize the important role played by each aspect of abuse and dependence—biological, psychological, social, and cultural—in determining who will and who will not have difficulties with these substances.

In a study that examined substance use among adolescents as a way to reduce stress (Chassin, Pillow, Curran, Molina, & Barrera, 1993), researchers compared a group of adolescents who had alcoholic parents with a group whose parents did not have drinking problems. The researchers found that just having a parent with alcohol dependence was a major factor in predicting who would use alcohol and other drugs. However, they also found that adolescents who reported negative affect, such as feeling lonely or being tense, were more likely than others to use drugs. The researchers further determined that the adolescents from both groups tended to use drugs as a way to cope with unpleasant feelings. This study and others (see, for example, Pardini, Lochman, & Wells, 2004) suggest that one contributing factor to adolescent drug use is the desire to escape from unpleasantness. It also suggests that to prevent people from using drugs we may need to address influences such as stress and anxiety, a strategy we discuss in our section on treatment.

Many people who use psychoactive substances experience a crash after being high. If people reliably crash, why don't they just stop taking drugs? One explanation is given by Solomon and Corbit in an interesting integration of both the positive and the negative reinforcement processes (Solomon, 1980; Solomon & Corbit, 1974). The *opponent-process theory* holds that an increase in positive feelings will be followed shortly by an increase in negative feelings. Similarly, an increase in negative feelings will be followed by a period of positive feelings (Ray, 2012). The opponent-process theory claims that this mechanism is strengthened with use and weakened by disuse. So a person who has been using a drug for some time will need more of it to achieve the same results (tolerance). At the same time, the negative feelings that follow drug use tend to intensify. For many people, this is the point at which the motivation for drug taking shifts from desiring the euphoric high to alleviating the increasingly unpleasant crash. Unfortunately, they come to believe that the best remedy is more of the same drug.

Researchers have also looked at substance abuse as a way of self-medicating for other problems (Bailey & Baillie, 2012). If people have difficulties with anxiety, for example, they may be attracted to barbiturates or alcohol because of their anxiety-reducing qualities. In one study, researchers were successful in treating a group of cocaine addicts who had ADHD with methylphenidate (Ritalin) (Dursteler et al., 2015; Levin, Evans, Brooks, & Garawi, 2007). They had hypothesized that these individuals used cocaine to help focus their attention. Once their ability to concentrate improved with the methylphenidate, the users reduced their use of cocaine.

Cognitive Dimensions

What people expect to experience when they use drugs influences how they react to them. A person who expects to be less inhibited when she drinks alcohol will act less inhibited whether she actually drinks alcohol or a placebo she thinks is alcohol (Bailey & Baillie, 2012). This observation about the influence of how we think about drug use has been labeled an *expectancy effect* and has received considerable research attention.

Expectancies develop before people actually use drugs, perhaps as a result of parents' and peers' drug use, advertising, and media figures who model drug use (Campbell & Oei, 2013). In an important study, students in Canada in grades 7 to 11 were questioned each year for three years about their thoughts about alcohol and marijuana use (Fulton, Krank, & Stewart, 2012; Young, 2013). Included were instructions for them to list three or four things they expected would happen if they used a particular substance. Positive expectancies about the effects of alcohol or marijuana use predicted who was more likely to use and increase their use of these drugs three years later. These results suggest that adolescents may begin drinking or using other drugs partly because they believe these substances will have positive effects.

Expectations appear to change as people have more experience with drugs, although their expectations are similar for alcohol, nicotine, cannabis, and cocaine (Simons, Dvorak, & Lau-Barraco, 2009; Young, 2013). Some evidence points to positive expectancies—believing you will feel good if you take a drug—as an indirect influence on drug problems. In other words, what these beliefs may do

is increase the likelihood you will take certain drugs, which in turn will increase the likelihood that problems will arise.

Once people stop taking drugs after prolonged or repeated use, powerful urges called "cravings" can interfere with efforts to remain off these drugs (Hollander & Kenny, 2012; Young, 2013). *DSM-5* includes cravings as one of the criteria for diagnosing a substance-related disorder. These urges seem to be triggered by factors such as the availability of the drug, contact with things associated with drug taking (for example, sitting in a bar), specific moods (for example, being depressed), or having a small dose of the drug. For example, one study used a virtual reality apparatus to simulate visual, auditory, and olfactory (an alcohol-dipped tissue) cues (Lee et al., 2009) for alcohol-dependent adults. The participants could choose among kinds of alcoholic beverages (e.g., beer, whiskey, or wine), snacks, and drinking environments (beer garden, restaurant, and pub). The researchers found significant increases in cravings for alcohol under these conditions (Lee et al., 2009). Research is under way to determine how cravings may work in the brain and if certain medications can be used to reduce these urges and help supplement treatment (Hollander & Kenny, 2012).

Social Dimensions

Exposure to psychoactive substances is a necessary prerequisite to their use and possible abuse, as previously discussed. In one large study, 820 adolescents (ages 14–17) were studied to assess what factors influenced the age at which they would have their first drink of alcohol (Kuperman et al., 2013). This study found several factors predicted early alcohol use including when their best friends started drinking, whether their family was at high risk for alcohol dependence, and the presence of behavior problems in these children.

Research suggests that drug-addicted parents spend less time monitoring their children than parents without drug problems (Dishion, Patterson, & Reid, 1988) and that this is an important contribution to early adolescent substance use (Kerr, Stattin, & Burk, 2010). When parents do not provide appropriate supervision, their children tend to develop friendships with peers who supported drug use (Van Ryzin, Fosco, & Dishion, 2012). Children influenced by drug use at home may be exposed to peers who use drugs as well. A self-perpetuating pattern seems to be associated with drug use that extends beyond the genetic influences we discussed previously.

How does our society view people who are dependent on drugs? This issue is of tremendous importance because it affects efforts to legislate the sale, manufacture, possession, and use of these substances. It also dictates how drug-dependent individuals are treated. Two views of substance-related disorders characterize contemporary thought:

the moral weakness and the disease models of dependence. According to the *moral weakness model of chemical dependence*, drug use is seen as a failure of self-control in the face of temptation; this is a psychosocial perspective. Proponents of this model see drug users as lacking the character or moral fiber to resist the lure of drugs. The *disease model of physiological dependence*, in contrast, assumes that drug use disorders are caused by an underlying physiological cause; this is a biological perspective. Those who ascribe to this model think that just as diabetes or asthma can't be blamed on the afflicted individuals, neither should drug use disorders. AA and similar organizations see drug use disorders as an incurable disease over which the addict has no control (Kelly, Stout, Magill, Tonigan, & Pagano, 2010).

Neither perspective does justice to the complex interrelationship between the psychosocial and biological influences that affect substance disorders. Viewing drug use as moral weakness leads to punishing those afflicted with the disorder, whereas a disease model includes seeking treatment for a medical problem. Messages that the disorder is out of their control can at times be counterproductive. A comprehensive view of substance-related disorders that includes both psychosocial and biological influences is needed for this important societal concern to be addressed adequately.

Cultural Dimensions

When we examine a behavior as it appears in different cultures, it is necessary to re-examine what is considered abnormal (Kohn, Wintrob, & Alarcón, 2009). Each culture has its own preferences for acceptable psychoactive drugs, as well as its own prohibitions for substances it finds unacceptable. Keep in mind that in addition to defining what is or is not acceptable, cultural norms affect the rates of substance use in important ways. For example, research suggests that alcohol may be more available in poorer Mexican towns (i.e., more stores or individuals selling alcohol), leading to higher rates of alcoholism in these areas (Parker, McCaffree, & Alaniz, 2013).

On the other hand, in certain cultures, including Korea, people are expected to drink alcohol heavily on certain social occasions (C. K. Lee, 1992). As we have seen before, exposure to these substances, in addition to social pressure for heavy and frequent use, may facilitate their abuse, and this may explain the high alcohol abuse rates in countries like Korea. This cultural influence provides an interesting natural experiment when exploring gene–environment interactions. People of Asian descent are more likely to have the ALDH2 gene, which produces a severe "flushing" effect (reddening and burning of the face) after drinking alcohol. This flushing effect was thought to be responsible for a relatively low rate of drinking in the population (de Wit & Phillips, 2012). However, between 1979 and 1992—when

In many cultures, alcohol is used as part of certain rituals, demonstrated in this photo of Masai elders drinking ceremonial beer.

increased drinking became socially expected—there was an increase in alcohol abuse (Higuchi *et al.*, 1994). The protective value of having the ALDH2 gene was diminished by the change in cultural norms (Rutter, Moffit, & Caspi, 2006).

Cultural factors not only influence the rates of substance abuse but also determine how it is manifested. Research indicates that alcohol consumption in Poland and Finland is relatively low, yet conflicts related to drinking and arrests for drunkenness in those countries are high compared with those in the Netherlands, which has about the same rate of alcohol consumption (Osterberg, 1986). Our discussion of expectancies may provide some insight into how the same amount of drinking can have different behavioral outcomes. Expectancies about the effects of alcohol use differ across cultures (for example, "Drinking makes me more aggressive" versus "Drinking makes me more withdrawn"); these differing expectancies may partially account for the variations in the consequences of drinking in Poland, Finland, and the Netherlands. Whether substance use is considered a harmful dysfunction often depends on the assumptions of the cultural group.

An Integrative Model

Any explanation of substance use disorders must account for the basic issue raised earlier in this chapter: Why do some people use drugs but not abuse them or become dependent? ● Figure 10.5 illustrates how the multiple influences we have discussed may interact to account for this process. Access to a drug is a necessary but not a sufficient condition for abuse or dependence. Exposure has many sources, including the media, parents, peers, and, indirectly, lack of supervision. Whether people use a drug depends also on social and cultural expectations, some encouraging and some discouraging, such as laws against possession or sale of the drug.

People use alcohol and drugs all over the world. However, the rates of use differ significantly across countries and cultures, due in part to availability and social norms. A survey of people from 17 countries around the world revealed that approximately 85% to 95% of people report using alcohol at some point in their lifetime (the U.S. rate is 92%), although the rates in Africa and the Middle East are significantly lower (40%–58%) (Degenhardt et al., 2008). The use of other drugs such as tobacco, cannabis, and cocaine are significantly lower across all countries; however, the rates in the United States are significantly higher for each of these drugs than in virtually all other countries studied. For instance, the rate of cannabis use is 0% to 19% in most countries, but is 42% in the United States (and New Zealand). The rate of cocaine use is 0% to 4% in every country except the United States, in which 16% of people report using cocaine at some point in their life. The exact reason for these higher rates of use in the United States are not known, but drug use

is significantly associated with higher income, and so availability of drugs and the accumulation of wealth in the United States may play a strong role.

Although the rate of alcohol and drug use varies across countries, some interesting similarities in use are found across many different countries. Young people use alcohol and drugs more than older people, and although men have historically been shown to use alcohol and drugs at much higher rates than women, women appear to be catching up. This is true for both alcohol use (Grucza, Bucholz, Rice, & Bierut, 2008; Grucza, Norberg, Bucholz, & Bierut, 2008) and for drug use more generally (Degenhardt et al., 2008). Many possible explanations exist for the observed change in rates of female alcohol and drug use, with the majority focusing on the fact that over the past several decades, women have achieved greater economic, social, and political status. More specifically, explanations included the following: (1) changes in occupational options for women (e.g., women are more likely to be employed

and may adopt the traditional male notion of alcohol as a reasonable reward for a day of hard work, or may be more exposed to opportunities/occasions for drinking); (2) changes in social roles for women (e.g., cohabitation is becoming more prevalent and has been associated with higher rates of drinking); and (3) changes in adherence to gender stereotypes (e.g., women no longer conform to meeting traditional roles put on them of being nurturing, caring, and emotional) (for additional explanations see the review by Plant et al., 2008). Although it seems to be more socially and culturally accepted for women to engage in such drinking (and drug use) behaviors, women still experience greater barriers to treatment and stigma than men with similar dependence. Studies are needed to better understand exactly why this change has occurred and to develop better methods for preventing such high rates of abuse and dependence in the United States and around the globe. ∎

● **Figure 10.5** An integrative model of substance-related disorders.

The path from drug use to abuse and dependence is more complicated (see Figure 10.5). As major stressors aggravate many disorders we have discussed, so do they increase the risk of abuse and dependence on psychoactive substances. Genetic influences may be of several types. Some individuals may inherit a greater sensitivity to the effects of certain drugs; others may inherit an ability to metabolize substances more quickly and are thereby able to tolerate higher (and more dangerous) levels (Young-Wolff, Enoch, & Prescott, 2011). Other psychiatric conditions may indirectly put someone at risk for substance abuse. Antisocial personality disorder, characterized by the frequent violation of social norms (see Chapter 11), is thought to include a lowered rate of arousal; this may account for the increased prevalence of substance abuse in this group. People with mood disorders or anxiety disorders may self-medicate by using drugs to relieve the negative symptoms of their disorder, and this may account for the high rates of substance abuse in this group.

We know also that continued use of certain substances changes the way our brains work through a process called *neuroplasticity*. With the continued use of substances such as alcohol, cocaine, or the other drugs we explore in this chapter, the brain reorganizes itself to adapt. Unfortunately, this change in the brain increases the drive to obtain the drug and decreases the desire for other nondrug experiences—both of which contribute to continued use and relapse (Russo *et al.*, 2010).

It is clear that abuse and dependence cannot be predicted from one factor, be it genetic, neurobiological, psychological, or cultural. For example, *some* people with the genes common to many with substance abuse problems do not become abusers. Many people who experience the most crushing stressors, such as abject poverty or bigotry and violence, cope without resorting to drug use. There are different pathways to abuse, and we are only now beginning to identify their basic outlines.

Once a drug has been used repeatedly, biology and cognition conspire to create dependence. Continual use of most drugs causes tolerance, which requires the user to ingest more of the drug to produce the same effect. Conditioning is also a factor. If pleasurable drug experiences are associated with certain settings, a return to such a setting will later cause urges to develop, even if the drugs themselves are not available.

10.3 Concept CHECK

Indicate whether these statements about the causes of substance-related disorders are true (T) or false (F):

1. _____ Negative reinforcement is involved in the continuance of drug use, because drugs often provide escape from pain, stress, panic, and so on.

2. _____ Research with both animals and humans indicates that substance abuse in general is affected by our genes, although not one particular gene.

3. _____ The media and parental influences have no effect on adolescent drug use; it is solely a peer pressure factor.

4. _____ The expectancy effect is illustrated when a person who expects to be less inhibited when drinking alcohol is given a placebo and acts or feels normally.

5. _____ To some extent, all psychoactive drugs provide a pleasurable experience, creating positive reinforcement.

Treatment of Substance-Related Disorders

▶ What psychological and medical treatments are available for substance-related disorders?

When we left Danny, he was in jail, awaiting the legal outcome of being arrested for vehicular manslaughter. At this point in his life, Danny needs more than legal help; he needs to free himself from his addiction to alcohol and cocaine. And the first step in his recovery has to come from him. Danny must admit he needs help, that he does indeed have a problem with drugs, and that he needs others to help him overcome his chronic dependence. The personal motivation to work on a drug problem appears to be important but not necessarily essential in the treatment of substance abuse (National Institute on Drug Abuse [NIDA], 2009). Unfortunately, although Danny's arrest seemed to shock him into realizing how serious his problems had become, he was not ready to confront them head-on.

Treating people who have substance-related disorders is a difficult task. Perhaps because of the combination of influences that often work together to keep people hooked, the outlook for those who are dependent on drugs is often not positive. You will see in the case of heroin dependence, for example, that a best-case scenario is often just trading one addiction (heroin) for another (methadone). And even people who successfully cease taking drugs may feel the urge to resume drug use all their lives.

Treatment for substance-related disorders focuses on multiple areas (Higgins *et al.*, 2014). Sometimes the first step is to help someone through the withdrawal process; typically, the ultimate goal is abstinence. In other situations, the goal is to get a person to maintain a certain level of drug use without escalating its intake, and sometimes it is geared toward preventing exposure to drugs. Because substance abuse arises from so many influences, it should not be surprising that treating people with substance-related disorders is not a simple matter of finding just the right drug or the best way to change thoughts or behavior.

Importantly, it is estimated that fewer than 25% of the people who have significant problems with substance use seek treatment for their problems (Dawson *et al.*, 2005). In order to reach out to these individuals, efforts are under way to put in place routine screenings for substance use problems in settings such as doctor's offices, hospital emergency rooms, and even in college and university health clinics. This community-wide approach is an important part of identifying difficulties and bringing treatment to those in need (Tucker, Murphy, & Kertesz, 2011).

We discuss the treatment of substance-related disorders as a group because treatments have so much in common. For example, many programs that treat people for dependence on a variety of substances also teach skills for coping with life stressors. Some biological treatments focus on how to cancel out the effects of the ingested substances. We discuss the obvious differences among substances as they arise.

Biological Treatments

There have been a variety of biologically based approaches designed primarily to change the way substances are experienced. In other words, scientists are trying to find ways to prevent people from experiencing the pleasant highs

associated with drug use or to find alternative substances that have some of the positive effects (for example, reducing anxiety) without their addictive properties. Table 10.1 lists the current recommended medical treatments for many of the more intractable substance dependence problems.

Agonist Substitution

Increased knowledge about how psychoactive drugs work on the brain has led researchers to explore ways of changing how they are experienced by people who are dependent on them. One method, **agonist substitution**, involves providing the person with a safe drug that has a chemical makeup similar to the addictive drug (therefore the name *agonist*). *Methadone* is an opiate agonist that is often given as a heroin substitute (Schwartz, Brooner, Montoya, Currens, & Hayes, 2010). When users develop a tolerance for methadone, however, it loses its analgesic and sedative qualities. Because heroin and methadone have *cross-tolerance*, meaning they act on the same neurotransmitter receptors, a heroin addict who takes methadone may become addicted to the methadone instead (Maremmani *et al.*, 2009). Research suggests that when addicts combine methadone with counseling, many reduce their use of heroin and engage in less criminal activity (Schwartz *et al.*, 2009). A newer agonist—buprenorphine—blocks the effects of opiates and seems to encourage better compliance than would a non-opiate or opiate antagonist (Strain *et al.*, 2009).

Addiction to cigarette smoking is also treated by a substitution process. The drug—**nicotine**—is provided to smokers in the form of gum, patch, inhaler, or nasal spray, which lack the carcinogens included in cigarette smoke; the dose is later tapered off to lessen withdrawal from the drug. In general, these replacement strategies help people stop smoking, although they work best with psychological

TABLE 10.1 | Medical Treatments

	Substance Treatment Goal	Treatment Approach
Nicotine	Reduce withdrawal symptoms and cravings	Nicotine replacement therapy (patch, gum, spray, lozenge, and inhaler)
	Reduce withdrawal symptoms and cravings	Bupropion (Zyban)
Alcohol	Reduce reinforcing effects of alcohol	Naltrexone
	Reduce alcohol craving in abstinent individuals	Acamprosate (Campral)
	Maintenance of abstinence	Disulfiram (Antabuse)
Cannabis		No specific medical interventions recommended
Cocaine		No specific medical interventions recommended
Opioids	Maintenance of abstinence	Methadone
	Maintenance of abstinence	Buprenorphine (Subutex)

SOURCE: From American Psychiatric Association. (2007). Practice guidelines for the treatment of patients with substance use disorders (2nd ed.). *American Journal of Psychiatry, 164* (Suppl.), 1–14.

therapy (Carpenter *et al.*, 2013; Hughes, 2009). The **nicotine patch** requires less effort and provides a steadier nicotine replacement (Hughes, 2009).

Antagonist Treatments

We described how many psychoactive drugs produce euphoric effects through their interaction with the neurotransmitter systems in the brain. What would happen if the effects of these drugs were blocked so that the drugs no longer produced the pleasant results? Would people stop using the drugs? **Antagonist drugs** block or counteract the effects of psychoactive drugs, and a variety of drugs that seem to cancel out the effects of opiates have been used with people dependent on a variety of substances. The most often prescribed opiate-antagonist drug, naltrexone, has had only limited success with individuals who are not simultaneously participating in a structured treatment program (Krupitsky & Blokhina, 2010). When it is given to a person who is dependent on opiates, it produces immediate withdrawal symptoms, an extremely unpleasant effect. A person must be free from these withdrawal symptoms completely before starting naltrexone, and because it removes the euphoric effects of opiates, the user must be highly motivated to continue treatment. Acamprosate also seems to decrease cravings in people dependent on alcohol, and it works best with highly motivated people who are also participating in psychosocial interventions (Kennedy *et al.*, 2010). The brain mechanisms for the effects of this drug are not well understood (Oslin & Klaus, 2009).

Overall, naltrexone or the other drugs being explored are not the magic bullets that would shut off the addict's response to psychoactive drugs and put an end to dependence. They do appear to help some drug abusers handle withdrawal symptoms and the cravings that accompany attempts to abstain from drug use; antagonists may therefore be a useful addition to other therapeutic efforts.

Aversive Treatment

In addition to looking for ways to block the euphoric effects of psychoactive drugs, clinicians in this area may prescribe drugs that make ingesting the abused substances extremely unpleasant. The expectation is that a person who associates the drug with feelings of illness will avoid using the drug. The most commonly known aversive treatment uses disulfiram (Antabuse) with people who have an alcohol use disorder (Ivanov, 2009). People who drink alcohol after taking Antabuse experience nausea, vomiting, and elevated heart rate and respiration. Ideally, Antabuse is taken each morning, before the desire to drink arises. Unfortunately, non-compliance is a major concern, and a person who skips the Antabuse for a few days is able to resume drinking (Ellis & Dronsfield, 2013).

Other Biological Approaches

Medication is often prescribed to help people deal with the often-disturbing symptoms of withdrawal. Clonidine, developed to treat hypertension, has been given to people withdrawing from opiates. Because withdrawal from certain prescribed medications such as sedative drugs can cause cardiac arrest or seizures, these drugs are gradually tapered off to minimize dangerous reactions. In addition, sedative drugs (benzodiazepines) are often prescribed to help minimize discomfort for people withdrawing from other drugs, such as alcohol (Sher, Martinez, & Littlefield, 2011).

Psychosocial Treatments

Most biological treatments for substance abuse show some promise with people who are trying to eliminate their drug habit. Not one of these treatments alone is successful for most people, however (Schuckit, 2009b). Most research indicates a need for social support or therapeutic intervention. Because so many people need help to overcome their substance disorder, a number of models and programs have been developed. Unfortunately, in no other area of psychology have unvalidated and untested methods of treatment been so widely accepted. A reminder: A program that has not been subject to the scrutiny of research *may* work, but the sheer number of people receiving services of unknown value is still cause for concern. We next review several therapeutic approaches that *have* been evaluated.

Inpatient Facilities

Inpatient facilities for people with substance abuse problems are designed to help people get through the initial withdrawal period and to provide supportive therapy so that they can go back to their communities (Morgan, 1981). However, such inpatient care can be extremely expensive (Bender, 2004). The question arises, then, as to how effective this type of care is compared with outpatient therapy that can cost 90% less. Research suggests there may be no difference between

....

agonist substitution A replacement of a drug on which a person is dependent with one that has a similar chemical makeup, an **agonist**. Used as a treatment for **substance dependence**.

nicotine Toxic and addictive substance found in tobacco leaves.

nicotine patch Patch placed on the skin that delivers **nicotine** to smokers without the carcinogens in cigarette smoke. Somewhat more successful than nicotine gum because it requires less effort by the wearer and delivers the drug more consistently; should be coupled with counseling to stop smoking and avoid **relapse**

antagonist drugs The medication that blocks or counteracts the effects of a psychoactive drug.

Alcoholics Anonymous and Its Variations

The most popular model for the treatment of substance abuse is a variation of the Twelve Steps program developed by Alcoholics Anonymous (AA). The foundation of AA is the notion that alcoholism is a disease and alcoholics must acknowledge their addiction to alcohol and its destructive power over them and look to a higher power to help them overcome their shortcomings. Central to the design of AA is its independence from the established medical community and the freedom it offers from the stigmatization of alcoholism (Denzin, 1987; Robertson, 1988). An important component is the social support it provides through group meetings.

Despite challenges conducting systematic research on AA because participants attend meetings anonymously and only when they feel the need to, there have been numerous attempts to evaluate the program's effect on alcoholism (McCrady & Tonigan, 2015). Research finds that those who regularly participate in AA activities—or other similar supportive approaches—and follow its guidelines carefully are more likely to have positive outcomes, such as reduced drinking and improved psychological health (Kelly, 2013; Zemore, Subbaraman, & Tonigan, 2013). Studies suggest that those who are more likely to engage with AA tend to have a more severe alcohol use problem and seem to be more committed to abstinence (McCrady & Tonigan, 2015). Thus, AA can be an effective treatment for highly motivated people with alcohol dependence. Research to date has not shown how AA compares to other treatments. However, preliminary evidence shows that AA can be helpful for individuals seeking to achieve total abstinence and may be more cost effective than other treatments. Researchers are still trying to understand exactly why AA and the 12-step program work, but it seems that social support plays an important role (McCrady & Tonigan, 2015).

Some individuals have a more mixed experience with AA and this includes agnostics and atheists, women, and minority groups (McCrady & Tonigan, 2015). Other groups now exist (e.g., Rational Recovery, Moderation Management, Women for Sobriety, SMART Recovery) for individuals who benefit from the social support of others but who may not want the abstinence-oriented 12-step program offered by groups modeled after AA (Tucker *et al.*, 2011).

Controlled Use

One of the tenets of AA is total abstinence; recovering alcoholics who have just one sip of alcohol are believed to have "slipped" until they again achieve abstinence. Some researchers question this assumption, however, and believe at least a portion of abusers of several substances (notably alcohol and nicotine) may be capable of becoming social users without resuming their abuse of these drugs.

In the alcoholism treatment field, the notion of teaching people **controlled drinking** is extremely controversial, partly because of a classic study showing partial success in teaching severe abusers to drink in a limited way (Sobell & Sobell, 1978). The participants were 40 male alcoholics in an alcoholism treatment program at a state hospital who were thought to have a good prognosis. The men were assigned either to a program that taught them how to drink in moderation (experimental group) or to a group that was abstinence oriented (control group). The researchers followed the men for more than two years, maintaining contact with 98% of them. During the second year after treatment, those who participated in the controlled drinking group were functioning well 85% of the time, whereas the men in the abstinence group were reported to be doing well only 42% of the time. Some men in both groups suffered serious relapses and required rehospitalization and some were incarcerated. The results of this study suggest that controlled drinking may be a viable alternative to abstinence for some alcohol abusers, although it clearly isn't a cure.

The controversy over this study began with a paper published in the prestigious journal *Science* (Pendery, Maltzman, & West, 1982). The authors reported they had contacted the men in the Sobell study after 10 years and found that only one of the 20 men in the experimental group maintained a pattern of controlled drinking. Although this re-evaluation made headlines and was the subject of a segment on the *60 Minutes* television show, it had a number of flaws (Marlatt, Larimer, Baer, & Quigley, 1993). Most serious was the lack of data on the abstinence group over the same 10-year follow-up period.

The controversy over the Sobell study still has a chilling effect on controlled drinking as a treatment of alcohol abuse in the United States. In contrast, controlled drinking is widely accepted as a treatment for alcoholism in the United Kingdom. Despite opposition, research on this approach has been conducted in the ensuing years (e.g., Orford & Keddie, 2006; van Amsterdam & van den Brink, 2013), and the results seem to show that controlled drinking is at least as effective as abstinence but that neither treatment is successful for 70% to 80% of patients over the long term—a rather bleak outlook for people with alcohol dependence problems.

Component Treatment

Most comprehensive treatment programs aimed at helping people with substance use disorder have a number of components thought to boost the effectiveness of the "treatment package" (NIDA, 2009). We saw in our review of biological treatments that their effectiveness is increased when psychologically based therapy is added. In aversion therapy, which uses a conditioning model, substance use is paired with something extremely unpleasant, such as a brief electric shock or feelings of nausea. For example, a person might be offered a drink of alcohol and receive a painful shock when the glass reaches his lips. The goal is to counteract the positive associations with substance use with negative associations. The negative associations can also be made by imagining unpleasant scenes in a technique called *covert sensitization* (Cautela, 1966); the person might picture herself beginning to snort cocaine and be interrupted with visions of herself becoming violently ill (Kearney, 2006).

One component that seems to be a valuable part of therapy for substance use is *contingency management* (Higgins *et al.*, 2014). Here, the clinician and the client together select the behaviors that the client needs to change and decide on the reinforcers that will reward reaching certain goals, perhaps money or small retail items like CDs. In a study of cocaine abusers, clients received cash vouchers (up to almost $2,000) for having cocaine-negative urine specimens (Higgins *et al.*, 2006). This study found greater abstinence rates among cocaine-dependent users with the contingency management approach and other skills training than among users in a more traditional counseling program that included a 12-step approach to treatment.

Another package of treatments is the *community reinforcement approach* (e.g., Campbell, Miele, Nunes, McCrimmon, & Ghitza, 2012). In keeping with the multiple influences that affect substance use, several facets of the drug problem are addressed to help identify and correct aspects of the person's life that might contribute to substance use or interfere with efforts to abstain. First, a spouse, friend, or relative who is not a substance user is recruited to participate in relationship therapy to help the abuser improve relationships with other important people. Second, clients are taught how to identify the antecedents and consequences that influence their drug taking. For example, if they are likely to use cocaine with certain friends, clients are taught to recognize the relationships and encouraged to avoid the associations. Third, clients are given assistance with employment, education, finances, or other social service areas that may help reduce their stress. Fourth, new recreational options help the person replace substance use with new activities. There is now strong empirical support for the effectiveness of this approach with alcohol and cocaine abusers (Higgins *et al.*, 2014).

Obstacles to successful treatment for substance use and dependence include a lack of personal awareness that one has a problem and an unwillingness to change. An increasingly common intervention approach that directly addresses these needs is referred to as *Motivational Enhancement Therapy (MET)* (NIDA, 2009). MET is based on the work of Miller and Rollnick (2012), who proposed that behavior change in adults is more likely with empathetic and optimistic counseling (the therapist understands the client's perspective and believes that he or she can change) and a focus on a personal connection with the client's core values (for example, drinking and its consequences interferes with spending more time with family). By reminding the client about what he or she cherishes most, MET intends to improve the individual's belief that any changes made (e.g., drinking less) will have positive outcomes (e.g., more family time) and the individual is therefore more likely to make the recommended changes. MET has been used to assist individuals with a variety of substance use problems, and it appears to be a useful component to add to psychological treatment (e.g., Manuel, Houck, & Moyers, 2012).

Cognitive-behavioral therapy (CBT) is an effective treatment approach for many psychological disorders and it is also one of the most well designed and studied approaches for treating substance dependence (Granillo, Perron, Jarman, & Gutowski, 2013). This treatment addresses multiple aspects of the disorder, including a person's reactions to cues that lead to substance use (for example, being among certain friends) and thoughts and behaviors to resist use. Another target of CBT addresses the problem of relapse. Marlatt and Gordon's (1985) **relapse prevention** treatment model looks at the learned aspects of dependence and sees relapse as a failure of cognitive and behavioral coping skills (Witkiewitz & Marlatt, 2004). Therapy involves helping people remove any ambivalence about stopping their drug use by examining their beliefs about the positive aspects of the drug ("There's nothing like a cocaine high") and confronting the negative consequences of its use ("I fight with my wife when I'm high"). High-risk situations are identified ("having extra money in my pocket"), and strategies are developed to deal with potentially problematic situations, as well as with the craving that arises from abstinence. Incidents of relapse are dealt with as occurrences from which the person can recover; instead of looking on these episodes as inevitably leading to more drug use, people in treatment are encouraged to see them as episodes brought on by temporary stress or a situation that can be changed. Research on this technique suggests that it may be particularly effective for alcohol problems (McCrady, 2014), as well as in treating a variety of other substance-related disorders (Marlatt & Donovan, 2005).

Prevention

Adolescents are at high risk for drug addiction due to their higher rates of experimentation with drugs. When done right, education about drugs' risks can lead to decreases in drugs of abuse (e.g., ecstasy and tobacco) (Volkow & Warren, 2015). However, over the past few years, the strategies for preventing substance abuse and dependence have shifted from education-based approaches (for example, teaching schoolchildren that drugs can be harmful) to more wide-ranging approaches, including changes in

controlled drinking An extremely controversial treatment approach to **alcohol** dependence, in which severe abusers are taught to drink in moderation.

relapse prevention An extremely controversial treatment approach to **alcohol** dependence, in which severe abusers are taught to drink in moderation.

the laws regarding drug possession and use and community-based interventions (Sher *et al.*, 2011). Many states, for example, have implemented education-based programs in schools to try to deter students from using drugs. The widely used Drug Abuse Resistance Education (DARE) program encourages a "no drug use" message through fear of consequences, rewards for commitments not to use drugs, and strategies for refusing offers of drugs. Unfortunately, several extensive evaluations suggest that this type of program may not have its intended effects (Pentz, 1999). Fortunately, more comprehensive programs that involve skills training to avoid or resist social pressures (such as peers) and environmental pressures (such as media portrayals of drug use) can be effective in preventing drug abuse among some. For example, one large-scale longitudinal study used a community-based intervention strategy to reduce binge drinking and alcohol-related injuries (for example, car crashes and assaults) (Holder *et al.*, 2000). Three communities were mobilized to encourage responsible beverage service (that is, not serving too much alcohol to bar patrons), limit alcohol access to underage drinkers, and increase local enforcement of drinking and driving laws to limit access to alcohol. People's self-reports of drinking too much and drinking and driving were fewer after the intervention, as were alcohol-related car accidents and assaults. These types of comprehensive programs may need to be replicated across communities and extended to more pervasive influences (for example, how drug use is portrayed in the media) to effect significant prevention results (Newton, Conrod, Teesson, & Faggiano, 2012).

It may be that our most powerful preventive strategy involves cultural change. Over the past 45 years or so, we have gone from a "I get high with a little help from my friends" society to one that champions statements like "Just say no to drugs." The social unacceptability of excessive drinking, smoking, and other drug use is probably responsible for this change. Implementing this sort of intervention is beyond the scope of one research investigator or even a consortium of researchers collaborating across many sites. It requires the cooperation of governmental, educational, and even religious institutions. We may need to rethink our approach to preventing drug use and abuse (Newton *et al.*, 2012).

10.4 Concept CHECK

Matching the examples below with the following terms: (a) dependent, (b) cross-tolerant, (c) agonist substitution, (d) antagonist, (e) relapse prevention, (f) controlled drinking, (g) aversion therapy, (h) covert sensitization, (i) contingency management, and (j) anonymous:

1. _____ is a controversial treatment for alcohol abuse because of a negative but flawed experimental finding, but also because it conflicts with the belief in total abstinence.

2. Methadone is used to help heroin addicts kick their habit in a method called _____.

3. _____ drugs block or counteract the effects of psychoactive drugs and are sometimes effective in treating addicts.

4. In _____ the clinician and the client work together to decide which behaviors the client needs to change and which reinforcers will be used as rewards for reaching set goals.

5. It has been difficult to evaluate rigorously the effectiveness of Alcoholics Anonymous, because the participants are _____.

6. In _____, substance use is paired with something extremely unpleasant (like alcohol and vomiting with Antabuse).

7. Heroin and methadone are _____, which means they affect the same neurotransmitter receptors.

8. The _____ model involves therapy that helps individuals remove ambivalence about stopping their drug use by examining their beliefs about the positive and negative aspects of drug use.

9. By imagining unpleasant scenes, the _____ technique helps the person associate the negative effects of the drug with drug use.

10. Unfortunately, the heroin addict may become permanently _____ on methadone.

Gambling Disorder

▶ What psychological and physiological processes lead to gambling disorders?

Gambling is growing in popularity in this country, and in many places it is a legal and acceptable form of entertainment. Perhaps as a result, **gambling disorder** affects an increasing number of people, with a lifetime estimate of approximately 1.9% of adult Americans (Ashley & Boehlke,

2012). Research suggests that among pathological gamblers, 14% have lost at least one job, 19% have declared bankruptcy, 32% have been arrested, and 21% have been incarcerated (Gerstein *et al.*, 1999). The *DSM-5* criteria for gambling disorder include the same pattern of urges we observe in the other substance-related disorders. Note too the parallels with substance dependence, with the need to gamble increasing amounts of money over time and the "withdrawal symptoms" such as restlessness and irritability when attempting to stop. These parallels to substance-related disorders led to the re-categorization of gambling disorder as an "Addictive Disorder" in *DSM-5* (Denis, Fatséas, & Auriacombe, 2012).

There is a growing body of research on the nature and treatment of gambling disorder. For example, work is under way to explore the biological origins of the urge to gamble among pathological gamblers. Research in this area and others (e.g., genetic research) show strong similarities in the biological origins of gambling disorders and substance use disorders. In one study, brain-imaging technology was used to observe brain function while gamblers observed videotapes of other people gambling (Potenza *et al.*, 2003). A decreased level of activity was observed in those regions of the brain that are involved in impulse regulation when compared with controls, suggesting an interaction between the environmental cues to gamble and the brain's response (which may be to decrease the ability to resist these cues). Studies have found that the ventromedial prefrontal cortex and orbitofrontal cortex do not function as normal in those with gambling disorder. Poor impulse control and risky decisions are both processes that involve ventromedial prefrontal cortex, and those individuals with higher problems in these areas also show poorer response to treatment and higher relapse rates (Yau, Yip, & Potenza, 2015).

Treatment of gambling problems is difficult. Those with gambling disorder exhibit a combination of characteristics—including denial of the problem, impulsivity, and continuing optimism ("One big win will cover my losses!")—that interfere with effective treatment. Pathological gamblers often experience cravings similar to people who are substance dependent (Grant, Odlaug, & Schreiber, 2015). Treatment is often similar to substance dependence treatment, and there is a parallel Gambler's Anonymous that incorporates the same 12-step program we discussed previously. However, the evidence of effectiveness for Gambler's Anonymous suggests that 70% to 90% drop out of these programs and that the desire to quit must be present before intervention (Ashley & Boehlke, 2012). Cognitive-behavioral interventions help reduce the symptoms of gambling disorder. Brief and full course treatments have both been found to help. Given the higher rates of impulsivity of those with these disorder and thus their high dropout rates from treatment, more research is starting to compare the brief versions to the full course ones (Grant *et al.*, 2015).

In addition to gambling disorder being included under the heading of "Addictive Disorders," *DSM-5* includes another potentially addictive behavior "Internet Gaming Disorder" as a condition for further study (American Psychiatric Association, 2013). The goal of including this potentially new category of addictive behavior is to encourage additional research on its nature and treatment.

DSM 5 — DISORDER CRITERIA SUMMARY
Gambling Disorder

A. Persistent and recurrent problematic gambling behavior leading to clinically significant impairment of distress, as indicated by the individual exhibiting four (or more) of the following in a 12-month period: (1) Needs to gamble with increasing amounts of money in order to achieve the desired excitement. (2) Is restless or irritable when attempting to cut down or stop gambling. (3) Has made repeated unsuccessful efforts to control, cut back, or stop gambling. (4) Is often preoccupied with gambling. (5) Often gambles when feeling distressed. (6) After losing money gambling, often returns another day to get even. (7) Lies to conceal the extent of involvement with gambling. (8) Has jeopardized or lost a significant relationship, job, or educational or career opportunity because of gambling. (9) Relies on others to provide money to relieve desperate financial situations caused by gambling. (10) The gambling behavior is not better explained by a manic episode.

Specify current severity:
Mild: four to five criteria met
Moderate: six to seven criteria met
Severe: eight to nine criteria met

From American Psychiatric Association. (2013). *Diagnostic and statistical manual of mental disorders* (5th ed.). Washington, DC.

Impulse-Control Disorders

▶ **What conditions are listed in *DSM-5* as impulse-control disorders?**

A number of the disorders we describe in this book start with an irresistible impulse—usually one that will ultimately be harmful to the person affected. Typically, the person experiences increasing tension leading up to the act and, sometimes, pleasurable anticipation of acting on the impulse. For example, paraphilias such as pedophilia (sexual attraction to children), eating disorders, and the substance-related disorders in this chapter often commence with temptations or desires that are destructive

....

gambling disorder Persistent and recurrent problematic gambling behavior leading to clinically significant impairment or distress.

but difficult to resist. *DSM-5* includes three additional impulse-control disorders: intermittent explosive disorder, kleptomania, and pyromania (Muresanu, Stan, & Buzoianu, 2012).

Intermittent Explosive Disorder

People with **intermittent explosive disorder** have episodes in which they act on aggressive impulses that result in serious assaults or destruction of property (Coccaro & McCloskey, 2010). Although it is unfortunately common among the general population to observe aggressive outbursts, when you rule out the influence of other disorders (for example, antisocial personality disorder, borderline personality disorder, a psychotic disorder, and Alzheimer's disease) or substance use, this disorder is not often diagnosed. In a rare but important large study of more than 9,000 people, researchers found that the lifetime prevalence of this disorder was 7.3% (Kessler *et al.*, 2006). This diagnosis is controversial and has been debated throughout the development of the *DSM*. One concern, among others, is that by validating a general category that covers aggressive behavior it may be used as a legal defense—insanity—for all violent crimes (Coccaro & McCloskey, 2010).

Research is at the beginning stages for intermittent explosive disorder and focuses on the brain regions involved as well as the influence of neurotransmitters such as serotonin and norepinephrine and testosterone levels, along with their interaction with psychosocial influences (stress, disrupted family life, and parenting styles). Recent studies have proposed that there is a disruption of the orbital frontal cortex's role (the "executive part" of the brain) in inhibiting amygdala activation (the "emotional part" of the brain) combined with changes in the serotonin system in those with this disorder (Yau *et al.*, 2015). Cognitive-behavioral interventions (for example, helping the person identify and avoid "triggers" for aggressive outbursts) and approaches modeled after drug treatments appear the most effective for these individuals, although few controlled studies yet exist (McCloskey, Noblett, Deffenbacher, Gollan, & Coccaro, 2008).

Kleptomania

The story of wealthy actress Winona Ryder stealing $5,500 worth of merchandise from Saks Fifth Avenue in Beverly Hills, California, in 2001 was as puzzling as it was titillating. Why risk a multimillion-dollar career over some clothes that she could easily afford? Was hers a case of **kleptomania**—a recurrent failure to resist urges to steal things that are not needed for personal use or their monetary value? This disorder appears to be rare, but it is not well studied, partly because of the stigma associated with identifying oneself as acting out this illegal behavior. Some studies suggest that the disorder may be more common in women and that it

typically starts in adolescence (Yau *et al.*, 2015). The patterns described by those with this disorder are similar—the person begins to feel a sense of tension just before stealing, which is followed by feelings of pleasure or relief while the theft is committed (Grant, Odlaug, & Kim, 2010). People with kleptomania score high on assessments of impulsivity, reflecting their inability to judge the immediate gratification of stealing compared with the long-term negative consequences (for example, arrest, embarrassment) (Grant & Kim, 2002). Patients with kleptomania often report having no memory (amnesia) about the act of shoplifting (Hollander, Berlin, & Stein, 2009). Brain-imaging research supports these observations, with one study finding damage in areas of the brain associated with poor decision making (inferior frontal regions) (Grant, Correia, & Brennan-Krohn, 2006).

There appears to be high comorbidity between kleptomania and mood disorders, and to a lesser extent with substance abuse and dependence (Grant *et al.*, 2010). Some refer to kleptomania as an "antidepressant" behavior, or a reaction on the part of some to relieve unpleasant feelings through stealing (Fishbain, 1987). To date, few reports of treatment exist, and these involve either behavioral interventions or use of antidepressant medication. In one exception, naltrexone—the opioid antagonist used in the treatment of alcoholism—was somewhat effective in reducing the urge to steal in persons diagnosed with kleptomania (Grant, Kim, & Odlaug, 2009).

Pyromania

Just as we know that someone who steals does not necessarily have kleptomania, it is also true that not everyone who sets fires is considered to have **pyromania**—an impulse-control disorder that involves having an irresistible urge to set fires. Again, the pattern parallels that of kleptomania, where the person feels a tension or an arousal before setting a fire and a sense of gratification or relief while the fire burns. These individuals will also be preoccupied with fires and the associated equipment involved in setting and putting out these fires (Dickens & Sugarman, 2012). Also rare, pyromania is diagnosed in only about 3% of arsonists (Lindberg, Holi, Tani, & Virkkunen, 2005), because arsonists can include people who set fires for monetary gain or revenge rather than to satisfy a physical or psychological urge. Because so few people are diagnosed with this disorder, research on etiology and treatment is limited (Dickens & Sugarman, 2012). Research that has been conducted follows the general group of arsonists (of which only a small percentage have pyromania) and examines the role of a family history of fire setting along with comorbid impulse disorders (antisocial personality disorder and alcoholism). Treatment is generally cognitive-behavioral and involves helping the person identify the signals that initiate the urges and teaching coping strategies to resist the temptation to start fires (Bumpass, Fagelman, & Brix, 1983; McGrath, Marshall, & Prior, 1979).

Match the following disorders with their corresponding symptoms: (a) gambling disorder, (b) intermittent explosive disorder, (c) kleptomania, and (d) pyromania:

1. This rarely diagnosed disorder is characterized by episodes of aggressive impulses and can sometimes be treated with cognitive-behavioral interventions, drug treatments, or both. _____

2. This disorder begins with the person feeling a sense of tension that is released and followed with pleasure after he has committed a robbery. _____

3. This disorder affects somewhere between 3% and 5% of the adult American population and is characterized by the need to gamble. _____

4. Individuals with this disorder are preoccupied with fires and the equipment involved in setting and putting out fires. _____

DSM 5 CONTROVERSY   Are Substance Dependency and Substance Abuse the Same?

One of the changes to *DSM-5* that caused concern among some in the field of substance-related disorders was dropping the distinction between dependence on a substance and abuse of that substance (e.g., Schuckit, 2012). Although there is general agreement that abusing a substance (e.g., binge drinking) and being dependent on that substance (e.g., increasing tolerance to alcohol and going through withdrawal symptoms if drinking is stopped) are different processes, research shows that, practically speaking, they tend to go together. In other words, if someone is routinely abusing a drug that person will likely become dependent on it (O'Brien, 2011). From a scientific point of view, therefore, there is an obvious difference between abuse and dependence, but

from a clinical perspective (which is the main function of the *DSM*) the argument was made that having these as separate diagnoses was more complicated than was necessary.

In addition, a second major change was the addition of "Addictive Disorder"—in specific, gambling disorder—to the substance-related disorders section. Here again the science suggests that the phenomena are quite similar with both substance-related disorders and gambling disorder showing patterns of dependence, cravings, and working on similar brain pathways (Ashley & Boehlke, 2012). However, this potentially opens up the category for the inclusion of many different kinds of "addictions." Other problems that cause real dysfunction

among some people include the new *DSM-5* disorder under further study ("Internet gaming disorder") (Block, 2008; Van Rooij, Schoenmakers, Vermulst, Van Den Eijnden, & Van De Mheen, 2011) and even "tanning addiction" (Poorsattar & Hornung, 2010), and they are being taken seriously as similar types of problems. It is likely that many activities have the potential for causing dependence because they activate the reward systems in our brains in much the same way as the substances described. The difference in whether or not they constitute a "disorder" may come back to whether or not they cause the harmful distress that is part of most psychological diagnoses. ●

---

intermittent explosive disorder The episodes during which a person acts on aggressive impulses that result in serious assaults or destruction of property.

kleptomania A recurrent failure to resist urges to steal things not needed for personal use or their monetary value.

pyromania An **impulse-control disorder** that involves having an irresistible urge to set fires.

Perspectives on Substance-Related and Addictive Disorders

What are substance-related and addictive disorders?

▶ In *DSM-5*, substance-related and addictive disorders include problems with the use of depressants (alcohol, barbiturates, and benzodiazepines), stimulants (amphetamines, cocaine, nicotine, and caffeine), opiates (heroin, codeine, and morphine), and hallucinogens (cannabis and LSD) as well as gambling.

Depressants, Stimulants, and Opioids

What are the physiological and psychological effects of depressants?

▶ Depressants are a group of drugs that decrease central nervous system activity. The primary effect is to reduce our levels of physiological arousal and help us relax. Included in this group are alcohol and sedative, hypnotic, and anxiolytic drugs, such as those prescribed for insomnia.

What are the physiological and psychological effects of stimulants?

▶ Stimulants, the most commonly consumed psychoactive drugs, include caffeine (in coffee, chocolate, and many soft drinks), nicotine (in tobacco products such as cigarettes), amphetamines, and cocaine. In contrast to the depressant drugs, stimulants make us more alert and energetic.

What are the physiological and psychological effects of opiates

▶ Opiates include opium, morphine, codeine, and heroin; they have a narcotic effect—relieving pain and inducing sleep. The broader term *opioids* is used to refer to the family of substances that includes these opiates and synthetic variations created by chemists (e.g., methadone) and the similarly acting substances that occur naturally in our brains (enkephalins, beta-endorphins, and dynorphins).

Cannabis-Related Disorders

What are the physiological and psychological effects of cannabis?

▶ **Cannabis (marijuana)** is the most routinely used illegal substance, with 5%–15% of people in western countries reporting regular use. Perhaps more than any other drug, however, cannabis can produce different reactions in people, including a sense of well-being, mood swings, and paranoia.

Hallucinogen-Related Disorders

What are the physiological and psychological effects of hallucinogenics?

▶ Hallucinogens essentially change the way the user perceives the world. Sight, sound, feelings, and even smell are distorted, sometimes in dramatic ways, in a person under the influence of drugs such as cannabis and LSD.

Other Drugs of Abuse

What are the physiological and psychological effects of other drugs, including inhalants, steroids, and designer drugs?

▶ A number of other substances are used by individuals to alter sensory experiences. The high associated with the use of inhalants resembles that of alcohol intoxication and usually includes dizziness, slurred speech, incoordination, euphoria, and lethargy. Steroid use differs from other drug use because the substance does not produce a desirable high but instead is used to enhance performance and body size. Designer drugs heighten a person's auditory and visual perception, as well as the senses of taste and touch.

Causes and Treatment of Substance-Related Disorders

What physiological and psychological processes lead to substance dependence?

▶ Most psychotropic drugs seem to produce positive effects by acting directly or indirectly on the dopaminergic mesolimbic system (the pleasure pathway). In addition, psychosocial factors such as expectations, stress, and cultural practices interact with the biological factors to influence drug use.

What psychological and medical treatments are available for substance-related disorders?

▶ Substance dependence is treated successfully only in a minority of those affected, and the best results reflect the motivation of the drug user and a combination of biological and psychosocial treatments.

▶ Programs aimed at preventing drug use may have the greatest chance of significantly affecting the drug problem.

Gambling Disorder

What psychological and physiological processes lead to gambling disorder?

▶ Problem gamblers display the same types of cravings and dependence as persons who have substance-related disorders.

▶ Similar brain systems appear to be involved with those addicted to gambling as seen in persons with substance-related disorders.

Impulse-Control Disorders

What conditions are listed in *DSM-5* as impulse-control disorders?

▶ In *DSM-5*, impulse-control disorders include three separate disorders: intermittent explosive disorder, kleptomania, and pyromania.

▮▮ Key Terms

substance-related and addictive disorders, 367
impulse-control disorders, 367
alcohol use disorder, 367
psychoactive substance, 368
substance use, 368
substance intoxication, 368
substance use disorders, 369
physiological dependence, 369
tolerance, 369
withdrawal, 369
substance dependence, 370
substance abuse, 370
depressants, 371
stimulants, 371
opiates, 371
hallucinogens, 371

other drugs of abuse, 371
gambling disorder, 371
alcohol, 371
alcohol-related disorders, 371
withdrawal delirium (delirium tremens/DTs), 373
Wernicke-Korsakoff syndrome, 373
fetal alcohol syndrome (FAS), 374
barbiturates, 375
benzodiazepines, 375
amphetamines, 377
amphetamine use disorders, 377
cocaine use disorders, 378
tobacco-related disorders, 380
caffeine-related disorders, 381
opioid-related disorders, 382

Cannabis (*Cannabis* sativa) (marijuana), 383
cannabis use disorders, 384
LSD (*d*-lysergic acid diethylamide), 385
hallucinogen use disorders, 385
hallucinogenic substances, 385
agonist substitution, 394
nicotine, 394
nicotine patch, 395
antagonist drugs, 395
controlled drinking, 396
relapse prevention, 397
gambling disorder, 398
intermittent explosive disorder, 400
kleptomania, 400
pyromania, 400

Answers to Concept Checks

10.1

Part A

1. c; 2. b; 3. d; 4. a

Part B

5. c; 6. d; 7. b; 8. a

10.2

1. False (the use of crack by pregnant mothers adversely affects only some babies); 2. True; 3. True;

4. False (cannabis produces the most variable reactions in people); 5. False (amphetamines are produced in labs); 6. True; 7. False (stimulants occur naturally)

10.3

1. T; 2. T; 3. F (all have an effect); 4. F (they would still act uninhibited); 5. T

10.4

1. f; 2. c; 3. d; 4. i; 5. j; 6. g; 7. b; 8. e; 9. h; 10. a

10.5

1. b; 2. c; 3. a; 4. d

Chapter Quiz

1. The definition of substance abuse according to the *DSM-5* is based on:
   a. how much of the substance is consumed per day
   b. how much of the substance is consumed per week
   c. how significantly the substance interferes with the user's life
   d. the type of substance used

2. _____ is the need for greater amounts of a drug to experience the same effect, whereas _____ is the negative physical response that occurs when a drug is not taken.
   a. Tolerance; withdrawal
   b. Delirium; withdrawal
   c. Dependence; tolerance
   d. Accommodation; abuse

3. Which of the following statements most accurately describes the relationship between gender and alcohol consumption?
   a. Women are more likely to use alcohol, but men are more likely to be heavy drinkers.

   b. Men are more likely to use alcohol, but women are more likely to be heavy drinkers.
   c. Women are more likely to use alcohol and be heavy drinkers.
   d. Men are more likely to use alcohol and be heavy drinkers.

4. Dr. Myers prescribes medication to help control a patient's seizures. The patient reports that the medication also makes her feel calm and helps her sleep. Dr. Myers most likely prescribed a(n):
   a. hallucinogen
   b. opiate
   c. benzodiazepine
   d. amphetamine

5. The primary neurotransmitter affected by cocaine is _____, whereas the primary neurotransmitter affected by opiates is _____.
   a. GABA; norepinephrine
   b. acetylcholine; GABA
   c. norepinephrine; dopamine
   d. dopamine; GABA

6. For marijuana users, "reverse tolerance" occurs when:

a. chronic use renders the user unable to feel high

b. a first-time user does not feel high

c. more pleasure from the drug is reported after repeated use

d. a chronic user experiences withdrawal symptoms

7. Gino is a recovering alcoholic. To help with his treatment, Gino's physician prescribed a drug that causes Gino to experience shortness of breath and severe vomiting if he drinks. What drug has the physician prescribed?

a. Antabuse

b. MDMA

c. amyl nitrate

d. PCP

8. One psychological component of addiction may involve taking a drug to avoid negative feelings associated with coming down from a high. What theory describes this use of substances to avoid worsening lows?

a. tolerance theory

b. substance cycle theory

c. opponent-process theory

d. polydependence theory

9. Research shows that the way individuals think about a drug influences the way they act when using the drug. This phenomenon is known as the:

a. tolerance paradigm

b. expectancy effect

c. dependency model

d. opponent-process theory

10. Carlos's psychiatrist treats him for cocaine abuse by delivering a shock when Carlos attempts to use cocaine, a treatment known as _____. In contrast, Lisa's therapist has her imagine having painful seizures at the same time that Lisa is thinking about using cocaine, a treatment known as _____.

a. aversion therapy; covert sensitization

b. contingency management; relapse prevention

c. narcotics anonymous; controlled use

d. agonist substitution; aversive treatment

(See Appendix A for answers.)

Exploring Substance Use Disorders

- Many kinds of problems can develop when people use and abuse substances that alter the way they think, feel, and behave.
- Once seen as due to personal weakness, drug abuse and dependence are now thought influenced by both biological and psychosocial factors.

Trigger

Social Influences
- Exposure to drugs—through media, peers, parents, or lack of parental monitoring—versus no exposure to drugs
- Social expectations and cultural norms for use
- Family/culture/society and peers (all or some) supportive versus unsupportive of drug use

Psychological Influences

Not to use:
- Fear of effects of drug use
- Decision not to use drugs
- Feeling of confidence and self-esteem without drug use

To use:
- Drug use for pleasure; association with "feeling good" (positive reinforcement)
- Drug use to avoid pain and escape unpleasantness by "numbing out" (negative reinforcement)
- Feeling of being in control
- Positive expectations/urges about what drug use will be like
- Avoidance of withdrawal symptoms
- Presence of other psychological disorders: mood anxiety, etc.

Causes

Drug Use and Drug Abuse

Biological Influences
- Inherited genetic vulnerability affects:
  – Body's sensitivity to drug (ADH gene)
  – Body's ability to metabolize drug (presence of specific enzymes in liver)
- Drugs activate natural reward center ("pleasure pathway") in brain
- Neuroplasticity increases drug-seeking and relapse

TREATMENT: BEST TO USE MULTIPLE APPROACHES

Psychosocial Treatments
- Aversion therapy—to create negative associations with drug use (shocks with drinking, imagining nausea with cocaine use)
- Contingency management to change behaviors by rewarding chosen behaviors
- Alcoholics Anonymous and its variations
- Inpatient hospital treatment (can be expensive)
- Controlled use
- Community reinforcement
- Relapse prevention

Biological Treatments
- Agonist substitution
  – Replacing one drug with a similar one (methadone for heroin, nicotine gum and patches for cigarettes)
- Antagonist substitution
  – Blocking one drug's effect with another drug (naltrexone for opiates and alcohol)
- Aversive treatments
  – Making taking drug very unpleasant (using Antabuse, which causes nausea and vomiting when mixed with alcohol, to treat alcoholism)
- Drugs to help recovering person deal with withdrawal symptoms (clonidine for opiate withdrawal, sedatives for alcohol, etc.)

TYPES OF DRUGS

	Examples	Effects
Depressants	Alcohol, barbiturates (sedatives: Amytal, Seconal, Nembutal), benzodiazepines (antianxiety: Valium, Xanax, Halcion)	- Decreased central nervous system activity - Reduced levels of body arousal - Relaxation
Stimulants	Amphetamines, cocaine, nicotine, caffeine	- Increased physical arousal - User feels more alert and energetic
Opiates	Heroin, morphine, codeine	- Narcotic—reduce pain and induce sleep and euphoria by mirroring opiates in the brain (endorphins, etc.)
Hallucinogens	Cannabis, LSD, Ecstasy	- Altered mental and emotional perception - Distortion (sometimes dramatic) of sensory perceptions

Exploring Impulse-Control Disorders

Characterized by inability to resist acting on a drive or temptation. Sufferers often perceived by society as having a problem simply due to a lack of "will."

TYPES OF IMPULSE-CONTROL DISORDERS

Disorder		Characteristics	Treatment
Intermittent Explosive	Ollyy/Shutterstock.com	■ Acting on aggressive impulses that result in assaults or destruction of property ■ Current research is focused on how neurotransmitters and testosterone levels interact with psychosocial influences (stress, parenting styles)	Cognitive-behavioral interventions (helping person identify and avoid triggers for aggressive outbursts) and approaches modeled after drug treatments appear most effective
Kleptomania	Robert Kneschke/Shutterstock.com	■ Recurring failure to resist urges to steal unneeded items ■ Feeling tense just before stealing, followed by feelings of pleasure or relief when committing the theft ■ High comorbidity with mood disorders and, to a lesser degree, with substance abuse/dependence	Behavioral interventions or antidepressant medication
Pyromania	Dale A Stork/Shutterstock.com	■ Irresistible urge to set fires ■ Feeling aroused prior to setting fire then a sense of gratification or relief while the fire burns ■ Rare; diagnosed in less than 4% of arsonists	Cognitive-behavioral interventions (helping person identify signals triggering urges, and teaching coping strategies to resist setting fires)

11

Personality Disorders

CHAPTER OUTLINE

An Overview of Personality Disorders

Aspects of Personality Disorders
Categorical and Dimensional Models
Personality Disorder Clusters
Statistics and Development
Gender Differences
Comorbidity
Personality Disorders under Study

Cluster A Personality Disorders

Paranoid Personality Disorder
Schizoid Personality Disorder
Schizotypal Personality Disorder

Cluster B Personality Disorders

Antisocial Personality Disorder
Borderline Personality Disorder
Histrionic Personality Disorder
Narcissistic Personality Disorder

Cluster C Personality Disorders

Avoidant Personality Disorder
Dependent Personality Disorder
Obsessive-Compulsive Personality
  Disorder

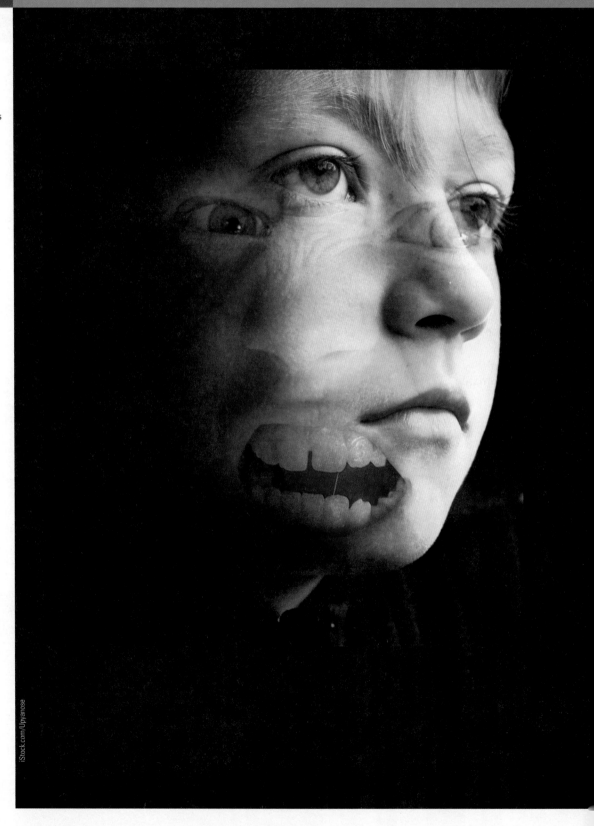

iStock.com/Upyanose

408

Use scientific reasoning to interpret behavior:	▶ Identify basic biological, psychological, and social components of behavioral explanations (e.g., inferences, observations, operational definitions, and interpretations) (APA SLO 2.1a) (*see textbook pages 416–419, 423–425, 428–429, 431, 433–435, 437*)
Engage in innovative and integrative thinking and problem solving:	▶ Describe problems operationally to study them empirically. (APA SLO 2.3a) (*see textbook pages 409–414*)
Describe applications that employ discipline-based problem solving:	▶ Correctly identify antecedents and consequences of behavior and mental processes (APA SLO 1.3c) Describe examples of relevant and practical applications of psychological principles to everyday life (APA SLO 1.3a) (*see textbook pages 409–437*)

* Portions of this chapter cover learning outcomes suggested by the American Psychological Association (2013) in its guidelines for the undergraduate psychology major. Chapter coverage of these outcomes is identified above by APA Goal and APA Suggested Learning Outcome (SLO).

An Overview of Personality Disorders

▶ **What are the essential features of personality disorders?**

We all think we know what a personality is. It's all the characteristic ways a person behaves and thinks: "Michael tends to be shy"; "Mindy likes to be dramatic"; "Juan is sensitive." When such personality characteristics interfere with relationships with others, cause the person distress, or in general disrupt activities of daily living, we consider these to be *personality disorders* (Skodol, 2012). In this chapter, we look at a number of personality disorders. First, we examine how we conceptualize personality disorders and the issues related to them; then we describe the disorders themselves.

Aspects of Personality Disorders

Unlike many of the disorders we have discussed, personality disorders are chronic; they do not come and go but originate in childhood and continue throughout adulthood (Widiger, 2012). Because these problems affect personality, they pervade every aspect of a person's life. For example, if a woman is overly suspicious (a sign of a possible paranoid personality disorder), this trait will affect almost everything she does, including her employment (she may change jobs often if she believes co-workers conspire against her), her relationships (she may not be able to sustain a relationship if she can't trust anyone), and even where she lives (she may move often if she suspects her landlords are out to get her).

A **personality disorder** is therefore a persistent pattern of emotions, cognitions, and behavior that results in enduring emotional distress for the person affected and/or for others and may cause difficulties with work and relationships (American Psychiatric Association, 2013). Note that individuals with personality disorders may not feel subjective distress; indeed, it may be others who acutely feel distress because of the actions of the person with the

disorder. This is common with antisocial personality disorder, because the individual may show a disregard for the rights of others yet exhibit no remorse (Hare, Neumann, & Widiger, 2012). In certain cases, someone other than the person with the personality disorder must decide whether the disorder is causing significant functional impairment because the affected person cannot make such a judgment.

DSM-5 lists 10 specific personality disorders. Although the prospects for treatment success for people who have personality disorders may be more optimistic than previously thought (Nelson, Beutler, & Castonguay, 2012), unfortunately, as you will see, many people who have personality disorders in addition to other psychological problems (for example, major depression) tend to do poorly in treatment.

Categorical and Dimensional Models

Most of us are sometimes suspicious of others and a little paranoid, dramatic, too self-involved, or reclusive. Fortunately, these characteristics do not last long or are not intense; they haven't significantly impaired how we live and work. People with personality disorders, however, display problem characteristics over extended periods and in many situations, which can cause emotional pain for themselves, others, or both (Widiger, 2012). Their difficulty, then, can be seen as one of *degree* rather than *kind;* in other words, the problems of people with personality disorders may just

....

personality disorder An enduring maladaptive pattern for relating to the environment and self, exhibited in a range of contexts that cause significant functional impairment or subjective distress.

be extreme versions of the problems many of us experience temporarily, such as being shy or suspicious (South, Oltmanns, & Krueger, 2011).

The distinction between problems of degree and problems of kind is usually described in terms of *dimensions* instead of *categories*. The issue that continues to be debated in the field is whether personality disorders are extreme versions of otherwise typical personality variations (dimensions) or ways of relating that are different from psychologically healthy behavior (categories) (Skodol, 2012). You can see the difference between dimensions and categories in everyday life. For example, we tend to look at gender categorically. Society generally views us as being in one category—"female"—or the other—"male." Yet many believe it is more accurate to look at gender in terms of dimensions. For example, we know that "male" and "female" may describe a range of choices in gender expression (e.g., personal grooming, attire, use of makeup and other body modifications). We could just as easily place people along a continuum of maleness and femaleness rather than in the absolute categories of male or female.

Many researchers and clinicians in this field see personality disorders as extremes on one or more personality dimensions. Yet because of the way people are diagnosed with the *DSM*, the personality disorders—like most other disorders—end up being viewed in categories. You have two choices—either you do ("yes") or you do not ("no") have a disorder. For example, either you have antisocial personality disorder or you don't. There is no "somewhat" when it comes to personality disorders.

There are advantages to using categorical models of behavior, the most important being their convenience. With simplification, however, come problems. One is that the mere act of using categories leads clinicians to reify them; that is, to view disorders as real "things," comparable to the realness of an infection or a broken arm. Some argue that personality disorders are not things that exist but points at which society decides a particular way of relating to the world has become a problem. There is the important unresolved issue again: Are personality disorders just an extreme variant of normal personality, or are they distinctly different disorders?

Some had proposed that the *DSM-5* personality disorders section be replaced or at least supplemented by a dimensional model (South *et al.*, 2011; Widiger, 2012) in which individuals would not only be given categorical diagnoses but also would be rated on a series of personality dimensions. Currently, there is an alternative model of personality disorders included in the section on "emerging measures and models" in *DSM-5* that is included for further study (American Psychiatric Association, 2013). This model focuses on a continuum of disturbances of "self" (i.e., how you view yourself and your ability to be self-directed) and interpersonal (i.e., your ability to empathize and be intimate with others) functioning. It remains to be seen how this alternative model will be used in the future.

Personality Disorder Clusters

DSM-5 divides the personality disorders into three groups, or clusters (American Psychiatric Association, 2013) (see Table 11.1). The cluster division is based on resemblance. Cluster A is called the odd or eccentric cluster; it includes paranoid, schizoid, and schizotypal personality disorders. Cluster B is the dramatic, emotional, or erratic cluster; it consists of antisocial, borderline, histrionic, and narcissistic personality disorders. Cluster C is the anxious or fearful cluster; it includes avoidant, dependent, and obsessive-compulsive personality disorders. We follow this order in our review.

Statistics and Development

An important population survey suggests that as many as one in 10 adults in the United States may have a diagnosable personality disorder (Lenzenweger, Lane, Loranger, & Kessler, 2007), which makes them relatively common (see Table 11.2). Numbers vary across countries, but worldwide about 6% of adults may have at least one personality disorder (Huang *et al.*, 2009). Differences in prevalence estimates may be the result of different survey methods: surveying people in clinical settings versus surveying the general population—even those not seeking assistance (Torgersen, 2012). Similarly, gender differences in the disorders—for example, more women were diagnosed with borderline personality disorder and more men identified with antisocial personality disorder—are highly variable when surveying the general population.

Personality disorders were thought to originate in childhood and continue into the adult years (Cloninger & Svakic, 2009). More sophisticated analyses suggest that personality disorders can remit over time (Zanarini, Frankenburg, Hennen, & Silk, 2006, 2014); however, they may be replaced by other personality disorders (Torgersen, 2012). In other words, a person could receive a diagnosis of one personality disorder at one point and then years later no longer meet the criteria for his original problem but now have characteristics of a second (or third) personality disorder. Our lack of information about such important features of personality disorders as their developmental course is a repeating theme. The gaps in our knowledge of the course of about half these disorders are visible in Table 11.2. One reason for this dearth of research is that many individuals do not seek treatment in the early phases of their disorder. This makes it difficult to study people with personality disorders from the beginning, although a few research studies have helped us understand the development of several disorders (Hecht, Cicchetti, Rogosch, & Crick, 2014).

TABLE 11.1 | Personality Disorders

Personality Disorder	Description
Cluster A—Odd or Eccentric Disorders	
Paranoid personality disorder	A pervasive distrust and suspiciousness of others such that their motives are interpreted as malevolent.
Schizoid personality disorder	A pervasive pattern of detachment from social relationships and a restricted range of expression of emotions in interpersonal settings.
Schizotypal personality disorder	A pervasive pattern of social and interpersonal deficits marked by acute discomfort with reduced capacity for close relationships, as well as by cognitive or perceptual distortions and eccentricities of behavior.
Cluster B—Dramatic, Emotional, or Erratic Disorders	
Antisocial personality disorder	A pervasive pattern of disregard for and violation of the rights of others.
Borderline personality disorder	A pervasive pattern of instability of interpersonal relationships, self-image, affects, and control over impulses.
Histrionic personality disorder	A pervasive pattern of excessive emotion and attention seeking.
Narcissistic personality disorder	A pervasive pattern of grandiosity (in fantasy or behavior), need for admiration, and lack of empathy.
Cluster C—Anxious or Fearful Disorders	
Avoidant personality disorder	A pervasive pattern of social inhibition, feelings of inadequacy, and hypersensitivity to negative evaluation.
Dependent personality disorder	A pervasive and excessive need to be taken care of, which leads to submissive and clinging behavior and fears of separation.
Obsessive-compulsive personality disorder	A pervasive pattern of preoccupation with orderliness, perfectionism, and mental and interpersonal control, at the expense of flexibility, openness, and efficiency.

SOURCE: Reprinted, with permission, from American Psychiatric Association. (2013). *Diagnostic and statistical manual of mental disorders* (5th ed.). Washington, DC: Author, © 2013 American Psychiatric Association.

TABLE 11.2 | Statistics and Development of Personality Disorders

Disorder	Prevalence*	Gender Differences*	Course
Paranoid personality disorder	In the clinical population: 6.3%–9.6%	Approximately equal among men and women	Insufficient information
	In the general population: 1.5%–1.8%		
Schizoid personality disorder	In the clinical population: 1.4%–1.9%	Slightly more common among men	Insufficient information
	In the general population: 0.9%–1.2%		
Schizotypal personality disorder	In the clinical population: 6.4%–5.7%	Slightly more common among men	Chronic; some go on to develop schizophrenia
	In the general population: 0.7%–1.1%		

(Continued)

Disorder	Prevalence*	Gender Differences*	Course
Antisocial personality disorder	In the clinical population: 3.9%–5.9%	Much more common among men	Dissipates after age 40 (Hare, McPherson, & Forth, 1988)
	In the general population: 1.0%–1.8%		
Borderline personality disorder	In the clinical population: 28.5%	Approximately equal among men and women	Symptoms gradually improve if individuals survive into their 30s (Zanarini *et al.*, 2006); approximately 6% die by suicide (Perry, 1993)
	In the general population: 1.4%–1.6%		
Histrionic personality disorder	In the clinical population: 8.0%–9.7%	Slightly more common among women	Chronic
	In the general population: 1.2%–1.3%		
Narcissistic personality disorder	In the clinical population: 5.1%–10.1%	Slightly more common among men	May improve over time (Cooper & Ronningstam, 1992; Gunderson, Ronningstam, & Smith, 1991)
	In the general population: 0.1%–0.8%		
Avoidant personality disorder	In the clinical population: 21.5%–24.6%	Slightly more common among women	Insufficient information
	In the general population: 1.4%–2.5%		
Dependent personality disorder	In the clinical population: 13.0%–15.0%	Much more common among women	Insufficient information
	In the general population: 0.9%–1.0%		
Obsessive-compulsive personality disorder	In the clinical population: 6.1%–10.5%	Slightly more common among men	Insufficient information
	In the general population: 1.9%–2.1%		

*Population data and gender data reported in Torgersen, S. (2012). Epidemiology. In T. A. Widiger (Ed.), *The Oxford handbook of personality disorders* (pp. 186–205). New York: Oxford University Press.

Gender Differences

Men diagnosed with a personality disorder tend to display traits characterized as more aggressive, structured, self-assertive, and detached, and women tend to present with characteristics that are more submissive, emotional, and insecure (Torgersen, 2012). It is not surprising, then, that antisocial personality disorder is present more often in males and dependent personality disorder more often in females. Historically, histrionic and borderline personality disorders were identified by clinicians more often in women (Dulit, Marin, & Frances, 1993; Stone,

1993), but according to more recent studies of their prevalence in the general population, equal numbers of males and females may have histrionic and borderline personality disorders (see Table 11.2). If this observation holds up in future studies, why have these disorders been predominantly diagnosed among females?

Do the disparities indicate differences between men and women in certain basic experiences that are genetic, sociocultural, or both, or do they represent biases on the part of the clinicians who make the diagnoses? Take, for example, a classic study by Maureen Ford and Thomas Widiger (1989), who sent fictitious case histories to clinical psychologists for diagnosis. One case described a person with *antisocial personality disorder*, which is characterized by irresponsible and reckless behavior and usually diagnosed in males; the other case described a person with *histrionic personality disorder*, which is characterized by excessive emotionality and attention seeking and more often diagnosed in females. The subject was identified as male in some versions of each case and as female in others, although everything else was identical. As the graph in ● Figure 11.1 shows, when the antisocial personality disorder case was labeled male, most psychologists gave the correct diagnosis. When the same case of antisocial personality disorder was labeled female, however, most psychologists diagnosed it as histrionic personality disorder

▲ Gender bias may affect the diagnosis of clinicians who associate certain behavioral characteristics with one sex or the other.

rather than antisocial personality disorder. In the case of histrionic personality disorder, being labeled a woman increased the likelihood of that diagnosis. Ford and Widiger (1989) concluded that the psychologists incorrectly diagnosed more women as having histrionic personality disorder.

This gender difference in diagnosis has also been criticized by other authors (see, for example, Kaplan, 1983) on the grounds that histrionic personality disorder, like several other personality disorders, is biased against females. As Kaplan (1983) points out, many features of histrionic personality disorder, such as overdramatization, vanity, seductiveness, and overconcern with physical appearance, are characteristic of the Western "stereotypical female." This disorder may simply be the embodiment of extremely "feminine" traits (Chodoff, 1982); branding such an individual mentally ill, according to Kaplan, reflects society's inherent bias against females.

The issue of gender bias in diagnosing personality disorder remains highly controversial (Liebman & Burnette, 2013). Remember, however, that just because certain disorders are observed more in men or women doesn't necessarily indicate bias (Lilienfeld, VanValkenburg, Larntz, & Akiskal, 1986). Widiger and Spitzer (1991) point out that the criteria for the disorder may themselves be biased *(criterion gender bias)*, or the assessment measures and the way they are used may be biased *(assessment gender bias)*. In general, the criteria themselves do not appear to have strong gender bias, although there may be some tendency for clinicians to use their own bias when using the criteria and therefore diagnose males and females differently (Oltmanns & Powers, 2012).

Comorbidity

Looking at Table 11.2 and adding up the prevalence rates across the personality disorders, you might conclude that up to 25% of all people are affected. In fact,

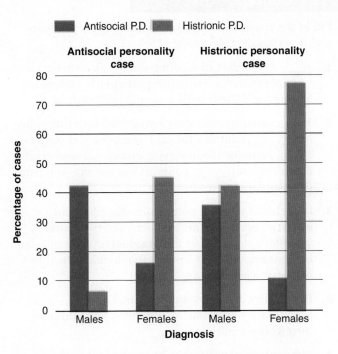

● **Figure 11.1** Gender bias in diagnosing personality disorders (P.D.). Data are shown for the percentage of cases clinicians rated as antisocial personality disorder or histrionic personality disorder, depending on whether the case was described as a male or a female. (From Ford, M. R., & Widiger, T. A. [1989]. Sex bias in the diagnosis of histrionic and antisocial personality disorders. *Journal of Consulting and Clinical Psychology, 57*, 301–305.)

the percentage of people in the population with a personality disorder is likely closer to 10% (Huang *et al.*, 2009; Lenzenweger *et al.*, 2007). What accounts for this discrepancy? A major concern with the personality disorders is that people tend to be diagnosed with more than one. The term *comorbidity* historically describes the condition in which a person has multiple diseases (Caron & Rutter, 1991). Disagreement is ongoing about whether the term should be used with psychological disorders because of the frequent overlap of different disorders (Skodol, 2005). In just one example, Zimmerman, Rothschild, and Chelminski (2005) conducted a study of 859 psychiatric outpatients and assessed how many had one or more personality disorders. Researchers found that a person with a particular personality disorder often also meets the criteria for other disorders. For example, a person identified with borderline personality disorder is also likely to receive diagnoses of paranoid, schizotypal, antisocial, narcissistic, avoidant, or dependent personality disorders.

Do people really tend to have more than one personality disorder? Are the ways we define these disorders inaccurate, and do we need to improve our definitions so that they do not overlap? Or did we divide the disorders in the wrong way, and do we need to rethink the categories? Complicating this issue is the phenomenon that people will change diagnoses over time (Torgersen, 2012). Such questions about comorbidity are just a few of the important issues faced by researchers who study personality disorders.

Personality Disorders under Study

Other personality disorders have been studied for inclusion in the *DSM*—for example, sadistic personality disorder, which includes people who receive pleasure by inflicting pain on others (Levesque, 2012), and passive-aggressive personality disorder, which includes people who are defiant and refuse to cooperate with requests—attempting to undermine authority figures (Wetzler & Jose, 2012). The existence of these disorders as distinct personality disorders remains controversial, so they were not included in *DSM-5* (Wetzler & Jose, 2012).

We now review the personality disorders currently in *DSM-5*, 10 in all. Table 11.3 provides a simplified look at how people with different personality disorders view the world.

TABLE 11.3 | Main Beliefs Associated with Specific Personality Disorders

Personality Disorder	Main Belief
Paranoid	I cannot trust people.
Schizotypal	It's better to be isolated from others.
Schizoid	Relationships are messy, undesirable.
Histrionic	People are there to serve or admire me.
Narcissistic	Since I am special, I deserve special rules.
Borderline	I deserve to be punished.
Antisocial	I am entitled to break rules.
Avoidant	If people knew the "real" me, they would reject me.
Dependent	I need people to survive and be happy.
Obsessive-compulsive	People should do better, try harder.

SOURCE: Reprinted with permission from Lobbestael, J., & Arntz, A. (2012). Cognitive contributions to personality disorders. In T. A. Widiger (Ed.), *The Oxford handbook of personality disorders* (p. 326). New York: Oxford University Press.

11.1 Concept CHECK

Fill in the blanks to complete the following statements about personality disorders:

1. _____ refers to meeting diagnostic criteria for multiple disorders, which is particularly common among individuals with personality disorders.

2. The personality disorders are divided into three clusters: _____ contains the odd or eccentric disorders; _____ contains the dramatic, emotional, and erratic disorders; and _____ contains the anxious and fearful disorders.

3. It's debated whether personality disorders are extreme versions of normal personality variations (therefore classified as dimensions) or ways of relating that are different from psychologically healthy behavior (classified as _____).

4. Personality disorders are described as _____ because they originate in childhood and continue throughout adulthood.

5. Although gender differences are evident in the research of personality disorders, some differences in the findings may be the result of _____.

▶ **What are the essential characteristics of odd or eccentric personality disorders?**

Three personality disorders—paranoid, schizoid, and schizotypal—share common features that resemble some of the psychotic symptoms seen in schizophrenia. These odd or eccentric personality disorders are described next.

Paranoid Personality Disorder

Although it is probably adaptive to be a little wary of other people, being too distrustful can interfere with making friends, working with others, and, in general, getting through daily interactions in a functional way. People with **paranoid personality disorder** are excessively mistrustful and suspicious of others, without any justification. They assume other people are out to harm or trick them; therefore, they tend not to confide in others. Consider the case of Jake.

Jake... • *Research Victim*

Jake grew up in a middle-class neighborhood, and although he never got in serious trouble, he had a reputation in school for arguing with teachers and classmates. After high school, he enrolled in a community college, but he flunked out after the first year. Jake's lack of success in school was partly attributable to his failure to take responsibility for his grades. He began to develop conspiracy theories about fellow students and professors, believing they worked together to see him fail. Jake bounced from job to job, complaining that his employers were spying on him.

At age 25—and against his parents' wishes—he moved out of his parents' home to a town out of state. Unfortunately, the letters Jake wrote home confirmed his parents' fears. He was becoming increasingly preoccupied with theories about people who were out to harm him, and had developed an elaborate theory that researchers working with the CIA drugged him as a child and implanted something in his ear that emitted microwaves. These microwaves, he believed, were causing him to develop cancer. Over two years, he became increasingly preoccupied with this theory, writing letters to authorities trying to convince them he was being slowly killed. After he threatened harm to local college administrators, his parents were contacted, and they brought him to a psychologist who diagnosed him with paranoid personality disorder and major depression.

Clinical Description

The defining characteristic of people with paranoid personality disorder is a pervasive unjustified distrust. Certainly, there may be times when someone is deceitful and "out to get you"; however, people with paranoid personality disorder are suspicious in situations in which most other people would agree their suspicions are unfounded. Even events that have nothing to do with them are interpreted as personal attacks (Bernstein & Useda, 2007; APA, 2013). These people would view a neighbor's barking dog or a delayed airline flight as a deliberate attempt to annoy them. Unfortunately, such mistrust often extends to people close to them and makes meaningful relationships difficult.

Suspiciousness and mistrust can show themselves in a number of ways. People with paranoid personality disorder may be argumentative, may complain, or may be quiet. This style of interaction is communicated, sometimes nonverbally, to others, often resulting in discomfort among those who come in contact with them. These individuals are sensitive to criticism and have an excessive need for autonomy (APA, 2013). Having this disorder increases the risk of suicide attempts and violent behavior, and these people tend to have a poor overall quality of life (Hopwood & Thomas, 2012).

DSM 5 DISORDER CRITERIA SUMMARY
Paranoid Personality Disorder

A. A pervasive distrust and suspiciousness of others such that their motives are interpreted as malevolent, beginning by early adulthood and present in a variety of contexts, as indicated by four (or more) of the following: (1) suspects, without sufficient basis, that others are exploiting, harming, or deceiving him or her, (2) is preoccupied with unjustified doubts about the loyalty or trustworthiness of friends or associates, (3) is reluctant to confide in others because of unwarranted fear that the information will be used maliciously against him or her, (4) reads hidden demeaning or threatening meanings into benign remarks or events, (5) persistently bears grudges, i.e., is unforgiving of insults, injuries, or slights, (6) perceives attacks on his or her character or reputation that are not apparent to others and is quick to react angrily or to counterattack, (7) has recurrent suspicions, without justification, regarding fidelity of spouse or sexual partner.

---

paranoid personality disorder A cluster A (odd or eccentric) **personality disorder** involving pervasive distrust and suspiciousness of others such that their motives are interpreted as malevolent.

B. Does not occur exclusively during the course of schizophrenia, a bipolar disorder or depressive disorder with psychotic features, or another psychotic disorder and is not attributable to the physiological effects of another medical condition.

Note: If criteria are met prior to the onset of schizophrenia, add "premorbid," i.e., "paranoid personality disorder (premorbid)."

From American Psychiatric Association. (2013). *Diagnostic and statistical manual of mental disorders* (5th ed.). Washington, DC.

Causes

In general, there appears to be a strong role for genetics in paranoid personality disorder (Kendler *et al.*, 2015) and there seems to be a relationship with schizophrenia (Bolinskey *et al.*, 2015), causing some to suggest eliminating paranoid personality disorder as a separate disorder from the *DSM* (Triebwasser, Chemerinski, Roussos, & Siever, 2013).

Psychological contributions to paranoid personality disorder are even less certain. Some psychologists point to the thoughts (or "schemas") of people with paranoid personality disorder as a way of explaining their behavior. One view is that people with this disorder have the following basic mistaken assumptions about others: "People are malevolent and deceptive," "They'll attack you if they get the chance," and "You can be okay only if you stay on your toes" (Lobbestael & Arntz, 2012). This is a maladaptive way to view the world, yet it seems to pervade every aspect of the lives of these individuals. Although we don't know why they develop these perceptions, some speculation is that the roots are in their early upbringing. Their parents may teach them to be careful about making mistakes and may impress on them that they are different from other people. This vigilance causes them to see signs that other people are deceptive and malicious (Triebwasser, Chemerinski, Roussos, & Siever, 2013).

Cultural factors have also been implicated in the disorder. Certain groups of people, such as prisoners, refugees, people with hearing impairments, and older adults, are thought to be particularly susceptible because of their unique experiences (Ryder, Sunohara, & Kirmayer, 2015; Raza, DeMarce, Lash, & Parker, 2014). Imagine how you might view other people if you were an immigrant who had difficulty with the language and the customs of your new culture. Other people laughing or talking quietly might be interpreted as somehow directed at you. Therefore, cognitive and cultural factors may interact to produce the suspiciousness observed in some people with paranoid personality disorder.

Treatment

Because people with paranoid personality disorder are mistrustful of everyone, they are unlikely to seek help when they need it, and they have difficulty developing trusting relationships necessary for successful therapy (Sarkar & Adshead, 2012; Skodol & Gunderson, 2008). When these individuals do seek therapy, the trigger is usually a crisis—such as Jake's threats to harm strangers—or other problems such as anxiety or depression (Kelly, Casey, Dunn, Ayuso-Mateos, & Dowrick, 2007).

Therapists try to provide an atmosphere conducive to developing a sense of trust (Bender, 2005). They often use cognitive therapy to counter the person's mistaken assumptions about others, focusing on changing the person's beliefs that all people are malevolent and cannot be trusted (Beck, Davis, & Freeman, 2015). However, a survey of mental health professionals indicated that only 11% of therapists who treat paranoid personality disorder thought these individuals would continue in therapy long enough to be helped (Quality Assurance Project, 1990).

Schizoid Personality Disorder

Do you know someone who is a "loner"? Someone who comes to class alone, sits alone, and leaves alone? Now, magnify this preference for isolation many times over and you can begin to grasp the impact of **schizoid personality disorder** (Hopwood & Thomas, 2012). People with this personality disorder show a pattern of detachment from social relationships and a limited range of emotions in interpersonal situations. They seem aloof, cold, and indifferent to other people. Consider the case of Mr. Z.

▲ People with paranoid personality disorder often believe that impersonal situations exist specifically to annoy or otherwise disturb them.

Andrej Andic/Shutterstock.com

Mr. Z... • *All on His Own*

A 39-year-old scientist was referred after his return from a tour of duty in Antarctica where he had stopped cooperating with others, had withdrawn to his room, and had begun drinking. Mr. Z. was orphaned at age four, raised by an aunt until age nine, and subsequently looked after by an aloof housekeeper. At university, he excelled at physics, but chess was his only contact with others. Throughout his life, he made no close friends and engaged primarily in solitary activities. Until the tour of duty in Antarctica, he had been successful in his research work in physics. He was now, some months after his return, drinking at least a bottle of Schnapps each day, and his work continued to deteriorate. He presented as self-contained and unobtrusive and was difficult to engage. He was at a loss to explain his colleagues' anger at his aloofness and appeared indifferent to their opinion. He did not appear to require any interpersonal relations, although he did complain of some tedium in his life and at one point during the interview became sad, expressing longing to see his uncle in Germany, his only living relation.

(Cases and excerpts reprinted, with permission of the Royal Australian and New Zealand College of Psychiatrists, from Quality Assurance Project (1990). Treatment outlines for paranoid, schizotypal and schizoid personality disorders. *Australian and New Zealand Journal of Psychiatry, 24*, 339–350.)

Clinical Description

Most individuals with schizoid personality disorder seem neither to desire nor to enjoy closeness with others, including sexual relationships. They appear cold and detached and do not seem affected by praise or criticism. Some, however, are sensitive to the opinions of others but are unwilling or unable to express this emotion. For them, social isolation may be painful. Unfortunately, homelessness appears to be prevalent among people with this disorder, perhaps as a result of their lack of friendships and lack of dissatisfaction about not having a sexual relationship (Rouff, 2000; Angstman & Rasmussen, 2011).

The social deficiencies of people with schizoid personality disorder are similar to those of people with paranoid personality disorder, although more extreme. As Beck and Freeman (1990, p. 125) put it, they "consider themselves to be observers rather than participants in the world around them." They do not seem to have the unusual thought processes that characterize the other disorders in Cluster A (Cloninger & Svakic, 2009). For example, people with paranoid and schizotypal personality disorders often have *ideas of reference*, mistaken beliefs that meaningless events relate just to them. In contrast, those with schizoid personality disorder share the social isolation, poor rapport, and constricted affect (showing neither positive nor negative emotion) seen in people with paranoid personality disorder. You will see in Chapter 12 that this distinction among psychotic-like symptoms is important to understanding people with schizophrenia.

Causes and Treatment

Childhood shyness is reported as a precursor to later adult schizoid personality disorder. It may be that this personality trait is inherited and serves as a determinant in the development of this disorder. Abuse and neglect in childhood are also reported among individuals with this disorder (Lobbestael, Arntz, & Bernstein, 2010; Carr, Keenleyside, & Fitzhenry, 2015). Research demonstrates significant overlap in the occurrence of autism spectrum disorder and schizoid personality disorder (Hummelen, Pedersen, Wilberg, & Karterud, 2014; Vannucchi *et al.*, 2014). It is possible that a biological dysfunction found in both autism and schizoid personality disorder combines with early learning or early problems with interpersonal relationships to produce the social deficits that define schizoid personality disorder (Hopwood & Thomas, 2012).

It is rare for a person with this disorder to request treatment except in response to a crisis such as extreme depression or losing a job (Kelly *et al.*, 2007). Therapists often begin treatment by pointing out the value in social relationships. The person with the disorder may even need to be taught the emotions felt by others to learn empathy (Skodol & Gunderson, 2008) and receive social skills training. The therapist takes the part of a friend or significant other in a technique known as role-playing and helps the patient practice establishing and maintaining relationships (Skodol & Gunderson, 2008). This type of social skills training is helped by identifying a social network—a person or people who will be supportive (Bender, 2005).

DSM 5 — DISORDER CRITERIA SUMMARY
Schizoid Personality Disorder

A. A pervasive pattern of detachment from social relationships and a restricted range of expression of emotions in interpersonal settings, beginning by early adulthood and present in a variety of contexts, as indicated by four (or more) of the following: (1) neither desires nor enjoys close relationships, including being part of a family, (2) almost always chooses solitary activities, (3) has little, if any, interest in having sexual experiences with another person, (4) takes pleasure in few, if any, activities, (5) lacks close friends or confidants other than first-degree relatives, (6) appears indifferent to the praise or criticism of others, (7) shows emotional coldness, detachment, or flattened affectivity.

B. Does not occur exclusively during the course of schizophrenia, a bipolar disorder or depressive disorder with psychotic features, another psychotic disorder, or autism spectrum disorder and is not attributable to the physiological effects of another medical condition.

Note: If criteria are met prior to the onset of schizophrenia, add "premorbid," e.g., "schizoid personality disorder (premorbid)."

From American Psychiatric Association. (2013). *Diagnostic and statistical manual of mental disorders* (5th ed.). Washington, DC.

....

schizoid personality disorder A cluster A (odd or eccentric) personality disorder featuring a pervasive pattern of detachment from social relationships and a restricted range of expression of emotions.

Schizotypal Personality Disorder

People with **schizotypal personality disorder** are typically socially isolated, like those with schizoid personality disorder. In addition, they behave in ways that would seem unusual to many of us, and they tend to be suspicious and to have odd beliefs (Chemerenski, Triebwasser, Roussos, & Siever, 2013; Rosell, Futterman, McMaster, & Siever, 2014). Schizotypal personality disorder is considered by some to be on a continuum (that is, on the same spectrum) with schizophrenia but without some of the more debilitating symptoms, such as hallucinations and delusions. In fact, because of this close connection, *DSM-5* includes this disorder under both the heading of a personality disorder and a schizophrenia spectrum disorder (American Psychiatric Association, 2013). Consider the case of Mr. S.

Mr. S... • *All on His Own*

Mr. S. was a 35-year-old chronically unemployed man who had been referred by a physician because of a vitamin deficiency. This was thought to have eventuated because Mr. S. avoided any foods that "could have been contaminated by machine." He had begun to develop alternative ideas about diet in his 20s and soon left his family and began to study an Eastern religion. "It opened my third eye; corruption is all about," he said.

He now lived by himself on a small farm, attempting to grow his own food, bartering for items he could not grow himself. He spent his days and evenings researching the origins and mechanisms of food contamination and had developed a small band that followed his ideas. He had never married and maintained little contact with his family. He had refused medication from the physician and became uneasy when the facts of his deficiency were discussed with him.

(Cases and excerpts reprinted, with permission of the Royal Australian and New Zealand College of Psychiatrists, from Quality Assurance Project, 1990. Treatment outlines for paranoid, schizotypal and schizoid personality disorders. *Australian and New Zealand Journal of Psychiatry, 24,* 339–350.)

Clinical Description

People given a diagnosis of schizotypal personality disorder have psychotic-like (but not psychotic) symptoms (such as believing everything relates to them personally), social deficits, and sometimes cognitive impairments or paranoia (Kwapil & Barrantes-Vidal, 2012). These individuals are often considered odd because of how they relate to others, how they think and behave, and even how they dress. They have *ideas of reference;* for example, they may believe that everyone on a passing city bus is talking about them, yet they may be able to acknowledge this is unlikely (Rosell *et al.*, 2014).

Again, some people with schizophrenia also have ideas of reference, but they are usually not able to "test reality" or see the illogic of their ideas.

Individuals with schizotypal personality disorder also have odd beliefs or engage in "magical thinking," believing, for example, that they are clairvoyant or telepathic (Furnham & Crump, 2014). In addition, they report unusual perceptual experiences, including such illusions as feeling the presence of another person when they are alone. Notice the subtle but important difference between *feeling* as if someone else is in the room and the more extreme perceptual distortion in people with schizophrenia who might report there *is* someone else in the room when there isn't. Unlike people who simply have unusual interests or beliefs, those with schizotypal personality disorder tend to be suspicious and have paranoid thoughts, express little emotion, and may dress or behave in unusual ways (for example, wear many layers of clothing in the summer or mumble to themselves) (Chemerinski *et al.*, 2013). Prospective research on children who later develop schizotypal personality disorder found that they tend to be passive and unengaged and are hypersensitive to criticism (Olin *et al.*, 1997).

Causes

Historically, the word *schizotype* was used to describe people who were predisposed to develop schizophrenia (Meehl, 1962; Rado, 1962). Schizotypal personality disorder is viewed by some to be one phenotype of a schizophrenia genotype. Recall that a *phenotype* is one way a person's genetics is expressed. A *genotype* is the gene or genes that make up a particular disorder. Depending on a variety of other influences, however, the way you turn out—your phenotype—may vary from other persons with a similar genetic makeup. Some people are thought to have "schizophrenia genes" (the genotype) yet, because of the relative lack of biological influences (for example, prenatal illnesses) or environmental stresses (for example, poverty, maltreatment), some will have the less severe schizotypal personality disorder (the phenotype) (Kwapil & Barrantes-Vidal, 2012).

The idea of a relationship between schizotypal personality disorder and schizophrenia arises partly from the way people with the disorders behave. Many characteristics of schizotypal personality disorder, including ideas of reference, illusions, and paranoid thinking, are similar but milder forms of behaviors observed among people with schizophrenia. Genetic research also seems to support a relationship. Family, twin, and adoption studies have shown an increased prevalence of schizotypal personality disorder among relatives of people with schizophrenia who do not also have schizophrenia themselves (Siever & Davis, 2004). These studies also tell us, however, that the environment can strongly influence schizotypal personality disorder. Some research suggests that schizotypal symptoms are strongly associated with childhood maltreatment among men, and this childhood maltreatment seems to result in posttraumatic stress disorder (PTSD) symptoms (see Chapter 4) among women (Berenbaum, Thompson, Milanak, Boden, & Bredemeier, 2008).

Cognitive assessment of people with this disorder points to mild-to-moderate decrements in their ability to perform on tests involving memory and learning, suggesting some damage in the left hemisphere (Siever & Davis, 2004). Other research, using magnetic resonance imaging, points to generalized brain abnormalities in those with schizotypal personality disorder (Lener et al., 2014; Modinos et al., 2009).

Treatment

People with schizotypal personality disorder who request clinical help often seek assistance due to anxiety or depression. Relatedly, the presence of schizotypal personality disorder significantly increases the risk for developing major depressive disorder even years later (Skodol et al., 2011). Treatment includes some of the medical and psychological treatments for depression (Cloninger & Svakic, 2009; Mulder, Frampton, Luty, & Joyce, 2009).

Controlled studies of attempts to treat people with schizotypal personality disorder are few. There is growing interest in treating this disorder, however, because it is being viewed as a precursor to schizophrenia (McClure et al., 2010). One study used a combination of approaches, including antipsychotic medication, community treatment (a team providing therapeutic services), and social skills training, to treat symptoms. Researchers found that this combination reduced their symptoms or postponed the onset of later schizophrenia (Nordentoft et al., 2006). Treating younger persons who have symptoms of schizotypal personality disorder with a combination of antipsychotic medication, cognitive behavior therapy, and social skills training to avoid the onset of schizophrenia is proving to be a promising prevention strategy (Graff, McClure, & Siever, 2014; Nordentoft et al., 2015).

11.2 Concept CHECK

Which personality disorders are described here?

1. Heidi trusts no one and wrongly believes other people want to harm her. She is sure her husband is secretly planning to leave her and take their three boys, although she has no proof. She no longer divulges any information to co-workers for fear that it will be used in a plot against her. She is usually tense and ready to argue about harmless comments made by family members. _____

2. Rebecca lives alone out in the country with her birds and has little contact with others. She is extremely concerned with pollution, fearing that harmful chemicals are in the air and water around her. She has developed her own water purification system and makes her own clothes. If it is necessary for her to go outside, she covers her body with excessive clothing and wears a facemask to avoid the contaminated air. _____

3. Doug is a college student who has no close friends. He comes to class every day and sits in a corner alone. Most students find him difficult to engage and complain about his lack of involvement in class activities, but he appears indifferent to what others say. He has never had a girlfriend, and expresses no desire to have sex. He is meeting with a therapist only because his family tricked him into going. _____

schizotypal personality disorder A cluster A (odd or eccentric) **personality disorder** involving a pervasive pattern of interpersonal deficits featuring acute discomfort with, and reduced capacity for, close relationships, as well as cognitive or perceptual distortions and eccentricities of behavior.

Cluster B Personality Disorders

▶ What are the essential characteristics of dramatic, emotional, or erratic personality disorders?

People diagnosed with the Cluster B personality disorders—antisocial, borderline, histrionic, and narcissistic—all have behaviors that have been described as dramatic, emotional, or erratic. These personality disorders are described next.

Antisocial Personality Disorder

People with **antisocial personality disorder** are among the most puzzling of the individuals a clinician will see in a practice and are characterized as having a history of failing to comply with social norms. They perform actions most of us would find unacceptable, such as stealing from friends and family. They also tend to be irresponsible, impulsive, and deceitful (De Brito & Hodgins, 2009). Robert Hare, a pioneer in the study of people with psychopathy (a subgroup of persons with antisocial personality disorder), describes them as "social predators who charm, manipulate, and ruthlessly plow their way through life, leaving a broad trail of broken hearts, shattered expectations, and empty wallets. Completely lacking in conscience and empathy, they selfishly take what they want and do as they please, violating social norms and expectations without the slightest sense of guilt or regret" (Hare, 1993, p. xi). Consider the case of Ryan.

Ryan... • *The Thrill Seeker*

I first met Ryan on his 17th birthday. Unfortunately, he was celebrating the event in a psychiatric hospital. He had been truant from school for several months and had gotten into trouble; the judge who heard his case had recommended psychiatric evaluation.

My first impression was that Ryan was cooperative and pleasant. He pointed out a tattoo on his arm that he had made himself, saying that it was a "stupid" thing to have done and that he now regretted it. He regretted many things and was looking forward to moving on with his life. I later found out that he was never truly remorseful for anything.

Our second interview was quite different. In the 48 hours since our first interview, Ryan had done a number of things that showed why he needed help. The most serious incident involved a 15-year-old girl named Ann who attended class with Ryan in the hospital school. Ryan had told her that he was going to get himself discharged, get in trouble, and be sent to the same prison Ann's father was in, where he would rape her father. Ryan's threat so upset Ann that she hit her

teacher and several of the staff. When I spoke to Ryan about this, he smiled slightly and said he was bored and that it was fun to upset Ann. When I asked whether it bothered him that his behavior might extend her stay in the hospital, he looked puzzled and said, "Why should it bother me? She's the one who'll have to stay in this hell hole!"

Ryan told me he loved PCP, or "angel dust," and that he would rather be dusted than anything else. He routinely made the two-hour trip to New York City to buy drugs in a dangerous neighborhood. He denied that he was ever nervous. This wasn't machismo; he really seemed unconcerned.

Ryan made little progress. I discussed his future in family therapy sessions and we talked about his pattern of showing supposed regret and remorse and then stealing money from his parents and going back onto the street. Most of our discussions centered on trying to give his parents the courage to say no to him and not to believe his lies. Ryan was eventually discharged to a drug rehabilitation program. Within four weeks, he had convinced his parents to take him home, and within two days he had stolen all their cash and disappeared; he apparently went back to his friends and to drugs.

When he was in his 20s, after one of his many arrests for theft, he was diagnosed as having antisocial personality disorder. His parents never summoned the courage to turn him out or refuse him money, and he continues to con them into providing him with a means of buying more drugs.

Clinical Description

Individuals with antisocial personality disorder tend to have long histories of violating the rights of others (Black, 2013; Hare et al., 2012). They are often described as being aggressive because they take what they want, indifferent to the concerns of other people. Lying and cheating seem to be second nature to them, and often they appear unable to tell the difference between the truth and the lies they make up to further their own goals. They show no remorse or concern over the sometimes devastating effects of their actions. Substance abuse is common in people with antisocial personality disorder and appears to be a lifelong pattern among these individuals (Hasin et al., 2011). The long-term outcome for people with antisocial personality disorder is usually poor, regardless of gender (Black, 2013;

Colman *et al.*, 2009). One classic study, for example, followed 1,000 delinquent and non-delinquent boys over a 50-year period (Laub & Vaillant, 2000). Many of the delinquent boys would today receive a diagnosis of conduct disorder, which you will see later may be a precursor to antisocial personality disorder in adults. The delinquent boys were more than twice as likely to die an unnatural death (for example, accident, suicide, or homicide) as their non-delinquent peers, which may be attributed to factors such as alcohol abuse and poor self-care (for example, infections and reckless behavior).

Antisocial personality disorder has had a number of names over the years: moral insanity, egopathy, sociopathy, and psychopathy. A great deal has been written about these labels; we focus on the two that have figured most prominently in psychological research: **psychopathy** and *DSM-5*'s antisocial personality disorder. There continues to be debate in the field if these really are two distinct disorders (Douglas *et al.*, 2015; Wall, Wygant, & Sellbom, 2015).

DSM 5 DISORDER CRITERIA SUMMARY
Antisocial Personality Disorder

A. A pervasive pattern of disregard for and violation of the rights of others, occurring since age 15 years, as indicated by three (or more) of the following: (1) failure to conform to social norms with respect to lawful behaviors, as indicated by repeatedly performing acts that are grounds for arrest, (2) deceitfulness, as indicated by repeated lying, use of aliases, or conning others for personal profit or pleasure, (3) impulsivity or failure to plan ahead, (4) irritability and aggressiveness, as indicated by repeated physical fights or assaults, (5) reckless disregard for safety of self or others, (6) consistent irresponsibility, as indicated by repeated failure to sustain consistent work behavior or honor financial obligations, (7) lack of remorse, as indicated by being indifferent to or rationalizing having hurt, mistreated, or stolen from another.

B. The individual is at least age 18 years.

C. There is evidence of conduct disorder with onset before age 15 years.

D. The occurrence of antisocial behavior is not exclusively during the course of schizophrenia or bipolar disorder.

From American Psychiatric Association. (2013). *Diagnostic and statistical manual of mental disorders* (5th ed.). Washington, DC.

Defining Criteria Hervey Cleckley (1941/1982), a psychiatrist who spent much of his career working with the "psychopathic personality," identified a constellation of 16 major characteristics, most of which are personality traits and are sometimes referred to as the "Cleckley criteria." Hare and his colleagues, building on the descriptive work of Cleckley, researched the nature of psychopathy (see, for example, Hare, 1970; Harpur, Hare, & Hakstian, 1989) and developed a 20-item checklist that serves as an assessment tool. Six of the criteria that Hare includes in his Revised Psychopathy Checklist (PCL-R) are as follows:

1. Glibness/superficial charm
2. Grandiose sense of self-worth
3. Pathological lying
4. Conning/manipulative
5. Lack of remorse or guilt
6. Callous/lack of empathy
   (Hare *et al.*, 2012, p. 480)

With some training, clinicians are able to gather information from interviews with a person, along with material from significant others or institutional files (for example, prison records), and assign the person scores on the checklist, with high scores indicating psychopathy (Hare & Neumann, 2006).

The Cleckley/Hare criteria focus primarily on underlying *personality traits* (for example, being self-centered or manipulative). Earlier versions of the *DSM* criteria for antisocial personality focused almost entirely on observable *behaviors* (for example, "impulsively and repeatedly changes employment, residence, or sexual partners"). *DSM-5*, however, moved closer to the trait-based criteria and includes some of the same language included in Hare's PCL-R (e.g., callousness, manipulativeness, and deceitfulness). Unfortunately, research on identifying persons with antisocial personality disorder suggests that this new definition reduces the reliability of the diagnosis (Regier *et al.*, 2013). Additional work will be needed to improve the reliability of this diagnosis while maintaining the core traits that characterize these individuals.

Antisocial Personality Disorder and Criminality Although Cleckley did not deny that many psychopaths are at greatly elevated risk for criminal and antisocial behaviors, he did emphasize that some have few or no legal or interpersonal difficulties. In other words, some psychopaths are not criminals and some do not display outward aggressiveness. What separates many in this group from those who get into trouble with the law may be their intelligence quotient (IQ). In a classic prospective, longitudinal study, White, Moffitt, and Silva (1989) followed almost 1,000 children, beginning at age five, to see what predicted antisocial behavior at age 15. They found that, of the five-year-olds determined to be at high risk for later delinquent

antisocial personality disorder A cluster B (dramatic, emotional, or erratic) personality disorder involving a pervasive pattern of disregard for and violation of the rights of others. Similar to the non-*DSM-5* label psychopathy but with greater emphasis on overt behavior than on personality traits.

psychopathy A non-*DSM-5* category similar to **antisocial personality disorder** but with less emphasis on overt behavior. Indicators include superficial charm, lack of remorse, and other personality characteristics.

behavior, 16% did indeed have run-ins with the law by the age of 15, and 84% did not. What distinguished these two groups? In general, the at-risk children with lower IQs were the ones who got in trouble. This suggests that having a higher IQ may help protect some people from developing more serious problems, or it may at least prevent them from getting caught.

Some psychopaths function quite successfully in certain segments of society (for example, politics, business, and entertainment). Because of the difficulty in identifying these people, such "successful" or "subclinical" psychopaths (who meet some of the criteria for psychopathy) have not been the focus of much research.

Identifying psychopaths among the criminal population seems to have important implications for predicting their future criminal behavior (Vitacco, Neumann, & Pardini, 2014). As you can imagine, having personality characteristics such as a lack of remorse and impulsivity can lead to difficulty staying out of trouble. In general, research has found that people who score high on measures of psychopathy commit crimes at a higher rate than those with lower scores and are at greater risk for more violent crimes and recidivism (repeating offenses) (e.g., Widiger, 2006), although some recent research has found psychopathy to be a less reliable predictor of criminality (Colins, Andershed, & Pardini, 2015).

Conduct Disorder

DSM-5 provides a separate diagnosis for children who engage in behaviors that violate society's norms: *conduct disorder*. It provides for the designation of two subtypes: *childhood-onset type* (the onset of at least one criterion characteristic of CD prior to age 10 years) or *adolescent-onset type* (the absence of any criteria characteristic of CD prior to age 10 years). An additional subtype, new to *DSM-5*, is called "with a callous-unemotional presentation" (Barry, Golmaryami, Rivera-Hudson, & Frick, 2012). This designation is an indication that the young person presents in a way that suggests personality characteristics similar to an adult with psychopathy.

Many children with conduct disorder—most often diagnosed in boys—become juvenile offenders and become involved with drugs. Data from long-term follow-up research indicate that many adults with antisocial personality disorder or psychopathy had conduct disorder as children (Robins, 1978; Kasen, Cohen, Skodol, Johnson, & Brook, 2014); the likelihood of an adult having antisocial personality disorder increases if, as a child, he or she had both conduct disorder and attention deficit/hyperactivity disorder (Biederman, Mick, Faraone, & Burback, 2001; Moffitt, Caspi, Rutter, & Silva, 2001). In many cases, the types of norm violations that an adult would engage in—irresponsibility regarding work or family—appear as younger versions in conduct disorder, such as truancy from

DSM 5 DISORDER CRITERIA SUMMARY
Conduct Disorder

A. A repetitive and persistent pattern of behavior in which the basic rights of others or major age-appropriate societal norms or rules are violated, as manifested by the presence of at least three of the following 15 criteria in the past 12 months from any of the categories below, with at least one criterion present in the past six months:

Aggression to People and Animals

1. Often bullies, threatens, or intimidates others.
2. Often initiates physical fights.
3. Has used a weapon that can cause serious physical harm to others (e.g., a bat, brick, broken bottle, knife, gun).
4. Has been physically cruel to people.
5. Has been physically cruel to animals.
6. Has stolen while confronting a victim (e.g., mugging, purse snatching, extortion, armed robbery).
7. Has forced someone into sexual activity.

Destruction of Property

8. Has deliberately engaged in fire setting with the intention of causing serious damage.
9. Has deliberately destroyed others' property (other than by fire setting).

Deceitfulness or Theft

10. Has broken into someone else's house, building, or car.
11. Often lies to obtain goods or favors or to avoid obligations (i.e., "cons" others).
12. Has stolen items of non-trivial value without confronting a victim (e.g., shoplifting, but without breaking and entering; forgery).

Serious Violations of Rules

13. Often stays out at night despite parental prohibitions, beginning before age 13 years.
14. Has run away from home overnight at least twice while living in the parental or parental surrogate home, or once without returning for a lengthy period.
15. Is often truant from school, beginning before age 13 years.

B. The disturbance in behavior causes clinically significant impairment in social, academic, or occupational functioning.

C. If the individual is age 18 years or older, criteria are not met for antisocial personality disorder.

From American Psychiatric Association. (2013). *Diagnostic and statistical manual of mental disorders* (5th ed.). Washington, DC.

school or running away from home. Some children with conduct disorder do feel remorseful about their behavior, which is why *DSM-5* included the qualifier "with a callous-unemotional presentation" in order to better differentiate these two groups.

Genetic Influences

Family, twin, and adoption studies all suggest a genetic influence on both antisocial personality disorder and criminality (Checknita *et al.*, 2015; Reichborn-Kjennerud *et al.*, 2015). For example, in a classic study, Crowe (1974) examined children whose mothers were felons and who were later adopted by other families, and compared them with adopted children of normal mothers. All were separated from their mothers as newborns, minimizing the possibility that environmental factors from their biological families were responsible for the results. Crowe found that the adopted offspring of felons had significantly higher rates of arrests, conviction, and antisocial personality than did the adopted offspring of normal mothers, which suggests at least some genetic influence on criminality and antisocial behavior.

Crowe found something else quite interesting, however: The adopted children of felons who themselves later became criminals had spent more time in interim orphanages than either the adopted children of felons who did not become criminals or the adopted children of normal mothers. As Crowe points out, this suggests a gene–environment interaction; in other words, genetic factors may be important only in the presence of certain environmental influences (alternatively, certain environmental influences are important only in the presence of certain genetic predispositions). Genetic factors may present a vulnerability, but actual development of criminality may require environmental factors, such as a deficit in early, high-quality contact with parents or parent surrogates.

If you remember back to Chapter 3, we introduced the concept of an *endophenotype*—underlying aspects of a disorder that might be more directly influenced by genes. In the case of antisocial personality disorder, gene researchers are looking for genetic differences that may influence factors such as serotonin and dopamine levels or the relative lack of anxiety or fear seen in these individuals (which we discuss next) (Hare *et al.*, 2012). Although this research is at its early stages, it is refining the search for genes—not for ones that "cause" antisocial personality disorder but for genes that create the unusual aspects of an antisocial personality, such as fearlessness, aggressiveness, impulsivity, and lack of remorse.

Neurobiological Influences

A great deal of research has focused on neurobiological influences that may be specific to antisocial personality disorder. One thing seems clear: General brain damage does not explain why some people become psychopaths or criminals; these individuals appear to score as well on neuropsychological tests as the rest of us (Hart, Forth, & Hare, 1990). Such tests are designed to detect only significant damage in the brain, however, and will not pick up subtle changes in chemistry or structure that could affect behavior.

Arousal Theories The fearlessness, seeming insensitivity to punishment, and thrill-seeking behaviors characteristic of those with antisocial personality disorder (especially those with psychopathy) sparked interest in what neurobiological processes might contribute to these unusual reactions. Early theoretical work on people with antisocial personality disorder emphasized two hypotheses: the underarousal hypothesis and the fearlessness hypothesis.

According to the *underarousal hypothesis*, psychopaths have abnormally low levels of cortical arousal (Sylvers, Ryan, Alden, & Brennan, 2009), which is the primary cause of their antisocial and risk-taking behaviors; they seek stimulation to boost their low levels of arousal. Researchers have examined childhood and adolescent psychophysiological predictors of adult antisocial behavior and criminality. Raine, Venables, and Williams (1990), for example, assessed a sample of 15-year-olds on a variety of autonomic and central nervous system variables. They found that future criminals had lower skin conductance activity, lower heart rate during rest periods, and more slow-frequency brain wave activity, all indicative of low arousal.

According to the *fearlessness hypothesis*, psychopaths possess a higher threshold for experiencing fear than most other individuals (Lykken, 1957, 1982). In other words, things that greatly frighten the rest of us have little effect on the psychopath (Syngelaki, Fairchild, Moore, Savage, & Goozen, 2013). According to proponents of this hypothesis, the fearlessness of the psychopath gives rise to all the other major features of the syndrome.

Theorists have tried to connect what we know about the workings of the brain with clinical observations of people with antisocial personality disorder, especially those with psychopathy. Several theorists have applied Jeffrey Gray's (1987) model of brain functioning to this population (Fowles, 1988; Quay, 1993). According to Gray, three major brain systems influence learning and emotional behavior: the behavioral inhibition system (BIS), the reward system, and the fight/flight system. Two of these systems, the BIS and the reward system, have been used to explain the behavior of people with psychopathy. The BIS is responsible for our ability to stop or slow down when we are faced with impending punishment, non-reward, or novel situations; activation of this system leads to anxiety and frustration. The BIS is thought to be located in the septohippocampal system and involves the noradrenergic and serotonergic neurotransmitter systems. The reward system is responsible for how we behave—in particular, our approach to positive rewards—and is associated with hope and relief. This system probably involves the dopaminergic system in the mesolimbic area of the brain, which we previously noted as the "pleasure pathway" for its role in substance use and abuse (see Chapter 10).

If you think about the behavior of psychopaths, the possible malfunctioning of these systems is clear. An imbalance between the BIS and the reward system may make

▲ Many prisons allow visits between inmates and their children, partly to help reduce later psychological problems in those children.

the fear and anxiety produced by the BIS less apparent and the positive feelings associated with the reward system more prominent (Hoppenbrouwers, Neumann, Lewis, & Johansson, 2015; Quay, 1993). Theorists have proposed that this type of neurobiological dysfunction may explain why psychopaths aren't anxious about committing the antisocial acts that characterize their disorder.

Researchers continue to explore how differences in neurotransmitter function (for example, serotonin) and neurohormone function (for example, androgens such as testosterone and the stress neurohormone cortisol) in the brains of these individuals can explain the callousness, superficial charm, lack of remorse, and impulsivity that characterize people with psychopathy. Integrative theories that link these differences to both genetic and environmental influences are just now beginning to be outlined (DeLisi & Vaughn, 2015; Hare *et al.*, 2012) and may lead to better understanding and treatments for this debilitating disorder.

Psychological and Social Dimensions

What goes on in the mind of a psychopath? In one of several studies of how psychopaths process reward and punishment, Newman, Patterson, and Kosson (1987) set up a card-playing task on a computer; they provided five-cent rewards and fines for correct and incorrect answers to psychopathic and non-psychopathic criminal offenders. The game was constructed so that at first players were rewarded about 90% of the time and fined only about 10% of the time. Gradually, the odds changed until the probability of getting a reward was 0%. Despite feedback that reward was no longer forthcoming, the psychopaths continued to play and lose, while those without psychopathy stopped playing. As a result of this and other studies, the researchers

hypothesized that once psychopaths set their sights on a reward goal, they are less likely than non-psychopaths to be deterred despite signs the goal is no longer achievable (Dvorak-Bertscha, Curtin, Rubinstein, & Newman, 2009). Again, considering the reckless and daring behavior of some psychopaths (robbing banks without a mask and getting caught immediately), failure to abandon an unattainable goal fits the overall picture.

Gerald Patterson's influential work suggests that aggression in children with antisocial personality disorder may escalate, partly as a result of their interactions with their parents (Granic & Patterson, 2006; Patterson, 1982). He found that the parents often give in to the problem behaviors displayed by their children. For example, a boy's parents ask him to make his bed and he refuses. One parent yells at the boy. The boy yells back and becomes abusive. At some point, his interchange becomes so aversive that the parent stops fighting and walks away, thereby ending the fight but also letting the son not make his bed. Giving in to these problems results in short-term gains for both the parent (calm is restored in the house) and the child (he gets what he wants), but it results in continuing problems. The child has learned to continue fighting and not give up, and the parent learns that the only way to "win" is to withdraw all demands. This "coercive family process" combines with other factors, such as genetic influences, parental depression, poor monitoring of their child's activities, and less parental involvement, to help maintain the aggressive behaviors (Chronis *et al.*, 2007; Patterson, DeBaryshe, & Ramsey, 1989). Coercive parenting—along with genetics—appears to be at least modestly involved with the callous-unemotional traits that seem related to later psychopathy (Waller *et al.*, 2015).

Although little is known about which environmental factors play a direct role in causing antisocial personality disorder and psychopathy (as opposed to childhood conduct disorders), evidence from adoption studies strongly suggests that shared environmental factors—that tend to make family members similar—are important to the etiology of criminality and perhaps antisocial personality disorder. For example, in the adoption study by Sigvardsson, Cloninger, Bohman, and von Knorring (1982), low social status of the adoptive parents increased the risk of non-violent criminality among females. Like children with conduct disorders, individuals with antisocial personality disorder come from homes with inconsistent parental discipline (see, for example, Robins, 1966).

Developmental Influences

As children move into adulthood, the forms of antisocial behaviors change—from truancy and stealing from friends to extortion, assaults, armed robbery, or other crimes. Fortunately, clinical lore, as well as scattered empirical reports (Robins, 1966), suggest that rates of antisocial behavior begin to decline rather markedly around the age of 40. In their classic study, Hare, McPherson, and Forth (1988) provided empirical support for this phenomenon. They examined the conviction rates of male psychopaths and male non-psychopaths who had been incarcerated for a variety of crimes. The researchers found that between the ages of 16 and 45 the conviction rates of non-psychopaths remained relatively constant. In contrast, the conviction rates of psychopaths remained relatively constant up until about 40, at which time they decreased markedly (see ●Figure 11.2). Why antisocial behavior often declines around middle age remains unanswered (Hare *et al.*, 2012).

An Integrative Model

How can we put all this information together to get a better understanding of people with antisocial personality disorder? Remember that the research just discussed sometimes involved people labeled as having antisocial personality disorder but at other times included people labeled as psychopathic or even criminals. Whatever the label, it appears these people have a genetic vulnerability to antisocial behaviors and personality traits.

One potential gene–environment interaction may be seen in the role of fear conditioning in children. If you remember back to Chapters 1 and 4, we discussed how we learn to fear things that can harm us (for example, a hot stove) through the pairing of an unconditioned stimulus

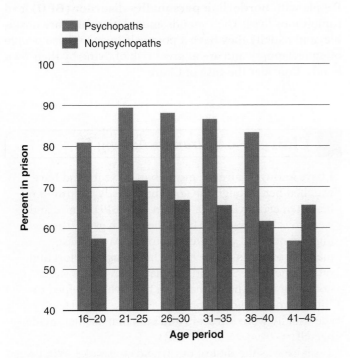

●**Figure 11.2** Lifetime course of criminal behavior in psychopaths and non-psychopaths. (Based on Hare, R. D., McPherson, L. M., & Forth, A. E. [1988]. Male psychopaths and their criminal careers. *Journal of Consulting and Clinical Psychology, 56,* 710–714.)

(e.g., heat from burner) and a conditioned stimulus (e.g., parent's warning to stay away), resulting in avoidance of the conditioned stimulus. But what if this conditioning is somehow impaired and you do not learn to avoid things that can harm you? An important study looked at whether abnormal responses to fear conditioning as a young child could be responsible for later antisocial behavior in adults (Gao, Raine, Venables, Dawson, & Mednick, 2010). This large 20-year study assessed fear conditioning in a group of 1,795 children at age three, and then looked to see who had a criminal record at age 23. They found that offenders showed significantly reduced fear conditioning at age three compared with matched comparison participants, with many of these children showing no fear conditioning at all. Deficits in amygdala functioning are thought to make individuals unable to recognize cues that signal threat, making them relatively fearless, which suggests that these children had problems in this area of the brain (Sterzer, 2010). These findings may point to a mechanism by which genetic influences (leading to damage in the amygdala) interact with environmental influences (learning to fear threats) to produce adults who are relatively fearless and therefore engage in behaviors that cause harm to themselves and others.

Biological influences further interact with other environmental experiences such as early childhood adversity. In a family that may already be under stress because of divorce or substance abuse, there may be an interaction style that encourages antisocial behavior on the part of the child (Thomas, 2009). The child's antisocial and impulsive behavior—partly caused by the child's difficult temperament and impulsivity (Chronis *et al.*, 2007; Kochanska, Aksan, & Joy, 2007)—alienates other children who might be good role models and attracts others who encourage antisocial behavior. These behaviors may also result in the child's dropping out of school and a poor occupational history in adulthood, which help create increasingly frustrating life circumstances that further incite acts against society (Thomas, 2009).

This is, admittedly, an abbreviated version of a complex scenario. The important element is that in this integrative model of antisocial behavior, biological, psychological, and cultural factors combine in intricate ways to create someone like Ryan.

Treatment

One of the major problems with treating people in this group is typical of numerous personality disorders: They rarely identify themselves as needing treatment. Because of this, and because they can be manipulative even with their therapists, most clinicians are pessimistic about the outcome of treatment for adults who have antisocial personality disorder, and there are few documented success stories (National Collaborating Centre for Mental Health, 2010). In general, therapists agree with incarcerating these people to deter future antisocial acts. One large study with violent offenders found that cognitive behavior therapy could reduce the likelihood of violence five years after treatment (Olver, Lewis, & Wong, 2013). Importantly, however, treatment success was negatively correlated with ratings on the PCL-R for traits of "selfish, callous, and remorseless use of others." In other words, the higher the score on this trait (which we have seen is related to psychopathy), the less successful this group was in refraining from violence after their treatment.

Clinicians also encourage identification of high-risk children so that treatment can be attempted before they become adults (National Collaborating Centre for Mental Health, 2010; Thomas, 2009). The most common treatment strategy for children involves parent training (Scott, Briskman, & O'Connor, 2014; Patterson, 1986). Parents are taught to recognize behavior problems early and to use praise and privileges to reduce problem behavior and encourage prosocial behaviors. Treatment studies typically show that these types of programs can significantly improve the behaviors of many children who display antisocial behaviors (Conduct Problems Prevention Research Group, 2010). A number of factors, however, put families at risk either for not succeeding in treatment or for dropping out early; these include cases with a high degree of family dysfunction, socioeconomic disadvantage, high family stress, a parent's history of antisocial behavior, and severe conduct disorder on the part of the child (Kaminski, Valle, Filene, & Boyle, 2008).

▲ Children with conduct disorder may become adults with antisocial personality disorder.

Catherine Ursillo/Science Source

Prevention

The aggressive behaviors of children are remarkably stable, meaning that children who hit, insult, and threaten others are likely to continue these behaviors as they age. Approaches to change this course are being implemented mainly in school settings and emphasize behavioral supports for good behavior and skills training to improve social competence (Reddy, Newman, De Thomas, & Chun, 2009). Research using parent training for young children (toddlers from 1 ½ to 2 ½ years) suggests that early intervention may be particularly helpful (Shaw, Dishion, Supplee, Gardner, & Arnds, 2006). Aggression can be reduced and social competence (for example, making friends) can be improved among young children, and these results generally are maintained over a few years (Conduct Problems Prevention Research, 2010; Reddy et al., 2009). One study found that the association between childhood conduct disorder and adult antisocial behavior was weaker among those adolescents who participated in high school sports (Samek, Elkins, Keyes, Iacono, & McGue, 2015). It is too soon to assess the impact of targeted prevention programs on adult antisocial behaviors typically observed among people with this personality disorder (Ingoldsby, Shelleby, Lane, & Shaw, 2012). Given the ineffectiveness of treatment for adults, however, prevention may be the best approach.

Borderline Personality Disorder

People with **borderline personality disorder (BPD)** lead tumultuous lives. Their moods and relationships are unstable, and usually they have a poor self-image. These people often feel empty and are at great risk of dying by their own hands. Consider the case of Claire.

Claire... • *A Stranger Among Us*

I have known Claire for more than 40 years and have watched her through the good but mostly bad times of her often erratic life as a person with BPD. Claire and I went to school together from the eighth grade through high school, and we've kept in touch. My earliest memory of her is of her hair, which was cut short and rather unevenly. She told me that when things were not going well, she cut her own hair, which helped to "fill the void." I later found out that the long sleeves she usually wore hid scars and cuts that she had made herself.

Claire was the first of our friends to smoke. What was unusual about this and her later drug use was not that they occurred or that they began early; it was that she didn't seem to use them to get attention, like everyone else. Claire was also one of the first whose parents divorced, and both of them seemed to abandon her emotionally. She later told me that her father was an alcoholic who had regularly beaten her and her mother. She did poorly in school and had a low opinion of herself. She often said she was stupid and ugly, yet she was neither.

Throughout our school years, Claire left town periodically, without any explanation. I learned later that she was in psychiatric facilities to get help with her suicidal depression. She often threatened to kill herself, although we didn't guess that she was serious.

In our later teens, we all drifted away from Claire. She had become increasingly unpredictable, sometimes berating us for a perceived slight ("You're walking too fast. You don't want to be seen with me!"), and at other times desperate to be around us. We were confused by her behavior. As we all grew older, the "void" she described in herself became overwhelming and eventually shut us all out.

Claire married twice, and both times had passionate but stormy relationships interrupted by hospitalizations. She tried to stab her first husband during a particularly violent rage. She tried a number of drugs but mainly used alcohol to "deaden the pain."

Now, in her 50s, things have calmed down, although she says she is rarely happy. Claire does feel a little better about herself and is doing well as a travel agent. Although she is seeing someone, she is reluctant to become involved because of her personal history. Claire was ultimately diagnosed with depression and BPD.

Clinical Description

BPD is one of the most common personality disorders observed in clinical settings; it is observed in every culture and is seen in about 1% to 2% of the general population (Torgersen, 2012). Claire's life illustrates the instability characteristic of people with BPD. They tend to have turbulent relationships, fearing abandonment but lacking control over their emotions (Hooley, Cole, & Gironde, 2012). They often engage in behaviors that are suicidal, self-mutilative, or both. Claire sometimes used her cigarette to burn herself, and she carved her initials in her arm. A significant proportion—nearly 10%—die by suicide (Gunderson, 2011; Björkenstam, Björkenstam, Holm, Gerdin, & Ekselius, 2015). Fortunately, the long-term outcome for people with BPD is encouraging (Zanarini, Frankenburg, Reich, & Fitzmaurice, 2012), with approximately nine out of ten patients achieving remission in the decade after seeking treatment (Gunderson et al., 2011; Keuroghlian et al., 2015).

People with BPD are often intense, going from anger to deep depression in a short time. Dysfunction in the area of emotion is sometimes considered one of the core features of BPD (Linehan & Dexter-Mazza, 2008) and is one of the best predictors of suicide in this group (McGirr et al., 2009). The characteristic of instability (in emotion, interpersonal relationships, self-concept, and behavior) is seen as a core feature with some describing this group as being "stably unstable" (Hooley et al., 2012). This instability extends to impulsivity, which can be seen in their drug abuse and self-mutilation. Although not so obvious as to why, the self-injurious behaviors, such as cutting, sometimes are described as tension-reducing by people who engage in these behaviors (McKenzie & Gross, 2014; Nock, 2010). Claire's empty feeling is also common; these people are sometimes described as chronically bored and have difficulties with their own identities (Linehan & Dexter-Mazza, 2008).

The mood disorders we discussed in Chapter 6 are common among people with BPD; one study of inpatients with this disorder found that more than 80% also had major depression and approximately 10% had bipolar II disorder (Zanarini et al., 1998). Eating disorders are also common, particularly bulimia (see Chapter 8): Approximately 25% of people with BPD also have bulimia, while 20% meet criteria for anorexia (Zanarini et al., 1998). Up to 64% of the people with BPD are also diagnosed with at least one substance use disorder (Zanarini et al., 1998). As with antisocial personality disorder, people with BPD tend to improve during their 30s and 40s, although they may continue to have difficulties into old age (Zanarini et al., 2012).

DSM 5 DISORDER CRITERIA SUMMARY
Borderline Personality Disorder

A pervasive pattern of instability of interpersonal relationships, self-image, and affects, and marked impulsivity, beginning by early adulthood and present in a variety of contexts, as indicated by five (or more) of the following:

1. Frantic efforts to avoid real or imagined abandonment. (Note: Do not include suicidal or self-mutilating behavior covered in Criterion 5.)

2. A pattern of unstable and intense interpersonal relationships characterized by alternating between extremes of idealization and devaluation.

3. Identity disturbance: markedly and persistently unstable self-image or sense of self.

4. Impulsivity in at least two areas that are potentially self-damaging (e.g., spending, sex, substance abuse, reckless driving, binge eating). (Note: Do not include suicidal or self-mutilating behavior covered in Criterion 5.)

5. Recurrent suicidal behavior, gestures, or threats, or self-mutilating behavior.

borderline personality disorder A cluster B (dramatic, emotional, or erratic) **personality disorder** involving a pervasive pattern of instability of interpersonal relationships, self-image, affect, and control over impulses.

6. Affective instability due to a marked reactivity of mood (e.g., intense episodic dysphoria, irritability, or anxiety usually lasting a few hours and only rarely more than a few days).

7. Chronic feelings of emptiness.

8. Inappropriate, intense anger or difficulty controlling anger (e.g., frequent displays of temper, constant anger, recurrent physical fights).

9. Transient, stress-related paranoid ideation or severe dissociative symptoms.

From American Psychiatric Association. (2013). *Diagnostic and statistical manual of mental disorders* (5th ed.). Washington, DC.

Causes

The results from numerous family studies suggest that BPD is more prevalent in families with the disorder and somehow linked with mood disorders (Amad, Ramoz, Thomas, Jardri, & Gorwood, 2014). Studies of monozygotic (identical) and dizygotic (fraternal) twins indicated a higher concordance rate among monozygotic twins, further supporting the role of genetics in the expression of BPD (Calati, Gressier, Balestri, & Serretti, 2013).

The emotional reactivity that is a central aspect of BPD has led researchers to look at this personality trait for clues about inherited influences (endophenotypes). Important genetic studies are investigating genes associated with the neurochemical serotonin because dysfunction in this system has been linked to the emotional instability, suicidal behaviors, and impulsivity seen in people with this disorder (Soloff, Chiappetta, Mason, Becker, & Price, 2014; Joyce, Stephenson, Kennedy, Mulder, & McHugh, 2013). This research is in its early stages, and there are, as yet, no solid answers for how genetic differences lead to the symptoms of BPD (Amad *et al.*, 2014).

Neuroimaging studies, designed to locate areas in the brain contributing to BPD, point to the limbic network (Schulze, Schmahl, & Niedtfeld, 2016: Stone, 2013). This area in the brain is involved in emotion regulation and dysfunctional serotonin neurotransmission, linking these findings with genetic research. Low serotonergic activity is involved with the regulation of mood and impulsivity, making it a target for extensive study in this group (Hooley *et al.*, 2012).

Cognitive factors in BPD are just beginning to be explored. How do people with this disorder process information, and does this contribute to their difficulties? One study that looked at the thought processes of these individuals asked people with and without BPD to look at words projected on a computer screen and try to remember some of the words and try to forget others (Korfine & Hooley, 2000). When the words were not related to the symptoms of BPD—for example, "celebrate," "charming," and "collect"—both groups performed equally well. However, when they were presented with words that might be relevant

▲ Borderline personality disorder is often accompanied by self-mutilation.

to the disorder—for example, "abandon," "suicidal," and "emptiness"—individuals with BPD remembered more of these words despite being instructed to forget them. This preliminary evidence for a memory bias may hold clues to the nature of this disorder and may someday be helpful in designing more effective treatment (Winter, Elzinga, & Schmahl, 2013; Baer, Peters, Eisenlohr-Moul, Geiger, & Sauer, 2012).

An important environmental risk factor in a gene–environment interaction explanation for BPD is the possible contribution of early trauma, especially sexual and physical abuse. Numerous studies show that people with BPD are more likely to report abuse than are healthy individuals or those with other psychiatric conditions (see, for example, Kuo, Khoury, Metcalf, Fitzpatrick, & Goodwill, 2015; Zanarini *et al.*, 2014). Unfortunately, these types of studies (based on recollection and a correlation between the two phenomena) do not tell us directly whether abuse and neglect cause later BPD. In an important study, researchers followed 500 children who had documented cases of physical and sexual abuse and neglect and compared them in adulthood with a control group (no history of reported abuse or neglect) (Widom, Czaja, & Paris, 2009). Significantly more abused and neglected children went on to develop BPD compared with controls. This finding is particularly significant for girls and women because girls are two or three times more likely to be sexually abused than boys (Bebbington *et al.*, 2009).

It is clear that a majority of people who receive the diagnosis of BPD have suffered terrible abuse or neglect from parents, sexual abuse, physical abuse by others, or a combination of these (Ball & Links, 2009). For those who have not reported such histories, some research is examining just how they could develop BPD. For example, factors such as temperament (emotional nature, such as being impulsive, irritable, or hypersensitive) or neurological impairments (being exposed prenatally to alcohol or drugs) and how they interact with parental styles may account for some cases of BPD (Graybar & Boutilier, 2002).

Symptoms of BPD have been observed among people who have gone through rapid cultural changes. The problems of identity, emptiness, fears of abandonment, and low anxiety threshold have been found in child and adult immigrants (Laxenaire, Ganne-Vevonec, & Streiff, 1982; Skhiri, Annabi, Bi, & Allani, 1982). These observations further support the possibility that prior trauma may, in some individuals, lead to BPD.

Remember, however, that a history of childhood trauma, including sexual and physical abuse, occurs in people with other disorders, such as schizoid personality disorder, somatic symptom disorder (see Chapter 5), panic disorder (see Chapter 4), and dissociative identity disorder (see Chapter 5). In addition, a portion of individuals with BPD have no apparent history of such abuse (Cloninger & Svakic, 2009). Although childhood sexual abuse and physical abuse and neglect seem to play an important role in the etiology of BPD (Zanarini & Wedig, 2014), neither appears to be necessary or sufficient to produce the syndrome.

An Integrative Model

Although there is no currently accepted integrative model for BPD, it is tempting to borrow from the work on anxiety disorders to outline a possible view. If you recall from Chapter 4, we describe the "triple vulnerability" theory (Barlow, 2002; Suárez, Bennett, Goldstein, & Barlow, 2008). The first vulnerability (or diathesis) is a generalized biological vulnerability. We can see the genetic vulnerability to emotional reactivity in people with BPD and how this affects specific brain function. The second vulnerability is a generalized psychological vulnerability. In the case of people with BPD, they tend to view the world as threatening and to react strongly to real and perceived threats. The third vulnerability is a specific psychological vulnerability, learned from early environmental experiences; this is where early trauma, abuse, or both may advance this sensitivity to threats. When a person is stressed, his or her biological tendency to be overly reactive interacts with the psychological tendency to feel threatened. This may result in the outbursts and suicidal behaviors commonly observed in this group. This preliminary model awaits validation and further research.

Treatment

In stark contrast to individuals with antisocial personality disorder, who rarely acknowledge requiring help, those with BPD appear quite distressed and are more likely to seek treatment even than people with anxiety and mood disorders (Bender *et al.*, 2014; Ansell, Sanislow, McGlashan, & Grilo, 2007). Reviews of research on the use of medical treatment for people with BPD suggest that symptomatic treatment can sometimes be helpful. For disturbances in affect (e.g., anger, sadness) a class of drugs known as mood stabilizers (e.g., some anticonvulsive and antipsychotic drugs) can be effective (Silk & Feurino III, 2012). Efforts to provide successful treatment are complicated by problems with drug abuse, compliance with treatment, and suicide attempts. As a result, many clinicians are reluctant to work with people who have BPD.

One of the most thoroughly researched cognitive-behavioral treatments was developed by Marsha Linehan (Linehan *et al.*, 2006; Linehan & Dexter-Mazza, 2008). This approach—called **dialectical behavior therapy (DBT)**—involves helping people cope with the stressors that seem to trigger suicidal behaviors and other maladaptive responses. Priority in treatment is first given to those behaviors that may result in harm (suicidal behaviors), then those behaviors that interfere with therapy, and, finally, those that interfere with the patient's quality of life. Weekly individual sessions provide support, and patients are taught how to identify and regulate their emotions. Problem solving is emphasized so that patients can handle difficulties more effectively. In addition, they receive treatment similar to that used for people with PTSD, in which prior traumatic events are reexperienced to help extinguish the fear associated with them (see Chapter 4). In the final stage of therapy, clients learn to trust their own responses rather than depend on the validation of others, sometimes by visualizing themselves not reacting to criticism (Lynch & Cuper, 2012).

Results from a number of studies suggest that DBT may help reduce suicide attempts, dropouts from treatment, and hospitalizations (Linehan *et al.*, 2015; Linehan & Dexter-Mazza, 2008; McMain, Guimond, Streiner, Cardish, & Links, 2013). A follow up of 39 women who received either DBT or general therapeutic support (called "treatment as usual") for one year showed that, during the first six months of follow up, the women in the DBT group were less suicidal, less angry, and better adjusted socially (Linehan & Kehrer, 1993). A growing body of evidence is now available to document the effectiveness of this approach to aid many individuals with this debilitating disorder (Linehan, 2014).

. . . .

dialectical behavior therapy (DBT) A promising treatment for **borderline personality disorder** that involves exposing the client to stressors in a controlled situation, as well as helping the client regulate **emotions** and cope with stressors that might trigger suicidal behavior.

How would you describe a woman who regularly exhibits unstable relationships (e.g., falls in and out of love quickly), problems with her self-identity (e.g., frequently changes her career goals), and impulsive decision making (e.g., goes on reckless shopping sprees)? Are these just "normal" behaviors, expressions, and decisions for a woman, or do they indicate the presence of a psychological disorder? *DSM-5* (APA, 2013) states that "a pervasive pattern of instability of interpersonal relationships, self-image, and affects, and marked impulsivity that begins by early adulthood and is present in a variety of contexts" is the primary feature of BPD (APA, 2013, p. 663). With this *DSM-5* understanding, the woman described here might be diagnosed with

BPD—a disorder that is predominately (75% of the time) found in women. This differential sex prevalence rate, and several of the criteria for BPD, have led to wide debate over the possibility of gender bias in the diagnosis of BPD.

From a socialization perspective, it has been argued that women are trained from a young age to be what our society calls *dependent* and can be more sensitive to criticism or rejection from others (e.g., girls are taught to place high emphasis on things such as relatedness and tend to view themselves through the appraisals of others) (Becker, 1997). Additionally, in attempting to understand how a BPD diagnosis affects women, feminist literature has argued that "the diagnosis of BPD is the latest manifestation of historical attempts

to explain away the strategies which some women use to survive and resist oppression and abuse, by describing these strategies as symptomatic of a disturbed personality/pathology" (Shaw & Proctor, 2005, p. 484). Both of these perspectives suggest that BPD is an unfair diagnosis: either pathologizing socialized expressions of gender or devaluing the experiences and expressions of women. However, diagnosing and treating such extreme behaviors may be the appropriate action. What do you think? Is it the case that extremes in socialized gender expression unfairly lead to labels of personality disorder and devaluation, or do such extreme expressions suggest unhealthiness and call for diagnosis and treatment? ■

Probably some of the most intriguing research we describe in this book involves using the techniques in brain imaging to see how psychological treatments influence brain function. One pilot study examined emotional reactions to upsetting photos (for example, pictures of women being attacked) in controls and in women with BPD (Schnell & Herpertz, 2007). This study found that among the women who benefited from treatment, arousal (in the amygdala and hippocampus) to the upsetting photos improved over time as a function of treatment. No changes occurred in controls or in women who did not have positive treatment experiences. This type of integrative research holds enormous promise for our understanding of BPD and the mechanisms underlying successful treatment.

Histrionic Personality Disorder

Individuals with **histrionic personality disorder** tend to be overly dramatic and often seem almost to be acting, which is why the term *histrionic*, which means theatrical in manner, is used. Consider the case of Pat.

Pat... • *Always Onstage*

When we first met, Pat seemed to radiate enjoyment of life. She was single, in her mid-30s, and was going to night school for her master's degree. She often dressed flamboyantly. During the day she taught children with disabilities, and when she didn't have class, she was

often out late on a date. When I first spoke with her, she enthusiastically told me how impressed she was with my work in the field of developmental disabilities and that she had been extremely successful in using some of my techniques with her students. She was clearly overdoing the praise, but who wouldn't appreciate such flattering comments?

Because some of our research included children in her classroom, I saw Pat often. Over a period of weeks, however, our interactions grew strained. She often complained of various illnesses and injuries (falling in the parking lot, twisting her neck looking out a window) that interfered with her work. She was disorganized, often leaving to the last minute tasks that required considerable planning. Pat made promises to other people that were impossible to keep but seemed to be aimed at winning their approval; when she broke the promise, she usually made up a story designed to elicit sympathy and compassion.

Pat often interrupted meetings about research to talk about her latest boyfriend. The boyfriends changed almost weekly, but her enthusiasm ("Like no other man I have ever met!") and optimism about the future ("He's the guy I want to spend the rest of my life with!") remained high for each of them. Wedding plans were seriously discussed with almost every one, despite their brief acquaintance. Pat was ingratiating, especially to the male teachers, who often helped her out of trouble she got into because of her disorganization.

When it became clear that she would probably lose her teaching job because of her poor performance, Pat managed to manipulate several of the male teachers and the assistant principal into recommending her for a new job in a nearby school district. A year later, she was still at the new school but had been moved twice to different classrooms. According to teachers she worked with, Pat still lacked close interpersonal relationships, although she described her current romantic relationship as "deeply involved." After a rather long period of depression, Pat sought help from a psychologist, who diagnosed her as also having histrionic personality disorder.

Clinical Description

People with histrionic personality disorder are inclined to express their emotions in an exaggerated fashion, for example, hugging someone they have just met or crying uncontrollably during a sad movie (Ferguson & Negy, 2014; Blashfield, Reynolds, & Stennett, 2012). They also tend to be vain, self-centered, and uncomfortable when they are not in the limelight. They are often seductive in appearance and behavior, and they are typically concerned about their looks. (Pat, for example, spent a great deal of money on unusual jewelry and was sure to point it out to anyone who would listen.) In addition, they seek reassurance and approval constantly and may become upset or angry when others do not attend to them or praise them. People with histrionic personality disorder also tend to be impulsive and have great difficulty delaying gratification.

The cognitive style associated with histrionic personality disorder is impressionistic (Beck, Freeman, & Davis, 2007), characterized by a tendency to view situations in global, black-and-white terms. Speech is often vague, lacking in detail, and characterized by exaggeration (APA, 2013; Nestadt *et al.*, 2009). For example, when Pat was asked about a date she had had the night before, she might say it was "amazing" but fail to provide more detailed information.

The high rate of this diagnosis among women versus men raises questions about the nature of the disorder and its diagnostic criteria (Boysen, Ebersole, Casner, & Coston, 2014). As we first discussed in the beginning of this chapter, there is some thought that the features of histrionic personality disorder, such as overdramatization, vanity, seductiveness, and overconcern with physical appearance, are characteristic of the Western "stereotypical female" and may lead to an overdiagnosis among women. Sprock (2000) examined this important question and found some evidence for a bias among psychologists and psychiatrists to associate the diagnosis with women rather than men.

Causes

Despite its long history, little research has been done on the causes or treatment of histrionic personality disorder. One hypothesis involves a possible relationship with antisocial personality disorder. Evidence suggests that histrionic personality and antisocial personality co-occur more often than chance would account for. Lilienfeld and colleagues (1986), for example, found that roughly two-thirds of people with a histrionic personality also met criteria for antisocial personality disorder. The evidence for this association has led to the suggestion (see, for example, Cloninger, 1978; Lilienfeld, 1992) that histrionic personality and antisocial personality may be sex-typed alternative expressions of the same unidentified underlying condition. Females with the underlying condition may be predisposed to exhibit a predominantly histrionic pattern, whereas males with the underlying condition may be predisposed to exhibit a predominantly antisocial pattern. Whether this association exists remains a controversial issue, however, and further research on this potential relationship is needed (Dolan & Völlm, 2009; Salekin, Rogers, & Sewell, 1997), particularly given that borderline personality disorder has also been conceptualized as a female variant of psychopathy (Sprague, Javdani, Sadeh, Newman, & Verona, 2012).

Treatment

Although a great deal has been written about ways of helping people with histrionic personality disorder, little of the

▲ People with histrionic personality disorder tend to be vain, extravagant, and seductive.

histrionic personality disorder A cluster B (dramatic, emotional, or erratic) **personality disorder** involving a pervasive pattern of excessive emotionality and attention seeking.

A pervasive pattern of excessive emotionality and attention seeking, beginning by early adulthood and present in a variety of contexts, as indicated by five (or more) of the following:

1. Is uncomfortable in situations in which he or she is not the center of attention.

2. Interaction with others is often characterized by inappropriate sexually seductive or provocative behavior.

3. Displays rapidly shifting and shallow expression of emotions.

4. Consistently uses physical appearance to draw attention to self.

5. Has a style of speech that is excessively impressionistic and lacking in detail.

6. Shows self-dramatization, theatricality, and exaggerated expression of emotion.

7. Is suggestible (i.e., easily influenced by others or circumstances).

8. Considers relationships to be more intimate than they actually are.

From American Psychiatric Association. (2013). *Diagnostic and statistical manual of mental disorders* (5th ed.). Washington, DC.

research demonstrates success (Cloninger & Svakic, 2009). A large part of therapy for these individuals usually focuses on the problematic interpersonal relationships. They often manipulate others through emotional crises, using charm, sex, seductiveness, or complaining (Beck *et al.*, 2007). People with histrionic personality disorder often need to be shown how the short-term gains derived from this interactional style result in long-term costs, and they need to be taught more appropriate ways of negotiating their wants and needs.

Narcissistic Personality Disorder

We all know people who think highly of themselves—perhaps exaggerating their real abilities. They consider themselves somehow different from others and deserving of special treatment. In **narcissistic personality disorder**, this tendency is taken to its extreme. In Greek mythology, Narcissus was a youth who spurned the love of Echo, so enamored was he of his own beauty. He spent his days admiring his own image reflected in a pool of water. Psychoanalysts, including Freud, used the term *narcissistic* to describe people who show an exaggerated sense of self-importance and are preoccupied with receiving attention (Ronningstam, 2012). Consider the case of Willie.

Willie... • *It's All About Me*

Willie was an office assistant in a small law firm. Now in his early 30s, Willie had an extremely poor job history. He never stayed employed at the same place for more than two years, and he spent considerable time working through temporary employment agencies. Your first encounter, however, would make you believe that he was extremely competent and that he ran the office. If you entered the waiting room, you were greeted by Willie, even though he wasn't the receptionist. He would be extremely solicitous, asking how he could be of assistance, offer you coffee, and ask you to make yourself comfortable in "his" reception area. Willie liked to talk, and any conversation was quickly redirected in a way that kept him the center of attention.

This type of ingratiating manner was welcomed at first but soon annoyed other staff. This was especially true when he referred to the other workers in the office as his staff, even though he was not responsible for supervising any of them. The conversations with visitors and staff often consumed a great deal of his time and the time of other staff, and this was becoming a problem. He quickly became controlling in his job—a pattern revealed in his other positions as well—eagerly taking charge of duties assigned to others. Unfortunately, he did not complete these tasks well, and this created a great deal of friction.

When confronted with any of these difficulties, Willie would first blame others. Ultimately, however, it would become clear that Willie's self-centeredness and controlling nature were at the root of many of the office inefficiencies. During a disciplinary meeting with all of the law firm's partners, an unusual step, Willie became explosively abusive and blamed them for being out to get him. He insisted that his performance was exceptional at all of his previous positions—something contradicted by his previous employers—and that they were at fault. After calming down, he revealed a previous drinking problem, a history of depression, and multiple family problems, all of which he believed contributed to any difficulties he experienced.

The firm recommended he be seen at a university clinic as a condition of his continued employment, where he was diagnosed with major depression as well as narcissistic personality disorder. Ultimately, his behavior—including lateness and incomplete work—resulted in his termination. In a revealing turn of events, Willie reapplied for another position at the same firm two years later. A mix-up in records failed to reveal his previous termination, but he lasted only three days—showing up late to work on his second and third days. He was convinced he could be successful, yet he could not change his behavior to conform to even the minimal standards needed to be successful at work.

Clinical Description

People with narcissistic personality disorder have an unreasonable sense of self-importance and are so preoccupied with themselves that they lack sensitivity and compassion for other people (Caligor, Levy, & Yeomans, 2015; Ronningstam, 2012). Their exaggerated feelings and their fantasies of greatness, called *grandiosity,* create a number of negative attributes. They require and expect a great deal of special attention—the best table in the restaurant, the illegal parking space in front of the movie theater. They also tend to use or exploit others for their own interests and show little empathy. When confronted with other successful people, they can be extremely envious and arrogant. And because they often fail to live up to their own expectations, they are often depressed.

Causes and Treatment

We start out as infants being self-centered and demanding, which is part of our struggle for survival. Part of the socialization process, however, involves teaching children empathy and altruism. Some writers, including Kohut (1971, 1977), believe that narcissistic personality disorder arises largely from a profound failure by the parents of modeling empathy early in a child's development. As a consequence,

the child remains fixated at a self-centered, grandiose stage of development. In addition, the child (and later the adult) becomes involved in an essentially endless and fruitless search for the ideal person who will meet her unfulfilled empathic needs.

Research on treatment options is extremely limited in both number of studies and reports of success (Ronningstam, 2014; Cloninger & Svakic, 2009; Dhawan, Kunik, Oldham, & Coverdale, 2010). When therapy is attempted with these individuals, it often focuses on their grandiosity, their hypersensitivity to evaluation, and their lack of empathy toward others (Campbell & Miller, 2011; Beck *et al.,* 2007). Cognitive therapy strives to replace their fantasies with a focus on the day-to-day pleasurable experiences that are truly attainable. Coping strategies such as relaxation training are used to help them face and accept criticism. Helping them focus on the feelings of others is also a goal. Because individuals with this disorder are vulnerable to severe depressive episodes, particularly in middle age, treatment is often initiated for the depression. It is impossible to draw any conclusions, however, about the impact of such treatment on the actual narcissistic personality disorder.

DSM 5 — DISORDER CRITERIA SUMMARY
Narcissistic Personality Disorder

A pervasive pattern of grandiosity (in fantasy or behavior), need for admiration, and lack of empathy, beginning by early adulthood and present in a variety of contexts, as indicated by five (or more) of the following:

1. Has a grandiose sense of self-importance (e.g., exaggerates achievements and talents, expects to be recognized as superior without commensurate achievements).

2. Is preoccupied with fantasies of unlimited success, power, brilliance, beauty, or ideal love.

3. Believes that he or she is "special" and unique and can only be understood by, or should associate with, other special or high-status people (or institutions).

4. Requests excessive admiration.

5. Has a sense of entitlement (i.e., unreasonable expectations of especially favorable treatment or automatic compliance with his or her expectations).

6. Is interpersonally exploitative (i.e., takes advantage of others to achieve his or her own ends).

7. Lacks empathy: is unwilling to recognize or identify with the feelings and needs of others.

8. Is often envious of others or believes that others are envious of him or her.

9. Shows arrogant, haughty behaviors or attitudes.

From American Psychiatric Association. (2013). *Diagnostic and statistical manual of mental disorders* (5th ed.). Washington, DC.

11.3 Concept CHECK

Correctly identify the type of personality disorder described here:

1. Elaine has low self-esteem and usually feels empty unless she does dangerous and exciting things. She is involved in drugs and has casual sex, even with strangers. She threatens to commit suicide if her boyfriend talks about leaving her, and alternates between passionately loving and hating him. _____

2. Lance is 19 and has been in trouble with the law for two years. He lies to his parents, vandalizes buildings, and fights with others. He shows no remorse for the people he injures or the grief he causes his parents. _____

3. Nancy thinks she is the best at everything. She thinks her performance is always excellent, and is critical of anyone else's success. She constantly looks for admiration and reassurance from others. _____

4. Samantha is known for being overly dramatic. She cries uncontrollably during sad movies, and she is vain and self-centered, interrupting many class conversations to discuss her personal life. _____

narcissistic personality disorder A cluster B (dramatic, emotional, or erratic) **personality disorder** involving a pervasive pattern of grandiosity in fantasy or behavior, need for admiration, and lack of **empathy**.

▶ What are the essential characteristics of anxious or fearful personality disorders?

People diagnosed with avoidant, dependent, and obsessive-compulsive disorders share common features with people who have anxiety disorders. These anxious or fearful personality disorders are described next.

Avoidant Personality Disorder

People with **avoidant personality disorder** are extremely sensitive to the opinions of others, and although they desire social relationships, their anxiety leads them to avoid such associations. Their extremely low self-esteem—coupled with a fear of rejection—causes them to be limited in their friendships and dependent on those they feel comfortable with (Eikenaes, Pedersen, &Wilberg, 2015; Sanislow, da Cruz, Gianoli, & Reagan, 2012). Consider the case of Jane.

Jane... • *Not Worth Noticing*

Jane was raised by an alcoholic mother who had borderline personality disorder and who abused her verbally and physically. As a child, Jane made sense of this abusive treatment by believing that she must be an intrinsically unworthy person to be treated so badly. In her late 20s, Jane still expected to be rejected when others found out she was unworthy and bad.

Jane was self-critical and thought people would not like her, that they would see she was a loser, and that she would have nothing to say. She became upset if she perceived that someone was reacting negatively or neutrally. If a sales clerk was slightly curt, Jane automatically thought it must be because she (Jane) was unworthy or unlikable. She then felt sad. When she received positive feedback from others, she discounted it. As a result, Jane had few friends and certainly no close ones.

(Case and excerpt reprinted, with permission, from Beck, A. T., & Freeman, A., 1990. *Cognitive therapy of personality disorders.* New York: Guilford Press, ©1990 Guilford Press.)

Clinical Description

Theodore Millon (1981), who initially proposed this diagnosis, notes that it is important to distinguish between individuals who are asocial because they are apathetic, affectively flat, and relatively uninterested in interpersonal relationships (comparable to what *DSM-5* terms schizoid personality disorder) and individuals who are asocial because they are interpersonally anxious and fearful of rejection. It is the latter who fit the criteria of avoidant personality disorder (Millon & Martinez, 1995). These individuals feel chronically rejected by others and are pessimistic about their future.

Causes

Some evidence has found that avoidant personality disorder is related to other subschizophrenia-related disorders, occurring more often in relatives of people who have schizophrenia (Fogelson *et al.*, 2010, 2007). A number of theories have been proposed that integrate biological and psychosocial influences as the cause of avoidant personality disorder. Millon (1981), for example, suggests that these individuals may be born with a difficult temperament or personality characteristics. As a result, their parents may reject them, or at least not provide them with enough early, uncritical love. This rejection, in turn, may result in low self-esteem and social alienation, conditions that persist into adulthood. Limited support exists for psychosocial influences in the cause of avoidant personality disorder. For example, Stravynski, Elie, and Franche (1989) questioned a group of people with avoidant personality disorder and a group of control participants about their early treatment by their parents. Those with the disorder remembered their parents as more rejecting, more guilt engendering, and less affectionate than the control group, suggesting parenting may contribute to the development of this disorder. Similarly, research has consistently found that these individuals are more likely to report childhood experiences of neglect, isolation, rejection, and conflict with others (Eikenaes, Egeland, Hummelen, & Wilberg, 2015; Meyer & Carver, 2000).

DSM 5 | DISORDER CRITERIA SUMMARY
Avoidant Personality Disorder

A pervasive pattern of social inhibition, feelings of inadequacy, and hypersensitivity to negative evaluation, beginning by early adulthood and present in a variety of contexts, as indicated by four (or more) of the following:

1. Avoids occupational activities that involve significant interpersonal contact because of fears of criticism, disapproval, or rejection.

2. Is unwilling to get involved with people unless certain of being liked.

3. Shows restraint within intimate relationships because of the fear of being shamed or ridiculed.

---

4. Is preoccupied with being criticized or rejected in social situations.

5. Is inhibited in new interpersonal situations because of feelings of inadequacy.

6. Views self as socially inept, personally unappealing, or inferior to others.

7. Is unusually reluctant to take personal risks or to engage in any new activities because they may prove embarrassing.

From American Psychiatric Association. (2013). *Diagnostic and statistical manual of mental disorders* (5th ed.). Washington, DC.

Treatment

There are a number of well-controlled studies on approaches to therapy for people with avoidant personality disorder (Leahy & McGinn, 2012). Behavioral intervention techniques for anxiety and social skills problems have had some success (e.g., Borge *et al.*, 2010; Emmelkamp *et al.*, 2006). Because the problems experienced by people with avoidant personality disorder resemble those of people with social phobia, many of the same treatments are used for both groups (see Chapter 4). Therapeutic alliance—the collaborative connection between therapist and client—appears to be an important predictor for treatment success in this group (Strauss *et al.*, 2006).

Dependent Personality Disorder

We all know what it means to be dependent on another person. People with **dependent personality disorder**, however, rely on others to make ordinary decisions as well as important ones, which results in an unreasonable fear of abandonment. Consider the case of Karen.

Karen... • *Whatever You Say*

Karen was a 45-year-old married woman who was referred for treatment by her physician for problems with panic attacks. During the evaluation, she appeared to be worried, sensitive, and naive. She was easily overcome with emotion and cried on and off throughout the session. She was also self-critical at every opportunity. For example, when asked how she got along with other people, she reported that "others think I'm dumb and inadequate," although she could give no evidence as to what made her think that. She reported that she didn't like school because "I was dumb" and that she always felt that she was not good enough.

Karen described staying in her first marriage for 10 years, even though "it was hell." Her husband had affairs and was verbally abusive. She tried to leave him but gave in to his repeated requests to return. She was finally able to divorce him, and shortly afterward she met and married her current husband, whom she described as kind, sensitive, and supportive. Karen stated that she preferred to have others make important decisions and agreed with other people to avoid conflict. She worried about being left alone without anyone to take care of her and reported feeling lost without other people's reassurance. She also reported that her feelings were easily hurt, so she worked hard not to do anything that might lead to criticism.

(Case and excerpt reprinted, with permission, from Beck, A. T., & Freeman, A. (1990). *Cognitive therapy of personality disorders*. New York: Guilford Press, © 1990 by Guilford Press.)

Clinical Description

Individuals with dependent personality disorder sometimes agree with other people when their own opinion differs so as not to be rejected (Bornstein, 2012). Their desire to obtain and maintain supportive and nurturant relationships may lead to their other behavioral characteristics, including submissiveness, timidity, and passivity. People with this disorder are similar to those with avoidant personality disorder in their feelings of inadequacy, sensitivity to criticism, and need for reassurance. However, people with dependent personality disorder respond by clinging to relationships (Disney, 2013; Bornstein, 2012). It is important to note that in certain cultures (e.g., East Asian Confucianism) dependence and submission may be viewed as a desired interpersonal state (Chen, Nettles, & Chen, 2009).

Causes and Treatment

We are all born dependent on other people for food, physical protection, and nurturance. Part of the socialization process in most cultures involves helping us live independently (Bornstein, 1992). It was thought that disruptions such as the early death of a parent or neglect or rejection by caregivers could cause people to grow up fearing abandonment (Stone, 1993). It also is clear, however, that genetic influences are important in the development of this disorder (e.g., Gjerde *et al.*, 2012). What is not yet understood are the physiological factors underlying this genetic influence and how they interact with environmental influences (Sanislow *et al.*, 2012).

avoidant personality disorder A cluster C (anxious or fearful) **personality disorder** featuring a pervasive pattern of social inhibition, feelings of inadequacy, and hypersensitivity to criticism.

dependent personality disorder A cluster C (anxious or fearful) **personality disorder** characterized by a person's pervasive and excessive need to be taken care of, a condition that leads to submissive and clinging behavior and fears of separation.

The literature for this disorder is mostly descriptive; little research exists to show whether a particular treatment is effective (Borge *et al.*, 2010; Paris, 2008). On the surface, because of their attentiveness and eagerness to give responsibility for their problems to the therapist, people with dependent personality disorder can appear to be ideal patients. That very submissiveness, however, negates one of the major goals of therapy, which is to make the person more independent and personally responsible (Leahy & McGinn, 2012). Therapy therefore progresses gradually as the patients develop confidence in their ability to make decisions independently (Beck *et al.*, 2007). There is a particular need for care that the patient does not become overly dependent on the therapist.

DSM 5 DISORDER CRITERIA SUMMARY
Dependent Personality Disorder

A pervasive and excessive need to be taken care of that leads to submissive and clinging behavior and fears of separation, beginning by early adulthood and present in a variety of contexts, as indicated by five (or more) of the following:

1. Has difficulty making everyday decisions without an excessive amount of advice and reassurance from others.

2. Needs others to assume responsibility for most major areas of his or her life.

3. Has difficulty expressing disagreement with others because of fear of loss of support or approval. (Note: Do not include realistic fears of retribution.)

4. Has difficulty initiating projects or doing things on his or her own (because of a lack of self-confidence in judgment or abilities rather than a lack of motivation or energy).

5. Goes to excessive lengths to obtain nurturance and support from others, to the point of volunteering to do things that are unpleasant.

6. Feels uncomfortable or helpless when alone because of exaggerated fears of being unable to care of himself or herself.

7. Urgently seeks another relationship as a source of care and support when a close relationship ends.

8. Is unrealistically preoccupied with fears of being left to take care of himself or herself.

From American Psychiatric Association. (2013). *Diagnostic and statistical manual of mental disorders* (5th ed.). Washington, DC.

Obsessive-Compulsive Personality Disorder

People who have **obsessive-compulsive personality disorder** are characterized by a fixation on things being done "the right way" (Diedrich & Voderholzer, 2015). Although many might envy their persistence and dedication, this preoccupation with details prevents them from completing much of anything. Consider the case of Daniel.

Daniel... • *Getting It Exactly Right*

Each day at exactly 8 A.M., Daniel arrived at his office at the university where he was a graduate student in psychology. On his way, he always stopped at the 7-Eleven for coffee and the *New York Times*. From 8 A.M. to 9:15 A.M., he drank his coffee and read the paper. At 9:15 A.M., he reorganized the files that held the hundreds of papers related to his doctoral dissertation, now several years overdue. From 10 a.m. until noon, he read one of these papers, highlighting relevant passages. Then he took the paper bag that held his lunch (always a peanut butter and jelly sandwich and an apple) and went to the cafeteria to purchase a soda and eat by himself. From 1 P.M. until 5 P.M., he held meetings, organized his desk, made lists of things to do, and entered his references into a new database program on his computer. At home, Daniel had dinner with his wife and then worked on his dissertation until after 11 P.M., although much of the time was spent trying out new features of his home computer.

Daniel was no closer to completing his dissertation than he had been 4.5 years ago. His wife was threatening to leave him because he was equally rigid about everything at home and she didn't want to remain in this limbo of graduate school forever. When Daniel eventually sought help from a therapist for his anxiety over his deteriorating marriage, he was diagnosed as having obsessive-compulsive personality disorder.

Clinical Description

Like many with this personality disorder, Daniel is work oriented, spending little time doing anything that isn't related to his graduate studies. Because of their general rigidity, these people tend to have poor interpersonal relationships (Samuels & Costa, 2012).

This personality disorder seems to be only distantly related to obsessive-compulsive disorder, one of the anxiety disorders we described in Chapter 4 (Samuels & Costa, 2012). People like Daniel tend not to have the obsessive thoughts and the compulsive behaviors seen in the like-named obsessive-compulsive disorder. Although people with the anxiety disorder sometimes show characteristics of the personality disorder, they show the characteristics of other personality disorders as well (for example, avoidant, histrionic, or dependent) (Melca, Yücel, Mendlowicz, de Oliviera-Souza, & Fontenelle, 2015; Trull, Scheiderer, & Tomko, 2012).

An intriguing theory suggests that the psychological profiles of many serial killers point to the role of obsessive-compulsive personality disorder. Ferreira (2000) notes that these individuals do not often fit the definition of someone with a severe mental illness—such as schizophrenia—but are "masters of control" in manipulating their victims. Their need to control all aspects of the crime fits the pattern of people with obsessive-compulsive personality disorder, and some combination of this disorder and unfortunate childhood experiences may lead to this disturbing behavior pattern. Obsessive-compulsive personality disorder may also play a role among some sex offenders—in particular, pedophiles. Brain-imaging research on pedophiles suggests that brain functioning in these individuals is similar to those with obsessive-compulsive personality disorder (Schiffer *et al.*, 2007). At the other end of the behavioral spectrum, it is also common to find obsessive-compulsive personality disorder among gifted children, whose quest for perfectionism can be quite debilitating (Nugent, 2000).

Causes and Treatment

There seems to be a moderate genetic contribution to obsessive-compulsive personality disorder (Gjerde *et al.*, 2015; Cloninger & Svakic, 2009). Some people may be predisposed to favor structure in their lives, but to reach the level it did in Daniel may require parental reinforcement of conformity and neatness.

Therapy often attacks the fears that seem to underlie the need for orderliness (Pinto, 2015). These individuals are often afraid that what they do will be inadequate, so they procrastinate and excessively ruminate about important issues and minor details alike. Therapists help the individual relax or use cognitive reappraisal techniques to reframe compulsive thoughts. This form of cognitive-behavioral therapy appears to be effective for people with this personality disorder (Svartberg, Stiles, & Seltzer, 2004).

DSM 5 DISORDER CRITERIA SUMMARY
Obsessive-Compulsive Personality Disorder

A pervasive pattern of preoccupation with orderliness, perfectionism, and mental and interpersonal control, at the expense of flexibility, openness, and efficiency, beginning by early adulthood and present in a variety of contexts, as indicated by four (or more) of the following:

1. Is preoccupied with details, rules, lists, order, organization, or schedules to the extent that the major point of the activity is lost.

2. Shows perfectionism that interferes with task completion (e.g., is unable to complete a project because his or her own overly strict standards are not met).

3. Is excessively devoted to work and productivity to the exclusion of leisure activities and friendships (not accounted for by obvious economic necessity).

4. Is over-conscientious, scrupulous, and inflexible about matters of morality, ethics, or values (not accounted for by cultural or religious identification).

5. Is unable to discard worn-out or worthless objects even when they have no sentimental value.

6. Is reluctant to delegate tasks or to work with others unless they submit to exactly his or her way of doing things.

7. Adopts a miserly spending style toward both self and others; money is viewed as something to be hoarded for future catastrophes.

8. Shows rigidity and stubbornness.

From American Psychiatric Association. (2013). *Diagnostic and statistical manual of mental disorders* (5th ed.). Washington, DC.

11.4 Concept CHECK

Match the following scenarios with the correct disorder:

1. During a therapy session, John gets up for a glass of water. Ten minutes later, he is still not back. He first had to clean the fountain area and neatly arrange the glasses before pouring his glass of water. _____

2. Whitney claims she is unintelligent and has no skills. She is also afraid to be alone and seeks constant reassurance from her family and friends. She says and does nothing about her cheating husband because she thinks that if she shows any resolve, she will be abandoned. _____

3. Mike has no social life because of his great fear of rejection. He disregards compliments and reacts excessively to criticism, which only feeds his pervasive feelings of inadequacy. Mike takes everything personally. _____

. . . .

obsessive-compulsive personality disorder A cluster C (anxious or fearful) **personality disorder** featuring a pervasive pattern of preoccupation with orderliness, perfectionism, and mental and interpersonal control at the expense of flexibility, openness, and efficiency.

CONTROVERSY   The Battle for the Personality Disorders

iscussion about the personality disorders in *DSM-5* included proposals for a number of major changes to this category. The elimination of the distinction between "Axis I" and "Axis II" disorders elevated the personality disorders into the mainstream of problems experienced by individuals. However, one of the biggest changes proposed was to completely eliminate five of the personality disorders (paranoid, schizoid, histrionic, avoidant, and dependent personality disorders). Instead, people previously diagnosed with these disorders would be identified as having a general personality disorder with the traits specified (e.g., suspiciousness, emotional liability, hostility, etc.). The rationale for their removal included a relative lack of research on these disorders and significant overlap among the disorders (comorbidity) (Skodol, 2012). In anticipation of this significant change, one set of researchers authored a paper with the title "The Death of Histrionic Personality Disorder" (Blashfield et al., 2012) and the personality disorders community of researchers in general was divided over this change (Pull, 2013). Ultimately, the final draft retained these disorders and left for a later time proposals for dealing with the problems of lack of research and specificity. This back and forth on how to carve up diagnoses exemplifies the difficulties that continue to exist for any diagnostic system, even after decades of arduous and dedicated research. ∎

SUMMARY

An Overview of Personality Disorders

What are the essential features of personality disorders?

▶ The personality disorders represent long-standing and ingrained ways of thinking, feeling, and behaving that can cause significant distress. Because people may display two or more of these maladaptive ways of interacting with the world, considerable disagreement remains over how to categorize the personality disorders.

▶ *DSM-5* includes 10 personality disorders that are divided into three clusters: Cluster A (odd or eccentric) includes paranoid, schizoid, and schizotypal personality disorders; Cluster B (dramatic, emotional, or erratic) includes antisocial, borderline, histrionic, and narcissistic personality disorders; and Cluster C (anxious or fearful) includes avoidant, dependent, and obsessive-compulsive personality disorders.

Cluster A Personality Disorders

What are the essential characteristics of odd or eccentric personality disorders?

▶ People with paranoid personality disorder are excessively mistrustful and suspicious of other people, without any justification. They tend not to confide in others and expect other people to do them harm.

▶ People with schizoid personality disorder show a pattern of detachment from social relationships and a limited range of emotions in interpersonal situations. They seem aloof, cold, and indifferent to other people.

▶ People with schizotypal personality disorder are typically socially isolated and behave in ways that would seem unusual to most of us. In addition, they tend to be suspicious and have odd beliefs about the world.

Cluster B Personality Disorders

What are the essential characteristics of dramatic, emotional, or erratic personality disorders?

▶ People with antisocial personality disorder have a history of failing to comply with social norms. They perform actions most of us would find unacceptable, such as stealing from friends and family. They also tend to be irresponsible, impulsive, and deceitful.

▶ In contrast to the DSM-5 criteria for antisocial personality, which focus almost entirely on observable behaviors (for example, impulsively and repeatedly changing employment, residence, or sexual partners), the related concept of psychopathy primarily reflects underlying personality traits (for example, self-centeredness or manipulativeness).

▶ People with borderline personality disorder lack stability in their moods and in their relationships with other people, and they usually have poor self-esteem. These individuals often feel empty and are at great risk of suicide.

- Individuals with histrionic personality disorder tend to be overly dramatic and often appear almost to be acting.
- People with narcissistic personality disorder think highly of themselves—beyond their real abilities. They consider themselves somehow different from others and deserving of special treatment.

Cluster C Personality Disorders

What are the essential characteristics of anxious or fearful personality disorders?

- People with avoidant personality disorder are extremely sensitive to the opinions of others and therefore avoid social relationships. Their extremely low self-esteem, coupled with a fear of rejection, causes them to reject the attention of others.

- Individuals with dependent personality disorder rely on others to the extent of letting them make everyday decisions, as well as major ones; this results in an unreasonable fear of being abandoned.
- People who have obsessive-compulsive personality disorder are characterized by a fixation on things being done "the right way." This preoccupation with details prevents them from completing much of anything.
- Treating people with personality disorders is often difficult because they usually do not see that their difficulties are a result of the way they relate to others.
- Personality disorders are important for the clinician to consider because they may interfere with efforts to treat more specific problems such as anxiety, depression, or substance abuse. Unfortunately, the presence of one or more personality disorders is associated with a poor treatment outcome and a generally negative prognosis.

Key Terms

personality disorder, 409
paranoid personality disorder, 415
schizoid personality disorder, 417
schizotypal personality disorder, 418
antisocial personality disorder, 420

psychopathy, 421
borderline personality disorder, 426
dialectical behavior
    therapy (DBT), 429
histrionic personality disorder, 430

narcissistic personality disorder, 432
avoidant personality disorder, 434
dependent personality disorder, 435
obsessive-compulsive personality
    disorder, 436

Answers to Concept Checks

11.1

1. comorbidity; 2. Cluster A, Cluster B, Cluster C; 3. categories; 4. chronic; 5. bias

11.2

1. paranoid; 2. schizotypal; 3. schizoid

11.3

1. borderline; 2. antisocial; 3. narcissistic; 4. histrionic

11.4

1. obsessive-compulsive; 2. dependent; 3. Avoidant

Chapter Quiz

1. The dimensional versus categorical debate over the nature of personality disorders can also be described as a debate between _____ and _____.
   a. diagnosis; prognosis
   b. state; trait
   c. degree; kind
   d. qualitative; quantitative

2. Some personality disorders are diagnosed more frequently in men than in women. One explanation for this difference is as follows:
   a. Symptoms are interpreted by clinicians in different ways depending on the gender of the person with the symptoms.
   b. Men are more likely to seek help from mental health professionals than women.
   c. Most clinicians are men, and they tend to see psychopathology more often in patients of the same gender as themselves.
   d. Because of hormonal differences, women are more likely to have acute disorders and men are more likely to have chronic personality disorders.

3. Genetic research and an overlap in symptoms suggest a common relationship between schizophrenia and:
   a. borderline personality disorder
   b. schizotypal personality disorder
   c. schizoid personality disorder
   d. antisocial personality disorder

4. Criteria for psychopathy emphasize _____, and criteria for antisocial personality disorder emphasize _____.
   a. behavior; personality
   b. personality; behavior
   c. criminal conduct; social isolation
   d. social isolation; criminal conduct

5. Which symptom is characteristic of persons with borderline personality disorder?
   a. impulsivity
   b. aloofness
   c. mania
   d. grandiosity

6. Which theory suggests psychopaths may engage in antisocial and risk-taking behavior to stimulate their cortical system?
   a. equifinality hypothesis
   b. transcortical magnetic stimulation hypothesis
   c. underarousal hypothesis
   d. equipotential hypothesis

7. Greeting a new acquaintance with effusive familiarity, crying uncontrollably during a movie, and trying to be the center of attention at a party are typical behaviors of someone with:
   a. borderline personality disorder
   b. narcissistic personality disorder
   c. histrionic personality disorder
   d. paranoid personality disorder

8. Which of the following statements is most true about borderline personality disorder?

 a. Childhood abuse is rare in people with borderline personality disorder.

 b. Borderline personality disorder is more frequently diagnosed in men than in women.

 c. Behaviors in borderline personality disorder overlap those seen in posttraumatic stress disorder.

 d. Borderline personality disorder is seldom accompanied by self-mutilation.

9. People with which personality disorder often exhibit childlike, egocentric behaviors?

 a. paranoid

 b. antisocial

 c. schizotypal

 d. narcissistic

10. An individual who is preoccupied with details, rules, organization, and scheduling to the extent that it interferes with daily functioning may have:

 a. obsessive-compulsive personality disorder

 b. narcissistic personality disorder

 c. antisocial personality disorder

 d. schizoid personality disorder

 (See Appendix A for answers.)

Exploring Personality Disorders

- People with personality disorders think and behave in ways that cause distress to themselves and/or the people who care about them.
- There are three main groups, or clusters, of personality disorders, which usually begin in childhood.

CLUSTER A
Odd or Eccentric

Gazelle Technologies

Paranoid
extreme suspicion

Psychological Influences
- Thoughts that people are malicious, deceptive, and threatening
- Behavior based on mistaken assumptions about others

Biological Influences
- Possible but unclear link with schizophrenia

Causes

Schizoid
social isolation

Psychological Influences
- Very limited range of emotions
- Apparently cold and unconnected
- Unaffected by praise or criticism

Biological Influences
- May be associated with lower density of dopamine receptors

Causes

Social/Cultural Influences
- "Outsiders" may be susceptible because of unique experiences (e.g., prisoners, refugees, people with hearing impairments, and the elderly)
- Parents' early teaching may influence

Treatment
- Difficult because of client's mistrust and suspicion
- Cognitive work to change thoughts
- Low success rate

Treatment
- Learning value of social relationships
- Social skills training with role playing

Social/Cultural Influences
- Preference for social isolation
- Lack of social skills
- Lack of interest in close relationships, including romantic or sexual

Schizotypal
suspicion and odd behavior

Psychological Influences
- Unusual beliefs, behavior, or dress
- Suspiciousness
- Believing insignificant events are personally relevant ("ideas of reference")
- Expressing little emotion
- Symptoms of major depressive disorder

Biological
- Genetic vulnerability for schizophrenia but without the biological or environmental stresses present in that disorder

Causes

Treatment
- Teaching social skills to reduce isolation and suspicion
- Medication (haloperidol) to reduce ideas of reference, odd communication, and isolation
- Low success rate

Social/Cultural Influences
- Preference for social isolation
- Excessive social anxiety
- Lack of social skills

CLUSTER C
Anxious or Fearful

Photodisc/Getty Images

Dependent
pervasive need to be taken care of

Psychological Influences
- Early "loss" of caretaker (death, rejection, or neglect) leads to fear of abandonment
- Timidity and passivity

Biological Influences
- Each of us born dependent for protection, food, and nurturance

Causes

Social/Cultural Influences
- Agreement for the sake of avoiding conflict
- Similar to Avoidant in
  - inadequacy
  - sensitivity to criticism
  - need for reassurance
  BUT
for those same shared reasons
- Avoidants withdraw
- Dependents cling

Treatment
- Very little research Appear as ideal clients
- Submissiveness negates independence

CLUSTER B Dramatic, Emotional, or Erratic

Narcissistic excessive interest in oneself

Psychological Influences

- May be influenced by lack of parental modeling of empathy
- Later this influences the child's ability to empathize with others

Biological Influences

- Unclear how biology plays a role in this disorder

Causes

Social/Cultural Influences

- Changes in societal norms that emphasize short-term hedonism, individualism, competitiveness, and success

Treatment

- Cognitive therapy to focus on the day-to-day pleasurable experiences that are attainable
- Teaching coaching strategies to use and accept criticism

Antisocial violation of others' rights

Psychological Influences

- Difficulty learning to avoid punishment
- Indifferent to concerns of others

Biological Influences

- Genetic vulnerability combined with environmental influences
- Abnormally low cortical arousal
- High fear threshold

Causes

Social/Cultural Influences

- Criminality
- Stress/exposure to trauma
- Inconsistent parental discipline
- Socioeconomic disadvantage

Treatment

- Seldom successful (incarceration instead)
- Parent training if problems are caught early
- Prevention through preschool programs

Borderline tumultuous instability

Psychological Influences

- Suicidal
- Erratic moods
- Impulsivity

Causes

Biological Influences

- Familial link to mood disorders
- Possibly inherited tendencies (impulsivity or volatility)

Treatment

- Dialectical behavior therapy (DBT) Medication:
  – tricyclic antidepressants
  – minor tranquilizers
  – lithium

Social/Cultural Influences

- Early trauma, especially sexual/physical abuse
- Rapid cultural changes (immigration) may trigger symptoms

Histrionic excessively emotional

Psychological Influences

- Vain and self-centered
- Easily upset if ignored
- Vague and hyperbolic
- Impulsive; difficulty delaying gratification

Biological Influences

- Possible link to antisocial disorder
  – women histrionic/men antisocial

Causes

Treatment

- Little evidence of success
- Rewards and fines
- Focus on interpersonal relations

Social/Cultural Influences

- Overly dramatic behavior attracts attention
- Seductive
- Approval-seeking

Avoidant inhibition

Psychological Influences

- Low self-esteem
- Fear of rejection, criticism leads to fear of attention
- Extreme sensitivity
- Resembles social phobia

Biological Influences

- Innate characteristics may cause rejection

Causes

Social/Cultural Influences

- Insufficient parental affection

Treatment

- Behavioral intervention techniques sometimes successful
  – systematic desensitization
  – behavioral rehearsal
- Improvements usually modest

Obsessive-Compulsive fixation on details

Biological Influences

- Distant relation to OCD
- Probable weak genetic role
  – predisposition to structure combined with parental reinforcement

Psychological Influences

- Generally rigid
- Dependent on routines
- Procrastinating

Causes

Social/Cultural Influences

- Very work-oriented
- Poor interpersonal relationships

Treatment

- Little information
- Therapy
  – attack fears behind need
  – relaxation or distraction techniques redirect compulsion to order

12 Schizophrenia Spectrum and Other Psychotic Disorders

CHAPTER OUTLINE

Perspectives on Schizophrenia
  Early Figures in Diagnosing
    Schizophrenia
  Identifying Symptoms

Clinical Description,
Symptoms, and Subtypes
  Positive Symptoms
  Negative Symptoms
  Disorganized Symptoms
  Historic Schizophrenia Subtypes
  Other Psychotic Disorders

Prevalence and Causes
of Schizophrenia
  Statistics
  Development
  Cultural Factors
  Genetic Influences
  Neurobiological Influences
  Psychological and Social Influences

Treatment of Schizophrenia
  Biological Interventions
  Psychosocial Interventions
  Treatment across Cultures
  Prevention

Eekhoff Picture Lab/Blend Images LLC

444

Use scientific reasoning to interpret behavior:	▶ Identify basic biological, psychological, and social components of behavioral explanations (e.g., inferences, observations, operational definitions, and interpretations). (APA SLO 2.1a) *(see textbook pages 457–466)*
Develop a working knowledge of the content domains of psychology:	▶ Summarize important aspects of history of psychology, including key figures, central concerns, methods used, and theoretical conflicts. (APA SLO 1.2c) *(see textbook pages 445–446,)*
Engage in innovative and integrative thinking and problem solving:	▶ Describe problems operationally to study them empirically. (APA SLO 2.3a) *(see textbook pages 446–452)*
Describe applications that employ discipline-based problem solving:	▶ Correctly identify antecedents and consequences of behavior and mental processes (APA SLO 1.3c). *(see textbook pages 457–466)* Describe examples of relevant and practical applications of psychological principles to everyday life. (APA SLO 1.3a) *(see textbook pages 467–472)*

* Portions of this chapter cover learning outcomes suggested by the American Psychological Association (2013) in its guidelines for the undergraduate psychology major. Chapter coverage of these outcomes is identified above by APA Goal and APA Suggested Learning Outcome (SLO).

Perspectives on Schizophrenia

▶ How is schizophrenia defined, and what symptoms are included in its diagnosis?

A middle-aged man walks the streets of New York City with aluminum foil on the inside of his hat so Martians can't read his mind. A young woman sits in her college classroom and hears the voice of God telling her she is a vile and disgusting person. You try to strike up a conversation with the super-market bagger, but he stares at you vacantly and will say only one or two words in a flat, toneless voice. Each of these people may have **schizophrenia**, the startling disorder characterized by a broad spectrum of cognitive and emotional dysfunctions including delusions and hallucinations, disorganized speech and behavior, and inappropriate emotions.

Schizophrenia is a complex syndrome that inevitably has a devastating effect on the lives of the person affected and on family members. This disorder can disrupt a person's perception, thought, speech, and movement: almost every aspect of daily functioning. People with these severe mental health problems are more likely to be stigmatized and discriminated against than those without schizophrenia (Corker *et al.*, 2015; Farelly *et al.*, 2014). And despite important advances in treatment, full recovery from schizophrenia has a low base rate of one in seven patients (Jääskeläinen *et al.*, 2013). In addition to the emotional costs, the financial drain is considerable. The annual cost of schizophrenia in the United States is estimated to exceed $60 billion when factors such as family caregiving, lost wages, and treatment are considered (Kennedy, Altar, Taylor, Degtiar, & Hornberger, 2014; Wu *et al.*, 2005). Because schizophrenia is so widespread, affecting approximately one of every 100 people at some point in their lives,

and because its consequences are so severe, research on its causes and treatment has expanded rapidly. Given the attention it has received, you would think the question "What is schizophrenia?" would by now be answered easily. It is not.

In this chapter, we explore this disorder and review efforts to determine whether schizophrenia is distinct or a combination of disorders. The search is complicated by the presence of subtypes: different presentations and combinations of symptoms such as hallucinations, delusions, and disorders of speech, emotion, and socialization. After discussing the characteristics of people with schizophrenia, we describe research into its causes and treatment.

Early Figures in Diagnosing Schizophrenia

In *Observations on Madness and Melancholy*, published in 1809, John Haslam portrayed what he called "a form of insanity." About the same time Haslam was writing his description in England, the French physician Philippe Pinel was writing about people we would describe as having schizophrenia (Pinel, 1801/1962, 1809). Some 50 years later, another physician, Benedict Morel, used the French term *démence* (loss of mind) *précoce* (early, premature) because the onset of the disorder is often during adolescence.

. . . .

schizophrenia A devastating psychotic disorder that may involve characteristic disturbances in thinking (**delusions**), perception (**hallucinations**), speech, **emotions**, and behavior.

Toward the end of the 19th century, the German psychiatrist Emil Kraepelin (1899) built on the writings of Haslam, Pinel, and Morel (among others) to give us what stands today as the most enduring description and categorization of schizophrenia. Two of Kraepelin's accomplishments are especially important. First, he combined several symptoms of insanity that had usually been viewed as reflecting separate and distinct disorders: **catatonia** (alternating immobility and excited agitation), **hebephrenia** (silly and immature emotionality), and **paranoia** (delusions of grandeur or persecution). Kraepelin thought these symptoms shared similar underlying features and included them under the Latin term **dementia praecox**.

In a second important contribution, Kraepelin (1898) distinguished dementia praecox from manic-depressive illness (now called bipolar disorder). For people with dementia praecox, an early age of onset and a poor outcome were characteristic; in contrast, these patterns were not essential to manic depression (Lewis, Escalona, & Keith, 2009). Kraepelin also noted the numerous symptoms in people with dementia praecox, including hallucinations, delusions, negativism, and stereotyped behavior.

A second major figure in the history of schizophrenia was Kraepelin's contemporary, Eugen Bleuler (1908), a Swiss psychiatrist who introduced the term *schizophrenia* (Berrios, 2011; Fusar-Poli & Politi, 2008). The label was significant because it signaled Bleuler's departure from Kraepelin on what he thought was the core problem. *Schizophrenia*, which comes from the combination of the Greek words for "split" *(skhizein)* and "mind" *(phren)*, reflected Bleuler's belief that underlying all the unusual behaviors shown by people with this disorder was an **associative splitting** of the basic functions of personality. This concept emphasized the "breaking of associative threads," or the destruction of the forces that connect one function to the next. Furthermore, Bleuler believed that a difficulty keeping a consistent train of thought characteristic of all people with this disorder led to the many and diverse symptoms they displayed. Whereas Kraepelin focused on early onset and poor outcomes, Bleuler highlighted what he believed to be the universal underlying problem. Unfortunately, the concept of "split mind" inspired the common but incorrect use of the term *schizophrenia* to mean split or multiple personality.

Identifying Symptoms

As you read about different disorders in this book, you have learned that a particular behavior, way of thinking, or emotion usually defines or is characteristic of each disorder. For example, depression always includes feelings of sadness, and panic disorder is always accompanied by intense feelings of anxiety. Surprisingly, this isn't the case for schizophrenia. Schizophrenia is a number of behaviors or symptoms that aren't necessarily shared by all people who are given this diagnosis.

Despite these complexities, researchers have identified clusters of symptoms that make up the disorder of schizophrenia. Later we describe these dramatic symptoms, such as seeing or hearing things that others do not (*hallucinations*) or having beliefs that are unrealistic, bizarre, and not shared by others in the same culture (*delusions*). But first, consider the following case of an individual who had an intense but relatively rare short-term episode of psychotic behavior.

Arthur... • *Saving the Children*

We first met 22-year-old Arthur at an outpatient clinic in a psychiatric hospital. Arthur's family was extremely concerned and upset by his unusual behavior and was desperately seeking help for him. They said that he was "sick" and "talking like a crazy man," and they were afraid he might harm himself.

Arthur had a normal childhood in a middle-class suburban neighborhood. His parents had been happily married until his father's death several years earlier. Arthur was an average student throughout school and had completed an associate's degree in junior college. His family seemed to think he regretted not continuing on to receive a bachelor's degree. Arthur had worked in a series of temporary jobs, and his mother reported that he seemed satisfied with what he was doing. He lived and worked in a major city, some 15 minutes from his mother and his married brother and sister.

Arthur's family said that about three weeks before he came to the clinic, he had started speaking strangely. He had been laid off from his job a few days before because of cutbacks and hadn't communicated with any of his family members for several days. When they next spoke with him, his behavior startled them. Although he had always been idealistic and anxious to help other people, he now talked about saving all the starving children in the world with his "secret plan." At first, his family assumed this was just an example of Arthur's sarcastic wit, but his demeanor changed to one of extreme concern and he spoke non-stop about his plans. He began carrying several spiral notebooks that he claimed contained his scheme for helping starving children; he said he would reveal it only at the right time to the right person. Suspecting that Arthur might be taking drugs, which could explain the sudden and dramatic change in his behavior, his family searched his apartment. Although they didn't find any evidence of drug use, they did find his checkbook and noticed a number of strange entries. Over the past several weeks, Arthur's handwriting had deteriorated, and he had written notes instead of the usual check information ("Start to begin now"; "This is important!"; "They must be saved"). He had also made unusual notes in several of his most prized books, a particularly alarming development given his reverence for these books.

As the days went on, Arthur showed dramatic changes in emotion, often crying and acting apprehensively. He stopped wearing socks and underwear and, despite the extremely cold weather, wouldn't wear a jacket when he went outdoors. At the family's insistence, he moved into his mother's apartment. He slept little, and kept the family up until the early morning. His mother said it was like being in a living nightmare. Each morning she would wake up with a knot in her stomach, not wanting to get out of bed because she felt so helpless to do anything to rescue Arthur from his obvious distress.

The family's sense of alarm grew as Arthur revealed more details of his plan. He said that he was going to the German embassy because that was the only place people would listen to him. He would climb the fence at night when everyone was asleep and present his plan to the German ambassador. Fearing that Arthur would be hurt trying to enter the embassy grounds, his family contacted a local psychiatric hospital, described Arthur's condition, and asked that he be admitted. Much to their surprise and disappointment, they were told that Arthur could commit himself but that they couldn't bring him in involuntarily unless he was in danger of doing harm to himself or others.

His family finally talked Arthur into meeting the staff at the outpatient clinic. In our interview, it was clear he was delusional, firmly believing in his ability to help all starving children. After some cajoling, I finally convinced him to let me see his books. He had written random thoughts (for example, "The poor, starving souls"; "The moon is the only place") and made drawings of rocket ships. Parts of his plan involved building a rocket ship that would go to the moon, where he would create a community for all malnourished children, a place where they could live and be helped. After a few brief comments on his plan, I began to ask him about his health.

"You look tired; are you getting enough sleep?"

"Sleep isn't really needed," he noted. "My plans will take me through, and then they can all rest."

"Your family is worried about you," I said. "Do you understand their concern?"

"It's important for all concerned to get together, to join together," he replied.

With that, he got up and walked out of the room and out of the building, after telling his family that he would be right back. After five minutes they went to look for him, but he had disappeared. He was missing for two days, which caused his family a great deal of concern about his health and safety. In an almost miraculous sequence of events, they found him walking the streets of the city. He acted as if nothing had happened. Gone were his notebooks and the talk of his secret plan.

We will never know exactly what happened to Arthur to make him behave so bizarrely and then recover so quickly and completely. Research that we discuss next may shed some light on schizophrenia and potentially help other Arthurs and their families.

Clinical Description, Symptoms, and Subtypes

▶ What are the distinctions among positive, negative, and disorganized symptoms of schizophrenia?
▶ What are the clinical characteristics of schizophrenia and other psychotic disorders?

The case of Arthur shows the range of problems experienced by people with schizophrenia or other psychotic disorders. The term **psychotic behavior** has been used to characterize many unusual behaviors, although in its strictest sense, it usually involves delusions (irrational beliefs) and/or hallucinations (sensory experiences in the absence of external events). Schizophrenia is one of the disorders that involve psychotic behavior; we describe others in more detail later.

Schizophrenia can affect all the functions we rely on each day. Before we describe the symptoms, it is important to look carefully at the specific characteristics of people who exhibit these behaviors, partly because we constantly see distorted images of people with schizophrenia. Evidence

catatonia A disorder of movement involving immobility or excited agitation.

hebephrenia A silly and immature emotionality, a characteristic of some types of **schizophrenia**.

paranoia People's irrational beliefs that they are especially important (**delusions of grandeur**) or that other people are seeking to do them harm.

dementia praecox The Latin term meaning premature loss of mind; an early label for what is now called **schizophrenia**, emphasizing the disorder's frequent appearance during adolescence.

associative splitting A separation among basic functions of human personality (for example, cognition, **emotion**, and perception) seen by some as the defining characteristic of **schizophrenia**.

psychotic behavior A severe **psychological disorder** category characterized by **hallucinations** and loss of contact with reality.

for violence among people with schizophrenia suggests that although they may be more likely to commit violent acts than the general population, traits such as anger and antisocial personality are better predictors of violence than psychosis (Skeem, Kennealy, Monahan, Peterson, & Appelbaum, 2016). Despite this information, the majority of characters with schizophrenia in English language movies between 1990 and 2010 were portrayed as violent, with more than one-third depicted as murderers and one-fourth as suicidal (Owen, 2012).

Schizophrenia spectrum disorder constitutes the group of diagnoses we cover in this chapter. Previous editions of the *DSM* struggled with this concept in its varied presentations over the years, and, as we describe in this chapter, *DSM-5* currently includes schizophrenia as well as other related psychotic disorders that fall under this heading (including schizophreniform, schizoaffective, delusional, and brief psychotic disorders). In addition, a personality disorder (schizotypal personality disorder, discussed in Chapter 11) is also considered to be included under this umbrella category of schizophrenia spectrum disorders. All of these difficulties seem to share features of extreme reality distortion (for example, hallucinations and delusions).

Mental health workers typically distinguish between *positive* and *negative symptoms* of schizophrenia. A third dimension, *disorganized symptoms*, also appears to be an important aspect of the disorder (Liddle, 2012). Positive symptoms generally refer to symptoms around distorted reality. Negative symptoms involve deficits in normal behavior in such areas as speech, blunted affect (or lack of emotional reactivity), and motivation (Foussias *et al.*, 2014). Disorganized symptoms include rambling speech, erratic behavior, and inappropriate affect (for example, smiling when you are upset). A diagnosis of schizophrenia requires that two or more positive, negative, and/or disorganized symptoms be present for at least one month, with at least one of these symptoms including delusions, hallucinations, or disorganized speech. *DSM-5* also includes a dimensional assessment that rates the severity of the individual's symptoms on a 0 to 4 scale with 0 indicating a symptom is not present, 1 indicating equivocal evidence (i.e., not sure), 2 indicating it is present but mild, 3 that it is present and moderate, and 4 that it is present and severe (American Psychiatric Association, 2013). A great deal of research has focused on the different symptoms of schizophrenia, each of which is described here in some detail.

Positive Symptoms

The **positive symptoms** of schizophrenia are the more obvious signs of psychosis, including delusions and hallucinations. Between 50% and 70% of people with schizophrenia experience hallucinations, delusions, or both (Lindenmayer & Khan, 2006).

Delusions

A belief that would be seen by most members of a society as a misrepresentation of reality is called a *disorder of thought content,* or a **delusion**. Because of its importance in schizophrenia, delusion has been called "the basic characteristic of madness" (Jaspers, 1963, p. 93). If, for example, you believe that squirrels are aliens sent to Earth on a reconnaissance mission, you would be considered delusional. The media often portray people with schizophrenia as believing they are famous or important people (such as Napoleon or Jesus Christ), although this is only one type of delusion. Arthur's belief that he could end starvation for all the world's children is also a *delusion of grandeur* (a mistaken belief that the person is famous or powerful) (Knowles, McCarthy-Jones, & Rowse, 2011).

A common delusion in people with schizophrenia is that others are "out to get them." Called *delusions of persecution,* these beliefs can be most disturbing. Other more unusual delusions include Capgras syndrome, in which the person believes someone he or she knows has been replaced by a double, and Cotard's syndrome, in which the person believes he or she is dead (Debruyne & Audenaert, 2012; Salvatore *et al.*, 2014). Why would someone come to believe such obviously improbable things? A number of theories exist and can be summarized into two themes—motivational or deficit theories (McKay, Langdon, & Coltheart, 2007). A *motivational view of delusions* would look at these beliefs as attempts to deal with and relieve anxiety and stress. A person develops "stories" around some issue—for example, a famous person is in love with her (erotomania)—that helps the person make sense of uncontrollable anxieties in a tumultuous world. Preoccupation with the delusion distracts the individual from the upsetting aspects of the world, such as hallucinations. In contrast, a *deficit view of delusion* sees these beliefs as resulting from brain dysfunction that creates these disordered cognitions or perceptions. Much work remains to develop an integrative account for these debilitating symptoms of schizophrenia (Howes & Murray, 2014).

Hallucinations

Have you ever thought you heard someone call your name, only to discover that no one was there? Did you ever think you saw something move by you, yet nothing did? We all have fleeting moments when we think we see or hear something that isn't there. For many people with schizophrenia, however, these perceptions are real and occur regularly. The experience of sensory events without any input from the surrounding environment is called a **hallucination**. The case of David illustrates the phenomena of hallucinations, as well as other disorders of thought that are common among people with schizophrenia.

David... • *Missing Uncle Bill*

David was 25-years-old when I met him; he had been living in a psychiatric hospital for about three years. He was a little overweight and of average height; he typically dressed in a T-shirt and jeans and tended to be active. I first encountered him while I was talking to another man who lived on the same floor. David interrupted us by pulling on my shoulder. "My Uncle Bill is a good man. He treats me well." Not wanting to be impolite, I said, "I'm sure he is. Maybe after I've finished talking to Michael here, we can talk about your uncle." David persisted, "He can kill fish with a knife. Things can get awfully sharp in your mind, when you go down the river. I could kill you with my bare hands—taking things into my own hands. . . . I know you know!" He was now speaking quickly and had gained emotionality, along with speed, as he spoke. I talked to him quietly until he calmed down for the moment; later, I looked into David's file for some information about his background.

David was brought up on a farm by his Aunt Katie and Uncle Bill. His father's identity is unknown and his mother, who had mental retardation, couldn't care for him. David, too, was diagnosed as having mental retardation, although his functioning was only mildly impaired, and he attended school. The year David's Uncle Bill died, his high school teachers first reported unusual behavior. David occasionally talked to his deceased Uncle Bill in class. Later, he became increasingly agitated and verbally aggressive toward others and was diagnosed as having schizophrenia. He managed to graduate from high school but never obtained a job after that; he lived at home with his aunt for several years. Although his aunt sincerely wanted him to stay with her, his threatening behavior escalated to the point that she requested he be seen at the local psychiatric hospital.

I spoke with David again and had a chance to ask him a few questions. "Why are you here in the hospital, David?" "I really don't want to be here," he told me. "I've got other things to do. The time is right, and you know, when opportunity knocks." He continued for a few minutes until I interrupted him. "I was sorry to hear that your Uncle Bill died a few years ago. How are you feeling about him these days?" "Yes, he died. He was sick and now he's gone. He likes to fish with me, down at the river. He's going to take me hunting. I have guns. I can shoot you, and you'd be dead in a minute."

David's conversational speech resembled a ball rolling down a rocky hill. Like an accelerating object, his speech gained momentum the longer he went on and, as if bouncing off obstacles, the topics almost always went in unpredictable directions. If he continued for too long, he often became agitated and spoke of harming others. David also told me that his uncle's voice spoke to him repeatedly. He heard other voices also, but he couldn't identify them or tell me what they said. We return to David's case later in this chapter when we discuss causes and treatments.

Hallucinations can involve any of the senses, although hearing things that aren't there, or *auditory hallucination*, is the most common form experienced by people with schizophrenia, with 70% of those with the diagnosis endorsing this type (Liddle, 2012; Waters *et al.*, 2012). David had frequent auditory hallucinations, usually of his uncle's voice. When David heard a voice that belonged to his Uncle Bill, he often couldn't understand what his uncle was saying;

positive symptoms A more overt symptom, such as a **delusion** or **hallucination**, displayed by some people with **schizophrenia**.

delusion A psychotic symptom involving disorder of thought content and presence of strong beliefs that are misrepresentations of reality.

hallucination A psychotic symptom of perceptual disturbance in which something is seen, heard, or otherwise sensed although it is not actually present.

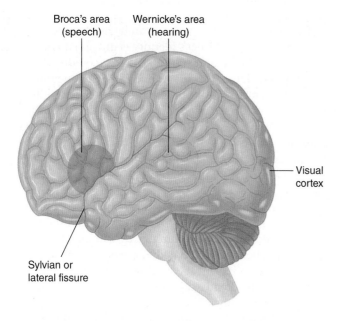

Broca's area (speech)   Wernicke's area (hearing)

Visual cortex

Sylvian or lateral fissure

● **Figure 12.1** Major areas of functioning of the cerebral cortex. In most people, only the left hemisphere is specialized for language.

on other occasions, the voice was clearer. "He told me to turn off the TV. He said, 'It's too damn loud, turn it down, turn it down.'" This is consistent with recent views of hallucinations as being related to metacognition or "thinking about thinking." In other words, metacognition is a phrase to describe examining your own thoughts. Most of us have had an occasional intrusive thought that we try not to focus on (for example, thinking, "I wish she were dead!" when you know that's not appropriate). People who experience hallucinations appear to have intrusive thoughts, but they believe they are coming from somewhere or someone else. They then worry about having these thoughts and engage in meta-worry—or worrying about worrying. Unfortunately, meta-worry has been linked to increased anxiety and depression symptoms for those suffering from hallucinations (Oosterhout, Krabbendam, Smeets, & Gaag, 2013).

Exciting research on hallucinations uses sophisticated brain-imaging techniques to try to localize these phenomena in the brain. In one of the first studies of its kind, researchers in London used single photon emission computed tomography (SPECT) to study the cerebral blood flow of men with schizophrenia who also had auditory verbal hallucinations and made a surprising discovery (McGuire, Shah, & Murray, 1993): the part of the brain most active during hallucinations was Broca's area (see ● Figure 12.1). This is surprising because Broca's

area is known to be involved in speech *production*, rather than language *comprehension*. Because auditory verbal hallucinations usually involve understanding the "speech" of others, you might expect more activity in Wernicke's area, which involves language comprehension. These observations support the metacognition theory that people who are hallucinating are *not* hearing the voices of others but are listening to their own thoughts or their own voices and cannot recognize the difference (Allen & Modinos, 2012). One possible explanation for this problem is referred to as poor "emotional prosody comprehension." Prosody is that aspect of our spoken language that communicates meaning and emotion through our pitch, amplitude, pauses, etc. We can often tell when a person is asking a question, for example, not just by the words themselves but also by the way it is said (e.g., "Hungry?"). Research suggests that emotional prosody is deficient in persons with auditory verbal hallucinations, contributing to the confusion both with others as well as when interpreting "inner voices" (Alba-Ferrara, Fernyhough, Weis, Mitchell, & Hausmann, 2012).

Negative Symptoms

In contrast to the active presentations that characterize the positive symptoms of schizophrenia, the **negative symptoms** usually indicate the absence or insufficiency of normal behavior. They include apathy, poverty of

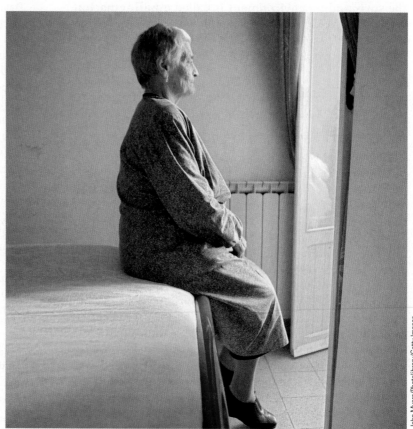

John Myers/Photolibrary/Getty Images

▲ Negative symptoms of schizophrenia include social withdrawal and apathy.

(i.e., limited) thought or speech, and emotional and social withdrawal, and approximately 25% of people with schizophrenia display these symptoms (Cohen, Natarajan, Araujo, & Solanki, 2013; Millan, Fone, Steckler, & Horan, 2014).

Avolition

Avolition is the inability to initiate and persist in activities. People with this symptom (also referred to as *apathy*) show little interest in performing even the most basic day-to-day functions, including those associated with personal hygiene.

Alogia

Alogia refers to the relative absence of speech. A person with alogia may respond to questions with brief replies that have little content and may appear uninterested in the conversation. Such deficiency in communication is believed to reflect a negative thought disorder rather than inadequate communication skills. Some researchers, for example, suggest that people with alogia may have trouble finding the right words to formulate their thoughts (Andreasen, 2012). Sometimes alogia takes the form of delayed comments or slow responses to questions. Talking with individuals who manifest this symptom can be extremely frustrating, making you feel as if you are "pulling teeth" to get them to respond.

Anhedonia

A related symptom is called **anhedonia**, the presumed lack of pleasure experienced by some people with schizophrenia. Like some mood disorders, anhedonia signals an indifference to activities that would typically be considered pleasurable, including eating, social interactions, and sexual relations.

Asociality

This symptom may seem similar to avolition or related to anhedonia. However, asociality has been recognized as a separate symptom of schizophrenia spectrum disorders. This symptom captures a lack of interest in social interactions (APA, 2013). Unfortunately, this symptom can also result from or be worsened by limited opportunities to interact with others, particularly for severely ill patients (Reddy, Horan, & Green, 2016).

Affective Flattening

Imagine that people wore masks at all times: You could communicate with them verbally, but you wouldn't be able to see their emotional reactions. Approximately one-quarter of the people with schizophrenia exhibit what is called **flat affect** (Lewis *et al.*, 2009; Simonsen *et al.*, 2012). They are similar to people wearing masks because they do not show emotions when you would normally expect them to. They may stare at you vacantly, speak in a flat and toneless manner, and seem unaffected by things going on around them. However, although they do not react openly to emotional situations, they may be responding on the inside.

Howard Berenbaum and Thomas Oltmanns (1992) compared people with schizophrenia who had flat (or "blunted") affect with those who did not. The two groups were shown clips from comedies and dramas selected to create emotional reactions in the viewer. Berenbaum and Oltmanns found that the people with flat affect showed little change in facial expression, although they reported experiencing the appropriate emotions. The authors concluded that the flat affect in schizophrenia may represent difficulty expressing emotion, not a lack of feeling. Researchers can now use computer analyses of facial expressions to more objectively assess the emotional expressiveness of people with disorders such as schizophrenia (Kring & Elis, 2013). One such study confirmed the difficulty of people with this disorder to express themselves properly with facial expressions (Hamm, Pinkham, Gur, Verma, & Kohler, 2014).

The expression of affect—or the lack of this expression—may be an important symptom of the development of schizophrenia. In a particularly innovative study, researchers videotaped high-risk children (those with one or more parents who had schizophrenia) eating lunch in 1972 and followed them up almost 20 years later (Schiffman *et al.*, 2004). The researchers were able to show that children who later went on to develop schizophrenia typically displayed less positive and more negative affect than those children who did not develop the disorder. This suggests that emotional expression may be one way to identify potential schizophrenia in children.

Disorganized Symptoms

Perhaps the least studied and therefore the least understood symptoms of schizophrenia are referred to as the "disorganized symptoms." These include a variety of erratic behaviors that affect speech, motor behavior, and emotional reactions. The prevalence of these behaviors among those with schizophrenia is unclear.

negative symptoms A less outgoing symptom, such as **flat affect** or poverty of speech, displayed by some people with **schizophrenia**.

avolition An inability to initiate or persist in important activities. Also known as *apathy*.

alogia A deficiency in the amount or content of speech, a disturbance often seen in people with **schizophrenia**.

anhedonia An inability to experience pleasure, associated with some **mood** and schizophrenic disorders.

flat affect An apparently emotionless demeanor (including toneless speech and vacant gaze) when a reaction would be expected.

Disorganized Speech

A conversation with someone who has schizophrenia can be particularly frustrating. If you want to understand what is bothering or upsetting this person, eliciting relevant information is especially difficult. For one thing, people with schizophrenia often lack *insight,* an awareness that they have a problem. In addition, they experience what Bleuler called "associative splitting" and what researcher Paul Meehl called "cognitive slippage" (Bleuler, 1908; Meehl, 1962). These phrases help describe the speech problems of people with schizophrenia: Sometimes they jump from topic to topic, and at other times they talk illogically. *DSM-5* uses the term **disorganized speech** to describe such communication problems. Let's go back to our conversation with David to demonstrate the symptom.

> THERAPIST: Why are you here in the hospital, David?
> DAVID: I really don't want to be here. I've got other things to do. The time is right, and you know, when opportunity knocks . . .

David didn't really answer the question he was asked. This type of response is called *tangentiality*—that is, going off on a tangent instead of answering a specific question. David also abruptly changed the topic of conversation to unrelated areas, a behavior that has variously been called *loose association* or *derailment* (Liddle, 2012).

> THERAPIST: I was sorry to hear that your Uncle Bill died a few years ago. How are you feeling about him these days?
> DAVID: Yes, he died. He was sick, and now he's gone. He likes to fish with me, down at the river. He's going to take me hunting. I have guns. I can shoot you, and you'd be dead in a minute.

Again, David didn't answer the question. It was unclear whether he didn't understand the question, couldn't focus his attention, or found it too difficult to talk about his uncle. You can see why people spend a great deal of time trying to interpret all the hidden meanings behind this type of conversation. Unfortunately, however, such analyses have yet to provide us with useful information about the nature of schizophrenia or its treatment.

Inappropriate Affect and Disorganized Behavior

Occasionally, people with schizophrenia display **inappropriate affect**, laughing or crying at improper times. Sometimes they exhibit bizarre behaviors such as hoarding objects or acting in unusual ways in public. People with schizophrenia engage in a number of other "active" behaviors that are usually viewed as unusual. For example, catatonia is one of the most curious symptoms in some individuals with schizophrenia; it involves motor dysfunctions that range

from wild agitation to immobility. *DSM-5* now includes catatonia as a separate schizophrenia spectrum disorder. On the active side of the continuum, some people pace excitedly or move their fingers or arms in stereotyped ways. At the other end of the extreme, people hold unusual postures, as if they were fearful of something terrible happening if they moved (**catatonic immobility**). This manifestation can also involve *waxy flexibility,* or the tendency to keep their bodies and limbs in the position they are put in by someone else.

Again, to receive a diagnosis of schizophrenia, a person must display two or more of the major symptoms for a significant portion of time for one month. At least one of the symptoms must include delusions, hallucinations, or disorganized speech. Depending on the combination of symptoms displayed, two people could receive the same diagnosis but behave differently, for example, one having marked hallucinations and delusions and the other displaying disorganized speech and some negative symptoms. Proper treatment depends on differentiating individuals in terms of their varying symptoms.

Historic Schizophrenia Subtypes

Three main types of schizophrenia have historically been identified: paranoid (delusions of grandeur or persecution), disorganized (or hebephrenic; silly and immature emotionality), and catatonic (alternate immobility and excited agitation). Although these categories continued to be used in *DSM-IV-TR,* they were dropped from the diagnostic criteria for *DSM-5* (American Psychiatric Association, 2013). Part of the rationale for omitting these subtypes was that they were not used frequently in clinical work, and the nature of an individual's symptoms can change over the course of his or her illness; so people could move from one category to another (Tandon *et al.*, 2013). The dimensional assessment

▲ Homeless people who suffer from schizophrenia often bear the additional burden of persecutory delusions, which interfere with outside efforts to help.

of severity is now used instead of the three schizophrenia subtypes (Pagsberg, 2013).

In the next section, we describe the disorders included under the broader heading of "Schizophrenia Spectrum and Other Psychotic Disorders."

Other Psychotic Disorders

The psychotic behaviors of some individuals do not fit neatly under the heading of schizophrenia as we have just described. Several other categories of disorders depict these significant variations. Remember that although people with related psychotic disorders display many of the characteristics of schizophrenia, these disorders differ significantly.

Schizophreniform Disorder

Some people experience the symptoms of schizophrenia for a few months only; they can usually resume normal lives. The symptoms sometimes disappear as the result of successful treatment, but they often do so for reasons unknown. The label **schizophreniform disorder** classifies these symptoms, but because relatively few studies are available on this disorder, data on important aspects of it are sparse. It appears, however, that the lifetime prevalence is approximately 0.2% (Erlich, Smith, Horwath, & Cournos, 2014). The *DSM-5* diagnostic criteria for schizophreniform disorder include onset of psychotic symptoms within four weeks of the first noticeable change in usual

---

DSM 5 — DISORDER CRITERIA SUMMARY
Schizophreniform Disorder

A. Two (or more) of the following, each present for a significant portion of time during a one-month period (or less if successfully treated). At least one of these must be (1), (2), or (3): (1) delusions, (2) hallucinations, (3) disorganized speech (e.g., frequent derailment or incoherence), (4) grossly disorganized or catatonic behavior, (5) negative symptoms.

B. An episode of the disorder lasts at least one month but less than six months.

C. Schizoaffective disorder and depressive or bipolar disorder with psychotic features have been ruled out.

D. The disturbance is not attributable to the physiological effects of a substance (e.g., a drug of abuse, a medication) or another medical condition.

Specify if:

With good prognostic features: This specifier requires the presence of at least two of the following features: onset of prominent psychotic symptoms within four weeks of the first noticeable change in usual behavior or functioning; confusion or perplexity; good premorbid social and occupational functioning; and absence of blunted or flat affect.

Without good prognostic features: This specifier is applied if two or more of the above features have not been present.

From American Psychiatric Association. (2013). *Diagnostic and statistical manual of mental disorders* (5th ed.). Washington, DC.

DSM 5 — DISORDER CRITERIA SUMMARY
Schizoaffective Disorder

A. An uninterrupted period of illness during which there is a major mood episode (major depressive or manic) concurrent with Criterion A of schizophrenia.

Note: The major depressive episode must include Criterion A1: Depressed mood.

B. Delusions or hallucinations for two or more weeks in the absence of a major mood episode (depressive or manic) during the lifetime duration of the illness.

C. Symptoms that meet criteria for a major mood episode are present for the majority of the total durance of the active and residual portions of the illness.

D. The disturbance is not attributable to the effects of a substance (e.g., a drug of abuse, a medication) or another medical condition.

From American Psychiatric Association. (2013). *Diagnostic and statistical manual of mental disorders* (5th ed.). Washington, DC.

---

behavior, confusion at the height of the psychotic episode, good *premorbid* (before the psychotic episode) social and occupational functioning, and the absence of blunted or flat affect (Garrabe & Cousin, 2012).

Schizoaffective Disorder

Historically, people who had symptoms of schizophrenia and who exhibited the characteristics of mood disorders (for example, depression or bipolar disorder) were lumped in the category of schizophrenia. Now, however, this mixed bag of problems is diagnosed as **schizoaffective disorder** (Tsuang, Stone, & Faraone, 2012). The prognosis is similar to the prognosis for people with schizophrenia—that is, individuals tend not to get better on their own and are likely to continue experiencing major life difficulties for many years. *DSM-5* criteria for schizoaffective disorder require, in addition to the presence of a mood disorder, delusions or hallucinations for at least two weeks in the absence of prominent mood symptoms (American Psychiatric Association, 2013).

....

disorganized speech A style of talking often seen in people with **schizophrenia**, involving incoherence and a lack of typical logic patterns.

inappropriate affect An emotional display that is improper for the situation.

catatonic immobility A disturbance of motor behavior in which the person remains motionless, sometimes in an awkward posture, for extended periods.

schizophreniform disorder A psychotic disorder involving the symptoms of **schizophrenia** but lasting less than 6 months.

flat affect An apparently emotionless demeanor (including toneless speech and vacant gaze) when a reaction would be expected.

schizoaffective disorder A psychotic disorder featuring symptoms of both **schizophrenia** and major **mood disorder**.

Delusional Disorder

Delusions are beliefs that are not generally held by other members of a society. The major feature of **delusional disorder** is a persistent belief that is contrary to reality, in the absence of other characteristics of schizophrenia. For example, a woman who believes without any evidence that co-workers are tormenting her by putting poison in her food may have a delusional disorder. This disorder is characterized by a persistent delusion that is not the result of an organic factor such as brain seizures or of any severe psychosis. Individuals with delusional disorder tend not to have flat affect, anhedonia, or other negative symptoms of schizophrenia; importantly, however, they may become socially isolated because they are suspicious of others. The delusions are often long-standing, sometimes persisting over several years (Munro, 2012).

DSM-5 recognizes the following delusional subtypes: erotomanic, grandiose, jealous, persecutory, and somatic.

DSM 5 DISORDER CRITERIA SUMMARY
Delusional Disorder

A. The presence of one (or more) delusions with a duration of one month or longer.

B. Criterion A for schizophrenia has never been met.

C. Apart from the impact of the delusion(s) or its ramifications, functioning is not markedly impaired, and behavior is not obviously bizarre or odd.

D. If manic or major depressive episodes have occurred, these have been brief relative to the duration of the delusional periods.

E. The disturbance is not attributable to the physiological effects of a substance or another medical condition and is not better explained by another mental disorder.

Specify whether:

Erotomanic type: delusion that another person is in love with the individual.

Grandiose type: delusion of having some great (but unrecognized) talent or insight or having made some important discovery.

Jealous type: delusion that the individual's spouse or lover is unfaithful.

Persecutory type: delusions that the individual is being conspired against, cheated, spied on, followed, poisoned or drugged, maliciously maligned, harassed, or obstructed in the pursuit of long-term goals.

Somatic type: delusions that involve bodily functions or sensations.

Mixed type: no delusional theme predominates.

Unspecified type: delusional belief cannot be clearly determined or is not described in the specific types (e.g., referential delusions without a prominent persecutory or grandiose component).

From American Psychiatric Association. (2013). *Diagnostic and statistical manual of mental disorders* (5th ed.). Washington, DC.

An *erotomanic type* of delusion is the irrational belief that one is loved by another person, usually of higher status. Some individuals who stalk celebrities appear to have erotomanic delusional disorder. The *grandiose type* of delusion involves believing in one's inflated worth, power, knowledge, identity, or special relationship to a deity or famous person (Knowles *et al.*, 2011). A person with the *jealous type* of delusion believes the sexual partner is unfaithful. The *persecutory type* of delusion involves believing oneself (or someone close) is being malevolently treated in some way. Finally, with the *somatic delusions* the person feels afflicted by a physical defect or general medical condition. Typically these delusions differ from the more bizarre types often found in people with schizophrenia because in delusional disorder *the imagined events could be happening but aren't* (for example, mistakenly believing you are being followed); in schizophrenia, however, delusions tend to fall in the bizarre category (for example, believing your brain waves broadcast your thoughts to other people around the world). *DSM-5* allows for one bizarre delusion in delusional disorder, which separates it from a diagnosis of schizophrenia, which requires more than one delusion to be present (Heckers *et al.*, 2013).

Previous versions of *DSM* included a separate delusional disorder—**shared psychotic disorder (folie à deux)**, the condition in which an individual develops delusions simply as a result of a close relationship with a delusional individual. The content and nature of the delusion originate with the partner and can range from the relatively bizarre, such as believing enemies are sending harmful gamma rays through your house, to the fairly ordinary, such as believing you are about to receive a major promotion despite evidence to the contrary. *DSM-5* now includes this type of delusion under delusional disorder with a specifier to indicate if the delusion is shared (American Psychiatric Association, 2013).

Delusional disorder seems to be relatively rare, affecting 24 to 60 people out of every 100,000 in the general population (de Portugal, González, Haro, Autonell, & Cervilla, 2008; Ibanez-Casas & Cervilla, 2012). Among those people with psychotic disorders in general, between 2% and 8% are thought to have delusional disorder (Vahia & Cohen, 2009; Blaney, 2015). Researchers can't be confident about the percentages because they know that many of these individuals have no contact with the mental health system.

The onset of delusional disorder is relatively late: The average age of first admission to a psychiatric facility is between 35 and 55 (Ibanez-Casas & Cervilla, 2012). Because many people with this disorder can lead relatively typical lives, they may not seek treatment until their symptoms become most disruptive. Delusional disorder seems to afflict more females than males (55% and 45%, respectively, of the affected population).

In a longitudinal study, Opjordsmoen (1989) followed 53 people with delusional disorder for an average of 30 years and found they tended to fare better in life than people with schizophrenia but not as well as those with some other psychotic disorders, such as schizoaffective disorder. About

80% of the 53 individuals had been married at some time, and half were employed, which demonstrates an ability to function relatively well despite delusions.

There is much conflicting evidence about either the biological or the psychosocial influences on delusional disorder (Ibanez-Casas & Cervilla, 2012). Research on families suggests that the characteristics of suspiciousness, jealousy, and secretiveness may occur more often among the relatives of people with delusional disorder than among the population at large, suggesting some aspect of this disorder may be inherited (Kendler & Walsh, 2007).

A number of other disorders can cause delusions, and their presence should be ruled out before diagnosing delusional disorder. For example, abuse of amphetamines, alcohol, and cocaine can cause delusions, as can brain tumors, Huntington's disease, and Alzheimer's disease (Blaney, 2015). *DSM-5* includes two categories of these disorders: **substance-induced psychotic disorder** and **psychotic disorder associated with another medical condition**—so that clinicians can qualify the nature of these difficulties.

Brief Psychotic Disorder

Recall the puzzling case of Arthur, who suddenly experienced the delusion that he could save the world and whose intense emotional swings lasted for only a few days. He

---

DSM 5 — DISORDER CRITERIA SUMMARY
Substance/Medication-Induced Psychotic Disorder

A. Presence of one or both of the following symptoms: (1) Delusions. (2) Hallucinations

B. There is evidence from the history, physical examination, or laboratory findings of both (1) and (2): (1) The symptoms in Criterion A developed during, or soon after substance intoxication or withdrawal or after exposure to a medication. (2) The involved substance/medication is capable of producing the symptoms in Criterion A.

C. The disturbance is not better explained by a psychotic disorder that is not substance/medication-induced.

   1. The symptoms preceded the onset of substance/ medication use; the symptoms persist for a substantial period of time (e.g., about one month) after the cessation of acute withdrawal or severe intoxication; or there is other evidence of an independent non-substance/medication-induced psychotic disorder (e.g., a history of recurrent non-substance/medication-related episodes).

D. The disturbance does not occur exclusively during the course of a delirium.

E. The disturbance causes clinically significant distress or impairment in social, occupational, or other important areas of functioning.

From American Psychiatric Association. (2013). *Diagnostic and statistical manual of mental disorders* (5th ed.). Washington, DC.

DSM 5 — DSM DISORDER CRITERIA SUMMARY
Psychotic Disorder Associated with Another Medical Condition

A. Prominent hallucinations or delusions.

B. There is evidence from the history, physical examination, or laboratory findings that the disturbance is the direct pathophysiological consequence of another medical condition.

C. The disturbance is not better explained by another mental disorder.

D. The disturbance does not occur exclusively during the course of a delirium.

From American Psychiatric Association. (2013). *Diagnostic and statistical manual of mental disorders* (5th ed.). Washington, DC.

---

would receive the *DSM-5* diagnosis of **brief psychotic disorder**, which is characterized by the presence of one or more positive symptoms such as delusions, hallucinations, or disorganized speech or behavior lasting one month or less. Individuals like Arthur regain their previous ability to function well in day-to-day activities. Brief psychotic disorder is often precipitated by extremely stressful situations.

Attenuated Psychosis Syndrome

Some individuals who start to develop psychotic symptoms such as hallucinations or delusions are often sufficiently distressed to seek help from mental health professionals. They can be at high risk for developing schizophrenia and may be at an early stage of the disorder (called prodromal). Although they may not meet the full criteria for schizophrenia, they may be good candidates for early intervention in an effort to prevent symptoms from worsening. To focus attention on these individuals, *DSM-5* is proposing a potentially new psychotic disorder for further study—**attenuated psychosis syndrome** (Fusar-Poli, Carpenter, Woods, & McGlashan, 2014).

shared psychotic disorder (folie à deux) A psychotic disturbance in which individuals develop a **delusion** similar to that of a person with whom they share a close relationship. Also known as *folie à deux*.

substance-induced psychotic disorder Psychosis caused by the ingestion of medications, psychoactive drugs, or toxins.

psychotic disorder associated with another medical condition Condition that is characterized by hallucinations or delusions and that is the direct result of another physiological disorder, such as stroke or brain tumor.

brief psychotic disorder A psychotic disturbance involving **delusions**, **hallucinations**, or **disorganized speech** or behavior but lasting less than 1 month; often occurs in reaction to a stressor.

attenuated psychosis syndrome Disorder involving the onset of psychotic symptoms such as hallucinations and delusions, which puts a person at high risk for schizophrenia; designated for further study by *DSM-5*.

DSM DISORDER CRITERIA SUMMARY
Brief Psychotic Disorder

A. Presence of one (or more) of the following symptoms. At least one of these must be (1), (2), or (3): (1) delusions, (2) hallucinations, (3) disorganized speech (e.g., frequent derailment or incoherence), (4) grossly disorganized or catatonic behavior.

Note: Do not include a symptom if it is a culturally sanctioned response

B. Duration of an episode of the disturbance is at least one day but less than one month, with eventual full return to premorbid level of functioning.

C. The disturbance is not better explained by major depressive or bipolar disorder with psychotic features or another psychotic disorder such as schizophrenia or catatonia, and is not attributable to the effects of a substance (e.g., a drug of abuse, a medication) or another medical condition.

From American Psychiatric Association. (2013). *Diagnostic and statistical manual of mental disorders* (5th ed.). Washington, DC.

12.1 Concept CHECK

Part A

Determine which symptoms or types of schizophrenia spectrum disorders are described in each scenario.

1. Jane has spent the past half hour staring in the mirror. As you approach her, she turns away and giggles. When you ask what she's laughing at, she answers, but you're having difficulty understanding what she says. _____

2. Drew has experienced hallucinations and bizarre delusions for the past four months. _____

3. Greg's cognitive skills and affect are relatively intact. He, however, often has delusions and hallucinations that convince him enemies are out to persecute him. _____

4. Alice usually holds an unusual posture and is sometimes seen grimacing. _____

5. Cameron has started to hear voices, and this is very disturbing to him. He told his parents and recognizes that he needs to see a mental health professional for help. _____

Part B

Diagnose the type of psychotic disorders described in each of the following. Choose from (a) schizophreniform disorder, (b) schizoaffective disorder, and (c) delusional disorder.

6. Lately Dom has become more isolated because he believes his co-workers are conspiring to get him fired. He becomes agitated whenever he sees a group of employees talking and laughing, because he believes that they are plotting against him. _____

7. Natalie reveals to her therapist that she hears numerous voices talking to her and giving her orders. Her doctor has just sent her to this therapist for what he believes to be a major depressive episode. She had begun to sleep all the time and contemplated suicide often. _____

8. If Shawn's schizophrenic symptoms disappeared after about four months and he returned to his normal life, what diagnosis might he have received? _____

Prevalence and Causes of Schizophrenia

▶ What are the potential genetic, neurobiological, developmental, and psychosocial risk factors for schizophrenia?

To uncover the causes of schizophrenia, researchers look in several areas: (1) the possible genes involved in schizophrenia, (2) the chemical action of the drugs that help many people with this disorder, (3) abnormalities in the working of the brains of people with schizophrenia, and (4) environmental risk factors that may precipitate the onset of the symptoms (Harrison, 2012; Murray & Castle, 2012). We now examine the nature of schizophrenia and learn how researchers have attempted to understand and treat people who have it.

Statistics

Worldwide, the lifetime prevalence rate of schizophrenia is roughly equivalent for men and women, and it is estimated to be 0.2% to 1.5% in the general population, which means the disorder will affect about 1% of the population at some point (Erlich *et al.*, 2014). Life expectancy is slightly less than average, partly because of the higher rate of suicide and accidents among people with schizophrenia. Although there is some disagreement about the distribution of schizophrenia between men and women, the difference between the sexes in age of onset is clear. For men, the likelihood of onset diminishes with age, but it can still first occur after the age of 75. The frequency of onset for women is lower than for men until age 36, when the relative risk for onset switches, with more women than men being affected later in life (Jablensky, 2012). Women appear to have more favorable outcomes than do men.

Development

The more severe symptoms of schizophrenia first occur in late adolescence or early adulthood, although we saw that there may be signs of the development of the disorder in early childhood (Murray & Castle, 2012). Children who go on to develop schizophrenia show early clinical features such as mild physical abnormalities, poor motor coordination, and mild cognitive and social problems (Golembo-Smith et al., 2012; Matheson et al., 2013). Unfortunately, these types of early problems are not specific enough to schizophrenia—meaning they could also be signs of other problems—to be able to say for sure that a particular child will later develop schizophrenia.

Up to 85% of people who later develop schizophrenia go through a **prodromal stage**—a one- to two-year period before the serious symptoms occur but when less severe yet unusual behaviors start to show themselves (Jablensky, 2012). These behaviors include ideas of reference (thinking insignificant events relate directly to them), magical thinking (believing they have special abilities such as being clairvoyant or telepathic), and illusions (such as feeling the presence of another person when they are alone). In addition, other symptoms are common, such as isolation, marked impairment in functioning, and a lack of initiative, interests, or energy (Addington et al., 2015).

Once symptoms begin to appear, it can take from two years to around 10 years before a person at high risk (e.g., has mild positive symptoms) meets full criteria for a psychotic disorder (Nelson et al., 2013). The highest period of risk for patients to develop a full-fledged psychotic disorder is during the first two years following their first displays of mild symptoms. Risk factors for going from high risk to developing the disorder include the length of duration of symptoms before seeking help, baseline functioning, as well as the presence of negative symptoms and disorganized symptoms (Addington et al., 2015, Nelson et al., 2013). Part of the delay in seeking help may be the result of hiding symptoms from others (sometimes because of increasing paranoia). Personality factors and the amount and quality of social support may also

play a role in the amount of time it takes a person to first seek treatment (Ruiz-Veguilla et al., 2012). Once treated, patients will often improve. Unfortunately, most will also go through a pattern of relapse and recovery (Emsley, Chiliza, Asmal & Harvey, 2013). This relapse rate is important when discussing the course of schizophrenia. For example, the data from one classic study show the course of schizophrenia among four prototypical groups (Zubin, Steinhauer, & Condray, 1992). About 22% of the group had one episode of schizophrenia and improved without lasting impairment. The remaining 78% experienced several episodes with differing degrees of impairment between them. People with schizophrenia have a poorer prognosis than those with most of the other disorders we describe in this book—including a high risk of suicide (Jablensky, 2012). ● Figure 12.2 graphically depicts the developmental course of schizophrenia.

Cultural Factors

Because schizophrenia is so complex, the diagnosis itself can be controversial. Some have argued that "schizophrenia" does not really exist but is a derogatory label for people who behave in ways outside the cultural norm (see, for example, Szasz, 1961). This concern takes us back to our discussions in the first chapter about the difficulty defining what is abnormal. Although the idea that schizophrenia exists only in the minds of mental health professionals is certainly provocative, this extreme view is contradicted by experience. We have had a great deal of contact with

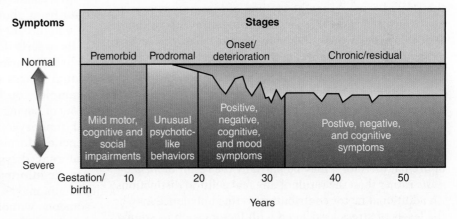

Natural history of schizophrenia

● **Figure 12.2** The longitudinal course of schizophrenia is depicted starting at birth through old age. The severity of the symptoms is showing on the left axis, and the changes in symptoms across each phase (premorbid, prodromal, onset, and chronic) are labeled. (Adapted from Lieberman, J. A., Perkins, D., Belger, A., Chakos, M., Jarskog, F., Boteva, K., & Gilmore, J. (2001). The early stages of schizophrenia: Speculations on pathogenesis, pathophysiology, and therapeutic approaches. *Biological Psychiatry, 50,* p. 885.)

prodromal stage Period of 1 to 2 years before serious symptoms of **schizophrenia** occur but when less severe yet unusual behaviors start to appear.

people who have this disorder and with their families and friends, and the tremendous amount of emotional pain resulting from schizophrenia gives definite credence to its existence. In addition, many people in widely diverging cultures have the symptoms of schizophrenia, which supports the notion that it is a reality for many people worldwide. Schizophrenia is thus universal, affecting all racial and cultural groups studied so far. There are even shared neuroanatomical similarities that provide evidence of schizophrenia's presence across individuals from different cultures (Gong et al., 2015).

However, the course and outcome of schizophrenia vary from culture to culture. For example, the stressors associated with significant political, social, and economic problems that are prevalent in many areas of Africa, Latin America, and Asia may contribute to poorer outcomes for people with schizophrenia in these countries (Jablensky, 2012). The lack of an adequate mental health infrastructure in low- and middle-income countries is also a problem for providing care to those suffering from schizophrenia. Efforts to increase several countries' capacity to care for those with schizophrenia have had some success in upper middle–income countries like China and Brazil (Patel, 2015). More initiatives focused on schizophrenia and other mental health disorders worldwide are starting to gain momentum.

In the United States, proportionately more African Americans receive the diagnosis of schizophrenia than Caucasians (Schwartz & Feisthamel, 2009). Research from both England and the United States suggests that people from devalued ethnic minority groups (Afro-Caribbean in England and African Americans and Puerto Ricans in the United States) may be victims of bias and stereotyping (Jones & Gray, 1986; Lewis, Croft-Jeffreys, & Anthony, 1990); in other words, they may be more likely to receive a diagnosis of schizophrenia than members of a dominant group. One prospective study of schizophrenia among different ethnic groups in London found that although the outcomes of schizophrenia appear similar across these groups, blacks were more likely to be detained against their will, brought to the hospital by police, and given emergency injections (Goater et al., 1999). The differing rates of schizophrenia, therefore, may be partially the result of *misdiagnosis* rather than the result of any real cultural distinctions. An additional factor contributing to this imbalance may be the levels of stress associated with factors such as stigma, isolation, and discrimination (Anglin, Lighty, Greenspoon, & Ellman, 2014; Pinto, Ashworth, & Jones, 2008).

Genetic Influences

We could argue that few areas of abnormal psychology so clearly illustrate the enormous complexity and intriguing mystery of genetic influences on behavior as does the phenomenon of schizophrenia (Murray & Castle, 2012). Despite the possibility that schizophrenia may be several different disorders, we can safely make one generalization: *Genes are responsible for making some individuals vulnerable to schizophrenia.* We look at a range of research findings from family, twin, adoptee, offspring of twins, and linkage and association studies. We conclude by discussing the compelling reasons that no one gene is responsible for schizophrenia; rather, multiple gene variances combine to produce vulnerability (Murray & Castle, 2012).

Family Studies

In 1938, Franz Kallmann published a major study of the families of people with schizophrenia (Kallmann, 1938). Kallmann examined family members of more than 1,000 people diagnosed with schizophrenia in a Berlin psychiatric hospital. He showed that the severity of the parent's disorder influenced the likelihood of the child's having schizophrenia: The more severe the parent's schizophrenia, the more likely the children were to develop it. Another observation was important: All forms of schizophrenia (for example, the historic categories such as catatonic and paranoid) were seen within the families. In other words, it does not appear that you inherit a predisposition for what was previously diagnosed as paranoid schizophrenia. Instead, you may inherit a general predisposition for schizophrenia that manifests in the same form or differently from that of your parent. More recent research confirms this observation and suggests that families that have a member with schizophrenia are at risk not just for schizophrenia alone or for all psychological disorders; instead, there appears to be some familial risk for a spectrum of psychotic disorders related to schizophrenia.

In a classic analysis, Gottesman (1991) summarized the data from about 40 studies of schizophrenia, as shown in ● Figure 12.3. The most striking feature of this graph is its orderly demonstration that the risk of having schizophrenia varies according to how many genes an individual shares with someone who has the disorder. For example, you have the greatest chance (approximately 48%) of having schizophrenia if it has affected your identical (monozygotic) twin, a person who shares 100% of your genetic information. Your risk drops to about 17% with a fraternal (dizygotic) twin, who shares about 50% of your genetic information. And having any relative with schizophrenia makes you more likely to have the disorder than someone without such a relative (about 1% if you have no relative with schizophrenia). Because family studies can't separate genetic influence from the impact of the environment, we use twin and adoption studies to help us evaluate the role of shared experiences in the cause of schizophrenia.

Twin Studies

If they are raised together, identical twins share 100% of their genes and 100% of their environment, whereas fraternal twins share only about 50% of their genes and 100% of their environment. If the environment is solely

▲ The Genain quadruplets all had schizophrenia but exhibited different symptoms over the years.

● **Figure 12.3** Risk of developing schizophrenia. (Based on Gottesman, I. I. (1991). *Schizophrenia genesis: The origins of madness.* New York, NY: W. H. Freeman.)

responsible for schizophrenia, we would expect little difference between identical and fraternal twins with regard to this disorder. If only genetic factors are relevant, both identical twins would always have schizophrenia (be concordant), and the fraternal twins would both have it about 50% of the time. Research from twin studies indicates that

the truth is somewhere in the middle (Braff *et al.*, 2007; van Os, Kenis, & Rutten, 2010).

In one of the most fascinating of "nature's experiments," identical quadruplets, all of whom have schizophrenia, have been studied extensively. Nicknamed the "Genain" quadruplets (from the Greek, meaning "dreadful gene"), these women have been followed by David Rosenthal and his colleagues at the National Institute of Mental Health for a number of years (Rosenthal, 1963). The fictitious names of the girls reported in studies of their lives—Nora, Iris, Myra, and Hester—represent the letters NIMH for the National Institute of Mental Health. In a sense, the women represent the complex interaction between genetics and environment. All four shared the same genetic predisposition, and all were brought up in the same particularly dysfunctional household; yet the time of onset for schizophrenia, the symptoms and diagnoses, the course of the disorder, and, ultimately, their outcomes, differed significantly from sister to sister.

One genetic explanation for these differences may be the presence of *de novo* mutations in the sisters. These are genetic mutations that can occur as a result of a mutation in a germ cell (egg or sperm) of one of the parents or, perhaps in the case of these sisters, in the fertilized egg after conception. The case of the Genain quadruplets also reveals an important consideration in studying genetic influences on behavior—*unshared environments* (Plomin, 1990). We tend to think that siblings, and especially identical multiples, are brought up exactly the same way. The impression is that "good" parents expose their children to favorable environments and "bad" parents give them unstable experiences. Even identical siblings can have different prenatal and family experiences and can therefore be exposed to varying degrees of biological and environmental stress. For example, Hester, one of the Genain sisters, was described by her disturbed parents as a habitual masturbator, and she had more social problems than her sisters as she grew up. Hester was the first to experience severe symptoms of schizophrenia, at age 18, but her sister Myra was not hospitalized until six years later. This unusual case demonstrates that even siblings who are close in every aspect of their lives can still have considerably different experiences physically and socially as they grow up, which may result in vastly different outcomes. A follow up on the lives of these women showed the progression of their disorder stabilized and in some cases improved when they were assessed at age 66 (Mirsky *et al.*, 2000).

Adoption Studies

Several adoption studies have distinguished the roles of the environment and genetics as they affect schizophrenia. The largest adoption study was conducted in Finland (Tienari, 1991). From a sample of almost 20,000 women with schizophrenia, the researchers found 190 children who had been given up for adoption. The data from this study support the idea that schizophrenia represents a spectrum of related disorders, all of which overlap genetically. If an adopted child had a biological mother with schizophrenia, that child had about a 5% chance of having the disorder (compared to about only 1% in the general population). However, if the biological mother had schizophrenia or one of the related psychotic disorders (for example, delusional disorder or schizophreniform disorder), the risk that the adopted child would have one of these disorders rose to about 22% (Tienari *et al.*, 2003; Tienari, Wahlberg, & Wynne, 2006). Even when raised away from their biological parents, children of parents with schizophrenia have a much higher chance of having the disorder themselves. At the same time, there appears to be a protective factor if these children are brought up in healthy supportive homes. In other words, a gene–environment interaction was observed in this study, with a good home environment reducing the risk of schizophrenia (Gilmore, 2010; Wynne *et al.*, 2006).

The Offspring of Twins

Twin and adoption studies strongly suggest a genetic component for schizophrenia, but what about children who develop schizophrenia even though their parents do not? For example, the study by Tienari and colleagues (2003, 2006) we just discussed found that 1.7% of the children with non-schizophrenic parents developed schizophrenia. Does this mean you can develop schizophrenia without "schizophrenic genes"? Or are some people carriers, having the genes for schizophrenia but for some reason not showing the disorder themselves? An important clue to this question comes from research on the children of twins with schizophrenia.

In a study begun in 1971 by Margit Fischer and later continued by Irving Gottesman and Aksel Bertelsen, 21 identical twin pairs and 41 fraternal twin pairs with a history of schizophrenia were identified, along with their children (Fischer, 1971; Gottesman & Bertelsen, 1989). The researchers wanted to determine the relative likelihood that a child would have schizophrenia if her parent did and if the parent's twin had schizophrenia but the parent did not. • Figure 12.4 illustrates the findings from this study. For example, if your parent is an identical (monozygotic) twin with schizophrenia, you have about a 17% chance of having the disorder yourself, a figure that holds if you are the child of an unaffected identical twin whose co-twin has the disorder.

On the other hand, look at the risks for the child of a fraternal (dizygotic) twin. If your parent is the twin with schizophrenia, you have about a 17% chance of having schizophrenia yourself. If your parent does not have schizophrenia but your parent's fraternal twin does, your risk is only about 2%. The data clearly indicate that you can have genes that predispose you to schizophrenia, not show the disorder yourself, but still pass on the genes to your children. In other words, you can be a "carrier" for schizophrenia. This is some of the strongest evidence yet that people

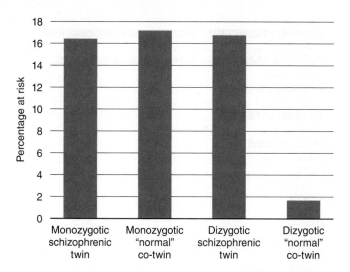

• **Figure 12.4** Risk for schizophrenia among children of twins.

are genetically vulnerable to schizophrenia. Remember, however, there is only a 17% chance of inheritance if your parent has schizophrenia, meaning that other factors help determine who will have this disorder.

Linkage and Association Studies

Genetic linkage and association studies rely on traits such as blood types (whose exact location on the chromosome is already known) inherited in families with the disorder you are looking for—in this case, schizophrenia. Because researchers have determined the location of the genes for these traits (called *marker genes*), they can make a guess about the location of the disorder genes inherited with them. To date, researchers have looked at several sites for genes that may be responsible for schizophrenia (Kirov & Owen, 2009). A recent study that combined one of the largest samples (i.e., 36,989 cases of individuals with schizophrenia and 113,075 controls) found many new genetic factors involved in schizophrenia. This further strengthens that genetic risk arises from a large number of common genes each with a small effect that might be detected by genome-wide association studies (Ripke *et al.*, 2014).

Endophenotypes Genetic research on schizophrenia is evolving, and the information on the findings from these sophisticated studies is now being combined with advances in our understanding of specific deficits found in people with this disorder. Remember, in complex disorders such as this, researchers are not looking for a "schizophrenia gene" or genes. Instead, researchers try to find basic processes that contribute to the behaviors or symptoms of the disorder and then find the gene or genes that cause these difficulties—a strategy called *endophenotyping* (Braff *et al.*, 2007).

Several potential candidates for endophenotypes for schizophrenia have been studied over the years. One of the more highly researched is called *smooth-pursuit eye movement,* or eye-tracking. Keeping their head still, typical people are able to track a moving pendulum, back and forth, with their eyes. The ability to track objects smoothly across the visual field is deficient in many people who have schizophrenia (Holzman & Levy, 1977; Iacono, Bassett, & Jones, 1988); it does not appear to be the result of drug treatment or institutionalization (Lieberman *et al.*, 1993). It also seems to be a problem for relatives of those with schizophrenia (Ivleva *et al.*, 2014). This abnormal eye-tracking ability decreases in likelihood the further a person is genetically from someone with schizophrenia. When all these observations are combined, they suggest an eye-tracking deficit may be an endophenotype for schizophrenia that could be used in further study.

Other such research focuses on the social, cognitive, and emotional deficits characteristic of schizophrenia. One study, for example, looked at multiple generations of families who had someone with schizophrenia (Gur *et al.*, 2007). They tested them on a variety of skills for identified cognitive deficits in areas we described previously—such as emotion identification—and showed that specific problems were inherited in the same manner as schizophrenia (suggesting that these cognitive deficits might be endophenotypes for schizophrenia). Currently, a number of endophenotypes are being explored by a large group of scientists (*The Consortium on the Genetics of Schizophrenia*) studying more than 1,200 individuals with schizophrenia and their families (Greenwood *et al.*, 2013).

Neurobiological Influences

The belief that schizophrenia involves a malfunctioning brain goes back as far as the writings of Kraepelin (1856–1926). It is therefore not surprising that a great deal of research has focused on the brain.

Dopamine

One of the most enduring yet controversial theories of the cause of schizophrenia involves the neurotransmitter *dopamine* (Harrison, 2012). In Chapter 2, we discussed the sensitivity of specific neurons to specific neurotransmitters and described how they cluster throughout the brain. The top of ● Figure 12.5 shows two neurons and the important

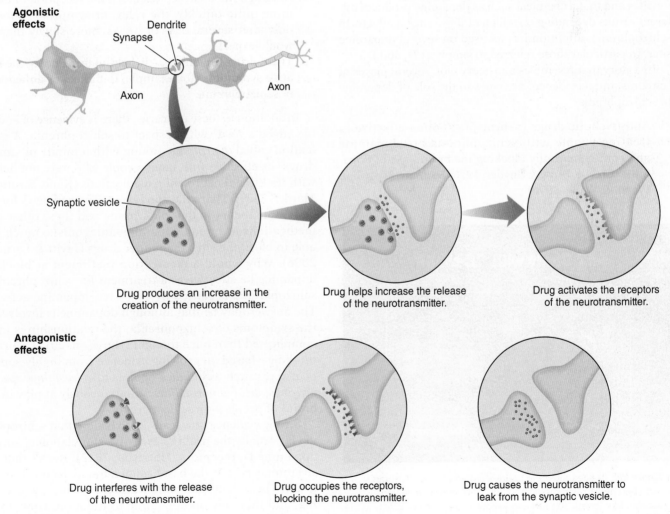

● **Figure 12.5** Some ways drugs affect neurotransmission.

synaptic gap that separates them. Neurotransmitters are released from the storage vessels (synaptic vesicles) at the end of the axon, cross the gap, and are taken up by receptors in the dendrite of the next axon. Chemical "messages" are transported in this way from neuron to neuron throughout the brain.

This process can be influenced in a number of ways, and the rest of Figure 12.5 illustrates some of them. The chemical messages can be increased by agonistic agents or decreased by antagonistic agents. Antagonistic effects slow or stop messages from being transmitted by preventing the release of the neurotransmitter, blocking uptake at the level of the dendrite, or causing leaks that reduce the amount of neurotransmitter released. On the other hand, agonistic effects assist with the transference of chemical messages and, if extreme, can produce too much neurotransmitter activity by increasing production or release of the neurotransmitter and by affecting more receptors at the dendrites.

What we've learned about antipsychotic medications points to the possibility that the dopamine system is too active in people with schizophrenia. The simplified picture in Figure 12.5 does not show that there are different receptor sites and that a chemical such as dopamine produces different results depending on which of those sites it affects. In schizophrenia, attention has focused on several dopamine sites, in particular those referred to simply as D_1 and D_2.

In a story that resembles a mystery plot, several pieces of "circumstantial evidence" are clues to the role of dopamine in schizophrenia:

1. Antipsychotic drugs (neuroleptics) often effective in treating people with schizophrenia are dopamine antagonists, partially blocking the brain's use of dopamine (Creese, Burt, & Snyder, 1976; Seeman, Lee, Chau Wong, & Wong, 1976).

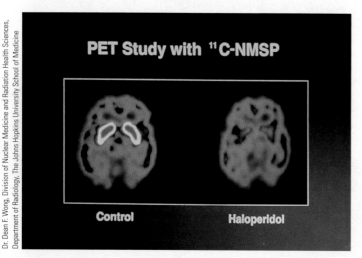

Dr. Dean F. Wong, Division of Nuclear Medicine and Radiation Health Sciences, Department of Radiology, The Johns Hopkins University School of Medicine

▲ These PET images show the brain of a man with schizophrenia who had never been medicated (left) and after he received haloperidol (right). The red and yellow areas indicate activity in the D2 receptors; haloperidol evidently reduced dopamine activity.

2. These neuroleptic drugs can produce negative side effects similar to those in Parkinson's disease, a disorder known to be caused by insufficient dopamine.
3. The drug L-dopa, a dopamine agonist used to treat people with Parkinson's disease, produces schizophrenia-like symptoms in some people (Davidson *et al.*, 1987).
4. Amphetamines, which also activate dopamine, can make psychotic symptoms worse in some people with schizophrenia (van Kammen, Docherty, & Bunney, 1982).

In other words, when drugs are administered that are known to increase dopamine (agonists), there is an increase in schizophrenic behavior; when drugs that are known to decrease dopamine activity (antagonists) are used, schizophrenic symptoms tend to diminish. Taking these observations together, researchers theorized that schizophrenia in some people was attributable to excessive dopamine activity.

Despite these observations, some evidence contradicts the dopamine theory (Javitt & Laruelle, 2006):

1. A significant number of people with schizophrenia are not helped by the use of dopamine antagonists.
2. Although the neuroleptics block the reception of dopamine quite quickly, the relevant symptoms subside only after several days or weeks, more slowly than we would expect.
3. These drugs are only partly helpful in reducing the negative symptoms (for example, flat affect or anhedonia) of schizophrenia.

In addition to these concerns, there is evidence of a "double-edged sword" with respect to schizophrenia. A medication called *olanzapine*—along with a family of similar drugs—is effective with many people who were not helped with traditional neuroleptic medications (Kane, Stroup, & Marder, 2009). That's the good news. The bad news for the dopamine theory is that olanzapine and these other new medications are weak dopamine antagonists, much less able to block the sites than other drugs (Javitt & Laruelle, 2006). Why would a medication inefficient at blocking dopamine be effective as a treatment for schizophrenia if schizophrenia is caused by excessive dopamine activity? The answer may be that although dopamine is involved in the symptoms of schizophrenia, the relationship is more complicated than once thought (Harrison, 2012). Current thinking—based on growing evidence from highly sophisticated research techniques—points to *at least three specific neurochemical abnormalities* simultaneously at play in the brains of people with schizophrenia.

Strong evidence now leads us to believe that schizophrenia is partially the result of excessive stimulation of striatal dopamine D_2 receptors (Harrison, 2012). Recall that the striatum is part of the basal ganglia found deep within the brain. These cells control movement, balance, and walking, and they rely on dopamine to function. How do we know that excessive stimulation of D_2 receptors is involved in schizophrenia? One clue is that the most effective antipsychotic drugs all share dopamine D_2 receptor antagonism—meaning they help block the stimulation of the D_2 receptors (Ginovart & Kapur, 2010). Using brain-imaging techniques such as SPECT, scientists can view the living brain of a person with schizophrenia and can observe how the newer, "second generation" antipsychotic medications work on these specific dopamine sites.

A second area of interest to scientists investigating the cause of schizophrenia is the observation of a deficiency in the stimulation of prefrontal dopamine D_1 receptors (Howes & Kapur, 2009). Therefore, while some dopamine sites may be overactive (for example, striatal D_2), a second type of dopamine site in the part of the brain that we use for thinking and reasoning (prefrontal D_1 receptors) appears to be less active and may account for other symptoms common in schizophrenia. As you will see later in this chapter, people with schizophrenia display a range of deficits in the prefrontal section of the brain, and this area may be less active in people with schizophrenia.

Finally, a third area of neurochemical interest involves research on alterations in prefrontal activity involving glutamate transmission (Harrison, 2012). Glutamate is an excitatory neurotransmitter that is found in all areas of the brain and is only now being studied in earnest. Just as we saw with dopamine (for example, D_1 and D_2 receptors), glutamate has different types of receptors, and the ones being studied for their role in schizophrenia are the *N*-methyl-d-aspartate (NMDA) receptors. And, just as researchers were led to the study of dopamine by observations from the effects of dopamine-specific drugs on behavior, the effects of certain drugs that affect NMDA receptors point to clues to schizophrenia. Two recreational drugs described in Chapter 10—phencyclidine (PCP) and ketamine—can result in psychotic-like behavior in people without schizophrenia and can exacerbate psychotic symptoms in those with schizophrenia. Both PCP and ketamine are also NMDA antagonists, suggesting that a deficit in glutamate or blocking of NMDA sites may be involved in some symptoms of schizophrenia (Goff & Coyle, 2001).

Research on these two neurotransmitters and their relationship to each other is complex and awaits further clarification. However, advances in technology are leading us closer to the clues behind this enigmatic disorder and closer still to better treatments.

Brain Structure

Evidence for neurological damage in people with schizophrenia comes from a number of observations. Many children with a parent who has the disorder, and who are therefore at risk, tend to show subtle but observable neurological problems, such as abnormal reflexes and inattentiveness (Buka, Seidman, Tsuang, & Goldstein, 2013). These difficulties are persistent: Adults who have schizophrenia show deficits in their ability to perform certain tasks and to

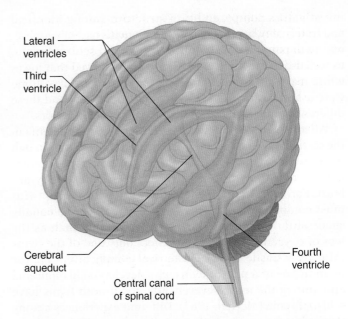

● **Figure 12.6** Location of the cerebrospinal fluid in the human brain. This extracellular fluid surrounds and cushions the brain and spinal cord. It also fills the four interconnected cavities (cerebral ventricles) within the brain and the central canal of the spinal cord.

attend during reaction time exercises (Cleghorn & Albert, 1990). Such findings suggest that brain damage or dysfunction may cause or accompany schizophrenia, although no one site is probably responsible for the whole range of symptoms (Harrison, 2012).

One of the most reliable observations about the brain in people with schizophrenia involves the size of the ventricles (see ● Figure 12.6). As early as 1927, these liquid-filled cavities showed enlargement in some brains examined in people with schizophrenia (Jacobi & Winkler, 1927). Since then, more sophisticated techniques have been developed for observing the brain, and in the dozens of studies conducted on ventricle size, the great majority show abnormally large lateral and third ventricles in people with schizophrenia (Harrison, 2012). Ventricle size may not be a problem, but the dilation (enlargement) of the ventricles indicates that adjacent parts of the brain either have not developed fully or have atrophied, thus allowing the ventricles to become larger.

Ventricle enlargement is not seen in everyone who has schizophrenia. Several factors seem to be associated with this finding. For example, enlarged ventricles are observed more often in men than in women (Abel, Drake, & Goldstein, 2010). Also, ventricles seem to enlarge in proportion to age and to the duration of the schizophrenia. One study found that individuals with schizophrenia who were exposed to influenza prenatally may be more likely to have enlarged ventricles (Takei, Lewis, Jones, Harvey, & Murray, 1996). In a study of ventricle size, researchers investigated the possible role of genetics (van Haren *et al.*, 2012). Using magnetic resonance imaging (MRI), investigators compared brain structure among identical and fraternal twin pairs in which both twins had schizophrenia, twin pairs in which only one twin had schizophrenia, as well as healthy twin pairs. The results showed that lower white matter volume and larger third ventricular volume were associated with the risk for schizophrenia, and these differences appeared to be influenced by genetic factors.

We touched on the concept of unshared environments in the section on genetics (Jang, 2005; Plomin, 1990). Although twins are identical genetically, they can experience a number of environmental differences, even before they are born. For instance, in the intrauterine environment, twins must compete for nutrients, and they may not be equally successful. In addition, birth complications, such as the loss of oxygen (anoxia), could affect only one of the twins (Murray & Castle, 2012). Obstetrical complications appear often in one of a pair of twins who develops schizophrenia and among the more severely affected if both twins have schizophrenia (McNeil, 1987). Different experiences among twins already predisposed to the disorder could damage the brain and cause the types of symptoms we associate with schizophrenia.

The frontal lobes of the brain have also interested researchers looking for structural problems associated with schizophrenia (Williams *et al.*, 2013). As we described in the section on neurotransmitters, this area may be less active in people with schizophrenia than in people without the disorder, a phenomenon sometimes known as *hypofrontality* (*hypo* means "less active," or "deficient"). Research by Weinberger and other scientists at the National Institute of Mental Health refined this observation, suggesting that deficient activity in a particular area of the frontal lobes, the dorsolateral prefrontal cortex (DLPFC), may be implicated in schizophrenia (Berman & Weinberger, 1990; Rasetti *et al.*, 2011). When people with and without schizophrenia are given tasks that involve the DLPFC, less activity (measured by cerebral blood flow) is recorded in the brains of those with schizophrenia. Also, it has been shown that there is less connectivity between this region and other brain regions, meaning the DLPFC is "communicating" less with other brain regions (Rasetti *et al.*, 2011). Follow-up studies show that some individuals with schizophrenia show *hyperfrontality* (that is, too much activity), indicating that the dysfunction is reliable, but hyperfrontality displays itself differently in different people (Callicott *et al.*, 2003; Garrity *et al.*, 2007).

It appears that several brain sites are implicated in the cognitive dysfunction observed among people with schizophrenia, especially the prefrontal cortex, various related cortical regions, and subcortical circuits, including the thalamus and the striatum (Shenton & Kubicki, 2009). Remember that this dysfunction seems to occur *before the onset* of schizophrenia. In other words, brain variations may develop progressively, beginning before the symptoms of the disorder are apparent, perhaps prenatally (Harrison, 2012).

Prenatal and Perinatal Influences

There is evidence that the prenatal (before birth) and perinatal (around the time of birth) environment are correlated with the development of schizophrenia (Murray & Castle, 2012). Fetal exposure to viral infection, pregnancy complications, and delivery complications are among the environmental influences that seem to affect whether someone develops schizophrenia.

Several studies have shown that schizophrenia may be associated with prenatal exposure to influenza, viruses, or infections. For example, Sarnoff Mednick and colleagues followed a large number of people after a severe Type A2 influenza epidemic in Helsinki, Finland, and found that those whose mothers were exposed to influenza during the second trimester of pregnancy were more likely to have schizophrenia than others (Cannon, Barr, & Mednick, 1991). This observation has been confirmed by some researchers (see, for example, O'Callaghan, Sham, Takei, Glover, & Murray, 1991; Venables, 1996) but not by others (Buchanan & Carpenter, 2005; Selten, Frissen, Lensvelt-Mulders, & Morgan, 2009). The indications that virus-like diseases may cause damage to the fetal brain, which later may cause the symptoms of schizophrenia, are suggestive and may help explain why some people with schizophrenia behave the way they do (Murray & Castle, 2012).

The evidence of pregnancy complications (for example, bleeding) and delivery complications (for example, asphyxia or lack of oxygen) and their relationship to later schizophrenia suggest, on the surface, that this type of environmental stress combined with genetic and other variables may trigger the expression of the disorder (Kotlicka-Antczak, Pawelczyk, Rabe-Jabłońska, Smigielski, & Pawelczyk, 2014; Suvisaari *et al.*, 2013). It is possible, however, that the genes carried by the fetus that make it vulnerable to schizophrenia may themselves contribute to the birth complications (van Os & Allardyce, 2009).

The chronic and early use of marijuana (cannabis) is also being studied as a potential influence on the onset of schizophrenia (Murray & Castle, 2012). Some research suggests that people who use marijuana in high doses have an increased likelihood of developing schizophrenia for those with CNR1 genotypes (Ho, Wassink, Ziebell, & Andreasen, 2011) and that people with schizophrenia are more likely to have a cannabis use disorder than individuals without schizophrenia (Corcoran *et al.*, 2008; Martins & Gorelick, 2011). However, the link between these two problems is not yet clearly understood, and there are conflicting findings about whether or not other factors may be responsible for this correlation (Murray & Castle, 2012).

Psychological and Social Influences

That one identical twin may develop schizophrenia and the other may not suggests that schizophrenia involves something in addition to genes. We know that early brain trauma, perhaps resulting from a second-trimester virus-like attack or obstetrical complications, may generate physical stress that contributes to schizophrenia. All these observations show clearly that schizophrenia does not fall neatly into a few simple causal packages. For instance, not all people with schizophrenia have enlarged ventricles, nor do they all have a hypofrontality or disrupted activity in their dopamine systems. The causal picture may be further complicated by psychological and social factors. We next look at research into psychosocial factors. Do emotional stressors or family interaction patterns *initiate* the symptoms of schizophrenia? If so, how might those factors cause people to relapse after a period of improvement?

Stress

Researchers have studied the effects of a variety of stressors on schizophrenia. Living in a large city, for example, is associated with an increased risk of developing schizophrenia (Boydell & Allardyce, 2012). Dohrenwend and Egri (1981) observed that otherwise healthy people who engage in combat during a war often display temporary symptoms that resemble those of schizophrenia. In a classic study, Brown and Birley (1968; Birley & Brown, 1970) examined people whose onset of schizophrenia could be dated within a week. These individuals had experienced a high number of stressful life events in the three weeks before they started showing signs of the disorder. In a large-scale study sponsored by the World Health Organization, researchers also looked at the role of life events in the onset of schizophrenia (Day *et al.*, 1987). This cross-national study confirmed the findings of Brown and Birley across eight research centers.

The *retrospective* nature of such research creates problems. Each study relies on after-the-fact reports, collected after the person showed signs of schizophrenia. One always wonders whether such reports are biased in some way and therefore misleading. At the same time, there are strong individual differences in how people experience the same life events, and people with schizophrenia may experience events differently than those without the disorder (Murray & Castle, 2012).

Do the symptoms of schizophrenia become worse as a result of stressful life experiences? This vulnerability–stress model of schizophrenia suggests that this is the case, and it may be helpful in predicting problems. One research study used a natural disaster—the 1994 Northridge, California, earthquake—to assess how people with schizophrenia would react to this stress when compared with those with bipolar disorder and healthy controls (Horan *et al.*, 2007). Both patient groups reported more stress-related symptoms compared with the controls; however, the people with schizophrenia reported lower levels of self-esteem after the disaster and were more likely to engage in avoidance coping (not thinking about the problem or becoming resigned to difficulties) than the other two groups. Research on sociocultural stress, such as poverty, homelessness, early life adversity, growing up in an urban environment, minority

group position, and the stress of being in a new country (van Os, Kenis, & Rutten, 2010; Lataster, Myin-Germeys, Lieb, Wittchen, & Van Os, 2012), suggests that these psychosocial stressors influence onset and possibly development of schizophrenia. Onset of symptoms usually happens as a result of environmental stressors, showing that these stressors may have their impact during sensitive periods in development. For example, stressors in early life may influence development of psychosis, possibly by increasing stressors later in life, making individuals more sensitive to later stressors, or both (Lataster *et al.*, 2012).

A simple vulnerability can develop into a severe disorder from the interchange between genes and the environment. For example, some studies now show that particular gene variances may predict which individuals with schizophrenia will be more likely to react negatively (such as relapse) with increased stress (Ascher-Svanum *et al.*, 2010). These types of studies point to how stress can impact people with schizophrenia, and may suggest useful treatments (such as cognitive-behavioral therapy to help them cope more appropriately) (Ascher-Svanum *et al.*, 2010).

Families and Relapse

A great deal of research has studied how interactions within the family affect people who have schizophrenia. For example, the term **schizophrenogenic mother** was used for a time to describe a mother whose cold, dominant, and rejecting nature was thought to cause schizophrenia in her children (Fromm-Reichmann, 1948). In addition, the term **double bind communication** was used to portray a communication style that produced conflicting messages, which, in turn, caused schizophrenia to develop (Bateson, 1959). Here, the parent presumably communicates messages that have two conflicting meanings; for example, a mother responds coolly to her child's embrace but says, "Don't you love me anymore?" when the child withdraws. Although these theories are no longer supported, they have been—and in some cases continue to be—destructive, producing guilt in parents who are persuaded that their early mistakes caused devastating consequences.

Recent work has focused more on how family interactions contribute not to the onset of schizophrenia but to relapse after initial symptoms are observed. Research has focused on a particular emotional communication style known as **expressed emotion (EE)**. This concept was

....

schizophrenogenic mother According to an obsolete, unsupported theory, a cold, dominating, and rejecting parent who was thought to cause **schizophrenia** in her offspring.

double bind communication According to an obsolete, unsupported theory, the practice of transmitting conflicting messages that was thought to cause **schizophrenia**.

expressed emotion (EE) Hostility, criticism, and over-involvement demonstrated by some families toward a family member with a **psychological disorder**. This can often contribute to the person's **relapse**.

formulated by George W. Brown and his colleagues in London. Following a sample of people who had been discharged from the hospital after an episode of schizophrenic symptoms, the researchers found that former patients who had limited contact with their relatives did better than the patients who spent longer periods with their families (Brown, 1959). Additional research results indicated that if the levels of criticism (disapproval), hostility (animosity), and emotional overinvolvement (intrusiveness) expressed by the families were high, patients tended to relapse (Brown, Monck, Carstairs, & Wing, 1962).

Other researchers have since found that ratings of high expressed emotion in a family are a good predictor of relapse among people with chronic schizophrenia (Cechnicki, Bielańska, Hanuszkiewicz, & Daren, 2013). If you have schizophrenia and live in a family with high expressed emotion, you are 3.7 times more likely to relapse than if you lived in a family with low expressed emotion (Kavanagh, 1992; Parker & Hadzi-Pavlovic, 1990). Here are examples of interviews that show how families of people with schizophrenia might communicate expressed emotion:

High Expressed Emotion

▸ I always say, "Why don't you pick up a book, do a crossword, or something like that to keep your mind off it." That's even too much trouble.

▸ I've tried to jolly him out of it and pestered him into doing things. Maybe I've overdone it, I don't know.

Low Expressed Emotion

▸ I know it's better for her to be on her own, to get away from me and try to do things on her own.
Whatever she does suits me.
I just tend to let it go because I know that when she wants to speak she will speak. (Hooley, 1985, p. 134)

This style suggests that families with high expressed emotion view the symptoms of schizophrenia as controllable and that the hostility arises when family members think that patients just do not want to help themselves (Hooley & Campbell, 2002; McNab, Haslam, & Burnett, 2007). The literature on expressed emotion is valuable to our understanding of why symptoms of schizophrenia recur and may show us how to treat people with this disorder and their families so that they do not experience further psychotic episodes (Cechnicki *et al.*, 2013).

An interesting issue that arises when studying family influences is whether what we see is unique to our culture or universal. Looking at expressed emotion across different cultures may help us learn whether expressed emotion is a *cause* of schizophrenia (Breitborde, López, & Kopelowicz, 2010; Kymalainen & Weisman de Mamani, 2008). Remember that the rate of schizophrenia is observed to be about the same worldwide, with a prevalence of about 1% in the global population. If a factor like high expressed emotion

in families is a causal agent, we should see the same rates in families across cultures; however, they differ, as you can see in ● Figure 12.7. These data come from an analysis of the concept of expressed emotion in several studies from India, Mexico, United Kingdom, and the United States (Jenkins & Karno, 1992). The differences suggest that there are cultural variations in how families react to someone with schizophrenia and their reactions do not cause the disorder (Singh, Harley, & Suhail, 2013). In addition, what may appear to be over-involvement in one culture may be viewed as supportive in other cultures.

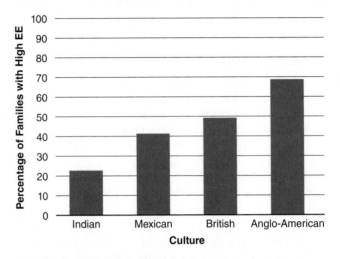

● **Figure 12.7** Cultural differences in expressed emotion.

12.2 Concept CHECK

Check your understanding of genetic vulnerability by filling in the blanks of the statements associated with family, twin, and adoption studies. Choose from (a) higher, (b) lower, (c) equal, (d) severity, (e) type, (f) identical twin, (g) specific, (h) fraternal twin, and (i) general.

1. The greatest risk of having schizophrenia is in those who have a(n) _____ or _____ with schizophrenia. Any relative with schizophrenia will make your chances of developing the disorder _____ than those of the general population.

2. Raised in a home other than that of their biological parents, adopted children of parents with schizophrenia have a(n) _____ chance of having the disorder themselves. Children of people with schizophrenia adopted into families without schizophrenia have a _____ than-average chance of having schizophrenia.

3. The likelihood of a child's having schizophrenia is influenced by the _____ of the parent's disorder. One may inherit a predisposition for _____ schizophrenia that is the same or different from that of the parent.

Treatment of Schizophrenia

▶ What are the goals of therapy for schizophrenia?

▶ What biological and psychosocial treatments for schizophrenia are available?

What do you do for someone who has delusions, hears his dead uncle's voice, or can't communicate complete thoughts? The search for help has taken many paths. In the Western world today, treatment usually begins with one of the neuroleptic drugs invaluable in reducing the symptoms of schizophrenia for many people. They are typically used with a variety of psychosocial treatments to reduce relapse, compensate for skills deficits, and improve cooperation for taking the medications (Cunningham Owens & Johnstone, 2012).

Biological Interventions

Researchers have assumed for more than 100 years that schizophrenia requires some form of biological intervention. Kraepelin, who so eloquently described dementia praecox in the late 19th century, saw the disorder as a brain disease. Lacking a biological treatment, he routinely recommended that the physician use "good patience, kindly disposition, and self-control" to calm excited patients (Nagel, 1991).

During the 1930s, several novel biological treatments were tried. One approach was to inject massive doses of insulin—the drug that given in smaller doses is used to

▲ An early 16th-century painting of psychosurgery, in which part of the brain is removed to treat mental illness.

treat diabetes—to induce comas in people suffering from schizophrenia. Insulin coma therapy was thought for a time to be helpful, but closer examination showed it carried great risk of serious illness and death. During this time, *psychosurgery*, including prefrontal lobotomies, was introduced, and in the late 1930s, electroconvulsive therapy (ECT) was advanced as a treatment for schizophrenia. As with earlier drastic treatments, initial enthusiasm for ECT faded because it was found not to be beneficial for most people with schizophrenia—although it is still used with a limited number of people today, sometimes in combination with antipsychotic medications (Zervas, Theleritis, & Soldatos, 2012). As we explained in Chapter 6, ECT is sometimes recommended for people who experience severe episodes of depression.

Antipsychotic Medications

A breakthrough in the treatment of schizophrenia came during the 1950s with the introduction of several drugs that relieved symptoms in many people (Cunningham Owens & Johnstone, 2012). Called *neuroleptics* (meaning "taking hold of the nerves"), these medications provided the first real hope that help was available for people with schizophrenia. When they are effective, neuroleptics help people think more clearly and reduce hallucinations and delusions. They work by affecting the positive symptoms (delusions, hallucinations, and agitation) and to a lesser extent the negative and disorganized ones, such as social deficits. Table 12.1 shows the classes of these drugs (based on their chemical structure) and their trade names.

Recall from our discussion of the dopamine theory of schizophrenia that the neuroleptics are dopamine antagonists. One of their major actions in the brain is to interfere with the dopamine neurotransmitter system. They can also affect other systems, however, such as the serotonergic and glutamate system. We are just beginning to understand the mechanisms by which these drugs work.

In general, each drug is effective with some people and not with others. Clinicians and patients often must go through a trial-and-error process to find the medication that works best, and some individuals do not benefit significantly from any of them. The earliest neuroleptic drugs, called conventional or first-generation antipsychotics (such as Haldol and Thorazine), are effective for approximately 60% to 70% of people who try them (Cunningham, Owens, & Johnstone, 2012). Many people are not helped by antipsychotics, however, or they experience unpleasant side effects. Fortunately, some people respond well to

Bridgeman Art Library, London/SuperStock

TABLE 12.1 | Commonly Used Antipsychotic Medications

Class	Example*	Degree of Extrapyramidal Side Effects**
Conventional Antipsychotics		
Phenothi-azines	Chlorpromazine/*Thorazine*	Moderate
	Fluphenazine/*Prolixin*	High
	Mesoridazine/*Serentil*	Low
	Perphenazine/*Trilafon*	High
	Thioridazine/*Mellaril*	Low
	Trifluoperazine/*Stelazine*	High
Butyrophe-none	Haloperidol/*Haldol*	High
Others	Loxapine/*Loxitane*	High
	Molindone/*Moban*	Low
	Thiothixene/*Navane*	High
Second-Generation Agents		
	Aripiprazole/*Abilify*	Low
	Clozapine/*Clozaril*	Low
	Olanzapine/*Zyprexa*	Low
	Quetiapine/*Seroquel*	Low
	Risperidone/*Risperdal*	Low
	Ziprasidone/*Geodon*	Low

* The trade name is in italics.

** Extrapyramidal side effects include a number of motor disorders such as uncontrollable limb movements or the inability to initiate motion.

SOURCE: Adapted from American Psychiatric Association. (2004). Practice guideline for the treatment of patients with schizophrenia, 2nd edition. *American Journal of Psychiatry, 161*(Suppl.), 1–56.

newer medications—sometimes called atypical or second-generation antipsychotics; the most common are risperidone and olanzapine. These newer drugs were in part developed to help patients who were previously unresponsive to medications. A comparison of multiple clinical trials shows better efficacy, though small, in preventing symptoms re-emergence for these newer drugs over the previous ones (Kishimoto *et al.*, 2013). Initially, it was thought that the newer drugs had fewer serious side effects than the conventional antipsychotics. However, two large-scale studies—one conducted in the United States (called the "Clinical Antipsychotic Trials of Intervention Effectiveness" or CATIE) (Stroup & Lieberman, 2010) and one in the United Kingdom (called the "Cost Utility of the Latest Antipsychotic Drugs in Schizophrenia Study" or CUtLASS) (Jones *et al.*, 2006)—found that the second-generation drugs were no more effective or better tolerated than the older drugs (Lieberman & Stroup, 2011). These results point out how important it is to carefully study the outcomes of all new treatments.

Non-compliance with Medication: Why?

Despite the optimism generated by the effectiveness of antipsychotics, they work only when they are taken properly, and many people with schizophrenia do not routinely take their medication. In the large-scale study we just mentioned, 74% of those studied had stopped taking their medications 18 months after initial use (Lieberman & Stroup, 2011).

A number of factors seem to be related to patients' non-compliance with a medication regimen, including negative doctor–patient relationships, cost of the medication, stigma, and poor social support (Haddad, Brain, & Scott, 2014). Not surprisingly, negative side effects are a major factor in patient refusal. Antipsychotics can produce a number of unwanted physical symptoms, such as grogginess, blurred vision, and dryness of the mouth. Because the drugs affect neurotransmitter systems, more serious side effects, called *extrapyramidal symptoms*, can also result (Cunningham, Owens, & Johnstone, 2012). These symptoms include the motor difficulties similar to those experienced by people with Parkinson's disease, sometimes called Parkinsonian symptoms. *Akinesia* is one of the most common; it includes an expressionless face, slow motor activity, and monotonous speech. Another extrapyramidal symptom is *tardive dyskinesia*, which involves involuntary movements of the tongue, face, mouth, or jaw and can include protrusions of the tongue, puffing of the cheeks, puckering of the mouth, and chewing movements. Tardive dyskinesia seems to result from long-term use of high doses of antipsychotic medication and is often irreversible. Studies have shown that up to 20% to 50% of all patients treated with antipsychotics develop tardive dyskenesia with lower risk for younger people (only 3% to 5% of younger people taking this medication display tardive dyskinesia, with the risk increasing over time) (Waln & Jankovic, 2013). These serious negative side effects have justifiably concerned people who otherwise benefit from the drugs.

To learn what patients themselves say, Windgassen (1992) questioned 61 people who had had recent onsets of schizophrenia. About half reported the feeling of sedation or grogginess as an unpleasant side effect. Other complaints included deterioration in the ability to think or concentrate (18%), problems with salivation (16%), and blurred vision (16%). Although a third of the patients felt the medications were beneficial, about 25% had a negative attitude toward them. A significant number of people who could benefit from antipsychotic medications find them unacceptable as a treatment, which may explain the relatively high rates of refusal and noncompliance (Sendt, Tracy, & Bhattacharyya, 2015; Yamada *et al.*, 2006).

Researchers have made this a major treatment issue in schizophrenia, realizing that medications can't be successful if they aren't taken regularly. Researchers hoped compliance rates would improve with the introduction of injectable medications. Instead of taking an oral antipsychotic every

▲ One of the major obstacles to drug treatment for schizophrenia is compliance. Patients discontinue their medication for a variety of reasons, including the negative side effects.

day, patients can have their medications injected every few weeks. Unfortunately, non-compliance remains an issue, primarily because patients do not return to the hospital or clinic for repeated doses (Kane *et al.*, 2009; Kishimoto *et al.*, 2012). Psychosocial interventions are now used not only to treat schizophrenia but also to increase medication-taking compliance by helping patients communicate better with professionals about their concerns.

Psychosocial Interventions

Historically, a number of psychosocial treatments have been tried for schizophrenia, reflecting the belief that the disorder results from problems in adapting to the world because of early experiences (Cunningham, Owens, & Johnstone, 2012). Today, few believe that psychological factors cause people to have schizophrenia or that traditional psychotherapeutic approaches will cure them. Nevertheless, you will see that psychological methods have an important role. Despite the great promise of drug treatment, the problems with ineffectiveness, inconsistent use, and relapse suggest that by themselves drugs may not be effective with many people. As with a number of the disorders discussed in this text, recent work in the area of psychosocial intervention has suggested the value of an approach that uses both kinds of treatment (Mueser & Marcello, 2011).

Until relatively recently, most people with severe and chronic cases of schizophrenia were treated in hospital settings. Gordon Paul and Robert Lentz conducted pioneering work in the 1970s at a mental health center in Illinois (Paul & Lentz, 1977). Borrowing from the behavioral approaches used by Ted Ayllon and Nate Azrin (1968), Paul and Lentz designed an environment for inpatients that encouraged appropriate socialization, participation in group sessions, and self-care such as bed making while discouraging violent outbursts. They set up an elaborate **token economy**, in which residents could earn access to meals and small

luxuries by behaving appropriately. A patient could, for example, buy cigarettes with the tokens he earned for keeping his room neat. On the other hand, a patient would be fined (lose tokens) for being disruptive or otherwise acting inappropriately. This incentive system was combined with a full schedule of daily activities. Paul and Lentz compared the effectiveness of applied behavioral (or social learning) principles with traditional inpatient environments. In general, they found that patients who went through their program did better than others on social, self-care, and vocational skills, and more of them could be discharged from the hospital.

During the years since 1955, many efforts have combined to halt the routine institutionalization of people with schizophrenia in the United States (Fakhoury & Priebe, 2007). This trend has occurred partly because of court rulings that limit involuntary hospitalization and partly because of the relative success of antipsychotic medication. The bad news is that policies of deinstitutionalization have often been ill conceived, with the result that many people who have schizophrenia or other serious psychological disorders are homeless—the number is estimated at between 150,000 and 200,000 people in the United States alone (Foster, Gable, & Buckley, 2012; Pearson, Montgomery, & Locke, 2009). The good news is that more attention is being focused on supporting these people in their communities, among their friends and families. The trend is away from creating better hospital environments and toward the perhaps more difficult task of addressing complex problems in the less predictable and insecure world outside. So far, only a small fraction of the growing number of homeless individuals with mental disorders is being helped.

▲ A mother is glad to have her daughter home from a psychiatric hospital, but acknowledges that "Now the real struggle begins."

One of the more insidious effects of schizophrenia is its negative impact on a person's ability to relate to other people. Although not as dramatic as hallucinations and delusions, problems with social skills can be the most visible impairment displayed by people with schizophrenia and can prevent them from getting and keeping jobs and making friends. Clinicians attempt to reteach social skills such as basic conversation, assertiveness, and relationship building

token economy A social learning behavior modification system in which individuals earn items they can exchange for desired rewards by displaying appropriate behaviors.

to people with schizophrenia (Mueser & Marcello, 2011). Therapists divide complex social skills into their component parts, which they model. Then the clients do role-playing and ultimately practice their new skills in the "real world," while receiving feedback and encouragement at signs of progress. The challenge of teaching social skills, as with all therapies, is to maintain the effects over a long period.

In addition to social skills, programs often teach a range of ways people can adapt to their disorder yet live in the community. At the Independent Living Skills Program at the University of California, Los Angeles, for example, the focus is on helping people take charge of their own care by such methods as identifying signs that warn of a relapse and learning how to manage their medication (Liberman, 2007). Preliminary evidence indicates that this type of training may help prevent relapses by people with schizophrenia, although longer-term outcome research is needed to see how long the effects last (Cunningham, Owens, & Johnstone, 2012).

Is there a role for new technologies in the diagnosis and treatment of schizophrenia? Creative researchers are answering this question in a number of exciting developments for the field. One study carried out at King's College in London tested the nature of paranoia in a virtual reality environment among groups with low paranoia, nonclinical paranoia, and those with persecutory delusions (Freeman, Pugh, Vorontsova, Antley, & Slater, 2010). Researchers constructed a virtual scene that depicts a London subway and created avatars as passengers that at times would look at the study participant. Across the groups, there were meaningful differences in levels of anxiety, worry, interpersonal sensitivity, and depression according to their previous levels of paranoia. Other research is using this technology to assist older persons with schizophrenia improve their cognitive and general motor skills (for example, by having them push away colorful balls that are floating toward them in a virtual world) (Chan, Ngai, Leung, & Wong, 2010). These virtual assessments and treatments provide clinicians with controllable and safer environments in which to study and treat persons with schizophrenia.

Another psychosocial intervention for schizophrenia is cognitive remediation aimed at improving cognitive processes, such as attention, executive functioning, and memory, all of which are associated with impairments over the course of schizophrenia. Impairment in these cognitive areas predicts patients' overall functioning and poor response to other treatments (e.g., psychological rehabilitation or social skills training) (Mueser, Deavers, Penn, & Cassisi, 2013). The intervention consists of cognitive practice exercises and learning cognitive strategies. This intervention seems to improve cognitive abilities and overall functioning, especially when combined with other treatments, such as psychological rehabilitation (Mueser et al., 2013). Also, studies suggest that patients' functioning improves more when a strategy-based approach is taken (Wykes, Huddy, Cellard, McGurk, & Czobor, 2011).

Cognitive-behavioral intervention on the negative symptoms seems to result in only modest improvements (Cella, Preti, Edwards, Dow, & Wykes, 2017).

In our discussion of the psychosocial influences on schizophrenia, we reviewed some work linking the person's social and emotional environments to the recurrence of schizophrenic episodes (McNab et al., 2007). It is logical to ask whether families could be helped by learning to reduce their level of expressed emotion and whether this would result in fewer relapses and better overall functioning for people with schizophrenia. Several studies have addressed these issues (Falloon et al., 1985; Hogarty et al., 1986, 1991), and behavioral family therapy has been used to teach the families of people with schizophrenia to be more supportive (Dixon & Lehman, 1995; Mueser, Liberman, & Glynn, 1990). Research on professionals who provide care for people who have schizophrenia, and who may display high levels of expressed emotion, is also an active area of study (Cunningham, Owens, & Johnstone, 2012).

In contrast to traditional therapy, behavioral family therapy resembles classroom education (Falloon, 2015; Lefley, 2009). Family members are informed about schizophrenia and its treatment, relieved of the myth that they caused the disorder, and taught practical facts about antipsychotic medications and their side effects. They are also helped with communication skills so that they can become more empathic listeners, and they learn constructive ways of expressing negative feelings to replace the harsh criticism that characterizes some family interactions. In addition, they learn problem-solving skills to help them resolve conflicts. Like the research on social skills training, outcome research suggests that the effects of behavioral family therapy are significant during the first year but less robust two years after intervention (Cunningham, Owens, & Johnstone, 2012). This type of therapy, therefore, must be ongoing if patients and their families are to benefit from it.

Adults with schizophrenia face great obstacles to maintaining gainful employment. Their social skills deficits make reliable job performance and adequate employee relationships a struggle. To address these difficulties, some programs focus on vocational rehabilitation, such as supportive employment. Supportive employment involves providing coaches who give on-the-job training, and these efforts can help some people with schizophrenia maintain meaningful jobs (Mueser & Marcello, 2010).

Where treatment occurs, it has expanded over the years from locked wards in large mental hospitals, to family homes, to local communities. In addition, the services have expanded to include self-advocacy and self-help groups. Former patients have organized programs such as Fountain House in New York City to provide mutual support. Psychosocial clubs have differing models, but all are "person centered" and focus on obtaining positive experiences through employment opportunities, friendship, and empowerment. Many see this consumer-run self-help model as an added component to more specific interventions such as social skills training, family intervention, and medical management of symptoms. Some research indicates that participation may help reduce relapses, but as it is also possible that those who participate may be a special group of individuals, it is difficult to interpret improvements (Davidson, Chinman, Sells, & Rowe, 2006; Goering *et al.*, 2006).

Because schizophrenia is a complex disorder that affects multiple areas of functioning, effective treatment is carried out at several levels. Table 12.2 lists six approaches to treatment that have proved effective in assisting these individuals to achieve higher quality lives. Probably the most extensively studied program is the assertive community treatment (ACT) program that grew out of work by researchers in Madison, Wisconsin (Swartz *et al.*, 2006). ACT involves using a multidisciplinary team of professionals to provide broad-ranging treatment across all domains, including medication management, psychosocial treatment, and vocational training and support. As you can see, one approach alone is not sufficient to address the many needs of people with schizophrenia and their families (Cunningham, Owens, & Johnstone, 2012; Mueser & Marcello, 2011).

Treatment across Cultures

Treatment of schizophrenia and its delivery differ from one country to another and across cultures within countries. For example, the vast majority of the Xhosa people of South Africa who have schizophrenia report using traditional healers who sometimes recommend the use of oral

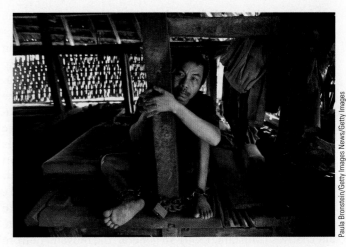

▲ Treatment for the symptoms of schizophrenia vary widely by culture—from humane approaches using empirically validated interventions to simply removing the person from society.

treatments to induce vomiting, enemas, and the slaughter of cattle to appease the spirits (Koen, Niehaus, Muller, & Laurent, 2008). Latinos may be less likely than other groups to seek help in institutional settings, relying instead on family support (Hernandez, Barrio, & Yamada, 2013; Liberman & Kopelowicz, 2009). Adapting treatments to make them culturally relevant—in this case, adding important relatives to the social skills training of Latinos with schizophrenia—is essential for effectiveness (Kopelowicz *et al.*, 2012).

In one interesting study, beliefs about symptoms and treatments were compared between British and Chinese populations (Furnham & Wong, 2007). Native Chinese

TABLE 12.2 | An Integrative Treatment Approach

Treatment	Description
Collaborative psychopharmacology	Using antipsychotic medications to treat the main symptoms of the disorder (hallucinations, delusions), as well as using other medications for secondary symptoms (for example, antidepressant medication for people with secondary depression)
Assertive community treatment	Providing support in the community, with emphasis on small caseloads for care providers, services in the community setting rather than a clinic, and 24-hour coverage
Family psychoeducation	Assisting family members, including educating them about the disorder and its management, helping them reduce stress and tension in the home, and providing social support
Supportive employment	Providing sufficient support before and during employment so that the person can find and keep a meaningful job
Illness management and recovery	Helping the individual become an active participant in treatment, including providing education about the disorder, teaching effective use of medication strategies for collaborating with clinicians, and coping with symptoms when they reoccur
Integrated dual-disorders treatment	Treating co-existing substance use

hold more religious beliefs about both the causes and the treatments of schizophrenia than those living in England—for example, endorsing statements such as "Schizophrenia is due to evil done in a previous life" and "Ancestor worship (burning candles and joss sticks) will help treat schizophrenia." These different beliefs translate into practice—with the British using more biological, psychological, and community treatments, and the Chinese relying more on alternative medicine (Furnham & Wong, 2007). Supernatural beliefs about the cause of schizophrenia among family members in Bali lead to limited use of antipsychotic medication in treatment (Kurihara, Kato, Reverger, & Gusti Rai Tirta, 2006). In many countries in Africa, people with schizophrenia are kept in prisons, primarily because of the lack of adequate alternatives (Mustafa, 1990). In general, the movement from housing people in large institutional settings to community care is ongoing in most Western countries.

Prevention

One strategy for preventing a disorder such as schizophrenia is to identify and treat children who may be at risk for getting the disorder later in life. In our discussion of genetics, we noted that approximately 17% of the children born to parents who have schizophrenia are likely themselves to develop the disorder. These high-risk children have been the focus of several studies.

A classic at-risk study was initiated in the 1960s by Sarnoff A. Mednick and Fini Schulsinger (1965, 1968). They identified 207 Danish children of mothers who had severe cases of schizophrenia and 104 control children born to mothers who had no history of the disorder. The average age of these children was about 15 when they were first identified, and the researchers followed them for 10 more years to determine whether any factors had predicted who would and would not develop schizophrenia. We have already discussed pregnancy and delivery-related complications. Mednick and Schulsinger also identified *instability of early family rearing environment,* which suggests that environmental influences may trigger the onset of schizophrenia (Cannon *et al.,* 1991). Poor parenting may place additional strain on a vulnerable person who is already at risk.

One approach to prevention of schizophrenia receiving increased attention is the treatment of persons in the prodromal stages of the disorder—mentioned previously as *attenuated psychosis syndrome.* Here the individual is beginning to show early mild signs of schizophrenia (e.g., hallucinations, delusions) but is aware of these changes. Efforts to intervene with these individuals are being investigated as a means of either stopping to progression of the disorder or preventing relapses (Cunningham, Owens, & Johnstone, 2012).

Discussing Diversity   Treatment and Understanding of Psychosis across Cultures

Although people in different parts of the world who are diagnosed with schizophrenia experience many of the same symptoms, the treatment they receive differs greatly depending on the culture in which they live. Some of these differences are not specific to the diagnosis of schizophrenia but instead result from differences in the mental health services each country provides. For instance, one study revealed that in a given year only 2% of people in Nigeria receive mental healthcare compared to 18% of those in the United States and that such differences are largely explained by the amount of money each country dedicates toward mental health services (Wang et al., 2007). Cultural differences also exist within each country as related to the treatment and understanding of schizophrenia specifically. One study, for example, found that the general public and physicians in the United

States were more accepting of those with schizophrenia than the same groups in Japan (Richards, Hori, Sartorius, & Kunugi, 2014). Hispanics diagnosed with schizophrenia in the United States appear less likely than other groups to seek help from formal institutional settings and instead receive support from their families (Dassori, Miller, & Saldana, 1995). Because of this focus on the family, treatments for schizophrenia among Hispanics are more likely to include relatives in the treatment process (Kopelowicz, Liberman, & Zarate, 2006).

Differences in treatment approaches around the world also are influenced to some degree by varying perspectives about the causes of schizophrenia. For instance, people from Eastern cultures (e.g., China) hold more religious beliefs about the causes of schizophrenia than those in Western cultures (e.g., the United Kingdom), with

those in the United Kingdom putting greater emphasis on biological and psychological factors (Furnham & Wong, 2007). These differences in beliefs about the causes of schizophrenia translate into differences in how schizophrenia is treated across cultures, with China relying more on alternative medicine approaches and the United Kingdom making greater use of biological and psychological treatments (Furnham & Wong, 2007). Many newer studies on the prediction and treatment of schizophrenia are being conducted across different cultures and countries (Bertelsen *et al.,* 2008; Cannon *et al.,* 2008). It is likely that studies taking this broader approach will lead to an enhanced understanding of the ways in which culture can influence the study, assessment, and treatment of this serious mental disorder. ∎

Read the descriptions and then match them to the following words: (a) olanzapine, (b) extrapyramidal symptoms, (c) serotonin, (d) dopamine, (e) metabolites, (f) token economy, (g) vocational rehabilitation, (h) social skills training, (i) behavioral family intervention.

1. Setting up an elaborate _____ in which patients are fined for disruptive or inappropriate behavior and rewarded for appropriate behavior is beneficial in hospitals.

2. In _____, clinicians attempt to re-teach such behaviors as basic conversation, assertiveness, and relationship building to people with schizophrenia.

3. Aside from social skills training, two psychosocial treatments for schizophrenia, _____ (teaching family members to be supportive) and _____ (teaching meaningful jobs), may be helpful.

4. Recent studies sometimes indicate that the relationship of the neurotransmitters _____ and _____ may explain some positive symptoms of schizophrenia.

5. Because antipsychotic medications may cause serious side effects, some patients stop taking them. One serious side effect is called _____, which may include Parkinsonian symptoms.

DSM 5 CONTROVERSY Attenuated Psychosis Syndrome

One of the most discussed changes in *DSM-5* related to schizophrenia spectrum and other psychotic disorders was the possible inclusion of a new diagnosis, *attenuated psychosis syndrome*. Recall that this diagnosis would be given to a person who is beginning to experience one or more of the symptoms of schizophrenia such as hallucinations or delusions but is aware that these are unusual experiences and are not typical for a healthy person (i.e., relatively intact reality testing). They are at high risk for having more severe symptoms as displayed in schizophrenia spectrum disorder. The argument for including this set of symptoms as a new disorder is that catching the person in these early stages might prove helpful for early intervention efforts (Pagsberg, 2013). It is possible that getting the symptoms under control before they become severe might save the person from years of suffering (Woods, Walsh, Saksa, & McGlashan, 2010).

On the other hand, some argued against focusing attention on this select group of individuals. From a public health perspective, some suggest that rather than limit prevention efforts to this group, that broader attention should be paid to the mental health status of the general population to screen for and provide services for any person showing signs of these disturbances (van Os, 2011). *DSM-5* "cut the baby in half" by including the disorder in its section "condition for further study." It remains to be seen if this set of criteria will eventually make its way into the *DSM* and what impact that will have on treatment and outcomes for those affected. •

SUMMARY

Perspectives on Schizophrenia

How is schizophrenia defined, and what symptoms are included in its diagnosis?

▶ Schizophrenia is a complex syndrome that has been recognized for many years. Perhaps the earliest and best description of this disorder was published in 1809 by John Haslam in his book *Observations on Madness and Melancholy*.

▶ A number of historic figures during the 19th and early 20th century contributed to the evolving definitions and possible causes of this spectrum of disorders.

Clinical Description, Symptoms, and Subtypes

What are the distinctions among positive, negative, and disorganized symptoms of schizophrenia?

What are the clinical characteristics of schizophrenia and other psychotic disorders?

▶ Schizophrenia is characterized by a broad spectrum of cognitive and emotional dysfunctions that include delusions and hallucinations, disorganized speech and behavior, and inappropriate emotions.

- The symptoms of schizophrenia can be divided into positive, negative, and disorganized. Positive symptoms are active manifestations of abnormal behavior, or an excess or distortion of normal behavior, and include delusions and hallucinations. Negative symptoms involve deficits in normal behavior on such dimensions as affect, speech, and motivation. Disorganized symptoms include rambling speech, erratic behavior, and inappropriate affect.
- Psychotic behaviors, such as hallucinations and delusions, characterize several other disorders; these include schizophreniform disorder (which includes people who experience the symptoms of schizophrenia for less than six months); schizoaffective disorder (which includes people who have symptoms of schizophrenia and who exhibit the characteristics of mood disorders, such as depression and bipolar affective disorder); delusional disorder (which includes people with a persistent belief that is contrary to reality, in the absence of the other characteristics of schizophrenia); and brief psychotic disorder (which includes people with one or more positive symptoms, such as delusions, hallucinations, or disorganized speech or behavior over the course of less than a month).
- A proposed new disorder—attenuated psychosis syndrome—includes one or more of the symptoms of schizophrenia such as hallucinations or delusions, but the individual is aware that these are unusual experiences and are not typical for a healthy person. This is included in the Appendix of *DSM-5* as a disorder in need of further study.

Prevalence and Causes of Schizophrenia

What are the potential genetic, neurobiological, developmental, and psychosocial risk factors for schizophrenia?

- A number of causative factors have been implicated for schizophrenia, including genetic influences, neurotransmitter imbalances, structural damage to the brain caused by a prenatal viral infection or birth injury, and psychological stressors.
- Relapse appears to be triggered by hostile and critical family environments characterized by high expressed emotion.

Treatment of Schizophrenia

What are the goals of therapy for schizophrenia?

What biological and psychosocial treatments for schizophrenia are available?

- Successful treatment for people with schizophrenia rarely includes complete recovery. The quality of life for these individuals can be meaningfully affected, however, by combining antipsychotic medications with psychosocial approaches, employment support, and community-based and family interventions.
- Treatment typically involves antipsychotic drugs that are usually administered with a variety of psychosocial treatments, with the goal of reducing relapse and improving skills in deficits and compliance in taking the medications. The effectiveness of treatment is limited, because schizophrenia is typically a chronic disorder.

Key Terms

schizophrenia, 445
catatonia, 446
hebephrenia, 446
paranoia, 446
dementia praecox, 446
associative splitting, 446
psychotic behavior, 447
positive symptoms, 448
delusion, 448
hallucination, 449
negative symptoms, 450
avolition, 451
alogia, 451

anhedonia, 451
flat affect, 451
disorganized speech, 452
inappropriate affect, 452
catatonic immobility, 452
schizophreniform disorder, 453
schizoaffective disorder, 453
delusional disorder, 454
shared psychotic disorder (folie à
    deux), 454
substance-induced psychotic
    disorder, 455

psychotic disorder associated with
    another medical condition, 455
brief psychotic disorder, 455
attenuated psychosis syndrome, 455
prodromal stage, 457
schizophrenogenic mother, 465
double bind communication, 465
expressed emotion (EE), 465
token economy, 469

Answers to Concept Checks

12.1

Part A

1. disorganized; 2. Schizophreniform disorder; 3. Delusional disorder; 4. catatonic; 5. Attenuated psychosis syndrome

Part B

6. c; 7. b; 8. a; 9. d

12.2

1. f, h, a; 2. a, a; 3. d, i

12.3

1. f; 2. h; 3. i, g; 4. d, c; 5. b

Chapter Quiz

1. One distinction used to characterize symptoms of schizophrenia divides them into what two broad categories?
   a. paranoid and catatonic
   b. episodic and chronic
   c. psychiatric and somatic
   d. positive and negative

2. Emotional and social withdrawal, apathy, and poverty of speech and thought are examples of what type of symptoms in schizophrenia?
   a. psychotic
   b. negative
   c. disorganized
   d. positive

3. Rhonda fears that her employer is trying to poison her with gas emitted from the overhead lights in her office. Given what you know about Rhonda's thoughts, what symptom of schizophrenia is she likely to have?
   a. catatonia
   b. disorganized thoughts and behaviors
   c. paranoia
   d. undifferentiated thoughts and behaviors

4. Which disorder is characterized by symptoms similar to those seen in schizophrenia but of shorter duration, often with successful remission of symptoms?
   a. schizophreniform disorder
   b. delusional disorder
   c. schizoaffective disorder
   d. bipolar disorder

5. Most people with schizophrenia:
   a. have multiple episodes that get progressively worse
   b. have only one episode with full recovery after it
   c. have episodes of alternating positive and negative symptoms
   d. have multiple episodes, with different degrees of impairment between episodes

6. Research on cultural factors and schizophrenia suggests that African Americans:
   a. may have higher rates than other ethnic groups because of misdiagnosis
   b. may have higher rates than other ethnic groups because they are exposed to more prejudice and bias
   c. may be more vulnerable to schizophrenia because of chromosomal differences
   d. with schizophrenia are more likely to experience negative symptoms than positive symptoms

7. Which sibling of an individual with schizophrenia is most likely to develop schizophrenia?

   a. monozygotic twin raised in the same home

   b. monozygotic twin raised in a different home

   c. dizygotic twin raised in the same home

   d. dizygotic twin raised in a different home

8. Which statement is true about antipsychotic medications and the treatment of schizophrenia?

   a. Antipsychotic medications are not as effective as psychosocial treatments.

   b. Different medications are effective with different people and to a different degree.

   c. All antipsychotic medications appear to be equally effective for all patients.

   d. Most patients go through a trial-and-error period to determine whether antipsychotic, antidepressant, or antianxiety medications are most effective for them.

9. Which type of psychosocial treatment has been most effective for treating the behavioral problems seen in schizophrenia?

   a. psychodynamic psychotherapy

   b. moral treatment

   c. psychosurgery

   d. token economies

10. Which two psychosocial interventions appear to be most helpful for people with schizophrenia?

   a. hypnosis and psychosurgery

   b. ECT and social skills training

   c. psychoanalytic psychotherapy and expressed emotion management

   d. family education and vocational rehabilitation

   (See Appendix A for answers.)

Exploring Schizophrenia

▶ Schizophrenia disrupts perception of the world, thought, speech, movement, and almost every other aspect of daily functioning.

▶ Usually chronic with a high relapse rate; complete recovery from schizophrenia is rare.

- Stressful, traumatic life event
- High expressed emotion (family criticism, hostility, and/or intrusion)
- Sometimes no obvious trigger

Trigger

Biological Influences

- Inherited tendency (multiple genes) to develop disease
- Prenatal/birth complications—viral infection during pregnancy/birth injury affect child's brain cells
- Brain chemistry (abnormalities in the dopamine and glutamate systems)
- Brain structure (enlarged ventricles)

Dynamic Graphics/Jupiter Images

Social Influences

- Environment (early family experiences) can trigger onset
- Culture influences interpretation of disease/symptoms (hallucinations, delusions)

Javier Pierini/Photodisc/Getty Images

Causes

Behavioral Influences

- **Positive symptoms:**
  —Active manifestations of abnormal behavior (delusions, hallucinations, disorganized speech, odd body movements, or catatonia)
- **Negative symptoms:**
  —Flat affect (lack of emotional expression)
  —Avolition (lack of initiative, apathy)
  —Alogia (relative absence in amount or content of speech)

Emotional and Cognitive Influences

- Interaction styles that are high in criticism, hostility, and emotional overinvolvement can trigger a relapse

TREATMENT OF SCHIZOPHRENIA

Treatment

Individual, Group, and Family Therapy	▪ Can help patient and family understand the disease and symptom triggers. ▪ Teaches families communication skills. ▪ Provides resources for dealing with emotional and practical challenges.
Social Skills Training	▪ Can occur in hospital or community settings. ▪ Teaches the person with schizophrenia social, self-care, and vocational skills.

Medications	▪ Taking neuroleptic medications may help people with schizophrenia to:
	  —Clarify thinking and perceptions of reality
	  —Reduce hallucinations and delusions
	▪ Drug treatment must be consistent to be effective. Inconsistent dosage may aggravate existing symptoms or create new ones.

Photos: Photodisc/Getty Images

SYMPTOMS OF SCHIZOPHRENIA

People with schizophrenia do not all show the same kinds of symptoms. Symptoms vary from person to person and may be cyclical. Common symptoms include:

Symptoms		
Delusions	Joshua Ets-Hokin/Photodisc/Getty Images	■ Unrealistic and bizarre beliefs not shared by others in the culture ■ May be delusions of grandeur (that you are really Mother Teresa or Napoleon) or delusions of persecution (the cyclist who believed her competitors were sabotaging her by putting pebbles in the road)
Hallucinations	Photodisc/Getty Images	■ Sensory events that aren't based on any external event (hearing voices, seeing people who have died) ■ Many have auditory hallucinations (David hears his dead uncle talking to him)
Disorganized Speech	Royalty Free/Corbis	■ Jumping from topic to topic ■ Talking illogically (not answering direct questions, going off on tangents) ■ Speaking in unintelligible words and sentences
Behavioral Problems	Dynamic Graphics/Jupiter Images	■ Pacing excitably, wild agitation ■ Catatonic immobility ■ Waxy flexibility (keeping body parts in the same position when they are moved by someone else) ■ Inappropriate dress (coats in the summer, shorts in the winter) ■ Inappropriate affect ■ Ignoring personal hygiene
Withdrawal	Photodisc/Getty Images	■ Lack of emotional response (flat speech, little change in facial expressions) ■ Apathy (little interest in day-to-day activities) ■ Delayed and brief responses in conversation ■ Loss of enjoyment in pleasurable activities (eating, socializing, sex)

13

Neurodevelopmental and Neurocognitive Disorders

CHAPTER OUTLINE

Overview of Neurodevelopmental Disorders

Attention-Deficit/ Hyperactivity Disorder

    Clinical Descriptions
    Statistics
    Causes
    Treatment for ADHD

Specific Learning Disorder

    Clinical Description
    Statistics
    Causes
    Treatment of Learning Disorders

Autism Spectrum Disorder

    Clinical Description
    Statistics
    Causes: Psychological and Social
        Dimensions
    Causes: Biological Dimensions
    Treatment of Autism Spectrum Disorder

Intellectual Disability (Intellectual Developmental Disorder)

    Clinical Description
    Statistics
    Causes
    Treatment of Intellectual Disability

Prevention of Neurodevelopmental Disorders

Overview of Neurocognitive Disorders

Delirium

    Clinical Description and Statistics
    Causes
    Treatment
    Prevention

Major and Mild Neurocognitive Disorders

    Clinical Description and Statistics
    Neurocognitive Disorder Due to
        Alzheimer's Disease
    Vascular Neurocognitive Disorder
    Other Medical Conditions That Cause
        Neurocognitive Disorder
    Substance/Medication-Induced
        Neurocognitive Disorder
    Causes of Neurocognitive Disorder
    Treatment
    Prevention

480

iStock.com/TrevOC

Use scientific reasoning to interpret behavior:	▸ Identify basic biological, psychological, and social components of behavioral explanations (e.g., inferences, observations, operational definitions, and interpretations). (APA SLO 2.1a) *(see textbook pages 482–483, 486–487, 490–491, 495–496, 500–503, 506, 511–516)*
Engage in innovative and integrative thinking and problem solving:	▸ Describe problems operationally to study them empirically. (APA SLO 2.3a) *(see textbook pages 482–485, 488–489, 492–494, 498–500, 505–506, 508–515)*
Describe applications that employ discipline-based problem solving:	▸ Correctly identify antecedents and consequences of behavior and mental processes (APA SLO 1.3c). *(see textbook pages 482–483, 486–487, 490–491, 495–496, 500–503, 506, 515–517)*
	▸ Describe examples of relevant and practical applications of psychological principles to everyday life. (APA SLO 1.3a) *(see textbook pages 482–483, 487–488, 491–492, 496–497, 503–504, 507, 517–520)*

* Portions of this chapter cover learning outcomes suggested by the American Psychological Association (2013) in its guidelines for the undergraduate psychology major. Chapter coverage of these outcomes is identified above by APA Goal and APA Suggested Learning Outcome (SLO).

Overview of Neurodevelopmental Disorders

▸ Why is knowledge of critical development stages important for understanding neurodevelopmental disorders?

Almost all disorders described in this book are developmental disorders in the sense that they change over time. Most disorders originate in childhood, although the full presentation of the problem may not manifest itself until much later. Disorders that show themselves early in life often persist as the person grows older, so the term *childhood disorder* may be misleading. Because the developmental disorders in this group are all believed to be neurologically based, *DSM-5* categorizes them as **neurodevelopmental disorders** (American Psychiatric Association, 2013). In this chapter, we cover those disorders that are revealed in a clinically significant way during a child's developing years and are of concern to families and educators. Remember, however, that these difficulties often persist through adulthood and are typically lifelong problems, not problems unique to children. Before we discuss specific disorders, we need to address the broad topic of development in relation to disorders usually first diagnosed in infancy, childhood, or adolescence. For example, what effect do the early disruptions in skills have on a child's later life? Does it matter when in the developmental period certain problems arise? Are disruptions in development permanent, thus making any hope for treatment doubtful?

Recall that in Chapter 2 we described developmental psychopathology as the study of how disorders arise and how they change with time (Nigg, 2015). Childhood is considered particularly important, because the brain changes significantly for several years after birth; this is also when critical developments occur in social, emotional, cognitive, and other important competency areas. These changes mostly follow a pattern: The child develops one skill before acquiring the next, and subsequent skills often build upon one another. Although this pattern of change is only one aspect of development, it is an important concept at this point because it implies that any disruption in the development of early skills will, by the very nature of this sequential process, disrupt the development of later skills. For example, some researchers believe that people with autism spectrum disorder suffer from a disruption in early social development, which prevents them from developing important social relationships, even with their parents (Durand, 2014). From a developmental perspective, the absence of early and meaningful social relationships has serious consequences. Children whose motivation to interact with others is disrupted may have a more difficult time learning to communicate; that is, they may not want to learn to speak if other people are not important to them. Researchers don't know whether a disruption in communication skills is a direct outcome of the disorder or a by-product of disrupted early social development.

Understanding this type of developmental relationship is important for several reasons. Knowing what processes are disrupted will help us understand the disorder better and may lead to more appropriate intervention strategies. It may be important to identify children with attention-deficit/hyperactivity disorder (ADHD), for example, because their

....

neurodevelopmental disorders Neurologically based disorders that are revealed in a clinically significant way during a child's developing years.

problems with impulsivity may interfere with their ability to create and maintain friendships, an important developmental consideration. Similarly, identifying a disorder such as autism spectrum disorder (ASD) at an early age is important for these children so that their social deficits can be addressed before they affect other skill domains, such as social communication. Too often, people see early and pervasive disruptions in developmental skills and expect a negative prognosis, with the problems predetermined and permanent. Remember, however, that biological and psychosocial influences continuously interact with each other. Therefore, even for disorders such as ADHD and ASD that have clear biological bases, the presentation of the disorder is different for each individual. Changes at the biological or the psychosocial level may reduce the impact of the disorder.

One note of caution is appropriate here. There is real concern in the profession, especially among developmental psychologists, that some workers in the field may view aspects of normal development as symptoms of abnormality. For example, *echolalia*, which involves repeating the speech of others, was once thought to be a sign of autism spectrum disorder. When we study the development of speech in children without disorders, however, we find that repeating what someone else says is an intermediate step in language development. In children with autism spectrum disorder, therefore, echolalia is just a sign of relatively delayed language skills and not a symptom of their disorder (Roberts, 2014). Knowledge of development is important for understanding the nature of psychological disorders.

With that caveat in mind, we now examine several disorders usually diagnosed first in infancy, childhood, or adolescence. We also examine *intellectual disability*, which involves considerable deficits in cognitive abilities. Communication and motor disabilities, which are also considered neurodevelopmental disorders, are described in Table 13.1.

TABLE 13.1 | Common Communication and Motor Disorders

Childhood-Onset Fluency Disorder			
Clinical Description	**Statistics**	**Etiology**	**Treatment**
A disturbance in speech fluency that includes a number of problems with speech, such as repeating syllables or words, prolonging certain sounds, making obvious pauses, or substituting words to replace ones that are difficult to articulate.	Occurs twice as often among boys as among girls. Begins most often in children by the age of six, and 98% of cases occur before the age of 10 (Maguire, Yeh, & Ito, 2012). Approximately 80% of children who stutter before they enter school will no longer stutter after they have been in school a year or so (Kroll & Beitchman, 2005).	Rather than anxiety causing childhood-onset fluency disorder, this problem makes people socially anxious (Ezrati-Vinacour & Levin, 2004). Multiple brain pathways appear to be involved, and genetic influences may be a factor (Maguire *et al.*, 2012).	Parents are counseled about how to talk to their children. *Regulated-breathing method* is a promising behavioral treatment in which the person is instructed to stop speaking when a stuttering episode occurs and then to take a deep breath (exhale, then inhale) before proceeding (Onslow, Jones, O'Brian, Packman, & Menzies, 2012). Altered auditory feedback (electronically changing speech feedback to people who stutter) can improve speech, as can using forms of self-monitoring, in which people modify their own speech for the words they stutter (Onslow *et al.*, 2012).
Language Disorder			
Clinical Description	**Statistics**	**Etiology**	**Treatment**
Limited speech in *all* situations. *Expressive language* (what is said) is significantly below *receptive language* (what is understood); the latter is usually average.	Occurs in 10% to 15% of children younger than three years of age (Johnson & Beitchman, 2005) and is almost five times as likely to affect boys as girls (Whitehurst *et al.*, 1988).	An unfounded psychological explanation is that the children's parents may not speak to them enough. A biological theory is that middle ear infection is a contributory cause.	May be self-correcting and may not require special intervention (Whitehurst *et al.*, 1988).

Social (Pragmatic) Communication Disorder

Clinical Description	Statistics	Etiology	Treatment
Difficulties with the social aspects of verbal and non-verbal communication, including verbosity, prosody, excessive switching of topics, and dominating conversations (Adams *et al.*, 2012). Does not have the restricted and repetitive behaviors found in ASD.	Exact estimates not yet available, but the number of cases identified appears to be rising with increasing awareness (Baird *et al.*, 2006; Bishop, 2000).	Limited information.	Individualized social skills training (e.g., modeling, role playing) with an emphasis on teaching important rules necessary for carrying on conversations with others (e.g., what is too much and too little information) (Adams *et al.*, 2012).

Tourette's Disorder

Clinical Description	Statistics	Etiology	Treatment
Involuntary motor movements *(tics)*, such as head twitching, or vocalizations, such as grunts, that often occur in rapid succession, come on suddenly, and happen in idiosyncratic or stereotyped ways. Vocal tics often include the involuntary repetition of obscenities.	Of all children, up to 20% show some tics during their growing years, and one to 10 children out of every 1,000 have Tourette's disorder (Jummani & Coffey, 2009). Usually develops before the age of 14. High comorbidity between tics and ADHD, as well as obsessive-compulsive disorder (Jummani & Coffey, 2009).	There are likely multiple vulnerability genes that influence the form and severity of tics (Jummani & Coffey, 2009).	*Psychological:* Self-monitoring, relaxation training, and habit reversal.

Adapted from (Durand, 2011)

Attention-Deficit/Hyperactivity Disorder

▶ What are the central defining features of attention deficit/hyperactivity disorder?

Do you know people who flit from activity to activity, who start many tasks but seldom finish one, who have trouble concentrating, and who don't seem to pay attention when others speak? These people may have **attention-deficit/hyperactivity disorder (ADHD)**, one of the most common reasons children are referred for mental health services in the United States. The primary characteristics of such people include a pattern of inattention, such as being disorganized or forgetful about school- or work-related tasks, or of hyperactivity and impulsivity. These deficits can significantly disrupt academic efforts, as well as social relationships. Consider the case of Danny.

Danny... • *The Boy Who Couldn't Sit Still*

Danny, a 9-year-old boy, was referred to us because of his difficulties at school and at home. Danny had a great deal of energy and loved playing most sports, especially baseball. Academically, his work was adequate,

attention-deficit/hyperactivity disorder (ADHD) Developmental disorder featuring maladaptive levels of inattention, excessive activity, and impulsiveness.

although his teacher reported that his performance was diminishing and she believed he would do better if he paid more attention in class. Danny rarely spent more than a few minutes on a task without some interruption: He would get up out of his seat, rifle through his desk, or constantly ask questions. His peers were frustrated with him because he was equally impulsive during their interactions. He never finished a game, and in sports he tried to play all positions simultaneously.

At home, Danny was considered a handful. His parents reported that they often scolded him for not carrying out some task, although the reason seemed to be that he forgot what he was doing rather than that he deliberately tried to defy them. They also said that, out of their own frustration, they sometimes grabbed him by the shoulders and yelled, "Slow down!" because his hyperactivity drove them crazy.

Clinical Description

Danny has many characteristics of ADHD. Like Danny, people with this disorder have a great deal of difficulty sustaining their attention on a task or activity (Barkley, 2015c). As a result, their tasks are often unfinished, and they often seem not to be listening when someone else is speaking. In addition to this serious disruption in attention, some people with ADHD display motor hyperactivity. Children with this disorder are often described as fidgety in school, unable to sit still for more than a few minutes. Danny's restlessness in his classroom was a considerable source of concern for his teacher and peers, who were frustrated by his impatience and excessive activity. In addition to hyperactivity and problems

sustaining attention, impulsivity—acting apparently without thinking—is a common complaint made about people with ADHD. For instance, during meetings at baseball practice, Danny often shouted responses to the coach's questions even before the coach had a chance to finish his sentence.

For ADHD, *DSM-5* differentiates two categories of symptoms. The first includes problems of *inattention*. People may appear not to listen to others; they may lose necessary school assignments, books, or tools; and they may not pay enough attention to details, making careless mistakes. The second category of symptoms includes *hyperactivity and impulsivity*. Hyperactivity includes fidgeting, having trouble sitting for any length of time, and always being on the go. Impulsivity includes blurting out answers before questions have been completed and having trouble waiting turns. Either the first (inattention) or the second and third (hyperactivity and impulsivity) set of symptoms must be present for someone to be diagnosed with ADHD (American Psychiatric Association, 2013). These different presentations are called *subtypes*, and they include the inattentive subtype (what some may call *ADD*, noting the absence of hyperactivity, although this is not an official diagnostic label), and the hyperactive/impulsive subtype. Other individuals meet criteria for both inattention and hyperactivity/impulsivity, and these individuals are labeled with the *combined* subtype.

Inattention, hyperactivity, and impulsivity often cause other problems that appear secondary to ADHD. Academic performance often suffers, especially as the child progresses in school. Children with ADHD are likely to be unpopular and rejected by their peers (McQuade & Hoza, 2015). This, too, may be the result of genetic factors as well as environmental influences such as a hostile home environment and gene–environment interactions. For example,

---

 Discussing Diversity ADHD across Age and Gender

ADHD is most often diagnosed among boys and among children and adolescents. This has led some to question whether this disorder looks different in girls and adults than it does in young boys or whether ADHD is simply less common in these groups. Most research to date on ADHD has used research samples made up mostly of young boys, which has made it difficult to determine frequency and symptoms of ADHD in girls and adults. Some have suggested that part of the reason for the focus on young boys is that many researchers and clinicians have paid more attention to symptoms of hyperactivity than to problems with inattention because the former are more disruptive and easily measurable

than the latter and that hyperactivity is more common in boys. So has ADHD been overlooked among girls and adults because the symptoms of this disorder look different in these groups?

Several recent large-scale studies have begun to shed light on this question. In one study, researchers at the Pediatric Psychopharmacology Unit at the Massachusetts General Hospital tested whether the symptoms of ADHD differ between boys and girls (Biederman *et al.*, 2001b). They found that girls with ADHD are more likely than boys to have the inattentive subtype and are less likely to have symptoms of hyperactivity, opposition, and other disruptive behaviors. A study by Fayyad and colleagues (2007) examined the

occurrence of ADHD among adults in 10 countries. This study revealed that 3.4% of adults report having ADHD, with a slightly higher rate found among men (4.1%) than among women (2.7%). Adult ADHD was found to be associated with significant levels of comorbidity and impairment at work. Moreover, few of those with adult ADHD reported receiving treatment for this problem (Fayyad *et al.*, 2007).

Studies such as these suggest that, although ADHD may look different among girls and adults, it does occur and is associated with problems in functioning and unmet need for treatment. It is hopeful that efforts to accurately identify and effectively treat this problem will lead to improvements in the life of those affected by ADHD. ∎

some research shows that having a specific genotype and psychosocial distress can predict ADHD in children (Barkley, 2015a; Nigg, Nikolas, & Burt, 2010).

Statistics

An important analysis of prevalence of ADHD suggests that the disorder is found in about 5.2% of the child populations across all regions of the world (Polanczyk, de Lima, Horta, Biederman, & Rohde, 2007). Boys are two to three times more likely to be diagnosed with ADHD than girls, and this discrepancy increases for children being seen in clinics (Owens, Cardoos, & Hinshaw, 2015; Spencer, Biederman, & Mick, 2007). The reason for this gender difference is largely unknown. It may be that adults are more tolerant of hyperactivity among girls, who tend to be less active than boys with ADHD. Boys tend to be more aggressive, which will more likely result in attention by mental health professionals (Rucklidge, 2010). Girls with ADHD, on the other hand, tend to display more behaviors referred to as "internalizing"—specifically, anxiety and depression (Owens *et al.*, 2015).

Children with ADHD are first identified as different from their peers around age three or four; their parents describe them as active, mischievous, slow to toilet train, and oppositional (Taylor, 2012). The symptoms of inattention, impulsivity, and hyperactivity become increasingly obvious during the school years. Despite the perception that children grow out of ADHD, their problems usually continue: it is estimated that about half of the children with ADHD have ongoing difficulties through adulthood (McGough, 2005). Over time, children with ADHD seem to be less impulsive, although inattention persists. During adolescence, the impulsivity manifests itself in different areas; for example, teens with ADHD are at greater risk for pregnancy and contracting sexually transmitted infections. They are also more likely to have driving difficulties, such as crashes; to be cited for speeding; and to have their licenses suspended (Barkley, 2015b; Fabiano & Schatz, 2015).

What happens to children and adolescents with ADHD as they become adults? Rachel Klein and her colleagues followed up on more than 200 boys with this disorder and reported on their status 33 years later (Klein *et al.*, 2012). When compared with a group without ADHD, the majority of these men (84%) were employed but in jobs with significantly lower positions than the comparison group. They also had 2.5 fewer years of education and were much less likely to hold higher degrees. These men were also more likely to be divorced and to have substance use problems and antisocial personality disorder (Klein *et al.*, 2012). In addition, the effects of their tendency to be impulsive may account for their increased risk of displaying risky driving, having a sexually transmitted disease, increased chance of having a head injury, and more emergency department admissions (Ramos Olazagasti *et al.*, 2013).

Diagnosing children with ADHD is complicated. Several other *DSM-5* disorders, also found in children, appear to overlap significantly with this disorder. Specifically,

---

DSM 5 DISORDER CRITERIA SUMMARY
Attention Deficit/Hyperactivity Disorder

A. A persistent pattern of inattention and/or hyperactivity–impulsivity that interferes with functioning or development, as characterized by (1) and/or (2):

1. **Inattention:** Six (or more) of the following symptoms have persisted for at least six months to a degree that is inconsistent with developmental level and that negatively impacts directly on social and academic/occupational activities:
   Note: The symptoms are not solely a manifestation of oppositional behavior, defiance, hostility, or failure to understand tasks or instructions. For older adolescents and adults (age 17 and older), at least five symptoms are required. (a) Often fails to give close attention to details or makes careless mistakes in schoolwork, at work, or during other activities; (b) often has difficulty sustaining attention in tasks or play activities; (c) often does not seem to listen when spoken to directly; (d) often does not follow through on instructions and fails to finish schoolwork, chores, or duties in the workplace; (e) often has difficulty organizing tasks and activities; (f) often avoids, dislikes, or is reluctant to engage in tasks that require sustained mental effort; (g) often loses things necessary for tasks or activities. (h) Is often easily distracted by extraneous stimuli (for older adolescents and adults, may include unrelated thoughts); (i) is often forgetful in daily activities.

2. **Hyperactivity and impulsivity:** Six (or more) of the following symptoms have persisted for at least six months to a degree that is inconsistent with developmental level and that negatively impacts directly on social and academic/occupational activities:
   Note: The symptoms are not solely a manifestation of oppositional behavior, defiance, hostility, or failure to understand tasks or instructions. For older adolescents and adults (age 17 and older), at least five symptoms are required. (a) Often fidgets with or taps hands or feet or squirms in seat; (b) often leaves seat in situations when remaining seated is expected; (c) often runs about or climbs in situations where it is inappropriate. (**Note:** In adolescents or adults, may be limited to feeling restless.) (d) often unable to play or engage in leisure activities quietly; (e) is often "on the go," acting as if "driven by a motor"; (f) often talks excessively; (g) often blurts out an answer before a question has been completed; (h) often has difficulty waiting his or her turn; (i) often interrupts or intrudes on others.

B. Several inattentive or hyperactive-impulsive symptoms were present prior to age 12 years.

C. Several inattentive or hyperactive-impulsive symptoms are present in two or more settings.

D. There is clear evidence that the symptoms interfere with, or reduce the quality of, social, academic, or occupational functioning.

E. The symptoms do not occur exclusively during the course of schizophrenia or another psychotic disorder and are not better explained by another mental disorder, substance intoxication, or withdrawal.

From American Psychiatric Association. (2013). *Diagnostic and statistical manual of mental disorders* (5th ed.). Washington, DC.

oppositional defiant disorder (ODD), conduct disorder, and bipolar disorder all have characteristics seen in children with ADHD (Toth, de Lacy, & King, 2016). ODD is a *DSM-5* disorder that includes behaviors such as "often loses temper," "argues with adults," "touchy and easily annoyed by others," and "often spiteful and vindictive" (Toth, de Lacy, & King, 2016). The impulsivity and hyperactivity observed in children with ADHD can manifest themselves in some of these symptoms.

Causes

ADHD is considered to be highly influenced by genetics. Researchers have known for some time that ADHD is more common in families in which one person has the disorder. For example, the relatives of children with ADHD have been found to be more likely to have ADHD themselves than would be expected in the general population (Fliers *et al.*, 2009). It is important to note that these families display an increase in psychopathology in general, including conduct disorder, mood disorders, anxiety disorders, and substance abuse (Barkley, 2015a). This research and the comorbidity in the children themselves suggest that some shared genetic deficits may contribute to the problems experienced by individuals with these disorders (Brown, 2009).

As with other disorders, researchers are finding that multiple genes are responsible for ADHD (Nikolas & Burt, 2010). In its simplest form, we tend to think of genetic "problems" in terms of having genes turned off (not making proteins) when they should be turned on and vice versa. Research on ADHD (and on other disorders) is finding that in many cases, however, mutations occur that either create extra copies of a gene on one chromosome or result in the deletion of genes (called **copy number variants**) (Martin, O'Donovan, Thapar, Langley, & Williams, 2015). Because our DNA is structured to function with corresponding or matching pairs of genes on each chromosome, the additions or deletions of genes result in disrupted development.

Most attention to date focuses on genes associated with the neurochemical dopamine, although norepinephrine, serotonin, and gamma-aminobutyric acid (GABA) are also implicated in the cause of ADHD.

As with several other disorders we've discussed, researchers are looking for endophenotypes, those basic deficits—such as specific attentional problems—characteristic of ADHD. The goal is to link these deficits to specific brain dysfunctions. Not surprisingly, specific areas of current interest for ADHD are the brain's attention system, working memory functions, inattentiveness, and impulsivity. Researchers are trying to tie specific genetic defects to these cognitive processes to make the link between genes and behavior. Some research indicates that poor "inhibitory control" (the ability to stop responding to a task when signaled) may be common among children with ADHD and their unaffected family members (siblings and parents) and

may be one genetic marker (an endophenotype) for this disorder (Goos, Crosbie, Payne, & Schachar, 2009; Nikolas & Nigg, 2015).

The strong genetic influence in ADHD does not rule out any role for the environment (Ficks & Waldman, 2009). In one of a growing number of gene–environment interaction studies of ADHD, researchers found that children with a specific mutation involving the dopamine system were more likely to exhibit the symptoms of ADHD if their mothers smoked during pregnancy (Kahn, Khoury, Nichols, & Lanphear, 2003; Russell, Ford, Williams, & Russell, 2016. Prenatal smoking seemed to interact with this genetic predisposition to increase the risk for hyperactive and impulsive behavior. Other research is pointing to additional environmental factors, such as maternal stress and alcohol use, and parental marital instability and discord, as involved in these gene–environment interactions (Barkley, 2015a; Ficks & Waldman, 2009). In addition, a variety of other pregnancy complications (for example, maternal alcohol consumption and low birth weight) may play a role in increasing the chance that a child with a genetic predisposition for ADHD will display the symptoms characteristic of this disorder (Barkley, 2006c).

A great deal of research on the structure and the function of the brain for children with ADHD has been conducted. In general, researchers know that the overall volume of the brain in those with ADHD is slightly smaller (3% to 4%) than in children without ADHD (Barkley, 2015a). A number of areas in the brains of those with ADHD appear affected, especially those involved in self-organizational abilities (Valera, Faraone, Murray, & Seidman, 2007). These changes seem less pronounced in persons who received medication (Taylor, 2012). In fact, a number of studies now point to a "growth enhancing effect" of stimulant medication, suggesting that brain development progresses in a more typical fashion in children receiving medication for ADHD versus those who do not (Frodl & Skokauskas, 2012; Rubia *et al.*, 2014).

A variety of toxins such as allergens and food additives have been considered as possible causes of ADHD. Some research suggests that there may be a small but measurable impact of artificial food colors and additives on the behavior of young children (Hurt & Arnold, 2015). One study found that three-year-old and eight- to nine-year-old children who consumed typical amounts of preservatives (sodium benzoate) and food colorings had increased levels of hyperactive behaviors (inattention, impulsivity, and overactivity) (McCann *et al.*, 2007). Other research points to the possible role of toxins such as the pesticides found in foods as contributing to an increased risk of ADHD (Barkley, 2015a; Bouchard, Bellinger, Wright, & Weisskopf, 2010).

Psychological and social dimensions of ADHD may further influence the disorder itself—especially how the child fares over time. Negative responses by parents, teachers, and peers to the affected child's impulsivity and hyperactivity

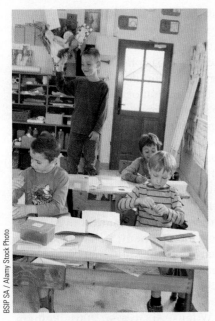

▲ A child with ADHD is likely to behave inappropriately regardless of the setting.

may contribute to feelings of low self-esteem, especially in children who are also depressed (Anastopoulos, Sommer, & Schatz, 2009). Years of constant reminders by teachers and parents to behave, sit quietly, and pay attention may create a negative self-image in these children, which, in turn, can negatively affect their ability to make friends, and these effects can last into adulthood (Murphy, 2015). Thus, the possible biological influences on impulsivity, hyperactivity, and attention, combined with attempts to control these children, may lead to rejection and consequent poor self-image. An integration of the biological and psychological influences on ADHD suggests that both need to be addressed when designing effective treatments (Barkley, 2015c).

Treatment of ADHD

Treatment for ADHD has proceeded on two fronts: psychosocial and biological interventions (Smith & Shapiro, 2015). Psychosocial treatments generally focus on broader issues such as improving academic performance, decreasing disruptive behavior, and improving social skills. Typically, the goal of biological treatments is to reduce the children's impulsivity and hyperactivity and to improve their attention skills. Current thinking in this area points to using parent- and/or teacher-delivered behavioral interventions for young children before attempting medication (Subcommittee on Attention-Deficit/Hyperactivity Disorder & Management, 2011).

Psychosocial Interventions

Researchers recommend various behavioral interventions to help children with ADHD at home and in school (Pfiffner & DuPaul, 2015; Robin, 2015). In general, the programs set such goals as increasing the amount of time the child remains seated, the number of math papers completed, or appropriate play with peers. Reinforcement programs reward the child for improvements and, at times, punish misbehavior with loss of rewards. Other parent education programs teach families how to respond constructively to

their child's behaviors and how to structure the child's day to help prevent difficulties (e.g., Loren *et al.*, 2015). Social skills training for these children also seems to be an important treatment component (Watson, Richels, Michalek, & Raymer, 2015). For adults with ADHD, cognitive-behavioral intervention to reduce distractibility and improve organizational skills appears helpful (Knouse, 2015). Most clinicians recommend a combination of approaches designed to individualize treatments for those with ADHD, targeting both short-term management issues (decreasing hyperactivity and impulsivity) and long-term concerns (preventing and reversing academic decline and improving social skills).

Biological Interventions

The first types of medication used for children with ADHD were stimulants. It is estimated that 3.5% of the children living in the United States are being treated with medication for symptoms of ADHD (Zuvekas & Vitiello, 2012). Drugs such as methylphenidate (Ritalin, Adderall) and several non-stimulant medications such as atomoxetine (Strattera), guanfacine (Tenex), and clonidine have proved helpful in reducing the core symptoms of hyperactivity and impulsivity and in improving concentration on tasks (Connor, 2015).

Originally, it seemed paradoxical or contrary to expect that children would calm down after taking a stimulant. However, on the same low doses, children and adults with and without ADHD react in the same way. It appears that stimulant medications reinforce the brain's ability to focus attention during problem-solving tasks (Connor, 2006). Although the use of stimulant medications remains controversial, especially for children, most clinicians recommend them temporarily, in combination with psychosocial interventions, to help improve children's social and academic skills.

The concerns over the use of stimulant medications now include their potential for abuse. In Chapter 10, we discussed that drugs such as Ritalin and Adderall are sometimes abused for their ability to create elation and reduce fatigue (Varga, 2012). And, the widespread misperception that use of these medications to improve academic performance (they are frequently used for this purpose on college campuses) and that they are harmless is also of concern (Watson, Arcona, & Antonuccio, 2015). This is particularly worrisome for children with ADHD because they are at increased risk for later substance abuse (Wagner & Pliszka, 2009). As mentioned previously, other non-stimulant drugs such as atomoxetine (Strattera) also appear effective for some children with ADHD. This drug is a selective norepinephrine-reuptake inhibitor and therefore does not produce the same "highs" when used in larger doses. Research

copy number variants Genes that are deleted as a result of mutations; these deletions may play a role in the development of ADHD and other disorders.

suggests that other drugs, such as some antidepressants (imipramine) and a drug used for treating high blood pressure (clonidine) may have similar effects as atomoxetine on people with ADHD (Connor, 2015). All these drugs seem to improve compliance and decrease negative behaviors in many children, and their effects do not usually last when the drugs are discontinued.

Psychopharmacogenetics is the study of how your genetic makeup influences your response to certain drugs. The hope for this field is that medications can be matched or even "designed" for individuals to better complement their specific needs (Jain, 2015). One study looked at the use of methylphenidate (Ritalin) for children and adolescents with ADHD (Polanczyk, Zeni et al., 2007). For those who had a specific gene defect, methylphenidate had a strong positive effect, especially on their problems with inattention. This was not the case for those with ADHD who did not have that gene defect. Currently, the use of drug treatments tends to be by trial and error. This new study holds the promise of potentially eliminating this guesswork by tailoring the treatment to the individual.

How effective is medication for children with ADHD? Unfortunately, some portions of children do not respond to medications. In addition, most children who do respond only show improvement in ability to focus their attention but do not show gains in the important areas of academics and social skills. In addition, the medications often result in unpleasant side effects, such as insomnia, drowsiness, or irritability (Connor, 2015).

Combined Approach to Treatment

To determine whether a combined approach to treatment is the most effective, a large-scale study initiated by the National Institute of Mental Health was conducted by six teams of researchers (Jensen et al., 2001). Labeled the Multimodal Treatment of Attention-Deficit/Hyperactivity Disorder (MTA) study, this 14-month study included 579 children who were randomly assigned to one of four groups. One group of the children received routine care without medication or specific behavioral interventions (community care). The three treatment groups consisted of medication management (usually methylphenidate), intensive behavioral treatment, and a combination of the two treatments. Initial reports from the study suggested that the combination of behavioral treatments and medication and medication alone were superior to behavioral treatment alone and community intervention for ADHD symptoms. For problems that went beyond the specific symptoms of ADHD, such as social skills, academics, parent–child relations, oppositional behavior, and anxiety or depression, results suggested slight advantages of combination over single treatments (medication management, behavioral treatment) and community care.

Some controversy surrounds the interpretation of these findings—specifically, whether the combination of behavioral and medical treatments is superior to medication alone (Biederman, Spencer, Wilens, & Greene, 2001; Pelham, 1999). One of the concerns surrounding the study was that although medication continued to be dispensed, the behavioral treatment was faded over time, which may account for the observed differences.

Practically, if there is no difference between these two treatments, most parents and therapists would opt for simply providing medication for these children because of its ease of use and lower time commitment (Connor, 2015). Behavioral interventions have the added benefit, however, of improving aspects of the child and family that are not directly affected by medication. Reinterpretations of the data from this large-scale study continue, and more research likely will be needed to clarify the combined and separate effects of these two approaches to treatment (Connor, 2015; Ollendick & Shirk, 2010). Despite these advances, however, children with ADHD continue to pose a considerable challenge to their families and to the educational system.

Specific Learning Disorder

▶ What is specific learning disorder, and how is it typically treated?

Because parents often invest a great deal of time, resources, and emotional energy to ensure their children's academic success, it can be upsetting when a child with no obvious intellectual deficits does not achieve as expected. In this section, we describe **specific learning disorder**—which is characterized by performance that is substantially below what would be expected given the person's age, intelligence quotient (IQ) score, and education (Pierce, 2016). We also look briefly at disorders that involve how we communicate. Consider the case of Alice.

Alice... • *Taking a Learning Disorder to College*

Alice, a 20-year-old college student, sought help because of her difficulty in several of her classes. She reported that she had been a good student until about the sixth grade, when her grades suffered significantly. Her teacher informed her parents that she wasn't working up to her potential and she needed to be better motivated. Alice had always worked hard in school but promised to try harder. However, with each report card, her mediocre grades made her feel worse about herself. She managed to graduate from high school, but by that time she felt she was not as bright as her friends.

Alice enrolled in a community college and again found herself struggling with the work. Over the years, she had learned several tricks that helped her study and at least get passing grades. She read the material in her textbooks aloud to herself; she had discovered that she could recall the material better this way than if she just read silently to herself.

After her sophomore year, Alice transferred to the university, which she found even more demanding and where she failed most of her classes. After our first meeting, I suggested that she be formally assessed to identify the source of her difficulty. As suspected, Alice had a specific learning disorder.

Scores from an IQ test placed her slightly above average, but she was assessed to have significant difficulties with reading. Her comprehension was poor, and she could not remember most of the content of what she read. We recommended that she continue with her trick of reading aloud, because her comprehension for what she heard was adequate. In addition, Alice was taught how to analyze her reading—that is, how to outline and take notes. She was encouraged to audiotape her lectures and play them back to herself as she drove. Although Alice did not become an A student, she was able to graduate from the university, and she now works with young children who themselves have learning disabilities.

Clinical Description

According to *DSM-5* criteria, Alice would be diagnosed as having a specific learning disorder (in her case especially in the area of reading), which is defined as a significant discrepancy between a person's academic achievement and what would be expected for someone of the same age—referred to by some as "unexpected underachievement" (Miciak, Fletcher, & Stuebing, 2016; Scanlon, 2013). More specifically, the criteria require that the person perform academically at a level significantly below that of a typical person of the same age, cognitive ability (as measured on an IQ test), and educational background. In addition, a diagnosis of specific learning disorder requires that the person's disability not be caused by a sensory difficulty, such as trouble with sight or hearing, and should not be the result of poor or absent instruction. Clinicians can use the specifiers for *disorders of reading, written expression, or mathematics* to highlight specific problems for remediation. As with other disorders, clinicians rate the disorder on levels of severity.

Historically, a specific learning disorder would be defined as a discrepancy of more than two standard deviations between achievement and IQ. There was considerable controversy, however, over using the discrepancy between IQ and achievement as part of the process of identifying children with learning disorders (Cavendish, 2013). Part of the criticism involves the delay between when learning problems occur and when they finally result in a large enough difference between IQ scores and achievement scores—which may not be measurable until later in a child's academic life. An alternative approach—called *response to intervention*—is now being used by many clinicians (Miciak *et al.*, 2016). It involves identifying a child as having a specific learning disorder when the response to a known effective intervention (for example, an early reading program) is significantly inferior to the performance by peers (Cavendish, 2013; Van-DerHeyden & Harvey, 2012). This provides an early warning system and focuses on providing effective instruction.

Statistics

The prevalence of specific learning disorders has been estimated between 5% and 15% across youth of various ages and cultures (American Psychological Association, 2013). In the United States, approximately 6.5 million students between the ages of three and 21 were receiving services for specific learning disorder between 2009 and 2010 (U.S. Department of Education, 2012). The frequency of this diagnosis appears to increase in wealthier regions of the country, suggesting that with better access to diagnostic services, more children are identified (see ● Figure 13.1). There do appear to be racial differences in the diagnosis of specific learning disorder (referred to as "disproportionality") (Bruce & Venkatesh, 2014; Cortiella & Horowitz, 2014). Approximately 1% of Caucasian children and 2.6% of black children were receiving services for problems with learning in 2001 (Bradley, Danielson, & Hallahan, 2002). It appears that societal views of disability, racism, and inequitable assessment are among the factors that contribute to disproportionality (Bruce & Venkatesh, 2014).

Difficulties with reading are the most common of the learning disorders and occur in some form in 7% of the general population (Pennington & Bishop, 2009; Peterson & Pennington, 2012). Mathematics disorder appears in approximately 5% to 6% of the population (Pierce, 2016), but there is limited information about the prevalence of disorder of written expression among children and adults. Students with learning disorders are more likely to drop out of school (Vogel & Reder, 1998; Kearney, 2008), more likely to be unemployed (Gerber, 2012), and more likely to have suicidal thoughts and attempt suicide (Daniel *et al.*, 2006). However, the negative outcomes for adults may be mitigated by providing the proper supports, such as having a positive relationship with caring adults and providing accommodations in postsecondary educational and employment settings (Gregg, 2013).

....

specific learning disorder Neurodevelopmental disorder characterized by academic performance that is substantially below what would be expected given the person's age, intelligence quotient (IQ) score, and education.

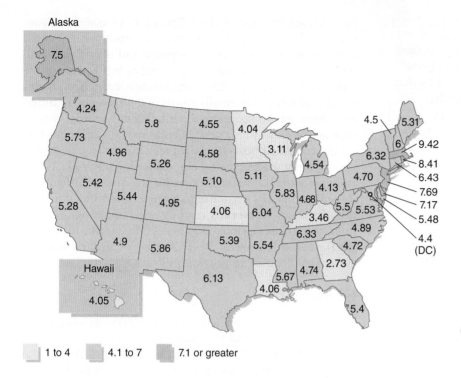

Alaska
7.5

4.24
5.8   4.55   4.04
5.73
4.96   4.58   3.11
5.26
5.42   5.10   5.11   4.54
5.28   5.44   4.95   5.83   4.13   4.70
         4.06   6.04   4.68   5.5   5.53
                        3.46
4.9   5.86   5.39   5.54   6.33   4.89
                                4.72
                        5.67   4.74   2.73
6.13   4.06

4.5   5.31
6   9.42
6.32   8.41
       6.43
4.70   7.69
       7.17
       5.48
       4.4
       (DC)

Hawaii
4.05

5.4

☐ 1 to 4   ☐ 4.1 to 7   ☐ 7.1 or greater

● **Figure 13.1** Uneven distribution. The highest percentages of schoolchildren diagnosed with learning disabilities are in the wealthiest states.

DSM 5 — DISORDER CRITERIA SUMMARY
Specific Learning Disorder

A. Difficulty learning and using academic skills, as indicated by the presence of at least one of the following symptoms that have persisted for at least six months, despite the provision of interventions that target those difficulties: (1) Inaccurate or slow and effortful word reading; (2) difficulty understanding the meaning of what is read; (3) difficulties with spelling; (4) difficulties with written expression; (5) difficulties mastering number sense, number facts, or calculation; (6) difficulties with mathematical reasoning (e.g., has severe difficulty applying mathematical concepts, facts, or procedures to solve quantitative problems).

B. The affected academic skills are substantially and quantifiably below those expected for the individual's chronological age and cause significant interference with academic or occupational performance, or with activities of daily living, as confirmed by individually administered standardized achievement measures and comprehensive clinical assessment. For individuals age 17 years and older, a documented history of impairing learning difficulties may be substituted for the standardized assessment.

C. The learning difficulties begin during school-age years but may not become fully manifest until the demands for those affected academic skills exceed the individual's limited capacities (e.g., as in timed tests, reading or writing lengthy complex reports for a tight deadline, excessively heavy academic loads).

D. The learning difficulties are not better accounted for by intellectual disabilities, uncorrected visual or auditory acuity, other mental or neurological disorders, psychosocial adversity, lack of proficiency in the language of academic instruction, or inadequate educational instruction.

A group of disorders loosely identified as *communication disorders* seems closely related to specific learning disorder (American Psychiatric Association, 2013). These disorders can appear deceptively benign, yet their presence early in life can cause wide-ranging problems later. For a brief overview of these disorders, which include **childhood-onset fluency disorder** (previously called **stuttering**) and **language disorder** (which combines *DSM-IV-TR* expressive and mixed receptive–expressive language disorders), see Table 13.1.

Causes

Theories about the causes of specific learning disorder include genetic, neurobiological, and environmental factors (Peterson & Pennington, 2012). It is clear that learning disorders run in families, and sophisticated family and twin studies bear this out (e.g., Christopher *et al.*, 2013). Yet, analyses of the genes involved suggest that many effects are not specific—meaning that there are not different genes responsible for reading disorders and mathematics disorders. Instead, there are genes that affect learning, and they may contribute to problems across domains (reading, mathematics, writing) (Petrill, 2013; Plomin & Kovas, 2005).

The different problems associated with learning themselves have different origins. For example, children (and adults) often have different problems associated with reading. Reading disorders are sometimes broken into problems with word recognition (difficulty decoding single words—sometimes called *dyslexia*), fluency (problems being able to read words and sentences smoothly and automatically), and comprehension (difficulty getting meaning from what is read) (Siegel & Mazabell, 2013; Tannock, 2009b). Most research to date focuses on problems with word recognition, and there is evidence that some develop these problems primarily through their genes, whereas others develop problems as a result of environmental factors (Siegel & Mazabell, 2013). At the same time, environmental influences such as the home reading habits of families can significantly affect outcomes—especially with skills such as word recognition—suggesting that reading to children at risk for reading disorders can lessen the impact of the genetic influence (Siegel & Mazabell, 2013).

Various forms of subtle brain impairment have also been thought responsible for learning disabilities; some of the earliest theories involve a neurological explanation (Hinshelwood, 1896). Research suggests structural, as well as functional, differences in the brains of people with learning disabilities. Specifically, three areas of the left hemisphere appear to be involved in problems with dyslexia (word recognition)—Broca's area (which affects articulation and word analysis), an area in the left parietotemporal area (which affects word analysis), and an area in the left occipitotemporal area (which affects recognizing word form) (Peterson & Pennington, 2012). A different area in the left hemisphere—the intraparietal sulcus—seems to be critical for the development of a sense of numbers and is implicated in mathematics disorder (Ashkenazi, Black, Abrams, Hoeft, & Menon, 2013).

▲ These functional MRI scans of composite data from six dyslexic adults and eight controls show a horizontal slice through the brain, with the face at the top. Imaging shows atypical brain activity associated with dyslexia. The scans were performed while subjects tracked a pattern of moving dots on a computer screen. A brain area (V5/MT) normally active during such motion tasks did not switch on in dyslexic subjects (right). Their brain activity was more similar to that of controls during a pattern recognition task (left).

In contrast, there is no current evidence for specific deficits responsible for disorders of written expression.

You saw that Alice persisted despite the obstacles caused by her specific learning disorder, as well as by the reactions of teachers and others. What helped her continue toward her goal when others choose, instead, to drop out of school? Psychological and motivational factors that have been reinforced by others seem to play an important role in the eventual outcome of people with learning disorders. Factors such as socioeconomic status, cultural expectations, parental interactions and expectations, and child management practices, together with existing neurological deficits and the types of support provided in the school, seem to determine outcome (Gregg, 2013).

Treatment of Learning Disorders

Learning disorders primarily require educational intervention. Biological (drug) treatment is typically restricted to those individuals who may also have comorbid ADHD. Educational efforts can be broadly categorized into (1) specific skills instruction, including instruction on vocabulary, finding the main idea, and finding facts in readings, and (2) strategy instruction, which includes efforts to improve cognitive skills through decision making and critical thinking (Fletcher, Lyon, Fuchs, & Barnes, 2006; Pierce, 2016).

Many programs are used to assist children with their problems related to learning. One approach that has received considerable research support is called Direct Instruction (Kame'enui, Fien, & Korgesaar, 2013). This program includes several components; among them are systematic instruction (using highly scripted lesson plans that place students together in small groups based on their progress) and teaching for mastery (teaching students until they understand all concepts). In addition, children are constantly assessed, and plans are modified based on progress. Direct Instruction and several related programs appear to significantly improve academic skills in children with specific learning disorder (Kame'enui et al., 2013).

How do these behavioral and educational approaches help children with reading difficulties? Research using brain-imaging technology is allowing us to answer this question. One study used functional magnetic resonance imaging (fMRI) scanning to compare how children with and without reading disorders processed simple tasks (Temple et al., 2003). The children with reading difficulties were then exposed to eight weeks of intensive training on a computer that helped them work on their auditory and language-processing skills. Not only did the children improve their reading skills, but also their brains started functioning in a way similar to the brains of their peers who were good readers. This and similar

childhood-onset speech fluency disorder (stuttering) Disturbance in the fluency and time patterning of speech (for example, sound and syllable repetitions or prolongations).

language disorder Getting one's meaning or message across to others (expressive language disorder), or understanding the message coming from others (receptive language disorder).

studies (Peterson & Pennington, 2012) mirror results seen with other disorders—namely, that behavioral interventions can change the way the brain works and that we can use such interventions to help individuals with problems.

13.1 Concept CHECK

Assign a label to each of the following cases: (a) ADHD, (b) social (pragmatic) communication disorder, (c) Tourette's disorder, or (d) specific learning disorder:

1. Trent's developmental disorder is characterized by uncontrollable yelps, sniffs, and grunting noises. _____

2. Ten-year-old Cole has trouble waiting his turn during games and does things seemingly without thinking. He often calls out answers in school, sometimes before the complete question is asked. _____

3. In school, 6-year-old Miley appears extremely awkward. She doesn't understand when other children are being sarcastic and misses many social communication cues. _____

4. Kelly was a good student until the sixth grade. Now, as a high school senior concerned about graduation, Kelly has sought help. She places above average on an IQ test but shows significant problems with reading and comprehension. _____

Autism Spectrum Disorder

▶ What are the major characteristics of autism spectrum disorder?

Autism spectrum disorder (ASD) is a neurodevelopmental disorder that affects how one perceives and socializes with others (Durand, 2014). *DSM-5* combined most of the disorders previously included under the umbrella term "pervasive developmental disorders" (e.g., autistic disorder, Asperger's disorder, and **childhood disintegrative disorder**) and included them into this one category (American Psychiatric Association, 2013). Moreover, **Rett disorder**, a genetic condition that affects mostly females and is characterized by hand wringing and poor coordination, is diagnosed as ASD with the qualifier "associated with Rett syndrome" or "associated with MeCP2 mutation" (the gene involved in Rett syndrome). And the designation "not otherwise specified," which was applied to other disorders prior to *DSM-5*, was deleted. A disorder new to *DSM-5*—social (pragmatic) communication disorder (see Table 13.1)—includes the difficulties in social communication seen in ASD, but without restricted, repetitive patterns of behavior. These individuals do not easily learn the social rules when communicating with others (e.g., interrupting, talking too loud, not listening to others). Certain individuals previously diagnosed with **pervasive developmental disorder—not otherwise specified** may fall into this category.

Clinical Description

Two major characteristics of ASD are expressed in *DSM-5*: 1) impairments in social communication and social interaction, and 2) restricted, repetitive patterns of behavior, interests, or activities (American Psychiatric Association, 2013). In addition, *DSM-5* recognizes that the impairments are present in early childhood and that they limit daily functioning. It is the degree of impairment in each of these characteristics that presumably distinguish individuals previously diagnosed with the separate disorders of autistic disorder, Asperger's disorder, and pervasive developmental disorder—not otherwise specified.

To accommodate the range of difficulties in the two symptom clusters (social/communication interaction and restricted, repetitive patterns of behavior, interests, or activities), *DSM-5* introduced three levels of severity: Level 1—"Requiring support," Level 2—"Requiring substantial support," and "Level 3—"Requiring very substantial support." Separate ratings are provided for social/communication interaction and for restricted interests and repetitive behaviors. Each level of support is described qualitatively and, as yet, has no quantitative equivalent. This subjectivity makes assigning the appropriate level of support needed somewhat problematic if the person with ASD does not perform at the extreme ends of these categories (Durand, 2014). Consider the case of Amy.

Amy... • *In Her Own World*

Amy, three-years-old, spends much of her day picking up pieces of lint. She drops the lint in the air and then watches intently as it falls to the floor. She also licks the back of her hands and stares at the saliva. She hasn't spoken yet and can't feed or dress herself. Several times a day, she screams so loudly that the neighbors at first thought she was being abused. She doesn't seem to be interested in her mother's love and affection but will take her mother's hand to lead her to the refrigerator. Amy likes to eat butter—whole pats of it, several at a time. Her mother uses the pats of butter that you get at some restaurants to help Amy learn and to keep her well-behaved. If Amy helps with dressing herself, or if she sits quietly for several minutes, her mother gives her some butter. Amy's mother knows that the butter isn't good for her, but it is the only thing that seems to get through to the child. The family's pediatrician has been concerned about Amy's developmental delays for some time and has recently suggested that she be evaluated by specialists. The pediatrician thinks Amy may have autism spectrum disorder, and the child and her family will probably need extensive support.

Impairment in Social Communication and Social Interaction

One of the defining characteristics of people with ASD is that they fail to develop age-appropriate social relationships (Davis & Carter, 2014). Amy never made friends among her peers and often limited her contact with adults to using them as tools—for example, taking the adult's hand to reach for something she wanted. Research on the symptoms of ASD including communication difficulties and social difficulties (which were listed independently as part of *DSM-IV-TR*) revealed the considerable overlap of these symptoms (Frazier *et al.*, 2012; Skuse, 2012). *DSM-5* combines these two areas into one general symptom cluster (social communication and social interaction). Difficulties with social communication and interaction are further defined by the inclusion of three aspects—problems with social reciprocity (a failure to engage in back-and-forth social interactions), non-verbal communication, and initiating and maintaining social relationships—all three of which must be present to be diagnosed with ASD.

Social reciprocity for individuals with more severe symptoms of ASD (previously diagnosed with autistic disorder) involves the inability to engage in **joint attention** (Gillespie-Lynch *et al.*, 2012; Schietecatte *et al.*, 2012). If a toddler without ASD sees a toy she likes, she might look at her mother, smile, look at the toy, and look at her mother again. This social act communicates not only interest in the toy but also the desire to share this interest with another person. This action is limited in persons with ASD. Among persons with milder symptoms of ASD (previously diagnosed with Asperger's disorder), this lack of social reciprocity might present itself as appearing self-focused and not showing interest in things other people care about.

Research using sophisticated eye-tracking technology shows how social deficits evolve as the person develops. In one classic study, scientists showed an adult man with ASD some scenes from movies and compared how he looked at social scenes with how a man without ASD did so (Klin, Jones, Schultz, Volkmar, & Cohen, 2002). You can see from

DSM 5 — DISORDER CRITERIA SUMMARY
Autism Spectrum Disorder

A. Persistent deficits in social communication and social interaction across multiple contexts, as manifested by the following, currently or by history:

1. Deficits in social-emotional reciprocity; ranging, for example from abnormal social approach and failure of normal back-and-forth conversation; to reduced sharing of interests, emotions, and affect; to failure to initiate or respond to social interactions.

2. Deficits in non-verbal communicative behaviors used for social interaction, ranging for example, from poorly integrated verbal and non-verbal communication; to abnormalities in eye contact and body language or deficits in understanding and use of gestures; to a total lack of facial expressions and non-verbal communication.

3. Deficits in developing, maintaining and understanding relationships, ranging for example, from difficulties adjusting behavior to suit various social contexts; to difficulties in sharing imaginative play and in making friends; to absence of interest in peers.

B. Restricted, repetitive patterns of behavior, interests, or activities, as manifested by at least two of the following, currently or by history: (1) stereotyped or repetitive motor movements, use of objects or, speech; (2) insistence on sameness, inflexible adherence to routines, or ritualized patterns of verbal or non-verbal behavior; (3) highly restricted, fixated interests that are abnormal in intensity or focus; (4) hyper- or hyporeactivity to sensory input or unusual interest in sensory aspects of the environment.

C. Symptoms must be present in the early developmental period (but may not become fully manifest until social demands exceed limited capacities, or may be masked by learned strategies in later life).

D. Symptoms cause clinically significant impairment in social, occupational, or other important areas of current functioning.

E. The disturbances are not better explained by intellectual disability (intellectual developmental disorder) or global developmental delay. Intellectual disability and autism spectrum disorder frequently co-occur; to make comorbid diagnoses of autism spectrum disorder and intellectual disability, social communication should be below that expected for general developmental level.

From American Psychiatric Association. (2013). *Diagnostic and statistical manual of mental disorders* (5th ed.). Washington, DC.

autism spectrum disorder (ASD) Neurodevelopmental disorder characterized by significant impairment in social interactions and communication and restricted patterns of behavior, interest, and activity.

childhood disintegrative disorder Pervasive developmental disorder involving severe regression in language, adaptive behavior, and motor skills after a 2- to 4-year period of normal development.

Rett disorder Progressive neurological developmental disorder featuring constant hand-wringing, **intellectual disability**, and impaired motor skills.

pervasive developmental disorder—not otherwise specified Wide-ranging, significant, and long-lasting dysfunctions that appear before the age of 18.

joint attention Attention shared by two persons toward an object after one person has indicated interest in the object to the other person; this social interaction is limited or absent in people with **autism spectrum disorder**.

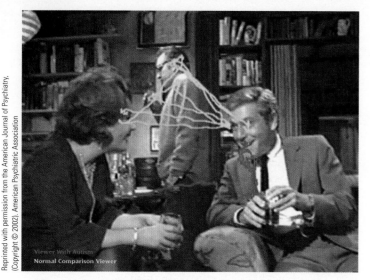

Researchers are exploring how people with autism view social interactions among other people. (From Klin, A., Jones, W., Schultz, R., Volkmar, F., & Cohen, D. (2002). Defining and quantifying the social phenotype in autism. *American Journal of Psychiatry, 159*, 895–908.)

Restricted, Repetitive Patterns of Behavior, Interests, or Activities

The more striking characteristics of ASD include *restricted, repetitive patterns of behavior, interests,* or *activities.* Amy appeared to like things to stay the same: She became extremely upset if even a small change was introduced (such as moving her toys in her room). This intense preference for the status quo has been called *maintenance of sameness.* Often, people with ASD spend countless hours in *stereotyped* and *ritualistic behaviors,* making such stereotyped movements as spinning around in circles, waving their hands in front of their eyes with their heads cocked to one side, or biting their hands (Durand, 2014). For individuals with less severe ASD, these behaviors can take the form of an almost obsessive interest in certain, very specific subjects (such as following airline schedules or memorizing ZIP codes). This tendency to be much more interested in esoteric facts than in people further helps to interfere with social relationships.

Statistics

Current estimates of the rates of ASD are based on the previous *DSM-IV-TR* and *ICD-10* criteria (Lord & Bishop, 2010). ASD was once thought to be a rare disorder (e.g., one in 10,000 births), although more recent estimates of its occurrence show an increase in its prevalence. For example, estimates as reported by the Centers for Disease Control and Prevention suggest that an average of one in 68 eight-year-old children in the United States had a diagnosis under the category of ASD (Centers for Disease Control and Prevention, 2014). The majority of the rise in the rates may be the result of changes between versions of the *DSM* (Miller *et al.*, 2013) as well as increased awareness on the part of professionals and the general public. The reasons behind these changes are complex, however, and other environmental factors (e.g., prenatal exposure to toxins) cannot yet be ruled out as partially contributing to the rise in rates (Frombonne *et al.*, 2011; Liu & Bearman, 2012).

Gender differences are apparent in ASD, with the average reported male to female estimate being 4.5 to one (Centers for Disease Control and Prevention, 2014). ASD appears to be a universal phenomenon, identified in every part of the world, including Sweden (Gillberg, 1984), Japan (Sugiyama & Abe, 1989), Russia (Lebedinskaya & Nikolskaya, 1993), and Hong Kong (Chung, Luk, & Lee, 1990).

People with ASD have a range of IQ scores. It is estimated that approximately 31% of individuals with ASD have intellectual disabilities (defined as an IQ score less than 70, comparable deficits in adaptive functioning, and present before the age of 18) (Centers for Disease Control and Prevention, 2014). The higher children score on IQ tests, the less likely they are to need extensive support by family members or people in the helping professions. Conversely, young children with ASD who score lower on IQ tests are more likely to be severely delayed in acquiring communication skills and to need a great deal of educational and social support as they grow older.

the photo that the man with ASD (indicated by the red lines) scanned non-social aspects of the scene (the actors' mouth and jacket), while the man without ASD looked at the socially meaningful sections (looking from eye to eye of the people conversing). This research suggests that people with ASD—for reasons not yet fully understood—may not be interested in social situations.

Deficits in non-verbal communication can involve problems with a range of actions in persons with severe forms of ASD (e.g., not pointing to things you want) and among those with milder forms of ASD (e.g., standing too close to someone). Individuals with the less severe form of ASD may also lack appropriate facial expressions or tone of voice (also known as **prosody**; Durand, 2014) when speaking or just give the appearance of general non-verbal awkwardness. Finally, the deficits in social reciprocity and non-verbal communication can combine to influence the third symptom—problems maintaining social relationships.

Approximately 25% of individuals with ASD do not develop speech proficiency sufficient to communicate their needs effectively (Anderson *et al.*, 2007). In those with some speech, sometimes their communication is unusual. Some repeat the speech of others, a pattern called echolalia, which we referred to earlier as a sign of delayed speech development. If you say, "My name is Eileen, what's yours?" they will repeat all or part of what you said: "Eileen, what's yours?" And often, not only are your words repeated, but so is your intonation. On the other end of the autism spectrum, these individuals can be very verbal, but because of the social deficits and their tendency to have restricted interests, they often have one-sided conversations about the topics they want to discuss.

Causes: Psychological and Social Dimensions

ASD is a complex condition that does not appear to have a single cause (Durand, 2014). Instead, a number of biological contributions may combine with psychosocial influences. Because historical context is important to research, it is helpful to examine past, as well as more recent, theories of ASD. (In doing this, we are departing from this book's usual format of providing biological dimensions first.)

Historically, ASD was wrongly seen as the result of failed parenting (Bettelheim, 1967; Tinbergen & Tinbergen, 1972). Mothers and fathers of children with the more severe form of ASD were characterized as perfectionistic, cold, and aloof (Kanner, 1949), with relatively high socioeconomic status (Allen, DeMyer, Norton, Pontius, & Yang, 1971; Cox, Rutter, Newman, & Bartak, 1975) and higher IQs than the general population (Kanner, 1943). Descriptions such as these inspired theories that held parents responsible for their children's unusual behaviors. These views were devastating to a generation of parents, who felt guilty and responsible for their children's problems. More sophisticated research using larger samples of children and families suggests that the parents of individuals with autism may not differ substantially from parents of children without disabilities (Bhasin & Schendel, 2007).

Other theories about the origins of ASD were based on the unusual speech patterns of some individuals—namely, their tendency to avoid first-person pronouns such as *I* and *me* and to use *he* and *she* instead. For example, if you ask a child with ASD, "Do you want something to drink?" he might say, "He wants something to drink" (meaning "I want something to drink"). This observation led some theorists to wonder whether ASD involves a lack of self-awareness (Goldfarb, 1963; Mahler, 1952). Theorists suggested that the withdrawal seen among people with ASD reflected a lack of awareness of their own existence.

Later research has shown, however, that some people with ASD do seem to have self-awareness (Lind & Bowler, 2009) and that it follows a developmental progression. Just like children without a disability, those with cognitive abilities below the level expected for a child of 18 to 24 months show little or no self-recognition, but people with more advanced abilities do demonstrate self-awareness. Self-concept may be lacking when people with ASD also have cognitive disabilities or delays, not because of the disorder itself.

Myths about people with ASD are perpetuated when the idiosyncrasies of the disorder are highlighted. These perceptions are furthered by portrayals such as Dustin Hoffman's in the movie *Rain Man*—his character could, for instance, instantaneously and accurately count hundreds of toothpicks falling to the floor. This type of exceptional mental ability—referred to as savant skills—does not occur in all individuals with ASD. It is estimated that approximately one-third of individuals with ASD have these unusual skills, although no persons with the more severe form of ASD appear to have savant abilities (Howlin, Goode, Hutton, & Rutter, 2010; Rutter & Pickles, 2015). These exceptional skills appear to be the result of possessing superior working memory and highly focused attention (Bennett & Heaton, 2012).

Causes: Biological Dimensions

Deficits in such skills as social communication and the characteristic restricted and repetitive behaviors and interests appear to be biological in origin. The role of biological influences on the origins of ASD, examined next, has received much empirical support.

Genetic Influences

It is evident that the genetics of ASD are highly complex (Wang *et al.*, 2015) with a moderate genetic heritability (Hallmayer *et al.*, 2011; Rutter, 2011a). Numerous genes on a number of our chromosomes have already been implicated in some way in the presentation of ASD (Li, Zou, & Brown, 2012). And as with other psychological disorders, many genes are involved, but each one has only a relatively small effect.

Families that have one child with ASD have about a 20% chance of having another child with the disorder (Ozonoff *et al.*, 2011). This rate is more than 100 times the risk in the general population, providing strong evidence of a genetic component in the disorder. The exact genes involved in the development of ASD remain elusive. One area that is receiving attention involves the genes responsible for the brain chemical oxytocin. Because oxytocin is shown to have a role in how we bond with others and in our social memory, researchers are looking at whether genes responsible for this neurochemical are involved with the disorder (Wermter *et al.*, 2010).

Neurobiological Influences

As in the area of genetics, many neurobiological influences are being studied to help explain the social communication and behavior problems observed in ASD (Fein, 2011). One intriguing theory involves research on the amygdala—the area of the brain involved in emotions such as anxiety and fear. Researchers studying the brains of people with ASD after they died note that adults with and without the disorder have an amygdala of about the same size but that those with ASD have fewer neurons in this structure (Schumann & Amaral, 2006). Earlier research showed that young children with ASD actually have a larger amygdala. The theory being proposed is that the amygdala in children with ASD is enlarged early in life—causing excessive anxiety and fear (perhaps contributing to their social withdrawal). With continued stress, the release of the stress hormone cortisol damages the amygdala, causing the relative absence of these

....

prosody Vocal characteristics such as tone and stress; people with **autism spectrum disorder** often have trouble recognizing and interpreting these vocal cues.

neurons in adulthood. The damaged amygdala may account for the different way people with ASD respond to social situations (Lombardo, Chakrabarti, & Baron-Cohen, 2009).

An additional neurobiological influence we mentioned in the section on genetics involves the neuropeptide oxytocin. Remember that this is an important social neurochemical that influences bonding and is found to increase trust and reduce fear. Some research on children with ASD found lower levels of oxytocin in their blood (Modahl *et al.*, 1998), and giving oxytocin to people with ASD improved their ability to remember and process information with emotion content (such as remembering happy faces), a problem that is symptomatic of ASD (Guastella *et al.*, 2010).

One highly controversial theory is that mercury—specifically, the mercury previously used as a preservative in childhood vaccines (thimerosal)—is responsible for the increases seen in ASD. Large epidemiological studies conducted in Denmark show that there is no increased risk of ASD in children who are vaccinated (Madsen *et al.*, 2002; Parker, Schwartz, Todd, & Pickering, 2004). Additional research shows that the number of vaccinations—also a cause of concern by some families—does not contribute to an increased risk of ASD (DeStefano, Price, & Weintraub, 2013). Despite this and other convincing evidence, the correlation between when a child is vaccinated for measles, mumps, and rubella (12–15 months) and when the symptoms of ASD first become evident (before three years), continues to fuel the belief by many families that there must be some connection. The negative consequence of this concern is that some parents are not vaccinating their children, and this is thought to contribute to a significant increase in cases of measles and mumps in the United States and other countries (Centers for Disease Control and Prevention, 2011).

Treatment of Autism Spectrum Disorder

One generalization that can be made about ASD is that no completely effective treatment exists. Attempts to eliminate the social communication problems experienced by these individuals have not been successful to date. Rather, most efforts at treating people with ASD focus on enhancing their communication and daily living skills and on reducing problem behaviors, such as tantrums and self-injury (Durand, 2014). We describe some of these approaches next, including important work on early intervention for young children with ASD.

Psychosocial Treatments

Problems with communication and language are among the defining characteristics of ASD. A significant portion of people with ASD often do not acquire meaningful speech; they tend either to have limited speech or to use unusual speech, such as echolalia. Teaching people to speak in a useful way is difficult. Think about how we teach languages: It mostly involves imitation. But a child who has ASD can't or won't imitate.

In the mid-1960s, the late Ivar Lovaas and his colleagues took a monumental first step toward addressing the difficulty of getting children with the more severe forms of ASD to imitate others verbally (Lovaas, Berberich, Perloff, & Schaeffer, 1966). They began by reinforcing a child with food and praise for making any sound while watching the teacher. After the child mastered that step, they reinforced the child only if she made a sound after the teacher made a request—such as the phrase, "Say 'ball'" (a procedure known as *discrimination training*). Once the child reliably made some sound after the teacher's request, the teacher used *shaping* to reinforce only approximations of the requested sound, such as the sound of the letter "b." This continued until the child could correctly respond to multiple requests, demonstrating imitation by copying the words or phrases made by the teacher. Once the children could imitate, speech was easier, and progress was made in teaching some of them to use labels, plurals, sentences, and other more complex forms of language (Lovaas, 1977).

More recently, several different approaches have "normalized" this type of teaching, bringing the instruction away from a desk with one child and one teacher to regular settings at home, in school, and in the community and attempting to use more child-directed versus adult-directed techniques (Durand, 2014). These **naturalistic teaching strategies** include arranging the environment so that the child initiates an interest (e.g., placing a favorite toy just out of reach), and this is used as a teaching opportunity (e.g., Say, "I want truck."). Various evidence-based treatment packages use aspects of this approach, including incidental teaching (McGee, Morrier, & Daly, 1999), pivotal response training (Koegel & Koegel, 2012), and milieu teaching (Hancock & Kaiser, 2012). These techniques seem to increase a variety of social communication skills among some children with more severe forms of ASD (Goldstein, 2002).

One of the most striking features of people with ASD is their unusual reactions to other people. Although social deficits are among the more obvious problems experienced

▲ Temple Grandin has a Ph.D. in animal science and a successful career designing humane equipment for handling livestock. She also has autism.

by people with autism, they can also be the most difficult to teach. A number of approaches are now used to teach social skills, including the use of peers who do not have ASD as trainers, and there is evidence that those with ASD can improve their socialization skills (Durand, 2014).

Lovaas and his colleagues at the University of California, Los Angeles, reported on their early intervention efforts with young children (Lovaas, 1987). They used intensive behavioral treatment for communication and social skills problems for 40 hours or more per week, which seemed to improve intellectual and educational functioning. Follow up suggests that these improvements are long lasting (Smith & Iadarola, 2015). Subsequent research on early intervention for toddlers with ASD include programs specifically targeting joint attention and play skills—the absence of which are some of the earliest signs of problematic social development. Focusing on these skills in the early years is important for helping the child develop more sophisticated social repertoires (Poon, Watson, Baranek, & Poe, 2012). A growing research base suggests that these skills can be facilitated among very young children with ASD (Lawton & Kasari, 2012; Wong & Kasari, 2012) and preliminary follow-up data suggest this approach may facilitate later development of language (Kasari, Gulsrud, Freeman, Paparella, & Hellemann, 2012). Some exciting research suggests that intensive early behavioral intervention may "normalize" the functioning of the developing brain in these children compared with children with ASD who do not receive this treatment (Dawson *et al.*, 2012; Voos *et al.*, 2013).

Individuals with less severe forms of ASD do not have the cognitive delays often found in persons with more severe forms, and can—with support—do well academically in school. However, their social difficulties and common comorbid problems (e.g., ADHD, anxiety) complicate their interactions with peers and teachers and can lead to disruptive behavior problems. A number of different programs exist to help school-aged children improve skills such as appropriate social interaction, problem-solving, self-control, recognizing emotions in others, expanding their often narrow range of interests, and improving their understanding of non-literal idioms (e.g., understanding that the phrase "get off my back" means something very different from its literal meaning) (e.g., Karkhaneh *et al.*, 2010; Koning, Magill-Evans, Volden, & Dick, 2011). This work is in its infancy, and future research should tell us how best to improve these abilities in persons with ASD.

Biological Treatments

Medical intervention has had little positive impact on the core symptoms of social and language difficulties (Durand, 2014). A variety of pharmacological treatments are used to decrease agitation, with the major tranquilizers and serotonin-specific reuptake inhibitors being most helpful (Greydanus, Kaplan, & Patel, 2015). Because ASD may result from a variety of deficits, it is unlikely that one drug will work for everyone with this disorder. Much current work is focused on finding pharmacological treatments for specific behaviors or symptoms.

Integrating Treatments

Early intervention for very young children with ASD holds the most hope for significant changes in the core symptoms of this disorder. The treatment of choice for older children and those not responsive to early intervention combines various approaches to the many facets of this disorder. For children, most therapy consists of school education with special psychological supports for problems with communication and socialization. Behavioral approaches have been most clearly documented as benefiting children in this area. Pharmacological treatments can help some of them temporarily. Parents also need support because of the great demands and stressors involved in living with and caring for such children. As children with ASD grow older, intervention focuses on efforts to integrate them into the community, often with supported living arrangements and work settings. Because the range of abilities of people with ASD is so great, however, these efforts differ dramatically. Some people are able to live in their own apartments with only minimal support from family members. Others, with more severe forms of cognitive impairment, require more extensive efforts to support them in their communities.

13.2 Concept CHECK

Determine how well you are able to diagnose the disorder in each of the following situations by labeling them (a) ASD requiring very substantial support, (b) ASD requiring support, (c) Rett disorder, (d) social (pragmatic) communication disorder:

1. At an early age, Dwight became preoccupied with geography and could name all of the state capitals. His speech development was not delayed, but he does not like to play with other children or to be touched or held. _____

2. Six-year-old Tangelique has a low IQ and enjoys sitting in the corner by herself, where she arranges her toys or spins around in circles. She is unable to communicate verbally. She throws tantrums when her routine is changed or when her parents try to get her to do something she doesn't want to do. _____

3. Six-year-old Megan experiences many problems in communicating and does not seem to understand the "rules" when speaking with other children. _____

4. Five-year-old Alicia has increasingly severe intellectual disability and is beginning to have trouble walking on her own. One of the characteristics of her disorder is constant hand-wringing. _____

naturalistic teaching strategies Instructional techniques that are used with children having neurodevelopmental disorders and that move away from traditional desk instruction toward more natural social interactions.

Intellectual Disability (Intellectual Developmental Disorder)

▶ How is intellectual disability defined, and what categories are used to classify intellectual disabilities?

Intellectual disability (ID) is a disorder evident in childhood as significantly below-average intellectual and adaptive functioning (Toth *et al.*, 2016). People with ID experience difficulties with day-to-day activities to an extent that reflects both the severity of their cognitive deficits and the type and amount of assistance they receive. *DSM-5* identifies difficulties in three domains: conceptual (e.g., skill deficits in areas such as language, reasoning, knowledge, and memory), social (e.g., problems with social judgment and the ability to make and retain friendships), and practical (e.g., difficulties managing personal care or job responsibilities) (American Psychiatric Association, 2013). Perhaps more than any other group you have studied in this text, people with ID have throughout history received treatment that can best be described as shameful (Scheerenberger, 1983). *DSM-IV-TR* previously used the term "mental retardation," but this was changed in *DSM-5* to "intellectual disability" (or intellectual developmental disorder) to be consistent with changes in terminology in this field (American Psychiatric Association, 2013).

The manifestations of ID are varied. Some individuals function quite well, even independently, in our complex society. Others with ID have significant cognitive and physical impairments and require considerable assistance to carry on day-to-day activities. Consider the case of James.

Gabriel Olsen/FilmMagic/Getty Images

▲ Lauren Potter (an actress with Down syndrome) played Becky Jackson in the popular television show *Glee*.

James... *Up to the Challenge*

James's mother contacted us because he was disruptive at school and at work. James was 17 and attended the local high school. He had Down syndrome and was described as likable and, at times, mischievous. He enjoyed skiing, bike riding, and other activities common among teenage boys. School administrators complained because James didn't participate in activities such as physical education, and at the work site that was part of his school program, he was often sullen, sometimes lashing out at the supervisors. They were considering moving him to a program with more supervision and less independence.

James's family had moved often during his youth, and they experienced striking differences in the way each community responded to James. In some school districts, he was placed in classes with other children his age, and his teachers were provided with additional assistance and consultation. In others, it was recommended that he be taught separately. Sometimes the school district had a special classroom in the school for children with intellectual disabilities. Other districts had programs in other towns, and James would have to travel an hour to and from school each day. Every time he was assessed in a new school, he received scores on his IQ tests in the range of 40 to 50, and each school gave him the same diagnosis: Down syndrome with moderate intellectual disability.

In high school, James had several academic classes in a separate classroom for children with learning problems, but he participated in some classes, such as gym, with students who did not have intellectual disability. His current difficulties in gym (not participating) and at work (being oppositional) were jeopardizing his placement in both programs. When I spoke with James's mother, she expressed frustration that the work program was beneath him because he was asked to do boring, repetitive work such as folding paper. James expressed a similar frustration, saying that he was treated like a baby. He could communicate fairly well when he wanted to, although he sometimes would become confused about what he wanted to say and it was difficult to understand everything he tried to articulate. On observing him at school and at work, and after speaking with his teachers, we realized that a common paradox had developed. James resisted work he thought was too easy. His teachers interpreted his resistance to mean that the work was too hard for him, and they gave him even simpler tasks. He resisted or protested more vigorously, and they responded with even more supervision and structure.

Clinical Description

People with ID display a broad range of abilities and personalities. Individuals like James, who have mild or moderate impairments, can, with proper preparation, carry out most of the day-to-day activities expected of any of us. Many can learn to use mass transportation, purchase groceries, and hold a variety of jobs. Those with more severe impairments may need help to eat, bathe, and dress themselves, although with proper training and support, they can achieve a degree of independence. These individuals experience impairments that affect most areas of functioning. Language and communication skills are often the most obvious. James was only mildly impaired in this area, needing help with articulation. In contrast, people with more severe forms of ID may never learn to use speech as a form of communication, requiring alternatives such as sign language or special communication devices to express even their most basic needs. Because many cognitive processes are adversely affected, individuals with intellectual disability have difficulty learning, the level of challenge depending on how extensive the cognitive disability is.

The *DSM-5* criteria for ID no longer include numeric cutoffs for IQ scores, which were present in previous versions. To be diagnosed with ID, a person must have significantly sub-average intellectual functioning, a determination made with one of several IQ tests with a cutoff score set by *DSM-5* of approximately 70. The American Association on Intellectual and Developmental Disabilities (AAIDD), which has its own, similar definition of intellectual disability, has a cutoff score of approximately 70 to 75 (Toth *et al.*, 2016).

The second criterion calls for concurrent deficits or impairments in adaptive functioning. In other words, scoring "approximately 70 or below" on an IQ test is not sufficient for a diagnosis of ID; a person must also have significant difficulty in areas such as communication, self-care, home living, social and interpersonal skills, use of community resources, self-direction, functional academic skills, work, leisure, health, and safety. To illustrate, although James had many strengths, such as his ability to communicate and his social and interpersonal skills (he had several good friends), he was not as proficient as other teenagers at caring for himself in areas such as home living, health, and safety or in academic areas. This aspect of the definition is important because it excludes people who can function quite well in society but for various reasons do poorly on IQ tests. For instance, someone whose primary language is not English may do poorly on an IQ test but may still function at a level comparable with those of peers. This person would not be considered to have ID even with a score of below 70 on the English-based IQ test.

The final criterion for ID is the age of onset. The characteristic below-average intellectual and adaptive abilities must be evident before the person is 18. This cutoff is designed to identify affected individuals when the brain is developing and therefore when any problems should become evident. The age criterion rules out the diagnosis of ID for adults who suffer from brain trauma or forms of dementia that impair their abilities. The age of 18 is somewhat arbitrary, but it is the age at which most children leave school, when our society considers a person an adult.

The imprecise definition of ID brings up an important issue: Intellectual disability, perhaps more than any of the other disorders, is defined by society. The cutoff score of 70 or 75 is based on a statistical concept (two or more standard deviations from the mean), not on qualities inherent in people who supposedly have ID. There is little disagreement about the diagnosis for people with the most severe disabilities; however, the majority of people diagnosed with ID are in the mild range of cognitive impairment. They need some support and assistance, but remember that the criteria for using the label of ID are based partly on a somewhat arbitrary cutoff score for IQ that can (and does) change with changing social expectations.

DSM 5 — DISORDER CRITERIA SUMMARY
Intellectual Disability (Intellectual Developmental Disorder)

Intellectual disability (intellectual developmental disorder) is a disorder with onset during the developmental period that includes both intellectual and adaptive functioning deficits in conceptual, social, and practical domains. The following three criteria must be met:

A. Deficits in intellectual functions, such as reasoning, problem solving, planning, abstract thinking, judgment, academic learning, and learning from experience, confirmed by both clinical assessment and individualized, standardized intelligence testing.

B. Deficits in adaptive functioning that result in failure to meet developmental and sociocultural standards for personal independence and social responsibility. Without ongoing support, the adaptive deficits limit functioning in one or more activities of daily life, such as communication, social participation, and independent living, across multiple environments such as home, school, work, and community.

C. Onset of intellectual and adaptive deficits during the developmental period.

From American Psychiatric Association. (2013). *Diagnostic and statistical manual of mental disorders* (5th ed.). Washington, DC.

---

intellectual disability (ID) A diagnosis received when one achieves a significantly below-average score on a test of intelligence and by limitations in the ability to function in areas of daily life. Significantly subaverage intellectual functioning paired with deficits in adaptive functioning such as self-care or occupational activities, appearing before age 18.

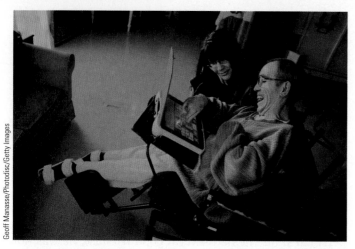

▲ Although this man cannot speak, he is learning to communicate with an eye-gaze board, pointing to or simply looking at the image that conveys his message.

People with ID differ significantly in their degree of disability. Almost all classification systems have differentiated these individuals in terms of their ability or on the cause of the ID (Holland, 2012). Traditionally, classification systems have identified four levels of ID: *mild*, which is identified by an IQ score between 50–55 and 70; *moderate*, with a range of 35–40 to 50–55; *severe*, ranging from 20–25 to 35–40; and *profound*, which includes people with IQ scores below 20–25. It is difficult to categorize each level of ID according to "average" individual achievements by people at each level. A person with severe or profound ID tends to have extremely limited formal communication skills (no spoken speech or only one or two words) and may require great or even total assistance in dressing, bathing, and eating. Yet people with these diagnoses have a range of skills that depend on training and the availability of other supports. Similarly, people like James, who have mild or moderate ID, should be able to live independently or with minimal supervision; again, however, their achievement depends partly on their education and the community support available to them.

Statistics

Approximately 90% of people with ID fall under the label of mild intellectual disability (IQ of 50 to 70). When you add individuals with moderate, severe, and profound ID (IQ below 50), the total population of people with this disorder represents approximately 1% to 3% of the general population (Toth *et al.*, 2016).

The course of ID is chronic, meaning that people do not go through periods of remission, such as with substance use disorders or anxiety disorders. The prognosis for people with this disorder varies considerably, however. Given appropriate training and support, individuals with less severe forms of ID can live relatively independent and productive lives. People with more severe impairments require more assistance to participate in work and community life.

Causes

There are literally hundreds of known causes of intellectual disability, including the following:

> *Environmental:* For example, deprivation, abuse, and neglect
> *Prenatal:* For instance, exposure to disease or drugs while still in the womb
> *Perinatal:* Such as difficulties during labor and delivery
> *Postnatal:* For example, infections and head injury

As we mentioned in Chapter 10, heavy use of alcohol among pregnant women can produce a disorder in their children called *fetal alcohol syndrome,* a condition that can lead to severe learning disabilities (Rangmar *et al.*, 2015). Other prenatal factors that can produce ID include the pregnant woman's exposure to disease and chemicals and poor nutrition. In addition, lack of oxygen (anoxia) during birth and malnutrition and head injuries during the developmental period can lead to severe cognitive impairments (Toth *et al.*, 2016).

Biological Dimensions

Most research on the causes of ID focuses on biological influences. We next look at biological dimensions that appear to be responsible for the more common forms of ID.

Genetic Influences Multiple genetic influences appear to contribute to ID, including chromosomal disorders (e.g., having an extra 21st chromosome, as in Down syndrome), single-gene disorders, mitochondrial disorders (defects in mitochondria, which are compartments found in most human cells that generate the majority of energy needed by the cells to function) and multiple genetic mutations (Toth *et al.*, 2016). A portion of the people with more severe ID have identifiable single-gene disorders, involving a *dominant gene* (which expresses itself when paired with a normal gene), a *recessive gene* (which expresses itself only when paired with another copy of itself), or an *X-linked gene* (present on the X or sex chromosome). Only a few dominant genes result in ID, probably because of natural selection: someone who carries a dominant gene that results in ID is less likely to have children and thus less likely to pass the gene to offspring. Therefore, this gene becomes less likely to continue in the population. Some people, however, especially those with mild ID, do marry and have children, thus passing on their genes.

Before we discuss known genetic causes of ID, it is important to recognize that as many as 30% of cases of ID have no identified etiology (Toth *et al.*, 2016). Important research using sophisticated genetic analysis techniques is pointing to genetic causes that went previously undetected. One study of children from Germany and Switzerland found that a variety of genetic mutations including *de novo* disorders (genetic mutations occurring in the sperm or egg or after fertilization) were present in those children with ID of unknown origin (Rauch *et al.*, 2012). This work is important not only because it helps identify new causes of ID but also because it helps explain why a child could have a genetically-based disorder without that mutation being present in either parent. Mutations in genetic material can occur at various points in development, and this helps explain the causes of previously puzzling cases of ID.

The next time you drink a diet soda, notice the warning, "Phenylketonurics: Contains Phenylalanine." This is a caution for people with the recessive disorder called **phenylketonuria (PKU)**, which affects one of every 10,000 newborns and is characterized by an inability to break down a chemical in our diets called phenylalanine (Schuck *et al.*, 2015; Toth *et al.*, 2016). Until the mid-1960s, the majority of people with this disorder had ID, seizures, and behavior problems, resulting from high levels of this chemical. Researchers developed a screening technique, however, that identifies the existence of PKU; infants are now routinely tested at birth, and any individuals identified with PKU can be successfully treated with a special diet that avoids the chemical phenylalanine. This is a rare example of the successful prevention of one form of ID.

Lesch-Nyhan syndrome, an X-linked disorder, is characterized by ID, signs of cerebral palsy (spasticity or tightening of the muscles), and self-injurious behavior, including finger- and lip-biting (Nyhan, 1978). Only males are affected, because a recessive gene is responsible; when it is on the X chromosome in males, it does not have a normal gene to balance it because males do not have a second X chromosome. Women with this gene are carriers and do not show any of the symptoms.

As our ability to detect genetic defects improves, more disorders will be identified genetically. The hope is that our increased knowledge will be accompanied by improvements in our ability to treat or, as in the case of PKU, prevent intellectual disability and other negative outcomes.

Chromosomal Influences Approximately 60 years ago the number of chromosomes—46—was correctly identified in human cells (Tjio & Levan, 1956). Three years later, researchers found that people with Down syndrome had an additional small chromosome (Lejeune, Gauthier, & Turpin, 1959). Since that time, a number of other chromosomal aberrations that result in ID have been identified. We describe Down syndrome and fragile X syndrome in some detail, but there are hundreds of other ways in which abnormalities among the chromosomes can lead to ID (Toth *et al.*, 2016).

Down syndrome, the most common chromosomal form of ID, was first identified by the British physician Langdon Down in 1866. The disorder is caused by the presence of an extra 21st chromosome and is therefore sometimes referred to as *trisomy 21*. For reasons not completely understood, during cell division, two of the 21st chromosomes stick together (a condition called nondisjunction), creating one cell with one copy that dies and one cell with three copies that divide to create a person with Down syndrome.

People with Down syndrome have characteristic facial features, including folds in the corners of their upwardly slanting eyes, a flat nose, and a small mouth with a flat roof that makes the tongue protrude somewhat. They also tend to have congenital heart malformations. Adults with Down syndrome also have a greatly increased risk of dementia of the Alzheimer's type (Wiseman *et al.*, 2015). This disorder among people with Down syndrome occurs earlier than usual (sometimes in their early 20s) and has led to the finding that at least one form of Alzheimer's disease is attributable to a gene on the 21st chromosome.

The incidence of children born with Down syndrome has been tied to maternal age: As the age of the mother increases, so does her chance of having a child with this disorder (see ● Figure 13.2). A woman at age 20 has a one in 2,000 chance of having a child with Down syndrome; at the age of 35, this risk increases to one in 500; and at the age of 45, it increases again to one in 18 births (Girirajan, 2009). Despite these numbers, many more children with Down syndrome are born to younger mothers simply because younger mothers have more children. The reason for the rise in incidence with maternal age is not clear. Some suggest that because a woman's ova (eggs) are all produced in youth, the older ones have been exposed to toxins, radiation, and other harmful substances over longer periods. This exposure may interfere with the normal meiosis (division) of the chromosomes, creating an extra 21st chromosome (Pueschel & Goldstein, 1991). It may also be that the hormonal changes that occur as women age contribute to this error in cell division (Pandya, Mevada, Patel, & Suthar, 2013).

. . . .

phenylketonuria (PKU) **Recessive gene** disorder involving the inability to break down a food chemical whose buildup causes **intellectual disability**, seizures, and behavior problems. PKU can be detected by infant screening and prevented by a specialized diet.

Lesch-Nyhan syndrome **X-linked gene** disorder characterized by **intellectual disability**, signs of cerebral palsy, and **self-injurious** behavior.

Down syndrome Type of **intellectual disability** caused by a chromosomal aberration (chromosome 21) and involving characteristic physical appearance. Also known as *trisomy 21*.

amniocentesis Prenatal medical procedure that allows the detection of abnormalities (for example, **Down syndrome**) in the developing fetus. It involves removal and analysis of amniotic fluid from the mother.

chorionic villus sampling (CVS) A genetic test conducted during early pregnancy that samples cells found in the placenta (chorionic villi) and assesses possible genetic or chromosomal problems in the villus.

● Figure 13.2 The increasing likelihood of Down syndrome with maternal age. (Based on data from Hook, E. B. (1982). Epidemiology of Down syndrome. In S. M. Pueschel & J. E. Rynders, Eds., *Down syndrome: Advances in biomedicine and the behavioral sciences* [pp. 11–88]. Cambridge, MA: Ware Press, © 1982 Ware University Press.)

For some time, it has been possible to detect the presence of Down syndrome through **amniocentesis**, a procedure that involves removing and testing a sample of the fluid that surrounds the fetus in the amniotic sac, and through **chorionic villus sampling (CVS)** in which a small piece of placenta tissue is removed and tested. These types of test are not always desirable because it is an invasive procedure (inserting a needle that could cause unwanted damage to the developing fetus). There are now more sophisticated tests of a mother's blood that can be used to detect Down syndrome as early as the first trimester of pregnancy (Abele *et al.*, 2015). The presence of this chromosomal abnormality does not convey information about the eventual severity of the disorder, however. Despite this lack of information, some estimate that a prenatal diagnosis of Down syndrome leads to a choice for an elective abortion more than 50% of the time (Natoli, Ackerman, McDermott, & Edwards, 2012).

Fragile X syndrome is a second common chromosomally related cause of ID (Clarke & Deb, 2012). As its name suggests, this disorder is caused by an abnormality on the X chromosome, a mutation that makes the tip of the chromosome look as though it were hanging from a thread, giving it the appearance of fragility (Lubs, Stevenson, & Schwartz, 2012). As with Lesch-Nyhan syndrome, which also involves the X chromosome, fragile X primarily affects males because they do not have a second X chromosome with a normal gene to balance out the mutation. Unlike Lesch-Nyhan carriers, however, women who carry fragile X syndrome commonly display mild-to-severe learning disabilities (Santoro, Bray, & Warren, 2012). Men with the disorder display moderate-to-severe levels of ID and have higher rates of hyperactivity, short attention spans, gaze avoidance, and perseverative speech (repeating the same words again and again). In addition, such physical characteristics as large ears, testicles, and head circumference are common. Estimates are that one of every 4,000 males and one of every 8,000 females are born with fragile X syndrome (Toth & King, 2010).

Psychological and Social Dimensions

Cultural influences that may contribute to ID can include abuse, neglect, and social deprivation. Sometimes referred to as **cultural–familial intellectual disability**, people with these characteristics are thought to have cognitive impairments that result from a combination of psychosocial and biological influences, although the specific mechanisms that lead to this type of ID are not yet understood. Fortunately, because of better child care systems and early identification of potential family difficulties, these cases are rare today (Kaski, 2012).

Treatment of Intellectual Disability

Biological treatment of ID is currently not a viable option. Generally, the treatment of individuals with ID parallels that of people with more severe forms of ASD, attempting to teach them the skills they need to become more productive and independent. For individuals with mild ID, intervention is similar to that for people with learning disorders. Specific learning deficits are identified and addressed to help the student improve such skills as reading and writing. At the same time, these individuals often need additional support to live in the community. For people with more severe disabilities, the general goals are the same; however, the level of assistance they need is often more extensive. Remember that the expectation for all people with ID is that they will in some way participate in community life, attend school and later hold a job, and have the opportunity for meaningful social relationships. Advances in electronic and educational technologies have made this goal realistic even for people with profound ID.

Individuals with ID can acquire skills through the many behavioral innovations first introduced in the early 1960s to teach such basic self-care as dressing, bathing, feeding, and toileting to people with even the most severe disabilities (Durand, 2014). The skill is broken into its component parts (a procedure called a *task analysis*), and people are taught each part in succession until they can perform the whole skill. Performance on each step is encouraged by praise and by access to objects or activities the people desire (reinforcers). Success in teaching these skills is usually measured by the level of independence people can attain by using them. Typically, most individuals, regardless of their disability, can be taught to perform some skills.

Communication training is important for people with ID. The goals of communication training differ, depending on the existing skills. For people with mild levels of ID, the goals may be relatively minor (for example, improving articulation) or more extensive (for example, organizing a conversation) (Berney, 2012; Heath, Ganz, Parker, Burke, & Ninci, 2015). Some, like James, have communication skills that are already adequate for day-to-day needs.

For individuals with the most severe disabilities, communication skills training can be particularly challenging, because they may have multiple physical or cognitive deficits that make spoken communication difficult or impossible. Creative researchers, however, use alternative systems that may be easier for these individuals, including sign language, used primarily by people with hearing disabilities, and *augmentative communication strategies*. Augmentative strategies may use picture books, teaching the person to make a request by pointing to a picture—for instance, pointing to a picture of a cup to request a drink (Heath *et al.*, 2015). A variety of computer-assisted devices including tablet computers can be programmed so that the individual presses a button to produce complete spoken sentences (for example, "Would you come here? I need your help."). People with limited communication skills can be taught to use these devices, which helps them reduce the frustration of not being able to relate their feelings and experiences to other people (Durand, 2011).

Concern is often expressed by parents, teachers, and employers that some people with ID can be physically or verbally aggressive or may hurt themselves. Considerable debate has ensued over the proper way to reduce these behavior problems; the most heated discussions involve whether to use painful punishers (Repp & Singh, 1990). Alternatives to punishment that may be equally effective in reducing behavior problems such as aggression and self-injury include teaching people how to communicate their need or desire for such things as attention that they seem to be getting with their problem behaviors (Durand, 2012). Important advances are being made in significantly reducing even severe behavior problems for some people.

In addition to ensuring that people with ID are taught specific skills, caretakers focus on supporting them in their communities. "Supported employment" involves helping an individual find and participate satisfactorily

....

fragile X syndrome Pattern of **abnormality** caused by a defect in the **X chromosome** resulting in **intellectual disability**, learning problems, and unusual physical characteristics.

cultural–familial intellectual disability Mild form of **intellectual disability** that may be caused largely by environmental influences.

▲ Today, great efforts are made to keep people with intellectual disability and other mental disorders in their homes and communities.

in a competitive job (Drake, Bond, & Becker, 2012). Research has shown not only that people with ID can be placed in meaningful jobs but also that, despite the costs associated with supported employment, it can be cost-effective (Cimera, 2012). The benefits to people who achieve the satisfaction of being a productive part of society are incalculable.

There is general agreement about *what* should be taught to people with ID. The controversy in recent years has been over *where* this teaching should take place. Should people with ID, especially the severe forms, be taught in specially designed separate classrooms or workshops, or should they attend their public schools and work at local businesses? Increasingly, teaching strategies to help these students learn are being used in regular classrooms and in preparing them to work at jobs in the community (Foley, Dyke, Girdler, Bourke, & Leonard, 2012).

Prevention of Neurodevelopmental Disorders

▶ What are major prevention efforts for the neurodevelopmental disorders?

Prevention efforts for the neurodevelopmental disorders outlined in this chapter are in their early stages. One such effort—early intervention—has been described for ASD and appears to hold promise for some children. In addition, early intervention can target and assist children who, because of inadequate environments, are at risk for developing cultural–familial ID (Eldevik, Jahr, Eikeseth, Hastings, & Hughes, 2010). The national Head Start program is one such effort at early intervention; it combines educational, medical, and social supports for these children and their families. One project identified a group of children shortly after birth and provided them with an intensive preschool program, along with medical and nutritional supports. This intervention continued until the children began formal education in kindergarten (Martin, Ramey, & Ramey, 1990). The researchers of this study found that for all but one of the children in a control group who received medical and nutritional support but not the intensive educational experiences, each had IQ scores below 85 at age three, but that three-year-olds in the experimental group all tested above 85. Such findings are important because they show the potential for creating a lasting impact on the lives of children with developmental disorders and their families.

A number of important questions remain regarding early intervention efforts. Not all children, for example, benefit significantly from such efforts, and future research will need to determine how best to identify children and families who will benefit from such programs, how early in the child's development programs should begin, and how long to continue these early intervention programs to produce desirable outcomes.

Given recent advances in genetic screening and technology, it may someday be possible to detect and correct genetic and chromosomal abnormalities; related ongoing research could fundamentally change our approach to children with developmental disorders. For example, one study used mice that were genetically engineered to model fragile X syndrome found in many individuals with ID (Suvrathan, Hoeffer, Wong, Klann, & Chattarji, 2010). Researchers found that they could improve the functioning of certain glutamate receptors in the amygdala of the mice with a drug that blocks these receptors. The results were more normalized functioning between these neurons, a potential early medical intervention for children with fragile X disorder (Krueger & Bear, 2011; Suvrathan, Hoeffer, Wong, Klann, & Chattarji, 2010). Someday, it may be possible for similar research to be performed prenatally on children identified as having syndromes associated with ID. For example, it may soon be possible to conduct prenatal gene therapy, where a developing fetus that has been screened for a genetic disorder may be the target of intervention before birth.

This prospect is not without its difficulties, however. Advances in biomedical technology will need support from psychological researchers to make sure that any treatments are carried out properly. For example, biological risk factors for several developmental disorders include malnutrition and exposure to toxins such as lead and alcohol. Although medical researchers can identify the role of these biological events in cognitive development, psychologists will need to support these efforts. Behavioral intervention for safety training (for example, involving lead-based paints in older homes), substance-use treatment and prevention, and behavioral medicine (for example, "wellness" efforts) are examples of crucial roles played by psychologists in helping to prevent certain developmental disorders.

Overview of Neurocognitive Disorders

▶ What are the defining features of neurocognitive disorders?

Whereas intellectual disability and specific learning disorder are believed to be present from birth, most neurocognitive disorders develop much later in life. In the rest of this chapter, we review two classes of cognitive disorders: *delirium*, an often temporary condition displayed as confusion and disorientation; and *mild or major neurocognitive disorder*, a progressive condition marked by gradual deterioration of a range of cognitive abilities.

Delirium

▶ What are the symptoms of and treatment for delirium?

The disorder known as **delirium** is characterized by impaired consciousness and cognition during the course of several hours or days. Consider the case of Mr. J.

Mr. J... • *Sudden Distress*

Mr. J., an older gentleman, was brought to the hospital emergency room. He didn't know his own name, and at times he didn't seem to recognize his daughter who was with him. Mr. J. appeared confused, disoriented, and a little agitated. He had difficulty speaking clearly and could not focus his attention to answer even the most basic questions. Mr. J.'s daughter reported that he had begun acting this way the night before, had been awake most of the time since then, was frightened, and seemed even more confused today. She told the nurse that this behavior was not normal for him, and she was worried that he was becoming "senile." She mentioned that his doctor had just changed his hypertension medication and wondered whether the new medication could be causing her father's distress. Mr. J. was ultimately diagnosed as having substance-induced delirium (a reaction to his new medication); once the medication was stopped, he improved significantly over the course of the next two days.

delirium Rapid-onset reduced clarity of consciousness and cognition, with confusion, disorientation, and deficits in memory and language.

Clinical Description and Statistics

People with delirium appear confused, disoriented, and out of touch with their surroundings. They cannot focus and sustain their attention on even the simplest tasks. There are marked impairments in memory and language (Meagher & Trzapacz, 2012). Mr. J. had trouble speaking; he was not only confused but also couldn't remember basic facts, such as his own name. As you saw, the symptoms of delirium do not come on gradually but develop over hours or a few days, and they can vary over the course of a day.

Delirium is estimated to be present in approximately 20% of older adults who are admitted into acute care facilities such as emergency rooms (Meagher & Trzapacz, 2012). It is most prevalent among older adults, people undergoing medical procedures, cancer patients, and people with acquired immune deficiency syndrome (AIDS). Once thought to be only a temporary problem, more recent work indicates that the effects of delirium may be more lasting (Cole, Ciampi, Belzile, & Zhong, 2009; Meagher, Adamis, Trzepacz, & Leonard, 2012). Some individuals continue to have problems on and off; some even lapse into a coma and may die. Many medical conditions that impair brain function have been linked to delirium, including intoxication by drugs and poisons; withdrawal from drugs such as alcohol and sedative, hypnotic, and anxiolytic drugs; infections; head injury; and various other types of brain trauma (Meagher & Trzapacz, 2012).

Causes

DSM-5 recognizes several causes of delirium among its subtypes. The diagnosis received by Mr. J.—substance-induced delirium—as well as delirium not otherwise

---

DSM 5 DISORDER CRITERIA SUMMARY
Delirium

A. A disturbance in attention (i.e., reduced ability to direct, focus, sustain, and shift attention) and awareness (reduced orientation to the environment).

B. The disturbance develops over a short period of time (usually hours to a few days), represents a change from baseline attention and awareness, and tends to fluctuate in severity during the course of a day.

C. An additional disturbance in cognition (e.g., memory deficit, disorientation, language, visuospatial ability, or perception).

D. The disturbances in Criteria A and C are not better explained by another pre-existing, established, or evolving neurocognitive disorder and do not occur in the context of a severely reduced level of arousal, such as coma.

E. There is evidence from the history, physical examination, or laboratory findings that the disturbance is a direct physiological consequence of another medical condition, substance intoxication or withdrawal, or exposure to a toxin, or is due to multiple etiologies.

From American Psychiatric Association. (2013). *Diagnostic and statistical manual of mental disorders* (5th ed.). Washington, DC.

---

specified include disruptions in the person's ability to direct, focus, sustain, and shift attention. Delirium may be experienced by children who have high fevers or who are taking certain medications (Smeets *et al.*, 2010). However, that delirium can be brought on by the improper use of medication is a particular problem for older adults, because they tend to use prescription medications more than any other age group. The risk of problems among the elderly is increased further because they tend to eliminate drugs from their systems less efficiently than younger individuals. It is not surprising, then, that adverse drug reactions resulting in hospitalization are almost six times higher among elderly people than in other age groups (Budnitz, Lovegrove, Shehab, & Richards, 2011; Olivier *et al.*, 2009). And it is believed that delirium is responsible for many of the falls that cause debilitating hip fractures in the elderly (Seitz, Adunuri, Gill, & Rochon, 2011; Stenvall *et al.*, 2006). Although there has been some improvement in the use of medication among older adults with physicians using more care with drug dosages and the use of multiple drugs, improper use continues to produce serious side effects, including symptoms of delirium (Budnitz *et al.*, 2011; Olivier *et al.*, 2009). Because possible combinations of illnesses and medications are so numerous, determining the cause of delirium is extremely difficult (Solai, 2009).

Delirium often occurs during the course of dementia; as many as 50% of people with dementia suffer at least one episode of delirium (Fong, Davis, Growdon, Albuquerque, & Inouye, 2015; Kwok, Lee, Lam, & Woo, 2008). Because many of the primary medical conditions can be treated, delirium is often reversed within a relatively short time. Yet, those who develop delirium while in the hospital have a one-and-a-half times increased risk for death in the following year, and this risk of mortality increases to two-to-four-times for those in critical care with delirium (Inouye, Westendorp, & Saczynski, 2014). However, factors other than medical conditions can trigger delirium. Age itself is an important factor; older adults are more susceptible to developing delirium as a result of mild infections or medication changes (Inouye *et al.*, 2014). Sleep deprivation, immobility, and excessive stress can also cause delirium (Solai, 2009).

Researchers studying the brain functioning of persons with and without delirium are beginning to understand the mechanisms underlying this disorder using fMRI scanning (Choi *et al.*, 2012; Slooter & de Groot, 2014). Although such research is potentially important for efforts to both prevent and treat delirium, there are potential ethical concerns. For example, a person experiencing delirium is not capable of providing informed consent for participating in such research and therefore someone else (e.g., a spouse or relative) must agree. In addition, fMRI testing can be anxiety-provoking for many people and is possibly frightening for someone already so disoriented (Gaudreau, 2012).

Treatment

The first step for the treatment of delirium is addressing underlying causes. For example, delirium brought on by withdrawal from alcohol or other drugs is usually treated with haloperidol or other antipsychotic medications. Infections, brain injury, and tumors are given the appropriate medical intervention, which often then resolves the accompanying delirium. The antipsychotic drugs haloperidol or olanzapine are also prescribed for individuals in acute delirium when the cause is unknown (Meagher & Trzapacz, 2012).

The recommended first line of treatment for a person experiencing delirium is psychosocial intervention. The goal of non-medical treatment is to reassure the individual to help him or her deal with the agitation, anxiety, and hallucinations of delirium. The inclusion of a family member in the care for patients with delirium may be a great comfort to the patient. Similarly, personal belongings such as photographs may also be a comforting intervention (Fearing & Inouye, 2009; van Munster & de Rooij, 2014). Also, a patient who is included in treatment decisions retains a sense of control that can aid in the patient's ability to cope with anxiety and agitation (Katz, 1993). This type of psychosocial treatment can help the person manage during this disruptive period until the medical causes are identified and addressed (Breitbart & Alici, 2012). Some evidence suggests that this type of support can also delay institutionalization for elderly patients (Rahkonen *et al.*, 2001).

Prevention

Proper medical care for illnesses and therapeutic drug monitoring can play significant roles in preventing delirium (Breitbart & Alici, 2012). For example, the increased number of older adults involved in managed care and patient counseling on drug use appear to have led to more appropriate use of prescription drugs among the elderly (U.S. General Accounting Office, 1995). In addition, structured multidisciplinary interventions that target the prevention of delirium during hospital stays in older patients are very effective (for more information see Hospital Elder Life Program; Inouye *et al.*, 2014). These programs are implemented by an interdisciplinary team of doctors, nurses, and volunteers and consist of re-orientating the patient, providing vision and hearing aids as needed, increasing sleep and physical activity, maintaining proper hydration and nutrition, involving the patient in therapeutic activities, and reducing dosages of psychoactive drugs. One downside is that these programs require a lot of resources from hospitals to put it into place consistently.

▲ Elderly patients with delirium in care facilities are often comforted by having their personal belongings nearby.

Angela Hampton Picture Library /Alamy Stock Photo

13.4 Concept CHECK

Match the terms with the following descriptions of delirium: (a) memory, (b) cause, (c) counseling, (d) confused, (e) elderly, and (f) trauma:

1. Managed care and patient _____ have been successful in preventing delirium in older adults.

2. Treatment of delirium depends on the _____ of the episode and can include medications, psychosocial intervention, or both.

3. Delirium severely affects people's _____, making tasks such as recalling one's own name difficult.

4. The _____ population is at the greatest risk of experiencing delirium resulting from improper use of medications.

5. Various types of brain _____, such as head injury or infection, have been linked to delirium.

6. People who suffer from delirium appear to be _____ or out of touch with their surroundings.

Major and Mild Neurocognitive Disorders

▶ What are the symptoms of and treatment for major and mild neurocognitive disorders?

Few things are more frightening than the possibility of one day not recognizing those you love, not being able to perform the most basic of tasks and, worse yet, being acutely aware of this failure of your mind. When family members show these signs, initially adult children often deny any difficulty, coming up with excuses ("I forget things, too") for their parents' failing abilities. **Major neurocognitive disorder** (previously labeled **dementia**) is a gradual deterioration of brain functioning that affects memory, judgment, language, and other advanced cognitive processes. **Mild neurocognitive disorder** is a new *DSM-5* disorder that was created to focus attention on the early stages of cognitive decline. Here the person has modest impairments in cognitive abilities but can, with some accommodations (for example, making extensive lists of things to do or creating elaborate schedules), continue to function independently.

Causes of neurocognitive disorders include several medical conditions and the abuse of drugs or alcohol that produce negative changes in cognitive functioning. Some of these conditions—for instance, infection or depression—can cause neurocognitive impairment, although it is often

DSM 5 DISORDER CRITERIA SUMMARY
Major Neurocognitive Disorder

A. Evidence of significant cognitive decline from a previous level of performance in one or more cognitive domains (complex attention, executive function, learning and memory, language, perceptual-motor, or social cognition) based on: (1) Concern of the individual, a knowledgeable informant, or the clinician that there has been a significant decline in cognitive function; and (2) A substantial impairment in cognitive performance, preferably documented by standardized neuropsychological testing or, in its absence, another quantified clinical assessment.

B. The cognitive deficits interfere with independence in everyday activities.

C. The cognitive deficits do not occur exclusively in the context of a delirium.

D. The cognitive deficits are not better explained by another mental disorder.

Specify whether due to:

Alzheimer's disease, Frontotemporal lobar degeneration, Lewy body disease, Vascular disease, Traumatic brain injury, Substance/medication use, HIV infection, Prion disease, Parkinson's disease, Huntington's disease, Another medical condition, Multiple etiologies, Unspecified.

From American Psychiatric Association. (2013). *Diagnostic and statistical manual of mental disorders* (5th ed.). Washington, DC.

DSM 5 DISORDER CRITERIA SUMMARY
Mild Neurocognitive Disorder

A. Evidence of modest cognitive decline from a previous level of performance in one or more cognitive domains (complex attention, executive function, learning and memory, language, perceptual motor, or social cognition) based on: (1) Concern of the individual, a knowledgeable informant, or the clinician that there has been a mild decline in cognitive function; and (2) A modest impairment in cognitive performance, preferably documented by standardized neuropsychological testing or, in its absence, another quantified clinical assessment.

B. The cognitive deficits do not interfere with capacity for independence in everyday activities.

C. The cognitive deficits do not occur exclusively in the context of a delirium.

D. The cognitive deficits are not better explained by another mental disorder.

Specify whether due to:

Alzheimer's disease, Frontotemporal lobar degeneration, Lewy body disease, Vascular disease, Traumatic brain injury, Substance/medication use, HIV infection, Prion disease, Parkinson's disease, Huntington's disease, Another medical condition, Multiple etiologies, Unspecified.

From American Psychiatric Association. (2013). *Diagnostic and statistical manual of mental disorders* (5th ed.). Washington, DC.

reversible through treatment of the primary condition. Some forms of the disorder, such as Alzheimer's disease, are at present irreversible. Although delirium and neurocognitive disorder can occur together, neurocognitive disorder has a gradual progression as opposed to delirium's acute onset; people with neurocognitive disorder are not disoriented or confused in the early stages, unlike people with delirium. Like delirium, however, neurocognitive disorder has many causes, including a variety of traumas to the brain such as stroke (which destroys blood vessels), syphilis and HIV, severe head injury, the introduction of certain toxic or poisonous substances, and diseases such as Parkinson's, Huntington's, and Alzheimer's. Consider the personal account by Pat Summitt, the most successful NCAA basketball coach of all time. She coached the Tennessee Lady Vols basketball team from 1974 to 2012—winning a record-setting 1,098 games—until her symptoms of neurocognitive disorder due to Alzheimer's disease prevented her from working with the team full-time. Unfortunately, Pat Summitt passed away in 2016 at the age of 64 as the result of complications due to Alzheimer's. Before she died she courageously wrote of her experiences with this disorder (Summitt, 2013).

Pat Summitt • *Grit and Determination*

At the age of 57, Pat Summitt was a successful basketball coach and mother, but she was beginning to experience lapses in her memory. Despite having cognitive difficulties, not all of her memories were lost to her in this initial stage of the disease. She began her memoir with the things she remembered:

> I remember the night my son was born. The doctor placed him on my chest and I said, "Hey, Tyler, I've been waitin' on you." (pp. 6–7)

Her memory for important experiences that occurred years ago remained intact. However, recent experiences and facts were more elusive. She then goes on to describe some of the things she no longer remembered:

> Sometimes, when I first wake up, I don't remember where I am. For a moment I'm disoriented and uneasy, and I have to lie there until it comes to me... I struggle to remember directions. There are moments when I'm driving to someplace I should know, and I have to ask, "Do I go left or right here?" (p. 7)

Many people who begin to have these cognitive difficulties retell these initial experiences as incredibly frightening. However, Summitt's reaction to her diagnosis and her doctor's recommendations show an incredible level of courage and strength:

> The doctor told me that given my diagnosis, frankly, he felt I could no longer work at all. I should step down immediately, because in his opinion the dementia would progress rapidly. I needed to quit, and get myself out of the public eye as quickly as possible, or I would "embarrass" myself and ruin my legacy. As he spoke, I felt my fist clench. It was all I could do not to lunge across the desk and drop him with one punch. Who did he think he was? Even if I had an irreversible brain disease—even if I did—what right did he have to tell me how to cope with it? Quit? Quit? (pp. 17–18)

She goes on to write about her unusually practical and optimistic perspective on having Alzheimer's disease—a view of this degenerative disease that should serve as a role model for the millions of people impacted by this disorder:

> Above all, I know that Alzheimer's has brought me to a point that I was going to arrive at someday anyway. With or without this diagnosis, I was going to experience diminishment. We all do. It's our fate.

> No, I can't size up a court of ten players anymore, see the clock out of one eye and the shifting schemes of opposing players with the other, and order up a countermove by hollering "Five!" or "Motion!" But I can suggest that people with mild to moderate stages of dementia have far more abilities than incapacities. I can suggest that just because certain circuits of memory or swiftness of synapses may fail, thought and awareness and consciousness do not. (p. 375)

Source: Summitt, P. H. (2013). *Sum it up: A thousand and ninety-eight victories, a couple of irrelevant losses, and a life in perspective.* New York: Crown Archetype.

Clinical Description and Statistics

Depending on the individual and the cause, the gradual progression of neurocognitive disorder may have somewhat different symptoms, although all aspects of cognitive functioning are eventually affected. In the initial stages, memory impairment is typically seen as an inability to register ongoing events. In other words, a person can remember how to talk and may remember events from many years ago but will have trouble remembering what happened in the past hour. For example, Pat Summitt had vivid recollections about her childhood but could not remember which direction to drive in familiar places.

Visuospatial skills are impaired among people with neurocognitive disorder. **Agnosia**, the inability to recognize and name objects, is one of the most familiar symptoms. **Facial agnosia**, the inability to recognize even familiar faces, can be extremely distressing to family members. A general deterioration of intellectual function results from impairment in memory, planning, and abstract reasoning.

Perhaps partly because people suffering from neurocognitive disorder are aware that they are deteriorating mentally, emotional changes often occur as well. Common side effects are delusions (irrational beliefs), depression, agitation, aggression, and apathy (Lovestone, 2012). It is difficult, however, to establish the cause-and-effect relationship. It is not known how much behavioral change is caused by progressive brain deterioration directly and how much is a result of the frustration and discouragement that inevitably accompany the loss of function and the isolation of "losing"

major neurocognitive disorder (dementia) Gradual deterioration of brain functioning that affects memory, judgment, language, and other advanced cognitive processes.

mild neurocognitive disorder Modest impairment in cognitive abilities that can be overcome with accommodations such as extensive lists or elaborate schedules.

agnosia Inability to recognize and name objects; may be a symptom of **dementia** or other brain disorders.

facial agnosia Type of **agnosia** characterized by a person's inability to recognize even familiar faces.

loved ones. Cognitive functioning continues to deteriorate until the person requires almost total support to carry out day-to-day activities. Ultimately, death occurs as the result of inactivity, combined with the onset of other illnesses, such as pneumonia.

Globally, it is estimated that one new case of major neurocognitive disorder is identified every seven seconds (Ferri *et al.*, 2005). Major neurocognitive disorder can develop at almost any age, although this disorder is more frequent in older adults. The methodology for estimating the number of those suffering from major neurocognitive disorder has resulted in sometimes diverging numbers (Launer, 2011). Current estimates in the United States suggest a prevalence of around five million people with major neurocognitive disorder (Alzheimer's Association, 2011), with rates of a little more than 5% in people older than 65 and 20% to 40% in those older than 85 (Richards & Sweet, 2009). The increasing number of people with just one form of neurocognitive disorder—due to Alzheimer's disease—is alarming. A dramatic rise in Alzheimer's disease is predicted through the year 2050 as larger numbers of people are expected to live beyond 85 years of age. ● Figure 13.3 illustrates how the prevalence of neurocognitive disorder due to Alzheimer's disease is projected to greatly increase in older adults, partly as a result of the increase of baby boomers who will become senior citizens (Hebert, Weuve, Scherr, & Evans, 2013). Among the eldest of adults, research on centenarians

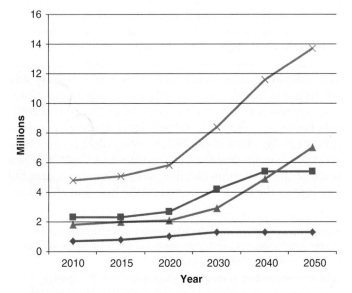

● **Figure 13.3** With the increasing numbers of persons living longer, the rate of Alzheimer's disease is predicted to escalate dramatically through the year 2050. (From Hebert, L. E., Weuve, J., Scherr, P. A., & Evans, D. A. (2013). Alzheimer disease in the United States (2010–2050) estimated using the 2010 census. *Neurology, 80*(19), 1778–1783.)

(people 100 years and older) indicates that up to 100% showed signs of neurocognitive disorder (Davey *et al.*, 2013; Imhof *et al.*, 2007). Neurocognitive disorder due to Alzheimer's disease rarely occurs in people under 45 years of age.

Estimates of the prevalence of the new *DSM-5* diagnosis— mild neurocognitive disorder—have been studied by the Einstein Aging Study at Yeshiva University (Katz *et al.*, 2012). Researchers recruited 1,944 adults aged 70 or older and assessed them for mild neurocognitive disorder as well as mild amnestic neurocognitive disorder in this group. This latter disorder—in its more severe state—was previously a separate *DSM* disorder (*amnestic disorder*) but has been folded into the general neurocognitive disorder group. Almost 10% of those over 70 had mild neurocognitive disorder, and 11.6% met the criteria for mild amnestic neurocognitive disorder. Race also seemed to be a factor with black men and women at higher risk for mild neurocognitive disorder than white men and women (Katz *et al.*, 2012).

A problem with confirming prevalence figures for neurocognitive disorder is that survival rates alter the outcomes. Because adults are generally living longer and are therefore more at risk of developing neurocognitive disorder, it is not surprising that the disorder is more prevalent. Incidence studies, which count the number of new cases in a year, may thus be the most reliable method for assessing the frequency of neurocognitive disorder, especially among the elderly. Research shows that the rate for new cases doubles with every five years of age after age 75. Many studies find greater increases of neurocognitive disorder among women (Carter, Resnick, Mallampalli, & Kalbarczyk, 2012). Neurocognitive disorder due to Alzheimer's disease may, as we discuss later, be more prevalent among women. Together, results suggest that neurocognitive disorder is relatively common among older adults, and the chances of developing it increase rapidly after the age of 75.

In addition to the human costs of neurocognitive disorder, the financial costs are staggering. Estimates of the costs of caring for people with neurocognitive disorder due to Alzheimer's disease are often quoted to be about $100 billion per year in the United States. One estimate indicates that the total worldwide societal cost of major neurocognitive disorder is more than $604 billion (Wimo *et al.*, 2013), including informal care and direct medical costs. Also, many times, family members care for an afflicted person around the clock, which is an inestimable personal and financial commitment (Lovestone, 2012).

DSM-5 identifies classes of neurocognitive disorder based on etiology: (1) Alzheimer's disease, (2) vascular injury, (3) frontotemporal degeneration, (4) traumatic brain injury, (5) Lewy body disease, (6) Parkinson's disease, (7) HIV infection, (8) substance use, (9) Huntington's disease, (10) prion disease, and (11) another medical condition. We emphasize neurocognitive disorder due to Alzheimer's disease because of its prevalence (almost half of those with neurocognitive disorder exhibit this type) and the relatively large amount of research conducted on its etiology and treatment.

Neurocognitive Disorder Due to Alzheimer's Disease

In 1907, the German psychiatrist Alois Alzheimer first described the disorder that bears his name. He wrote of a 51-year-old woman who had a "strange disease of the cerebral cortex" that manifested as progressive memory impairment and other behavioral and cognitive problems, including suspiciousness (Richards & Sweet, 2009). He called the disorder an "atypical form of senile dementia"; thereafter, it was referred to as **Alzheimer's disease**.

The *DSM-5* diagnostic criteria for **neurocognitive disorder due to Alzheimer's disease** include multiple cognitive deficits that develop gradually and steadily. Predominant are impairment of memory, orientation, judgment, and reasoning. The inability to integrate new information results in failure to learn new associations. Individuals with Alzheimer's disease forget important events and lose objects. Their interest in non-routine activities narrows. They tend to lose interest in others and, as a result, become more socially isolated. As the disorder progresses, they can become agitated, confused, depressed, anxious, or even combative. Many of these difficulties become more pronounced late in the day—in a phenomenon referred to as "sundowner syndrome"—perhaps as a result of fatigue or a disturbance in the brain's biological clock (Ferrazzoli, Sica, & Sancesario, 2013; Lemay & Landreville, 2010).

People with neurocognitive disorder due to Alzheimer's disease also display one or more other cognitive disturbances, including aphasia (difficulty with language), apraxia (impaired motor functioning), agnosia (failure to recognize objects), or difficulty with activities such as planning, organizing, sequencing, or abstracting information. These cognitive impairments have a serious negative impact on social and occupational functioning, and they represent a significant decline from previous abilities.

In the past, a definitive diagnosis of Alzheimer's disease could be made only after an autopsy determined that certain characteristic types of damage were present in the brain. There is now growing evidence, however, that the use of sophisticated brain scans along with new chemical tracers may soon be able to help clinicians identify the presence of Alzheimer's disease before the significant declines in cognitive abilities (through a project called the Alzheimer's Disease Neuroimaging Initiative [ADNI]) or death (Douaud *et al.*, 2013; Weiner *et al.*, 2012). In addition, research on the presence of certain markers for Alzheimer's (e.g., beta amyloid—the substance in the amyloid plaques found in the brains of persons with this disease) in spinal fluid also appears to increase the accuracy of a diagnosis (Vanderstichele *et al.*, 2012). Currently, to make a diagnosis without direct examination of the brain, a simplified version of a mental status exam is used to assess language and memory problems.

Cognitive deterioration with Alzheimer's disease is slow during the early and later stages but more rapid during the middle stages (Ito *et al.*, 2011; Richards & Sweet, 2009). The average survival time is estimated to be about four to eight years, although many individuals live dependently for more than 20 years. In some forms, the disease can occur relatively early, during the 40s or 50s (sometimes referred to as *early onset*), but it usually appears during the 60s or 70s. Alzheimer's disease is believed to afflict more than 5.3 million Americans and millions more worldwide (Alzheimer's Association, 2015).

Some early research on prevalence suggested that Alzheimer's disease may occur more often in people who are poorly educated (Amieva *et al.*, 2014; Fratiglioni *et al.*, 1991). Greater impairment among uneducated people might indicate a much earlier onset, suggesting that Alzheimer's disease causes intellectual dysfunction that in turn hampers educational efforts. Or there could be something about intellectual achievement that prevents or delays the onset of symptoms of the disorder. Later research seems to confirm the latter explanation. It appears that educational level may predict a delay in the observation of symptoms (Amieva *et al.*, 2014). Unfortunately, people who attain a higher level of education also decline more rapidly once the symptoms become more severe (Scarmeas, Albert, Manly, & Stern, 2006), suggesting that education does not prevent Alzheimer's disease but just provides a buffer period of better functioning. Educational attainment may somehow create a mental "reserve," a learned set of skills that helps someone cope longer with the cognitive deterioration that marks the beginning of neurocognitive deficits. Some people may adapt more successfully than others and thus escape detection longer. This tentative hypothesis may prove useful in designing treatment strategies, especially during the early stages of the disorder.

Tim Beddow/Science Source

▲ The PET scan of a brain afflicted with Alzheimer's disease (left) shows significant tissue deterioration in comparison with a normal brain (right).

Alzheimer's disease Disease of the cerebral cortex that causes an atypical form of senile dementia, discovered in 1906 by German **psychiatrist** Alois Alzheimer.

neurocognitive disorder due to Alzheimer's disease Condition resulting from a disease that develops most often in people 50 and older, characterized by multiple cognitive defects that develop gradually and steadily.

A biological version of this theory—the cognitive reserve hypothesis—suggests that the more synapses a person develops throughout life, the more neuronal death must take place before the signs of dementia are obvious (Farias *et al.*, 2012). Mental activity that occurs with education presumably builds up this reserve of synapses and serves as an initial protective factor in the development of the disorder. It is likely that both skill development and the changes in the brain with education may contribute to how quickly the disorder progresses.

Research suggests that Alzheimer's disease may be more prevalent among women (Alzheimer's Association, 2015; Craig & Murphy, 2009), even when women's higher survival rate is factored into the statistics. A tentative explanation involves the hormone estrogen. Women lose estrogen as they grow older, so perhaps estrogen is protective against the disease. A large and important study—the Women's Health Initiative Memory Study—looked at hormone use among women and its effect on Alzheimer's disease (Lobo, 2013; Shumaker *et al.*, 2004). In its initial findings, the study followed women over age 65 using a type of combined estrogen plus progestin known as Prempro and, contrary to the belief that giving women estrogen would decrease their chance of developing neurocognitive disorder, they observed an *increased* risk for Alzheimer's disease (Coker *et al.*, 2010; Maki & Henderson, 2012). More research is ongoing into the individual effects of these two types of hormones on dementia.

Finally, there appear to be questions about the prevalence of Alzheimer's disease according to cultural and/or racial identity. Early research seemed to suggest that certain populations (such as those with Japanese, Nigerian, certain Native American, and Amish backgrounds) were less likely to be affected (for example, see Pericak-Vance *et al.*, 1996; Rosenberg *et al.*, 1996). Similarly, prevalence rates of Alzheimer's disease in low- and middle-income countries have also been reportedly lower than higher-income countries (Sosa-Ortiz, Acosta-Castillo, & Prince, 2012). More recent work indicates, however, that some of these differences may be due to lower numbers in those who seek assistance (possibly due to stigma as well high levels of social care from family members), as well as differences in education, and how the disorders were measured (Sosa-Ortiz *et al.*, 2012; Wilson *et al.*, 2010). Alzheimer's disease is found in roughly the same numbers across all ethnic groups, with one study finding a slightly lower rate among American Indians (Weiner, Hynan, Beekly, Koepsell, & Kukull, 2007). As you will see, findings like these help bring us closer to understanding the causes of this devastating disease.

Vascular Neurocognitive Disorder

Each year, 500,000 people die from strokes (any diseases or traumas to the brain that result in restriction or cessation of blood flow). Although stroke is the third-leading cause of death in the United States, many people survive, but one potential long-term consequence can be severely debilitating. **Vascular neurocognitive disorder** is a progressive brain disorder that is a common cause of neurocognitive deficits. It is one of the more common causes of neurocognitive disorder (Erkinjuntti, 2012).

The word *vascular* refers to blood vessels. When the blood vessels in the brain are blocked or damaged and no longer carry oxygen and other nutrients to certain areas of brain tissue, damage results. Because multiple sites in the brain can be damaged, the profile of degeneration—the particular skills that are impaired—differs from person to person. *DSM-5* lists as criteria for vascular neurocognitive disorder cognitive disturbances such as declines in speed of information processing and executive functioning (e.g., complex decision-making) (Erkinjuntti, 2012). In contrast, those with Alzheimer's disease have memory problems as their initial cognitive disturbance.

The prevalence of vascular neurocognitive disorder is approximately 1.5% in people 70 to 75 years of age and increases to 15% for those over the age of 80 (Neugroschi, Kolevzon, Samuels, & Marin, 2005). The risk for men is slightly higher than among women, and this has been reported in many developed and developing countries (Kalaria *et al.*, 2008). The relatively high rate of cardiovascular disease among men in general may account for their increased risk of vascular neurocognitive disorder. The onset of vascular dementia is typically more sudden than the onset for Alzheimer's, probably because the disorder is the result of stroke, which inflicts brain damage immediately. The outcome, however, is similar for people with both types: Ultimately, they will require formal nursing care until they succumb to an infectious disease such as pneumonia, to which they are susceptible because of weakening of the immune system.

Other Medical Conditions That Cause Neurocognitive Disorder

A number of other neurological and biochemical processes can lead to neurocognitive disorder. *DSM-5* identifies eight specific causes in addition to Alzheimer's disease and vascular damage: frontotemporal degeneration, traumatic brain injury, Lewy body disease, Parkinson's disease, HIV infection, substance use, Huntington's disease, and prion disease. In addition, a final category—neurocognitive disorder due to another medical condition—is provided for other causes. Other medical conditions that can lead to neurocognitive disorder include normal pressure hydrocephalus (excessive water in the cranium, resulting from brain shrinkage), hypothyroidism (an underactive thyroid gland), brain tumor, and vitamin B12 deficiency. There is increasing recognition of neurocognitive disorder among athletes who receive repeated blows to the head. In the past, this type of neurocognitive disorder was referred to as *dementia pugilistica* (which suggested that it was restricted to boxers or pugilists) but it is currently referred to as *chronic traumatic encephalopathy (CTE)*. CTE is caused by repetitive **head trauma** that can provoke distinctive neurodegeneration (Baugh *et al.*, 2012). In their effect on cognitive ability, all of these disorders are comparable to the other forms of neurocognitive disorder we have discussed so far.

Frontotemporal neurocognitive disorder is an overarching term used to categorize a variety of brain disorders that damage the frontal or temporal regions of the brain—areas that affect personality, language, and behavior (Gustafson & Brun, 2012). *DSM-5* identifies two variants of frontotemporal neurocognitive disorder—through declines in appropriate behavior (e.g., socially inappropriate actions, apathy, making poor judgments) or language (e.g., problems with speech, finding the right word, naming objects). One of the disorders in this category of neurocognitive disorders is **Pick's disease**, a rare neurological condition—occurring in about 5% of those people with neurocognitive impairment—that produces symptoms similar to that of Alzheimer's disease. The course of this disease is believed to last from five to 10 years and appears to have a genetic component (Gustafson & Brun, 2012). Pick's disease usually occurs relatively early in life—during a person's 40s or 50s—and is therefore considered an example of early onset neurocognitive disorder.

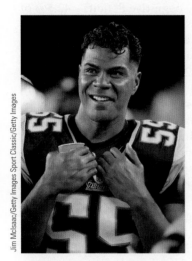

▲ Junior Seau was an NFL star football player who committed suicide in 2012. The National Institutes of Health—at the request of his family—determined through an examination of his brain that he had abnormalities consistent with repetitive blows to the head, which resulted in chronic traumatic encephalopathy (CTE).

Severe trauma to the head causes the brain to sustain lasting injuries (called **traumatic brain injury** or **TBI**), which can lead to neurocognitive disorder (Fleminger, 2012). **Neurocognitive disorder due to traumatic brain injury** includes symptoms that persist for at least a week following the trauma, including executive dysfunction (e.g., difficulty planning complex activities) and problems with learning and memory. Those that are at greatest risk for TBI are teens and young adults, especially accompanied by alcohol abuse or lower socio-economic class (Fleminger, 2012). Traffic accidents, assaults, falls, and suicide attempts are common causes, as is being exposed to bomb blasts in combat.

The second most common type of neurocognitive disorders (after Alzheimer's disease) is **neurocognitive disorder due to Lewy body disease** (Aarsland, Ballard, Rongve, Broadstock, & Svenningsson, 2012; McKeith *et al.*, 2005). Lewy bodies are microscopic deposits of a protein that damage brain cells over time. The signs of this disorder come on gradually and include impairment in alertness and attention, vivid visual hallucinations, and motor impairment as seen in Parkinson's disease. In fact, there is some overlap between this disorder and **neurocognitive disorder due to Parkinson's disease** (Mindham & Hughes, 2012).

Parkinson's disease is a degenerative brain disorder that affects about 100 to 300 people in every 100,000 people worldwide, though estimates vary widely due to challenges in diagnosing the disorder (Wirdefeldt, Adami, Cole, Trichopoulos, & Mandel, 2011). Motor problems are characteristic among people with Parkinson's disease, who tend to have stooped posture, slow body movements (called *bradykinesia*), tremors, and jerkiness in walking. The voice is also affected; afflicted individuals speak in a soft monotone. The changes in motor movements are the result of damage to dopamine pathways. Because dopamine is involved in complex movement, a reduction in this neurotransmitter makes affected individuals increasingly unable to control their muscle movements, which leads to tremors and muscle weakness.

▲ Both Michael J. Fox and the late Muhammed Ali, pictured here, devoted time and celebrity status to efforts to cure Parkinson's disease – and both Fox and Ali's lives were severely affected by the degenerative disease.

vascular neurocognitive disorder Progressive brain disorder involving loss of cognitive functioning, caused by blockage of blood flow to the brain, that appears concurrently with other neurological signs and symptoms.

head trauma Injury to the head and, therefore, to the brain, typically caused by accidents; can lead to cognitive impairments, including memory loss.

frontotemporal neurocognitive disorder Condition that damages the frontal or temporal regions of the brain; behavior or language is negatively affected.

Pick's disease Rare neurological disorder that results in **presenile dementia**.

traumatic brain injury (TBI) Brain damage caused by a blow to the head or other trauma that injures the brain and results in diminished neurocognitive capacity.

neurocognitive disorder due to traumatic brain injury Condition resulting from jarring of the brain caused by a blow to the head or other impact; symptoms persist for at least a week after the initial trauma.

neurocognitive disorder due to Lewy body disease Neurological impairment that affects people with Lewy body disease, in which protein deposits damage brain cells and gradually cause motor impairments and loss of alertness.

neurocognitive disorder due to Parkinson's disease Disorder characterized by progressive decline in motor movements; results from damage to dopamine pathways.

Parkinson's disease Degenerative brain disorder principally affecting motor performance (for example, tremors and stooped posture) associated with reduction in **dopamine**. **Dementia** may be a result as well.

In addition to degeneration of these pathways, Lewy bodies are also present in the brains of affected persons. The course of the disease varies widely, with some individuals functioning well with treatment. It is estimated that about 75% of people who survive more than 10 years with Parkinson's disease develop neurocognitive disorder; conservative estimates place the rate at four to six times that found in the general population (Aarsland & Kurz, 2010; Svenningsson, Westman, Ballard, & Aarsland, 2012).

The **human immunodeficiency virus type 1 (HIV-1)**, which causes AIDS, can also cause neurocognitive disorder (called **neurocognitive disorder due to HIV infection**) (Maj, 2012). This impairment seems to be independent of the other infections that accompany HIV; in other words, the HIV infection itself seems to be responsible for the neurological impairment. The early symptoms of neurocognitive disorder resulting from HIV are cognitive slowness, impaired attention, and forgetfulness. Affected individuals also tend to be clumsy, to show repetitive movements such as tremors and leg weakness, and to become apathetic and socially withdrawn.

Like neurocognitive disorder from Parkinson's disease and several other causes, neurocognitive disorder resulting from HIV is sometimes referred to as *subcortical dementia*, because it affects primarily the inner areas of the brain, below the outer layer called the cortex (Clifford & Ances, 2013). The distinction between cortical (including neurocognitive disorder due to Alzheimer's disease) and subcortical dementia is important because of the different expressions of neurocognitive disorder in these two categories (see Table 13.2). **Aphasia**, which involves impaired language skills, occurs among people with neurocognitive disorder due to Alzheimer's disease but not among people with subcortical dementia. In contrast, people with subcortical dementia are more likely to experience severe depression and anxiety than those with neurocognitive disorder due to Alzheimer's disease. In general, motor skills including speed and coordination are impaired early on among those with subcortical dementia. The differing patterns of impairment can be attributed to the different areas of the brain affected by the disorders causing the neurocognitive disorder.

Huntington's disease is a genetic disorder that initially affects motor movements, typically in the form of *chorea*, involuntary limb movements (Pringsheim *et al.*, 2012). People with Huntington's disease can live for 20 years after the first signs of the disease appear, although skilled nursing care is often required during the final stages. Just as with Parkinson's disease, only a portion of people with Huntington's disease go on to display cognitive deficits—42.5% of new Huntington's disorder cases also present with *mild* cognitive impairment (Robbins & Cools, 2014). Estimates of how many individuals go on to develop neurocognitive disorders vary widely from 20% to 80%—although some researchers believe that all patients with Huntington's disease would eventually display neurocognitive impairments if they lived long enough (Marsh & Margolis, 2009). **Neurocognitive disorder due to Huntington's disease** also follows the subcortical pattern.

The search for the gene responsible for Huntington's disease reads like a detective story. For some time, researchers have known that the disease is inherited as an autosomal dominant disorder, meaning that approximately 50% of the offspring of an adult with Huntington's disease will develop the disease. Since 1979, behavioral scientist Nancy Wexler and a team of researchers have been studying the largest known extended family in the world afflicted by Huntington's disease in small villages in Venezuela. Using genetic linkage analysis techniques (see Chapter 3), these researchers first mapped the deficit to an area on chromosome 4 (Gusella *et al.*, 1983) and then identified the elusive gene (Huntington's Disease Collaborative Research Group, 1993). Finding that one gene that causes a disease is unusual; research on other inherited mental disorders typically points to multiple gene (polygenic) influences.

Neurocognitive disorder due to prion disease is a rare progressive neurodegenerative disorder caused by

TABLE 13.2 | Characteristics of Neurocognitive Disorders

Characteristic	Dementia of the Alzheimer's Type	Subcortical Dementias
Language	Aphasia (difficulties with articulating speech)	No aphasia
Memory	Both recall and recognition are impaired	Impaired recall; normal or less impaired recognition
Visuospatial skills	Impaired	Impaired
Mood	Less severe depression and anxiety	More severe depression and anxiety
Motor speed	Normal	Slowed
Coordination	Normal until late in the progression	Impaired

SOURCE: Adapted, with permission of Oxford University Press, from Cummings, J. L. (Ed.) (1990). *Subcortical dementia.* New York, NY: Oxford University Press, © 1990 Jeffrey L. Cummings.

"prions"—proteins that can reproduce themselves and cause damage to brain cells leading to neurocognitive decline (Collinge, 2012). Unlike other infectious agents such as bacteria or viruses, prions are thought by some to have no DNA or RNA that can be destroyed by chemicals or radiation. As a result, there is no known treatment for prion disease, and the course of this disorder is always fatal. On the positive side, prions are not contagious in humans and have only been contracted through cannibalism (causing kuru) or accidental inoculations (e.g., through blood transfusions from an infected person) (Collinge, 2012). One type of prion disease, **Creutzfeldt-Jakob disease**, is believed to affect only one in every million individuals (Heath *et al.*, 2010; Sikorska, Knight, Ironside, & Liberski, 2012). An alarming development in the study of Creutzfeldt-Jakob disease is the finding of 10 cases of a new variant that may be linked to bovine spongiform encephalopathy, more commonly referred to as "mad cow disease" (Ebringer, 2015; Neugroschi *et al.*, 2005). This discovery led to a ban on exporting beef from the United Kingdom for a number of years because the disease might be transmitted from infected cattle to humans. We do not yet have definitive information about the link between mad cow disease and the new form of Creutzfeldt-Jakob disease (Wiggins, 2009).

Substance/Medication-Induced Neurocognitive Disorder

Prolonged drug use, especially combined with poor diet, can damage the brain and, in some circumstances, can lead to neurocognitive disorder. This impairment unfortunately lasts beyond the period involved in intoxication or withdrawal from these substances.

As many as 50% to 70% of chronic heavy alcohol users show cognitive impairment (Sico *et al.*, 2014), and 7% of those with an alcohol use disorder also meet criteria for a neurocognitive disorder (Neugroschi *et al.*, 2005). The long-term abuse of a number of drugs can lead to symptoms of neurocognitive disorder, including alcohol, inhalants such as glue or gasoline, and sedative, hypnotic, and anxiolytic drugs. These drugs pose a threat because they create physiological dependence, making it difficult for a user to stop ingesting them. The resulting brain damage can be permanent and can cause the same symptoms as seen in neurocognitive disorder due to Alzheimer's type. The *DSM-5* criteria for **substance/medication-induced neurocognitive disorder** are essentially the same as many of the other forms of neurocognitive disorder; they include memory impairment and at least one of the following cognitive disturbances: aphasia (language disturbance), apraxia (inability to carry out motor activities despite intact motor function), agnosia (failure to recognize or identify objects despite intact sensory function), or a disturbance in executive functioning (such as planning, organizing, sequencing, and abstracting).

Causes of Neurocognitive Disorder

A complete description of what is known about the origins of this type of brain impairment is beyond the scope of this book, but we highlight some insights available for more common forms of this disorder.

Biological Influences

As you have seen, neurocognitive disorder can be caused by a number of processes. The most common cause of neurocognitive disorder, Alzheimer's disease, is also the most mysterious. Because of its prevalence and our relative ignorance about the factors responsible for it, Alzheimer's disease has held the attention of many researchers who are trying to find the cause and ultimately a treatment or cure for this devastating condition.

What do we know about Alzheimer's disease? After the death of the patient he described as having a "strange disease of the cerebral cortex," Alois Alzheimer performed an autopsy. He found that the brain contained large numbers of tangled, strand-like filaments within the brain cells (referred to as *neurofibrillary tangles*). This type of damage occurs in everyone with Alzheimer's disease. A second type of degeneration results from gummy protein deposits—called *amyloid plaques* (also referred to as *neuritic* or *senile plaques*)—that accumulate between the neurons in the brains of people with this disorder. Amyloid plaques are also found in older adults who do not have symptoms of neurocognitive disorder, but they have far fewer of them than do individuals with Alzheimer's disease (Richards & Sweet, 2009). Both forms of damage—neurofibrillary

human immunodeficiency virus type 1 (HIV-1) Disease that causes AIDS.

neurocognitive disorder due to HIV infection Less common type of neurocognitive disorder that affects people who have HIV; may lead to impaired thinking in advanced stages.

aphasia Impairment or loss of language skills resulting from brain damage caused by **stroke**, **Alzheimer's disease**, or other illness or trauma.

huntington's disease Genetic disorder marked by involuntary limb movements and progressing to **dementia**.

neurocognitive disorder due to Huntington's disease Neurological disorder that follows a subcortical pattern and is notable for causing involuntary limb movements.

neurocognitive disorder due to prion disease Rare progressive neurodegenerative disorder caused by prions, proteins that can reproduce themselves and cause damage to brain cells.

creutzfeldt-Jakob disease Extremely rare condition that causes **dementia**.

substance/medication-induced neurocognitive disorder Brain damage caused by prolonged use of drugs, often in combination with a poor diet.

tangles and amyloid plaques—accumulate over the years and are believed to produce the characteristic neurocognitive disorders we have been describing (Weiner et al., 2012).

These two types of degeneration affect extremely small areas and can be detected only by a microscopic examination of the brain. As mentioned earlier, scientists are close, however, to developing the neuroimaging technology and measures to assess amyloid proteins in spinal fluid that may soon detect the early development of these types of brain cell damage without having to rely on an autopsy (Weiner et al., 2012). In addition to having neurofibrillary tangles and amyloid plaques, over time the brains of many people with Alzheimer's disease atrophy (shrink) to a greater extent than would be expected through normal aging (Lovestone, 2012). Because brain shrinkage has many causes, however, only by observing the tangles and plaques can a diagnosis of Alzheimer's disease be properly made.

Rapid advances are being made toward uncovering the genetic bases of Alzheimer's disease (e.g., Seshadri et al., 2010). As with most other behavioral disorders we have examined, multiple genes seem to be involved in the development of Alzheimer's disease. Table 13.3 illustrates what we know so far.

Some genes that are now identified are **deterministic**, meaning that if you have one of these genes you have a nearly 100% chance of developing Alzheimer's disease (Bettens, Sleegers, & Van Broeckhoven, 2010). Deterministic genes such as the precursor gene for small proteins called *amyloid beta peptides* (also referred to as beta-amyloid or A(b) and the *Presenilin 1* and *Presenilin 2* genes will inevitably lead to Alzheimer's disease, but, fortunately, these genes are also rare in the general population. For treatment purposes, this means that even if researchers can find a way to prevent these genes from leading to Alzheimer's disease, it will only help a relatively small number of people. On the other hand, some genes—including the *apolipoprotein E4 (apo E4)* gene—are known as **susceptibility** genes. These genes only slightly increase the risk of developing Alzheimer's disease, but in contrast to the deterministic genes, these are more common in the general population (Lovestone,

2012). If future research can find ways to interfere with the *apo E4* gene, many people will be helped.

Although closing in on the genetic origins of Alzheimer's disease has not brought immediate treatment implications, researchers are nearer to understanding how the disease develops, which may result in medical interventions. Genetic research has advanced our knowledge of how the amyloid plaques develop in the brains of people with Alzheimer's disease and may hold a clue to its origins. In the core of the plaques is a solid waxy substance made up of a peptide called amyloid beta or Ab. Just as cholesterol buildup on the walls of blood vessels chokes the blood supply, deposits of Ab are believed by some researchers to cause the cell death associated with Alzheimer's disease (Lovestone, 2012). An important question, then, is "Why does this protein accumulate in the brain cells of some people but not of others?"

For all disorders described in this book, we have identified the role of biological, psychological, or both types of stressors as partially responsible for the onset of the disorder. Does neurocognitive disorder due to Alzheimer's disease—which appears to be a strictly biological event—follow the same pattern? One of the leading candidates for an external contributor to this disorder is head trauma. As we have seen, it appears that repeated blows to the head can bring on neurocognitive disorder (chronic traumatic encephalopathy or CTE). Head trauma may be one of the stressors that initiate the onset of neurocognitive disorder of varying types. Other such stressors include having diabetes, high blood pressure, or herpes simplex virus-1 (Richards & Sweet, 2009). As with each of the disorders discussed, psychological and biological stressors may interact with physiological processes to produce Alzheimer's disease.

Psychological and Social Influences

Although few would claim that psychosocial influences directly cause the type of brain deterioration seen in people with neurocognitive disorder, they may help determine onset and course. For example, a person's lifestyle may involve

TABLE 13.3 | Genetic Factors in Alzheimer's Disease

Gene	Chromosome	Age of Onset (years)
APP	21	43 to 59
Presenilin 1	14	33 to 60
Presenilin 2	1	50 to 90
apo E4	19	60

AAP = amyloid precursor protein; *apo E4* = apolipoprotein E4.

SOURCE: Lovestone, S. (2012). Dementia: Alzheimer's disease. In M. G. Gelder, N. C. Andreasen, J. J. Lopez Jr. & J. R. Geddes (Eds.), *New Oxford textbook of psychiatry* (2nd. ed., Vol. 1, pp. 333–343). New York: Oxford University Press.

▲ Nancy Wexler headed the team of scientists who found the gene for Huntington's disease.

contact with factors that can cause neurocognitive disorder. You saw, for instance, that substance abuse can lead to neurocognitive disorder and, as we discussed previously, whether a person abuses drugs is determined by a combination of biological and psychosocial factors. In the case of vascular neurocognitive disorder, a person's biological vulnerability to vascular disease will influence the chances of strokes that can lead to this form of disorder. Lifestyle issues such as diet, exercise, and stress influence cardiovascular disease and therefore help determine who experiences vascular neurocognitive disorder (see Chapter 7).

Cultural factors may also affect this process. For example, hypertension and strokes are more prevalent among African Americans and subgroups of Asian Americans than non-Hispanic whites (Howard *et al.*, 2013; King, Mainous III, & Geesey, 2007). This may explain why vascular neurocognitive disorder is also more often observed in members of these groups. Neurocognitive disorder caused by head trauma and malnutrition are relatively prevalent in preindustrial rural societies (Del Parigi, Panza, Capurso, & Solfrizzi, 2006). Not getting enough of vitamins B$_9$ and B$_{12}$ in particular seems to lead to neurocognitive disorder, although the process is as yet unknown (Michelakos *et al.*, 2013). These findings suggest that occupational safety (such as protecting workers from head injuries) and economic conditions influencing diet also affect the prevalence of certain forms of neurocognitive disorders. It is apparent that psychosocial factors help influence who does and who does not develop certain forms of neurocognitive disorder.

Psychosocial factors themselves influence the course of neurocognitive disorder. Recall that educational attainment may affect the onset of dementia (Amieva *et al.*, 2014). Having certain skills may help some people cope better than others with the early stages of neurocognitive disorder. The early stages of confusion and memory loss may be better tolerated in cultures with lowered expectations of older adults. In certain cultures, including the Chinese, younger people are expected to take the demands of work and care

from older adults after a certain age, and symptoms of dementia are viewed as a sign of normal aging (Sun, Ong, & Burnette, 2012; Hinton, Guo, Hillygus, & Levkoff, 2000). Neurocognitive disorder may go undetected for years in these societies (Sosa-Ortiz *et al.*, 2012).

Treatment

For many of the disorders discussed in other chapters, treatment prospects are fairly good. Clinicians can combine various strategies to reduce suffering significantly. Even when treatment does not bring expected improvements, mental health professionals have usually been able to stop problems from progressing. This is not the case in the treatment of neurocognitive disorder.

One factor preventing major advances in the treatment of neurocognitive disorder is the nature of the damage caused by this disorder. The brain contains billions of neurons, many more than are used. Damage to some can be compensated for by others because of plasticity. There is a limit to where and how many neurons can be destroyed, however, before vital functioning is disrupted. Researchers are closing in on how to use the brain's natural process of regeneration to potentially reverse the damage caused in neurocognitive disorder (e.g., Wright, Kawas, & Harding, 2015). Currently, however, with extensive brain damage, no known treatment can restore lost abilities. The goals of treatment therefore become (1) trying to prevent certain conditions, such as substance abuse or strokes, that may bring on neurocognitive disorder; (2) trying to delay the onset of symptoms to provide better quality of life; and (3) attempting to help these individuals and their caregivers cope with the advancing deterioration. Most efforts in treating neurocognitive disorder have focused on the second and third goals, with biological treatments aimed at stopping the cerebral deterioration and psychosocial treatments directed at helping patients and caregivers cope.

A troubling statistic further clouds the tragic circumstances of neurocognitive disorder. In one study, more than 60% of caregivers of people with neurocognitive disorder—usually relatives—have the symptoms characteristic of one or more anxiety disorders (55% of these caregivers had anxiety) and/or clinical depression (37% of the caregivers had depression) (Joling *et al.*, 2015). Compared with the public, these caregivers use more psychotropic medications (designed to reduce symptoms of various psychological disorders) and report stress symptoms at three times the normal rate. Caring for people with neurocognitive disorder, especially in its later stages, is clearly a trying experience. In fact, there is some evidence to suggest that the stress associated with caring for a person with neurocognitive

deterministic In genetics, **genes** that lead to nearly a 100% chance of developing the associated disorder. These are rare in the population.

susceptibility In genetics, **genes** that only slightly increase the risk of developing the disorder, but in contrast to the **deterministic** genes, these are more common in the population.

disorder may place the caregiver at greatly increased risk for developing neurocognitive disorder themselves (Norton et al., 2010). As a result, clinicians are becoming increasingly sensitive to the needs of these caregivers, and research is now exploring interventions that are easy to disseminate (such as over the internet) to assist them in caring for people with neurocognitive disorder. Preliminary results from such interventions are promising and have important implications for the caregivers of the "baby-boomer" generation (Blom, Bosmans, Cuijpers, Zarit, & Pot, 2013).

Biological Treatments

Neurocognitive disorder resulting from known infectious diseases, nutritional deficiencies, and depression can be treated if it is caught early. Unfortunately, however, no known treatment exists for the types of neurocognitive disorder that account for the vast majority of cases. Neurocognitive disorder caused by stroke, Parkinson's disease, or Huntington's disease is not currently treatable, because there is no effective treatment for the primary disorder. However, exciting research in several related areas has brought us closer to helping individuals with these forms of neurocognitive disorder. A substance that may help preserve and perhaps restore neurons—glial cell–derived neurotrophic factor—may someday be used to help reduce or reverse the progression of degenerative brain diseases (Lu, Nagappan, Guan, Nathan, & Wren, 2013). Researchers are also looking into the possible benefits of transplanting stem cells (fetal brain tissue) into the brains of people with such diseases. Initial results from these studies are still preliminary but appear promising (Pen & Jensen, 2016). Neurocognitive disorder brought on by strokes may now be more preventable by new drugs that help prevent much of the damage inflicted by the blood clots characteristic of stroke (Erkinjuntti, 2012). Most current attention is on a treatment for dementia of the Alzheimer's type, because it affects so many people. Here, too, however, success has been modest at best.

Much work has been directed at developing drugs that will enhance the cognitive abilities of people with neurocognitive disorder due to Alzheimer's type. Many seem to be effective initially, but long-term improvements have not been observed in placebo-controlled studies (Richards & Sweet, 2009). Several drugs (called *cholinesterase inhibitors*) have had a modest impact on cognitive abilities in some patients and include donepezil (Aricept), rivastigmine (Exelon), and galantamine (Reminyl) (Trinh, Hoblyn, Mohanty, & Yaffe, 2003). These drugs prevent the breakdown of the neurotransmitter acetylcholine (which is deficient in people with Alzheimer's disease), thus making more acetylcholine available to the brain. Research suggests that, when using these drugs, people's cognitive abilities improve to the point where they were six months earlier (Kimchi & Lyketos, 2015). But the gain is not permanent. Even people who respond positively do not stabilize but continue to

experience the cognitive decline associated with Alzheimer's disease. In addition, if they stop taking the drug—as almost three-quarters of the patients do because of negative side effects such as liver damage and nausea—they lose even that six-month gain (Kimchi & Lyketos, 2015). Newer drugs are being investigated that target the beta amyloid (plaques) in the brain, and it is hoped that these advances will provide a positive prognosis for this disease (Lukiw, 2012; McClam, Marano, Rosenberg, & Lyketsos, 2015).

Several other medical approaches are being explored to slow the course of Alzheimer's disease. Initial research suggested that *Ginkgo biloba* (maidenhair) may produce modest improvements in the memory of people with Alzheimer's disease, but other studies have not replicated this benefit (Vellas et al., 2012). Similarly, a few large studies have found that among individuals with moderately severe impairment, high doses of vitamin E (2,000 international units per day) delayed progression compared with a placebo (Dysken et al., 2014; Sano et al., 1997), but it did not prevent the development of the disease. Further research, in fact, indicates that taking high doses of vitamin E may actually increase mortality and therefore this intervention is no longer recommended (Richards & Sweet, 2009). Modest slowing of the progression of the disease also may be obtained by introducing exercise to patients (Paillard, Rolland, & de Souto Barreto, 2015). To date, however, no medical interventions are available that directly treat and therefore stop the progression of the conditions that cause the cerebral damage in Alzheimer's disease.

Medical interventions for neurocognitive disorder also include the use of drugs to help with some associated symptoms. A variety of antidepressants are commonly recommended to alleviate the depression and anxiety that often accompany the cognitive decline. Antipsychotic medication is sometimes used for those who become unusually agitated (Richards & Sweet, 2009).

Other researchers are targeting vaccines that would potentially treat and prevent—rather than just delay—the symptoms of Alzheimer's disease. Much of the research is attempting to get the immune system to attack the process that overproduces the small proteins (Ab) that lead to cell death. More recent research with humans and animals indicates that there may be several vaccines that could be effective in preventing the damage caused by Ab formation and therefore represent the first glimmer of hope for patients and their families (Davtyan et al., 2013).

Psychosocial Treatments

Psychosocial treatments are now receiving a great deal of attention for their ability to delay the onset of severe cognitive decline. These efforts focus on enhancing the lives of people with neurocognitive disorder, as well as those of their families.

People with neurocognitive disorder can be taught skills to compensate for their lost abilities. Some researchers have evaluated formal adaptations to help people in the early stages of neurocognitive disorder. Michelle Bourgeois (2007) created "memory wallets" to help people with Alzheimer's disease carry on conversations. On white index cards inserted into a wallet are printed declarative statements such as, "My husband John and I have three children," or "I was born on January 6, 1921, in Pittsburgh." With advances in technology such as tablet computers that can be programmed to "speak" for the person, adaptations such as these help people communicate with others, help them remain aware of their surroundings, and can reduce the frustration that comes with the awareness of their own decline (Fried-Oken et al., 2012).

Cognitive stimulation seems to be an effective method for delaying the onset of the more severe cognitive effects of this disorder (Aguirre, Woods, Spector, & Orrell, 2013; Woods, Aguirre, Spector, & Orrell, 2012). These activities include word games, tests of memory of faces, and practice with numbers (for example, how much change back you would receive from a purchase). These types of skill-building exercises can maintain cognitive activity and improve the quality of life in those patients when compared with controls (Choi & Twamley, 2013).

Individuals with advanced neurocognitive disorder are not able to feed, bathe, or dress themselves. They cannot communicate with or recognize even familiar family members. They may wander away from home and become lost. Because they are no longer aware of social stigma, they may engage in public displays of sexual behavior, such as masturbation. They may be frequently agitated or even physically violent. To help both the person with dementia and the caregiver, researchers have explored interventions for dealing with these consequences of the disorder (Lovestone, 2012).

For example, some research indicates that a combination of exercise for patients and instruction for caregivers on how to handle behavior problems can improve the overall health and the depression in people with Alzheimer's disease (Potter, Ellard, Rees, & Thorogood, 2011; Teri et al., 2003).

Of great concern is the tendency of people with neurocognitive disorder to wander. Sometimes they wind up in places or situations that may be dangerous (for example, stairwells or the

▲ A resident of an assistive living facility practices cognitive stimulation using one of several computer-based systems

street). Sometimes the person may be tied to a chair or bed, or sedated, to prevent roaming. Unfortunately, physical and medical restraint has its own risks, including additional medical complications; it also adds greatly to the loss of control and independence that already plague the person with neurocognitive disorder. Psychological treatment as an alternative to restraint sometimes involves providing cues for people to help them safely navigate around their home or other areas. New innovations in surveillance technology—creating a "smart home" that can monitor the location of the patient and warn caregivers—may provide more peace of mind for those who care for these patients. At the same time, ethical concerns are being raised about the use of this technology because of its ability to invade privacy (Bharucha et al., 2009; Chung, Demiris, & Thompson, 2016).

Someone with neurocognitive disorder can become agitated and sometimes verbally and physically aggressive. In these situations, medical intervention is often used, although many times with only modest results (Testad, Ballard, Brønnick, & Aarsland, 2010). Some research suggests that teaching communication skills in a manner similar to programs for persons with autism spectrum disorder (Durand, 2012) may help reduce aggressive behavior in persons with neurocognitive disorder (Livingston et al., 2014). In addition, caregivers are often given assertiveness training to help them deal with hostile behaviors. Some caregivers may either passively accept all criticism inflicted by the person with neurocognitive disorder, which increases stress, or become angry and aggressive in return. This last response is of particular concern because of the potential for elder abuse. Withholding food or medication or inflicting physical abuse is most common among caregivers of elderly people who have cognitive deficits. Research has also shown that elder abuse occurs in nursing homes and assisted living, with neglect and emotional abuse being the most common in these settings (Castle, Ferguson-Rome, & Teresi, 2015; Post, Page, Conner, & Prokhorov, 2010). It is important to teach caregivers how to handle stressful circumstances so that they do not escalate into abusive situations.

In general, families of people with mild to moderate neurocognitive disorder can benefit from supportive counseling to help them cope with the frustration, depression, guilt, and loss that take a heavy emotional toll. Despite numerous studies aimed at supporting caregivers, however, the results to date remain weak and additional work is needed to determine how best to support these individuals (Schoenmakers, Buntinx, & DeLepeleire, 2010; Tremont et al., 2015).

Early on, caregivers need basic information on the causes and treatment of neurocognitive disorder, financial and legal issues, and locating help for the patient and the family. As the disorder progresses, and the affected person requires increasing amounts of assistance, caregivers will need help managing behavioral difficulties (wandering away or violent outbursts) and developing effective ways to communicate with the patient. Clinicians also assist the family with decisions about hospitalizations and, finally, help them adjust during bereavement. However, the best methods to help caregivers help others are still being explored (Peeters, Van Beek, Meerveld, Spreeuwenberg, & Francke, 2010; Zabalegui et al., 2014).

Prevention

You can imagine that it is difficult to study prevention efforts for neurocognitive disorder because of the need to follow individuals for long periods to see whether the efforts are effective. One major study conducted in Sweden—where socialized medicine provides complete medical histories of all residents—looked at many of the risk factors and protective factors under study today (Fratiglioni & Qiu, 2009; Fratiglioni, Winblad, & von Strauss, 2007). Through interviews and medical histories, they came to three major conclusions: control your blood pressure, do not smoke, and lead an active physical and social life. These recommendations came out as the major factors that individuals can change—because you cannot change your genetics, for example—that will decrease the chances of developing neurocognitive disorder (Rizzuto, Orsini, Qiu, Wang, & Fratiglioni, 2012). Additional prevention research is ongoing, and there may be other potentially fruitful research areas that can lead to the successful prevention of this devastating disorder.

DSM 5 CONTROVERSY   Losing a Valued Label

One of the most talked about and debated changes in the *DSM-5* was the elimination of separate categories for "autistic disorder" and "Asperger's disorder"—which were present in *DSM-IV*. The rationale behind this reorganization of the separate autism related disorders under one rubric was that ASDs could be reliably distinguished from other disorders, but within this category there were considerable inconsistencies (Frazier et al., 2012; Rutter, 2011b). In other words, it was not always clear if someone had a milder form of autistic disorder (e.g., with more speech) or whether it was Asperger's disorder. They all share the pervasive deficits in social communication skills as well as the restricted patterns of behaviors. It was argued that the main differences among the disorders are ones involving the severity of the symptoms, language level, and levels of intellectual deficit and therefore could be grouped together as autism spectrum disorder—with varying degrees of severity.

One of the first concerns was that these new criteria might exclude some individuals who previously met *DSM-IV* criteria and, in turn, it might result in the denial of treatment services for those left out. This concern was precipitated by researchers who evaluated cases that received a *DSM-IV* diagnosis of autism or a related disorder and tried to see how many would now fall into the new ASD category (McPartland, Reichow, & Volkmar, 2012). Their initial findings caused considerable alarm since they concluded that almost 40% of individuals would not meet the *DSM-5* criteria. Although subsequent analyses found this number to be lower (e.g., approximately 9% in one study; Huerta, Bishop, Duncan, Hus, & Lord, 2012), there remains a concern that some individuals will no longer be eligible for needed services.

In addition to the concern about combining this disorder into the generic autism spectrum disorder, many of those individuals who have been previously diagnosed with Asperger's disorder feel that this decision takes away part of their identity (Pellicano & Stears, 2011). Rather than feeling shame or embarrassment about receiving this diagnosis, a good number of these individuals embrace their distinctiveness. Some advocate for seeing these differences in terms of "neurodiversity," or viewing their "disorder" as just a different and not abnormal way to view the world (Armstrong, 2010; Singer, 1999). In fact, the word "Aspies" is sometimes used with pride by individuals with this label (e.g., Beardon & Worton, 2011) and those who do not have this disorder are often referred to as "neurotypical"—sometimes in a negative way. It is likely that despite the elimination of Asperger's disorder from *DSM-5*, some in this community will continue to hold on to the label with pride.

SUMMARY

Overview of Neurodevelopmental Disorders

Why is knowledge of critical development stages important for understanding neurodevelopmental disorders?

▶ Developmental psychopathology is the study of how disorders arise and change with time. These changes usually follow a pattern, with the child mastering one skill before acquiring the next. This aspect of development is important because it implies that any disruption in the acquisition of early skills will, by the very nature of the developmental process, also disrupt the development of later skills.

Attention-Deficit/Hyperactivity Disorder

What are the central defining features of attention deficit/hyperactivity disorder?

▶ The primary characteristics of people with attention-deficit/hyperactivity disorder (ADHD) are a pattern of inattention (such as not paying attention to school- or work-related tasks), impulsivity, and/or hyperactivity. These deficits can significantly disrupt academic efforts and social relationships.

Specific Learning Disorder

What is specific learning disorder, and how is it typically treated?

▶ *DSM-5* describes specific learning disorder as academic performance that is substantially below what would be expected given the person's age, intelligence quotient (IQ) score, and education. These problems can be seen as difficulties with reading, mathematics, and/or written expression. All are defined by performance that falls far short of expectations based on intelligence and school preparation.

▶ Communication and motor disorders seem closely related to specific learning disorder. They include childhood speech fluency disorder (stuttering), a disturbance in speech fluency; language disorder, limited speech in all situations but without the types of cognitive deficits that lead to language problems in people with intellectual disability or one of the pervasive developmental disorders; and Tourette's disorder, which includes involuntary motor movements such as head twitching and vocalizations such as grunts that occur suddenly, in rapid succession, and in idiosyncratic or stereotyped ways.

Autism Spectrum Disorder

What are the major characteristics of autism spectrum disorder?

▶ People with ASD all experience trouble progressing in language, socialization, and cognition. This is not a relatively minor problem (like specific learning disorder) but is a condition that significantly affects how individuals live and interact with others.

▶ ASD is a childhood disorder characterized by significant impairment in social communication skills and restricted, repetitive patterns of behavior, interests, or activities. This disorder does not have a single cause; instead, a number of biological conditions may contribute, and these, in combination with psychosocial influences, result in the unusual behaviors displayed by people with ASD.

▶ Impressive advances have been made in improving outcomes for many young children with ASD using early intervention programs. Treatment for older children involves behavioral interventions focused on their social communication deficits and the restricted, repetitive patterns of behavior, interests, or activities.

Intellectual Disability (Intellectual Developmental Disorder)

How is intellectual disability defined, and what categories are used to classify intellectual disabilities?

▶ The definition of intellectual disability has three parts: significantly sub-average intellectual functioning, concurrent deficits or impairments in present adaptive functioning, and an onset before the age of 18.

▶ Down syndrome is a type of ID caused by the presence of an extra 21st chromosome. It is possible to detect the presence of Down syndrome in a fetus through a process known as amniocentesis.

▶ Two other types of ID are common: fragile X syndrome, which is caused by a chromosomal abnormality of the tip of the X chromosome, and cultural–familial intellectual disability, a rare problem resulting from adverse environmental conditions.

Prevention of Neurodevelopmental Disorders

What are major prevention efforts for the neurodevelopmental disorders?

▶ Prevention efforts for the neurodevelopmental disorders are in their early stages. These efforts include early intervention. Although many children can make significant progress if interventions are initiated early in life, not all children benefit significantly from such efforts. Given recent advances in genetic screening and technology, it may someday be possible to detect and correct genetic and chromosomal abnormalities.

Overview of Neurocognitive Disorders

What are the defining features of neurocognitive disorders?

▶ Most neurocognitive disorders develop much later in life. Two classes of neurocognitive disorders exist: *delirium* and *mild or major neurocognitive disorder*.

Delirium

What are the symptoms of delirium?

▶ Delirium is a temporary state of confusion and disorientation that can be caused by brain trauma, intoxication by drugs or poisons, surgery, and a variety of other stressful conditions, especially among older adults.

Major and Mild Neurocognitive Disorders

What are the symptoms of and treatment for major and mild neurocognitive disorders?

▶ Major neurocognitive disorder is a progressive and degenerative condition marked by gradual deterioration of a range of cognitive abilities including memory, language, and planning, organizing, sequencing, and abstracting information.

▶ Mild neurocognitive disorder is a condition in which there are early signs of cognitive decline such that it begins to interfere with activities of daily living.

▶ Alzheimer's disease is the leading cause of neurocognitive disorder, affecting approximately four million people in the United States; there is currently no known cause or cure.

▶ To date, there is no effective treatment for the irreversible neurocognitive disorder caused by Alzheimer's disease, Lewy bodies, vascular disease, Parkinson's disease, Huntington's disease, and various less common conditions that produce progressive cognitive impairment. Treatment often focuses on helping patients cope with the continuing loss of cognitive skills and helping caregivers deal with the stress of caring for affected individuals.

▬▬ Key Terms

neurodevelopmental disorders, 481
attention-deficit/hyperactivity disorder (ADHD), 483
Tourette's disorder, 523
copy number variants, 486
specific learning disorder, 488
childhood—onset fluency disorder (stuttering), 490
language disorder, 490
autism spectrum disorder (ASD), 492
childhood disintegrative disorder, 492
Rett disorder, 492
pervasive developmental disorder—not otherwise specified, 492
joint attention, 493
prosody, 494
naturalistic teaching strategies, 496
intellectual disability (ID), 498
phenylketonuria (PKU), 501
Lesch-Nyhan syndrome, 501
Down syndrome, 501
amniocentesis, 502

chorionic villus sampling (CVS), 502
fragile X syndrome, 502
cultural–familial intellectual disability, 503
delirium, 505
major neurocognitive disorder (dementia), 508
mild neurocognitive disorder, 508
agnosia, 509
facial agnosia, 509
Alzheimer's disease, 511
neurocognitive disorder due to Alzheimer's disease, 511
vascular neurocognitive disorder, 512
head trauma, 513
frontotemporal neurocognitive disorder, 513
Pick's disease, 513
traumatic brain injury (TBI), 513
neurocognitive disorder due to traumatic brain injury, 513

neurocognitive disorder due to Lewy body disease, 513
neurocognitive disorder due to Parkinson's disease, 513
Parkinson's disease, 513
human immunodeficiency virus type 1 (HIV-1), 514
neurocognitive disorder due to HIV infection, 514
aphasia, 514
Huntington's disease, 514
neurocognitive disorder due to Huntington's disease, 514
neurological disorder due to prion disease, 515
Creutzfeldt-Jakob disease, 515
substance/medication-induced neurocognitive disorder, 515
deterministic, 516
susceptibility, 516

Answers to Concept Checks

13.1

1. c; 2. a; 3. b; 4. d; 5. a

13.2

1. b; 2. a; 3. d; 4. c

13.3

1. profound, pervasive support; 2. moderate, limited support; 3. severe, extensive support; 4. mild, intermittent support

13.4

1. c; 2. b; 3. a; 4. e; 5. f; 6. d

13.5

1. b; 2. c; 3. a; 4. substance-induced neurocognitive disorder; 5. vascular neurocognitive disorder; 6. neurocognitive disorder due to Alzheimer's disease.

Chapter Quiz

1. According to the *DSM-5,* the symptoms that are characteristic of ADHD are:
   a. inattention and hyperactivity/impulsivity
   b. echolalia and hyperactivity/impulsivity
   c. hallucinations and delusions
   d. obsessions and compulsions

2. Echolalia is characterized by which of the following behaviors?
   a. continuously reading the same sentence or words
   b. repeating the speech of others
   c. mimicking the movements of others
   d. staring ahead without blinking for long periods

3. Behavioral techniques are often used to address communication problems that occur with autism. _____ involves rewarding the child for progressive approximations of speech, and _____ involves rewarding the child for making sounds that the teacher requests.
   a. Shaping; discrimination training
   b. Modeling; syntax training
   c. Imitating; expression training
   d. Processing; academic training

4. Research has shown that ADHD in children is associated with:
   a. chronic neglect
   b. having an alcoholic father
   c. maternal smoking during pregnancy
   d. death of a parent in early childhood

5. Which of the following is NOT a recommended treatment for persons with specific learning disorder?
   a. instruction on vocabulary
   b. finding facts in readings
   c. efforts to improve cognitive skills through decision making and critical thinking
   d. medical intervention

6. _____ is a form of intellectual disability caused by the presence of an extra 21st chromosome.
   a. Down syndrome
   b. Fragile X syndrome
   c. PKU syndrome
   d. Fetal alcohol syndrome

7. Joe has a mild intellectual disability. His therapist is teaching him a skill by breaking it down into its component parts. Joe's therapist is implementing what technique?
   a. skills treatment   c. component processing
   b. biofeedback   d. task analysis

8. _____ is characterized by acute confusion and disorientation; whereas _____ is marked by deterioration in a broad range of cognitive abilities.
   a. Delirium; amnesia
   b. Amnesia; delirium
   c. Major neurocognitive disorder; delirium
   d. Delirium; major neurocognitive disorder

9. Which disorder can be diagnosed definitively only at autopsy by the presence of large numbers of amyloid plaques and neurofibrillary tangles?
   a. vascular neurocognitive disorder
   b. neurocognitive disorder due to Alzheimer's disease
   c. delirium
   d. neurocognitive disorder due to Parkinson's disease

10. Psychological and social influences are important to consider when studying neurocognitive disorders because they:
    a. can accelerate the type of brain damage seen in this disease
    b. provide a rationale for psychopharmacological intervention
    c. may help determine the time of onset and course of dementia
    d. can be used to reverse the progression of Alzheimer's disease

(See Appendix A for answers.)

Exploring Neurodevelopmental Disorders

Disorders that appear early in life disrupt the normal course of development.

▶ Interrupting or preventing the development of one skill impedes mastery of the skill that is normally acquired next.

▶ Knowing what skills are disrupted by a particular disorder is essential to developing appropriate intervention strategies.

COGNITION

LANGUAGE

SOCIALIZATION

Photos: Photodisc/Getty Images

Infancy   **Childhood**   **Adolescence**

TYPES OF NEURODEVELOPMENTAL DISORDERS

		Description	Causes	Treatment
Attention-Deficit/Hyperactivity Disorder (ADHD)	Suzanne Tucker/Shutterstock.com	■ Inattentive, overactive, and impulsive behavior ■ Disrupted schooling and relationships ■ Symptoms may change with maturity, but problems persist. ■ More prevalent in boys than girls	■ Research suggests hereditary factor ■ Abnormal neurology ■ Possible link with maternal smoking ■ Negative responses by others create low self-esteem.	■ Biological (medication) – improves compliance – decreases negative behaviors – effects not long term ■ Psychological (behavioral) – goal setting and reinforcement
Specific Learning Disorder	Courtesy of Laureate Learning Systems Inc.	■ Reading, math, and written expression fall behind IQ, age, and education. ■ May also be accompanied by ADHD	■ Theories assume genetic, neurobiological, and environmental factors.	■ Education intervention – basic processing – cognitive and behavioral skills

		Types	Description	Treatment
Communication and Motor Disorders Closely related to learning disorders, but comparatively benign. Early appearance, wide range of problems later in life	Photodisc/Getty Images	**Childhood Onset Fluency Disorder (Stuttering)**	Disturbance in speech fluency (repeating words, prolonging sounds, extended pauses)	■ Psychological ■ Pharmacological
		Language Disorder	Limited speech in all situations	■ Psychological ■ Some cases may be self-correcting
		Social (Pragmatic) Communication Disorder	Problems with the social aspects of verbal and nonverbal communication	■ Psychological
		Tourette's Disorder	Involuntary motor movements (tics), such as physical twitches or vocalizations	■ Psychological ■ Pharmacological

PERVASIVE DEVELOPMENTAL DISORDERS

Autism Spectrum Disorder

Description	Causes	Treatment

■ Severely impaired social communication
■ Restricted, repetitive patterns of behavior, interests, or activities
■ Symptoms often develop before 36 months of age.
■ Manifests across a wide range of functioning, from individuals who have limited communication skills to those who can converse with others but lack the social pragmatic skills to be able to make and maintain meaningful social relationships.
	■ Little conclusive data
	■ Numerous biological factors
	  – clear genetic component
	  – evidence of brain damage (cognitive deficits) combined with psychosocial influences
		■ Behavioral focus
		  – communication
		  – socialization
		  – living skills
		■ Inclusive schooling
		■ Temporary benefits from medication

INTELLECTUAL DISABILITY

Description	Causes	Treatment

■ Adaptive and intellectual functioning significantly below average
■ Language and communication impairments
■ Wide range of impairment—from mild to profound—in daily activities (90% of affected individuals have mild impairments).
	■ Hundreds of identified factors
	  – genetic
	  – prenatal
	  – perinatal
	  – postnatal
	  – environmental
	■ Nearly 75% of cases cannot be attributed to any known cause.
		■ No biological intervention
		■ Behavioral focus similar to that for autism
		■ Prevention
		  – genetic counseling
		  – biological screening
		  – maternal care

Exploring Neurocognitive Disorders

◗ When the brain is damaged, the effects are irreversible, accumulating until learning, memory, or consciousness are obviously impaired.

◗ Neurocognitive disorders develop much later than intellectual disability and other learning disorders, which are believed to be present at birth.

TYPES OF NEUROCOGNITIVE DISORDERS

		Description	Causes (subtypes)	Treatment
Delirium		■ Impaired consciousness and cognition for several hours or days – confusion, disorientation, inability to focus ■ Most prevalent among older adults, people with AIDS, and patients on medication	■ Delirium due to a general medical condition ■ Substance-induced delirium ■ Delirium due to multiple etiologies ■ Delirium not otherwise specified	■ Pharmacological – benzodiazepines – antipsychotics ■ Psychosocial – reassurance – presence of personal objects – inclusion in treatment decisions

Todd Pearson/DigitalVision/Getty Images

Photodisc/Getty Images

Major and Mild Neurocognitive Disorders

- Gradual deterioration of brain functioning that affects judgment, memory, language, and other advanced cognitive processes
- Caused by medical condition or drug abuse
- Some forms are irreversible; some are resolved by treatment of primary condition.

TYPES OF NEUROCOGNITIVE DISORDERS

		Description	Causes	Treatment
Neurocognitive Disorder due to Alzheimer's Disease	 Christian Martinez Kempin/E+/Getty Images 	■ Increasing memory impairment and other multiple behavioral and cognitive deficits, affecting language, motor functioning, ability to recognize people or things, and/or planning ■ Most prevalent neurocognitive disorder ■ Subject of most research	■ Progressive brain damage, evident in neurofibrillary tangles and neuritic plaque, confirmed by autopsy but assessed by simplified mental status exam ■ Involves multiple genes	■ No cure so far, but hope lies in genetic research and amyloid protein. ■ Management may include lists, maps, and notes to help maintain orientation. ■ New medications that prevent acetylcholine breakdown and vitamin therapy delay but do not stop progression of decline.
Substance-induced Neurocognitive Disorder	 Photodisc/Getty Images	■ Caused by brain damage due to prolonged drug use, especially in combination with poor diet, as in alcohol dependency; other substances may include inhalants, and the sedative, hypnotic, and anxiolytic drugs ■ Treatment focuses on prevention.		
Vascular Neurocognitive Disorder	 Photodisc/Getty Images	■ Permanent deterioration due to blocked or damaged blood vessels in the brain (stroke) ■ Symptoms include declines in speed of information processing and executive functioning (e.g., complex decision making) and may also include problems with walking and weakness of limbs. ■ Treatment focuses on coping.		

Neurocognitive Disorders Due to Other Medical Conditions	Simon Fraser/Royal Victoria Infirmary, Newcastle upon Tyne/Science Source	■ Similar in effect to other cognitive disorders, but caused by:
		  – head trauma
		  – Lewy bodies, HIV, Parkinson's, Huntington's, Pick's, or Creutzfeldt-Jakob disease
		  – hydrocephalus, hypothyroidism, brain tumor, and vitamin B12 deficiency
		■ Treatment of primary condition is sometimes possible.		

14 Mental Health Services: Legal and Ethical Issues

CHAPTER OUTLINE

Civil Commitment
Criteria for Civil Commitment
Procedural Changes Affecting Civil Commitment
An Overview of Civil Commitment

Criminal Commitment
The Insanity Defense
Reactions to the Insanity Defense
Therapeutic Jurisprudence
Competence to Stand Trial
Duty to Warn
Mental Health Professionals as Expert Witnesses

Patients' Rights and Clinical Practice Guidelines
The Right to Treatment
The Right to Refuse Treatment
The Rights of Research Participants
Evidence-Based Practice and Clinical Practice Guidelines

SpeedKingz/Shutterstock.com

528

Describe applications that employ discipline-based problem solving:

▶ Describe examples of relevant and practical applications of psychological principles to everyday life. (APA SLO 1.3a) *(see textbook pages 530–531, 541–544)*

▶ Articulate how psychological principles can be used to explain social issues, address pressing societal needs, and inform public policy. (APA SLO 1.3A) *(see textbook pages 532–534, 535–540)*

* Portions of this chapter cover learning outcomes suggested by the American Psychological Association (2013) in its guidelines for the undergraduate psychology major. Chapter coverage of these outcomes is identified above by APA Goal and APA Suggested Learning Outcome (SLO).

We begin this chapter with a return to Arthur, whom we described in Chapter 12 as having psychotic symptoms.

Arthur... • *A Family's Dilemma*

As you remember, Arthur was brought to our clinic by family members because he was speaking and acting strangely. He talked incessantly about his "secret plan" to save all the starving children in the world. His family's concern intensified when Arthur said he was planning to break into the German embassy and present his plan to the German ambassador. Alarmed by his increasingly inappropriate behavior and fearing he would be hurt, the family was astounded to learn they could not force him into a psychiatric hospital. Arthur could admit himself—which was not likely, given his belief that nothing was wrong with him—but they had no power to admit him involuntarily unless he was in danger of doing harm to himself or others. Even if they sincerely believed some harm might be forthcoming, this wasn't sufficient reason to admit him involuntarily. The family coped with this emergency as best they could for several weeks until the worst of Arthur's behaviors began to diminish.

Why wouldn't the mental health facility admit Arthur, who was clearly in need of help? Why couldn't his family authorize the mental health facility to act? What would have happened if Arthur had entered the embassy and hurt or killed someone? Would he have gone to jail, or would he have received help from the mental health community? These are just a few of the issues that surface when we try to balance the rights of people who have psychological disorders with the responsibilities of society to provide care.

Mental health professionals face such questions daily. They must both diagnose and treat people and consider individual and societal rights and responsibilities. As we describe how systems of ethics and legal concepts have developed, remember they change with time and with shifting societal and political perspectives on mental illness. How we treat people with psychological disorders is partly a function of how society views these people. For example, do people with mental illness need help and protection, or does society need protection from them? As public opinion about people with mental illness changes, so do the relevant laws and legal and ethical issues affect both research and practice.

Civil Commitment

▶ How does the legal concept of mental illness differ from a clinically diagnoses psychological disorder?

▶ What is the relationship between dangerousness and mental illness?

▶ What are the interactions among mental illness, deinstitutionalization, and homelessness?

Laws have been designed to protect people who display abnormal behavior and to protect society. Often, achieving this protection is a delicate balancing act, with the scales sometimes thought to be tipped in favor of the rights of individuals and at other times in favor of society. For example, each state has **civil commitment laws** that detail when a person can be legally declared to have a mental illness and be placed in a hospital for treatment

civil commitment laws Legal proceeding that determines a person is mentally disordered and may be hospitalized, even involuntarily.

(Nunley, Nunley, Cutleh, Dentingeh, & McFahland, 2013). When Arthur's family tried to have him involuntarily committed to a mental health facility, hospital officials decided that because he was not in imminent danger of hurting himself or others he could not be committed against his will. In this case, the laws protected Arthur from involuntary commitment, but they also put him and others at potential risk by not compelling him to get help.

Civil commitment laws in the United States date back to the late 19th century. Before this time, almost all people with severe mental illness were cared for by family members or the community or were left to care for themselves. An alarming trend accompanied the development of a large public hospital system devoted to treating such individuals: involuntary commitment of people for reasons unrelated to mental illness (Simon & Shuman, 2009). There were even instances in which women were committed to psychiatric hospitals by their husbands simply for holding differing personal or political views. In the 1800s, Mrs. E. P. W. Packard crusaded for better civil commitment laws after being involuntarily confined to a psychiatric hospital for three years because her husband felt her religious views were "dangerous to the spiritual interests of his children and the community" (Packard & Olsen, 1871; p. 11).

Criteria for Civil Commitment

Historically, states have permitted commitment when several conditions have been met: (1) The person has a "mental illness" and is in need of treatment, (2) the person is dangerous to himself or herself or others, or (3) the person is unable to care for himself, a situation considered a "grave disability." How these conditions are interpreted has varied over the years and has always been controversial. Two types of authority permit the government to take actions that are against a citizen's will: police power and *parens patriae*

("state or country as the parent") power. Under police power, the government takes responsibility for protecting the public health, safety, and welfare and can create laws and regulations to ensure this protection. Criminal offenders are held in custody if they are a threat to society. The state applies *parens patriae* power when citizens are not likely to act in their own best interest; for example, to commit individuals with severe mental illness to mental health facilities when it is believed that they might be harmed because they are unable to secure the basic necessities of life, such as food and shelter (grave disability), or because they do not recognize their need for treatment (Nunley *et al.*, 2013).

A person in need of help can always voluntarily request admission to a mental health facility. When an individual does not voluntarily seek help but others feel that treatment or protection is necessary, however, the formal process of civil commitment can be initiated. The specifics of this process differ from state to state, but it usually begins with a petition by a relative or mental health professional to a judge. The court may then request an examination to assess psychological status, ability for self-care, need for treatment, and potential for harm. The judge considers this information and decides whether commitment is appropriate. This process is similar to other legal proceedings, and the person under question has all the rights and protections provided by the law. In most states, the person can even request that a jury hear the evidence and make a determination. In all cases, the person must be notified that the civil commitment proceedings are taking place, must be present during the trial, must have representation by an attorney, and can examine the witnesses and request an independent evaluation. These safeguards are built into the civil commitment process to guarantee the rights of the person being examined and to ensure that no one is involuntarily committed to a psychiatric facility for other than legitimate reasons.

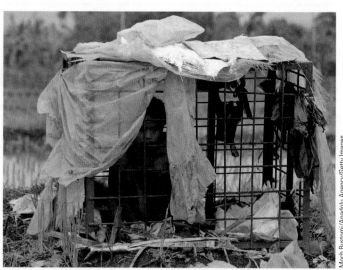

▲ People with mental illness are treated differently in different cultures.

Another route to civil commitment is being adopted by some states: court-ordered assisted outpatient treatment (AOT) (Nunley *et al.*, 2013). In this option, the person with severe mental illness agrees to receive treatment as a condition for continuing to live in the community. These AOT laws provide a balance between the individual's right to live independently and the community's concerns about safety (Nunley *et al.*, 2013).

In emergency situations, when there is clearly immediate danger, a short-term commitment can be made without the formal proceedings required of a civil commitment. Family members or sometimes police officers certify that the person presents a "clear and present danger" to herself or to others (Nunley *et al.*, 2013). Arthur's family was unsuccessful in having him admitted on an emergency basis because it was not clear that anyone was in immediate danger, only that someone might be hurt. Again, deciding what is a "clear and present danger" sometimes requires subjective judgment from the court and mental health professionals.

Defining Mental Illness

Mental illness is a legal concept, typically meaning severe emotional or thought disturbances that negatively affect an individual's health and safety. Each state has its own definition. For example, in New York, "'Mental illness means an affliction with a mental disease or mental condition which is manifested by a disorder or disturbance in behavior, feeling, thinking, or judgment to such an extent that the person afflicted requires care, treatment and rehabilitation" (*New York Mental Hygiene Law*, 1992). In contrast, in Connecticut, "'Mentally ill person' means a person who has a mental or emotional condition that has substantial adverse effects on his or her ability to function and who requires care and treatment, and specifically excludes a person who is an alcohol-dependent person or a drug-dependent person" (Connecticut General Statutes Annotated, 1992). Many states exclude cognitive disability or substance-related disorders from the definition of mental illness.

Mental illness is *not* synonymous with psychological disorder; in other words, receiving a diagnosis according to the *Diagnostic and Statistical Manual (DSM-5)* does not necessarily mean that a person's condition fits the legal definition of mental illness. Although the *DSM* is quite specific about criteria that must be met for diagnosis, there is considerable ambiguity about what constitutes a "mental condition" or what are "adverse effects on his or her ability to function." This allows flexibility in making decisions individually, but it also maintains the possibility of subjective impression and bias as influences on these decisions.

Dangerousness

Assessing whether someone is a danger to self or others is a critical determinant of the civil commitment process. **Dangerousness** is a particularly controversial concept to

▲ The government can exert parens patriae to protect people from hurting themselves.

describe people with mental illness: according to popular opinion, people who are mentally ill are more dangerous than those who are not (Kobau, DiIorio, Chapman, & Delvecchio, 2010; Schomerus *et al.*, 2012). Although this conclusion is questionable, it is still widespread, partly because of sensational media reports. Such views are important to the process of civil commitment if they bias a determination of dangerousness and unfairly link it with severe mental illness.

The results of research on dangerousness and mental illness are often mixed, but evidence points to a moderately increased rate of violence among people with mental illness (Elbogen & Johnson, 2009; Elbogen, Dennis, & Johnson, in press). Closer examination of this kind of research reveals that although having a mental illness generally does increase the likelihood of future violence, specific factors such as a high anger predisposition, recent stressors (e.g., victimization) and substance use are likely responsible for the increased risk of violence (Elbogen

mental illness Term formerly used to mean psychological disorder but less preferred because it implies that the causes of the disorder can be found in a medical disease process.

dangerousness Tendency to violence that, contrary to popular opinion, is not more likely among mental patients.

et al., in press). It is also the presence of these risk factors that may predict the reoccurrence of perpetrated violent crimes by individual with mental illness.

Unfortunately, the widely held misperception that people with mental illness are more dangerous may differentially affect ethnic minorities (Vinkers, de Vries, van Baars, & Mulder, 2010). Black males are often perceived as dangerous, even when they don't exhibit any violent behavior, which may partly explain why black individuals are overrepresented among those who are involuntarily committed to state psychiatric institutions (Lindsey, Joe, Muroff, & Ford, 2010).

How do you determine whether a person is dangerous to others? How accurate are mental health professionals at predicting who will and who will not later be violent? The answers bear directly on the process of civil commitment, as well as on protection for society. If we can't accurately predict dangerousness, how can we justify involuntary commitment?

Numerous risk assessment tools are routinely used to determine if someone is likely to be dangerous to society, including the Psychopathy Checklist-Revised (PCL-R) (Hare & Vertommen, 2003; Neumann, Johansson, & Hare, 2013) used to identify persons with psychopathy. Evidence from numerous studies suggest that these tools are best at identifying persons at low risk of being violent but only marginally successful at accurately detecting who will be violent at a later point (Fazel, Singh, Doll, & Grann, 2012). Mental health professionals can identify groups of people who are at greater risk than the general population for being violent—such as having a previous history of both violence and drug or alcohol dependence—and can so advise the court. What clinicians cannot yet do is predict with certainty whether a particular person will or will not become violent.

Procedural Changes Affecting Civil Commitment

Clearly, there are significant problems with the process of civil commitment. In particular, deciding whether a person has a mental illness or is dangerous requires considerable subjective judgment and, because of varying legal language, this determination can differ from state to state. These problems have resulted in a number of significant legal developments.

The Supreme Court and Civil Commitment

In 1957, the parents of Kenneth Donaldson had him committed to the Florida State Hospital for treatment of paranoid schizophrenia. Donaldson was not considered dangerous, yet, despite repeated offers of placement in a halfway house or with a friend, Dr. O'Connor, the superintendent of the hospital, refused to release him for almost 15 years, during which Donaldson received virtually no treatment (Donaldson, 1976). Donaldson successfully sued Dr. O'Connor for damages, winning $48,500. In deciding the case, the Supreme Court found that "a State cannot constitutionally confine . . . a non-dangerous individual who is capable of surviving safely in freedom by himself or with the help of willing and responsible family and friends" (O'Connor v. Donaldson, 1975).

Here, and in a subsequent decision known as Addington v. Texas (1979), the Supreme Court said that more than just a promise of improving quality of life is required to commit someone involuntarily. If non-dangerous people with mental illness can survive in the community with the help of others, they should not be detained against their will. Needing treatment or having a grave disability was not sufficient to commit someone involuntarily with a mental illness. The effect of this decision substantially limited the government's ability to commit individuals unless they were dangerous (Nunley et al., 2013).

Criminalization

Because of the tightened restrictions on involuntary commitment that prevailed in the 1960s and 1970s, many people who would normally have been committed to mental health facilities for treatment were instead being handled by the criminal justice system. In other words, people with severe mental illness were now living in the community, but many were not receiving the mental health services they needed and would eventually run afoul of the legal system because of their behavior. This "criminalization" of the mentally ill was of great concern because the criminal justice system was not prepared to care for these individuals (Chaimowitz, 2012; Lamb, 2009). Family members were increasingly frustrated that they couldn't obtain treatment for their loved ones, who were instead languishing in jail without help.

Deinstitutionalization and Homelessness

In addition to criminalization, two other trends emerged at this time, starting in the 1980s: an increase in the number of people who were homeless and **deinstitutionalization**, the movement of people with severe mental illness out of institutions. Remember that homelessness is not exclusively a problem of the mentally ill. The estimates of psychological disorders among those who are homeless vary, in part because of the difficulty in tracking these individuals. Best estimates suggest that diagnoses of severe mental illness (for example, schizophrenia and bipolar disorder) among homeless persons are about 30% (Substance Abuse and Mental Health Services Administration, 2011). For reasons not yet fully understood, ethnicity may also play a part in who among people with mental illness becomes homeless. In a large study in San Diego County, for example, Latinos and Asian Americans with mental illness were less likely to become homeless, but African Americans were more likely to be homeless (Folsom et al., 2005).

▲ Larry Hogue was involuntarily committed to a psychiatric hospital because, homeless and under the influence of drugs (left), he terrorized residents of a New York City neighborhood for years. Once off drugs (right), Hogue was able to control himself.

Information on the characteristics of people who are homeless is important because it provides us with clues about why people become homeless, and it dispels the notion that all homeless people have mental health problems. For a time, homelessness was blamed on strict civil commitment criteria and deinstitutionalization (Colp, 2009; Nooe & Patterson, 2010); that is, policies to severely limit who can be involuntarily committed, the limits placed on the hospital stays of people with severe mental illness, and the concurrent closing of large psychiatric hospitals were held responsible for the substantial increase in homelessness during the 1980s. Although a sizable percentage of homeless people have mental illness, the rise in homelessness is also the result of such economic factors as increased unemployment and a shortage of low-income housing (Nooe & Patterson, 2010). Yet the perception that civil commitment restrictions and deinstitutionalization caused homelessness resulted in movements to change commitment procedures.

Reforms in civil commitment that made it more difficult to commit someone involuntarily occurred at the same time the policy of deinstitutionalization was closing large psychiatric hospitals (Nunley *et al.*, 2013). Deinstitutionalization had two goals: (1) to close the large state mental hospitals and (2) to create a network of community mental health centers where the released individuals could be treated. Although the first goal appears to have been substantially accomplished, with about a 75% decrease in the number of hospitalized patients (Kiesler & Sibulkin, 1987), the essential goal of providing alternative community care appears not to have been attained. Instead, there was **transinstitutionalization**, or the movement of people with severe mental illness from large psychiatric hospitals to nursing homes or other group residences, including jails and prisons, many of which provide only marginal services (Lamb & Weinberger, 2009; Primeau, Bowers, Harrison, & XuXu, 2013). Because of the deterioration in care for many people who had previously been served by the mental hospital system, deinstitutionalization is largely considered a failure.

Reactions to Strict Commitment Procedures

Arthur's psychotic reaction and his family's travails in trying to get help occurred during the mid-1970s, a time characterized by greater concern for individual freedom than for society's rights and by the belief that people with mental illness were not properly served by being forced into treatment. Others, however, especially relatives of afflicted people, felt that by not coercing some individuals into treatment, the system was sanctioning their mental decline and placing them at grave risk of harm. The culmination of a number of factors—such as the lack of success with deinstitutionalization, the rise in homelessness, and the criminalization of people with severe mental illness—gave rise to a backlash against their perceived causes, including the strict civil commitment laws. The case of Joyce Brown captures this clash of concerns between individual freedoms for people with mental illness and society's responsibility to treat them.

Joyce Brown... • *Homeless but Not Helpless*

During a 1988 winter emergency in New York City, Mayor Ed Koch ordered that all homeless people who appeared to be mentally ill should be involuntarily committed to a mental health facility for their protection. He used the legal principle of *parens patriae* to justify this action, citing the need to protect these individuals from the cold and from themselves. One of the people who was taken off the streets, 40-year-old Joyce Brown, was picked up against her will and admitted to Bellevue Hospital, where she received a diagnosis of paranoid schizophrenia. She had been homeless for some time, swearing at people as they walked by; at one point, she adopted the name Billie Boggs after a New York television personality with whom she fantasized a relationship. Supported by the New York Civil Liberties Union, Brown contested her commitment and was released after three months (Tushnet, 2008).

This case is important because it illustrates the conflicting interests over civil commitment. Brown's family had for some

deinstitutionalization Systematic removal of people with severe **mental illness** or **intellectual disability** from institutions like psychiatric hospitals.

transinstitutionalization Movement of people with severe mental illness from large psychiatric hospitals to smaller group residences.

time been concerned about her well-being and had tried unsuccessfully to have her involuntarily committed. Although she had never hurt anyone or tried to commit suicide, they felt that living on the streets of New York City was too hazardous, and they feared for her welfare. Brown chose not to seek treatment and resisted efforts to place her in alternative settings. At times, she could be quite articulate in making a case for her freedom of choice. Only weeks after she was released from the hospital, she was again living on the streets.

Rulings such as *O'Connor v. Donaldson* and *Addington v. Texas* had argued that mental illness and dangerousness should be criteria for involuntary commitment. Because of cases like Brown's and concerns about homelessness and criminalization, however, a movement emerged calling for a return to broader civil procedures that would permit commitment not only of those who showed dangerousness to self or others, but also of individuals in need of treatment and those with grave disability—and not dangerous—an opinion that continues to be shared by many today (Gordon, 2015). Groups including the National Alliance on Mental Illness, a coalition of family members of people with mental illness, argued for legal reform to make involuntary commitment easier—an emotional response to the failure to protect and treat people with mental illness. Several states in the late 1970s and early 1980s changed their civil commitment laws in an attempt to address these concerns. Whereas people were previously detained because of violence, they were now admitted under *parens patriae* powers; also, whereas most admissions had been voluntary, they were now involuntary. Hospitals began to fill up because of longer stays and repeated admissions

and they accepted only involuntary admissions; therefore, the result of easing the procedure for involuntarily committing people with mental illness was only to change the authority under which they were admitted.

The special case of sex offenders has attracted attention in recent years, and the issue of how to treat repeat offenders is at the heart of the concerns over civil commitment. In the years between 1930 and 1960, some states passed "sexual psychopath laws" that provided hospitalization instead of incarceration, but for an indefinite period (Saleh, Malin, Grudzinskas Jr., & Vitacco, 2010). Sex offenders (rapists and pedophiles) could be civilly committed until they demonstrated that treatment was effective. However, because treatment is often unsuccessful when attempted with uncooperative clients and because public opinion moved from a priority to treat to a priority to punish, these laws were repealed or went unused. Recent efforts have focused on incarcerating sex offenders for their crimes and, if they are judged still dangerous at the end of their sentences, civilly committing them. Confinement of this type was viewed by the court as acceptable because it was seen as treatment, even though the justices conceded that such treatment is often ineffective (Zonana & Buchanan, 2009). Some are concerned that these laws give the government too much latitude in using civil commitment (as opposed to incarceration) just to keep certain individuals away from others in society (La Fond, 2005). However, those who are incarcerated and released from prison face many legal restrictions (e.g., housing) that may have negative effects by limiting rehabilitation and reintegration into society (Bonnar-Kidd, 2010).

Discussing Diversity   Mental Illness, Homelessness, and Culture

Mental disorders are associated with significant psychological distress and impairment but also can have a huge negative impact on people's ability to earn a living and carry out their day-to-day activities (Hipes, Lucas, Phelan, & White, 2016) . It is estimated that mental disorders cost U.S. society approximately $193.2 billion per year, with 75% of this because of lost earnings among those with serious mental illness and 25% because of not being employed as a result of having a mental illness (Kessler et al., 2008).

Some negative effects of mental disorders seem to hit some groups harder than others. One study of 10,340 residents of San Diego, California, found that 15% of patients receiving treatment for a serious mental illness had an episode of homelessness in

the past year and, more importantly, that African American patients were at significantly higher risk of homelessness than all other patients (Folsom et al., 2005). Also, Latino and Asian American patients were at significantly lower risk of homelessness relative to Caucasian and African American patients. These differences remained even after controlling for differences in the rates of psychiatric disorders, substance abuse, medical benefits, and overall level of functioning (Folsom et al., 2005). The researchers suggest that this difference may be the result not of ethnicity but of cultural differences in the availability of social and community resources for each group—with Latinos and Asian Americans offering higher levels of support and resources than Caucasian and African Americans.

Another potential explanation is that differences exist in the treatments provided to these groups and that these differences could influence patients' ability to find housing and regular employment. In support of this view, a study by Kuno and Rothbard (2002) revealed that African American Medicaid recipients are significantly less likely than Caucasian recipients to receive newer and more effective antipsychotic treatments. Although the exact reasons for these differences are not currently known, these studies make it clear that gaining greater clarity about the interactions of mental illness, occupational function, homelessness, and culture must be a top priority for mental health researchers and clinicians. ∎

An Overview of Civil Commitment

What should the criteria be for involuntarily committing someone with severe mental illness to a mental health facility? Should imminent danger to self or others be the only justification, or should society act as a parent and coerce people who appear to be in distress and in need of asylum or safety? How do we address the concerns of families like Arthur's who see their loved ones overcome by psychological problems? And what of our need not to be verbally harassed by people like Joyce Brown? When do these rights take precedence over the rights of an individual to be free from unwanted incarceration? It is tempting to conclude that the legal system has failed to address these issues and reacts only to the political whims of the times.

From another point of view, however, the periodic change in laws is a sign of a healthy system that responds to the limitations of previous decisions. The reactions by the Supreme Court in the 1970s to the coercive and arbitrary nature of civil commitment were as understandable as more recent attempts to make it easier to commit people in obvious need of help. As the consequences of these changes become apparent, the system responds to correct injustices. Although improvements may seem excruciatingly slow and may not always correctly address the issues in need of reform, the fact that laws can be changed should make us optimistic that the needs of individuals and of society can ultimately be addressed through the courts.

Criminal Commitment

▶ What are the legal standards for invoking the insanity defense and determining competency to stand trial?

What would have happened if Arthur had been arrested for trespassing on embassy grounds or if he had hurt or killed someone in his effort to present his plan for saving starving children? Would he have been held responsible for his actions, given his obvious disturbed mental state? How would a jury have responded to him when he seemed fine just several days later? If he was not responsible for his behavior then, why does he seem so normal now?

These questions are of enormous importance as we debate whether people should be held responsible for their criminal behavior despite the possible presence of mental illness. **Criminal commitment** is the process by which people are held because (1) they have been accused of committing a crime and are detained in a mental health facility until they can be assessed as fit or unfit to participate in legal proceedings against them, or (2) they have been found not guilty of a crime by reason of insanity.

The Insanity Defense

The purpose of our criminal justice system is to protect our lives, our liberty, and our pursuit of happiness, but not all people are punished for criminal behavior. The law recognizes that, under certain circumstances, people are not responsible for their behavior and it would be unfair and perhaps ineffective to punish them. Current views originate from a case recorded more than 150 years ago in England. Daniel M'Naghten today might receive the diagnosis of paranoid schizophrenia. He held the delusion that the English Tory party was persecuting him, and he set out to kill

....

criminal commitment Legal procedure by which a person found not guilty of a crime by reason of **insanity** must be confined in a psychiatric hospital.

TABLE 14.1 | Important Factors in the Evolution of the Insanity Defense

Factor	Date	Quotation
M'Naghten rule	1843	[I]t must be clearly proved that at the time of committing the act, the party accused was labouring under such a defect of reason, from disease of the mind, as not to know the nature and quality of the act he was doing; or if he did know it, that he did not know he was doing what was wrong. (101 Cl. & F. 200, 8 Eng. Rep. 718, H.L. 1843)
Durham rule	1954	An accused is not criminally responsible if his unlawful act was the product of mental disease or mental defect. (*Durham v. United States*, 1954)
American Law Institute (ALI) rule	1962	1. A person is not responsible for criminal conduct if at the time of such conduct as a result of mental disease or defect he lacks substantial capacity either to appreciate the criminality (wrongfulness) of his conduct or to conform his conduct to the requirements of law. 2. As used in the Article, the terms "mental disease or defect" do not include an abnormality manifested only by repeated criminal or otherwise antisocial conduct. (American Law Institute, 1962)
Diminished capacity	1978	Evidence of abnormal mental condition would be admissible to affect the degree of crime for which an accused could be convicted. Specifically, those offenses requiring intent or knowledge could be reduced to lesser included offenses requiring only reckless or criminal neglect. (New York State Department of Mental Hygiene, 1978)
Insanity Defense Reform Act	1984	A person charged with a criminal offense should be found not guilty by reason of insanity if it is shown that, as a result of mental disease or mental retardation, he was unable to appreciate the wrongfulness of his conduct at the time of his offense. (American Psychiatric Association, 1983, p. 685)

SOURCE: Reprinted, with permission, from Silver, E., Cirincione, C., & Steadman, H. J. (1994). Demythologizing inaccurate perceptions of the insanity defense. *Law and Human Behavior, 18,* 63–70, © 1994 Plenum Press.

the British prime minister. He mistook the man's secretary for the prime minister and killed the secretary instead. In what has become known as the M'Naghten rule, the English court decreed that people are not responsible for their criminal behavior if they do not know what they are doing or if they don't know that what they are doing is wrong. This ruling was, in essence, the beginning of the *insanity defense* (see Table 14.1). For more than 100 years, this rule was used to determine culpability when a person's mental state was in question.

In the intervening years, other standards have been introduced to modify the M'Naghten rule because many critics felt that simply relying on an accused person's knowledge of right or wrong was too limiting and a broader definition was needed (Simon & Shuman, 2009). Mental illness alters not only a person's cognitive abilities but also that person's emotional functioning, and mental health professionals believed the entire range of functioning should be taken into account when a person's responsibility was determined. One influential decision, known as the Durham rule, was based on the case *Durham v. United States* (1954). The Durham rule broadened the criteria for responsibility from knowledge of right or wrong to state that the "accused is not criminally responsible if his unlawful act was the product of mental disease or mental defect" (see Table 14.1). This decision was initially hailed by mental health professionals because it allowed them to

present to a judge or jury a complete picture of the person with mental illness. Unfortunately, it was soon apparent that mental health professionals did not have the expertise to assess reliably whether a person's mental illness caused the criminal behavior in question and therefore that decisions were being based on unscientific opinions (Gunn & Wheat, 2012). Although the Durham rule is no longer used, it caused a re-examination of the criteria used in the insanity defense.

An influential study of the question surrounding the definition of culpability was conducted around the same time as the Durham decision by a group of attorneys, judges, and law scholars who belonged to the American Law Institute (ALI). Their challenge was to develop criteria for determining whether a person's mental competence makes him or her answerable for criminal behavior. The ALI first reaffirmed the importance of distinguishing the behavior of people with mental illness from that of people without mental disorders. Its members pointed out that the threat of punishment was unlikely to deter someone who had severe mental illness; the group's position was that these individuals should instead be treated until they improve and should then be released. The ALI concluded that people are not responsible for their criminal behavior if, because of their mental illness, they cannot recognize the inappropriateness of their behavior or control it (American Law Institute, 1962). The criteria shown in Table 14.1, known as the ALI test, stipulate that a person must either be unable to distinguish right from wrong—as set forth in the M'Naghten rule—or be incapable of self-control to be shielded from legal consequences.

The ALI also included provisions for the concept of **diminished capacity** (see Table 14.1), which holds that people's ability to understand the nature of their behavior and therefore their criminal intent can be diminished by their mental illness. The theory of criminal intent—otherwise called *mens rea*, or having a "guilty mind"—is important legally because to convict someone of a crime, there must be proof of the physical act *(actus rea)* and the mental state *(mens rea)* of the person committing the act (Gunn & Wheat, 2012). For example, if a woman accidentally hits someone who steps in front of her car and the person subsequently dies, the woman would not be held criminally responsible; although a person was killed, there was no criminal intent—the driver didn't deliberately hit the person and attempt murder. The diminished capacity concept proposes that a person with mental illness who commits a criminal offense may not, because of the illness, have criminal intent and therefore cannot be held responsible.

Reactions to the Insanity Defense

Judicial rulings through the 1960s and 1970s regarding criminal responsibility parallel the course of civil commitment. An effort was made to focus on the needs of people with mental illness who also broke the law, providing mental health treatment instead of punishment. The successful use of concepts such as *insanity* or *diminished capacity* in criminal cases alarmed large segments of the population, however. Without question, the case that prompted the strongest outrage against the insanity defense and the most calls for its abolition is that of John W. Hinckley, Jr. (Zapf, Zottoli, & Pirelli, 2009). On March 31, 1981, as President Ronald Reagan walked out of the Washington Hilton Hotel, Hinckley fired several shots, hitting and seriously wounding the president, a Secret Service agent, a police officer, and James Brady, the president's press secretary. In an instant, Secret Service agents tackled and disarmed Hinckley. Hinckley was obsessed with actress Jodie Foster; he claimed he tried to kill the president to impress her. Hinckley was judged by a jury to be not guilty by reason of insanity (NGRI), using the ALI standard. The verdict sent shock waves throughout the country and legal community (Zapf *et al.*, 2009).

Although the insanity defense had already been criticized in the United States, about 75% of the states substantially changed their insanity defense rules after Hinckley's verdict, making it more difficult to use this defense (Simon & Shuman, 2014). As you have seen before, such impulses often are based more on emotion than on fact. Highly publicized cases, such as those of Hinckley, Charles Manson, Jeffrey Dahmer, and Ted Kaczynski, have led many people to associate mental illness with violence, thereby creating an unfavorable public perception of the insanity defense. One telephone survey study found that 91% of people who responded agreed with the statement, "judges and juries have a hard time telling whether the defendants are really sane or insane" (Hans, 1986). Almost 90% agreed the "insanity plea is a loophole that allows too many guilty people to go free."

Is there hard evidence that the insanity defense is used too often? A study of the public's impression of the insanity defense compared it with the actual use of the defense and its outcomes (Silver, Cirincione, & Steadman, 1994). As Table 14.2 shows, the public's perception that this defense is used in 37% of all felony cases is a gross overestimate; the actual figure is less than 1%. The public also overestimates how often the defense is successful, as well as how often people judged NGRI are set free. People tend to underestimate the length of hospitalization of those who are acquitted. In contrast to public perceptions, the length of time a person is confined to a hospital after being judged

TABLE 14.2 | Comparison of Public Perceptions with the Actual Occurrence of the Insanity Defense

	Public Perception (%)	Actual Occurrence (%)
Use of Insanity Defense		
Felony indictments resulting in an insanity plea	37.0	0.9
Insanity pleas resulting in acquittal	44.0	26.0
Disposition of Insanity Acquittees		
Insanity acquittees sent to a mental hospital	50.6	84.7
Insanity acquittees set free	25.6	15.3
Conditional release		11.6
Outpatient		2.6
Release		1.1
Length of Confinement of Insanity Acquittees (in months)		
All crimes	21.8	32.5
Murder		76.4

SOURCE: Reprinted, with permission, from Silver, E., Cirincione, C., & Steadman, H. J. (1994). Demythologizing inaccurate perceptions of the insanity defense. *Law and Human Behavior, 18,* 63–70, © 1994 Plenum Press.

diminished capacity Evidence of an abnormal mental condition in people that causes criminal charges against them requiring intent or knowledge to be reduced to lesser offenses requiring only reckless or criminal neglect.

NGRI may exceed the time the person would have spent in jail had that person been convicted of the crime (Simon & Shuman, 2014). Hinckley, for example, was a patient in St. Elizabeth's Hospital for more than 30 years and only recently in 2016 was he released. Other research shows that individuals with mental illness who are found guilty of *non-violent* crimes can be committed more than eight times as long as those people without mental illness placed in prison (Perlin, 2000). In contrast to public perception, people with mental illness apparently do not often "beat the rap" as a result of being judged NGRI.

Despite evidence that it is not used excessively and does not result in widespread early release of dangerous individuals, major changes were made in the criteria for the insanity defense after the Hinckley verdict. Both the American Psychiatric Association (1983) and the American Bar Association (1984) recommended modifications, moving back toward M'Naghten-like definitions. Shortly afterward, Congress passed the Insanity Defense Reform Act of 1984, which incorporated these suggestions and made successful use of the insanity defense more difficult.

Another attempt at reforming the insanity plea has been to replace the NGRI verdict with a verdict of guilty but mentally ill (GBMI) (Kimonis, 2015; Torry & Billick, 2010). Although there are several versions of the GBMI verdict, the shared premise is that the consequences for a person ruled GBMI are different from those for a person who is NGRI. People found to be NGRI are not sent to prison but are evaluated at a psychiatric facility until such time as they are judged ready for release. A person determined to be no longer mentally ill must be released. If Arthur had committed a crime and was found NGRI, because his brief psychotic disorder was quickly resolved, he would probably have been released immediately. In contrast, one version of the GBMI verdict in theory allows the system both to treat and to punish the individual. The person found guilty is given a prison term just as if there were no question of mental illness. Whether the person is incarcerated in prison or in a mental health facility is decided by legal authorities. If the person recovers from mental illness before the sentence

has passed, that person can be confined in prison for the maximum length of the term. If Arthur were found GBMI under this system, he could serve a full prison sentence, even though his mental illness was resolved. This version of GBMI has been adopted by a number of states (Simon & Shuman, 2014).

The second version of GBMI is even harsher for the mentally ill offender. Convicted individuals are imprisoned, and prison authorities may provide mental health services if they are available. The verdict itself is simply a declaration by the jury that the person was mentally ill at the time the crime was committed and does not result in differential treatment for the perpetrator. Idaho, Montana, and Utah have abandoned the insanity defense altogether and have adopted this version of GBMI ("The Evolving Insanity Defense," 2006).

Currently, the type of verdicts available (NGRI versus GBMI) depends on the laws of the particular state where the crimes were committed. Overall, some estimate that there are more than three times the number of people with severe mental illness in jails than in hospitals, pointing to the consequences of these changes in mental health laws (Torrey, Eslinger, Lamb, & Pavle, 2010). ● Figure 14.1 illustrates how people with severe mental illness are increasingly being placed in prisons rather than in special mental health facilities. The percentage of placements in prisons is approaching rates comparable to that of those more than 150 years ago, before adequate services were available.

▲ Jared Loughner, who shot Congresswoman Gabrielle Giffords and killed six other people, was forcibly medicated to make him fit to stand trial for his crimes. He ultimately pleaded guilty and received a sentence of life in prison without parole.

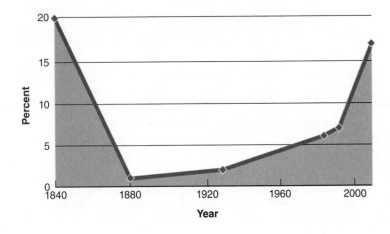

● **Figure 14.1** The percentage of jail and prison inmates with serious mental illness. The graph shows the increasing trend over the past few decades to incarcerate people with severe mental illness rather than to provide treatment. From Torrey, E., Eslinger, S., Lamb, R., & Pavle, J. (2010). *More mentally ill persons are in jails and prisons than hospitals: A survey of the states* (p. 13). Arlington, VA: Treatment Advocacy Center.

Therapeutic Jurisprudence

When individuals with psychological disorders break the law, they may now find themselves in one of a variety of "problem-solving courts" (Ahern & Coleman-Eufinger, 2013; Goodale, Callahan, & Steadman, 2013). For example, today in many states you can find drug treatment courts, domestic violence courts, and mental health courts, among others. These problem-solving courts are based on the concept of therapeutic jurisprudence—in essence, using what we know about behavior change to help people in trouble with the law. In drug treatment court, for example, a judge might be assigned to all criminal cases involving drug-addicted defendants. The judge would have the leeway to delay sentencing under the condition that the accused obtained and held a job for six months, received drug treatment, and remained drug free. Similarly, a defendant in a mental health court might be helped by referrals to programs in the community and involvement of family members. Rather than simply trying to decide between prison and freedom, the court can serve as an instrument of social change. This evolving concept may provide effective alternatives in the criminal justice system for people with severe mental illness.

Society has long recognized the need to identify criminals who may not be in control of their behavior and who may not benefit from simple incarceration. The challenge is in trying to do what may be impossible: determining whether the person knew what she was doing, knew right from wrong, and could control her behavior. Mental health professionals cannot assess mental health retrospectively. An additional dilemma is the desire, on the one hand, to provide care to people with mental illness and, on the other, to treat them as responsible individuals. Finally, we must resolve the simultaneous and conflicting interests of wanting to assist people with mental illness and wanting to be protected from them. The recent trend of using problem-solving courts may be one way to address these concerns. We must reach a national consensus about the basic value of people with mental illness to decide how they should be dealt with legally.

Competence to Stand Trial

Before people can be tried for a criminal offense, they must be able to understand the charges against them and to assist with their own defense, criteria outlined by the Supreme Court in *Dusky v. United States* (1960). Thus, in addition to interpreting a person's state of mind during the criminal act, experts must also anticipate the person's state of mind during the subsequent legal proceedings. A person could be ruled NGRI because of his mental illness at the time of the criminal act yet still be competent to stand trial, a situation that would have occurred in Arthur's case had he committed a crime.

A person determined to be incompetent to stand trial typically loses the authority to make decisions and faces commitment. Because a trial requires a determination of **competence**, most people with obvious and severe impairments who commit crimes are never tried. Some observers estimate that for every person who receives a verdict of NGRI, 45 others are committed to a mental health facility with a diagnosis of severe mental illness (Butler, 2006). The length of stay is the time it takes the committed person to regain competence. Because this period can be drawn out, the courts have ruled it cannot be indefinite and that, after a reasonable amount of time, the person must be found competent, set free, or committed under civil law (*Jackson v. Indiana*, 1972). Laws are often not precise in their language, and the phrase "reasonable amount of time" is open to a great deal of interpretation.

A final issue relates to the legal concept of burden of proof, the weight of evidence needed to win a case. In decisions of competence to stand trial, an important ruling placed responsibility on the defendant to provide the burden of proof—in this case, that she is incompetent to stand trial (*Medina v. California*, 1992). Again, public concern that dangerous individuals with mental illness are routinely acquitted and let loose on society after committing multiple violent offenses flies in the face of the facts. More realistically, a person with mental illness commits a non-violent crime and receives treatment through legal actions, such as the competence proceedings.

Duty to Warn

What are the responsibilities of professionals who suspect that someone with whom they are working may hurt or even kill another person? Must they contact the appropriate authority or the person who may be harmed, or are they forbidden to discuss information disclosed during therapy sessions?

These issues were the subject of a tragic case known as *Tarasoff v. Regents of the University of California* (1974, 1976). In 1969, Prosenjit Poddar, a graduate student at the University of California, Berkeley, killed a fellow student, Tatiana Tarasoff, who had previously rejected his romantic advances. At the time of the murder, he was being seen by two therapists at the University Health Center and had received a diagnosis of paranoid schizophrenia. At his last session, Poddar hinted that he was going to kill Tarasoff. His therapist believed this threat was serious and contacted the campus police, who investigated the allegation and received assurances from Poddar that he would leave Tarasoff alone. Weeks later, after repeated attempts to contact her, Poddar shot and stabbed Tarasoff until she died.

After learning of the therapists' role in the case, Tarasoff's family sued the university, the therapists, and the university police, saying they should have warned Tarasoff that she was in danger. The court agreed, and the Tarasoff case has been

....

competence Ability of legal defendants to participate in their own defense and understand the charges and the roles of the trial participants.

used ever since as a standard for therapists concerning their **duty to warn** a client's potential victims. Related cases have further defined the role of the therapist in warning others (Johnson, Persad, & Sisti, 2014; Mason, Worsley, & Coyle, 2010). Courts have generally ruled that the threats must be specific. In *Thompson v. County of Alameda* (1980), the California Supreme Court ruled that a therapist does not have a duty to warn when a person makes non-specific threats against non-specific people. It is difficult for therapists to know their exact responsibilities for protecting third parties from their clients. Good clinical practice dictates that any time they are in doubt they should consult with colleagues.

Mental Health Professionals as Expert Witnesses

Judges and juries often have to rely on **expert witnesses**, individuals who have specialized knowledge, to assist them in making decisions (Mullen, 2010). We have alluded to several instances in which mental health professionals serve in such a capacity, providing information about a person's dangerousness or ability to understand and participate in the defense. The public perceives expert witnesses ambivalently. On one hand, they see the value of persuasive expert testimony in educating a jury; on the other, they see expert witnesses as "hired guns" whose opinions suit the side that pays their bills (Simon & Shuman, 2009). How reliable are the judgments of mental health professionals who act as expert witnesses?

To take one example, in deciding whether someone should be civilly committed, the assessor must determine the person's potential for future violence. Research suggests that mental health professionals can make reliable predictions of dangerousness over the short term, for two to 20 days after the evaluation (Scott *et al.*, 2008). They have not, however, been able to make reliable predictions of violence after longer periods (Fazel *et al.*, 2012). It seems that the assessment tools that professionals use to assess danger may impact accuracy. Assessment tools that were designed to assess danger of violence in specific groups of patients (e.g., juvenile offenders) were more accurate than general assessment tools (Singh, Grann, & Fazel, 2011). A second area in which mental health professionals are often asked to provide consultation is in assigning a diagnosis. Recent revisions of diagnostic criteria have addressed this issue directly, helping clinicians make diagnoses that are generally reliable. Remember, however, that the legal definition of mental illness is not matched by a comparable disorder in *DSM-5*. Therefore, statements about whether someone has a "mental illness" reflect determinations made by the court, not by mental health professionals.

Mental health professionals appear to have expertise in identifying *malingering* and in assessing competence. Remember that to malinger is to fake or grossly exaggerate symptoms, usually to be absolved from blame. For

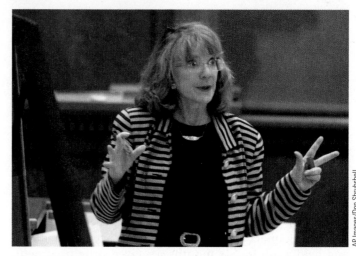

▲ Elizabeth Loftus, a psychologist at the University of California, Irvine and an expert in human memory, testifies during the pretrial hearing of former White House official Lewis "Scooter" Libby.

example, a person might claim to have been actively hallucinating at the time of the crime and therefore not responsible. Research indicates that the Minnesota Multiphasic Personality Inventory test is mostly accurate in revealing malingering in people claiming to have serious mental illness. The examiners look for true symptoms, but ones people with mental illness rarely report. Malingerers, in their rush to fake their illness, will often overreport these problems, perhaps to convince others they are mentally ill (Sellbom, Toomey, Wygant, Kucharski, & Duncan, 2010; Tarescavage, Wygant, Gervais, & Ben-Porath, 2013). Mental health professionals also appear capable of providing reliable information about a person's competence, or ability to understand and assist with a defense (Shulman, Cohen, Kirsh, Hull, & Champine, 2007). Overall, mental health professionals can provide judges and juries with reliable and useful information in certain areas (Scott *et al.*, 2008).

The research described here does not indicate how accurate expert testimony is under everyday conditions. In other words, under the right circumstances experts can make accurate determinations of the short-term risks that a person will commit an act of violence, is faking certain symptoms, or is competent to stand trial and of what diagnosis should be made. Still, other factors conspire to influence expert testimony. Personal and professional opinions that exceed the competence of the expert witness can influence what information is or is not presented, as well as how it is relayed to the court (Drogin, Commons, Gutheil, Meyer, & Norris, 2012). For instance, if the expert witness believes generally that people should not be involuntarily committed to mental health facilities, this opinion will likely influence how the witness presents clinical information in civil commitment court proceedings.

Check your understanding of criminal commitment by identifying the following concepts: (a) competence to stand trial, (b) diminished capacity, (c) American Law Institute rule, (d) Durham rule, (e) M'Naghten rule, (f) malingering, (g) expert witness, and (h) duty to warn:

1. The defendant does not go to trial because she is unable to understand the proceedings and assist in the defense. _____

2. The person could not distinguish between right and wrong at the time of the crime. _____

3. The person is not responsible for the crime if he is not able to appreciate the wrongfulness of behavior caused by mental disease or defect. _____

4. One of my clients threatened his mother's life during his session today. Now I must decide whether I have a(n) _____.

5. A mental disorder could lessen a person's ability to understand criminal behavior and to form criminal intent. _____

6. Dr. Z testified in court that the defendant was faking and exaggerating symptoms to evade responsibility. Dr. Z is acting as a(n) _____, and the defendant is _____.

7. The person is not criminally responsible if the crime was the result of "mental disease or mental defect." _____

Patients' Rights and Clinical Practice Guidelines

▶ What are the key rights of patients in the mental health system?

Until about 40 years ago, people in mental health facilities were accorded few rights. What treatment they received and whether they could make phone calls, send and receive mail, or have visitors were typically decided by hospital personnel who rarely consulted with the patient. Abuses of this authority, however, led to legal action and subsequent rulings by the courts concerning the rights of people in these facilities.

The Right to Treatment

One of the most fundamental rights of people in mental health facilities is the right to treatment (Bloch & Green, 2012). Starting in the early 1970s, a series of class-action lawsuits (filed on behalf of many individuals) helped establish the rights of people with mental illness and mental retardation. A landmark case, *Wyatt v. Stickney* (1972), grew out of a lawsuit filed by the employees of large institutions in Alabama who were fired because of funding difficulties. The case also established the minimum standards that facilities had to meet in relation to the people who were hospitalized. Among the standards set by *Wyatt v. Stickney* were minimum staff–patient ratios and physical requirements, such as a certain number of showers and toilets for a given number of residents. The case also mandated that facilities make positive efforts to attain treatment goals for their patients. *Wyatt v. Stickney* went further and expanded on a concept called the "least restrictive alternative," indicating that, wherever possible, people should be provided with care and treatment in the least confining and limiting environment possible.

Despite this movement to secure treatment for people in mental health facilities, a gap was left as to what constituted proper treatment. The case of *Youngberg v. Romeo* (1982) reaffirmed the need to treat people in non-restrictive settings but essentially left to professionals the decision about the type of treatment to be provided. This concerned patient advocates because, historically, leaving treatment to professional judgment has not always resulted in the intended end for the people in need of help. In 1986, Congress provided a number of safeguards by passage of the Protection and Advocacy for Mentally Ill Individuals Act (Woodside & Legg, 1990), which established a series of protection and advocacy agencies in each state to investigate allegations of abuse and neglect and to act as legal advocates.

The Right to Refuse Treatment

One of the most controversial issues in mental health today is the right of people, especially those with severe mental illness, to refuse treatment (Bloch & Green, 2012; Simon & Shuman, 2014). In recent times, the argument has centered on the use of antipsychotic medications. On one side of the issue are the mental health professionals who believe that, under certain circumstances, people with severe mental illness are not capable of making a decision in their own best interest and that the clinician is therefore responsible for providing treatment, despite the protestations of

duty to warn Mental health professional's responsibility to break confidentiality and notify the potential victim whom a client has specifically threatened.

expert witnesses Person who because of special training and experience is allowed to offer opinion testimony in legal trials.

the affected people. On the other side, patients and their advocates argue that all people have a fundamental right to make decisions about their own treatment, even if doing so is not in their own best medical interests.

Although this controversy is not yet resolved, one court case has responded to a related question: Can people be "forced" to become competent to stand trial? This is an interesting dilemma: If people facing criminal charges are delusional or have such frequent severe hallucinations that they cannot fully participate in the legal proceedings, can they be forced against their will to take medication to reduce these symptoms, thereby making them competent to stand trial? A Supreme Court ruling, *Riggins v. Nevada* (1992), stated that, because of the potential for negative side effects (such as the involuntary motor movements associated with tardive dyskinesia), people cannot be forced to take antipsychotic medication. Other rulings, however, make allowances for involuntary medication following a *Harper* hearing ("Washington v. Harper," 1990)—a due process hearing that allows mental health professionals to argue for the merits of medication use and the patient to provide a counterargument. This process was used to involuntarily medicate Jared Loughner—the man who eventually pleaded guilty to 19 charges of murder and attempted murder for a 2011 attack in Tucson, Arizona, in which U.S. Representative Gabrielle Giffords was severely injured and six other people were killed.

The Rights of Research Participants

In general, people who participate in psychological research have the following rights (American Psychological Association, 2010a, 2010b):

1. The right to be informed about the purpose of the research study
2. The right to privacy
3. The right to be treated with respect and dignity
4. The right to be protected from physical and mental harm
5. The right to choose to participate or to refuse to participate without prejudice or reprisals
6. The right to anonymity in the reporting of results
7. The right to the safeguarding of their records

These rights are particularly important for people with psychological disorders who may not be able to understand them fully (Bloch & Green, 2012). One of the most important concepts in research is that those who participate must be fully informed about the risks and benefits of the study. Simple consent is not sufficient; it must be *informed consent*, or formal agreement by the subject to participate after being fully apprised of all important aspects of the study, including any possibility of harm. An important case underlines the significance of informed consent and the sometimes-grey areas that exist in applied research.

In 1988, 23-year-old Greg Aller signed a consent form agreeing to participate in a treatment study at the University of California at Los Angeles (UCLA) Neuropsychiatric Institute (Willwerth, 1993). Since the previous year, Greg had experienced vivid and frightening hallucinations and delusions about space aliens. His parents had contacted UCLA for assistance. They learned that the university was initiating a study to evaluate people in the early stages of schizophrenia. If Greg participated, he could receive extremely expensive drug therapy and counseling free. After taking the drug Prolixin for three months as part of the study, he improved dramatically; the hallucinations and delusions were gone.

Although overjoyed with the results, Greg's parents were concerned about the second phase of the study, which involved taking him off the medication. They were reassured by the researchers that this was an important and normal part of treatment for people with schizophrenia and that the potential for negative side effects of taking the drug for too long was great. They were also told the researchers would put Greg back on the medication if he grew considerably worse without it.

Toward the end of 1989, Greg was slowly taken off the drug, and he soon started having delusions about former President Ronald Reagan and space aliens. Although his deterioration was obvious to his parents, Greg did not indicate to the researchers that he needed the medication or tell them of his now-continuous hallucinations and delusions. Greg continued to deteriorate, at one point threatening to kill his parents. After several more months, Greg's parents persuaded him to ask for more medication. Although better than he was earlier, Greg has still not returned to the much-improved state he achieved following his first round of medication.

◀ Greg Aller (right, with his parents) participated in a drug study at UCLA and suffered a severe relapse of psychotic symptoms when medication was withdrawn. He and his family subsequently raised the issue of informed consent for such research.

Mojgan B. Azimi

This case highlights the conflicts that can arise when researchers attempt to study important questions in psychopathology. The controversy emerging from this case should be an added warning to researchers about their responsibilities to people who participate in their studies and their obligation to design added safeguards to protect the welfare of their study subjects. Some are now exploring methods to assess formally whether participants with mental illness fully understand the risks and benefits associated with these studies (e.g., Harmell, Palmer, & Jeste, 2012; Palmer, Savla, Roesch, & Jeste, 2013).

Evidence-Based Practice and Clinical Practice Guidelines

As described throughout this book, evidence has accumulated on the effectiveness of psychological treatments for specific disorders both in research clinics and in clinics that serve the public directly (Barlow, Bullis, Comer, & Ametaj, 2013; IOM, 2015). When this evidence is put in the form of recommendations on how to treat a particular problem, these recommendations are called clinical practice guidelines (Hollon *et al.*, 2014; IOM, 2011). In 1989, legislation established a new branch of the federal government called the Agency for Health Care Policy and Research. In 1999, this agency was reauthorized by Congress and renamed the Agency for Healthcare Research and Quality. The purpose of this agency is to establish uniformity in the delivery of effective health and mental health-care and to communicate to practitioners, policy makers, and patients alike throughout the country the latest developments in treating certain disorders effectively. The agency is also responsible for research into improving systems for the delivery of health and mental health services. Now with the passage in 2010 of legislation to provide a form of national health insurance in the United States (the Patient Protection and Affordable Care Act or "Obamacare"), making health-care more efficient and effective is more important than ever.

The government hopes not only to reduce costs by eliminating unnecessary or ineffective treatments but also to facilitate the utilization of effective interventions based on the latest research evidence (IOM, 2015). In recent years, governments have allocated billions of dollars to facilitate dissemination and implementation of evidence-based psychological treatments in various health-care systems such as the Veterans Health Administration in the United States and the National Health Service in the United Kingdom (McHugh & Barlow, 2010, 2012). Treating people effectively—alleviating their pain and distress—is the most important way to reduce health-care costs because these individuals will no longer request one treatment after another in an unending search for relief. To this end, as part of the ACA, Congress enabled the Patient-Centered Outcomes Research Institute to facilitate research on which treatments for what conditions are most effective, and to disseminate this information widely (Dickersin, 2010).

Anticipating the importance of this trend and the necessity that clinical practice guidelines be sound and valid, a task force of the American Psychological Association composed a template, or set, of principles for constructing and evaluating guidelines for clinical interventions for both psychological disorders and psychosocial aspects of physical disorders. The task force decided that clinical practice guidelines for specific disorders should be constructed on the basis of two simultaneous considerations, or axes: the clinical efficacy axis and the clinical utility axis. The **clinical efficacy axis** is a consideration of the scientific evidence to determine whether the intervention in question is effective when compared with an alternative treatment or with no treatment in a controlled clinical research context.

To determine clinical efficacy, experiments called clinical trials must establish whether the intervention in question is better than no therapy, better than a non-specific therapy, or better than an alternative therapy. Clinicians might also rely on information collected from various clinics where a large number of practitioners are treating the disorder in question. If these clinicians collect systematic data on the outcomes of their patients, they can ascertain how many are "cured," how many improve somewhat without recovering, and how many fail to respond to the intervention. Such data are referred to as *quantified clinical observations* or *clinical replication series*. Finally, a *clinical consensus* of leading experts is also a valuable source of information, although not as valuable as data from quantified clinical observations or randomized controlled trials (in which individuals are assigned randomly to a treatment or a control condition to evaluate the efficacy of the treatment).

The **clinical utility axis** is concerned with external validity, the extent to which an internally valid intervention is effective in different settings or under different circumstances from those where it was tested, and how easily it can be disseminated and implemented in those settings. For example, will patients accept the intervention and comply with its requirements, and is it relatively easy to administer? A second issue on the clinical utility axis is generalizability, which refers to the extent to which an intervention is effective with patients of differing backgrounds (ethnicity, age, or sex), as well as in different settings (inpatient, outpatient, or community) or with different therapists. Again, an intervention could be effective in a research setting with one group of patients but generalize poorly across different ethnic groups. In summary, a treatment can be highly effective as determined by the clinical efficacy axis, but unless the treatment is widely generalizable, feasible, and cost-effective, it is unlikely to be disseminated or implemented. For a summary of these two axes, see Table 14.3.

....

clinical efficacy axis One of a proposed set of guidelines for evaluating clinical interventions on the evidence of their effectiveness (compare with **clinical utility axis**).

clinical utility axis One of a proposed set of guidelines for evaluating clinical interventions by whether they can be applied effectively and cost effectively in real clinical settings (compare with **clinical efficacy axis**).

TABLE 14.3 | Overview of Template for Constructing Psychological Intervention Guidelines

Clinical Efficacy (Internal Validity)	Clinical Utility (External Validity)

A. Better than alternative therapy (randomized controlled trials, or RCTs)
B. Better than non-specific therapy (RCTs)
C. Better than no therapy (RCTs)
D. Quantified clinical observations
E. Clinical consensus
  1. Strongly positive
  2. Mixed
  3. Strongly negative
  4. Contradictory evidence
	A. Feasibility
	  1. Patient acceptability (cost, pain, duration, side effects, and so on)
	  2. Patient choice in face of relatively equal efficacy
	  3. Probability of compliance
	  4. Ease of dissemination (number of practitioners with competence, requirements for training, opportunities for training, need for costly technologies or additional support personnel, and so on)
	B. Generalizability
	  1. Patient characteristics
	    a. Cultural background issues
	    b. Gender issues
	    c. Developmental level issues
	  2. Other relevant patient characteristics
	    a. Therapist characteristics
	    b. Issues of robustness when applied in practice settings with different time frames, and so on
	  3. Contextual factors regarding setting in which treatment is delivered
	C. Costs and benefits
	  1. Costs of delivering intervention to individual and society
	  2. Costs to individual and society of withholding intervention

Note: Confidence in treatment efficacy is based on both (a) absolute and relative efficacy of treatment and (b) quality and replicability of studies in which this judgment is made.

Note: Confidence in clinical utility as reflected on these three dimensions should be based on systematic and objective methods and strategies for assessing these characteristics of treatment as they are applied in actual practice. In some cases, randomized controlled trials will exist. More often, data will be in the form of quantified clinical observations (clinical replication series) or other strategies, such as health economic calculations.

SOURCE: American Psychological Association Board of Professional Affairs Task Force on Psychological Intervention Guidelines. (1995). *Template for developing guidelines: Interventions for mental disorders and psychosocial aspects of physical disorders*. Approved by APA Council of Representatives, February 1995. Washington, D.C.: American Psychological Association.

In 2010, the American Psychological Association decided to develop its own set of clinical practice guidelines on providing the best evidence-based psychological care for people with psychological disorders (Hollon *et al.*, 2014).

In Chapter 1, we reviewed various activities that make up the role of scientist-practitioners in the mental health professions, who take a scientific approach to their clinical work to provide the most effective assessment procedures and interventions. Changes in the delivery of mental health services are likely to be accompanied by considerable disruption, because this is a major system that affects millions of people. But the change will also bring opportunities. Scientist-practitioners will contribute to the process of guidelines development in several ways. For example, as attempts are made to assess the clinical utility or external validity of interventions, the collected experience of thousands of mental health professionals will be immensely valuable. Most information relevant to clinical utility or external validity will be collected by these clinicians in the course of their practice. Thus, they will truly fulfill the scientist-practitioner role to the benefit of patients being treated for mental health issues.

14.3 Concept CHECK

Identify the following situation using one of these terms: (a) informed consent, (b) refuse treatment, (c) clinical utility, (d) clinical efficacy, and (e) reduce costs:

1. Recently, clinical practice guidelines were established on two axes. The _____ axis is a consideration of the scientific evidence to determine whether the intervention in question is effective.

2. The _____ axis is concerned with an intervention's effectiveness in the clinical setting where it will be applied, not in the research setting.

3. The clinical researcher knows the potential for harm of the participants is slight but is nevertheless careful to tell them about it and asks them whether they agree to give their _____.

4. Clinical practice guidelines are designed to safeguard clients and _____.

5. The Supreme Court ruling in Riggins v. Nevada helped support a patient's right to _____.

SUMMARY

Civil Commitment

How does the legal concept of mental illness differ from a clinically diagnoses psychological disorder?

▶ Civil commitment laws determine the conditions under which a person may be certified legally to have a mental illness and therefore to be placed in a hospital, sometimes in conflict with the person's own wishes.

▶ Historically, states have permitted commitment when several conditions have been met: (1) the person has a mental illness and is in need of treatment, (2) the person is dangerous to himself or to others, or (3) the person is unable to care for himself.

▶ *Mental illness* as used in legal system language is not synonymous with *psychological disorder;* each state has its own definition of mental illness, usually meant to include people with severe disturbances that negatively affect their health and safety.

What is the relationship between dangerousness and mental illness?

▶ Having a mental illness does not seem to increase the likelihood of dangerousness, that is, that a person will commit violent acts in the future, although having symptoms of hallucinations and delusions does seem to indicate more risk for behaving violently.

What are the interactions among mental illness, deinstitutionalization, and homelessness?

▶ The combination of the lack of success with deinstitutionalization, which has resulted instead in transinstitutionalization; the rise in homelessness; and the criminalization of people with severe mental illness led to a backlash against the perceived causes of these factors, including the strict civil commitment laws.

Criminal Commitment

What are the legal standards for invoking the insanity defense and determining competency to stand trial?

▶ Criminal commitment is the process by which people are held for one of two reasons: (1) They have been accused of committing a crime and are detained in a mental health facility until they can be determined fit or unfit to participate in legal proceedings against them, or (2) they have been found not guilty of a crime by reason of insanity.

▶ The insanity defense is defined by a number of legal rulings: The M'Naghten rule states that people are not responsible for criminal behavior if they do not know

what they are doing, or if they do know and they don't know it is wrong. The Durham rule broadened the criteria for responsibility from knowledge of right or wrong to the presence of a "mental disease or defect." The American Law Institute criteria concluded that people were not responsible for their criminal behavior if, because of their mental illness, they lacked either the cognitive ability to recognize the inappropriateness of their behavior or the ability to control their behavior.

▶ The concept of diminished capacity holds that people's ability to understand the nature of their behavior and therefore their criminal intent could be lessened by their mental illness.

▶ A determination of competence must be made before an individual can be tried for a criminal offense: To stand trial, people must be competent—able to understand the charges against them and to assist with their own defense.

▶ Duty to warn is a standard that sets forth the responsibility of the therapist to warn potential victims that a client may attempt to hurt or kill them.

▶ Individuals who have specialized knowledge and who assist judges and juries in making decisions, especially about such issues as competence and malingering, are called expert witnesses.

Patients' Rights and Clinical Practice Guidelines

What are the key rights of patients in the mental health system?

▶ One of the more fundamental rights of patients in mental health facilities is their right to treatment. By contrast, a great deal of controversy exists over whether all patients are capable of making a decision to refuse treatment. This is an especially difficult dilemma in the case of antipsychotic medications that may improve patients' symptoms but bring with them severe negative side effects.

▶ Subjects who participate in any research study must be fully informed of the risks and benefits and formally give their informed consent to indicate they have been fully informed.

▶ Clinical practice guidelines can play a major role in providing information about types of interventions that are likely to be effective for a specific disorder, thereby setting the stage for evidence-based practice. Critical to such a determination are measures of clinical efficacy (internal validity) and clinical utility (external validity).

Key Terms

civil commitment laws, 529
mental illness, 531
dangerousness, 531
deinstitutionalization, 532

transinstitutionalization, 533
criminal commitment, 535
diminished capacity, 537
competence, 539

duty to warn, 540
expert witnesses, 540
clinical efficacy axis, 543
clinical utility axis, 543

Answers to Concept Checks

14.1

1. mental disorder; 2. dangerous;
3. grave disability; 4. legal;
5. deinstitutionalization;
6. transinstitutionalization

14.2

1. a; 2. e; 3. c; 4. h; 5. b; 6. g, f;
7. d

14.3

1. d; 2. c; 3. a; 4. e; 5. b

Chapter Quiz

1. According to a recent review by La Fond and Durham, since the 1960s mental health law in the United States has followed what pattern?

   a. a commitment to protecting society, followed by a shift in emphasis to protecting the individual

   b. a commitment to protecting the individual, followed by a shift in emphasis to protecting society

   c. a consistent protection of the individual above protection of society

   d. a consistent protection of society above protection of the individual

2. Sally has stopped eating because of her delusional belief that extraterrestrial aliens are trying to poison her. Because of her symptoms, Sally is placed in a psychiatric hospital involuntarily based on what civil authority?

   a. malingering

   b. uninformed consent

   c. police power

   d. *parens patriae*

3. Which statement is true regarding the relationship between mental illness and dangerousness?

   a. Men with mental illness who are Hispanic are more likely to be dangerous than men with mental illness from other ethnic groups.

   b. People with mental illness are more likely to be dangerous if they have been committed to a mental health facility against their will.

   c. Women with mental illness are more likely to be dangerous than women without mental illness.

   d. Most studies suggest that people with mental illness without hallucinations or delusions are no more likely to be dangerous than people without mental illness.

4. One goal of taking people out of mental health facilities (deinstitutionalization) was to:

   a. create mental health centers in the community that could provide a network of supportive treatments

   b. reduce the need for civil commitments, which had become too ethically complex

   c. allow families to provide more intensive care in more familiar environments

   d. test the effectiveness of new antipsychotic medications that had just been developed

5. The M'Naghten rule incorporated what criterion to determine whether a person's mental state influenced guilt or innocence?

   a. whether the act was within the individual's control

   b. whether an "average citizen" would excuse the act

   c. whether the individual knew that the act committed was wrong

   d. whether the individual felt remorse for the act

6. "Diminished capacity" is a legal concept that proposes that when people with mental illness commit a crime they may lack:

   a. intent

   b. guilt

   c. remorse

   d. memory

7. Research regarding use of the not guilty by reason of insanity (NGRI) defense has found that:

a. the public underestimates how often people use the defense in felony cases

b. the public overestimates how often people use this defense successfully

c. the public underestimates how often people who use the defense are set free

d. the public overestimates how long people who are judged NGRI are confined to a hospital

8. The guilty but mentally ill (GBMI) verdict is different from the NGRI verdict in that:

a. only in GBMI are people assumed to have no knowledge that what they did was wrong

b. people convicted of GBMI can be treated successfully for their mental illness yet still serve a full term in prison

c. people convicted of GBMI can be taken to prison, but they must receive treatment for their mental illness

d. people convicted of GBMI are detained in psychiatric hospitals, not prisons

9. An individual who commits a crime but is judged to be incompetent to stand trial may be:

a. immediately released

b. sent to prison without a trial

c. committed to a mental health facility until he is competent

d. committed to a mental health facility indefinitely

10. According to the Tarasoff verdict, a therapist can release confidential information about a client when:

a. the therapist suspects the client may be dangerous, even though a threat has not been made

b. the client has made a non-specific threat but the client has a history of violent behavior

c. the client poses a threat to the safety of a specific individual

d. the client has made any threat of violence, even a non-specific threat

(See Appendix A for answers.)

Appendix

A: Answers to Chapter Quizzes

Chapter 1 (pages 28–29)
1. b 2. c 3. d 4. a 5. d 6. b 7. b 8. c 9. d 10. c

Chapter 2 (page 68)
1. b 2. b 3. d 4. d 5. b 6. b 7. c 8. c 9. d 10. c

Chapter 3 (pages 115–116)
1. c 2. b 3. a 4. d 5. a 6. d 7. b 8. c 9. a 10. c

Chapter 4 (pages 169–170)
1. c 2. a 3. b 4. d 5. d 6. a 7. c 8. a 9. a 10. d

Chapter 5 (page 197)
1. d 2. a 3. c 4. d 5. b 6. b 7. b 8. a 9. d 10. d

Chapter 6 (pages 244–245)
1. b 2. c 3. a 4. a 5. c 6. b 7. b 8. d 9. c 10. a

Chapter 7 (pages 278–279)
1. a 2. a 3. d 4. c 5. a 6. c 7. a 8. b 9. c 10. a

Chapter 8 (pages 322–323)
1. b 2. d 3. a 4. b 5. b 6. a 7. d 8. b 9. b 10. c

Chapter 9 (page 363)
1. b 2. b 3. d 4. c 5. c 6. d 7. a 8. c 9. c 10. a

Chapter 10 (pages 404–405)
1. c 2. a 3. d 4. c 5. d 6. c 7. a 8. c 9. b 10. a

Chapter 11 (pages 438–439)
1. c 2. a 3. b 4. b 5. a 6. c 7. c 8. c 9. d 10. a

Chapter 12 (pages 476–477)
1. d 2. b 3. c 4. a 5. d 6. a 7. A 8. b 9. d 10. d

Chapter 13 (page 524)
1. a 2. b 3. a 4. c 5. b 6. a 7. D 8. d 9. b 10. c

Chapter 14 (pages 546–547)
1. b 2. d 3. d 4. a 5. c 6. a 7. b 8. b 9. c 10. c

abnormal behavior Actions that are unexpected and often evaluated negatively because they differ from typical or usual behavior.

actigraph Small electronic device that is worn on the wrist like a watch and records body movements. This device can be used to record sleep–wake cycles.

action potentials Short periods of electrical activity at the membrane of a neuron, responsible for the transmission of signals within the neuron.

acute pain Pain that typically follows an injury and disappears once the injury heals or is effectively treated.

acute stress disorder Severe reaction immediately following a terrifying event, often including amnesia about the event, emotional numbing, and **derealization**. Many victims later develop **posttraumatic stress** disorder.

adjustment disorders Clinically significant emotional and behavioral symptoms in response to one or more specific stressors.

adoption studies In genetics research, the study of first-degree relatives reared in different families and environments. If they share common characteristics, such as a disorder, this finding suggests that those characteristics have a genetic component.

affect Conscious, subjective aspect of an **emotion** that accompanies an action at a given time.

agnosia Inability to recognize and name objects; may be a symptom of **dementia** or other brain disorders.

agonist In **neuroscience**, a chemical substance that effectively increases the activity of a **neurotransmitter** by imitating its effects.

agonist substitution A replacement of a drug on which a person is dependent with one that has a similar chemical makeup, an **agonist**. Used as a treatment for **substance dependence**.

agoraphobia Anxiety about being in places or situations from which escape might be difficult.

AIDS-related complex (ARC) Group of minor health problems such as weight loss, fever, and night sweats that appears after HIV infection but before development of full-blown AIDS.

alcohol By-product of the fermentation of yeasts, sugar, and water; the most commonly used and abused **depressant** substance.

alcohol-related disorders Cognitive, biological, behavioral, and social problems associated with **alcohol** use and abuse.

alcohol use disorder A cognitive, biological, behavioral, and social problem associated with **alcohol** use and abuse.

alogia A deficiency in the amount or content of speech, a disturbance often seen in people with **schizophrenia**.

alters Shorthand term for *alter ego,* one of the different personalities or identities in **dissociative identity disorder**.

Alzheimer's disease Disease of the cerebral cortex that causes an atypical form of senile dementia, discovered in 1906 by German **psychiatrist** Alois Alzheimer.

amniocentesis Prenatal medical procedure that allows the detection of abnormalities (for example, **Down syndrome**) in the developing fetus. It involves removal and analysis of amniotic fluid from the mother.

amphetamine use disorders Psychological, biological, behavioral, and social problems associated with **amphetamine** use and abuse.

amphetamines **Stimulant** medication used to treat hypersomnia by keeping the person awake during the day, and to treat **narcolepsy,** including sudden onset episodes, by suppressing **rapid eye movement sleep.**

analogue models Approach to research that employs subjects who are similar to clinical clients, allowing replication of a clinical problem under controlled conditions.

anhedonia An inability to experience pleasure, associated with some **mood** and schizophrenic disorders.

animal phobia Unreasonable, enduring **fear** of animals or insects that usually develops early in life.

anorexia nervosa Eating disorder characterized by recurrent food refusal, leading to dangerously low body weight.

antagonist In **neuroscience**, a chemical substance that decreases or blocks the effects of a **neurotransmitter**.

antagonist drugs The medication that blocks or counteracts the effects of a psychoactive drug.

antigens Foreign material that enters the body, including bacteria and parasites.

antisocial personality disorder A cluster B (dramatic, emotional, or erratic) **personality disorder** involving a pervasive pattern of disregard for and violation of the rights of others. Similar to the non-*DSM-IV-TR* label **psychopathy** but with greater emphasis on overt behavior than on personality traits.

anxiety **Mood** state characterized by marked **negative affect** and bodily symptoms of tension in which a person apprehensively anticipates future danger or misfortune. Anxiety may involve feelings, behaviors, and physiological responses.

aphasia Impairment or loss of language skills resulting from brain damage caused by **stroke**, **Alzheimer's disease**, or other illness or trauma.

association studies Research strategy for comparing **genetic markers** in groups of people with and without a particular disorder.

associative splitting A separation among basic functions of human personality (for example, cognition, **emotion**, and perception) seen by some as the defining characteristic of **schizophrenia**.

attachment disorders Developmentally inappropriate behaviors in which a child is unable or unwilling to form normal attachment relationships with caregiving adults.

attention-deficit/hyperactivity disorder (ADHD) Developmental disorder featuring maladaptive levels of inattention, excessive activity, and impulsiveness.

attenuated psychosis syndrome Disorder involving the onset of psychotic symptoms such as hallucinations and delusions, which puts a person at high risk for schizophrenia; designated for further study by *DSM-5.*

autism spectrum disorder (ASD) Neurodevelopmental disorder characterized by significant impairment in social interactions and communication and restricted patterns of behavior, interest, and activity.

autoimmune disease Condition in which the body's **immune system** attacks healthy tissue rather than **antigens**.

avoidant personality disorder A cluster C (anxious or fearful) **personality disorder** featuring a pervasive pattern of social inhibition, feelings of inadequacy, and hypersensitivity to criticism.

avolition An inability to initiate or persist in important activities. Also known as *apathy*.

barbiturates A sedative (and addictive) drug such as Amytal, Seconal, or Nembutal that is used as a sleep aid.

bariatric surgery Surgical approach to extreme **obesity,** usually accomplished by stapling the stomach to create a small stomach pouch or bypassing the stomach through gastric bypass surgery.

baseline Measured rate of a behavior before introduction of an intervention that allows comparison and assessment of the effects of the intervention.

behavior therapy Array of therapeutic methods based on the principles of behavioral and **cognitive science**, as well as principles of learning as applied to clinical problems. It considers specific behaviors rather than inferred conflicts as legitimate targets for change.

behavioral assessment Measuring, observing, and systematically evaluating (rather than inferring) the client's thoughts, feelings, and behavior in the actual problem situation or context.

behavioral inhibition system (BIS) Brain circuit in the **limbic system** that responds to threat signals by inhibiting activity and causing **anxiety**.

behavioral medicine Interdisciplinary approach applying behavioral science to the prevention, **diagnosis**, and treatment of medical problems. Also known as *psychosomatic medicine*.

behavioral model Explanation of human behavior, including dysfunction, based on principles of learning and adaptation derived from experimental psychology.

behaviorism Explanation of human behavior, including dysfunction, based on principles of learning and adaptation derived from experimental psychology.

benzodiazepines An antianxiety drug such as Valium, Xanax, Dalmane, or Halcion also used to treat insomnia. Effective against **anxiety** (and, at high potency, **panic disorder**), benzodiazepines show some side effects, such as some cognitive and motor impairment, and may result in **substance dependence**. **Relapse** rates are extremely high when such a drug is discontinued.

binge Relatively brief episode of uncontrolled, excessive consumption, usually of food or **alcohol**.

binge-eating disorder (BED) Pattern of eating involving distress-inducing **binges** not followed by purging behaviors; being considered as a new *DSM* diagnostic category.

biofeedback Use of physiological monitoring equipment to make individuals aware of their own bodily functions, such as blood pressure or brain waves, that they cannot normally access, with the purpose of controlling these functions.

bipolar I disorder Alternation of **major depressive episodes** with full **manic episodes**.

bipolar II disorder Alternation of **major depressive episodes** with **hypomanic episodes** (not full **manic episodes**).

blood–injection–injury phobia Unreasonable **fear** and avoidance of exposure to blood, injury, or the possibility of an injection. Victims experience fainting and a drop in blood pressure.

body dysmorphic disorder (BDD) **Somatoform disorder** featuring a disruptive preoccupation with some imagined defect in appearance ("imagined ugliness").

borderline personality disorder A cluster B (dramatic, emotional, or erratic) **personality disorder** involving a pervasive pattern of instability of interpersonal relationships, self-image, affect, and control over impulses.

brain circuits **Neurotransmitter** current or neural pathway in the brain.

breathing-related sleep disorders Sleep disruption leading to excessive sleepiness or insomnia, caused by a breathing problem such as interrupted **(sleep apnea)** or labored **(hypoventilation)** breathing.

brief psychotic disorder A psychotic disturbance involving **delusions**, **hallucinations**, or **disorganized speech** or behavior but lasting less than 1 month; often occurs in reaction to a stressor.

bulimia nervosa Eating disorder involving recurrent episodes of uncontrolled excessive **(binge)** eating followed by compensatory actions to remove the food (for example, deliberate vomiting, laxative abuse, and excessive exercise).

caffeine-related disorders Cognitive, biological, behavioral, and social problems associated with the use and abuse of caffeine.

cancer Category of often-fatal medical conditions involving abnormal cell growth and malignancy.

Cannabis (*Cannabis* sativa) (marijuana) See **marijuana**.

cannabis use disorders A problematic pattern of cannabis use leading to clinically significant impairment or distress.

cardiovascular disease Afflictions in the mechanisms, including the heart, blood vessels, and their controllers, responsible for transporting blood to the body's tissues and organs. Psychological factors may play important roles in such diseases and their treatments.

case study method Research procedure in which a single person or small group is studied in detail. The method does not allow conclusions about cause-and-effect relationships, and findings can be generalized only with great caution (contrast with **single-case experimental design**).

castration anxiety In **psychoanalysis**, the **fear** in young boys that they will be mutilated genitally because of their lust for their mothers.

catatonia A disorder of movement involving immobility or excited agitation.

catatonic immobility A disturbance of motor behavior in which the person remains motionless, sometimes in an awkward posture, for extended periods.

catharsis Rapid or sudden release of emotional tension thought to be an important factor in psychoanalytic therapy.

childhood disintegrative disorder **Pervasive developmental disorder** involving severe regression in language, adaptive behavior, and motor skills after a 2- to 4-year period of normal development.

childhood—onset fluency disorder (stuttering) Disturbance in the fluency and time patterning of speech (for example, sound and syllable repetitions or prolongations).

chorionic villus sampling (CVS) A genetic test conducted during early pregnancy that samples cells found in the placenta (chorionic villi) and assesses possible genetic or chromosomal problems in the villus.

chronic fatigue syndrome (CFS) Incapacitating exhaustion following only minimal exertion, accompanied by fever, headaches, muscle and joint pain, depression, and **anxiety**.

chronic pain Enduring pain that does not decrease over time; may occur in muscles, joints, and the lower back; and may be caused by enlarged blood vessels or degenerating or cancerous tissue. Other significant factors are social and psychological.

circadian rhythm sleep disorders Sleep disturbances resulting in sleepiness or insomnia, caused by the body's inability to synchronize its sleep patterns with the current pattern of day and night.

circumplex model A model describing different emotions as points in a 2-dimensional space of valence and arousal.

civil commitment laws Legal proceeding that determines a person is mentally disordered and may be hospitalized, even involuntarily.

classical (or pure) categorical approach **Classification** method founded on the assumption of clear-cut differences among disorders, each with a different known cause. Also known as *pure categorical approach*.

classical conditioning Fundamental learning process first described by Ivan Pavlov. An event that automatically elicits a response is paired with another stimulus event that does not (a neutral stimulus). After repeated pairings, the neutral stimulus becomes a **conditioned stimulus** that by itself can elicit the desired response.

classification Assignment of objects or people to categories on the basis of shared characteristics.

clinical assessment Systematic evaluation and measurement of psychological, biological, and social factors in a person presenting with a possible **psychological disorder**.

clinical description Details of the combination of behaviors, thoughts, and feelings of an individual that make up a particular disorder.

clinical efficacy axis One of a proposed set of guidelines for evaluating clinical interventions on the evidence of their effectiveness (compare with **clinical utility axis**).

clinical significance Degree to which research findings have useful and meaningful applications to real problems.

clinical utility axis One of a proposed set of guidelines for evaluating clinical interventions by whether they can be applied effectively and cost effectively in real clinical settings (compare with **clinical efficacy axis**).

cocaine use disorders Cognitive, biological, behavioral, and social problems associated with the use and abuse of **cocaine**.

cognitive science Field of study that examines how humans and other animals acquire, process, store, and retrieve information.

cognitive therapy Treatment approach that involves identifying and altering negative thinking styles related to **psychological disorders** such as depression and **anxiety** and replacing them with more positive beliefs and attitudes—and, ultimately, more adaptive behavior and coping styles.

cohort effect Observation that people of different age groups differ in their values and experiences.

cohorts Participants in each age group of a study with a **cross-sectional design**.

collective unconscious Accumulated wisdom of a culture collected and remembered across generations, a psychodynamic concept introduced by Carl Jung.

comorbidity Presence of two or more disorders in an individual at the same time.

comparative treatment research **Outcome research** that contrasts two or more treatment methods to determine which is most effective.

competence Ability of legal defendants to participate in their own defense and understand the charges and the roles of the trial participants.

complicated grief Grief characterized by debilitating feelings of loss and emotions so painful that a person has trouble resuming a normal life; designated for further study as a disorder by *DSM-5*.

compulsions Repetitive, ritualistic, time-consuming behavior or mental act a person feels driven to perform.

confound Any factor occurring in a study that makes the results uninterpretable because its effects cannot be separated from those of the variables being studied.

confounding variable Variable in a research study that was not part of the intended design and that may contribute to changes in the **dependent variable**.

control group Group of individuals in a study who are similar to the experimental subjects in every way but are not exposed to the treatment received by the experimental group. Their presence allows for a comparison of the differential effects of the treatment.

controlled drinking An extremely controversial treatment approach to **alcohol** dependence, in which severe abusers are taught to drink in moderation.

conversion disorder Physical malfunctioning, such as blindness or paralysis, suggesting neurological impairment but with no organic pathology to account for it.

copy number variants Genes that are deleted as a result of mutations; these deletions may play a role in the development of ADHD and other disorders.

coronary heart disease (CHD) Blockage of the arteries supplying blood to the heart muscle; a major cause of death in Western culture, with social and psychological factors involved.

correlation Degree to which two variables are associated. In a **positive correlation**, the two variables increase or decrease together. In a **negative correlation**, one variable decreases as the other increases.

correlation coefficient Computed statistic reflecting the strength and direction of any association between two variables. It can range from 21.00 through 0.00 (indicating no association) to 11.00, with the absolute value indicating the strength and the sign reflecting the direction.

course Pattern of development and change of a disorder over time.

covert sensitization Cognitive-behavioral intervention to reduce unwanted behaviors by having clients imagine the extremely aversive consequences of the behaviors and establish negative rather than positive associations with them.

Creutzfeldt-Jakob disease Extremely rare condition that causes **dementia**.

criminal commitment Legal procedure by which a person found not guilty of a crime by reason of **insanity** must be confined in a psychiatric hospital.

cross-generational effect Limit on the **generalizability** of longitudinal research because the group under study may differ from others in culture and experience.

cross-sectional design Methodology to examine a characteristic by comparing individuals of different ages (contrast with **longitudinal design**).

cultural–familial intellectual disability Mild form of **intellectual disability** that may be caused largely by environmental influences.

cyclothymic disorder Chronic (at least 2 years) **mood disorder** characterized by alternating **mood** elevation and depression levels that are not as severe as **manic** or **major depressive episodes**.

dangerousness Tendency to violence that, contrary to popular opinion, is not more likely among mental patients.

defense mechanisms Common pattern of behavior, often an adaptive coping style when it occurs in moderation, observed in response to a particular situation. Psychoanalytic theory suggests that defense mechanisms are **unconscious** processes originating in the **ego**.

deinstitutionalization Systematic removal of people with severe **mental illness** or **intellectual disability** from institutions like psychiatric hospitals.

delayed ejaculation Disorder in which a man achieves orgasm only with great difficulty.

delirium Rapid-onset reduced clarity of consciousness and cognition, with confusion, disorientation, and deficits in memory and language.

delusion A psychotic symptom involving disorder of thought content and presence of strong beliefs that are misrepresentations of reality.

delusional disorder A psychotic disorder featuring a persistent belief contrary to reality (**delusion**) but no other symptoms of **schizophrenia**.

dementia praecox The Latin term meaning premature loss of mind; an early label for what is now called **schizophrenia**, emphasizing the disorder's frequent appearance during adolescence.

dependent personality disorder A cluster C (anxious or fearful) **personality disorder** characterized by a person's pervasive and excessive need to be taken care of, a condition that leads to submissive and clinging behavior and fears of separation.

dependent variable In an experimental study, the phenomenon that is measured and expected to be influenced (compare with **independent variable**).

depersonalization-derealization disorder **Dissociative disorder** in which feelings of depersonalization are so severe they dominate the client's life and prevent normal functioning.

depressants A **psychoactive substance** that results in behavioral sedation; such substances include **alcohol** and the sedative, hypnotic, and anxiolytic drugs.

depressive cognitive triad Thinking errors by depressed people negatively focused in three areas: themselves, their immediate world, and their future.

derealization Situation in which the individual loses a sense of the reality of the external world.

deterministic In genetics, **genes** that lead to nearly a 100% chance of developing the associated disorder. These are rare in the population.

diagnosis Process of determining whether a **presenting problem** meets the established criteria for a specific **psychological disorder**.

dialectical behavior therapy (DBT) A promising treatment for **borderline personality disorder** that involves exposing the client to stressors in a controlled situation, as well as helping the client regulate **emotions** and cope with stressors that might trigger suicidal behavior.

diathesis–stress model Hypothesis that both an inherited tendency (a **vulnerability**) and specific stressful conditions are required to produce a disorder.

dimensional approach Method of categorizing characteristics on a continuum rather than on a binary, either-or, or all-or-none basis.

diminished capacity Evidence of an abnormal mental condition in people that causes criminal charges against them requiring intent or knowledge to be reduced to lesser offenses requiring only reckless or criminal neglect.

directionality Possibility that when two variables, A and B, are correlated variable A causes variable B or variable B causes variable A.

disinhibited social engagement disorder Condition in which a child shows no inhibitions whatsoever in approaching adults.

disorder of arousal Category of sleep disorder during NREM sleep that includes **sleepwalking** and **sleep terrors.**

disorganized speech A style of talking often seen in people with **schizophrenia**, involving incoherence and a lack of typical logic patterns.

disruptive mood dysregulation disorder Condition in which a child has chronic negative moods such as anger and irritability without any accompanying mania.

dissociative amnesia Dissociative disorder featuring the inability to recall personal information; usually of a stressful or traumatic nature.

dissociative disorder Disorder in which individuals feel detached from themselves or their surroundings and feel reality, experience, and identity may disintegrate.

dissociative fugue Dissociative disorder featuring sudden, unexpected travel away from home, along with an inability to recall the past, sometimes with assumption of a new identity.

dissociative identity disorder (DID) Disorder in which as many as 100 personalities or fragments of personalities coexist within one body and mind. Formerly known as *multiple personality disorder.*

dissociative trance Altered state of consciousness in which people firmly believe they are possessed by spirits; considered a disorder only where there is distress and dysfunction.

dopamine Neurotransmitter whose generalized function is to activate other neurotransmitters and to aid in exploratory and pleasure-seeking behaviors (thus balancing

serotonin). A relative excess of dopamine is implicated in **schizophrenia** (although contradictory evidence suggests the connection is not simple), and its deficit is involved in **Parkinson's disease**.

double bind communication According to an obsolete, unsupported theory, the practice of transmitting conflicting messages that was thought to cause **schizophrenia**.

double-blind control Procedure in **outcome research** that prevents bias by ensuring that neither the subjects nor the providers of the experimental treatment know who is receiving treatment and who is receiving a **placebo**.

double depression Severe **mood disorder** typified by **major depressive episodes** superimposed over a background of **dysthymic disorder**.

Down syndrome Type of **intellectual disability** caused by a chromosomal aberration (chromosome 21) and involving characteristic physical appearance. Also known as *trisomy 21*.

dream analysis Psychoanalytic therapy method in which dream content is examined as symbolic of **id** impulses and **intrapsychic conflicts**.

duty to warn Mental health professional's responsibility to break confidentiality and notify the potential victim whom a client has specifically threatened.

dyssomnias Problems in getting to sleep or in obtaining sufficient quality sleep.

effect size A statistical process that eliminates how large a change in measure occurred. Often used before and after a clinical treatment to determine its relative success.

ego In **psychoanalysis**, the psychic entity responsible for finding realistic and practical ways to satisfy **id** drives.

ego psychology Psychoanalytic theory that emphasizes the role of the **ego** in development and attributes **psychological disorders** to failure of the ego to manage impulses and internal conflicts. Also known as *self-psychology*.

electroconvulsive therapy (ECT) Biological treatment for severe, chronic depression involving the application of electrical impulses through the brain to produce seizures. The reasons for its effectiveness are unknown.

electroencephalogram (EEG) Measure of electrical activity patterns in the brain, taken through electrodes placed on the scalp.

emotion Pattern of action elicited by an external event and a feeling state, accompanied by a characteristic physiological response.

endogenous (natural) opioids Substance occurring naturally throughout the body that functions like a **neurotransmitter** to shut down pain sensation even in the presence of marked tissue damage. These opioids may contribute to psychological problems such as eating disorders. Also known as an *endorphin* or *enkephalin*.

endophenotypes Genetic mechanism that contributes to the underlying problems causing the symptoms and difficulties experienced by people with **psychological disorders**.

epidemiology **Psychopathology** research method examining the prevalence, distribution, and consequences of disorders in populations.

epigenetics The study of factors other than inherited DNA sequence, such as new learning or stress, that alter the phenotypic expression of **genes**.

equifinality **Developmental psychopathology** principle that a behavior or disorder may have several causes.

erectile disorder Recurring inability in some men to attain or maintain adequate penile erection until completion of sexual activity.

essential hypertension High blood pressure with no verifiable physical cause, which makes up the overwhelming majority of high blood pressure cases.

etiology Cause or source of a disorder.

excitatory Causing excitation. Activating.

excoriation Recurrent, difficult-to-control picking of one's skin leading to significant impairment or distress.

exhibitionistic disorder Sexual gratification attained by exposing genitals to unsuspecting strangers.

exorcism Religious ritual that attributes disordered behavior to possession by demons and seeks to treat the individual by driving the demons from the body.

experiment Research method that can establish causation by manipulating the variables in question and controlling for alternative explanations of any observed effects.

expert witnesses Person who because of special training and experience is allowed to offer opinion testimony in legal trials.

expressed emotion (EE) Hostility, criticism, and over-involvement demonstrated by some families toward a family member with a **psychological disorder**. This can often contribute to the person's **relapse**.

external validity Extent to which research findings generalize, or apply, to people and settings not involved in the study.

extinction Learning process in which a response maintained by **reinforcement** in **operant conditioning** or pairing in **classical conditioning** decreases when that reinforcement or pairing is removed; also the procedure of removing that reinforcement or pairing.

facial agnosia Type of **agnosia** characterized by a person's inability to recognize even familiar faces.

factitious disorder Non-existent physical or **psychological disorder** deliberately faked for no apparent gain except, possibly, sympathy and attention.

false negative Assessment error in which no pathology is noted (that is, test results are negative) when one is actually present.

false positive Assessment error in which pathology is reported (that is, test results are positive) when none is actually present.

familial aggregation Extent to which a disorder would be found among a patient's relatives.

family studies Genetic study that examines patterns of traits and behaviors among relatives.

fear **Emotion** of an immediate alarm reaction to present danger or life-threatening emergencies.

female orgasmic disorder Recurring delay or absence of orgasm in some women following a normal sexual excitement phase, relative to their prior experience and current stimulation. Also known as inhibited orgasm (female).

female sexual interest/arousal disorder Recurrent inability in some women to attain or maintain adequate lubrication and sexual excitement swelling responses until completion of sexual activity.

fetal alcohol syndrome (FAS) A pattern of problems, including learning difficulties, behavior deficits, and characteristic physical flaws, resulting from heavy drinking by the victim's mother when she was pregnant with the victim.

fetishistic disorder Long-term, recurring, intense sexually arousing urges, fantasies, or behavior that involve the use of nonliving, unusual objects and that cause distress or impairment in life functioning.

fight/flight system (FFS) **Brain circuit** in animals that when stimulated causes an immediate alarm-and-escape response resembling human **panic**.

flat affect An apparently emotionless demeanor (including toneless speech and vacant gaze) when a reaction would be expected.

flight or fight response Biological reaction to alarming stressors that musters the body's resources (for example, blood flow and respiration) to resist or flee a threat.

fragile X syndrome Pattern of **abnormality** caused by a defect in the **X chromosome** resulting in **intellectual disability**, learning problems, and unusual physical characteristics.

free association Psychoanalytic therapy technique intended to explore threatening material repressed into the **unconscious**. The patient is instructed to say whatever comes to mind without censoring.

frontotemporal neurocognitive disorder Condition that damages the frontal or temporal regions of the brain; behavior or language is negatively affected.

frotteuristic disorder **Paraphilic disorder** in which the person gains sexual gratification by rubbing against unwilling victims in crowds from which they cannot escape.

gambling disorder Persistent and recurrent problematic gambling behavior leading to clinically significant impairment or distress.

gamma-aminobutyric acid (GABA) **Neurotransmitter** that reduces activity across the **synaptic cleft** and thus inhibits a range of behaviors and **emotions**, especially generalized **anxiety**.

gender dysphoria Psychological dissatisfaction with biological gender, a disturbance in the sense of identity as a male or female. The primary goal is not sexual arousal but rather to live the life of the opposite gender.

gender nonconformity A phenomenon in which pre-pubescent children do not identify with their biological sex, but instead identify strongly with the gender of the opposite sex and display varying degrees of behavior more characteristic of the opposite sex.

gene–environment correlation model Hypothesis that people with a genetic predisposition for a disorder may also have a genetic tendency to create environmental risk factors that promote the disorder.

general adaptation syndrome (GAS) Sequence of reactions to sustained **stress** described by Hans Selye. These stages are alarm, resistance, and exhaustion, which may lead to death.

generalizability Extent to which research results apply to a range of individuals not included in the study.

generalized amnesia Loss of memory of all personal information, including identity.

generalized anxiety disorder (GAD) **Anxiety** disorder characterized by intense, uncontrollable, unfocused, chronic, and continuous worry that is distressing and unproductive, accompanied by physical symptoms of tenseness, irritability, and restlessness.

genes Long deoxyribonucleic acid (DNA) molecule, the basic physical unit of heredity that appears as a location on a chromosome.

genetic linkage analysis Study that seeks to match the inheritance pattern of a disorder to that of a **genetic marker**. This helps researchers establish the location of the **gene** responsible for the disorder.

genetic markers Inherited characteristic for which the chromosomal location of the responsible **gene** is known.

genito-pelvic pain/penetration disorder Sexual dysfunction in which a woman experiences pain or difficulty with penetration during intercourse; may include **vaginismus.**

genotypes Specific genetic makeup of an individual.

glutamate Amino acid **neurotransmitter** that excites many different **neurons**, leading to action.

hallucination A psychotic symptom of perceptual disturbance in which something is seen, heard, or otherwise sensed although it is not actually present.

hallucinogen use disorders Cognitive, biological, behavioral, and social problems associated with the use and abuse of hallucinogenic substances.

hallucinogens Any **psychoactive substance**, such as **LSD** or **marijuana**, that can produce **delusions, hallucinations, paranoia**, and altered sensory perception.

head trauma Injury to the head and, therefore, to the brain, typically caused by accidents; can lead to cognitive impairments, including memory loss.

health psychology Subfield of **behavioral medicine** that studies psychological factors important in health promotion and maintenance.

hebephrenia A silly and immature emotionality, a characteristic of some types of **schizophrenia**.

heterosexual behavior Sexual activity with members of the opposite gender.

histrionic personality disorder A cluster B (dramatic, emotional, or erratic) **personality disorder** involving a pervasive pattern of excessive emotionality and attention seeking.

homosexual behavior Sexual activity with members of the same gender.

hormone Chemical messenger produced by the endocrine glands.

human genome project Ongoing scientific attempt to develop a comprehensive map of all human **genes**.

human immunodeficiency virus type 1 (HIV-1) Disease that causes AIDS.

Huntington's disease Genetic disorder marked by involuntary limb movements and progressing to **dementia**.

hypersomnolence disorders Sleep dysfunction involving an excessive amount of sleep that disrupts normal routines.

hypertension Major risk factor for **stroke** and heart and kidney disease that is intimately related to psychological factors. Also known as *high blood pressure*.

hypomanic episode Less severe and less disruptive version of a **manic episode** that is one of the criteria for several **mood disorders**.

hypothesis Educated guess or statement to be tested by research.

id In **psychoanalysis**, the **unconscious** psychic entity present at birth representing basic drives.

idiographic strategy A close and detailed investigation of an individual emphasizing what makes that person unique. (Compare with **nomothetic strategy**.)

illness anxiety disorder Somatic symptom disorder (previously known as *somatoform disorder*) involving severe **anxiety** over belief in having a disease process without any evident physical cause.

immune system Body's means of identifying and eliminating any foreign materials (for example, bacteria, parasites, and even transplanted organs) that enter.

implicit memory Condition of memory in which a person cannot recall past events despite acting in response to them.

impulse-control disorders A disorder in which a person acts on an irresistible, but potentially harmful, impulse.

inappropriate affect An emotional display that is improper for the situation.

incest Deviant sexual attraction (**pedophilia**) directed toward a family member; often the attraction of a father toward a daughter who is maturing physically.

incidence Number of new cases of a disorder appearing during a specific period (compare with **prevalence**).

independent variable Phenomenon manipulated by the experimenter in a study and expected to influence the **dependent variable**.

informed consent Ethical requirement whereby research subjects agree to participate in a study only after they receive full disclosure about the nature of the study and their own role in it.

inhibitory Causing inhibition. Suppressing.

insomnia disorder Condition in which insufficient sleep interferes with normal functioning.

integrated grief Grief that evolves from acute grief into a condition in which the individual accepts the finality of a death and adjusts to the loss.

intellectual disability (ID) A diagnosis received when one achieves a significantly below-average score on a test of intelligence and by limitations in the ability to function in areas of daily life. Significantly subaverage intellectual functioning paired with deficits in adaptive functioning such as self-care or occupational activities, appearing before age 18.

intelligence quotient (IQ) Score on an intelligence test estimating a person's deviation from average test performance.

intermittent explosive disorder The episodes during which a person acts on aggressive impulses that result in serious assaults or destruction of property.

internal validity Extent to which the results of a study can be attributed to the **independent variable** after confounding alternative explanations have been ruled out.

interpersonal psychotherapy (IPT) Brief treatment approach that emphasizes resolution of interpersonal problems and stressors, such as role disputes in marital conflict, forming relationships in marriage, or a new job. It has demonstrated effectiveness for such problems as depression.

intrapsychic conflicts In psychoanalytic theory, a struggle among the **id**, **ego**, and **superego**.

introspection Early, nonscientific approach to the study of psychology involving systematic attempts to report thoughts and feelings that specific stimuli evoked.

inverse agonist In **neuroscience**, a chemical substance that produces effects opposite those of a particular **neurotransmitter**.

joint attention Attention shared by two persons toward an object after one person has indicated interest in the object to the other person; this social interaction is limited or absent in people with **autism spectrum disorder**.

kleptomania A recurrent failure to resist urges to steal things not needed for personal use or their monetary value.

labeling Applying a name to a phenomenon or a pattern of behavior. The label may acquire negative connotations or be applied erroneously to the person rather than that person's behaviors.

language disorder Getting one's meaning or message across to others (expressive language disorder), or understanding the message coming from others (receptive language disorder).

learned helplessness Martin Seligman's theory that people become anxious and depressed when they make an attribution that they have no control over the **stress** in their lives (whether or not they do in reality).

learned helplessness theory of depression Martin Seligman's theory that people become anxious and depressed when they make an attribution that they have no control over the **stress** in their lives (whether or not they actually have control).

Lesch-Nyhan syndrome X-linked gene disorder characterized by **intellectual**

disability, signs of cerebral palsy, and **self-injurious** behavior.

level Degree of behavior change with different interventions (for example, high or low).

localized or selective amnesia Memory loss limited to specific times and events, particularly traumatic events.

longitudinal designs Systematic study of changes in the same individual or group examined over time (contrast with **cross-sectional design**).

LSD (d-lysergic acid diethylamide) The most common hallucinogenic drug; a synthetic version of the grain fungus ergot.

maintenance treatment Combination of continued **psychosocial treatment**, medication, or both designed to prevent **relapse** following therapy.

major depressive disorder Mood disorder involving one *(single episode)* or more (separated by at least 2 months without depression, *recurrent*)

major depressive episode Most common and severe experience of depression, including feelings of worthlessness, disturbances in bodily activities such as sleep, loss of interest, and inability to experience pleasure, persisting at least 2 weeks.

major neurocognitive disorder (dementia) Gradual deterioration of brain functioning that affects memory, judgment, language, and other advanced cognitive processes.

male hypoactive sexual desire disorder Dysfunction in which a man feels distress from having little or no sexual interest.

malingering Deliberate faking of a physical or **psychological disorder** motivated by gain.

mania Period of abnormally excessive elation or euphoria associated with some **mood disorders**.

mental hygiene movement Mid-19th-century effort to improve care of the mentally disordered by informing the public of their mistreatment.

mental illness Term formerly used to mean **psychological disorder** but less preferred because it implies that the causes of the disorder can be found in a medical disease process.

mental status exam Relatively coarse preliminary test of a client's judgment, orientation to time and place, and emotional and mental state; typically conducted during an initial interview.

microsleeps Short, seconds-long periods of sleep that occur in people who have been deprived of sleep.

mild neurocognitive disorder Modest impairment in cognitive abilities that can be overcome with accommodations such as extensive lists or elaborate schedules.

mixed features Condition in which the individual experiences both elation and depression or **anxiety** at the same time. Also known as *dysphoric manic episode* or *mixed manic episode*.

modeling (also observational learning) Learning through observation and imitation of the behavior of other individuals and consequences of that behavior.

mood Enduring period of emotionality.

mood disorders One of a group of disorders involving severe and enduring disturbances in emotionality ranging from elation to severe depression.

mood-stabilizing drug A medication used in the treatment of **mood disorders**, particularly bipolar disorder, that is effective in preventing and treating pathological shifts in mood.

moral therapy Psychosocial approach in the 19th century that involved treating patients as normally as possible in normal environments.

multidimensional integrative approach Approach to the study of **psychopathology** that holds **psychological disorders** are always the products of multiple interacting causal factors.

multiple baseline Single-case experimental design in which measures are taken on two or more behaviors or on a single behavior in two or more situations. A particular intervention is introduced for each at different times. If behavior change is coincident with each introduction, this is strong evidence the intervention caused the change.

narcissistic personality disorder A cluster B (dramatic, emotional, or erratic) **personality disorder** involving a pervasive pattern of grandiosity in fantasy or behavior, need for admiration, and lack of **empathy**.

narcolepsy Sleep disorder involving sudden and irresistible sleep attacks.

natural environment phobia Fear of situations or events in nature, especially heights, **storms, and water.**

naturalistic teaching strategies Instructional techniques that are used with children having neurodevelopmental disorders and that move away from traditional desk instruction toward more natural social interactions.

negative correlation Association between two variables in which one increases as the other decreases.

negative symptoms A less outgoing symptom, such as **flat affect** or poverty of speech, displayed by some people with **schizophrenia**.

neurocognitive disorder due to Alzheimer's disease Condition resulting from a disease that develops most often in people 50 and older, characterized by multiple cognitive defects that develop gradually and steadily.

neurocognitive disorder due to HIV infection Less common type of neurocognitive disorder that affects people who have HIV; may lead to impaired thinking in advanced stages.

neurocognitive disorder due to Huntington's disease Neurological disorder that follows a subcortical pattern and is notable for causing involuntary limb movements.

neurocognitive disorder due to Lewy body disease Neurological impairment that affects people with Lewy body disease, in which protein deposits damage brain cells and gradually cause motor impairments and loss of alertness.

neurocognitive disorder due to Parkinson's disease Disorder characterized by progressive decline in motor movements; results from damage to dopamine pathways.

neurocognitive disorder due to prion disease Rare progressive neurodegenerative disorder caused by prions, proteins that can reproduce themselves and cause damage to brain cells.

neurocognitive disorder due to traumatic brain injury Condition resulting from jarring of the brain caused by a blow to the head or other impact; symptoms persist for at least a week after the initial trauma.

neurodevelopmental disorders Neurologically based disorders that are revealed in a clinically significant way during a child's developing years.

neurohormones Hormone that affects the brain and is increasingly the focus of study in **psychopathology**.

neuroimaging Sophisticated computer-aided procedure that allows nonintrusive examination of nervous system structure and function.

neuron Individual nerve cell responsible for transmitting information.

neuropsychological test Assessment of brain and nervous system functioning by testing an individual's performance on behavioral tasks.

neuroscience Study of the nervous system and its role in behavior, thoughts, and **emotions.**

neurosis (*plural* neuroses) Obsolete psychodynamic term for a **psychological disorder** thought to result from an **unconscious** conflict and the **anxiety** it causes. Plural is *neuroses*.

neurotransmitters Chemical that crosses the **synaptic cleft** between nerve cells to transmit impulses from one **neuron** to the next. Relative excess or deficiency of neurotransmitters is involved in several **psychological disorders**.

nicotine Toxic and addictive substance found in tobacco leaves.

nicotine patch Patch placed on the skin that delivers **nicotine** to smokers without the carcinogens in cigarette smoke. Somewhat more successful than nicotine gum because it requires less effort by the wearer and delivers the drug more consistently; should be coupled with counseling to stop smoking and avoid **relapse**.

night eating syndrome Consuming a third or more of daily food intake after the evening meal and getting out of bed at least once during the night to have a high-calorie snack. In the morning, however, individuals with night eating syndrome are not hungry and do not usually eat breakfast. These individuals do not **binge** during their night eating and seldom purge.

nightmares Frightening and anxiety-provoking dreams occurring during **rapid eye movement sleep**. The individual recalls the bad dreams and recovers alertness and orientation quickly.

nomenclature In a naming system or **nosology**, the actual labels or names that are applied. In **psychopathology**, these include **mood disorders** and eating disorders.

nomothetic strategy Identification and examination of large groups of people with the same disorder to note similarities and develop general laws.

norepinephrine (also noradrenaline) Neurotransmitter active in the **central** and **peripheral nervous systems**, controlling heart rate, blood pressure, and respiration, among other functions. Because of its role in the body's alarm reaction, it may also contribute generally and indirectly to **panic attacks** and other disorders. Also known as *noradrenaline*.

nosology **Classification** and naming system for medical and psychological phenomena.

obesity Excess of body fat resulting in a body mass index (BMI, a ratio of weight to height) of 30 or more.

object relations Modern development in psychodynamic theory involving the study of how children incorporate the memories and values of people who are close and important to them.

obsessions Recurrent intrusive thought or impulse the client seeks to suppress or neutralize while recognizing it is not imposed by outside forces.

obsessive-compulsive disorder (OCD) **Anxiety** disorder involving unwanted, persistent, intrusive thoughts and impulses, as well as repetitive actions intended to suppress them.

obsessive-compulsive personality disorder A cluster C (anxious or fearful) **personality disorder** featuring a pervasive pattern of preoccupation with orderliness, perfectionism, and mental and interpersonal control at the expense of flexibility, openness, and efficiency.

opiates An addictive **psychoactive substance** such as heroin, **opium**, or **morphine** that causes temporary euphoria and analgesia (pain reduction).

opioid-related disorders Cognitive, biological, behavioral, and social problems associated with the use and abuse of **opiates** and their synthetic variants.

orgasmic reconditioning Learning procedure to help clients strengthen appropriate patterns of sexual arousal by pairing appropriate stimuli with the pleasurable sensations of masturbation.

other drugs of abuse Other substances that are abused but do not fit easily into one of the common categories including inhalants, anabolic steroids, and other over-the-counter and prescription medications.

panic Sudden, overwhelming fright or terror.

panic attack Abrupt experience of intense **fear** or discomfort accompanied by several physical symptoms, such as dizziness or heart palpitations.

panic control treatment (PCT) **Cognitive–behavioral treatment** for **panic attacks**, involving gradual exposure to feared somatic sensations and modification of perceptions and attitudes about them.

panic disorder (PD) Recurrent unexpected panic attacks accompanied by concern about future attacks and/or a lifestyle change to avoid future attacks.

paranoia People's irrational beliefs that they are especially important (**delusions of grandeur**) or that other people are seeking to do them harm.

paranoid personality disorder A cluster A (odd or eccentric) **personality disorder** involving pervasive distrust and suspiciousness of others such that their motives are interpreted as malevolent.

paraphilic disorders Sexual disorders and deviations in which sexual arousal occurs almost exclusively in the context of inappropriate objects or individuals.

parasomnias **Abnormal behaviors** such as **nightmares** or **sleepwalking** that occur during sleep.

Parkinson's disease Degenerative brain disorder principally affecting motor performance (for example, tremors and stooped posture) associated with reduction in **dopamine**. **Dementia** may be a result as well.

patient uniformity myth Tendency to consider all members of a category as more similar than they are, ignoring their individual differences.

pedophilia Paraphilia involving strong sexual attraction toward children.

persistent depressive disorder (dysthymia) **Mood disorder** involving persistently depressed **mood**, with low self-esteem, **withdrawal**, pessimism, or despair, present for at least 2 years, with no absence of symptoms for more than 2 months.

personality disorder An enduring maladaptive pattern for relating to the environment and self, exhibited in a range of contexts that cause significant functional impairment or subjective distress.

personality inventories Self-report questionnaire that assesses personal traits by asking respondents to identify descriptions that apply to themselves.

person-centered therapy Therapy method in which the client, rather than the counselor, primarily directs the course of discussion, seeking self-discovery and self-responsibility.

pervasive developmental disorder—not otherwise specified Wide-ranging, significant, and long-lasting dysfunctions that appear before the age of 18.

phenotypes Observable characteristics or behaviors of an individual.

phenylketonuria (PKU) Recessive gene disorder involving the inability to break down a food chemical whose buildup causes **intellectual disability**, seizures, and behavior problems. PKU can be detected by infant screening and prevented by a specialized diet.

phobia **Psychological disorder** characterized by marked and persistent **fear** of an object or situation.

physiological dependence the use of increasingly greater amounts of the drug to experience the same effect (**tolerance**) and a negative physical response when the substance is no longer ingested.

Pick's disease Rare neurological disorder that results in **presenile dementia**.

placebo control groups In **outcome research**, a **control group** that does not receive the experimental manipulation but is given a similar procedure with an identical expectation of change, allowing the researcher to assess any **placebo effect**.

placebo effect Behavior change resulting from the person's expectation of change rather than from the experimental manipulation itself.

polysomnographic (PSG) evaluation Assessment of sleep disorders in which a client sleeping in the lab is monitored for heart, muscle, respiration, brain wave, and other functions.

positive correlation Association between two variables in which one increases as the other increases.

positive symptoms A more overt symptom, such as a **delusion** or **hallucination**, displayed by some people with **schizophrenia**.

posttraumatic stress disorder (PTSD) Enduring, distressing emotional disorder that follows exposure to a severe helplessness-or fear-inducing threat. The victim reexperiences the trauma, avoids stimuli associated with it, and develops a numbing of responsiveness and an increased vigilance and arousal.

premature ejaculation Recurring ejaculation before the person wishes it, with minimal sexual stimulation.

premenstrual dysphoric disorder Clinically significant emotional problems that can occur during the premenstrual phase of the reproductive cycle of a woman.

prepared learning Ability adaptive for evolution, allowing certain associations to be learned more readily than others.

presenting problem Original complaint reported by the client to the therapist. The actual treated problem may be a modification derived from the presenting problem.

prevalence Number of people displaying a disorder in the total population at any given time (compare with **incidence**).

primary insomnia Difficulty in initiating, maintaining, or gaining from sleep; not related to other medical or psychological problems.

proband In genetics research, the individual displaying the trait or characteristic being studied.

prodromal stage Period of 1 to 2 years before serious symptoms of **schizophrenia** occur but when less severe yet unusual behaviors start to appear.

prognosis Predicted development of a disorder over time.

projective tests Psychoanalytically based measure that presents ambiguous stimuli to clients on the assumption that their responses can reveal their **unconscious** conflicts. Such tests are inferential and lack high **reliability** and **validity**.

prosody Vocal characteristics such as tone and stress; people with **autism spectrum disorder** often have trouble recognizing and interpreting these vocal cues.

prototypical approach System for categorizing disorders using both essential, defining characteristics and a range of variation on other characteristics.

psychoactive substance Substances, such as a drug, that alter **mood** or behavior.

psychoanalysis Assessment and therapy pioneered by Sigmund Freud that emphasizes exploration of, and insight into, **unconscious** processes and conflicts.

psychoanalyst Therapist who practices **psychoanalysis** after earning either an M.D. or a Ph.D. degree and receiving additional specialized postdoctoral training.

psychoanalytic model Complex and comprehensive theory originally advanced by Sigmund Freud that seeks to account for the development and structure of personality, as well as the origin of **abnormal behavior**, based primarily on inferred inner entities and forces.

psychodynamic psychotherapy Contemporary version of **psychoanalysis** that still emphasizes **unconscious** processes and conflicts but is briefer and more focused on specific problems.

psychological autopsy Postmortem psychological profile of a suicide victim constructed from interviews with people who knew the person before death.

psychological disorder Psychological dysfunction associated with distress or impairment in functioning that is not a typical or culturally expected response.

psychological factors affecting medical condition the presence of a diagnosed medical condition that is adversely affected (increased in frequency or severity) by one or more psychological or behavioral factors.

psychoncology Study of psychological factors involved in the **course** and treatment of **cancer**.

psychoneuroimmunology (PNI) Study of psychological influences on the neurological responding involved in the body's immune response.

psychopathology Scientific study of **psychological disorders**.

psychopathy A non-*DSM-IV-TR* category similar to **antisocial personality disorder** but with less emphasis on overt behavior. Indicators include superficial charm, lack of remorse, and other personality characteristics.

psychophysiological assessment Measurement of changes in the nervous system reflecting psychological or emotional events such as **anxiety**, **stress**, and sexual arousal.

psychosexual stages of development Psychoanalytic concept of the sequence of phases a person passes through during development. Each stage is named for the location on the body where **id** gratification is maximal at that time.

psychosocial treatment Treatment practices that focuses on social and cultural factors (such as family experience), as well as psychological influences. These approaches include cognitive, behavioral, and interpersonal methods.

psychotic behavior A severe **psychological disorder** category characterized by **hallucinations** and loss of contact with reality.

psychotic disorder associated with another medical condition Condition that is characterized by hallucinations or delusions and that is the direct result of another physiological disorder, such as stroke or brain tumor.

purging techniques In the eating disorder **bulimia nervosa,** the self-induced vomiting or laxative abuse used to compensate for excessive food ingestion.

pyromania An **impulse-control disorder** that involves having an irresistible urge to set fires.

randomization Method for placing individuals into research groups that assures each an equal chance of being assigned to any group, thus eliminating any systematic differences across groups.

rapid eye movement (REM) sleep Periodic intervals of sleep during which the eyes move rapidly from side to side, and dreams occur, but the body is inactive.

reactive attachment disorder Attachment disorder in which a child with disturbed behavior neither seeks out a caregiver nor responds to offers of help from one; fearfulness and sadness are often evident.

rebound insomnia In a person with insomnia, the worsened sleep problems that can occur when medications are used to treat insomnia and then withdrawn.

recurrent Repeatedly occurring.

reinforcement In **operant conditioning**, consequences for behavior that strengthen it or increase its frequency. Positive reinforcement involves the contingent delivery of a desired consequence. Negative reinforcement is the contingent escape from an aversive consequence. Unwanted behaviors may result from reinforcement of those behaviors or the failure to reinforce desired behaviors.

relapse prevention The extending therapeutic progress by teaching the client how to cope with future troubling situations.

relaxation response Active components of meditation methods, including repetitive thoughts of a sound to reduce distracting thoughts and closing the mind to other intruding thoughts, that decrease the flow of **stress hormones** and **neurotransmitters** and cause a feeling of calm.

reliability Degree to which a measurement is consistent—for example, over time or among different raters.

repeated measurement When responses are measured on more than two occasions (not just before and after intervention) to assess **trends**.

research design Plan of experimentation used to test a **hypothesis**.

retrospective information Literally "the view back;" data collected by examining records or recollections of the past. It is limited by the accuracy, **validity**, and thoroughness of the sources.

Rett disorder Progressive neurological developmental disorder featuring constant hand-wringing, **intellectual disability**, and impaired motor skills.

reuptake Action by which a **neurotransmitter** is quickly drawn back into the discharging **neuron** after being released into a **synaptic cleft**.

rheumatoid arthritis Painful, degenerative disease in which the **immune system** essentially attacks itself, resulting in stiffness, swelling, and even destruction of the joints. **Cognitive–behavioral treatments** can help relieve pain and stiffness.

schizoaffective disorder A psychotic disorder featuring symptoms of both **schizophrenia** and major **mood disorder**.

schizoid personality disorder A cluster A (odd or eccentric) **personality disorder** featuring a pervasive pattern of detachment from social relationships and a restricted range of expression of **emotions**.

schizophrenia A devastating psychotic disorder that may involve characteristic disturbances in thinking (**delusions**), perception (**hallucinations**), speech, **emotions**, and behavior.

schizophreniform disorder A psychotic disorder involving the symptoms of **schizophrenia** but lasting less than 6 months.

schizophrenogenic mother According to an obsolete, unsupported theory, a cold, dominating, and rejecting parent who was thought to cause **schizophrenia** in her offspring.

schizotypal personality disorder A cluster A (odd or eccentric) **personality disorder** involving a pervasive pattern of interpersonal deficits featuring acute discomfort with, and reduced capacity for, close relationships, as well as cognitive or perceptual distortions and eccentricities of behavior.

scientist-practitioner Mental health professional expected to apply scientific methods to his or her work. A scientist–practitioner must know the latest research on **diagnosis** and treatment, must evaluate his or her methods for effectiveness, and may generate research to discover information about disorders and their treatment.

self-actualizing Process emphasized in humanistic psychology in which people strive to achieve their highest potential against difficult life experiences.

self-efficacy Perception of having the ability to cope with **stress** or challenges.

self-monitoring Action by which clients observe and record their own behaviors as either an assessment of a problem and its change or a treatment procedure that makes them more aware of their responses. Also known as *self-observation*.

self-psychology See **ego psychology**.

separation anxiety disorder Excessive, enduring **fear** in some children that harm will come to them or their parents while they are apart.

sequential design Combination of **cross-sectional** and **longitudinal designs** involving repeated study of different **cohorts** over time.

serotonin **Neurotransmitter** involved in processing of information and coordination of movement, as well as inhibition and restraint. It also assists in the regulation of eating, sexual, and aggressive behaviors, all of which may be involved in different **psychological disorders**. Its interaction with **dopamine** is implicated in **schizophrenia**.

sex reassignment surgery Surgical procedures to alter a person's physical anatomy to conform to that person's psychological gender identity.

sexual dysfunction Sexual disorder in which the client finds it difficult to function adequately while having sex.

sexual masochism **Paraphilia** in which sexual arousal is associated with experiencing pain or humiliation.

sexual sadism **Paraphilia** in which sexual arousal is associated with inflicting pain or humiliation.

shaping In **operant conditioning**, the development of a new response by reinforcing successively more similar versions of that response. Both desirable and undesirable behaviors may be learned in this manner.

shared psychotic disorder (folie à deux) A psychotic disturbance in which individuals develop a **delusion** similar to that of a person with whom they share a close relationship. Also known as *folie à deux*.

single-case experimental designs Research tactic in which an **independent variable** is manipulated for a single individual, allowing cause-and-effect conclusions but with limited **generalizability** (contrast with **case study method**).

situational phobia **Anxiety** involving enclosed places (for example, claustrophobia) or public transportation (for example, **fear** of flying).

sleep apnea Disorder involving brief periods when breathing ceases during sleep.

sleep efficiency (SE) Percentage of time actually spent sleeping of the total time spent in bed.

sleep terrors Episodes of apparent awakening from sleep, accompanied by signs of **panic,** followed by disorientation and amnesia for the incident. These occur during **nonrapid eye movement sleep** and so do not involve frightening dreams.

sleepwalking (somnambulism) **Parasomnia** that involves leaving the bed during **nonrapid eye movement sleep**. See also **somnambulism**.

social anxiety disorder (SAD) Extreme, enduring, irrational **fear** and avoidance of social or performance situations.

social phobia Extreme, enduring, irrational **fear** and avoidance of social or performance situations.

somatic symptom disorder Disorder involving extreme and long-lasting focus on multiple physical symptoms for which no medical cause is evident.

specific learning disorder Neurodevelopmental disorder characterized by academic performance that is substantially below what would be expected given the person's age, intelligence quotient (IQ) score, and education.

specific phobia Unreasonable **fear** of a specific object or situation that markedly interferes with daily life functioning.

standardization Process of establishing specific norms and requirements for a measurement technique to ensure it is used consistently across measurement occasions. This includes instructions for administering the measure, evaluating its findings, and comparing these to data for large numbers of people.

statistical significance Small probability of obtaining the observed research findings by chance.

stimulants A **psychoactive substance** that elevates **mood**, activity, and alertness; such substances include **amphetamines,** caffeine, **cocaine,** and **nicotine.**

stress Body's physiological response to a stressor, which is any event or change that requires adaptation.

stroke/cerebral vascular accident (CVA) Temporary blockage of blood vessels supplying the brain, or a rupture of vessels in the brain, resulting in temporary or permanent loss of brain functioning.

substance abuse A pattern of **psychoactive substance** use leading to significant distress or impairment in social and occupational roles and in hazardous situations.

substance dependence A maladaptive pattern of substance use characterized by the need for increased amounts to achieve the desired effect, negative physical effects when the substance is withdrawn, unsuccessful efforts to control its use, and substantial effort expended to seek it or recover from its effects. Also known as *addiction*.

substance intoxication A physiological reaction, such as impaired judgment and motor ability, as well as **mood** change, resulting from the ingestion of a **psychoactive substance.**

substance use The ingestion of psychoactive substances in moderate amounts that does not significantly interfere with social, educational, or occupational functioning.

substance use disorders When the recurrent use of alcohol and/or drugs causes clinically and functionally significant impairment, such as health problems, disability, and failure to meet major responsibilities at work, school, or home.

substance/medication-induced neurocognitive disorder Brain damage caused by prolonged use of drugs, often in combination with a poor diet.

substance-induced psychotic disorder Psychosis caused by the ingestion of medications, psychoactive drugs, or toxins.

substance-related and addictive disorders Range of problems associated with the use and abuse of drugs such as **alcohol, cocaine,** heroin, and other substances people use to alter the way they think, feel, and behave. These are extremely costly in human and financial terms.

suicidal attempts Effort made to kill oneself.

suicidal ideation Serious thoughts about committing suicide.

suicidal plans The formulation of a specific method of killing oneself.

superego In **psychoanalysis,** the psychic entity representing the internalized moral standards of parents and society.

susceptibility In genetics, **genes** that only slightly increase the risk of developing the disorder, but in contrast to the **deterministic** genes, these are more common in the population.

synaptic cleft Space between nerve cells where chemical transmitters act to move impulses from one **neuron** to the next.

systematic desensitization Behavioral therapy technique to diminish excessive **fears,** involving gradual exposure to the feared stimulus paired with a positive coping experience, usually relaxation.

taxonomy System of naming and **classification** (for example, of specimens) in science.

terminal button The end of an axon (of a neuron) where neurotransmitters are stored before release.

testability Ability of a **hypothesis,** for example, to be subjected to scientific scrutiny and to be accepted or rejected, a necessary condition for the hypothesis to be useful.

tobacco-related disorders Cognitive, biological, behavioral, and social problems associated with the use and abuse of **nicotine.**

token economy A social learning behavior modification system in which individuals earn items they can exchange for desired rewards by displaying appropriate behaviors.

tolerance The need for increased amounts of a substance to achieve the desired effect, and a diminished effect with continued use of the same amount.

Tourette's disorder Developmental disorder featuring multiple dysfunctional motor and vocal **tics.**

transference Psychoanalytic concept suggesting that clients may seek to relate to the therapist as they do to important authority figures, particularly their parents.

transinstitutionalization Movement of people with severe **mental illness** from large psychiatric hospitals to smaller group residences.

transvestic disorder **Paraphilia** in which individuals, usually males, are sexually aroused or receive gratification by wearing clothing of the opposite sex.

traumatic brain injury (TBI) Brain damage caused by a blow to the head or other trauma that injures the brain and results in diminished neurocognitive capacity.

trend Direction of change of a behavior or behaviors (for example, increasing or decreasing).

trichotillomania People's urge to pull out their own hair from anywhere on the body, including the scalp, eyebrows, and arm.

twin studies In genetics research, the comparison of twins with unrelated or less closely related individuals. If twins, particularly monozygotic twins who share identical **genotypes,** share common characteristics such as a disorder, even if they were reared in different environments, then strong evidence of genetic involvement in those characteristics exists.

type A behavior pattern Cluster of behaviors including excessive competitiveness, time-pressured impatience, accelerated speech, and anger, originally thought to promote high risk for heart disease.

type B behavior pattern Cluster of behaviors including a relaxed attitude, indifference to time pressure, and less forceful ambition; originally thought to promote low risk for heart disease.

unconditional positive regard Acceptance by the counselor of the client's feelings and actions without judgment or condemnation.

unconscious Part of the psychic makeup that is outside the awareness of the person.

vaginismus Recurring involuntary muscle spasms in the outer third of the vagina that interfere with sexual intercourse.

validity Degree to which a technique measures what it purports to measure.

variability Degree of change in a phenomenon over time.

vascular neurocognitive disorder Progressive brain disorder involving loss of cognitive functioning, caused by blockage of blood flow to the brain, that appears concurrently with other neurological signs and symptoms.

voyeuristic disorder Paraphilic disorder in which sexual arousal is derived from observing unsuspecting individuals undressing or naked.

vulnerability Susceptibility or tendency to develop a disorder.

Wernicke-Korsakoff syndrome Organic brain syndrome resulting from prolonged heavy **alcohol** use, involving confusion, unintelligible speech, and loss of motor coordination. It may be caused by a deficiency of thiamine, a vitamin metabolized poorly by heavy drinkers.

withdrawal A severely negative physiological reaction to removal of a **psychoactive substance**, which can be alleviated by the same or a similar substance.

withdrawal delirium (delirium tremens/DTs) The frightening hallucinations and body tremors that result when a heavy drinker withdraws from **alcohol**. Also known as *delirium tremens (DT)*.

withdrawal design Removing a treatment to note whether it has been effective. In **single-case experimental designs**, a behavior is measured **(baseline)**, an **independent variable** is introduced (intervention), and then the intervention is withdrawn. Because the behavior continues to be measured throughout (**repeated measurement**), any effects of the intervention can be noted.

References

Aaronson, C. J., Shear, M. K., Goetz, R. R., Allen, L. B., Barlow, D. H., White, K. S., & Gorman, J. M. (2008). Predictors and time course of response among panic disorder patients treated with cognitive-behavioral therapy. *Journal of Clinical Psychiatry, 69*(3), 418–424.

Aarsland, D., & Kurz, M. W. (2010). The epidemiology of dementia associated with Parkinson's disease. *Journal of the Neurological Sciences, 289*(1–2), 18–22.

Aarsland, D., Ballard, C., Rongve, A., Broadstock, M., & Svenningsson, P. (2012). Clinical trials of dementia with Lewy bodies and Parkinson's disease dementia. *Current Neurology and Neuroscience Reports, 12*(5), 492–501.

Abbey, S. E., & Garfinkel, P. E. (1991). Neurasthenia and chronic fatigue syndrome: The role of culture in the making of a diagnosis. *American Journal of Psychiatry, 148*, 1638–1646.

Abbott, D. W., de Zwaan, M., Mussell, M. P., Raymond, N. C., Seim, H. C., Crow, S. J., & Mitchell J. E. (1998). Onset of binge eating and dieting in overweight women: Implications for etiology, associated features and treatment. *Journal of Psychosomatic Research, 44*, 367–374.

Abbott, S. M., Soca, R., & Zee, P. C. (2014). Circadian rhythm sleep disorders. In *Primary Care Sleep Medicine* (pp. 297–309). New York, NY: Springer.

Abdul-Hamid, W. K., & Stein, G. (2012). The Surpu: Exorcism of antisocial personality disorder in ancient Mesopotamia. *Mental Health, Religion & Culture*. doi: 10.1080/13674676.2012.713337

Abel, G. G. (1989). Behavioral treatment of child molesters. In A. J. Stunkard & A. Baum (Eds.), *Perspectives in behavioral medicine: Eating, sleeping and sex* (pp. 223–242). Hillsdale, NJ: Erlbaum.

Abel, G. G., Barlow, D. H., Blanchard, E. B., & Guild, D. (1977). The components of rapists' sexual arousal. *Archives of General Psychiatry, 34*, 895–903.

Abel, G. G., Becker, J. V., Cunningham-Rathner, J., Mittelman, M., & Rouleau, J. L. (1988). Multiple paraphilic diagnoses among sex offenders. *Bulletin of the American Academy of Psychiatry and Law, 16*, 153–168.

Abel, K. M., Drake, R., & Goldstein, J. M. (2010). Sex differences in schizophrenia. *International Review of Psychiatry, 22*(5), 417–428.

Abela, J. R., & Hankin, B. L. (2011). Rumination as a vulnerability factor to depression during the transition from early to middle adolescence: A multiwave longitudinal study. *Journal of Abnormal Psychology, 120*(2), 259–271.

Abela, J. R., & Skitch, S. A. (2007). Dysfunctional attitudes, self-esteem, and hassles: Cognitive vulnerability to depression in children of affectively ill parents. *Behaviour Research and Therapy, 45*(6), 1127–1140.

Abela, J. R., Stolow, D., Mineka, S., Yao, S., Zhu, X. Z., & Hankin, B. L. (2011). Cognitive vulnerability to depressive symptoms in adolescents in urban and rural Hunan, China: A multiwave longitudinal study. *Journal of Abnormal Psychology, 120*(4), 765–778.

Abele, H., Wagner, P., Sonek, J., Hoopmann, M., Brucker, S., Artunc-Ulkumen, B., & Kagan, K. O. (2015). First trimester ultrasound screening for Down syndrome based on maternal age, fetal nuchal translucency and different combinations of the additional markers nasal bone, tricuspid and ductus venosus flow. *Prenatal Diagnosis, 35*(12), 1182–1186.

Abrahamson, D. J., Barlow, D. H., Sakheim, D. K., Beck, J. G., & Athanasiou, R. (1985). Effects of distraction on sexual responding in functional and dysfunctional men. *Behavior Therapy, 16*, 503–515.

Abramowitz, J. S., & Jacoby, R. J. (2015). Obsessive-compulsive and related disorders: A critical review of the new diagnostic class. *Annual Review of Clinical Psychology, 11*, 165–186.

Abramowitz, J. S., Taylor, S., & McKay, D. (2012). Exposure-based treatment for obsessive compulsive disorder. In G. Steketee (Ed.), *The Oxford handbook of obsessive compulsive and spectrum disorders* (pp. 322–364). New York, NY: Oxford University Press.

Abramson, L. Y., Metalsky, G. I., & Alloy, L. B. (1989). Hopelessness depression: A theory-based subtype of depression. *Psychological Review, 96*(2), 358–372.

Abramson, L. Y., Seligman, M. E. P., & Teasdale, J. D. (1978). Learned helplessness in humans: Critique and reformulation. *Journal of Abnormal Psychology, 87*, 49–74.

Abse, D. W. (1987). *Hysteria and related mental disorders: An approach to psychological medicine.* Bristol, UK: Wright.

Adachi, Y., Sato, C., Nishino, N., Ohryoji, F., Hayama, J., & Yamagami, T. (2009). A brief parental education for shaping sleep habits in 4-month-old infants. *Clinical Medicine & Research, 7*(3), 85–92. doi: 10.3121/cmr.2009.814

Adams, C., Lockton, E., Freed, J., Gaile, J., Earl, G., McBean, K., & Law, J. (2012). The Social Communication Intervention Project: A randomized controlled trial of the effectiveness of speech and language therapy for school-age children who have pragmatic and social communication problems with or without autism spectrum disorder.

International Journal of Language & Communication Disorders, 47(3), 233–244. doi: 10.1111/j.1460-6984.2011.00146.x

Adams, T. D., Davidson, L. E., Litwin, S. E., Kolotkin, R. L., LaMonte, M. J., Pendleton, R. C., & Hunt, S. C. (2012). Health benefits of gastric bypass surgery after 6 years. *JAMA: Journal of the American Medical Association, 308*(11), 1122–1131. doi: 10.1001/2012.jama.11164

Adams, T. D., Gress, R. E., Smith, S. C., Halverson, R. C., Simper, S. C., Rosamond, W. D., & Hunt, S. C. (2007). Long-term mortality after gastric bypass surgery. *New England Journal of Medicine, 357*(8), 753–761.

Addington v. Texas, 99 S. Ct. 1804 (1979). Addington, J., Liu, L., Buchy, L., Cadenhead, K. S., Cannon, T. D., Cornblatt, B. A., & Woods, S. W. (2015). North American prodrome longitudinal study (NAPLS 2): the prodromal symptoms. *The Journal of Nervous and Mental Disease, 203*(5), 328–335.

Addis, M. E. (2008). Gender and depression in men. *Clinical Psychology: Science and Practice, 15*(3), 153–168.

Ader, R., & Cohen, N. (1975). Behaviorally conditioned immunosuppression. *Psychosomatic Medicine, 37*, 333–340.

Ader, R., & Cohen, N. (1993). Psychoneuroimmunology: Conditioning and stress. *Annual Review of Psychology, 44*, 53–85.

Adler, C. M., Côte, G., Barlow, D. H., & Hillhouse, J. J. (1994). *Phenomenological relationships between somatoform, anxiety, and psychophysiological disorders.* Unpublished manuscript.

Adler, N. E. (2013). Health disparities taking on the challenge. *Perspectives on Psychological Science, 8*(6), 679–681.

Afari, N., & Buchwald, D. (2003). Chronic fatigue syndrome: A review. *American Journal of Psychiatry, 160*, 221–236.

Agatisa, P., Matthews, K., Bromberger, J., Edmundowicz, D., Chang, Y., & Sutton-Tyrell, K. (2005). Coronary and aortic calcification in women with major depression history. *Archives of Internal Medicine, 165*, 1229–1236.

Aggarwal, N. K., Nicasio, A. V., DeSilva, R., Boiler, M., & Lewis-Fernández, R. (2013). Barriers to implementing the *DSM-5* cultural formulation interview: A qualitative study. *Culture, Medicine, and Psychiatry, 37*(3), 505–533.

Agras, W. S. (1987). *Eating disorders: Management of obesity, bulimia, and anorexia nervosa.* Elmsford, NY: Pergamon.

Agras, W. S. (2001). The consequences and costs of eating disorders. *Psychiatric Clinics of North America, 24*, 371–379.

Agras, W. S., Sylvester, D., & Oliveau, D. (1969). The epidemiology of common fears and phobia. *Comprehensive Psychiatry, 10*, 151–156.

Agras, W. S., Telch, C. F., Arnow, B., Eldredge, K., & Marnell, M. (1997). One year follow-up of cognitive-behavioral therapy of obese individuals with binge eating disorder. *Journal of Consulting and Clinical Psychology, 65*, 343–347.

Agras, W. S., Walsh, B. T., Fairburn, C. G., Wilson, G. T., & Kraemer, H. C. (2000). A multicenter comparison of cognitive-behavioral therapy and interpersonal psychotherapy for bulimia nervosa. *Archives of General Psychiatry, 57*, 459–466.

Agras W. S., Hammer, L. D., Huffman L. C., Mascola, A., Bryson, S. W. , & Danaher, C. (2012). Improving healthy eating in families with a toddler at risk for overweight: A cluster randomized controlled trial. *Journal of Developmental and Behavioral Pediatrics, 33*(7), 529–534.

Aguirre, E., Woods, R. T., Spector, A., & Orrell, M. (2013). Cognitive stimulation for dementia: a systematic review of the evidence of effectiveness from randomised controlled trials. *Ageing Research Reviews, 12*(1), 253–262.

Ahern, R. W., & Coleman-Eufinger, C. (2013). New promises: Specialized dockets as partnerships between treatment and the criminal justice system. In K. Yeager, D. Cutler, D. Svendsen, & G. M. Sills (Eds.), *Modern community mental health: An interdisciplinary approach* (pp. 475–483). New York, NY: Oxford University Press.

Ahima, R. S., & Lazar, M. A. (2013). The health risk of obesity—better metrics imperative. *Science, 341*(6148), 856–858.

Ahlers, C. J., Schaefer, G. A., Mundt, I. A., Roll, S., Englert, H., Willich, S. N., & Beier, K. M. (2011). How unusual are the contents of paraphilias? Paraphilia-associated sexual arousal patterns in a community based sample of men. *Journal of Sexual Medicine, 8*(5), 1362–1370.

Ahmed, A. O., Green, B. A., Goodrum, N. M., Doane, N. J., Birgenheir, D., & Buckley, P. F. (2013). Does a latent class underlie schizotypal personality disorder? Implications for schizophrenia. *Journal of Abnormal Psychology, 122*, 475–491. doi:10.1037/a0032713

Ahmed, I., & Thorpy, M. (2012). Narcolepsy and idiopathic hypersomnia. In M. S. Badr (Ed.), *Essentials of sleep medicine: An approach for clinical pulmonology* (pp. 297–314). New York, NY: Humana Press.

Aikins, D. E., & Craske, M. G. (2001). Cognitive theories of generalized anxiety disorder. *Psychiatric Clinics of North America, 24*, 57–74.

Akiskal, H. (2006). Special issue on circular insanity and beyond: Historic contributions of French psychiatry to contemporary concepts and research on bipolar disorder. *Journal of Affective Disorders, 96*, 141–143.

Akiskal, H. S. (2009). Dysthymia, cyclothymia, and hyperthymia. In M. G. Gelder, N. C. Andreasen, J. J. López-Ibor Jr., & J. R. Geddes (Eds.), *New Oxford textbook of psychiatry* (2nd ed., Vol. 1, pp. 680–692). Oxford, UK: Oxford University Press.

Akiskal, H. S., & Cassano, G. B. (Eds.) (1997). *Dysthymia and the spectrum of chronic depressions*. New York, NY: Guilford.

al'Absi, M., & Wittmers, L. E., Jr. (2003). Enhanced adrenocortical responses to stress in hypertension-prone men and women. *Annals of Behavioral Medicine, 25*, 25–33.

Alba-Ferrara, L., Fernyhough, C., Weis, S., Mitchell, R. L. C., & Hausmann, M. (2012). Contributions of emotional prosody comprehension deficits to the formation of auditory verbal hallucinations in schizophrenia. *Clinical Psychology Review, 32*(4), 244–250. doi: 10.1016/j.cpr.2012.02.003

Albano, A. M., & Barlow, D. H. (1996). Breaking the vicious cycle: Cognitive-behavioral group treatment for socially anxious youth. In E. D. Hibbs & P. S. Jensen (Eds.), *Psychosocial treatments for child and adolescent disorders* (pp. 43–62). Washington, DC: American Psychological Association.

Albano, A. M., & Hack, S. (2004). Children and adolescents. In R. G. Heimberg, C. L. Turk, & D. S. Mennin (Eds.), *Generalized anxiety disorder: Advances in research and practice* (pp. 383–408). New York, NY: Guilford.

Albano, A. M., Chorpita, B. F., & Barlow, D. H. (1996). Childhood anxiety disorders. In E. J. Mash & R. A. Barkley (Eds.), *Child psychopathology* (pp. 196–241). New York, NY: Guilford.

Albano, A. M., Miller, P. P., Zarate, R., Côté, G., & Barlow, D. H. (1997). Behavioral assessment and treatment of PTSD in prepubertal children: Attention to development factors and innovative strategies in the case study of a family. *Cognitive and Behavioral Practice, 4*, 245–262.

Albert, C., Chae, C., Rexrode, K., Manson, J., & Kawachi, I. (2005). Phobic anxiety and risk of coronary heart disease and sudden cardiac among women. *Circulation, 111*, 480–487.

Albertini, R. S., & Phillips, K. A. (1999). Thirty-three cases of body dysmorphic disorder in children and adolescents. *Journal of the American Academy of Child and Adolescent Psychiatry, 38*(4), 453–459.

Albon, T., & Schneider, S. (2007). Psychotherapy of childhood anxiety disorders: A meta-analysis. *Psychother Psychosom, 76*, 15–24.

Albright, J. A., Stevens, S. A., & Beussman, D. J. (2012). Detecting ketamine in beverage residues: Application in date rape detection. *Drug Testing and Analysis, 4*(5), 337–341. doi: 10.1002/dta.335

Alda, M. (2015). Lithium in the treatment of bipolar disorder: Pharmacology and pharmacoge-netics. *Molecular Psychiatry, 20*, 661–670.

Alessi, S. M., Roll, J. M., Reilly, M. P., & Johanson, C. E. (2002). Establishment of a diazepam preference in human volunteers following a differential-conditioning history of placebo versus diazepam choice. *Experimental and Clinical Psychopharmacology, 10*, 77–83.

Alexander, F. G. (1939). Emotional factors in essential hypertension: Presentation of a tentative hypothesis. *Psychosomatic Medicine, 1*, 175–179.

Alexander, F. G. (1950). *Psychosomatic medicine*. New York, NY: Norton.

Alexander, F. G., & Selesnick, S. T. (1966). *The history of psychiatry: An evaluation of psychiatric thought and practice from prehistoric times to the present*. New York, NY: Harper & Row.

Alexopoulos, G., Katz, I., Bruce, M., Heo, M., Have, T., Raue, P., Reynolds, C. F., III., (2005). Remission in depressed geriatric primary care patients: A report from the PROSPECT study. *American Journal of Psychiatry, 162*, 718–724.

Alexopoulos, G. S. (2005). Depression in the elderly. *Lancet, 365*, 1961–1970.

Ali, S. R., Liu, W. M., & Humedian, M. (2004). Islam 101: Understanding the religion and therapy implications. *Professional Psychology: Research and Practice, 35*(6), 635.

Alim, T. N., Feder, A., Graves, R. E., Wang, Y., Weaver, J., Westphal, M., & Charney, D. S. (2008). Trauma, resilience, and recovery in a high-risk African-American population. *The American Journal of Psychiatry, 165*(12), 1566–1575.

Allan, R. & Ungar, M. (2014). Resilience-building interventions with children, adolescents, and their families. In S. Prince-Embury & D. H., Saklofske (Eds.). *Resilience Interventions for Youth in Diverse Populations* (pp. 447–462). New York, NY: Springer.

Allen, J., DeMyer, M. K., Norton, J. A., Pontius, W., & Yang, G. (1971). Intellectuality in parents of psychotic, subnormal, and normal children. *Journal of Autism and Childhood Schizophrenia, 1*(3), 311–326.

Allen, J. J., & Movius, H. L. (2000). The objective assessment of amnesia in dissociative identity disorder using event-related potentials. *International Journal of Psychophysiology, 38*, 21–41.

Allen, J. L., Lavallee K. L., Herren C., Ruhe, K., & Schneider, S. (2010). DSM-IV criteria for childhood separation anxiety disorder: Informant, age, and sex differences. *Journal of Anxiety Disorders, 24*(8), 946–952. doi: 10.1016/j.janxdis.2010.06.022

Allen, K., Bloscovitch, J., & Mendes, W. B. (2002). Cardiovascular reactivity in the presence of pets, friends, and spouses: The truth about cats and dogs. *Psychosomatic Medicine, 64*, 727–739.

Allen, K. L., Byrne, S. M., Oddy, W. H., & Crosby, R. D. (2013). *DSM–IV–TR* and *DSM-5* eating disorders in adolescents: Prevalence, stability, and psychosocial correlates in a population-based sample of male and female adolescents. *Journal of Abnormal Psychology, 122*(3), 720–732.

Allen, L. A., Woolfolk, R. L., Escobar, J. I., Gara, M. A., & Hamer, R. M. (2006). Cognitive-behavioral therapy for somatization disorder: A randomized controlled trial. *Archives of Internal Medicine, 166*(14), 1512–1518.

Allen, L. B., White, K. S., Barlow, D. H., Shear, M. K., Gorman, J. M., & Woods, S. W. (2010). Cognitive-behavior therapy (CBT) for panic disorder: Relationship of anxiety and depression comorbidity with treatment outcome. *Journal of Psychopathology & Behavioral Assessment, 32*(2), 185–192.

Allen, L. S., & Gorski, R. A. (1992). Sexual orientation and the size of the anterior commissure in the human brain. *Proceedings of the National Academy of Science, 89*, 7199–7202.

Allen, N. J., & Barres, B. A. (2009). Neuroscience: Glia—more than just brain glue. *Nature, 457*(7230), 675–677.

Allen, P., & Modinos, G. (2012). Structural neuro-imaging in psychotic patients with auditory verbal hallucinations. In J. D. Blom & I. E. C. Sommer (Eds.), *Hallucinations* (pp. 251–265). New York, NY: Springer.

Allender, S., Peto, V., Scarborough, P., Boxer, A., and Rayner, M. (2007). *Coronary heart disease statistics*. Oxford, England: British Heart Foundation & Stroke Association.

Aller, R., & Aller, G. (1997). An institutional response to patient/family complaints. In A. E. Shamoo (Ed.), *Ethics in neuro-biological research with human subjects: The Baltimore Conference on Ethics* (pp. 155–172). Amsterdam, The Netherlands: Gordon and Breach.

Alloy, L., & Abramson, L. (2006). Prospective incidence of first onsets and recurrences of depression in individuals at high and low cognitive risk for depression. *Journal of Abnormal Psychology, 115*, 145–156.

Alloy, L., Abramson, L. Y., Hogan, M. E., Whitehouse, W. G., Rose, D. T., Robinson, M. S., & Lapkin, J. B. (2000). The Temple-Wisconsin cognitive vulnerability to depression project: Lifetime history of axis I psychopathology in individuals at high and low cognitive risk for depression. *Journal of Abnormal Psychology, 109*, 403–418.

Alloy, L., Abramson, L., Safford, S., & Gibb, B. (2006). The cognitive vulnerability to depression (CVD) project: Current findings and future directions. In L. B. Alloy & J. H. Riskind (Eds.), *Cognitive vulnerability to emotional disorders* (pp. 33–61). Hillsdale, NJ: Erlbaum.

Alloy, L. B., & Abramson, L. Y. (2010). The role of the behavioral approach system (BAS) in bipolar spectrum disorders. *Current Directions in Psychological Science, 19*(3), 189–194.

Alloy, L. B., Abramson, L. Y., Urosevic, S., Bender, R. E., & Wagner, C. A. (2009). Longitudinal predictors of bipolar spectrum disorders: A behavioral approach system (BAS) perspective. *Clinical Psychology* (New York), *16*(2), 206–226.

Alloy, L. B., Bender, R. E., Whitehouse, W. G., Wagner, C. A., Liu, R. T., Grant, D. A., & Abramson, L. Y. (2012). High Behavioral Approach System (BAS) sensitivity, reward responsiveness, and goal-striving predict first onset of bipolar spectrum disorders: A prospective behavioral high-risk design. *Journal of Abnormal Psychology, 121*(2), 339–351.

Alloy, L. B., Nusslock, R., & Boland, E. M. (2015). The development and course of bipolar spectrum disorders: An integrated reward and circadian rhythm dysregulation model. *Annual Review of Clinical Psychology, 11*, 213.

Alpers, G. W. (2009). Ambulatory assessment of panic disorder and specific phobia. *Psychological Assessment, 21*, 476–485.

Alter, H. J., Mikovits, J. A., Switzer, W. M., Ruscetti, F. W., Lo, S. C., Klimas, N., . . . Lipkin, W. I. (2012). A multicenter blinded analysis indicates no association between chronic fatigue syndrome/myalgic encephalomyelitis and either xenotropic murine leukemia virus-related virus or polytropic murine leukemia virus. *MBio, 3*(5), e0026612.

Althof, S. (2006). The psychology of premature ejaculation: Therapies and consequences. *Journal of Sexual Medicine, 3*, 324–331.

Althof, S. E. (2007). Treatment of rapid ejaculation: Psychotherapy, pharmacotherapy, and combined therapy. In S. R. Leiblum (Ed.), *Principles and practice of sex therapy* (4th ed., pp. 212–240). New York, NY: Guilford.

Altman, M., & Wilfley, D. E. (2015). Evidence update on the treatment of overweight and obesity in children and adolescents. *Journal of Clinical Child & Adolescent Psychology, 44*(4), 521–537.

Altshuler, L. L., Kupka, R. W., Hellemann, G., Frye, M. A., Sugar, C. A., McElroy, S. L., & Suppes, T. (2010). Gender and depressive symptoms in 711 patients with bipolar disorder evaluated prospectively in the Stanley Foundation bipolar treatment outcome network. *American Journal of Psychiatry, 167*(6), 708–715.

Alzheimer's Association. (2011). Alzheimer's dis-ease facts and figures. *Alzheimer's & Dementia: The Journal of the Alzheimer's Association, 7*, 208–244.

Alzheimer's Association, (2015). 2015 Alzheimer's disease facts and figures. *Alzheimer's & Dementia* (Vol. 11). Chicago, IL: Alzheimer's Association.

Amad, A., Ramoz, N., Thomas, P., Jardri, R., & Gorwood, P. (2014). Genetics of borderline personality disorder: systematic review and proposal of an integrative model. *Neuroscience & Biobehavioral Reviews, 40*, 6–19.

Amat, J., Baratta, B. V., Paul, E., Bland, S. T., Watkins, L. R., & Maier, S. F. (2005). Medial prefrontal cortex determines how stressor controllability affects behavior and dorsal raphe nucleus. *Nature Neuroscience, 8*, 365–371.

American Bar Association Standing Committee on Association Standards for Criminal Justice. (1984). *Criminal justice and mental health standards*. Chicago, IL: Author.

American College of Obstetricians and Gynecologists. (2002). Clinical management guidelines for obstetricians–gynecologists: Premenstrual syndrome. *ACOG Practice Bulletin*. No. 15. Washington, DC: American College of Obstetricians and Gynecologists.

American Law Institute. (1962). *Model penal code: Proposed official draft*. Philadelphia, PA: Author.

American Psychiatric Association. (1980). *Diagnostic and statistical manual of mental disorders* (3rd ed.). Washington, DC: Author.

American Psychiatric Association. (1983). American Psychiatric Association statement on the insanity defense. *American Journal of Psychiatry, 140*, 681–688.

American Psychiatric Association. (2000a). *Diagnostic and statistical manual of mental disorders* (4th ed., text revision). Washington, DC: Author.

American Psychiatric Association. (2000b). Substance use disorders: Alcohol, cocaine, opioids. In *Practice guidelines for the treatment of psychiatric disorders: Compendium 2000* (pp. 139–238). Washington, DC: Author.

American Psychiatric Association. (2004). Practice guideline for the treatment of patients with schizophrenia (2nd ed.). *American Journal of Psychiatry, 161*(Suppl.), 1–56.

American Psychiatric Association. (2006). Practice guideline for the psychiatric evaluation of adults (2nd ed.). *American Journal of Psychiatry, 163*(Suppl.), 1–36.

American Psychiatric Association. (2007). Practice guidelines for the treatment of patients with substance use disorders (2nd ed.). *American Journal of Psychiatry, 164*(Suppl.), 1–14.

American Psychiatric Association. (2010). Clinical practice guidelines. *American Journal of Psychiatry, 167*(10).

American Psychiatric Association Practice Guideline. (2010). *Practice guideline for the treatment of patients with major depressive disorder* (3rd ed.). Washington, DC: American Psychiatric Association. Retrieved from http://www.psychiatryonline.com/pracGuide/pracGuideTopic_7.aspx

American Psychiatric Association. (2010a). *APA practice guidelines for treatment of patients with eating disorders* (3rd ed.). Retrieved from http://www.psychiatryonline.com/content.aspx?aID5138866

American Psychiatric Association. (2010b). DSM-5 Development: Sleep–Wake Disorders. Retrieved November 6, 2012, from http://www.dsm5.org/ProposedRevision/Pages/Sleep-WakeDisorders.aspx

American Psychiatric Association. (2013). *Diagnostic and statistical manual of mental disorders* (5th ed.). Washington, D.C.: Author.

American Psychological Association. (2002a). Ethical principles of psychologists and code of conduct. *American Psychologist, 57*, 1060–1073.

American Psychological Association. (2010a). 2010 Amendments to the 2002 "Ethical principles of psychologists and code of conduct." *American Psychologist, 65*(5), 493–493.

American Psychological Association. (2010b). Report of the ethics committee, 2009. *American Psychologist, 65*(5), 483–492.

American Psychological Association. (2012). *The APA guidelines for the undergraduate psychology major version 2.0*. Washington, D: American Psychological Association.

American Psychological Association. (2013). *APA guidelines for the undergraduate psychology major*. Washington, DC: Author.

American Psychological Association Presidential Task Force. (2006). Evidence-based practice in psychology. *American Psychologist, 61*, 271–285.

American Psychological Association Task Force on Gender Identity and Gender Variance. (2008). *Report of the Task Force on Gender Identity and Gender Variance*. Washington, DC: Author.

American Society of Plastic Surgeons. (2012). National cosmetic procedures. Retrieved from http://www.plasticsurgery.org/news-and-resources/2012-plastic-surgery-statistics.html

Ames, G. E., Patel, R. H., McMullen, J. S., Thomas, C. S., Crook, J. E., Lynch, S. A., & Lutes, L. D. (2014). Improving maintenance of lost weight following a commercial liquid meal replacement program: a preliminary study. *Eating Behaviors, 15*(1), 95–98.

Amieva, H., Mokri, H., Le Goff, M., Meillon, C., Jacqmin-Gadda, H., Foubert-Samier, A., . . . Dartigues, J. F. (2014). Compensatory mechanisms in higher-educated subjects with Alzheimer's disease: a study of 20 years of cognitive decline. *Brain, 137*(4), 1167–1175.

Anandam, A., Akinnusi, M., Kufel, T., Porhomayon, J., & El-Solh, A. A. (2013). Effects of dietary weight loss on obstructive sleep apnea: a meta-analysis. *Sleep and Breathing, 17*(1), 227–234.

Anastopoulos, A., Sommer, J., & Schatz, N. (2009). ADHD and family functioning. *Current Attention Disorders Reports, 1*(4), 167–170. doi: 10.1007/s12618-009-0023-2

Andersen, B. L., & Cyranowski, J. M. (1994). Women's sexual self-schema. *Journal of Personality and Social Psychology, 67*(6), 1079–1100.

Andersen, B. L., Cyranowski, J. M., & Espindle, D. (1999). Men's sexual self-schema. *Journal of Personality and Social Psychology, 76*(4), 645–661.

Andersen, B. L., Farrar, W. B., Golden-Kreutz, D., Emery, C. F., Glaser, R., Crespin, T., & Carson, W. E., III. (2007). Distress reduction from a psychological intervention contributes to improved health for cancer patients. *Brain, Behavior, and Immunity, 21*, 953–961.

Andersen, B. L., Yang, H., Farrar, W. B., Golden-Kreutz, D. M., Emery, C. F., Thornton, L. M., & Carson, W. E., III. (2008). Psychologic intervention improves survival for breast cancer patients: A randomized clinical trial. *Cancer, 113*, 3450–3458.

Anderson, D. K., Lord, C., Risi, S., DiLavore, P. S., Shulman, C., Thurm, A., & Pickles, A. (2007). Patterns of growth in verbal abilities among children with autism spectrum disorder. *Journal of Consulting and Clinical Psychology, 75*(4), 594–604.

Anderson, J. L., Sellbom, M., Wygant, D. B., Salekin, R. T., & Krueger, R. F. (2014). Examining the associations between DSM-5 Section III antisocial personality disorder traits and psychopathy in community and university samples. *Journal of Personality Disorders, 28*(5), 675–697.

Andersson, E., Hedman, E., Enander, J., Djurfeldt, D. R., Ljótsson, B., Cervenka, S., . . . Rück, C. (2015). D-Cycloserine vs placebo as adjunct to cognitive behavioral therapy for Obsessive-compulsive disorder and interaction with antidepressants: A randomized clinical trial. *JAMA Psychiatry, 72*(7):659–667.

Andrasik, F. (2000). Biofeedback. In D. I. Mostofsky & D. H. Barlow (Eds.), *The management of stress and anxiety in medical disorders* (pp. 66–83). Needham Heights, MA: Allyn & Bacon.

Andreasen, N. C. (1987). Creativity and mental illness: Prevalence rates in writers and their first-degree relatives. *American Journal of Psychiatry, 144*(10), 1288–1292.

Andreasen, N. C. (2012). Schizophrenia: A conceptual history. In M. G. Gelder, N. C. Andreasen, J. J. Lopez-Ibor, Jr., & J. R. Geddes (Eds.), *New Oxford textbook of psychiatry* (2nd. ed., Vol. 1, pp. 521–526). New York, NY: Oxford University Press.

Andrews, G., Hobbs, M. J., Borkovec, T. D., Beesdo, K., Craske, M. G., Heimberg, R. G., & Stanley, M. A. (2010). Generalized worry disorder: A review of DSM-IV generalized anxiety disorder and options for DSM-V. *Depression and Anxiety, 27*(2), 134–147. doi: 10.1002/da.20658

Aneshensel, C. S., Pearlin, L. I., Mullan, J. T., Zarit, S. H., & Whitlatch, C. J. (1995). *Profiles in caregiving: The unexpected career.* San Diego, CA: Academic.

Anglin, D. M., Lighty, Q., Greenspoon, M., & Ellman, L. M. (2014). Racial discrimination is associated with distressing subthreshold positive psychotic symptoms among US urban ethnic minority young adults. *Social Psychiatry and Psychiatric Epidemiology, 49*(10), 1545–1555.

Angst, J. (2009). Course and prognosis of mood disorders. In M. G. Gelder, N. C. Andreasen, J. J. López-Ibor, Jr., & J. R. Geddes (Eds.), *New Oxford textbook of psychiatry* (2nd ed., Vol. 1, pp. 665–669). Oxford, UK: Oxford University Press.

Angst, J., & Grobler, C. (2015) Unipolar mania: A necessary diagnostic concept. *European Archives of Psychiatry and Clinical Neuroscience, 265*, 273–280.

Angst, J., & Sellaro, R. (2000). Historical perspectives and natural history of bipolar disorder. *Biological Psychiatry, 48*(6), 445–457.

Angst, J., Cui, L. H., Swendsen, J., Rothen, S., Cravchik, A., & Merikangas, K. R. (2010). Major depressive disorder with subthreshold bipolarity in the National Comorbidity Survey Replication. *American Journal of Psychiatry, 167*(10), 1194–1201.

Angst, J. Azorin, J.-M., Bowden, C. L., Perugi, G., Vieta, E., Gamma, A., & Young, A. H. (2011). Prevalence and characteristics of undiagnosed bipolar disorders in patients with a major depressive episode. *Archives of General Psychiatry, 68*(8), 791–798.

Angstman, K. B., & Rasmussen, N. H. (2011). Personality disorders: review and clinical application in daily practice. *American Family Physician, 84*(11), 1253.

Anisman, H., Zaharia, M. D., Meaney, M. J., & Merali, Z. (1998). Do early life events permanently alter behavioral and hormonal responses to stressors? *International Journal of Developmental Neuroscience, 16*(3–4), 149–164.

Ansell, E., Sanislow, C., McGlashan, T., & Grilo, C. (2007). Psychosocial impairment and treatment utilization by patients with border-line personality disorder, other personality disorders, mood and anxiety disorders, and a healthy comparison group. *Comprehensive Psychiatry, 48*(4), 329–336.

Anson, M., Veale, D., & de Silva, P. (2012). Social-evaluative versus self-evaluative appearance concerns in body dysmorphic disorder. *Behavior Research and Therapy, 50*(12), 753–760. doi: 10.1016/j.brat.2012.09.003

Anton, B., & Leff, L. P. (2006). A novel bivalent morphine/heroin vaccine that prevents relapse to heroin addiction in rodents. *Vaccine, 24*(16), 3232–3240.

Antoni, M. H. (2012). *Stress, coping, and health in HIV/AIDS.* The Oxford Handbook of Stress, Heath, and Coping. Oxford, UK: Oxford University Press.

Antoni, M. H., & Lutgendorf, S. (2007). Psychosocial factors and disease progression in cancer. *Current Directions in Psychological Science, 16*, 42–46.

Antoni, M. H., Cruess, D. G., Cruess, S., Lutgendorf, S., Kumar, M., Ironson, G., & Schneiderman, N. (2000). Cognitive-behavioral stress management intervention effects on anxiety, 24-hr urinary norepinephrine output, and T-cytotoxic/suppressor cells over time among symptomatic HIV-infected gay men. *Journal of Consulting and Clinical Psychology, 68*, 31–45.

Antoni, M. H., Lechner, S., Diaz, A., Vargas, S., Holley, H., Phillips, K., & Blombery, B. (2009). Cognitive behavioral stress management effects on psychosocial and psychological adaptation in women undergoing treatment for breast cancer. *Brain, Behavior, and Immunity, 23*, 580–591.

Antoni, M. H., Lechner, S., Kazi, A., Wimberly, S., Sifre, T., Urcuyo, K., & Carver, C. S. (2006). How stress management improves quality of life after treatment for breast cancer. *Journal of Consulting and Clinical Psychology, 74*, 1143–1152.

Antony, M. M., & Barlow, D. H. (2002). Specific phobias. In D. H. Barlow, *Anxiety and its disorders: The nature and treatment of anxiety and panic* (2nd ed.). New York, NY: Guilford.

Antony, M. M., & Barlow, D. H. (Eds.). (2010). *Handbook of assessment and treatment planning for psychological disorders* (2nd ed.). New York, NY: Guilford.

Antony, M. M., Brown, T. A., & Barlow, D. H. (1997a). Heterogeneity among specific phobia types in DSM-IV. *Behavior Research and Therapy, 35*, 1089–1100.

Antony, M. M., Brown, T. A., & Barlow, D. H. (1997b). Response to hyperventilation and 5.5% CO2 inhalation of subjects with types of specific phobia, panic disorder, or no mental disorder. *American Journal of Psychiatry, 154*, 1089–1095.

Antony, M. M., Craske, M. G., & Barlow, C. H. (2006). *Mastering your fears and phobias: Workbook.* New York, NY: Oxford University Press.

Aouizerate, B., Rotge, J., Martin-Guehl, C., Cuny, E., Rougier, A., Guehl, D., & Tignol, J. (2006). A systematic review of psychsurgical treatments for obsessive-compulsive disorder: Does deep brain stimulation represent the future trend in psychosurgery? *Clinical Neuropsychiatry, 3*(6), 391–403.

Apfelbaum, B. (2000). Retarded ejaculation: A much misunderstood syndrome. In S. R. Leiblum & R. C. Rosen (Eds.), *Principles and practice of sex therapy* (3rd ed., pp. 205–241). New York, NY: Guilford.

Arai, J. A., Li, S., Hartley, D. M., & Feig, L. A. (2009). Transgenerational rescue of a genetic defect in long-term potentiation and memory formation by juvenile enrichment. *The Journal of Neuroscience, 29*(5), 1496–1502.

Arcelus J., Mitchell, A. J., Wales, J., & Nielsen, S. (2011). Mortality rates in patients with anorexia nervosa and other eating disorders: A meta-analysis of 36 studies. *Archives of General Psychiatry, 68*(7), 724–731. doi: 10.1001/archgenpsychiatry.2011.74

Arenkiel, B. R., & Ehlers, M. D. (2009). Molecular genetics and imaging technologies for circuit-based neuroanatomy. *Nature, 461*(7266), 900–907.

Agras, W. S., Lock, J., Brandt, H., Bryson, S. W., Dodge, E., Halmi, K. A.. & Woodside, B. (2014). Comparison of 2 family therapies for adolescent anorexia nervosa: a randomized parallel trial. *JAMA Psychiatry, 71*(11), 1279–1286.

Armbruster, D., Mueller, A., Moser, D. A., Lesch, K. P., Brocke, B., & Kirschbaum, C. (2009). Interaction effect of D4 dopamine receptor gene and serotonin transporter promoter polymorphism on the cortisol stress response. *Behavioral Neuroscience, 123*(6), 1288–1295.

Armstrong, T. (2010). *Neurodiversity: Discovering the extraordinary gifts of autism, ADHD, dyslexia, and other brain differences.* Boston: Da Capo Press.

Aronow, E., Weiss, K. A., & Reznikoff, M. (2013). *A practical guide to the Thematic Apperception Test: The TAT in clinical practice.* London: Routledge.

Arria, A. M., Garnier-Dykstra, L. M., Cook, E. T., Caldeira, K. M., Vincent, K. B., Baron, R. A., & O'Grady, K. E. (2013). Drug use patterns in young adulthood and post-college employment. *Drug and Alcohol Dependence, 127* (1–3), 23–30. doi: http://dx.doi.org/10.1016/j.drugalcdep.2012.06.001

Arrindell, W. A., Eisemann, M., Richter, J., Oei, T. P. S., Caballo, V. E., van der Ende, J., & Hudson, B. L. (2003a). Phobic anxiety in 11 nations Part I: Dimensional constancy of the five-factor model. *Behaviour Research and Therapy, 41*, 461–479.

Arrindell, W. A., Eisemann, M., Richter, J., Oei, T. P. S., Caballo, V. E., van der Ende, J., & Zaldívar, F. (2003b). Masculinity–feminity as a national characteristic and its relationship with national agoraphobic fear levels: Fodor's sex role hypothesis revitalized. *Behaviour Research and Therapy, 41*, 795–807.

Arterburn, D. E., & Fisher, D. P. (2014). The current state of the evidence for bariatric surgery. *Journal of the American Medical Association, 312*(9), 898–899.

Arterburn, D. E., Olsen, M. K., Smith, V. A., Livingston, E. H., Van Scoyoc, L., Yancy, W. S., . . . Maciejewski, M. L. (2015). Association between bariatric surgery and long-term survival. *Journal of the American Medical Association, 313*(1), 62–70.

Asberg, M., Nordstrom, P., & Traskman-Bendz, L. (1986). Cerebrospinal fluid studies in suicide: An overview. *Annals of the American Academy of Science, 487*, 243–255.

Ascher-Svanum, H., Zhu, B., Faries, D. E., Salkever, D., Slade, E. P., Peng, X., & Conley, R. R. (2010). The cost of relapse and the predictors of relapse in the treatment of schizophrenia. *BMC Psychiatry, 10*(1), 2.

Aschoff, J., & Wever, R. (1962). Spontanperiodik des Menschen die Ausschulus aller Zeitgeber. *Die Naturwissenschaften, 49*, 337–342.

Ashare, R. L., Karlawish, J. H., Wileyto, E. P., Pinto, A., & Lerman, C. (2012). APOE _4, an Alzheimer's disease susceptibility allele, and smoking cessation. *The Pharmacogenomics Journal*. doi: 10.1038/tpj.2012.49

Ashkenazi, S., Black, J. M., Abrams, D. A., Hoeft, F., & Menon, V. (2013). Neurobiological underpinnings of math and reading learning disabilities. *Journal of Learning Disabilities*. doi: 10.1177/0022219413483174

Ashley, L. L., & Boehlke, K. K. (2012). Pathological gambling: A general overview. *Journal of Psychoactive Drugs, 44*(1), 27–37. doi: 10.1080/02791072.2012.662078

Askew, C., Hagel, A., & Morgan, J. (2015). Vicarious learning of children's social-anxiety-related fear beliefs and emotion Stroop bias. *Emotion, 15*, 501–510.

Asmundson, G. J., & Carleton, R. N. (2009). Fear of pain. In M. M. Antony & M. B. Stein (Eds.), *Oxford handbook of anxiety and related disorders* (pp. 551–561). Oxford, UK: Oxford University Press.

Asnaani, A., Gutner, C., Hinton, D., & Hofmann, S. G. (2009). Panic disorder, panic attacks, and panic attack symptoms across race-ethnic groups: Results of the Collaborative Psychiatric Epidemiology Survey. *CNS Neuroscience and Therapeutics, 15*, 249–254.

Asnaani, A., Richey, J. A., Dimaite, R., Hinton, D. E., & Hofmann, S. G. (2010). A cross-ethnic comparison of lifetime prevalence rates of anxiety disorders. *Journal of Nervous and Mental Disease, 198*(8), 551–555. doi: 10.1097/NMD.0b013e3181ea169f

Assumpção, A. A., Garcia, F. D., Garcia, H. D., Bradford, J. M., & Thibaut, F. (2014). Pharmacologic treatment of paraphilias. *Psychiatric Clinics of North America, 37*(2), 173–181.

Attia, E., & Roberto, C. A. (2009). Should amenorrhea be a diagnostic criterion for anorexia nervosa? *International Journal of Eating Disorders, 42*(7), 581–589.

Attie, I., & Brooks-Gunn, J. (1995). The development of eating regulation across the life span. In D. Cicchetti & D. J. Cohen (Eds.), *Developmental psychopathology* (Vol. 2) (pp. 332–368). New York, NY: Wiley.

Augedal, A. W., Hansen, K. S., Kronhaug, C. R., Harvey, A. G., & Pallesen, S. (2013). Randomized controlled trials of psychological and pharmacological treatments for nightmares: A meta-analysis. *Sleep Medicine Reviews 17*(2), 143–152. doi: 10.1016/j.smrv.2012.06.001

Aurora, R. N., Zak, R. S., Auerbach, S. H., Casey, K. R., Chowdhuri, S., Karippot, A., & Bista, S. R. (2010). Best practice guide for the treatment of nightmare disorder in adults. *Journal of Clinical Sleep Medicine: JCSM: Official Publication of the American Academy of Sleep Medicine, 6*(4), 389.

Auyeng, B., Baron-Cohen, S., Ashwin, E., Knickmeyer, R., Taylor, K., Hackett, G., & Hines, M. (2009). Fetal testosterone predicts sexually differentiated childhood behavior in girls and boys. *Psychological Science, 20*, 144–148.

Ayala, E. S., Meuret, A. E., & Ritz, T. (2009). Treatments for blood-injury-injection phobia: A critical review of current evidence. *Journal of Psychiatric Research, 43*(15), 1235–1242.

Ayearst, L. E., & Bagby, R. M. (2010). Evaluating the psychometric properties of psychological measures. In M. M. Antony & D. H. Barlow (Eds.), *Handbook of assessment and treatment planning for psychological disorders* (2nd ed.). New York, NY: Guilford.

Ayers, C. R., Thorp, S. R., & Wetherell, J. L. (2009). Anxiety disorders and hoarding in older adults. In M. M. Antony & M. B. Stein (Eds.), *Oxford handbook of anxiety and related disorders.* (pp. 625–635). New York, NY: Oxford University Press.

Ayers, C. R., Saxena, S., Golshan, S., & Wetherell, J. L. (2010). Age at onset and clinical features of late life compulsive hoarding. *International Journal of Geriatric Psychiatry, 25*(2), 142–149. doi: 10.1002/gps.2310

Ayllon, T., & Azrin, N. H. (1968). *The token economy: A motivational system for therapy and rehabilitation.* New York, NY: Appleton-Century-Crofts.

Azmitia, E. C. (1978). The serotonin-producing neurons of the midbrain median and dorsal raphe nuclei. In L. Iverson, S. Iverson, & S. Snyder (Eds.), *Handbook of psychopharmacology: Vol. 9. Chemical pathways in the brain* (pp. 233–314). New York, NY: Plenum.

Babyak, M., Blumenthal, J. A., Herman, S., Khatri, P., Doraiswamy, M., Moore, K., & Krishnan, K. R. (2000). Exercise treatment for major depression: Maintenance of therapeutic benefit at 10 months. *Psychosomatic Medicine, 62*, 633–638.

Bach, A. K., Barlow, D., & Wincze, J. (2004). The enhancing effects of manualized treatment for erectile dysfunction among men using slide-nafil: A preliminary investigation. *Behaviour Therapy, 35*, 55–73.

Bach, A. K., Brown, T. A., & Barlow, D. H. (1999). The effects of false negative feedback on efficacy expectancies and sexual arousal in sexually functional males. *Behavior Therapy, 30*, 79–95.

Bach, A. K., Wincze, J. P., & Barlow, D. H. (2001). Sexual dysfunction. In D. H. Barlow (Ed.), *Clinical handbook of psychological disorders: A step-by-step treatment manual* (3rd ed., pp. 562–608). New York, NY: Guilford.

Badr, M. S. (2012). Central sleep apnea. In M. S. Badr (Ed.), *Essentials of sleep medicine* (pp. 219–232). New York: Humana Press.

Baek, J. H., Eisner, L. R., & Nierenberg, A. A. (2014). Epidemiology and course of unipolar mania: Results from the National Epidemiologic Survey on Alcohol and Related Conditions (NESARC). *Depression and Anxiety, 31*, 746–755.

Baer, R. A., Peters, J. R., Eisenlohr-Moul, T. A., Geiger, P. J., & Sauer, S. E. (2012). Emotion-related cognitive processes in borderline personality disorder: a review of the empirical literature. *Clinical Psychology Review, 32*(5), 359–369.

Bailey, J. A. (2009). Addressing common risk and protective factors can prevent a wide range of adolescent risk behaviors. *Journal of Adolescent Health, 45*(2), 107–108.

Bailey, J. M. (2003). *The man who would be queen: The science of gender-bending and transsexualism.* Washington, DC: National Academy.

Bailey, J. M., & Benishay, D. S. (1993). Familial aggregation of female sexual orientation. *American Journal of Psychiatry, 150*(2), 272–277.

Bailey, J. M., & Pillard, R. C. (1991). A genetic study of male sexual orientation. *Archives of General Psychiatry, 48,* 1089–1096.

Bailey, J. M., Pillard, R. C., Dawood, K., Miller, M. B., Farrer, L. A., Trivedi, S., & Murphy, R. L. (1999). A family history study of male sexual orientation using three independent samples. *Behavior Genetics, 29,* 79–86.

Bailey, J. M., Pillard, R. C., Neale, M. C., & Agyei, Y. (1993). Heritable factors influence sexual orientation in women. *Archives of General Psychiatry, 50,* 217–223.

Bailey, R. C., & Baillie, A. J. (2012). The relationship between placebo alcohol and affect: Motives for drinking. *Drug and Alcohol Review, 32*(2), 162–169. doi: 10.1111/j.1465-3362.2012.00500.x

Baird, G., Simonoff, E., Pickles, A., Chandler, S., Loucas, T., Meldrum, D., & Charman, T. (2006). Prevalence of disorders of the autism spectrum in a population cohort of children in South Thames: The Special Needs and Autism Project (SNAP). *The Lancet, 368*(9531), 210–215.

Baker, C. D., & DeSilva, P. (1988). The relationship between male sexual dysfunction and belief in Zilbergeld's myths: An empirical investigation. *Sexual and Marital Therapy, 3*(2), 229–238.

Baldessarini, R., Pompili, M., & Tondo, L. (2006). Suicidal risk in antidepressant drug trials. *Archives of General Psychiatry, 63,* 246–248.

Baldwin, J. D., & Baldwin, J. I. (1989). The socialization of homosexuality and heterosexuality in a non-Western society. *Archives of Sexual Behavior, 18,* 13–29.

Baldwin, R. (2009). Mood disorders in the elderly. In M. G. Gelder, N. C. Andreasen, K. J. López-Ibor, Jr., & J. R. Geddes (Eds.), *New Oxford textbook of psychiatry* (2nd ed., Vol. 2, pp. 1550–1558). Oxford, UK: Oxford University Press.

Ball, J., & Links, P. (2009). Borderline personality disorder and childhood trauma: Evidence for a causal relationship. *Current Psychiatry Reports, 11*(1), 63–68. doi: 10.1007/s11920-009-0010-4

Ballantyne, J. C. (2012). Opioids and other analgesics. In J. C. Verster, K. Brady, M. Galanter, & P. Conrod (Eds.), *Drug abuse and addiction in medical illness* (pp. 241–250). New York, NY: Springer.

Balon, R. (2006). SSRI-associated sexual dysfunction. *American Journal of Psychiatry, 163,* 1504–1512.

Balon, R., Segraves, R., & Clayton, A. (2007). Issues for DSM-V: Sexual dysfunction, disorder, or variation along normal distribution— Toward rethinking DSM criteria of sexual dysfunctions. *American Journal of Psychiatry, 164,* 198–200.

Balter, M. (2015). Can epigenetics explain the homosexuality puzzle? *Science, 350*(6257), 148.

Bancroft, J. (1989). *Human sexuality and its problems* (2nd ed.). New York, NY: Churchill Livingstone.

Bancroft, J. (1994). Homosexual orientation: The search for a biological basis. *British Journal of Psychiatry, 164,* 437–440.

Bancroft, J. (1997). Sexual problems. In D. M. Clark & C. G. Fairburn (Eds.), *Science and practice of cognitive behavior therapy* (pp. 243–257). New York, NY: Oxford University Press.

Bancroft, J., Loftus, J., & Long, J. S. (2003). Distress about sex: A national survey of women in heterosexual relationships. *Archives of Sexual Behavior, 32,* 193–208.

Bandelow, B., Krause, J., Wedekind, D., Broocks, A., Hajak, G., & Ruther, E. (2005). Early traumatic life events, parental attitudes, family history, and birth risk factors in patients with border-line personality disorder and healthy controls. *Psychiatry Research, 134,* 169–179.

Bandura, A. (1973). *Aggression: A social learning analysis.* Englewood Cliffs, NJ: Prentice Hall.

Bandura, A. (1986). *Social foundations of thought and action: A social cognitive theory.* Englewood Cliffs, NJ: Prentice Hall.

Bandura, A., O'Leary, A., Taylor, C. B., Gauthier, J., & Gossard, D. (1987). Perceived self-efficacy and pain control: Opioid and nonopioid mechanisms. *Journal of Personality and Social Psychology, 53,* 563–571.

Bar-Haim, Y., Larry, D., Pergamin, L., Bakermans-Kranenburg, M. J., Van Ijzendoorn, M. H. (2007). Threat-related attentional bias in anxious and non-anxious individuals: A meta-analytic study. *Psychological Bulletin, 133,* 1–24.

Barclay, N. L., & Gregory, A. M. (2013). Quantitative genetic research on sleep: a review of normal sleep, sleep disturbances and associated emotional, behavioural, and health-related difficulties. *Sleep Medicine Reviews, 17*(1), 29–40.

Bardone-Cone, A. M., Schaefer, L. M., Maldonado, C. R., Fitzsimmons, E. E., Harney, M. B., Lawson, M. A., . . . Smith, R. (2010). Aspects of self-concept and eating disorder recovery: What does the sense of self look like when an individual recovers from an eating disorder? *Journal of Social and Clinical Psychology, 29*(7), 821–846.

Bargh, J. A., & Chartrand, T. L. (1999). The unbearable automaticity of being. *American Psychologist, 54,* 462–479.

Barik, J., Marti, F., Morel, C., Fernandez, S. P., Lanteri, C., Godeheu, G., & Tronche, F. (2013). Chronic stress triggers social aversion via glucocorticoid receptor in dopaminoceptive neurons. *Science, 339*(6117), 332–335. doi: 10.1126/science.1226767

Barker, C., Pistrang, N., & Elliot, R. (2015). *Research methods in clinical psychology.* West Sussex, UK: John Wiley and Sons Inc.

Barkley, R. A. (1990). *Attention-deficit hyperactivity disorder: A handbook for diagnosis and treatment.* New York, NY: Guilford.

Barkley, R. A. (2006a). ADHD in adults: Developmental course and outcome of children with ADHD, and ADHD in clinic-referred adults. In R. A. Barkley (Ed.), *Attention-deficit hyperactivity disorder: A handbook for diagnosis and treatment* (3rd ed., pp. 248–296). New York, NY: Guilford.

Barkley, R. A. (2006b). Etiologies. In R. A. Barkley (Ed.), *Attention-deficit hyperactivity disorder: A handbook for diagnosis and treatment* (3rd ed., pp. 219–247). New York, NY: Guilford.

Barkley, R. A. (2015a). Etiologies of ADHD. In R. A. Barkley (Ed.), *Attention-deficit hyperactivity disorder: A handbook for diagnosis &* *treatment* (4th ed., pp. 356–390). New York, NY: The Guilford Press.

Barkley, R. A. (2015b). Health problems and related impairments in children and adults with ADHD. In R. A. Barkley (Ed.), *Attention-deficit hyperactivity disorder: A handbook for diagnosis & treatment* (4th ed., pp. 267–313). New York, NY: The Guilford Press.

Barkley, R. A. (Ed.). (2015c). *Attention-deficit hyperactivity disorder: A handbook for diagnosis & treatment* (4th ed.). New York, NY: The Guilford Press.

Barlow, D. H. (1986). Causes of sexual dysfunction: The role of anxiety and cognitive interference. *Journal of Consulting and Clinical Psychology, 54,* 140–148.

Barlow, D. H. (1988). *Anxiety and its disorders: The nature and treatment of anxiety and panic.* New York, NY: Guilford.

Barlow, D. H. (1991). Disorders of emotion. *Psychological Inquiry, 2*(1), 58–71.

Barlow, D. H. (2000). Unraveling the mysteries of anxiety and its disorders from the perspective of emotion theory. *American Psychologist, 55,* 1245–1263.

Barlow, D. H. (2002). *Anxiety and its disorders: The nature and treatment of anxiety and panic* (2nd ed.). New York, NY: Guilford.

Barlow, D. H. (2004). Covert sensitization for paraphilia. In D. Wedding & R. J. Corsini (Eds.), *Case studies in psychotherapy* (4th ed., pp. 105–113). Belmont, CA: Thomson. (Reprinted from *Covert conditioning casebook* (1st ed., pp. 187–207) by J. R. Cautela & A. J. Kearney, Eds., 1993, Belmont, CA: Brooks/Cole.

Barlow, D. H., & Craske, M. G. (2007). *Mastery of your anxiety and panic* (4th ed.). New York, NY: Oxford University Press.

Barlow, D. H., & Lehman, C. L. (1996). Advances in the psychosocial treatment of anxiety disorders: Implications for national health care. *Archives of General Psychiatry, 53,* 727–735.

Barlow, D. H., & Liebowitz, M. R. (1995). Specific and social phobias. In H. I. Kaplan & B. J. Sadock (Eds.), *Comprehensive textbook of psychiatry: VI* (pp. 1204–1217). Baltimore, MD: Williams & Wilkins.

Barlow, D. H., & Nock, M. K. (2009). Why can't we be more idiographic in our research? *Perspectives on Psychological Science, 4,* 19–21.

Barlow, D. H., & Wincze, J. P. (1980). Treatment of sexual deviations. In S. R. Leiblum & L. A. Pervin (Eds.), *Principles and practice of sex therapy* (pp. 347–375). New York, NY: Guilford.

Barlow, D. H., Allen, L. B., & Basden, S. (2007). Psychological treatments for panic disorders, phobias, and generalized anxiety disorder. In P. E. Nathan & J. M. Gorman (Eds.), *A guide to treatments that work* (3rd ed.). New York, NY: Oxford University Press.

Barlow, D. H., Allen, L. B., & Choate, M. L. (2004). Toward a unified treatment for emotional disorders. *Behavior Therapy, 35,* 205–230.

Barlow, D. H., Becker, R., Leitenberg, H., & Agras, W. S. (1970). A mechanical strain gauge for recording penile circumference change. *Journal of Applied Behavior Analysis, 3,* 73–76.

Barlow, D. H., Brown, T. A., & Craske, M. G. (1994). Definitions of panic attacks and panic disorder in DSM-IV: Implications for research. *Journal of Abnormal Psychology, 103*, 553–554.

Barlow, D. H., Bullis, J. R., Comer, J. S., & Ametaj, A. A. (2013). Evidence-based psychological treatments: An update and a way forward. In S. Nolen-Hoeksema, T. D. Cannon, & T. Widiger (Eds.), *Annual Review of Clinical Psychology* (Vol. 9, pp. 1–27). Palo Alto, CA: Annual Reviews.

Barlow, D. H., Chorpita, B. F., & Turovsky, J. (1996). Fear, anxiety, and disorders of emotion. In D. A. Hope (Ed.), *Perspectives on anxiety, panic and fear* (The 43rd Annual Nebraska Symposium on Motivation) (pp. 251–328). Lincoln, NE: Nebraska University Press.

Barlow, D. H., Ellard, K. K., Sauer-Zavala, S., Bullis, J. R., & Carl, J. R. (2014). The origins of neuroticism. *Perspectives on Psychological Science, 9*, 481–496.

Barlow, D. H., Farchione, T. J., Fairholme, C. P., Ellard, K. K., Boisseau, C. L., Allen, L. B., & Ehrenreich-May, J. (2012b). *Unified protocol for the transdiagnostic treatment of emotional disorders* (Therapist Guide). New York, NY: Oxford University Press.

Barlow, D. H., Gorman, J. M., Shear, K. M., & Woods, S. W. (2000). Cognitive-behavioral therapy, imipramine, or their combination for panic disorder: A randomized controlled trial. *JAMA: Journal of the American Medical Association, 283*(19), 2529–2536.

Barlow, D. H., Hayes, S. C., & Nelson, R. O. (1984). *The scientist practitioner: Research and accountability in clinical and educational settings.* Boston, MA: Allyn & Bacon.

Barlow, D. H., Levitt, J. T., & Bufka, L. F. (1999). The dissemination of empirically supported treatments: A view to the future. *Behaviour Research and Therapy, 37*(Suppl. 1), S147–162.

Barlow, D. H., Moscovitch, D. A., & Micco, J. A. (2004). Psychotherapeutic interventions for phobias: A review. In M. Maj, H. S. Akiskal, J. L. Lopez-Ibor, & A. Okasha (Eds.), *Phobias.* (pp.179–210). Hoboken, NJ: Wiley.

Barlow, D. H., Nock, M. K., & Hersen, M. (2009). *Single case experimental designs: Strategies for studying behavior change* (3rd ed.). New York, NY: Allyn & Bacon.

Barlow, D. H., Pincus, D. B., Heinrichs, N., & Choate, M. L. (2003). Anxiety disorders. In I. B. Weiner (Series Ed.), G. S. Stricker & T. A. Widiger (Vol. Eds.), *Handbook of psychology.* Hoboken, NJ: Wiley.

Barlow, D. H., Rapee, R. M., & Parini, S. (2014). *10 steps to mastering Stress: A lifestyle approach.* New York, NY: Oxford University Press.

Barlow, D. H., Sakheim, D. K., & Beck, J. G. (1983). Anxiety increases sexual arousal. *Journal of Abnormal Psychology, 92*, 49–54.

Barlow, D. H., Sauer-Zavala, S., Carl, J. R., Bullis, J. R. & Ellard, K. K. (2014). The nature, diagnosis, and treatment of neuroticism: Back to the future. *Clinical Psychological Science, 2*, 344–365.

Barmish, A. J., & Kendall, P. C. (2005). Should parents be co-clients in cognitive behavioral therapy for anxious youth? *Journal of Clinical Child and Adolescent Psychology, 34*(3), 69–581. doi: 10.1207/s15374424jccp3403

Barnard, A. (2000, September 12). When plastic surgeons should just say "no." *Boston Globe,* pp. E1, E3.

Barnhofer, T., Crane, C., Brennan, K., Duggan, D. S., Crane, R. S., Eames, C., Radford, S., Silverton, S., Fennell, M. J., Williams, J. M., (2015). Mindfulness-based cognitive therapy (MBCT) reduces the association between depressive symptoms and suicidal cognitions in patients with a history of suicidal depression. *J Consult Clin Psychol, 83*(6):1013–1020.

Baron, M., Risch, N., Hamburger, R., Mandel, B., Kushner, S., Newman, M.. Belmaker, R. H. (1987). Genetic linkage between X-chromosome markers and bipolar affective illness. *Nature, 326*(6110), 289–292.

Barrett, L. F. (2009). Variety is the spice of life: A psychological construction approach to understanding variability in emotion. *Cognition and Emotion, 23*(7), 1284–1306.

Barrett, L. F. (2012). Emotions are real. *Emotion, 12*(3), 413–429. doi: 10.1037/a0027555

Barry, C. T., Golmaryami, F. N., Rivera-Hudson, N., & Frick, P. J. (2012). Evidence-based assessment of conduct disorder: Current considerations and preparation for DSM-5. *Professional Psychology: Research and Practice, 44*(1), 56–63.

Barsky, A. J., & Ahern, D. K. (2005). Cognitive behavior therapy for hypochondriasis: A randomized controlled trial. *JAMA: Journal of the American Medical Association, 291*, 1464–1470.

Barsky, A. J., Orav, E., & Bates, D. (2005). Somatization increases medical utilization and costs independent of psychiatric and medical comorbidity. *Archives of General Psychiatry, 62*, 903–910.

Barthelemy, O. J., Richardson, M.A., Rose-Jacobs, R., Forman, L. S., Cabral, H. J. & Frank, D. A. (2016). Effects of intrauterine substance and postnatal violence expo-sure on aggression in children. *Aggressive Behavior, 42*, 209–221.

Bartholomew, R. E., Wessely, S., & Rubin, G. J. (2012). Mass psychogenic illness and the social network: Is it changing the pattern of outbreaks? *Journal of the Royal Society of Medicine, 105*(12), 509–512.

Bartlett, N., & Vasey, P. (2006). A retrospective study of childhood gender-atypical behavior in Samoan Fa'afafine. *Archives of Sexual Behavior, 35*, 695–666.

Bartlik, B., & Goldberg, J. (2000). Female sexual arousal disorder. In S. R. Leiblum & R. C. Rosen (Eds.), *Principles and practice of sex therapy* (3rd ed., pp. 85–117). New York, NY: Guilford.

Basson, R. (2007). Sexual desire/arousal disorders in women. In S. R. Leiblum (Ed.), *Principles and practice of sex therapy* (4th ed., pp. 25–53). New York, NY: Guilford.

Basson, R., Wierman, M., van Lankveld, J., & Brotto, L. (2010). Summary of the recommendations on sexual dysfunctions in women. *Journal of Sexual Medicine, 7*(1, pt. 2), 314–326.

Bateson, G. (1959). Cultural problems posed by a study of schizophrenic process. In A. Auerback (Ed.), *Schizophrenia: An integrated approach* (pp. 125–148). New York, NY: Ronald.

Baugh, C. M., Stamm, J. M., Riley, D. O., Gavett, B. E., Shenton, M. E., Lin, A., . . . Stern, R. A. (2012). Chronic traumatic encephalopathy: neurodegeneration following repetitive concussive and subconcussive brain trauma. *Brain Imaging and Behavior, 6*(2), 244–254.

Baumann, M. H. (2014). Awash in a sea of 'bath salts': Implications for biomedical research and public health. *Addiction, 109*(10), 1577–1579.

Baumann, M. H., Partilla, J. S., Lehner, K. R., Thorndike, E. B., Hoffman, A. F., Holy, M., & Brandt, S. D. (2013). Powerful cocaine-like actions of 3, 4-methylene-dioxypyrovalerone (MDPV), a principal constituent of psychoactive 'bath salts' products. *Neuropsychopharmacology, 38*(4), 552–562.

Baxter, L.R .(1992). Neuroimaging studies of obsessive compulsive disorder. *Psychiatric Clinics of North America, 15*(4):871–884.

Beach, S. R., & O'Leary, K. D. (1992). Treating depression in the context of marital discord: Outcome and predictors of response of marital therapy versus cognitive therapy. *Behavior Therapy, 23*(4), 507–528.

Beach, S. R. H., Jones, D. J., & Franklin, K. J. (2009). Marital, family, and interpersonal therapies for depression in adults. In I. H. Gotlib & C. L. Hammen (Eds.), *Handbook of depression* (2nd ed., pp. 624–641). New York, NY: Guilford.

Beach, S. R. H., Sandeen, E. E., & O'Leary, K. D. (1990). Depression in marriage: A model for etiology and treatment. In D. H. Barlow (Ed.), *Treatment manuals for practitioners* (pp. 53–86). New York, NY: Guilford.

Beals, J., Manson, S., Whitesell, N., Mitchell, C., Novins, D., Simpson, S., & Spicer, P. (2005). Prevalence of major depressive episode in two American Indian reservation populations: Unexpected findings with a structured interview. *American Journal of Psychiatry, 162*, 1713–1722.

Bear, R. E., Fitzgerald, P., Rosenfeld, J. V., & Bittar, R. G. (2010). Neurosurgery for obsessive-compulsive disorder: Contemporary approaches. *Journal of Clinical Neuroscience, 17*(1), 1–5. doi: 10.1016/j.jocn. 2009.02.043

Beard, G. M. (1869). Neurasthenia or nervous exhaustion. *Boston Medical Surgical Journal, 3*, 217–221.

Beardon, L., & Worton, D. (2011). *Aspies on mental health: Speaking for ourselves.* London, U.K.: Jessica Kingsley.

Beardslee, W. R., Brent, D. A., Weersing, V. R., Clarke, G. N., Porta, G., Hollon, S. D., . . . Garber, J. (2013). Prevention of depression in at-risk adolescents: Longer-term effects. *Journal of American Medical Association Psychiatry, 70*, 1161–1170.

Beaver, K. M., Barnes, J. C., May, J. S., & Schwartz, J. A. (2011). Psychopathic personality traits, genetic risk, and gene-environment correlations. *Criminal Justice and Behavior, 38*(9), 896–912.

Bebbington, P., Cooper, C., Minot, S., Brugha, T., Jenkins, R., Meltzer, H., Dennis, M. (2009). Suicide attempts, gender, and sexual abuse: Data from the 2000 British Psychiatric Morbidity Survey. *American Journal of Psychiatry, 166*(10), 1135.

Bech, P. (2009). Clinical features of mood disorders and mania. In M. G. Gelder, N. C. Andreasen, J. J. López-Ibor, Jr., & J. R. Geddes (Eds.), *New Oxford textbook of psychiatry* (2nd ed., Vol. 1, pp. 632–637). Oxford, UK: Oxford University Press.

Beck, A. T. (1967). *Depression: Clinical, experimental and theoretical aspects.* New York, NY: Harper & Row.

Beck, A. T. (1976). *Cognitive therapy and the emotional disorders.* New York, NY: International Universities Press.

Beck, A. T. (1986). Hopelessness as a predictor of eventual suicide. *Annals of the New York Academy of Science, 487,* 90–96.

Beck, A. T., & Freeman, A. (1990). *Cognitive therapy of personality disorders.* New York, NY: Guilford.

Beck, A.T., Davis, D. D., & Freeman, A., Eds. (2015). *Cognitive therapy of personality disorders* (3rd ed.) New York, NY: Guilford.

Beck, A. T., Epstein, N., & Harrison, R. (1983). Cognitions, attitudes and personality dimensions in depression. *British Journal of Cognitive Psychotherapy, 1*(1), 1–16.

Beck, A. T., Freeman, A., & Davis, D. D. (2007). *Cognitive therapy of personality disorders* (2nd ed.). New York, NY: Guilford.

Beck, J. G. (1993). Vaginismus. In W. O'Donohue & J. H. Geer (Eds.), *Handbook of sexual dysfunctions: Assessment and treatment* (pp. 381–397). Boston, MA: Allyn & Bacon.

Beck, J. G., & Averill, P. M. (2004). Older adults. In R. G. Heimberg, C. L. Turk, & D. S. Mennin (Eds.), *Generalized anxiety disorder: Advances in research and practice* (pp. 409–433). New York, NY: Guilford.

Beck, J. G., & Stanley, M. A. (1997). Anxiety disorders in the elderly: The emerging role of behavior therapy. *Behavior Therapy, 28,* 83–100.

Beck, J. G., & Sloan, D. M. (Eds.). (2012). *The Oxford handbook of traumatic stress disorders.* New York, NY: Oxford University Press.

Becker, C. B., Smith, L. M., & Ciao, A. C. (2005). Reducing eating disorder risk factors in sorority members: A randomized trial. *Behavior Therapy, 36,* 245–253.

Becker, J. T., Mestre, L. T., Ziolko, S., & Lopez, O. L. (2007). Gene-environment interactions with cognition in late life and compression of morbidity. *American Journal of Psychiatry, 164*(6), 849–852.

Becker, J. V. (1990). Treating adolescent sexual offenders. *Professional Psychology: Research and Practice, 21,* 362–365.

Becvar, D. S. (2013). *Handbook of family resilience.* New York, NY: Springer.

Beekman, A. T., Geerlings, S. W., Deeg, D. J., Smit, J. H., Schoevers, R. S., de Beurs, E., & van Tilberg, W. (2002). The natural history of late-life depression: A 6-year prospective study in the community. *Archives of General Psychiatry, 59,* 605–611.

Beesdo, K., Pine, D. S., Lieb, R., & Wittchen, H.-U. (2010). Incidence and risk patterns of anxiety and depressive disorders and categorization of generalized anxiety disorder. *Archives of General Psychiatry, 67*(1), 47–57.

Beesdo-Baum, K., Klotsche, J., Knappe, S., Craske, M. G., LeBeau, R. T., Hoyer, J., & Wittchen, H.-U. (2012). Psychometric properties of the dimensional anxiety scales for DSM-5 in an unselected sample of German treatment seeking patients. *Depression and Anxiety, 29*(12), 1014–1024.

Béjot, Y., Juenet, N., Garrouty, R., Maltaverne, D., Nicolleau, L., Giroud, M., & Didi-Roy, R. (2010). Sexsomnia: An uncommon variety of parasomnia. *Clinical Neurology and Neurosurgery, 112*(1), 72–75.

Belik, S. L., Sareen, J., & Stein, M. B. (2009). Anxiety disorders and physical comorbidity. In M. M. Antony & M. B. Stein (Eds.), *Oxford handbook of anxiety and related disorders.* (pp. 596–610). New York, NY: Oxford University Press.

Bell, C. C., Dixie-Bell, D. D., & Thompson, B. (1986). Further studies on the prevalence of isolated sleep paralysis in black subjects. *Journal of the National Medical Association, 78*(7), 649–659.

Bell, I. R. (1994). Somatization disorder: Health care costs in the decade of the brain. *Biological Psychiatry, 35,* 81–83.

Bellak, L. (1975). *The thematic apperception test, the children's apperception test, and the senior apperception technique in clinical use* (3rd ed.). New York, NY: Grune & Stratton.

Ben Itzchak, E., Lahat, E., Burgin, R., & Zachor, A. D. (2008). Cognitive, behavior and intervention outcome in young children with autism. *Research in Developmental Disabilities, 29*(5), 447–458.

Ben-Porath, Y. S., & Tellegen, A. (2008). *MMPI-2-RF: Manual for administration, scoring and interpretation.* Minnesota: University of Minnesota Press.

Benbadis, R. R., & Allen-Hauser, W. (2000). An estimate of the prevalence of psychogenic non-epileptic seizures. *Seizure, 9*(4), 280–281.

Bender, D. S. (2005). Therapeutic alliance. In J. M. Oldham, A. E. Skodol, & D. S. Bender (Eds.), *Textbook of personality disorders* (pp. 405–420). Washington, DC: American Psychiatric Publishing.

Bender, D. S., Dolan, R. T., Skodol, A. E., Sanislow, C. A., Dyck, I. R., McGlashan, T. H., . . . Gunderson, J. G. (2014). Treatment utilization by patients with personality disorders. *American Journal of Psychiatry.*

Bender, E. (2004). Data show wide variation in addiction treatment costs. *Psychiatric News, 39,* 11.

Benjamin, C. L., Harrison, J. P., Settipani, C. A., Brodman, D. M., & Kendall, P. C. (2013). Anxiety and related outcomes in young adults 7 to 19 years after receiving treatment for child anxiety. *Journal of Consulting and Clinical Psychology, 81,* 865.

Bennett, E., & Heaton, P. (2012). Is talent in autism spectrum disorders associated with a specific cognitive and behavioural phenotype? *Journal of Autism and Developmental Disorders, 42*(12), 2739–2753.

Bennett, K., Shepherd, J., & Janca, A. (2013). Personality disorders and spirituality. *Current Opinion in Psychiatry, 26*(1), 79–83.

Benowitz, N. (2008). Neurobiology of nicotine addiction: Implications for smoking cessation treatment. *The American Journal of Medicine, 121* (4A), S3–S10.

Benson, H. (1975). *The relaxation response.* New York, NY: William Morrow.

Benson, H. (1984). *Beyond the relaxation response.* New York, NY: Times Books.

Berenbaum, H., & Oltmanns, T. F. (1992). Emotional experience and expression in schizophrenia and depression. *Journal of Abnormal Psychology, 101,* 37–44.

Berenbaum, H., Thompson, R. J., Milanak, M. E., Boden, M. T., & Bredemeier, K. (2008). Psychological trauma and schizotypal personality disorder. *Journal of Abnormal Psychology, 117*(3), 502–519.

Berghöfer, A., Pischon, T., Reinhold, T., Apovian, C. M., Sharma, A. M., & Willich, S. N. (2008). Obesity prevalence from a European perspective: A systematic review. *BMC Public Health, 8,* 200.

Berkman, L. F., & Syme, S. L. (1979). Social networks, host resistance, and mortality: A nine-year follow-up study of Alameda county residents. *American Journal of Epidemiology, 109,* 186.

Berman, A. L. (2009). Depression and suicide. In I. H. Gotlib & C. L. Hammen (Eds.), *Handbook of depression* (2nd ed., pp. 510–530). New York, NY: Guilford.

Berman, A. L., & Jobes, D. A. (1991). *Adolescent suicide: Assessment and intervention.* Washington, DC: American Psychological Association.

Berman, J. R., Berman, L. A., Toler, S. M., Gill, J., Haughie, S., for the Sildenafil Study Group. (2003). Safety and efficacy of sildenafil citrate for the treatment of female sexual arousal disorder: A double-blind, placebo controlled study. *The Journal of Urology, 170,* 2333–2338.

Berman, K. F., & Weinberger, D. R. (1990). Lateralization of cortical function during cognitive tasks: Regional cerebral blood flow studies of normal individuals and patients with schizophrenia. *Journal of Neurology, Neurosurgery and Psychiatry, 53,* 150–160.

Berman, M. E., McCloskey, M. S., Fanning, J. R., Schumacher, J. A., & Coccaro, E. F. (2009). Serotonin augmentation reduces response to attack in aggressive individuals. *Psychological Science, 20*(6), 714–720. doi: 10.1111/j.1467-9280.2009.02355.x

Bernat, J. A., Calhoun, K. S., & Adams, H. E. (1999). Sexually aggressive and nonaggressive men: Sexual arousal and judgments in response to acquaintance rape and consensual analogues. *Journal of Abnormal Psychology, 108,* 662–673.

Berner, L. A., Shaw, J. A., Witt, A. A., & Lowe, M. R. (2013). The relation of weight suppression and body mass index to symptomatology and treatment response in anorexia nervosa. *Journal of Abnormal Psychology, 122*(3), 694–708.

Berney, T. P. (2012). Methods of treatment. In M. G. Gelder, N. C. Andreasen, J. J. Lopez-Ibor, Jr., & J. R. Geddes (Eds.), *New Oxford textbook of psychiatry* (2nd. ed., Vol. 2, pp. 1871–1877). New York, NY: Oxford University Press.

Bernstein, D. M., & Loftus, E. F. (2009). How to tell if a particular memory is true or false. *Perspectives on Psychological Science, 4*(4), 370–374.

Bernstein, D. P., & Useda, J. (2007). Paranoid personality disorder. In W. O'Donohue, K. Fowler, & S. Lilienfeld (Eds.), *Personality disorders: Toward the DSM-V* (pp. 41–62). Thousand Oaks, CA: Sage.

Berntsen, D., Johannessen, K. B., Thornsen, Y. D., Bertelsen, M., Hoyle, R. H., & Rubin, D. C. (2012). Peace and war: Trajectories of posttraumatic stress disorder symptoms before, during, and after military deployment in Afghanistan. *Psychological Science, 23*, 1557–1565.

Berridge, K. C., & Kringelbach, M. L. (2015). Pleasure systems in the brain. *Neuron, 86*(3), 646–664.

Berrios, G. E. (2011). Eugen Bleuler's place in the history of psychiatry. *Schizophrenia Bulletin, 37*(6), 1095–1098.

Berton, O., McClung, C. A., DiLeone, R. J., Krishnan, V., Renthal, W., Russo, S. J., & Nestler, E. J. (2006). Essential role of BDNF in the mesolimbic dopamine pathway in social defeat stress. *Science, 311*, 864–868.

Bettelheim, B. (1967). *The empty fortress*. New York, NY: Free Press.

Bettens, K., Sleegers, K., & Van Broeckhoven, C. (2010). Current status on Alzheimer disease molecular genetics: From past, to present, to future. *Human Molecular Genetics, 19*(R1), R4–11.

Bhagwanjee, A., Parekh, A., Paruk, Z., Petersen, I., & Subedar, H. (1998). Prevalence of minor psychiatric disorders in an adult African rural community in South Africa. *Psychological Medicine, 28*, 1137–1147.

Bharucha, A., Anand, V., Forlizzi, J., Dew, M., Reynolds, C., III, Stevens, S., Wactlar, H. (2009). Intelligent assistive technology applications to dementia care: Current capabilities, limitations, and future challenges. *The American Journal of Geriatric Psychiatry: Official Journal of the American Association for Geriatric Psychiatry, 17*(2), 88.

Bhasin, T., & Schendel, D. (2007). Sociodemographic risk factors for autism in a U.S. metropolitan area. *Journal of Autism and Developmental Disorders, 37*, 667–677.

Biederman, J., Faraone, S. V., Wozniak, J., Mick, E., Kwon, A., Cayton, G. A., & Clark, S. V. (2005). Clinical correlates of bipolar disorder in a large, referred sample of children and adolescents. *Journal of Psychiatric Research, 39*(6), 611–622.

Biederman, J., Mick, E., Faraone, S. V., Spencer, T., Wilens, T. E., & Wozniak, J. (2000). Pediatric mania: A developmental subtype of bipolar disorder? *Biological Psychiatry, 48*(6), 458–466.

Biederman, J., Spencer, T., Wilens, T., & Greene, R. (2001). Attention-deficit/hyperactivity disorder. In G. O. Gabbard (Ed.), *Treatment of psychiatric disorders* (3rd ed., Vol. 1, pp. 145–176). Washington, DC: American Psychiatric Publishing.

Bierut, L. J., Heath, A. C., Bucholz, K. K., Dinwiddie, S. H., Madden, P. A., Statham, D. J., & Martin, N. G. (1999). Major depressive disorder in a community-based twin sample: Are there different genetic and environmental contributions for men and women? *Archives of General Psychiatry, 56*(6), 557–563.

Billy, J. O. G., Tanfer, K., Grady, W. R., & Klepinger, D. H. (1993). The sexual behavior of men in the United States. *Family Planning Perspectives, 25*, 52–60.

Binder, E. B., Bradley, R. G., Liu, W., Epstein, M. P., Deveau, T. C., Mercer, K. B., & Ressler, K. J. (2008). Association of FKBP5 polymorphisms and childhood abuse with risk of posttraumatic stress disorder symptoms in adults. *JAMA: Journal of the American Medical Association, 299*(11), 1291–1305.

Binik, Y. M. (2010). The DSM diagnostic criteria for dyspareunia. *Archives of Sexual Behavior, 39*, 292–303.

Binik, Y. M., Bergeron, S., & Kalifé, S. (2007). Dyspareunia and vaginismus: So-called sexual pain. In S. R. Leiblum (Ed.), *Principles and practice of sex therapy* (4th ed., pp. 124–156). New York, NY: Guilford.

Binzer, M., Andersen, P. M., & Kullgren, G. (1997). Clinical characteristics of patients with motor disability due to conversion disorder: A prospective control group study. *Journal of Neurology, Neurosurgery, and Psychiatry, 63*(1), 83–88.

Birkmeyer, J. D., Finks, J. F., O'Reilly, A., Oerline, M., Carlin, A. M., Nunn, A. R., . . . Birkmeyer, N. J. (2013). Surgical skill and complication rates after bariatric surgery. *New England Journal of Medicine, 369*(15), 1434–1442.

Birley, J., & Brown, G. W. (1970). Crisis and life changes preceding the onset or relapse of acute schizophrenia: Clinical aspects. *British Journal of Psychiatry, 16*, 327–333.

Birmaher, B., Axelson, D., Goldstein, B., Strober, M., Gill, M. K., Hunt, J., & Keller, M. (2009). Four-year longitudinal course of children and adolescents with bipolar spectrum disorders: The Course and Outcome of Bipolar Youth (COBY) study. *American Journal of Psychiatry, 166*(7), 795–804.

Bishop, D. V. M. (2000). Pragmatic language impairment: A correlate of SLI, a distinct subgroup, or part of the autistic continuum. In D. V. M. Bishop & L. B. Leonard (Eds.), *Speech and language impairments in children: Causes, characteristics, intervention and outcome* (pp. 99–113). East Sussex, UK: Psychology Press.

Björkenstam, E., Björkenstam, C., Holm, H., Gerdin, B., & Ekselius, L. (2015). Excess cause-specific mortality in in-patient-treated individuals with personality disorder: 25-year nationwide population-based study. *The British Journal of Psychiatry, 207*(4):339–345.

Bjorntorp, P. (1997). Obesity. *Lancet, 350*, 423–426. Black, D. W. (2013). *Bad Boys, Bad Men: Confronting Antisocial Personality Disorder (Sociopathy)*. New York: Oxford University Press.

Black, J. A., White, B., Viner, R. M., & Simmons, R. K. (2013). Bariatric surgery for obese children and adolescents: a systematic review and meta-analysis. *Obesity Reviews, 14*(8), 634–644.

Blacker, D. (2005). Psychiatric rating scales. In B. J. Sadock & V. A. Sadock (Eds.), *Kaplan & Sadock's comprehensive textbook of psychiatry* (pp. 929–955). Philadelphia, PA: Lippincott Williams & Wilkins.

Blagys, M. D., & Hilsenroth, M. J. (2000). Distinctive features of short-term psychodynamic–interpersonal psychotherapy: A review of the comparative psychotherapy process literature. *Clinical Psychology: Science and Practice, 7*, 167–188.

Blair, K., Shaywitz, J., Smith, B. W., Rhodes, R., Geraci, M., Jones, M., & Pine, D. S. (2008). Response to emotional expressions in generalized social phobia and generalized anxiety disorder: Evidence for separate disorders. *American Journal of Psychiatry, 165*(9), 1193–1202. doi: 10.1176/appi.ajp.2008.07071060

Blanchard, E. B. (1992). Psychological treatment of benign headache disorders. Special issue: Behavioral medicine: An update for the 1990s. *Journal of Consulting and Clinical Psychology, 60*(4), 537–551.

Blanchard, E. B., & Andrasik, F. (1982). Psychological assessment and treatment of headache: Recent developments and emerging issues. *Journal of Consulting and Clinical Psychology, 50*(6), 859–879.

Blanchard, E. B., & Epstein, L. H. (1977). *A biofeedback primer*. Reading, MA: Addison-Wesley.

Blanchard, R. (2008). Sex ration of older siblings in heterosexual and homosexual, right-handed and non-right-handed men. *Archives of Sexual Behavior, 37*, 977–981.

Blanchard, R. (2010). The DSM diagnostic criteria for pedophilia. *Archives of Sexual Behavior, 39*, 304–314.

Blanchard, R., & Bogaert, A. (1996). Homosexuality in men and number of older brothers. *American Journal of Psychiatry, 153*, 27–31.

Blanchard, R., & Bogaert, A. (1998). Birth order in homosexual versus heterosexual sex offenders against children, pubescents, and adults. *Archives of Sexual Behavior, 27*(6), 595–603.

Blanchard, R., & Steiner, B. W. (1992). *Clinical management of gender identity disorders in children and adults*. Washington, DC: American Psychiatric Press.

Blanco, C., Goodwin, R., Liebowitz, M. R., Schmidt, A. B., Lewis-Fernandez, R., & Olfson, M. (2004). Use of psychotropic medications for patients with office visits who receive a diagnosis of panic disorder. *Medical Care, 42*(12), 1242–1246.

Blanco, C., Rubio, J., Wall, M., Wang, S., Jiu, C. J., & Kendler, K. S. (2014). Risk factors for anxiety disorders: Common and specific effects in a national sample, *Depression and Anxiety, 31*, 756–774.

Blanco, C., Vesga-Lopez, O., Stewart, J. W., Liu, S.-M., Grant, B. F., & Hasin, D. S. (2012). Prevalence, correlates, comorbidity and treatment-seeking among individuals with a lifetime major depressive episode with and without atypical features: Results from the National Epidemiologic Survey on Alcohol and Related Conditions. *Journal of Clinical Psychiatry, 73*(2), 224–232.

Blaney, P. H. (2015). Paranoid and delusional disorders. In P.H. Blaney, R. F. Krueger, Robert F. & T. Millon (Eds), *Oxford textbook of psychopathology* (3rd ed., pp. 383–417). New York, NY: Oxford University Press.

Blasco-Fontecilla, H. (2013). On suicide clusters: More than contagion. *The Australian and New Zealand Journal of Psychiatry, 47*(5), 490–491.

Blascovich, J., Spencer, S. J., Quinn, D., & Steele, B. (2001). African Americans and high blood pressure: The role of stereotype threat. *Psychological Science, 12*(3), 225–229.

Blascovich, J., & Tomaka, J. (1996). The biopsychosocial model of arousal regulation. *Advances in Experimental Social Psychology, 28*, 1–51.

Blashfield, R. K., Keeley, J. W., Flanagan, E. H., & Miles, S. R. (2014). The cycle of classification: *DSM-I* through *DSM-5*. *Annual review of clinical psychology, 10*, 25–51. doi: 10.1146/annurev-clinpsy-032813-153639

Blashfield, R. K., Reynolds, S. M., & Stennett, B. (2012). The death of histrionic personality disorder. In T. A. Widiger (Ed.), *The Oxford handbook of personality disorders* (pp. 603–627). New York, NY: Oxford University Press.

Blazer, D. G. (2003). Depression in late life: Review and commentary. *Journal of Gerontology – Series A Biological Sciences and Medical Science, 58*, 249–265.

Blazer, D. G., & Hybels, C. F. (2009). Depression in later life: Epidemiology, assessment, impact, and treatment. In I. H. Gotlib & C. L. Hammen (Eds.), *Handbook of depression* (2nd ed., pp. 492–509). New York, NY: Guilford.

Blazer, D. G., George, L., & Hughes, D. (1991). The epidemiology of anxiety disorders: An age comparison. In C. Salzman & B. Liebowitz (Eds.), *Anxiety disorders in the elderly* (pp. 17–30). New York, NY: Springer.

Blehar, M. C., & Rosenthal, N. E. (1989). Seasonal affective disorder and phototherapy. *Archives of General Psychiatry, 46*, 469–474.

Bleiberg, K. L., & Markowitz, J. C. (in press). Interpersonal psychotherapy for depression. In D. H. Barlow (Ed.), *Clinical handbook of psychological disorders: A step-by-step treatment manual* (5th ed.). New York, NY: Guilford.

Bleuler, E. (1908). Die prognose der dementia praecox (schizophreniegruppe). *Allgemeine Zeitschrift für Psychiatrie, 65*, 436–464.

Bleuler, E. (1911). *Dementia praecox or the group of schizophrenias* (J. Zinkin, Trans.). New York, NY: International Universities Press.

Bleuler, E. (1924). *Textbook of psychiatry* (A. A. Brill, Trans.). New York, NY: Macmillan.

Bliss, E. L. (1984). A symptom profile of patients with multiple personalities including MMPI results. *Journal of Nervous and Mental Diseases, 172*, 197–211.

Bloch, M., Schmidt, P. J., & Rubinow, D. R. (2014). Premenstrual syndrome: Evidence for symptom stability across cycles. *American Journal of Psychiatry, 154*(12), 1741–1746.

Bloch, M. H., Landeros-Weisenberger, A., Rosario, M. C., Pittenger, C., & Leckman, J. F. (2008). Meta-analysis of the symptom structure of obsessive-compulsive disorder. *American Journal of Psychiatry, 165*(12), 1532–1542. doi: 10.1176/appi.ajp.2008.08020320

Bloch, S., & Green, S. (2012). Psychiatric ethics. In M. G. Gelder, N. C. Andreasen, J. J. LopezIbor, Jr., & J. R. Geddes (Eds.), *New Oxford textbook of psychiatry* (2nd. ed., Vol. 1, pp. 28–32). New York, NY: Oxford University Press.

Block, J. J. (2008). Issues for DSM-V: Internet addiction. *American Journal of Psychiatry, 165*(3), 306–307. doi: 10.1176/appi.ajp.2007.07101556

Blom, M. M., Bosmans, J. E., Cuijpers, P., Zarit, S. H., & Pot, A. M. (2013). Effectiveness and cost-effectiveness of an internet intervention for family caregivers of people with dementia: design of a randomized controlled trial. *BMC Psychiatry, 13*(1), 1.

Bloom, F. E., & Kupfer, D. J. (1995). *Psychopharmacology: The fourth generation of progress*. New York, NY: Raven.

Bloom, F. E., Nelson, C. A., & Lazerson, A. (2001). *Brain, mind, & behavior* (3rd ed.). New York, NY: Worth.

Blumenthal, J. A., Sherwood, A., Babyak, M., Watkins, L., Waugh, R., Georgiades, A., & Hinderliter, A. (2005). Effects of exercise and stress management training on markers of cardiovascular risk in patients with ischemic heart disease. *JAMA: Journal of the American Medical Association, 293*, 1626–1634.

Blumenthal, S. J. (1990). An overview and synopsis of risk factors, assessment, and treatment of suicidal patients over the life cycle. In S. J. Blumenthal & D. J. Kupfer (Eds.), *Suicide over the life cycle: Risk factors, assessment and treatment of suicidal patients* (pp. 685–734). Washington, DC: American Psychiatric Press.

Blumenthal, S. J., & Kupfer, D. J. (1988). Clinical assessment and treatment of youth suicide. *Journal of Youth and Adolescence, 17*, 1–24.

Blundell, J. E. (2002). The psychobiological approach to appetite and weight control. In K. D. Brownell & C. G. Fairburn (Eds.), *Eating disorders and obesity: A comprehensive handbook* (2nd ed., pp. 13–20). New York, NY: Guilford.

Boardman, J. D., Barnes, L. L., Wilson, R. S., Evans, D. A., & de Leon, C. F. M. (2012). Social disorder, APOE-E4 genotype, and change in cognitive function among older adults living in Chicago. *Social Science & Medicine, 74*(10), 1584–1590. doi: http://dx.doi.org/10.1016/j.socscimed.2012.02.012

Bob, P. (2003). Dissociation and neuroscience: History and new perspectives. *International Journal of Neuroscience, 113*, 903–914.

Bockoven, J. S. (1963). *Moral treatment in American psychiatry*. New York, NY: Springer.

Bockting, C. L., Hollon, S. D., Jarrett, R. B., Kuyken, W., & Dobson, K. (2015). A lifetime approach to major depressive disorder: The contributions of psychological interventions in preventing relapse and recurrence. *Clinical Psychology Review, 41*, 16–25.

Bodell, L. P., & Keel, P. K. (2015). Weight suppression in bulimia nervosa: Associations with biology and behavior. *Journal of Abnormal Psychology, 124*(4), 994–1002.

Boden, J. M., Fergusson, D. M., & Horwood, L. J. (2012). Alcohol misuse and violent behavior: Findings from a 30-year longitudinal study. *Drug and Alcohol Dependence, 122*(1), 135–141.

Bodlund, O., & Kullgren, G. (1996). Transsexualism—General outcome and prognostic factors: A five-year follow-up study of nineteen transsexuals in the process of changing sex. *Archives of Sexual Behavior, 25*, 303–316.

Bodnar, R. J. (2012). Endogenous opiates and behavior. *Peptides, 38*(2), 463–522.

Boehm, J. K., & Kubzansky, L. D. (2012). The heart's content: The association between positive psychological well-being and cardiovascular health. *Psychological bulletin, 138*(4), 655–691.

Bøen, H., Dalgard, O. S., & Bjertness, E. (2012). The importance of social support in the associations between psychological distress and somatic health problems and socioeconomic factors among older adults living at home: A cross sectional study. *BMC Geriatrics, 12*(1), 27.

Bogaert, A. F., & Skorska, M. (2011). Sexual orientation, fraternal birth order, and the maternal immune hypothesis: A review. *Frontiers in Neuroendocrinology, 32*(2), 247–254.

Bogan, R. K., Roth, T., Schwartz, J., & Miloslavsky, M. (2014). Time to response with sodium oxybate for the treatment of excessive daytime sleepiness and cataplexy in patients with narcolepsy. Journal of clinical sleep medicine: *JCSM: official publication of the American Academy of Sleep Medicine, 11*(4), 427–432.

Bogart, A. F. (2010). Physical development and sexual orientation in men and women: An analysis of NATSL-2000. *Archives of Sexual Behavior, 39*, 110–116.

Bögels, S. M., Alden, L., Beidel, D. C., Clark, L. A., Pine, D. S., Stein, M. B., & Voncken, M. (2010). Social anxiety disorder: Questions and answers for the DSM-V. *Depression and Anxiety, 27*(2), 168–189. doi: 10.1002/da.20670

Boland, R. J., & Keller, M. B. (2009). Course and outcome of depression. In I. H. Gotlib & C. L. Hammen (Eds.), *Handbook of depression* (2nd ed., pp. 23–43). New York, NY: Guilford.

Bolinskey, P. K., James, A. V., Cooper-Bolinskey, D., Novi, J. H., Hunter, H. K., Hudak, D. V., . . . Lenzenweger, M. F. (2015). Revisiting the blurry boundaries of schizophrenia: Spectrum disorders in psychometrically identified schizotypes. *Psychiatry Research, 225*(3), 335–340.

Bonanno, G. (2006). Is complicated grief a valid construct? *Clinical Psychology Science Practice, 13*, 129–134.

Bonanno, G., & Kaltman, S. (1999). Toward an integrative perspective on bereavement. *Psychological Bulletin, 125*(6), 1004–1008.

Bonanno, G. A., & Kaltman, S. (2001). The varieties of grief experience. *Clinical Psychology Review, 21*, 705–734.

Bonanno, G., Wortman, C., & Nesse, R. (2004). Prospective patterns of resilience and maladjustment during widowhood. *Psychology and Aging, 19*, 260–271.

Bonanno, G. A., (2004). Loss, trauma, and human resilience: Have we underestimated the human capacity to thrive after extremely aversive events? *American Psychologist, 59*, 20–28.

Bond, A., & Lader, M. (2012). Anxiolytics and sedatives. In J. C. Verster, K. Brady, M. Galanter, & P. Conrod (Eds.), *Drug abuse and addiction in medical illness: Causes, con-sequences and treatment* (pp. 231–239). New York, NY: Springer.

Bongaarts, J., & Over, M. (2010). Global HIV/AIDS policy in transition. *Science, 328*, 1359–1360.

Bonnar-Kidd, K. K. (2010). Sexual offender laws and prevention of sexual violence or recidivism. *American Journal of Public Health, 100*(3), 412–419.

Booij, L., & Van der Does, A. J. (2007). Cognitive and serotonergic vulnerability to depression: Convergent findings. *Journal of Abnormal Psychology, 116*(1), 86–94.

Boon, S., & Draijer, N. (1993). Multiple personality disorder in the Netherlands: A clinical investigation of 71 cases. *American Journal of Psychiatry, 150,* 489–494.

Boone, L., Soenens, B., Vansteenkiste, M., & Braet, C. (2012). Is there a perfectionist in each of us? An experimental study on perfectionism and eating disorder symptoms. *Appetite, 59*(2), 531–540.

Boot, W. R., Simons, D. J., Stothart, C., & Stutts, C. (2013). The pervasive problem with placebos in psychology why active control groups are not sufficient to rule out placebo effects. *Perspectives on Psychological Science, 8*(4), 445–454. doi: 10.1177/1745691613491271

Borg, L., Buonora, M., Butelman, E. R., Ducat, E., Ray, B. M., & Kreek, M. J. (2015). The pharmacology of opioids. In R. K. Ries, D. A. Fiellin, S. C. Miller, & R. Saitz (Eds.), *The ASAM principles of addiction medicine* (5th Ed., pp. 135–150). New York, NY: Wolters Kluwer.

Borge, F.-M., Hoffart, A., Sexton, H., Martinsen, E., Gude, T., Hedley, L. M., & Abrahamsen, G. (2010). Pre-treatment predictors and in-treatment factors associated with change in avoidant and dependent personality disorder traits among patients with social phobia. *Clinical Psychology & Psychotherapy, 17*(2), 87–99.

Borgelt, L. M., Franson, K. L., Nussbaum, A. M., & Wang, G. S. (2013). The pharmacologic and clinical effects of medical cannabis. *Pharmacotherapy: The Journal of Human Pharmacology and Drug Therapy, 33*(2), 195–209.

Borges, G., Nock, M. K., Abad, J. M. H., Hwang, I., Sampson, N. A., Alonso, J., & Kessler, R. C. (2010). Twelve month prevalence of and risk factors for suicide attempts in the WHO World Mental Health Surveys. *The Journal of Clinical Psychiatry, 71*(12), 1617–1628.

Borkovec, T. D., & Costello, E. (1993). Efficacy of applied relaxation and cognitive-behavioral therapy in the treatment of generalized anxiety disorder. *Journal of Consulting and Clinical Psychology, 61*(4), 611–619.

Borkovec, T. D., & Hu, S. (1990). The effect of worry on cardiovascular response to phobic imagery. *Behaviour Research and Therapy, 28,* 69–73.

Borkovec, T. D., & Ruscio, A. (2001). Psychotherapy for generalized anxiety disorder. *Journal of Clinical Psychiatry, 62,* 37–45.

Borkovec, T. D., Alcaine, O. M., & Behar, E. (2004). Avoidance theory of worry and generalized anxiety disorder. In R. G. Heimberg, C. L. Turk, & D. S. Mennin (Eds.), *Generalized anxiety disorder: Advances in research and practice* (pp. 77–108). New York, NY: Guilford.

Borkovec, T. D., Shadick, R., & Hopkins, M. (1991). The nature of normal and pathological worry. In R. M. Rapee & D. H. Barlow (Eds.), *Chronic anxiety, generalized anxiety disorder, and mixed anxiety depression.* New York, NY: Guilford.

Bornstein, R. F. (1992). The dependent personality: Developmental, social, and clinical perspectives. *Psychological Bulletin, 112,* 3–23.

Bornstein, R. F. (2012). Dependent personality disorder. In T. A. Widiger (Ed.), *The Oxford handbook of personality disorders* (pp. 505–526). New York, NY: Oxford University Press.

Borodinsky, L. N., Root, C. M., Cronin, J. A., Sann, S. B., Gu, X., & Spitzer, N. C. (2004). Activity dependent homeostatic specification of transmitter expression in embryonic neurons. *Nature, 429,* 523–530.

Boskind-Lodahl, M. (1976). Cinderella's stepsisters: A feminist perspective on anorexia nervosa and bulimia. *Signs, 2,* 342–356.

Bosson, J. K., Parrott, D. J., Swan, S. C., Kuchynka, S. L., & Schramm, A. T. (2015). A dangerous boomerang: Injunctive norms, hostile sexist attitudes, and male-to-female sexual aggression. *Aggressive Behavior, 41*(6), 580–593.

Bouchard, C. (2002). Genetic influences on body weight and shape. In K. D. Brownell & C. G. Fairburn (Eds.), *Eating disorders and obesity: A comprehensive handbook* (2nd ed., pp. 21–26). New York, NY: Guilford.

Bouchard, M. F., Bellinger, D. C., Wright, R. O., & Weisskopf, M. G. (2010). Attention-deficit/hyperactivity disorder and urinary metabolites of organophosphate pesticides. *Pediatrics, 125*(6), e1270–1277.

Bouchard, T. J., Jr., Lykken, D. T., McGue, M., Segal, N. L., & Tellegen, A. (1990). Sources of human psychological differences: The Minnesota study of twins reared apart. *Science, 250,* 223–228.

Bouman, T. K. (2014). Psychological treatments for hypochondriasis: A narrative review. *Current Psychiatry Reviews, 10,* 58–69.

Bourgeois, M. S. (1992). Evaluating memory wallets in conversations with persons with dementia. *Journal of Speech and Hearing Research, 35,* 1344–1357.

Bourgeois, M. S. (2007). *Memory books and other graphic cuing systems: Practical communication and memory aids for adults with dementia.* Baltimore, MD: Health Professions.

Bouton, M. E. (2005). Behavior systems and the contextual control of anxiety, fear, and panic. In L. Feldman Barrett, P. Niedenthal, & P. Winkielman (Eds.), *Emotion: Conscious and unconscious* (pp. 205–227). New York, NY: Guilford.

Bouton, M. E., Mineka, S., & Barlow, D. H. (2001). A modern learning-theory perspective on the etiology of panic disorder. *Psychological Review, 108,* 4–32.

Bower, B. (1999). Personality conflicts: A clinical upstart elbows its way into the personality-assessment fray. *Science News, 156,* 88–90.

Bower, J. E., Moskowitz, J. T., & Epel, E. (2009). Is benefit finding good for your health? Pathways linking positive life changes after stress and physical health outcomes. *Current Directions in Psychological Science, 18,* 337–341.

Bowers, J. S., & Marsolek, C. J. (2003). *Rethinking implicit memory.* New York, NY: Oxford University Press.

Bowlby, J. (1980). *Attachment and loss.* New York, NY: Basic Books.

Bowman, E. S., & Coons, P. M. (2000). The differential diagnosis of epilepsy, pseudoseizures, dissociative identity disorder, and dissociative disorder not otherwise specified. *Bulletin of the Menninger Clinic, 64,* 164–180.

Boyce, N. (2011). Suicide clusters: The undiscovered country. *The Lancet, 378*(9801), 1452.

Boydell, J., & Allardyce, J. (2011). Does urban density matter? In A. S. David, S. Kapur, P. McGuffin, & R. M. Murray (Eds.), *Schizophrenia: The final frontier—A festschrift for Robin M. Murray* (pp. 273–280). New York, NY: Routledge.

Boyer, P., & Liénard, P. (2008). Ritual behavior in obsessive and normal individuals: Moderating anxiety and reorganizing the flow of action. *Current Directions in Psychological Science, 17*(4), 291–294.

Boysen, G., Ebersole, A., Casner, R., & Coston, N. (2014). Gendered mental disorders: Masculine and feminine stereotypes about mental disorders and their relation to stigma. *The Journal of Social Psychology, 154*(6), 546–565.

Bradford, A., & Meston, C. M. (2006). The impact of anxiety on sexual arousal in women. *Behaviour Research and Therapy, 44,* 1067–1077.

Bradford, A., & Meston, C. M. (2011). Sex and gender disorders. In D. H. Barlow (Ed.), *Oxford handbook of clinical psychology.* New York, NY: Oxford University Press.

Bradford, J. (1997). Medical interventions in sexual deviance. In D. R. Laws & W. O'Donohue (Eds.), *Sexual deviance: Theory, assessment and treatment* (pp. 449–464). New York, NY: Guilford.

Bradley, B. P., Mogg, K., White, J., Groom, C., & de Bono, J. (1999). Attentional bias for emotional faces in generalized anxiety disorder. *British Journal of Clinical Psychology, 38,* 267–278.

Bradley, R., Danielson, L., & Hallahan, D. P. (Eds.). (2002). *Identification of learning disabilities: Research to practice.* Mahwah, NJ: Erlbaum.

Bradley, R. G., Binder, E. B., Epstein, M. P., Tang, Y., Nair, H. P., Liu, W., & Ressler, K. J. (2008). Influence of child abuse on adult depression: Moderation by the corticotropin-releasing hormone receptor gene. *Archives of General Psychiatry, 65*(2), 190–200.

Bradley, W. (1937). The behavior of children receiving Benzedrine. *American Journal of Psychiatry, 94,* 577–585.

Brady, J. P., & Lind, D. L. (1961). Experimental analysis of hysterical blindness. *Archives of General Psychiatry, 4,* 331–339.

Braff, D., Schork, N. J., & Gottesman, I. I. (2007). Endophenotyping schizophrenia. *American Journal of Psychiatry, 164,* 705–707.

Brakefield, T. A., Mednick, S. C., Wilson, H. W., De Neve, J. E., Christakis, N. A., & Fowler, J. H. (2014). Same-sex sexual attraction does not spread in adolescent social networks. *Archives of Sexual Behavior, 43*(2), 335–344.

Brand, B., Classen, C., Lanins, R., Loewenstein, R., McNary, S., Pain, C., & Putnam, F. (2009). A naturalistic study of dissociative identity disorder and dissociative disorder not otherwise specified patients treated by community clinicians. *Psychological Trauma: Theory, Research, Practice, and Policy, 1*(2), 153–171.

Brannigan, G. G., & Decker, S. L. (2006). The Bender-Gestalt II. *American Journal of Orthopsychiatry, 76*(1), 10–12.

Brawman-Mintzer, O. (2001). Pharmacologic treatment of generalized anxiety disorder. *Psychiatric Clinics of North America, 24*, 119–137.

Bray, G. A. (2012). Diet and exercise for weight loss. *Journal of American Medical Association, 307*(24), 2641–2642.

Breckenridge, J., Salter, M., & Shaw, E. (2012). *Use and abuse: Understanding the intersections of childhood abuse, alcohol and drug use and mental health.* Sydney, Australia: University of New South Wales.

Breitbart, W., & Alici, Y. (2012). Evidence-based treatment of delirium in patients with cancer. *Journal of Clinical Oncology, 30*(11), 1206–1214. doi: 10.1200/jco.2011.39.8784

Breitborde, N. J., López, S. R., & Kopelowicz, A. (2010). Expressed emotion and health outcomes among Mexican-Americans with schizophrenia and their caregiving relatives. *The Journal of Nervous and Mental Disease, 198*(2), 105–109.

Bremner, J. D. (1999). Does stress damage the brain? *Biological Psychiatry, 45*, 797–805.

Bremner, J. D., Randall, P. R., Scott, T. M., Bronen, R. A., Seibyl, J. P., Southwick, S. M., & Innis, R. R. (1995). MRI-based measurement of hippocampal volume in patients with combat-related posttraumatic stress disorder. *American Journal of Psychiatry, 152*, 973–981.

Brenes, G. A., Miller, M. E., Stanley, M. A., Williamson, J. D., Knudson, M., & McCall, W. V. (2009). Insomnia in older adults with generalized anxiety disorder. *American Journal of Geriatric Psychiatry, 17*, 465–472.

Brenner, D. E., Kukull, W. A., van Belle, G., Bowen, J. D., McCormick, W. C., Teri, L., & Larson, E. B. (1993). Relationship between cigarette smoking and Alzheimer's disease in a population-based case-control study. *Neurology, 43*, 293–300.

Brent, D., & Birmaher, B. (2009). Paediatric mood disorders. In M. G. Gelder, N. C. Andreasen, J. J. López-Ibor, Jr., & J. R. Geddes (Eds.), *New Oxford textbook of psychiatry* (2nd ed., Vol. 2, pp. 1669–1680). Oxford, UK: Oxford University Press.

Brent, D., Emslie, G., Clarke, G., Wagner, K. D., Asarnow, J. R., Keller, M., & Zelazny, J. (2008). Switching to another SSRI or to venlafaxine with or without cognitive behavioral therapy for adolescents with SSRI-resistant depression: The TORDIA randomized controlled trial. *JAMA: Journal of the American Medical Association, 299*(8), 901–913.

Brent, D., Melhem, N., Donohoe, M. B., & Walker, M. (2009). The incidence and course of depression in bereaved youth 21 months after the loss of a parent to suicide, accident, or sudden natural death. *American Journal of Psychiatry, 166*(7), 786–794.

Brent, D. A., & Kolko, D. J. (1990). The assessment and treatment of children and adolescents at risk for suicide. In S. J. Blumenthal & D. J. Kupfer (Eds.), *Suicide over the life cycle: Risk factors, assessment and treatment of suicidal patients.* Washington, DC: American Psychiatric Press.

Brent, D. A., & Mann, J. J. (2005). Family genetic studies, suicide, and suicidal behavior. *American Journal of Medical Genetics, 133*(1), 13–24.

Brent, D. A., Brunwasser, S. M., Hollon, S. D., Weersing, V. R., Clarke, G. N., Beardless, W. R., Gladstone, T. R. G., Porta, G., Lynch, F. L., Iyengar, S., & Garber, J. (2015). Effect of a cognitive-behavioral prevention program on depression 6 years after implementation among at-risk adolescents: A randomized clinical trial. *JAMA Psychiatry, 72*, 1110–1118.

Brent, D. A., Melhem, N. M., Oquendo, M., Burke, A., Birmaher, B., Stanley, B., Biernesser, C., Keilp, J., Kalka, D., Ellis, S., Porta, G., Zelazny, J., Iyengar, S., & Mann, J. J. (2015). Familial pathways to early-onset suicide attempt: A 5.6-year prospective study. *JAMA Psychiatry, 72*, 160–168.

Brent, D. A., Oquendo, M., Birmaher, B., Greenhill, L., Kolko, D., Stanley, B., & Mann, J. J. (2002). Familial pathways to early-onset suicide attempt risk for suicidal behavior in offspring of mood-disordered suicide attempters. *Archives of General Psychiatry, 59*, 801–807.

Brent, D. A., Oquendo, M., Birmaher, B., Greenhill, L., Kolko, D., Stanley, B., & Mann, J. J. (2003). Peripubertal suicide attempts in offspring of suicide attempters with siblings concordant for suicidal behavior. *American Journal of Psychiatry, 160*, 1486–1493.

Brent, D. A., Perper, J. A., Goldstein, C. E., Kolko, D. J., Allan, M. J., Allman, C. J., & Zellenak, J. P. (1988). Risk factors for adolescent suicide: A comparison of adolescent suicide victims with suicidal inpatients. *Archives of General Psychiatry, 45*, 581–588.

Brentjens, M. H., Yeung-Yue, K. A., Lee, P. C., & Tyring, S. K. (2003). Recurrent genital herpes treatments and their impact on quality of life. *Pharmacoeconomics, 21*, 853–863.

Breslau, N. (2012). Epidemiology of posttraumatic stress disorder in adults. In J. G. Beck & D. M. Sloan (Eds.), *The Oxford handbook of traumatic stress disorders* (pp. 84–97). New York, NY: Oxford University Press.

Breslau, N., Davis, G. C., & Andreski, M. A. (1995). Risk factors for PTSD-related traumatic events: A prospective analysis. *American Journal of Psychiatry, 152*, 529–535.

Breslau, N., Lucia, V. C., & Alvarado, G. F. (2006). Intelligence and other predisposing factors in exposure to trauma and posttraumatic stress disorder. *Archives of General Psychiatry, 63*, 1238–1245.

Breuer, J., & Freud, S. (1957). *Studies on hysteria.* New York, NY: Basic Books. (Original work published 1895.)

Brewer, S., Gleditsch, S. L., Syblik, D., Tietjens, M. E., & Vacik, H. W. (2006). Pediatric anxiety: Child life intervention in day surgery. *Journal of Pediatric Nursing, 21*, 13–22.

Brewerton, T. D., Rance, S. J., Dansky, B. S., O'Neil, P. M., & Kilpatrick, D. G. (2014). A comparison of women with child-adolescent versus adult onset binge eating: Results from the National Women's Study. *International Journal of Eating Disorders, 47*(7), 836–843.

Britton, J. C., & Rauch, S. L. (2009). Neuroanatomy and neuroimaging of anxiety disorders. In M. Antony & M. B. Stein (Eds.), *Oxford handbook of anxiety and related disorders* (pp. 97–110). Oxford, UK: Oxford University Press.

Britton, J. C., Grillon, C., Lissek, S., Norcross, M. A., Szuhany, K., Chen, G., Ernst, M., Nelson, E. E., Leibenluft, E., Shechner, T., & Pine, D. S. (2013). Response to learned threat: An fMRI study in adolescent and adult anxiety. *American Journal of Psychiatry, 170*, 1195–1204.

Brody, A. L., Saxena, S., Stoessel, P., Gillies, L. A., Fairbanks, L. A., Alborzian, S., & Baxter, L. R., Jr. (2001). Regional brain metabolic changes in patients with major depression treated with either paroxetine or interpersonal therapy. *Archives of General Psychiatry, 48*, 631–640.

Brody, H., & Miller, F. G. (2011). Lessons from recent research about the placebo effect—from art to science. *JAMA: Journal of the American Medical Association, 306*(23), 2612–2613. doi: 10.1001/jama.2011.1850

Brody, M. J., Walsh, B. T., & Devlin, M. J. (1994). Binge eating disorder: Reliability and validity of a new diagnostic category. *Journal of Consulting and Clinical Psychology, 62*, 381–386.

Broft, A., Berner, L. A., & Walsh, B. T. (2010). Pharmacotherapy for bulimia nervosa. In C. M. Grilo & J. E. Mitchell (Eds.), *The treatment of eating disorders: A clinical handbook.* (pp. 388–401). New York, NY: Guilford.

Bromet, E., Andrade, L. H., Hwang, I., Sampson, N. A., Alonso, J., de Girolamo, G., & Kessler, R. C. (2011). Cross-national epidemiology of DSM-IV major depressive episode. *BMC Medicine, 9*(1), 90.

Brondolo, E., Grantham, K. I., Karlin, W., Taravella, J., Mencia-Ripley, A., Schwartz, J. E., & Contrada, R. J. (2009). Trait hostility and ambulatory blood pressure among traffic enforcement agents: The effects of stressful social interactions. *Journal of Occupational Health Psychology, 14*(2), 110–121.

Brotman, M. A., Schmajuk, M., Rich, B. A., Dickstein, D. P., Guyer, A. E., Costello, E. J., & Leibenluft, E. (2006). Prevalence, clinical correlates, and longitudinal course of severe mood dysregulation in children. *Biological Psychiatry, 60*(9), 991–997.

Brotto, L. A. (2006). Psychologic-based desire and arousal disorders: Treatment strategies and outcome results. In I. Goldstein, C. M. Meston, S. R. Davis, & A. M. Traish (Eds.), *Women's sexual function and dysfunction: Study, diagnosis, and treatment* (pp. 441–448). New York, NY: Taylor and Francis.

Brotto, L. A. (2010). The DSM diagnostic criteria for hypoactive sexual desire disorder in women. *Archives of Sexual Behavior, 39*, 222–239.

Brotto, L. (2015). Filbanserin. *Archives of Sexual Behavior, 44*(8), 2103–2105. doi 10.1007/s10508-015-0643-9

Brotto, L., & Luria, M. (2014). *Sexual interest/arousal disorder in women.* In Y. M. Binik & K. S. K. Hall (Eds.). Principles and Practice of Sex Therapy 5th edition (pp. 17–42). New York, NY: The Guildford Press.

Broude, G. J., & Greene, S. J. (1980). Cross-cultural codes on 20 sexual attitudes and practices. In H. Barry, III, & A. Schlegel

(Eds.), *Cross-cultural samples and codes* (pp. 313–333). Pittsburgh, PA: University of Pittsburgh Press.

Broughton, R., Billings, R., & Cartwright, R. (1994). Homicidal somnambulism: A case report. *Sleep, 17*, 253–264.

Broughton, R. J. (2000). NREM arousal parasomnias. In M. H. Kryger, T. Roth, & W. C. Dement (Eds.), *Principles and practice of sleep medicine* (3rd ed., pp. 693–706). Philadelphia, PA: W. B. Saunders.

Brown, A., Scales, U., Beever, W., Rickards, B., Rowley, K., & O'Dea, K. (2012). Exploring the expression of depression and distress in aboriginal men in central Australia: A qualitative study. *BMC Psychiatry, 12*(1), 97.

Brown, D. R., Ahmed, F., Gary, L. E., & Milburn, M. G. (1995). Major depression in a community sample of African Americans. *American Journal of Psychiatry, 152*, 373–378.

Brown, G. W. (1959). Experiences of discharged chronic schizophrenic mental hospital patients in various types of living group. *Millbank Memorial Fund Quarterly, 37*, 105–131.

Brown, G. W., & Birley, J. L. T. (1968). Crisis and life change and the onset of schizophrenia. *Journal of Health and Social Behavior, 9*, 203–214.

Brown, G. W., Monck, E. M., Carstairs, G. M., & Wing, J. K. (1962). Influence of family life on the course of schizophrenic illness. *British Journal of Preventive and Social Medicine, 16*, 55–68.

Brown, J., & Finn, P. (1982). Drinking to get drunk: Findings of a survey of junior and senior high school students. *Journal of Alcohol and Drug Education, 27*, 13–25.

Brown, M. M., Bell, D. S., Jason, L. A., Christos, C., & Bell, D. E. (2012). Understanding long term outcomes of chronic fatigue syndrome. *Journal of Clinical Psychology, 68*(9), 1028–1035.

Brown, P. L. (2006, December 2). Supporting boys or girls when the line isn't clear. *New York Times.* Retrieved from http://www.nytimes.com/2006/12/02/us/02child.html

Brown, R. J., & Lewis-Fernandez, R. (2011). Culture and conversion disorder: Implications for DSM-5. *Psychiatry, 74*(3), 187–206. doi: 10.1521/psyc.2011.74.3.187

Brown, T. A., & Barlow, D. H. (2005). Dimensional versus categorical classification of mental disorders in the fifth edition of the diagnostic and statistical manual of mental disorders and beyond: Comment on the special section. Special issue: Toward a dimensionally based taxonomy of psychopathology. *Journal of Abnormal Psychology, 114*(4), 551–556.

Brown, T. A., & Barlow, D. H. (2009). A proposal for a dimensional classification system based on the shared features of the DSM-IV anxiety and mood disorders: Implications for assessment and treatment. *Psychological Assessment, 21*(3), 256–271.

Brown, T. A., & Barlow, D. H. (2014). *Anxiety and related disorders interview schedule for DSM-5 (ADIS-5L): Client interview schedule.* New York, NY: Oxford University Press.

Brown, T. A., & Barlow, D. H. (in press). *Anxiety Disorders Interview Schedule for DSM-5 (AVIS.5).* New York, NY: Oxford University Press.

Brown, T. A., & Naragon-Gainey, K. (2013). Evaluation of the unique and specific contributions of dimensions of the triple vulnerability model to the prediction of DSM-IV anxiety and mood disorder constructs. *Behavior Therapy, 44*(2), 277–292.

Brown, T. A., Barlow, D. H., & Liebowitz, M. R. (1994). The empirical basis of generalized anxiety disorder. *American Journal of Psychiatry, 15*(9), 1272–1280.

Brown, T. A., Campbell, L. A., Lehman, C. L., Grisham, J. R., & Mancill, R. B. (2001). Current and lifetime comorbidity of the DSM-IV anxiety and mood disorders in a large clinical sample. *Journal of Abnormal Psychology.*

Brown, T. A., Chorpita, B. F., & Barlow, D. H. (1998). Structural relationships among dimensions of the DSM-IV anxiety and mood disorders and dimensions of negative affect, positive affect, and autonomic arousal. *Journal of Abnormal Psychology, 107*(2), 179–192.

Brown, T. A., Marten, P. A., & Barlow, D. H. (1995). Discriminant validity of the symptoms comprising the DSM-III-R and DSM-IV associated symptom criterion of generalized anxiety disorder. *Journal of Anxiety Disorders, 9*, 317–328.

Brown, T. A., White, K. S., & Barlow, D. H. (2005). A psychometric reanalysis of the Albany panic and phobia questionnaire. *Behaviour Research and Therapy, 43*, 337–355.

Brown, T. E. (Ed.). (2009). *ADHD comorbidities: Handbook for ADHD complications in children and adults.* Arlington, VA: American Psychiatric Publishing.

Brown, W. M., Finn, C. J., Cooke, B. M., & Breedlove, S. M. (2002). Differences in finger length ratios between self-identified "butch" and "femme" lesbians. *Archives of Sexual Behavior, 31*, 123–127.

Browne, H. A., Hansen, S. N., Buxbaum, J. D., Gair, S. L., Nissen, J. B., Nikolajsen, K. H., Schendel, D. E., Reichenberg, A., Parner, E. T., & Grice, D. E. (2015). Familial clustering of tic disorders and obsessive-compulsive disorder. *JAMA psychiatry, 72*, 359–366.

Brownell, K. D. (1991). Dieting and the search for the perfect body: Where physiology and culture collide. *Behavior Therapy, 22*, 1–12.

Brownell, K. D. (2002). Eating disorders in athletes. In K. D. Brownell & C. G. Fairburn (Eds.), *Eating disorders and obesity: A comprehensive handbook* (2nd ed., pp. 191–196). New York, NY: Guilford.

Brownell, K. D. (2003). *Food fight: The inside story of the food industry, America's obesity crisis and what we can do about it.* New York, NY: McGraw-Hill.

Brownell, K. D., & Fairburn, C. G. (Eds.) (1995). *Eating disorders and obesity: A comprehensive handbook.* New York, NY: Guilford.

Brownell, K. D., & Frieden, T. R. (2009). Ounces of prevention—the public policy case for taxes on sugared beverages. *New England Journal of Medicine, 360*(18), 1805–1808.

Brownell, K. D. & Ludwig, D. S. (2011). The supplemental nutrition assistance program, soda, and USDA policy: Who benefits? *Journal of American Medical Association, 306*, 1370–1371.

Brownell, K. D., & Rodin, J. (1994). The dieting maelstrom: Is it possible and advisable to lose weight? *American Psychologist, 49*(9), 781–791.

Brownell, K. D., & Yach, D. (2005). The battle of the bulge. *Foreign Policy,* 26–27.

Brownell, K. D., Farley, T., Willett, W. C., Popkin, B. M., Chaloupka, F. J., Thompson, J. W., & Ludwig, D. S. (2009). The public health and economic benefits of taxing sugar-sweetened beverages. *New England Journal of Medicine, 361*(16), 1599–1605.

Brownell, K. D., Hayes, S. C., & Barlow, D. H. (1977). Patterns of appropriate and deviant sexual arousal: The behavioral treatment of multiple sexual deviations. *Journal of Consulting and Clinical Psychology, 45*(6), 1144–1155.

Brownell, K. D., Kersh, R., Ludwig, D. S., Post, R. C., Puhl, R. M., Schwartz, M. B., & Willett, W. C. (2010). Personal responsibility and obesity: A constructive approach to a controversial issue. *Health Affairs, 29*(3), 379–387.

Bruce, M. L. (2002). Psychosocial risk factors for depressive disorders in late life. *Biological Psychiatry, 52*, 175–184.

Bruce, M. L., & Kim, K. M. (1992). Differences in the effects of divorce on major depression in men and women. *American Journal of Psychiatry, 149*(7), 914–917.

Bruce, S. E., Yonkers, K. A., Otto, M. W., Eisen, J. L., Weisberg, R. B., Pagano, M., & Keller, M. B. (2005). Influence of psychiatric comorbidity on recovery and recurrence in generalized anxiety disorder, social phobia, and panic disorder: A 12-year prospective study. *American Journal of Psychiatry, 162*, 1179–1187.

Bruce, S. M., & Venkatesh, K. (2014). Special education disproportionality in the United States, Germany, Kenya, and India. *Disability & Society, 29*(6), 908–921. doi: 10.1080/09687599.2014.880330

Bruch, H. (1973). *Eating disorders: Obesity, anorexia nervosa, and the person within.* New York, NY: Basic Books.

Bruch, H. (1985). Four decades of eating disorders. In D. M. Garner & P. E. Garfinkel (Eds.), *Handbook of psychotherapy for anorexia nervosa and bulimia* (pp. 7–18). New York, NY: Guilford.

Bruch, M. A., & Heimberg, R. G. (1994). Differences in perceptions of parental and personal characteristics between generalized and non-generalized social phobics. *Journal of Anxiety Disorders, 8*, 155–168.

Bruck, M., Ceci, S., Francouer, E., & Renick, A. (1995). Anatomically detailed dolls do not facilitate preschoolers' reports of a pediatric examination involving genital touching. *Journal of Experimental Psychology: Applied, 1*, 95–109.

Brunoni, A. R., Valiengo, L., Baccaro, A., Zanao, T., de Oliveira, J. F., Goulart, A., & Fregni, F. (2013). The sertraline versus electrical current therapy for treating depression clinical study: Results from a factorial, randomized, controlled trial. *JAMA Psychiatry, 70*(4), 383–391.

Bryant, R. A. (2010). The complexity of complex PTSD. *American Journal of Psychiatry, 167*, 879–881.

Bryant, R. A., Moulds, M. L., & Nixon, R. V. D. (2003). Cognitive behavior therapy of acute stress disorder: A four-year follow-up. *Behaviour Research and Therapy, 41*, 489–494.

Bryant, R. A., & Das, P. (2012). The neural circuitry of conversion disorder and its recovery. *Journal of Abnormal Psychology, 121*(1), 289–296. doi: 10.1037/a0025076

Bryant, R. A., Kenny, L., Joscelyne, A., Rawson, N., Maccallum, F., Cahill, C., Hopwood, S., Aderka, I., & Nickerson, A. (2014). Treating prolonged grief disorder: A randomized clinical trial. *JAMA Psychiatry, 71*, 1332–1339.

Bryant, R. A., Friedman, M. J., Spiegel, D., Ursano, R., & Strain, J. (2011). A review of acute stress disorder in DSM-5. *Depression and Anxiety, 28*(9), 802–817. doi: 10.1002/da.20737

Bryant, R. A., O'Donnell, M. L., Creamer, M., McFarlane, A., & Silove, D. (2013). A multisite analysis of the fluctuating course of posttraumatic stress disorder. *JAMA Psychiatry, 70*, 839–846.

Buchanan, R. W., & Carpenter, W. T. (2005). Schizophrenia and other psychotic disorders. In B. J. Sadock & V. A. Sadock (Eds.), *Kaplan & Sadock's comprehensive textbook of psychiatry* (pp. 1329–1345). Philadelphia, PA: Lippincott, Williams & Wilkins.

Buchwald, A. M., & Rudick-Davis, D. (1993). The symptoms of major depression. *Journal of Abnormal Psychology, 102*(2), 197–205.

Buchwald, H., Avidor, Y., Braunwald, E., Jensen, M. D., Pories, W., Fahrbach, K., & Schoelles, K. (2004). Bariatric surgery: A systematic review and meta-analysis. *JAMA: Journal of the American Medical Association, 292*, 1724–1737.

Buckingham-Howes, S., Berger, S. S., Scaletti, L. A., & Black, M. M. (2013). Systematic review of prenatal cocaine exposure and adolescent development. *Pediatrics, 131* (6), e1917–e1936.

Budnitz, D. S., Lovegrove, M. C., Shehab, N., & Richards, C. L. (2011). Emergency hospitalizations for adverse drug events in older Americans. *New England Journal of Medicine, 365*(21), 2002–2012.

Bufferd, S. J., Dougherty, L. R., Carlson, G. A., Rose, S., Klein, D. N. (2012). Psychiatric disorders in preschoolers: Continuity from ages 3 to 6. *American Journal of Psychiatry, 169*, 1157–1164.

Buffum, J. (1982). Pharmacosexology: The effects of drugs on sexual function—A review. *Journal of Psychoactive Drugs, 14*, 5–44.

Buhle, J. T., Stevens, B. L., Friedman, J. J., & Wager, T. D. (2012). Distraction and placebo: two separate routes to pain control. *Psychological Science, 23*(3), 246–253.

Buhlmann, U., Reese, H. E., Renaud, S., & Wilhelm, S. (2008). Clinical considerations for the treatment of body dysmorphic disorder with cognitive-behavioral therapy. *Body Image, 5*(1), 39–49.

Buka, S. L., Seidman, L. J., Tsuang, M. T., & Goldstein, J. M. (2013). The New England family study high-risk project: Neurological impairments among offspring of parents with schizophrenia and other psychoses. *American Journal of Medical Genetics Part B: Neuropsychiatric Genetics, 162*(7), 653–660.

Bulik, C. M., Sullivan, P. F., & Kendler, K. S. (2000). An empirical study of the classification of eating disorders. *American Journal of Psychiatry, 157*(6), 886–895.

Bulik, C. M., Sullivan, P. F., Tozzi, F., Furberg, H., Lichtenstin, P., & Pedersen, N. L. (2006). Prevalence, heritability, and prospective risk factors, for anorexia nervosa. *Archives of General Psychiatry, 63*(3), 305–312.

Bulik, C. M., Thornton, L., Pinheiro, A. P., Plotnicov, K., Klump, K. L., Brandt, H., . . . Kaye, W. H. (2008). Suicide attempts in anorexia nervosa. *Psychosomatic Medicine, 70*(3), 378–383.

Bumpass, E. R., Fagelman, F. D., & Brix, R. J. (1983). Intervention with children who set fires. *American Journal of Psychotherapy, 37*(3), 328–345.

Burgess, C. R., & Scammell, T. E. (2012). Narcolepsy: neural mechanisms of sleepiness and cataplexy. *The Journal of Neuroscience, 32*(36), 12305–12311.

Burkhalter, H., Wirz-Justice, A., Denhaerynck, K., Fehr, T., Steiger, J., Venzin, R. M., . . . De Geest, S. (2015). The effect of bright light therapy on sleep and circadian rhythms in renal transplant recipients: A pilot randomized, multicentre wait-list controlled trial. *Transplant International, 28*(1), 59–70.

Burnette, M. M., Koehn, K. A., Kenyon-Jump, R., Hutton, K., & Stark, C. (1991). Control of genital herpes recurrences using progressive muscle relaxation. *Behavior Therapy, 22*, 237–247.

Burnham, M. M., & Gaylor, E. E. (2011). Sleep environments of young children in post-industrial societies. In M. El-Sheikh (Ed.), *Sleep and development: Familial and sociocultural considerations* (pp. 195–218). New York, NY: Oxford University Press.

Burns, J. W., Glenn, B., Bruehl, S., Harden, R. N., & Lofland, K. (2003). Cognitive factors influence outcome following multidisciplinary chronic pain treatment: A replication and extension of a cross-lagged panel analysis. *Behaviour Research and Therapy, 41*, 1163–1182.

Burns, J. W., Nielson, W. R., Jensen, M. P., Heapy, A., Czlapinski, R., & Kerns, R. D. (2015). Specific and general therapeutic mechanisms in cognitive behavioral treatment of chronic pain. *Journal of Consulting and Clinical Psychology, 83*(1), 1–11.

Burri, A., Spector, T., & Rahman, Q. (2013). A discordant monozygotic twin approach to testing environmental influences on sexual dysfunction in women. *Archives of Sexual Behavior, 42*(6), 961–972.

Burton, R. (1977). *Anatomy of melancholy.* (Reprint edition). New York, NY: Random House. (Original work published 1621.)

Busatto, G. F. (2013). Structural and functional neuroimaging studies in major depressive disorder with psychotic features: A critical review. *Schizophrenia Bulletin, 39*(4), 776–786. doi: 10.1093/schbul/sbt054

Buscher, A. L., & Giordano, T. P. (2010). Gaps in knowledge in caring for HIV survivors long-term. *JAMA: Journal of the American Medical Association, 304*, 340–341.

Bushman, B. J. (1993). Human aggression while under the influence of alcohol and other drugs: An integrative research review. *Psychological Science, 2*, 148–152.

Butcher, J. N. (2009). Clinical personality assessment: History, evolution, contemporary models, and practical applications. In J. N. Butcher (Ed.), *Oxford handbook of personality assessment* (pp. 5–21). New York, NY: Oxford University Press.

Butcher, J. N., Graham, J. R., Williams, C. L., & Ben-Porath, Y. S. (1990). *Development and use of the MMPI-2 content scales.* Minneapolis, MN: University of Minnesota Press.

Butler, B. (2006). NGRI revisited: Venirepersons' attitudes toward the insanity defense. *Journal of Applied Social Psychology, 36*, 1833–1847.

Butler, L. D., Duran, R. E. F., Jasiukaitis, P., Koopman, C., & Spiegel, D. (1996). Hypnotizability and traumatic experience: A diathesis stress model of dissociative symptomatology. *American Journal of Psychiatry, 153*, 42–63.

Buysse, D. J., Strollo, P. J., Black, J. E., Zee, P. G., & Winkelman, J. W. (2008). Sleep disorders. In R. E. Hales, S. C. Yudofsky, & G. O. Gabbard (Eds.), *The American Psychiatric Publishing textbook of psychiatry* (5th ed., pp. 921–969). Arlington, VA: American Psychiatric Publishing.

Buzzella, B. A., Ehrenreich-May, J. T., & Pincus, D. B. (2011). Comorbidity and family factors associated with selective mutism. *Child Development Research, 2011*, 1–9.

Bye, E. K. (2007). Alcohol and violence: Use of possible confounders in a time-series analysis. *Addiction, 102*, 369–376.

Byers, A. L., Yaffe, K., Covinsky, K. E., Friedman, M. B., & Bruce, M. L. (2010). High occurrence of mood and anxiety disorders among older adults: The National Comorbidity Survey Replication. *Archives of General Psychiatry, 67*(5), 489–496. doi: 10.1001/archgenpsychiatry.2010.35

Byne, W., & Parsons, B. (1993). Human sexual orientation: The biologic theories reappraised. *Archives of General Psychiatry, 50*, 228–239.

Byne, W., Lasco, M. S., Kemether, E., Edgar, M. A., Morgello, S., Jones, L. B., & Tobet, S. (2000). The interstitial nuclei of the human anterior hypothalamus: An investigation of sexual variation in volume and cell size, number and density. *Brain Research, 856*, 254–258.

Byne, W., Bradley, S. J., Coleman, E., Eyler, A. E., Green, R., Menvielle, E. J., & Tompkins, D. A. (2012). Report of the American Psychiatric Association Task Force on treatment of gender identity disorder. *Archives of Sexual Behavior, 41*(4), 759–796.

Byrd, A. L., Loeber, R., & Pardini, D. A. (2014). Antisocial behavior, psychopathic features and abnormalities in reward and punishment processing in youth. *Clinical Child and Family Psychology Review, 17*(2), 125–156.

Byrne, D., & Schulte, L. (1990). Personality dispositions as mediators of sexual responses. *Annual Review of Sex Research, 1*, 93–117.

Byrne, E. M., Johnson, J., McRae, A. F., Nyholt, D. R., Medland, S. E., Gehrman, P. R., & Chenevix-Trench, G. (2012). A genome-wide association study of caffeine-related sleep disturbance: Confirmation of a role for a common variant in the adenosine receptor. *Sleep, 35*(7), 967–975.

Caballero, B. (2007). The global epidemic of obesity: An overview. *Epidemiologic Reviews, 29*, 1–5.

Caballo, V. E., Salazar, I. C., Irurtia, M. J., Olivares, P., & Olivares, J. (2014). The relationship between social skills and social anxiety and personality styles/disorders. *Behavioral Psychology, 22*, 401–422.

Cacioppo, J. T., Amaral, D. G., Blanchard, J. J., Cameron, J. L., Carter, C. S., Crews, D., & Quinn, K. J. (2007). Social neuroscience: Progress and implications for mental health. *Perspectives on Psychological Science, 2*(2), 99–123.

Cacioppo, J. T., & Patrick, W. (2008). *Loneliness: Human nature and the need for social connection.* New York, NY: Norton.

Cadoret, R. J. (1978). Psychopathology in the adopted-away offspring of biologic parents with antisocial behavior. *Archives of General Psychiatry, 35*, 176–184.

Cadoret, R. J., Yates, W. R., Troughton, E., Woodworth, G., & Stewart, M. A. (1995). Genetic-environment interaction in the genesis of aggressivity and conduct disorders. *Archives of General Psychiatry, 52*, 916–924.

Cafri, G., Yamamiya, Y., Brannick, M., & Thompson, J. K. (2005). The influence of sociocultural factors on body image: A meta-analysis. *Clinical Psychology: Science and Practice, 12*, 421–433.

Caglayan, A. O. (2010). Genetic causes of syndromic and non-syndromic autism. *Developmental Medicine & Child Neurology, 52*(2), 130–138. doi: 10.1111/j.1469-8749.2009.03523.x

Cain, A. S., Epler, A. J., Steinley, D., & Sher, K. J. (2010). Stability and change in patterns of concerns related to eating, weight, and shape in young adult women: A latent transition analysis. *Journal of Abnormal Psychology, 119*(2), 255–267.

Cain, V. S., Johannes, C. B., Avis, N. E., Mohr, B., Schocken, M., Skurnick, J., & Ory, M. (2003). Sexual functioning and practices in a multi-ethnic study of midlife women: Baseline results from SWAN. *Journal of Sex Research, 40*(3), 266–276.

Calabrese, J., Shelton, M., Rapport, D., Youngstrom, E., Jackson, K., Bilali, S., & Findling, R. L. (2005). A 20-month, double-blind, maintenance trial of lithium versus divalproex, in rapid-cycling bipolar disorder. *American Journal of Psychiatry, 162*, 2152–2161.

Calamari, J. E., Chik, H. M., Pontarelli, N. K., & DeJong, B. L. (2012). Phenomenology and epidemiology of obsessive compulsive disorder. In G. Steketee (Ed.), *The Oxford handbook of obsessive compulsive and spectrum disorders* (pp. 11–47). New York, NY: Oxford University Press.

Calamari, J. E., Wiegartz, P. S., Riemann, B. C., Cohen, R. J., Greer, A., Jacobi, D. M., & Carmin, C. (2004). Obsessive-compulsive disorder subtypes: An attempted replication and extension of symptom-based taxonomy. *Behavior Research and Therapy, 42*, 647–670.

Calati, R., Gressier, F., Balestri, M., & Serretti, A. (2013). Genetic modulation of borderline personality disorder: systematic review and meta-analysis. *Journal of Psychiatric Research, 47*(10), 1275–1287.

Caligor, E., Levy, K. N., & Yeomans, F. E. (2015). Narcissistic personality disorder: diagnostic and clinical challenges. *American Journal of Psychiatry, 172*(5).

Callahan, L. A., McGreevy, M. A., Cirincione, C., & Steadman, H. (1992). Measuring the effects of the guilty but mentally ill (GBMI) verdict: Georgia's 1982 GBMI reform. *Law and Human Behavior, 16*, 447–462.

Callanan, V. J., & Davis, M. S. (2012). Gender differences in suicide methods. *Social Psychiatry and Psychiatric Epidemiology, 47*(6), 857–869.

Callicott, J. H., Mattay, V. S., Verchinski, B. A., Marenco, S., Egan, M. F., & Weinberger, D. R. (2003). Complexity of prefrontal cortical dysfunction in schizophrenia: More than up or down. *American Journal of Psychiatry, 160*, 2209–2215.

Cameron, N. M., Champagne, F. A., Parent, C., Fish, E. W., Ozaki-Kuroda, K., & Meaney, M. J. (2005). The programming of individual differences in defensive responses and reproductive strategies in the rat through variations in maternal care. *Neuroscience and Biobehavioral Reviews, 29*, 843–865.

Campbell, A. N., Miele, G. M., Nunes, E. V., McCrimmon, S., & Ghitza, U. E. (2012). Web-based, psychosocial treatment for substance use disorders in community treatment settings. *Psychological Services, 9*(2), 212.

Campbell, J. M., & Oei, T. P. (2010). A cognitive model for the intergenerational transference of alcohol use behavior. *Addictive Behaviors, 35*(2), 73–83. doi: 10.1016/j.addbeh.2009.09.013

Campbell, J., & Oei, T. P. (2013). The intergenerational transference of addiction. In P.M. Miller, A.W. Blume, D.J. Kavanagh, K.M. Kampman, M.E. Bates, M.E. Larimer, N. M. Petry, P. De Witte, & S.A. Ball (Eds), *Principles of addiction: Comprehensive addictive behaviors and disorders*, (Vol.1, 313–322). Waltham, MA: Elsevier Academic Press.

Campbell, W. K., & Miller, J. D. (2011). *The hand-book of narcissism and narcissistic personality disorder: Theoretical approaches, empirical findings, and treatments.* Hoboken, NJ: John Wiley & Sons.

Campbell-Sills, L., & Brown, T. A. (2010). Generalized anxiety disorder. In M. M. Antony & D. H. Barlow (Eds.), *Handbook of assessment and treatment planning for psychological disorders* (2nd ed., pp. 224–266). New York, NY: Guilford.

Campbell-Sills, L., Ellard, K. K., & Barlow, D. H. (2015). Emotion regulation in anxiety disorders. In J. J. Gross (Ed.), *Handbook of Emotion Regulation* (2nd ed.). New York, NY: Guilford.

Campo, J. A., Nijman, H., Merckelbach, H., & Evers, C. (2003). Psychiatric comorbidity of gender identity disorders: A survey among Dutch psychiatrists. *American Journal of Psychiatry, 160*, 1332–1336.

Campo, J. V., & Negrini, B. J. (2000). Case study: Negative reinforcement and behavioral management of conversion disorder. *Journal of the American Academy of Child and Adolescent Psychiatry, 39*(6), 787–790.

Canli, T., & Lesch, K.-P. (2007). Long story short: The serotonin transporter in emotion regulation and social cognition. *Nature Neuroscience, 10*, 1103–1109.

Cannon, T. D., Barr, C. E., & Mednick, S. A. (1991). Genetic and perinatal factors in the etiology of schizophrenia. In E. F. Walker (Ed.), *Schizophrenia: A life-course developmental perspective* (pp. 9–31). New York, NY: Academic.

Cannon, W. B. (1929). *Bodily changes in pain, hunger, fear and rage* (2nd ed.). New York, NY: Appleton-Century-Crofts.

Cannon, W. B. (1942). Voodoo death. *American Anthropologist, 44*, 169–181.

Cantor, J. M., Blanchard, R., Paterson, A. D., & Bogaert, A. F. (2002). How many gay men owe their sexual orientation to fraternal birth order? *Archives of Sexual Behavior, 31*, 63–71.

Capobianco, D. J., Swanson, J. W., & Dodick, D. W. (2001). Medication-induced (analgesic rebound) headache: Historical aspects and initial descriptions of the North American experience. *Headache, 41*, 500–502.

Cardeña, E., & Carlson, E. (2011). Acute stress disorder revisited. *Annual Review of Clinical Psychology, 7*, 245–267. doi: 10.1146/annurev-clinpsy-032210-104502

Cardeña, E., Lewis-Fernandez, R., Bear, D., Pakianathan, I., & Spiegel, D. (1996). Dissociative disorders. In T. A. Widiger, A. J. Frances, H. A. Pincus, R. Ross, M. B. First, & W. W. Davis (Eds.), *DSM-IV sourcebook* (Vol. 2, pp. 973–1005). Washington, DC: American Psychiatric Press.

Cardeña, E. A., & Gleaves, D. H. (2003). Dissociative disorders: Phantoms of the self. In M. Hersen & S. M. Turner (Eds.), *Adult psychopathology and diagnosis* (4th ed., pp. 476–404). Hoboken, NJ: Wiley.

Cardi, V., Esposito, M., Clarke, A., Schifano, S., & Treasure, J. (2015). The impact of induced positive mood on symptomatic behaviour in eating disorders. An experimental, AB/BA crossover design testing a multimodal presentation during a test-meal. *Appetite, 87*, 192–198.

Carlo, G., Knight, G. P., Roesch, S. C., Opal, D., & Davis, A. (2014). Personality across cultures: A critical analysis of Big Five research and current directions. In F. T. L. Leong, L. Comas-Díaz, G. C. Nagayama Hall, V. C. McLoyd, & J. E. (Eds.) *APA handbook of multicultural psychology, Vol. 1: Theory and research*, (pp. 285–298). Washington, DC: American Psychological Association.

Carlson, G. A. (1990). Annotation: Child and adolescent mania—Diagnostic considerations. *Journal of Child Psychology and Psychiatry, 31*(3), 331–341.

Carlson, G. A., & Klein, D. N. (2014). How to understand divergent views on bipolar disorder in youth. *Annual Review of Clinical Psychology, 10*, 529–551.

Carlson, G. A., & Meyer S. E. (2006). Phenomenology and diagnosis of bipolar disorder in children, adolescents, and adults: Complexities and developmental issues. *Development and Psychopathology, 18*, 939–969.

Caron, C., & Rutter, M. (1991). Comorbidity in childhood psychopathology: Concepts, issues, and research strategies. *Journal of Child Psychology and Psychiatry, 32*, 1063–1080.

Carpenter, A. L., Pulfiafico, A. C., Kurtz, S. M., Pincus, D. B., & Comer, J. S. (2014). Extending parent-child interaction therapy for early childhood internalizing problems: New advances for ana overlooked population. *Clinical Child and Family Psychology Review, 17*, 340–356.

Carpenter, M. J., Jardin, B. F., Burris, J. L., Mathew, A. R., Schnoll, R. A., Rigotti, N. A., & Cummings, K. M. (2013). Clinical strategies to enhance the efficacy of nicotine replacement therapy for smoking cessation: a review of the literature. *Drugs, 73*(5), 407–426.

Carpenter, W. T., & van Os, J. (2011). Should attenuated psychosis syndrome be a DSM-5 diagnosis? *American Journal of Psychiatry, 168*(5), 460–463.

Carpentier, M., Silovsky, J., & Chaffin, M. (2006). Randomized trial of treatment for children with sexual behavior problems: Ten-year follow-up. *Journal of Consulting and Clinical Psychology, 74*, 482–488.

Carr, A., Keenleyside, M., & Fitzhenry, M. (2015). *The Waterford Mental Health Survey.* University College Dublin School of Psychology, Health Services Executive.

Carr, E. G., & Durand, V. M. (1985). Reducing behavior problems through functional communication training. *Journal of Applied Behavior Analysis, 18*, 111–126.

Carrico, A. W., & Antoni, M. H. (2008). Effects of psychological interventions on neuroendocrine hormone regulation and immune states in HIV-positive persons: A review of randomized controlled trials. *Psychosomatic Medicine, 70*, 575–584.

Carrier, S., Brock, G. B., Pommerville, P. J., Shin, J., Anglin, G., Whittaker, S., & Beasley, C. M., Jr. (2005). Efficacy and safety of oral tadalafil in the treatment of men in Canada with erectile dysfunction: A randomized, double-blind, parallel, placebo-controlled clinical trial. *Journal of Sexual Medicine, 2*, 685–698.

Carroll, B. J., Feinberg, M., Greden, J. F., Haskett, R. F., James, N. M., Steiner, M., & Tarika, J. (1980). Diagnosis of endogenous depression: Comparison of clinical, research, and neuroendocrine criteria. *Journal of Affective Disorders, 2*, 177–194.

Carroll, B. J., Martin, F. I., & Davies, B. (1968). Resistance to suppression by dexamethasone of plasma 11-O.H.C.S. levels in severe depressive illness. *British Medical Journal, 3*, 285–287.

Carroll, R. A. (2007). Gender dysphoria and trans-gender experiences. In S. R. Leiblum (Ed.), *Principles and practice of sex therapy* (4th ed., pp. 477–508). New York, NY: Guilford.

Carson, R. C. (1991). Discussion: Dilemmas in the pathway of DSM-IV. *Journal of Abnormal Psychology, 100*, 302–307.

Carson, R. C. (1996). Aristotle, Galileo, and the *DSM* taxonomy: The case of schizophrenia. *Journal of Consulting and Clinical Psychology, 64*(6), 1133–1139.

Carstensen, L. L., Charles, S. T., Isaacowitz, D., & Kennedy, Q. (2003). Life-span personality development and emotion. In R. J. Davidson, K. Scherer, & H. H. Goldsmith (Eds.), *Handbook of affective sciences* (pp. 931–951). Oxford, UK: Oxford University Press.

Carstensen, L. L., Turan, B. Scheibe, S., Ram, N., Ersner-Hershfield, H., Samanez-Larkin, G. R., Brooks, K. P., & Nesselroad, J. R. (2011). Emotional experience improves with age: Evidence based on over 10 years of experience sampling. *Psychology and Aging, 26*, 21–33.

Carter, C. L., Resnick, E. M., Mallampalli, M., & Kalbarczyk, A. (2012). Sex and gender differences in Alzheimer's disease: Recommendations for future research. *Journal of Women's Health, 21*(10), 1018–1023.

Carter, J. C., & Fairburn, C. G. (1998). Cognitive-behavioral self-help for binge eating disorder: A controlled effectiveness study. *Journal of Consulting and Clinical Psychology, 66*, 616–623.

Carter, J. C., McFarlane, T. L., Bewell, C., Olmsted, M. P., Woodside, D. B., Kaplan, A. S., & Crosby, R. D. (2009). Maintenance treatment for anorexia nervosa: A comparison of cognitive behavior therapy and treatment as usual. *International Journal of Eating Disorders, 42*(3), 202–207.

Carter, J. S., Garber, J., Cielsa, J., & Cole, D. (2006). Modeling relations between hassles and internalizing and externalizing symptoms in adolescents: A four-year prospective study. *Journal of Abnormal Psychology, 115*, 428–442.

Carter, J. S., & Garber, J. (2011). Predictors of the first onset of a major depressive episode and changes in depressive symptoms across adolescence: Stress and negative cognitions. *Journal of Abnormal Psychology, 120*(4), 779–796.

Carter, R. M., Wittchen, H.-U., Pfister, H., & Kessler, R. C. (2001). One-year prevalence of subthreshold and threshold DSM-IV generalized anxiety disorder in a nationally representative sample. *Depression & Anxiety, 13*, 78–88.

Cartwright, R. D. (2006). Sleepwalking. In T. Lee-Chiong (Ed.), *Sleep: A comprehensive handbook* (pp. 429–433). Hoboken, NJ: Wiley.

Carvalho, M., Carmo, H., Costa, V., Capela, J., Pontes, H., Remião, F., & Bastos, M. D. (2012). Toxicity of amphetamines: An update. *Archives of Toxicology, 86*(8), 1167–1231. doi: 10.1007/s00204-012-0815-5

Carver, C. S., Johnson, S. L., & Joormann, J. (2009). Two-mode models of self-regulation as a tool for conceptualizing effects of the serotonin system in normal behavior and diverse disorders. *Current Directions in Psychological Science, 18*(4), 195–199.

Caspi, A., McClay, J., Moffitt, T. E., Mill, J., Martin, J., Craig, I. W., & Poulton, R. (2002). Role of genotype in the cycle of violence in maltreated children. *Science, 297*, 851–853.

Caspi, A., Sugden, K., Moffitt, T. E., Taylor, A., Craig, I. W., Harrington, H., & Poulton, R. (2003). Influence of life stress on depression: Moderation by a polymorphism in the 5-HTT gene. *Science, 301*, 386–389.

Cassano, G., Rucci, P., Frank, E., Fagiolini, A., Dell'Osso, L., Shear, K., & Kupfer, D. J. (2004). The mood spectrum in unipolar and bipolar disorder: Arguments for a unitary approach. *American Journal of Psychiatry, 161*, 1264–1269.

Cassidy, F., Yatham, L. N., Berk, M., & Grof, P. (2008). Pure and mixed manic subtypes: A review of diagnostic classification and validation. *Bipolar Disorders, 10*, 131–143.

Castell, B. D., Kazantzis, N., & Moss-Morris, R. E. (2011). Cognitive behavioral therapy and graded exercise for chronic fatigue syndrome: A meta-analysis. *Clinical Psychology: Science and Practice, 18*(4), 311–324.

Castle, N., Ferguson-Rome, J. C., & Teresi, J. A. (2015). Elder abuse in residential long-term care: An update to the 2003 National Research Council Report. *Journal of Applied Gerontology, 34*(4), 407–443.

Castonguay, L. G., Eldredge, K. L., & Agras, W. S. (1995). Binge eating disorder: Current state and directions. *Clinical Psychology Review, 15*, 815–890.

Castro, F. G., & Nieri, T. (2010). Cultural factors in drug use etiology: Concepts, methods, and recent findings. In L. M. Scheier (Ed.), *Handbook of drug use etiology: Theory, methods, and empirical findings* (pp. 305–324). Washington, DC: American Psychological Association.

Cautela, J. R. (1966). Treatment of compulsive behavior by covert sensitization. *Psychological Record, 16*, 33–41.

Cautela, J. R. (1967). Covert sensitization. *Psychological Reports, 20*, 459–468.

Cavendish, W. (2013). Identification of learning disabilities: Implications of proposed DSM-5 criteria for school-based Assessment. *Journal of Learning Disabilities, 46*(1), 52–57. doi: 10.1177/0022219412464342

Cechnicki, A., Bielańska, A., Hanuszkiewicz, I., & Daren, A. (2013). The predictive validity of Expressed Emotions (EE) in schizophrenia. A 20-year prospective study. *Journal of Psychiatric Research, 47*(2), 208–214. doi: http://dx.doi.org/10.1016/j.jpsychires.2012.10.004

Ceci, S. J. (1995). False beliefs: Some developmental and clinical considerations. In D. L. Schacter (Ed.), *Memory distortion: How minds, brains, and societies reconstruct the past* (pp. 91–125). Cambridge, MA: Harvard University Press.

Ceci, S. J. (2003). Cast in six ponds and you'll reel in something: Looking back on 25 years of research. *American Psychologist, 58*, 855–867.

Cederlöf, M., Thornton, L. M., Baker, J., Lichtenstein, P., Larsson, H., Rück, C., . . . Mataix-Cols, D. (2015). Etiological overlap between obsessive-compulsive disorder and anorexia nervosa: a longitudinal cohort, multigenerational family and twin study. *World Psychiatry, 14*(3), 333–338.

Celio, A. A., Winzelberg, A. J., Dev, P., & Taylor, C. B. (2002). Improving compliance in on-line, structured self-help programs: Evaluation of an eating disorder prevention program. *Journal of Psychiatric Practice, 8*, 14–20.

Celio, A. A., Zabinski, M. F., & Wilfley, D. E. (2002). African American body images. In T. F. Cash & T. Pruzinsky (Eds.), *Body image: A handbook of theory, research and clinical practice* (pp. 234–242). New York, NY: Guilford.

Cella, M., Preti, A., Edwards, C., Dow, T. & Wykes, T. (2017). Cognitive remediation for negative symptoms of schizophrenia: A network meta-analysis. *Clinical Psychology Review, 52*, 43–51. Doi:http://dx.doi.org/10.1016/j.cpr.2016.11.009

Centers for Disease Control, National Center for Health Statistics. (2014). *Multiple cause-of-death data, 1999–2013*. Retrieved from http: //wonder.cdc.gov.ezproxy.bu.edu/mcd.html.

Centers for Disease Control and Prevention. (2007). Cigarette smoking among adults—United States, 2006. *Morbidity and Mortality Weekly Report* [serial online]; 56(44): 1157–1161. Retrieved from http://www.cdc.gov/mmwr/preview/mmwrhtml/mm5644a2.htm

Centers for Disease Control and Prevention. (2008). Annual smoking-attributable mortality, year, and potential life lost, and productivity losses—United States, 2000–2004. *Morbidity and Mortality Weekly Report* [serial online]; 57(45): 1226–1228. Retrieved from http://www.cdc.gov/mmwr/preview/mmwrhtml/mm5745a3.htm

Centers for Disease Control and Prevention. (2010a). *Diagnosis of HIV infection and AIDS in the United States and dependent areas, 2008* (HIV Surveillance Report, Volume 20). Retrieved from http://www.cdc.gov/hiv/surveillance/resources/reports/2008report/index.htm

Centers for Disease Control and Prevention. (2010b). Fatal injury data. Retrieved from http://www.cdc.gov/injury/wisqars/fatal.html

Centers for Disease Control and Prevention. (2010c). Web-based Injury Statistics Query and Reporting System (WISQARS). Retrieved from http://www.cdc.gov/ncipc/wisqars

Centers for Disease Control and Prevention. (2011a). Prevalence of hypertension and controlled hypertension—United States, 2005–2008. *Morbidity and Mortality Weekly Report, 60*(1), 94–97.

Centers for Disease Control and Prevention. (2011b). Measles—United States, January–May 20, 2011. *Morbidity and Mortality Weekly Report, 60*(20), 666–668.

Centers for Disease Control and Prevention. (2012). Prevalence of autism spectrum disorders—Autism and Developmental Disabilities Monitoring Network, 14 sites, United States, 2008. *Morbity and Mortality Weekly Report, 61*(SS-03), 1–19. Retrieved from http://www.cdc.gov/mmwr/preview/mmwrhtml/ss6103a1.htm?s_cid=ss6103a1_e

Centers for Disease Control and Prevention. (2013a). *National Center for Health Statistics, State and Local Area Integrated Telephone Survey. 2011–2012 National Survey of Children's Health*. Rockville, MD: U.S. Department of Health and Human Services.

Centers for Disease Control and Prevention. (2013b). Human immunodeficiency virus (HIV) disease death rates among men aged 25–54 years, by race and age group—national vital statistics. *Morbidity and Mortality Weekly Report, 62*(9), 175.

Centers for Disease Control and Prevention. (2013c). Suicide among adults aged 35–64 Years—United States, 1999–2010. *Morbidity and Mortality Weekly Report, 62*(17), 321–325.

Centers for Disease Control and Prevention. (2014). *Prevalence of Autism Spectrum Disorders Among Children 8 Years — Autism and Developmental Disabilities Monitoring Network, 11 Sites, United States, 2010*.MMWR 2014;63, (No. SS-02):1–19. Retrieved from: http://www.cdc.gov/mmwr/preview/mmwrhtml/ss6103a1.htm?s_cid=ss6103a1_e

Centers for Disease Control and Prevention (2015). *Incidence, prevalence, and cost of sexually transmitted infections in the United States*. http://www.cdc.gov/std/herpes/std-fact-herpes-detailed.htm.

Cha, C. B., Najmi, S., Park, J. M., Finn, C. T., & Nock, M. J. (2010). Attentional bias toward suicide-related stimuli predicts suicidal behavior. *Journal of Abnormal Psychology, 119*, 616–622.

Chaimowitz, G. (2012). The criminalization of people with mental illness. *Canadian Journal of Psychiatry, 57*(2), 129.

Chalder, T., Deary, V., Husain, K., & Walwyn, R. (2010). Family-focused cognitive behavior therapy versus psycho-education for chronic fatigue syndrome in 11-to 18-year-olds: A randomized controlled treatment trial. *Psychological Medicine, 40*(8), 1269–1279.

Chalder, T., Cleare, A., & Wessely, S. (2000). The management of stress and anxiety in chronic fatigue syndrome. In D. I. Mostofsky & D. H. Barlow (Eds.), *The management of stress and anxiety in medical disorders* (pp. 160–179). Needham Heights, MA: Allyn & Bacon.

Chamberlain, S. R., Menzies, L., Hampshire, A., Suckling, J., Fineberg, N. A., Campo, N., & Sahakien, B. J. (2008). Orbitofrontal dysfunction in patients with Obsessive-compulsive disorder and their unaffected relatives. *Science, 321*, 421–422.

Chamberlain, S. R., Menzies, L., Sahakian, B. J., & Fineberg, N. A. (2007). Lifting the veil on trichotillomania. *American Journal of Psychiatry, 164*, 568–574.

Chan, C., Ngai, E., Leung, P., & Wong, S. (2010). Effect of the adapted virtual reality cognitive training program among Chinese older adults with chronic schizophrenia: A pilot study. *International Journal of Geriatric Psychiatry, 25*(6), 643–649.

Chandra, A., Mosher, W. D., & Casey, C. (2011). *Sexual behavior, sexual attraction, and sexual identity in the United States: data from the 2006-2008 National Survey of Family Growth*. Atlanta, GA: U.S. Department of Health and Human Services, Centers for Disease Control and Prevention, National Center for Health Statistics.

Chaouloff, F., & Groc, L. (2010). Temporal modulation of hippocampal excitatory transmission by corticosteroids and stress. *Frontiers in Neuroendocrinology*. Advance online publication. 32(1), 25–42 doi: 10.1016/j.yfrne.2010.07.004

Chapman, A. L., Dixon-Gordon, K. L., Butler, S. M., & Walters, K. N. (2015). Emotional reactivity to social rejection versus a frustration induction among persons with borderline personality features. *Personality Disorders: Theory, Research, and Treatment, 6*(1), 88.

Charland, L. C. (2008). A moral line in the sand: Alexander Crichton and Philippe Pinel on the psychopathology of the passions. In L. C. Charland & P. Zachar (Eds.), *Fact and value in emotion* (pp. 15–34). Amsterdam, The Netherlands: John Benjamins.

Charland, L. C. (2010). Science and morals in the affective psychopathology of Philippe Pinel. *History of Psychiatry, 21*(1), 38–53.

Charles, S. T., & Carstensen, L. L. (2010). Social and emotional aging. *Annual Review of Psychology, 61*, 383–409.

Charney, D. S. (2004). Psychobiological mechanisms of resilience and vulnerability: Implications for successful adaptation to extreme stress. *The American Journal of Psychiatry, 161*(2), 195–216.

Charney, D. S., & Drevets, W. C. (2002). Neuro-biological basis of anxiety disorders. In K. L. Davis, D. Charney, J. T. Coyle, & C. Nemeroff (Eds.), *Neuropsychopharmacology: The fifth generation of progress* (pp. 901–951). Philadelphia, PA: Lippincott Williams & Wilkins.

Charney, D. S., Barlow, D. H., Botteron, K., Cohen, J. D., Goldman, D., Raquel, E. G., & Zalcman, S. J. (2002). Neuroscience research agenda to guide development of a pathophysiologically based classification system. In D. J. Kupfer, M. B. First, & D. A. Regier (Eds.), *A research agenda for DSM-V* (pp. 31–83). Washington, DC: American Psychiatric Association.

Charney, D. S., Woods, S. W., Price, L. H., Goodman, W. K., Glazer, W. M., & Heninger, G. R. (1990). Noradrenergic dysregulation in panic disorder. In J. C. Ballenger (Ed.), *Neurobiology of panic disorder* (pp. 91–105). New York, NY: Wiley-Liss.

Chartrand, H., Sareen, J., Toews, M., & Bolton, J. M. (2012). Suicide attempts versus nonsuicidal self-injury among individuals with anxiety disorders in a nationally representative sample. *Depression and Anxiety, 29*, 172–179.

Chassin, L., Pillow, D. R., Curran, P. J., Molina, B. S. G., & Barrera, M. (1993). Relation of parental alcoholism to early adolescent substance use: A test of three mediating mechanisms. *Journal of Abnormal Psychology, 102*, 3–19.

Chassin, L., Presson, C. C., Rose, J. S., & Sherman, S. J. (2001). From adolescence to adulthood: Age-related changes in beliefs about cigarette smoking in a Midwestern community sample. *Health Psychology, 20*(5), 377–386.

Chasson, G. S., Buhlmann, U., Tolin, D. F., Rao, S. R., Reese, H. E., Welsh, K. S., & Wilhelm, S. (2010). Need for speed: Evaluating slopes of OCD recovery in behavior therapy enhanced with d-cycloserine. *Behavior Research and Therapy, 48*, 675–679.

Chavez, M., & Insel, T. R. (2007). Eating disorders: National Institute of Mental Health perspective. *American Psychologist, 62*, 159–166.

Check, J. R. (1998). Munchausen syndrome by proxy: An atypical form of child abuse. *Journal of Practical Behavioral Health, 4*, 340–345.

Checknita, D., Maussion, G., Labonté, B., Comai, S., Tremblay, R. E., Vitaro, F., . . . Turecki, G. (2015). Monoamine oxidase A gene promoter methylation and transcriptional downregulation in an offender population with antisocial personality disorder. *The British Journal of Psychiatry, 206*(3), 216–222.

Chemerinski, E., Triebwasser, J., Roussos, P., & Siever, L. J. (2013). Schizotypal personality disorder. *Journal of Personality Disorders, 27*(5), 652–679.

Chen, M. C., Hamilton, J. P., & Gotlib, I. H. (2010). Decreased hippocampal volume in healthy girls at risk of depression. *Archives of General Psychiatry, 67*(3), 270–276.

Chen, Y., Nettles, M. E., & Chen, S.-W. (2009). Rethinking dependent personality disorder: Comparing different human relatedness in cultural contexts. *Journal of Nervous and Mental Disease, 197*(11), 793–800.

Chesney, M. A. (1986, November). *Type A behavior: The biobehavioral interface.* Keynote address presented at the annual meeting of the Association for Advancement of Behavior Therapy, Chicago.

Cheung, F. M. (1995). Facts and myths about somatization among the Chinese. In T. Y. Lin, W. S. Tseng, & E. K. Yeh (Eds.), *Chinese societies and mental health* (pp. 156–166). Hong Kong: Oxford University Press.

Cheung, F. M. (2012). Mainstreaming culture in psychology. *American Psychologist, 67*(8), 721–730. doi: 10.1037/a0029876

Cheung, F. M., van de Vijver, F. J., & Leong, F. T. (2011). Toward a new approach to the study of personality in culture. *American Psychologist, 66*(7), 593–603. doi: 10.1037/a0022389

Cheung, Y., Law, C., Chan, B., Liu, K., & Yip, P. (2006). Suicidal ideation and suicidal attempts in a population based study of Chinese people: Risk attributable to hopelessness, depression, and social factors. *Journal of Affective Disorders, 90,* 193–199.

Chevalier, J. M., & Buckles, D. J. (2013). *Participatory action research: Theory and methods for engaged inquiry.* New York, NY: Routledge.

Chida, Y., & Mao, X. (2009). Does psychosocial stress predict symptomatic herpes simplex virus recurrence? A meta-analytic investigation on prospective studies. *Brain, Behavior, and Immunity, 23,* 917–925.

Chida, Y., & Steptoe, A. (2009). The association of anger and hostility with future coronary heart disease: A meta-analytic review of prospective evidence. *Journal of the American College of Cardiology, 53*(11), 936–946.

Chida, Y., & Steptoe, A. (2010). Greater cardiovascular responses to laboratory mental stress are associated with poor subsequent cardiovascular risk status: A meta-analysis of prospective evidence. *Hypertension, 55*(4), 1026–1032.

Chioqueta, A., & Stiles, T. (2004). Suicide risk in patients with somatization disorder. *Crisis: The Journal of Crisis Intervention and Suicide Prevention, 25*(1), 3–7.

Chisuwa, N., & O'Dea, J. A. (2010). Body image and eating disorders amongst Japanese adolescents: A review of the literature. *Appetite, 54,* 5–15.

Chivers, M. L., & Bailey, J. M. (2000). Sexual orientation of female-to-male transsexuals: A comparison of homosexual and nonhomosexual types. *Archives of Sexual Behavior, 29*(3), 259–279.

Chivers, M. L., Rieger, G., Latty, E., & Bailey, M. (2004). A sex difference in the specificity of sexual arousal. *Psychological Science, 15,* 736–744.

Chmielewski, M., Clark, L. A., Bagby, R. M., & Watson, D. (2015). Method matters: Understanding diagnostic reliability in *DSM-IV* and *DSM-5. Journal of Abnormal Psychology, 124*(3), 764–769. http://dx.doi.org/10.1037/abn0000069

Cho, H. J., Lavretsky, H., Olmstead, R., Levin, M. J., Oxman, M. N., & Irwin, M. R. (2008). Sleep disturbance and depression recurrence in community-dwelling older adults: A prospective study. *American Journal of Psychiatry, 165*(12), 1543–1550.

Choate, M. L., Pincus, D. B., Eyberg, S. M., & Barlow, D. B. (2005). Parent–child interaction therapy for treatment of separation anxiety disorder: A pilot study. *Cognitive and Behavioral Practice, 12*(1), 126–135.

Chobanian, A. V., Bakris, G. L., Black, H. R., Cushman, W. C., Green, L. A., Izzo, J. L., & National High Blood Pressure Education Program Coordinating Committee. (2003). Seventh report of the Joint National Committee on prevention, detection, evaluation, and treatment of high blood pressure. *Hypertension, 42,* 1206–1252.

Chodoff, P. (1982). Hysteria in women. *American Journal of Psychiatry, 139,* 545–551.

Choi, J., & Twamley, E. W. (2013). Cognitive rehabilitation therapies for Alzheimer's disease: A review of methods to improve treatment engagement and self-efficacy. *Neuropsychology Review, 23*(1), 48–62. doi: 10.1007/s11065-013-9227-4

Choi, S.-H., Lee, H., Chung, T.-S., Park, K.-M., Jung, Y.-C., Kim, S. I., & Kim, J.-J. (2012). Neural network functional connectivity during and after an episode of delirium. *American Journal of Psychiatry, 169*(5), 498–507. doi: 10.1176/appi.ajp.2012.11060976

Chorpita, B. F., & Barlow, D. H. (1998). The development of anxiety: The role of control in the early environment. *Psychological Bulletin, 124*(1), 3–21.

Chosak, A., Marques, L., Greenberg, J. L., Jenike, E., Dougherty, D. D., & Wilhelm, S. (2008). Body dysmorphic disorder and Obsessive-compulsive disorder: Similarities, differences and the classification debate. *Expert Review of Neurotherapeutics, 8*(8), 1209–1218.

Christakis, N. A., & Fowler, J. H. (2007). The spread of obesity in a large social network over 32 years. *New England Journal of Medicine, 357*(4), 370–379.

Christopher, J. C., Wendt, D. C., Marecek, J., & Goodman, D. M. (2014). Critical cultural awareness: Contributions to a globalizing psychology. *American Psychologist, 69*(7), 645–655.

Christopher, M. E., Hulslander, J., Byrne, B., Samuelsson, S., Keenan, J. M., Pennington, B., & Olson, R. K. (2013). Modeling the etiology of individual differences in early reading development: Evidence for strong genetic influences. *Scientific Studies of Reading, 17*(5), 350–368.

Chronis, A. M., Lahey, B. B., Pelham, W. E., Jr., Williams, S. H., Baumann, B. L., Kipp, H., & Rathouz, P. J. (2007). Maternal depression and early positive parenting predict future conduct problems in young children with attention-deficit/hyperactivity disorder. *Developmental Psychology, 43,* 70–82.

Chung, J., Demiris, G., & Thompson, H. J. (2016). Ethical Considerations Regarding the Use of Smart Home Technologies for Older Adults: An Integrative Review. *Annual Review of Nursing Research, 34*(1), 155–181.

Chung, S. Y., Luk, S. L., & Lee, P. W. H. (1990). A follow-up study of infantile autism in Hong Kong. *Journal of Autism and Developmental Disorders, 20,* 221–232.

Chung, T., & Martin, C. S. (2009). Subjective stimulant and sedative effects of alcohol during early drinking experiences predict alcohol involvement in treated adolescents. *Journal of Studies on Alcohol and Drugs, 70*(5), 660–667.

Cicchetti, D. (1991). A historical perspective on the discipline of developmental psychopathology. In J. Rolf, A. S. Masten, D. Cicchetti, K. H. Nuechterlein, & S. Weintraub (Eds.), *Risk and protective factors in the development of psychopathology* (pp. 2–28). New York, NY: Cambridge University Press.

Cimera, R. E. (2012). The economics of supported employment: What new data tell us. *Journal of Vocational Rehabilitation, 37*(2), 109.

Ciraulo, D. A., Barlow, D. H., Gulliver, S. B., Farchione, T., Morissette, S. B., Kamholz, B. W., Eisenmenger, K., Brown, B., Devine, E., Brown, T. A., & Knapp, C. M. (2013). The effects of venlafaxine and cognitive behavioral therapy alone and combined in the treatment of co-morbid alcohol use-anxiety disorders. *Behaviour Research and Therapy, 51,* 729–735.

Clance, P. R., & Imes, S. A. (1978). The imposter phenomenon in high achieving women: Dynamics and therapeutic intervention. *Psychotherapy: Theory, Research & Practice, 15*(3), 241–247.

Clancy, S. A., McNally, R. J., Schacter, D. L., Lenzenweger, M. F., & Pitman, R. K. (2002). Memory distortion in people reporting abduction by aliens. *Journal of Abnormal Psychology, 111,* 455–461.

Clark, C. J., Henderson, K. M., de Leon, C. F., Guo, H., Lunos, S., Evans, D. A., & Everso Rose, S. A. (2012). Latent constructs in psychosocial factors associated with cardiovascular disease: An examination by race and sex. *Frontiers in Psychiatry, 3,* 5.

Clark, D. A., & O'Connor, K. (2005). Thinking is believing: Ego-dystonic intrusive thoughts in obsessive-compulsive disorder. In D. A. Clark (Ed.), *Intrusive thoughts in clinical disorders* (pp. 145–174). New York, NY: Guilford.

Clark, D. A., & Rhyno, S. (2005). Unwanted intrusive thoughts in nonclinical individuals: Implications for clinical disorders. In D. A. Clark (Ed.), *Intrusive thoughts in clinical disorders* (pp. 1–29). New York, NY: Guilford.

Clark, D. M. (1986). A cognitive approach to panic. *Behaviour Research and Therapy, 24,* 461–470.

Clark, D. M. (1996). Panic disorder: From theory to therapy. In P. Salkovskis (Ed.), *Frontiers of cognitive therapy* (pp. 318–344). New York, NY: Guilford.

Clark, D. M., Ehlers, A., Hackman, A., McManus, F., Fennell, M., Grey, N., & Wild, J. (2006). Cognitive therapy versus exposure and applied relaxation in social phobia: A randomized controlled trial. *Journal of*

Consulting and Clinical Psychology, 74, 568–578.

Clark, D. M., Ehlers, A., McManus, F., Hackman, A., Fennell, M. J. V., Campbell, H., & Louis, B. (2003). Cognitive therapy versus fluoxetine in generalized social phobia: A randomized placebo-controlled trial. *Journal of Consulting and Clinical Psychology, 71,* 1058–1067.

Clark, D. M., Salkovskis, P. M., Hackmann, A., Middleton, H., Anastasiades, P., & Gelder, M. (1994). A comparison of cognitive therapy, applied relaxation and imipramine in the treatment of panic disorder. *British Journal of Psychiatry, 164*(6), 759–769.

Clark, L. A. (2005). Temperament as a unifying basis for personality and psychopathology [Special issue]. *Journal of Abnormal Psychology, 114,* 505–521.

Clark, R. (2003). Parental history of hypertension and coping responses predict blood pressure changes in black college volunteers undergoing a speaking task about perceptions of racism. *Psychosomatic Medicine, 65,* 1012–1019.

Clarke, D. M., & Deb, S. (2012). Syndromes causing intellectual disability. In M. G. Gelder, N. C. Andreasen, J. J. Lopez Jr. & J. R. Geddes (Eds.), *New Oxford Textbook of Psychiatry* (2nd. ed., Vol. 2, pp. 1838–1848). New York, NY: Oxford University Press.

Clarkin, J. F., Howieson, D. B., & McClough, J. (2008). The role of psychiatric measures in assessment and treatment. In R. E. Hales, S. C. Yudofsky, & G. O. Gabbard (Eds.), *The American Psychiatric Publishing textbook of psychiatry* (5th ed., pp. 73–110). Arlington, VA: American Psychiatric Publishing.

Clayton, A. H., Croft, H. A., & Handiwala, L. (2014). Antidepressants and sexual dysfunction: Mechanisms and clinical implications. *Postgraduate Medicine, 126*(2), 91–99.

Clayton, E. W. (2015). Beyond myalgic encephalomyelitis/chronic fatigue syndrome: An IOM report on redefining an illness. *JAMA, 313*(11), 1101–1102.

Cleckley, H. M. (1982). *The mask of sanity* (6th ed.). St. Louis, MO: Mosby. (Original work published 1941.)

Cleghorn, J. M., & Albert, M. L. (1990). Modular disjunction in schizophrenia: A framework for a pathological psychophysiology. In A. Kales, C. N. Stefanis, & J. A. Talbot (Eds.), *Recent advances in schizophrenia* (pp. 59–80). New York, NY: Springer-Verlag.

Clement, U. (1990). Surveys of heterosexual behavior. *Annual Review of Sex Research, 1,* 45–74.

Clementz, B. A., & Sweeney, J. A. (1990). Is eye movement dysfunction a biological marker for schizophrenia? A methodological review. *Psychological Bulletin, 108,* 77–92.

Clifford, D. B., & Ances, B. M. (2013). HIV-associated neurocognitive disorder. *The Lancet Infectious Diseases, 13*(11), 976–986.

Cloninger, C. R. (1978). The link between hysteria and sociopathy: An integrative model of pathogenesis based on clinical, genetic, and neurophysiological observations. In H. S. Akiskal & W. L. Webb (Eds.), *Psychiatric diagnosis: Exploration of biological predictors* (pp. 189–218). New York, NY: Spectrum.

Cloninger, C. R., & Svakic, D. M. (2009). Personality disorders. In B. J. Sadock, V. A. Sadock, & P. Ruiz (Eds.), *Kaplan & Sadock's comprehensive textbook of psychiatry* (9th ed., Vol. II, pp. 2197–2240). Philadelphia, PA: Lippincott Williams & Wilkins.

Closser, M. H. (1992). Cocaine epidemiology. In T. R. Kosten & H. D. Kleber (Eds.), *Clinician's guide to cocaine addiction: Theory, research, and treatment* (pp. 225–240). New York, NY: Guilford.

Coates, T. J. (1990). Strategies for modifying sexual behavior for primary and secondary prevention of HIV disease. *Journal of Consulting and Clinical Psychology, 58*(1), 57–69.

Cobb, S. (1976). Social support as a moderator of life stress. *Psychosomatic Medicine, 38,* 300.

Cobham, V. E., Dadds, M. R., Spence, S. H., & McDermott, B. (2010). Parental anxiety in the treatment of childhood anxiety: A different story three years later. *Journal of Clinical Child and Adolescent Psychology, 39*(3), 410–420. PMID 20419581

Coccaro, E. F. (2012). Intermittent explosive disorder as a disorder of impulsive aggression for DSM-5. *American Journal of Psychiatry, 169*(6), 577–588.

Coccaro, E. F., & McCloskey, M. (2010). Intermittent explosive disorder: Clinical aspects. In E. Aboujaoude & L. M. Koran (Eds.), *Impulse control disorders* (pp. 221–232). New York, NY: Cambridge University Press.

Cocores, J. A., Miller, N. S., Pottash, A. C., & Gold, M. S. (1988). Sexual dysfunction in abusers of cocaine and alcohol. *American Journal of Drug and Alcohol Abuse, 14,* 169–173.

Coderre, T. J., Katz, J., Vaccarino, A. L., & Melzack, R. (1993). Contribution of central neuroplasticity to pathological pain: Review of clinical and experimental evidence. *Pain, 52,* 259–285.

Coe, C. L. (2010). Immunity in primates within a psychobiological perspective. In Demas, G. E., & Nelson, R. J. (Eds.) *Ecoimmunology.* New York, NY: Oxford University Press.

Cohen, A. S., Barlow, D. H., & Blanchard, E. B. (1985). Psychophysiology of relaxation-associated panic attacks. *Journal of Abnormal Psychology, 94,* 98.

Cohen, C. I., Natarajan, N., Araujo, M., & Solanki, D. (2013). Prevalence of negative symptoms and associated factors in older adults with schizophrenia spectrum disorder. *American Journal of Geriatric Psychiatry, 21*(2), 100–107. doi: 10.1097/JGP.1090b1013e3182447b3182443

Cohen, D., & Pressman, S. D. (2006). Positive affect and health. *Current Directions in Psychological Science, 15,* 122–125.

Cohen, J. (2002). Confronting the limits of success. *Science, 296,* 2320–2324.

Cohen, J. (2011). AIDS research: Complexity surrounds HIV prevention advances. *Science, 333*(6041), 393.

Cohen, J. B., & Reed, D. (1985). Type A behavior and coronary heart disease among Japanese men in Hawaii. *Journal of Behavioral Medicine, 8,* 343–352.

Cohen, J. S., Edmunds, J. M., Brodman, D. M., Benjamin, C. L., & Kendall, P. C. (2012). Using self-monitoring: Implementation of collaborative empiricism in cognitive-behavioral therapy. *Cognitive and Behavioral Practice. 20*(4), 419–428. doi: 10.1016/j.cbpra.2012.06.002

Cohen, L., Soares, C., Vitonis, A., Otto, M., & Harlow, B. (2006). Risk for new onset of depression during the menopausal transition. *Archive General Psychiatry, 63,* 385–390.

Cohen, S. (1996). Psychological stress, immunity, and upper respiratory infections. *Current Directions in Psychological Science, 5,* 86–90.

Cohen, S., & Herbert, T. B. (1996). Health psychology: Psychological factors and physical disease from the perspective of human psychoneuro-immunology. *Annual Review of Psychology, 47,* 113–142.

Cohen, S., & Janicki-Deverts, D. (2009). Can we improve our physical health by altering our social networks? *Perspectives on Psychological Science, 4,* 375–378.

Cohen, S., Doyle, W. J., & Skoner, D. P. (1999). Psychological stress, cytokine production, and severity of upper respiratory illness. *Psychosomatic Medicine, 61,* 175–180.

Cohen, S., Doyle, W. J., Skoner, D. P., Fireman, P., Gwaltney, J. M., Jr., & Newsome, J. T. (1995). State and trait negative affect as predictors of objective and subjective symptoms of respiratory viral infections. *Journal of Personality and Social Psychology, 68,* 159–169.

Cohen, S., Doyle, W. J., Turner, R., Alper, C. M., & Skoner, D. P. (2003). Sociability and susceptibility to the common cold. *Psychological Science, 14*(5), 389–395.

Cohen, S., Doyle, W., Skoner, D. P., Rabin, B. S., & Gwaltney, J. M. (1997). Social ties and susceptibility to the common cold. *JAMA: Journal of the American Medical Association, 277,* 1940–1944.

Cohen-Kettenis, P. T., & Pfäfflin, F. (2010). The DSM diagnostic criteria for gender identity disorder in adolescents and adults. *Archives of Sexual Behavior, 39,* 499–513.

Coker, L. H., Espeland, M. A., Rapp, S. R., Legault, C., Resnick, S. M., Hogan, P., . . . Shumaker, S. A. (2010). Postmenopausal hormone therapy and cognitive outcomes: The Women's Health Initiative Memory Study (WHIMS). *The Journal of Steroid Biochemistry and Molecular Biology, 118*(4–5), 304–310.

Cole, M. G., Ciampi, A., Belzile, E., & Zhong, L. (2009). Persistent delirium in older hospital patients: A systematic review of frequency and prognosis. *Age and Ageing, 38*(1), 19–26.

Cole, S. W. (2008). Psychosocial influences on HIV-1 disease progression: Neural, endocrine, and virologic mechanisms. *Psychosomatic Medicine, 70,* 562–568.

Cole, S. W. (2011). Socioenvironmental effects on gene expression. In K. S. Kendler, S. Jaffee, & D. Romer (Eds.), *The dynamic genome and mental health: The role of genes and environments in youth development* (pp. 195–228). New York, NY: Oxford University Press.

Coleman, E., Bockting, W. O., & Gooren, L. (1993). Homosexual and bisexual identity in sex-reassigned female-to-male transsexuals. *Archives of Sexual Behavior, 22,* 37–50.

Coleman, E., Colgan, P., & Gooren, L. (1992). Male cross-gender behavior in Myanmar (Burma): A description of the acault. *Archives of Sexual Behavior, 21*(3), 313–321.

Colins, O. F., Andershed, H., & Pardini, D. A. (2015). Psychopathic traits as predictors of future criminality, intimate partner aggression, and substance use in young adult men. *Law & Human Behavior, 39*(6), 547–558.

Colles, S. L., & Dixon, J. B. (2012). The relationship of night eating syndrome with obesity, bariatric surgery, and physical health. In J. D. Lundgren, K. C. Allison, & A. J. Stunkard (Eds.), *Night eating syndrome: Research, assessment and treatment* (pp. 85–107). New York, NY: Guilford.

Colles, S. L., Dixon, J. B., & O'Brien, P. E. (2007). Night eating syndrome and nocturnal snacking: Association with obesity, binge eating, and psychological distress. *International Journal of Obesity, 31*, 1722–1730.

Collinge, J. (2012). Prion disease. In M. G. Gelder, N. C. Andreasen, J. J. Lopez, Jr., & J. R. Geddes (Eds.), *New Oxford textbook of psychiatry* (2nd. ed., Vol. 1, pp. 351–361). New York, NY: Oxford University Press.

Collinge, J., Whitfield, J., McKintosh, E., Beck, J., Mead, S., Thomas, D. J., & Alpers, M. P. (2006). Kuru in the 21st century: An acquired human prion disease with very long incubation periods. *Lancet, 367*(9528), 2068–2074.

Collinge, J., Whitfield, J., McKintosh, E., Frosh, A., Mead, S., Hill, A. F., . . . Alpers, M. P. (2008). A clinical study of kuru patients with long incubation periods at the end of the epidemic in Papua New Guinea. Philosophical Transactions of the Royal Society of London B: *Biological Sciences, 363*(1510), 3725–3739.

Colloca, L., Lopiano, L., Lanotte, M., & Benedetti, F. (2004). Overt versus covert treatment for pain, anxiety, and Parkinson's disease. *Lancet Neurology, 3*(11), 679–684. doi: 10.1016/S1474-4422(04)00908-1

Colman, I., Murray, J., Abbott, R., Maughan, B., Kuh, D., Croudace, T., & Jones, P. B. (2009). Outcomes of conduct problems in adolescence: 40 year follow-up of national cohort. *British Medical Journal, 338*, a2981.

Colp, R. (2009). History of psychiatry. In B. J. Sadock, V. A. Sadock, & P. Ruiz (Eds.), *Kaplan & Sadock's comprehensive textbook of psychiatry* (9th ed., Vol. II, pp. 4474–4509). Philadelphia, PA: Lippincott Williams & Wilkins.

Comas-Diaz, L. (1981). Puerto Rican *espiritismo* and psychotherapy. *American Journal of Orthopsychiatry, 51*(4), 636–645.

Comer, J. S., Blanco, C., Hasin, D. S., Liu, S.-M., Grant, B. F., Turner, J. B., & Olfson, M. (2011). Health-related quality of life across the anxiety disorders: results from the national epidemiologic survey on alcohol and related conditions (NESARC). *Journal of Clinical Psychiatry, 72*, 43–50.

Comer, J. S., Mojtabai, R., & Olfson, M. (2011). National trends in the antipsychotic treatment of psychiatric outpatients with anxiety disorders. *American Journal of Psychiatry, 168*, 1057–1065.

Compare, A., Bigi, R., Orrego, P. S., Proietti, R., Grossi, E., & Steptoe, A. (2013). Type d personality is associated with the development of stress cardiomyopathy following emotional triggers. *Annals of Behavioral Medicine, 45*(3), 299–307.

Compas, B. E., Boyer, M., Stanger, C., Colletti, R., & Thomsen, A. (2006). Latent variable analysis of coping, anxiety/depression, and somatic symptoms in adolescents with chronic pain. *Journal of Consulting and Clinical Psychology, 74*, 1132–1142.

Compas, B. E., Forehand, R., Keller, G., Champion, J. E., Rakow, A., Reeslund, K. L., & Cole, J. D. A. (2009). Randomized controlled trial of a family cognitive-behavioral preventive intervention for children of depressed parents. *Journal of Consulting and Clinical Psychology, 77*(6), 1007–1020.

Compas, B. E., Oppedisano, G., Connor, J. K., Gerhardt, C. A., Hinden, B. R., Achenbach, T. M., & Hammen, C. (1997). Gender differences in depressive symptoms in adolescence: Comparison of national samples of clinically referred and nonreferred youths. *Journal of Consulting and Clinical Psychology, 65*, 617–626.

Compton, S. N., Peris, T. S., Almirall, D., Birmaher, B., Sherrill, J., Kendall, P. C., . . . Albano, A. M. (2014). Predictors and moderators of treatment response in childhood anxiety disorders: results from the CAMS trial. *Journal of Consulting and Clinical Psychology, 82*(2), 212–224.

Compton, W. M., Boyle, M., & Wargo, E. (2015). Prescription opioid abuse: problems and responses. *Preventive Medicine, 80*, 5–9.

Condon, W., Ogston, W., & Pacoe, L. (1969). Three faces of Eve revisited: A study of transient microstrabismus. *Journal of Abnormal Psychology, 74*, 618–620.

Conduct Problems Prevention Research Group. (2010). The effects of a multiyear universal social-emotional learning program: The role of student and school characteristics. *Journal of Consulting and Clinical Psychology, 78*(2), 156–168.

Connecticut General Statutes Annotated, 319: Part II, 17a-495 (1992). Connor, D. F. (2006). Stimulants. In R. A. Barkley (Ed.), *Attention-deficit hyperactivity disorder: A handbook for diagnosis and treatment* (3rd ed., pp. 608–647). New York, NY: Guilford.

Connor, D. F. (2015). Stimulant and nonstimulant medications for childhood ADHD. In R. A. Barkley (Ed.), *Attention-deficit hyperactivity disorder: A handbook for diagnosis & treatment* (4th ed., pp. 666–685). New York, NY: The Guilford Press.

Conti, C. R., Pepine, C. J., & Sweeney, M. (1999). Efficacy and safety of sildenafil citrate in the treatment of erectile dysfunction in patients with ischemic heart disease. *American Journal of Cardiology, 83*, 29C–34C.

Convit, A. (2012). Obesity is associated with structural and functional brain abnormalities: Where do we go from here? *Psychosomatic Medicine, 74*, 673–674.

Conwell, Y., Duberstein, P. R., & Caine, E. D. (2002). Risk factors for suicide in later life. *Biological Psychiatry, 52*, 193–204.

Conwell, Y., Duberstein, P. R., Cox, C., Hermmann, J. H., Forbes, N. T., & Caine, E. D. (1996). Relationships of age and axis I diagnoses in victims of completed suicide: A psychological autopsy study. *American Journal of Psychiatry, 153*, 1001–1008.

Cook, P. J. (1993). The matter of tobacco use. *Science, 262*, 1750–1751.

Cookson, C. (2009). Confronting our fear: Legislating beyond battered woman syndrome and the law of self-defense in Vermont. *Vermont Law Review, 34*, 415.

Coolidge, F., Thede, L., & Young, S. (2002). The heritability of gender identity disorder in a child and adolescent twin sample. *Behavior Genetics, 32*, 251–257.

Coolidge, F. L., Marle, P. D., Rhoades, C. S., Monaghan, P., & Segal, D. L. (2013). Psychometric properties of a new measure to assess autism spectrum disorder in DSM-5. *American Journal of Orthopsychiatry, 83*(1), 126.

Coons, P. M. (1994). Confirmation of childhood abuse in child and adolescent cases of multiple personality disorder not otherwise specified. *Journal of Nervous & Mental Disease, 182*, 461–464.

Coons, P. M., Bowman, E. S., Kluft, R. P., & Milstein, V. (1991). The cross cultural occurrence of NPD: Additional cases from a recent survey. *Dissociation, 4*, 124–128.

Cooper, A. J. (1988). Sexual dysfunction and cardiovascular disease. *Stress Medicine, 4*, 273–281.

Cooper, A. M., & Ronningstam, E. (1992). Narcissistic personality disorder. In A. Tasman & M. B. Riba (Eds.), *Review of psychiatry* (Vol. 11, pp. 80–97). Washington, DC: American Psychiatric Press.

Cooper, J., Kapur, N., Webb, R., Lawlor, M., Guthrie, E., Mackway-Jones, K., & Appleby, L. (2005). Suicide after deliberate self-harm: A 4-year cohort study. *American Journal of Psychiatry, 162*, 297–303.

Cooper, N. S., Feder, A., Southwick, S. M., & Charney, D. S. (2007). Resilience and vulnerability to trauma: Psychobiological mechanisms. In D. Romer & E. F. Walker (Eds.), *Adolescent psychopathology and the developing brain: Integrating brain and prevention science* (pp. 347–372). New York, NY: Oxford University Press.

Cooper, S.-A., & Smiley, E. (2012). Prevalence of intellectual disabilities and epidemiology of mental ill-health in adults with intellectual disabilities. In M. G. Gelder, N. C. Andreasen, J. J. Lopez-Ibor, & J. R. Geddes (Eds.), *New Oxford textbook of psychiatry* (2nd. ed., Vol. 2, pp. 1825–1829). New York, NY: Oxford University Press.

Cooperberg, J., & Faith, M. S. (2004). Treatment of obesity II: Childhood and adolescent obesity. In J. K. Thompson (Ed.), *Handbook of eating disorders and obesity* (pp. 443–450). New York, NY: Wiley.

Cope, M. B., Fernandez, J. R., & Allison, D. (2004). Genetic and biological risk factors. In J. K. Thompson (Ed.), *Handbook of eating disorders and obesity* (pp. 323–338). New York, NY: Wiley.

Cope, N., Eicher, J. D., Meng, H., Gibson, C. J., Hager, K., Lacadie, C., & Gruen, J. R. (2012). Variants in the DYX2 locus are associated with altered brain activation in reading-related brain regions in subjects with reading disability. *NeuroImage, 63*(1), 148–156. doi: http:// dx.doi.org/10.1016/j.neuroimage.2012.06.037

Copeland, W. E., Shanahan, L., Egger, H., Angold, A., & Costello, E. J. (2014). Adult diagnostic and functional outcomes of DSM-5 disruptive mood dysregulation disorder. *American Journal of Psychiatry, 171*, 668–674.

Coplan, J. D., Trost, R. C., Owens, M. J., Cooper, T. B., Gorman, J. M., Nemeroff, C. B., & Rosenblum, L. A. (1998). Cerebrospinal fluid concentrations of somatostatin and biogenic amines in grown primates reared by mothers exposed to manipulated foraging conditions. *Archives of General Psychiatry, 55*, 473–477.

Corcoran, C. M., Kimhy, D., Stanford, A., Khan, S., Walsh, J., Thompson, J., & Malaspina, D. (2008). Temporal association of cannabis use with symptoms in individuals at clinical high risk for psychosis. *Schizophrenia Research, 106*, 286–293.

Corker, E. A., Beldie, A., Brain, C., Jakovljevic, M., Jarema, M., Karamustafalioglu, O., . . . Waern, M. (2015). Experience of stigma and discrimination reported by people experiencing the first episode of schizophrenia and those with a first episode of depression: The FEDORA project. *International Journal of Social Psychiatry, 61*(5), 438–445.

Correll, C. U., Hauser, M., Auther, A. M., & Cornblatt, B. A. (2010). Research in people with psychosis risk syndrome: A review of the current evidence and future directions. *Journal of Child Psychology and Psychiatry, 51*(4), 390–431.

Corrigan, P. W., Druss, B. G., & Perlick, D. A. (2014). The impact of mental illness stigma on seeking and participating in mental health care. *Psychological Science in the Public Interest, 15*(2), 37–70. doi: 10.1177/1529100614531398

Corson, P. W., & Andersen, A. E. (2002). Body image issues among boys and men. In T. F. Cash & T. Pruzinsky (Eds.), *Body image: A handbook of theory, research and clinical practice* (pp. 192–199). New York, NY: Guilford.

Cortiella, C., & Horowitz, S. H. (2014). *The State of Learning Disabilities: Facts, Trends and Emerging Issues* (3rd ed.). New York, NY: National Center for Learning Disabilities.

Cortoni, F., & Gannon, T. A. (2011). Female sexual offenders. In D. P. Boer, R. Eher, L. A. Craig, L. H. Miner, & F. Pfafflin (eds.). *International perspectives on the assessment and treatment of sex offenders: Theory, practice and research,* (pp. 35–54). New York, NY: John Wiley & Sons.

Cortoni, F., & Gannon, T. A. (2016). Female Sexual Offenders: An Overview. In A. Phenix & H. M. Hoberman (Eds.). *Sexual Offending* (pp. 213–224). New York, NY: Springer.

Coryell, W., Endicott, J., & Keller, M. (1992). Rapid cycling affective disorder: Demo-graphics, diagnosis, family history, and course. *Archives of General Psychiatry, 49*, 126–131.

Coryell, W., Endicott, J., Maser, J. D., Keller, M. B., Leon, A. C., & Akiskal, H. S. (1995). Long-term stability of polarity distinctions in the affective disorders. *American Journal of Psychiatry, 152*, 385–390.

Coryell, W., Solomon, D., Turvey, C., Keller, M., Leon, A. C., Endicott, J., & Mueller, T. (2003). The long-term course of rapid-cycling bipolar disorder. *Archives of General Psychiatry, 60*, 914–920.

Costa, E. (1985). Benzodiazepine-GABA interactions: A model to investigate the neurobiology of anxiety. In A. H. Tuma & J. D. Maser (Eds.), *Anxiety and the anxiety disorders*. Hillsdale, NJ: Erlbaum.

Costa e Silva, J. A., & De Girolamo, G. (1990). Neurasthenia: History of a concept. In N. Sartorius, D. Goldberg, G. De Girolamo, J. A. Costa e Silva, Y. Lecrubier, & U. Wittchen (Eds.), *Psychological disorders in general medical settings* (pp. 699–81). Toronto, Canada: Hogrefe and Huber.

Costa Jr, P. T., & McCrae, R. R. (2013). The five-factor model of personality and its relevance to personality disorders. *Personality and Personality Disorders: The Science of Mental Health, 7*, 17.

Costantino, A., Cerpolini, S., Alvisi, S., Morselli, P. G., Venturoli, S., & Meriggiola, M. C. (2013). A prospective study on sexual function and mood in female-to-male transsexuals during testosterone administration and after sex reassignment surgery. *Journal of Sex & Marital Therapy, 39*(4), 321–335.

Cottone, P., Sabino, V., Roberto, M., Bajo, M., Pockros, L., Frihauf, J. B., & Zorrilla, E. P. (2009). CRF system recruitment mediates dark side of compulsive eating. *PNAS: Proceedings of the National Academy of Sciences of the United States of America, 106*, 20016–20020.

Courchesne, E. (1997). Brainstem, cerebellar and limbic neuroanatomical abnormalities in autism. *Current Opinion in Neurobiology, 7*, 269–278.

Courcoulas, A. P. (2012). Progress in filling the gaps in bariatric surgery. *JAMA: Journal of the American Medical Association, 308*, 1160–1161. doi: 10.1001/jama.2012.12337

Courcoulas, A. P., Christian, N. J., Belle, S. H., Berk, P. D., Flum, D. R., Garcia, L., . . . Wolfe, B. M. (2013). Weight change and health outcomes at 3 years after bariatric surgery among individuals with severe obesity. *JAMA, 310*(22), 2416–2425.

Cowley, G., & Spingen, K. (1990, March). The promise of Prozac. *Newsweek, 115*(13), 38.

Cox, A., Rutter, M., Newman, S., & Bartak, L. (1975). A comparative study of infantile autism and specific developmental receptive language disorder: II. Parental characteristics. *British Journal of Psychiatry, 126*, 146–159.

Cox, A. C., Weed, N. C., & Butcher, J. N. (2009). The MMPI-2: History, interpretation, and clinical issues. In J. N. Butcher (Ed.), *Oxford handbook of personality assessment* (pp. 250–276). New York, NY: Oxford University Press.

Cox, B. C., Swinson, R. P., Schulman, I. D., Kuch, K., & Reikman, J. T. (1993). Gender effects in alcohol use in panic disorder with agoraphobia. *BRAT, 31*(4), 413–416.

Coyne, J. C., Stefanek, M., & Palmer, S. C. (2007). Psychotherapy and survival in cancer: The conflict between hope and evidence. *Psychological Bulletin, 133*, 367–394.

Cozanitis, D. A. (2004). One hundred years of barbiturates and their saint. *Journal of the Royal Society of Medicine, 97*, 594–598.

Crabbe, J. C., Wahlsten, D., & Dudek, B. C. (1999). Genetics of mouse behavior: Interactions with laboratory environment. *Science, 284*, 1670–1672.

Craddock, N., & Jones, I. (2001). Molecular genetics of bipolar disorder. *British Journal of Psychiatry, 41*, 128–133.

Crago, M., Shisslak, C. M., & Estes, L. S. (1997). Eating disturbances among American minority groups: A review. *The International Journal of Eating Disorders, 19*, 239–248.

Craig, M. C., & Murphy, D. G. M. (2009). Alzheimer's disease in women. *Best Practice & Research Clinical Obstetrics & Gynaecology, 23*(1), 53–61.

Craighead, W. E., Hart, A. B., Craighead, L. W., & Ilardi, S. S. (2002). Psychosocial treatments for major depressive disorder. In P. E. Nathan & J. M. Gorman (Eds.), *A guide to treatments that work* (2nd ed., pp. 245–261). New York, NY: Oxford University Press.

Craske, M. G., & Barlow, D. H. (1988). A review of the relationship between panic and avoidance. *Clinical Psychology Review, 8*, 667–685.

Craske, M. G., & Barlow, D. H. (2006). *Mastery of your anxiety and worry*. New York, NY: Oxford University Press.

Craske, M. G., & Barlow, D. H. (2014). Panic disorder and agoraphobia. In D. H. Barlow, *Clinical handbook of psychological disorders* (pp. 1–61). New York, NY: Guilford Press.

Craske, M. G., & Rowe, M. K. (1997). Nocturnal panic. *Clinical Psychology: Science & Practice, 4*, 153–174.

Craske, M. G., Antony, M. M., & Barlow, D. H. (2006). *Mastering your fears and phobias: Therapist guide*. New York, NY: Oxford University Press.

Craske, M. G., Barlow, D. H., Clark, D. M., Curtis, G. C., Hill, E. M., Himle, J. A., & Warwick, H. M. C. (1996). Specific (simple) phobia. In T. A. Widiger, A. J. Frances, H. A. Pincus, R. Ross, M. B. First, & W. W. Davis (Eds.), *DSM-IV sourcebook* (Vol. 2, pp. 473–506). Washington, DC: American Psychiatric Association.

Craske, M. G., Brown, T. A., & Barlow, D. H. (1991). Behavioral treatment of panic disorder: A two-year follow-up. *Behavior Therapy, 22*, 289–304.

Craske, M. G., Hermans, D., & Vansteenwegen, D. (2006). *Fear and learning*. Washington, DC: American Psychological Association.

Craske, M. G., Kircanski, K., Epstein, A., Wittchen, H.-U., Pine, D. S., Lewis-Fernández, R., & Hinton, D. (2010). Panic disorder: A review of DSM-IV panic disorder and proposals for DSM-V. *Depression and Anxiety, 27*(2), 93–112.

Craske, M. G., Lang, A. J., Mystkowski, J. L., Zucker, B. G., & Bystritsky, A. (2002). Does nocturnal panic represent a more severe form of panic disorder? *Journal of Nervous and Mental Disease, 190*, 611–618.

Craske, M. G., Rauch, S. L., Ursano, R., Prenoveau, J., Pine, D. S., & Zinbarg, R. E. (2009). What is an anxiety disorder? *Depression and Anxiety, 26*, 1066–1085.

Craske, M. G., Stein, M. B., Sullivan, G., Sherbourne, C., Bystritsky, A., Rose, R. D., & Roy-Byrne, P. (2011). Disorder-specific impact of coordinated anxiety learning and management treatment for anxiety disorders in primary care. *Archives* of *General Psychiatry, 68*, 378–388. doi: 10.1001/archgenpsychiatry.2011.25

Crawford, N. (2003). ADHD: A women's issue. *Monitor on Psychology, 35*, 28–30.

Creed, F., & Barsky, A. (2004). A systematic review of the epidemiology of somatisation disorder and hypochondriasis. *Journal of Psychosomatic Research, 56*, 391–408.

Creese, I., Burt, D. R., & Snyder, S. H. (1976). Dopamine receptor binding predicts clinical and pharmacological potencies of antischizophrenic drugs. *Science, 192*, 481–483.

Cremniter, D., Jamin, S., Kollenbach, K., Alvarez, J. C., Lecrubier, Y., Gilton, A., & Spreux-Varoquaux, O. (1999). CSF 5-HIAA levels are lower in impulsive as compared to nonimpulsive violent suicide attempts and control subjects. *Biological Psychiatry, 45*(12), 1572–1579.

Crerand, C., Sarwer, D., Magee, L., Gibbons, L., Lowe, M., Bartlett, S., & Whitaker, L. A. (2004). Rate of body dysmorphic disorder among patients seeking facial plastic surgery. *Psychiatric Annals, 34*, 958–965.

Crichton, P., & Morey, S. (2003). Treating pain in cancer patients. In D. C. Turk & R. J. Gatchel (Eds.), *Psychological approaches to pain management: A practitioner's handbook* (2nd ed., pp. 501–514). New York, NY: Guilford.

Crisp, A. H., Callender, J. S., Halek, C., & Hsu, L. K. G. (1992). Long-term mortality in anorexia nervosa: A 20-year follow-up of the St. George's and Aberdeen cohorts. *British Journal of Psychiatry, 161*, 104–107.

Cristancho, M. A., Kocsis, J. H., & Thase, M. E. (2012). Dysthymic disorder and other chronic depressions. *FOCUS, 10*, 422–427.

Critelli, J. W., & Bivona, J. M. (2008). Women's erotic rape fantasies: An evaluation of theory and research. *Journal of Sex Research, 45*, 57–70.

Critser, G. (2003). *Fat land: How Americans became the fattest people in the world*. Boston, MA: Houghton Mifflin.

Croen, L. A., Najjar, D. V., Fireman, B., & Grether, J. K. (2007). Maternal and paternal age and risk of autism spectrum disorders. *Archives of Pediatrics & Adolescent Medicine, 161*(4), 334.

Crouse, K. (2013, January 3). A fun-loving, carefree, spirit becomes the face of anxiety. *New York Times*. Retrieved from http://www.nytimes.com/2013/01/04/sports/golf/charlie-beljan-lives-a-life-of-high-anxiety-and-low-golf-scores.html?pagewanted=all

Crow, S. J., Mitchell, J. E., Roerig, J. D., & Steffen, K. (2009). What potential role is there for medication treatment in anorexia nervosa? *International Journal of Eating Disorders, 42*(1), 1–8.

Crow, S. J., Thuras, P., Keel, P. K., & Mitchell, J. E. (2002). Long-term menstrual and reproductive function in patients with bulimia nervosa. *American Journal of Psychiatry, 159*, 1048–1050.

Crowe, R. R. (1974). An adoption study of antisocial personality. *Archives of General Psychiatry, 31*, 785–791.

Crowley, T., Richardson, D., & Goldmeir, D. (2006). Recommendation for the management of vaginismus: BASHH special interest group for sexual dysfunction. *International Journal of STD and AIDS, 17*, 14–18.

Crump, C., Sundquist, K., Winkleby, M.A., Sundquist, J. (2013). Comorbidities and mortality in bipolar disorder: A Swedish national cohort study. *JAMA Psychiatry, 70*(9):931–939.

Csordas, T. J. (2015). Cultural phenomenology and psychiatric illness. In L. J. Kirmayer, R. Lemelson, & C. A. Cummings (Eds.). *Re-visioning psychiatry: Cultural phenomenology, critical neuroscience, and global mental health* (117–140). New York, NY: Cambridge University Press.

Cuffee, Y., Ogedegbe, C., Williams, N. J., Ogedegbe, G., & Schoenthaler, A. (2014). Psychosocial risk factors for hypertension: An update of the literature. *Current hypertension reports, 16*(10), 1–11.

Cuijpers, P. (2015). Psychotherapies for adult depression: Recent developments. *Current Opinion in Psychiatry, 28*, 24–29.

Cuijpers, P., Beekman, A. T., & Reynolds III, C. F. (2012). Preventing depression: A global priority. *JAMA: The Journal of the American Medical Association, 307*(10), 1033–1034.

Cuijpers, P., Geraedts, A. S., van Oppen, P., Andersson, G., Markowitz, J. C., & van Straten, A. (2011). Interpersonal psychotherapy for depression: a meta-analysis. *American Journal of Psychiatry, 168*(6), 581–592.

Cuijpers, P., Sijbrandji, M., Koole, S., Huibers, M., Berking, M., & Andersson, G. (2014). Psychological treatment of generalized anxiety disorder: A meta-analysis. *Clinical Psychology Review, 34*, 130–140.

Cummings, J. L. (Ed.). (1990). *Subcortical dementia*. New York, NY: Oxford University Press.

Cunningham, J., Yonkers, K. A., O'Brien, S., & Eriksson, E. (2009). Update on research and treatment of premenstrual dysphoric disorder. *Harvard Review of Psychiatry, 17*(2), 120–137.

Cunningham Owens, D. G., & Johnstone, E. C. (2012). Treatment and management of schizophrenia. In M. G. Gelder, N. C. Andreasen, J. J. López-Ibor, Jr., & J. R. Geddes (Eds.), *New Oxford textbook of psychiatry* (2nd. ed., Vol. 1, pp. 578–595). New York, NY: Oxford University Press.

Curatolo, P., Bombardieri, R., & Jozwiak, S. (2008). Tuberous sclerosis. *The Lancet, 372*(9639), 657–668.

Currier, J. M., Neimeyer, R. A., & Berman, J. S. (2008). The effectiveness of psychotherapeutic interventions for bereaved persons: A comprehensive quantitative review. *Psychological Bulletin, 134*(5), 648–661.

Curtis, G. C., Hill, E. M., & Lewis, J. A. (1990*). Heterogeneity of DSM-III-R simple phobia and the simple phobia/agoraphobia boundary: Evidence from the ECA study*. Preliminary report to the Simple Phobia subcommittee of the DSM-IV Anxiety Disorders Work Group.

Curtis, G. C., Himle, J. A., Lewis, J. A., & Lee, Y-J. (1989*). Specific situational phobias: Variant of agoraphobia?* Paper requested by the Simple Phobia subcommittee of the DSM-IV Anxiety Disorders Work Group.

Cuthbert, B. N. (2014). The RDoC framework: facilitating transition from ICD/DSM to dimensional approaches that integrate neuroscience and psychopathology. *World Psychiatry, 13*(1), 28–35.

Cyranowski, J. M., Aarestad, S. L., & Andersen, B. L. (1999). The role of sexual self-schema in a diathesis-stress model of sexual dysfunction. *Applied & Preventative Psychology, 8*, 217–228.

Cyranowski, J. M., Frank, E., Young, E., & Shear, M. K. (2000). Adolescent onset of the gender difference in lifetime rates of major depression. *Archives of General Psychiatry, 57*, 21–27.

D'Hulst, C., Atack, J. R., & Kooy, R. F. (2009). The complexity of the GABAAA receptor shapes unique pharmacological profiles. *Drug Discovery Today, 14*(17–18), 866–875. doi: 10.1016/j.drudis.2009.06.009

D'Onofrio, B. M., Turkheimer, E., Emery, R. E., Slutske, W. S., Heath, A. C., Madden, P. A., & Martin, N. G. (2006). A genetically informed study of the processes underlying the association between parental marital instability and offspring adjustment. *Developmental Psychology, 42*, 486–499.

D'Onofrio, B. M., Rickert, M. E., Langström, N., Donahue, K. L., Coyne, C. A., Larsson, H., & Rathouz, P. J. (2012). Familial confounding of the association between maternal smoking during pregnancy and offspring substance use and problems. *JAMA Psychiatry, 69*(11), 1140–1150.

Daamen, A. P., Penning, R., Brunt, T., & Verster, J. C. (2012). Cocaine. In J. C. Verster, K. Brady, M. Galanter, & P. Conrod (Eds.), *Drug abuse and addiction in medical illness* (pp. 163–173). New York, NY: Springer.

Dalack, G. W., Glassman, A. H., & Covey, L. S. (1993). Nicotine use. In D. L. Dunner (Ed.), *Current psychiatric therapy* (pp. 114–118). Philadelphia, PA: W. B. Saunders.

Dalenberg, C. J., Brand, B. L., Gleaves, D. H., Dorahy, M. J., Loewenstein, R. J., Cardeña, E., Frewen, P. A., Carlson, E. B., Spiegel, D. (2012). Evaluation of the evidence for the trauma and fantasy models of dissociation. *Psychological Bulletin, 138*(3), 550–588.

Dalle Grave, R., Calugi, S., Doll, H. A., & Fairburn, C. G. (2013). Enhanced cognitive behaviour therapy for adolescents with anorexia nervosa: An alternative to family therapy? *Behaviour Research and Therapy, 51*, R9–R12.

Daly, R. J. (1983). Samuel Pepys and post traumatic stress disorder. *British Journal of Psychiatry, 143*, 64–68.

Damasio, A. (2007). Neuroscience and ethics: Intersections. *American Journal of Bioethics, 7*(1), 3–7.

Dan, O., Sagi-Schwartz, A., Bar-haim, Y., & Eshel, Y. (2011). Effects of early relationships on children's perceived control: A longitudinal study. *International Journal of Behavioral Development, 35*(5), 449–456.

Dana, R. H. (1996). The Thematic Apperception Test (TAT). In C. S. Newmark (Ed.), *Major psychological assessment instruments* (pp. 166–205). Boston, MA: Allyn & Bacon.

Daniel, S. S., Walsh, A. K., Goldston, D. B., Arnold, E. M., Reboussin, B. A., & Wood, F. B. (2006). Suicidality, school dropout, and reading problems among adolescents. *Journal of Learning Disabilities, 39*, 507–514.

Daniels, A., Adams, N., Carroll, C., & Bei-necke, R. (2009). A conceptual model for behavioral health and primary care integration: Emerging challenges and strategies for improving international mental health services. *International Journal of Mental Health*, 38(1), 100–112.

Dansinger, M. L., Gleason, J. A., Griffith, J. L., Selker, H. P., & Schaefer, E. J. (2005). Comparison of the Atkins, Ornish, Weight Watchers, and Zone diets for weight loss and heart disease risk reduction: A randomized trial. *JAMA: Journal of the American Medical Association*, 293, 43–53.

Darcangelo, S. (2008). Fetishism: Psychopathology and theory. In D. R. Laws & W. T. O'Donohue (Eds.), *Sexual deviance: Theory, assessment, and treatment* (2nd ed., pp. 108–118). New York, NY: Guilford.

Darwin, C. R. (1872). *The expression of emotions in man and animals*. London, UK: John Murray.

Davey, A., Dai, T., Woodard, J. L., Miller, L. S., Gondo, Y., Johnson, M. A., . . . Stabler, S. P. (2013). Profiles of cognitive functioning in a population-based sample of centenarians using factor mixture analysis. *Experimental Aging Research*, 39(2), 125–144.

Davey, G. (2006). Cognitive mechanisms in fear acquisition and maintenance. In M. G. Craske, D. Hermans, & D. Vansteenwegen (Eds.), *Fear and learning from basic processes to clinical implications.* (pp. 99–116). Washington, DC: American Psychological Association.

David Klonsky, E., Kotov, R., Bakst, S., Rabinowitz, J., & Bromet, E. J. (2012). Hopelessness as a predictor of attempted suicide among first admission patients with psychosis: A 10-year cohort study. *Suicide and Life-Threatening Behavior*, 42(1), 1–10.

Davidson, A. J., Sellix, M. T., Daniel, J., Yamazaki, S., Menaker, M., & Block, G. D. (2006). Chronic jet-lag increases mortality in aged mice. *Current Biology*, 16, R914–R916.

Davidson, J. R. T., Foa, E. B., & Huppert, J. D. (2004). Fluoxetine, comprehensive Cognitive behavioral therapy, and placebo in generalized social phobia. *Archives of General Psychiatry*, 61, 1005–1013.

Davidson, K., MacGregor, M. W., Stuhr, J., Dixon, K., & MacLean, D. (2000). Constructive anger verbal behavior predicts blood pressure in a population-based sample. *Health Psychology*, 19, 55–64.

Davidson, K. W., Mostofsky, E., & Whang, W. (2010). Don't worry, be happy: Positive affect and reduced 10-year incident coronary heart disease: The Canadian Nova Scotia Health Survey. *European Heart Journal*, 31(9), 1065–1070.

Davidson, L., Chinman, M., Sells, D., & Rowe, M. (2006). Peer support among adults with serious mental illness: a report from the field. *Schizophrenia Bulletin*, 32(3), 443–450.

Davidson, M., Keefe, R. S. E., Mohs, R. C., Siever, L. J., Losonczy, M. F., Horvath, T. B., & Davis, K. L. (1987). L-Dopa challenge and relapse in schizophrenia. *American Journal of Psychiatry*, 144, 934–938.

Davidson, R., Pizzagalli, D., Nitschke, J., & Putnam, K. (2002). Depression: Perspectives from affective neuroscience. *Annual Review of Psychology*, 53, 545–574.

Davidson, R. J. (1993). Cerebral asymmetry and emotion: Methodological conundrums. *Cognition and Emotion*, 7, 115–138.

Davidson, R. J., Pizzagalli, D. A., & Nitschke, J. B. (2009). Representation and regulation of emotion in depression: Perspectives from affective neuroscience. In I. H. Gotlib & C. L. Hammen (Eds.), *Handbook of depression* (2nd ed., pp. 218–248). New York, NY: Guilford.

Davidson, S. L. (2014). Relationship between Childhood Conduct Disorder and Antisocial Personality Disorder in Adulthood: An Argument in Favor of Mandatory Life Sentences without Parole for Juvenile Homicide Offenders. *Law and Psychology Review*, 39, 239.

Davies, M. N., Verdi, S., Burri, A.,Trzaskowski, M., Lee, M., Hettema, J. M., Jansen, R., Boomsma, D. I., & Spector, T. D. (2015). Generalized anxiety disorder: A twin study of genetic architecture, genome-wide association and differential gene expression. *PlosOne*, 10(8), e0134865

Davis, C., Levitan, R. D., Kaplan, A. S., Carter, J., Reid, C., Curtis, C., & Kennedy, J. L. (2007). Dopamine transporter gene (DAT1) associated with appetite suppression to methylphenidate in a case–control study of binge eating disorder. *Neuropsychopharmacology*, 32(10), 2199–2206.

Davis, L. (2014). Paraphilic Disorders in Women: Mental Illness or a Reaction to Untreated Trauma?. In N. L., Ishibashi (Eds.). *Arguing with the DSM-5: Reflections for the perspective of social work*, (pp. 29–39). Lulu.com: Chicago, Il.

Davis, M. (2002). Neural circuitry of anxiety and stress disorders. In K. L. Davis, D. Charney, J. T. Coyle, & C. Nemeroff (Eds.), *Neuropsychopharmacology: The fifth generation of progress* (pp. 901–930). Philadelphia, PA: Lippincott Williams & Wilkins.

Davis, N. O., & Carter, A. S. (2014). Social development in autism. In F. Volkmar, S. Rogers, R. Paul, & K. A. Pelphrey (Eds.), *Handbook of autism and pervasive developmental disorders* (4th ed., pp. 212–229). New York, NY: Wiley.

Davison, G. C. (1968). Elimination of a sadistic fantasy by a client-controlled counter-conditioning technique: A case study. *Journal of Abnormal Psychology*, 73, 91–99.

Davison, S., & Janca, A. (2012). Personality disorder and criminal behaviour: what is the nature of the relationship? *Current Opinion in Psychiatry*, 25(1), 39–45.

Davtyan, H., Ghochikyan, A., Petrushina, I., Hovakimyan, A., Davtyan, A., Poghosyan, A., . . . Larsen, A. K. (2013). Immunogenicity, efficacy, safety, and mechanism of action of epitope vaccine (Lu AF20513) for Alzheimer's disease: prelude to a clinical trial. *The Journal of Neuroscience*, 33(11), 4923–4934.

Dawson, D. A., Grant, B. F., Stinson, F. S., Chou, P. S., Huang, B., & Ruan, W. J. (2005). Recovery from DSM-IV alcohol dependence: United States, 2001–2002. *Addiction*, 100, 281–292.

Dawson, D. A., Goldstein, R. B., & Grant, B. F. (2012). Differences in the profiles of DSM-IV and DSM-5 alcohol use disorders: Implications for clinicians. *Alcoholism: Cinical and Experimental Research*, 37(Suppl.S1), E305–E313. doi: 10.1111/j.1530-0277.2012.01930.x

Dawson, G., Jones, E. J. H., Merkle, K., Venema, K., Lowy, R., Faja, S., & Webb, S. J. (2012). Early behavioral intervention is associated with normalized brain activity in young children with autism. *Journal of the American Academy of Child and Adolescent Psychiatry*, 51(11), 1150–1159.

Dawson, M., Mottron, L., & Gernsbacher, M. (2008). Learning in autism. In J. H. Byrne & H. L. Roediger (Eds.), *Learning and memory: A comprehensive reference: Cognitive psychology* (pp. 759–772). New York, NY: Elsevier.

Day, R., Nielsen, J. A., Korten, A., Ernberg, G., Dube, K. C., Gebhart, J., & Olatawura, M. (1987). Stressful life events preceding the acute onset of schizophrenia: A cross-national study from the World Health Organization. *Cultural Medicine and Psychiatry*, 11, 123–205.

de Azeredo, L. A., Rovaris, D. L., Mota, N. R., Polina, E. R., Marques, F. Z., Contini, V., . . . Grevet, E. H. (2014). Further evidence for the association between a polymorphism in the promoter region of SLC6A3/DAT1 and ADHD: findings from a sample of adults. *European Archives of Psychiatry and Clinical Neuroscience*, 264(5), 401–408.

De Backer, G., Kittel, F., Kornitzer, M., & Dramaix, M. (1983). Behavior, stress, and psychosocial traits as risk factors. *Preventative Medicine*, 12, 32–36.

De Brito, S. A., & Hodgins, S. (2009). Antisocial personality disorder. In M. McMurran & R. C. Howard (Eds.), *Personality, personality disorder and violence: An evidence based approach* (pp. 133–154). New York, NY: Wiley.

De Dios, J. A. A., & Brass, S. D. (2012). New and unconventional treatments for obstructive sleep apnea. *Neurotherapeutics*, 9(4), 702–709.

de Kleine, R. A., Hendriks, G. J., Kusters, W. J., Broekman, T. G., & van Minnen, A. (2012): A randomized placebo-controlled trial of d-cycloserine to enhance exposure therapy for posttraumatic stress disorder. *Biological Psychiatry*, 71, 962–968.

de Lissovoy, V. (1961). Head banging in early childhood. *Child Development*, 33, 43–56.

de Portugal, E., González, N., Haro, J. M., Autonell, J., & Cervilla, J. A. (2008). A descriptive case-register study of delusional disorder. *European Psychiatry*, 23(2), 125–133.

De Raedt, R., Vanderhasselt, M.-A., & Baeken, C. (2015). Neurostimulation as an intervention for treatment resistant depression: From research on mechanisms towards targeted neurocognitive strategies. *Clinical Psychology Review*, 41, 61–69.

de Wit, H., & Phillips, T. J. (2012). Do initial responses to drugs predict future use or abuse? *Neuroscience & Biobehavioral Reviews*, 36(6), 1565–1576. doi: http://dx.doi.org/10.1016/j.neubiorev.2012.04.005

de Zambotti, M., Claudatos, S., Inkelis, S., Colrain, I. M., & Baker, F. C. (2015). Evaluation of a consumer fitness-tracking device to assess sleep in adults. *Chronobiology International*, 32(7), 1024–1028.

Deakin, J. F. W., & Graeff, F. G. (1991). Critique: 5-HT and mechanisms of defence. *Journal of Psychopharmacology, 5*(4), 305–315.

Deale, A., Chalder, T., Marks, I., & Wessely, S. (1997). Cognitive behavior therapy for chronic fatigue syndrome: A randomized controlled trial. *American Journal of Psychiatry, 154*, 408–414.

Deale, A., Husain, K., Chalder, T., & Wessely, S. (2001). Long-term outcome of cognitive behavioral therapy versus relaxation therapy for chronic fatigue syndrome: A 5-year follow-up study. *American Journal of Psychiatry, 158*, 2038–2042.

Debruyne, H., & Audenaert, K. (2012). Towards understanding Cotard's syndrome: An overview. *Neuropsychiatry, 2*(6), 481–486.

Decety, J., & Skelly, L. R. (2013). The neural underpinnings of the experience of empathy: Lessons for psychopathy. In K. N. Ochsner & S. M. Kosslyn (Eds.), *The Oxford handbook of cognitive neuroscience, volume 2: The cutting edges* (pp. 228–243). New York, NY: Oxford University Press.

Deckersbach, T., Moshier, S. J., Tuschen-Caffier, B., & Otto, M. W. (2011). Memory dysfunction in panic disorder: An investigation of the role of chronic benzodiazepine use. *Depression and Anxiety, 28*, 999–1007. doi: 10.1002/da.20891

Deckersbach, T., Peters, A. T., Sylvia, L., Urdahl, A., Magalhães, P. V., Otto, M. W., . . . Nierenberg, A. (2014). Do comorbid anxiety disorders moderate the effects of psychotherapy for bipolar disorder? Results from STEP-BD. *American Journal of Psychiatry, 171*(2), 178–186.

Del Parigi, A., Panza, F., Capurso, C., & Solfrizzi, V. (2006). Nutritional factors, cognitive decline, and dementia. *Brain Research Bulletin, 69*(1), 1–19.

DeLamater, J., & Sill, M. (2005). Sexual desire in latter life. *Journal of Sex Research, 42*, 138–149.

Delano-Wood, L., & Abeles, N. (2005). Late-life depression: Detection, risk, reduction, and somatic intervention. *Clinical Psychology Science Practice, 12*, 207–217.

DeLisi, M., & Vaughn, M. G. (2015). Ingredients for criminality require genes, temperament, and psychopathic personality. *Journal of Criminal Justice, 43*(4), 290–294.

Delizonna, L. L., Wincze, J. P., Litz, B. T., Brown, T. A., & Barlow, D. H. (2001). A comparison of subjective and physiological measures of mechanically produced and erotically produced erections. (Or, is an erection an erection?) *Journal of Sex and Marital Therapy, 27*, 21–31.

Dell, P. F. (1998). Axis II pathology in outpatients with dissociative identity disorder. *Journal of Nervous and Mental Disease, 186*(6), 352–356.

Dell, P. F., & O'Neil, J. A. (Eds.). (2009). *Dissociation and the dissociative disorders.* New York, NY: Routledge.

Dembroski, T. M., & Costa, P. T., Jr. (1987). Coronary prone behavior: Components of the Type A pattern and hostility. *Journal of Personality, 55*(2), 211–235.

Demers, C. H., Bogdan, R., & Agrawal, A. (2014). The genetics, neurogenetics and pharmacogenetics of addiction. *Current Behavioral Neuroscience Reports, 1*(1), 33–44.

Denis, C., Fatséas, M., & Auriacombe, M. (2012). Analyses related to the development of DSM-5 criteria for substance use related disorders: 3. An assessment of pathological gambling criteria. *Drug and Alcohol Dependence, 122*(1–2), 22–27. doi: http://dx.doi.org/10.1016/j.drugalcdep.2011.09.006

Dent, M. F., & Bremner, J. D. (2009). Pharmacotherapy for posttraumatic stress disorder and other trauma-related disorders. In M. M. Antony & M. B. Stein (Eds.), *Oxford handbook of anxiety and related disorders.* (pp. 405–416). New York, NY: Oxford University Press.

Denys, D., Mantione, M., Figee, M., van den Munckhof, P., Koerselman, F., Westenberg, H., & Schuurman, R. (2010). Deep brain stimulation of the nucleus accumbens for treatment-refractory Obsessive-compulsive disorder. *Archives of General Psychiatry, 67*(10), 1061–1068. doi: 10.1001/archgenpsychiatry.2010.122

Denzin, N. K. (1987). *The recovering alcoholic.* Newbury Park, CA: Sage.

Depue, R. A., Luciana, M., Arbisi, P., Collins, P., & Leon, A. (1994). Dopamine and the structure of personality: Relation of agonist-induced dopamine activity to positive emotionality. *Journal of Personality and Social Psychology, 67*, 485–498.

DeRogatis, L. R., Komer, L., Katz, M., Moreau, M., Kimura, T., Garcia, M. J., & . . . Pyke, R. (2012). Treatment of Hypoactive Sexual Desire Disorder in premenopausal women: Efficacy of flibanserin in the VIOLET Study. *Journal of Sexual Medicine, 9*, 1074–1085. doi:10.1111/j.1743-6109.2011.02626.x

Dersh, J., Polatin, P. B., & Gatchel, R. J. (2002). Chronic pain and psychopathology: Research findings and theoretical considerations. *Psychosomatic Medicine, 64*, 773–786.

DeRubeis, R., Gelfand, L. A., Tang, T. Z., & Simons, A. D. (1999). Medications versus cognitive behavior therapy for severely depressed outpatients: Mega-analysis of four randomized comparisons. *American Journal of Psychiatry, 156*, 1007–1013.

DeRubeis, R., Hollon, S., Amsterdam, J., Shelton, R., Young, P., & Gallop, R. (2005). Cognitive therapy vs. medications in the treatment of moderate to severe depression. *Archives of General Psychiatry, 62*, 409–416.

Desantis, A., & Hane, A. (2010). "Adderall is definitely not a drug": Justifications for the illegal use of ADHD stimulants. *Substance Use & Misuse, 45*(1–2), 31–46.

DeStefano, F., Price, C. S., & Weintraub, E. S. (2013). Increasing exposure to antibody-stimulating proteins and polysaccharides in vaccines is not associated with risk of autism. *Journal of Pediatrics, 163*(2), 561–567. doi: http://dx.doi.org/10.1016/j.jpeds.2013.02.001

Devanand, D. P. (2002). Comorbid psychiatric disorders in late life depression. *Biological Psychiatry, 52*, 236–242.

Deveci, A., Taskin, O., Dinc, G., Yilmaz, H., Demet, M. M., Erbay-Dundar, P., & Ozman, E. (2007). Prevalence of pseudoneurologic conversion disorder in an urban community in Manisa, Turkey. *Social Psychiatry and Psychiatric Epidemiology, 42*(11), 857–864.

DeWall, C. N., MacDonald, G., Webster, G. D., Masten, C. L., Baumeister, R. F., Powell, C., & Eisenberger, N. I. (2010). Acetaminophen reduces social pain: Behavioral and neural evidence. *Psychological Science, 21*, 931–937.

DeWitt, D. J., Adlaf, E. M., Offord, D. R., & Ogborne, A. C. (2000). Age at first alcohol use: A risk factor for the development of alcohol disorders. *American Journal of Psychiatry, 157*, 745–750.

Dhawan, N., Kunik, M. E., Oldham, J., & Coverdale, J. (2010). Prevalence and treatment of narcissistic personality disorder in the community: A systematic review. *Comprehensive Psychiatry, 51*(4), 333–339. doi: 10.1016/j.comppsych.2009.09.003

Dhejne, C., Öberg, K., Arver, S., & Landén, M. (2014). An analysis of all applications for sex reassignment surgery in Sweden, 1960–2010: Prevalence, incidence, and regrets. *Archives of Sexual Behavior, 43*(8), 1535–1545.

Diamond, L. M. (2007). A dynamical systems approach to the development and expression of female same-sex sexuality. *Perspectives on Psychological Science, 2*, 142–161.

Diamond, L. M. (2012). The desire disorder in research on sexual orientation in women: Contributions of dynamical systems theory. *Archives of Sexual Behavior, 41*(1), 73–83.

Diamond, L. M., Butterworth, M. R., & Savin-Williams, R. C. (2011). Working with sexual-minority individuals. In D. H. Barlow (Ed.), *Oxford handbook of clinical psychology.* New York, NY: Oxford University Press.

Diamond, M. (1995). Biological aspects of sexual orientation and identity. In L. Diamant & R. D. McAnulty (Eds.), *The psychology of sexual orientation, behavior, and identity.* Westport, CT: Greenwood Press.

Diamond, M., & Sigmundson, K. (1997). Sex reassignment at birth: Long-term review and clinical implications. *Archives of Pediatric and Adolescent Medicine, 151*, 298–304.

Dick, D. M. (2011). Gene-environment interaction in psychological traits and disorders. *Annual Review of Clinical Psychology, 7*, 383–409. doi: 10.1146/annurev-clinpsy-032210-104518

Dickens, G., & Sugarman, P. (2012). Adult firesetters: Prevalence, characteristics and psychopathology. In G. L. Dickens, P. A. Sugarman & T. A. Gannon (Eds.), *Firesetting and mental health: Theory, research and practice* (pp. 3–27). London, UK: RCPsych Publications.

Dickens, W. T., Turkheimer, E., & Beam, C. (2011). The social dynamics of the expression of genes for cognitive ability. In K. S. Kendler, S. Jaffee, & D. Romer (Eds.), *The dynamic genome and mental health: The role of genes and environments in youth development* (pp. 103–127). New York, NY: Oxford University Press.

Dickersin, K. (2010). To reform U.S. health care, start with systematic reviews. *Science, 329*, 516.

DiClemente, R. J., Crittenden, C. P., Rose, E., Sales, J. M., Wingood, G. M., Crosby, R. A., & Salazar, L. F. (2008). Psychosocial predictors of HIV-associated sexual behaviors and the efficacy of prevention interventions in adolescents at-risk for HIV infection: What works and what doesn't work? *Psychosomatic Medicine, 70,* 598–605.

DiClemente, R. J., Wingwood, G. M., Harrington, K. F., Lang, D. L., Davies, S. L., Hook, E. W., & Robillard, A. (2004). Efficacy of an HIV prevention intervention for African American adolescent girls: A randomized controlled trial. *JAMA: Journal of the American Medical Association, 292,* 171–179.

Diedrich, A., & Voderholzer, U. (2015). Obsessive– compulsive personality disorder: A current review. *Current Psychiatry Reports, 17*(2), 1–10.

Diener, E. (2000). Subjective well-being: The science of happiness, and a proposal for a national index. *American Psychologist, 55,* 34–43.

Diener, E., Oishi, S., & Lucas, R. E. (2003). Personality, culture, and subjective well-being: Emotional and cognitive evaluations of life. *Annual Review of Psychology, 54,* 403–425.

Dimberg, U., & Öhman, A. (1983). The effects of directional facial cues on electrodermal conditioning to facial stimuli. *Psychophysiology, 20,* 160–167.

Dimidjian, S., Barrera Jr., M., Martell, C., Muñoz, R. F., Lewinsohn, P. M. (2011). The origins and current status of behavioral activation treatments for depression. *Annual Review of Clinical Psychology, 7,* 1–38.

Dimidjian, S., Martell, C., Herman-Dunn, R., & Hubley, S. (in press). Behavior activation for depression. In D. H. Barlow (Ed.), *Clinical handbook of psychological disorders: A step-by-step treatment manual* (5th ed.). New York, NY: Guilford.

Dimon, L. (2013). What witchcraft is Facebook? *The Atlantic.* Retrieved October 19, 2015 from http: //www.theatlantic.com/health/archive/2013/09/what-witchcraft-is-facebook/279499/

Dimsdale, J. E., Creed, F., Escobar, J., Sharpe, M., Wulsin, L., Barsky, A., Lee, S., Irwin, M. R., & Levenson, J. (2013) Somatic symptom disorder: An important change in *DSM. Journal of Psychosomatic Research, 75,* 223–228.

DiNardo, P. A., Guzy, L. T., Jenkins, J. A., Bak, R. M., Tomasi, S. F., & Copeland, M. (1988). Etiology and maintenance of dog fears. *Behaviour Research and Therapy, 26,* 241–244.

Dinnel, D. L., Kleinknecht, R. A., & Tanaka-Matsumi, J. (2002). A cross-cultural comparison of social phobia symptoms. *Journal of Psychopathology and Behavioral Assessment, 24,* 75–82.

Dishion, T. J., Patterson, G. R., & Reid, J. R. (1988). Parent and peer factors associated with drug sampling in early adolescence: Implications for treatment. In E. R. Rahdert & J. Gabowski (Eds.), *Adolescent drug abuse: Analyses of treatment research* (NIDA Research Monograph No. 77, DHHS Publication No. ADM88-1523, pp. 69–93). Rockville, MD: National Institute on Drug Abuse.

Disney, K. L. (2013). Dependent personality disorder: A critical review. *Clinical Psychology Review, 33*(8), 1184–1196.

Dixon, L. B., & Lehman, A. F. (1995). Family interventions for schizophrenia. *Schizophrenia Bulletin, 21,* 631–643.

Dixon-Gordon, K. L., Weiss, N. H., Tull, M. T., DiLillo, D., Messman-Moore, T., & Gratz, K. L. (2015). Characterizing emotional dysfunction in borderline personality, major depression, and their co-occurrence. *Comprehensive Psychiatry, 62,* 187–203.

Djernes, J. K. (2006). Prevalence and predictors of depression in populations of elderly: A review. *Acta Psychiatrica Scandinavica, 113*(5), 372–387.

Docter, R. F., & Prince, V. (1997). Transvestism: A survey of 1032 cross-dressers. *Archives of Sexual Behavior, 26,* 589–605.

Doehrmann, O., Ghosh, S. S., Polli, F. E., Reynolds, G. O., Whitfield-Gabrieli, S., Hofmann, S. G., Pollack, M., & Gabrieli, J. D. (2013). Predicting treatment response in social anxiety disorder from functional magnetic resonance imaging. *JAMA Psychiatry, 70,* 87–97.

Dogan, S. (2009). Vaginismus and accompanying sexual dysfunctions in a Turkish clinical sample. *Journal of Sexual Medicine, 6,* 184–192.

Dohrenwend, B. P., & Dohrenwend, B. S. (1981). Socioenvironmental factors, stress and psychopathology. *American Journal of Community Psychology, 9*(2), 128–164.

Dohrenwend, B. P., & Egri, G. (1981). Recent stressful life events and episodes of schizophrenia. *Schizophrenia Bulletin, 7,* 12–23.

Dohrenwend, B. P., Turner, J. B., & Turse, N. A. (2006). The psychological risks of Vietnam for U.S. veterans: A revisit with new data and methods. *Science, 313,* 979–982.

Dohrenwend, B. P. Yager, T. J., Wall, M. M., & Adams, B. G. (2012). The roles of combat exposure, personal vulnerability, and involve-ment in harm to civilians or prisoners in Vietnam-war-related posttraumatic stress disorder. *Clinical Psychological Science, 1,* 223–238.

Dolan, M., & Völlm, B. (2009). Antisocial personality disorder and psychopathy in women: A literature review on the reliability and validity of assessment instruments. *International Journal of Law and Psychiatry, 32*(1), 2–9.

Dominé, F., Berchtold, A., Akré, C., Michaud, P.-A., & Suris, J.-C. (2009). Disordered eating behaviors: What about boys? *Journal of Adolescent Health, 44*(2), 111–117.

Domino, E. F. & Miller, S. C. (2015). The pharmacology of dissociatives. In R.K. Ries, D.A. Fiellin, S.C. Miller, & R. Saitz (Eds.), *The ASAM principles of addiction medicine* (5th Ed., pp. 256–266). New York, NY: Wolters Kluwer.

Domschke, K., & Dannlowski, U. (2010). Imaging genetics of anxiety disorders. *NeuroImage, 53,* 822–831.

Donaldson, K. (1976). *Insanity inside out.* New York, NY: Crown.

Donath, C., Gräßel, E., Baier, D., Pfeiffer, C., Bleich, S., & Hillemacher, T. (2012). Predictors of binge drinking in adolescents: ultimate and distal factors—a representative study. *BMC Public Health, 12*(1), 263–278.

Douaud, G., Menke, R. A. L., Gass, A., Monsch, A. U., Rao, A., Whitcher, B., & Smith, S. (2013). Brain microstructure reveals early abnormalities more than two years prior to clinical progression from mild cognitive impairment to Alzheimer's disease. *The Journal of Neuroscience, 33*(5), 2147–2155.

Dougall, N., Maayan, N., Soares-Weiser, K., McDermott, L. M., & McIntosh, A. (2015). Transcranial magnetic stimulation for schizophrenia. *Schizophrenia Bulletin, 41*(6), 1220–1222.

Dougherty, D. D., Rauch, S. L., & Jenike, M. A. (2012). Pharmacological treatments for obsessive compulsive disorder. In G. Steketee (Ed.), *The Oxford handbook of obsessive compulsive and spectrum disorders* (pp. 291–306). New York, NY: Oxford University Press.

Douglas, K. S., Guy, L. S., & Hart, S. D. (2009). Psychosis as a risk factor for violence to others: A meta-analysis. *Psychological Bulletin, 135*(5), 679–706. doi: 10.1037/a0016311

Douglas, K. S., Nikolova, N. L., Kelley, S. E., Edens, J. F., Cutler, B. L. (Ed.), & Zapf, P. A. (Ed.). (2015). *APA handbook of forensic psychology, Vol. 1: Individual and situational influences in criminal and civil contexts.* Washington, DC: American Psychological Association.

Douzgou, S., Breen, C., Crow, Y. J., Chandler, K., Metcalfe, K., Jones, E., & Clayton-Smith, J. (2012). Diagnosing fetal alcohol syndrome: new insights from newer genetic technologies. *Archives of Disease in Childhood, 97*(9), 812–817. doi: 10.1136/archdischild-2012-302125

Dowling, N., Smith, D., & Thomas, T. (2007). A comparison of individual and group cognitive-behavioural treatment for female pathological gambling. *Behaviour Research and Therapy, 45*(9), 2192–2202.

Dragioti, E., Dimoliatis, I., Fountoulakis, K. N., & Evangelou, E. (2015). A systematic appraisal of allegiance effect in randomized controlled trials of psychotherapy. *Annals of General Psychiatry, 14*(1), 25–33. doi:10.1186/s12991-015-0063-1

Drake, R., Bond, G. & Becker, D. (2012). *Individual placement and support: An evidence-based approach to supported employment.* New York, NY: Oxford.

Drogin, E. Y., Commons, M. L., Gutheil, T. G., Meyer, D. J., & Norris, D. M. (2012). "Certainty" and expert mental health opinions in legal proceedings. *International Journal of Law and Psychiatry, 35*(5–6), 348–353. doi: http://dx.doi.org/10.1016/j.ijlp.2012.09.002

Drummond, K. D., Bradley, S. J., Peterson-Badali, M., & Zucker, K. J. (2008). A follow-up study of girls with gender identity disorder. *Developmental Psychology, 44,* 34–45.

Dubovsky, S. L. (1983). Psychiatry in Saudi Arabia. *American Journal of Psychiatry, 140*(11), 1455–1459.

Duclos, J., Vibert, S., Mattar, L., & Godart, N. (2012). Expressed emotion in families of patients with eating disorders: a review of the literature. *Current Psychiatry Reviews, 8*(3), 183–202.

Dugas, M. J., Schwartz, A., & Francis, K. (2012). Intolerance of uncertainty, fear of anxiety, and adolescent worry. *Journal of Abnormal Child Psychology, 40,* 863–870.

Dulit, R. A., Marin, D. B., & Frances, A. J. (1993). Cluster B personality disorders. In D. L. Dunner (Ed.), *Current psychiatric therapy* (pp. 405–411). Philadelphia, PA: W. B. Saunders.

Duman, R. (2004). Depression: A case of neuronal life and death? *Biological Psychiatry, 56,* 140–145.

Dummit, E. S., 3rd, Klein, R. G., Tancer, N. K., Asche, B., Martin, J., & Fairbanks, J. A. (1997). Systematic assessment of 50 children with selective mutism. *Journal of the American Academy of Child and Adolescent Psychiatry, 36*(5), 653–660. doi: 10.1097/00004583-199705000-00016

Dunlop, B. W., & Nemeroff, C. B. (2007). The role of dopamine in the pathophysiology of depression. *Archives of General Psychiatry, 64*(3), 327–337.

DuPaul, G. J., Gormley, M. J., & Laracy, S. D. (2013). Comorbidity of LD and ADHD: Implications of DSM-5 for assessment and treatment. *Journal of Learning Disabilities, 46*(1), 43–51. doi: 10.1177/0022219412464351

Durand, V. M. (1990). *Severe behavior problems: A functional communication training approach.* New York, NY: Guilford.

Durand, V. M. (1998). *Sleep better: A guide to improving the sleep of children with special needs.* Baltimore, MD: Paul H. Brookes.

Durand, V. M. (1999). Functional communication training using assistive devices: Recruiting natural communities of reinforcement. *Journal of Applied Behavior Analysis, 32*(3), 247–267.

Durand, V. M. (2001). Future directions for children and adolescents with mental retardation. *Behavior Therapy, 32,* 633–650.

Durand, V. M. (2006). Sleep terrors. In J. E. Fisher & W. T. O'Donohue (Eds.), *Evidence-based psychotherapy* (pp. 654–659). Reno, NV: Springer.

Durand, V. M. (2008). *When children don't sleep well: Interventions for pediatric sleep disorders, Therapist guide.* New York, NY: Oxford University Press.

Durand, V. M. (2011). Disorders of development. In D.H. Barlow, (Ed.), *Oxford handbook of clinical psychology* (pp., 551–573). New York: Oxford University Press.

Durand, V. M. (2012). Functional communication training: Treating challenging behavior. In P. Prelock & R. McCauley (Eds.), *Treatment of autism spectrum disorders: Evidence-based intervention strategies for communication & social interaction* (pp. 107–138). Baltimore, MD: Paul H. Brookes.

Durand, V.M. (2014a). *Autism spectrum disorder: A clinical guide for general practitioners.* Washington, D.C.: American Psychological Association.

Durand, V. M. (2014b). *Disorders of development.* In D. H. Barlow (Ed.), Oxford handbook of clinical psychology: Revised edition (pp. 558–581). New York: Oxford University.

Durand, V. M. (2014c). *Sleep better!: A guide to improving sleep for children with special needs (revised edition).* Baltimore, MD: Paul H. Brookes.

Durand, V. M., & Carr, E. G. (1992). An analysis of maintenance following functional communication training. *Journal of Applied Behavior Analysis, 25*(4), 777–794.

Durand, V. M., & Hieneman, M. (2008). *Helping parents with challenging children: Positive family intervention, Facilitator's guide.* New York, NY: Oxford University Press.

Durand, V. M., & Mindell, J. A. (1999). Behavioral intervention for childhood sleep terrors. *Behavior Therapy, 30,* 705–715.

Durand, V. M., & Wang, M. (2011). Clinical trials. In J. C. Thomas & M. Hersen (Eds.), *Understanding research in clinical and counseling psychology,* (pp. 201–228). New York, NY: Routledge.

Durand, V. M., Hieneman, M., Clarke, S., Wang, M., & Rinaldi, M. (2013). Positive family intervention for severe challenging behavior I: A multi-site randomized clinical trial. *Journal of Positive Behavior Interventions, 15*(3), 133–143.

Durant, C., Christmas, D., & Nutt, D. (2010). The pharmacology of anxiety. *Current Topics in Behavioral Neurosciences, 2,* 303–330.

Durham, M. L., & La Fond, J. Q. (1985). The empirical consequences and policy implications of broadening the statutory criteria for civil commitment. *Yale Law and Policy Review, 3,* 395–446.

Durham v. United States, 214 F.2d, 862, 874-875 (D.C. Cir., 1954). Durkheim, E. (1951). *Suicide: A study in sociology.* (J. A. Spaulding & G. Simpson, Trans.). New York, NY: Free Press.

Durkin, M. S., Maenner, M. J., Newschaffer, C. J., Lee, L. C., Cunniff, C. M., Daniels, J. L., & Zahorodny, W. (2008). Advanced parental age and the risk of autism spectrum disorder. *American Journal of Epidemiology, 168*(11), 1268–1276.

Dürsteler, K. M., Berger, E. M., Strasser, J., Caflisch, C., Mutschler, J., Herdener, M., & Vogel, M. (2015). Clinical potential of methylphenidate in the treatment of cocaine addiction: a review of the current evidence. *Substance abuse and rehabilitation, 6,* 61–74.

Dusky v. United States, 362 U.S. 402 (1960). Dusseldorp, E., van Elderen, T., Maes, S., Meulman, J., & Kraaij, V. (1999). A meta-analysis of psychoeducational programs for coronary heart disease patients. *Health Psychology, 18,* 506–519.

Dustin, M. L., & Long, E. O. (2010). Cytotoxic immunological synapses. *Immunological Review, 235,* 24–34.

Dvorak-Bertscha, J., Curtin, J., Rubinstein, T., & Newman, J. (2009). Psychopathic traits moderate the interaction between cognitive and affective processing. *Psychophysiology, 46*(5), 913.

Dysken, M. W., Sano, M., Asthana, S., Vertrees, J. E., Pallaki, M., Llorente, M., . . . Prieto, S. (2014). Effect of vitamin E and memantine on functional decline in Alzheimer disease: the TEAM-AD VA cooperative randomized trial. *JAMA, 311*(1), 33–44.

Dzau, V. J., & Pizzo, P. A. (2014). Relieving Pain in America: Insights from an Institute of Medicine committee. *JAMA, 312*(15), 1507–1508.

Eaker, E. D., Pinsky, J., & Castelli, W. P. (1992). Myocardial infarction and coronary death among women: Psychosocial predictors from a 20-year follow-up of women in the Framingham study. *American Journal of Epidemiology, 135,* 854–864.

Eastman, C. I., Young, M. A., Fogg, L. F., Liu, L., & Meaden, P. M. (1998). Bright light treatment of winter depression: A placebo-controlled trial. *Archives of General Psychiatry, 55*(10), 883–889.

Eaton, W. W., Kessler, R. C., Wittchen, H.-U., & McGee, W. J. (1994). Panic and panic disorder in the United States. *American Journal of Psychiatry, 151,* 413–420.

Eaton, W. W., Shao, H., Nestadt, G., Lee, H. B., Bienvenu, O. J., & Zandi, P. (2008). Population-based study of first onset and chronicity in major depressive disorder. *Archives of General Psychiatry, 65*(5), 513–520.

Ebigno, P. (1982). Development of a culture-specific screening scale of somatic complaints indicating psychiatric disturbance. *Culture, Medicine, and Psychiatry, 6*(1), 29–43.

Ebigno, P. O. (1986). A cross sectional study of somatic complaints of Nigerian females using the Enugu Somatization Scale. *Culture, Medicine, and Psychiatry, 10,* 167–186.

Ebringer, A. (2015). *Creutzfeldt-Jakob Disease and its variants.* In Multiple sclerosis, mad cow disease and acinetobacter (pp. 141–152). London, UK: Springer International Publishing.

Eckman, T. A., Wirshing, W. C., Marder, S. R., Liberman, R. P., Johnston-Cronk, K., Zimmermann, K., & Mintz, J. (1992). Techniques for training schizophrenic patients in illness self-management: A controlled trial. *American Journal of Psychiatry, 149,* 1549–1555.

Eddy, K. T., Dorer, D. J., Franko, D. L., Tahilani, K., Thompson-Brenner, H., & Herzog, D. B. (2008). Diagnostic crossover in anorexia nervosa and bulimia nervosa: Implications for DSM-V. *American Journal of Psychiatry, 165*(2), 245–250.

Eddy, K. T., Keel, P. K., Dorer, D. J., Delinsky, S. S., Franko, D. L., & Herzog, D. B. (2002). A longitudinal comparison of anorexia nervosa subtypes. *International Journal of Eating Disorders, 31,* 191–201.

Edwards, A. C., & Kendler, K. S. (2012). A twin study of depression and nicotine dependence: Shared liability or causal relationship? *Journal of Affective Disorders, 142*(1–3), 90–97. doi: http://dx.doi.org/10.1016/j.jad.2012.03.048

Edwards, A. J. (1994). *When memory fails: Helping the Alzheimer's and dementia patient.* New York, NY: Plenum Press.

Edwards, G. (2012). "The Evil Genius of the Habit": DSM-5 seen in historical context. *Journal of Studies on Alcohol and Drugs, 73*(4), 699.

Edwards, R. R., Campbell, C., Jamison, R. N., & Wiech, K. (2009). The neurobiological underpinnings of coping with pain. *Current Directions in Psychological Science, 18,* 237–241.

Eelen, P., & Vervliet, B. (2006). Fear conditioning and clinical implications: What can we learn from the past? In M. G. Craske, D. Hermans, & D. Vansteenwegen, *Fear and learning: From basic processes to clinical implications* (pp. 17–35). Washington, DC: American Psychological Association.

Eftekhari, A., Ruzek, J. L., Crowley, J. J., Rosen, C. S., Greenbaum, M. A., & Karlin, B. E. (2013). Effectiveness of national implementation of prolonged exposure therapy in veterans affairs care. *JAMA Psychiatry, 70,* 949–955.

Egan, B. M., Zhao, Y., & Axon, R. N. (2010). US trends in prevalence, awareness, treatment, and control of hypertension. *JAMA: Journal of the American Medical Association, 303,* 2043–2050.

Egeland, J. A., Gerhard, D. S., Pauls, D. L., Sussex, J. N., Kidd, K. K., Alien, C. R., . . . Housman, D. E. (1987). Bipolar affective disorders linked to DNA markers on chromosome 11. *Nature, 325*(6107), 783–787.

Ehlers, A., & Clark, D. M. (2003). Early psychological interventions for adult survivors of trauma: A review. *Biological Psychiatry, 53,* 817–826.

Ehlers, A., Clark, D. M., Hackmann, A., McManus, F., Fennell, M., Herbert, C., & Mayou, R. (2003). A randomized controlled trial of cognitive therapy, a self-help booklet, and repeated assessments as early interventions for post-traumatic stress disorder. *Archives of General Psychiatry, 60,* 1024–1032.

Ehlers, A., Hackmann, A., Grey, N., Wild, J., Liness, S., Albert, I., Deale, A., Stott, R., & Clark, D. M. (2014). A randomized controlled trial of 7-day intensive and standard weekly cognitive therapy for PTSD and emotion-focused supportive therapy. *American Journal of Psychiatry, 171,* 294–304.

Ehlers, A., Hofmann, S. G., Herda, C. A., & Roth, W. T. (1994). Clinical characteristics of driving phobia. *Journal of Anxiety Disorders, 8,* 323–339.

Ehrenreich, J. T., Goldstein, C. R., Wright, L. R., & Barlow, D. H. (2009). Development of a unified protocol for the treatment of emotional disorders in youth. *Child & Family Behavior Therapy, 31*(1), 20–37.

Ehrhardt, A. A., & Meyer-Bahlburg, H. F. L. (1981). Effects of prenatal sex hormones on gender-related behavior. *Science, 211,* 1312–1318.

Ehrhardt, A. A., Meyer-Bahlburg, H. F. L., Rosen, L. R., Feldman, J. F., Veridiano, N. P., Zimmerman, I., & McEwen, B. (1985). Sexual orientation after prenatal exposure to exogenous estrogen. *Archives of Sexual Behavior, 14*(1), 57–77.

Eikenaes, I., Egeland, J., Hummelen, B., & Wilberg, T. (2015). Avoidant Personality Disorder versus Social Phobia: The Significance of Childhood Neglect. *PloS one, 10*(3), e0122846.

Eikenæs, I., Pedersen, G., & Wilberg, T. (2016). Attachment styles in patients with avoidant personality disorder compared with social phobia. *Psychology and Psychotherapy: Theory, Research and Practice. 89*(3), 245–260.

Eisenberger, N. I. (2012). The neural bases of social pain: Evidence for shared representations with physical pain. *Psychosomatic Medicine, 74*(2), 126–135.

Eisler, I., Dare, C., Hodes, M., Russell, G. F. M., Dodge, E., & Le Grange, D. (2000). Family therapy for adolescent anorexia nervosa: The results of a controlled comparison of two family interventions. *Journal of Child Psychology and Psychiatry, 41,* 727–736.

Ekstrand, M. L., & Coates, T. J. (1990). Maintenance of safer sexual behaviors and predictors of risky sex: The San Francisco men's health study. *American Journal of Public Health, 80,* 973–977.

El-Gabalawy, R., Mackenzie, C. S., Thibodeau, M. A., Asmundson, G. J. G., & Sareen, J. (2013). Health anxiety disorders in older adults: Conceptualizing complex conditions in late life. *Clinical Psychology Review, 33,* 1096–1105.

Elbedour, S., Shulman, S., & Kedem, P. (1997). Children's fears: Cultural and developmental perspectives. *Behavior Research and Therapy, 35,* 491–496.

Elbogen, E., & Johnson, S. (2009). The intricate link between violence and mental disorder: Results from the National Epidemiologic Survey on Alcohol and Related Conditions. *Archives of General Psychiatry, 66*(2), 152.

Elbogen, E. B., Dennis, P. A., & Johnson, S. C. (In press). Beyond mental illness targeting stronger and more direct pathways to violence. *Clinical Psychological Science.*

Eldevik, S., Jahr, E., Eikeseth, S., Hastings, R. P., & Hughes, C. J. (2010). Cognitive and adaptive behavior outcomes of behavioral intervention for young children with intellectual disability. *Behavior Modification, 34*(1), 16–34.

Eley, T. C. (2011). The interplay between genes and environment in the development of anxiety and depression. In K. S. Kendler, S. Jaffee, & D. Romer (Eds.), *The dynamic genome and mental health: The role of genes and environments in youth development* (pp. 229–254). New York, NY: Oxford University Press.

Ellard, K. K. (2013). *An examination of the neural correlates of emotion acceptance versus worry in generalized anxiety disorder.* (Unpublished doctoral dissertation). Boston, MA: Boston University.

Ellason, J. W., & Ross, C. A. (1997). Two-year follow up of inpatients with dissociative identity disorder. *American Journal of Psychiatry, 154,* 832–839.

Ellis, P. M., & Dronsfield, A. T. (2013). Antabuse's diamond anniversary: Still sparkling on? *Drug and Alcohol Review, 32*(4), 342–344.

Emery, C. F., Anderson, D. R., & Andersen, B. L. (2011). Psychological interventions in health care settings. In D. H. Barlow (Ed.), *Oxford handbook of clinical psychology.* (pp. 701–716). New York, NY: Oxford University Press.

Emmelkamp, P. M. G., Benner, A., Kuipers, A., Feiertag, G. A., Koster, H. C., & van Apeldoorn, F. J. (2006). Comparison of brief dynamic and cognitive-behavioural therapies in avoidant personality disorder. *The British Journal of Psychiatry, 189*(1), 60–64.

Emsley, R., Chiliza, B., Asmal, L., & Harvey, B. H. (2013). The nature of relapse in schizophrenia. *BMC Psychiatry, 13*(1), 50.

England, P., & Bearak, J. (2014). The sexual double standard and gender differences in attitudes toward casual sex among US university students. *Demographic Research, 30,* 1327–1338.

Epperson, C. N., Steiner, M., Hartlage, S. A., Eriksson, E., Schmidt, P. J., Jones, I., & Yonkers, K. A. (2012). Premenstrual dysphoric disorder: Evidence for a new category for DSM-5. *American Journal of Psychiatry, 169*(5), 465–475.

Epstein, D. R., Sidani, S., Bootzin, R. R., & Belyea, M. J. (2012). Dismantling multicomponent behavioral treatment for insomnia in older adults: A randomized controlled trial. *Sleep, 35*(6), 797–805.

Epstein, L. H., Myers, M. D., Raynor, H., & Saelens, B. E. (1998). Treatment of pediatric obesity. *Pediatrics, 101,* 554–570.

Eranti, S., Mogg, A., Pluck, G., Landau, S., Purvis, R., Brown, R. G., & McLoughlin, D. M. (2007). A randomized, controlled trial with 6-month follow-up of repetitive transcranial magnetic stimulation and electroconvulsive therapy for severe depression. *American Journal of Psychiatry, 164*(1), 73–81.

Erath, S. A., Bierman, K. L., & Conduct Problems Prevention Research Group. (2006). Aggressive marital conflict, maternal harsh punishment, and child aggressive-disruptive behavior: Evidence for direct and mediated relations. *Journal of Family Psychology, 20,* 217–226.

Erikson, E. (1982). *The life cycle completed.* New York, NY: Norton.

Erkinjuntti, T. (2012). Vascular dementia. In M. G. Gelder, N. C. Andreasen, J. J. Lopez-Ibor, Jr., & J. R. Geddes (Eds.), *New Oxford textbook of psychiatry* (2nd. ed., Vol. 1, pp. 375–384). New York, NY: Oxford University Press.

Erlich, M. D., Smith, T. E., Horwath, E., & Cournos, F. (2014). Schizophrenia and other psychotic disorders. In J. L. Cutler (Ed), *Psychiatry* (pp. 97–128). New York, NY: Oxford University Press.

Eroglu, C., & Barres, B. A. (2010). Regulation of synaptic connectivity by glia. *Nature, 468*(7321), 223–231. doi: 10.1038/nature09612

Eron, L., & Huesmann, R. (1990). The stability of aggressive behavior: Even unto the third generation. In M. Lewis & S. Miller (Eds.), *Handbook of developmental psychopathology* (pp. 147–156). New York, NY: Plenum.

Ersche, K. D., Jones, P. S., Williams, G. B., Robbins, T. W., & Bullmore, E. T. (2012). Cocaine dependence: A fast-track for brain ageing? *Molecular Psychiatry. 18,* 134–135. doi: http://www.nature.com/mp/journal/vaop/ncurrent/suppinfo/mp201231s1.html

Escobar, J. I., Gara, M. A., Diaz-Martinez, A. M., Interian, A., Warman, M., Allen, L. A., & Rodgers, D. (2007). Effectiveness of a time-limited cognitive behavior therapy type intervention among primary care patients with medically unexplained symptoms. *Annals of Family Medicine, 5*(4), 328–335.

Escobar, M. J., Huepe, D., Decety, J., Sedeño, L., Messow, M. K., Baez, S., . . . Schröeder, J. (2014). Brain signatures of moral sensitivity in adolescents with early social deprivation. *Scientific Reports, 4.*

Eser, D., Schule, C., Baghai, T. C., Romeo, E., & Rupprecht, R. (2006). Neuroactive steroids in depression and anxiety disorders: Clinical studies. *Neuroendocrinology, 84*(4), 244–254.

Eslinger, P. J., & Damasio, A. R. (1985). Severe disturbance of higher cognition after bilateral frontal lobe ablation: Patient EVR. *Neurology, 35,* 1731–1741.

Esparza-Romero, J., Valencia, M. E., Urquidez-Romero, R., Chaudhari, L. S., Hanson, R. L., Knowler, W. C., . . . Schulz, L. O. (2015). Environmentally driven increases in type 2 diabetes and obesity in Pima Indians and non-Pimas in Mexico over a 15-year period: the Maycoba Project. *Diabetes Care, 38*(11), 2075–2082.

Essex, M. J., Klein, M. H., Slattery, M. J., Goldsmith, H. H., & Kalin, N. H. (2010). Early risk factors and developmental pathways to chronic high inhibition and social anxiety disorder in adolescence. *American Journal of Psychiatry, 167*(1), 40–46. doi: 10.1176/appi.ajp.2009.07010051

Eth, S. (1990). Posttraumatic stress disorder in childhood. In M. Hersen & C. G. Last (Ed.), *Handbook of child and adult psychopathology: A longitudinal perspective.* Elmsford, NY: Pergamon Press.

Etkin, A., & Schatzberg, A. F. (2011). Common abnormalities and disorder-specific compensation during implicit regulation of emotional processing in generalized anxiety and major depressive disorders. *American Journal of Psychiatry, 168*(9), 968–978.

Etter, J. (2009). Dependence on the nicotine gum in former smokers. *Addictive Behaviors, 34*(3), 246–251.

Ettinger, A. B., Devinsky, O., Weisbrot, D. M., Ramakrishna, R. K., & Goyal, A. (1999). A comprehensive profile of clinical, psychiatric, and psychosocial characteristics of patients with psychogenic nonepileptic seizures. *Epilepsia, 40*(9), 1292–1298.

Evans, R. M., Emsley, C. L., Gao, S., Sahota, A., Hall, K. S., Farlow, M. R., Hendrie, H. (2000). Serum cholesterol, APOE genotype, and the risk of Alzheimer's disease: A population-based study of African Americans. *Neurology, 54*, 240–242.

Exner, J. E. (2003). *The Rorschach: A comprehensive system. Basic foundations and principles of interpretation* (4th ed.). New York, NY: Wiley.

Eysenck, H. J. (Ed.) (1967). *The biological basis of personality.* Springfield, IL: Charles C. Thomas.

Ezrati-Vinacour, R., & Levin, I. (2004). The relationship between anxiety and stuttering: A multidimensional approach. *Journal of Fluency Disorders, 29*(2), 135–148.

Ezzati, M., & Riboli, E. (2012). Can noncommunicable diseases be prevented? Lessons from studies of populations and individuals. *Science, 337*(6101), 1482–1487.

Ezzel, C. (1993). On borrowed time: Long-term survivors of HIV-l infection. *Journal of NIH Research, 5*, 77–82.

Fabiano, G. A., & Schatz, N. K. (2015). Driving risk interventions for teens with ADHD. In R. A. Barkley (Ed.), *Attention-deficit hyperactivity disorder: A handbook for diagnosis & treatment* (4th ed., pp. 705–727). New York, NY: The Guilford Press.

Fagan, P. J., Wise, T. N., Schmidt, C. W., & Berlin, M. D. (2002). Pedophilia. *JAMA: Journal of the American Medical Association, 288*, 2458–2465.

Fagundes, C. P., & Way, B. (2014). Early-life stress and adult inflammation. *Current Directions in Psychological Science, 23*(4), 277–283.

Fagundes, C. P., Glaser, R., Johnson, S. L., Andridge, R. R., Yang, E. V., Di Gregorio, M. P., & Kiecolt-Glaser, J. K. (2012). Basal cell carcinoma: Stressful life events and the tumor environment. *Archives of General Psychiatry, 69*(6), 618–626.

Fahrner, E. M. (1987). Sexual dysfunction in male alcohol addicts: Prevalence and treatment. *Archives of Sexual Behavior, 16*(3), 247–257.

Failer, J. L. (2002). *Who qualifies for rights? Homelessness, mental illness, and civil commitment.* Ithaca, NY: Cornell University Press.

Fairburn, C. G. (1985). Cognitive-behavioral treatment for bulimia. In D. M. Garner & P. E. Garfinkel (Eds.), *Handbook of psychotherapy for anorexia nervosa and bulimia* (pp. 160–192). New York, NY: Guilford.

Fairburn, C. G. (2008). *Cognitive behavior therapy and eating disorders.* New York, NY: Guilford.

Fairburn, C. G. (2013). *Overcoming binge eating* (2nd ed.). New York, NY: Guilford.

Fairburn, C. G., & Bohn, K. (2005). Eating disorder NOS (EDNOS): An example of the troublesome 'not otherwise specified' (NOS) category in DSM-IV. *Behaviour Research and Therapy, 43*(6), 691–701.

Fairburn, C. G., & Brownell, K. D. (2002). *Eating disorders and obesity: A comprehensive handbook* (2nd ed.). New York, NY: Guilford.

Fairburn, C. G., & Cooper, Z. (1993). The eating disorder examination. In C. G. Fairburn & G. T. Wilson (Eds.), *Binge eating: Nature, assessment, and treatment.* (pp. 317–360). New York, NY: Guilford.

Fairburn, C. G., Cooper, Z., Doll, H. A., O'Connor, M. E., Bohn, K., Hawker, D. M., Palmer, R. L. (2009). Transdiagnostic cognitive-behavioral therapy for patients with eating disorders: A two-site trial with 60-week follow-up. *American Journal of Psychiatry, 166*, 311–319.

Fairburn, C. G., & Cooper, Z. (in press). Eating disorders: A transdiagnostic protocol. In D. H. Barlow (Ed.), *Clinical handbook of psychological disorders: A step-by-step treatment manual* (5th ed.). New York, NY: Guilford.

Fairburn, C. G., Agras, W. S., & Wilson, G. T. (1992). The research on the treatment of bulimia nervosa: Practical and theoretical implications. In G. H. Anderson & S. H. Kennedy (Eds.), *The biology of feast and famine: Relevance to eating disorders* (pp. 317–340). New York, NY: Academic Press.

Fairburn, C. G., Cooper, Z., & Cooper, P. J. (1986). The clinical features and maintenance of bulimia nervosa. In K. D. Brownell & J. P. Foreyt (Eds.), *Handbook of eating disorders: Physiology, psychology, and treatment of obesity, anorexia, and bulimia* (pp. 389–404). New York, NY: Basic Books.

Fairburn, C. G., Cooper, Z., & Shafran, R. (2003). Cognitive behavior therapy for eating disorders: A "transdiagnostic" theory and treatment. *Behaviour Research and Therapy, 41*, 509–528.

Fairburn, C. G., Cooper, Z., Bohn, K., O'Connor, M. E., Doll, H. A., & Palmer, R. L. (2007). The severity and status of eating disorder NOS: Implications for DSM-V. *Behavior Research and Therapy, 45*, 1705–1715.

Fairburn, C. G., Cooper, Z., Doll, H. A., & Davies, B. A. (2005). Identifying dieters who will develop an eating disorder: A prospective, population-based study. *American Journal of Psychiatry, 162*, 2249–2255.

Fairburn, C. G., Cooper, Z., Doll, H. A., & Welch, S. L. (1999). Risk factors for anorexia nervosa: Three integrated case-control comparisons. *Archives of General Psychiatry, 56*, 468–476.

Fairburn, C. G., Cooper, Z., Doll, H. A., Norman, P., & O'Connor, M. (2000). The natural course of bulimia nervosa and binge eating disorder in young women. *Archives of General Psychiatry, 57*, 659–665.

Fairburn, C. G., Cooper, Z., Doll, H. A., Palmer, R. L., Dalle Grave, R. (2013). Enhanced cognitive behaviour therapy for adults with anorexia nervosa: A UK-Italy study. *Behaviour Research and Therapy, 51*(1), R2–R8.

Fairburn, C. G., Cowen, P. J., & Harrison, P. J. (1999). Twin studies and the etiology of eating disorders. *International Journal of Eating Disorders, 26*(4), 349–358.

Fairburn, C. G., Doll, H. A., Welch, S. L., Hay, P. J., Davies, B. A., & O'Connor, M. E. (1998). Risk factors for binge eating disorder. *Archives of General Psychiatry, 55*, 425–432.

Fairburn, C. G., Jones, R., Peveler, R. C., Hope, R. A., & O'Connor, M. (1993). Psychotherapy and bulimia nervosa: The longer-term effects of interpersonal psychotherapy, behaviour therapy and cognitive behaviour therapy. *Archives of General Psychiatry, 50*, 419–428.

Fairburn, C. G., Shafran, R., & Cooper, Z. (1999). A cognitive behavioural theory of anorexia nervosa. *Behaviour Research and Therapy, 37*, 1–13.

Fairburn, C. G., Stice, E., Cooper, Z., Doll, H. A., Norman, P. A., & O'Connor, M. E. (2003). Understanding persistence in bulimia nervosa: A 5-year naturalistic study. *Journal of Consulting and Clinical Psychology, 71*, 103–109.

Fairburn, C. G., Welch, S. L., Doll, S. A., Davies, B. A., & O'Connor, M. E. (1997). Risk factors for bulimia nervosa: A community-based case-control study. *Archives of General Psychiatry, 54*, 509–517.

Fairholme, C. P., Boisseau, C. L., Ellard, K. K., Ehrenreich, J. T., & Barlow, D. H. (2010). Emotions, emotion regulation, and psychological treatment: A unified perspective. In A. M. Kring & D. M. Sloan (Eds.), *Emotion regulation and psychopathology: A transdiagnostic approach to etiology and treatment* (pp. 283–309). New York, NY: Guilford.

Fakhoury, W., & Priebe, S. (2007). Deinstitutionalization and reinstitutionalization: Major changes in the provision of mental healthcare. *Psychiatry, 6*(8), 313–316. doi: 10.1016/j.mppsy.2007.05.008

Fallon, A. E., & Rozin, P. (1985). Sex differences in perceptions of desirable body shape. *Journal of Abnormal Psychology, 94*, 102–105.

Fallon, B. A., Altamash, I., Qureshi, A. I., Schneier, F. R., Sanchez-Lacay, A., Vermes, D., & Liebowitz, M. R. (2003). An open trial of fluvoxamine for hypochondriasis. *Psychosomatics, 44*, 298–303.

Falloon, I. R. (Ed.). (2015). *Handbook of behavioural family therapy.* London, UK: Routledge.

Falloon, I. R. H., Boyd, J. L., McGill, C. W., Williamson, M., Razani, J., Moss, H. B., & Simpson, G. M. (1985). Family management in the prevention of morbidity of schizophrenia. *Archives of General Psychiatry, 42*, 887–896.

Falloon, I. R. H., Brooker, C., & Graham-Hole, V. (1992). Psychosocial interventions for schizophrenia. *Behaviour Change, 9*, 238–245.

Fang, A., & Hofmann, S. G. (2010). Relationship between social anxiety disorder and body dysmorphic disorder. *Clinical Psychology Review, 30,* 1040–1048.

Fang, A., & Wilhelm, S. (2015). Clinical features, cognitive biases, and treatment of body dysmorphic disorder. *Annual Review of Clinical Psychology, 11,* 187–212.

Farias, S. T., Chand, V., Bonnici, L., Baynes, K., Harvey, D., Mungas, D., & Reed, B. (2012). Idea density measured in late life predicts subsequent cognitive trajectories: Implications for the measurement of cognitive reserve. *The Journals of Gerontology Series B: Psychological Sciences and Social Sciences, 67*(6), 677–686. doi: 10.1093/geronb/gbr162

Farnam, F., Janghorbani, M., Merghati-Khoei, E., & Raisi, F. (2014). Vaginismus and its correlates in an Iranian clinical sample. *International Journal of Impotence Research, 26*(6), 230–234.

Farrelly, S., Clement, S., Gabbidon, J., Jeffery, D., Dockery, L., Lassman, F., . . . Thornicroft, G. (2014). Anticipated and experienced discrimination amongst people with schizophrenia, bipolar disorder and major depressive disorder: A cross sectional study. *BMC Psychiatry, 14*(1), 157.

Fatemi, S. H., Aldinger, K. A., Ashwood, P., Bauman, M. L., Blaha, C. D., Blatt, G. J., & Welsh, J. P. (2012). Consensus paper: Pathological role of the cerebellum in autism. *Cerebellum, 11*(3), 777–807. doi: 10.1007/s12311-012-0355-9

Fauci, A. S., & Folkers, G. K. (2012). Toward an AIDS-free generation. *JAMA: Journal of the American Medical Association, 308*(4), 343–344.

Faurholt-Jepsen, M., Frost, M., Ritz, C., Christensen, E. M., Jacoby, A. S., Mikkelsen, R. L., . . . Kessing, L. V. (2015). Daily electronic self-monitoring in bipolar disorder using smartphones–the MONARCA I trial: a randomized, placebo-controlled, single-blind, parallel group trial. *Psychological Medicine, 45*(13):2691–2704.

Fausto-Sterling, A. (2000a). The five sexes, revisited. *The Sciences, 40*(4), 19–23.

Fausto-Sterling, A. (2000b). *Sexing the body.* New York, NY: Basic.

Fausto-Sterling, A. (2015). Intersex: Concept of multiple sexes is not new. *Nature, 519*(7543), 291–291.

Fava, G. A., Grandi, S., Rafanelli, C., Fabbri, S., & Cazzaro, M. (2000). Explanatory therapy in hypochondriasis. *Journal of Clinical Psychiatry, 61*(4), 317–322.

Fava, G. A., Ruini, C., Rafanelli, C., Finos, L., Conti, S., & Grandi, S. (2004). Six-year outcome of cognitive behavior therapy for prevention of recurrent depression. *American Journal of Psychiatry, 161,* 1872–1876.

Fawzy, F. I., Cousins, N., Fawzy, N. W., Kemeny, M. E., Elashoff, R., & Morton, D. (1990). A structured psychiatric intervention for cancer patients: I. Changes over time in methods of coping and affective disturbance. *Archives of General Psychiatry, 47,* 720–728.

Fawzy, F. I., Kemeny, M. E., Fawzy, N. W., Elashoff, R., Morton, D., Cousins, N., & Fahey, J. L. (1990). A structured psychiatric intervention for cancer patients: II. Changes over time in immunological measures. *Archives of General Psychiatry, 47,* 729–735.

Fazel, S., Singh, J. P., Doll, H., & Grann, M. (2012). Use of risk assessment instruments to predict violence and antisocial behaviour in 73 samples involving 24,827 people: Systematic review and meta-analysis. *BMJ: British Medical Journal, 345,* e4692. doi: http: //dx.doi.org/10.1136/bmj.e4692

Fearing, M. A., & Inouye, S. K. (2009). Delirium. In D. G. Blazer & D. C. Steffens (Eds.), *The American Psychiatric Publishing textbook of geriatric psychiatry* (4th ed., pp. 229–242). Arlington, VA: American Psychiatric Publishing.

Federoff, J. P., Fishell, A., & Federoff, B. (1999). A case series of women evaluated for paraphilic sexual disorders. *Canadian Journal of Human Sexuality, 8*(2), 127–140.

Fein, D. A. (2011). *The neuropsychology of autism.* New York, NY: Oxford University Press.

Feinberg, M., & Carroll, B. J. (1984). Biological "markers" for endogenous depression: Effect of age, severity of illness, weight loss and polarity. *Archives of General Psychiatry, 41,* 1080–1085.

Feingold, B. F. (1975). *Why your child is hyperactive.* New York, NY: Random House.

Feinstein, C., & Phillips, J. M. (2006). Developmental disorders of communication, motor skills, and learning. In M. K. Dulcan & J. M. Wiener (Eds.), *Essentials of child and adolescent psychiatry* (pp. 203–231). Washington, DC: American Psychiatric Publishing.

Feldman, H. A., Goldstein, I., Hatzichristou, D. G., Krane, R. J., & McKunlay, J. B. (1994). Impotence and its medical and psychosocial correlates: Results of the Massachusetts Male Aging Study. *Journal of Urology, 151,* 54–61.

Feldman, M. B., & Meyer, I. H. (2007). Childhood abuse and eating disorders in gay and bisexual men. *International Journal of Eating Disorders, 40*(5), 418–423.

Feldman, M. D., & Christensen, J. F. (Eds.). (2014). *Behavioral medicine: A guide for clinical practice,* 4th edition. McGraw-Hill Medical.

Fergus, T. A., & Valentiner, D. P. (2010). Disease phobia and disease conviction are separate dimensions underlying hypochondriasis. *Journal of Behavior Therapy and Experimental Psychiatry, 41,* 438–444.

Ferguson, C. J., & Negy, C. (2014). Development of a brief screening questionnaire for histrionic personality symptoms. *Personality and Individual Differences, 66,* 124–127.

Fergusson, D., & Woodward, L. J. (2002). Mental health, educational, and social role outcomes of adolescents with depression. *Archives of General Psychiatry, 59,* 225–231.

Fergusson, D., Horwood, J., Ridder, E., & Beautrais, A. (2005). Subthreshold depression in adolescence and mental health outcomes in adulthood. *Archives of General Psychiatry, 62,* 66–72.

Ferrazzoli, D., Sica, F., & Sancesario, G. (2013). Sundowning Syndrome: A possible marker of frailty in Alzheimer's disease? *CNS & Neurological Disorders-Drug Targets (Formerly Current Drug Targets-CNS & Neurological Disorders), 12*(4), 525–528.

Ferreira, C. (2000). Serial killers: Victims of compulsion or masters of control? In D. H. Fishbein (Ed.), *The science, treatment, and prevention of antisocial behaviors: Application to the criminal justice system* (pp. 15-1–15-18). Kingston, NJ: Civic Research Institute.

Ferri, C. P., Prince, M., Brayne, C., Brodaty, H., Fratiglioni, L., Ganguli, M., & Scazufca, M. (2005). Global prevalence of dementia: A Delphi consensus study. *The Lancet, 366*(9503), 2112–2117. doi: http://dx.doi.org/10.1016/S0140-6736(05)67889-0

Ferster, C. B. (1961). Positive reinforcement and behavioral deficits of autistic children. *Child Development, 32,* 437–456.

Ferster, C. B., & Skinner, B. F. (1957). *Schedules of reinforcement.* New York, NY: Appleton-Century-Crofts.

Fertuck, E. A., Jekal, A., Song, I., Wyman, B., Morris, M. C., Wilson, S. T., & Stanley, B. (2009). Enhanced "Reading the Mind in the Eyes" in borderline personality disorder compared to healthy controls. *Psychological Medicine, 39*(12), 1979–1988.

Feusner, J. D., Phillips, K. A., & Stein, D. J. (2010). Olfactory reference syndrome: Issues for DSM-V. *Depression and Anxiety, 27*(6), 592–599. doi: 10.1002/da.20688

Ficks, C., & Waldman, I. (2009). Gene-environment interactions in attention-deficit/hyperactivity disorder. *Current Psychiatry Reports, 11*(5), 387–392. doi: 10.1007/s11920-009-0058-1

Ficks, C. A., & Waldman, I. D. (2014). Candidate genes for aggression and antisocial behavior: a meta-analysis of association studies of the 5HTTLPR and MAOA-uVNTR. *Behavior Genetics, 44*(5), 427–444.

Field, A. E., Cheung, L., Wolf, A. M., Herzog, D. B., Gortmaker, S. L., & Colditz, G. A. (1999). Exposure to the mass media and weight concerns among girls. *Pediatrics, 103,* e36.

Field, A. E., Sonneville, K. R., Crosby, R. D., Swanson, S. A., Eddy, K. T., Camargo, C. A., . . . Micali, N. (2014). Prospective associations of concerns about physique and the development of obesity, binge drinking, and drug use among adolescent boys and young adult men. *JAMA Pediatrics, 168*(1), 34–39.

Fielder, R. L., Carey, K. B., & Carey, M. P. (2013). Are hookups replacing romantic relationships? A longitudinal study of first-year female college students. *Journal of Adolescent Health, 52*(3), 657–659.

Fields, B. W., & Fristad, M. A. (2009). Assessment of childhood bipolar disorder. *Clinical Psychology: Science and Practice, 16*(2), 166–181.

Fileborn, B., Thorpe, R., Hawkes, G., Minichiello, V., Pitts, M., & Dune, T. (2015). Sex, desire and pleasure: Considering the experiences of older Australian women. *Sexual and Relationship Therapy, 30*(1), 117–130.

Filippi, M. (Ed.). (2015). *Oxford textbook of neuro-imaging.* Oxford, UK: Oxford University Press.

Fincham, F. D., Beach, S. R. H., Harold, G. T., & Osborne, L. N. (1997). Marital satisfaction and depression: Different causal relationships for men and women? *Psychological Science, 8*(5), 351–357.

Fineberg, N. A., Potenza, M. N., Chamberlain, S. R., Berlin, H. A., Menzies, L., Bechara, A., & Hollander, E. (2010). Probing compulsive and impulsive behaviors, from animal models to endophenotypes: A narrative review. *Neuropsychopharmacology, 35*(3), 591–604.

Finger, S., & Zaromb, F. (2006). Benjamin Franklin and shock-induced amnesia. *American Psychologist, 61*, 240–248.

Finkenbine, R., & Miele, V. J. (2004). Globus hystericus: A brief review. *General Hospital Psychiatry, 26*, 78–82.

First, M. B., & Pincus, H. A. (2002). The DSM-IV text revision: Rationale and potential impact on clinical practice. *Psychiatric Services, 53*, 288–292.

Fischer, M. (1971). Psychoses in the offspring of schizophrenic monozygotic twins and their normal co-twins. *British Journal of Psychiatry, 118*, 43–52.

Fishbain, D. A. (1987). Kleptomania as risk-taking behavior in response to depression. *American Journal of Psychotherapy, 41*, 598–603.

Fisher, C. B., & Vacanti-Shova, K. (2012). The responsible conduct of psychological research: An overview of ethical principles, APA Ethics Code standards, and federal regulations. In S. J. Knapp, M. C. Gottlieb, M. M. Handelsman, & L. D. VandeCreek (Eds.), *APA handbook of ethics in psychology, Vol 2: Practice, teaching, and research* (pp. 335–369). Washington, DC: American Psychological Association.

Fisher, P. L., & Wells, A. (2009). Psychological models of worry and generalized anxiety disorder. In M. M. Antony & M. B. Stein (Eds.), *Oxford handbook of anxiety and related disorders* (pp. 225–237). New York, NY: Oxford University Press.

Fiske, A., Wetherell, J. L., & Gatz, M. (2009). Depression in older adults. *Annual Review of Clinical Psychology, 5*, 363–389.

Fitts, S. N., Gibson, P., Redding, C. A., & Deiter, P. J. (1989). Body dysmorphic disorder: Implications for its validity as a DSM-III-R clinical syndrome. *Psychological Reports, 64*, 655–658.

Flaherty, J. H. (2011). The evaluation and management of delirium among older persons. *Medical Clinics of North America, 95*(3), 555–577.

Flanagan, J. (2015). Epigenome-wide association studies (EWAS): Past, present, and future. In M. Verma (Ed.), *Cancer Epigenetics* (Vol. 1238, pp. 51–63). New York, NY: Springer.

Flegal, K. M., Carroll, M. D., Kit, B. K., & Ogden, C. L. (2012). Prevalence of obesity and trends in the distribution of body mass index among US adults, 1999–2010. *JAMA: Journal of the American Medical Association, 307*(5), 491–497.

Flegal, K. M., Kit, B. K., Orpana, H., & Graubard, B. I. (2013). Association of all-cause mortality with overweight and obesity using standard body mass index categories: A systematic review and meta-analysis. *JAMA: Journal of the American Medical Association, 309*(1), 71–82. doi: 10.1001/jama.2012.113905

Flegal, K. M., Kruszon-Moran, D., Carroll, M. D., Fryar, C. D., & Ogden, C. L. (2016). Trends in obesity among adults in the United States, 2005 to 2014. *JAMA, 315*(21), 2284–2291.

Flegal, K. M., Carroll, M. D., Ogden, C. L., & Curtin, L. R. (2010). Prevalence and trends in obesity among US adults, 1999–2008. *JAMA: Journal of the American Medical Association, 303*(3), 235–241.

Flegal, K. M., Graubard, B. I., Williamson, D. F., & Gail, M. H. (2005). Excess deaths associated with underweight, overweight, and obesity. *JAMA: Journal of the American Medical Association, 293*, 1861–1867.

Fleischer, M., Schäfer, M., Coogan, A., Häßler, F., & Thome, J. (2012). Sleep disturbances and circadian CLOCK genes in borderline personality disorder. *Journal of Neural Transmission, 119*(10), 1105–1110. doi: 10.1007/s00702-012-0860-5

Fleminger, S. (2012). The neuropsychiatry of head injury. In M. G. Gelder, N. C. Andreasen, J. J. Lopez-Ibor, Jr., & J. R. Geddes (Eds.), *New Oxford Textbook of Psychiatry* (2nd ed., Vol. 1, pp. 387–399). New York, NY: Oxford University Press.

Flemming, K. (2010). The use of morphine to treat cancer-related pain: A synthesis of quantitative and qualitative research. *Journal of Pain and Symptom Management, 39*(1), 139–154.

Fletcher, J. M., Lyon, G. R., Fuchs, L. S., & Barnes, M. A. (2007). *Learning disabilities: From identification to intervention*. New York, NY: Guilford.

Fletcher, R. B., & Hattie, J. (2011). *Intelligence and intelligence testing*. New York, NY: Routledge.

Fliers, E., Vermeulen, S., Rijsdijk, F., Altink, M., Buschgens, C., Rommelse, N., & Franke, B. (2009). ADHD and poor motor performance from a family genetic perspective. *Journal of the American Academy of Child & Adolescent Psychiatry, 48*(1), 25–34.

Flint, A., Schaffer, A., Meyers, B., Rothschild, A., & Mulsant, B. (2006). Research assessment of patients with psychotic depression: The STOP-PD approach. *Psychiatric Annals, 36*, 48–56.

Flint, J. (2009). Molecular genetics. In M. G. Gelder, N. C. Andreasen, J. J. Lopez-Ibor, Jr., & J. R. Geddes (Eds.), *New Oxford textbook of psychiatry* (2nd ed., Vol. 1, pp. 222–233). Oxford, UK: Oxford University Press.

Flor, H., & Turk, D. C. (2011). *Chronic Pain: An Integrated Biobehavioral Approach*. Seattle, WA: International Association for the Study of Pain Press.

Flor, H., Elbert, T., Kenecht, S., Weinbruch, C., Pantev, C., Birbaumer, N., & Taub, E. (1995). Phantom limb pain as a perceptual correlate of cortical reorganization following arm amputation. *Nature, 375*, 482–484.

Flores, B., & Schatzberg, A. (2006). Psychotic depression. In D. J. Stein, D. J. Kupfer, & A. F. Schatzberg (Eds.). *The American Psychiatric Publishing textbook of mood disorders* (pp. 561–571). Arlington, VA: American Psychiatric Publishing.

Flynn, J. R. (1984). The mean IQ of Americans: Massive gains 1932 to 1978. *Psychological Bulletin, 95*, 29–51.

Foa, E. B., Gillihan, S. J., & Bryant, R. A. (2013). Challenge and successes in dissemination of evidence-based treatment for posttraumatic stress: Lessons learned from prolonged exposure therapy for PTSD. *Psychological Science in the Public Interest (Supplement), 14*, 65–11.

Foa, E. B., Jenike, M., Kozak, M. J., Joffe, R., Baer, L., Pauls, D., & Turner, S. M. (1996). Obsessive-compulsive disorder. In T. A. Widiger, A. J. Frances, H. A. Pincus, M. R. Ross, M. B. First, & W. W. Davis (Eds.), *DSM-IV sourcebook* (Vol. 2, pp. 549–576). Washington, DC: American Psychiatric Association.

Foa, E. B., Liebowitz, M. R., Kozak, M. J., Davies, S., Campeas, R., Franklin, M. E., & Tu, X. (2005). Randomized, placebo-controlled trial of exposure and ritual prevention, clomipramine, and their combination in the treatment of obsessive-compulsive disorder. *American Journal of Psychiatry, 162*, 151–161.

Foa, E. B., McLean, C. P., Capaldi, S., & Rosenfield, D. (2013). Prolonged exposure vs. supportive counseling for sexual abuse-related PTSD in adolescent girls: A ranomized controlled trial. *JAMA, 310*, 2650–2657.

Fogelson, D. L., Asarnow, R. A., Sugar, C. A., Subotnik, K. L., Jacobson, K. C., Neale, M. C., . . . Nuechterlein, K. H. (2010). Avoidant personality disorder symptoms in first-degree relatives of schizophrenia patients predict performance on neurocognitive measures: the UCLA family study. *Schizophrenia Research, 120*(1), 113–120.

Fogelson, D. L., Nuechterlein, K. H., Asarnow, R. A., Payne, D. L., Subotnik, K. L., Jacobson, K. C., & Kendler, K. S. (2007). Avoidant personality disorder is a separable schizophrenia-spectrum personality disorder even when controlling for the presence of paranoid and schizotypal personality disorders: The UCLA family study. *Schizophrenia Research, 91*, 192–199.

Foley, E., Baillie, A., Huxter, M., Price, M., & Sinclair, E. (2010). Mindfulness-based cognitive therapy for individuals whose lives have been affected by cancer: A randomized controlled-trial. *Journal of Consulting and Clinical Psychology, 78*, 72–79.

Foley, K. R., Dyke, P., Girdler, S., Bourke, J., & Leonard, H. (2012). Young adults with intellectual disability transitioning from school to post-school: A literature review framed within the ICF. *Disability and Rehabilitation, 34*(20), 1747–1764.

Folsom, D. P., Hawthorne, W., Lindamer, L., Gilmer, T., Bailey, A., Golshan, S., & Jeste, D. V. (2005). Prevalence and risk factors for homelessness and utilization of mental health services among 10,340 patients with serious mental illness in a large public mental health system. *American Journal of Psychiatry, 162*, 370–376.

Folstein, M. F., Folstein, S. E., & McHugh, P. R. (1975). "Mini-mental state": a practical method for grading the cognitive state of patients for the clinician. *Journal of Psychiatric Research, 12*(3), 189–198.

Fong, T. G., Davis, D., Growdon, M. E., Albuquerque, A., & Inouye, S. K. (2015). The interface between delirium and dementia in elderly adults. *The Lancet Neurology, 14*(8), 823–832.

Forand, N. R., & Derubeis, R. J. (2013). Pretreatment anxiety predicts patterns of change in cognitive behavioral therapy and medications for depression. *Journal of Consulting and Clinical Psychology, 81*(5), 774–782. doi: 10.1037/a0032985

Ford, C., & Beach, F. (1951). *Patterns of sexual behavior*. New York, NY: Harper & Row.

Ford, E. S, Croft, J. B., Posner, S. F., Goodman, R. A., & Giles, W. H. (2013). Co-Occurrence of Leading Lifestyle-Related Chronic Conditions Among Adults in the United States, 2002-2009. *Preving Chronic Disease, 2013* Apr 25;10:E6. http://www.cdc.gov/pcd/issues/2013/12_0316.htm

Ford, H., & Cortoni, F. (2008). Sexual deviance in females: Assessment and treatment. In D. R. Laws & W. T. O'Donohue (Eds.), *Sexual deviance: Theory, assessment, and treatment* (2nd ed., pp. 508–526). New York, NY: Guilford.

Ford, J. B., Sutter, M. E., Owen, K. P., & Albertson, T. E. (2014). Volatile substance misuse: an updated review of toxicity and treatment. *Clinical Reviews in Allergy & Immunology, 46*(1), 19–33.

Ford, M. R., & Widiger, T. A. (1989). Sex bias in the diagnosis of histrionic and antisocial personality disorders. *Journal of Consulting and Clinical Psychology, 57,* 301–305.

Fordyce, W. E. (1988). Pain and suffering: A reappraisal. *American Psychologist, 43*(4), 276–283.

Fortes, I. S., Paula, C. S., Oliveira, M. C., Bordin, I. A., de Jesus Mari, J., & Rohde, L. A. (2015). A cross-sectional study to assess the prevalence of DSM-5 specific learning disorders in representative school samples from the second to sixth grade in Brazil. *European Child & Adolescent Psychiatry,* 1–13.

Forti, G., Corona, G., Vignozzi, L. & Maggi, M. (2011) Testosterone and Other Hormonal Therapies (Antiestrogen, DHEA, Thyroid Hormones) for Erectile Dysfunction. In M. Maggi (Eds). *Hormonal Therapy for Male Sexual Dysfunction* (pp. 42–54). Oxford, UK: Wiley-Blackwell.

Foster, A., Gable, J., & Buckley, J. (2012). Home-lessness in schizophrenia. *The Psychiatric Clinics of North America, 35*(3), 717.

Foussias, G., Agid, O., Fervaha, G., & Remington, G. (2014). Negative symptoms of schizophrenia: clinical features, relevance to real world functioning and specificity versus other CNS disorders. *European Neuropsychopharmacology, 24*(5), 693–709.

Fournier, J. C., DeRubeis, R. J., Hollon, S. D., Dimidjian, S., Amsterdam, J. D., Shelton, R. C., & Fawcett, J. (2010). Antidepressant drug effects and depression severity: A patient-level meta-analysis. *JAMA: Journal of the American Medical Association, 303*(1), 47–53.

Fowler, J. C. (2012). Suicide risk assessment in clinical practice: Pragmatic guidelines for imperfect assessments. *Psychotherapy, 49*(1), 81–90.

Fowles, D. C. (1988). Psychophysiology and psychopathy: A motivational approach. *Psychophysiology, 25,* 373–391.

Fox, E., & Damjanovic, L. (2006) The eyes are sufficient to produce a threat superiority effect. *Emotion, 6,* 534–539.

Foy, D. W., Resnick, H. S., Sipprelle, R. C., & Carroll, E. M. (1987). Premilitary, military and postmilitary factors in the development of combat related posttraumatic stress disorder. *The Behavior Therapist, 10,* 3–9.

Frances, A. (2009). Whither DSM-V? *British Journal of Psychiatry, 195,* 391–392.

Frances, A. (2010, February 11). Opening pandora's box: The 19 worst suggestions for DSM-5. *Psychiatric Times.*

Frances, A., & Widiger, T. A. (1986). Methodological issues in personality disorder diagnosis. In T. Millon & G. L. Klerman (Eds.), *Contemporary directions in psychopathology: Toward the DSM-IV* (pp. 381–400). New York, NY: Guilford.

Frances, A. J. (2012). DSM 5 is guide not bible— Ignore its ten worst changes. *Psychology Today.* Retrieved from http://www.psychologytoday.com/blog/dsm5-in-distress/201212/dsm-5-is-guide-not-bible-ignore-its-ten-worst-changes/comments

Frances, A. J., & Widiger, T. (2012). Psychiatric diagnosis: Lessons from the *DSM-IV* past and cautions for the *DSM-5* future. In S. Nolen-Hoeksema, T.D. Cannon, & T. Widiger (Eds.), *Annual review of clinical psychology* (Vol. 8, pp. 109–130). Palo Alto, CA: Annual Reviews.

Francis, D., Diorio, J., Liu, D., & Meaney, M. J. (1999). Nongenomic transmission across generations of maternal behavior and stress responses in the rat. *Science, 286,* 1155–1158.

Francis, D. D., Diorio, J., Plotsky, P. M., & Meaney, M. J. (2002). Environmental enrichment reverses the effects of maternal separation on stress reactivity. *Journal of Neuroscience, 22,* 7840–7843.

Frank, E., Anderson, C., & Rubinstein, D. (1978). Frequency of sexual dysfunction in "normal" couples. *New England Journal of Medicine, 299,* 111–115.

Frank, E., Nimgaonkar, V. L., Philips, M. L., & Kupfer, D. J. (2015). All the world's a (clinical) stage: Rethinking bipolar disorder from a longitudinal perspective. *Molecular Psychiatry, 20,* 23–31.

Frank, E., Swartz, H. A., Mallinger, A. G., Thase, M. E., Weaver, E. V., & Kupfer, D. J. (1999). Adjunctive psychotherapy for bipolar disorder: Effects of changing treatment modality. *Journal of Abnormal Psychology, 108*(4), 579–587.

Franklin, J. E., & Frances, R. J. (1999). Alcohol and other psychoactive substance use disorders. In R. E. Hales, S. C. Yudofsky, & J. A. Talbott (Eds.), *Textbook of psychiatry* (3rd ed., pp. 363–423). Washington, DC: American Psychiatric Press.

Franklin, K. A., & Lindberg, E. (2015). Obstructive sleep apnea is a common disorder in the population—a review on the epidemiology of sleep apnea. *Journal of Thoracic Disease, 7*(8), 1311.

Franklin, M. E., & Foa, E. B. (2014). Obsessive-compulsive disorder. In D. H. Barlow (Ed.), *Clinical handbook of psychological disorders: A step-by-step treatment manual* (5th ed.). New York, NY: Guilford.

Franko, D. L., Keshaviah, A., Eddy, K. T., Krishna, M., Davis, M. C., Keel, P. K., & Herzog, D. B. (2013). A longitudinal investigation of mortality in anorexia nervosa and bulimia nervosa. *American Journal of Psychiatry, 170*(8), 917–925.

Franko, D. L., Wonderlich, S. A., Little, D., & Herzog, D. B. (2004). Diagnosis and classification of eating disorders. In J. K. Thompson (Ed.), *Handbook of eating disorders and obesity* (pp. 58–80). New York, NY: Wiley.

Franko, D. L., Thompson-Brenner, H., Thompson, D. R., Boisseau, C. L., Davis, A., Forbush, K. T., & Wilson, G. T. (2012). Racial/ethnic differences in adult participants in randomized clinical trials of binge eating disorder. *Journal of Consulting and Clinical Psychology, 80,* 186–195.

Frasure-Smith, N., & Lesperance, F. (2005). Depression and coronary heart disease: Complex synergism of mind, body, and environment. *Current Directions in Psychological Science, 14,* 39–43.

Frasure-Smith, N., Lesperance, F., Juneau, M., Talajic, M., & Bourassa, M. G. (1999). Gender, depression, and one-year prognosis after myocardial infarction. *Psychosomatic Medicine, 61,* 26–37.

Fratiglioni, L., & Qiu, C. (2009). Prevention of common neurodegenerative disorders in the elderly. *Experimental Gerontology, 44*(1), 46–50.

Fratiglioni, L., Grut, M., Forsell, Y., Viitanen, M., Grafstrom, M., Holmen, K., & Winblad, B. (1991). Prevalence of Alzheimer's disease and other dementias in an elderly urban population: Relationship with age, sex and education. *Neurology, 41,* 1886–1892.

Fratiglioni, L., Winblad, B., & von Strauss, E. (2007). Prevention of Alzheimer's disease and dementia: Major findings from the Kungsholmen Project. *Physiology & Behavior, 92*(1–2), 98–104.

Frazier, T. W., Youngstrom, E. A., Speer, L., Embacher, R., Law, P., Constantino, J. N., & Eng, C. (2012). Validation of proposed DSM-5 criteria for autism spectrum disorder. *Journal of the American Academy of Child & Adolescent Psychiatry, 51*(1), 28–40. e23. doi: 10.1016/j.jaac.2011.09.021

Fredrikson, M., & Matthews, K. A. (1990). Cardiovascular responses to behavioral stress and hypertension: A meta-analytic review. *Annals of Behavioral Medicine, 12*(1), 30–39.

Fredrikson, M., Annas, P., & Wik, G. (1997). Parental history, aversive exposure and the development of snake and spider phobia in women. *Behavior Research and Therapy, 35,* 23–28.

Freedman, M., King, J., & Kennedy, E. (2001). Popular diets: A scientific review. *Obesity Research, 9*(Suppl.), S1–S38.

Freeman, D., Pugh, K., Vorontsova, N., Antley, A., & Slater, M. (2010). Testing the continuum of delusional beliefs: An experimental study using virtual reality. *Journal of Abnormal Psychology, 119*(1), 83–92.

Freeman, E., Sammel, M., Lin, H., & Nelson, D. (2006). Associations of hormones and menopausal status with depressed mood in women with no history of depression. *Archive General Psychiatry, 63,* 375–382.

Freeman, E. W., Rickels, K., Sammel, M. D., Lin, H., & Sondheimer, S. J. (2009). Time to relapse after short-or long-term treatment of severe premenstrual syndrome with sertraline. *Archives of General Psychiatry, 66*(5), 537–544.

Freinkel, A., Koopman, C., & Spiegel, D. (1994). Dissociative symptoms in media eyewitnesses of an execution. *American Journal of Psychiatry, 151,* 1335–1339.

French-Belgian Collaborative Group. (1982). Ischemic heart disease and psychological patterns: Prevalence and incidence studies in Belgium and France. *Advances in Cardiology, 29,* 25–31.

Frenda, S. J., Nichols, R. M., & Loftus, E. F. (2011). Current issues and advances in misinformation research. *Current Directions in Psychological Science, 20*(1), 20–23. doi: 10.1177/0963721410396620

Freud, A. (1946). *Ego and the mechanisms of defense*. New York, NY: International Universities Press.

Freud, S. (1974). On coca. In R. Byck (Ed.), *Cocaine papers by Sigmund Freud* (pp. 49–73). New York, NY: Stonehill. (Original work published 1885.)

Freund, K., Seto, M. C., & Kuban, M. (1996). Two types of fetishism. *Behaviour Research and Therapy, 34*, 687–694.

Frick, P. J. (2012). Developmental pathways to conduct disorder: Implications for future directions in research, assessment, and treatment. *Journal of Clinical Child & Adolescent Psychology, 41*(3), 378–389. doi: 10.1080/15374416.2012.664815

Fridlund, A. J., Beck, H. P., Goldie, W. D., & Irons, G. (2012). Little Albert: A neurologically impaired child. *History of Psychology, 15*(4), 302–327.

Friedberg, F., & Sohl, S. (2009). Cognitive-behavior therapy in chronic fatigue syndrome: Is improvement related to physical activity? *Journal of Clinical Psychology, 65*, 423–442.

Fried-Oken, M., Rowland, C., Daniels, D., Dixon, M., Fuller, B., Mills, C., & Oken, B. (2012). AAC to support conversation in persons with moderate Alzheimer's disease. *Augmentative and Alternative Communication, 28*(4), 219–231.

Friedl, M. C., & Draijer, N. (2000). Dissociative disorders in Dutch psychiatric inpatients. *American Journal of Psychiatry, 157*(6), 1012–1013.

Friedman, A. F., Bolinskey, P. K., Levak, R. W., & Nichols, D. S. (2014). *Psychological Assessment with the MMPI-2/MMPI-2-RF*. London, UK: Routledge.

Friedman, J. M. (2009). Obesity: Causes and control of excess body fat. *Nature, 459*(7245), 340–342.

Friedman, M., & Rosenman, R. H. (1959). Association of specific overt behavior pattern with blood and cardiovascular findings. *JAMA: Journal of the American Medical Association, 169*, 1286.

Friedman, M., & Rosenman, R. H. (1974). *Type A behavior and your heart*. New York, NY: Knopf.

Friedman, M. J. (2009). Phenomenology of post-traumatic stress disorder and acute stress disorder. In M. M. Antony & M. B. Stein (Eds.), *Oxford handbook of anxiety and related disorders* (pp. 65–72). New York, NY: Oxford University Press.

Friedman, M. J., Resick, P. A., Bryant, R. A., Strain, J., Horowitz, M., & Spiegel, D. (2011). Classification of trauma and stressor-related disorders in DSM-5. *Depression and Anxiety, 28*(9), 737–749. doi: 10.1002/da.20845

Fritz, C. O., Morris, P. E., & Richler, J. J. (2012). Effect size estimates: Current use, calculations, and interpretation. *Journal of Experimental Psychology: General, 141*(1), 2–18.

Frodl, T., & Skokauskas, N. (2012). Meta-analysis of structural MRI studies in children and adults with attention deficit hyperactivity disorder indicates treatment effects. *Acta Psychiatrica Scandinavica, 125*(2), 114–126.

Frombonne, E., Quirke, S., & Hagen, A. (2011). Epidemiology of pervasive developmental disorders. In D. G. Amaral, G. Dawson, & D. Geschwind (Eds.), *Autism spectrum disorders* (pp. 90–111). New York, NY: Oxford University Press.

Fromm-Reichmann, F. (1948). Notes on the development of treatment of schizophrenics by psychoanalytic psychotherapy. *Psychiatry, 11*, 263–273.

Frost, R. O., & Rasmussen, J. L. (2012). Phenomenology and characteristics of compulsive hoarding. In G. Steketee (Ed.), *The Oxford handbook of obsessive compulsive and spectrum disorders* (pp. 70–88). New York, NY: Oxford University Press.

Frost, R. O., Patronek, G., & Rosenfield, E. (2011). Comparison of object and animal hoarding. *Depression and Anxiety, 28*(10), 885–891. doi: 10.1002/da.20826

Frost, R. O., Steketee, G., & Tolin, D. F. (2012). Diagnosis and assessment of hoarding disorder. *Annual Review of Clinical Psychology, 8*, 219–242. doi: 10.1146/annurev-clinpsy-032511-143116

Frühauf, S., Gerger, H., Schmidt, H. M., Munder, T., & Barth, J. (2013). Efficacy of psychological interventions for sexual dysfunction: a systematic review and meta-analysis. *Archives of Sexual Behavior, 42*(6), 915–933.

Fugl-Meyer, A. R., & Sjogren Fugl-Meyer, K. (1999). Sexual disabilities, problems, and satisfaction in 18–74 year old Swedes. *Scandinavian Journal of Sexology, 3*, 79–105.

Fuji, D. E., Tsushima, V., Murakami-Brundage, J., & Kamath, V. (2014). *Assessing for schizophrenia in Asian Americans. In guide to psychological assessment with Asians* (pp. 305–326). New York, NY: Springer.

Fukuda, K., Straus, S. E., Hickie, I., Sharpe, M. B., Dobbins, J. G., & Komaroff, A. L. (1994). Chronic fatigue syndrome: A comprehensive approach to its diagnosis and management. *Annals of Internal Medicine, 121*, 953–959.

Fullana, M. A., Mataix-Cols, D., Caspi, A., Harrington, H., Grisham, J. R., Moffitt, T. E., & Poulton, R. (2009). Obsessions and compulsions in the community: Prevalence, interference, help-seeking, developmental stability, and co-occurring psychiatric conditions. *American Journal of Psychiatry, 166*(3), 329–336. doi: 10.1176/appi.ajp.2008.08071006

Fulton, J. J., Kiel, E. J., Tull, M. T., & Gratz, K. L. (2014). Associations between perceived parental overprotection, experiential avoidance, and anxiety. *Journal of Experimental Psychopathology, 5*, 200–211. doi: 10.5127/jep.034813

Fulton, H. G., Krank, M. D., & Stewart, S. H. (2012). Outcome expectancy liking: A self-generated, self-coded measure predicts adolescent substance use trajectories. *Psychology of Addictive Behaviors, 26*(4), 870.

Furberg, H., Olarte, M., Afari, N., Goldberg, J., Buchwald, D., & Sullivan, P. (2005). The prevalence of self-reported chronic fatigue in a U.S. twin registry. *Journal of Psychosomatic Research, 59*, 283–290.

Furman, W., & Collibee, C. (2014). Sexual activity with romantic and nonromantic partners and psychosocial adjustment in young adults. *Archives of Sexual Behavior, 43*(7), 1327–1341.

Furnham, A., & Crump, J. (2014). A bright side, facet analysis of Schizotypal Personality Disorder: The relationship between the HDS Imaginative Factor, the NEO-PI-R personality trait facets in a large adult sample. *Thinking Skills and Creativity, 11*, 42–47.

Furnham, A., & Wong, L. (2007). A cross-cultural comparison of British and Chinese beliefs about the causes, behaviour manifestations and treatment of schizophrenia. *Psychiatry Research, 151*, 123–138.

Furr, J. M., Tiwari, S., Suveg, C., & Kendall, P. C. (2009). Anxiety disorders in children and adolescents. In M. M. Antony & M. B. Stein (Eds.), *Oxford handbook of anxiety and related disorders* (pp. 636–656). New York, NY: Oxford University Press.

Furr, J. M., Comer, J. S., Sacks, H., Chan, P. T., Kerns, C. E., Feinberg, L., & Kurtz, S.M.S. (2012, November). *The Boston University Brave Buddies Program: A replication of the Brave Buddies intensive, outpatient treatment program for children with selective mutism*. Paper presented at the 46th annual meeting of the Association for Behavioral and Cognitive Therapies, National Harbor, MD.

Fusar-Poli, P., & Politi, P. (2008). Paul Eugen Bleuler and the birth of schizophrenia (1908). *American Journal of Psychiatry, 165*(11), 1407. doi: 10.1176/appi.ajp.2008.08050714

Fusar-Poli, P., Carpenter, W. T., Woods, S. W., & McGlashan, T. H. (2014). Attenuated psychosis syndrome: ready for DSM-5.1? *Annual Review of Clinical Psychology, 10*, 155–192.

Fushimi, N., Wang, L., Ebisui, S., Cai, S., & Mikage, M. (2008). Studies of ephedra plants in Asia. Part 4.1. Morphological differences between Ephedra sinica Stapf and E. intermedia Schrenk et C.A. Meyer, and the botanical origin of Ma-huang produced in Qinghai Province. *Journal of Traditional Medicines, 25*(3), 61–66.

Fyer, A., Liebowitz, M., Gorman, J., Compeas, R., Levin, A., Davies, S., et al. (1987). Discontinuation of alprazolam treatment in panic patients. *American Journal of Psychiatry, 144*, 303–308.

Fyer, A. J., Mannuzza, S., Chapman, T. F., Liebowitz, M. R., & Klein, D. F. (1993). A direct interview family study of social phobia. *Archives of General Psychiatry, 50*, 286–293.

Fyer, A. J., Mannuzza, S., Gallops, M. S., Martin, L. Y., Aaronson, C., Gorman, J. M., et al. (1990). Familial transmission of simple phobias and fears: A preliminary report. *Archives of General Psychiatry, 47*, 252–256.

Gagnon, J. H. (1990). The explicit and implicit use of the scripting perspective in sex research. *Annual Review of Sex Research, 1*, 1–43.

Galatzer-Levy, I. R., & Bonanno, G. A. (2014). Optimism and death predicting the course and consequences of depression trajectories in response to heart attack. *Psychological Science, 25*, 2177–2178.

Galea, S., Ahern, J., Resnick, H., Kilpatrick, D., Bucuvalas, M., Gold, J., and Vlahov, D. (2002). Psychological sequelae of the September 11 terrorist attacks in New York City. *New England Journal of Medicine, 346*, 982–987.

Gallagher, M. W., Bentley, K. H., & Barlow, D. H. (2014). Perceived control and vulnerability to anxiety disorders: A meta-analytic review. *Cognitive Therapy and Research, 38,* 571–584.

Gallant, A. R., Lundgren, J., & Drapeau, V. (2012). The night-eating syndrome and obesity. *Obesity Reviews, 13*(6), 528–536.

Galletta, A. (2013). *Mastering the semi-structured interview and beyond: From research design to analysis and publication.* New York, NY: NYU Press.

Gallo, L., & Matthews, K. (2003). Understanding the association between socioeconomic status and physical health: Do negative emotions play a role? *Psychological Bulletin, 129,* 10–51.

Gandaglia, G., Briganti, A., Jackson, G., Kloner, R. A., Montorsi, F., Montorsi, P., & Vlachopoulos, C. (2014). A systematic review of the association between erectile dysfunction and cardiovascular disease. *European Urology, 65*(5), 968–978.

Ganguli, M., Blacker, D., Blazer, D. G., Grant, I., Jeste, D. V., Paulsen, J. S., & Sachdev, P. S. (2011). Classification of neurocognitive disorders in DSM-5: A work in progress. *American Journal of Geriatric Psychiatry, 19*(3), 205–210.

Gansler, D. A., McLaughlin, N. C., Iguchi, L., Jerram, M., Moore, D. W., Bhadelia, R., et al. (2009). A multivariate approach to aggression and the orbital frontal cortex in psychiatric patients. *Psychiatry Research: Neuroimaging, 171*(3), 145–154.

Gao, Y., Raine, A., Venables, P. H., Dawson, M. E., & Mednick, S. A. (2010). Association of poor childhood fear conditioning and adult crime. *American Journal of Psychiatry, 167*(1), 56–60. doi: 10.1176/appi.ajp.2009.09040499

Garber, J., & Carter, J. S. (2006). Major depression. In R. T. Ammerman (Ed.), *Comprehensive handbook of personality and psychopathology. Volume III: Child psychopathology* (pp. 165–216). Hoboken, NJ: Wiley.

Garber, J., Clarke, G. N., Weersing, V. R., Beardslee, W. R., Brent, D. A., Gladstone, T. R., & Iyengar, S. (2009). Prevention of depression in at-risk adolescents: A randomized controlled trial. *JAMA: Journal of the American Medical Association, 301*(21), 2215–2224.

Garber, J., Gallerani, C. M., & Frankel, S. A. (2009). Depression in children. In I. H. Gotlib & C. L. Hammen (Eds.), *Handbook of depression* (2nd ed., pp. 405–443). New York, NY: Guilford.

Garcia, G., Kincannon, H. T., Poston Jr, D. L., & Walther, C. S. (2014). *Patterns of Sexual Activity in China and the United States.* In D. L. Poston, Jr., W.S. Yang, & D. N. Farris (Eds.), The Family and Social Change in Chinese Societies (pp. 99–116). Amsterdam, The Netherlands: Springer.

Garcia, J., McGowan, B. K., & Green, K. F. (1972). Biological constraints on conditioning. In A. H. Black & W. F. Prokasy (Eds.), *Classical conditioning II: Current research and theory.* New York, NY: Appleton-Century-Crofts.

Garcia-Campayo, J., Claraco, L. M., Sanz-Carrillo, C., Arevalo, E., & Monton, C. (2002). Assessment of a pilot course on the management of somatization disorder for family doctors. *General Hospital Psychiatry, 24,* 101–105.

Garcia-Lopez, L.J., Olivares, J., Beidel, D., Albano, A., Turner, S., & Rosa, A. (2006). Efficacy of three treatment protocols for adolescents with social anxiety disorder: A 5-year follow-up assessment. *Journal of Anxiety Disorders, 20*(2), 175–191. doi: 10.1016/j.janxdis.2005.01.003

Gardiner, C., Kiazand, A., Alhassan, S., Soowon, K., Stafford, R., Balise, R., & King, A. C. (2007). Comparison of the Atkins, Zone, Ornish, and LEARN diets for change in weight and related risk factors among over-weight premenopausal women. *JAMA: Journal of the American Medical Association, 297,* 969–977.

Garfield, A. F., & Zigler, E. (1993). Adolescent suicide prevention: Current research and social policy implications. *American Psychologist, 48*(2), 169–182.

Garfinkel, P. E. (1992). Evidence in support of attitudes to shape and weight as a diagnostic criterion of bulimia nervosa. *International Journal of Eating Disorders, 11*(4), 321–325.

Garland, E. L., Howard, M. O., Vaughn, M. G., & Perron, B. E. (2011). Volatile substance misuse in the United States. *Substance Use & Misuse, 46*(Suppl. 1), 8–20.

Garlow, S., & Nemeroff, C. B. (2003). Neurobiology of depressive disorders. In R. J. Davidson, K. R. Scherer, & H. H. Goldsmith (Eds.), *Handbook of affective sciences* (pp. 1021–1043). New York, NY: Oxford University Press.

Garlow, S., Boone, E., Li, W., Owens, M., & Nemeroff, C. (2005). Genetic analysis of the hypothalamic corticotrophin releasing factor system. *Endocrinology, 146,* 2362–2368.

Garmezy, N., & Rutter, M. (Eds.) (1983). *Stress, coping and development in children.* New York, NY: McGraw-Hill.

Garner, D. M., & Fairburn, C. G. (1988). Relationship between anorexia nervosa and bulimia nervosa: Diagnostic implications. In D. M. Garner & P. E. Garfinkel (Eds.), *Diagnostic issues in anorexia nervosa and bulimia nervosa.* New York, NY: Brunner/Mazel.

Garner, D. M., Garfinkel, P. E., Rockert, W., & Olmsted, M. P. (1987). A prospective study of eating disturbances in the ballet. Ninth World Congress of the International College of Psychosomatic Medicine, Sydney, Australia. *Psychotherapy and Psychosomatics, 48*(1–4), 170–175.

Garnier-Dykstra, L. M., Caldeira, K. M., Vincent, K. B., O'Grady, K. E., & Arria, A. M. (2012). Nonmedical use of prescription stimulants during college: Four-year trends in exposure opportunity, use, motives, and sources. *Journal of American College Health, 60*(3), 226–234. doi: 10.1080/07448481.2011.589876

Garrabe, J., & Cousin, F. R. (2012). Acute and transient psychotic disorders. In M. G. Gelder, N. C. Andreasen, J. J. Lopez-Ibor, Jr., & J. R. Geddes (Eds.), *New Oxford textbook of psychiatry* (2nd. ed., Vol. 1, pp. 602–608). New York, NY: Oxford University Press.

Garrity, A. G., Pearlson, G. D., McKiernan, K., Lloyd, D., Kiehl, K. A., & Calhoun, V. D. (2007). Aberrant "default mode" functional connectivity in schizophrenia. *American Journal of Psychiatry, 164*(3), 450–457.

Gatchel, R. (2005). *Clinical essentials of pain management.* Washington, DC: American Psychological Association.

Gatchel, R. J., & Dersh, J. (2002). Psychological disorders and chronic pain: Are there cause-and-effect relationships? In D. C. Turk & R. J. Gatchel (Eds.), *Psychological approaches to pain management: A practitioner's handbook* (2nd ed., pp. 30–51). New York, NY: Guilford.

Gatchel, R. J., & Turk, D. C. (Eds.) (1999). *Psychosocial factors in pain: Critical perspectives.* New York, NY: Guilford.

Gatchel, R. J., Peng, Y. B., Peters, M. L., Fuchs, P. N., & Turk, D. C. (2007). The biopsychosocial approach to chronic pain: Scientific advances and future directions. *Psychological Bulletin, 133,* 581–624.

Gaudreau, J.-D. (2012). Insights into the neural mechanisms underlying delirium. *American Journal of Psychiatry, 169*(5), 450–451. doi: 10.1176/appi.ajp.2012.12020256 Gavin, A. M. (2003). The asylum at Quaise: Nantucket's antebellum poor farm. *Historic Nantucket, 52*(4), 17–20.

Gavin, N. I., Gaynes, B. N., Lohr, K. N., Meltzer-Brody, S., Gartlehner, G., & Swinson, T. (2005). Perinatal depression—A systematic review of prevalence and incidence. *Obstetrics and Gynecology, 106*(5), 1071–1083.

Gaw, A. C. (2008). Cultural issues. In R. E. Hales, S. C. Yudofsky, & G. O. Gabbard (Eds.), *The American Psychiatric Publishing textbook of psychiatry* (5th ed., pp. 1529–1547). Arlington, VA: American Psychiatric Publishing.

Ge, X., Conger, R., & Elder, G. (1996). Coming of age too early: Pubertal influences on girls' vulnerability to psychological distress. *Child Development, 67,* 3386–3400.

Gearhardt, A. N., Bragg, M. A., Pearl, R. L., Schvey, N. A., Roberto, C. A., & Brownell, K. D. (2012). Obesity and public policy. In S. Nolen-Hoeksema, T. D. Cannon, & T. Widiger (Eds.), *Annual review of clinical psychology* (Vol. 8, pp. 404–430). Palo Alto, CA: Annual Reviews.

Gearhardt, A. N., Yokum, S., Orr, P. T., Stice, E., Corbin, W. R., & Brownell, K. D. (2011). Neural correlates of food addiction. *Archives of General Psychiatry, 68*(8), 808–815.

Gearhart, J. P. (1989). Total ablation of the penis after circumcision electrocautery: A method of management and long term follow-up. *Journal of Urology, 42,* 789–801.

Geer, J. H., Morokoff, P., & Greenwood, P. (1974). Sexual arousal in women: The development of a measurement device for vaginal blood volume. *Archives of Sexual Behavior, 3,* 559–564.

Gelernter, J., & Stein, M. B. (2009). Heritability and genetics of anxiety disorders. In M. M. Antony & M. B. Stein (Eds.), *Oxford handbook of anxiety and related disorders.* Oxford, UK: Oxford University Press.

Geller, B., Cooper, T. B., Graham, D. L., Fetaer, H. M., Marsteller, F. A., & Wells, J. M. (1992). Pharmacokinetically designed double blind placebo controlled study of nortriptyline in 6–12 year olds with major depressive disorder: Outcome: Nortriptyline and hydroxynortriptyline plasma levels; EKG, BP and side effect measurements. *Journal of the American Academy of Child and Adolescent Psychiatry, 31,* 33–44.

Gendron, M., & Feldman Barrett, L. (2009). Reconstructing the past: A century of ideas about emotion in psychology. *Emotion Review, 1*(4), 316–339.

Generations United. (2006). *Meth and child welfare: Promising solutions for children, their parents and grandparents.* Washington, DC: Author.

George, M. S., Taylor, J. J., & Short, E. B. (2013). The expanding evidence base for rTMS of depression. *Current Opinions in Psychiatry, 26,* 13–18.

Geraerts, E., Lindsay, D. S., Merckelbach, H., Jelicic, M., Raymaekers, L., Arnold, M. M., & Schooler, J. S. (2009). Cognitive mechanisms underlying recovered memory experiences of childhood sexual abuse. *Psychological Science, 20,* 92–98.

Gerard, D. L. (1997). Chiarugi and Pinel considered: Soul's brain/person's mind. *Journal of the History of the Behavioral Sciences, 33*(4), 381–403.

Gerber PJ: The impact of learning disabilities on adulthood: a review of the evidenced-based literature for research and practice in adult education. *Journal of Learning Disabilities, 45*(1), 31–46, 201210.1177/00222194114266858

Gershon, E. S., Kelsoe, J. R., Kendler, K. S., & Watson, J. D. (2001). It's time to search for susceptibility genes for major mental illnesses. *Science, 294,* 5.

Gerstein, D. R., Volberg, R. A., Toce, M. T., Harwood, H., Johnson, R. A., & Bule, T., & Tucker, A. (1999). *Gambling impact and behavior study: Report to the national gambling impact study commission.* Chicago, IL: National Opinion Research Center at the University of Chicago.

Geschwind, D. H. & Flint, J. (2015). Genetics and genomics of psychiatric disease. *Science, 349,* 1489–1494.

Gesquiere, L. R., Learn, N. H., Simao, M. C. M., Onyango, P. O., Alberts, S. C., & Altmann, J. (2011). Life at the top: Rank and stress in wild male baboons. *Science, 333*(6040), 357–360.

Giannotti, F., & Cortesi, F. (2009). Family and cultural influences on sleep development. *Child and Adolescent Psychiatric Clinics of North America, 18*(4), 849–861. doi: 10.1016/j.chc.2009.04.003

Gibbons, R., Hur, K., Bhaumik, D., & Mann, J. (2006). The relationship between antidepressant prescription rates and rate of early adolescent suicide. *American Journal of Psychiatry, 163,* 1898–1904.

Giedke, H., & Schwarzler, F. (2002). Therapeutic use of sleep deprivation in depression. *Sleep Medicine Reviews, 6,* 361–377.

Gielen, A., & McDonald, E. M., & Shields, W. (20154). Unintentional home injuries across the life span: Problems and solutions. *Annual Review of Public Health, 36,* 231–253.

Gielen, A.C., Sleet, D., & DiClemente, R. (Eds). 2006. *Injury and violence prevention: Behavioral science theories, methods, and applications.* San Francisco, CA: Jossey-Bass.

Giesbrecht, T., Lynn, S. J., Lilienfeld, S. O., & Merckelbach, H. (2008). Cognitive processes in dissociation: An analysis of core theoretical assumptions. *Psychological Bulletin, 134*(5), 617–647.

Giesbrecht, T., Smeets, T., Leppink, J., Jelicic, M., & Merckelbach, H. (2007). Acute dissociation after 1 night of sleep loss. *Journal of Abnormal Psychology, 116*(3), 599–606.

Giese-Davis, J., Collie, K., Rancourt, K. M., Neri, E., Kraemer, H. C., & Spiegel, D. (2011). Decrease in depression symptoms is associated with longer survival in patients with metastatic breast cancer: A secondary analysis. *Journal of Clinical Oncology, 29*(4), 413–420.

Gillberg, C. (1984). Infantile autism and other childhood psychoses in a Swedish urban region: Epidemiological aspects. *Journal of Child Psychology and Psychiatry, 25,* 35–43.

Gillespie, C. F., & Nemeroff, C. B. (2007). Corticotropin-releasing factor and the psychobiology of early-life stress. *Current Directions in Psychological Science, 16*(2), 85–89.

Gillespie-Lynch, K., Sepeta, L., Wang, Y., Marshall, S., Gomez, L., Sigman, M., & Hutman, T. (2012). Early childhood predictors of the social competence of adults with autism. *Journal of Autism and Developmental Disorders, 42*(2), 161–174. doi: 10.1007/s10803-011-1222-0

Gilmore, J. H. (2010). Understanding what causes schizophrenia: A developmental perspective. *American Journal of Psychiatry, 167*(1), 8–10. doi: 10.1176/appi.ajp.2009.09111588

Giltay, E., Geleijnse, J., Zitman, F., Hoekstra, T., & Schouten, E. (2004). Dispositional optimism and all-cause and cardiovascular mortality in a prospective cohort of elderly Dutch men and women. *Archives of the General Psychiatry, 61,* 1126–1135.

Ginovart, N., & Kapur, S. (2010). Dopamine receptors and the treatment of schizophrenia. In K. A. Neve (Ed.), *The dopamine receptors* (2nd ed., pp. 431–477). New York, NY: Humana Press.

Ginsburg, G. S., & Silverman, W. K. (2000). Gender role orientation and fearfulness in children with anxiety disorders. *Journal of Anxiety Disorders, 14*(1), 57–67.

Ginsburg, G. S., Becker, E. M., Keeton, C. P., Sakolsky, D., Piacentini, J., Albano, A. M., ... Kendall, P.C. (2014). Naturalistic follow-up of youths treated for pediatric anxiety disorders. *JAMA Psychiatry, 71,* 310.

Ginsburg, G. S., Drake, K. L., Tein, J-Y, Teetsel, R., & Riddle, M. A. (2015). Preventing onset of anxiety disorders in offspring of anxious parents: A randomized controlled trial of a family-based intervention. *American Journal of Psychiatry, 172,* 1207–1214.

Girault, J. A., & Greengard, P. (2004). The neurobiology of dopamine signaling. *Archives of Neurology, 61*(5), 641–644.

Girirajan, S. (2009). Parental-age effects in Down syndrome. *Journal of Genetics, 88*(1), 1–7. doi: 10.1007/s12041-009-0001-6

Gislason, I. L. (1988). Eating disorders in childhood (ages 4 through 11 years). In B. J. Blinder, B. F. Chaitin, & R. S. Goldstein (Eds.), *The eating disorders: Medical and psychological bases of diagnosis and treatment* (pp. 285–293). New York, NY: PMA.

Gitlin, M. J. (2009). Pharmacotherapy and other somatic treatments for depression. In I. H. Gotlib & C. L. Hammen (Eds.), *Handbook of depression* (2nd ed., pp. 554–585). New York, NY: Guilford.

Gjerde, L. C., Czajkowski, N., Røysamb, E., Ørstavik, R. E., Knudsen, G. P., Østby, K., & Reichborn-Kjennerud, T. (2012). The heritability of avoidant and dependent personality disorder assessed by personal interview and questionnaire. *Acta Psychiatrica Scandinavica, 126*(6), 448–457. doi: 10.1111/j.1600-0447.2012.01862.x

Gjerde, L. C., Czajkowski, N., Røysamb, E., & Knudsen, G. P. (2015). A longitudinal, population-based twin study of avoidant and obsessive-compulsive personality disorder traits from early to middle adulthood. *Psychological Medicine, 45*(16), 3539–3548.

Glaser, R., & Kiecolt-Glaser, J. K. (2005). Stress-induced immune dysfunction: Implications for health. *Nature Reviews Immunology, 5*(3), 243–251.

Glaser, R., Kennedy, S., Lafuse, W. P., Bonneau, R. H., Speicher, C. E., Hillhouse, J., & Kiecolt-Glaser, J. K. (1990). Psychological stress-induced modulation of IL-2 receptor gene expression and IL-2 production in peripheral blood leukocytes. *Archives of General Psychiatry, 47,* 707–712.

Glaser, R., Rice, J., Sheridan, J., Fertel, R., Stout, J., Speicher, C., et al. (1987). Stress-related immune suppression: Health implications. *Brain, Behavior, and Immunity, 1,* 7–20.

Glasper, E. R., Schoenfeld, T. J., & Gould, E. (2012). Adult neurogenesis: Optimizing hippocampal function to suit the environment. *Behavioural Brain Research, 227*(2), 380–383.

Glaus, J., Vandeleur, C., Gholam-Rezaee, M., Castelao, E., Perrin, M., Rothen, S., & Preisig, M. (2012). Atypical depression and alcohol misuse are related to the cardiovascular risk in the general population. *Acta Psychiatrica Scandinavica, 1–12.*

Gleason, M. M., Fox, N. A., Drury, S., Smyke, A., Egger, H. L., Nelson, C. A., 3rd, & Zeanah, C. H. (2011). Validity of evidence-derived criteria for reactive attachment disorder: Indiscriminately social/disinhibited and emotionally withdrawn/inhibited types. *Journal of the American Academy of Child and Adolescent Psychiatry, 50*(3), 216–231. e3. doi: 10.1016/j.jaac.2010.12.012

Gleaves, D. H. (1996). The sociocognitive model of dissociative identity disorder: A reexamination of the evidence. *Psychological Bulletin, 120,* 42–59.

Gleaves, D. H., Smith, S. M., Butler, L. D., & Spiegel, D. (2004). False and recovered memories in the laboratory and clinic: A review of experimental and clinical evidence. *Clinical Psychology: Science and Practice. 11*(1), 3–28.

Goater, N., King, M., Cole, E., Leavey, G., Johnson-Sabine, E., Blizard, R., & Hoar, A. (1999). Ethnicity and outcomes of psychosis. *British Journal of Psychiatry, 175,* 34–42.

Godart, N. T., Perdereau, F., Rein, Z., Berthoz, S., Wallier, J., Jeammet, P., & Falment, M. F. (2007). Comorbidity studies of eating disorders and mood disorders. Critical review of the literature. *Journal of Affective Disorders, 97*(1–3), 37–49.

Goel, M. S., McCarthy, E. P., Phillips, R. S., & Wee, C. C. (2004). Obesity among U.S. immigrant subgroups by duration of residence. *JAMA: Journal of the American Medical Association, 292,* 2860–2867.

Goel, A. K., Talwar, D., & Jain, S. K. (2015). Evaluation of short-term use of nocturnal nasal continuous positive airway pressure for a clinical profile and exercise capacity in adult patients with obstructive sleep apneahypopnea syndrome. *Lung India, 32*(3), 225.

Goering, P., Durbin, J., Sheldon, C. T., Ochocka, J., Nelson, G., & Krupa, T. (2006). Who uses consumer-run self-help organizations? *American Journal of Orthopsychiatry, 76,* 367–373.

Goff, D. C., & Coyle, J. T. (2001). The emerging role of glutamate in the pathophysiology and treatment of schizophrenia. *American Journal of Psychiatry, 158,* 1367–1377.

Gold, J. H. (1997). Premenstrual dysphoric disorder: What's that? *JAMA: Journal of the American Medical Association, 278,* 1024–1025.

Gold, J. H. (1999). Premenstrual dysphoric disorder: An update. *Journal of Practical Psychiatry and Behavioral Health, 5,* 209–215.

Gold, J. H., Endicott, J., Parry, B. L., Severino, S. K., Stotland, N., & Frank, E. (1996). Late luteal phase dysphoric disorder. In T. A. Widiger, A. J. Frances, H. A. Pincus, Ross, R., First, M. B., & Davis, W. W. (Eds.), *DSM-IV sourcebook* (Vol. 2, pp. 317–394). Washington, DC: American Psychiatric Association.

Gold, S. N., & Seibel, S. L. (2009). Treating dissociation: A contextual approach. In P. F. Dell & J. A. O'Neil (Eds.), *Dissociation and the dissociative disorders: DSM-V and beyond.* (pp. 625–636). New York, NY: Routledge/Taylor & Francis Group.

Goldberg, D., & Fawcett, J. (2012). The importance of anxiety in both major depression and bipolar disorder. *Depression and Anxiety, 29*(6), 471–478.

Goldberg, J. F., Perlis, R. H., Bowden, C. L., Thase, M. E., Miklowitz, D. J., Marangell, L. B., Sachs, G. S. (2009). Manic symptoms during depressive episodes in 1,380 patients with bipolar disorder: Findings from the STEP-BD. *American Journal of Psychiatry, 166*(2), 173–181.

Golden, C. J., Hammeke, T. A., & Purisch, A. D. (1980). *The Luria-Nebraska Battery manual.* Palo Alto, CA: Western Psychological Services.

Golden, R., Gaynes, B., Ekstrom, R., Hmaer, R., Jacobsen, F., Nemeroff, C. B. (2005). The efficacy of light therapy in the treatment of mood disorders: A review and meta-analysis of the evidence. *American Journal of Psychiatry, 162,* 656–662.

Goldfarb, W. (1963). Self-awareness in schizophrenic children. *Archives of General Psychiatry, 8,* 63–76.

Goldin, P. R., Manber, T., Hakimi, S., Canli, T., & Gross, J. J. (2009). Neural bases of social anxiety disorder: Emotional reactivity and cognitive regulation during social and physical threat. *Archives of General Psychiatry, 66*(2), 170–180.

Goldin, P. R., Ziv, M., Jazaieri, H., Hahn, K., Heimberg, R., & Gross, J. J. (2013). Impact of cognitive behavioral therapy for social anxiety disorder on the neural dynamics of cognitive reappraisal of negative self-beliefs: randomized clinical trial. *JAMA Psychiatry, 70*(10), 1048–1056.

Goldman, N., Glei, D. A., Lin, Y., & Weinstein, M. (2010). The serotonin transporter polymorphism (5-HTTLPR): Allelic variation and links with depressive symptoms. *Depression and Anxiety, 27*(3), 260–269.

Goldmeier, D., Garvey, L., & Barton, S. (2008). Does chronic stress lead to increased rates of recurrences of genital herpes?—A review of the psychoneuroimmunilogical evidence. *International Journal of STD and AIDS, 19,* 359–362.

Goldschmidt, A. B., Hilbert, A., Manwaring, J. L., Wilfley, D. E., Pike, K. M., Fairburn, C. G., & Striegel-Moore, R. (2010). The significance of overvaluation of shape and weight in binge eating disorder. *Behaviour Research and Therapy, 48*(3), 187–193.

Goldstein, G., & Shelly, C. (1984). Discriminative validity of various intelligence and neuropsychological tests. *Journal of Consulting and Clinical Psychology, 52,* 383–389.

Goldstein, H. (2002). Communication intervention for children with autism: A review of treatment efficacy. *Journal of Autism and Developmental Disorders, 32*(5), 373–396. doi: 10.1023/a:1020589821992

Goldstein, I., Lue, T. F., Padma-Nathan, H., Rosen, R. C., Steers, W. D., & Wicker, P. A., for the Sildenafil Study Group. (1998). Oral sildenafil in the treatment of erectile dysfunction. *New England Journal of Medicine, 338,* 1397–1404.

Goldstein, J. M., & Lewine, R. R. J. (2000). Overview of sex differences in schizophrenia: Where have we been and where do we go from here? In D. J. Castle, J. McGrath, & J. Kulkarni (Eds.), *Women and schizophrenia* (pp. 111–143). Cambridge, UK: Cambridge University Press.

Goldstein, S., & Brooks, R. B. (Eds.). (2013). *Handbook of resilience in children* (2nd ed.). New York, NY: Springer.

Goldston, D., Reboussin, B., & Daniel, S. (2006). Predictors of suicide attempts: State and trait components. *Journal of Abnormal Psychology, 115,* 842–849.

Goldston, D. B., Molock, S. D., Whitbeck, L. B., Murakami, J. L., Zayas, L. H., & Hall, G. C. N. (2008). Cultural considerations in adolescent suicide prevention and psychosocial treatment. *American Psychologist, 63*(1), 14–31.

Golembo-Smith, S., Schiffman, J., Kline, E., Sørensen, H. J., Mortensen, E. L., Stapleton, L., . . . Mednick, S. (2012). Premorbid multivariate markers of neurodevelopmental instability in the prediction of adult schizophrenia-spectrum disorder: a high-risk prospective investigation. *Schizophrenia Research, 139*(1), 129–135.

Golier, J., Yehuda, R., Lupien, S., Harvey, P., Grossman, R., & Elkin, A. (2002). Memory performance in Holocaust survivors with posttraumatic stress disorder. *American Journal of Psychiatry, 159,* 1682–1688.

Gomez-Caminero, A., Blumentals, W. A., Russo, L., Brown, R. R., & Castilla-Puentes, R. (2005). Does panic disorder increase the risk of coronary heart disease? A cohort study of a national managed care database. *Psychosomatic Medicine, 67,* 688–691.

Gomez-Gil, E., Steva, I., Almaraz, M. C., Pasara, E., Segovia, S., & Guillamon, A. (2010). Familiality of gender identity disorder in non-twin siblings. *Archives of Sexual Behavior, 39,* 546–552.

Gong, Q., Dazzan, P., Scarpazza, C., Kasai, K., Hu, X., Marques, T. R., . . . David, A. S. (2015). A neuroanatomical signature for schizophrenia across different ethnic groups. *Schizophrenia Bulletin,* sbv109.

Gonzalez, J. S., Batchelder, A. W., Psaros, C. P., & Safren, S. A. (2011). Depression and HIV/AIDS treatment nonadherence: A review and meta-analysis. *Journal of Acquired Immune Deficiency Syndromes, 58*(2), 181–187.

Gonzalez, J. S., Hendriksen, E. S., Collins, E. M., Duran, R. E., & Safren, S. A. (2009). Latinos and HIV/AIDS: Examining factors related to disparity and identifying opportunities for psychosocial intervention research. *AIDS and Behavior, 13*(3), 582–602.

Good, B. J., & Kleinman, A. M. (1985). Culture and anxiety: Cross-cultural evidence for the patterning of anxiety disorders. In A. H. Tuma & J. D. Maser (Eds.), *Anxiety and the anxiety disorders* (pp. 297–313). Hillsdale, NJ: Erlbaum.

Goodale, G., Callahan, L., & Steadman, H. J. (2013). Law and psychiatry: What can we say about mental health courts today? *Psychiatric Services, 64*(4), 298–300.

Goodkin, K., Baldewicz, T. T., Asthana, D., Khamis, I., Blaney, N. T., Kumar, M., & Shapshak, P. (2001). A bereavement support group intervention affects plasma burden of human immunodeficiency virus type 1. Report of a randomized controlled trial. *Journal of Human Virology, 4,* 44–54.

Goodman, G. S., Ghetti, S., Quas, J. A., Edelstein, R. S., Alexander, K. W., Redlich, A. D., Cordon, I. M., & Jones, D. P. H. (2003). A prospective study of memory for child sexual abuse: New findings relevant to the repressed/lost memory controversy. *Psychological Science, 14*(2), 113–118.

Goodman, G. S., Quas, J. A., & Ogle, C. M. (2010). Child maltreatment and memory. *Annual Reviews of Psychology, 61,* 325–351. doi: 10.1146/annurev.psych.093008.100403

Goodman, R., & Scott, S. (2012). Sleep disorders. In R. Goodman & S. Scott (Eds.), *Child and adolescent psychiatry* (3rd ed., pp. 163–170). Goodnough, A. (2002). Post-9/11 pain found to linger in young minds. Available at http://www.nytimes.com/2002/05/02/health/02SCHO.html?todaysheadlines

Goodrick, S. (2014). Defining narcolepsy. *The Lancet Neurology, 13*(6), 542.

Goodwin, D. W., & Gabrielli, W. F. (1997). Alcohol: Clinical aspects. In J. H. Lowinson, P. Ruiz, R. B. Millman, & J. G. Langrod (Eds.), *Substance abuse: A comprehensive textbook* (pp. 142–148). Baltimore, MD: Williams & Wilkins.

Goodwin, D. W., & Guze, S. B. (1984). *Psychiatric diagnosis* (3rd ed.). New York, NY: Oxford University Press.

Goodwin, F. K., & Ghaemi, S. N. (1998). Understanding manic-depressive illness. *Archives of General Psychiatry, 55*(1), 23–25.

Goodwin, F. K., & Jamison, K. R. (Eds.) (2007). *Manic depressive illness: Bipolar disorders and recurrent depression* (2nd ed.). New York, NY: Oxford University Press.

Goodwin, F. K., Fireman, B., Simon, G. E., Hunkeler, E. M., Lee, J., & Revicki, D. (2003). Suicide risk in bipolar disorder during treatment with lithium and divalproex. *JAMA: Journal of the American Medical Association, 290*, 1467–1473.

Goodwin, G. M. (2009). Neurobiological aetiology of mood disorders. In M. G. Gelder, N. C. Andreasen, J. J. Lopez-Ibor, Jr., & J. R. Geddes (Eds.), *New Oxford textbook of psychiatry* (2nd ed., Vol. 1, pp. 658–664). Oxford, UK: Oxford University Press.

Goodwin, P. J., Leszcz, M., Ennis, M., Koopmans, J., Vincent, L., Guther, H., & Hunter, J. (2001). The effect of group psychosocial support on survival in metastatic breast cancer. *New England Journal of Medicine, 345*, 1719–1726.

Goos, L. M., Crosbie, J., Payne, S., & Schachar, R. (2009). Validation and extension of the endophenotype model in ADHD patterns of inheritance in a family study of inhibitory control. *American Journal of Psychiatry, 166*(6), 711–717.

Gordis, E. (2000). Alcohol, the brain, and behavior: Mechanisms of addiction. *Alcohol Research & Health, 24*(1), 12–15.

Gordon, J. A. (2002). Anxiolytic drug targets: Beyond the usual suspects. *Journal of Clinical Investigation, 110*(7), 915–917.

Gordon, S. (2015). The danger zone: How the dangerousness standard in civil commitment proceedings harms people with serious mental illness. *Utah Law Review*, paper 911.

Gordon, L., Joo, J. E., Powell, J. E., Ollikainen, M., Novakovic, B., Li, X., & Saffery, R. (2012). Neonatal DNA methylation profile in human twins is specified by a complex interplay between intrauterine environmental and genetic factors, subject to tissue-specific influence. *Genome Research, 22*(8), 1395–1406. doi: 10.1101/gr.136598.111

Gore-Felton, C., & Koopman, C. (2008). Behavioral mediation of the relationship between psychosocial factors and HIV disease progression. *Psychosomatic Medicine, 70*, 569–574. Gorenstein, E. E., & Newman, J. P. (1980). Disinhibitory psychopathology: A new perspective and a model for research. *Psychological Review, 87*, 301–315.

Gotlib, I. H., & Abramson, L. Y. (1999). Attributional theories of emotion. In T. Dagleish & M. J. Power (Eds.), *Handbook of cognition and emotion* (pp. 613–636). Chichester, UK: Wiley.

Gotlib, I. H., & Hammen, C. L. (2009). *Handbook of depression* (2nd ed.). New York, NY: Guilford.

Gotlib, I. H., & Joormann, J. (2010). Cognition and depression: Current status and future directions. *Annual Review of Clinical Psychology, 6*, 285–312.

Gotlib, I. H., & Krasnoperova, E. (1998). Biased information processing as a vulnerability factor for depression. *Behavior Therapy, 29*, 603–617.

Gotlib, I. H., & Nolan, S. A. (2001). Depression. In A. S. Bellack & M. Hersen (Eds.), *Psychopathology in adulthood* (2nd ed., pp. 252–277). Boston, MA: Allyn & Bacon.

Gotlib, I. H., Joormann, J., & Foland-Ross, L. C. (2014). Understanding familial risk for depression: A 25-year perspective. *Perspectives on Psychological Science, 9*, 94–108.

Gotlib, I. H., Ranganath, C., & Rosenfeld, J. P. (1998). Frontal EEG alpha asymmetry, depression, and cognitive functioning. *Cognition and Emotion, 12*, 449–478.

Gotlib, I. H., Roberts, J. E., & Gilboa, E. (1996). Cognitive interference in depression. In I. G. Sarason, G. R. Pierce, & B. R. Sarason (Eds.), *Cognitive interference: Theories, methods, and findings* (pp. 347–377). Mahwah, NJ: Erlbaum.

Gottesman, I. I. (1991). *Schizophrenia genesis: The origins of madness*. New York, NY: W. H. Freeman.

Gottesman, I. I., & Bertelsen, A. (1989). Dual mating studies in psychiatry: Offspring of inpatients with examples from reactive (psychogenic) psychoses. *International Review of Psychiatry, 1*, 287–296.

Gottfredson, L., & Saklofske, D. H. (2009). Intelligence: Foundations and issues in assessment. *Canadian Psychology/Psychologie canadienne, 50*(3), 183–195.

Gottlieb, G. (1998). Normally occurring environmental and behavioral influences on gene activity: From central dogma to probabilistic epigenesis. *Psychological Review, 105*, 492–802.

Gould, M. (1990). Suicide clusters and media exposure. In S. J. Blumenthal & D. J. Kupfer (Eds.), *Suicide over the life cycle: Risk factors, assessment and treatment of suicidal patients* (pp. 517–532). Washington, DC: American Psychiatric Press.

Gould, M., Marrocco, F., Kleinman, M., Thomas, J., Mostkoff, K., Cote, J., & Davies, M. (2005). Evaluating iatrogenic risk of youth suicide screening programs. *JAMA: Journal of the American Medical Association, 293*, 1635–1643.

Gould, M. S. (2001). Suicide and the media. *Annals of the New York Academy of Sciences, 932*, 200–221; discussion 221–224.

Gould, M. S., Greenberg, T., Velting, D. M., & Shaffer, D. (2003). Youth suicide risk and preventive interventions: A review of the past 10 years. *Journal of the American Academy of Child and Adolescent Psychiatry, 42*(4), 386–405.

Gould, S. J. (1991). The chain of reason versus the chain of thumbs. In *Bully for brontosaurus: Reflections in natural history* (pp. 182–197). New York, NY: Norton.

Goyal, M., Singh, S., Sibinga, E. M., Gould, N. F., Rowland-Seymour, A., Sharma, R., . . . Haythornwaite, J. A. (2014). Meditation programs for psychological stress and well-being: A systematic review and meta-analysis. *JAMA Internal Medicine, 174*(3), 357–368.

Grabbe, K. L., & Bunnell, R. (2010). Reframing HIV prevention in sub-saharan Africa using couple-centered approaches. *JAMA: Journal of the American Medical Association, 304*, 346–347.

Grabe, S., & Hyde, J. S. (2006). Ethnicity and body dissatisfaction among women in the United States: A meta-analysis. *Psychological Bulletin, 132*, 622–640.

Grabe, S., Ward, L. M., & Hyde, J. S. (2008). The role of the media in body image concerns among women: A meta-analysis of experimental and correlational studies. *Psychological Bulletin, 134*(3), 460–476.

Grados, M. A., Riddle, M. A., Samuels, J. F., Liang, K-Y., Hoehn-Saric, R., Bienvenu, O. J., & Nestadt, J. (2001). The familial phenotype of obsessive-compulsive disorder in relation to tic disorders: The Hopkins OCD family study. *Biological Psychiatry, 50*, 559–565.

Grady-Weliky, T. (2003). Premenstrual dysphoric disorder. *New England Journal of Medicine, 345*, 433–438.

Graeff, F. G. (1993). Role of 5-ht in defensive behavior and anxiety. *Review in the Neurosciences, 4*, 181–211.

Graeff, F. G. (2004). Serotonin, the periaqueductal gray and panic. *Neuroscience and Biobehavioral Reviews, 28*, 239–259.

Graff, F. S., McClure, M. M., & Siever, L. J. (2014). Remediation and Cognitive Enhancers in Schizotypal Personality Disorder. *Current Treatment Options in Psychiatry, 1*(4), 369–375.

Graham, C. A. (2010). The DSM criteria for female orgasmic disorder. *Archives of Sexual Behavior, 39*, 256–270.

Granic, I., & Patterson, G. R. (2006). Toward a comprehensive model of antisocial development: A dynamic systems approach. *Psychological Review, 113*, 101–131.

Granillo, M. T., Perron, B. E., Jarman, C., & Gutowski, S. M. (2013). Cognitive behavioral therapy with substance use disorders: Theory, evidence, and practice. In M. G. Vaughn & B. E. Perron (Eds.), *Social work practice in the addictions* (pp. 101–118). New York, NY: Springer.

Grant, B., Chou, S., Goldstein, R., Huang, B., Stinson, F., Saha, T., & Pickering, R, P. (2008). Prevalence, correlates, disability, and comorbidity of DSM-IV borderline personality disorder: Results from the Wave 2 National Epidemiologic Survey on Alcohol and Related Conditions. *The Journal of Clinical Psychiatry, 69*(4), 533.

Grant, B. F., Hasin, D. S., Stinson, F. S., Dawson, D. A., Ruan, J., Goldstein, R. B., Smith, S. M., Saha, T. D., & Huang, B. (2005). Prevalence, correlates, comorbidity, and comparative disability of *DSM-IV* generalized anxiety disorder in the USA: Results from the National Epidemiological Survey of Alcohol and Related Conditions. *Psychological Medicine, 35*, 747–759.

Grant, B. F., Stinson, F. S., Dawson, D. A., Chou, S. P., DuFour, M. C., Compton, W., . . . Kaplan, K. (2004). Prevalence and co-occurrence of substance use disorders and independent mood and anxiety disorders: Results from the national survey on alcohol and related conditions. *Archives of General Psychiatry, 61*, 807–816.

Grant, I., Patterson, T. L., & Yager, J. (1988). Social supports in relation to physical health and symptoms of depression in the elderly. *American Journal of Psychiatry, 145*(10), 1254–1258.

Grant, J. E., & Kim, S. W. (2002). Temperament and early environmental influences in kleptomania. *Comprehensive Psychiatry, 43*, 223–229.

Grant, J. E., Correia, S., & Brennan-Krohn, T. (2006). White matter integrity in kleptomania: A pilot study. *Psychiatry Research: Neuroimaging, 147*, 233–237.

Grant, K. E., Compas, B. E., Thurm, A. E., McMahon, S. D., & Gipson, P. Y. (2004). Stressors and child and adolescent psychopathology: Measurement issues and prospective effects. *Journal of Clinical Child and Adolescent Psychology, 33*(2), 412–425.

Grant, J. E. (2003). Family history and psychiatric comorbidity in persons with kleptomania. *Comprehensive Psychiatry, 44*(6), 437–441.

Grant, J. E., Kim, S. W., & Odlaug, B. L. (2009). A double-blind, placebo-controlled study of the opiate antagonist, naltrexone, in the treatment of kleptomania. *Biological Psychiatry, 65*(7), 600–606.

Grant, J. E., Odlaug, B. L., & Kim, S. W. (2010). Kleptomania: Clinical characteristics and relationship to substance use disorders. *The American Journal of Drug and Alcohol Abuse, 36*(5), 291–295.

Grant, J.E., Odlaug, B. L. & Schreiber, L.R.N. (2015). Pathologic gambling: Clinical characteristics and treatment. In R.K. Ries, D.A. Fiellin, S.C. Miller, & R. Saitz (Eds.), *The ASAM principles of addiction medicine* (5th Ed., pp. 575–587). New York, NY: Wolters Kluwer.

Grant, J. E., Stein, D. J., Woods, D. W., & Keuthen, N. J. (Eds.). (2012). *Trichotillomania, skin picking, and other body-focused repetitive behaviors.* Arlington, VA: American Psychiatric Publishing.

Gratten, J., Wray, N. R., Keller, M. C., & Visscher, P. M. (2014). Large-scale genomics unveils the genetic architecture of psychiatric disorders. *Nature Neuroscience, 17*, 782–790.

Gray, J. A. (1982). *The neuropsychology of anxiety.* New York, NY: Oxford University Press.

Gray, J. A. (1985). Issues in the neuropsychology of anxiety. In A. H. Tuma & J. D. Maser (Eds.), *Anxiety and the anxiety disorders* (pp. 5–25). Hillside, NJ: Erlbaum.

Gray, J. A. (1987). *The psychology of fear and stress* (2nd ed.). New York, NY: Cambridge University Press.

Gray, J. A., & Buffery, A. W. H. (1971). Sex differences in emotional and cognitive behavior in mammals including man: Adaptive and neural bases. *Acta Psychologica, 35*, 89–111.

Gray, J. A., & McNaughton, N. (1996). The neuropsychology of anxiety: Reprise. In D. A. Hope (Ed.), *Perspectives on anxiety, panic and fear* (The 43rd Annual Nebraska Symposium on Motivation) (pp. 61–134). Lincoln, NE: Nebraska University Press.

Gray, J. A., & McNaughton, N. (2003). *The neuropsychology of anxiety: An enquiry into the function of the septo-hippocampal system.* Oxford, UK: Oxford University Press.

Graybar, S. R., & Boutilier, L. R. (2002). Nontraumatic pathways to borderline personality disorder. *Psychotherapy: Theory / Research/Practice/Training, 39*, 152–162.

Grazzi, L., Andrasik, F., D'Amico, D., Leone, M., Usai, S., Kass, S. J., & Bussone, G. (2002). Behavioral and pharmacologic treatment of transformed migraine with analgesic overuse: Outcome at 3 years. *Headache, 42*, 483–490.

Grebb, J. A., & Carlsson, A. (2009). Introduction and considerations for a brain-based diagnostic system in psychiatry. In B. J. Sadock, V. A. Sadock, & P. Ruiz (Eds.), *Kaplan & Sadock's comprehensive textbook of psychiatry* (9th ed., Vol. I, pp. 1–5). Philadelphia, PA: Lippincott Williams & Wilkins.

Greely, H., & Simpson, J. R. (2012). *Neuroimaging in forensic psychiatry: From the clinic to the courtroom.* New York, NY: Wiley.

Green, B. L., Grace, M. C., Lindy, J. D., Titchener, J. L., & Lindy, J. G. (1983). Levels of functional impairment following a civilian disaster: The Beverly Hills Supper Club fire. *Journal of Consulting and Clinical Psychology, 51*, 573–580.

Green, C. R., Ndao-Brumblay, S. K., & Hart-Johnson, T. (2009). Sleep problems in a racially diverse chronic pain population. *The Clinical Journal of Pain, 25*(5), 423–430.

Green, R. (1987). *The "sissy boy syndrome" and the development of homosexuality.* New Haven, CT: Yale University Press.

Green, R., & Money, J. (1969). *Transsexualism and sex reassignment.* Baltimore, MD: Johns Hopkins Press.

Green McDonald, P., O'Connell, M., & Suls, J. (2015). Cancer control falls squarely within the province of the psychological sciences. *American Psychologist, 70*(2), 61.

Greenberg, B. D., Rauch, S. L., & Haber, S. N. (2010). Invasive circuitry-based neurotherapeutics: Stereotactic ablation and deep brain stimulation for OCD. *Neuropsychopharmacology, 35*(1), 317–336. doi: 10.1038/npp.2009.128

Greenberg, D. R., & LaPorte, D. L. (1996). Racial differences in body type preferences of men for women. *International Journal of Eating Disorders, 19*, 275–278.

Greenberg, H. R. (2005). Impulse-control disorders not elsewhere classified. In B. J. Sadock & V. A. Sadock (Eds.), *Kaplan & Sadock's comprehensive textbook of psychiatry* (8th ed., pp. 2035–2054). Philadelphia, PA: Lippincott, Williams & Wilkins.

Greenough, W. T., Withers, G. S., & Wallace, C. S. (1990). Morphological changes in the nervous system arising from behavioral experience: What is the evidence that they are involved in learning and memory? In L. R. Squire & E. Lindenlaub (Eds.), *The biology of memory, Symposia Medica Hoescht 23* (pp. 159–183). Stuttgart/New York, NY: Schattauer Verlag.

Greenwood, T. A., Lazzeroni, L. C., Calkins, M. E., Freedman, R., Green, M. F., Gur, R. E., ... Radant, A. D. (2016). Genetic assessment of additional endophenotypes from the Consortium on the Genetics of Schizophrenia Family Study. *Schizophrenia Research, 170*(1), 30–40.

Greenwood, T. A., Lazzeroni, L. C., Murray, S. S., Cadenhead, K. S., Calkins, M. E., Dobie, D. J., . . . Braff, D. L. (2014). Analysis of 94 candidate genes and 12 endophenotypes for schizophrenia from the Consortium on the Genetics of Schizophrenia. *American Journal of Psychiatry, 168*(9), 930–946. http://dx.doi.org/10.1176/appi.ajp.2011.10050723

Greenwood, T. A., Swerdlow, N. R., Gur, R. E., Cadenhead, K. S., Calkins, M. E., Dobie, D. J., & Braff, D. L. (2013). Genome-wide linkage analyses of 12 endophenotypes for schizophrenia from the Consortium on the Genetics of Schizophrenia. *American Journal of Psychiatry, 170*(5), 521–532.

Greeven, A., Van Balkom, A., Visser, S., Merkelbach, J., Van Rood, Y., Van Dyck, R., & Spinhoven, P. (2007). Cognitive behavior therapy and paroxetine in the treatment of hypochondriasis: A randomized controlled trial. *American Journal of Psychiatry, 164*, 91–99.

Gregg, N. (2013). Adults with learning disabilities: Factors contributing to persistence. In H. L. Swanson, K. R. Harris, & S. Graham (Eds.), *Handbook of learning disabilities* (2nd ed., pp. 85–103). New York, NY: Guilford.

Gregoire, A. (1992). New treatments for erectile impotence. *British Journal of Psychiatry, 160*, 315–326.

Greydanus, D. E., Kaplan, G., & Patel, D. R. (2015). Pharmacology of autism spectrum disorder. In S. H. Fatemi (Ed.), *Molecular basis of autism* (pp. 173–194). New York, NY: Springer.

Griffith, E. E. H., English, T., & Mayfield, U. (1980). Possession, prayer and testimony: Therapeutic aspects of the Wednesday night meeting in a black church. *Psychiatry, 43*(5), 120–128.

Griffiths, R., Richards, W., Johnson, M., McCann, U., & Jesse, R. (2008). Mystical-type experiences occasioned by psilocybin mediate the attribution of personal meaning and spiritual significance 14 months later. *Journal of Psychopharmacology, 22*(6), 621.

Griffiths, R. R., Richards, W. A., McCann, U., & Jesse, R. (2006). Psilocybin can occasion mystic-type experiences having substantial and sustained personal meaning and spiritual significance. *Psychopharmacology, 187*, 268–283.

Grilo, C. M., Crosby, R. D., Wilson, G. T., & Masheb, R. M. (2012). 12-Month follow-up of fluoxetine and cognitive behavioral therapy for binge eating disorder. *Journal of Consulting and Clinical Psychology, 80*(6), 1108–1113.

Grilo, C. M., Masheb, R. M., & White, M. A. (2010). Significance of overvaluation of shape/weight in binge-eating disorder: Comparative study with overweight and bulimia nervosa. *Obesity, 18*, 499–504.

Grilo, C. M., Masheb, R. M., & Wilson, G. T. (2001). Subtyping binge eating disorder. *Journal of Consulting and Clinical Psychology, 69*, 1066–1072.

Grilo, C. M., Masheb, R. M., & Wilson, G. T. (2005). Efficacy of cognitive behavioral therapy and fluoxetine for the treatment of binge eating disorder: A randomized double-blind placebo-controlled comparison. *Biological Psychiatry, 57*(3), 301–309.

Grilo, C. M., Masheb, R. M., & Wilson, G. T. (2006). Rapid response to treatment for binge eating disorder. *Journal of Consulting and Clinical Psychology, 74*, 602–613.

Grilo, C. M., Masheb, R. M., Wilson, G. T., Gueorguieva, R., & White, M. A. (2011). Cognitive-behavioral therapy, behavioral weight loss, and sequential treatment for obese patients with binge-eating disorder: A randomized controlled trial. *Journal of Consulting and Clinical Psychology, 79*(5), 675–685.

Grinspoon, L., & Bakalar, J. B. (1980). Drug dependence: Non-narcotic agents. In H. I. Kaplan, A. M. Freedman, & B. J. Sadock (Eds.), *Comprehensive textbook of psychiatry* (3rd ed., pp. 1614–1629). Baltimore, MD: Williams & Wilkins.

Grisham, J., Frost, R. O., Steketee, G., Kim, H. J., & Hood, S. (2006). Age of onset of compulsive hoarding. *Journal of Anxiety Disorders, 20,* 675–686.

Grisham, J. R., & Barlow, D. H. (2005). Compulsive hoarding: Current research and theory. *Journal of Psychopathology and Behavioral Assessment, 27,* 45–52.

Grisham, J. R., Norberg, M. M., & Certoma, S. P. (2012). Treatment of compulsive hoarding. In G. Steketee (Ed.), *The Oxford handbook of obsessive compulsive and spectrum disorders* (pp. 422–435). New York, NY: Oxford University Press.

Grizenko, N., Fortier, M.-E., Zadorozny, C., Thakur, G., Schmitz, N., Duval, R., & Joober, R. (2012). Maternal stress during pregnancy, ADHD symptomatology in children and genotype: Gene-environment interaction. *Journal of the Canadian Academy of Child and Adolescent Psychiatry, 21*(1), 9.

Gross, J. J. (in press). *Handbook of emotion regulation* (2nd ed.). New York, NY: Guilford.

Grossardt, B. R., Bower, J. H., Geda, Y. E., Colligan, R. C., & Rocca, W. A. (2009). Pessimistic, anxious, and depressive personality traits predict all-cause mortality: The Mayo Clinic Cohort Study of Personality and Aging. *Psychosomatic Medicine, 71,* 491–160.

Grossman, C. I., Purcell, D. W., Rotheram-Borus, M. J., & Veniegas, R. (2013). Opportunities for HIV combination prevention to reduce racial and ethnic health disparities. *American Psychologist, 68*(4), 237–246.

Grosz, H. J., & Zimmerman, J. (1965). Experimental analysis of hysterical blindness: A follow-up report and new experimental data. *Archives of General Psychiatry, 13,* 255–260.

Grosz, H. J., & Zimmerman, J. (1970). A second detailed case study of functional blindness: Further demonstration of the contribution of objective psychological laboratory data. *Behavior Therapy, 1,* 115–123.

Gruber, J., Johnson, S. L., Oveis, C., & Keltner, D. (2008). Risk for mania and positive emotional responding: Too much of a good thing? *Emotion, 8*(1), 23–33.

Gu, D., Kelly, T. N., Wu. X., Chen, J., Samet, J. M., Huang, J. F., & He, J. (2009). Mortality attributable to smoking in China. *New England Journal of Medicine, 360,* 150–159.

Guastella, A. J., Einfeld, S. L., Gray, K. M., Rinehart, N. J., Tonge, B. J., Lambert, T. J., Hickie, I. (2010). Intranasal oxytocin improves emotion recognition for youth with autism spectrum disorders. *Biological Psychiatry, 67*(7), 692–694.

Guedeney, N. (2007). Withdrawal behavior and depression in infancy. *Infant Mental Health Journal, 28,* 393–408.

Guilleminault, C. (1989). Clinical features and evaluation of obstructive sleep apnea. In M. H. Kryger, T. Roth, & W. C. Dement (Eds.), *Principles and practice of sleep medicine* (pp. 552–558). Philadelphia, PA: W. B. Saunders.

Gulliksson, M., Burell, G., Vessby, B., Lundin, L., Toss, H., & Svärdsudd, K. (2011). Randomized controlled trial of cognitive behavioral therapy vs standard treatment to prevent recurrent cardiovascular events in patients with coronary heart disease: Secondary Prevention in Uppsala Primary Health Care project (SUPRIM). *Archives of Internal Medicine, 171*(2), 134–140.

Gündel, H., O'Connor, M. F., Littrell, L., Fort, C., & Lane, R. D. (2003). Functional neuroanatomy of grief: An FMRI study. *American Journal of Psychiatry, 160,* 1946–1953.

Gunderson, J. G. (2011). Borderline personality disorder. *New England Journal of Medicine, 364,* 2037–2042.

Gunderson, J. G., Ronningstam, E., & Smith, L. E. (1991). Narcissistic personality disorder: A review of data on DSM-III-R descriptions. *Journal of Personality Disorders, 5,* 167–177.

Gunderson, J. G., Stout, R. L., McGlashan, T. H., Shea, M. T., Morey, L.C., ... & Zanarini, M.C. (2011). Ten-year course of borderline personality disorder: psychopathology and function from the Collaborative Longitudinal Personality Disorders study. *Archives of General Psychiatry, 68*(8), 827–837.

Gunn, M., & Wheat, K. (2012). General principles of law relating to people with mental disorder. In M. G. Gelder, N. C. Andreasen, J. J. Lopez-Ibor, Jr., & J. R. Geddes (Eds.), *New Oxford Textbook of Psychiatry* (2nd. ed., Vol. 2, pp. 1895–1907). New York, NY: Oxford University Press.

Gunnar, M. R., & Fisher, P. A. (2006). Bringing basic research on early experience and stress neurobiology to bear on preventive interventions for neglected and maltreated children. *Development and Psychopathology, 18*(3), 651–677.

Gunnar, M. R., Hostinar, C. E., Sanches, M. M., Tottenam, N., & Sullivan, R. M. (2015). Parental buffering of fear and stress neurobiology: Reviewing parallels across rodent, monkey, and human models. *Social Neuroscience, 10,* 474–478.

Gupta, S., & Bonanno, G. A. (2011). Complicated grief and deficits in emotional expressive flexibility. *Journal of Abnormal Psychology, 120*(3), 635–643.

Gur, R. E., Nimgaonkar, V. L., Almasy, L., Calkins, M. E., Ragland, J. D., Pogue-Geile, M. F., & Gur, R. C. (2007). Neurocognitive endophenotypes in a multiplex multigenerational family study of schizophrenia. *American Journal of Psychiatry, 164,* 813–819.

Guralnik, O., Giesbrecht, T., Knutelska, M., Sirroff, B., & Simeon, D. (2007). Cognitive functioning in depersonalization disorder. *Journal of Nervous and Mental Disease, 195*(12), 983–988.

Guralnik, O., Schmeidler, J., & Simeon, D. (2000). Feeling unreal: Cognitive processes in depersonalization. *American Journal of Psychiatry, 157*(1), 103–109.

Gureje, O. (2004). What can we learn from a cross-national study of somatic distress? *Journal of Psychosomatic Research, 56,* 409–412.

Gureje, O., Simon, G. E., Ustun, T. B., & Goldberg, D. P. (1997). Somatization in cross-cultural perspective: A World Health Organization study in primary care. *American Journal of Psychiatry, 154,* 989–995.

Gurvits, T. V., Shenton, M. E., Hokama, H., Ohta, H., Lasko, N. B., Gilbertson, M. W., & Pitman, R. K. (1996). Magnetic resonance imaging study of hippocampal volume in chronic, combat-related posttraumatic stress disorder. *Biological Psychiatry, 40,* 1091–1099.

Gusella, J. F., Wexler, N. S., Conneally, P. M., Naylor, S. L., Anderson, M. A., Tanzi, R. E., & Martin, J. B. (1983). A polymorphic DNA marker genetically linked to Huntington's disease. *Nature, 306,* 234–239.

Gustad, J., & Phillips, K. A. (2003). Axis I comorbidity in body dysmorphic disorder. *Comprehensive Psychiatry, 44,* 270–276.

Gustafson, L., & Brun, A. (2012). Frontotemporal dementias. In M. G. Gelder, N. C. Andreasen, J. J. Lopez-Ibor, Jr., & J. R. Geddes (Eds.), *New Oxford Textbook of Psychiatry* (2nd. ed., Vol. 1, pp. 344–350). New York, NY: Oxford University Press.

Guttmannova, K., Bailey, J. A., Hill, K. G., Lee, J. O., Hawkins, J. D., Woods, M. L., & Catalano, R. F. (2011). Sensitive periods for adolescent alcohol use initiation: Predicting the lifetime occurrence and chronicity of alcohol problems in adulthood. *Journal of Studies on Alcohol and Drugs, 72*(2), 221–231.

Guze, S. B., Cloninger, C. R., Martin, R. L., & Clayton, P. J. (1986). A follow-up and family study of Briquet's syndrome. *British Journal of Psychiatry, 149,* 17–23.

Hackett, T. P., & Cassem, N. H. (1973). Psychological adaptation to convalescence in myocardial infarction patients. In J. P. Naughton, H. K. Hellerstein, & I. C. Mohler (Eds.), *Exercise testing and exercise training in coronary heart disease.* New York, NY: Academic Press.

Haddad, P. M., Brain, C., & Scott, J. (2014). Nonadherence with antipsychotic medication in schizophrenia: challenges and management strategies. *Patient Related Outcome Measures, 5,* 43–62.

Hadland, S. E., Austin, S. B., Goodenow, C. S., & Calzo, J. P. (2014). Weight misperception and unhealthy weight control behaviors among sexual minorities in the general adolescent population. *Journal of Adolescent Health, 54*(3), 296–303.

Hadley, S., Kim, S., Priday, L., & Hollander, E. (2006). Pharmacologic treatment of body dysmorphic disorder. *Primary Psychiatry, 13,* 61–69.

Haeffel, G. J., & Hames, J. L. (2014). Cognitive vulnerability to depression can be contagious. *Clinical Psychological Science, 2,* 75–85.

Haenen, M. A., de Jong, P. J., Schmidt, A. J. M., Stevens, S., & Visser, L. (2000).

Hypochondriacs' estimation of negative outcomes: Domain-specificity and responsiveness to reassuring and alarming information. *Behaviour Research and Therapy, 38*, 819–833.

Hahn, T., Kircher, T., Straube, B., Wittchen, H-U., Konrad, C., Ströhle, A., . . . Lueken, U. (2015). Predicting treatment response to cognitive behavioral therapy in panic disorder with agoraphobia by integrating local neural information. *JAMA Psychiatry, 72*, 68–74.

Hall, D. E., Eubanks, L., Meyyazhagan, S., Kenney, R. D., & Cochran Johnson, S. (2000). Evaluation of covert video surveillance in the diagnosis of Munchausen syndrome by proxy: Lessons from 41 cases. *Pediatrics, 6*, 1305–1312.

Hall, K. (2007). Sexual dysfunction and childhood sexual abuse: Gender differences and treatment implications. In S. R. Leiblum (Ed.), *Principles and practice of sex therapy* (4th ed., pp. 350–378). New York, NY: Guilford.

Hall, L. S., & Love, C. T. (2003). Finger-length ratios in female monozygotic twins discordant for sexual orientation. *Archives of Sexual Behavior, 32*, 23–28.

Halliburton, A. E., & Bray, B. C. (2016). Long-Term Prevalence and Demographic Trends in US Adolescent Inhalant Use: Implications for Clinicians and Prevention Scientists. *Substance Use & Misuse*, 1–14.

Hallmayer, J., Cleveland, S., Torres, A., Phillips, J., Cohen, B., Torigoe, T., & Smith, K. (2011). Genetic heritability and shared environmental factors among twin pairs with autism. *Archives of General Psychiatry*, archgenpsychiatry. 2011.2076 v2011.

Hamer, D. H., Hu, S., Magnuson, V. L., Hu, N., & Pattatucci, A. M. (1993). A linkage between DNA markers on the X chromosome and male sexual orientation. *Science, 261*, 321–327.

Halmi, K. A., Bellace, D., Berthod, S., Ghosh, S., Berrettini, W., Brandt, H. A., . . . Strober, M. (2012). An examination of early childhood perfectionism across anorexia nervosa subtypes. *International Journal of Eating Disorders, 45*(6), 800–807.

Hamilton, J. L., Stange, J. P., Abramson, L. Y., & Alloy, L. B. (in press). Stress and the development of cognitive vulnerabilities to depression explain sex differences in depressive symptoms during adolescence. *Clinical Psychological Science*, 2167702614545479.

Hamm, J., Pinkham, A., Gur, R. C., Verma, R., & Kohler, C. G. (2014). Dimensional information-theoretic measurement of facial emotion expressions in schizophrenia. *Schizophrenia Research and Treatment, 2014*, ID 243907.

Hammen, C. (2005). Stress and depression. *Annual Review of Clinical Psychology, 1*, 293–319.

Hammen, C. (2009). Children of depressed parents. In I. H. Gotlib & C. Hammen (Eds.), *Handbook of depression* (2nd ed., pp. 275–297). New York, NY: Guilford.

Hammen, C., & Keenan-Miller, D. (2013). In G. Stricker, T. A. Widiger, & I. B. Weiner (Eds.), *Handbook of psychology, Volume 8: Clinical psychology* (pp. 121–146). Hoboken, NJ: Wiley.

Hammer, S., Saag, M., Scheechter, M., Montaner, J., Schooley, R., Jacobsen, D., & the International AIDS Society-USA Panel. (2006). Treatment for adult HIV infection: 2006 recommendations of the International AIDS Society-USA panel. *JAMA: Journal of the American Medical Association, 296*, 827–843.

Hampton, T. (2010). Depression care effort brings dramatic drop in large HMO population's suicide rate. *JAMA: Journal of the American Medical Association, 303*(19), 1903–1905.

Hancock, T. B., & Kaiser, A. P. (2012). Implementing enhanced milieu teaching with children who have autism spectrum disorders. In P. A. Prelock & R. J. McCauley (Eds.), *Treatment of autism spectrum disorders: Evidence based-intervention strategies for communication and social interactions* (pp. 163–187). Baltimore, MD: Paul H. Brookes.

Hankin, B. L., & Abramson, L. Y. (2001). Development of gender differences in depression: An elaborated cognitive vulnerability–transactional stress theory. *Psychological Bulletin, 127*, 773–796.

Hankin, B. L., Wetter, E., & Cheely, C. (2007). Sex differences in adolescent depression: A developmental psychopathological approach. In J. R. Z. Abela & B. L. Hankin (Eds.), *Handbook of depression in children and adolescents* (pp. 377–414). New York, NY: Guilford.

Hanlon, E. C., & Van Cauter, E. (2011). Quantification of sleep behavior and of its impact on the cross-talk between the brain and peripheral metabolism. *Proceedings of the National Academy of Sciences, 108*(Supplement 3), 15609–15616. doi: 10.1073/pnas.1101338108

Hanna, G. L. (1995). Demographic and clinical features of obsessive-compulsive disorder in children and adolescents. *Journal of the American Academy of Child and Adolescent Psychiatry, 34*, 19–27.

Hannema, S., Schagen, S., Hoekzema, E., Kreukels, B., Veltman, D., Cohen-Kettenis, P., & Bakker, J. (2014). *Brain Structure and Function in Gender Dysphoric Adolescents.* Poster presented at 53rd Annual ESPE Meeting, Dublin, Ireland.

Hans, V. P. (1986). An analysis of public attitudes toward the insanity defense. *Criminology, 4*, 393–415.

Hanson, R. K., Gordon, A., Harris, A. J. R., Marques, J. K., Murphy, W., Quinsey, V. L., & Seto, M. C. (2002). First report on the collaborative outcome data project on the effectiveness of psychological treatment for sex offenders. *Sexual Abuse: A Journal of Research and Treatment, 14*, 169–194.

Hanson, R. K., Steffy, R. A., & Gauthier, R. (1993). Long-term recidivism of child molesters. *Journal of Consulting and Clinical Psychology, 61*, 646–652.

Hantouche, E., Akiskal, H., Azorin, J., Chatenet-Duchene, L., & Lancrenon, S. (2006). Clinical and psychometric characterization of depression in mixed mania: A report from the French National Cohort of 1090 manic patients. *Journal of Affective Disorders, 96*, 225–232.

Hara, K., Adachi, N., Akanuma, N., Ito, M., Okazaki, M., Matsubara, R., . . . Onuma, T. (2015). Dissociative experiences in epilepsy: Effects of epilepsy-related factors on pathological dissociation. *Epilepsy and Behavior, 44*, 185–191.

Harbert, T. L., Barlow, D. H., Hersen, M., & Austin, J. B. (1974). Measurement and modification of incestuous behavior: A case study. *Psychological Reports, 34*, 79–86.

Harburg, E., Kaciroti, N., Gleiberman, L., Julius, M., & Schork, M. A. (2008). Marital pair anger-coping types may act as an entity to affect mortality: Preliminary findings from a prospective study (Tecumseh, Michigan, 1971– 1988). *Journal of Family Communication, 8*(1), 44–61.

Hardie, T. L., Moss, H. B., & Lynch, K. G. (2006). Genetic correlations between smoking initiation and smoking behaviors in a twin sample. *Addictive Behaviors, 31*(11), 2030–2037.

Hare, R. D. (1970). *Psychopathy: Theory and research.* New York, NY: Wiley.

Hare, R. D. (1993). *Without conscience: The disturbing world of the psychopaths among us.* New York, NY: Pocket Books.

Hare, R. D., & Neumann, C. S. (2006). The PCL-R assessment of psychopathology: Development, structural properties, and new directions. In C. J. Patrick (Ed.), *Handbook of psychopathy* (pp. 58–88). New York, NY: Guilford.

Hare, R. D., & Vertommen, H. (2003). *The Hare psychopathy checklist—revised.* Toronto, Canada: Multi-Health Systems.

Hare, R. D., McPherson, L. M., & Forth, A. E. (1988). Male psychopaths and their criminal careers. *Journal of Consulting and Clinical Psychology, 56*, 710–714.

Hare, R. D., Neumann, C. S., & Widiger, T. A. (2012). Psychopathy. In T. A. Widiger (Ed.), *The Oxford handbook of personality disorders* (pp. 478–504). New York, NY: Oxford University Press.

Hariri, A. R., Mattay, V. S., Tessitore, A., Kolachana, B., Fera, F., Goldman, D., & Weinberger, D. R. (2002). Serotonin transporter genetic variation and the response of the human amygdala. *Science, 297*, 400–402.

Harmell, A. L., Palmer, B. W., & Jeste, D. V. (2012). Preliminary study of a web-based tool for enhancing the informed consent process in schizophrenia research. *Schizophrenia Research, 141*(2–3), 247–250. doi: http://dx.doi.org/10.1016/j.schres.2012.08.001

Harmer, C. J. (2008). Serotonin and emotional processing: Does it help explain antidepressant drug action? *Neuropharmacology, 55*(6), 1023–1028.

Harmer, C. J., O'Sullivan, U., Favaron, E., Massey-Chase, R., Ayres, R., Reinecke, A., & Cowen, P. J. (2009). Effect of acute antidepressant administration on negative affective bias in depressed patients. *The American Journal of Psychiatry, 166*(10), 1178–1184.

Harper, L. V. (2005). Epigenetic inheritance and the intergenerational transfer of experience. *Psychological Bulletin, 131*, 340–360.

Harpur, T. J., Hare, R. D., & Hakstian, A. R. (1989). Two-factor conceptualization of psychopathy: Construct validity and assessment implications. *Psychological Assessment: A Journal of Consulting and Clinical Psychology, 1*, 6–17.

Harrison, B. J., Pujol, J., Cardoner, N., Deus, J., Alonso, P., Lopez-Sola, M., & Soriano-Mas, C. (2013). Brain corticostriatal systems and the major clinical symptom dimensions of obsessive-compulsive disorder. *Biological Psychiatry, 73*(4), 321–328. doi: 10.1016/j.biopsych.2012.10.006

Harrison, P. J. (2012). The neurobiology of schizophrenia. In M. G. Gelder, N. C. Andreasen, J. J. Lopez-Ibor, Jr., & J. R. Geddes (Eds.), *New Oxford Textbook of Psychiatry* (2nd. ed., Vol. 1, pp. 561–568). New York, NY: Oxford University Press.

Hart, S. D., Forth, A. E., & Hare, R. D. (1990). Performance of criminal psychopaths on selected neuropsychological tests. *Journal of Abnormal Psychology, 99*, 374–379.

Harte, C. B. & Meston, C. M. (2008a). Acute effects of nicotine on physiological and subjective sexual arousal in nonsmoking men: A randomized, double-blind, placebo-controlled trial. *The Journal of Sexual Medicine, 5*(1), 110–121.

Harte, C. B. & Meston, C. M. (2008b). The inhibitory effects of nicotine on physiological sexual arousal in nonsmoking women: Results from a randomized, double-blind, placebocontrolled, cross-over trial. *The Journal of Sexual Medicine, 5*(5), 1184–1197.

Hartlage, S. A., Freels, S., Gotman, N., & Yonkers, K. (2012). Criteria for premenstrual dysphoric disorder: Secondary analyses of relevant data sets. *Archives of General Psychiatry, 69*(3), 300–305.

Harvey, A. G. (2008). Sleep and circadian rhythms in bipolar disorder: Seeking synchrony, harmony, and regulation. *The American Journal of Psychiatry, 165*(7), 820–829.

Harvey, A. G., Soehner, A. M., Kaplan, K. A., Hein, K., Lee, J., Kanady, J., . . . Buysse, D. J. (2015). Treating insomnia improves mood state, sleep, and functioning in bipolar disorder: A pilot randomized controlled trial. *Journal of Consulting and Clinical Psychology, 83*, 564–577.

Harvey, A. G., Talbot, L. S., & Gershon, A. (2009). Sleep disturbance in bipolar disorder across the lifespan. *Clinical Psychology: Science and Practice, 16*(2), 256–277.

Harvey, P. D., & Bowie, C. R. (2013). Schizophrenia spectrum conditions. In I. B. Weiner (Series Ed.), G. Stricker & T. A. Widiger (Vol. Eds.), *Handbook of psychology: Vol. 8, Clinical psychology* (pp. 240–261). Hoboken, NJ: John Wiley & Sons.

Harvey, S. B., & Wessely, S. (2009). Chronic fatigue syndrome: Identifying zebras among the horses. *BMC Medicine, 7*, 58. doi: 10.1186/1741-7015-7-58

Harvey, S. B., Wadsworth, M., Wessely, S., & Hotopf, M. (2008). Etiology of chronic fatigue syndrome: Testing popular hypotheses using a national birth cohort study. *Psychosomatic Medicine, 70*, 488–495.

Hasin, D., Fenton, M. C., Skodol, A., Krueger, R., Keyes, K., . . . Grant, B. Personality disorders and the 3-year course of alcohol, drug, and nicotine use disorders. *Archives of General Psychiatry, 68*(11), 1158–1167.

Hasin, D., Goodwin, R., Stinson, F., & Grant, B. (2005). Epidemiology of major depressive disorder. *Archives of General Psychiatry, 62*, 1097–1106.

Hasin, D. S. (2012). Combining abuse and dependence in DSM-5. *Journal of studies on alcohol and drugs, 73*(4), 702–704.

Haslam, J. (1976). *Observations on madness and melancholy*. New York, NY: Arno Press. (Original work published in 1809.)

Hatfield, E., Cacioppo, J. T., & Rapson, R. L. (1994). *Emotional contagion*. Cambridge: Cambridge University Press.

Hathaway, S. R., & McKinley, J. C. (1943). *Manual for the Minnesota Multiphasic Personality Inventory*. New York, NY: Psychological Corporation.

Haukkala, A., Konttinen, H., Laatikainen, T., Kawachi, I., & Uutela, A. (2010). Hostility, anger control, and anger expression as predictors of cardiovascular disease. *Psychosomatic Medicine, 72*(6), 556–562.

Hauner, K. K., Mineka, S., Voss, J. L., & Paller, K. A. (2012). Exposure therapy triggers lasting reorganization of neural fear processing. *Proceedings of the National Academy of Sciences of the United States, 109*(23), 9203–9208. doi: 10.1073/pnas.1205242109

Hausteiner, C., Klupsch, D., Emeny, R., Baumert, J., Ladwig, K. H., & Investigators (2010). Clustering of negative affectivity and social inhibition in the community: Prevalence of type D personality as a cardiovascular risk marker. *Psychosomatic Medicine, 72*(2), 163–171.

Hawes, D. J., Helyer, R., Herlianto, E. C., & Willing, J. (2013). Borderline personality features and implicit shame-prone self-concept in middle childhood and early adolescence. *Journal of Clinical Child & Adolescent Psychology, 42*(3), 302–308. doi: 10.1080/15374416.2012.723264

Hawkley, L. C., & Cacioppo, J. T. (2007). Aging and loneliness: Downhill quickly? *Current Directions in Psychological Science, 16*, 187–191.

Hawkley, L. C., Thisted, R. A., Masi, C. M., & Cacioppo, J. T. (2010). Loneliness predicts increased blood pressure: 5-year cross-lagged analyses in middle-aged and older adults. *Psychology and Aging, 25*(1), 132–141.

Hawton, K. (1995). Treatment of sexual dysfunctions of sex therapy and other approaches. *British Journal of Psychiatry, 167*, 307–314.

Hawton, K., Houston, K., Haw, C., Townsend, E., & Harriss, L. (2003). Comorbidity of axis I and axis II disorders in patients who attempted suicide. *American Journal of Psychiatry, 160*, 1494–1500.

Hay, P. J., & Fairburn, C. (1998). The validity of the DSM-IV scheme for classifying bulimic eating disorders. *International Journal of Eating Disorders, 23*, 7–15.

Hay, P. J., & Hall, A. (1991). The prevalence of eating disorders in recently admitted psychiatric in-patients. *British Journal of Psychiatry, 159*, 562–565.

Hayes, S. C., Barlow, D. H., & Nelson-Gray, R. O. (1999). *The scientist-practitioner: Research and accountability in the age of managed care* (2nd ed.). Boston, MA: Allyn & Bacon.

Hayes-Skelton, S. A., Roemer, L., & Orsillo, S. M. (2013), A randomized clinical trial comparing an acceptance-based behavior therapy to applied relaxation for generalized anxiety disorder. *Journal of Consulting and Clinical Psychology, 81*, 761–773.

Haynes, S. G., & Matthews, K. A. (1988). Area review: Coronary-prone behavior: Continuing evolution of the concept: Review and methodologic critique of recent studies on type A behavior and cardiovascular disease. *Annals of Behavioral Medicine, 10*(2), 47–59.

Haynes, S. G., Feinleib, M., & Kannel, W. B. (1980). The relationship of psychosocial factors to coronary heart disease in the Framingham study: III. Eight-year incidence of coronary heart disease. *American Journal of Epidemiology, 111*, 37–58.

Haynes, S. N., O'Brien, W., & Kaholokula, J. (2011). *Behavioral assessment and case formulation*. New York, NY: Wiley.

Haynes, S. N., Yoshioka, D. T., Kloezeman, K., & Bello, I. (2009). Clinical applications of behavioral assessment. In J. N. Butcher (Ed.), *Oxford handbook of personality assessment* (pp. 226–249). New York: Oxford University Press.

Haynos, A. F., & Fruzzetti, A. E. (2011). Anorexia nervosa as a disorder of emotion dysregulation: Evidence and treatment implications. *Clinical Psychology: Science and Practice, 18*(3), 183–202.

Hazell, P., O'Connell, D., Heathcote, D., Robertson, J., & Henry, D. (1995). Efficacy of tricyclic drugs in treating child and adolescent depression: A meta-analysis. *British Medical Journal, 8*, 897–901.

Hazlett-Stevens, H., & Bernstein, D. A. (2012). Relaxation. In W. T. O'Donohue & J. E. Fisher (Eds.), *Cognitive Behavior Therapy: Core Principles for Practice* (pp. 105–132). Hoboken, NJ: Wiley

Heath, A. K., Ganz, J. B., Parker, R., Burke, M., & Ninci, J. (2015). A Meta-analytic Review of Functional Communication Training Across Mode of Communication, Age, and Disability. *Review Journal of Autism and Developmental Disorders, 2*(2), 155–166.

Heath, C. A., Cooper, S. A., Murray, K., Lowman, A., Henry, C., MacLeod, M. A., . . . Will, R. G. (2010). Validation of diagnostic criteria for variant Creutzfeldt-Jakob disease. *Annals of Neurology, 67*(6), 761–770.

Hebert, L. E., Weuve, J., Scherr, P. A., & Evans, D. A. (2013). Alzheimer disease in the United States (2010–2050) estimated using the 2010 census. *Neurology, 80*(19), 1778–1783.

Hecht, K. F., Cicchetti, D., Rogosch, F. A., & Crick, N. R. (2014). Borderline personality features in childhood: The role of subtype, developmental timing, and chronicity of child maltreatment. *Development and Psychopathology, 26*(03), 805–815.

Heckers, S., Barch, D. M., Bustillo, J., Gaebel, W., Gur, R., Malaspina, D., . . . Van Os, J. (2013). Structure of the psychotic disorders classification in DSM-5. *Schizophrenia Research, 150*(1), 11–14.

Heim, C., Plotsky, P., & Nemeroff, C. (2004). Importance of studying the contributions of early adverse experience to neurobiological findings in depression. *Neuropsychopharmacology, 29,* 641–648.

Heim, C., Wagner, D., Maloney, E., Papanicolaou, D., Dimitris, A., Solomon, L., & Reeves, W. C. (2006). Early adverse experience and risk for chronic fatigue syndrome. *Archives of General Psychiatry, 63,* 1258–1266.

Heiman, J. R. (2000). Orgasmic disorders in women. In S. R. Leiblum & R. C. Rosen (Eds.), *Principles and practice of sex therapy* (3rd ed., pp. 118–153). New York, NY: Guilford.

Heiman, J. R. (2007). Orgasmic disorders in women. In S. R. Leiblum (Ed.), *Principles and practice of sex therapy* (4th ed., pp. 84–123). New York, NY: Guilford.

Heiman, J. R., & LoPiccolo, J. (1983). Clinical outcome of sex therapy: Effects of daily versus weekly treatment. *Archives of General Psychiatry, 40,* 443–449.

Heiman, J. R., & LoPiccolo, J. (1988). *Becoming orgasmic: A sexual and personal growth program for women* (rev. ed.). New York, NY: Prentice Hall.

Heiman, J. R., & Meston, C. M. (1997). Empirically validated treatment for sexual dysfunction. *Annual Review of Sex Research, 8,* 148–195.

Heimberg, R. G., & Magee, L. (2014). Social anxiety disorder. In D. H. Barlow (Ed.), *Clinical handbook of psychological disorders: A step-by-step treatment manual* (5th ed.). New York, NY: Guilford

Heintzelman, S. J., & King, L. A. (2014). (The Feeling of) Meaning-as-information. *Personality and Social Psychology Review,* 1088868313518487.

Helgeson, V. (2005). Recent advances in psychosocial oncology. *Journal of Consulting and Clinical Psychology, 73,* 268–271.

Heller, W., & Nitschke, J. B. (1997). Regional brain activity in emotion: A framework for understanding cognition in depression. *Cognition and Emotion, 11*(5–6), 737–661.

Helzer, J. E., Wittchen, H.-U., Krueger, R. F., & Kraemer, H. C. (2008). Dimensional options for DSM-V: The way forward. In J. E. Helzer, H. C. Kraemer, R. F. Krueger, H.-U. Wittchen, P. J. Sirovatka, & D. A. Regier (Eds.), *Dimensional approaches in diagnostic classification: Refining the research agenda for DSM-V* (pp. 115–127). Washington, D.C.: American Psychiatric Association.

Helzer, J. E., Kraemer, H. C., Krueger, R. F., Wittchen, H.-U., Sirovatka, P. J., & Regier, D. A. (Eds.) (2008). *Dimensional approaches in diagnostic classification: Refining the research agenda for DSM-V.* Washington, DC: American Psychiatric Association.

Henderson, K. E., & Brownell, K. D. (2004). The toxic environment and obesity: Contribution and cure. In J. K. Thompson (Ed.), *Handbook of eating disorders and obesity* (pp. 339–348). New York, NY: Wiley.

Hendriks, G. J., Kampman, M., Keijsers, G. P., Hoogduin, C. A., & Voshaar, R. C. O. (2014). Cognitive-behavioral therapy for panic disorder with agoraphobia in older people: A comparison with younger patients. *Depression and Anxiety, 31,* 669–677.

Henquet, C., Krabbendam, L., Spauwen, J., Kaplan, C., Lieb, R., Wittchen, H.-U., & van Os, J. (2005). Prospective cohort study of cannabis use, predisposition for psychosis, and psychotic symptoms in young people. *British Medical Journal, 330,* 11.

Herbert, T. B., & Cohen, S. (1993). Depression and immunity: A meta-analytic review. *Psychological Bulletin, 113*(3), 472–486.

Herdt, G. H. (1987). *The Sambia: Ritual and gender in New Guinea.* New York, NY: Holt, Rinehart and Winston.

Herdt, G. H., & Stoller, R. J. (1989). Commentary to "The socialization of homosexuality and heterosexuality in a non-Western society." *Archives of Sexual Behavior, 18,* 31–34.

Herlitz, C. A., & Forsberg, M. (2010). Sexual behavior and risk assessment in different age cohorts in the general population of Sweden (1989-2007). *Scandinavian Journal of Public Health, 38,* 32–39.

Hermans, E. J., Henckens, M. J. A. G., Joels, M., & Fernandez, G. (2014). Dynamic adaptation of large-scale brain networks in response to acute stressors. *Trends in Neurosciences, 37,* 304–314.

Hermans, E. J., van Marle, H. J., Ossewaarde, L., Henckens, M. J., Qin, S., van Kesteren, M. T., & Fernández, G. (2011). Stress-related noradrenergic activity prompts large-scale neural network reconfiguration. *Science, 334*(6059), 1151–1153. doi: 10.1126/science.1209603

Hernandez, M., Barrio, C., & Yamada, A. M. (2013). Hope and burden among Latino families of adults with schizophrenia. *Family Process, 52*(4), 697–708.

Heron, J., Barker, E. D., Joinson, C., Lewis, G., Hickman, M., Munafò, M., & Macleod, J. (2013). Childhood conduct disorder trajectories, prior risk factors and cannabis use at age 16: birth cohort study. *Addiction, 108*(12), 2129–2138.

Hershberger, S., & Segal, N. (2004). The cognitive, behavioral, and personality profiles of a male monozygotic triplet set discordant for sexual orientation. *Archives of Sexual Behavior, 33,* 497–514.

Herzog, D. B., Dorer, D. J., Keel, P. K., Selwyn, S. E., Ekeblad, E. R., Flores, A. T., & Keller, M. B. (1999). Recovery and relapse in anorexia and bulimia nervosa: A 7.5-year follow-up study. *Journal of the American Academy of Child and Adolescent Psychiatry, 38*(7), 829–837.

Heshka, S., Anderson, J. W., Atkinson, R. L., Greenway, F. L., Hill, J. O., Phinney, S. D., & Pi-Sunyer, F. X. (2003). Weight loss with self-help compared with a structured commercial program: A randomized trial. *JAMA: Journal of the American Medical Association, 289,* 1792–1798.

Hetherington, M. M., & Cecil, J. E. (2010). Gene-environment interactions in obesity. *Forum of Nutrition, 63,* 195–203.

Hettema, J. M., Neale, M. C., & Kendler, K. S. (2001). A review and meta-analysis of the genetic epidemiology of anxiety disorders. *American Journal of Psychiatry, 158,* 1568–1578.

Hettema, J. M., Prescott, C. A., Myers, J. M., Neale, M. C., & Kendler, K. S. (2005). The structure of genetic and environmental risk factors for anxiety disorders in men and women. *Archives of General Psychiatry, 62,* 182–189.

Heylens, G., De Cuypere, G., Zucker, K. J., Schelfaut, C., Elaut, E., Vanden Bossche, H., . . . T'Sjoen, G. (2012). Gender identity disorder in twins: A review of the case report literature. *The Journal of Sexual Medicine, 9*(3), 751–757.

Higgins, S. T., Heil, S. H., Dantona, R., Donham, R., Matthews, M., & Badger, G. J. (2006). Effects of varying the monetary value of voucher-based incentives on abstinence achieved during and following treatment among cocaine-dependent outpatients. *Addiction, 102,* 271–281.

Higgins, S. T., Sigmon, S. C., & Heil, S. H. (2014). Drug use disorders. In D. H. Barlow (Ed.), *Clinical handbook of psychological disorders: A step-by-step treatment manual.* New York, NY: Guilford.

Higuchi, S., Matsushita, S., Imazeki, H., Kinoshita, T., Takagi, S., & Kono, H. (1994). Aldehyde dehydrogenase genotypes in Japanese alcoholics. *Lancet, 343,* 741–742.

Hilgard, E. R. (1992). Divided consciousness and dissociation. *Consciousness & Cognition, 1,* 16–31.

Hilbert, A., Hildebrandt, T., Agras, W. S., Wilfley, D. E., & Wilson, G. T. (2015). Rapid response in psychological treatments for binge eating disorder. *Journal of Consulting and Clinical Psychology, 83*(3), 649–654.

Hill, C. (2011). Practitioner Review: Effective treatment of behavioural insomnia in children. *Journal of Child Psychology and Psychiatry, 52*(7), 731–740.

Hill, K. G., Bailey, J. A., Hawkins, J. D., Catalano, R. F., Kosterman, R., Oesterle, S., & Abbott, R. D. (2014). The onset of STI diagnosis through age 30: Results from the Seattle Social Development Project intervention. *Prevention Science, 15*(1), 19–32.

Hiller, W., Fichter, M. M., & Rief, W. (2003). A controlled treatment study of somatoform disorders including analysis of healthcare utilization and cost-effectiveness. *Journal of Psychosomatic Research, 54,* 369–380.

Hiller, W., Leibbrand, R., Rief, W., & Fichter, M. (2005). Differentiating hypochondriasis from panic disorder. *Journal of Anxiety Disorders, 19,* 29–49.

Hillis, A. E. (2014). Inability to empathize: brain lesions that disrupt sharing and understanding another's emotions. *Brain, 137*(4), 981–997.

Hindmarch, I. (1990). Cognitive impairment with anti-anxiety agents: A solvable problem? In D. Wheatley (Ed.), *The anxiolytic jungle: Where, next?* (pp. 49–61). Chichester, UK: Wiley.

Hinshaw, S. P., & Stier, A. (2008). Stigma as related to mental disorders. *Annual Review of Clinical Psychology, 4,* 367–393.

Hinshelwood, J. A. (1896). A case of dyslexia: A peculiar form of word-blindness. *Lancet, 2,* 1451–1454.

Hinton, D., Pich, V., Chhean, D., Pollack, M. H., & Barlow, D. H. (2004). Olfactory-triggered panic attacks among Cambodian refugees attending a psychiatric clinic. *General Hospital Psychiatry, 26*(5), 390–397.

Hinton, D., Pollack, M. H., Pich, V., Fama, J. M., & Barlow, D. H. (2005). Orthostatically induced panic attacks among Cambodian refugees: Flashbacks, catastrophic cognitions, and associated psychopathology. *Cognitive Behavioral Practice, 12,* 301–311.

Hinton, D. E., & Good, B. J. (Eds.). (2009). *Culture and panic disorder.* Stanford: Stanford University Press.

Hinton, D. E., Chong, R., Pollack, M. H., Barlow, D. H., & McNally, R. J. (2008). Ataque de nervios: Relationship to anxiety sensitivity and dissociation predisposition. *Depression and Anxiety, 25,* 489–495.

Hinton, D. E., Hofmann, S. G., Pitman, R. K., Pollack, M. H., & Barlow, D. H. (2008). The panic attack-posttraumatic stress disorder model: Applicability to orthostatic panic among Cambodian refugees. *Cognitive Behavioral Therapy, 37*(2), 101–16.

Hinton, D. E., Lewis-Fernandez, R., & Pollack, M. H. (2009). A model of the generation of ataque de nervios: The role of fear of negative affect and fear of arousal symptoms. *CNS Neuroscience Therapeutics, 15*(3), 264–275.

Hinton, D. E., Park, L., Hsia, C., Hofmann, S., & Pollack, M. H. (2009). Anxiety disorder presentations in Asian populations: A review. *CNS Neuroscience & Therapeutics, 15*(3), 295–303.

Hinton, L., Guo, Z., Hillygus, J., & Levkoff, S. (2000). Working with culture: A qualitative analysis of barriers to the recruitment of Chinese-American family caregivers for dementia research. *Journal of Cross-Cultural Gerontology, 15*(2), 119–137. doi: 10.1023/A:1006798316654

Hirschfeld, D. R., Rosenbaum, J. F., Biederman, J., Bolduc, E. A., Farone, S. V., Snidman, N., & Kagan, J. (1992). Stable behavioral inhibition and its association with anxiety disorder. *Journal of the American Academy of Child and Adolescent Psychiatry, 31,* 103–111.

Hirschfeld, R. M. A., Keller, M. M., Panico, S., Arons, B. S., Barlow, D., Davidoff, F., & Wyatt, R. J. (1997). The National Depressive and Manic-Depressive Association consensus statement on the undertreatment of depression. *JAMA: Journal of the American Medical Association, 277*(4), 333–340.

Hirshkowitz, M., Seplowitz, R. G., & Sharafkhaneh, A. (2009). Sleep disorders. In B. J. Sadock, V. A. Sadock, & P. Ruiz (Eds.), *Kaplan & Sadock's comprehensive textbook of psychiatry* (9th ed., Vol. I, pp. 2150–2177). Philadelphia, PA: Lippincott Williams & Wilkins.

Hitchcock, P. B., & Mathews, A. (1992). Interpretation of bodily symptoms in hypochondriasis. *Behaviour Research and Therapy, 30*(3), 223–234.

Hlastala, S. A., Kotler, J. S., McClellan, J. M., & McCauley, E. A. (2010). Interpersonal and social rhythm therapy for adolescents with bipolar disorder: Treatment development and results from an open trial. *Depression and Anxiety, 27*(5), 457–464.

Ho, B. C., Wassink, T. H., Ziebell, S., & Andreasen, N. C. (2011). Cannabinoid receptor 1 gene polymorphisms and marijuana misuse interactions on white matter and cognitive deficits in schizophrenia. *Schizophrenia Research, 128*(1), 66–75.

Hodgson, K., & McGuffin, P. (2013). The genetic basis of depression. *Current Topics in Behavioral Neurosciences, 14,* 81–99.

Hoek, H. W. (2002). The distribution of eating disorders. In K. D. Brownell & C. G. Fairburn (Eds.), *Eating disorders and obesity: A comprehensive handbook* (2nd ed., pp. 207–211). New York, NY: Guilford.

Hoek, H. W., van Harten, P. N., Hermans, K., M. E., Katzman, M. A., Matroos, G. E., & Susser, E. S. (2005). The incidence of anorexia nervosa on Curacao. *American Journal of Psychiatry, 162,* 748–752.

Hoffman, B., Papas, R., Chatkoff, D., & Kerns, R. (2007). Meta-analysis of psychological interventions for chronic low back pain. *Health Psychology, 26,* 1–9.

Hoffman, R. E., Boutros, N. N., Hu, S., Berman, R. M., Krystal, J. H., & Charney, D. S. (2000). Transcranial magnetic stimulation and auditory hallucinations in schizophrenia. *Lancet, 355,* 1073–1075.

Hoffman, R. E., Hawkins, K. A., Gueorguieva, R., Boutros, N. N., Rachid, F., Carroll, K., & Krystal, J. H. (2003). Transcranial magnetic stimulation of left temporoparietal cortex and medication-resistant auditory hallucinations. *Archives of General Psychiatry, 60,* 49–56.

Hofmann, S. G. (2007a). Enhancing exposure-based therapy from a translational research perspective. *Behaviour Research and Therapy, 45*(9), 1987–2001.

Hofmann, S. G. (2007b). Cognitive factors that maintain social anxiety disorder: A comprehensive model and its treatment implications. *Cognitive Behaviour Therapy, 36*(4), 195–209.

Hofmann, S. G. (2014). D-cycloserine for treating anxiety disorders: Making good exposures better and bad exposures worse. *Depression and Anxiety, 31,* 175.

Hofmann, S. G., & Barlow, D. H. (1996). Ambulatory psychophysiological monitoring: A potentially useful tool when treating panic relapse. *Cognitive and Behavioral Practice, 3,* 53–61.

Hofmann, S. G., & Barlow, D. H. (2002). Social phobia (social anxiety disorder). In D. H. Barlow, *Anxiety and its disorders: The nature and treatment of anxiety and panic* (2nd ed.). New York, NY: Guilford.

Hofmann, S. G., & Hinton, D. E. (2014). Cross-cultural aspects of anxiety disorders. *Current Psychiatry Reports, 16,* 450.

Hofmann, S. G., & Otto, M. W. (2008). *Cognitive-behavior therapy of social anxiety disorder: Evidence-based and disorder specific treatment techniques.* New York, NY: Routledge.

Hofmann, S. G., Sawyer, A. T., Witt, A., & Oh, D. (2010). The effect of mindfulness-based therapy on anxiety and depression: A meta-analytic review. *Journal of Consulting and Clinical Psychology, 78,* 169–183.

Hofmann, S. G., & Smits, J. A. (2008). Cognitive-behavioral therapy for adult anxiety disorders: A meta-analysis of randomized placebo-controlled trials. *Journal of Clinical Psychiatry, 69*(4), 621–632.

Hofmann, S. G., Alpers, G. W., & Pauli, P. (2009). Phenomenology of panic and phobic disorders. In M. M. Antony & M. B. Stein (Eds.), *Oxford handbook of anxiety and related disorders* (pp. 34–46). New York, NY: Oxford University Press.

Hofmann, S. G., Asnaani, A., & Hinton, D. E. (2010). Cultural aspects in social anxiety and social anxiety disorder. *Depression and Anxiety, 27*(12), 1117–1127.

Hofmann, S. G., Asnaani, A., Vonk, J. J., Sawyer, A. T., & Fang, A. (2012). The efficacy of cognitive behavioral therapy: A review of meta-analyses. *Cognitive Therapy and Research, 36,* 427–440.

Hofmann, S. G., Lehman, C. L., & Barlow, D. H. (1997). How specific are specific phobias? *Journal of Behavior Therapy and Experimental Psychiatry, 28,* 233–240.

Hofmann, S. G., Moscovitch, D. A., Litz, B. T., Kim, H.-J., Davis, L., & Pizzagalli, D. A. (2005). The worried mind: Autonomic and prefrontal activation during worrying. *Emotion, 5,* 464–475.

Hofmann, S. G., Meuret, A. E., Smitts, J. A. J., Simon, N. M., Pollack, M. H., Eisenmenger, K., & Otto, M. W. (2006). Augmentation of exposure therapy with D-cycloserine for social anxiety disorder. *Archives of General Psychiatry, 63*(3), 298–304.

Hofmann, S. G., Sawyer, A. T., & Asnaani, A. (2012). D-cycloserine as an augmentation strategy for cognitive behavioral therapy of anxiety disorders: An update. *Current Pharmaceutical Design, 18*(35), 5659–5662.

Hofmann, S. G., Sawyer, A. T., Witt, A., & Oh, D. (2010). The effect of mindfulness-based therapy on anxiety and depression: A meta-analytic review. *Journal of Consulting and Clinical Psychology, 78,* 169–183.

Hofmann, S. G., Smits, J. A., Rosenfield, D., Simon, N., Otto, M. W., Meuret, A. E., & Pollack, M. H. (2013). D-cycloserine as an augmentation strategy with cognitive-behavioral therapy for social anxiety disorder. *American Journal of Psychiatry, 170*(7), 751–758. doi: 10.1176/appi.ajp.2013

Hogarty, G. E., Anderson, C. M., Reiss, D. J., Kornblith, S. J., Greenwald, D. P., Javna, C. D., & Madonia, M. J. (1986). Family psychoeducation, social skills training, and maintenance chemotherapy in the aftercare treatment of schizophrenia: I. One year effects of a controlled study on relapse and expressed emotion. *Archives of General Psychiatry, 43,* 633–642.

Hogarty, G. E., Anderson, C. M., Reiss, D. J., Kornblith, S. J., Greenwald, D. P., Ulrich, R. F., Carter, M., & The Environmental–Personal Indicators in the Course of Schizophrenia (EPICS) Research Group. (1991). Family psychoeducation, social skills training, and maintenance chemotherapy in the aftercare treatment of schizophrenia. *Archives of General Psychiatry, 48,* 340–347.

Holden, C. (2005). Obesity in the east. *Science, 307,* 38.

Holder, H. D., Gruenewald, P. J., Ponicki, W. R., Treno, A. J., Grube, J. W., Saltz, R. F., & Roeper, P. (2000). Effect of community-based interventions on high-risk drinking and alcohol-related injuries. *JAMA: Journal of the American Medical Association, 284,* 2341–2347.

Holland, A. J. (2012). Classification, diagnosis, psychiatric assessment, and needs assessment. In M. G. Gelder, N. C. Andreasen, J. J. Lopez-Ibor, Jr., & J. R. Geddes (Eds.), *New Oxford textbook of psychiatry* (2nd. ed., Vol. 2, pp. 1819–1824). New York, NY: Oxford University Press.

Holland, J. M., & Gallagher-Thompson, D. (2011). Interventions for mental health problems in later life. In D. H. Barlow (Ed.), *Oxford handbook of clinical psychology* (pp. 810–836). New York, NY: Oxford University Press.

Hollander, E., Allen, A., Kwon, J., Aronowitz, B., Schmeidler, J., Wong, C., & Simeon, D. (1999). Clomipramine vs. desipramine crossover trial in body dysmorphic disorder: Selective efficacy of a serotonin reuptake inhibitor in imagined ugliness. *Archives of General Psychiatry, 56*(11), 1033–1039.

Hollander, E., Berlin, H. A., & Stein, D. J. (2009). Impulse-control disorders not elsewhere classified. In J. A. Bourgeois, R. E. Hales, J. S. Young, & S. C. Yudofsky (Eds.), *The American Psychiatric Publishing Board review guide for psychiatry* (pp. 469–482). Arlington, VA: American Psychiatric Publishing.

Hollander, J. A., & Kenny, P. J. (2012). Compulsive drug use and brain reward systems. In J. C. Verster, K. Brady, M. Galanter, & P. Conrod (Eds.), *Drug Abuse and Addiction in Medical Illness* (pp. 63–72). New York, NY: Springer.

Hollis, J. F., Connett, J. E., Stevens, V. J., & Greenlick, M. R. (1990). Stressful life events, Type A behavior, and the prediction of cardiovascular and total mortality over six years. *Journal of Behavioral Medicine, 13*(3), 263–280.

Hollon, S. D. (2011). Cognitive and behavior therapy in the treatment and prevention of depression. *Depression and Anxiety, 28*(4), 263–266.

Hollon, S. D., & Dimidjian, S. (2009). Cognitive and behavioral treatment of depression. In I. H. Gotlib & C. L. Hammen (Eds.), *Handbook of depression* (2nd ed., pp. 586–603). New York, NY: Guilford.

Hollon, S. D., Areán, P. A., Craske, M. G., Crawford, K. A., Kivlahan, D. R., Magnavita, J. J., . . . Kurtzman, H. (2014). Development of Clinical Practice Guidelines. *Annual Review of Clinical Psychology, 10*(1), 213–241. doi: doi:10.1146/annurev-clinpsy-050212-185529

Hollon, S. D, DeRubeis, R. J., Fawcett, J., Amsterdam, J. D., Shelton, R. C., Zajecka, J., Young, P. R., & Gallop, R. (2014). Effect of cognitive therapy with antidepressant medications vs antidepressants alone on the rate of recovery in major depressive disorder: A randomized clinical trial. *JAMA Psychiatry, 71,* 1157–1164.

Hollon, S. D., DeRubeis, R. J., Shelton, R. C., Amsterdam, J. D., Salomon, R. M., O'Reardon, J. P., & Gallop, R. (2005). Prevention of relapse following cognitive therapy vs. medications in moderate to severe depression. *Archives of General Psychiatry, 62,* 417–422.

Hollon, S. D., Stewart, M. O., & Strunk, D. (2006). Cognitive behavior therapy has enduring effects in the treatment of depression and anxiety. *Annual Review of Psychology, 57,* 285–315.

Holroyd, K. A., & Penzien, D. B. (1986). Client variables in the behavioral treatment of current tension headache: A meta-analytic review. *Journal of Behavioral Medicine, 9,* 515–536.

Holroyd, K. A., Andrasik, F., & Noble, J. (1980). A comparison of EMG biofeedback and a credible pseudotherapy in treating tension headache. *Journal of Behavioral Medicine, 3,* 29–39.

Holroyd, K. A., Penzien, D. B., Hursey, K. G., Tobin, D. L., Rogers, L., Holm, J. E., & Chila, A. G. (1984). Change mechanisms in EMG biofeedback training. Cognitive changes underlying improvements in tension headache. *Journal of Consulting and Clinical Psychology, 52,* 1039–1053.

Holt-Lunstad, J., Birmingham, W. A., & Light, K. C. (2008). Influence of a "warm touch" support enhancement intervention among married couples on ambulatory blood pressure, oxytocin, alpha amylase, & cortisol. *Psychosomatic Medicine, 70,* 976–985.

Holt-Lunstad, J., Smith, T. B., & Layton, J. B. (2010). Social relationships and mortality risk: A meta-analytic review. *PLoS Med, 7*(7), e1000316. doi: 10.1371/journal.pmed.1000316

Holzman, P. S., & Levy, D. L. (1977). Smooth pursuit eye movements and functional psychoses: A review. *Schizophrenia Bulletin, 3,* 15–27.

Hook, E. B. (1982). Epidemiology of Down syndrome. In S. M. P. J. E. Rynders (Ed.), *Down syndrome: Advances in biomedicine and the behavioral sciences* (pp. 11–88). Cambridge, MA: Ware Press.

Hooley, J. M. (1985). Expressed emotion: A review of the critical literature. *Clinical Psychology Review, 5,* 119–139.

Hooley, J. M., & Campbell, C. (2002). Control and controllability: Beliefs and behaviour in high and low expressed emotion relatives. *Psychological Medicine, 32,* 1091–1099.

Hooley, J. M., Cole, S. H., & Gironde, S. (2012). Borderline personality disorder. In T. A. Widiger (Ed.), *The Oxford handbook of personality disorders* (pp. 409–436). New York, NY: Oxford University Press.

Hoon, P. W., Wincze, J. P., & Hoon, E. F. (1977). A test of reciprocal inhibition: Are anxiety and sexual arousal in women mutually inhibitory? *Journal of Abnormal Psychology, 86,* 65–74.

Hoppenbrouwers, S., Neumann, C. S., Lewis, J., & Johansson, P. (2015). A latent variable analysis of the Psychopathy Checklist–Revised and behavioral inhibition system/behavioral activation system factors in North American and Swedish offenders. *Personality Disorders: Theory, Research, and Treatment, 6*(3), 251–260.

Hopwood, C. J., & Thomas, K. M. (2012). Paranoid and schizoid personality disorders. In T. A. Widiger (Ed.), *The Oxford handbook of personality disorders* (pp. 582–602). New York, NY: Oxford University Press.

Horan, W. P., Ventura, J., Mintz, J., Kopelowicz, A., Wirshing, D., Christian-Herman, J., Foy, D., & Liberman, R. P. (2007). Stress and coping responses to a natural disaster in people with schizophrenia. *Psychiatry Research, 151,* 77–86.

Horowitz, J., & Garber, J. (2006). The prevention of depressive symptoms in children and adolescents: A meta-analytic review. *Journal of Consulting and Clinical Psychology, 74,* 401–415.

Horwath, E., & Weissman, M. (1997). Epidemiology of anxiety disorders across cultural groups. In S. Friedman (Ed.), *Cultural issues in the treatment of anxiety* (pp. 21–39). New York, NY: Guilford.

Horwath, E., & Weissman, M. M. (2000). The epidemiology and cross-national presentation of obsessive-compulsive disorder. *Psychiatric Clinics of North America, 23*(3), 493–507.

Hostinar, C. E., Sullivan, R. M., & Gunnar, M. R. (2013, April 22). Psychobiological mechanisms: Review of animal models and human studies across development. *Psychological Bulletin.* Advance online publication.

House, J. S., Landis, K. R., & Umberson, D. (1988). Social relationships and health. *Science, 241,* 540–545.

House, J. S., Robbins, C., & Metzner, H. M. (1982). The association of social relationships and activities with mortality: Prospective evidence from the Tecumseh community health study. *American Journal of Epidemiology, 116,* 123.

Houston, B. K., Chesney, M. A., Black, G. W., Cates, D. S., & Hecker, M. H. L. (1992). Behavioral clusters and coronary heart disease risk. *Psychosomatic Medicine, 54*(4), 447–461.

Howard, G., Lackland, D. T., Kleindorfer, D. O., Kissela, B. M., Moy, C. S., Judd, S. E., . . . Howard, V. J. (2013). Racial differences in the impact of elevated systolic blood pressure on stroke risk. *JAMA Internal Medicine,173*(1), 46–51.

Howe, M. L. (2007). Children's emotional false memories. *Psychological Science, 18*(10), 856–860.

Howell, M. (2012). Parasomnias: An updated review. *Neurotherapeutics, 9*(4), 753–775. doi: 10.1007/s13311-012-0143-8

Howes, O. D., & Kapur, S. (2009). The dopamine hypothesis of schizophrenia: Version III— The final common pathway. *Schizophrenia Bulletin, 35*(3), 549–562. doi: 10.1093/schbul/sbp006

Howes, O. D., & Murray, R. M. (2014). Schizophrenia: an integrated sociodevelopmental-cognitive model. *The Lancet, 383*(9929), 1677–1687.

Howes, O. D., Kambeitz, J., Kim, E., Stahl, D., Slifstein, M., Abi-Dargham, A., & Kapur, S. (2012). The nature of dopamine dysfunction in schizophrenia and what this means for treatment: meta-analysis of imaging studies. *Archives of General Psychiatry, 69*(8), 776–786.

Howland, R. H., Rush, A. J., Wisniewski, S. R., Trivedi, M. H., Warden, D., Fava, M., & Gallop, R. (2009). Concurrent anxiety and substance use disorders among outpatients with major depression: Clinical features and effect on treatment outcome. *Drug and Alcohol Dependence, 99*(1-3), 248–260.

Howlin, P., Goode, S., Hutton, J., & Rutter, M. (2010). Savant skills in autism: Psychometric approaches and parental reports. In F. Happé & U. Frith (Eds.), *Autism and talent* (pp. 13–24). New York, NY: Oxford University Press.

Hser, Y. I., Evans, E., Grella, C., Ling, W., & Anglin, D. (2015). Long-term course of opioid addiction. *Harvard Review of Psychiatry, 23*(2), 76–89.

Hsu, L. K. G. (1988). The outcome of anorexia nervosa: A reappraisal. *Psychological Medicine, 18,* 807–812.

Hsu, L. K. G. (1990). *Eating disorders*. New York, NY: Guilford.

Hsu, L. K. G., & Zimmer, B. (1988). Eating disorders in old age. *International Journal of Eating Disorders, 7*, 133–138.

Huang, Y., Kotov, R., de Girolamo, G., Preti, A., Angermeyer, M., Benjet, C., & Kessler, R. C. (2009). DSM-IV personality disorders in the WHO World Mental Health Surveys. *The British Journal of Psychiatry, 195*(1), 46–53. doi: 10.1192/bjp.bp.108.058552

Huang, Y. C., Lin, C. C., Hung, Y. Y., & Huang, T. L. (2013). Rapid relief of catatonia in mood disorder by lorazepam and diazepam. *Biomedical Journal, 36*(1), 35–39.

Hubert, N. C., Jay, S. M., Saltoun, M., & Hayes, M. (1988). Approach-avoidance and distress in children undergoing preparation for painful medical procedures. *Journal of Clinical Child Psychology, 17*(3), 194–202.

Hucker, S. J. (1997). Sexual sadism: Psychopathology and theory. In D. R. Laws & W. T. O'Donohue (Eds.), *Sexual deviance: Theory, assessment, and treatment* (pp. 194–209). New York, NY: Guilford.

Hucker, S. J. (2008). Sexual masochism: Psychopathology and theory. In D. R. Laws & W. T. O'Donohue (Eds.), *Sexual deviance: Theory, assessment, and treatment* (2nd ed., pp. 250–263). New York, NY: Guilford.

Hudson, J. I., Hiripi, E., Pope, H. G., Jr., & Kessler, R. C. (2007). The prevalence and correlates of eating disorders in the national comorbidity survey replication. *Biological Psychiatry, 61*, 348–358.

Hudson, J. I., Lalonde, J. K., Berry, J. M., Pindych, L. J., Bulik, C. M., Crow, S. J., & Pope, H. G. (2006). Binge-eating disorder as a distinct familial phenotype in obese individuals. *Archives of General Psychiatry, 63*, 313–319.

Hudson, J. I., Mangweth, B., Pope, H. G., Jr., De Col, C., Hausmann, A., Gutweniger, S., & Tsaung, M. T. (2003). Family study of affective spectrum disorder. *Archives of General Psychiatry, 60*, 170–177.

Huerta, M., Bishop, S. L., Duncan, A., Hus, V., & Lord, C. (2012). Application of DSM-5 criteria for autism spectrum disorder to three samples of children with DSM-IV diagnoses of pervasive developmental disorders. *American Journal of Psychiatry, 169*(10), 1056–1064.

Hughes, J. R. (2009). Nicotine-related disorders. In B. J. Sadock, V. A. Sadock, & P. Ruiz (Eds.), *Kaplan & Sadock's comprehensive textbook of psychiatry* (9th ed., Vol. I, pp. 1353–1360). Philadelphia, PA: Lippincott Williams & Wilkins.

Hummelen, B., Pedersen, G., Wilberg, T., & Karterud, S. (2014). Poor Validity of the DSM-IV Schizoid Personality Disorder Construct as a Diagnostic Category. *Journal of Personality Disorders*, 1–13.

Humphrey, L. L. (1989). Observed family interactions among subtypes of eating disorders using structural analysis of social behavior. *Journal of Consulting and Clinical Psychology, 57*, 206–214.

Hunsley, J., & Mash, E. J. (2011). Evidence based assessment. In D. H. Barlow (Ed.), *Oxford handbook of clinical psychology*. (pp. 76–97). New York, NY: Oxford University Press.

Hunt, W. A. (1980). History and classification. In A. E. Kazdin, A. S. Bellack, & M. Hersen (Eds.), *New perspectives in abnormal psychology*. New York, NY: Oxford University Press.

Hunter, E., Sierra, M., & David, A. (2004). The epidemiology of depersonalisation and derealisation: A systematic review. *Social Psychiatry and Psychiatric Epidemiology, 39*, 9–18.

Hunter, J. A., Jr., & Mathews, R. (1997). Sexual deviance in females. In D. R. Laws & W. T. O'Donohue (Eds.), *Sexual deviance: Theory, assessment, and treatment* (pp. 465–490). New York, NY: Guilford.

Huntington's Disease Collaborative Research Group. (1993). A novel gene containing a trinucleotide repeat that is expanded and unstable on Huntington's disease chromosomes. *Cell, 72*, 971–983.

Huntjens, R. J., Peters, M., Woertman, L., Bovenschen, L., Loes, M., Martin, R., & Postma, A. (2006). Inter-identity amnesia in dissociative identity disorder: A simulated memory impairment? *Psychological Medicine, 36*, 857–863.

Huntjens, R. J., Postma, A., Hamaker, E. L., Woertman, L., van der Hart, O., & Peters, M. (2002). Perceptual and conceptual priming in patients with dissociative identity disorder. *Memory & Cognition, 30*, 1033–1043.

Huntjens, R. J., Postma, A., Peters, M., Woertman, L., & van der Hart, O. (2003). Interidentity amnesia for neutral, episodic information in dissociative identity disorder. *Abnormal Psychology*, 112, 290–297.

Huppert, J. D. (2009). Anxiety disorders and depression comorbidity. In M. M. Antony & M. B. Stein (Eds.), *Oxford handbook of anxiety and related disorders* (pp. 576–586). New York, NY: Oxford University Press.

Hurt, S. W., Schnurr, P. P., Severino, S. K., Freeman, E. W., Gise, L. H., Rivera-Tovar, A., & Steege, J. F. (1992). Late luteal phase dys-phoric disorder in 670 women evaluated for premenstrual complaints. *American Journal of Psychiatry, 149*(4), 525–530.

Hurt, E., & Arnold, L. E. (2015). Dietary management of ADHD. In R. A. Barkley (Ed.), *Attention-deficit hyperactivity disorder: A handbook for diagnosis & treatment* (4th ed., pp. 630–640). New York, NY: The Guilford Press.

Hutchinson, D. M., & Rapee, R. M. (2007). Do friends share similar body image and eating problems? The role of social networks and peer influences in early adolescence. *Behaviour Research and Therapy, 45*(7), 1557–1577.

Hyde, L. W., Shaw, D. S., & Hariri, A. R. (2013). Understanding youth antisocial behavior using neuroscience through a developmental psychopathology lens: review, integration, and directions for research. *Developmental Review, 33*(3), 168–223.

Hyman, S. E. (2009). How adversity gets under the skin. *Nature Neuroscience, 12*(3), 241–243.

Hyman, S. E. (2010). The diagnosis of mental disorders: The problem of reification. *Annual Review of Clinical Psychology, 6*, 155–179. doi:10.1146/annurev.clinpsy.3.022806.091532

Hypericum Depression Trial Study Group. (2002). Effect of *Hypericum perforatum* (St John's wort) in major depressive disorder: A randomized controlled trial. *JAMA: Journal of the American Medical Association, 287*, 1853–1854.

Iacono, W. G., Bassett, A. S., & Jones, B. D. (1988). Eye tracking dysfunction is associated with partial trisomy of chromosome 5 and schizophrenia. *Archives of General Psychiatry, 45*(12), 1140–1141.

Iacovino, J. M., Jackson, J. J., & Oltmanns, T. F. (2014). The relative impact of socioeconomic status and childhood trauma on Black-White differences in paranoid personality disorder symptoms. *Journal of Abnormal Psychology,123*(1), 225.

Ibanez-Casas, I., & Cervilla, J. A. (2012). Neuropsychological research in delusional disorder: A comprehensive review. *Psychopathology, 45*(2), 78–95.

Ikramuddin, S., & Livingston, E. H. (2013). New insights on bariatric surgery outcomes. *JAMA, 310*(22), 2401–2402.

Imhof, A., Kovari, E., von Gunten, A., Gold, G., Rivara, C.-B., Herrmann, F. R., & Giannakopoulos, P. (2007). Morphological substrates of cognitive decline in nonagenarians and centenarians: A new paradigm? *Journal of the Neurological Sciences, 257*(1–2), 72–79.

Ingoldsby, E. M., Shelleby, E., Lane, T., & Shaw, D. S. (2012). Extrafamilial contexts and children's conduct problems. In V. Maholmes & R. B. King (Eds.), *The Oxford handbook of poverty and child development* (pp. 404–422). New York, NY: Oxford University Press.

Ingram, R., Miranda, J., & Segal, Z. (2006). Cognitive vulnerability to depression. In L. B. Alloy and J. H. Riskind (Eds.)., *Cognitive vulnerability to emotional disorders* (pp. 63–91). Mahwah, NJ: Erlbaum.

Inouye, S. K., Westendorp, R. G., & Saczynski, J. S. (2014). Delirium in elderly people. *The Lancet, 383*(9920), 911–922.

Insel, T., Cuthbert, B., Garvey, M., Heinssen, R., Pine, D. S., Quinn, K., . . . Wang, P. (2010). Research domain criteria (RDoC): Toward a new classification framework for research on mental disorders. *American Journal of Psychiatry, 167*(7), 748–751. http://dx.doi.org/10.1176/appi.ajp.2010.09091379

Insel, T. R. (1992). Toward a neuroanatomy of obsessive-compulsive disorder. *Archives of General Psychiatry, 49*, 739–744.

Insel, T. R. (2006). Beyond efficacy: The STAR*D trial. *American Journal of Psychiatry, 163*, 5–7.

Insel, T. R. (2009). Translating scientific opportunity into public health impact: A strategic plan for research on mental illness. *Archives of General Psychiatry, 66*(2), 128–133.

Insel, T. R. (2014). The NIMH research domain criteria (RDoC) project: precision medicine for psychiatry. *American Journal of Psychiatry, 171*(4), 395–397.

Insel, T. R., Scanlan, J., Champoux, M., & Suomi, S. J. (1988). Rearing paradigm in a nonhuman primate affects response to B-CCE challenge. *Psychopharmacology, 96*, 81–86.

Institute of Medicine. (1999). *Reducing the burden of injury: Advancing prevention and treatment*. Washington, DC: National Academies Press.

Institute of Medicine. (2001). *Crossing the quality chasm: A new health system for the 21st century.* Washington, DC: National Academies Press.

Institute of Medicine. (2002). *Reducing suicide: A national imperative.* Washington, DC: National Academies Press.

IOM. (2011). *Clinical Practice Guidelines We Can Trust.* Washington, DC: The National Academies Press.

IOM. (2015). *Psychosocial interventions for mental and substance use disorders: A framework for establishing evidence-based standards.* Washington, DC: The National Academies Press.

Iribarren, C., Sidney, S., Bild, D. E., Liu, K., Markovitz, J. H., Roseman, J. M., & Matthews, K. (2000). Association of hostility with coronary artery calcification in young adults. *JAMA: Journal of the American Medical Association, 283*(19), 2546–2551.

Ironson, G., Taylor, C. B., Boltwood, M., Bartzokis, T., Dennis, C., Chesney, M., & Segal, G. M. (1992). Effects of anger on left ventricular ejection fraction in coronary artery disease. *American Journal of Cardiology, 70,* 281–285.

Isaacowitz, D., Smith, T. T., & Carstensen, L. L. (2003). Socioemotional selectivity, positive bias, and mental health among trauma survivors in old age. *Ageing International, 28,* 181–199.

Isenberg-Grzeda, E., Kutner, H. E., & Nicolson, S. E. (2012). Wernicke-Korsakoff-syndrome: Under-recognized and under-treated. *Psychosomatics, 53*(6), 507–516. doi: http: //dx.doi.org/10.1016/j.psym.2012.04.008

Ito, K., Corrigan, B., Zhao, Q., French, J., Miller, R., Soares, H., . . . Fullerton, T. (2011). Disease progression model for cognitive deterioration from Alzheimer's Disease Neuroimaging Initiative database. *Alzheimer's & Dementia, 7*(2), 151–160.

Ivanov, I. (2009). Disulfiram and acamprosate. In B. J. Sadock, V. A. Sadock, & P. Ruiz (Eds.), *Kaplan & Sadock's comprehensive textbook of psychiatry* (9th ed., Vol. II, pp. 3099–3105). Philadelphia, PA: Lippincott Williams & Wilkins.

Iverson, L. (2006). Neurotransmitter transporters and their impact on the development of psychopharmacology. *British Journal of Pharmacology, 147*(Suppl. 1), S82–S88.

Ivleva, E. I., Moates, A. F., Hamm, J. P., Bernstein, I. H., O'Neill, H. B., Cole, D., . . . Tamminga, C. A. (2014). Smooth pursuit eye movement, prepulse inhibition, and auditory paired stimuli processing endophenotypes across the schizophrenia-bipolar disorder psychosis dimension. *Schizophrenia Bulletin, 40*(3), 642–652.

Izard, C. E. (1992). Basic emotions, relations among emotions, and emotion–cognition relations. *Psychological Review, 99*(3), 561–565.

Jääskeläinen, E., Juola, P., Hirvonen, N., McGrath, J. J., Saha, S., Isohanni, M., . . . Miettunen, J. (2013). A systematic review and meta-analysis of recovery in schizophrenia. *Schizophrenia Bulletin, 39*(6), 1296–1306.

Jablensky, A. (2012). Epidemiology of schizophrenia. In M. G. Gelder, N. C. Andreasen,

J.J. Lopez-Ibor, Jr., & J. R. Geddes (Eds.), *New Oxford Textbook of Psychiatry* (2nd. ed., Vol. 1, pp. 540–553). New York, NY: Oxford University Press.

Jackson, C., Brown, J. D., & L'Engle, K. L. (2007). R-rated movies, bedroom televisions, and initiation of smoking by white and black adolescents. *Archives of Pediatrics & Adolescent Medicine, 161,* 260–268.

Jackson, G., Rosen, R., Kloner, R., & Kostis, J. (2006). The second Princeton consensus on sexual dysfunction and cardiac risk: New guidelines for sexual medicine. *Journal of Sexual Medicine, 3*(1), 28–36.

Jackson, J. S., Knight, K. M., & Rafferty, J. A. (2010). Race and unhealthy behaviors: Chronic stress, the HPA axis, and physical and mental health disparities over the life course. *American Journal of Public Health, 100*(5), 933–939. doi: 10.2105/AJPH.2008.143446

Jackson, T., & Chen, H. (2011). Risk factors for disordered eating during early and middle adolescence: Prospective evidence from mainland Chinese boys and girls. *Journal of Abnormal Psychology, 120*(2), 454–464.

Jackson v. Indiana, 406 U.S. 715 (1972). Jacobi, W., & Winkler, H. (1927). Encephalographische studien an chronischen schizophrenen. *Archives fur Psychiarrie und Nervenkrunkheiten, 81*(1), 299–332.

Jacobson, N. S., Dobson, K. S., Truax, P. A., Addis, M. E., Koerner, K., Gollan, J. K., & Prince, S. E. (1996). A component analysis of cognitive-behavioral treatment for depression. *Journal of Consulting and Clinical Psychology, 64,* 295–304.

Jacobson, N. S., Fruzzetti, A. E., Dobson, K., Whisman, M., & Hops, H. (1993). Couple therapy as a treatment for depression: II. The effects of relationship quality and therapy on depressive relapse. *Journal of Consulting and Clinical Psychology, 61*(3), 516–519.

Jacobson, N. S., Martell, C. R., & Dimidjian, S. (2001). Behavioral activation treatment for depression: Returning to contextual roots. *Clinical Psychology: Science and Practice, 8*(3), 255–270.

Jacobsen, P. B., & Andrykowski, M. A. (2015). Tertiary prevention in cancer care: Understanding and addressing the psychological dimensions of cancer during the active treatment period. *American Psychologist, 70*(2), 134–145.

Jaffe, J. H., Rawson, R. A., & Ling, W. (2005). Cocaine-related disorders. In B. J. Sadock & V. A. Sadock (Eds.), *Kaplan & Sadock's comprehensive textbook of psychiatry* (8th ed., pp. 1220–1238). Philadelphia, PA: Lippincott, Williams & Wilkins.

Jaffee, S. (2011). Genotype-environment correlations: Definitions, methods of measurement, and implications for research on adolescent psychopathology. In K. S. Kendler, S. Jaffee, & D. Romer (Eds.), *The dynamic genome and mental health: The role of genes and environments in youth development* (pp. 79–102). New York, NY: Oxford University Press.

Jager, G. (2012). Cannabis. In J. C. Verster, J. Brady, M. Galanter, & P. Conrod (Eds.), *Drug abuse and addiction in medical illness* (pp. 151–162). New York, NY: Springer.

Jain, K. K. (2015). Personalized management of psychiatric disorders. In K. K. Jain (Ed.), *Textbook of personalized medicine* (2nd ed., pp. 461–478). New York, NY: Springer.

Jakicic, J. M., Tate, D. F., Lang, W., Davis, K. K., Polzien, K., Rickman, A. D., & Finkelstein, E. A. (2012). Effect of a stepped-care intervention approach on weight loss in adults: A randomized clinical trial. *JAMA: Journal of the American Medical Association, 307*(24), 2617–2626.

James, B. O., Jenkins, R., & Lawani, A. O. (2012). Depression in primary care: the knowledge, attitudes and practice of general practitioners in Benin City, Nigeria. *South African Family Practice, 54*(1), 55–60.

James, P. A., Oparil, S., Carter, B. L., Cushman, W. C., Dennison-Himmelfarb, C., Handler, J., Lackland, D. T., . . . Ortiz, E. (2014). 2014 evidence-based guideline for the management of high blood pressure in adults: report from the panel members appointed to the Eighth Joint National Committee (JNC 8). *JAMA, 311*(5), 507–520.

Jamison, K. R. (1989). Mood disorders and patterns of creativity in British writers and artists. *Psychiatry, 52*(2), 125–134.

Jamison, K. R. (1993). *Touched with fire: Manic depressive illness and the artistic temperament.* New York, NY: Macmillan.

Jamison, R. N., & Virts, K. L. (1990). The influence of family support on chronic pain. *Behaviour Research and Therapy, 28*(4), 283–287.

Jang, K. L. (2005). *The behavioral genetics of psychopathology: A clinical guide.* Mahwah, NJ: Lawrence Erlbaum Associates.

Jang, S. H., Kim, D. I., & Choi, M. S. (2014). Effects and treatment methods of acupuncture and herbal medicine for premenstrual syndrome/premenstrual dysphoric disorder: systematic review. *BMC Complementary and Alternative Medicine, 14*(1), 11. doi:10.1186/1472-6882-14-11

Jannini, E. A., Burri, A., Jern, P., & Novelli, G. (2015). Genetics of human sexual behavior: Where we are, where we are going. *Sexual Medicine Reviews, 3*(2), 65–77.

Jansen, A. G., Mous, S. E., White, T., Posthuma, D., & Polderman, T. J. (2015). What twin studies tell us about the heritability of brain development, morphology, and function: A review. *Neuropsychology Review, 25*(1), 27–46.

Janszky, I., Ahnve, S., Lundberg, I., & Hemmingsson, T. (2010). Early-onset depression, anxiety, and risk of subsequent coronary heart disease: 37-year follow-up of 49,321 young Swedish men. *Journal of the American College of Cardiology, 56*(1), 31–37.

Jarrett, R. B., Minhajuddin, A., Gershenfeld, H., Friedman, E. S., & Thase, M. E. (2013). Preventing depressive relapse and recurrence in higher-risk cognitive therapy responders: a randomized trial of continuation phase cognitive therapy, fluoxetine, or matched pill placebo. *JAMA Psychiatry, 70,* 1152–1160.

Jason, L. A., Fennell, P. A., & Taylor, R. R. (2003). *Handbook of chronic fatigue syndrome.* Hoboken, NJ: Wiley.

Jason, L. A., Richman, J. A., Rademaker, A. W., Jordan, K. M., Plioplys, A. V., Taylor, R. R., & Plioplys, S. (1999). A community-based study of chronic fatigue syndrome. *Archives of Internal Medicine, 159*, 2129–2137.

Jason, L. A., Roesner, N., Porter, N., Parenti, B., Mortensen, J., & Till, L. (2010). Provision of social support to individuals with chronic fatigue syndrome. *Journal of Clinical Psychology, 66*, 249–258.

Jaspers, K. (1963). *General psychopathology* (J. Hoenig & M. W. Hamilton, Trans.). Manchester, UK: Manchester University Press.

Jaussent, I., Dauvilliers, Y., Ancelin, M. L., Dartigues, J. F., Tavernier, B., Touchon, J., & Besset, A. (2011). Insomnia symptoms in older adults: Associated factors and gender differences. *The American Journal of Geriatric Psychiatry, 19*(1), 88.

Javitt, D. C., & Laruelle, M. (2006). Neuro-chemical theories. In J. A. Lieberman, T. S. Stroup, & D. O. Perkins (Eds.), *The American Psychiatric Publishing textbook of schizophrenia* (pp. 85–116). Washington, DC: American Psychiatric Publishing.

Javitt, D. C., & Zukin, S. R. (2009). Phencyclidine (or phencyclidine-like)-related disorders. In B. J. Sadock, V. A. Sadock, & P. Ruiz (Eds.), *Kaplan & Sadock's comprehensive textbook of psychiatry* (9th ed., Vol. I, pp. 1337–1397). Philadelphia, PA: Lippincott Williams & Wilkins.

Jellinek, E. M. (1946). Phases in the drinking histories of alcoholics. *Quarterly Journal of Studies on Alcohol, 7*, 1–88.

Jellinek, E. M. (1952). Phases of alcohol addiction. *Quarterly Journal of Studies on Alcohol, 13*, 673–684.

Jellinek, E. M. (1960). *The disease concept of alcohol*. New Brunswick, NJ: Hillhouse Press.

Jenike, M. A., Baer, L., Ballantine, H. T., Martuza, R. L., Tynes, S., Giriunas, I., & Cassem, N. H. (1991). Cingulotomy for refractory obsessive-compulsive disorder: A long-term follow-up of 33 patients. *Archives of General Psychiatry, 48*, 548–555.

Jenkins, J. H., & Karno, M. (1992). The meaning of expressed emotion: Theoretical issues raised by cross-cultural research. *American Journal of Psychiatry, 149*, 9–21.

Jenni, O. G., & O'Connor, B. B. (2005). Children's sleep: An interplay between culture and biology. *Pediatrics, 115*(1), 204–216. doi: 10.1542/peds.2004-0815B

Jennings, W. G., & Reingle, J. M. (2012). On the number and shape of developmental/life-course violence, aggression, and delinquency trajectories: A state-of-the-art review. *Journal of Criminal Justice, 40*(6), 472–489.

Jensen, E., Schmidt, E., Pedersen, B., & Dahl, R. (1991). Effect on smoking cessation of silver acetate, nicotine and ordinary chewing gum. *Psychopharmacology, 104*(4), 470–474.

Jensen, H. M., Gron, R., Lidegaard, O., Pedersen, L. H., Andersen, P. K., & Kessing, L. V. (2013). Maternal depression, antidepressant use in pregnancy and Apgar scores in infants. *British Journal of Psychiatry, 202*(5), 347–351.

Jensen, P. S., Hinshaw, S. P., Swanson, J. M., Greenhill, L. L., Conners, C. K., Arnold, L. E., & Wigal, T. (2001). Findings from the NIMH Multimodal Treatment Study of ADHD (MTA): Implications and applications for primary care providers. *Journal of Developmental and Behavioral Pediatrics, 22*(1), 60–73.

Jiang, W., Samad, Z., Boyle, S., Becker, R. C., Williams, R., Kuhn, C., & Velazquez, E. J. (2013). Prevalence and clinical characteristics of mental stress-induced myocardial ischemia in patients with coronary heart disease. *Journal of the American College of Cardiology, 61*(7), 714–722.

Jiann, B. P., Su, C. C., Yu, C. C., Wu, T. T., & Huang, J. K. (2009). Risk factors for individual domains of female sexual function. *The Journal of Sexual Medicine, 6*(12), 3364–3375.

Jilek, W. G. (1982). Altered states of consciousness in North American Indian ceremonials. *Ethos, 10*(4), 326–343.

Jindal, R. D., Thase, M. E., Fasiczka, A. L., Friedman, E. S., Buysse, D. J., Frank, E., & Kupfer, D.J. (2002). Electroencephalographic sleep profiles in single-episode and recurrent unipolar forms of major depression: II. Comparison during remission. *Biological Psychiatry, 1*, 230–236.

Jockin, V., McGue, M., & Lykken, D. T. (1996). Personality and divorce: A genetic analysis. *Journal of Personality and Social Psychology, 71*, 288–299.

Joe, S., Baser, R., Breeden, G., Neighbors, H., & Jackson, J. (2006). Prevalence of and risk factors for lifetime suicide attempts among blacks in the United States. *JAMA: Journal of the American Medical Association, 296*, 2112–2123.

Johannes, C. B., Araujo, A. B., Feldman, H. A., Derby, C. A., Kleinman, K. P., & McKinlay, J. B. (2000). Incidence of erectile dysfunction in men 40 to 69 years old: Longitudinal results from the Massachusetts male aging study. *Journal of Urology, 163*, 460–463.

Johansson, A., Sundbom, E., Höjerback, T., & Bodlund, O. (2010). A five-year follow-up study of Swedish adults with gender identity disorder. *Archives of Sexual Behavior, 39*(6), 1429–1437.

Johnson, A. M., Mercer, C. H., Erens, B., Copas, A. J., McManus, S., Wellings, K., & Field, J. (2001). Sexual behaviour in Britain: Partnerships, practices, and HIV risk behaviours. *The Lancet, 358*, 1835–1842.

Johnson, A. M., Wadsworth, J., Wellings, K., Bradshaw, S., & Field, J. (1992). Sexual lifestyles and HIV risk. *Nature, 360*, 410–412.

Johnson, C. J., & Beitchman, J. H. (2005). Expressive language disorder. In B. J. Sadock & V. A. Sadock (Eds.), *Kaplan & Sadock's comprehensive textbook of psychiatry* (pp. 3136–3142). Philadelphia, PA: Lippincott, Williams & Wilkins.

Johnson, J. G., Cohen, P., Kasen, S., & Brook, J. S. (2002). Eating disorders during adolescence and the risk for physical and mental disorders during early adulthood. *Archives of General Psychiatry, 59*, 545–552.

Johnson, J. G., Cohen, P., Kasen, S., & Brook, J. S. (2006). Dissociative disorders among adults in the community, impaired functioning, and Axis I and Axis II comorbidity. *Journal of Psychiatric Research, 40*, 131–140.

Johnson, J. G., Cohen, P., Pine, D. S., Klein, D. F., Kasen, S., & Brook, J. S. (2000). Association between cigarette smoking and anxiety disorders during adolescence and early adulthood. *JAMA: Journal of the American Medical Association, 284*, 2348–2351.

Johnson, J. G., Weissman, M. M., & Klerman, G. L. (1990). Panic disorder, comorbidity and suicide attempts. *Archives of General Psychiatry, 47*, 805–808.

Johnson, R., Persad, G., & Sisti, D. (2014). The Tarasoff rule: The implications of interstate variation and gaps in professional training. *Journal of the American Academy of Psychiatry and the Law Online, 42*(4), 469–477.

Johnson, S. L., & Miller, I. (1997). Negative life events and time to recovery from episodes of bipolar disorder. *Journal of Abnormal Psychology, 106*(3), 449–457.

Johnson, S. L., Cuellar, A. K., & Miller, C. (2009). Bipolar and unipolar depression: A comparison of clinical phenomenology, biological vulnerability, and psychosocial predictors. In I. H. Gotlib & C. L. Hammen (Eds.), *Handbook of depression* (2nd ed., pp. 142–162). New York, NY: Guilford.

Johnson, S. L., Cuellar, A. K., Ruggero, C., Winett-Perlman, C., Goodnick, P., White, R., & Miller, I. (2008). Life events as predictors of mania and depression in bipolar I disorder. *Journal of Abnormal Psychology, 117*(2), 268–277.

Johnson, S. L., Gruber, J. L., & Eisner, L. R. (2007). Emotion and bipolar disorder. In J. Rottenberg & S. L. Johnson (Eds.), *Emotion and psychopathology* (pp. 123–150). Washington, DC: American Psychological Association.

Johnson, S. L., Winett, C. A., Meyer, B., Greenhouse, W. J., & Miller, I. (1999). Social support and the course of bipolar disorder. *American Psychological Association, 180*(4), 558–566.

Johnson, W., Turkheimer, E., Gottesman, I. I., & Bouchard, T. J., Jr. (2009). Beyond heritability: Twin studies in behavioral research. *Current Directions in Psychological Science, 18*(4), 217–220.

Johnston, B. C., Kanters, S., Bandayrel, K., Wu, P., Naji, F., Siemieniuk, R. A., . . . Mills, E. J. (2014). Comparison of weight loss among named diet programs in overweight and obese adults: A meta-analysis. *JAMA, 312*(9), 923–933.

Johnston, C. A., Rost, S., Miller-Kovach, K., Moreno, J. P., & Foreyt, J. P. (2013). Multi-component access to a commercially available weight loss program: A randomized controlled trial. *The FASEB Journal, 27*(1_MeetingAbstracts), 851–852.

Johnston, L. D., O'Malley, P. M., Bachman, J. G., & Schulenberg, J. E. (2012). *Monitoring the future: National survey results on drug use, 1975-2011. Volume II: College Students & Adults Ages 19-50.* Ann Arbor MI: Institute for Social Research, University of Michigan.

Joiner, T., Kalafat, J., Draper, J., Stokes, H., Knudson, M., Berman, A. L., & McKeon, R. (2007). Establishing standards for the assessment of suicide risk among callers to the national suicide prevention lifeline. *Suicide and Life-Threatening Behavior, 37*(3), 353–365.

Joiner, T. E., Jr. (1997). Shyness and low social support as interactive diatheses, with loneliness as mediator: Testing an interpersonal– personality view of vulnerability to depressive symptoms. *Journal of Abnormal Psychology, 106*(3), 386–394.

Joiner, T. E. (2014). *The perversion of virtue: Understanding murder-suicide.* New York, NY: Oxford University Press.

Joiner, T. E., Jr. (1999). A test of interpersonal theory of depression in youth psychiatric inpatients. *Journal of Abnormal Child Psychology, 27*(1), 77–85.

Joiner, T. E., Jr., & Rudd, M. D. (1996). Toward a categorization of depression-related psychological constructs. *Cognitive Therapy and Research, 20*, 51–68.

Joiner, T. E., Jr., & Rudd, M. D. (2000). Intensity and duration of suicidal crises vary as a function of previous suicide attempts and negative life events. *Journal of Consulting and Clinical Psychology, 68*(5), 909–916.

Joiner, T. E., Jr., & Timmons, K. A. (2009). Depression in its interpersonal context. In I. H. Gotlib & C. L. Hammen (Eds.), *Handbook of depression* (2nd ed., pp. 322–339). New York, NY: Guilford.

Joiner, T. E., Jr., Heatherton, T. F., & Keel, P. K. (1997). Ten year stability and predictive validity of five bulimia-related indicators. *American Journal of Psychiatry, 154*, 1133–1138.

Joling, K. J., van Marwijk, H. W., Veldhuijzen, A. E., van der Horst, H. E., Scheltens, P., Smit, F., & van Hout, H. P. (2015). The two-year incidence of depression and anxiety disorders in spousal caregivers of persons with dementia: who is at the greatest risk? *The American Journal of Geriatric Psychiatry, 23*(3), 293–303.

Jones, B. E., & Gray, B. A. (1986). Problems in diagnosing schizophrenia and affective disorders in blacks. *Hospital and Community Psychiatry, 37*, 61–65.

Jones, J. C., & Barlow, D. H. (1990). The etiology of posttraumatic stress disorder. *Clinical Psychology Review, 10*, 299–328.

Jones, P., Barnes, T., Davies, L., Dunn, G., Lloyd, H., Hayhurst, K., & Lewis, S. W. (2006). Randomized controlled trial of the effect on quality of life of second-vs first-generation antipsychotic drugs in schizophrenia: Cost Utility of the Latest Antipsychotic Drugs in Schizophrenia Study (CUtLASS 1). *Archives of General Psychiatry, 63*(10), 1079.

Jones, R. T. (2009). Hallucinogen-related disorders. In B. J. Sadock, V. A. Sadock, & P. Ruiz (Eds.), *Kaplan & Sadock's comprehensive textbook of psychiatry* (9th ed., Vol. I, pp. 1331–1340). Philadelphia, PA: Lippincott Williams & Wilkins.

Joo, E. Y., Yoon, C. W., Koo, D. L., Kim, D., & Hong, S. B. (2012). Adverse effects of 24 hours of sleep deprivation on cognition and stress hormones. *Journal of Clinical Neurology, 8*(2), 146–150.

Joormann, J. (2009). Cognitive aspects of depression. In I. H. Gotlib & C. L. Hammen (Eds.), *Handbook of depression* (2nd ed., pp. 298–321). New York, NY: Guilford.

Jordan, B. D., Relkin, N. R., Ravdin, L. D., Jacobs, A. R., Bennett, A., & Gandy, S. (1997). Apolipoprotein E Epsilon 4 associated with chronic traumatic brain injury in boxing. *JAMA: Journal of the American Medical Association, 278*, 136–140.

Joyce, P. R., Stephenson, J., Kennedy, M., Mulder, R. T., & McHugh, P. C. (2013). The presence of both serotonin 1A receptor (HTR1A) and dopamine transporter (DAT1) gene variants increase the risk of borderline personality disorder. *Frontiers in Genetics, 4*, 313.

Joyner, M. J., Charkoudian, N., & Wallin, B. G. (2010). Sympathetic nervous system and blood pressure in humans: Individualized patterns of regulation and their implications. *Hypertension, 56*(1), 10–16.

Judd, L. L. (2000). Course and chronicity of unipolar major depressive disorder: Commentary on Joiner. *Child Psychology Science and Practice, 7*(2), 219–223.

Judd, L. L. (2012). Dimensional paradigm of the long-term course of unipolar major depressive disorder. *Depression and Anxiety, 29*(3), 167–171.

Judd, L. L., Akiskal, H., Schettler, P., Coryell, W., Endicott, J., Maser, J., & Keller, M. B. (2003). A prospective investigation of the natural history of the long-term weekly symptomatic status of bipolar II disorder. *Archives of General Psychiatry, 60*, 261–269.

Judge, B., & Rusyniak, D. (2009). Illicit drugs I: Amphetamines. In M. R. Dobbs (Ed.), *Clinical neurotoxicology: Syndromes, substances, environments, expert consult* (pp. 303–313). Philadelphia, PA: WB Saunders.

Judge, C., O'Donovan, C., Callaghan, G., Gaoatswe, G., & O'Shea, D. (2014). Gender dysphoria–prevalence and co-morbidities in an Irish adult population. *Frontiers in Endocrinology, 5*(87), 1–5.

Juliano, L. M., Ferré, S. & Griffiths, R. R. (2015). Tha pharmacology of caffeine. In R. K. Ries, D.A. Fiellin, S. C. Miller, & R. Saitz (Eds.), *The ASAM principles of addiction medicine* (5th Ed., pp. 180–200). New York, NY: Wolters Kluwer.

Jummani, R., & Coffey, B. J. (2009). Tic disorders. In B. J. Sadock, V. A. Sadock, & P. Ruiz (Eds.), *Kaplan & Sadock's comprehensive textbook of psychiatry* (9th ed., Vol. II, pp. 3609–3623). Philadelphia, PA: Lippincott Williams & Wilkins.

Junginger, J. (1997). Fetishism: Assessment and treatment. In D. R. Laws & W. O'Donohue (Eds.), *Sexual deviance: Theory, assessment and treatment* (pp. 92–110). New York, NY: Guilford.

Kafka, M. P. (2010). The DSM diagnostic criteria for fetishism. *Archives of sexual behavior, 39*(2), 357–362.

Kafka, M. P., & Hennen, J. (2003). Hypersexual desire in males: Are males with paraphilias difference from males with paraphilia-related disorders? *Sexual Abuse: A Journal of Research & Treatment, 4*, 307–321.

Kagan, J. (2014a). Temperamental contributions to the development of psychological profiles: Basic issues. In S. G. Hofmann and P. D. DiBartolo (Eds.), *Social anxiety: Clinical, developmental, and social perspectives (third edition)* (pp. 377–418). Amsterdam, The Netherlands: Elsevier/Academic Press.

Kagan, J. (2014b). Temperamental contributions to the development of psychological profiles: I. Two candidates. In S. G. Hofmann and P. D. DiBartolo (Eds.), *Social anxiety: Clinical, developmental, and social perspectives (third edition)* (pp. 419–450). Amsterdam, The Netherlands: Elsevier/Academic Press.

Kahler, C. W., Litvin Bloom, E., Leventhal, A. M. & Brown, R. A. (2015). Behavioral interventions in smoking cessation. In R. K. Ries, D. A. Fiellin, S. C. Miller, & R. Saitz (Eds.), *The ASAM principles of addiction medicine* (5th Ed., pp. 894–911). New York, NY: Wolters Kluwer.

Kahn, R. S., Khoury, J., Nichols, W. C., & Lanphear, B. P. (2003). Role of dopamine transporter genotype and maternal prenatal smoking in childhood hyperactive-impulsive, inattentive, and oppositional behaviors. *The Journal of Pediatrics, 143*(1), 104–110.

Khan, S., King, A. P., Abelson, J. L., & Liberzon, I. (2009). Neuroendocrinology of anxiety disorders. In M. M. Antony & M. B. Stein (Eds.), *Oxford handbook of anxiety and related disorders* (pp. 111–122). New York: Oxford University Press.

Kaiser, J. (2006). Differences in immune cell "brakes" may explain chimp–human split on AIDS. *Science Magazine, 312*, 672–673.

Kalaria, R., Maestre, G., Arizaga, R., Friedland, R., Galasko, D., Hall, K., & Potocnik, F. (2008). Alzheimer's disease and vascular dementia in developing countries: Prevalence, management, and risk factors. *Lancet Neurology, 7*(9), 812.

Kalat, J. W. (2013). *Biological psychology* (11th ed.). Belmont, CA: Wadsworth, Cengage Learning.

Kalivas, P. W. (2005). New directions pharmacotherapy for addiction or can we forget to be addicted? *Clinical Neuroscience Research, 5*, 147–150.

Kallmann, F. J. (1938). *The genetics of schizophrenia.* New York, NY: Augustin.

Kalra, G., Christodoulou, G., Jenkins, R., Tsipas, V., Christodoulou, N., Lecic-Tosevski, D., . . . Bhugra, D. (2012). Mental health promotion: guidance and strategies. *European Psychiatry, 27*(2), 81–86. doi:10.1016/j.eurpsy.2011.10.001

Kame'enui, E. J., Fien, H., & Korgesaar, J. (2013). Direct instruction as *eo nomine* and contronym: Why the right words and the details matter. In H. L. Swanson, K. R. Harris, & S. Graham (Eds.), *Handbook of learning disabilities* (2nd ed.). New York, NY: Guilford.

Kamen, C., Tejani, M. A., Chandwani, K., Janelsins, M., Peoples, A. R., Roscoe, J. A., & Morrow, G. R. (2014). Anticipatory nausea and vomiting due to chemotherapy. *European Journal of Pharmacology, 722*, 172–179.

Kaminski, J. W., Valle, L., Filene, J., & Boyle, C. (2008). A meta-analytic review of components associated with parent training program effectiveness. *Journal of Abnormal Child Psychology, 36*(4), 567–589.

Kanai, R., Bahrami, B., Roylance, R., & Rees, G. (2012). Online social network size is reflected in human brain structure. *Proceedings of the Royal Society: Biological Sciences, 279*(1732), 1327–1334. doi: 10.1098/rspb.2011.1959

Kanaya, T., & Ceci, S. (2012). The impact of the Flynn effect on LD diagnoses in special education. *Journal of Learning Disabilities, 45*(4), 319–326. doi: 10.1177/0022219410392044

Kanaya, T., Scullin, M. H., & Ceci, S. J. (2003). The Flynn effect and U.S. policies: The impact of rising IQ scores on American society via mental retardation diagnoses. *American Psychologist, 58,* 778–790.

Kanayama, G., Barry, S., & Pope, H. G. (2006). Body image and attitudes toward male roles in anabolic–androgenic steroid users. *American Journal of Psychiatry, 163,* 697–703.

Kandel, E. R., Schwartz, J., & Jessell, T. M. (2000). *Principles of neural science* (4th ed.). New York, NY: McGraw-Hill.

Kane, J. M., Stroup, S., & Marder, S. R. (2009). Schizophrenia: Pharmacological treatment. In B. J. Sadock, V. A. Sadock, & P. Ruiz (Eds.), *Kaplan & Sadock's comprehensive textbook of psychiatry* (9th ed., Vol. I, pp. 1547–1556). Philadelphia, PA: Lippincott Williams & Wilkins.

Kanigel, R. (1988, October/November). Nicotine becomes addictive. *Science Illustrated, 2,* 19–21.

Kanner, L. (1943). Autistic disturbances of affective contact. *Nervous Child, 2,* 217–250.

Kanner, L. (1949). Problems of nosology and psychodynamics of early infantile autism. *American Journal of Orthopsychiatry, 19,* 416–426.

Kanner, L., & Eisenberg, L. (1955). Notes on the follow-up studies of autistic children. In P. H. J. Zubin (Ed.), *Psychopathology of childhood* (pp. 227–239). New York, NY: Grune & Stratton.

Kansas v. Hendricks, 117 S. Ct. 2072 (1997).

Kaplan, H. S. (1979). *Disorders of sexual desire.* New York, NY: Brunner/Mazel.

Kaplan, M. (1983). A woman's view of DSM-III. *American Psychologist, 38,* 786–792.

Kaplan, S. A., Reis, R. B., Kohn, I. J., Ikeguchi, E. F., Laor, E., Te, A. E., & Martins, A. C. (1999). Safety and efficacy of sildenafil in postmenopausal women with sexual dysfunction. *Urology, 53,* 481–486.

Kaptchuk, T. J., Kelley, J. M., Conboy, L. A., Davis, R. B., Kerr, C. E., & Lembo, A. J. (2008). Components of placebo effect: Randomised controlled trial in patients with irritable bowel syndrome. *BMJ, 336*(7651), 999–1003. doi: 10.1136/bmj.39524.439618.25

Kariuki-Nyuthe, C. & Stein, D. J. (2015). Anxiety and related disorders and physical illness. *Key Issues in Mental Health, 179,* 81–97.

Karg, K., Burmeister, M., Shedden, K., & Sen, S. (2011). The serotonin transporter promoter variant (5-HTTLPR), stress, and depression meta-analysis revisited: Evidence of genetic moderation. *Archives of General Psychiatry, 68*(5), 444–454. doi: 10.1001/archgenpsychiatry.2010.189

Karkhaneh, M., Clark, B., Ospina, M. B., Seida, J. C., Smith, V., & Hartling, L. (2010). Social Stories™ to improve social skills in children with autism spectrum disorder. *Autism, 14*(6), 641–662. doi: 10.1177/1362361310373057

Karlin, B. E., Trockel, M., Spira, A. P., Taylor, C. B., & Manber, R. (2015). National evaluation of the effectiveness of cognitive behavioral therapy for insomnia among older versus younger veterans. *International Journal of Geriatric Psychiatry, 30*(3), 308–315.

Kasari, C., Gulsrud, A., Freeman, S., Paparella, T., & Hellemann, G. (2012). Longitudinal follow-up of children with autism receiving targeted interventions on joint attention and play. *Journal of the American Academy of Child & Adolescent Psychiatry, 51*(5), 487–495. doi: http://dx.doi.org/10.1016/j.jaac.2012.02.019

Kasen, S., Cohen, P., Skodol, A. E., Johnson, J. G., & Brook, J. S. (1999). Influence of child and adolescent psychiatric disorders on young adult personality disorder. *American Journal of Psychiatry, 156*(10), 1529–1535.

Kasindorf, J. (1988, May 2). The real story of Billie Boggs: Was Koch right—Or the civil libertarians? *New York,* pp. 36–44.

Kaski, M. (2012). Aetiology of intellectual disability: General issues and prevention. In M. G. Gelder, N. C. Andreasen, J. J. Lopez-Ibor, Jr., & J. R. Geddes (Eds.), *New Oxford textbook of psychiatry* (2nd. ed., Vol. 2, pp. 1830–1837). New York, NY: Oxford University Press.

Kaslow, N. J., Davis, S. P., & Smith, C. O. (2009). Biological and psychosocial interventions for depression in children and adolescents. In I. H. Gotlib & C. L. Hammen (Eds.), *Handbook of depression* (2nd ed., pp. 642–672). New York, NY: Guilford.

Kass, A. E., Trockel, M., Safer, D. L., Sinton, M. M., Cunning, D., Rizk, M. T., . . . Taylor, C. B. (2014). Internet-based preventive intervention for reducing eating disorder risk: A randomized controlled trial comparing guided with unguided self-help. *Behaviour Research and Therapy, 63,* 90–98.

Kass, D. J., Silvers, F. M., & Abrams, G. M. (1972). Behavioral group treatment of hysteria. *Archives of General Psychiatry, 26,* 42–50. Kato, K., Sullivan, P., Evengard, B., & Pederson, N. (2006). Premorbid predictors of chronic fatigue. *Archives of General Psychiatry, 63,* 1267–1272.

Katon, W. (1993). Somatization disorder, hypochondriasis, and conversion disorder. In D. L. Dunner (Ed.), *Current psychiatric therapy* (pp. 314–320). Philadelphia, PA: W. B. Saunders.

Katon, W. J. (2003). Clinical and health services relationships between major depression, depressive symptoms, and general medical illness. *Biological Psychiatry, 54,* 216–226.

Katz, I. R. (1993). Delirium. In D. L. Dunner (Ed.), *Current psychiatric therapy* (pp. 65–73). Philadelphia, PA: W. B Saunders.

Katz, J., & Gagliese, L. (1999). Phantom limb pain: A continuing puzzle. In R. J. Gatchel & D. C. Turk (Eds.), *Psychosocial factors in pain: Critical perspectives* (pp. 284–300). New York, NY: Guilford.

Katz, M., DeRogatis, L. R., Ackerman, R., Hedges, P., Lesko, L., Garcia, M. J., & Sand, M. (2013). Efficacy of flibanserin in women with hypoactive sexual desire disorder: Results from the BEGONIA trial. *Journal Of Sexual Medicine, 10,* 1807–1815. doi:10.1111/jsm.12189

Katz, M. J., Lipton, R. B., Hall, C. B., Zimmerman, M. E., Sanders, A. E., Verghese, J., & Derby, C. A. (2012). Age-specific and sex-specific prevalence and incidence of mild cognitive impairment, dementia, and Alzheimer dementia in blacks and whites: A report from the Einstein Aging Study. *Alzheimer Disease & Associated Disorders, 26*(4), 335–343. doi: 310.1097/WAD.1090b1013e31823dbcfc

Kaufman, C. E., Beals, J., Croy, C., Jiang, L., Novins, D. K., & The AI-SUPERPFP Team (2013). Multilevel context of depression in two American Indian tribes. *Journal of Consulting and Clinical Psychology, 81,* 1040–1051.

Kaufman, J. C. (2001). The Sylvia Plath effect: Mental illness in eminent creative writers. *The Journal of Creative Behavior, 35,* 37–50.

Kaufman, J. C. (2002). Creativity and confidence: Price of achievement. *American Psychologist, 57,* 375–376.

Kaufman, J. C., & Baer, J. (2002). I bask in dreams of suicide: Mental illness, poetry, and women. *Review of General Psychology, 6,* 271–286.

Kavale, K. A., & Forness, S. R. (1983). Hyperactivity and diet treatment: A meta-analysis of the Feingold hypothesis. *Journal of Learning Disabilities, 16,* 324–330.

Kavanagh, D. J. (1992). Recent developments in expressed emotion and schizophrenia. *British Journal of Psychiatry, 160,* 601–620.

Kay, C., & Green, J. (2013). Reactive attachment disorder following early maltreatment: Systematic evidence beyond the institution. *Journal of Abnormal Child Psychology, 41*(4), 571–586. doi: 10.1007/s10802-012-9705-9

Kaye, W. (2008). Neurobiology of anorexia and bulimia nervosa. *Physiology and Behavior, 94*(1), 121–135.

Kaye, W. H., Bulik, C. M., Thornton, L., Barbarich, N., Masters, K., & Price Foundation Collaborative Group. (2014). Comorbidity of anxiety disorders with anorexia and bulimia nervosa. *American Journal of Psychiatry, 161*(12), 2215–2221.

Kaye, W. H., Weltzin, T. E., Hsu, L. K. G., McConaha, C. W., & Bolton, B. (1993). Amount of calories retained after binge eating and vomiting. *American Journal of Psychiatry, 150*(6), 969–971.

Kazak, A. E., & Noll, R. B. (2015). The integration of psychology in pediatric oncology research and practice: Collaboration to improve care and outcomes for children and families. *American Psychologist, 70*(2), 146–158.

Kazak, A. E., Boeving, C. A., Alderfer, M. A., Hwang, W., & Reilly, A. (2005). Posttraumatic stress symptoms during treatment in parents of children with cancer. *Journal of Clinical Oncology, 23,* 7405–7410.

Kazdin, A. E. (2011). *Single-case research designs: Methods for clinical and applied settings.* New York: Oxford University Press.

Keane, T. M., & Barlow, D. H. (2002). Post-traumatic stress disorder. In D. H. Barlow, *Anxiety and its disorders: The nature and treatment of anxiety and panic.* (2nd ed., pp. 418–453). New York, NY: Guilford.

Keane, T. M., & Miller, M. W. (2012). Future of classification in posttraumatic stress disorder. In J. G. Beck & D. M. Sloan (Eds.), *The Oxford handbook of traumatic stress disorders* (pp. 54–66). New York, NY: Oxford University Press.

Keane, T. M., Marx, B. P., Sloan, D. M., & DePrince, A. (2011). Trauma, dissociation, and post-traumatic stress disorder. In D. H. Barlow (Ed.), *The Oxford handbook of clinical psychology* (pp. 359–386). New York, NY: Oxford University Press.

Kearney, A. J. (2006). A primer of covert sensitization. *Cognitive and Behavioral Practice, 13*(2), 167–175. doi: 10.1016/j.cbpra.2006.02.002

Kearney, C. A., Albano, A. M., Eisen, A. R., Allan, W. D., & Barlow, D. H. (1997). The phenomenology of panic disorder in youngsters: An empirical study of a clinical sample. *Journal of Anxiety Disorders, 11*(10), 49–62.

Kearns, M. C., Ressler, K. J., Zatzick, D., & Rothbaum, B. O. (2012). Early interventions for PTSD: A review. *Depression and Anxiety, 29*, 833–842. doi: 10.1002/da.21997

Keck, P. E., & McElroy, S. L. (2002). Pharmacological treatments for bipolar disorder. In P. E. Nathan & J. M. Gorman (Eds.), *A guide to treatments that work* (2nd ed., pp. 277–299). New York, NY: Oxford University Press.

Keefe, D. L. (2002). Sex hormones and neural mechanisms. *Archives of Sexual Behavior, 31*(5), 401–403.

Keefe, F. J., & France, C. R. (1999). Pain: Biopsychosocial mechanisms and management. *Current Directions in Psychological Science, 8*, 137–141.

Keefe, F. J., Dunsmore, J., & Burnett, R. (1992). Behavioral and cognitive-behavioral approaches to chronic pain: Recent advances and future directions. Special issue: Behavioral medicine: An update for the 1990s. *Journal of Consulting and Clinical Psychology, 60*(4), 528–536.

Keel, P. K., & Forney, K. J. (2013). Psychosocial risk factors for eating disorders. *International Journal of Eating Disorders, 46*(5), 433–439.

Keel, P. K., Brown, T. A., Holland, L. A., & Bodell, L. P. (2012). Empirical classification of eating disorders. *Annual Review of Clinical Psychology, 8*, 381–404.

Keel, P. K., Dorer, D. J., Eddy, K. T., Franko, D., Charatan, D. L., & Herzog, D. B. (2003). Predictors of mortality in eating disorders. *Archives of General Psychiatry, 60*, 179–183.

Keel, P. K., Fichter, M., Quadfleig, N., Bulik, C. M., Baxter, M. G., Thornton, L., & Kaye, W. H. (2004). Application of a latent class analysis to empirically define eating disorder phenotypes. *Archives of General Psychiatry, 61*, 192–200.

Keel, P. K., Heatherton, T. F., Dorer, D. J., Joiner, T, E., & Zalta, A. K. (2006). Point prevalence of bulimia nervosa in 1982, 1992, and 2002. *Psychological Medicine, 36*, 119–127.

Keel, P. K., Mitchell, J. E., Miller, K. B., Davis, T. L., & Crow, S. J. (2000). Predictive validity of bulimia nervosa as a diagnostic strategy. *American Journal of Psychiatry 157*(1), 136–138.

Keilitz, I. (1987). Researching and reforming the insanity defense. *Rutgers Law Review, 39*, 289–322.

Keitner, G. I., Ryan, C. E., Miller, I. W., Kohn, R., Bishop, D. S., & Epstein, N. B. (1995). Role of the family in recovery and major depression. *American Journal of Psychiatry, 152*, 1002–1008.

Keller, M. B., & Wunder, J. (1990). Bipolar disorder in childhood. In M. Hersen & C. G. Last (Eds.), *Handbook of child and adult psychopathology: A longitudinal perspective.* Elmsford, NY: Pergamon Press.

Keller, M. B., Klein, D. N., Hirschfeld, R. M. A., Kocsis, J. H., McCullough, J. P., Miller, I., & Marin, D. B. (1995). Results of the DSM-IV mood disorders field trial. *American Journal of Psychiatry, 152*, 843–849.

Keller, M. B., Lavori, P. W., Endicott, J., Coryell, W., & Klerman, G. L. (1983). "Double depression": Two year follow-up. *American Journal of Psychiatry, 140*(6), 689–694.

Keller, M. B., McCollough, J. P., Klein, D. N., Arnow, B., Dunner, D. L., Gelenberg, A. J., & Zajecka, J. (2000). A comparison of nefazodone, the cognitive behavioral-analysis system of psychotherapy, and their combination for the treatment of chronic depression. *New England Journal of Medicine, 342*(20), 1462–1470.

Kellner, C. H., Greenberg, R. M., Murrough, J. W., Bryson, E. O., Briggs, M. C., & Pasculli, R. M. (2012). ECT in treatment-resistant depression. *American Journal of Psychiatry, 169*(12), 1238–1244.

Kellner, D. (2008). Media spectacle and the "massacre at Virginia Tech." In B. Agger & T. W. Luke (Eds.), *There is a gunman on campus: Tragedy and terror at Virginia Tech* (pp. 29–54). Lanham, MD: Rowman & Littlefield.

Kellner, R. (1992). Diagnosis and treatments of hypochondriacal syndromes. *Psychosomatics, 33*(3), 278–279.

Kelly, B. D., Casey, P., Dunn, G., Ayuso-Mateos, J. L., & Dowrick, C. (2007). The role of personality disorder in "difficult to reach" patients with depression: Findings from the ODIN study. *European Psychiatry, 22*, 153–159.

Kelly, J. F. (2013). Alcoholics Anonymous science update: Introduction to the special issue. *Substance Abuse, 34*(1), 1–3. doi: 10.1080/08897077.2012.691447

Kelly, J. F., Stout, R. L., Magill, M., Tonigan, J. S., & Pagano, M. E. (2010). Mechanisms of behavior change in alcoholics anonymous: Does Alcoholics Anonymous lead to better alcohol use outcomes by reducing depression symptoms? *Addiction, 105*(4), 626–636.

Kelly, M. P., Strassberg, D. S., & Kircher, J. R. (1990). Attitudinal and experiential correlates of anorgasmia. *Archives of Sexual Behavior, 19*(2), 165–177.

Kelly, P., & Frosch, E. (2012). Recognition of delirium on pediatric hospital services. *Psychosomatics, 53*(5), 446–451.

Kemeny, M. E. (2003). The psychobiology of stress. *Current Directions in Psychological Science, 12*(4), 124–129.

Kemp, S. (1990). *Medieval psychology.* New York, NY: Greenwood Press.

Kendall, P. C., & Comer, J. S. (2014). Research methods in clinical psychology: Updated edition. In D. H. Barlow (Ed.), *Oxford handbook of clinical psychology* (pp. 52–75). New York, NY: Oxford University.

Kendall, P. C., & Peterman, J. S. (2015). CBT for adolescents with anxiety: Mature yet still developing. *American Journal of Psychiatry, 172*, 519–530.

Kendall, P. C., Hudson, J. L., Gosch, E., Flannery-Schroeder, E., & Suveg, C. (2008). Cognitive behavioral therapy for anxiety disordered youth: A randomized clinical trial evaluating child and family modalities. *Journal of Consulting and Clinical Psychology, 76*(2), 282–297. doi: 10.1037/0022-006X.76.2.282

Kendler, K., & Walsh, D. (2007). Schizophreniform disorder, delusional disorder and psychotic disorder not otherwise specified: Clinical features, outcome and familial psychopathology. *Acta Psychiatrica Scandinavica, 91*(6), 370–378.

Kendler, K. S. (2001). Twin studies of psychiatric illness. *Archives of General Psychiatry, 58*, 1005–1013.

Kendler, K. S. (2005). Psychiatric genetics: A methodological critique. In N. C. Andreasen (Ed.), *Research advances in genetics and genomics: Implications for psychiatry* (pp. 5–25). Washington, DC: American Psychiatric Publishing.

Kendler, K. S. (2006). Reflections on the relationship between psychiatric genetics and psychiatric nosology. *American Journal of Psychiatry, 163*, 1138–1146.

Kendler, K. S. (2011). A conceptual overview of gene-environment interaction and correlation in a developmental context. In K. S. Kendler, S. Jaffee, & D. Romer (Eds.), *The dynamic genome and mental health: The role of genes and environments in youth development* (pp. 5–28). New York, NY: Oxford University Press.

Kendler, K. S. (2013). What psychiatric genetics has taught us about the nature of psychiatric illness and what is left to learn. *Molecular Psychiatry, 18*(10), 1058–1066. doi: 10.1038/mp.1013.50

Kendler, K. S., & Gardner, C. O. (2010). Dependent stressful life events and prior depressive episodes in the prediction of major depression: the problem of causal inference in psychiatric epidemiology. *Archives of General Psychiatry, 67*(11), 1120–1127.

Kendler, K. S., & Gardner, C. O. (2014). Sex differences in the pathways to major depression: A study of opposite-sex twin Pairs. *American Journal of Psychiatry, 171*, 426–435.

Kendler, K. S., & Prescott, C. A. (2006). *Genes, environment, and psychopathology: Understanding the causes of psychiatric and substance use disorders.* New York, NY: Guilford.

Kendler, K. S., Aggen, S. H., & Neale, M. C. (2013). Evidence for multiple genetic factors underlying DSM-IV criteria for major depression. *JAMA Psychiatry, 70*(6), 599–607. doi: 10.1001/jamapsychiatry.2013.751

Kendler, K. S., Aggen, S. H., & Patrick, C. J. (2013). Familial influences on conduct disorder reflect 2 genetic factors and 1 shared environmental factor. *JAMA Psychiatry, 70*(1), 78–86.

Kendler, K. S., Aggen, S. H., Neale, M. C., Knudsen, G. P., Krueger, R. F., Tambs, K., . . . Reichborn-Kjennerud, T. (2015). A longitudinal twin study of cluster A personality disorders. *Psychological Medicine, 45*(07), 1531–1538.

Kendler, K. S., Chen, X., Dick, D., Maes, H., Gillespie, N., Neale, M. C., & Riley, B. (2012). Recent advances in the genetic epidemiology and molecular genetics of substance use disorders. *Nature Neuroscience, 15*(2), 181–189. doi: 10.1038/nn.3018.

Kendler, K. S., Czajkowski, N., Tambs, K., Torgersen, S., Aggen, S. H., Neale, M. C., & Reichborn-Kjennerud, T. (2006). Dimensional representations of DSM-IV cluster A personality disorders in a population-based sample of Norwegian twins: A multivariate study. *Psychological Medicine, 36,* 1583–1591.

Kendler, K. S., Gatz, M., Gardner, C. O., & Pedersen, N. L. (2007). Clinical indices of familial depression in the Swedish Twin Registry. *Acta Psychiatrica Scandinavica, 115*(3), 214–220.

Kendler, K. S., Heath, A. C., Martin, N. G., & Eaves, L. J. (1987). Symptoms of anxiety and symptoms of depression: Same genes, different environments? *Archives of General Psychiatry, 44*(5), 451–457.

Kendler, K. S., Hettema, J. M., Butera, F., Gardner, C. O., & Prescott, C. A. (2003). Life event dimensions of loss, humiliation, entrapment, and danger in the prediction of onsets of major depression and generalized anxiety. *Archives of General Psychiatry, 60,* 789–796.

Kendler, K. S., Jacobson, K. C., Prescott, C. A., & Neale, M. C. (2003). Specificity of genetic and environmental risk factors for use and abuse/dependence of cannabis, cocaine, hallucinogens, sedatives, stimulants, and opiates in male twins. *American Journal of Psychiatry, 160,* 687–695.

Kendler, K. S., Jaffee, S., & Romer, D. (2011). *The dynamic genome and mental health: The role of genes and environments in youth development.* New York, NY: Oxford University Press.

Kendler, K. S., Karkowski, L. M., & Prescott, C. A. (1999a). The assessment of dependence in the study of stressful life events: Validation using a twin design. *Psychological Medicine, 29*(6), 1455–1460.

Kendler, K. S., Karkowski, L. M., & Prescott, C. A. (1999b). Causal relationship between stressful life events and the onset of major depression. *American Journal of Psychiatry, 156*(6), 837–841.

Kendler, K. S., Kessler, R. C., Walters, E. E., MacLean, C., Neale, M. C., Heath, A. C., & Eaves, L. J. (1995). Stressful life events, genetic liability, and onset of an episode of major depression in women. *American Journal of Psychiatry, 152,* 833–842.

Kendler, K. S., Kuhn, J., Vittum, J., Prescott, C. A., & Riley, B. (2005). The interaction of stressful life events and a serotonin transporter polymorphism in the prediction of episodes of major depression. *Archives of General Psychiatry, 62,* 529–535.

Kendler, K. S., Larsson Lönn, S., Morris, N. A., Sundquist, J., Långström, N., & Sundquist, K. (2014). A Swedish national adoption study of criminality. *Psychological Medicine, 44*(09), 1913–1925.

Kendler, K. S., MacLean, C., Neale, M., Kessler, R., Heath, A., & Eaves, L. (1991). The genetic epidemiology of bulimia nervosa. *American Journal of Psychiatry, 148*(12), 1627–1637.

Kendler, K. S., Myers, J., & Prescott, C. A. (2005). Sex differences in the relationship between social support and risk for major depression: A longitudinal study of opposite-sex twin pairs. *American Journal of Psychiatry, 162,* 250–256.

Kendler, K. S., Myers, J., & Zisook, S. (2008). Does bereavement-related major depression differ from major depression associated with other stressful life events? *American Journal of Psychiatry, 165*(11), 1449–1455.

Kendler, K. S., Neale, M. C., Kessler, R. C., Heath, A. C., & Eaves, L. J. (1992a). Generalized anxiety disorder in women: A population-based twin study. *Archives of General Psychiatry, 49,* 267–272.

Kendler, K. S., Neale, M. C., Kessler, R. C., Heath, A. C., & Eaves, L. J. (1992b). Major depression and generalized anxiety disorder: Same genes, (partly) different environments? *Archives of General Psychiatry, 49,* 716–722.

Kendler, K. S., Neale, M. C., Heath, C., & Eaves, L. J. (1993). A longitudinal twin study of 1-year prevalence of major depression in women. *Archives of General Psychiatry, 50,* 843–852.

Kendler, K. S., Neale, M. C., MacLean, C. J., Heath, A. C., Eaves, L. J., & Kessler, R. C. (1993). Smoking and major depression: A causal analysis. *Archives of General Psychiatry, 50,* 36–43.

Kendrick, D., Young, B., Mason-Jones, A.J., Ilyas, N., Achana, F.A., et al. (2012). Home safety education and provision of safety equipment for injury prevention. *Cochrane Database Syst. Rev. 9*:CD005014.

Kennard, B. D., Clarke, G. N., Weersing, V. R., Asarnow, J. R., Shamseddeen, W., Porta, G., & Brent, D. A. (2009). Effective components of TORDIA cognitive–behavioral therapy for adolescent depression: Preliminary findings. *Journal of Consulting and Clinical Psychology, 77*(6), 1033–1041.

Kennedy, K. A., & Barlow, D. H. (in press). The Unified Protocol for Transdiagnostic Treatment of Emotional Disorders: An introduction. In T. J. Farchione, & D. H. Barlow (Eds.), *Applications of the Unified Protocol for Transdiagnostic Treatment of Emotional Disorders.* New York: Oxford University Press.

Kennedy, J. L., Altar, C. A., Taylor, D. L., Degtiar, I., & Hornberger, J. C. (2014). The social and economic burden of treatment-resistant schizophrenia: A systematic literature review. *International Clinical Psychopharmacology, 29*(2), 63–76.

Kennedy, S. (2000). Psychological factors and immunity in HIV infection: Stress, coping, social support, and intervention outcomes. In D. I. Mostofsky & D. H. Barlow (Eds.), *The management of stress and anxiety in medical disorders* (pp. 194–205). Needham Heights, MA: Allyn & Bacon.

Kennedy, S. H., Giacobbe, P., Rizvi, S. J., Placenza, F. M., Nishikawa, Y., Mayberg, H. S., & Lozano, A. M. (2011). Deep brain stimulation for treatment-resistant depression: Follow-up after 3 to 6 years. *American Journal of Psychiatry, 168*(5), 502–510.

Kennedy, S. H., Konarski, J. Z., Segal, Z. V., Lau, M. A., Bieling, P. J., McIntyre, R. S., & Mayberg, H. S. (2007). Differences in brain glucose metabolism between responders to CBT and venlafaxine in a 16-week randomized controlled trial. *The American Journal of Psychiatry, 164*(5), 778–788.

Kennedy, W. K., Leloux, M., Kutscher, E. C., Price, P. L., Morstad, A. E., & Carnahan, R. M. (2010). Acamprosate. *Expert Opinion on Drug Metabolism & Toxicology, 6*(3), 363–380.

Kerns, R. D., Rosenberg, R., & Otis, J. D. (2002). Self-appraised problem solving and pain-relevant social support as predictors of the experience of chronic pain. *Annals of Behavioral Medicine, 24,* 100–105.

Kerns, R. D., Sellinger, J., & Goodin, B. R. (2011). Psychological treatment of chronic pain. *Annual Review of Clinical Psychology, 7,* 411–434.

Kerr, M., Stattin, H., & Burk, W. J. (2010). A reinterpretation of parental monitoring in longitudinal perspective. *Journal of Research on Adolescence, 20*(1), 39–64. doi: 10.1111/j.1532-7795.2009.00623.x

Kersting, A., Brahler, E., Glaesmer, H., & Wagner, B. (2011). Prevalence of complicated grief in a representative population-based sample. *Journal of Affective Disorders, 131*(1–3), 339–343.

Keski-Rahkonen, A., Hoek, H. W., Susser, E. S., Linna, M. S., Sihvola, E., Raevuori, A., & Rissanen, A. (2007). Epidemiology and course of anorexia nervosa in the community. *American Journal of Psychiatry, 164*(8), 1259–1265.

Kessler, R. C. (2006). The epidemiology of depression among women. In C. Keyes & S. Goodman (Eds.), *A handbook for the social, behavioral, and biomedical sciences: Women and depression* (pp. 22–37). New York, NY: Cambridge University Press.

Kessler, R. C., & Bromet, E. J. (2013). The epidemiology of depression across cultures. *Annual Review of Public Health, 34,* 119–138.

Kessler, R. C., Avenevoli, S., Costello, H., Georgiades, K., Green, J. G., Gruber, M. J., & Merikangas, K. R. (2012). Prevalence, persistence, and sociodemographic correlates of DSM-IV disorders in the National Comorbidity Survey Replication Adolescent Supplement. *Archives of General Psychiatry, 69*(4), 372–380. doi: 10.1001/archgenpsychiatry.2011.160

Kessler, R. C., Coccaro, E. F., Fava, M., Jaeger, S., Jin, R., & Walters, E. (2006). The prevalence and correlates of DSM-IV intermittent explosive disorder in the National Comorbidity Survey Replication. *Archives of General Psychiatry, 63*(6), 669–679.

Kessler, R. C., & Wang, P. S. (2009). Epidemiology of depression. In I. H. Gotlib & C. L. Hammen (Eds.), *Handbook of depression* (2nd ed., pp. 5–22). New York, NY: Guilford.

Kessler, R. C., Avenevoli, S., & Ries Merikangas, K. (2001). Mood disorders in children and adolescents: An epidemiologic perspective. *Biological Psychiatry, 49*(12), 1002–1014.

Kessler, R. C., Berglund, P., Borges, G., Nock, M., & Wang, P. (2005). Trends in suicide ideation, plans, gestures, and attempts in the United States, 1990–1992 to 2001–2003. *JAMA: Journal of the American Medical Association, 293,* 2487–2495.

Kessler, R. C., Berglund, P., Demler, O., Jin, R., Merikangas, K. R., & Walters, E. E. (2005). Lifetime prevalence and age-of-onset distributions of DSM-IV disorders in the National Comorbidity Survey Replication. *Archives of General Psychiatry, 62*, 593–602.

Kessler, R. C., Berglund, P., Demler, O., Jin, R., Koretz, D., Merikangas, K. R., & National Comorbidity Survey Replication. (2003). The epidemiology of major depressive disorder: Results from the National Comorbidity Survey Replication (NCS-R). *JAMA: Journal of the American Medical Association, 289*, 3095–3105.

Kessler, R. C., Chiu, W. T., Demler, O., & Walters, E. E. (2005). Prevalence, severity, and comorbidity of 12-month DSM-IV disorders in the National Comorbidity Survey replication. *Archives of General Psychiatry, 62*, 617–627.

Kessler, R. C., Chiu, W. T., Jin, R., Ruscio, A. M., Shear, K., & Walters, E. E. (2006). The epidemiology of panic attacks, panic disorder, and agoraphobia in the National Comorbidity Survey Replication. *Archives of General Psychiatry, 63*(4), 415–424. doi: 10.1001/archpsyc.63.4.415

Kessler, R. C., Galea, S., Jones, R. T., & Parker, H. A. (2006). *Mental illness and suicidality after Hurricane Katrina.* Bulletin of the World Health Organization (WHO Publication No. 06-033019).

Kessler, R. C., McGonagle, K. A., Zhao, S., Nelson, C. B., Hughes, M., Eshleman, S., & Kendler, K. S. (1994). Lifetime and 12-month prevalence of DSM-III-R psychiatric disorders among persons aged 15–54 in the United States: Results from the National Comorbidity Survey. *Archives of General Psychiatry, 5*, 8–19.

Kessler, R. C., Petukhova, M., Sampson, N.A., Zaslavsky, A.M., & Wittchen, H.U. (2012). Twelve-month and lifetime prevalence and lifetime morbid risk of anxiety and mood disorders in the United States. *International Journal of Methods in Psychiatric Research, 21*, 169.

Keuroghlian, A. S., Gunderson, J. G., Pagano, M. E., Markowitz, J. C., Ansell, E. B., Shea, M. T., . . . Stout, R. L. (2015). Interactions of Borderline Personality Disorder and Anxiety Disorders Over 10 Years. *The Journal of Clinical Psychiatry, 76*(11), 1–478.

Keys, A., Brozek, J., Henschel, A., Michelson, O., & Taylor, H. L. (1950). *The biology of human starvation* (Vol. 1). Minneapolis MN: University of Minnesota Press.

Khachaturian, Z. S. (2007). Alzheimer's 101. *Alzheimer's and Dementia, 3*, 1–2.

Khan, S., King, A.P., Abelson, J.L, & Liberzon, I. (2009). Neuroendocrinology of anxiety disorders. In M. M. Antony & M. B. Stein (Eds.), *Oxford handbook of anxiety and related disorders.* Oxford, UK: Oxford University Press.

Khokhar, J., Ferguson, C., Zhu, A., & Tyndale, R. (2010). Pharmacogenetics of drug dependence: Role of gene variations in susceptibility and treatment. *Annual Review of Pharmacology and Toxicology, 50*(1), 39–61.

Khoury, B., Lecomte, T., Fortin, G., Masse, M., Therien, P., Bouchard, V., . . . Hofmann, S. G. (2013). Mindfulness-based therapy: A comprehensive meta-analysis. *Clinical Psychology Review, 33*, 763–771.

Kiecolt-Glaser, J. K., & Newton, T. L. (2001). Marriage and health: His and hers. *Psychological Bulletin, 127*, 475–503.

Kiecolt-Glaser, J. K., Loving, T., Stowell, J., Malarkey, W., Lemeshow, S., & Dickinson, S., & Glaser, R. (2005). Hostile marital interactions, proinflammatory cytokine production, and wound healing. *Archives of General Psychiatry, 62*, 1377–1384.

Kiesler, C. A., & Sibulkin, A. E. (1987). *Mental hospitalization: Myths and facts about a national crisis.* Beverly Hills, CA: Sage.

Kiesler, D. J. (1966). Some myths of psychotherapy research and the search for a paradigm. *Psychological Bulletin, 65*, 110–136.

Kihlstrom, J. F. (1992). Dissociation and dissociations: A commentary on consciousness and cognition. *Consciousness & Cognition, 1*, 47–53.

Kihlstrom, J. F. (1997). Memory, abuse, and science. *American Psychologist, 52*, 994–995.

Kihlstrom, J. F. (2005a). Dissociative disorders. In S. Nolen-Hoeksema, T. D. Cannon, & T. Widiger (Eds.), *Annual review of clinical psychology* (Vol. 1). Palo Alto, CA: Annual Reviews.

Kihlstrom, J. F. (2005b). Dissociative disorders. *Annual Review of Clinical Psychology, 1*, 227–253.

Kihlstrom, J. F., Glisky, M. L., & Anguilo, M. J. (1994). Dissociative tendencies and dissociative disorders. *Journal of Abnormal Psychology, 103*, 117–124.

Killerman, S. (2015). Retrieved from: http://itspronouncedmetrosexual.com/2013/01/a-comprehensive-list-of-lgbtq-term-definitions/

Killgore, W. D. S., Cotting, D. I., Thomas, J. L., Cox, A. L., McGurk, D., Vo, A. H., & Hoge, C. W. (2008). Post-combat invincibility: Violent combat experiences are associated with increased risk-taking propensity following deployment. *Journal of Psychiatric Research, 42*(13), 1112–1121. doi: 10.1016/j.jpsychires.2008.01.001

Kilpatrick, D. G., Resnick, H. S., & Friedman, M. J. (2010). National Stressful Events Survey PTSD Short Scale (NSESSS-PTSD).

Kilpatrick, D. G., Koenen, K. C., Ruggiero, K. J., Acierno, R., Galea, S., Resnick, H. S., & Gelernter, J. (2007). The serotonin transporter genotype and social support and moderation of posttraumatic stress disorder and depression in hurricane-exposed adults. *The American Journal of Psychiatry, 164*(11), 1693–1699.

Kilzieh, N., & Akiskal, H. S. (1999). Rapid-cycling bipolar disorder: An overview of research and clinical experience. *Psychiatric Clinics of North America, 22*(3), 585–607.

Kim, E. D., & Lipshultz, L. I. (1997, April 15). Advances in the treatment of organic erectile dysfunction. *Hospital Practice*, 101–120.

Kim, H. F., Schulz, P. E., Wilde, E. A., & Yudofsky, S. C. (2008). Laboratory testing and imaging studies in psychiatry. In R. E. Hales, S. C. Yudofsky, & G. O. Gabbard (Eds.), *The American Psychiatric Publishing textbook of psychiatry* (5th ed., pp. 19–72). Arlington, VA: American Psychiatric Publishing.

Kim, J. M., & López, S. R. (2014). The expression of depression in Asian Americans and European Americans. *Journal of Abnormal Psychology, 123*, 745–763.

Kimchi, E.Z. & Lyketos, C. G. (2015). Dementia and milder cognitive symptoms. In D.C. Steffens, D. G. Blazer, & M. E. Thakur (Eds.), *The American Psychiatric Publishing textbook of geriatric psychiatry* (5th ed., pp.177–242). Washington, D.C.: American Psychiatric Publishing.

Kimonis, E. R. (2015). Insanity defense/guilty but mentally ill. In *The Encyclopedia of Clinical Psychology.* Hoboken, NJ: John Wiley & Sons.

King, D. E., Mainous III, A. G., & Geesey, M. E. (2007). Turning back the clock: Adopting a healthy lifestyle in middle age. *The American Journal of Medicine, 120*(7), 598–603.

King, D. W., King, L. A., Foy, D. W., & Gudanowski, D. M. (1996). Prewar factors in combat related posttraumatic stress disorder: Structural equation modeling with a national sample of female and male Vietnam veterans. *Journal of Consulting and Clinical Psychology, 64*, 520–531.

King, L. A., Pless, A. P., Schuster, J. L., Potter, C. M., Park, C. L., Spiro, A., & King, D. W. (2012). Risk and protective factors for traumatic stress disorder. In J. G. Beck & D. M. Sloan (Eds.), *The Oxford handbook of traumatic stress disorders* (pp. 333–346). New York, NY: Oxford University Press.

King, M., & Wexler, D. (2010). Therapeutic jurisprudence. In J. M. Brown & E. A. Campbell (Eds.), *The Cambridge handbook of forensic psychology* (pp. 126–132). Cambridge, UK: Cambridge University Press.

Kinzie, J. D., Leung, P. K., Boehnlein, J., & Matsunaga, D. (1992). Psychiatric epidemiology of an Indian village: A 19-year replication study. *Journal of Nervous and Mental Disease, 180*(1), 33–39.

Kirmayer, L. J., & Sartorius, N. (2007). Cultural models and somatic syndromes. *Psychosomatic Medicine, 69*(9), 832–840.

Kirmayer, L. J., & Weiss, M. (1993). *On cultural considerations for somatoform disorders in the DSM-IV.* In cultural proposals and supporting papers for DSM-IV. Submitted to the DSM-IV Task Force by the Steering Committee, NIMH-Sponsored Group on Culture and Diagnosis.

Kirmayer, L. J., Looper, K. J., & Taillefer, S. (2003). Somatoform disorders. In M. Hersen & S. M. Turner (Eds.), *Adult psychopathology and diagnosis* (4th ed., pp. 420–475). New York, NY: Wiley.

Kirov, G., & Owen, M. J. (2009). Genetics of schizophrenia. In B. J. Sadock, V. A. Sadock, & P. Ruiz (Eds.), *Kaplan & Sadock's comprehensive textbook of psychiatry* (9th ed., Vol. I, pp. 1462–1475). Philadelphia, PA: Lippincott Williams & Wilkins.

Kishimoto, T., Agarwal, V., Kishi, T., Leucht, S., Kane, J. M., & Correll, C. U. (2013). Relapse prevention in schizophrenia: a systematic review and meta-analysis of second-generation antipsychotics versus first-generation antipsychotics. *Molecular Psychiatry, 18*(1), 53–66.

Kishimoto, T., Robenzadeh, A., Leucht, C., Leucht, S., Watanabe, K., Mimura, M., . . . Correll, C. U. (2012). Long-acting injectable vs oral antipsychotics for relapse prevention in schizophrenia: A meta-analysis of randomized trials. *Schizophrenia Bulletin*, sbs150.

Kistner, J. A. (2009). Sex differences in child and adolescent psychopathology: An introduction to the special section. *Journal of Clinical Child and Adolescent Psychology, 38*(4), 453–459.

Kivimaki, M., Nyberg, S. T., Batty, G. D., Fransson, E. I., Heikkila, K., Alfredsson, L., & Consortium, I. P.-W. (2012). Job strain as a risk factor for coronary heart disease: a collaborative meta-analysis of individual participant data. *Lancet, 380*(9852), 1491–1497.

Kjernisted, K. D., Enns, M. W., & Lander, M. (2002). An open-label clinical trial of nefazodone in hypochondriasis. *Psychosomatics, 43*, 290–294.

Klaus, K., Rief, W., Brähler, E., Martin, A., Glaesmer, H., & Mewes, R. (2015). Validating psychological classification criteria in the context of somatoform disorders: A one- and four-year follow-up. *Journal of Abnormal Psychology, 124*(4):1092–1101.

Klein, D. F. (1989). The pharmacological validation of psychiatric diagnosis. In L. Robins & J. Barrett (Eds.), *Validity of psychiatric diagnosis*. New York, NY: Raven Press.

Klein, D. N. (2008). Classification of depressive disorders in the DSM-V: Proposal for a two-dimension system. *Journal of Abnormal Psychology, 117*(3), 552–560.

Klein, D. N. (2010). Chronic depression: Diagnosis and classification. *Current Directions in Psychological Science, 19*(2), 96–100.

Klein, D. N., Glenn, C. R., Kosty, D. B., Seeley, J. R., Rohde, P., & Lewinsohn, P. M. (2013). Predictors of first lifetime onset of major depressive disorder in young adulthood. *Journal of Abnormal Psychology, 122*, 1–6.

Klein, D. N., Lewinsohn, P. M., Rohde, P., Seeley, J. R., & Durbin, C. E. (2002). Clinical features of major depressive disorder in adolescents and their relatives: Impact on familial aggregation, implications for phenotype definition, and specificity of transmission. *Journal of Abnormal Psychology, 111*, 98–106.

Klein, D. N., Schwartz, J. E., Rose, S., & Leader, J. B. (2000). Five-year course and outcome of dysthymic disorder: A prospective, naturalistic follow-up study. *American Journal of Psychiatry, 157*(6), 931–939.

Klein, D. N., Shankman, S., & Rose, S. (2006). Ten-year prospective follow-up study of the naturalistic course of dysthymic disorder and double depression. *American Journal of Psychiatry, 163*, 872–880.

Klein, D. N., Taylor, E. B., Dickstein, S., & Harding, K. (1988). The early–late onset distinction in DSM-III-R dysthymia. *Journal of Affective Disorders, 14*(1), 25–33.

Klein, R. G., Mannuzza, S., Ramos Olazagasti, M. A., Roizen, E., Jesse A. Hutchison, J. A., . . . Castellanos, F. X. (2012). Clinical and functional outcome of childhood attention-deficit/hyperactivity disorder 33 years later. *Archives of General Psychiatry, 69*(12), 1295–1303. doi: 10.1001/archgenpsychiatry.2012.271

Kleinknecht, R. A., Dinnel, D. L., Kleinknecht, E. E., Hiruma, N., & Harada, N. (1997). Cultural factors in social anxiety: A comparison of social phobia symptoms and *taijin kyofusho*. *Journal of Anxiety Disorders, 11*, 157–177.

Kleinman, A. (1986). *Social origins of distress and disease: Depression, neurasthenia, and pain in modern China*. New Haven, CT: Yale University Press.

Kleinman, A. (2004). Culture and depression. *New England Journal of Medicine, 351*, 951–953.

Kleinplatz, F. J., Moser, C., & Lev, A. I. (2012). Sex and gender identity disorders. In I. B. Weiner, G. Stricker, & T. A. Widiger (Eds.), *Handbook of psychology, clinical psychology* (2nd ed., Vol. 8, pp. 171–192). Hoboken, NJ: Wiley.

Kleinstäuber, M., Witthöft, M., & Hiller, W. (2011). Efficacy of short-term psychotherapy for multiple medically unexplained physical symptoms: A meta-analysis. *Clinical Psychology Review, 31*, 146–160.

Klerman, G. L., & Weissman, M. M. (1989). Increasing rates of depression. *JAMA: Journal of the American Medical Association, 261*, 2229–2235.

Klerman, G. L., Weissman, M. M., Rounsaville, B. J., & Chevron, E. S. (1984). *Interpersonal psychotherapy of depression*. New York, NY: Basic Books.

Klimas, N., Koneru, A. O., & Fletcher, M. A. (2008). Overview of HIV. *Psychosomatic Medicine, 70*, 523–530.

Klin, A., Jones, W., Schultz, R., Volkmar, F., & Cohen, D. (2002). Defining and quantifying the social phenotype in autism. *American Journal of Psychiatry, 159*, 895–908.

Kluft, R. P. (1984). Treatment of multiple personality disorder. *Psychiatric Clinics of North America, 7*, 9–29.

Kluft, R. P. (1991). Multiple personality disorder. In A. Tasman & S. W. Goldinger (Eds.), *Review of psychiatry* (Vol. 10). Washington, DC: American Psychiatric Press.

Kluft, R. P. (1996). Treating the traumatic memories of patients with dissociative identity disorder. *American Journal of Psychiatry, 153*, 103–110.

Kluft, R. P. (1999). Current issues in dissociative identity disorder. *Journal of Practical Psychology and Behavioral Health, 5*, 3–19.

Kluft, R. P. (2009). A clinician's understanding of dissociation: Fragments of an acquaintance. In P. F. Dell & J. A. O'Neil (Eds.), *Dissociation and the dissociative disorders*. New York, NY: Routledge.

Klump, K. L., Kaye, W. H., & Strober, M. (2001). The evolving genetic foundations of eating disorders. *The Psychiatric Clinics of North America, 24*, 215–225.

Klump, K. L., Racine, S. E., Hildebrandt, B., Burt, S. A., Neale, M., Sisk, C. L., . . . Keel, P. K. (2014). Influences of Ovarian Hormones on Dysregulated Eating A Comparison of Associations in Women With Versus Women Without Binge Episodes. *Clinical Psychological Science, 2*(5), 545–559.

Klumpp, H., Fitzgerald, D. A., & Phan, K. L. (2013). Neural predictors and mechanisms of cognitive behavioral therapy on threat processing in social anxiety disorder. *Progress in Neuro-Psychopharmacology & Biological Psychiatry, 45*, 83–91.

Knapp, S. J., Gottlieb, M. C., Handelsman, M. M., & VandeCreek, L. D. (2012a). *APA handbook of ethics in psychology, Vol 1: Moral foundations and common themes*. Washington, DC: American Psychological Association.

Knapp, S. J., Gottlieb, M. C., Handelsman, M. M., & VandeCreek, L. D. (2012b). *APA handbook of ethics in psychology, Vol 2: Practice, teaching, and research*. Washington, DC: American Psychological Association.

Knappe, S., Beesdo-Baum, K., Nocon, A., & Wittchen, H.-U. (2012). Re-examining the differential familial liability of agoraphobia and panic disorder. *Depression and Anxiety, 29*(11), 931–938.

Knoop, H., Prins, J. B., Moss-Morris, R., & Bleijenberg, G. (2010). The central role of cognitive processes in the perpetuation of chronic fatigue syndrome. *Journal of Psychosomatic Research, 68*, 489–494.

Knopik, V. S., Bidwell, L. C., Flessner, C., Nugent, N., Swenson, L., Bucholz, K. K., . . . Heath, A. C. (2014). DSM-IV defined conduct disorder and oppositional defiant disorder: an investigation of shared liability in female twins. *Psychological Medicine, 44*(05), 1053-1064.

Knouse, L. E. (2015). Cognitive-behavioral therapies for ADHD. In R. A. Barkley (Ed.), *Attention-deficit hyperactivity disorder: A handbook for diagnosis & treatment* (4th ed., pp. 757–773). New York, NY: The Guilford Press.

Knowles, R., McCarthy-Jones, S., & Rowse, G. (2011). Grandiose delusions: A review and theoretical integration of cognitive and affective perspectives. *Clinical Psychology Review, 31*(4), 684–696. doi: 10.1016/j.cpr.2011.02.009

Ko, H-C., Lee, L-R., Chang, R-B., & Huang, K-E. (1996). Comorbidity of premenstrual depression and postpartum blues among Chinese women. *Biological Psychiatry, 39*, 648.

Kobau, R., DiIorio, C., Chapman, D., & Delvecchio, P. (2010). Attitudes about mental illness and its treatment: Validation of a generic scale for public health surveillance of mental illness associated stigma. *Community Mental Health Journal, 46*(2), 164–176.

Koch, P., Mansfield, P., Thurau, D., & Carey, M. (2005). "Feeling frumpy": The relationship between body image and sexual response changes in midlife women. *Journal of Sex Research, 42*, 215–223.

Kochanska, G., Aksan, N., & Joy, M. E. (2007). Children's fearfulness as a moderator of parenting in early socialization: Two longitudinal studies. *Developmental Psychology, 43*, 222–237.

Kochman, F. J., Hantouche, E. G., Ferrari, P., Lancrenon, S., Bayart, D., & Akiskal, H. S. (2005). Cyclothymic temperament as a prospective predictor of bipolarity and suicidality in children and adolescents with major depressive disorder. *Journal of Affective Disorders, 85*, 181–189.

Koegel, R. L., & Koegel, L. K. (2012). *The PRT pocket guide: Pivotal response treatment for autism spectrum disorders*. Baltimore, MD: Paul H. Brookes.

Koen, L., Niehaus, D., Muller, J., & Laurent, C. (2008). Use of traditional treatment methods in a Xhosa schizophrenia population. *South African Medical Journal, 93*(6), 443.

Kogon, M. M., Biswas, A., Pearl, D., Carlson, R. W. L., & Spiegel, D. (1997). Effects of medical and psychotherapeutic treatment on the survival of women with metastatic breast carcinoma. *Cancer, 80*, 225–230.

Kohn, R., Wintrob, R. M., & Alarcón, R. D. (2009). Transcultural psychiatry. In B. J. Sadock, V. A. Sadock, & P. Ruiz (Eds.), *Kaplan & Sadock's comprehensive textbook of psychiatry* (9th ed., Vol. I, pp. 734–753). Philadelphia, PA: Lippincott Williams & Wilkins.

Kohut, H. (1971). *The analysis of self*. New York, NY: International Universities Press.

Kohut, H. (1977). *The restoration of the self*. Chicago, IL: University of Chicago Press.

Kolb, B., & Whishaw, I. Q. (1998). Possible regeneration of rat medial front cortex following neonatal frontal lesions. *Behavioral Brain Research, 91*, 127–141.

Kolb, B., Gibb, R., & Gorny, G. (2003). Experience-dependent changes in dendritic arbor and spine density in neocortex vary qualitatively with age and sex. *Neurobiology of Learning & Memory, 79*, 1–10.

Kolb, B., Gibb, R., & Robinson, T. E. (2003). Brain plasticity and behavior. *Current Directions in Psychological Science, 12*(1), 1–5.

Kolla, B. P., Auger, R., & Morgenthaler, T. (2012). Circadian rhythm sleep disorders. *ChronoPhysiology and Therapy, 2*, 19–34.

Kollei, I., Schieber, K., de Zwaan, M., Svitak, M., & Martin, A. (2013). Body dysmorphic disorder and nonweight-related body image concerns in individuals with eating disorders. *International Journal of Eating Disorders, 46*(1), 52–59. doi: 10.1002/eat.22067

Kollins, S. (2008). ADHD, substance use disorders, and psychostimulant treatment: Current literature and treatment guidelines. *Journal of Attention Disorders, 12*(2), 115.

Kong, L. L., Allen, J. J., & Glisky, E. L. (2008). Interidentity memory transfer in dissociative identity disorder. *Journal of Abnormal Psychology, 117*(3), 686–692.

Koning, C., Magill-Evans, J., Volden, J., & Dick, B. (2011 September 15). Efficacy of cognitive behavior therapy-based social skills intervention for school-aged boys with autism spectrum disorders. *Research in Autism Spectrum Disorders*. doi: 10.1016/j.rasd.2011.07.011

Koob, A. (2009). *The root of thought*. Upper Saddle River, NJ: FT Press.

Kopelowicz, A., Zarate, R., Wallace, C. J., Liberman, R. P., Lopez, S. R., & Mintz, J. (2012). The ability of multifamily groups to improve treatment adherence in Mexican Americans with schizophrenia. *Archives of General Psychiatry, 69*(3), 265.

Koran, L. M., Abujaoude, E., Large, M. D., & Serpe, R. T. (2008). The prevalence of body dysmorphic disorder in the United States adult population. *CNS Spectrums, 13*(4), 316–322.

Korfine, L., & Hooley, J. M. (2000). Directed forgetting of emotional stimuli in borderline personality disorder. *Journal of Abnormal Psychology, 109*, 214–221.

Kosberg, J. I., Kaufman, A. V., Burgio, L. D., Leeper, J. D., & Sun, F. (2007). Family caregiving to those with dementia in rural Alabama: Racial similarities and differences. *Journal of Aging and Health, 19*, 3–21.

Kovacs, M., Akiskal, H. S., Gatsonis, C., & Parrone, P. L. (1994). Childhood-onset dysthymic disorder. *Archives of General Psychiatry, 51*, 365–374.

Kovacs, M., Goldston, D., & Gatsonis, C. (1993). Suicidal behaviors and childhood-onset depressive disorders: A longitudinal investigation. *Journal of the American Academy of Child and Adolescent Psychiatry, 32*, 8–20.

Kotlicka-Antczak, M., Pawełczyk, A., Rabe-Jabłońska, J., Śmigielski, J., & Pawełczyk, T. (2014). Obstetrical complications and Apgar score in subjects at risk of psychosis. *Journal of Psychiatric Research, 48*(1), 79–85.

Kraemer, H. C. (2014). The reliability of clinical diagnoses: State of the art. *Annual Review of Clinical Psychology, 10*, 111–130. doi: 10.1146/annurev-clinpsy-032813-153739

Kraepelin, E. (1898). *The diagnosis and prognosis of dementia praecox*. Paper presented at the 29th Congress of Southwestern German Psychiatry, Heidelberg.

Kraepelin, E. (1899). *Kompendium der psychiatrie* (6th ed.). Leipzig, Germany: Abel.

Kraepelin, E. (1913). *Psychiatry: A textbook for students and physicians*. Leipzig, Germany: Barth.

Kraepelin, E. (1919). *Dementia praecox and paraphrenia* (R. M. Barclay & G. M. Robertson, Trans.). New York, NY: R. E. Krieger.

Kral, J. G. (2002). Surgical interventions for obesity. In K. D. Brownell & C. G. Fairburn (Eds.), *Eating disorders and obesity: A comprehensive handbook* (2nd ed., pp. 510–515). New York, NY: Guilford.

Krenek, M., & Maisto, S. A. (2013). Life events and treatment outcomes among individuals with substance use disorders: A narrative review. *Clinical Psychology Review, 33*(3), 470–483. doi: http://dx.doi.org/10.1016/j.cpr.2013.01.012

Kring, A. M. (2012). Emotion deficits in people with schizophrenia. *Annual Review of Clinical Psychology, 9*, 409–433.

Kring, A. M., & Elis, O. (2013). Emotion deficits in people with schizophrenia. Annual review of clinical psychology, 9, 409–433.

Kring, A. M., & Sloan, D. M. (2010). *Emotion regulation and psychopathology: A transdiagnostic approach to etiology and treatment*. New York, NY: Guilford.

Kroenke, K. (2007). Efficacy of treatment for somatoform disorders: A review of randomized controlled trials. *Psychosomatic Medicine, 69*(9), 881–888.

Kroll, R., & Beitchman, J. H. (2009). Stuttering. In B. J. Sadock, V. A. Sadock, & P. Ruiz (Eds.), *Kaplan & Sadock's comprehensive textbook of psychiatry* (9th ed., Vol. II, pp. 3528–3533). Philadelphia, PA: Lippincott Williams & Wilkins.

Krueger, D. D., & Bear, M. F. (2011). Toward fulfilling the promise of molecular medicine in fragile X syndrome. *Annual Review of Medicine, 62*, 411.

Krueger, R. B. (2010a). The DSM diagnostic criteria for sexual sadism. *Archives of Sexual Behavior, 39*(2), 325–345.

Krueger, R. B. (2010b). The DSM diagnostic criteria for sexual masochism. *Archives of sexual behavior, 39*(2), 346–356.

Krueger, R. B., & Kaplan, M. S. (2015). Paraphilic Disorders. In A. Tasman, J. Kay, J. A. Lieberman, M. B. First, & M. B. Riba (Eds.). *Psychiatry, Fourth Edition* (pp.1749–1758). Chichester, UK: John Wiley & Sons, Ltd.

Krueger, R. F., Hopwood, C. J., Wright, A. G., & Markon, K. E. (2014). *DSM-5* and the path toward empirically based and clinically useful conceptualization of personality and psychopathology. *Clinical Psychology: Science and Practice, 21*(3), 245–261. doi: 10.1111/cpsp.12073

Krueger, R. F., & Markon, K. E. (2014). The role of the *DSM-5* personality trait model in moving toward a quantitative and empirically based approach to classifying personality and psychopathology. *Annual Review of Clinical Psychology, 10*, 477–501. doi: 10.1146/annurev-clinpsy-032813-153732

Krueger, R. F., Markon, K. E., Patrick, C. J., & Iacono, W. G. (2005). Externalizing psychopathology in adulthood: A dimensional-spectrum conceptualization and its implications for DSM-V. *Journal of Abnormal Psychology, 114*(4), 537–550. doi:10.1037/0021-843x.114.4.537

Krueger, R. F., Watson, D., & Barlow, D. H. (2005). Introduction to the special section: Toward a dimensionally based taxonomy of psychopathology [Special issue]. *Journal of Abnormal Psychology, 114*, 491–493.

Krug, E. G., Kresnow, M.-J., Peddicord, J. P., Dahlberg, L. L., Powell, K. E., Crosby, A. E., & Annest, J. L. (1998). Suicide after natural disasters. *New England Journal of Medicine, 338*(6), 373–378.

Krupitsky, E., & Blokhina, E. (2010). Long-acting depot formulations of naltrexone for heroin dependence: A review. *Current Opinion in Psychiatry, 23*(3), 210.

Kuehn, B. M. (2010). Sibutramine warning. *JAMA: Journal of the American Medical Association, 303*, 322.

Kumpulainen, K. (2002). Phenomenology and treatment of selective mutism. *CNS Drugs, 16*(3), 175–180.

Kuo, W. H., Gallo, J. J., & Tien, A. Y. (2001). Incidence of suicide ideation and attempts in adults: The 13-year follow-up of a community sample in Baltimore, Maryland. *Psychological Medicine, 31*, 1181–91.

Kuo, J. R., Khoury, J. E., Metcalfe, R., Fitzpatrick, S., & Goodwill, A. (2015). An examination of the relationship between childhood emotional abuse and borderline personality disorder features: The role of difficulties with emotion regulation. *Child Abuse and Neglect, 39*, 147–155.

Kuperman, S., Chan, G., Kramer, J. R., Wetherill, L., Bucholz, K. K., Dick, D., & Schuckit, M. A. (2013). A model to determine the likely age of an adolescent's first drink of alcohol. *Pediatrics, 131*(2), 242–248. doi: 10.1542/peds.2012-0880

Kupfer, D. J. (1995). Sleep research in depressive illness: Clinical implications—A tasting menu. *Biological Psychiatry, 38*, 391–403.

Kupfer, D. J., First, M. B., & Regier, D. A. (2002). *A research agenda for DSM-V*. Washington, DC: American Psychiatric Association.

Kupfer, D. J., Frank, E., & Ritchey, F. C. (2015). Staging bipolar disorder: What data and what models are needed? *Lancet Psychiatry, 6*, 564–570.

Kupka, R., Luckenbaugh, D., Post, R., Suppes, T., Altshuler, L., Keck, P., & Nolen, W. A. (2005). Comparison of rapid-cycling and non-rapid-cycling bipolar disorder based on prospective mood ratings in 539 outpatients. *American Journal of Psychiatry, 162*, 1273–1280.

Kurihara, T., Kato, M., Reverger, R., & Gusti Rai Tirta, I. (2006). Beliefs about causes of schizophrenia among family members: A community-based survey in Bali. *Psychiatric Services, 57,* 1795–1799.

Kurtz, M. M., & Richardson, C. L. (2012). Social cognitive training for schizophrenia: A meta-analytic investigation of controlled research. *Schizophrenia Bulletin, 38*(5), 1092–1104.

Kurtz, T. W. (2010). Genome-wide association studies will unlock the genetic basis of hypertension: Con side of the argument. *Hypertension, 56*(6), 1021–1025.

Kuyken, W., Hayes, R., Barrett, B., Byng, R., Dalgleish, T., Kessler, D., . . . Byford, S. (2015). Effectiveness and cost-effectiveness of mindfulness-based cognitive therapy compared with maintenance antidepressant treatment in the prevention of depressive relapse or recurrence (PREVENT): a randomised controlled trial. *Lancet, 386,* 63–73.

Kwapil, T. R., & Barrantes-Vidal, N. (2012). Schizotypal personality disorder: An integrative review. In T. A. Widiger (Ed.), *The Oxford handbook of personality disorders* (pp. 437– 477). New York, NY: Oxford University Press.

Kwok, T., Lee, J., Lam, L., & Woo, J. (2008). Vitamin B12 supplementation did not improve cognition but reduced delirium in demented patients with vitamin B12 deficiency. *Archives of Gerontology and Geriatrics, 46*(3), 273–282.

Kymalainen, J., & Weisman de Mamani, A. G. (2008). Expressed emotion, communication deviance, and culture in families of patients with schizophrenia: A review of the literature. *Cultural Diversity and Ethnic Minority Psychology, 14*(2), 85–91.

La Fond, J. Q. (2005). *Preventing sexual violence: How society should cope with sex offenders.* Washington, DC: American Psychological Association.

La Fond, J. Q., & Durham, M. L. (1992). *Back to the asylum: The future of mental health law and policy in the United States.* New York, NY: Oxford University Press.

La Greca, A. M., & Prinstein, M. J. (2002). Hurricanes and earthquakes. In A. N. La Greca, W. K. Silverman, & M. C. Roberts (Eds.), *Helping Children Cope with Disasters and Terrorism* (Vol. 1, pp. 107–138). Washington, DC: American Psychological Association.

La Greca, A. M., Silverman, W. K., Lai, B., & Jaccard, J. (2010). Hurricane-related exposure experiences and stressors, other life events, and social support: Concurrent and prospective impact on children's persistent posttraumatic stress symptoms. *Journal of Consulting and Clinical Psychology, 78,* 794–805. doi: 10.1037/a0020775

Laan, E. & Tiefer, L. (2014). *The sham drug idea of the year: Pink Viagra.* L. A. Times. Retrieved from http://www.latimes.com/opinion/op-ed/la-oe-laan-tiefer-pink-viagra-20141114-story.html

Lacey, J. H. (1992). The treatment demand for bulimia: A catchment area report of referral rates and demography. *Psychiatric Bulletin, 16,* 203–205.

Lack, L. C., Gradisar, M., Van Someren, E. J. W., Wright, H. R., & Lushington, K. (2008). The relationship between insomnia and body temperatures. *Sleep Medicine Reviews, 12*(4), 307–317.

Lader, M., & Sartorius, N. (1968). Anxiety in patients with hysterical conversion symptoms. *Journal of Neurology, Neurosurgery, and Psychiatry, 31,* 490–495.

Lader, M. H. (1975). *The psychophysiology of mental illness.* London, UK: Routledge & Kegan Paul.

Laing, R. D. (1967). *The politics of experience.* New York, NY: Pantheon.

Lakes, K., Vaughan, E., Jones, M., Burke, W., Baker, D., & Swanson, J. (2012). Diverse perceptions of the informed consent process: Implications for the recruitment and participation of diverse communities in the National Children's Study. *American Journal of Community Psychology, 49*(1), 215–232. doi: 10.1007/s10464-011-9450-1

Lakin, M. M., Montague, D. K., Vanderbrug Medendorp, S., Tesar, L., & Schover, L. R. (1990). Intracavernous injection therapy: Analysis of results and complications. *Journal of Urology, 143,* 1138–1141.

Lalumière, M. L., Blanchard, R., & Zucker, K. J. (2000). Sexual orientation and handedness in men and women: A meta-analysis. *Psychological Bulletin, 126,* 575–592.

Lam, R. W., & Lavitan, R. D. (2000). Pathophysiology of seasonal affective disorder: A review. *Journal of Psychiatry and Neuroscience, 25,* 469–480.

Lam, R., Levitt, A., Levitan, R., Enns, M., Morehouse, R., Michalak, E., & Tam, S. E. (2006). The Can-Sad study: A randomized controlled trial of the effectiveness of light therapy and fluoxetine in patients with winter seasonal affective disorder. *American Journal of Psychiatry, 163,* 805–812.

Lam, T. H., Ho, S. Y., Hedley, A. J., Mak, K. H., & Peto, R. (2001). Mortality and smoking in Hong Kong: Case-control study of all adult deaths in 1998. *British Medical Journal, 323,* 361–362.

Lamb, H. R. (2009). Reversing criminalization. *American Journal of Psychiatry, 166*(1), 8–10. doi: 10.1176/appi.ajp.2008.08101515

Lamb, H. R., & Weinberger, L. E. (2009). Criminalization of persons with severe mental illness. In B. J. Sadock, V. A. Sadock, & P. Ruiz (Eds.), *Kaplan & Sadock's comprehensive textbook of psychiatry* (9th ed., Vol. II, pp. 4380–4395). Philadelphia, PA: Lippincott Williams & Wilkins.

Lamberg, L. (2003). All night diners: Researchers take a new look at night eating syndrome. *JAMA: Journal of the American Medical Association, 290,* 1442.

Lamis, D. A., Malone, P. S., Langhinrichsen-Rohling, J., & Ellis, T. E. (2010). Body investment, depression, and alcohol use as risk factors for suicide proneness in college students. *Crisis: The Journal of Crisis Intervention and Suicide Prevention, 31*(3), 118–127.

Landis, S., & Insel, T. R. (2008, November 7). The "neuro" in neurogenetics. *Science, 322,* 821.

Lang, P. J. (1985). The cognitive psychophysiology of emotion: Fear and anxiety. In A. H. Tuma & J. D. Maser (Eds.), *Anxiety and the anxiety disorders.* Hillsdale, NJ: Erlbaum.

Lang, P. J. (1995). The emotion probe: Studies of motivation and attention. *American Psychologist, 50,* 372–385.

Lang, P. J., Bradley, M. M., & Cuthbert, B. N. (1998). Emotion, motivation, and anxiety: Brain mechanisms and psychophysiology. *Biological Psychiatry, 44,* 1248–1263.

Långström, N., & Seto, M. (2006). Exhibitionistic and voyeuristic in a Swedish national population survey. *Archives of Sexual Behavior, 35,* 427–435.

Långström, N., & Zucker, K. (2005). Transvestic fetishism in the general population: Prevalence and correlates. *Journal of Sex & Marital Therapy, 31,* 87–95.

Långström, N., Rahman, Q., Carlström, E., & Lichtenstein, P. (2010). Genetic and environmental effects on same-sex sexual behavior: A population study of twins in Sweden. *Archives of Sexual Behavior, 39,* 75–80.

Lanius, R. A., Brand, B., Vermetten, E., Frewen, P. A., & Spiegel, D. (2012). The dissociative subtype of posttraumatic stress disorder: Rationale, clinical and neurobiological evidence, and implications. *Depression and Anxiety, 29,* 701–708. doi: 10.1002/da.21889

Lapierre, S., Erlangsen, A., Waern, M., De Leo, D., Oyama, H., Scocco, P., & Quinnett, P. (2011). A systematic review of elderly suicide prevention programs. *Crisis: The Journal of Crisis Intervention and Suicide Prevention, 32*(2), 88–98.

Larsen, B. A., Darby, R. S., Harris, C. R., Nelkin, D. K., Milam, P. E., & Christenfeld, N. J. (2012). The immediate and delayed cardiovascular benefits of forgiving. *Psychosomatic Medicine, 74*(7), 745–750. doi: 10.1097/PSY.0b013e31825fe96c

Larson, N. C., Barger, S. D., & Sydeman, S. J. (2013). Type D personality is not associated with coronary heart disease risk in a North American sample of retirement-aged adults. *International Journal of Behavioral Medicine, 20*(2), 277–285.

Lasch, C. (1978). *The culture of narcissism: American life in an age of diminishing expectations.* New York, NY: W. W. Norton.

Lataster, J., Myin-Germeys, I., Lieb, R., Wittchen, H. U., & Van Os, J. (2012). Adversity and psychosis: A 10-year prospective study investigating synergism between early and recent adversity in psychosis. *Acta Psychiatrica Scandinavica, 125*(5), 388–399.

Latfi, R., Kellum, J. M., DeMaria, E. J., & Sugarman, H. J. (2002). Surgical treatment of obesity. In T. A. Wadden & A. J. Stunkard (Eds.), *Handbook of obesity treatment* (pp. 339–356). New York, NY: Guilford.

Lau, J. Y. F., & Eley, T. C. (2010). The genetics of mood disorders. *Annual Review of Clinical Psychology, 6,* 313–337.

Laub, J. H., & Vaillant, G. E. (2000). Delinquency and mortality: A 50-year follow-up study of 1,000 delinquent and nondelinquent boys. *American Journal of Psychiatry, 157,* 96–102.

Laumann, E., Gagnon, J., Michael, R., & Michaels, S. (1994). *The social organization of sexuality: Sexual practices in the United*

States. Chicago, IL: University of Chicago Press.

Laumann, E., Paik, A., & Rosen, R. C. (1999). Sexual dysfunction in the United States. Prevalence and predictors. *JAMA: Journal of the American Medical Association, 281,* 537–544.

Laumann, E., Paik, A., Glasser, D., Kang, J., Wang, T., Levinson, B., & Gingell, C. (2006). A cross-national study of subjective sexual well-being among older women and men: Findings from the global study of sexual attitudes and behaviors. *Archives of Sexual Behavior, 35,* 145–161.

Laumann, E. O., Nicolosi, A., Glasser, D. B., Paik, A., Gingell, C., Moreira, E., & Wang, T. (2005). Sexual problems among women and men aged 40-80 years: Prevalence and correlates identified by the Global Study of Sexual Attitudes and Behaviors. *International Journal of Impotence Research, 17,* 39–57.

Launer, L. J. (2011). Counting dementia: there is no one "best" way. *Alzheimer's & Dementia, 7*(1), 10–14.

Lauriello, J., Bustillo, J. R., & Keith, S. J. (2005). Schizophrenia: Scope of the problem. In B. J. Sadock & V. A. Sadock (Eds.), *Kaplan & Sadock's comprehensive textbook of psychiatry* (pp. 1345–1354). Philadelphia, PA: Lippincott, Williams & Wilkins.

Lawrence, A. (2005). Sexuality before and after male-to-female sex reassignment surgery. *Archives of Sexual Behavior, 34,* 147–166.

Lawrence, A. A. (2013). Debating the Meaning of Autogynephilia. In A. A. Lawrence (Eds.). *Men Trapped in Men's Bodies* (pp. 95–110; 161–178). New York, NY: Springer.

Laws, D. R., & O'Donohue, W. (Eds.) (1997). *Sexual deviance: Theory, assessment and treatment.* New York, NY: Guilford.

Laws, D. R., & O'Donohue, W. T. (2008). Introduction. In D. R. Laws & W. T. O'Donohue (Eds.), *Sexual deviance: Theory, assessment, and treatment* (2nd ed., pp. 1–20). New York, NY: Guilford.

Lawton, K., & Kasari, C. (2012). Teacher-implemented joint attention intervention: Pilot randomized controlled study for pre-schoolers with autism. *Journal of Consulting and Clinical Psychology, 80*(4), 687.

Laxenaire, M., Ganne-Vevonec, M. O., & Streiff, O. (1982). Les problèmes d'identité chez les enfants des migrants. *Annales Medico-Psychologiques, 140,* 602–605.

Lazare, D. (1989, October 14). Drugs 'R' Us. *In These Times,* 12–13.

Lazarus, R. S. (1968). Emotions and adaptation: Conceptual and empirical relations. In W. J. Arnold (Ed.), *Nebraska Symposium on Motivation* (Vol. 16). Lincoln, NE: University of Nebraska Press.

Lazarus, R. S. (1991). Progress on a cognitive-motivational relational theory of emotion. *American Psychologist, 46*(8), 819–834.

Lazarus, R. S. (1995). Psychological stress in the workplace. In R. Crandall & P. L. Perrewe (Eds.), *Occupational stress: A handbook* (pp. 3–14). Philadelphia, PA: Taylor & Francis.

Le Foll, B., Gallo, A., Le Strat, Y., Lu, L., & Gorwood, P. (2009). Genetics of dopamine receptors and drug addiction: A comprehensive review. *Behavioural Pharmacology, 20*(1), 1–17.

le Grange, D., Crosby, R. D., Rathouz, P. J., & Leventhal, B. L. (2007). A randomized controlled comparison of family-based treatment and supportive psychotherapy for adolescent bulimia nervosa. *Archives of General Psychiatry, 64*(9), 1049–1056.

le Grange, D., Lock, J., Loeb, K., & Nicholls, D. (2010). Academy for eating disorders position paper: The role of the family in eating disorders. *International Journal of Eating Disorders, 43,* 1–5.

Leahy, R. L., & McGinn, L. K. (2012). Cognitive therapy for personality disorders. In T. A. Widiger (Ed.), *The Oxford handbook of personality disorders* (pp. 727–750). New York, NY: Oxford University Press.

LeBeau, R., Bogels, S., Moller, E., & Craske, M. (2015). Integrating dimensional assessment and categorical diagnosis in *DSM-5*: The benefits and challenges of the paradigm shift for the anxiety disorders. *Psychopathology Review, 2*(1), 83–99.

LeBeau, R., Mischel, E., Resnick, H., Kilpatrick, D., Friedman, M., & Craske, M. (2014). Dimensional assessment of posttraumatic stress disorder in *DSM-5. Psychiatry Research, 218*(1), 143–147. doi:10.1016/j.psychres.2014.03.032

LeBeau, R. T., Glenn, D., Liao, B., Wittchen, H.-U., Beesdo-Baum, K., Ollendick, T., & Craske, M. G. (2010). Specific phobia: A review of DSM-IV specific phobia and preliminary recommendations for DSM-V. *Depression and Anxiety, 27*(2), 148–167.

LeBeau, R. T., Glenn, D. E., Hanover, L. N., Beesdo-Baum, K., Wittchen, H.-U., & Craske, M. G. (2012). A dimensional approach to measuring anxiety for DSM-5. *International Journal of Methods in Psychiatric Research, 21*(4), 258–272.

LeBeau, R. T., Mischel, E. R., Simpson, H. B., Mataix-Cols, D., Phillips, K. A., Stein, D. J., & Craske, M. G. (2013). Preliminary assessment of obsessive–compulsive spectrum disorder scales for *DSM-5. Journal of Obsessive-Compulsive and Related Disorders, 2*(2), 114–118.

Lebedinskaya, K. S., & Nikolskaya, O. S. (1993). Brief report: Analysis of autism and its treatment in modern Russian defectology. *Journal of Autism and Developmental Disorders, 23,* 675–697.

Lechner, S., Antoni, M. (2004). Posttraumatic growth and group based intervention for persons dealing with cancer: What have we learned so far? *Psychological Inquiry, 15,* 35–41.

Leckman, J. F., Denys, D., Simpson, H. B., Mataix-Cols, D., Hollander, E., Saxena, S., & Stein, D. (2010). Obsessive-compulsive disorder: A review of the diagnostic criteria and possible subtypes and dimensional specifiers for DSM-V. *Depression and Anxiety, 27*(6), 507–527. doi: 10.1002/da.20669

Leckman, J. F., Grice, D. E., Boardman, J., Zhang, H., Vitali, A., Bondi, C., & Pauls, D. (1997). Symptoms of obsessive-compulsive disorder. *American Journal of Psychiatry, 154,* 911–917.

Lecrubier, Y., Bakker, A., Dunbar, G., & the Collaborative Paroxetine Panic Study Investigators. (1997). A comparison of paroxetine, clomipramine and placebo in the treatment of panic disorder. *Acta Psychiatrica Scandinavica, 95,* 145–152.

Lecrubier, Y., Judge, R., & the Collaborative Paroxetine Panic Study Investigators. (1997). Long term evaluation of paroxetine, clomipramine and placebo in panic disorder. *Acta Psychiatrica Scandinavica, 95,* 153–160.

Ledford, H. (2015). First cancer-fighting virus approved. *Nature, 526,* 622–623.

LeDoux, J. E. (1996). *The emotional brain: The mysterious underpinnings of emotional life.* New York, NY: Simon & Schuster.

LeDoux, J. E. (2002). *Synaptic self: How our brains become who we are.* New York, NY: Penguin Books.

LeDoux, J. (2015). *Anxious: Using the brain to understand and treat fear and anxiety.* New York, NY: Viking.

Lee, C. C., Czaja, S. J., & Schulz, R. (2010). The moderating influence of demographic characteristics, social support, and religious coping on the effectiveness of a multicomponent psychosocial caregiver intervention in three racial ethnic groups. *The Journals of Gerontology Series B: Psychological Sciences and Social Sciences, 65B*(2), 185–194.

Lee, C. K. (1992). Alcoholism in Korea. In J. Helzer & G. Canino (Eds.), *Alcoholism—North America, Europe and Asia: A coordinated analysis of population data from ten regions* (pp. 247–262). London, U.K.: Oxford University Press.

Lee, M., Martin-Ruiz, C., Graham, A., Court, J., Jaros, E., Perry, R., & Perry, E. (2002). Nicotinic receptor abnormalities in the cerebellar cortex in autism. *Brain, 125,* 1483–1495.

Lee, M. A., & Shlain, B. (1992). *Acid dreams: The complete social history of LSD: The CIA, the sixties, and beyond.* New York, NY: Grove Press.

Lee, S. H., Han, D. H., Oh, S., Lyoo, I. K., Lee, Y. S., Renshaw, P. F., & Lukas, S. (2009). Quantitative electroencephalographic (qEEG) correlates of craving during virtual reality therapy in alcohol-dependent patients. *Pharmacology Biochemistry and Behavior, 91*(3), 393–397. doi: 10.1016/j.pbb.2008.08.014

Lee, T. M., Chen, E. Y., Chan, C. C., Paterson, J. G., Janzen, H. L., & Blashko, C. A. (1998). Seasonal affective disorder. *Clinical Psychology: Science and Practice, 5,* 275–290.

Lefley, H. (2009). *Family psychoeducation in serious mental illness: Models, outcomes, applications.* New York, NY: Oxford University Press.

Lefrancois, G. R. (1990). *The lifespan* (3rd ed.). Belmont, CA: Wadsworth.

Le Grange, D., Lock, J., Agras, W. S., Bryson, S. W., & Jo, B. (2015). Randomized Clinical Trial of Family-Based Treatment and Cognitive-Behavioral Therapy for Adolescent Bulimia Nervosa. *Journal of the American Academy of Child & Adolescent Psychiatry, 54*(11), 886–894.

Lehman, B. J., Taylor, S. E., Kiefe, C. I., & Seeman, T. E. (2009). Relationship of early life stress and psychological functioning to blood pressure in the CARDIA study. *Health Psychology, 28*(3), 338–346.

Leibbrand, R., Hiller, W., & Fichter, M. M. (2000). Hypochondriasis and somatization: Two distinct aspects of somatoform disorders? *Journal of Clinical Psychology*, 56, 63–72.

Leibenluft, E. (2011). Severe mood dysregulation, irritability, and the diagnostic boundaries of bipolar disorder in youths. *American Journal of Psychiatry*, 168(2), 129–142.

Leibenluft, E., & Rich, B. A. (2008). Pediatric bipolar disorder. *Annual Review of Clinical Psychology*, 4, 163–187.

Leiblum, S. R. (2010). *Treating sexual desire disorders: A clinical casebook*. New York, NY: Guilford.

Leiblum, S. R., & Rosen, R. C. (Eds.) (2000). *Principles and practice of sex therapy* (3rd ed.). New York, NY: Guilford.

Leitenberg, H., Detzer, M. J., & Srebnik, D. (1993). Gender differences in masturbation and the relation of masturbation experience in preadolescence and/or early adolescence to sexual behavior and sexual adjustment in young adulthood. *Archives of Sexual Behavior*, 22(2), 87–98.

Lejeune, J., Gauthier, M., & Turpin, R. (1959). Étude des chromosomes somatiques de neuf enfants mongoliens. *Comptes Rendus Hebdomadaires des Séances de l' Académie des Sciences. D: Sciences Naturelles (Paris)*, 248, 1721–1722.

Lemay, M., & Landreville, P. (2010). Verbal agitation in dementia: The role of discomfort. *American Journal of Alzheimer's Disease and Other Dementias*, 25(3), 193–201. doi: 10.1177/1533317509356687.

Lener, M. S., Wong, E., Tang, C. Y., Byne, W., Goldstein, K. E., Blair, N. J., . . . Hazlett, E. A. (2014). White matter abnormalities in schizophrenia and schizotypal personality disorder. *Schizophrenia Bulletin*, 41(1), 300–310.

Lenze, E. J., Miller, A. R., Munir, Z. B., Pornoppadol, C., & North, C. S. (1999). Psychiatric symptoms endorsed by somatization disorder patients in a psychiatric clinic. *Annals of Clinical Psychiatry*, 11(2), 73–79.

Lenze E. J., Mulsant B. H., Shear M.K., Schulberg H. C., Dew M. A., Begley A. E., . . . Reynolds C. F. 3rd. (2000). Comorbid anxiety disorders in depressed elderly patients. *Am J Psychiatry*, 157(5):722–728.

Lenzenweger, M., Lane, M., Loranger, A., & Kessler, R. (2007). DSM-IV personality disorders in the National Comorbidity Survey Replication. *Biological Psychiatry*, 62(6), 553–564.

Lenzenweger, M. F., & Dworkin, R. H. (1996). The dimensions of schizophrenia phenomenology. Note one or two, at least three, perhaps four. *British Journal of Psychiatry*, 168, 432–440.

Lenzenweger, M. F., McLachlan, G., & Rubin, D. B. (2007). Resolving the latent structure of schizophrenia endophenotypes using expectation-maximization-based finite mixture modeling. *Journal of Abnormal Psychology*, 116, 16–29.

Lerner, R., Kibler, J. L. & Zeichner, S. B. (2013). Relationship between mindfulness-based stress reduction and immune function in cancer and HIV/AIDS. *Cancer and Clinical Oncology*, 2(1), 62–72.

Leserman, J. (2008). Role of depression, stress, and trauma in HIV disease progression. *Psychosomatic Medicine*, 70, 539–545.

Leserman, J., Petitto, J. M., Golden, R. N., Gaynes, B. N., Gu, H., Perkins, D. O., & Evans, D. L. (2000). Impact of stressful life events, depression, social support, coping, and cortisol on progression to AIDS. *American Journal of Psychiatry*, 157, 1221–1228.

Leuchter, A. F., Cook, I. A., Witte, E. A., Morgan, M., & Abrams, M. (2002). Changes in brain function of depressed subjects during treatment with placebo. *American Journal of Psychiatry*, 159(1)122–129.tf vtcr c

LeVay, S. (1991). A difference in hypothalamic structure between heterosexual and homo-sexual men. *Science*, 253, 1034–1037.

Levenston, G. K., Patrick, C. J., Bradley, M. M., & Lang, P. J. (2000). The psychopath as observer: emotion and attention in picture processing. *Journal of Abnormal Psychology*, 109(3), 373.

Leventhal, A. M., & Zvolensky, M. J. (2015). Anxiety, depersssion, and cigarette smoking: A transdiagnostc vulnerability framework to understand emotion-smoking comorbidity. *Psychological Bulletin*, 141, 176–212.

Levesque, R. J. (2012). Sadistic personality disorder. In *Encyclopedia of Adolescence* (pp. 2445–2446). New York, NY: Springer.

Levin, F. R., Evans, S. M., Brooks, D. J., & Garawi, F. (2007). Treatment of cocaine dependent treatment seekers with adult ADHD: Double-blind comparison of methylphenidate and placebo. *Drug and Alcohol Dependence*, 87, 20–29.

Levine, J. A., Lanningham-Foster, L. M., McCrady, S. K., Krizan, A. C., Olson, L. R., Kane, P. H., . . . Clark, M. M. (2005). Interindividual variation in posture allocation: Possible role in human obesity. *Science*, 307, 584–586.

Levine, M. P., & Smolak, L. (1996). Media as a context for the development of disordered eating. In L. Smolak, M. P. Levine, & R. Striegel-Moore (Eds.), *The developmental psychopathology of eating disorders: Implications for research, prevention, and treatment* (pp. 235–257). Mahwah, NJ: Erlbaum.

Levine, S. B., (2015). Filbanserin. *Archives of Sexual Behavior*, 44(8), 2107–2109. doi: 10.1007/s10508-015-0617-y

Levinson, D. F. (2009). Genetics of major depression. In I. H. Gotlib & C. L. Hammen (Eds.), *Handbook of depression* (2nd ed., pp. 165–186). New York, NY: Guilford.

Levitt, A., & Boyle, M. (2002). The impact of latitude on the prevalence of seasonal depression. *Canadian Journal of Psychiatry*, 46, 650–654.

Levitt, A. J., Joffe, R. T., Moul, D. F., Lam, R. W., Teicher, M. H., Lebegue, B., & Buchanan, A. (1993). Side effects of light therapy in seasonal affective disorder. *American Journal of Psychiatry*, 150, 650–652.

Levy, B. R., Slade, M. D., Kunkel, S. R., & Kasl, S. V. (2002). Longevity increased by positive self-perceptions of aging. *Journal of Personality and Social Psychology*, 83, 261–270.

Levy, K. B., O'Grady, K. E., Wish, E. D., & Arria, A. M. (2005). An in-depth qualitative examination of the ecstasy experience: Results of a focus group with Ecstasy-using

college students. *Substance Use and Misuse*, 40(9–10), 1427–1441. doi: 10.1081/ja-200066886

Lewinsohn, P. M., Allen, N. B., Seeley, J. R., & Gotlib, I. H. (1999). First onset versus recurrence of depression: Differential processes of psychosocial risk. *Journal of Abnormal Psychology*, 108(3), 483–489.

Lewis, B. A., Statt, E., & Marcus, B. H. (2011). Behavioral interventions in public health settings: Physical activity, weight loss, and smoking. In D. H. Barlow (Ed.), *Oxford handbook of clinical psychology* (pp. 717–738). New York, NY: Oxford University Press.

Lewis, D. O., Yeager, C. A., Swica, Y., Pincus, J. H., & Lewis, M. (1997). Objective documentation of child abuse and dissociation in 12 murderers with dissociative identity disorder. *American Journal of Psychiatry*, 154, 1703–1710.

Lewis, F. M., Brandt, P. A., Cochrane, B. B., Griffith, K. A., Grant, M., Haase, J. E., . . . Shands, M. E. (2015). The Enhancing Connections Program: A six-state randomized clinical trial of a cancer parenting program. *Journal of Consulting and Clinical Psychology*, 83(1), 1–12.

Lewis, G., Croft-Jeffreys, C., & Anthony, D. (1990). Are British psychiatrists racist? *British Journal of Psychiatry*, 157, 410–415.

Lewis, G., David, A., Andreasson, S., & Allsbeck, P. (1992). Schizophrenia and city life. *Lancet*, 340, 137–140.

Lewis, S., Escalona, R., & Keith, S. J. (2009). Phenomenology of schizophrenia. In B. J. Sadock, V. A. Sadock, & P. Ruiz (Eds.), *Kaplan & Sadock's comprehensive textbook of psychiatry* (9th ed., Vol. I, pp. 1433–1451). Philadelphia, PA: Lippincott Williams & Wilkins.

Lewis, T., DiLillo, D., & Peterson, L. (2004). Parental beliefs regarding developmental benefits of childhood injuries. *American Journal of Health Behavior*, 28(Suppl. 1) S61–S68.

Lewis, T. T., Everson-Rose, S. A., Powell, L. H., Matthews, K. A., Brown, C., & Wesley, D. (2006). Chronic exposure to everyday discrimination and coronary artery calcification in African-American women: The SWAN heart study. *Psychosomatic Medicine*, 68, 362–368.

Lewis-Fernández, R., Hinton, D. E., Laria, A. J., Patterson, E. H., Hofmann, S. G., Craske, M. G., & Liao, B. (2010). Culture and the anxiety disorders: Recommendations for DSM-V. *Depression and Anxiety*, 27(2), 212–229.

Lewy, A. J., & Sack, R. L. (1987). Light therapy of chronobiological disorders. In A. Halaris (Ed.), *Chronobiology and psychiatric disorders* (pp. 181–206). New York, NY: Elsevier.

Lewy, A. J., Bauer, V. K., Cutler, N. L., Ahmed, S., Thomas, K. H., Blood, M. L., & Letham Jackson, J. M. (1998). Morning vs. evening light treatment of patients with winter depression. *Archives of General Psychiatry*, 55, 890–896.

Lewy, A. J., Kern, H. E., Rosenthal, N. E., & Wehr, T. A. (1982). Bright artificial light treatment of a manic-depressive patient with a seasonal mood cycle. *American Journal of Psychiatry, 139*, 1496–1498.

Lewy, A. J., Tutek, J., Havel, L. L., & Nikia, M. N. (2014). The role of circadian rhythms, light and melatonin in SAD and nonseasonal affective and anxiety disorders. *Current Psychiatry Reviews, 10*, 214–222.

Leyfer, O., & Brown, T.A. (2011). The anxiety-depression spectrum. In D. H. Barlow (Ed.), *Oxford handbook of clinical psychology* (pp. 279–293). New York, NY: Oxford University Press.

Lezak, M. D., Howieson, D. B., Bigler, E. D., & Tranel, D. (2012). *Neuropsychological assessment* (5th ed.). New York, NY: Oxford University Press.

Li, X., Zou, H., & Brown, W. T. (2012). Genes associated with autism spectrum disorder. *Brain Research Bulletin, 88*(6), 543–552. doi: 10.1016/j.brainresbull.2012.05.017

Liberman, R., & Kopelowicz, A. (2009). Training skills for illness self-management in the rehabilitation of schizophrenia: A family-assisted program for Latinos in California. *Salud Mental, 31*, 93–105.

Liberman, R. P. (2007). Dissemination and adoption of social skills training: Social validation of an evidence-based treatment for the mentally disabled. *Journal of Mental Health, 16*, 595–623.

Liddell, H. S. (1949). The role of vigilance in the development of animal neurosis. In P. Hoch & J. Zubin (Eds.), *Anxiety.* New York, NY: Grune & Stratton.

Liddle, P. F. (2012). Descriptive clinical features of schizophrenia. In M. G. Gelder, N. C. Andreasen, J. J. Lopez-Ibor, Jr., & J. R. Geddes (Eds.), *New Oxford textbook of psychiatry* (2nd. ed., Vol. 1, pp. 526–531). New York, NY: Oxford University Press.

Lieb, R. (2015). Epidemiological perspectives on comorbidity between substance use disorders and other mental disorders. In G. Dom & F. Moggy (Eds), *Co-occurring addictive and psychiatric disorders* (pp. 3–12). Berlin, Germany: Springer Heidelberg.

Lieb, R., Wittchen, H-U., Hofler, M., Fuetsch, M., Stein, M. B., & Merikangas, K. R. (2000). Parental psychopathology, parenting styles, and the risk of social phobia in offspring. *Archives of General Psychiatry, 57*, 859–866.

Lieb, R., Zimmermann, P., Friis, R. H., Hofler, M., Tholen, S., & Wittchen, H.-U. (2002). The natural course of DSM-IV somatoform disorders and syndromes among adolescents and young adults: A prospective-longitudinal community study. *European Psychiatry, 17*, 321–331.

Lieberman, J. A., & Stroup, T. S. (2011). The NIMH-CATIE schizophrenia study: What did we learn? *American Journal of Psychiatry, 168*(8), 770–775. doi: 10.1176/appi.ajp.2011.11010039

Lieberman, J. A., Jody, D., Alvir, J. M. J., Ashtari, M., Levy, D. L., Bogerts, B., & Cooper, T. (1993). Brain morphology, dopamine, and eye-tracking abnormalities in first-episode schizophrenia. *Archives of General Psychiatry, 50*, 357–368.

Lieberman, J. A., Perkins, D., Belger, A., Chakos, M., Jarskog, F., Boteva, K., & Gilmore, J. (2001). The early stages of schizophrenia: Speculations on pathogenesis, pathophysiology, and therapeutic approaches. *Biological Psychiatry, 50*, 885.

Liebeskind, J. (1991). Pain can kill. *Pain, 44*, 3–4.

Liebman, R. E., & Burnette, M. (2013). It's not you, it's me: An examination of clinician-and client-level influences on counter-transference toward borderline personality disorder. *American Journal of Orthopsychiatry, 83*(1), 115–125. doi: 10.1111/ajop.12002

Liebowitz, M. R., Schneier, F., Campeas, R., Hollander, E., Hatterer, J., Fyer, A., Gully, R. (1992). Phenelzine vs. atenolol in social phobia: A placebo controlled comparison. *Archives of General Psychiatry, 49*, 290–300.

Lilenfeld, L. R. R., Wonderlich, S., Riso, L. P., Crosby, R., & Mitchell, J. (2006). Eating disorders and personality: A methodological and empirical review. *Clinical Psychology Review, 26*, 299–320.

Lilienfeld, S. O. (1992). The association between antisocial personality and somatization disorders: A review and integration of theoretical models. *Clinical Psychology Review, 12*, 641–662.

Lilienfeld, S. O. (2014). *DSM-5:* Centripetal scientific and centrifugal antiscientific forces. *Clinical Psychology: Science and Practice, 21*(3), 269–279. doi: 10.1111/cpsp.12075

Lilienfeld, S. O., & Hess, T. H. (2001). Psychopathic personality traits and somatization: Sex differences and the mediating role of negative emotionality. *Journal of Psychopathology and Behavioral Assessment, 23*, 11–24.

Lilienfeld, S. O., & Lynn, S. J. (2003). Dissociative identity disorder: Multiple personalities, multiple controversies. In S. O. Lilienfeld, S. J. Lynn, & J. M. Lohr (Eds.), *Science and pseudoscience in clinical psychology* (pp. 109–142). New York, NY: Guilford.

Lilienfeld, S. O., & Marino, L. (1995). Mental disorder as a Roschian concept: A critique of Wakefield's 'harmful dysfunction' analysis. *Journal of Abnormal Psychology, 104*(3), 411–420.

Lilienfeld, S. O., & Marino, L. (1999). Essentialism revisited: Evolutionary theory and the concept of mental disorder. *Journal of Abnormal Psychology, 108*, 400–411.

Lilienfeld, S. O., Kirsch, I., Sarbin, T. R., Lynn, S. J., Chaves, J. F., & Ganaway, G. K. (1999). Dissociative identity disorder and the sociocognitive model: Recalling the lessons of the past. *Psychological Bulletin, 125*(5), 507–523.

Lilienfeld, S. O., VanValkenburg, C., Larntz, K., & Akiskal, H. S. (1986). The relationship of histrionic personality to antisocial personality and somatization disorders. *American Journal of Psychiatry, 143*, 718–722.

Lima, E. N., Stanley, S., Kaboski, B., Reitzel, L. R., Richey, A., Castro, Y., & Jakobsons, L. J. (2005). The incremental validity of the MMPI-2: When does therapist access not enhance treatment outcome? *Psychological Assessment, 17*(4), 462–468.

Lin, K. M., Hwu, H. G., & Tsuang, M. T. (2012). Schizophrenia and other psychosis in Asians and Asian Americans. In E. C. Chang (Ed.), *Handbook of Adult Psychopathology in Asians: Theory, Diagnosis, and Treatment* (p. 83). New York, NY: Oxford University Press.

Lind, S., & Bowler, D. (2009). Delayed self-recognition in children with autism spectrum disorder. *Journal of Autism and Developmental Disorders, 39*(4), 643–650. doi: 10.1007/s10803-008-0670-7

Lindau, S. T., Schumm, L. P., Laumann, E. O., Levinson, W., O'Muircheartaigh, C. A., & Waite, L. J. (2007). A study of sexuality and health among older adults in the United States. *New England Journal of Medicine, 357*(8), 762–774.

Lindberg, N., Holi, M. M., Tani, P., & Virkkunen, M. (2005). Looking for pyromania: Characteristics of a consecutive sample of Finnish male criminals with histories of recidivist fire-setting between 1973 and 1993. *BMC Psychiatry, 5*(1), 47–52.

Lindblad, F., & Hjern, A. (2010). ADHD after fetal exposure to maternal smoking. *Nicotine & Tobacco Research, 12*(4), 408–415.

Lindenmayer, J., & Khan, A. (2006). Psychopathology. In J. A. Lieberman, T. S. Stroup & D. O. Perkins (Eds.), *Textbook of schizophrenia* (pp. 187–221). Washington, DC: American Psychiatric Publishing.

Lindsey, M., Joe, S., Muroff, J., & Ford, B. (2010). Social and clinical factors associated with psychiatric emergency service use and civil commitment among African-American youth. *General Hospital Psychiatry, 32*, 300–309.

Linehan, M., Comtois, K., Murray, A., Brown, M., Gallop, R., Heard, H., & Lindenboim, N. (2006). Two-year randomized controlled trial and follow-up of dialectical behavior therapy vs therapy by experts for suicidal behaviors and borderline personality disorder. *Archives of General Psychiatry, 63*(7), 757.

Linehan, M., Schmidt, H., Dimeff, L., Craft, J., Kanter, J., & Comtois, K. (1999). Dialectical behavior therapy for patients with borderline personality disorder and drug-dependence. *American Journal on Addictions, 8*(4), 279–292.

Linehan, M. M. (2015). *DBT® Skills Training Manual.* New York: Guilford.

Linehan, M. M., & Dexter-Mazza, E. T. (2008). Dialectical behavior therapy for borderline personality disorder. In D. H. Barlow (Ed.), *Clinical handbook of psychological disorders* (4th ed., pp. 365–420). New York, NY: Guilford.

Linehan, M. M., & Kehrer, C. A. (1993). Borderline personality disorder. In D. H. Barlow (Ed.), *Clinical handbook of psychological disorders: A step by step treatment manual* (pp. 396–441). New York, NY: Guilford.

Linton, S. J., Kecklund, G., Franklin, K. A., Leissner, L. C., Sivertsen, B., Lindberg, E., . . . Björkelund, C. (2015). The effect of the work environment on future sleep disturbances: a systematic review. *Sleep Medicine Reviews, 23*, 10–19.

Liotti, M., Mayberg, H. S., McGinnis, S., Brannan, S. L., & Jerabek, P. (2002). Unmasking disease-specific cerebral blood flow abnormalities: Mood challenge in patients with remitted unipolar depression. *American Journal of Psychiatry, 159*, 1807–1808.

Lipchik, G. L., Holroyd, K. A., & Nash, J. M. (2002). Cognitive-behavioral management of recurrent headache disorders: A minimal-therapist-contact approach. In D. C. Turk & R. J. Gatchel (Eds.), *Psychological approaches to pain management: A practitioner's handbook* (2nd ed.) (pp. 365–389). New York, NY: Guilford.

Lissek, S., & Grillon, C. (2012). Learning models of PTSD. In J. G. Beck & D. M. Sloan (Eds.), *The Oxford handbook of traumatic stress disorders* (pp. 175–190). New York, NY: Oxford University Press.

Lissek, S., Kaczkurkin, A. N., Rabin, S., Geraci, M., Pine, D. S., & Grillon, C. (2014). Generalized anxiety disorder is associated with overgeneralization of classically conditioned fear. *Biological psychiatry, 75*(11), 909–915.

Litvin, E. B., Ditre, J. W., Heckman, B. W., & Brandon, T. H. (2012). Nicotine. In J. C. Verster, K. Brady, M. Galanter, & P. Conrod (Eds.), *Drug abuse and addiction in medical illness* (pp. 137–150). New York, NY: Springer.

Litz, B. T., Salters-Pedneault, K., Steenkamp, M., Hermos, J. A., Bryant, R. A., Otto, M. W., & Hofmann, S. G. (2012). A randomized placebo-controlled trial of d-cycloserine and exposure therapy for post-traumatic stress disorder. *Journal of Psychiatric Research, 46,* 1184–1190.

Liu, K., & Bearman, P. S. (2012, September 19). Focal points, endogenous processes, and exogenous shocks in the autism epidemic. *Sociological Methods & Research.* doi: 10.1177/0049124112460369

Livhits, M., Mercado, C., Yermilov, I., Parikh, J. A., Dutson, E., Mehran, A., . . . Gibbons, M. M. (2012). Preoperative predictors of weight loss following bariatric surgery: systematic review. *Obesity Surgery, 22*(1), 70–89.

Livesley, W. J., & Jang, K. L. (2008). The behavioral genetics of personality disorder. *Annual Review of Clinical Psychology, 4,* 247–274.

Livesley, W. J., Jang, K. L., & Vernon, P. A. (1998). Phenotypic and genotypic structure of traits delineating personality disorder. *Archives of General Psychiatry, 55,* 941–948.

Livingston, E. H. (2007). Obesity, mortality, and bariatric surgery death rates. *JAMA: Journal of the American Medical Association, 298*(20), 2406–2408.

Livingston, E. H. (2010). Surgical treatment of obesity in adolescence. *JAMA: Journal of the American Medical Association, 303*(6), 559–560.

Livingston, E. H. (2012). Inadequacy of BMI as an indicator for bariatric surgery. *Journal of American Medical Association, 307,* 88–89.

Llewellyn, C. H., Trzaskowski, M., van Jaarsveld, C. H., Plomin, R., & Wardle, J. (2014). Satiety mechanisms in genetic risk of obesity. *JAMA Pediatrics, 168*(4), 338–344.

Lloyd, E. A. (2005). *The case of the female orgasm: Bias in the science of evolution.* Cambridge, MA: Harvard University Press.

Lo, S. C., Pripuzova, N., Li, B., Komaroff, A. L., Hung, G. C., Wang, R., & Alter, H. J. (2010). Detection of MLV-related virus gene sequences in blood of patients with chronic fatigue syndrome and healthy blood donors. *Proceedings of the National Academy of Sciences, 107*(36), 15874–15879.

Lo, S. C., Pripuzova, N., Li, B., Komaroff, A. L., Hung, G. C., Wang, R., & Alter, H. J. (2012). Retraction for Lo et al., Detection of MLV-related virus gene sequences in blood of patients with chronic fatigue syndrome and healthy blood donors. *Proceedings of the National Academy of Sciences of the United States of America, 109*(1), 346–346.

Lobbestael, J., & Arntz, A. (2012). Cognitive contributions to personality disorders. In T. A. Widiger (Ed.), *The Oxford handbook of personality disorders* (pp. 325–344). New York, NY: Oxford University Press.

Lobbestael, J., Arntz, A. & Bernstein, D. P. (2010). Disentangling the relationship between different types of childhood maltreatment and personality disorders. *Journal of Personality Disorders, 24,* 285–295.

Lobo, R. A. (2013). Where are we 10 years after the Women's Health Initiative? *The Journal of Clinical Endocrinology & Metabolism, 98*(5), 1771–1780.

Lochner, C., Grant, J. E., Odlaug, B. L., Woods, D. W., Keuthen, N. J., & Stein, D. J. (2012). DSM-5 field survey: Hair-pulling disorder (trichotillomania). *Depression and Anxiety, 29,* 1025–1031. doi: 10.1002/da.22011

Lock, J., Le Grange, D., Agras, W. S., & Dare, C. (2001). *Treatment manual for anorexia nervosa: A family-based approach.* New York, NY: Guilford.

Lock, J., Le Grange, D., Agras, W. S., Fitzpatrick, K. K., Jo, B., Accurso, E., . . . Stainer, M. (2015). Can adaptive treatment improve outcomes in family-based therapy for adolescents with anorexia nervosa? Feasibility and treatment effects of a multi-site treatment study. *Behaviour Research and Therapy, 73,* 90–95.

Lock, J., Le Grange, D., Agras, S., Moye, A., Byrson, S. W., & Jo, B. (2010). Randomized clinical trial comparing family-based treatment with adolescent-focused individual therapy for adolescents with anorexia nervosa. *Archives of General Psychiatry, 67*(10), 1025–1032.

Loehlin, J. C. (1992). *Genes and environment in personality development.* Newbury Park, CA: Sage. Loehlin, J., McFadden, D., Medland, S., & Martin, N. (2006). Population differences in finger-length ratios: Ethnicity or latitude? *Archives of Sexual Behavior, 35,* 739–742.

Loftus, E., & Davis, D. (2006). Recovered memories. *Annual Review of Clinical Psychology, 2,* 469–498.

Loftus, E. F. (2003). Make-believe memories. *American Psychologist, 58,* 867–873.

Loftus, E. F., Coan, J. A., & Pickrell, J. E. (1996). Manufacturing false memories using bits of reality. In L. Reder (Ed.), *Implicit memory and meta-cognition* (pp. 195–220). Mahwah, NJ: Erlbaum.

Logan, C. (2009). Sexual deviance in females: Psychopathology and theory. In D. R. Laws & W. T. O'Donohue (Eds.), *Sexual deviance: Theory, assessment, and treatment* (2nd ed., pp. 486–507). New York, NY: Guilford.

Lombardi, V. C., Ruscetti, F. W., Gupta, J. D., Pfost, M. A., Hagen, K. S., Peterson, D. L., . . . Mikovits, J. A. (2009). Detection of an infectious retrovirus, XMRV, in blood cells of patients with chronic fatigue syndrome. *Science, 326*(5952), 585–589.

Lombardo, M. V., Chakrabarti, B., & Baron-Cohen, S. (2009). The amygdala in autism: not adapting to faces? *American Journal of Psychiatry, 166*(4), 395–397.

Lonczak, H. S. P., Abbott, R. D. P., Hawkins, J. D. P., Kosterman, R. P., & Catalano, R. F. P. (2002). Effects of the Seattle Social Development Project on sexual behavior, pregnancy, birth, and sexually transmitted disease outcomes by age 21 years. *Archives of Pediatrics & Adolescent Medicine, 156*(5), 438–447.

Loomans, E. M., Hofland, L., van der Stelt, O., van der Wal, M. F., Koot, H. M., Van den Bergh, B. R. H., & Vrijkotte, T. G. M. (2012). Caffeine intake during pregnancy and risk of problem behavior in 5-to 6-year-old children. *Pediatrics, 130*(2), e305–e313. doi: 10.1542/peds.2011-3361

López, S. R., & Guarnaccia, P. J. (2012). Cultural dimensions of psychopathology: The social world's impact on mental disorders. In J. E. Maddux & B. A. Winstead (Eds.), *Psychopathology: Foundations for a contemporary understanding* (pp. 45–68). New York, NY: Routledge.

LoPiccolo, J., Heiman, J. R., Hogan, D. R., & Roberts, C. W. (1985). Effectiveness of single therapists versus cotherapy teams in sex therapy. *Journal of Consulting and Clinical Psychology, 53*(3), 287–294.

Lord, C., & Bishop, S. L. (2010). Autism spectrum disorders. *Social Policy Report, 24*(2), 3–21.

Loren, R. E. A., Vaughn, A. J., Langberg, J. M., Cyran, J. E. M., Proano-Raps, T., Smolyansky, B. H., . . . Epstein, J. N. (2015). Effects of an 8-session behavioral parent training group for parents of children with ADHD on child impairment and parenting confidence. *Journal of Attention Disorders, 19*(2), 158–166. doi: 10.1177/1087054713484175

Lösel, F., & Schmucker, M. (2005). The effectiveness of treatment for sexual offenders: A comprehensive meta-analysis. *Journal of Experimental Criminology, 1,* 117–146.

Lovaas, O. I. (1977). *The autistic child: Language development through behavior modification.* New York, NY: Irvington.

Lovaas, O. I. (1987). Behavioral treatment and normal educational and intellectual functioning in young autistic children. *Journal of Consulting and Clinical Psychology, 55,* 3–9.

Lovaas, O. I., Berberich, J. P., Perloff, B. F., & Schaeffer, B. (1966). Acquisition of imitative speech by schizophrenic children. *Science, 151,* 705–707.

Lovallo, W. R. (2010). Cardiovascular responses to stress and disease outcomes: a test of the reactivity hypothesis. *Hypertension, 55*(4), 842–843.

Lovestone, S. (2012). Dementia: Alzheimer's disease. In M. G. Gelder, N. C. Andreasen, J. J. Lopez-Ibor, Jr., & J. R. Geddes (Eds.), *New Oxford textbook of psychiatry* (2nd. ed., Vol. 1, pp. 333–343). New York, NY: Oxford University Press.

Lovibond, P. (2006). Fear and avoidance: An integrated expectancy model. In M. G. Craske, D. Hermans, & D. Vansteenwegen, *Fear and learning: From basic processes to clinical implications* (pp. 117–132). Washington, DC: American Psychological Association.

Lowe, M. R., Miller-Kovach, K., Frie, N., & Phelan, S. P. (1999). An initial evaluation of a commercial weight loss program: Short-term effects on weight, eating behavior, and mood. *Obesity Research, 7*, 51–59.

Lozano, A. M., Giacobbe, P., Hamani, C., Rizvi, S. J., Kennedy, S. H., Kolivakis, T. T., . . . Mayberg, H. S. (2012). A multicenter pilot study of sub-callosal cingulate area deep brain stimulation for treatment-resistant depression. *Journal of Neurosurgery, 116*, 15–22.

Lu, B., Nagappan, G., Guan, X., Nathan, P. J., & Wren, P. (2013). BDNF-based synaptic repair as a disease-modifying strategy for neurodegenerative diseases. *Nature Reviews Neuroscience, 14*(6), 401–416.

Lubinski, D. (2004). Introduction to the special section of cognitive abilities: 100 years after Spearman's (1904) "'General intelligence,' objectively determined and measured." *Journal of Personality and Social Psychology, 86*, 96–111.

Lubs, H. A., Stevenson, R. E., & Schwartz, C. E. (2012). Fragile X and X-linked intellectual disability: Four decades of discovery. *The American Journal of Human Genetics, 90*(4), 579–590. doi: http://dx.doi.org/10.1016/j.ajhg.2012.02.018

Luby, J. L. (2012). Dispelling the "They'll Grow Out of It" myth: Implications for intervention. *American Journal of Psychiatry, 169*, 1128–1129.

Luby, J. L., Gaffrey, M. S., Tillman, R., April, L. M., Belden, A. C. (2014). Trajectories of preschool disorders to full DSM depression at school age and early adolescence: Continuity of preschool depression. *American Journal of Psychiatry, 171*, 768–776.

Luby, J. L., Mrakotsky, C., Heffelfinger, A., Brown, K., Hessler, M., & Spitznagel, E. (2003). Modification of DSM-IV criteria for depressed preschool children. *American Journal of Psychiatry, 160*, 1169–1172.

Ludescher, B., Leitlein, G., Schaefer, J. E., Vanhoeffen, S., Baar, S., Machann, J., & Eschweiler, G. (2009). Changes of body composition in bulimia nervosa: Increased visceral fat and adrenal gland size. *Psychosomatic Medicine, 71*(1), 93–97.

Ludwig, A., Brandsma, J., Wilbur, C., Bendfeldt, F., & Jameson, D. (1972). The objective study of a multiple personality. *Archives of General Psychiatry, 26*, 298–310.

Ludwig, A. M. (1995). *The price of greatness: Resolving the creativity and madness controversy.* New York, NY: Guilford Publications.

Ludwig, D. S. (2012). Weight loss strategies for adolescents: A 14-year-old struggling to lose weight. *JAMA: Journal of the American Medical Association, 307*, 498–508.

Lugnegård, T., Hallerbäck, M. U., & Gillberg, C. (2012). Personality disorders and autism spectrum disorders: what are the connections? *Comprehensive Psychiatry, 53*(4), 333–340.

Lukiw, W. J. (2012). Amyloid beta (Ab) peptide modulators and other current treatment strategies for Alzheimer's disease (AD). *Expert Opinion on Emerging Drugs, 17*(1), 43–60.

Lundgren, J. D., Allison, K. C., & Stunkard, A. J. (Eds.)(2012). *Night eating syndrome: Research, assessment and treatment.* New York, NY: Guilford.

Lundh, L.-G., & Öst, L.-G. (1996). Recognition bias for critical faces in social phobics. *BRAT, 34*, 787–794.

Lundstrom, B., Pauly, I., & Walinder, J. (1984). Outcome of sex reassignment surgery. *Acta Psychiatrica Scandinavica, 70*, 289–294.

Lurigio, A., & Harris, A. (2009). Mental illness, violence, and risk assessment: An evidence-based review. *Victims & Offenders, 4*(4), 341–347.

Lussier, P., & Piché, L. (2008). Frotteurism: Psychopathology and theory. In D. R. Laws & W. T. O'Donohue (Eds.), *Sexual deviance: Theory, assessment, and treatment* (2nd ed., pp. 131–149). New York, NY: Guilford.

Lutgendorf, S., Costanzo, E., & Siegel, S. (2007). Psychosocial influences in oncology: An expanded model of biobehavioral mechanisms. In R. Ader, R. Glaser, N. Cohen, & M. Irwin (Eds.), *Psychoneuroimmunology* (4th ed., pp. 869–895). New York, NY: Academic Press.

Lutgendorf, S. K., & Andersen, B. L. (2015). Biobehavioral approaches to cancer progression and survival: Mechanisms and interventions. *American Psychologist, 70*(2), 186–197

Lutgendorf, S. K., Antoni, M. H., Ironson, G., Klimas, N., Kumar, M., Starr, K., & Schneiderman, N. (1997). Cognitive-behavioral stress management decreases dysphoric mood and herpes simplex virus-type 2 antibody titers in symptomatic HIV-seropositive gay men. *Journal of Consulting and Clinical Psychology, 65*, 31–43.

Lydiard, R. B., Brawman-Mintzer, O., & Ballenger, J. C. (1996). Recent developments in the psychopharmacology of anxiety disorders. *Journal of Consulting & Clinical Psychology, 64*, 660–668.

Lyketsos, C. G., & Olin, J. (2002). Depression in Alzheimer's disease: Overview and treatment. *Biological Psychiatry, 52*, 243–252.

Lykken, D. T. (1957). A study of anxiety in the sociopathic personality. *Journal of Abnormal and Social Psychology, 55*, 6–10.

Lykken, D. T. (1982). Fearlessness: Its carefree charms and deadly risks. *Psychology Today, 16*, 20–28.

Lynam, D. R., & Vachon, D. D. (2012). Antisocial personality disorder in DSM-5: Missteps and missed opportunities. *Personality Disorders: Theory, Research, and Treatment, 3*(4), 483–495. doi: 10.1037/per0000006

Lynch, F. L., Dickerson, J. F., Clarke, G., Vitiello, B., Porta, G., Wagner, K. D., & Brent, D. (2011). Incremental cost-effectiveness of combined therapy vs medication only for youth with selective serotonin reuptake inhibitor-resistant depression: Treatment of SSRI-resistant depression in adolescents trial findings. *Archives of General Psychiatry, 68*(3), 253.

Lynch, S. K., Turkheimer, E., D'Onofrio, B. M., Mendle, J., Emery, R. E., Slutske, W. S., & Martin, N. G. (2006). A genetically informed study of the association between harsh punishment and offspring behavioral problems. *Journal of Family Psychology, 20*, 190–198.

Lynch, T. R., & Cuper, P. F. (2012). Dialectical behavior therapy of borderline and other personality disorders. In T. A. Widiger (Ed.), *The Oxford handbook of personality disorders* (pp. 785–793). New York, NY: Oxford University Press.

Lynn, S. J., Lilienfeld, S. O., Merckelbach, H., Giesbach T., McNally, R. J., Loftus, E. F., Bruck, M., Garry M., & Malaktaris, A. (2014). The trauma model of dissociation: Inconvenient truths and stubborn fictions. Comment on Dahlberg et al. (2012). *Psychological Bulletin, 140*, 896–910.

Lyons, M. J., Eisen, S. A., Goldberg, J., True, W., Lin, N., Meyer, J. M., & Tsuang, M. T. (1998). A registry-based twin study of depression in men. *Archives of General Psychiatry, 55*, 468–472.

Lyons, M. J., True, W. R., Eisen, S. A., Goldberg, J., Meyer, J. M., Faraone, S. V., & Tsuang, M. (1995). Differential heritability of adult and juvenile antisocial traits. *Archives of General Psychiatry, 52*, 906–915.

Lyons, M. J., York, T. P., Franz, C. E., Grant, M. D., Eaves, L. J., Jacobson, K. C., & Kremen, W. S. (2009). Genes determine stability and the environment determines change in cognitive ability during 35 years of adulthood. *Psychological Science, 20*(9), 1146–1152.

Lyubomirsky, S. (2001). Why are some people happier than others? The role of cognitive and motivational processes in well-being. *American Psychologist, 56*, 239–249.

Ma, S., Hoang, M. A., Samet, J. M., Wang, J., Mei, C., Xu, X., & Stillman, F. A. (2008). Myths and attitudes that sustain smoking in China. *Journal of Health Communication, 13*, 654–666.

Maccallum, F. & Bryant, R. A. (2011). Imagining the future in complicated grief. *Depression and Anxiety, 28*(8), 658–665.

Macdonald, P. T., Waldorf, D., Reinarman, C., & Murphy, S. (1988). Heavy cocaine use and sexual behavior. *Journal of Drug Issues, 18*, 437–455.

MacDougall, J. M., Dembroski, T. M., Dimsdale, J. E., & Hackett, T. P. (1985). Components of Type A, hostility, and anger-in: Further relationships to angiographic findings. *Health Psychology, 4*(2), 137–152.

Mace, C. J. (1992). Hysterical conversion II: A critique. *British Journal of Psychiatry, 161*, 378–389.

Macedo, M., Marques, A., & Queirós, C. (2015). Virtual reality in assessment and treatment of schizophrenia: a systematic review. *Jornal Brasileiro de Psiquiatria, 64*(1), 70–81.

Maciejewski, P., Zhang, B., Block, S., & Prigerson, H. (2007). An empirical examination of the stage theory of grief. *JAMA: Journal of the American Medical Association, 297*(7), 716–723.

MacKinnon, D. F., Zandi, P. P., Gershon, E. S., Nurnberger, J. I., & DePaulo, J. R. (2003). Association of rapid mood switching with panic disorder and familial panic risk in familial bipolar disorder. *American Journal of Psychiatry, 160*, 1696–1698.

MacLeod, C., & Mathews, A. M. (1991). Cognitive-experimental approaches to the emotional disorders. In P. R. Martin (Ed.), *Handbook of behavior therapy and psychological science: An integrative approach* (pp. 116–150). Elmsford, NY: Pergamon Press.

Macleod, J., Oakes, R., Copello, A., Crome, I., Egger, M., & Hickman, M., & Davey Smith, G. (2004). Psychological and social sequelae of cannabis and other illicit drug use by young people: A systematic review of longitudinal, general population studies. *Lancet, 363*, 1579–1588.

Macy, J. T., Chassin, L., & Presson, C. C. (2012). The association between implicit and explicit attitudes toward smoking and support for tobacco control measures. *Nicotine & Tobacco Research.* doi: 10.1093/ntr/nts117

Madsen, K. M., Hviid, A., Vestergaard, M., Schendel, D., Wohlfahrt, J., Thorsen, P., & Melbye, M. (2002). A population-based study of measles, mumps, and rubella vaccination and autism. *New England Journal of Medicine, 347*, 1477–1482.

Magee, W. J., Eaton, W. W., Wittchen, H.-U., McGonagle, K. A., & Kessler, R. C. (1996). Agoraphobia, simple phobia, and social phobia in the National Comorbidity Survey. *Archives of General Psychiatry, 53*, 159–168.

Magne-Ingvar, U., Ojehagen, A., & Traskman-Bendz, L. (1992). The social network of people who attempt suicide. *Acta Psychiatrica Scandinavica, 86*, 153–158.

Magruder, K., Serpi, T., Kimerling, R., Kilbourne, A. M., Collins, J. F., Cypel, Y., Frayne, S. M., Furey, J., Huang, G. D., Gleason, T., Reinhard, M. J., Spiro, A., & Kang, H. (2015). Prevalence of posttraumatic stress disorder in Vietnam-era women veterans: The health of Vietnam-era Women's Study (HealthVIEWS). *JAMA Psychiatry, 72*, 1127–1134.

Maguire, G. A., Yeh, C. Y., & Ito, B. S. (2012). Overview of the diagnosis and treatment of stuttering. *Journal of Experimental & Clinical Medicine, 4*(2), 92–97.

Maher, B. A., & Maher, W. B. (1985a). Psychopathology: I. From ancient times to the eighteenth century. In G. A. Kimble & K. Schlesinger (Eds.), *Topics in the history of psychology* (pp. 251–294). Hillsdale, NJ: Erlbaum.

Maher, B. A., & Maher, W. B. (1985b). Psychopathology: II. From the eighteenth century to modern times. In G. A. Kimble & K. Schlesinger (Eds.), *Topics in the history of psychology* (pp. 295–329). Hillsdale, NJ: Erlbaum.

Maher, J. J. (1997). Exploring alcohol's effects on liver function. *Alcohol Health & Research World, 21*, 5–12.

Mahler, M. (1952). On childhood psychosis and schizophrenia: Autistic and symbiotic infantile psychosis. *Psychoanalytic Study of the Child, 7*, 286–305.

Mahoney, D. F., Purtilo, R. B., Webbe, F. M., Alwan, M., Bharucha, A. J., Adlam, T. D., Becker S. A. (2007). In-home monitoring of persons with dementia: Ethical guidelines for technology research and development. *Alzheimer's & Dementia, 3*(3), 217–226.

Mai, F. (2004). Somatization disorder: A practical review. *Canadian Journal of Psychiatry, 49*, 652–662.

Maier, S. F., & Seligman, M. E. (1976). Learned helplessness: Theory and evidence. *Journal of Experimental Psychology: General, 105*(1), 3–46.

Mainz, V., Schulte-Rüther, M., Fink, G. R., Herpertz-Dahlmann, B., & Konrad, K. (2012). Structural brain abnormalities in adolescent anorexia nervosa before and after weight recovery and associated hormonal changes. *Psychosomatic Medicine, 74*, 574–582.

Maj, M., Pirozzi, R., Magliano, L., & Bartoli, L. (2002). The prognostic significance of "switching" in patients with bipolar disorder: A 10-year prospective follow-up study. *American Journal of Psychiatry, 159*, 1711–1717.

Maj, M. (2008). Depression, bereavement and "understandable" intense sadness: Should the DSM-IV approach be revised? *American Journal of Psychiatry, 165*(11), 1373–1375.

Maj, M. (2012). Dementia due to HIV disease. In M. G. Gelder, N. C. Andreasen, J. J. Lopez-Ibor, Jr., & J. R. Geddes (Eds.), *New Oxford textbook of psychiatry* (2nd. ed., Vol. 1, pp. 384–386). New York, NY: Oxford University Press.

Maki, P. M., & Henderson, V. W. (2012). Hormone therapy, dementia, and cognition: the Women's Health Initiative 10 years on. *Climacteric, 15*(3), 256–262.

Malatesta, V. J., & Adams, H. E. (2001). Sexual dysfunctions. In H. E. Adams & P. B. Sutker (Eds.), *Comprehensive handbook of psychopathology* (3rd ed., pp. 713–748). New York, NY: Kluwer Academic/Plenum.

Malavige, L. S., & Jayawickrema, S. (2015). Premature ejaculation and its management. *Sri Lanka Journal of Diabetes Endocrinology and Metabolism, 5*(1), 13–19.

Maldonado, J. R., Butler, L. D., & Spiegel, D. (1998). Treatments for dissociative disorders. In P. E. Nathan & J. M. Gorman (Eds.), *A guide to treatments that work*. New York, NY: Oxford University Press.

Maletzky, B. (2002). The paraphilias: Research and treatment. In P. E. Nathan & J. M. Gorman (Eds.), *A guide to treatments that work* (2nd ed., pp. 525–557). New York, NY: Oxford University Press.

Maletzky, B. M. (1991). *Treating the sexual offender*. Newbury Park, CA: Sage.

Malm, H., Sourander, A., Gissler, M., Gyllenberg, D., Hinkka-Yli-Salomäki, S., McKeague, I. W., . . . Brown, A. S. (2015). Pregnancy complications following prenatal exposure to SSRIs or maternal psychiatric disorders: Results from population-based national register data. *American Journal of Psychiatry.* doi: 10.1176/appi.ajp.2015.14121575

Manber, R., Edinger, J. D., Gress, J. L., San Pedro-Salcedo, M. G., Kuo, T. F., & Kalista, T. (2008). Cognitive behavioral therapy for insomnia enhances depression outcome in patients with comorbid major depressive disorder and insomnia. *Sleep, 31*(4), 489–495.

Mancuso, S., Knoesen, N., & Castle, D.J. (2010). Delusional vs. nondelusional body dysmorphic disorder. *Comprehensive Psychiatry, 51*(2), 177–182.

Mandalos, G. E., & Szarek, B. L. (1990). Dose-related paranoid reaction associated with fluoxetine. *Journal of Nervous and Mental Disease, 178*(1), 57–58.

Mandell, D. S., Thompson, W. W., Weintraub, E. S., DeStefano, F., & Blank, M. B. (2005). Trends in diagnosis rates for autism and ADHD at hospital discharge in the context of other psychiatric diagnoses. *Psychiatric Services, 56*(1), 56–62. doi: doi:10.1176/appi.ps.56.1.56

Manicavasagar, V., Marnane, C., Pini, S., Abelli, M., Rees, S., Eapen, V., & Silove, D. (2010). Adult separation anxiety disorder: A disorder comes of age. *Current Psychiatry Reports, 12*(4), 290–297. doi: 10.1007/s11920-010-0131-9

Mann, J., Apter, A., Bertolote, J., Beautrais, A., Currier, D., Haas, A., & Hendin, H. (2005). Suicide prevention strategies: A systematic review. *JAMA: Journal of the American Medical Association, 294*, 2064–2074.

Mann, J. J., Brent, D. A., & Arango, V. (2001). The neurobiology and genetics of suicide and attempted suicide: A focus on the serotonergic system. *Neuropsychopharmacology, 24*(5), 467–477.

Mann, J. J., Malone, K. M., Diehl, D. J., Perel, J., Cooper, T. B., & Mintun, M. A. (1996). Demonstration in vivo of reduced serotonin responsivity in the brain of untreated depressed patients. *American Journal of Psychiatry, 153*, 174–182.

Mann, J. J., Waternaux, C., Haas, G. L., & Malone, K. M. (1999). Toward a clinical model of suicidal behavior in psychiatric patients. *American Journal of Psychiatry, 156*(2), 181–189.

Mann, K., Klingler, T., Noe, S., Röschke, J., Müller, S., & Benkert, O. (1996). Effects of yohimbine on sexual experiences and nocturnal penile tumescence and rigidity in erectile dysfunction. *Archives of Sexual Behavior, 25*, 1–16.

Mann, T., Tomiyama, A. J., & Ward, A. (2015). Promoting Public Health in the Context of the "Obesity Epidemic" False Starts and Promising New Directions. *Perspectives on Psychological Science, 10*(6), 706–710.

Manne, S. L., & Ostroff, J. S. (2008). *Coping with breast cancer: A couples-focused group intervention: Therapist guide*. New York, NY: Oxford University Press.

Manni, R., Ratti, M. T., & Tartara, A. (1997). Nocturnal eating: Prevalence and features in 120 insomniac referrals. *Sleep, 20*, 734–738.

Mannino, D. M., Klevens, R. M., & Flanders, W. D. (1994). Cigarette smoking: An independent risk factor for impotence? *American Journal of Epidemiology, 140*, 1003–1008.

Manson, J. E., Willett, W. C., Stampfer, M. J., Colditz, G. A., Hunter, D. J., Hankinson, S. E., & Speizer, F. E. (1995). Body weight and mortality among women. *New England Journal of Medicine, 333*, 677–685.

Manson, S. M., & Good, B. J. (1993, January). *Cultural considerations in the diagnosis of DSM-IV mood disorders.* Cultural proposals and supporting papers for DSM-IV. Submitted to the DSM-IV Task Force by the Steering Committee, NIMH-Sponsored Group on Culture and Diagnosis.

Månsson, K. N. T., Carlbring, P., Frick, A., Engman, J., Olsson, C. J., Bodlund, O.,

Furmark, T., & Andersson, G. (2013). Altered neural correlates of affective processing after internet-delivered cognitive behavior therapy for social anxiety disorder. *Psychiatry Research, 214*(3), 229–237.

Mantovani, A., Pavlicova, M., Avery, D., Nahas, Z., McDonald, W. M., Wajdik, C. D., & Lisanby, S. H. (2012). Long-term efficacy of repeated daily prefrontal transcranial magnetic stimulation (TMS) in treatment-resistant depression. *Depression and Anxiety, 29*(10), 883–890.

Manuel, J. K., Houck, J. M., & Moyers, T. B. (2012). The impact of significant others in motivational enhancement therapy: Findings from Project MATCH. *Behavioural and cognitive psychotherapy, 40*(3), 297.

Marangell, L., Rush, A., George, M., Sackheim, H., Johnson, C, Husain, M., & Lisanby, S. H. (2002). Vagus nerve stimulation (VNS) for major depressive episodes: One year outcomes. *Biological Psychiatry, 51*, 280–287.

March, J. S., & Vitiello, B. (2009). Clinical messages from the Treatment for Adolescents with Depression Study (TADS). *American Journal of Psychiatry, 166*(10), 1118–1123.

Marcus, E. (2010). *Why suicide? Questions and answers about suicide, suicide prevention and coping with the suicide of someone you Know.* New York, NY: Harper Collins.

Marcus, S. C., & Olfson, M. (2010). National trends in the treatment for depression from 1998 to 2007. *Archives of General Psychiatry, 67*(12), 1265–1273.

Maremmani, I., Pacini, M., Pani, P. P., Popovic, D., Romano, A., Maremmani, A. G. I., & Perugi, G. (2009). Use of street methadone in Italian heroin addicts presenting for opioid agonist treatment. *Journal of Addictive Diseases, 28*(4), 382–388.

Markon, K. E. (2013). Epistemological pluralism and scientific development: An argument against authoritative nosologies. *Journal of Personality Disorders, 27*(5), 554–579.

Marks, I. M. (1969). *Fears and phobias.* New York, NY: Academic.

Marks, I. M. (1985). Behavioural treatment of social phobia. *Psychopharmacology Bulletin, 21*, 615–618.

Marlatt, G. A., & Gordon, J. R. (1985). *Relapse prevention: Maintenance strategies in the treatment of addictive behaviors.* New York, NY: Guilford.

Marlatt, G. A., Larimer, M. E., Baer, J. S., & Quigley, L. A. (1993). Harm reduction for alcohol problems: Moving beyond the controlled drinking controversy. *Behavior Therapy, 24*, 461–504.

Marlatt, G. A., & Donovan, D. M. (2005). *Relapse prevention: Maintenance strategies in the treatment of addictive behaviors.* New York, NY: Guilford.

Marmar, C. R., Schlenger, W., Henn-Haase, C., Qian, M., Purchia, E., Li, M., . . . Kulka, R. A. (2015). Course of posttraumatic stress disorder 40 years after the Vietnam war. Findings from the National Vietnam Veterans Longitudinal Study. *JAMA Psychiatry, 72*, 875–881.

Marmot, M. G., & Syme, S. L. (1976). Acculturation and coronary heart disease in Japanese Americans. *American Journal of Epidemiology, 104*, 225–247.

Marques, J. K., Wiederanders, M., Day, D. M., Nelson, C., & van Ommeren, A. (2005). Effects of a relapse prevention program on sexual recidivism: Final results from California's Sex Offender Treatment and Evaluation Project (SOTEP). *Sexual Abuse: A Journal of Research and Treatment, 17*(1), 79–107.

Marques, L., Alegria, M., Becker, A. E., Chen, C.-N., Fang, A., Chosak, A., & Diniz, J. B. (2011). Comparative prevalence, correlates of impairment, and service utilization for eating disorders across US ethnic groups: Implications for reducing ethnic disparities in health care access for eating disorders. *International Journal of Eating Disorders, 44*(5), 412–420.

Marques, M. M., De Gucht, V. Gouveia, M. J., Leal, I., & Maes, S. (2015). Differential effects of behavioral interventions with a graded physical activity componenet in patients suffering from chronic fatigue (syndrome): An updated systematic review and meta-analysis. *Clinical Psychology Review, 40*, 123–137.

Marsac, M. L., Kassam-Adams, N., Hildenbrand, A. K., Kohser, K. L., & Winston, F. K. (2011). After the injury: Initial evaluation of a web-based intervention for parents of injured children. *Health Education Research, 26*(1), 1–12.

Marsh, L., & Margolis, R. L. (2009). Neuro-psychiatric aspects of movement disorders. In B. J. Sadock, V. A. Sadock, & P. Ruiz (Eds.), *Kaplan & Sadock's comprehensive textbook of psychiatry* (9th ed., Vol. I, pp. 481–503). Philadelphia, PA: Lippincott Williams & Wilkins.

Marsh, R., Horga, G., Wang, Z., Wang, P., Klahr, K. W., Berner, L. A., & Peterson, B. S. (2011). An fMRI study of self-regulatory control and conflict resolution in adolescents with bulimia nervosa. *American Journal of Psychiatry, 168*, 1210–1220.

Marshall, W. L. (1997). Pedophilia: Psychopathology and theory. In D. R. Laws & W. O'Donohue (Eds.), *Sexual deviance: Theory, assessment and treatment* (pp. 152–174). New York, NY: Guilford.

Marshall, W. L., & Barbaree, H. E. (1990). An integrated theory of the etiology of sexual offending. In W. L. Marshall, D. R. Laws, & H. E. Barbaree (Eds.), *Handbook of sexual assault: Issues, theories, and treatment of the offender* (pp. 257–725). New York, NY: Plenum.

Marshall, W. L., Barbaree, H. E., & Christophe, D. (1986). Sexual offenders against female children: Sexual preferences for age of victims and type of behavior. *Canadian Journal of Behavioral Science, 18*, 424–439.

Marteau, T. M., Hollands, G. J., & Fletcher, P. C. (2012). Changing human behavior to prevent disease: The importance of targeting automatic processes. *Science, 337*(6101), 1492–1495.

Marten, P. A., Brown, T. A., Barlow, D. H., Borkovec, T. D., Shear, M. K., & Lydiard, R. B. (1993). Evaluation of the ratings comprising the associated symptom criterion of DSM-III-R generalized anxiety disorder. *Journal of Nervous and Mental Disease, 181*(11), 676–682.

Martens, E. J., de Jonge, P., Na, B., Cohen, B. E., Lett, H., & Whooley, M. A. (2010). Scared to death? Generalized anxiety disorder and cardiovascular events in patients with stable coronary heart disease. *Archives of General Psychiatry, 67*, 750–758.

Martensson, B., Petterson, A., Berglund,L., & Ekselius, L. (2015). Bright white light therapy in depression: A critical review of the evidence. *Journal of Affective Disorders, 182*, 1–7.

Martin, I. (1983). Human classical conditioning. In A. Gale & J. A. Edward (Eds.), *Physiological correlates of human behavior: Vol. 2. Attention and performance.* London, UK: Academic Press.

Martin, J., O'Donovan, M. C., Thapar, A., Langley, K., & Williams, N. (2015). The relative contribution of common and rare genetic variants to ADHD. *Transl Psychiatry, 5*, e506. doi: 10.1038/tp.2015.5

Martin, P. R., & MacLeod, C. (2009). Behavioral management of headache triggers: avoidance of triggers is an inadequate strategy. *Clinical Psychology Review, 29*, 483–495.

Martin, P. R., Reece, J., Callan, M., MacLeod, C., Kaur, A., Gregg, K., & Goadsby, P. J. (2014). Behaviorl management of the triggers of recurrent headache: A randomized controlled trial. *Behavioural Research and Therapy, 61*, 1–11.

Martin, S. D., Martin, E., Rai, S. S., Richardson, M. A., & Royall, R. (2001). Brain blood flow changes in depressed patients treated with interpersonal psychotherapy or venlafaxine hydrochloride. *Archives of General Psychiatry, 58*, 641–648.

Martin, S. L., Ramey, C. T., & Ramey, S. L. (1990). The prevention of intellectual impairment in children of impoverished families: Findings of a randomized trial of educational daycare. *American Journal of Public Health, 80*, 844–847.

Martin-Pichora, A. L., & Antony, M. M. (2011). Successful treatment of olfactory reference syndrome with cognitive behavioral therapy: A case study. *Cognitive and Behavioral Practice, 18*, 545–554.

Martinez, A. G., Piff, P. K., Mendoza-Denton, R., & Hinshaw, S. P. (2011). The power of a label: Mental illness diagnoses, ascribed humanity, and social rejection. *Journal of Social and Clinical Psychology, 30*(1), 1–23. doi: 10.1521/jscp.2011.30.1.1

Martinez, M. A., & Craighead, L. W. (2015). Toward Person (ality)-Centered Treatment: How Consideration of Personality and Individual Differences in Anorexia Nervosa May Improve Treatment Outcome. *Clinical Psychology: Science and Practice, 22*(3), 296–314.

Martínez-Fernández, E., Aragón-Poce, F., Márquez-Espinós, C., Pérez-Pérez, A., Pérez-Bustamante, F., & Torres-Morera, L. (2002). The history of opiates. In J. C. Diz, A. Franco, D. R. Bacon, J. Ruprehr, & J. Alvarez (Eds.), *The history of anesthesia: Proceedings of the fifth International Symposium on the History of Anesthesia, Santiago, Spain, September 19–23, 2001* (pp. 75–77). Amsterdam, The Netherlands: Elsevier Science.

Martins, S. S., & Gorelick, D. A. (2011). Conditional substance abuse and dependence by diagnosis of mood or anxiety disorder or schizophrenia in the US population. *Drug and Alcohol Dependence, 119*(1), 28–36.

Maser, J. D. (1985). List of phobias. In A. H. Tuma & J. D. Maser (Eds.), *Anxiety and the anxiety disorders*. Hillsdale, NJ: Erlbaum.

Maser, J. D., Kaelber, C., & Weise, R. E. (1991). International use and attitudes toward DSM-III and DSM-III-R: Growing consensus in psychiatric classification. *Journal of Abnormal Psychology, 100*(3), 271–279.

Masia-Warner, C., Klein, R. G., Dent, H. C., Fisher, P. H., Alvir, J., Albano, A., & Guardino, M. (2005). School-based intervention for adolescents with social anxiety disorder: Results of a controlled study. *Journal of Abnormal Child Psychology, 33*(6), 707–722. doi: 10.1007/s10802-005-7649-z

Mason, F. L. (1997). Fetishism: Psychopathology and theory. In D. R. Laws & W. O'Donohue (Eds.), *Sexual deviance: Theory, assessment and treatment* (pp. 75–91). New York, NY: Guilford.

Mason, T., Worsley, A., & Coyle, D. (2010). Forensic multidisciplinary perspectives of Tarasoff liability: A vignette study. *Journal of Forensic Psychiatry & Psychology, 21*(4), 549–554.

Master, S. L., Eisenberger, N. I., Taylor, S. E., Naliboff, B. D., Shirinyan, D., & Lieberman, M. D. (2009). A picture's worth: Partner photographs reduce experimentally induced pain. *Psychological Science, 20*, 1316–1318.

Masters, W. H., & Johnson, V. E. (1966). *Human sexual response*. Boston, MA: Little, Brown.

Masters, W. H., & Johnson, V. E. (1970). *Human sexual inadequacy*. Boston, MA: Little, Brown.

Mataix-Cols, D., Boman, M., Monzani, B., Rück, C., Serlachius, E., Långström, N., & Lichtenstein, P. (2013). Population-based, multigenerational family clustering study of obsessive-compulsive disorder. *JAMA psychiatry, 70*, 709–717.

Mataix-Cols, D., Frost, R. O., Pertusa, A., Clark, L. A., Saxena, S., Leckman, J. F., & Wilhelm, S. (2010). Hoarding disorder: A new diagnosis for DSM-V? *Depression and Anxiety, 27*(6), 556–572. doi: 10.1002/da.20693

Matheson, S. L., Vijayan, H., Dickson, H., Shepherd, A. M., Carr, V. J., & Laurens, K. R. (2013). Systematic meta-analysis of childhood social withdrawal in schizophrenia, and comparison with data from at-risk children aged 9–14 years. *Journal of Psychiatric Research, 47*(8), 1061–1068.

Mathew, S. J., & Hoffman, E. J. (2009). Pharmacotherapy for generalized anxiety disorder. In M. M. Antony & M. B. Stein (Eds.), *Oxford handbook of anxiety and related disorders* (pp. 350–363). New York, NY: Oxford University Press.

Mathews, C.A. (2009). Phenomenology of obsessive-compulsive disorder. In M. M. Antony & M. B. Stein (Eds.), *Oxford handbook of anxiety and related disorders*. Oxford, UK: Oxford University Press.

Matsubayashi, T., Sawada, Y., & Ueda, M. (2012). Natural disasters and suicide: Evidence from Japan. *Social Science & Medicine, 82*, 126–133.

Matsumoto, D. (1996). *Culture and psychology*. Pacific Grove, CA: Brooks/Cole.

Matthews, K. (2005). Psychological perspectives on the development of coronary heart disease. *American Psychologist, 60*, 780–796.

Matthews, K. A. (2013). Matters of the heart: Advancing psychological perspectives on cardiovascular diseases. *Perspectives on Psychological Science, 8*, 676–678.

Matthews, K. A. (1988). Coronary heart disease and Type A behaviors: Update on and alternative to the Booth-Kewley and Friedman (1987) quantitative review. *Psychological Bulletin, 104*(3), 373–380.

Matthews, K. A., Schott, L. L., Bromberger, J., Cyranowski, J., Everson-Rose, S. A., & Sowers, M. F. (2007). Associations between depressive symptoms and inflammatory/hemostatic markers in women during the menopausal transition. *Psychosomatic Medicine, 69*, 124–130.

Matthews-Ewald, M. R., Zullig, K. J., & Ward, R. M. (2014). Sexual orientation and disordered eating behaviors among self-identified male and female college students. *Eating Behaviors, 15*(3), 441–444.

Mattis, S. G., & Ollendick, T. H. (2002). Non-clinical panic attacks in late adolescence prevalence and associated psychopathology. *Journal of Anxiety Disorders, 16*, 351–367.

Matza, L. S., Revicki, D. A., Davidson, J. R., & Stewart, J. W. (2003). Depression with atypical features in the National Comorbidity Survey: Classification, description, and consequences. *Archives of General Psychiatry, 60*, 817–826.

Mauler, B. I., Hamm, A. O., Weike, A. I., & Tuschen-Caffier, B. (2006). Affect regulation and food intake in bulimia nervosa: Emotional responding to food cues after deprivation and subsequent eating. *Journal of Abnormal Psychology, 115*, 567–579.

Maust, D., Cristancho, M., Gray, L., Rushing, S., Tjoa, C., & Thase, M. E. (2012). *Psychiatric rating scales*. In T. E. Schlaepfer & C. B. Nemeroff (eds.). Handbook of Clinical Neurology (pp. 227–237) Amsterdam, The Netherlands: Elsevier

Maxwell, J. C., & Brecht, M.-L. (2011). Methamphetamine: Here we go again? *Addictive Behaviors, 36*(12), 1168–1173. doi: 10.1016/j.addbeh.2011.07.017

Mayberg, H., Lozano, A., Voon, V., McNeely, H., Seminowicz, D., Hanani, C., & Kennedy, S. H. (2005). Deep brain stimulation for treatment resistant depression. *Neuron, 45*, 651–660.

Mayou, R., Phil, M., Kirmayer, L., Simon, G., Kroenke, G., & Sharpe, M. (2005). Soma-to-form disorders: Time for a new approach in DSM-V. *American Journal of Psychiatry, 162*, 847–855.

Mayville, S., Katz, R. C., Gipson, M. T., & Cabral, K. (1999). Assessing the prevalence of body dysmorphic disorder in an ethnically diverse group of adolescents. *Journal of Child and Family Studies, 8*(3), 357–362.

Mazure, C. M. (1998). Life stressors as risk factors in depression. *Clinical Psychology: Science and Practice, 5*(3), 291–313.

Mazure, C. M., Bruce, M. L., Maciejewski, P. K., & Jacobs, S. C. (2000). Adverse life events and cognitive-personality characteristics in the prediction of major depression and antidepressant response. *American Journal of Psychiatry, 157*(6), 896–903.

Mbata, G., & Chukwuka, J. (2012). Obstructive sleep apnea hypopnea syndrome. *Annals of Medical and Health Sciences Research, 2*(1), 74–77.

McCabe, M., & Wauchope, M. (2005). Behavioral characteristics of men accused of rape: Evidence for different types of rapists. *Archives of Sexual Behavior, 34*, 241–253.

McCabe, R., Antony, M. M., Summerfeldt, L. J., Liss, A., & Swinson, R. P. (2003). Preliminary examination of the relationship between anxiety disorders in adults and self-reported history of teasing or bullying experiences. *Cognitive Behaviour Therapy, 32*, 187–193.

McCabe, S. E., West, B. T., Teter, C. J., & Boyd, C. J. (2012). Co-ingestion of prescription opioids and other drugs among high school seniors: Results from a national study. *Drug and Alcohol Dependence, 126*(1–2), 65–70. doi: http://dx.doi.org/10.1016/j.drugalcdep.2012.04.017

McCaffery, J. M., Papandonatos, G. D., Stanton, C., Lloyd-Richardson, E. E., & Niaura, R. (2008). Depressive symptoms and cigarette smoking in twins from the national longitudinal study of adolescent health. *Health Psychology, 27* (3, Suppl. 1), S207–S215.

McCaffrey, R. J., Lynch, J. K., & Westervelt, H. J. (2011). Clinical neuropsychology. In D. H. Barlow (Ed.), *Oxford handbook of clinical psychology* (pp. 680–700). New York, NY: Oxford University.

McCann, D., Barrett, A., Cooper, A., Crumpler, D., Dalen, L., Grimshaw, K., & Prince, E. (2007). Food additives and hyperactive behaviour in 3-year-old and 8/9-year-old children in the community: A randomised, double-blinded, placebo-controlled trial. *The Lancet, 370*(9598), 1560–1567.

McCann, U. D., & Ricaurte, G. A. (2009). Amphetamine (or amphetamine-like)-related disorders. In B. J. Sadock, V. A. Sadock, & P. Ruiz (Eds.), *Kaplan & Sadock's comprehensive textbook of psychiatry* (9th ed., Vol. I, pp. 1288–1296). Philadelphia, PA: Lippincott Williams & Wilkins.

McCann, U. D., Sgambati, F. P., Schwartz, A. R., & Ricaurte, G. A. (2009). Sleep apnea in young abstinent recreational MDMA ("ecstasy") consumers. *Neurology, 73*(23), 2011–2017.

McClam, T. D., Marano, C. M., Rosenberg, P. B., & Lyketsos, C. G. (2015). Interventions for neuropsychiatric symptoms in neurocognitive impairment due to Alzheimer's disease: A Review of the Literature. *Harvard Review of Psychiatry, 23*(5), 377–393.

McClearn, G. E., Johansson, B., Berg, S., Pedersen, N. L., Ahern, F., Petrill, S. A., & Plomin, R. (1997). Substantial genetic influence on cognitive abilities in twins 80 or more years old. *Science, 276*, 1560–1563.

McClellan, J., & King, M. C. (2010). Genomic analysis of mental illness: A changing landscape. *JAMA: Journal of the American Medical Association, 303*(24), 2523–2524.

McClellan, J., Kowatch, R., & Findling, R. L. (2007). Practice parameter for the assessment and treatment of children and adolescents with bipolar disorder. *Journal of the American Academy of Child and Adolescent Psychiatry, 46*(1), 107–125.

McCloskey, M. S., Noblett, K. L., Deffenbacher, J. L., Gollan, J. K., & Coccaro, E. F. (2008). Cognitive-behavioral therapy for intermittent explosive disorder: A pilot randomized clinical trial. *Journal of Consulting and Clinical Psychology, 76*(5), 876–886.

McClure, M., Harvey, P., Goodman, M., Triebwasser, J., New, A., Koenigsberg, H., & Siever, L. J. (2010). Pergolide treatment of cognitive deficits associated with schizotypal personality disorder: Continued evidence of the importance of the dopamine system in the schizophrenia spectrum. *Neuropsychopharmacology, 35*, 1356–1362.

McCrady, B. S. (2014). Alcohol use disorders. In D. H. Barlow (Ed.), *Clinical handbook of psychological disorders: A step-by-step treatment manual*. New York, NY: Guilford.

McCrady, B. S. & Tonigan, J.S. (2015). Recent research into the Twelve-Step programs. In R.K. Ries, D.A. Fiellin, S.C. Miller, & R. Saitz (Eds.), *The ASAM principles of addiction medicine* (5th Ed., pp. 1043–1059). New York, NY: Wolters Kluwer.

McCrae, R., & Costa P., Jr., (2008). The five-factor theory of personality. In O. P. John, R. W. Robins, & L. A. Pervin (Eds.), *Handbook of personality: Theory and research* (3rd ed., pp. 159–181). New York, NY: Guilford.

McCrae, R. R. (2002). NEO PI-R data from 36 cultures: Further intercultural comparisons. In R. McCrae & J. Allik (Eds.), *The five-factor model of personality across cultures* (pp. 105–126). New York, NY: Kluwer Academic/Plenum.

McCullough, J. P., Jr. (2000). *Treatment for chronic depression: Cognitive Behavioral Analysis System of Psychotherapy (CBASP)*. New York, NY: Guilford.

McCullough, J. P., Jr. (in press). Introduction and state-of-the-art issues for CBASP. In M. Belz, F. Caspar & E. Schramm (Eds.), *CBASP in Practice: Basic concepts and new developments*. Munich, Germany: Elsevier.

McCullough, J. P., Jr., Klein, D. N., Keller, M. B., Holzer, C. E., III, Davis, S. M., Kornstein, S. G., & Harrison, W. M. (2000). Comparison of DSM-III-R chronic major depression and major depression superimposed on dysthymia (double depression): Validity of the distinction. *Journal of Abnormal Psychology, 109*, 419–427.

McEwen, B. S., & Magarinos, A. M. (2004). Does stress damage the brain? In J. M. Gorman, *Fear and anxiety: The benefits of translational research* (pp. 23–45). Washington, DC: American Psychiatric Publishing.

McFadden, D., Loehlin, J., Breedlove, S., Lippa, R., Manning, J., & Rahman, Q. (2005). A reanalysis of five studies on sexual orientation and the relative length of the 2nd and 4th fingers (the 2D: 4D ratio). *Archives of Sexual Behavior, 34*, 341–356.

McGee, G. G., Morrier, M. J., & Daly, T. (1999). An incidental teaching approach to early intervention for toddlers with autism. *Research and Practice for Persons with Severe Disabilities, 24*(3), 133–146.

McGirr, A., Paris, J., Lesage, A., Renaud, J., & Turecki, G. (2009). An examination of DSM-IV borderline personality disorder symptoms and risk for death by suicide: A psychological autopsy study. *Canadian Journal of Psychiatry, 54*(2), 87.

McGoldrick, M., Loonan, R., & Wohlsifer, D. (2007). Sexuality and culture. In S. R. Leiblum (Ed.), *Principles and practice of sex therapy* (4th ed., pp. 416–441). New York, NY: Guilford.

McGough, J. J. (2005). Adult manifestations of attention-deficit/hyperactivity disorder. In B. J. Sadock & V. A. Sadock (Eds.), *Kaplan & Sadock's comprehensive textbook of psychiatry* (pp. 3198–3204). Philadelphia, PA: Lippincott, Williams & Wilkins.

McGovern, M. P., Xie, H., Segal, S. R., Siembab, L., & Drake, R. E. (2006). Addiction treatment services and co-occurring disorders: Prevalence estimates, treatment practices, and barriers. *Journal of Substance Abuse Treatment, 31*(3), 267–275.

McGovern, P. E. (2007). *Ancient wine: The search for the origins of viniculture*. Princeton, NJ: Princeton University Press.

McGrath, P., Marshall, P. G., & Prior, K. (1979). A comprehensive treatment program for a fire setting child. *Journal of Behavior Therapy and Experimental Psychiatry, 10*(1), 69–72.

McGrath, R. E., & Carroll, E. J. (2012). The current status of "projective" "tests." In H. Cooper, P. M. Camic, D. L. Long, A. T. Panter, D. Rindskopf, & K. Sher (Eds.), *APA handbook of research methods in psychology, Vol 1: Foundations, planning, measures, and psychometrics* (pp. 329–348). Washington, D.C.: American Psychological Association.

McGue, M., & Lykken, D. T. (1992). Genetic influence on risk of divorce. *Psychological Science, 3*(6), 368–373.

McGuffin, P., Rijsdijk, F., Andrew, M., Sham, P., Katz, R., & Cardno, A. (2003). The heritability of bipolar affective disorder and the genetic relationship to unipolar depression. *Archives of General Psychiatry, 60*, 497–502.

McGuire, J. F., Piacentini, J., Scahill, L., Woods, D. W., Villarreal, R., Wilhelm, S., . . . Peterson, A. L. (2015). Bothersome tics in patients with chronic tic disorders: Characteristics and individualized treatment response to behavior therapy. *Behaviour Research and Therapy, 70*, 56–62.

McGuire, P. K., Shah, G. M. S., & Murray, R. M. (1993). Increased blood flow in Broca's area during auditory hallucinations in schizophrenia. *Lancet, 342*, 703–706.

McHugh, R. K. (2015). Treatment of co-occurring anxiety disorders and substance use disorders. *Harvard Review of Psychiatry, 23*, 99–111.

McHugh, R. K., & Barlow, D. H. (2010). The dissemination and implementation of evidence-based psychological treatments: A review of current efforts. *American Psychologist, 65*, 73–84.

McHugh, R. K., & Barlow, D. H., Eds. (2012). *Dissemination and implementation of evidence-based psychological interventions*. New York, NY: Oxford University Press.

McKay, D., Todaro, J., Neziroglu, F., Campisi, T., Moritz, E. K., & Yaryura-Tobias, J. A. (1997). Body dysmorphic disorder: A preliminary evaluation of treatment and maintenance using exposure with response prevention. *Behaviour Research and Therapy, 35*, 67–70.

McKay, R., & Dennett, D. (2010). The evolution of misbelief. *Behavioral and Brain Sciences, 32*(6), 493–510.

McKay, R., Langdon, R., & Coltheart, M. (2007). Models of misbelief: Integrating motivational and deficit theories of delusions. *Consciousness and Cognition, 16*(4), 932–941.

McKeith, I. G., Dickson, D. W., Lowe, J., Emre, M., O'Brien, J. T., Feldman, H., & Perry, E. K. (2005). Diagnosis and management of dementia with Lewy bodies: Third report of the DLB consortium. *Neurology, 65*(12), 1863–1872.

McKenna, B. S., & Eyler, L. T. (2012). Overlapping prefrontal systems involved in cognitive and emotional processing in euthymic bipolar disorder and following sleep deprivation: A review of functional neuroimaging studies. *Clinical Psychology Review, 32*(7), 650–663. doi: 10.1016/j.cpr.2012.07.003

McKenzie, K. C., & Gross, J. J. (2014). Nonsuicidal self-injury: an emotion regulation perspective. *Psychopathology, 47*(4), 207–219.

McKenzie, S. J., Williamson, D. A., & Cubic, B. A. (1993). Stable and reactive body image disturbances in bulimia nervosa. *Behavior Therapy, 24*, 195–207.

McKetin, R., Coen, A., & Kaye, S. (2015). A comprehensive review of the effects of mixing caffeinated energy drinks with alcohol. *Drug and Alcohol Dependence, 151*, 15–30.

McLaughlin, N. C. R., & Greenberg, B. D. (2012). In G. Steketee (Ed.), *The Oxford handbook of obsessive compulsive and spectrum disorders* (pp. 307–321). New York, NY: Oxford University Press.

McLean, P., & Taylor, S. (1992). Severity of unipolar depression and choice of treatment. *Behaviour Research and Therapy, 30*(5), 443–451.

McMain, S., Links, P. S., Guimond, T., Wnuk, S., Eynan, R., Bergmans, Y., & Warwar, S. (2013). An exploratory study of the relationship between changes in emotion and cognitive processes and treatment outcome in borderline personality disorder. *Psychotherapy Research, 23*(6), 658–673.

McMain, S. F., Guimond, T., Streiner, D. L., Cardish, R. J., & Links, P. S. (2014). Dialectical behavior therapy compared with general psychiatric management for borderline personality disorder: clinical outcomes and functioning over a 2-year follow-up. *American Journal of Psychiatry, 169*, 650–671.

McNab, C., Haslam, N., & Burnett, P. (2007). Expressed emotion, attributions, utility beliefs, and distress in parents of young people with first episode psychosis. *Psychiatry Research, 151*, 97–106.

McNally, R. (2003). *Remembering trauma*. Cambridge, MA: Belknap Press.

McNally, R. J. (1996). Cognitive bias in the anxiety disorders. In D. A. Hope (Ed.), *Perspectives on anxiety, panic and fear* (The 43rd Annual Nebraska Symposium on Motivation) (pp. 211–250). Lincoln, NE: Nebraska University Press.

McNally, R. J. (1999). EMDR and mesmerism: A comparative historical analysis. *Journal of Anxiety Disorders, 13*, 225–236.

McNally, R. J. (2011). *What is mental illness?* Cambridge, MA: Harvard University Press.

McNally, R. J., & Geraerts, E. (2009). A new solution to the recovered memory debate. *Perspectives on Psychological Science, 4*(2), 126–134.

McNally, R. J. (2012a). Explaining "memories" of space alien abduction and past lives: An experimental psychopathology approach. *Journal of Experimental Psychopathology, 3*(1), 2–16.

McNally, R. J. (2012b). Are we winning the war against posttraumatic stress disorder? *Science, 336*(6083), 872–874. doi: 10.1126/science.1222069

McNeil, T. F. (1987). Perinatal influences in the development of schizophrenia. In H. Helmchen & F. A. Henn (Eds.), *Biological perspectives of schizophrenia* (pp. 125–138). New York, NY: Wiley.

McPartland, J. C., Reichow, B., & Volkmar, F. R. (2012). Sensitivity and specificity of proposed DSM-5 diagnostic criteria for autism spectrum disorder. *Journal of the American Academy of Child & Adolescent Psychiatry, 51*(4), 368–383. doi: 10.1016/j.jaac.2012.01.007

McQuade, J. D., & Hoza, B. (2015). Peer relationships of children with ADHD. In R. A. Barkley (Ed.), *Attention-deficit hyperactivity disorder: A handbook for diagnosis & treatment* (4th ed., pp. 210–222). New York, NY: The Guilford Press.

McWilliams, J. M., Meara, E., Zaslavsky, A. M., & Ayanian, J. Z. (2009). Differences in control of cardiovascular disease and diabetes by race, ethnicity, and education: U.S. trends from 1999 to 2006 and effects of Medicare coverage. *Annals of Internal Medicine, 150*(8), 505–515.

Mead, G. E., Morley, W., Campbell, P., Greig, C. A., McMurdo, M., & Lawlor, D. A. (2009). Exercise for depression. *Cochrane Database of Systematic Reviews, 3*, CD004366. doi: 10.1002/14651858.CD004366.pub4

Meagher, D., & Trzapacz, P. (2012). Delirium. In M. G. Gelder, N. C. Andreasen, J. J. Lopez-Ibor, Jr., & J. R. Geddes (Eds.), *New Oxford textbook of psychiatry* (2nd. ed., Vol. 1, pp. 325–333). New York, NY: Oxford University Press.

Meagher, D., Adamis, D., Trzepacz, P., & Leonard, M. (2012). Features of subsyndromal and persistent delirium. *The British Journal of Psychiatry, 200*(1), 37–44.

Meaney, M. J., & Szyf, M. (2005). Maternal care as a model for experience-dependent chromatin plasticity? *Trends in Neurosciences, 28*(9), 456–463.

Means, M. K., & Edinger, J. D. (2006). Non-pharmacologic therapy of insomnia. In T. Lee-Chiong (Ed.), *Sleep: A comprehensive handbook* (pp. 133–136). Hoboken, NJ: Wiley.

Mechoulam, R., & Parker, L. A. (2013). The endo-cannabinoid system and the brain. *Annual Review of Psychology, 64*, 21–47.

Medina v. California, 112 S. Ct. 2575 (1992).

Mednick, S. A., & Schulsinger, F. (1965). A longitudinal study of children with a high risk for schizophrenia: A preliminary report. In S. Vandenberg (Ed.), *Methods and goals in human behavior genetics* (pp. 255–296). New York, NY: Academic Press.

Mednick, S. A., & Schulsinger, F. (1968). Some premorbid characteristics related to break-down in children with schizophrenic mothers. *Journal of Psychiatric Research, 6*, 267–291.

Meehl, P. E. (1945). The dynamics of "structured" personality tests. *Journal of Clinical Psychology, 1*, 296–303.

Meehl, P. E. (1962). Schizotaxia, schizotypy, schizophrenia. *American Psychologist, 17*, 827–838.

Meehl, P. E. (1989). Schizotaxia revisited. *Archives of General Psychiatry, 46*, 935–944.

Mehler, P. S., Birmingham, L. C., Crow, S. J., & Jahraus, J. P. (2010). Medical complications of eating disorders. In C. M. Grilo & J. E. Mitchell (Eds.), *The treatment of eating disorders: A clinical handbook* (pp. 66–80). New York, NY: Guilford.

Melamed, B. G., & Siegel, L. J. (1975). Reduction of anxiety in children facing hospitalization and surgery by use of filmed modeling. *Journal of Consulting and Clinical Psychology, 43*(4), 511–521.

Melca, I. A., Yücel, M., Mendlowicz, M. V., de Oliveira-Souza, R., & Fontenelle, L. F. (2015). The correlates of obsessive–compulsive, schizotypal, and borderline personality disorders in obsessive–compulsive disorder. *Journal of Anxiety Disorders, 33*, 15–24.

Melhem, N. M., Porta, G., Shamseddeen, W., Payne, M. W., & Brent, D. A. (2011). Grief in adolescents bereaved by sudden parental death. *Archives of General Psychiatry, 68*(9), 911–919.

Meltzer-Brody, S., Stuebe, A., Dole, N., Savitz, D., Rubinow, D., & Thorp, J. (2011). Elevated corticotropin releasing hormone (CRH) during pregnancy and risk of postpartum depression (PPD). *Journal of Clinical Endocrinology & Metabolism, 96*(1), E40–E47.

Melzack, R. (1999). From the gate to the neuromatrix. *Pain* (Suppl. 6), S121–S126.

Melzack, R. (2005). Evolution of the neuromatrix theory of pain. *Pain Practice, 5*, 85–94.

Melzack, R., & Wall, P. D. (1965). Pain mechanisms: A new theory. *Science, 150*, 971–979.

Melzack, R., & Wall, P. D. (1982). *The challenge of pain.* New York, NY: Basic Books.

Mennes, C. E., Ben Abdallah, A., & Cottler, L. B. (2009). The reliability of self-reported cannabis abuse, dependence and withdrawal symptoms: Multisite study of differences between general population and treatment groups. *Addictive Behaviors, 34*(2), 223–226. doi: 10.1016/j.addbeh.2008.10.003

Menza, M. (2006). STAR*D: The results begin to roll in. *American Journal of Psychiatry, 163*, 1123–1125.

Mercer, K. B., Orcutt, H. K., Quinn, J. F., Fitzgerald, C. A., Conneely, K. N., Barfield, R. T., & Ressler, K. J. (2012). Acute and posttraumatic stress symptoms in a prospective gene x environment study of a university campus shooting. *Archives of General Psychiatry, 69*(1), 89–97. doi: 10.1001/archgenpsychiatry.2011.109

Meredith, S. E., Juliano, L. M., Hughes, J. R., & Griffiths, R. R. (2013). Caffeine use disorder: a comprehensive review and research agenda. *Journal of Caffeine Research, 3*(3), 114–130.

Merens, W., Willem Van der Does, A. J., & Spinhoven, P. (2007). The effects of serotonin manipulations on emotional information processing and mood. *Journal of Affective Disorders, 103*(1–3), 43–62.

Merikangas, K. R., & Pato, M. (2009). Recent developments in the epidemiology of bipolar disorder in adults and children: Magnitude, correlates, and future directions. *Clinical Psychology: Science and Practice, 16*(2), 121–133.

Merikangas, K. R., & Risch, N. (2014). Will the genomics revolution revolutionize psychiatry?. *American Journal of Psychiatry 160*(4), 625–635. http://dx.doi.org/10.1176/appi.ajp.160.4.625

Merikangas, K. R., Akiskal, H. S., Angst, J., Greenberg, P. E., Hirschfeld, R. M., Petukhova, M., & Kessler, R. C. (2007). Lifetime and 12-month prevalence of bipolar spectrum disorder in the National Comorbidity Survey Replication. *Archives of General Psychiatry, 64*(5), 543–552.

Merikangas, K. R., Cui, L., Kattan, G., Carlson, G. A., Youngstrom, E. A., & Angst, J. (2012). Mania with and without depression in a community sample of US adolescents. *Archives of General Psychiatry, 69*(9), 943–951.

Merikangas, K. R., Jin, R., He, J. P., Kessler, R. C., Lee, S., Sampson, N. A., & Zarkov, Z. (2011). Prevalence and correlates of bipolar spectrum disorder in the World Mental Health Survey Initiative. *Archives of General Psychiatry, 68*(3), 241–251.

Mermin, J., & Fenton, K. A. (2012). The future of HIV prevention in the United States. *JAMA: Journal of the American Medical Association, 308*(4), 347–348.

Meston, C. M., & Gorzalka, B. B. (1995). The effects of sympathetic activation on physiological and subjective sexual arousal in women. *Behaviour Research and Therapy, 33*, 651–664.

Meston, C. M. & Lorenz, T. A. (2013). Physiological stress responses predict sexual functioning and satisfaction differently in women who have and have not been sexually abused in childhood. *Psychological Trauma: Theory, Research, Practice, and Policy, 5*(4), 350–358.

Meuret, A. E., Rosenfield, D., Wilhelm, F. H., Zhou, E., Conrad, A., Ritz, T., & Roth, W. T. (2011). Do unexpected panic attacks occur spontaneously? *Biological Psychiatry, 70*, 985–991. doi: 10.1016/j.biopsych.2011.05.027

Meyer, A. J., Nash, J. D., McAlister, A. L., Maccoby, M., & Farquhar, J. W. (1980). Skills training in a cardiovascular health education campaign. *Journal of Consulting and Clinical Psychology, 2*, 129–142.

Meyer, B., & Carver, C. S. (2000). Negative childhood accounts, sensitivity and pessimism: A study of avoidant personality disorder features in college students. *Journal of Personality Disorders, 14*, 233–248.

Meyer-Bahlburg, H., Dolezal, C., Baker, S., Carlson, A., Obeid, J., & New, M. (2004). Prenatal androgenization affects gender-related behavior but not gender identity in 5–12 year old girls with congenital adrenal hyperplasia. *Archives of Sexual Behavior, 33*, 97–104.

Meyer-Bahlburg, H. F. (2010). From mental disorder to iatrogenic hypogonadism: Dilemmas in conceptualizing gender identity variants as psychiatric conditions. *Archives of Sexual Behavior, 39*(2), 461–476.

Meyerowitz, B. E. (1983). Postmastectomy coping strategies and quality of life. *Health Psychology, 2,* 117–132.

Mezick, E. J., Matthews, K. A., Hall, M., Kamarck, T. W., Strollo, P. J., Buysse, D. J., & Reis, S. E. (2010). Low life purpose and high hostility are related to an attenuated decline in nocturnal blood pressure. *Health Psychology, 29*(2), 196–204.

Mezzich, J. E., Kleinman, A., Fabrega, H., Jr., Good, B., Johnson-Powell, G., Lin, K. M., & Parron, D. (1992). *Cultural proposals for DSM-IV.* Submitted to the DSM-IV Task Force by the Steering Committee, NIMH-Sponsored Group on Culture and Diagnosis.

Michalak, J., Schultze, M., Heidenreich, T., & Schramm, E. (2015). A randomized controlled trial on the efficacy of mindfulness-based cognitive therapy and a group version of cognitive behavioral analysis system for chronically depressed patients. *Journal of Consulting and Clinical Psychology, 83,* 951–963.

Michelakos, T., Kousoulis, A. A., Katsiardanis, K., Dessypris, N., Anastasiou, A., Katsiardani, K.-P., & Petridou, E. T. (2013). Serum folate and B12 levels in association with cognitive impairment among seniors: Results from the VELESTINO study in Greece and meta-analysis. *Journal of Aging and Health, 25*(4), 589–616. doi: 10.1177/0898264313482488

Michultka, D. M., Blanchard, E. B., Appelbaum, K. A., Jaccard, J., & Dentinger, M. P. (1989). The refractory headache patient: II. High medication consumption (analgesic rebound) head-ache. *Behaviour Research and Therapy, 27,* 411–420.

Miciak, J., Fletcher, J. M., & Stuebing, K. K. (2016). Accuracy and validity of methods for identifying learning disabilities in a response-to-intervention service delivery framework. In S. R. Jimerson, M. K. Burns, & A. M. VanDerHeyden (Eds.), *Handbook of response to intervention: The science and practice of multi-tiered systems of support* (pp. 421–440). New York, NY: Springer.

Mihura, J. L., Meyer, G. J., Dumitrascu, N., & Bombel, G. (2012). The validity of individual Rorschach variables: Systematic reviews and meta-analyses of the Comprehensive System. *Psychological Bulletin 139*(3), 548–605. doi: 10.1037/10029406

Miklowitz, D. J. (2014). Bipolar disorder. In D. H. Barlow (Ed.), *Clinical handbook of psychological disorders: A step-by-step treatment manual* (5th ed.). New York, NY: Guilford.

Miklowitz, D. J., George, E. L., Richards, J. A., Simoneau, T. L., & Suddath, R. L. (2003). A randomized study of family-focused psycho-education and pharmacotherapy in the outpatient management of bipolar disorder. *Archives of General Psychiatry, 60,* 904–912.

Miklowitz, D. J., Otto, M. W., Frank, E., Reilly-Harrington, N. A., Wisniewski, S. R., Kogan, J. N., Nierenberg, A. A., . . . Sachs, G. S., (2007). Psychosocial treatments for bipolar depression: a 1-year randomized trial from the Systematic Treatment Enhancement Program. *Arch Gen Psychiatry, 64*(4):419–426.

Miklowitz, D. J., Schneck, C. D., Singh, M. K., Taylor, D. O., George, E. L., Cosgrove, M. E.,

Howe, M. E., Dickinson, L. M., Garber, J., & Chang, K. D. (2013). Early intervention for symptomatic youth for bipolar disorder: A randomized trial of family-focused therapy. *Journal of the American Academy of Child and Adolescent Psychiatry, 52,* 121–131.

Mill, J. (2011). Epigenetic effects on gene function and their role in mediating gene-enviroment interactions. In K. S. Kendler, S. Jaffee, & D. Romer (Eds.), *The dynamic genome and mental health: The role of genes and environments in youth development* (pp. 145–171). New York, NY: Oxford University Press.

Millan, M. J., Fone, K., Steckler, T., & Horan, W. P. (2014). Negative symptoms of schizophrenia: Clinical characteristics, pathophysiological substrates, experimental models and prospects for improved treatment. *European Neuropsychopharmacology, 24*(5), 645–692.

Millar, H. R., Qrdell, F., Vyvyan, J. P., Naji, S. A., Prescott, G. J., & Eagles, J. M. (2005). Anorexia nervosa mortality in northeast Scotland 1965–1999. *American Journal of Psychiatry, 162,* 753–757.

Miller, G. (2011). Social neuroscience. Why loneliness is hazardous to your health. *Science, 331*(6014), 138–140. doi: 10.1126/science.331.6014.138

Miller, G., & Blackwell, E. (2006). Turning up the heat: Inflammation as a mechanism linking chronic stress, depression, and heart disease. *Current Directions in Psychological Science, 15,* 269–277.

Miller, I. W., & Norman, W. H. (1979). Learned helplessness in humans: A review and attribution-theory model. *Psychological Bulletin, 86*(1), 93–118.

Miller, I. W., Norman, W. H., & Keitner, G. I. (1989). Cognitive-behavioral treatment of depressed inpatients: Six-and twelve-month follow-up. *American Journal of Psychiatry, 146,* 1274–1279.

Miller, J., Bilder, D., Farley, M., Coon, H., Pinborough-Zimmerman, J., Jenson, W., & McMahon, W. (2013). Autism spectrum disorder reclassified: A second look at the 1980s Utah/UCLA Autism Epidemiologic Study. *Journal of Autism and Developmental Disorders 43*(1), 200–210. doi: 10.1007/s10803-012-1566-0

Miller, M. W., Wolf, E. J., Keane, T. M. (2014). Posttraumatic stress disorder in DSM-5: New criteria and controversies. *Clinical Psychology: Science and Practice, 21,* 208–220.

Miller, N. E. (1969). Learning of visceral and glandular responses. *Science, 163,* 434–445.

Miller, S. D. (1989). Optical differences in cases of multiple personality disorder. *Journal of Nervous and Mental Disease, 177*(8), 480–486.

Miller, T. Q., Smith, T. W., Turner, C. W., Guijarro, M. L., & Hallet, A. J. (1996). A meta-analytic review of research on hostility and physical health. *Psychological Bulletin, 119*(2), 322–348.

Miller, W. R., & Hester, R. K. (1986). Inpatient alcoholism treatment: Who benefits? *American Psychologist, 41,* 794–805.

Miller, W. R., & Rollnick, S. (2002). *Motivational interviewing: Lessons preparing people for change.* New York, NY: Guildford.

Miller, W.R. & Rollnick, S. (2012). *Motivational interviewing: Helping people change.* New York, NY: Guilford Press.

Millon, T. (1981). *Disorders of personality: DSM-III, Axis II.* New York, NY: Wiley.

Millon, T. (1991). Classification in psychopathology: Rationale, alternatives, and standards. *Journal of Abnormal Psychology, 100*(3), 245–261.

Millon, T. (2004). *Masters of the mind.* Hoboken, NJ: Wiley.

Millon, T., & Martinez, A. (1995). Avoidant personality disorder. In W. J. Livesley (Ed.), *The DSM-IV personality disorders* (pp. 218–233). New York, NY: Guilford.

Mills, P. J., Adler, K. A., Dimsdale, J. E., Perez, C. J., Ziegler, M. G., Ancoli-Israel, S., & Grant, I. (2004). Vulnerable caregivers of Alzheimer disease patients have a deficit in beta 2-adrenergic receptor sensitivity and density. *American Journal of Geriatric Psychiatry, 12,* 281–286.

Mindell, J. A., & Owens, J. A. (2015). *A clinical guide to pediatric sleep: diagnosis and management of sleep problems* (3rd ed.). Philadelphia, PA: Lippincott Williams & Wilkins.

Mindham, R. H. S., & Hughes, T. A. (2012). Dementia in Parkinson's disease. In M. G. Gelder, N. C. Andreasen, J. J. Lopez-Ibor, Jr., & J. R. Geddes (Eds.), *New Oxford textbook of psychiatry* (2nd. ed., Vol. 1, pp. 368–371). New York, NY: Oxford University Press.

Mineka, S. (1985). The frightful complexity of the origins of fears. In F. R. Bruch & J. B. Overmier (Eds.), *Affect, conditioning, and cognition: Essays on the determinants of behavior.* Hillsdale, NJ: Erlbaum.

Mineka, S., & Sutton, J. (2006). In M. G. Craske, D. Hermans, & D. Vansteenwegen, *Fear and learning: From basic processes to clinical implications* (pp. 75–97), Washington, DC: American Psychological Association.

Mineka, S., Watson, D., & Clark, L. A. (1998). Comorbidity of anxiety and unipolar mood disorders. *Annual Review of Psychology, 49,* 377–412.

Mineka, S., & Zinbarg, R. (1996). Conditioning and ethological models of anxiety disorders: Stress-in-dynamic-context anxiety models. In D. A. Hope (Ed.), *Perspectives on anxiety, panic and fear* (The 43rd Annual Nebraska Symposium on Motivation) (pp. 135–210). Lincoln, NE: Nebraska University Press.

Mineka, S., & Zinbarg, R. (1998). Experimental approaches to understanding the mood and anxiety disorders. In J. Adair (Ed.), *Advances in psychological research, Vol. 2: Social, personal, and cultural aspects* (pp. 429–454). Hove, UK: Psychology Press/Erlbaum.

Mineka, S., & Zinbarg, R. (2006). A contemporary learning theory perspective on the etiology of anxiety disorders. *American Psychologist, 61,* 10–26.

Minino, A. M., Arias, E., Kochanek, K. D., Murphy, S. L., & Smith, B. L. (2002). Deaths: Final data for 2000. *National Vital Statistics Reports, 50,* 1–119.

Minuchin, S., Rosman, B. L., & Baker, L. (1978). *Psychosomatic families*. Cambridge, MA: Harvard University Press.

Mirsky, A. F., Bieliauskas, L. A., French, L. M., van Kammen, D. P., Jonsson, E., & Sedvall, G. (2000). A 39-year follow-up of the Genain quadruplets. *Schizophrenia Bulletin, 26*, 699–708.

Mistry, H., Bhugra, D., Chaleby, K., Khan, F., & Sauer, J. (2009). Veiled communication: is uncovering necessary for psychiatric assessment? *Transcultural Psychiatry, 46*(4), 642–650. doi: 10.1177/1363461509351366

Mitchell, D. C., Knight, C. A., Hockenberry, J., Teplansky, R., & Hartman, T. J. (2014). Beverage caffeine intakes in the US. *Food and Chemical Toxicology, 63*, 136–142.

Mitchell, W. B., DiBartolo, P. M., Brown, T. A., & Barlow, D. H. (1998). Effects of positive and negative mood on sexual arousal in sexually functional males. *Archives of Sexual Behavior, 27*(2), 197–207.

Mobbs, D., Lau, H., Jones, O., & Frith, C. (2009). Law, responsibility, and the brain. In N. Murphy, G. Ellis, & T. O'Connor (Eds.), *Downward causation and the neurobiology of free will* (pp. 243–260). New York, NY: Springer.

Mock, S. E., & Eibach, R. P. (2012). Stability and change in sexual orientation identity over a 10-year period in adulthood. *Archives of Sexual Behavior, 41*(3), 641–648.

Modahl, C., Green, L., Fein, D., Morris, M., Waterhouse, L., Feinstein, C., & Levin, H. (1998). Plasma oxytocin levels in autistic children. *Biological Psychiatry, 43*, 270–277.

Modinos, G., Mechelli, A., Ormel, J., Groenewold, N., Aleman, A., & McGuire, P. (2009). Schizotypy and brain structure: A voxel-based morphometry study. *Psychological Medicine, 40*, 1423–1431.

Modrego, P. J. (2010). Depression in Alzheimer's disease. Pathophysiology, diagnosis, and treatment. *Journal of Alzheimer's Disease, 21*, 1077–1087.

Moene, F. C., Landberg, E. H., Hoogduin, K. A., Spinhoven, P., Hertzberger, L. I., Kleyweg, R. P., & Weeda, J. (2000). Organic syndromes diagnosed as conversion disorder: Identification and frequency in a study of 85 patients. *Journal of Psychosomatic Research, 49*, 7–12.

Moene, F. C., Spinhoven, P., Hoogduin, K. A., & van Dyck, R. (2002). A randomised controlled clinical trial on the additional effect of hypnosis in a comprehensive treatment programme for in-patients with conversion disorder of the motor type. *Psychotherapy and psychosomatics, 71*, 66–76.

Moene, F. C., Spinhoven, P., Hoogduin, K. A., & van Dyck, R. (2003). A randomized controlled clinical trial of a hypnosis-based treatment for patients with conversion disorder, motor type. *International Journal of Clinical and Experimental Hypnosis, 51*(1), 29–50.

Moffitt, T. E., Caspi, A., Rutter, M., & Silva, P. A. (2001). *Sex differences in antisocial behaviour: Conduct disorder, delinquency, and violence in the Dunedin longitudinal study*. Cambridge, UK: Cambridge University Press.

Mogg, K., Bradley, B. P., Millar, N., & White, J. (1995). A follow-up study of cognitive bias in generalized anxiety disorder. *BRAT, 33*, 927–935.

Mogg, K., Philippot, P., & Bradley, B. P. (2004). Selective attention to angry faces in clinical social phobia. *Journal of Abnormal Psychology, 113*, 160–165.

Mogil, J. S., Sternberg, W. F., Kest, B., Marek, P., & Liebeskind, J. C. (1993). Sex differences in the antagonism of swim stress-induced analgesia: Effects of gonadectomy and estrogen replacement. *Pain, 53*, 17–25.

Mohlman, J., Bryant, C., Lenze, E. J., Stanley, M. A., Gum, A., Flit, A., & Craske, M. G. (2012). Improving recognition of late life anxiety disorders in Diagnostic and Statistical Manual of Mental Disorders, Fifth Edition: Observations and recommendations of the Advisory Committee to the Lifespan Disorders Work Group. *International Journal of Geriatric Psychiatry, 27*, 549–556. doi: 10.1002/gps.2752

Moll K, Kunze S, Neuhoff N, Bruder J, Schulte-Körne G (2014) Specific Learning Disorder: Prevalence and Gender Differences. *PLoS ONE 9*(7): e103537.

Money, J., & Ehrhardt, A. (1972). *Man and woman, boy and girl*. Baltimore, MD: Johns Hopkins University Press.

Monroe, S. M., & Reid, M. W. (2009). Life stress and major depression. *Current Directions in Psychological Science, 18*(2), 68–72.

Monroe, S. M., Kupfer, D. J., & Frank, E. (1992). Life stress and treatment course of recurrent depression: I. Response during index episode. *Journal of Consulting and Clinical Psychology, 60*(5), 718–724.

Monroe, S. M., Roberts, J. E., Kupfer, D. J., & Frank, E. (1996). Life stress and treatment course of recurrent depression: II. Postrecovery associations with attrition, symptom course, and recurrence over 3 years. *Journal of Abnormal Psychology, 105*(3), 313–328.

Monroe, S. M., Rohde, P., Seeley, J. R., & Lewinsohn, P. M. (1999). Life events and depression in adolescence: For first onset of major depressive disorder. *Journal of Abnormal Psychology, 108*(4), 606–614.

Monroe, S. M., Slavich, G. M., & Georgiades, K. (2009). The social environment and life stress in depression. In I. H. Gotlib & C. L. Hammen (Eds.), *Handbook of depression* (2nd ed., pp. 340–360). New York, NY: Guilford.

Monson, C. M., Fredman, S. J., Macdonald, A., Pukay-Martin, N. D., Resick, P. A., & Schnurr, P. P. (2012). Effect of cognitive-behavioral couple therapy for PTSD: A randomized controlled trial. *Journal of American Medical Association, 308*, 700–709. doi: 10.1001/jama.2012.9307

Monson, C. M., Resick, P. A., & Rizvi, S. L. (2014). Posttraumatic stress disorder. In D.H. Barlow (Ed.), *Clinical handbook of psychological disorders: A step-by-step treatment manual* (5th ed.). New York, NY: Guilford.

Montejo-Gonzalez, A. L., Liorca, G., Izquierdo, J. A., Ledesma, A., Bousono, M., Calcedo, A., & Vincens, E. (1997). SSRI-induced sexual dysfunction: Fluoxetine, paroxetine, sertraline, and fluvoxamine in a prospective, multicenter, and descriptive clinical study of 344 patients. *Journal of Sex and Marital Therapy, 23*, 176–194.

Moore, D. S. (2001). *The dependent gene: The fallacy of "nature vs. nurture."* New York, NY: Henry Holt.

Moore, M. (2012). Behavioral sleep problems in children and adolescents. *Journal of Clinical Psychology in Medical Settings, 19*(1), 77–83.

Moreno, A., Azar, M., Warren, N., Dickerson, T., Koob, G., & Janda, K. (2010). A critical evaluation of a nicotine vaccine within a self-administration behavioral model. *Molecular pharmaceutics, 7*(2), 431–441.

Moreno, C., Laje, G., Blanco, C., Jiang, H., Schmidt, A. B., & Olfson, M. (2007). National trends in the outpatient diagnosis and treatment of bipolar disorder in youth. *Archives of General Psychiatry, 64*(9), 1032–1039.

Morenz, B., & Becker, J. (1995). The treatment of youthful sexual offenders. *Applied & Preventive Psychology, 4*, 247–256.

Morey, L. C., & Ochoa, E. S. (1989). An investigation of adherence to diagnostic criteria: Clinical diagnosis of the DSM-III personality disorders. *Journal of Personality Disorders, 3*(3), 180–192.

Morey, J. N., Boggero, I. A., Scott, A. B., & Segerstrom, S. C. (2015). Current directions in stress and human immune function. *Current Opinion in Psychology, 5*, 13–17.

Morgan, D. (2007). The rationale for an immunological approach to Alzheimer's therapeutics. In A. C. Cuello (Ed.), *Pharmacological mechanisms in Alzheimer's therapeutics* (pp. 141–148). New York, NY: Springer.

Morgan, H. W. (1981). *Drugs in America: A social history, 1800–1980*. Syracuse, NY: Syracuse University Press.

Morin, C. M., & Benca, R. (2012). Chronic insomnia. *The Lancet, 379*(9821), 1129–1141. doi: 10.1016/s0140-6736(11)60750-2

Morin, C. M., Savard, J., & Ouellet, M. C. (2012). Nature and treatment of insomnia. In I. B. Weiner, A. M. Nezu, C. M. Nezu, & P. A. Geller (Eds.), *Handbook of psychology, Health psychology* (Vol. 9, pp. 318–339).

Morokoff, P. J., & Heiman, J. R. (1980). Effects of erotic stimuli on sexually functional and dysfunctional women: Multiple measures before and after sex therapy. *Behaviour Research and Therapy, 18*, 127–137.

Morrato, E. H., & Allison, D. B. (2012). FDA approval of obesity drugs: A difference in risk-benefit perceptions. *JAMA: Journal of the American Medical Association, 308*, 1097–1098. doi: 10.1001/jama.2012.10007

Morris, J. K., Cook, D. G., & Shaper, A. G. (1994). Loss of employment and mortality. *British Medical Journal, 308*, 1135–1139.

Morris, J. S., Öhman, A., & Dolan, R. J. (1998). Conscious and unconscious emotion learning in the human amygdala. *Nature, 393*, 467–470.

Morrison, A. S. & Heimberg, R. G. (2013). Social anxiety and social anxiety disorder. *Annual Review of Clinical Psychology, 9*, 249–274.

Morrow, G. R., & Dobkin, P. L. (1988). Anticipatory nausea and vomiting in cancer patients undergoing chemotherapy treatment: Prevalence, etiology, and behavioral interventions. *Clinical Psychology Review, 8*, 517–556.

Mortberg, E., Clark, D. M., & Bejerot, S. (2011). Intensive group cognitive therapy and individual cognitive therapy for social phobia: Sustained improvement at 5-year follow-up. *Journal of Anxiety Disorders, 25,* 994–1000. doi: 10.1016/j.janxdis.2011.06.007

Mosher, D. L., & Sirkin, M. (1984). Measuring a macho personality constellation. *Journal of Research in Personality, 18,* 150–163.

Mosher, W. D., Chandra, A., & Jones, J. (2005). Sexual behavior and selected health measures: Men and women 15–44 years of age, United States, 2002. *Advance Data from Vital and Health Statistics, 362,* 1–55. Hyattsville, MD: National Center for Health Statistics.

Moskowitz, A. (2004). "Scared stiff": Catatonia as an evolutionary based fear response. *Psychological Review, 111,* 984–1002.

Mostofsky, D. I., & Barlow, D. H. (Eds.) (2000). *The management of stress and anxiety in medical disorders.* Needham Heights, MA: Allyn & Bacon.

Mucha, T. F., & Reinhardt, R. F. (1970). Conversion reactions in student aviators. *American Journal of Psychiatry, 127,* 493–497.

Mueller, T., Keller, M. B., Leon, A. C., Solomon, D. A., Shea, M. T., Coryell, W., & Endicott, J. (1996). Recovery after 5 years of unremitting major depressive disorder. *Archives of General Psychiatry, 53,* 794–799.

Mueser, K. T., & Berenbaum, H. (1990). Psychodynamic treatment of schizophrenia: Is there a future? *Psychological Medicine, 20,* 253–262.

Mueser, K. T., & Marcello, S. (2011). Schizophrenia. In D. H. Barlow (Ed.), *Oxford handbook of clinical psychology* (pp. 469–503). New York, NY: Oxford University.

Mueser, K. T., Deavers, F., Penn, D. L., & Cassisi, J. E. (2013). Psychosocial treatments for schizophrenia. *Annual Review of Clinical Psychology, 9,* 465–497.

Mueser, K. T., Liberman, R. P., & Glynn, S. M. (1990). Psychosocial interventions in schizophrenia. In A. Kales, C. N. Stefanis, & J. A. Talbott (Eds.), *Recent advances in schizophrenia* (pp. 213–235). New York, NY: Springer-Verlag.

Mufson, L., Pollack-Dorta, K., Wickramaratne, P., Nomura, Y., Olfson, M., & Weismann, M. (2004). A randomized effectiveness trial of interpersonal psychotherapy for depressed adolescents. *Archives of General Psychiatry, 61,* 577–584.

Muhuri, P.K., Gfroerer, J.C., Davies, M.C. (2013). *Associations of nonmedical pain reliever use and initiation of heroin use in the United States Center for Behavioral Health Statistics and Quality.* Retrieved from http:// www.samhsa. gov/data/2k13/DataReview/ DR006/nonmedical-pain-reliever-use-2013.htm.

Mulder, R., Frampton, C., Luty, S., & Joyce, P. (2009). Eighteen months of drug treatment for depression: Predicting relapse and recovery. *Journal of Affective Disorders, 114*(1–3), 263–270.

Mullany, B., Barlow, A., Goklish, N., Larzelere-Hinton, F., Cwik, M., Craig, M., & Walkup, J. T. (2009). Toward understanding suicide among youths: Results from the White Mountain Apache tribally mandated suicide surveillance system, 2001–2006. *American Journal of Public Health, 99*(10), 1840–1848.

Mullen, P. (2010). The psychiatric expert witness in the criminal justice system. *Criminal Behaviour and Mental Health, 20*(3), 165–176.

Mumford, D. B., Whitehouse, A. M., & Platts, M. (1991). Sociocultural correlates of eating disorders among Asian schoolgirls in Bradford. *British Journal of Psychiatry, 158,* 222–228.

Munder, T., Flückiger, C., Gerger, H., Wampold, B. E., & Barth, J. (2012). Is the allegiance effect an epiphenomenon of true efficacy differences between treatments? A meta-analysis. *Journal of Counseling Psychology, 59*(4), 631–637.

Munjack, D. J. (1984). The onset of driving phobias. *Journal of Behavior Therapy and Experimental Psychiatry, 15,* 305–308.

Muñoz, R. F., Le, H.-N., Clarke, G. N., Barrera, A. Z., & Torres, L. D. (2009). Preventing first onset and recurrence of major depressive episodes. In I. H. Gotlib & C. L. Hammen (Eds.), *Handbook of depression* (2nd ed., pp. 533–553). New York, NY: Guilford.

Muñoz, R. F., Beardslee, W. R., Leykin, Y. (2012). Major depression can be prevented. *American Psychologist, 67*(4), 285–295.

Muñoz, R. F., Cuijpers, P., Smit, F., Barrera, A. Z., & Leykin, Y. (2010). Prevention of major depression. *Annual Review of Clinical Psychology, 6,* 181–212.

Munro, A. (2012). Persistent delusional symptoms and disorders. In M. G. Gelder, N. C. Andreasen, J. J. Lopez-Ibor, Jr., & J. R. Geddes (Eds.), *New Oxford textbook of psychiatry* (2nd. ed., Vol. 1, pp. 609–628). New York, NY: Oxford University Press.

Muresanu, D. F., Stan, A., & Buzoianu, A. (2012). Neuroplasticity and impulse control disorders. *Journal of the Neurological Sciences, 316*(1–2), 15–20. doi: http://dx.doi.org/10.1016/j.jns.2012.01.016

Muris, P., & Field, A. P. (2010). The role of verbal threat information in the development of childhood fear. "Beware the Jabberwock." *Clinical Child and Family Psychology Review, 13,* 129–150.

Murphy, J. A., & Byrne, G. J. (2012). Prevalence and correlates of the proposed DSM-5 diagnosis of chronic depressive disorder. *Journal of Affective Disorders, 139,* 172–180.

Murphy, K. R. (2015). Psychological counseling of adults with ADHD. In R. A. Barkley (Ed.), *Attention-deficit hyperactivity disorder: A handbook for diagnosis & treatment* (4th ed., pp. 741–756). New Yok: The Guilford Press.

Murphy, S. L., Xu, J., & Kochanek, K. D. (2013). *Deaths: Final data for 2010.* National Vital Statiscctics Reports, 61,(4). Murphy, T. K., Storch, E. A., Lewin, A. B., Edge, P. J., & Goodman, W. K. (2012). Clinical factors associated with pediatric autoimmune neuropsychiatric disorders associated with streptococcal infections. *Journal of Pediatrics, 160,* 314–319. doi: 10.1016/j.jpeds.2011.07.012

Murphy, W. D., & Page, I. J. (2008). Exhibitionism: Psychopathology and theory. In D. R. Laws & W. T. O'Donohue (Eds.), *Sexual deviance: Theory, assessment, and treatment* (2nd ed., pp. 61–75). New York, NY: Guilford.

Murray, R. M., & Castle, D. J. (2012). Genetic and environmental risk factors for schizophrenia. In M. G. Gelder, N. C. Andreasen, J. J. LopezIbor, Jr., & J. R. Geddes (Eds.), *New Oxford textbook of psychiatry* (2nd. ed., Vol. 1, pp. 553–561). New York, NY: Oxford University Press.

Mustafa, G. (1990). Delivery systems for the care of schizophrenic patients in Africa-Sub-Sahara. In A. Kales, C. N. Stefanis, & J. A. Talbot (Eds.), *Recent advances in schizophrenia* (pp. 353–371). New York, NY: Springer-Verlag.

Mustanski, B. S., Bailey, J. M., & Kaspar, S. (2002). Dermatoglyphics, handedness, sex, and sexual orientation. *Archives of Sexual Behavior, 31,* 113–122.

Mustian, K. M., Devine, K., Ryan, J. L., Janelsins, M. C., Sprod, L. K., Peppone, L. J., Candelario, G. D., Mohile, S. G., & Morrow, G. R. (2011). Treatment of nausea and vomiting during chemotherapy. *U.S. Oncology & Hematology, 7*(2), 91–97.

My-pro-ana. (2013). Home page. Retrieved July 19, 2013, from http://www.myproana.com/

Myers, J. K., Weissman, M. M., Tischler, C. E., Holzer, C. E., III, Orvaschel, H., Anthony, J. C., & Stoltzman, R. (1984). Six-month prevalence of psychiatric disorders in three communities. *Archives of General Psychiatry, 41,* 959–967.

Nagayama Hall, G. C. (1995). The preliminary development of theory-based community treatment for sexual offenders. *Professional Psychology: Research and Practice, 26*(5), 478–483.

Nagel, D. B. (1991). Psychotherapy of schizophrenia: 1900–1920. In J. G. Howells (Ed.), *The concept of schizophrenia: Historical perspectives* (pp. 191–201). Washington, DC: American Psychiatric Press.

Najavits, L. M. (2007). Psychosocial treatments for posttraumatic stress disorder. In P. E. Nathan & J. M. Gorman (Eds.), *A guide to treatments that work* (3rd ed.). New York, NY: Oxford University Press.

Nakajima, M., & al'Absi, M. (2012). Predictors of risk for smoking relapse in men and women: A prospective examination. *Psychology of Addictive Behaviors, 26*(3), 633–637.

Narrow, W. E., Clarke, D. E., Kuramoto, S. J., Kraemer, H. C., Kupfer, D. J., Greiner, L., & Regier, D. A. (2013). *DSM-5 field trials in the United States and Canada, Part III: Development and reliability testing of a cross-cutting symptom assessment for DSM-5. American Journal of Psychiatry, 170*(1), 71–82.

Nash, W. P., Boasso, A. M., Steenkamp, M. M., Larson, J. L., Lubin, R. E., & Litz, B. T. (2014). Posttraumatic stress in deployed marines: Prospective trajectories of early adaptation. *Journal of Abnormal Psychology, 124,* 155–171.

Nasser, M. (1988). Eating disorders: The cultural dimension. *Social Psychiatry and Psychiatric Epidemiology, 23,* 184–187.

National Collaborating Centre for Mental Health. (2009). *Borderline personality disorder: The NICE GUIDELINE on treatment and management, Clinical practice guideline no. 78.* London, UK: British Psychological Society & Royal College of Psychiatrists.

National Institute of Drug Abuse (2013) ([field_ revisiondate_1]). MDMA (Ecstasy or Molly) Retrieved from http://www .drugabuse.gov/ publications/drugfacts/ mdma-ecstasy-or -molly on September 14,

2014 National Institute of Mental Health. (2003). *Breaking ground, breaking through: The strategic plan for mood disorders research* (NIH Publication No. 03-5121). Washington, DC: U.S. Government Printing Office.

National Institute on Alcohol Abuse and Alcoholism. (1997). *Alcohol alert: Alcohol-metabolism* (No. 35, PH 371). Bethesda, MD: Author.

National Institute on Drug Abuse (NIDA). (2009). *Principles of addiction treatment: A research-based guide, 2nd edition* (NIH Publication No. 09-4180). Rockville, MD: National Institute on Drug Abuse.

National Safety Council. (2013). Estimating the cost of unintentional injuries. Retrieved from http://www.nsc.org/news_resources/injury_and_death_statistics/Pages/EstimatingtheCostsofUnintentional Injuries.aspx

National Sleep Foundation. (2005). *2005 sleep in America poll*. Washington, DC: Author.

National Sleep Foundation. (2009). *2009 sleep in America poll*. Washington, DC: Author.

Natoli, J. L., Ackerman, D. L., McDermott, S., & Edwards, J. G. (2012). Prenatal diagnosis of Down syndrome: A systematic review of termination rates (1995–2011). *Prenatal diagnosis, 32*(2), 142–153.

Navarrete, C. D., Olsson, A., Ho, A. K., Mendes, W. B., Thomsen, L., & Sidanius, J. (2009). Fear extinction to an outgroup face: The role of target gender. *Psychological Science, 20*(2), 155–158. doi: 10.1111/j.1467-9280.2009.02273.x

Neal-Barnett, A. M., & Smith, J., Sr. (1997). African Americans. In S. Friedman (Ed.), *Cultural issues in the treatment of anxiety* (pp. 154–174). New York, NY: Guilford.

Neimeyer, R. A., & Currier, J. M. (2009). Grief therapy: Evidence of efficacy and emerging directions. *Current Directions in Psychological Science, 18*(6), 352–356.

Nelles, W. B. N., & Barlow, D. H. (1988). Do children panic? *Clinical Psychology Review, 8*(4), 359–372.

Nelson, B., Yuen, H. P., Wood, S. J., Lin, A., Spiliotacopoulos, D., Bruxner, A., . . . Francey, S. M. (2013). Long-term follow-up of a group at ultra high risk ("prodromal") for psychosis: The PACE 400 study. *JAMA Psychiatry, 70*(8), 793–802.

Nelson, D. L., Beutler, L. E., & Castonguay, L. G. (2012). Psychotherapy integration in the treatment of personality disorders: A commentary. *Journal of Personality Disorders, 26*(1), 7–16.

Nelson, R. O., & Barlow, D. H. (1981). Behavioral assessment: Basic strategies and initial procedures. In D. H. Barlow (Ed.), *Behavioral assessment of adult disorders*. New York, NY: Guilford.

Nemeroff, C. (2004). Early-life adversity, CRF dysregulation, and vulnerability to mood and anxiety disorders. *Psychopharmacology Bulletin, 38*, 14–20.

Nemeroff, C. B. (2013). Psychoneuroimmunoendocrinology: The biological basis of mind-body physiology and pathophysiology. *Depression and Anxiety, 30*(4), 285–287.

Nepon, J., Belik, S. L., Bolton, J., & Sareen, J. (2010). The relationship between anxiety disorders and suicide attempts: Findings from the national epidemiologic survey on alcohol and related conditions. *Depression and Anxiety, 27*, 791–798.

Nestadt, G., Romanoski, A., Chahal, R., Merchant, A., Folstein, M., Gruenberg, E., McHugh, P. R. (2009). An epidemiological study of histrionic personality disorder. *Psychological Medicine, 20*(2), 413–422.

Nestler, E. J., Hyman, S. E., & Malenka, R. C. (2008). *Molecular neuropharmacology* (2nd ed.). New York, NY: McGraw-Hill.

Neubauer, D. (2009). New directions in the pharmacologic treatment of sleep disorders. *Primary Psychiatry, 16*(2), 52–58.

Neugroschi, J. A., Kolevzon, A., Samuels, S. C., & Marin, D. B. (2005). Dementia. In B. J. Sadock & V. A. Sadock (Eds.), *Kaplan & Sadock's comprehensive textbook of psychiatry* (pp. 1068–1093). Philadelphia, PA: Lippincott, Williams & Wilkins.

Neumann, C. S., Johansson, P. T., & Hare, R. D. (2013). The Psychopathy Checklist-Revised (PCL-R), low anxiety, and fearlessness: A structural equation modeling analysis. *Personality Disorders: Theory, Research, and Treatment, 4*(2), 129–137.

Neumark-Sztainer, D., & Eisenberg, M. E. (2014). Body Image Concerns, Muscle-Enhancing Behaviors, and Eating Disorders in Males. *JAMA, 312*(20), 2156–2157.

Neumark-Sztainer, D., & Haines, J. (2004). Psychosocial and behavioral consequences of obesity. In J. K. Thompson (Ed.), *Handbook of eating disorders and obesity* (pp. 349–371). New York, NY: Wiley.

Neumark-Sztainer, D., Wall, M., Larson, N. I., Eisenberg, M. E., & Loth, K. (2011). Dieting and disordered eating behaviors from adolescence to young adulthood: findings from a 10-year longitudinal study. *Journal of the American Dietetic Association, 111*(7), 1004–1011.

Nevsimalova, S. (2009). Narcolepsy in childhood. *Sleep Medicine Reviews, 13*(2), 169–180. doi: 10.1016/j.smrv.2008.04.007

New York Mental Hygiene Law § 1.03 (20) (1992).

Newman, M. G., Castonguay, L. G., Borkovec, T. D., Fisher, A. J., Boswell, J. F., Szkodny, L. E., & Nordberg, S. S. (2011). A randomized controlled trial of cognitive-behavioral therapy for generalized anxiety disorder with integrated techniques from emotion-focused and interpersonal therapies. *Journal of Consulting and Clinical Psychology, 79*(2), 171–181. doi: 10.1037/a0022489

Newman, J. P., Patterson, C. M., & Kosson, D. S. (1987). Response perseveration in psychopaths. *Journal of Abnormal Psychology, 96*, 145–148.

Newman, J. P., Widom, C. S., & Nathan, S. (1985). Passive-avoidance in syndromes of disinhibition: Psychopathy and extraversion. *Journal of Personality and Social Psychology, 50*, 624–630.

Newton, N. C., Conrod, P., Teesson, M., & Faggiano, F. (2012). School-based alcohol and other drug prevention. In J. C. Verster, K. Brady, M. Galanter, & P. Conrod (Eds.), *Drug abuse and addiction in medical illness* (pp. 545–560). New York, NY: Springer.

Neylan, T. C., Reynolds, C. F., III, & Kupfer, D. J. (2003). Sleep disorders. In R. E. Hales & S. C. Yudofsky (Eds.), *Textbook of clinical psychiatry* (4th ed., pp. 975–1000). Washington, DC: American Psychiatric Publishing.

Nezu, C. M., Nezu, A. M., Friedman, S. H., Houts, P. S., DelliCarpini, L., Bildner, C., & Faddis, S. (1999). Cancer and psychological distress: Two investigations regarding the role of social problem-solving. *Journal of Psychosocial Oncology, 16*(3–4), 27–40.

Ng, B. Y., Yap, A. K., Su, A., Lim, D., & Ong, S. H. (2002). Personality profiles of patients with dissociative trance disorder in Singapore. *Comprehensive psychiatry, 43*, 121–126.

Ng, M., Fleming, T., Robinson, M., Thomson, B., Graetz, N., Margono, C., . . . Gupta, R. (2014). Global, regional and national prevalence of overweight and obesity in children and adults 1980-2013: A systematic analysis. *Lancet (London, England), 384*(9945), 766–781.

Nicassio, P. M., Greenberg, M. A. & Motivala, S. J. (2010). Clinical psychology and health psychology: Toward an integrated perspective on health. In J. M. Suls, Davidson, K. W., & Kaplan, R. M. (Eds.) *Handbook of health psychology and behavioral medicine*. New York, NY: Guilford.

Nichols, D. S. (2011). *Essentials of MMPI-2 assessment* (2nd ed.). Hoboken, NJ: Wiley.

Nierenberg, A. A., Fava, M., Trivedi, M. H., Wisniewski, S. R., Thase, M. E., McGrath, P. J., & Rush, A. J. (2006). Comparison of lithium and T3 augmentation following two failed medication treatments for depression: A STAR*D report. *The American Journal of Psychiatry, 163*(9), 1519–1530.

Nierenberg, A. A., Akiskal, H. S., Angst, J., Hirschfeld, R. M., Merikangas, K. R., Petukhova, M., & Kessler, R. C. (2010). Bipolar disorder with frequent mood episodes in the National Comorbidity Survey Replication (NCS-R). *Molecular Psychiatry, 15*(11), 1075–1087.

Nierenberg, A. A., Friedman, E. S., Bowden, C. L., Sylvia, L. G., Thase, M. E., Ketter, T., & Calabrese, J. R. (2013). Lithium treatment moderate-dose use study (LiTMUS) for bipolar disorder: A randomized comparative effectiveness trial of optimized personalized treatment with and without lithium. *American Journal of Psychiatry, 170*(1), 102–110.

Nigg, J. T. (2015). Editorial: The shape of the nosology to come in developmental psychopathology. *Journal of Child Psychology and Psychiatry, 56*(4), 397–399. doi: 10.1111/jcpp.12408

Nigg, J. T., Nikolas, M., & Burt, S. A. (2010). Measured gene-by-environment interaction in relation to Attention-Deficit/Hyperactivity Disorder. *Journal of the American Academy of Child & Adolescent Psychiatry, 49*(9), 863–873. doi: 10.1016/j.jaac.2010.01.025

Nijmeijer, J. S., Minderaa, R. B., Buitelaar, J. K., Mulligan, A., Hartman, C. A., & Hoekstra, P. J. (2008). Attention-deficit/hyperactivity disorder and social dysfunctioning. *Clinical Psychology Review, 28*(4), 692–708.

Nijs, J., Paul, L., & Wallman, K. (2008). Chronic fatigue syndrome: An approach combining self-management with graded exercise to avoid exacerbations. *Journal of Rehabilitation Medicine, 40*, 241–247.

Nikolas, M., & Burt, S. (2010). Genetic and environmental influences on ADHD symptom dimensions of inattention and hyperactivity: A meta-analysis. *Journal of Abnormal Psychology, 119*(1), 1.

Nikolas, M. A., & Nigg, J. T. (2015). Moderators of neuropsychological mechanism in Attention-Deficit Hyperactivity Disorder. *Journal of Abnormal Child Psychology, 43*(2), 271–281. doi: 10.1007/s10802-014-9904-7

Nisbett, R. E., & Ross, L. (1980). *Human inference: Strategies and shortcomings in social judgment.* New York, NY: Century.

Nivard, M. G., Dolan, C. V., Kendler, K. S., Kan, K.-J., Willemsen, G., Van Beijsterveldt, C. E. M. . . . Boomsma, D. I. (2015). Stability in symptoms of anxiety and depression as a function of genotype and environment: A longitudinal twin study from ages 3 to 63 years. *Psychological Medicine, 45,* 1039–1049.

Nivoli, A. M., Murru, A., & Vieta, E. (2010). Lithium: Still a cornerstone in the long-term treatment in bipolar disorder? *Neuropsychobiology, 62*(1), 27–35.

Nock, M., & Kessler, R. (2006). Prevalence of and risk factors for suicide attempts versus suicide gestures: Analysis of the National Comorbidity Survey. *Journal of Abnormal Psychology, 115,* 616–623.

Nock, M. K. (2010). Self-injury. *Annual Review of Clinical Psychology, 6,* 339–363.

Nock, M. K., Borges, G., Bromet, E. J., Alonso, J., Angermeyer, M., Beautrais, A., & Williams, D. (2008). Cross-national prevalence and risk factors for suicidal ideation, plans and attempts. *British Journal of Psychiatry, 192*(2), 98–105.

Nock, M. K., Borges, G., Bromet, E. J., Cha, C. B., Kessler, R. C., & Lee, S. (2008). Suicide and suicidal behavior. *Epidemiologic Reviews, 30,* 133–154.

Nock, M. K., Cha, C. B., & Dour, H. J. (2011). Disorders of impulse-control and self-harm. In D. H. Barlow (Ed.), *Oxford handbook of clinical psychology* (pp. 504–529). New York, NY: Oxford University.

Nock, M. K., Hwang, I., Sampson, N. A., & Kessler, R. C. (2010). Mental disorders, comorbidity and suicidal behavior: Results from the National Comorbidity Survey Replication. *Molecular Psychiatry, 15,* 868–876.

Nock, M. K., Kazdin, A. E., Hiripi, E., & Kessler, R. C. (2006). Prevalence, subtypes, and correlates of DSM-IV conduct disorder in the National Comorbidity Survey Replication. *Psychological Medicine, 36*(05), 699–710.

Nock, M. K., Park, J. M., Finn, C. T., Deliberto, T. L., Dour, H. J., & Banaji, M. R. (2010). Measuring the suicidal mind: Implicit cognition predicts suicidal behavior. *Psychological Science, 21*(4), 511–517.

Nock, M. K., Cha, C. B., & Dour, H. J. (2011). Disorders of impulse-control and self-harm. In D. H. Barlow (Ed.), *Handbook of clinical psychology.* (pp. 504–529). New York, NY: Oxford University Press.

Nofzinger, E. A., Schwartz, C. F., Reynolds, C. F., Thase, M., Jennings, J. R., Frank, E., & Kupfer, D. J. (1994). Affect intensity and phasic REM sleep in depressed men before and after treatment with cognitive-behavior therapy. *Journal of Consulting and Clinical Psychology, 62,* 83–91.

Nolen-Hoeksema, S. (1990). *Sex differences in depression.* Stanford, CA: Stanford University Press.

Nolen-Hoeksema, S. (2000). Further evidence for the role of psychosocial factors in depression chronicity. *Clinical Psychology: Science and Practice, 7*(2), 224–227.

Nolen-Hoeksema, S., & Hilt, L. M. (2009). Gender differences in depression. In I. H. Gotlib & C. L. Hammen (Eds.), *Handbook of depression* (2nd ed., pp. 386–404). New York, NY: Guilford.

Nolen-Hoeksema, S., Girgus, J. S., & Seligman, M. E. P. (1992). Predictors and consequences of childhood depressive symptoms: A 5-year longitudinal study. *Journal of Abnormal Psychology, 101*(3), 405–422.

Nolen-Hoeksema, S., Wisco, B. E., & Lyubomirsky, S. (2008). Rethinking rumination. *Perspectives on Psychological Science, 3*(5), 400–424.

Nooe, R. M., & Patterson, D. A. (2010). The ecology of homelessness. *Journal of Human Behavior in the Social Environment, 20*(2), 105–152.

Nordentoft, M., Melau, M., Iversen, T., Petersen, L., Jeppesen, P., Thorup, A., . . . Jørgensen, P. (2015). From research to practice: how OPUS treatment was accepted and implemented throughout Denmark. *Early Intervention in Psychiatry, 9*(2), 156–162.

Nooe, R. M., & Patterson, D. A. (2010). The ecology of homelessness. *Journal of Human Behavior in the Social Environment, 20*(2), 105–152.

Nordentoft, M., Thorup, A., Petersen, L., Ohlenschlaeger, J., Melau, M., Christensen, T. O., & Jeppesen, P. (2006). Transition rates from schizotypal disorder to psychotic disorder for first-contact patients included in the opus trial: A randomized clinical trial of integrated treatment and standard treatment. *Schizophrenia Research, 83,* 29–40.

Normile, D. (2009). Asia grapples with unexpected wave of HIV infections. *Science, 27,* 1174.

Norrholm, S. D., & Ressler, K. J. (2009). Genetics of anxiety and trauma-related disorders. *Neuroscience, 164*(1), 272–287.

Norris, A. L., Marcus, D. K., & Green, B. A. (2015). Homosexuality as a discrete class. *Psychological Science, 26*(12), 1843–1853.

Norton, G. R., Harrison, B., Hauch, J., & Rhodes, L. (1985). Characteristics of people with infrequent panic attacks. *Journal of Abnormal Psychology, 94,* 216–221.

Norton, M. C., Smith, K. R., Østbye, T., Tschanz, J. T., Corcoran, C., Schwartz, S., & Welsh-Bohmer, K. A. (2010). Greater risk of dementia when spouse has dementia? The Cache County Study. *Journal of the American Geriatrics Society, 58*(5), 895–900.

Novak, B. (2010). Kleptomania and the law. In E. Aboujaoude (Ed.), *Impulse control disorders* (pp. 45–50). New York, NY: Cambridge University Press.

Noyes, R., & Kletti, R. (1977). Depersonalization in response to life-threatening danger. *Comprehensive Psychiatry, 18,* 375–384.

Noyes, R., Garvey, M. J., Cook, B., & Suelzer, M. (1991). Controlled discontinuation of benzodiazepine treatment for patients with panic disorder. *American Journal of Psychiatry, 148,* 517–523.

Noyes, R., Stuart, S. P., Langbehn, D. R., Happel, R. L., Longley, S. L., Muller, B. A., Yagla, S. J. (2003). Test of an interpersonal model of hypochondriasis. *Psychomatic Medicine, 65,* 292–300.

Noyes, R., Watson, D., Carney, C., Letuchy, E., Peloso, P., Black, D., & Doebbeling, B. N. (2004). Risk factors for hypochondriacal concerns in a sample of military veterans. *Journal of Psychosomatic Research, 57,* 529–539.

Noyes, R., Jr., Stuart, S. P., & Watson, D. B. (2008). A reconceptualization of the somatoform disorders. *Psychosomatics, 49*(1), 14–22.

Ntika, M., Sakellariou, I., Kefalas, P., & Stamatopoulou, I. (2014, June). Experiments with emotion contagion in emergency evacuation simulation. In *Proceedings of the 4th International Conference on Web Intelligence, Mining and Semantics (WIMS14)* (p. 49). ACM.

Nugent, S. A. (2000). Perfectionism: Its manifestations and classroom-based interventions. *Journal of Secondary Gifted Education, 11,* 215–221.

Nunes, K. L., Hermann, C. A., Malcom, J. R., & Lavoie, K. (2013). Childhood sexual victimization, pedophilic interest, and sexual recidivism. *Child Abuse & Neglect, 37*(9), 703–711.

Nunes, P., Wenzel, A., Borges, K., Porto, C., Caminha, R., & de Oliveira, I. (2009). Volumes of the hippocampus and amygdala in patients with borderline personality disorder: A meta-analysis. *Journal of Personality Disorders, 23*(4), 333–345.

Nunley, W., Nunley, B., Cutleh, D. L., Dentingeh, J., & McFahland, B. (2013). Involuntary civil commitment. In K. Yeager, D. Cutler, D. Svendsen, & G. M. Sills (Eds.), *Modern community mental health: An interdisciplinary approach* (pp. 49–61). New York, NY: Oxford University Press.

Nurnberger, J. I. (2012). Genetics of bipolar disorder: Where we are and where we are going. *Depression and Anxiety, 29,* 991–993.

Nurnberger, J. I., & Gershon, E. S. (1992). Genetics. In E. S. Paykel (Ed.), *Handbook of affective disorders* (pp. 126–145). New York, NY: Guilford.

Nusslock, R., Harmon-Jones, E., Alloy, L. B., Urosevic, S., Goldstein, K., & Abramson, L. Y. (2012). Elevated left mid-frontal cortical activity prospectively predicts conversion to bipolar I disorder. *Journal of Abnormal Psychology, 121*(3), 592–601.

Nyhan, W. L. (1978). The Lesch-Nyhan syndrome. *Developmental Medicine and Child Neurology, 20,* 376–387.

Nzwalo, H., Ferreira, L., Peralta, R., & Bentes, C. (2013). Sleep-related eating disorder secondary to zolpidem. *BMJ Case Reports,* bcr2012008003.

O'Brien, C. (2011). Addiction and dependence in DSM-V. *Addiction, 106*(5), 866–867.

O'Brien, M. E., Clark, R. A., Besch, C. L., Myers, L., & Kissinger, P. (2003). Patterns and correlates of discontinuation of the initial HAART regimen in an urban outpatient cohort. *Journal of Acquired Immune Deficiency Syndrome, 34*(4), 407–414.

O'Brien, P. E., Sawyer, S. M., Laurie, C., Brown, W. A., Skinner, S., Veit, F., & Dixon, J. B. (2010). Laparoscopic adjustable gastric banding in severely obese adolescents: A randomized trial. *JAMA: Journal of the American Medical Association, 303*(6), 519–526.

O'Brien, P. M., Backstrom, T., Brown, C., Dennerstein, L., Endicott, J., Epperson, C. N., & Yonkers, K. (2011). Towards a consensus on diagnostic criteria, measurement and trial design of the premenstrual disorders: The ISPMD Montreal consensus. *Archives of Women's Mental Health, 14*(1), 13–21. doi: 10.1007/s00737-010-0201-3

O'Callaghan, E., Sham, P., Takei, N., Glover, G., & Murray, R. M. (1991). Schizophrenia after prenatal exposure to 1957 A2 influenza epidemic. *Lancet, 337*, 1248–1250.

O'Carroll, P. W. (1990). Community strategies for suicide prevention and intervention. In S. J. Blumenthal & D. J. Kupfer (Eds.), *Suicide over the life cycle: Risk factors, assessment and treatment of suicidal patients.* Washington, DC: American Psychiatric Press.

O'Connor, M. F., Wellisch, D. K., Stanton, A. L., Eisenberger, N. I., Irwin, M. R., & Lieberman, M. D. (2008). Craving love? Enduring grief activates brain's reward center. *Neuroimage, 42*(2), 969–972.

O'Connor v. Donaldson, 95 S. Ct. 2486 (1975).

O'Donnell, M. L., Varker, T., Creamer, M., Fletcher, S., McFarlane, A. C., Silove, D., & Forbes, D. (2013). Exploration of delayed-onset posttraumatic stress disorder after severe injury. *Psychosomatic Medicine, 75*, 68–75. doi: 10.1097/PSY.0b013e3182761e8b

O'Donovan, A., Tomiyama, A. J., Lin, J., Puterman, E., Adler, N. E., Kemeny, M., & Epel, E. S. (2012). Stress appraisals and cellular aging: A key role for anticipatory threat in the relationship between psychological stress and telomere length. *Brain, Behavior and Immunity, 26*(4), 573–579.

O'Hara, M. W., & McCabe, J. E. (2013). Postpartum depression: Current status and future directions. *Annual Review of Clinical Psychology, 9*, 379–407.

O'Hara, M. W., Stuart, S., Gorman, L. L., & Wenzel, A. (2000). Efficacy of interpersonal psychotherapy for postpartum depression. *Archives of General Psychiatry, 57*, 1039–1045.

Oades, R. D. (1985). The role of noradrenaline in tuning and dopamine in switching between signals in the CNS. *Neuroscience and Biobehavioral Reviews, 9*, 261–282.

Oakley, D. A., & Halligan, P. W. (2009). Hypnotic suggestion and cognitive neuroscience. *Trends in Cognitive Sciences, 13*(6), 264–270.

Oar, E. L., Farrell, L. J., Waters, A. M., Conlon, E. G., & Ollendick, T. H. (2015). One session treatment for pediatric blood-injection-injury phobia: A controlled multiple baseline trial. *Behaviour Research and Therapy, 73*, 131–142.

Ochsner, K. N., Ray, R. R., Hughes, B., McRae, K., Cooper, J. C., Weber, J., & Gross, J. J. (2009). Bottom-up and top-down processes in emotion generation: Common and distinct neural mechanisms.

Psychological Science, 20(11), 1322–1331. doi: 10.1111/j.1467-9280.2009.02459.x

Odlaug, B. L., & Grant, J. E. (2012). Pathological skin picking. In J. E. Grant, D. J. Stein, D. W. Woods, N. J. Keuthen (Eds.), *Trichotillomania, skin picking, and other body-focused repetitive behaviors* (pp. 21–41). Arlington, VA: American Psychiatric Publishing.

Ogden, C. L., Carroll, M. D., Curtin, L. R., Lamb, M. M., & Flegal, K. M. (2010). Prevalence of high body mass index in US children and adolescents, 2007–2008. *JAMA: Journal of the American Medical Association, 303*(3), 242–249.

Ogden, C. L., Carroll, M. D., Curtin, L. R., McDowell, M. A., Tabak, C. J., & Flegal, K. M. (2006). Prevalence of overweight and obesity in the United States, 1999–2004. *JAMA: Journal of the American Medical Association, 295*, 1549–1555.

Ogden, C. L., Carroll, M. D., Kit, B. K., & Flegal, K. M. (2012). Prevalence of obesity and trends in body mass index among US children and adolescents, 1999–2010. *JAMA: Journal of American Medical Association, 307*, 483–490.

Ogden, C. L., Carroll, M. D., Kit, B. K., & Flegal, K. M. (2014). Prevalence of childhood and adult obesity in the United States, 2011-2012. *JAMA, 311*(8), 806–814.

Ogden, C. L., Carroll, M. D., Lawman, H. G., Fryar, C. D., Kruszon-Moran, D., Kit, B. K., & Flegal, K. M. (2016). Trends in obesity prevalence among children and adolescents in the United States, 1988-1994 through 2013-2014. *JAMA, 315*(21), 2292–2299.

Ohayon, M. M., & Schatzberg, A. F. (2002). Pre-valence of depressive episodes with psychotic features in the general population. *American Journal of Psychiatry, 159*, 1855–1861.

Ohayon, M. M., & Schatzberg, A. F. (2003). Using chronic pain to predict depressive morbidity in the general population. *Archives of General Psychiatry, 60*, 39–47.

Ohayon, M. M., Dauvilliers, Y., & Reynolds, C. F. (2012). Operational definitions and algorithms for excessive sleepiness in the general population: Implications for DSM-5 nosology. *Archives of General Psychiatry, 69*(1), 71–79. doi: 10.1001/archgenpsychiatry.2011.1240

Öhman, A. (1996). Preferential pre-attentive processing of threat in anxiety: Preparedness and attentional biases. In R. Rapee (Ed.), *Current controversies in the anxiety disorders* (pp. 253–290). New York, NY: Guilford.

Öhman, A., & Dimberg, U. (1978). Facial expressions as conditioned stimuli for electrodermal responses: A case of preparedness? *Journal of Personality and Social Psychology, 36*(11), 1251–1258.

Öhman, A., & Mineka, S. (2001). Fears, phobias, and preparedness: Toward an evolved model of fear and fear learning. *Psychological Review, 108*(3), 483–522.

Öhman, A., Flykt, A., & Lundqvist, D. (2000). Unconscious emotion: Evolutionary perspective, psychophysiological data, and neuro-psychological mechanisms. In R. Lane & L. Nadel (Eds.), *The cognitive neuroscience of emotion* (pp. 296–327). New York, NY: Oxford University Press.

Okazaki, S., Okazaki, M., & Sue, S. (2009). Clinical personality assessment with Asian Americans. In J. N. Butcher (Ed.), *Oxford handbook of personality assessment* (pp. 377–395). New York, NY: Oxford University Press.

olde Hartman, T. C., Borghuis, M. S., Lucassen, P. L., van de Laar, F. A., Speckens, A. E., & van Weel, C. (2009). Medically unexplained symptoms, somatisation disorder and hypochondriasis: Course and prognosis. A systematic review. *Journal of Psychosomatic Research, 66*(5), 363–377.

Oldenburg, B., de Courten, M. & Frean, E. (2010). The contribution of health psychology to the advancement of global health. In J. M. Suls, K. W. Davidson, & R. M. Kaplan, (Eds.), *Handbook of health psychology and behavioral medicine.* New York, NY: Guilford.

Olds, J. (1956). Pleasure centers in the brain. *Scientific American, 195*, 105–116.

Olds, J., & Milner, P. M. (1954). Positive reinforcement produced by electrical stimulation of septal area and other regions of rat brain. *Journal of Comparative and Physiological Psychology, 47*, 419–427.

Olfson, M., King, M. & Schoenbaum, M. (2015). Benzodiazepine use in the United States. *JAMA Psychiatry, 72*, 136–142.

Olfson, M., Marcus, S., & Schaffer, D. (2006). Antidepressant drug therapy and suicide in severely depressed children and adolescents. *Archives of General Psychiatry, 63*, 865–872.

Olfson, M., Shaffer, D., Marcus, S. C., & Greenberg, T. (2003). Relationship between antidepressant medication treatment and suicide in adolescents. *Archives of General Psychiatry, 60*, 978–82.

Olin, S. S., Raine, A., Cannon, T. D., Parnas, J., Schulsinger, F., & Mednick, S. A. (1997). Childhood behavior precursors of schizotypal personality disorder. *Schizophrenia Bulletin, 23*, 93–103.

Olivardia, R., Pope, H. G., & Hudson, J. I. (2000). Muscle dysmorphia in male weightlifters: A case-control study. *American Journal of Psychiatry, 157*, 1291–1296.

Oliver, M. B., & Hyde, J. S. (1993). Gender differences in sexuality: A meta-analysis. *Psychological Bulletin, 114*(1), 29–51.

Olives, C., Myerson, R., Mokdad, A. H., Murray, C. J., & Lim, S. S. (2013). Prevalence, awareness, treatment, and control of hypertension in United States counties, 2001–2009. *PLoS One, 8*(4), e60308.

Olivier, P., Bertrand, L., Tubery, M., Lauque, D., Montastruc, J.-L., & Lapeyre-Mestre, M. (2009). Hospitalizations because of adverse drug reactions in elderly patients admitted through the emergency department: A prospective survey. *Drugs & Aging, 26*(6), 475–482.

Ollendick, T. H., & Muris, P. (2015). The scientific legacy of Little Hans and Little Albert: Future directions for research on specific phobias in youth. *Journal of Clinical Child and Adolescent Psychology, 44*, 689–706.

Ollendick, T. H., & Shirk, S. R. (2010). Clinical interventions with children and adolescents: Current status, future directions. In D. H. Barlow (Ed.), *Oxford handbook of clinical psychology* (pp. 762–788). New York, NY: Oxford University Press.

Olmstead, S. B., Pasley, K., & Fincham, F. D. (2013). Hooking up and penetrative hookups: Correlates that differentiate college men. *Archives of Sexual Behavior, 42*(4), 573–583.

Olsen, S., Smith, S. S., Oei, T. P. S., & Douglas, J. (2012). Motivational interviewing (MINT) improves continuous positive airway pressure (CPAP) acceptance and adherence: A randomized controlled trial. *Journal of Consulting and Clinical Psychology, 80*(1), 151.

Olson, K. R., Key, A. C., & Eaton, N. R. (2015). Gender cognition in transgender children. *Psychological Science, 26*, 476–474.

Oltmanns, T. F., & Powers, A. D. (2012). Gender and personality disorders. In T. A. Widiger (Ed.), *The Oxford handbook of personality disorders* (pp. 206–218). New York, NY: Oxford University Press.

Olver, M. E., Lewis, K., & Wong, S. C. P. (2013). Risk reduction treatment of high-risk psychopathic offenders: The relationship of psychopathy and treatment change to violent recidivism. *Personality Disorders: Theory, Research, and Treatment, 4*(2), 160–167.

Omalu, B. I., Ives, D. G., Buhari, A. M., Lindner, J. L., Schauer, P. R., Wecht, C. H., & Kuller, L. H. (2007). Death rates and causes of death after bariatric surgery for Pennsylvania residents, 1995 to 2004. *Archives of Surgery, 142*(10), 923–928; discussion 929.

Onslow, M., Jones, M., O'Brian, S., Packman, A., & Menzies, R. (2012). Stuttering. In P. Sturmey & M. Hersen (Eds.), *Handbook of evidence-based practice in clinical psychology* (Vol. 1, pp. 185–208). New York, NY: John Wiley & Sons, Inc.

Opara, F., Hawkins, K., Sundaram, A., Merchant, M., Rasmussen, S. & Holmes, L., Jr. (2013). Impact of comorbidities onracial/ethnic disparities in hypertension in the United States. *ISRN Public Health, 2013*, e967518. doi: 10.1155/2013/967518.

Opjordsmoen, S. (1989). Delusional disorders: I. Comparative long-term outcome. *Acta Psychiatrica Scandinavica, 80*, 603–612.

Oquendo, M., Galfalvy, H., Russo, S., Ellis, S., Grunebaum, M., Burke, A., & Mann, J. J. (2004). Prospective study of clinical predictors of suicidal acts after a major depressive episode in patients with major depressive disorder or bipolar disorder. *American Journal of Psychiatry, 161*, 1433–1441.

The Oregon Research Institute. (2013). *eBody Project*. Retrieved from https://www.ebodyproject.org/

Orford, J., & Keddie, A. (2006). Abstinence or controlled drinking in clinical practice: A test of the dependence and persuasion hypotheses. *Addiction, 81*(4), 495–504.

Organization for Economic Co-operation and Development (2012). *Obesity Update 2012*. Retrieved from http://www.oecd.org/health/49716427.pdf

Orne, M. T., Dinges, D. F., & Orne, E. C. (1984). On the differential diagnosis of multiple personality in the forensic context. *International Journal of Clinical and Experimental Hypnosis, 32*, 118–169.

Orsillo, S. M., & Roemer, L. (2011). *The mindful way through anxiety: Break free from chronic worry and reclaim your life*. New York, NY: Guilford.

Orth-Gomer, K., Schneiderman, N., Wang, H. X., Walldin, C., Blom, M., & Jernberg, T. (2009). Stress reduction prolongs life in women with coronary disease: The Stockholm Women's Intervention Trial for Coronary Heart Disease (SWITCHD). *Circulation Cardiovascular Quality and Outcomes, 2*(1), 25–32.

Ortin, A., Lake, A. M., Kleinman, M., & Gould, S. (2012). Sensation seeking as risk factor for suicidal ideation and suicide attempts in adolescence. *Journal of Affective Disorders, 143*, 214–222.

Oslin, D. W., & Klaus, J. R. (2009). Drug and alcohol abuse. In B. J. Sadock & V. A. Sadock (Eds.), *Kaplan & Sadock's comprehensive textbook of psychiatry* (9th ed., Vol. 2, pp. 4088–4095). Philadelphia, PA: Lippincott Williams & Wilkins.

Öst, L. G. (1985). Mode of acquisition of phobias. *Acta Universitatis Uppsaliensis* (Abstracts of Uppsala Dissertations from the Faculty of Medicine), *529*, 1–45.

Öst, L. G. (1989). Blood phobia: A specific phobia subtype in DSM-IV. Paper requested by the Simple Phobia subcommittee of the DSM-IV Anxiety Disorders Work Group.

Öst, L. G. (1992). Blood and injection phobia: Background and cognitive, physiological, and behavioral variables. *Journal of Abnormal Psychology, 101*(1), 68–74.

Öst, L. G., & Sterner, U. (1987). Applied tension: A specific behavioural method for treatment of blood phobia. *Behaviour Research and Therapy, 25*, 25–30.

Öst, L. G., Svensson, L., Hellström, K., & Lindwall, R. (2001). One-session treatment of specific phobia in youths: A randomized clinical trial. *Journal of Consulting and Clinical Psychology, 69*, 814–824.

Osterberg, E. (1986). Alcohol-related problems in cross-national perspectives: Results of the ISACE study. Special issue: Alcohol and culture: Comparative perspectives from Europe and America. (T. Babot, Ed.). *Annals of the New York Academy of Sciences, 472*, 10–20.

Oswalt, S. B., & Wyatt, T. J. (2013). Sexual health behaviors and sexual orientation in a US national sample of college students. *Archives of Sexual Behavior, 42*(8), 1561–1572.

Otis, J., Macdonald, A., & Dobscha, A. (2006). Integration and coordination of pain management in primary care. *Journal of Clinical Psychology, 62*, 1333–1343.

Otis, J. D., & Pincus, D. B. (2008). Chronic pain. In B. A. Boyer & I. Paharia (Eds.), *Comprehensive handbook of clinical health psychology* (pp. 349–370). Hoboken, NJ: Wiley.

Otis, J. D., Pincus, D. B., & Murawksi, M. E. (2011). Cognitive behavioral therapy in pain management. In M. E. Ebert & R. D. Kerns (Eds.), *Behavioral and psychopharmacological therapeutics in pain management* (pp. 184–200). New York, NY: Cambridge University Press.

Otto, M. W., & Applebaum, A. J. (2011). The nature and treatment of bipolar disorder and the bipolar spectrum. In D. H. Barlow (Ed.), *Handbook of clinical psychology*. New York, NY: Oxford University Press.

Otto, M. W., Behar, E., Smits, J. A. J., & Hofmann, S. G. (2009). Combining pharmacological and cognitive behavioral therapy in the treatment of anxiety disorders. In M. M. Antony & M. B. Stein (Eds.), *Oxford handbook of anxiety and related disorders* (pp. 429–440). New York, NY: Oxford University Press.

Otto, M. W., Reilly-Harrington, N. A., Knauz, R. O., Henin, A., Kogan, J. N., & Sachs, G. S. (2008a). *Managing bipolar disorder: A cognitive-behavioral approach. (Therapist Guide)*. New York, NY: Oxford University Press.

Otto, M. W., Reilly-Harrington, N. A., Knauz, R. O., Henin, A., Kogan, J. N., & Sachs, G. S. (2008b). *Managing bipolar disorder: A cognitive-behavioral approach. (Workbook)*. New York, NY: Oxford University Press.

Otto, M. W., Tolin, D. F., Simon, N. M., Pearlson, G. D., Basden, S., Meunier, S. A., & Pollack, M. H. (2010). Efficacy of D-cycloserine for enhancing response to cognitive-behavior therapy for panic disorder. *Biological Psychiatry, 67*(4), 365–370.

Oude Luttikhuis, H., Baur, L., Jansen, H., Shrewsbury, V. A., O'Malley, C., Stolk, R. P., & Summerbell, C. D. (2009). Interventions for treating obesity in children: Review. *Cochrane Database System Review, 1*: CD001871.

Ouellet-Morin, I., Boivin, M., Dionne, G., Lupien, S. J., Arseneault, L., Barr, R. G., & Tremblay, R. E. (2008). Variations in heritability of cortisol reactivity to stress as a function of early familial adversity among 19-month-old twins. *Archives of General Psychiatry, 65*(2), 211–218.

Overeem, S., & Reading, P. (Eds.). (2010). *Sleep disorders in neurology: A practical approach*. New York, NY: Wiley-Blackwell.

Ovsiew, F. (2005). Neuropsychiatry and behavioral neurology. In B. J. Sadock & V. A. Sadock (Eds.), *Kaplan & Sadock's comprehensive text-book of psychiatry* (pp. 323–349). Philadelphia, PA: Lippincott Williams & Wilkins.

Owen, J., & Fincham, F. D. (2011). Effects of gender and psychosocial factors on "friends with benefits" relationships among young adults. *Archives of Sexual Behavior, 40*(2), 311–320.

Owen, J. J., Rhoades, G. K., Stanley, S. M., & Fincham, F. D. (2010). "Hooking up" among college students: Demographic and psychosocial correlates. *Archives of Sexual Behavior, 39*, 653–663.

Owen, P. R. (2012). Portrayals of schizophrenia by entertainment media: a content analysis of contemporary movies. *Psychiatric Services, 63* (7), 655–659.

Owens, E. B., Cardoos, S. L., & Hinshaw, S. P. (2015). Developmental progression and gender differences among individuals with ADHD. In R. A. Barkley (Ed.), *Attention-deficit hyperactivity disorder: A handbook for diagnosis & treatment* (4th ed., pp. 223–255). New York, NY: The Guilford Press.

Owens, M., Goodyer, I. M., Wilkinson, P., Bhardwaj, A., Abbott, R., Croudace, T., & Sahakian, B. J. (2012). 5-HTTLPR and early childhood adversities moderate cognitive and emotional processing in adolescence. *PLoS One, 7(11)*, e48482. doi: 10.1371/journal.pone.0048482

Owens, Mulchahey, Taylor, Maloney, Dearborn, & Weiss 2009 ref from Chapter 9, MSP 8

Ozbay, F., Johnson, D. C., Dimoulas, E., Morgan, A., III, Charney, D., & Southwick, S. (2007). Social support and resilience to stress: From neurobiology to clinical practice. *Psychiatry, 4*(5), 35–40.

Ozonoff, S., Young, G. S., Carter, A., Messinger, D., Yirmiya, N., Zwaigenbaum, L., & Stone, W. L. (2011). Recurrence risk for autism spectrum disorders: A baby siblings research consortium study. *Pediatrics, 128*(3), e488–e495. doi: 10.1542/peds.2010-2825

Pace-Schott, E.F., Germain, A. Milad, M.R. (2015). Effects of sleep on memory for conditioned fear and fear extinction. *Psychological Bulletin, 141*, 835.

Packard, E. P. W., & Olsen, S. N. B. (1871). *The prisoners' hidden life, or insane asylums unveiled: As demonstrated by the report of the investigating committee of the legislature of Illinois, together with Mrs. Packard's coadjutors' testimony.* Chicago, IL: J. N. Clarke.

Padmanabhan, S., Caulfield, M., & Dominiczak, A. F. (2015). Genetic and molecular aspects of hypertension. *Circulation Research, 116*(6), 937–959.

Page, A. C., & Martin, N. G. (1998). Testing a genetic structure of blood–injury–injection fears. *American Journal of Medical Genetics (Neuropsychiatric Genetics), 81*, 377–384.

Page, G. G., Ben-Eliyahu, S., Yirmiya, R., & Liebeskind, J. C. (1993). Morphine attenuates surgery-induced enhancement of metastatic colonization in rats. *Pain, 54*(1), 21–28.

Pagsberg, A. K. (2013). Schizophrenia spectrum and other psychotic disorders. *European Child & Adolescent Psychiatry, 22*(1), 3–9. doi: 10.1007/s00787-012-0354-x

Pahlajani, G., Raina, R., Jones, S., Ali, M., & Zippe, C. (2012). Vacuum erection devices revisited: Its emerging role in the treatment of erectile dysfunction and early penile rehabilitation following prostate cancer therapy. *The Journal of Sexual Medicine, 9*(4), 1182–1189.

Paillard, T., Rolland, Y., & de Souto Barreto, P. (2015). Protective effects of physical exercise in Alzheimer's disease and Parkinson's disease: A narrative review. *Journal of Clinical Neurology, 11*(3), 212–219.

Palace, E. M. (1995). Modification of dysfunctional patterns of sexual response through autonomic arousal and false physiological feedback. *Journal of Consulting and Clinical Psychology, 63*, 604–615.

Palace, E. M., & Gorzalka, B. B. (1990). The enhancing effects of anxiety on arousal in sexually dysfunctional and functional women. *Journal of Abnormal Psychology, 99*(4), 403–411.

Palamar, J. J., & Barratt, M. J. (2016). Synthetic cannabinoids: undesirable alternatives to natural marijuana. *The American Journal of Drug and Alcohol Abuse*, Advance online publication. doi:# 10.3109/00952990.2016.1139584.

Palmer, B. W., Savla, G. N., Roesch, S. C., & Jeste, V. (2013). Changes in capacity to consent over time in patients involved in psychiatric research. *The British Journal of Psychiatry, 202*(6), 454–458.

Pan, A., Sun, Q., Okereke, O. I., Rexrode, K. M., & Hu, F. B. (2011). Depression and risk of stroke morbidity and mortality: A meta-analysis and systematic review. *JAMA: Journal of the American Medical Association, 306*(11), 1241–1249.

Pan, L., Blanck, H. M., Sherry, B., Dalenius, K., & Grummer-Strawn, L. M. (2012). Trends in the prevalence of extreme obesity among US preschool-aged children living in low-income families, 1998–2010. *JAMA: Journal of American Medical Association, 308*, 2563–2565.

Pandya, N. H., Mevada, A., Patel, V., & Suthar, M. (2013). Study of effects of advanced maternal age related risks for Down syndrome & other trisomies. *International Journal of Biomedical and Advance Research, 4*(2), 123–127.

Paniagua, F. A., & Yamada, A. M. (Eds.). (2013). *Handbook of multicultural mental health: Assessment and treatment of diverse populations.* Academic Press.

Pantaleo, G., Graziosi, C., & Fauci, A. S. (1993). The immunopathogenesis of human immunodeficiency virus infection. *New England Journal of Medicine, 328*, 327–335.

Panza, F., Frisardi, V., Seripa, D., Logroscino, G., Santamato, A., Imbimbo, B. P., & Solfrizzi, V. (2012). Alcohol consumption in mild cognitive impairment and dementia: Harmful or neuroprotective? *International Journal of Geriatric Psychiatry, 27*(12), 1218–1238. doi: 10.1002/gps.3772

Papadopoulos, F. C., Ekbom, A., Brandt, L., & Ekselius, L. (2009). Excess mortality, causes of death and prognostic factors in anorexia nervosa. *British Journal of Psychiatry, 194*(1), 10–17.

Papazoglou, A., Jacobson, L. A., McCabe, M., Kaufmann, W., & Zabel, T. A. (2014). To ID or not to ID? Changes in classification rates of intellectual disability using DSM-5. *Mental Retardation, 52*(3), 165–174.

Papillo, J. F., & Shapiro, D. (1990). The cardiovascular system. In J. T. Cacioppo & L. G. Tassinaryo (Eds.), *Principles of psychophysiology: Physical, social, and inferential elements.* New York, NY: Cambridge University Press.

Paquette, V., Lévesque, J., Mensour, B., Leroux, J-M., Beudoin, G., Bourgouin, P., Beauregard, M. (2003). "Change the mind and you change the brain": Effects of cognitive-behavioral therapy on the neural correlates of spider phobia. *Neuroimage, 18*, 401–409.

Parcesepe, A. M., & Cabassa, L. J. (2013). Public stigma of mental illness in the United States: A systematic literature review. *Administration and Policy in Mental Health and Mental Health Services Research, 40*(5), 384–399.

Parchi, P., Capellari, S., & Gambetti, P. (2012). Fatal familial and sporadic insomnia. In W. Dickson & R. O. Weller (Eds.), *Neurodegeneration: The molecular pathology of dementia and movement disorders* (2nd ed., pp. 346–349). Oxford, UK: Wiley-Blackwell.

Pardini, D., Lochman, J., & Wells, K. (2004). Negative emotions and alcohol use initiation in high-risk boys: The moderating effect of good inhibitory control. *Journal of Abnormal Child Psychology, 32*, 505–518.

Pardini, D. A., Frick, P. J., & Moffitt, T. E. (2010). Building an evidence base for DSM-5 conceptualizations of oppositional defiant disorder and conduct disorder: Introduction to the special section. *Journal of Abnormal Psychology, 119*(4), 683–688.

Paris, J. (2008). Clinical trials of treatment for personality disorders. *Psychiatric Clinics of North America, 31*(3), 517–526. doi: 10.1016/j.psc.2008.03.013

Park, C. L., Edmondson, D., Fenster, J. R., & Blank, T. O. (2008). Meaning making and psychological adjustment following cancer: The mediating roles of growth, life meaning, and restored just-world beliefs. *Journal of Consulting and Clinical Psychology, 76*, 863–875.

Park, D. C. (2007). Eating disorders: A call to arms. *American Psychologist, 62*, 158.

Parker, G., & Hadzi-Pavlovic, D. (1990). Expressed emotion as a predictor of schizophrenic relapse: An analysis of aggregated data. *Psychological Medicine, 20*, 961–965.

Parker, G., McCraw, S., Blanch, B., Hadzi-Pavlovic, D., Synnot, H., & Rees, A. (2013). Discriminating melancholic and non-melancholic depression by prototypic clinical features. *Journal of Affective Disorders, 144*, 199–207.

Parker, G., McCraw, S., & Fletcher, K. (2012). Cyclothymia. *Depression and Anxiety, 29*(6), 487–494.

Parker, R. N., McCaffree, K. J., & Alaniz, M. L. (2013). Alcohol availability and violence among Mexican American youth. In R. N. Parker & K. J. McCaffree (Eds.), *Alcohol and violence: The nature of the relationship and the promise of prevention* (pp. 31–38). Plymouth, U.K.: Lexington.

Parker, S., Schwartz, B., Todd, J., & Pickering, L. (2004). Thimerosal-containing vaccines and autistic spectrum disorder: A critical review of published original data. *Pediatrics, 114*(3), 793.

Parkinson, L., & Rachman, S. (1981a). Intrusive thoughts: The effects of an uncontrived stress. *Advances in Behaviour Research and Therapy, 3*, 111–118.

Parkinson, L., & Rachman, S. (1981b). Speed of recovery from an uncontrived stress. *Advances in Behaviour Research and Therapy, 3*, 119–123.

Parner, E. T., Baron-Cohen, S., Lauritsen, M. B., Jørgensen, M., Schieve, L. A., Yeargin-Allsopp, M., & Obel, C. (2012). Parental age and autism spectrum disorders. *Annals of Epidemiology, 22*(3), 143–150.

Parrott, A. C. (2012). MDMA and LSD. In J. C. Verster, K. Brady, M. Galanter, & P. Conrod (Eds.), *Drug abuse and addiction in medical illness* (pp. 175–188). New York, NY: Springer.

Parrott, D. J., Tharp, A. T., Swartout, K. M., Miller, C. A., Hall, G. C. N., & George, W. H. (2012). Validity for an integrated laboratory analogue of sexual aggression and bystander intervention. *Aggressive Behavior, 38*(4), 309–321. doi: 10.1002/ab.21429

Parry-Jones, B., & Parry-Jones, W. L. (2002). History of bulimia and bulimia nervosa. In K. D. Brownell & C. G. Fairburn (Eds.), *Eating disorders and obesity: A comprehensive handbook* (2nd ed., pp. 145–150). New York, NY: Guilford.

Parry-Jones, W. L., & Parry-Jones, B. (1994). Implications of historical evidence for the classification of eating disorders. *British Journal of Psychiatry, 165,* 287–292.

Pasewark, R. A., & Seidenzahl, D. (1979). Opinions concerning the insanity plea and criminality among mental patients. *Bulletin of the American Academy of Psychiatry and Law, 7,* 199–202.

Passie, T. & Halpern, J. H. (2015). The pharmacology of hallucinogens. In R.K. Ries, D.A. Fiellin, S.C. Miller, & R. Saitz (Eds.), *The ASAM principles of addiction medicine* (5th Ed., pp. 235–255). New York, NY: Wolters Kluwer.

Patel, S. R., White, D. P., Malhotra, A., Stanchina, M. L., & Ayas, N. T. (2003). Continuous positive airway pressure therapy for treating gess in a diverse population with obstructive sleep apnea: Results of a meta-analysis. *Archives of Internal Medicine, 163*(5), 565–571. doi: 10.1001/archinte.163.5.565

Patrick, D., Althof, S., Pryor, J., Rosen, R., Rowland, D., Ho, K., & Jamieson, C. (2005). Premature ejaculation: An observational study of men and their partners. *Journal of Sexual Medicine, 2,* 358–367.

Patterson, G. R. (1982). *Coercive family process.* Eugene, OR: Castalia.

Patterson, G. R. (1986). Performance models for antisocial boys. *American Psychologist, 41,* 432–444.

Patterson, G. R., DeBaryshe, B. D., & Ramsey, E. (1989). A developmental perspective on antisocial behavior. *American Psychologist, 44,* 329–335.

Patton, G. C., Johnson-Sabine, E., Wood, K., Mann, A. H., & Wakeling, A. (1990). Abnormal eating attitudes in London school girls—A prospective epidemiological study: Outcome at twelve month follow-up. *Psychological Medicine, 20,* 383–394.

Paul, G. L., & Lentz, R. J. (1977). *Psychosocial treatment of chronic mental patients: Milieu versus social learning programs.* Cambridge, MA: Harvard University Press.

Paul, T., Schroeter, K., Dahme, B., & Nutzinger, D. O. (2002). Self-injurious behavior in women with eating disorders. *American Journal of Psychiatry, 159,* 408–411.

Paulesu, E., Démonet, J. F., Fazio, F., McCrory, E., Chanoine, V., Brunswick, N., & Frith, U. (2001). Dyslexia: Cultural diversity and biological unity. *Science, 291*(5511), 2165–2167. doi: 10.1126/science.1057179

Pauli, P., & Alpers, G. W. (2002). Memory bias in patients with hypochondriasis and somatoform pain disorder. *Journal of Psychosomatic Research, 52,* 45–53.

Paulson, J. F., & Bazemore, S. D. (2010). Prenatal and postpartum depression in fathers and its association with maternal depression: A meta-analysis. *JAMA: Journal of the American Medical Association, 303*(19), 1961–1969.

Paxton, S. J., Schutz, H. K., Wertheim, E. H., & Muir, S. L. (1999). Friendship clique and peer influences on body image concerns, dietary restraint, extreme weight-loss behaviors, and binge eating in adolescent girls. *Journal of Abnormal Psychology, 108*(2), 255–266.

Paykel, E. S., & Scott, J. (2009). Treatment of mood disorders. In M. G. Gelder, N. C. Andreasen, J. López-Ibor, Jr., & J. R. Geddes (Eds.), *New Oxford textbook of psychiatry* (2nd ed., Vol. 1, pp. 669–680). Oxford, UK: Oxford University Press.

Payne, K., Reissing, E., Lahaie, M., Binik, Y., Amsel, R., & Khalife, S. (2005). What is sexual pain? A critique of DSM's classification of dyspareunia and vaginismus. In D. Karasic & J. Drescher (Eds.), *Sexual and gender diagnoses of the Diagnostic and Statistical Manual (DSM): A reevaluation* (pp. 141–154). New York, NY: Haworth.

Payne, L. A., White., K. S., Gallagher, M. W., Woods, S. W., Shear, M. K., Gorman, J. M., Farchione, T. J., & Barlow, D. H. (2016). Second-stage treatments for relative non-responders to cognitive-behavioral therapy (CBT) for panic disorder with or without agoraphobia: Continued CBT versus SSRI: A randomized controlled trial. *Depression and Anxiety, 33,* 392–399.

Payne, L. A., White, K. S., Gallagher, M. W., Woods, S. W., Shear, K. M., Gorman, J. M., Farchione, T. J., & Barlow, D. H. (in press). Second-stage treatments for relative non-responders to cognitive-behavioral therapy (CBT) for panic disorder with or without agoraphobia—Continued CBT versus paroxetine: A randomized controlled trial. *Depression and Anxiety.*

Peall, K. J., & Robertson, N. P. (2014). Narcolepsy: environment, genes and treatment. *Journal of Neurology, 261*(8), 1644–1646.

Pearlstein, T. (2010). Premenstrual dysphoric disorder: Out of the appendix. *Archives of Women's Mental Health, 13*(1), 21–23.

Pearlstein, T., & Steiner, M. (2008). Premenstrual dysphoric disorder: Burden of illness and treatment update. *Journal of Psychiatry & Neuroscience, 33*(4), 291–301.

Pearlstein, T., Yonkers, K. A., Fayyad, R., & Gillespie, J. A. (2005). Pretreatment pattern of symptom expression in premenstrual dysphoric disorder. *Journal of Affective Disorder, 85,* 275–282.

Pearson, C., Montgomery, A., & Locke, G. (2009). Housing stability among homeless individuals with serious mental illness participating in Housing First programs. *Journal of Community Psychology, 37*(3), 404–417.

Pearson, C. M., Wonderlich, S. A., & Smith, G. T. (2015). A Risk and Maintenance Model for Bulimia Nervosa: From Impulsive Action to Compulsive Behavior, *Psychological Review, 122*(3), 516–533.

Peat, C., Mitchell, J. E., Hoek, H. W., & Wonderlich, S. A. (2009). Validity and utility of subtyping anorexia nervosa. *International Journal of Eating Disorders, 42*(7), 590–594.

Peat, C. M., Peyerl, N. L., & Muehlenkamp, J. J. (2008). Body image and eating disorders in older adults: A review. *The Journal of General Psychology, 135*(4), 343–358.

Pedersen, C. B., & Mortensen, P. B. (2006). Are the cause(s) responsible for urban-rural differences in schizophrenia risk rooted in families or in individuals? *American Journal of Epidemiology, 163*(11), 971–978.

Pedersen, N. L. (2010). Reaching the limits of genome-wide significance in Alzheimer disease: Back to the environment. *JAMA: Journal of the American Medical Association, 303*(18), 1864–1865.

Peeters, J., Van Beek, A., Meerveld, J., Spreeuwenberg, P., & Francke, A. (2010). Informal caregivers of persons with dementia, their use of and needs for specific professional support: A survey of the National Dementia Programme. *BMC Nursing, 9*(1), 9. doi: 10.1186/1472-6955-9-9

Pehlivanturk, B., & Unal, F. (2002). Conversion disorder in children and adolescents: A 4-year follow-up study. *Journal of Psychosomatic Research, 52,* 187–191.

Pelham, W. E., Jr. (1999). The NIMH Multimodal Treatment Study for attention-deficit hyperactivity disorder: Just say yes to drugs alone? *Canadian Journal of Psychiatry, 44,* 981–990.

Pellicano, E., & Stears, M. (2011). Bridging autism, science and society: Moving toward an ethically informed approach to autism research. *Autism Research, 4*(4), 271–282. doi: 10.1002/aur.201

Pellowski, J. A., Kalichman, S. C., Matthews, K. A., & Adler, N. (2013). A pandemic of the poor: Social disadvantage and the U.S. HIV epidemic. *American Psychologist, 68*(4), 197–209.

Pen, A. E., & Jensen, U. B. (2016). Current status of treating neurodegenerative disease with induced pluripotent stem cells. *Acta Neurologica Scandinavica.* doi: 10.1111/ane.12545. [Epub ahead of print]

Penders, T. M., Gestring, R. E., & Vilensky, D. A. (2012). Intoxication delirium following use of synthetic cathinone derivatives. *The American Journal of Drug and Alcohol Abuse, 38*(6), 616–617.

Pendery, M. L., Maltzman, I. M., & West, L. J. (1982). Controlled drinking by alcoholics? New findings and a reevaluation of a major affirmative study. *Science, 217,* 169–175.

Penedo, F. J., Antoni, M. H., & Schneiderman, N. (2008). *Cognitive-behavioral stress management for prostate cancer recovery: Facilitator guide.* New York, NY: Oxford University Press.

Peng, T. (2008, November 23). Out of the Shadows. *Newsweek.*

Pennington, B., & Bishop, D. (2009). Relations among speech, language, and reading disorders. *Annual Review of Psychology, 60,* 283–306.

Pentz, M. A. (1999). Prevention. In M. Galanter & H. D. Kleber (Eds.), *Textbook of substance abuse treatment* (2nd ed., pp. 535–544). Washington, DC: American Psychiatric Press.

Peplau, L. A. (2003). Human sexuality: How do men and women differ? *Current Directions in Psychological Science, 12,* 37–40.

Perea, G., & Araque, A. (2007). Astrocytes potentiate transmitter release at single hippocampal synapses. *Science, 317,* 1083–1087.

Pereira, D. B., Antoni, M. H., Danielson, A., Simon, T., Efantis-Potter, J., Carver, C. S., & O'Sullivan, M. J. (2003). Stress as a predictor of symptomatic genital herpes virus recurrence in women with human immunodeficiency virus. *Journal of Psychosomatic Research, 54*(3), 237–244.

Pérez-Fuentes, G., Olfson, M., Villegas, L., Morcillo, C., Wang, S., & Blanco, C. (2013). Prevalence and correlates of child sexual abuse: A national study. *Comprehensive Psychiatry, 54*(1), 16–27.

Perez-Sales, P. (1990). Camptocormia. *British Journal of Psychiatry, 157*, 765–767.

Pericak-Vance, M. A., Johnson, C. C., Rimmler, J. B., Saunders, A. M., Robinson, L. C., D'Hondt, E. G., & Haines, J. L. (1996). Alzheimer's disease and apolipoprotein E-4 allele in an Amish population. *Annals of Neurology, 39*, 700–704.

Peris, T. S., Compton, S. N., Kendall, P. C., Birmaher, B., Sherrill, J., March, J., . . . Piacentini, J. (2015). Trajectories of change in youth anxiety during cognitive—behavior therapy. *Journal of Consulting and Clinical Psychology, 83*(2), 239.

Perkonigg, A., Pfister, H., Stein, M. B., Hofler, M., Lieb, R., Maercker, A., & Wittchen, H.-U. (2005). Longitudinal course of posttraumatic stress disorder and posttraumatic stress disorder symptoms in a community sample of adolescents and young adults. *American Journal of Psychiatry, 162*, 1320–1327.

Perlin, M. L. (2000). *The hidden prejudice: Mental disability on trial.* Washington, DC: American Psychological Association.

Perlis, M. L., Smith, L. J., Lyness, J. M., Matteson, S. R., Pigeon, W. R., Jungquist, C. R., & Tu, X. (2006). Insomnia as a risk factor for onset of depression in the elderly. *Behavioral Sleep Medicine, 4*(2), 104–113.

Perneczky, R., Wagenpfeil, S., Lunetta, K. L., Cupples, L. A., Green, R. C., DeCarli, C., & Kurz, A. (2009). Education attenuates the effect of medial temporal lobe atrophy on cognitive function in Alzheimer's disease: The MIRAGE Study. *Journal of Alzheimer's Disease, 17*(4), 855–862.

Perrault, R., Carrier, J., Desautels, A., Montplaisir, J., & Zadra, A. (2014). Electroencephalographic slow waves prior to sleepwalking episodes. *Sleep Medicine, 15*(12), 1468–1472.

Perron, B., & Howard, M. (2009). Adolescent inhalant use, abuse, and dependence. *Addiction, 104*(7), 1185–1192.

Perry, J. C. (1993). Longitudinal studies of personality disorders. *Journal of Personality Disorders, 7*, 63–85.

Perry, J. C., & Bond, M. (2012). Change in defense mechanisms during long-term dynamic psychotherapy and five-year outcome. *American Journal of Psychiatry, 169*(9), 916–925.

Perry, J. C., & Bond, M. (2014). Change in defense mechanisms during long-term dynamic psychotherapy and five-year outcome. *American Journal of Psychiatry, 169*(9), 916–925.

Person, D. C., & Borkovec, T. D. (1995, August). *Anxiety disorders among the elderly: Patterns and issues.* Paper presented at the 103rd annual meeting of the American Psychological Association. New York.

Perugi, G., Angst, J., Azorin, J. M., Bowden, C., Vieta, E., & Young, A. H. (2013). Is comorbid borderline personality disorder in patients with major depressive episode and bipolarity a developmental subtype? Findings from the international BRIDGE study. *Journal of Affective Disorders, 144*, 72–78.

Petersen, J. L., & Hyde, J. S. (2010). A meta-analytic review of research on gender differences in sexuality, 1993-2007. *Psychological Bulletin, 136*, 21–38.

Petersen, R. C., Smith, G. E., Waring, S. C., Ivnik, R. J., Tangalos, E. G., & Kokmen, E. (1999). Mild cognitive impairment: Clinical characterization and outcome. *Archives of Neurology, 56*(3), 303–308. doi: 10.1001/archneur.56.3.303

Peterson, L., & Roberts, M. C. (1992). Complacency, misdirection, and effective prevention of children's injuries. *American Psychologist, 47*(8), 1040–1044.

Peterson, L., & Thiele, C. (1988). Home safety at school. *Child and Family Behavior Therapy, 10*(1), 1–8.

Peterson, R. L., & Pennington, B. F. (2012). Developmental dyslexia. *The Lancet, 379*(9830), 1997–2007. doi: http://dx.doi.org/10.1016/S0140-6736(12)60198-6

Petit, D., Pennestri, M. H., Paquet, J., Desautels, A., Zadra, A., Vitaro, F., . . . Montplaisir, J. (2015). Childhood sleepwalking and sleep terrors: a longitudinal study of prevalence and familial aggregation. *JAMA Pediatrics, 169*(7), 653–658.

Petrill, S. A. (2013). Behavioral genetics, learning abilities, and disabilities. In H. L. Swanson, R. Harris, & S. Graham (Eds.), *Handbook of learning disabilities* (2nd ed., pp. 293–306). New York, NY: Guilford.

Petrovic, P., Kalso, E., Petersson, K. M., & Ingvar, M. (2002). Placebo and opioid analgesia— imaging a shared neuronal network. *Science, 295*(5560), 1737–1740.

Petry, N. M., & O'Brien, C. P. (2013). Internet gaming disorder and the *DSM-5. Addiction, 108*(7), 1186–1187. doi: 10.1111/add.12162

Pfiffner, L. J., & DuPaul, G. J. (2015). Treatment of ADHD in school settings. In R. A. Barkley (Ed.), *Attention-deficit hyperactivity disorder: A handbook for diagnosis & treatment* (4th ed., pp. 596–629). New York, NY: The Guilford Press.

Phé, V., & Rouprêt, M. (2012). Erectile dysfunction and diabetes: a review of the current evidence-based medicine and a synthesis of the main available therapies. *Diabetes & metabolism, 38*(1), 1–13.

Phelan, S., & Wadden, T. A. (2004). Behavioral assessment of obesity. In J. K. Thompson (Ed.), *Handbook of eating disorders and obesity* (pp. 393–420). New York, NY: Wiley.

Philips, H. C., & Grant, L. (1991). Acute back pain: A psychological analysis. *Behaviour Research and Therapy, 29*, 429–434.

Phillips, K. A. (1991). Body dysmorphic disorder: The distress of imagined ugliness. *American Journal of Psychiatry, 148*, 1138–1149.

Phillips, K. A. (2005). *The broken mirror: Understanding and treating body dysmorphic disorder* (Rev. & expanded ed.). New York, NY: Oxford University Press.

Phillips, K. A., & Stout, R. (2006). Association in the longitudinal course of body dysmorphic disorder with major depression, obsessive compulsive disorder, and social phobia. *Journal of Psychiatric Research, 40*, 360–369.

Phillips, K. A., Albertini, R. S., & Rasmussen, S. A. (2002). A randomized placebo-controlled trial of fluoxetine in body dysmorphic disorder. *Evidence-Based Mental Health, 5*, 119.

Phillips, K. A., Dufresne, R. G., Wilkel, C. S., & Vittorio, C. C. (2000). Rate of body dysmorphic disorder in dermatology patients. *Journal of the American Academy of Dermatology, 42*, 436–441.

Phillips, K. A., Grant, J., Siniscalchi, J., & Albertini, R. S. (2001). Surgical and nonpsychiatric medical treatment of patients with body dysmorphic disorder. *Psychosomatics, 42*, 504–510.

Phillips, K. A., McElroy, S. L., Keck, P. E., Jr., Pope, H. G., Jr., & Hudson, J. I. (1993). Body dysmorphic disorder: 30 cases of imagined ugliness. *American Journal of Psychiatry, 150*, 302–308.

Phillips, K. A., Menard, W., & Fay, C. (2006). Gender similarities and differences in 200 individuals with body dysmorphic disorder. *Comprehensive Psychiatry, 47*, 77–87.

Phillips, K. A., Menard, W., Fay, C., & Pagano, M. E. (2005). Psychosocial functioning and quality of life in body dysmorphic disorder. *Comprehensive Psychiatry, 46*(4), 254–260.

Phillips, K. A., Menard, W., Fay, C., & Weisberg, R. (2005). Demographic characteristics, phenomenology, comorbidity, and family history in 200 individuals with body dysmorphic disorder. *Psychosomatics, 46*, 317–325.

Phillips, K. A., Menard, W., Pagano, M., Fay, C., & Stout, R. (2006). Delusional versus nondelusional body dysmorphic disorder: Clinical features and course of illness. *Journal of Psychiatric Research, 40*, 95–104.

Phillips, K. A., Pagano, M., Menard, W., & Stout, R. (2006). A 12-month follow-up study of the course of body dysmorphic disorder. *American Journal of Psychiatry, 163*, 907–912.

Phillips, K. A., Pinto, A., Hart, A. S., Coles, M. E., Eisen, J. L., Menard, W., & Rasmussen, S. A. (2012). A comparison of insight in body dysmorphic disorder and obsessive-compulsive disorder. *Journal of Psychiatric Research, 46*, 1293–1299. doi: 10.1016/j.jpsychires.2012.05.016

Phillips, K. A., Wilhelm, S., Koran, L. M., Didie, E., Fallon, B., Feusner, J., & Stein, D. J. (2010). Body dysmorphic disorder: Some key issues for DSM-V. *Depression and Anxiety, 27*, 573–591. doi: 10.1002/da.20709.

Phillips, K. A., Yen, S., & Gunderson, J. G. (2003). Personality disorders. In R. E. Hales & S. C. Yudofsky (Eds.), *Textbook of clinical psychiatry* (4th ed., pp. 804–832). Washington, DC: American Psychiatric Publishing.

Phillips, L. J., Francey, S. M., Edwards, J., & McMurray, N. (2007). Stress and psychosis: Towards the development of new models of investigation. *Clinical Psychology Review, 27*, 307–317.

Phillips, M. R., Li, X., & Zhang, Y. (2002). Suicide rates in China, 1995–99. *Lancet, 359*, 835–840.

Phillips, M. R., Shen, Q., Liu, X., Pritker, S., Streiner, D., Conner, K., & Yang, G. (2007). Assessing depressive symptoms in persons who die of suicide in mainland China. *Journal of Affective Disorders, 98*, 73–82.

Pierce, K. (2016). Neurodevelopmental disorders: Specific learning disorder, communication disorders, and motor disorders. In M. K. Dulcan (Ed.), *Dulcan's Textbook of Child and Adolescent Psychiatry* (2nd ed., pp. 157–171). Arlington, VA: American Psychiatric Publishing.

Pierce, K. A., & Kirkpatrick, D. R. (1992). Do men lie on fear surveys? *Behaviour Research and Therapy, 30,* 415–418.

Pike, K. M., & Rodin, J. (1991). Mothers, daughters, and disordered eating. *Journal of Abnormal Psychology, 100*(2), 198–204.

Pike, K. M., Hoek, H. W., & Dunne, P. E. (2014). Cultural trends and eating disorders. *Current Opinion in Psychiatry, 27*(6), 436–442.

Pike, K. M., Walsh, B. T., Vitousek, K., Wilson, G. T., & Bauer, J. (2003). Cognitive behavior therapy in the posthospitalization treatment of anorexia nervosa. *American Journal of Psychiatry, 160,* 2046–2048.

Pincus, D. B., Santucci, L. C., Ehrenreich, J. T., & Eyberg, S. M. (2008). The implementation of modified parent-child interaction therapy for youth with separation anxiety disorder. *Cognitive and Behavioral Practice, 15*(2), 118–125.

Pinel, P. (1962). *A treatise on insanity.* New York, NY: Hafner. (Original work published in 1801.)

Pinel, P. H. (1809). *Traité medico-philosophique sur l'aliénation mentale.* Paris, France: J. A. Brosson.

Pinto, A. (2015). Treatment of Obsessive-compulsive personality disorder. In *Clinical Handbook of Obsessive-Compulsive and Related Disorders* (pp. 415–429). Springer International Publishing.

Pinto, R., Ashworth, M., & Jones, R. (2008). Schizophrenia in black Caribbeans living in the UK: An exploration of underlying causes of the high incidence rate. *The British Journal of General Practice, 58*(551), 429.

Piomelli, D. (2003). The molecular logic of endocannabinoid signalling. *Nature Reviews: Neuroscience, 4*(11), 873–884.

Piomelli, D. (2014). More surprises lying ahead. The endocannabinoids keep us guessing. *Neuropharmacology, 76,* 228–234.

Pisetsky, E. M., Thornton, L. M., Lichtenstein, P., Pedersen, N. L., & Bulik, C. M. (2013). Suicide attempts in women with eating disorders. *Journal of Abnormal Psychology, 122*(4), 1042–1056.

Pizzagalli, D. A. (2014). Depression, stress, and anhedonia: Toward a synthesis and integrated model. *Annual Review of Clinical Psychology, 10,* 393–432.

Pletcher, M. J., Vittinghoff, E., Kalhan, R., Richman, J., Safford, M., Sidney, S., & Kertesz, S. (2012). Association between marijuana exposure and pulmonary function over 20 years. *JAMA: Journal of the American Medical Association, 307*(2), 173–181. doi: 10.1001/jama.2011.1961

Pliszka, S. R. (2015). Comorbid psychiatric disorders in children with ADHD. In R. A. Barkley (Ed.), *Attention-deficit hyperactivity disorder: A handbook for diagnosis & treatment* (4th ed., pp. 140–168). New York, NY: The Guilford Press.

Plomin, R. (1990). The role of inheritance in behavior. *Science, 248,* 183–188.

Plomin, R., & Davis, O. S. P. (2009). The future of genetics in psychology and psychiatry: Microarrays, genome-wide association, and non-coding RNA. *Journal of Child Psychology and Psychiatry, 50*(1–2), 63–71.

Plomin, R., & Kovas, Y. (2005). Generalist genes and learning disabilities. *Psychological Bulletin, 131*(4), 592–617.

Plomin, R., DeFries, J. C., McClearn, G. E., & Rutter, M. (1997). *Behavioral genetics: A primer* (3rd ed.). New York, NY: Freeman.

Plomin, R., McClearn, G. E., Smith, D. L., Skuder, P., Vignetti, S., Chorney, M. J., & McGuffin, P. (1995). Allelic association between 100 DNA markers and high versus low IQ. *Intelligence, 21,* 31–48.

Pocock, S. J. (2013). *Clinical trials: a practical approach.* Hoboken, NJ: John Wiley & Sons.

Podewils, L. J., Guallar, E., Kuller, L. H., Fried, L. P., Lopez, O. L., Carlson, M., & Lyketsos, C. G. (2005). Physical activity, APOE genotype, and dementia risk: Findings from the Cardiovascular Health Cognition Study. *American Journal of Epidemiology, 161,* 639–651.

Polanczyk, G., de Lima, M. S., Horta, B. L., Biederman, J., & Rohde, L. A. (2007). The worldwide prevalence of ADHD: A systematic review and metaregression analysis. *American Journal of Psychiatry, 164,* 942–948.

Polanczyk, G., Zeni, C., Genro, J. P., Guimaraes, A. P., Roman, T., Hutz, M. H., & Rohde, L. A. (2007). Association of the adrenergic a2A receptor gene with methylphenidate improvement of inattentive symptoms in children and adolescents with attention-deficit/hyperactivity disorder. *Archives of General Psychiatry, 64,* 218–224.

Polivy, J., & Herman, C. P. (2002). Dieting and its relation to eating disorder. In K. D. Brownell & C. G. Fairburn (Eds.), *Eating disorders and obesity: A comprehensive handbook* (2nd ed., pp. 83–86). New York, NY: Guilford.

Polivy, J. M., & Herman, C. P. (1993). Etiology of binge eating: Psychological mechanisms. In C. G. Fairburn & G. T. Wilson (Eds.), *Binge eating: Nature, assessment, and treatment.* New York, NY: Guilford.

Pollack, M. H. (2005). The pharmacotherapy of panic disorder. *Journal of Clinical Psychiatry, 66,* 23–27.

Pollack, M. H., & Simon, N. M. (2009). Pharmacotherapy for panic disorder and agoraphobia. In M. M. Antony & M. B. Stein (Eds.), *Oxford handbook of anxiety and related disorders* (pp. 295–307). New York, NY: Oxford University Press.

Polloway, E. A., Schewel, R., & Patton, J. R. (1992). Learning disabilities in adulthood: Personal perspectives. *Journal of Learning Disabilities, 25,* 520–522.

Polonsky, D. C. (2000). Premature ejaculation. In S. R. Leiblum & R. C. Rosen (Eds.), *Principles and practice of sex therapy* (3rd ed., pp. 305–332). New York, NY: Guilford.

Pompili, M., Serafini, G., Innamorati, M., Biondi, M., Siracusano, A., Di Giannantonio, M., & Möller-Leimkühler, A. M. (2012). Substance abuse and suicide risk among adolescents. *European Archives of Psychiatry and Clinical Neuroscience, 262*(6), 469–485.

Pompili, M., Serafini, G., Innamorati, M., Möller-Leimkühler, A. M., Giupponi, G., Girardi, P., & Lester, D. (2010). The hypothalamic-pituitary-adrenal axis and serotonin abnormalities: A selective overview for the implications of suicide prevention. *European Archives of Psychiatry and Clinical Neuroscience, 260*(8), 583–600.

Ponseti, J., Granert, O., Jansen, O., Wolff, S., Beier, K., Neutze, J., & Bosinski, H. (2012). Assessment of pedophilia using hemodynamic brain response to sexual stimuli. *Archives of General Psychiatry, 69*(2), 187.

Poon, K., Watson, L., Baranek, G., & Poe, M. D. (2012). To what extent do joint attention, imitation, and object play behaviors in infancy predict later communication and intellectual functioning in ASD? *Journal of Autism and Developmental Disorders, 42*(6), 1064–1074. doi: 10.1007/s10803-011-1349-z

Poorsattar, S., & Hornung, R. (2010). Tanning addiction: Current trends and future treatment. *Expert Review of Dermatology, 5*(2), 123–125.

Pope, C., Pope, H., Menard, W., Fay, C., Olivardia, R., & Phillips, K. (2005). Clinical features of muscle dysmorphia among males with body dysmorphic disorder. *Body Image, 4,* 395–400.

Pope, H. G., Jr., Oliva, P. S., Hudson, J. I., Bodkin, J. A., & Gruber, A. J. (1999). Attitudes toward DSM-IV dissociative disorders diagnoses among board-certified American psychiatrists. *American Journal of Psychiatry, 156*(2), 321–323.

Pope, H. G., Jr., & Kanayama, G. (2012). Anabolic– androgenic steroids. In J. C. Verster, K. Brady, M. Galanter, & P. Conrod (Eds.), *Drug Abuse and Addiction in Medical Illness* (pp. 251–264). New York, NY: Springer.

Pope, H. G., Jr., Cohane, G. H., Kanayama, G., Siegel, A. J., & Hudson, J. I. (2003). Testosterone gel supplementation for men with refractory depression: A randomized, placebo-controlled trial. *The American Journal of Psychiatry, 160*(1), 105–111.

Pope, H. G., Jr., Gruber, A. J., Mangweth, B., Bureau, B., deCol, C., Jouvent, R., & Hudson, J. I. (2000). Body image perception among men in three countries. *American Journal of Psychiatry, 157,* 1297–1301.

Pope Jr, H. G., Gruber, A. J., Mangweth, B., Bureau, B., Jouvent, R., & Hudson, J. I. (2014). Body image perception among men in three countries. *American Journal of Psychiatry, 157*(8), 1297–1301.

Pope, K. S. (1996). Memory, abuse and science: Questioning claims about the false memory syndrome epidemic. *American Psychologist, 51,* 957–974.

Pope, K. S. (1997). Science as careful questioning: Are claims of a false memory syndrome epidemic based on empirical evidence? *American Psychologist, 52,* 997–1006.

Poppa, T., & Bechara, A. (2015). A neural perspective of immoral behavior and psychopathy. *AJOB Neuroscience, 6*(3), 15–24.

Portenoy, R., & Mathur, G. (2009). Cancer pain. In S.-C. J. Yeung, C. P. Escalante, & R. F. Gagel (Eds.), *Medical care of the cancer patient* (pp. 60–71). Shelton, CT: PMPH USA Ltd.

Post, L., Page, C., Conner, T., & Prokhorov, A. (2010). Elder abuse in long-term care: Types, patterns, and risk factors. *Research on Aging, 32*(3), 323.

Post, R. M. (1992). Transduction of psychosocial stress into the neurobiology of recurrent affective disorder. *American Journal of Psychiatry, 149*(8), 999–1010.

Post, R. M., Rubinow, D. R., Uhde, T. W., Roy-Byrne, P. P., Linnoila, M., Rosoff, A., & Cowdry, R. (1989). Dysphoric mania: Clinical and biological correlates. *Archives of General Psychiatry, 46,* 353–358.

Potenza, M. N., Steinberg, M. A., Skudlarski, P., Fulbright, R. K., Lacadie, C. M., Wilber, M. K., & Wexler, B. E. (2003). Gambling urges in pathological gambling: A functional magnetic resonance imaging study. *Archives of General Psychiatry, 60*, 828–836.

Potter, R., Ellard, D., Rees, K., & Thorogood, M. (2011). A systematic review of the effects of physical activity on physical functioning, quality of life and depression in older people with dementia. *International Journal of Geriatric Psychiatry, 26*(10), 1000–1011.

Poulsen, S., Lunn, S., Daniel, S. I. F., Folke, S., Mathiesen, B. B., Katznelson, H., & Fairburn, C. G. (2014). A randomized controlled trial of psychoanalytic psychotherapy versus cognitive behavior therapy for bulimia nervosa. *American Journal of Psychiatry, 171*, 109–116.

Powell, R. A., & Howell, A. J. (1998). Effectiveness of treatment for dissociative identity disorder. *Psychological Reports, 83*, 483–490.

Powers, A. D., Gleason, M. E., & Oltmanns, T. F. (2013). Symptoms of borderline personality disorder predict interpersonal (but not independent) stressful life events in a community sample of older adults. *Journal of Abnormal Psychology, 122*(2), 469.

Prause, N., & Janssen, E. (2006). Blood flow: Vaginal photoplethysmography. In Goldstein, I., Meston, C. M., Davis, S. R., & Traish, A. M. (Eds.), *Women's sexual function and dysfunction: Study, diagnostic and treatment* (pp. 359–367). New York, NY: Taylor and Francis.

Prelior, E. F., Yutzy, S. H., Dean, J. T., & Wetzel, D. (1993). Briquet's syndrome, dissociation and abuse. *American Journal of Psychiatry, 150*, 1507–1511.

Prenoveau, J. M., Craske, M. G., Liao, B., & Ornitz, E. M. (2013). Human fear conditioning and extinction: Timing is everything... or is it? *Biological psychology, 92*(1), 59–68.

President's New Freedom Commission on Mental Health. (2003). *Achieving the promise: Transforming mental health care in America— Final report* (DHHS Pub. No. SMA-03-3832). Rockville, MD: Substance Abuse and Mental Health Services Administration.

Presley, C. A., & Meilman, P. W. (1992). *Alcohol and drugs on American college campuses: A report to college presidents.* Carbondale: Southern Illinois University Press.

Presnall, N., Webster-Stratton, C. H., & Constantino, J. N. (2014). Parent training: Equivalent improvement in externalizing behavior for children with and without familial risk. *Journal of the American Academy of Child & Adolescent Psychiatry, 53*(8), 879–887.

Price, A. M. H., Wake, M., Ukoumunne, O. C., & Hiscock, H. (2012). Outcomes at six years of age for children with infant sleep problems: Longitudinal community-based study. *Sleep Medicine, 13*(8), 991–998. doi: 10.1016/j.sleep.2012.04.014

Price, J. R., Mitchell, E., Tidy, E., & Hunot, V. (2008). Cognitive behaviour therapy for chronic fatigue syndrome in adults. *Cochrane Database of Systematic Reviews, 3*, CD001027. doi: 10.1002/14651858. CD001027.pub2

Price, S. R., Hilchey, C. A., Darredeau, C., Fulton, H. G., & Barrett, S. P. (2010). Energy drink co-administration is associated with increased reported alcohol ingestion. *Drug and Alcohol Review, 29*(3), 331–333.

Pridal, C. G., & LoPiccolo, J. (2000). Multielement treatment of desire disorders: Integration of cognitive, behavioral and systemic therapy. In R. Leiblum & R. C. Rosen (Eds.), *Principles and practice of sex therapy* (3rd ed., pp. 57–81). New York, NY: Guilford.

Prince, M. (1906–1907). Hysteria from the point of view of dissociated personality. *Journal of Abnormal Psychology, 1*, 170–187.

Primeau, A., Bowers, T. G., Harrison, M. A., & XuXu. (2013). Deinstitutionalization of the mentally ill: Evidence for transinstitutionalization from psychiatric hospitals to penal institutions. *Comprehensive Psychology, 2*(1), Article-2.

Pringsheim, T., Wiltshire, K., Day, L., Dykeman, J., Steeves, T., & Jette, N. (2012). The incidence and prevalence of Huntington's disease: A systematic review and meta-analysis. *Movement Disorders, 27*(9), 1083–1091.

Prins, J., van der Meer, J., & Bleijenberg, G. (2006). Chronic fatigue syndrome. *Lancet, 367*, 346–355. pro-ana-nation. (2010). Home page. Retrieved April 28, 2010, from http://www.proana-nation.com/v1/index.php

Proulx, T., & Heine, S. J. (2009). Connections from Kafka: Exposure to meaning threats improves implicit learning of an artificial grammar. *Psychological Science, 20*(9), 1125–1131.

Pruzinsky, T. (1988). Collaboration of plastic surgeon and medical psychotherapist: Elective cosmetic surgery. *Medical Psychotherapy, 1*, 1–13.

Pueschel, S. M., & Goldstein, A. (1991). Genetic counseling. In J. L. Matson & J. A. Mulick (Eds.), *Handbook of mental retardation* (2nd ed., pp. 279–291). Elmsford, NY: Pergamon Press.

Pugliese, M. T., Weyman-Daun, M., Moses, N., & Lifshitz, F. (1987). Parental health beliefs as a cause of nonorganic failure to thrive. *Pediatrics, 80*, 175–182.

Puhan, M. A., Suarez, A., Cascio, C. L., Zahn, A., Heitz, M., & Braendli, O. (2006). Didgeridoo playing as alternative treatment for obstructive sleep apnoea syndrome: randomised controlled trial. *BMJ 332*(7536), 266–270.

Puliafico, A. C., Comer, J. S., & Pincus, D. B. (2012). Adapting parent-child interaction therapy to treat anxiety disorders in young children. *Child and Adolescent Psychiatry Clinics of North America, 21*, 607–619.

Pulkki-Raback, L., Kivimäki, M., Ahola, K., Joutsenniemi, K., Elovainio, M., & Virtanen, M. (2012). Living alone and antidepressant medication use: A prospective study in a working-age population. *BMC Public Health, 12*(1), 236. doi: 10.1186/1471-2458-12-236

Pull, C. B. (2013). Too few or too many? Reactions to removing versus retaining specific personality disorders in DSM-5. *Current Opinion in Psychiatry, 26*(1), 73–78.

Purdy, D., & Frank, E. (1993). Should postpartum mood disorders be given a more prominent or distinct place in DSM-IV? *Depression, 1*, 59–70.

Pury, C. L. S., & Mineka, S. (1997). Covariation bias for blood–injury stimuli and aversion outcomes. *Behavior Research and Therapy, 35*, 35–47.

Putnam, F. W. (1991). Dissociative phenomena. In A. Tasman & S. M. Goldinger (Eds.), *American Psychiatric Press review of psychiatry* (Vol. 10). Washington, DC: American Psychiatric Press.

Putnam, F. W. (1992). Altered states: Peeling away the layers of a multiple personality. *Sciences, 32*(6), 30–36.

Putnam, F. W. (1997). *Dissociation in children and adolescents: A developmental perspective.* New York, NY: Guilford.

Putnam, F. W., & Loewenstein, R. J. (1993). Treatment of multiple personality disorder: A survey of current practices. *American Journal of Psychiatry, 150*, 1048–1052.

Putnam, F. W., Guroff, J. J., Silberman, E. K., Barban, L., & Post, R. M. (1986). The clinical phenomenology of multiple personality disorder: Review of 100 recent cases. *Journal of Clinical Psychiatry, 47*, 285–293.

Puzziferri, N., Roshek, T. B., Mayo, H. G., Gallagher, R., Belle, S. H., & Livingston, E. H. (2014). Long-term follow-up after bariatric surgery: a systematic review. *JAMA, 312*(9), 934–942.

Quality Assurance Project. (1990). Treatment outlines for paranoid, schizotypal and schizoid personality disorders. *Australian and New Zealand Journal of Psychiatry, 24*, 339–350.

Quay, H. C. (1993). The psychobiology of under-socialized aggressive conduct disorder: A theoretical perspective. *Development and Psychopathology, 5*, 165–180.

Quinsey, V. L. (2010). Coercive paraphilic disorder. *Archives of Sexual Behavior, 39*, 405–410. Quoidbach, J., Gilbert, D. T., & Wilson, T. D. (2013). The end of history illusion. *Science, 339*(6115), 96–98. doi: 10.1126/science.1229294

Rabe, S., Zoellner, T., Beauducel, A., Maercker, A., & Karl, A. (2008). Changes in brain electrical activity after cognitive behavioral therapy for posttraumatic stress disorder in patients injured in motor vehicle accidents. *Psychosomatic Medicine, 70*(1), 13–19.

Rabins, P. V. (2006). *Guideline watch: Practice guidelines for the treatment of patients with Alzheimer's disease and other dementias of late life.* Washington, DC: American Psychiatric Association.

Rabins, P. V., & Lyketsos, C. G. (2011). A commentary on the proposed DSM revision regarding the classification of cognitive disorders. *American Journal of Geriatric Psychiatry, 19*(3), 201–204.

Rachman, S. (1978). *Fear and courage.* San Francisco: W. H. Freeman.

Rachman, S. (1991). Neo-conditioning and the classical theory of fear acquisition. *Clinical Psychology Review, 11*, 155–173.

Rachman, S. (2006). *Fear of contamination.* New York, NY: Oxford University Press.

Rachman, S., & de Silva, P. (1978). Abnormal and normal obsessions. *Behaviour Research and Therapy, 16*, 233–248.

Rachman, S., & Hodgson, R. (1968). Experimentally induced "sexual fetishism": Replication and development. *Psychological Record, 18*(1), 25–27.

Racine, S. E., & Wildes, J. E. (2015). Dynamic longitudinal relations between emotion regulation difficulties and anorexia nervosa symptoms over the year following intensive treatment. *Journal of Clinical and Consulting Psychology, 83*(4), 785–795.

Rado, S. (1962). Theory and therapy: The theory of schizotypal organization and its application to the treatment of decompensated schizotypal behavior. In S. Rado (Ed.), *Psychoanalysis of behavior* (Vol. 2, pp. 127–140). New York, NY: Grune & Stratton.

Radomsky, A. S., & Taylor, S. (2005). Subtyping OCD: Prospects and problems. *Behavior Therapy, 36*, 371–379.

Rahkonen, T., Eloniemi-Sulkava, U., Paanila, S., Halonen, P., Sivenius, J., & Sulkava, R. (2001). Systematic intervention for supporting community care of elderly people after a delirium episode. *International Psychogeriatrics, 13*(1), 37–49.

Raine, A., Venables, P. H., & Williams, M. (1990). Relationships between central and autonomic measures of arousal at age 15 years and criminality at age 24 years. *Archives of General Psychiatry, 47*, 1003–1007.

Raison, C. L., Klein, H. M., & Steckler, M. (1999). The moon and madness reconsidered. *Journal of Affective Disorders, 53*(1), 99–106.

Rakison, D. H. (2009). Does women's greater fear of snakes and spiders originate in infancy? *Evolution and Human Behavior, 30*(6), 438–444.

Ramachandran, V. S. (1993). Filling in the gaps in perception II: Scotomas and phantom limbs. *Current Directions in Psychological Science, 2*, 56–65.

Ramchandani, P., Stein, A., Evans, J., O'Connor, T., & the ALSPAC Study Team. (2005). Paternal depression in the postnatal period and child development: A prospective population study. *Lancet, 365*, 2201–2205.

Ramos Olazagasti, M. A., Klein, R. G., Mannuzza, S., Belsky, E. R., Hutchison, J. A., Lashua-Shriftman, E. C., & Xavier Castellanos, F. (2013). Does childhood attention-deficit/hyperactivity disorder predict risk-taking and medical illnesses in adulthood? *Journal of the American Academy of Child & Adolescent Psychiatry, 52*(2), 153–162.e154. doi: http://dx.doi.org/10.1016/j.jaac.2012.11.012

Ramrakha, S., Paul, C., Bell, M. L., Dickson, N., Moffitt, T. E., & Caspi, A. (2013). The relationship between multiple sex partners and anxiety, depression, and substance dependence disorders: A cohort study. *Archives of Sexual Behavior, 42*(5), 863–872.

Ramsawh, H. J., Morgentaler, A., Covino, N., Barlow, D. H., & DeWolf, W. C. (2005). Quality of life following simultaneous placement of penile prosthesis with radical prostatectomy. *Journal of Urology, 174*(4, Part 1 of 2), 1395–1398.

Ramsawh, H., Raffa, S. D., White, K. S., & Barlow, D. H. (2008). Risk factors for isolated sleep paralysis in an African American sample: A preliminary study. *Behavior Therapy 39*(4), 386–397. doi: 10.1016/j.beth.2007.11.002.

Rangmar, J., Hjern, A., Vinnerljung, B., Strömland, K., Aronson, M., & Fahlke, C. (2015). Psychosocial outcomes of fetal alcohol syndrome in adulthood. *Pediatrics, 135*(1), e52–e58.

Ranjith, G., & Mohan, R. (2004). Dhat syndrome: A functional somatic syndrome? (Letter to the editor). *British Journal of Psychiatry*, pp. 200–209.

Ranson, M. B., Nichols, D. S., Rouse, S. V., & Harrington, J. L. (2009). Changing or replacing an established psychological assessment standard: Issues, goals, and problems with special reference to recent developments in the MMPI-2. In J. N. Butcher (Ed.), *Oxford handbook of personality assessment* (pp. 112–139). New York, NY: Oxford University Press.

Rapee, R. M., & Melville, L. F. (1997). Recall of family factors in social phobia and panic disorder: Comparison of mother and offspring reports. *Depression and Anxiety, 5*, 7–11.

Rapee, R. M., Schniering, C. A., & Hudson, J. L. (2009). Anxiety disorders during childhood and adolescence: Origins and treatment. *Annual Review of Clinical Psychology, 5*, 311–341.

Rapkin, A. J., Chang, L. C., & Reading, A. E. (1989). Mood and cognitive style in premenstrual syndrome. *Obstetrics and Gynecology, 74*, 644–649. Rasetti, R., Sambataro, F., Chen, Q., Callicott, J. H., Mattay, V. S., & Weinberger, D. R. (2011). Altered cortical network dynamics: a potential intermediate phenotype for schizophrenia and association with ZNF804A. *Archives of General Psychiatry, 68*(12), 1207–1217.

Rasmussen, S. A., & Eisen, J. L. (1990). Epidemiology of obsessive-compulsive disorder. *Journal of Clinical Psychiatry, 51*, 10–14.

Rasmusson, A. M., Anderson, G. M., Krishnan-Sarin, S., Wu, R., & Paliwal, P. (2006). A decrease in plasma DHEA to cortisol ratio during smoking abstinence may predict relapse: A preliminary study. *Psychopharmacology, 186*, 473–480.

Rassin, E., & Koster, E. (2003). The correlation between thought–action fusion and religiosity in a normal sample. *Behaviour Research and Therapy, 41*, 361–368.

Rathod, N. H., Addenbrooke, W. M., & Rosenbach, A. F. (2005). Heroin dependence in an English town: 33-year follow-up. *British Journal of Psychiatry, 187*, 421–425.

Rauch, A., Wieczorek, D., Graf, E. R., Wieland, T., Endele, S., Schwarzmayr, T., & Strom, T., M. (2012). Range of genetic mutations associated with severe non-syndromic sporadic intellectual disability: An exome sequencing study. *The Lancet, 380*(9854), 1674–1682.

Rauch, S. A. M., King, A. P., Abelson, J., Tuerk, P. W., Smith, E., Rothbaum, B. O., Clifton, E., Defever, A, & Liberzon, I. (2014). Biological and symptom changes in posttraumatic disorder treatment: A randomized clinical trial. *Depression and Anxiety, 32*, 204–212.

Rauch, S. L., Phillips, K. A., Segal, E., Markis, N., Shin, L. M., Whalen, P. J., & Kennedy, D. N. (2003). A preliminary morphometric magnetic resonance imaging study of regional brain volumes in body dysmorphic disorder. *Psychiatry Research, 122*, 13–19.

Ravussin, E., Valencia, M. E., Esparza, J., Bennett, P. H., & Schulz, L. O. (1994). Effects of a traditional lifestyle on obesity in Pima Indians. *Diabetes Care, 17*, 1067–1074.

Ray, L. A. (2012). Clinical neuroscience of addiction: Applications to psychological science and practice. *Clinical Psychology: Science and Practice, 19*(2), 154–166. doi: 10.1111/j.1468-2850.2012.01280.x

Ray, W. A., Gurwitz, J., Decker, M. D., & Kennedy, D. L. (1992). Medications and the safety of the older driver: Is there a basis for concern? Special issue: Safety and mobility of elderly drivers: II. *Human Factors, 34*(1), 33–47.

Raymond, N. C., Coleman, E., Ohlerking, F., Christenson, G. A., & Miner, M. (1999). Psychiatric comorbidity in pedophilic sex offenders. *American Journal of Psychiatry, 156*, 786–788.

Rayner, K. E., Schniering, C. A., Rapee, R. M., Taylor, A., & Hutchinson, D. M. (2012). Adolescent girls' friendship networks, body dissatisfaction, and disordered eating: Examining selection and socialization processes. *Journal of Abnormal Psychology, 122*(1), 93–104. doi: 10.1037/a0029304

Raza, G. T., DeMarce, J. M., Lash, S. J., & Parker, J. D. (2014). Paranoid Personality Disorder in the United States: The Role of Race, Illicit Drug Use, and Income. *Journal of Ethnicity in Substance Abuse, 13*(3), 247–257.

Razran, G. (1961). The observable unconscious and the inferable conscious in current Soviet psychophysiology: Interoceptive conditioning, semantic conditioning, and the orienting reflex. *Psychological Review, 68*, 81–150.

Rea, M., Tompson, M. C., & Miklowitz, D. J. (2003). Family-focused treatment versus individual treatment for bipolar disorder: Results of a randomized clinical trial. *Journal of Consulting and Clinical Psychology, 71*, 482–492.

Reames, B. N., Finks, J. F., Bacal, D., Carlin, A. M., & Dimick, J. B. (2014). Changes in bariatric surgery procedure use in Michigan, 2006-2013. *JAMA, 312*(9), 959–961.

Reas, D. L., & Grilo, C. M. (2014). Current and emerging drug treatments for binge eating disorder. *Expert Opinion on Emerging Drugs, 19*(1), 99–142.

Rebocho, M. F., & Silva, P. (2014). Target selection in rapists: The role of environmental and contextual factors. *Aggression and Violent Behavior, 19*(1), 42–49.

Record, N. B., Onion, D. K., Prior, R. E., Dixon, D. C., Record, S. S., Fowler, F. L., Cayer, G. R., Amos, C. I., & Pearson, T. A. (2015). Community-wide cardiovascular disease prevention programs and health outcomes in a rural county, 1970-2010. *JAMA, 313*(2), 147–155.

Redd, W. H., & Andrykowski, M. A. (1982). Behavioral intervention in cancer treatment: Controlling aversion reactions to chemotherapy. *Journal of Consulting and Clinical Psychology, 50*, 1018–1029.

Reddy, L. A., Newman, E., De Thomas, C. A., & Chun, V. (2009). Effectiveness of school-based prevention and intervention programs for children and adolescents with emotional disturbance: A meta-analysis. *Journal of School Psychology, 47*(2), 77–99.

Reddy, L. F., Horan, W. P., & Green, M. F. (2016). Motivational deficits and negative symptoms in schizophrenia: Concepts and assessments. *Current Topics in Behavioral Neuroscience, 27*, 357–373.

Reeves, G. M., Nijjar, G. V., Langenberg, P., Johnson, M. A., Khabazghazvini, B., Sleemi, A., & Postolache, T. T. (2012). Improvement in depression scores after 1 hour of light therapy treatment in patients with seasonal affective disorder. *The Journal of Nervous and Mental Disease, 200*(1), 51–54.

Regier, D. A., Narrow, W. E., Kuhl, E. A., & Kupfer, D. J. (2009). The conceptual development of DSM-V. *American Journal of Psychiatry, 166*(6), 645–650.

Regier, D. A., Narrow, W. E., Clarke, D. E., Kraemer, H. C., Kuramoto, S. J., Kuhl, E. A., & Kupfer, D. J. (2013). DSM-5 field trials in the United States and Canada, part II: Test-retest reliability of selected categorical diagnoses. *American Journal of Psychiatry, 170*(1), 59–70.

Rehm, J., Marmet, S., Anderson, P., Gual, A., Kraus, L., Nutt, D. J., . . . Wiers, R. W. (2013). Defining substance use disorders: Do we really need more than heavy use? *Alcohol and Alcoholism, 48*(6), 633–640.

Reichenberg, A., Gross, R., Weiser, M., Bresnahan, M., Silverman, J., Harlap, S., Lubin, G. (2006). Advancing paternal age and autism. *Archives of General Psychiatry, 63*(9), 1026.

Reichborn-Kjennerud, T., Czajkowski, N., Ystrøm, E., Ørstavik, R., Aggen, S. H., Tambs, K., . . . Kendler, K. S. (2015). A longitudinal twin study of borderline and antisocial personality disorder traits in early to middle adulthood. *Psychological Medicine, 45*(14), 3121–3131.

Reilly-Harrington, N. A., Alloy, L. B., Fresco, D. M., & Whitehouse, W. G. (1999). Cognitive styles and life events interact to predict bipolar and unipolar symptomatology. *Journal of Abnormal Psychology, 108*(4), 567–578.

Reilly-Harrington, N. A., Deckersbach, T., Knauz, R., Wu, Y., Tran, T., Eidelman, P., & Nierenberg, A. A. (2007). Cognitive behavioral therapy for rapid-cycling bipolar disorder: A pilot study. *Journal of Psychiatric Practice, 13*(5), 291–297.

Reiman, E. M., Webster, J. A., Myers, A. J., Hardy, J., Dunckley, T., Zismann, V. L., & Stephan, D. (2007). GAB2 alleles modify Alzheimer's risk in APOE ´4 carriers. *Neuron, 54*(5), 713–720.

Reiss, S. (1991). Expectancy model of fear, anxiety and panic. *Clinical Psychology Review, 11*, 141–153.

Reitan, R. M., & Davison, I. A. (1974). *Clinical neuropsychology: Current status and applications.* Washington, DC: V. H. Winston.

Rekers, G. A., Kilgus, M., & Rosen, A. C. (1990). Long-term effects of treatment for gender identity disorder of childhood. *Journal of Psychology & Human Sexuality, 3*(2), 121–153.

Rentz, D. M., Parra Rodriguez, M. A., Amariglio, R., Stern, Y., Sperling, R., & Ferris, S. (2013). Promising developments in neuropsychological approaches for the detection of preclinical Alzheimer's disease: a selective review. *Alzheimers Research & Therapy, 5*(6), 58. Report of the Advisory Panel on Alzheimer's

Disease. (1995). *Alzheimer's disease and related dementias: Biomedical update.* U.S. Department of Health and Human Services. Washington, DC: U.S. Government Printing Office.

Repp, A. C., & Singh, N. N. (1990). *Perspectives on the use of nonaversive and aversive interventions for persons with developmental disabilities.* Sycamore, IL: Sycamore.

Rescorla, R. A. (1988). Pavlovian conditioning: It's not what you think it is. *American Psychologist, 43*(3), 151–160.

Resick, P. A., Williams, L. F., Suvak, M. K., Monson, C. M., & Gradus, J. L. (2012). Long-term outcomes of cognitive-behavioral treatments for posttraumatic stress disorder among female rape survivors. *Journal of Consulting and Clinical Psychology, 80*, 201–210. doi: 10.1037/a0026602

Ressler, K. J., & Rothbaum, B. O. (2013). Augmenting obsessive-compulsive disorder treatment from brain to mind. *JAMA Psychiatry, 70*, 1129–1131.

Reynolds, C. F., III. (2009). Prevention of depressive disorders: A brave new world. *Depression and Anxiety, 26*(12), 1062–1065.

Reynolds, C. F. (2011). Troubled sleep, troubled minds, and DSM-5. *Archives of General Psychiatry, 68*(10), 990–991. doi: 10.1001/archgenpsychiatry.2011.104 Rhebergen, D., & Graham, R. (2014). The re-labelling of dysthymic disorder to persistent depressive disorder in DSM-5: Old wine in new bottles? *Current Opinions in Psychiatry, 27*, 27–31.

Ricciardelli, L. A., & McCabe, M. P. (2004). A biopsychosocial model of disordered eating and the pursuit of muscularity in adolescent boys. *Psychological Bulletin, 130*, 170–205.

Rice, G., Anderson, C., Risch, N., & Ebers, G. (1999). Male homosexuality: Absence of linkage to microsatellite markers at Xq28. *Science, 284*, 665–667.

Rice, M. E., & Harris, G. T. (2002). Men who molest their sexually immature daughters: Is a special explanation required? *Journal of Abnormal Psychology, 111*, 329–339.

Richards, R., Kinney, D. K., Lunde, I., Benet, M., & Merzel, A. P. C. (1988). Creativity in manic depressives, cyclothymes, their normal relatives, and control subjects. *Journal of Abnormal Psychology, 97*(3), 281–288.

Richards, S. S., & Sweet, R. A. (2009). Dementia. In B. J. Sadock, V. A. Sadock, & P. Ruiz (Eds.), *Kaplan & Sadock's comprehensive textbook of psychiatry* (9th ed., Vol. I, pp. 1167–1198). Philadelphia, PA: Lippincott Williams & Wilkins.

Richardson, G., Goldschmidt, L., & Willford, J. (2009). Continued effects of prenatal cocaine use: Preschool development. *Neurotoxicology and Teratology, 31*(6), 325–333.

Richardson, G. S. (2006). Shift work sleep disorder. In T. Lee-Chiong (Ed.), *Sleep: A comprehensive handbook* (pp. 395–399). Hoboken, NJ: Wiley.

Richters, J., de Visser, R. O., Badcock, P. B., Smith, A. M., Rissel, C., Simpson, J. M., & Grulich, A. E. (2014). Masturbation, paying for sex, and other sexual activities: the Second Australian Study of Health and Relationships. *Sexual Health, 11*(5), 461–471.

Rickels, K., Rynn, M., Ivengar, M., & Duff, D. (2006). Remission of generalized anxiety disorder: A review of the paroxetine clinical

trials database. *Journal of Clinical Psychiatry, 67*, 41–47.

Rickels, K., Schweizer, E., Case, W. G., & Greenblatt, D. J. (1990). Long-term therapeutic use of benzodiazepines: I. Effects of abrupt discontinuation. *Archives of General Psychiatry, 47*, 899–907.

Ridenour, T. A., & Howard, M. O. (2012). Inhalants abuse: Status of etiology and intervention. In J. C. Verster, K. Brady, M. Galanter, & P. Conrod (Eds.), *Drug abuse and addiction in medical illness* (pp. 189–199). New York, NY: Springer.

Riding, A. (1992, November 17). New catechism for Catholics defines sins of modern world. *New York Times*, pp. A1, A16.

Ridley, N. J., Draper, B., & Withall, A. (2013). Alcohol-related dementia: An update of the evidence. *Alzheimers Research & Therapy, 5*(3), 1–8.

Rief, W., & Martin, A. (2014). How to use the new *DSM-5* somatic symptom disorder diagnosis in research and practice: A critical evaluation and a proposal for modifications. *Annual Review of Clinical Psychology, 10*, 339–367.

Rief, W., Hiller, W., & Margraf, J. (1998). Cognitive aspects of hypochondriasis and the somatization syndrome. *Journal of Abnormal Psychology, 107*, 587–595.

Rieger, G., & Savin-Williams, R. C. (2012). Gender nonconformity, sexual orientation, and psychological well-being. *Archives of Sexual Behavior, 41*(3), 611–621.

Riemann, D., Berger, M., & Voderholzer, U. (2001). Sleep and depression—Results from psychobiological studies: An overview. *Biological Psychology, 57*, 67–103.

Riggins v. Nevada, 112 S. Ct. 1810 (1992).

Riggs, J. E. (1993). Smoking and Alzheimer's disease: Protective effect or differential survival bias? *Lancet, 342*, 793–794.

Riihimäki, K., Vuorilehto, M., Melartin, T., Haukka, J., & Isometsä, E. (2013). Incidence and predictors of suicide attempts among primary-care patients with depressive disorders: A 5-year prospective study. *Psychological Medicine*, 1–12.

Ripke, S., Neale, B. M., Corvin, A., Walters, J. T., Farh, K. H., Holmans, P. A., . . . Pers, T. H. (2014). Biological insights from 108 schizophrenia-associated genetic loci. *Nature, 511*(7510), 421.

Risch, N., Herrell, R., Lehner, T., Liang, K. Y., Eaves, L., Hoh, J., & Merikangas, K. R. (2009). Interaction between the serotonin transporter gene (5-HTTLPR), stressful life events, and risk of depression: A meta-analysis. *Journal of American Medical Association, 301*(23), 2462–2471. doi: 10.1001/jama.2009.878

Ritsner, M. S., & Gottesman, I.I.(2011). The schizophrenia construct after 100 years of challenges. In M. S. Ritsner (Ed), *Handbook of schizophrenia spectrum disorders* (Vol 1, pp. 1–44). Heidelberg, Germany: Springer.

Ritterband, L. M., Thorndike, F. P., Gonder-Frederick, L. A., Magee, J. C., Bailey, E. T., Saylor, D. K., Morin, C. M. (2009). Efficacy of an internet-based behavioral intervention for adults with insomnia. *Arch Gen Psychiatry, 66*(7), 692–698. doi: 10.1001/archgenpsychiatry.2009.66

Ritz, T., Meuret, A. E., & Ayala, E. S. (2010). The psychophysiology of blood-injection-injury phobia: Looking beyond the diphasic response. *International Journal of Psychophysiology, 78*, 50–67.

Riva, P., Romero Lauro, L. J., Dewall, C. N., & Bushman, B. J. (2012). Buffer the pain away: Stimulating the right ventrolateral prefrontal cortex reduces pain following social exclusion. *Psychological Science, 23*(12), 1473–1475.

Rivera-Tovar, A. D., & Frank, E. (1990). Late luteal phase dysphoric disorder in young women. *American Journal of Psychiatry, 147*, 1634–1636.

Rivera-Tovar, A. D., Pilkonis, P., & Frank, E. (1992). Symptom patterns in late luteal-phase dysphoric disorder. *Journal of Psychopathology and Behavioral Assessment, 14*, 189–199.

Rizzuto, D., Orsini, N., Qiu, C., Wang, H.-X., & Fratiglioni, L. (2012). Lifestyle, social factors, and survival after age 75: Population based study. *BMJ: British Medical Journal, 345*, e5568.

Ro, A., Geronimus, A., Bound, J., Griffith, D., & Gee, G. (2015). Cohort and Duration Patterns Among Asian Immigrants: Comparing Trends in Obesity and Self-Rated Health. *Biodemography and Social Biology, 61*(1), 65–80.

Robbins, T. W., & Cools, R. (2014). Cognitive deficits in Parkinson's disease: a cognitive neuroscience perspective. *Movement Disorders, 29*(5), 597–607.

Roberts, A., Cash, T., Feingold, A., & Johnson, B. (2006). Are black–white differences in females' body dissatisfaction decreasing? A meta-analytic review. *Journal of Consulting and Clinical Psychology, 74*, 1121–1131.

Roberts, J. M. (2014). Echolalia and language development in children with autism. In J. Arciuli & J. Brock (Eds.), *Communication in Autism* (Vol. 11, pp. 55–74). Philadelphia: John Benjamins Publishing Company.

Roberts, R. E., Kaplan, G. A., Shema, S. J., & Strawbridge, W. J. (1997). Does growing old increase the risk for depression? *American Journal of Psychiatry, 154*, 1384–1390.

Roberts, R. E., Roberts, C. R., & Chen, I. G. (2000). Ethnocultural differences in sleep complaints among adolescents. *The Journal of Nervous and Mental Disease, 188*, 222–229.

Roberts, W., Milich, R., & Barkley, R. A. (2015). Primary symptoms, diagnostic criteria, sub-typing, and prevalence of ADHD. In R. A. Barkley (Ed.), *Attention-deficit hyperactivity disorder: A handbook for diagnosis & treatment* (4th ed., pp. 51–80). New York, NY: The Guilford Press.

Robertson, D., Snarey, J., Ousley, O., Harenski, K., Bowman, F. D., Gilkey, R., Kilts, C. (2007). The neural processing of moral sensitivity to issues of justice and care. *Neuropsychologia, 45*(4), 755–766.

Robertson, N. (1988). *Getting better: Inside Alcoholics Anonymous.* New York, NY: William Morrow.

Robin, A. L. (2015). Training families of adolecents with ADHD. In R. A. Barkley (Ed.), *Attention-deficit hyperactivity disorder: A handbook for diagnosis & treatment* (4th ed., pp. 537–568). New York, NY The Guilford Press.

Robinaugh, D. J., & McNally, R. J. (2013). Remembering the past and envisioning the future in bereaved adults with and without complicated grief. *Clinical Psychological Science, 1*(3), 290–300. doi: 10.1177/2167702613476027.

Robins, L. N. (1966). *Deviant children grown up: A sociological and psychiatric study of sociopathic personality.* Baltimore, MD: Williams & Wilkins.

Robins, L. N. (1978). Sturdy childhood predictors of adult antisocial behavior: Replications from longitudinal studies. *Psychological Medicine, 8*, 611–622.

Robinson, G. E., Fernald, R. D., & Clayton, D. F. (2008, November 7). Genes and social behavior. *Science, 322*, 896–899.

Robinson, R. G., Jorge, R. E., Moser, D. J., Acion, L., Solodkin, A., Small, S. L., & Arndt, S. (2008). Escitalopram and problem-solving therapy for prevention of post-stroke depression: A randomized controlled trial: Correction. *JAMA: Journal of the American Medical Association, 301*(10).

Robles, T., Glaser, R., & Kiecolt-Glaser, J. (2005). Out of balance: A new look at chronic stress, depression, and immunity. *Current Directions in Psychological Science, 14*, 111–115.

Rock, C. L., Flatt, S. W., Sherwood, N. E., Karanja, N., Pakiz, B., & Thomson, C. A. (2010). Effect of a free prepared meal and incentivized weight loss program on weight loss and weight loss maintenance in obese and overweight women: A randomized controlled trial. *JAMA: Journal of American Medical Association, 304*, 1803–1810.

Rockney, R. M., & Lemke, T. (1992). Casualties from a junior–senior high school during the Persian Gulf war: Toxic poisoning or mass hysteria? *Developmental and Behavioral Pediatrics, 13*(5), 339–342.

Rodin, J., & Langer, E. J. (1977). Long-term effects of a controlled relevant intervention with the institutionalized aged. *Journal of Personality and Social Psychology, 35*(12), 897–902.

Rodin, J., & Salovey, P. (1989). Health psychology. *Annual Review of Psychology, 40*, 533–579.

Rodrigue, K. M., Rieck, J. R., Kennedy, K. M., Devous, M. D., Diaz-Arrastia, R., & Park, D. C. (2013). Risk factors for b-amyloid deposition in healthy aging: vascular and genetic effects. *JAMA Neurology, 70*(5), 600–606.

Roelofs, K., Keijsers, G. P., Hoogduin, K. A., Naring, G. W., & Moene, F. C. (2002). Childhood abuse in patients with conversion disorder. *American Journal of Psychiatry, 159*, 1908–1913.

Roemer, L., & Orsillo, S. M. (2013). An acceptance-based behavioral therapy for generalized anxiety disorder. In D. H. Barlow (Ed.), *Clinical handbook of psychological disorders: A step-by-step treatment manual* (5th ed.). New York, NY: Guilford.

Roemer, L., Orsillo, S. M., & Barlow, D. H. (2002). Generalized anxiety disorder. In D. H. Barlow, *Anxiety and its disorders: The nature and treatment of anxiety and panic* (2nd ed.). New York, NY: Guilford.

Rohan, K. J. (2009). *Coping with the seasons: A cognitive-behavioral approach to seasonal affective disorder: Therapist guide.* New York, NY: Oxford University Press.

Rohan, K. J., Roecklein, K. A., Lacy, T. J., & Vacek, P. M. (2009). Winter depression recurrence one year after cognitive-behavioral therapy, light therapy, or combination treatment. *Behavioral Therapy, 40*(3), 225–238.

Rohan, K. J., Roecklein, K. A., Tierney Lindsey, K., Johnson, L. G., Lippy, R. D., Lacy, T. M., & Barton, F. B. (2007). A randomized controlled trial of cognitive-behavioral therapy, light therapy, and their combination for seasonal affective disorder. *Journal of Consulting and Clinical Psychology, 75*, 489–500.

Rohan, K. J., Sigmon, S. T., & Dorhofer, D. M. (2003). Cognitive-behavioral factors in seasonal affective disorder. *Journal of Consulting and Clinical Psychology, 71*, 22–30.

Rohan, M. J., Meyerhoff, J., Ho, S. Y., Evans, M., Postolache, T. T., & Vacek, P. M. (2015). Outcomes one and two winters following cognitive-behavioral therapy or light therapy for seasonal affective disorder. *American Journal of Psychiatry.* doi: appiajp201515060773

Rohde, P., Lewinsohn, P. M., Klein, D. N., Seeley, J. R., & Gau, J. M. (2013). Key characteristics of major depressive disorder occurring in childhood, adolescence, emerging adulthood, and adulthood. *Clinical Psychological Science, 1*(1), 41–53.

Roid, G. H. (2003). *Stanford-binet intelligence scales (SB5).* Rolling Meadows, IL: Riverside.

Roid, G. H., & Pomplun, M. (2005). Interpreting the Stanford-Binet intelligence scales (5th ed.). In D. P. Flanagan & P. L. Harrison (Eds.), *Contemporary intellectual assessment: Theories, tests, and issues* (2nd ed., pp. 325–343). New York, NY: Guilford.

Rojo, L., Conesa, L., Bermudez, O., & Livianos, L. (2006). Influence of stress in the onset of eating disorders: Data from a two stage epidemiologic controlled study. (2006). *Psychosomatic Medicine, 68*, 628–635.

Rollman, B. L., Belnap, B. H., Mazumdar, S., Houck, P. R., Zhu, F., Gardner, W., & Shear, M. K. (2005). A randomized trial to improve the quality of treatment for panic and generalized anxiety disorders in primary care. *Archives of General Psychiatry, 62*, 1332–1341. doi: 10.1001/archpsyc.62.12.1332

Romanelli, R. J., Wu, F. M., Gamba, R., Mojtabai, R., & Segal, J. B. (2014). Behavioral therapy and serotonin reuptake inhibitor pharmacotherapy in the treatment of obsessive-compulsive disorder: A systematic review and meta-analysis of head-to-head randomized controlled trials, *Depression and Anxiety, 31*, 641–652.

Ronningstam, E. (2012). Narcissistic personality disorder: The diagnostic process. In T. A. Widiger (Ed.), *The Oxford handbook of personality disorders* (pp. 527–548). New York, NY: Oxford University Press.

Ronningstam, E. (2014). Introduction to the special series on "Narcissistic personality disorder—New perspectives on diagnosis and treatment." *Personality Disorders: Theory, Research, and Treatment, 5*(4), 419.

Room, R., & Greenfield, T. (2006). Alcoholics Anonymous, other 12-step movements and psychotherapy in the US population, 1990. *Addiction, 88*(4), 555–562.

Root, T. L., Pinheiro, A. P., Thornton, L., Strober, M., Fernandez-Aranda, F., Brandt, H., & Bulk, C. M. (2010). Substance use disorders in women with anorexia nervosa. *International Journal of Eating Disorders, 43*(1), 14–21.

Rorabaugh, W. J. (1991). Alcohol in America. *OAH Magazine of History, 6*(2), 17–19.

Rorschach, H. (1951). *Psychodiagnostics.* New York, NY: Grune & Stratton. (Original work published 1921.)

Roscoe, J. A., Morrow, G. R., Aapro, M. S., Molassiotis, A., & Olver, I. (2011). Anticipatory nausea and vomiting. *Support Care Cancer, 19*(10), 1533–1538.

Rosell, D. R., Futterman, S. E., McMaster, A., & Siever, L. J. (2014). Schizotypal personality disorder: a current review. *Current Psychiatry Reports, 16*(7), 1–12.

Rosellini, A. J., Boettcher, H., Brown, T. A., & Barlow, D. H. (2015). A transdiagnostic temperament-phenotype profile approach to emotional disorder classification: An update. *Psychopathology Review, 2*(1), 110–128.

Rosen, J. C., Reiter, J., & Orosan, P. (1995). Cognitive-behavioral body image therapy for body dysmorphic disorder. *Journal of Consulting Clinical Psychology, 63*, 263–269.

Rosen, R., Janssen, E., Wiegel, M., Bancroft, J., Althof, S., Wincze, J., & Barlow, D. H. (2006). Psychological and interpersonal correlates in men with erectile dysfunction and their partners: A pilot study of treatment outcome with sildenafil. *Journal of Sex & Marital Therapy, 32*, 215–234.

Rosen, R., Wing, R., Schneider, S., & Gendrano, N. (2005). Epidemiology of erectile dysfunction: The role of medical comorbidities and lifestyle factors. *Urological Clinics of North America, 32*, 403–417.

Rosen, R. C. (2000). Medical and psychological interventions for erectile dysfunction: Toward a combined treatment approach. In S. R. Leiblum & R. C. Rosen (Eds.), *Principles and practice of sex therapy* (3rd ed., pp. 276–304). New York, NY: Guilford.

Rosen, R. C. (2007). Erectile dysfunction: Integration of medical and psychological approaches. In S. R. Leiblum (Ed.), *Principles and practice of sex therapy* (4th ed., pp. 277–312). New York, NY: Guilford.

Rosen, R. C., & Beck, J. G. (1988). *Patterns of sexual arousal: Psychophysiological processes and clinical applications.* New York, NY: Guilford.

Rosen, R. C., Connor, M. K., Miyasato, G., Link, C., Shifren, J. L., Fisher, W. A., . . . Schobelock, M. J. (2012). Sexual desire problems in women seeking healthcare: a novel study design for ascertaining prevalence of hypoactive sexual desire disorder in clinic-based samples of US women. *Journal of Women's Health, 21*(5), 505–515.

Rosenberg, R. N., Richter, R. W., Risser, R. C., Taubman, K., Prado-Farmer, I., Ebalo, E., & Schellenberg, G. D. (1996). Genetic factors for the development of Alzheimer's disease in the Cherokee Indian. *Archives of Neurology, 53*, 997–1000.

Rosengren, A., Tibblin, G., & Wilhelmsen, L. (1991). Self-perceived psychological stress and incidence of coronary artery disease in middle-aged men. *American Journal of Cardiology, 68*, 1171–1175.

Rosenman, R. H., Brand, R. J., Jenkins, C. D., Friedman, M., Straus, R., & Wurm, M. (1975). Coronary heart disease in the Western Collaborative Group Study: Final follow-up experience of 8 years. *JAMA: Journal of the American Medical Association, 233*, 872–877.

Rosenthal, D. (Ed.). (1963). *The Genain quadruplets: A case study and theoretical analysis of heredity and environment in schizophrenia.* New York, NY: Basic Books.

Rosenthal, M., Gratz, K., Kosson, D., Cheavens, J., Lejuez, C., & Lynch, T. (2008). Borderline personality disorder and emotional responding: A review of the research literature. *Clinical Psychology Review, 28*(1), 75–91.

Rosenthal, P. A., & Rosenthal, S. (1984). Suicidal behavior by preschool children. *American Journal of Psychiatry, 141*, 520–525.

Rösler, A., & Witztum, M. D. (1998). Treatment of men with paraphilia with a long-acting analogue of gonadotropin-releasing hormone. *New England Journal of Medicine, 338*, 416–422.

Ross, A. O., & Pelham, W. E. (1981). Child psycho-pathology. *Annual Review of Psychology, 32*, 243–278.

Ross, C. A. (1997). *Dissociative identity disorder.* New York, NY: Wiley.

Ross, C. A. (2009). Dissociative amnesia and dissociative fugue. In P. F. Dell & J. A. O'Neil (Eds.), *Dissociation and the dissociative disorders* (pp. 429–434). New York, NY: Routledge. Ross, C. A., Anderson, G., Fleisher, W. P., & Norton, G. R. (1991). The frequency of multiple personality disorder among psychiatric inpatients. *American Journal of Psychiatry, 148*, 1717–1720.

Ross, C. A., Miller, S. D., Reagor, P., Bjornson, L., Fraser, G. A., & Anderson, G. (1990). Structured interview data on 102 cases of multiple personality disorder from four centers. *American Journal of Psychiatry, 147*, 596–601.

Rossow, I., & Bye, E. K. (2012). The problem of alcohol-related violence: An epidemiological and public health perspective. In M. McMurran (Ed.), *Alcohol-related violence* (pp. 1–18). Chichester, UK: Wiley.

Rothbaum, B. O., Price, M., Jovanovic, T., Norrholm, S. D., Gerardi, M., Dunlop, B., . . . Ressler, K. J. (2014): A randomized, double-blind evaluation of D-cycloserine or alprazolam combined with virtual reality exposure therapy for posttraumatic stress disorder in Iraq and Afghanistan War veterans. *American Journal of Psychiatry, 171*, 640–648.

Rothblum, E. D. (2002). Gay and lesbian body images. In T. F. Cash & T. Pruzinsky (Eds.), *Body image: A handbook of theory, research and clinical practice* (pp. 257–265). New York, NY: Guilford.

Rothschild, A. J. (2013). Challenges in the treatment of major depressive disorder with psychotic features. *Schizophrenia Bulletin, 39*(4), 787–796. doi: 10.1093/schbul/sbt046

Rottenberg, J., & Johnson, S. L. (2007). *Emotion and psychopathology: Bridging affective and clinical science.* Washington, DC: American Psychological Association.

Rotton, J., & Kelly, I. W. (1985). Much ado about the full moon: A meta-analysis of lunar-lunacy research. *Psychological Bulletin, 97*(2), 286–306.

Rouff, L. (2000). Schizoid personality traits among the homeless mentally ill: A quantitative and qualitative report. *Journal of Social Distress and the Homeless, 9*, 127–141.

Roush, W. (1997). Herbert Benson: Mind–body maverick pushes the envelope. *Science, 276*, 357–359.

Rowe, J. B. (2010). Conversion disorder: Understanding the pathogenic links between emotion and motor systems in the brain. *Brain, 133*(Pt 5), 1295–1297.

Rowell, E. A., & Rowell, R. (1939). *On the trail of marihuana: The weed of madness.* Mountain View, CA: Pacific Press.

Roy, A. K., Lopes, V., & Klein, R. G. (2014). Disruptive mood dysregulation disorder: A new diagnostic approach to chronic irritability in youth. *American Journal of Psychiatry, 171*, 918–924.

Roy-Byrne, P. P., & Katon, W. (2000). Anxiety management in the medical setting: Rationale, barriers to diagnosis and treatment, and proposed solutions. In D. I. Mostofsky & D. H. Barlow (Eds.), *The management of stress and anxiety in medical disorders* (pp. 1–14). Needham Heights, MA: Allyn & Bacon.

Rubia, K., Alegria, A. A., Cubillo, A. I., Smith, A. B., Brammer, M. J., & Radua, J. (2014). Effects of stimulants on brain function in Attention-Deficit/Hyperactivity Disorder: A systematic review and meta-analysis. *Biological Psychiatry, 76*(8), 616–628. doi: 10.1016/j.biopsych.2013.10.016

Rubin, R. T. (1982). Koro (Shook Yang): A culture-bound psychogenic syndrome. In C. T. H. Friedmann & R. A. Fauger (Eds.), *Extraordinary disorders of human behavior* (pp. 155–172). New York, NY: Plenum Press.

Rubio, J. M., Markowitz, J. C., Alegria, A., Perez-Fuentes, G., Liu, S.-M., Lin, K.-H., & Blanco, C. (2011). Epidemiology of chronic and nonchronic major depressive disorder: Results from the national epidemiology survey on alcohol and related conditions. *Depression and Anxiety, 28*, 622–631.

Ruchkin, V., Schwab-Stone, M., Jones, S., Cicchetti, D. V., Koposov, R., & Vermeiren, R. (2005). Is posttraumatic stress in youth a culture-bound phenomenon? A comparison of symptom trends in selected U.S. and Russian communities. *American Journal of Psychiatry, 162*, 538–544.

Rück, C., Karlsson, A., Steele, J. D., Edman, G., Meyerson, B. A., Ericson, K., & Svanborg, P. (2008). Capsulotomy for obsessive-compulsive disorder: Long-term follow-up of 25 patients. *Archives of General Psychiatry, 65*(8), 914–921. doi: 10.1001/archpsyc.65.8.914.

Rucklidge, J. J. (2010). Gender differences in attention-deficit/hyperactivity disorder. *The Psychiatric Clinics of North America, 33*(2), 357–373.

Rudaz, M., Craske, M. G., Becker, E. S., Ledermann, T., & Margraf, J. (2010). Health anxiety and fear of fear in panic disorder and agoraphobia vs. social phobia: A prospective longitudinal study. *Depression and Anxiety, 27*, 404–411.

Rudd, M. D., Joiner, Y., & Rajab, M. H. (2001). *Treating suicidal behavior.* New York, NY: Guilford.

Rudd, M. D., Rajab, M. H., Orman, D. T., Stulman, D. A., Joiner, T., & Dixon, W. (1996). Effectiveness of an outpatient intervention targeting suicidal young adults: Preliminary results. *Journal of Consulting and Clinical Psychology, 64,* 179–190.

Rudolph, K. D. (2009). Adolescent depression. In I. H. Gotlib & C. L. Hammen (Eds.), *Handbook of depression* (2nd ed., pp. 444–466). New York, NY: Guilford.

Ruffin, R., Ironson, G., Fletcher, M. A., Balbin, E., & Schneiderman, N. (2012). Health locus of control beliefs and healthy survival with AIDS. *International Journal of Behavioral Medicine, 19*(4), 512–517.

Ruiz, F. S., Andersen, M. L., Martins, R. C. S., Zager, A., Lopes, J. D., & Tufik, S. (2012). Immune alterations after selective rapid eye movement or total sleep deprivation in healthy male volunteers. *Innate Immunity, 18*(1), 44–54.

Ruiz-Veguilla, M., Luisa Barrigón, M., Diaz, F. J., Ferrin, M., Moreno-Granados, J., Dolores Salcedo, M., & Gurpegui, M. (2012). The duration of untreated psychosis is associated with social support and temperament. *Psychiatry Research, 200*(2–3), 687–692. doi: http:// dx.doi.org/10.1016/j.psychres.2012.03.024

Rupprecht, R., Rammes, G., Eser, D., Baghai, T. C., Schule, C., Nothdurfter, C., & Kucher, K. (2009). Translocator protein (18 kD) as target for anxiolytics without benzodiazepine-like side effects. *Science, 325*(5939), 490–493.

Rusch, N., Lieb, K., Gottler, I., Hermann, C., Schramm, E., Richter, H., & Bohus, M. (2007). Shame and implicit self-concept in women with borderline personality disorder. *American Journal of Psychiatry, 164*(3), 500–508.

Ruscio, J. (2004). Diagnoses and the behaviors they denote: A critical evaluation of the labeling theory of mental illness. *Scientific Review of Mental Health Practice, 3,* 5–22.

Russell, A.E., Ford, T., Williams, R. & Russell, G. (2016). The association between socioeconomic disadvantage and attention deficit/hyperactivity disorder (ADHD): A systematic review. *Child Psychiatry & Human Development, 47* (3), 440–458.

Rush, A. (2007). STAR *D: What have we learned? *American Journal of Psychiatry, 164,* 201–204.

Rush, A. J., Erman, M. K., Giles, D. E., Schlesser, A., Carpenter, G., Vasavada, N., & Roffwarg, H. P. (1986). Polysomnographic findings in recently drug-free and clinically remitted depressed patients. *Archives of General Psychiatry, 43,* 878–884.

Rush, A. J., Giles, D. E., Schlesser, M. A., Orsulak, P. J., Weissenburger, J. E., Fulton, C. L., & Roffwarg, P. (1997). Dexamethasone response, thyrotro-pin-releasing hormone stimulation, rapid eye movement latency, and subtypes of depression. *Biological Psychiatry, 41,* 915–928.

Rush, B. (1812). *Medical inquiries and observations upon the diseases of the mind.* Philadelphia, PA: Kimber and Richardson.

Russell, A. E., Ford, T., Williams, R., & Russell, G. (in press). The association between socioeconomic disadvantage and Attention Deficit /Hyperactivity Disorder (ADHD): A systematic review. *Child Psychiatry & Human Development,* 1–19. doi: 10.1007/s10578-015-0578-3

Russell, G. (2009). Disorders of eating: Anorexia nervosa. In M. G. Gelder, N. C. Andreasen, J. J. López-Ibor, Jr., & J. R. Geddes (Eds.), *New Oxford textbook of psychiatry* (2nd ed., pp. 777–800). New York, NY: Oxford University Press.

Russell, G. F. M. (1979). Bulimia nervosa: An ominous variant of anorexia nervosa. *Psychological Medicine, 9,* 429–448.

Russell, G. F. M. (2009). Disorders of Eating: Anorexia Nervosa. In M. G. Gelder, N. C. Andreasen, J. J. López-Ibor, Jr., & J. R. Geddes (Eds.), *New Oxford textbook of psychiatry* (2nd ed., pp. 777–800). New York, NY: Oford University Press.

Russell, G. F. M., Szmukler, G. I., Dare, C., & Eisler, I. (1987). An evaluation of family therapy in anorexia nervosa and bulimia nervosa. *Archives of General Psychiatry, 44,* 1047–1056.

Russo, S. J., Dietz, D. M., Dumitriu, D., Morrison, J. H., Malenka, R. C., & Nestler, E. J. (2010). The addicted synapse: mechanisms of synaptic and structural plasticity in nucleus accumbens. *Trends in neurosciences, 33*(6), 267–276.

Rutledge, T., Groesz, L., Linke, S., Woods, G., & Herbst, K. (2011). Behavioural weight management for the primary careprovider. *Obesity Reviews, 12*(5), e290–e297.

Rutter, M. (2002). The interplay of nature, nurture, and developmental influences: The challenge ahead for mental health. *Archives of General Psychiatry, 59,* 996–1000.

Rutter, M. (2006). *Genes and behavior: Nature–nurture interplay.* Oxford, UK: Blackwell.

Rutter, M. (2010). Gene-environment interplay. *Depression and Anxiety, 27*(1), 1–4.

Rutter, M. (2011a). Progress in understanding autism: 2007–2010. *Journal of Autism and Developmental Disorders, 41*(4), 395–404. doi: 10.1007/s10803-011-1184-2

Rutter, M. (2011b). Research review: Child psychiatric diagnosis and classification: Concepts, findings, challenges and potential. *Journal of Child Psychology and Psychiatry, 52*(6), 647–660. doi: 10.1111/j.1469-7610.2011.02367.x

Rutter, M., & Giller, H. (1984). *Juvenile delinquency: Trends and perspectives.* New York, NY: Guilford.

Rutter, M., Moffitt, T. E., & Caspi, A. (2006). Gene–environment interplay and psychopathology: Multiple varieties but real effects. *Journal of Child Psychology and Psychiatry, 47,* 226–261.

Rutter, M., & Pickles, A. (2016). Annual Research Review: Threats to the validity of child psychiatry and psychology. *Journal of Child Psychology and Psychiatry 57*(3), 398–416.

Ruzek, J. I. (2012). Community-based early intervention with trauma survivors. In J. G. Beck & D. M. Sloan (Eds.), *The Oxford handbook of traumatic stress disorders* (pp. 347–362). New York, NY: Oxford University Press.

Ruzek, J. I., Karlin, B. E., & Zeiss, A. (2012). Implementation of evidence-based psychological treatments in the Veterans Health Administration. In R. K. McHugh & D. H. Barlow (Eds.), *Dissemination and implementation of evidence-based psychological interventions* (pp. 78–96). New York, NY: Oxford University Press.

Ryan, D. H., & Kushner, R. (2010). The state of obesity and obesity research. *JAMA: Journal of American Medical Association, 304,* 1835–1836.

Ryan, W. D. (1992). The pharmacologic treatment of child and adolescent depression. *Psychiatric Clinics of North America, 15,* 29–40.

Ryder, A. G., Sunohara, M., & Kirmayer, L. J. (2015). Culture and personality disorder: from a fragmented literature to a contextually grounded alternative. *Current opinion in psychiatry, 28*(1), 40–45.

Ryder, A. G., Yang, J., Zhu, X., Yao, S., Yi, J., Heine, S. J., & Bagby, R. M. (2008). The cultural shaping of depression: Somatic symptoms in China, psychological symptoms in North America? *Journal of Abnormal Psychology, 117*(2), 300–313.

Saab, P. G., Llabre, M. M., Hurwitz, B. E., Frame, C. A., Reineke, I., Fins, A. I., & Schneiderman, N. (1992). Myocardial and peripheral vascular responses to behavioral challenges and their stability in black and white Americans. *Psychophysiology, 29*(4), 384–397.

Sachdev, P. S., Blacker, D., Blazer, D. G., Ganguli, M., Jeste, D. V., Paulsen, J. S., & Petersen, R. C. (2014). Classifying neurocognitive disorders: The DSM-5 approach. *Nature Reviews Neurology, 10*(11), 634–642.

Sachs, G. S., & Rush, A. J. (2003). Response, remission, and recovery in bipolar disorders: What are the realistic treatment goals? *Journal of Clinical Psychiatry, 64,* 18–22.

Sachs, G. S., Nierenberg, A. A., Calabrese, J. R., Marangell, L. B., Wisniewski, S. R., Gyulai, L., & Thase, M. E. (2007). Effectiveness of adjunctive antidepressant treatment for bipolar depression. *New England Journal of Medicine, 356*(17), 1711–1722.

Sack, R. L., Auckley, D., Auger, R. R., Carskadon, M. A., Wright, K. P., Jr., Vitiello, M. V., & American Academy of Sleep Medicine. (2007). Circadian rhythm sleep disorders: Part II, Advanced sleep phase disorder, delayed sleep phase disorder, free-running disorder, and irregular sleep-wake rhythm. *Sleep, 30*(11), 1484–1501.

Sackeim, H. A., & Devanand, D. P. (1991). Dissociative disorders. In M. Hersen & S. M. Turner (Eds.), *Adult psychopathology & diagnosis* (2nd ed., pp. 279–322). New York, NY: Wiley.

Sackeim, H. A., Nordlie, J. W., & Gur, R. C. (1979). A model of hysterical and hypnotic blindness: Cognition, motivation and awareness. *Journal of Abnormal Psychology, 88,* 474–489.

Sackett, D. L., Strauss, S. E., Richardson, W. S., Rosenberg, W., & Haynes, R. B. (2000). *Evidence-based medicine: How to practice and teach EBM* (2nd ed.). London, UK: Churchill Livingstone.

Sacks, H., Comer, J. S., Pincus, D. B., Comacho, M., & Hunter, L. (2013). Effective interventions for students with separation anxiety disorder. In C. Franklin, M.B. Harris, & P. Allen-Meares (Eds.), *The school services sourcebook* (2nd ed.). New York, NY: Oxford University Press.

Sacks, J. A., Comer, J. S., Furr, J. M., Pincus, D. B., & Kurtz, S. M. S. (2011, November). *Daily speech changes across an intensive group behavioral treatment program for early childhood selective mutism.* Poster presented at the 45th annual meeting of the Association of Behavioral and Cognitive Therapies, Child and Adolescent Anxiety Special Interest Group Exposition. Toronto, Canada.

Sadler, C., & Sugai, G. (2009). Effective behavior and instructional support: A district model for early identification and prevention of reading and behavior problems. *Journal of Positive Behavior Interventions, 11*(1), 35–46. doi: 10.1177/1098300708322444

Safford, M. M., Brown, T. M., Muntner, P. M., Durant, R. W., Glasser, S., Halanych, J. H., . . . Howard, G. (2012). Association of race and sex with risk of incident acute coronary heart disease events. *JAMA, 308*(17), 1768–1774.

Sahler, O., Fairclough, D., Phipps, S., Mukhern, R., Dolgin, M., & Noll, R. (2005). Using problem solving skills training to reduce negative affectivity in mothers of children with newly diagnosed cancer: Report of a multisite randomized trial. *Journal of Consulting and Clinical Psychology, 73*, 272–283.

Saigh, P. A. (1984). Pre-and postinvasion anxiety in Lebanon. *Behavior Therapy, 15*, 185–190.

Sakheim, D. K., Barlow, D. H., Abrahamson, D. J., & Beck, J. G. (1987). Distinguishing between organogenic and psychogenic erectile dysfunction. *Behaviour Research and Therapy, 25*, 379–390.

Saleh, F., Malin, H., Grudzinskas, A., Jr., & Vitacco, M. (2010). Paraphilias with co-morbid psychopathy: The clinical and legal significance to sex offender assessments. *Behavioral Sciences & the Law, 28*(2), 211–223.

Salekin, R. T. (2006). Psychopathy in children and adolescents: Key issues in conceptualization and assessment. In C. J. Patrick (Ed.), *Handbook of psychopathy* (pp. 389–414). New York, NY: Guilford.

Salekin, R. T., Rogers, R., & Sewell, K. W. (1997). Construct validity of psychopathy in a female offender sample: A multi-trait– multimethod evaluation. *Journal of Abnormal Psychology, 106*(4), 576–585. doi: 10.1037/0021-843x.106.4.576

Salkovskis, P., Warwick, H., & Deale, A. (2003). Cognitive-behavioral treatment for severe and persistent health anxiety. *Brief Treatment and Crisis Intervention, 3*, 353–367.

Salkovskis, P. M., & Campbell, P. (1994). Thought suppression induces intrusion in naturally occurring negative intrusive thoughts. *Behaviour Research and Therapy, 32*(1), 1–8.

Sallet, J., Mars, R. B., Noonan, M. P., Andersson, J. L., O'Reilly, J. X., & Rushworth, M. F. (2011). Social network size affects neural circuits in macaques. *Science, 334*(6056), 697–700. doi: 10.1126/science.1210027

Salvatore, P., Bhuvaneswar, C., Tohen, M., Khalsa, H. M., Maggini, C., & Baldessarini, R. J. (2014). Capgras' syndrome in first-episode psychotic disorders. *Psychopathology, 47*(4), 261–269.

Samek, D. R., Elkins, I. J., Keyes, M. A., Iacono, W. G., & McGue, M. (2015). High school sports involvement diminishes the association between childhood conduct disorder and adult antisocial behavior. *Journal of Adolescent Health, 57*(1), 107–112.

Samson, L., & Janssen, E. (2014). Sexual and affective responses to same-and opposite-sex stimuli in heterosexual and homosexual men: Assessment and manipulation of visual attention. *Archives of Sexual Behavior, 43*(5), 917–930.

Samueli, S., Abraham, K., Dressler, A., Groeppel, G., Jonak, C., Muehlebner, A., . . . Feucht, M. (2015). Tuberous Sclerosis Complex: new criteria for diagnostic work-up and management. *Wiener klinische Wochenschrift, 127*(15–16), 619–630. doi: 10.1007/s00508-015-0758-y

Samuels, J., & Costa, P. T. (2012). Obsessive-compulsive personality disorder. In T. A. Widiger (Ed.), *The Oxford handbook of personality disorders* (pp. 566–581). New York, NY: Oxford University Press.

Sanderson, W. C., & Barlow, D. H. (1990). A description of patients diagnosed with DSM-III-R generalized anxiety disorder. *Journal of Nervous and Mental Disease, 178*, 588–591.

Sandin, B., Chorot, P., Santed, M., & Valiente, R. (2004). Differences in negative life events between patients with anxiety disorders, depression and hypochondriasis. *Anxiety, Stress & Coping: An International Journal, 17*, 37–47.

Sanislow, C. A., da Cruz, K. L., Gianoli, M. O., & Reagan, E. M. (2012). Avoidant personality disorder, traits, and type. In T. A. Widiger (Ed.), *The Oxford handbook of personality disorders* (pp. 549–565). New York, NY: Oxford University Press.

Sanislow, C. A., Quinn, K. J., & Sypher, I. (2015). NIMH Research Domain Criteria (RDoC). *The encyclopedia of clinical psychology.* Hoboken, NJ: John Wiley & Sons, Inc. doi: 10.1002/9781118625392.wbecp541

Sankey, A., Hill, C., Brown, J., Quinn, L., & Fletcher, A. (2006). A follow-up study of chronic fatigue syndrome in children and adolescents: Symptoms persistence and school absenteeism. *Clinical Child Psychology and Psychiatry, 11*, 126–138.

Sano, M., Ernesto, C., Thomas, R. G., Klauber, M. R., Schafer, K., Grundman, M., & Thal, L. J. (1997). A controlled trial of selegiline, alpha-tocopherol, or both as treatment for Alzheimer's disease. *New England Journal of Medicine, 336*, 1216–1222.

Santarelli, L., Saxe, M., Gross, C., Surget, A., Battaglia, F., Dulawa, S., & Hen, R. (2003). Requirement of hippocampal neurogenesis for the behavioral effects of antidepressants. *Science, 301*, 805–809.

Santoro, M. R., Bray, S. M., & Warren, S. T. (2012). Molecular mechanisms of fragile X syndrome: A twenty-year perspective. *Annual Review of Pathology: Mechanisms of Disease, 7*, 219–245.

Santosa, C. M., Strong, C. M., Nowakowska, C., Wang, P. W., Rennicke, C. M., & Ketter, T. A. (2007). Enhanced creativity in bipolar disorder patients: A controlled study. *Journal of Affective Disorders, 100*(1–3), 31–39.

Santosh, P. J. (2009). Medication for children and adolescents: Current issues. In M. G. Gelder, C. Andreasen, J. J. Lopez-Ibor, Jr., & J. R. Geddes (Eds.), *New Oxford textbook of psychiatry* (2nd ed., Vol. 2, pp. 1793–1798). Oxford, UK: Oxford University Press.

Santry, H. P., Gillen, D. L., & Lauderdale, D. S. (2005). Trends in bariatric surgical procedures. *JAMA: Journal of the American Medical Association, 294*, 1909–1917.

Santucci, L. C., Ehrenreich, J. T., Trosper, S. E., Bennett, S. M., & Pincus, D. B. (2009). Development and preliminary evaluation of a one-week summer treatment program for separation anxiety disorder. *Cognitive and Behavioral Practice, 16*, 317–331. doi: 10.1016/j.cbpra.2008.12.005

Sapolsky, R. (2004). Is impaired neurogenesis relevant to the affective symptoms of depression? *Biological Psychiatry, 56*, 137–139.

Sapolsky, R. M. (1990). Stress in the wild. *Scientific American, 262*, 116–123.

Sapolsky, R. M. (2000). Genetic hyping. *The Sciences, 40*(2), 12–15.

Sapolsky, R. M. (2002). *A primate's memoir.* New York, NY: Simon & Schuster.

Sapolsky, R. M. (2007). Stress, stress-related disease, and emotional regulation. In J. J. Gross (Ed.), *Handbook of emotion regulation* (pp. 606–615). New York, NY: Guilford.

Sapolsky, R. M., & Meaney, M. J. (1986). Maturation of the adrenal stress response: Neuroendocrine control mechanisms and the stress hyporesponsive period. *Brain Research Review, 11*, 65–76.

Sapolsky, R. M., & Ray, J. C. (1989). Styles of dominance and their endocrine correlates among wild, live baboons. *American Journal of Primatology, 18*(1), 1–13.

Sarbin, T., & Mancuso, J. (1980). *Schizophrenia: Medical diagnosis or moral verdict?* Elmsford, NY: Pergamon Press.

Sareen, J., Jacobi, F., Cox, B. J., Belik, S., Clara, I., & Stein, B. M. (2006). Disability and poor quality of life associated with comorbid anxiety disorders and physical conditions. *Archives of Internal Medicine, 166*, 2109–2116.

Sari, Y., Johnson, V. R., & Weedman, J. M. (2011). Role of the serotonergic system in alcohol dependence: from animal models to clinics. *Progress in Molecular Biology and Translational Science, 98*, 401–443.

Sarkar, A. & Adshead, G., Eds. (2012). *Clinical Topics in Personality Disorder.* London: RJPsych Publications.

Sarrel, P. M., & Masters, W. H. (1982). Sexual molestation of men by women. *Archives of Sexual Behavior, 11*, 117–131.

Sarwer, D. B., Foster, G. D., & Wadden, T. A. (2004). Treatment of obesity I: Adult obesity. In J. K. Thompson (ed.), *Handbook of eating disorders and obesity* (pp. 421–442). New York, NY: Wiley.

Saudino, J. J., Pedersen, N. L., Lichenstein, P., McClearn, G. E., & Plomin, R. (1997). Can personality explain genetic influence on life events? *Journal of Personality & Social Psychology, 72*(1), 196–206.

Saudino, K. J., & Plomin, R. (1996). Personality and behavioral genetics: Where have we been and where are we going? *Journal of Research in Personality, 30*, 335–347.

Saudino, K. J., Plomin, R., & DeFries, J. C. (1996). Tester-rated temperament at 14, 20, and 24 months: Environmental change and genetic continuity. *British Journal of Developmental Psychology, 14,* 129–144.

Savard, J., Savard, M.-H., & Morin, C. M. (2011). Insomnia. In M. M. Antony & D. H. Barlow (Eds.), *Handbook of assessment and treatment planning for psychological disorders* (2nd ed. (pp. 633–670). New York, NY: Guilford.

Savin-Williams, R. (2006). Who's gay? Does it matter? *Current Directions in Psychological Science, 15,* 40–44.

Saxe, G. N., Stoddard, F., Hall, E., Chawla, N., Lopez, C., Sheridan, R., & Yehuda, R. (2005). Pathways to PTSD: Part I. Children with burns. *American Journal of Psychiatry, 162,* 1299–1304.

Saxe, G. N., van der Kolk, B. A., Berkowitz, R., Chinman, G., Hall, K., Leiberg, G., & Schwartz, J. (1993). Dissociative disorders in psychiatric inpatients. *American Journal of Psychiatry, 150,* 1037–1042.

Saxena, S., & Prasad, K. (1989). DSM-III subclassifications of dissociative disorders applied to psychiatric outpatients in India. *American Journal of Psychiatry, 146,* 261–262.

Saxena, S., Winograd, A., Dunkin, J. J., Maidment, K., Rosen, R., Vapnik, T., & Bystritsky, A. (2001). A retrospective review of clinical characteristics and treatment response in body dysmorphic disorder versus Obsessive-compulsive disorder. *Journal of Clinical Psychiatry, 62,* 67–72.

Scanlon, D. (2013). Specific learning disability and its newest definition: Which is comprehensive? and which is insufficient? *Journal of Learning Disabilities, 46*(1), 26–33. doi: 10.1177/0022219412464342

Scarmeas, N., Albert, S. M., Manly, J. J., & Stern, Y. (2006). Education and rates of cognitive decline in incident Alzheimer's disease. *Journal of Neurology, Neurosurgery, and Psychiatry, 77*(3), 308–316.

Schacter, D. L., Chiu, P., & Ochsner, K. N. (1993). Implicit memory: A selective review. *Annual Review of Neuroscience, 16,* 159–182.

Schaffer, A., Isometsä, E. T., Tondo, L. H., Moreno, D., Turecki, G., Reis, C., . . . Yatham, L. N. (2015). International Society for Bipolar Disorders Task Force on Suicide: Meta-analyses and meta-regression of correlates of suicide attempts and suicide deaths in bipolar disorder. *Bipolar Disorders, 17,* 1–16.

Scharfstein, L. A., Beidel, D., Finnell, L. R., Distler, A., & Carter, N. T. (2011). Do pharmacological and behavioral interventions differentially affect treatment outcome for children with social phobia? *Behavior Modification, 35*(5), 451–467. Doi: 10.1177/0145445511408590

Schatzberg, A. (2000). New indications for anti-depressants. *Journal of Clinical Psychiatry, 61*(Suppl. 11), 9–17.

Schatzberg, A., Rush, J., Arnow, B., Banks, P., Blalock, J., Borian, F., . . . Keller, M. B. (2005). Chronic depression: Medication (Nefazodone) or psychotherapy (CBASP) is effective when the other is not. *Archives of General Psychiatry, 62,* 513–520.

Scheerenberger, R. C. (1983). *A history of mental retardation.* Baltimore, MD: Paul H. Brookes.

Scheidt, P. C., Harel, Y., Trumble, A. C., Jones, D. H., Overpeck, M. D., & Bijur, P. E. (1995). The epidemiology of nonfatal injuries among U.S. children and youth. *American Journal of Public Health, 85,* 932–938.

Scheidt, P. C., Overpeck, M. D., Trifiletti, L. B., & Cheng, T. (2000). Child and adolescent injury research in 1998: A summary of abstracts submitted to the Ambulatory Pediatrics Association and the American Public Health Association. *Archives of Pediatrics and Adolescent Medicine, 154,* 442–445.

Scheier, M. F., Matthews, K. A., Owens, J. F., Magovern, G. J., Sr., Lefebvre, R. C., Abbott, R. A., & Carver, C. S. (1989). Dispositional optimism and recovery from coronary artery bypass surgery: The beneficial effects on physical and psychological well-being. *Journal of Personality and Social Psychology, 57*(6), 1024–1040.

Schenck, C. H., Arnulf, I., & Mahowald, M. W. (2007). Sleep and sex: What can go wrong? A review of the literature on sleep related disorders and abnormal sexual behaviors and experiences. *Sleep, 30*(6), 683.

Schiavi, R. C. (1990). Chronic alcoholism and male sexual dysfunction. *Journal of Sex and Marital Therapy, 16,* 23–33.

Schiavi, R. C., White, D., Mandeli, J., & Levine, A. C. (1997). Effect of testosterone administration on sexual behavior and mood in men with erectile dysfunction. *Archives of Sexual Behavior, 26,* 231–241.

Schietecatte, I., Roeyers, H., & Warreyn, P. (2012). Exploring the nature of joint attention impairments in young children with autism spectrum disorder: Associated social and cognitive skills. *Journal of Autism and Developmental Disorders, 42*(1), 1–12. doi: 10.1007/s10803-011-1209-x

Schiffer, B., Peschel, T., Paul, T., Gizewski, E., Forsting, M., Leygraf, N., & Krueger, T. H. C. (2007). Structural brain abnormalities in the frontostriatal system and cerebellum in pedophilia. *Journal of Psychiatric Research, 41,* 753–762.

Schiffman, J., Walker, E., Ekstrom, M., Schulsinger, F., Sorensen, H., & Mednick, S. (2004). Childhood videotaped social and neuromotor precursors of schizophrenia: A prospective investigation. *American Journal of Psychiatry, 161*(11), 2021–2027.

Schildkraut, J. J. (1965). The catecholamine hypothesis of affective disorders: A review of supporting evidence. *American Journal of Psychiatry, 122,* 509–522.

Schiller, C., & Allen, P. J. (2005). Follow-up of infants prenatally exposed to cocaine. *Pediatric Nursing, 31,* 427–436.

Schlosser, R. W., & Koul, R. K. (2015). Speech output technologies in interventions for individuals with autism spectrum disorders: A scoping review. *Augmentative and Alternative Communication, 31*(4), 285–309.

Schmaling, K. B., Fiedelak, J. I., Katon, W. J., Bader, J. O., & Buchwald, D. S. (2003). Prospective study of the prognosis of unexplained chronic fatigue in a clinic-based cohort. *Psychosomatic Medicine, 65,* 1047–1054.

Schmidt, U., Lee, S., Beecham, J., Perkins, S., Treasure, J., Yi, I., & Eisler, I. (2007). A randomized controlled trial of family therapy and cognitive behavior therapy guided self-care for adolescents with bulimia nervosa and related disorders. *American Journal of Psychiatry, 164*(4), 591–598.

Schneck, C., Miklowitz, D., Calabrese, J., Allen, M., Thomas, M., Wisniewski, S., & Sachs, G. S. (2004). Phenomenology of rapid-cycling bipolar disorder: Data from the first 500 participants in the systematic treatment enhancement program. *American Journal of Psychiatry, 161,* 1902–1908.

Schneck, C. D., Miklowitz, D. J., Miyahara, S., Araga, M., Wisniewski, S., Gyulai, L., & Sachs, G. S. (2008). The prospective course of rapid-cycling bipolar disorder: Findings from the STEP-BD. *American Journal of Psychiatry, 165*(3), 370–377; quiz 410.

Schneider, S., Blatter-Meunier, J., Herren, C., In-Albon, T., Adornetto, C., Meyer, A., & Lavallee, K. L. (2013). The efficacy of a family-based cognitive-behavioral treatment for separation anxiety disorder in children aged 8–13: A randomized comparison with a general anxiety program. *Journal of Consulting and Clinical Psychology, 81,* 932.

Schneiderman, N. (2004). Psychosocial, behavioral, and biological aspects of chronic diseases. *Current Directions in Psychological Science, 13,* 247–251.

Schneier, F. R., Neria, Y., Pavlicova, M., Hembree, E., Suh, E. J., Amsel, L., & Marshall, R. D. (2012). Combined prolonged exposure therapy and paroxetine for PTSD related to the World Trade Center attack: A randomized controlled trial. *American Journal of Psychiatry, 169,* 80–88. doi: 10.1176/appi.ajp.2011.11020321

Schnell, K., & Herpertz, S. C. (2007). Effects of dialectic-behavioral-therapy on the neural correlates of affective hyperarousal in border-line personality disorder. *Journal of Psychiatric Research, 41,* 837–847.

Schoenbach, V. J., Kaplan, B. H., Fredman, L., & Kleinbaum, D. G. (1986). Social ties and mortality in Evans County, Georgia. *American Journal of Epidemiology, 123,* 577.

Schoenberg, M. R., Marsh, P. J., & Benbadis, S. R. (2012). Where are somatoform disorders going? An update on the DSM-V. *Expert Review of Neurotherapeutics, 12,* 1371–1374. doi: 10.1586/ern.12.136

Schoeneman, T. J. (1977). The role of mental illness in the European witchhunts of the sixteenth and seventeenth centuries: An assessment. *Journal of the History of the Behavioral Sciences, 13,* 337–351.

Schoenmakers, B., Buntinx, F., & DeLepeleire, J. (2010). Supporting the dementia family care-giver: The effect of home care intervention on general well-being. *Aging & Mental Health, 14*(1), 44–56.

Schomerus, G., Schwahn, C., Holzinger, A., Corrigan, P. W., Grabe, H. J., Carta, M. G., & Angermeyer, M. C. (2012). Evolution of public attitudes about mental illness: A systematic review and meta-analysis. *Acta Psychiatrica Scandinavica, 125*(6), 440–452.

Schredl, M. (2010). Nightmare frequency and nightmare topics in a representative German sample. *European Archives of*

Psychiatry and Clinical Neuroscience, 260(8), 565–570.

Schreiner-Engel, P., & Schiavi, R. C. (1986). Lifetime psychopathology in individuals with low sexual desire. *Journal of Nervous and Mental Disease, 174,* 646–651.

Schuck, P. F., Malgarin, F., Cararo, J. H., Cardoso, F., Streck, E. L., & Ferreira, G. C. (2015). Phenylketonuria pathophysiology: On the role of metabolic alterations. *Aging and disease, 6*(5), 390–399.

Schuckit, M. A. (1994). Low level of response to alcohol as a predictor of future alcoholism. *American Journal of Psychiatry, 151,* 184–189.

Schuckit, M. A. (1998). Biological, psychological and environmental predictors of alcoholism risk: A longitudinal study. *Journal of Studies on Alcohol, 59,* 485–494.

Schuckit, M. A. (2009b). Alcohol-use disorders. *The Lancet, 373*(9662), 492–501.

Schuckit, M. A. (2012). Editor's corner: Editorial in reply to the comments of Griffith Edwards. *Journal of Studies on Alcohol and Drugs, 73*(4), 521.

Schuckit, M. A. (2014a). A brief history of research on the genetics of alcohol and other drug use disorders. *Journal of Studies on Alcohol and Drugs: Supplement, 75*(Suppl. 17), 59–67.

Schuckit, M. A. (2014b). Recognition and management of withdrawal delirium (delirium tremens). *New England Journal of Medicine, 371*(22), 2109–2113.

Schuckit, M. A., Smith, T. L., Anthenelli, R., & Irwin, M. (1993). Clinical course of alcoholism in 636 male inpatients. *American Journal of Psychiatry, 150,* 786–792.

Schulberg, H. C., Block, M. R., Madonia, M. J., Scott, C. P., Rodriguez, E., Imber, S. D., & Coulehan, J. L. (1996). Treating major depression in primary care practice: Eight-month clinical outcomes. *Archives of General Psychiatry, 53,* 913–919.

Schulz, R., Drayer, R. A., & Rollman, B. L. (2002). Depression as a risk factor for non-suicide mortality in the elderly. *Biological Psychiatry, 52,* 205–225.

Schulze, L., Schmahl, C., & Niedtfeld, I. (2016). Neural correlates of disturbed emotion processing in borderline personality disorder: a multimodal meta-analysis. *Biological psychiatry, 79*(2), 97–106.

Schumann, C. M., & Amaral, D. G. (2006). Stereological analysis of amygdala neuron number in autism. *Journal of Neuroscience, 26,* 7674–7679.

Schurger, A., Pereira, F., Treisman, A., & Cohen, J. D. (2010). Reproducibility distinguishes conscious from nonconscious neural representations. *Science, 327,* 97–99.

Schutter, D. J. (2009). Antidepressant efficacy of high-frequency transcranial magnetic stimulation over the left dorsolateral prefrontal cortex in double-blind sham-controlled designs: A meta-analysis. *Psychological Medicine, 39*(1), 65–75.

Schwalberg, M. D., Barlow, D. H., Alger, S. A., & Howard, L. J. (1992). Comparison of bulimics, obese binge eaters, social phobics, and individuals with panic disorder or comorbidity across DSM-III-R anxiety. *Journal of Abnormal Psychology, 101,* 675–681.

Schwartz, A. J. (2011). Rate, relative risk, and method of suicide by students at 4-year colleges and universities in the United States, 2004–2005 through 2008–2009. *Suicide and Life-Threatening Behavior, 41*(4), 353–371.

Schwartz, B. I., Mansbach, J. M., Marion, J. G., Katzman, D. K., & Forman, S. (2008). Variations in admission practices for adolescents with anorexia nervosa: North American sample. *Journal of Adolescent Health, 43*(5), 425–431.

Schwartz, I. M. (1993). Affective reactions of American and Swedish women to the first premarital coitus: A cross-cultural comparison. *Journal of Sex Research, 30*(1), 18–26.

Schwartz, M. B., & Brownell, K. D. (2007). Actions necessary to prevent childhood obesity: Creating the climate for change. *Journal of Law, Medicine, & Ethics, 35,* 78–89.

Schwartz, M. S., & Andrasik, F. (Eds.) (2003). *Biofeedback: A practitioner's guide* (3rd ed.). New York, NY: Guilford.

Schwartz, P. J., Brown, C., Wehr, T. A., & Rosenthal, N. E. (1996). Winter seasonal affective disorder: A follow-up study of the first 59 patients of the National Institute of Mental Health seasonal studies program. *American Journal of Psychiatry, 153,* 1028–1036.

Schwartz, R., & Feisthamel, K. (2009). Disproportionate diagnosis of mental disorders among African American versus European American clients: Implications for counseling theory, research, and practice. *Journal of Counseling & Development, 87*(3), 295–301.

Schwartz, R. P., Brooner, R. K., Montoya, I. D., Currens, M., & Hayes, M. (2010). A 12-year follow-up of a methadone medical maintenance program. *The American Journal on Addictions, 8*(4), 293–299.

Schwartz, R. P., Jaffe, J. H., O'Grady, K. E., Das, B., Highfield, D. A., & Wilson, M. E. (2009). Scaling-up interim methadone maintenance: Treatment for 1,000 heroin-addicted individuals. *Journal of Substance Abuse Treatment, 37*(4), 362–367. doi: 10.1016/j.jsat.2009.04.002

Schwarzkopf, D. S., & Rees, G. (2010). Brain activity to rely on? *Science, 327,* 43–44.

Scoriels, L., Jones, P. B., & Sahakian, B. J. (2013). Modafinil effects on cognition and emotion in schizophrenia and its neurochemical modulation in the brain. *Neuropharmacology, 64,* 168–184.

Scott, C. L., Hilty, D. M., & Brook, M. (2003). Impulse-control disorders not elsewhere classified. In R. E. Hales & S. C. Yudofsky (Eds.), *Textbook of clinical psychiatry* (4th ed., pp. 781–802). Washington, DC: American Psychiatric Publishing.

Scott, C. L., Quanbeck, C. D., & Resnick, P. J. (2008). Assessment of dangerousness. In R. E. Hales, S. C. Yudofsky, & G. O. Gabbard (Eds.), *The American Psychiatric Publishing textbook of psychiatry* (5th ed., pp. 1655–1672). Arlington, VA: American Psychiatric Publishing.

Scott, J. E., & Dixon, L. B. (1995). Psychological interventions for schizophrenia. *Schizophrenia Bulletin, 21,* 621–630.

Scott, K. M., Lim, C., Al-Hamzawi, A., Alonso, J., Bruffaerts, R., Caldas-de-Almeida, J. M., . . . Kessler R.C. (in press). Association of mental disorders with subsequent chronic physical conditions: World mental health surveys from 17 countries. *JAMA Psychiatry.* doi: 10.1001/jamapsychiatry.2015.2688

Scott, S., Briskman, J., & O'Connor, T. G. (2014). Early prevention of antisocial personality: long-term follow-up of two randomized controlled trials comparing indicated and selective approaches. *American Journal of Psychiatry, 171*(6), 649–657.

Sedlak, T. W., & Kaplin, A. I. (2009). Novel neurotransmitters. In B. J. Sadock, V. A. Sadock, & P. Ruiz (Eds.), *Kaplan & Sadock's comprehensive textbook of psychiatry* (9th ed., Vol. I, pp. 102–118). Philadelphia, PA: Lippincott Williams & Wilkins.

Seedat, S., Scott, K. M., Angermeyer, M. C., Berglund, P., Bromet, E. J., Brugha, T. S., & Kessler, R. C. (2009). Cross-national associations between gender and mental disorders in the WHO World Mental Health Surveys. *Archives of General Psychiatry, 66*(7), 785.

Seeman, P., Lee, T., Chau Wong, M., & Wong, K. (1976). Antipsychotic drug doses and neuroleptic/dopamine receptors. *Nature, 261,* 717–719.

Segal, N. (2006). Two monozygotic twin pairs discordant for female to male transsexualism. *Archives of Sexual Behavior, 35,* 347–358.

Segal, Z. V., Williams, J. M. G., Teasdale, J. D. (2002). *Mindfulness-based cognitive therapy for depression: A new approach to preventing relapse.* New York, NY: Guilford.

Segal, Z. V., Bieling, P., Young, T., MacQueen, G., Cooke, R., Martin, L., & & Levitan, R. D. (2010). Antidepressant monotherapy vs sequential pharmacotherapy and mindfulness-based cognitive therapy, or placebo, for relapse prophylaxis in recurrent depression. *Archives of General Psychiatry, 67*(12), 1256.

Segerstrom, S. C., & Sephton, S. E. (2010). Optimistic expectancies and cell-mediated immunity: The role of positive affect. *Psychological Science, 21,* 448–455.

Seglem, K. B., Waaktaar, T., Ask, H., & Torgersen, S. (2015). Genetic and environmental influences on adolescents' smoking involvement: a multi-informant twin study. *Behavior Genetics, 45*(2), 171–180.

Segraves, R., & Althof, S. (1998). Psychotherapy and pharmacotherapy of sexual dysfunctions. In P. E. Nathan & J. M. Gorman (Eds.), *A guide to treatments that work* (pp. 447–471). New York, NY: Oxford University Press.

Segraves, R., & Woodard, T. (2006). Female hypoactive sexual desire disorder: History and current status. *Journal of Sexual Medicine, 3,* 408–418.

Seib, D. R., & Martin-Villalba, A. (2015). Neurogenesis in the normal ageing hippocampus: A mini-review. *Gerontology, 61*(4), 327–335.

Seitz, D. P., Adunuri, N., Gill, S. S., & Rochon, P. A. (2011). Prevalence of dementia and cognitive impairment among older adults with hip fractures. *Journal of the American Medical Directors Association, 12*(8), 556–564.

Seligman, M. E. P. (1971). Phobias and preparedness. *Behavior Therapy, 2,* 307–320.

Seligman, M. E. P. (1975). *Helplessness: On depression, development and death.* San Francisco, CA: W. H. Freeman.

Seligman, M. E. P. (1998). *Learned optimism* (2nd ed.). New York, NY: Simon & Schuster.

Seligman, M. E. P. (2002). *Authentic happiness: Using the new positive psychology to realize your potential for lasting fulfillment.* New York, NY: Free Press/Simon & Schuster.

Seligman, M. E. P., Schulman, P., DeRubeis, R. J., & Hollon, S. D. (1999). The prevention of depression and anxiety. *Prevention and Treatment, 2,* 8.

Sellbom, M., Toomey, J. A., Wygant, D. B., Kucharski, L. T., & Duncan, S. (2010). Utility of the MMPI–2–RF (restructured form) validity scales in detecting malingering in a criminal forensic setting: A known-groups design. *Psychological Assessment, 22*(1), 22–31.

Selten, J. P., Frissen, A., Lensvelt-Mulders, G., & Morgan, V. A. (2009). Schizophrenia and 1957 pandemic of influenza: meta-analysis. *Schizophrenia Bulletin,* sbp147.

Selye, H. (1936). A syndrome produced by diverse noxious agents. *Nature, 138,* 32.

Selye, H. (1950). *The physiology and pathology of exposure to stress.* Montreal, Canada: Acta.

Semans, J. H. (1956). Premature ejaculation: A new approach. *Southern Medical Journal, 49,* 353–358.

Semple, R. J., & Burke, C.A. (2012). Mindfulness based treatment for children and adolescents. In P. C. Kendall (Ed.), *Child and adolescent therapy: Cognitive-behavioral procedures* (4th ed., pp. 411–426). New York, NY: Guilford.

Sendt, K. V., Tracy, D. K., & Bhattacharyya, S. (2015). A systematic review of factors influencing adherence to antipsychotic medication in schizophrenia-spectrum disorders. *Psychiatry Research, 225*(1), 14–30.

Serefoglu, E. C. & Saitz, T. R. (2012). New insights on premature ejaculation: a review of definition, classification, prevalence and treatment. *Asian J Androl, 14*(6), 822–829.

Seshadri, S., Fitzpatrick, A. L., Ikram, M. A., DeStefano, A. L., Gudnason, V., Boada, M., & Breteler, M. M. (2010). Genome-wide analysis of genetic loci associated with Alzheimer disease. *JAMA: Journal of the American Medical Association, 303*(18), 1832–1840.

Seto, M., Cantor, J., & Blanchard, R. (2006). Child pornography offenses are a valid diagnostic indicator of pedophilia. *Journal of Abnormal Psychology, 115,* 610–615.

Seto, M. C. (2009). Pedophilia. In S. Nolen-Hoeksema, T. D. Cannon, & T. Widiger, (Eds.), *Annual review of clinical psychology* (Vol. 5, pp. 391–408). Palo Alto, CA: Annual Reviews.

Seto, M. C. (2012). Is pedophilia a sexual orientation? *Archives of Sexual Behavior, 41*(1), 231–236.

Seto, M. C., Kingston, D. A., & Bourget, D. (2014). Assessment of the Paraphilias. *Psychiatric Clinics of North America, 37*(2), 149–161.

Seto, M. C., Lalumière, M. L., Harris, G. T., & Chivers, M. L. (2012). The sexual responses of sexual sadists. *Journal of abnormal psychology, 121,* 739–753.

Severino, S. K., & Moline, M. L. (1989). *Premenstrual syndrome: A clinician's guide.* New York, NY: Guilford.

Shaffer, D. R. (1993). *Developmental psychology: Childhood and adolescence* (3rd ed.). Pacific Grove, CA: Brooks/Cole.

Shafran, R., Cooper, Z., & Fairburn, C. G. (2002). Clinical perfectionism: A cognitive-behavioural analysis. *Behaviour Research Therapy, 40,* 773–791.

Shafran, R., Lee, M., Payne, E., & Fairburn, C. G. (2006). The impact of manipulating personal standards on eating attitudes and behaviour. *Behaviour Research and Therapy, 44,* 897–906.

Shalev, A. Y., Ankri, Y., Israeli-Shalev, Y., Peleg, T., Adessky, R., & Freedman, S. (2012). Prevention of posttraumatic stress disorder by early treatment: Results from the Jerusalem Trauma Outreach and Prevention study. *Archives of General Psychiatry, 69,* 166–176. doi: 10.1001/archgenpsychiatry.2011.127

Shamloul, R. & Ghanem, H. (2013). Erectile dysfunction. *The Lancet, 381*(9861), 153–165.

Shapiro, D. (1974). Operant-feedback control of human blood pressure: Some clinical issues. In P. A. Obrist, A. H. Black, J. Brener, & L. V. DiCara (Eds.), *Cardiovascular psychophysiology: Current issues in response mechanisms, biofeedback, and methodology.* Chicago, IL: Aldine.

Shapiro, J. R., Berkman, N. D., Brownley, K. A., Sedway, J. A., Lohr, K. N., & Bulik, C. M. (2007). Bulimia nervosa treatment: A systematic review of randomized controlled trials. *International Journal of Eating Disorders, 40*(4), 321–336.

Sharma, M. P., & Manjula, M. (2013). Behavioral and psychological management of somatic symptom disorder: An overview. *International Review of Psychiatry, 25,* 116–124.

Sharpe, M. (1992). Fatigue and chronic fatigue syndrome. *Current Opinion in Psychiatry, 5,* 207–212.

Sharpe, M. (1993). *Chronic fatigue syndrome* (pp. 298–317). Chichester, UK: Wiley.

Sharpe, M. (1997). Chronic fatigue. In D. M. Clark & C. G. Fairburn (Eds.), *Science and practice of cognitive behavior therapy* (pp. 381–414). Oxford, UK: Oxford University Press.

Sharpe, M., Clements, A., Hawton, K., Young, A., Sargent, P., & Cowen, P. (1996). Increased prolactin response to buspirone in chronic fatigue syndrome. *Journal of Affective Disorders, 41,* 71–76.

Sharpless, B. A. & Barber, J. P. (2011). Lifetime prevalence rates of sleep paralysis: A systematic review. *Sleep Medicine Reviews, 15,* 311–315.

Sharpless, B., & Doghramji, K. (2015). *Sleep Paralysis: Historical, Psychological, and Medical Perspectives.* Oxford University Press.

Shatkin, J. P., & Ivanenko, A. (2009). Pediatric sleep disorders. In B. J. Sadock, V. A. Sadock, & P. Ruiz (Eds.), *Kaplan & Sadock's comprehensive textbook of psychiatry* (9th ed., Vol. I, pp. 3903–3908). Philadelphia, PA: Lippincott Williams & Wilkins.

Shaw, D. S., Dishion, T. J., Supplee, L., Gardner, F., & Arnds, K. (2006). Randomized trial of a family-centered approach to the prevention of early conduct problems: 2-year effects of the family check-up in early childhood. *Journal of Consulting and Clinical Psychology, 74,* 1–9.

Shaw, J., & Porter, S. (2015). Constructing rich false memories of committing crime. *Psychological Science, 26,* 291–301.

Shear, K., Jin, R., Ruscio, A. M., Walters, E. E., & Kessler, R. C. (2006). Prevalence and correlates of estimated DSM-IV child and adult separation anxiety disorder in the National Comorbidity Survey Replication. *American Journal of Psychiatry, 163*(6), 1074–1083. doi: 10.1176/appi.ajp.163.6.107

Shear, M. K. (2012). Getting straight about grief. *Depression and Anxiety, 29,* 461–464.

Shear, M. K., Brown, T. A., Barlow, D. H., Money, R., Sholomskas, D. E., Woods, S. W., & Papp, L. A. (1997). Multicenter collaborative panic disorder severity scale. *American Journal of Psychiatry, 154,* 1571–1575.

Shear, M. K., Simon, N., Wall, M., Zisook, S., Neimeyer, R., Duan, N., & Keshaviah, A. (2011). Complicated grief and related bereavement issues for DSM-5. *Depression and Anxiety, 28,* 103–117.

Shear, M. K., Wang, Y., Skritskaya, N., Duan, N., Mauro, C., & Ghesquiere, A. (2014). Treatment of complicated grief in elderly persons: A randomized clinical trial. *JAMA Psychiatry, 71,* 1287–1295.

Sheets, E. S., & Craighead, W. E. (2014). Comparing chronic interpersonal and non-interpersonal stress domains as predictors of depression recurrence in emerging adults. *Behaviour Research and Therapy, 63,* 36–42.

Sheikh, J. I. (1992). Anxiety and its disorders in old age. In J. E. Birren, K. Sloan, & G. D. Cohen (Eds.), *Handbook of mental health and aging* (pp. 410–432). New York, NY: Academic Press.

Shen, B., Avivi, Y. E., Todaro, J. F., Spiro, A., III., Laurenceau, J., Ward, K. D., & Niaura, R. (2008). Anxiety characteristics independently and prospectively predict myocardial infarction in men: The unique contribution of anxiety among psychologic factors. *Journal of the American College of Cardiology, 51,* 113–119.

Shenton, M. E., & Kubicki, M. (2009). Structural brain imaging in schizophrenia. In B. J. Sadock, V. A. Sadock, & P. Ruiz (Eds.), *Kaplan & Sadock's comprehensive textbook of psychiatry* (9th ed., Vol. I, pp. 1494–1507). Philadelphia, PA: Lippincott Williams & Wilkins.

Sheperis, C. J., Lionetti, T. M., & Snook, J. (2015). Substance-related disorders. In B. Flamez & C. J. Sheperis (Eds), *Diagnosing and treating children and adolescents: A guide for mental health professionals* (pp. 413–440). Hoboken, NJ: Wiley & Sons.

Sheppes, G., Luria, R., Fukuda, K., & Gross, J. J. (2013). There's more to anxiety than meets the eye: Isolating threat-related attentional engagement and disengagement biases. *Emotion, 13,* 520–528.

Sher, K. J., Martinez, J. A., & Littlefield, A. K. (2011). Alcohol use and alcohol use disorders. In D. H. Barlow (Ed.), *Oxford handbook of clinical psychology.* New York, NY: Oxford University.

Sherbourne, C. D., Hays, R. D., & Wells, K. B. (1995). Personal and psychosocial risk factors for physical and mental health outcomes and course of depression among depressed patients. *Journal of Consulting and Clinical Psychology, 63,* 345–355.

Shin, L. M., & Liberzon, I. (2010). The neurocircuitry of fear, stress, and anxiety disorders. *Neuropsychopharmacology, 35*(1), 169–191.

Shin, L. M., Lasko, N. B., Macklin, M. L., Karpf, R. D., Milad, M. R., Orr, S. P., & Pitman, R. K. (2009). Resting metabolic activity in the cingulate cortex and vulnerability to posttraumatic stress disorder. *Archives of General Psychiatry, 66*(10), 1099–1107. doi: 10.1001/archgenpsychiatry.2009.138

Shin, L. M., Shin, P. S., Heckers, S., Krangel, T. S., Macklin, M. L., Orr, S. P., & Rauch, S. L. (2004). Hippocampal function in post-traumatic stress disorder. *Hippocampus, 14,* 292–300.

Shingleton, R. M., Thompson-Brenner, H., Thompson, D. R., Pratt, E. M., & Franko, D. L. (2015). Gender differences in clinical trials of binge eating disorder: An analysis of aggregated data. *Journal of Consulting and Clinical Psychology, 83*(2), 382–386.

Shneidman, E. S. (1989). Approaches and commonalities of suicide. In R. F. W. Diekstra, R. Mariss, S. Platt, A. Schmidtke, & G. Sonneck (Eds.), *Suicide and its prevention: The role of attitude and imitation. Advances in Suicidology* (Vol. 1). Leiden, Netherlands: E. J. Brill.

Shneidman, E. S., Farberow, N. L., & Litman, R. E. (Eds.) (1970). *The psychology of suicide.* New York, NY: Science House.

Shulman, K. I., Cohen, C. A., Kirsh, F. C., Hull, I. M., & Champine, P. R. (2007). Assessment of testamentary capacity and vulnerability to undue influence. *American Journal of Psychiatry, 164*(5), 722–727.

Shumaker, S. A., Legault, C., Kuller, L., Rapp, S. R., Thal, L., Lane, D. S., Coker, L. H., & Women's Health Initiative Memory Study. (2004). Conjugated equine estrogens and incidence of probable dementia and mild cognitive impairment in postmenopausal women: Women's Health Initiative Memory Study. *JAMA: Journal of the American Medical Association, 291,* 3005–3007.

Sibrava, N. J., Beard, C., Bjornsson, A. S., Moitra, E., Weisberg, R. B., & Keller, M. B. (2013). Two-year course of generalized anxiety disorder, social anxiety disorder, and panic disorder in a longitudinal sample of African American adults. *Journal of Consulting and Clinical Psychology, 81,* 1052.

Sico, J.J., Amin, H., Sorokin, A., Volpe, D. C., Hamid, H., Machado, D., ... Brust, J. C. M. (2014). Neurologic disorders related to alcohol and other drug use. In R. K. Ries, D. A. Fiellin, S. C. Miller, & R. Saitz (Eds.), *The ASAM principles of addiction medicine,* (5th ed., pp. 1178–1194). New York, NY: Wolters Kluwer.

Siddiqui, F., & D'Ambrosio, C. (2012). Sleep disorders in older patients. In M. Pisani (Ed.), *Aging and lung disease* (pp. 173–188). New York: Humana Press.

Siegel, L. S., & Mazabell, S. (2013). Basic cognitive processes and reading disabilities. In H. L. Swanson, K. R. Harris, & S. Graham (Eds.), *Handbook of learning disabilities* (2nd ed., pp. 186–213). New York, NY: Guilford.

Sierra, M., & Berrios, G. E. (1998). Depersonalization: Neurobiological perspectives. *Society of Biological Psychiatry, 44,* 898–908.

Sierra, M., Senior, C., Dalton, J., McDonough, M., Bond, A., Phillips, M. L., & David, A. S. (2002). Autonomic response in depersonalization disorder. *Archives of General Psychiatry, 59,* 833–838.

Siever, L. J., & Davis, K. L. (2004). The pathophysiology of schizophrenia disorders: Perspectives from the spectrum. *American Journal of Psychiatry, 161,* 398–413.

Siever, L. J., Davis, K. L., & Gorman, L. K. (1991). Pathogenesis of mood disorders. In K. Davis, H. Klar, & J. T. Coyle (Eds.), *Foundations of psychiatry.* Philadelphia, PA: W. B. Saunders.

Siffre, M. (1964). *Beyond time* (H. Briffaul, Trans.). New York, NY: McGraw-Hill.

Sigafoos, J., Green, V. A., Schlosser, R., O'Reilly, M. F., Lancioni, G. E., Rispoli, M., Lang, R. (2009). Communication intervention in Rett syndrome: A systematic review. *Research in Autism Spectrum Disorders, 3*(2), 304–318. doi: 10.1016/j.rasd.2008.09.006

Sikorska, B., Knight, R., Ironside, J. W., & Liberski, P. P. (2012). Creutzfeldt-Jakob disease. In S.I. Ahmad (ed), *Neurodegenerative diseases* (pp. 76–90). New York, NY: Springer US.

Silberg, J. L., Maes, H., & Eaves, L. J. (2012). Unraveling the effect of genes and environment in the transmission of parental antisocial behavior to children's conduct disturbance, depression and hyperactivity. *Journal of Child Psychology and Psychiatry, 53*(6), 668–677.

Silk, K. R., & Feurino III, L. (2012). Psychopharmacology of personality disorders. In T. A. Widiger (Ed.), *The Oxford handbook of personality disorders* (pp. 713–726). New York, NY: Oxford University Press.

Silove, D. M., Marnane, C. L., Wagner, R., Manicavasagar, V. L., & Rees, S. (2010). The prevalence and correlates of adult separation anxiety disorder in an anxiety clinic. *BMC Psychiatry, 10,* 21.

Silver, E., Cirincione, C., & Steadman, H. J. (1994). Demythologizing inaccurate perceptions of the insanity defense. *Law and Human Behavior, 18,* 63–70.

Silverman, W. K., & La Greca, A. M. (2002). Children experiencing disasters: Definitions, reactions and predictors of outcomes. In A. N. La Greca, W. K. Silverman, & M. C. Roberts (Eds.), *Helping children cope with disasters and terrorism* (Vol. 1, pp. 11–33). Washington, DC: American Psychological Association.

Silverman, W. K., & Rabian, B. (1993). Simple phobias. *Child and Adolescent Psychiatric Clinics of North America, 2,* 603–622.

Silverstone, T. (1985). Dopamine in manic depressive illness: A pharmacological synthesis. *Journal of Affective Disorders, 8*(3), 225–231.

Simeon, D. (2009). Neurobiology of depersonalization disorder. In P. F. Dell & J. A. O'Neil (Eds.), *Dissociation and the dissociative disorders* (pp. 367–372). New York, NY: Routledge. Simeon, D., & Abugal, J. (2006).

Feeling unreal: Depersonalization disorder and the loss of the self. Oxford, UK: Oxford University Press.

Simeon, D., Guralnik, O., Hazlett, E. A., Spiegel-Cohen, J., Hollander, E., & Buchsbaum, M. S. (2000). Feeling unreal: A PET study of depersonalization disorder. *American Journal of Psychiatry, 157,* 1782–1788.

Simeon, D., Guralnik, O., Knutelska, M., Hollander, E., & Schmeidler, J. (2001). Hypothalamic–pituitary–adrenal axis dysregulation in depersonalization disorder. *Neuropsychopharmacology, 25,* 793–795.

Simeon, D., Guralnik, O., Schmeidler, J., & Knutelska, M. (2004). Fluoxetine therapy in depersonalization disorder: Randomised controlled trial. *British Journal of Psychiatry, 185,* 31–36.

Simeon, D., Knutelska, M., Nelson, D., & Guralnik, O. (2003). Feeling unreal: A depersonalization disorder update of 117 cases. *Journal of Clinical Psychiatry, 64,* 990–997.

Simmons, R., & Blyth, D. (1987). *Moving into adolescence: The impact of pubertal change and school context.* New York, NY: Aldine de Gruyter.

Simms, L. J., Prisciandaro, J. J., Krueger, R. F., & Goldberg, D. P. (2012). The structure of depression, anxiety, and somatic symptoms in primary care. *Psychological Medicine, 42,* 15–28.

Simon, G. (2006). How can we know whether anti-depressants increase suicide risk? *American Journal of Psychiatry, 163,* 1861–1863.

Simon, G. E., Gureje, O., & Fullerton, C. (2001). Course of hypochondriasis in an international primary care study. *General Hospital Psychiatry, 23,* 51–55.

Simon, G. E., von Koff, M., Saunders, K., Miglioretti, D. L., Crane, P. K., van Belle, G., & Kessler, R. C. (2006). Association between obesity and psychiatric disorders in the U.S. adult population. *Archives of General Psychiatry, 63,* 824–830.

Simon, N. M. (2012). Is complicated grief a post-loss stress disorder? *Depression and Anxiety, 29,* 541–544.

Simon, N. M. (2013). Treating complicated grief. *JAMA, 310,* 416–423.

Simon, R. I., & Shuman, D. W. (2008). Psychiatry and the law. In R. E. Hales, S. C. Yudofsky, & G. O. Gabbard (Eds.), *The American Psychiatric Publishing textbook of psychiatry* (5th ed., pp. 1555–1599). Arlington, VA: American Psychiatric Publishing.

Simon, R. I., & Shuman, D. W. (2009). Clinical-legal issues in psychiatry. In B. J. Sadock, V. A. Sadock, & P. Ruiz (Eds.), *Kaplan & Sadock's comprehensive textbook of psychiatry* (9th ed., Vol. II, pp. 4427–4439). Philadelphia, PA: Lippincott Williams & Wilkins.

Simon, R. I. & Shuman, D. W. (2014). Clinical issues in psychiatry and the law. In R. E. Hales, S. C. Yudofsky, & L. Weiss Roberts (Eds), *The American Psychiatric Publishing textbook of psychiatry* (6th ed., pp.175–204). Washington, DC: American Psychiatric Publishing, Inc.

Simon, W., & Gagnon, J. H. (1986). Sexual scripts: Permanence and change. *Archives of Sexual Behavior, 15*(2), 97–120.

Simoneau, T. L., Miklowitz, D. J., Richards, J. A., Saleem R., & George, E. L. (1999). Bipolar disorder and family communication: Effects of a psychoeducational treatment program. *Journal of Abnormal Psychology, 108*, 588–597.

Simonetti, J. A., Mackelprang, J. L., Rowhani-Rahbar, A., Zatzick, D., & Rivara, F. P. (2015). Psychiatric comorbidity, suicidality, and in-home firearm access among a nationally representative sample of adolescents. *JAMA Psychiatry, 72*, 152–159.

Simons, J. S., Dvorak, R. D., & Lau-Barraco, C. (2009). Behavioral inhibition and activation systems: Differences in substance use expectancy organization and activation in memory. *Psychology of Addictive Behaviors, 23*(2), 315–328. doi:10.1037/a0015834

Simpson, G. K., Tate, R. L., Whiting, D. L., & Cotter, R. E. (2011). Suicide prevention after traumatic brain injury: A randomized controlled trial of a program for the psychological treatment of hopelessness. *The Journal of Head Trauma Rehabilitation, 26*(4), 290–300.

Simpson, H. B., Foa, E. B., Liebowitz, M. R., Huppert, J. D., Cahill, S., Maher, M. J., . . . Campeas, R. (2013). Cognitive-behavioral therapy vs. resperidone for augmenting serotonin reuptake inhibitors in obsessive-compulsive disorder: A randomized clinical trial. *JAMA Psychiatry, 70*, 1190–1199.

Singer, J. (1999). "Why can't you be normal for once in your life?" From a "problem with no name" to the emergence of a new category of difference. In M. Corker & S. French (Eds.), *Disability discourse* (pp. 59–67). Buckingham, U.K.: Open University Press.

Singer, M., & Flannery, D. J. (2000). The relationship between children's threats of violence and violent behaviors. *Archives of Pediatrics and Adolescent Medicine, 154*, 785–790.

Singh, J. P., Grann, M., & Fazel, S. (2011). A comparative study of violence risk assessment tools: A systematic review and metaregression analysis of 68 studies involving 25,980 participants. *Clinical Psychology Review, 31*(3), 499–513.

Singh, S., Basu, D., Kohli, A., & Prabhakar, S. (2009). Auditory P300 event-related potentials and neurocognitive functions in opioid dependent men and their brothers. *American Journal on Addictions, 18*(3), 198–205.

Singh, S. P., Harley, K., & Suhail, K. (2013). Cultural specificity of emotional overinvolvement: A systematic review. *Schizophrenia Bulletin, 39*(2), 449–463. doi: 10.1093/schbul/sbr170

Sisask, M., & Värnik, A. (2012). Media roles in suicide prevention: A systematic review. *International Journal of Environmental Research and Public Health, 9*(1), 123–138.

Sit, D., Rothschild, A. J., & Wisner, K. L. (2006). A review of postpartum psychosis. *Journal of Womens Health, 15*(4), 352–368.

Sjöström, L., Peltonen, M., Jacobson, P., Sjöström, C. D., Karason, K., Wedel, H., . . . Carlsson, L. M. S. (2012). Bariatric surgery and long-term cardiovascular events. *JAMA: Journal of American Medical Association, 307*, 56–65.

Skeem, J., Kennealy, P., Monahan, J., Peterson, J., & Appelbaum, P. (2016). Psychosis uncommonly and inconsistently precedes violence among high-risk individuals. *Clinical Psychological Science, 4*(1), 40–49.

Skhiri, D., Annabi, S., Bi, S., & Allani, D. (1982). Enfants d'immigrés: Facteurs de liens ou de rupture? *Annales Medico-Psychologiques, 140*, 597–602.

Skidmore, R., Linsenmeier, J., & Bailey, J. (2006). Gender nonconformity and psychological distress in lesbians and gay men. *Archives of Sexual Behavior, 35*, 685–697.

Skinner, B. F. (1938). *The behavior of organisms: An experimental analysis.* Appleton-Century. Oxford: England.

Skinner, B. F. (1948). *Walden two.* New York, NY: Macmillan.

Skinner, B. F. (1971). *Beyond freedom and dignity.* New York, NY: Knopf.

Skodol, A. E. (2005). Manifestations, clinical diagnosis, and comorbidity. In J. M. Oldham, A. E. Skodol, & D. S. Bender (Eds.), *Textbook of personality disorders* (pp. 57–87). Washington, DC: American Psychiatric Publishing.

Skodol, A. E. (2012). Personality disorders in DSM-5. *Annual Review of Clinical Psychology, 8*, 317–344.

Skodol, A. E., Bender, D. S., Morey, L. C., Clark, L. A., Oldham, J. M., Alarcon, R. D., & Siever, L. J. (2011). Personality disorder types proposed for DSM-5. *Journal of Personality Disorders, 25*(2), 136–169.

Skodol, A. E., & Gunderson, J. G. (2008). Personality disorders. In R. E. Hales, S. C. Yudofsky, & G. O. Gabbard (Eds.), *The American Psychiatric Publishing textbook of psychiatry* (5th ed., pp. 821–860). Arlington, VA: American Psychiatric Publishing.

Skodol, A. E., Grilo, C. M., Keyes, K. M., Geier, T., Grant, B. F., & Hasin, D. S. (2011). Relationship of personality disorders to the course of major depressive disorder in a nationally representative sample. *American Journal of Psychiatry, 168*(3), 257–264.

Skuse, D. H. (2012). DSM-5's conceptualization of autistic disorders. *Journal of the American Academy of Child and Adolescent Psychiatry, 51*(4), 344–346. doi: 10.1016/j.jaac.2012.02.009

Slavich, G. M., & Irwin, M. R. (2014). From stress to inflammation and major depressive disorder: A social signal transduction theory of depression. *Psychological Bulletin, 140*, 774–815.

Sleet, D. A., Hammond, R., Jones, R., Thomas, N., & Whitt, B. (2003). Using psychology for injury and violence prevention in the community. In R. H. Rozensky, N. G. Johnson, C. D. Goodheart, & R. Hammond (Eds.), *Psychology builds a healthy world* (pp. 185–216). Washington, DC: American Psychological Association.

Slooter, A. J. C., & de Groot, J.-C. (2014). Neuroimaging of delirium. In R. A. J. O. Dierckx, A. Otte, E. F.J. de Vries, A. van Waarde (Eds), *PET and SPECT in psychiatry* (pp. 463–470). Berlin, Germany: Springer Berlin Heidelberg.

Slotema, C. W., Aleman, A., Daskalakis, Z. J., & Sommer, I. E. (2012). Meta-analysis of repetitive transcranial magnetic stimulation in the treatment of auditory verbal hallucinations: Update and effects after one month. *Schizophrenia Research, 142*(1–3), 40–45. doi: http://dx.doi.org/10.1016/j.schres.2012.08.025

Smeets, G., de Jong, P. J., & Mayer, B. (2000). If you suffer from a headache, then you have a brain tumour: Domain-specific reasoning "bias" and hypochondriasis. *Behaviour Research and Therapy, 38*, 763–776.

Smith, B. H., & Shapiro, C. J. (2015). Combined treatments for ADHD. In R. A. Barkley (Ed.), *Attention-deficit hyperactivity disorder: A handbook for diagnosis & treatment* (4th ed., pp. 686–704). New York, NY: The Guilford Press.

Smith, D. E., Marcus, M. D., & Kaye, W. (1992). Cognitive-behavioral treatment of obese binge eaters. *International Journal of Eating Disorders, 12*, 257–262.

Smith, Frederick H. (2008). *The archaeology of alcohol and drinking.* Gainesville, FL: University of Florida Press.

Smith, G. A., & Hall, J. A. (1982). Evaluating Michigan's guilty but mentally ill verdict: An empirical study. *Journal of Law Reform, 16*, 75–112.

Smith, G. P., & Gibbs, J. (2002). Peripheral physiological determinants for eating and body weight. In K. D. Brownell & C. G. Fairburn (Eds.), *Eating disorders and obesity: A comprehensive handbook* (2nd ed., pp. 8–12). New York, NY: Guilford.

Smith, G. T., & Oltmanns, T. F. (2009). Scientific advances in the diagnosis of psychopathology: Introduction to the special section. *Psychological Assessment, 21*(3), 241–242.

Smith, G. T., Simmons, J. R., Flory, K., Annus, A. M., & Hill, K. K. (2007). Thinness and eating expectancies predict subsequent binge-eating and purging behavior among adolescent girls. *Journal of Abnormal Psychology, 116*, 188–197.

Smith, T., Horwath, E., & Cournos, F. (2010). Scizophrenia and other psychotic disorders. In J. L. Cutler & E. R. Marcus (Eds.), *Psychiatry* (2nd ed., pp. 101–131). New York, NY: Oxford University Press.

Smith, T., & Iadarola, S. (2015). Evidence base update for autism spectrum disorder. *Journal of Clinical Child & Adolescent Psychology, 44*(6), 897–922. doi: 10.1080/15374416.2015.1077448

Smith, T. C., Ryan, M. A., Wingard, D. L., Slymen, D. J., Sallis, J. F., Kritz-Silverstein, D., & Millennium Cohort Study Team (2008). New onset and persistent symptoms of post-traumatic stress disorder self reported after deployment and combat exposures: Prospective population based US military cohort study. *BMJ: British Medical Journal, 336*(7640), 366–371. doi: 10.1136/bmj.39430.638241.AE

Smith, T. W. (1992). Hostility and health: Current status of a psychosomatic hypothesis. *Health Psychology, 11*(3), 139–150.

Smith, W., Noonan, C., & Buchwald, D. (2006). Mortality in a cohort of chronically fatigued patients. *Psychological Medicine, 36*, 1301–1306.

Smitherman, T. A., Burch, R., Sheikh, H., & Loder, E. (2013). The prevalence, impact, and treatment of migraine and severe headaches in the United States: A review of statistics from national surveillance studies. *Headache, 53*(3), 427–436.

Smolak, L., & Levine, M. P. (1996). Adolescent transitions and the development of eating problems. In L. Smolak, M. P. Levine, & R. Striegel-Moore (Eds.), *The developmental psychopathology of eating disorders: Implications for research, prevention, and treatment* (pp. 207–233). Mahwah, NJ: Erlbaum.

Smoller, J. W. (2013). Disorders and borders: Psychiatric genetics and nosology. American Journal of Medical Genetics, Part B: *Neuropsychiatric Genetics, 162*, 559–578.

Smoller, J. W., Block, S. R., & Young, M. M. (2009). Genetics of anxiety disorders: The complex road from DSM to DNA. *Depression and Anxiety, 26*(11), 965–975. doi: 10.1002/da.20623

Smoller, J. W., Yamaki, L. H., & Fagerness, J. A. (2005). The corticotropin-releasing hormone gene and behavioral inhibition in children at risk for panic disorder. *Biological Psychiatry, 57*, 1485–1492.

Snelling, J., Sahai, A., & Ellis, H. (2003). Attitudes of medical and dental students to dissection. *Clinical Anatomy, 16*, 165–172.

Snowdon, D. A., Kemper, S. J., Mortimer, J. A., Greiner, L. H., Wekstein, D. R., & Markesbery, W. R. (1996). Linguistic ability in early life and cognitive function and Alzheimer's disease in late life: Findings from the nun study. *JAMA: Journal of the American Medical Association, 275*(7), 528–532.

Snyder, J. S., Soumier, A., Brewer, M., Pickel, J., & Cameron, H. A. (2011). Adult hippocampal neurogenesis buffers stress responses and depressive behaviour. *Nature, 476*(7361), 458–U112.

Snyder, L. (2012). American College of Physicians ethics manual. *Annals of Internal Medicine, 156*(1_Part_2), 73–104. doi:10.7326/0003-4819-156-1-201201031-00001

Snyder, S. H. (1976). The dopamine hypothesis of schizophrenia: Focus on the dopamine receptor. *American Journal of Psychiatry, 133*, 197–202.

Snyder, S. H. (1981). Opiate and benzodiazepine receptors. *Psychosomatics, 22*(11), 986–989.

Snyder, S. H., Burt, D. R., & Creese, I. (1976). Dopamine receptor of mammalian brain: Direct demonstration of binding to agonist and antagonist states. *Neuroscience Symposia, 1*, 28–49.

Sobell, M. B., & Sobell, L. C. (1978). *Behavioral treatment of alcohol problems*. New York, NY: Plenum Press.

Sobell, M. B., & Sobell, L. C. (1993). *Problem drinkers: Guided self-change treatment*. New York, NY: Guilford.

Society for Research in Child Development. (2007). *Ethical standards for research with children*. Available from www.srcd.org/ethicalstandards.html.

Soeiro-de-Souza, M. G., Dias, V. V., Bio, D. S., Post, R. M., & Moreno, R. A. (2011). Creativity and executive function across manic, mixed and depressive episodes in bipolar I disorder. *Journal of Affective Disorders, 135*(1–3), 292–297.

Sohn, C., & Lam, R. (2005). Update on the biology of seasonal affective disorder. *CNS Spectrums, 10*, 635–646.

Sohn, M., & Bosinski, H. A. G. (2007). Gender identity disorders: Diagnostic and surgical aspects. *Journal of Sexual Medicine, 4*, 1193–1208.

Solai, L. K. K. (2009). Delirium. In B. J. Sadock, V. A. Sadock, & P. Ruiz (Eds.), *Kaplan & Sadock's comprehensive textbook of psychiatry* (9th ed., Vol. I, pp. 1153–1167). Philadelphia, PA: Lippincott Williams & Wilkins.

Soloff, P. H., Chiappetta, L., Mason, N. S., Becker, C., & Price, J. C. (2014). Effects of serotonin-2A receptor binding and gender on personality traits and suicidal behavior in borderline personality disorder. *Psychiatry Research: Neuroimaging, 222*(3), 140–148.

Soloff, P. H., Lynch, K. G., Kelley, T. M., Malone, K. M., & Mann, J. J. (2000). Characteristics of suicide attempts of patients with major depressive episode and border-line personality disorder: A comparative study. *American Journal of Psychiatry, 157*(4), 601–608.

Solomon, D. A., Leon, A. C., Coryell, W. H., Endicott, J., Li, C., Fiedorowicz, J. G., & Keller, M. B. (2010). Longitudinal course of bipolar I disorder: Duration of mood episodes. *Archives of General Psychiatry, 67*(4), 339–347.

Solomon, D. A., Leon, A. C., Endicott, J., Coryell, W. H., Mueller, T. I., Posternak, M. A., & Keller, M. B. (2003). Unipolar mania over the course of a 20-year follow-up study. *American Journal of Psychiatry, 160*, 2049–2051.

Solomon, R. L. (1980). The opponent-process theory of acquired motivation: The costs of pleasure and the benefits of pain. *American Psychologist, 35*, 691–712.

Solomon, R. L., & Corbit, J. D. (1974). An opponent process theory of motivation: I. Temporal dynamics of affect. *Psychological Review, 81*, 119–145.

Soreca, I., Frank, E., & Kupfer, D. J. (2009). The phenomenology of bipolar disorder: What drives the high rate of medical burden and determines long-term prognosis? *Depression and Anxiety, 26*(1), 73–82.

Sorkin, A., Weinshall, D., Modai, I., & Peled, A. (2006). Improving the accuracy of the diagnosis of schizophrenia by means of virtual reality. *American Journal of Psychiatry, 163*, 512–520.

Sosa-Ortiz, A. L., Acosta-Castillo, I., & Prince, M. J. (2012). Epidemiology of dementias and Alzheimer's disease. *Archives of Medical Research, 43*(8), 600–608.

Souery, D., Zaninotto, L., Calati, R., Linotte, S., Mendlewicz, J., Sentissi, O., & Serretti, A. (2012). Depression across mood disorders: Review and analysis in a clinical sample. *Comprehensive Psychiatry, 53*, 24–38.

South, S. C., Oltmanns, T. F., & Krueger, R. F. (2011). The spectrum of personality disorders. In D. H. Barlow (Ed.), *Oxford handbook of clinical psychology* (pp. 530–550). New York, NY: Oxford University.

Spangler, D. L., Simons, A. D., Monroe, S. M., & Thase, M. E. (1996). Gender differences in cognitive diathesis-stress domain match: Implications for differential pathways to depression. *Journal of Abnormal Psychology, 105*, 653–657.

Spangler, D. L., Simons, A. D., Monroe, S. M., & Thase, M. E. (1997). Comparison of cognitive models of depression: Relationships between cognitive constructs and cognitive diathesis-stress match. *Journal of Abnormal Psychology, 106*, 395–403.

Spanos, N. P. (1996). *Multiple identities and false memories: A sociocognitive prospective*. Washington, DC: American Psychological Association.

Spanos, N. P., Cross, P. A., Dickson, K., & DuBreuil, S. C. (1993). Close encounters: An examination of UFO experiences. *Journal of Abnormal Psychology, 102*, 624–632.

Spanos, N. P., Weeks, J. R., & Bertrand, L. D. (1985). Multiple personality: A social psychological perspective. *Journal of Abnormal Psychology, 92*, 362–376.

Speisman, R. B., Kumar, A., Rani, A., Foster, T. C., & Ormerod, B. K. (2013). Daily exercise improves memory, stimulates hippocampal neurogenesis and modulates immune and neuroimmune cytokines in aging rats. *Brain, Behavior and Immunity, 28*, 25–43. doi: 10.1016/j.bbi.2012.09.013.

Spencer, T. J., Biederman, J., & Mick, E. (2007). Attention-deficit/hyperactivity disorder: Diagnosis, lifespan, comorbidities, and neurobiology. *Ambulatory Pediatrics, 7*(1, Suppl. 1), 73–81.

Spiegel, D. (2010). Dissociation in DSM-5. *Journal of Trauma and Dissociation, 11*(3), 261–265.

Spiegel, D. (2013). Tranceformations: Hypnosis in brain and body. *Depression and Anxiety, 30*, 342–352.

Spiegel, D., Bloom, J. R., Kramer, H. C., & Gotheil, E. (1989). Effect of psychosocial treatment on survival of patients with metastatic breast cancer. *Lancet, 14*, 888–891.

Spiegel, D., Lewis-Fernandez, R., Lanius, R., Vermetten, E., Simeon, D., & Friedman, M. (2013). Dissociative disorders in DSM-5. *Annual Review of Clinical Psychology, 9*, 299–326.

Spiegel, D., Loewenstein, R. J., Lewis-Fernandez, R., Sar, V., Simeon, D., Vermetten, E., & Dell, P. F. (2011). Dissociative disorders in DSM-5. *Depression and Anxiety, 28*, 824–852. doi: 10.1002/da.20874

Spielberger, C. D., & Frank, R. G. (1992). Injury control: A promising field for psychologists. *American Psychologist, 47*(8), 1029–1030.

Spielman, A. J., & Glovinsky, P. (1991). The varied nature of insomnia. In P. J. Hauri (Ed.), *Case studies in insomnia* (pp. 1–15). New York, NY: Plenum Press.

Spinella, M. (2005). Mood in relation to sub-clinical symptoms. *International Journal of Neuroscience, 115*, 433–443.

Spinelli, M. G., & Endicott, J. (2003). Controlled clinical trial of interpersonal psychotherapy versus parenting education program for depressed pregnant women. *American Journal of Psychiatry, 160*, 555–562.

Spinelli, S., Chefer, S., Suomi, S. J., Higley, J. D., Barr, C. S., & Stein, E. (2009). Early-life stress induces long-term morphologic changes in primate brain. *Archives of General Psychiatry, 66*(6), 658–665.

Spira, A., Bajos, N., Bejin, A., Beltzer, N., Bozon, M., Ducot, M., & Touzard, H. (1992). AIDS and sexual behavior in France. *Nature, 360*, 407–409.

Spitzer, C., Spelsberg, B., Grabe, H. J., Mundt, B., & Freyberger, H. J. (1999). Dissociative experiences and psychopathology in conversion disorders. *Journal of Psychosomatic Research, 46*(3), 291–294.

Spitzer, R. L. (1999). Harmful dysfunction and the DSM definition of mental disorder. *Journal of Abnormal Psychology, 108,* 430–432.

Spitzer, R. L., Yanovski, S. Z., Wadden, T., Wing, R., Marcus, M., Stunkard, A., & Horne, R. L. (1993). Binge eating disorder: Its further validation in a multi-site study. *International Journal of Eating Disorders, 13,* 137–153.

Spoont, M. R. (1992). Modulatory role of serotonin in neural information processing: Implications for human psychopathology. *Psychological Bulletin, 112*(2), 330–350.

Sprague, J., Javdani, S., Sadeh, N., Newman, J. P., & Verona, E. (2012). Borderline personality disorder as a female phenotypic expression of psychopathy? *Personality Disorders: Theory, Research, and Treatment, 3*(2), 127.

Sprock, J. (2000). Gender-typed behavioral examples of histrionic personality disorder. *Journal of Psychopathology and Behavioral Assessment, 22,* 107–122.

Spurrell, E. B., Wilfley, D. E., Tanofsky, M. B., & Brownell, K. D. (1997). Age of onset for binge eating: Are there different pathways to binge eating? *International Journal of Eating Disorders, 21,* 55–65.

Srivastava, S., Childers, M. E., Baek, J. H., Strong, C. M., Hill, S. J., Warsett, K. S., & Ketter, T. A. (2010). Toward interaction of affective and cognitive contributors to creativity in bipolar disorders: A controlled study. *Journal of Affective Disorders, 125,* 27–34.

Staal, W. G., Pol, H. E. H., Schnack, H. G., Hoogendoorn, M. L. C., Jellema, K., & Kahn, R. S. (2000). Structural brain abnormalities in patients with schizophrenia and their healthy siblings. *American Journal of Psychiatry, 157,* 416–421.

Stahl, S. M. (2008). *Stahl's essential psychopharmacology* (3rd ed.). New York, NY: Cambridge University Press.

Stall, R., McKusick, L., Wiley, J., Coates, T. J., & Ostrow, D. G. (1986). Alcohol and drug use during sexual activity and compliance with safe sex guidelines for AIDS. *Health Education Quarterly, 13,* 359–371.

Stamm, J. M., Bourlas, A. P., Baugh, C. M., Fritts, N. G., Daneshvar, D. H., Martin, B. M., . . . Stern, R. A. (2015). Age of first exposure to football and later-life cognitive impairment in former NFL players. *Neurology, 84*(11), 1114–1120.

Stangier, U., Hilling, C., Heidenreich, T., Risch, A. K., Barocka, A., Schlösser, R., . . . Hautzinger, M. (2013). Maintenance Cognitive-Behavioral Therapy and Manualized Psychoeducation in the Treatment of Recurrent Depression: A Multicenter Prospective Randomized Controlled Trial. *American Journal of Psychiatry, 170,* 624–632.

Stangier, U., Schramm, E., Heidenreich, T., Berger, M., & Clark, D. M. (2011). Cognitive therapy vs. interpersonal therapy in social anxiety disorder: A randomized controlled trial. *Archives of General Psychiatry, 68,* 692–700. doi: 10.1001/archgenpsychiatry.2011.67

Stanley, M. A., Beck, J. G., Novy, D. M., Averill, P. M., Swann, A. C., Diefenbach, G. J., & Hopko, D. R. (2003). Cognitive-behavioral treatment of late-life generalized anxiety disorder. *Journal of Consulting and Clinical Psychology, 71*(2), 309–319.

Stanley, M. A., Wilson, N. L., Novy, D. M., Rhoades, H. M., Wagener, P. D., Greisinger, A. J., & Kunik, M. E. (2009). Cognitive behavior therapy for generalized anxiety disorder among older adults in primary care: A randomized clinical trial. *JAMA: Journal of the American Medical Association, 301*(14), 1460–1467. doi: 10.1001/jama.2009.458

Stappenbeck, C. A., Hellmuth, J. C., Simpson, T., & Jakupcak, M. (2014). The effects of alcohol problems, PTSD, and combat exposure on nonphysical and physical aggression among Iraq and Afghanistan war veterans. *Psychological Trauma: Theory, Research, Practice, and Policy, 6*(1), 65–72.

Starkman, M. N., Giordani, B., Gebarski, S. S., Berent, S., Schork, M. A., & Schteingart, D. E. (1999). Decrease in cortisol reverses human hippocampal atrophy following treatment of Cushing's disease. *Biological Psychiatry, 46,* 1595–1602.

State v. Campanaro, Nos. 632-79, 1309-79, 1317-79, 514-80, & 707-80 (S. Ct. N. J. Criminal Division, Union County 1980).

Stathopoulou, G., Powers, M. B., Berry, A. C., Smits, J. A. J., & Otto, M. W. (2006). Exercise interventions for mental health: A quantitative and qualitative review. *Clinical Psychology: Science and Practice, 13*(2), 179–193.

Steiger, A. (2008). Hormones and sleep. In S. R. Pandi-Perumal & J. Verster (Eds.), *Sleep disorders: Diagnosis and therapeutics* (pp. 457–466). Boca Raton, FL: Taylor & Francis.

Steiger, H., Bruce, K. R., & Groleau, P. (2011). Neural circuits, neurotransmitters, and behavior: Serotonin and temperament in bulimic syndromes. *Current Topics in Behavioral Neurosciences, 6,* 125–138.

Steiger, H., Bruce, K. R., Israël, M. (2013). Eating disorders: Anorexia nervosa, bulimia nervosa, and binge eating disorder. In I. B. Weiner (Series Ed.), G. Stricker & T. A. Widiger (Vol. Eds.), *Handbook of psychology: Vol. 8 Clinical psychology* (pp. 147–170). Hoboken, NJ: Wiley.

Stein, D. J., Phillips, K. A., Bolton, D., Fulford, K. W. M., Sadler, J. Z., & Kendler, K.S. (2010). What is a mental/psychiatric disorder? From DSM-IV to DSM-V. *Psychological Medicine, 40*(11), 1759–1765.

Stein, M., Hilsenroth, M., Slavin-Mulford, J., & Pinsker, J. (2011). *Social Cognition and Object Relations Scale: Global Rating Method (SCORS-G).* Unpublished manuscript, Massachusetts General Hospital and Harvard Medical School, Boston, MA, 1(2).

Stein, M. B., Goldin, P. R., Sareen, J., Zorrilla, L. T., & Brown, G. G. (2002). Increased amygdala activation to angry and contemptuous faces in generalized social phobia. *Archives of General Psychiatry, 59,* 1027–1034.

Stein, M. B., Liebowitz, M. R., Lydiard, R. B., Pitts, C. D., Bushnell, W., & Gergel, I. (1998). Paroxetine treatment of generalized social phobia (social anxiety disorder). A randomized clinical trial. *JAMA: Journal of the American Medical Association, 280,* 708–713.

Stein, M. B., Schork, N. J., & Gelernter, J. (2007). Gene-by-environment (serotonin transporter and childhood maltreatment) interaction for anxiety sensitivity, an intermediate phenotype for anxiety disorders. *Neuropsychopharmacology, 33*(2), 312–319.

Stein, M. I. (1978). Thematic apperception test and related methods. In B. B. Wolman (Ed.), *Clinical diagnosis of mental disorders: A handbook* (pp. 179–235). New York, NY: Plenum Press.

Steinberg, A. B., & Phares, V. (2001). Family functioning, body image, and eating disturbances. In J. K. Thompson & L. Smolak (Eds.), *Body image, eating disorders, and obesity in youth: Assessment, prevention and treatment* (127–147). Washington, DC: American Psychological Association.

Steinglass, P., Weisstub, E., & Kaplan De-Nour, A. K. (1988). Perceived personal networks as mediators of stress reactions. *American Journal of Psychiatry, 145,* 1259–1264.

Steketee, G., & Barlow, D. H. (2002). Obsessive-compulsive disorder. In D. H. Barlow, *Anxiety and its disorders: The nature and treatment of anxiety and panic* (2nd ed.). New York, NY: Guilford.

Steketee, G., & Frost, R. O. (2007a). *Compulsive hoarding and acquiring: Client workbook.* New York, NY: Oxford University Press.

Steketee, G., & Frost, R. O. (2007b). *Compulsive hoarding and acquiring: Therapist guide.* New York, NY: Oxford University Press.

Steketee, G., Gibson, A., Frost, R. O., Alabiso, J., Arluke, A., & Patronek, G. (2011). Characteristics and antecedents of people who hoard animals: An exploratory comparative interview study. *Review of General Psychology, 15*(2), 114–124.

Steketee, G., Quay, S., & White, K. (1991). Religion and guilt in OCD patients. *Journal of Anxiety Disorders, 5,* 359–367.

Stellos, K., Panagiota, V., Sachsenmaier, S., Trunk, T., Straten, G., Leyhe, T., . . . Laske, C. (2010). Increased circulating progenitor cells in Alzheimer's disease patients with moderate to severe dementia: Evidence for vascular repair and tissue regeneration? *Journal of Alzheimer's Disease, 19*(2), 591–600.

Stenvall, M., Olofsson, B., Lundstrom, M., Svensson, O., Nyberg, L., & Gustafson, Y. (2006). Inpatient falls and injuries in older patients treated for femoral neck fracture. *Archives of Gerontology and Geriatrics, 43*(3), 389–399.

Steptoe, A., & Wardle, J. (2012). Enjoying life and living longer. *Archives of Internal Medicine, 172*(3), 273–275. doi: 10.1001/archinternmed.2011.1028

Sterzer, P. (2010). Born to be criminal? What to make of early biological risk factors for criminal behavior. *American Journal of Psychiatry, 167*(1), 1–3. doi:10.1176/appi.ajp.2009.09111601

Stevens, R. G., & Zhu, Y. (2015). Electric light, particularly at night, disrupts human circadian rhythmicity: is that a problem? *Philosophical Transactions of the Royal Society of London B: Biological Sciences, 370*(1667), 20140120.

Stewart, S. E., Jenike, E., & Jenike, M. A. (2009). Biological treatment for obsessive-compulsive disorder. In M. M. Antony & M. B. Stein (Eds.), *Oxford handbook of anxiety and related disorders* (pp. 375–390). New York, NY: Oxford University Press.

Stice, E., & Shaw, H. (2004). Eating disorder prevention programs: A meta-analytic review. *Psychological Bulletin, 130*, 206–227.

Stice, E., Akutagawa, D., Gaggar, A., & Agras, W. S. (2000). Negative affect moderates the relation between dieting and binge eating. *International Journal of Eating Disorders, 27*, 218–229.

Stice, E., Cameron, R. P., Killen, J. D., Hayward, C., & Taylor, C. B. (1999). Naturalistic weight-reduction efforts prospectively predict growth in relative weight and onset of obesity among female adolescents. *Journal of Consulting and Clinical Psychology, 67*, 967–974.

Stice, E., Marti, C. N., & Rohde, P. (2013). Prevalence, incidence, impairment, and course of the proposed DSM-5 eating disorder diagnoses in an 8-year prospective community study of young women. *Journal of Abnormal Psychology, 122*(2), 445–457.

Stice, E., Marti, C. N., Shaw, H., & Jaconis, M. (2009). An 8-year longitudinal study of the natural history of threshold, subthreshold, and partial eating disorders from a community sample of adolescents. *Journal of Abnormal Psychology, 118*(3), 587–597.

Stice, E., Ng, J., & Shaw, H. (2010). Risk factors and prodromal eating pathology. *Journal of Child Psychology and Psychiatry and Allied Disciplines, 51*(4), 518–525.

Stice, E., Presnell, K., Shaw, H., & Rohde, P. (2005). Psychological and behavioral risk factors for obesity onset in adolescent girls: A prospective study. *Journal of Consulting and Clinical Psychology, 73*, 195–202.

Stice, E., Rohde, P., Butryn, M. L., Shaw, H., & Marti, C. N. (2015). Effectiveness Trial of a Selective Dissonance-based Eating Disorder Prevention Program with Female College Students: Effects at 2-and 3-Year Follow-up. *Behaviour Research and Therapy, 71*, 21–26.

Stice, E., Rohde, P., Durant, S., & Shaw, H. (2012). A preliminary trial of a prototype internet dissonance-based eating disorder prevention program for young women with body image concerns. *Journal of Consulting and Clinical Psychology, 80*, 907–916.

Stice, E., Rohde, P., Shaw, H., & Marti, C. N. (2012). Efficacy trial of a selective prevention program targeting both eating disorder symptoms and unhealthy weight gain among female college students. *Journal of Consulting and Clinical Psychology, 80*, 164–170.

Stice, E., Shaw, H., & Marti, C. N. (2006). A meta-analytic review of obesity prevention programs for children and adolescents: The skinny on interventions that work. *Psychological Bulletin, 132*(5), 667–691.

Stice, E., Shaw, H., & Marti, C. N. (2007). A meta-analytic review of eating disorder prevention programs: Encouraging findings. *Annual Review of Clinical Psychology, 3*, 207–231.

Stinson, F. S., Dawson, D. A., Goldstein, R. B., Chou, S. P., Huang, B., Smith, S. M., & Pickering, R. P. (2008). Prevalence, correlates, disability, and comorbidity of DSM-IV narcissistic personality disorder: Results from the Wave 2 National Epidemiologic Survey on Alcohol and Related Conditions. *Journal of Clinical Psychiatry, 69*(7), 1033.

Stokes, A., & Preston, S. H. (2016). Revealing the burden of obesity using weight histories. *Proceedings of the National Academy of Sciences, 113*(3), 572–577.

Stoller, R. J. (1976). Two feminized male American Indians. *Archives of Sexual Behavior, 5*, 529–538.

Stone, A. B., Pearlstein, T. B., & Brown, W. A. (1991). Fluoxetine in the treatment of late luteal phase dysphoric disorder. *Journal of Clinical Psychiatry, 52*(7), 290–293.

Stone, J., Carson, A., Aditya, H., Prescott, R., Zaubi, M., Warlow, C., Sharpe, M. (2009). The role of physical injury in motor and sensory conversion symptoms: A systematic and narrative review. *Journal of Psychosomatic Research, 66*(5), 383–390.

Stone, J., Carson, A., Duncan, R., Coleman, R., Roberts, R., Warlow, C., . . . Sharpe, M. (2009). Symptoms 'unexplained by organic disease' in 1144 new neurology out-patients: How often does the diagnosis change at follow-up? *Brain, 132*(Pt 10), 2878–2888.

Stone, J., Kotoula, V., Dietrich, C., De Simoni, S., Krystal, J. H., & Mehta, M. A. (2015). Perceptual distortions and delusional thinking following ketamine administration are related to increased pharmacological MRI signal changes in the parietal lobe. *Journal of Psychopharmacology, 29*(9), 1025–1028.

Stone, J., LaFrance, W. C., Levenson, J. L., & Sharpe, M. (2010). Issues for DSM-5: Conversion disorder. *American Journal of Psychiatry, 167*, 626–627.

Stone, J., Smyth, R., Carson, A., Lewis, S., Prescott, R., Warlow, C., & Sharpe, M. (2005). Systematic review of misdiagnosis of conversion symptoms and hysteria. *British Medical Journal, 331*, no pagination specified.

Stone, J., Smyth, R., Carson, A., Warlow, C., & Sharpe, M. (2006). La belle indifference in conversion symptoms and hysteria: Systematic review. *British Journal of Psychiatry, 188*, 204–209.

Stone, M. H. (1993). Cluster C personality disorders. In D. L. Dunner (Ed.), *Current psychiatric therapy* (pp. 411–417). Philadelphia, PA: W. B. Saunders.

Stone, M. H. (2013). A new look at borderline personality disorder and related disorders: hyper-reactivity in the limbic system and lower centers. *Psychodynamic Psychiatry, 41*(3), 437–466.

Strain, E. C. (2009). Substance-related disorders. In B. J. Sadock, V. A. Sadock, & P. Ruiz (Eds.), *Kaplan & Sadock's comprehensive textbook of psychiatry* (9th ed., Vol. I, pp. 1237–1268). Philadelphia, PA: Lippincott Williams & Wilkins.

Strain, E. C., Lofwall, M. R., & Jaffe, J. H. (2009). Opioid-related disorders. In B. J. Sadock, V. A. Sadock, & P. Ruiz (Eds.), *Kaplan & Sadock's comprehensive textbook of psychiatry* (9th ed., Vol. I, pp. 1360–1387). Philadelphia, PA: Lippincott Williams & Wilkins.

Strain, J. J., & Friedman, M. J. (2011). Considering adjustment disorders as stress response syndromes for DSM-5. *Depression and Anxiety, 28*, 818–823. doi: 10.1002/da.20782

Stratta, P., Capanna, C., Riccardi, I., Carmassi, C., Piccinni, A., Dell'Osso, L., & Rossi, A. (2012). Suicidal intention and negative spiritual coping one year after the earthquake of L'Aquila (Italy). *Journal of Affective Disorders, 136*(3), 1227–1231.

Straus, S. E., Tosato, G., Armstrong, G., Lawley, T., Preble, O. T., Henle, W., & Blaese, R. M. (1985). Persisting illness and fatigue in adults with evidence of Epstein Barr virus infection. *Annals of Internal Medicine, 102*, 7–16.

Strauss, J. L., Hayes, A. M., Johnson, S. L., Newman, C. F., Brown, G. K., Barber, J. P., & Beck, A. T. (2006). Early alliance, alliance ruptures, and symptom change in a nonrandomized trial of cognitive therapy for avoidant and obsessive-compulsive personality disorders. *Journal of Consulting and Clinical Psychology, 74*, 337–345.

Stravynski, A., Elie, R., & Franche, R. L. (1989). Perception of early parenting by patients diagnosed with avoidant personality disorder: A test of the overprotection hypothesis. *Acta Psychiatrica Scandinavica, 80*, 415–420.

Striegel-Moore, R. H., & Franko, D. L. (2002). Body image issues among girls and women. In T. F. Cash & T. Pruzinsky (Eds.), *Body image: A handbook of theory, research and clinical practice* (pp. 183–191). New York, NY: Guilford.

Striegel-Moore, R. H., & Franko, D. L. (2008). Should binge eating disorder be included in the DSM-V? A critical review of the state of the evidence. *Annual Review of Clinical Psychology, 4*, 305–324.

Striegel-Moore, R. H., Cachelin, F. M., Dohm, F. A., Pike, M., Wilfley, D. E., & Fairburn, C. G. (2001). Comparison of binge eating disorder and bulimia nervosa in a community sample. *International Journal of Eating Disorders, 29*, 157–165.

Striegel-Moore, R. H., Dohm, F. A., Kraemer, H. C., Taylor, C. B., Daniels, S., Crawford, P. B., & Schreiber, G. B. (2003). Eating disorders in white and black women. *American Journal of Psychiatry, 160*, 1326–1331.

Striegel-Moore, R. H., Franko, D. L., & Garcia, J. (2009). The validity and clinical utility of night eating syndrome. *International Journal of Eating Disorders, 42*(8), 720–738.

Striegel-Moore, R. H., Silberstein, L. R., & Rodin, J. (1986). Toward an understanding of risk factors for bulimia. *American Psychologist, 3*, 246–263.

Striegel-Moore, R. H., Silberstein, L. R., & Rodin, J. (1993). The social self in bulimia nervosa: Public self-consciousness, social anxiety, and perceived fraudulence. *Journal of Abnormal Psychology, 102*(2), 297–303.

Striegel-Moore, R. H., Wilson, G. T., DeBar, L., Perrin, N., Lynch, F., Rosselli, F., &

Kraemer, H.C. (2010). Cognitive behavioral guided self-help for the treatment of recurrent binge eating. *Journal of Consulting and Clinical Psychology, 78*(3), 312–321.

Striegel-Moore, R., Rosselli, F., Wilson, G., Perrin, N., Harvey, K., & DeBar, L. (2010). Nocturnal eating: Association with binge eating, obesity, and psychological distress. *Clinical Psychology & Psychotherapy, 11*, 13.

Strike, P. C., & Steptoe, A. (2005). Behavioral and emotional triggers of acute coronary syndromes: A systematic review and critique. *Psychosomatic Medicine, 67*, 179–186.

Strober, M. (2002). Family–genetic perspectives on anorexia nervosa and bulimia nervosa. In K. D. Brownell & C. G. Fairburn (Eds.), *Eating disorders and obesity: A comprehensive handbook* (2nd ed., pp. 212–218). New York, NY: Guilford.

Strober, M., Freeman, R., Lampert, C., Diamond, J., & Kaye, W. (2000). Controlled family study of anorexia nervosa and bulimia nervosa: Evidence of shared liability and transmission of partial syndromes. *American Journal of Psychiatry, 157*, 393–401.

Stroebe, M., Stroebe, W., & Abakoumkin, G. (2005). The broken heart: Suicidal ideation in bereavement. *American Journal of Psychiatry, 162*, 2178–2180.

Strokoff, J., Owen, J., & Fincham, F. D. (2014). Diverse reactions to hooking up among US university students. *Archives of Sexual Behavior, 44*(4), 935–943.

Strong, C. M., Nowakowska, C., Santosa, C. M., Wang, P. W., Kraemer, H. C., & Ketter, T. A. (2007). Temperament-creativity relationships in mood disorder patients, healthy controls and highly creative individuals. *Journal of Affective Disorders, 100*(1–3), 41–48.

Stroup, T. S., & Lieberman, J. A. (Eds.). (2010). *Antipsychotic trials in schizophrenia: The CATIE project*. Cambridge, UK: Cambridge University Press.

Stunkard, A., Allison, K., & Lundgren, J. (2008). Issues for DSM-V: Night eating syndrome. *American Journal of Psychiatry, 165*(4), 424.

Suarez, E. C., Lewis, J. G., & Kuhn, C. (2002). The relation of aggression, hostility, and anger to lipopolysaccharide-stimulated tumor necrosis factor (TNF) by blood monocytes from normal men. *Behavior and Immunity, 16*, 675–684.

Suárez, L., Bennett, S., Goldstein, C., & Barlow, D. H. (2009). Understanding anxiety disorders from a "triple vulnerabilities" framework. In M. M. Antony & M. B. Stein (Eds.), *Oxford handbook of anxiety and related disorders* (pp. 153–172). New York, NY: Oxford University Press.

Subcommittee on Attention-Deficit/Hyperactivity Disorder, Steering Committee on Quality Improvement, & Management. (2011). ADHD: Clinical practice guidelines for the diagnosis, evaluation, and treatment of attention-deficit/hyperactivity disorder in children and adolescents. *Pediatrics, 128*(5), 1007–1022. doi: 10.1542/peds.2011-2654

Subramanian, S., Bandopadhyay, D., Mishra, P. K., Mathew, M., & John, M. (2010). Design and development of non-fibrillar amyloid b as a potential Alzheimer vaccine. *Biochemical and Biophysical Research Communications, 394*(2), 393–397.

Substance Abuse and Mental Health Services Administration. (2014). *Results from the 2013 National Survey on Drug Use and Health: Summary of National Findings,* NSDUH Series H-48, HHS Publication No. (SMA) 14-4863. Rockville, MD: Substance Abuse and Mental Health Services Administration.

Substance Abuse and Mental Health Services Administration, Office of Applied Studies. (2002). *Emergency department trends from the Drug Abuse Warning Network, final estimates 1994–2001.* (DAWN Series D-21, DHHS Publication No. (SMA) 02-3635). Rockville, MD: Author.

Substance Abuse and Mental Health Services Administration, Office of Applied Studies. (2009). *Results from the 2008 National Survey on Drug Use and Health: National findings* (NSDUH Series H-36, DHHS Publication No. (SMA) 09-4434). Rockville, MD: Author.

Substance Abuse and Mental Health Services Administration. (2011, July). Current statistics on the prevalence and characteristics of people experiencing homelessness in the United States. Retrieved May 12, 2013, from http://homeless.samhsa.gov/ResourceFiles/hrc_factsheet.pdf

Substance Abuse and Mental Health Services Administration (SAMHSA). (2011). *The DAWN Report: Trends in Emergency Department Visits Involving Underage Alcohol Use: 2005 to 2009.* Rockville, MD: Substance Abuse and Mental Health Services Administration; 2011.

Substance Abuse and Mental Health Services Administration. (2012). *Results from the 2011 National Survey on Drug Use and Health: Summary of national findings* (NSDUH Series H-44, DHHS Publication No. (SMA) 12-4713). Rockville, MD: Author.

Substance Abuse and Mental Health Services Administration (SAMHSA). (2013). *National Survey on Drug Use and Health (NSDUH). Table 2.41B—Alcohol Use in Lifetime, Past Year, and Past Month among Persons Aged 18 or Older, by Demographic Characteristics: Percentages, 2012 and 2013.* Available at: http://www.samhsa.gov/data/sites/default/files/NSDUH-DetTabsPDFWHTML2013/Web/HTML/NSDUH-DetTabsSect2 peTabs1to42-2013.htm#tab2.41b

Substance Abuse and Mental Health Services Administration. (2014). *National Survey on Drug Use and Health.* Retrieved from: http://www.samhsa.gov/data/sites/default/files/NSDUH-FRR1-2014/NSDUH-FRR1-2014.pdf

Sue, S., Yan Cheng, J. K., Saad, C. S., & Chu, J. P. (2012). Asian American mental health: A call to action. *American Psychologist, 67*(7), 532.

Sugiyama, T., & Abe, T. (1989). The prevalence of autism in Nagoya, Japan: A total population study. *Journal of Autism and Developmental Disorders, 19*, 87–96.

Sullivan, G. M., & LeDoux, J. E. (2004). Synaptic self: Conditioned fear, developed adversity, and the anxious individual. In J. M. Gorman (Ed.), *Fear and anxiety: The benefits of translational research* (pp. 1–22). Washington, DC: American Psychiatric Publishing.

Sullivan, G. M., Kent, J. M., & Coplan, J. D. (2000). The neurobiology of stress and anxiety. In D. I. Mostofsky & D. H. Barlow (Eds.), *The management of stress and anxiety in medical disorders* (pp. 15–35). Needham Heights, MA: Allyn & Bacon.

Sullivan, P. F., Neale, M. C., Kendler, K. S. (2000). Genetic epidemiology of major depression: Review and meta-analysis, *American Journal of Psychiatry, 157*, 1552–1562.

Sullivan, S. (2012). Update on emerging drugs for insomnia. *Expert Opinion on Emerging Drugs, 17*(3), 295–298. doi: 10.1517/14728214.2012.693158

Sullivan, S., & Guilleminault, C. (2009). Emerging drugs for insomnia: New frontiers for old and novel targets. *Expert Opinion on Emerging Drugs, 14*(3), 411–422.

Sulloway, F. (1979). *Freud, biologist of the mind.* London, UK: Burnett.

Suls, J., & Bunde, J. (2005). Anger, anxiety, and depression as risk factors for cardiovascular disease: The problems and implications of overlapping affective dispositions. *Psychological Bulletin, 131*, 260–300.

Summerfeldt, L. J., Kloosterman, P. H., & Antony, M. M. (2010). Structured and semi-structured interviews. In M. M. Antony & D. H. Barlow (Eds.), *Handbook of assessment and treatment planning for psychological disorders* (2nd ed.). New York, NY: Guilford.

Summitt, P. H. (2013). *Sum it up: A thousand and ninety-eight victories, a couple of irrelevant losses, and a life in perspective.* New York, NY: Crown Archetype.

Sun, F., Ong, R., & Burnette, D. (2012). The influence of ethnicity and culture on dementia caregiving a review of empirical studies on Chinese Americans. *American Journal of Alzheimer's disease and Other Dementias, 27*(1), 13–22.

Sun, J. (2011). Seasonality of suicide in Shandong, China, 991–2009: Associations with gender, age, area and methods of suicide. *Journal of Affective Disorders, 135*(1–3), 258–266.

Sun, N., Li, Y., Cai, Y., Chen, J., Shen, Y., Sun, J., & Zhang, K. (2012). A comparison of melancholic and nonmelacholic recurrent major depression in Han Chinese women. *Depression and Anxiety, 29*, 4–9.

Suomi, S. J. (1999). Attachment in rhesus monkeys. In J. Cassidy & P. Shaver (Eds.), *Handbook of attachment: Theory, research, and clinical applications* (pp. 181–197). New York, NY: Guilford.

Suomi, S. J. (2000). A biobehavioral perspective on developmental psychopathology. In A. J. Sameroff, J. Lewis, & S. M. Miller (Eds.), *Handbook of developmental psychopathology* (pp. 237–256). New York, NY: Kluwer Academic/Plenum.

Sutherland, K., & Cistulli, P. A. (2015). Recent advances in obstructive sleep apnea pathophysiology and treatment. *Sleep and Biological Rhythms, 13*(1), 26–40.

Sutin, A. R., Stephan, Y., & Terracciano, A. (2015). Weight Discrimination and Risk of Mortality. *Psychological Science, 26*(11), 1803–1811.

Sutin, A. R., Terracciano, A., Milaneschi, Y., An, Y., Ferrucci, L., & Zonderman, A. B. (2013). The trajectory of depressive symptoms across the adult life span. *JAMA Psychiatry, 70,* 803–811.

Suvrathan, A., Hoeffer, C. A., Wong, H., Klann, E., & Chattarji, S. (2010). Characterization and reversal of synaptic defects in the amygdala in a mouse model of fragile X syndrome. *Proceedings of the National Academy of Sciences, 107*(25), 11591–11596.

Suvisaari, J. M., Taxell-Lassas, V., Pankakoski, M., Haukka, J. K., Lönnqvist, J. K., & Häkkinen, L. T. (2013). Obstetric complications as risk factors for schizophrenia spectrum psychoses in offspring of mothers with psychotic disorder. *Schizophrenia Bulletin, 39*(5), 1056–1066.

Svartberg, M., Stiles, T. C., & Seltzer, M. H. (2004). Randomized, controlled trial of the effectiveness of short-term dynamic psychotherapy and cognitive therapy for cluster C personality disorders. *American Journal of Psychiatry, 161,* 810–817.

Svenningsson, P., Westman, E., Ballard, C., & Aarsland, D. (2012). Cognitive impairment in patients with Parkinson's disease: diagnosis, biomarkers, and treatment. *The Lancet Neurology, 11*(8), 697–707.

Svetkey, L. P., Stevens, V. J., Brantley, P. J., Appel, L. J., Hollis, J. F., Loria, C. M., & Aicher, K. (2008). Comparison of strategies for sustaining weight loss: The weight loss maintenance randomized controlled trial. *JAMA: Journal of the American Medical Association, 299*(10), 1139–1148.

Swann, A. C., Lafer, B., Perugi, G., Frye, M., Bauer, M., Bahk, W.-M., & Suppes, T. (2013). Bipolar mixed states: An international society for bipolar disorders task force report on symptom structure, course of illness, and diagnosis. *American Journal of Psychiatry, 170*(1), 31–42.

Swanson, S. A., Crow, S. J., Le Grange, D., Swendsen, J., & Merikangas, K. R. (2011). Prevalence and correlates of eating disorders in adolescents. *Archives of General Psychiatry, 68,* 714–723.

Swartz, M., Blazer, D., George, L., & Landerman, R. (1986). Somatization disorder in a community population. *American Journal of Psychiatry, 143,* 1403–1408.

Swartz, M. S., Lauriello, J., & Drake, R. E. (2006). Psychosocial therapies. In J. A. Lieberman, T. S. Stroup, & D. O. Perkins (Eds.), *The American Psychiatric Publishing textbook of schizophrenia* (pp. 327–340). Washington, DC: American Psychiatric Publishing.

Swedo S. E., Leckman J. F., & Rose, N. R. (2012). From research subgroup to clinical syndrome: Modifying the PANDAS criteria to describe PANS (pediatric acute-onset neuropsychiatric syndrome). *Pediatrics & Therapeutics, 2*(2), 1–8. doi: 10.4172/2161-0665.1000113

Swedo, S. E., Pleeter, J. D., Richter, D. M., Hoffman, C. L., Allen, A. J., Hamburger, S. D., & Rosenthal, N. E. (1995). Rates of seasonal affective disorder in children and adolescents. *American Journal of Psychiatry, 152,* 1016–1019.

Swendeman, D., Ramanathan, N., Baetscher, L., Medich, M., Scheffler, A., Comulada, W. S., & Estrin, D. (2015). Smartphone self-monitoring to support self-management among people living with HIV: perceived benefits and theory of change from a mixed-methods randomized pilot study. *JAIDS Journal of Acquired Immune Deficiency Syndromes, 69,* S80–S91.

Sylvers, P., Ryan, S., Alden, S., & Brennan, P. (2009). Biological factors and the development of persistent criminality. In J. Savage (Ed.), *The development of persistent criminality* (pp. 141–162). New York, NY: Oxford University Press.

Syngelaki, E. M., Fairchild, G., Moore, S. C., Savage, J. C., & Goozen, S. H. M. (2013). Fearlessness in juvenile offenders is associated with offending rate. *Developmental Science, 16*(1), 84–90.

Sysko, R., & Wilson, G. T. (2011). Eating disorders. In D. H. Barlow (Ed.), *Handbook of clinical psychology.* (pp. 387–404). New York, NY: Oxford University Press.

Szasz, T. (1961). *The myth of mental illness: Foundations of a theory of personal conduct.* New York, NY: Hoeber-Harper.

Takahasi, T. (1989). Social phobia syndrome in Japan. *Comprehensive Psychiatry, 30,* 45–52.

Takei, N., Lewis, S., Jones, P., Harvey, I., & Murray, R. M. (1996). Prenatal exposure to influenza and increased cerebrospinal fluid spaces in schizophrenia. *Schizophrenia Bulletin, 22,* 521–534.

Talbot, L. S., Stone, S., Gruber, J., Hairston, I. S., Eidelman, P., & Harvey, A. G. (2012). A test of the bidirectional association between sleep and mood in bipolar disorder and insomnia. *Journal of Abnormal Psychology, 121*(1), 39–50.

Tan, E. S. (1980). Transcultural aspects of anxiety. In G. D. Burrows & B. Davies (Eds.), *Handbook of studies on anxiety.* Amsterdam, The Netherlands: Elsevier/North-Holland.

Tandon, R., & Carpenter, W. T. (2012). DSM-5 status of psychotic disorders: 1 year prepublication. *Schizophrenia Bulletin, 38*(3), 369–370. doi: 10.1093/schbul/sbs048

Tandon, R., Gaebel, W., Barch, D. M., Bustillo, J., Gur, R. E., Heckers, S., . . . Van Os, J. (2013). Definition and description of schizophrenia in the DSM-5. *Schizophrenia research, 150*(1), 3–10.

Tannock, R. (2009a). Mathematics disorder. In B. J. Sadock, V. A. Sadock, & P. Ruiz (Eds.), *Kaplan & Sadock's comprehensive textbook of psychiatry* (9th ed., Vol. II, pp. 3485–3493). Philadelphia, PA: Lippincott Williams & Wilkins.

Tannock, R. (2009b). Reading disorder. In B. J. Sadock, V. A. Sadock, & P. Ruiz (Eds.), *Kaplan & Sadock's comprehensive textbook of psychiatry* (9th ed., Vol. II, pp. 3475–3485). Philadelphia, PA: Lippincott Williams & Wilkins.

Tapert, S. F., & Jacobus, J. (2012). Neurotoxic effects of alcohol in adolescence. *Annual review of clinical psychology, 9*(1). Tarasoff v. Regents of University of California ("Tarasoff I"), 529 P.2d 553 (Cal. S. Ct. 1974). Tarasoff v. Regents of University of California ("Tarasoff II"), 551 P.2d 334 (Cal. S. Ct. 1976).

Tarescavage, A. M., Wygant, D. B., Gervais, R. O., & Ben-Porath, Y. S. (2013). Association between the MMPI-2 Restructured Form (MMPI-2-RF) and malingered neurocognitive dysfunction among non-head injury disability claimants. *The Clinical Neuropsychologist, 27*(2), 313–335.

Tarullo, A. R., & Gunnar, M.R. (2006). Child maltreatment and the developing HPA axis. *Hormones and Behavior, 50,* 632–639.

Tau, G. Z., & Peterson, B. S. (2010). Normal development of brain circuits. *Neuropsychopharmacology, 35*(1), 147–168.

Taylor, D., Gehrman, P., Dautovich, N. D., Lichstein, K. L., & McCrae, C. S. (2014). Causes of Insomnia. In D. Taylor, P. Gehrman, N. D. Dautovich, K. L. Lichstein, & C. S. McCrae (Eds.), *Handbook of Insomnia* (pp. 11–27). New York, NY: Springer.

Taylor, E. (2012). Attention deficit and hyperkinetic disorders in childhood and adolescence. In M. G. Gelder, N. C. Andreasen, J. J. Lopez-Ibor, Jr., & J. R. Geddes (Eds.), *New Oxford textbook of psychiatry* (2nd. ed., Vol. 2, pp. 1643–1654). New York, NY: Oxford University Press.

Taylor, G. T., Maloney, S., Dearborn, J., & Weiss, J. (2009). Hormones in the mentally disturbed brain: Steroids and peptides in the development and treatment of psychopathology. *Central Nervous System Agents in Medicinal Chemistry, 9,* 331–360.

Taylor, J., & Lang, A. R. (2006). Psychopathy and substance use disorders. In C. J. Patrick (Ed.), *Handbook of psychopathy* (pp. 495–511). New York, NY: Guilford.

Taylor, R. R., Jason, L. A., Richman, J. A., Torres-Harding, S. R., King, C., & Song, S. (2003). Epidemiology. In L. A. Jason, P. A. Fennell, & R. R. Taylor (Eds.), *Handbook of chronic fatigue syndrome* (pp. 3–25). Hoboken, NJ: Wiley.

Taylor, S., & Asmundson, G. J. G. (2004). *Treating health anxiety: A cognitive behavioral approach.* New York, NY: Guilford.

Taylor, S., & Asmundson, G. J. G. (2009). Hypochondriasis and health anxiety. In M. M. Antony & M. B. Stein (Eds.), *Oxford handbook of anxiety and related disorders* (pp. 525–540). Oxford, UK: Oxford University Press.

Taylor, S., Abramowitz, J. S., McKay, D., & Cuttler, C. (2012). Cognitive approaches to understanding obsessive compulsive and related disorders. In G. Steketee (Ed.), *The Oxford handbook of obsessive compulsive and spectrum disorders* (pp. 233–252). New York, NY: Oxford University Press.

Taylor, S., Asmundson, G., & Coons, M. (2005). Current directions in the treatment of hypochondriasis. *Journal of Cognitive Psychotherapy: An International Quarterly, 19,* 285–304.

Taylor, S., Thordarson, D. S., Jang, K. L., & Asmundson, G. J. (2006). Genetic and environmental origins of health anxiety: A twin study. *World Psychiatry, 5*(1), 47–50.

Taylor, S. E. (2002). *The tending instinct: How nurturing is essential to who we are and how we live.* New York, NY: Henry Holt.

Taylor, S. E. (2006). Tend and befriend: Biobehavioral bases of affiliation under stress. *Current Directions in Psychological Science, 15*(6), 273–277.

Taylor, S. E. (2009). *Health psychology* (7th ed.). New York, NY: McGraw-Hill.

Taylor, S. E., Klein, L. C., Lewis, B. P., Gruenewald, T. L., Gurung, R. A. R., & Updegraff, J. A. (2000). Biobehavioral responses to stress in females: Tend-and-befriend, not fight-or-flight. *Psychological Review, 107*, 411–429.

Taylor, S. E., Repetti, R. L., & Seeman, T. (1997). Health psychology: What is an unhealthy environment and how does it get under the skin? *Annual Review of Psychology, 48*, 411–447.

Tazici, O. (2014). Unipolar mania: A distinct entity. *Journal of Affective Disorders, 152–154*, 52–56.

Teachman, B.A., Joormann, J., Steinman, S. A., & Gotlib, I. H. (2012). Automaticity in anxiety disorders and depressive disorder. *Clinical Psychology Review, 32*, 575–603.

Teasdale, J. D. (1993). Emotion and two kinds of meaning: Cognitive therapy and applied cognitive science. *Behaviour Research and Therapy, 31*(4), 339–354.

Teasdale, J. D., Scott, J., Moore, R. G., Hayhurst, H., Pope, M., & Paykel, E. S. (2001). How does cognitive therapy prevent relapse in residual depression? Evidence from a controlled trial. *Journal of Consulting and Clinical Psychology, 69*, 347–357.

Teasdale, J. D., Segal, Z. V., Williams, J. M., Ridgeway, V. A., Soulsby, J. M., & Lau, M. A. (2000). Prevention of relapse/recurrence in major depression by mindfulness-based cognitive therapy. *Journal of Consulting and Clinical Psychology, 4*, 615–623.

Teh, C. F., Zaslavsky, A. M., Reynolds, C. F., & Cleary, P. D. (2009). Effect of depression treatment on chronic pain outcomes. *Psychosomatic Medicine, 72*, 61–67.

Teicher, M. H., Glod, C., & Cole, J. O. (1990). Emergence of intense suicidal preoccupation during fluoxetine treatment. *American Journal of Psychiatry, 147*(1), 207–210.

Telch, C. F., & Agras, W. S. (1993). The effects of a very low calorie diet on binge eating. *Behavior Therapy, 24*, 177–193.

Telch, M. J., Lucas, J. A., & Nelson, P. (1989). Nonclinical panic in college students: An investigation of prevalence and symptomatology. *Journal of Abnormal Psychology, 98*, 300–306. Telch, M. J., Rosenfield, D., Lee, H.-J., & Pai, A. (2012). Emotional reactivity to a single inhalation of 35% carbon dioxide and its association with later symptoms of posttraumtic stress disorders and anxiety n soldiers deployed to Iraq. *Archives of General Psychiatry, 69*, 1161–1168.

Temoshok, L. R., Wald, R. L., Synowski, S., & Garzino-Demo, A. (2008). Coping as a multisystem construct associated with pathways mediating HIV-relevant immune function and disease progression. *Psychosomatic Medicine, 70*, 555–561.

Temple, E., Deutisch, G. K., Poldrack, R. A., Miller, S. L., Tallal, P., Merzenich, M. M., Gabrieli, J. (2003). Neural deficits in children with dyslexia ameliorated by behavioral remediation: Evidence from functional MRI. *Proceedings of the National Academy of Sciences, 100*, 2860–2865.

Tenhula, W. N., Bellack, A. S., & Drake, R. E. (2009). Schizophrenia: Psychosocial approaches. In B. J. Sadock, V. A. Sadock, & P. Ruiz (Eds.), *Kaplan & Sadock's comprehensive textbook of psychiatry* (9th ed., Vol. I, pp. 1557–1572). Philadelphia, PA: Lippincott Williams & Wilkins.

ter Kuile, M. M., Melles, R., de Groot, H. E., Tuijnman-Raasveld, C. C., & van Lankveld, J. J. (2013). Therapist-aided exposure for women with lifelong vaginismus: A randomized waiting-list control trial of efficacy. *Journal of Consulting and Clinical Psychology, 81*(6), 1127–1136.

ter Kuile, M., van Lankveld, J., Jacques, J., de Groot, E., Melles, R., Neffs, J., & Zanbergen, M. (2007). Cognitive-behavioral therapy for women with lifelong vaginismus: Process and prognostic factors. *Behaviour Research and Therapy, 45*, 359–373.

Teri, L., Gibbons, L. E., McCurry, S. M., Logsdon, R. G., Buchner, D. M., Barlow, W. E., & Larson, E. B. (2003). Exercise plus behavioral management in patients with Alzheimer disease: A randomized controlled trial. *JAMA: Journal of the American Medical Association, 290*(15), 2015–2022.

Terman, J. S., Terman, M., Lo, E., & Cooper, T. B. (2001). Circadian time of morning light administration and therapeutic response in winter depression. *Archives of General Psychiatry, 58*, 69–75.

Terman, M., Terman, J. S., & Ross, D. C. (1998). A controlled trial of timed bright light and negative air ionization of treatment of winter depression. *Archives of General Psychiatry, 55*, 875–882.

Testad, I., Ballard, C., Brønnick, K., & Aarsland, D. (2010). The effect of staff training on agitation and use of restraint in nursing home residents with dementia: A single-blind, randomized controlled trial. *The Journal of Clinical Psychiatry, 71*(1), 80.

Teti, D. M., & Crosby, B. (2012). Maternal depressive symptoms, dysfunctional cognitions, and infant night waking: The role of maternal nighttime behavior. *Child Development, 83*(3), 939–953. doi: 10.1111/j.1467-8624.2012.01760.x

Thaker, G. K., & Avila, M. (2003). Schizophrenia, V: Risk markers. *American Journal of Psychiatry, 160*, 1578.

Thapar, A., & McGuffin, P. (2009). Quantitative genetics. In M. G. Gelder, N. C. Andreasen, J. J. Lopez-Ibor, Jr., & J. R. Geddes (Eds.), *New Oxford textbook of psychiatry* (2nd ed., Vol. 1, pp. 212–221). Oxford, UK: Oxford University Press.

Thase, M. E. (1990). Relapse and recurrence in unipolar major depression: Short-term and long-term approaches. *Journal of Clinical Psychiatry, 51*(Suppl. 6), 51–57.

Thase, M. E. (2005). Major depressive disorder. In F. Andrasik (Ed.), *Comprehensive handbook of personality and psychopathology. Volume 2: Adult psychopathology* (pp. 207–230). New York, NY: Wiley.

Thase, M. E. (2009). Neurobiological aspects of depression. In I. H. Gotlib & C. L. Hammen (Eds.), *Handbook of depression* (2nd ed., pp. 187–217). New York, NY: Guilford. Thase, M. E., & Denko, T. (2008). Pharmacotherapy of mood disorders. *Annual Review of Clinical Psychology, 4*, 53–91.

Thase, M. E., & Kupfer, D. J. (1996). Recent developments in the pharmacotherapy of mood disorders. *Journal of Consulting and Clinical Psychology, 64*, 646–659.

Thase, M. E., Simons, A. D., & Reynolds, C. F., III. (1996). Abnormal electroencephalographic sleep profiles in major depression. *Archives of General Psychiatry, 53*, 99–108.

Thayer, J. F., Friedman, B. H., & Borkovec, T. D. (1996). Autonomic characteristics of generalized anxiety disorder and worry. *Biological Psychiatry, 39*, 255–266.

The Evolving Insanity Defense. (2006). *ABA Journal, 92*, 37.

Thibodeau, M. A., Welch, P. G., Sareen, J., & Asmundson, G. L. G. (2013). Anxiety disorders are independently associated with suicide ideation and attempts: Propensity score matching in two epidemiological samples. *Depression and Anxiety, 30*, 947–954.

Thirthalli, J., & Rajkumar, R. P. (2009). Statistical versus clinical significance in psychiatric research—An overview for beginners. *Asian Journal of Psychiatry, 2*(2), 74–79.

Thomas, C. R. (2009). Oppositional defiant disorder and conduct disorder. In M. K. Dulcan (Ed.), *Dulcan's textbook of child and adolescent psychiatry* (pp. 223–239). Arlington, VA: American Psychiatric Publishing.

Thompson v. County of Alameda, 614 P.2d 728 (Cal. S. Ct. 1980). Thompson, J. K., & Kinder, B. (2003). Eating disorders. In M. Hersen & S. Turner (Eds.), *Handbook of adult psychopathology* (4th ed., pp. 555–582). New York, NY: Plenum.

Thompson, J. K., & Stice, E. (2001). Thin-idea internalization: Mounting evidence for a new risk factor for body-image disturbance and eating pathology. *Current Directions in Psychological Science, 11*, 181–183.

Thompson, J. R., Bradley, V. J., Buntinx, W. H. E., Schalock, R. L., Shogren, K. A., Snell, M. E., & Yeager, M. (2009). Conceptualizing supports and the support needs of people with intellectual disability. *Intellectual and Developmental Disabilities, 47*(2), 135–146.

Thompson, M. A., Aberg, J. A., Cahn, P., Montaner, J. S. G., Rizzardini, G., Telenti, A., & Schooley, R. T. (2010). Antiretroviral treatment of adult HIV infection. *JAMA: Journal of the American Medical Association, 304*, 321–333.

Thompson, M. A., Mugavero, M. J., Amico, K. R., Cargill, V. A., Chang, L. W., Gross, R., & Nachega, J. B. (2012). Guidelines for improving entry into and retention in care and anti-retroviral adherence for persons with HIV: Evidence-based recommendations from an International Association of Physicians in AIDS Care panel. *Annals of Internal Medicine, 156*(11), 817–833, W-284–W-294.

Thompson-Brenner, H., Boisseau, C. L., & St. Paul, M. S. (2011). Representations of ideal figure-size in *Ebony* magazine: A content analysis. *Body Image, 8*(4), 373–378.

Thompson-Brenner, H., Glass, S., & Westen, D. (2003). A multidimensional meta-analysis of psychotherapy for bulimia nervosa. *Clinical Psychology: Science and Practice, 10*, 269–287.

Thoresen, C. E., & Powell, L. H. (1992). Type A behavior pattern: New perspectives on theory, assessment and intervention. Special issue: Behavioral medicine: An update for the 1990s. *Journal of Consulting and Clinical Psychology, 60*(4), 595–604.

Thorlton, J., Colby, D. A., & Devine, P. (2014). Proposed actions for the US Food and Drug Administration to implement to minimize adverse effects associated with energy drink consumption. *American Journal of Public Health, 104*(7), 1175–1180.

Thorndike, A. N., Riis, J., Sonnenberg, L. M., & Levy, D. E. (2014). Traffic-light labels and choice architecture: promoting healthy food choices. *American journal of Preventive Medicine, 46*(2), 143–149.

Thorndike, A. N., Sonnenberg, L., Riis, J., Barraclough, S., & Levy, D. E. (2012). A 2-phase labeling and choice architecture intervention to improve healthy food and beverage choices. *American Journal of Public Health, 102*(3), 527–533.

Thorpe, G. L., & Burns, L. E. (1983). *The agoraphobic syndrome*. New York, NY: Wiley.

Thurston, R. C., & Kubzansky, L. D. (2009). Women, loneliness, and incident coronary heart disease. *Psychosomatic Medicine, 71*(8), 836–842.

Thyer, B. A. (1993). Childhood separation anxiety disorder and adult-onset agoraphobia: Review of evidence. In C. Last (Ed.), *Anxiety across the lifespan: A developmental perspective* (pp. 128–145). New York, NY: Springer.

Tienari, P. (1991). Interaction between genetic vulnerability and family environment: The Finnish adoptive family study of schizophrenia. *Acta Psychiatrica Scandinavica, 84,* 460–465.

Tienari, P., Wahlberg, K.-E., & Wynne, L. C. (2006). Finnish adoption study of schizophrenia: Implications for family interventions. *Families, Systems & Health, 24,* 442–451.

Tienari, P., Wynne, L. C., Laksy, K., Moring, J., Nieminen, P., & Sorri, A., & Wahlberg, K. E. (2003). Genetic boundaries of the schizophrenia spectrum: Evidence from the Finnish adoptive family study of schizophrenia. *American Journal of Psychiatry, 160,* 1567–1594.

Tienari, P., Wynne, L. C., Moring, J., Lahti, I., Naarala, M., Sorri, A., & Moring, J. (1994). The Finnish adoptive family study of schizophrenia: Implications for family research. *British Journal of Psychiatry, 23*(Suppl. 164), 20–26.

Tiggemann, M. (2002). Media influences on body image development. In T. F. Cash & T. Pruzinsky (Eds.), *Body image: A handbook of theory, research and clinical practice* (pp. 91–98). New York, NY: Guilford.

Tiggemann, M., & Lynch, J. E. (2001). Body image across the life span in adult women: The role of self-objectification. *Developmental Psychology, 37,* 243–253.

Timimi, S., & Taylor, E. (2004). ADHD is best understood as a cultural construct. *British Journal of Psychiatry, 184,* 8–9.

Timlett, A. (2013). Controlling bizarre delusions. *Schizophrenia Bulletin, 39*(2), 244–246. doi: 10.1093/schbul/sbs137

Tinbergen, E. A., & Tinbergen, N. (1972). *Early childhood autism: An ethological approach.* Berlin, Germany: Parey.

Tingelstad, J. B. (1991). The cardiotoxicity of the tricyclics. *Journal of the American Academy of Child and Adolescent Psychiatry, 30,* 845–846.

Tishelman, A. C., Kaufman, R., Edwards-Leeper, L., Mandel, F. H., Shumer, D. E., & Spack, N. P. (2015). Serving transgender youth: Challenges, dilemmas, and clinical examples. *Professional Psychology: Research and Practice, 46*(1), 37–45.

Tishler, C. L., Reiss, N. S., & Rhodes, A. R. (2007). Suicidal behavior in children younger than twelve: A diagnostic challenge for emergency department personnel. *Academic Emergency Medicine, 14*(9), 810–818.

Tjio, J. H., & Levan, A. (1956). The chromosome number of man. *Hereditas, 42,* 1–6.

Tober, D. M., & Budiani, D. (2014). Introduction: Why Islam health and body? *Body and Society, 13*(3), 1–13.

Todaro, J. F., Shen, B., Raffa, S. D., Tilkemeier, P. L., & Niaura, R. (2007). Prevalence of anxiety disorders in men and women with established coronary heart disease. *Journal of Cardiopulmonary Rehabilitation and Prevention, 27,* 86–91.

Tolin, D. F. (2011). Challenges and advances in treating hoarding. *Journal of Clinical Psychology, 67,* 451–455. doi: 10.1002/jclp.20796

Tolin, D. F., Frost, R. O., Steketee, G., & Muroff, J. (2015). Cognitive behavioral therapy for hoarding disorder: A meta-analysis. *Depression and Anxiety, 32,* 158–166.

Tolin, D. F., Stevens, M. C., Villavicencio, A. L., Norberg, M. M., Calhoun, V. D., Frost, R. O., & Pearlson, G. D. (2012). Neural mechanisms of decision making in hoarding disorder. *Archives of General Psychiatry, 69,* 832–841. doi: 10.1001/archgenpsychiatry.2011.1980

Tomarken, A., & Keener, A. (1998). Frontal brain asymmetry and depression: A self-regulatory perspective. *Cognition and Emotion, 12,* 387–420.

Tomarken, A., Dichter, G., Garber, J., & Simien, C. (2004). Relative left frontal hypo-activation in adolescents at risk for depression. *Biological Psychology, 67,* 77–102.

Tomenson, B., McBeth, J., Chew-Graham, C. A., MacFarlane, G., Davies, I., Jackson, J., & Creed, F. H. (2012). Somatization and health anxiety as predictors of health care use. *Psychosomatic Medicine, 74*(6), 656–664. doi: 10.1097/PSY.0b013e31825cb140

Tondo, L., Jamison, K. R., & Baldessarini, R. J. (1997). Effect of lithium maintenance on suicidal behavior in major mood disorders. In D. M. Stoff & J. J. Mann (Eds.), *The neurobiology of suicide: From the bench to the clinic* (Vol. 836, pp. 339–351). New York, NY: Academy of Sciences.

Toomey, R., Faraone, S. V., Simpson, J. C., & Tsuang, M. T. (1998). Negative, positive, and disorganized symptom dimensions in schizophrenia, major depression, and bipolar disorder. *Journal of Nervous and Mental Disorders, 186,* 470–476.

Torgersen, S. (1986). Genetics of somatoform disorder. *Archives of General Psychiatry, 43,* 502–505.

Torgersen, S. (2012). Epidemiology. In T. A. Widiger (Ed.), *The Oxford handbook of personality disorders* (pp. 186–205). New York, NY: Oxford University Press.

Torrey, E., Eslinger, S., Lamb, R., & Pavle, J. (2010). *More mentally ill persons are in jails and prisons than hospitals: A survey of the states.* Arlington, VA: Treatment Advocacy Center.

Tortorella, A., Fabrazzo, M., Monteleone, A. M., Steardo, L., & Monteleone, P. (2014). The role of drug therapies in the treatment of anorexia and bulimia nervosa: A review of the literature. *Journal of Psychopathology, 20,* 50–65.

Torry, Z., & Billick, S. (2010). Overlapping universe: Understanding legal insanity and psychosis. *Psychiatric Quarterly,* 1–10.

Toth, K., & King, B. H. (2010). Intellectual disability (mental retardation). In M. K. Dulcan (Ed.), *Dulcan's textbook of child and adolescent psychiatry* (5th ed., pp. 151–172). Arlington, VA: American Psychiatric Publishing.

Toth, K., de Lacy, N., & King, B. H. (2016). Intelectual disability. In M. K. Dulcan (Ed.), *Dulcan's Textbook of Child and Adolescent Psychiatry* (2nd ed., pp. 105–133). Arlington, VA: American Psychiatric Publishing.

Toth, S. L., Harris, L. S., Goodman, G. S., & Cicchetti, D. (2011). Influence of violence and aggression on children's psychological development: Trauma, attachment, and memory. In P. R. Shaver & M. Mikulincer (Eds.), *Human aggression and violence: Causes, manifestations, and consequences* (pp. 351–365). Washington, DC: American Psychological Association. doi: 10.1037/12346-019

Tovote, P., Fadok, J. P., & Lüthi, A. (2015). Neuronal circuits of fear and anxiety. *Nature Reviews Neuroscience, 16,* 317–331.

Townsend, J. M., & Wasserman, T. H. (2011). Sexual hookups among college students: Sex differences in emotional reactions. *Archives of Sexual Behavior, 40*(6), 1173–1181.

Tracey, S. A., Chorpita, B. F., Douban, J., & Barlow, D. H. (1997). Empirical evaluation of DSM-IV generalized anxiety disorder criteria in children and adolescents. *Journal of Clinical Child Psychology, 26,* 404–414.

Trauer, J. M., Qian, M. Y., Doyle, J. S., Rajaratnam, S. M., & Cunnington, D. (2015). Cognitive Behavioral Therapy for Chronic Insomnia: A Systematic Review and Meta-analysis. *Annals of Internal Medicine, 163*(3), 191–204.

Treatment for Adolescents with Depression Study Team (TADS). (2004). Fluoxetine, cognitive-behavioral therapy, and their combination for adolescents with depression. *JAMA: Journal of the American Medical Association, 292,* 807–820.

Treatment for Adolescents with Depression Study Team. (2009). The Treatment for Adolescents with Depression Study (TADS): Outcomes over 1 year of naturalistic follow-up. *American Journal of Psychiatry, 166,* 1141–1149.

Tremont, G., Davis, J. D., Papandonatos, G. D., Ott, B. R., Fortinsky, R. H., Gozalo, P., . . . Bishop, D. S. (2015). Psychosocial telephone intervention for dementia caregivers: A randomized, controlled trial. *Alzheimer's & Dementia, 11*(5), 541–548.

Triebwasser, J., Chemerinski, E., Roussos, P., & Siever, L. J. (2013). Paranoid personality disorder. *Journal of Personality Disorders, 27*(6), 795–805.

Trinh, N., Hoblyn, J., Mohanty, S., & Yaffe, K. (2003). Efficacy of cholinesterase inhibitors in the treatment of neuropsychiatric symptoms and functional impairment in Alzheimer disease: A meta-analysis. *JAMA, 289*(2), 210–216. doi: 10.1001/jama.289.2.210

Trivedi, M., Rush, A., Wisniewski, S., Nierenberg, A., Warden, D., Ritz, L., & STAR*D Study Team. (2006). Evaluation of outcomes with citalopram for depression using measurement-based care in STAR *D: Implications for clinical practice. *American Journal of Psychiatry, 163,* 28–40.

True, W. R., Rice, J., Eisen, S. A., Heath, A. C., Goldberg, J., Lyons, M. J., & Nowak, J. (1993). A twin study of genetic and environmental contributions to liability for posttraumatic stress symptoms. *Archives of General Psychiatry, 50,* 257–264.

Trull, T.J., Carpenter, R. W., & Widiger, T. A. (2013). Personality disorders. In I. B. Weiner (Series Ed.), G. Stricker & T. A. Widiger (Vol. Eds.), *Handbook of psychology: Vol. 8 Clinical psychology* (pp. 94–120). Hoboken, NJ: John Wiley & Sons.

Trull, T. J., Scheiderer, E. M., & Tomko, R. L. (2012). Axis II comorbidity. In T. A. Widiger (Ed.), *The Oxford handbook of personality disorders* (pp. 566–581). New York, NY: Oxford University Press.

Truong, T., Liquet, B., Menegaux, F., Plancoulaine, S., Laurent-Puig, P., Mulot, C., . . . Guénel, P. (2014). Breast cancer risk, nightwork, and circadian clock gene polymorphisms. *Endocrine-related cancer, 21*(4), 629–638.

Tsai, A. C., Lucas, M., & Kawachi, I. (2015). Association between social integration and suicide among women in the United States. *JAMA Psychiatry, 72,* 987.

Tsai, G. E., Condie, D., Wu, M. T., & Chang, I. W. (1999). Functional magnetic resonance imaging of personality switches in a woman with dissociative identity disorder. *Harvard Review of Psychiatry, 7*(2), 119–122.

Tsao, J. C. I., Mystkowski, J. L., Zucker, B. G., & Craske, M. G. (2002). Effects of cognitive-behavioral therapy for panic disorder on comorbid conditions: Replication and extension. *Behavior Therapy, 33,* 493–509.

Tsuang, M. T., Stone, W. S., & Faraone, S. V. (2012). Schizoaffective and schizotypal disorders. In M. G. Gelder, N. C. Andreasen, J. J. Lopez-Ibor, Jr., & J. R. Geddes (Eds.), *New Oxford textbook of psychiatry* (2nd. ed., Vol. 1, pp. 595–602). New York, NY: Oxford University Press.

Tuchman, B. (1978). *A distant mirror.* New York, NY: Ballantine Books.

Tucker, J. A., Murphy, J. G., & Kertesz, S. G. (2011). Substance use disorders. In M. Antony & D. H. Barlow (Eds.), *Handbook of assessment and treatment planning for psychological disorders* (2nd ed.). New York, NY: Guilford.

Turk, D. C., & Monarch, E. S. (2002). Biopsychosocial perspective on chronic pain. In D. C. Turk & R. J. Gatchel (Eds.), *Psychological approaches to pain management: A practitioner's handbook* (2nd ed., pp. 3–29). New York, NY: Guilford.

Turkheimer, E. (1998). Heritability and biological explanation. *Psychological Review, 105,* 782–791.

Turkheimer, E., & Waldron, M. C. (2000). Nonshared environment: A theoretical, methodological, and quantitative review. *Psychological Bulletin, 126,* 78–108.

Turkheimer, E., Haley, A., Waldron, M., D'Onofrio, B., & Gottesman, I. I. (2003). Socioeconomic status modifies heritability of IQ in young children. *Psychological Science, 14,* 623–628.

Turner, C., Spinks, A., McClure, R., Nixon, J. (2004). Community-based interventions for the prevention of burns and scalds in children. *Cochrane Database Syst. Rev.* 3:CD004335

Turner, J., Mancl, L., & Aaron, L. (2006). Short-and long-term efficacy of brief cognitive behavioral therapy for patients with chronic temporomandibular disorder pain: A randomized, controlled trial. *Pain, 121,* 181–194.

Turner, S. M., Beidel, D. C., & Jacob, R. G. (1994). Social phobia: A comparison of behavior therapy and atenolol. *Journal of Consulting Psychology, 62,* 350–358.

Turovsky, J., & Barlow, D. H. (1996). Generalized anxiety disorder. In J. Margraf (Ed.), *Textbook of behavior therapy* (pp. 87–106). Berlin, Germany: Springer-Verlag.

Tushnet, M. (2008). Who qualifies for rights? [Review of the book *Homelessness, mental illness and civil commitment*]. *The Journal of Politics, 66*(02), 626–628.

Tyler, D. B. (1955). Psychological changes during experimental sleep deprivation. *Diseases of the Nervous System, 16,* 293–299.

Tylš, F., Páleníček, T., & Horáček, J. (2014). Psilocybin–summary of knowledge and new perspectives. *European Neuropsychopharmacology, 24*(3), 342–356.

Tynes, L. L., White, K., & Steketee, G. S. (1990). Toward a new nosology of Obsessive-compulsive disorder. *Comprehensive Psychiatry, 31,* 465–480. U.S. Department of Education, National Center for Education Statistics. (2012). *Digest of education statistics, 2011*(NCES 2012-001).

U.S. Department of Energy Office of Science. (2009). *Human genome project information.* Retrieved from http://www.ornl.gov/sci/techresources/Human_Genome/home.shtml

U.S. Department of Health and Human Services. (1991). *Health and behavior research.* National Institutes of Health: Report to Congress.

U.S. General Accounting Office. (1995). *Prescription drugs and the elderly: Many still receive potentially harmful drugs despite recent improvements.* (GOA/HEHS-95-152). United States General Accounting Office: Report to Congress.

Uchino, B. N. (2009). Understanding the link between social support and physical health: A life-span perspective with emphasis on the separability of perceived and received support. *Perspectives on Psychological Science, 4,* 236–255.

Uddin, M., Amstadter, A. B., Nugent, N. R., & Koenen, K. C. (2012). Genetics and genomics of posttraumatic stress disorder. In J. G. Beck & D. M. Sloan (Eds.), *The Oxford handbook of traumatic stress disorders* (pp. 143–158). New York, NY: Oxford University Press.

Uebelacker, L., & Whisman, M. (2006). Moderators of the association between relationship discord and major depression in a national population-based sample. *Journal of Family Psychology, 20,* 40–46.

Uehara, T., Yamasaki, T., Okamoto, T., Koike, T., Kan, S., Miyauchi, S., & Tobimatsu, S. (2013). Efficiency of a "small-world" brain network depends on consciousness level: A resting-state fMRI study. *Cerebral Cortex.* doi: 10.1093/cercor/bht004

Uhde, T. (1994). The anxiety disorder: Phenomenology and treatment of core symptoms and associated sleep disturbance. In M. Kryger, T. Roth, & W. Dement (Eds.), *Principles and practice of sleep medicine* (pp. 871–898). Philadelphia, PA: Saunders.

Uher, R. (2011). Gene-enviroment interactions. In K. S. Kendler, S. Jaffee, & D. Romer (Eds.), *The dynamic genome and mental health: The role of genes and environments in youth development* (pp. 29–58). New York, NY: Oxford University Press.

Uleman, J. S., Saribay, S. A., & Gonzalez, C. M. (2008). Spontaneous inferences, implicit impressions, and implicit theories. *Annual Review of Psychology, 59,* 329–360.

UNAIDS (2009). *AIDS epidemic update 2009.* Geneva: Joint United Nations Programme on HIV/AIDS (UNAIDS). Retrieved from http://www.who.int/hiv/pub/epidemiology / epidemic/en/index.html

Unger, J. B., Yan, L., Chen, X., Jiang, X., Azen, S., Qian, G., & Johnson, C. (2001). Adolescent smoking in Wuhan, China: Baseline data from the Wuhan Smoking Prevention Trial. *American Journal of Preventive Medicine, 21*(3), 162–169.

Unutzer, J., Katon, W., Callahan, C. M., Williams, J. W., Hunkeler, E., Harpole, L., & Langston, C. (2002). Collaborative care management of late-life depression in the primary care setting: A randomized controlled trial. *JAMA: Journal of the American Medical Association, 288,* 2836–2845.

Urbina, S. (2014). *Essentials of psychological testing.* Hoboken, NJ: John Wiley & Sons.

Ursano, R. J., Sonnenberg, S. M., & Lazar, S. G. (2008). Psychodynamic psychotherapy. In R. E. Hales, S. C. Yudofsky, & G. O. Gabbard (Eds.), *The American Psychiatric Publishing textbook of psychiatry* (5th ed., pp. 1171– 1190). Arlington, VA: American Psychiatric Publishing.

U.S. Department of Health and Human Services. The Health Consequences of Smoking—50 Years of Progress: A Report of the Surgeon General. Atlanta, GA:

U.S. Department of Health and Human Services, Centers for Disease Control and Prevention, National Center for Chronic Disease Prevention and Health Promotion, Office on Smoking and Health, 2014. http://www.surgeongeneral.gov/library/reports/50-years-of-progress/exec-summary.pdf

Ussher, J. M. (2013). Diagnosing difficult women and pathologising femininity: Gender bias in psychiatric nosology. *Feminism & Psychology, 23*(1), 63–69.

Vachon, D. D., Lynam, D. R., Widiger, T. A., Miller, J. D., McCrae, R. R., & Costa, P. T. (2013). Basic Traits Predict the Prevalence of Personality Disorder Across the Life Span The Example of Psychopathy. *Psychological Science, 24*(5), 698–705.

Vahia, I. V., & Cohen, C. I. (2009). Schizophrenia and delusional disorders. In B. J. Sadock, V. A. Sadock, & P. Ruiz (Eds.), *Kaplan & Sadock's comprehensive textbook of psychiatry* (9th ed., Vol. II, pp. 4073– 4081). Philadelphia, PA: Lippincott Williams & Wilkins.

Vaillant, G. E. (1979). Natural history of male psychological health. *New England Journal of Medicine, 301*, 1249–1254.

Vaillant, G. E. (1992). *Ego mechanisms of defense: A guide for clinicians and researchers.* Washington, D.C.: American Psychiatric Press.

Vaillant, G. E. (2012). Lifting the field's "repression" of defenses. *American Journal of Psychiatry, 169*(9), 885–887.

Valchev, V. H., Nel, J. A., Van de Vijver, F. J., Meiring, D., De Bruin, G. P., & Rothmann, S. (2013). Similarities and differences in implicit personality concepts across Ethno-cultural groups in South Africa. *Journal of Cross-Cultural Psychology, 44*(3), 365–388.

Valera, E. M., Faraone, S. V., Murray, K. E., & Seidman, L. J. (2007). Meta-analysis of structural imaging findings in attention-deficit/hyperactivity disorder. *Biological Psychiatry, 61*, 1361–1369.

Valtonen, H. M., Suominen, K., Mantere, O., Leppämäki, S., Arvilommi, P., & Isometsä, E. (2007). Suicidal behaviour during different phases of bipolar disorder. *Journal of Affective Disorders, 97*, 101–107.

Van Ameringen, M., Mancini, C., Patterson, B., & Simpson, W. (2009). Pharmacotherapy for social anxiety disorder: An update. *The Israel Journal of Psychiatry and Related Sciences, 46*(1), 53–61.

van Amsterdam, J., & van den Brink, W. (2013). Reduced-risk drinking as a viable treatment goal in problematic alcohol use and alcohol dependence. *Journal of Psychopharmacology, 27*(11), 987–997.

van Beijsterveldt, C., Hudziak, J., & Boomsma, D. (2006). Genetic and environmental influences on cross-gender behavior and relation to behavior problems: A study of Dutch twins at ages 7 and 10 years. *Archives of Sexual Behavior, 35*, 647–658.

van der Hart, O., & Nijenhuis, E. R. S. (2009). Dissociative disorders. In P. H. Blaney & T. Millon (Eds.), *Oxford textbook of psychopathology* (2nd ed., pp. 452–481). New York, NY: Oxford University Press.

van der Kloet, D., Giesbrecht, T., Lynn, S. J., Merckelbach, H., & de Zutter, A. (2012). Sleep normalization and decrease in dissociative experiences: Evaluation in an inpatient sample. *Journal of Abnormal Psychology, 121*, 140–150. doi: 10.1037/a0024781

van der Meer, L., Sutherland, D., O'Reilly, M. F., Lancioni, G. E., & Sigafoos, J. (2012). A further comparison of manual signing, picture exchange, and speech-generating devices as communication modes for children with autism spectrum disorders. *Research in Autism Spectrum Disorders, 6*(4), 1247–1257.

van Dongen, J., Ehli, E. A., Slieker, R. C., Bartels, M., Weber, Z. M., Davies, G. E., . . . Boomsma, D. I. (2014). Epigenetic variation in monozygotic twins: a genome-wide analysis of DNA methylation in buccal cells. *Genes, 5*(2), 347–365. doi:10.3390/genes5020347

van Duijil, M., Cardena, E., & de Jong, J. (2005). The validity of DSM-IV dissociative disorders in southwest Uganda. *Transcultural Psychiatry, 42*, 219–241.

Van Dycke, K. C., Rodenburg, W., van Oostrom, C. T., van Kerkhof, L. W., Pennings, J. L., Roenneberg, T., . . . van der Horst, G. T. (2015). Chronically Alternating Light Cycles Increase Breast Cancer Risk in Mice. *Current Biology, 25*(14), 1932–1937.

van Haren, N. E., Rijsdijk, F., Schnack, H. G., Picchioni, M. M., Toulopoulou, T., Weisbrod, M., . . . Boomsma, D. I. (2012). The genetic and environmental determinants of the association between brain abnormalities and schizophrenia: the schizophrenia twins and relatives consortium. *Biological Psychiatry, 71*(10), 915–921.

van Hoeken, D., Veling, W., Sinke, S., Mitchell, J. E., & Hoek, H. W. (2009). The validity and utility of subtyping bulimia nervosa. *International Journal of Eating Disorders, 42*(7), 595–602.

van Kammen, D. P., Docherty, J. P., & Bunney, W. E. (1982). Prediction of early relapse after pimozide discontinuation by response to d-amphetamine during pimozide treatment. *Biological Psychiatry, 17*, 223–242.

van Laar, M., Volkerts, E., & Verbaten, M. (2001). Subchronic effects of the GABA-agonist lorazepam and the 5-HT2A/2C antagonist ritanserin on driving performance, slow wave sleep and daytime sleepiness in healthy volunteers. *Psychopharmacology (Berlin), 154*, 189–197.

van Munster, B. C., & de Rooij, S. E. (2014). Delirium: A synthesis of current knowledge. *Clinical Medicine, 14*(2), 192–195.

Van Orden, K. A., Witte, T. K., Cukrowicz, K. C., Braithwaite, S. R., Selby, E. A., & Joiner, T. E., Jr. (2010). The interpersonal theory of suicide. *Psychological Review, 117*(2), 575–600.

van Os, J. (2011). Should attenuated psychosis syndrome be a DSM-5 diagnosis? *American Journal of Psychiatry, 168*(5), 460–463.

van Os, J., & Allardyce, J. (2009). The clinical epidemiology of schizophrenia. In B. J. Sadock, V. A. Sadock, & P. Ruiz (Eds.), *Kaplan & Sadock's comprehensive textbook of psychiatry* (9th ed., Vol. I, pp. 1475–1487). Philadelphia, PA: Lippincott Williams & Wilkins.

van Os, J., Kenis, G., & Rutten, B. P. (2010). The environment and schizophrenia. *Nature, 468*(7321), 203–212.

van Overveld, M., de Jong, P. J., & Peters, M. L. (2011). The Multi-Dimensional Blood/Injury Phobia Inventory: Its psychometric properties and relationship with disgust propensity and disgust sensitivity. *Journal of Anxiety Disorders, 25*(3), 319–325. doi: http://dx.doi.org/10.1016/j.janxdis.2010.10.004

Van Praag, H. M., & Korf, J. (1975). Central monamine deficiency in depressions: Causative of secondary phenomenon? *Pharmakopsychiatr Neuropsychopharmakol, 8*, 322–326.

Van Rooij, A. J., Schoenmakers, T. M., Vermulst, A. A., Van Den Eijnden, R. J. J. M., & Van De Mheen, D. (2011). Online video game addiction: Identification of addicted adolescent gamers. *Addiction, 106*(1), 205–212. doi: 10.1111/j.1360-0443.2010.03104.x

Van Ryzin, M. J., Fosco, G. M., & Dishion, T. J. (2012). Family and peer predictors of substance use from early adolescence to early adulthood: An 11-year prospective analysis. *Addictive Behaviors, 37*(12), 1314–1324. doi: 10.1016/j.addbeh.2012.06.020

Vander Wal, J. S. (2012). Night eating syndrome: a critical review of the literature. *Clinical Psychology Review, 32*(1), 49–59.

VanDerHeyden, A., & Harvey, M. (2012). Using data to advance learning outcomes in schools. *Journal of Positive Behavior Interventions.* doi: 10.1177/1098300712442387

Vanderstichele, H., Bibl, M., Engelborghs, S., Le Bastard, N., Lewczuk, P., Molinuevo, J. L., & Blennow, K. (2012). Standardization of preanalytical aspects of cerebrospinal fluid biomarker testing for Alzheimer's disease diagnosis: A consensus paper from the Alzheimer's Biomarkers Standardization Initiative. *Alzheimer's & Dementia, 8*(1), 65–73. doi: http://dx.doi.org/10.1016/j.jalz.2011.07.004

Vanitallie, T. B., & Lew, E. A. (1992). Assessment of morbidity and mortality risk in the overweight patient. In T. A. Wadden and T. B. Vanitallie (Eds.), *Treatment of the seriously obese patient.* New York, NY: Guilford.

Vannucchi, G., Masi, G., Toni, C., Dell'Osso, L., Marazziti, D., & Perugi, G. (2014). Clinical features, developmental course, and psychiatric comorbidity of adult autism spectrum disorders. *CNS Spectrums, 19*(02), 157–164.

van't Veer-Tazelaar, P. J., van Marwijk, H. W. J., van Oppen, P., van Hout, H. P. J., van der Horst, H. E., Cuijpers, P., & Beekman, A. T. (2009). Stepped-care prevention of anxiety and depression in late life: A randomized controlled trial. *Archives of General Psychiatry, 66*(3), 297–304.

Varga, M. D. (2012). Adderall abuse on college campuses: A comprehensive literature review. *Journal of Evidence-Based Social Work, 9*(3), 293–313.

Vasterling, J. J., Brailey, K., Constans, J. I., & Sotker, P. B. (1998). Attention and memory dysfunction in posttraumatic stress disorders. *Neuropsychology, 12*(1), 125–133.

Vazsonyi, A. T., Ksinan, A., Mikuška, J., & Jiskrova, G. (2015). The Big Five and adolescent adjustment: An empirical test across six cultures. *Personality and Individual Differences, 83*, 234–244.

Vazques, G. H., Holtzman, J. N., Tondo, L., & Baldessarini, R. J. (2015). Efficacy and tolerability of treatment for bipolar depression. *Journal of Affective Disorders, 183*, 258–262.

Veale, D. (2000). Outcome of cosmetic surgery and "DIY" surgery inpatients with body dysmorphic disorder. *Psychiatric Bulletin, 24*(6), 218–221.

Veale, D., & Riley, S. (2001). Mirror, mirror on the wall, who is the ugliest of them all? The psychopathology of mirror gazing in body dysmorphic disorder. *Behaviour Research and Therapy, 39*, 1381–1393.

Veale, D., Boocock, A., Gournay, K., Dryden, W., Shah, F., & Walburn, J. (1996). Body dysmorphic disorder: A survey of 50 cases. *British Journal of Psychiatry, 169*, 196–201.

Veale, D., Ennis, M., & Lambrou, C. (2002). Possible association of body dysmorphic disorder with an occupation or education in art and design. *American Journal of Psychiatry, 159*, 1788–1790.

Veale, D., Gournay, K., Dryden, W., Boocock, A., Shah, F., Willson, R., & Walburn, J. (1996). Body dysmorphic disorder: A cognitive behavioral model and pilot randomized control trial. *Behaviour Research and Therapy, 34,* 717–729.

Veith, I. (1965). Hysteria: *The history of a disease.* Chicago: University of Chicago Press. Vellas, B., Coley, N., Ousset, P. J., Berrut, G., Dartigues, J. F., Dubois, B., . . . Touchon, J. (2012). Long-term use of standardised Ginkgo biloba extract for the prevention of Alzheimer's disease (GuidAge): a randomised placebo-controlled trial. *The Lancet Neurology, 11*(10), 851–859.

Venables, P. H. (1996). Schizotypy and maternal exposure to influenza and to cold temperature: The Mauritius study. *Journal of Abnormal Psychology, 105,* 53–60.

Venables, N. C., Hall, J. R., & Patrick, C. J. (2014). Differentiating psychopathy from antisocial personality disorder: A triarchic model perspective. *Psychological Medicine, 44*(05), 1005–1013.

Verma, K. K., Khaitan, B. K., & Singh, O. P. (1998). The frequency of sexual dysfunction in patients attending a sex therapy clinic in North India. *Archives of Sexual Behavior, 27,* 309–314.

Vermetten, E., Schmahl, C., Lindner, S., Loewenstein, R., & Bremner, J. (2006). Hippocampal and amygdalar volumes in dissociative identity disorder. *American Journal of Psychiatry, 163,* 630–636.

Vermund, S. H., Sheldon, E. K., & Sidat, M. (2015). Southern Africa: The highest priority region for HIV prevention and care interventions. *Current HIV/AIDS Report, 12,* 191–195.

Vernberg, E. M., LaGreca, A. M., Silverman, W. K., & Prinstein, M. J. (1996). Prediction of posttraumatic stress symptoms in children after Hurricane Andrew. *Journal of Abnormal Psychology, 105,* 237–248.

Viana, A. G., Beidel, D. C., & Rabian, B. (2009). Selective mutism: A review and integration of the last 15 years. *Clinical Psychology Review, 29*(1), 57–67. doi: 10.1016/j.cpr.2008.09.009

Viguera, A. C., Tondo, L., Koukopoulos, A. E., Reginaldi, D., Lepri, B., & Baldessarini, R. (2011). Episodes of mood disorders in 2,252 pregnancies and postpartum periods. *American Journal of Psychiatry, 168*(11), 1179–1185.

Vingerhoets, A. J. J. M., Rottenberg, J., Cevaal, A., & Nelson, J. K. (2007). Is there a relationship between depression and crying? A review. *Acta Psychiatrica Scandinavica, 115,* 340–351.

Vinkers, D., de Vries, S., van Baars, A., & Mulder, C. (2010). Ethnicity and dangerousness criteria for court ordered admission to a psychiatric hospital. *Social Psychiatry and Psychiatric Epidemiology, 45*(2), 221–224.

Virag, R. (1999). Indications and early results of sildenafil (Viagra) in erectile dysfunction. *Urology, 54,* 1073–1077.

Vitacco, M. J., Neumann, C. S., & Caldwell, M. F. (2010). Predicting antisocial behavior in high-risk male adolescents: Contributions of psychopathy and instrumental violence. *Criminal Justice and Behavior, 37*(8), 833–846.

Vitacco, M. J., Neumann, C. S., & Pardini, D. A. (2014). Predicting future criminal offending in a community-based sample of males

using self-reported psychopathy. *Criminal Justice and Behavior, 41*(3), 345–363.

Vitiello, B., & Lederhendler, I. (2000). Research on eating disorders: Current status and future prospects. *Biological Psychiatry, 47,* 777–786.

Vogel, S. A., & Reder, S. (1998). Educational attainment of adults with learning disabilities. In A. A. Vogel & S. Reder (Eds.), *Learning disabilities, literacy, and adult education* (pp. 5–28). Baltimore, MD: Paul H. Brookes.

Vohs, K. D., Bardone, A. M., Joiner, T. E., Jr., Abramson, L. Y., & Heatherton, T. F. (1999). Perfectionism, perceived weight status, and self-esteem interact to predict bulimic symptoms: A model of bulimic symptom development. *Journal of Abnormal Psychology, 108,* 695–700.

Voigt, K., Nagel, A., Meyer, B., Langs, G., Braukhaus, C., & Lowe, B. (2010). Towards positive diagnostic criteria: A systematic review of somatoform disorder diagnoses and suggestions for future classification. *Journal of Psychosomatic Research, 68*(5), 403–414.

Voigt, K., Wollburg, E., Weinmann, N., Herzog, A., Meyer, B., Langs, G., & Lowe, B. (2012). Predictive validity and clinical utility of DSM-5 somatic symptom disorder—Comparison with DSM-IV somatoform disorders and additional criteria for consideration. *Journal of Psychosomatic Research, 73*(5), 345–350. doi: 10.1016/j.jpsychores.2012.08.020

Volkow, N. D., Baler, R. D., Compton, W. M., & Weiss, S. R. (2014). Adverse health effects of marijuana use. *New England Journal of Medicine, 370*(23), 2219–2227.

Volkow, N. D., Wang, G. J., Kollins, S. H., Wigal, T. L., Newcorn, J. H., Telang, F., & Swanson, J. M. (2009). Evaluating dopamine reward pathway in ADHD: Clinical implications. *JAMA: Journal of the American Medical Association, 302*(10), 1084–1091.

Voon, V., Gallea, C., Hattori, N., Bruno, M., Ekanayake, V., & Hallett, M. (2010). The involuntary nature of conversion disorder. *Neurology, 74*(3), 223–228.

Voos, A., Pelphrey, K., Tirrell, J., Bolling, D., Wyk, B., Kaiser, M., & Ventola, P. (2013). Neural mechanisms of improvements in social motivation after pivotal response treatment: Two case studies. *Journal of Autism and Developmental Disorders, 43*(1), 1–10. doi: 10.1007/s10803-012-1683-9

Vriends, N., Pfaltz, M. C., Novianti, P., & Hadiyono, J. (2013). Taijin kyofusho and social anxiety and their clinical relevance in Indonesia and Switzerland. *Frontiers in Psychology, 4,* 3. doi: 10.3389/fpsyg.2013.00003

Vrshek-Schallhorn, S., Stroud, C.B., Mineka, S., Hammen, C., Zinbarg, R.E., Wolitzky-Taylor, K., Craske, M.G. (2015). Chronic and episodic interpersonal stress as statistically unique predictors of depression in two samples of emerging adults. *Journal of Abnormal Psychology, 124*(4), 918.

Waddell, J., Morris, R. W., & Bouton, M. E. (2006). Effects of bed nucleus of the stria terminalis lesions on conditioned anxiety: Aversive conditioning with long-duration conditional stimuli and reinstatement of extinguished fear. *Behavioral Neuroscience, 120,* 324–336.

Wadden, T. A., & Osei, S. (2002). The treatment of obesity: An overview. In T. A. Wadden & A. J. Stunkard (Eds.), *Handbook of obesity treatment* (pp. 229–248). New York, NY: Guilford.

Wadden, T. A., Brownell, K. D., & Foster, G. D. (2002). Obesity: Responding to the global epidemic. *Journal of Consulting and Clinical Psychology, 70,* 510–525.

Wadden, T. A., Butryn, M. L., Hong, P. S., & Tsai, A. G. (2014). Behavioral treatment of obesity in patients encountered in primary care settings: a systematic review. *JAMA, 312*(17), 1779–1791.

Wade, T. D., Bulik, C. M., Prescott, C. A., & Kendler, K. S. (2004). Sex influences on shared risk factors for bulimia nervosa and other psychiatric disorders. *Archives of General Psychiatry, 61,* 251–256.

Wade, T. D., Tiggemann, M., Bulik, C. M., Fairburn, C. G., Wray, N. R., & Martin, N. G. (2008). Shared temperament risk factors for anorexia nervosa: A twin study. *Psychosomatic Medicine, 70*(2), 239–244.

Wager, T. (2005). The neural bases of placebo effects in pain. *Current Directions in Psychological Science, 14,* 175–179.

Wagner, B. M. (1997). Family risk factors for child and adolescent suicidal behavior. *Psychological Bulletin, 121,* 246–298.

Wagner, G., Penelo, E., Wanner, C., Gwinner, P., Trofaier, M. L., Imgart, H., . . . Karwautz, A. F. (2013). Internet-delivered cognitive–behavioural therapy v. conventional guided self-help for bulimia nervosa: long-term evaluation of a randomised controlled trial. *The British Journal of Psychiatry, 202*(2), 135–141.

Wagner, D., Becker, B., Koester, P., Gouzoulis-Mayfrank, E., & Daumann, J. (2012). A prospective study of learning, memory, and executive function in new MDMA users. *Addiction, 108*(1), 136–145. doi: 10.1111/j.1360-0443.2012.03977.x

Wagner, K. D., & Pliszka, S. R. (2009). Treatment of child and adolescent disorders. In A. F. Schatzberg & C. B. Nemeroff (Eds.), *The American Psychiatric Publishing textbook of psychopharmacology* (4th ed., pp. 1309–1372). Arlington, VA: American Psychiatry Publishing.

Wakefield, J. C. (1999). Evolutionary versus prototype analyses of the concept of disorder. *Journal of Abnormal Psychology, 108,* 3, 374–399.

Wakefield, J. C. (2003). Dysfunction as a factual component of disorder. *Behavior Research and Therapy, 41,* 969–990.

Wakefield, J. C. (2009). Mental disorder and moral responsibility: Disorders of personhood as harmful dysfunctions, with special reference to alcoholism. *Philosophy, Psychiatry, & Psychology, 16*(1), 91–99.

Wakefield, J.C., Schmitz, M. F., First, M. B., & Horwitz, A. V. (2007). Extending the bereavement exclusion for major depression to other losses: Evidence from the national comorbidity survey. *Archives of General Psychiatry, 64,* 433–440

Walker, D. L., Ressler, K. J., Lu, K.-T., & Davis, M. (2002). Facilitation of conditioned fear extinction by systemic administration or intra-amygdala infusions of D-cycloserine assessed with fear-potentiated startle. *Journal of Neuroscience, 22,* 2343–2351.

Walkup, J. T., Albano, A. M., Piacentini, J., Birmaher, B., Compton, S. N., Sherrill, J. T., & Kendall, P. C. (2008). Cognitive behavioral therapy, sertraline, or a combination in childhood anxiety. *New England Journal of Medicine, 359*(26), 2753–2766. doi: 10.1056/NEJMoa0804633

Wall, T. D., Wygant, D. B., & Sellbom, M. (2015). Boldness explains a key difference between psychopathy and antisocial personality disorder. *Psychiatry, Psychology and Law, 22*(1), 94–105.

Wallace, C. S., Kilman, V. L., Withers, G. S., & Greenough, W. T. (1992). Increases in dendritic length in occipital cortex after 4 days of differential housing in weanling rats. *Behavioral and Neural Biology, 58*, 64–68.

Wallace, J., & O'Hara, M. W. (1992). Increases in depressive symptomatology in the rural elderly: Results from a cross-sectional and longitudinal study. *Journal of Abnormal Psychology, 101*(3), 398–404.

Waller, N. G., & Ross, C. A. (1997). The prevalence and biometric structure of pathological dissociation in the general population: Taxometric and behavior genetic findings. *Journal of Abnormal Psychology, 106*, 499–510.

Waller, N. G., Putnam, F. W., & Carlson, E. B. (1996). Types of dissociation and dissociative types: A taxometric analysis of dissociative experiences. *Psychological Methods, 1*, 300–321.

Waller, R., Dotterer, H. L., & Hyde, L. W. (2015). A Gene-Environment Approach to Understanding Youth Antisocial Behavior. *Emerging Trends in the Social and Behavioral Sciences: An Interdisciplinary, Searchable, and Linkable Resource.* 1–33.

Waller, R., Gardner, F., Hyde, L. W., Shaw, D. S., Dishion, T. J., & Wilson, M. N. (2012). Do harsh and positive parenting predict parent reports of deceitful-callous behavior in early childhood? *Journal of Child Psychology and Psychiatry, 53*(9), 946–953.

Waller, R., Gardner, F., Shaw, D. S., Dishion, T. J., Wilson, M. N., & Hyde, L. W. (2015). Callous-unemotional behavior and early-childhood onset of behavior problems: the role of parental harshness and warmth. *Journal of Clinical Child & Adolescent Psychology, 44*(4), 655–667.

Waln, O., & Jankovic, J. (2013). An update on tardive dyskinesia: From phenomenology to treatment. *Tremor and Other Hyperkinetic Movements, 3*, pii: tre-03-161-4138-1.

Walsh, B. T. (1991). Fluoxetine treatment of bulimia nervosa. *Journal of Psychosomatic Research, 35*, 471–475.

Walsh, B. T. (1995). Pharmacotherapy of eating disorders. In K. D. Brownell & C. G. Fairburn (Eds.), *Eating disorders and obesity: A comprehensive handbook* (pp. 313–317). New York, NY: Guilford.

Walsh, B. T. (2010). Eating disorders in DSM-V: Review of existing literature (Part 3). *International Journal of Eating Disorders, 43*(2), 97.

Walsh, B. T., Agras, W. S., Devlin, M. J., Fairburn, C. G., Wilson, G. T., Kahn, C., & Chally, M. K. (2000). Fluoxetine for bulimia nervosa following poor response to psychotherapy. *American Journal of Psychiatry, 157*, 1332–1334.

Walsh, B. T., Hadigan, C. M., Devlin, M. J., Gladis, M., & Roose, S. P. (1991). Long-term outcome of antidepressant treatment of bulimia nervosa. *Archives of General Psychiatry, 148*, 1206–1212.

Walsh, B. T., Kaplan, A. S., Attia, E., Olmsted, M., Parides, M., Carter, J. C., & Rockert, W. (2006). Fluoxetine after weight restoration in anorexia nervosa. *JAMA: Journal of the American Medical Association, 295*, 2605–2612.

Walsh, B. T., Wilson, G. T., Loeb, K. L., Devlin, M. J., Pike, K. M., Roose, S. P., Fleiss, J., & Waternaux, C. (1997). Medication and psychotherapy in the treatment of bulimia nervosa. *American Journal of Psychiatry, 154*, 523–531.

Walsh, J. K., Mayleben, D., Guico-Pabia, C., Vandormael, K., Martinez, R., & Deacon, S. (2008). Efficacy of the selective extrasynaptic GABA A agonist, gaboxadol, in a model of transient insomnia: A randomized, controlled clinical trial. *Sleep Medicine, 9*(4), 393–402.

Walsh, K., Danielson, C. K., McCauley, J. L., Saunders, B. E., Kilpatrick, D. G., & Resnick, H. S. (2012). National prevalence of post-traumatic stress disorder among sexually revictimized adolescent, college, and adult household-residing women. *Archives of General Psychiatry, 69*(9), 935–942. doi: 10.1001/archgenpsychiatry.2012.132

Walters, E. E., & Kendler, K. S. (1995). Anorexia nervosa and anorexia-like syndromes in a population based female twin sample. *American Journal of Psychiatry, 152*, 64–71.

Wan, M., Abel, K., & Green, J. (2008). The transmission of risk to children from mothers with schizophrenia: A developmental psychopathology model. *Clinical Psychology Review, 28*(4), 613–637.

Wan, Y. Y. (2010). Multitasking of helper T cells. *Immunology, 130*, 166–171.

Wang, H., Troy, L. M., Rogers, G. T., Fox, C. S., McKeown, N. M., Meigs, J. B., & Jacques, P. F. (2014). Longitudinal association between dairy consumption and changes of body weight and waist circumference: *The Framingham Heart Study. International Journal of Obesity, 38*(2), 299–305. doi:10.1038/ijo.2013.78

Wang, P. S., Berglund, P., Olfson, M., Pincus, H. A., Wells, K. B., & Kessler, R. C. (2005). Failure and delay in initial treatment contact after first onset of mental disorders in the national comorbidity survey replication. *Archives of General Psychiatry, 62*, 603–613.

Wang, P. S., Bohn, R. L., Glynn, R. J., Mogun, H., & Avorn, J. (2001). Hazardous benzodiazepine regimens in the elderly: Effects of half-life, dosage, and duration on risk of hip fracture. *American Journal of Psychiatry, 158*, 892–898.

Wang, S. (2006). Contagious behavior. *Psychological Science, 19*, 22–26.

Wang, S., & Blazer, D.G. (2015). Depression and cognition in the elderly. *Annual Review of Clinical Psychology, 11*, 331.

Wang, T., Collet, J.-P., Shapiro, S., & Ware, M. A. (2008). Adverse effects of medical cannabinoids: A systematic review. *CMAJ, 178*(13), 1669–1678. doi: 10.1503/cmaj.071178

Wang, X., Wang, D., & Shen, J. (2006). The effects of social support on depression in the aged. *Chinese Journal of Clinical Psychology, 14*, 73.

Wang, Y., Wang, P., Xu, X., Goldstein, J., McConkie, A., Cheung, S. W., & Jiang, Y.-H. (2015). Genetics of autism spectrum disorders: The opportunity and challenge in the genetics clinic. In S. H. Fatemi (Ed.), *Molecular basis of autism* (pp. 33–66). New York, NY: Springer.

Wang, Z., Baker, D. G., Harrer, J., Hamner, M., Price, M., & Amstadter, A. (2011). The relationship between combat-related posttraumatic stress disorder and the 5-HTTLPR/rs25531 polymorphism. *Depression and Anxiety, 28*, 1067–1073. doi: 10.1002/da.20872

Wang, Z., Neylan, T. C., Mueller, S. G., Lenoci, M., Truran, D., Marmar, C. R., & Schuff, N. (2010). Magnetic resonance imaging of hippocampal subfields in posttraumatic stress disorder. *Archives of General Psychiatry, 67*(3), 296–303. doi: 10.1001/archgenpsychiatry.2009.205

Ward, M. M., Swan, G. E., & Chesney, M. A. (1987). Arousal-reduction treatments for mild hypertension: A meta-analysis of recent studies. *Handbook of Hypertension, 9*, 285–302.

Ward, T., & Beech, A. R. (2008). An integrated theory of sexual offending. In D. R. Laws & W. T. O'Donohue (Eds.), *Sexual deviance: Theory, assessment, and treatment* (2nd ed., pp. 21–36). New York, NY: Guilford.

Warshaw, M. G., Dolan, R. T., Keller, M. B. (2000). Suicidal behavior in patients with current or past panic disorder: Five years of prospective data from the Harvard/Brown Anxiety Research Program. *American Journal of Psychiatry, 157*, 1876–1878.

Warwick, H. M., & Salkovskis, P. M. (1990). Hypochondriasis. *Behavior Research Therapy, 28*, 105–117.

Washington v. Harper, 494 U.S. 210 C.F.R. (1990).

Waters, E., de Silva-Sanigorski, A., Hall, B. J., Brown, T. Campbell, K. J., Gao, Y., & Summerbell, C. D. (2011). Interventions for preventing obesity in children. *Cochrane Database System Review, 12*: CD001871.

Waters, F., Allen, P., Aleman, A., Fernyhough, C., Woodward, T. S., Badcock, J. C., . . . Vercammen, A. (2012). Auditory hallucinations in schizophrenia and nonschizophrenia populations: a review and integrated model of cognitive mechanisms. *Schizophrenia Bulletin, 38*(4), 683–693.

Watson, G. L., Arcona, A. P., & Antonuccio, D. O. (2015). The ADHD drug abuse crisis on American college campuses. *Ethical Human Psychology and Psychiatry, 17*(1), 5–21.

Watson, J. B. (1913). Psychology as a behaviorist views it. *Psychology Review, 20*, 158–177.

Watson, S. M. R., Richels, C., Michalek, A. P., & Raymer, A. (2015). Psychosocial treatments for ADHD: A systematic appraisal of the evidence. *Journal of Attention Disorders, 19*(1), 3–10. doi: 10.1177/1087054712447857

Weaver, J. C. G., Cervoni, N., Champagne, F. A., D'Alessio, A. C., Charma, S., Seckl, J., & Meaney, M. J. (2004). Epigenetic programming by maternal behavior. *Nature Neuroscience, 7*, 847–854.

Wechsler, H., Lee, J.E., Kuo, M., Seibring, M., Nelson, T.F., & Lee, H. (2002). Trends in college binge drinking during a period of increased prevention efforts: Findings from 4 Harvard School of Public Health College Alcohol Study surveys: 1993–2001. *Journal of American College Health, 50*(5):203–217.

Weck, F., Neng, J. M. B., Richtberg, S., Jakob, M., & Stangier, U. (2015). Cognitive therapy versus exposure therapy for hypochondriasis (health anxiety): A randomized controlled trial. *Journal of Consulting and Clinical Psychology, 83*, 665–676.

Weems, C. F., Silverman, W. K., & La Greca, A. M. (2000). What do youths referred for anxiety problems worry about?: Worry and its relation to anxiety and anxiety disorders in children and adolescents. *Journal of Abnormal Child Psychology, 28*, 63–72.

Wegner, D. (1989). *White bears and other unwanted thoughts.* New York, NY: Viking.

Wehr, T. A., Duncan, W. C., Jr., Sher, L., Aeschbach, D., Schwartz, P. J., Turner, E. H., & Rosenthal, N. E. (2001). A circadian signal of change of season in patients with seasonal affective disorder. *Archives of General Psychiatry, 58*, 1108–1114.

Weight Watchers International. (2010). Company overview. Retrieved from http://www.weightwatchersinternational.com/phoenix.zhtml?c5130178&p5irol-irhome

Weinberg, M. S., Lottes, I. L., & Shaver, F. M. (1995). Swedish or American youth: Who is more permissive? *Archives of Sexual Behavior, 24*, 409–437.

Weinberger, D. R., Berman, K. F., & Chase, T. N. (1988). Mesocortical dopaminergic function and human cognition. *Annals of the New York Academy of Sciences, 537*, 330–338.

Weiner, D. B. (1979). The apprenticeship of Philippe Pinel: A new document, 'Observations of Citizen Pussin on the insane.' *The American Journal of Psychiatry, 136*(9), 1128–1134.

Weiner, D. N. (1996). *Premature ejaculation: An evaluation of sensitivity to erotica.* Unpublished doctoral dissertation, State University of New York, Albany.

Weiner, L., & Avery-Clark, C. (2014). Sensate Focus: clarifying the Masters and Johnson's model. *Sexual and Relationship Therapy, 29*(3), 307–319.

Weiner, M. F., Hynan, L. S., Beekly, D., Koepsell, T. D., & Kukull, W. A. (2007). Comparison of Alzheimer's disease in American Indians, whites, and African Americans. *Alzheimer's & Dementia, 3*(3), 211–216.

Weiner, M. W., Aisen, P. S., Jack, Jr., C. R., Jagust, W. J., Trojanowski, J. Q., Shaw, L., & Schmidt, M. (2010). The Alzheimer's Disease Neuroimaging Initiative: Progress report and future plans. *Alzheimer's and Dementia, 6*(3), 202–211, e207.

Weiner, M. W., Veitch, D. P., Aisen, P. S., Beckett, L. A., Cairns, N. J., Green, R. C., & Trojanowski, J. Q. (2012). The Alzheimer's Disease Neuroimaging Initiative: A review of papers published since its inception. *Alzheimer's & Dementia, 8*(1, Supplement), S1–S68. doi: http://dx.doi.org/10.1016/j.jalz.2011.09.172

Weinstock, H., Berman, S., & Cates, W. (2004). Sexually transmitted diseases in American youth: Incidence and prevalence estimates. *Perspectives on Sexual and Reproductive Health, 36*, 6–10.

Weisberg, R. B., Maki, K. M., Culpepper, L., & Keller, M. B. (2005). Is anyone really 1.1.D.?: The occurrence and course of mixed anxiety-depressive disorder in a sample of primary care patients. *Journal of Nervous and Mental Disease, 193*(4), 223–230.

Weisburg, R. B., Brown, T. A., Wincze, J. P., & Barlow, D. H. (2001). Causal attributions and male sexual arousal: The impact of attributions for a bogus erectile difficulty on sexual arousal, cognitions, and affect. *Journal of Abnormal Psychology, 110*(2), 324–334.

Weiser, M. (2011). Early intervention for schizophrenia: The risk-benefit ratio of antipsychotic treatment in the prodromal phase. *American Journal of Psychiatry, 168*(8), 761–763. doi: 10.1176/appi.ajp.2011.11050765

Weiskrantz, L. (1980). Varieties of residual experience. *Quarterly Journal of Experimental Psychology, 32*, 365–386.

Weiskrantz, L. (1992, September/October). Unconscious vision: The strange phenomenon of blindsight. *The Sciences*, pp. 23–28.

Weiss, B., & Garber, J. (2003). Developmental differences in the phenomenology of depression. *Development and Psychopathology, 15*, 403–430.

Weiss, L. G., Locke, V., Pan, T., Harris, J. G., Saklofske, D. H., & Prifitera, A. (2015). WISC-V Use in Societal Context. In L. G. Weiss, D. H. Saklofske, J. A. Holdnack & A. Prifitera (Eds.), *WISC-V Assessment and Interpretation: Scientist-Practitioner Perspectives*, 123–176. San Diego, CA: Elsevier.

Weiss, R. D., & Iannucci, R. A. (2009). Cocaine-related disorders. In B. J. Sadock, V. A. Sadock, & P. Ruiz (Eds.), *Kaplan & Sadock's comprehensive textbook of psychiatry* (9th ed., Vol. I, pp. 1318–1331). Philadelphia, PA: Lippincott Williams & Wilkins.

Weisse, C. S., Pato, C. W., McAllister, C. G., Littman, R., & Breier, A. (1990). Differential effects of controllable and uncontrollable acute stress on lymphocyte proliferation and leukocyte percentages in humans. *Brain, Behavior, and Immunity, 4*, 339–351.

Weissman, M. (1995). *Mastering depression: A patient's guide to interpersonal psychotherapy.* New York, NY: Oxford University Press.

Weissman, M., Bland, R., Canino, G., Greenwald, S., Hwo, H., Lee, C., & Eng-Kung, Y. (1994). The cross national epidemiology of obsessive compulsive disorder. *Journal of Clinical Psychiatry, 55*, 5–10.

Weissman, M., Wickramaratne, P., Nomura, Y., Verdeli, H., Pilowsky, D., Grillon, C., & Bruder, G. (2005). Families at high and low risk for depression: A 3-generation study. *Archives of General Psychiatry, 62*, 29–36.

Weissman, M. M., & Olfson, M. (1995). Depression in women: Implications for health care research. *Science, 269*, 799–801.

Weissman, M. M., Bland, R. C., Canino, G. J., Greenwald, S., Hwu, H. G., Lee, C. K., & et al. (1994). The cross national epidemiology of obsessive compulsive disorder. The Cross National Collaborative Group. *Journal of Clinical Psychiatry, 55*(Suppl.), 5–10.

Weissman, M. M., Bruce, M. L., Leaf, P. J., Florio, L. P., & Holzer, C. (1991). Affective disorders. In L. N. Robins & D. A. Regier (Eds.), *Psychiatric disorders of America: The epidemiologic catchment area study* (pp. 53–80). New York, NY: Free Press.

Weissman, M. M., Klerman, G. L., Markowitz, J. S., & Ouellette, R. (1989). Suicidal ideation and suicide attempts in panic disorder and attacks. *New England Journal of Medicine, 321*, 1209–1214.

Weissman, M. M., Wolk, S., Wickramaratne, P., Goldstein, R. B., Adams, P., Greenwald, S., & Steinberg, D. (1999). Children with prepubertal-onset major depressive disorder and anxiety grow up. *Archives of General Psychiatry, 56*, 794–801.

Weitz, E. S., Hollon, S. D., Twisk, J., van Straten, A., Huibers, M. J., David, D., . . . Cuijpers, P. (in press). Baseline depression severity as moderator of depression outcomes between cognitive behavioral therapy vs pharmacotherapy: An individual patient data meta-analysis. *JAMA Psychiatry.* doi:10.1001/jamapsychiatry.2015.1516

Weitze, C., & Osburg, S. (1996). Transsexualism in Germany: Empirical data on epidemiology and application of the German transsexuals' act during its first ten years. *Archives of Sexual Behavior, 25*, 409–465.

Welch, P. G., Carleton, R. N., & Asmundson, G. J. (2009). Measuring health anxiety: Moving past the dichotomous response option of the original Whiteley Index. *Journal of Anxiety Disorders, 23*, 1002–1007. doi: 10.1016/j.janxdis.2009.05.006

Welham, J., Scott, J., Williams, G., Najman, J., Bor, W., O'Callaghan, M., McGrath, J. (2008). Emotional and behavioural antecedents of young adults who screen positive for non-affective psychosis: A 21-year birth cohort study. *Psychological Medicine, 39*(4), 625–634.

Wells, A.,Welford, M., King, P., Papageorgiou, C., Wisely, J., & Mendel, E. (2010). A pilot randomized trial of metacognitive therapy vs applied relaxation in the treatment of adults with generalized anxiety disorder. *Behaviour Research and Therapy, 48*, 429–434.

Wells, B., & Twenge, J. (2005). Changes in young people's sexual behavior and attitudes, 1943–1999: A cross-temporal meta-analysis. *Review of General Psychology, 9*, 249–261.

Wells, D. L., & Ott, C. A. (2011). The "new" marijuana. *The Annals of Pharmacotherapy, 45*(3), 414–417. doi: 10.1345/aph.1P580

Wells, K. B., Stewart, A., Hays, R. D., Burnam, M. A., Rogers, W., Daniels, M., & Ware J. (1989). The functioning and well-being of depressed patients: Results from the medical outcomes study. *JAMA: Journal of the American Medical Association, 262*(7), 914–919.

Wermter, A.-K., Kamp-Becker, I., Hesse, P., Schulte-Körne, G., Strauch, K., & Remschmidt, H. (2010). Evidence for the involvement of genetic variation in the *oxytocin receptor gene (OXTR)* in the etiology of autistic disorders on high-functioning level. *American Journal of Medical Genetics Part B: Neuropsychiatric Genetics, 153B*(2), 629–639.

Werner, K. B., Few, L. R., & Bucholz, K. K. (2015). Epidemiology, Comorbidity, and Behavioral Genetics of Antisocial Personality Disorder and Psychopathy. *Psychiatric Annals, 45*(4), 195.

Westen, D. (1991). Social cognition and object relations. *Psychological Bulletin, 109,* 429–455.

Wetherell, J. L., Ayers, C. R., Nuevo, R., Stein, M. B., Ramsdell, J., & Patterson, T. L. (2010). Medical conditions and depressive, anxiety, and somatic symptoms in older adults with and without generalized anxiety disorder. *Aging and Mental Health, 14,* 764–768.

Wetherell, J. L., Gatz, M., & Craske, M. G. (2003). Treatment of generalized anxiety disorder in older adults. *Journal of Consulting and Clinical Psychology, 71,* 31–40.

Wetherell, J. L., Lenze, E. J., & Stanley, M. (2005). Evidence-based treatment of geriatric anxiety disorders. *Psychiatric Clinics of North America, 28,* 871–896.

Wetherell, J. L., Thorp, S. R., Patterson, T. L., Golshan, S., Jeste, D. V., & Gatz, M. (2004). Quality of life in geriatric generalized anxiety disorder: A preliminary investigation. *Journal of Psychiatric Research, 38,* 305–312.

Wetzler, S., & Jose, A. (2012). Passive-aggressive personality disorder: The demise of a syndrome. In T. A. Widiger (Ed.), *The Oxford handbook of personality disorders* (pp. 674–693). New York, NY: Oxford University Press.

Wexler, N. S. (2012). Huntington's disease: Advocacy driving science. *Annual Review of Medicine, 63,* 1–22.

Wheeler, J., Newring, K. A. B., Draper, C. (2008). Transvestic fetishism: Psychopathology and theory. In D. R. Laws & W. T. O'Donohue (Eds.), *Sexual deviance: Theory, assessment, and treatment* (2nd ed., pp. 286–304). New York, NY: Guilford.

Whisman, M., Weinstock, L., & Tolejko, N. (2006). Marriage and depression. In L. M. Corey & S. Goodman (Eds.), *A handbook for the social, behavioral, and biomedical sciences* (pp. 219–240). Boulder, CO: Cambridge University Press.

Whisman, M. A., Johnson, D. P., & Smolen, A. (2011). Dysfunctional attitudes and the serotonin transporter promoter polymorphism (5-HTTLPR). *Behavior Therapy, 42*(2), 300–305.

Whitbourne, S. K., & Skultety, K. M. (2002). Body image development: Adulthood and aging. In A. M. Cash & T. Pruzinsky (Eds.), *Body image: A handbook of theory, research, and clinical practice* (pp. 83–90). New York, NY: Guilford.

White, A., & Hingson, R. (2014). The burden of alcohol use: Excessive alcohol consumption and related consequences among college students. *Alcohol Research: Current Reviews, 35*(2), 201–218.

White, J. L., Moffitt, T. E., & Silva, P. A. (1989). A prospective replication of the protective effects of IQ in subjects at high risk for juvenile delinquency. *Journal of Consulting and Clinical Psychology, 57,* 719–724.

White, K. S., & Barlow, D. H. (2002). In D. H. Barlow (Ed.), *Anxiety and its disorders: The nature and treatment of anxiety and panic* (2nd ed.). New York, NY: Guilford.

White, K. S., Brown, T. A., Somers, T. J., & Barlow, D. H. (2006). Avoidance behavior in panic disorder: The moderating influence of perceived control. *Behaviour Research and Therapy, 44,* 147–157.

White, K. S., Payne, L. A., Gorman, J. M., Shear, M. K., Woods, S. W., Saksa, J. R., & Barlow, D. H. (2013). Does maintenance CBT contribute to long-term treatment response of panic disorder with or without agoraphobia? A randomized controlled clinical trial. *Journal of Consulting and Clinical Psychology, 81,* 47–57.

White, P. D., Goldsmith, K. A., Johnson, A. L., Potts, L., Walwyn, R., DeCesare, J. C., & Group, P. T. M. (2011). Comparison of adaptive pacing therapy, cognitive behavior therapy, graded exercise therapy, and specialist medical care for chronic fatigue syndrome (PACE): A randomised trial. *Lancet, 377*(9768), 823–836.

White, W., & Kurtz, E. (2008). Twelve defining moments in the history of Alcoholics Anonymous. In M. Galanter & L. A. Kaskutas (Eds.), *Research on Alcoholics Anonymous and spirituality in addiction recovery: The twelve-step program model, spiritually oriented recovery, twelve-step membership, effectiveness and outcome research* (pp. 37–57). New York, NY: Springer Verlag.

Whitehurst, G. J., Fischel, J. E., Lonigan, C. J., Valdez-Menchaca, M. C., DeBaryshe, B. D., & Caulfield, M. B. (1988). Verbal interaction in families of normal and expressive-language-delayed children. *Developmental Psychology, 24,* 690–699.

Whiteside, U., Bittinger, J. N., Kilmer, J. R., Lostutter, T. W. & Larimer, M. E. (2015). College student drinking. In R.K. Ries, D.A. Fiellin, S.C. Miller, & R. Saitz (Eds.), *The ASAM principles of addiction medicine* (5th Ed., pp. 562–574). New York, NY: Wolters Kluwer.

Whitfield-Gabrieli, S., Ghosh, S. S., Nieto-Castanon, A., Saygin, Z., Doehrmann, O., Chai, X. J., . . . Gabrieli, J. D. E. (in press). Brain connectomics predict response to treatment in social anxiety disorder. *Molecular Psychiatry, 21*(5), 680–685.

Whitnam, F. L., Diamond, M., & Martin, J. (1993). Homosexual orientation in twins: A report on 61 pairs and three triplet sets. *Archives of Sexual Behavior, 22*(3), 187–206.

Whittal, M. L., Agras, W. S., & Gould, R. A. (1999). *Behavior Therapy, 30,* 117–135.

Whittal, M. L., & Robichaud, M. (2012). Cognitive treatment for OCD. In G. Steketee (Ed.), *The Oxford handbook of obsessive compulsive and spectrum disorders* (pp. 345–364). New York, NY: Oxford University Press.

Whooley, M. A., & Wong, J. M. (2013). Depression and cardiovascular disorders. *Annual Review of Clinical Psychology, 9,* 327–354.

Whooley, M. A., de Jonge, P., Vittinghoff, E., Otte, C., Moos, R., Carney, R. M., & Browner, W. S. (2008). Depressive symptoms, health behaviors, and risk of cardiovascular events in patients with coronary heart disease. *JAMA: Journal of the American Medical Association, 300,* 2379–2388.

Widaman, K. F. (2009). Phenylketonuria in children and mothers: Genes, environments, behavior. *Current Directions in Psychological Science, 18*(1), 48c52.

Widiger, T. A. (1991). Personality disorder dimensional models proposed for the DSM-IV. *Journal of Personality Disorders, 5,* 386–398.

Widiger, T. A. (2006). Psychopathy and DSM-IV psychopathology. In C. J. Patrick (Ed.), *Handbook of psychopathy* (pp. 156–171). New York, NY: Guilford.

Widiger, T. A. (2011). The DSM-5 dimensional model of personality disorder: Rationale and empirical support. *Journal of Personality Disorders, 25*(2), 222–234.

Widiger, T. A. (2012). Historical developments and current issues. In T. A. Widiger (Ed.), *The Oxford handbook of personality disorders* (pp. 13–34). New York, NY: Oxford University Press.

Widiger, T.A. (2013). Classification and diagnosis: Historical development and contemporary issues. In J. Maddux & B. Winstead (Eds.), *Psychopathology: Foundations for a contemporary understanding* (3rd ed.). New York, NY: Erlbaum.

Widiger, T. A., & Coker, L. A. (2003). Mental disorders as discrete clinical conditions: Dimensional versus categorical classification. In M. Hersen & S. M. Turner (Eds.), *Adult psychopathology and diagnosis* (4th ed., pp. 3–35). New York, NY: Wiley.

Widiger, T. A., & Crego, C. (2013). Diagnosis and classification. In I. B. Weiner (Series Ed.), G. Stricker & T. A. Widiger (Vol. Eds.), *Handbook of psychology: Vol. 8 Clinical psychology* (pp. 3–18). Hoboken, NJ: John Wiley & Sons.

Widiger, T. A., & Edmundson, M. (2011). Diagnoses, dimensions, and DSM V. In D. H. Barlow (Ed.), *Handbook of clinical psychology.* New York, NY: Oxford University Press.

Widiger, T. A., & Samuel, D. B. (2005). Diagnostic categories or dimensions? A question for the diagnostic and statistical manual of mental disorders (5th ed.). *Journal of Abnormal Psychology, 114,* 494–504.

Widiger, T. A., & Sankis, L. M. (2000). Adult psychopathology: Issues and controversies. *Annual Review of Psychology, 51,* 377–404.

Widiger, T. A., & Simonsen, E. (2005). Alternative dimensional models of personality disorder: Finding a common ground. *Journal of Personality Disorders, 19*(2), 110–130.

Widiger, T. A., & Spitzer, R. L. (1991). Sex bias in the diagnosis of personality disorders: Conceptual and methodological issues. *Clinical Psychology Review, 11,* 1–22.

Widiger, T. A., Cadoret, R., Hare, R., Robins, L., Rutherford, M., Zanarini, M., . . . Hart, S. (1996). DSM—IV antisocial personality disorder field trial. *Journal of Abnormal Psychology, 105*(1), 3.

Widiger, T. A., Frances, A. J., Pincus, H. A., Ross, R., First, M. B., Davis, W., & Kline, M. (Eds.) (1998). *DSM-IV sourcebook* (Vol. 4). Washington, DC: American Psychiatric Association.

Widiger, T. A., Livesley, W. J., & Clark, L. A. (2009). An integrative dimensional classification of personality disorder. *Psychological Assessment, 21*(3), 243–255.

Widiger, T., & Trull, T. (2007). Plate tectonics in the classification of personality disorder: Shifting to a dimensional model. *American Psychologist, 62*(2), 71.

Widom, C. S. (1977). A methodology for studying noninstitutionalized psychopaths. *Journal of Consulting and Clinical Psychology, 45,* 674–683.

Widom, C. S. (1984). Sex roles, criminality, and psychopathology. In C. S. Widom (Ed.),

Sex roles and psychopathology (pp. 183–217). New York, NY: Plenum Press.

Widom, C. S., Czaja, S. J., & Paris, J. (2009). A prospective investigation of borderline personality disorder in abused and neglected children followed up into adulthood. *Journal of Personality Disorders, 23*(5), 433–446.

Wiebe, S. T., Cassoff, J., & Gruber, R. (2012). Sleep patterns and the risk for unipolar depression: A review. *Nature and Science of Sleep, 4*, 63–71.

Wiech, K., Ploner, M., & Tracey, I. (2008). Neurocognitive Aspects of Pain Perception. *Trends in Cognitive Sciences, 12*, 306–313.

Wiegel, M. (2008). *Women who sexually abuse minors: Description and instrument validation*. (Unpublished doctoral dissertation). Boston University, Boston, MA.

Wiegel, M., Scepkowski, L., & Barlow, D. (2006). Cognitive and affective processes in female sexual dysfunctions. In I. Goldstein, C. Meston, S. Davis, & A. Traish (Eds.), *Women's sexual function and dysfunction: Study, diagnosis and treatment* (pp. 85–92). London, UK: Taylor & Francis.

Wiegel, M., Wincze, J. P., & Barlow, D. H. (2002). Sexual dysfunction. In M. M. Antony & D. H. Barlow (Eds.), *Handbook of assessment and treatment planning for psychological disorders* (pp. 481–522). New York, NY: Guilford.

Wiger, D. E., & Mooney, N. B. (2015). Mental Status Exam. In R. L. Cautin (Eds.), *The Encyclopedia of Clinical Psychology* (1–5). Hoboken, NJ : John Wiley & Sons. doi 10.1002/9781118625392.wbecp104

Wiggins, R. (2009). Prion stability and infectivity in the environment. *Neurochemical Research, 34*(1), 158–168.

Wiklander, M., Samuelsson, M., Jokinen, J., Nilsonne, Å., Wilczek, A., Rylander, G., & Åsberg, M. (2012). Shame-proneness in attempted suicide patients. *BMC Psychiatry, 12*(1), 50.

Wilcox, H. C., Arria, A. M., Caldeira, K. M., Vincent, K. B., Pinchevsky, G. M., & O'Grady, K. E. (2010). Prevalence and predictors of persistent suicide ideation, plans, and attempts during college. *Journal of Affective Disorders, 127*(1), 287–294.

Wilcox, H. C., Storr, C. L., & Breslau, N. (2009). Posttraumatic stress disorder and suicide attempts in a community sample of urban American young adults. *Archives of General Psychiatry, 66*(3), 305–311. doi: 10.1001/archgenpsychiatry.2008.557

Wilfley, D. E., & Rodin, J. (1995). Cultural influences on eating disorders. In K. D. Brownell & C. G. Fairburn (Eds.), *Eating disorders and obesity: A comprehensive handbook*. New York, NY: Guilford, pp. 78–82.

Wilfley, D. E., Welch, R., Stein, R. I., Spurrell, E. B., Cohen, L. R., Saelens, B. E., & Matt, G. E. (2002). A randomized comparison of group cognitive-behavioral and group interpersonal psychotherapy for treatment of overweight individuals with binge-eating disorder. *Archives of General Psychiatry, 59*, 713–721.

Wilhelm, S., Buhlmann, U., Tolin, D. F., Meunier, S. A., Pearlson, G. D., Reese, H. E., . . . Rauch, S. L. (2008). Augmentation of behavior therapy with D-cycloserine for obsessive-compulsive disorder. *American Journal of Psychiatry. 165*, 335–341.

Wilhelm, S., Otto, M. W., Lohr, B., & Deckersbach, T. (1999). Cognitive behavior group therapy for body dysmorphic disorder: A case series. *Behaviour Research and Therapy, 37*, 71–75.

Wilk, K., & Hegerl, U. (2010). Time of mood switches in ultra-rapid cycling disorder: A brief review. *Psychiatry Research, 180*, 1–4.

Williams, C. J., & Weinberg, M. S. (2003). Zoophilia in men: A study of sexual interest in animals. *Archives of Sexual Behavior, 32*, 523–535.

Williams, J., Hadjistavropoulos, T., & Sharpe, D. (2006). A meta-analysis of psychological and pharmacological treatments for body dysmorphic disorder. *Behaviour Research and Therapy, 44*, 99–111.

Williams, J. M. G., Teasdale, J. D., Segal, Z. V., & Kabat-Zinn, J. (2007). *The mindful way through depression: Freeing yourself from chronic unhappiness*. New York, NY: Guilford.

Williams, L. (1994). Recall of childhood trauma: A prospective study of women's memories of child sexual abuse. *Journal of Consulting and Clinical Psychology, 62*, 1167–1176.

Williams, M. R., Chaudhry, R., Perera, S., Pearce, R. K. B., Hirsch, S. R., Ansorge, O., . . . Maier, M. (2013). Changes in cortical thickness in the frontal lobes in schizophrenia are a result of thinning of pyramidal cell layers. *European Archives of Psychiatry and Clinical Neuroscience, 263*(1), 25–39.

Williams, R. B., & Schneiderman, N. (2002). Resolved: Psychosocial interventions can improve clinical outcomes in organic disease (Pro). *Psychosomatic Medicine, 64*, 552–557.

Williams, R. B., Barefoot, J. C., & Schneiderman, N. (2003). Psychosocial risk factors for cardiovascular disease; More than one culprit at work. *JAMA: Journal of the American Medical Association, 290*, 2190–2192.

Williams, R. B., Marchuk, D. A., Gadde, K. M., Barefoot, J. C., Grichnik, K., Helms, M. J., & Siegler, I.C. (2001). Central nervous system serotonin function and cardiovascular responses to stress. *Psychosomatic Medicine, 63*, 300–305.

Willwerth, J. (1993, August 30). Tinkering with madness. *Time*, pp. 40–42.

Wilson, B. M., Mickes, L., Stolarz-Fantino, S., Evrard, M., & Fantino, E. (2015). Increased false-memory susceptibility after mindfulness meditation. *Psychological Science, 26*, 1567–1573.

Wilson, G. T., & Fairburn, C. G. (2007). Treatments for eating disorders. In P. E. Nathan & J. M. Gorman (Eds.), *A guide to treatments that work* (3rd ed., pp. 579–610). New York, NY: Oxford University Press.

Wilson, G. T., & Zandberg, L. (2012). Cognitive-behavioral guided self-help for eating disorders: Effectiveness and scalability. *Clinical Psychology Review, 32*, 343–357.

Wilson, G. T., Loeb, K. L., Walsh, B. T., Labouvie, E., Petkova, E., Liu, S., & Waternaux, C. (1999). Psychological versus pharmacological treatments of bulimia nervosa: Predictors and processes of change. *Journal of Consulting and Clinical Psychology, 67*, 451–459.

Wilson, G. T., Wilfley, D. E., Agras, W. S., & Bryson, S. W. (2010). Psychological treatments of binge eating disorder. *Archives of General Psychiatry, 67*(1), 94–101.

Wilson, R. S., Aggarwal, N. T., Barnes, L. L., Mendes de Leon, C. F., Hebert, L. E., & Evans, D. A. (2010). Cognitive decline in incident Alzheimer disease in a community population. *Neurology, 74*(12), 951–955.

Wimo, A., Jönsson, L., Bond, J., Prince, M., Winblad, B., & Alzheimer's Disease International. (2013). The worldwide economic impact of dementia 2010. *Alzheimer's & Dementia, 9*(1), 1–11.

Winchel, R. M., Stanley, B., & Stanley, M. (1990). Biochemical aspects of suicide. In S. J. Blumenthal & D. J. Kupfer (Eds.), *Suicide over the life cycle: Risk factors, assessment and treatment of suicidal patterns* (pp. 97–126). Washington, DC: American Psychiatric Press.

Wincze, J. P. (2009). *Enhancing sexuality: A problem-solving approach to treating dysfunction: Therapist guide* (2nd ed). New York, NY: Oxford University Press.

Wincze, J. P., & Carey, M. P. (2001). *Sexual dysfunction: A guide for assessment and treatment*. New York, NY: Guilford.

Wincze, J. P., & Weisberg, R. B. (2015). *Sexual dysfunction: A guide for assessment and treatment*. New York, NY: Guilford Publications

Wincze, J. P., Bach, A., & Barlow, D. H. (2008). Sexual dysfunction. In D. H. Barlow (Ed.), *Clinical handbook of psychological disorders: A step-by-step treatment manual* (4th ed., pp. 615–661). New York, NY: Guilford.

Windgassen, K. (1992). Treatment with neuroleptics: The patient's perspective. *Acta Psychiatrica Scandinavica, 86*, 405–410.

Wing, J. K., Cooper, J. E., & Sartorius, N. (1974). *The measurement and classification of psychiatric symptoms*. Cambridge, UK: Cambridge University Press.

Wing, R. R. (2010). Treatment options for obesity: Do commercial weight loss programs have a role? *Journal of American Medical Association, 304*, 1837–1838.

Winkelman, J. W. (2006). Efficacy and tolerability of open-label topiramate in the treatment of sleep-related eating disorder: A retrospective case series. *Journal of Clinical Psychiatry, 67*, 1729–1734.

Winter, A. (1998). *Mesmerized powers of mind in Victorian Britain*. Chicago, IL: University of Chicago Press.

Winter, D., Elzinga, B., & Schmahl, C. (2013). Emotions and memory in borderline personality disorder. *Psychopathology, 47*(2), 71–85.

Winters, R. W., & Schneiderman, N. (2000). Anxiety and coronary heart disease. In D. I. Mostofsky & D. H. Barlow (Eds.), *The management of stress and anxiety in medical disorders* (pp. 206–219). Needham Heights, MA: Allyn & Bacon.

Winzelberg, A. J., Eppstein, D., Eldredge, K. L., Wilfley, D., Dasmahapatra, R., Dev, P., & Taylor, C. B. (2000). Effectiveness of an Internet-based program for reducing risk factors for eating disorders. *Journal of Consulting and Clinical Psychology, 68,* 346–350.

Winzelberg, A. J., Taylor, C. B., Sharpe, T., Eldredge, K. L., Dev, P., & Constantinou, P. S. (1998). Evaluation of a computer-mediated eating disorder intervention program. *International Journal of Eating Disorders, 24,* 339–349.

Wirdefeldt, K., Adami, H. O., Cole, P., Trichopoulos, D., & Mandel, J. (2011). Epidemiology and etiology of Parkinson's disease: A review of the evidence. *European Journal of Epidemiology, 26*(1), 1–58.

Wirz-Justice, A. (1998). Beginning to see the light. *Archives of General Psychiatry, 55,* 861–862.

Wise, M. G., Hilty, D. M., & Cerda, G. M. (2001). Delirium due to a general medical condition, delirium due to multiple etiologies, and delirium not otherwise specified. In G. O. Gabbard (Ed.), *Treatment of psychiatric disorders* (3rd ed., Vol. 1, pp. 387–412). Washington, DC: American Psychiatric Publishing.

Wiseman, F. K., Al-Janabi, T., Hardy, J., Karmiloff-Smith, A., Nizetic, D., Tybulewicz, V. L., . . . Strydom, A. (2015). A genetic cause of Alzheimer disease: mechanistic insights from Down syndrome. *Nature Reviews Neuroscience, 16,* 564–574.

Wiseman, F. K., Alford, K. A., Tybulewicz, V. L. J., & Fisher, E. M. C. (2009). Down syndrome—recent progress and future prospects. *Human Molecular Genetics, 18*(R1), R75–83.

Wisner, K. L, Bogen, D. L., Sit, D., McShea, M., Hughes, C., Rizzo, D., . . . Wisniewski, S. W. (2013). Does fetal exposure to SSRIs or maternal depression impact infant growth? *American Journal of Psychiatry, 170*(5), 485–493.

Wisner, K. L., Moses-Kolko, E. L., & Sit, D. K. (2010). Postpartum depression: A disorder in search of a definition. *Archives of Women's Mental Health, 13*(1), 37–40.

Wisner, K. L., Parry, B. L., & Piontek, C. M. (2002). Postpartum depression. *New England Journal of Medicine, 347,* 194–199.

Wisner, K. L., Sit, D. K. Y., McShea, M. C., Rizzo, D., Zoretich, R. A., Hughes, C., L. . . . Hanusa, B. H. (2013). Onset timing, thoughts of self-harm, and diagnoses in postpartum women with screen-positive depression findings. *JAMA Psychiatry, 70*(5), 490–498.

Witherington, R. (1988). Suction device therapy in the management of erectile impotence. *Urologic Clinics of North America, 15,* 123–128.

Witkiewitz, K., & Marlatt, G. A. (2004). Relapse prevention for alcohol and drug problems: That was Zen, this is Tao. *American Psychologist, 59,* 224–235.

Wittchen, H.-U. (2002). Generalized anxiety disorder: Prevalence, burden, and cost to society. *Depression and Anxiety, 16,* 162–171.

Wittchen, H.-U. (2012). The burden of mood disorders. *Science, 338,* 15.

Wittchen, H.-U., Gloster, A. T., Beesdo-Baum, K., Fava, G. A., & Craske, M. G. (2010). Agoraphobia: A review of the diagnostic classificatory position and criteria. *Depression and Anxiety, 27,* 113–133.

Wittchen, H.-U., Knäuper, B., & Kessler, R. C. (1994). Lifetime risk of depression. *British Journal of Psychiatry, 165*(Suppl. 26), 116–122.

Wittchen, H.-U., Zhao, S., Kessler, R. C., & Eaton, W. W. (1994). DSM-III-R generalized anxiety disorder in the national comorbidity survey. *Archives of General Psychiatry, 51,* 355–364.

Witthöft, M., & Hiller, W. (2010). Psychological approaches to origins and treatments of somatoform disorders. *Annual Review of Clinical Psychology, 6,* 257–283.

Wittstein, I., Thiemann, D., Lima, J., Baughman, K., Sculman, S., Gerstenblith, G., & Champion, H. C. (2005). Neurohumoral features of myocardial stunning due to sudden emotional stress. *New England Journal of Medicine, 352,* 539–548.

Wolf, E. J., Lunney, C. A., Miller, M. W., Resick, P. A., Friedman, M. J., & Schnurr, P. P. (2012). The dissociative subtype of PTSD: A replication and extension. *Depression and Anxiety, 29,* 679–688. doi: 10.1002/da.21946

Wolf, E. J., Miller, M. W., Reardon, A. F., Ryabchenko, K. A., Castillo, D., & Freund, R. (2012). A latent class analysis of dissociation and posttraumatic stress disorder: Evidence for a dissociative subtype. *Archives of General Psychiatry, 69,* 698–705. doi: 10.1001/archgenpsychiatry.2011.1574

Wolf, M. M. (1978). Social validity: The case for subjective measurement or how applied behavior analysis is finding its heart. *Journal of Applied Behavior Analysis, 11,* 203–214.

Wolf-Maier, K., Cooper, R. S., Banegas, J. R., Giampaoli, S., Hense, H., Joffres, M., & Vescio, F. (2003). Hypertension prevalence and blood pressure levels in 6 European countries, Canada, and the United States. *JAMA: Journal of the American Medical Association, 289,* 2362–2369.

Wolfe, B. M., & Belle, S. H. (2014). Long-term risks and benefits of bariatric surgery: A research challenge. *JAMA, 312*(17), 1792–1793.

Wolff, K. (2012). Ketamine. In J. C. Verster, K. Brady, M. Galanter & P. Conrod (Eds.), *Drug Abuse and Addiction in Medical Illness* (pp. 201–211). New York, NY: Springer.

Wolitzky-Taylor, K. B., Castriotta, N., Lenze, E. J., Stanley, M. A., & Craske, M. G. (2010). Anxiety disorders in older adults: A comprehensive review. *Depression and Anxiety, 27*(2), 190–211. doi: 10.1002/da.20653

Wollburg, E., Voigt, K., Braukhaus, C., Herzog, A., & Lowe, B. (2013). Construct validity and descriptive validity of somatoform disorders in light of proposed changes for the DSM-5. *Journal of Psychosomatic Research, 74*(1), 18–24. doi: 10.1016/j.jpsychores.2012.09.015

Wolpe, J. (1958). *Psychotherapy by reciprocal inhibition.* Stanford, CA: Stanford University Press.

Wonderlich, S. A., Gordon, K. H., Mitchell, J. E., Crosby, R. D., & Engel, S. G. (2009). The validity and clinical utility of binge eating disorder. *International Journal of Eating Disorders, 42*(8), 687–705.

Wong, C., & Kasari, C. (2012). Play and joint attention of children with autism in the preschool special education classroom. *Journal of Autism and Developmental Disorders, 42*(10), 2152–2161. doi: 10.1007/s10803-012-1467-2

Wood, J. M., Garb, H. N., Nezworski, M. T., Lilienfeld, S. O., & Duke, M. C. (2015). A second look at the validity of widely used Rorschach indices: Comment on Mihura, Meyer, Dumitrascu, and Bombel (2013). *Psychology Bulletin, 141*(1):236–249.

Woodman, C. L., Noyes, R., Black, D. W., Schlosser, S., & Yagla, S. J. (1999). A 5-year follow-up study of generalized anxiety disorder and panic disorder. *Journal of Nervous and Mental Disease, 187,* 3–9.

Woods, B., Aguirre, E., Spector, A. E., & Orrell, M. (2012). Cognitive stimulation to improve cognitive functioning in people with dementia. *Cochrane Database Systematic Review, 2,* CD005562.

Woods, E. R., Lin, Y. G., Middleman, A., Beckford, P., Chase, L., & DuRant, R. H. (1997). The associations of suicide attempts in adolescents. *Pediatrics, 99,* 791–796.

Woods, S. W., Miller, T. J., Davidson, L., Hawkins, K. A., Sernyak, M. J., & McGlashan, T. H. (2001). Estimated yield of early detection of prodromal or first episode patients by screening first-degree relatives of schizophrenic patients. *Schizophrenia Research, 52,* 21–27.

Woods, S. W., Walsh, B. C., Saksa, J. R., & McGlashan, T. H. (2010). The case for including attenuated psychotic symptoms syndrome in DSM-5 as a psychosis risk syndrome. *Schizophrenia Research, 123*(2–3), 199.

Woodside, M. R., & Legg, B. H. (1990). Patient advocacy: A mental health perspective. *Journal of Mental Health Counseling, 12,* 38–50.

Woolfolk, R. L., & Allen, L. A. (2011). Somatoform and physical disorders. In D. H. Barlow (Ed.), *Oxford handbook of clinical psychology* (pp. 334–358). New York, NY: Oxford University Press.

Worell, J., & Remer, P. (1992). *Feminist perspectives in therapy: An empowerment model for women.* New York, NY: Wiley.

Workman, J. L., Barha, C. K., & Galea, L. A. M. (2012). Endocrine substrates of cognitive and affective changes during pregnancy and postpartum. *Behavioral Neuroscience, 126*(1), 54–72.

World Health Organization. (1992). *The ICD-10 classification of mental and behavioural disorders: Clinical descriptions and diagnostic guidelines.* Geneva, Switzerland: World Health Organization.

World Health Organization. (2000). *Women and HIV/AIDS: Fact sheet no. 242.* Retrieved from http://www.who.int/inf-fs/en/fact242.html

World Health Organization. (2001). *Mental Health: New Understanding, New Hope.* Geneva, Switzerland: World Health Organization.

World Health Organization. (2003). Global summary of the HIV/AIDS epidemic, December 2003. Retrieved from http://www.who.int/hiv/pub/epidemiology/epi2003/en

World Health Organization. (2004). *Global status report on alcohol 2004* (2nd ed.). Geneva, Switzerland: World Health Organization.

World Health Organization. (2011). Mental health atlas: 2011. Italy: World Health Organization. doi:10.1093/schbul/sbp137

Wright, J. (2009). *Address unknown: The homeless in America*. New Brunswick, NJ: Transaction. Wright, J. P., Tibbetts, S. G., & Daigle, L. E. (2015). *Criminals in the making: Criminality across the life course*. Sage Publications.

Wright, J. W., Kawas, L. H., & Harding, J. W. (2015). The development of small molecule angiotensin IV analogs to treat Alzheimer's and Parkinson's diseases. *Progress in Neurobiology, 125*, 26–46.

Wu, E., Birnbaum, H., Shi, L., Ball, D., Kessler, R., Moulis, M., Aggarwal, J. (2005). The economic burden of schizophrenia in the United States in 2002. *Journal of Clinical Psychiatry, 66*(9), 1122–1129.

Wu, F. (2009). *Suicide and Justice: A Chinese Perspective*. New York, NY: Routledge.

Wu, L.-T., Blazer, D. G., Li, T.-K., & Woody, G. E. (2011). Treatment use and barriers among adolescents with prescription opioid use disorders. *Addictive Behaviors, 36*(12), 1233–1239. doi: 10.1016/j.addbeh.2011.07.033

Wu, L.-T., Parrott, A., Ringwalt, C., Patkar, A., Mannelli, P., & Blazer, D. (2009). The high prevalence of substance use disorders among recent MDMA users compared with other drug users: Implications for intervention. *Addictive Behaviors, 34*(8), 654–661.

Wulfert, E., Franco, C., Williams, K., Roland, B., & Maxson, J. H. (2008). The role of money in the excitement of gambling. *Psychology of Addictive Behaviors, 22*(3), 380–390.

Wulfert, E., Maxson, J., & Jardin, B. (2009). Cuespecific reactivity in experienced gamblers. *Psychology of Addictive Behaviors, 23*(4), 731–735. doi: 10.1037/a0017134

Wyatt v. Stickney, 344 F. Supp. 373 (Ala. 1972).

Wykes, T., Huddy, V., Cellard, C., McGurk, S. R., & Czobor, P. (2011). A meta-analysis of cognitive remediation for schizophrenia: methodology and effect sizes. *American Journal of Psychiatry, 168*, 472–485.

Wyllie, E., Glazer, J. P., Benbadis, S., Kotagal, P., & Wolgamuth, B. (1999). Psychiatric features of children and adolescents with pseudoseizures. *Archives of Pediatrics and Adolescent Medicine, 153*, 244–248.

Wynick, S., Hobson, R. P., & Jones, R. B. (1997). Psychogenic disorders of vision in childhood ("visual conversion reaction"): Perspectives from adolescence: A research note. *Journal of Child Psychology and Psychiatry, 38*(3), 375–379.

Wynne, L. C., Tienari, P., Nieminen, P., Sorri, A., Lahti, I. O., Moring, J., & Miettunen, J. (2006). I. Genotype-environment interaction in the schizophrenia spectrum: Genetic liability and global family ratings in the Finnish Adoption Study. *Family Process, 45*(4), 419–434.

Xing, G., Zhang, L., Russell, S., & Post, R. (2006). *Schizophrenia Research, 84*, 36–56.

Yach, D., Struckler, D., & Brownell, K. D. (2006). Epidemiologic and economic consequences of the global epidemics of obesity and diabetes. *Nature Medicine, 12(1)*, 62–66.

Yamada, K., Watanabe, K., Nemoto, N., Fujita, H., Chikaraishi, C., Yamauchi, K., & Kanba, S. (2006). Prediction of medication noncompliance in outpatients with schizophrenia: 2-year follow-up study. *Psychiatry Research, 141*, 61–69.

Yamamoto, J., Silva, A., Sasao, T., Wang, C., & Nguyen, L. (1993). Alcoholism in Peru. *American Journal of Psychiatry, 150*, 1059–1062.

Yan, L. L., Liu, K., Matthews, K. A., Daviglus, M. L., Ferguson, T. F., & Kiefe, C. I. (2003). Psychosocial risk factors and risk of hypertension: The coronary artery risk development in young adults (CARDIA) study. *JAMA: Journal of the American Medical Association, 290*, 2138–2148.

Yanez, B., Edmondson, D., Stanton, A. L., Park, C. L., Kwan, L., Ganz, P. A., & Blank, T. O. (2009). Facets of spirituality as predictors of adjustment to cancer: Relative contributions of having faith and finding meaning. *Journal of Consulting and Clinical Psychology, 77*, 730–741.

Yanovski, S. Z., & Yanovski, J. A. (2014). Long-term drug treatment for obesity: A systematic and clinical review. *JAMA, 311*(1), 74–86.

Yates, P. M., Hucker, S. J., & Kingston, D. A. (2008). Sexual sadism: Psychopathology and theory. In D. R. Laws & W. T. O'Donohue (Eds.), *Sexual deviance: Theory, assessment, and treatment* (2nd ed., pp. 213–230). New York, NY: Guilford.

Yatham, L. N., Kennedy, S., O'Donovan, C., Parikh, Sagar, V., MacQueen, G., & Beaulieu, S. (2006). Canadian Network for Mood and Anxiety Treatments (CANMAT) guidelines for the management of patients with bipolar disorder: Update 2007. *Bipolar Disorders, 8*, 721–739.

Yatham, L. N., Liddle, P. F., Sossi, V., Erez, J., Vafai, N., Lam, R. W., & Blinder, S. (2012). Positron emission tomography study of the effects of tryptophan depletion on brain serotonin2 receptors in subjects recently remitted from major depression. *Archives of General Psychiatry, 69*(6), 601–609.

Yau, Y. H.C., Yip, S.W. & Potenza, M.N. (2015). Understanding "behavioral addictions": insights from research. In R.K. Ries, D.A. Fiellin, S.C. Miller, & R. Saitz (Eds.), *The ASAM principles of addiction medicine* (5th Ed., pp. 55–81). New York, NY: Wolters Kluwer.

Yeaton, W. H., & Bailey, J. S. (1978). Teaching pedestrian safety skills to young children: An analysis and one-year follow-up. *Journal of Applied Behavior Analysis, 11*, 315–329.

Yeh, S.-R., Fricke, R. A., & Edwards, D. H. (1996, January 19). The effect of social experience on serotonergic modulation of escape circuit of crayfish. *Science, 271*, 355–369.

Yehuda, R., Pratchett, L., & Pelcovitz, M. (2012). Biological contributions to PTSD: Differentiating normative from pathological response. In J. G. Beck & D. M. Sloan (Eds.), *The Oxford handbook of traumatic stress disorders* (pp. 159–174). New York, NY: Oxford University Press.

Yen, S., Johnson, J., Costello, E., & Simpson, E. (2009). A 5-day dialectical behavior therapy partial hospital program for women with borderline personality disorder: Predictors of outcome from a 3-month follow-up study. *Journal of Psychiatric Practice, 15*(3), 173.

Yeo, G. S., & Heisler, L. K. (2012). Unraveling the brain regulation of appetite: lessons from genetics. *Nature Neuroscience, 15*(10), 1343–1349.

Yerkes, R. M., & Dodson, J. D. (1908). The relation of strength of stimulus to rapidity of habit-formation. *Journal of Comparative Neurology and Psychology, 18*, 459–482.

Yim, I. S., Glynn, L. M., Dunkel-Schetter, C., Hobel, C. J., Chicz-DeMet, A., & Sandman, C. A. (2009). Risk of postpartum depressive symptoms with elevated corticotropin-releasing hormone in human pregnancy. *Archives of General Psychiatry, 66*(2), 162–169.

Yin, R. K. (2012). *Applications of case study research* (3rd ed.). Thousand Oaks, CA: Sage.

Yonkers, K. A., Kornstein, S. G., Gueorguieva, R., Merry, B., Van Steenburgh, K., & Altemus, M. (2015). Symptom-onset dosing of sertraline for the treatment of premenstrual dysphoric disorder: A randomized clinical trial. *JAMA Psychiatry, 72*(10):1037–1044.

Yonkers, K. A., Warshaw, M., Massion, A. O., & Keller, M. B. (1996). Phenomenology and course of generalized anxiety disorder. *British Journal of Psychiatry, 168*, 308–313.

Yoo, J. A., & Huang, C. C. (2012). The effects of domestic violence on children's behavior problems: Assessing the moderating roles of poverty and marital status. *Children and Youth Services Review, 34*(12), 2462–2473.

Young, A. M., & Herling, S. (1986). Drugs as reinforcers: Studies in laboratory animals. In S. R. Goldberg & I. P. Stolerman (Eds.), *Behavioral analysis of drug dependence* (pp. 9–67). Orlando, FL: Academic Press.

Young, J. E., Rygh, J. L., Weinberger, A. D., & Beck, A. T. (in press). Cognitive therapy for depression. In D. H. Barlow (Ed.), *Clinical handbook of psychological disorders: A step-by-step treatment manual* (5th ed.). New York, NY: Guilford.

Young, R. M. (2013). Cravings and expectancies. In P.M. Miller, A.W. Blume, D.J. Kavanagh, K.M. Kampman, M.E. Bates, M.E. Larimer, N. M. Petry, P. De Witte, & S.A. Ball (Eds), *Principles of addiction: Comprehensive addictive behaviors and disorders*, (Vol.1, 425–434). Waltham, MA: Elsevier Academic Press.

Young-Wolff, K. C., Enoch, M.-A., & Prescott, C. A. (2011). The influence of gene-environment interactions on alcohol consumption and alcohol use disorders: A comprehensive review. *Clinical Psychology Review, 31*(5), 800–816. doi: 10.1016/j.cpr.2011.03.005

Youngberg v. Romeo, 457 U.S. 307 (1982).

Youngstrom, E. A. (2009). Definitional issues in bipolar disorder across the life cycle. *Clinical Psychology: Science and Practice, 16*(2), 140–160.

Yu, X., Tam, W. W., Wong, P. T., Lam, T. H., & Stewart, S. M. (2012). The Patient Health Questionnaire-9 for measuring depressive symptoms among the general population in Hong Kong. *Comprehensive Psychiatry, 53*(1), 95–102. doi:10.1016/j.comppsych.2010.11.002

Zabalegui, A., Hamers, J. P., Karlsson, S., Leino-Kilpi, H., Renom-Guiteras, A., Saks,

K., . . . Cabrera, E. (2014). Best practices interventions to improve quality of care of people with dementia living at home. *Patient Education and Counseling, 95*(2), 175–184.

Zachar, P., & Kendler, K. S. (2014). A diagnostic and statistical manual of mental disorders history of premenstrual dysphoric disorder. *The Journal of Nervous and Mental Disease, 202*(4), 346–352. doi: 10.1097/NMD.0000000000000128

Zadra, A., & Donderi, D. C. (2000). Nightmares and bad dreams: Their prevalence and relationship to well-being. *Journal of Abnormal Psychology, 109,* 273–281.

Zajonc, R. B. (1984). On the primacy of affect. *American Psychologist, 39*(2), 117–123.

Zajonc, R. B. (1998). Emotions. In D. Gilbert, S. T. Fiske, & G. Lindzey (Eds.), *Handbook of social psychology* (Vol. 1, 4th ed., pp. 591–632). New York, NY: McGraw-Hill.

Zakowski, S. G., McAllister, C. G., Deal, M., & Baum, A. (1992). Stress, reactivity, and immune function in healthy men. *Health Psychology, 11,* 223–232.

Zanarini, M. C., & Wedig, M. M. (2014). Childhood adversity and the development of borderline personality disorder. In *Handbook of Borderline Personality Disorder in Children and Adolescents* (pp. 265–276). New York, NY: Springer.

Zanarini, M. C., Frankenburg, F. R., Dubo, E. D., Sickel, A. E., Trikha, A., Levin, A., . . . Prifitera, A. (2015). WISC-V Use in Societal Context. In L. G. Weiss, D. H. Saklofske, J. A. Holdnack & A. Prifitera (Eds.), *WISC-V Assessment and Interpretation: Scientist-Practitioner Perspectives*, 123–176. San Diego, CA: Elsevier.

Zanarini, M. C., Frankenburg, F. R., Hennen, J., Reich, D. B., & Silk, K. R. (2006). Prediction of the 10-year course of borderline personality disorder. *American Journal of Psychiatry, 163,* 827–832.

Zanarini, M. C., Frankenburg, F. R., Reich, D. B., & Fitzmaurice, G. (2012). Attainment and stability of sustained symptomatic remission and recovery among patients with borderline personality disorder and axis II comparison subjects: a 16-year prospective follow-up study. *American Journal of Psychiatry, 169*(5), 476–483.

Zanarini, M. C., Frankenburg, F. R., & Fitzmaurice, G. M. (2014). Severity of anxiety symptoms reported by borderline patients and Axis II comparison subjects: description and prediction over 16 years of prospective follow-up. *Journal of Personality Disorders, 28*(6), 767–777.

Zanarini, M. C., Reichman, C. A., Frankenburg, F. R., Reich, D. B., & Fitzmaurice, G. (2010). The course of eating disorders in patients with borderline personality disorder: A 10-year follow-up study. *International Journal of Eating Disorders, 43*(3), 226–232.

Zapf, P., Zottoli, T., & Pirelli, G. (2009). Insanity in the courtroom: Issues of criminal responsibility and competency to stand trial. In D. A. Krauss & J. D. Lieberman (Eds.), *Psychological expertise in court: Psychology in the courtroom* (pp. 79–101). Surrey, England: Ashgate.

Zautra, A., Johnson, L., & Davis, M. (2005). Positive affect as a source of resilience for women in chronic pain. *Journal of Consulting and Clinical Psychology, 73,* 212–220.

Zeanah, C. H., & Gleason, M. M. (2010). *Reactive attachment disorders: A review for DSM-V.* Retrieved December 29, 2010 from http:// stage.dsm5.org/Proposed%20Revision%20 Attachments/APA%20DSM-5%20 Reactive%20 Attachment%20Disorder%20 Review.pdf

Zemore, S. E., Subbaraman, M., & Tonigan, J. S. (2013). Involvement in 12-step activities and treatment outcomes. *Substance Abuse, 34*(1), 60–69. doi: 10.1080/08897077.2012.691452

Zervas, I. M., Theleritis, C., & Soldatos, C. R. (2012). Using ECT in schizophrenia: A review from a clinical perspective. *World Journal of Biological Psychiatry, 13*(2), 96–105.

Zhai, L., Zhang, H., & Zhang, D. (2015). Sleep duration and depression among adults: A meta-analysis of prospective studies. *Depression and Anxiety, 32,* 644–670.

Zhang, H., & Cai, B. (2003). The impact of tobacco on lung health in China. *Respirology, 8,* 17–21.

Zheng, G., Yang, Y., Zhu, X., & Elston, R. C. (2012). *Analysis of genetic association studies.* New York, NY: Springer.

Zhou, J. N., Hofman, M. A., Gooren, L. J., & Swaab, D. F. (1995). A sex difference in the human brain and its relation to transsexuality. *Nature, 378,* 68–70.

Zigler, E., & Hodapp, R. M. (1986). *Understanding mental retardation.* Cambridge, UK: Cambridge University Press.

Zilbergeld, B. (1999). *The new male sexuality.* New York, NY: Bantam Books.

Zilboorg, G., & Henry, G. (1941). *A history of medical psychology.* New York, NY: W. W. Norton.

Zillmann, D. (1983). Arousal and aggression. In R. G. Geen & E. Donnerstein (Eds.), *Aggression: Theoretical and empirical reviews* (Vol. 1, pp. 75–102). New York, NY: Academic Press.

Zimmerman, M., & Mattia, J. I. (1998). Body dys-morphic disorder in psychiatric outpatients: Recognition, prevalence, comorbidity, demographic, and clinical correlates. *Comprehensive Psychiatry, 39*(5), 265–270.

Zimmerman, M., Rothschild, L., & Chelminski, I. (2005). The prevalence of DSM-IV personality disorders in psychiatric outpatients. *American Journal of Psychiatry, 162,* 1911–1918.

Zinbarg, R. E., & Barlow, D. H. (1996). Structure of anxiety and the anxiety disorders: A hierarchical model. *Journal of Abnormal Psychology, 105,* 181–193.

Zinbarg, R. E., Barlow, D. H., Liebowitz, M. R., Street, L., Broadhead, E., Katon, W., & Kraemer, H. (1998). The DSM-IV field trial for mixed anxiety-depression. In T. A. Widiger, A. J. Frances, H. A. Pincus, R. Ross, M. B. First, W. Davis, & M. Kline (Eds.), *DSM-IV sourcebook* (Vol. 4, pp. 735–799). Washington, DC: American Psychiatric Association.

Zinbarg, R. E., Barlow, D. H., Liebowitz, M., Street, L., Broadhead, E., Katon, W., & Kraemer, H. (1994). The DSM-IV field trial for mixed anxiety depression. *American Journal of Psychiatry, 151,* 1153–1162.

Zinbarg, R. E., Craske, M. G., & Barlow, D. H. (2006). *Mastery of your anxiety and worry: Therapist guide.* New York, NY: Oxford University Press.

Zingmond, D. S., McGory, M. L., & Ko, C. Y. (2005). Hospitalization before and after gastric bypass surgery. *JAMA: Journal of the American Medical Association, 294,* 1918–1924.

Zisook, S., Corruble, E., Duan, N., Inglewicz, A., Karam, E., Lanouette, N., & Young, I. T. (2012). The bereavement exclusion and DSM-5. *Depression and Anxiety, 29,* 425–443.

Zonana, H., & Buchanan, A. (2009). Ethical issues in the treatment of sex offenders. In F. M. Saleh, A. J. Grudzinskas, J. M. Bradford, & B. D. M. (Eds.), *Sex offenders: Identification, risk assessment, treatment, and legal issues* (pp. 425–440). New York, NY: Oxford University Press.

Zou, L., Chen, W., Shao, S., Sun, Z., Zhong, R., Shi, J., & Song, R. (2012). Genetic variant in KIAA0319, but not in DYX1C1, is associated with risk of dyslexia: An integrated meta-analysis. *American Journal of Medical Genetics Part B: Neuropsychiatric Genetics, 159B*(8), 970–976. doi: 10.1002/ajmg.b.32102

Zubieta, J., Bueller, J., Jackson, L., Scott, D., Xu, Y., & Koeppe, R., & Stohler, C. S. (2005). Placebo effects mediated by endogenous opioid activity on u-opioid receptors. *Journal of Neuroscience, 25,* 7754–7762.

Zubin, J., Steinhauer, S. R., & Condray, R. (1992). Vulnerability to relapse in schizophrenia. *British Journal of Psychiatry, 161,* 13–18.

Zuccato, C., & Cattaneo, E. (2009). Brain-derived neurotrophic factor in neurodegenerative diseases. *Nature Reviews Neurology, 5*(6), 311–322.

Zuchner, S., Cuccaro, M. L., Tran-Viet, K. N., Cope, H., Krishnan, R. R., Pericak-Vance, M. A., & Ashley-Koch, A. (2006). SLITRK1 mutations in trichotillomania. *Molecular Psychiatry, 11,* 887–889.

Zucker, K. J. (2005). Measurement of psychosexual differentiation. *Archives of Sexual Behavior, 34,* 375–388.

Zucker, K. J. (2010). The DSM diagnostic criteria for gender identity disorder in children. *Archives of Sexual Behavior, 39,* 477–498.

Zuvekas, S. H., & Vitiello, B. (2012). Stimulant medication use in children: A 12-year perspective. *American Journal of Psychiatry, 169*(2), 160–166. doi: doi:10.1176/appi.ajp.2011.11030387

Zwahlen, M., & Egger, M. (2006). *Progression and mortality of untreated HIV-positive individuals living in resource-limited settings: Update of literature review and evidence synthesis* (UNAIDS Obligation HQ/05/42204). Retrieved from http://data.unaids.org/pub/ periodical/2006/zwahlen_unaids_hq_05_422204_2007_en.pdf

Zwaigenbaum, L., Bryson, S., & Garon, N. (2013). Early identification of autism spectrum disorders. *Behavioural Brain Research, 251,* 133–146.

A

Aaron, L., 222, 273
Aarsland, D., 513, 514, 519
Abakoumkin, G., 206
Abbey, S. E., 269
Abbott, D. W., 107, 288, 314
Abe, T., 494
Abel, G. G.., 306, 348, 353, 463
Abela, J. R., 223, 224, 225
Abele, H., 502
Abeles, N.., 213, 214, 227
Abrahamson, D. J., 338
Abramowitz, J. S., 153, 157
Abrams, D. A., 491
Abramson, L., 55, 213, 220, 221, 222, 223, 224, 225, 226, 296
Abujaoude, E., 160
Ackerman, D. L., 502
Acosta-Castillo, I., 512
Adami, H. O., 513
Adamis, D., 506
Adams, B. G., 149, 305, 348, 483
Addenbrooke, W. M., 383
Addis, M. E., 224
Ader, R., 256
Aditya, H., 180, 183
Adlaf, E. M., 375
Adler, A., 20
Adler, C. M., 252, 257
Adshead, G., 416
Adunuri, N., 506
Afari, N., 268, 270
Agatisa, P., 263
Aggarwal, N. K., 89
Aggen, S. H., 216, 308
Agras, W. S., 137, 288, 293, 298, 299, 300, 301, 305, 338
Agrawal, A., 388
Aguirre, E., 519
Agyei, Y., 331
Ahern, D. K., 178, 539
Ahlers, C. J., 359
Ahmed, A. O., 91, 212, 312
Ahnve, S., 264
Akinnusi, M., 315
Akiskal, H., 205, 211, 413
Akré, C., 289
Aksan, N., 425
al'Absi, M., 380
Alaniz, M. L., 391
Alarcón, R. D., 391
Alba-Ferrara, L., 450
Albano, A. M., 128, 138, 144, 147, 156
Albert, C., 463, 511
Albertini, R. S., 159, 160, 161
Albertson, T. E., 386
Albright, J. A., 375
Albuquerque, A., 506
Alcaine, O. M., 127
Alda, M., 229
Alden, S., 423
Alderfer, M. A., 260
Alegria, A., 204

Alessi, S. M., 389
Alexander, F. G., 9, 12, 14, 249
Alexopoulos, G., 213, 229
Alfred Adler, 20
Alhassoon, 306
Ali, S. R., 109
Alici, Y., 507
Allani, D., 429
Allardyce, J., 63, 464, 465
Allen, L. B., 43, 61, 123, 128, 140, 160, 161, 173, 176, 179, 183, 190, 232, 331, 450, 495
Allender, S., 262
Allison, D., 303, 304, 305
Alloy, L., 213, 220, 221, 222, 223, 225, 226
Allsbeck, P., 63
Almklov, 306
Alonso, J., 236, 238
Alper, C. M., 254
Alpers, G. W., 137, 141, 142, 177
Altar, C. A., 445
Alter, H. J., 268
Althof, S., 336, 343, 344
Altman, M., 305
Altshuler, L. L., 212
Alvarado, G. F., 150
Alzheimer's Association, 558, 560, 561, 510, 512
Amad, A., 428
Amaral, D. G., 495
Amat, J., 150
American Law Institute (ALI), 587, 536
American Psychiatric Association, 5, 33, 63, 70, 76, 85, 87, 88, 89, 118, 173, 176, 181, 185, 188, 203, 227, 228, 229, 230, 241, 284, 300, 311, 317, 338, 345, 347, 355, 358, 369, 370, 381, 385, 386, 399, 409, 410, 415, 418, 430, 431, 448, 451, 452, 453, 454, 481, 484, 489, 490, 492, 498, 538, 542
Ames, G. E., 304
Ametaj, A. A., 543
Amieva, H., 511, 517
Amstadter, A. B., 149, 308
Anandam, A., 315
Anastopoulos, A., 487
Ances, B. M., 514
Andersen, A. E., 183, 259, 273, 294, 330
Andershed, H., 422
Anderson, C., 267, 380, 494
Anderson, D. K., 290
Andersson, E., 145
Andrasik, F., 271
Andreasen, N. C., 451, 464
Andreasson, S., 63
Andreski, M. A., 149
Andrews, G., 126
Andrykowski, M. A., 259
Anglin, D., 383, 458
Angold, A., 209
Angst, J., 203, 204, 211
Angstman, K. B., 417
Anguilo, M., 191
Anna Freud, 20
Annabi, S., 429
Annas, P., 57

Annus, A. M., 291
Ansell, E., 429
Anson, M., 161
Anthony, D., 144, 458
Antley, A., 470
Antoni, M., 251, 258, 259
Antonuccio, D. O., 487
Antony, M. M., 34, 71, 74, 137, 140
Apfelbaum, B., 336
Appelbaum, K. A., 448
Applebaum, A. J., 211, 234
Arai, J. A., 41
Araque, A., 43
Araujo, M., 451
Arbisi, P., 51
Arcelus, J., 283, 284
Arcona, A. P., 487
Arenkiel, B. R., 48
Armbruster, D., 51
Armstrong, T., 520
Arnds, K., 426
Arnold, L. E., 486
Arnow, B., 299
Arntz, A., 416, 417
Arnulf, I., 319
Aronow, E., 77
Arria, A. M., 369, 377
Arrindell, W. A., 130, 137, 140
Arteburn, 305
Aryer, 358
Ascher-Svanum, H., 465
Aschoff, J., 313
Ashkenazi, S., 491
Ashley, L. L., 398, 399, 401
Ashworth, M., 458
Asmal, L., 457
Asmundon, 178
Asmundson, G., 175, 176, 177, 178
Asnaani, A., 61, 122, 142
Assumpção, A. A., 353
Attia, E., 288
Attie, I., 291, 295
Audenaert, K., 449
Augedal, A. W., 317
Auger, R., 314
Auriacombe, M., 399
Aurora, R. N., 317
Austin, S. B., 294
Autonell, J., 454
Auyeng, B., 331, 357
Avenevoli, S., 213
Averill, P. M., 125
Avery-Clark, C., 343
Avorn, J., 127
Ayala, E. S., 34, 139, 140
Ayanian, J. Z., 261
Ayas, N. T., 315
Ayearst, L. E., 72
Ayers, C. R., 126, 138, 163
Ayllon, T., 469
Ayuso-Mateos, J. L., 416
Azmitia, E. C., 49
Azrin, N. H., 469

Babyak, M., 232
Bach, A., 333, 338, 341, 342, 344
Bachman, J. G., 374
Bader, J. O., 269
Badr, M. S., 313
Baek, J. H., 203
Baer, J., 396, 428
Bagby, R. M., 72, 86
Baghai, T. C., 49
Bailey, J., 107, 330, 331, 355, 357, 390
Baillie, A., 259, 390
Baird, G., 483
Baker, C. D., 295, 308
Bakker, A., 133
Bakshi, 356
Balbin, E., 258
Baldessarini, R., 229, 230
Baldwin, J. D., 214, 350
Baler, R. D., 384
Balestri, M., 428
Ball, J., 429
Ballantyne, J. C., 383
Ballard, C., 513, 514, 519
Ballenger, J. C., 157
Balon, R., 333, 339
Balter, M., 331
Bancroft, J., 330, 331, 333, 345, 346
Bandura, A., 56, 254, 266
Baranek, G., 497
Barban, L., 189
Barbaree, H. E., 349, 350
Barber, J. P., 132
Barclay, X., 317
Bardone, A. M., 296
Bardone-Cone, A. M., 296
Barefoot, J. C., 263
Barger, S. D., 264, 308
Bargh, J. A., 57
Barik, J., 54
Barker, C., 76
Barkley, R. A., 484, 485, 486, 487
Barlow, D. H., 6, 11, 34, 54, 55, 56, 57, 59, 61, 71, 72, 74, 83, 84, 86, 89, 90, 91, 100, 102, 118, 119, 120, 122, 123, 125, 126, 127, 128, 129, 130, 131, 132, 133, 134, 135, 136, 137, 138, 140, 141, 142, 144, 147, 149, 150, 154, 156, 157, 162, 177, 178, 184, 203, 209, 217, 218, 220, 221, 224, 225, 232, 251, 253, 263, 272, 333, 338, 340, 341, 342, 344, 345, 346, 348, 350, 351, 429, 543, 133, 134
Barmish, A. J., 144
Barnard, A., 161
Barnes, J. C., 491
Barnhofer, T., 231
Baron, M., 106
Baron-Cohen, S., 496
Barr, C. E., 464
Barraclough, S., 305
Barrantes-Vidal, N., 418
Barratt, M. J., 384
Barrera, A. Z., 203, 389
Barres, B. A., 43
Barrett, L. F., 58, 381
Barrio, C., 471
Barry, C. T., 293, 422
Barsaglini, 52
Barsky, A., 176, 178, 179, 175, 176
Bartak, L., 495
Barth, J., 343
Bartholomew, R. E., 11
Bartlett, N., 357
Barton, S., 251
Basden, S., 128

Bassett, A. S., 461
Basson, R., 335, 344
Batchelder, A. W., 258
Bates, D., 176
Bateson, G., 465
Bauer, J., 299
Baugh, C. M., 512
Baumann, M. H., 387
Baumert, J., 264
Baxter, L. R., 52, 121
Beach, F., 223, 225, 329
Beals, J., 212, 215
Beam, C., 37
Bear, D., 52, 504
Bearak, J., 329
Beardon, L., 520
Beardslee, W. R., 214, 232, 234
Bearman, P. S., 494
Beaulieu, S., 51
Beautrais, A., 214
Bebbington, P., 428
Bech, P., 203
Beck, J. G., 23, 125, 128, 151, 222, 231, 239, 337, 338, 416, 417, 431, 432, 433, 436
Becker, B., 93, 132, 291, 338, 353, 378, 428, 430, 504
Becvar, D. S., 65
Beech, A. R., 350, 351, 356
Beekly, D., 512
Beekman, A. T., 213, 214, 233
Beesdo, K., 126
Beesdo-Baum, K., 6, 129
Behar, E., 127, 133
Beidel, D. C., 144, 145
Beitchman, J. H., 482
Bejerot, S., 145
Béjot, Y., 319
Bell, C. C., 268
Bellinger, D. C., 486
Bello, I., 75
Belzile, E., 506
Ben Abdallah, A., 384
Benbadis, R. R., 183
Benca, R., 309
Bender, D. S., 220, 395, 416, 417, 429
Bendfeldt, F., 188
Benedetti, F., 53
Ben-Eliyahu, S., 270
Benetti, 52
Benishay, D. S., 331
Benjamin, C. L., 76, 144
Bennett, S. M., 429, 495
Ben-Porath, Y. S., 80, 540
Benson, H., 272
Bentes, C., 315
Bentley, K. H., 122
Berberich, J. P., 496
Berchtold, A., 289
Berenbaum, H., 419, 451
Berger, M., 144, 218
Berghöfer, A., 303
Berglund, L., 125, 126, 130, 137, 138, 142, 149, 155, 156
Berkman, L. F., 62
Berlin, H. A., 348, 400
Berman, A. L., 49, 206, 227, 228, 236, 237, 239, 240, 242, 464
Bermudez, O., 297
Bernat, J. A., 348
Berner, L. A., 288, 298
Berney, T. P., 503
Bernstein, D. A., 83, 193, 415, 417
Berrios, G. E., 185, 446
Berry, A. C., 232
Bertelsen, A., 460, 472

Berton, O., 54
Bertrand, L. D., 189
Besch, C. L., 258
Bettelheim, B., 495
Bettens, K., 516
Beussman, D. J., 375
Beutler, L. E., 409
Bhagwanjee, A., 125
Bharucha, A., 519
Bhasin, T., 495
Bhattacharyya, S., 468
Bhaumik, D., 227
Bhugra, D., 109
Bi, S., 429
Biederman, J., 208, 422, 484, 485, 488
Bielan´ska, 466
Bierut, L. J., 216, 392
Bigler, E. D., 81
Billick, S., 538
Billings, R., 318
Billy, J. O. G., 327
Binder, E. B., 39
Binik, Y. M., 337, 338
Binzer, M., 183
Birkmeyer, J. D., 305
Birley, J., 465
Birmaher, B., 211, 213, 218
Birmingham, L. C., 286
Bishop, D., 483, 489, 494, 520
Biswas, A., 259
Bittar, R. G., 52
Bittinger, J. N., 374
Bixler, 309
Bjertness, E., 236
Björkenstam, C., 427
Bjorntorp, P., 303
Black, D. W., 263, 305, 420, 491
Blackwell, E., 250, 254
Blagys, M. D., 21
Blair, K., 143
Blanchard, E. B., 271, 331, 346, 347, 348, 349
Blanck, H. M., 302
Blanco, C., 133, 204
Blaney, P. H., 454, 455
Blank, T. O., 259
Blasco-Fontecilla, H., 240
Blascovich, J., 253
Blashfield, R. K., 5, 85, 86, 91, 431, 438
Blazer, D. G., 138, 214, 229
Bleiberg, K. L., 232
Bleijenberg, G., 268
Bleuler, E., 452
Bloch, M., 154, 155, 541, 542
Block, J. J., 401
Blokhina, E., 395
Blom, M. M., 518
Bloom, F. E., 48, 258
Blumenthal, J. A., 60, 236, 262
Blundell, J. E., 304
Blyth, D., 224
Bockoven, J. S., 15, 16
Bockting, C. L., 355
Boden, J. M., 375, 419
Bodkin, J. A., 190
Bodnar, R. J., 266
Boehlke, K. K., 398, 399, 401
Boehm, J. K., 261
Boehnlein, J., 215
Boen, 236
Boettcher, H., 90
Boeving, C. A., 260
Bogaert, A., 331
Bogan, R. K., 315
Bogdan, R., 388

Bogels, S., 6, 85
Bögels, S. M., 145
Bohman, 424
Bohn, K., 127
Boiler, M., 89
Boisseau, C. L., 59, 61, 292
Boland, E. M., 204, 205, 206, 220
Bolinskey, P. K., 416
Bolton, B., 286
Bombel, G., 77
Bonanno, G., 206, 214
Bond, A., 49, 375, 376, 504
Bongaarts, J., 257
Bolinskey, P. K., 80
Bonnar-Kidd, K. K., 534
Boocock, A., 159, 160
Boomsma, D., 356
Boone, E., 296
Boot, W. R., 111
Borg, L., 382
Borge, F.-M., 435, 436
Borgelt, L. M., 384
Borges, G., 236, 237, 238
Borkovec, T. D., 126, 127
Bornstein, R. F., 435
Boskind-Lodahl, M., 289
Bosmans, J. E., 518
Bouchard, C., 37, 105, 304, 486
Bouman, T. K., 178
Bourke, J., 504
Bourgeois, M., 519
Boutilier, L. R., 429
Bouton, M. E., 55, 119, 122, 132
Bower, J. E., 259, 263
Bowers, J. S., 533
Bowie, C. R., 91
Bowler, D., 495
Boxer, A., 262
Boyce, N., 240
Boydell, J., 63, 465
Boyer, P., 155
Boyle, C., 382, 426
Boysen, G., 431
Bradford, A., 333, 337, 338, 339, 340, 343, 344,
       350, 353
Bradley, B. P., 126, 357, 489
Bradshaw, S., 328
Brady, J. P., 183
Braet, C., 296
Braff, D., 459, 460
Brahler, E., 206
Brailey, K., 150
Brain, C., 468
Brakefield, T. A., 331
Brand, B., 147, 195
Brandon, T. H., 380
Brandsma, J., 188
Brandt, L., 283
Brannick, M., 292
Brannigan, G. G., 81
Braukhaus, C., 176
Brawman-Mintzer, O., 128, 157
Bray, B. C., 304, 386, 502
Brecht, M.-L., 378
Breckenridge, J., 389
Bredemeier, K., 419
Breitbart, W., 507
Breitborde, N. J., 466
Bremner, J., 150, 152, 192
Brenes, G. A., 125
Brennan, P., 423
Brennan-Krohn, T., 400
Brent, D., 213, 218, 232, 234, 238, 239
Breslau, N., 149, 150

Breuer, J., 57
Brewer, M., 218, 259
Brewerton, T. D., 288
Briskman, J., 426
Britton, J. C., 122, 217
Brix, R. J., 400
Broadstock, M., 513
Brodman, D. M., 76, 144
Brody, A. L., 53
Broekman, T. G., 152
Broft, A., 298
Bromet, E., 212, 215, 224, 236, 237, 238
Brondolo, E., 261, 262
Brønnick, K., 519
Brook, J. S., 164, 185, 301, 422
Brooks, D. J., 65, 390
Brooks-Gunn, J., 291, 295
Brooner, R. K., 394
Brotman, M. A., 208
Brotto, L., 333, 344
Broude, G. J., 330
Broughton, R., 318
Brown, A., 74, 86, 89, 90, 91, 118, 119, 123, 125, 126,
       137, 162, 182, 183, 203, 212, 215, 217, 219,
       220, 225, 242, 268, 269, 338, 380, 465, 466,
       486, 495
Browne, H. A., 155
Brownell, K. D., 286, 292, 294, 302, 303, 304, 305,
       345, 352
Bruce, K. R., 123, 126, 213, 214, 223, 224, 283,
       296, 489
Bruch, H., 144, 295
Bruck, M., 193
Bruehl, S., 265
Brun, A., 513
Brunoni, A. R., 230
Brush, 372
Bryant, R. A., 62, 148, 183, 206
Bryson, S., 106, 300, 301
Buchanan, A., 464, 534
Bucholz, K. K., 392
Buchwald, A. M., 268, 269, 270, 305
Buckles, D. J., 112
Buckley, J., 469
Budiani, D., 109
Budnitz, D. S., 506
Buffum, J., 340
Buhle, J. T., 268
Buka, S. L., 463
Bulik, C. M., 288, 295, 296
Bullis, J. R., 54, 61, 162, 253, 543
Bullmore, E. T., 380
Bumpass, E. R., 400
Bunde, J., 263
Bunnell, R., 275
Bunney, W. E., 462
Buntinx, F., 519
Burback, L., 422
Burch, R., 267
Burk, W. J., 390
Burke, C. A., 47, 503
Burkhalter, X., 315
Burmeister, M., 39
Burnett, P., 466
Burnette, D., 413, 517
Burnham, M. M., 310
Burns, J. W., 130, 265, 266
Burri, A., 331, 341
Burt, D. R., 51, 462, 485, 486
Burwell, 291
Buscher, A. L., 258
Bushman, B. J., 375
Butcher, J. N., 76, 80
Butera, F., 220

Butler, B., 190, 191, 192, 539
Butryn, M. L., 301, 304
Butterworth, M. R., 328
Buysse, D. J., 311
Buzoianu, A., 400
Buzzella, B. A., 145
Bye, E. K., 375
Byers, A. L., 126, 213
Byne, W., 358, 359
Byrne, D., 204, 340, 381
Bystritsky, A., 131

C
Caballero, B., 302, 304
Cabassa, L. J., 90
Cabral, H. J., 160
Cacioppo, J. T., 11, 56, 59, 63, 249, 254, 261
Cafri, G., 292
Cain, A. S., 289
Caine, E. D., 214, 236
Calabrese, J., 230
Calamari, J. E., 155, 156
Calati, R., 428
Caldeira, K. M., 377
Calhoun, K. S., 309, 348
Caligor, E., 433
Callahan, L., 539
Callanan, V. J., 236
Callicott, J. H., 464
Calugi, S., 301
Calzo, J. P., 294
Camargo, C. A., 289
Cameron, H. A., 218
Campbell, A. N., 123, 157, 390, 397, 433, 466
Campbell-Sills, L., 59, 61, 125, 126, 232
Canli, T., 120
Cannon, T. D., 61, 464, 472
Cantor, J., 331, 349
Capaldi, S., 151
Capobianco, D. J., 273
Capurso, C., 517
Carbaugh, 257
Cardeña, E., 148, 186, 188, 190
Cardi, V., 94
Cardish, R. J., 429
Cardoos, S. L., 485
Carey, K. B., 121, 329, 341
Carl, J. R., 54, 61, 162, 253
Carlat, 289, 294
Carleton, R. N., 175
Carlson, E., 148, 191, 259
Carlström, E., 331
Caron, C., 414
Carpenter, A. L., 91, 145, 234, 395, 455, 464
Carr, A., 110, 417
Carrico, A. W., 258
Carrier, S., 318, 344
Carroll, B. J., 77, 149, 284, 302, 358
Carson, A., 180, 182, 183
Carstairs, G. M., 466
Carstensen, L. L., 63, 64, 65
Carter, A. S., 219, 220, 221, 222, 300, 493, 510
Cartwright, R., 318
Carvalho, M., 377, 378
Carver, C. S., 251, 434
Case, W. G., 127
Casey, P., 416
Cash, T., 160
Casner, R., 431
Caspi, A., 36, 38, 40, 41, 49, 391, 422
Cassem, N. H., 274
Cassisi, J. E., 470
Cassoff, J., 306

Castell, B. D., 270
Castelli, W. P., 263
Castle, D. J., 456, 457, 458, 464, 465, 519
Castonguay, L. G., 288, 409
Castriotta, N., 130
Catalano, R. F. P., 107
Cates, D. S., 263
Caufrield, 261
Cautela, J. R., 351, 397
Cavendish, W., 489
Cazzaro, M., 178
CBT-i, 316
Cechnicki, A., 466
Ceci, S., 193
Cecil, J. E., 304
Cederlöf, M., 288
Celio, A. A., 290
Cella, M., 470
Cellard, C., 470
Centers for Disease Control and Prevention (CDC),
        236, 251, 260, 274, 382, 494, 496
Cervilla, J. A., 454, 455
Cevaal, A., 203
Cha, C. B., 236, 237, 241
Chaimowitz, G., 532
Chakrabarti, B., 496
Chalder, T., 270
Chaleby, K., 109
Chamberlain, S. R., 164
Champine, P. R., 540
Champoux, M., 53
Chan, B., 239, 470
Chandra, A., 327, 328
Chang, I. W., 190
Chaouloff, F., 252
Chapman, A. L., 144, 531
Charkoudian, N., 261
Charland, L. C., 306
Charles, S. T., 63, 64, 65
Charney, D. S., 50, 65
Chartrand, H., 57
Chassin, L., 108, 389
Chasson, G. S., 145
Chatkoff, D., 273
Chattarji, S., 504
Chau Wong, M., 462
Chavez, M., 283
Check, J. R., 181
Checknita, D., 423
Cheely, C., 65
Chelminski, I., 414
Chemerinski, E., 416, 418
Chen, H., 218, 435
Cheng, T., 274
Chesney, M., 60, 263, 273
Cheung, F. M., 239
Chevalier, J. M., 112
Chhean, D., 121, 138
Chiappetta, L., 428
Chida, Y., 251, 261, 262, 263
Chik, H. M., 155
Chiliza, B., 457
Chinman, M., 471
Chisuwa, N., 284
Chiu, P., 57, 125, 130, 132, 142, 149, 155, 212
Chivers, M. L., 330, 348, 355
Chmielewski, M., 86
Cho, H. J., 99
Choate, M. L., 61, 140, 141, 232
Chobanian, A. V., 260n
Chodoff, P., 413
Choi, J., 506, 519
Chong, R., 131
Chorot, P., 178

Chorpita, B. F., 91, 122, 126, 150, 221, 224, 225
Chosak, A., 159
Christakis, N. A., 304
Christensen, J. F., 250
Christenson, G. A., 345
Christmas, D., 120
Christophe, D., 349
Christopher, J. C., 108, 490
Christos, C., 268
Chronis, A. M., 424, 425
Chukwuka, J., 313
Chun, V., 426
Chung, J., 308, 375, 494, 519
Ciampi, A., 506
Ciaranello, 48
Cicchetti, D., 65, 410
Cielsa, J., 220
Cimera, R. E., 504
Ciraulo, D. A., 123
Cirincione, C., 537
Cistulli, X., 315
Clance, P. R., 296
Clancy, S. A., 193
Clark, D. A., 154
Clark, D. M., 132, 144, 145, 151, 269
Clark, L. A., 86, 91, 120
Clark, R., 261
Clark, R. A., 258
Clarke, A., 75, 94, 110, 213, 502
Clarkin, J. F., 76, 77, 234
Claudatos, S., 308
Clayton, A., 177, 269, 333
Cleary, P. D., 265
Cleghorn, J. M., 463
Clemenson, 54
Clement, U., 329
Clifford, D. B., 514
Cloninger, C. R., 177, 410, 417, 419, 424, 429, 431,
        432, 433, 437
Closser, M. H., 379
Coan, J. A., 193
Coates, T. J., 275
Cobb, S., 63
Cobham, V. E., 144
Coccaro, E. F., 49, 400
Cochrane, B. B., 57
Cocores, J. A., 340
Coderre, T. J., 271
Coe, C. L., 251, 254, 256
Coen, A., 375
Coffey, B. J., 483
Cohen, A. S., 63, 76, 185, 214, 249, 254, 256, 257, 258,
        263, 301, 422, 451, 454, 493, 540
Cohen-Kettenis, P. T., 354
Coker, L. H., 512
Colby, D. A., 381
Cole, D., 37, 220, 227, 256, 258, 427, 506, 513
Coleman, E., 345, 355
Coleman-Eufinger, C., 539
Colgan, P., 355
Colibazzi, 59
Colins, O. F., 422
Colles, S. L., 303
Collet, J.-P., 384
Collibee, C., 329
Collier, 63
Colligan, R. C., 263
Collinge, J., 515
Collins, E. M., 51
Colloca, L., 53
Colman, I., 421
Colp, R., 109, 533
Colrain, I. M., 308
Coltheart, M., 449

Comacho, M., 141
Comer, J. S., 99, 133, 141, 145, 543
Commons, M. L., 540
Compare, A., 262, 264
Compas, B. E., 65, 274
Compton, S. N., 382, 384
Condie, D., 190
Condon, W., 190
Condray, R., 457
Conduct Problems Prevention Research Group, 426
Conesa, L., 297
Conger, R., 224
Conlon, E. G., 140
Connecticut General Statutes Annotated, 531
Conner, T., 519
Connett, J. E., 263
Connor, D. F., 487, 488
Conrod, P., 398
Constans, J. I., 150
Conti, C. R., 344
Convit, A., 284
Conwell, Y., 214, 236, 239
Cook, B., 127
Coolidge, F., 356
Cools, R., 514
Coons, M., 178, 193, 195
Cooper, A. J., 339
Cooper, A. M., 412
Cooper, J., 239
Cooper, J. E., 72
Cooper, Z., 285, 286, 287, 288, 289, 290, 295, 296,
        298, 299, 300
Cooperberg, J., 305
Cope, M. B., 304
Copeland, W. E., 209
Copen, 327
Corbit, J. D., 389
Corcoran, C. M., 464
Corker, E. A., 445
Correia, S., 400
Corrigan, P. W., 109
Corson, P. W., 294
Cortesi, F., 310
Cortiella, C., 489
Coryell, W., 211
Costa e Silva, J. A., 263, 436
Costantino, A., 358
Costanzo, E., 258
Costello, E., 209
Coston, N., 431
Côté, G., 147
Cotter, R. E., 239
Cottler, L. B., 384
Cottone, P., 293
Courcoulas, A. P., 305
Cournos, F., 453
Courtney, 267
Cousin, F. R., 453
Coverdale, J., 433
Covey, L. S., 380
Covinsky, K. E., 126, 213
Cowen, P. J., 295
Cowley, G., 227
Cox, A., 80, 495
Coyle, D., 463, 540
Crabbe, J. C., 40
Crago, M., 290
Craig, M. C., 512
Craighead, L. W., 223, 296
Craske, M. G., 6, 22, 85, 119, 120, 127, 128, 129, 130,
        131, 132, 133, 134, 135, 137, 138, 140, 176
Creed, F., 176
Creese, I., 51, 462
Crego, C., 5, 91

Cremniter, D., 238
Crerand, C., 161
Crichton, P., 273
Crick, N. R., 410
Cristancho, M. A., 204
Croft-Jeffreys, C., 458
Crosbie, J., 486
Crosby, B., 288, 296, 299, 309, 310
Crow, S. J., 286, 288, 298
Crowe, R. R., 423
Crowley, T., 338
Crump, C., 211, 418
Cubic, B. A., 296
Cuffee, Y., 261, 262
Cuijpers, P., 232, 233, 518
Cunningham Owens, D. G., 467, 468, 469, 470, 471, 472
Cunnington, X., 316
Cuper, P. F., 429
Curran, P. J., 389
Currens, M., 394
Currier, J. M., 206
Curtin, J., 302, 424
Curtis, G. C., 137
Cuthbert, B. N., 26
Cutleh, D. L., 530
Cuttler, 157
Cyranowski, J. M., 224, 330, 342
Czaja, S. J., 428
Czobor, P., 470

D

Daamen, A. P., 378, 380
Dadds, M. R., 144
Dahlenberg, 192
Dahme, B., 296
Dalack, G. W., 380
Dalenius, K., 302
Dalgard, O. S., 236
Dalle Grave, R., 301
Daly, R. J., 496
Damashek, 274
Damasio, A., 52
D'Ambrosio, C., 316
Daniel, S., 239, 489
Danielson, A., 251, 489
Dansky, B. S., 288
Darcangelo, S., 346
Dare, C., 298, 301
Daren, A., 466
Darredeau, C., 381
Das, P., 183
Dassori, 472
Daumann, J., 93, 378
Dautovich, N. D., 309
Dauvilliers, Y., 306
Davey, A., 510
David, A. S., 63, 184
David Klonsky, E., 239
Davidson, J. R. T., 145, 225, 264, 314, 462, 471
Davies, B., 126, 294, 382
Davila, 223, 225
Davis, K. L., 36, 47, 126, 145, 149, 192, 193, 194, 229, 236, 287, 416, 418, 419, 431, 493, 506
Davison, G. C., 81, 348
Davtyan, H., 518
Dawson, D. A., 370, 394, 425, 497
Day, R., 352, 465
De Backer, G., 263
de Bono, J., 126
De Brito, S. A., 420
de Courten, M., 251
de Groot, H. E., 506

de Groot, J.-C., 343
De Gucht, V., 270
de Jong, J., 176, 188
de Kleine, R. A., 152
de Lacy, N., 486
de Lima, M. S., 485
de Lissovoy, V., 436
de Portugal, E., 454
De Raedt, R., 230
de Rooij, S. E., 507
de Silva, P., 161
de Souto Barreto, P., 518
De Thomas, C. A., 426
de Vries, S., 532
de Wit, H., 391
de Zambotti, M., 308
de Zutter, A., 192
de Zwaan, M., 160
Deale, A., 270, 273
Dean, J. T., 48
Dearborn, J., 252
Deavers, F., 470
Deb, S., 502
DeBaryshe, B. D., 424
Debruyne, H., 449
Decker, M. D., 81, 127
Deckersbach, T., 88, 135, 160
Deffenbacher, J. L., 400
DeFries, J. C., 217
Degenhardt, 392
Degtiar, I., 445
Deiter, P. J., 159
DeJong, B. L., 155
Del Parigi, A., 517
Delano-Wood, L., 213, 214, 227
DeLepeleire, J., 519
DeLisi, M., 98, 424
Delizonna, L. L., 344
Dell, P. F., 184
Delvecchio, P., 531
DeMarce, J. M., 416
DeMaria, E. J., 305
DeMartini, 121
Dembroski, T. M., 60, 263
Demers, C. H., 388
Demiris, G., 519
Demler, O., 125, 126, 130, 137, 138, 142, 149, 155, 212, 200, 156
DeMyer, M. K., 495
Deng, 54
Denis, C., 399
Denko, T., 227, 228, 230
Dennis, M., 531
Dent, M. F., 152
Dentingeh, J., 530
Denys, D., 52
Denzin, N. K., 396
DePrince, A., 146, 184
Depue, R. A., 51
DeRogatis, L. R., 344
Dersh, J., 175, 265
DeRubeis, R., 229, 233
Desautels, X., 318
DeSilva, P., 89, 342
DeStefano, F., 496
Devanand, D. P., 186, 187, 190, 191, 214
Deveci, A., 182
Devine, P., 381
DeWall, C. N., 268
DeWitt, D. J., 375
Dexter-Mazza, E. T., 427, 429
Dhawan, N., 433
Dhejne, C., 358
Diamond, J., 295, 328, 330, 331, 357

Dick, D. M., 38, 497
Dickens, G., 37, 40, 400
Dickersin, K., 543
Diedrich, A., 436
Diener, E., 56, 61
DiIorio, C., 531
Dimaite, R., 142
Dimberg, U., 143
Dimidjian, S., 203, 225, 232
Dimoliatis, I., 99
Dimon, L., 11
Dimsdale, J. E., 60, 173
DiNardo, P. A., 139
Dinges, D. F., 189
Dinnel, D. L., 142
Diorio, J., 40, 121
Dirks, 309
Dishion, T. J., 390, 426
Disney, K. L., 435
Ditre, J. W., 380
Dixon, J. B., 303, 470
Djernes, J. K., 214
Dobkin, P. L., 22
Docherty, J. P., 462
Docter, R. F., 347
Dodick, D. W., 273
Doehrmann, O., 53, 144
Dogan, S., 342, 357
Dohnt, 309
Dohrenwend, B. P., 149, 465
Dolan, M., 57, 431
Doll, H., 294, 301, 532
Dominé, F., 289
Dominiczak, A. F., 261
Domino, E. F., 387
Donaldson, K., 532
Donderi, D. C., 317
D'Onofrio, B. M., 37, 96, 380
Donovan, D. M., 397
Dorer, D. J., 284
Douaud, G., 511
Dougherty, D. D., 157
Douglas, J., 421
Douzgou, S., 374
Dow, T., 470
Dowrick, C., 416
Doyle, W. J., 63, 254, 316
Dragioti, E., 99
Draijer, N., 191
Drake, K. L., 144, 463, 504
Dramaix, M., 263
Drapeau, V., 303
Draper, B., 346, 373
Drayer, R. A., 214
Drevets, W. C., 50
Drogin, E. Y., 540
Dronsfield, A. T., 395
Drummond, K. D., 306, 357
Druss, B. G., 109
Dubovsky, S. L., 109
Duberstein, P. R., 214, 236
Dubovsky, S. L., 109
Ducios, 295
Dudai, 54
Dudek, B. C., 40
Duff, D., 127
Dufresne, R. G., 160
Dugas, M. J., 128
Duke, M. C., 77
Dulit, R. A., 412
Duman, R., 218
Dumitrascu, N., 77
Dummit, E. S., 145
Duncan, A., 182, 520, 540
Dunlop, B. W., 51, 217

Dunn, G., 416
Dunne, P. E., 291
DuPaul, G. J., 487
Duran, R. E., 191
Durand, V. M., 75, 94, 98, 103, 110, 131, 310, 315, 316, 317, 318, 481, 492, 494, 495, 496, 497, 503, 519
Durant, C., 120, 301
Durkheim, E., 237
Dürsteler, K. M., 390
Dusseldorp, E., 262
Dustin, M. L., 255
Dvorak, R. D., 390
Dvorak-Bertscha, J., 424
Dyke, P., 504
Dysken, M. W., 518

E

Eaker, E. D., 263
Eaton, N. R., 126, 130, 138, 204, 358
Eaves, L. J., 216, 217
Ebersole, A., 431
Ebigno, P., 109, 179
eBody Project, 301
Ebringer, A., 515
Eddy, K. T., 287, 290, 298, 301
Edinger, J. D., 316
Edmondson, D., 259
Edmunds, J. M., 76
Edmundson, M., 85, 86, 91
Edwards, A. C., 53, 265, 266, 369, 470, 502
Eelen, P., 55
Efantis-Potter, J., 251
Eftekhari, A., 151
Egan, B. M., 260
Egeland, J., 106
Egger, H., 209, 257
Egri, G., 465
Ehlers, A., 48, 138, 151
Ehrenreich, J. T., 59, 61, 141, 209
Ehrenreich-May, J. T., 145
Ehrhardt, A., 356
Eibach, R. P., 330, 331
Eikenaes, I., 434
Eikeseth, S., 504
Eisen, A. R., 156
Eisenberg, L., 293, 294
Eisenberger, N. I., 268
Eisenlohr-Moul, T. A., 428
Eisler, I., 298, 301
Eisner, L. R., 203, 220
Ekbom, A., 283
Ekelund, 51
Ekselius, L., 283, 427
Ekstrand, M. L., 275
Elbogen, E., 531
Elder, G., 224
Eldevik, S., 504
Eldredge, K. L., 288, 299
Eley, T. C., 39, 216, 217, 220
El-Gabalawy, R., 176
Elie, R., 434
Elis, O., 451
Elkins, I. J., 426
Ellard, D., 54, 59, 61, 122, 123, 162, 232, 253, 519
Ellason, J. W., 195
Elliot, R., 76
Ellis, H., 239, 395
Ellman, L. M., 458
Elovainio, M., 51
El-Solh, A. A., 315
Elzinga, B., 428

Emeny, R., 264
Emery, C. F., 259, 262, 263
Emmelkamp, P. M. G., 435
Emsley, R., 457
Engel, S. G., 288
England, P., 329
Ennis, M., 160
Enoch, M.-A., 393
Epel, E., 259
Epler, A. J., 289
Epperson, C. N., 207
Epstein, L. H., 271
Eranti, S., 230
Erik Erikson, E., 20, 64
Erkinjuntti, T., 512, 518
Erlich, M. D., 453, 456
Eroglu, C., 43
Ersche, K. D., 380
Ervin, 63
Escalona, R., 446
Escobar, J. I., 176
Eser, D., 49
Eslinger, P. J., 52, 538
Esparza-Romero, J., 304
Espindle, D., 330
Esposito, M., 94
Essex, M. J., 120, 143
Estes, L. S., 290
Eth, S., 147
Euling, 267
Evangelou, E., 99
Evans, D. A., 383, 390, 510
Evengard, B., 269
Evrard, M., 20
Exner, J. E., 77
Eyberg, S. M., 141
Ezrati-Vinacour, R., 482
Ezzati, M., 249, 250
Ezzel, C., 258

F

Fabbri, S., 178
Fabiano, G. A., 485
Fadok, J. P., 119
Fagan, P. J., 348, 350, 352, 353
Fagelman, F. D., 400
Faggiano, F., 398
Fagundes, C. P., 258, 259
Fairburn, C. G., 283, 285, 286, 287, 288, 289, 290, 292, 294, 295, 296, 298, 299, 300, 301
Fairchild, G., 423
Fairholme, C. P., 59, 61
Faith, M. S., 305
Fakhoury, W., 469
Fallon, A. E., 178, 292
Falloon, I. R., 470
Fama, J. M., 121
Fang, A., 61, 122, 158, 161
Fanning, J. R., 49
Fantino, E., 192
Faraone, S. V., 422, 453, 486
Farberow, N. L., 238
Farelly, 445
Farias, S. T., 512
Farnam, F., 342
Farquhar, J. W., 276
Farrell, L. J., 140
Fatséas, M., 399
Fauci, A. S., 251, 257, 258
Faurholt-Jepsen, M., 76
Fausto-Sterling, A., 359
Fava, G. A., 129, 178, 227, 229

Fay, C., 159, 160
Fayyad, R., 484
Fazel, S., 532, 540
Fearing, M. A., 507
Feig, L. A., 41
Fein, D. A., 495
Feingold, A., 160
Feinleib, M., 262
Feldman, H. A., 250, 289, 294, 335
Felmingham
Fenster, J. R., 259
Fenton, K. A., 251, 258, 275
Fergus, T. A., 176
Ferguson, C., 388, 431
Ferguson-Rome, J. C., 519
Fergusson, D., 214, 375
Fernandez, J. R., 120, 304
Fernandez-Mendoza, 309
Fernyhough, C., 450
Ferrazzoli, D., 511
Ferré, S., 381
Ferreira, C., 315, 436
Ferri, C. P., 510
Ferster, C. B., 24
Feurino III, L., 429
Ficks, C., 486
Fiedelak, J. I., 269
Field, A. E., 139, 289, 291, 293, 301, 328
Fielder, R. L., 329
Fields, B. W., 213, 214
Fien, H., 491
Fileborn, B., 334
Filene, J., 426
Filippi, M., 81, 82
Fincham, F. D., 223, 329
Fineberg, N. A., 48, 164
Fink, G. R., 296
Finkenbine, R., 180
Finn, C. J., 241
First, M. B., 87, 88, 241
Fischer, M., 460
Fishbain, D. A., 400
Fisher, C. B., 127, 305
Fiske, A., 213, 214, 218, 229, 236
Fitts, S. N., 159
Fitzgerald, D. A., 52, 144
Fitzhenry, M., 417
Fitzmaurice, G., 427
Fitzpatrick, S., 428
Flanagan, E. H., 5, 105, 106
Flanders, W. D., 340
Flannery-Schroeder, E., 144
Flegal, K. M., 284, 302
Fleminger, S., 513
Flemmin, 370
Fletcher, A., 80, 211, 249, 257, 258, 268, 489, 491
Fliers, E., 486
Flint, A., 36, 37
Flor, H., 265, 271
Flory, K., 291
Flykt, A., 59
Foa, E. B., 145, 157, 158
Foa150
Fogelson, D. L., 434
Foland-Ross, L. C., 222
Foley, E., 259, 504
Folkers, G. K., 251, 257, 258
Folsom, D. P., 532, 534
Fone, K., 451
Fong, T. G., 506
Fontenelle, L. F., 436
Forand, N. R., 229
Ford, B., 251, 329, 386, 413, 486, 532

Ford, M., 413
Fordyce, W. E., 265
Foreyt, J. P., 304
Forman, S., 300
Forney, K. J., 292
Fort, C., 207
Forth, A. E., 423, 425
Fosco, G. M., 390
Foster, A., 218, 302, 469
Fountoulakis, K. N.,, 99
Fournier, J. C., 227, 232
Foussias, G., 448
Fowler, J. C., 240, 304
Fowles, D. C., 423
Fox, E., 241
Foy, D. W., 149
Frampton, C., 419
France, C. R., 265, 271
Frances, A., 89, 91, 319, 375, 412
Franche, R. L., 434
Francis, D., 40, 121, 128
Francke, A., 520
Francouer, E., 193
Frank, E., 218, 220, 224, 229, 230, 234, 274
Frank, R. G., 332
Frankel, S. A., 205
Frankenburg, F. R., 410, 427
Franklin, J. E., 157, 223, 313, 375
Franko, D. L., 283, 284, 285, 288, 291, 300
Franson, K. L., 384
Fratiglioni, L., 511, 520
Frazier, T. W., 493, 520
Frean, E., 251
Fredrikson, M., 57, 261
Freels, S., 208
Freeman, A., 214, 295, 416, 417, 431, 470, 497
French-Belgian Collaborative Group, 263
Frenda, S. J., 194
Freud, A., 20
Freud, S., 57, 173, 237
Frewen, P. A., 147
Frick, P. J., 422
Fricke, R. A., 53
Fridlund, A. J., 23
Frie, N., 304
Friedberg, F., 270
Frieden, T. R., 305
Friedl, M. C., 191
Friedman, A. F., 80, 126, 146, 148, 149, 150, 152, 213, 233, 262, 268, 304
Friedman, B. H., 262
Fried-Oken, M., 519
Frissen, A., 464
Fristad, M. A., 213, 214
Fritz, C. O., 94
Frodl, T., 486
Frombonne, E., 494
Frost, R. O., 162, 163
Frühauf, S., 343
Fruzzetti, A. E., 296
Fryar, C. D., 302
Fu, 267
Fuchs, L. S., 491
Fugl-Meyer, A. R., 333
Fuji, D. E., 109
Fullana, M. A., 155
Fulton, H. G., 122, 381, 390
Furberg, H., 268
Furman, W., 329
Furnham, A., 418, 471, 472
Furr, J. M., 125, 128
Fusar-Poli, P., 446, 455
Futterman, S. E., 418
Fyer, A., 133, 137

G

Gaag, 450
Gable, J., 469
Gage, 54
Gagliese, L., 265
Gagnon, J., 341
Gail, M. H., 284
Galatzer-Levy, I. R., 214
Galea, L. A. M., 149
Gallagher, M. W., 122
Gallagher- Thompson, D., 63, 254
Gallant, A. R., 303
Gallerani, C. M., 205
Galletta, A., 74
Gallo, A., 50, 236, 264
Gamba, R., 158
Gandaglia, G., 339
Ganne-Vevonec, M. O., 429
Gansler, D. A., 52
Ganz, J. B., 503
Gao, Y., 425
Gara, M. A., 176
Garawi, F., 390
Garb, H. N., 77
Garber, J., 205, 213, 214, 218, 219, 220, 221, 222, 232, 233
Garcia, F. D., 63, 329, 353
Garcia-Lopez, L. J., 144
Gardner, C. O., 216, 219, 220, 224, 426
Garfield, 242
Garfinkel, P. E., 269, 286, 294
Garland, E. L., 386
Garlipp, 63
Garner, D. M., 283, 294
Garnier-Dykstra, L. M., 377
Garon, N., 106
Garrabe, J., 453
Garrity, A. G., 464
Garvey, L., 127, 251
Gary, L. E., 212
Garzino-Demo, A., 258
Gatchel, R., 175, 265, 266
Gatsonis, C., 205, 237
Gatz, M., 128, 213, 216
Gau, J. M., 205
Gaudreau, J.-D., 506
Gauthier, M., 501
Gaylor, E. E., 310
Ge, X., 224
Gearhardt, A. N., 302, 303, 304
Geda, Y. E., 263
Geer, J. H., 338
Geesey, M. E., 517
Gehrman, P., 309
Geiger, P. J., 428
Geleijnse, J., 264
Gelernter, J., 121
Gendrano, N., 335
George, E. L., 138, 230, 234
George, L. W., 219
Geraerts, E., 193
Gerard, D. L., 15
Gerber, P. J., 489
Gerdin, B., 427
Gerger, H., 343
Germain150
Gershenfeld, H., 233
Gershon, A., 216
Gershon, E. S., 37
Gerstein, D. R., 398
Gervais, R. O., 540
Gesquiere, L. R., 252

Gfroerer, J. C., 382
Ghaemi, S. N., 220, 229
Ghanem, H., 335
Ghitza, U. E., 397
Giannotti, F., 310
Gianoli, M. O., 434
Gibb, B., 64, 65, 223
Gibbons, R., 227
Gibbs, J., 304
Gibson, P., 159
Giedke, H., 218
Gielen, A. C., 275
Giesbrecht, T., 20, 184, 185, 189, 191, 192
Giese-Davis, J., 258, 259
Gifford, 267
Gill, S. S., 506
Gillberg, C., 494
Giller, H., 96
Gillespie-Lynch, K., 493
Gillham, 232
Gilman, 241, 291
Gilmore, J. H., 460
Giltay, E., 264
Ginovart, N., 463
Ginsburg, G. S., 144
Giordano, T. P., 258
Gipson, M. T., 160
Girdler, S., 504
Girgus, J. S., 221
Girirajan, S., 501
Gironde, S., 427
Gitlin, M. J., 227, 228, 230
Gjerde, L. C., 435, 437
Gladue, 331
Glaesmer, H., 206
Glasper, E. R., 218
Glass, S., 299
Glassman, A. H., 380
Glazer, J. P., 183
Gleaves, D. H., 186, 190, 191
Gleditsch, S. L., 259
Gleiberman, L., 60
Glenn, B., 265
Glick, 234
Glisky, E. L., 190, 191
Glod, C., 227
Gloster, A. T., 129
Glover, G., 464
Glovinsky, P., 310
Glynn, R. J., 127, 470
Goater, N., 458
Godart, N., 288, 295
Goel, M. S., 313
Goering, P., 471
Goff, D. C., 463
Gold, J. H., 195, 340
Goldberg, D., 176, 179
Golden, C. J., 81
Goldfarb, W., 495
Goldie, W. D., 23
Goldmeier, D., 251
Goldmeir, D., 338
Goldsmith, H. H., 120
Goldstein, A., 65, 81, 209, 335, 344, 370, 429, 463, 496, 501
Goldston, D., 236, 237, 239
Golembo-Smith, S., 457
Golier, J., 150
Gollan, J. K., 400
Golmaryami, F. N., 422
Golshan, S., 163
Gomez-Gil, E., 356
Gong, Q., 458
Gonzalez, C. M., 57, 258

González, N., 454
Good, B. J., 138, 215
Goodale, G., 539
Goode, S., 495
Goodenow, C. S., 294
Goodin, B. R., 271
Goodman, D. M., 108, 193, 194, 317
Goodrick, X. X., 312
Goodwill, A., 428
Goodwin, F. K., 52, 203, 211, 220, 229, 234
Gooren, L., 355
Goos, L. M., 486
Goozen, S. H. M., 423
Gordis, E., 389
Gordon, J. A., 288, 397, 534
Gore-Felton, C., 258
Gorelick, D. A., 464
Gorman, J. M., 134
Gorny, G., 64
Gorski, R. A., 331
Gorwood, P., 50, 428
Gosch, E., 144
Gotheil, E., 258
Gotlib, I. H., 213, 218, 222, 225
Gotman, N., 208
Gottesman, I. I., 37, 105, 458, 460
Gottfredson, L., 81
Gottlieb, M. C., 112
Gould, E., 218, 239, 240, 298
Gournay, K., 160
Gouveia, M. J., 270
Gouzoulis-Mayfrank, E., 93, 378
Goyal, A., 272
Grabbe, K. L., 275
Grabe, H. J., 292
Grace, M. C., 148
Gradisar, M., 309
Gradus, J. L., 152
Graeff, F. G., 121
Graff, F. S., 419
Graham, C. A., 80, 204, 333, 336
Grandi, S., 178
Granic, I., 424
Granillo, M. T., 397
Grann, M., 532, 540
Grant, B., 63, 126, 161, 164, 203, 219, 265, 370, 374, 399, 400
Gratten, J., 120
Gratz, K. L., 122
Graubard, B. I., 284
Gray, B. A., 50, 120, 121, 458
Graybar, S. R., 429
Gray, J. A., 423
Graziosi, C., 257
Grazzi, L., 274
Green, B. A., 148, 153, 308, 331, 356, 357, 451, 541, 542
Greenberg, B. D., 158, 228, 240, 290
Greenblatt, D. J., 127
Greene, R., 330, 488
Greenlick, M. R., 263
Greenough, W. T., 54
Greenspoon, M., 458
Greenwood, P., 104, 338, 461
Greeven, A., 179
Gregg, N., 489, 491
Gregoire, A., 344
Gregory, X., 317
Grella, C., 383
Gressier, F., 428
Greydanus, D. E., 497
Griebel, 49
Griffith, E. E. H., 188
Griffiths, R., 381, 385

Grillon, C., 150
Grilo, C., 289, 296, 298, 300, 429
Grisham, J., 123, 162, 163
Grobler, C., 203
Groc, L., 252
Groleau, P., 296
Groom, C., 126
Gross, J. J., 58, 59, 60, 427
Grossardt, B. R., 263
Grossman, C. I., 275
Grosz, H. J., 182
Growdon, M. E., 506
Gruber, A. J., 190, 220, 226, 306
Grucza, 392
Grudzinskas, A. Jr., 534
Grummer-Strawn, L. M., 302
Gu, D., 276
Guan, X., 518
Guarnaccia, P. J., 107, 108
Guastella, A. J., 496
Guedeney, N., 213
Gueorguieva, R., 300
Guijarro, M. L., 261
Guild, D., 348
Guilleminault, C., 49
Guimond, T., 429
Gulliksson, M., 262
Gulsrud, A., 497
Gündel, H., 207
Gunderson, J. G., 416, 417, 427
Gunn, M., 536, 537
Gunnar, M. R., 122, 150, 259
Guo, Z., 517
Gupta, S., 206
Gur, R. C., 451, 461
Guralnik, O., 185
Gureje, O., 179
Guroff, J. J., 189
Gurvits, T. V., 150
Gurwitz, J., 127
Gusella, J. F., 514
Gustad, J., 159, 160
Gustafson, L., 513
Gusti Rai Tirta, I., 472
Gutheil, T. G., 540
Gutowski, S. M., 397
Guze, S. B., 177
Gwaltney, J. M., 63

H
Haber, S. N., 158
Hack, S., 128
Hackett, T. P., 60, 274
Haddad, P. M., 468
Hadland, S. E., 294
Hadley, S., 160
Hadzi-Pavlovic, D., 466
Haeffel, G. J., 220
Haenen, M. A., 176, 177
Haines, J., 302
Hakstian, A. R., 421
Haley, A., 37
Hall, A., 284, 341
Hallahan, D. P., 489
Haller, 53
Hallet, A. J., 261
Halliburton, A. E., 386
Hallmayer, J., 495
Halmi, K. A., 296
Halpern, J. H., 385, 386
Hamburg, 291
Hamer, D. H., 176

Hames, J. L., 220
Hamilton, J. L., 213, 218
Hamm, A. O., 296, 451
Hammeke, T. A., 81
Hammen, C., 213, 217, 219, 222, 229, 230, 233
Hammer, S., 257, 258
Hampton, T., 242
Hancock, T. B., 496
Handelsman, M. M., 112
Haney, 60
Hankin, B. L., 65, 224, 225
Hanlon, E. C., 306
Hanna, G. L., 156
Hans, V. P., 537
Hansen, K. S., 317
Hanson, R. K., 352
Hantouche, E., 238
Hanuszkiewicz, I., 466
Harada, N., 142
Harburg, E., 60
Harden, R. N., 265
Hardie, T. L., 387
Harding, J. W., 517
Hare, R. D., 409, 420, 421, 423, 424, 425, 532
Hariri, A. R., 36
Harley, K., 466
Harlow, B., 214
Harmell, A. L., 542
Harmer, C. J., 48, 49
Haro, J. M., 454
Harold, G. T., 223
Harpur, T. J., 421
Harrington, J. L., 80
Harris, G. T., 219, 225, 348, 349, 352
Harrison, B., 144, 295, 456, 461, 462, 463, 464, 533
Hart, A. B., 423
Harte, C. B., 340
Hart-Johnson, T., 308
Hartlage, S. A., 208
Hartley, D. M., 41
Hartman, T. J., 176, 381
Harvey, A. G., 91, 218, 220, 269, 270, 317, 457, 463, 489
Hasin, D., 203, 212, 215, 420
Haslam, N., 466
Hastings, R. P., 504
Hatfield, E., 11, 59
Hattie, J., 80
Hatzichristou, D. G., 335
Haukka, J., 237
Haukkala, A., 261
Hauner, K. K., 140
Hausmann, M., 450
Hausteiner, C., 264
Havekes, 306
Hawkins, J. D. P., 107
Hawkley, L. C., 249, 254, 261
Hawton, K., 334, 335
Hay, P. J., 284, 286
Hayes, M., 6, 259, 345, 394
Hayes-Skelton, S. A., 128
Hayley, 308
Haynes, R. B., 75, 76, 262, 263
Haynos, A. F., 296
Hays, R. D., 225
Hazell, P., 65
Hazlett-Stevens, H., 83
Heath, A. C., 216, 217, 503, 515
Heathcote, D., 65
Heatherton, T. F., 284, 296
Heaton, P., 495
Hebert, L. E., 510
Hecht, K. F., 410
Hecker, M. H. L., 263

Heckers, S., 454
Heckman, B. W., 380
Hedley, A. J., 276
Heidenreich, T., 144, 231
Heil, S. H., 369
Heim, C., 269
Heiman, J. R., 336, 343
Heimberg, R. G., 141, 144
Heinrichs, N., 140
Heisler, L. K., 304
Hellemann, G., 497
Heller, W., 48
Hellman, 331
Hellmuth, J. C., 389
Hemmingsson, T., 264
Henckens, M. J. A. G., 120
Henderson, K. E., 303, 304, 512
Hendriks, G. J., 152
Hendrix, Jimi, 367
Henen, 178
Hennen, J., 345, 410
Henry, D., 15, 65
Hepworth, 219
Herbert, T. B., 254, 256
Herda, C. A., 138
Herdt, G. H., 330
Herling, S., 389
Herman, C. P., 295
Herman-Dunn, R., 225
Hermann, C. A., 350
Hermans, D., 120
Hernandez, M., 471
Heron, J., 384
Herpertz, S. C., 430
Herpertz-Dahlmann, B., 296
Herren, C., 140
Hersen, M., 100
Herzog, A., 176, 285, 289, 291
Heshka, S., 304
Hetherington, M. M., 304
Hettema, J. M., 37, 126, 220
Heylens, G., 356
Hieneman, M., 75, 110
Higgins, S. T., 369, 394, 397
Higuchi, S., 391
Hilchey, C. A., 381
Hildenbrand, A. K., 275
Hilgard, E. R., 57
Hill, C., 107, 137, 268, 291, 316
Hiller, W., 174, 176, 177, 178, 179, 309
Hillygus, J., 517
Hilsenroth, M., 21, 77
Hilt, L. M., 224
Hilty, D. M., 164
Hindmarch, I., 127
Hingson, R., 374
Hinshaw, S. P., 64, 90, 485
Hinton, D., 121, 131, 138, 142, 517
Hipes, 534
Hirschfeld, D. R., 143, 227
Hirshkowitz, M., 311
Hiruma, N., 142
Hitchcock, P. B., 177
Hlastala, S. A., 234
Ho, B. C., 276, 464
Hoblyn, J., 518
Hockenberry, J., 381
Hodgins, S., 420
Hodgson, K., 216, 350
Hoeffer, C. A., 504
Hoeft, F., 491
Hoek, H. W., 286, 287, 291
Hoekstra, T., 264
Hoffman, A. F., 127, 128, 273

Hofmann, S. G., 59, 60, 61, 122, 126, 128, 131, 133, 136, 137, 138, 141, 142, 144, 145, 161, 231, 272
Hogarty, G. E., 470
Holden, C., 303
Holder, H. D., 398
Holi, M. M., 400
Holland, A. J., 63, 254, 500
Hollander, E., 160, 185, 390, 400
Hollands, G. J., 249
Hollis, J. F., 263
Hollon, S. D., 133, 232, 233, 543, 544
Holm, H., 427
Holmes, L., 49
Holroyd, K. A., 267, 271
Holtzman, J. N., 229
Holzman, P. S., 461
Hong, P. S., 304, 306
Horney, Karen, 20
Hooley, J. M., 427, 428, 466
Hopkins, M., 127
Hopwood, C. J., 86, 415, 416, 417
Horácek, J., 385
Horan, W. P., 451, 465
Hori, 472
Hornberger, J. C., 445
Hornung, R., 401
Horowitz, J., 232, 489
Horta, B. L., 485
Horwath, E., 156, 453
Horwitz, A. V., 241
Horwood, J., 214, 375
Hospital Elder Life Program, 507
Hostinar, C. E., 122, 259
Hotopf, M., 269
Houck, J. M., 397
House, J. S., 62, 63
Houston, B. K., 263
Howard, L. J., 386, 517
Howe, M. L., 193
Howell, A. J., 195, 319
Howes, O. D., 449, 463
Howieson, D. B., 76, 81
Howland, R. H., 88
Howlin, P., 495
Hoza, B., 484
Hser, Y. I., 383
Hsia, C., 138
Hsu, L. K. G., 286, 287, 295, 300
Hu, N., 126
Huang, C. C., 96, 410, 414
Hubert, N. C., 259
Hubley, S., 225
Hucker, S. J., 347
Huddy, V., 470
Hudson, J. I., 140, 144, 190, 217, 286, 289, 290, 294
Hudziak, J., 356
Huerta, M., 520
Hughes, C. J., 138, 381, 395, 504, 513
Hull, I. M., 234, 540
Humedian, M., 109
Hummelen, B., 417, 434
Hunsley, J., 77
Hunt, W. A., 14
Hunter, E., 141, 184
Huntington's Disease Collaborative Research Group, 514
Huntjens, R. J., 190
Huppert, J. D., 123, 145
Hur, K., 227
Hurt, E., 486
Hus, V., 520
Husain, K., 270
Hutchinson, D. M., 293
Hutton, J., 495

Huxter, M., 259
Hwang, I., 239, 260
Hybels, C. F., 214, 229
Hyde, J. S., 292, 329, 330
Hyman, S. E., 37, 47, 91
Hynan, L. S., 512

I

Iacono, W. G., 426, 461
Iadarola, S., 497
Iannucci, R. A., 380
Ibanez-Casas, I., 454, 455
Imes, S. A., 296
Ingoldsby, E. M., 426
Inkelis, S., 308
Inouye, S. K., 506, 507
Insel, T., 26, 41, 91, 228, 229, 283
Inse, Thomas, 52l
Institute of Medicine, 69, 266, 342,242, 264
Institute of Medicine National Safety Council, 274
IOM, 543
IRB Fisher, 112
Irons, G., 23
Ironside, J. W., 515
Ironson, G., 60, 263
Irwin, M., 217
Isaacowitz, D., 65
Isenberg-Grzeda, E., 373
Isometsä, E., 237
Israël, M., 283
Ito, B. S., 482, 511
Ivanenko, A., 318
Ivanov, I., 395
Ivengar, M., 127
Iverson, L., 47
Ivleva, E. I., 461

J

Jaarsveid, 304
Jablensky, A., 457, 458
Jaccard, J., 150
Jackson v. Indiana, 339
Jacob, R. G., 144
Jacobsen, P. B., 259
Jacobson, K. C., 225, 232, 388
Jacoby, R. J., 153
Jaconis, M., 289
Jaffee, S., 39, 216, 220
Jager, G., 383, 384
Jahr, E., 504
Jahraus, J. P., 286
Jain, K. K., 313, 488
Jakicic, J. M., 304
Jakob, M., 178
Jakupcak, M., 389
James, B. O., 109, 260
Jameson, D., 188
Jamison, K. R., 211, 229, 230, 234, 265
Janca, A., 348
Jang, K. L., 177, 464
Janghorbani, M., 342
Janicki-Deverts, D., 249, 254
Jankiewicz, 257
Jankovic, J., 468
Jannini, E. A., 331
Jansen, A. G., 105
Janssen, E., 330, 338
Janszky, I., 264
Jardri, R., 428
Jarman, C., 397
Jarrett, R. B., 233
Jasiukaitis, P., 191

Jason, L. A., 268, 270
Jaspers, K., 448
Jaussent, I., 309
Javdani, S., 431
Javitt, D. C., 387, 462
Jay, S. M., 259
Jayawickrema, S., 340, 343
Jeffrey, 423
Jelicic, M., 184
Jellinek, E. M., 374
Jenike, E., 157, 158
Jenkins, J. H., 109, 466
Jenness, 225
Jensen, E., 229, 488, 518
Jensen, H. M.
Jern, P., 331
Jesse, R., 385
Jeste, D. V., 542
Jiang, W., 262
Jilek, W. G., 188
Jin, R., 125, 126, 130, 140
Jindal, R. D., 218
Jo, B., 301
Jobes, D. A., 237
Jockin, V., 39
Joe, S., 532
Joels, M., 120
Johanson, C. E., 389
Johansson, A., 358, 424, 532
John, M. B., 23
Johnson, A. M., 328
Johnson, B., 160
Johnson, C. J., 482
Johnson, D. P., 217, 225
Johnson, J. G., 121, 185, 191, 301, 422
Johnson, M., 385
Johnson, R., 540
Johnson, S. L., 61, 220, 223, 226, 531
Johnson, W., 105, 211, 218
Johnson, V. E., 96, 332, 342–343
Johnson, V. R., 372
Johnson-Sabine, E., 293
Johnston, B. C., 304, 309, 374
Johnstone, E. C., 467, 468, 469, 470, 471, 472
Joiner, T., 223, 239, 240, 242, 284, 296
Joling, K. J., 517
Jones, E. J. H., 149, 150, 223, 241, 327, 328, 344, 380, 458, 461, 463, 468, 482, 493
Jones, Mary Cover, 23
Joo, E. Y., 306
Joormann, J., 222
Joplin, Janis, 367
Jose, A., 414
Joslyn, 372
Joy, M. E., 425
Joyce, P., 419, 428
Joyner, M. J., 261
Judd, L. L., 204, 205, 211
Judge, B., 133
Juliano, L. M., 381
Julius, M., 60
Jummani, R., 483
Jung, C., 20
Junginger, J., 346

K

Kabat-Zinn, J., 231
Kaciroti, N., 60
Kaelber, C., 88
Kafka, M. P., 345, 346
Kagan, J., 143
Kahler, C. W., 380
Kahn, R. S., 486

Kaholokula, J., 75
Kaiser, A. P., 258, 270, 496
Kaiser, J., 257
Kalaria, R., 512
Kalbarczyk, A., 510
Kalichman, S. C., 257
Kalin, N. H., 120
Kalra, G., 106
Kamath, V., 109
Kame'enui, E. J., 491
Kamen, C., 22
Kaminski, J. W., 426
Kanayama, G., 293, 294, 387
Kandel, E. R., 38, 54, 57, 58
Kane, J. M., 462, 469
Kannel, W. B., 262
Kanner, L., 495
Kaplan De-Nour, A. K., 344, 345, 413, 497
Kaplin, A. I., 384
Kapur, S., 463
Karg, K., 39, 48
Karkhaneh, M., 497
Karlin, B. E., 98
Karno, M., 466
Karterud, S., 417
Kasari, C., 497
Kasen, S., 185, 301, 422
Kaski, M., 503
Kasl, S. V., 56
Kaslow, N. J., 229, 232
Kass, A. E., 301
Kassam-Adams, N., 275
Kates, 257
Kato, K., 269, 472
Katon, W., 126, 177, 269
Katz, I. R., 160, 265, 271, 344, 507, 510
Katzman, D. K., 300
Kaufmann, W., 212
Kavanagh, D. J., 466
Kawachi, I., 225, 261
Kawas, L. H., 517
Kay, C., 153
Kaye, S., 286, 287, 288, 295, 296, 299, 375
Kazak, A. E., 259, 260
Kazantzis, N., 270
Kazdin, A. E., 100
Keane, T. M., 146, 149, 150, 184, 195
Kearney, A. J., 397, 489
Kearns, M. C., 152
Keddie, A., 396
Keefe, D. L., 265, 271, 356
Keel, P. K., 284, 288, 291, 292
Keeley, J. W., 5
Keenan, J. M., 217, 222r
Keenan-Miller, D., 219, 229, 230
Keenleyside, M., 417
Kefalas, P., 11
Kehrer, C. A., 429
Keith, S. J., 446
Keitner, G. I., 225
Keller, M. B., 120, 204, 205, 206, 233
Kellner, C. H., 178, 230
Kellum, J. M., 305
Kelly, B. D., 239, 391, 396, 416, 417
Kelsey, 48
Keltikangas-Jarvinen, 51
Keltner, D., 226
Kemeny, M. E., 253
Kemp, S., 9, 10, 12
Kendall, P. C., 76, 99, 122, 125, 144
Kendler, K.S. , 5, 36, 37, 38, 39, 41, 126, 216, 217, 219, 220, 224, 225, 295, 296, 297, 308, 388, 416, 455
Kendrick, D., 275
Kenis, G., 459, 465

Kennard, B. D., 232
Kennealy, P., 448
Kennedy, D. L., 53, 91, 127, 230, 251, 258, 395, 428, 445
Kenny, P. J., 390
Kerns, R., 265, 271, 272, 273
Kerr, M., 390
Kersting, A., 206
Kertesz, S. G., 394
Kessler, R. C., 118, 121, 125, 126, 130, 132, 137, 138, 140, 142, 149, 155, 156, 203, 204, 205, 212, 213, 215, 216, 217, 224, 236, 237, 239, 400, 410, 534
Kest, B., 267
Keuroghlian, A. S., 427
Keuthen, N. J., 164
Key, A. C., 358
Keyes, M. A., 426
Keyes, A.
Khan, A., 109, 448
Khokhar, J., 388
Khoury, B., 128, 231, 272, 428, 486
Kibler, J. L., 258
Kiecolt-Glaser, J. K., 254
Kiefe, C. I., 261
Kiel, E. J., 122
Kiesler, C. A., 95, 533
Kihlstrom, J. F., 57, 184, 189, 190, 191, 194
Killgore, W. D. S., 389
Kilmer, J. R., 374
Kilpatrick, D. G., 39, 288
Kim, K. M., 83, 126, 160, 215, 223, 224, 306, 400
Kimchi, E. Z., 518
Kimonis, E. R., 538
Kincannon, H. T., 329
King, B. H., 126, 128, 150, 216, 375, 486, 503, 517
Kinzie, J. D., 215
Kirkpatrick, D. R., 308
Kirmayer, L. J., 177, 179, 183, 416
Kirov, G., 460
Kirsh, F. C., 540
Kishimoto, T., 468, 469
Kissinger, P., 258
Kistner, J. A., 62
Kit, B. K., 284, 302
Kittel, F., 263
Kivimaki, M., 51
Klann, E., 504
Klaus, J. R., 87, 395
Klein, D. F., 120, 144, 204, 205, 208, 220, 485
Kleinknecht, E. E., 142
Kleinman, A., 61, 215, 239
Kleinplatz, F. J., 336, 337, 339
Kleinstäuber, M., 178
Klevens, R. M., 340
Klimas, N., 257, 258
Klin, A., 493
Kloezeman, K., 75
Kloner, R., 339
Kloosterman, P. H., 74
Kluft, R. P., 189, 190, 191, 194, 195
Klump, K. L., 291, 295, 296, 297
Klumpp, H., 144
Klupsch, D., 264
Knapp, S. J., 112
Knight, C. A., 381, 515
Knouse, L. E., 487
Knowles, R., 448, 454
Knudson, M., 125
Knutelska, M., 185
Knutson, 306
Ko, C. Y., 305
Koban, 265
Kobau, R., 531

Koch, P., 341
Kochanska, G., 425
Kochman, F. J., 211
Kocsis, J. H., 204
Koegel, L. K., 496
Koelling, 63
Koen, L., 471
Koenen, K. C., 149
Koepsell, T. D., 512
Koester, P., 93, 378
Kogon, M. M., 259
Kohler, C. G., 451
Kohn, R., 391
Kohser, K. L., 275
Kohut, H., 20, 433
Kolb, B., 64, 65
Kolevzon, A., 512
Kolla, B. P., 314
Kollei, I., 160
Koneru, A. O., 257
Kong, L. L., 60, 190
Koning, C., 497
Konrad, K., 296
Konttinen, H., 261
Koo, D. L., 306
Koob, A., 43
Koopman, C., 191, 258
Kopelowicz, A., 466, 471, 472
Koran, L. M., 160
Korf, J., 217
Korfine, L., 428
Korgesaar, J., 491
Kornitzer, M., 263
Kosson, D. S., 424
Koster, E., 157
Kosterman, R. P., 107
Kostis, J., 339
Kotagal, P., 183
Kotler, J. S., 234
Kotlicka-Antczak, M., 464
Kovacs, M., 205, 237
Kovas, Y., 490
Kraaij, V., 262
Krabbendam, L., 450
Kraemer, H. C., 86, 299
Kral, J. G., 305
Kramer, H. C., 258
Krane, R. J., 335
Krank, M. D., 390
Krenek, M., 375
Kreutzmann, 306
Kring, A. M., 451
Krishnan-Sarin, S., 380
Kroenke, K., 178
Kronhaug, C. R., 317
Krueger, D. D., 86, 87, 90, 91, 176, 345, 347, 348, 410, 504
Krug, E. G., 239
Krupitsky, E., 395
Kruszon-Moran, D., 302
Kubicki, M., 464
Kubzansky, L. D., 261
Kucharska-Newton, 60
Kucharski, L. T., 540
Kufel, T., 315
Kuhl, E. A., 5
Kuhn, J., 225
Kuile, B., 343
Kukull, W. A., 512
Kullgren, G., 183
Kumar, A., 218
Kumpulainen, K., 145
Kunik, M. E., 433
Kunkel, S. R., 56

Kuno, 534
Kuo, J. R., 236, 237, 428
Kuperman, S., 390
Kupfer, D. J., 5, 87, 218, 220, 228
Kurihara, T., 472
Kurtz, E., 145, 261
Kurz, M. W., 514
Kusters, W. J., 152
Kutner, H. E., 373
Kuyken, W., 231, 272
Kwapil, T. R., 418
Kwok, T., 506
Kymalainen, J., 466

L

La Fond, J. Q., 534
La Greca, A. M., 125, 147, 150
Laan, E., 344
Laatikainen, T., 261
Lacey, J. H., 284
Lader, M., 49, 375, 376
Ladwig, K. H., 264
LaFrance, W. C., 180
Lai, B., 150
Laird, 64
Lake, A. M., 239
Lakes, K., 111
Lakin, M. M., 344
Lalumiere, M. L., 348
Lam, L., 109, 219, 276, 506
Lamb, H. R., 302, 532, 533, 538
Lambrou, C., 160
Lamis, D. A., 239
Lampert, C., 295
Landén, M., 358
Landeros-Weisenberger, A., 154
Landis, K. R., 41, 63
Landreville, P.
Lane, M., 207, 410, 426
Lang, A. J., 131
Langdon, R., 449
Langer, E. J., 126
Langh-inrichsen-Rohling, J., 239
Langley, K., 486
Långström, N., 331, 346, 347
Lanius, R. A., 147
Lanotte, M., 53
Lanphear, B. P., 486
Lapierre, S., 242
LaPorte, D. L., 290
Large, M. D., 160
Larimer, M. E., 374, 396
Larntz, K., 413
Larsen, B. A., 60
Larson, J. L., 264
Laruelle, M., 462
Lash, S. J., 416
Lataster, J., 465
Latfi, R., 305
Latty, E., 330
Lau, H., 216, 217
Laub, J. H., 421
Lau-Barraco, C., 390
Laumann, E., 334, 335, 336, 337, 338, 340, 341
Launer, L. J., 510
Laurent, C., 471
Lavallee, K. L., 140
Lavoie, K., 350
Law, C., 239
Lawani, A. O., 109
Lawrence, A., 347
Laws, D. R., 352
Lawton, K., 497

Laxenaire, M., 429
Lazarus, R. S., 60
Lazerson, A., 48
Le Foll, B., 50
Le Grange, D., 295, 299, 301
Le Strat, Y., 50
Leader, J. B., 205
Leahy, R. L., 435, 436
Leal, I., 270
LeBeau, R., 6, 85, 88, 89, 136, 137, 140
Lebedinskaya, K. S., 494
Leckman, J. F., 154, 155
Lecrubier, Y., 133
Lederhendler, I., 290, 296
Ledermann, T., 132
Ledford, H., 256
LeDoux, J., 48, 49, 50, 59, 118, 120, 121
Lee, C. K., 60, 150, 296, 390, 462, 494, 506
Lee, H.-J. C. K., 391
Lefley, H., 470
Lefrancois, G. R., 92
Legg, B. H., 541
Lehman, A. F., 123, 136, 261, 470
Lehrer, 21
Leibenluft, E., 208, 213
Leiblum, S. R., 333, 334, 335
Leitenberg, H., 338
Lejeune, J., 501
Lemay, M., 511
Lemke, T., 11
Lener, M. S., 419
Lensvelt-Mulders, G., 464
Lentz, R. J., 469
Lenze, E. J., 130, 214
Lenzenweger, M., 193, 410, 414
Leon, A., 51
Leonard, H., 504, 506
Leppink, J., 184
Lerner, R., 258
Lesch, K. P., 120
Leserman, J., 63, 258
Leung, P., 215, 470
Levak, R. W., 80
Levan, A., 501
LeVay, S., 331
Levenson, J. L., 180
Leventhal, A. M., 121, 299, 380
Levesque, R. J., 414
Levin, F. R., 390, 482
Levine, A. C., 292, 296, 304, 344
Levinson, D. F., 216
Levkoff, S., 517
Levy, B. R., 56, 305, 378, 433, 461
Lewinsohn, P. M., 203, 205, 219, 220
Lewis, S. W., 63, 137, 251, 260, 274, 424, 426, 446, 451, 458, 463
Lewis, D. O., 182
Lewis, F. M.
Lewis- Fernández, R., 89, 131, 182, 183
Leyfer, O., 162, 217
Leykin, Y., 232
Lezak, M. D., 81
Li, S., 41, 495
Liao, B., 22, 309
Liberman, R., 470, 471, 472
Liberski, P. P., 515
Liberzon, I., 122
Lichstein, K. L., 309
Lichtenstein, P., 331
Liddle, P. F., 448, 449, 452
Lieb, R., 126, 144, 370, 465
Liebenluft, 208
Lieberman, J. A., 461, 468
Liebeskind, J., 265, 267, 270

Liebman, R. E., 413
Liebowitz, M. R., 137, 144
Liénard, P., 155
Lifshitz, F., 293
Lighty, Q., 458
Lilenfeld, L. R. R., 5, 90, 184, 190, 194, 296, 413, 431
Lillienfeld, 77, 85, 87
Lim, D., 188, 260
Lima, E. N., 128
Lin, C. C., 204, 214
Lind, D. L., 183, 308, 495
Lindberg, N., 313, 400
Lindenmayer, J., 448
Lindner, S., 192
Lindsey, M., 532
Lindy, J. D., 148
Linehan, M., 427, 429
Ling, W., 383
Links, P., 429
Linsenmeier, J., 357
Linton, X., 314
Lionetti, T. M., 371
Lipchik, G. L., 267
Lippa, R., 57
Lipshultz, L. I., 344
Liss, A., 144
Lissek, S., 150
Lissek 21
Litman, R. E., 238
Little, D., 285
Littlefield, A. K., 395
Littrell, L., 207
Litvin Bloom, E., 380
Litz, B. T., 126
Liu, D., 40, 109, 204, 239, 494
Livesley, W. J., 91
Livhits, M., 305
Livianos, L., 297
Livingston, E. H., 305, 519
Llewellyn, C. H., 304
Lloyd, E. A., 336
Lo, E., 268
Lobbestael, J., 416, 417
Lobo, R. A., 512
Lochman, J., 389
Lochner, C., 164
Lock, J., 295, 301
Locke, G., 469
Loder, E., 267
Loeb, K., 295
Loewenstein, R. J., 192, 195
Lofland, K., 265
Loftus, E. F., 20, 193, 194, 333
Lohr, B., 160
Lombardi, V. C., 268
Lombardo, M. V., 496
Lonczak, H. S. P., 107
Long, E. O., 255, 333
Loomans, E. M., 381
Loonan, R., 330
Looper, K. J., 177
Lopes, V., 208
Lopez, O. L., 108, 215, 466
Lopiano, L., 53
LoPiccolo, J., 334, 343
Loranger, A., 410
Lord, C., 494, 520
Loren, R. E. A., 487
Lorenz, T. A., 341
Lösel, F., 352
Lostutter, T. W., 374
Lovaas, O. I., 496, 497
Lovallo, W. R., 252
Lovato, 309

Lovegrove, M. C., 506
Lovestone, S., 509, 510, 516, 519
Lowe, B., 176, 288, 304
Lozano, A. M., 230
Lu, B., 50, 145, 518
Lubs, H. A., 502
Luby, J. L., 213
Lucas, J. A., 61, 225, 534
Lucia, V. C., 150
Luciana, M., 51
Ludescher, B., 286
Ludwig, A., 188, 190, 304, 305
Luk, S. L., 494
Lukiw, W. J., 518
Lundberg, I., 264
Lundgren, J., 303
Lundh, L.-G., 143
Lundquist, 59
Lunney, C. A., 147
Luria, M., 333
Lussier, P., 346
Lutgendorf, S. K., 258, 259
Lüthi, A., 119
Luttikhuis, Oude, 305
Luty, S., 419
Lydiard, R. B., 126, 157
Lyketsos, C. G., 214, 518
Lykken, D. T., 37, 39, 423
Lynch, F. L., 96, 239, 291, 387, 429
Lynn, S. J., 20, 184, 192, 194
Lyon, G. R., 491
Lyons, M. J., 37, 105, 216
Lyubomirsky, S., 56, 224

M

Ma, S., 276
MacCallum, 206
Maccoby, M., 276
Macdonald, P. T., 340
MacDougall, J. M., 60
Mace, C. J., 180
Maciejewski, P., 206
Mackenzie, C. S., 176
MacLeod, C., 273
Macleod, J., 384
Macy, J. T., 108
Madsen, K. M., 496
Maeng, 62
Maes, H., 262, 270
Magarinos, A. M., 150
Magee, W. J., 130, 138, 142, 144
Magill, M., 391
Magill-Evans, J., 497
Magne-Ingvar, U., 237
Magruder, K., 148
Maguire, G. A., 482
Maher, B. A., 9, 12, 15, 372
Mahler, M., 495
Mahowald, M. W., 319
Maier, S. F., 55
Mainous III, A. G., 517
Mainz, V., 296, 300
Maisto, S. A., 375
Maj, M., 241, 514
Mak, K. H., 276
Maki, K. M., 512
Malavige, L. S., 340, 343
Malcom, J. R., 350
Maldonado, J. R., 190, 195
Malenka, R. C., 47
Maletzky, B., 352, 353
Malhotra, A., 315
Malin, H., 534

Mallampalli, M., 510
Mallan, 57
Malm, H., 229
Malone, K. M., 239
Maloney, S., 252
Maltzman, I. M., 396
Manber, R., 98
Mancill, R. B., 123
Mancini, C., 144
Mancl, L., 273
Mandalos, G. E., 227
Mandel, J., 513
Manicavasagar, V., 140
Manjula, M., 178
Manly, J. J., 511
Mann, A. H., 227, 238, 239, 242, 284, 293, 304
Mann, J., 237
Manni, R., 319
Mannino, D. M., 340
Mansbach, J., 300
Mansfield, P., 341
Manson, J., 215, 302
Månsson, K. N. T., 144
Mantovani, A., 230
Manuel, J. K., 397
Mao, X., 251
Marangell, L., 230
Marano, C. M., 518
Marcello, S., 469, 470, 471
Marcus, B. H., 227, 228, 236, 251, 299, 300
Marder, S. R., 462
Marecek, J., 108
Marek, P., 267
Maremmani, A. G. I., 394
Margolis, R. L., 514
Margraf, J., 132, 174
Marin, D. B., 412, 512
Marinelli, 53
Marino, L., 5
Marion, J. G.,, 300
Markon, K. E., 86, 90, 91
Markowitz, J. S., 204, 232
Marks, I., 142
Marlatt, G. A., 396, 397
Marmot, M. G., 263
Marnane, C. L., 140
Marnell, M., 299
Marques, A., 270, 290, 291, 352
Marsac, M. L., 275
Marsh, L., 296, 514
Marshall, P. G., 349, 350, 352, 400
Marteau, T. M., 249
Martell, C., 203, 225, 232
Marten, P. A., 125, 126
Martens, E. J., 263
Marti, C. N., 289, 301
Martin, A., 52, 139, 160, 177, 273, 375, 486, 504
Martinez, A., 90, 296, 395, 434
Martins, S. S., 464
Marx, B. P., 146, 184
Maser, J. D., 88, 136
Mash, E. J., 77
Masheb, R. M., 289, 296, 300
Masi, C. M., 261
Maslow, Abraham, 22
Mason, F. L., 345, 428, 540
Master, S. L., 266
Masters, W. H., 96
Masters, William, 342
Mataix-Cols, D., 155
Matheson, S. L., 457
Mathew, S. J., 127, 128
Mathews, A., 154, 177
Mathur, G., 370

Matsubayashi, T., 239
Matsumoto, D., 263
Matsunaga, D., 215
Mattar, L., 295
Matthews, K., 257, 261, 262, 263, 264
Matthews-Ewald, M. R., 289
Mattia, J. I., 159, 160
Mattis, S. G., 132
Mauler, B. I., 296
Maust, D., 76
Maxwell, J. C., 378
Mayberg, H., 230
Mayford, 54
Mayou, R., 194
Mayville, S., 160
Mazabell, S., 491
Mbata, G., 313
McAlister, A. L., 276
McCabe, J. E., 144, 289
McCaffree, K. J., 391
McCall, W. V., 125
McCann, D., 378, 385, 486
McCarthy-Jones, S., 448
McCauley, E. A., 234
McClam, T. D., 518
McClearn, G. E., 37, 217
McClellan, J., 216
McCloskey, M., 49, 400
McClough, J., 76
McClure, M., 419
McConaha, C. W., 286
McCrady, B. S., 374, 396, 397
McCrae, C. S., 309
McCraw, S., 211
McCrimmon, S., 397
McCullough, J. P., 206, 231, 233
McCutcheon, 53
McDermott, B., 144, 502
McDonald, E. M., 259, 275
McEwen, B. S., 46, 150
McFahland, B., 530
McGee, G. G., 496
McGinn, L. K., 435, 436
McGirr, A., 427
McGlashan, T., 429, 455, 473
McGoldrick, M., 330, 341, 342
McGonagle, K. A., 138
McGory, M. L., 305
McGough, J. J., 485
McGrath, P., 77, 400
McGue, M., 37, 39, 426
McGuffin, P., 216
McGuire, J. F., 155, 450
McGurk, S. R., 470
McHugh, P. C., 131, 428, 543
McKay, D., 157, 160, 449
McKeith, I. G., 513
McKenzie, K. C., 296, 427
McKetin, R., 375
McKunlay, J. B., 335
McKusick, L., 275
McLaughlin, N. C. R., 158
McLean, C. P., 151
McMain, S., 429
McMaster, A., 418
McNab, C., 466, 470
McNally, R., 4, 5, 121, 131, 148, 192, 193, 194, 206
McNaughton, N., 50, 120, 121
McNeil, T. F., 464
McPartland, J. C., 520
McPherson, L. M., 425
McQuade, J. D., 484
McWilliams, J. M., 261
Mead, G. E., 232

Meagher, D., 506, 507
Meaney, M. J., 37, 40, 121, 252
Means, M. K., 316
Meara, E., 261
Mechelli, A., 52
Mechoulam, R., 384
Medendorp, Vanderbrug, 344
Mednick, S. A., 425, 464
Mednick, Sarnoff A., 472
Meehl, P. E., 90, 418, 452
Meerlo, 306
Meerveld, J., 520
Mehler, P. S., 286, 288
Meilman, P. W., 374
Melamed, B. G., 259
Melartin, T., 237
Melca, I. A., 436
Melville, L. F., 144
Melzack, R., 266, 271
Menard, W., 159, 160
Mendel, E., 128
Mendlowicz, M. V., 436
Mendoza-Denton, R., 90
Mennes, C. E., 384
Menon, V., 491
Menzies, L., 164, 482
Merckelbach, H., 20, 184
Meredith, S. E., 381
Merens, W., 49
Merghati-Khoei, E., 342
Merikangas, K. R., 106, 130, 204, 211, 212, 213
Mermin, J., 251, 258, 275
Meston, C. M., 333, 337, 338, 339, 340, 341, 343, 344, 350
Metalsky, G. I., 221
Metcalfe, K., 428
Metzner, H. M., 62
Meulman, J., 262
Meuret, A. E., 34, 122, 139, 140
Mevada, A., 501
Meyer, I. H., 77, 276, 289, 294, 434, 540
Meyer-Bahlburg, H., 356, 358
Meyerowitz, B. E., 274
Mezick, E. J., 261
Mezzich, J. E., 188
Micco, J. A., 140
Michael, R., 341
Michaels, S., 341
Michalak, J., 231
Michalek, A. P., 487
Michaud, P.-A., 289
Michelakos, T., 517
Miciak, J., 489
Mick, E., 422, 485
Mickes, L., 20
Miele, G. M., 180, 397
Mihura, J. L., 77
Miklowitz, D. J., 234, 235
Miklowitz 233
Milad, M. R., 62, 151
Milanak, M. E., 419
Milburn, N. G., 212
Miles, S. R., 5
Mill, J., 40, 41
Millan, M. J., 451
Millar, H. R., 283
Miller, S. C., 53, 55, 62, 125, 146, 147, 220, 221, 250, 254, 261, 263, 340, 387, 397, 433, 472, 494
Miller-Kovach, K., 304
Millon, T., 15, 86, 434
Mills, P. J., 254
Milner, P. M., 388
Miloslavsky, M., 315
Mindell, J. A., 306, 312

Mindham, R. H. S., 513
Mineka, S., 55, 57, 122, 127, 140, 143
Miner, M., 345
Minhajuddin, A., 233
Minino, A. M., 236
Minuchin, S., 298
Mirsky, A. F., 459
Mistry, H., 109
Mitchell, A. J., 283, 286, 287, 288, 296, 298, 381, 450
Mock, S. E., 330, 331
Modahl, C., 496
Modinos, G., 419, 450
Modrego, P. J., 214
Moffitt, 36, 421, 422
Mogg, K., 126, 143
Mogil, J. S., 267
Mogun, H., 127
Mohan, R., 179
Mohanty, S., 518
Mohlman, J., 130
Mohr, B., 47
Mojtabai, R., 133, 158
Mokdad, A. H., 260
Molina, B. S. G., 389
Moller, E., 6, 85
Monahan, J., 448
Monarch, E. S., 273
Monck, E. M., 466
Money, J., 356
Monroe, S. M., 219, 220, 223, 225
Monson, C. M., 151, 152
Montague, D. K., 344
Montgomery, A., 469
Montoya, I. D., 394
Montplaisir, X., 318
Mooney, N. B., 71
Moore, D. S., 40, 41, 219, 310, 423
Moreno, A., 208, 304
Morey, J. N., 273
Morgan, C. A., 395, 464
Morgenthaler, T., 314
Morin, C. M., 308, 309, 310, 316
Morokoff, P., 338
Morrato, E. H., 305
Morrier, M. J., 496
Morris, J. S., 57, 94
Morrison, A. S., 141
Morrow, G. R., 22
Mörtberg, E., 145
Moscovitch, D. A., 126, 140
Moses, N., 293
Mosher, D. L., 327, 328
Moshier, S. J., 135
Moskowitz, A., 259
Moss, H. B., 387
Moss-Morris, R., 270
Mostofsky, D. I., 251, 264
Motivala, S. J., 250
Mous, S. E., 105
Moyers, T. B., 397
Mucha, T. F., 182
Muehlenkamp, J. J., 291
Mueller, T., 205
Mueser, K. T., 469, 470, 471
Muhuri, P. K., 382
Muir, S. L., 293
Mulchahey, 252
Mulder, C., 419, 428, 532
Mullany, B., 236
Mullen, P., 540
Muller, J., 471
Mumford, D. B., 290, 291
Munder, T., 343
Muñoz, R. F., 203, 232

Name Index • I-13

Munro, A., 454
Murakami-Brundage, J., 109
Murawski, 265
Muresanu, D. F., 400
Muris, P., 120, 139
Muroff, J., 163, 532
Murphy, D. G. M., 204, 340, 346, 394, 487, 512
Murray, K. E., 63, 260, 449, 450, 456, 457, 458, 463, 464, 465, 486
Murru, A., 229
Mustafa, G., 472
Mustian, K. M., 23
Myers, J., 37, 126, 130, 135, 224, 258
Myerson, R., 260
Myin-Germeys, I., 465
My-pro-ana, 284
Mystkowski, J. L., 131

N

Nagappan, G., 518
Nagel, D. B., 467
Najmi, S., 241
Nakajima, M., 380
Nanda, 356
Narrow, W. E., 5, 88
Nash, J. D., 267, 276
Nasser, M., 290, 291
Natarajan, N., 451
Nathan, P. J., 518
National Center for Health Statistics, 382
National Collaborating Centre for Mental Health, 425, 426
National Institute of Drug Abuse, 378
National Institute of Mental Health, 229
National Institute on AlcoholDrug Abuse (NIDA), 393
Natoli, J. L., 502
Navarrete, C. D., 143
Ndao-Brumblay, S. K., 308
Neale, M. C., 37, 126, 216, 217, 331, 388
Negy, C., 431
Neimeyer, R. A., 206
Nelles, W. B. N., 130
Nelson, B., 6, 48, 185, 203, 214, 352, 409, 457
Nelson, C., 71
Nelson-Gray, R. O., 6
Nemeroff, C., 51, 217, 225, 259
Neng, J. M. B., 178
Nesse, R., 206
Nestadt, G., 431
Nestler, E. J., 47
Nettles, M. E., 435
Neubauer, D., 315
Neugroschi, J. A., 512, 515
Neumann, C. S., 409, 421, 422, 424, 532
Neumark-Sztainer, D., 293, 294, 302
Nevsimalova, S., 315
Newman, C. F., 424, 426, 431, 495
Newring, K. A. B., 346
Newton, N. C., 254, 398
Nezworski, M. T., 77
Ng, J., 188, 295, 303
Ngai, E., 470
Nicasio, A. V., 89
Nicassio, P. M., 250
Nicholls, D., 295
Nichols, D. S., 78, 79, 80, 486
Nicolson, S. E., 373
NIDA, 396, 397
Niedtfeld, I., 428
Niehaus, D., 471
Nielsen, S., 283, 388
Nierenberg, A. A., 46, 203

Nigg, J. T., 481, 485, 486
Nijs, J., 270
Nikolas, M., 485, 486
Nikolskaya, O. S., 494
Ninci, J., 503
Nivard, M. G., 220
Nivoli, A. M., 229
Noble, J., 271
Noblett, K. L., 400
Nock, M. K., 84, 100, 164, 236, 237, 238, 239, 241, 427
Nolan, S. A., 213
Nolen-Hoeksema, S., 221, 224
Noll, R. B., 259
Nooe, R. M., 533
Noonan, C., 269
Norberg, M. M., 392
Nordentoft, M., 419
Norman, P., 55, 221
Normile, D., 257
Norrholm, S. D., 149, 150
Norris, A. L., 540
Norton, G. R., 495, 518
Novelli, G., 331
Noyes, R., 127, 177, 178, 194
Ntika, M., 11
Nugent, N. R., 437
Nunes, E. V., 350, 397
Nunley, B., 530, 531, 532, 533
Nurnberger, J. I., 216
Nussbaum, A. M., 384
Nusslock, R., 220
Nutt, D., 120, 385
Nutzinger, D. O., 296
Nyhan, W. L., 501
Nzwalo, H., 315

O

Oar, E. L., 140
Öberg, 358
O'Brien, P. E., 75, 258, 303, 305, 370, 401, 482
O'Callaghan, E., 464
O'Carroll, P. W., 240
Ochsner, K. N., 57, 122
O'Connell, M., 65, 259
O'Connor, M., 154, 206, 207, 426
O'Dea, K., 284
Odlaug, B. L., 164, 399, 400
O'Donnell, M. L., 148
O'Donohue, W. T., 352
O'Donovan, A., 486
Oei, T. P., 390
Offord, D. R., 375
Ogborne, A. C., 375
Ogden, C. L., 284, 302, 303
Ogle, C. M., 194
O'Grady, K. E., 377, 378
Ogston, W., 190
Oh, D., 128, 231
O'Hara, M. W., 214
Ohayon, M. M., 265, 306
Ohlerking, F., 345
Öhman, A., 57, 59, 143
Oishi, S., 61
Ojehagen, A., 237
Okazaki, S., 79
O'Kearney, 310
Oldenburg, B., 251
Oldham, J., 433
Olds, J., 388
Olfson, M., 126, 133, 227, 228, 375
Olin, J., 214, 418
Oliva, P. S., 190
Olivardia, R., 294

Oliveau, D., 137
Oliver, M. B., 329
Olives, C., 260
Olivier, P., 506
Ollendick, T. H., 120, 132, 140, 488
Olmstead, S. B., 329
Olmsted, M.,, 294
Olson, R. K., 358
Oltmanns, T. F., 410, 413, 451
Olver, I., 426
O'Malley, P. M., 374
O'Neil, J. A., 184, 288
Ong, R., 188, 517
Onslow, M., 482
Oosterhout, 450
Opjordsmoen, S., 454
Oquendo, M., 239
Orav, E., 176
Orff, 306
Orford, J., 396
Organization for Economic Co-operation and Development, 303
Ormerod, B. K., 218
Orne, E. C., 189
Ornitz, E. M., 22
Orosan, P., 160
Orrell, M., 519
Orsillo, S. M., 126, 127, 128
Orsini, N., 520
Orth-Gomer, K., 262
Ortin, A., 239
Osborne, L. N., 223
Osburg, S., 355
Osei, S., 304
Oslin, D. W., 395
Öst, L.-G., 34, 139, 140, 143
Osterberg, E., 391
Ostrow, D. G., 275
Oswalt, S. B., 330
Otis, J. D., 265, 271, 273
Otte, C., 47
Otto, M., 133, 135, 144, 160, 211, 214, 232, 234
Ouellet-Morin, I., 40, 41
Oveis, C., 226
Over, M., 257
Overeem, S., 313
Overpeck, M. D., 274
Ovsiew, F., 83
Owen, J., 329, 386, 448, 460
Owens, E. B., 120, 252, 306, 312, 467, 468, 469, 470, 471, 472, 485
Ozbay, F., 65
Ozonoff, S., 495

P

Pace-Schott, E. F., 150
Packman, A., 482
Pacoe, L., 190
Padmanabhan, S., 261
Pagano, M., 160, 391
Page, A. C., 139, 270, 346, 519
Pagsberg, A. K., 453, 473
Pahlajani, G., 344
Pai, A., 150
Paik, A., 334
Paillard, T., 518
Palamar, J. J., 384
Pálenícek, T., 385
Paliwal, P., 380
Paller, K. A., 140
Pallesen, S., 317
Palmer, B. W., 542
Pan, A., 263, 302

Pandya, N. H., 501
Paniagua, F. A., 109
Pantaleo, G., 257
Panza, F., 373, 517
Papadopoulos, F. C., 283, 284
Papageorgiou, C., 128
Paparella, T., 497
Papas, R., 273
Papillo, J. F., 260
Paquette, V., 140
Parcesepe, A. M., 90
Pardini, D., 389, 422
Parekh, A., 125
Parini, S., 272
Paris, J., 428, 436
Park, C. L., 138, 241, 259
Parker, G., 149, 211, 384, 391, 416, 466, 496, 503
Parkinson, L., 156, 157
Parrone, P. L., 205
Parrott, A. C., 385
Parry-Jones, B., 289
Paruk, Z., 125
Pasley, K., 329
Passie, T., 385, 386
Patel, D. R., 315, 458, 497, 501
Paterson, A. D., 331
Pato, C. W., 209, 212, 213
Patrick, C. J., 337
Patterson, B., 63, 144, 390, 424, 426, 533
Patton, G. C., 293
Paul, G. L., 270, 296, 469
Pauli, P., 137, 141, 142, 177
Pavle, J., 538
Pawelczyk, 464
Paxton, S. J., 293
Paykel, E. S., 232
Payne, E., 135, 296, 486
Peall, K. J., 312
Pearl, D., 259
Pearson, C., 295, 469
Peat, C., 287, 291
Pech, 310
Pedersen, B., 216, 417, 434
Pederson, N., 63, 269
Peeters, J., 520
Pelcovitz, M., 150
Pelham, W. E., 488
Pellicano, E., 520
Pellowski, J. A., 257
Pen, A. E., 518
Penas-Lledo, 295
Pendery, M. L., 396
Peng, T., 284
Penn, D. L., 470
Pennington, B. F., 489, 490, 491, 492
Pentz, M. A., 398
Penzien, D. B., 271
Pepine, C. J., 344
Peplau, L. A., 330
Peralta, R., 315
Perea, G., 43
Pereira, D. B., 251
Perez, C. J., 204
Pérez-Fuentes, G., 348
Perez-Sales, P., 182
Pericak-Vance, M. A., 512
Peris, T. S., 100
Perlick, D. A., 109
Perlin, M. L., 538
Perloff, B. F., 496
Perrault, X., 318
Perron, B. E., 386, 397
Persad, G., 540
Perugi, G., 239

Peterman, J. S., 122
Peters, J. R., 190, 428
Petersen, I., 125, 329, 330
Peterson, L., 48, 274, 448, 489, 490, 491, 492
Peterson-Badali, M., 357
Petit, X., 318, 319
Peto, R., 262, 276
Petrill, S. A., 490
Pettersson-Yeo, 52
Petukhova, M., 118, 121, 137
Peyeri, 291
Pfäfflin, F., 354
Pfiffner, L. J., 487
Phan, K. L., 144
Phelan, S., 304, 534
Phelps, 52
Philips, H. C., 265
Phillips, J. M., 158, 159, 160, 161, 185, 186, 391
Pich, V., 138
Piché, L., 346
Pickel, J., 218
Pickering, R. P., 496
Pickles, A., 495
Pickrell, J. E., 193
Pierce, K., 488, 489, 491
Piff, P. K., 90
Pike, K. M., 291, 295, 299
Pillard, R. C., 331
Pillow, D. R., 389
Pincus, D. B., 88, 140, 141, 145, 265, 271, 273
Pine, D. S., 126
Pinkham, A., 451
Pinkser, 77
Pinsky, J., 263
Pinto, A., 437, 458
Piomelli, D., 384
Pirelli, G., 537
Pistrang, N., 76
Pitman, R. K., 193
Pittenger, C., 154
Pizzagalli, D., 126, 203
Plant, 392
Platts, M., 290, 291
Pletcher, M. J., 384
Pliszka, S. R., 487
Plomin, R., 36, 105, 217, 304, 459, 464, 490
Plotsky, P., 121
Pocock, S. J., 98
Poe, M. D., 497
Polanczyk, G., 485, 488
Polatin, P. B., 175
Polderman, T. J., 105
Politi, P., 446
Polivy, J., 295
Pollack, M. H., 121, 131, 133, 138
Pompili, M., 238, 239
Ponseti, J., 351
Pontarelli, N. K., 155
Pontius, W., 495
Poon, K., 497
Poorsattar, S., 401
Pope, C., 160, 190, 194, 293, 294, 387
Porhomayon, J., 315
Portenoy, R., 370
Post, L., 189, 220, 519
Posthuma, D., 105
Postma, A., 190
Poston Jr, D. L., 329
Pot, A. M., 518
Potenza, M. N., 399
Pottash, A. C., 340
Potter, R., 519
Poulsen, S., 299
Powell, L. H., 195

Powers, A. D., 232, 413
Pratchett, L., 150
Pratt, E. M., 300
Prause, N., 338
Prenoveau, J. M., 22
Prescott, C. A., 37, 126, 220, 224, 388, 393
Presley, C. A., 374
Presnell, K., 304
Pressman, S. D., 254
Presson, C. C., 108
Preston, S. H., 284, 302
Preti, A., 470
Price, C. S., 259, 381, 428, 496
Pridal, C. G., 334
Priday, L., 160
Priebe, S., 469
Primeau, A., 533
Prince, M., 347, 512
Pringsheim, T., 514
Prins, J., 268
Prinstein, M. J., 150
Prior, K., 400
Prisciandaro, J. J., 176
Proctor, 430
Prokhorov, A., 519
Pruzinsky, T., 161
Psaros, C. P., 258
Pueschel, S. M., 501
Pugh, K., 470
Pugliese, M. T., 293
Puhan, X., 315
Puliafico, A. C., 141, 145
Pulkki-Råbåck, L., 63
Pulkki-Råback, 225
Pull, C. B., 438
Purcell, D. W., 275
Purdon, 154
Purisch, A. D., 81
Pury, C. L. S., 57
Putnam, F. W., 189, 190, 191, 192, 195

Q

Qian, X., 316
Qiu, C., 520
Quality Assurance Project, 457, 416
Quas, J. A., 194
Quay, H. C., 157, 423, 424
Quigley, L. A., 396
Quinn, D., 268
Quinsey, V. L., 348

R

Rabe, S., 464
Rabian, B., 138, 145
Rabin, B. S., 63
Rachman, S., 148, 155, 156, 157, 350
Racine, S. E., 300
Rado, S., 418
Rafanelli, C., 178
Rahkonen, T., 507
Rahman, Q., 331, 341
Raina, R., 344
Raine, A., 423, 425
Raisi, F., 342
Rajab, M. H., 242
Rajaratnam, X., 316
Rajkumar, R. P., 94
Rakison, D. H., 57
Ramachandran, V. S., 265
Ramey, C. T., 504
Ramos Olazagasti, M. A., 485
Ramoz, N., 428

Ramrakha, S., 329
Ramsey, E., 424
Rance, S. J., 288
Rangmar, J., 500
Rani, A., 218
Ranjith, G., 179
Ranson, M. B., 80
Rapee, R. M., 140, 144, 272, 293
Rapson, R. L., 11, 59
Rasetti, R., 464
Rasmussen, J. L., 156, 162, 417
Rasmusson, A. M., 380
Rassin, E., 157
Rathod, N. H., 383
Rathouz, P. J., 299
Ratti, M. T., 319
Rauch, A., 150, 157, 158, 159, 217, 501
Ravindranathan, 372
Ray, J. C., 127, 253, 370, 372, 388, 389
Raymer, A., 487
Raymond, N. C., 345
Rayner, K. E., 23, 262, 293, 296
Raza, G. T., 416
Razran, G., 122
Rea, M., 234
Reading, A. E., 313
Reagan, E. M., 434
Reas, D. L., 298
Rebocho, M. F., 348
Reboussin, B., 239
Redding, C. A., 159
Reddy, L. A., 426, 451
Reder, S., 489
Reed, B., 263
Rees, G., 140, 519
Regier, D. A., 5, 87, 89, 91, 421
Rehm, J., 369
Reich, D. B., 427
Reichborn-Kjennerud, T., 423
Reichow, B., 520
Reid, J. R., 219, 390
Reilly, A., 389
Reilly-Harrington, N. A., 234
Reinarman, C., 340
Reinhardt, R. F., 182
Reiss, S., 122, 236
Reitan, R. M., 81
Reiter, J., 160
Remer, P., 80
Renick, A., 193
Repp, A. C., 503
Rescorla, R. A., 22, 55
Resick, P. A., 151, 152
Resnick, E. M., 149, 510
Ressler, K. J., 145, 149, 150, 152, 158
Reverger, R., 472
Reynolds, C. F., 233, 265, 306, 431
Reznikoff, M., 77
Rhebergen, D.
Rhoades, C. S., 329
Rhodes, A. R., 236
Riboli, E., 249, 250
Ricaurte, G. A., 378
Ricciardelli, L. A., 289
Rice, G., 349, 352, 392
Rich, B. A., 208, 213
Richards, J. A., 234, 385, 472, 506, 510, 511, 515, 516, 518
Richardson, C. L., 338
Richels, C., 487
Richey, J. A., 142
Richler, J. J., 94
Richtberg, S., 178
Richters, J., 329

Rickels, K., 127
Ridder, E., 214
Riddle, M. A., 144
Ridenour, T. A., 386
Riding, A., 367
Ridley, N. J., 373
Rief, W., 174, 176, 177
Rieger, G., 330, 358
Riemann, D., 218
Ries Merikangas, K., 213
Riihimäki, K., 24
Riis, J., 305
Riley, B., 159
Rinaldi, M., 75, 110
Ripke, S., 460
Risch, N., 106
Riso, L. P., 296
Ritterband, L. M., 316
Ritz, T., 34, 139, 140
Rivera-Hudson, N., 422
Rizvi, S. L., 151
Rizzuto, D., 520
Robbins, C., 62, 380, 514
Roberto, C. A., 288
Roberts, A., 160, 220, 274, 482
Robertson, D., 65, 312, 396
Robichaud, M., 158
Robin, A. L., 487
Robinaugh, D. J., 206
Robins, L. N., 422, 424
Robinson, G. E., 65
Robles, T., 253, 254
Rocca, W. A., 263
Rochon, P. A., 506
Rockert, W., 294
Rockney, R. M., 11
Rodin, J., 126, 263, 291, 292, 295, 296
Roelofs, K., 183
Roemer, L., 126, 127, 128, 216, 220
Roerig, J. D., 298
Roesch, S. C., 542
Rogers, R., 22, 431
Rogers, Carl, 22
Rogosch, F. A., 410
Rohde, P., 205, 213, 219, 220, 301, 304, 485
Roid, G. H., 80
Rojo, L., 297
Roll, J. M., 389
Rolland, Y., 518
Rollman, B. L., 128, 214
Rollnick, S., 397
Romanelli, R. J., 158
Romeo, E., 49
Rongve, A., 513
Ronningstam, E., 432, 433
Root, T. L., 288
Rosalie, 23
Rosario, M. C., 154
Rose, J. S., 108, 205
Rosell, D. R., 418
Rosellini, A. J., 90, 91
Rosen, A. C., 160, 334, 335, 339, 342, 343, 344
Rosenbach, A. F., 383
Rosenbaum, J. F., 227
Rosenberg, P. B., 265, 512, 518
Rosenfeld, J. P., 52
Rosenfield, D., 150, 151
Rosenman, R. H., 262
Rosenthal, D., 236, 459
Ross, A. O., 186, 190, 191, 192, 195
Rossow, I., 375
Rost, S., 304
Roth, W. T., 138, 315
Rothbard, 534

Rothbaum, B. O., 151, 152, 158
Rothblum, E. D., 62, 289
Rotheram-Borus, M. J., 275
Rothschild, A., 414
Rottenberg, J., 61
Rouff, L., 417
Rouse, S. V., 80
Rousseau, 257
Roussos, P., 416, 418
Rowe, J. B., 131, 182, 183, 471
Rowse, G., 448
Roy, A. K., 208
Roy-Byrne, P. P., 126
Rozin, P., 292
Rubia, K., 486
Rubin, G. J., 11, 179
Rubinstein, T., 424
Rubio, J., 204
Rück, C., 158
Rucklidge, J. J., 485
Rudaz, M., 132
Rudd, M. D., 223, 239, 242
Rudolph, K. D., 213
Ruffin, R., 258
Ruhe, K., 140
Ruiz, F. S., 306
Ruiz-Veguilla, M., 457
Rupprecht, R., 49
Ruscio, A. M., 140
Rush, A. J., 218, 228, 230
Rush, B., 218, 228, 230
Russell, A. E., 283, 286, 287, 288, 289, 293, 295, 296, 298, 300, 486
Russo, L., 393
Rutten, B. P., 459, 465
Rutter, M., 36, 37, 39, 41, 64, 96, 217, 391, 414, 422, 495, 520
Ruzek, J. I., 150
Ryan, D. H., 423
Ryder, A. G., 215, 267, 416
Ryder, Winona, 400
Rygh, J. L., 222
Rynn, M., 127

S
Saab, P. G., 261
Sachs, G. S.
Sack, R. L., 315
Sackeim, H. A., 186, 188, 190, 191
Sacks, H., 141
Saczynski, J. S., 506
Sadeh, N., 431
Safford, M. M., 223
Safren, S. A., 258
Sahakian, B. J., 164
Sahler, O., 260
Saitz, T. R., 337
Sakellariou, I., 14
Sakellariou, I., 11
Sakheim, D. K., 338
Saklofske, D. H., 81
Saksa, J. R., 473
Saldana, 472
Saleem, R., 234
Saleh, F., 534
Salekin, R. T., 431
Salkovskis, P., 157, 177
Sallet, J., 54
Salovey, P., 263
Salter, M., 389
Saltoun, M., 259
Salvatore, P., 449
Samek, D. R., 426

SAMHSA, 374, 376, 379, 382, 383
Sammel, M., 214
Sampson, N. A., 121, 239
Samson, L., 330
Samuels, J., 436, 512
Sancesario, G., 511
Sanches, M. M., 122
Sandin, B., 53, 178
Sanislow, C., 429, 434, 435
Sankey, A., 268
Sankis, L. M., 5
Sano, M., 518
Santarelli, L., 218
Santed, M., 178
Santoro, M. R., 502
Santosh, P. J., 65
Santucci, L. C., 141
Sapolsky, R. M., 4, 40, 252, 253
Sareen, J., 176
Sari, Y., 372
Saribay, S. A., 57
Sarkar, A., 416
Sartorius, N., 52, 472
Sartorius 71
Sarwer, D. B., 304, 305
Sauer, J., 109, 428
Sauer, S. E., 54
Sauer-Zavala, S., 61, 162, 253
Savage, J. C., 423
Savard, J., 316
Savin-Williams, R., 328, 331, 355, 358
Savla, G. N., 542
Sawada, Y., 239
Sawyer, A. T., 61, 122, 128, 231
Saxe, G. N., 149, 191
Saxena, S., 160, 163
Scales, U., 215
Scanlon, D., 489
Scarborough, P., 262
Scarmeas, N., 511
Scepkowski, L., 340
Schachar, R., 486
Schacter, D. L., 57, 193
Schaeffer, B., 496
Schaffer, D., 211, 227
Schatz, N. K., 485, 487
Schatzberg, A., 127, 265
Scheerenberger, R. C., 498
Scheiderer, E. M., 436
Scheidt, P. C., 274
Scheier, M. F., 274
Schenck, C. H., 319
Schendel, D., 495
Scherr, P. A., 510
Schiavi, R. C., 334, 340
Schieber, K., 160
Schietecatte, I., 493
Schifano, S., 94
Schiffer, B., 437
Schiffman, J., 451
Schmahl, C., 192, 428
Schmaling, K. B., 269
Schmeidler, J., 185
Schmidt, A. B., 176, 343, 348
Schmitz, M. F., 241
Schmucker, M., 352
Schneider, S., 140, 144, 185, 335
Schneiderman, N., 254, 258, 261, 263
Schneier, F. R., 152
Schnell, K., 430
Schniering, C. A., 140, 293
Schoenbaum, M., 126, 375
Schoeneman, T. J., 9
Schoenfeld, T. J., 218

Schoenmakers, B., 401, 519
Schomerus, G., 531
Schork, M. A., 60, 121
Schouten, E., 264
Schover, L. R., 344
Schramm, A. T., 144, 231
Schredl, M., 317
Schreiber, G. B., 399
Schreiner-Engel, P., 334
Schroeter, K., 296
Schuck, P. F., 501
Schuckit, M. A., 372, 373, 375, 389, 395, 401
Schule, C., 49
Schulenberg, J. E., 374
Schulman, P., 233
Schulsinger, F., 472
Schulte, C., 340
Schulte-Rüther, M., 296
Schultz, R., 493
Schultze, M., 231
Schulz, L. O., 83, 214
Schulze, L., 428
Schumacher, J. A., 49
Schumann, C. M., 495
Schutter, D. J., 230
Schutz, H. K., 293
Schwartz, A. J., 52, 128, 205, 237, 271, 300, 303, 304, 315, 394, 496, 502
Schwarzler, F., 218
Schweizer, E., 127
Scott, C. L., 121, 164, 232, 253, 254, 317, 426, 468, 540
Sedlak, T. W., 384
Seedat, S., 224
Seeley, J. R., 205, 219, 220
Seeman, P., 261, 462
Segal, D. L., 37, 158, 231
Segerstrom, S. C., 254, 256
Seglem, K. B., 387
Segraves, R., 333, 343, 344
Seibel, S. L., 195
Seidman, L. J., 463, 486
Seitz, D. P., 506
Selesnick, S. T., 9, 12, 14
Seligman, M. E., 55, 57, 221, 233
Sellaro, R., 211
Sellbom, M., 421, 540
Sellinger, J., 271
Sells, D., 471
Selten, J. P., 464
Seltzer, M. H., 437
Selye, H., 251
Semans, J. H., 343
Sen, S., 39
Sendt, K. V., 468
Sephton, S. E., 254, 256
Seplowitz, R. G., 311
Serefoglu, E. C., 337
Serpe, R. T., 160
Serretti, A., 428
Seshadri, S., 516
Seto, M., 346, 348, 349, 353
Settipani, C. A., 144
Sewell, K. W., 431
Shadick, R., 127
Shaffer, D., 64, 228, 240
Shafran, R., 295, 296
Shah, G. M. S., 450
Shalev, A. Y., 151
Sham, P., 464
Shamloul, R., 335
Shanahan, L., 209
Shapiro, C. J., 260, 384, 487
Sharafkhaneh, A., 311
Sharma, M. P., 178

Sharpe, D., 49, 180, 270
Sharpe, M., 269
Sharpless, B. A., 132
Shatkin, J. P., 318
Shaw, D. S., 288, 289, 295, 301, 304, 389, 426, 430
Shear, K., 126, 130, 134, 140, 206, 224, 241
Shedden, K., 39
Sheets, E. S., 223
Shehab, N., 506
Sheikh, H., 138, 267
Sheldon, E. K., 257
Shelleby, E., 426
Shelly, C., 81
Shen, B., 225, 263
Shenton, M. E., 464
Sheperis, C. J., 371
Sher, K. J., 274, 289, 395, 398
Sherbourne, C. D., 225
Sherman, S. J., 108
Sherry, B., 302
Shields, W., 275
Shin, L. M., 122, 150
Shingleton, R. M., 300
Shirk, S. R., 488
Shisslak, C. M., 290
Shneidman, E. S., 238
Short, E. B., 230
Shulman, C., 540
Shumaker, S. A., 512
Shuman, D. W., 530, 537, 538, 540, 541
Sibrava, N. J., 131
Sibulkin, A. E., 533
Sica, F., 511
Sico, J. J., 515
Sidat, M., 257
Siddiqui, F., 316
Siegel, A. J., 258, 259, 491
Sierra, M., 184, 185
Siever, L. J., 416, 418, 419
Siffre, M., 313
Sigmon, S. C., 369
Sigmund Freud, 13
Sigmundson, K., 357, 421
Sikorska, B., 515
Silberman, E. K., 189
Silberstein, L. R., 291, 296
Silk, K. R., 410, 429
Silove, D., 140
Silva, P., 348, 421, 422
Silver, E., 537
Silverman, W. K., 125, 138, 147, 150
Silverstone, T., 217
Simeon, D., 185
Simmons, J. R., 224, 291, 305
Simms, L. J., 176
Simon, G., 133, 179, 206, 228, 251, 530, 536, 537, 538, 540, 541
Simoneau, T. L., 234
Simonetti, J. A., 235
Simons, A. D., 111, 223, 390
Simonsen, E., 451
Simpson, E., 144, 158, 239, 389
Sinclair, E., 259
Singer, J., 520
Singh, J. P., 466, 503, 532, 540
Siniscalchi, J., 161
Sinke, S., 286
Sipprelle, R. C., 149
Sirroff, B., 185
Sisask, M., 240
Sisti, D., 540
Sjogren Fugl-Meyer, K., 333
Skeem, J., 448
Skeldon, 309

Skey, 80
Skhiri, D., 429
Skidmore, W., 357
Skinner, B. F., 24
Skodol, A. E., 409, 410, 414, 416, 417, 419, 422, 438
Skokauskas, N., 486
Skoner, D. P., 63, 254
Skorska, M., 331
Skultety, K. M., 291
Skuse, D. H., 493
Slade, M. D., 56
Slater, M., 470
Slattery, M. J., 120
Slavich, G. M., 217
Slavin-Mulford, J., 77
Sleegers, K., 516
Sloan, D. M., 146, 151, 184
Slooter, A. J. C., 506
Smeets, G., 184, 450, 506
Smigielski, J., 464
Smith, C. O., 65, 148, 229, 261, 263, 269, 291, 295, 296, 299, 304, 316, 453, 487, 497
Smitherman, T. A., 267
Smits, J. A., 133, 232
Smolak, L., 292, 296
Smolen, A., 217, 225
Smollen, 225
Smoller, J. W., 120
Snook, J., 371
Snyder, J. S., 51, 111, 218, 462
Soares, C., 214
Sobell, L. C., 374, 396
Soca, X., 314
Soenens, B., 296
Sohl, S., 270
Sohn, C., 219
Solai, L. K. K., 506
Solanki, D., 451
Soldatos, C. R., 467
Solfrizzi, V., 517
Soloff, P. H., 239, 428
Solomon, D. A., 389
Sommer, I. E., 487
Sonnenberg, L., 305
Soreca, I., 218, 219, 220
Sosa-Ortiz, A. L., 512, 517
Sotker, P. B., 150
Souery, D., 204
Soumier, A., 218
South, S. C., 410
Spangler, D. L., 223
Spanos, N. P., 189, 190
Spector, A., 341, 519
Speisman, R. B., 218
Spence, S. H., 144
Spencer, S. J., 485, 488
Spiegel, D., 147, 148, 184, 185, 186, 187, 188, 190, 191, 192, 258, 259
Spielberger, C. D.
Spielman, A. J., 310
Spinella, M., 155
Spinelli, M. G., 54, 289
Spinhoven, P., 49
Spira, A., 98, 328
Spitzer, C., 413
Sprague, J., 431
Spreeuwenberg, P., 520
Springen, 227
Sprock, J., 431
Spurrell, E. B., 288
St. Paul, M. S., 292
Stahl, S. M., 48, 51
Stall, R., 275
Stamatpoulou, 11

Stan, A., 400
Stanchina, M. L., 315
Stange, J. P., 213
Stangier, U., 144, 178, 234
Stanley, B., 125, 128, 130, 329
Stanley, S., 128
Stappenbeck, C. A., 389
Starr, K., 223
Stathopoulou, G., 232
Statt, E., 251
Stattin, H., 390
Steadman, H., 537, 539
Stears, M., 520
Steckler, M., 451
Steffen, K.298
Steiger, A., 283, 284, 286, 289, 291, 295, 296, 297, 306
Stein, D. J., 5, 77, 121, 144, 164, 400
Steinhauer, S. R., 457
Steinley, D., 289
Steketee, G., 154, 156, 157, 159, 162, 163
Stennett, B., 431
Stenvall, M., 506
Stephan, Y., 303
Stephenson, J., 428
Steptoe, A., 56, 261, 262, 263
Stern, Y., 511
Sternberg, W. F., 267
Sterner, U., 140
Sterzer, P., 425
Stevens, B. L., 176, 263, 268, 314, 375
Stevenson, R. E., 502
Stewart, J. W., 109, 157, 232, 233, 390
Stice, E., 286, 289, 290, 292, 293, 295, 296, 301, 304
Stier, A., 64, 90
Stiles, T., 437
Stinson, F., 203
Stoessel, P., 52
Stohart, 111
Stokes, 284, 302
Stolarz-Fantino, S., 20
Stoller, R. J., 330, 355
Stone, A. B., 180, 181, 182, 183, 412, 428, 435, 453
Stout, R., 159, 160, 161, 391
Strain, E. C., 148, 152, 372, 387, 388, 394
Stratta, P., 239
Strauss, J. L., 435
Stravynski, A., 434
Streiff, O. 429
Streiner, D. L., 429
Striegel-Moore, R., 286, 288, 291, 296, 300, 303
Strike, P. C., 263
Strober, M., 295
Stroebe, M., 206
Strokoff, J., 329
Stroud, C. B., 223
Stroup, S., 462, 468
Strunk, D., 232, 233
Stuart, S., 194
Stuckler, 303
Stuebing, K. K., 489
Stunkard, A., 303
Stutts, C., 111
Su, A., 188
Suarez, E. C., 60
Suárez, L., 54, 150, 156, 429
Subbaraman, M., 396
Subedar, H., 125
Substance Abuse and Mental Health Services Administration, 97, 367, 532
Suddath, R. L., 234
Sue, S., 78
Suelzer, M., 127
Sugarman, H. J., 305, 400
Sugiyama, T., 494

Suhail, K., 466
Sullivan, G. M., 48, 49, 50, 122, 216, 259, 269
Suls, J., 259, 263
Summerfeldt, L. J., 74, 144
Summitt, P. H., 508
Sun, F., 236, 517
Sundquist, J., 211
Sunohara, M., 416
Suomi, S. J., 40, 53
Supplee, L., 426
Suthar, M., 501
Sutherland, D., 315
Sutin, A. R., 205, 303
Sutter, M. E., 386
Suvak, M. K., 152
Suveg, C., 125, 144
Suvisaari, J. M., 464
Suvrathan, A., 504
Svakic, D. M., 410, 417, 419, 429, 432, 433, 437
Svartberg, M., 437
Svenningsson, P., 513, 514
Svitak, M., 160
Swan, G. E., 273
Swann, A. C., 204
Swanson, J. W., 273, 286, 288, 289
Swartz, M. S., 471
Sweeney, J. A., 344
Sweet, R. A., 510, 511, 515, 516, 518
Swenderman, 76
Swinson, R. P., 144
Syblik, D., 259
Sydeman, S. J., 264
Sylvers, P., 423
Sylvester, D.:, 137
Syme, S. L., 62, 263
Syngelaki, E. M., 423
Synowski, S., 258
Sysko, R., 285, 286, 288, 298, 299
Szarek, B. L., 227
Szasz, T., 457
Szmukler, G. I., 298
Szyf, M., 37

T

Taillefer, S., 177
Takei, N., 463, 464
Talbot, L. S., 218
Talwar, X., 313
Tam, W. W., 109
Tan, E. S., 61, 138
Tanaka-Matsumi, J., 142
Tandon, R., 452
Tani, P., 400
Tannock, R., 491
Tanofsky, M. B., 288
Tarescavage, A. M. 540
Tartara, A., 319
Tarullo, A. R., 150
Tate, R. L., 239
Tau, G. Z., 48
Taylor, D. 62, 98, 157, 177, 178, 230, 250, 252, 254, 256, 258, 260, 261, 262, 264, 265, 266, 269, 271, 272, 274, 293, 309, 445, 485, 486
Taylor, C. B., 274
Teasdale, J. D., 55, 60, 61, 221, 231, 233
Teesson, M., 398
Teetsel, R. 144
Teh, C. F., 265
Teicher, M. H., 227
Tein, J-Y, Teetsel, R., 144
Telch, C. F., 132, 150, 293, 299
Tellegen, A., 37, 80
Temoshok, L. R., 258

Temple, E., 491
Teplansky, R., 381
Teresi, J. A., 519
Teri, L., 519
Terracciano, A., 303
Tesar, L., 344
Testad, I., 519
Teti, D. M., 309, 310
Thapar, A., 486
Thase, M. E., 204, 217, 218, 223, 225, 227, 228, 229, 230, 231, 233
Thayer, J. F., 126
Thede, L., 356
Theleritis, C., 467
Thibaut, F., 353
Thibodeau, M. A.,, 176
Thirthalli, J., 94
Thisted, R. A., 261
Thomas, K. M., 413, 415, 416, 417, 425, 426, 428
Thompson, W. W., 257, 258, 292, 300, 419, 519
Thompson-Brenner, H., 292, 299
Thordarson, D. S., 177
Thorlton, J., 381
Thorndike, A. N., 305
Thorogood, M., 519
Thorpe, G. L., 126, 130
Thorpy, M., 312
Thuras, P., 288
Thurau, D., 341
Tiefer, L., 344
Tien, A. Y., 236
Tienari, P., 40, 459, 460
Tietjens, M. E., 259
Tiggemann, M., 291
Timmons, K. A., 223
Tinbergen, E. A., 495
Tingelstad, J. B., 229
Tishelman, A. C., 358
Tishler, C. L., 236
Titchener, J. L., 148
Tiwari, S., 125
Tjio, J. H., 501
Tober, D. M., 109
Todd, J., 496
Tolejko, N., 223
Tolin, D. F., 162, 163
Tomaka, J., 253
Tomenson, B., 175
Tomiyama, A. J., 284, 304a
Tomko, R. L., 436
Tompson, M. C., 234
Tondo, L., 229, 230
Tonigan, J. S., 391, 396
Toomey, J. A., 540
Torgersen, S., 387, 410, 412, 414, 427
Torrey, E., 538
Torry, Z., 538
Toth, K., 193, 194, 486, 498, 499, 500, 501, 503
Tottenam, N., 122
Tovote, P., 119, 120
Townsend, E., 329
Tracey, S. A., 295
Tracy, D. K., 468
Tranel, D., 81
Traskman-Bendz, L., 237
Trauer, X., 316
Treasure, J., 94
Treatment for Adolescents with Depression Study [TADS] Team, 229
Tremont, G., 519
Trichopoulos, D., 513
Triebwasser, J., 416, 418
Trifiletti, L. B.,, 274
Trinh, N., 518

Trivedi, M., 228
Trockel, M., 98
True, W. R., 149
Trull, T., 91, 436
Truong, X., 314
Trzapacz, P., 506, 507
Trzaskowski, M., 304
Trzepacz, P., 506
Tsai, A. C., 190, 225, 304
Tsuang, M. T., 453, 463
Tsushima, V., 109
Tuchman, B., 9, 10
Tucker, J. A., 394, 396
Tuke, W., 15, 63
Tuijnman-Raasveld, C. C., 343
Tull, M. T., 122
Turk, D. C., 265, 271, 273
Turkheimer, E., 37, 40, 105
Turner, C., 144, 149, 254, 261, 273
Turovsky, J., 126, 127
Turpin, R., 501
Turse, N. A., 149
Tuschen-Caer, B., 296
Tus-chen-Caffier, B. 135
Tushnet, M., 533
Twamley, E. W., 519
Twenge, J., 329
Tylš, F., 385, 386
Tyndale, R., 388
Tynes, L. L., 159

U

Uchino, B. N., 251, 254
Uddin, M., 149
Ueda, M., 239
Uehara, T., 58
Uhde, T., 131
Uleman, J. S., 57
Umberson, D., 63
Unger, J. B., 276
Unutzer, J., 229
Urbina, S., 71
Urosevic, S., 220
Ursano, R., 148
US Department of Education, 489
US Department of Energy Office of Science, 36
US Department of Health and Human Services, 251
Useda, J., 415
Ustun, T. B., 179
Utela, 261

V

Vacanti-Shova, K., 112
Vaccarino, A. L., 271
Vacik, H. W., 259
Vahia, I. V., 454
Vaillant, G. E., 421
Vaillant, G., 253
Valentiner, D. P., 176
Valera, E. M., 486
Valiente, R., 178
Valle, L., 426
Valtonen, H. M., 211
Van Ameringen, M., 144
van Amsterdam, J., 396
van Baars, A., 532
Van Beek, A., 520
van Beijsterveldt, C., 356
Van Broeckhoven, C., 516
van den Brink, W., 396
Van Den Eijnden, R. J. J. M., 401
van der Hart, O., 190

van der Kloet, D., 20
van der Meer, J., 268
van Dongen, J., 105
van Duijil, M., 188
van Dycke, 314
van Elderen, T., 262
van Haren, N. E., 463
van Hoeken, D., 286
van Kammen, D. P., 462
van Laar, M., 127
van Lankveld, J., 343
van Minnen, A., 152
van Munster, B. C., 507
van Ommeren, A., 352
van Orden, K. A., 239
Van Os, J., 465
van Overveld, M. O., 459, 464, 465, 473
Van Praag, H. M., 217
Van Rooij, A. J., 401
Van Ryzin, M. J., 390
Vande-Creek, 112
Vander Wal, J. S., 303
VanDerHeyden, A., 489
Vanderstichele, H., 511
Vannucchi, G., 417
Vansteenkiste, M., 296
VanValkenburg, C., 413
Varga, M. D., 487
Värnik, A., 238, 240
Vasey, P., 357
Vassos, 63
Vasterling, J. J., 150
Vaughn, M. G., 386, 424
Vazques, G. H., 229
Veale, D., 159, 160, 161
Veith, I., 10
Veling, W., 286
Vellas, B., 518
Velting, D. M., 240
Venables, N. C., 423, 425, 464
Veniegas, R., 275
Venkatesh, K., 489
Verbaten, M., 127
Verma, K. K., 451
Vermetten, E., 147, 192
Vermulst, A. A., 401
Vermund, S. H., 257
Vernberg, E. M., 150
Verona, E., 431
Vertommen, H., 532
Vervliet, B., 55
Vgontzas, 309
Viana, A. G., 145
Vibert, S., 295
Vieta, E., 229
Viikari, 51
Vincent, K. B., 377
Viner, R. M., A. J., 305
Vingerhoets
Vinkers, D., 532
Virag, R., 344
Virkkunen, M., 400
Virts, K. L., 265
Visscher, P. M., 120
Visser, L., 176
Vitacco, M., 422, 534
Vitiello, B., 290, 296, 487
Vitonis, A., 214
Vitousek, K., 299
Vittorio, C. C., 160
Voderholzer, U., 218, 436
Voderhozer, 306
Vogel, S. A., 489
Vohs, K. D., 296

Voigt, K., 175, 176, 194
Volden, J., 497
Volkerts, E., 127
Volkmar, F., 493, 520
Volkow, N. D., 51, 384, 387, 388, 397
Völlm, B., 431
von Knorring, 424
von Strauss, E., 520
Vonk, J. J., 122
Voos, A., 497
Vorontsova, N., 470
Voss, J. L., 140
Vrshek-Schallhorn, S., 223
Vuorilehto, M., 24

W

Waaktaar, T., 387
Wadden, T. A., 302, 304
Wade, T. D., 295
Wadsworth, M., 269
Wadsworth, J., 328
Wager, T., 265, 267, 268
Wagner, B., 206
Wagner, B. M., 239
Wagner, C. A., 220
Wagner, D., 93, 387
Wagner, K. D., 487
Wahlberg, K. E., 460
Wahlsten, D., 40
Wakefield, J. C., 5, 241
Wakeling, A., 293
Wald, R. L., 258
Waldman, I., 486
Waldorf, D., 340
Waldron, M., 37, 40
Wales, J., 283
Walker, D. L., 145
Wall, M., 149, 207
Wall, P. D., 266
Wall, T. D., 421
Wallace, C. S., 54
Waller, R., 424
Waller, N. G., 191, 192, 194
Wallin, B. G., 261
Wallman, K., 270
Waln, O., 468
Walsh, B. C., 473
Walsh, B. T., 291, 298, 299
Walsh, D., 455
Walsh, K., 149
Walters, E. E., 125, 126, 130, 140, 212, 295, 296
Walther, C. S., 329
Wan, Y. Y., 255
Wang, G. S., 384
Wang, H., 108
Wang, H.-X., 520
Wang, M., 75, 94, 98, 110
Wang, P. S., 127, 142, 203, 204, 205, 212
Wang, S., 11, 59, 214
Wang, T., 384
Wang, X., 225
Wang, Y., 495
Ward, A., 273, 284, 292, 304, 350, 351
Wardle, J., 56
Ware, M. A., 384
Wargo, E., 382
Warren, S. T., 387, 388, 397, 502
Warwick, H., 177
Wasserman, T. H., 329
Wassink, T. H., 464
Waters, A. M., 140, 304, 449
Watson, D. B., 37, 86, 91, 194, 487, 497
Way, B., 256

Weaver, J. C. G., 40
Weck, F., 178
Wedig, M. M., 429
Weed, N. C., 80
Weedman, J. M., 372
Weeks, J. R., 189
Weems, C. F., 125
Wegner, D., 157
Weike, A. I., 296
Weinberg, M. S., 345
Weinberger, A. D., 222, 464, 533
Weiner, D. B., 343, 511, 512, 516
Weinstock, H., 223
Weintraub, E. S., 496
Weis, S., 450
Weisberg, R., 159, 160, 333, 335, 336, 341, 343, 351
Weisburg, R. B., 338, 339, 340
Weise, R. E., 88
Weisfeld, 267
Weiskrantz, L., 57, 182
Weisman de Mamani, A. G., 466
Weiss, B., 77, 80, 179, 252, 380, 384
Weisskopf, M. G., 486
Weissman, M., 156, 216, 232
Weitze, C., 355
Welch, P. G., 287, 296
Welford, M., 128
Wellings, K., 328
Wells, A., 127, 128, 225, 329, 384, 389
Weltzin, T. E., 286
Wendt, D. C., 108
Wermter, A.-K., 495
Wertheim, E. H., 293
Wessely, S., 11, 269, 270
West, B. T., 396
Westen, D., 77, 299
Westendorp, R. G., 506
Westman, E., 514
Wetherell, J. L., 125, 126, 128, 163, 213
Wetter, E., 65
Wetzler, S., 414
Weuve, J., 510
Wever, R., 313
Weyman-Daun, M., 293
Whang, W., 264
Wheat, K., 536, 537
Wheeler, J., 346
Whisman, M., 217, 223, 225
Whitbourne, S. K., 291
White, K., 105, 126, 129, 132, 157, 159, 270, 289, 300, 305, 315, 372, 374, 421, 534
Whiteford, 121
Whitehouse, A. M., 290, 291
Whitehurst, G. J., 482
Whiteside, U., 374
Whitfield-Gabrieli, S., 52, 53,144
Whiting, D. L., 239
Whittal, M. L., 158, 298
Whooley, M. A., 214, 263
Widiger, T., 5, 85, 86, 88, 89, 91, 409, 410, 413, 422
Widiger, T. A. Crego, 4
Widom, C. S., 428
Wiebe, S. T., 306
Wiederanders, M., 352
Wiegel, M., 338, 340, 342
Wiger, D. E., 72
Wiggins, R., 515
Wik, G., 57
Wilberg, T., 417, 434
Wilbur, C., 188
Wilcox, H. C., 237
Wilde, E. A., 83
Wildes, J. E., 300

Wilens, T., 488
Wiley, D. E., 275
Wilfley, D. E., 288, 290, 300, 305
Wilhelm, S., 145, 158, 160
Wilkel, C. S., 160
Willem Van der Does, A. J., 49
Williams, C. J., 60, 80, 152, 160, 193, 231, 263, 274, 345, 380, 423, 464, 486
Williamson, D. A., 125, 284, 296
Willwerth, J., 542
Wilner, 234
Wilson, B. M., 20, 285, 286, 288, 289, 296, 298, 299, 300, 512
Wimo, A., 510
Winblad, B., 520
Wincze, J. P., 333, 335, 336, 337, 338, 339, 340, 341, 342, 343, 344, 346, 350, 351
Windgassen, K., 468
Wing, J. K., 72, 304, 335, 466
Winkelman, J. W., 319
Winkleby, M. A., 211
Winston, F. K., 275
Winter, A., 17, 428
Winters, R. W., 261
Wintrob, R. M., 391
Winzelberg, A. J., 301
Wirdefeldt, K., 513
Wisco, B. E., 224
Wise, T. N., 348
Wisely, J., 128
Wiseman, F. K., 501
Wish, E. D., 378
Withall, A., 373
Witherington, R., 344
Withers, G. S., 54
Witkiewitz, K., 397
Witt, A., 128, 231, 288
Wittchen, H-U., 118, 121, 126, 129, 130, 138, 214, 465
Witthöft, M., 176, 177, 178, 179
Wittstein, I., 262
Woertman, L., 190
Wohlsifer, D., 330
Wolf, E. J., 146, 147
Wolff, K., 387
Wolf-Maier, K., 260
Wolgamuth, B., 183
Wolitzky-Taylor, K. B., 130
Wollburg, E., 176, 194
Wonderlich, S., 285, 287, 288, 295, 296
Wong, C., 109, 214, 261, 426, 462, 470, 471, 472, 497, 504
Woo, J., 506
Wood, J. M., 77, 293
Woods, D. W., 134, 164, 239, 455, 473, 519
Woodside, M. R., 541
Woodward, L. J., 214, 267
Wooley, 261
Woolfolk, R. L., 160, 161, 173, 176, 179, 183
Worell, J., 80
World Health Organization, 64, 92, 96, 88, 236, 275, 374
Worsley, A., 540
Wortman, C., 206
Worton, D., 520
Wray, N. R., 120
Wren, P., 518
Wright, A. G., 86, 209, 486, 517
Wu, E., 158, 190, 236, 380, 445
Wyatt, T. J., 330
Wygant, D. B., 421, 540
Wykes, T., 470
Wyllie, E., 183
Wynne, L. C., 460

X

Xuxu, W., 533

Y

Yach, D., 303
Yaffe, K., 126, 213, 518
Yager, J., 63, 149
Yamada, A. M., 109, 319, 468, 471
Yan, L., 261
Yanez, B., 259
Yang, G., 495
Yanovski, J. A., 304, 305
Yap, A. K., 188
Yatham, L. N., 217, 230
Yau, Y. H. C., 399, 400
Yeh, C. Y., 53, 54, 482
Yehuda, R., 150
Yeo, G. S., 304
Yeomans, F. E., 433
Yiend, 56
Yin, R. K., 96
Yip, P., 239, 399
Yirmiya, R., 270
Yonkers, K., 208
Yoo, J. A., 96
Yoon, C. W., 306
Yoshioka, D. T., 75
Young, A. H., 222, 224, 225, 231, 356, 389, 390

Youngstrom, E. A., 213
Young-Wolff, K. C., 393
Yu, C. C., 109
Yücel, M., 436
Yudofsky, S. C., 83

Z

Zabalegui, A., 520
Zabinski, M. F., 290
Zachar, P., 5
Zadra, A., 317, 318
Zajonc, R. B., 59
Zalta, A. K., 284
Zanarini, M. C., 410, 427, 428, 429
Zandberg, L., 300
Zapf, P. A., 537
Zarate, R., 147, 472
Zarit, S. H., 518
Zaslavsky, A. M., 118, 121, 261, 265
Zatzick, D., 152
Zautra, A., 265
Zee, X., 314
Zeichner, S. B., 258
Zemore, S. E., 396
Zeni, C., 488
Zervas, I. M., 467
Zhai, L., 218
Zhang, D., 18

Zhang, H., 218
Zhao, S., 126
Zhong, R., 506
Zhu, Y., 314
Zhu, A., 388
Ziebell, S., 464
Zigler, E., 242
Zilbergeld, B., 342
Zilboorg, G., 10, 15
Zimmerman, M., 159, 160, 414
Zimmerman, J., 182
Zinbarg, R., 88, 127, 143
Zingmond, D. S., 305
Zippe, C., 344
Zisook, S., 241
Zitman, F., 264
Zonana, H., 534
Zottoli, T., 537
Zou, H., 495
Zubieta, J., 267
Zubin, J., 457
Zuchner, S., 164
Zucker, B. G., 131
Zucker, K. J., 333, 347, 357
Zukin, S. R., 387
Zuvekas, S. H., 487
Zvolensky, M. J., 121
Zwahlen, M., 257
Zwaigenbaum, L., 106

A

Abnormal behavior
    biological tradition, 11–15
    defined, 4
    historical conceptions, 8–9
    integrative approach, 25–26
    models of, 8–9
    problematic, 4
    psychological tradition, 15–25
    supernatural tradition, 9–11
Acamprosate, 394, 395
Acquired immune deficiency syndrome. *See*
        HIV/AIDS
Actigraph, 307
Action potentials, 43
Action tendency, 59
Actus rea, 537
Acute onset, 7
Acute pain, 264, 265
Acute stress disorder, 148–149, 185
Addington v. Texas, 532, 534
ADH. *See* Alcohol dehydrogenase (ADH)
ADHD. *See* Attention deficit/hyperactivity
        disorder (ADHD)
Adjustment disorders, 152–153
Adler, Alfred, 20, 22
Adolescents
    bulimia, 289–290
    conduct disorder in, 422–423
    conversion disorder in, 183
    mood disorders and, 212–213
    obese, 302–303
    schizophrenia onset in, 457
    somatic symptom disorder and, 176
    suicides by, 237, 238
Adoption studies, 104–105, 459–460
Adrenal cortex, 217
Adrenaline. *See* Epinephrine
Advanced sleep phase type, 314
Advanced syphilis, 12
Affect
    defined, 59, 73
    inappropriate, 452
    mental status exam and, 73
Affective flattening, 451
Age
    ADHD onset, 485–486
    BDD onset, 160
    bipolar disorders, 211
    blood–injection–injury phobia onset, 137
    depression onset, 205–206, 214
    eating disorder onset, 289–290, 291
    illness anxiety disorder onset, 176
    intellectual disability onset, 499
    IQ scores and, 80
    maternal, Down syndrome and, 502
    mature, 20

mood disorder onset, 213–214
neurocognitive disorder onset, 510
schizophrenia onset, 457
somatic symptom disorder onset, 176
specific phobia onset, 137
Agency for Health Care Policy and
        Research, 543
Agency for Healthcare Research and
        Quality, 543
Agnosia, 509
Agonist substitution, 394–395
Agonists, 48
Agoraphobia
    case study, 129
    clinical description of, 129–130
    defined, 128
    development of, 129–130, 132
    diagnostic criteria, 131
    evolution of, 137
    features of, 131
    situational avoidance and, 130
    statistics, 130–131
    treatment of, 134–135
AIDS. *See* HIV/AIDS
AIDS-related complex (ARC), 257
    antisocial personality disorder, 423–424
    pedophilic disorder and, 349
Akinesia, 468
Alarm reaction, 150
Alcohol
    blood concentrations, 373
    body absorption of, 371, 372
    metabolism of, 372
    response to, 388–389
Alcohol abuse
    aggression and, 375
    clinical description, 371
    diagnostic criteria, 372
    early alcohol use and, 375
    effects of, 371–374
    origins of, 371
    progression of, 374–375
    sexual dysfunction and, 339–340
    statistics, 374
    suicide and, 239
    treatments for, 393–394
Alcohol-related disorders
    aggression and, 375
    clinical description, 371
    diagnostic criteria, 372
    early alcohol use and, 375
    effects of, 371–374
    origins of, 371
    progression of, 374–375
    sexual dysfunction and, 339–340
    statistics, 374
    suicide and, 239

treatments for, 393–394
Alcoholics Anonymous, 396
ALDH2 gene, 391
Allegiance effect, 99
Alleles, 38–39
Alogia, 451
Alpha-adrenergic receptors, 50
Alpha waves, 83
Alprazolam, 133
Alters, 188
Altruistic suicide, 237
Alzheimer's disease
    biological factors, 515–516
    clinical description of, 511
    insomnia disorder and, 308
    neurocognitive disorder due to, 551–552
    statistics, 509–510
    studies of, 511–512
    treatments for, 518–520
    vaccines for, 518
American Association on Intellectual
        and Development Disabilities
        (AAIDD), 499
American Journal of Insanity, 13
American Law Institute (ALI) rule, 536
Amino acids, 48
Amitriptyline (Elavil), 228
Amok, 187
Amnestic disorders
    neurocognitive disorder and, 510
    types of, 185–186
Amniocentesis, 501, 502
Amphetamine use disorders, 377
Amphetamines
    characterization of, 377–378
    dopamine and, 378
    intoxication, 377–378
    recreational use of, 378
Amygdala, 45, 67
Amyloid beta peptides, 516
Amyloid plaques, 515–516
Anabolic-androgenic steroids, 293–294, 387
Analogue models, 94
Anandamide, 384
Angina pectoris, 262
Anhedonia, 203, 451
Animal phobias, 137
Anna O., 17, 57, 96
Anomic suicides, 237
Anomie, 237
Anorexia nervosa
    AIDS-associated, 384
    associated psychological
        disorders, 288
    case study, 286–287
    characterization of, 286–288
    clinical description of, 287–288

course of, 289
cultural factors, 291
defined, 283
disorder criteria for, 288
drug treatments for, 300–301
medical consequences of, 288
treatments for, 300–301
Antabuse. *See* Disulfiram
Antagonist drugs, 395
Antagonist treatments, 395
Antagonists, 48
Antibodies, 255
Anticipated course, 7
Antidepressants. *See also specific drugs*
effectiveness of, 227–228
increase in therapeutic use of, 229
mood disorders, 227–229
most commonly prescribed, 228
Antigens, 255–256
Antipsychotic drugs. *See also specific drugs*
commonly used, 468
development of, 468
effectiveness of, 462–463
noncompliance with, 468–469
side effects, 467–468
Antisocial personality disorder
arousal theories for, 423–424
case studies, 420
clinical description of, 420–422
conduct disorder and, 422
criminality in, 421–422
defining criteria, 421
developmental influences, 424–425
diagnosis, reliability of, 420
disorder criteria for, 421, 422
gender differences in, 412, 413
genetic influences, 423
integrative model for, 425
neurobiological influences, 423–424
prevention of, 426
psychopathy in, 421
psychosocial factors, 424
substance abuse and, 370
treatments for, 425–426
Anxiety
case study, 221
castration, 19
conversion disorder and, 182–183
cultural influences on, 121
defined, 118
effects of, 118–119
fear and, 118–119
neurobiology of, 122
panic and, 61, 130
stress and, 253–254
Anxiety and Related Disorders Interview Schedule for DSM-5 (ADIS-5), 74
Anxiety disorders, 118. *See also* Panic disorders
biological contributions, 120–122
brain structure and, 120
causes of, 120–123
characterization of, 59
children with, 7
comorbidity of, 123
cultural influences on, 121
depression and, 214

emerging conceptions of, 162–163
generalized, 124–128
genetic factors, 217
illness anxiety disorder and, 175–179
insomnia disorder and, 309–310
integrated model for, 122–123
panic and, 61, 130
physical disorders and, 123
psychological factors, 122
social factors, 122
social phobias, 141–146
specific phobia, 135–140
suicide and, 239
summary, 164–166
terms, definitions of, 118–120
Anxiety sensitivity, 122, 126
Anxiolytic drugs, 376, 515
Aphasia, 514
Apolipoprotein E4 (apo E4), 516
Appearance, mental status exam and, 72
Arbitrary inference, 222
ARC. *See* AIDS-related complex (ARC)
Arousal
Asclepiad Temples, 15
Asociality, 451
Asperger's disorder, 492–493, 520. *See also* Autism spectrum disorder
Assertiveness training, 273
Assessment. *See* Clinical assessment
Assessment gender bias, 413
Association studies, 105–106, 460–461
Associative splitting, 446, 452
Asylum reform, 16
Asylums, 16
Ataques de nervios, 89, 131
Atherosclerosis, 262, 264
Atomoxetine, 487–488
Attachment disorders, 152
Attention deficit/hyperactivity disorder (ADHD)
adults with, 487
age and, 484
biological interventions, 487–488
case study, 483–484
causes of, 486–487
clinical description, 484–485
defined, 483
diagnosis of, 484–486
disorder criteria for, 485
gender and, 484
learning disorders and, 491
mood disorders and, 214
psychosocial interventions, 487
statistics, 485–486
treatments for, 487–488
Attenuated psychosis syndrome, 455, 472
Attribution, 55
Atypical behavior, 4–5
Auditory hallucinations, 85, 449
Augmentative communication strategies, 503
Autism spectrum disorder, 492
Asperger's disorder *vs.*, 520
biological factors, 495–496
case study, 492–493
causes, 495–496
characteristics of, 492
clinical description, 492–494

defined, 492
disorder criteria for, 493
genetic influences, 495
history of, 493–494
neurobiological factors, 495–496
psychosocial factors, 495
social communication impairment in, 493–494
social interaction impairment in, 493–494
statistics, 494
treatments for, 496–497
Autogynephilia, 347
Autohypnotic model, 192
Autonomic inflexibility, 126
Autonomic nervous system, 46
Autonomic restrictors, 126
Aversive treatment, 395
Avoidant personality disorder
case study, 434
causes of, 434
clinical description, 411, 434
disorder criteria for, 434–435
treatments for, 435
Avolition, 451
Axons, 42–43

B

Barbiturates. *See also specific drugs*
clinical description of, 375–376
defined, 375
statistics, 376
Bariatric surgery, 305
Basal ganglia, 45
Baseline, 101
B cells, 255
BDD. *See* Body dysmorphic disorder (BDD)
BED. *See* Binge-eating disorder (BED)
Behavior. *See also* Health-related behavior
abstinence, 370
across cultures, 104–111
assessment of, 75, 84
disorganized, 452
drug-seeking, 370
genes, developments, 37
heterosexual, 328
homosexual, 328
mental status exam and, 72
modification of, 275
nongenomic inheritance of, 40–41
personality disorder and, 410
rating scales, 76
researching over time, 106–108
types, 262
Behavioral approach system (BAS), 226
Behavioral assessment, 75–76
Behavioral inhibition system (BIS), 121, 423
Behavioral medicine, 250
Behavioral model
behaviorism and, 23–24
classical conditioning, 22–23
contributions of, 25
defined, 22
operant conditioning, 24–25
therapy origins, 24

Behaviorism, 16, 23–24
The Behavior of Organisms (Skinner), 24
Behavior rating scales, 76
Behavior therapy, 24
Bender Visual–Motor Gestalt Test, 81
Benzodiazepines, 14, 49
   clinical description of, 375–376
   defined, 375
   GABA, 49
   GAD, 126–127
   Insomnia and, 315
   panic disorders, 135
   statistics, 376
Beta-adrenergic receptors, 50
Beta amyloid, 516
Beta-blockers, 50, 144
Bianchi, Kenneth, 189
Binge-eating disorder (BED)
   characterization, 324
   controversial *DSM-5* inclusion of, 319
   cultural factors, 290–291
   defined, 283
   disorder criteria for, 289
   drug treatment for, 289–290
   statistics, 289–290
   treatments for, 299–300
Binge-eating/purging type of anorexia
   nervosa, 287
Biofeedback, 83, 271
Biological model
   ADHD, 487–488
   American, 13
   anxiety disorders, 120–122
   autism, 495–496
   Chinese, 12
   consequences of, 14–15
   defined, 8
   DID and, 192
   eating disorders, 295–296
   Greek, 11–12
   intellectual disability, 500–503
   mood disorders, 216–219
   nineteenth century, 12–14
   neurocognitive disorder, 487–488
   panic disorders and, 132
   PTSD, 149–150
   Roman, 11–12
   substance-related disorders, 387–389
   treatment development, 14
Bipolar disorders. *See also* Mania
   case studies, 209–210
   defining criteria for, 210
   disorder criteria for, 210
   duration of, 211
   emotions and, 61
   identifying features of, 209
   onset of, 211
   psychological treatments for, 234–235
   rapid-cycling specifier, 213
   sleep and mood in, 218–219
   stress and, 220
   type I and II, 210
BIS. *See* Behavioral inhibition system (BIS)
Bisexuality, 357
Bleuler, Eugen, 446
Blind sight, 57, 182

Blood–injection–injury phobia, 3, 33–34,
   136–137, 140
Bloodletting, 12
Blood-Oxygen-Level-Dependent fMRI
   (BOLD-fMRI), 82
Blood pressure, 136–137, 260–261
BMI. *See* Body mass index (BMI)
Body dysmorphic disorder (BDD)
   case study, 158
   causes of, 160–161
   clinical description, 159
   defects location, 159
   disorder criteria for, 159
   history of, 159
   OCD and, 159, 160–161
   plastic surgery and, 161
   statistics, 159–160
   treatment for, 160–161
Body mass index (BMI), 284, 302
Body weight. *See also* Obesity
   assessment of, 284–285
   concerns with, 301
   control, case study, 284–285
   cultural factors, 290–291
   dieting and gain in, 293
   gender comparisons, 292
   surgery to reduce, 304
   weight loss programs, 304–305
BOLD-fMRI. *See* Blood-Oxygen-Level-
   Dependent fMRI (BOLD-fMRI)
Borderline personality disorder
   case study, 426–427
   causes of, 428–429
   clinical description of, 427
   disorder criteria for, 427–428
   integrative model for, 429
   treatments for, 429–430
Brady, James, 537
Bradykinesia, 513
Brain circuits, 48
Brain development neurotrophic factor
   (BDNF), 54
Brain functioning
   ADHD, 486–487
   alcohol use and, 388–389
   delirium and, 505–506
   depersonalization-derealization disorder
   and, 185
   learning disorders and, 491
   psychopathy and, 424
Brain stem, 44–45
Brain structure. *See also specific regions*
   anxiety disorders and, 120
   components, 44–45, 47
   divisions, 45
   implications for, 51–52
   mood disorders and, 218–219
   neuroimaging of, 81–82
   psychosocial influences on, 52–53
   schizophrenia, 463–464
   schizotypal personality disorder and, 419
Breathalyzer test, 372
Breathing-related sleep disorders
   defined, 312
   treatments for, 315–316
   types of, 312–313

Breuer, Josef, 17, 57, 96
Brief psychotic disorder, 455
Briquet's syndrome. *See* Somatoform
   disorders
Broca's area, 450
Bulimia nervosa, 62
   associated psychological disorders, 286
   case study, 284–285
   clinical description, 285–286
   course of, 290
   defined, 283
   disorder criteria for, 285
   drug treatments for, 298
   features of, 285
   gender differences, 62
   medical consequences of, 286
   statistics, 289–290
   treatments for, 299
Bupropion, 437

C

Caffeine use disorder, 381
CAH. *See* Congenital adrenal hyperplasia
   (CAH)
Callous-unemotional presentation, 422
Cancer, 258–260
Cannabinoids, 384
Cannabis use disorders, 384
Carbamazepine, 230
Cardiovascular disease, 260–264
   anger and, 262–263
   chronic negative emotions, role of,
     263–264
   coronary heart disease, 262–263
   hypertension, 260–262
Case study method, 96
Castration anxiety, 19
Cataplexy, 312, 315
Catatonia, 446
Catatonic immobility, 452
Categorical approaches, 85
Catharsis, 17, 151
Catholic Church, 11, 348, 367
CAT scan. *See* Computerized axial
   tomography (CAT) scan
Caudate nucleus, 45
Cause and effect, 220
CBASP. *See* Cognitive-Behavioral Analysis
   System of Psychotherapy (CBASP)
CBGT. *See* Cognitive-behavioral group
   therapy (CBGT)
CBT. *See* Cognitive-behavioral therapy
   (CBT)
Central nervous system (CNS), 41–43
   amphetamine effects on, 417–18
   components of, 4143
   function of, 41
Central sleep apnea, 313
   disorder criteria for, 313
Cerebellum, 44–45
Cerebral cortex, 45, 46
   subdivisions and primary functions of, 46
Cerebral vascular accidents (CVAs), 260
CFS. *See* Chronic fatigue syndrome (CFS)
Charcot, Jean-Martin, 17

Charles VI, 10, 12, 25
CHD. *See* Coronary heart disease (CHD)
Chemical transporter, 38
Childhood disintegrative disorder, 492
Childhood-onset fluency disorder, 482, 490
Children. *See also* Developmental disorders
    antisocial personality disorder in, 421–422
    anxiety in, 7
    conduct disorder in, 422–423
    eating disorders in, 291
    false memories of, 193
    fluency disorder in, 482
    GAD in, 125
    gender nonconformity, treatment of, 358–359
    mood disorders in, 212–213
    obese, 302
    OCD in, 155
    panic in, 7
    PTSD in, 149-150
    at risk for crime, 422
    schizophrenic, 472
    separation anxiety disorder in, 140–141
    sexual abuse of, 349
    sleep habits of, 310
    smoking by, 275–276
    suicides by, 237
Children's Apperception Test (CAT), 77
Choleric person, 12
Cholinesterase inhibitors, 518
Chorionic villus sampling (CVS), 502
Chromosomes
    Alzheimer's disease and, 516
    intellectual disability and, 501–503
    sex, 36
Chronic course, 7
Chronic fatigue syndrome (CFS)
    characterization, 268–270
    complex-specific model of, 269
    definition of, 268
    good outcomes for, 269
    inclusion criteria, 268
    treatment of, 270
Chronic pain
    biological aspects of, 266
    CFS and, 268–270
    denial for, 274
    drugs for, 273–274
    gender differences, 267–268
    overview, 264–265
    psychological aspects of, 265–266
    psychosexual factors, 264–266
    reduction, comprehensive approach to, 272–273
    reserve capacity model, 264
    social aspects of, 265–266
    stress reduction, 273–274
    types of, 264–265
Chronic stress, 217, 252, 254
Chronic traumatic encephalopathy (CTE), 512, 516
Cialis, 344
Cigarette smoking
    addiction to, 380
    agonist substitution, 394

    in China, 275–276
    prenatal, ADHD and, 486
Cingulate gyrus, 45
Circadian rhythms, 218–219
Circadian rhythm sleep disorders
    characterization of, 314
    disorder criteria for, 314
    research on, 314
    types of, 314
Circumplex model, 59
Civil commitment
    case study, 533, 585
    changes affecting, 532–534
    criminalization, 532
    criteria for, 530–532
    dangerousness defined in, 531–532
    defined, 581
    deinstitutionalization effects, 532–533
    history of, 582
    homelessness, 532–533
    legal rulings on, 584
    mental illness, defined in, 531
    overview of, 535
    strict, 533–534
    Supreme Court and, 532
Classical approach, 85
Classical categorical approaches, 85
Classical conditioning, 22–23
Classification, 84
Claustrophobia, 137
Cleckley, Hervey, 421
Cleckley criteria, 421
Clinical assessment. *See also* Diagnosis
    behavior, 75–76
    case study, 70–71
    concepts of, 71–72
    intelligence testing, 80–81
    interviews, 72–74
    neuroimaging, 81–82
    neuropsychological testing, 81
    observations, 75–76
    physical examination, 74–75
    process of, 70
    psychological testing, 76–81
    psychophysiological, 82–83
    self-monitoring, 76
    summary, 113–114
Clinical description, 6–7
    alcohol-related disorders, 371
    anorexia nervosa, 287–288
    antisocial personality disorder, 420–421
    attention-deficit/hyperactivity disorder (ADHD), 484–485
    autism spectrum disorder (ASD), 492
    avoidant personality disorder, 434
    BDD, 159
    BPD, 427
    bulimia nervosa, 285–286
    conversion disorders, 180
    delirium, 506
    dependent personality disorder, 435
    depressive disorders, 204
    dissociative identity disorder (DID), 188
    GAD, 125
    histrionic personality disorder, 431
    insomnia disorder, 308

    intellectual disability (ID), 499–500
    major neurocognitive disorder, 509–510
    narcissistic personality disorder, 433
    obsessive-compulsive disorder (OCD), 154–155
    obsessive-compulsive personality disorder, 436
    panic disorder (PD), 129–130
    paranoid personality disorder, 415
    paraphilic disorders, 345
    PTSD, 146–148
    schizoid personality disorder, 417
    schizotypal personality disorder, 418
    sedative-, hypnotic-, or anxiolytic-related disorders, 375–376
    social anxiety disorder (social phobia), 141–142
    somatic symptom disorder, 176
    specific learning disorder, 489
    specific phobia, 135–137
Clinical efficacy axis, 543
Clinical practice guidelines, 541–544
Clinical psychologists, 6
Clinical significance, 94–95
Clinical trials, 98
Clinical utility axis, 543
Clonidine, 395
Cluster A personality disorders
    exploration of, 438
    paranoid, 415–416
    schizoid, 416–417
    schizotypal, 418–419,
Cluster B personality disorders
    antisocial personality, 420–426
    borderline, 426–430
    exploration of, 438–439
    histrionic, 430–432
    narcissistic, 432–433
Cluster C personality disorders
    avoidant, 434–435
    dependent, 435–436
    exploration of, 439
    OCD, 436–437
CNS. *See* Central nervous system (CNS)
Cocaine use disorder, 378–380
Cognitive-Behavioral Analysis System of Psychotherapy (CBASP), 231, 233
Cognitive-behavioral model, 22
Cognitive-behavioral therapy (CBT)
    anorexia nervosa, 300
    BED, 299–300
    brain structure and, 52
    bulimia nervosa, 299
    conversion disorder, 183
    depression, 233
    erectile dysfunction, 344
    GAD, 128
    illness anxiety disorder, 179
    mood disorders, 230–231
    panic disorders, 134–135
    sleep disorders, 317
    somatic symptom disorder, 178
    substance abuse, 397
Cognitive science, 55–58
Cohort effect, 107
Cohorts, 107

Collective unconscious, 20
Commitment. *See* Civil commitment; Criminal commitment
Communication disorders, 448, 483, 490, 492. *See also specific disorder*
Community reinforcement, 397
Comorbidity
  ADHD, 486
  anxiety disorders, 123
  defined, 89
  mood disorders, 214
  personality disorders, 413–414
  physical disorders, 123
Comparative treatment research, 99–100
Complex-specific model, 269
Complicated grief, 206–207
Component treatment, 396–397
Comprehensive system, 77
Compulsions, 154–156
Computerized axial tomography (CAT) scan, 81
Concurrent validity, 72
Conditioned response, 23
Conditioned stimulus, 23
Conditioning, 22
  classical, 22–23
  cognitive processes and, 55
  examples of, 55
  function of, 55
  operant, 24–25
Conduct disorder, 214, 422
  adolescent onset type, 422
  childhood onset type, 422
  disorder criteria for, 465
Confound, 93
Confounding variable, 93
Construct validity, 87
Content validity, 87
Contingency management, 397
Continuous positive air pressure (CPAP) machine, 315
Control groups
  defined, 94
  function of, 99
  placebo, 99
  randomized, 94
Controlled drinking, 396
Conversion disorder (functional neurological symptom disorder)
  case study, 180, 182
  causes, 182–183
  clinical description of, 180
  disorder criteria for, 180
  statistics, 182
  treatment of, 183
Conversion hysteria, 173
Coping styles, 21
Copy number variants, 486
Coronary heart disease (CHD)
  characterization of, 262
  chronic negative emotions and, 263–264
  psychosocial factors, 262
  type A behavior pattern, 262–263
  type B behavior pattern, 262–263
Correlation
  coefficient, 96

defined, 96
designs, 96
directionality, 97
interpretation issues in, 96–98
negative, 97
positive, 96
types of, 96–97
Corticotropin-releasing factor (CRF)
  anxiety disorders and, 120
  PTSD and, 150
  stress and, 252
Cortisol, 47, 217–218, 252–253
Counseling psychologists, 6
Countertransference, 21
Covert sensitization, 351
CPAP. *See* Continuous positive air pressure (CPAP) machine
Creutzfeldt-Jakob disease, 515
CRF. *See* Corticotropin-releasing factor (CRF)
Criminal commitment
  defined, 535
  insanity defenses, 535–538
  NGRI, 537–539
  therapeutic jurisprudence, 539
  trial competency and, 539
Criterion gender bias, 413
Criterion validity, 87
Cross-cultural factors
  alcohol metabolism, 374–375
  BDD, 160–161
  behavior, 108–109
  characteristics of, 108–109
  children's sleep, 309
  cigarette smoking, 276
  dimensional models, 409–410
  dissociative trance disorder, 192
  DSM-5 and, 88–89
  eating disorders, 290–291
  mood disorders and, 215, 223–225
  obesity, 304
  OCD and, 157
  panic disorders, 131
  paranoid personality disorder, 416
  personality disorders, 409
  psychopathology and, 61–62
  schizophrenia, 458
  schizophrenia treatment, 471–472
  schizotypal personality disorder, 418
  sexual dysfunction, 340–342
  sexuality, 330
  social phobia and, 143
  specific phobia and, 138
  substance abuse, 391
  suicide, 236
Cross-fostering, 40
Cross-generational effect, 108
Cross-sectional designs, 107
CTE. *See* Chronic traumatic encephalopathy (CTE)
Cued panic attack, 119
Cultural–familial intellectual disability, 503
Cultural formulation, 89
CVAs. *See* Cerebral vascular accidents (CVAs)
CVS. *See* Chorionic villus sampling (CVS)

Cyclothymic disorder, 211
Cyproterone acetate, 353

D
Dahmer, Jeffrey, 537
Dangerousness, 531–532
DARE. *See* Drug Abuse Resistance Education (DARE)
DBT. *See* Dialectical behavior therapy (DBT)
D-cycloserine (DCS), 145
Death, leading causes of, 250
Defense mechanisms
  adaptive, 18
  defined, 18
  examples of, 19
  maladaptive, 18
  use of, 19
Deinstitutionalization, 532–533
Delayed ejaculation disorder, 336, 337
Delayed sleep phase type, 314
Delirium
  case study, 505
  causes, 506
  clinical description of, 506
  defined, 505
  disorder criteria for, 506
  prevention of, 507
  statistics, 506
  treatment for, 507
Delirium tremens (DTs), 373
Delta waves, 83
Delusions
  characterization of, 448–449
  defined, 448
  disorders, 454–455
  grandeur, 446, 448
  types of, 454–455
Dementia. *See* Major neurocognitive disorder
Dementia praecox, 87, 446
Dementia pugilistica, 512
Demons, 9
Dendrites, 42
Denial
  defined, 19
  as means of coping, 274
De novo mutations, 459
Dependence. *See* Substance dependence
Dependent personality disorders
  case study, 435
  causes of, 435–436
  clinical description of, 435
  cultural differences, 435
  disorder criteria for, 436
  treatment for, 435–436
Dependent variable, 92–93
Depersonalization, 184
Depersonalization-derealizationdisorder, 185
Depo-Provera. *See* Cyproterone acetate; Medroxyprogesterone
Depressants
  alcohol as, 371–375
  anxiolytic substances, 375–376

characterization of, 371
hypnotic substances, 375–376
sedatives, 375–376
Depression
  ADHD and, 488
  age onset, 214
  anorexia nervosa-associated, 288
  anxiety disorders and, 214
  bulimia nervosa-associated, 286
  case studies, 201–202, 235
  cognitive vulnerability for, 223
  combined treatments for, 233
  double, 204
  emotion and, 61
  experience of, 246
  genetic factors, 216–217
  grief and, 206–207, 243
  learned helplessness theory of, 221–222
  nicotine withdrawal and, 380
  overview of, 204–206
  relapse prevention, 233–234
  stressful life events and, 219, 254, 258
  stress hypothesis of, 218
  supernatural explanation for, 9
Depressive cognitive triad, 222
Depressive disorders. *See also specific
    disorder*
  bipolar, 209–211
  case study, 205
  clinical description, 204–205
  double depression, 204
  duration, 205–206
  grief *vs.*, 206–207, 243
  mood disorders *vs.*, 212–213
  onset, 205–206
Derailment, 73
Derealization, 184
Descriptive validity, 72
Desensitization, 24
Designer drugs, 378, 386–387
Development. *See also* Life-span
    development
  abnormal *vs.* normal, 482
  agoraphobia, 128–129, 134
  anti-psychotic drugs, 467–469
  eating disorders, 291
  hypothesis, 92–93
  intelligence testing, 80
  MMPI, 78–80
  operant conditioning, 24–25
  personality disorders, 411–412
  positive strategies for, 106
  psychopathy, 424
  psychosexual stages, 19
  schizophrenia, 457
  sexual orientation, 330–331
Developmental disorders
  ADHD, 483–488
  autism spectrum disorder, 492–497
  case study of, 483–484
  exploration of, 524–525
  intellectual disability, 498–504
  learning, 488–492
  overview of, 481–483
  prevention of, 504–505
  specific learning disorder, 488–492
  summary, 521–522

Developmental psychology, 7
Developmental psychopathology, 7
Dhat, 179
Diagnosis, 70. *See also specific disorder*
  categorical approach, 85–86
  classification issues, 85
  dimensional approach, 85–86
  labeling and, 90
  pre-1980 system, 87
  prototypical approach, 86
  reliability of, 86–87
  stigma and, 90
  strategies, 84–85
  summary, 113
  validity of, 87
Diagnostic and Statistical Manual (DSM-I),
    87
*Diagnostic and Statistical Manual
    (DSM-II),* 87
*Diagnostic and Statistical Manual (DSM-III/
    III-R),* 87–88
*Diagnostic and Statistical Manual (DSM-IV/
    IV-TR),* 88, 123, 284
Diagnostic and Statistical Manual (DSM-5),
    5, 70, 88–90, 113, 173, 531
  assessment criteria, 70–71
  case study, 88–89
  classification changes in, 194
  criticism of, 89–90
  cultural factors, 88–89
  Cultural Formulation Interview, 89
  cultural/social considerations in, 89
  defense mechanisms, 18–19
  multiaxial format in, 88
  sadism criteria, 347–348
Dialectical behavior therapy (DBT), 429
Diastolic blood pressure, 260
Diathesis, 38
Diathesis–stress model
  defined, 38
  for gene–environment
      interaction, 38–39
  landmark study of, 38–39
  processes, 38
DID. *See* Dissociative identity disorder
    (DID)
Diet
  weight gain when dieting, 293–294
  weight loss programs, 304–305
Dimensional approach, 85–86
Dimethyltryptamine (DMT), 385
Diminished capacity, 536, 537
Direct experience, 138–139
Direct instruction, 491
Directionality, 97
Discrimination training, 496
Disinhibited social engagement disorder,
    153
Disorder of arousal, 307, 317
Disorder of thought content, 448
Disorganized speech, 452
Displacement, 18, 19
Disruptive mood dysregulation disorder,
    207, 208–209
  disorder criteria for, 209
Dissociation, 57, 173
Dissociative disorders

amnesia, 185–188
anesthetics, 387
case study, 188
common characteristics among, 199
defined, 173
depersonalization-derealization, 185
DID, 188–195
fugue, 186–187
summary, 196
trance, 188
types of, 185
Dissociative fugue, 186–187
Dissociative identity disorder (DID)
  biological contributions, 192
  case studies, 188, 189
  causes, 191
  characteristics of, 189
  clinical description, 188
  disorder criteria for, 189
  faking of, 189–190
  real memories and false, 192–194
  statistics, 190–191
  suggestibility and, 191–192
  treatment for, 194–195
Dissociative trance disorder, 188
Distress, 4
Disulfiram, 394, 395
Dix, Dorothea, 16, 31
DMT. *See* Dimethyltryptamine (DMT)
DNA, 36, 40, 259, 486, 515
DNA microarrays, 36
Dominant genes, 500
Dopamine, 43
  ADHD and, 486
  characterization of, 50–51
  cocaine and, 378–380
  drug interaction with, 461–463
  function of, 50–51
  pathways, 50–51
  schizophrenia and, 461–463, 467
Dorsal horns of the spinal column, 266
Double bind communication, 465
Double-blind control, 99
Double-blind placebo control, 99
Double depression, 204–205
Down, Langdon, 501
Down syndrome, 104, 498, 501–502
Dracula hormone. *See* Melatonin
Dramatic behavior. *See* Cluster B
personality disorders
Dream analysis, 20
Drug Abuse Resistance Education (DARE),
    398
Drug holidays, 102
*DSM. See specific version of the Diagnostic
    and Statistical Manual*
DST. *See* Dexamethasone suppression
    test (DST)
DTs. *See* Delirium tremens (DTs)
Durham rule, 536
Durham v. United States, 536
Dusky v. United States, 539
Duty to warn, 539–540
Dyslexia, 491
Dyssomnias, 306, 307
Dysthymia. *See* Persistent depressive
    disorder (dysthymia)

E

Eating disorders
  anorexia nervosa. *See* Anorexia nervosa
  BED. *See* Binge-eating disorder (BED)
  biological dimensions, 295–296
  bulimia nervosa, 284–286, 299
  case studies, 295, 299
  causes of, 292–298
  cultural influences on, 291
  developmental considerations, 291
  dieting and, 295
  drug treatments, 298
  exploration of, 324
  family factors in, 295
  integrative model for, 297–298
  obesity and, 284, 293, 302–305
  overview of, 283–284
  prevalence estimates, 290
  prevention of, 301
  psychological dimensions of, 296–297
  psychological treatments for, 298–301
  social dimensions, 292–295
  treatments for, 298–301
  types of, 283–283
Eccentric behavior. *See* Cluster A
      personality disorders
Echolalia, 482, 494
ECT. *See* Electroconvulsive therapy
EEG. *See* Electroencephalogram (EEG)
Effect size, 94
Ego, 18
Ego and the Mechanisms of Defense
      (A. Freud), 30
Egoistic suicides, 237
Ego psychology, 20
Ejaculation
  delayed, 333, 336
  premature, 332, 333, 336, 337
  retrograde, 336
Elavil. *See* Amitriptyline
Elderly
  anxiety among, 130, 214
  depression and, 214
  GAD prevalence among, 126
  mood disorders and, 212–213
  suicide among, 236, 242
Electra complex, 19
Electrocardiogram, 307
Electroconvulsive therapy (ECT), 14, 230,
      247
  as schizophrenia treatment, 467
Electrodermal responding, 83
Electroencephalogram (EEG)
  defined, 82
  patterns, 82–83
  sleep disorders and, 307
Electrolyte imbalance, 286
Electromyogram, 307
Electrooculogram, 307
Emotional behavior. *See* Cluster B
personality disorders
Emotional disorders, 59. *See also* Mood
      disorders
Emotional prosody comprehension, 450
Emotion contagion, 11
Emotions

chronic negative, 263–264
  components, 59–60
  contagion, 11
  defined, 59
  disorders of, 59. *See also* Mood disorders
  fear, 58–59
  function of, 59
  and psychopathology, 61
Empathy, 22
Endocrine system, 46, 217–218
Endogenous opioids, 266
Endophenotypes, 104, 460–461, 486
Endophenotyping, 460
Endorphins. *See* Endogenous opioids
Environment
    ADHD and, 486
    –gene interaction, 38–40
    learning disorders and, 490
    psychopathy and, 424
    sleep disorders and, 315
Epidemiological research
    application of, 97–98
    defined, 97
    goal of, 97
Epidemiology, 97
Epigenetics, 40–41
Epinephrine, 46
Episodic course, 7
Equifinality, principle of, 65
Erectile disorder, 334–335
Erectile dysfunction, 334–335, 341
Ergotism, 385
Erikson, Erik, 20
Erotic films, 340
Erotophobia, 340
ERP. *See* Event-related potential (ERP)
Erratic behavior. *See* Cluster B personality
      disorders
Essential hypertension, 260–261
*Ethical Principles of Psychologists and Code
      of Conduct*, 112
Ethics, 111–112, 114
Etiology, 7–8, 482–483
Event-related potential (ERP), 83
Evidence-based instruction, 316
Evidence-based practice (EBP), 543–544
Evil eye, 61–62
Evoked potential. *See*
      Electroencephalogram (EEG)
Excitatory neurotransmitters, 463
Excitement, 253–254
Excoriation, 164
Exhibitionistic disorder, 346, 347
Exner, John, 77
Exorcism, 9
Expectancy effect, 390
Expected (cued) panic attack, 119
Experiments
    comparative treatment, 99–100
    control groups, 99
    defined, 98
    group designs, 98
    single-case designs, 100–103
Expert witnesses, 540
Explanatory therapy, 178
Explicit memory, 57

Exposure and response prevention, 52, 160
Exposure and ritual prevention, 157
Expressed emotion, 465–466
Expressive language disorder, 490
External validity, 92, 93–94
Extinction, 23
Extrapyramidal symptoms, 468
Eysenck, Hans, 24

F

Face validity, 77
Facial agnosia, 509
Factitious disorders, 174, 181, 182
False memory syndrome, 193
False negatives, 81
False positives, 81
Familial aggregation, 87
Familial factors
    borderline personality disorder
      and, 428–429
    characterization of, 104
    eating disorders, 295
    psychopathy, 425
    schizophrenia and, 458, 465–466
    substance abuse, 387–388
    suicide, 238
FAS. *See* Fetal alcohol syndrome (FAS)
Fatalistic suicides, 237
Fearlessness hypothesis, 423
Fears. *See also* Cluster C personality
      disorders
    cultural aspects of, 61–64
    defined, 118
    emotions of, 58–61
    evolutionary and social influences, 63
    physiology of, 58–59
    prevalence of, 138
    purpose, 58–59
    reaction to, 119–120
Female orgasmic disorder, 336, 337
Female sexual interest/arousal disorder,
      333–334
    disorder criteria for, 335
Fetal alcohol syndrome (FAS), 374, 500
Fetishistic disorder, 346
FFS. *See* Fight/flight system (FFS)
Fight/flight system (FFS), 121
Fixation, 19
Flat affect, 451
Flibanserin, 344
Flight or fight response, 58
Flight of ideas, 203
Fluency disorder in children, 482, 490
Fluoxetine, 227–229, 298
fMRI. *See* Functional magnetic resonance
      imaging (fMRI)
Folie à deux, 454
Food taxes, 305
Forebrain, 44–45
Formal observation, 75
Foster, Jodie, 537
Fox, Michael J., 513
Fragile X syndrome, 501–503
Franklin, Benjamin, 223
Fraternal birth order hypothesis, 331

Free association, 20
Frenzy witchcraft, 187
Freud, Anna, 18, 20
Freud, Sigmund, 13, 16–20, 22, 24, 55, 57, 96, 118, 173, 180, 182–183, 237, 432
  basic observations of, 17
  defense mechanism theory of, 18–19
  free association, 20
  mind structure theory of, 18
  psychosexual theory of, 19
Fright disorders, 61
Frigo phobia, 138
Fromm, Erich, 20
Frontal lobes, 127, 464
Frontotemporal neurocognitive disorders, 513
Frotteuristic disorder, 346, 347
Fugue, dissociative, 186–187
Functional communication training
  defined, 103, 110
  intellectual disabled children, 504
Functional genomics, 388
Functional magnetic resonance imaging (fMRI), 58, 190
Functional neurological symptom disorder, 180–184

G

GABA. *See* Gamma-aminobutyric acid (GABA)
GABA-benzodiazepine system, 120, 132
GAD. *See* Generalized anxiety disorder (GAD)
Galen, 11–12
Galvanic skin response (GSR), 83
Gambling disorder, 371, 398–399
Gamma-aminobutyric acid (GABA), 43
  ADHD and, 486
  alcohol use and, 372–373
  anxiety disorders and, 120
  anxiolytic substance, 376
  benzodiazepines and, 49
  characterization of, 49
  function of, 49
  glutamate and, 49
  hypnotic substances, 376
  sedatives, 376
  stress response and, 256
  substance abuse and, 387
Gamma-hydroxybutyrate (GHB), 387
Gate control theory of pain, 266
GBMI. *See* Guilty but mentally ill (GBMI)
Gender differences
  ADHD, 485
  Alzheimer's disease, 512
  antisocial personality disorder, 412
  BDD, 182
  body sizes, 292
  bulimia nervosa, 62, 289–290
  in casual sex, 329–330
  chronic pain, 267–268
  depression, 62
  exposure therapy for PTSD, 62
  response to, 62
  histrionic personality disorder, 431

homosexuality attitudes of, 329
insomnia disorder, 309
mood disorders, 62, 223–225
OCD, 62
panic attack, 130
personality disorders, 412–413
psychopathology and, 62
schizophrenia, 457
sex reassignment surgery, 358
sexual dysfunction, 333
sexuality, 329–330
somatic symptom disorder, 177
Gender dysphoria, 327, 354
  case studies, 354, 356–357
  causes of, 356
  defined, 327, 354
  defining criteria for, 355
  disorder criteria for, 354–355
  exploration of, 364–365
  treatments for, 358–359
Gender nonconformity, 357, 358–359
Gender roles, 62
Gene–environment correlation model, 39–40, 220
Gene–environment interaction
  adoption studies, 104–105
  Alzheimer's disease, 516
  borderline personality disorder and, 428
  conduct disorder, 423
  diathesis–stress model for, 38–39
  twin studies, 105
Generalizability, 94
Generalized amnesia, 186
Generalized anxiety disorder (GAD)
  cardiac vagal tone and, 126
  case study, 124–125
  causes, 126–127
  clinical description of, 125
  disorder criteria for, 125
  integrative model of, 127
  onset, 126
  statistics, 125–126
  symptoms of, 125
  treatment for, 127–128
Generalized biological vulnerability, 123, 126, 139, 143, 331
Generalized psychological vulnerability
  anxiety, 123, 143
  panic disorders, 133
  PTSD, 150–151
General paresis, 13
Genes, 36. *See also* Chromosomes
  Alzheimer's disease-associated, 516
  behavior, developments, 37
  depression/anxiety link, 217
  diathesis–stress model, 38–39
  effects of, 36
  environment and, 38–40
  expression of, 37
  gene–environment correlation model, 39–40
  independent influences, 40
  nature of, 36–37
  substance abuse, 367–368, 391
Gene therapy, 345, 504
Genetic linkage analysis, 105–106

Genetic markers, 106
Genetics. *See also* Genes
  ADHD, 486
  Alzheimer's disease, 516
  analyses, 105–106
  antisocial personality disorder, 423
  autism spectrum disorder, 495
  borderline personality disorder, 428
  family studies, 104–106
  hypersomnolence disorder, 311–312
  intellectual disability, 500–503
  mood disorders, 216–217
  schizophrenia, 458–461
  schizotypal personality disorder, 419–420
  somatic symptom disorder, 177
  study of, 104–106
  substance abuse, 387–388
  substance-related disorders, 387–388
  twin studies. *See* Twin studies
Genital herpes, 250–251
Genito-pelvic pain/penetration disorder, 337, 338
Genome, 36, 104
Genotypes, 104
GHB. *See* Gamma-hydroxybutyrate (GHB)
Ginkgo biloba, 518
Glia cells, 43
Globus hystericus, 180
Glucocorticoid, 37, 54
Glutamate, 43, 49, 463
  alcohol use and, 372
Graduated extinction, 316
Grandeur, delusions of, 12, 446, 448
Grandiosity, 433
Grave disability, 530, 534
Grey, John P., 12, 13–14, 25
Grief, 206–207, 241
GSR. *See* Galvanic skin response (GSR)
Guided imagery relaxation, 316
Guilty but mentally ill (GBMI), 538
Gynecomastia, 358

H

HAART. *See* Highly active antiretroviral therapy (HAART)
Hair pulling disorder, 164
Hallucinations
  characterization of, 449
  defined, 73, 449
  SPECT imaging of, 450
  treatments for, 467
  types of, 449–450
Hallucinogen use disorder, 385–386
Hallucinogens, 371, 385–386
Halstead-Reitan Neuropsychological Battery, 81
Hara-kiri, 237
Harper hearing, 542
Haslam, John, 445–446
Head trauma, 512, 516–517
Health promotion, 106
Health psychology
  AIDS, 257–258
  behavior types, 262–263
  biofeedback, 271

Health psychology (continued)
 cancer, 258–260
 CFS and, 268–270
 CHD, 262–263
 chronic pain, 264–270
 defined, 250
 exploration of, 280–281
 importance of, 250
 meditation, 272
 overview of, 249–250
 relaxation, 272
 summary, 277
Health-related behavior. See also Stress
 AIDS example, 251
 focus on, 250–251
Heart attack, 262
Heart disease, 60
Hebephrenia, 446
Helper T cells, 255
"Herbal incense," 384
Hermaphroditism, 355
Heterosexual behavior, 328
Hierarchy of needs, 22
Highly active antiretroviral therapy
  (HAART), 257–258
Hinckley, John W., Jr., 537–538
Hindbrain, 44
Hippocampus
 defined, 45
 mood disorders and, 218
 stress and, 218, 252
Hippocrates, 11–13
Hippocratic Corpus, 11
Histrionic personality disorder
 case study, 430–431
 causes, 431
 clinical description of, 431
 disorder criteria for, 432
 gender differences, 431
 treatment for, 431–432
HIV/AIDS
 behavioral patterns and, 251
 characterization of, 251
 death rates from, 257
 epidemiological studies of, 111
 immune system and, 256
 marijuana and, 384
 neurocognitive disorder due to, 514–515
 disorder criteria for, 564
 prevention, 275
 psychosocial factors, 257–258
Hoarding disorder, 161–163
Homelessness, 532–533
Homosexual behavior, 328
Hormones, 46. See also specific hormone
Horney, Karen, 20
HPA. See Hypothalamic–pituitary–
  adrenocortical (HPA) axis
5-HTT gene, 38
Human genome project, 104
Human immunodeficiency virus. See HIV/
  AIDS
Humanistic psychology, 22
Humanistic theory, 22
Human Sexual Inadequacy (Masters and
  Johnson), 342

Humoral theory of disorders, 12
Huntington's disease, 36, 512
 neurocognitive disorder due to, 514
5-hydroxytryptamine (5HT), 49
Hyperfrontality, 464
Hypersomnolence disorder, 311–312
Hypertension, 260–262
 characterization of, 260–262
 essential, 260
 minorities and, 260–261
 neurobiological causes, 261–262
 physiological measures for treating, 83
 prevalence of, 260–261
 psychological factors, 249, 261–262
Hypnagogic hallucinations, 312
Hypnosis, 17
Hypnotic drugs, 318, 376
Hypnotic trance, 192
Hypochondriasis. See Illness anxiety
  disorder
Hypofrontality, 464, 465
Hypomanic episode, 203
Hypothalamic–pituitary–adrenocortical
  (HPA) axis, 47
 anxiety disorders and, 120
 mood disorders and, 217
 PTSD and, 150
 stress and, 252
Hypothalamus, 45, 313
Hypothesis
 defined, 92
 development of, 92–93. See also specific
  hypotheses
Hypoventilation, 312, 313
Hypoxiphilia, 348
Hysteria, 12, 13, 173

I
ICD-10. See International Classification of
  Diseases (ICD-10)
Id, 18
Ideas of reference, 73, 159, 417, 418
Idiographic strategy, 84
Illness anxiety disorder, 173, 175
 case study, 175–176
 causes of, 176–178
 clinical description, 176
 disorder criteria for, 176
 statistics, 176
 treatment for, 178–179
Imaginal exposure, 151
Imipramine (Tofranil), 134, 488
Immune system
 AIDS. See HIV/AIDS
 defined, 254
 function of, 255–256
 stress and, 254–255
Immunoglobulins, 255
Impairment, concept of, 4
Implicit memory, 57
Impulse-control disorders
 characterization of, 400
 defined, 367
 exploration of, 407
 gambling disorder, 398–399

intermittent explosive, 400
 kleptomania, 400
 pyromania, 400
 trichotillomania, 164
Impulsivity
 ADHD, 484, 486
 biological factors, 486
 suicide and, 239
Inappropriate affect, 452
Inattention, 484–485
Incest, 348–349
Incidence, defined, 7, 97
Independent Living Skills Program, 470
Independent variable, 92, 93, 98–99
Indicated prevention, 107
Inferiority complex, 20
Informal observation, 75
Information transmission, 139
Informed consent, 111–112, 542
Inhalant use disorder, 386
Inheritance, nongenomic, 40–41
Inhibitory neurotransmitters, 43
Injury prevention, 274–275
Inpatient facilities, 395–396
Insanity defense. See Not guilty by reason
  of insanity (NGRI)
Insanity Defense Reform Act, 538
Insidious onset, 7
Insight, 17
Insomnia
 environmental treatments, 315
 medical treatments, 315
 preventing, 317
 psychological treatments, 316
 rebound, 310
Insomnia disorder
 case study, 308
 causes of, 309–310
 clinical description, 308
 integrative model of, 310
 statistics, 308–309
Institutionalization policies, 469
Institutional review board (IRB), 111–112
Insulin shock therapy, 14
Integrated grief, 206
Integrative model
antisocial personality disorder, 425
 anxiety disorders, 122–123
 borderline personality disorder, 429–430
 brain function studies, 53–54
 case study, 34–35
 characterization of, 25
 eating disorders, 297–298
 generalized anxiety disorder, 128
 hypochondriasis, 177
 insomnia disorder, 310, 311
 mood disorders, 225–226
 multidimensional, 34–35
 panic disorders, 134–135
 schizophrenia treatment, 471–472
 substance abuse, 391–393
 suicidal behavior, 240
Intellectual disability
 biological dimensions, 500–503
 case study, 498
 causes of, 500–503

chromosomal influences, 501–503
clinical description, 499–500
communication skills and, 499
defined, 498
degrees of, 500
de novo disorders and, 501
disorder criteria for, 499
Down syndrome, 501–502
fragile X syndrome, 502–503
genetic influences, 500–501
Lesch-Nyhan syndrome, 501
psychosocial dimensions, 503
social dimensions, 503
statistics, 500
treatments for, 503–504
Intellectual functioning, 73
Intelligence quotient (IQ)
antisocial personality disorder and, 421
calculation of, 80
intellectual disability, 499
specific learning disorders and, 488
Intelligence testing, 80–81
Intermittent explosive disorder, 400
Internal validity, 92, 93–94
International Classification of Diseases (ICD-10), 88
International Classification of Diseases and Related Health Problems (ICD), 87
Interoceptive avoidance, 130
Interpersonal and social rhythm therapy (IPSRT), 234
Interpersonal psychotherapy (IPT), 225
bulimia nervosa, 299
defined, 232
depression, 232
mood disorders, 232
Interpersonal theory of suicide, 239
Interrater reliability, 72, 77
Intersexuality, 355, 359
Intervention guidelines, 544
Interviews
clinical assessment, 72–74
function of, 72–74
mental status exam, 72–74
mood disorder, 286
motivational, 352
semistructured clinical, 74
sexual behavior, 338
Intoxication
alcohol, 371–375, 386
amphetamine, 377–378
anxiolytic drugs, 376
cannabis, 383–384
characterization of, 368–369
disorder criteria for, 370–371
hypnotic drugs, 371
opioid, 382
sedative, 371
substance, 368–369
Intrapsychic conflicts, 18, 21
Introspection, 23
Inverse agonists, 48
IPSRT. *See* Interpersonal and social rhythm therapy (IPSRT)
IPT. *See* Interpersonal psychotherapy (IPT)

IQ. *See* Intelligence quotient (IQ)
IRB. *See* Institutional review board (IRB)
Irregular sleep–wake type, 314
Ischemia, 262
Isolated sleep paralysis, 132

J

Jackson v. Indiana, 539
Jet lag sleep disorder, 220, 310, 314
Jones, Mary Cover, 23
Jung, Carl, 20, 22

K

K2, 384
Kaczynski, Ted, 537
Ketamine, 387, 463
Killer T cells, 255
Kleptomania, 400
Kohut, Heinz, 20, 433
Koro, 63, 179
Kraepelin, Emil, 14, 87, 446
Kyol goeu, 179

L

Labeling, 90, 305
La belle indifférence, 183
Lady Gaga, 4, 5
Language disorder, 482, 490
Law of effect, 24
Learned alarms, 132
Learned helplessness, 55–56, 221
Learned optimism, 55
Learning disorders
causes of, 490–491
clinical description of, 489
disorder criteria for, 490
statistics, 489–490
treatments for, 491
Lesch-Nyhan syndrome, 501, 502
Leukocytes, 255
Levitra, 344, 345
Lewy body disease, neurocognitive disorder due to, 512, 513
Libido, 18
Life-span development, 7
focus of, 64–65
mood disorder and, 213–214
principles of, 64–65
Life-span developmental psychopathology, 7
Light therapy, 247
Limbic system, 45, 120–122, 252
Linkage studies, 37, 106, 460–461
Lithium, 229
Lithium carbonate, 229
LL. *See* Long allele (LL)
LLPDD. *See* Late luteal phase dysphoric disorder (LLPDD)
Localized amnesia, 186
Long allele (LL), 38, 39
Longitudinal designs, 107–108
Loose association, 73
LSD (*d*-lysergic acid diethylamide), 385
Lunatic, 11

Luria-Nebraska Neuropsychological Battery, 81
Lymphocytes, 255, 256
Lysergic acid amide, 385

M

Macrophages, 255
Magical thinking, 418, 457
Magnetic resonance imaging (MRI), 81, 463–464
Maintenance treatment, 233
Major depressive disorders, 204
recurrent, 233
genetic factors, 217
Major depressive episodes, 204
defined, 202
disorder criteria for, 86, 203
duration of, 203
length of, 204, 211
Major neurocognitive disorder. *See also* Neurocognitive disorder
alcohol abuse and, 373
biological treatments, 518
causes of, 515–517
characteristics of, 514
classes of, 510
clinical description of, 509–510
defined, 508
disorder criteria for, 508
exploration of, 527
prevention of, 520
psychosocial factors, 516–517
psychosocial treatments, 518–520
statistics, 509–510
subcortical, 514
substance induced, 515
treatments for, 517–520
Male hypoactive sexual desire disorder, 333
Malingerers, 181, 190, 540
Malingering, 180, 540
Mania
biological dimensions, 216–219
circadian rhythms and, 218–219
cultural differences, 215
cultural dimensions, 223–225
defined, 203
duration of, 205–206
ECT for, 230
emotion and, 61
experience of, 246
familial influences, 216–217
genetic factors, 216–217
integrative theory of, 225–226
learned helplessness and, 221
life-span developmental influences, 213–214
medications for, 227–230
negative cognitive styles and, 222–223
neurotransmitter systems, 217
onset of, 211
overview of, 202–203
prevalence of, 212–215
prevention of, 232–233
psychological dimensions, 219–223
severe, 213

Mania *(continued)*
  sleep and, 218–219
  social support for, 223–225
  structure of, 203–204
  summary, 243
  TMS for, 230
  treatments for, 247
  understanding, 201–202
  vagus nerve stimulation for, 230
Manic depressive psychosis, 87
Manic episodes, 203–204
Manipulating a variable, 98
Mann, Horace, 16
Manson, Charles, 537
Mantra, 272
MAO inhibitors, 227, 228
Marijuana
  disorders related to, 383–384
  medical, 384
  reactions to, 383–384
  sexual pleasure and, 340
  synthetic, 384
  use of, 383–384
Marker genes, 460
Marriage and family therapists, 6
Maslow, Abraham, 22
Masochism, 347–348
Mass hysteria, 10–11
Masturbation, 329, 330, 335, 336, 350
Mathematics disorders, 490
Mature stage, 20
MBCT. *See* Mindfulness-based cognitive
    therapy (MBCT)
MDMA. *See*
    Methylenedioxymethamphetamine
    (MDMA)
Medical condition, psychological factors
    affecting, 179–180
Medication-induced psychotic disorder, 455
Medina v. California, 539
Meditation, 272
Medroxyprogesterone, 353
Medulla, 44
Melancholic features/symptoms, 216, 219
Melancholic personality, 12
Melancholy, 9–10, 12. *See also* Depression
Melatonin, 314
Memory
  dissociative fugue and, 186
  explicit, 57
  false, 192–194
  PTSD and, 151–152
Memory B cells, 255
Memory T cells, 255
Mens rea, 537
Mental health counselors, 6
Mental health law
  civil commitment, 529–535
  clinical practice, 543–544
  clinical practice guidelines, 543–544
  criminal commitment, 535–540
  overview, 529–530
  patients' rights, 541–544
  research, 111–112
  summary, 545
Mental hygiene movement, 16

Mental illness
  criminal commitment, 535–540
  criminalization of, 532, 535–540
  defined, 531
Mental retardation. *See* Intellectual
    disability
Mental status exam, 72–74
  categories of, 72–73
  components of, 74
  confidentiality in, 74
  defined, 72
  interpretation of, 73
Mescaline, 385
Mesmer, Anton, 16–17
Meta-cognitions, 128
Methadone, 394
Methylene-dioxymethamphetamine
    (MDMA), 378
  hypothesis-testing of, 93
  3,4-methylenedioxypyrovalerone
    (MDPV), 387
Methylphenidate, 315, 390, 487, 488
Microsleeps, 308
Midbrain, 45
Mild neurocognitive disorder. *See also*
    Neurocognitive disorder
  biological treatments, 518
  causes of, 515–517
  characteristics of, 514
  classes of, 510
  clinical description of, 509–510
  defined, 508
  disorder criteria for, 508
  exploration of, 524
  prevention of, 520
  psychosocial factors, 516–517
  psychosocial treatments, 518–520
  statistics, 509–510
  subcortical, 514
  substance induced, 515
  treatments for, 517–520
Mind, structure of, 18
Mindfulness-based cognitive therapy
    (MBCT), 231
Minnesota Multiphasic Personality
    Inventory (MMPI)
  development of, 78
  malingering detection by, 540
  profile form, 79
  research on, 80
  scales of, 78
Mixed features specifier, 204
Mixed reuptake inhibitors, 227, 228
Mixed sleep apneas, 313
MMPI. *See* Minnesota Multiphasic
    Personality Inventory (MMPI)
M'Naghten rule, 536–537
Mob psychology, 11
Modafinil, 315
Modeling, 56
Molecular genetics, 36
Mongoloidism. *See* Down syndrome
Monoamine oxidase (MAO) inhibitors, 227
Monoamines, 48
Mood, 59
  mental status exam and, 73

Mood disorders, 59. *See also* Bipolar
    disorder; Depression
  biological dimensions, 216–219
  case study, 201–202
  causes of, 215–226
  defining, 201–202
  depression and, 202–203
  integrative model of, 225–226
  mania and, 202–203
  prevalence of, 212–215
  prevention, 233–234
  psychological dimensions, 219–223
  sociocultural dimensions, 223–225
  structure of, 203–204
  treatment of, 227–235
Mood-stabilizing drug, 229
Moral principles, 18
Moral therapy, 15–16
Morel, Benedict, 445
Motivational Enhancement Therapy
    (MET), 397
Motivational interviewing, 352
MRI. *See* Magnetic resonance imaging
    (MRI)
MSG. *See* Monosodium glutamate (MSG)
Multiaxial format, 88
Multidimensional integrative approach, 33
Multiple baselines, 102–103
Multiple personality disorder. *See*
    Dissociative identity disorder (DID)
Munchausen syndrome by proxy, 181
Muscle relaxation techniques, 271, 272
Mutism, selective, 145–146
Myocardial infarction, 160, 262
Myocardial stunning, 262
Myocardium, 262

N
Naltrexone, 388, 395, 400
Narcissistic personality disorders
  case study, 432
  causes of, 433
  clinical description of, 433
  disorder criteria for, 433
  treatments for, 433
Narcolepsy, 312
National Health Service, 543
National Institute of Mental Health
    (NIMH), 26, 91, 134, 459
Natural environment phobia, 137
Naturalistic teaching strategies, 496
Natural opioids, 266
Negative cognitive styles, 221, 222–223
Negative correlation, 97
Negative reinforcement, 388, 389–390
Nervous system
  central. *See* Central nervous system
  divisions of, 41
  neurotransmitters and, 252
  peripheral. *See* Peripheral nervous
      system
Neurobiological factors. *See also* Brain
    functioning; Brain structure
  antisocial personality disorder, 423–424
  anxiety, 122

autism spectrum disorder, 495–496
hypertension, 261
panic, 122
schizophrenia, 461–464
sexual dysfunctions, 340
substance abuse, 388–389
Neurocognitive disorders. *See also specific disorder*
Alzheimer's disease, 511–512
causes of, 515–520
classes of, 510
delirium, 505–507
due to traumatic brain injury, 513
exploration of, 578
HIV/AIDS-related, 514
Huntington's disease-related, 514
major, 508–520
medical condition-associated, 512–515
mild, 508–520, 522
Parkinson's disease, 513–514
Pick's disease, 513
overview of, 505
prion disease-related, 514–515
substance/medication-induced, 515
summary, 522
vascular, 512
Neurodevelopmental disorders, 481–483
Neurofibrillary tangles, 515, 516
Neurohormones, 217
Neuroimaging
brain functioning, 82
brain structure, 81–82
defined, 81
Neuroleptics, 14, 462, 467
Neurons, 42–43
transmission of information, 48
Neuroplasticity, 393
Neuropsychological testing, 81
Neuroscience, 41
Neuroses, 19
Neurosis, 20, 87, 173
Neurosurgery, 52, 153, 158
Neurotransmitters, 47–51. *See also specific biochemicals*
abnormal activity of, 48
defined, 43
discovery of, 49
excitatory, 43
inhibitory, 43
mood disorders and, 217
paths of, 48
release of, 48
types of, 48–51
NGRI. *See* Not guilty by reason of insanity (NGRI)
Nicotine
characterization of, 380
negative effects of, 380
withdrawal, 380
Nicotine patch, 395
Nicotine use disorder, 380–. *See also* Cigarette smoking
Night eating syndrome, 303
Nightmare disorders, 317–318
NIMH. *See* National Institute of

Mental Health (NIMH) NMDA. *See* N-methyl-d-aspartate (NMDA)
N-methyl-d-aspartate (NMDA), 463
Nocturnal eating syndrome, 319
Nocturnal panic, 131–132
Nomenclature, 84
Nomothetic strategy, 84
Non-demand pleasuring, 342–343
Non-24-hour sleep–wake type, 314
Nonrapid eye movement (NREM), 312
Noradrenaline. *See* Norepinephrine
Norepinephrine, 43, 50
Norepinephrine pathways, 50
Normal behavior
in childhood, 481
sexuality, 327–331
social standard of, 5
Nosology, 84
Not culturally expected behavior, 4–5
Not guilty by reason of insanity (NGRI)
factors in, 538
vs. guilty but mentally ill, 538
history of, 537–538
public reactions to, 539
reform efforts, 538
NREM. *See* Nonrapid eye movement (NREM)

O

Obesity
causes of, 304
defined, 284, 285
eating disorders and, 284
eating patterns and, 303–304
onset of, 293
statistics, 302–303
treatments for, 304–305
Object relations, 20
Observational assessment, 75
Observational learning, 56
Observations on Madness and Melancholy (Haslam), 445
Obsessions, 154–155
Obsessive-compulsive disorder (OCD), 73
anorexia nervosa-associated, 288
BDD and, 159, 160
brain functioning, 54–55
case study, 154
causes, 156–157
clinical description, 154–155
defined, 153
disorder criteria for, 154
hoarding and, 161–162
statistics, 155–156
tic disorder and, 155
treatment for, 157–158
types of, 154–155
Obsessive-compulsive personality disorder
case study, 436
causes of, 437
clinical description of, 436–437
disorder criteria for, 437
pedophiles and, 437
serial killers and, 436–437
treatment for, 437

Obstructive sleep apnea hypopnea syndrome, 313
Occipital lobe, 45
OCD. *See* Obsessive-compulsive disorder (OCD)
O'Connor v. Donaldson, 532, 534
Odd behavior. *See* Cluster A personality disorders
Oedipus complex, 19
Oedipus Rex, 19
Olanzapine, 462
Oncology, 258
Operant conditioning, 24–25
Operant control of pain, 265, 266
Operational definition, 76
Opiates, 371
Opioid-related disorders
characterization of, 382–383
marijuana, 382
withdrawal from, 382
Opioids, 382
endogenous, 266
Opioid use disorder, 382, 383
Opponent-process theory, 389
Oppositional defiant disorder (ODD), 485
Orbital front cortex, , 52
Oresme, Nicholas, 9
Orgasm disorders, 335–337
Orgasmic reconditioning, 352
Overgeneralization, 222

P

Pain. *See also* Acute pain; Chronic pain
medication, 274
reduction program, 272–273
sexual, 337–338
Pain behaviors, 265
Pa-leng, 138
Panic
anxiety disorders and, 53, 61, 128
defined, 119
neurobiology of, 122
nocturnal, 131–132
psychological aspects, 122
stress and, 122
Panic attacks
case study, 119
causes of, 120–123
defined, 119
disorder criteria for, 119
expected, 119
gender differences, 130
prevalence of, 130
types, 119
unexpected, 119
Panic control treatment (PCT), 134
Panic disorders. *See also* Anxiety disorders
case study, 129
causes of, 132
in childhood, 7
clinical description of, 129–130
cultural factors, 131
disorder criteria for, 131
evolution of, 142–143
psychological intervention for, 133–134

Panic disorders *(continued)*
   statistics, 130–131
   treatments for, 132–135
Papaverine, 344
Paracelsus, 11
Paradoxical intention, 316
Paranoia
   cocaine-induced, 378
   defined, 446
   virtual reality treatment for, 470
Paranoid personality disorder
   case study, 415–416
   causes of, 416
   clinical description of, 415
   disorder criteria for, 415
   treatments for, 416
Paraphilia
   exploration of, 364
   paraphilic disorder *vs.*, 359
Paraphilic disorders
   assessment of, 351–353
   case studies, 346–347, 349, 350
   causes of, 349–351
   clinical description of, 345–351
   comorbidity and, 345
   defined, 345
   drug treatments for, 353
   exhibitionistic disorder, 346
   fetishistic disorder, 346
   gender differences, 349
   incest, 348–349
   masochism, 347–348
   paraphilia *vs.*, 359
   pedophilic disorder, 348–349
   sadism, 347–348
   transvestic disorder, 346–347
   treatment of, 351–353
   voyeuristic disorder, 346
Parasomnias
   characterization of, 306, 317–319
   types of, 317–318
Parasympathetic nervous system, 46, 47
Parens patriae, 530, 533, 534
Parietal lobe, 45
Parkinson's disease, 51
   Biological treatment, 518
   neurocognitive disorder due to, 513–514
Paroxetine, 127, 135, 179
Passive-aggressive personality disorder, 414
Patient Protection and Affordable Care
   Act, 543
Patients' rights, 541–544
Patient uniformity myth, 95
Pavlov, Ivan, 16, 22–23
Paxil. *See* Paroxetine
PCP. *See* Phencyclidine (PCP)
PCT. *See* Panic control treatment (PCT)
Pedophilic disorder, 348–349
Penetration disorder, 337, 338
Penile prostheses, 344
Penile strain gauge, 338
Penis envy, 19
Performance scales, 80
Periodic limb movement disorder, 309
Peripheral nervous system (PNS), 41, 45–47
Persecution, delusions of, 448

Persecutory type of delusions, 454
Persistent depressive disorder (dysthymia)
   characterization of, 204
   DSM IV, 204, 206
   duration of, 212
   subtypes of, 212
Personality disorders. *See also specific*
      disorder
   aspects of, 409
   beliefs about, 414
   categorical models, 409–410
   cluster A, 415–419
   cluster B, 420–433
   cluster C, 434–437
   clusters, 410
   comorbidity, 413–414
   development of, 411–412
   diagnostic overlap of, 414
   dimensional models, 409–410
   DSM-5, 409, 434
   exploration of, 442–443
   gender differences, 412–413
   new studies on, 414
   overview of, 409–414
   statistics, 410–412
   summary, 438–439
Personality inventories, 77–80
   neuropsychological testing, 81
   popularity of, 78
   types of, 77–80
Person-centered therapy, 22
Pervasive developmental disorders, 492
PET. *See* Positron emission tomography
      (PET) scan
Phantom limb pain, 265
Phase advances, 315
Phase delays, 315
Phencyclidine (PCP), 385, 463
Phenotypes, 104, 418
Phenylalanine, 501
Phenylketonuria (PKU), 501
Phii pob, 188
Phlegmatic personality, 12
Phobias. *See also specific types of phobias*
   blood–injection–injury, 3
   case study, 3–4
   causes of, 34–35
   cultural aspects of, 61–62
   defined, 3
   social, 141–146
   specific, 135–141
   symptoms, 18–19
Phony pills. *See* Placebos
Phototherapy, 315
Physical disorders. *See also specific diseases*
   ancient treatments for, 12
   behavior modification for, 274–276
   characterization of, 249
   deaths associated with, 250
   delirium in, 505
   injury prevention, 274–275
   psychosocial effects of, 257–270
   psychosocial treatments for, 270–276
   sexual dysfunction and, 339–340
Stanford three community study, 276
Physical examinations, 74–75

Pick's disease, 513
Pinel, Philippe, 15, 17, 446
Pivloktoq, 187
PKU. *See* Phenylketonuria (PKU)
Placebo control groups, 99
Placebo effect, 99
   on brain function, 53
Plastic surgery, 161
Pleasure center, 388
Pleasure principle, 18
PMDD. *See* Premenstrual dysphoric
      disorder (PMDD)
PNI. *See* Psychoneuroimmunology (PNI)
PNS. *See* Peripheral nervous system (PNS)
Poddar, Prosenjit, 539
Polygenic effect, 36
Polysomnographic (PSG) evaluation, 306
Pons, 67
Positive correlation, 96
Positive development strategies, 106
Positive psychology, 56
Positive reinforcement, 389
Positron emission tomography (PET)
      scan, 82
Possession, 10
Postpartum onset specifier, 220
Posttraumatic stress disorder (PTSD)
   case study, 147
   causes of, 149–151
   clinical description, 146–148
   DBT for, 429
   disorder criteria for, 148
   DID and, 191
   statistics, 148–149
   stress diathesis model and, 149
   symptoms, 147
   treatments for, 151–152
Pragmatic communication disorder, 492
Predictive validity, 72, 87
Prefrontal cortex, 45
Prefrontal lobotomies, 467
Premature ejaculation, 336–337
Premenstrual dysphoric disorder (PMDD),
      207–208
   disorder criteria for, 208
Premenstrual symptoms (PMS), 207
Prepared learning, 57
Presenilin 1 and 2, 516
Presenting problem, 6
Prevalence, defined, 7, 97
Prevention
   antisocial personality disorder, 426
   delirium, 507
   depression relapse, 233–234
   eating disorders, 301
   exposure and response, 52
   exposure and ritual, 157
   HIV/AIDS, 275
   indicated, 107
   injury, 274–275
   mood disorders, 232–233
   neurocognitive disorder, 520
   neurodevelopmental disorders, 504–505
   relapse, 252, 397
   research, 106–108
   schizophrenia, 472

selective, 107
sleep disorders, 317
substance-related disorders, 397–398
universal strategies, 107
Primary care settings, 176
Primary insomnia, 308
Primary process, 18
Prion disease, neurocognitive disorder due to, 514–515
Privileged communication, 73
Proband, 104, 216
Problem-solving courts, 539
Process research, 100
Prognosis, 7, 84
Progressive muscle relaxation, 272
Progressive relaxation, 316
Projection, 19
Projective testing, 76–77
Prostaglandin, 344
Protection and Advocacy for Mentally Ill Individuals Act, 541
Prototypical approach, 86
Prozac. See Fluoxetine
Psilocybin, 385–386
Psyche, defined, 8
Psychiatric nurses, 6
Psychiatric social workers
   duty to warn, 540
   education of, 6
   as expert witnesses, 540
Psychiatrists,6
Psychiatry: A Textbook for Students and Physicians (Kraepelin), 87
Psychoactive substances, 368
Psychoanalysis, 16
Psychoanalyst, 21
   duty to warn, 540
   as expert witnesses, 540
Psychoanalytic model, 17
Psychoanalytic psychotherapy, 20–21
Psychoanalytic theory, 16–22
   characterization of, 18
   defense mechanisms, 18–19
   mind structures, 18
   pioneers in, 16–17
   post-Freudian, 19–20
   practitioners, 21
   psychodynamic psychotherapy, 20–21
   psychosexual stages, 19–
Psychodynamic psychotherapy, 21
Psychological autopsy, 238
Psychological disorders
   case study, 3–4
   categorization of, 4–6
   defined, 3, 4
Psychological dysfunction, 4
Psychological factors affecting medical condition, 179–180
Psychological harm, 112
Psychological model, 8
Psychological testing
   Intelligence testing, 80–81
   personality inventories, 77–80
   projective, 76–77
   purpose of, 76

types of, 76
Psychological tradition
   anxiety disorders and, 122
   asylum reform, 16
   behavioral model, 22–25
   bipolar disorder, 234–235
   eating disorders, 296–297, 298–301
   historical origins of, 15
   humanistic theory, 22
   mood disorders, 230–233
   moral therapy, 15–16
   panic disorders and, 133–134
   psychoanalytic theory, 16–17
   schizophrenia, 464–466
   sexual dysfunction, 340
   sleep disorders, 316
   substance abuse, 389–390
Psychologists, 6
Psychomotor retardation, 72
Psychoncology, 258
Psychoneuroendocrinology, 46
Psychoneuroimmunology (PNI), 256
Psychopathology
   biological tradition, 11–14
   brain structure and, 44–45
   clinical description of, 6–7
   CNS and, 41–43
   cognitive processes and, 55
   conditioning and, 55
   cultural factors, 61–62
   defined, 6
   developmental, 7
   emotions and, 58–61
   etiology, 7–8
   events time line, 30–31
   genetic factors, 36–41
   global incidence of, 64
   integrative approach, 25
   life-span development and, 7, 64–65
   neurotransmitters and, 47–48
   one-dimensional vs. multidimensional models, 34–35
   PNS and, 45–47
   practitioners, 6
   psychological tradition, 15–25
   social effects and, 62–64
   summary, 26
   supernatural tradition, 9–11
Psychopathy, 421
Psychopharmacogenetics, 488
Psychophysiological assessment, 82–83, 338
Psychophysiological disorders, 249
Psychophysiology, 82
Psychosexual stages, 19
Psychosis, 13
Psychosocial factors
   antisocial personality disorder, 424
   attention deficit/hyperactivity disorder, 487CHD and, 263–264
   autism spectrum disorder, 496–497
   brain function/structure, 52–54
   cancer, 258–260
   coronary heart disease, 262
   HIV/AIDS, 257–258

intellectual disability, 503–504
neurocognitive disorder, 517, 516–517
neurotransmitter systems, 53–54
physical disorders, 257–270
psychopathy, 424
schizophrenia, 469–471
Psychosocial treatments
   for ASD, 496–497
   defined, 15
   for neurocognitive disorder, 518–520
   of physical disorders, 270–276
   of schizophrenia, 469–471
   sexual dysfunction, 342–344
   substance abuse, 395–397
Psychosomatic medicine, 249
Psychosurgery, 52, 153, 158, 467
Psychotherapy by Reciprocal Inhibition (Wolpe), 96
Psychotic behavior, 447
Psychotic disorder associated with medical condition, 455
Psychotic features specifiers, 220
PTSD. See Posttraumatic stress disorder (PTSD)
Purging techniques, 285
Pyromania, 400

Q
Quantitative genetics, 36

R
Rachman, Stanley, 24
Randomization, 94
Randomized clinical trial, 110
Rape
   date, 375
   PTSD and, 149
   sadistic, 348
   sexual arousal in, 348
   social factors, 340, 353
Rapid-cycling specifier, 230, 234
Rapid eye movement (REM) sleep, 218
   defined, 306
   mood disorders and, 218
   narcolepsy and, 312
   panic disorders and, 131
Rationalization, 19
Rauwolfia serpentine (reserpine), 14
Rave, 10
Rayner, Rosalie, 23
Reaction formation, 19
Reactive attachment disorder, 153
Reactivity, 76
Reading disorders, 490, 491
Reagan, Ronald, 537, 542
Reality principle, 18
Rebound insomnia, 310
Receptors, 42
Recessive genes, 36, 500, 501
Reciprocal gene–environment model, 39
Reinforcement, 24
Relapse prevention, 233–234, 352, 397
Relaxation response, 272
Relaxation techniques, 272

Reliability, 72, 86–87
REM sleep. *See* Rapid eyemovement
    (REM) sleep
Repeated measurements
    defined, 100
    process of, 100–101
    trends and, 100–101
    variability and, 100–101
Replication, 110
Repression, 19
Research. *See also specific disorders*
    basic concepts, 92–94
    behavior across cultures, 108–109
    behavior over time, 106–108
    correlation, 96–98
    design, 92
    epidemiological, 97–98
    ethics and, 111–112
    experimental, 98–100
    government regulation of, 542
    individual cases, 95–96
    participants' rights in, 112, 542
    power of, 109–110
    in psychopathology, 92–95
    replication in, 110
    statistical vs. clinical significance, 94–95
    study components, 92–94
    summary, 113
Reserve capacity model, 264
Response to intervention, 489
Reticular activating system, 45
Retrograde ejaculation, 336
Retrospective information, 107
Rett disorder, 492
Reuptake, 48
Riggins v. Nevada, 542
Ritalin. *See* Methylphenidate
Rogers, Carl, 22
Rorschach inkblot test, 76–77
Ryder, Winona, 400

S

SAD. *See* Seasonal affective disorder (SAD)
Sadism, 347–348
Saint Vitus's Dance, 10
Sakel, Manfred, 14
Salpêtrière Hospital, 17
Same-sex arousal patterns, 355
Sanguine, 12
Scheduled awakenings, 318
Schedules of reinforcement, 24
Schizoaffective disorder, 453
Schizoid personality disorder
    case study, 416–417
    causes, 417
    clinical description, 417
    diagnostic criteria for, 417
    treatment, 417
Schizophrenia
    adoption studies, 459–460
    association studies, 460–461
    avoidant personality disorder and,
        434–435
    biological interventions, 467–469

case studies, 446–447
clinical descriptions of, 447–456
development of, 457
diagnostic criteria for, 448
disorganized symptoms, 451–452
dopamine and, 461–463
early symptom identification, 446–448
endophenotypes, 460–461
exploration of, 478
history of, 452–453
institutionalization and, 469
integrative treatment of, 471
linkage studies, 460–461
negative symptoms, 450–451
neurobiological factors, 461–464
paranoid personality disorder and,
    415–416
positive symptoms, 448–450
prenatal influences, 464
prevention of, 472
prodromal stages, treatment during, 472
psychological interventions, 464–467
psychosocial interventions, 469–471
relapse, 465–466
related disorders, 452–455
schizotypal personality disorder and,
    418–419
social skills programs, 470
statistics, 456–457
summary, 473–474
symptoms, 447–456, 479
treatments for, 471–472, 478
twin offspring studies, 460
twin studies, 458–459
virtual reality treatment for, 470
Schizophrenia genes, 418
Schizophrenia spectrum disorders, 448,
    451
Schizophreniform disorder, 453
Schizophrenogenic mother, 465
Schizotypal personality disorder, 448
    case study, 418
    causes, 418–419
    clinical description of, 418
    schizophrenia *vs.*, 448
    treatments for, 419
Scientist-practitioners, 6
Script theory of sexual functioning, 341
SE. *See* Sleep efficiency (SE)
Seasonal affective disorder (SAD), 218
Secondary process, 18
Sedatives, 375–376
Selective amnesia, 186
Selective mutism, 145
Selective prevention, 107
Selective-serotonin reuptake inhibitors
    (SSRIs)
    illness anxiety disorder, 179
    mood disorders, 227
    panic disorders, 133
    social phobia, 144–145
    use of, 50
Self-actualizing, 22
Self-efficacy, 254
Self-monitoring, 76

Self-psychology, 20
Semistructured clinical interviews, 74
Senior Apperception Test (SAT), 77
Sensate focus, 342
Sense of control, 253
Sensorium, 73
Separation anxiety disorder, 140–141
Septum, 45
Sequential design, 108
Serial killers, 436
Serotonin, 38, 43
    characterization of, 49–50
    function of, 49–50
    pathways, 49
    SSRIs. *See* Selective-serotonin reuptake
        inhibitors (SSRIs)
    suicide and, 239
Sex chromosomes, 36
Sex ratio, 7
Sex reassignment surgery, 358
Sexsomnia, 319
Sexual abuse, 192
Sexual arousal disorder
    case study, 334
    prevalence of, 335
    types of, 335
Sexual assault. *See* Rape
Sexual confusion, 347
Sexual desire disorders, 333–334
Sexual dysfunction
    alcohol abuse and, 339–340
    arousal disorder, 334–335
    biological factors, 339–340
    case studies, 334, 336–337
    categories of, 333
    causes of, 339–342
    desire disorders, 333–334
    exploration of, 365
    interviews, 338
    medical examination for, 338
    medical treatments, 344
    orgasm disorders, 335–337
    overview of, 332–338
    psychological factors, 342
    psychophysiological assessment, 338
    psychosocial treatments, 342–344
    sociocultural factors, 340–342
    summary, 345
    treatments for, 342–344
Sexual response cycle, 332–333
Sexual self-schemas, 330
Sexuality
    cultural differences, 330
    gender differences, 329–330
    male practices, 327–328
    normal, 327–329
    summary, 360
Sexually transmitted infections (STI), 485.
        See also HIV/AIDS
Sexual orientation, 330–331
Sexual pain disorder, 337–338
Sexual psychopath laws, 534
Shaping, 25
Shared psychotic disorder, 454
Shift work type sleep disorder, 314

Shinkeishitsu, 142, 179
Short allele (SS), 38
Sildenafil, 344
Single blind group, 99
Single-case designs
concept of, 100
experiments, 98–103
repeated measurements in, 100–101
withdrawal designs, 101–102
Single photon emission computed
tomography (SPECT), 82
Sinoaortic baroreflex arc, 34
Situational phobia, 137
Situation-exposure tasks, 134
Sizemore, Chris Costner, 190
Skinner, B. F., 16, 24–25
Skin picking disorder, 164
Sleep apnea, 309, 311, 313
central, 313
panic disorders and, 132
Sleep attacks, 313
Sleep disorders
breathing-related, 312–131
categories of, 307
environmental treatments for, 315
hypersomnolence disorder, 311–312
insomnia disorder. *See* Insomnia disorder
medical treatments for, 315
mood disorders and, 218–219
narcolepsy, 312
non-rapid eye movement in, 318
overview of, 306–308
parasomnias, 317–319
prevention of, 317
psychological treatments for, 316
rapid eye movement in, 306
summary, 320
Sleep efficiency (SE), 308
Sleep habits, 317
Sleep hygiene, 317
Sleep paralysis, 312
Sleep-related hypoventilation, 313
Sleep terrors, 131, 317
Sleepwalking disorder, 318
SMD. *See* Severe mood disorders (SMD)
Smooth-pursuit eye movement, 460–461
Social anxiety disorder. *See* Social phobia
Social communication disorder,
482–483
Social factors
anxiety disorders, 123
eating disorders, 292–294
mood disorders and, 225
sexual dysfunction, 340–342
specific phobias, 139–140
substance-related disorders, 390–391
Social learning, 56
Social learning model, 22
Social phobias
case studies, 141
causes, 142–144
clinical description of, 141–142
diagnostic criteria for, 142
statistics, 142
treatment for, 144–145

Social relationships, 63–64. *See also*
Psychosocial factors
Social validity, 94
Social workers. *See* Psychiatric social
workers
Somatic delusions, 454
Somatic nervous system, 45
Somatic symptom disorder, 12, 173
case study, 174–175
causes of, 176–178
diagnostic criteria for, 175
history of, 174–175
statistics, 176
treatment for, 178–179
Somatic symptom disorders (previously
somatoform disorders)
BDD, 158–161
common characteristics among, 198
conversion disorder, 180–183
defined, 173
factitious disorder, 181
illness anxiety disorder. *See* Illness
anxiety disorder
mood disorders and, 215
summary, 196
Somnambulism, 318
Soul, defined, 8
Specific learning disorders, 488
case study, 488–489
causes of, 490–491
clinical description, 489
diagnostic criteria for, 490
statistics, 489–490
treatments for, 491
Specific phobias
causes of, 138–140
clinical description, 135–137
diagnostic criteria for, 136
statistics, 137–138
treatments for, 140–141
types of, 136–137
Specific psychological vulnerability, 123
SPECT. *See* Single photon emission computed tomography (SPECT)
Speech, disorganized, 452
"Spice," 384
SS. *See* Short allele (SS)
SSRIs. *See* Selective-serotonin reuptake
inhibitors (SSRIs)
Standardization, 73
Stanford-Binet test, 80
Stanford three community study, 276
Statistical significance, 94–95
Stem cells, 518
STI. *See* Sexually transmitted
infections (STI)
Stimulants, 371
ADHD treatment with, 487
amphetamines, 377–378
caffeine, 381
cocaine, 378–380
opioids, 382–383
tobacco, 380
Stimulus generalization, 22
St. John's wort. *See* Hypericum

Strattera. *See* Atomoxetine
Stress
anxiety and, 253
bipolar disorder and, 220
case study, 272
causes of, 252–253
conversion disorder and, 180
defined, 251
depression and, 219–220, 253–254
excitement and, 253–254
illness anxiety disorder and, 178
immune response and, 254–255
panic and, 122
physiology of, 251–252
schizophrenia and, 465
stages of, 251
suicide and, 239–240
supernatural explanation for, 9–10
tend and befriend response, 62
Stress hormones, 252
Stress hypothesis, 217
Stressor-related disorders, 146. *See also*
specific disorder
Stress physiology, 251
Stress reduction
comprehensive approach to, 272–273
drugs for, 273–274
Striatum, 462
Strokes, 260
Stroop color-naming paradigm, 58
Stuttering, 490
Subcortical dementia, 514
Sublimation, 18, 19
Substance abuse. *See also specific*
substances
defined, 371
sexual dysfunction and, 339–340
substance dependency *vs.*, 401
Substance dependence
abuse *vs.*, 401
characterization of, 370–371
defined, 371
disease model of, 391
moral weakness of, 391
nicotine, 380
statistics, 374
substance abuse *vs.*, 401
Substance-induced psychotic disorder, 455
Substance intoxication, 369
Substance/medication-induced
neurocognitive disorder, 515
Substance-related disorders. *See also*
specific substances
abuse, 370
anabolic-androgenic steroids, 387
anesthetic associated, 387
biological factors, 387–389
biological treatments for, 394–395
case study, 368
causes of, 387–393
cognitive factors, 390
cultural factors, 391
defined, 367
dependence, 370
depressant-associated, 371–376

Substance-related disorders *(continued)*
  diagnostic issues, 370–371
  exploration of, 406
  integrative model, 391–393
  intoxication, 368–369
  involvement levels, 368–370
  neurobiological factors, 388–389
  neurocognitive disorder, 515
  prevention of, 397–398
  psychological factors, 389–390
  psychosocial treatments for, 395–397
  sexual dysfunction and, 339–340
  social factors, 390–391
  stimulant-associated, 377–381
  summary, 402–403
  treatments for, 393–398
Substance use, 369
Subthreshold, 89
Suggestibility, 191–192
Suicidal attempts, 236
Suicidal ideation, 236
Suicidal plans, 236
Suicides
  causes, 237
  DBT and, 429
  interpersonal theory of, 239
  paranoid personality disorder and, 415
  planning of, 236
  risk factors for, 238–240
  statistics, 236–237
  treatment for, 240–242
  types, 237
Sundowner syndrome, 511
Superego, 18
Supernatural model, 8
Supernatural tradition
  case study, 10
  demons and, 9
  mass hysteria, 10–11
  melancholy, 9–10
  possession and, 10
  stress and, 9–10
  witches and, 9
Suppressor T cells, 255
Suprachiasmatic nucleus, 313
Supreme Court rulings, 542
Susceptibility genes, 516
Sustained stress, 251
Susto, 61
Sympathetic nervous system, 46, 47
Symptom substitution, 21
Synapses, 42
Synaptic cleft, 43
Synthetic marijuana, 384
Syphilis, 12–13
Systematic desensitization, 24
Systolic blood pressure, 260

T

*Taijin kyo*fusho, 142, 161
Tarantism, 10
Tarasoff, Tatiana, 539
Tarasoff v. Regents of the University of California, 539
Tardive dyskinesia, 468
Task analysis, 503

TAT. *See* Thematic Apperception Test (TAT)
Taxonomy, 84, 85
TBI. *See* Traumatic brain injury (TBI)
T cells, 255
Temporal lobe, 45
Tend and befriend response, 62
Terminal button, 43
Testability, 93
Testosterone, 353
Tetrahydrocannabinols (THC), 384
Test–retest reliability, 72
Thalamus, 45
Thanatos, 18
Thematic Apperception Test (TAT), 77
Therapeutic alliance, 21
Therapeutic jurisprudence, 539
Thompson v. County of Alameda, 540
Thorndike, Edward L., 24
Thought–action fusion, 157
Thought processes, 73
The Three Faces of Eve, 190
Threshold, 89, 109, 289
Thyroxine, 46
Tic disorder, 155
Time-limited course, 7
TMS. *See* Transcranial magnetic stimulation (TMS)
Tobacco-related disorder, 380–381
Tobacco, use of, 381
Token economy, 469
Tolerance, 369, 385
Top-down change, 53
Tourette's disorder, 155, 483, 524
Trance, dissociative, 188
Transcranial magnetic stimulation (TMS), 230
Transference, 21
Transinstitutionalization, 533
Transsexuals, 358
Transvestic disorder, 346–347
Trauma, 146. *See also specific disorder*
  head, 512
  PTSD and, 148. *See also* Posttraumatic stress disorder (PTSD)
  treatment for, 151–152
Traumatic brain injury (TBI), 513
  neurocognitive disorder due to, 513
Treatment groups, 99
Treatment outcome, 100
Treatment process, 100
Tremors, 51
Trends, 100
Trichotillomania, 164
Tricyclic antidepressants, 228
Triple vulnerability theory, 123
Trisomy 21, 501
Tuke, William, 15
Twelve Steps program, 396
Twin studies, 105
  antisocial personality disorder, 423
  complications in, 105
  eating disorders, 295
  function of, 105
  genetic factors, 37
  mood disorders, 216
  PTSD, 149
  schizophrenia, 458–459

sexual orientation, 331
substance abuse, 387
Type A behavior pattern, 262
Type B behavior pattern, 262
Type D personality, 264

U

Unconditional positive regard, 22
Unconditioned response, 23
Unconditioned stimulus, 23
Unconscious, 17, 57–58
Unconscious vision, 57
Uncued panic attack, 119
Underarousal hypothesis, 423
Unexpected (uncued) panic attack, 119
Unipolar mood disorder, 203
Universal prevention strategies, 107

V

Vacuum device therapy, 344
Vaginal photoplethysmograph, 338
Vaginismus, 337
Vagus nerve stimulation, 230
Validity, 72, 87, 92
Valproate (Divalproex), 230
Variables, 98
Vascular neurocognitive disorder, 512
Vasovagal syncope, 34
Ventricle enlargement, 463
Veterans Health Administration, 543
Viagra. *See* Sildenafil
Vicarious experience, 138
Vinvusa, 188
von Meduna, Joseph, 14
Voyeuristic disorder, 346
Vulnerability
  anxiety-associated, 123
  biological, 123
  depression-associated, 223
  diathesis–stress model, 38–39
  generalized psychological, 123
  sexual orientation, 331
  specific psychological, 123

W

Watson, John B., 16, 23
Wechsler Adult Intelligence Scale (WAIS-IV), 80
Wechsler Intelligence Scale for Children (WISC-V), 80
Wechsler Preschool and Primary Scale of Intelligence (WPPSI-IV), 80
Weight. *See* Body Weight
Weight loss programs, 304
Wernicke-Korsakoff syndrome, 373
Witches, 9
Withdrawal
  cocaine, 380
  delirium, 369
  designs, 101–102
  nicotine, 380–381
  opioids, 382
Wolpe, Joseph, 24
Written expression disorders, 489
Wyatt v. Stickney, 541

X

Xanax. *See* Alprazolam
X chromosomes, 36
X-linked gene, 500

Y

Yang, 12, 138
Y chromosomes, 36
Yin, 12, 138
Youngberg v. Romeo, 541

Z

Zoloft. *See* Sertraline
Zyban, 394

DSM-5 CLASSIFICATIONS

Neurodevelopmental Disorders

Intellectual Disabilities

Intellectual Disability (Intellectual Developmental Disorder)/Global Developmental Delay/Unspecified Intellectual Disability (Intellectual Developmental Disorder)

Communication Disorders

Language Disorder/Speech Sound Disorder/Childhood-Onset Fluency Disorder (Stuttering)/Social (Pragmatic) Communication Disorder/Unspecified Communication Disorder

Autism Spectrum Disorder

Autism Spectrum Disorder

Attention-Deficit/Hyperactivity Disorder

Attention-Deficit/Hyperactivity Disorder/ Other Specified Attention-Deficit/ Hyperactivity Disorder/Unspecified Attention-Deficit/Hyperactivity Disorder

Specific Learning Disorder

Motor Disorders

Developmental Coordination Disorder/ Stereotypic Movement Disorder

Tic Disorders

Tourette's Disorder/Persistent (Chronic) Motor or Vocal Tic Disorder/Provisional Tic Disorder/Other Specified Tic Disorder/Unspecific Tic Disorder

Other Neurodevelopmental Disorders

Other Specified Neurodevelopmental Disorder/Unspecified Neurodevelopmental Disorder

Schizophrenia Spectrum and other Psychotic Disorders

Schizotypal (Personality) Disorder
Delusional Disorder
Brief Psychotic Disorder
Schizophreniform Disorder
Schizophrenia
Schizoaffective Disorder
Substance/Medication-Induced Psychotic Disorder
Psychotic Disorder Due to Another Medical Condition
Catatonia Associated with Another Mental Disorder
Catatonic Disorder due to Another Medical Condition
Unspecified Catatonia
Other Specified Schizophrenia Spectrum and Other Psychotic Disorder
Unspecified Schizophrenia Spectrum and Other Psychotic Disorder

Bipolar and Related Disorders

Bipolar I Disorder/Bipolar II Disorder/ Cyclothymic Disorder/Substance/ Medication-Induced Bipolar and Related Disorder/Bipolar and Related Disorder Due to Another Medical Condition/ Other Specified Bipolar and Related Disorder/Unspecified Bipolar and Related Disorder

Depressive Disorders

Disruptive Mood Dysregulation Disorder/ Major Depressive Disorder/Persistent Depressive Disorder (Dysthymia)/ Premenstrual Dysphoric Disorder/ Substance/Medication-Induced Depressive Disorder/Depressive Disorder Due to Another Medical Condition/ Other Specified Depressive Disorder/ Unspecified Depressive Disorder

Anxiety Disorders

Separation Anxiety Disorder/Selective Mutism/Specific Phobia/Social Anxiety Disorder (Social Phobia)/ Panic Disorder/Panic Attack Specifier/ Agoraphobia/Generalized Anxiety Disorder/Substance/Medication-Induced Anxiety Disorder/Anxiety Disorder Due to Another Medical Condition/Other Specified Anxiety Disorder/Unspecified Anxiety Disorder

Obsessive-Compulsive and Related Disorders

Obsessive-Compulsive Disorder/Body Dysmorphic Disorder/Hoarding Disorder/Trichotillomania (Hair-Pulling Disorder)/Excoriation (Skin-Picking) Disorder/Substance/Medication-Induced Obsessive-Compulsive and Related Disorder/Obsessive-Compulsive and Related Disorder Due to Another Medical Condition/Other Specified Obsessive-Compulsive and Related Disorder/Unspecified Obsessive-Compulsive and Related Disorder

Trauma- and Stressor-Related Disorders

Reactive Attachment Disorder/Disinhibited Social Engagement Disorder/Post-traumatic Stress Disorder (includes Posttraumatic Stress Disorder for Children 6 Years and Younger)/Acute Stress Disorder/Adjustment Disorders/ Other Specified Trauma- and Stressor-Related Disorder/Unspecified Trauma- and Stressor-Related Disorder

Dissociative Disorders

Dissociative Identity Disorder/Dissociative Amnesia/Depersonalization/ Derealization Disorder/Other Specified Dissociative Disorder/Unspecified Dissociative Disorder

Somatic Symptom and Related Disorders

Somatic Symptom Disorder/Illness Anxiety Disorder/Conversion Disorder (Functional Neurological Symptom Disorder)/Psychological Factors Affecting Other Medical Conditions/ Factitious Disorder (includes Factitious Disorder Imposed on Self, Factitious Disorder Imposed on Another)/Other Specified Somatic Symptom and Related Disorder/Unspecified Somatic Symptoms and Related Disorder

Feeding and Eating Disorders

Pica/Rumination Disorder/Avoidant/ Restrictive Food Intake Disorder/ Anorexia Nervosa (Restricting type, Binge-eating/Purging type)/Bulimia Nervosa/Binge-Eating Disorder/Other Specified Feeding or Eating Disorder/ Unspecified Feeding or Eating Disorder

Elimination Disorders

Enuresis/Encopresis/Other Specified Elimination Disorder/Unspecified Elimination Disorder

Sleep-Wake Disorders

Insomnia Disorder/Hypersomnolence Disorder/Narcolepsy

Breathing-Related Sleep Disorders

Obstructive Sleep Apnea Hypopnea/
Central Sleep Apnea/Sleep-Related
Hypoventilation/Circadian Rhythm
Sleep-Wake Disorders

Parasomnias

Non-Rapid Eye Movement Sleep Arousal
Disorders/Nightmare Disorder/Rapid
Eye Movement Sleep Behavior Disorder/
Restless Legs Syndrome/Substance/
Medication-Induced Sleep Disorder/
Other Specified Insomnia Disorder/
Unspecified Insomnia Disorder/Other
Specified Hypersomnolence Disorder/
Unspecified Hypersomnolence Disorder/
Other Specified Sleep-Wake Disorder/
Unspecified Sleep-Wake Disorder

Sexual Dysfunctions

Delayed Ejaculation/Erectile Disorder/
Female Orgasmic Disorder/Female
Sexual Interest/Arousal Disorder/
Genito-Pelvic Pain/Penetration
Disorder/Male Hypoactive Sexual Desire
Disorder/Premature (Early) Ejaculation/
Substance/Medication-Induced Sexual
Dysfunction/Other Specified Sexual
Dysfunction/Unspecified Sexual
Dysfunction

Gender Dysphoria

Gender Dysphoria/Other Specified
Gender Dysphoria/Unspecified
Gender Dysphoria

Disruptive, Impulse-Control, and Conduct Disorders

Oppositional Defiant Disorder/Intermittent
Explosive Disorder/Conduct Disorder/
Antisocial Personality Disorder/
Pyromania/Kleptomania/Other
Specified Disruptive, Impulse-Control,
and Conduct Disorder/Unspecified
Disruptive, Impulse-Control, and
Conduct Disorder

Substance-Related and Addictive Disorders

Substance-Related Disorders

Alcohol-Related Disorders: Alcohol Use
Disorder/Alcohol Intoxication/Alcohol
Withdrawal/Other Alcohol-Induced
Disorders/Unspecified Alcohol-Related
Disorder

Caffeine-Related Disorders: Caffeine
Intoxication/Caffeine Withdrawal/Other
Caffeine-Induced Disorders/Unspecified
Caffeine-Related Disorder

Cannabis-Related Disorders: Cannabis
Use Disorder/Cannabis Intoxication/
Cannabis Withdrawal/Other Cannabis-
Induced Disorders/Unspecified
Cannabis-Related Disorder

Hallucinogen-Related Disorders:
Phencyclidine Use Disorders/
Other Hallucinogen Use Disorder/
Phencyclidine Intoxication/Other
Hallucinogen Intoxication/Hallucinogen
Persisting Perception Disorder/Other
Phencyclidine-Induced Disorders/
Other Hallucinogen-Induced Disorders/
Unspecified Phencyclidine-Related
Disorders/Unspecified Hallucinogen-
Related Disorders

Inhalant-Related Disorders: Inhalant Use
Disorder/Inhalant Intoxication/Other
Inhalant-Induced Disorders/Unspecified
Inhalant-Related Disorders

Opioid-Related Disorders: Opioid Use
Disorder/Opioid Intoxication/Opioid
Withdrawal/Other Opioid-Induced
Disorders/Unspecified Opioid-Related
Disorder

Sedative-, Hypnotic-, or Anxiolytic-
Related Disorders: Sedative, Hypnotic,
or Anxiolytic Use Disorder/Sedative,
Hypnotic, or Anxiolytic Intoxication/
Sedative, Hypnotic, or Anxiolytic
Withdrawal/Other Sedative-, Hypnotic-,
or Anxiolytic-Induced Disorders/
Unspecified Sedative-, Hypnotic-,
or Anxiolytic-Related Disorder

Stimulant-Related Disorders: Stimulant
Use Disorder/Stimulant Intoxication/
Stimulant Withdrawal/Other Stimulant-
Induced Disorders/Unspecified
Stimulant-Related Disorder

Tobacco-Related Disorders: Tobacco Use
Disorder/Tobacco Withdrawal/Other
Tobacco-Induced Disorders/Unspecified
Tobacco-Related Disorder

Other (or Unknown) Substance-Related
Disorders: Other (or Unknown)
Substance Use Disorder/Other (or
Unknown) Substance Intoxication/Other
(or Unknown) Substance Withdrawal/
Other (or Unknown) Substance-Induced
Disorders/Unspecified Other (or
Unknown) Substance-Related Disorder

Non-Substance-Related Disorders

Gambling Disorder

Neurocognitive Disorders

Delirium

Major and Mild Neurocognitive Disorders

Major or Mild Neurocognitive Disorder
Due to Alzheimer's Disease
Major or Mild Frontotemporal
Neurocognitive Disorder
Major or Mild Neurocognitive Disorder
with Lewy Bodies
Major or Mild Vascular Neurocognitive
Disorder
Major or Mild Neurocognitive Disorder
Due to Traumatic Brain Injury
Substance/Medication-Induced Major or
Mild Neurocognitive Disorder
Major or Mild Neurocognitive Disorder
Due to HIV Infection
Major or Mild Neurocognitive Disorder
Due to Prion Disease
Major or Mild Neurocognitive Disorder
Due to Parkinson's Disease
Major or Mild Neurocognitive Disorder
Due to Huntington's Disease
Major or Mild Neurocognitive Disorder
Due to Another Medical Condition
Major and Mild Neurocognitive Disorders
Due to Multiple Etiologies
Unspecified Neurocognitive Disorder

Personality Disorders

Cluster A Personality Disorders

Paranoid Personality Disorder/Schizoid
Personality Disorder/Schizotypal
Personality Disorder

Cluster B Personality Disorders

Antisocial Personality Disorder/Borderline
Personality Disorder/Histrionic
Personality Disorder/Narcissistic
Personality Disorder

Cluster C Personality Disorders

Avoidant Personality Disorder/Dependent
Personality Disorder/Obsessive-
Compulsive Personality Disorder

Other Personality Disorders

Personality Change Due to Another
Medical Condition/Other Specified
Personality Disorder/Unspecified
Personality Disorder